WHO WAS WHO
A CUMULATED INDEX
1897–1990

WHO'S WHO

An annual biographical dictionary
first published in 1849

WHO WAS WHO

Published by
A & C BLACK

WHO WAS WHO

A
CUMULATED
INDEX
1897–1990

A & C BLACK
LONDON

FIRST PUBLISHED 1991
A & C BLACK (PUBLISHERS) LIMITED
35 BEDFORD ROW LONDON WC1R 4JH

COPYRIGHT © 1991 A & C BLACK (PUBLISHERS) LTD

ISBN 0–7136–3457–X

PRINTED AND BOUND IN GREAT BRITAIN
BY WILLIAM CLOWES LTD, BECCLES AND LONDON

PREFACE

THIS INDEX has been prepared to give easy access to the eight volumes of *Who Was Who* for those who may come upon a name, in newspapers, journals, diaries or memoirs, which was obviously so familiar to the writer that he saw no need to explain it; for those who know that an entry should appear in one of the eight volumes, but do not know which volume—because the date of death is not to hand; for researchers in social and political history. The entries thus brought into one list are far from uniform; they range from very brief to expansive, from very personal to official in tone; but they are alike in that they were compiled, for the most part, by their subjects, published in their lifetimes, and sent for correction each year. They give at worst a clue, at best a full answer, to the enquirer seeking to turn a name into a person.

In the ninety-four years of publication recorded there have been many changes, not so much of editorial policy as in the sort of person whose name and career attracted general public interest. *Who's Who* has reflected this interest faithfully; an invitation to have an entry has always signified the compilers' response thereto, rather than the capricious accolade sometimes supposed.

In the earlier days of *Who's Who* consistency seems, not surprisingly, to have been thought relatively unimportant. The result is a wide variety of forms of heading to entries, which required adaptation to fit into a single list. A form has been chosen for the Index which leaves no doubt as to which entry is referred to, but which is not necessarily exactly as printed in the book. Individuals preferred to appear under styles such as The MacDermot, or, in the case of titles, with forms or numberings not now regarded as correct. They spelt their names (for example) M'Taggart, Mactaggart or McTaggart. Where it is conceivable that a name might be hard to find a cross-reference is given, as it is to the part of a double surname under which an entry appears from the other part. There are also cross-references from pseudonyms, maiden names, married names, and other forms appearing in entries.

For hereditary peerages the Index gives the title only; where for any reason one holder of the title is missing from the sequence this is indicated. For life peerages, courtesy titles, and the titles of Lords of Session it gives the forenames and family name also; life peers have a cross-reference under their former names if these differ from their eventual title, and Lords of Session also have a cross-reference to their judicial titles from their family names and forenames. Baronets appear in alphabetical order among other entries; if there are two or more baronetcies of the same surname they are distinguished by the date of creation, and any missing from the sequences are noted.

In the case of names preceded by prefixes such as von or de, which may appear under the prefix or under the main part of the name in *Who Was Who*, the Index gives them as they appear in the book with no cross-reference to the other possible form.

It has always been necessary to include some entries in Addenda to the volumes of *Who Was Who*, because the compilers did not learn of the deaths in question until the main part of the volumes had been completed; such entries are transferred to the appropriate volume when a new edition is published, and in these cases both appearances of the entry are indexed. Where entries appear in the Addenda they are distinguished by (A) after the volume number. There were, however, occasions, particularly in the earlier years, when an entry was removed from *Who's Who* and included in *Who Was Who* by mistake; when the mistake was discovered the entry was returned to *Who's Who* but remained also, wrongly, in *Who Was Who*. In these cases the earlier, incorrect, appearance of the name has not been indexed. In the course of preparation of the Index a number of entries have been found without a date of death appended or with incomplete names. Where possible the dates and names have been discovered and included; they are added to the volumes of *Who Was Who* as new editions are published.

It is normal for entries once included in *Who's Who* to remain until death, but there has been one major exception to this. In 1943 the paper shortage was so acute that, even though the book was treated generously by the authorities, it became necessary to reduce the number of entries sharply. Very few of those entries then deleted were ever returned to *Who's Who*, and they do not appear in *Who Was Who*.

A

A. K. H. B; *see* Boyd, Very Rev. A. K. H.
Aalto, Alvar; *see* Aalto, H. A. H.
Aalto, (Hugo) Alvar (Henrik), 1898–1976, vol. VII
Aaltonen, Wäinö Valdemar, 1894–1966, vol. VI
Aaron, Richard Ithamar, 1901–1987, vol. VIII
Aarons, Sir Daniel Sidney, 1885–1983, vol. VIII
Abadie, Major Eustace Henry Egremont, 1877–1914, vol. I
Abadie, Captain George Howard Fanshawe, 1873–1904, vol. I
Abadie, Maj.-Gen. Henry Richard, 1841–1915, vol. I
Abady, Jacques, 1872–1964, vol. VI
Abayomi, Sir Kofo Adekunle, 1896–1979, vol. VII
Abbas, Kuli Khan (Nawab), 1864–1938, vol. III
Abbay, Col Bryan Norman, 1881–1947, vol. IV
Abbay, Rev. Richard, 1844–1924, vol. II
Abbe, Cleveland, 1838–1916, vol. II
Abbey, Edwin Austin, 1852–1911, vol. I
Abbey, Lt-Col Walter Bulmer Tate, 1872–1949, vol. IV
Abbey, William Henry, 1864–1943, vol. IV
Abbiss, Sir George, 1884–1966, vol. VI
Abbot, Charles Greeley, 1872–1973, vol. VII
Abbot, Dermot Charles Hyatt, 1908–1990, vol. VIII
Abbot, Dame Elsie Myrtle, 1907–1983, vol. VIII
Abbot, Lt-Col Frederick William, 1862–1942, vol. IV
Abbott, Albert, 1872–1950, vol. IV
Abbott, Albert Holden, 1871–1934, vol. III
Abbott, Alexander Crever, 1860–1935, vol. III
Abbott, Arthur, 1879–1955, vol. V
Abbott, Arthur William, 1893–1986, vol. VIII
Abbott, Hon. Sir Charles (Arthur Hillas) Lempriere, 1889–1960, vol. V
Abbott, Charles Lydiard Aubrey, 1886–1975, vol. VII
Abbott, Charles Theodore, *died* 1956, vol. V
Abbott, Claude Colleer, 1889–1971, vol. VII
Abbott, Hon. Douglas Charles, 1899–1987, vol. VIII
Abbott, Edwin, 1878–1947, vol. IV
Abbott, Rev. Edwin Abbott, 1838–1926, vol. II
Abbott, Rev. Eric Symes, 1906–1983, vol. VIII
Abbott, Evelyn Robins, 1873–1950, vol. IV
Abbott, Francis Charles, 1867–1938, vol. III
Abbott, Frank Frost, 1860–1924, vol. II
Abbott, Brig.-Gen. Henry Alexius, 1849–1924, vol. II
Abbott, Rt Rev. Henry Pryon Almon, 1881–1945, vol. IV
Abbott, Col Rev. Preb. Herbert Alldridge, 1881–1962, vol. VI
Abbott, Col Herbert Edward Stacy, 1855–1939, vol. III
Abbott, John Sutherland, 1900–1979, vol. VII
Abbott, Hon. Sir Joseph Palmer, 1842–1901, vol. I

Abbott, Brig.-Gen. Leonard Henry, 1875–1949, vol. IV
Abbott, Rev. Lyman, 1835–1922, vol. II
Abbott, Sir Myles John, 1906–1984, vol. VIII
Abbott, Percival William Henry, 1869–1954, vol. V
Abbott, Lt-Col Percy Phipps, 1869–1940, vol. III
Abbott, Brig. Reginald Stuart, 1882–1964, vol. VI
Abbott, Rt Rev. Robert Crowther, 1869–1927, vol. II
Abbott, Thomas Charles, *died* 1927, vol. II
Abbott, Rev. Thomas Kingsmill, *died* 1912, vol. I
Abbott, Rev. Thomas Kingsmill, 1829–1913, vol. I
Abbott, William, 1891–1963, vol. VI
Abdool Raoof, Khan Bahadur Sir Muhammad, *died* 1947, vol. IV
Abdoolcader, Sir Husein Hasanally, 1890–1974, vol. VII
Abdul, Sir Husain Sahib, Khan Bahadur Mirza, vol. III
Abdul Maliki, Alhaji, 1914–1969, vol. VI
Abdul Qaiyum, Nawab Sir Sahibzada, 1866–1937, vol. III
Abdul Rahman Putra, Tunku (Prince), 1903–1990, vol. VIII
Abdul Razak bin Hussein, Hon. Tun Haji, 1922–1976, vol. VII
Abdulrahman Khan, Ameer of Afghanistan, *died* 1901, vol. I
Abdussamad Khan, Sahibzada Sir, 1874–1943, vol. IV
Abdy, Sir Anthony Charles Sykes, 3rd Bt, 1848–1921, vol. II
Abdy, Brig.-Gen. Anthony John, 1856–1924, vol. II
Abdy, Sir Henry Beadon, 4th Bt, 1854–1921, vol. II
Abdy, Richard Combe, *died* 1938, vol. III
Abdy, Sir Robert Henry Edward, 5th Bt, 1896–1976, vol. VII
Abdy, Sir William Neville, 2nd Bt, 1844–1910, vol. I
à Beckett, Ada Mary; *see* à Beckett, Mrs T. A.
à Beckett, Sir Albert, 1840–1904, vol. I
A'Beckett, Arthur William, 1844–1909, vol. I
A'Beckett, Hon. Sir Thomas, 1837–1919, vol. II
à Beckett, Mrs Thomas Archibald, (Ada Mary à Beckett), 1872–1948, vol. IV
Abel, Arthur Lawrence, 1895–1978, vol. VII
Abel, Sir Frederick Augustus, 1st Bt, 1826–1902, vol. I
Abel, Henry George, 1875–1945, vol. IV
Abel Smith, Sir Alexander, 1904–1980, vol. VII
Abel Smith, Vice Adm. Sir Conolly; *see* Abel Smith, Sir E. M. C.
Abel Smith, Desmond, 1892–1974, vol. VII
Abel Smith, Vice Adm. Sir (Edward Michael) Conolly, 1899–1985, vol. VIII

Abel-Smith, Geoffrey Samuel, 1871–1926, vol. II
Abel-Smith, Brig.-Gen. Lionel, 1870–1946, vol. IV
Abel Smith, Reginald Henry Macaulay, 1890–1964, vol. VI
Abell, Sir George Edmond Brackenbury, 1904–1989, vol. VIII
Abell, George Foster, 1875–1946, vol. IV
Abell, Lt-Col Robert Lloyd, 1889–1957, vol. V
Abell, Thomas Bertrand, 1880–1956, vol. V
Abell, Sir Westcott Stile, 1877–1961, vol. VI
Abend, Hallett, 1884–1955, vol. V
Abensur, Isaac Aaron, 1861–1937, vol. III
Abeokuta, The Alake of, (Ademola II), Sir Ladapo Ademola, 1873–1962, vol. VI
Aberconway, 1st Baron, 1850–1934, vol. III
Aberconway, 2nd Baron, 1879–1953, vol. V
Abercorn, 2nd Duke of, 1838–1913, vol. I
Abercorn, 3rd Duke of, 1869–1953, vol. V
Abercorn, 4th Duke of, 1904–1979, vol. VII
Abercorn, Dowager Duchess of; (Rosalind Cecilia Caroline), 1869–1958, vol. V
Abercrombie, Captain Alexander Ralph, 1896–1918, vol. II
Abercrombie, Col Charles Murray, 1874–1933, vol. III
Abercrombie, George Francis, 1896–1978, vol. VII
Abercrombie, Sir John Robertson, 1888–1960, vol. V
Abercrombie, Lascelles, 1881–1938, vol. III
Abercrombie, Sir (Leslie) Patrick, 1879–1957, vol. V
Abercrombie, Michael, 1912–1979, vol. VII
Abercrombie, Nigel James, 1908–1986, vol. VIII
Abercrombie, Sir Patrick; see Abercrombie, Sir L. P.
Abercrombie, Peter Henderson, 1867–1950, vol. IV
Abercromby, 4th Baron, 1838–1917, vol. II
Abercromby, 5th Baron, 1841–1924, vol. II
Abercromby, Bt-Col Sir George William, 8th Bt, 1886–1964, vol. VI
Abercromby, Sir Robert Alexander, 9th Bt, 1895–1972, vol. VII
Aberdare, 2nd Baron, 1851–1929, vol. III
Aberdare, 3rd Baron, 1885–1957, vol. V
Aberdeen, David du Rieu, 1913–1987, vol. VIII
Aberdeen and Temair, 1st Marquess of, 1847–1934, vol. III
Aberdeen and Temair, 2nd Marquis of, 1879–1965, vol. VI
Aberdeen and Temair, 3rd Marquis of, 1883–1972, vol. VII
Aberdeen and Temair, 4th Marquess of, 1908–1974, vol. VII
Aberdeen and Temair, 5th Marquess of, 1913–1984, vol. VIII
Aberdeen and Temair, Marchioness of; (Ishbel Maria), 1857–1939, vol. III
Abergavenny, 1st Marquess of, 1826–1915, vol I
Abergavenny, 2nd Marquess of, 1853–1927, vol. II
Abergavenny, 3rd Marquess of, 1854–1938, vol. III
Abergavenny, 4th Marquess of, 1883–1954, vol. V
Aberhart, Hon. William, 1878–1943, vol. IV
Abernethy, James Smart, 1907–1976, vol. VII
Abertay, 1st Baron, 1875–1940, vol. III
Abinash Chandra Sen, Rai Bahadur, 1870–1922, vol. II
Abingdon, 7th Earl of, 1836–1928, vol. II

Abinger, 4th Baron, 1871–1903, vol. I
Abinger, 5th Baron, 1872–1917, vol. II
Abinger, 6th Baron, 1876–1927, vol. II
Abinger, 7th Baron, 1878–1943, vol. IV
Ablett, Thomas Robert, died 1945, vol. IV
Abney, Sir William de Wiveleslie, 1843–1921, vol. II
Abrahall, Rt Rev. Anthony Leigh Egerton H.; see Hoskyns-Abrahall
Abrahall, Bennet H.; see Hoskyns-Abrahall.
Abrahall, Sir Theo Chandos H.; see Hoskyns-Abrahall.
Abraham, Ashley Perry, 1876–1951, vol. V
Abraham, Rt Rev. C. T., 1857–1945, vol. IV
Abraham, Rt Rev. Charles John, 1814–1903, vol. I
Abraham, Edgar Gaston Furtado, 1880–1955, vol. V
Abraham, George Dixon, 1872–1965, vol. VI
Abraham, Gerald Ernest Heal, 1904–1988, vol. VIII
Abraham, James Johnston, 1876–1963, vol VI
Abraham, Sir John Bradley, 1881–1945, vol. IV
Abraham, John Conrad, 1889–1939, vol. III
Abraham, Louis Arnold, 1893–1983, vol. VIII
Abraham, Rt Rev. Philip Selwyn, 1897–1955, vol. V
Abraham, Phineas Simon, died 1921, vol. II
Abraham, Robert John Elliot, 1927–1985, vol. VIII
Abraham, William, 1840–1915, vol. I
Abraham, Rt. Hon. William, 1842–1922, vol. II
Abraham, Maj.-Gen. Sir William Ernest Victor, 1897–1980, vol. VII
Abrahams, Sir Adolphe, 1883–1967, vol. VI
Abrahams, Major Sir Arthur Cecil, 1878–1944, vol. IV
Abrahams, Bertram, 1870–1908, vol. I
Abrahams, Sir Charles Myer, 1914–1985, vol. VIII
Abrahams, Doris Caroline; see Brahms, Caryl
Abrahams, Gerald, 1907–1980, vol. VII
Abrahams, Harold Maurice, 1899–1978, vol. VII
Abrahams, Israel, 1858–1925, vol. II
Abrahams, Sir Lionel, 1869–1919, vol. II
Abrahams, Louis Barnett, 1839–1918, vol. II
Abrahams, Rt Hon. Sir Sidney Solomon, 1885–1957, vol. V
Abrahamson, Sir Martin Arnold, 1870–1962, vol. VI
Abram, Sir George Stewart, 1866–1928, vol. II
Abram, John Hill, died 1933, vol. III
Abramson, Major Albert, 1876–1944, vol. IV
Abruzzi, Duke of; Prince Luigi Amedeo Giuseppé Maria Ferdinando Francesco, 1873–1933, vol. III
Abubakr, Seiyid Sir, bin Sheik al Kaf, 1885–1965, vol. VI
Achard, Marcel, 1899–1974, vol. VII
Acharya, Sir Vijaya Ragahava, 1875–1953, vol. V
Acheampong, Ignatius Kutu, 1931–1979, vol. VII
Acheson, Capt. Albert Edward, 1862–1945, vol. IV
Acheson, Andrew Basil, 1895–1959, vol. V
Acheson, Anne Crawford, died 1962, vol. VI
Acheson, Dean, 1893–1971, vol. VII
Acheson, Maj.-Gen. Hon. Edward Archibald Brabazon, 1844–1921, vol. II
Acheson, Edward Goodrich, 1856–1931, vol. III
Acheson, Sir James Glasgow, 1889–1973, vol. VII
Acheson, Hon. Patrick George Edward Cavendish-, 1883–1957, vol. V
Achurch, Janet, (Janet Achurch Sharp), died 1916, vol. II

Ackerley, Rev. Frederick George, 1871–1954, vol. V
Ackermann, Gerald, 1876–1960, vol. V(A), vol. VI
Ackerman, Myron, 1913–1985, vol. VIII
Ackers, Benjamin St John, 1839–1915, vol. I
Ackland, Robert Craig, *died* 1923, vol. II
Ackland, William Alfred, 1875–1940, vol. III(A), vol. IV
Ackland, Major William Robert, 1863–1949, vol. IV
Acklom, Captain Cecil Ryther, 1872–1937, vol. III
Acklom, Maj. Spencer, *died* 1918, vol. II
Ackner, Brian Gerard Conrad, 1918–1966, vol. VI
Ackner, Conrad Adolf, 1880–1976, vol. VII
Ackroyd, Sir Cuthbert Lowell, 1st Bt, 1892–1973, vol. VII
Ackroyd, Dame (Dorothy) Elizabeth, 1910–1987, vol. VIII
Ackroyd, Sir Edward James, 1838–1904, vol. I
Ackroyd, Dame Elizabeth; *see* Ackroyd, Dame D. E.
Ackroyd, Thomas Raven, 1861–1946, vol. IV
Acland, Col Alfred Dyke, 1858–1937, vol. III
Acland, Sir Antony Guy, 5th Bt (*cr* 1890), 1916–1983, vol. VIII
Acland, Arthur Geoffrey Dyke, 1909–1964, vol. VI
Acland, Rt Hon. Sir Arthur Herbert Dyke, 13th Bt (*cr* 1644), 1847–1926, vol. II
Acland, Lt-Gen. Arthur Nugent F.; *see* Floyer-Acland.
Acland, Sir (Charles) Thomas Dyke, 12th Bt (*cr* 1644), 1842–1919, vol. II
Acland, Engr-Rear-Adm. Edward Leopold Dyke, 1878–1968, vol. VI
Acland, F. A., 1861–1950, vol. IV(A), vol. V
Acland, Rt Hon. Sir Francis Dyke, 14th Bt (*cr* 1644), 1874–1939, vol. III
Acland, Captain Frank Edward Dyke, 1857–1943, vol. IV
Acland, Henry Dyke, 1867–1942, vol. IV
Acland, Sir Henry Wentworth Dyke, 1st Bt (*cr* 1890), 1815–1900, vol. I
Acland, Captain Sir Hubert Guy Dyke, 4th Bt (*cr* 1890), 1890–1978, vol. VII
Acland, Sir (Hugh) John (Dyke), 1904–1981, vol. VIII
Acland, Col Sir Hugh Thomas Dyke, 1874–1956, vol. V
Acland, Sir John; *see* Acland, Sir H. J. D.
Acland, Sir Reginald Brodie Dyke, 1856–1924, vol. II
Acland, Rt Rev. Richard Dyke, 1881–1954, vol. V
Acland, Sir Richard Thomas Dyke, 15th Bt, 1906–1990, vol. VIII
Acland, Theodore Dyke, 1851–1931, vol. III
Acland, Rev. Theodore William Gull, 1890–1960, vol. V
Acland, Sir Thomas; *see* Acland, Sir C. T. D.
Acland, Rt Hon. Sir Thomas Dyke, 11th Bt (*cr* 1644), 1809–1898, vol. I
Acland, Adm. Sir William Alison Dyke, 2nd Bt (*cr* 1890), 1847–1924, vol. II
Acland, Sir William Henry Dyke, 3rd Bt (*cr* 1890), 1888–1970, vol. II
Acland-Troyte, Lt-Col Sir Gilbert John, 1876–1964, vol. VI
Acomb, Henry Waldo, 1891–1962, vol. VI
A'Court-Repington, Lt-Col Charles; *see* Repington.

A'Court-Repington, Charles Henry Wyndham, 1819–1903, vol. I
Acton, 1st Baron, 1834–1902, vol. I
Acton, 2nd Baron, 1870–1924, vol. II
Acton, 3rd Baron, 1907–1989, vol. VIII
Acton, Hon. Sir Edward, 1865–1945, vol. IV
Acton, Dame (Ellen) Marian, 1887–1971, vol. VII
Acton, Fitzmaurice, 1874–1921, vol. II
Acton, Frederick, 1845–1933, vol. III
Acton, Harry Burrows, 1908–1974, vol. VII
Acton, Lt-Col Hugh William, 1883–1935, vol. III
Acton, John Adams, *died* 1910, vol. I
Acton, Dame Marian, *see* Acton, Dame E. M.
Acton, Murray A.; *see* Adams-Acton.
Acton, Maj.-Gen. Thomas Heward, 1917–1977, vol. VII
Acton, Lt-Col William Maxwell, 1878–1939, vol. III
Acutt, Sir Keith (Courtney), 1909–1986, vol. VIII
Acworth, Captain Bernard, 1885–1963, vol. VI
Acworth, Harry Arbuthnot, 1849–1933, vol. III
Acworth, Col Louis Raymond, 1872–1934, vol. III
Acworth, Sir William Mitchell, 1850–1925, vol. II
Adair, Maj.-Gen. Sir Allan Henry Shafto, 6th Bt, 1897–1988, vol. VIII
Adair, Arthur Robin, 1913–1981, vol. VIII
Adair, Cecil; *see* Everett-Green, Evelyn.
Adair, Adm. Charles Henry, 1851–1920, vol. II
Adair, Sir Charles William, 1822–1897, vol. I
Adair, Mrs Cornelia, *died* 1922, vol. II
Adair, Edward Robert, 1888–1967, vol. VI
Adair, Sir Frederick Edward Shafto, 4th Bt, 1860–1915, vol. I
Adair, Gilbert Smithson, 1896–1979, vol. VII
Adair, Sir Hugh Edward, 3rd Bt, 1815–1902, vol. I
Adair, Brig.-Gen. Hugh Robert, 1863–1946, vol. IV
Adair, Sir (Robert) Shafto, 5th Bt, 1862–1949, vol. IV
Adair, Sir Shafto; *see* Adair, Sir R. S.
Adair, Rear-Adm. Thomas Benjamin Stratton, *died* 1928, vol. II
Adair, Gen. Sir William Thompson, 1850–1931, vol. III
Adam, Hon. Lord; James Adam, 1824–1914, vol. I
Adam, Hon. Sir Alexander Duncan Grant, 1902–1986, vol. VIII
Adam, Sir Charles Elphinstone, 1st Bt (*cr* 1882), 1859–1922, vol. II
Adam, Charles Fox Frederick, 1852–1913, vol. I
Adam, Captain Charles Keith, 1891–1971, vol. VII
Adam, Colin Gurdon Forbes, 1889–1982, vol. VIII
Adam, Rev. David Stow, 1859–1925, vol. II
Adam, Edwin, 1862–1931, vol. III
Adam, Eric Graham Forbes, 1888–1925, vol. II
Adam, Sir Frank Forbes, 1st Bt (*cr* 1917), 1846–1926, vol. II
Adam, Maj.-Gen. Frederick Archibald, 1860–1924, vol. II
Adam, Frederick Edward Fox, 1887–1969, vol. VI
Adam, Major Frederick Loch, 1864–1907, vol. I
Adam, Mrs George, (H. Pearl Adam), 1882–1957, vol. V
Adam, George Jefferys, 1883–1930, vol. III
Adam, H. Pearl; *see* Adam, Mrs George.
Adam, Captain Herbert Algernon, 1872–1920, vol. II
Adam, J. Millen, 1853–1941, vol. IV

Adam, James, 1860–1907, vol. I
Adam, Sir James, 1870–1949, vol. IV
Adam, John Hunter, 1882–1958, vol. IV
Adam, Mme Juliette, 1836–1936, vol. III
Adam, Karl, 1876–1966, vol. VI
Adam, Kenneth, 1908–1978, vol. VII
Adam, Neil Kensington, 1891–1973, vol. VII
Adam, Patrick William, 1854–1929, vol. III
Adam, Randle R.; see Reid-Adam.
Adam, General Sir Ronald Forbes, 2nd Bt (cr 1917), 1885–1982, vol. VIII
Adam, Major William Augustus, 1865–1940, vol. III
Adami, John George, 1862–1926, vol. II
Adami, Sir Leonard Christian, 1874–1952, vol. V
Adamic, Louis, 1899–1951, vol. V
Adams, 1st Baron, 1890–1960, vol. V
Adams, Alexander Annan, 1884–1955, vol. V
Adams, Air Vice-Marshal Alexander Annan, 1908–1990, vol. VIII
Adams, Hon. Alexander Samuel, 1861–1937, vol. III
Adams, Allen; see Adams, Allender S.
Adams, Allender Steele, (Allen), 1946–1990, vol. VIII
Adams, Rev. Arthur, 1852–1926, vol. II
Adams, Arthur Henry, 1872–1936, vol. III
Adams, Sir Arthur Robert, 1861–1937, vol. III
Adams, Beale, died 1939, vol. III
Adams, Bernard, died 1965, vol. VI
Adams, Brooks, 1848–1927, vol. II
Adams, Captain Bryan Fullerton, 1887–1971, vol VII
Adams, Charles Edward, 1870–1945, vol. IV
Adams, Charles Francis, 1835–1915, vol. I
Adams, Charles Kingsley, 1899–1971, vol. VII
Adams, Colin Wallace Maitland, 1928–1990, vol. VIII
Adams, Air Cdre Cyril Douglas, 1897–1988, vol. VIII
Adams, Dartrey; see Adams, H. D. C.
Adams, David, 1871–1943, vol. IV
Adams, David Morgan, 1875–1942, vol. IV
Adams, Miss E. Proby, died 1945, vol. IV
Adams, Ephraim Douglass, 1865–1930, vol. III
Adams, Sir Ernest Charles, 1886–1974, vol. VII
Adams, Col Francis, 1874–1945, vol. IV
Adams, Sir Francis Boyd, 1888–1974, vol. VII
Adams, Rev. Francis John, 1858–1929, vol. III
Adams, Frank; see Adams, J. F.
Adams, Frank Dawson, 1859–1942, vol. IV
Adams, Frederick James, 1885–1957, vol. V
Adams, George Burton, 1851–1925, vol. II
Adams, George Francis, 1870–1921, vol. II
Adams, Col Gofton Gee, 1861–1936, vol. III
Adams, Sir Grantley Herbert, 1898–1971, vol. VII
Adams, Major Sir Hamilton John G.; see Goold-Adams.
Adams, (Harold) Richard, 1912–1978, vol. VII
Adams, Harry William, 1868–1947, vol. IV
Adams, Henry, 1846–1935, vol. III
Adams, Henry Carter, 1851–1921, vol. II
Adams, Henry Charles, 1873–1952, vol. V
Adams, Col Sir Henry Edward Fane G.; see Goold-Adams.
Adams, Captain Henry George Homer, 1879–1960, vol. V
Adams, Ven. Henry Joseph, 1870–1946, vol. IV

Adams, Comdr Henry William Allen, 1884–1962, vol. VI
Adams, Herbert, 1858–1945, vol. IV
Adams, Herbert, 1874–1958, vol. V
Adams, Herbert Louis, 1910–1972, vol. VII
Adams, (Howard) Dartrey (Charles), 1897–1958, vol. V
Adams, James Alexander, died 1930, vol. III
Adams, James Elwin Cokayne, 1876–1961, vol. VI
Adams, James Truslow, 1878–1949, vol. IV
Adams, James Whyte Leitch, 1909–1983, vol. VIII
Adams, Rev. James Williams, 1839–1903, vol. I
Adams, Comdr Sir Jameson Boyd, 1880–1962, vol. VI
Adams, Sir John, 1857–1934, vol. III
Adams, John, 1872–1950, vol. IV
Adams, Sir John Bertram, 1920–1984, vol. VIII
Adams, Sir John Coode-, 1859–1934, vol. III
Adams, J(ohn) Frank, 1930–1989, vol. VIII
Adams, Ven. John Michael G.; see Goold-Adams.
Adams, Rt Hon. John Michael Geoffrey Manningham, 1931–1985, vol. VIII
Adams, John Roland, 1894–1961, vol. VI
Adams, (John) Roland, 1900–1983, vol. VIII
Adams, Captain Joseph Ebenezer, 1878–1926, vol. II
Adams, Joseph Robert George, 1859–1919, vol. II
Adams, Katharine; see Webb, Katharine.
Adams, Louis, 1853–1931, vol. III
Adams, Marcus Algernon, 1875–1959, vol. V
Adams, Mary Grace Agnes, 1898–1984, vol. VIII
Adams, Sir Maurice Edward, 1901–1982, vol. VIII
Adams, Col Noel Percy, 1882–1954, vol. V
Adams, Paul, 1903–1972, vol. VII
Adams, Philip Edward Homer, 1879–1948, vol. IV
Adams, Rev. Reginald Arthur, 1864–1939, vol. III
Adams, Rev. Reginald Samuel, died 1928, vol. II
Adams, Richard; see Adams, H. R.
Adams, Richard, 1846–1908, vol. I
Adams, Robert, 1917–1984, vol. VIII
Adams, Maj.-Gen. Sir Robert Bellew, 1856–1928, vol. II
Adams, Roland; see Adams, J. R.
Adams, Rev. Canon Samuel Trerice, died 1936, vol. III
Adams, Samuel Vyvyan Trerice, 1900–1951, vol. V
Adams, Sherman, 1899–1986, vol. VIII
Adams, Sidney Herbert; see Sidney, Herbert.
Adams, Stanley John, 1893–1965, vol. VI
Adams, Stephen; see Maybrick, Michael.
Adams, Sydney, 1905–1980, vol. VII
Adams, Sir Theodore Samuel, 1885–1961, vol. VI
Adams, Thomas, died 1929, vol. III
Adams, Thomas, 1871–1940, vol. III
Adams, Sir Walter, 1906–1975, vol. VII
Adams, Most Rev. Walter Robert, 1877–1957, vol. V
Adams, Walter Sydney, 1876–1956, vol. V
Adams, Wilfrid George, 1885–1936, vol. III
Adams, William B.; see Bridges-Adams.
Adams, William Dacres, 1864–1951, vol. V
Adams, William Davenport, 1851–1904, vol. I
Adams, William George Stewart, 1874–1966, vol. VI
Adams, William Grylls, 1836–1915, vol. I
Adams, William Henry, 1844–1928, vol. II, vol. III

Adams, Rev. Canon William John Telia Phythian P.; see Phythian-Adams.

Adams, Rear-Adm. William Leslie Graham, 1901–1963, vol. VI

Adams, William Thomas, 1884–1949, vol. IV

Adams-Acton, Gladstone Murray, 1886–1971, vol. VII

Adams-Beck, John Melliar, 1909–1979, vol. VII

Adams-Connor, Captain Harry George, 1859–1939, vol. III

Adamson, Very Rev. Alexander Campbell, 1921–1983, vol. VIII

Adamson, Lt-Col Charles Henry Ellison, 1846–1930, vol. III

Adamson, Estelle Inez Ommanney, 1910–1990, vol. VIII

Adamson, Sir Harvey, 1854–1941, vol. IV

Adamson, Col Henry Mackenzie, 1861–1939, vol. III

Adamson, Horatio George, 1865–1955, vol. V

Adamson, Mrs Jennie Laurel, died 1962, vol. VI

Adamson, John, 1865–1918, vol. II

Adamson, John, 1886–1969, vol. VI

Adamson, Sir John Ernest, 1867–1950, vol. IV

Adamson, John Evans, 1884–1961, vol. VI

Adamson, Col John George, 1855–1932, vol. III

Adamson, John William, 1857–1947, vol. IV

Adamson, Joy-Friederike Victoria, 1910–1980, vol. VII

Adamson, Sir Kenneth Thomas, 1904–1976, vol. VII

Adamson, Lawrence Arthur, 1860–1932, vol. III

Adamson, Robert, 1852–1902, vol. I

Adamson, Lt-Col and Hon. Col Robert Hay, 1869–1936, vol. III

Adamson, Robert Stephen, 1885–1965, vol. VI

Adamson, William, 1830–1910, vol. I

Adamson, Sir William, 1832–1917, vol. II

Adamson, Rt Hon. William, 1863–1936, vol. III

Adamson, William Murdoch, 1881–1945, vol. IV

Adcock, (Arthur) St John, 1864–1930, vol. III

Adcock, Sir Frank Ezra, 1886–1968, vol. VI

Adcock, Sir Hugh, 1847–1920, vol. II

Adcock, St John; see Adcock, A. St J.

Adcock, Sir Robert Henry, 1899–1990, vol. VIII

Addams, Jane, 1860–1935, vol. III

Addams Williams, Christopher, 1877–1944, vol. IV

Adderley, Sir Augustus John, 1835–1905, vol. I

Adderley, Hubert John Broughton-, 1860–1931, vol. III

Adderley, Hon. and Rev. James Granville, 1861–1942, vol. IV

Adderley, Hon. Reginald Edmund, 1857–1934, vol. III

Addington, 2nd Baron, 1842–1915, vol. I

Addington, 3rd Baron, 1883–1966, vol. VI

Addington, 4th Baron, 1884–1971, vol. VII

Addington, 5th Baron, 1930–1982, vol. VIII

Addinsell, Richard Stewart, 1904–1977, vol. VII

Addis, Sir Charles Stewart, 1861–1945, vol. IV

Addis, Sir John Mansfield, 1914–1983, vol. VIII

Addis, Sir William, 1901–1978, vol. VII

Addis, Rev. William Edward, 1844–1917, vol. II

Addison, 1st Viscount, 1869–1951, vol. V

Addison, 2nd Viscount, 1904–1976, vol. VII

Addison, Adm. Sir (Albert) Percy, 1875–1952, vol. V

Addison, D'Arcy Wentworth, 1872–1955, vol. V

Addison, Air Vice-Marshal Edward Barker, 1898–1987, vol. VIII

Addison, Maj.-Gen. George Henry, 1876–1964, vol. VI

Addison, Sir James, 1879–1949, vol. IV

Addison, John Edmund Wentworth, 18380–1907, vol. I

Addison, Sir Joseph, 1879–1953, vol. V

Addison, Brig. Leonard Joseph Lancelot, 1902–1975, vol. VII

Addison, Margaret E. T., 1868–1940, vol. III(A), vol. IV

Addison, Oswald Lacy, 1874–1942, vol. IV

Addison, Adm. Sir Percy; see Addison, Adm. Sir A. P.

Addison, Hon. William, 1890–1966, vol. VI

Addison, William Innes, 1857–1912, vol. I

Addison, Rev. William Robert Fountaine, died 1962, vol. VI

Addison-Smith, Chilton Lind, 1875–1955, vol. V

Addison-Smith, George Lind, 1870–1934, vol. III

Addleshaw, Very Rev. George William Outram, 1906–1982, vol. VIII

Addleshaw, John Lawrence, 1902–1989, vol. VIII

Addy, Sidney Oldall, 1848–1933, vol. III

Adeane, Baron (Life Peer); Michael Edward Adeane, 1910–1984, vol. VIII

Adeane, Charles Robert Whorwood, 1863–1943, vol. IV

Adeane, Col Sir Robert Philip Wyndham, 1905–1979, vol. VII

Adeler, Max, (Charles Heber Clark), 1841–1915, vol. I

Adenauer, Konrad, 1876–1967, vol. VI

Adeney, Bernard, died 1966, vol. VI

Adeney, Walter Frederick, 1849–1920, vol. II

Aderemi I; see Ife.

Adermann, Rt Hon. Sir Charles Frederick, 1896–1979, vol. VII

Adey, (Arthur) Victor, 1912–1990, vol. VIII

Adey, Victor; see Adey, A. V.

Adey, William James, 1874–1956, vol. V

Adie, Edward Percival, 1890–1977, vol. VII

Adie, William John, 1886–1935, vol. III

Adie-Shepherd, Harold Richard Bowman, 1904–1979, vol. VII

Adjaye, Sir Edward; see Asafu-Adaye.

Adkin, Harry Kenrick K.; see Knight-Adkin.

Adkin, Rev. Walter Kenrick K.; see Knight-Adkin.

Adkins, Sir Ryland; see Adkins, Sir W. R. D.

Adkins, Sir (William) Ryland Dent, 1862–1925, vol. II

Adlam, George Henry Joseph, 1876–1946, vol. IV

Adlam, Lt-Col Tom Edwin, 1893–1975, vol. VII

Adler, Alfred, 1870–1937, vol. III

Adler, Cyrus, 1863–1940, vol. III

Adler, Elkan Nathan, 1861–1946, vol. IV

Adler, Felix, 1851–1933, vol. III

Adler, Very Rev. Hermann, 1839–1911, vol. I

Adler, Lawrence James, 1931–1988, vol. VIII

Adler, Rev. Michael, 1868–1944, vol. IV

Adler, Miss N., died 1950, vol. IV

Adler, Saul, 1895–1966, vol. VI

Adlercron, Brig.-Gen. Rodolph Ladeveze, 1873–1966, vol. VI

Adoo, Juius S.; *see* Sarkodee-Adoo.

Adorian, Paul, 1905–1983, vol. VIII

Adrian, 1st Baron, 1889–1977, vol. VII

Adrian, Alfred Douglas, 1845–1922, vol. II

Adrian, Frederick Obadiah, 1836–1909, vol. I

Adrian, Lady; (Hester Agnes), 1899–1966, vol. VI

Adrian, Max, 1903–1973, vol. VII

Adshead, Prof. Stanley Davenport, 1868–1946, vol. IV

Ady, Julia, (Mrs Henry Ady), *died* 1924, vol. II

Adye, Frederick James, 1874–1945, vol. IV

Adye, Maj.-Gen. Sir John, 1857–1930, vol. III

Adye, Gen. Sir John (Miller), 1819–1900, vol. I

Adye, Col Walter, 1858–1915, vol. I

Æ; *see* Russell, G.W.

Aehrenthal, Count Alois, 1854–1912, vol. I

Aelen, Most Rev. John, 1853–1929, vol. III

Aeron-Thomas, Gwilym Ewart, 1885–1958, vol. V

Affleck, Sir Frederick Danby James, 8th Bt, 1856–1939, vol. III

Affleck, Sir James Ormiston, *died* 1922, vol. II

Affleck, John Barr, 1878–1941, vol. IV

Affleck, Sir Robert, 7th Bt, 1852–1919, vol. II

Afghanistan, Ameer of; *see* Abdulrahman Khan.

Aflalo, Frederick George, 1870–1918, vol. II

Afsur-Ul-Mulk, Afsur-ud-Dowla, Afsur Jung, Mirza Mahomed Ali Beg, Khan Bahadur, Nawab, Maj.-Gen., *died* 1930, vol. III

Aga Khan (III), HH Rt Hon. Aga Sultan Sir Mohomed Shah, 1877–1957, vol. V

Agar, Sir Arthur Kirwan, 1877–1942, vol. IV

Agar, Captain Augustus Willington Shelton, 1890–1968, vol. VI

Agar, Charles Phipp, 1886–1963, vol. VI

Agar, Col Edward, 1859–1930, vol. III

Agar, Sir Francis, 1859–1934, vol. III

Agar, Hon. Francis William Arthur, 1873–1936, vol. III

Agar, Herbert Sebastian, 1897–1980, vol. VII

Agar, Lt-Col John Arnold Shelton, *died* 1951, vol. V

Agar, Wilfred Eade, 1882–1951, vol. V

Agar-Robartes, Hon. Thomas Charles Reginald, 1880–1915, vol. I

Agarwala, Sir Clifford Manmohan, 1890–1964, vol. VI

Agassiz, Alexander, 1835–1910, vol. I

Agate, James Evershed, 1877–1947, vol. IV

Aggey, Most Rev. John Kwao Amuzu, 1908–1972, vol. VII

Aghnides, Thanassis, 1889–1984, vol. VIII

Aglen, Anthony John, 1911–1984, vol. VIII

Aglen, Ven. Anthony Stocker, 1836–1908, vol. I

Aglen, Sir Francis Arthur, 1869–1932, vol. III

Aglen, John; *see* Aglen, A. J.

Aglionby, Col Arthur, 1832–1911, vol. I

Aglionby, Rev. Canon Francis Keyes, 1848–1937, vol. III

Aglionby, Rt Rev. John Orfeur, 1884–1963, vol. VI

Agnew, Alan Graeme, 1887–1962, vol. V

Agnew, Sir Andrew, 1882–1955, vol. V

Agnew, Sir Andrew Noel, 9th Bt (*cr* 1629), 1850–1928, vol. II

Agnew, (Sir) Fulque Melville Gerald Noel, 10th Bt (*cr* 1629), 1900–1975, vol. VII

Agnew, Sir George William, 2nd Bt (*cr* 1895), 1852–1941, vol. IV

Agnew, Sir Geoffrey William Gerald, 1908–1986, vol. VIII

Agnew, Comdr Hugh Ladas, 1894–1975, vol. VII

Agnew, Hon. Sir James Wilson, 1815–1901, vol. I

Agnew, Hon. John Hume, 1863–1908, vol. I

Agnew, Sir John Stuart, 3rd Bt (*cr* 1895), 1879–1957, vol. V

Agnew, Sir Norris Montgomerie, 1895–1973, vol. VII

Agnew, Sir Patrick Dalreagle, 1868–1925, vol. II

Agnew, Comdr Sir Peter Garnett, 1st Bt, 1900–1990, vol. VIII

Agnew, Philip Leslie, 1863–1938, vol. III

Agnew, Col Quentin Graham Kinnaird, 1861–1937, vol. III

Agnew, Sir Robert David Garrick, 1930–1987, vol. VIII

Agnew, Sir Stair, 1831–1916, vol. II

Agnew, Sir William, 1st Bt (*cr* 1895), 1825–1910, vol. I

Agnew, Vice-Adm. Sir William Gladstone, 1898–1960, vol. V

Agnew, William Lockett, 1858–1918, vol. II

Agnew, Sir William Thomas Fischer, 1847–1903, vol. I

Agnon, Shmuel Yosef Halevi, 1888–1970, vol. VI

Agostini, L. E., 1858–1918, vol. II

Agron, Gershon, 1893–1959, vol. V

Agronsky, Gershon; *see* Agron, G.

Aguet, Gustave Charles, *died* 1927, vol. II

Ahearne, Christopher Dominic, 1886–1964, vol. VI

Ahern, Maj.-Gen. Donal Maurice, 1911–1966, vol. VI

Ahern, Maj.-Gen. Timothy Michael Richard, 1908–1980, vol. VII

Aherne, Rev. David, 1871–1941, vol. IV

Ahlefeldt-Laurvig, Count Preben Ferdinand, 1872–1946, vol. IV

Ahlmann, Hans Wilhelmson, 1889–1974, vol. VII

Ahmad, Hon. Ahsanuddin, 1849–1918, vol. II

Admad, Maulvi Sir Nizam-ud-Din-Niwab Nizamat Jung Bahadur, 1871–1955, vol. V

Ahmad, Maulvi Sir Rafiuddin, 1865–1954, vol. V

Admad, Sir Zia-Uddin, 1879–1947, vol. IV

Admad Khan, Sardar Sahibzada Sir Sultan, 1864–1936, vol. III

Admed, Fakhruddin Ali, 1905–1977, vol. VII

Ahmed, Kabeerud-Din, 1888–1939, vol. III(A), vol. IV

Ahmed, Sir Syed Sultan, 1880–1963, vol. VI

Aicard, Jean, 1848–1921, vol. II

Aickin, Very Rev. George Ellis, *died* 1937, vol. III

Aickin, Hon. Sir Keith Arthur, 1916–1982, vol. VIII

Aickin, Thomas Reginald, 1886–1948, vol. IV(A)

Aidé, Charles Hamilton, 1826–1906, vol. I

Aiers, David Pascoe, 1922–1983, vol. VIII

Aiken, Conrad Potter, 1889–1973, vol. VII

Aiken, Frank, 1898–1983, vol. VIII

Aiken, John Elliott, 1909–1971, vol. VII

Aiken, John Macdonald, *died* 1961, vol. VI

Aikenhead, Brig. David Francis, 1895–1955, vol. V

Aikins, Hon. Sir James Albert Manning, 1851–1929, vol. III

Aikman, Sir Alexander, 1886–1968, vol. VI

Aikman, David Wann, 1863–1931, vol. III

Aikman, George, 1830–1905, vol. I

Aikman, Robert Gordon, 1905–1962, vol. VI

Aikman, Sir Robert Smith, 1844–1917, vol. II

Aikman, Col Thomas S. G. H. Robertson-, 1860–1948, vol. IV

Ailesbury, 5th Marquess of, 1842–1911, vol. I

Ailesbury, 6th Marquess of, 1873–1961, vol. VI

Ailesbury, 7th Marquess of, 1904–1974, vol. VII

Ailsa, 3rd Marquess of, 1847–1938, vol. III

Ailsa, 4th Marquess of, 1872–1943, vol. IV

Ailsa, 5th Marquess of, 1875–1956, vol. V

Ailsa, 6th Marquess of, 1882–1957, vol. V

Ailwyn, 1st Baron, 1855–1924, vol. II

Ailwyn, 2nd Baron, 1886–1936, vol. III

Ailwyn, 3rd Baron, 1887–1976, Vol. VII

Ailwyn, 4th Baron, 1896–1988, vol. VIII

Ainger, Rev. Alfred, 1837–1904, vol. I

Ainger, Arthur Campbell, 1841–1919, vol. II

Ainley, Eric Stephen, 1918–1986, vol. VIII

Ainley, Henry Hinchcliffe, 1879–1945, vol. IV

Ainley-Walker, Ernest William, 1871–1955, vol. V

Ainscough, Sir Thomas Martland, 1886–1976, vol. VII

Ainsley, John William, 1899–1976, vol. VII

Ainslie, Ainslie Douglas, 1838–1929, vol. III

Ainslie, Ven. Alexander Colvin, *died* 1903, vol. I

Ainslie, Lt-Col Charles Marshall, 1878–1940, vol. III

Ainslie, Charlotte, 1863–1960, vol. V

Ainslie, Grant Duff Douglas, 1865–1948, vol. IV

Ainslie, Lt-Col Henry Sandys, 1869–1948, vol. IV

Ainslie, James Percival, 1899–1973, vol. VII

Ainslie, Rev. Richard Montague, 1858–1924, vol. II

Ainsworth, Alfred Richard, 1879–1959, vol. V

Ainsworth, Bt Col Charles, 1874–1956, vol. V

Ainsworth, David, 1842–1906, vol. I

Ainsworth, Harry, 1888–1965, vol. VI

Ainsworth, John, 1864–1946, vol. IV

Ainsworth, Sir John Francis, 3rd Bt, 1912–1981, vol. VIII

Ainsworth, Sir John Stirling, 1st Bt, 1844–1923, vol. II

Ainsworth, Maj.-Gen. Sir Ralph Bignell, 1875–1952, vol. V

Ainsworth, Mrs Robert; *see* Brunskill, Muriel.

Ainsworth, Sir Thomas, 2nd Bt, 1886–1971, vol. VII

Ainsworth, Lt-Col William John, 1873–1945, vol. IV

Ainsworth-Davis, James Richard, 1861–1934, vol. III

Ainsworth-Davis, John Creyghton, 1895–1976, vol. VII

Ainsworth Dickson, Thomas, 1881–1935, vol. III

Aird, Ian, 1905–1962, vol. VI

Aird, Sir John, 1st Bt, 1833–1911, vol. I

Aird, Sir John, 2nd Bt, 1861–1934, vol. III

Aird, Sir John, 1855–1938, vol. III

Aird, Col Sir John Renton, 3rd Bt, 1898–1973, vol. VII

Aird, Ronald, 1902–1986, vol. VIII

Airedale, 1st Baron, 1835–1911, vol. I

Airedale, 2nd Baron, 1863–1944, vol. IV

Airedale, 3rd Baron, 1882–1958, vol. V

Airey, Sir Edwin, 18780–1955, vol. V

Airey, Paymr Rear-Adm. Frederick W. I., 1861–1922, vol. II

Airey, Harold M.; *see* Morris-Airey.

Airey, Col Henry Parke, 1844–1911, vol. I

Airey, Sir James Talbot, 1812–1898, vol. I

Airey, John Robinson, *died* 1937, vol. III

Airey, Col Robert Berkeley, 1874–1933, vol. III

Airey, Lt-Gen. Sir Terence Sydney, 1900–1983, vol. VIII

Airlie, 8th Earl of, 1856–1900, vol. I

Airlie, 12th (*de facto* 9th) Earl of, 1893–1968, vol. VI

Airlie, Countess of; (Mabell Frances Elizabeth), 1866–1956, vol. V

Airy, Anna, 1882–1964, vol. VI

Airy, Rev. Basil Reginald, 1845–1924, vol. II

Airy, Osmund, 1845–1928, vol. III

Airy, Wilfrid, *died* 1925, vol. II

Aitchison, Rt Hon. Lord; Craigie Mason Aitchison, 1882–1941, vol. IV

Aitchison, Gen. Charles Terrington, 1825–1919, vol. II

Aitchison, Craigie Mason; *see* Aitchison, Rt Hon. Lord.

Aitchison, Sir David, 1892–1975, vol. VII

Aitchison, George, 1825–1910, vol. I

Aitchison, George, 1877–1954, vol. V

Aitchison, James, 1899–1968, vol. VI

Aitchison, James Edward Tierney, 1835–1898, vol. I

Aitchison, Patrick Edward, 1881–1945, vol. IV

Aitchison, Sir Stephen, 1st Bt, 1863–1942, vol. IV

Aitchison, Sir Stephen Charles de Lancey, 3rd Bt, 1923–1958, vol. V

Aitchison, Sir Walter de Lancey, 2nd Bt, 1892–1953, vol. V

Aitken, Alexander Craig, 1895–1967, vol. VI

Aitken, Sir Arthur Percival Hay, (Sir Peter Aitken), 1905–1984, vol. VIII

Aitken, Rt Rev. Aubrey; *see* Aitken, Rt Rev. W. A.

Aitken, Cecil Edward, 1888–1959, vol. V

Aitken, Charles, 1869–1936, vol. III

Aitken, Edward Hamilton, 1851–1909, vol. I

Aitken, George Atherton, 1860–1917, vol. II

Aitken, George Benjamin Johnston, *died* 1942, vol. IV

Aitken, George Lewis, 1864–1940, vol. III

Aitken, Henry, 1851–1931, vol. III

Aitken, Ian Hugh, 1919–1986, vol. VIII

Aitken, Hon. J. G. W., *died* 1921, vol. II

Aitken, Sir James, 1880–1948, vol. IV

Aitken, James Hume, 1890–1955, vol. V

Aitken, Janet Kerr, 1886–1982, vol. VIII

Aitken, John, *died* 1919, vol. II

Aitken, John E., *died* 1957, vol. V

Aitken, John Hobson, 1851–1923, vol. II

Aitken, Col John James, 1878–1946, vol. IV

Aitken, Sir (John William) Max, 2nd Bt, 1910–1985, vol. VIII

Aitken, Sir Max; *see* Aitken, Sir J. W. M.

Aitken, Major Nigel Woodford, 1882–1963, vol. VI

Aitken, Sir Peter; *see* Aitken, Sir A. P. H.

Aitken, Sir Robert, 1863–1924, vol. II

Aitken, Rev. Canon Robert Aubrey, 1870–1941, vol. IV

Aitken, Robert Grant, 1864–1951, vol. V

Aitken, Air Vice-Marshal (Robert) Stanley, 1896–1982, vol. VIII

Aitken, Air Vice-Marshal Stanley; see Aitken, Air Vice-Marshal R. S.

Aitken, Stephen Rowan, 1883–1943, vol. IV

Aitken, Col William, 1846–1917, vol. II

Aitken, Rt Rev. William Aubrey, 1911–1985, vol. VIII

Aitken, Rev. William Hay Macdowall Hunter, 1841–1927, vol. II

Aitken, Sir William Traven, 1905–1964, vol. VI

Aiton, Sir Arthur; see Aiton, Sir J. A.

Aiton, Sir (John) Arthur, 1864–1950, vol. IV

Aiyangar, Sir Venbakam B.; see Bashyam Aiyangar.

Aiyar, Sir C. P. R.; see Ramaswami Aiyar.

Aiyar, N. Chandrasekhara, 1888–1957, vol. V

Aiyar, Sir Theagaraja; see Sadasiva Aiyar.

Aiyer, Sir Pazhamarneri Sundaram Sivaswamy, 1864–1946, vol. IV

Ajasa, Sir Kitoyi, 1866–1937, vol. III

Akbar, Hon. M. T., 1880–1944, vol. IV(A)

Aked, Charles Frederic, 1864–1941, vol. IV

Akeley, Carl Ethan, 1864–1926, vol. II

Akenhead, David, 1894–1978, vol. VII

Akenhead, Rev. Edmund, died 1931, vol. III

Akerman, John Camille, died 1950, vol. IV

Akerman, Hon. Sir John William, 1825–1905, vol. I

Akerman, Air Vice-Marshal Walter Joseph Martin, 1901–1964, vol. VI

Akerman, Maj.-Gen. William Philip Jopp, 1888–1971, vol. VII

Akers, Sir Wallace Alan, 1888–1954, vol. V

Akhurst, Captain Algernon Frederic, 1893–1972, vol. VII

Akrill-Jones, Rev. Canon David, 1868–1945, vol. IV

Alabaster, Sir Chaloner, 1838–1898, vol. I

Alabaster, Sir Chaloner Grenville, 1880–1958, vol. V

Alagappa Chettiar, Sir Ramanatha, 1909–1957, vol. V

Alam, Hon. Anthony Alexander, 1898–1983, vol. VIII

Alanbrooke, 1st Viscount, 1883–1963, vol. VI

Alanbrooke, 2nd Viscount, 1920–1972, vol. VII

Alba, 17th Duque de, 1878–1953, vol. V

Alban, Sir Frederick John, 1882–1965, vol. VI

Alban Davies, Jenkin, 1901–1968, vol. VI

Albanesi, Mme, (Effie Henderson), 1859–1936, vol. III

Albani, Dame Emma, 1852–1930, vol. III

Albee, Ernest, 1865–1927, vol. II

Albemarle, 8th Earl of, 1858–1942, vol. IV

Albemarle, 9th Earl of, 1882–1979, vol. VII

Albert-Buisson, François, 1881–1961, vol. VI

Albertini, Luigi, 1871–1941, vol. IV

Alberts, Col Johannes Joachim, 1872–1947, vol. IV

Albery, Sir Bronson James, 1881–1971, vol. VII

Albery, Sir Donald Arthur Rolleston, 1914–1988, vol. VIII

Albery, Sir Irving James, 1879–1967, vol. VI

Albery, Michael James, 1910–1975, vol. VII

Albrecht, Ralph Gerhart, 1896–1985, vol. VIII

Albright, George Stacey, 1855–1945, vol. IV

Albright, William Foxwell, 1891–1971, vol. VII

Albu, Sir George, 1st Bt, 1857–1935, vol. III

Albu, Major Sir George Werner, 2nd Bt, 1905–1963, vol. VI

Albu, Leopold, died 1938, vol. III

Alcazar, Sir Henry Albert, 1860–1930, vol. III

Alchin, Gordon, died 1947, vol. IV

Alcock, Lt-Col Alfred William, 1859–1933, vol. III

Alcock, Charles William, 1842–1907, vol. I

Alcock, Henry, 1886–1948, vol. IV

Alcock, Rev. Preb. John Mark, died 1955, vol. V

Alcock, Captain Sir John William, 1892–1919, vol. II

Alcock, Nathaniel Henry, 1871–1913, vol. I

Alcock, Reginald, 1868–1944, vol. IV

Alcock, Sir Rutherford, 1809–1897, vol. I

Alcock, Sir Walter Galpin, 1861–1947, vol. IV

Alcorn, George Oscar, 1850–1930, vol. III

Aldam, Col William St Andrew W.; see Warde-Aldam.

Aldanov, Mark, 1889–1957, vol. V

Alden, Henry Mills, 1836–1919, vol. II

Alden, John Hewlett, 1900–1976, vol. VII

Alden, Sir Percy, 1865–1944, vol. IV

Aldenham, 1st Baron, 1819–1907, vol. I

Aldenham, 2nd Baron, 1846–1936, vol. III

Aldenham, 3rd Baron, 1879–1939, vol. III

Aldenham, 4th Baron, and Hunsdon of Hunsdon, 2nd Baron, 1888–1969, vol. VI

Aldenham, 5th Baron, 1922–1986, vol. VIII

Alder, Kurt, 1902–1958, vol. V

Alder, Wilfred, died 1962, vol. VI

Alderdice, Hon. Frederick Charles, 1872–1936, vol. III

Alderman, Edwin Anderson, 1861–1931, vol. III

Alderman, Harry Graham, 1895–1962, vol. VI

Alderman, Major Robert Edward, 1887–1934, vol. III

Alderman, Col Walter William, 1874–1935, vol. III

Aldersey, Captain Ralph, 1890–1971, vol. VII

Alderson, Rt Rev. Cecil William, 1900–1968, vol. VI

Alderson, Sir Charles Henry, 1831–1913, vol. I

Alderson, Sir Edward Hall, 1864–1951, vol. V

Alderson, Lt-Gen. Sir Edwin Alfred Hervey, 1859–1927, vol. II

Alderson, Rev. Frederick Cecil, 1836–1907, vol.I

Alderson, Sir George Beeton, 1844–1926, vol. II

Alderson, Sir Harold George, 1891–1978, vol. VII

Alderson, Michael Rowland, 1931–1988, vol. VIII

Alderson, Vice-Adm. William John Standly, died 1946, vol. IV

Alderton, George Edwin Lisle, 1888–1969, vol. VI(AII)

Aldham, Rev. Canon Vernon Harcourt, 1843–1929, vol. III

Aldin, Cecil Charles Windsor, 1870–1935, vol. III

Aldington, Charles, 1862–1922, vol. II

Aldington, Hubert Edward, 1883–1967, vol. VI

Aldington, John Norman, 1905–1987, vol. VIII

Aldington, Richard, 1892–1962, vol. VI

Aldous, Guy Travers, 1906–1981, vol. VIII

Aldred-Brown, George Ronald Pym, 1896–1946, vol. IV

Aldren Turner, John William; see Turner.

Aldrich, Gertrude; see Lawrence, G.

Aldrich, Adm. Pelham, 1844–1930, vol. III

Aldrich, Thomas Bailey, 1836–1906, vol. I

Aldrich, Winthrop Williams, 1885–1974, vol. VII

Aldrich-Blake, Dame Louisa Brandreth, 1865–1925, vol. II

Aldridge, Lt-Col Arthur Russell, 1864–1947, vol. IV

Aldridge, Sir Frederick, 1891–1966, vol. VI

Aldridge, John Arthur Malcolm, 1905–1983, vol. VIII

Aldridge, Major John Barttelot, 1871–1909, vol. I

Aldridge, Very Rev. John Mullings, *died* 1920, vol. II

Aldridge, Leonard, 1892–1952, vol. V

Aldworth, Lt-Col William, 1855–1900, vol. I

Alec-Smith, Col Rupert Alexander, 1913–1983, vol. VIII

Aleixandre, Vicente Pio Marcelino Cirilo, 1898–1984, vol. VIII

Alekhine, Alexander; *see* Alekhine, A. A.

Alekhine, (Aljechin) Alexander, 1892–1946, vol. IV

Alers Hankey, Richard Lyons, 1906–1969, vol. VI

Alexander of Hillsborough, 1st Earl, 1885–1965, vol. VI

Alexander of Hillsborough, Countess; (Esther Ellen), 1877–1969, vol. VI

Alexander of Tunis, 1st Earl, 1891–1969, vol. VI

Alexander, Mrs; *see* Hector, Annie Alexander.

Alexander, Alexander, 1849–1928, vol. II

Alexander, Rev. Archibald, 1874–1942, vol. IV

Alexander, Rev. Archibald Browning Drysdale, 1855–1931, vol. III

Alexander, Arthur Harvey, 1843–1905, vol. I

Alexander, Col Aubrey de Vere, 1849–1923, vol. II

Alexander, Boyd, 1873–1910, vol. I

Alexander, Lt-Col Boyd Francis, 1834–1917, vol. II

Alexander, Charles, *see* Alexander, R. C.

Alexander, Brig.-Gen. Charles Henry, 1856–1946, vol. IV

Alexander, Charles McCallon, 1867–1920, vol. II

Alexander, Rear-Adm. Charles Otway, 1888–1970, vol. VI

Alexander, Maj.-Gen. Sir Claud, 1st Bt (*cr* 1886), 1831–1899, vol. I

Alexander, Sir Claud, 2nd Bt (*cr* 1886), 1867–1945, vol. IV

Alexander, Conel Hugh O'Donel, 1909–1974, vol. VII

Alexander, Conel W. O'D. L., 1879–1920, vol. II

Alexander, Cyril Wilson, 1879–1947, vol. IV

Alexander, Sir Darnley Arthur Raymond, 1920–1989, vol. VIII

Alexander, David, *died* 1944, vol. IV

Alexander, David, 1906–1972, vol. VII

Alexander, David Lindo, 1842–1922, vol. II

Alexander, Sir Desmond William Lionel C.; *see* Cable-Alexander.

Alexander, Sir Douglas, 1st Bt (*cr* 1921), 1864–1949, vol. IV

Alexander, Sir Douglas Hamilton, 2nd Bt, 1900–1983, vol. VIII

Alexander, Major Dudley Henry, 1863–1931, vol. III

Alexander, Duncan Hubert David, 1911–1985, vol. VIII

Alexander, Edward Bruce, 1872–1955, vol. V

Alexander, Maj.-Gen. Edward Currie, 1875–1964, vol. VI

Alexander, Edwin, 1870–1926, vol. II

Alexander, Eleanor Jane, *died* 1939, vol. III

Alexander, Ernest Edward, 1872–1946, vol. IV

Alexander, Maj.-Gen. Ernest Wright, 1870–1934, vol. III

Alexander, Lt-Col Francis David, 1878–1956, vol. V

Alexander, Sir Frank Samuel, 1st Bt (*cr* 1945), 1881–1959, vol. V

Alexander, Frederick Matthias, 1869–1955, vol. V

Alexander, Frederick William, 1859–1937, vol. III

Alexander, Sir George, 1858–1918, vol. II

Alexander, George Edward, 1865–1931, vol. III

Alexander, Gilchrist Gibb, 1871–1958, vol. V

Alexander, Harold Vincent, 1886–1950, vol. IV

Alexander, Col Harvey, 1859–1936, vol. III

Alexander, Lt-Col Heber Maitland, 1881–1942, vol. IV

Alexander, Henry, 1841–1914, vol. I

Alexander, Sir Henry, 1875–1940, vol. III

Alexander, Henry Clay, 1902–1969, vol. VI

Alexander, Henry Joachim, 1897–1988, vol. VIII

Alexander, Maj.-Gen. Henry Lethbridge, 1878–1944, vol. IV

Alexander, Maj.-Gen. Henry Templer, 1911–1977, vol. VII

Alexander, Herbert, 1874–1946, vol. IV

Alexander, Lt-Col Hon. Herbrand Charles, 1888–1965, vol. VI

Alexander, James Browning, 1888–1962, vol. VI

Alexander, Rt Hon. Sir James Ulick F. C.; *see* Alexander, Rt Hon. Sir Ulick.

Alexander, Very Rev. John, 1833–1908, vol. I

Alexander, Hon. John, 1876–1941, vol. IV

Alexander, Col John Donald, 1867–1922, vol. II

Alexander, John W., 1856–1915, vol. I

Alexander, Joseph Gundry, 1848–1918, vol. II

Alexander, Sir Lionel Cecil William, 6th Bt (*cr* 1809), 1885–1956, vol. V

Alexander, Lt-Col Maurice, 1889–1945, vol. IV

Alexander, Nell Haigh, 1915–1986, vol. VIII

Alexander, Peter, *died* 1969, vol. VI

Alexander, Reginald Gervase, 1859–1916, vol. II

Alexander, (Richard) Charles, 1884–1968, vol. VI

Alexander, Robert, *died* 1923, vol. II

Alexander, Lt-Col Robert Donald Thain, 1878–1969, vol. VI

Alexander, Robert Edward, 1874–1946, vol. IV

Alexander, Maj.-Gen. Ronald Okeden, 1888–1949, vol. IV

Alexander, Samuel, 1859–1938, vol. III

Alexander, Rev. Sidney Arthur, 1866–1948, vol. IV

Alexander, Sir Sidney Robert, 1863–1929, vol. III

Alexander, Stanley Walker, 1895–1980, vol. VII

Alexander, Thomas, *died* 1933, vol. III

Alexander, Thomas Hood Wilson, 1878–1941, vol. IV

Alexander, Rt Hon. Sir Ulick, 1889–1973, vol. VII

Alexander, Walter, 1895–1964, vol. VI

Alexander, Most Rev. William, 1824–1911, vol. I

Alexander, William, *died* 1921, vol. II

Alexander, Brig.-Gen. Sir William, 1874–1954, vol. V

Alexander, William Cleverly, 1840–1916, vol. II

Alexander, Rev. William Menzies, *died* 1929, vol. III

Alexander, Lt-Col William Nathaniel Stuart, 1874–1956, vol. V

Alexander, Col Hon. William Sigismund Patrick, 1895–1972, vol. VII
Alexander-Sinclair, Adm. Sir Edwyn Sinclair, 1865–1945, vol. IV
Alexander-Sinclair, John Alexis Clifford Cerda, 1906–1988, vol. VIII
Alexandrowicz, Charles Henry, 1902–1975, vol. VII
Alfieri, Ernest, 1864–1913, vol. I
Alfieri, Maj.-Gen. Frederick John 1892–1961, vol. VI
Alford, Rt Rev. Charles Richard, 1816–1898, vol. I
Alford, Rev. Preb. Charles Symes Leslie, 1885–1963, vol. VI
Alford, Sir Edward Fleet, 1850–1905, vol. I
Alford, (Edward) John (Gregory), 1890–1960, vol. V(A)
Alford, Lt-Col Henry, *died* 1955, vol. V
Alford, Rev. Henry Powell, *died* 1921, vol. II
Alford, John; *see* Alford, E. J. G.
Alford, Rev. Josiah George, 1847–1924, vol. II
Alford, Sir Robert Edmund, 1904–1979, vol. VII
Algar, Claudius Randleson, 1900–1988, vol. VIII
Algeo, Sir Arthur, 1903–1967, vol. VI
Alger, John Goldworth, 1836–1907, vol. I
Algie, Sir Ronald Macmillan, 1888–1978, vol. VII
Ali, Abdullah Yusuf, 1872–1953, vol. V
Ali, Khan Bahadur Nawab Sir Chaudri Fazal, *died* 1942, vol. IV
Ali, (Chaudri) Mohamad, 1905–1980, vol. VII
Ali, Mir Aula, *died* 1898, vol. I
Ali, Mohamad; *see* Ali, C. M.
Ali, Mohammed, 1909–1963, vol. VI
Ali, Rt Hon. (Syed) A.; *see* Ameer-Ali.
Ali, Syed Waris A.; *see* Ameer Ali.
Ali, Sir Torick A.; *see* Ameer Ali.
Ali Chowdhuri, Hon. Nawab Bahadur Syed Nawab, 1863–1929, vol. III
Ali-Rajpur, Raja of, 1881–1948, vol. IV(A), vol. V
Alice, HRH Princess; *see* Athlone, Countess of.
Alington, 1st Baron, 1825–1904, vol. I
Alington, 2nd Baron, 1859–1919, vol. II
Alington, 3rd Baron, 1896–1940, vol. III
Alington, Adrian Richard, 1895–1958, vol. V
Alington, Vice-Adm. Argentine Hugh, 1876–1945, vol. IV
Alington, Adm. Arthur Hildebrand, 1839–1925, vol. II
Alington, Very Rev. Cyril Argentine, 1872–1955, vol. V
Alington, Hon. Mrs Cyril, (Hester Margaret), 1874–1958, vol. V
Alington, Hon. Hester Margaret; *see* Alington, Hon. Mrs Cyril.
Alison, Sir Archibald, 2nd Bt, 1826–1907, vol. I
Alison, Sir Archibald, 3rd Bt, 1862–1921, vol. II
Alison, Comdr Sir Archibald, 4th Bt, 1888–1967, vol. VI
Alison, David, *died* 1955, vol. V
Alison, Sir Frederick Black, 5th Bt, 1893–1970, vol. VI
Alison, John, 1861–1952, vol. V
Alker, Thomas, 1904–1981, vol. VIII
Allan of Kilmahew, Baron (Life Peer); Robert Alexander Allan, 1914–1979, vol. VII
Allan, Albert, 1893–1948, vol. IV

Allan, Archibald Russell Watson, 1878–1959, vol. V
Allan, Arthur Percy, 1868–1927, vol. II
Allan, Charles Edward, 1861–1929, vol. III
Allan, Donald James, 1907–1978, vol. VII
Allan, Douglas Alexander, 1896–1967, vol. VI
Allan, F. L., 1893–1964, vol. VI
Allan, Francis John, 1858–1932, vol. III
Allan, George William, 1860–1940, vol. III
Allan, Sir Harold Egbert, 1894–1953, vol. V
Allan, Sir Henry Marshman H.; *see* Havelock-Allan.
Allan, Sir Henry Ralph Moreton H.; *see* Havelock-Allan.
Allan, Captain Henry Samuel, 1892–1979, vol. VII
Allan, Sir Henry Spencer Moreton H.; *see* Havelock-Allan.
Allan, Hugh A., 1857–1938, vol. III
Allan, Col Sir Hugh Montagu, 1860–1951, vol. V
Allan, Rev. J. B., 1873–1932, vol. III
Allan, Janet Laurie, 1892–1985, vol. VIII
Allan, Hon. John, 1866–1936, vol. III
Allan, John, *died* 1955, vol. V
Allan, John, 1927–1979, vol. VII
Allan, John Arthur Briscoe, 1911–1981, vol. VIII
Allan, Captain John Steele, 1889–1979, vol. VII (AII)
Allan, Maud, *died* 1956, vol. V
Allan, Philip Bertram Murray, 1884–1973, vol. VII
Allan, Sir Robert George, 1879–1972, vol. VII
Allan, Robert W., *died* 1942, vol. IV
Allan, Maj.-Gen. William, 1832–1918, vol. II
Allan, Sir William, 1837–1903, vol. I
Allan, Lt-Col William David, 1879–1961, vol. VI
Allan, William Nimmo, 1896–1984, vol. VIII
Allanby, Ven. Christopher Gibson, *died* 1917, vol. II
Allanson, Col Cecil John Lyons, 1877–1943, vol. IV
Allanson, Harry Llewelyn Lyons, 1876–1955, vol. V
Allard, Sir George Mason, 1866–1953, vol. V
Allard, Hon. Jules, 1859–1945, vol. IV
Allardyce, Elsie Elizabeth, (Lady Allardyce), *died* 1962, vol. VI
Allardyce, Brig. John Grahame Buchanan, 1878–1949, vol. IV
Allardyce, Robert Moir, 1882–1951, vol. V
Allardyce, Sir William Lamond, 1861–1930, vol. III
Allason, Maj.-Gen. Sir Richard B.; *see* Bannatine-Allason.
Allason, Brig.-Gen. Walter, 1875–1960, vol. V
Allberry, Albert Spenser, 1880–1949, vol. IV
Allbon, Charles F., 1856–1926, vol. II, vol. III
Allbutt, Rt Hon. Sir Clifford; *see* Allbutt, Rt Hon. Sir T. C.
Allbutt, Rt Hon. Sir (Thomas) Clifford, 1836–1925, vol. II
Allchin, Sir Geoffrey Cuthbert, 1895–1968, vol. VI
Allchin, Thomas, 1848–1936, vol. III
Allchin, Sir William Henry, 1846–1911, vol. I
Allcock, Rev. Arthur Edmund, 1851–1924, vol. II
Allcock, John Gladding Major, 1905–1986, vol. VIII
Allcott, Walter Herbert, 1880–1951, vol. V
Allcroft, Herbert John, 1865–1911, vol. I
Allcroft, Sir Philip M.; *see* Magnus-Allcroft.
Allden, John Eric, 1886–1949, vol. IV
Allderidge, Charles Donald, 1889–1958, vol. V
Alldis, Rev. Canon John, 1849–1930, vol. III
Alldridge, Thomas Joshua, 1847–1916, vol. II

Alldritt, Walter, 1918–1990, vol. VIII

Allegro, John Marco, 1923–1988, vol. VIII

Allen of Fallowfield, Baron (Life Peer); Alfred Walter Henry Allen, 1914–1985, vol. VIII

Allen of Hurtwood, 1st Baron, 1889–1939, vol. III

Allen of Hurtwood, Lady; (Marjory), 1897–1976, vol. VII

Allen, A. Stuart, 1890–1957, vol. V

Allen, Sir (Albert) George, 1888–1956, vol. V

Allen, Hon. Alfred Ernest, 1912–1987, vol. VIII

Allen, Brig.-Gen. Alfred James Whitacre, 1857–1939, vol. III

Allen, Arthur Acland, 1868–1939, vol. III

Allen, Arthur Cecil, 1887–1981, vol. VIII

Allen, Maj.-Gen. Arthur Samuel, 1894–1959, vol. V

Allen, Rev. Barten Wilcockson, *died* 1940, vol. III

Allen, Basil Copleston, 1870–1935, vol. III

Allen, Benjamin, 1845–1929, vol. III

Allen, Rear-Adm. Sir Bertram Cowles, 1875–1957, vol. V

Allen, Sir Carleton Kemp, 1887–1966, vol. VI

Allen, Lt-Col Carleton Woodford, 1878–1938, vol. III

Allen, Col Sir Charles, 1852–1920, vol. II

Allen, Air Vice-Marshal Charles Edward Hamilton, 1899–1975, vol. VII

Allen, Charles Francis Egerton, 1847–1927, vol. II

Allen, Major Rt Hon. Charles Peter, 1861–1930, vol. III

Allen, Charles Peter Selwyn, 1917–1977, vol. VII

Allen, Charles Turner, 1877–1958, vol. V

Allen, Clabon Walter, 1904–1987, vol. VIII

Allen, Clarence Edgar, 1871–1951, vol. V

Allen, Sir Denis; *see* Allen, Sir W. D.

Allen, Derek Fortrose, 1910–1975, vol. VII

Allen, Sir Donald Richard, 1894–1983, vol. VIII

Allen, Edgar Johnson, 1866–1942, vol. IV

Allen, Edgar Malpas, 1883–1967, vol. VI

Allen, Lt-Col Edward, 1859–1933, vol. III

Allen, Edward H.; *see* Heron-Allen.

Allen, Col Edward Watts, 1883–1965, vol. VI

Allen, Edwin Hopkins, 1878–1967, vol. VI

Allen, Ernest Joshua, 1871–1955, vol. V

Allen, Sir Ernest King, 1864–1937, vol. III

Allen, F. M.; *see* Downey, Edmund.

Allen, Sir Francis Raymond, 2nd Bt, 1910–1939, vol. III

Allen, Frank, 1874–1965, vol. VI

Allen, Sir Frederick Charles, 1st Bt, 1864–1934, vol. III

Allen, Frederick Lewis, 1890–1954, vol. V

Allen, Frederick Martin Brice, 1898–1972, vol. VII

Allen, Rt Rev. Geoffrey Francis, 1902–1982, vol. VIII

Allen, Sir George; *see* Allen, Sir A. G.

Allen, Engr Rear-Adm. George Bennett, 1888–1948, vol. IV

Allen, George Berney, 1862–1917, vol. II

Allen, George Cyril, 1900–1982, vol. VIII

Allen, Rev. George Kendall, 1883–1975, vol. VII

Allen, Sir George Oswald Browning, 1902–1989, vol. VIII

Allen, George Thomas, 1852–1940, vol. III

Allen, Sir George Vance, 1894–1970, vol. VI

Allen, Rt Rev. Gerald Burton, 1885–1956, vol. V

Allen, Godfrey; *see* Allen, W. G.

Allen, Grant, 1848–1899, vol. I

Allen, Rear-Adm. Hamilton Colclough, 1883–1964, vol. VI

Allen, Harold Major, 1911–1977, vol. VII

Allen, Harold Tuckwell, 1879–1950, vol. IV

Allen, Sir Harry Brookes, 1854–1926, vol. II

Allen, Harry Epworth, 1894–1958, vol. V

Allen, Henry George, *died* 1908, vol. I

Allen, Brig. Henry Isherwood, 1887–1979, vol. VII

Allen, Henry Seymour, 1847–1928, vol. II

Allen, Maj.-Gen. Henry Tureman, 1859–1930, vol. III

Allen, Herbert Stanley, 1873–1954, vol. V

Allen, Herbert Warner, 1881–1968, vol. VI

Allen, Rev. Canon Herbert William, *died* 1944, vol. IV

Allen, Hervey, 1889–1949, vol. IV

Allen, Lt-Col Hugh Morris, 1867–1932, vol. III

Allen, Sir Hugh Percy, 1869–1946, vol. IV

Allen, Inglis, 1879–1943, vol. IV

Allen, Jack, 1905–1984, vol. VIII

Allen, Very Rev. James, 1802–1897, vol. I

Allen, Col Hon. Sir James, 1885–1942, vol. IV

Allen, James Godfrey Colquhoun, 1904–1982, vol. VIII

Allen, James Lane, 1849–1925, vol. II

Allen, Vice-Adm. John Derwent, 1875–1958, vol. V

Allen, John Edsall, 1861–1944, vol. IV

Allen, John Ernest, 1872–1962, vol. VI

Allen, John Romilly, 1847–1907, vol. I

Allen, Sir John Sandeman, 1865–1935, vol. III

Allen, Col John Sandeman, 1892–1949, vol. IV

Allen, Col John Woolley, 1865–1942, vol. IV

Allen, Leslie Holdsworth, 1879–1964, vol. VI

Allen, Comdt Mary Sophia, 1878–1964, vol. VI

Allen, Maurice; *see* Allen, W. M.

Allen, Sir Milton Pentonville, 1888–1981, vol. VIII

Allen, Col Newton Seymour, 1957–1934, vol. III

Allen, Norman Percy, 1903–1972, vol. VII

Allen, Sir Oswald Coleman, 1887–1959, vol. V

Allen, Percy Stafford, 1869–1933, vol. III

Allen, Maj.-Gen. Ralph Edward, 1946–1910, vol. I

Allen, Raymond Cecil, 1872–1937, vol. III

Allen, Raymond Seaforth Stirling, 1905–1974, vol. VII

Allen, Rev. Richard Watson, 1833–1914, vol. I

Allen, Richard William, 1876–1921, vol. II

Allen, Sir Richard William, 1867–1955, vol. V

Allen, Captain Robert Calder, 1812–1903, vol. I

Allen, Lt-Col Robert Candlish, 1881–1942, vol. IV

Allen, Col Robert Franklin, 1860–1916, vol. II

Allen, Maj.-Gen. Robert Hall, 1886–1981, vol. VIII

Allen, Sir Roger, 1909–1972, vol. VII

Allen, Brig. Ronald Lewis, 1916–1986, vol. VIII

Allen, Sir Ronald Wilberforce, 1889–1936, vol. III

Allen, Sir Roy George Douglas, 1906–1983, vol. VIII

Allen, Col Sir Stephen Shepherd, 1882–1964, vol. VI

Allen, Sydney Scholefield, 1898–1974, vol. VII

Allen, Rev. Thomas, 1837–1912, vol. I

Allen, Very Rev. Thomas, 1873–1927, vol. II

Allen, Sir Thomas, 1864–1943, vol. IV

Allen, Thomas Carleton, 1852–1927, vol. II

Allen, Thomas Palmer, 1899–1979, vol. VII

Allen, W(alter) Godfrey, 1891–1986, vol. VIII
Allen, Sir Walter Macarthur, 1870–1943, vol. IV
Allen, Wilfred Baugh, 1849–1922, vol. II
Allen, William, 1892–1941, vol. IV
Allen, William, 1870–1945, vol. IV
Allen, Major William Barnsley, 1892–1933, vol. III
Allen, Sir (William) Denis, 1910–1987, vol. VIII
Allen, William Edward David, 1901–1973, vol. VII
Allen, William Gilbert, 1892–1970, vol. VI
Allen, Sir William Guilford, 1898–1977, vol. VII
Allen, William Henry, 1844–1926, vol. II
Allen, Lt-Col Sir William James, 1866–1947, vol. IV
Allen, Major William Lynn, 1871–1914, vol. I
Allen, (William) Maurice, 1908–1988, vol. VIII
Allen, William Philip, 1888–1958, vol. V
Allen, William Shepherd, 1831–1915, vol. I
Allen, Rev. Willoughby Charles, 1867–1953, vol. V
Allen-Williams, Brig.-Gen. Sir Arthur John 1869–1949, vol. IV
Allenby, 1st Viscount, 1861–1936, vol. III
Allenby, 2nd Viscount, 1903–1984, vol. VIII
Allenby, Captain Frederick Claude Hynman, 1864–1934, vol. III
Allenby, Adm. Reginald Arthur, 1861–1936, vol. III
Allendale, 1st Baron, 1829–1907, vol. I
Allendale, 1st Viscount, 1860–1923, vol. II
Allendale, 2nd Viscount, 1890–1956, vol. V
Allerton, 1st Baron, 1840–1917, vol. II
Allerton, 2nd Baron, 1867–1925, vol. II
Allerton, Air Cdre Ord Denny, 1902–1977, vol. VII
Allerton, Reginald John, 1898–1990, vol. VIII
Alletson, Major G. C., died 1928, vol. II
Alleyne, Maj.-Gen. Sir James, died 1899, vol. I
Alleyne, Sir John Gay Newton, 3rd Bt, 1820–1912, vol. I
Alleyne, Captain Sir John Meynell, 4th Bt, 1889–1983, vol. VIII
Allfrey, Lt-Gen. Sir Charles Walter, 1895–1964, vol. VI
Allfrey, Major Edward Mortimer, 1886–1957, vol. V
Allfrey, Captain Maurice Charles, 1916–1942, vol. IV
Allgeyer, Rt Rev. Emile Auguste, 1856–1924, vol. II
Allgood, Maj.-Gen. George, 1827–1907, vol. I
Allgood, Brig.-Gen. William Henry Loraine, 1868–1957, vol. V
Allhusen, (Augustus) Henry (Eden), 1867–1925, vol. II
Allhusen, Beatrice May, died 1918, vol. II
Allhusen, Lt-Col. Frederick Henry, 1872–1957, vol. V
Allhusen, Henry; see Allhusen, A. H. E.
Allhusen, William Hutt, 1845–1923, vol. II
Allies, Mary H. A., 1852–1927, vol. II
Allighan, Garry, born 1900, vol. VII(AII)
Allin, Norman, 1884–1973, vol. VII
Allin, Samuel John Henry Wallis, 1871–1933, vol. III
Allingham, Helen, (Mrs William Allingham), 1848–1926, vol. II
Allingham, Herbert William, died 1904, vol. I
Allingham, Margery Louise, 1904–1966, vol. VI
Allingham, Mrs William; see Allingham, H.
Allinson, Adrian Paul, 1890–1959, vol. V
Allinson, Air Vice-Marshal Norman Stuart, 1904–1984, vol. VIII
Allison, Sir Charles William, 1886–1972, vol. VII

Allison, Rev. David, died 1940, vol. III
Allison, James, 1865–1951, vol. V
Allison, James Anthony, 1915–1976, vol. VII
Allison, Sir John; see Allison, Sir W. J.
Allison, Captain John Hamilton, 1902–1968, vol. VI
Allison, John William, died 1934, vol. III
Allison, Rt Rev. Oliver Claude, 1908–1989, vol. VIII
Allison, Philip Rowland, 1907–1974, vol. VII
Allison, Ralph Victor, 1900–1987, vol. VIII
Allison, Sir Richard John, 1869–1958, vol. V
Allison, Richard Sydney, 1899–1978, vol. VII
Allison, Sir Robert Andrew, 1838–1926, vol. II
Allison, William, 1851–1925, vol. II
Allison, Sir (William) John, 1903–1966, vol. VI
Alliston, Sir Frederick Prat, 1832–1912, vol. I
Allitsen, Frances, (Mary Frances Bumpus), 1849–1912, vol. I
Allitt, Sir (John) William, 1896–1972, vol. VII
Allitt, Sir William; see Allitt, Sir J. W.
Allix, Charles Peter, 1842–1920, vol. II
Allman, George James, 1812–1898, vol. I
Allman, George Johnston, 1824–1904, vol. I
Allman, Robert, 1854–1917, vol. II, vol. III
Allmand, Arthur John, 1885–1951, vol. V
Allnutt, Col Edward Bruce, 1885–1972, vol. VII
Allnutt, Rev. George Herbert, 1843–1919, vol. II
Allom, Sir Charles Carrick, 1865–1947, vol. IV
Allott, Eric Newmarch, 1899–1980, vol. VII
Allport, Alfred, 1867–1949, vol. IV
Allsebrook, George Clarence, 1877–1957, vol. V
Allsop, Hon. Sir James Joseph Whittlesea, 1887–1963, vol. VI
Allsop, Kenneth, 1920–1973, vol. VII
Allsop, Lt-Col William Gillian, 1874–1951, vol. V
Allsop, Hon. Alfred Percy, 1861–1929, vol. III
Allsopp, Cecil Benjamin, 1904–1989, vol. VIII
Allsopp, Hon. Frederic Ernest, 1857–1928, vol. II
Allsopp, Hon. George Higginson, 1846–1907, vol. I
Allsopp, Captain Hon. Herbert Tongue, 1855–1920, vol. II
Allsopp, Samuel Ranulph, 1899–1975, vol. VII
Allsup, Major Edward Saunders, 1879–1928, vol. II
Allt, Wilfrid Greenhouse, 1889–1969, vol. VI
Allum, Frederick Warner, 1869–1963, vol. VI
Allum, Horace Benjamin, 1884–1966, vol. VI
Allum, Sir John Andrew Charles, 1889–1972, vol. VII
Allward, Walter Seymour, 1876–1955, vol. V
Allwood, James, died 1933, vol. III
Allwork, Rev. Robert Long, 1863–1919, vol. II
Allworthy, Rev. Thomas Bateson, 1879–1964, vol. VI
Alma-Tadema, Miss Anna, died 1943, vol. IV
Alma-Tadema, Laura Theresa, (Lady Alma-Tadema), died 1909, vol. I
Alma-Tadema, Miss Laurence, died 1940, vol. III
Alma-Tadema, Sir Lawrence, 1836–1912, vol. I
Almedingen, Edith Martha, 1898–1971, vol. VII
Almond, Hely Hutchinson, 1837–1903, vol. I
Almond, Sir James, 1891–1964, vol. VI
Almond, Hon. Col Ven. John Macpherson, 1872–1939, vol. III(A), vol. IV
Almond, W. Douglas, died 1916, vol. II
Alness, 1st Baron, 1868–1955, vol. V
Alpass, Joseph Herbert, 1873–1969, vol. VI
Alpe, Frank Theodore, died 1952, vol. V

12

Alsop, James Willcox, 1846–1921, vol. II
Alsop, Ralph, *died* 1950, vol. IV
Alstead, Robert, 1873–1946, vol. IV
Alston, Alexander Rowland, 1863–1945, vol. IV
Alston, Rt Rev. Arthur Fawssett, 1872–1954, vol. V
Alston, Rt Hon. Sir Beilby Francis, 1868–1929, vol. III
Alston, Sir Charles Ross, 1862–1937, vol. III
Alston, Sir Francis Beilby, 1820–1905, vol. I
Alston, Brig.-Gen. Francis George, 1878–1961, vol. VI
Alston, Hilda, (Lady Alston), *died* 1945, vol. IV
Alston, Captain Hubert George, 1866–1939, vol. III
Alston, Leonard, 1875–1953, vol. V
Alston, Brig. Llewilyn Arthur Augustus, 1890–1968, vol. VI
Alston, Rowland Crewe, 1852–1933, vol. III
Alston Roberts West, Gen. Sir Michael Montgomerie; *see* West.
Alt, Col William John, 1840–1908, vol. I
Altham, Captain Edward, 1882–1950, vol. IV
Altham, Lt-Gen. Sir Edward Altham, 1856–1943, vol. IV
Altham, Harry Surtees, 1888–1965, vol. VI
Althaus, Frederick Rudolph, 1895–1975, vol. VII
Althaus, Friedrich, 1829–1897, vol. I
Altman, Sir Albert Joseph, 1839–1912, vol. I
Alton, Ernest Henry, *died* 1952, vol. V
Alton, Sir Francis Cooke, 1856–1926, vol. II
Altrincham, 1st Baron, 1879–1955, vol. V
Alty, Thomas, 1899–1982, vol. VIII
Alun Roberts, Robert, 1894–1969, vol. VI
Aluwihare, Sir Richard, 1895–1976, vol. VII
Alvarez, Justin Charles William, 1859–1934, vol. III
Alvarez, Luis Walter, 1911–1988, vol. VIII
Alvarez de Rocafuarte, Marguerite; *see* D'Alvarez, Madame.
Alverstone, 1st Viscount, 1842–1915, vol. I
Alves, Duncan Elliott, 1870–1940, vol. III
Alves, Lt-Col Henry Malcolm Jerome, 1883–1940, vol. III
Alvin, Juliette Louise, *died* 1982, vol. VIII
Alvingham, 1st Baron, 1889–1955, vol. V
Alvord, Clarence Walworth, 1868–1928, vol. II
Alwar, HH Raj Rishi Shri Sewai Sir Jey Singhji Veerendra Shiromani Dev, Bharat Dharam Prabhakar, Maharaj of, 1882–1937, vol. III
Alwyn, William, 1905–1985, vol. VIII
Aly Khan, Shah, 1911–1960, vol. V
Amaldi, Edoardo, 1908–1989, vol. VIII
Amand de Mendieta, Rev. Emmanuel Alexandre, 1907–1976, vol. VII
Amar Singh, Gen. Raja Sir, 1864–1909, vol. I
Amarjit Singh, Lt-Col Maharajkumar, 1893–1944, vol. IV
Ambedkar, Bhimrao Ramji, 1893–1956, vol. V
Ambler, Air Vice-Marshal Geoffrey Hill, 1904–1978, vol. VII
Ambler, Harry, 1908–1988, vol. VIII
Ambrose, Robert, 1855–1940, vol. III
Ambrose, Brig. Robert Denis, 1896–1974, vol. VII
Ambrose, William, 1832–1908, vol. I
Amcotts, Lt-Comdr John C.; *see* Cracroft-Amcotts.

Amcotts, Lt-Col Sir Weston C.; *see* Cracroft-Amcotts.
Ameer-Ali, Rt Hon. (Syed), 1849–1928, vol. II
Ameer Ali, (Syed) Waris, 1886–1975, vol. VII
Ameer Ali, Sir Torick, 1891–1975, vol. VII
Amers, Maj.-Gen. John Henry, 1904–1990, vol. VIII
Amery, Rt Hon. Leopold Stennett, 1873–1955, vol. V
Amery, William Bankes, 1883–1951, vol. V
Ames, Sir Cecil Geraint, 1897–1977, vol. VII
Ames, Frederick, 1836–1918, vol. II
Ames, Sir Herbert Brown, 1863–1954, vol. V
Ames, Jennifer; *see* Greig, Maysie.
Ames, John Richard Woodland, 1872–1947, vol. IV
Ames, Lt-Col Oswald Henry, 1862–1927, vol. II
Ames, Percy W., 1853–1919, vol. II
Amherst, 3rd Earl, 1836–1910, vol. I
Amherst, 4th Earl, 1856–1927, vol. II
Amherst of Hackney, 1st Baron, 1835–1909, vol. I
Amherst of Hackney, Baroness (2nd in line), 1857–1919, vol. II
Amherst of Hackney, 3rd Baron, 1912–1980, vol. VII
Amherst, Rev. Hon. Percy Arthur, 1839–1910, vol. I
Amherst, Hon. Sybil Margaret, *died* 1926, vol. II
Ami, Henry M., 1858–1931, vol. III
Amies, Sir Arthur Barton Pilgrim, 1902–1976, vol. VII
Amigo, Most Rev. Peter E., 1864–1949, vol. IV
Amin, All Hajj Mohammud; *see* Keane, John Fryer Thomas.
Ammon, 1st Baron, 1873–1960, vol. V
Amod, Thakor of, Sardar Nawab Sir Naharsinhji Ishwarsinhji, *died* 1945, vol. IV
Amor, Arthur Joseph, 1897–1966, vol. VI
Amoroso, Emmanuel Ciprian, 1901–1982, vol. VIII
Amory, 1st Viscount, 1899–1981, vol. VIII
Amory, Sir Ian Murray Heathcoat Heathcoat-, 2nd Bt, 1865–1931, vol. III
Amory, Major Sir John Heathcoat-, 3rd Bt, 1894–1972, vol. VII
Amory, Sir John Heathcoat H.; *see* Heathcoat-Amory.
Amory, Sir William H.; *see* Heathcoat Amory.
Amos, Major Herbert Gilbert Maclachlan, 1866–1924, vol. II
Amos, Sir Maurice Sheldon, 1872–1940, vol. III
Amphlett, Major Charles Grove, 1862–1921, vol. II
Amphlett, Richard Holmden, 1847–1925, vol. II
Ampthill, 2nd Baron, 1869–1935, vol. III
Ampthill, 3rd Baron, 1896–1973, vol. VII
Ampthill, Lady; (Margaret), 1874–1957, vol. V
Amshewitz, J. H., 1882–1942, vol. IV
Amulree, 1st Baron, 1860–1942, vol. IV
Amulree, 2nd Baron, 1900–1983, vol. VIII
Amundsen, Captain Roald, 1872–1928, vol. II
Amwell, 1st Baron, 1876–1966, vol. VI
Amwell, 2nd Baron; Frederick Norman Montagne, 1912–1990, vol. VIII
Amyand, Arthur; *see* Haggard, Major E.A.
Amyot, Lt-Col Hon. George Elie, 1856–1940, vol. III
Amyot, Lt-Col John Andrew, 1867–1940, vol. III
Ancaster, 1st Earl of, 1830–1910, vol. I
Ancaster, 2nd Earl of, 1867–1951, vol. V
Ancaster, 3rd Earl of, 1907–1983, vol. VIII
Anda, Géza, 1921–1976, vol. VII

13

Anderson, Hon. Lord; Andrew Macbeth Anderson, 1862–1936, vol. III

Anderson, Dame Adelaide Mary, 1868–1936, vol. III

Anderson, Sir Alan Garrett, 1877–1952, vol. V

Anderson, Alan Orr, 1879–1958, vol. V

Anderson, Alexander, 1850–1904, vol. I

Anderson, Alexander, (Surfaceman), 1845–1909, vol. I

Anderson, Alexander, 1858–1936, vol. III

Anderson, Alexander, 1888–1954, vol. V

Anderson, Maj.-Gen. Alexander Dingwall, 1843–1916, vol. II

Anderson, Sir Alexander Greig, 1885–1961, vol. VI

Anderson, Sir Alexander James, 1879–1965, vol. VI

Anderson, Alexander Knox, 1892–1955, vol. V

Anderson, Alexander Richard, *died* 1933, vol. III

Anderson, Maj.-Gen. Alexander Vass, 1895–1963, vol. VI

Anderson, Maj.-Gen. Alfred, 1842–1909, vol. I

Anderson, Andrew Macbeth; *see* Anderson, Hon. Lord.

Anderson, Andrew Newton, 1880–1950, vol. IV

Anderson, Archibald Stirling Kennedy, 1887–1972, vol. VII

Anderson, Arthur Emilius David, 1886–1967, vol. VI

Anderson, Arthur Ingham, 1916–1976, vol. VII

Anderson, Sir Arthur Robert, 1860–1924, vol. II

Anderson, Maj.-Gen. Arthur William Leslie, 1842–1929, vol. III

Anderson, Sir Athol Lancelot, 1875–1955, vol. V

Anderson, Sir Austin Innes, 1897–1973, vol. VII

Anderson, Brig.-Gen. Austin Thomas, *died* 1949, vol. IV

Anderson, Lt-Col Barton Edward, 1881–1927, vol. II

Anderson, C. Goldsborough, 1865–1936, vol. III

Anderson, Charles, 1876–1944, vol. IV

Anderson, Major Charles, 1886–1954, vol. V

Anderson, Lt-Gen. Sir Charles Alexander, 1857–1940, vol. III

Anderson, Charles Buxton, 1879–1953, vol. V

Anderson, Lt-Col Charles Groves Wright, 1897–1988, vol. VIII

Anderson, Charles Martin, 1918–1961, vol. VI

Anderson, Rt Rev. Charles Palmerston, 1865–1930, vol. III

Anderson, Clinton Presba, 1895–1975, vol. VII

Anderson, Sir Colin Skelton, 1904–1980, vol. VII

Anderson, Daniel Elie, *died* 1928, vol. II

Anderson, Gen. David, 1821–1909, vol. I

Anderson, Sir David, 1880–1953, vol. V

Anderson, David; *see* Hon. Lord St Vigeans.

Anderson, David Dick, 1889–1980, vol. VII

Anderson, David Fyfe, 1904–1988, vol. VIII

Anderson, David Martin, 1880–1955, vol. V

Anderson, Adm. Sir (David) Murray, 1874–1936, vol. III

Anderson, David Steel, 1902–1986, vol. VIII

Anderson, Sir David Stirling, 1895–1981, vol. VIII

Anderson, Lt-Gen. Sir Desmond Francis, 1885–1967, vol. VI

Anderson, Sir Donald Forsyth, 1906–1973, vol. VII

Anderson, Sir Donald George, 1917–1975, vol. VII

Anderson, Sir Duncan Law, 1901–1980, vol. VII

Anderson, Edith Muriel, (Lady Anderson), 1878–1958, vol. V

Anderson, Col Edmund Bullar, 1857–1935, vol. III

Anderson, Sir Edward Arthur, 1908–1979, vol. VII

Anderson, Rev. Edward Erskine, 1872–1950, vol. IV

Anderson, Lt-Col Edward Philip, 1883–1934, vol. III

Anderson, Edward William, 1901–1981, vol. VIII

Anderson, Elizabeth Garrett, 1836–1917, vol. II

Anderson, Emily, 1891–1962, vol. VI

Anderson, Col Eric Litchfield Brooke, 1889–1959, vol. V

Anderson, Eric Oswald, 1870–1935, vol. III

Anderson, Rt Rev. Ernest Augustus, 1859–1945, vol. IV

Anderson, Major Ernest Chester, 1863–1913, vol. I

Anderson, Lt-Col Francis, 1888–1925, vol. II

Anderson, Sir Francis, 1858–1941, vol. IV

Anderson, Brig.-Gen. Sir Francis James, *died* 1920, vol. II

Anderson, Francis Sheed, 1897–1966, vol. VI

Anderson, Frank, 1889–1959, vol. V

Anderson, Sir Frederick, 1884–1961, vol. VI

Anderson, Rev. Frederick Ingall, *died* 1961, vol. VI

Anderson, Lt-Col Frederick Jasper, 1886–1957, vol. V

Anderson, Sir George, 1845–1923, vol. II

Anderson, Sir George, 1876–1943, vol. IV

Anderson, Dr George Cranston, 1879–1944, vol. IV

Anderson, George David, 1913–1983, vol. VIII

Anderson, Major George Denis, 1885–1971, vol. VII

Anderson, George Henry Garstin, 1896–1959, vol. V

Anderson, Hon. George James, 1860–1935, vol. III

Anderson, George Knox, 1854–1941, vol. IV

Anderson, Sir Gilmour M.; *see* Menzies Anderson.

Anderson, Lt-Col Guy Willoughby, 1885–1949, vol. IV

Anderson, Gen. Harry Cortlandt, 1826–1921, vol. II

Anderson, Lt-Gen. Sir Hasting; *see* Anderson, Lt-Gen. Sir W. H.

Anderson, Rev. Hector David, 1906–1989, vol. VIII

Anderson, Henry Aiken, 1851–1936, vol. III

Anderson, Major Henry Graeme, 1882–1925, vol. II

Anderson, Lt-Col Henry Stewart, 1872–1961, vol. VI

Anderson, Gen. Sir Horace Searle, 1833–1907, vol. I

Anderson, Hugh Alfred, 1867–1933, vol. III

Anderson, Hugh Fraser, 1910–1986, vol. VIII

Anderson, Sir Hugh Kerr, 1865–1928, vol. II

Anderson, Ian, 1891–1970, vol. VI

Anderson, J. Wemyss, 1868–1930, vol. III

Anderson, James, 1881–1915, vol. I

Anderson, James, 1857–1932, vol. III

Anderson, Col James, 1872–1955, vol. V

Anderson, James B., 1886–1938, vol. III

Anderson, Col James Dalgliesh, 1877–1947, vol. IV

Anderson, James Drummond, 1852–1920, vol. II

Anderson, Sir James Drummond, 1886–1968, vol. VI

Anderson, James Maitland, 1852–1927, vol. II

Anderson, James Stirling, 1891–1976, vol. VII

Anderson, Hon. James Thomas Milton, 1878–1946, vol. IV

Anderson, James Wallace, *born* 1848, vol. II

Anderson, John, 1833–1900, vol. I

Anderson, John, 1840–1910, vol. I

Anderson, Sir John, 1858–1918, vol. II

Anderson, Sir John, 1852–1924, vol. II

Anderson, John, 1886–1935, vol. III

Anderson, Lt-Col John, 1852–1936, vol. III

Anderson, John, 1855–1938, vol. III

Anderson, Sir John, 1st Bt (cr 1920), 1878–1963, vol. VI

Anderson, Sir John, 1908–1965, vol. VI

Anderson, John, 1896–1984, vol. VIII

Anderson, Gen. Sir John D'Arcy, 1908–1988, vol. VIII

Anderson, Most Rev. John George, 1866–1943, vol. IV

Anderson, John George Clark, 1870–1952, vol. V

Anderson, John Gerard, 1836–1912, vol. I

Anderson, John Hubback, 1883–1950, vol. IV

Anderson, Rt Rev. John Ogle, 1912–1969, vol. VI

Anderson, John Stuart, 1908–1990, vol. VIII

Anderson, John William Stewart, 1874–1920, vol. II

Anderson, Joseph, 1832–1916, vol. II

Anderson, Major Joseph Ringland, 1894–1961, vol. VI

Anderson, Rev. K. C., vol. II

Anderson, Gen. Sir Kenneth Arthur Noel, 1891–1959, vol. V

Anderson, Hon. Sir Kenneth McColl, 1909–1985, vol. VIII

Anderson, Sir Kenneth Skelton, 1st Bt (cr 1919), 1866–1942, vol. IV

Anderson, Dame Kitty, 1903–1979, vol. VII

Anderson, Maj.-Gen. Louis Edward, 1861–1941, vol. IV

Anderson, Louisa Garrett, 1873–1943, vol. IV

Anderson, Mark Louden, 1895–1961, vol. VI

Anderson, Martin Cynicus, 1854–1932, vol. III

Anderson, Mary Reid; see Macarthur, M. R.

Anderson, Sir Maurice Abbot, 1861–1938, vol. III

Anderson, Maxwell, 1888–1959, vol. V

Anderson, Captain Sir Maxwell Hendry Maxwell-, 1879–1951, vol. V

Anderson, Melville Best, 1851–1933, vol. III

Anderson, Adm. Sir Murray; see Anderson, Adm. Sir D. M.

Anderson, Maj.-Gen. Nelson Graham, 1875–1945, vol. IV

Anderson, Lt-Col Sir Neville, 1881–1963, vol. VI

Anderson, Ven. Nicol Keith, 1882–1953, vol. V

Anderson, Air Vice-Marshal Norman Russel, died 1948, vol. IV

Anderson, Col Patrick Campbell, 1894–1965, vol. VI

Anderson, Peter Corsar, 1871–1955, vol. V

Anderson, Peter John, died 1926, vol. II

Anderson, Richard John, 1848–1914, vol. I

Anderson, Lt-Gen. Sir Richard Neville, 1907–1979, vol. VII

Anderson, Sir Robert, 1841–1918, vol. II

Anderson, Sir Robert, 1st Bt (cr 1911), 1837–1921, vol. II

Anderson, Sir Robert Albert, 1866–1942, vol. IV

Anderson, Robert Bernerd, 1910–1989, vol. VIII

Anderson, Major Robert Grenville G.; see Gayer-Anderson.

Anderson, Brig. Robert Heath, 1882–1940, vol. III

Anderson, Brig.-Gen. Sir Robert Murray McCheyne, 1867–1940, vol. III(A), vol. IV

Anderson, Rt Hon. Sir Robert Newton, 1871–1948, vol. IV

Anderson, Sir Robert Rowand, 1834–1921, vol. II

Anderson, Roger Charles, 1883–1976, vol. VII

Anderson, Col Rowland James Percy, 1873–1950, vol. IV

Anderson, Major Roy Dunlop, 1878–1932, vol. III

Anderson, Rudolph Martin, 1876–1961, vol. VI

Anderson, Rupert Darnley, 1859–1944, vol. IV

Anderson, Samuel Boyd, 1878–1934, vol. III

Anderson, Sherwood, died 1941, vol. IV

Anderson, Stanley, 1884–1966, vol. VI

Anderson, Brig.-Gen. Stuart Milligan, 1879–1954, vol. V

Anderson, Tempest, 1846–1913, vol. I

Anderson, Theodore Farnworth, 1901–1979, vol. VII

Anderson, Thomas, 1844–1926, vol. II

Anderson, Thomas, 1904–1990, vol. VIII

Anderson, Thomas Alexander Harvie, died 1953, vol. V

Anderson, Thomas David, 1853–1932, vol. III

Anderson, Col Thomas Gayer G.; see Gayer-Anderson.

Anderson, Sir Thomas M'Call, 1836–1908, vol. I

Anderson, Thomas Scott, 1853–1919, vol. II

Anderson, Brig. Thomas Stephen James, 1909–1969, vol. VI

Anderson, Maj.-Gen. Thomas Victor, 1881–1972, vol. VII

Anderson, Lt-Gen. Sir (Warren) Hastings, 1872–1930, vol. III

Anderson, Maj.-Gen. Warren Melville, 1894–1973, vol. VII

Anderson, Sir William, 1835–1898, vol. I

Anderson, William, 1842–1900, vol. I

Anderson, William, 1831–1913, vol. I

Anderson, Col William, 1886–1944, vol. IV

Anderson, William, 1889–1955, vol. V

Anderson, William Alexander, 1890–1971, vol. VII

Anderson, Maj.-Gen. William Beaumont, 1877–1959, vol. V.

Anderson, William Blair, 1877–1959, vol. V

Anderson, Col William Campbell, 1868–1926, vol. II

Anderson, Brig.-Gen. William Christian, 1867–1942, vol. IV

Anderson, William Crawford, 1877–1919, vol. II

Anderson, William Galloway Macdonald, 1905–1978, vol. VII

Anderson, William Geddes, 1858–1932, vol. III

Anderson, Brig. William Henniker, 1880–1958, vol. V

Anderson, Sir William Hewson, 1897–1968, vol. VI

Anderson, Sir William John, 1846–1908, vol. I

Anderson, Rt Rev. William Louis, 1892–1972, vol. VII

Anderson, Lt-Col William Maurice, 1873–1946, vol. IV

Anderson, Lt-Col William Menzies, 1883–1940, vol. III

Anderson, Col William Patrick, 1851–1927, vol. II

Anderson, Col William Robert le Geyt, 1850–1908, vol. I

Anderson, William Thomas, 1872–1948, vol. IV

Anderson, Very Rev. W(illiam) White, 1888–1956, vol. V

Anderson-Morshead, Lt-Col Rupert Henry, *died* 1918, vol. II

Andersson, Lt-Col Sir (Charles) Llewellyn, 1861–1948, vol. IV

Andersson, Lt-Col Sir Llewellyn; *see* Andersson, Lt-Col Sir C. L.

Anderton, Sir Francis Robert Ince, 1859–1950, vol. IV

Anderton, Francis Swithin, 1868–1909, vol. I

Anderton, Col Geoffrey, 1902–1981, vol. VIII

Andoe, Vice-Adm. Sir Hilary Gustavus, 1841–1905, vol. I

Andrade, Edward Neville da Costa, 1887–1971, vol. VII

André, Brig. James Richard Glencoe, 1899–1981, vol. VIII

Andreades, Andrew, 1876–1935, vol. III

Andreae, Herman Anton, 1876–1965, vol. VI

Andrew, Rt Rev. Agnellus Matthew, 1908–1987, vol. VII

Andrew, Alistair Hugh, 1908–1947, vol. IV

Andrew, George, 1873–1956, vol. V

Andrew, Engr-Capt. George Edward, 1869–1945, vol. IV

Andrew, Rev. Sir (George) Herbert, 1910–1985, vol. VIII

Andrew, Rev. Sir Herbert; *see* Andrew, Rev. Sir G. H.

Andrew, Ian Graham, 1893–1962, vol. VI

Andrew, Sir John, 1896–1968, vol. VI

Andrew, John Harold, 1887–1961, vol. VI

Andrew, Brig. Leslie Wilton, 1897–1969, vol. VI

Andrew, Col Richard Hynman, 1885–1964, vol. VI

Andrew, Samuel Ogden, 1868–1952, vol. V

Andrew, Walter Jonathan, *died* 1934, vol. III

Andrew, William Monro, 1895–1973, vol. VII

Andrew, Rev. Canon William Shaw, 1884–1963, vol. VI

Andrewes, Antony, 1910–1990, vol. VIII

Andrewes, Sir Christopher Howard, 1896–1988, vol. VIII

Andrewes, David; *see* Andrewes, E. D. E.

Andrewes, Edward David Eden, 1909–1990, vol. VIII

Andrewes, Major Francis Edward, 1878–1920, vol. II

Andrewes, Sir Frederick William, 1859–1932, vol. III

Andrewes, Rev. Canon Gerrard Thomas, 1855–1941, vol. IV

Andrewes, Rev. John Brereton, *died* 1920, vol. II

Andrewes, Adm. Sir William Gerrard, 1899–1974, vol. VII

Andrews, Albert Andrew, 1896–1976, vol. VII

Andrews, (Arthur) John (Francis), 1906–1984, vol. VIII

Andrews, Lt-Col Cecil Rollo Payton, 1870–1951, vol. V

Andrews, Rev. Charles Freer, 1871–1940, vol. III

Andrews, Charles M'Lean, 1863–1943, vol. IV

Andrews, Charles William, 1866–1924, vol. II

Andrews, Cyril Frank Wilton, 1892–1978, vol. VII

Andrews, Éamonn, 1922–1987, vol. VIII

Andrews, Edward Gordon, *died* 1915, vol. II

Andrews, Sir Edwin Arthur C.; *see* Chapman-Andrews.

Andrews, Hon. Elisha Benjamin, 1844–1917, vol. II

Andrews, Ernest Clayton, 1870–1948, vol. IV

Andrews, Sir Ernest Herbert, 1873–1961, vol. VI

Andrews, Captain Francis Arthur Lavington, 1869–1944, vol. IV

Andrews, Rev. George Whitefield, 1833–1931, vol. III

Andrews, Harry Fleetwood, 1911–1989, vol. VIII

Andrews, Harry Thomson, 1897–1985, vol. VIII

Andrews, Henry Russell, 1871–1942, vol. IV

Andrews, Rev. Herbert T., 1864–1928, vol. II

Andrews, Hugh, *died* 1926, vol. II

Andrews, Rt Hon. Sir James, 1st Bt, 1877–1951, vol. V

Andrews, James Frank, 1848–1922, vol. II

Andrews, James Peter, 1902–1968, vol. VI

Andrews, John Alban, *died* 1964, vol. VI

Andrews, John; *see* Andrews, A. J. F.

Andrews, John Launcelot, 1893–1968, vol. VI

Andrews, Rt Hon. Sir John Lawson Ormrod, 1903–1986, vol. VIII

Andrews, Rt Hon. John Miller, 1871–1956, vol. V

Andrews, Air Vice-Marshal John Oliver, 1896–1989, vol. VIII

Andrews, Joseph Ormond, 1873–1909, vol. I

Andrews, Rev. Canon Leonard Martin, 1886–1989, vol. VIII

Andrews, Lewis Yelland, 1896–1937, vol. III

Andrews, Sir Linton; *see* Andrews, Sir W. L.

Andrews, Rev. Canon Martin; *see* Andrews, Rev. Canon L. M.

Andrews, Norman Roy F.; *see* Fox-Andrews.

Andrews, Surgeon Captain Octavius William, 1865–1936, vol. III

Andrews, Rear-Adm. Robert Walter Benjamin, 1876–1965, vol. VI

Andrews, Roland Stuart, 1897–1961, vol. VI

Andrews, Roy Chapman, 1884–1960, vol. V

Andrews, Stanley George B.; *see* Burt-Andrews.

Andrews, Thomas, 1847–1907, vol. I

Andrews, Rt Hon. Thomas, 1843–1916, vol. II

Andrews, Rt Rev. Walter, 1852–1932, vol. III

Andrews, Wilfrid, 1892–1975, vol. VII

Andrews, William, 1848–1908, vol. I

Andrews, Rt Hon. William Drennan, 1832–1924, vol. II

Andrews, William Horner, 1887–1953, vol. V

Andrews, Sir (William) Linton, 1886–1972, vol. VII

Andrews, Winifred Agnes, 1918–1983, vol. VIII

Andrews-Speed, James, 1876–1939, vol. III

Andric, Ivo, 1892–1975, vol. VII

Andrus, Brig.-Gen. Thomas Alchin, 1872–1959, vol. V

Anethan, Baroness Albert d', *died* 1935, vol. III

Aney, Madhao Shrihari, 1880–1968, vol. VI

Angas, Sir (John) Keith, 1900–1977, vol. VII

Angas, Sir Keith; *see* Angas, Sir J. K.

Angas, Major Lawrence Lee Bazley, 1893–1973, vol. VII

Angel, John, 1881–1960, vol. V

Angell, Col Frederick John, 1861–1922, vol. II

Angell, James Burrill, 1829–1916, vol. II

Angell, James Rowland, 1869–1949, vol. IV

Angell, Sir Norman, 1874–1967, vol. VI

Angellier, Auguste Jean, 1848–1911, vol. I

Angers, Hon. Sir Auguste Réal, 1837–1919, vol. II

Angers, Hon. Eugène-Réal, 1883–1956, vol. V

Angier, Sir Theodore Vivian Samuel, 1843–1935, vol. III

Anglesey, 4th Marquess of, 1835–1898, vol. I

Anglesey, 5th Marquess of, 1875–1905, vol. I

Anglesey, 6th Marquess of, 1885–1947, vol. IV

Angless, Violet B.; *see* Brunton-Angless.

Anglin, Arthur H., 1850–1934, vol. III

Anglin, Arthur Whyte, 1867–1955, vol. V

Anglin, Rt Hon. Francis Alexander, 1865–1933, vol. III

Angliss, Dame Jacobena Victoria Alice, 1897–1980, vol. VII(AII)

Angliss, Hon. Sir William Charles, 1865–1957, vol. V

Angst, Sir Henry, 1847–1922, vol. II

Angus, Alfred Henry, 1873–1957, vol. V

Angus, Col Edmund Graham, 1889–1983, vol. VIII

Angus, Henry Brunton, 1867–1927, vol. II

Angus, J. Mortimer, 1850–1945, vol. IV

Angus, Richard Bladworth, 1831–1922, vol. II

Angus, Rev. Samuel, 1881–1943, vol. IV

Angus, Brig. Tom Hardy, 1899–1984, vol. VIII

Angus, Sir William, 1841–1912, vol. I

Angus, Col William Mathwin, 1851–1934, vol. III

Angwin, Col Sir (Arthur) Stanley, 1883–1959, vol. V

Angwin, Hugh Thomas Moffitt, 1888–1949, vol. IV

Angwin, Col Sir Stanley; *see* Angwin, Col Sir A. S.

Angwin, Hon. William Charles, 1863–1944, vol. IV

Anley, Brig.-Gen. Barnett Dyer Lempriere Gray, 1873–1954, vol. V

Anley, Brig.-Gen. Frederick Gore, 1864–1936, vol. III

Anley, Col Henry Augustus, 1864–1942, vol. IV

Anley, Major Philip Francis Ross, 1874–1956, vol. V

Ann, Sir Edwin Thomas, 1852–1913, vol. I

Annaly, 3rd Baron, 1857–1922, vol. II

Annaly, 4th Baron, 1885–1970, vol. VI

Annaly, 5th Baron, 1927–1990, vol. VIII

Annamunthodo, Sir Harry, 1920–1986, vol. VIII

Annan, Robert, 1885–1981, vol. VIII

Annan, William, 1872–1952, vol. V

Annand, James, 1843–1906, vol. I

Annandale, Charles, 1843–1915, vol. I

Annandale, Nelson; *see* Annandale, T. N.

Annandale, Thomas, 1838–1907, vol. I

Annandale, (Thomas) Nelson, 1876–1924, vol. II

Anne, Ernest Lambert Swinburne, 1852–1939, vol. III

Anne, George Charlton, 1886–1960, vol. V

Annesley, 5th Earl, 1831–1908, vol. I

Annesley, 6th Earl, 1884–1914, vol. I

Annesley, 7th Earl, 1861–1934, vol. III

Annesley, 8th Earl, 1894-1957, vol. V

Annesley, 9th Earl, 1900–1979, vol. VII

Annesley, Captain Hon. Arthur, 1880–1914, vol. I

Annesley, Lt-Gen. Sir Arthur Lyttelton L.; *see* Lyttelton-Annesley.

Annesley, Col Arthur Stephen Robert, 1869–1939, vol. III

Annesley, Lt-Col James Howard Adolphus, 1868–1919, vol. I

Annesley, Captain John Campbell, 1895–1964, vol. VI

Annesley, Lt-Col William Henry, 1876–1934, vol. III

Annesley, Major William Richard Norton, 1863–1914, vol. I

Annett, Engr-Captain George Lewis, 1887–1980, vol. VII

Annett, Henry Edward, 1871–1945, vol. IV(A), vol. V

Annigoni, Pietro, 1910–1988, vol. VIII

Anningson, Bushell, *died* 1916, vol. II

Annois, Leonard Lloyd, 1906–1966, vol. VI

Anns, Bryan Herbert, 1929–1975, vol. VII

Anouilh, Jean, 1910–1987, vol. VIII

Anrep, Gleb V., 1891–1955, vol. V

Anscomb, Major Allen-Mellers, *born* 1849, vol. II

Ansell, Rev. Preb. George Frederick James, 1886–1951, vol. V

Ansell, James Lawrence Bunting, 1912–1978, vol. VII

Ansell, John, 1874–1948, vol. IV

Ansell, William Henry, 1872–1959, vol. V

Ansell, William James David, 1858–1920, vol. II

Ansermet, Ernest, 1883–1969, vol. VI

Ansett, Sir Reginald Myles, 1909–1981, vol. VIII

Anslow, 1st Baron, 1850–1933, vol. III

Anson, Viscount; Thomas William Arnold Anson, 1913–1958, vol. V

Anson, Rt Rev. and Hon. Adelbert John Robert, 1840–1909, vol. I

Anson, Captain Hon. Alfred, 1876–1944, vol. IV

Anson, Rear-Adm. Algernon Horatio, 1854–1913, vol. I

Anson, Maj.-Gen. Sir Archibald Edward Harbord, 1826–1925, vol. II

Anson, Adm. Charles Eustace, 1859–1940, vol. III

Anson, Hon. Claud, 1864–1947, vol. IV

Anson, Sir Denis George William, 4th Bt, 1888–1914, did not have an entry in Who's Who.

Anson, Sir Edward Reynell, 6th Bt, 1902–1951, vol. V

Anson, Hon. Frederic William, 1862–1917, vol. II

Anson, Lt-Col Hon. Sir George Augustus, 1857–1947, vol. IV

Anson, George H., *died* 1957, vol. V

Anson, Ven. George Henry Greville, *died* 1898, vol. I

Anson, Sir (George) Wilfrid, 1893–1974, vol. VII

Anson, Rev. Harold, 1867–1954, vol. V

Anson, Sir John Henry Algernon, 5th Bt, 1897–1918, vol. II

Anson, Sir Wilfrid; *see* Anson, Sir G. W.

Anson, Rt Hon. Sir William Reynell, 3rd Bt, 1843–1914, vol. I

Ansorge, Sir Eric Cecil, 1887–1977, vol. VII

Ansorge, William John, 1850–1913, vol. I

Anstead, Rudolph David, 1876–1962, vol. VI

Anstey, Most Rev. Arthur Henry, *died* 1955, vol. V

Anstey, Brig. Edgar Carnegie, 1882–1958, vol. V

Anstey, Edgar Harold Macfarlane, 1907–1987, vol. VIII

Anstey, F.; *see* Guthrie, T.A.

Anstey, Hon. Frank, 1865–1940, vol. III

Anstey, Gilbert Tomkins, 1889–1974, vol. VII

Anstey, Percy, 1876–1920, vol. II

Anstey, Vera, 1889–1976, vol. VII

Anstey, Engr-Rear-Adm. William John, 1860–1936, vol. III

Anstice, Hon. Col Sir Arthur, 1846–1929, vol. III

Anstice, Vice-Adm. Sir Edmund Walter, 1899–1979, vol. VII

Anstice, Lt-Col Sir Robert Henry, 1843–1922, vol. II

Anstie, James, 1836–1924, vol. II

Anstruther, Brig. Alexander Meister, 1902–1969, vol. VI

Anstruther, Arthur Wellesley, 1864–1938, vol. III

Anstruther, Col Charles Frederick St Clair, 1855–1925, vol. II

Anstruther, Hon. Dame Eva Isabella Henrietta, 1869–1935, vol. III

Anstruther, George Elliot, 1870–1940, vol. III

Anstruther, Henry Torrens, 1860–1926, vol. II

Anstruther, Col Philip Noel, 1891–1960, vol. V

Anstruther, Sir Ralph William, 6th Bt (*cr* 1694), 1858–1934, vol. III

Anstruther, Adm. Robert Hamilton, 1862–1938, vol. III

Anstruther, Lt-Col Robert Hamilton Lloyd-, 1841–1914, vol. I

Anstruther, Sir Windham Charles James Carmichael, 8th Bt (*cr* 1700 and 1798), 1824–1898, vol. I

Anstruther, Sir Windham Eric Francis Carmichael-, 11th Bt (*cr* 1700 and 1798), 1900–1980, vol. VII

Anstruther, Sir Windham Frederick Carmichael-, 10th Bt (*cr* 1700 and 1798), 1902–1928, vol. II

Anstruther, Sir Windham Robert Carmichael, 9th Bt (*cr* 1700 and 1798), 1877–1903, vol. I

Anstruther-Gough-Calthorpe, Sir FitzRoy Hamilton, 1st Bt, 1872–1957, vol. V

Anstruther-Gough-Calthorpe, Brig. Sir Richard Hamilton, 2nd Bt, 1908–1985, vol. VIII

Anstruther-Gray, Lt-Col William, 1859–1938, vol. III

Anstruther-Gray, William John St Clair; *see* Baron Kilmany.

Anstruther-Thomson, John, 1818–1904, vol. I

Antelme, Hon. Sir Celicourt, 1818–1899, vol. I

Anthonisz, James Oliver, 1860–1921, vol. II

Anthonisz, Peter Daniel, 1822–1903, vol. I

Anthony, C. L.; *see* Smith, Dodie.

Anthony, Henry Montesquieu, 1873–1949, vol. IV

Anthony, Herbert Douglas, 1892–1968, vol. VI

Anthony, Irvin, 1890-1971, vol. VII

Anthony, Sir John, *died* 1935, vol. III

Anthony, Philip Arnold, 1873–1949, vol. IV

Anthony, Maj.-Gen. Richard William, 1874–1940, vol. III

Anthony, Maj.-Gen. William Samuel, 1874–1943, vol. IV

Antill, Maj.-Gen. John Macquarie, 1866–1937, vol. III

Antony, Jonquil, 1912–1980, vol. VII

Antrim, 11th Earl of, 1851–1918, vol. II

Antrim, 12th Earl of, 1878–1932, vol. III

Antrim, 13th Earl of, 1911–1977, vol. VII

Antrobus, Sir Cosmo Gordon, 5th Bt, 1859–1939, vol. III

Antrobus, Dame Edith Marion, 1862–1944, vol. IV

Antrobus, Sir Edmund, 3rd Bt, 1818–1899, vol. I

Antrobus, Sir Edmund, 4th Bt, 1848–1915, vol. I

Antrobus, Edward Gream, 1860–1940, vol. III

Antrobus, John Coutts, 1829–1916, vol. II

Antrobus, Maurice Edward, 1895–1985, vol. VIII

Antrobus, Captain Sir Philip Humphrey, 6th Bt, 1876–1968, vol. VI

Antrobus, Sir Reginald Laurence, 1853–1942, vol. IV

Antrobus, Lt-Col Ronald Henry, 1891–1980, vol. VII

Anwyl, Sir Edward, 1866–1914, vol. I

Anwyl, Rev. John Bodvan, 1875–1949, vol. IV(A), vol. V

Anwyl-Davies, Thomas, 1891–1971, vol. VII

Anwyl-Passingham, Col Augustus Mervyn Owen, 1880–1955, vol. V

Anzon Caccamisi, Baronne; *see* Marchesi, Blanche

Aoki, Viscount, 1844–1914, vol. I

Apcar, Sir Apcar Alexander, 1851–1913, vol. I

Ap Ellis, Gp Captain Augustine, 1886–1969, vol. VI

Aplin, Harold D'Auvergne, 1879–1958, vol. V

Aplin, Major John George Orlebar, *died* 1915, vol. I

Aplin, Col Philip John Hanham, 1858–1927, vol. II

Aplin, Col Stephen Lushington, 1863–1940, vol. III

Appelbe, Brig.-Gen. Edward Benjamin, 1855–1935, vol. III

Apperley, (George Owen) Wynne, 1884–1960, vol. V

Apperley, Newton Wynne, 1846–1925, vol. II

Apperley, Wynne; *see* Apperley, G. O. W.

Apperley, Sir Aldred, 1839–1913, vol. I

Apperly, Herbert, *died* 1932, vol. III

Apperson, George Latimer, 1857–1937, vol. III

Appleby, Sir Alfred, 1866–1952, vol. V

Appleby, Lt-Col Charles Bernard, 1905–1975, vol. VII

Appleby, Maj.-Gen. David Stanley, 1918–1989, vol. VIII

Appleby, Lt-Col John Pringle, 1891–1966, vol. VI

Appleby, Sir Robert Rowland, 1887–1966, vol. VI

Applegarth, Robert, 1834–1924, vol. II

Appleton, Arthur Beeny, *died* 1950, vol. IV

Appleton, Sir Edward Victor, 1892–1965, vol. VI

Appleton, George Webb, 1845–1909, vol. I

Appleton, Brig. Gilbert Leonard, 1894–1970, vol. VI

Appleton, Rev. Richard, 1849–1909, vol. I

Appleton, William, 1846–1906, vol. I

Appleton, Sir William, 1889–1958, vol. V

Appleton, William Archibald, 1859–1940, vol. III

Appleton, William Thomas, 1859–1930, vol. III

Appleyard, Maj.-Gen. Frederick Ernest, 1829–1911, vol. I

Appleyard, Col Kenelm Charles, 1894–1967, vol. VI

Appleyard, Rollo, 1867–1943, vol. IV

Applin, Captain Arthur, *died* 1949, vol. IV

Applin, Lt-Col Reginald Vincent Kempenfelt, 1869–1957, vol. V

Apponyi, Count Albert, 1846–1933, vol. III

Apps, Rear-Adm. Edgar Stephen, 1893–1958, vol. V

Apps, Engr-Captain William Richard, 1862–1947, vol. IV

ap Rhys Pryce, Gen. Sir Henry Edward, 1874–1950, vol. IV

Apsey, Sir John, 1859–1930, vol. III

Apsley, Lord; Allen Algernon Bathurst, 1895–1942, vol. IV

Apsley, Lady; (Violet Emily Mildred), 1895–1966, vol. VI

Apthorp, Major Shirley East, 1882–1937, vol. III

Arabi, Sayed Ahmed Pasha, 1841–1911, vol. I

Aragon, Louis, 1897–1982, vol. VIII

Arbab Dost Muhammad Khan, Khan Bahadur Sir, *died* 1931, vol. III

Arber, Agnes, (Mrs E. A. Newell Arber), 1879–1960, vol. V

Arber, Mrs E. A. Newell; *see* Arber, Agnes.

Arber, Edward, 1836–1912, vol. I
Arber, Edward Alexander Newell, 1870–1918, vol. II
Arberry, Arthur John, 1905–1969, vol. VI
Arbuckle, Hon. Sir William, 1839–1915, vol. I
Arbuckle, Sir William Forbes, 1902–1966, vol. VI
Arbuthnot, Brig. Alexander George, 1873–1961, vol. VI
Arbuthnot, Sir Alexander John, 1822–1907, vol. I
Arbuthnot, Sir Charles George, 1824–1899, vol. I
Arbuthnot, Charles George, 1846–1928, vol. II
Arbuthnot, Vice-Adm. Charles Ramsay, 1850–1913, vol. I
Arbuthnot, Clifford William Ernest, 1885–1974, vol. VII
Arbuthnot, Brig.-Gen. Sir Dalrymple, 5th Bt, 1867–1941, vol. IV
Arbuthnot, Captain Ernest Kennaway, 1876–1945, vol. IV
Arbuthnot, Adm. Sir Geoffrey Schomberg, 1885–1957, vol. V
Arbuthnot, Ven. George, 1846–1922, vol. II
Arbuthnot, Sir George Gough, 1847–1929, vol. III
Arbuthnot, Gerald Archibald, 1872–1916, vol. II
Arbuthnot, Maj.-Gen. Henry Thomas, 1834–1919, vol. II
Arbuthnot, Sir Hugh Fitz-Gerald, 7th Bt, 1922–1983, vol. VIII
Arbuthnot, James Woodgate, 1848–1927, vol. II
Arbuthnot, Major John Bernard, 1875–1950, vol. IV
Arbuthnot, Major Sir Robert Dalrymple, 6th Bt, 1919–1944, vol. IV
Arbuthnot, Robert Edward Vaughan, 1871–1922, vol. II
Arbuthnot, Rear-Adm. Sir Robert Keith, 4th Bt, 1864–1916, vol. II
Arbuthnot, Robert Wemyss Muir, 1889–1962, vol. VI
Arbuthnot-Leslie of Warthill, William, 1878–1956, vol. V
Arbuthnott, 11th Viscount of, 1845–1914, vol. I
Arbuthnott, 12th Viscount of, 1849–1917, vol. II
Arbuthnott, 13th Viscount of, 1847–1920, vol. II
Arbuthnott, 14th Viscount of, 1882–1960, vol. V
Arbuthnott, 15th Viscount of, 1897–1966, vol. VI
Arbuthnott, Hon. David, 1820–1901, vol. I
Arbuthnott, John Campbell, 1858–1923, vol. II
Arbuthnott, Robert, 1900–1980, vol. VII
Arcedeckne-Butler, Maj.-Gen. St John Desmond, 1896–1959, vol. V
Arch, Joseph, 1826–1919, vol. II
Archambeault, Hon. Sir Horace, 1857–1918, vol. II
Archambeault, Rt Rev. Joseph Alfred, 1859–1913, vol. I
Archbold, William Arthur Jobson, 1865–1947, vol. IV
Archdale, Brig. Arthur Somerville, 1882–1948, vol. IV
Archdale, Rt Hon. Edward, 1850–1916, vol. II
Archdale, Rt Hon. Sir Edward Mervyn, 1st Bt, 1853–1943, vol. IV
Archdale, Rev. Canon Eyre William Preston, 1871–1955, vol. IV
Archdale, Helen Alexander, 1876–1949, vol. IV
Archdale, Brig.-Gen. Hugh James, 1854–1921, vol. II
Archdale, Vice-Adm. Sir Nicholas Edward, 2nd Bt, 1881–1955, vol. V

Archdale, Major Theodore Montgomery, 1873–1918, vol. II
Archdale, Rev. Thomas Hewan, *died* 1924, vol. II
Archdall, Rev. Canon Henry Kingsley, 1886–1976, vol. VII
Archdall, Rt Rev. Mervyn, 1833–1913, vol. I
Archer, Allan; *see* Archer, H. A. F. B.
Archer, Sir Archibald, 1902–1983, vol. VIII
Archer, Lt-Col Charles, 1861–1941, vol. IV
Archer, Adm. Sir Ernest Russell, 1891–1958, vol. V
Archer, Francis Kentdray, 1882–1962, vol. VI
Archer, Sir Geoffrey Francis, 1882–1964, vol. VI
Archer, George, 1896–1960, vol. V
Archer, Sir Gilbert, 1882–1948, vol. IV
Archer, Maj.-Gen. Gilbert Thomas Lancelot, 1903–1986, vol. VIII
Archer, Major Henry, 1883–1917, vol. II
Archer, (Henry) Allan (Fairfax Best), 1887–1950, vol. IV
Archer, Captain Hugh Edward Murray, 1879–1930, vol. III
Archer, James, 1822–1904, vol. I
Archer, Col James Henry L.; *see* Lawrence-Archer.
Archer, Sir John, 1860–1949, vol. IV
Archer, John Beville, 1893–1949, vol. IV
Archer, John Mark, 1908–1965, vol. VI
Archer, Wing Comdr John Oliver, 1887–1968, vol. VI
Archer, Norman Ernest, 1892–1970, vol. VI
Archer, Richard Lawrence, 1874–1953, vol. V
Archer, Col Samuel Arthur, 1871–1943, vol. IV
Archer, Thomas, 1823–1905, vol. I
Archer, Walter E., 1855–1917, vol. II
Archer, William, 1856–1924, vol. II
Archer, William George, 1907–1979, vol. VII
Archer, William John, 1861–1934, vol. III
Archer-Hind, Richard Dacre, 1849–1910, vol. I
Archer Houblon, Mrs Doreen, 1899–1977, vol. VII
Archer-Houblon, Col George Bramston; *see* Houblon.
Archer-Jackson, Lt-Col Basil, 1884–1965, vol. VI
Archer-Shee, Lt-Col Sir Martin, 1873–1935, vol. III
Archey, Sir Gilbert Edward, 1890–1974, vol. VII
Archibald, 1st Baron, 1898–1975, vol. VII
Archibald, Col (temp. Brig.) Gordon King, *died* 1942, vol. IV
Archibald, James, 1863–1946, vol. IV
Archibald, James Montgomery, 1920–1983, vol. VIII
Archibald, Very Rev. John, *died* 1916, vol. II
Archibald, John Gordon, 1885–1970, vol. VI
Archibald, Hon. John Sprott, 1843–1932, vol. III
Archibald, Myles, 1898–1961, vol. VI
Archibald, Raymond Clare, 1875–1957, vol. V
Archibald, Sir Robert George, 1880–1953, vol. V
Archibald, Sir William Frederick Alphonse, 1846–1922, vol. II
Arcot, Prince of, 1882–1952, vol. V
Ardagh, Lt-Col George Hutchings, 1863–1930, vol. III
Ardagh, Maj.-Gen. Sir John Charles, 1840–1907, vol. I
Arden, Lt-Col John Henry Morris, 1875–1918, vol. II
Arden-Clarke, Sir Charles Noble, 1898–1962, vol. VI
Arden-Close, Col Sir Charles Frederick, 1865–1952, vol. V

Arden Wood, William Henry Heton, 1858–1932, vol. III

Ardilaun, 1st Baron, 1840–1915, vol. I

Ardill, Rev. John Roche, *died* 1947, vol. IV(A)

Arditi, Luigi, 1822–1903, vol. I

Ardizzone, Edward Jeffrey Irving, 1900–1979, vol. VII

Ardron, John, 1843–1919, vol. II

Ardwall, Hon. Lord; Andrew Jameson, 1845–1911, vol. I

Arenberg, Auguste Louis Alberic, Prince D', 1837–1924, vol. II

Arendzen, Rev. John, 1873–1954, vol. V

Arensky, Antony Stepanovich, 1861–1906, vol. I

Argenti, Philip Pandely, 1891–1974, vol. VII

Argles, Rev. Canon George Marsham, 1841–1920, vol. II

Argyle, Lt-Col Edward Percy, 1875–1935, vol. III

Argyle, Hon. Sir Stanley Seymour, 1867–1940, vol. III

Argyll, 8th Duke of, 1823–1900, vol. I

Argyll, 9th Duke of, 1845–1914, vol. I

Argyll, 10th Duke of, 1872–1949, vol. IV

Argyll, 11th Duke of, 1903–1973, vol. VII

Aria, Mrs, 1866–1931, vol. III

Arias, Roberto Emilio, 1918–1989, vol. VIII

Ariff, Sir Kamil Mohamed, 1893–1960, vol. V

Aris, Lt-Col Charles John, 1874–1931, vol. III

Aris, Ernest Alfred, 1882–1963, vol. VI

Aris, Major Herbert, 1868–1952, vol. V

Arisugawa, Prince Takehito, 1862–1913, vol. I

Arkell, Rev. Anthony John, 1898–1980, vol. VII

Arkell, Captain Sir Noël; *see* Arkell, Captain Sir T. N.

Arkell, Reginald, *died* 1959, vol. V

Arkell, Captain Sir (Thomas) Noël, 1893–1981, vol. VIII

Arkell, William Joscelyn, 1904–1958, vol. V

Arkle, Harry, 1893–1973, vol. VII

Arkwright, Rev. Ernest Henry, 1868–1950, vol. IV

Arkwright, Esme Francis Wigsell, 1882–1934, vol. III

Arkwright, Francis, 1846–1915, vol. II

Arkwright, Frederic Charles, 1853–1923, vol. II

Arkwright, John Hungerford, 1833–1905, vol. I

Arkwright, John Peter, 1864–1931, vol. III

Arkwright, Sir John Stanhope, 1872–1954, vol. V

Arkwright, Sir Joseph Arthur, 1864-1944, vol. IV

Arkwright, Richard, 1835–1918, vol. II

Arkwright, Maj.-Gen. Robert Harry Bertram, 1903–1971, vol. VII

Arkwright, William, 1857–1925, vol. II

Arlen, Michael, 1895–1956, vol. V

Arlen, Stephen Walter, 1913–1972, vol. VII

Arliss, George, 1868–1946, vol. IV

Arliss, Vice-Adm. Stephen Harry Tolson, 1895–1954, vol. V

Armaghdale, 1st Baron, 1850–1924, vol. II

Armand, Louis, 1905–1971, vol. VII

Armbruster, Charles Hubert, 1874–1957, vol. V

Armer, Sir Frederick; *see* Armer, Sir I. F.

Armer, Sir (Isaac) Frederick, 1891–1982, vol. VIII

Armes, Col Reginald John, 1876–1948, vol. IV

Armfelt, Roger Noel, 1897–1955, vol. V

Armfield, Constance, (Mrs Maxwell Armfield); *see* Smedley, Constance.

Armfield, Maxwell Ashby, 1881–1972, vol. VII

Armitage, Captain Albert Borlase, 1864–1943, vol. IV

Armitage, Sir Arthur Llewellyn, 1916–1984, vol. VIII

Armitage, Bernard William, 1890–1976, vol. VII

Armitage, Sir Cecil; *see* Armitage, Sir S. C.

Armitage, Captain Sir Cecil Hamilton, 1869–1933, vol. III

Armitage, Cecil Henry, 1877–1955, vol. V

Armitage, Gen. Sir (Charles) Clement, 1881–1973, vol. VII

Armitage, Major Charles Leathley, 1871–1951, vol. V

Armitage, Gen. Sir Clement; *see* Armitage, Gen. Sir Charles C.

Armitage, Rev. Cyril Moxon, 1900–1966, vol. VI

Armitage, Brig.-Gen. Edward Hume, 1859–1949, vol. IV

Armitage, Elkanah, 1844–1929, vol. III

Armitage, Ella Sophia, 1841–1931, vol. III

Armitage, Francis Paul, 1875–1953, vol. V

Armitage, Frank, 1872–1955, vol. V

Armitage, Rev. George, 1856–1948, vol. IV

Armitage, Hugh Traill, 1881–1963, vol. VI

Armitage, John, 1910–1980, vol. VII

Armitage, Robert, 1866–1944, vol. IV

Armitage, Rev. Robert, 1857–1954, vol. V

Armitage, Sir Robert Perceval, 1906–1990, vol. VIII

Armitage, Sir (Stephen) Cecil, 1889–1962, vol. VI

Armitage, Valentine Leathley, 1888–1964, vol. VI

Armitage, Ven. William James, 1860–1929, vol. III

Armitage-Smith, George, *died* 1923, vol. II

Armitage-Smith, Sir Sydney Armitage, 1876–1932, vol. III

Armitstead, 1st Baron, 1824–1915, vol. I

Armitstead, Ven. John Hornby, 1868–1941, vol. IV

Armitstead, Rev. John Richard, 1829–1918, vol. II

Armour, Donald John, *died* 1933, vol. III

Armour, Eric Norman, 1877–1934, vol. III

Armour, George Denholm, 1864–1949, vol. IV

Armour, Rev. James Brown, 1842–1928, vol. II

Armour, Hon. John Douglas, 1830–1903, vol. I

Armour, Jonathan Ogden, 1863–1927, vol. II

Armour, Margaret; *see* MacDougall, Margaret.

Armour, Rev. Samuel Crawford, 1839–1929, vol. III

Armour, Rt Rev. Thomas Makinson, 1890–1963, vol. VI

Armour, William, 1903–1979, vol. VII

Armour-Hannay, Samuel Beveridge, 1856–1919, vol. II

Arms, John Taylor, 1887–1953, vol. V

Armstead, Henry Hugh, 1828–1905, vol. I

Armstrong, 1st Baron *cr* 1887, 1810–1900, vol. I (up to the 5th edition of vol. I this entry is headed in error by the first three lines of the following entry: Armstrong, Sir Alexander)

Armstrong, 1st Baron *cr* 1903, 1863–1941, vol. IV

Armstrong, 2nd Baron *cr* 1903, 1892–1972, vol. VII

Armstrong, 3rd Baron, 1919–1987, vol. VIII

Armstrong of Sanderstead, Baron (Life Peer); William Armstrong, 1915–1980, vol. VII

Armstrong, Sir Alexander, 1818–1899, vol. I

Armstrong, Sir Alfred Norman, 1899–1966, vol. VI

Armstrong, Sir Andrew Harvey, 3rd Bt, 1866–1922, vol. II

Armstrong, Anthony (A. A.); *see* Willis, A. A.

Armstrong, Sir Andrew St Clare, 5th Bt, 1912–1987, vol. VIII

Armstrong, Arthur Henry, 1893–1972, vol. VII

Armstrong, Arthur Leopold, 1888–1973, vol. VII

Armstrong, Col Bertie Harold Olivier, 1873–1950, vol. IV

Armstrong, Brig. Charles Douglas, 1897–1985, vol. VIII

Armstrong, Sir Charles Herbert, 1862–1949, vol. IV

Armstrong, Brig.-Gen. Charles Johnstone, 1872–1934, vol. III

Armstrong, Christopher Wyborne, 1899–1986, vol. VIII

Armstrong, Rev. Canon Claude Blakeley, 1889–1982, vol. VIII

Armstrong, David, *see* Clewes, Winston.

Armstrong, Edmond Arrenton, 1899–1966, vol. VI

Armstrong, Edmund Clarence Richard, 1879–1923, vol. II

Armstrong, Rev. Sir Edmund Frederick, 2nd Bt, 1836–1899, vol. I

Armstrong, Edmund La Touche, 1864–1946, vol. IV

Armstrong, Edward, 1846–1928, vol. II

Armstrong, Lt-Col Edward, 1869–1951, vol. V

Armstrong, Maj.-Gen. Edward Francis Hunter, 1834–1917, vol. II

Armstrong, Edward Frankland, 1878–1945, vol. IV

Armstrong, Hon. Ernest Howard, vol. III

Armstrong, F. A. W. T., 1849–1920, vol. II

Armstrong, Francis Edwin, 1879–1921, vol. II

Armstrong, Sir Francis Philip, 3rd Bt, 1871–1944, vol. IV

Armstrong, Major Francis Savage Nesbitt S.; *see* Savage-Armstrong.

Armstrong, Francis William, 1919–1988, vol. VIII

Armstrong, Frederick Ernest, 1884–1962, vol. VI

Armstrong, Captain Sir George Carlyon Hughes, 1st Bt, 1836–1907, vol. I

Armstrong, George Eli, 1854–1933, vol. III

Armstrong, Sir George Elliot, 2nd Bt, 1866–1940, vol. III

Armstrong, George Francis S.; *see* Savage-Armstrong.

Armstrong, George Frederick, 1842–1900, vol. I

Armstrong, George Gilbert, 1870–1945, vol. IV

Armstrong, George James, 1901–1972, vol. VII

Armstrong, Col Gerald Denne, 1865–1931, vol. III

Armstrong, Sir Gloster; *see* Armstrong, Sir H. G.

Armstrong, Sir Godfrey, 1882–1964, vol. VI

Armstrong, Hamilton Fish, 1893–1973, vol. VII

Armstrong, Captain Harold Courtenay, 1892–1943, vol. IV

Armstrong, Sir (Harry) Gloster, 1861–1938, vol. III

Armstrong, Rt Hon. Henry Bruce, 1844–1943, vol. IV

Armstrong, Henry Edward, 1848–1937, vol. III

Armstrong, Rev. James, *died* 1928, vol. II

Armstrong, James Shelley Phipps, 1899–1971, vol. VII

Armstrong, John, 1893–1973, vol. VII

Armstrong, Surg.-Dentist John Alexander, 1862–1928, vol. II

Armstrong, John Anderson, 1910–1990, vol. VIII

Armstrong, Brig. John Cardew, 1887–1953, vol. V

Armstrong, Col John Cecil, 1870–1961, vol. VI

Armstrong, Sir John Dunamace H.; *see* Heaton-Armstrong.

Armstrong, John Elliot, 1875–1962, vol. VI

Armstrong, Vice-Adm. John Garnet, 1870–1949, vol. IV

Armstrong, Hon. John Ignatius, 1908–1977, vol. VII

Armstrong, Most Rev. John Ward, 1915–1987, vol. VIII

Armstrong, John Warneford Scobell, 1877–1960, vol. V

Armstrong, Katharine Fairlie, 1892–1969, vol. VI

Armstrong, Louis Daniel, 1900–1971, vol. VII

Armstrong, Martin Donisthorpe, 1882–1974, vol. VII

Armstrong, Rt Rev. Mervyn, 1906–1984, vol. VIII

Armstrong, Dame Nellie; *see* Melba, Dame Nellie.

Armstrong, Sir Nesbitt William, 4th Bt, 1875–1953, vol. V

Armstrong, Col Oliver Carleton, 1859–1932, vol. III

Armstrong, Sir Richard Harold, 1874–1950, vol. IV

Armstrong, Gen. St George Bewes, 1871–1956, vol. V

Armstrong, Samuel, 1878–1959, vol. V

Armstrong, Rev. Simon Carter, 1856–1942, vol. IV

Armstrong, Thomas, 1832–1911, vol. I

Armstrong, Thomas, 1899–1978, vol. VII

Armstrong, Thomas Graves Lowry Herbert, 1856–1940, vol. III

Armstrong, Rt Rev. Thomas Henry, 1857–1930, vol. III

Armstrong, Thomas Mandeville Emerson, 1869–1922, vol. II

Armstrong, Wallace Edwin, 1896–1980, vol. VII

Armstrong, Sir Walter, 1850–1918, vol. II

Armstrong, Rev. Walter H., 1873–1949, vol. IV

Armstrong, William, 1882–1952, vol. V

Armstrong, William Charles H.; *see* Heaton-Armstrong.

Armstrong, Hon. William Drayton, 1861–1936, vol. III

Armstrong, William George, 1859–1941, vol. IV

Armstrong, Sir William Herbert Fletcher, 1892–1950, vol. IV

Armstrong Cowan, Sir Christopher; *see* Cowan, Sir C. G. A.

Armstrong-Jones, Sir Robert; *see* Jones.

Armstrong-Jones, Ronald Owen Lloyd, 1899–1966, vol. VI

Armytage, Rev. Canon Duncan, 1889–1954, vol. V

Armytage, Sir George, 5th Bt, 1819–1899, vol. I

Armytage, Brig.-Gen. Sir George Ayscough, 7th Bt, 1872–1953, vol. V

Armytage, Sir George John, 6th Bt, 1842–1918, vol. II

Armytage, Captain Sir John Lionel, 8th Bt, 1901–1983, vol. VIII

Armytage, Percy, 1853–1934, vol. III

Armytage, Rear-Adm. Reginald William, 1903–1984, vol. VIII

Armytage, Lt-Col Vivian Bartley G.; *see* Green-Armytage.

Arnason, Frú Barbara; *see* Moray Williams, B.

Arnaud, Emile, 1864–1921, vol. II

Arnaud, Yvonne, 1895–1958, vol. V
Arnavon, Jacques, 1877–1949, vol. IV
Arnell, Charles Christopher, 1881–1948, vol. IV
Arnett, Edward John, died 1940, vol. III
Arney, Frank Douglas, 1899–1983, vol. VIII
Arnheim, Edward Henry Silberstein Von, died 1925, vol. II
Arnison, William Christopher, 1837–1899, vol. I
Arno, Peter, 1906–1968, vol. VI
Arnold, 1st Baron, 1878–1945, vol. IV
Arnold, Sir Alfred, 1835–1908, vol. I
Arnold, Col Alfred James, 1866–1933, vol. III
Arnold, Maj.-Gen. Allan Cholmondeley, 1893–1962, vol. VI
Arnold, Sir Arthur, 1833–1902, vol. I
Arnold, Arthur, 1891–1961, vol. VI
Arnold, Bening Mourant, 1884–1955, vol. V
Arnold, Denis Midgley, 1926–1986, vol. VIII
Arnold, Edmund George, 1865–1939, vol. III
Arnold, Edward Augustus, 1857–1942, vol. IV
Arnold, Edward Carleton, died 1949, vol. IV
Arnold, Edward Vernon, 1857–1926, vol. II
Arnold, Sir Edwin, 1832–1904, vol. I
Arnold, Edwin Lester, died 1935, vol. III
Arnold, Sir Frederick Blackmore, 1906–1968, vol. VI
Arnold, George Frederick, died 1917, vol. II
Arnold, Henry Fraser James Coape-, 1846–1923, vol. II
Arnold, Gen. of the Army Henry H., 1886–1950, vol. IV
Arnold, Rev. Henry James Lawes, 1854–1928, vol. II
Arnold, Lt-Col Herbert Tollemache, 1867–1943, vol. IV
Arnold, Ivor Deiniol Osborn, 1895–1952, vol. V
Arnold, Major John Effingham, 1882–1939, vol. III
Arnold, John Oliver, 1858–1930, vol. III
Arnold, Ralph Crispian Marshall, 1906–1970, vol. VI
Arnold, Reginald Edward, 1853–1938, vol. III
Arnold, Ronald Nathan, 1908–1963, vol. VI
Arnold, Col Stanley, 1844–1906, vol. I
Arnold, Thomas, 1823–1900, vol. I
Arnold, Thomas George, 1866–1944, vol. IV
Arnold, Thomas James, 1879–1945, vol. IV
Arnold, Sir Thomas Walker, 1864–1930, vol. III
Arnold, Thurman Wesley, 1891–1969, vol. VI
Arnold, Tom, (Thomas Charles Arnold), died 1969, vol. VI
Arnold, Sir William Henry, 1903–1973, vol. VII
Arnold, William R., 1872–1929, vol. III
Arnold-Forster, Rear-Adm. Forster Delafield, 1876–1958, vol. V
Arnold-Forster, Major Francis Anson, 1890–1966, vol. VI
Arnold-Forster, Comdr Hugh Christopher, 1890–1965, vol. VI
Arnold-Forster, Rt Hon. Hugh Oakeley, 1855–1909, vol. I
Arnoldi, Frank, born 1848, vol. III
Arnoldi, Col Frank Fauquier, 1889–1953, vol. V
Arnott, Most Rev. Felix Raymond, 1911–1988, vol. VIII
Arnott, Rev. Henry, died 1931, vol. III
Arnott, James Fullarton, 1914–1982, vol. VIII
Arnott, Sir John, 1st Bt, 1817–1898, vol. I

Arnott, John, 1871–1942, vol. IV
Arnott, Sir John Alexander, 2nd Bt, 1853–1940, vol. III
Arnott, Col John Maclean, 1869–1945, vol. IV
Arnott, Sir John Robert Alexander, 5th Bt, 1927–1981, vol. VIII
Arnott, Sir Lauriston John, 3rd Bt, 1890–1958, vol. V
Arnott, Leonard, 1887–1943, vol. IV
Arnott, Sir Robert John, 4th Bt, 1896–1966, vol. VI
Arnott, Maj.-Gen. Stanley, 1888–1972, vol. VII
Arnott, Brig.-Gen. William, 1860–1929, vol. III
Arnould, Francis Graham, 1875–1941, vol. IV
Aron, Raymond Claude Ferdinand, 1905–1983, vol. VIII
Aron, Robert, 1905–1975, vol. VII
Aronson, Victor Rees, 1880–1951, vol. V
Arp, Jean Hans, 1887–1966, vol. VI
Arran, 5th Earl of, 1839–1901, vol. I
Arran, 6th Earl of, 1868–1958, vol. V
Arran, 7th Earl of, 1903–1958, vol. II
Arran, 8th Earl of, 1910–1983, vol. VIII
Arrhenius, Svante August, 1859–1927, vol. II
Arrol, Sir William, 1839–1913, vol. I
Arrow, Gilbert John, 1873–1948, vol. IV
Arrowsmith, Hugh, 1888–1972, vol. VII
Arrowsmith, Rev. Preb. Walter Gordon, 1888–1964, vol. VI
Arrowsmith-Brown, Lt-Col James Arnold, 1882–1937, vol. III
Arsenault, Hon. Aubin Edmond, 1870–1969, vol. VI
Artemus Jones, Sir Thomas; see Jones.
Arthur, Sir Allan, 1857–1923, vol. II
Arthur, Hon. Sir Basil Malcolm, 5th Bt, 1928–1985, vol. VIII
Arthur, Col Sir Charles Gordon, 1884–1953, vol. V
Arthur, Major Christopher Geoffrey, 1882–1943, vol. IV
Arthur, Donald Ramsay, 1917–1984, vol. VIII
Arthur, Sir Geoffrey George, 1920–1984, vol. VIII
Arthur, Sir George Compton Archibald, 3rd Bt, 1860–1946, vol. IV
Arthur, Sir George Malcolm, 4th Bt, 1908-1949, vol. IV
Arthur, Col John Maurice, 1877–1954, vol. V
Arthur, Captain Leonard Robert Sunskersett, 1864–1903, vol. I
Arthur, Col Lionel Francis, 1876–1952, vol. V
Arthur, Sir (Oswald) Raynor, 1905–1973, vol. VII
Arthur, Sir Raynor; see Arthur, Sir O. R.
Arthur, Hon. Richard, 1865–1932, vol. III
Artsibashev, Michel Petrovitch, 1878–1927, vol. II
Arunachalam, Sir Ponnambalam, 1853–1924, vol. II
Arundale, George Sydney, 1878–1945, vol. IV
Arundel and Surrey, Earl of; Philip Joseph Mary Fitzalan-Howard, 1879–1902, vol. I
Arundel, Sir Arundel Tagg, 1843–1929, vol. III
Arundell of Wardour, 12th Baron, 1831–1906, vol. I
Arundell of Wardour, 13th Baron, 1834–1907, vol. I
Arundell of Wardour, 14th Baron, 1859–1921, vol. II
Arundell of Wardour, 15th Baron, 1861–1939, vol. III
Arundell of Wardour, 16th Baron, 1907–1944, vol. IV
Arundell, Dennis Drew, 1898–1988, vol. VIII
Arundell, Brig. Sir Robert Duncan Harris, 1904–1989, vol. VIII

Arup, Sir Ove Nyquist, 1895–1988, vol. VIII

Arur Singh, Sir Sardar Bahadur Sardar, 1863–1926, vol. II

Arwyn, Baron (Life Peer); Arwyn Randall Arwyn, 1897–1978, vol. VII

Asafu-Adjaye, Sir Edward Okyere, 1903–1976, vol. VII

Asbury, William, 1889–1961, vol. VI

Asch, Sholem, 1880–1957, vol. V

Asche, Oscar, 1872–1936, vol. III

Ascoli, Frank David, 1883–1958, vol. V

Ascroft, Peter Byers, 1906–1965, vol. VI

Ascroft, Robert, 1847–1899, vol. I

Ascroft, Sir William, 1832–1916, vol. II

Ascroft, Sir William Fawell, 1876–1954, vol. V

Ash, Audrey B., *died* 1958, vol. V

Ash, Edwin Lancelot Hopewell-, 1881–1964, vol. VI

Ash, Rt Rev. Fortescue Leo, 1882–1956, vol. V

Ash, Graham Baron, 1889–1980, vol. VII

Ash, Major William Claudius Casson, 1870–1916, vol. II

Ashbee, C. R., 1863–1942, vol. IV

Ashbolt, Sir Alfred Henry, 1870–1930, vol. III

Ashbourne, 1st Baron, 1837–1913, vol. I

Ashbourne, 2nd Baron, 1868–1942, vol. IV

Ashbourne, 3rd Baron, 1901–1983, vol. VIII

Ashbridge, Sir Noel, 1889–1975, vol. VII

Ashbrook, 7th Viscount, 1830–1906, vol. I

Ashbrook, 8th Viscount, 1836–1919, vol. II

Ashbrook, 9th Viscount, 1870–1936, vol. III

Ashburner, Maj.-Gen. George Elliot, 1820–1907, vol. I

Ashburner, Lt-Col Lionel Forbes, 1874–1923, vol. II

Ashburner, Lionel Robert, 1827–1907, vol. I

Ashburner, Walter, 1864–1936, vol. III

Ashburnham, 5th Earl of, 1840–1913, vol. I

Ashburnham, 6th Earl of, 1855–1924, vol. II

Ashburnham, Sir Anchitel, 8th Bt, 1828–1899, vol. I

Ashburnham, Sir Anchitel Piers, 9th Bt; *see* Ashburnham-Clement.

Ashburnham, Sir Cromer, 1831–1917, vol. II

Ashburnham, Sir Fleetwood, 11th Bt, 1869–1953, vol. V

Ashburnham, Hon. John, 1845–1912, vol. I

Ashburnham, Sir Reginald, 10th Bt, 1865–1944, vol. IV

Ashburnham-Clement, Sir Anchitel Piers, 9th Bt, 1861–1935, vol. III

Ashburton, 5th Baron, 1866–1938, vol. III

Ashburton, Lady; (Louisa), *died* 1903, vol. I

Ashby, Arthur Wilfred, 1886–1953, vol. V

Ashby, Col George Ashby, 1856–1937, vol. III

Ashby, Hugh Tuke, 1880–1952, vol. V

Ashby, Sir James William Murray, 1822–1911, vol. I

Ashby, Dame Margery Irene C.; *see* Corbett Ashby.

Ashby, Very Rev. Paul Ogilvie, 1867–1937, vol. III

Ashby, Robert Claude, 1876–1963, vol. VI

Ashby, Thomas, 1874–1931, vol. III

Ashby-Sterry, Joseph, *died* 1917, vol. II

Ashcombe, 1st Baron, 1828–1917, vol. II

Ashcombe, 2nd Baron, 1867–1947, vol. IV

Ashcombe, 3rd Baron, 1899–1962, vol. VI

Ashcroft, Alex Hutchinson, 1887–1963, vol. VI

Ashcroft, (Charles) Neil, 1937–1984, vol. VIII

Ashcroft, D(udley) Walker, 1904–1963, vol. VI

Ashcroft, Neil; *see* Ashcroft, C. N.

Ashcroft, Thomas, 1890–1961, vol. VI

Ashdown, Baron (Life Peer); Arnold Silverstone, 1911–1977, vol. VII

Ashdown, Arthur Durham, 1872–1953, vol. V

Ashdown, Sir Curtis George, 1876–1933, vol. III

Ashdown, Sir George Henry, 1857–1924, vol. II

Ashdown, Rt Rev. Hugh Edward, 1904–1977, vol. VII

Ashe, Rear-Adm. Edward Percy, 1852–1914, vol. I

Ashenheim, Sir Neville Noel, 1900–1984, vol. VIII

Asher, Alexander, 1835–1905, vol. I

Asher, Amy, (Mrs Peter Asher); *see* Shuard, A.

Asher, Sir Augustus Gordon Grant, 1861–1930, vol. III

Asher, Florence May, 1888–1977, vol. VII

Asher, Samuel Garcia, 1868–1938, vol. III

Asherson, Nehemiah, 1897–1989, vol. VIII

Ashfield, Percy John, 1870–1946, vol. IV

Ashford, Bailey K., *died* 1934, vol. III

Ashford, Sir Cyril Ernest, 1867–1951, vol. V

Ashford, Hon. William George, 1874–1925, vol. II

Ashkanasy, Maurice, 1901–1971, vol. VII

Ashley; *see* Harinden, A. E.

Ashley, Lord; Anthony Ashley-Cooper, 1900–1947, vol. IV

Ashley, Rt Hon. (Anthony) Evelyn Melbourne, 1836–1907, vol. I

Ashley, Hon. Cecil, 1849–1932, vol. III

Ashley, Rt Hon. Evelyn Melbourne; *see* Ashley, Rt Hon. A. E. M.

Ashley, Francis Noel, 1884–1976, vol. VII

Ashley, Lt-Col Frank, 1870–1923, vol. II

Ashley, Frederick Morewood, 1846–1933, vol. III

Ashley, Henry V., 1872–1945, vol. IV

Ashley, Sir Percy Walter Llewellyn, 1876–1945, vol. IV

Ashley, Walter, 1893–1937, vol. III

Ashley, Sir William James, 1860–1927, vol. II

Ashley-Brown, Ven. William, 1887–1970, vol. VI

Ashley-Scarlett, Lt-Col Henry, 1886–1976, vol. VII

Ashlin, George C., 1837–1922, vol. II

Ashmall, Rev. Francis James, 1856–1948, vol. IV

Ashman, Sir Frederick Herbert, 2nd Bt, 1875–1916, vol. II

Ashman, Sir Herbert, 1st Bt, 1854–1914, vol. I

Ashmead-Bartlett, Ellis, 1881–1931, vol. III

Ashmead-Bartlett, Sir Ellis; *see* Bartlett.

Ashmole, Bernard, 1894–1988, vol. VIII

Ashmore, Hon. Lord; John Wilson, 1857–1932, vol. III

Ashmore, Sir Alexander Murray, 1855–1906, vol. I

Ashmore, Maj.-Gen. Edward Bailey, 1872–1953, vol. V

Ashmore, Major Edwin James Caldwell, 1893–1959, vol. V

Ashmore, Vice-Adm. Leslie Haliburton, 1893–1974, vol. VII

Ashmore, William Caldwell, 1866–1931, vol. III

Ashton, 1st Baron, 1842–1930, vol. III

Ashton, Baroness; (Florence Maude), 1856–1944, vol. IV

Ashton of Hyde, 1st Baron, 1855–1933, vol. III

Ashton of Hyde, 2nd Baron, 1901–1983, vol. VIII

Ashton, Algernon Bennet Langton, 1859–1937, vol. III

Ashton, Arthur Jacob, 1855–1925, vol. II

Ashton, Sir (Arthur) Leigh (Bolland), 1897–1983, vol. VIII

Ashton, Lt-Col Edward Malcolm, 1895–1978, vol. VII

Ashton, Ellis, 1919–1985, vol. VIII

Ashton, Lt-Gen. Ernest Charles, 1873–1957, vol. V

Ashton, Sir Frederick William Mallandaine, 1904–1988, vol. VIII

Ashton, Gilbert, 1896–1981, vol. VIII

Ashton, Harry, 1882–1952, vol. V

Ashton, Helen, (Mrs Arthur Jordan), 1891–1958, vol. V

Ashton, Captain Henry Gordon Gooch, 1870–1951, vol. V

Ashton, Sir Hubert, 1898–1979, vol. VII

Ashton, Hon. James, 1864–1939, vol. III

Ashton, Engr Rear-Adm. James, 1883–1951, vol. V

Ashton, Rt Rev. John William, 1866–1964, vol. VI

Ashton, Julian Rossi, 1851–1942, vol. IV

Ashton, Sir Leigh; *see* Ashton, Sir A. L. B.

Ashton, Margaret, 1856–1937, vol. III

Ashton, Sir Ralph Percy, 1860–1921, vol. II

Ashton, Teddy; *see* Clarke, Charles Allen.

Ashton, Rt Hon. Thomas, 1844–1927, vol. II

Ashton, Thomas Southcliffe, 1889–1968, vol. VI

Ashton, Sir William, 1881–1963, vol. VI

Aston-Gwatkin, Frank Trelawny Arthur, 1889–1976, vol. VII

Ashton-Gwatkin, Rev. Walter Henry Trelawny; *see* Gwatkin.

Ashtown, 3rd Baron, 1868–1946, vol. IV

Ashtown, 4th Baron, 1897–1966, vol. VI

Ashtown, 5th Baron, 1901–1979, vol. VII

Ashtown, 6th Baron, 1931–1990, vol. VIII

Ashwanden, Col Sydney William Louis, 1878–1947, vol. IV

Ashwell, Maj. Arthur Lindley, 1886–1986, vol. VIII

Ashwell, Lena, *died* 1957, vol. V

Ashwin, Sir Bernard Carl, 1896–1975, vol. VII

Ashworth, Ernest Horatio, 1870–1934, vol. III

Ashworth, Harold Kenneth, 1903–1978, vol. VII

Ashworth, James Hartley, 1874–1936, vol. III

Ashworth, Sir John Percy, 1906–1975, vol. VII

Ashworth, Philip Arthur, 1853–1921, vol. II

Ashworth, Air Comdt Dame Veronica Margaret, 1910–1977, vol. VII

Aske, Sir Robert William, 1st Bt, 1872–1954, vol. V

Askew, Claude Arthur, *died* 1917, vol. II

Askew, Herbert Royston, 1891–1986, vol. VIII

Askew, William George, 1890–1968, vol. VI

Askew-Robertson, Watson, 1834–1907, vol. I

Askew Robertson, William Haggerston, 1868–1942, vol. IV

Askey, Arthur Bowden, 1900–1982, vol. VIII

Askin, Hon. Sir Robert William, 1909–1981, vol. VIII

Askuran, Sir Shantidas, 1882–1950, vol. IV(A), vol. V

Askwith, 1st Baron, 1861–1942, vol. IV

Askwith, Lady; (Ellen), *died* 1962, vol. VI

Askwith, Arthur Vivian, 1893–1971, vol. VII

Askwith, Rev. Edward Harrison, 1864–1946, vol. IV

Askwith, Col Henry Francis, 1865–1938, vol. III

Askwith, Rt Rev. Wilfred Marcus, 1890–1962, vol. VI

Askwith, Ven. William Henry, 1843–1911, vol. I

Aslett, Alfred, 1847–1928, vol. II

Aslin, Charles Herbert, 1893–1959, vol. V

Aslin, Elizabeth Mary, 1923–1989, vol. VIII

Asman, Rev. Harry Newbitt, 1877–1950, vol. IV

Aspden, Hartley, 1858–1940, vol. III

Aspell, Sir John, 1854–1938, vol. III

Aspinall, Sir Algernon Edward, 1871–1952, vol. V

Aspinall, Arthur, 1901–1972, vol. VII

Aspinall, Butler, 1861–1935, vol. III

Aspinall, Sir John Audley Frederick, 1851–1937, vol. III

Aspinall, John Bridge, 1877–1932, vol. III

Aspinall, Major John Ralph, 1878–1947, vol. IV

Aspinall, Ven. Noël Lake, 1861–1934, vol. III

Aspinall, Lt-Col Robert Lowndes, 1869–1916, vol. II

Aspinall, Lt-Col Robert Stivala, 1895–1954, vol. V

Aspinall, William Briant Philip, 1912–1988, vol. VIII

Aspinall-Oglander, Brig.-Gen. Cecil Faber, 1878–1959, vol. V

Asquith of Bishopstone, Baron (Life Peer); Cyril Asquith, 1890–1954, vol. V

Asquith of Yarnbury, Baroness (Life Peeress); Helen Violet Bonham Carter, 1887–1969, vol. VI

Asquith, Hon. Anthony, 1902–1968, vol. VI

Asquith, Hon. Arthur Melland, 1883–1939, vol. III

Asquith, Lady Cynthia, *died* 1960, vol. V

Asquith, Cyril Edward, 1902–1967, vol. VI

Asquith, Hon. Herbert, 1881–1947, vol. IV

Asquith, Raymond, 1878–1916, vol. II

Asser, Gen. Sir John; *see* Asser, Gen. Sir J. J.

Asser, Gen. Sir (Joseph) John, 1867–1949, vol. IV

Asser, Brig.-Gen. Verney, 1873–1944, vol. IV

Assheton, Ralph, 1830–1907, vol. I

Assheton, Sir Ralph Cockayne, 1st Bt, 1860–1955, vol. V

Assheton, Richard, 1863–1915, vol. I

Assheton-Smith, Sir Charles Garden, 1st Bt, 1851–1914, vol. I

Assheton-Smith, George William Duff, 1848–1904, vol. I

Astaire, Fred, 1899–1987, vol. VIII

Astbury, Arthur Ralph, 1880–1973, vol. VII

Astbury, Lt-Comdr Frederick Wolfe, 1872–1954, vol. V

Astbury, Rev. George, *died* 1926, vol. II

Astbury, Sir George, 1902–1985, vol. VIII

Astbury, Rev. Canon (Harold) Stanley, 1889–1962, vol. VI

Astbury, Herbert Arthur, 1870–1968, vol. VI

Astbury, Rt Hon. Sir John Meir, 1860–1939, vol. III

Astbury, Norman Frederick, 1908–1987, vol. VIII

Astbury, Rev. Canon Stanley; *see* Astbury, Rev. Canon H. S.

Astbury, William Thomas, 1898–1961, vol. VI

Astell, Maj.-Gen. Charles Edward, *died* 1901, vol. I

Astell, Richard John Vereker, 1890–1969, vol. VI

Astell, Captain Somerset Charles Godfrey Fairfax, 1866–1917, vol. II

Astell Hohler, Thomas Sidney, 1919–1989, vol. VIII

Asterley Jones, Philip; *see* Jones.

Astley, Bertram Frankland Frankland-Russell-, 1857–1904, vol. I
Astley, Major Delaval Graham L'Estrange, 1868–1951, vol. V
Astley, Henry Jacob Delaval Frankland-Russell-, 1888–1912, vol. I
Astley, Hubert Delaval, 1860–1925, vol. II
Astley, Rev. Hugh John Dukinfield, 1856–1930, vol. III
Astley, Kathleen Mary; see Astley, Mrs Reginald.
Astley, Mrs Reginald, (Kathleen Mary Astley), 1880–1973, vol. VII
Astley, Reginald Basil, 1862–1942, vol. IV
Astley-Corbett, Sir Francis Edmund George, 4th Bt, 1859–1939, vol. III
Astley-Corbett, Sir (Francis) Henry (Rivers), 5th Bt, 1915–1943, vol. IV
Astley-Corbett, Sir Henry; see Astley-Corbett, Sir F. H. R.
Astley-Rushton, Vice-Adm. Edward Astley; see Rushton.
Aston, Alfred Withall, 1852–1929, vol. III
Aston, Arthur Vincent, 1896–1981, vol. VIII
Aston, Rev. Canon Basil, 1880–1957, vol. V
Aston, Bernard Cracroft, 1871–1951, vol. V
Aston, Sir Christopher Southcote, 1920–1982, vol. VIII
Aston, Francis William, 1877–1945, vol. IV
Aston, Maj.-Gen. Sir George Grey, 1861–1938, vol. III
Aston, Theodore, died 1910, vol. I
Aston, Thomas William, 1922–1981, vol. VIII
Aston, William George, 1841–1911, vol. I
Astor, 1st Viscount, 1848–1919, vol. II
Astor, 2nd Viscount, 1879–1952, vol. V
Astor, 3rd Viscount, 1907–1966, vol. VI
Astor, Viscountess; (Nancy); 1879–1964, vol. VI
Astor of Hever, 1st Baron, 1886–1971, vol. VI
Astor of Hever, 2nd Baron, 1918–1984, vol. VIII
Astor, Hon. John, 1923–1987, vol. VIII
Astor, John Jacob, 1864–1912, vol. I
Astor, Hon. Michael Langhorne, 1916–1980, vol. VII
Asturias, Miguel Angel, 1899–1974, vol. VII
Atatürk, Kamâl, 1881–1938, vol. III
Atcherley, Air Vice-Marshal David Francis William, 1904–1952, vol. V
Atcherley, Col Sir Llewellyn William, 1871–1954, vol. V
Atcherley, Air Marshal Sir Richard Llewellyn Roger, 1904–1970, vol. VI
Atchison, Major Charles Ernest, 1875–1917, vol. II
Atchley, Chewton, 1850–1922, vol. II
Atchley, Shirley Clifford, 1871–1936, vol. III
Athaide, Most Rev. Dominic Romuald, 1909–1982, vol. VIII
Athawes, Edward James, died 1902, vol. I
Athelstan-Johnson, Wilfrid, 1876–1939, vol. III
Athenagoras, Archbishop, (Archbishop of Thyateira), died 1962, vol. VI
Athenagoras, Spyrou, 1886–1972, vol. VII
Athenagoras, Theodoritos, 1912–1979, vol. VII
Atherley, Major Evelyn George Hammond, 1852–1935, vol. III
Atherley-Jones, Llewellyn Archer, 1851–1929, vol. III

Atherton, Gertrude Franklin, died 1948, vol. IV
Atherton, Ray, 1885–1960, vol. V
Atherton, Col Thomas James, 1856–1920, vol. II
Athill, Charles Harold, died 1922, vol. II
Athill, Lt-Col Francis Remi Imbert, 1880–1958, vol. V
Athlone, 1st Earl of, 1874–1957, vol. V
Athlone, Countess of, (HRH Princess Alice), 1883–1981, vol. VIII
Athlumney, 6th Baron, 1865–1929, vol. III
Atholl, 7th Duke of, 1840–1917, vol. II
Atholl, 8th Duke of, 1871–1942, vol. IV
Atholl, 9th Duke of, 1879–1957, vol. V
Atholl, Duchess of; (Katharine Marjory), died 1960, vol. V
Atholstan, 1st Baron, 1848–1938, vol. III
Atkey, Sir Albert (Reuben), 1867–1947, vol. IV
Atkey, Oliver Francis Haynes, died 1960, vol. V
Atkin, Baron (Life Peer); James Richard Atkin, 1867–1944, vol. IV
Atkin, Charles, died 1934, vol. III
Atkin, Peter Wilson, 1859–1931, vol. III
Atkins, Maj.-Gen. Sir Alban Randell Crofton, 1870–1926, vol. II
Atkins, Alexander Robert; see Atkins, R.
Atkins, Charles Norman, 1885–1960, vol. V
Atkins, Col Ernest Clive, 1870–1953, vol. V
Atkins, Frederick Anthony, 1864–1929, vol. III
Atkins, Sir Hedley John Barnard, 1905–1983, vol. VIII
Atkins, Henry Gibson, 1871–1942, vol. IV
Atkins, Ian Robert, 1912–1979, vol. VII
Atkins, Sir Ivor Algernon, 1869–1953, vol. V
Atkins, Col Sir John, 1875–1963, vol. VI
Atkins, John Black, 1871–1954, vol. V
Atkins, John Spencer, 1905–1987, vol. VIII
Atkins, John William Hey, 1874–1951, vol. V
Atkins, Malcolm Ramsay, 1881–1960, vol. V
Atkins, Robert, 1886–1972, vol. VII
Atkins, Thomas Frederick B.; see Burnaby-Atkins.
Atkins, William Ringrose Gelston, 1884–1959, vol. V
Atkins, Sir William Sydney Albert, 1902–1989, vol. VIII
Atkinson, Baron (Life Peer); John Atkinson, 1844–1932, vol. III
Atkinson, Major Sir Arthur Joseph, died 1959, vol. V
Atkinson, Brig.-Gen. Ben, 1872–1942, vol. IV
Atkinson, Brooks; see Atkinson, J. B.
Atkinson, Cecil Hewitt, 1894–1954, vol. V
Atkinson, Hon. Cecil Thomas, 1876–1919, vol. II
Atkinson, Ven. Charles Frederic, 1855–1942, vol. IV
Atkinson, Charles Milner, 1854–1920, vol. II
Atkinson, Hon. Sir Cyril, 1874–1967, vol. VI
Atkinson, Donald, 1886–1963, vol. VI
Atkinson, Rev. Edward, died 1915, vol. I
Atkinson, Ven. Edward Dupré, 1855–1937, vol. III
Atkinson, Sir Edward Hale Tindal, 1878–1957, vol. V
Atkinson, Surgeon-Captain Edward Leicester, 1882–1929, vol. III
Atkinson, Sir Edward Tindal, 1847–1930, vol. III
Atkinson, Major Edward William, 1873–1920, vol. II
Atkinson, Lt-Gen. Sir Edwin Henry de Vere, 1867–1947, vol. IV
Atkinson, Rt Hon. Sir Fenton, 1906–1980, vol. VII

Atkinson, Brig.-Gen. Francis Garnett, 1857–1941, vol. IV

Atkinson, Frank Buddle, 1866–1953, vol. V

Atkinson, Frank Stuart, 1899–1971, vol. VII

Atkinson, George, *died* 1941, vol. IV

Atkinson, Major George Prestage, 1885–1929, vol. III

Atkinson, Henry John Farmer-, 1828–1913, vol. I

Atkinson, Rev. Canon Henry Sadgrove, *died* 1927, vol. II

Atkinson, Henry Tindal, *died* 1918, vol. II

Atkinson, Rev. J. Augustus, *died* 1911, vol. I

Atkinson, Lt-Col John, *died* 1945, vol. IV

Atkinson, Sir (John) Kenneth, 1905–1989, vol. VIII

Atkinson, John Mitford, 1856–1917, vol. II

Atkinson, Sir John Nathaniel, 1857–1931, vol. III

Atkinson, Maj.-Gen. John Richard Breeks, 1844–1926, vol. II

Atkinson, (Justin) Brooks, 1894–1984, vol. VIII

Atkinson, Sir Kenneth; *see* Atkinson, Sir J. K.

Atkinson, Maj.-Gen. Sir Leonard Henry, 1910–1990, vol. VIII

Atkinson, Meredith, 1883–1929, vol. III

Atkinson, Robert, 1883–1952, vol. V

Atkinson, Thomas Dinham, 1864–1948, vol. IV

Atkinson, Thomas John Day, 1882–1949, vol. IV

Atkinson, Vivian Buchanan, 1886–1960, vol. V

Atkinson, Sir William Nicholas, 1850–1930, vol. III

Atkinson-Willes, Adm. Sir George Lambart, 1847–1921, vol. II

Atlay, James Beresford, 1860–1912, vol. I

Atlay, Rev. Marcus Ethelbert, *died* 1934, vol. III

Atlay, Sir Wilfrid, 1866–1929, vol. III

Atta, Nana Sir Ofori, 1881–1943, vol. IV

Attenborough, Charles Leete, 1853–1937, vol. III

Attenborough, Frederick L., 1887–1973, vol. VII

Attenborough, James, 1884–1984, vol. VIII

Attenborough, Walter Annis, 1850–1932, vol. III

Atterbury, Sir Frederick, 1853–1919, vol. II

Attewell, Humphry Cooper, 1894–1972, vol. VII

Attfield, John, 1835–1911, vol. I

Atthill, Major Anthony William Maunsell, 1861–1926, vol. II

Atthill, Lombe, 1827–1910, vol. I

Attlee, 1st Earl, 1883–1967, vol. VI

Attlee, Wilfrid Henry Waller, 1876–1962, vol. VI

Attwater, Harry Lawrence, 1885–1961, vol. VI

Attwell, Mabel Lucie, (Mrs Harold Earnshaw), 1879–1964, vol. VI

Attwood, Harold Augustus F.; *see* Freeman-Attwood.

Attygalle, Sir Nicholas, 1894–1970, vol. VI(AII)

Atukorala, Nandasara Wijetilaka, 1915–1969, vol. VI

Atwater, Albert William, 1856–1929, vol. III

Atwood, Clare, 1866–1962, vol. VI

Aubin, Charles Walter Duret, 1894–1972, vol. VII

Auboyneau, Adm. Philippe Marie Joseph Raymond, 1899–1961, vol. VI

Aubrey, Henry Miles W.; *see* Windsor-Aubrey.

Aubrey, Brig. Herbert Arthur Reginald, 1883–1954, vol. V

Aubrey, Rev. Melbourn Evans, 1885–1957, vol. V

Aubrey, Sir Stanley James, 1883–1962, vol. VI

Aubrey, William Hickman Smith, 1858–1916, vol. II

Aubrey-Fletcher, Rt Hon. Sir Henry; *see* Fletcher.

Aubrey-Fletcher, Major Sir Henry Lancelot, 6th Bt, 1887–1969, vol. VI

Aubrey-Fletcher, Sir Lancelot, 5th Bt, 1846–1937, vol. III

Auchinleck, Field-Marshal Sir Claude John Eyre, 1884–1981, vol. VIII

Auchinleck, William Douglas, 1848–1932, vol. III

Auchmuty, James Johnston, 1909–1981, vol. VIII

Auckland, 5th Baron, 1859–1917, vol. II

Auckland, 6th Baron, 1895–1941, vol. IV

Auckland, 7th Baron, 1891–1955, vol. V

Auckland, 8th Baron, 1892–1957, vol. V

Auden, George Augustus, 1872–1957, vol. V

Auden, Henry William, 1867–1940, vol. III

Auden, Rev. Thomas, 1836–1920, vol. II

Auden, Wystan Hugh, 1907–1973, vol. VII

Audette, Hon. Louis Arthur, 1856–1942, vol. IV

Audiffret-Pasquier, Duc d', (Edmé Armand Gaston), 1823–1905, vol. I

Audland, Brig. Edward Gordon, 1896–1976, vol. VII

Audley, Baroness (22nd in line), 1858–1942, vol. IV

Audley, 23rd Baron, 1913–1963, vol. VI

Audley, Baroness (24th in line), 1911–1973, vol. VII

Audsley, Matthew Thomas, 1891–1975, vol. VII

Auer, Leopold, 1845–1930, vol. III

Aufrecht, Theodor, 1821–1907, vol. I

Augagneur, Victor, 1855–1931, vol. III

Aulard, Alphonse, 1849–1928, vol. II

Auld, Maj.-Gen. Robert, 1848–1911, vol. I

Auld, Lt-Col Samuel James Manson, 1884–1963, vol. VI

Ault, Norman, 1880–1950, vol. IV

Aumonier, Stacy, 1887–1928, vol. II

Aung, Maung Myat Tun, *died* 1920, vol. II

Auric, Georges, 1899–1983, vol. VIII

Auriol, Vincent, 1884–1966, vol. VI

Aurobindo, Sri, 1872–1950, vol. IV

Austen, Gen. Sir Alfred Reade G.; *see* Godwin-Austen.

Austen, Col Arthur Robert, 1860–1939, vol. III

Austen, Major Ernest Edward, 1867–1938, vol. III

Austen, Rev. George, 1839–1933, vol. III

Austen, Harold Cholmley Mansfield, 1878–1975, vol. VII

Austen, Harold William Colmer, 1868–1943, vol. IV

Austen, Henry Haversham G.; *see* Godwin-Austen.

Austen, Sir William Chandler R.; *see* Roberts-Austen.

Austen, Winifred M. L., *died* 1964, vol. VI

Austen-Cartmell, James; *see* Cartmell.

Austen-Leigh, Rev. Augustus, 1840–1905, vol. I

Austen-Leigh, Charles Edward, 1833–1916, vol. II

Austen-Leigh, Richard Arthur, 1872–1961, vol. VI

Austin, 1st Baron, 1866–1941, vol. IV

Austin, Alfred, 1835–1913, vol. I

Austin, Maj.-Gen. Arthur Bramston, 1893–1967, vol. VI

Austin, Hon. Austin Albert, 1855–1925, vol. II

Austin, Vice-Adm. Sir Francis Murray, 1881–1953, vol. V

Austin, Frederic, 1872–1952, vol. V

Austin, Frederick Britten, 1885–1941, vol. IV

Austin, George Wesley, 1891–1975, vol. VII

Austin, Sir Harold Bruce Gardiner, 1877–1943, vol. IV
Austin, Sir Herbert, 1867–1929, vol. III
Austin, Brig.-Gen. Herbert Henry, 1868–1937, vol. III
Austin, James Valentine, 1850–1914, vol. I
Austin, Sir John, 1st Bt, 1824–1906, vol. I
Austin, Sir John Byron Fraser, 3rd Bt, 1897–1981, vol. VIII
Austin, Brig.-Gen. John Gardiner, died 1956, vol. V
Austin, John Langshaw, 1911–1960, vol. V
Austin, Sir John Worroker, died 1980, vol. VII(AII)
Austin, Mary Hunter, died 1934, vol. III
Austin, Dame (Mary) Valerie (Hall), 1900–1986, vol. VIII
Austin, Michael, 1855–1916, vol. II
Austin, Reginald McPherson, 1887–1950, vol. IV
Austin, Richard, 1903–1989, vol. VIII
Austin, Robert Sargent, 1895–1973, vol. VII
Austin, Roland, 1874–1954, vol. V
Austin, Roland Gregory, 1901–1974, vol. VII
Austin, Sumner Francis, 1888–1981, vol. VIII
Austin, Sir Thomas, 1887–1976, vol. VII
Austin, Thomas Aitken, 1895–1982, vol. VIII
Austin, Dame Valerie; see Austin, Dame M. V. H.
Austin, Warren Robinson, 1877–1962, vol. VI
Austin, Sir William Michael Byron, 2nd Bt, 1871–1940, vol. III
Austin, Sir William Ronald, 4th Bt, 1900–1989, vol. VIII
Austral, Florence, 1894–1968, vol. VI
Auswild, Sir James Frederick John, 1908–1985, vol. VIII
Auten, Captain Harold, died 1964, vol. VI
Auty, Robert, 1914–1978, vol. VII
Ava, Earl of; Archibald James Leofric Temple Blackwood, 1863–1900, vol. I
Avebury, 1st Baron, 1834–1913, vol. I
Avebury, 2nd Baron, 1858–1929, vol. III
Avebury, 3rd Baron, 1915–1971, vol. VII
Aveling, Arthur Francis, 1893–1954, vol. V
Aveling, Charles, 1873–1959, vol. V
Aveling, Claude, 1869–1943, vol. IV
Aveling, Francis Arthur Powell, 1875–1941, vol. IV
Avenol, Joseph Louis Anne, 1879–1952, vol. V
Averill, Most Rev. Alfred Walter, 1865–1957, vol. V
Averill, Leslie Cecil Lloyd, 1897–1981, vol. VIII
Avery, Charles Harold, 1867–1943, vol. IV
Avery, David Robert, 1921–1983, vol. VIII
Avery, Brig. Henry Esau, 1885–1961, vol. VI
Avery, Major Leonard, died 1953, vol. V
Avery, Thomas, 1862–1940, vol. III
Avery, Sir William Beilby, 1st Bt, 1854–1908, vol. I
Avery, Sir William Eric Thomas, 2nd Bt, 1890–1918, vol. II
Aves, Ernest, 1857–1917, vol. II
Aves, Dame Geraldine Maitland, 1898–1986, vol. VIII
Avezathe, Gerald Henry, 1889–1966, vol. VI
Avgherinos, George, 1906–1989, vol. VIII
Avis, John, 1851–1936, vol. III
Avon, 1st Earl of, 1897–1977, vol. VII
Avon, 2nd Earl of, 1930–1985, vol. VIII
Avonmore, 6th Viscount, 1866–1910, vol. I

Avory, Rt Hon. Sir Horace Edmund, 1851–1935, vol. III
Awbery, Stanley Stephen, 1888–1969, vol. VI
Awdry, Rev. Charles Hill, died 1910, vol. I
Awdry, Sir Richard Davis, 1843–1916, vol. II
Awdry, Rt Rev. William, 1842–1910, vol. I
Axford, Surg.-Rear-Adm. Walter Godfrey, 1861–1942, vol. IV
Axon, Sir Albert Edwin, 1898–1974, vol. VII
Axon, William Edward Armytage, 1846–1913, vol. I
Ayala, Ramon Pérez de, 1880–1962, vol. VI
Aydelotte, Frank, 1880–1956, vol. V
Ayer, Sir Alfred Jules, 1910–1989, vol. VIII
Ayers, Charles William, 1880–1965, vol. VI
Ayers, Hon. Sir Henry, 1821–1897, vol. I
Ayers, Herbert Wilfred, 1889–1986, vol. VIII
Ayers, Engineer Captain Robert Bell, 1863–1940, vol. III
Ayerst, Rev. George Haughton, 1863–1931, vol. III
Ayerst, Rev. William, 1830–1904, vol. I
Aykroyd, Sir Aldred Hammond, 2nd Bt (cr 1920), 1894–1965, vol. VI
Aykroyd, Sir Frederic Alfred, 1st Bt (cr 1929), 1873–1949, vol. IV
Aykroyd, Wallace Ruddell, 1899–1979, vol. VII
Aykroyd, Sir William Henry, 1st Bt (cr 1920), 1865–1947, vol. IV
Aylen, Rt Rev. Charles Arthur William, 1882–1972, vol. VII
Aylen, Helena Constance; see Romanne-James.
Ayles, Rev. Herbert Henry Baker, 1861–1940, vol. III
Ayles, Walter Henry, 1879–1953, vol. V
Aylesford, 8th Earl of, 1851–1924, vol. II
Aylesford, 9th Earl of, 1908–1940, vol. III(A), vol. IV
Aylesford, 10th Earl of, 1886–1958, vol. V
Aylesworth, Hon. Sir Allen Bristol, 1854–1952, vol. V
Ayliff, Henry Kiell, died 1949, vol. IV
Ayling, Sir William Bock, 1867–1946, vol. IV
Aylmer, 7th Baron, 1814–1901, vol. I
Aylmer, 8th Baron, 1842–1923, vol. II
Aylmer, 9th Baron, 1880–1970, vol. VI(AII)
Aylmer, 10th Baron, 1883–1974, vol. VII
Aylmer, 11th Baron, 1886–1977, vol. VII
Aylmer, 12th Baron, 1907–1982, vol. VIII
Aylmer, Sir Arthur Percy Fitzgerald, 12th Bt (cr 1622), 1858–1928, vol. II
Aylmer, Col Edmund Kendal Grimston, 1859–1931, vol. III
Aylmer, Sir Felix, 1889–1979, vol. VII
Aylmer, Sir Fenton Gerald, 15th Bt, 1901–1987, vol. VIII
Aylmer, Lt-Gen. Sir Fenton John, 13th Bt (cr 1622), 1862–1935, vol. III
Aylmer, Sir Gerald (Arthur) Evans-Freke, 14th Bt (cr 1622), 1869–1939, vol. III
Aylmer, Gerald Percy Vivian, 1856–1936, vol. III
Aylmer, Rear-Adm. Henry Evans-Freke, 1878–1933, vol. III
Aylmer-Jones, Sir Felix E.; see Aylmer, Sir Felix.
Aylward, Florence, 1862–1950, vol. IV
Aylward, Francis, 1911–1978, vol. VII
Aylwen, Sir George, 1st Bt, 1880–1967, vol. VI
Aynsley, Vice-Adm. Charles Murray, 1821–1901, vol. I

Aynsley, Sir Charles Murray M.; *see* Murray-Aynsley.

Aynsley, George Ayton, 1896–1981, vol. VIII

Ayre, Sir Amos Lowrey, 1885–1952, vol. V

Ayre, Captain Leslie Charles Edward, 1886–1979, vol. VII

Ayre, Sir Wilfrid, 1890–1971, vol. VII

Ayres, Sir Reginald John, 1900–1966, vol. VI

Ayres, Ruby Mildred, 1883–1955, vol. V

Ayrton, Hertha, *died* 1923, vol. II

Ayrton, Maxwell; *see* Ayrton, O.M.

Ayrton, Michael, 1921–1975, vol. VII

Ayrton, (Ormrod) Maxwell, *died* 1960, vol. V

Ayrton, William Edward, 1847–1908, vol. I

Ayscough, Florence, *died* 1942, vol. IV

Ayscough, John; *see* Bickerstaffe-Drew, Rt Rev. Mgr Count F. B. D.

Ayscough, Rev. Thomas Ayscough, 1830–1920, vol. II

Ayson, Hugh Fraser, 1884–1948, vol. IV

Aytoun, Col Andrew, 1860–1945, vol. IV

Ayub Khan, Field-Marshal Mohammad; *see* Khan, Field-Marshal M. A.

Azariah, Rt Rev. Vedanayakam Samuel, 1874–1945, vol. IV

Azcarate y Florez, Pablo de, 1890–1971, vol. VII

Azizuddin Ahmad, Kazi Sir, 1861–1940, vol. III

Azizul Huque, Khan Bahadur Sir M., 1892–1947, vol. IV

Azopardi, James Frendo, 1866–1938, vol. III

Azopardi, Sir Vincent Frendo, 1865–1919, vol. II

B

Ba, Sir Maung, *died* 1937, vol. III

Baba, Hon. Sir Khem Singh Beda, 1830–1905, vol. I

Babb, S. Nicholson, 1874–1957, vol. V

Babbage, Maj.-Gen. Henry Prevost, 1824–1918, vol. II

Babbitt, Irving, 1865–1933, vol. III

Baber, Edward Cresswell, *died* 1910, vol. I

Baber, Lt-Col John Barton, 1892–1967, vol. VI

Baber Shum Shere Jung Bahadur Rana, General, 1888–1960, vol. V

Babington, Rt Hon. Sir Anthony Brutus, 1877–1972, vol. VII

Babington, Col David Melville, 1863–1929, vol. III

Babington, Captain Gervase, 1890–1948, vol. IV

Babington, Lt-Gen. Sir James Melville, 1854–1936, vol. III

Babington, Air Marshal Sir John Tremayne; *see* Tremayne, Air Marshal Sir J. T.

Babington, Air Marshal Sir Philip, 1894–1965, vol. VI

Babington, Very Rev. Richard, 1869–1952, vol. V

Babington, Ven. Richard Hamilton, 1901–1984, vol. VIII

Babington, Col Stafford Charles, 1866–1951, vol. V

Babington Smith, Michael James, 1901–1984, vol. VIII

Babonau, Col Alexander Frederick, 1882–1949, vol. IV

Babtie, Lt-Gen. Sir William, 1859–1920, vol. II

Baby-Casgrain, Hon. Col Hon. Joseph Philippe; *see* Casgrain.

Bacchus, Captain Roy, 1883–1951, vol. V

Bach, Guido R., *died* 1905, vol. I

Bacharach, Alfred Louis, 1891–1966, vol. VI

Bachauer, Gina, (Mrs Alex Sherman), 1913–1976, vol. VII

Bache, Miss Constance, 1846–1903, vol. I

Bacheller, Irving, 1859–1950, vol. IV(A), vol. V

Bacher, William, 1850–1913, vol. I

Back, Ven. Hugh Cairns Alexander, 1863–1928, vol. II

Back, Ivor, *died* 1951, vol. V

Back, Ronald Eric George, 1926–1989, vol. VIII

Backhaus, Wilhelm, 1884–1969, vol. VI

Backhouse, Sir Edmund Trelawny, 2nd Bt, 1873–1944, vol. IV

Backhouse, Col Edward Henry Walford, 1895–1973, vol. VII

Backhouse, Major Sir John Edmund, 3rd Bt, 1909–1944, vol. IV

Backhouse, Sir Jonathan Edmund, 1st Bt, 1849–1918, vol. II

Backhouse, Lt-Col Julius Batt, 1854–1911, vol. I

Backhouse, Lt-Col Miles Roland Charles, 1878–1962, vol. VI

Backhouse, Adm. Oliver, 1876–1943, vol. IV

Backhouse, Adm. of the Fleet Sir Roger Roland Charles, 1878–1939, vol. III

Backhouse, Thomas Mercer, 1903–1955, vol. V

Bacon, Benjamin Wisner, 1860–1932, vol. III

Bacon, Sir Edmund Castell, 13th Bt, 1903–1982, vol. VIII

Bacon, Sir Edward Denny, 1860–1938, vol. III

Bacon, Edwin Munroe, 1844–1916, vol. II

Bacon, Frederic, 1880–1943, vol. IV

Bacon, Frederick Joseph, 1853–1929, vol. III

Bacon, Gertrude, (Mrs T. J. Foggitt), 1874–1949, vol. IV

Bacon, Sir Hickman Beckett, 11th Bt, 1855–1945, vol. IV

Bacon, Janet Ruth, 1891–1965, vol. VI

Bacon, John Henry Frederick, 1865–1914, vol. I

Bacon, John Mackenzie, 1846–1904, vol. I

Bacon, Sir Nicholas Henry, 12th Bt, 1857–1947, vol. IV

Bacon, Sir Ranulph Robert Maunsell, 1906–1988, vol. VIII

Bacon, Adm. Sir Reginald Hugh Spencer, 1863–1947, vol. IV

Bacon, Sir Roger Sewell, 1895–1962, vol. VI

Bacon, Comdr Sidney Kendrick, 1871–1950, vol. IV

Bacot, Arthur William, 1866–1922, vol. II

Badcock, Gen. Sir Alexander Robert, 1844–1907, vol. I

Badcock, Brig.-Gen. Francis Frederick, 1867–1926, vol. II

Badcock, Brig. Gerald Eliot, 1883–1966, vol. VI

Badcock, Isaac, 1842–1906, vol. I

Badcock, Jasper Capper, 1840–1924, vol. II

Badcock, Paymaster Captain Kenneth Edgar, 1886–1947, vol. IV

Baddeley, Angela; *see* Clinton-Baddeley, M. A.

Baddeley, Col Charles Edward, 1861–1923, vol. II

Baddeley, Sir Frank Morrish, 1874–1966, vol. VI

Baddeley, Hermione, 1908–1986, vol. VIII

Baddeley, Sir John Beresford, 3rd Bt, 1899–1979, vol. VII

Baddeley, John Halkett, 1920–1972, vol. VII

Baddeley, Sir John James, 1st Bt, 1842–1926, vol. II

Baddeley, Hon. John Marcus, 1881–1953, vol. V

Baddeley, Sir (John) William, 2nd Bt, 1869–1951, vol. V

Baddeley, Sir Vincent Wilberforce, 1874–1961, vol. VI

Baddeley, Sir William; *see* Baddeley, Sir J. W.

Badè, William Frederic, 1871–1936, vol. III

Badel, Alan, 1923–1982, vol. VIII

Badeley, 1st Baron, 1874–1951, vol. V

Badeley, Rt Rev. Walter Hubert, 1894–1960, vol. V

Baden-Powell, 1st Baron, 1857–1941, vol. IV

Baden-Powell, 2nd Baron, 1913–1962, vol. VI

Baden-Powell, Lady; (Olave St Clair), 1889–1977, vol. VII

Baden-Powell, Agnes, 1858–1945, vol. IV

Baden-Powell, Major Baden Fletcher Smyth, 1860–1937, vol. III

Baden-Powell, Baden Henry, 1841–1901, vol. I

Baden-Powell, Frank Smyth, 1850–1933, vol. III

Baden-Powell, Sir George Smyth, 1847–1898, vol. I

Baden-Powell, (Henry) Warington (Smyth), 1847–1921, vol. II

Baden-Powell, Warington; *see* Baden-Powell, H. W. S.

Badenoch, Sir (Alexander) Cameron, 1889–1973, vol. VII

Badenoch, Sir Cameron; *see* Badenoch, Sir A. C.

Badenoch, Rev. George Roy, 1830–1912, vol. I

Bader, Group Captain Sir Douglas Robert Steuart, 1910–1982, vol. VIII

Bader, Hubert Eugène, 1902–1936, vol. III

Badger, Rev. Canon George Edwin, 1868–1948, vol. IV

Badgerow, Sir George W., 1872–1937, vol. III

Badham, Edward Leslie, *died* 1944, vol. IV

Badham, Rev. Leslie Stephen Ronald, 1908–1975, vol. VII

Badham-Thornhill, Col George, 1876–1958, vol. V

Badley, John Haden, 1865–1967, vol. VI

Badmin, Stanley Roy, 1906–1989, vol. VIII

Badock, Sir Stanley Hugh, 1867–1945, vol. IV

Badock, Sir Walter, 1854–1931, vol. III

Baekeland, Leo Hendrik, 1863–1944, vol. IV

Baerlein, Edgar Max, 1879–1971, vol. VII

Baerlein, Henry, 1875–1960, vol. V, vol. VI

Bagchi, Satischandra, 1882–1939, vol. III(A), vol. IV

Bagenal, Hope; *see* Bagenal, P. H. E.

Bagenal, (Philip) Hope (Edward), 1888–1979, vol. VII

Baggaley, Ernest James, 1900–1978, vol. VII

Baggallay, Claude, 1853–1906, vol. I

Baggallay, Ernest, 1850–1931, vol. III

Baggallay, Rev. Frederick, 1855–1928, vol. II

Baggallay, Lt-Col Richard Romer Claude, 1884–1975, vol. VII

Bagge, Sir Alfred Thomas, 3rd Bt, 1843–1916, vol. II

Bagge, Sir Alfred William Francis, 4th Bt, 1875–1939, vol. III

Bagge, Sir John Alfred Picton, 6th Bt, 1914–1990, vol. VIII

Bagge, Sir (John) Picton, 5th Bt, 1877–1967, vol. VI

Bagge, Sir Picton; *see* Bagge, Sir J. P.

Bagge, Major Sir Richard Ludwig, 1872–1933, vol. III

Bagge, Stephen Salisbury, 1859–1950, vol. IV

Baggott, Ven. Louis John, 1891–1965, vol. VI

Baghot de la Bere, Stephen, 1877–1927, vol. II

Bagley, Desmond Simon, 1923–1983, vol. VIII

Bagley, Edward Albert Ashton, 1876–1961, vol. VI

Bagnall, Hon. Sir Arthur; *see* Bagnall, Hon. Sir W. A.

Bagnall, Colin; *see* Bagnall, F. C.

Bagnall, Frank Colin, 1909–1989, vol. VIII

Bagnall, Sir John, 1888–1954, vol. V

Bagnall, Rt Rev. Walter Edward, 1903–1984, vol. VIII

Bagnall, Hon. Sir (William) Arthur, 1917–1976, vol. VII

Bagnall-Wild, Ralph Bagnall, 1845–1925, vol. II

Bagnall-Wild, Brig.-Gen. Ralph Kirkby, 1873–1953, vol. V

Bagnold, Col Arthur Henry, 1854–1943, vol. IV

Bagnold, Enid, (Lady Jones), 1889–1981, vol. VIII

Bagnold, Brig. Ralph Alger, 1896–1990, vol. VIII

Bagot, 4th Baron, 1857–1932, vol. III

Bagot, 5th Baron, 1866–1946, vol. IV

Bagot, 6th Baron, 1877–1961, vol. VI

Bagot, 7th Baron, 1894–1973, vol. VII

Bagot, 8th Baron, 1897–1979, vol. VII

Bagot, Sir Alan Desmond, 1st Bt, 1896–1920, vol. II

Bagot, Col Charles Hervey, 1847–1911, vol. I

Bagot, Sir Charles Samuel, 1828–1906, vol. I

Bagot, (Sir) Josceline FitzRoy (1st Bt, but died before the passing under the Great Seal of the Patent of Baronetage), 1854–1913, vol. I

Bagot, Richard, 1860–1921, vol. II

Bagot, Theodosia, (Lady Bagot), 1865–1940, vol. III

Bagot, Major Hon. Walter Lewis, 1864–1927, vol. II

Bagot-Chester, Col Heneage Charles, 1836–1912, vol. I

Bagrit, Sir Leon, 1902–1979, vol. VII

Bagshawe, Arthur Clement, 1874–1937, vol. III

Bagshawe, Sir Arthur William Garrard, 1871–1950, vol. IV

Bagshawe, Most Rev. Edward Gilpin, 1829–1915, vol. I

Bagshawe, Edward Leonard, 1876–1955, vol. V

Bagshawe, Francis John Edward, 1877–1953, vol. V

Bagshawe, Col Frederick William, 1868–1945, vol. IV

Bagshawe, Lt-Col Herbert Vale, 1874–1962, vol. VI

Bagshawe, Thomas Wyatt, 1901–1976, vol. VII

Bagshawe, William Henry Gunning, 1825–1901, vol. I

Bagster, Robert, 1847–1924, vol. II

Baguley, Sir John Minty, 1880–1964, vol. VI

Bagwell, John, 1874–1946, vol. IV

Bagwell, Lt-Col John, 1884–1949, vol. IV

Bagwell, Richard, 1840–1918, vol. II

Bahadur Shamsher Jang Bahadur Rana, Commanding-General, 1892–1977, vol. VII

Bahauddin Khan, Resaldar Major, 1833–1901, vol. I
Bahawalpur, Ameer of, 1904–1966, vol. VI
Bahawalpur, Nawab of, 1883–1907, vol. I
Bahr, Sir Philip M; see Manson-Bahr.
Bahrain, Ruler of; HH Shaikh Sir Hamed bin Isa Al Khalifah, 1874–1942, vol. IV
Bahrain, Ruler of, HH Shaikh Sulman bin Hamad Al Khalifah, died 1961, vol. VI
Baig, Mirza Sir Abbas Ali, died 1932, vol. III
Baigent, Rt Rev. Mgr William Joseph, 1857–1930, vol. III
Baikie, Alfred, 1861–1947, vol. IV
Bailkie, Brig.-Gen. Sir Hugh Archie Dundas Simpson-, 1871–1924, vol. II
Baikie, Rev. James, 1866–1931, vol. III
Baildon, Henry Bellyse, died 1907, vol. I
Bailey, Sir Abe, 1st Bt, 1864–1940, vol. III
Bailey, Col Alfred John, 1867–1940, vol. III
Bailey, Arnold Savage, 1881–1935, vol. III
Bailey, Arthur, 1903–1979, vol. VII
Bailey, Arthur Charles John, 1886–1951, vol. V
Bailey, Captain Arthur Harold, 1873–1925, vol. II
Bailey, Charles Thomas Peach, 1882–1968, vol. VI
Bailey, Cyril, 1871–1957, vol. V
Bailey, Rev. (Derrick) Sherwin, 1910–1984, vol. VIII
Bailey, Sir Donald Coleman, 1901–1985, vol. VIII
Bailey, Lt-Col Edmund Wyndham-Grevis, 1858–1920, vol. II
Bailey, Sir Edward Battersby, 1881–1965, vol. VI
Bailey, Ernest Edmond, 1907–1956, vol. V
Bailey, Lt-Col Francis William, 1871–1932, vol. III
Bailey, Lt-Col Frederick George Glyn, 1880–1951, vol. V
Bailey, Frederick Manson, 1827–1915, vol. I
Bailey, Lt-Col Frederick Marshman, 1882–1967, vol. VI
Bailey, George Buchanan, 1898–1969, vol. VI
Bailey, Air Cdre George Cyril, 1890–1972, vol. VII
Bailey, Sir George Edwin, 1879–1965, vol. VI
Bailey, Sir George Leader, 1882–1953, vol. V
Bailey, George Leo, 1901–1979, vol. VII
Bailey, Gertrude Mary, 1870–1941, vol. IV
Bailey, Hamilton, 1894–1961, vol. VI
Bailey, Rev. Henry, 1815–1906, vol. I
Bailey, Henry Christopher, 1878–1961, vol. VI
Bailey, Hon. Herbert Crawshay, died 1936, vol. III
Bailey, Horace Thomas, 1852–1945, vol. IV
Bailey, Miss (Irene) Temple, died 1953, vol. V
Bailey, Sir James, 1840–1910, vol. I
Bailey, James Vincent, 1908–1984, vol. VIII
Bailey, John, 1889–1957, vol. V
Bailey, Sir John, 1898–1969, vol. VI
Bailey, John Cann, 1864–1931, vol. III
Bailey, John E., 1897–1958, vol. V
Bailey, John Frederick, 1866–1938, vol. III
Bailey, Rev. J(ohn) H(enry) Shackleton, 1875–1956, vol. V
Bailey, Sir John Milner, 2nd Bt, 1900–1946, vol. IV
Bailey, John Walter, 1845–1930, vol. III
Bailey, Kenneth, 1909–1963, vol. VI
Bailey, Kenneth Claude, 1896–1951, vol. V
Bailey, Sir Kenneth Hamilton, 1898–1972, vol. VII
Bailey, Liberty Hyde, 1858–1954, vol. V
Bailey, Lionel Danyers, 1879–1967, vol. VI

Bailey, Philip James, 1816–1902, vol. I
Bailey, Sir Reginald Greenwood, 1894–1953, vol. V
Bailey, Richard William, 1885–1957, vol. V
Bailey, Sir Rowland, 1852–1930, vol. III
Bailey, Sidney Alfred, 1886–1972, vol. VII
Bailey, Rev. Sherwin; see Bailey, Rev. D. S.
Bailey, Adm. Sir Sidney Robert, 1882–1942, vol. IV
Bailey, Stanley John, 1901–1980, vol. VII
Bailey, Miss Temple; see Bailey, I. T.
Bailey, Victor Albert, 1895–1964, vol. VI
Bailey, Hon. Brig.-Gen. Vivian Telford, 1868–1938, vol. III
Bailey, Walter M.; see Milne-Bailey.
Bailey, Wilfrid Norman, 1893–1961, vol. VI
Bailey, Rt Hon. William Frederick, 1857–1917, vol. II
Bailey, Sir William Henry, 1838–1913, vol. I
Bailey, William Henry, born 1855, vol. II
Bailey, Sir William Thomas, 1873–1949, vol. IV
Bailhache, Sir Clement Meacher, 1856–1924, vol. II
Bailie, Thomas, 1885–1957, vol. V
Bailie, Maj.-Gen. Thomas Maubourg, 1844–1918, vol. II
Baillet-Latour, Comte de; Henry, 1876–1942, vol. IV
Baillie, Sir Adrian William Maxwell, 6th Bt, 1898–1947, vol. IV
Baillie, Rev. Albert Victor, 1864–1955, vol. V
Baillie, Col Augustus Charles, 1861–1939, vol. III
Baillie, Rev. Donald Macpherson, 1887–1954, vol. V
Baillie, Sir Duncan Colvin, 1856–1919, vol. II
Baillie, Col Duncan Gus, 1872–1968, vol. VI
Baillie, Hon. Evan; see Baillie, Hon. G. E. M.
Baillie, Sir Frank, 1875–1921, vol. II
Baillie, Lt-Col Frederick David M.; see Murray Baillie.
Baillie, Sir Gawaine George Stuart, 5th Bt, 1893–1914, vol. I
Baillie, Hon. (George) Evan (Michael), 1894–1941, vol. IV
Baillie, George Henry, 1901–1970, vol. VI(AII)
Baillie, Col Hugh Frederick, 1879–1941, vol. IV
Baillie, Dame Isobel, 1895–1983, vol. VIII
Baillie, Sir James Black, 1872–1940, vol. III
Baillie, Gen. James Cadogan Parkison, 1835–1928, vol. II
Baillie, James Evan Bruce, 1859–1931, vol. III
Baillie, Very Rev. John, 1886–1960, vol. V
Baillie, John Gilroy, 1896–1960, vol. V
Baillie, John Strachan, 1896–1989, vol. VIII
Baillie, Lady Maud Louisa Emma, 1896–1975, vol. VII
Baillie, Sir Robert Alexander, 4th Bt, 1859–1907, vol. I
Baillie, Ronald Hugh, 1863–1948, vol. IV
Baillie-Gage, Thomas Robert; see Gage.
Baillie-Grohman, Vice-Adm. Harold Tom, 1888–1978, vol. VII
Baillie-Grohman, William A., 1851–1921, vol. II(A)
Baillie-Hamilton, Hon. Charles William, 1900–1939, vol. III
Baillie-Hamilton, Sir William Alexander, 1844–1920, vol. II
Baillie Reynolds, Paul Kenneth; see Reynolds.
Baillie-Saunders, Margaret, 1873–1949, vol. IV

Baillieu, 1st Baron, 1889–1967, vol. VI
Baillieu, 2nd Baron, 1915–1973, vol. VII
Baillon, Maj.-Gen. Joseph Aloysius, 1895–1951, vol. V
Baily, Francis Evans, *died* 1962, vol. VI
Baily, Francis Gibson, 1868–1945, vol. IV
Baily, J. T. Herbert, 1865–1914, vol. I
Baily, Rev. Johnson, 1835–1915, vol. I
Baily, Leslie, 1906–1976, vol. VII
Baily, Robert Edward Hartwell, 1885–1973, vol. VII
Bain, Sir (Albert) Ernest, 1875–1939, vol. III
Bain, Alexander, 1818–1903, vol. I
Bain, Cyril William Curtis, 1895–1987, vol. VIII
Bain, David, 1855–1933, vol. III
Bain, Donald Charles, 1913–1964, vol. VI
Bain, Sir Ernest; *see* Bain, Sir A. E.
Bain, Francis William, 1863–1940, vol. III
Bain, Sir Frederick, 1889–1950, vol. IV
Bain, Sir James, 1817–1898, vol. I
Bain, James Robert, 1851–1913, vol. I
Bain, Kenneth Bruce Findlater; *see* Findlater, Richard.
Bain, Robert Nisbet, 1854–1909, vol. I
Bain, William Alexander, 1905–1971, vol. VII
Bain-Marais, Colin, 1893–1942, vol. IV
Bainbridge, Col Sir Edmond, 1841–1911, vol. I
Bainbridge, Maj.-Gen. Sir (Edmund) Guy (Tulloch), 1867–1943, vol. IV
Bainbridge, Emerson, 1845–1911, vol. I
Bainbridge, Francis Arthur, 1874–1921, vol. II
Bainbridge, Maj.-Gen. Frederick Thomas, 1834–1915, vol. I
Bainbridge, Maj.-Gen. Sir Guy; *see* Bainbridge, Maj.-Gen. Sir E. G. T.
Bainbridge, Herbert William, 1862–1940, vol. III
Bainbridge, Rev. Howard Gurney D.; *see* Daniell-Bainbridge.
Bainbridge, Rear-Adm. John Hugh, 1845–1901, vol. I
Bainbridge, Col Norman Bruce, 1869–1935, vol. III
Bainbridge, Brig.-Gen. Percy Agnew, 1864–1934, vol. III
Bainbridge, Brig.-Gen. William Frank, 1873–1953, vol. V
Bainbrigge, Rev. Philip Thomas, *died* 1919, vol. II
Baines, Ven. Albert, *died* 1951, vol. V
Baines, Sir Frank, 1877–1933, vol. III
Baines, Frederick Ebenezer, 1832–1911, vol. I
Baines, Rt Rev. Frederick Samuel, *died* 1939, vol. III
Baines, Rt Rev. Henry Wolfe, 1905–1972, vol. VII
Baines, Hubert, 1874–1953, vol. V
Baines, Lt-Col J. C., 1876–1928, vol. II
Baines, Sir Jervoise Athelstane, 1847–1925, vol. II
Baines, Matthew Talbot, 1863–1925, vol. II
Baines, William, 1899–1922, vol. II
Baines, William Henry, 1879–1958, vol. V
Bainton, Edgar Leslie, 1880–1956, vol. V
Bairamian, Sir Vahé Robert, 1900–1984, vol. VIII
Baird, Sir Alexander, 1st Bt (*cr* 1897), 1849–1920, vol. II
Baird, Brig.-Gen. Alexander Walter Frederic, 1876–1931, vol. III
Baird, Rev. Andrew Cumming, 1883–1940, vol. III
Baird, Col Andrew Wilson, 1842–1908, vol. I
Baird, Sir David, 3rd Bt (*cr* 1809), 1832–1913, vol. I

Baird, Sir David, 4th Bt (*cr* 1809), 1865–1941, vol. IV
Baird, Gen. Sir Douglas; *see* Baird, Gen. Sir H. B. D.
Baird, Douglas H., *died* 1940, vol. III
Baird, Sir Dugald, 1899–1986, vol. VIII
Baird, Edith Elina Helen, *died* 1924, vol. II
Baird, Brig.-Gen. Edward William David, 1864–1956, vol. V
Baird, Rear-Adm. Sir George Henry, 1871–1924, vol. II
Baird, Hon. George Thomas, 1847–1917, vol. II
Baird, Gen. Sir (Harry Beauchamp) Douglas, 1877–1963, vol. VI
Baird, James Craig, 1906–1973, vol. VII
Baird, Sir James Hozier Gardiner, 9th Bt (*cr* 1695), 1883–1966, vol. VI
Baird, John, 1906–1965, vol. VI
Baird, John George Alexander, 1854–1917, vol. II
Baird, Sir John Kennedy Erskine, 1832–1908, vol. I
Baird, John L., 1888–1946, vol. IV
Baird, May Deans, (Lady Baird), 1901–1983, vol. VIII
Baird, Percy Johnstone, 1877–1956, vol. V
Baird, Sir Robert Hugh Hanley, 1855–1934, vol. III
Baird, William, 1848–1918, vol. II
Baird, Major Sir William, 1874–1956, vol. V
Baird, William Arthur, 1879–1933, vol. III
Baird, William George, 1889–1975, vol. VII
Baird, William James, 1893–1961, vol. VI
Baird, Sir William James Gardiner, 8th Bt (*cr* 1695), 1854–1921, vol. II
Baird, Sir William MacDonald, 1881–1946, vol. IV
Baird-Smith, David, *died* 1951, vol. V
Bairnsfather, Captain Bruce, 1888–1959, vol. V
Bairnsfather, Captain George Edward Beckwith, 1855–1945, vol. IV
Bairstow, Arthur William, 1855–1943, vol. IV
Bairstow, Sir Edward C., 1874–1946, vol. IV
Bairstow, Sir Leonard, 1880–1963, vol. VI
Bajpai, Sir Girja Shankar, 1891–1954, vol. V
Bajpai, Sir Seetla Prasad, Rai Bahadur, 1865–1947, vol. IV
Baker, Baron (Life Peer); John Fleetwood Baker, 1901–1985, vol. VIII
Baker, Rev. Albert Edward, 1884–1962, vol. VI
Baker, Alfred, *died* 1942, vol. IV
Baker, Sir Alfred, 1870–1943, vol. IV
Baker, Alfred Thomas, 1873–1936, vol. III
Baker, Alfreda Helen, 1897–1984, vol. VIII
Baker, Mrs Alice, *died* 1935, vol. III
Baker, Allan; *see* Baker, J. F. A.
Baker, Alma; *see* Baker, C. A.
Baker, Andrew Clement, 1842–1913, vol. I
Baker, Arthur, 1861–1939, vol. III
Baker, Major Arthur Brander, 1868–1918, vol. II
Baker, Arthur Harold, 1890–1962, vol. VI
Baker, Arthur Lemprière Lancey, 1905–1986, vol. VIII
Baker, Brig.-Gen. Arthur Slade, 1863–1943, vol. IV
Baker, Sir Augustine FitzGerald, 1851–1922, vol. II
Baker, Sir Benjamin, 1840–1907, vol. I
Baker, Lt-Col (Bernard) Granville, 1870–1957, vol. V
Baker, Bevan Braithwaite B.; *see* Bevan-Baker.
Baker, Air Marshal Sir Brian Edmund, 1896–1979, vol. VII

Baker, Bryant, 1881–1970, vol. VI
Baker, Vice-Adm. Casper Joseph, 1852–1918, vol. II
Baker, Baker, Col Cecil Norris, 1869–1934, vol. III
Baker, Charles, 1851–1934, vol. III
Baker, (Charles) Alma, 1857–1941, vol. IV
Baker, Charles Ernest S.; see Smalley-Baker.
Baker, Charles Gaffney, 1907–1969, vol. VI
Baker, Charles Henry Collins, 1880–1959, vol. V
Baker, Charles Maurice, 1872–1952, vol. V
Baker, Colin Lewis Gilbert, 1913–1982, vol. VIII
Baker, Lt-Col Sir Dodington George Richard S.; see Sherston-Baker.
Baker, Rt Rev. Donald, 1882–1968, vol. VI
Baker, Doris Manning, died 1971, vol. VII
Baker, Edmund Wilfrid, 1869–1953, vol. V
Baker, Edward Charles Stuart, 1864–1944, vol. IV
Baker, Lt-Col Edward Mervyn, 1875–1925, vol. II
Baker, Rev. Edward Morgan, 1874–1940, vol. III
Baker, Sir Edward Norman, 1857–1913, vol. I
Baker, Major Edwin Godfrey Phipps, 1885–1963, vol. VI
Baker, Rev. Eric Wilfred, 1899–1973, vol. VII
Baker, Ernest A., 1869–1941, vol. IV
Baker, Brig. Euston Edward Francis, 1895–1981, vol. VIII
Baker, Flora May, 1882–1949, vol. IV
Baker, Francis Douglas, 1884–1958, vol. V
Baker, Frederick Grenfell, died 1930, vol. III
Baker, Sir Frederick Spencer Arnold, 1885–1963, vol. VI
Baker, Field-Marshal Sir Geoffrey Harding, 1912–1980, vol. VII
Baker, Col George, 1840–1910, vol. I
Baker, George Arthur, 1885–1976, vol. VII
Baker, Hon. George Barnard, 1834–1910, vol. I
Baker, Air Vice-Marshal George Brindley Aufrere, 1894–1968, vol. VI
Baker, George Edwin, 1876–1960, vol. V
Baker, George Fisher, 1840–1931, vol. III
Baker, Rt Hon. Sir George Gillespie, 1910–1984, vol. III
Baker, George Philip, 1879–1951, vol. V
Baker, Sir George Sherston, 4th Bt (cr 1796), 1846–1923, vol. II
Baker, Lt-Col Granville; see Baker, Lt-Col B. G.
Baker, Granville Edwin Lloyd L.; see Lloyd-Baker.
Baker, Rt Hon. Harold Trevor, 1877–1960, vol. V
Baker, Henry, 1893–1975, vol. VII
Baker, Henry Frederick, died 1956, vol. V
Baker, Hon. Sir Henry Seymour, 1890–1968, vol. VI
Baker, Henry William Clinton-; see Clinton-Baker.
Baker, H(enry) Wright, 1893–1969, vol. VI
Baker, Sir Herbert, 1862–1946, vol. IV
Baker, Herbert Arthur, 1875–1946, vol. IV
Baker, Herbert Brereton, 1862–1935, vol. III
Baker, Sir Humphrey Dodington Benedict S.; see Sherston-Baker.
Baker, J. Percy, 1859–1930, vol. III
Baker, Sir Jack Croft, 1894–1962, vol. VI
Baker, James, 1847–1920, vol. II
Baker, Adm. Sir Lewis C.; see Clinton-Baker.
Baker, James H., 1848–1925, vol. II
Baker, Lt-Gen. James Mitchell, 1878–1956, vol. V
Baker, Maj.-Gen. Jasper, 1877–1964, vol. VI

Baker, Joanna Constance, (Mrs Noel Baker); see Scott-Moncrieff, J. C.
Baker, Sir John, 1828–1909, vol. I
Baker, Sir John, 1861–1939, vol. III
Baker, John, 1867–1939, vol. III
Baker, John Alfred, 1882–1957, vol. V
Baker, (John Frederic) Allan, 1903–1987, vol. VIII
Baker, John Gilbert, 1834–1920, vol. II
Baker, Rt Rev. John Gilbert Hindley, 1910–1986, vol. VIII
Baker, Ven. John Percy, 1871–1947, vol. IV
Baker, John Randal, 1900–1984, vol. VIII
Baker, Air Chief Marshal Sir John Wakeling, 1897–1978, vol. VII
Baker, Sir Joseph; see Baker, Sir S. J.
Baker, Joseph Allen, 1852–1918, vol. II
Baker, Julian Levett, 1873–1958, vol. V
Baker, Lawrence James, 1827–1921, vol. II
Baker, Adm. Sir Lewis C.; see Clinton-Baker.
Baker, Newton Diehl, 1871–1937, vol. III
Baker, Olive Katherine Lloyd L.; see Lloyd-Baker.
Baker, Oliver, 1856–1939, vol. III
Baker, Percy M., 1872–1935, vol. III
Baker, Peter Frederick, 1939–1987, vol. VIII
Baker, Lt-Col Sir Randolf Littlehales, 4th Bt (cr 1802), 1879–1959, vol. V
Baker, Ray Stannard, 1870–1946, vol. IV
Baker, Reginald George Gillam, 1887–1971, vol. VII
Baker, Reginald Tustin, 1900–1966, vol. VI
Baker, Hon. Sir Richard Chaffey, 1842–1911, vol. I
Baker, Richard St Barbe, 1889–1982, vol. VIII
Baker, Richard Thomas, 1854–1941, vol. VI
Baker, Major Robert Joseph, 1857–1931, vol. III
Baker, Sir Rowland, 1908–1983, vol. VIII
Baker, Sir (Stanislaus) Joseph, 1898–1989, vol. VIII
Baker, Rev. Stanley, 1868–1950, vol. IV
Baker, Sir Stanley, 1928–1976, vol. VII
Baker, Stephen Leonard, 1888–1978, vol. VII
Baker, Rev. Sir Talbot Hastings Bendall, 3rd Bt (cr 1802), 1820–1900, vol. I
Baker, Sir Thomas, died 1926, vol. II
Baker, Col Thomas MacDonald, 1894–1976, vol. VII
Baker, Lt-Gen. Thomas Norris, 1833–1915, vol. I
Baker, Walter John, 1876–1930, vol. III
Baker, Walter Reginals, 1852–1929, vol. III
Baker, Will C., vol. III
Baker, Rev. William, 1841–1910, vol. I
Baker, William, 1849–1920, vol. II
Baker, Ven. William Arthur, 1870–1950, vol. IV
Baker, Sir William Frederick, 1844–1929, vol. III
Baker, Ven. William George, died 1923, vol. II
Baker, Adm. William Henry Baker, 1862–1932, vol. III
Baker, Lt-Gen. Sir William Henry Goldney, 1888–1964, vol. VI
Baker, Rev. William James Furneaux Vashon, 1851–1932, vol. III
Baker, Rt Rev. William Scott, 1902–1990, vol. VIII
Baker, Sir William Thomas Webb, 1873–1948, vol. IV
Baker, Rev. William Wing Carew, 1860–1930, vol. III
Baker-Carr, Brig.-Gen. Christopher D'Arcy Bloomfield Saltern, 1878–1949, vol. IV

Baker-Carr, Major Robert George Teesdale, 1867–1931, vol. III

Baker-Wilbraham, Sir George Barrington; *see* Wilbraham.

Baker-Wilbraham, Sir Philip Wilbraham; *see* Wilbraham.

Baker Wilbraham, Sir Randle John; *see* Wilbraham.

Bakewell, James Herbert, *died* 1931, vol. III

Bakewell, Robert Donald, 1899–1982, vol. VIII

Bakker, Cornelis Jan, 1904–1960, vol. V

Bakst, Léon, 1868–1924, vol. II

Balanchine, George Melitonovitch, 1904–1983, vol. VIII

Balasinor, Nawab of, 1894–1945, vol. IV

Balbo, Maresciallo dell'Aria Italo, 1896–1940, vol. III

Balch, Emily Greene, 1867–1961, vol. VI

Balchin, Brig. Nigel Marlin, 1908–1970, vol. VI

Balcon, Sir Michael, 1896–1977, vol. VII

Bald, Major Alfred Campbell, *died* 1905, vol. I

Bald, Lt-Col John Arthur, 1876–1960, vol. V

Bald, Robert Cecil, 1901–1965, vol. VI

Balderston, John Lloyd, 1889–1954 vol. V

Baldock, Maj.-Gen. Thomas Stanford, 1854–1937, vol. III

Baldock, William, 1850–1933, vol. III

Baldrey, Lt-Col Frank Shelson Headon, 1869–1935, vol. III

Baldry, Alfred Lys, 1858–1939, vol. III

Baldry, Walter Burton Burton-; *see* Burton-Baldry.

Baldwin of Bewdley, 1st Earl, 1867–1947, vol. IV

Baldwin of Bewdley, 2nd Earl, 1899–1958, vol. V

Baldwin of Bewdley, 3rd Earl, 1904–1976, vol. VII

Baldwin, Sir Archer Ernest, 1883–1966, vol. VI

Baldwin, Rev. Edward Curtis, 1844–1941, vol. IV

Baldwin, Ernest H. F., 1909–1969, vol. VI

Baldwin, Engr-Rear-Adm. George William, 1871–1955, vol. V

Baldwin, Brig.-Gen. Guy Melfort, 1865–1945, vol. IV

Baldwin, Sir Harry, 1862–1931, vol. III

Baldwin, James Arthur, 1924–1987, vol. VIII

Baldwin, James Mark, 1861–1934, vol. III

Baldwin, Air Marshal Sir John Eustace Arthur, 1892–1975, vol. VII

Baldwin, Lt-Col Sir John Grey, 1867–1939, vol. III

Baldwin, John Herbert Lacy, 1863–1945, vol. IV

Baldwin, Joseph Mason, 1878–1945, vol. IV

Baldwin, Nelson Mills, 1923–1980, vol. VII

Baldwin, Hon. Simeon Eben, 1840–1927, vol. II

Baldwin-Webb, Col James, *died* 1940, vol. III

Bale, Edwin, 1838–1923, vol. II

Bale, Hon. Sir Henry, 1854–1910, vol. I

Balerno, Baron (Life Peer); Alick Drummond Buchanan-Smith, 1898–1984, vol. VIII

Balewa, Alhaji Rt Hon. Sir Abubakar T.; *see* Tafawa Balewa.

Balfour, 1st Earl of, 1848–1930, vol. III

Balfour, 2nd Earl of, 1853–1945, vol. IV

Balfour, 3rd Earl of, 1902–1968, vol. VI

Balfour of Burleigh, 6th Lord, 1849–1921, vol. II

Balfour of Burleigh, 11th (*de facto* 7th) Lord, 1883–1967, vol. VI

Balfour of Inchrye, 1st Baron, 1897–1988, vol. VIII

Balfour, Alfred, 1885–1963, vol. VI

Balfour, Brig.-Gen. Sir Alfred Granville, 1858–1936, vol. III

Balfour, Alice Blanche, *died* 1936, vol. III

Balfour, Sir Andrew, 1873–1931, vol. III

Balfour, Ven. Andrew Jackson, 1845–1923, vol. II

Balfour, Col. Arthur Macintosh, 1862–1936, vol. III

Balfour, Charles Barrington, 1862–1921, vol. II

Balfour, Major Charles James, 1889–1939, vol. III

Balfour, Captain Christopher Egerton, 1872–1907, vol. I

Balfour, David, 1903–1989, vol. VIII

Balfour, Edward, 1849–1927, vol. II

Balfour, Brig. Edward William Sturgis, 1884–1955, vol. V

Balfour, Col Eustace James Anthony, *died* 1911, vol. I

Balfour, Lady Frances, 1858–1931, vol. III

Balfour, Lt-Col Francis Cecil Campbell, 1884–1965, vol. V

Balfour, Rt Rev. Francis Richard Townley, 1846–1924, vol. II

Balfour, Lt-Col Frederick Robert Stephen, 1873–1945, vol. IV

Balfour, George, 1872–1941, vol. IV

Balfour, Sir Graham, 1858–1929, vol. III

Balfour, Henry, 1863–1939, vol. III

Balfour, Sir Isaac Bayley, 1853–1922, vol. II

Balfour, Hon. James, 1830–1913, vol. I

Balfour, Hon. James Moncreiff, 1878–1960, vol. V

Balfour, James William, 1827–1907, vol. I

Balfour, Sir John, 1894–1983, vol. VIII

Balfour, Col John Edmond Heugh, 1863–1952, vol. V

Balfour, Lt-Col Kenneth Robert, 1863–1936, vol. III

Balfour, Margaret Ida, *died* 1945, vol. IV

Balfour, Lt-Col Oswald Herbert Campbell, *died* 1953, vol. V

Balfour, Patrick; *see* Kinross, 3rd Baron.

Balfour, Lt-Gen. Sir Philip Maxwell, 1898–1977, vol. VIII

Balfour, Sir Robert, 1st Bt, 1844–1929, vol. III

Balfour, Rev. Robert Gordon, 1826–1905, vol. I

Balfour, Col William Edward Ligonier, 1855–1934, vol. III

Balfour-Browne, John Hutton; *see* Browne.

Balfour-Browne, Vincent R., *died* 1963, vol. VI

Balfour-Browne, William Alex Francis, 1874–1967, vol. VI

Balfour-Lynn, Stanley, 1922–1986, vol. VIII

Balfour-Melville, Leslie Melville, 1854–1937, vol. III

Baliol Scott, Edward, 1873–1963, vol. VI

Baliol Scott, Napier, 1903–1956, vol. V

Baline, Israel; *see* Berlin, Irving.

Ball, Alan Hugh, 1924–1987, vol. VIII

Ball, Sir Albert, 1862–1946, vol. IV

Ball, Sir Arthur; *see* Ball, Sir C. A. K.

Ball, Air Vice-Marshall Sir Benjamin, 1912–1977, vol. VII

Ball, Sir (Charles) Arthur (Kinahan), 2nd Bt, 1877–1945, vol. IV

Ball, Sir Charles Bent, 1st Bt, 1851–1916, vol. II

Ball, Charles Francis, 1869–1933, vol. III

Ball, Major Charles James Prior, 1893–1973, vol. VII

Ball, Rev. Charles Richard, *died* 1918, vol. II

Ball, E. Bruce, 1873–1944, vol. IV

Ball, Sir Edmund Lancaster, 1883–1971, vol. VII
Ball, Ernest, *died* 1927, vol. II
Ball, Eustace Alfred R.; *see* Reynolds-Ball.
Ball, Major George Joseph, 1880–1952, vol. V
Ball, Sir (George) Joseph, 1885–1961, vol. VI
Ball, Sir George Thomas T.; *see* Thalben-Ball.
Ball, Harry Standish, 1888–1941, vol. IV
Ball, James Barry, *died* 1926, vol. II
Ball, Sir James Benjamin, 1867–1920, vol. II
Ball, James Dyer, 1847–1919, vol. II
Ball, John, 1861–1940, vol. III
Ball, John, 1872–1941, vol. IV
Ball, Rt Hon. John Thomas, 1815–1898, vol. I
Ball, Sir Joseph; *see* Ball, Sir G. J.
Ball, Rev. Kenneth Vernon James, 1906–1986, vol. VIII
Ball, Sir Nigel Gresley, 3rd Bt, 1892–1978, vol. VII
Ball, Robert Edward, 1911–1990, vol. VIII
Ball, Sir Robert Stawell, 1840–1913, vol. I
Ball, Thomas, 1846–1922, vol. II
Ball, Very Rev. Thomas Isaac, *died* 1916, vol. II
Ball, Walter William Rouse, 1850–1925, vol. II
Ball, Wilfrid, 1853–1917, vol. II
Ball, Willet, 1873–1962, vol. VI
Ball, William Antony, 1904–1973, vol. VII
Ball, Sir William Girling, *died* 1945, vol. IV
Ball, Sir William Valentine, 1874–1960, vol. V
Ballance, Sir Charles Alfred, 1856–1936, vol. III
Ballance, Rear-Adm. Frank Arthur, 1902–1978, vol. VII
Ballance, Sir Hamilton Ashley, 1867–1936, vol. III
Ballantine-Dykes, Col Frescheville Hubert; *see* Dykes.
Ballantrae, Baron (Life Peer); Bernard Edward Fergusson, 1911–1980, vol. VII
Ballantyne, Alexander Hanson, 1911–1983, vol. VIII
Ballantyne, Archibald Morton, 1908–1977, vol. VII
Ballantyne, Arthur James, 1876–1954, vol. V
Ballantyne, Colin Sandergrove, 1908–1988, vol. VIII(A)
Ballantyne, Air Vice-Marshal Gordon Arthur, 1900–1981, vol. VIII
Ballantyne, Sir Henry, 1855–1941, vol. IV
Ballantyne, Henry, 1912–1983, vol. VIII
Ballantyne, Horatio, 1871–1956, vol. V
Ballantyne, John Andrew, 1912–1960, vol. V
Ballantyne, John William, 1861–1923, vol. II
Ballard, Albert, 1888–1969, vol. VI
Ballard, Ven. Arthur Henry, 1912–1984, vol. VIII
Ballard, Lt-Col Basil W.; *see* Woods Ballard.
Ballard, Bristow Guy, 1902–1975, vol. VII
Ballard, Brig.-Gen. Colin Robert, 1868–1941, vol. IV
Ballard, Edward, 1820–1897, vol. I
Ballard, Rev. Frank, *died* 1931, vol. III
Ballard, Rev. Frank Hewett, *died* 1959, vol. V
Ballard, Adm. George Alexander, 1862–1948, vol. IV
Ballard, Geoffrey Horace, 1927–1990, vol. VIII
Ballard, Henry, 1840–1919, vol. II
Ballard, Brig. James Archibald William, 1905–1978, vol. VII
Ballard, Philip Boswood, 1865–1950, vol. IV
Ballentine, Maj.-Gen. John Steventon, 1897–1965, vol. VI
Ballin, Ada S., *died* 1906, vol. I

Ballingall, Lt-Col Henry Miller, 1878–1936, vol. III
Ballinger, Sir John, 1860–1933, vol. III
Ballou, Henry Arthur, 1872–1937, vol. III
Balls, William Lawrence, 1882–1960, vol. V
Bally, Maj.-Gen. John Ford, 1845–1912, vol. I
Balmain, Pierre Alexandre, 1914–1982, vol. VIII
Balme, Archibald Hamilton, *died* 1942, vol. IV
Balme, David Mowbray, 1912–1989, vol. VIII
Balme, Harold, *died* 1953, vol. V
Balmforth, Rev. Canon Henry, 1890–1977, vol. VII
Balogh, Baron (Life Peer); Thomas Balogh, 1905–1985, vol. VIII
Balrampur, Maharaja Bahadur of, 1879–1921, vol. II
Balsdon, John Percy Vyvian Dacre, 1901–1977, vol. VII
Balston, Thomas, 1883–1967, vol. VI
Baly, Edward Charles Cyril, 1871–1948, vol. IV
Balzani, Count Ugo, 1847–1916, vol. II
Bam, Lt-Col Pieter Canzius van Blommestein; *see* Stewart-Bam of Ards.
Bamber, Col Charles James, 1855–1941, vol. IV
Bamber, John, 1915–1976, vol. VII
Bamber, Captain Wyndham Lerrier, *died* 1924, vol. II
Bambridge, Sir George, 1883–1961, vol. VI
Bambridge, Henry James, 1881–1956, vol. V
Bambridge, Rev. Joseph John, *died* 1923, vol. II
Bambridge, Thomas, vol. III
Bamfield, Lt-Gen. Albert Henry, 1830–1908, vol. I
Bamfield, Maj.-Gen. Harold John Kinahan, *died* 1959, vol. V
Bamford, Major Edward, 1887–1928, vol. II
Bamford, Sir Eric St John, 1891–1957, vol. V
Bamford, Lt-Col Harry William Morrey, 1882–1968, vol. VI
Bamford, Percival Clifford, 1886–1960, vol. V
Bamford, Rt Rev. Thomas Ambrose, 1861–1945, vol. VI
Bamford-Slack, Sir John, 1857–1909, vol. I
Bampton, Rev. Joseph M., 1854–1933, vol. III
Banarji, Hon. Sir Pramada Charan, *died* 1930, vol. III
Banatvala, Col Sir Hormasjee Eduljee, 1859–1932, vol. III
Banbury of Southam, 1st Baron, 1850–1936, vol. III
Banbury of Southam, 2nd Baron, 1915–1981, vol. VIII
Banbury, Brig.-Gen. Walter Edward, 1863–1927, vol. II
Bancroft, Claude Keith, 1885–1919, vol. I:
Bancroft, Edgar Addison, 1857–1925, vol. II
Bancroft, Elias, *died* 1924, vol. II
Bancroft, George Pleydell, 1868–1956, vol. V
Bancroft, Hubert Howe, 1832–1918, vol. II
Bancroft, Marie Effie, (Lady Bancroft), 1839–1921, vol. II
Bancroft, Sir Oswald Lawrance, 1888–1964, vol. VI
Bancroft, Sir Squire Bancroft, 1841–1926, vol. II
Bandaranaike, Sir Solomon Dias, 1862–1946, vol. IV
Bandaranaike, Solomon West Ridgeway Dias, 1899–1959, vol. V
Bandon, 4th Earl of, 1850–1924, vol. II
Bandon, 5th Earl of, 1904–1979, vol. VII
Bandon, Countess of; (Georgina), 1853–1942, vol. IV
Banerjea, A. C., 1894–1979, vol. VII

Banerjea, Pramathanath, 1881–1960, vol. V(A)
Banerjea, Sir Surendranath, 1848–1925, vol. II
Banerjee, Sir Gooroo Dass, 1844–1919, vol. II
Banerjee, Rabindra Nath, 1895–1985, vol. VIII
Banerjee, Sarat Chandra, 1870–1932, vol. III
Banerji, Sir Albion Rajkumar, 1871–1950, vol. IV
Banerji, Amiya Charan, 1891–1968, vol. VI(AII)
Banes, George Edward, 1828–1907, vol. I
Banfield, John William, died 1945, vol. IV
Banfield, Col Rees John Francis, 1850–1926, vol. II
Banford, Leslie Jackson, died 1961, vol. VI
Bangor, 5th Viscount, 1828–1911, vol. I
Bangor, 6th Viscount, 1868–1950, vol. IV
Bangs, John Kendrick, 1862–1922, vol. II
Banham, Prof. (Peter) Reyner, 1922–1988, vol. VIII
Banham, Prof. Reyner; see Banham, Prof. P. R.
Banister, Col Fitzgerald Muirson, 1853–1928, vol. II
Banister, George Henry, died 1934, vol. III
Banister, John Bright, 1880–1938, vol. III
Banister, Rt Rev. William, 1855–1928, vol. II
Bankart, Sir Alfred Seymour, 1870–1933, vol. III
Bankart, Surg. Rear-Adm. Sir Arthur Reginald, 1868–1943, vol. IV
Bankart, Arthur Sydney Blundell, 1879–1951, vol. V
Bankart, Vice-Adm. Sir (George) Harold, 1893–1964, vol. VI
Bankart, Vice-Adm. Sir Harold; see Bankart, Vice-Adm. Sir G. H.
Bankes, Rev. Eldon Surtees, 1829–1915, vol. I
Bankes, Henry John Ralph, 1902–1981, vol. VIII
Bankes, Rt Hon. Sir John Eldon, 1854–1946, vol. IV
Bankes, Ralph George Scott, 1900–1948, vol. IV
Bankes, Ralph Vincent, 1867–1921, vol. II
Bankes, Robert Wynne, 1887–1975, vol. VII
Bankes, Walter Ralph, 1853–1904, vol. I
Bankes-Williams, Ivor Maredydd, 1896–1974, vol. VII
Bankole-Jones, Sir Samuel; see Jones.
Banks, A(rthur) Leslie, 1904–1989, vol. VIII
Banks, Col Hon. Charles Arthur, 1885–1961, vol. VI
Banks, Col Cyril, 1901–1969, vol. VI
Banks, Sir Donald, 1891–1975, vol. VII
Banks, Edward Bernard, 1901–1968, vol. VI
Banks, Elizabeth, died 1938, vol. III
Banks, Air Cdre Francis Rodwell, 1898–1985, vol. VIII
Banks, Mrs George Linnaeus, 1821–1897, vol. I
Banks, Lt-Col Henry John Archibald, 1869–1939, vol. III
Banks, Isabella; see Banks, Mrs George Linnaeus
Banks, James Dallaway, 1917–1985, vol. VIII
Banks, Sir John Garnett, 1889–1974, vol. VII
Banks, Rev. John Shaw, 1835–1917, vol. II
Banks, Sir John Thomas, died 1908, vol. I
Banks, Leslie James, 1890–1952, vol. V
Banks, Sir Reginald Mitchell, 1880–1940, vol. III
Banks, Rev. Samuel John Sherbrooke, 1861–1941, vol. IV
Banks, Sir Thomas Macdonald; see Banks, Sir Donald.
Banks, Captain William Eric, 1900–1986, vol. VIII
Banks, Sir William Mitchell, 1842–1904, vol. I
Banks-Davis, Henry John, 1867–1936, vol. III

Bannatine-Allason, Maj.-Gen. Sir Richard, 1855–1940, vol. III
Bannatyne, Rev. Colin A., 1849–1920, vol. II
Bannatyne, Maj.-Gen. Neil Charles, 1880–1970, vol. VI
Bannatyne, Sir Robert Reid, 1875–1956, vol. V
Banner, Sir George Knowles H.; see Harmood-Banner.
Banner, Major Sir Harmood H.-; see Harmood-Banner.
Banner, Hubert Stewart, 1891–1964, vol. VI
Banner, Sir John Sutherland H.; see Harmood-Banner.
Bannerman of Kildonan, Baron (Life Peer); John MacDonald Bannerman, 1901–1969, vol. VI
Bannerman, Sir Alexander, 11th Bt, 1871–1934, vol. III
Bannerman, Sir (Alexander) Patrick, 14th Bt, 1933–1989, vol. VIII
Bannerman, Lt-Col Sir Arthur D'Arcy Gordon, 12th Bt, 1866–1955, vol. V
Bannerman, Charles Edward Woolhouse, 1884–1943, vol. IV
Bannerman, David Armitage, 1886–1979, vol. VII
Bannerman, Lt-Col Sir Donald Arthur Gordon, 13th Bt, 1899–1989, vol. VIII
Bannerman, Sir George, 10th Bt, 1827–1901, vol. I
Bannerman, Rt Hon. Sir Henry C.; see Campbell-Bannerman.
Bannerman, Sir Patrick; see Bannerman, Sir A. P.
Bannerman, Gen. William, 1828–1914, vol. I
Bannerman, Maj.-Gen. William Burney, 1858–1924, vol. II
Banning, Lt-Col Stephen Thomas, 1859–1935, vol. III
Bannister, Rev. Arthur Thomas, 1862–1936, vol. III
Bannister, Charles Olden, 1876–1955, vol. V
Bannister, Frank Kenneth, 1909–1975, vol. VII
Bannister, Frederick Allan, 1901–1970, vol. VI
Bannister, Grace, died 1986, vol. VIII
Bannister, Rev. Henry Marriott, 1854–1919, vol. II
Banon, Brig.-Gen. Frederick Lionel, 1862–1950, vol. IV
Bansda, ex-Maharaja Saheb of, 1888–1951, vol. V
Banswara, Maharawal of, 1888–1944, vol. IV(A), vol. V
Banta, Arthur Mangun, 1877–1946, vol. IV(A), vol. V
Banting, Sir Frederick Grant, 1891–1941, vol. IV
Banting, Air Vice-Marshal George Gaywood, 1898-1973, vol. VII
Bantock, George Granville, died 1913, vol. I
Bantock, Sir Granville, 1868–1946, vol. IV
Banton, George, 1856–1932, vol. III
Banwell, Sir (George) Harold, 1900–1982, vol. VIII
Banwell, Godwin Edward, 1897–1981, vol. VIII
Banwell, Sir Harold; see Banwell, Sir G. H.
Barbé, Louis A., 1845–1926, vol. II
Barbenson, Nicholas Peter Le Cocq, 1838–1928, vol. II
Barber, Alan Theodore, 1905–1985, vol. VIII
Barber, Arthur Vavasour, died 1957, vol. V
Barber, Rev. Benjamin Aquila, 1876–1946, vol. IV
Barber, Charles Alfred, 1860–1933, vol. III

Barber, Lt-Col Charles Harrison, 1877–1965, vol. VI
Barber, Lt-Gen. Sir Colin Muir, 1897–1964, vol. VI
Barber, Donald, 1905–1957, vol. V
Barber, Ven. Edward, 1841–1914, vol. I
Barber, Sir (Edward) Fairless, 1873–1958, vol. V
Barber, Elizabeth; see Barber, M. E.
Barber, Eric Arthur, 1888–1965, vol. VI
Barber, Sir Fairless; see Barber, Sir E. F.
Barber, Maj.-Gen. Frederick Charles, died 1908, vol. I
Barber, Maj.-Gen. George Walter, 1868–1951, vol. V
Barber, Sir George William, 1858–1945, vol. IV
Barber, Harold Wordsworth, 1886–1955, vol. V
Barber, Sir Henry; see Barber, Sir W. H.
Barber, Sir Herbert William, 1887–1978, vol. VII
Barber, Horace Newton, 1914–1971, vol. VII
Barber, Captain James William, died 1962, vol. VI
Barber, Leslie Claud Seton, 1894–1968, vol. VI
Barber, Mary, 1911–1965, vol. VI
Barber, (Mary) Elizabeth, 1911–1979, vol. VII
Barber, Noël John Lysberg, 1909–1988, vol. VIII
Barber, Ohio C., 1841–1920, vol. II
Barber, Percival Ellison, died 1959, vol. V
Barber, Sir Philip; see Barber, Sir T. P.
Barber, Philip Stanley, 1895–1973, vol. VII
Barber, Samuel, 1910–1981, vol. VIII
Barber, Rev. Thomas Gerard, died 1952, vol. V
Barber, Sir (Thomas) Philip, 1st Bt (cr 1960), 1876–1961, vol. VI
Barber, William Charles, died 1921, vol. II
Barber, William David, died 1952, vol. V
Barber, W(illiam) Edmund, died 1958, vol. V
Barber, Sir (William) Henry, 1st Bt (cr 1924), 1860–1927, vol. II
Barber, Rev. William Theodore Aquila, 1858–1945, vol. IV
Barber-Starkey, William Joseph Starkey, 1847–1924, vol. II
Barberton, Ivan Graham Mitford-, 1896–1976, vol. VII
Barbier, Paul, died 1921, vol. II
Barbier, Paul, 1873–1947, vol. IV
Barbieri, Bishop Guido Bastiani Pascucci, 1836–1910, vol. I
Barbirolli, Sir John Giovanni Battista, 1899–1970, vol. VI
Barbour, A. H. Freeland, 1856–1927, vol. II
Barbour, Sir David Miller, 1841–1928, vol. II
Barbour, George, 1841–1919, vol. II
Barbour, George Brown, 1890–1977, vol. VII(AII)
Barbour, George Freeland, 1882–1946, vol. IV
Barbour, Harold Adrian Milne, 1874–1938, vol. III
Barbour, Rt Hon. Sir John Milne, 1st Bt, 1868–1951, vol. V
Barbour, Major Robert, 1876–1928, vol. II
Barbusse, Henri, 1873–1935, vol. III
Barchard, Col Charles Henry, 1828–1902, vol. I
Barclay, Alexander, 1896–1987, vol. VIII
Barclay, Alfred Ernest, 1876–1949, vol. IV
Barclay, Sir Cecil; see Barclay, Sir R. C. de B.
Barclay, Rt Hon. Sir Colville Adrian de Rune, 1869–1929, vol. III
Barclay, Brig. Cyril Nelson, 1896–1979, vol. VII
Barclay, Edward Exton, 1860–1948, vol. IV

Barclay, Florence Louisa, 1862–1920, vol. II
Barclay, Sir George Head, 1862–1921, vol. II
Barclay, Sir Harry John, 1861–1933, vol. III
Barclay, Col Henry Albert, 1858–1947, vol. IV
Barclay, Hugh Gurney, 1851–1936, vol. III
Barclay, Rev. Humphrey Gordon, died 1955, vol. V
Barclay, Rev. James, 1844–1920, vol. II
Barclay, John, 1845–1936, vol. III
Barclay, John Stephen, 1908–1968, vol. VI
Barclay, Major Maurice Edward, 1886–1962, vol. VI
Barclay, Sir Noton; see Barclay, Sir R. N.
Barclay, Col Reginald, 1861–1945, vol. IV
Barclay, Robert, 1837–1913, vol. I
Barclay, Robert Buchanan, 1843–1919, vol. II
Barclay, Sir (Robert) Cecil de Belzim, 13th Bt, 1862–1930, vol. III
Barclay, Robert Francis, 1867–1948, vol. IV
Barclay, Robert Leatham, 1869–1939, vol. III
Barclay, Sir (Robert) Noton, 1872–1957, vol. V
Barclay, Sir Robert Wyvill, 1880–1951, vol. V
Barclay, Theodore David, 1906–1981, vol. VIII
Barclay, Sir Thomas, 1839–1921, vol. II
Barclay, Rev. Thomas, 1849–1935, vol. III
Barclay, Sir Thomas, 1853–1941, vol. IV
Barclay, William, 1907–1978, vol. VII
Barclay, William Singer, 1871–1947, vol. IV
Barclay-Harvey, Sir (Charles) Malcolm, 1890–1969, vol. VI
Barclay-Harvey, Sir Malcolm; see Barclay-Harvey, Sir C. M.
Barclay-Smith, Edward, died 1945, vol. IV
Barclay-Smith, (Ida) Phyllis, died 1980, vol. VII
Barclay-Smith, Phyllis; see Barclay-Smith, I. P.
Barcroft, John Coleraine Hanbury, 1908–1958, vol. V
Barcroft, Sir Joseph, 1872–1947, vol. IV
Barcŷnska, Countess Hélène Armiger Barclay, died 1930, vol. III
Bardill, Ralph William, 1876–1935, vol. III
Bardoux, Jacques, 1874–1959, vol. V
Bardsley, Rt Rev. Cyril Charles Bowman, 1870–1940, vol. III
Bardsley, Rev. Ernest John, 1868–1948, vol. IV
Bardsley, Rt Rev. John Wareing, 1835–1904, vol. I
Bardsley, Rev. Joseph Udell Norman, 1868–1928, vol. II
Bardsley, Robert Vickers, 1890–1952, vol. V
Bardswell, Charles William, 1832–1902, vol. I
Bardswell, Hugh Rosser, 1874–1962, vol. VI
Bardswell, Noel Dean, 1871–1938, vol. III
Bardwell, Thomas Newman Frederick, 1850–1931, vol. III
Bardwell, Captain William Scot, 1892–1968, vol. VI
Bare, Lt-Col Alfred Raymund, 1886–1967, vol. VI
Bare, Captain Arnold Edwin, 1880–1917, vol. II
Barea, Arturo, 1897–1957, vol. V
Barefoot, Lt-Col George Henry, 1864–1924, vol. II
Barff, Rev. Albert, died 1913, vol. I
Barff, Henry Ebenezer, 1857–1925, vol. II
Barff, Rev. Henry Tootai, 1834–1917, vol. II
Barff, Stafford Edward Douglas, 1909–1976. vol. VII
Barfoot, Most Rev. Walter Foster, 1893–1978, vol. VII
Barford, Edward, 1898–1980, vol. VII
Barge, Lt-Col Kenneth, 1883–1971, vol. VII

Barger, George, 1878–1939, vol. III
Bargone, Frédéric Charles; see Farrère, Claude.
Barham, Col Arthur Saxby, 1869–1952, vol. V
Barham, Ven. Charles Mitchell, died 1935, vol. III
Barham, Rt Rev. E(dward) Lawrence, 1901–1973, vol. VII
Barham, Sir George, 1836–1913, vol. I
Barham, George Titus, 1860–1937, vol. III
Baria, Raja of, 1886–1949, vol. IV
Barillon, Rt Rev. Emile, 1860–1935, vol. III
Baring, Sir Charles Christian, 2nd Bt, 1898–1990, vol. VIII
Baring, Brig.-Gen. Hon. Everard, 1865–1932, vol. III
Baring, Hon. Francis Henry, 1850–1915, vol. I
Baring, Sir Godfrey, 1st Bt, 1871–1957, vol. V
Baring, Godfrey Nigel Everard, 1870–1934, vol. III
Baring, Major Hon. Guy Victor, 1873–1916, vol. II
Baring, Harold Herman John, 1869–1927, vol. II
Baring, Hon. Hugo, 1876–1949, vol. IV
Baring, Sir Mark, 1916–1988, vol. VIII
Baring, Wing Comdr Hon. Maurice, 1874–1945, vol. IV
Baring, Walter, 1844–1915, vol. I
Baring, Hon. Windham, 1880–1922, vol. II
Baring-Gould, Sabine, 1834–1924, vol. II
Bark, Sir Peter, 1869–1937, vol. III
Barke, Allen; see Barke, J. A.
Barke, James Allen, 1903–1990, vol. VIII
Barker, Alan; see Barker, W. A.
Barker, Aldred Farrer, 1868–1964, vol. VI
Barker, Sir Alport; see Barker, Sir T. W. A.
Barker, Anthony Raine, 1880–1963, vol. VI
Barker, Arthur Edward James, died 1916, vol. II
Barker, Lt-Col Arthur James, 1918–1981, vol. VIII
Barker, Augustine, 1887–1937, vol. III
Barker, Bertie Thomas Percival, 1877–1961, vol. VI
Barker, Cecil; see Barker, H. C. J.
Barker, Sir (Charles Frederic) James, 1914–1980, vol. VII
Barker, Col Charles William Panton, 1857–1926, vol. II
Barker, Air Vice-Marshal Clifford Cockcroft, 1909–1977, vol. VII
Barker, Captain Sir David W., 1858–1941, vol. IV
Barker, Denis William Knighton, 1908–1981, vol. VIII
Barker, Dennis Albert, 1926–1989, vol. VIII
Barker, Douglas William Ashley, 1905–1978, vol. VII
Barker, Edward Harrison, 1851–1919, vol. II
Barker, Eric Leslie, 1912–1990, vol. VIII
Barker, Sir Ernest, 1874–1960, vol. V
Barker, Col Ernest Francis William, 1877–1961, vol. VI
Barker, Gen. Sir Evelyn Hugh, 1894–1983, vol. VIII
Barker, Sir Francis Henry, 1865–1922, vol. II
Barker, Col Sir Francis William James, 1841–1924, vol. II
Barker, Lt-Col Frederic Allan, 1882–1959, vol. V
Barker, Hon. Sir Frederic Eustace, 1838–1916, vol. II
Barker, Lt-Col Frederick George, 1866–1951, vol. V
Barker, Maj.-Gen. Sir George, 1849–1930, vol. III
Barker, George, 1858–1936, vol. III(A), vol. IV
Barker, Gen. Sir George Digby, 1833–1914, vol. I

Barker, Rev. Canon Gilbert David, 1882–1958, vol. V
Barker, Harley Granville G.; see Granville-Barker.
Barker, (Harold) Cecil James, 1893–1974, vol. VII
Barker, Helen G.; see Granville-Barker.
Barker, Sir Henry Edward, 1872–1942, vol. IV
Barker, Henry James, 1852–1934, vol. III(A), vol. IV
Barker, Sir Herbert Atkinson, 1869–1950, vol. IV
Barker, Hugh Purslove, 1909–1984, vol. VIII
Barker, J. Ellis, 1870–1948, vol. IV
Barker, Sir James; see Barker, Sir C. F. J.
Barker, Sir John, 1st Bt, 1840–1914, vol. I
Barker, John, died 1970, vol. VI
Barker, John Edward, 1832–1912, vol. I
Barker, Lt-Col John Stafford, 1879–1959, vol. V
Barker, Maj.-Gen. John Stewart Scott, 1853–1918, vol. II
Barker, Very Rev. Joseph, 1834–1924, vol. II
Barker, Lancelot Elliot, 1908–1972, vol. VII
Barker, Lewellys F., 1867–1943, vol. IV
Barker, Brig. Lewis Ernest Stephen, 1895–1981, vol. VIII
Barker, Dame Lilian Charlotte, 1874–1955, vol. V
Barker, Louis William, 1879–1954, vol. V
Barker, Mary Ann, (Lady Barker); see Broome, M. A.
Barker, Lt-Gen. Michael George Henry, 1884–1960, vol. V
Barker, Rev. Peter, died 1937, vol. III
Barker, Lt-Col Randle Barnett-, 1870–1918, vol. II
Barker, Sir Rayner Childe, 1858–1945, vol. IV
Barker, Maj.-Gen. Richard Ernest, 1888–1962, vol. VI
Barker, Sir Robert Beacroft, 1890–1960, vol. V, vol. VI
Barker, Lt-Col Robert Hewitt, 1887–1961, vol. VI
Barker, Captain Roland Auriol, 1892–1954, vol. V
Barker, Ronald Ernest, 1920–1976, vol. VII
Barker, Sir Ross; see Barker, Sir W. R.
Barker, Rev. Rowland Vectis, 1846–1926, vol. II
Barker, Dame Sara Elizabeth, 1904–1973, vol. VII
Barker, Sydney George, 1887–1942, vol. IV
Barker, Thomas Vipond, 1881–1931, vol. III
Barker, Sir (Thomas William) Alport, died 1956, vol. V
Barker, Tom Battersby, died 1968, vol. VI
Barker, Sir (Wilberforce) Ross, 1874–1957, vol. V
Barker, Very Rev. William, 1838–1917, vol. II
Barker, (William) Alan, 1923–1988, vol. VIII
Barker, Lt-Col William Arthur John, 1879–1924, vol. II
Barker, Lt-Col William George, 1894–1930, vol. III
Barker, William Henry, 1882–1929, vol. III
Barker, Wright, died 1941, vol. IV
Barker-Benfield, Brig. Karl Vere, 1892–1969, vol. VI
Barker-Mill, William Claude Frederick V.; see Vaudrey-Barker-Mill.
Barkla, Charles Glover, 1877–1944, vol. IV
Barkley, Alben William, 1877–1956, vol. V
Barkley, Brenda Edith, (Mrs Harry Barkley); see Ryman, B. E.
Barkley, Col Macdonald, 1871–1956, vol. V
Barkley, William Henry, 1869–1942, vol. IV
Barkly, Sir Henry, 1815–1898, vol. I

Barkway, Rt Rev. James Lumsden, 1878–1968, vol. VI

Barlas, Sir Richard Douglas, 1916–1982, vol. VIII

Barlee, Sir Kenneth William, *died* 1956, vol. V

Barley, Frederick, *died* 1915, vol. I

Barley, Lt-Col Leslie John, 1890–1979, vol. VII

Barling, Sir Gilbert; *see* Barling, Sir H. G.

Barling, Sir (Harry) Gilbert, 1st Bt, 1855–1940, vol. III

Barling, Joseph, *born* 1839, vol. III

Barling Lt-Col Seymour Gilbert, *died* 1960, vol. V

Barlow, Sir Alan; *see* Barlow, Sir J. A. N.

Barlow, Rt Hon. Sir Anderson M.; *see* Montague-Barlow.

Barlow, Adm. Charles James, 1848–1921, vol. II

Barlow, Rt Rev. Christopher George, 1858–1915, vol. I

Barlow, Disney Charles, 1880–1965, vol. VI

Barlow, Francis John, 1869–1940, vol. III

Barlow, Sir Frank Herbert, 1918–1979, vol. VII

Barlow, George Thomas, 1865–1919, vol. II

Barlow, Harold Everard Monteagle, 1899–1989, vol. VIII

Barlow, Rev. Henry Theodore Edward, 1863–1906, vol. I

Barlow, Sir Hilaro William Wellesley, 5th Bt (*cr* 1803), 1861–1941, vol. IV

Barlow, Horace M., 1884–1954, vol. V

Barlow, James, 1921–1973, vol. VII

Barlow, Sir (James) Alan (Noel), 2nd Bt (*cr* 1900), 1881–1968, vol. VI

Barlow, Rev. James William, 1826–1913, vol. I

Barlow, Jane, 1857–1917, vol. II

Barlow, Çol John, *died* 1924, vol. II

Barlow, John, 1853–1943, vol. IV(A)

Barlow, Sir John Denman, 2nd Bt, 1898–1986, vol. VIII

Barlow, Sir John Emmott, 1st Bt (*cr* 1907), 1857–1932, vol. III

Barlow, Percy, 1867–1931, vol. III

Barlow, Ralph Mitford Marriott, 1904–1977, vol. VII

Barlow, Sir Richard Hugh, 6th Bt (*cr* 1803), 1904–1946, vol. IV

Barlow, Sir Richard Wellesley, 4th Bt (*cr* 1803), 1836–1904, vol. I

Barlow, Sir Robert, 1891–1976, vol. VII

Barlow, Thomas Bradwall, 1900–1988, vol. VIII

Barlow, Sir Thomas Dalmahoy, 1st Bt (*cr* 1900), 1845–1945, vol. IV

Barlow, Sir Thomas D., 1883–1964, vol. VI

Barlow, Walter Sydney L.; *see* Lazarus-Barlow.

Barlow, William, 1834–1915, vol. I

Barlow, William, 1845–1934, vol. III

Barlow, William Henry, 1812–1902, vol. I

Barltrop, Ernest William, 1893–1957, vol. V

Barman, Christian August, 1898–1980, vol. VII

Barnaby, Sir Nathaniel, 1829–1915, vol. I

Barnard, 9th Baron, 1854–1918, vol. II

Barnard, 10th Baron, 1888–1964, vol. VI

Barnard, Andrew Bigoe, 1862–1928, vol. II

Barnard, Beverley Gayer, 1916–1973, vol. VII

Barnard, Sir Charles Loudon, 1823–1902, vol. I

Barnard, Rev. Charles William, *died* 1928, vol. II

Barnard, Brig.-Gen. Cyril Darcy Vivien C.; *see* Cary-Barnard.

Barnard, Sir Edmund Broughton, 1856–1930, vol. III

Barnard, Eric, 1891–1980, vol. VII

Barnard, Francis Pierrepont, 1854–1931, vol. III

Barnard, Hon. Sir Frank Stillman, 1856–1936, vol. III

Barnard, Vice-Adm. Sir Geoffrey, 1902–1974, vol. VII

Barnard, George Grey, 1863–1938, vol. III

Barnard, George Henry, 1868–1948, vol. IV

Barnard, Sir Henry William, 1891–1981, vol. VIII

Barnard, Sir Herbert, 1831–1920, vol. II

Barnard, Howard Clive, 1884–1985, vol. VIII

Barnard, Brig.-Gen. John Henry, 1846–1901, vol. I

Barnard, Joseph Edwin, *died* 1949, vol. IV

Barnard, Joseph Terence Owen, 1872–1936, vol. III

Barnard, Leonard William, 1870–1951, vol. V

Barnard, Rev. Percy Mordaunt, 1868–1941, vol. IV

Barnard, Thomas Theodore, 1898–1983, vol. VIII

Barnard, Hon. William Edward, 1886–1958, vol. V

Barnard, William George, 1892–1956, vol. V

Barnard, Maj.-Gen. William Osborne, 1838–1920, vol. II

Barnard, William Tyndall, 1855–1923, vol. II

Barnardiston, Col Nathaniel, 1832–1916, vol. II

Barnardiston, Maj.-Gen. Nathaniel Walter, 1858–1919, vol. II

Barnardiston, Lt-Col Samuel John Barrington, 1875–1924, vol. II

Barnardo, Fleming; *see* Barnardo, F. A. F.

Barnardo, (Frederick Adolphus) Fleming, 1874–1962, vol. VI

Barnardo, Thomas John, 1845–1905, vol. I

Barnato, Henry Isaac, *died* 1908, vol. I

Barnato, Woolf, 1895–1948, vol. IV

Barnby, 1st Baron, 1841–1929, vol. III

Barnby, 2nd Baron, 1884–1982, vol. VIII

Barne, Rt Rev. George Dunsford, 1879–1954, vol. V

Barne, Major Miles, 1874–1917, vol. II

Barne, Brig. William Bradley Gosset, 1880–1951, vol. V

Barneby, William Theodroe, 1873–1946, vol. IV

Barnell, Herbert Rex, 1907–1973, vol. VII

Barnes, Alexander, 1855–1924, vol. II

Barnes, Alfred Edward, 1881–1956, vol. V

Barnes, Rt Hon. Alfred John, 1887–1974, vol. VII

Barnes, Alfred Schwartz, 1868–1949, vol. IV

Barnes, Anthony Charles, 1891–1974, vol. VII

Barnes, Gen. Ardley Henry Falwasser, 1837–1910, vol. I

Barnes, Arthur Chapman, 1891–1985, vol. VIII

Barnes, Rev. Canon Arthur Hubert, *died* 1952, vol. V

Barnes, Arthur Kentish, 1872–1954, vol. V

Barnes, Rt Rev. Mgr Arthur Stapylton, 1861–1936, vol. III

Barnes, Barry K., (Nelson Barry Mackintosh Barnes), 1906–1965, vol. VI

Barnes, Bernard, 1890–1950, vol. IV

Barnes, Bertie Frank, 1888–1965, vol. VI

Barnes, Captain Charles Roper Gorell, 1896–1918, vol. II

Barnes, Edwin Clay, 1864–1941, vol. IV

Barnes, Eric Cecil, 1899–1987, vol. VIII

Barnes, Air Cdre Eric Delano, 1900–1957, vol. V
Barnes, Rt Rev. Ernest William, 1874–1953, vol. V
Barnes, Fancourt, *died* 1908, vol. I
Barnes, Frank, *died* 1960, vol. V
Barnes, Col Frank Purcell, 1880–1956, vol. V
Barnes, Sir Frederic Gorell, 1856–1939, vol. III
Barnes, Frederick Dallas, 1843–1899, vol. I
Barnes, Rt Hon. George Nicoll, 1859–1940, vol. III
Barnes, Sir George Reginald, 1904–1960, vol. V
Barnes, Sir George Stapylton, 1858–1946, vol. IV
Barnes, Harold Charles Edward, 1871–1940, vol. III
Barnes, Harold William, 1912–1981, vol. VIII
Barnes, Major Harry, 1870–1935, vol. III
Barnes, Harry Cheetham, 1898–1961, vol. VI(AII)
Barnes, Harry Elmer, 1889–1968, vol. VI
Barnes, Sir Harry Jefferson, 1915–1982, vol. VIII
Barnes, Henry, 1842–1921, vol. II
Barnes, Howard Turner, 1873–1950, vol. IV(A)
Barnes, Sir Hugh Shakespear, 1853–1940, vol. III
Barnes, Major Humphry Aston, 1900–1940, vol. III
Barnes, Col James, 1866–1936, vol. III
Barnes, Sir James Horace, 1891–1969, vol. VI
Barnes, Sir (James) Sidney, 1881–1952, vol. V
Barnes, John Frederick Evelyn, 1851–1925, vol. II
Barnes, John Morrison, 1913–1975, vol. VII
Barnes, Sir Kenneth Ralph, 1878–1957, vol. V
Barnes, Nelson Barry Mackintosh, *see* Barnes, Barry K.
Barnes, Col Osmond, 1834–1930, vol. III
Barnes, Rev. Peter, 1856–1921, vol. II
Barnes, Maj.-Gen. Sir Reginald Walter Ralph, 1871–1946, vol. IV
Barnes, Richard Cumberland, 1912–1970, vol. VI(AII)
Barnes, Sir Sidney; *see* Barnes, Sir J. S.
Barnes, Stanley, 1875–1955, vol. V
Barnes, Sir Thomas James, 1888–1964, vol. VI
Barnes, Hon. Walter Henry, 1858–1933, vol. III
Barnes, Walter Mayhew, 1871–1950, vol. IV
Barnes, Air Vice-Marshal William Edward, 1897–1958, vol. V
Barnes, Rev. William Emery, 1859–1939, vol. III
Barnes, Sir William Lethbridge G.; *see* Gorell Barnes.
Barnes, Winston Herbert Frederick, 1909–1990, vol. VIII
Barnes-Lawrence, Rev. Arthur Evelyn, 1851–1931, vol. III
Barnes-Lawrence, Herbert Cecil, 1852–1921, vol. II
Barnetson, Baron (Life Peer); William Denholm Barnetson, 1917–1981, vol. VIII
Barnetson, Maj.-Gen. James Craw, 1907–1984, vol. VIII
Barnett, Lt-Col Alfred George, 1883–1955, vol. V
Barnett, Alfred John, 1857–1943, vol. IV
Barnett, Rev. Arthur Thomas, 1858–1941, vol. IV
Barnett, Sir Ben Lewis, 1894–1979, vol. VII
Barnett, Cecil Guy, 1881–1959, vol. V
Barnett, Charles Edward, 1848–1937, vol. III
Barnett, Cyril Harry, 1919–1970, vol. VI
Barnett, Rev. Ernest Judd, 1859–1955, vol. V
Barnett, Sir Geoffrey Morris, 1902–1970, vol. VI
Barnett, George Aldred, *died* 1903, vol. I
Barnett, Col George Henry, 1880–1942, vol. IV
Barnett, Sir George Percy, 1894–1965, vol. VI

Barnett, Guy; *see* Barnett, N. G.
Barnett, Harry Villiers, 1858–1928, vol. II
Barnett, Dame Henrietta; *see* Barnett, Dame M. H.
Barnett, Dame Henrietta Octavia, 1851–1936, vol. III
Barnett, Lt-Col Henry N.; *see* Norman Barnett.
Barnett, Rev. Herbert, 1851–1937, vol. III
Barnett, John Francis, 1837–1916, vol. II
Barnett, Lionel David, 1871–1960, vol. V
Barnett, Sir Louis Edward, 1865–1946, vol. IV
Barnett, Dame (Mary) Henrietta, 1905–1985, vol. VIII
Barnett, Rev. Maurice, 1917–1980, vol. VII
Barnett, (Nicolas) Guy, 1928–1986, vol. VIII
Barnett, Percy Arthur, 1858–1941, vol. IV
Barnett, Richard David, 1909–1986, vol. VIII
Barnett, Major Sir Richard Whieldon, 1863–1930, vol. III
Barnett, Rev. Samuel Augustus, 1844–1913, vol. I
Barnett, Rev. T. Ratcliffe, 1868–1946, vol. IV
Barnett-Barker, Lt-Col Randle; *see* Barker.
Barnett-Clarke, Very Rev. Charles William, *died* 1916, vol. II
Barnewall, Sir John Robert, 11th Bt, 1850–1936, vol. III
Barnewall, Sir Reginald Aylmer John de Barneval, 10th Bt, 1838–1909, vol. I
Barnewall, Sir Reginald J., 12th Bt, 1888–1961, vol. VI
Barnewall, Hon. Reginald Nicholas Francis, 1897–1918, vol. II
Barnham, Henry Dudley, 1854–1936, vol. III
Barnhill, Alexander Perley, 1863–1935, vol. III
Barnicoat, John Wallis, 1814–1905, vol. I
Barnie, Marian, (Mrs Donald Barnie); *see* Veitch, Marian.
Barnish, Captain Geoffrey Howard, 1887–1941, vol. IV
Barns, Rev. John Wintour Baldwin, 1912–1974, vol. VII
Barns, Thomas Alexander, 1881–1930, vol. III
Barnsley, Alan Gabriel; *see* Fielding, Gabriel.
Barnsley, Brig.-Gen. Sir John, 1858–1926, vol. II
Barnsley, Maj.-Gen. Robert Eric, 1886–1968, vol. VI
Barnsley, (William) Edward, 1900–1987, vol. VIII
Barnston, Sir Harry, 1st Bt, 1870–1929, vol. III
Barnwell, Col Ralph Ernest, 1895–1984, vol. VIII
Baroda, HH Maharaja Gaekwar Sir Sayaji Rao III, 1863–1939, vol. III
Baroda, Maharaja of, 1908–1968, vol. VI
Baroja Nessi, Pio, (Don Pio Baroja), 1872–1956, vol. V
Baron, Sir Barclay Josiah, *died* 1919, vol. II
Baron, Bernhard, 1850–1929, vol. III
Baron, Sir Bernhard; *see* Baron, Sir L. B.
Baron, Colin, 1921–1987, vol. VIII
Baron, Cyril Faudel Joseph, 1903–1978, vol. VII
Baron, Sir Edward Samson, 1892–1962, vol. VI
Baron, Sir (Louis) Bernhard, 1st Bt, 1876–1934, vol. III
Baron-Suckling, Rev. Charles William, 1862–1944, vol. IV
Barotseland, Litunga of, 1888–1968, vol. VI
Barr, Alexander Wallace, 1886–1949, vol. IV
Barr, Alfred Hamilton, jun., 1902–1981, vol. VIII

Barr, Amelia Edith, 1831–1919, vol. II

Barr, Archibald, 1855–1931, vol. III

Barr, Lt-Col Sir David William Keith, 1846–1916, vol. II

Barr, Sir George William, 1881–1956, vol. V

Barr, Comdr James, 1855–1937, vol. III

Barr, Sir James, 1849–1938, vol. III

Barr, Rev. James, 1862–1949, vol. IV

Barr, Sir James, 1884–1952, vol. V

Barr, James Angus Evan Abbot, 1862–1923, vol. II

Barr, James Gordon, 1908–1963, vol. VI

Barr, John, 1859–1940, vol. III

Barr, Mark, 1871–1950, vol. IV

Barr, Robert, *died* 1912, vol. I

Barr, Thomas, 1846–1916, vol. II

Barr, Venie, *died* 1947, vol. IV

Barr Smith, Sir Tom Elder, 1904–1968, vol. VI

Barraclough, Frank, 1901–1974, vol. VII

Barraclough, Geoffrey, 1908–1984, vol. VIII

Barraclough, Henry, 1894–1982, vol. VIII

Barraclough, Sir Henry; *see* Barraclough, Sir S. H. E.

Barraclough, Brig. Sir John Ashworth, *died* 1981, vol. VIII

Barraclough, Sir (Samuel) Henry (Egerton), 1874–1958, vol. V

Barran, Sir John, 1st Bt, 1821–1905, vol. I

Barran, Sir John Leighton, 3rd Bt, 1904–1974, vol. VII

Barran, Sir John Nicholson, 2nd Bt, 1872–1952, vol. V

Barran, Sir Rowland Hirst, 1858–1949, vol. IV

Barrand, Arthur Rhys, 1861–1941, vol. IV

Barratt, Sir Albert, 1860–1941, vol. IV

Barratt, Air Chief Marshal Sir Arthur Sheridan, 1891–1966, vol. VI

Barratt, Sir Charles, 1910–1971, vol. VII

Barratt, Captain Sir Francis Henry Godolphin L., 2nd Bt; *see* Layland-Barratt.

Barratt, Sir Francis Layland-, 1st Bt, 1860–1933, vol. III

Barratt, Col Herbert James, 1858–1952, vol. V

Barratt, John Arthur, 1857–1944, vol. IV

Barratt, John Oglethorpe Wakelin, 1862–1956, vol. V

Barratt, Reginald, 1861–1917, vol. II

Barratt, Major Stanley George Reeves E.; *see* Elton-Barratt.

Barratt, Sir Sydney, 1898–1975, vol. VII

Barratt, Rev. Thomas H., 1870–1951, vol. V

Barratt, Maj.-Gen. William Cross, 1862–1940, vol. III

Barratt, William Donald, 1883–1955, vol. V

Barraud, Francis, *died* 1924, vol. II

Barrell, Francis Richard, 1860–1915, vol. I

Barrère, Jean-Bertrand Marie, 1914–1985, vol. VIII

Barres, Maurice, 1862–1923, vol. II

Barret, Rt Rev. John Patrick, 1878–1946, vol. IV

Barrett, Major Alexander Gould, 1866–1954, vol. V

Barrett, Anthony Arthur, 1930–1986, vol. VIII

Barrett, Field Marshal Sir Arthur Arnold, 1857–1926, vol. III

Barrett, Sir Arthur George, 1895–1984, vol. VIII

Barrett, Ashley William, *died* 1939, vol. III

Barrett, Lt-Col Cyril Charles Johnson, 1884–1933, vol. III

Barrett, Col Dacre Lennard, 1858–1941, vol. IV

Barrett, Rev. Daniel William, *died* 1925, vol. II

Barrett, Edith Helen, *died* 1939, vol. III

Barrett, Brig.-Gen. Edward Alfred M.; *see* Moulton-Barrett.

Barrett, Edward Ivo Medhurst, 1879–1950, vol. IV

Barrett, Edwin Cyril Geddes, 1909–1986, vol. VIII

Barrett, Florence Elizabeth, (Lady Barrett), *died* 1945, vol. IV

Barrett, Francis E. H. Joyce, *died* 1925, vol. II

Barrett, Frank, 1848–1926, vol. II

Barrett, Frank Ashley, *died* 1954, vol. V

Barrett, Rev. George Slatyer, 1839–1916, vol. II

Barrett, Col Henry Walter, 1857–1949, vol. IV

Barrett, Herbert Roper, 1873–1943, vol. IV

Barrett, Rev. Hugh S.; *see* Scott-Barrett.

Barrett, Hugh T.; *see* Tufnell-Barrett.

Barrett, Lt-Col Sir James Williams, 1862–1945, vol. IV

Barrett, Col John Cridlan, 1897–1977, vol. VII

Barrett, Group Captain John Francis Tufnell, 1898–1941, vol. IV

Barrett, Norman Rupert, 1903–1979, vol. VII

Barrett, Robert John, 1861–1942, vol. IV

Barrett, Thomas J., 1841–1914, vol. I

Barrett, William, 1863–1931, vol. III

Barrett, Very Rev. William Edward Colvile, 1880–1956, vol. V

Barrett, Sir William Fletcher, 1844–1925, vol. II

Barrett, Sir William Scott, 1843–1921, vol. II

Barrett, Wilson, 1846–1904, vol. I

Barrett-Lennard, Sir Fiennes, *died* 1963, vol. VI

Barrett-Lennard, Lt-Col John, 1863–1935, vol. III

Barrett-Lennard, Sir Richard Fiennes; *see* Lennard.

Barrett-Lennard, Sir Thomas, 2nd Bt; *see* Lennard.

Barrett-Lennard, Sir Thomas, 3rd Bt; *see* Lennard.

Barrett-Lennard, Sir Thomas Richard F.; *see* Lennard.

Barrie, Alexander Baillie, 1906–1957, vol. V

Barrie, Sir Charles, 1840–1921, vol. II

Barrie, Derek Stiven Maxwelton, 1907–1989, vol. VIII

Barrie, Rt Hon. Hugh Thom, 1860–1922, vol. II

Barrie, James, 1862–1932, vol. III

Barrie, Sir James Matthew, 1st Bt, 1860–1937, vol. III

Barrie, Sir Walter, 1901–1988, vol. VIII

Barringer, Paul Brandon, 1857–1941, vol. IV

Barrington, 8th Viscount, 1825–1901, vol. I

Barrington, 9th Viscount, 1848–1933, vol. III

Barrington, 10th Viscount, 1873–1960, vol. V

Barrington, 11th Viscount, 1908–1990, vol. VIII

Barrington, Hon. Bernard; *see* Barrington, Hon. W. B. L.

Barrington, Hon. Sir (Bernard) Eric (Edward), 1847–1918, vol. II

Barrington, Sir Charles Bacon, 6th Bt, 1902–1980, vol. VII(AII)

Barrington, Sir Charles Burton, 5th Bt, 1848–1943, vol. IV

Barrington, Charles George, 1827–1911, vol. I

Barrington, Claud, 1893–1960, vol. V

Barrington, E.; *see* Beck, L. A.

Barrington, Emilie Isabel, *died* 1933, vol. III

Barrington, Hon. Sir Eric; *see* Barrington, Hon. Sir B. E. E.

Barrington, Ernest James William, 1909–1985, vol. VIII

Barrington, John Harcourt, 1907–1973, vol. VII

Barrington, Sir Kenneth Charles Peto, 1911–1987, vol. VIII

Barrington, Hon. Rupert Edward Selborne, 1877–1975, vol. VII

Barrington, Sir Vincent Hunter Barrington K.; *see* Kennett-Barrington.

Barrington, Hon. (Walter)Bernard (Louis), 1876–1959, vol. V

Barrington, Hon. Sir William Augustus Curzon, 1842–1922, vol. II

Barrington-Fleet, George Rutland, 1853–1922, vol. II

Barrington-Kennett, Lt-Col Brackley Herbert Barrington, 1846–1919, vol. II

Barrington-Ward, Frederick Temple, 1880–1938, vol. III

Barrington-Ward, John Grosvenor, 1894–1946, vol. IV

Barrington-Ward, Sir Lancelot Edward, 1884–1953, vol. V

Barrington-Ward, Rev. Mark James, *died* 1924, vol. II

Barrington-Ward, Sir Michael; *see* Barrington-Ward, Sir V. M.

Barrington-Ward, Robert M'Gowan, 1891–1948, vol. IV

Barrington-Ward, Sir (Victor) Michael, 1887–1972, vol. VII

Barrios, Benjamin, 1878–1929, vol. III

Barritt, Sir David Thurlow, 1903–1990, vol. VIII

Barron, Claud Alexander, 1871–1948, vol. IV

Barron, Donovan Allaway, 1907–1980, vol. VII

Barron, Elwyn Alfred, *died* 1929, vol. III

Barron, Evan Macleod, 1879–1965, vol. VI

Barron, Maj.-Gen. Frederick Wilmot, 1880–1963, vol. VI

Barron, Gladys Caroline, *died* 1967, vol. VI

Barron, Maj.-Gen. Sir Harry, 1847–1921, vol. II

Barron, Sir Henry Page-Turner, 2nd Bt, 1824–1900, vol. I

Barron, James, 1847–1919, vol. II

Barron, Brig.-Gen. Netterville Guy, 1867–1945, vol. IV

Barron, Oswald, 1868–1939, vol. III

Barron, Wilfrid Philip S.; *see* Shepherd-Barron.

Barron, Col Willie Netterville, 1872–1930, vol. III

Barrow, Albert Boyce, *died* 1939, vol. III

Barrow, Sir Alfred, 1850–1928, vol. II

Barrow, Adm. Arthur, 1853–1914, vol. I

Barrow, Col Arthur Frederick, 1850–1903, vol. I

Barrow, Rear-Adm. Benjamin Wingate, 1878–1966, vol. VI

Barrow, Gen. Sir Edmund George, 1852–1934, vol. III

Barrow, Rt Hon. Errol Walton, 1920–1987, vol. VIII

Barrow, Sir Francis Laurence John, 4th Bt, 1862–1950, vol. IV

Barrow, Gen. Sir George de Symons, 1864–1959, vol. V

Barrow, Maj.-Gen. Harold Percy Waller, 1876–1957, vol. V

Barrow, John, 1808–1898, vol. I

Barrow, Sir John Croker, 3rd Bt, 1833–1900, vol. I

Barrow, Rev. Canon John Harrison, 1881–1981, vol. VIII

Barrow, Hon. Sir Malcolm Palliser, 1900–1973, vol. VII

Barrow, Oscar Theodore, 1854–1937, vol. III

Barrow, Sir Reuben Vincent, 1838–1918, vol. II

Barrow, Sir Samuel, 1859–1935, vol. III

Barrow, Walter, 1867–1954, vol. V

Barrow, Sir Wilfrid John Wilson Croker, 5th Bt, 1897–1960, vol. V

Barrowclough, Rt Hon. Sir Harold Eric, 1894–1972, vol. VII

Barrows, William Leonard, 1905–1976, vol. VII

Barrs, Alfred George, 1853–1934, vol. III

Barry, Rt Rev. Alfred, 1826–1910, vol. I

Barry, Brig. Arthur Gordon, 1885–1942, vol. IV

Barry, Lt-Col Arthur John, 1859–1944, vol. IV

Barry, Lt-Col Cecil Charles Stewart, 1867–1933, vol. III

Barry, Charles, 1887–1963, vol. VI

Barry, Charles David, *died* 1928, vol. II

Barry, Rt Hon. Charles Robert, 1825–1897, vol. I

Barry, Adm. Sir Claud Barrington, 1891–1951, vol. V

Barry, Sir (Claude) Francis, 3rd Bt, 1883–1970, vol. VI

Barry, David Thomas, 1870–1955, vol. V

Barry, (Donald Angus) Philip, 1920–1987, vol. VIII

Barry, E. L. M.; *see* Milner-Barry.

Barry, Edward, 1852–1927, vol. II(A), vol. III

Barry, Lt-Col Edward, 1896–1952, vol. V

Barry, Sir Edward Arthur, 2nd Bt, 1858–1949, vol. IV

Barry, Sir Francis; *see* Barry, Sir C. F.

Barry, Sir Francis Tress, 1st Bt, 1825–1907, vol. I

Barry, Rt Rev. (Frank) Russell, 1890–1976, vol. VII

Barry, Sir Gerald Reid, 1898–1968, vol. VI

Barry, Geraldine Mary, 1897–1978, vol. VII

Barry, Rear-Adm. Sir Henry Deacon, 1849–1908, vol. I

Barry, Rt Rev. Hugh Van Lynden O.; *see* Otter-Barry.

Barry, Iris, 1895–1969, vol. VI

Barry, Hon. Lt-Col James, *died* 1920, vol. II

Barry, Major James D., *died* 1941, vol. IV

Barry, Hon. Jeremiah Hayes, 1858–1946, vol. IV

Barry, Rt Rev. John, 1875–1938, vol. III

Barry, John Arthur, 1850–1911, vol. I

Barry, Sir John Edmond, 1828–1919, vol. II

Barry, Hon. Sir John Vincent William, 1903–1969, vol. VI

Barry, Sir John Wolfe Wolfe-, 1836–1918, vol. II

Barry, Michael, (James Barry Jackson), 1910–1988, vol. VIII

Barry, Norman, 1916–1984, vol. VIII

Barry, Sir Patrick Redmond, 1898–1972, vol. VII

Barry, Philip; *see* Barry, D. A. P.

Barry, Ralph Brereton, 1856–1920, vol. II

Barry, Redmond, 1866–1913, vol. I

Barry, Richard Fitzwilliam, 1861–1916, vol. II(A), vol. III

Barry, Sir Rupert Rodney Francis Tress, 4th Bt, 1910–1977, vol. VII
Barry, Rt Rev. Russell; *see* Barry, Rt Rev. F. R.
Barry, Col Stanley Leonard, 1873–1943, vol. IV
Barry, Col Thomas David Collis, *died* 1943, vol. IV
Barry, Rt Rev.Thomas Francis, 1841–1920, vol. II
Barry, Most Rev. William, 1872–1929, vol. III
Barry, Rt Rev. Mgr William Francis, 1849–1930, vol. III
Barry, William James, 1864–1952, vol. V
Barry, William Whitmore O.; *see* Otter-Barry.
Barry-Doyle, Rt Rev. Mgr Richard; *see* Doyle.
Barrymore, 1st Baron, 1843–1925, vol. II
Barrymore, Ethel, 1879–1959, vol. V
Barrymore, John, 1882–1942, vol. IV
Barrymore, Lionel, 1878–1954, vol. V
Barson, Derek Emmanuel, 1922–1980, vol. VII
Barstow, Maj.-Gen. Arthur Edward, 1888–1942, vol. IV
Barstow, Sir George Lewis, 1874–1966, vol. VI
Barstow, Maj.-Gen. Henry, 1876–1952, vol. V
Barstow, Major John Nelson, 1890–1936, vol. III
Barstow, Mrs Montague; *see* Baroness Orczy
Barstow, Percy Gott, 1883–1969, vol. VI
Barter, Lt-Gen. Sir Charles St Leger, 1857–1931, vol. III
Barter, Captain Frederick, *died* 1953, vol. V
Barter, Geoffrey Herbert, 1901–1952, vol. V
Barter, Rev. Herbert Francis Treseder, 1869–1949, vol. IV
Barter, John Wilfred, 1917–1983, vol. VIII
Barter, Sir Percy, 1886–1975, vol. VII
Barter, Sir Richard, 1837–1916, vol. II
Barth, Lt-Col Sir Jacob William, 1871–1941, vol. IV
Barth, Karl, 1886–1968, vol. VI
Bartholomé, Albert, 1848–1928, vol. II
Bartholomew, Maj.-Gen. Arthur Wollaston, 1878–1945, vol. IV
Bartholomew, Sir Clarence Edward, 1879–1946, vol. IV
Bartholomew, Col Hugh John, 1871–1938, vol. III
Bartholomew, James Rankin, 1887–1951, vol. V(A)
Bartholomew, John, 1870–1937, vol. III
Bartholomew, John, 1890–1962, vol. VI
Bartholomew, John Eric, (Eric Morecambe), 1926–1984, vol. VIII
Bartholomew, John George, 1860–1920, vol. II
Bartholomew, Gen. Sir William Henry, 1877–1962, vol. VI
Barthorpe, Major Sir Frederick James, *died* 1942, vol. IV
Bartington, Dennis Walter, 1901–1985, vol. VIII
Bartle, Anita, *died* 1962, vol. VI
Bartleet, Rev. Edwin Berry, 1872–1946, vol. IV
Bartleet, Rev. Samuel Edwin, 1835–1924, vol. II
Bartleman, Maj.-Gen. Woodburn Francis, 1840–1924, vol. II
Bartlet, James Vernon, 1863–1940, vol. III
Bartlet, Rev. T. J., 1833–1915, vol. I
Bartlett, Lt-Col Alfred James Napier, 1884–1956, vol. V
Bartlett, Ven. Arthur Robert, 1851–1923, vol. II
Bartlett, Lt-Col Sir Basil Hardington, 2nd Bt, 1905–1985, vol. VIII

Bartlett, Cdre Charles Alfred, 1868–1945, vol. IV
Bartlett, Sir Charles John, 1889–1955, vol. V
Bartlett, Rev. Charles Oldfeld, 1858–1937, vol. III
Bartlett, (Charles) Vernon (Oldfeld), 1894–1983, vol. VIII
Bartlett, Sir David; *see* Bartlett, Sir H. D. H.
Bartlett, Rt Rev. David Daniel, 1900–1977, vol. VII
Bartlett, Rev. Canon Donald Mackenzie Maynard, 1873–1969, vol. VI
Bartlett, Ellis A.; *see* Ashmead-Bartlett.
Bartlett, Sir Ellis Ashmead-, 1849–1902, vol. I
Bartlett, Sir Frederic Charles, 1886–1969, vol. VI
Bartlett, George Bertram, 1880–1944, vol. IV
Bartlett, Sir (Henry) David (Hardington), 3rd Bt, 1912–1989, vol. VIII
Bartlett, Sir Herbert Henry, 1st Bt, 1842–1921, vol. II
Bartlett, Humphrey Edward Gibson, 1880–1951, vol. V
Bartlett, Joseph Leslie, 1889–1968, vol. VI
Bartlett, Paul Wayland, 1865–1925, vol. II
Bartlett, Peter Geoffrey, 1922–1986, vol. VIII
Bartlett, Vernon; *see* Bartlett, C. V. O.
Bartlett, W. H., 1858–1932, vol. III
Bartlett-Burdett-Coutts, Rt Hon. William Lehman Ashmead; *see* Burdett-Coutts.
Bartley, Lt-Col Bryan Cole, *died* 1968, vol. VI
Bartley, Sir Charles, 1882–1968, vol. VI
Bartley, Sir George Christopher Trout, 1842–1910, vol. I
Bartley, Sir John, 1886–1954, vol. V
Bartley, Patrick, 1909–1956, vol. V
Bartley, William, 1885–1961, vol. VI
Bartley-Denniss, Lt-Col Cyril Edmund Bartley, 1882–1955, vol. V
Bartley-Denniss, Sir Edmund Robert Bartley, 1854–1931, vol. III
Bartók, Béla, 1881–1945, vol. IV
Bartolo, Hon. Sir Augustus, 1883–1937, vol. III
Bartolomé, Adm. Sir Charles Martin de, 1871–1941, vol. IV
Barton, Arthur Edward Victor, 1892–1983, vol. VIII
Barton, Most Rev. Arthur William, 1881–1962, vol. VI
Barton, Arthur Willoughby, 1899–1976, vol. VII
Barton, Lt-Col Baptist Johnston, 1876–1944, vol. IV
Barton, Major Basil Kelsey, 1879–1958, vol. V
Barton, Cecil James Juxon Talbot, 1891–1980, vol. VII
Barton, Cecil Molyneux, 1883–1962, vol. VI
Barton, Major Charles Gerard, 1860–1919, vol. II
Barton, Sir Charles Newton, 1907–1987, vol. VIII
Barton, Lt-Col Charles Walter, 1876–1950, vol. IV
Barton, Clarence, 1892–1957, vol. V
Barton, Rt Hon. Sir (Dunbar) Plunket, 1st Bt, 1853–1937, vol. III
Barton, Rt Hon. Sir Edmund, 1849–1920, vol. II
Barton, Edwin Alfred, 1863–1953, vol. V
Barton, Edwin Henry, 1858–1925, vol. II
Barton, Adm. Ernest Gillbe, 1861–1938, vol. III
Barton, Captain Francis Rickman, 1865–1947, vol. IV
Barton, Frederick Sherbrooke, 1895–1969, vol. VI
Barton, Maj.-Gen. Sir Geoffry, 1844–1922, vol. II
Barton, Rev. George Aaron, 1859–1942, vol. IV

Barton, George Alexander Heaton, 1865–1924, vol. II
Barton, George Samuel Horace, 1883–1962, vol. VI
Barton, Guy Trayton, 1908–1977, vol. VII
Barton, Sir Harold Montague, 1882–1962, vol. VI
Barton, Ven. Harry Douglas, 1898–1968, vol. VI
Barton, Lt-Col Sir Henry Baldwin, 1869–1952, vol. V
Barton, Sir John George, 1850–1937, vol. III
Barton, Rt Rev. Mgr John Mackintosh Tilney, 1898–1977, vol. VII
Barton, John Saxon, 1875–1961, vol. VI
Barton, Joseph Edwin, 1875–1959, vol. V
Barton, Lt-Col Leslie Eric, 1889–1952, vol. V
Barton, Col Maurice Charles, 1852–1939, vol. III
Barton, Rt Hon. Sir Plunket; *see* Barton, Rt Hon. Sir D. P.
Barton, Richard, 1850–1927, vol. II
Barton, Lt-Col Richard Lionel, 1875–1942, vol. IV
Barton, Robert Childers, 1881–1975, vol. VII
Barton, Rose, *died* 1929, vol. III
Barton, Samuel Saxon, *died* 1957, vol. V
Barton, Sir Sidney, 1876–1946, vol. IV
Barton, Sidney James, 1909–1986, vol. VIII
Barton, Rev. Walter John, *died* 1955, vol. V
Barton, Wilfred Alexander, 1880–1953, vol. V
Barton, Sir William, 1862–1957, vol. V
Barton, William Henry, 1869–1928, vol. II
Barton, Lt-Col William Hugh, 1874–1945, vol. IV
Barton, Sir William Pell, 1871–1956, vol. V
Bartram, Rev. Henry, 1849–1934, vol. III
Bartram, Sir Robert Appleby, 1835–1925, vol. II
Barttelot, Adm. Sir Brian Herbert Fairbairn, 1867–1942, vol. IV
Barttelot, Major Sir Walter Balfour, 3rd Bt, 1880–1918, vol. II
Barttelot, Lt-Col Sir Walter de Stopham, 4th Bt, 1904–1944, vol. IV
Barttelot, Sir Walter George, 2nd Bt, 1855–1900, vol. I
Barty, James Webster, 1841–1915, vol. I
Baruch, Bernard Mannes, 1870–1965, vol. VI
Barwell, Rev. Arthur Henry Sanxay, 1834–1913, vol. I
Barwell, Claud Foster, 1912–1971, vol. VII
Barwell, Harold Shuttleworth, 1875–1959, vol. V
Barwell, Hon. Sir Henry Newman, 1877–1959, vol. V
Barwick, George Frederick, 1853–1931, vol. III
Barwick, Sir John Storey, 1st Bt, 1840–1915, vol. I
Barwick, Sir John Storey, 2nd Bt, 1876–1953, vol. V
Barwick, Sir Richard Llewellyn, 3rd Bt, 1916–1979, vol. VII
Barzellotti, Giacomo, 1844–1917, vol. II
Basden, Rev. George Thomas, 1873–1944, vol. IV
Basedow, Herbert, 1881–1933, vol. III
Bashford, Ernest Francis, 1873–1923, vol. II
Bashford, Sir Henry Howarth, 1880–1961, vol. VI
Bashford, Rt Rev. James W., 1849–1919, vol. II
Bashford, John Laidlay, *died* 1908, vol. I
Bashford, Major Lindsay; *see* Bashford, Major R. J. L.
Bashford, Major (Radcliffe James) Lindsay, 1881–1921, vol. II
Bashyam Aiyangar, Sir Venbakam, *died* 1908, vol. I
Basing, 2nd Baron, 1860–1919, vol. II

Basing, 3rd Baron, 1890–1969, vol. VI
Basing, 4th Baron, 1903–1983, vol. VIII
Baskcomb-Harrison, Captain Henry Neville; *see* Harrison.
Baskerville, Beatrice; *see* Guichard, B. C.
Baskerville, Rev. Charles Gardiner, 1830–1921, vol. II
Baskerville, Lt-Col Charles Herbert Lethbridge, 1860–1946, vol. IV
Baskerville, Geoffrey, 1870–1944, vol. IV
Baskerville, Rev. Canon George Knyfton, 1867–1941, vol. IV
Baskerville, Ralph Hopton, 1883–1918, vol. II
Baskett, Charles H., 1872–1953, vol. V
Baskett, Sir Ronald Gilbert, 1901–1972, vol. VII
Basnett, Baron (Life Peer); David Basnett, 1924–1989, vol. VIII
Bason, Fred, (Frederick Thomas Bason), 1907–1973, vol. VII
Bass, Hamar Alfred, 1842–1898, vol. I
Bass, John Stuart, 1905–1954, vol. V
Bass, Col Philip de Salis, 1862–1936, vol. III
Bass, Sir William Arthur Hamar, 2nd Bt, 1879–1952, vol. V
Bassano, 3rd Duc de, 1844–1906, vol. I
Basser, Sir Adolph, 1887–1964, vol. VI
Basset, Alfred Barnard, 1854–1930, vol. III
Bassett, Arthur Francis, 1873–1950, vol. IV
Bassett, Maj.-Gen. Richard Augustin Marriott, 1891–1954, vol. V
Basset, Ronald Lambart, 1898–1972, vol. VII
Bassett, Arthur Tilney, 1869–1964, vol. VI
Bassett, George Arthur, 1884–1971, vol. VII
Bassett, Henry, 1881–1965, vol. VI
Bassett, Herbert Harry, 1874–1939, vol. III(A), vol. IV
Bassett, John Harold, *died* 1974, vol. VII
Bassett, John Spencer, 1867–1928, vol. II
Bassett, Ralph Henry, 1896–1962, vol. VII
Bassett, Sir Walter Eric, 1892–1978, vol. VII
Bassett Smith, Guy; *see* Bassett Smith, N. G.
Bassett Smith, (Newlands) Guy, 1910–1984, vol. VIII
Bassett-Smith, Surg.-Rear-Adm. Sir Percy William, 1861–1927, vol. II
Bastable, Charles F., 1855–1945, vol. IV
Bastard, Bt Col Reginald, 1880–1960, vol. V
Bastard, Rev. William Pollexfen, 1832–1915, vol. I
Bastian, Henry Charlton, 1837–1915, vol. I
Bastin, Brig. David Terence, 1904–1982, vol. VIII
Bastin, Maj.-Gen. George Edward Restalic, 1902–1960, vol. V
Bastyan, Lt-Gen. Sir Edric Montague, 1903–1980, vol. VII
Bastyan, Maj.-Gen. Kenneth Cecil Orville, 1906–1975, vol. VII
Basu, Bhupendra Nath, 1859–1924, vol. II
Basu, Hon. Bijay Kumar, 1885–1937, vol. III
Batchelor, Alfred Alexander Meston, 1901–1982, vol. VIII
Batchelor, Rev. Alfred Williams, 1864–1961, vol. VI
Batchelor, Denzil Stanley, 1906–1969, vol. VI
Batchelor, Hon. Egerton Lee, 1865–1911, vol. I
Batchelor, Ferdinand Campion, *died* 1916, vol. II
Batchelor, Francis Malcolm, 1865–1937, vol. III

Batchelor, George Frederick Grant, 1902–1984, vol. VIII

Batchelor, Col Gordon Guthrie Malcolm, 1908–1976, vol. VII

Batchelor, John Stanley, 1905–1987, vol. VIII

Batchelor, Meston; *see* Batchelor, A. A. M.

Batchelor, Sir Stanley Lockhart, 1868–1938, vol. III

Batchelor, Lt-Col Vivian Allan, 1882–1960, vol. V

Bate, Ven. Alban F., 1893–1986, vol. VIII

Bate, Col Albert Louis Frederick, 1862–1924, vol. II

Bate, Maj.-Gen. (Alfred) Christopher, 1927–1980, vol. VII

Bate, Maj.-Gen. Christopher; *see* Bate, Maj.-Gen. A. C.

Bate, Captain Claude Lindsay, *died* 1957, vol. V

Bate, Edward Raoul, 1859–1948, vol. IV

Bate, Francis, *died* 1950, vol. IV

Bate, Henry; *see* Bate, I. H.

Bate, Sir Henry Newel, 1828–1917, vol. II

Bate, Very Rev. Herbert Newell, 1871–1941, vol. IV

Bate, (Isaac) Henry, 1899–1986, vol. VIII

Bate, John Pawley, 1857–1921, vol. II

Bate, Percy, 1868–1913, vol. I

Bate, Col Thomas Elwood Lindsay, 1852–1937, vol. III

Bate, Brig.-Gen. Thomas Reginald Fraser, 1881–1964, vol. VI

Bate, Dame Zara Kate, 1909–1989, vol. VIII

Bate-Smith, Edgar Charles, 1900–1989, vol. VIII

Bateman, 2nd Baron, 1826–1901, vol. I

Bateman, 3rd Baron, 1856–1931, vol. III

Bateman, Sir Alfred Edmund, 1844–1929, vol. III

Bateman, Alys, *died* 1924, vol. II

Bateman, Rev. Arthur Fitzroy D.; *see* Dobbie-Bateman.

Bateman, Arthur Leonard, 1879–1957, vol. V

Bateman, Brig.-Gen. Bernard Montague, 1865–1937, vol. III

Bateman, Sir Charles Harold, 1892–1986, vol. VIII

Bateman, Maj.-Gen. Donald Roland Edwin Rowan, 1901–1969, vol. VI

Bateman, Edward Louis, 1834–1909, vol. I

Bateman, Francis John Harvey, *died* 1920, vol. II

Bateman, Sir Frederic, 1824–1904, vol. I

Bateman, George Cecil, 1882–1963, vol. VI

Bateman, Lt-Col Harold Henry, 1888–1974, vol. VII

Bateman, Harry, 1882–1946, vol. IV

Bateman, Henry Mayo, 1887–1970, vol. VI

Bateman, James, *died* 1959, vol. V

Bateman, John, 1839–1910, vol. I

Bateman, Rev. William Fairbairn La Trobe-, 1845–1926, vol. II

Bateman, Rev. William Henry Fraser, 1855–1923, vol. II

Bateman-Champain, Brig.-Gen. Hugh Frederick, 1869–1933, vol. III

Bateman-Champain, Rt Rev. John Norman, 1880–1950, vol. IV

Bateman-Hanbury, Rev. Hon. Arthur Allen, 1829–1919, vol. II

Bateman-Hanbury, Captain Hon. Charles Stanhope Melville, 1877–1931, vol. III

Bateman-Hanbury, Major Edward Reginald, 1859–1907, vol. I

Bater, Rev. Alfred Brenchly, *died* 1933, vol. III

Bates, Sir Alfred, 1897–1979, vol. VII

Bates, Arlo, 1850–1918, vol. II

Bates, Arthur Henry, *died* 1947, vol. IV

Bates, Lt-Col Austin Graves, 1891–1961, vol. VI

Bates, Major Cecil Robert, 1882–1935, vol. III

Bates, Brig.-Gen. Sir (Charles) Loftus, 1863–1951, vol. V

Bates, Sir Darrell; *see* Bates, Sir J. D.

Bates, Rt Hon. Sir Dawson; *see* Bates, Rt Hon. Sir R. D.

Bates, Sir Edward Bertram, 3rd Bt (*cr* 1880), 1877–1903, vol. I

Bates, Sir Edward Percy, 2nd Bt (*cr* 1880), 1845–1899, vol. I

Bates, Air-Vice-Marshal Eric Cecil, 1906–1975, vol. VII

Bates, Brig.-Gen. Francis Stewart Montague, 1876–1954, vol. V

Bates, Frederic Alan, 1884–1957, vol. V

Bates, Harry, 1851–1899, vol. I

Bates, Harry Stuart, 1893–1985, vol. VIII

Bates, Henry Montague, 1849–1928, vol. II

Bates, Henry Thomas Roy, 1902–1958, vol. V

Bates, Herbert Ernest, 1905–1974, vol. VII

Bates, Sir (Julian) Darrell, 1913–1989, vol. VIII

Bates, Leslie Fleetwood, 1897–1978, vol VII

Bates, Air Vice-Marshal Sir Leslie John Vernon, 1896–1966, vol. VI

Bates, Brig.-Gen. Sir Loftus; *see* Bates, Brig.-Gen. Sir C. L.

Bates, Ven. Mansel Harry, 1912–1980, vol. VII

Bates, Oric, 1883–1918, vol. II

Bates, Sir Percy Elly, 4th Bt (*cr* 1880), 1879–1946, vol. IV

Bates, Rt Hon. Sir (Richard) Dawson, 1st Bt (*cr* 1937), 1876–1949, vol. IV

Bates, Rev. Canon T., 1842–1911, vol. I

Bates, Thorpe, 1883–1958, vol. V

Bateson, Sir Alexander Dingwall, 1866–1935, vol. III

Bateson, Lt-Col David Mayhew, 1906–1975, vol. VII

Bateson, Sir Dingwall Latham, 1898–1967, vol. VI

Bateson, Frederick Wilse, 1901–1978, vol. VII

Bateson, Col John Holgate, 1880–1956, vol.V

Bateson, Rev. Joseph Harger, 1865–1935, vol. III

Bateson, Mary, 1865–1906, vol. I

Bateson, Air Vice-Marshal Robert Norman, 1912–1986, vol. VIII

Bateson, Rear-Adm. Stuart Latham, 1898–1980, vol.VII

Bateson, Williams, 1861–1926, vol. II

Batey, Charles Edward, 1893–1981, vol. VIII

Batey, Joseph, 1867–1949, vol. IV

Batey, Rowland William John S.; *see* Scott-Batey.

Bath, 5th Marquess of, 1862–1946, vol. IV

Bath, Engr-Rear-Adm. George Clark, 1862–1925, vol. II

Bath, Hon. Thomas Henry, 1875–1956, vol. V

Bather, Elizabeth Constance, 1904–1988, vol. VIII

Bather, Francis Arthur, 1863–1934, vol. III

Bather, Ven. Henry Francis, 1832–1905, vol. I

Bather, Rear-Adm. Rowland Henry, 1873–1961, vol. VI

Batho, Sir Charles Albert, 1st Bt, 1872–1938, vol. III

Batho, Cyril, 1885–1951, vol. V
Batho, Edith Clara, 1895–1986, vol. VIII
Batho, Sir Maurice Benjamin, 2nd Bt, 1910–1990, vol. VIII
Bathurst, 7th Earl, 1864–1943, vol. IV
Bathurst, Lt-Col Hon. (Allen) Benjamin, 1872–1947, vol. IV
Bathurst, Lt-Col Hon. Benjamin; *see* Bathurst, Lt-Col Hon. A. B.
Bathurst, Charles, 1836–1907, vol. I
Bathurst, Ven. Frederick, *died* 1910, vol. I
Bathurst, Major Sir Frederick Edward William Hervey-, 5th Bt, 1870–1956, vol. V
Bathurst, Sir Frederick Thomas Arthur Hervey, 4th Bt, 1833–1900, vol. I
Bathurst, Hon. William Ralph Seymour, 1903–1970, vol. VI
Batiffol, Pierre Henry, 1861–1929, vol. III
Batley, Mabel Terry; *see* Lewis, M. T.
Batson, Col Herbert, 1853–1941, vol. IV
Batson, Reginald George, 1885–1974, vol. VII
Batt, Rear-Adm. Charles Ernest, 1874–1958, vol. V
Batt, Francis Raleigh, 1890–1961, vol. VI
Batt, Lt-Col Reginald Cossley, 1872–1952, vol. V
Batt, Lt-Col William Elliott, 1882–1971, vol. VII
Batt, William Loren, 1885–1965, vol. VI
Battcock, Col Grenville Arthur, 1882–1964, vol. VI
Batten, Adm.Alexander William Chisholm, 1851–1925, vol. II
Batten, Edith Mary, 1905–1985, vol. VIII
Batten, Frederick Eustace, 1865–1918, vol. II
Batten, (Harry) Mortimer, 1888–1958, vol. V
Batten, Col Herbert Cary George, 1849–1926, vol. II
Batten, Col Herbert Copeland Cary, 1884–1963, vol. VI
Batten, Herbert Ernest, 1877–1950, vol. IV
Batten, Jean Gardner, 1909–1982, vol. VIII
Batten, Sir John Kaye, 1865–1938, vol. III
Batten, Col John Mount, 1843–1916, vol. II
Batten, John Winterbotham, 1831–1901, vol. I
Batten, Lauriston Leonard, 1863–1934, vol. III
Batten, Mortimer; *see* Batten, H. M.
Batten, Maj.-Gen. Richard Hutchison, 1908–1972, vol. VII
Batterbee, Sir Harry Fagg, 1880–1976, vol. VII
Battersby, Edmund James, 1911–1978, vol. VII
Battersby, Rev. Preb. Gerald William, 1911–1961, vol. VI
Battersby, Henry Francis Prevost, *died* 1949, vol. IV
Battersby, Maj.-Gen. John Prevost, 1826–1917, vol. II
Battersby, Maj.-Gen. Thomas Preston, *died* 1941, vol. IV
Battersby, Thomas Stephenson Francis, 1855–1933, vol. III
Battersea, 1st Baron, 1843–1907, vol. I
Battersea, Lady; (Constance), 1843–1931, vol. III
Battershill, Sir William Denis, 1896–1959, vol. V
Battey, Mrs E. J.; *see* White, E. E. McI.
Batthyany-Strattmann, HSH Edmund, 1826–1914, vol. I
Battine, Lt-Col Reginald St Clair, 1869–1942, vol. IV
Battiscombe, Rear-Adm. Albert Henry William, 1831–1918, vol. II

Battistini, Mattia, 1858–1928, vol. II
Battle, George Frederick Newsum, 1897–1966, vol. VI
Battle, Richard John Vulliamy, 1907–1982, vol. VIII
Battle, William Henry, *died* 1936, vol. III
Battley, John Rose, 1880–1952, vol. V
Batty, Archibald Douglas George Staunton, 1877–1961, vol. VI
Batty, Rt Rev. Basil Staunton, *died* 1952, vol. V
Batty, Rt Rev. Francis de Witt, 1879–1961, vol. VI
Batty, Herbert, 1849–1923, vol. II
Batty, James Henly, 1868–1946, vol. IV
Batty, Tom, 1906–1980, vol. VII
Batty-Smith, Henry, *died* 1927, vol. II
Battye, Maj.-Gen. Arthur, 1839–1909, vol. I
Battye, Aubyn Bernard Rochfort T.; *see* Trevor-Battye.
Battye, Col Basil Condon, 1882–1932, vol. III
Battye, Lt-Col Clinton Wynyard, 1874–1917, vol. II
Battye, Maj.-Gen. Henry Doveton, 1833–1915, vol. I
Battye, Brig. Ivan Urmston, 1875–1953, vol. V
Battye, James Sykes, 1871–1954, vol. V
Battye, Lt-Col Montague M'Pherson, 1836–1929, vol. III
Battye, Major Richmond Keith Molesworth, 1905–1958, vol. V
Battye, Maj.-Gen. Stuart Hedley Molesworth, 1907–1987, vol. VIII
Battye, Lt-Col Walter Rothney, 1874–1943, vol. IV
Baty, Charles Witcomb, 1900–1979, vol. VII
Baty, Thomas, 1869–1954, vol. V
Bauchop, Lt-Col Arthur, 1871–1915, vol. I
Baud, Rt Rev. Joseph A., 1890–1980, vol. VII(AII)
Baudains, Captain George La Croix, 1892–1942, vol. IV
Baudains, Captain Philip, 1836–1909, vol. I
Baudouin, Charles, 1893–1963, vol. VI
Baudoux, Most Rev. Maurice, 1902–1988, vol. VIII
Baudrillart, Cardinal Henri Marie Alfred, 1859–1942, vol. IV
Bauer, Louis Hopewell, 1888–1964, vol. VI(AII)
Baugh, Charles Herbert, 1881–1953, vol. V
Baugh, Captain George Johnstone, 1862–1924, vol. II
Baughan, Edward Algernon, 1865–1938, vol. III
Baughan, William Frederick, 1834–1908, vol. I
Baulkwill, Sir Pridham; *see* Baulkwill, Sir R. P.
Baulkwill, Sir (Reginald) Pridham, 1895–1974, vol. VII
Baulkwill, Rev. William Robert Kellaway, 1860–1915, vol. I
Baum, Vicki, 1896–1960, vol. V
Baumann, Arthur Anthony, 1856–1936, vol. III
Baume, Eric; *see* Baume, F. E.
Baume, Frederick Ehrenfried, (Eric Baume), 1900–1967, vol. VI
Baumer, Lewis C. E., 1870–1963, vol. VI
Baverstock, Rev. Alban Henry, 1871–1950, vol. IV
Bavin, John Thomas, *died* 1937, vol. III
Bavin, Hon. Sir Thomas Rainsford, 1874–1941, vol. IV
Bawden, Edward, 1903–1989, vol. VIII
Bawden, Sir Frederick Charles, 1908–1972, vol. VII
Bax, Sir Arnold Edward Trevor, 1883–1953, vol. V

Bax, Clifford, 1886–1962, vol. VI
Bax, Ernest Belfort, 1854–1926, vol. II
Bax, Adm. Robert Nesham, *died* 1969, vol. VI
Bax, Rodney Ian Shirley, 1920–1983, vol. VIII
Bax-Ironside, Sir Henry George Outram, 1859–1929, vol. III
Baxendale, Col Joseph Francis Noel, 1877–1957, vol. V
Baxendale, Joseph William, 1848–1915, vol. I
Baxter, Alexander Duncan, 1908–1988, vol. VIII
Baxter, Sir (Arthur) Beverley, 1891–1964, vol. VI
Baxter, Cdre Sir Arthur James, 1890–1951, vol. V
Baxter, Sir Beverley; *see* Baxter, Sir A. B.
Baxter, Charles William, 1895–1969, vol. VI
Baxter, Frederick William, 1897–1980, vol. VII
Baxter, George Herbert, 1894–1962, vol. VI
Baxter, Sir George Washington, 1st Bt, 1853–1926, vol. II
Baxter, Herbert James, 1900–1974, vol. VII
Baxter, James, 1886–1964, vol. VI
Baxter, James Houson, 1894–1973, vol. VII
Baxter, James Sinclair, *died* 1933, vol. III
Baxter, James Thomson, 1925–1985, vol. VIII
Baxter, John Babington Macaulay, 1868–1946, vol. IV
Baxter, Sir (John) Philip, 1905–1989, vol. VIII
Baxter, Rev. Michael Paget, 1834–1910, vol. I
Baxter, Sir Philip; *see* Baxter, Sir J. P.
Baxter, Sir Thomas, 1878–1951, vol. V
Baxter, Thomas Tennant, 1894–1947, vol. IV
Baxter, William, 1911–1979, vol. VII
Baxter, Sir William James, 1845–1918, vol. II
Baxter, Wynne Edwin, 1844–1920, vol. II
Bayard, Brig.-Gen. Reginald, 1860–1925, vol. II
Bayer, Sir Horace, 1878–1965, vol. VI
Bayes, Gilbert, 1872–1952, vol. V
Bayes, Walter, 1869–1956, vol. V
Bayfield, Rev. Matthew Albert, 1852–1922, vol. II
Bayford, 1st Baron, 1867–1940, vol. III
Bayford, Major Edmund Heseltine, 1873–1942, vol. IV
Bayford, Robert Augustus, 1838–1922, vol. II
Bayford, Robert Frederic, 1871–1951, vol. V
Baykov, Alexander M., 1899–1963, vol. VI
Baylay, Brig.-Gen. Sir Atwell Charles, 1879–1957, vol. V
Baylay, Brig.-Gen. Frederick, 1865–1956, vol. V
Bayles, Herbert Laurence, 1886–1940, vol. III
Bayley, Col Arthur George, 1878–1949, vol. IV
Bayley, Charles Butterworth, 1876–1926, vol. II
Bayley, Charles Clive, 1864–1923, vol. II
Bayley, Sir Charles Stuart, 1854–1935, vol. III
Bayley, Lt-Col Edward Charles, 1867–1924, vol. II
Bayley, Brig.-Gen. Gerald Edward, 1874–1955, vol. V
Bayley, Sir H. Dennis R.; *see* Readett-Bayley.
Bayley, Lt-Col Hadrian, *died* 1931, vol. III
Bayley, Sir John, 1852–1952, vol. V
Bayley, Maj.-Gen. Kennett, 1903–1967, vol. VI
Bayley, Col Lionel Seton, 1875–1940, vol. III
Bayley, Sir Lyttelton Holyoake, 1827–1910, vol. I
Bayley, Sir Steuart Colvin, 1836–1925, vol. II
Bayley, Lt-Col Steuart Farquharson, 1863–1938, vol. III

Bayley, Thomas, 1846–1906, vol. I
Bayley, Vernon Thomas, 1908–1966, vol. VI
Bayley, Victor, 1880–1972, vol. VII
Bayliffe, Col Alfred Danvers, 1873–1942, vol. IV
Baylis, Rev. Frederick, *died* 1935, vol. III
Baylis, Harry Arnold, 1889–1972, vol. VII
Baylis, Lilian Mary, 1874–1937, vol. III
Baylis, Thomas Henry, 1817–1908, vol. I
Bayliss, Edwin, 1894–1971, vol. VII
Bayliss, Col George Sheldon, 1900–1984, vol. VIII
Bayliss, William, 1886–1963, vol. VI
Bayliss, Sir William Maddock, 1860–1924, vol. II
Bayliss, Sir Wyke, 1835–1906, vol. I
Bayly, Lt-Col Abingdon Robert, 1871–1952, vol. V
Bayly, Ada Ellen, 1857–1903, vol. I
Bayly, Maj.-Gen. Sir Alfred William Lambart, 1856–1928, vol. II
Bayly, Edward, 1865–1934, vol. III
Bayly, Major Edward Archibald Theodore, 1877–1959, vol. V
Bayly, Francis Albert, *died* 1911, vol. I
Bayly, Hugh Wansey, 1873–1946, vol. IV
Bayly, Gen. John, 1821–1905, vol. I
Bayly, Adm. Sir Lewis, 1857–1938, vol. III
Bayly, Col Richard Kerr, 1838–1903, vol. I
Bayly, William Reynolds, 1867–1937, vol. III
Bayne, Charles Gerwien, 1860–1947, vol. IV
Bayne, Charles S., 1876–1952, vol. V
Bayne, Charles Walter, 1872–1937, vol. III
Bayne, Ven. Percy Matheson, 1865–1942, vol. IV
Bayne, Rt Rev. Stephen Fielding, Jr, 1908–1974, vol. VII
Bayne, Thomas Wilson, 1845–1931, vol. III
Bayne, William, *died* 1922, vol. II
Bayne-Jardine, Brig. Christian West, 1888–1959, vol. V
Baynes, Rt Rev. Arthur Hamilton, 1854–1942, vol. IV
Baynes, Sir Christopher William, 4th Bt, 1847–1936, vol. III
Baynes, Dorothy Julia C.; *see* Colston-Baynes.
Baynes, Edward Stuart Augustus, 1889–1972, vol. VII
Baynes, Edward William, 1880–1962, vol. VI
Baynes, Frederic William Wilberforce, 1889–1967, vol. VI
Baynes, Frederick, 1848–1917, vol. II
Baynes, Lt-Gen. George Edward, 1823–1906, vol. I
Baynes, Helton Godwin, 1882–1943, vol. IV
Baynes, Hon. Joseph, 1842–1925, vol. II
Baynes, Keith Stuart, 1887–1977, vol. VII
Baynes, Norman Hepburn, 1877–1961, vol. VI
Baynes, Robert Edward, 1849–1921, vol. II
Baynes, Sir Rory Malcolm Stuart, 6th Bt, 1886–1979, vol. VII
Baynes, Sir William Edward Colston, 5th Bt, 1876–1971, vol. VII
Baynes, Sir William John Walter, 3rd Bt, 1820–1897, vol. I
Baynham, Brig. Cuthbert Theodore, 1889–1966, vol. VI
Baynham, Tom, 1904–1985, vol. VIII
Baynham, Captain Sir Walter de Mouchet, 1876–1936, vol. III

Bazarrabusa, Byabasakuzi Timothy, 1912–1966, vol. VI

Bazeley, Rev. William, 1843–1925, vol. II

Bazell, Charles Ernest, 1909–1984, vol. VIII

Bazett, Henry Cuthbert, 1885–1950, vol. IV

Bazin, Germain René Michel, 1901–1990, vol. VIII

Bazin, René François Nicolas Marie, *died* 1932, vol. III

Bazire, Rev. Canon Reginald Victor, 1900–1990, vol. VIII

Bazley, Sir Thomas Sebastian, 2nd Bt, 1829–1919, vol. II

Bazley-White, John, 1847–1927, vol. II

Bea, HE Cardinal Agostino, 1881–1968, vol. VI

Beach, Charles Fisk, 1854–1934, vol. III

Beach, Col Gerald, 1881–1955, vol. V

Beach, Rex, 1887–1949, vol. IV

Beach, Col Thomas Boswall, 1866–1941, vol. IV

Beach, Lady Victoria Alexandrina H.; *see* Hicks-Beach.

Beach, William Frederick H.; *see* Hicks Beach.

Beach, Maj.-Gen. William Henry, 1871–1952, vol. V

Beach, Major William Whitehead H.; *see* Hicks Beach.

Beach, William Wither Bramston H.; *see* Hicks-Beach.

Beachcomber; *see* Morton, J. C. A. B. M.

Beachcroft, Sir Charles Porten, 1871–1927, vol. II

Beachcroft, Maurice; *see* Beachcroft, P. M.

Beachcroft, Sir Melvill; *see* Beachcroft, Sir R. M.

Beachcroft, (Philip) Maurice, 1879–1969, vol. VI

Beachcroft, Sir (Richard) Melvill, 1846–1926, vol. II

Beachcroft, Thomas Owen, 1902–1988, vol. VIII

Beadle, George Wells, 1903–1989, vol. VIII

Beadle, Sir Gerald Clayton, 1899–1976, vol. VII

Beadle, Rt Hon. Sir Hugh; *see* Beadle, Rt Hon. Sir T. H. W.

Beadle, James Prinsep Barnes, 1863–1947, vol. IV

Beadle, Rt Hon. Sir (Thomas) Hugh (William), 1905–1980, vol. VII

Beadnell, Surg. Rear-Adm. Charles Marsh, 1872–1947, vol. IV

Beadnell, Hugh John Llewellyn, 1874–1944, vol. IV

Beadon, Lt-Col Henry Cecil, 1869–1959, vol. V

Beadon, Bt Col Lancelot Richmond, 1875–1922, vol. II

Beadon, Col Roger Hammet, 1887–1945, vol. IV

Beaglehole, John Cawte, 1901–1971, vol. VII

Beak, Maj.-Gen. Daniel Marcus William, 1891–1967, vol. VI

Beak, George Bailey, 1872–1934, vol. III

Beal, Vice-Adm. Alister Francis, 1875–1962, vol. VI

Beal, Charles, 1841–1921, vol. II

Beal, Col Henry, 1843–1905, vol. I

Beal, Col Robert, *died* 1907, vol. I

Beal, Rev. T. Gilbert, 1865–1948, vol. IV

Beale, Charles Gabriel, *died* 1912, vol. I

Beale, Dame Doris Wilfred, 1889–1971, vol. VII

Beale, Dorothea, 1831–1906, vol. I

Beale, Evelyn Martin Lansdowne, 1928–1985, vol. VIII

Beale, George Galloway, 1868–1936, vol. III

Beale, Lt-Col Henry Yelverton, 1860–1930, vol. III

Beale, Hon. Sir Howard; *see* Beale, Hon. Sir O. H.

Beale, Sir John Field, 1874–1935, vol. III

Beale, Lionel Smith, 1828–1906, vol. I

Beale, Sir Louis Bernhardt George Stephen, 1879–1971, vol. VII

Beale, Hon. Sir (Oliver) Howard, 1898–1983, vol. VIII

Beale, Percival Spencer, 1906–1981, vol. VIII

Beale, Peter; *see* Beale, Percival S.

Beale, Peyton Todd Bowman, 1864–1957, vol. V

Beale, Sir Samuel Richard, 1881–1964, vol. VI

Beale, Sir William Phipson, 1st Bt, 1839–1922, vol. II

Beale-Browne, Brig.-Gen. Desmond John Edward, 1870–1953, vol. V

Beales, Arthur Charles Frederick, 1905–1974, vol. VII

Beales, Hugh Lancelot, 1889–1988, vol. VIII

Beales, Lance; *see* Beales, H. L.

Beales, Reginald Edwin, 1909–1980, vol. VII

Beall, Lt-Col Edward Metcalfe, 1877–1950, vol. IV

Beall, Captain George, 1840–1918, vol. II

Beals, Carlyle Smith, 1899–1979, vol. VII

Beaman, Bt Lt-Col Ardern Arthur Hulme, 1886–1950, vol. IV

Beaman, Ardern George Hulme, 1857–1929, vol. III

Beaman, Sir Frank Clement Offley, 1858–1928, vol. III

Beaman, Lt-Col Winfrid Kelsey, *died* 1929, vol. III

Beament, Brig. Arthur Warwick, 1898–1966, vol. VI

Beamish, Wing-Comdr Francis Victor, 1903–1942, vol. IV

Beamish, Air Marshal Sir George Robert, 1905–1967, vol. VI

Beamish, Rear-Adm. Henry Hamilton, 1829–1901, vol. I

Beamish, Rear-Adm. Tufton Percy Hamilton, 1874–1951, vol. V

Beamish, Tufton Victor Hamilton; *see* Baron Chelwood.

Bean, Rev. Alexander Henry Stillingfleet, 1849–1929, vol. III

Bean, Ven. Arthur Selwyn, 1886–1981, vol. VIII

Bean, Charles Edwin Woodrow, 1879–1968, vol. VI

Bean, Sir Edgar Layton, 1893–1977, vol. VII

Bean, Sir George, 1855–1924, vol. II

Bean, Hon. Sir George Joseph, 1915–1973, vol. VII

Bean, John Harper, 1885–1963, vol. VI

Bean, Robert Ernest, 1935–1987, vol. VIII

Bean, Thomas Ernest, 1900–1983, vol. VIII

Bean, William Jackson, 1863–1947, vol. IV

Beane, Sir Francis Adams, 1872–1959, vol. V

Beaney, Alan, 1905–1985, vol. VIII

Beanland, Maj.-Gen. Douglas, 1893–1963, vol. VI

Beanlands, Rev. Arthur John, 1857–1917, vol. II

Bearblock, Engr Rear-Adm. Charles William John, 1865–1929, vol. III

Bearcroft, Col Edward Hugh, 1852–1932, vol. III

Bearcroft, Adm. John Edward, 1851–1931, vol. III

Beard, Charles A., 1874–1948, vol. IV

Beard, Charles Thomas, 1858–1918, vol. II

Beard, Maj.-Gen. Edmund Charles, 1894–1974, vol. VII

Beard, Lt-Col George John Allen, *died* 1922, vol. II

Beard, James Robert, 1885–1962, vol. VI

Beard, John, 1871–1950, vol. IV

Beard, John Stanley Coombe, 1890–1970, vol. VI

Beard, Sir Lewis, 1858–1933, vol. III
Beard, Paul, 1901–1989, vol. VIII
Beard, Paul Michael, 1930–1989, vol. VIII
Beard, Sidney Hartnoll, 1862–1938, vol. III
Beard, Wilfred Blackwell, 1892–1967, vol. VI
Beardmore, Rt Rev. Harold, 1898–1968, vol. VI
Beards, Samuel Arthur, *died* 1975, vol. VII
Beardsell, Sir William Arthur, 1865–1940, vol. III
Beardsley, Aubrey, 1874–1898, vol. I
Beardsworth, Air Vice-Marshal George Braithwaite, 1904–1959, vol. V
Beare, Daniel Robert O'S.; *see* O'Sullivan-Beare.
Beare, Ernest Edwin, 1877–1956, vol. V
Beare, John Isaac, *died* 1918, vol. II
Beare, Josias Crocker, 1881–1962, vol. VI
Beare, Sir Thomas Hudson, 1859–1940, vol. III
Beare, William, 1900–1963, vol. VI
Bearn, Edward Gordon, 1887–1945, vol. IV
Bearn, Col Frederic Arnot, 1890–1981, vol. VIII
Bearne, Catherine Mary, *died* 1923, vol. II
Bearne, Lt-Col Lewis Collinwood, 1878–1940, vol. III
Bearsted, 1st Viscount, 1853–1927, vol. II
Bearsted, 2nd Viscount, 1882–1948, vol. IV
Bearsted, 3rd Viscount, 1909–1986, vol. VIII
Beasley, Cyril George, 1901–1956, vol. V
Beasley, Sir (Horace) Owen (Compton), 1877–1960, vol. V
Beasley, Rt Hon. John Albert, 1895–1949, vol. IV
Beasley, Sir Owen; *see* Beasley, Sir H. O. C.
Beath, John Henry, 1835–1904, vol. I
Beaton, Lt-Col Angus John, 1858–1945, vol. IV
Beaton, Arthur Charles, 1904–1990, vol. VIII
Beaton, Sir Cecil Walter Hardy, 1904–1980, vol. VII
Beaton, Surg. Rear-Adm. Douglas Murdo, 1901–1990, vol. VIII
Beaton, John Angus, 1909–1987, vol. VIII
Beatson, Col Charles Henry, 1851–1938, vol. III
Beatson, Maj.-Gen. Finlay Cochrane, 1855–1933, vol. III
Beatson, Sir George Thomas, 1848–1933, vol. III
Beatson, Maj.-Gen. Sir Stuart Brownlow, 1854–1914, vol. I
Beatson-Bell, Col John, 1866–1929, vol. III
Beattie, Lt-Col Alexander Elder, 1888–1951, vol. V
Beattie, Rt Hon. Sir Andrew, *died* 1923, vol. II
Beattie, Sir Carruthers; *see* Beattie, Sir J. C.
Beattie, Charles Innes, 1875–1952, vol. V
Beattie, Colin Panton, 1902–1987, vol. VIII
Beattie, Francis, 1885–1945, vol. IV
Beattie, Sir James, 1861–1933, vol. III
Beattie, James Martin, 1868–1955, vol. V
Beattie, John, *died* 1960, vol. V
Beattie, John, 1899–1976, vol. VII
Beattie, Sir (John) Carruthers, 1866–1946, vol. IV
Beattie, Brig. Joseph Hamilton, 1903–1985, vol. VIII
Beattie, Captain Kenneth Adair, 1883–1940, vol. III
Beattie, Rt Rev. Philip Rodger, 1912–1960, vol. V
Beattie, Robert, 1873–1940, vol. III
Beattie, Captain Stephen Halden, 1908–1975, vol. VII
Beattie, William, 1903–1986, vol. VIII
Beattie, Hon. Col Rev. William, 1873–1943, vol. IV
Beattie-Brown, William, 1831–1909, vol. I

Beatty, 1st Earl, 1871–1936, vol. III
Beatty, 2nd Earl, 1905–1972, vol. VII
Beatty, Sir (Alfred) Chester, 1875–1968, vol. VI
Beatty, (Alfred) Chester, 1907–1983, vol. VIII
Beatty, Major Charles Harold Longfield, 1870–1917, vol. II
Beatty, Sir Chester; *see* Beatty, Sir A. C.
Beatty, Chester; *see* Beatty, A. C.
Beatty, Sir Edward Wentworth, 1877–1943, vol. IV
Beatty, Maj.-Gen. Sir Guy Archibald Hastings, 1870–1954, vol. V
Beatty, Haslitt Michael, *died* 1916, vol. II
Beatty, James, 1870–1947, vol. IV
Beatty, Sir Kenneth James, *died* 1966, vol. VI
Beatty, Brig.-Gen. Lionel Nicholson, 1867–1929, vol. III
Beatty, Pakenham Thomas, 1855–1930, vol. III
Beatty, Rose Mabel, 1879–1932, vol. III
Beatty, Wallace, 1853–1923, vol. III
Beatty, Wing-Comdr William Dawson, 1884–1941, vol. IV
Beaty-Pownall, Adm. Charles Pipon, 1872–1938, vol. III
Beaubien, Hon. Charles Philippe, 1870–1949, vol. IV
Beaubien, De Gaspé, 1881–1969, vol. VI(AII)
Beaubien, Justine Lacoste, (Mme L. de G. Beaubien), 1877–1967, vol. VI
Beauchamp, 7th Earl, 1872–1938, vol. III
Beauchamp, 8th Earl, 1903–1979, vol. VII
Beauchamp, Sir Brograve Campbell, 2nd Bt (*cr* 1911), 1897–1976, vol. VII
Beauchamp, Sir Douglas Clifford, (Sir Peter Beauchamp), 2nd Bt, 1903–1983, vol. VIII
Beauchamp, Sir Edward, 1st Bt (*cr* 1911), 1849–1925, vol. II
Beauchamp, Col Sir Frank, 1st Bt (*cr* 1918), 1866–1950, vol. IV
Beauchamp, Guy, 1902–1981, vol. VIII
Beauchamp, Sir Harold, 1858–1938, vol. III
Beauchamp, Rt Rev. Mgr Henry, 1884–1948, vol. IV
Beauchamp, Henry King, 1866–1907, vol. I
Beauchamp, Col Sir Horace George Proctor-, 6th Bt (*cr* 1744), 1856–1915, vol. I
Beauchamp, Rev. Sir Ivor Cuthbert Proctor-, 8th Bt (*cr* 1744), 1900–1971, vol. VII
Beauchamp, Rev. Sir Montagu Harry Proctor-, 7th Bt (*cr* 1744), 1860–1939, vol. III
Beauchamp, Sir Peter; *see* Beauchamp, Sir D. C.
Beauchamp, Sir Reginald William Proctor-, 5th Bt (*cr* 1744), 1853–1912, vol. I
Beauchamp, Sir Sydney, 1861–1921, vol. II
Beauchesne, Arthur, 1876–1959, vol. V
Beauclerk, Lord William de Vere, 1883–1954, vol. V
Beauclerk, William Nelthorpe, 1849–1908, vol. I
Beaufort, 8th Duke of, 1824–1899, vol. I
Beaufort, 9th Duke of, 1847–1924, vol. II
Beaufort, 10th Duke of, 1900–1984, vol. VIII
Beaufort, Sir Leicester Paul, 1853–1926, vol. II
Beaufoy, Henry Mark, 1887–1958, vol. V
Beaufoy, Mark Hanbury, 1854–1922, vol. II
Beaufoy, Samuel Leslie George, 1899–1961, vol. VI
Beauman, Brig.-Gen. Archibald Bentley, 1888–1977, vol. VII

Beauman, Wing Comdr Eric Bentley, 1891–1989, vol. VIII

Beaumarchais, Jacques Delarüe Caron de, 1913–1979, vol. VII

Beaumont, Baroness (11th in line), 1894–1971, vol. VII

Beaumont, Cyril William, 1891–1976, vol. VII

Beaumont, Rev. Francis Morton, 1838–1915, vol. I

Beaumont, Air Cdre Frank, 1896–1968, vol. VI

Beaumont, Sir George Arthur Hamilton, 11th Bt, 1881–1933, vol. III

Beaumont, George Ernest, 1888–1974, vol. VII

Beaumont, Sir George Howland William, 10th Bt, 1851–1914, vol. I

Beaumont, Henry Frederick, 1833–1913, vol. I

Beaumont, Sir Henry Hamond Dawson, 1867–1949, vol. IV

Beaumont, Hon. Hubert, 1864–1922, vol. II

Beaumont, Captain Hubert, *died* 1948, vol. IV

Beaumont, Hugh, 1908–1973, vol. VII

Beaumont, James Buchan, 1925–1973, vol. VII

Beaumont, Rt Hon. Sir John William Fisher, 1877–1974, vol. VII

Beaumont, Kenneth Macdonald, 1884–1965, vol. VI

Beaumont, Adm. Sir Lewis Anthony, 1847–1922, vol. II

Beaumont, Michael Wentworth, 1903–1958, vol. V

Beaumont, Hon. Ralph Edward Blackett, 1901–1977, vol. VII

Beaumont, Roberts, *born* 1862, vol. II

Beaumont, Somerset Archibald, 1836–1921, vol. II

Beaumont, W(illiam) Comyns, 1879–1955, vol. V

Beaumont, Sir William Henry, 1851–1930, vol. III

Beaumont, William Worby, 1848–1929, vol. III

Beaumont-Nesbitt, Maj.-Gen. Frederick George, 1893–1971, vol. VII

Beaumont-Thomas, Col Lionel, 1893–1942, vol. IV

Beaurepaire, Sir Frank, 1891–1956, vol. V

Beauvoir, Simone Lucie Ernestine Marie Bertrand de, 1908–1986, vol. VIII

Beavan, Arthur Henry, 1844–1907, vol. I

Beavan, Margaret, *died* 1931, vol. III

Beavan, Rt Rev. Frederic Hicks, 1855–1941, vol. IV

Beaver, Sir Hugh Eyre Campbell, 1890–1967, vol. VI

Beaver, James Addams, 1837–1914, vol. I

Beaverbrook, 1st Baron, 1879–1964, vol. VI

Beavis, Arthur Beagley, 1867–1934, vol. III

Beavis, David, 1913–1987, vol. VIII

Beavis, Maj.-Gen. Leslie Ellis, 1895–1975, vol. VII

Beazeley, Lt-Col George Adam, 1870–1961, vol. VI

Beazley, Sir (Charles) Raymond, 1868–1955, vol. V

Beazley, Col Sir Geoffrey; *see* Beazley, Col Sir J. G. B.

Beazley, Sir Hugh Loveday, 1880–1964, vol. VI

Beazley, Col Sir (James) Geoffrey (Brydon), 1884–1962, vol. VI

Beazley, Sir John Davidson, 1885–1970, vol. VI

Beazley, John Godfrey, 1885–1948, vol. IV

Beazley, Patrick Langford, 1859–1923, vol. II

Beazley, Sir Raymond; *see* Beazley, Sir C. R.

Beazley, Lt-Col Walter Edwin, 1886–1969, vol. VI

Bebb, Rev. Llewellyn John Montfort, 1862–1915, vol. I

Bebbington, Bernard Nicolas, 1910–1980, vol. VII

Bebbington, Rev. John Henry, died 1936, vol. III

Bebel, Ferdinand August, 1840–1913, vol. I

Beberrua, 3rd Count of, born 1839, vol. III

Bech, Joseph, 1887–1975, vol. VII

Becher, Maj.-Gen. Andrew Cracroft, 1858–1929, vol. III

Becher, Dame Ethel Hope, 1867–1948, vol. IV

Becher, Sir Eustace William Windham Wrixon-, 4th Bt, 1859–1934, vol. III

Becher, Lt-Col Henry Wrixon-, 1866–1951, vol. V

Becher, Sir John Wrixon-, 3rd Bt, 1828–1914, vol. I

Becher, Rear-Adm. Otto Humphrey, 1908–1977, vol. VII

Becher, Gen. Septimus Harding, 1817–1908, vol. I

Béchervaise, Albert Eric, 1884–1969, vol. VI

Beck, Col Hon. Sir Adam, 1857–1925, vol. II

Beck, Sir (Arthur) Cecil (Tyrrell), 1878–1932, vol. III

Beck, Arthur Clement, 1865–1949, vol. IV

Beck, Sir Cecil; *see* Beck, Sir A. C. T.

Beck, Lt-Col Charles Harrop, 1861–1910, vol. I

Beck, Conrad, *died* 1944, vol. IV

Beck, Diana Jean Kinloch, 1902–1956, vol. V

Beck, Edward Anthony, 1848–1916, vol. II

Beck, Maj.-Gen. Edward Archibald, 1880–1974, vol. VI

Beck, Rev. Edward Josselyn, 1832–1924, vol. II

Beck, Egerton, 1858–1941, vol. IV

Beck, Rev. Frederick John, *died* 1922, vol. II

Beck, Most Rev. George Andrew, 1904–1978, vol. VII

Beck, Harvey Mortimer, 1868–1948, vol. IV

Beck, Hon. James Montgomery, 1861–1936, vol. III

Beck, Hon. Sir Johannes Henricus Meiring, 1855–1919, vol. II

Beck, John Melliar A.; *see* Adams-Beck.

Beck, Mrs L. Adams, *died* 1931, vol. III

Beck, Hon. Nicholas Du Bois Dominic, 1857–1928, vol. II

Beck, Captain Oliver Lawrence, *died* 1947, vol. IV

Beck, Sir Raymond, 1861–1953, vol. V

Beck, Very Rev. William Ernest, 1884–1957, vol. V

Beck, William Hopkins, 1892–1957, vol. V

Becke, George Louis, 1848–1913, vol. I

Becke, Major Sir Jack, 1878–1962, vol. VI

Becke, Brig.-Gen. John Harold Whitworth, 1879–1949, vol. IV

Becker, Sir Ellerton; *see* Becker, Sir J. E.

Becker, Sir Frederick Edward Robert, 1871–1936, vol. III

Becker, Harry Thomas Alfred, 1892–1980, vol. VII

Becker, Sir (Jack) Ellerton, 1904–1979, vol. VII

Becker, Neal Dow, 1883–1955, vol. V

Becker, Sir Walter Frederick, 1855–1927, vol. II

Beckett, Angus; *see* Beckett, J. A.

Beckett, Arthur, *died* 1943, vol. IV

Beckett, Brig.-Gen. Charles Edward, 1849–1925, vol. II

Beckett, Maj.-Gen. Clifford Thomason, 1891–1972, vol. VII

Beckett, Sir Eric; *see* Beckett, Sir W. E.

Beckett, Sir Eric Frederick, 1895–1971, vol. VII

Beckett, Geoffrey Bernard, 1903–1965, vol. VI

Beckett, Hon. Sir Gervase; *see* Beckett, Hon. Sir W. G.

Beckett, Harold, 1891–1952, vol. V
Beckett, James, 1891–1970, vol. VI
Beckett, John Angus, 1909–1990, vol. VIII
Beckett, Lt-Col John Douglas Mortimer, 1881–1918, vol. II
Beckett, John Warburton, 1894–1964, vol. VI(AII)
Beckett, Noel George Stanley, 1916–1990, vol. VIII
Beckett, Richard Henry, 1882–1981, vol. VIII
Beckett, Ronald Brymer, 1891–1970, vol. VI
Beckett, Hon. Rupert Evelyn, 1870–1955, vol. V
Beckett, Samuel Barclay, 1906–1989, vol. VIII
Beckett, Col Stephen, 1840–1921, vol. II
Beckett, Captain Walter Napier Thomason, 1893–1941, vol. IV
Beckett, Walter Ralph Durie, 1864–1917, vol. II
Beckett, Sir (William) Eric, 1896–1966, vol. VI
Beckett, Hon. Sir (William) Gervase, 1st Bt, 1866–1937, vol. III
Beckett, Brig.-Gen. William Thomas Clifford, 1862–1956, vol. V
Beckles, Rt Rev. Edward Hyndman, *died* 1902, vol. I
Beckles, Gordon, 1901–1954, vol. V
Beckwith, Brig.-Gen. Arthur Thackeray, 1875–1942, vol. IV
Beckwith, Edward George Ambrose, *died* 1935, vol. III
Beckwith, Air Vice-Marshal William Flint, 1913–1971, vol. VII
Beckwith-Smith, Maj.-Gen. Merton, 1890–1942, vol. IV
Bective, Countess of; (Alice), *died* 1928, vol. II
Bedale, Rev. Frederick, *died* 1924, vol. II
Bedale, Rear-Adm. Sir John Leigh, 1891–1964, vol. VI
Bedale, Rev. Stephen Frederick Burstal, 1888–1961, vol. VI
Beddall, Maj.-Gen. Walter Samuel, 1894–1973, vol. VII
Beddard, Arthur Philip, *died* 1939, vol. III
Beddard, Frank Evers, 1858–1926, vol. II
Beddard, Frederick Denys, 1917–1985, vol. VIII
Beddington, Brig. Sir Edward Henry Lionel, 1884–1966, vol. VI
Beddington, Frances Ethel, (Mrs Claude Beddington), *died* 1963, vol. VI
Beddington, Gerald Ernest, 1867–1958, vol. V
Beddington, Jack, 1893–1959, vol. V
Beddington, Nadine Dagmar, 1915–1990, vol. VIII
Beddington, Reginald, 1877–1962, vol. VI
Beddington, Maj.-Gen. William Richard, 1893–1975, vol. VII
Beddington-Behrens, Sir Edward, 1897–1968, vol. VI
Beddoe, Jack Eglinton, 1914–1990, vol. VIII
Beddoe, John, 1826–1911, vol. I
Beddome, Col Richard Henry, *died* 1910, vol. I
Beddow, Lt-Col Arnold Bellamy, 1883–1965, vol. VI
Beddy, James Patrick, 1900–1976, vol. VII
Beddy, Brig. Percy Langdon, *died* 1945, vol. IV
Bedell, Frederick, 1868–1958, vol. V(A)
Bedells, Charles Herbert, 1862–1943, vol. IV
Bedford, 11th Duke of, 1858–1940, vol. III
Bedford, 12th Duke of, 1888–1953, vol. V
Bedford, Duchess of; (Mary du Caurroy), 1865–1937, vol. III

Bedford, Vice-Adm. Arthur Edward Frederick, 1881–1949, vol. IV
Bedford, Lt-Col Sir Charles Henry, 1866–1931, vol. III
Bedford, Davis Evan, 1898–1978, vol. VII
Bedford, Adm. Sir Frederick George Denham, 1838–1913, vol. I
Bedford, Henry Hall, 1847–1930, vol. III
Bedford, Herbert, 1867–1945, vol. IV
Bedford, Mrs Herbert; *see* Lehmann, Liza.
Bedford, James Douglas Hardy, 1884–1960, vol. V
Bedford, John, 1903–1980, vol. VII
Bedford, Leslie Herbert, 1900–1989, vol. VIII
Bedford, Richard Perry, 1883–1967, vol. VI
Bedford, Maj.-Gen. Sir Walter George Augustus, 1858–1922, vol. II
Bedford, Rev. William Campbell Riland, 1852–1922, vol. II
Bedford, Rev. William Kirkpatrick Riland, 1826–1905, vol. I
Bedi, Raja Sir Baba Gurbukhsh Singh, *died* 1945, vol. IV
Bedier, Joseph, 1864–1938, vol. III
Bedingfeld, Sir Henry Edward P.; *see* Paston-Bedingfeld.
Bedingfeld, Sir Henry George P.; *see* Paston-Bedingfeld.
Bednall, Maj.-Gen. Sir (Cecil Norbury) Peter, 1895–1982, vol. VIII
Bednall, Maj.-Gen. Sir Peter; *see* Bednall, Maj.-Gen. Sir C. N. P.
Bedson, Peter Phillips, 1853–1943, vol. IV
Bedson, Sir Samuel Phillips, 1886–1969, vol. VI
Bedwell, Cyril Edward Alfred, *died* 1950, vol. IV
Bedwell, Rev. Francis, *died* 1925, vol. II
Bedwell, Horace, 1868–1954, vol. V
Beebe, (Charles) William, 1877–1962, vol.VI
Beebe, William; *see* Beebe, C. W.
Beeby, Sir George Stephenson, 1869–1942, vol. IV
Beech, Francis William, 1885–1969, vol. VI
Beech, Lt-Col John Robert, 1860–1915, vol. I
Beecham, Sir Adrian Welles, 3rd Bt, 1904–1982, vol. VIII
Beecham, Sir Joseph, 1st Bt, 1848–1916, vol. II
Beecham, Sir Thomas, 2nd Bt, 1879–1961, vol. VI
Beecher, Most Rev. Leonard James, 1906–1987, vol. VIII
Beecher, Rev. Patrick A., 1870–1940, vol. III
Beecher, Willis Judson, 1838–1912, vol. I
Beechey, Rev. St Vincent, 1841–1905, vol. I
Beeching, Baron (Life Peer); Richard Beeching, 1913–1985, vol. VIII
Beeching, Maj.-Gen. Frank, 1839–1916, vol. II
Beeching, Very Rev. Henry Charles, 1859–1919, vol. II
Beechman, Captain Alec; *see* Beechman, Captain N. A.
Beechman, Captain Nevil Alexander, (Captain Alec Beechman), *died* 1965, vol. VI
Beeding, Francis; *see* Saunders, H. A. St G.
Beeck, Sir Marcus Truby, 1923–1986, vol. VIII
Beeman, Christina May, *died* 1935, vol. III
Beeman, Engr Rear-Adm.Sir Robert, *died* 1963, vol. VI

Beeman, Brig. William Gilbert, 1884–1953, vol. V
Beer, Sir Frederick Tidbury T.; *see* Tidbury-Beer.
Beer, Harry, 1896–1970, vol. VI
Beer, Ven. Henry, 1844–1937, vol. III
Beer, Col James Henry Elias, 1848–1925, vol. II
Beer, Mrs Nellie, 1900–1988, vol. VIII
Beer Bikram Singh, Rajkumar, *died* 1923, vol. II
Beerbohm, Sir Max, 1872–1956, vol. V
Beere, Mrs Bernard, (Fanny Mary), 1856–1915, vol. I
Beernaert, Auguste Marie François, 1829–1912, vol. I
Beery, Wallace, 1885–1949, vol. IV
Beesley, Dodie, (Mrs A. M. Beesley); *see* Smith, D.
Beesly, Edward Spenser, 1831–1915, vol. I
Beesly, Lewis Rowland, 1912–1978, vol. VII
Beeson, Cyril Frederick Cherrington, 1889–1975, vol. VII
Beeston, Col Joseph Livesley, 1859–1921, vol. II
Beet, Rev. Joseph Agar, 1840–1924, vol. II
Beetham, Sir Edward Betham, 1905–1979, vol. VII
Beeton, Alan, 1880–1942, vol. IV
Beeton, Sir Mayson, *died* 1947, vol. IV
Beeton, William Hugh, 1903–1976, vol. VII
Beets, Nicolaas, 1814–1903, vol. I
Beevor, Charles Edward, 1854–1908, vol. I
Beevor, Sir Hugh Reeve, 5th Bt, 1858–1939, vol. III
Beevor, Rt Rev. Humphry, 1903–1965, vol. VI
Beevor, John Grosvenor, 1905–1987, vol. VIII
Beevor, Comdr Sir Thomas Lubbock, 6th Bt, 1897–1943, vol. IV
Beevor, Lt-Col Walter Calverley, 1858–1927, vol. II
Begas, Reinhold, 1831–1911, vol. I
Begbie, Maj.-Gen. Elphinstone Waters, 1842–1915, vol. I
Begbie, Col Francis Warburton, 1864–1922, vol. II
Begbie, Major George Edward, 1868–1907, vol. I
Begbie, Harold, 1871–1929, vol. III
Begbie, Rt Rev. Herbert Gordon Smirnoff, 1905–1973, vol. VII
Begbie, Ven. Herbert Smirnoff, 1871–1951, vol. V
Begbie, Sir James, 1859–1934, vol. III
Begg, Col Charles Mackie, *died* 1919, vol. II
Begg, Ferdinand Faithfull, 1847–1926, vol. II
Begg, Rt Rev. Ian Forbes, 1910–1989, vol. VIII
Begg, Jean, 1887–1971, vol. VII
Begg, John Henderson, 1844–1911, vol. I
Begg, Col Robert B.; *see* Burns-Begg.
Begg, Rev William H.; *see* Henderson-Begg.
Beggs, Engr-Captain James, *died* 1949, vol. IV
Beggs, Hon. Theodore, 1859–1940, vol. III
Begin, His Eminence Cardinal Louis Nazaire, 1840–1925, vol. II
Behan, Brendan, 1923–1964, vol. VI
Behan, Sir Harold Garfield, 1901–1979, vol. VII(AII)
Behan, Sir John Clifford Valentine, 1881–1957, vol. V
Beharrell, Sir Edward; *see* Beharrell, Sir G. E.
Beharrel, Sir George; *see* Beharrell, Sir J. G.
Beharrel, Sir (George) Edward, 1899–1972, vol. VII
Beharrell, Sir (John) George, 1873–1959, vol. V
Behr, Fritz Bernhard, 1842–1927, vol. II
Behram, Sir Jehangir Bomonji B.; *see* Bomon-Behram.
Behrend, George L., 1868–1950, vol. IV
Behrens, Sir Charles, 1848–1925, vol. II
Behrens, Major Clive, 1871–1935, vol. III

Behrens, Edgar Charles, 1885–1975, vol. VII
Behrens, Sir Edward B.; *see* Beddington-Behrens.
Behrens, Gustav, 1846–1936, vol. III
Behrens, Sir Leonard Frederick, 1890–1978, vol. VII
Behrens, Walter, 1856–1922, vol. II
Behrman, Samuel Nathaniel, 1893–1973, vol. VII
Behrman, Simon, 1902–1988, vol. VIII
Beibitz, Rev. Joseph Hugh, 1868–1936, vol. III
Beilby, Sir George Thomas, 1850–1924, vol. II
Beinart, Ben Zion, 1914–1979, vol. VII
Beique, Hon. Frederic Liguori, 1845–1933, vol. III
Beirne, Hon. Thomas Charles, 1860–1949, vol. IV
Beit, Alfred, 1853–1906, vol. I
Beit, Sir Otto John, 1st Bt, 1865–1930, vol. III
Beith, Maj.-Gen. John Hay, 1876–1952, vol. V
Beith, Hon. Robert, 1843–1922, vol. II
Béjot, Eugène, *died* 1931, vol. III
Békésy, Dr Georg von, 1899–1972, vol. VII
Beland, Hon. Henri, 1869–1935, vol. III
Belasco, David, 1859–1931, vol. III
Belch, Alexander, *died* 1967, vol. VI
Belchem, David; *see* Belchem, Maj.-Gen. R. F. K.
Belchem, Maj.-Gen. Ronald Frederick King, (David), 1911–1981, vol. VIII
Belcher, Rev. Arthur Hayes, 1876–1947, vol. IV
Belcher, Sir Charles Frederic, 1876–1970, vol. VI
Belcher, Captain Douglas Walter, 1889–1953, vol. V
Belcher, Major Ernest Albert, 1871–1949, vol. IV
Belcher, George Frederick Arthur, 1875–1947, vol. IV
Belcher, Lt-Col Harold Thomas, 1875–1917, vol. II
Belcher, John, 1841–1913, vol. I
Belcher, John William, 1905–1964, vol. VI
Belcher, Major Robert, 1849–1919, vol. II
Belcher, Rev. Thomas Waugh, 1831–1910, vol. I
Belcher, Rt Rev. Wilfrid Bernard, *died* 1963, vol. VI
Belcourt, Hon Napoleon Antoine, 1860–1932, vol. III
Belden, Rev. Albert David, 1883–1964, vol. VI
Belfield, Sir Henry Conway, 1855–1923, vol. II
Belfield, Lt-Gen. Sir Herbert Eversley, 1857–1934, vol. III
Belfield, Lt-Col Sydney, 1862–1946, vol. IV
Belfield, Major William Seymour, *died* 1924, vol. II(A), vol. III
Belfrage, Leif Axel Lorentz, 1910–1990, vol. VIII
Belfrage, Sydney Henning, 1871–1950, vol. IV
Belgion, (Harold) Montgomery, 1892–1973, vol. VII
Belgion, Montgomery; *see* Belgion, H. M.
Belgrave, Sir Charles Dalrymple, 1894–1969, vol. VI
Belhaven and Stenton, 10th Lord, 1840–1920, vol. II
Belhaven and Stenton, 11th Lord, 1871–1950, vol. IV
Belhaven and Stenton, 12th Lord, 1903–1961, vol. VI
Belhaven, Master of; Hon. Ralph Gerard Alexander Hamilton, 1883–1918, vol. II
Belilios, Emanuel Raphael, 1837–1905, vol. I
Belisario, John Colquhoun, 1900–1976, vol. VII
Béliveau, Most Rev. Arthur, 1870–1955, vol. V
Beljame, Alexandre, *died* 1906, vol. I
Belk, John Thomas, 1837–1901, vol. I
Belk, Lt-Col William, 1869–1952, vol. V
Bell, Adam Carr, 1847–1912, vol. I
Bell, Captain Adolphus Edmund, 1850–1927, vol. II
Bell, Adrian Hanbury, 1901–1980, vol. VII
Bell, Alexander Foulis, 1876–1940, vol. III

Bell, Alexander Graham, 1847–1922, vol. II
Bell, Andrew Beatson, 1831–1913, vol. I
Bell, Andrew James, 1856–1932, vol. III
Bell, Lt-Comdr Archibald Colquhoun, died 1958, vol. V
Bell, Archibald Græme, 1868–1948, vol. IV
Bell, Rev. Archibald William, 1870–1938, vol. III
Bell, Sir Arthur Capel Herbert, 1904–1977, vol. VII
Bell, Arthur Doyne Courtenay, 1900–1970, vol. VI
Bell, Arthur George, died 1916, vol. II
Bell, Maj.-Gen. Arthur Henry, 1871–1956, vol. V
Bell, Col Arthur Hugh, 1878–1968, vol.VI
Bell, Maj.-Gen. Sir Arthur Lynden L.; see Lynden-Bell.
Bell, Arthur William, 1868–1935, vol. III
Bell, Aubrey FitzGerald, 1881–1950, vol. IV
Bell, Rev. Benjamin, 1845–1930, vol. III
Bell, Sir (Bernard) Humphrey, died 1959, vol. V
Bell, Bertram Charles, 1893–1941, vol. IV
Bell, Sir Charles Alfred, 1870–1945, vol. IV
Bell, Rev. Canon Charles Carlyle, 1868–1954, vol. V
Bell, Rev. Charles Dent, 1818–1898, vol. I
Bell, Charles Francis, 1871–1966, vol. VI
Bell, Charles Frederick Moberly, 1847–1911, vol. I
Bell, Captain Charles Leigh de Hauteville, 1903–1972, vol. VII
Bell, Sir Charles William, 1907–1988, vol. VIII
Bell, Sir Charles William M.; see Morrison-Bell.
Bell, Claude Waylen, 1891–1964, vol. VI
Bell, Sir Claude William Hedley M.; see Morrison-Bell.
Bell, Clive, 1881–1964, vol. VI
Bell, Sir Clive M.; see Morrison-Bell.
Bell, Cyril Francis, 1883–1957, vol. V
Bell, Sir Douglas James, 1904–1974, vol. VII
Bell, Sir Eastman, 2nd Bt (cr 1909), 1884–1955, vol. V
Bell, Edward, 1844–1926, vol. II
Bell, Col Edward, 1866–1937, vol. III
Bell, Edward Allen, 1884–1959, vol. V
Bell, Col Edward Horace Lynden L.; see Lynden-Bell.
Bell, (Edward) Percy, 1902–1987, vol. VIII
Bell, Sir (Edward) Peter (Stubbs), 1902–1957, vol. V
Bell, Edward Price, 1869–1943, vol. IV
Bell, Enid Moberly, 1881–1967, vol. VI
Bell, Eric Temple, 1883–1960, vol. V
Bell, Ernest, 1851–1933, vol. III
Bell, Sir Ernest Albert Seymour, died 1955, vol. V
Bell, Lt-Col Ernest FitzRoy M.; see Morrison-Bell.
Bell, Lt-Col Eustace Widdrington M.; see Morrison-Bell.
Bell, Eva Mary, died 1959, vol. V
Bell, Hon. Sir Francis Dillon, died 1898, vol. I
Bell, Sir Francis Gordon, 1887–1970, vol. VI
Bell, Rt Hon. Sir Francis Henry Dillon, 1851–1936, vol. III
Bell, Francis Jeffrey, died 1924, vol. II
Bell, Frank, 1878–1961, vol. VI
Bell, Sir Frederick Archibald, 1891–1972, vol. VII
Bell, Col Frederick Charles, 1883–1971, vol. VII
Bell, Captain Frederick Secker, 1897–1973, vol. VII
Bell, Lt-Col Frederick William, died 1954, vol. V
Bell, Geoffrey Foxall, 1896–1984, vol. VIII
Bell, Hon. George Alexander, 1856–1927, vol. II

Bell, Rev. George Charles, died 1913, vol. I
Bell, Rev. Canon George Fancourt, 1874–1952, vol. V
Bell, George Howard, 1905–1986, vol. VIII
Bell, Col George James Hamilton, 1861–1930, vol. VII
Bell, Col Hon. Sir George John, 1872–1944, vol. IV
Bell, Rt Rev. George Kennedy Allen, 1883–1958, vol. V
Bell, Rev. Preb. George Milner, 1872–1947, vol. IV
Bell, George Trafford, 1913–1984, vol. VIII
Bell, Gertrude Margaret Lowthian, 1868–1926, vol. II
Bell, Grace Effingham Laughton, (Mrs Harry Graham Bell), died 1875, vol. VII
Bell, Major Graham Airdrie, 1874–1929, vol. III
Bell, Harold Arthur, 1918–1978, vol. VII
Bell, Sir (Harold) Idris, 1879–1967, vol. VI
Bell, Lt-Col Sir Harold W.; see Wilberforce-Bell.
Bell, Harry, 1899–1984, vol. VIII
Bell, Harry Charles Purvis, 1851–1937, vol. III
Bell, Mrs Harry Graham; see Bell, G. E. L.
Bell, Rev. Henry, 1838–1919, vol. II
Bell, Sir Henry, 1st Bt (cr 1909), 1848–1931, vol. III
Bell, Henry, died 1935, vol. III
Bell, Henry McGrady, 1880–1958, vol. V
Bell, Lt-Col Henry Stanley, 1874–1949, vol. IV
Bell, (Henry Thomas) Mackenzie, 1856–1930, vol. III
Bell, Henry Thurburn Montague, 1873–1949, vol. IV
Bell, Herbert Clifford Francis, 1881–1966, vol. VI
Bell, Herbert Wright, 1857–1936, vol. III
Bell, Sir Hesketh, 1864–1952, vol. V
Bell, Sir Hugh, 2nd Bt (cr 1885), 1844–1931, vol. III
Bell, Sir Hugh Francis, 4th Bt (cr 1885), 1923–1970, vol. VI
Bell, Sir Humphrey; see Bell, Sir B. H.
Bell, Sir Idris; see Bell, Sir H. I.
Bell, Isaac, 1879–1964, vol. VI
Bell, Sir (Isaac) Lowthian, 1st Bt (cr 1885), 1816–1904, vol. I
Bell, James, 1825–1908, vol. I
Bell, Rev. James, died 1918, vol. II
Bell, Sir James, 1st Bt (cr 1895), 1850–1929, vol. III
Bell, Sir James, 1866–1937, vol. III
Bell, Sir James, 1878–1948, vol. IV
Bell, James, 1872–1955, vol. V
Bell, James Alan, 1894–1968, vol. VI
Bell, Maj.-Gen. Sir James Alexander, 1856-1926, vol. II
Bell, Rev. James Allen, died 1934, vol. III
Bell, James Mackintosh, 1877–1934, vol. III
Bell, James Young, 1877–1966, vol. VI
Bell, Sir John, 2nd Bt (cr 1895), 1876–1943, vol. IV
Bell, John, 1890–1958, vol. V
Bell, Very Rev. John, 1898–1983, vol. VIII
Bell, Col John B.; see Beatson-Bell.
Bell, Sir John Charles, 1st Bt (cr 1908), 1844–1924, vol. II
Bell, John Elliott, 1886–1985, vol. VIII
Bell, Sir John Ferguson, 1856–1937, vol. III
Bell, John Joy, 1871–1934, vol. III
Bell, John Keble, 1875–1928, vol. II
Bell, John Stewart, 1928–1990, vol. VIII
Bell, Ven. John White, died 1928, vol. II(A), vol. III

Bell, Lt-Col John William, 1844–1928, vol. II
Bell, Sir John William Anderson, 1873–1938, vol. III
Bell, Joseph, 1837–1911, vol. I
Bell, Joseph, 1899–1989, vol. VIII
Bell, Hon. Joshua Thomas, 1863–1911, vol. I
Bell, Julia, 1879–1979, vol. VII
Bell, Rev. Kenneth Norman, 1884–1951, vol. V
Bell, Laird, 1883–1965, vol. VI
Bell, Lilian, died 1929, vol. III
Bell, Louis, 1864–1923, vol. II
Bell, Sir Lowthian; see Bell, Sir I. L.
Bell, Mackenzie; see Bell, H. T. M.
Bell, Col Mark Sever, 1843–1906, vol. I
Bell, Mrs Mary Taylor Watson, died 1943, vol. IV
Bell, Lt-Col Matthew Gerald Edward, 1871–1926, vol. II
Bell, Col Sir Maurice Hugh Lowthian, 3rd Bt (cr 1885), 1871–1944, vol. IV
Bell, Nancy R. E., died 1933, vol. III
Bell, Rev. Sir Nicholas Dodd Beatson, 1867–1936, vol. III
Bell, Norris Garrett, 1860–1937, vol. III
Bell, Oliver, 1898–1952, vol. V
Bell, Percy; see Bell, E. P.
Bell, Sir Peter; see Bell, Sir E. P. S.
Bell, Maj.-Gen. Peter Harvey, 1886–1963, vol. VI
Bell, P(hilip) Ingress, 1900–1986, vol. VIII
Bell, Richard, 1859–1930, vol. III
Bell, Robert, 1841–1917, vol. II
Bell, Robert, 1845–1926, vol. II
Bell, Robert, 1863–1937, vol. III
Bell, Robert Anning, 1863–1933, vol. III
Bell, Sir Robert Duncan, 1878–1953, vol. V
Bell, Robert Stanley Warren, 1871–1921, vol. II
Bell, Sir Ronald McMillan, 1914–1982, vol. VIII
Bell, Sir Stanley, 1899–1972, vol. VII
Bell, Very Rev. Thomas, 1820–1917, vol. II
Bell, Sir Thomas, 1865–1952, vol. V
Bell, Sir Thomas Hugh; see Bell, Sir Hugh.
Bell, Thomas Reid Davys, died 1948, vol. IV
Bell, Hon. Valentine Græme, 1839–1908, vol. I
Bell, Rev. Vicars Walker, 1904–1988, vol. VIII
Bell, Walter George, died 1942, vol. IV
Bell, Col William, 1829–1913, vol. I
Bell, Rev. William, died 1918, vol. II
Bell, William, 1860–1946, vol. IV
Bell, William Abraham, 1841–1920, vol. II
Bell, William B.; see Blair-Bell.
Bell, Lt-Col William Cory Heward, 1875–1961, vol. VI
Bell, Rev. Canon William Godfrey, 1880–1953, vol. V
Bell, Sir William James, 1859–1913, vol. I
Bell-Irving, Lt-Col Andrew, 1855–1929, vol. III
Bell-Irving, James Jardine, 1859–1936, vol. III
Bell-Irving, John, 1846–1925, vol. II
Bell-Smith, Frederic Marlett, 1846–1923, vol. II
Bell-Smyth, Brig.-Gen. John Ambard, 1868–1922, vol. II
Bellairs, Angus d'Albini, 1918–1990, vol. VIII
Bellairs, Comdr Carlyon, 1871–1955, vol. V
Bellairs, Hamon D'Albini, died 1932, vol. III
Bellairs, Rear-Adm. Roger Mowbray, 1884–1959, vol. V

Bellairs, Lt-Gen. Sir William, 1828–1913, vol. I
Bellamy, Albert, died 1931, vol. III
Bellamy, Albert Alexander, (Alec), 1914–1981, vol. VIII
Bellamy, Alec; see Bellamy, Albert A.
Bellamy, Basil Edmund, 1914–1989, vol. VIII
Bellamy, Charles Vincent, 1867–1938, vol. III
Bellamy, Dennis, 1894–1964, vol. VI
Bellamy, Edward, 1850–1898, vol. I
Bellamy, Rev. James, 1819–1909, vol. I
Bellamy, Sir Joseph Arthur, 1845–1918, vol. II
Bellamy, Lionel John, 1916–1982, vol. VIII
Bellamy, Lt-Col Robert, 1871–1927, vol. II
Bellamy, Brig. Robert Hugh, 1910–1972, vol. VII
Bellars, Rear-Adm. Edward Gerald Hyslop, 1894–1955, vol. V
Bellasis, Edward, 1852–1922, vol. II
Bellasis, Captain Richard O.; see Oliver-Bellasis.
Bellenger, Captain Rt Hon. Frederick John, 1894–1968, vol. VI
Bellerby, Rev. Alfred Courthope Benson, 1888–1979, vol. VII
Bellerby, Major John Rotherford, 1896–1977, vol. VII
Belleroche, Albert de, 1864–1944, vol. IV
Bellessort, André, 1861–1942, vol. IV
Bellew, 3rd Baron, 1855–1911, vol. I
Bellew, 4th Baron, 1857–1935, vol. III
Bellew, 5th Baron, 1889–1975, vol. VII
Bellew, 6th Baron, 1890–1981, vol. VIII
Bellew, Sir Arthur John G.; see Grattan-Bellew.
Bellew, Lt-Col Sir Charles Christopher G.; see Grattan-Bellew.
Bellew, Captain Edward Donald, 1882–1961, vol. VI
Bellew, Sir Henry Christopher G.; see Grattan-Bellew.
Bellew, Hon. Richard Eustace, 1858–1933, vol. III
Belley, Hon. L. G., 1863–1930, vol. III
Bellhouse, Sir Gerald, 1867–1946, vol. IV
Bellingham, Sir (Alan) Henry, 4th Bt, 1846–1921, vol. II
Bellingham, Brig.-Gen. Sir Edward Henry Charles Patrick, 5th Bt, 1879–1956, vol. V
Bellingham, Sir Henry; see Bellingham, Sir A. H.
Bellingham, Sir Roger Carroll Patrick Stephen, 6th Bt, 1911–1973, vol. VII
Bellman, Sir Harold, 1886–1963, vol. VI
Bello, Alhaji Sir Ahmadu, 1909–1966, vol. VI
Belloc, Hilaire; see Belloc, J. H. P.
Belloc, (Joseph) Hilaire (Pierre), 1870–1953, vol. V
Belloc, Marie Adelaide, (Mrs Belloc Lowndes), 1868–1947, vol. IV
Bellot, Hugh Hale, 1890–1969, vol. VI
Bellot, Hugh Hale Leigh, 1860–1928, vol. II
Bellville, Captain George Ernest, 1879–1967, vol. VI
Belmont, August, 1853–1924, vol. II
Belmont, Perry, 1851–1947, vol. IV
Belmore, 4th Earl of, 1835–1913, vol. I
Belmore, 5th Earl of, 1870–1948, vol. IV
Belmore, 6th Earl of, 1873–1949, vol. IV
Belmore, 7th Earl of, 1913–1960, vol. V
Beloe, Vice-Adm. Sir (Isaac) William (Trant), 1909–1966, vol. VI
Beloe, Robert, 1905–1984, vol. VIII

Beloe, Rev. Robert Douglas, 1868–1931, vol. III
Beloe, Vice-Adm. Sir William; *see* Beloe, Vice-Adm. Sir I. W. T.
Belper, 2nd Baron, 1840–1914, vol. I
Belper, 3rd Baron, 1883–1956, vol. V
Belsey, Sir Francis Flint, 1837–1914, vol. I
Belshaw, Edward, *died* 1916, vol. II
Belstead, 1st Baron, 1882–1958, vol. V
Belt, Comdr Francis Walter, 1862–1938, vol. III
Belton, Rev. Francis George, *died* 1962, vol. VI
Belton, Leslie James, 1897–1949, vol. IV
Bemelmans, Ludwig, 1898–1962, vol. VI
Bemont, Charles, 1848–1939, vol. III(A), vol. IV
Bemrose, Sir Henry Howe, 1827–1911, vol. I
Bemrose, Sir John Maxwell; *see* Bemrose, Sir Max.
Bemrose, Sir Max, (John Maxwell), 1904–1986, vol. VIII
Ben-Gurion, David, 1886–1973, vol. VII
Benares, Maharajah Bahadur of, 1855–1931, vol. III
Benares, Maharaja of, 1874–1939, vol. III
Benas, Bertram Benjamin Baron, *died* 1968, vol. VI
Benavente, Jacinto, 1866–1954, vol. V
Benbow, Sir Henry, 1838–1916, vol. II
Bence-Jones, Col Philip Reginald, 1897–1972, vol. VII
Bence-Lambert, Col Guy Lenox, 1856–1930, vol. III
Benckendorff, Count de, Alexandre, 1849–1917, vol. II
Bencraft, Sir Henry William Russell, 1858–1943, vol. IV
Benda, Wladyslaw Theodor, 1873–1948, vol. IV, vol. V
Bendall, Cecil, 1856–1906, vol. I
Bendall, Ernest Alfred, 1846–1924, vol. II
Bendall, Col Frederic William Duffield, 1882–1953, vol. V
Bender, Rev. A. P., 1863–1937, vol. III
Bender, William Edward Gustave, 1885–1961, vol. VI
Bendern, Count; Arnold Maurice, 1879–1968, vol. VI
Bendit, Gladys; *see* Presland, John.
Benecke, Paul V. M., 1868–1944, vol. IV
Benedict, Ruth Fulton, 1887–1948, vol. IV
Benedite, Leonce, *died* 1925, vol. II
Benes, Dr Eduard, 1884–1948, vol. IV
Benét, Stephen Vincent,. 1898–1943, vol. IV
Benét, William Rose, 1886–1950, vol. IV
Benett, Lt-Col Henry Cleeve, 1877–1941, vol. IV
Beney, Frederick William, 1884–1986, vol. VIII
Benfield, Brig. Karl Vere B.; *see* Barker-Benfield.
Benger, Berenger, 1868–1935, vol. III
Bengough, Guy Dunstan, 1876–1945, vol. IV
Bengough, Maj.-Gen. Sir Harcourt Mortimer, 1837–1922, vol. II
Benham, Frederic Charles Courtenay, *died* 1962, vol. VI
Benham, Sir Gurney; *see* Benham, Sir W. G.
Benham, Rev. William, 1831–1910, vol. I
Benham, Sir William Blaxland, 1860–1950, vol. IV
Benham, Sir (William)Gurney, 1859–1944, vol. IV
Benians, Ernest Alfred, 1880–1952, vol. IV
Benin, Oba of; Akenzua II; Godfrey Okoro, 1899–1978, vol. VII
Benjamin, Arthur, 1893–1960, vol. V
Benjamin, Sir Benjamin, 1834–1905, vol. I

Benjamin, Lewis S., 1874–1932, vol. III
Benjamin, Louis Edmund, 1865–1935, vol. III
Benjamin-Constant, Jean Joseph, 1845–1902, vol. I
Benka-Coker, Sir Salako Ambrosius, 1900–1965, vol. VI
Benn, Alfred William, 1843–1916, vol. II
Benn, Engr Rear-Adm. Edward Piercy St John, 1872–1947, vol. IV
Benn, Sir Ernest John Pickstone, 2nd Bt (*cr* 1914), 1875–1954, vol. V
Benn, Ion Bridges Hamilton, 1887–1956, vol. V
Benn, Captain Sir Ion Hamilton, 1st Bt (*cr* 1920), 1863–1961, vol. VI
Benn, Sir John Andrews, 3rd Bt, 1904–1984, vol. VIII
Benn, Sir John Williams, 1st Bt (*cr* 1914), 1850–1922, vol. II
Benn, Lt-Col Robert Arthur Edward, 1867–1940, vol. III
Bennet, Sir Edward, 1880–1958, vol. V
Bennet, Edward Armstrong, *died* 1977, vol. VII
Bennet, Maj.-Gen. John, 1893–1976, vol. VII
Bennet-Clark, Thomas Archibald, 1903–1975, vol. VII
Bennett, 1st Viscount, 1870–1947, vol. IV
Bennett of Edgbaston, 1st Baron, 1880–1957, vol. V
Bennett, Sir Albert Edward, 1900–1972, vol. VII
Bennett, Sir Albert James, 1st Bt, 1872–1945, vol. IV
Bennett, Alexander John Munro, 1868–1943, vol. IV
Bennett, Lt-Col Alfred Charles, *died* 1915, vol. I
Bennett, Alfred Gordon, 1901–1962, vol. VI
Bennett, Col Alfred Joshua, 1865–1946, vol. IV
Bennett, Alfred Rosling, 1850–1928, vol. II
Bennett, Alfred William, 1833–1902, vol. I
Bennett, Andrew Percy, 1866–1943, vol. IV
Bennett, Arnold; *see* Bennett, E. A.
Bennett, Sir Arnold Lucas, 1908–1983, vol. VIII
Bennett, Arthur, 1862–1931, vol. III
Bennett, Cecil Harry Andrew, 1898–1967, vol. VI
Bennett, Engr-Rear-Adm. Cecil Reginald Percival, 1896–1976, vol. VII
Bennett, Sir Charles Alan, 1877–1943, vol. IV
Bennett, Lt-Col Charles Hugh, 1867–1932, vol. III
Bennett, Lt-Col Sir C(harles) Wilfrid, 2nd Bt, 1898–1952, vol. V
Bennett, Sir Courtenay Walter, 1855–1937, vol. III
Bennett, Cyril, 1928–1976, vol. VII
Bennett, Daniel, 1900–1985, vol. VIII
Bennett, Air Vice-Marshal Donald Clifford Tyndall, 1910–1986, vol. VIII
Bennett, Edward Hallaran, 1837–1907, vol. I
Bennett, (Enoch) Arnold, 1867–1931, vol. III
Bennett, Sir Ernest Nathaniel, *died* 1947, vol. IV
Bennett, Captain (Eugene) Paul, 1892–1970, vol. VI
Bennett, Sir Francis Sowerby, 1863–1950, vol. VI
Bennett, Very Rev. Frank Selwyn Macaulay, 1866–1947, vol. IV
Bennett, Rt Rev. Frederick Augustus, 1872–1950, vol. IV
Bennett, Rev. Frederick George, *died* 1937, vol. III
Bennett, Frederick Henry C.; *see* Curtis-Bennett.
Bennett, Captain Geoffrey Martin, 1909–1983, vol. VIII
Bennett, Geoffrey Thomas, *died* 1943, vol. IV
Bennett, Rev. George, 1855–1930, vol. III

Bennett, Rt Rev. George Henry, 1875–1946, vol. IV
Bennett, George John, 1863–1930, vol. III
Bennett, George Lovett, 1846–1916, vol. II
Bennett, George Macdonald, 1892–1959, vol. V
Bennett, George Wheatley, 1845–1921, vol. II
Bennett, Lt-Gen. Gordon; *see* Bennett, Lt-Gen. H. G.
Bennett, Henry Currie L.; *see* Leigh-Bennett.
Bennett, Sir Henry Curtis, 1846–1913, vol. I
Bennett, Lt-Gen. (Henry) Gordon, 1887–1962, vol. VI
Bennett, Sir Henry Honywood C.; *see* Curtis-Bennett.
Bennett, Rev. Henry Leigh, 1833–1912, vol. I
Bennett, Henry Stanley, 1889–1972, vol. VII
Bennett, Jack Arthur Walter, 1911–1981, vol. VIII
Bennett, James, 1912–1984, vol. VIII
Bennett, James Allan Jamieson, 1903–1973, vol. VII
Bennett, James Gordon, 1841–1918, vol. II
Bennett, Engr Rear-Adm. James Martin Cameron, *died* 1922, vol. II
Bennett, Jill, 1929–1990, vol. VIII
Bennett, Joan, 1896–1986, vol. VIII
Bennett, Joan Geraldine, 1910–1990, vol. VIII
Bennett, Sir John, 1814–1897, vol. I
Bennett, Sir John, 1876–1948, vol. IV
Bennett, John, 1909–1975, vol. VII
Bennett, Sir John (Cecil) Sterndale, 1895–1969, vol. VI
Bennett, John Colburn, 1897–1969, vol. VI
Bennett, Hon. Sir John R., 1866–1941, vol. IV
Bennett, John Reginald William, 1888–1971, vol. VII
Bennett, John Sloman, 1914–1990, vol. VIII
Bennett, John Still, 1911–1970, vol. VI
Bennett, Sir John Thorne Masey, 1894–1949, vol. IV
Bennett, John Wheeler W.; *see* Wheeler-Bennett.
Bennett, Sir John Wheeler W.; *see* Wheeler-Bennett.
Bennett, Kenneth Geoffrey, 1911–1974, vol. VII
Bennett, Sir Noel C.; *see* Curtis-Bennett.
Bennett, Sir Norman Godfrey, 1870–1947, vol. IV
Bennett, Captain Paul; *see* Bennett, Captain E. P.
Bennett, Percy Raymond L.; *see* Leigh-Bennett.
Bennett, Sir Reginald, *died* 1944, vol. IV
Bennett, Reginald Robert, 1879–1966, vol. VI
Bennett, Rex George, 1885–1972, vol. VII
Bennett, Robert Augustus, 1855–1929, vol. III
Bennett, Maj.-Gen. Roland Anthony, 1899–1974, vol. VII
Bennett, Rev. Canon Ronald Du Pré G.; *see* Grange-Bennett.
Bennett, Seymour John 1848–1930, vol. III
Bennett, T. C. S.; *see* Sterndale-Bennett.
Bennett, T. Izod, 1887–1946, vol. IV
Bennett, Thomas Henry, *died* 1900, vol. I
Bennett, Sir Thomas Jewell, 1852–1925, vol. II
Bennett, Sir Thomas Penberthy, 1887–1980, vol. VII
Bennett, Comdr Thomas William, 1872–1939, vol. III
Bennett, Thomas William Westropp, 1867–1962, vol. VI
Bennett, Hon. Walter, 1864–1934, vol. III
Bennett, Lt-Col Sir Wilfrid; *see* Bennett, Lt-Col Sir C. W.
Bennett, Col William, 1835–1912, vol. I
Bennett, William, 1854–1935, vol. III
Bennett, William, 1873–1937, vol. III

Bennett, William Exall Tempest, 1858–1937, vol. III
Bennett, Sir William Gordon, *died* 1982, vol. VIII
Bennett, William H., 1859–1925, vol. II
Bennett, William Hart, 1861–1918, vol. II
Bennett, Sir William Henry, 1852–1931, vol. III
Bennett, Sir William James, 1896–1971, vol. VII
Bennett-Edwards, Mrs; *see* Edwards, Mrs B.
Bennett-Goldney, Francis, 1865–1918, vol. II
Benney, Ernest Alfred Sallis, 1894–1966, vol. VI
Benning, Captain Charles Stuart, 1884–1924, vol. II
Bennion, Claud, 1886–1976, vol. VII
Bennison, John; *see* Bennison, R. J.
Bennison, (Robert) John, 1928–1989, vol. VIII
Benoit, Pierre, 1886–1962, vol. VI
Benoy, Brig. James Francis, 1896–1972, vol. VII
Benoy, Maj.-Gen. John Meredith, 1896–1977, vol. VII
Benskin, Gladys Sheffield, (Mrs Joseph Benskin), 1888–1978, vol. VII
Benskin, Col Joseph, 1883–1953, vol. V
Bensley, Benjamin Arthur, 1875–1934, vol. III
Bensley, Col Clement Henry, 1870–1940, vol. III
Bensley, Edward von Blomberg, 1863–1939, vol. III
Bensly, Rev. William James, 1874–1943, vol. IV
Benson, Arthur Christopher, 1862–1925, vol. II
Benson, Sir Arthur Edward Trevor, 1907–1987, vol. VIII
Benson, Arthur Henry, 1852–1912, vol. I
Benson, Rev. Sir (Clarence) Irving, 1897–1980, vol. VII(AII)
Benson, Air Cdre Constantine Evelyn, *died* 1960, vol. V
Benson, Rear-Adm. Cyril Herbert Gordon, 1884–1974, vol. VII
Benson, Edward Frederic, 1867–1940, vol. III
Benson, Maj.-Gen. Edward Riou, 1903–1985, vol. VIII
Benson, Hon. (Eleanor) Theodora Roby, 1906–1968, vol. VI
Benson, Sir Frank, 1878–1952, vol. V
Benson, Sir Frank Robert, 1858–1939, vol. III
Benson, Frank Weston, 1862–1951, vol. V
Benson, Maj.-Gen. Sir Frederick William, 1849–1916, vol. II
Benson, Sir George, 1889–1973, vol. VII
Benson, Guy Holford, 1888–1975, vol. VII
Benson, Hon. Lt-Col Henry Wightman, 1855–1935, vol. III
Benson, Rev. Sir Irving; *see* Benson, Rev. Sir C. I.
Benson, Sir J. Hawtrey, 1843–1931, vol. III
Benson, James Bourne, 1848–1930, vol. III
Benson, Rev. John Peter, *died* 1944, vol. IV
Benson, Margaret J., *died* 1936, vol. III
Benson, Rev. Niale Shane Trevor, 1911–1980, vol. VII
Benson, Percy George Reginald, 1872–1961, vol. VI
Benson, Surg.-Gen. Percy Hugh, 1852–1933, vol. III
Benson, Philip de Gylpyn, 1883–1931, vol. III
Benson, Preston, 1896–1975, vol. VII
Benson, Col Ralph Hawtrey Rohde, 1880–1943, vol. IV
Benson, Sir Ralph Sillery, 1851–1920, vol. II
Benson, Lt-Col Sir Rex Lindsay, 1889–1968, vol. IV
Benson, Rev. Richard Meux, 1824–1915, vol. I

Benson, Brig.-Gen. Riou Philip, 1863–1939, vol. III
Benson, Brig. Robert, 1881–1952, vol. V
Benson, Vice-Adm. Robert Edmund Ross, *died* 1927, vol. II
Benson, Robert Henry, 1850–1929, vol. III
Benson, Very Rev. Mgr Robert Hugh, 1871–1914, vol. I
Benson, Col Starling Meux, 1846–1933, vol. III
Benson, Stella, 1892–1933, vol. III
Benson, Hon. Theodora; *see* Benson, Hon. E. T. R.
Benson, Ven. Thomas M., *died* 1921, vol. II
Benson, Col Wallace, *died* 1951, vol. V
Benson, William Arthur Smith, 1854–1924, vol. II
Benson, William Denman, 1848–1919, vol. II
Benson, Col William George Sackville, 1861–1954, vol. V
Benson, William John, *died* 1941, vol. IV
Benson, William Noël, 1885–1957, vol. V
Benstead, Sir John, 1897–1979, vol. VII
Bensusan, Samuel Levy, 1872–1958, vol. V
Bent, Col Arthur Milton, 1870–1940, vol. III
Bent, Col Charles Edward, 1880–1955, vol. V
Bent, Rear-Adm. Eric Ritchie, 1888–1949, vol. IV
Bent, James Theodore, 1852–1897, vol. I
Bent, Mabel Virginia Anna, (Mrs Theodore Bent), *died* 1929, vol. III
Bent, Mrs Theodore; *see* Bent, M. V. A.
Bent, Hon. Sir Thomas, 1838–1909, vol. I
Bentall, Gerald Chalmers, 1903–1971, vol. VII
Benthall, Sir Edward Charles, 1893–1961, vol. VI
Benthall, Major John Lawrence, 1868–1947, vol. IV
Benthall, Michael Pickersgill, 1919–1974, vol. VII
Bentham, Ethel, *died* 1931, vol. III
Bentham, George Jackson, 1863–1929, vol. III
Bentham, Percy George, 1883–1936, vol. III
Bentinck, Baron Adolph Willem Carel, 1905–1970, vol. VI
Bentinck, Arthur Harold Walter, *died* 1964, vol. VI
Bentinck, Lt-Col Lord Charles C.; *see* Cavendish-Bentinck.
Bentinck, Rev. Charles D., 1866–1940, vol. III
Bentinck, Rev. Sir Charles Henry, 1879–1955, vol. V
Bentinck, Frederick Cavendish-, 1856–1948, vol. IV
Bentinck, Lord Henry Cavendish, 1863–1931, vol. III
Bentinck, Lady Norah, *died* 1939, vol. III
Bentinck, Adm. Sir Rudolph Walter, 1869–1947, vol. IV
Bentinck, Baron Walter Guy, 1864–1957, vol. V
Bentinck, Lord William Augustus Cavendish-, 1865–1903, vol. I
Bentinck, Count William Charles Philip Otho, 1848–1912, vol. I
Bentley, Alfred, *died* 1923, vol. II
Bentley, Arthur Owen, 1898–1943, vol. IV
Bentley, Bertram Henry, 1873–1946, vol. IV
Bentley, Charles Albert, 1873–1949, vol. IV
Bentley, Rt Rev. David Williams Bentley, *died* 1970, vol. VI
Bentley, Edmund Clerihew, 1875–1956, vol. V
Bentley, Col Francis I., 1868–1938, vol. III
Bentley, Frederic Herbert, 1905–1980, vol. VII
Bentley, Nicolas Clerihew, 1907–1978, vol. VII
Bentley, Phyllis Eleanor, 1894–1977, vol. VII

Bentley, Richard, 1854–1936, vol. III
Bentley, Walter Owen, 1888–1971, vol. III
Bentley-Buckle, Lt-Col Arthur William; *see* Buckle.
Bentliff, Hubert David, 1891–1953, vol. V
Bentliff, Walter David, 1859–1940, vol. III
Benton, Gordon William, 1893–1983, vol. VIII
Benton, Sir John, 1850–1927, vol. II
Benton, William, 1900–1973, vol. VII
Bentwich, Helen Caroline, (Mrs Norman Bentwich), 1892–1972, vol. VII
Bentwich, Herbert, 1856–1932, vol. III
Bentwich, Norman de Mathos, 1883–1971, vol. VII
Benuarrat, 7th Baron of, 1870–1935, vol. III
Benyon, Sir Henry Arthur, 1st Bt, 1884–1959, vol. V
Benyon, James Herbert, 1849–1935, vol. III
Benyon, Vice-Adm. Richard, 1892–1968, vol. VI
Benziger, August, 1867–1955, vol. V
Benzinger, Immanuel G. A., *born* 1865, vol. III
Beoku-Betts, Sir Ernest Samuel, 1895–1957, vol. V
Beovich, Most Rev. Matthew, 1896–1981, vol. VIII
Berar, State of; Gen. HH the Prince of, 1907–1970, vol. VI (AII)
Berard, Victor, 1864–1931, vol. III
Bercovici, Konrad, *died* 1961, vol. VI
Berendsen, Sir Carl August, 1890–1973, vol. VII
Berens, Alexander Augustus, 1842–1926, vol. II
Berens, Herbert Cecil Benyon, 1908–1981, vol. VIII
Berenson, Bernhard, 1865–1959, vol. V
Beresford, 1st Baron, 1846–1919, vol. II
Beresford, Ven. Alfred Richard Angland, *died* 1936, vol. III
Beresford, Cecil Hugh W., *died* 1912, vol. I
Beresford, Col Charles Edward de la Poer, 1850–1921, vol. II
Beresford, Rev. Charles John, 1868–1936, vol. III
Beresford, Denis R. P.; *see* Pack-Beresford.
Beresford, Eric George Harold, 1901–1983, vol. VIII
Beresford, George de la Poer, 1831–1906, vol. I
Beresford, Maj.-Gen. Sir George de la Poer, *died* 1964, vol. VI
Beresford, Jack, 1899–1977, vol. VII
Beresford, Rev. John, 1839–1918, vol. II
Beresford, John Baldwyn, 1888–1940, vol. III
Beresford, Maj.-Gen. John Beresford, *born* 1828, vol. II
Beresford, John Davys, 1873–1947, vol. IV
Beresford, John George M.; *see* Massy-Beresford.
Beresford, John Stuart, 1845–1926, vol. II
Beresford, Lord Marcus de la Poer, 1848–1922, vol. II
Beresford, Marcus Henry de la Poer, 1857–1934, vol. III
Beresford, Lt-Gen. Mostyn de la Poer, 1835–1911, vol. I
Beresford, Hon. Seton Robert de la Poer Horsley, 1868–1928, vol. II
Beresford, Tristram de la Poer, 1887–1962, vol. VI
Beresford, Lady William, *died* 1909, vol. I
Beresford, Lord William Leslie de la Poer, 1847–1900, vol. I
Beresford-Peirse, Major Sir Henry Bernard de la Poer, 4th Bt, 1875–1949, vol. IV
Beresford-Peirse, Sir Henry Campbell de la Poer, 5th Bt, 1905–1972, vol. VII

Beresford-Peirse, Sir Henry Monson de la Poer, 3rd Bt, 1850–1926, vol. II

Beresford-Peirse, Lt-Gen. Sir Noel Monson de la Poer, 1887–1953, vol. V

Beresford-Peirse, Rev. Richard Windham de la Poer, 1876–1952, vol. V

Beresford-Peirse, Rev. Canon Windham de la Poer, 1858–1940, vol. III

Berg, Alban, 1885–1935, vol. III

Bergel, Franz, 1900–1987, vol. VIII

Berger, Francesco, 1834–1933, vol. III

Berget, Baron Alphonse, 1860–1933, vol. III

Bergh, Rt Rev. Frederick Thomas, 1840–1924, vol. II

Bergholt, Ernest George Binckes, 1856–1925, vol. II

Bergin, John Alexander, 1920–1986, vol. VIII

Bergin, Kenneth Glenny, 1911–1981, vol. VIII

Bergin, Osborn Joseph, *died* 1950, vol. IV

Bergin, William, 1864–1942, vol. IV

Bergius, Friedrich Karl Rudolph, 1884–1949, vol. IV

Bergman, Ingrid, 1915–1982, vol. VIII

Bergne, Sir John Henry Gibbs, 1842–1908, vol. I

Bergner, Elisabeth, 1900–1986, vol. VIII

Bergson, Henri Louis, 1859–1941, vol. IV

Beringer, Oscar, 1844–1922, vol. II

Beringer, Mrs Oscar, 1856–1936, vol. III

Berkeley, 8th Earl, 1865–1942, vol. IV

Berkeley, Baroness (15th in line), 1840–1899, vol. I

Berkeley, Baroness (16th in line), 1875–1964, vol. VI

Berkeley, Rt Rev. Alfred Pakenham, 1862–1938, vol. III

Berkeley, Lt-Col Arthur Mowbray, 1870–1937, vol. III

Berkeley, Lt-Col Christopher Robert, 1877–1959, vol. V

Berkeley, Sir Comyns, 1865–1946, vol. IV

Berkeley, Sir Ernest James Lennox, 1857–1932, vol. III

Berkeley, Essex Digby, 1843–1936, vol. III

Berkeley, Maj.-Gen. Frederick George, 1841–1906, vol. I

Berkeley, Sir George, 1819–1905, vol. I

Berkeley, Sir Henry Spencer, 1851–1918, vol. II

Berkeley, Maj.-Gen. James Cavan, 1839–1926, vol. II

Berkeley, Sir Lennox Randal Francis, 1903–1989, vol. VIII

Berkeley, Sir Maurice Julian, *died* 1931, vol. III

Berkeley, Captain Reginald Cheyne, 1890–1935, vol. III

Berkeley, Robert Valentine, 1853–1940, vol. III

Berkeley, Stanley, *died* 1909, vol. I

Berkin, John Phillip, 1905–1979, vol. VII

Berle, Adolf Augustus, 1895–1971, vol. VII

Berlin, Irving, 1888–1989, vol. VIII

Berliner, Emile, 1851–1929, vol. III

Berlyn, Alfred, *died* 1936, vol. III

Berlyn, Mrs Alfred, *died* 1943, vol. IV

Berlyn, Bernard Henry Alfred Forbes, 1886–1936, vol. III

Bermingham, Engr-Rear-Adm. Cecil Henry Alec, 1870–1938, vol. III

Bernacchi, Louis Charles, 1876–1942, vol. IV

Bernacchi, Michael Louis, 1911–1983, vol. VIII

Bernadotte, Count Folke, 1895–1948, vol. IV

Bernal, Frederic, 1828–1924, vol. II

Bernal, Lt-Col Greville Hugh Woodlee, *died* 1922, vol. II

Bernal, John Desmond, 1901–1971, vol. VII

Bernal, Ralph, 1867–1938, vol. III

Bernard, Albert Victor, 1885–1955, vol. V

Bernard, Andrew Milroy F.; *see* Fleming-Bernard.

Bernard, Anthony, 1891–1963, vol. VI

Bernard, Hon. Charles Brodrick Amyas, 1904–1977, vol. VII

Bernard, Sir Charles Edward, 1837–1901, vol. I

Bernard, Sir Dallas Gerald Mercer, 1st Bt, 1888–1975, vol. VII

Bernard, Lt-Gen. Sir Denis Kirwan, 1882–1956, vol. V

Bernard, Col Sir Edgar Edwin, 1866–1931, vol. III

Bernard, Rev. Edward Russell, 1842–1921, vol. II

Bernard, Rt Rev. Eustace Anthony M.; *see* Morrogh Bernard.

Bernard, Francis Georgius, 1908–1978, vol. VII

Bernard, Lt-Col Francis Tyringham H.; *see* Higgins Bernard.

Bernard, Jean-Jacques, 1888–1972, vol. VII

Bernard, Most Rev. and Rt Hon. John Henry, 1860–1927, vol. II

Bernard, Col Joseph Francis, 1871–1953, vol. V

Bernard, Oliver Percy, 1881–1939, vol. III

Bernard, Percy Brodrick, 1844–1912, vol. I

Bernard, Lt-Col Ronald Percy Hamilton, 1875–1921, vol. II

Bernard, Col Ronald Playfair St Vincent, 1888–1943, vol. IV

Bernard, Rev. Thomas Dehany, 1815–1904, vol. I

Bernard, Adm. Vivian Henry Gerald, 1868–1934, vol. III

Bernard, Lt-Col William Kingsmill, 1872–1933, vol. III

Bernays, Charles Arrowsmith, 1862–1940, vol. III

Bernays, Comdr Leopold Arthur, *died* 1917, vol. II

Bernays, Lewis Adolphus, 1831–1908, vol. I

Bernays, Lewis Edward, 1886–1972, vol. VII

Bernays, Robert Hamilton, 1902–1945, vol. IV

Berners, Baroness (7th in line), 1835–1917, vol. II

Berners, 8th Baron, 1855–1918, vol. II

Berners, 14th (*de facto* 9th) Baron, 1883–1950, vol. IV

Berners, John Anstruther, *died* 1934, vol. III

Berners, Brig.-Gen. Ralph Abercrombie, 1871–1949, vol. IV

Berney, Sir Henry, 1862–1953, vol. V

Berney, Sir Henry Hanson, 9th Bt, 1843–1907, vol. I

Berney, Captain Sir Thomas Reedham, 10th Bt, 1893–1975, vol. VII

Berney-Ficklin, Maj.-Gen. Horatio Pettus Mackintosh, 1892–1961, vol. VI

Bernhardt, Sarah, 1845–1923, vol. II

Bernier, Captain Joseph Elzear, 1852–1934, vol. III

Bernier, Hon. Michel Esdras, 1841–1921, vol. II

Bernier, Hon. Thomas Alfred, 1844–1909, vol. I

Bernstein, Cecil George, 1904–1981, vol. VIII

Bernstein, Henri, 1876–1953, vol. V

Bernstein, Leonard, 1918–1990, vol. VIII

Bernstorff, Count John, 1862–1939, vol. III

Berrangé, Major Christian Anthony Lawson, 1864–1922, vol. II

Berridge, Harold, 1872–1949, vol. IV
Berridge, Sir Thomas Henry Devereux, 1857–1924, vol. II
Berrie, John Archibald Alexander, 1887–1962, vol. VI
Berrow, William Lewis, 1862–1928, vol. II
Berry, Alan Percival, 1926–1983, vol. VIII
Berry, Lt-Col Alfred Eugene, 1869–1932, vol. III
Berry, Hon. Sir Anthony George, 1925–1984, vol. VIII
Berry, Arthur, 1862–1929, vol. III
Berry, Rev. Charles Albert, 1852–1899, vol. I
Berry, Rev. Edward Arthur, 1871–1949, vol. IV
Berry, (Frances) May Dickinson, 1857–1934, vol. III
Berry, Sir George Andreas, 1853–1940, vol. III
Berry, Hon. Sir Graham, 1822–1904, vol. I
Berry, Harry, 1890–1982, vol. VIII
Berry, Henry, 1883–1956, vol. V
Berry, Henry Fitz-Patrick, *born* 1847, vol. II
Berry, Sir (Henry) Vaughan, 1891–1979, vol. VII
Berry, Very Rev. Hugh Frederick, *died* 1961, vol. VI (AII)
Berry, Prof. Jack, 1918–1980, vol. VII (AII)
Berry, Sir James, 1860–1946, vol. IV
Berry, John Stanley, 1915–1975, vol. VII
Berry, John William Edward, 1901–1971, vol. VII
Berry, Col Hon. Julian, 1920–1988, vol. VIII
Berry, Martha McChesney, 1866–1942, vol. IV
Berry, May Dickinson; *see* Berry, F. M. D.
Berry, Michael Francis, 1906–1988, vol. VIII
Berry, Lady Pamela Margaret Elizabeth; *see* Hartwell, Lady.
Berry, Richard James Arthur, 1867–1962, vol. VI
Berry, Robert, 1825–1903, vol. I
Berry, Rev. Sidney Malcolm, 1881–1961, vol. VI
Berry, Rt Rev. Thomas Sterling, 1854–1931, vol. III
Berry, Trevor T.; *see* Thornton-Berry.
Berry, Sir Vaughan; *see* Berry, Sir H. V.
Berry, Sir Walter Wheeler, 1857–1933, vol. III
Berry, Sir William John, 1865–1937, vol. III
Berry, Hon. Sir William Bisset-, 1839–1922, vol. II
Berry, William Grinton, 1873–1926, vol. II
Berryman, Lt-Gen. Sir Frank Horton, 1894–1981, vol. VIII
Berryman, Sir Frederick Henry, 1869–1952, vol. V
Berryman, John, 1914–1972, vol. VII
Berryman, Montague Levander, 1899–1974, vol. VII
Berteau, Francis Cyrus, 1856–1945, vol. IV
Berteaux, Henry Maurice, 1852–1911, vol. I
Bertenshaw, Eric Strickland, 1888–1957, vol. V
Berthon, Rear-Adm. Charles Pierre, 1893–1965, vol. VI
Berthon, Rev. Edward Lyon, 1813–1899, vol. I
Berthon, Henry Edward, 1862–1948, vol. IV
Berthoud, Edward Henry, 1876–1955, vol. V
Berthoud, Sir Eric Alfred, 1900–1989, vol. VIII
Berthoulat, Georges, 1859–1930, vol. III
Bertie of Thame, 1st Viscount, 1844–1919, vol. II
Bertie of Thame, 2nd Viscount, 1878–1954, vol. V
Bertie, Rev. Hon. Alberic Edward, 1846–1928, vol. II
Berties, Major Hon. Arthur Michael, 1886–1957, vol. V
Berties, Lt-Col Hon. George Aubrey Vere, 1850–1926, vol. II

Bertie, Col Hon. Reginal Henry, 1856–1950, vol. IV
Bertillon, Alponse, 1853–1914, vol. I
Bertouch, Baroness de, Beatrice, *died* 1931, vol. III
Bertram, Brig.-Gen. Sir Alexander, 1853–1926, vol. II
Bertram, Anthony, 1897–1978, vol. VII
Bertram, Sir Anton, 1869–1937, vol. III
Bertram, Douglas Somerville, 1913–1988, vol. VIII
Bertram, Edith, (Lady Bertram), *died* 1959, vol. V
Bertram, Francis George Lawder, 1875–1938, vol. III
Bertram, Sir George Clement, 1841–1915, vol. I
Bertram, Julius, 1866–1944, vol. IV
Bertram, Louis John, 1859–1940, vol. III
Bertram, Neville Rennie, 1909–1974, vol. VII
Bertram, Lt-Col William Robert, 1888–1970, vol. VI
Bertrand, Cavalier Léon, 1897–1980, vol. VII
Bertrand, Louis Marie Emile, 1866–1941, vol. IV
Beruete y Moret, Aureliano de, 1878–1922, vol. II (A), vol. III
Berwick, 7th Baron, 1847–1897, vol. I
Berwick, 8th Baron, 1877–1947, vol. IV
Berwick, 9th Baron, 1897–1953, vol. V
Berwick, T., 1826–1915, vol. I
Berwick, William Edward Hodgson, 1888–1944, vol. IV
Besant, Annie, 1847–1933, vol. III
Besant, Arthur Digby, 1869–1960, vol. V
Besant, Sir Walter, 1836–1901, vol. I
Besant, William Henry, 1828–1917, vol. II
Besicovitch, Abram Samoilovitch, 1891–1970, vol. VI
Besier, Rudolf, 1878–1942, vol. IV
Besley, Edward Thomas Edmonds, 1826–1901, vol. I
Besley, Rev. Walter Philip, 1870–1934, vol. III
Besly, Ernest Francis Withers, 1891–1965, vol. VI
Besly, Maurice, 1888–1945, vol. IV
Besnard, Paul Albert, 1849–1934, vol. III
Bessborough, 7th Earl of, 1821–1906, vol. I
Bessborough, 8th Earl of, 1851–1920, vol. II
Bessborough, 9th Earl of, 18880–1956, vol. V
Bessell, Peter Joseph, 1921–1985, vol. VIII
Bessell-Browne, Brig.-Gen. Alfred Joseph; *see* Browne.
Bessemer, Sir Henry, 1813–1898, vol. I
Best, Charles Herbert, 1899–1978, vol. VII
Best, Edna, 1900–1974, vol. VII
Best, Elsdon, 1856–1931, vol. III
Best, George Percival, 1872–1953, vol. V
Best, Captain Humphrey Willie, 1884–1959, vol. V
Best, Hon. James William, 1882–1960, vol. V
Best, Rev. John Dugdale, 1856–1933, vol. III
Best, Sir John Victor Hall, 1894–1972, vol. VII
Best, Ven. Joseph, 1880–1965, vol. VI
Best, Hon. Margaret, 1872–1941, vol. IV
Best, Adm. Hon. Sir Matthew Robert, 1878–1940, vol. III
Best, Rt Hon. Richard, *died* 1939, vol. III
Best, Richard Irvine, 1872–1959, vol. V
Best, Hon. Robert Rainy, 1834–1903, vol. I
Best, Hon. Sir Robert Wallace, 1856–1946, vol. IV
Best, Sir Thomas Alexander Vans, 1870–1941, vol. IV
Best, Rear-Adm. Thomas William, 1915–1984, vol. VIII

Best-Shaw, Sir John James Kenward, 9th Bt, 1895–1984, vol. VIII

Beste, Captain Sir Henry Aloysius Bruno D.; *see* Digby-Beste.

Besterman, Theodore Deodatus Nathaniel, 1904–1976, vol. VII

Beswick, Baron (Life Peer); Frank Beswick, 1912–1987, vol. VIII

Betham, Lt-Col Sir Geoffrey Lawrence, 1889–1963, vol. VI

Betham, Brig.-Gen. Robert Mitchell, 1864–1939, vol. III

Betham-Edwards, Matilda; *see* Edwards.

Bethel, Albert, *born* 1874, vol. III

Bethell, 1st Baron, 1861–1945, vol. IV

Bethell, 2nd Baron, 1902–1965, vol. VI

Bethell, 3rd Baron, 1928–1967, vol. VI

Bethell, Captain Adrian, 1890–1941, vol. IV

Bethell, Hon. (Albert) Victor, 1864–1927, vol. II

Bethell, Adm. Hon. Sir Alexander Edward, 1855–1932, vol. III

Bethell, Col Alfred Bryan, 1875–1956, vol. V

Bethell, Maj.-Gen. Donald Andrew Douglas Jardine, (Drew), 1921–1988, vol. VIII

Bethell, Maj.-Gen. Drew; *see* Bethell, Maj.-Gen. Donald A. D. J.

Bethell, Col Edward Hugh, 1854–1940, vol. III

Bethell, George Richard, 1849–1919, vol. II

Bethell, Brig.-Gen. Henry Arthur, 1861–1939, vol. III

Bethell, Maj.-Gen. Sir (Hugh) Keppel, 1882–1947, vol. IV

Bethell, Maj.-Gen. Sir Keppel; *see* Bethell, Maj.-Gen. Sir H. K.

Bethell, Hon. Richard, 1883–1929, vol. III

Bethell, Sir Thomas Robert, *died* 1957, vol. V

Bethell, Hon. Victor; *see* Bethell, Hon. A.V.

Bethell, William, 1847–1926, vol. II

Bethune, Rev. Charles James Stewart, 1838–1932, vol. III

Bethune, Lt.-Gen. Sir Edward Cecil, 1855–1930, vol. III

Bethune, Francis John, 1860–1954, vol. V

Bethune, Lt-Col Henry Alexander, 1866–1946, vol. IV

Bethune, Henry Leonard, 1858–1939, vol. III

Bethune, Rev. John Walter, 1882–1960, vol. V

Bethune, Strachan, 1821–1910, vol. I

Bethune-Baker, Rev. James Franklin, 1861–1951, vol. V

Betjeman, Sir John, 1906–1984, vol. VIII

Betjemann, Gilbert H., 1840–1921, vol. II

Bett, Rev. Henry, 1876–1953, vol. V

Bett, Surg. Rear-Adm. William, 1863–1946, vol. IV

Bettany, Frederick George, 1868–1942, vol. IV

Betteridge, Don; *see* Newman, Bernard.

Bettington, Gp Captain (Arthur) Vere, 1881–1950, vol. IV

Bettington, Cp Captain Vere; *see* Bettington, Gp Captain A. V.

Bettmann, Siegfried, 1863–1951, vol. V

Betts, Mrs E. M.; *see* Hayes, Gertrude.

Betts, Edward William, 1881–1980, vol. VII

Betts, Captain Ernest Edward Alexander, 1877–1951, vol. V

Betts, Sir Ernest Samuel B.; *see* Beoku-Betts.

Betts, Frederick Pimlott, 1853–1930, vol. III

Betts, James Anthony, 1897–1980, vol. VII

Betts, Reginald Robert, 1903–1961, vol. VI

Betts, William Andrew, 1866–1945, vol. IV

Betty, Vice-Adm. Arthur K.; *see* Kemmis Betty.

Betty, Lt-Col Paget K.; *see* Kemmis Betty.

Betuel, Herbert William Norman, 1908–1980, vol. VII

Beuttler, Brig. V. O., 1886–1948, vol. IV

Bevan, Sir Alfred Henry, 1837–1900, vol. I

Bevan, Rt Hon. Aneurin, 1897–1960, vol. V

Bevan, Anthony Ashley, 1859–1933, vol. III

Bevan, Bill; *see* Bevan, C. W. L.

Bevan, Cecil Wilfrid Luscombe, (Bill), 1920–1989, vol. VIII

Bevan, Cosmo, 1863–1935, vol. III

Bevan, Sir David Martyn E.; *see* Evans Bevan.

Bevan, Rt Rev. Edward Latham, 1861–1934, vol. III

Bevan, Edwyn Robert, 1870–1943, vol. IV

Bevan, Francis Augustus, 1840–1919, vol. II

Bevan, Frederick Charles, *born* 1856, vol. III

Bevan, Captain George Parker, 1878–1920, vol. II

Bevan, Ven. Henry Edward James, 1854–1935, vol. III

Bevan, Ven. Hugh Henry Molesworth, 1884–1970, vol. VI

Bevan, Janet; *see* Baroness Lee of Asheridge.

Bevan, John Henry, 1894–1978, vol. VII

Bevan, John Sage, 1900–1978, vol. VII

Bevan, Lawrence Emlyn Douglas, 1903–1972, vol. VII

Bevan, Leonard, 1926–1990, vol. VIII

Bevan, Major Rev. Llewelyn David, 1842–1918, vol. II

Bevan, Hon. Dame Maud Elizabeth, 1856–1944, vol. IV

Bevan, Percy Archibald Thomas, 1909–1981, vol. VIII

Bevan, Rear-Adm. Sir Richard Hugh Loraine, 1885–1976, vol. VII

Bevan, Robert Alexander Polhill, 1901–1974, vol. VII

Bevan, Stuart James, *died* 1935, vol. III

Bevan, Wilfred, 1866–1940, vol. III

Bevan, Ven. William Latham, 1821–1908, vol. I

Bevan-Baker, Bevan Braithwaite, 1890–1963, vol. VI

Bevan-Lewis, William, 1847–1929, vol. III

Bevenot, Clovis, *died* 1925, vol. II

Beveridge, 1st Baron, 1879–1963, vol. VI

Beveridge, Lady; (Janet), 1876–1959, vol. V

Beveridge, Alexander William Morton, *died* 1959, vol. V

Beveridge, Maj.-Gen. Arthur Joseph, 1893–1959, vol. V

Beveridge, Erskine, 1851–1920, vol. II

Beveridge, Rev. John, 1857–1943, vol. IV

Beveridge, Maj.-Gen. Sir Wildred William Ogilvy, 1864–1962, vol. VI

Beverley, Rt Rev. Alton Ray, 1884–1956, vol. V

Beverley, Frank, 1880–1972, vol. VII

Beverley, Vice-Adm. Sir (William) York (La Roche), 1895–1982, vol. VIII

Beverley, Vice-Adm. Sir York; *see* Beverley, Vice-Adm. Sir W. Y. La R.

Bevers, Edmund Cecil, 1876–1961, vol. VI
Beves, Donald Howard, 1896–1961, vol. VI
Beves, Brig.-Gen. Percival Scott, 1868–1924, vol. II
Beville, Lt-Col Charles Hamilton, 1865–1934, vol. III
Beville, Lt-Col Francis Granville, 1867–1923, vol. II
Beville, Gen. Sir Goerge Francis, 1837–1913, vol. I
Bevin, Rt Hon. Ernest, 1881–1951, vol. V
Bevin, Dame Florence Anne, 1882–1968, vol. VI
Bevir, Sir Anthony, 1895–1977, vol. VII
Bevir, Vice-Adm. Oliver, 1891–1967, vol. VI
Bewerunge, Rev. Henry, *born* 1862, vol. II
Bewes, Lt-Col Arthur Edward, 1871–1922, vol. II
Bewes, Wyndham Austis, 1857–1942, vol. IV
Bewick, Ralph Martin, 1861–1934, vol. III
Bewick-Copley, Brig.-Gen. Sir Robert Calverley Alington Bewicke, 1855–1923, vol. II
Bewley, Col Alfred William, 1866–1939, vol. III
Bewley, Sir Edmund Thomas, 1837–1908, vol. I
Bewley, Henry, 1860–1945, vol. IV
Bewley, Thomas Kenneth, 1890–1943, vol. IV
Bewley, William Fleming, 1891–1976, vol. VII
Bewoor, Sir Gurunath Venkatesh, *died* 1950, vol. IV
Bews, John William, 1884–1938, vol. III
Bewsher, Brig. Frederick William, 1886–1950, vol. IV
Bewsher, Paul, 1894–1966, vol. VI
Bewsher, Lt-Col William Dent, 1868–1942, vol. IV
Bex, Charles James, *died* 1940, vol. III
Beyen, Johan Willem, 1897–1976, vol. VII
Beyers, Brig.-Gen. Hon. Christian Frederick, 1869–1914, vol. I
Beyers, Hon. Fredrik William, 1867–1938, vol. III
Beyfus, Gilbert Hugh, 1885–1960, vol. V
Beynon, Albert Gwyn, 1908–1978, vol. VII
Beynon, Major Godfrey Evan Schaw P.; *see* Protheroe-Beynon.
Beynon, Brig.-Gen. Henry Lawrence Norman, 1868–1950, vol. IV
Beynon, Sir John Wyndham, 1st Bt, 1864–1944, vol. IV
Beynon, Maj.-Gen. Sir William George Lawrence, 1866–1955, vol. V
Bezzant, Rev. Canon James Stanley, 1897–1967, vol. VI
Bhabha, H. J., 1852–1941, vol. IV
Bhabha, Homi Jehangir, 1909–1966, vol. VI
Bhagat, Lt-Gen. Premindra Singh, 1918–1975, vol. VII
Bhalja, Govardhan Shankerlal, 1895–1948, vol. IV (A), vol. V
Bhan, Suraj, 1904–1980, vol. VII (AII)
Bhandari, Rai Bahadur Sir Gopal Das, 1860–1927, vol. II
Bhandarkar, Devadatta Ramkrishna, 1875–1950, vol. IV (A), vol. V
Bhandarkar, Sir Ramkrishna Gopal, 1837–1925, vol. II
Bhanot, Harnam Dass, 1897–1948, vol. IV
Bharatpur, Maharaja of, 1899–1929, vol. III
Bhatawadekar, Sir Bhalchandra Krishna, *born* 1852, vol. III
Bhatnagar, Sir Shanti Swarupa, 1895–1955, vol. V
Bhatt, Ramchandra Madhavram, 1874–1936, vol. III
Bhavnagar, HH Maharaja of, 1875–1919, vol. II

Bhopal, HH Nawab Shah Jahan Begum, 1838–1901, vol. I
Bhopal, HH Nawab Sultan Jehan Begum, 1858–1930, vol. III
Bhopal, Ruler of, 1894–1960, vol. V
Bhore, Sir Joseph William, 1878–1960, vol. V
Bhownagree, Sir Mancherjee Merwanjee, 1851–1933, vol. III
Bhutan, Maharajah of, 1861–1926, vol. II
Bhutto, Zulfikar Ali, 1928–1979, vol. VII
Biagi, Guido, 1855–1925, vol. II
Biancardi, Lt Col Nicola G.; *see* Grech-Biancardi.
Bibby, Major Sir (Arthur) Harold, 1st Bt, 1889–1986, vol. VIII
Bibby, Arthur Wilson, 1846–1935, vol. III
Bibby, Major Brian; *see* Bibby, Major F. B. F.
Bibby, Cyril, 1914–1987, vol. VIII
Bibby, Frank, 1857–1923, vol. II
Bibby, Major (Frank) Brian (Frederic), 1893–1929, vol. III
Bibby, Major Sir Harold; *see* Bibby, Major Sir A. H.
Bibby, John Hartley, 1864–1938, vol. III
Bibby, Joseph, 1851–1940, vol. III
Bibby, Samuel Leslie, 1897–1985, vol. VIII
Bibesco, Prince Antoine, 1878–1951, vol. V
Bice, Hon. Sir John George, 1853–1923, vol. II
Bicester, 1st Baron, 1867–1956, vol. V
Bicester, 2nd Baron, 1898–1968, vol. VI
Bickerdyke, John, (Charles Henry Cook), 1858–1933, vol. III
Bickerstaffe, Sir John, 1848–1930, vol. III
Bickerstaffe-Drew, Rt Rev. Mgr Count Francis Browning Drew, 1858–1928, vol. II
Bickersteth, Rt Rev. Edward, 1850–1897, vol. I
Bickersteth, Rt Rev. Edward Henry, 1825–1906, vol. I
Bickersteth, Rev. Canon Edward Monier, 1882–1976, vol. VII
Bickersteth, Geoffrey Langdale, 1884–1974, vol. VII
Bickersteth, John Burgon, 1888–1979, vol. VII
Bickersteth, John Joseph, 1850–1932, vol. III
Bickersteth, John Richard, 1897–1967, vol. VI
Bickersteth, Rev. Kenneth Julian Faithfull, 1885–1962, vol. VI
Bickersteth, Rev. Montagu Cyril, 1858–1936, vol. III
Bickersteth, Robert Alexander, 1862–1924, vol. II
Bickersteth, Rev. Samuel, 1857–1937, vol. III
Bickerton, Alexander William, 1842–1929, vol. III
Bickerton, John Myles, 1894–1977, vol. VII
Bickerton, Reginald Ernest, 1870–1949, vol. IV
Bicket, Sir Alexander, 1853–1931, vol. III
Bicket, Brig.-Gen. William Neilson, 1883–1978, vol. VII
Bickford, Adm. Andrew Kennedy, 1844–1927, vol. II
Bickford, Major Arthur Louis, 1870–1916, vol. II
Bickford, Brig.-Gen. Edward, 1861–1949, vol. IV
Bickford, Rt Rev. Mgr Francis P., 1889–1968, vol. VI
Bickford, Captain William George Hastings, *died* 1932, vol. III
Bickford, Rev. William Pennington, 1874–1941, vol. IV
Bickford, Col William Wilfrid, 1871–1951, vol. V
Bickley, Francis Lawrance, 1885–1976, vol. VII
Bickley, William Gee, 1893–1969, vol. VI

Bicknell, Rev. Edward John, *died* 1934, vol. III
Bicknell, Lt-Col Henry Percy Frank, 1879–1940, vol. III
Bidault, Georges, 1899–1983, vol. VIII
Bidder, George Parker, 1863–1953, vol. V
Bidder, Maurice McClean, 1879–1934, vol. III
Biddle, A. J. Drexel, 1874–1948, vol. IV
Biddle, Maj.-Gen. Anthony J. Drexel, 1896–1961, vol. VI
Biddle, Francis, 1886–1968, vol. VI
Biddle, Major Fred Leslie, 1885–1917, vol. II
Biddle, Maj.-Gen. John, 1859–1936, vol. III
Biddle, Sir Reginald Poulton, 1888–1970, vol. VI
Biddlecombe, Rev. Stuart Holman, 1879–1944, vol. IV
Biddulph, 1st Baron, 1834–1923, vol. II
Biddulph, 2nd Baron, 1869–1949, vol. IV
Biddulph, 3rd Baron, 1898–1972, vol. VII
Biddulph, 4th Baron, 1931–1988, vol. VIII
Biddulph, Assheton, 1850–1916, vol. II
Biddulph, Sir Francis Henry, 9th Bt, 1882–1980, vol. VII
Biddulph, Brig.-Gen. Harry, 1872–1952, vol. V
Biddulph, Lt-Col Hope, 1866–1940, vol. III
Biddulph, Gen. Sir Michael Anthony Shrapnel, 1823–1904, vol. I
Biddulph, Gen. Sir Robert, 1835–1918, vol. II
Biddulph, Sir Stuart Royden, 10th Bt, 1908–1986, vol. VIII
Biddulph, Sir Theophilus George, 8th Bt, 1874–1948, vol. IV
Biddulph, Thomas Henry Stillingfleet, 1846–1919, vol. II
Bidie, Surg.-Gen. George, 1830–1913, vol. I
Bidlake, Rev. Walter, 1865–1938, vol. III
Bidwell, Rt Rev. Edward John, 1866–1941, vol. IV
Bidwell, Hayward John, 1849–1931, vol. III
Bidwell, Leonard Arthur, 1865–1912, vol. I
Bidwell, Rt Rev. Mgr Manuel John, *died* 1930, vol. III
Bidwell, Rear-Adm. Roger Edward Shelford, 1899–1968, vol. VI
Bidwell, Shelford, 1848–1909, vol. I
Bierbach, Martin, 1926–1984, vol. VIII
Bierer, Joshua, 1901–1984, vol. VIII
Biermans, Rt Rev. John Henry Mary, 1871–1941, vol. IV
Biernacki, Roderick Korneli, *died* 1943, vol. IV
Biffen, Sir Rowland, 1874–1949, vol. IV
Bigelow, John, 1817–1911, vol. I
Bigelow, Melville Madison, 1846–1921, vol. II
Bigelow, Poultney, 1855–1954, vol. V
Bigg, Rev. Charles, 1840–1908, vol. I
Bigg, Henry Robert Heather, 1853–1911, vol. I
Bigg, Wilfred Joseph, 1897–1983, vol. VIII
Biggam, Maj.-Gen. Sir Alexander Gordon, 1888–1963, vol. VI
Biggar, Maj.-Gen. James Lyons, 1856–1922, vol. II
Biggar, Oliver Mowat, 1876–1948, vol. IV
Biggart, Sir John Henry, 1905–1979, vol. VII
Biggart, Sir Thomas, *died* 1949, vol. IV
Bigge, Sir Amherst S.; *see* Selby-Bigge, Sir L. A.
Bigge, Sir John Amherst S.; *see* Selby-Bigge.

Bigge, Col Thomas Arthur Hastings, 1866–1955, vol. V
Bigge, Maj.-Gen. Thomas Scovell, 1837–1914, vol. I
Bigge, Sir William Egelric, *died* 1916, vol. II
Bigger, Sir Edward Coey, 1861–1942, vol. IV
Bigger, Joseph Warwick, 1891–1951, vol. V
Biggs, Sir (Albert) Ashley, *died* 1938, vol. III
Biggs, Sir Arthur Worthington, 1846–1928, vol. II
Biggs, Sir Ashley; *see* Biggs, Sir A. A.
Biggs, Christopher Thomas Ewart E.; *see* Ewart-Biggs.
Biggs, George Nixon, 1881–1922, vol. II
Biggs, Col Henry Vero, 1860–1925, vol. II
Biggs, Hermann M., 1859–1923, vol. II
Biggs, Vice-Adm. Sir Hilary Worthington, 1905–1976, vol. VII
Biggs, Rt Rev. Huyshe Wolcott Y.; *see* Yeatman-Biggs.
Biggs, Leonard Vivian, 1873–1944, vol. IV
Biggs, Sir Lionel William, 1906–1985, vol. VIII
Biggs-Davison, Sir John Alec, 1918–1988, vol. VIII
Bigham, Hon. Sir (Frank) Trevor R., 1876–1954, vol. V
Bigham, Hon. Sir Trevor; *see* Bigham, Hon. Sir F. T. R.
Bigland, Alfred, 1855–1936, vol. III
Bigland, Eileen Anne Carstairs, (Mrs E. W. Bigland), 1898–1970, vol. VI
Bigland, Ernest Frank, 1913–1985, vol. VIII
Bigland, Rt Rev. Mgr John, 1871–1945, vol. IV
Bigland, Percy, *died* 1926, vol. II
Bignold, Sir Arthur, 1839–1915, vol. I
Bignold, Sir (Charles) Robert, 1892–1970, vol. VI
Bignold, Sir Robert; *see* Bignold, Sir C. R.
Bigsby, Sydney Herbert, 1885–1946, vol. IV
Bigsworth, Air Cdre Arthur Wellesley, 1885–1961, vol. VI
Bigwood, Sir Cecil, 1863–1947, vol. IV
Bigwood, James, 1839–1919, vol. II
Bijawar State, HH Bharat Dharm-indu Maharajah Sawai Sir Sawant Singh Bahadur, 1877–1940, vol. III (A), vol. IV
Bikaner, Maharajah of; General HH Maharajadhiraj Sri Ganga Singbji Bahadur, 1880–1943, vol. IV
Bikaner, Maharajah of; Lt-Gen. HH Maharajadhiraj Raj Rajeshwar Narendra Shiromani (Sri Sadul Singhji Bahadur), 1902–1950, vol. IV
Bikaner, Maharaja of; Karni Singhji Bahadur, 1924–1988, vol. VIII
Bilainkin, George, 1903–1981, vol. VIII
Bilaspur (Kehlur) State, Chief HH Raja Bije Chand, 1873–1931, vol. III
Bilbrough, Rt Rev. Harold Ernest, 1867–1950, vol. IV
Biles, Sir John Harvard, 1854–1933, vol. III
Bilgrami, Syed Akeel, Nawab Sir Akeel Jung Bahadur, 1874–1945, vol. IV
Bilgrami, Sayyid Ali, Shamsul Ulama, 1853–1911, vol. I
Bilgrami, Syed Hossain, 1842–1926, vol. II
Bilgrami, Sayyid Sir Mehdi Husain, Nawab Mahdi Yar Jang Bahadur, *died* 1948, vol. IV
Biliotti, Sir Alfred, 1833–1915, vol. II
Bilkey, Paul Ernest, 1878–1962, vol. VI
Bill, Charles, 1843–1915, vol. I

Bill, Comdr Robert, 1910–1987, vol. VIII
Bill, Rt Rev. Sydney Alfred, 1884–1964, vol. VI
Billam, John Bertram Hardy, 1920–1986, vol. VIII
Bille, Frank Ernest, 1832–1918, vol. II
Billen, Rev. Albert Victor, *died* 1961, vol. VI
Billett, Rev. Canon Frederick, *died* 1941, vol. IV
Billimoria, Sir Shapoorjee, 1877–1958, vol. V
Billing, Rt Rev. Claudius, *died* 1898, vol. I
Billing, N. Pemberton, 1880–1948, vol. IV
Billingham, Col John Alfred Lawrence, 1868–1955, vol. V
Billinghurst, Alfred John, 1880–1963, vol. VI
Billings, Rear-Adm. Frederick Stewart, 1900–1980, vol. VII
Billington, Mary Frances, *died* 1925, vol. II
Billington, Ray Allen, 1903–1981, vol. VIII
Billington, William, *died* 1932, vol. III
Billington, Lt-Col Lawson, 1882–1954, vol. V
Billmeir, Jack Albert, 1900–1963, vol. VI
Billson, Alfred, 1839–1907, vol. I
Billson, Hon. Alfred Arthur, 1858–1930, vol. III
Billson, Herbert George, 1871–1938, vol. III
Bilney, Air Vice-Marshal Christopher Neil Hope, 1898–1988, vol. VIII
Bilsborrow, Most Rev. James Romanus, 1862–1931, vol. III
Bilsborrow, Rt Rev. John, 1837–1903, vol. I
Bilsland, 1st Baron, 1892–1970, vol. VI
Bilsland, Sir William, 1st Bt, 1847–1921, vol. II
Bilton, Lt-Col Lewis Leonard, *died* 1954, vol. V
Bilton, Percy, 1896–1983, vol. VIII
Binchy, Daniel A., 1900–1989, vol. VIII
Binder, Sir Bernhard Heymann, 1876–1966, vol. VI
Bindley, Rev. Thomas Herbert, 1861–1931, vol. III
Bindloss, Harold, 1866–1945, vol. IV
Bindoff, Stanley Thomas, 1908–1980, vol. VII
Bing, Geoffrey Henry Cecil, 1909–1977, vol. VII
Bing, Gertrud, 1892–1964, vol. VI
Bingen, Sir Eric Albert, 1898–1972, vol. VII
Bingham, Col Sir Albert Edward, 2nd Bt, 1868–1945, vol. IV
Bingham, Hon. Albert Yelverton, 1840–1907, vol. I
Bingham, Captain Alexander Gordon, 1873–1933, vol. III
Bingham, Rear-Adm. Hon. Barry; *see* Bingham, Rear-Adm. Hon. E. B. S.
Bingham, Maj.-Gen. Hon. Sir Cecil Edward, 1861–1934, vol. III
Bingham, Col Charles Henry Marion, 1873–1957, vol. V
Bingham, Lt-Col Hon. Denis; *see* Bingham, Lt-Col Hon. J. D. Y.
Bingham, Rear-Adm. Hon. (Edward) Barry (Stewart), 1881–1939, vol. III
Bingham, Maj.-Gen. Hon. Sir Francis Richard, 1863–1935, vol. III
Bingham, James, 1916–1990, vol. VIII
Bingham, Lt-Col Hon. (John) Denis (Yelverton), *died* 1940, vol. III
Bingham, Sir John Edward, 1st Bt, 1839–1915, vol. I
Bingham, Lionel John, 1878–1919, vol. II
Bingham, Brig.-Gen. Oswald Buckley Bingham Smith-, 1868–1949, vol. IV
Bingham, Lt-Col Ralph Charles, 1885–1977, vol. VII

Bingham, Rear-Adm. Hon. Richard, 1847–1924, vol. II
Bingham, Robert Porter, 1903–1982, vol. VIII
Bingham, Robert Worth, 1871–1937, vol. III
Bingham, Lt-Col Samuel, *died* 1941, vol. IV
Bingley, 1st Baron, 1870–1947, vol. IV
Bingley, Adm. Sir Alexander Noel Campbell, 1905–1972, vol. VII
Bingley, Lt-Gen. Sir Alfred Horsford, 1865–1944, vol. IV
Bingley, Henry Campbell Alchorne, *died* 1939, vol. III
Bingley, Col Robert Albert Glanville, 1902–1976, vol. VII
Binnall, Rev. Canon Peter Blannin Gibbons, 1907–1980, vol. VII
Binney, Anthony Lockhart, 1890–1973, vol. VII
Binney, Lt-Col Edward Victor, 1885–1942, vol. IV
Binney, Sir Frederick George; *see* Binney, Sir G.
Binney, Sir George, 1900–1972, vol. VII
Binney, Adm. Sir Hugh; *see* Binney, Adm. Sir T. H.
Binney, James, 1868–1935, vol. III
Binney, Captain Ralph Douglas, 1888–1944, vol. IV
Binney, Adm. Sir (Thomas) Hugh, 1883–1953, vol. V
Binney, Rev. William Hibbert, 1857–1916, vol. II
Binnie, Sir Alexander Richardson, 1839–1917, vol. II
Binnie, Rev. Alfred Jonathan, *died* 1926, vol. II
Binnie, Alfred Maurice, 1901–1986, vol. VIII
Binnie, Geoffrey Morse, 1908–1989, vol. VIII
Binnie, James, 1842–1930, vol. III
Binnie, Thomas Inglis, 1874–1954, vol. V
Binnie, William James Eames, 1867–1949, vol. IV
Binning, Col Lord; George Baillie-Hamilton, 1856–1917, vol. II
Binning, Sir Arthur William, 1861–1931, vol. III
Binning, Lt-Col Joseph, 1845–1913, vol. I
Binns, Arthur, 1861–1952, vol. V
Binns, Sir Arthur Lennon, 1891–1971, vol. VII
Binns, Asa, 1873–1946, vol. IV
Binns, Sir Bernard Ottwell, 1898–1953, vol. V
Binns, Edward Ussher Elliott E.; *see* Elliott-Binns.
Binns, Sir Frank, 1898–1954, vol. V
Binns, Surg. Rear-Adm. George Augustus, 1918–1990, vol. VIII
Binns, Howard Reed, 1909–1987, vol. VIII
Binns, John, 1914–1986, vol. VIII
Binns, Joseph, 1900–1975, vol. VII
Binns, Kenneth, 1882–1969, vol. VI
Binns, Kenneth Johnstone, 1912–1987, vol. VIII
Binns, Rev. Leonard Elliott Elliott-, 1885–1963, vol. VI
Binns, Percy, *died* 1920, vol. II
Binny, Graham, *died* 1929, vol. III
Binny, Major Steuart Scott, 1871–1916, vol. II
Binstead, Arthur Morris, 1861–1914, vol. I
Binstead, Herbert Ernest, 1869–1937, vol. III
Binstead, Mary, *died* 1928, vol. II
Binyon, Basil, 1885–1977, vol. VII
Binyon, Laurence; *see* Binyon, R. L.
Binyon, (Robert) Laurence, 1869–1943, vol. IV
Bion, Frederick Fleetwood, 1870–1949, vol. IV
Birch, Sir Alan; *see* Birch, Sir J. A.
Birch, Albert Edward Henry, 1868–1954, vol. V
Birch, Sir Arthur, 1837–1914, vol. I

Birch, Claude Churchill, 1846–1940, vol. III
Birch, David; see Birch, W. H. D.
Birch, De Burgh, 1852–1937, vol. III
Birch, Col Edward Massy, 1875–1964, vol. VI
Birch, Sir Ernest Woodford, 1857–1929, vol. III
Birch, (Evelyn) Nigel (Chetwode); see Baron Rhyl.
Birch, Francis Lyall, 1889–1956, vol. V
Birch, George Henry, 1842–1904, vol. I
Birch, Henry William, 1854–1927, vol. II
Birch, Gen. Sir (James Frederick) Noel, 1865–1939, vol. III
Birch, Major James Richard Kemmis, 1859–1907, vol. I
Birch, Sir (John) Alan, 1909–1961, vol. VI
Birch, Rev. John George, born 1839, vol. II
Birch, John Henry Stopford, died 1949, vol. IV
Birch, Nigel; see Baron Rhyl.
Birch, Gen. Sir Noel; see Birch, Gen. Sir J. F. N.
Birch, Lt-Col Percy Yates, 1884–1939, vol. III
Birch, S. J. Lamorna, 1869–1955, vol. V
Birch, Walter de Gray, 1842–1924, vol. II
Birch, (William Henry) David, 1894–1968, vol. VI
Birch, Wyndham Lindsay, 1879–1950, vol. IV
Birch-Reynardson, Col Charles; see Reynardson.
Birch-Reynardson, Lt-Col Henry T.; see Reynardson.
Birchall, Sir John Dearman, 1875–1941, vol. IV
Birchall, Sir Raymond; see Birchall, Sir W. R.
Birchall, Sir (Walter) Raymond, 1888–1968, vol. VI
Bircham, Sir Bernard Edward H.; see Halsey-Bircham.
Bircham, Sir Bertram Okeden, 1877–1961, vol. VI
Bircham, Major Humphry Francis William, 1875–1916, vol. II
Birchenough, Charles, 1882–1973, vol. VII
Birchenough, Very Rev. Godwin, 1880–1953, vol. V
Birchenough, Sir Henry, 1st Bt, 1853–1937, vol. III
Birchenough, Mabel, (Lady Birchenough), died 1936, vol. III
Bird, Sir Alfred Frederick, 1849–1922, vol. II
Bird, Archibald John, 1872–1939, vol. III
Bird, Col Arthur James Glover, 1883–1962, vol. VI
Bird, Hon. Bolton Stafford, 1840–1924, vol. II
Bird, Sir Charles Hayward, 1862–1944, vol. IV
Bird, Christopher John, 1855–1922, vol. II
Bird, Lt-Gen. Sir Clarence August, 1885–1986, vol. VIII
Bird, Cuthbert Hilton G.; see Golding-Bird.
Bird, Sir C(yril) Handley, 1896–1969, vol. VI
Bird, Rt Rev. Cyril Henry G.; see Golding-Bird.
Bird, (Cyril) Kenneth, 1887–1965, vol. VI
Bird, Sir Cyril Pangbourne, 1906–1984, vol. VIII
Bird, Sir Donald Geoffrey, 3rd Bt, 1906–1963, vol. VI
Bird, Elliott Beverley S.; see Steeds-Bird.
Bird, Eric Leslie, 1894–1965, vol. VI
Bird, Sir Ernest Edward, 1877–1945, vol. IV
Bird, Ernest Roy, 1883–1933, vol. III
Bird, Sir F. Hugh W. S.; see Stonehewer Bird.
Bird, Air Vice-Marshal Frank Ronald, 1918–1983, vol. VIII
Bird, Col Frederic Dougan, 1858–1929, vol. III
Bird, Captain Frederic Godfrey, 1868–1919, vol. II
Bird, Gen. Sir George Corrie, 1838–1907, vol. I
Bird, (George William) Terence, 1914–1985, vol. VIII
Bird, Harington; see Bird, J. A. H.

Bird, Sir Harry, 1862–1944, vol. IV
Bird, Sir Henry Busby, 1856–1929, vol. III
Bird, Henry Edward, 1830–1908, vol. I
Bird, Isabella Lucy; see Bishop, Mrs I. L.
Bird, Sir James, 1863–1925, vol. II
Bird, Squadron Comdr Sir James, 1883–1946, vol. IV
Bird, Rev. James Grant, died 1920, vol. II
Bird, James William Fairbridge, 1858–1938, vol. III
Bird, (John Alexander) Harington, died 1936, vol. III
Bird, John Louis Warner, 1929–1983, vol. VIII
Bird, Rev. John Turnbull, 1862–1930, vol. III
Bird, Lt-Col John Wilfred, 1872–1938, vol. III
Bird, Kenneth; see Bird, C. K.
Bird, Captain Oliver, 1880–1963, vol. VI
Bird, Lt-Col Robert, 1866–1918, vol. II
Bird, Sir Robert Bland, 2nd Bt, 1876–1960, vol. V
Bird, Rev. Samuel William Elderfield, died 1926, vol. II
Bird, Col Spencer Godfrey, 1854–1926, vol. II
Bird, Col Stanley, 1864–1938, vol. III
Bird, Col Stanley George, 1837–1905, vol. I
Bird, Terence; see Bird, G. W. T.
Bird, Terence Frederick, 1906–1979, vol. VII
Bird, Tom, died 1932, vol. III
Bird, Veronica, 1932–1986, vol. VIII
Bird, Maj.-Gen. Sir Wilkinson Dent, 1869–1943, vol. IV
Bird, Sir William Barrott Montfort, 1855–1950, vol. IV
Bird, William Seymour, 1846–1919, vol. II
Birdwood, 1st Baron, 1865–1951, vol. V
Birdwood, 2nd Baron, 1899–1962, vol. VI
Birdwood, Lt-Col George Christopher McDowall, 1863–1944, vol. IV
Birdwood, Sir George Christopher Molesworth, 1832–1917, vol. II
Birdwood, Herbert Mills, 1837–1907, vol. I
Birgi, Muharrem Nuri, 1908–1986, vol. VIII
Birkbeck, Sir Edward, 1st Bt, 1838–1907, vol. I
Birkbeck, Geoffrey, 1875–1954, vol. V
Birkbeck, Harold Edward, 1902–1977, vol. VII
Birkbeck, Henry, 1853–1930, vol. III
Birkbeck, Major Henry Anthony, 1885–1956, vol. V
Birkbeck, Col Oliver, 1893–1952, vol. V
Birkbeck, Maj.-Gen. Theodore Henry, 1911–1976, vol. VII
Birkbeck, Maj.-Gen. Sir William Henry, 1863–1929, vol. III
Birkbeck, William John, 1859–1916, vol. II
Birkenhead, 1st Earl of, 1872–1930, vol. III
Birkenhead, 2nd Earl of, 1907–1975, vol. VII
Birkenhead, 3rd Earl of, 1936–1985, vol. VIII
Birkenruth, Adolphus, 1861–1940, vol. III
Birkett, 1st Baron, 1883–1962, vol. VI
Birkett, George William Alfred, 1908–1988, vol. VIII
Birkett, Brig.-Gen. Herbert Stanley, 1864–1942, vol. IV
Birkett, Brig. Richard Maule, 1882–1942, vol. IV
Birkett, Sir Thomas William, 1871–1957, vol. V
Birkin, Sir Alexander Russell, 4th Bt, 1861–1942, vol. IV
Birkin, Sir Charles Lloyd, 5th Bt, 1907–1985, vol. VIII
Birkin, Lt-Col Charles Wilfrid, 1865–1932, vol. III

Birkin, Sir Henry Ralph Stanley, 3rd Bt, 1896–1933, vol. III
Birkin, Air Cdre James Michael, 1912–1985, vol. VIII
Birkin, Lt-Col Richard Leslie, 1863–1936, vol. III
Birkin, Sir Stanley; see Birkin, Sir T. S.
Birkin, Sir Thomas Isaac, 1st Bt, 1831–1922, vol. II
Birkin, Sir (Thomas) Stanley, 2nd Bt, 1857–1931, vol. III
Birkinshaw, Air Cdre George William, 1896–1977, vol. VII
Birmyre, Sir Archibald, 1st Bt, 1875–1935, vol. III
Birks, Falconer Moffat, 1885–1960, vol. V
Birks, Maj.-Gen. Horace Leslie, 1897–1985, vol. VIII
Birley, Lt-Col Bevil Langton, 1884–1943, vol. IV
Birley, Sir Frank, 1883–1940, vol. III
Birley, James Leatham, 1884–1934, vol. III
Birley, Leonard, 1875–1951, vol. V
Birley, Norman Pellew, 1891–1980, vol. VII
Birley, Captain Sir Oswald Hornby Joseph, 1880–1952, vol. V
Birley, Mrs Percy Langton, 1875–1956, vol. V
Birley, Col Richard Kennedy, 1845–1914, vol. I
Birley, Sir Robert, 1903–1982, vol. VIII
Birley, Rt Rev. Thomas Howard, 1864–1949, vol. IV
Birmingham, George A.; see Hannay, Rev. James O.
Birnage, Arthur, 1874–1953, vol. V
Birnam, Hon. Lord; (Thomas) David King Murray, 1884–1955, vol. V
Birnie, Col Eugene St John, 1900–1976, vol. VII
Birnie, Captain Harry Charles, 1882–1943, vol. IV
Biron, Sir Chartres, 1863–1940, vol. III
Biron, Sir (Moshe Chaim Efraim) Philip, 1909–1981, vol. VIII
Biron, Sir Philip; see Biron, Sir M. C. E. P.
Birrell, Rt Hon. Augustine, 1850–1933, vol. III
Birrell, Col Edwin Thomas Fairweather, 1874–1944, vol. IV
Birrell, Hon. Frederick William, died 1939, vol. III
Birrell, John, 1836–1902, vol. I
Birrell-Gray, Major William; see Gray, Major W. B.
Birsay, Hon. Lord; Harald Robert Leslie, 1905–1982, vol. VIII
Birt, Francis Bradley B.; see Bradley-Birt.
Birt, Guy Capper, 1884–1972, vol. VII
Birt, Rev. Canon Roderick Harold Capper, 1882–1975, vol. VII
Birt, Sir William, 1834–1911, vol. I
Birtchnell, Sir Cyril Augustine, 1887–1967, vol. VI
Birtwistle, Brig.-Gen. Arthur, 1877–1937, vol. III
Birtwistle, George, 1877–1929, vol. III
Birtwistle, Ivor Treharne, 1892–1976, vol. VII
Bisat, William S., 1886–1973, vol. VII
Bischoff, Thomas Hume, 1886–1951, vol. V
Bischoffesheim, Henry Louis, 1829–1908, vol. I
Biscoe, Rev. Cecil Earle T.; see Tyndale-Biscoe.
Biscoe, Lt-Col Sir Hugh Vincent, 1881–1932, vol. III
Biscoe, Brig.-Gen. Julian Dallas Tyndale T.; see Tyndale-Biscoe.
Biscoe, Walter Treweeke, 1892–1969, vol. VI
Biscoe, Lt-Gen. William Walters, 1841–1920, vol. II
Bisdee, Lt-Col John Hutton, 1869–1930, vol. III
Bisgood, Joseph John, 1861–1927, vol. II
Bishop, Maj.-Gen. Sir Alec; see Bishop, Maj.-Gen. Sir W. H. A.

Bishop, Ann, 1899–1990, vol. VIII
Bishop, Arthur Henry Burdick, died 1969, vol. VI
Bishop, Edward Stanley; see Baron Bishopston.
Bishop, Lt-Comdr Francis Charles, 1905–1965, vol. VI
Bishop, Sir (Frank) Patrick, 1900–1972, vol. VII
Bishop, Frederic Sillery, died 1913, vol. I
Bishop, Captain Frederick Edward, 1872–1931, vol. III
Bishop, George Walter, 1886–1965, vol. VI
Bishop, Sir Harold, 1900–1983, vol. VIII
Bishop, Henry, died 1939, vol. III
Bishop, Rev. Hugh William Fletcher, 1907–1989, vol. VIII
Bishop, Mrs Isabella Luey, 1832–1904, vol. I
Bishop, John, 1828–1913, vol. I
Bishop, Joseph Bucklin, 1847–1928, vol. II
Bishop, Julius, 1855–1932, vol. III
Bishop, Laurence Arthur, 1895–1954, vol. V
Bishop, Matilda Ellen, 1844–1913, vol. I
Bishop, Sir Patrick; see Bishop, Sir F. P.
Bishop, Peter Maxwell Farrow, 1904–1979, vol. VII
Bishop, Richard Evelyn Donohue, 1925–1989, vol. VIII
Bishop, Hon. Robert Kirby, 1853–1930, vol. III
Bishop, Ronald Eric, 1903–1989, vol. VIII
Bishop, Theodore Bendysh Watson, 1886–1967, vol. VI
Bishop, W. Follen, 1856–1936, vol. III
Bishop, Walter Frederick, 1879–1955, vol. V
Bishop, Rev. William; see Bishop, Rev. H. W. F.
Bishop, Air Marshal William Avery, 1894–1956, vol. V
Bishop, Maj.-Gen. Sir (William Henry) Alexander, (Alec), 1897–1984, vol. VIII
Bishop, Sir William Poole, 1894–1977, vol. VII
Bishop, William Thomas, 1901–1982, vol. VIII
Bishopston, Baron (Life Peer); Edward Stanley Bishop, 1920–1984, vol. VIII
Bismarck, Prince Herbert von, 1849–1904, vol. I
Bispham, David, 1857–1921, vol. II
Bispham, James Webb, died 1956, vol. V
Biss, Godfrey Charles D'Arcy, 1909–1989, vol. VIII
Bisschop, Willem Roosegaarde, 1866–1944, vol. IV
Bisseker, Rev. Harry, 1878–1965, vol. VI
Bisset, Vice-Adm. Arthur William La Touche, 1892–1956, vol. V
Bisset, Captain Sir James Gordon Partridge, 1883–1967, vol. VI
Bisset, Sir Murray, 1876–1931, vol. III
Bisset, Col Sir William Sinclair Smith, 1843–1916, vol. II
Bisset-Berry, Hon. Sir William; see Berry.
Bisset-Smith, George Tulloch, 1863–1922, vol. II
Bissett, Maj.-Gen. Frederic William Lyon, 1888–1961, vol. VI
Bisson, Laurence Adophus, 1897–1965, vol. VI
Biswambhar Ray, Rai Bahadur (Vidyabenode), 1855–1930, vol. III
Biswas, Rt Rev. Nirod Kumar, 1905–1948, vol. IV
Bithell, Jethro, 1878–1962, vol. VI
Bizet, George; see Bisset-Smith, George Tulloch.
Bjoerling, Jussi, 1911–1960, vol. V
Björnson, Björnstjerne, 1832–1910, vol. I

Björnsson, Henrik Sveinsson, 1914–1985, vol. VIII

Blache, Jules Adolphe Lucien, 1893–1970, vol. VI

Blache-Fraser, Louis Nathaniel, 1904–1987, vol. VIII

Blachford, Lady; (Georgiana Mary), *died* 1900, vol. I

Black, Baron (Life Peer); William Rushton Black, 1893–1984, vol. VIII

Black, Sir Alec, 1st Bt (*cr* 1918), 1872–1942, vol. IV

Black, Alexander William, 1859–1906, vol. I

Black, Andrew, 1850–1916, vol. II

Black, Sir Archibald Campbell, *died* 1962, vol. VI

Black, Rt Hon. Arthur, 1888–1968, vol. VI

Black, Arthur John, 1855–1936, vol. III

Black, Sir Arthur William, 1863–1947, vol. IV

Black, Charles Crofton, 1880–1937, vol. III

Black, Lt-Col Claud Hamilton Griffith, *died* 1946, vol. IV

Black, Colin Mackenzie, 1877–1943, vol. IV

Black, Davidson, 1884–1934, vol. III

Black, Donald Harrison, 1899–1978, vol. VII

Black, Ebenezer Charlton, 1861–1927, vol. II

Black, Francis, *died* 1939, vol. III

Black, Sir Frederick William, 1863–1930, vol. III

Black, Hon. George, 1873–1965, vol. VI

Black, Major George Cumine Strahan, 1882–1951, vol. V

Black, George Joseph, 1918–1984, vol. VIII

Black, George Norman, 1907–1955, vol. V

Black, Rev. Canon Gibson James Hunter Monahan, 1867–1950, vol. IV

Black, Gordon, 1923–1990, vol. VIII

Black, Sir Harold, 1914–1981, vol. VIII

Black, Henry, 1875–1960, vol. V, vol. VI

Black, Sir Hermann David, 1905–1990, vol. VIII

Black, Hervey Stuart; *see* Black, I. H. S.

Black, Rev. Hugh, 1868–1953, vol. V

Black, Hugo LaFayette, 1886–1971, vol. VII

Black, (Ian) Hervey Stuart, 1908–1986, vol. VIII

Black, Rt Rev. James, 1894–1968, vol. VI

Black, Very Rev. James Macdougall, 1879–1949, vol. IV

Black, James Watt, 1840–1918, vol. II

Black, John Bennett, 1883–1964, vol. VI

Black, Col John Campbell Lamont, 1869–1950, vol. IV

Black, Sir John Paul, 1895–1965, vol. VI

Black, John Stewart, 1865–1930, vol. III

Black, John Sutherland, 1846–1923, vol. II

Black, John Wycliffe, 1862–1951, vol. V

Black, Kenneth, 1879–1959, vol. V

Black, Kenneth Oscar, 1910–1987, vol. VIII

Black, Ladbroke Lionel Day, 1877–1940, vol. III

Black, Sir Misha, 1910–1977, vol. VII

Black, Robert Alastair Lucien, 1921–1967, vol. VI

Black, Sir Robert Andrew Stransham, 2nd Bt, 1902–1979, vol. VII

Black, Sir Robert James, 1st Bt (*cr* 1922), 1860–1925, vol. II

Black, Sir Samuel, 1830–1910, vol. I

Black, Sydney, 1908–1968, vol. VI

Black, Thomas Porteous, 1878–1915, vol. I

Black, Maj.-Gen. Walter Clarence, 1867–1930, vol. III

Black, William, 1841–1898, vol. I

Black, Hon. William Anderson, 1847–1934, vol. III

Black, Maj.-Gen. William Campbell, 1846–1931, vol. III

Black, William Charles, 1890–1959, vol. V (A)

Black, William George, 1857–1932, vol. III

Black, William John, 1872–1941, vol. IV

Black, Maj.-Gen. Sir Wilsone, 1837–1909, vol. I

Black-Hawkins, (Clive) David, 1915–1983, vol. VIII

Black-Hawkins, David; *see* Black-Hawkins, C. D.

Blackadder, William, 1877–1940, vol. III

Blackader, Alexander Dougall, 1847–1932, vol. III

Blackader, Maj.-Gen. Charles Guinand, 1869–1921, vol. II

Blackall, Sir Henry William Butler, 1889–1981, vol. VIII

Blackbourne, Rev. Jacob, 1862–1936, vol. III

Blackburn, Hon. Lord; Robert Francis Leslie Blackburn, 1864–1944, vol. IV

Blackburn, Sir Arthur Dickinson, 1887–1970, vol. VI

Blackburn, Brig. Arthur Seaforth, 1892–1960, vol. V

Blackburn, Barbara; *see* Blackburn, E. B.

Blackburn, Lt-Col Sir Charles Bickerton, 1874–1972, vol. VII

Blackburn, Lt-Col Charles Cautley, 1867–1938, vol. III

Blackburn, (Evelyn) Barbara, 1898–1981, vol. VIII

Blackburn, Fred, 1902–1990, vol. VIII

Blackburn, Henry, 1830–1897, vol. I

Blackburn, Col John Edward, 1851–1927, vol. II

Blackburn, Maurice McCrae, 1880–1944, vol. IV

Blackburn, Hon. Sir Richard Arthur, 1918–1987, vol. VIII

Blackburn, Robert Francis Leslie; *see* Blackburn, Hon. Lord.

Blackburn, Sir Thomas, *died* 1974, vol. VII

Blackburn, Vernon, *died* 1907, vol. I

Blackburn, William Ernest, 1873–1951, vol. V

Blackburne, Lt-Col Charles Harold, 1876–1918, vol. II

Blackburne, Rev. Foster Grey, *died* 1909, vol. I

Blackburne, Gertrude Mary Ireland, 1861–1951, vol. V

Blackburne, Very Rev. Harry William, 1878–1963, vol. VI

Blackburne, Joseph Henry, 1841–1924, vol. II

Blackburne, Sir Kenneth William, 1907–1980, vol. VII

Blackburne, Very Rev. Lionel Edward, 1874–1951, vol. V

Blackburne, Col Robert Ireland, 1850–1930, vol. III

Blackden, Col Leonard Shadwell, 1863–1937, vol. III

Blacker, Carlos Paton, 1895–1975, vol. VII

Blacker, Edward Carew, 1863–1932, vol. III

Blacker, Col Frederick St John, 1881–1942, vol. IV

Blacker, Sir George, 1865–1948, vol. IV

Blacker, Maj.-Gen. George Patrick Demaine, 1906–1974, vol. VII

Blacker, Harold Alfred Cecil, 1889–1944, vol. IV

Blacker, L(atham) V(alentine) Stewart, *died* 1964, vol. VI

Blacker, Lt-Col Stewart William Ward, 1865–1935, vol. II

Blacket, Wilfred, 1859–1937, vol. III

Blackett, Baron (Life Peer); Patrick Maynard Stuart Blackett, 1897–1974, vol. VII

Blackett, Sir Basil Phillott, 1882–1935, vol. III
Blackett, Sir Charles Douglas, 9th Bt, 1904–1968, vol. VI
Blackett, Sir Edward William, 7th Bt, 1831–1909, vol. I
Blackett, Adm. Henry, 1867–1952, vol. V
Blackett, Sir Hugh Douglas, 8th Bt, 1873–1960, vol. V
Blackett, Rev. Selwyn, 1854–1935, vol. III
Blackett, Col William Cuthbert, 1859–1935, vol. III
Blackett Ord, Ven. Charles Edward, 1858–1931, vol. III
Blackford, 1st Baron, 1862–1947, vol. IV
Blackford, 2nd Baron, 1887–1972, vol. VII
Blackford, 3rd Baron, 1923–1977, vol. VII
Blackford, 4th Baron, 1962–1988, vol. VIII
Blackham, Maj.-Gen. Robert James, *died* 1951, vol. V
Blackie, Rt Rev. Ernest Morell, 1867–1943, vol. IV
Blackie, John Ernest Haldane, 1904–1985, vol. VIII
Blackie, Margery Grace, 1898–1981, vol. VIII
Blackie, Walter Wilfrid, 1860–1953, vol. V
Blacking, Randoll; *see* Blacking, W. H. R.
Blacking, (William Henry) Randoll, 1889–1958, vol. V
Blackledge, Geoffrey Glynn, 1894–1964, vol. VI
Blackledge, Rev. Canon George Robert, 1868–1935, vol. III
Blackley, Travers Robert, 1899–1982, vol. VIII
Blackley, Rev. William Lewery, 1830–1902, vol. I
Blacklock, Maj.-Gen. Cyril Aubrey, 1870–1936, vol. III
Blacklock, Donald Breadalbane, 1879–1955, vol. V
Blacklock, John William Stewart, *died* 1973, vol. VII
Blacklock, Captain Ronald William, 1889–1987, vol. VIII
Blackman, Aylward Manley, 1883–1956, vol. V
Blackman, Rear-Adm. Charles Maurice, 1890–1981, vol. VIII
Blackman, Frederick Frost, 1866–1947, vol. IV
Blackman, Geoffrey Emett, 1903–1980, vol. VII
Blackman, Moses, 1908–1983, vol. VIII
Blackman, Raymond Victor Bernard, 1910–1989, vol. VIII
Blackman, Vernon Herbert, 1872–1967, vol. VI
Blackman, Winifred Susan, *died* 1950, vol. IV
Blackmore, Sir Charles Henry, 1880–1967, vol. VI
Blackmore, Col Lindsay William Saul, 1896–1973, vol. VII
Blackmore, Richard Doddridge, 1825–1900, vol. I
Blackmur, Richard Palmer, 1904–1965, vol. VI
Blackshaw, J. F., 1875–1943, vol. IV
Blackshaw, James William, 1895–1983, vol. VIII
Blackshaw, Maurice Bantock, 1903–1975, vol. VII
Blackshaw, Rev. William, 1866–1953, vol. V
Blackton, James Stuart, 1875–1941, vol. IV
Blackwell, Sir Basil Henry, 1889–1984, vol. VIII
Blackwell, Sir (Cecil) Patrick, 1881–1944, vol. IV
Blackwell, Elizabeth, 1821–1910, vol. I
Blackwell, Sir Ernley Robertson Hay, 1868–1941, vol. IV
Blackwell, Francis Samuel, 1869–1951, vol. V
Blackwell, Major Francis Victor, *died* 1928, vol. II
Blackwell, John Humphrey, 1895–1979, vol. VII

Blackwell, John Kenneth, 1914–1986, vol. VIII
Blackwell, Sir Patrick; *see* Blackwell, Sir C. P.
Blackwell, Richard, 1918–1980, vol. VII
Blackwell, Thomas Francis, 1838–1907, vol. I
Blackwell, Thomas Francis, 1912–1983, vol. VIII
Blackwell, Thomas Geoffrey, 1884–1943, vol. IV
Blackwell, Maj.-Gen. William Richard, 1877–1946, vol. IV
Blackwood, Lt-Col Albemarle Price, 1881–1921, vol. II
Blackwood, Algernon Henry, 1869–1951, vol. V
Blackwood, Lord Basil; *see* Blackwood, Lord I.B.G.T.
Blackwood, Rt Rev. Donald Burns, 1884–1967, vol. VI (AII)
Blackwood, Sir Francis, 4th Bt, 1838–1924, vol. II
Blackwood, Sir Francis Elliot Temple, 6th Bt, 1901–1979, vol. VII
Blackwood, Captain Frederick Herbert, 1885–1926, vol. II
Blackwood, George William, 1876–1942, vol. IV
Blackwood, Sir Henry Palmer Temple, 5th Bt, 1896–1948, vol. IV
Blackwood, Lord (Ian) Basil (Gawaine Temple), 1870–1917, vol. II
Blackwood, James H., 1878–1951, vol. V
Blackwood, Dame Margaret, 1909–1986, vol. VIII
Blackwood, Captain Maurice Baldwin Raymond, 1882–1941, vol. IV
Blackwood, Sir Robert Rutherford, 1906–1982, vol. VIII
Blackwood, William, 1836–1912, vol. I
Blackwood, William, 1878–1958, vol. V
Blackwood, William, 1911–1990, vol. VIII
Blackwood-Price, Rev. Canon Edward Hyde, 1875–1940, vol. III
Blades, Hon. Lord; Daniel Patterson Blades, 1888–1959, vol. V
Blades, Daniel Patterson; *see* Blades, Hon. Lord.
Blades, Major Walter William, 1863–1943, vol. IV
Bladin, Air Vice-Marshal Francis Masson, 1898–1978, vol. VII
Bladon, Air Cdre Graham Clarke, 1899–1967, vol. VI
Blagden, Charles Otto, 1864–1949, vol. IV
Blagden, Rt Rev. Claude Martin, 1874–1952, vol. V
Blagden, Rev. Henry, 1832–1922, vol. II
Blagden, John Basil, 1901–1964, vol. VI
Blagden, Sir John Ramsay, 1908–1985, vol. VIII
Blagrove, Col Henry John, 1854–1925, vol. II
Blaikie, Leonard, 1873–1951, vol. V
Blaikie, Walter Biggar, 1847–1928, vol. II
Blaikie, Rev. William Garden, 1820–1899, vol. I
Blaikley, John Barnard, 1906–1975, vol. VII
Blaiklock, George, 1856–1943, vol. IV
Blain, Hon. Sir Eric Herbert, 1904–1969, vol. VI
Blain, Sir Herbert Edwin, 1870–1942, vol. IV
Blain, William, *died* 1908, vol. I
Blain, Sir William Arbuthnot, 1833–1911, vol. I
Blaine, Sir Charles Frederick, *died* 1915, vol. I
Blaine, Brig. Charles Herbert, 1883–1958, vol. V
Blaine, Sir Robert Stickney, *died* 1897, vol. I
Blair; *see* Blair-Fish, W. W.
Blair, Alexander, 1864–1944, vol. IV

Blair, Lt-Col Alexander Stevenson, 1865–1936, vol. III

Blair, Hon. Andrew George, 1844–1907, vol. I

Blair, Rev. Andrew Hamish, 1901–1981, vol. VIII

Blair, Andrew James Fraser, (Hamish Blair), 1872–1935, vol. III

Blair, Hon. Sir Archibald William, 1875–1952, vol. V

Blair, Brig.-Gen. Arthur, 1869–1947, vol. IV

Blair, Charles Neil Molesworth, 1910–1988, vol. VIII

Blair, Gen. Charles Renny, 1837–1912, vol. I

Blair, Charles Samuel, 1859–1939, vol. III

Blair, David, 1932–1976, vol. VII

Blair, David Arthur, 1917–1985, vol. VIII

Blair, Rt Rev. Sir David H.; *see* Hunter-Blair.

Blair, Douglas MacColl, 1940–1990, vol. VIII

Blair, Duncan MacCallum, 1896–1944, vol. IV

Blair, Captain Sir Edward H.; *see* Hunter-Blair.

Blair, Dame Emily Mathieson, 1892–1963, vol. VI

Blair, Eric Arthur; *see* Orwell, George.

Blair, Brig.-Gen. Everard Macleod, 1866–1939, vol. III

Blair, Col Frederick Gordon, 1852–1943, vol. IV

Blair, George William S.; *see* Scott Blair.

Blair, Hamish; *see* Blair, A. J. F.

Blair, Rev. Canon Harold Arthur, 1902–1985, vol. VIII

Blair, Gen. James, 1828–1905, vol. I

Blair, Sir James H.; *see* Hunter Blair.

Blair, Col James Molesworth, 1880–1925, vol. II

Blair, James Richard, 1890–1958, vol. V

Blair, Hon. Sir James William, 1871–1944, vol. IV

Blair, Kenneth Gloyne, 1882–1952, vol. V

Blair, Rt Rev. Laurence Frederick Devaynes, *died* 1925, vol. II

Blair, Oliver Robin, 1925–1975, vol. VII

Blair, Patrick James, 1865–1932, vol. III

Blair, Col Sir Patrick James, 1892–1972, vol. VII

Blair, Peter H.; *see* Hunter Blair.

Blair, Sir Reginald, 1st Bt, 1881–1962, vol. VI

Blair, Sir Robert, 1859–1935, vol. III

Blair, Robert Kerr, 1876–1942, vol. IV

Blair, Maj.-Gen. Walter Charles H.; *see* Hunter-Blair.

Blair, Very Rev. William, 1830–1916, vol. II

Blair-Bell, William, 1871–1936, vol. III

Blair-Cunynghame, Sir James Ogilvy, 1913–1990, vol. VIII

Blair-Fish, Wallace Wilfrid, 1889–1968, vol. VI

Blais, Rt Rev. Andrew Albert, 1842–1919, vol. II

Blaize, Rt Hon. Herbert Augustus, 1918–1989, vol. VIII

Blake, Captain Sir Acton; *see* Blake, Captain Sir H. A.

Blake, Sir Arthur Ernest, 1869–1935, vol. III

Blake, Arthur John J.; *see* Jex-Blake.

Blake, Col Arthur Maurice, *born* 1852, vol. II

Blake, Lt-Col Arthur O'Brien ffrench, 1879–1973, vol. VII

Blake, Comdr Sir Cuthbert Patrick, 6th Bt (*cr* 1772), 1885–1975, vol. VII

Blake, Hon. Edward, 1833–1912, vol. I

Blake, Sir Edward; *see* Blake, Sir F. E. C.

Blake, Edwin Holmes, 1873–1956, vol. V

Blake, Sir Ernest Edward, 1845–1920, vol. II

Blake, Eugene Carson, 1906–1985, vol. VIII

Blake, Sir Francis Douglas, 1st Bt (*cr* 1907), 1856–1940, vol. III

Blake, Sir (Francis) Edward (Colquhoun), 2nd Bt (*cr* 1907), 1893–1950, vol. IV

Blake, Francis Gilman, 1887–1952, vol. V

Blake, Vice-Adm. Sir Geoffrey, 1882–1968, vol. VI

Blake, George, 1893–1961, vol. VI

Blake, Lt-Col Sir (George) Reginald, 1882–1949, vol. IV

Blake, Maj.-Gen. Gilbert Alan, 1887–1971, vol. VII

Blake, Henrietta J.; *see* Jex-Blake.

Blake, Sir Henry Arthur, 1840–1918, vol. II

Blake, Henry E.; *see* Elliott-Blake.

Blake, Gen. Henry William, 1815–1908, vol. I

Blake, Henry Wollaston, 1815–1899, vol. I

Blake, Captain Sir (Herbert) Acton, 1857–1926, vol. II

Blake, Herbert Frederick, 1866–1946, vol. IV

Blake, Jack Percy, *died* 1950, vol. IV

Blake, Rev. James Edward Huxley, 1863–1933, vol. III

Blake, Rev. James Martindale, 1863–1934, vol. III

Blake, Rev. John Frederick, 1839–1906, vol. I

Blake, Sir John Lucian, 1898–1954, vol. V

Blake, John William, 1911–1987, vol. VIII

Blake, Katharine J.; *see* Jex-Blake.

Blake, Louisa Brandreth A.; *see* Aldrich-Blake.

Blake, Col Maurice Charles Joseph, 1837–1917, vol. II

Blake, Major Napoleon Joseph Rodolph, 1853–1926, vol. II

Blake, Nicholas; *see* Day-Lewis, Cecil.

Blake, Sir Patrick James Graham, 5th Bt (*cr* 1772), 1861–1930, vol. III

Blake, Lt-Col Sir Reginald; *see* Blake, Lt-Col Sir G. R.

Blake, Sophia J.; *see* Jex-Blake.

Blake, Lt-Col Terence Joseph Edward, 1886–1921, vol. II

Blake, Sir Thomas Patrick Ulick John Harvey, 15th Bt (*cr* 1622), 1870–1925, vol. II

Blake, Very Rev. Thomas William J.; *see* Jex-Blake.

Blake, Sir Ulick Temple, 16th Bt (*cr* 1622), 1904–1963, vol. VI

Blake, Vernon, 1875–1930, vol. III

Blake, Brig.-Gen. William Alan, 1878–1959, vol. V

Blake-Daly, John Archer; *see* Daly.

Blake-Humfrey, Rev. John, 1847–1930, vol. III

Blake-Reed, Sir John Seymour, 1882–1966, vol. VI

Blakelock, Denys Martin, 1901–1970, vol. VI

Blakely, Hon. Arthur, 1886–1972, vol. VII

Blakely, Colin George Edward, 1930–1987, vol. VIII

Blakeman, Joan, (Mrs L. T. Blakeman); *see* Woodward, Joan.

Blakeman, John, 1881–1942, vol. IV

Blakeman, Leslie Thompson, 1904–1975, vol. VII

Blakemore, Alan, 1919–1989, vol. VIII

Blakemore, Frederick, 1906–1955, vol. V

Blakeney, Edward Henry, *died* 1955, vol. V

Blakeney, Frederick Joseph, 1913–1990, vol. VIII

Blakeney, Col Herbert Norwood, 1871–1946, vol. IV

Blakeney, Rev. Richard, 1857–1946, vol. IV

Blakeney, Rev. Robert Bibby, 1865–1948, vol. IV

Blakeney, Brig.-Gen. Robert Byron Drury, 1872–1952, vol. V

Blakeney, Col William Edward Albemarle, *died* 1942, vol. IV

Blakenham, 1st Viscount, 1911–1982, vol. VIII

Blaker, Cedric, 1889–1965, vol. VI

Blaker, Harry Rowsell, 1872–1953, vol. V

Blaker, Sir John George, 1st Bt, 1854–1926, vol. II

Blaker, Nathaniel Robert, 1921–1990, vol. VIII

Blaker, Sir Reginald, 2nd Bt, 1900–1975, vol. VII

Blaker, Richard, 1893–1940, vol. III

Blaker, Richard Henry, 1866–1940, vol. III

Blaker, Col William Frederick, 1877–1933, vol. III

Blakesley, Major Henry J., *died* 1931, vol. III

Blakesley, Thomas H., 1847–1929, vol. III

Blakeway, Ven. Charles Edward, 1868–1922, vol. II

Blakeway, Lt-Col Sir Denys Brooke, 1870–1933, vol. III

Blakeway, John Denys, 1918–1986, vol. VIII

Blakeway, Brig.-Gen. John Prestwich, 1867–1936, vol. III

Blakey, James, 1851–1929, vol. III

Blakiston, Sir Arthur Frederick, 7th Bt, 1892–1974, vol. VII

Blakiston, Sir (Arthur) Norman (Hunter), 8th Bt, 1899–1977, vol. VII

Blakiston, Sir Charles Edward, 6th Bt, 1862–1941, vol. IV

Blakiston, Cuthbert Harold, 1879–1949, vol. IV

Blakiston, Rev. Cyril Ralph Noel, 1880–1941, vol. IV

Blakiston, Rev. Herbert Edward Douglas, 1862–1942, vol. IV

Blakiston, Sir Horace Nevile, 5th Bt, 1861–1936, vol. III

Blakiston, John Frnacis, 1882–1965, vol. IV

Blakiston, Sir Norman; *see* Blakiston, Sir A. N. H.

Blakiston, Wilfrid Robert Louis, 1876–1955, vol. V

Blakiston-Houston, Major Charles, 1868–1935, vol. III

Blakiston-Houston, John, 1829–1920, vol. II

Blakiston-Houston, Maj.-Gen. John, 1881–1959, vol. V

Blamey, Col Edwin Herbert, 1877–1936, vol. III

Blamey, Field Marshal Sir Thomas Albert, 1884–1951, vol. V

Blampied, Edmund, 1886–1966, vol. VI

Blanc, Edmond, 1861–1920, vol. II

Blanc, Sir Henry Jules, 1831–1911, vol. I

Blanc, Hippolyte Jean, 1844–1917, vol. II

Blanche, Rt Rev. Gustave, 1848–1916, vol. II

Blanche, Jaques Emile, 1862–1942, vol. IV

Blanco, Alfredo Ernesto, 1877–1945, vol. IV

Blanco White, Amber, 1887–1981, vol. VIII

Blanco White, George Rivers; *see* White.

Bland, Charles Heber, 1886–1966, vol. VI

Bland, E.; *see* Nesbit, E.

Bland, E. Beatrice, 1868–1951, vol. V

Bland, Brig.-Gen. Edward Humphry, 1866–1945, vol. IV

Bland, Edward Maltby, 1878–1946, vol. IV

Bland, Rev. Edward Michael, 1851–1936, vol. III

Bland, Francis Armand, 1882–1967, vol. VI

Bland, Francis Lawrence, 1873–1941, vol. IV

Bland, Sir (George) Nevile Maltby, 1886–1972, vol. VII

Bland, Lt-Col John Edward Michael, 1899–1976, vol. VII

Bland, John Otway Percy, 1863–1945, vol. IV

Bland, Sir Nevile; *see* Bland, Sir G. N. M.

Bland, Robert Norman, 1859–1948, vol. IV

Bland, Sir Thomas Maltby, 1906–1968, vol. VI

Bland, William Archdale, 1862–1934, vol. III

Bland, Col William St Colum, 1868–1950, vol. IV

Bland-Sutton, Sir John, 1st Bt, 1855–1936, vol. III

Blandford, Marchioness of; (Albertha Frances Anne), 1847–1932, vol. III

Blandford, George Fielding, 1829–1911, vol. I

Blandford, Laurence James, 1876–1944, vol. IV

Blandford, Hon. Sydney Dara, 1868–1929, vol. III

Blandy, Beatrice Charlotte, *died* 1950, vol. IV

Blandy, Sir Edmond Nicolas, *died* 1942, vol. IV

Blandy, Air Cdre Lyster Fettiplace, 1874–1964, vol. VI

Blandy, Richard Denis, 1891–1964, vol. VI

Blane, Brig.-Gen. Charles Forbes, 1859–1930, vol. III

Blane, Comdr Sir Charles Rodney, 4th Bt, 1879–1916, vol. II

Blane, Gilbert Gordon, 1851–1928, vol. II

Blane, Lt-Gen. Sir Seymour John, 3rd Bt, 1833–1911, vol. I

Blane, Thomas Andrew, 1881–1940, vol. III

Blane, William, 1864–1936, vol. III

Blanesborough, Baron (Life Peer); Robert Younger, 1861–1946, vol. IV

Blaney, Thomas, 1823–1903, vol. I

Blanford, William Thomas, 1832–1905, vol. I

Blank, Abraham Lewis, 1891–1967, vol. VI

Blankenberg, Sir Reginald Andrew, 1876–1960, vol. V (A)

Blantyre, 12th Baron, 1818–1900, vol. I

Blaserna, Pietro, *died* 1918, vol. II

Blatch, Sir William Bernard, 1887–1965, vol. VI

Blatchford, Robert, 1851–1943, vol. IV

Blatherwick, Col Sir Thomas, 1887–1950, vol. IV

Blathwayt, Raymond, 1855–1935, vol. III

Blathwayt, Robert Wynter, 1850–1936, vol. III

Blaxland, Maj.-Gen. Alan Bruce, 1892–1963, vol. VI

Blaxland, Rev. George Cuthbert, 1852–1930, vol. III

Blaxland, Vice-Adm. John Edric, 1847–1935, vol. III

Blaxter, Kenneth William, 1895–1964, vol. VI

Blaydes, Frederick Henry Marvell, 1818–1908, vol. I

Blaylock, Col Harry Woodburn, 1878–1928, vol. II

Bleackley, Horace William, 1868–1931, vol. III

Bleackley, Engr Rear-Adm. Hubert, 1886–1950, vol. IV

Blease, W. Lyon, 1884–1963, vol. VI

Bleasdale, Raymond John, 1924–1982, vol. VIII

Bleck, Edward Charles, 1861–1919, vol. II

Bledisloe, 1st Viscount, 1867–1958, vol. V

Bledisloe, 2nd Viscount, 1899–1979, vol. VII

Blee, David, 1899–1979, vol. VII

Blegen, Carl William, 1887–1971, vol. VII

Blelloch, Ian William, 1901–1982, vol. VIII

Blencowe, Rev. Alfred James, *died* 1928, vol. II

Blenkin, Very Rev. George Wilfrid, 1861–1924, vol. II

Blenkinsop, Maj.-Gen. Sir Alfred Percy, 1865–1936, vol. III

Blenkinsop, Arthur, 1911–1979, vol. VII

Blenkinsop, Edward Robert Kaye, 1871–1954, vol. V

Blenkinsop, Maj.-Gen. Sir Layton John, 1862–1942, vol. IV

Blennerhassett, Sir Arthur Charles Francis Bernard, 5th Bt, 1871–1915, vol. I

Blennerhassett, Col Blennerhassett Montgomerie, 1849–1926, vol. II

Blennerhassett, Sir Marmaduke Charles Henry Joseph, 6th Bt, 1902–1940, vol. III

Blennerhassett, Rt Hon. Sir Rowland, 4th Bt, 1839–1909, vol. I

Blennerhassett, Rowland Ponsonby, 1850–1913, vol. I

Blennerhassett, William Lewis Rowland Paul Sebastian, 1882–1958, vol. V

Bleriot, Louis, 1872–1936, vol. III

Blewett, Francis Richard, *born* 1869, vol. II

Blewett, Maj.-Gen. Robert Sidney, 1931–1987, vol. VIII

Blewitt, Maj.-Gen. William Edward, 1854–1939, vol. III

Bligh, Sir Edward Clare, 1887–1976, vol. VII

Bligh, John Murray, *died* 1968, vol. VI

Bligh, Sir Timothy James, 1918–1969, vol. VI

Blight, Francis James, 1858–1935, vol. III

Blind, Karl, 1826–1907, vol. I

Blind, Rudolf, 1850–1916, vol. II

Blindell, Sir James, 1884–1937, vol. III

Bliss, 4th Baron, 1869–1926, vol. II

Bliss, Sir Arthur Edward Drummond, 1891–1975, vol. VII

Bliss, Major Charles, 1871–1914, vol. I

Bliss, Cuthbert Vivian, 1878–1963, vol. VI

Bliss, Col Ernest William, 1869–1934, vol. III

Bliss, Sir Henry William, 1840–1919, vol. II

Bliss, Rev. Howard S., 1860–1920, vol. II

Bliss, Rev. John Worthington, 1832–1917, vol. II

Bliss, Joseph, 1853–1939, vol. III

Bliss, Kathleen Mary, (Mrs Rupert Bliss), 1908–1989, vol. VIII

Bliss, Brig. Philip Wheeler, 1887–1966, vol. VI

Bliss, Gen. Tasker Howard, 1853–1930, vol. III

Bliss, Col Thomas Gordon, 1869–1949, vol. IV

Bliss, Rev. William Henry, 1834–1919, vol. II

Bliven, Bruce, 1889–1977, vol. VII

Blixen Finecke, Karen; *see* Dinesen, Isak.

Bloch, Ernest, 1880–1959, vol. V

Bloch, Felix, 1905–1983, vol. VIII

Bloch, Jean de, *died* 1902, vol. I

Bloch, Sir Maurice, *died* 1964, vol. VI

Bloch, Olaf F., *died* 1944, vol. IV

Block, Sir Adam Samuel James, 1856–1941, vol. IV

Block, Brig. Allen Prichard, 1899–1973, vol. VII

Block, Comdr Leslie Kenneth Allen, 1906–1980, vol. VII

Blockey, Air Vice-Marshal Paul Sandland, 1905–1963, vol. VI

Blodget, Cornelia Otis, (Mrs A. S. Blodget); *see* Skinner, C. O.

Blofeld, Rev. Stuart, 1872–1950, vol. IV

Blofeld, Thomas Calthorpe, 1836–1908, vol. I

Blofield, Edgar Glanville, 1899–1981, vol. VIII

Blois, Captain Sir Gervase Ralph Edmund, 10th Bt, 1901–1968, vol. VI

Blois, Sir Ralph Barrett Macnaghten, 9th Bt, 1866–1950, vol. IV

Blois-Johnson, Lt-Col Thomas Gordon; *see* Johnson.

Blom, Eric Walter, 1888–1959, vol. V

Blomefield, Edward Hugh, 1852–1938, vol. III

Blomefield, Peregrine Maitland, 1917–1988, vol. VIII

Blomefield, Sir Thomas Edward Peregrine, 5th Bt, 1907–1984, vol. VIII

Blomefield, Sir Thomas Wilmot Peregrine, 4th Bt, 1848–1928, vol. II

Blomfield, Arthur Conran, 1863–1935, vol. III

Blomfield, Sir Arthur William, 1829–1899, vol. I

Blomfield, Maj.-Gen. Charles James, 1855–1928, vol. II

Blomfield, Charles James, *died* 1932, vol. III

Blomfield, Douglas John, 1885–1979, vol. VII

Blomfield, Joseph, 1870–1948, vol. IV

Blomfield, Sir Reginald, 1856–1942, vol. IV

Blomfield, Wing Comdr Richard Graham, 1890–1940, vol. III

Blomfield, Rear-Adm. Sir Richard Massie, 1835–1921, vol. II

Blomfield, Maj.-Gen. Valentine, 1898–1980, vol. VII

Blomfield, Rev. William Ernest, 1862–1934, vol. III

Blommers, Johannes Bernardus, 1845–1914, vol. I

Blond, Neville, 1896–1970, vol. VI

Blondin, Lt-Col Hon. Pierre Edouard, 1874–1943, vol. IV

Blood, Alexander, *died* 1933, vol. III

Blood, Gen. Sir Bindon, 1842–1940, vol. III

Blood, Sir Hilary Rudolph Robert, 1893–1967, vol. VI

Blood, Lancelot Ivan Neptune Lloyd-, 1896–1951, vol. V

Blood, Brig. William Edmund Robarts, 1897–1976, vol. VII

Blood, Brig. William Holcroft, 1887–1976, vol. VII

Blood-Smyth, Rev. William A., 1853–1940, vol. IV

Bloom, Ursula Harvey, (Mrs Gower Robinson), 1892–1984, vol. VIII

Bloomer, Rt Rev. Thomas, 1894–1984, vol. VIII

Bloomfield, Lady; (Georgiana), 1822–1905, vol. I

Bloomfield, Sir John Stoughton, 1901–1989, vol. VIII

Bloomfield, Maurice, 1855–1928, vol. II (A), vol. III

Blore, Rev. George John, 1835–1916, vol. II

Blore, Lt-Col Herbert Richard, 1871–1955, vol. V

Blosse, Sir David Edward L.; *see* Lynch-Blosse.

Blosse, Sir Henry L.; *see* Lynch-Blosse.

Blosse, Sir Robert Cyril Lynch-, 13th Bt, 1887–1951, vol. V

Blosse, Sir Robert Geoffrey Lynch-, 14th Bt, 1915–1963, vol. VI

Blosse, Sir Robert Lynch, 12th Bt, 1861–1942, vol. IV

Blouet, Léon Paul; *see* O'Rell, Max

Blough, Roger Miles, 1904–1985, vol. VIII

Bloundelle-Burton, John Edward, *died* 1917, vol. II

Blount, Austin Ernest, 1870–1954, vol. V

Blount, Air Vice-Marshal Charles Hubert Boulby, 1893–1940, vol. IV

Blount, Col Edward Augustine, *died* 1936, vol. III

Blount, Sir Edward Charles, 1809–1905, vol. I

Blount, Edward Francis Riddell-, 1865–1943, vol. IV
Blount, Sir Edward Robert, 11th Bt, 1884–1978, vol. VII
Blount, Vice-Adm. George Ronald, 1877–1964, vol. VI
Blount, Lt-Gen. Harold, 1881–1967, vol. VI
Blount, Sir Walter Aston, 10th Bt, 1876–1958, vol. V
Blount, Sir Walter de Sodington, 9th Bt, 1833–1915, vol. I
Blow, Detmar, 1867–1939, vol. III
Blow, Horatio John Hooper, 1855–1933, vol. III
Blow, Very Rev. Norman John, 1915–1950, vol. IV (A), vol. V
Blow, Sydney, died 1961, vol. VI
Blowers, Arthur R., 1868–1954, vol. V
Blowitz, Henri Georges Stephane Adolphe Opper de, 1832–1903, vol. I
Bloxam, John Astley, died 1926, vol. II
Blucher von Wahlstatt, Prince; see Wahlstatt.
Blucke, Air Vice-Marshal Robert Stewart, 1897–1988, vol. VIII
Bluett, Maj.-Gen. Douglas, 1897–1981, vol. VIII
Blum, Léon, 1872–1950, vol. IV
Blumberg, Gen. Sir Herbert Edward, 1869–1934, vol. III
Blumenfeld, Ralph David, 1864–1948, vol. IV
Blumenthal, George, 1858–1941, vol. IV
Blumenthal, Jacques, 1829–1908, vol. I
Blumhardt, J. F., died 1922, vol. II
Blundell, Lt-Col Bryan Seymour Moss-, 1878–1932, vol. III
Blundell, Charles Joseph W.; see Weld-Blundell.
Blundell, Sir Denis; see Blundell, Sir E. D.
Blundell, Rev. Canon E. K., 1886–1961, vol. VI
Blundell, Edward, 1842–1932, vol. III
Blundell, Sir (Edward) Denis, 1907–1984, vol. VIII
Blundell, Mrs Francis, died 1930, vol. III
Blundell, Francis Nicholas, 1880–1936, vol. III
Blundell, Col Frederick Blundell Moss, 1873–1964, vol. VI
Blundell, Henry B. H.; see Blundell-Hollinshead-Blundell.
Blundell, Henry Seymour Moss-, 1871–1947, vol. IV
Blundell, Col John Eyles, 1843–1931, vol. III
Blundell, Lionel Alleyne, 1910–1975, vol. VII
Blundell, Maj.-Gen. Richard H. B.; see Blundell-Hollinshead-Blundell.
Blundell, Sir Robert Henderson, 1901–1967, vol. IV
Blundell-Hollinshead-Blundell, Henry, 1831–1906, vol. I
Blundell-Hollinshead-Blundell, Maj.-Gen. Richard, 1835–1912, vol. I
Blunden, Edmund Charles, 1896–1974, vol. VII
Blunden, Sir John, 5th Bt, 1880–1923, vol. II
Blunden, Sir William, 4th Bt, 1840–1923, vol. II
Blunden, Sir William, 6th Bt, 1919–1985, vol. VIII
Blundstone, Ferdinand V., 1882–1951, vol. V
Blunt, Rev. Alexander Colvin, died 1920, vol. II
Blunt, Rt Rev. Alfred Walter Frank, 1879–1957, vol. V
Blunt, Lt-Col Allan St John, 1880–1931, vol. III
Blunt, Anthony Frederick, 1907–1983, vol. VIII
Blunt, Arthur Powlett, 1883–1946, vol. IV
Blunt, Col Charles Jasper, died 1933, vol. III

Blunt, Christopher Evelyn, 1904–1987, vol. VIII
Blunt, Col Conrad Edward Grant, 1868–1948, vol. IV
Blunt, Davenport Fabian Cartwright, died 1965, vol. VI
Blunt, Denzil Layton, 1891–1968, vol. VI
Blunt, Sir Edward Arthur Henry, 1877–1941, vol. IV
Blunt, Col Ernest, 1851–1932, vol. III
Blunt, Brig. Gerald Charles Gordon, 1883–1967, vol. VI
Blunt, Sir John Elijah, 1832–1916, vol. II
Blunt, Captain Sir John Harvey, 8th Bt, 1839–1922, vol. II
Blunt, Sir John Harvey, 9th Bt, 1872–1938, vol. III
Blunt, Sir John Lionel Reginald, 10th Bt, 1908–1969, vol. VI
Blunt, John Silvester, 1874–1943, vol. IV
Blunt, Reginald, 1857–1944, vol. IV
Blunt, Sir Richard David Harvey, 11th Bt, 1912–1975, vol. VII
Blunt, Rt Rev. Richard Lefevre, 1833–1910, vol. I
Blunt, Wilfrid Jasper Walter, 1901–1987, vol. VIII
Blunt, Wilfrid Scawen, 1840–1922, vol. II
Blunt, Sir William, 7th Bt, 1826–1902, vol. I
Blunt, Rear-Adm. William Frederick, 1870–1928, vol. II
Blyde, Sir Henry Ernest, 1896–1984, vol. VIII
Blyth, 1st Baron, 1841–1925, vol. II
Blyth, 2nd Baron, 1868–1943, vol. IV
Blyth, 3rd Baron, 1905–1977, vol. VII
Blyth, Alexander Wynter, died 1921, vol. II
Blyth, Alfred Carleton, 1865–1936, vol. III
Blyth, Benjamin Hall, 1849–1917, vol. II
Blyth, Lt-Col Charles Frederick Tolmé, 1868–1950, vol. IV
Blyth, Charles Henry, 1916–1986, vol. VIII
Blyth, Rt Rev. George Francis Popham, died 1914, vol. I
Blyth, Lt-Col James, 1869–1925, vol. II
Blyth, James, 1864–1933, vol. III
Blyth, James Pattison C.; see Currie-Blyth.
Blyth, Ormond Alfred, 1879–1947, vol. IV
Blyth, Robert Henderson, 1919–1970, vol. VI
Blyth, Rev. Thomas Allen, 1844–1913, vol. I
Blythe, Ernest, 1889–1975, vol. VII
Blythe, Wilfred Lawson, 1896–1975, vol. VII
Blythswood, 1st Baron, 1837–1908, vol. I
Blythswood, 2nd Baron, 1839–1916, vol. II
Blythswood, 3rd Baron, 1845–1918, vol. II
Blythswood, 4th Baron, 1870–1929, vol. III
Blythswood, 5th Baron, 1877–1937, vol. III
Blythswood, 6th Baron, 1881–1940, vol. III
Blythswood, 7th Baron, 1919–1940, vol. III
Blyton, Baron (Life Peer); William Reid Blyton, 1899–1987, vol. VIII
Blyton, Enid Mary, 1897–1968, vol. VI
Boag, Sir George Townsend, 1884–1969, vol. VI
Board, Air Cdre Andrew George, 1878–1973, vol. VII
Board, Sir (Archibald) Vyvyan, 1884–1973, vol. VII
Board, Ernest, 1877–1934, vol. III
Board, Peter, 1858–1945, vol. IV
Board, Sir Vyvyan; see Board, Sir A. V.
Board, Sir William John, 1869–1946, vol. IV
Boardman, Adm. Frederick Ross, 1843–1927, vol. II

Boardman, Paymaster Captain John Cogswell, *died* 1942, vol. IV

Boas, Franz, 1858–1942, vol. IV

Boas, Frederick S., 1862–1957, vol. V

Boas, Guy, 1896–1966, vol. VI

Boas, Leslie, 1912–1988, vol. VIII

Boase, Alan Martin, 1902–1982, vol. VIII

Boase, Lt-Gen. Allan Joseph, 1894–1964, vol. VI

Boase, Arthur Joseph, 1901–1986, vol. VIII

Boase, Col George Orlebar, 1881–1966, vol. VI

Boase, Thomas Sherrer Ross, 1898–1974, vol. VII

Boase, William Norman, 1870–1938, vol. III

Bockett, Herbert Leslie, 1905–1977, vol. VII (AII)

Bocquet, Guy Sutton, 1882–1961, vol. VI

Bocquet, (Roland) Roscoe (Charles), 1839–1920, vol. II

Boddam, Maj.-Gen. Welby Wraughton, 1832–1906, vol. I

Boddam-Whetham, Rear-Adm. Edye Kington, 1887–1944, vol. IV

Boddam-Whetham, Major Sydney A., 1885–1925, vol. II

Boddie, Donald Raikes, 1917–1984, vol. VIII

Boddie, George Frederick, 1900–1985, vol. VIII

Boddie, Rear-Adm. Ronald Charles, 1886–1967, vol. VI

Boddington, Rev. Edward Henry, *died* 1920, vol. II

Boddis, Alfred Charles, 1895–1958, vol. V

Bode, Major Louis William, 1860–1936, vol. III

Boden, Rev. Charles John, 1853–1937, vol. III

Bodenham-Lubienski, Count Louis, 1852–1909, vol. I

Bodenstein, Helgard Dewald Johannes, 1881–1943, vol. IV

Bodet, Jaime T.; *see* Torres Bodet.

Bodington, Rev. Charles, 1836–1918, vol. II

Bodington, Ven. Eric James, 1862–1929, vol. III

Bodington, Sir Nathan, 1848–1911, vol. I

Bodinnar, Sir John Francis, *died* 1958, vol. V

Bodkin, Sir Archibald Henry, 1862–1957, vol. V

Bodkin, Gilbert Edwin, 1886–1955, vol. V

Bodkin, Matthias M'Donnell, 1850–1933, vol. III

Bodkin, Thomas Patrick, 1887–1961, vol. VI

Bodkin, Fr William, 1867–1930, vol. III

Bodkin, Hon. Sir William Alexander, 1883–1964, vol. VI

Bodle, Brig.-Gen. William, 1855–1924, vol. II

Bodley, George Frederick, 1827–1907, vol. I

Bodley, John Edward Courtenay, 1853–1925, vol. II

Bodley Scott, Sir Ronald, 1906–1982, vol. VIII

Body, Rev. George, 1840–1911, vol. I

Body, Maj.-Gen. Kenneth Marten, 1883–1973, vol. VII

Boegner, Marc, 1881–1970, vol. VI

Boehm Boteler, Sir Edgar Collins; *see* Boteler.

Boevey, Sir Francis Hyde Crawley-, 6th Bt, 1868–1928, vol. II

Boevey, Sir Lance (Launcelot Valentine Hyde) C.; 7th Bt; *see* Crawley-Boevey.

Boevey, Sir Thomas Hyde Crawley, 5th Bt, 1837–1912, vol. I

Boffa, Sir Paul, 1890–1962, vol. VI

Bogard, Humphrey de Forest, 1899–1957, vol. V

Boger, Lt-Col Dudley Coryndon, *died* 1935, vol. III

Boger, Major R. W., 1868–1910, vol. I

Bogert, Clarence Atkinson, 1864–1949, vol. IV

Bogert, Ven. James John, 1835–1920, vol. II

Boggis-Rolfe, Douglass Horace, 1874–1966, vol. VI

Boggon, Roland Hodgson, 1903–1983, vol. VIII

Bogle, Very Rev. Andrew Nisbet, *died* 1957, vol. V

Bogle, Lt-Col John Savile, 1872–1940, vol. III

Bogle, Lockhart, *died* 1900, vol. I

Bogle-Smith, Col Steuart, 1859–1921, vol. II

Bohane, (Albert) Edward, 1873–1940, vol. III

Bohane, Edward; *see* Bohane, A. E.

Boheman, Erik, 1895–1979, vol. VII (AII)

Bohlen, Charles Eustis, 1904–1974, vol. VI

Bohr, Niels Henrik David, 1885–1962, vol. VI

Boileau, Sir Edmond Charles, 7th Bt, 1903–1980, vol. VII

Boileau, Col Etienne Ronald Partridge, 1870–1947, vol. IV

Boileau, Sir Francis George Manningham, 2nd Bt, 1830–1900, vol. I

Boileau, Sir Francis James, 5th Bt, 1871–1945, vol. IV

Boileau, Col Francis William, 1835–1915, vol. I

Boileau, Col Frank Ridley Farrer, 1867–1914, vol. I

Boileau, Sir Gilbert George Benson, 6th Bt, 1898–1978, vol. VII

Boileau, Brig.-Gen. Guy Hamilton, 1870–1962, vol. VI

Boileau, Hugh Evan Ridley, 1906–1952, vol. V

Boileau, Sir Maurice Colborne, 3rd Bt, 1865–1937, vol. III

Boileau, Sir Raymond Frederic, 4th Bt, 1868–1942, vol. IV

Boillot, Félix, 1880–1961, vol. VI

Bois, Col John, 1881–1941, vol. IV

Bois, Sir Stanley, 1864–1938, vol. III

Boisragon, Col Guy Hudleston, 1864–1931, vol. III

Boissier, Arthur Paul, 1882–1953, vol. V

Boissier, Rev. George John, 1857–1929, vol. III

Boissier, Léopold, 1893–1968, vol. VI

Boissier, Marie Louis Gaston, 1823–1908, vol. I

Boito, Arrigo, 1842–1918, vol. II

Bojer, Johan, 1872–1959, vol. V

Bok, Edward William, 1863–1930, vol. III

Bolam, Rev. Cecil Edward, 1875–1960, vol. V

Bolam, Sir Robert, *died* 1939, vol. III

Boland, Bridget, 1913–1988, vol. VIII

Boland, Sir (Edward) Rowan, 1898–1972, vol. VII

Boland, Frederick Henry, 1904–1985, vol. VIII

Boland, Harry, *died* 1922, vol. II

Boland, John Pius, 1870–1958, vol. V

Boland, Sir Rowan; *see* Boland, Sir E. R.

Bolden, John Leonard, 1841–1929, vol. III

Boldero, Sir Harold Esmond Arnison, 1889–1960, vol. VI

Boldrewood, Rolf, (Thomas Alexander Browne), 1826–1915, vol. I

Bole, Hon. W. Norman, 1846–1923, vol. II

Boles, Lt-Col Dennis Coleridge, 1885–1958, vol. V

Boles, Lt-Col Sir Dennis Fortescue, 1st Bt, 1861–1935, vol. III

Boles, Sir Gerald Fortescue, 2nd Bt, 1900–1945, vol. IV

Boles, Rev. Richard Henry, 1855–1929, vol. III

Bolingbroke, 5th Viscount, **and St John,** 6th Viscount, 1820–1899, vol. I

Bolingbroke, 6th Viscount, **and St John,** 7th Viscount, 1896–1974, vol. VII

Bolingbroke, Leonard George, 1859–1927, vol. II

Bolitho, Lt-Col Sir Edward Hoblyn Warren, *died* 1969, vol. VI

Bolitho, Hector; *see* Bolitho, Henry H.

Bolitho, (Henry) Hector, 1897–1974, vol. VII

Bolitho, Captain Richard John Bruce, 1889–1965, vol. VI

Bolitho, Thomas Bedford, 1835–1915, vol. I

Bolitho, Thomas Robins, 1840–1925, vol. II

Bolitho, Lt-Col William Edward Thomas, 1862–1919, vol. II

Böll, Heinrich Theodor, 1917–1985, vol. VIII

Bolland, Robert William, 1915–1974, vol. VII

Bollard, Hon. R. F., *died* 1927, vol. II

Bolling, Cunliffe Lawrance, 1898–1938, vol. III

Bols, Hon. Maj.-Gen. Eric Louis, 1904–1985, vol. VIII

Bols, Major Louis Jean, 1867–1909, vol. I

Bols, Lt-Gen. Sir Louis Jean, 1867–1930, vol. III

Bolsover, George Henry, 1910–1990, vol. VIII

Bolst, Captain Clifford Charles Alan Lawrence E.; *see* Erskine-Bolst.

Bolster, Francis, *died* 1941, vol. IV

Bolster, Rev. Robert Crofts, *died* 1918, vol. II

Bolster, Captain Thomas Charles Carpenter, *died* 1955, vol. V

Bolt, Rev. G. H., 1863–1947, vol. IV

Bolt, George Thomas, 1900–1971, vol. VII

Bolte, Dame Edith Lilian, (Lady Bolte), *died* 1986, vol. VIII

Bolte, Hon. Sir Henry Edward, 1908–1990, vol. VIII

Bolter, Albert Ernest, 1856–1933, vol. III

Bolton, 4th Baron, 1845–1922, vol. II

Bolton, 5th Baron, 1869–1944, vol. IV

Bolton, 6th Baron, 1900–1963, vol. VI

Bolton, Arthur Thomas, 1864–1945, vol. IV

Bolton, Charles, *died* 1947, vol. IV

Bolton, Brig. Charles Arthur, 1882–1964, vol. VI

Bolton, Rev. Charles Nelson, 1844–1918, vol. II

Bolton, Charles walter, 1850–1919, vol. II

Bolton, Lt-Col Edward Frederick, 1897–1977, vol. VII

Bolton, Edward Richards, 1878–1939, vol. III

Bolton, Sir Edwin, 1st Bt, 1858–1931, vol. III

Bolton, Elizabeth, 1878–1961, vol. VI

Bolton, Sir Frederic, 1851–1920, vol. II

Bolton, Gambier, *died* 1928, vol. II

Bolton, Col Geoffrey George Hargreaves, 1894–1983, vol. VIII

Bolton, Sir George Lewis French, 1900–1982, vol. VIII

Bolton, Guy, 1884–1979, vol. VII

Bolton, Herbert, *died* 1936, vol. III

Bolton, Sir (Horatio) Norman, 1875–1965, vol. VI

Bolton, Captain Sir Ian Frederick Cheney, 2nd Bt, 1889–1982, vol. VIII

Bolton, John, 1925–1986, vol. VIII

Bolton, Sir John Brown, 1902–1980, vol. VII (AII)

Bolton, Joseph Cheney, 1819–1901, vol. I

Bolton, Joseph Shaw, 1867–1946, vol. IV

Bolton, Louis Hamilton, 1884–1953, vol. V

Bolton, Sir Norman; *see* Bolton, Sir H. N.

Bolton, Percy, 1889–1981, vol. VIII

Bolton, Thomas Dolling, 1841–1906, vol. I

Bolton, Thomas Henry, 1841–1916, vol. II

Bolton, Brig.-Gen. William Kinsey, 1861–1941, vol. IV

Bomanji, Sir Dhunjibhoy, *died* 1937, vol. III

Bomford, Surg.-Gen. Sir Gerald, 1851–1915, vol. I

Bomford, Sir Hugh, 1882–1939, vol. III

Bomford, Richard Raymond, 1907–1981, vol. VIII

Bomon-Behram, Sir Jehangir Bomonji, 1868–1949, vol. IV

Bompas, Cecil Henry, 1868–1956, vol. V

Bompas, Henry Mason, 1836–1909, vol. I

Bompas, Rt Rev. William Carpenter, 1834–1906, vol. I

Bonaparte, Hon. Charles Joseph, 1851–1921, vol. II

Bonaparte, HIH Prince Roland, 1858–1924, vol. II

Bonaparte-Wyse, Andrew Nicholas, 1870–1940, vol. III

Bonar, Henry Alfred Constant, 1861–1935, vol. III

Bonar, James, 1852–1941, vol. IV

Bonavia, Hon. Edgar, 1868–1927, vol. II

Boncour, Joseph P.; *see* Paul-Boncour.

Bond, Arthur, 1907–1989, vol. VIII

Bond, Carrie Jacobs-, 1862–1946, vol. IV

Bond, Brig.-Gen. Charles Earbery, 1877–1953, vol. V

Bond, Charles John, *died* 1939, vol. III

Bond, Rev. Charles Watson, 1839–1922, vol. II

Bond, Lt-Col Chetwynd Rokeby Alfred, 1863–1944, vol. IV

Bond, Engr Captain Edmund Edward, 1865–1943, vol. IV

Bond, Edward, 1844–1920, vol. II

Bond, Sir Edward Augustus, 1815–1898, vol. I

Bond, Francis, *died* 1918, vol. II

Bond, Maj.-Gen. Sir Francis George, 1856–1930, vol. III

Bond, Frederick Bligh, 1864–1945, vol. IV

Bond, George, 1906–1988, vol. VIII

Bond, Maj.-Gen. George Alexander, 1901–1987, vol. VIII

Bond, Henry, 1853–1938, vol. III

Bond, Henry Coulson, 1864–1937, vol. III

Bond, Sir Hubert, 1870–1945, vol. IV

Bond, Col James Henry Robinson, 1871–1943, vol. IV

Bond, Ven. John, 1841–1912, vol. I

Bond, Maj.-Gen. John Arthur Mallock, 1891–1959, vol. V

Bond, John Wentworth Garneys, 1865–1948, vol. IV

Bond, Joshua Walter MacGeough, 1831–1905, vol. I

Bond, Lt-Gen. Sir Lionel Vivian, 1884–1961, vol. VI

Bond, Maurice Francis, 1916–1983, vol. VIII

Bond, Ralph Norman, 1900–1984, vol. VIII

Bond, Sir Ralph Stuart, 1871–1968, vol. VI

Bond, Lt-Col Reginald Copleston, 1866–1936, vol. III

Bond, Surg. Vice-Adm. Sir Reginald St George Smallridge, 1872–1955, vol. V

Bond, Maj.-Gen. Richard Lawrence, 1890–1979, vol. VII

Bond, Richard Warwick, 1857–1943, vol. IV

Bond, Rt Hon. Sir Robert, 1857–1927, vol. II

Bond, Rev. Robert, *died* 1952, vol. V

Bond, Stanley Shaw, 1877–1943, vol. IV
Bond, Sir Walter Adrian M.; *see* Macgeough Bond.
Bond, Walter Fitzgerald; *see* Fitzgerald, Walter.
Bond, Most Rev. William Bennett, 1815–1906, vol. I
Bond, Maj.-Gen. William Dunn, 1836–1919, vol. II
Bond, William Langley, 1873–1947, vol. IV
Bond, William Linskill, 1892–1950, vol. IV
Bond, William Ralph Garneys, 1880–1952, vol. V
Bondfield, Rt Hon. Margaret Grace, 1873–1953, vol. V
Bone, Sir David William, 1874–1959, vol. V
Bone, Rev. Frederic James, 1844–1917, vol. II
Bone, Gertrude Helena, (Lady Bone), *died* 1962, vol. VI
Bone, Engr-Rear-Adm. Howard, 1869–1955, vol. V
Bone, Captain Howard Francis, 1908–1981, vol. VIII
Bone, James, 1872–1962, vol. VI
Bone, John Wardle, 1869–1949, vol. IV
Bone, Sir Muirhead, 1876–1953, vol. V
Bone, Phyllis Mary, 1894–1972, vol. VII
Bone, Group Captain Reginald John, 1888–1972, vol. VII
Bone, Stephen, 1904–1958, vol. V
Bone, William Arthur, 1871–1938, vol. III
Bonet Maury, Amy-Gaston, 1842–1919, vol. II
Bonfield, John Martin, 1915–1976, vol. VII
Bonham, Lt-Col Charles Barnard, 1871–1943, vol. IV
Bonham, Major Sir Eric Henry, 3rd Bt, 1875–1937, vol. III
Bonham, Sir George Francis, 2nd Bt, 1847–1927, vol. II
Bonham, Col John, 1834–1928, vol. II
Bonham, Major Walter Floyd, 1869–1905, vol. I
Bonham-Carter, Alfred, *died* 1910, vol. I
Bonham-Carter, Sir (Arthur) Desmond, 1908–1985, vol. VIII
Bonham-Carter, Arthur Thomas, 1869–1916, vol. II
Bonham-Carter, Gen. Sir Charles, 1876–1955, vol. V
Bonham Carter, Rear-Adm. Sir Christopher Douglas, 1907–1975, vol. VII
Bonham-Carter, Air Cdre David William Frederick, 1901–1974, vol. VII
Bonham-Carter, Sir Desmond; *see* Bonham-Carter, Sir A. D.
Bonham-Carter, Sir Edgar, 1870–1956, vol. V
Bonham Carter, Helen Violet; *see* Baroness Asquith of Yarnbury.
Bonham-Carter, Ian Malcolm 1882–1953, vol. V
Bonham Carter, Sir Maurice, 1880–1960, vol. V
Bonham-Carter, Adm. Sir Stuart Sumner, 1889–1972, vol. VII
Bonheur, Rosa, (Marie Rosalie Bonheur), 1822–1899, vol. I
Bonhote, Rev. Edward Frederic, 1888–1972, vol. VII
Boni, Giacomo, 1859–1925, vol. II
Boniwell, Martin Charles, 1883–1967, vol. VI
Bonn, Leo, 1850–1929, vol. III
Bonn, Sir Max J., 1877–1943, vol. IV
Bonnar, John Calderwood, 1888–1956, vol. V
Bonnat, Leon, *died* 1922, vol. II
Bonner, Rev. Carey, 1859–1938, vol. III
Bonner, Charles George, 1884–1951, vol. V
Bonner, Sir George Albert, 1862–1952, vol. V
Bonner, Hypatia Bradlaugh, 1858–1935, vol. III

Bonner, Captain Singleton, 1879–1917, vol. II
Bonner-Smith, David; *see* Smith.
Bonnet, Georges, 1889–1973, vol. VII
Bonnetard, Sir France; *see* Bonnetard, Sir N. P. F.
Bonnetard, Sir (Nicholas Patrick) France, 1907–1969, vol. VI
Bonney, Rev. Edwin, 1873–1946, vol. IV
Bonney, Rev. Thomas George, 1833–1923, vol. II
Bonney, Victor, *died* 1953, vol. V
Bonsal, Stephen, 1865–1951, vol. V
Bonsall, Arthur Charles, 1859–1924, vol. II (A), vol. III
Bonsall, Major Hugh Edward, 1863–1928, vol. II
Bonser, Rev. Henry, 1884–1966, vol. VI
Bonser, Rt Hon. Sir John Winfield, 1847–1914, vol. I
Bonser, Wilfrid, 1887–1971, vol. VII
Bonsey, Henry Dawes, *died* 1919, vol. II
Bonsey, Rev. William, 1845–1909, vol. I
Bonsor, Sir Bryan Cosmo, 3rd Bt, 1916–1977, vol. VII
Bonsor, Sir Cosmo; *see* Bonsor, Sir H. C. O.
Bonsor, Sir (Henry) Cosmo (Orme), 1st Bt, 1848–1929, vol. III
Bonsor, Major Sir Reginald, 2nd Bt, 1879–1959, vol. V
Bonus, Maj.-Gen. Joseph, 1836–1926, vol. II
Bonus, Col William John, 1862–1943, vol. IV
Bonvalot, Pierre Gabriel, 1853–1933, vol. III
Bonwick, Alfred James, 1883–1949, vol. IV
Bonython, Hon. Sir (John) Langdon, 1848–1939, vol. III
Bonython, Sir (John) Lavington, 1875–1960, vol. V
Bonython, Sir Lavington; *see* Bonython, Sir J. L.
Booker, Lt-Col George Edward Nussey, *died* 1938, vol. III
Booker, Sir William Lane, 1824–1905, vol. I
Bookey, Col John Trench Brownrigg, 1847–1921, vol. II
Boome, Brig.-Gen. Edward Herbert, 1865–1945, vol. IV
Boon, Sir Geoffrey Pearl, 1888–1970, vol. VI
Boon, Quartermaster George, 1846–1927, vol. II
Boon, John, 1859–1928, vol. II
Boord, Sir Arthur; *see* Boord, Sir W. A.
Boord, Sir Richard William, 3rd Bt, 1907–1975, vol. VII
Boord, Sir (Thomas) William, 1st Bt, 1838–1912, vol. I
Boord, Sir William; *see* Boord, Sir T. W.
Boord, Sir (William) Arthur, 2nd Bt, 1862–1928, vol. II
Boos, Sir Werner James, 1911–1974, vol. VII
Boose, Major James Rufus, 1859–1936, vol. III
Boosey, Leslie Arthur, 1887–1979, vol. VII
Boot, Rev. Alfred, 1854–1937, vol. III
Boot, Henry Albert Howard, 1917–1983, vol. VIII
Boot, Sir Horace, 1873–1943, vol. IV
Boot, William Henry James, *died* 1918, vol. II
Booth, Alfred, 1893–1965, vol. VI
Booth, Sir Alfred Allen, 1st Bt (*cr* 1916), 1872–1948, vol. IV
Booth, Sir Arthur; *see* Booth, Sir G. A. W.
Booth, Bramwell; *see* Booth, W. B.

Booth, Mrs Bramwell, (Florence Eleanor), 1861–1957, vol. V
Booth, Catherine B.; see Bramwell-Booth.
Booth, Rt Hon. Charles, 1840–1916, vol. II
Booth, Charles, 1868–1938, vol. III
Booth, Sir Charles H., 1853–1939, vol. III
Booth, Hon. Charles Lutley S.; see Sclater-Booth.
Booth, Sir Charles Sylvester, 1897–1970, vol. VI
Booth, Edgar Harold, 1893–1963, vol. VI
Booth, Dame Edith; see Evans, Dame Edith.
Booth, Eva G.; see Gore-Booth.
Booth, Evangeline Cory, died 1950, vol. IV
Booth, Florence Eleanor; see Booth, Mrs Bramwell.
Booth, Rear-Adm. Sir Francis Fitzgerald H.; see Haworth-Booth.
Booth, Frederick Handel, 1867–1947, vol. IV
Booth, Sir (George) Arthur (Warrington), 1879–1972, vol. VII
Booth, George Macaulay, 1877–1971, vol. VII
Booth, Sir Henry William Gore-, 5th Bt (cr 1760), 1843–1900, vol. I
Booth, James William, died 1953, vol. V
Booth, John Bennion, 1880–1961, vol. VI
Booth, John Reginald Trevor, 1883–1963, vol. VI
Booth, Most Rev. Joseph John, 1886–1965, vol. VI
Booth, Sir Josslyn (Augustus Richard) Gore-, 6th Bt (cr 1760), 1869–1944, vol. IV
Booth, Very Rev. Lancelot Parker, died 1925, vol. II
Booth, Leonard William, 1856–1923, vol. II
Booth, Mary Booth, 1885–1969, vol. VI
Booth, Sir Michael Savile G.; see Gore-Booth.
Booth, Major Sir Paul, 1884–1963, vol. VI
Booth, Sir Philip, 2nd Bt (cr 1916), 1907–1960, vol. V
Booth, S. Lawson, died 1928, vol. II
Booth, W. S., 1896–1972, vol. VII
Booth, Col Hon. Walter Dashwood S.; see Sclater-Booth.
Booth, Walter Reynolds, 1891–1963, vol. VI
Booth, Rev. William, 1829–1912, vol. I
Booth, (William) Bramwell, 1856–1929, vol. III
Booth-Gravely, Sir Walter, 1882–1971, vol. VII
Booth Tucker, Frederick St George de Lautour, 1853–1929, vol. III
Boothby, Baron, (Life Peer); Robert John Graham Boothby, 1900–1986, vol. VIII
Boothby, Basil; see Boothby, E. B.
Boothby, Sir Brooke, 11th Bt, 1856–1913, vol. I
Boothby, Sir Charles Francis, 12th Bt, 1858–1926, vol. II
Boothby, (Evelyn) Basil, 1910–1990, vol. VIII
Boothby, Captain Evelyn Leonard Beridge, 1876–1937, vol. III
Boothby, Captain Frederick Lewis Maitland, 1881–1940, vol. III
Boothby, Guy Newell, 1867–1905, vol. I
Boothby, Rev. Sir Herbert Cecil, 13th Bt, 1863–1935, vol. III
Boothby, Comdr Hubert Basil, 1863–1941, vol. IV
Boothby, Sir Hugo Robert Brooke, 15th Bt, 1907–1986, vol. VIII
Boothby, Josiah, 1837–1916, vol. II
Boothby, Sir Robert Tuite, 1871–1941, vol. IV
Boothby, Sir Seymour William Brooke, 14th Bt, 1866–1951, vol. V

Boothby, Cdre William Osbert, 1866–1913, vol. I
Boothe, Clare; see Luce, Mrs Henry R.
Boothman, Air Chief Marshal Sir John Nelson, 1901–1957, vol. V
Boothroyd, (Edith) Hester, (Mrs Francis Boothroyd), 1915–1983, vol. VIII
Boothroyd, Hester, (Mrs Francis Boothroyd); see Boothroyd, E. H.
Boothroyd, (John) Basil, 1910–1988, vol. VIII
Booty, Arthur Ernest, 1875–1932, vol. III
Booty, Vice-Adm. Edward Leonard, 1871–1949, vol. IV
Boppe, Lucien, 1834–1909, vol. I
Bor, Gen. James Henry, 1857–1914, vol. I
Bor, Max; see Adrian, Max.
Bor, Norman Loftus, 1893–1972, vol. VII
Borah, William Edgar, 1865–1940, vol. III
Boraston, Sir John, 1851–1920, vol. II
Boraston, Lt-Col John Herbert, 1885–1969, vol. VI
Borchgrevink, Carsten E., 1864–1934, vol. III
Bordeaux, Henry, 1870–1963, vol. VI
Borden, Rev. Byron Crane, 1850–1929, vol. III
Borden, Hon. Sir Frederick William, 1847–1917, vol. II
Borden, Henry, 1901–1989, vol. VIII
Borden, Mary, (Lady Spears), died 1968, vol. VI
Borden, Rt Hon. Sir Robert Laird, 1854–1937, vol. III
Border, Hugh William, 1890–1981, vol. VIII
Bordes, Charles, 1865–1909, vol. I
Bordet, Jules Jean Baptiste Vincent, 1870–1961, vol. VI
Bordonaro, Antonio Chiaramonte, 1877–1932, vol. III
Boreel, Sir Alfred, 12th Bt, 1883–1964, vol. VI
Boreel, Sir Francis William Robert, 11th Bt, 1882–1941, vol. IV
Boreel, Sir Jacob Willem Gustaaf, 10th Bt, 1852–1937, vol. III
Boreham, Ven. Frederick, 1888–1966, vol. VI
Borenius, Tancred, 1885–1948, vol. IV
Borg, Sir George, 1887–1954, vol. V
Borg, Raphael, 1840–1903, vol. I
Borg Olivier, George, 1911–1980, vol. VII
Borgeaud, Charles, 1861–1940, vol. III
Borges, Jorge Luis, 1899–1986, vol. VIII
Boring, Edwin Garrigues, 1886–1968, vol. VI
Borland, John Ernest, died 1937, vol. III
Borland, Captain John MacInnes, 1869–1946, vol. IV
Borland, Kenneth Alexander, died 1948, vol. IV
Borland, Rev. William, 1867–1945, vol. IV
Born, Max, 1882–1970, vol. VI
Borneman, Roy Ernest, 1904–1983, vol. VIII
Borradaile, Col George William, 1838–1927, vol. II
Borradaile, Brig.-Gen. Harry Benn, 1860–1948, vol. IV
Borradaile, Lancelot Alexander, 1872–1945, vol. IV
Borradaile, Rev. Robert Hudson, died 1914, vol. I
Borrajo, Edward Marto, 1853–1909, vol. I
Borrett, Adm. George Holmes, died 1952, vol. V
Borrett, Maj.-Gen. Herbert Charles, 1841–1919, vol. II
Borrett, Lt-Gen. Sir Oswald Cuthbert, 1878–1950, vol. IV

Borrie, Peter Forbes, 1918–1984, vol. VIII

Borrowes, Sir Erasmus Dixon, 9th Bt, 1831–1898, vol. I

Borrowes, Sir Eustace Dixon, 11th Bt, 1866–1939, vol. III

Borrowes, Lt-Col Sir Kildare Dixon, 10th Bt, 1852–1924, vol. II

Borschette, Albert, 1920–1976, vol. VII

Borthwick, 17th Baron, 1867–1910, vol. I

Borthwick, Albert William, *died* 1937, vol. III

Borthwick, Lt-Col Alexander, 1839–1914, vol. I

Borthwick, Captain Alfred Edward, 1871–1955, vol. V

Borthwick, Algernon Malcolm, 1907–1975, vol. VII

Borthwick, Brig.-Gen. Francis Henry, 1883–1977, vol. VII

Borthwick, Henry, 1868–1937, vol. III

Borthwick, Sir Thomas, 1st Bt, 1835–1912, vol. I

Borthwick, Sir Thomas Banks, 2nd Bt; *see* Whitburgh.

Borthwick, William Henry, 1832–1928, vol. II

Borton, Air Vice-Marshal Amyas Eden, 1886–1969, vol. VI

Borton, Lt-Col Arthur Drummond, 1883–1933, vol. III

Borton, Col Charles Edward, 1857–1924, vol. II

Borton, Neville Travers, 1870–1938, vol. III

Borwick, 1st Baron, 1845–1936, vol. III

Borwick, 2nd Baron, 1880–1941, vol. IV

Borwick, 3rd Baron, 1886–1961, vol. VI

Borwick, Lt-Col George Oldroyd, 1879–1964, vol. VI

Borwick, Leonard, 1868–1925, vol. II

Borwick, Lt-Col Malcolm, 1882–1957, vol. V

Borwick, Lt-Col Michael George, 1916–1986, vol. VIII

Borwick, Lt-Col Sir Thomas Faulkner, 1890–1981, vol. VIII

Bosanquet, Sir Albert; *see* Bosanquet, Sir F. A.

Bosanquet, Bernard, 1848–1923, vol. II

Bosanquet, Bernard James Tindal, 1877–1936, vol. III

Bosanquet, Charles Ian Carr, 1903–1986, vol. VIII

Bosanquet, Adm. Sir Day Hort, 1843–1923, vol. II

Bosanquet, Sir (Frederick) Albert, 1837–1923, vol. II

Bosanquet, Major George Richard Bosanquet S.; *see* Smith-Bosanquet.

Bosanquet, Adm. George Stanley, 1835–1914, vol. I

Bosanquet, Helen, 1860–1925, vol. II

Bosanquet, Captain Henry Theodore Augustus, 1870–1959, vol. V

Bosanquet, Sir Oswald Vivian, 1866–1933, vol. III

Bosanquet, Robert Carr, 1871–1935, vol. III

Bosanquet, Robert Holford Macdowall, *died* 1912, vol. I

Bosanquet, Sir Ronald Courthope; *see* Bosanquet, Sir S. R. C.

Bosanquet, Sir (Samuel) Ronald Courthope, 1868–1952, vol. V

Bosanquet, Theodora, 1880–1961, vol. VI

Bosanquet, Vivian Henry Courthope, 1872–1943, vol. IV

Bosanquet, William Cecil, *died* 1941, vol. IV

Boscawen, Rt Hon. Sir Arthur Sackville Trevor G.; *see* Griffith-Boscawen.

Boscawen, Major Hon. George Edward, 1888–1918, vol. II

Boscawen, Hon. Hugh le Despencer, 1844–1908, vol. I

Boscawen, Hon. John Richard De Clare, 1860–1915, vol. I

Bosch, Carl, 1874–1940, vol. III

Bosch, Baron Jean van den, 1910–1985, vol. VIII

Bose, Sir Bipin Krishna, 1851–1933, vol. III

Bose, Rai Bahadur C.; *see* Chunilal Bose.

Bose, Sir Jagadis Chunder, 1858–1937, vol. III

Bose, Sir Kailas Chandra, Rai Bahadur, *died* 1927, vol. II

Bose, (L. M.) Vivian, 1891–1983, vol. VIII

Bose, Satyendranath, 1894–1974, vol. VII

Bose, Vivian; *see* Bose, L. M. V.

Bossom, Baron (Life Peer); Alfred Charles Bossom, 1881–1965, vol. VI

Bostock, Rev. Charles, 1869–1943, vol. IV

Bostock, Geoffrey, 1880–1961, vol. VI

Bostock, Henry, *died* 1923, vol. II

Bostock, Henry John, 1870–1956, vol. V

Bostock, Hon. Hewitt, 1864–1930, vol. III

Bostock, John, 1916–1977, vol. VII

Bostock, Col John Southey, 1875–1930, vol. III

Bostock, Samuel, *died* 1938, vol. III

Bostock, Air Vice-Marshal William Dowling, 1892–1968, vol. VI

Boston, 6th Baron, 1860–1941, vol. IV

Boston, 7th Baron, 1889–1958, vol. V

Boston, 8th Baron, 1897–1972, vol. VII

Boston, 9th Baron, 1897–1978, vol. VII

Boston, Sir Henry (Josiah) Lightfoot, 1898–1969, vol. VI

Boston, Lucy Maria, 1892–1990, vol. VIII

Boswall, Sir George Lauderdale H.; *see* Houstoun-Boswall.

Boswall, Sir George Reginald H.; *see* Houstoun-Boswall.

Boswall, Major Sir Gordon H.; *see* Houstoun-Boswall.

Boswall, Sir Thomas H.; *see* Houstoun-Boswall.

Boswall, Sir (Thomas) Randolph H.; *see* Houstoun-Boswall.

Boswall, Sir William Evelyn H.; *see* Houstoun-Boswall.

Boswell, Alexander Bruce, 1884–1962, vol. VI

Boswell, Arthur Radcliffe, *born* 1838, vol. II

Boswell, Maj.-Gen. John James, 1835–1908, vol. I

Boswell, Captain Lennox Albert Knox, 1898–1975, vol. VII

Boswell, Percy George Hamnall, 1886–1960, vol. V

Bosworth, George Herbert, 1896–1979, vol. VII

Bosworth, George Simms, 1916–1986, vol. VIII

Bosworth, Col William John, 1858–1923, vol. II

Bosworth-Smith, Nevil Digby, 1886–1964, vol. VI

Bosworth Smith, Reginald Montagu, 1872–1944, vol. IV

Boteler, Sir Edgar Collins Boehm, 2nd Bt, 1869–1928, vol. II

Botha, Colin Graham, 1883–1973, vol. VII

Botha, Rt Hon. Louis, 1863–1919, vol. II

Botham, Arthur William, 1874–1963, vol. VI

Bothamley, Rev. Hilton, *died* 1919, vol. II

Bothamley, Rev. Canon Westley, 1861–1933, vol. III
Bothe, Walther Wilhelm Georg Franz, 1891–1957, vol. V
Bott, Alan John, *died* 1952, vol. V
Bott, Lt-Col Robert Henry, 1882–1938, vol. III
Botteley, James, *born* 1839, vol. III
Botterell, Percy Dumville, 1880–1952, vol. V
Bottome, Phyllis, (Mrs A. E. Forbes Dennis), 1884–1963, vol. VI
Bottomley, Albert Ernest, 1873–1950, vol. IV
Bottomley, Sir Cecil; *see* Bottomley, Sir W. C.
Bottomley, Edwin, *died* 1929, vol. III
Bottomley, Gordon, 1874–1948, vol. IV
Bottomley, Col Herbert, 1866–1926, vol. II (A), vol. III
Bottomley, James H., 1857–1934, vol. III
Bottomley, James Thomson, 1845–1926, vol. II
Bottomley, John Mellor, 1888–1960, vol. V (A)
Bottomley, Air Chief Marshal Sir Norman Howard, 1891–1970, vol. VI
Bottomley, William Beecroft, 1863–1922, vol. II
Bottomley, Sir (William) Cecil, 1878–1954, vol. V
Bottrall, (Francis James) Ronald, 1906–1989, vol. VIII
Bottrall, Ronald; *see* Bottrall, F. J. R.
Boucaut, Hon. Sir James Penn, 1831–1916, vol. II
Bouch, Thomas, 1882–1963, vol. VI
Bouchard, Hon. T. Damien, *died* 1962, vol. VI
Bouche-Leclercq, Auguste, 1842–1923, vol. II
Boucher, Lt-Col Benjamin Hamilton, 1864–1928, vol. II
Boucher, Rev. Charles Estcourt, 1856–1940, vol. III
Boucher, Maj.-Gen. Sir Charles Hamilton, 1898–1951, vol. V
Boucher, Rear-Adm. Maitland Walter Sabine, 1888–1963, vol. VI
Boucher, Maj.-Gen. Valentine, 1904–1961, vol. VI
Boucherett, Emilia Jessie, 1825–1905, vol. I
Bouchier, Air Vice-Marshal Sir Cecil Arthur, 1895–1979, vol. VII
Boucicault, Dion, 1859–1929, vol. III
Boughey, Rev. Anchitel Harry Fletcher, 1849–1936, vol. III
Boughey, Charles Lovell Fletcher, 1887–1934, vol. III
Boughey, Sir Francis, 8th Bt, 1848–1927, vol. II
Boughey, Rev. Sir George, 5th Bt, 1837–1910, vol. I
Boughey, Col George Fletcher Ottley, 1844–1918, vol. II
Boughey, Sir George Menteth, 9th Bt, 1879–1959, vol. V
Boughey, Maj.-Gen. John, 1845–1932, vol. III
Boughey, Sir Richard James, 10th Bt, 1925–1978, vol. VII
Boughey, Rev. Sir Robert, 7th Bt, 1843–1921, vol. II
Boughey, Sir Thomas Fletcher, 4th Bt, 1836–1906, vol. I
Boughey, Sir William Fletcher, 6th Bt, 1840–1912, vol. I
Boughton, Rev. Canon Charles Henry Knowler, 1883–1943, vol. IV
Boughton, Sir Charles Henry Rouse-, 11th Bt, 1825–1906, vol. I
Boughton, Sir Edward Hotham Rouse-, 13th Bt, 1893–1963, vol. VI

Boughton, George Henry, 1833–1905, vol. I
Boughton, Michael Linnell Gerald, 1925–1990, vol. VIII
Boughton, Rutland, 1878–1960, vol. V
Boughton, Sir William St Andrew Rouse-, 12th Bt, 1853–1937, vol. III
Boughton-Knight, Charles Andrew R.; *see* Rouse-Boughton-Knight.
Bougle, C., *died* 1940, vol. III
Bouguereau, Adolphe William, 1825–1905, vol. I
Boulanger, Nadia Juliette, 1887–1979, vol. VII
Bould, John, 1855–1938, vol. III
Boulden, Rev. Alfred William, 1849–1920, vol. II
Boulenger, Charles L., 1885–1940, vol. III
Boulenger, Edward George, 1888–1946, vol. IV
Boulenger, George Albert, *died* 1937, vol. III
Boulger, Demetrius Charles, 1853–1928, vol. II
Boulger, Dorothy Henrietta, 1847–1923, vol. II
Boulger, George Simonds, 1853–1922, vol. II
Boulnois, Charles, 1832–1912, vol. II
Boulnois, Edmund, 1838–1911, vol. I
Boult, Sir Adrian Cedric, 1889–1983, vol. VIII
Boulter, Eric Thomas, 1917–1989, vol. VIII
Boulter, Rev. Canon John Sidney, 1890–1969, vol. VI
Boulter, Robert, 1885–1973, vol. VII
Boulter, Stanley Carr, 1852–1917, vol. II
Boulter, Rev. Walter Easton, 1874–1936, vol. III
Boulting, John Edward, 1913–1985, vol. VIII
Boulton, A. C. Forster, 1862–1949, vol. IV
Boulton, Lt-Col Aubrey Holmes, 1882–1932, vol. III
Boulton, Major Charles Percy, 1867–1916, vol. II
Boulton, Sir (Denis Duncan) Harold (Owen), 3rd Bt (*cr* 1905), 1892–1968, vol. VI
Boulton, Edward Henry Brooke, 1897–1982, vol. VIII
Boulton, Major Sir Edward John, 2nd Bt (*cr* 1944), 1907–1982, vol. VIII
Boulton, Maj.-Gen. Harold, 1872–1955, vol. V
Boulton, Sir Harold; *see* Boulton, Sir D. D. H. O.
Boulton, Sir Harold Edwin, 2nd Bt (*cr* 1905), 1859–1935, vol. III
Boulton, Norman Savage, 1899–1984, vol. VIII
Boulton, Percy, 1840–1909, vol. I
Boulton, Sir Samuel Bagster, 1st Bt (*cr* 1905), 1830–1918, vol. II
Boulton, Sidney, 1855–1932, vol. III
Boulton, Very Rev. Walter, 1901–1984, vol. VIII
Boulton, William Savage, 1867–1954, vol. V
Boulton, Sir William Whytehead, 1st Bt (*cr* 1944), 1873–1949, vol. IV
Boumphrey, Geoffrey Maxwell, 1894–1969, vol. VI
Bouquet, Rev. Alan Coates, 1884–1976, vol. VII
Bourcard, Gustave Amaury René, 1846–1925, vol. II (A), vol. III
Bourcart, Charles Daniel, 1860–1940, vol. III
Bourchier, Arthur, 1864–1927, vol. II
Bourchier, Rev. Basil Graham, 1881–1934, vol. III
Bourchier, Lt-Gen. Eustace Fane, 1822–1902, vol. I
Bourchier, Sir George, 1821–1898, vol. I
Bourchier, James David, 1850–1920, vol. II
Bourchier, Col Hon. Murray William James, 1881–1937, vol. III
Bourchier, Violet, (Mrs Arthur Bourchier); *see* Vanbrugh, Violet.

Bourchier, Very Rev. William Chadwick, *died* 1924, vol. II

Bourdelle, Antoine; *see* Bourdelle, E. A.

Bourdelle, (Emile) Antoine, 1861–1929, vol. III

Bourdillon, Sir Bernard Henry, 1883–1948, vol. IV

Bourdillon, Francis Bernard, 1883–1970, vol. VI

Bourdillon, Francis William, 1852–1921, vol. II

Bourdillon, Sir James Austin, 1848–1913, vol. I

Bourdillon, Lancelot Gerard, 1888–1950, vol. IV

Bourdillon, Robert Benedict, 1889–1971, vol. VII

Bourgeois, Emile, 1857–1934, vol. III

Bourgeois, Jeanne; *see* Mistinguett.

Bourgeois, Léon Victor Auguste, 1851–1925, vol. II

Bourget, Paul, 1852–1935, vol. III

Bourinot, Sir John George, 1837–1903, vol. I

Bourke, Hon. Algernon Henry, 1854–1922, vol. II

Bourke, Ven. Cecil Frederick Joseph, *died* 1910, vol. I

Bourke, Edmund, 1857–1939, vol. III

Bourke, Maj.-Gen. Sir George Deane, 1852–1936, vol. III

Bourke, Rev. Hon. George Wingfield, 1829–1903, vol. I

Bourke, Major Sir Harry L.; *see* Legge-Bourke.

Bourke, Lt-Col Henry Beresford, 1855–1921, vol. II

Bourke, John Francis, 1889–1967, vol. VI

Bourke, Lt-Col John Joseph, 1865–1933, vol. III

Bourke, Matthew J., *died* 1936, vol. III

Bourke, Hon. Maurice Archibald, 1853–1900, vol. I

Bourke, Sir Paget John, 1906–1983, vol. VIII

Bourke, Lt-Comdr Roland, 1885–1958, vol. V

Bourke, Hon. Terence Theobald, 1865–1923, vol. II

Bourke, Gp Captain Ulick John Deane, 1884–1948, vol. IV

Bourke-White, Margaret, 1906–1971, vol. VII

Bourne, Baron (Life Peer); Geoffrey Kemp Bourne, 1902–1982, vol. VIII

Bourne, Gen. Sir Alan George Barwys, 1882–1967, vol. VI

Bourne, Aleck William, 1886–1974, vol. VII

Bourne, Sir Alfred Gibbs, 1859–1940, vol. III

Bourne, Rev. Charles William, 1846–1927, vol. II

Bourne, Edward John, 1922–1974, vol. VII

Bourne, His Eminence Cardinal Francis, 1861–1935, vol. III

Bourne, Sir Frederick Chalmers, 1891–1977, vol. VII

Bourne, Sir Frederick Samuel Augustus, 1854–1940, vol. III

Bourne, Geoffrey, 1893–1970, vol. VI

Bourne, Lt Col Geoffrey Howard, 1909–1988, vol. VIII

Bourne, George; *see* Sturt, G.

Bourne, Rev. George Hugh, *died* 1925, vol. II

Bourne, Gilbert Charles, 1861–1933, vol. III

Bourne, Sir (Henry) Roland (Murray), 1874–1931, vol. III

Bourne, Hugh Clarence, *died* 1909, vol. I

Bourne, Kenneth Morison, 1893–1968, vol. VI

Bourne, Captain Rt Hon. Robert Croft, 1888–1938, vol. III

Bourne, Sir Roland; *see* Bourne, Sir H. R. M.

Bourne, Stafford, 1900–1986, vol. VIII

Bourne, Thomas Johnstone, 1864–1947, vol. IV

Bourne, Rev. William St Hill, 1846–1929, vol. III

Bourns, Newcome Whitelaw, *died* 1927, vol. II

Bousfield, Edward George Paul, 1880–1957, vol. V

Bousfield, Guy William John, 1893–1974, vol. VII

Bousfield, Rt Rev. Henry Brougham, 1832–1902, vol. I

Bousfield, Lt-Col Henry Richings, 1863–1930, vol. III

Bousfield, Col Hugh Delabere, 1872–1951, vol. V

Bousfield, Sir William, 1842–1910, vol. I

Bousfield, William Robert, 1854–1943, vol. IV

Boussac, Marcel, 1889–1980, vol. VII

Boustead, Rev. Canon Harry Wilson, 1858–1942, vol. IV

Boustead, Col Sir Hugh; *see* Boustead, Col Sir J. E. H.

Boustead, Col Sir (John Edmund) Hugh, 1895–1980, vol. VII

Boutens, Dr Peter Cornelis, 1870–1943, vol. IV

Boutflour, Robert, 1890–1961, vol. VI

Boutflower, Rt Rev. Cecil Henry, 1863–1942, vol. IV

Boutflower, Rev. Douglas Samuel, *died* 1940, vol. III

Boutroux, Emile, 1845–1921, vol. II

Boutwood, Rear-Adm. Laurence Arthur, 1898–1982, vol. VIII

Bouveret, Pascal Adolph Jean D.; *see* Dagnan-Bouveret.

Bouverie, Rev. Hon. Bertrand P.; *see* Pleydell-Bouverie.

Bouverie, Hon. Duncombe P.; *see* Pleydell-Bouverie.

Bouverie, Col Hon. Stuart P.; *see* Pleydell-Bouverie.

Bouverie-Pusey, Philip Francis, *died* 1933, vol. III

Bovell, Sir (Conrad Swire) Kerr, 1913–1973, vol. VII

Bovell, Sir Henry Alleyne, 1854–1938, vol. III

Bovell, Vice-Adm. Henry Cecil, 1893–1963, vol. VI

Bovell, John Redman, 1855–1928, vol. II (A), vol. III

Bovell, Sir Kerr; *see* Bovell, Sir C. S. K.

Bovell-Jones, Thomas Boughton, 1906–1967, vol. VI

Bovenschen, Sir Frederick Carl, 1884–1977, vol. VII

Bovey, Henry Taylor, *died* 1912, vol. I

Bovill, Major Anthony Charles Stevens, 1888–1943, vol. IV

Bovill, Charles Harry, 1878–1918, vol. II

Bovill, Edward William, 1892–1966, vol. VI

Boville, Thomas Cooper, 1860–1948, vol. IV

Bowater, Sir Dudley; *see* Bowater, Sir T. D. B.

Bowater, Sir Eric Vansittart, 1895–1962, vol. VI

Bowater, Major Sir Frank Henry, 1st Bt (*cr* 1939), 1866–1947, vol. IV

Bowater, Sir Frederick William, 1867–1924, vol. II

Bowater, Sir Ian Frank, 1904–1982, vol. VIII

Bowater, Sir Noël Vansittart, 2nd Bt (*cr* 1939) 1892–1984, vol. VIII

Bowater, Sir Rainald Vansittart, 2nd Bt (*cr* 1914), 1888–1945, vol. IV

Bowater, Sir (Thomas) Dudley Blennerhassett, 3rd Bt (*cr* 1914), 1889–1972, vol. VII

Bowater, Sir (Thomas) Vansittart, 1st Bt (*cr* 1914), 1862–1938, vol. III

Bowater, Sir Vansittart; *see* Bowater, Sir T. V.

Bowater, Sir William Henry, 1855–1932, vol. III

Bowcher, Frank, *died* 1938, vol. III

Bowdell, Wilfred, 1913–1989, vol. VIII

Bowden, Baron (Life Peer); Bertram Vivian Bowden, 1910–1989, vol. VIII

Bowden, Maj. Aubrey Henry, 1895–1987, vol. VIII

Bowden, Sir Frank, 1st Bt, 1848–1921, vol. II

Bowden, Captain Frank Lake, 1863–1906, vol. I
Bowden, Frank Philip, 1903–1968, vol. VI
Bowden, Major George Robert Harland, 1873–1927, vol. II
Bowden, Rev. Canon Guy Arthur George, 1909–1974, vol. VII
Bowden, Sir Harold, 2nd Bt, 1880–1960, vol. V
Bowden, Col James Hubert Thomas C.; see Cornish-Bowden.
Bowden, Lt-Col John, died 1948, vol. IV
Bowden, Kenneth Frank, 1916–1989, vol. VIII
Bowden, Norman Henry Martin, 1879–1968, vol. VI
Bowden, Richard Charles, 1887–1988, vol. VIII
Bowden, Vivian Gordon, 1884–1942, vol. IV
Bowden, Walter, 1859–1919, vol. II
Bowden, William Douglas, 1875–1944, vol. IV
Bowden-Smith, Adm. Sir Nathaniel, 1838–1921, vol. II
Bowden Smith, Vice-Adm. William, 1874–1962, vol. VI
Bowdler, Audley; see Bowdler, W. A.
Bowdler, Lt-Col Basil Wilfred Bowdler, 1873–1960, vol. V
Bowdler, Col Cyril William Bowdler, 1839–1918, vol. II
Bowdler, (William) Audley, 1884–1969, vol. VI
Bowdler-Henry, Cyril; see Henry.
Bowdon, John Erdeswick B.; see Butler-Bowdon.
Bowell, Hon. Sir Mackenzie, 1823–1917, vol. II
Bowen, Sir Albert, 1st Bt, 1858–1924, vol. II
Bowen, Lt-Col Alfred John Hamilton, 1885–1917, vol. II
Bowen, Arthur Charles M.; see Mainwaring-Bowen.
Bowen, Col Arthur Winniett Nunn, died 1964, vol. VI
Bowen, Catherine Drinker, died 1973, vol. VII
Bowen, Hon. Sir Charles Christopher, 1830–1917, vol. II
Bowen, Major Charles Otway Cole, 1867–1910, vol. I
Bowen, Rev. David, died 1928, vol. II (A), vol. III
Bowen, David, 1885–1950, vol. IV
Bowen, Edmund John, 1898–1980, vol. VII
Bowen, Major Sir Edward Crowther, 2nd Bt, 1885–1937, vol. III
Bowen, Edward Ernest, 1836–1901, vol. I
Bowen, Elizabeth Dorothea Cole, 1899–1973, vol. VII
Bowen, Sir George Bevan, 1858–1940, vol. III
Bowen, Rt Hon. Sir George Ferguson, 1821–1899, vol. I
Bowen, Col Herbert Walter, 1870–1944, vol. IV
Bowen, Col Hildred Edward W.; see Webb-Bowen.
Bowen, Horace George, died 1902, vol. I
Bowen, Ian; see Bowen, Ivor I.
Bowen, Ira Sprague, 1898–1973, vol. VII
Bowen, Ivor, died 1934, vol. III
Bowen, Ivor, 1902–1984, vol. VIII
Bowen, (Ivor) Ian, 1908–1984, vol. VIII
Bowen, James Bevan, 1828–1905, vol. I
Bowen, Air Cdre James Bevan, 1883–1969, vol. VI
Bowen, Sir John Cuthbert Grenside, 1860–1932, vol. III
Bowen, Sir John Edward Mortimer, 3rd Bt, 1918–1939, vol. III
Bowen, Sir John Poland, died 1955, vol. V

Bowen, Sir (John) William, 1876–1965, vol. VI
Bowen, Majorie; see Long, M. G.
Bowen, Norman Levi, 1887–1956, vol. V
Bowen, Owen, 1873–1967, vol. VI
Bowen, Sir Thomas Frederic Charles, 4th Bt, 1921–1989, vol. VIII
Bowen, Air Vice-Marshal Sir Tom Ince W.; see Webb-Bowen.
Bowen, Trevor Alfred, died 1964, vol. VI
Bowen, Sir William; see Bowen, Sir J. W.
Bowen, Lt-Col William Allan, 1879–1937, vol. III
Bowen, Hon. and Rev. William Edward, 1862–1938, vol. III
Bowen, William Henry, died 1963, vol. VI
Bowen, William Herbert, 1843–1937, vol. III
Bowen, Maj.-Gen. William Oswald, 1898–1961, vol. VI
Bowen, York, 1884–1961, vol. VI
Bowen-Buscarlet, Air Vice-Marshal Sir Willett Amalric Bowen, 1898–1967, vol. VI
Bowen-Davies, Alan, 1907–1974, vol. VII
Bowen-Jones, Sir John Bowen; see Jones.
Bowen-Rowlands, Ernest Brown, 1866–1951, vol. V
Bower, Sir Alfred Louis, 1st Bt, 1858–1948, vol. IV
Bower, Sir Edmund Ernest N.; see Nott-Bower.
Bower, Sir Frank, 1894–1982, vol. VIII
Bower, Frederick Orpen, 1855–1948, vol. IV
Bower, Lt-Col George Haddon, 1871–1950, vol. IV (A)
Bower, George Spencer, 1854–1928, vol. II
Bower, Sir Graham John, 1848–1933, vol. III
Bower, Maj.-Gen. Sir Hamilton, 1858–1940, vol. III
Bower, Sir John D.; see Dykes Bower.
Bower, Comdr John Graham, 1886–1940, vol. III
Bower, Sir John Reginald Hornby N.; see Nott-Bower.
Bower, Norman, 1907–1990, vol. VIII
Bower, Sir Percival, 1880–1948, vol. IV
Bower, Rev. Richard, 1845–1911, vol. I
Bower, Major Sir Robert Lister, 1860–1929, vol. III
Bower, Comdr Robert Tatton, 1894–1975, vol. VII
Bower, Lt-Gen. Sir Roger Herbert, 1903–1990, vol. VIII
Bower, Sir (William) Guy N.; see Nott-Bower.
Bower, Captain Sir William N.; see Nott-Bower.
Bowerbank, Sir Fred Thompson, 1880–1960, vol. V
Bowering, John, 1894–1973, vol. VII
Bowerley, Amelia M., died 1916, vol. II
Bowerley, Walter, 1876–1952, vol. V
Bowerman, Rt Hon. Charles William, 1851–1947, vol. IV
Bowerman, Brig. John Francis, 1893–1983, vol. VIII
Bowers, Sir Edward Hardman, 1854–1914, vol. I
Bowers, Frederick Gatus, 1882–1937, vol. III
Bowers, Rt Rev. John Phillips Allcot, 1854–1926, vol. II
Bowers, Ven. Percy Harris, 1856–1922, vol. II
Bowers, Col Percy Lloyd, 1879–1943, vol. IV
Bowes, Frederick, 1867–1958, vol. V
Bowes, Sir (Harold) Leslie, 1893–1988, vol. VIII
Bowes, Col Hugh, died 1952, vol. V
Bowes, Sir Leslie; see Bowes, Sir H. L.
Bowes, Robert Kenneth, 1904–1958, vol. V
Bowes, Brig.-Gen. William Hely, 1858–1932, vol. III

Bowes-Lyon, Hon. Sir David, 1902–1961, vol. VI
Bowes-Lyon, Hon. Francis, 1856–1948, vol. IV
Bowes-Lyon, Maj.-Gen. Sir (Francis) James (Cecil), 1917–1977, vol. VII
Bowes-Lyon, Captain Geoffrey Francis, 1886–1951, vol. V
Bowes-Lyon, Maj.-Gen. Sir James; *see* Bowes-Lyon, Maj.-Gen. Sir F. J. C.
Bowes-Lyon, Hon. John, 1886–1930, vol. III
Bowes-Lyon, Hon. Michael Claude Hamilton, 1893–1953, vol. V
Bowes Lyon, Captain Ronald George, 1893–1960, vol. V
Bowhill, Air Chief Marshal Sir Frederick William, 1880–1960, vol. V
Bowie, James Alexander, 1888–1949, vol. IV
Bowie, John, *died* 1941, vol. IV
Bowie, Robert Forbes, 1860–1940, vol. III
Bowie, Sir William Tait, 1876–1949, vol. IV
Bowker, Sir James; *see* Bowker, Sir R. J.
Bowker, Sir Leslie Cecil Blackmore, *died* 1965, vol. VI
Bowker, Sir (Reginald) James, 1901–1983, vol. VIII
Bowker, Lt-Col William James, 1869–1931, vol. III
Bowlby, Sir Anthony Alfred, 1st Bt, 1855–1929, vol. III
Bowlby, Arthur Salvin, 1872–1932, vol. III
Bowlby, Captain Cuthbert Francis Bond, 1895–1969, vol. VI
Bowlby, (Edward) John (Mostyn), 1907–1990, vol. VIII
Bowlby, Hon. Mrs Geoffrey, (Lettice), 1885–1988, vol. VIII
Bowlby, Rev. Henry Thomas, 1864–1940, vol. III
Bowlby, John; *see* Bowlby, E. J. M.
Bowlby, Hon. Lettice; *see* Bowlby, Hon. Mrs Geoffrey.
Bowle, Horace Edgar, 1886–1978, vol. VII
Bowle, John Edward, 1905–1985, vol. VIII
Bowle-Evans, Maj.-Gen. Charles Harford, 1867–1942, vol. IV
Bowler, Air Vice-Marshal Thomas Geoffrey, 1895–1974, vol. VII
Bowles, Baron (Life Peer); Francis George Bowles, 1902–1970, vol. VI
Bowles, Dame Ann P.; *see* Parker-Bowles.
Bowles, Chester, 1901–1986, vol. VIII
Bowles, Maj.-Gen. Frederick Augustus, 1851–1931, vol. III
Bowles, Maj.-Gen. Frederick Gilbert, *died* 1947, vol. IV
Bowles, George Frederic Stewart, 1877–1955, vol. V
Bowles, Hon. Brig.-Gen. Henry, 1854–1932, vol. III
Bowles, Sir Henry Ferryman, 1st Bt, 1858–1943, vol. IV
Bowles, Thomas Gibson, 1844–1922, vol. II
Bowley, Sir Arthur Lyon, 1869–1957, vol. V
Bowling, Paymaster-in-Chief Thomas Henry Lovelace, 1839–1922, vol. II
Bowling, Air Vice-Marshal Victor Swanton, 1908–1971, vol. VII
Bowly, Rev. Charles Henry, 1845–1913, vol. I
Bowly, Col William Arthur Travell, 1880–1957, vol. V

Bowman, Alexander, *died* 1941, vol. IV
Bowman, Archibald Allan, 1883–1936, vol. III
Bowman, Herbert Lister, 1874–1942, vol. IV
Bowman, Humphrey Ernest, 1879–1965, vol. VI
Bowman, Isaiah, 1878–1950, vol. IV
Bowman, Sir James, 1st Bt, 1898–1978, vol. VII
Bowman, Laurence George, 1866–1950, vol. IV
Bowman, Rev. Sir Paget Mervyn, 3rd Bt, 1873–1955, vol. V
Bowman, Patrick; *see* Bowman, T. P.
Bowman, Robert Ritchie, 1883–1970, vol. VI (AII)
Bowman, Thomas, *died* 1945, vol. IV
Bowman, (Thomas) Patrick, 1915–1987, vol. VIII
Bowman, Sir William Paget, 2nd Bt, 1845–1917, vol. II
Bowman-Manifold, Maj.-Gen. Sir (Michael) Graham Egerton; *see* Manifold.
Bown, Rev. George Herbert, 1871–1918, vol. II
Bowra, Cecil Arthur Verner, 1869–1947, vol. IV
Bowra, Sir (Cecil) Maurice, 1898–1971, vol. VII
Bowra, Sir Maurice; *see* Bowra, Sir C. M.
Bowran, Rev. John George, 1869–1946, vol. IV
Bowring, Sir Charles Calvert, 1872–1945, vol. IV
Bowring, Sir (Charles) Clement, 1844–1907, vol. I
Bowring, Sir Clement; *see* Bowring, Sir C. C.
Bowring, Edgar Alfred, 1826–1911, vol. I
Bowring, Rev. Edgar Francis, 1854–1931, vol. III
Bowring, Hon. Sir Edgar Rennie, 1858–1943, vol. IV
Bowring, Edgar Rennie, 1899–1982, vol. VIII
Bowring, Sir Frederick Charles, 1857–1936, vol. III
Bowring, Col Frederick Thomas Nelson Spratt, 1847–1934, vol. III
Bowring, Adm. Humphrey Wykeham, 1874–1952, vol. V
Bowring, Lewin Bentham, 1824–1910, vol. I
Bowring, Theodore Louis, 1901–1967, vol. VI
Bowring, Sir Thomas Benjamin, 1847–1915, vol. I
Bowring, Walter Andrew, 1875–1950, vol. IV
Bowring, Walter Armiger, 1874–1931, vol. III
Bowring, Sir William Benjamin, 1st Bt, 1837–1916, vol. II
Bowron, Sir Edward, 1857–1923, vol. II
Bowser, Ernest William, 1887–1969, vol. VI (AII)
Bowser, Hon. Sir John, 1856–1936, vol. III
Bowser, Rev. Sidney W., 1853–1928, vol. II
Bowser, William John, 1867–1933, vol. III
Bowstead, Rev. Canon Christopher J. K., 1844–1924, vol. II
Bowstead, John, 1897–1969, vol. VI
Bowyear, Vice-Adm. George le Geyt, 1817–1903, vol. I
Bowyear, Henry William Thomas, 1852–1936, vol. III
Bowyer, Sir Eric Blacklock, 1902–1964, vol. VI
Bowyer, Sir George Henry, 9th and 5th Bt, 1870–1950, vol. IV
Bowyer, John Francis, 1893–1974, vol. VII
Bowyer-Smijth, Sir William; *see* Smijth.
Bowyer-Smyth, Sir Alfred John; *see* Smyth.
Bowyer-Smyth, Captain Sir Philip Weyland; *see* Smyth.
Box, Charles Richard, *died* 1951, vol. V
Box, Rev. George Herbert, 1869–1933, vol. III
Box, Sydney, 1907–1983, vol. VIII

Boxall, Sir Alleyne Alfred, 1st Bt, 1855–1927, vol. II
Boxall, Col Sir Alleyne Percival, 2nd Bt, 1882–1945, vol. IV
Boxall, Col Sir Charles Gervaise, 1852–1914, vol. I
Boxall, William Percival Gratwicke, 1848–1931, vol. III
Boxer, (Charles) Mark (Edward), 1931–1988, vol. VIII
Boxer, Maj.-Gen. Edward M., *died* 1898, vol. I
Boxer, Rear-Adm. Henry Percy, 1885–1961, vol. VI
Boxer, Captain Herbert Martyn, 1882–1962, vol. VI
Boxer, Mark; *see* Boxer, C. M. E.
Boxshall, Col Henry Edwin, 1863–1936, vol. III
Boxwell, Lt-Col Ambrose, 1876–1959, vol. V
Boyagian, Henry Samuel Rogers, 1875–1947, vol. IV
Boyce, Arthur Cyril, 1867–1942, vol. IV
Boyce, Austin Alexander Rodney, 1870–1948, vol. IV (A)
Boyce, Col Charles Edward, 1882–1963, vol. VI
Boyce, Air Vice-Marshal Clayton Descou Clement, 1907–1987, vol. VIII
Boyce, Ven. Francis Bertie, 1884–1931, vol. III
Boyce, Francis Stewart, 1872–1940, vol. III
Boyce, Air Cdre George Harold, 1894–1975, vol. VII
Boyce, Gilbert L.; *see* Leighton-Boyce, Guy G.
Boyce, Guy Gilbert L.; *see* Leighton-Boyce.
Boyce, Sir (Harold) Leslie, 1st Bt, 1895–1955, vol. V
Boyce, Brig.-Gen. Harry Augustus, 1870–1954, vol. V
Boyce, Sir Leslie; *see* Boyce, Sir H. L.
Boyce, Sir Richard Leslie, 2nd Bt, 1929–1968, vol. VI
Boyce, Robert Henry, 1834–1909, vol. I
Boyce, Sir Rubert William, 1863–1911, vol. I
Boyce, Sarah, 1863–1939, vol. III
Boyce, Rev. Walter, 1853–1936, vol. III
Boyce, Maj.-Gen. Sir William George Bertram, 1868–1937, vol. III
Boycott, Arthur Edwin, 1877–1938, vol. III
Boycott, Rev. Desmond M.; *see* Morse-Boycott.
Boycott, Lt-Col T. A. W.; *see* Wight-Boycott.
Boyd of Merton, 1st Viscount, 1904–1983, vol. VIII
Boyd, Alexander Michael, 1905–1973, vol. VII
Boyd, Alexander Stuart, 1854–1930, vol. III
Boyd, Sir Alexander William K.; *see* Keown-Boyd.
Boyd, Alfred Ernest, *died* 1949, vol. IV
Boyd, Very Rev. Andrew Kennedy Hutchison, 1825–1899, vol. I
Boyd, Sir Archibald John, 1888–1959, vol. V
Boyd, Ven. Charles, 1842–1914, vol. I
Boyd, Col Charles Augustus R.; *see* Rochfort-Boyd.
Boyd, Charles Walter, 1869–1919, vol. II
Boyd, David Runciman, 1872–1955, vol. V
Boyd, Adm. Sir Denis William, 1891–1965, vol. VI
Boyd, Sir Donald James, 1877–1953, vol. V
Boyd, Douglas Thornley, 1896–1964, vol. VI
Boyd, Edmund Blaikie, 1894–1946, vol. IV
Boyd, Edward Charles Percy, 1871–1949, vol. IV
Boyd, Ernest, 1887–1946, vol. IV
Boyd, Francis Darby, 1866–1922, vol. II
Boyd, Rev. Francis Leith, 1856–1927, vol. II
Boyd, Frank M., 1863–1950, vol. IV
Boyd, Maj.-Gen. Sir Gerald Farrell, 1877–1930, vol. III
Boyd, Rev. Halbert Johnstone, 1872–1957, vol. V

Boyd, Sir Harry Robert, 1876–1940, vol. III
Boyd, Henry, 1831–1922, vol. II
Boyd, Henry, *died* 1942, vol. IV
Boyd, Lt-Col Henry Alexander, 1877–1943, vol. IV
Boyd, Lt-Col Henry Charles R.; *see* Rochfort-Boyd.
Boyd, Rev. Herbert Buchanan, *died* 1941, vol. IV
Boyd, Maj.-Gen. Ian Herbert Fitzgerald, 1907–1978, vol. VII
Boyd, James, 1888–1944, vol. IV
Boyd, James, 1888–1963, vol. VI
Boyd, James, *died* 1970, vol. VI
Boyd, James Dixon, 1907–1968, vol. VI
Boyd, Sir John, *died* 1967, vol. VI
Boyd, Hon. Sir John Alexander, 1837–1916, vol. II
Boyd, Col John Alexander, 1857–1931, vol. III
Boyd, Sir John McFarlane, 1917–1989, vol. VIII
Boyd, Sir John Smith, 1886–1963, vol. VI
Boyd, Brig. Sir John Smith Knox, 1891–1981, vol. VIII
Boyd, Maj.-Gen. Julius Middleton, 1837–1919, vol. II
Boyd, Lachlan Macpherson, 1904–1980, vol. VII
Boyd, Martin à Beckett, 1893–1972, vol. VII
Boyd, Mary Stuart, *died* 1937, vol. III
Boyd, Maurice James, 1911–1979, vol. VII
Boyd, Col Mossom Archibald, 1860–1943, vol. IV
Boyd, Air Vice-Marshal Owen Tudor, 1889–1944, vol. IV
Boyd, Robert, 1890–1959, vol. V
Boyd, Rt Rev. Robert McNeil, 1890–1958, vol. V
Boyd, Ven. Robert Wallace, *died* 1921, vol. II
Boyd, Sidney Arthur, 1880–1966, vol. VI
Boyd, Ven. Sydney Adolphus, 1857–1947, vol. IV
Boyd, Col Thomas Crawford, 1886–1967, vol. VI
Boyd, Thomas Herbert, 1890–1941, vol. IV
Boyd, Thomas J. L. Stirling, 1886–1973, vol. VII
Boyd, Sir Thomas Jamieson, 1818–1902, vol. I
Boyd, Rt Hon. Sir Walter, 1st Bt, 1833–1918, vol. II
Boyd, Sir Walter Herbert, 2nd Bt, 1867–1948, vol. IV
Boyd, William, 1867–1961, vol. VI (AII)
Boyd, William, 1874–1962, vol. VI
Boyd, William, 1885–1984, vol. VIII
Boyd, Rev. William Grenville, 1867–1941, vol. IV
Boyd Carpenter, Major Sir Archibald Boyd, 1873–1937, vol. III
Boyd-Carpenter, Henry John, 1865–1923, vol. II
Boyd-Carpenter, Captain John Peers, 1871–1936, vol. III
Boyd Carpenter, Rt Rev. William, 1841–1918, vol. II
Boyd-Moss, Brig.-Gen. Lionel Boyd, 1875–1940, vol. III
Boyd Neel, Louis; *see* Neel.
Boyd Orr, 1st Baron, 1880–1971, vol. VII
Boyd-Rochfort, Sir Cecil Charles, 1887–1983, vol. VIII
Boyd-Rochfort, Captain George Arthur, 1880–1940, vol. III
Boyd-Wilson, Edwin John, 1886–1973, vol. VII
Boyden, Rev. A. H., *died* 1940, vol. III (A), vol. IV
Boyer, Hon. Arthur, 1851–1922, vol. II
Boyer, Rear-Adm. (S) George Christopher Aubin, 1862–1949, vol. IV
Boyer, Sir Richard James Fildes, 1891–1961, vol. VI
Boyes, Charles Edward, 1866–1920, vol. II

Boyes, Sir George Thomas Henry, *died* 1910, vol. I

Boyes, Rear-Adm. Hector, 1881–1960, vol. V

Boyes, John, 1912–1985, vol. VIII

Boyes, Maj.-Gen. John Edward, 1843–1915, vol. I

Boyes, John Henry, 1886–1958, vol. V

Boyle of Handsworth, Baron (Life Peer); Edward Charles Gurney Boyle, 1923–1981, vol. VIII

Boyle, Sir Alexander George, 1872–1943, vol. IV

Boyle, Adm. Hon. Sir Algernon Douglas Edward Harry, 1871–1949, vol. IV

Boyle, Air Cdre Archibald Robert, 1887–1949, vol. IV

Boyle, (Arthur) Brian, 1913–1965, vol. VI

Boyle, Brian; *see* Boyle, A. B.

Boyle, Sir Cavendish, 1849–1916, vol. II

Boyle, Col Cecil Alexander, 1888–1941, vol. IV

Boyle, Sir Courtenay, 1845–1901, vol. I

Boyle, Daniel, 1859–1925, vol. II

Boyle, Rev. Desmond; *see* Boyle, Rev. J. D.

Boyle, Sir Edward, 1st Bt, 1849–1909, vol. I

Boyle, Sir Edward, 2nd Bt, 1878–1945, vol. IV

Boyle, Rear-Adm. Edward Courtney, 1883–1967, vol. VI

Boyle, Comdr Edward Louis Dalrymple, 1864–1923, vol. II

Boyle, Very Rev. George David, 1828–1901, vol. I

Boyle, Harry, 1863–1937, vol. III

Boyle, Captain Harry Lumsden, *died* 1955, vol. V

Boyle, Henry Edmund Gaskin, 1875–1941, vol. IV

Boyle, Captain James, 1850–1931, vol. III

Boyle, James, 1863–1936, vol. III

Boyle, John Andrew, 1916–1978, vol. VII

Boyle, Air Cdre Hon. John David, 1884–1974, vol. VII

Boyle, Rev. (John) Desmond, 1897–1982, vol. VIII

Boyle, John R., 1870–1936, vol. III

Boyle, Sir Lawrence, 1920–1989, vol. VIII

Boyle, Col Lionel Richard Cavendish, 1851–1920, vol. II

Boyle, Sir Richard Gurney, 4th Bt, 1930–1983, vol. VIII

Boyle, Richard Vicars, 1822–1908, vol. I

Boyle, Maj.-Gen. Robert, 1823–1899, vol. I

Boyle, Robert Colquhoun, 1877–1934, vol. III

Boyle, Vice-Adm. Hon. Robert Francis, 1863–1922, vol. II

Boyle, Robert William, 1883–1955, vol. V

Boyle, Brig.-Gen. Roger Courtenay, 1863–1944, vol. IV

Boyle, Vincent, 1891–1956, vol. V

Boyle, Hon. Walter John Harry, 1869–1939, vol. III

Boyle, Lt-Col Hon. William George, 1830–1908, vol. I

Boyle, William Lewis, 1859–1918, vol. II

Boyle, Rev. William Skinner, 1844–1915, vol. I

Boyne, 8th Viscount, 1830–1907, vol. I

Boyne, 9th Viscount, 1864–1942, vol. IV

Boyne, Robert John, *died* 1938, vol. III

Boynton, Sir Griffith Henry, 12th Bt, 1894–1937, vol. III

Boynton, Sir Griffith Wilfrid Norman, 13th Bt, 1889–1966, vol. VI

Boynton, Sir Henry Somerville, 11th Bt, 1844–1899, vol. I

Boynton, Captain Thomas Lamplugh W.; *see* Wickham-Boynton.

Boys, Sir Charles Vernon, 1855–1944, vol. IV

Boys, Sir Francis Theodore, 1870–1952, vol. V

Boys, Geoffrey Vernon, 1893–1945, vol. IV

Boys, Guy Ponsonby, 1871–1950, vol. IV

Boys, Henry Ward, 1874–1955, vol. V

Boys, Rt Rev. John, 1900–1972, vol. VII

Boys, Brig.-Gen. Reginald Harvey Henderson, 1867–1945, vol. IV

Boys-Smith, Winifred L., *died* 1939, vol. III

Boyson, Sir John Alexander, 1846–1926, vol. II

Boyton, Sir James, 1855–1926, vol. II

Bozman, Geoffrey Stephen, 1896–1973, vol. VII

Braadland, Erik, 1910–1988, vol. VIII

Brabant, Maj.-Gen. Sir Edward Yewd, 1839–1914, vol. I

Brabant, Rev. Frank Herbert, 1892–1972, vol. VII

Brabazon of Tara, 1st Baron, 1884–1964, vol. VI

Brabazon of Tara, 2nd Baron, 1910–1974, vol. VII

Brabazon, Maj.-Gen. Sir John Palmer, 1843–1922, vol. II

Brabin, Sir Daniel James, 1913–1975, vol. VII

Brabner, Rupert Arnold, 1911–1945, vol. IV

Brabourne, 2nd Baron, 1857–1909, vol. I

Brabourne, 3rd Baron, 1885–1915, vol. I

Brabourne, 4th Baron, 1863–1933, vol. III

Brabourne, 5th Baron, 1895–1939, vol. III

Brabourne, 6th Baron, 1922–1943, vol. IV

Brabrook, Sir Edward William, 1839–1930, vol. III

Braby, Frederick Cyrus, 1897–1983, vol. VIII

Brace, Col Henry Fergusson, 1888–1948, vol. IV

Brace, Sir Ivor Llewellyn, 1898–1952, vol. V

Brace, Rt Hon. William, 1865–1947, vol. IV

Bracegirdle, Rear-Adm. Sir Leighton Seymour, 1881–1970, vol. VI (AII)

Bracewell, Rev. Canon William, 1872–1954, vol. V

Bracewell-Smith, Sir George, (Sir Guy); *see* Smith.

Bracewell-Smith, Sir Guy; *see* Smith.

Bracewell-Smith, Sir Guy, 3rd Bt, 1952–1983, vol. VIII

Bracken, 1st Viscount, 1901–1958, vol. V

Bracken, Clio Hinton, *died* 1925, vol. II

Bracken, Sir Geoffrey Thomas Hirst, 1879–1951, vol. V

Brackenbury, Arthur Jocelyn, 1876–1935, vol. III

Brackenbury, Rev. Basil V. F., 1889–1965, vol. VI

Brackenbury, Sir Cecil Fabian, 1881–1958, vol. V

Brackenbury, Rt Hon. Gen. Sir Henry, 1837–1914, vol. I

Brackenbury, Sir Henry Britten, 1866–1942, vol. IV

Brackenbury, Col Henry Langton, 1868–1920, vol. II

Brackenbury, Hereward Irenius, *died* 1938, vol. III

Brackenbury, Adm. John William, 1842–1918, vol. II

Brackenbury, Laura, 1868–1937, vol. III

Brackenbury, Col Maule Campbell, 1844–1915, vol. I

Brackenridge, Sir Alexander, 1893–1964, vol. VI

Brackett, Oliver, 1875–1941, vol. IV

Brackley, Air Cdre Herbert George, 1894–1948, vol. IV

Bradbeer, Sir Albert Frederick, 1890–1963, vol. VI

Bradbury, 1st Baron, 1872–1950, vol. IV

Bradbury, (Elizabeth) Joyce, 1918–1989, vol. VIII

Bradbury, John Buckley, 1841–1930, vol. III

Bradbury, Joyce; *see* Bradbury, E. J.
Bradbury, Surg. Rear-Adm. William, 1884–1966, vol. VI
Bradby, Godfrey Fox, 1863–1947, vol. IV
Braddell, Darcy; *see* Braddell, T. A. D.
Braddell, Dorothy Adelaide, 1889–1981, vol. VIII
Braddell, Octavius Henry, 1843–1921, vol. II
Braddell, Sir Roland St John, 1880–1966, vol. VI
Braddell, (Thomas Arthur) Darcy, 1884–1970, vol. VI
Braddell, Sir Thomas de Multon Lee, 1856–1927, vol. II
Braddock, Mrs Elizabeth Margaret, 1899–1970, vol. VI
Braddock, Geoffrey Frank, 1881–1966, vol. VI
Braddock, Thomas, 1887–1976, vol. VII
Braddon, Rt Hon. Sir Edward Nicholas Coventry, 1829–1904, vol. I
Braddon, Hon. Sir Henry Yule, 1863–1955, vol. V
Braddon, Mary Elizabeth, (Mrs John Maxwell), 1837–1915, vol. I
Brade, Sir Reginald Herbert, 1864–1933, vol. III
Bradfield, Lt-Gen. Sir Ernest W. C., 1880–1963, vol. VI
Bradfield, Rt Rev. Harold William, 1898–1960, vol. V
Bradfield, John Job Crew, 1867–1943, vol. IV
Bradfield, William Walter, 1879–1925, vol. II
Bradford, 3rd Earl of, 1819–1898, vol. I
Bradford, 4th Earl of, 1845–1915, vol. I
Bradford, 5th Earl of, 1873–1957, vol. V
Bradford, 6th Earl of, 1911–1981, vol. VIII
Bradford, Rev. E. E., 1860–1944, vol. IV
Bradford, Adm. Sir Edward Eden, 1858–1935, vol. III
Bradford, Major Sir Edward Montagu Andrew, 3rd Bt (*cr* 1902), 1910–1952, vol. V
Bradford, Col Sir Edward Ridley Colborne, 1st Bt (*cr* 1902), 1836–1911, vol. I
Bradford, Ernle, 1922–1986, vol. VIII
Bradford, Lt-Col Sir Evelyn Ridley, 2nd Bt (*cr* 1902), 1869–1914, vol. I
Bradford, Sir James, 1841–1930, vol. III
Bradford, Sir John Ridley Evelyn, 4th Bt (*cr* 1902), 1941–1954, vol. V
Bradford, Sir John Rose, 1st Bt (*cr* 1931), 1863–1935, vol. III
Bradford, Ven. Richard Bleaden, 1913–1980, vol. VII
Bradford, Rev. Robert John, 1941–1981, vol. VIII
Bradford, Lt-Col Roland Boys, 1892–1917, vol. II
Bradford, Samuel Clement, 1878–1948, vol. IV
Bradford, Sir Thomas Andrews, 1886–1966, vol. VI
Bradford, Wat; *see* Woodgate, W. B.
Bradford, William Vincent, 1883–1974, vol. VII
Bradford, Lt-Gen. Wilmot Henry, 1815–1914, vol. I
Brading, Brig. Norman Baldwin, 1896–1990, vol. VIII
Bradley, Miss; *see* Field, Michael.
Bradley, Albert James, 1899–1972, vol. VII
Bradley, Andrew Cecil, 1851–1935, vol. III
Bradley, Arthur Granville, 1850–1943, vol. IV
Bradley, Col Sir (Augustus) Montague, 1865–1953, vol. V
Bradley, Brig.-Gen. Charles Edward, 1852–1931, vol. III
Bradley, Rev. Charles Lister, 1880–1957, vol. V

Bradley, Col Edward de Winton Herbert, 1889–1964, vol. VI
Bradley, Francis Ernest, *died* 1933, vol. III
Bradley, Francis Herbert, 1846–1924, vol. II
Bradley, Rear-Adm. Frederic Cyril, 1888–1957, vol. V
Bradley, Lt-Col Frederick Gardner, 1860–1935, vol. III
Bradley, Gladys Lilian, *died* 1978, vol. VII
Bradley, Harry, 1897–1982, vol. VIII
Bradley, Henry, 1845–1923, vol. II
Bradley, Herbert, 1856–1923, vol. II
Bradley, Herbert Dennis, 1878–1934, vol. III
Bradley, Air Marshal Sir John Stanley Travers, 1888–1982, vol. VIII
Bradley, Sir Kenneth Granville, 1904–1977, vol. VII
Bradley, Leslie Ripley, 1892–1968, vol. VI
Bradley, Col Sir Montague; *see* Bradley, Col Sir A. M.
Bradley, General of the Army Omar Nelson, 1893–1981, vol. VIII
Bradley, Orlando Charnock, 1871–1937, vol. III
Bradley, Peter Colley S.; *see* Sylvester-Bradley.
Bradley, Reginald Livingstone, 1894–1977, vol. VII
Bradley, Lt-Col Robert Anstruther, *died* 1965, vol. VI
Bradley, Thomas John, 1857–1936, vol. III
Bradley, Thomas Losco, 1869–1930, vol. III
Bradley, William, 1903–1972, vol. VII
Bradley-Birt, Francis Bradley, 1874–1963, vol. VI
Bradley-Williams, Col William Picton, 1890–1981, vol. VIII
Bradly, Henry George, 1876–1938, vol. III
Bradnack, Brian Oswald, 1898–1973, vol. VII
Bradney, George Preston, 1877–1959, vol. V
Bradney, Col Sir Joseph Alfred, 1859–1933, vol. III
Bradshaw, Mrs Albert S., *died* 1938, vol. III
Bradshaw, Surg.-Maj.-Gen. Sir (Alexander) Frederick, 1834–1923, vol. II
Bradshaw, Brig.-Gen. Charles Richard, 1873–1940, vol. III
Bradshaw, Constance H., *died* 1961, vol. VI
Bradshaw, Eric, 1909–1961, vol. VI
Bradshaw, Evelyn, 1862–1952, vol. V
Bradshaw, Surg.-Maj.-Gen. Sir Frederick; *see* Bradshaw, Surg.-Maj.-Gen. A. F.
Bradshaw, George Fagan, 1887–1960, vol. V
Bradshaw, Brig. George Rowley, 1898–1976, vol. VII
Bradshaw, Harold Chalton, 1893–1943, vol. IV
Bradshaw, Maj.-Gen. Laurence Julius Elliott, 1857–1929, vol. III
Bradshaw, Octavius, 1845–1928, vol. II
Bradshaw, Thomas R., 1857–1927, vol. II
Bradshaw, Thornton Frederick, 1917–1988, vol. VIII
Bradshaw, William, 1844–1927, vol. II
Bradshaw, Sir William, 1876–1955, vol. V
Bradshaw, William Graham, 1861–1941, vol. IV
Bradshaw, Maj.-Gen. William Pat Arthur, 1897–1966, vol. VI
Bradshaw-Isherwood, Christopher William; *see* Isherwood.
Bradshaw-Isherwood, John Henry; *see* Isherwood.
Bradstock, Major George, *died* 1966, vol. VI

Bradstreet, Sir Edmond Simon, 6th Bt, 1820–1905, vol. I

Bradstreet, Sir Edward Simon Victor, 7th Bt, 1856–1924, vol. II

Bradwell, Baron (Life Peer); Thomas Edward Neil Driberg, 1905–1976, vol. VII

Brady, Sir Andrew N.; *see* Newton-Brady.

Brady, Sir Francis William, 2nd Bt, 1824–1909, vol. I

Brady, George Stewardson, 1832–1921, vol. II

Brady, Major Gerald Charles Jervis, *died* 1941, vol. IV

Brady, Rev. Canon Henry Westby, 1884–1934, vol. III

Brady, Patrick Joseph, 1868–1943, vol. IV

Brady, Sir Robert Maziere, 3rd Bt, 1854–1909, vol. I

Brady, Sir Thomas Francis, 1824–1904, vol. I

Brady, Thomas John Bellingham, 1841–1910, vol. I

Brady, Major Sir William Longfield, 4th Bt, 1864–1927, vol. II

Brækstad, H. L., 1845–1915, vol. I

Bragg, Sir Lawrence; *see* Bragg, Sir W. L.

Bragg, Sir William Henry, 1862–1942, vol. IV

Bragg, Sir (William) Lawrence, 1890–1971, vol. VII

Bragge, Rev. Charles Albert, *died* 1923, vol. II

Braham, Dudley Disraeli, 1875–1951, vol. V

Braham, Harry Vincent, 1886–1938, vol. III

Brahms, Caryl, (Doris Caroline Abrahams), 1901–1982, vol. VIII

Braidwood, Harold Lithgow, 1872–1949, vol. IV

Brailey, William A., *died* 1915, vol. I

Brailsford, Frederick, 1903–1985, vol. VIII

Brailsford, Henry Noel, 1873–1958, vol. V

Brailsford, John William, 1918–1988, vol. VIII

Brain, 1st Baron, 1895–1966, vol. VI

Brain, Dennis, 1921–1957, vol. V

Brain, Sir Francis William Thomas, 1855–1921, vol. II

Brain, Sir Hugh Gerner, 1890–1976, vol. VII

Brain, Lawrence L.; *see* Lewton-Brain.

Brain, Reginald T., 1894–1971, vol. VII

Brain, Ronald, 1914–1989, vol. VIII

Braine, Brig. Herbert Edmund Reginald Rubens, 1876–1942, vol. IV

Braine, John Gerard, 1922–1986, vol. VIII

Braintree, 1st Baron, 1884–1961, vol. VI

Brais, (François) Philippe, 1894–1972, vol. VII

Brais, Philippe; *see* Brais, F. P.

Braithwaite, Major Sir Albert Newby, 1893–1959, vol. V

Braithwaite, Charles, *died* 1941, vol. IV

Braithwaite, Air Vice-Marshal Francis Joseph St George, 1907–1956, vol. V

Braithwaite, Col Francis Powell, 1875–1952, vol. V

Braithwaite, Major John, 1871–1940, vol. III

Braithwaite, Sir John Bevan, 1884–1973, vol. VII

Braithwaite, Sir Joseph Gurney, 1st Bt, 1895–1958, vol. V

Braithwaite, Vice-Adm. Lawrence Walter, 1878–1961, vol. VI

Braithwaite, Dame Lilian, 1873–1948, vol. IV

Braithwaite, Rev. Philip Richard Pipon, 1849–1933, vol. III

Braithwaite, Richard Bevan, 1900–1990, vol. VIII

Braithwaite, Robert, 1824–1917, vol. II

Braithwaite, Gen. Sir Walter Pipon, 1865–1945, vol. IV

Braithwaite, Warwick, 1896–1971, vol. VII

Braithwaite, William Charles, 1862–192, vol. II

Braithwaite, Brig.-Gen. William Garnett, 1870–1937, vol. III

Braithwaite, William John, 1875–1938, vol. III

Brake, Sir Francis, 1889–1960, vol. V

Brake, Brig.-Gen. Herbert Edward John, 1866–1936, vol. III

Brakenridge, Col Francis John, 1871–1955, vol. V

Brakspear, Sir Harold, 1870–1934, vol. III

Braley, Rev. Evelyn Foley, 1884–1963, vol. VI

Bramah, David, 1875–1947, vol. IV

Bramah, Ernest, *died* 1942, vol. IV

Brambell, Francis William Rogers, 1901–1970, vol. VI

Bramble, Courtenay Parker, 1900–1987, vol. VIII

Bramble, Paymaster Rear-Adm. James, 1850–1930, vol. III

Brame, John Samuel Strafford, 1871–1952, vol. V

Brameld, Rev. William Arthur, *died* 1922, vol. II

Bramley, Frank, 1857–1915, vol. I

Bramley, Fred, 1874–1925, vol. II

Bramley, Rev. Henry Ramsden, 1833–1917, vol. II

Bramley-Moore, Rev. William, 1831–1918, vol. II

Brampton, 1st Baron, 1817–1907, vol. I

Bramsdon, Sir Thomas Arthur, 1857–1935, vol. III

Bramston, Sir John, 1832–1921, vol. II

Bramston, Rev. John Trant, *died* 1931, vol. III

Bramwell, Sir Byrom, 1847–1931, vol. III

Bramwell, Edward George, 1865–1944, vol. IV

Bramwell, Edwin, 1873–1952, vol. V

Bramwell, Sir Frederick Joseph, 1st Bt, 1818–1903, vol. I

Bramwell, John Crighton, 1889–1976, vol. VII

Bramwell, John Milne, 1852–1925, vol. II

Bramwell-Booth, Catherine, 1883–1987, vol. VIII

Bramwell Davis, Maj.-Gen. Ronald Albert, 1905–1974, vol. VII

Branch, Sir (Charles Ernest) St John, *died* 1939, vol. III

Branch, James, 1845–1918, vol. II

Branch, Sir St John; *see* Branch, Sir C. E. St J.

Branch, Ven. Samuel Edmund, 1861–1932, vol. III

Brancker, Air Vice-Marshal Sir Sefton; *see* Brancker, Air Vice-Marshal Sir W. S.

Brancker, Air Vice-Marshal Sir (William) Sefton, 1877–1930, vol. III

Brand, 1st Baron, 1878–1963, vol. VI

Brand, Sir Alfred; *see* Brand, Sir W. A.

Brand, Hon. Arthur George, 1853–1917, vol. II

Brand, Hon. Charles, 1855–1912, vol. I

Brand, Maj.-Gen. Charles Henry, 1873–1961, vol. VI

Brand, (Charles) Neville, 1895–1951, vol. V

Brand, Air Vice-Marshal Sir (Christopher Joseph) Quintin, 1893–1968, vol. VI

Brand, Sir David, 1837–1908, vol. I

Brand, Hon. Sir David, 1912–1979, vol. VII

Brand, Col David Ernest, 1884–1948, vol. IV

Brand, Ferdinand, 1846–1922, vol. II

Brand, Sir Harry F., 1873–1951, vol. V

Brand, Adm. Hon. Sir Hubert George, 1870–1955, vol. V

Brand, James, 1843–1907, vol. I
Brand, Engr-Captain James John Cantley, 1880–1952, vol. V
Brand, Lt-Col John Charles, 1885–1929, vol. III
Brand, Neville; *see* Brand, C. N.
Brand, Air Vice-Marshal Sir Quintin; *see* Brand, Air Vice-Marshal Sir C. J. Q.
Brand, Hon. Roger, 1880–1945, vol. IV
Brand, Rear-Adm. Hon. Thomas Seymour, 1847–1916, vol. II
Brand, Sir (William) Alfred, 1888–1979, vol. VII (AII)
Brandeis, Louis Dembitz, 1856–1941, vol. IV
Brander, George Maconachie, 1906–1977, vol. VII
Brander, Col Herbert Ralph, 1861–1933, vol. III
Brander, Maj.-Gen. Maxwell Spieker, 1884–1972, vol. VII
Brander, William Browne, 1880–1951, vol. V
Brandes, George, 1842–1927, vol. II
Brandin, Louis M., 1874–1940, vol. III
Brandis, Sir Dietrich, 1824–1907, vol. I
Brandon, Very Rev. Lowther E., *died* 1933, vol. III
Brandon, Col Oscar Gilbert, 1876–1968, vol. VI
Brandon, Rev. Samuel George Frederick, 1907–1971, vol. VII
Brandon, Captain Vivian R., 1882–1944, vol. IV
Brandram, Rosina, *died* 1907, vol. I
Brandt, William, (Bill Brandt), 1904–1983, vol. VIII
Branfill Harrison, Col Cholmeley Edward Carl; *see* Harrison.
Branfoot, Surg.-Gen. Sir Arthur Mudge, 1848–1914, vol. I
Brangwyn, Sir Frank, 1867–1956, vol. V
Branly, Edouard, 1844–1940, vol. III
Branner, John Casper, 1850–1922, vol. II
Brannigan, Owen, 1908–1973, vol. VII
Branson, Col Sir Douglas Stephenson, 1893–1981, vol. VIII
Branson, Rt Hon. Sir George Arthur Harwin, 1871–1951, vol. V
Branson, William Philip Sutcliffe, 1874–1950, vol. IV
Brant, Richard William, 1852–1934, vol. III
Branthwaite, Robert Welsh, 1859–1929, vol. III
Braque, Georges, 1882–1963, vol. VI
Brash, James Couper, 1886–1958, vol. V
Brash, William Bardsley, 1877–1952, vol. V
Brasher, William Kenneth, 1897–1972, vol. VII
Braslau, Sophie, *died* 1935, vol. III
Brasnett, Rev. Bertrand Rippington, 1893–1988, vol. VIII
Brass, Sir Leslie Stuart, 1891–1958, vol. V
Brassey, 1st Earl, 1836–1918, vol. II
Brassey, 2nd Earl, 1863–1919, vol. II
Brassey of Apethorpe, 1st Baron, 1870–1958, vol. V
Brassey of Apethorpe, 2nd Baron, 1905–1967, vol. VI
Brassey, Albert, 1844–1918, vol. II
Brassey, Lt-Col Edgar Hugh, 1878–1946, vol. IV
Brassey, Captain Harold Ernest, 1877–1916, vol. II
Brassey, Col Sir Hugh Trefusis, 1915–1990, vol. VIII
Brassey, Captain Robert Bingham, 1875–1946, vol. IV
Brassington, William Salt, 1859–1939, vol. III
Brattain, Walter Houser, 1902–1987, vol. VIII

Bratton, Rt Rev. Theodore Du Bose, 1862–1944, vol. IV
Braude, Ernest Alexander Rudolph, 1922–1956, vol. V
Braudel, Fernand, 1902–1985, vol. VIII
Braun, Adolphe Armand, 1869–1938, vol. III
Braund, Sir Henry Benedict Linthwaite, 1893–1969, vol. VI
Braunholtz, Eugen Gustav Wilhelm, 1859–1941, vol. IV
Braunholtz, Gustav Ernst Karl, 1887–1967, vol. VI
Braunholtz, Hermann Justus, 1888–1963, vol. VI
Bray, Maj.-Gen. Sir Claude Arthur, 1858–1934, vol. III
Bray, Sir Denys de Saumarez, 1875–1951, vol. V
Bray, Sir Edward, 1849–1926, vol. II
Bray, Sir Edward Hugh, 1874–1950, vol. IV
Bray, Francis Edmond, 1882–1950, vol. IV
Bray, Frederick, 1895–1977, vol. VII
Bray, Col George Arthur Theodore, 1864–1933, vol. III
Bray, Col Hubert Alaric, 1867–1935, vol. III
Bray, Captain Sir Jocelyn, 1880–1964, vol. VI
Bray, Rt Rev. Patrick Albert, 1883–1953, vol. V
Bray, Sir Reginald More, 1842–1923, vol. II
Bray, Brig.-Gen. Robert Napier, 1872–1921, vol. II
Bray, Gen. Sir Robert Napier Hubert Campbell, 1908–1983, vol. VIII
Bray, Ronald William Thomas, 1922–1984, vol. VIII
Braybrooke, 5th Baron, 1823–1902, vol. I
Braybrooke, 6th Baron, 1827–1904, vol. I
Braybrooke, 7th Baron, 1855–1941, vol. IV
Braybrooke, 8th Baron, 1918–1943, vol. IV
Braybrooke, 9th Baron, 1897–1990, vol. VIII
Brayden, William Henry, 1865–1933, vol. III
Braye, 5th Baron, 1849–1928, vol. II
Braye, 6th Baron, 1874–1952, vol. V
Braye, 7th Baron, 1902–1985, vol. VIII
Braye, Philip George, 1894–1956, vol. V
Brayley, Baron (Life Peer); (John) Desmond Brayley. 1917–1977, vol. VII
Brayn, Sir Richard, 1850–1912, vol. I
Brayne, Albert Frederic Lucas, 1884–1970, vol. VI
Brayne, Charles Valentine, 1877–1964, vol. VI
Brayne, Frank Lugard, 1882–1952, vol. V
Brayshay, Sir Maurice William, 1883–1959, vol. V
Brazel, Claude Hamilton, 1894–1959, vol. V
Brazendale, George William, 1909–1990, vol. VIII
Brazier-Creagh, Col George Washington, 1858–1942, vol. IV
Brazil, Angela, 1868–1947, vol. IV
Braza, Pierre Paul François Camille de, Count de Savorgnan, 1852–1905, vol. I
Brazier, Rt Rev. Percy James, 1903–1989, vol. VIII
Breadalbane, 1st Marquis of, 1851–1922, vol. II
Breadalbane, 8th Earl of, 1885–1923, vol. II
Breadalbane and Holland, 9th Earl of, 1889–1959, vol. V
Breading, Lt-Col George Remington, 1877–1942, vol. IV
Breadner, Air Chief Marshall Lloyd Samuel, 1894–1952, vol. V
Breadner, Robert Walker, 1865–1935, vol. III

Breakey, Air Vice-Marshal John Denis, *died* 1965, vol. VI

Breaks, Rear-Adm. James, 1895–1968, vol. VI

Breakspear, W. A., *died* 1914, vol. I

Brealey, William Ramsden, 1889–1949, vol. IV

Brearley, Sir Norman, 1890–1989, vol. VIII

Breasted, James Henry, 1865–1935, vol. III

Brebner, Sir Alexander, 1883–1979, vol. VII

Brebner, Arthur, 1870–1922, vol. II

Brebner, John Bartlet, 1895–1957, vol. V

Brebner, Percy James, 1864–1922, vol. II

Brechin, Sir Herbert Archbold, 1903–1979, vol. VII

Brecknock, Marjorie Countess of, (Marjorie Minna), 1900–1989, vol. VIII

Brecon, 1st Baron, 1905–1976, vol. VII

Bredin, George Richard Frederick, 1899–1983, vol. VIII

Bredius, Abraham, 1855–1946, vol. IV

Bredon, Sir Robert Edward, 1846–1918, vol. II

Bree, Rt Rev. Herbert, 1828–1899, vol. I

Bree, Ven. William, 1822–1917, vol. II

Breech, Ernest Robert, 1897–1978, vol. VII

Breeks, Brig.-Gen. Richard William, 1863–1920, vol. II

Breen, Air Marshal John Joseph, 1896–1964, vol. VI

Breen, Timothy Florence, 1885–1966, vol. VI

Breene, Very Rev. Richard Simmons, 1886–1974, vol. VII

Breese, Air-Cdre Charles Dempster, 1889–1941, vol. IV

Breese, Major Charles Edward, 1867–1932, vol. III

Breithaupt, Hon. Louis Orville, 1890–1960, vol. V

Brema, Marie, 1856–1925, vol. II

Bremer, Walther Erich Emanuel Friedrich, 1887–1926, vol. II

Bremner, Alexander, 1890–1944, vol. IV

Bremner, Brig.-Gen. Arthur Grant, 1867–1950, vol. IV (A)

Bremner, Lt-Col Claude E. U., 1891–1965, vol. VI

Bremner, Captain Donald, 1864–1935, vol. III

Bremond, L'Abbé Henri, 1865–1933, vol. III

Brenan, Byron, 1847–1927, vol. II

Brenan, (Edward Fitz-) Gerald, 1894–1987, vol. VIII

Brenan, Gerald; *see* Brenan, E. F.

Brenan, James, 1837–1907, vol. I

Brenan, Sir John Fitzgerald, 1883–1953, vol. V

Brenan, John Patrick Micklethwait, 1917–1985, vol. VIII

Brenan, Terence Vincent, 1887–1974, vol. VII

Brenchley, Winifred Elsie, 1883–1953, vol. V

Brend, William A., 1873–1944, vol. IV

Brennan, Charles John, 1876–1972, vol. VII

Brennan, Hon. Frank, *died* 1950, vol. IV

Brennan, Joseph, 1887–1976, vol. VII

Brennan, Louis, 1852–1932, vol. III

Brennan, Lt-Gen. Michael, *died* 1986, vol. VIII

Brennan, Very Rev. Nicholas J., 1854–1928, vol. II

Brennan, Maj.-Gen. William Brian Francis, 1907–1977, vol. VII

Brent, Rt Rev. Charles Henry, 1862–1929, vol. III

Brentano, Heinrich von, 1904–1964, vol. VI

Brentford, 1st Viscount, 1865–1932, vol. III

Brentford, 2nd Viscount, 1896–1958, vol. V

Brentford, 3rd Viscount, 1902–1983, vol. VIII

Brereton, Alfred, 1849–1926, vol. II

Brereton, Austin, 1862–1922, vol. II

Brereton, Cloudesley, 1863–1937, vol. III

Brereton, Brig.-Gen. Edward Fitzgerald, *died* 1937, vol. III

Brereton, Very Rev. Eric Hugh, 1889–1962, vol. VI

Brereton, Bt Lt-Col Frederick Sadleir, 1872–1957, vol. V

Brereton, John Le Gay, 1871–1933, vol. III

Brereton, Maud Adeline Cloudesley-, *died* 1946, vol. IV

Brereton, Reginald Hugh, 1861–1944, vol. IV

Brereton, William Westropp, 1845–1924, vol. II

Bressey, Sir Charles Herbert, 1874–1951, vol. V

Breteuil, Marquis de; Henri Charles Joseph, 1848–1916, vol. II

Bretherton, Frederick S.; *see* Stapleton-Bretherton.

Bretherton, Major George Howard, 1860–1904, vol. I

Breton, Jules, 1827–1906, vol. I

Breton, Virginie Demont, 1859–1935, vol. III

Bretscher, Egon, 1901–1973, vol. VII

Brett, Arthur Cyril Adair, 1882–1936, vol. III

Brett, Sir Cecil Michael Wilford, 1852–1938, vol. III

Brett, Major Charles Arthur Hugh, 1865–1914, vol. I

Brett, Sir Charles Henry, 1839–1926, vol. II

Brett, Cyril Templeton, 1885–1960, vol. V

Brett, Francis William, 1885–1936, vol. III

Brett, Lt-Gen. George Howard, 1886–1963, vol. VI

Brett, George Platt, 1858–1936, vol. III

Brett, George Platt, jun., 1893–1984, vol. VIII

Brett, George Sidney, 1879–1944, vol. IV

Brett, Sir Henry, 1843–1927, vol. II

Brett, Henry James, 1878–1963, vol. VI

Brett, Very Rev. Henry Robert, 1868–1932, vol. III

Brett, James; *see* Brett, L. J.

Brett, John, 1831–1902, vol. I

Brett, Lt-Col John Aloysius, 1879–1955, vol. V

Brett, Sir Lionel, 1911–1990, vol. VIII

Brett, (Louis) James, 1910–1975, vol. VII

Brett, Lt-Col Hon. Maurice Vyner Baliol, 1882–1934, vol. III

Brett, Hon. Robert George, 1851–1929, vol. III

Brett, Brig. Rupert John, 1890–1963, vol. VI

Brett, Sir Wilford, 1824–1901, vol. I

Brett, William Bailie, 1889–1947, vol. IV

Brett-James, Antony; *see* Brett-James, E. A.

Brett-James, (Eliot) Antony, 1920–1984, vol. VIII

Brett Young, Francis; *see* Young, F. B.

Brettell, Frederick Gilbert, 1884–1965, vol. VI

Bretton, Very Rev. William Frederick, 1909–1971, vol. VII

Breuil, Abbé Henri Édouard Prosper, 1877–1961, vol. VI

Breul, Karl Herman, 1860–1932, vol. III

Breun, J. E., 1862–1921, vol. II

Brevitt, Sir Horatio, 1847–1933, vol. III

Brew, Robert John, 1838–1911, vol. I

Brewer, Sir (Alfred) Herbert, 1865–1928, vol. II

Brewer, David J., *died* 1910, vol. I

Brewer, Rev. Ebenezer Cobham, 1810–1897, vol. I

Brewer, Rev. Edward, *died* 1922, vol. II

Brewer, Frank, 1915–1987, vol. VIII

Brewer, Sir Henry Campbell, 1885–1963, vol. VI

Brewer, Sir Herbert; *see* Brewer, Sir A. H.

Brewer, Rt Rev. Leigh Richmond, 1839–1916, vol. II
Brewerton, Elmore, 1867–1962, vol. VI
Brewill, Lt-Col Arthur William, 1861–1923, vol. II
Brewin, Arthur Winbolt, 1867–1946, vol. IV
Brewin, Elizabeth Maud, (Mrs P. K. Brewin); *see* Pepperell, E. M.
Brewis, Captain Charles Richard Wynn, 1874–1953, vol. V
Brewis, (Henry) John, 1920–1989, vol. VIII
Brewis, John; *see* Brewis, H. J.
Brewis, John Fenwick, 1910–1986, vol. VIII
Brewis, Rev. John Salusbury, 1902–1972, vol. VII
Brewis, Nathaniel Thomas, *died* 1924, vol. II
Brewitt, Rev. James C., 1843–1905, vol. I
Brews, Alan; *see* Brews, R. A.
Brews, (Richard) Alan, 1902–1965, vol. VI
Brewster, Adolph Brewster, 1854–1937, vol. III
Brewster, Rt Rev. Benjamin, 1860–1941, vol. IV
Brewster, Rt Rev. Chauncey Bunce, 1848–1941, vol. IV
Brewster, Edward John, *died* 1931, vol. III
Brewster, Kingman, 1919–1988, vol. VIII
Brewster, Willoughby Staples, 1860–1932, vol. III
Brewtnall, Edward Frederick, 1846–1902, vol. I
Breymann, Dr Hermann Wilhelm, *died* 1910, vol. I
Brezhnev, Leonid Ilyich, 1906–1982, vol. VIII
Brian, Percy Wragg, 1910–1979, vol. VII
Briance, John Albert, 1915–1989, vol. VIII
Briand, Aristide, 1862–1932, vol. III
Briant, Bruce Edgar Dutton, 1895–1959, vol. V
Briant, Frank, 1865–1934, vol. III
Brice, Arthur John Hallam Montefiore, *died* 1927, vol. II
Brice, Rev. Edward Henry, *died* 1952, vol. V
Brice, Seward, 1846–1914, vol. I
Brickdale, Sir Charles F.; *see* Fortescue-Brickdale.
Brickdale, Eleanor F.; *see* Fortescue-Brickdale.
Brickdale, John Matthew F.; *see* Fortescue-Brickdale.
Brickell, Daniel Francis Horseman, 1893–1967, vol. VI
Bricker, John William, 1893–1986, vol. VIII
Brickman, Brig. Ivan Pringle, 1891–1980, vol. VII
Brickwell, Alfred James, 1870–1937, vol. III
Brickwood, Sir John, 1st Bt, 1852–1932, vol. III
Brickwood, Sir Rupert Redvers, 2nd Bt, 1900–1974, vol. VII
Bridge, Ann, (Lady O'Malley), 1891–1974, vol. VII
Bridge, Adm. Sir (Arthur) Robin (Moore), 1894–1971, vol. VII
Bridge, Brig. Charles Edward Dunscomb, 1886–1961, vol. VI
Bridge, Brig.-Gen. Sir Charles Henry, 1852–1926, vol. II
Bridge, Adm. Sir Cyprian Arthur George, 1839–1924, vol. II
Bridge, Frank, 1879–1941, vol. IV
Bridge, Sir Frederick, 1844–1924, vol. II
Bridge, George Wilfred, 1894–1971, vol. VII
Bridge, Sir John, 1824–1900, vol. I
Bridge, John Crosthwaite, 1877–1947, vol. IV
Bridge, Joseph Cox, 1853–1929, vol. III
Bridge, Joseph James Rabnett, 1875–1959, vol. V
Bridge, Peter Gonzalez, 1885–1942, vol. IV

Bridge, Adm. Sir Robin; *see* Bridge, Adm. Sir A. R. M.
Bridge, Roy Arthur Odell, 1911–1978, vol. VII
Bridge, Maj.-Gen. Thomas Field Dunscomb, 1847–1934, vol. III
Bridge, Thomas William, 1848–1909, vol. I
Bridgeford, Lt-Gen. Sir William, 1894–1971, vol. VII
Bridgeman, 1st Viscount, 1864–1935, vol. III
Bridgeman, 2nd Viscount, 1896–1982, vol. VIII
Bridgeman, Viscountess; (Caroline Beatrix), *died* 1961, vol. VI
Bridgeman, Brig.-Gen. Hon. Francis Charles, 1846–1917, vol. II
Bridgeman, Adm. Sir Francis Charles Bridgeman-, 1848–1929, vol. III
Bridgeman, Hon. Geoffrey John Orlando, 1898–1974, vol. VII
Bridgeman, Col Hon. Henry George Orlando, 1882–1972, vol. VII
Bridgeman, Hon. Sir Maurice Richard, 1904–1980, vol. VII
Bridgeman, Reginald Francis Orlando, 1884–1968, vol. VI
Bridgeman-Bridgeman, Adm. Sir Francis Charles; *see* Bridgeman.
Bridger, Rev. John, *died* 1911, vol. I
Bridges, 1st Baron, 1892–1969, vol. VI
Bridges, Col Arthur Holroyd, 1871–1953, vol. V
Bridges, Daisy Caroline, 1894–1972, vol. VII
Bridges, Sir Ernest Arthur, 1880–1953, vol. V
Bridges, Col Francis Doveton, 1871–1954, vol. V
Bridges, Col George, *died* 1962, vol. VI
Bridges, Rev. Sir George Talbot, 1818–1899, vol. I
Bridges, Lt-Gen. Sir (George) Tom (Molesworth), 1871–1939, vol. III
Bridges, Rear-Adm. Henry Dalrymple, 1881–1955, vol. V
Bridges, Col James Whiteside, 1863–1930, vol. III
Bridges, John Gourlay, 1901–1985, vol. VIII
Bridges, John Henry, 1832–1906, vol. I
Bridges, John Henry, 1852–1925, vol. II
Bridges, Lt-Col Lionel Forbes, 1871–1937, vol. III
Bridges, Robert, 1844–1930, vol. III
Bridges, Robert, 1858–1941, vol. IV
Bridges, Roy, 1885–1952, vol. V
Bridges, Lt-Gen. Sir Tom; *see* Bridges, Lt-Gen. Sir G. T. M.
Bridges, Rear-Adm. Walter Bogue, 1843–1917, vol. II
Bridges, Brig.-Gen. William Throsby, 1861–1915, vol. I
Bridges-Adams, William, 1889–1965, vol. VI
Bridgewater, Francis Matthew, 1851–1915, vol. I
Bridgford, Col Sir Robert, 1836–1905, vol. I
Bridgford, Brig.-Gen. Robert James, 1869–1954, vol. V
Bridgland, Albert Stanford, *died* 1944, vol. IV
Bridgland, Sir Aynsley Vernon, 1893–1966, vol. VI
Bridgman, Leonard Logoz, 1895–1980, vol. VII
Bridgman, Percy Williams, 1882–1961, vol. VI
Bridie, James, (O. H. Mavor), 1888–1951, vol. V
Bridport, 1st Viscount, 1814–1904, vol. I
Bridport, 2nd Viscount, 1839–1924, vol. II
Bridport, 3rd Viscount, 1911–1969, vol. VI

Briercliffe, Sir Rupert, 1889–1975, vol. VII
Brierley, Col Sir Charles Isherwood, 1879–1940, vol. III
Brierley, Edgar, 1858–1927, vol. II
Brierley, Col Geoffrey Teale, *died* 1961, vol. VI
Brierley, Captain Henry, 1897–1981, vol. VIII
Brierley, J., 1843–1914, vol. I
Brierley, Rev. Canon John, 1886–1964, vol. VI
Brierley, William Broadhurst, 1889–1963, vol. VI
Brierly, James Leslie, 1881–1955, vol. V
Brieux, Eugene, 1858–1932, vol. III
Briffa, Col Alfred, 1868–1952, vol. V
Briffault, Robert Stephen, 1876–1948, vol. IV
Brigden, James Bristock, 1887–1950, vol. IV(A)
Brigg, Sir John, 1834–1911, vol. I
Briggs, Albert William, 1900–1971, vol. VII
Briggs, Sir (Alfred) George (Ernest), 1900–1976, vol. VII
Briggs, Arthur Beecham, 1883–1937, vol. III
Briggs, Prof. Charles Augustus, 1841–1913, vol. I
Briggs, Lt-Gen. Sir Charles James, 1865–1941, vol. IV
Briggs, Adm. Sir Charles John, 1858–1951, vol. V
Briggs, D. H. Currer, 1893–1974, vol. VII
Briggs, Lt-Col Ernest, 1881–1947, vol. IV
Briggs, Ernest Edward, 1866–1913, vol. I
Briggs, Sir Francis Arthur, 1902–1983, vol. VIII
Briggs, Sir George; *see* Briggs, Sir A. G. E.
Briggs, George Edward, 1893–1985, vol. VIII
Briggs, Rev. Canon George Wallace, 1875–1959, vol. V
Briggs, Harold; *see* Briggs, W. J. H.
Briggs, Captain Harold Douglas, 1877–1944, vol. IV
Briggs, Lt-Gen. Sir Harold Rawdon, 1894–1952, vol. V
Briggs, Hon. Sir Henry, *born* 1844, vol. II
Briggs, Henry, 1883–1935, vol. III
Briggs, Henry, *died* 1944, vol. IV
Briggs, James, 1855–1933, vol. III
Briggs, Sir John Henry, 1808–1897, vol. I
Briggs, Martin Shaw, 1882–1977, vol. VII
Briggs, Col Norman, 1891–1960, vol. V
Briggs, Percy,1903–1980, vol. VII
Briggs, Rev. Rawdon, 1853–1936, vol. III
Briggs, Brig. Rawdon, 1892–1960, vol. V
Briggs, Maj.-Gen. Raymond, 1895–1985, vol. VIII
Briggs, Thomas, 1847–1934, vol. III
Briggs, (W. J.) Harold, 1870–1945, vol. IV
Briggs, Waldo Raven, 1883–1956, vol. V
Briggs, William, 1861–1932, vol. III
Briggs, Col William Hilton, 1871–1951, vol. V
Brighouse, Harold, 1882–1958, vol. V
Brighouse, Sir Samuel, *died* 1940, vol. III
Bright, Alfred Ernest, 1869–1938, vol. III
Bright, Allan Heywood, 1862–1941, vol. IV
Bright, Sir Charles, 1863–1937, vol. III
Bright, Charles Edward, 1829–1915, vol. I
Bright, Sir Charles Hart, 1912–1983, vol. VIII
Bright, Ernest Henry, 1864–1937, vol. III
Bright, Mrs Golding; *see* Egerton, George.
Bright, Ven. Hugh, 1867–1935, vol. III
Bright, Rt Rev. Humphrey Penderell, 1903–1964, vol. VI
Bright, Rt Hon. Jacob, 1821–1899, vol. I

Bright, James Franck, 1832–1920, vol. II
Bright, John Albert, 1848–1924, vol. II
Bright, Sir Joseph, 1849–1918, vol. II
Bright, Mary Chavelita; *see* Egerton, George.
Bright, Brig-Gen. Reginald Arthur, 1870–1942, vol. IV
Bright, Major Richard George Tyndall, 1872–1944, vol. IV
Bright, Rev. William, 1824–1901, vol. I
Bright, William Robert, 1857–1908, vol. I
Brighten, Lt-Col Edgar William, 1880–1966, vol. VI
Brightman, Rev. Frank Edward, 1856–1932, vol. III
Brightmore, A. W., 1864–1927, vol. II
Brigstocke, Charles Reginald, 1876–1951, vol. V
Brigstocke, Geoffrey Reginald William, 1917–1974, vol. VII
Brigstocke, George Edward, *died* 1971, vol. VII
Brill, Abraham Arden, 1874–1948, vol. IV
Brillant, Jules-André, 1888–1973, vol. VII
Brimacombe, Richard William, 1867–1930, vol. III
Brimble, Lionel John Farnham, 1904–1965, vol. VI
Brims, Charles William, 1877–1944, vol. IV
Brinckman, Col Sir Roderick Napoleon, 5th Bt, 1902–1985, vol. VIII
Brinckman, Major Sir Theodore Ernest Warren, 4th Bt, 1898–1954, vol. V
Brinckman, Col Sir Theodore Francis, 3rd Bt, 1862–1937, vol. III
Brinckman, Sir Theodore Henry, 2nd Bt, 1830–1905, vol. I
Brind, Adm. Sir (Eric James) Patrick, 1892–1963, vol. VI
Brind, George Walter Richard, 1911–1988, vol. VIII
Brind, Gen. Sir John Edward Spencer, 1878–1954, vol. V
Brind, Adm. Sir Patrick; *see* Brind, Adm. Sir E. J. P.
Brindle, Harry, *died* 1976, vol. VII
Brindle, Rt Rev. Robert, 1837–1916, vol. II
Brindley, Harold Hulme, 1865–1944, vol. IV
Brine, Edgar, 1856–1932, vol. III
Brink, Lt-Gen. George Edwin, 1889–1971, vol. VII
Brinkley, Captain Frank, 1841–1912, vol. I
Brinkley, Captain John Turner, 1855–1928, vol. II
Brinkworth, George Harold, 1906–1989, vol. VIII
Brinson, Derek Neilson, 1921–1974, vol. VII
Brinson, J. Paul, *died* 1927, vol. II
Brinton, Denis Hubert, 1902–1986, vol. VIII
Brinton, Maj. Sir (Esme) Tatton (Cecil), 1916–1985, vol. VIII
Brinton, Lt-Col John Chaytor, 1867–1956, vol. V
Brinton, Selwyn, *died* 1940, vol. III
Brinton, Major Sir Tatton; *see* Brinton, Major Sir E. T. C.
Brisbane, Arthur, 1864–1936, vol. III
Brisbane, Sir (Hugh) Lancelot, 1893–1966, vol. VI
Brisbane, Sir Lancelot; *see* Brisbane, Sir H. L.
Brisco, Sir Aubrey Hylton, 6th Bt, 1873–1957, vol. V
Brisco, Sir Hylton Musgrave Campbell, 7th Bt, 1886–1968, vol. VI
Brisco, Sir Hylton Ralph, 5th Bt, 1871–1922, vol. II
Brisco, Sir Musgrave Horton, 4th Bt, 1833–1909, vol. I
Briscoe, Sir Alfred Leigh, 2nd Bt, 1870–1921, vol. II
Briscoe, Arthur John Trevor, 1873–1943, vol. IV

Briscoe, Sir Charlton; *see* Briscoe, Sir J. C.

Briscoe, Major Edward William, 1857–1928, vol. II

Briscoe, Captain Henry Villiers, 1896–1983, vol. VIII

Briscoe, Henry Vincent Aird, 1888–1961, vol. VI

Briscoe, Hugh Kynaston, 1879–1956, vol. V

Briscoe, Sir (John) Charlton, 3rd Bt, 1874–1960, vol. V

Briscoe, Sir John James, 1st Bt, 1836–1919, vol. II

Briscoe, John Potter, 1848–1926, vol. II

Briscoe, Percy Charles, *died* 1951, vol. V

Briscoe, Captain Richard George, 1893–1957, vol. V

Briscoe, William Richard Brunskill, 1855–1930, vol. III

Brise, Archibald Weyland R.; *see* Ruggles-Brise.

Brise, Col Sir Edward Archibald R.; *see* Ruggles-Brise.

Brise, Sir Evelyn John R.; *see* Ruggles-Brise.

Brise, Maj.-Gen. Sir Harold Goodeve R.; *see* Ruggles-Brise.

Brise, Col Sir Samuel Ruggles, 1825–1899, vol. I

Brisson, Adolphe, *died* 1925, vol. II

Brisson, Henri, 1835–1912, vol. I

Brisson, Rosalind, (Mrs F. Brisson); *see* Russell, R.

Bristol, 3rd Marquis of, 1834–1907, vol. I

Bristol, 4th Marquis of, 1863–1951, vol. V

Bristol, 5th Marquess of, 1870–1960, vol. V

Bristol, 6th Marquess of, 1915–1985, vol. VIII

Bristol, Hon. Edmund, 1861–1927, vol. II

Bristol, Major Everett, 1888–1976, vol. VII

Bristow, Sir Charles Holditch, 1887–1967, vol. VI

Bristow, Ernest, 1873–1968, vol. VI

Bristow, Frederick George, *died* 1945, vol. IV

Bristow, Very Rev. John, *died* 1909, vol. I

Bristow, Rev. Richard Rhodes, *died* 1914, vol. I

Bristow, Sir Robert Charles, 1880–1966, vol. VI

Bristow, Walter Rowley, 1882–1947, vol. IV

Bristowe, Ethel Susan Graham, 1866–1952, vol. V

Bristowe, Samuel Botelen, *died* 1897, vol. I

Bristowe, William Syer, 1901–1979, vol. VII

Brittain, Alida Luisa, (Lady Brittain), *died* 1943, vol. IV

Brittain, Rev. Canon Arthur Henry Barrett, 1854–1911, vol. I

Brittain, Frederick, *died* 1969, vol. VI

Brittain, Sir Harry Ernest, 1873–1974, vol. VII

Brittain, Sir Herbert, 1894–1961, vol. VI

Brittain, John, 1849–1913, vol. I

Brittain, Vera, 1896–1970, vol. VI

Brittain, Rear-Adm. Wilfred Geoffrey, 1903–1979, vol. VII

Brittain, William Henry, 1835–1922, vol. II

Brittain, William James, 1905–1977, vol. VII

Brittan, Maj.-Gen. Charles Gisborne, 1860–1939, vol. III

Britten, Baron (Life Peer); (Edward) Benjamin Britten, 1913–1976, vol. VII

Britten, Benjamin; *see* Baron Britten.

Britten, Brig. Charles Richard, 1894–1984, vol. VIII

Britten, Comdr Sir Edgar Theophilus, 1874–1936, vol. III

Britten, Forester Richard John, 1928–1977, vol. VII

Britten, James, 1846–1924, vol. II

Britten, Rear-Adm. Richard Frederick, 1843–1910, vol. I

Brittlebank, Lt-Col Joseph William Forster, 1876–1944, vol. IV

Britton, Major Arthur Henry Daniel, 1875–1934, vol. III

Britton, Hon. Byron Moffat, 1833–1921, vol. II

Britton, Brig. Edwin John James, 1880–1955, vol. V

Britton, George Bryant, 1863–1929, vol. III

Britton, Hubert Thomas Stanley, 1892–1960, vol. V

Britton, Rev. Canon John, 1881–1948, vol. IV

Britton, Karl William, 1909–1983, vol. VIII

Britton, Major Philip William Poole C.; *see* Carlyon-Britton.

Brittorous, Brig. Francis Gerard Russell, 1896–1974, vol. VII

Broad, Lt-Gen. Sir Charles Noel Frank, 1882–1976, vol. VII

Broad, Charlie Dunbar, 1887–1971, vol. VII

Broad, Francis Alfred, 1874–1956, vol. V

Broad, George Alexander, 1844–1915, vol. I

Broad, Philip, 1903–1966, vol. VI

Broad, William Henry, 1875–1948, vol. IV

Broadbent, A., *died* 1919, vol. II(A), vol. III

Broadbent, Albert, 1867–1912, vol. I

Broadbent, Benjamin, 1850–1925, vol. II

Broadbent, Maj.-Gen. Sir Edward Nicholson, 1875–1944, vol. IV

Broadbent, Captain Harvey William, 1864–1942, vol. IV

Broadbent, Henry, 1852–1935, vol. III

Broadbent, Col John, 1872–1938, vol. III

Broadbent, Sir John, 2nd Bt, 1865–1946, vol. IV

Broadbent, Col John Edward, 1845–1931, vol. III

Broadbent, Joseph Edward, 1883–1948, vol. IV

Broadbent, Walter, *died* 1951, vol. V

Broadbent, Sir William Francis, 3rd Bt, 1904–1987, vol. VIII

Broadbent, Sir William Henry, 1st Bt, 1835–1907, vol. I

Broadbridge, 1st Baron, 1869–1952, vol. V

Broadbridge, 2nd Baron, 1895–1972, vol. VII

Broadbridge, Stanley Robertson, 1828–1978, vol. VII

Broadfoot, Col Archibald, 1843–1926, vol. II

Broadfoot, Hon. Sir Walter James, 1881–1965, vol. VI

Broadfoot, Major William, 1841–1922, vol. II

Broadhead, Rt Rev. Mgr Joseph, 1860–1929, vol. III

Broadhurst, Sir Edward Tootal, 1st Bt, 1858–1922, vol. II

Broadhurst, George H., 1866–1952, vol. V

Broadhurst, Henry, 1840–1911, vol. I

Broadhurst, Mary Aadelaide, *died* 1928, vol. II

Broadley, Alexander Meyrick, 1847–1916, vol. II

Broadley, Henry Broadley Harrison-, 1853–1914, vol. I

Broadley, Sir Herbert, 1892–1983, vol. VIII

Broadmead, Sir Philip Mainwaring, 1893–1977, vol. VII

Broadrick, Edward George, 1864–1929, vol. III

Broadus, Edmund Kemper, 1876–1936, vol. III

Broadway, Sir Alan Brice, 1873–1948, vol. IV

Broadway, Leonard Marsham, 1903–1974, vol. VII

Broadwood, Brig.-Gen. Arthur, 1849–1928, vol. II

Broadwood, Bertha Marion, 1846–1935, vol. III

Broadwood, Captain Evelyn Henry Tschudi, 1889–1975, vol. VII

Broadwood, Lt-Gen. Robert George, 1862–1917, vol. II

Broatch, Surg. Rear-Adm. George Thomas, 1862–1945, vol. IV

Broatch, James, 1900–1986, vol. VIII

Brock, Baron (Life Peer); Russell Claude Brock, 1903–1980, vol. VII

Brock, Alan Francis C.; *see* Clutton-Brock.

Brock, Lt-Col Alec Walter Saumarez, 1878–1949, vol. IV

Brock, Arthur C.; *see* Clutton-Brock.

Brock, Charles Edmund, 1870–1938, vol. III

Brock, Captain Donald Carey, 1891–1970, vol. VI

Brock, Dame Dorothy; *see* Brock, Dame M. D.

Brock, Adm. Sir Frederic Edward Errington, 1854–1929, vol. III

Brock, Brig.-Gen. Henry Jenkins, 1870–1933, vol. III

Brock, Air Cdre Henry Le Marchant, 1889–1946, vol. VI

Brock, Henry Matthew, 1875–1960, vol. V

Brock, Sir Laurence George 1879–1949, vol. IV

Brock, Dame (Madeline) Dorothy, 1886–1969, vol. VI

Brock, Adm. of the Fleet Sir Osmond de Beauvoir, 1869–1947, vol. IV

Brock, Rear-Adm. Patrick Willet, 1902–1988, vol. VIII

Brock, Reginald Walter, 1874–1935, vol. III

Brock, Sir Thomas, 1847–1922, vol. II

Brockbank, A. E., 1862–1958, vol. V

Brockbank, (John) Philip, 1922–1989, vol. VIII

Brockbank, Philip; *see* Brockbank, J. P.

Brockbank, Russell Partridge, 1913–1979, vol. VII

Brockbank, William, 1900–1984, vol. VIII

Brocket, 1st Baron, 1866–1934, vol. III

Brocket, 2nd Baron, 1904–1967, vol. VI

Brockholes, John William F.; *see* Fitzherbert-Brockholes.

Brockholes, William Joseph F.; *see* Fitzherbert-Brockholes.

Brockhurst, Gerald Leslie, 1890–1978, vol. VII

Brockie, Thomas, 1906–1976, vol. VII

Brockington, Rev. Alfred Allen, 1872–1938, vol. III

Brockington, Leonard Walter, 1888–1966, vol. VI

Brockington, Sir William Allport, 1871–1959, vol. V

Brocklebank, Sir Aubrey, 3rd Bt, 1873–1929, vol. III

Brocklebank, Sir (Clement) Edmund (Royds), 1882–1949, vol. IV

Brocklebank, Sir Edmund; *see* Brocklebank, Sir C. E. R.

Brocklebank, Captain Henry Cyril Royds, 1874–1957, vol. V

Brocklebank, Major John Jasper, 1875–1942, vol. IV

Brocklebank, Sir John Montague, 5th Bt, 1915–1974, vol. VII

Brocklebank, Mary Petrena; *see* Brocklebank, Mrs Thomas.

Brocklebank, Sir Thomas, 1st Bt, 1814–1906, vol. I

Brocklebank, Sir Thomas, 2nd Bt, 1848–1911, vol. I

Brocklebank, Thomas, 1841–1919, vol. II

Brocklebank, Mrs Thomas, (Mary Petrena Brocklebank), 1849–1937, vol. III

Brocklebank, Sir Thomas Aubrey Lawies, 4th Bt, 1899–1953, vol. V

Brocklehurst, Charles Douglas Fergusson P.; *see* Phillips Brocklehurst.

Brocklehurst, Rev. Canon George, 1868–1946, vol. IV

Brocklehurst, Captain Henry Dent, 1855–1932, vol. III

Brocklehurst, Major John Henry Dent-, 1882–1949, vol. IV

Brocklehurst, Sir John Ogilvy, 3rd Bt, 1926–1981, vol. VIII

Brocklehurst, Mary D.; *see* Dent-Brocklehurst.

Brocklehurst, Sir Philip Lancaster, 1st Bt, 1827–1904, vol. I

Brocklehurst, Sir Philip Lee, 2nd Bt, 1887–1975, vol. VII

Brocklehurst, Robert Walter Douglas Phillips, 1861–1948, vol. IV

Brocklehurst, William Brocklehurst, 1851–1929, vol. III

Brockman, Brig.-Gen. David Henry D.; *see* Drake-Brockman.

Brockman, Sir Digby Livingstone D.; *see* Drake-Brockman.

Brockman, Maj.-Gen. Edmund Alfred D.; *see* Drake-Brockman.

Brockman, Sir Edward Lewis, 1865–1943, vol. IV

Brockman, Edward Phillimore, *died* 1977, vol. VII

Brockman, Engr Rear-Adm. Henry Stafford, 1884–1958, vol. V

Brockman, Sir Henry Vernon D.; *see* Drake-Brockman.

Brockman, Lt-Col Ralph Evelyn D.; *see* Drake-Brockman.

Brockman, Ralph St Leger, 1889–1975, vol. VII

Brockway, Baron (Life Peer); (Archibald) Fenner Brockway, 1888–1988, vol. VIII

Brockwell, Esca Powys Butler, *died* 1934, vol. III

Brockwell, Rev. Canon John Cornthwaite, 1843–1927, vol. II

Brockwell, Maurice Walter, 1869–1958, vol. V

Broderick, Sir John Joyce, 1882–1933, vol. III

Broderick, Brig. Ralph Aalexander, 1888–1971, vol. VII

Brodetsky, Selig, 1888–1954, vol. V

Brodeur, Hon. Louis Philippe, 1862–1924, vol. II

Brodeur, Rear-Adm. Victor Gabriel, 1892–1976, vol. VII

Brodhurst, Henry William Frederick Cottingham, 1856–1943, vol. IV

Brodhurst, James George Joseph P.; *see* Penderel-Brodhurst.

Brodie, Captain Sir Benjamin Collins, 4th Bt, 1888–1971, vol VII

Brodie, Sir Benjamin Vincent Sellon, 3rd Bt, 1862–1938, vol. III

Brodie, Captain Ewen James, 1878–1914, vol. I

Brodie, George Bernard, 1839–1919, vol. II

Brodie, Harry Cunningham, 1875–1956, vol. V

Brodie of Brodie, Ian, 1868–1943, vol. IV

Brodie, Rabbi Sir Israel, 1895–1979, vol. VII

Brodie, John A., 1858–1934, vol. III

Brodie, Rt Rev. Matthew Joseph, 1864–1943, vol. IV

Brodie, Neil, 1900–1968, vol. VI
Brodie, Peter Ewen, 1914–1989, vol. VIII
Brodie, Very Rev. Peter Philip, 1916–1990, vol. VIII
Brodie, Thomas Gregor, 1866–1916, vol. II
Brodie, Thomas Vernor Alexander, 1907–1975, vol. VII
Brodie, Bt Major Walter Lorrain, 1884–1918, vol. II
Brodrick, Rev. Hon. Alan, 1840–1909, vol. I
Brodrick, Alan Houghton, died 1973, vol. VII
Brodrick, Hon. Arthur Grenville, 1868–1934, vol. III
Brodrick, Hon. George Charles, 1831–1903, vol. I
Brodrick, Sir Thomas, 1856–1925, vol. II
Brodrick, William John Henry, 1874–1964, vol. VI
Brodrick, Brig. William Le Couteur, 1888–1973, vol. VII
Brodsky, Adolph, 1851–1929, vol. III
Brogan, Colm, 1902–1977, vol. VII
Brogan, Sir Denis William, 1900–1974, vol. VII
Broglie, Duc de, Maurice, 1875–1960, vol. V
Broke-Smith, Brig. Philip William Lilian, 1882–1963, vol. VI
Bromage, Lt-Col John Aldhelm Raikes, 1891–1955, vol. V
Bromby, Rt Rev. Charles Henry, 1814–1907, vol. I
Bromet, Air Vice-Marshal Sir Geoffrey Rhodes, 1891–1983, vol. VIII
Bromet, Mary (Mrs Alfred Bromet); see Pownall, Mary.
Bromfield, Rev. George Henry Worth, 1842–1920, vol. II
Bromfield, Major Harry Hickman, 1869–1916, vol. II
Bromfield, Louis, 1896–1956, vol. V
Bromfield, William, 1868–1950, vol IV
Bromhead, Lt-Col Alfred Claude, 1876–1963, vol. VI
Bromhead, Sir Benjamin Denis Gonville, 5th Bt, 1900–1981, vol. VIII
Bromhead, Col Sir Benjamin Parnell, 4th Bt, 1838–1935, vol. III
Bromhead, Col Charles James, 1840–1922, vol. II
Bromilow, Maj.-Gen (David) George, 1884–1959, vol. V
Bromilow, Maj.-Gen. George; see Bromilow, Maj.-Gen. D. G.
Bromilow, Brig.-Gen. Walter, 1863–1939, vol. III
Bromilow, Rev. William E., 1857–1929, vol. III
Bromley, Rear-Adm. Sir Arthur, 8th Bt, 1876–1961, vol. VI
Bromley, Rear-Adm. Arthur Charles Burgoyne, died 1909, vol. I
Bromley, Sir Henry, 5th Bt, 1849–1905, vol. I
Bromley, Sir John, 1849–1915, vol. I
Bromley, John, 1876–1945, vol. IV
Bromley, Lancelot, 1885–1949, vol. IV
Bromley, Sir Maurice, 7th Bt; see Bromley-Wilson.
Bromley, Sir Robert, 6th Bt, 1874–1906, vol. I
Bromley, Sir Rupert Howe, 9th Bt, 1910–1966, vol. VI
Bromley, Sir Thomas Eardley, 1911–1987, vol. VIII
Bromley-Davenport, Dame Lilian Emily Isabel Jane, 1878–1972, vol. VII
Bromley-Davenport, Mrs Muriel Coomber, 1879–1956, vol. V
Bromley-Davenport, Lt-Col Sir Walter Henry, 1903–1989, vol. VIII

Bromley-Davenport, Brig.-Gen. Sir William, 1862–1949, vol. IV
Bromley-Derry, Henry, 1885–1954, vol. V
Bromley-Martin, Granville Edward, died 1941, vol. IV
Bromley-Wilson, Sir Maurice, 7th Bt, 1875–1957, vol. V
Brommage, Joseph Charles, 1897–1972, vol. VII
Brommelle, Norman Spencer, 1915–1989, vol. VIII
Bromwich, Engr Rear-Adm. George Herbert, 1871–1965, vol. VI
Bromwich, T. J. I'anson, died 1929, vol. III
Bronk, Detlev Wulf, 1897–1975, vol. VII
Bronowski, Jacob, 1908–1974, vol. VII
Bronson, Howard Logan, 1878–1968, vol. VI
Broodbank, Sir Joseph Guinness, 1857–1944, vol. IV
Brook, Rev. Canon Alfred Eyre-, died 1949, vol. IV
Brook, Barnaby; see Brooks, W. C.
Brook, Caspar, 1920–1983, vol. VIII
Brook, Charles, 1866–1930, vol. III
Brook, Clive, 1887–1974, vol. II
Brook, Rev. David, 1854–1933, vol. III
Brook, Donald Charles, 1894–1976, vol. VII
Brook, Sir Dryden, 1884–1971, vol. VI
Brook, Maj.-Gen. Edmund Smith, 1845–1910, vol. I
Brook, Edward Jonas, 1865–1924, vol. II
Brook, Captain Edward William, 1895–1963, vol. VI
Brook, Lt-Col Sir Frank, 1883–1960, vol. V
Brook, George Leslie, 1910–1987, vol. VIII
Brook, Herbert Arthur, 1855–1925, vol. II
Brook, Cdre James Kenneth, 1889–1976, vol. VII
Brook, John Herbert, 1912–1963, vol. VI
Brook, Bt Col Reginald James, 1885–1965, vol. VI
Brook, Rt Rev. Richard, 1880–1969, vol. VI
Brook, Rev. Victor John Knight, 1887–1974, vol. VII
Brook, Air Vice-Marshal William Arthur Darville, 1901–1953, vol. V
Brook-Jackson, Rev. Canon Edwin, 1877–1936, vol. III
Brooke of Cumnor, Baron (Life Peer); Henry Brooke, 1903–1984, vol. VIII
Brooke of Oakley, 1st Baron, 1869–1944, vol. IV
Brooke, Rev. Alan England, 1863–1939, vol. III
Brooke, Sir (Arthur) Douglas, 4th Bt (cr 1822), 1865–1907, vol. I
Brooke, Captain Basil Richard, 1882–1929, vol. III
Brooke, Vice-Adm. Basil Charles Barrington, 1895–1983, vol. VIII
Brooke, Sir Basil Stanlake, 5th Bt (cr 1822); see Brookeborough, 1st Viscount.
Brooke, Rear-Adm. Sir Basil Vernon, 1876–1945, vol. IV
Brooke, (Bernard) Jocelyn, 1908–1966, vol. VI
Brooke, Lt-Gen. Sir Bertram Norman Sergison-, 1880–1967, vol. VI
Brooke, Sir Charles Anthony Johnson; see Sarawak, Rajah of.
Brooke, Col. Louis, 1868–1938, vol. III
Brooke, Sir Charles Vyner, 1874–1963, vol. VI
Brooke, Brig.-Gen. Christopher Robert Ingham, 1869–1948, vol. IV
Brooke, Sir Douglas; see Brooke, Sir A. D.
Brooke, Sir Edward Geoffrey de C.; see de Capell Brooke.

Brooke, Lt-Col Edward William Saurin, 1873–1954, vol. V

Brooke, Emma Frances, *died* 1926, vol. II

Brooke, Sir Francis Hugh, 2nd Bt (*cr* 1903), 1882–1954, vol. V

Brooke, Rt Rev. Francis Key, 1852–1918, vol. II

Brooke, Rt Hon. Frank, 1851–1920, vol. II

Brooke, Maj.-Gen. Frank Hastings, 1909–1982, vol. VIII

Brooke, Maj-Gen. Geoffrey Francis Heremon, 1884–1966, vol. VI

Brooke, Sir George Cecil Francis, 3rd Bt (*cr* 1903), 1916–1982, vol. VIII

Brooke, George Cyril, 1884–1934, vol. III

Brooke, Lt-Col George Frank, *born* 1878, vol. II

Brooke, Sir George Frederick, 1st Bt (*cr* 1903), 1849–1926, vol. II

Brooke, Gilbert Edward, 1873–1936, vol. III

Brooke, Col Harry Morris Mitchelson, 1868–1934, vol. III

Brooke, Captain Sir Harry Vesey, 1845–1921, vol. II

Brooke, Brig.-Gen. Hugh Fenwick, 1871–1948, vol. IV

Brooke, Humphrey; *see* Brooke, T. H.

Brooke, Rev. James Mark Saurin, 1842–1918, vol. II

Brooke, Jocelyn; *see* Brooke, B. J.

Brooke, John, 1912–1987, vol. VIII

Brooke, Sir John Arthur, 1st Bt (*cr* 1919), 1844–1920, vol. II

Brooke, John Henry, *died* 1902, vol. I

Brooke, John Kendall, 1856–1939, vol. III

Brooke, Sir John Reeve, 1880–1937, vol. III

Brooke, Major Sir John Weston, 3rd Bt (*cr* 1919), 1911–1983, vol. VIII

Brooke, Ven. Joshua Ingham, 1836–1906, vol. I

Brooke, Gp-Captain Kennedy Gerard, 1882–1959, vol. V

Brooke, Leonard Leslie, 1862–1940, vol. III

Brooke, Brig.-Gen. Lionel Godolphin, 1849–1931, vol. III

Brooke, Margaret, (Lady Brooke); *see* Sarawak, Ranee of.

Brooke, Nevile John, 1891–1968, vol. VI

Brooke, Sir (Norman) Richard (Rowley), 1910–1989, vol. VIII

Brooke, Lt-Col Ralph, 1900–1982, vol. VIII

Brooke, Sir Richard; *see* Brooke, Sir N. R. R.

Brooke, Ven. Richard, *died* 1926, vol. II

Brooke, Sir Richard Christopher, 9th Bt (*cr* 1662), 1888–1981, vol. VIII

Brooke, Col Richard Edward Frederic H.; *see* Howard-Brooke.

Brooke, Sir Richard Marcus, 8th Bt (*cr* 1662), 1850–1920, vol. II

Brooke, Major Sir Robert Weston, 2nd Bt (*cr* 1919), 1885–1942, vol. IV

Brooke, Col Ronald George, 1866–1930, vol. III

Brooke, Rev. Stopford Augustus, 1832–1916, vol. II

Brooke, Stopford W. W., 1859–1938, vol. III

Brooke, Sir Thomas, 1st Bt (*cr* 1899), 1830–1908, vol. I

Brooke, (Thomas) Humphrey, 1914–1988, vol. VIII

Brooke, Major Victor Reginald, 1873–1914, vol. I

Brooke, Brig. Walter Headfort, 1887–1975, vol. VII

Brooke, Sir William Robert, 1842–1924, vol. II

Brooke, Willie, 1896–1939, vol. III

Brooke, Zachary Nugent, 1883–1946, vol. IV

Brooke-Hitching, Sir Thomas Henry, 1858–1926, vol. II

Brooke-Hunt, Violet, *died* 1910, vol. I

Brooke-Pechell, Sir Alexander; *see* Brooke-Pechell, Sir A. A.

Brooke-Pechell, Sir (Augustus) Alexander, 7th Bt, 1857–1937, vol. III

Brooke-Pechell, Sir George Samuel; *see* Pechell.

Brooke-Pechell, Sir Samuel George; *see* Pechell.

Brooke-Popham, Air Chief Marshal Sir Robert; *see* Popham.

Brookeborough, 1st Viscount, 1888–1973, vol. VII

Brookeborough, 2nd Viscount, 1922–1987, vol. VIII

Brooker, Brig.-Gen. Edward Part, 1866–1946, vol. IV

Brooker, William, 1918–1983, vol. VIII

Brookes, Hon. and Rev. Edgar Harry, 1897–1979, vol. VII

Brookes, Captain Sir Ernest Geoffrey, 1889–1969, vol. VI

Brookes, Ernest Roy, 1904–1972, vol. VII

Brookes, Air Vice-Marshal Hugh Hamilton, 1904–1988, vol. VIII

Brookes, Mabel Balcombe, (Lady Brookes), *died* 1975, vol. VII

Brookes, Sir Norman Everard, 1877–1968, vol. VI

Brookes, Warwick, *died* 1935, vol. III

Brookfield, Col Arthur Montagu, 1853–1940, vol. III

Brookfield, Charles Hallam Elton, 1857–1913, vol. I

Brookfield, G. Piers, 1894–1975, vol. VII

Brooking, Allan John, 1934–1980, vol. VII

Brooking, Maj.-Gen. Sir Harry Triscott, 1864–1944, vol. IV

Brooking, Adm. Patrick W. B., 1896–1964, vol. VI

Brookman, Sir George, 1853–1927, vol. II

Brooks, Sir (Arthur) David, 1864–1930, vol. III

Brooks, Captain Arthur William, 1887–1941, vol. IV

Brooks, Collin; *see* Brooks, W. C.

Brooks, Gen. Sir Dallas; *see* Brooks, Gen. Sir R. A. D.

Brooks, Sir David; *see* Brooks, Sir A. D.

Brooks, Eric St John; *see* Brooks, W. E. St J.

Brooks, Ernest Walter, 1863–1955, vol. V

Brooks, Hon. Mrs Florence, *died* 1934, vol. III

Brooks, Francis, 1861–1936, vol. III

Brooks, Ven. Frederick Richard, *died* 1912, vol. I

Brooks, Frederick Tom, 1882–1952, vol. V

Brooks, Rt Rev. Gerald Henry, 1905–1974, vol. VII

Brooks, Herbert, 1842–1918, vol. II

Brooks, Iris Mary, *died* 1971, vol. VII

Brooks, James, 1825–1901, vol. I

Brooks, Sir James Henry, 1863–1941, vol. IV

Brooks, John Birtwhistle Tyrrell, 1889–1962, vol. VI

Brooks, Hon. Marshall Jones, 1855–1944, vol. IV

Brooks, Oliver, 1920–1985, vol. VIII

Brooks, Ralph Terence St J.; *see* St John-Brooks.

Brooks, Gen. Sir (Reginald Alexander) Dallas, *died* 1966, vol. VI

Brooks, Ronald Clifton, 1899–1980, vol. VII

Brooks, Sydney, 1872–1937, vol. III

Brooks, Thomas Judson, 1880–1958, vol. V

Brooks, Lt-Col T(homas) Marshall, 1893–1967, vol. VI

Brooks, Van Wyck, 1886–1963, vol. VI

Brooks, Hon. William, 1858–1937, vol. III

Brooks, (William) Collin, 1893–1959, vol. V

Brooks, Sir William Cunliffe, 1st Bt, 1819–1900, vol. I

Brooks, (William) Eric St John, 1883–1955, vol. V

Brooksbank, Sir Edward Clitherow, 1st Bt, 1858–1943, vol. IV

Brooksbank, Col Sir (Edward) William, 2nd Bt, 1915–1983, vol. VIII

Brooksbank, Kenneth, 1915–1990, vol. VIII

Brooksbank, Col Sir William; *see* Brooksbank, Col Sir E. W.

Brooksby; *see* Elmhirst, Capt. E. P.

Broom, Cyril George Mitchell, 1889–1968, vol. VI

Broom, Sir James Thomson, 1866–1931, vol. III

Broom, Robert, 1866–1951, vol. V

Brooman-White, Major Charles James, 1883–1954, vol. V

Brooman-White, Richard Charles, 1912–1964, vol. VI

Broome, Viscount; Henry Franklin Chevallier Kitchener, 1878–1928, vol. II

Broome, Francis Napier, 1891–1980, vol. VII(AII)

Broome, Harold Holkar, 1875–1958, vol. V

Broome, Mary Ann, (Lady Broome), *died* 1911, vol. I

Broome, Maj.-Gen. Ralph Champneys, 1860–1915, vol. I

Broome, Hon. William, 1852–1930, vol. III

Broomfield, Sir Robert Stonehouse, 1882–1957, vol. V

Brophy, John, 1899–1965, vol. VI

Bros, James Reader White, 1841–1923, vol. II

Brosio, Manlio, 1897–1980, vol. VII

Broster, Dorothy Kathleen, *died* 1950, vol. IV

Broster, Lennox Ross, *died* 1965, vol. VI

Brotchie, James Rayner, 1909–1956, vol. V

Brotherhood, Stanley, 1876–1938, vol. III

Brotherston, Sir John Howie Flint, 1915–1985, vol. VIII

Brotherton, 1st Baron, 1856–1930, vol. III

Brotherton, Charles Frederick Ratcliffe, 1882–1949, vol. IV

Brotherton, Harry George, 1890–1980, vol. VII(AII)

Brotherton, John, 1867–1941, vol. IV

Brough, Maj.-Gen. Alan, 1876–1956, vol. V

Brough, Bennett Hooper, 1860–1908, vol. I

Brough, Bertram C., *died* 1938, vol. III

Brough, Charles Allan La Touche, *died* 1925, vol. II

Brough, Major John, *died* 1917, vol. II

Brough, John, 1917–1984, vol. VIII

Brough, Joseph, 1852–1925, vol. II

Brough, Lionel, 1836–1909, vol. I

Brough, Mary Bessie, 1863–1937, vol. III

Brough, Robert, 1872–1905, vol. I

Broughall, Rt Rev. Lewis Wilmot Bovell, 1876–1958, vol. V

Brougham and Vaux, 3rd Baron, 1836–1927, vol. II

Brougham and Vaux, 4th Baron, 1909–1967, vol. VI

Brougham, Harold de Vaux, 1858–1930, vol. III

Brougham, Very Rev. Henry, 1827–1913, vol. I

Brougham, Captain Hon. Henry, 1883–1927, vol. II

Brougham, James Rigg, 1826–1919, vol. II

Broughshane, 1st Baron, 1872–1953, vol. V

Broughton, Sir Alfred Davies Devonsher, 1902–1979, vol. VII

Broughton, Major Sir Delves; *see* Broughton, Major Sir H. J. D.

Broughton, Sir Delves Louis, 10th Bt, 1857–1914, vol. I

Broughton, Sir Henry Delves, 9th Bt, 1808–1899, vol. I

Broughton, Rev. Henry Ellis, *died* 1924, vol. II

Broughton, Major Sir (Henry John) Delves, 11th Bt, 1888–1942, vol. IV

Broughton, Leonard Gaston, 1864–1936, vol. III

Broughton, Miss Rhoda, 1840–1920, vol. II

Broughton, Urban Hanlon, 1857–1929, vol. III

Broughton-Adderley, Hubert John; *see* Adderley.

Broughton-Head, Leslie Charles, *died* 1961, vol. VI

Broun, Sir (James) Lionel, 11th Bt, 1875–1962, vol. VI

Broun, John Alexander, 1856–1935, vol. III

Broun, Sir Lionel; *see* Broun, Sir J. L.

Broun, Sir William, 10th Bt, 1848–1918, vol. II

Broun Lindsay, Major Sir (George) Humphrey (Maurice), 1888–1964, vol. VI

Broun Lindsay, Major Sir Humphrey; *see* Broun Lindsay, Major Sir G. H. M.

Brounger, Captain Kenneth, 1881–1942, vol. IV

Brounger, Richard Ernest, 1849–1922, vol. II

Brousson, Louis Maurice, *died* 1920, vol. II

Brouwer, Luitzen Egbertus Jan, 1881–1966, vol. VI

Browder, Earl Russell, 1891–1973, vol. VII

Browell, Col William Basil, 1870–1935, vol. III

Browett, Sir Leonard, 1884–1959, vol. V

Brown, Baron (Life Peer); Wilfred Banks Duncan Brown, 1908–1985, vol. VIII

Brown, A. Curtis, 1866–1945, vol. IV

Brown, Rev. A. Douglas, 1874–1940, vol. III

Brown, Adrian John, 1852–1919, vol. II

Brown, Alan Brock, 1911–1980, vol. VII

Brown, Alan Grahame, 1913–1972, vol. VII

Brown, Brig. Alan Ward, 1909–1971, vol. VII

Brown, Albert Joseph, 1861–1938, vol. III

Brown, Hon. Alexander, 1851–1926, vol. II

Brown, Alexander Crum, 1838–1922, vol. II

Brown, Col Alexander Denis B.; *see* Burnett-Brown.

Brown, Sir Alexander Hargreaves, 1st Bt, 1844–1922, vol. II

Brown, Alexander Kellock, 1849–1922, vol. II

Brown, Alfred Barratt, 1887–1947, vol. IV

Brown, Alfred Reginald R.; *see* Radcliffe-Brown.

Brown, Sir Alfred W., 1883–1955, vol. V

Brown, Sir Algernon; *see* Brown, Sir T. A.

Brown, Allan, 1884–1969, vol. VI

Brown, Anthony Geoffrey Hopwood G.; *see* Gardner-Brown.

Brown, Anthony George C.; *see* Clifton-Brown.

Brown, Rev. Archibald Geikie, 1844–1922, vol. II

Brown, Armitage Noel B.; *see* Bryan-Brown.

Brown, Sir Arnesby; *see* Brown, Sir J. A. A.

Brown, Arthur, 1884–1939, vol. III

Brown, Arthur, 1921–1979, vol. VII

Brown, Rev. Arthur Ernest, 1882–1952, vol. V

Brown, Wing Comdr Arthur James, 1884–1949, vol. IV

Brown, Lt-Col Arthur Miles W,; *see* Weber-Brown.

Brown, Sir Arthur W.; *see* Whitten-Brown.
Brown, Ashley Geikie, *died* 1957, vol. V
Brown, Major Cecil, *born* 1867, vol. II
Brown, Cecil Jermyn, 1886–1945, vol. IV
Brown, Air Vice-Marshal Cecil Leonard Morley, 1895–1955, vol. V
Brown, Cedric C.; *see* Clifton Brown.
Brown, Charles, 1849–1929, vol. III
Brown, Charles, 1884–1940, vol. III
Brown, Rev. Charles, 1855–1947, vol. IV
Brown, Sir Charles Gage, 1826–1908, vol. I
Brown, Charles Herbert, 1868–1942, vol. IV
Brown, Sir (Charles) James Officer, 1897–1984, vol. VIII
Brown, Lt-Col Charles John, *died* 1939, vol. III
Brown, Adm. Charles Randall, 1899–1983, vol. VIII
Brown, Col Charles Turner, 1875–1939, vol. III(A), vol. IV
Brown, Christopher Wilson, 1891–1949, vol. IV
Brown, Col Claude R.; *see* Russell-Brown.
Brown, Captain Claude Wreford W.; *see* Wreford-Brown.
Brown, Air Vice-Marshal Colin Peter, 1898–1965, vol. VI
Brown, David, *died* 1935, vol. III
Brown, Rt Rev. David Alan, 1922–1982, vol. VIII
Brown, David Hownam, 1879–1961, vol. VI
Brown, Derek Ernest D.; *see* Denny-Brown.
Brown, Douglas James, 1925–1989, vol. VIII
Brown, Eden Tatton, 1877–1961, vol. VI
Brown, Dame Edith Mary, 1864–1956, vol. V
Brown, Sir Edward, 1851–1939, vol. III
Brown, Edward Clifton C.; *see* Clifton-Brown.
Brown, Edward Percy, 1911–1972, vol. VII
Brown, Edward Thomas, 1879–1943, vol. IV
Brown, Edwin Percy, 1917–1990, vol. VIII
Brown, Eric, *died* 1939, vol. III
Brown, Maj.-Gen. Eric Gilmour, 1900–1967, vol. VI
Brown, Ernest, 1878–1949, vol. IV
Brown, Rt Hon. Ernest, 1881–1962, vol. VI
Brown, Lt-Col Ernest C.; *see* Craig-Brown.
Brown, Rev. Ernest Faulkner, 1854–1933, vol. III
Brown, Ernest William, 1866–1938, vol. III
Brown, (Everard) Kenneth, 1879–1958, vol. V
Brown, F. Gregory, 1887–1941, vol. IV
Brown, Rev. Francis, 1849–1916, vol. II
Brown, Vice-Adm. Francis Clifton,1874–1963, vol. VI
Brown, Francis David Wynyard, 1915–1967, vol. VI
Brown, Francis Y.; *see* Yeats-Brown.
Brown, Sir Frank, 1857–1931, vol. III
Brown, Sir Frank Herbert, 1868–1959, vol. V
Brown, Frank James, 1865–1958, vol. V
Brown, Frank Leslie, 1896–1977, vol. VII
Brown, Frank Percival, 1877–1958, vol. V
Brown, Frederick, 1851–1941, vol. IV
Brown, Adm. Frederick Dundas G.; *see* Gilpin-Brown.
Brown, Col Frederick John, 1857–1941, vol. IV
Brown, Lt-Col Geoffrey Benedict C.; *see* Clifton-Brown.
Brown, George, *born* 1844, vol. II
Brown, George, 1847–1934, vol. III
Brown, George, 1872–1946, vol. IV

Brown, George Alfred; *see* Baron George-Brown
Brown, George Clifford, 1879–1944, vol. IV
Brown, George Edward, 1872–1934, vol. III
Brown, Rt Rev. George Francis G.; *see* Graham Brown.
Brown, Rear-Adm. George Herbert Hempson, 1893–1977, vol. VII
Brown, Rev. George James C.; *see* Cowley-Brown.
Brown, Sir (George) Lindor, 1903–1971, vol. VII
Brown, George Mackenzie, 1869–1946, vol. IV
Brown, Col Sir George McLaren, 1865–1939, vol. III
Brown, George Ronald Pym A.; *see* Aldred-Brown
Brown, Sir George Thomas, 1827–1906, vol. I
Brown, Hon. George William, 1860–1919, vol. II
Brown, Gerard Baldwin, 1849–1932, vol. III
Brown, Gilbert Alexander M.; *see* Murray-Brown.
Brown, Gordon, 1921–1985, vol. VIII
Brown, H. Harris, 1864–1948, vol. IV
Brown, Major Harold, *died* 1918, vol. II
Brown, Harold, 1895–1969, vol. VI
Brown, Harold Arrowsmith, *died* 1968, vol. VI
Brown, Engr Vice-Adm. Sir Harold Arthur, 1878–1968, vol. VI
Brown, Harold George, 1876–1949, vol. IV
Brown, Harold John, 1899–1975, vol. VII
Brown, Sir Harry Percy, 1878–1967, vol. VI
Brown, Haydn, *died* 1936, vol. III
Brown, Helen Gilman, 1869–1942, vol. IV
Brown, Major Henry Coddington, 1876–1958, vol. V
Brown, Sir Henry Isaac Close, 1874–1962, vol. VI
Brown, Sir Herbert, 1869–1946, vol. IV
Brown, Herbert Charles, 1874–1940, vol. III (A), vol. IV
Brown, Herbert Macauley Sandes, 1897–1987, vol. VIII
Brown, Horace T., 1848–1925, vol. II
Brown, Horatio Robert Forbes, 1854–1926, vol. II
Brown, Brig.-Gen. Howard Clifton, 1868–1946, vol. IV
Brown, Hubert Sydney, 1898–1949, vol. IV
Brown, Ivor John Carnegie, 1891–1974, vol. VII
Brown, J. H.; *see* Hullah-Brown.
Brown, Rt Hon. James, 1862–1939, vol. III
Brown, James, *died* 1941, vol. III
Brown, James Alan Calvert, 1922–1984, vol. VIII
Brown, Sir James Officer; *see* Brown, Sir C. J. O.
Brown, Lt-Col James Arnold A.; *see* Arrowsmith-Brown.
Brown, James Arthur Kinnear, 1902–1971, vol. VII
Brown, Sir James Birch, 1888–1968, vol. VI
Brown, Lt-Col James C.; *see* Cross Brown
Brown, James Campbell, *died* 1910, vol. I
Brown, James Clifton, 1841–1917, vol. II
Brown, Hon. James Drysdale, 1850–1922, vol. II
Brown, James Duff, 1862–1914, vol. I
Brown, Major James Pearson, 1868–1942, vol. IV
Brown, Sir James Raitt, 1892–1979, vol. VII
Brown, Brig. James Sutherland, 1881–1951, vol. V
Brown, Rev. (James) Wilson (Davy), 1839–1922, vol. II
Brown, Jethro; *see* Brown, W. J.
Brown, John, 1844–1905, vol. I
Brown, Very Rev. John, 1850–1919, vol. II

Brown, John, 1830–1922, vol. II
Brown, Sir John, *died* 1928, vol. II
Brown, Lt-Gen. Sir John, 1880–1958, vol. V
Brown, John, 1890–1977, vol. VII
Brown, John A. H.; *see* Harvie-Brown.
Brown, Sir (John Alfred) Arnesby, 1866–1955, vol. V
Brown, John Cecil, 1911–1983, vol. VIII
Brown, Paymaster-Commander John Edwin Ambrose, 1879–1931, vol. III
Brown, John Francis Seccombe, 1917–1989, vol. VIII
Brown, John Frank, 1856–1941, vol. IV
Brown, Captain Sir John Hargreaves P.; *see* Pigott-Brown.
Brown, John James Graham, *died* 1925, vol. II
Brown, John Macdonald, *died* 1935, vol. III
Brown, Sir John McLeavy, 1842–1926, vol. II
Brown, John Macmillan, 1846–1935, vol. III
Brown, John Mason, 1900–1969, vol. VI
Brown, Very Rev. John Pierce, 1843–1925, vol. II
Brown, Sir John Rankine, *died* 1946, vol. IV
Brown, John T. T.; *died* 1933, vol. III
Brown, Rev. John Thomas, 1860–1929, vol. III
Brown, John Wesley, 1873–1944, vol. IV
Brown, Rev. Johnston Carnegie, 1862–1930, vol. III
Brown, Joseph, 1809–1902, vol. I
Brown, Sir Joseph, *died* 1919, vol. II
Brown, Joseph Pearce, 1850–1936, vol. III
Brown, Kenneth; *see* Brown, E. K.
Brown, Sir Kenneth Alfred Leader, 1906–1978, vol. VII
Brown, Laurence Morton, 1854–1910, vol. I
Brown, Leonard Graham, 1888–1950, vol. IV
Brown, Air Vice-Marshal Sir Leslie Oswald, 1893–1978, vol. VII
Brown, Lilian Kate Rowland-, 1863–1959, vol. V
Brown, Lilian Mabel Alice, (Lady Richmond Brown), *died* 1946, vol. IV
Brown, Sir Lindor; *see* Brown, Sir G. L.
Brown, Maj.-Gen. Llewellyn; *see* Brown, Maj.-Gen. R. L.
Brown, Mary M. Annesley, 1856–1932, vol. III
Brown, Maud Frances F.; *see* Forrester-Brown.
Brown, Sir Melville Richmond, 3rd Bt, 1866–1944, vol. IV
Brown, Meredith Jemima, *died* 1908, vol. I
Brown, Michael George Harold, 1907–1969, vol. VI
Brown, Montagu Y.; *see* Yeats-Brown.
Brown, Nicol Paton, 1853–1934, vol. III
Brown, Rev. Nigel Mackenzie M.; *see* Morgan-Brown.
Brown, Lt-Col Sir Norman Seddon S.; *see* Seddon-Brown.
Brown, Ormond John, 1922–1989, vol. VIII
Brown, Lt-Col Oscar, 1864–1932, vol. III
Brown, Rev. Canon Oscar Henry, 1896–1982, vol. VIII
Brown, Pamela Mary, 1917–1975, vol. VII
Brown, Sir Percival, 1901–1962, vol. VI
Brown, Percy, 1872–1955, vol. V
Brown, Captain Percy George, 1874–1954, vol. V
Brown, Brig.-Gen. Percy Wilson, 1876–1954, vol. V
Brown, Sir Peter Boswell, 1866–1948, vol. IV
Brown, Peter Hume, 1850–1918, vol. II
Brown, Raymond Gordon, 1912–1962, vol. VI

Brown, Reginald, *died* 1936, vol. III
Brown, Reginald Francis, 1910–1985, vol. VIII
Brown, Maj.-Gen. (Reginald) Llewellyn, 1895–1983, vol. VIII
Brown, Richard, 1844–1910, vol. I
Brown, Richard King, 1864–1942, vol. IV
Brown, Sir Robert Charles, 1836–1925, vol. II
Brown, Robert Cunyngham, 1867–1945, vol. IV
Brown, Major Sir Robert Hanbury, 1849–1926, vol. II
Brown, Robert J.; *see* Jardine-Brown.
Brown, Robert Neal R.; *see* Rudmose-Brown.
Brown, Robert Sidney, 1889–1959, vol. V
Brown, Lt-Col Robert Tilbury, 1873–1928, vol. II
Brown, Robson Christie, 1898–1971, vol. VII
Brown, Ronald David S.; *see* Stewart-Brown.
Brown, Ronald S.; *see* Stewart-Brown.
Brown, Rt Rev. Russel Featherstone, 1900–1988, vol. VIII
Brown, Samuel Edward, 1868–1929, vol. III
Brown, Sir Samuel Harold, 1903–1965, vol. VI
Brown, Samuel Lombard, *died* 1939, vol. III
Brown, Sidney George, 1873–1948, vol. IV
Brown, Spencer C.; *see* Curtis Brown.
Brown, Sir Stuart Kelson, 1885–1952, vol. V
Brown, Rear-Adm. Sydney, 1899–1970, vol. VI
Brown, Rev. Sydney Lawrence, 1880–1947, vol. IV
Brown, T. Austen, *died* 1924, vol. II
Brown, Sir (Thomas) Algernon, 1900–1960, vol. V
Brown, Thomas Brown R.; *see* Rudmose-Brown.
Brown, Thomas C.; *see* Craig-Brown.
Brown, Thomas Edwin Burton, 1833–1911, vol. I
Brown, Thomas G.; *see* Graham Brown.
Brown, Thomas James; *see* Brown, Tom.
Brown, Thomas Julian, 1923–1987, vol. VIII
Brown, Rt Hon. Thomas Watters, 1879–1944, vol. IV
Brown, Tom, (Thomas James Brown), 1886–1970, vol. VI
Brown, Air Cdre Sir Vernon, 1889–1986, vol. VIII
Brown, Hon. Villiers, 1843–1915, vol. I
Brown, Vincent, *died* 1933, vol. III
Brown, Walter, 1886–1957, vol. V
Brown, Walter Graham S.; *see* Scott-Brown.
Brown, Lt-Col Walter Henry, 1867–1928, vol. II
Brown, Walter Hugh, *died* 1950, vol. IV
Brown, Sir Walter L.; *see* Langdon-Brown.
Brown, Walter Russell, 1879–1966, vol. VI
Brown, William, 1850–1929, vol. III
Brown, William, 1856–1945, vol. IV
Brown, William, 1881–1952, vol. V
Brown, William, 1888–1975, vol. VII
Brown, Ven. William A.; *see* Ashley-Brown.
Brown, William Adams, 1865–1943, vol. IV
Brown, William B.; *see* Beattie-Brown.
Brown, Brig.-Gen. William Baker, 1864–1947, vol. IV
Brown, Sir William Barrowclough, 1893–1947, vol. IV
Brown, Maj.-Gen. William Douglas Elmes, 1913–1984, vol. VIII
Brown, Rt Rev. William F., 1862–1951, vol. V
Brown, Very Rev. William Henry, *died* 1924, vol. II
Brown, William Henry, 1845–1918, vol. II
Brown, Rt Rev. Mgr William Henry, 1852–1934, vol. III

Brown, William Herbert, *died* 1927, vol. II
Brown, Col Sir William James, 1832–1918, vol. II
Brown, Very Rev. William James, 1889–1970, vol. VI
Brown, (William) Jethro, 1868–1930, vol. III
Brown, William John, 1894–1960, vol. V
Brown, William John, 1911–1977, vol. VII
Brown, William Lowe L.; *see* Lowe-Brown.
Brown, William Marshall, 1868–1936, vol. III
Brown, Rt Rev. William Montgomery, 1855–1937, vol. III
Brown, Sir William Nicholson, 1865–1939, vol. III
Brown, Sir William R.; *see* Robson Brown.
Brown, Sir William Richmond, 2nd Bt, 1840–1906, vol. I
Brown, Sir William Roger, 1831–1902, vol. I
Brown, Sir William Scott, 1890–1968, vol. VI
Brown, Sir William Slater, 1845–1917, vol. II
Brown, Rev. William Tom, 1865–1939, vol. III
Brown, Rev. Wilson; *see* Brown, Rev. J. W. D.
Browne, Col Abraham Walker, 1854–1939, vol. III
Browne, Hon. Sir Albert, 1860–1923, vol. II
Browne, Captain Alexander Crawford, *died* 1942, vol. IV
Browne, Maj. Alexander Simon Cadogan, 1895–1987, vol. VIII
Browne, Alfred John J.; *see* Jukes-Browne.
Browne, Brig.-Gen. Alfred Joseph Bessell-, 1877–1947, vol. IV
Browne, Lt-Col Alfred Percy, 1868–1930, vol. III
Browne, Maj.-Gen. Andrew Smythe Montague, 1836–1916, vol. II
Browne, Lt-Gen. Sir Arthur George Frederic, 1851–1935, vol. III
Browne, Rt Rev. Arthur Heber, 1864–1951, vol. V
Browne, Rt Rev. Arthur Henry Howe, *died* 1961, vol. VI
Browne, Arthur Scott, 1866–1946, vol. IV
Browne, Rev. Barrington Gore, *died* 1914, vol. I
Browne, Sir Benjamin Chapman, 1839–1917, vol. II
Browne, Maj.-Gen. Beverley Wood, *died* 1948, vol. IV
Browne, Rev. Bevil; *see* Browne, Rev. W. B.
Browne, Sir Buckston; *see* Browne, Sir G. B.
Browne, Charles Edward, *born* 1861, vol. III
Browne, Sir Charles Ernest Christopher, 1871–1953, vol. V
Browne, Charles Macaulay, 1846–1911, vol. I
Browne, Col Charles Michael, 1878–1929, vol. III
Browne, Lt-Col Cuthbert Garrard, 1883–1951, vol. V
Browne, Daniel F., *died* 1913, vol. I
Browne, Denis, 1903–1965, vol. VI
Browne, Sir Denis John Wolko, 1892–1967, vol. VI
Browne, Brig.-Gen. Desmond John Edward B.; *see* Beale-Browne.
Browne, Brig. Dominick Andrew Sidney, 1904–1982, vol. VIII
Browne, Edith A., *died* 1963, vol. VI
Browne, Sir Edmond, 1857–1928, vol. II
Browne, Maj.-Gen. Edward George, 1863–1952, vol. V
Browne, Edward Granville, 1862–1926, vol. II
Browne, Sir (Edward) Humphrey, 1911–1987, vol. VIII
Browne, Edward Raban C.; *see* Cave-Browne.

Browne, E(lliott) Martin, 1900–1980, vol. VII
Browne, Col Sir Eric G.; *see* Gore-Browne.
Browne, Francis James, *died* 1863, vol. VI
Browne, Sir Francis G.; *see* Gore-Browne.
Browne, Major Frederick Macdonnell, 1873–1915, vol. I
Browne, George, *died* 1919, vol. II
Browne, Sir (George) Buckston, 1850–1945, vol. IV
Browne, Maj.-Gen. George Fitzherbert, 1851–1935, vol. III
Browne, Rt Rev. George Forrest, 1833–1930, vol. III
Browne, Col George Herbert Stewart, 1866–1944, vol. IV
Browne, Rev. George Rickards, 1854–1921, vol. II
Browne, George Sinclair, 1880–1946, vol. IV
Browne, George Stephenson, *died* 1970, vol. VI
Browne, Sir George Washington, 1853–1939, vol. III
Browne, Comdr Godfrey G.; *see* Gore-Browne.
Browne, Gordon Frederick, 1858–1932, vol. III
Browne, Sir Granville St John O.; *see* Orde Browne.
Browne, Hablot Robert Edgar, 1905–1984, vol. VIII
Browne, Hamilton Edward, 1860–1933, vol. III
Browne, Harold Carlyon Gore, 1844–1919, vol. II
Browne, Col Harold William Alexander Francis C.; *see* Crichton-Browne.
Browne, Henry Doughty, *died* 1907, vol. I
Browne, Henry George G.; *see* Gore-Browne.
Browne, Rev. Henry J., 1853–1941, vol. IV
Browne, Gen. Henry Ralph, 1828–1917, vol. II
Browne, Henry William Langley, 1848–1928, vol. II
Browne, Maj.-Gen. Herbert Jose Pierson, 1872–1953, vol. V
Browne, Gen. Horace Albert, 1832–1914, vol. I
Browne, Sir Humphrey; *see* Browne, Sir E. H.
Browne, Maj.-Gen. James, 1840–1917, vol. II
Browne, Brig. James Clendinning, 1878–1953, vol. V
Browne, Sir James C.; *see* Crichton-Browne.
Browne, Gen. Sir James Frankfort Manners, 1823–1911, vol. I
Browne, John Campbell McClure, 1912–1978, vol. VII
Browne, John Edward Stevenson, 1910–1976, vol. VII
Browne, Brig.-Gen. John Gilbert, 1878–1968, vol. VI
Browne, John Hutton Balfour-, 1845–1921, vol. II
Browne, Sir John Walton, 1845–1923, vol. II
Browne, Major John William, 1857–1938, vol. III
Browne, Julius Basil, 1892–1947, vol. IV
Browne, Kathleen A., *died* 1943, vol. IV
Browne, Rev. Laurence Edward, 1887–1986, vol. VIII
Browne, Leonard Foster, 1887–1960, vol. V
Browne, Maurice, 1881–1955, vol. V
Browne, Col Maurice, 1884–1961, vol. VI
Browne, Most Rev. Michael, *died* 1980, vol. VII
Browne, His Eminence Cardinal Michael David, 1887–1971, vol. VII
Browne, Nassau Blair, *died* 1940, vol. III(A), vol. IV
Browne, Philip Austin, 1898–1961, vol. VI
Browne, Sir Philip Henry, 1877–1950, vol. IV
Browne, Maj.-Gen. Reginald Spencer, 1856–1943, vol. IV
Browne, Richard Charles, 1911–1980, vol. VII
Browne, Rt Rev. Robert, 1844–1935, vol. III

Browne, Col Samuel Haslett, 1850–1933, vol. III
Browne, Gen. Sir Samuel James, 1824–1901, vol. I
Browne, Col Sherwood Dighton, 1862–1947, vol. IV
Browne, Dame Sidney Jane, 1850–1941, vol. IV
Browne, Stanley George, 1907–1986, vol. VIII
Browne, Lt-Col Sir Stewart G.; *see* Gore-Browne.
Browne, Maj.-Gen. Swinton John, 1837–1914, vol. I
Browne, Thomas Alexander; *see* Boldrewood, R.
Browne, Sir Thomas Anthony G.; *see* Gore Browne.
Browne, Air Marshal Sir Thomas Arthur W.; *see* Warne-Browne.
Browne, Thomas George, 1888–1963, vol. VI
Browne, Ven. Thomas Robert, 1889–1978, vol. VII
Browne, Tom, 1872–1910, vol. I
Browne, Vincent R. B.; *see* Balfour-Browne.
Browne, Major Walter Hamilton, 1875–1933, vol. III
Browne, Ven. Walter Marshall, 1885–1959, vol. V
Browne, Rt Rev. Wilfred G.; *see* Gore-Browne.
Browne, William, 1838–1924, vol. II
Browne, William Alex Francis B.; *see* Balfour-Browne.
Browne, Rev. (William) Bevil, 1845–1928, vol. II
Browne, Maj.-Gen. William C.; *see* Cave-Browne.
Browne, Lt-Col William Percy, 1893–1972, vol. VII
Browne, Surg.-Gen. William Richard, 1850–1924, vol. II
Browne, Wynyard Barry, 1911–1964, vol. VI
Browne-Cave, Sir Clement Charles C.; *see* Cave-Browne-Cave.
Browne-Cave, Rev. Sir Genille C.; *see* Cave-Browne-Cave.
Browne-Cave, Air Vice-Marshal Henry Meyrick C.; *see* Cave-Browne-Cave.
Browne-Cave, Sir Mylles C.; *see* Cave.
Browne-Cave, Captain Sir Reginald Ambrose C,; *see* Cave-Browne-Cave.
Browne-Cave, Sir Rowland Henry C.; *see* Cave-Browne-Cave.
Browne-Cave, Sir Thomas C.; *see* Cave-Browne-Cave.
Browne-Cave, Wing Comdr Thomas Reginald C.; *see* Cave-Browne-Cave.
Browne Clayton, Hon. Brig.-Gen. Robert Clayton, 1870–1939, vol. III
Browne-Mason, Col Hubert Oliver Browne, 1872–1930, vol. III
Browne-Synge-Hutchinson, Col Edward Douglas, 1861–1940, vol. III
Browne-Wilkinson, Rev. Arthur Rupert, 1889–1961, vol. VI
Brownell, Franklin; *see* Brownell, P. F.
Brownell, (Peleg) Franklin, 1857–1946, vol. IV
Brownell, Reginald Samuel, 1893–1961, vol. VI
Brownell, William Crary, 1851–1928, vol. II
Brownfield, Vice-Adm. Leslie Newton, 1901–1968, vol. VI
Brownfield, Surg. Rear-Adm. Owen Deane, 1891–1955, vol. V
Browning, Mrs Adeline Elizabeth, 1869–1950, vol. IV
Browning, Amy Katherine, 1881–1978, vol. VII
Browning, Andrew, 1889–1972, vol. VII
Browning, Carl Hamilton, 1881–1972, vol. VII
Browning, Rev. Charles William, 1855–1930, vol. III
Browning, Colin Arrott Robertson, 1833–1908, vol. I

Browning, Dame Daphne, (Lady Browning); *see* du Maurier, Dame Daphne.
Browning, Lt-Gen. Sir Frederick Arthur Montague, 1896–1965, vol. VI
Browning, Lt-Col Frederick Henry, *died* 1929, vol. III
Browning, Col George Dansey-, 1870–1941, vol. IV
Browning, Col George William, 1901–1981, vol. VIII
Browning, Lt-Col Herbert Arrott, 1861–1951, vol. V
Browning, Sir Jeffrey, 1862–1933, vol. III
Browning, Maj.-Gen. Langley, 1891–1974, vol. VII
Browning, Col Montague Charles 1837–1905, vol. I
Browning, Adm. Sir Montague Edward, 1863–1947, vol. IV
Browning, Oscar, 1837–1923, vol. II
Browning, Robert, 1902–1974, vol. VII
Browning, Sidney, *died* 1928, vol. II
Browning, Lt-Col Winthrop Benjamin, 1855–1934, vol. III
Brownjohn, Gen. Sir Nevil Charles Dowell, 1897–1973, vol. VII
Brownlee, John Donald Mackenzie, *died* 1969, vol. VI
Brownlee, John Edward, 1884–1961, vol. VI
Brownlees, Sir Anthony Culling, 1817–1897, vol. I
Brownlie, James Thomas, 1865–1938, vol. III
Brownlow, 3rd Earl, 1844–1921, vol. II
Brownlow, 5th Baron, 1867–1927, vol. II
Brownlow, 6th Baron, 1899–1978, vol. VII
Brownlow, Lt-Col Celadon Charles, 1843–1925, vol. II
Brownlow, Field-Marshal Sir Charles Henry, 1831–1916, vol. II
Brownlow, Col Charles William, 1862–1924, vol. II
Brownlow, Brig.-Gen. d'Arcy Charles, 1869–1938, vol. III
Brownlow, Lt-Gen. Henry Alexander, 1831–1914, vol. I
Brownlow, Rt Rev. William Robert, 1830–1901, vol. I
Brownlow, Maj.-Gen. William Vesey, 1841–1926, vol. II
Brownrigg, Rt Rev. Abraham, 1836–1928, vol. II
Brownrigg, Charles Edward, 1865–1942, vol. IV
Brownrigg, Vice-Adm. Sir Douglas Egremont Robert, 4th Bt, 1867–1939, vol. III
Brownrigg, Henry John Brodrick, 1828–1904, vol. I
Brownrigg, Adm. Sir (Henry John) Studholme, 1882–1943, vol. IV
Brownrigg, Sir Henry Moore, 3rd Bt, 1819–1900, vol. I
Brownrigg, Very Rev. John Studholme, 1841–1930, vol. III
Brownrigg, Col Metcalfe Studholme, 1845–1924, vol. II
Brownrigg, Adm. Sir Studholme; *see* Brownrigg, Adm. Sir H. J. S.
Brownrigg, Captain Thomas Marcus, 1902–1967, vol. IV
Brownrigg, Lt-Gen. Sir W. Douglas S., 1886–1946, vol. IV
Bruce of Melbourne, 1st Viscount, 1883–1967, vol. VI
Bruce, Vice-Adm. Alan Cameron, 1873–1947, vol. IV
Bruce, Alastair Henry, 1900–1988, vol. VIII
Bruce, Alexander, 1854–1911, vol. I
Bruce, Alexander, 1836–1920, vol. II
Bruce, Rev. Alexander Balmain, 1831–1899, vol. I

Bruce, Sir Alexander Carmichael, 1850–1926, vol. II
Bruce, Hon. Alice Moore, 1867–1951, vol. V
Bruce, Col Andrew Macrae, 1842–1920, vol. II
Bruce, Sir Charles, 1836–1920, vol. II
Bruce, Lt-Col Charles Edward, 1876–1950, vol. IV
Bruce, Brig.-Gen. Hon. Charles Granville, 1866–1939, vol. III
Bruce, Charles Mathewes, 1875–1939, vol. III
Bruce, Very Rev. Charles Saul, died 1913, vol. I
Bruce, Brig.-Gen. Clarence Dalrymple, 1862–1934, vol. III
Bruce, Rev. David, died 1911, vol. I
Bruce, Maj.-Gen. Sir David, 1855–1931, vol. III
Bruce, Col Hon. David, 1888–1964, vol. VI
Bruce, David Kirkpatrick Este, 1898–1977, vol. VII
Bruce, Rev. Douglas William, 1885–1953, vol. V
Bruce, Col Edward, 1850–1911, vol. I
Bruce, Eric Henry Stuart, 1855–1935, vol. III
Bruce, Rev. Francis Rosslyn Courtenay, 1871–1956, vol. V
Bruce, Frederick Fyvie, 1910–1990, vol. VIII
Bruce, Rt Hon. Sir Gainsford, 1834–1912, vol. I
Bruce, George Gordon, 1891–1976, vol. VII
Bruce, Col Sir Gerald Trevor, 1872–1953, vol. V
Bruce, Adm. Sir Henry Harvey, 1862–1948, vol. IV
Bruce, Rt Hon. Sir Henry Hervey, 3rd Bt (cr 1804), 1820–1907, vol. I
Bruce, Henry James, 1880–1951, vol. V
Bruce, Lt-Gen. Sir Henry Le Geyt, 1824–1899, vol. I
Bruce, Hon. Henry Lyndhurst, 1881–1915, vol. I
Bruce, Herbert, 1877–1935, vol. III
Bruce, Col Hon. Herbert Alexander, died 1963, vol. VI
Bruce, Captain Sir Hervey John William, 6th Bt (cr 1804), 1919–1971, vol. VII
Bruce, Sir Hervey Juckes Lloyd, 4th Bt (cr 1804), 1843–1919, vol. II
Bruce, Sir Hervey Ronald, 5th Bt (cr 1804), 1872–1924, vol. II
Bruce, Howard, 1879–1961, vol. VI
Bruce, Adm. Sir James Andrew Thomas, 1846–1921, vol. II
Bruce, John, 1837–1907, vol. I
Bruce, Sir John, 1905–1975, vol. VII
Bruce, Maj.-Gen. John Geoffrey, 1896–1972, vol. VII
Bruce, Hon. John Hamilton, 1889–1964, vol. VI
Bruce, John Mitchell, 1846–1929, vol. III
Bruce, Joseph Percy, 1861–1934, vol. III
Bruce, Marcus James Henry, 1890–1956, vol. V
Bruce, Sir Michael William Selby, 11th Bt (cr 1629), 1894–1957, vol. V
Bruce, Mildred Mary; see Bruce, Hon. Mrs V.
Bruce, Hon. Randolph; see Bruce, Hon. Robert R.
Bruce, Richard Isaac, 1840–1924, vol. II
Bruce, Col Robert, 1825–1899, vol. I
Bruce, Rev. Robert, 1829–1908, vol. I
Bruce, Rev. Robert, died 1915, vol. I
Bruce, Sir Robert, 1855–1931, vol. III
Bruce, Robert, died 1949, vol. IV
Bruce, Sir Robert, 1871–1955, vol. V
Bruce, Major Hon. Robert, 1882–1959, vol. V
Bruce, Robert Elton Spencer, 1936–1971, vol. VII
Bruce of Sumburgh, Robert Hunter Wingate, 1907–1983, vol. VIII

Bruce, Hon. (Robert) Randolph, 1863–1942, vol. IV
Bruce, Rev. Rosslyn; see Bruce, Rev. F. R. C.
Bruce, Tamara, (Mrs H. J. Bruce); see Karsavina, T.
Bruce, Brig.-Gen. Thomas, died 1966, vol. VI
Bruce, Thomas Dundas Hope, 1885–1940, vol. III
Bruce, Hon. Mrs Victor, (Mildred Mary), 1895–1990, vol. VIII
Bruce, Hon. Victoria Alexandrina Katherine, 1898–1951, vol. V
Bruce, Sir Wallace, 1878–1944, vol. IV
Bruce, Captain Wilfrid Montagu, 1874–1953, vol. V
Bruce, Ven. William Conybeare, died 1919, vol. II
Bruce, Sir William Cuningham, 9th Bt (cr 1629), 1825–1906, vol. I
Bruce, William Ironside, died 1921, vol. II
Bruce, William Napier, 1858–1936, vol. III
Bruce, William Speirs, 1867–1921, vol. II
Bruce, Rev. William Straton, 1846–1933, vol. III
Bruce, Sir William Waller, 10th Bt (cr 1629), 1856–1912, vol. I
Bruce-Chwatt, Leonard Jan, 1907–1989, vol. VIII
Bruce-Gardner, Sir Charles, 1st Bt, 1887–1960, vol. V
Bruce-Gardyne, Baron (Life Peer); John, (Jock), Bruce-Gardyne, 1930–1990, vol. VIII
Bruce-Joy, Albert, died 1924, vol. II
Bruce Lockhart, John Macgregor, 1914–1990, vol. VIII
Bruce Lockhart, Rab Brougham, 1916–1990, vol. VIII
Bruce Lockhart, Sir Robert Hamilton, 1887–1970, vol. VI
Bruce Mitford, Terence; see Mitford.
Bruce-Porter, Sir (Harry Edwin) Bruce, 1869–1948, vol. IV
Bruce-Williams, Maj.-Gen. Sir Hugh Bruce; see Williams.
Bruche, Maj.-Gen. Sir Julius Henry, 1873–1961, vol. VI
Bruchesi, Most Rev. Paul, 1855–1939, vol. III
Brudenell, George Lionel Thomas, 1880–1962, vol. VI
Bru-de-Wold, Col Hilmar Theodore, 1842–1913, vol. I
Bruen, Adm. Edward Francis, 1866–1952, vol. V
Bruen, Rt Hon. Henry, 1828–1912, vol. I
Bruford, Robert, 1868–1939, vol. III
Bruford, Walter Horace, 1894–1988, vol. VIII
Brugha, Cathal; see Burgess, Charles.
Bruhl, L. Burleigh, 1861–1942, vol. IV
Brühl, Paul, born 1855, vol. III
Bruhn, Erik Belton Evers, 1928–1986, vol. VIII
Brummer, Rev. Nicolaas Johannes, 1866–1947, vol. IV
Brumwell, George Murray, 1872–1963, vol. VI
Brumwell, Rev. Percy Middleton, 1881–1963, vol. VI
Brun, Constantin, 1860–1945, vol. IV
Brunault, Rt Rev. Joseph Simon-Hermann, 1857–1937, vol. III
Brundage, Avery, 1887–1975, vol. VII
Brundle, Frank Walter, 1890–1963, vol. VI
Brundrett, Sir Frederick, 1894–1974, vol. VII
Brundrit, Reginald Grange, 1883–1960, vol. V
Brune, Charles Glynn P.; see Prideaux-Brune.
Brune, Col Charles Robert P.; see Prideaux-Brune.

Brune, Sir Humphrey Ingelram P.; *see* Prideaux-Brune.

Bruneau, Hon. Arthur Aimé, 1864–1940, vol. III(A), vol. IV

Bruneau, Louis Charles Bonaventure Alfred, 1857–1934, vol. III

Brunel, Adrian Hope, 1892–1958, vol. V

Brunetiere, Ferdinand, 1849–1906, vol. I

Brunger, Captain Robert, 1893–1918, vol. II

Brüning, Heinrich, 1885–1970, vol. VI

Brunker, Brig.-Gen. Capel Molyneux, 1858–1936, vol. III

Brunker, Edward George, 1871–1951, vol. V

Brunker, Maj.-Gen. Sir James Milford Sutherland, 1854–1942, vol. IV

Brunner, Emil, 1889–1966, vol. VI

Brunner, Ernst August, *died* 1920, vol. II

Brunner, Sir Felix John Morgan, 3rd Bt, 1897–1982, vol. VIII

Brunner, Rt Rev. George, 1889–1969, vol. VI

Brunner, Sir John Fowler, 2nd Bt, 1865–1929, vol. III

Brunner, Rt Hon. Sir John Tomlinson, 1st Bt, 1842–1919, vol. II

Brunner, Roscoe, 1871–1926, vol. II

Brunot, Ferdinand, *died* 1938, vol. III

Brunskill, Catherine Lavinia Bennett, 1891–1981, vol. VIII

Brunskill, Brig. George Stephen, 1891–1982, vol. VIII

Brunskill, Maj.-Gen. Gerald, 1897–1964, vol. VI

Brunskill, Gerald FitzGibbon, 1866–1918, vol. II

Brunskill, Hubert Fawcett, 1873–1951, vol. V

Brunskill, Lt-Col John Handfield, 1875–1940, vol. III

Brunskill, Muriel, 1899–1980, vol. VII

Brunskill, Ven. Thomas Redmond, 1870–1936, vol. III

Brunt, Sir David, 1886–1965, vol. VI

Brunt, Robert Nigel Bright, 1902–1982, vol. VIII

Bruntnell, Albert, 1866–1929, vol. III

Brunton, Frederick William, 1879–1953, vol. V

Brunton, Sir (James) Stopford (Lauder), 2nd Bt, 1884–1943, vol. IV

Brunton, John Stirling, 1903–1977, vol. VII

Brunton, Sir Lauder; *see* Brunton, Sir T. L.

Brunton, Sir Stopford; *see* Brunton, Sir J. S. L.

Brunton, Sir (Thomas) Lauder, 1st Bt, 1844–1916, vol. II

Brunton, Sir William, 1867–1938, vol. III

Brunton-Angless, Violet, 1878–1951, vol. V

Brunwin-Hales, Rev. Canon G. T., 1859–1932, vol. III

Brunyate, Sir James Bennett, 1871–1951, vol. V

Brunyate, Sir William Edwin, 1867–1943, vol. IV

Brush, Lt-Col Edward James Augustus Howard, (Peter), 1901–1984, vol. VIII

Brush, Lt-Col Peter; *see* Brush, Lt-Col E. J. A. H.

Bruton, Charles Lamb, 1890–1969, vol. VI

Bruton, Rear-Adm. Charles William, 1875–1952, vol. V

Bruton, Sir James, 1848–1933, vol. III

Brutton, Charles Phipps, 1899–1964, vol. VI

Bruxner, Lt-Col Sir Michael Frederick, 1882–1970, vol. VI(AII).

Bruyne, Pieter Louis de, 1845–1917, vol. II

Bryan, Sir Andrew Meikle, 1893–1988, vol. VIII

Bryan, Charles Walter Gordon, 1883–1954, vol. V

Bryan, Denzil Arnold, 1909–1987, vol. VIII

Bryan, George Hartley, 1864–1928, vol. II

Bryan, Col Sir Herbert, 1865–1950, vol. IV

Bryan, Rev. J. Ingram, 1868–1953, vol. V

Bryan, Walter Burr-, *died* 1940, vol. III

Bryan, Col William Booth, *died* 1914, vol. I

Bryan, William Jennings, 1860–1925, vol. II

Bryan, Willoughby Guy, 1911–1987, vol. VIII

Bryan-Brown, Armitage Noel, 1900–1968, vol. VI

Bryans, Rev. John Lonsdale, 1853–1945, vol. IV

Bryant, Sir Arthur, 1899–1985, vol. VIII

Bryant, Charles David Jones, 1883–1937, vol. III

Bryant, Charles William, *died* 1935, vol. III

Bryant, Sir Francis Morgan, 1859–1938, vol. III

Bryant, Frederick, 1878–1942, vol. IV

Bryant, Frederick Beadon, 1858–1922, vol. II

Bryant, Col Frederick Carkeet, 1879–1956, vol. V

Bryant, Lt-Col George Herbert, 1883–1952, vol. V

Bryant, Captain Henry Grenville, 1872–1915, vol. I

Bryant, J. H., 1867–1906, vol. I

Bryant, Marguerite, (Mrs Munn), 1870–1962, vol. VI

Bryant, Sophie, 1850–1922, vol. II

Bryant, Thomas, 1828–1914, vol. I

Bryce, 1st Viscount, 1838–1922, vol. II

Bryce, Viscountess; (Elizabeth Marion), *died* 1939, vol. III

Bryce, Alexander Joshua Caleb, 1868–1940, vol. III

Bryce, Lt-Col Edward Daniel, 1879–1936, vol. III

Bryce, Rev. George, 1844–1931, vol. III

Bryce, James McKie, *died* 1946, vol. IV

Bryce, John Annan, 1844–1923, vol. II

Bryce, Thomas Hastie, 1862–1946, vol. IV

Bryce, William Kirk, 1867–1954, vol. V

Bryceson, Sir Arthur Benjamin, 1861–1943, vol. IV

Bryden, Henry Anderson, 1854–1937, vol. III

Bryden, Robert, 1865–1939, vol. III

Bryden, Sir William James, 1909–1986, vol. VIII

Brydon, James Herbert, 1881–1960, vol. V

Bryher, (Annie) Winifred, 1894–1983, vol. VIII

Bryher, Winifred; *see* Bryher, A. W.

Brymer, Ven. Frederick Augustus, *died* 1917, vol. II

Brymer, William Ernest, 1840–1909, vol. I

Brymner, William, *born* 1855, vol. III

Bryson, Charles; *see* Barry, Charles.

Bryson, George Murray, 1904–1970, vol. VI

Buber, Martin, 1878–1965, vol. VI

Buccleuch, 6th Duke of, **and Queensberry,** 8th Duke of, 1831–1914, vol. I

Buccleuch, 7th Duke of, **and Queensberry,** 9th Duke of, 1864–1935, vol. III

Buccleuch, 8th Duke of, **and Queensberry,** 10th Duke of, 1894–1973, vol. VII

Buchan, 13th Earl of, 1815–1899, vol. I

Buchan, 14th Earl of, 1850–1934, vol. III

Buchan, 15th Earl of, 1878–1960, vol. V

Buchan, 16th Earl of, 1899–1984, vol. VIII

Buchan, Hon. Alastair Francis, 1918–1976, vol. VII

Buchan, Alexander, 1829–1907, vol. I

Buchan, Anna, *died* 1948, vol. IV

Buchan, Lt-Col Charles Forbes, 1869–1954, vol. V

Buchan, Brig. David Adye, 1890–1950, vol. IV

Buchan, Captain James Ivory, 1885–1958, vol. V

Buchan, John; *see* Tweedsmuir, 1st Baron.

Buchan, Brig.-Gen. Lawrence, 1847–1909, vol. I

Buchan, Norman Findlay, 1922–1990, vol. VIII

Buchan, Priscilla Jean Fortescue; *see* Baroness Tweedsmuir of Belhelvie.

Buchan-Hepburn, Sir Archibald, 4th Bt, 1852–1929, vol. III

Buchan-Hepburn, Sir John Karslake Thomas, 5th Bt, 1894–1961, vol. VI

Buchanan, Most Rev. Alan Alexander, 1907–1984, vol. VIII

Buchanan, Sir Alexander Wellesley George Thomas L.; *see* Leith-Buchanan.

Buchanan, Captain Angus, 1886–1954, vol. V

Buchanan, Lt-Col Arthur Louis Hamilton, 1866–1925, vol. II

Buchanan, Arthur William Patrick, 1870–1939, vol. III

Buchanan, Major Sir Charles James, 4th Bt, 1899–1984, vol. VIII

Buchanan, Sir David Carrick Robert C.; *see* Carrick-Buchanan.

Buchanan, David William Ramsay C.; *see* Carrick-Buchanan.

Buchanan, Hon. Sir (Ebenezer) John, 1844–1930, vol. III

Buchanan, Brig. Edgar James Bernard, 1892–1979, vol. VII

Buchanan, Sir Eric Alexander, 3rd Bt, 1848–1928, vol. II

Buchanan, George, 1827–1906, vol. I

Buchanan, Rt Hon. George, 1890–1955, vol. V

Buchanan, Sir George Cunningham, 1865–1940, vol. III

Buchanan, Sir George Hector L.; *see* Leith-Buchanan.

Buchanan, Sir George Hector Macdonald L.; *see* Leith-Buchanan.

Buchanan, George Henry Perrott, 1904–1989, vol. VIII

Buchanan, Sir George Seaton, 1869–1936, vol. III

Buchanan, Rt Hon. Sir George William, 1854–1924, vol. II

Buchanan, Lt-Gen. Henry James, 1830–1903, vol. I

Buchanan, Rear-Adm. Herbert James, 1902–1965, vol. VI

Buchanan, J. Courtney, 1877–1949, vol. IV

Buchanan, Jack, (Walter John), 1890–1957, vol. V

Buchanan, Sir James, 2nd Bt, 1840–1901, vol. I

Buchanan, Rev. John, *died* 1945, vol. IV

Buchanan, Hon. Sir John; *see* Buchanan, Hon. Sir E. J.

Buchanan, Sir John Cecil Rankin, 1896–1976, vol. VII

Buchanan, John Lee, 1831–1922, vol. II

Buchanan, John Nevile, 1887–1969, vol. VI

Buchanan, Sir John Scoular, 1883–1966, vol. VI

Buchanan, John Young, 1844–1925, vol. II

Buchanan, Joseph Andrew William, *died* 1929, vol. III

Buchanan, Maj.-Gen. Sir Kenneth Gray, 1880–1973, vol. VII

Buchanan, Brig.-Gen. Kenneth James, 1863–1933, vol. III

Buchanan, Leslie, 1868–1943, vol. IV

Buchanan, Lewis Mansergh, 1836–1908, vol. I

Buchanan, Rev. Louis George, 1871–1952, vol. V

Buchanan, Milton Alexander, 1878–1952, vol. V

Buchanan, Major Sir Reginald Narcissus M.; *see* Macdonald-Buchanan.

Buchanan, Robert, 1841–1901, vol. I

Buchanan, Robert J. M., *died* 1925, vol. II

Buchanan, Rev. Robert M., 1871–1945, vol. IV

Buchanan, Robert Ogilvie, 1894–1980, vol. VII

Buchanan, Ven. Thomas Boughton, 1833–1924, vol. II

Buchanan, Rt Hon. Thomas Ryburn, 1846–1911, vol. I

Buchanan, Hon. Sir Walter Clarke, 1838–1924, vol. II

Buchanan, Sir Walter James, 1861–1924, vol. II

Buchanan, Walter John; *see* Buchanan, Jack.

Buchanan, Hon. William A., 1876–1954, vol. V

Buchanan-Dunlop, Col Henry Donald, 1878–1950, vol. IV

Buchanan-Dunlop, Captain David Kennedy, 1911–1985, vol. VIII

Buchanan-Jardine, Captain Sir John William; *see* Jardine.

Buchanan-Riddell, Sir John Walter; *see* Riddell.

Buchanan-Riddell, Sir Walter Robert; *see* Riddell.

Buchanan-Smith, Alick Drummond; *see* Baron Balerno.

Buchanan-Smith, Sir Walter, 1879–1944, vol. IV

Buchanan-Wollaston, Vice-Adm. Herbert Arthur; *see* Wollaston.

Bucher, Gen. Sir Francis Robert Roy; *see* Bucher, Gen. Sir R.

Bucher, Fredrick Newell, *died* 1964, vol. VI

Bucher, Gen. Sir Roy, 1895–1980, vol. VII

Buchheim, Charles Adolphus, 1828–1900, vol. I

Büchler, Adolph, 1867–1939, vol. III

Buchman, Frank N. D., 1878–1961, vol. VI

Buck, Sir Edward Charles, 1838–1916, vol. II

Buck, Edward Clarke, 1873–1950, vol. IV(A)

Buck, Sir Edward John, *died* 1948, vol. IV

Buck, George Stucley; *see* Stucley, Sir G. S.

Buck, Leslie William, 1915–1984, vol. VIII

Buck, Pearl Sydenstricker, 1892–1973, vol. VII

Buck, Sir Percy Carter, 1871–1947, vol. IV

Buck, Sir Peter Henry, *died* 1951, vol. V

Buckee, Henry Thomas, 1913–1989, vol. VIII

Buckell, Sir Robert, 1841–1925, vol. II

Buckeridge, Surg. Rear-Adm. Guy Leslie, 1877–1944, vol. IV

Buckham, Bernard, 1882–1963, vol. VI

Buckham, Sir George Thomas, 1863–1928, vol. II

Buckhurst, John William, 1853–1943, vol. IV

Buckingham and Chandos, Duchess of; (Alice Anne), *died* 1931, vol. III

Buckingham, Rev. Frederick Finney, *died* 1934, vol. III

Buckingham, George Somerset, 1903–1989, vol. VIII

Buckingham, Sir Henry Cecil, 1867–1931, vol. III

Buckingham, Col Sir James, 1843–1912, vol. I

Buckingham, John, 1894–1982, vol. VIII

Buckinghamshire, 7th Earl of, 1860–1930, vol. III

Buckinghamshire, 8th Earl of, 1906–1963, vol. VI

Buckinghamshire, 9th Earl of, 1901–1983, vol. VIII

Buckland, 1st Baron, 1877–1928, vol. II

Buckland, Captain Arthur Edgar, 1890–1969, vol. VI
Buckland, Charles Edward, 1847–1941, vol. IV
Buckland, Geoffrey Ronald Aubert, 1889–1968, vol. VI
Buckland, Brig. Gerald Charles Balfour, 1884–1967, vol. VI
Buckland, Sir Henry, 1870–1957, vol. V
Buckland, Sir Philip Lindsay, 1874–1952, vol. V
Buckland, Maj.-Gen. Sir Reginald Ulick Henry, 1864–1933, vol. III
Buckland, Sir Thomas, 1848–1947, vol. IV
Buckland, William Warwick, 1859–1946, vol. IV
Buckle, Comdr Archibald Walter, died 1927, vol. II
Buckle, Lt-Col Arthur William Bentley-, 1860–1923, vol. II
Buckle, Maj.-Gen. Charles Randolph, 1835–1920, vol. II
Buckle, Maj.-Gen. Christopher Reginald, 1862–1952, vol. V
Buckle, Adm. Claude Edward, 1839–1930, vol. III
Buckle, Col Cuthbert, 1885–1971, vol. VII
Buckle, George Earle, 1854–1935, vol. III
Buckle, John, 1867–1925, vol. II
Buckle, Rev. Martin Brereton, 1853–1915, vol. I
Buckle, Major Matthew Perceval, 1869–1914, vol. I
Buckler, Georgina Grenfell, (Mrs William Buckler), died 1953, vol. V
Buckler, William Hepburn, 1867–1952, vol. V
Buckleton, Sir Henry, 1864–1934, vol. III
Buckley, Abel, 1835–1908, vol. I
Buckley, Lt-Col Albert, 1877–1965, vol. VI
Buckley, Col Arthur Dashwood Bulkeley, 1860–1915, vol. I
Buckley, Brig.-Gen. Basil Thorold, 1874–1954, vol. V
Buckley, Charles William, 1874–1955, vol. V
Buckley, Sir Edmund, 1st Bt, 1834–1910, vol. I
Buckley, Sir Edmund, 2nd Bt, 1861–1919, vol. II
Buckley, Edward Dunscombe Henry, 1860–1931, vol. III
Buckley, Ven. Eric Rede, 1868–1948, vol. IV
Buckley, Rev. Felix J., 1834–1911, vol. I
Buckley, Rear-Adm. Frederic Arthur, 1887–1952, vol. V
Buckley, Lt-Col George Alexander Maclean, 1866–1937, vol. III
Buckley, Howard; see Buckley, W. H.
Buckley, Maj.-Gen. Sir Hugh Clive, 1880–1962, vol. VI
Buckley, Rev. James Monroe, 1836–1920, vol. II
Buckley, Ven. James Rice, 1849–1924, vol. II
Buckley, John J., 1863–1939, vol. III
Buckley, John Joseph Cronin, 1904–1972, vol. VII
Buckley, Rev. Jonathan Charles, died 1927, vol. II
Buckley, Llewellyn Eddison, 1866–1944, vol. IV
Buckley, Lt-Col Neville, 1867–1953, vol. V
Buckley, Rear-Adm. Peter Noel, 1909–1988, vol. VIII
Buckley, Robert Burton, 1847–1927, vol. II
Buckley, Hon. Dame Ruth Burton, 1898–1986, vol. VIII
Buckley, Ven. Thomas Richard, 1859–1936, vol. III
Buckley, Wilfred, 1873–1933, vol. III
Buckley, William, 1859–1937, vol. III
Buckley, (William) Howard, 1909–1974, vol. VII

Buckley, Lt-Col William Howell, 1896–1981, vol. VIII
Buckley, Brig. William Percy, 1887–1968, vol. VI
Buckman, Edwin, 1841–1930, vol. III
Buckman, Rosina, died 1948, vol. IV
Buckmaster, 1st Viscount, 1861–1934, vol. III
Buckmaster, 2nd Viscount, 1890–1974, vol. VII
Buckmaster, Charles A., 1854–1949, vol. IV
Buckmaster, Engr Rear-Adm. Frederick Henry, 1883–1947, vol. IV
Buckmaster, George Alfred, 1859–1937, vol. III
Buckmaster, Martin A., 1862–1960, vol. V
Bucknall, Lt-Gen. Gerard Corfield, 1894–1980, vol. VII
Bucknill, Rt Hon. Sir Alfred Townsend, 1880–1963, vol. VI
Bucknill, Sir John Alexander-Strachey, 1873–1926, vol. II
Bucknill, Sir John Charles, 1817–1897, vol. I
Bucknill, Peter Thomas, 1910–1987, vol. VIII
Bucknill, Rt Hon. Sir Thomas Townsend, 1845–1915, vol. I
Buckrose, J. E., died 1931, vol. III
Buckston, George Moreton, 1881–1942, vol. IV
Buckston, Rev. Henry, 1834–1916, vol. II
Buckton, Baron (Life Peer); Samuel Storey, 1896–1978, vol. VII
Buckton, Ernest James, 1883–1973, vol. VII
Buckton, Ven. Thomas Frederick, 1858–1933, vol. III
Buckworth-Herne-Soame, Sir Charles; see Soame.
Buckworth-Herne-Soame, Sir Charles Burnett; see Soame.
Buday, George, 1907–1990, vol. VIII
Budd, Alfred, died 1927, vol. II
Budd, Sir Cecil Lindsay, 1865–1945, vol. IV
Budd, Hon. Sir Harry Vincent, 1900–1979, vol. VII
Budd, Herbert Ashwin, 1881–1950, vol. IV
Budd, John Wreford, 1838–1922, vol. II
Budd, Stanley Alec, 1931–1989, vol. VIII
Budden, Rev. Charles William, 1878–1952, vol. V
Budden, Lt-Col F. H., 1887–1953, vol. V
Budden, Henry Ebenezer, 1871–1944, vol. IV
Budden, Lionel, 1891–1966, vol. VI
Budden, Lionel Bailey, 1887–1956, vol. V
Buddo, Hon. David, 1856–1937, vol. III
Budge, Sir Ernest A. Wallis, 1857–1934, vol. III
Budge, Sir Henry Sinclair Campbell, 1874–1946, vol. IV
Budge, Rev. Ronald Henderson Gunn, 1909–1976, vol. VII
Budgen, Rear-Adm. Douglas Adams, died 1947, vol. IV
Budgett, Hubert Maitland, 1882–1951, vol. V
Budworth, Maj.-Gen. Charles Edward Dutton, 1869–1921, vol. II
Budworth, Rev. Richard Dutton, 1867–1937, vol. III
Buell, Lt-Col William Senkler, 1868–1941, vol. IV
Buer, Mabel Craven, 1881–1942, vol. IV
Buesst, Captain Aylmer, 1883–1970, vol. VI
Buffey, Brig. William, 1899–1984, vol. VIII
Buganda, Kabaka (King) of, 1896–1939, vol. III
Buganda, HH The Kabaka of, 1924–1969, vol. VI
Buhl, Frants Peter William, 1850–1932, vol. III
Buhler, Robert, 1916–1989, vol. VIII

Buick, Thomas Lindsay, *died* 1938, vol. III
Buisson, Ferdinand Édouard, 1841–1932, vol. III
Buisson, François A.; *see* Albert-Buisson.
Buist, Comdr Colin, 1896–1981, vol. VIII
Buist, Maj.-Gen. David Simson, 1829–1908, vol. I
Buist, Col Herbert John Martin, 1868–1956, vol. V
Buist, H(ugo) Massac, 1878–1966, vol. VI
Buist, Robert Cochrane, 1860–1939, vol. III
Bülbring, Edith, 1903–1990, vol. VIII
Bulfin, Gen. Sir Edward Stanislaus, 1862–1939, vol. III
Bulganin, Marshal Nikolai Alexandrovich, 1895–1975, vol. VII
Bulkeley, Lt-Col C. Rivers, 1840–1934, vol. III
Bulkeley, Lt-Col Henry Charles, 1860–1938, vol. III
Bulkeley, John Pierson, *died* 1958, vol. V
Bulkeley, Sir Richard Henry Williams-, 12th Bt, 1862–1942, vol. IV
Bulkeley, Captain Thomas Henry Rivers, 1876–1914, vol. I
Bulkeley-Evans, William, 1870–1952, vol. V
Bulkeley-Owen, Rev. Thomas M. Bulkeley, *died* 1910, vol. I
Bull, A. J., 1875–1950, vol. IV
Bull, Amy Frances, 1902–1982, vol. VIII
Bull, Archibald William Major, 1888–1970, vol. VI
Bull, Bartle, 1902–1950, vol. IV
Bull, George, 1864–1929, vol. III
Bull, Sir George, 3rd Bt, 1906–1986, vol. VIII
Bull, George Lucien, 1876–1972, vol. VII
Bull, Sir Graham MacGregor, 1918–1987, vol. VIII
Bull, Hedley Norman, 1932–1985, vol. VIII
Bull, Henry Cecil Herbert, 1892–1964, vol. VI
Bull, James William Douglas, 1911–1987, vol. VIII
Bull, Rev. Paul Bertie, 1864–1942, vol. IV
Bull, René, *died* 1942, vol. IV
Bull, Sir Stephen John, 2nd Bt, 1904–1942, vol. IV
Bull, Rt Hon. Sir William, 1st Bt, 1863–1931, vol. III
Bull, William Charles, 1858–1933, vol. III
Bull, William Perkins, 1870–1948, vol. IV
Bullard, Maj.-Gen. Colin, 1900–1981, vol. VIII
Bullard, Sir Edward Crisp, 1907–1980, vol. VII
Bullard, Sir Harry, 1841–1903, vol. I
Bullard, John Eric, 1903–1961, vol. VI
Bullard, Rev. John Vincent, 1869–1941, vol. IV
Bullard, Sir Reader William, 1885–1976, vol. VII
Bullard, Lt-Gen. Robert Lee, 1861–1947, vol. IV
Bulleid, C. H., 1883–1956, vol. V
Bulleid, G. Lawrence, 1858–1933, vol. III
Bulleid, Oliver Vaughan Snell, 1882–1970, vol. VI
Bullen, Arthur Henry, 1857–1920, vol. II
Bullen, Frank Thomas, 1857–1915, vol. II
Bullen, Rt Rev. Herbert Guy, 1896–1937, vol. III
Bullen, Keith Edward, 1906–1976, vol. VII
Bullen, Percy Sutherland, 1867–1958, vol. V
Bullen-Smith, Col George Moultrie, 1870–1934, vol. III
Buller, Sir Alexander, 1834–1903, vol. I
Buller, Arthur Henry Reginald, 1874–1944, vol. IV
Buller, Arthur Tremayne, 1850–1917, vol. II
Buller, Dame (Audrey Charlotte) Georgiana, 1883–1953, vol. V
Buller, Charles William Dunbar-, 1847–1924, vol. II

Buller, Rear-Adm. Francis Alexander Waddilove, 1879–1943, vol. IV
Buller, Dame Georgiana; *see* Buller, Dame A. C. G.
Buller, Adm. Sir Henry Tritton, 1873–1960, vol. V
Buller, Brig.-Gen. Hon. Sir Henry Y.; *see* Yarde-Buller.
Buller, Major Herbert Cecil, 1882–1916, vol. II
Buller, Lt-Col John Dashwood, 1878–1961, vol. VI
Buller, Lt-Col Sir Mervyn Edward M.; *see* Manningham-Buller.
Buller, Sir Morton Edward Manningham-, 2nd Bt, 1825–1910, vol. I
Buller, Ralph Buller H.; *see* Hughes-Buller.
Buller, Gen. Rt Hon. Sir Redvers Henry, 1839–1908, vol. I
Buller, Sir Walter Lawry, 1838–1906, vol. I
Buller, Lt-Col Walter Thomas More, 1886–1938, vol. III
Buller, Hon. Walter Y.; *see* Yarde-Buller.
Bullerwell, William, 1916–1977, vol. VII
Bullett, Gerald William, 1893–1958, vol. V
Bulley, Rt Rev. Cyril; *see* Bulley, Rt Rev. S. C.
Bulley, Rt Rev. Sydney Cyril, 1907–1989, vol. VIII
Bullin, Major Sir Reginald, 1879–1969, vol. VI
Bullinger, Ethelbert William, 1837–1913, vol. I
Bullitt, William Christian, 1891–1967, vol. VI
Bulloch, Rev. James Boyd Prentice, 1915–1981, vol. VIII
Bulloch, John Malcolm, 1867–1938, vol. III
Bulloch, William, 1868–1941, vol. IV
Bullock, Rev. Charles, 1829–1911, vol. I
Bullock, Charles, *died* 1952, vol. V
Bullock, Sir Christopher Llewellyn, 1891–1972, vol. VII
Bullock, Lt-Col Edward George T.; *see* Troyte-Bullock.
Bullock, Sir Ernest, 1890–1979, vol. VII
Bullock, Ernest Henry, 1911–1957, vol. V
Bullock, Fred, 1878–1946, vol. IV
Bullock, Frederick Shore, 1847–1914, vol. I
Bullock, Lt-Gen. Sir George Mackworth, 1851–1926, vol. II
Bullock, Guy Henry, 1887–1956, vol. V
Bullock, Captain Sir (Harold) Malcolm, 1st Bt, 1890–1966, vol. VI
Bullock, Brig. Humphry, 1899–1959, vol. V
Bullock, Kenneth, 1901–1985, vol. VIII
Bullock, Captain Sir Malcolm; *see* Bullock, Captain Sir H. M.
Bullock, Ralph, 1868–1946, vol. IV
Bullock, Rev. Richard, 1839–1918, vol. II
Bullock, Samuel, 1844–1922, vol. II
Bullock, Shan F., 1865–1935, vol. III
Bullock, Thomas Lowndes, 1845–1915, vol. I
Bullock, Walter Ll., 1890–1944, vol. IV
Bullock, Ven. William, 1885–1944, vol. IV
Bullock, Willoughby, 1882–1950, vol. IV
Bullock-Marsham, Brig. Francis William; *see* Marsham.
Bullock-Marsham, Robert H.; *see* Marsham.
Bullock-Webster, Rev. George Russell, 1858–1934, vol. III
Bullough, Geoffrey, 1901–1982, vol. VIII
Bullough, Sir George, 1st Bt, 1870–1939, vol. III

Bullough, Major Ian, *died* 1936, vol. III
Bulman, Henry Herbert, 1871–1928, vol. II
Bulman, Oliver Meredith Boone, 1902–1974, vol. VII
Bulman, Paul Ward Spencer, 1896–1963, vol. VI
Bulmer, Edward Frederick, 1865–1941, vol. IV
Bulmer, James Alfred, *died* 1914, vol. I
Bulmer, Sir James William, 1881–1936, vol. III
Bulstrode, Herbert Timbrell, *died* 1911, vol. I
Bulteel, Major Sir John Crocker, 1890–1956, vol. V
Bulwer, Gen. Sir Edward Earle Gascoyne, 1829–1910, vol. I
Bulwer, Sir Henry Ernest Gascoyne, 1836–1914, vol. I
Bulwer, James Redfoord, 1820–1899, vol. I
Bulwer, William Dering Earle, 1856–1915, vol. I
Bulwer, Brig.-Gen. William Earle Gascoyne Lytton, 1829–1910, vol. I
Bulyea, George Hedley Vicars, 1859–1928, vol. II
Bumpus, Mary Frances; *see* Allitsen, Frances.
Bumstead, Kenneth, 1908–1987, vol. VIII
Bun Behari Kapur, Raja Bahadur, 1853–1924, vol. II
Bunbury, Cecil Edward Francis, 1864–1932, vol. III
Bunbury, Sir Charles Henry Napier, 11th Bt (*cr* 1681), 1886–1963, vol. VI
Bunbury, Evelyn James, 1888–1965, vol. VI
Bunbury, Brig. Francis Ramsay St Pierre, 1910–1990, vol. VIII
Bunbury, Sir Henry Charles John, 10th Bt (*cr* 1681), 1855–1930, vol. III
Bunbury, Sir Henry Noel, 1876–1968, vol. VI
Bunbury, Maj.-Gen. Sir Herbert Napier, 1851–1922, vol. II
Bunbury, Sir (John) William Napier, 12th Bt, 1915–1985, vol. VIII
Bunbury, Rev. Sir John Richardson, 3rd Bt (*cr* 1787), 1813–1909, vol. I
Bunbury, Sir Mervyn William Richardson-, 4th Bt (*cr* 1787), 1874–1952, vol. V
Bunbury, Brig. Noël Louis St Pierre, 1890–1971, vol. VII
Bunbury, Rt Rev. Thomas, *died* 1907, vol. I
Bunbury, Brig.-Gen. Vesey Thomas, 1859–1934, vol. III
Bunbury, Sir William; *see* Bunbury, Sir J. W. N.
Bunbury, Maj.-Gen. William Edwin, 1858–1925, vol. II
Bunce, John Thackray, 1828–1899, vol. I
Bunch, John L., *died* 1941, vol. IV
Bunche, Ralph Johnson, 1904–1971, vol. VII
Bund, John William W.; *see* Willis-Bund.
Bundey, Hon. Sir Henry; *see* Bundey, Hon. Sir W. H.
Bundey, Hon. Sir (William) Henry, 1838–1909, vol. I
Bundi, HH Maharao Raja, 1869–1927, vol. II
Bundi, HH Maharao Raja of, 1893–1945, vol. IV
Bundy, Edgar, *died* 1922, vol. II
Bune, John, *died* 1925, vol. II
Bunin, Ivan Alexseyevich, 1870–1953, vol. V
Bunker, Lt-Col Sidney Waterfield, 1889–1968, vol. VI
Bunn, Charles William, 1905–1990, vol. VIII
Bunning, Arthur John Farrant, 1895–1968, vol. VI
Bunning, Herbert, 1863–1937, vol. III
Bunny, Rupert Charles Wolston, 1864–1947, vol. IV
Bunoz, Rt Rev. Emile Marie, 1864–1945, vol. IV
Bunt, Rev. Frederick Darrell, 1902–1977, vol. VII

Buntine, James Robertson, 1841–1920, vol. II
Bunting, Basil, 1900–1985, vol. VIII
Bunting, D. G.; *see* George, Daniel.
Bunting, Sir Percy William, 1836–1911, vol. I
Buñuel, Luis, 1900–1983, vol. VIII
Burbank, Luther, 1849–1926, vol. II
Burbidge, Rev. Frederick William, 1840–1915, vol. I
Burbidge, Frederick William Thomas, 1847–1905, vol. I
Burbidge, Hon. George W., *died* 1908, vol. I
Burbidge, Sir John Richard Woodman, 4th Bt, 1930–1974, vol. VII
Burbidge, Percy William, 1891–1984, vol. VIII
Burbidge, Sir Richard, 1st Bt, 1847–1917, vol. II
Burbidge, Sir Richard Grant Woodman, 3rd Bt, 1897–1966, vol. VI
Burbidge, Sir (Richard) Woodman, 2nd Bt, 1872–1945, vol. IV
Burbidge, Sir Woodman; *see* Burbidge, Sir R. W.
Burbury, Samuel Hawksley, 1831–1911, vol. I
Burch, Cecil Reginald, 1901–1983, vol. VIII
Burch, Maj.-Gen. Frederick Whitmore, 1893–1977, vol. VII
Burch, Maj.-Gen. Geoffrey, 1923–1990, vol. VIII
Burch, George James, 1852–1914, vol. I
Burch, Lt-Col William Edward Scarth, *died* 1940, vol. III
Burchardt, Frank A., 1902–1958, vol. V
Burchnall, Joseph Langley, 1892–1975, vol. VII
Burckhardt, Charles James, 1891–1974, vol. VII
Burd, Rev. Frederick, 1826–1915, vol. I
Burd, Rev. Prebendary John, 1828–1918, vol. II
Burd, Rt Rev. Walter, 1888–1939, vol. III
Burden, 1st Baron, 1885–1970, vol. VI
Burden, Sqn Ldr Sir Frederick Frank Arthur, 1905–1987, vol. VIII
Burden, Frederick Parker, 1874–1971, vol. VII
Burden, Major Geoffrey Noel, 1898–1990, vol. VIII
Burden, Col Henry, 1867–1953, vol. V
Burder, Brig.-Gen. Ernest Sumner, 1866–1946, vol. IV
Burder, Sir John Henry, 1900–1988, vol. VIII
Burdett, Sir Charles Coventry, 9th Bt (*cr* 1665), 1902–1940, vol. III
Burdett, Sir Francis, 8th Bt (*cr* 1618), 1869–1951, vol. V
Burdett, Sir Henry, 1847–1920, vol. II
Burdett, Sir Henry Aylmer, 10th Bt (*cr* 1665), 1881–1943, vol. IV
Burdett, Osbert, 1885–1936, vol. III
Burdett, Scott Langshaw, 1897–1961, vol. VI
Burdett-Coutts, Baroness (1st in line), 1814–1906, vol. I
Burdett-Coutts, Rt Hon. William Lehman Ashmead Bartlett-, 1851–1921, vol. II
Burditt, George Frederick, 1862–1933, vol. III
Burdon, Sir Ernest, 1881–1957, vol. V
Burdon, Major Sir John Alder, 1866–1933, vol. III
Burdon, Rt Rev. John Shaw, 1826–1907, vol. I
Burdon, Rowland, 1857–1944, vol. IV
Burdon-Sanderson, Sir John Scott, 1st Bt, 1828–1905, vol. I(A)
Burdwan, Maharajadhiraja Bahadur of, 1881–1941, vol. IV

Bureau, Jacques, 1860–1933, vol. III
Buret, Captain Theobald John Claud P.; *see* Purcell-Buret.
Burford, George Henry, 1856–1937, vol. III
Burge, Sir Charles Henry, 1846–1921, vol. II
Burge, Rt Rev. Hubert Murray, 1862–1925, vol. II
Burge, James Charles George, 1906–1990, vol. VIII
Burge, Milward Rodon Kennedy, 1894–1968, vol. VI
Burger, Schalk William, *died* 1918, vol. II
Burges, Lt-Col Dan, 1873–1946, vol. IV
Burges, Ven. Ernest Travers, 1851–1921, vol. II
Burges, Col Ynyr Henry, 1834–1908, vol. I
Burgess, Arthur Henry, 1874–1948, vol. II
Burgess, Arthur James Wetherall, 1879–1957, vol. V
Burgess, Charles, (Cathal Brugha), 1874–1922, vol. II
Burgess, Lt-Col Charles Roscoe, 1874–1966, vol. VI(AII)
Burgess, Clarkson Leo, 1902–1975, vol. VII
Burgess, Duncan, 1850–1917, vol. II
Burgess, Rev. Francis, 1879–1948, vol. IV
Burgess, (Frank) Gelett, 1866–1951, vol. V
Burgess, Rt Rev. Frederick, 1853–1925, vol. II
Burgess, Frederick George, *died* 1951, vol. V
Burgess, Frederick William, 1855–1945, vol. IV
Burgess, Gelett; *see* Burgess, F. G.
Burgess, Geoffrey, 1906–1972, vol. VII
Burgess, Rt Hon. Henry Givens, 1859–1937, vol. III
Burgess, Herbert Edward, 1863–1948, vol. IV
Burgess, James, 1832–1916, vol. II
Burgess, James John Haldane, 1862–1927, vol. II
Burgess, John Bagnold, 1830–1897, vol. I
Burgess, Sir John Lawie, 1912–1987, vol. VIII
Burgess, Norman Francis Clifford, 1902–1940, vol. III
Burgess, Robert Nelson, 1867–1945, vol. IV
Burgess, Russell Brian, 1931–1979, vol. VII
Burgess, Sir Thomas Arthur Collier, 1906–1977, vol. VII
Burgess, Thomas Joseph Workman, 1849–1926, vol. II
Burgess, Hon. William Henry, 1847–1917, vol. II
Burgess, William Leslie, 1886–1954, vol. V
Burgess, Maj.-Gen. Sir William Livingstone Hatchwell S,; *see* Sinclair-Burgess.
Burgett, Rt Rev. Arthur Edward, 1869–1942, vol. IV
Burgh, 5th Baron, 1866–1926, vol. II
Burgh, 8th (otherwise 6th) Baron, 1906–1959, vol. V
Burghard, Frédéric François, 1864–1947, vol. IV
Burghard, Rear-Adm. Geoffrey Frederic, 1900–1981, vol. VIII
Burghclere, 1st Baron, 1846–1921, vol. II
Burghclere, Lady; (Winifred Henrietta Christina), 1864–1933, vol. III
Burgin, Rt Hon. Edward Leslie, 1887–1945, vol. IV
Burgin, George B., 1856–1944, vol. IV
Burgis, Sir Edwin Cooper, 1878–1966, vol. VI
Burgis, Lawrence Franklin, 1892–1972, vol. VII
Burgmann, Rt Rev. Ernest Henry, 1885–1967, vol. VI
Burgoyne, Lt-Col Sir Alan Hughes, 1880–1929, vol. III
Burgoyne, Major Gerald Achilles, 1874–1936, vol. III
Burgoyne, Sir John, 1875–1969, vol. VI
Burgoyne, Col Sir John Montagu, 10th Bt, 1832–1921, vol. II

Burhop, Eric Henry Stoneley, 1911–1980, vol. VII
Burke, Rt Rev. Mgr Alfred Edward, 1862–1927, vol. II
Burke, Sir Aubrey Francis, 1904–1989, vol. VIII
Burke, Col Bernard Bruce, 1876–1938, vol. III
Burke, Major Charles James, 1882–1917, vol. II
Burke, Desmond Peter Meredyth, 1912–1987, vol. VIII
Burke, Edmund Haviland, *died* 1914, vol. I
Burke, Edmund Tytler, 1888–1941, vol. IV
Burke, Captain Sir Gerald Howe, 7th Bt (*cr* 1797), 1893–1954, vol. V
Burke, Lt-Col Gerald Tyler, 1882–1952, vol. V
Burke, Harold Arthur, 1852–1942, vol. IV
Burke, Sir Henry Farnham, 1859–1930, vol. III
Burke, Sir Henry George, 5th Bt (*cr* 1797), 1859–1910, vol. I
Burke, Henry Lardner, 1850–1927, vol. II
Burke, Col Herbert Francis Lardner, 1883–1950, vol. IV
Burke, Captain James Henry Thomas, 1853–1902, vol. I
Burke, Sir John, *died* 1922, vol. II
Burke, John Barclay, 1924–1983, vol. VIII
Burke, John Benjamin Butler, 1871–1946, vol. IV
Burke, Kathleen, 1887–1958, vol. V
Burke, Rt Rev. Maurice Francis, 1845–1923, vol. II
Burke, Lt-Col Sir Richard John Charles, 1878–1960, vol. V
Burke, Sir Ronald; *see* Burke, Sir U. R.
Burke, Sir Theobald Hubert, 13th Bt (*cr* 1628), 1833–1909, vol. I
Burke, Thomas, 1886–1945, vol. IV
Burke, Sir Thomas Mallachy, 6th Bt (*cr* 1797), 1864–1913, vol. I
Burke, Thomas Michael, 1870–1949, vol. IV
Burke, Sir Thomas Stanley, 8th Bt, 1916–1989, vol. VIII
Burke, Sir (Ulick) Roland, 1872–1958, vol. V
Burke, Wilfrid Andrew, *died* 1968, vol. VI
Burke-Gaffney, Maj.-Gen. Edward Sebastian, 1900–1981, vol. VIII
Burkett, Sir William Robert, 1840–1908, vol. I
Burkhardt, Col Valentine Rodolphe, 1884–1967, vol. IV
Burkhart, Harvey J., 1864–1946, vol. IV
Burkill, Isaac Henry, 1870–1965, vol. VI
Burkitt, Col Bernard Maynard H.; *see* Humble-Burkitt.
Burkitt, Francis Crawford, 1864–1935, vol. III
Burkitt, Francis Holy, 1880–1952, vol. V
Burkitt, Miles Crawford, 1890–1971, vol. VII
Burkitt, Ven. Robert Scott Bradshaw, 1857–1940, vol. III(A), vol. IV
Burkitt, Robert William, 1908–1976, vol. VII
Burland, Col Jeffrey Hale, 1861–1914, vol. I
Burland, John Burland H.; *see* Harris-Burland.
Burland, Col William Watt, 1877–1935, vol. III
Burleigh, Bennet, *died* 1914, vol. I
Burleigh, Captain Cecil Wills, 1870–1940, vol. III
Burleigh, Very Rev. John H. S., 1894–1985, vol. VIII
Burleson, Rt Rev. Hugh Latimer, 1865–1933, vol. III
Burlingame, Edward Livermore, 1848–1922, vol. II
Burls, Sir Edwin Grant, 1844–1926, vol. II

Burlton, Lt-Col Philip Sykes Murphy, 1865–1950, vol. IV

Burman, Sir John Bedford, 1867–1941, vol. IV

Burmester, Adm. Sir Rudolf Miles, 1875–1956, vol. V

Burn, Col Alexander Henderson, 1885–1949, vol. IV

Burn, Very Rev. Andrew Ewbank, 1864–1927, vol. II

Burn, Lt-Col Charles Pelham Maitland, 1880–1925, vol. II

Burn, Sir Clive; see Burn, Sir R. C. W.

Burn, Dugald Stuart, 1877–1951, vol. V

Burn, Duncan Lyall, 1902–1988, vol. VIII

Burn, Sir George, 1847–1932, vol. III

Burn, Col Harold Septimus, died 1970, vol. VI

Burn, Sir Harry Harrison, 1888–1961, vol. VI

Burn, Brig.-Gen. Henry Pelham, 1882–1958, vol. V

Burn, Rev. John Henry, 1858–1937, vol. III

Burn, Sir Joseph, 1871–1950, vol. IV

Burn, Joshua Harold, 1892–1981, vol. VIII

Burn, Sir Richard, 1871–1947, vol. IV

Burn, Rev. Robert, 1829–1904, vol. I

Burn, Rodney Joseph, 1899–1984, vol. VIII

Burn, Sir (Roland) Clive (Wallace), 1882–1955, vol. V

Burn, Sir Sidney, 1881–1963, vol. VI

Burn, William Laurence, 1904–1966, vol. VI

Burn-Murdoch, Hector, 1881–1958, vol. V

Burn-Murdoch, Rev. Canon James McGibbon, 1828–1904, vol. I

Burn-Murdoch, Maj.-Gen. Sir John Francis, 1859–1931, vol. III

Burn-Murdoch, W. G., 1862–1939, vol. III

Burnaby, Major Algernon Edwyn, 1868–1938, vol. III

Burnaby, Davy; see Burnaby, G. D.

Burnaby, Lt-Col Eustace Beaumont, 1842–1916, vol. II

Burnaby, (George) Davy, 1881–1949, vol. IV

Burnaby, Lt-Col Hugo Beaumont, 1874–1916, vol. II

Burnaby, Rev. John, 1891–1978, vol. VII

Burnaby-Atkins, Thomas Frederick, 1836–1918, vol. II

Burnage, Col Granville John, 1858–1945, vol. IV

Burnand, Sir Francis Cowley, 1836–1917, vol. II

Burnand, Sir Frank; see Burnand, Sir R. F.

Burnand, Sir (Richard) Frank, 1887–1969, vol. VI

Burnand, Victor Wyatt, 1868–1940, vol. III

Burnard, Major Charles Francis, 1876–1931, vol. III

Burne, Lt-Col Alfred Higgins, 1886–1959, vol. V

Burne, Gen. Henry Knightley, 1825–1901, vol. I

Burne, Sir Lewis Charles, 1898–1978, vol. VII

Burne, Lt-Col Lindsay Eliott Lumley, 1877–1944, vol. IV

Burne, Col Newdigate Halford Marriot, 1872–1950, vol. IV(A), vol. V

Burne, Maj.-Gen. Sir Owen Tudor, 1837–1909, vol. I

Burne, Brig.-Gen. Rainald Owen, 1871–1923, vol. II

Burne, Richard Higgins, 1868–1953, vol. V

Burne, Ven. Richard Vernon Higgins, 1882–1970, vol. IV

Burne-Jones, Sir Edward Coley, 1st Bt, 1833–1898, vol. I

Burne-Jones, Sir Philip, 2nd Bt, 1861–1926, vol. II

Burnell, Lt-Col Charles Desborough, 1876–1969, vol. VI

Burnell-Nugent, Brig.-Gen. Frank, 1880–1942, vol. IV

Burnes, Sheila; see Bloom, Ursula.

Burnet, Rev. Amos, 1857–1926, vol. II

Burnet, Sir (Frank) Macfarlane, 1899–1985, vol. VIII

Burnet, John, 1863–1928, vol. II

Burnet, Sir John James, 1857–1938, vol. III

Burnet, John Rudolph Wardlaw, 1886–1941, vol. IV

Burnet, Sir Robert William, 1851–1931, vol. III

Burnett of Leys, Major Sir Alexander Edwin, 14th Bt (cr 1626), 1881–1959, vol. V

Burnett, Col Allan Harrington, 1884–1966, vol. VI

Burnett, Cecil Ross, 1872–1933, vol. III

Burnett, Gen. Sir Charles John, 1843–1915, vol. I

Burnett, Brig.-Gen. Charles Kenyon, 1868–1950, vol. IV

Burnett, Air Chief Marshal Sir Charles Stuart, 1882–1945, vol. IV

Burnett, Sir David, 1st Bt (cr 1913), 1851–1930, vol. III

Burnett, Sir Digby Vere, died 1958, vol. V

Burnett, Maj.-Gen. Edward John Sidney, 1921–1978, vol. VII

Burnett, Sir (Edward) Napier, 1872–1923, vol. II

Burnett, Mrs Frances (Eliza) Hodgson, 1849–1924, vol. II

Burnett, George Murray, 1921–1980, vol. VII

Burnett, Dame Ivy C.; see Compton-Burnett.

Burnett of Leys, Maj.-Gen. Sir James Lauderdale Gilbert, 13th Bt (cr 1626), 1880–1953, vol. V

Burnett, Major John Chaplyn, 1863–1943, vol. IV

Burnett, Brig. John Curteis, 1882–1968, vol. VI

Burnett, John George, 1876–1962, vol. VI

Burnett, Col Sir Leslie Trew, 2nd Bt (cr 1913), 1884–1955, vol. V

Burnett, Dame Maud, 1863–1950, vol. IV

Burnett, Lt-Col Maurice John Brownless, 1904–1988, vol. VIII

Burnett, Sir Napier; see Burnett, Sir E. N.

Burnett, Adm. Sir Robert Lindsay, 1887–1959, vol. V

Burnett, Lt-Col Robert Richardson, 1897–1975, vol. VII

Burnett of Leys, Sir Thomas, 12th Bt (cr 1626), 1840–1926, vol. II

Burnett, William Freshfield, 1865–1935, vol. III

Burnett, William George Esterbrooke, 1886–1978, vol. VII

Burnett-Brown, Col Alexander Denis, 1894–1966, vol. VI

Burnett-Hitchcock, Lt-Gen. Sir Basil Ferguson; see Hitchcock.

Burnett-Stuart, George Eustace, 1876–1938, vol. III

Burnett-Stuart, Gen. Sir John Theodosius, 1875–1958, vol. V

Burney, Sir Anthony George Bernard, 1909–1989, vol. VIII

Burney, Lt-Col Arthur Edward Cave, 1883–1931, vol. III

Burney, Admiral of the Fleet Sir Cecil, 1st Bt, 1858–1929, vol. III

Burney, Ven. Charles, died 1907, vol. I

Burney, Charles, 1840–1912, vol. I

Burney, Comdr Sir (Charles) Dennistoun, 2nd Bt, 1888–1968, vol. VI

Burney, Rev. Charles Fox, 1868–1925, vol. II
Burney, Comdr Sir Dennistoun; *see* Burney, Comdr Sir C. D.
Burney, Brig.-Gen. Herbert Henry, 1858–1932, vol. III
Burney, Brig.-Gen. Percy de Sausmarez, 1863–1934, vol. III
Burney, Sydney Bernard, *died* 1951, vol. V
Burnham, 1st Baron, 1833–1916, vol. II
Burnham, 1st Viscount (and 2nd Baron), 1862–1933, vol. III
Burnham, 3rd Baron, 1864–1943, vol. IV
Burnham, 4th Baron, 1890–1963, vol. VI
Burnham, Lady; (Marie Enid), *died* 1979, vol. VII
Burnham, Cecil, 1887–1965, vol. VI
Burnham, Forbes; *see* Burnham, L. F. S.
Burnham, James, 1905–1987, vol. VIII
Burnham, John Charles, 1866–1943, vol. IV
Burnham, (Linden) Forbes (Sampson), 1923–1985, vol. VIII
Burnie, James, 1882–1975, vol. VII
Burniston, Surg. Rear-Adm. Hugh Somerville, 1870–1962, vol. VI
Burnley, James, *died* 1919, vol. II
Burns, Sir Alan Cuthbert, 1887–1980, vol. VII
Burns, Arthur F., 1904–1987, vol. VIII
Burns, Bryan Hartop, 1896–1984, vol. VIII
Burns, Cecil Delisle, 1879–1942, vol. IV
Burns, Cecil Laurence, 1863–1929, vol. III
Burns, Sir Charles Ritchie, 1898–1985, vol. VIII
Burns, David, 1884–1969, vol. VI
Burns, Lt-Gen. Eedson Louis Millard, 1897–1985, vol. VIII
Burns, George, 1903–1970, vol. VI
Burns, Henry Stuart Mackenzie, 1900–1971, vol. VII
Burns, Col Hon. Sir James, 1846–1923, vol. II
Burns, James, 1859–1929, vol. III
Burns, Rev. James, 1865–1948, vol. IV
Burns, Rt Hon. John, 1858–1943, vol. IV
Burns, John George, 1880–1950, vol. IV
Burns, Brig. Lionel Bryan Douglas, 1895–1966, vol. VI
Burns, Sir Malcolm McRae, 1910–1986, vol. VIII
Burns, Very Rev. Michael John, 1863–1949, vol. IV
Burns, Philip Leonard, 1896–1968, vol. VI
Burns, Robert, 1869–1941, vol. IV
Burns, Robert, 1859–1951, vol. V
Burns, Robert, 1912–1971, vol. VII
Burns, Rev. Thomas, 1853–1938, vol. III
Burns, Sir Wilfred, 1923–1984, vol. VIII
Burns, William, 1884–1970, vol. VI
Burns, William Alexander, 1921–1972, vol. VII
Burns-Begg, Col Robert, 1872–1918, vol. II
Burns-Lindow, Lt-Col Isaac William, 1868–1946, vol. IV
Burnside, Rev. Frederick, *died* 1904, vol. I
Burnside, Helen Marion, 1844–1923, vol. II
Burnside, Robert Bruce, 1862–1929, vol. III
Burnside, Rev. Walter Fletcher, 1874–1949, vol. IV
Burnside, William, 1852–1927, vol. II
Burnside, William Snow, *died* 1920, vol. II
Burntwood, Baron (Life Peer); Julian Ward Snow, 1910–1982, vol. VIII
Burnyeat, William John Dalzell, 1874–1916, vol. II

Burpee, Lawrence Johnston, 1873–1946, vol. IV
Burr, Alfred, 1855–1952, vol. V
Burr, Rear-Adm. John Leslie, 1847–1917, vol. II
Burr, Malcolm, 1878–1954, vol. V
Burr-Bryan, Walter; *see* Bryan, W. B.
Burra, Edward, 1905–1976, vol. VII
Burrage, Alfred McLelland, 1889–1956, vol. V
Burrard, Major Sir Gerald, 8th Bt, 1888–1965, vol. VI
Burrard, Col Harry George, 1871–1963, vol. VI
Burrard, Sir Harry Paul, 6th Bt, 1846–1933, vol. III
Burrard, Col Sir Sidney Gerald, 7th Bt, 1860–1943, vol. IV
Burrard, Col William Dutton, 1861–1938, vol. III
Burrell, Sir Charles Raymond, 6th Bt, 1848–1899, vol. I
Burrell, Harry James, 1873–1945, vol. IV
Burrell, Vice-Adm. Sir Henry MacKay, 1904–1988, vol. VIII
Burrell, John; *see* Burrell, R. J.
Burrell, John Glyn, 1912–1984, vol. VIII
Burrell, John Percy, 1910–1972, vol. VII
Burrell, Joseph Frederick, 1909–1983, vol. VIII
Burrell, Lancelot S. T., 1883–1938, vol. III
Burrell, Hon. Martin, 1858–1938, vol. III
Burrell, Sir Merrik Raymond, 7th Bt, 1877–1957, vol. V
Burrell, Percy Saville, 1871–1958, vol. V
Burrell, Robert Eric, 1890–1968, vol. VI
Burrell, (Robert) John, 1923–1985, vol. VIII
Burrell, Sir Walter Raymond, 8th Bt, 1903–1985, vol. VIII
Burrell, Sir William, 1861–1958, vol. V
Burridge, Frederick Vango, 1869–1945, vol. IV
Burridge, Captain Robert Archibald Morison, *died* 1957, vol. V
Burrington, Arthur, *died* 1924, vol. II
Burrough, Adm. Sir Harold Martin, 1888–1977, vol. VII
Burroughes, Dorothy Mary Burroughes-, *died* 1963, vol. VI
Burroughs, Edgar Rice, 1875–1950, vol. IV
Burroughs, Rt Rev. Edward Arthur, 1882–1934, vol. III
Burroughs, Lt-Gen. Sir Frederick William Traill, 1831–1905, vol. I
Burroughs, John, 1837–1921, vol. II
Burroughs, Ronald Arthur, 1917–1980, vol. VII
Burroughs, Rev. William Edward, 1845–1931, vol. III
Burroughs-Fowler, Walter, *died* 1930, vol. III
Burrow, Edward John, 1869–1935, vol. III
Burrow, Harold, 1903–1987, vol. VIII
Burrow, Joseph le Fleming, 1888–1967, vol. VI
Burrow, Thomas, 1909–1986, vol. VIII
Burrowes, Lt-Col Algernon St Leger, 1847–1925, vol. II
Burrowes, Rt Rev. Arnold Brian, 1896–1963, vol. VI
Burrowes, Brig.-Gen. Arnold Robinson, 1867–1949, vol. IV
Burrowes, Herbert Alleyne Nathanael, 1870–1933, vol. III
Burrowes, Thomas Cosby, 1856–1925, vol. II(A), vol. III
Burrowes, Thomas Fraser, *died* 1947, vol. IV

Burrowes, William Henry Aglionby, *died* 1922, vol. II

Burrows, Albert, 1919–1972, vol. VII

Burrows, Alfred John, *died* 1957, vol. V

Burrows, Christine Mary Elizabeth, 1872–1959, vol. V

Burrows, Col Edmund Augustine, 1855–1927, vol. II

Burrows, Sir Ernest Pennington, 3rd Bt, 1851–1917, vol. II

Burrows, Rev. Francis Henry, 1857–1928, vol. II

Burrows, Sir Frederick Abernethy, 2nd Bt, 1845–1904, vol. I

Burrows, Sir Frederick John, 1887–1973, vol. VII

Burrows, Gen. George Reynolds Scott, 1827–1917, vol. II

Burrows, George Thomas, 1876–1949, vol. IV

Burrows, Harold, 1875–1955, vol. V

Burrows, Harold Jackson, 1902–1981, vol. VIII

Burrows, Very Rev. Hedley Robert, 1887–1983, vol. VIII

Burrows, Comdr Henry Montagu, 1899–1979, vol. VII

Burrows, Brig. Hollis Martin, 1884–1952, vol. V

Burrows, Sir John; *see* Burrows, Sir R. J. F.

Burrows, Rt Rev. Leonard Hedley, 1857–1940, vol. III

Burrows, Lionel Burton, 1883–1970, vol. VI

Burrows, Rev. Millar, 1889–1980, vol. VII

Burrows, Captain Montagu, 1819–1905, vol. I

Burrows, Lt-Gen. Montagu Brocas, 1894–1967, vol. VI

Burrows, Sir Robert Abraham, 1884–1964, vol. VI

Burrows, Sir (Robert) John (Formby), 1901–1987, vol. VIII

Burrows, Sir Roland, 1882–1952, vol. V

Burrows, Ronald Montagu, 1867–1920, vol. II

Burrows, Sir Stephen Montagu, 1856–1935, vol. III

Burrows, Theodore Arthur, 1857–1929, vol. III

Burrows, Rt Rev. Winfrid Oldfield, 1858–1929, vol. III

Burry, Bessie P.; *see* Pullen-Burry.

Burstall, Aubrey Frederic, 1902–1984, vol. VIII

Burstall, Frederick William, 1865–1934, vol. III

Burstall, Lt-Gen. Sir Henry Edward, 1870–1945, vol. IV

Burstall, Sara Annie, 1859–1939, vol. III

Burston, Maj.-Gen. Sir Samuel Roy, 1888–1960, vol. V

Burt, Brig.-Gen. Alfred, 1875–1949, vol. IV

Burt, Alfred LeRoy, 1888–1971, vol. VII

Burt, Sir Bryce Chudleigh, 1881–1943, vol. IV

Burt, Sir Charles, 1832–1913, vol. I

Burt, Charles Kingley J.; *see* Johnstone-Burt.

Burt, Clive Stuart Saxon, 1900–1981, vol. VIII

Burt, Sir Cyril Lodowic, 1883–1971, vol. VII

Burt, Sir George Mowlem, 1884–1964, vol. VI

Burt, Rear-Adm. Gerald George Percy, 1888–1965, vol. VI

Burt, Henry, 1844–1940, vol. III

Burt, Rev. Henry Chadwick, 1871–1959, vol. V(A)

Burt, Sir Henry Parsall, 1857–1936, vol. III

Burt, Hugh Armitage, 1911–1976, vol. VII

Burt, Col John Marshall, 1860–1931, vol. III

Burt, Sir John Mowlem, 1845–1918, vol. II

Burt, Joseph Barnes, *died* 1953, vol. V

Burt, Leonard James, 1892–1983, vol. VIII

Burt, Octavius, 1849–1940, vol. III

Burt, Hon. Septimus, 1847–1919, vol. II

Burt, Rt Hon. Thomas, 1837–1922, vol. II

Burt-Andrews, Stanley George, 1908–1990, vol. VIII

Burtchaell, Lt-Gen. Sir Charles Henry, 1866–1932, vol. III

Burtchaell, George Dames, 1853–1921, vol. II

Burton, 1st Baron, 1837–1909, vol. I

Burton, Baroness (2nd in line), 1873–1962, vol. VI

Burton, Alan Chadburn, 1904–1979, vol. VII

Burton, Rev. Arthur Daniel, 1852–1933, vol. III

Burton, Arthur Davis, 1887–1962, vol. VI

Burton, Maj.-Gen. Benjamin, 1855–1921, vol. II(A), vol. III

Burton, Sir Bunnell Henry, 1858–1943, vol. IV

Burton, Sir Charles William Cuffe, 5th Bt, 1823–1902, vol. I

Burton, Claud Peter Primrose, 1916–1957, vol. V

Burton, Brig. Colin, 1883–1945, vol. IV

Burton, Donald, 1892–1966, vol. VI

Burton, Brig.-Gen. Edmund Boteler, 1861–1942, vol. IV

Burton, Rev. Canon Edwin Hubert, 1870–1925, vol. II

Burton, Eli Franklin, 1879–1948, vol. IV

Burton, Rev. Ernest De Witt, 1856–1925, vol. II

Burton, Gen. Sir Fowler, 1822–1904, vol. I

Burton, Sir Francis Charles Edward D.; *see* Denys-Burton.

Burton, Frank Ernest, 1865–1948, vol. IV

Burton, Sir Frederick William, 1816–1900, vol. I

Burton, Captain Sir Geoffrey Duke, 1893–1954, vol. V

Burton, Sir Geoffrey Pownall, 1884–1972, vol. VII

Burton, Rt Rev. George Ambrose, 1852–1931, vol. III

Burton, Major Sir Gerald Arthur Fowler, 1869–1930, vol. III

Burton, Captain Gerard William, 1879–1915, vol. I

Burton, Harold, 1901–1966, vol. VI

Burton, Harold Hitz, 1888–1964, vol. VI

Burton, Rt Hon. Henry, 1866–1935, vol. III

Burton, Henry, 1907–1952, vol. V

Burton, Rev. Henry Darwin, 1858–1943, vol. IV

Burton, Col Henry Walter, 1876–1947, vol. IV

Burton, Rev. Canon Humphrey Philipps Walcot, 1888–1957, vol. V

Burton, John Adam Gib, 1888–1962, vol. VI

Burton, John Edward B.; *see* Bloundelle-Burton.

Burton, John Frederick, 1870–1937, vol. III

Burton, Rev. John James, 1849–1927, vol. II

Burton, Rev. John Richard, 1847–1939, vol. III

Burton, Rt Rev. Lewis William, 1852–1940, vol. III(A), vol. IV

Burton, Sir Montague, 1885–1952, vol. V

Burton, Neil Edward David, 1930–1990, vol. VIII

Burton, Sir Pomeroy, 1869–1947, vol. IV

Burton, Brig.-Gen. Reginald George, 1864–1951, vol. V

Burton, Richard, 1925–1984, vol. VIII

Burton, Brig.-Gen. St George Edward William, *died* 1943, vol. IV

Burton, Rt Rev. Spence, 1881–1966, vol. VI

Burton, William, *died* 1954, vol. V
Burton, Sir William James Miller, 1862–1946, vol. IV
Burton, Sir William Parker, 1864–1942, vol. IV
Burton-Baldry, Walter Burton, 1888–1940, vol. III
Burton-Chadwick, Sir Peter; *see* Burton-Chadwick, Sir R.
Burton-Chadwick, Sir Robert, 1st Bt, 1869–1951, vol. V
Burton-Chadwick, Sir Robert, (Sir Peter Burton-Chadwick), 2nd Bt, 1911–1983, vol. VIII
Burton-Fanning, Frederick William, 1863–1937, vol. III
Burtt Davy, Joseph, 1870–1940, vol. III
Burwash, Lachlin Taylor, 1874–1940, vol. III
Burwash, Rev. Nathanael, 1839–1918, vol. II
Bury, Viscount; Derek William Charles Keppel, 1911–1968, vol. VI
Bury, Lt-Col Charles Kenneth Howard, 1883–1963, vol. VI
Bury, Francis George, *died* 1926, vol. II
Bury, Sir George, 1866–1958, vol. V
Bury, George Wyman, 1874–1920, vol. II
Bury, Rt Rev. Herbert, *died* 1933, vol. III
Bury, John Bagnell, 1861–1927, vol. II
Bury, Judson Sykes, *died* 1944, vol. IV
Bury, Hon. Leslie Harry Ernest, 1913–1986, vol. VIII
Bury, Lindsay Edward, 1882–1952, vol. V
Bury, Oliver R. H., *died* 1946, vol. IV
Bury, Ralph Frederic, 1876–1954, vol. V
Bury, Rev. William, 1839–1920, vol. II
Buscarlet, Air Vice-Marshal Sir Willett Amalric Bowen B.; *see* Bowen-Buscarlet.
Busch, Adolf, 1891–1952, vol. V
Busch, Fritz, 1890–1951, vol. V
Bush, Hon. Sir Brian Drex, 1925–1989, vol. VIII
Bush, Douglas; *see* Bush, J. N. D.
Bush, Captain Eric Wheler, 1899–1985, vol. VIII
Bush, Frank Whittaker, 1825–1903, vol. I
Bush, Harry, 1883–1957, vol. V
Bush, Col Harry Stebbing, 1871–1942, vol. IV
Bush, Ian Elcock, 1928–1986, vol. VIII
Bush, Irving T., 1869–1948, vol. IV
Bush, Col (James) Paul, 1857–1930, vol. III
Bush, Rear-Adm. James Tobin, 1874–1949, vol. IV
Bush, (John Nash) Douglas, 1896–1983, vol. VIII
Bush, Brig.-Gen. John Ernest, 1858–1943, vol. IV
Bush, Col Paul; *see* Bush, Col J. P.
Bush, Adm. Sir Paul Warner, 1855–1930, vol. III
Bush, Raymond G. W., 1885–1972, vol. VII
Bush, Reginald Edgar James, 1869–1956, vol. V
Bush, Robert Edwin, 1855–1939, vol. III
Bush, Ronald Paul, 1902–1986, vol. VIII
Bush, Rev. Thomas Cromwell, *died* 1919, vol. II
Bush, Vannevar, 1890–1974, vol. VII
Bushby, Sir Edmund Fleming, 1879–1943, vol. IV
Bushby, Geoffrey Henry, 1899–1935, vol. III
Bushby, Henry Jeffreys, 1820–1903, vol. I
Bushby, Thomas, *died* 1916, vol. II
Bushby, Walter Edwin, 1889–1963, vol. VI
Bushe, Sir Grattan; *see* Bushe, Sir H. G.
Bushe, Sir (Henry) Grattan, 1886–1961, vol. VI
Bushe, Robert Gervase, 1851–1927, vol. II
Bushe, Seymour Coghill Hort, 1853–1922, vol. II

Bushe, Brig.-Gen. Thomas Francis, 1858–1951, vol. V
Bushe-Fox, Joscelyn Plunket, 1880–1954, vol. V
Bushe-Fox, Loftus Henry Kendal, 1863–1916, vol. II
Bushe-Fox, Patrick Loftus, 1907–1982, vol. VIII
Bushell, Stephen Wootton, 1844–1908, vol. I
Bushell, W. F., 1885–1974, vol. VII
Bushell, Rev. William Done, 1838–1917, vol. II
Bushman, Maj.-Gen. Sir Henry Augustus, 1841–1930, vol. III
Bushnell, Frank George, 1868–1941, vol. IV
Bushnell, Geoffrey Hext Sutherland, 1903–1978, vol. VII
Bushnell, George Herbert, 1896–1973, vol. VII
Busia, Kofi Abrefa, 1913–1978, vol. VII
Busk, Air Cdre Clifford Westly, 1898–1970, vol. VI
Busk, Sir Douglas Laird, 1906–1990, vol. VIII
Busk, Sir Edward Henry, 1844–1926, vol. II
Busk, Henrietta, 1845–1936, vol. III
Busk, Mrs Mary, 1854–1935, vol. III
Busoni, Ferruccio Benvenuto, 1866–1924, vol. II
Bussau, Hon. Sir (Albert) Louis, 1884–1947, vol. IV
Bussau, Hon. Sir Louis; *see* Bussau, Hon. Sir A. L.
Bussé, John, 1903–1956, vol. V
Bussell, Rev. Frederick William, 1862–1944, vol. IV
Bussell, Ven. William, *died* 1936, vol. III
Bussey, Ernest William, 1891–1958, vol. V
Bussey, Harry Youngman, 1858–1951, vol. V
Bussy, (George Francis) Philip, 1871–1933, vol. III
Bussy, Philip; *see* Bussy, G. F. P.
Bustamante, Rt Hon. and Exc. Sir Alexander; *see* Bustamante, Rt Hon. and Exc. Sir W. A.
Bustamante, Rt Hon. and Exc. Sir (William) Alexander, 1884–1977, vol. VII
Busteed, Bde-Surgeon Henry Elmsley, 1833–1912, vol. I
Buston, Brig.-Gen. Philip Thomas, 1853–1938, vol. III
Buswell, Col Ferberd Richard, *died* 1937, vol. III
Buswell, Ven. Henry Dison, 1839–1940, vol. III
Buszard, Marston Clarke, 1837–1921, vol. II
Butchart, Bt Lt-Col Henry Jackson, 1882–1971, vol. VII
Butcher, Arthur Douglas Deane, 1884–1944, vol. IV
Butcher, Very Rev. Charles Henry, 1833–1907, vol. I
Butcher, Maj.-Gen. Sir George James, 1860–1939, vol. III
Butcher, Sir Herbert Walter, 1st Bt, 1901–1966, vol. VI
Butcher, Paymaster Captain Reginald, 1880–1935, vol. III
Butcher, Rt Rev. Reginald Albert Claver, 1905–1975, vol. VII
Butcher, Samuel Henry, 1850–1910, vol. I
Butcher, William Deane, 1846–1919, vol. II
Bute, 3rd Marquess of, 1847–1900, vol. I
Bute, 4th Marquess of, 1881–1947, vol. IV
Bute, 5th Marquess of, 1907–1956, vol. V
Butement, William Alan Stewart, 1904–1990, vol. VIII
Butland, Sir Jack Richard, *died* 1982, vol. VIII
Butler of Saffron Walden, Baron (Life Peer); Richard Austen Butler, 1902–1982, vol. VIII
Butler, Rev. Alexander Douglas, *died* 1926, vol. II

Butler, Alfred J., 1850–1936, vol. III
Butler, Alfred Trego, 1880–1946, vol. IV
Butler, Col Arnold Charles Paul, 1890–1973, vol. VII
Butler, Arthur Gardiner, 1844–1925, vol. II
Butler, Col Arthur Graham, 1872–1949, vol. IV
Butler, Rev. Arthur Gray, 1831–1909, vol. I
Butler, (Arthur) Hugh (Montagu), 1873–1943, vol. IV
Butler, Arthur John, 1844–1910, vol. I
Butler, Arthur Stanley, 1854–1923, vol. II
Butler, Arthur Stanley George, 1888–1965, vol. VI
Butler, Lt-Col Arthur Townley, 1867–1948, vol. IV
Butler, Rt Rev. (Basil) Christopher, 1902–1986, vol. VIII
Butler, Lt-Col Charles Henry, 1881–1941, vol. IV
Butler, Sir (Charles) Owen, 1896–1968, vol. VI
Butler, Rt Rev. Christopher; see Butler, Rt Rev. B. C.
Butler, Rt Rev. Cuthbert; see Butler, Rt Rev. E. C.
Butler, Sir Cyril Kendall, 1864–1936, vol. III
Butler, Rev. Dugald, 1862–1926, vol. II
Butler, Rt Rev. (Edward) Cuthbert, 1858–1934, vol. III
Butler, Sir Edwin John, 1874–1943, vol. IV
Butler, Eliza Marian, 1885–1959, vol. V
Butler, Elizabeth, (Lady Butler), 1846–1933, vol. III
Butler, Maj.-Gen. Ernest Reuben Charles, 1864–1959, vol. V
Butler, Esmond Unwin, 1922–1989, vol. VIII
Butler, Captain Hon. Francis Almeric, 1872–1925, vol. II
Butler, Frank Chatterton, 1907–1984, vol. VIII
Butler, Frank Hedges, 1855–1928, vol. II
Butler, Sir Frederick George Augustus, 1873–1961, vol. VI
Butler, Sir Geoffrey, 1887–1929, vol. III
Butler, Maj.-Gen. Geoffrey Ernest, 1905–1981, vol. VIII
Butler, Sir George Beresford, 1857–1924, vol. II
Butler, George Grey, 1852–1935, vol. III
Butler, Sir Gerald Snowden, 1885–1969, vol. VI
Butler, Sir Harcourt; see Butler, Sir S. H.
Butler, Sir Harold Beresford, 1883–1951, vol. V
Butler, Harold Edgeworth, 1878–1951, vol. V
Butler, Harold Edwin, 1893–1973, vol. VII
Butler, Maj.-Gen. Henry, died 1907, vol. I
Butler, Rev. Henry Montagu, 1833–1918, vol. II
Butler, Herbert William, 1897–1971, vol. VII
Butler, Rev. Hercules Scott, 1850–1928, vol. II
Butler, Hon. (Horace) Somerset Edmond, 1903–1962, vol. VI
Butler, Hugh; see Butler, A. H. M.
Butler, Hugh Montagu, 1890–1972, vol. VII
Butler, Hugh Myddleton, 1857–1943, vol. IV
Butler, Lt-Col Humphrey, 1894–1953, vol. V
Butler, James Bayley, died 1964, vol. VI
Butler, Sir James Ramsay Montagu, 1889–1975, vol. VII
Butler, Rev. Lord (James) Theobald Bagot John, 1852–1929, vol. III
Butler, John Alfred Valentine, 1899–1977, vol. VII
Butler, Captain John Fitzhardinge Paul, 1888–1916, vol. II
Butler, Josephine Elizabeth, 1828–1906, vol. I
Butler, Kathleen Teresa Blake, 1883–1950, vol. IV

Butler, Brig.-Gen. Hon. Lesley James Probyn, 1876–1955, vol. V
Butler, Lionel Harry, 1923–1981, vol. VIII
Butler, Maria, 1868–1901, vol. I
Butler, Matthew Joseph, 1856–1933, vol. III
Butler, Gen. Sir Mervyn Andrew Haldane, 1913–1976, vol. VII
Butler, Mildred, died 1941, vol. IV
Butler, Hon. Sir Milo Broughton, 1906–1979, vol. VII
Butler, Sir Montagu Sherard Dawes, 1873–1952, vol. V
Butler, Sir Nevile Montagu, 1893–1973, vol. VII
Butler, Nicholas Murray, 1862–1947, vol. IV
Butler, Sir Owen; see Butler, Sir C. O.
Butler, Lt-Col Patrick Richard, 1880–1967, vol. VI
Butler, Sir Paul Dalrymple, 1886–1955, vol. V
Butler, Pierce Essex O'B.; see O'Brien-Butler.
Butler, Reg, (Reginald Cotterell Butler), 1913–1981, vol. VIII
Butler, Sir Reginald; see Butler, Sir R. R. F.
Butler, Comdr Sir (Reginald) Thomas, 2nd Bt (cr 1922), 1901–1959, vol. V
Butler, Hon. Sir Richard, 1850–1925, vol. II
Butler, Col Richard Barry, died 1957, vol. V
Butler, Lt-Col Richard F.; see Fowler-Butler.
Butler, Lt-Gen. Sir Richard Harte Keatinge, 1870–1935, vol. III
Butler, Richard Jago, 1884–1931, vol. III
Butler, Hon. Sir Richard Layton, 1885–1966, vol. IV
Butler, Sir Richard Pierce, 11th Bt (cr 1628), 1872–1955, vol. V
Butler, Richard William, 1844–1928, vol. II
Butler, Maj.-Gen. Robert Henry F.; see Fowler-Butler.
Butler, Sir (Robert) Reginald Frederick, 1st Bt (cr 1922), 1866–1933, vol. III
Butler, Major Hon. Robert Thomas Rowley Probyn, 1882–1938, vol. III
Butler, Rudolph Maximilian, 1872–1943, vol. IV
Butler, Maj.-Gen. St John Desmond A.; see Arcedeckne-Butler.
Butler, Samuel, 1835–1902, vol. I
Butler, Slade, died 1923, vol. II
Butler, Hon. Somerset; see Butler, Hon. H. S. E.
Butler, Sir (Spencer) Harcourt, 1869–1938, vol. III
Butler, Spencer Perceval, 1828–1915, vol. I
Butler, Maj.-Gen. Stephen Seymour, 1880–1964, vol. VI
Butler, Col Sydney George, 1874–1940, vol. III
Butler, Rev. Lord Theobold; see Butler, Rev. Lord J. T. B. J.
Butler, Maj.-Gen. Hon. Theobald Patrick Probyn, 1884–1970, vol. VI
Butler, Theobald Richard Fitzwalter, 1894–1976, vol. VII
Butler, Thomas, died 1937, vol. III
Butler, Comdr Sir Thomas; see Butler, Comdr Sir R. T.
Butler, Major Thomas Adair, 1836–1901, vol. I
Butler, Captain Sir Thomas Dacres, 1845–1937, vol. III
Butler, Thomas Harrison, 1871–1945, vol. IV

Butler, Sir Thomas Pierce, 10th Bt (*cr* 1628), 1836–1909, vol. I

Butler, Rear-Adm. Vernon Saumarez, 1885–1954, vol. V

Butler, Victor Spencer, 1900–1969, vol. VI

Butler, William F. T., *died* 1930, vol. III

Butler, Rt Hon. Sir William Francis, 1838–1910, vol. I

Butler, Brig-Gen. William John Chesshyre, 1864–1946, vol. IV

Butler, Sir William Waters, 1st Bt (*cr* 1926), 1866–1939, vol. III

Butler-Bowdon, John Erdeswick, 1850–1929, vol. III

Butler Brockwell, Esca Powys; *see* Brockwell, E. P. B.

Butler-Henderson, Hon. Eric Brand, 1884–1953, vol. V

Butler-Smythe, Albert Charles, 1852–1936, vol. III

Butlin, Sir Henry Guy Trentham, 2nd Bt, 1893–1916, vol. II

Butlin, Sir Henry Tretham, 1st Bt, 1845–1912, vol. I

Butlin, Sir William, 1851–1923, vol. II

Butlin, Sir William Edmund, 1899–1980, vol. VII

Butt, Sir Alfred, 1st Bt, 1878–1962, vol. VI

Butt, Charles Sinclair, 1900–1973, vol. VII

Butt, Dame Clara Ellen, 1873–1936, vol. III

Butt, John Everett, 1906–1965, vol. VI

Butt, Most Rev. Joseph, 1869–1944, vol. IV

Buttenshaw, Hon. Ernest Albert, 1876–1950, vol. IV, vol. V

Butter, Archibald Edward, 1874–1928, vol. II

Butterfield, Fred, *died* 1935, vol. III

Butterfield, Sir Frederick William Louis d'Hilliers Roosevelt Theodore, *died* 1943, vol. IV

Butterfield, Sir Harry Durham, 1898–1976, vol. VII

Butterfield, Sir Herbert, 1900–1979, vol. VII

Butterfield, Robert William Fitzmaurice, 1889–1967, vol. VI

Butterfield, William, 1814–1900, vol. I

Butters, Sir John Henry, 1885–1969, vol. VI

Butterworth, Alan, 1864–1937, vol. III

Butterworth, Sir Alexander-Kaye, 1854–1946, vol. IV

Butterworth, Arthur Reginald, 1850–1924, vol. II

Butterworth, Comdr Henry, 1866–1926, vol. II

Butterworth, Reginald, 1879–1951, vol. V

Butterworth, Col Reginald Francis Amherst, 1876–1960, vol. V

Butterworth, Hon. W. Walton, 1903–1975, vol. VII

Butti, Rt Rev. Mgr Peter L., *died* 1932, vol. III

Buttigieg, Anton, 1912–1983, vol. VIII

Buttle, Gladwin Albert Hurst, 1899–1983, vol. VIII

Button, Frederick Stephen, 1873–1948, vol. IV

Button, Howard, 1875–1965, vol. VI

Button, Sir Howard Stransom, 1873–1943, vol. IV

Buttrose, Murray, 1903–1987, vol. VIII

Butts, S., *died* 1906, vol. I

Buxton, 1st Earl, 1853–1934, vol. III

Buxton, Countess; (Mildred Anne), *died* 1955, vol. V

Buxton, Alfred Fowell, 1854–1952, vol. V

Buxton, Alfred St Clair, 1854–1920, vol. II

Buxton, Major Anthony, 1881–1970, vol. VI

Buxton, Comdr Bernard, 1882–1923, vol. II

Buxton, Charles Roden, 1875–1942, vol. IV

Buxton, Denis Alfred Jex, 1895–1964, vol. VI

Buxton, Maj. Desmond Gurney, 1898–1987, vol. VIII

Buxton, Dudley Wilmot, *died* 1931, vol. III

Buxton, Edward Gurney, 1865–1929, vol. III

Buxton, Edward North, 1840–1924, vol. II

Buxton, Francis William, 1847–1911, vol. I

Buxton, Geoffrey Powell, 1852–1929, vol. III

Buxton, Gladys, 1891–1971, vol. VII

Buxton, Rt Rev. Harold Jocelyn, 1880–1976, vol. VII

Buxton, Henry Fowell, 1876–1949, vol. IV

Buxton, James Basil, *died* 1954, vol. V

Buxton, John Henry, 1849–1934, vol. III

Buxton, Col John Lawrence, 1877–1951, vol. V

Buxton, Leonard Halford Dudley, 1889–1939, vol. III

Buxton, Lionel Gurney, 1876–1962, vol. VI

Buxton, Patrick Alfred, 1892–1955, vol. V

Buxton, Richard; *see* Shanks, Edward.

Buxton, Captain Richard Gurney, 1887–1972, vol. VII

Buxton, Dame Rita Mary, 1900–1982, vol. VIII

Buxton, Robert Vere, 1883–1953, vol. V

Buxton, Captain Roden Henry Victor, 1890–1970, vol. VI

Buxton, St John Dudley, 1891–1981, vol. VIII

Buxton, Sir Thomas Fowell, 3rd Bt, 1837–1915, vol. I

Buxton, Sir Thomas Fowell, 5th Bt, 1889–1945, vol. IV

Buxton, Sir (Thomas Fowell) Victor, 4th Bt, 1865–1919, vol. II

Buxton, Sir Victor; *see* Buxton, Sir T. F. V.

Buxton, William Leonard, 1894–1964, vol. VI

Buzacott, Charles Hardie, 1835–1918, vol. II

Buzacott, William James, 1866–1937, vol. III

Buzzard, Rear-Adm. Sir Anthony Wass, 2nd Bt, 1902–1972, vol. VII

Buzzard, Lt-Col Charles Norman, 1873–1961, vol. VI

Buzzard, Sir (Edward) Farquhar, 1st Bt, 1871–1945, vol. IV

Buzzard, Brig.-Gen. Frank Anstie, 1875–1950, vol. IV

Buzzard, John Huxley, 1912–1984, vol. VIII

Buzzard, Thomas, 1831–1919, vol. II

Byam, Maj.-Gen. William, 1841–1906, vol. I

Byam, William, 1882–1963, vol. VI

Byam Shaw, Glencairn Alexander, 1904–1986, vol. VIII

Byass, Bt Col Sir Geoffrey Robert Sidney, 2nd Bt, 1895–1976, vol. VII

Byass, Col Harry Nicholl, 1863–1956, vol. V

Byass, Sir Sidney Hutchinson, 1st Bt, 1862–1929, vol. III

Byatt, Edwin, 1888–1948, vol. IV

Byatt, Sir Horace Archer, 1875–1933, vol. III

Byers, Baron (Life Peer); Charles Frank Byers, 1915–1984, vol. VIII

Byers, Sir John William, *died* 1920, vol. II

Byers, Joseph Austen, 1895–1977, vol. VII

Byers, Mrs Margaret, *died* 1912, vol. I

Byford, Donald, 1898–1981, vol. VIII

Byford, Sir John, 1860–1931, vol. III

Byles, William Hounsom, 1872–1928, vol. II

Byles, Sir William Pollard, 1839–1917, vol. II

Byng, 1st Viscount, 1862–1935, vol. III

Byng, Lt-Col Hon. Antony Schomberg, 1876–1934, vol. III

Byng, Col Hon. Charles Cavendish George, 1849–1918, vol. II

Byng, Hon. Ivo Francis, 1874–1949, vol. IV

Byng, L. C.; *see* Crammer-Byng.

Byng, Major Hon. Lionel Francis George, 1858–1915, vol. I

Byng, Lady Mary Elizabeth Agnes; *see* Mauny-Talvande, Countess of.

Byng, Hon. Sydney, 1844–1920, vol. II

Bynner, Witter, 1881–1968, vol. VI

Byrd, Rear-Adm. Richard E., 1888–1957, vol. V

Byrde, Ven. Louis, *died* 1917, vol. II

Byrne, Alfred, 1882–1956, vol. V

Byrne, Brian Oswald D., *see* Byrne, Donn.

Byrne, Donn, 1889–1928, vol. II

Byrne, Sir Edmund Widdrington, 1844–1904, vol. I

Byrne, Most Rev. Edward J., 1872–1940, vol. III

Byrne, Rt Rev. Mgr Frederick, *born* 1834, vol. II

Byrne, Col Frederick Joseph, 1873–1929, vol. III

Byrne, Col Henry, 1840–1915, vol. I

Byrne, Rt Rev. Herbert Kevin, 1884–1978, vol. VII

Byrne, Rt Rev. James, 1870–1938, vol. III

Byrne, James Patrick, 1854–1935, vol. III

Byrne, Lt-Col John Dillon, 1875–1925, vol. II

Byrne, Brig.-Gen. Sir Joseph Aloysius, 1874–1942, vol. IV

Byrne, Hon. Sir Laurence Austin, 1896–1965, vol. VI

Byrne, Louis Campbell, *died* 1923, vol. II

Byrne, Muriel St Clare, 1895–1983, vol. VIII

Byrne, Patrick Sarsfield, 1913–1980, vol. VII

Byrne, Rev. Peter, *born* 1840, vol. II

Byrne, Air Cdre Reginald, 1888–1965, vol. VI

Byrne, Richard, *died* 1942, vol. IV

Byrne, Rt Hon. Sir William Patrick, 1859–1935, vol. III

Byrnes, James Francis, 1879–1972, vol. VII

Byrnes, Hon. Sir Percy Thomas, 1893–1973, vol. VII

Byrnes, Hon. Thomas Joseph, 1860–1898, vol. I

Byrom, Charles Reginald, 1878–1952, vol. V

Byrom, Thomas Emmett, 1871–1956, vol. V

Byron, 9th Baron, 1855–1917, vol. II

Byron, 10th Baron, 1861–1949, vol. IV

Byron, 11th Baron, 1903–1983, vol. VIII

Byron, 12th Baron, 1899–1989, vol. VIII

Byron, Captain Augustus William, 1856–1939, vol. III

Byron, Paymaster Rear-Adm. Charles Edgar, *died* 1940, vol. III

Byron, Edmund, 1843–1921, vol. II

Byron, Brig.-Gen. John, 1872–1944, vol. IV

Byron, Brig.-Gen. Hon. John Joseph, *died* 1935, vol. III

Byron, Col Richard, 1870–1939, vol. III

Byron, Robert, 1905–1941, vol. IV

Byrt, Albert Henry, 1881–1966, vol. VI

Bythesea, Rear-Adm. John, 1827–1906, vol. I

Bywater, Hector Charles, 1884–1940, vol. III

Bywater, Ingram, 1840–1914, vol. I

Bywater, Thomas Lloyd, 1905–1979, vol. VII

Bywaters, Hubert William, 1881–1966, vol. VI

C

Cabell, James Branch, 1879–1958, vol. V

Cable, 1st Baron, 1859–1927, vol. II

Cable, Boyd, *died* 1943, vol. IV

Cable, Eric Grant, 1887–1970, vol. VI

Cable, George Washington, 1844–1925, vol. II

Cable-Alexander, Sir Desmond William Lionel, 7th Bt, 1910–1988, vol. VIII

Caborne, Captain Warren Frederick, 1849–1924, vol. II

Cabot, Sir Daniel Alfred Edmond, 1888–1974, vol. VII

Cabot, Lt-Col Hugh, 1872–1945, vol. IV

Cabrol, Rt Rev. Fernand, 1855–1937, vol. III

Caccamisi, Baronne Anzon; *see* Marchesi, Blanche

Caccia, Baron (Life Peer); Harold Anthony Caccia, 1905–1990, vol. VIII

Caccia, Anthony Mario Felix, 1869–1962, vol. VI

Caclamanos, Demetrius, 1872–1949, vol. IV

Cacoyannis, Hon. Sir Panayotis Loizou, 1893–1980, vol. VII

Cadbury, Barrow, 1862–1958, vol. V

Cadbury, Edward, 1873–1948, vol. IV

Cadbury, Sir Egbert, 1893–1967, vol. VI

Cadbury, Dame Elizabeth Mary, (Mrs George Cadbury), 1858–1951, vol. V

Cadbury, George, 1839–1922, vol. II

Cadbury, Henry Joel, 1883–1974, vol. VII

Cadbury, Henry Tylor, 1882–1952, vol. V

Cadbury, Jocelyn Benedict Laurence, 1946–1982, vol. VIII

Cadbury, Laurence John, 1889–1982, vol. VIII

Cadbury, Paul Strangman, 1895–1984, vol. VIII

Caddell, Col Henry Mortimer, 1875–1944, vol. IV

Caddy, Adrian, 1879–1966, vol. VI

Caddy, Col Hector Osman, 1882–1935, vol. III

Cade, Sir Stanford, 1895–1973, vol. VII

Cadell, Alan, 1841–1921, vol. II

Cadell, Lt-Gen. Charles Alexander Elliott, 1888–1951, vol. V

Cadell, Francis Campbell Boileau, 1883–1937, vol. III

Cadell, Lt-Col Harry Ernest, 1867–1939, vol. III

Cadell, Henry Moubray, 1860–1934, vol. III

Cadell of Grange, Col Henry Moubray, 1892–1967, vol. VI

Cadell, Sir Patrick Robert, 1871–1961, vol. VI

Cadell, Sir Robert, 1825–1897, vol. I

Cadell, Col Thomas, 1835–1919, vol. II

Cadenhead, James, 1858–1927, vol. II

Cadge, William, *died* 1903, vol. I

Cadic, Edouard, 1858–1914, vol. I

Cadman, 1st Baron, 1877–1941, vol. IV

Cadman, 2nd Baron, 1909–1966, vol. VI

Cadman, Hon. Sir Alfred Jerome, *died* 1905, vol. I
Cadman, James, 1878–1947, vol. IV
Cadman, John Heaton, 1839–1906, vol. I
Cadman, Rev. Samuel Parkes, 1864–1936, vol. III
Cadman, Rev. William Healey, 1891–1965, vol. VI
Cadogan, 5th Earl, 1840–1915, vol. I
Cadogan, 6th Earl, 1869–1933, vol. III
Cadogan, Rt Hon. Sir Alexander George Montagu, 1884–1968, vol. VI
Cadogan, Hon. Sir Edward Cecil George, 1880–1962, vol. VI
Cadogan, Hon. Frederick William, 1821–1904, vol. I
Cadogan, Hon. William George Sydney, 1879–1914, vol. I
Cadoux, Cecil John, 1883–1947, vol. IV
Cadzow, Sir Norman James Kerr, 1912–1981, vol. VIII
Cafe, T. Watt, 1856–1925, vol. II
Cafe, Gen. William Martin, 1826–1906, vol. I
Caffery, Jefferson, 1886–1974, vol. VII
Caffieri, H., *died* 1932, vol. III
Caffyn, Brig. Sir Edward Roy, 1904–1990, vol. VIII
Caffyn, Kathleen Mannington, *died* 1926, vol. II
Caffyn, Sir Sydney Morris, 1901–1976, vol. VII
Cage, Edward Edwin Henry, 1912–1984, vol. VIII
Cahal, Dennis Abraham, 1921–1983, vol. VIII
Cahan, Hon. Charles Hazlitt, 1861–1944, vol. IV
Cahan, J(ohn) Flint, 1912–1961, vol. VI
Cahill, Rt Rev. John Baptist, 1841–1910, vol. I
Cahill, Sir (Joseph) Robert, 1879–1953, vol. V
Cahill, Patrick Richard, 1912–1990, vol. VIII
Cahill, Sir Robert; *see* Cahill, Sir J. R.
Cahill, Most Rev. Thomas Vincent, 1913–1978, vol. VII
Cahill, Lt-Col William Geoffrey, 1854–1931, vol. III
Cahn, Charles Montague, 1900–1985, vol. VIII
Cahn, Sir Julien, 1st Bt, *died* 1944, vol. IV
Cahusac, Col William Fremantle, 1857–1930, vol. III
Caie, John Morrison, 1878–1949, vol. IV
Caillard, Alfred, 1841–1900, vol. I
Caillard, Sir Vincent Henry Penalver, 1856–1930, vol. III
Caillaux, Joseph, *died* 1944, vol. IV
Cain, Sir Ernest, 2nd Bt, 1891–1969, vol. VI
Cain, Georges, *died* 1919, vol. II
Cain, John Cannell, 1871–1921, vol. II
Cain, Sir Jonathan Robert, 1869–1938, vol. III
Cain, Major Robert Henry, 1909–1974, vol. VII
Cain, Sir William, 1st Bt, 1864–1924, vol. II
Caine, Sir Derwent Hall, 1st Bt, 1891–1971, vol. VII
Caine, Gordon Ralph H.; *see* Hall Caine.
Caine, Sir Hall, 1853–1931, vol. III
Caine, William, 1873–1925, vol. II
Caine, William Ralph Hall, 1856–1939, vol. III
Caine, Willaim Sproston, 1842–1903, vol. I
Caines, Clement Guy, 1882–1952, vol. V
Caird, Sir Andrew, 1870–1956, vol. V
Caird, David, 1863–1934, vol. III
Caird, Edward, 1835–1908, vol. I
Caird, Francis M., *died* 1926, vol. II
Caird, Rev. George Bradford, 1917–1984, vol. VIII
Caird, Sir James, 1st Bt (*cr* 1928), 1864–1954, vol. V
Caird, Sir James Key, 1st Bt (*cr* 1913), 1837–1916, vol. II

Caird, Very Rev. John, 1820–1898, vol. I
Caird, Mrs Mona, *died* 1932, vol. III
Cairncross, Maj.-Gen. John, 1835–1914, vol. I
Cairnes, Captain William Elliot, 1862–1902, vol. I
Cairnes, William Plunket, 1857–1925, vol. II
Cairney, John, 1898–1966, vol. VI
Cairns, 3rd Earl, 1863–1905, vol. I
Cairns, 4th Earl, 1865–1946, vol. IV
Cairns, 5th Earl, 1909–1989, vol. VIII
Cairns, Rt Hon. Sir David Arnold Scott, 1902–1987, vol. VIII
Cairns, Very Rev. David Smith, 1862–1946, vol. IV
Cairns, Sir Hugh William Bell, 1896–1952, vol. V
Cairns, James, 1885–1939, vol. III
Cairns, John, 1859–1923, vol. II
Cairns, John Arthur Robert, *died* 1933, vol. III
Cairns, Sir Joseph Foster, 1920–1981, vol. VIII
Cairns, Julia, (Mrs Paul Davidson), 1893–1985, vol. VIII
Cairns, T., *died* 1908, vol. I
Cairns, William Murray, 1866–1949, vol. IV
Caithness, 17th Earl of, 1857–1914, vol. I
Caithness, 18th Earl of, 1862–1947, vol. IV
Caithness, 19th Earl of, 1906–1965, vol. VI
Cakobau, Ratu Sir Etuate Tui-Vanuavou Tugi, 1908–1973, vol. VII
Cakobau, Ratu Sir George Kadavulevu, 1911–1989, vol. VIII
Caldecot, Ivone K.; *see* Kirkpatrick-Caldecot.
Caldecote, 1st Viscount, 1876–1947, vol. IV
Caldecott, Rev. Alfred, 1850–1936, vol. III
Caldecott, Andrew; *see* Caldecott, J. A.
Caldecott, Sir Andrew, 1884–1951, vol. V
Caldecott, Lt-Col Ernest Lawrence, 1874–1927, vol. II
Caldecott, Maj.-Gen. Francis James, 1842–1926, vol. II
Caldecott, (John) Andrew, 1924–1990, vol. VIII
Calder, Alexander, 1898–1976, vol. VII
Calder, George, 1894–1968, vol. VI
Calder, George Alexander, 1859–1945, vol. IV
Calder, James, 1869–1940, vol. III
Calder, Col (Hon.) James, 1898–1968, vol. VI
Calder, Hon. James Alexander, 1868–1956, vol. V
Calder, Sir James Charles, 1869–1962, vol. VI
Calder, James William, 1914–1975, vol. VII
Calder, Sir John Alexander, 1889–1974, vol. VII
Calder, Air Vice-Marshal Malcolm Frederick, 1907–1978, vol. VII (AII)
Calder, (Peter) Ritchie; *see* Baron Ritchie-Calder.
Calder, Ritchie; *see* Baron Ritchie-Calder.
Calder, Robert, 1838–1912, vol. I
Calder, Ven. William, 1848–1923, vol. II
Calder, Sir William Moir, 1881–1960, vol. V
Calder-Marshall, Sir Robert, 1877–1955, vol. V
Calderbank, Philip Hugh, 1919–1988, vol. VIII
Calderon, George, 1868–1915, vol. I
Calderon, Philip Hermogenes, 1833–1898, vol. I
Calderon, W. Frank, 1865–1943, vol. IV
Calderwood, Henry, 1830–1897, vol. I
Calderwood, W. L., 1865–1950, vol. IV
Caldicott, Hon. Sir John Moore, 1900–1986, vol. VIII

Caldwell, Alexander Francis Somerville, 1873–1940, vol. III
Caldwell, Erskine, 1903–1987, vol. VIII
Caldwell, Francis, 1860–1934, vol. III
Caldwell, Maj.-Gen. Frederick Crofton H.; *see* Heath-Caldwell.
Caldwell, Godfrey David, 1920–1985, vol. VIII
Caldwell, Rt Hon. James, 1839–1925, vol. II
Caldwell, John, 1903–1974, vol. VII
Caldwell, John Foster, 1892–1981, vol. VIII
Caldwell, Peter Christopher, 1927–1979, vol. VII
Caldwell, Robert Nixon, 1888–1967, vol. VI
Caldwell, Col Robert Townley, 1843–1914, vol. I
Caldwell, Taylor, 1900–1985, vol. VIII
Caldwell, Thomas Fisher, 1866–1940, vol. III
Caldwell, William, 1863–1942, vol. IV
Caledon, 4th Earl of, 1846–1898, vol. I
Caledon, 5th Earl of, 1885–1968, vol. VI
Caledon, 6th Earl of, 1920–1980, vol. VII
Calhoun, Eleanor; *see* Lazarovich-Hrebelianovich.
Calkin, Lance, 1859–1936, vol. III
Call, Frank Oliver, 1878–1956, vol. V
Callaghan, Sir Alfred John, 1865–1940, vol. III
Callaghan, Maj.-Gen. Cecil Arthur, 1890–1967, vol. VI
Callaghan, Admiral of the Fleet Sir George Astley, 1852–1920, vol. II
Callaghan, Morley Edward, 1903–1990, vol. VIII
Callahan, James Morton, 1864–1956, vol. V
Callan, John Bartholomew, 1882–1951, vol. V
Callander, Lt-Gen. Sir Colin Bishop, 1897–1979, vol. VII
Callander, George Frederick William, 1848–1916, vol. II
Callander, Sir James, 1877–1952, vol. V
Callander, John Graham, 1873–1938, vol. III
Callander, Thomas, 1877–1959, vol. V
Callander, Major William Henry Burn, 1890–1967, vol. VI
Callas, Maria, 1923–1977, vol. VII
Callaway, Charles, 1838–1915, vol. I
Callaway, Air Vice-Marshal William Bertram, 1889–1974, vol. VII
Callcott, F. T., *died* 1923, vol. II
Callender, Hugh Longbourne, 1863–1930, vol. III
Callender, Lt-Col David Aubrey, 1868–1953, vol. V
Callender, Eustace Maud, 1864–1952, vol. V
Callender, Sir Geoffrey Arthur Romaine, 1875–1946, vol. IV
Callender, Sir Thomas Octavius, 1855–1938, vol. III
Calley, Hon. Maj.-Gen. Thomas Charles Pleydell, 1856–1932, vol. III
Callow, Charles Thomas Cheslyn, 1852–1933, vol. III
Callow, Graham, 1894–1960, vol. V
Callow, Robert Kenneth, 1901–1983, vol. VIII
Callow, William, 1812–1908, vol. I
Callwell, Maj.-Gen. Sir Charles Edward, 1859–1923, vol. II
Calman, William Thomas, 1871-1952, vol. V
Calmette, Leon Charles Albert, 1863–1933, vol. III
Calnan, Denis, *died* 1939, vol. III
Calry, 6th Count de, 1854–1950, vol. IV (A), vol. V
Calthorpe, 6th Baron, 1829–1910, vol. I
Calthorpe, 7th Baron, 1831–1912, vol. I

Calthorpe, 8th Baron, 1862–1940, vol. III
Calthorpe, 9th Baron, 1924–1945, vol. IV
Calthorpe, Sir FitzRoy Hamilton A. G.; *see* Anstruther-Gough-Calthorpe.
Calthorpe, Hon. Frederick Somerset Gough-, 1892–1935, vol. III
Calthorpe, Brig. Sir Richard Hamilton A. G.; *see* Anstruther-Gough-Calthorpe.
Calthorpe, Admiral of the Fleet Hon. Sir Somerset Arthur Gough-, 1864–1937, vol. III
Calthrop, Sir Cathrop Guy Spencer, 1st Bt, 1870–1919, vol. II
Calthrop, Col Christopher William C.; *see* Carr-Calthrop.
Calthrop, Dion Clayton, 1878–1937, vol. III
Calve, Emma, 1866–1942, vol. IV
Calver, Sir Robert Henry Sherwood, *died* 1963, vol. VI
Calverley, 1st Baron, 1877–1955, vol. V
Calverley, 2nd Baron, 1914–1971, vol. VII
Calverley, Joseph Ernest Goodfellow, 1872–1953, vol. V
Calvert, Albert Frederick, 1872–1946, vol. IV
Calvert, Albert Spencer, 1897–1953, vol. V
Calvert, Archibald Motteux, 1827–1906, vol. I
Calvert, Mrs Charles, 1836–1921, vol. II
Calvert, Edwin George Bleakley, *died* 1976, vol. VII
Calvert, Rt Rev. George Reginald, 1900–1976, vol. VII
Calvert, Hubert, 1875–1961, vol. VI
Calvert, James, *died* 1932, vol. III
Calvert, Lt-Col John Telfer, *died* 1944, vol. IV
Calvert, Sir Joseph, 1853–1931, vol. III
Calvert, Rear-Adm. Thomas Frederick Parker, 1883–1938, vol. III
Calvert, William Archibald, 1868–1943, vol. IV
Calvert, William Robinson, 1882–1949, vol. IV
Calvert-Jones, Maj.-Gen. Percy George, 1894–1977, vol. VII
Calvino, Italo, 1923–1985, vol. VIII
Calwell, Rt Hon. Arthur Augustus, 1896–1973, vol. VII
Cam, Helen Maud, 1885–1968, vol. VI
Camacho, Sir Maurice Vivian, 1885–1941, vol. IV
Cambage, Richard Hind, 1859–1928, vol. II
Camber-Williams, Rev. Robert, 1860–1924, vol. II
Cambon, Paul, 1843–1924, vol. II
Cambon, Roger Paul Jules, 1881–1970, vol. VI
Cambridge, 2nd Duke of, 1819–1904, vol. I
Cambridge, 1st Marquess of, 1868–1927, vol. II
Cambridge, 2nd Marquess of, 1895–1981, vol. VIII
Cambridge, Ada, 1844–1926, vol. II
Cambridge, Sir Arthur Wallace P.; *see* Pickard-Cambridge.
Cambridge, Elizabeth; *see* Hodges, Barbara K.
Cambridge, Rev. Octavius P.; *see* Pickard-Cambridge.
Cambridge, William Adair P.; *see* Pickard-Cambridge.
Camden, 4th Marquess of, 1872-1943, vol. IV
Camden, 5th Marquess, 1899–1983, vol. VIII
Came, William Gerald, 1889–1984, vol. VIII

Cameron of Balhousie, Baron (Life Peer); Marshal of the Royal Air Force Neil Cameron, 1920–1985, vol. VIII

Cameron, Rev. A. D., *died* 1946, vol. IV

Cameron, Alexander Gordon, 1886–1944, vol. IV

Cameron, Lt-Gen. Sir Alexander Maurice, 1898–1986, vol. VIII

Cameron, Alexander T., 1882–1947, vol. IV

Cameron, Rev. Allan Thomas, 1870–1932, vol. III

Cameron, Archibald, 1902–1964, vol. VI

Cameron, Gen. Sir Archibald Rice, 1870–1944, vol. IV

Cameron, Rev. Archibald Stuart, *died* 1936, vol. III

Cameron, Col Aylmer, 1833–1909, vol. I

Cameron, Basil; *see* Cameron, G. B.

Cameron, (Caroline) Emily, (Mrs Lovett Cameron), *died* 1921, vol. II

Cameron, Major Cecil Aylmer, 1883–1924, vol. II

Cameron, Sir Charles, 1st Bt, 1841–1924, vol. II

Cameron, Charles, 1886–1968, vol. VI

Cameron, Sir Charles Alexander, 1830–1921, vol. II

Cameron, Rev. Charles Leslie L.; *see* Lovett-Cameron.

Cameron, Charlotte, *died* 1946, vol. IV

Cameron, Sir Cornelius, 1896–1975, vol. VII

Cameron, Col Hon. Cyril St Clair, 1857–1941, vol. IV

Cameron, Vice-Adm. Cyril St Clair, 1879–1973, vol. VII

Cameron, Sir David Young, 1865–1945, vol. IV

Cameron of Lochiel, Donald, 1835–1905, vol. I

Cameron, Donald Andreas, 1856–1936, vol. III

Cameron, Sir Donald Charles, 1872–1948, vol. IV

Cameron, Lt-Col Sir Donald Charles, 1879–1960, vol. V (A), vol. VI

Cameron, Sir Donald Charles, 1877–1962, vol. VI

Cameron, Lt-Col Donald Hay, 1867–1932, vol. III

Cameron, Hon. Donald Norman, *died* 1931, vol. III

Cameron, Maj.-Gen. Donald Roderick, 1834–1921, vol. II

Cameron of Lochiel, Col Sir Donald Walter, 1876–1951, vol. V

Cameron, Hon. Sir Douglas Colin, 1854–1921, vol. II

Cameron, Sir Edward John, 1858–1947, vol. IV

Cameron, Edward Robert, 1857–1931, vol. III

Cameron, Elizabeth Dorothea Cole, (Mrs Alan Charles Cameron); *see* Bowen, E. D. C.

Cameron, Emily; *see* Cameron, C. E.

Cameron, Lt-Col Ewan Cornwallis, 1865–1932, vol. III

Cameron, Sir Ewen, 1841–1908, vol. I

Cameron of Lundavra, Col Ewen Allan, 1877–1958, vol. V

Cameron, Hon. Sir Ewen Paul, 1892–1964, vol. VI

Cameron, Finlay James, 1880–1954, vol. V

Cameron, (George) Basil, 1884–1975, vol. VII

Cameron, Lt-Col George Cecil Minett Sorell-, 1871–1947, vol. IV

Cameron, Ven. George Henry, 1861–1940, vol. III

Cameron, Gordon Campbell, 1937–1990, vol. VIII

Cameron, Hector Charles, 1878–1958, vol. V

Cameron, Sir Hector Clare, 1843–1928, vol. II

Cameron, Hugh, 1835–1918, vol. II

Cameron, Col Hugh Alan, 1871–1929, vol. III

Cameron, Irving Heward, 1855–1933, vol. III

Cameron, Isabella Douglas, *died* 1945, vol. IV

Cameron, James; *see* Cameron, M. J. W.

Cameron, Col James Black, 1882–1946, vol. IV

Cameron, Sir James Davidson Stuart, 1900–1969, vol. VI

Cameron, James Nield, 1884–1960, vol. V

Cameron, James Spottiswoode, *died* 1918, vol. II

Cameron, John, 1873–1960, vol. V

Cameron, Sir John, 2nd Bt, 1903–1968, vol. VI

Cameron, John Donald, 1858–1923, vol. II

Cameron, Adm. John Ewen, 1874–1939, vol. III

Cameron, John Forbes, 1873–1952, vol. V

Cameron, John Gordon Patrick, 1885–1970, vol. VI

Cameron, Rev. John Kennedy, 1860–1944, vol. IV

Cameron, Col John Philip, 1879–1950, vol. IV

Cameron, John Robson, 1845–1907, vol. I

Cameron, Brig. John S.; *see* Sorel Cameron.

Cameron, Col Kenneth, 1863–1939, vol. III (A), vol. IV

Cameron, Mrs Lovett; *see* Cameron, C. E.

Cameron, Captain Ludovick Charles Richard Duncombe-Jewell, 1866–1947, vol. IV

Cameron, Malcolm Graeme, 1857–1925, vol. II

Cameron, (Mark) James (Walter), 1911–1985, vol. VIII

Cameron, Matthew Brown, 1867–1952, vol. V

Cameron, Major Sir Maurice Alexander, 1855–1936, vol. III

Cameron, Murdoch, *died* 1930, vol. III

Cameron, Maj.-Gen. Neville John Gordon, 1873–1955, vol. V

Cameron, Brig. Orford Somerville, 1878–1958, vol. V

Cameron, Robert, 1825–1913, vol. I

Cameron, Maj.-Gen. Roderic Duncan, 1893–1975, vol. VII

Cameron, Sir Roderick William, 1825–1900, vol. I

Cameron, Sir Roy, 1899–1966, vol. VI

Cameron, Samuel J., 1878–1959, vol. V

Cameron, Thomas Wright Moir, 1894–1980, vol. VII (AII)

Cameron, William, *died* 1954, vol. V

Cameron, Gen. Sir William Gordon, 1827–1913, vol. I

Cameron, William Lochiel Sapte Lovett, 1854–1938, vol. III

Cameron, Rt Rev. William Mouat, 1854–1915, vol. I

Cameron-Head, Francis Somerville Cameron, 1896–1957, vol. V

Cameron-Head, James, 1851–1922, vol. II

Cameron-Ramsay-Fairfax-Lucy, Major Sir Brian Fulke; *see* Fairfax-Lucy.

Cameron-Ramsay-Fairfax-Lucy, Sir Henry William; *see* Fairfax-Lucy.

Cameron-Swan, Captain Donald, 1863–1951, vol. V

Camidge, Rt Rev. Charles Edward, 1838–1911, vol. I

Camilleri, Emanuel, 1887–1968, vol. VI (AII)

Camilleri, Rt Rev. Giovanni M., *born* 1843, vol. II

Camilleri, Sir Luigi A., 1892–1989, vol. VIII

Camm, Dom Bede, 1864–1942, vol. IV

Camm, John Sutcliffe, 1925–1985, vol. VIII

Camm, Sir Sydney, 1893–1966, vol. VI

Cammaerts, Emile, *died* 1953, vol. V

Cammell, Major Gerald Arthur, 1889–1933, vol. III

Cammidge, Percy John, 1872–1956, vol. V (A)

Camoys, 4th Baron, 1856–1897, vol. I
Camoys, 5th Baron, 1884–1968, vol. VI
Camoys, 6th Baron, 1913–1976, vol. VII
Camp, Harold Robert, 1893–1968, vol. VI
Camp, Instr Captain J., 1877–1962, vol. VI
Camp, Samuel James, 1876–1936, vol. III
Campagnac, E. T., *died* 1952, vol. V
Campbell, Alan Johnston, 1895–1982, vol. VIII
Campbell, Captain Alexander, 1839–1914, vol. I
Campbell, Sir Alexander, 6th Bt (*cr* 1667), 1841–1914, vol. I
Campbell, Lt-Col Alexander, 1881–1941, vol. IV
Campbell, Alexander, *died* 1961, vol. VI
Campbell, Sir Alexander, 1892–1963, vol. VI
Campbell, Brig. Alexander Donald Powys, 1894–1974, vol. VII
Campbell, Maj.-Gen. Sir (Alexander) Douglas, 1899–1980, vol. VII
Campbell, Lt-Col Alexander George, 1889–1936, vol. III
Campbell, Maj.-Gen. Alexander Henry Edward, 1835–1929, vol. III
Campbell, Alexander McCulloch, 1879–1955, vol. V
Campbell, Sir Alexander Thomas Cockburn-, 5th Bt (*cr* 1821), 1872–1935, vol. III
Campbell, Adm. Alexander Victor, 1874–1957, vol. V
Campbell, Lt-Col Sir Alexander William Dennistoun, 4th Bt (*cr* 1831), 1848–1931, vol. III
Campbell, Maj.-Gen. Alfred Edward, 1901–1973, vol. VII
Campbell, Alistair, 1907–1974, vol. VII
Campbell, Very Rev. Andrew James, 1875–1950, vol. IV
Campbell, Hon. Angus Dudley, 1895–1967, vol. VI
Campbell, Lord Archibald, 1846–1913, vol. I
Campbell, Lady Archibald; (Janey Sevilla), *died* 1923, vol. II
Campbell, Hon. Archibald, 1846–1913, vol. I
Campbell, Archibald, 1877–1963, vol. VI
Campbell, Sir Archibald Augustus Ava, 4th Bt (*cr* 1831), 1879–1916, vol. II
Campbell, Sir Archibald Ava, 3rd Bt (*cr* 1831), 1844–1913, vol. I
Campbell, Archibald Duncan, 1919–1975, vol. VII
Campbell, Rt Rev. Archibald Ean, 1856–1921, vol. II
Campbell, Maj.-Gen. Archibald Edwards, 1834–1921, vol. II
Campbell, Sir Archibald Henry, 1870–1948, vol. IV
Campbell, Archibald Hunter, 1902–1989, vol. VIII
Campbell, Major Archibald James Hamilton Douglas, 1884–1936, vol. III
Campbell of Achalader, Brig. Archibald Pennant, 1896–1983, vol. VIII
Campbell, Rt Rev. Archibald Rollo G.; *see* Graham-Campbell.
Campbell, Sir Archibald Spencer Lindsey, 5th Bt (*cr* 1808), 1852–1941, vol. IV
Campbell, Archibald Y., 1885–1958, vol. V
Campbell, Sir Archibald Young Gipps, 1872–1957, vol. V
Campbell, Arnold Everitt, 1906–1980, vol. VII (AII)
Campbell, Lt-Col Aylmer MacIver, 1837–1915, vol. I
Campbell, Beatrice Stella; *see* Campbell, Mrs Patrick.
Campbell, Brig. Sir Bruce Atta, 1888–1954, vol. V

Campbell, Lt-Col Hon. Sir Cecil James Henry, 1891–1952, vol. V
Campbell, Vice-Adm. Sir Charles, 1847–1911, vol. I
Campbell, Charles Arthur, 1897–1974, vol. VII
Campbell, Charles Douglas, 1905–1975, vol. VII
Campbell, Sir (Charles) Duncan Macnair, 2nd Bt (*cr* 1939), 1906–1954, vol. V
Campbell, Lt-Col Charles Ferguson, *died* 1925, vol. II
Campbell, Charles Graham, 1880–1971, vol. VII
Campbell, Lt-Col Charles Lionel Kirwan, 1873–1918, vol. II
Campbell, Sir Charles Ralph, 11th Bt (*cr* 1628), 1850–1919, vol. II
Campbell, Sir Charles Ralph, 12th Bt (*cr* 1628), 1881–1948, vol. IV
Campbell, Hon. Sir Charles Rudolph, 1885–1969, vol. VI
Campbell, Charles Sandwith, 1858–1923, vol. II
Campbell, Charles Stewart, 1875–1942, vol. IV
Campbell, Charles William, 1861–1927, vol. II
Campbell, Captain Claude Henry, 1878–1916, vol. II
Campbell, Lady Colin, *died* 1911, vol. I
Campbell, Rev. Colin, 1848–1931, vol. III
Campbell, Colin, 1851–1933, vol. III
Campbell, Sir Colin, 1891–1979, vol. VII
Campbell, Colin Algernon, 1874–1957, vol. V
Campbell, Ven. Colin Arthur Fitzgerald, 1863–1916, vol. II
Campbell, Col Colin Charles, 1842–1929, vol. III
Campbell, Colin George, 1852–1911, vol. I
Campbell, Colin George Pelham, 1872–1955, vol. V
Campbell, Sir David, 1889–1978, vol. VII
Campbell, Rt Hon. Sir David Callender, 1891–1963, vol. VI
Campbell, Gen. Sir David Graham Muschet, 1869–1936, vol. III
Campbell, Col David Wilkinson, 1832–1903, vol. I
Campbell, Most Rev. Donald Alphonsus, 1894–1963, vol. VI
Campbell, Ven. Donald F., 1886–1933, vol. III
Campbell, Donald Malcolm, 1921–1967, vol. VI
Campbell, Dorothy, (Mrs Alan Campbell); *see* Parker, D.
Campbell, Maj.-Gen. Sir Douglas; *see* Campbell, Maj.-Gen. Sir A. D.
Campbell, Douglas Colin, 1891–1957, vol. V
Campbell, Douglas Graham, 1867–1918, vol. II
Campbell, Douglas Mason, 1905–1978, vol. VII
Campbell, Lt-Col Duncan, 1880–1954, vol. V
Campbell, Sir Duncan Alexander Dundas, 3rd Bt (*cr* 1831), 1856–1926, vol. II
Campbell, Major Duncan Elidor, *died* 1930, vol. III
Campbell, Captain Duncan Lorn, 1881–1923, vol. II
Campbell, Sir Duncan John Alfred, 5th Bt (*cr* 1831), 1854–1932, vol. III
Campbell, Captain Duncan Lorn, 1881–1923, vol. II
Campbell, Sir Duncan Macnair; *see* Campbell, Sir C. D. M.
Campbell, Col Edmund George, 1893–1972, vol. VII
Campbell, Rev. Edward Fitzhardinge, 1880–1957, vol. V
Campbell, Sir Edward Taswell, 1st Bt (*cr* 1939), 1879–1945, vol. IV

Campbell, Captain Sir Eric Francis Dennistoun, 6th Bt (cr 1831), 1892–1963, vol. VI

Campbell, Major Hon. Eric Octavius, 1885–1918, vol. II

Campbell, Esther Helen, (Mrs Mungo Campbell); see McCracken, E. H.

Campbell, Evan Roy, 1908-1980, vol. VII

Campbell, Ewen, 1897-1975, vol. VII

Campbell, Sir Francis Alexander, 1852–1911, vol. I

Campbell, Sir Francis Joseph, 1832–1914, vol. I

Campbell, Col Frederick, 1843–1926, vol. II

Campbell, Gen. Sir Frederick, 1860–1943, vol. IV

Campbell, Maj.-Gen. Frederick Lorn, 1850–1931, vol. III

Campbell, George Archibald, 1875–1964, vol. VI

Campbell, Engr Captain George Douglas, 1884–1972, vol. VII

Campbell, Col George Frederick Colin, 1858–1937, vol. III

Campbell, Lord George Granville, 1850–1915, vol. I

Campbell, Sir George Ilay, 6th Bt (cr 1808), 1894–1967, vol. VI

Campbell, George James, 1842–1931, vol. III

Campbell, Brig.-Gen. George Polding, 1864–1928, vol. II

Campbell, Sir George Riddoch, 1887–1965, vol. VI

Campbell, Col George Tupper Campbell C.; see Carter-Campbell.

Campbell, Vice-Adm. George William McOran, 1877–1948, vol. IV

Campbell, Sir George William Robert, 1835–1905, vol. I

Campbell, Sir Gerald, 1879–1964, vol. VI

Campbell, Gerald FitzGerald, 1862–1933, vol. III

Campbell, Gertrude Elizabeth; see Campbell, Lady Colin.

Campbell, Vice-Adm. Gordon, 1886–1953, vol. V

Campbell, Sir Gordon Huntly, 1864–1953, vol. V

Campbell, Grace Margaret; see Wilson, G.M.

Campbell, Gen. Gunning Morehead, died 1920, vol. II

Campbell, Major Sir Guy Colin, 4th Bt (cr 1815), 1885–1960, vol. V

Campbell, Lt-Col Sir Guy Theophilus, 3rd Bt (cr 1815), 1854–1931, vol. III

Campbell, H. Donald, 1879–1969, vol. VI

Campbell, Sir Harold Alfred Maurice, 1892–1959, vol. V

Campbell, Harold Ernest, 1902–1980, vol. VII

Campbell, Captain Sir Harold George, 1888–1969, vol. VI

Campbell, Harry, died 1938, vol. III

Campbell, Lt-Col Harry La Trobe, born 1881, vol. II

Campbell, Brig. Hector, 1877–1972, vol. VII

Campbell, Sir Henry, 1856–1924, vol. II

Campbell, Henry Alexander, 1851–1907, vol. I

Campbell, Rt Rev. and Rt Hon. Henry Colville M.; see Montgomery Campbell.

Campbell, Adm. Sir Henry Hervey, 1865–1933, vol. III

Campbell, Rear-Adm. Henry John Fletcher, 1837–1914, vol. I

Campbell, Henry Johnstone, 1859–1935, vol. III

Campbell, Lt-Col Hon. Henry Walter, 1835–1910, vol. I

Campbell, Ven. Herbert Ernest, died 1930, vol. III

Campbell, Brig.-Gen. Herbert M.; see Montgomery-Campbell.

Campbell, Ian George Hallyburton, 1909–1986, vol. VIII

Campbell, Ian McIntyre, 1915–1982, vol. VIII

Campbell, Col Hon. Ian Malcolm, 1883–1962, vol. VI

Campbell of Airds, Bt Col Ian Maxwell, 1870–1954, vol. V

Campbell, Vice-Adm. Sir Ian Murray Robertson, 1898–1980, vol. VII

Campbell, Sir Ian Vincent Hamilton, 7th Bt (cr 1831), 1895–1978, vol. VII

Campbell, Ignatius Roy Dunnachie, 1901–1957, vol. V

Campbell, Captain Hon. Ivan, 1859–1917, vol. II

Campbell, Sir James, 5th Bt (cr 1667), 1818–1903, vol. I

Campbell, Sir James, 1842–1925, vol. II

Campbell, James, 1895–1957, vol. V

Campbell, Rt Hon. James Alexander, 1825–1908, vol. I

Campbell, Maj.-Gen. James Alexander, 1886–1964, vol. VI

Campbell, James Argyll, 1884–1944, vol. IV

Campbell, Sir James Clark, 1882–1964, vol. VI

Campbell, Rear-Adm. James Douglas, 1882–1954, vol. V

Campbell, James Duncan, 1833–1907, vol. I

Campbell, James Grant, 1914–1989, vol. VIII

Campbell, James Hugh, 1889–1934, vol. III

Campbell, Sir (James) Keith, 1928–1983, vol. VIII

Campbell, James Lang, 1858–1936, vol. III

Campbell, Sir James Macnabb, 1846–1903, vol. I

Campbell, Very Rev. James Montgomery, 1859–1937, vol. III

Campbell, James Reid, 1930–1985, vol. VIII

Campbell, Dame Janet Mary, died 1954, vol. V

Campbell, Surg.-Maj. John, 1817–1904, vol. I

Campbell, Lt-Col John, 1872–1928, vol. II

Campbell, Sir John, 1862–1929, vol. III

Campbell, Maj.-Gen. John, 1871–1941, vol. IV

Campbell, Sir John, 1874–1944, vol. IV

Campbell, Mrs John; see Campbell, May Eudora.

Campbell, Sir John Alexander Coldstream, 7th Bt (cr 1667), 1877–1960, vol. V

Campbell, Captain Hon. John Beresford, 1866–1915, vol. I

Campbell, Lt-Col Sir John Bruce Stuart, 2nd Bt (cr 1913), 1877–1943, vol. IV

Campbell, John Dermot, 1898–1945, vol. IV

Campbell, John Edward, 1862–1924, vol. II

Campbell, Lt-Col John Edward Robert, 1855–1936, vol. III

Campbell, John Gordon Drummond, 1864–1935, vol. III

Campbell, Brig.-Gen. John Hasluck, died 1921, vol. II

Campbell, Lt-Col John Hay, 1871–1946, vol. IV

Campbell, Sir John Home-Purves Hume-, 1879–1960, vol. V

Campbell, Sir John Johnston, 1897–1983, vol. VIII

Campbell, Sir John Logan, 1817–1912, vol. I

Campbell, Rev. John McLeod, *died* 1961, vol. VI

Campbell, John Macmaster, 1859–1939, vol. III

Campbell, (John) Maurice (Hardman), 1891–1973, vol. VII

Campbell, J(ohn) Menzies, 1887–1974, vol. VII

Campbell, John Ross, 1894–1969, vol. VI

Campbell, Sir John Stratheden, 1863–1928, vol. II

Campbell, Brig.-Gen. John Vaughan, 1876–1944, vol. IV

Campbell, Maj.-Gen. Sir John William, 1st Bt (*cr* 1913) (styled 8th, of Ardnamurchan), 1836–1915, vol. I

Campbell, Rev. Joseph William Robert, 1853–1935, vol. III

Campbell, Dame Kate Isabel, 1899–1986, vol. VIII

Campbell, Sir Keith; *see* Campbell, Sir J. K.

Campbell, Kenneth, *died* 1943, vol. IV

Campbell of Strachur, Lt-Col Kenneth John, 1878–1965, vol. VI

Campbell, Lt-Col Kenneth Rankin, 1863–1931, vol. III

Campbell, Lawson; *see* Campbell, W. L.

Campbell, Brig.-Gen. Leslie Warner Yule, 1867–1946, vol. IV

Campbell, Captain Leveson Granville Byron Alexander, 1881–1951, vol. V

Campbell, Rev. Lewis, 1830–1908, vol. I

Campbell, Lloyd, *died* 1950, vol. IV

Campbell, Maj.-Gen. Lorn Robert Henry Dick, 1846–1913, vol. I

Campbell, Sir Louis Hamilton, 14th Bt (*cr* 1628), 1885–1970, vol. VI

Campbell, Sir Malcolm, 1848–1935, vol. III

Campbell, Major Sir Malcolm, 1885–1948, vol. IV

Campbell, Col Rev. Malcolm Sydenham Clarke, 1863–1949, vol. IV

Campbell, Hon. Sir Marshall, 1849–1918, vol. II

Campbell, Maurice; *see* Campbell, J. M. H.

Campbell, May Eudora, (Mrs John Campbell), *died* 1975, vol. VII

Campbell, Lt-Col Montagu Douglas, 1852–1916, vol. II

Campbell, Mungo, 1900–1983, vol. VIII

Campbell, Sir Nigel Leslie, *died* 1948, vol. IV

Campbell, Sir Norman Dugald Ferrier, 13th Bt (*cr* 1628), 1883–1968, vol. VI

Campbell, Sir Norman Montgomery Abercromby, 10th Bt (*cr* 1628), 1846–1901, vol. I

Campbell, Norman Robert, 1880–1949, vol. IV

Campbell, Lt-Col Norman St Clair, 1877–1949, vol. IV

Campbell, Mrs Patrick, 1865–1940, vol. III

Campbell, Patrick; *see* Glenavy, 3rd Baron.

Campbell, Percy Gerald Cadogan, 1878–1960, vol. V(A), vol. VI (AI)

Campbell, Peter, 1856–1951, vol. V

Campbell, Sir Ralph Abercromby, 1906–1989, vol. VIII

Campbell, Lt-Col Hon. Ralph Alexander, 1877–1945, vol. IV

Campbell, Rev. Reginald John, 1867–1956, vol. V

Campbell, (Renton) Stuart, 1908–1966, vol. VI

Campbell, Richard Hamilton, *died* 1923, vol. II

Campbell, Richard Mitchelson, 1897–1974, vol. VII

Campbell, Very Rev. Richard Stewart Dobbs, *died* 1913, vol. I

Campbell, Richard Vary, 1840–1901, vol. I

Campbell, Maj.-Gen. Robert Dallas, 1832–1916, vol. II

Campbell, Robert Garrett, 1858–1931, vol. III

Campbell, Brig. Robert Morris, 1883–1949, vol. IV

Campbell, Col Sir Robert Neil, 1854–1928, vol. II

Campbell, Robert Peel William, 1853–1929, vol. III

Campbell, Robert Richmond, 1901–1972, vol. VII

Campbell, Lt-Col Robert Wemyss, *died* 1939, vol. III

Campbell, Robin Francis, 1912–1985, vol. VIII

Campbell, Maj.-Gen. Robin Hasluck, 1894–1964, vol. VI

Campbell, Sir Rollo Frederick G.; *see* Graham-Campbell.

Campbell, Col Ronald Bruce, 1878–1963, vol. VI

Campbell, Rt Hon. Sir Ronald Hugh, 1883–1953, vol. V

Campbell, Rt Hon. Sir Ronald Ian, 1890–1983, vol. VIII

Campbell, Major Roy Neil Boyd, 1884–1950, vol. IV

Campbell, Samuel George, 1861–1926, vol. II

Campbell, Sidney George, 1875–1956, vol. V

Campbell, Sidney Scholfield, 1909–1974, vol. VII

Campbell, Lt-Col Spurgeon, 1870–1935, vol. III

Campbell, Rev Canon Stephen, *died* 1918, vol. II

Campbell, Stuart; *see* Campbell, R. S.

Campbell, Sybil, 1889–1977, vol. VII

Campbell, Hon. Thane A., 1895–1978, vol. VII

Campbell, Thomas Joseph, *died* 1946, vol. IV

Campbell, Ven. Thomas Robert Curwen, 1843–1911, vol. I

Campbell, Maj.-Gen. Victor David Graham, 1905–1990, vol. VIII

Campbell, Lt-Gen. Sir Walter, 1864–1936, vol. III

Campbell, Captain Sir Walter Douglas Somerset, 1853–1919, vol. II

Campbell, Lt-Col Sir Walter Fendall, 1894–1973, vol. VII

Campbell, Walter Stanley, 1887–1957, vol. V

Campbell, Gen. Sir William, 1847–1918, vol. II

Campbell, Rev. William, 1841–1921, vol. II

Campbell, William, 1889–1953, vol. V

Campbell, William, 1895–1976, vol. VII

Campbell, William; *see* Skerrington, Hon. Lord.

Campbell, Sir William Andrewes Ava, 5th Bt (*cr* 1831), 1880–1949, vol. IV

Campbell, Major William Charles, *died* 1958, vol. V

Campbell, William Gordon, 1891–1974, vol. VII

Campbell, Maj.-Gen. William Henry McNeile V.; *see* Verschoyle-Campbell.

Campbell, Col William Kentigern Hamilton, 1865–1917, vol. II

Campbell, Major William Lachlan, *died* 1937, vol. III

Campbell, (William) Lawson, 1890–1970, vol. VI

Campbell, Brig.-Gen. William MacLaren, 1864–1924, vol. II

Campbell, William Middleton, 1849–1919, vol. II

Campbell, Brig.-Gen. William Nevile, 1863–1933, vol. III

Campbell, Lt-Gen. Sir William Pitcairn, 1856–1933, vol. III

Campbell, Major William Robinson, 1879–1915, vol. I

Campbell-Bannerman, Rt Hon. Sir Henry, 1836–1908, vol. I

Campbell-Colquhoun, William Erskine, 1866–1922, vol. II

Campbell Golding, Frederick; see Golding.

Campbell-Johnston, Malcolm, 1871–1931, vol. III

Campbell-Orde, Sir John William Powlett; see Orde.

Campbell-Orde, Major Sir Simon Arthur; see Orde.

Campbell-Preston, Hon. Mrs Angela, 1910–1981, vol. VIII

Campbell-Purdie, Cora Gwendolyn Jean, (Wendy), 1925–1985, vol. VIII

Campbell-Purdie, Wendy; see Campbell-Purdie, C. G. J.

Campbell-Smith, Walter; see Smith.

Campbell Swinton, Brig. Alan Henry; see Swinton.

Campbell-Walter, Rear-Adm. Keith McNeil, 1904–1976, vol. VII

Camperdown, 3rd Earl of, 1841–1918, vol. II

Camperdown, 4th Earl of, 1845–1933, vol. III

Campinchi, César, 1882–1941, vol. IV

Campion, 1st Baron, 1882–1958, vol. V

Campion, Bernard, died 1952, vol. V

Campion, Cecil; see Campion, J. C.

Campion, Col Douglas John Montriou, 1883–1963, vol. VI

Campion, George, 1846–1926, vol. II

Campion, George Goring, 1862–1946, vol. IV

Campion, Rev. Canon Herbert Roper, 1868–1941, vol. IV

Campion, Rear-Adm. Hubert, 1825–1900, vol. I

Campion, (John) Cecil, 1907–1971, vol. VII

Campion, Sidney Ronald, 1891–1978, vol. VII

Campion, Col William Henry, 1836–1923, vol. II

Campion, William Magan, died 1898, vol. I

Campion, Col Sir William Robert, 1870–1951, vol. V

Campling, Rev. Canon William Charles, 1888–1973, vol. VII

Campney, Hon. Ralph Osborne, 1894–1967, vol. VI

Camps, Francis Edward, 1905–1972, vol. VII

Camrose, 1st Viscount, 1879–1954, vol. V

Camsell, Charles, 1876–1958, vol. V

Camus, Albert, 1913–1960, vol. V

Cana, Frank Richardson, 1865–1935, vol. III

Canaway, Arthur Pitcairn, 1857–1949, vol. IV

Canby, Henry Seidel, 1878–1961, vol. VI

Cancellor, Henry Lannoy, 1862–1929, vol. III

Candau, Marcolino Gomes, 1911–1983, vol. VIII

Candler, Edmund, 1874–1926, vol. II

Candlish, Joseph John, 1855–1913, vol. I

Candy, Rear-Adm. Algernon Henry Chester, 1877–1959, vol. V

Candy, Air Vice-Marshal Charles Douglas, 1912–1985, vol. VIII

Candy, Sir Edward Townshend, 1854–1913, vol. I

Candy, George, 1841–1899, vol. I

Candy, Major Henry Augustus, 1842–1911, vol. I

Candy, Hugh Charles Herbert, died 1935, vol. III

Candy, Maj.-Gen. Ronald Herbert, died 1972, vol. VII

Cane, Arthur Beresford, 1864–1939, vol. III

Cane, Sir Cyril Hubert, 1891–1959, vol. V

Cane, Lucy Mary, (Mrs Arthur Beresford Cane), died 1926, vol. II

Cane, Robert Alexander Gordon, 1893–1975, vol. VII

Canfield, Cass, 1897–1986, vol. VIII

Canfield, Dorothy, (Dorothea Frances Canfield Fisher), 1879–1958, vol. V

Canfield, James Hulme, 1847–1909, vol. I

Canham, Brian John, 1930–1990, vol. VIII

Canham, Erwin Dain, 1904–1982, vol. VIII

Canham, Ven. Thomas Henry, died 1947, vol. IV

Cann, Hon. John Henry, 1860–1940, vol. III

Cann, Percy Walter, 1884–1973, vol. VII

Cann, Robert John, 1901–1983, vol. VIII

Cann, Sir William Moore, 1856–1947, vol. IV

Cannan, Charles, 1858–1919, vol. II

Cannan, Edwin, 1861–1935, vol. III

Cannan, Gilbert, 1884–1955, vol. V

Cannan, Maj.-Gen. James Harold, 1882–1976, vol. VII

Cannan, Joanna, (Mrs H. J. Pullein-Thompson), 1898–1961, vol. VI

Cannell, John, vol. III

Canney, Maurice Arthur, 1872–1942, vol. IV

Canning, Col Albert, 1861–1960, vol. V

Canning, Hon. Albert Stratford George, 1832–1916, vol. II

Canning, Rev. Clifford Brooke, 1882–1957, vol. V

Canning, Hon. Conway Stratford George, 1854–1926, vol. II

Canning, Sir Ernest R., 1876–1966, vol. VI

Canning, Frederick, 1882–1968, vol. VI

Canning, Hugh, died 1927, vol. II

Canning, Sir Samuel, 1823–1908, vol. I

Canning, Victor, 1911–1986, vol. VIII

Cannon, Annie Jump, 1863–1941, vol. IV

Cannon, George Harry Franklyn, 1885–1966, vol. VI

Cannon, Henry White, 1850–1934, vol. III

Cannon, Herbert Graham, 1897–1963, vol. VI

Cannon, James, 1864–1944, vol. IV

Cannon, Hon. Lawrence Arthur Dumoulin, 1877–1939, vol. III

Cannon, Lawrence John, 1852–1921, vol. II

Cannon, Sir Leslie, 1920–1970, vol. VI

Cannon, Air Vice-Marshal Leslie William, 1904–1986, vol. VIII

Cannon, Hon. Lucien, 1887–1950, vol. IV

Cannon, Walter Bradford, 1871–1945, vol. IV

Cannot, Brig.-Gen. Fernand Gustave Eugene, 1873–1941, vol. IV

Canny, Sir Gerald Bain, 1881–1954, vol. V

Canny, Col James Clare Macnamara, 1877–1942, vol. IV

Cant, Rev. Canon Reginald Edward, 1914–1987, vol. VIII

Cantan, Major Henry Thomas, 1868–1916, vol. II

Cantelli, Guido, 1920–1956, vol. V

Canter, Bernard Hall, 1906–1969, vol. VI

Canterbury, 4th Viscount, 1839–1914, vol. I

Canterbury, 5th Viscount, 1879–1918, vol. II

Canterbury, 6th Viscount, 1872–1941, vol. IV

Cantlie, Adm. Sir Colin, 1888–1967, vol. VI

Cantlie, Sir James, 1851–1926, vol. II

Cantlie, Sir Keith, 1886–1977, vol. VII

Cantlie, Lt-Gen. Sir Neil, 1892–1975, vol. VII
Canton, William, 1845–1926, vol. II
Cantor, Eddie, 1892–1964, vol. VI
Cantrell, Robert, 1849–1936, vol. III
Cantwell, Most Rev. John Joseph, 1874–1947, vol. IV
Canuck, Janey; *see* Murphy, Emily F.
Canziani, Estella Louisa Michaela, 1887–1964, vol. VI
Capablanca, José R., 1888–1942, vol. IV
Cape, Captain Charles Scarvell, *born* 1866, vol. III
Cape, Col Edmund Graves Meredith, 1878–1962, vol. VI
Cape, (Herbert) Jonathan, 1879–1960, vol. V
Cape, Jonathan; *see* Cape, H. J.
Cape, Thomas, 1868–1947, vol. IV
Capek, Karel, 1890–1938, vol. III
Capel, Air Vice-Marshal Arthur John, 1894–1979, vol. VII
Capel, Hon. Reginald Algernon, 1830–1906, vol. I
Capel, Mgr Thomas John, 1836–1911, vol. I
Capel Cure, Col Herbert; *see* Cure.
Capell, Col Algernon Essex, 1869–1952, vol. V
Capell, Richard, 1885–1954, vol. V
Capellini, Giovanni, *born* 1833, vol. II
Capener, Norman Leslie, 1898–1975, vol. VII
Capes, Bernard, *died* 1918, vol. II
Capes, Rev. William Wolfe, 1834–1914, vol. I
Capewell, Arthur, 1902–1957, vol. V
Capey, Reco, 1895–1961, vol. VI
Capon, Norman Brandon, 1892–1975, vol. VII
Capon, Maj.-Gen. Philip John Lauriston, 1902–1964, vol. VI
Caporn, Arthur Cecil, 1884–1953, vol. V
Capote, Truman, 1924–1984, vol. VIII
Cappel, Sir Albert James Leppoc, 1836–1924, vol. II
Cappel, Edward Louis, 1856–1936, vol. III
Cappel, Daniel Fowler, 1900–1976, vol. VII
Capper, Alfred Octavius, *died* 1921, vol. II
Capper, Major Charles Francis, 1902–1964, vol. VI
Capper, David Sing, *died* 1926, vol. II
Capper, Sir Derrick; *see* Capper, Sir W. D.
Capper, John Brainerd, 1855–1936, vol. III
Capper, Maj.-Gen. Sir John Edward, 1861–1955, vol. V
Capper, Stewart Henbest, 1859–1925, vol. II
Capper, Maj.-Gen. Sir Thompson, 1863–1915, vol. I
Capper, Col William, 1856–1934, vol. III
Capper, Sir (William) Derrick, 1912–1977, vol. VII
Cappon, James, 1854–1939, vol. III
Capps, Frederick Cecil Wray, 1898–1970, vol. VI
Capron, Athol John, 1859–1937, vol. III
Capron, Frederick Hugh, 1857–1955, vol. V
Caproni, Gianni, 1886–1957, vol. V
Capus, Alfred; *see* Capus, V. M. A.
Capus, (Vincent Marie) Alfred, 1858–1922, vol. II
Caradon, Baron (Life Peer); Hugh Mackintosh Foot, 1907–1990, vol. VIII
Carados; *see* Edwards, G. Spencer
Carbery, 9th Baron, 1868–1898, vol. I
Carbery, 10th Baron, 1892–1970, vol. VI (AII)
Carbery, Col Andrew Robert Dillon, 1868–1948, vol. IV
Carberry, Sir John Edward Doston, 1893–1977, vol. VII (AII)

Carbone, Sir Guiseppe, 1839–1913, vol. I
Carbonell, Rev. Canon Francis Rohde, 1849–1919, vol. II
Carbutt, Lt-Col Clive Lancaster, 1876–1948, vol. IV
Carcano, Miguel Angel, 1889–1978, vol. VII
Card, Wilfrid Ingram, 1908–1985, vol. VIII
Cardale, Vice-Adm. Charles Searle, 1841–1904, vol. I
Cardell, John, 1857–1937, vol. III (A)
Cardell, J(ohn) D(ouglas) Magor, 1896–1966, vol. VI
Cardell-Oliver, Hon. Dame (Annie) Florence (Gillies), 1876–1965, vol. VI
Cardell-Oliver, Hon. Dame Florence; *see* Cardell-Oliver, Hon. Dame A. F. G.
Carden, Major D'Arcy Vandeleur, 1892–1936, vol. III
Carden, Major Sir Frederick Henry Walter, 3rd Bt (*cr* 1887), 1873–1966, vol. VI
Carden, Sir Frederick Walter, 2nd Bt (*cr* 1887), 1833–1909, vol. I
Carden, Major Henry Charles, 1855–1915, vol. I
Carden, Sir Herbert, *died* 1941, vol. IV
Carden, Col John, 1870–1915, vol. I
Carden, Rev. John, 1882–1934, vol. III
Carden, Sir John Craven, 5th Bt (*cr* 1787), 1854–1931, vol. III
Carden, Captain Sir John Valentine, 6th Bt (*cr* 1787), 1892–1935, vol. III
Carden, Sir Lionel Edward Gresley, 1851–1915, vol. I
Carden, Col Louis Peile, 1860–1942, vol. IV
Carden, Adm. Sir Sackville Hamilton, 1857–1930, vol. III
Carden Roe, Brig. William, 1894–1977, vol. VII
Cardew, Sir Alexander Gordon, 1861–1937, vol. III
Cardew, Claud Ambrose, 1870–1959, vol. V
Cardew, Evelyn Roberta, (Lady Cardew), *died* 1953, vol. V
Cardew, Col Sir Frederic, 1839–1921, vol. II
Cardew, Rev. Prebendary Frederic Anstruther, 1866–1942, vol. IV
Cardew, Lt-Col George Ambrose, *died* 1941, vol. IV
Cardew, Col George Hereward, 1861–1949, vol. IV
Cardew, Michael Ambrose, 1901–1983, vol. VIII
Cardiff, Brig. Ereld Boteler Wingfield, 1909–1988, vol. VIII
Cardigan and Lancastre, Countess of; (Adeline Louise Maria), 1825–1915, vol. I
Cardin, James Joseph, 1839–1917, vol. II
Cardinale, Most Rev. Hyginus Eugene, 1916–1983, vol. VIII
Cardinall, Sir Allan Wolsey, 1887–1956, vol. V
Cardon, Philip Vincent, 1889–1965, vol. VI
Cardot, Rt Rev. Alexander, 1857–1925, vol. II
Cardozo, Benjamin N., 1870–1938, vol. III
Cardozo, Henry O'Connell, 1839–1905, vol. I
Carducci, Giosue, 1835–1907, vol. I
Cardus, Sir Neville, 1889–1975, vol. VII
Cardwell, Sir David, 1920–1982, vol. VIII
Cardwell, George, 1882–1962, vol. VI
Cardwell, Rev. John Henry, 1842–1921, vol. II
Care, Henry Clifford, 1892–1979, vol. VII
Carew, 3rd Baron, 1860–1923, vol. II
Carew, 4th Baron, 1863–1926, vol. II
Carew, 5th Baron, 1860–1927, vol. II

Carew, Charles Robert Sydenham, 1853–1939, vol. III

Carew, Major George Albert Lade, 1862–1937, vol. III

Carew, Sir Henry Palk, 9th Bt, 1870–1934, vol. III

Carew, Mrs James; *see* Terry, Dame Ellen.

Carew, James Laurence, *died* 1903, vol. I

Carew, Lt-Gen. Sir Reginald Pole, 1849–1924, vol. II

Carew, Major Robert John Henry, 1888–1982, vol. VIII

Carew, Sir Thomas Palk, 10th Bt, 1890–1976, vol. VII

Carew, William Desmond, 1899–1981, vol. VIII

Carew, William James, 1890–1990, vol. VIII

Carew-Gibson, Harry Frederick, 1869–1953, vol. V

Carew Hunt, Rear-Adm. Geoffrey Harry, 1917–1979, vol. VII

Carew Hunt, Captain Roland Cecil, 1880–1959, vol. V

Carew-Hunt, Lt-Col Thomas Edward, 1874–1950, vol. IV

Carey, Rev. Albert Darell T.; *see* Tupper-Carey.

Carey, Brig.-Gen. Arthur Basil, 1872–1961, vol. VI

Carey, Sir Bernard Sausmarez, 1864–1919, vol. II

Carey, Maj.-Gen. Carteret Walter, 1853–1932, vol. III

Carey, Cecil William Victor, 1887–1976, vol. VII

Carey, Chapple G.; *see* Gill-Carey.

Carey, Charles William, 1862–1943, vol. IV

Carey, Clive; *see* Carey, F. C. S.

Carey, Maj.-Gen. Constantine Phipps, 1835–1906, vol. I

Carey, Denis, 1909–1986, vol. VIII

Carey, (Francis) Clive (Savill), 1883–1968, vol. VI

Carey, Frank Stanton, 1860–1928, vol. II

Carey, Maj.-Gen. George Glas Sandeman, 1867–1948, vol. IV

Carey, Gordon Vero, 1886–1969, vol. VI

Carey, Brig.-Gen. Harold Eustace, 1874–1944, vol. IV

Carey, Col Herbert Clement, 1865–1948, vol. IV

Carey, Herbert Simon, 1856–1947, vol. IV

Carey, Rt Rev. Kenneth Moir, 1908–1979, vol. VII

Carey, Maj.-Gen. Laurence Francis de Vic, 1904–1972, vol. VII

Carey, Lionel Mohun, 1911–1988, vol. VIII

Carey, Very Rev. Michael Sausmarez, 1913–1985, vol. VIII

Carey, Brig.-Gen. Octavius William, 1865–1938, vol. III

Carey, Rosa Nouchette, 1840–1909, vol. I

Carey, Sir Thomas Godfrey, 1832–1906, vol. I

Carey, Sir Victor Gosselin, 1871–1957, vol. V

Carey, Captain Walter, *died* 1932, vol. III

Carey, Rt Rev. Walter Julius, 1875–1955, vol. V

Carey, Brig. Walter Louis John, 1872–1953, vol. V

Carey, Lt-Col Wilfrid Leathes de Mussenden, 1881–1937, vol. III

Carey, Col William, 1833-1905, vol. I

Carey, Sir Willoughby Langer, 1875–1933, vol. III

Carey Evans, Lady Olwen Elizabeth, 1892–1990, vol. VIII

Carey Taylor, Alan; *see* Taylor.

Cargill, Featherston, 1870–1959, vol. V

Cargill, Air Comdt Dame Helen Wilson, 1896–1969, vol. VI

Cargill, Sir (Ian) Peter (Macgillivray), 1915–1981, vol. VIII

Cargill, Sir John Traill, 1st Bt, 1867–1954, vol. V

Cargill, Lionel Vernon, *died* 1955, vol. V

Cargill, Sir Peter; *see* Cargill, Sir I. P. M.

Cargill Thompson, William David James, 1930–1978, vol. VII

Carill-Worsley, Philip Ernest T.; *see* Tindal-Carill-Worsley.

Carington, Herbert Hanbury Smith-, 1851–1917, vol. II

Carington, Neville Woodford S.; *see* Smith-Carington.

Carington, Lt-Col Rt Hon. Sir William Henry Peregrine, 1845–1914, vol. I

Carisbrooke, 1st Marquess of, 1886–1960, vol. V

Carkeek, Sir Arthur, 1861–1933, vol. III

Carlaw, John, *died* 1934, vol. III

Carlebach, Col Sir Philip, 1873–1949, vol. IV

Carles, William Richard, 1848–1929, vol. III

Carless, Albert, *died* 1936, vol. III

Carleston, Hadden Hamilton, 1904–1986, vol. VIII

Carleton, Hon. Brig.-Gen. Frank Robert Crofton, 1856–1924, vol. II

Carleton, Brig.-Gen. Frederick Montgomerie, 1867–1922, vol. II

Carleton, Ven. George Dundas, 1877–1961, vol. VI

Carleton, Major Guy Audouin, 1859–1941, vol. IV

Carleton, Gen. Henry Alexander, 1814–1900, vol. I

Carleton, Rev. James George, 1848–1918, vol. II

Carleton, John Dudley, 1908–1974, vol. VII

Carleton, Brig.-Gen. Lancelot Richard, 1861–1937, vol. III

Carleton, Brig.-Gen. Mongtomery Launcelot, 1861–1942, vol. IV

Carleton, Maj.-Gen. Richard Langford L.; *see* Leir-Carleton.

Carlier, Edmond William Wace, 1861–1940, vol. III

Carlile, Sir Edward, 1845–1917, vol. II

Carlile, Sir (Edward) Hildred, 1st Bt (*cr* 1917), 1852–1942, vol. IV

Carlile, Sir Hildred; *see* Carlile, Sir E. H.

Carlile, Rev. John Charles, *died* 1941, vol. IV

Carlile, Sir Walter; *see* Carlile, Sir W. W.

Carlile, Sir (William) Walter, 1st Bt (*cr* 1928), 1862–1950, vol. IV

Carlile, Rev. Wilson, 1847–1942, vol. IV

Carlill, Harold Flamank, 1875–1959, vol. V

Carlill, Hildred, *died* 1942, vol. IV

Carlin, Gaston, *died* 1922, vol. II

Carline, George, 1855–1920, vol. II

Carline, Sydney W., 1888–1929, vol. III

Carling, Sir Ernest Rock, 1877–1960, vol. V

Carling, Rt Hon. Sir John, 1828–1911, vol. I

Carlingford, 1st Baron, 1823–1898, vol. I

Carlisle, 9th Earl of, 1843–1911, vol. I

Carlisle, 10th Earl of, 1867–1912, vol. I

Carlisle, 11th Earl of, 1895–1963, vol. VI

Carlisle, Rt Hon. Alexander Montgomery, 1854–1926, vol. II

Carlisle, Rt Rev. Arthur, 1881–1943, vol. IV

Carlisle, Lt-Col Denton; *see* Carlisle, Lt-Col J. C. D.

Carlisle, Engr Rear-Adm. Frank Scott, 1882–1941, vol IV

Carlisle, Lt-Col (John Charles) Denton, 1888–1972, vol. VII

Carlisle, Kenneth Ralph Malcolm, 1908–1983, vol. VIII

Carlisle, R. H., 1865–1941, vol. IV

Carlos, Don; Duke of Madrid, 1848–1909, vol. I

Carlow, Viscount; George Lionel Seymour, 1907–1944, vol. IV

Carlow, Charles Augustus, died 1954, vol. V

Carlton, Sir Arthur, died 1931, vol. III

Carlton, C. Hope, 1889–1951, vol. V

Carlyle, Rev. Alexander James, 1861–1943, vol. IV

Carlyle, Edward Irving, 1871–1952, vol. V

Carlyle, Sir Robert Warrand, 1859–1934, vol. III

Carlyon, Sir Alexander Keith, 1848–1936, vol. III

Carlyon, Thomas Symington, 1902–1982, vol. VIII

Carlyon-Britton, Major Philip William Poole, 1863–1938, vol. III

Carman, Bliss, 1861–1929, vol. III

Carmichael, 1st Baron, 1859–1926, vol. II

Carmichael, Alexander, died 1912, vol. I

Carmichael, Captain Hon. Ambrose Campbell, 1872–1953, vol. V

Carmichael, Claude Dundas James, 1862–1915, vol. I

Carmichael, Sir Duncan, 1866–1923, vol. II

Carmichael, Sir Eardley Charles William G. C.; see Gibson-Craig-Carmichael.

Carmichael, Edward Arnold, 1896–1978, vol. VII

Carmichael, Rev. Frederic Falkiner, 1831–1919, vol. II

Carmichael, Sir George, 1866–1936, vol. III

Carmichael, George Chapman, 1924–1970, vol. VI

Carmichael, Captain Sir Henry Thomas G. C.; see Gibson-Craig-Carmichael.

Carmichael, James, 1846–1927, vol. II

Carmichael, Sir James, 1858–1934, vol. III

Carmichael, James, 1894–1966, vol. VI

Carmichael, James, died 1972, vol. VII

Carmichael, James Armstrong Gordon, 1913–1990, vol. VIII

Carmichael, Lt-Col Sir James Forrest Halkett, 1868–1934, vol. III

Carmichael, Sir James Morse, 3rd Bt, 1844–1902, vol. I

Carmichael, John Murray G.; see Gibson-Carmichael.

Carmichael, Leonard, 1898–1973, vol. VII

Carmichael, Mary, died 1935, vol. III

Carmichael, Mary Gertrude, (Lady Carmichael), died 1941, vol. IV

Carmichael, Montgomery, 1857–1936, vol. III

Carmichael, Norman Scott, 1883–1951, vol. V

Carmichael, Sir William G. C.; see Gibson-Craig-Carmichael, Sir A. H. W.

Carmichael Anstruther, Sir Windham Charles James; see Anstruther.

Carmichael-Anstruther, Sir Windham Eric Francis; see Anstruther.

Carmichael-Anstruther, Sir Windham Frederick; see Anstruther.

Carmichael-Anstruther, Sir Windham Robert; see Anstruther.

Carmichael-Ferrall, John, 1855–1923, vol. II

Carmody, Sir Alan Thomas, 1920–1978, vol. VII (AII)

Carmody, Very Rev. William P., died 1938, vol. III

Carmont, Hon. Lord; John Francis Carmont, 1880–1965, vol. VI

Carmont, John Francis; see Carmont, Hon. Lord.

Carnac, Charles James R.; see Rivett-Carnac.

Carnac, Sir Claud James R.; see Rivett-Carnac.

Carnac, Rev. Sir George R.; see Rivett-Carnac.

Carnac, Sir Henry George Crabbe R.; see Rivett-Carnac.

Carnac, Vice-Adm. James William R.; see Rivett-Carnac.

Carnac, Col John Henry R.; see Rivett-Carnac.

Carnac, Col Percy Temple R.; see Rivett-Carnac.

Carnac, Sir William Percival R.; see Rivett-Carnac.

Carnarvon, 5th Earl of, 1866–1923, vol. II

Carnarvon, 6th Earl of, 1898–1987, vol. VIII

Carncross, Hon. Sir Walter Charles Frederick, 1855–1940, vol. III

Carnduff, Sir Herbert William Cameron, 1862–1915, vol. I

Carne, Col James Power, 1906–1986, vol. VIII

Carnegie, Andrew, 1835–1919, vol. II

Carnegie, Hon. Charles, 1883–1906, vol. I

Carnegie, Col David, 1868–1949, vol. IV

Carnegie, Air Vice-Marshal David Vaughan, 1897–1964, vol. VI

Carnegie, Hon. David Wynford, 1871–1900, vol. I

Carnegie, Lt-Col Hon. Douglas George, 1870–1937, vol. III

Carnegie, Sir Francis, 1874–1946, vol. IV

Carnegie, Lady Helena Mariota, 1865–1943, vol. IV

Carnegie, Rt Hon. Sir Lancelot Douglas, 1861–1933, vol. III

Carnegie, Louise, (Mrs Andrew Carnegie), 1857–1946, vol. IV

Carnegie, Rev. William Hartley, 1860–1936, vol. III

Carnegy, Gen. Alexander, 1829–1900, vol. I

Carnegy, Col Charles Gilbert, 1864–1928, vol. II

Carnegy of Lour, Lt-Col Elliott; see Carnegy of Lour, Lt-Col U. E. C.

Carnegy, Rev. Canon Patrick Charles Alexander, 1893–1969, vol. VI

Carnegy, Maj.-Gen. Sir Philip Mainwaring, 1858–1927, vol. II

Carnegy of Lour, Lt-Col (Ughtred) Elliott (Carnegy), 1886–1973, vol. VII

Carner, Mosco, 1904–1985, vol. VIII

Carney, Most Rev. James F., 1915–1990, vol. VIII

Carney, Adm. Robert Bostwick, 1895–1990, vol. VIII

Carnochan, John Golder, 1910–1981, vol. VIII

Carnock, 1st Baron, 1849–1928, vol. II

Carnock, 2nd Baron, 1883–1952, vol. V

Carnock, 3rd Baron, 1884–1982, vol. VIII

Carnwath, 12th Earl of, 1847–1910, vol. I

Carnwath, 15th (de facto 13th) Earl of, 1883–1931, vol. III

Carnwath, 16th (de facto 14th) Earl of, 1851–1941, vol. IV

Carnwath, Thomas, 1878–1954, vol. V

Caröe, Sir Athelstan; see Caröe, Sir E. A. G.

Caröe, Sir (Einar) Athelstan (Gordon), 1903–1988, vol. VIII

Caroe, Sir Olaf Kirkpatrick, 1892–1981, vol. VIII

Caroe, William Douglas, 1857–1938, vol. III

Carolus-Duran, Emile Auguste, 1838–1917, vol. II

Caron, Hon. Joseph Edouard, 1866–1930, vol. III

Caron, Hon. Sir Joseph Philippe Rene Adolphe, 1842–1908, vol. I

Carozzi, Joseph L., 1866–1933, vol. III

Carpendale, Vice-Adm. Sir Charles Douglas, 1874–1968, vol. VI

Carpendale, Major Frederic Maxwell-, 1887–1958, vol. V

Carpenter, Captain Alfred, 1847–1925, vol. II

Carpenter, Vice-Adm. Alfred Francis Blakeney, 1881–1955, vol. V

Carpenter, Major Sir Archibald Boyd B.; *see* Boyd Carpenter.

Carpenter, Charles Claude, 1858–1938, vol. III

Carpenter, Brig.-Gen. Charles Murray, 1870–1942, vol. IV

Carpenter, David, 1866–1935, vol. III

Carpenter, Edward, 1844–1929, vol. III

Carpenter, Sir Eric Ashton, 1896–1973, vol. VII

Carpenter, Geoffrey Douglas Hale, 1882–1953, vol. V

Carpenter, George, 1859–1910, vol. I

Carpenter, Lt-Gen. George, 1877–1952, vol. V

Carpenter, Rev. George Herbert, 1865–1939, vol. III

Carpenter, George Lyndon, 1872–1948, vol. IV

Carpenter, Sir H. C. Harold, 1875–1940, vol. III

Carpenter, Ven. Harry William, 1854–1936, vol. III

Carpenter, Henry John B.; *see* Boyd-Carpenter.

Carpenter, Ven. Horace John, 1887–1965, vol. VI

Carpenter, Rev. J. Estlin, 1844–1927, vol. II

Carpenter, Rev. James Nelson, *died* 1949, vol. IV (A), vol. V

Carpenter, John MacGregor Kendall K.; *see* Kendall-Carpenter.

Carpenter, Maj.-Gen. John Owen, 1894–1967, vol. VI

Carpenter, Captain John Peers B.; *see* Boyd-Carpenter.

Carpenter, Percy Frederick, 1901–1964, vol. VI

Carpenter, Percy Henry, 1879–1962, vol. VI

Carpenter, Rhys, 1889–1980, vol. VII

Carpenter, Rev. Spencer Cecil, 1877–1959, vol. V

Carpenter, Trevor Charles, 1917–1986, vol. VIII

Carpenter, Adm. Hon. Walter Cecil, 1834–1904, vol. I

Carpenter, Sir Walter Randolph, 1877–1954, vol. V

Carpenter, Rt Rev. William B.; *see* Boyd Carpenter.

Carpenter-Garnier, John, 1839–1926, vol. II

Carpenter-Garnier, Rt Rev. Mark Rodolph, 1881–1969, vol. VI

Carpentier, Général d'Armée Marcel Maurice, 1895–1977, vol. VII

Carpmael, Kenneth S., 1885–1975, vol. VII

Carpmael, Raymond, 1875–1950, vol. IV

Carr, Alwyn C. E., *died* 1940, vol. III

Carr, Sir Arthur Strettell C.; *see* Comyns Carr.

Carr, Sir Bernard; *see* Carr, Sir F. B.

Carr, Sir Cecil Thomas, 1878–1966, vol. VI

Carr, Rt Rev. Charles Lisle, 1871–1942, vol. IV

Carr, Air Marshal Sir (Charles) Roderick, 1891–1971, vol. VII

Carr, Charles Telford, 1905–1976, vol. VII

Carr, Brig.-Gen. Christopher D'Arcy Bloomfield Saltern B.; *see* Baker-Carr.

Carr, Cyril Eric, 1926–1981, vol. VIII

Carr, David, 1847–1920, vol. II

Carr, Denis Edward Bernard, 1920–1981, vol. VIII

Carr, Rev. Edmund, 1826–1916, vol. II

Carr, Edward Arthur, 1903–1966, vol. VI

Carr, Col Edward Elliott, 1854–1926, vol. II

Carr, Edward Hallett, 1892–1982, vol. VIII

Carr, Sir Emsley, 1867–1941, vol. IV

Carr, Francis Howard, 1874–1969, vol. VI

Carr, Frank Arnold, 1873–1942, vol. IV

Carr, Sir (Frederick) Bernard, 1893–1981, vol. VIII

Carr, Rev. Frederick Robert, 1869–1952, vol. V

Carr, George Shadwell Quartano, 1866–1905, vol. I

Carr, Gilbert Harry, 1884–1954, vol. V

Carr, Harry Lascelles, 1907–1943, vol. IV

Carr, Lt-Col Henry Arbuthnot, 1872–1951, vol. V

Carr, Adm. Henry John, 1839–1914, vol. I

Carr, Henry Lambton, 1899–1988, vol. VIII

Carr, Henry Lascelles, 1841–1902, vol. I

Carr, Henry Marvell, 1894–1970, vol. VI

Carr, Herbert Reginald Culling, 1896–1986, vol. VIII

Carr, Herbert Wildon, 1857–1931, vol. III

Carr, Maj.-Gen. Howard, 1863–1944, vol. IV

Carr, Howard, 1880–1960, vol. V

Carr, Sir Hubert Winch, 1877–1955, vol. V

Carr, J. W. Comyns, 1849–1916, vol. II

Carr, Rev. James Haslewood, 1831–1915, vol. I

Carr, Sir James Henry Brownlow, 1913–1984, vol. VIII

Carr, Hon. John, 1819–1913, vol. I

Carr, John Dickson, *died* 1977, vol. VII

Carr, John Walter, 1862–1942, vol. IV

Carr, John Wesley, 1862–1939, vol. III

Carr, Lt-Gen. Laurence, 1886–1954, vol. V

Carr, Michael, 1947–1990, vol. VIII

Carr, Norman Alexander, 1899–1970, vol. VI

Carr, Rev. Owen Charles, *died* 1929, vol. III

Carr, Major Robert George Teesdale B.; *see* Baker-Carr.

Carr, Air Marshal Sir Roderick; *see* Carr, Air Marshal Sir C. R.

Carr, Rupert Ellis, 1910–1974, vol. VII

Carr, Theodore; *see* Carr, W. T.

Carr, Most Rev. Thomas Joseph, 1839–1917, vol. II

Carr, Rev. Walter Raleigh, 1843–1907, vol. I

Carr, Sir William, 1872–1949, vol. IV

Carr, Sir William Emsley, 1912–1977, vol. VII

Carr, Brig. William Greenwood, 1901–1982, vol. VIII

Carr, Rev. William Henry, 1857–1932, vol. III

Carr, Surg. Rear-Adm. William James, 1883–1966, vol. VI

Carr, Col William Moncrieff, 1886–1956, vol. V

Carr, Sir William St John, 1848–1928, vol. II

Carr, (William) Theodore, 1866–1931, vol. III

Carr-Calthrop, Col Christopher William, 1844–1934, vol. III

Carr-Gomm, Francis Culling, 1834–1919, vol. II

Carr-Gomm, Hubert William Culling, 1877–1939, vol. III

Carr-Hall, Col Ralph Ellis; *see* Hall.

Carr-Saunders, Sir Alexander Morris, 1886–1966, vol. VI

Carr-White, Maj.-Gen. Percy, 1856–1934, vol. III

Carrara, Arthur Charles, *died* 1949, vol. IV

Carre, Major Ralph G. Riddell, 1868–1941, vol. IV

Carrel, Alexis, 1873–1944, vol. IV

Carreras, Sir James, 1909–1990, vol. VIII

Carrick, 5th Earl of, 1835–1901, vol. I

Carrick, 6th Earl of, 1851–1909, vol. I

Carrick, 7th Earl of, 1873–1931, vol. III

Carrick, 8th Earl of, 1903–1957, vol. V

Carrick, Alexander, *died* 1966, vol. VI

Carrick-Buchanan, Sir David Carrick Robert, 1825–1904, vol. I

Carrick-Buchanan, David William Ramsay, 1834–1925, vol. II

Carrier, Philippe Leslie Caro, 1893–1975, vol. VII

Carrigan, William, *died* 1951, vol. V

Carrington, 4th Baron, 1852–1929, vol. III

Carrington, 5th Baron, 1891–1938, vol. III

Carrington, Charles Edmund, 1897–1990, vol. VIII

Carrington, Brig. Charles Ronald Brownlow, 1880–1948, vol. IV

Carrington, Very Rev. Charles Walter, 1859–1941, vol. IV

Carrington, Maj.-Gen. Sir Frederick, 1844–1913, vol. I

Carrington, Lt-Gen. Sir Harold; *see* Carrington, Lt-Gen. Sir R. H.

Carrington, Very Rev. Henry, 1814–1906, vol. I

Carrington, Vice-Adm. John Walsh, 1879–1964, vol. VI

Carrington, Sir John Worrell, 1847–1913, vol. I

Carrington, Most Rev. Philip, 1892–1975, vol. VII

Carrington, Richard, 1921–1971, vol. VII

Carrington, Lt-Gen. Sir (Robert) Harold, 1882–1964, vol. VI

Carrington, Roger Clifford, 1905–1971, vol. VII

Carrington, Sir William Speight, 1904–1975, vol. VII

Carritt, David; *see* Carritt, H. D. G.

Carritt, Edgar Frederick, 1876–1964, vol. VI

Carritt, (Hugh) David (Graham), 1927–1982, vol. VIII

Carroll, Sir Alfred Thomas, (Sir Turi Carroll), 1890–1975, vol. VII

Carroll, Rt Rev. Francis P., 1890–1967, vol. VI

Carroll, Francis Patrick, 1887–1955, vol. V

Carroll, Col Frederick Fitzgerald, *died* 1932, vol. III

Carroll, Hon. Henry George, 1865–1939, vol. III

Carroll, Sir James, *died* 1905, vol. I

Carroll, Hon. Sir James, 1857–1926, vol. II

Carroll, Sir John Anthony, 1899–1974, vol. VII

Carroll, Most Rev. John J., 1865–1949, vol. IV

Carroll, Brig.-Gen. John William Vincent, 1869–1927, vol. II

Carroll, Lewis, (Rev. Charles L. Dodgson), 1832–1898, vol. I

Carroll, Madeleine, 1906–1987, vol. VIII

Carroll, Paul Vincent, 1900–1968, vol. VI

Carroll, Sydney Wentworth, 1877–1958, vol. V

Carroll, Sir Turi; *see* Carroll, Sir Alfred Thomas.

Carroll, Rev. William Alexander, 1863–1935, vol. III

Carron, Baron (Life Peer); William John Carron, 1902–1969, vol. VI

Carrow, Comdr John Hinton, 1890–1973, vol. VII

Carruthers, Adam, 1857–1937, vol. III

Carruthers, Agnes Lucy Mary, 1872–1961, vol. VI

Carruthers, (Alexander) Douglas (Mitchell), *died* 1962, vol. VI

Carruthers, Engr-Rear-Adm. David John, 1867–1940, vol. III

Carruthers, Douglas; *see* Carruthers, A. D. M.

Carruthers, Lt-Col Francis John, 1868–1945, vol. IV

Carruthers, Lt-Col James, 1876–1936, vol. III

Carruthers, Rev. James E., 1848–1932, vol. III

Carruthers, John Bennett, 1869–1910, vol. I

Carruthers, Hon. Sir Joseph Hector M'Neil, 1857–1932, vol. III

Carruthers, Brig.-Gen. Robert Alexander, 1862–1945, vol. IV

Carruthers, Violet Rosa; *see* Markham, V. R.

Carruthers, William, 1830–1922, vol. II

Carruthers, Sir William, 1858–1936, vol. III

Carse, William Mitchell, 1899–1987, vol. VIII

Carslaw, Horatio Scott, 1870–1954, vol. V

Carson, Baron (Life Peer); Rt Hon. Sir Edward Henry Carson, 1854–1935, vol. III

Carson, Col Charles John Lloyd, 1866–1953, vol. V

Carson, Sir Charles William Charteris, 1874–1945, vol. IV

Carson, Hon. Edward, 1920–1987, vol. VIII

Carson, Brig. Sir Frederick, 1886–1960, vol. V

Carson, Herbert William, 1870–1930, vol. III

Carson, Howard Adams, 1842–1931, vol. III

Carson, Maj.-Gen. Sir John Wallace, 1864–1922, vol. II

Carson, Rev. Joseph, *died* 1898, vol. I

Carson, Lionel, 1873–1937, vol. III

Carson, Murray, 1865–1917, vol. II

Carson, Sir Norman John, 1877–1964, vol. VI

Carson, Rachel Louise, 1907–1964, vol. VI

Carson, Thomas Henry, 1843–1917, vol. II

Carson, Captain Hon. Walter Seymour, 1890–1946, vol. IV

Carswell, Catherine Roxburgh, 1879–1946, vol. IV

Carswell, Donald, 1882–1940, vol. III

Cart de Lafontaine, Lt-Col Henry Philip L., 1884–1963, vol. VI

Cartan, Elie Joseph, 1869–1951, vol. V

Carte, D'Oyly; *see* Carte, R. D.

Carte, (Richard) D'Oyly, 1844–1901, vol. I

Carte, Rupert D'Oyly; *see* D'Oyly Carte.

Carte, Col Thomas Elliott, 1861–1945, vol. IV

Carter, Albert Charles Robinson, 1864–1957, vol. V

Carter, Albert Thomas, 1861–1946, vol. IV

Carter, Alexander Scott, 1879–1969, vol. VI (AII)

Carter, Alfred B.; *see* Bonham-Carter.

Carter, Alfred Henry, 1849–1918, vol. II

Carter, Col Alfred Henry, 1856–1934, vol. III

Carter, Ven. Anthony Basil, 1881–1942, vol. IV

Carter, Sir Archibald; *see* Carter, Sir R. H. A.

Carter, Sir (Arthur) Desmond B.; *see* Bonham-Carter.

Carter, Arthur Herbert, 1890–1979, vol. VII

Carter, Hon. Arthur John, 1847–1917, vol. II

Carter, Arthur Thomas B.; *see* Bonham-Carter.

Carter, Major Aubrey John, 1872–1914, vol. I

Carter, Barry Robin Octavius, 1928–1981, vol. VIII

Carter, Maj.-Gen. Beresford Cecil Molyneux, 1872–1923, vol. II

Carter, Captain (S) Bernard, 1885–1954, vol. V

Carter, Gen. Sir Charles B.; see Bonham-Carter.

Carter, Brig.-Gen. Charles Herbert Philip, 1864–1943, vol. IV

Carter, Rev. Charles Sydney, 1876–1963, vol. VI

Carter, Sir Christopher Douglas B.; see Bonham Carter.

Carter, Rev. Cyril Robert, 1863–1930, vol. III

Carter, Air Cdre David William Frederick B.; see Bonham Carter.

Carter, Desmond, died 1939, vol. III

Carter, Hon. Sir Douglas Julian, 1908–1988, vol. VIII

Carter, Col Duncan Campbell, 1856–1942, vol. IV

Carter, Sir Edgar B.; see Bonham-Carter.

Carter, Edward Henry, 1876–1953, vol. V

Carter, Edward Julian, 1902–1982, vol. VIII

Carter, Edward Robert Erskine, 1923–1982, vol. VIII

Carter, Col Ernest Augustus Frederick, 1858–1934, vol. III

Carter, Ernestine Marie, 1906–1983, vol. VIII

Carter, Maj.-Gen. Sir Evan Eyare, 1866–1933, vol. III

Carter, Brig.-Gen. Francis Charles, 1858–1931, vol. III

Carter, Rev. Francis Edward, 1851–1935, vol. III

Carter, Francis Edward, 1886–1977, vol. VII

Carter, Frank W., 1870–1933, vol. III

Carter, Sir Frank Willington, 1865–1945, vol. IV

Carter, Franklin, 1837–1919, vol. II

Carter, Frederick, died 1967, vol. VI

Carter, Sir Frederick Bowker Terrington, 1819–1900, vol. I

Carter, Frederick William, 1870–1952, vol. V

Carter, Geoffrey William, 1909–1989, vol. VIII

Carter, Sir George John, 1860–1922, vol. II

Carter, George Stuart, 1893–1969, vol. VI

Carter, Sir Gerald Francis, 1881–1959, vol. V

Carter, Sir Gilbert Thomas G.; see Gilbert-Carter.

Carter, Lt-Col Godfrey Lambert, 1868–1932, vol. III

Carter, Lt-Col Sir Gordon, 1853–1941, vol. IV

Carter, Harry Graham, 1901–1982, vol. VIII

Carter, Col Harry Molyneux, 1850–1914, vol. I

Carter, Rev. Henry, 1874–1951, vol. V

Carter, Rev. Henry Child, 1875–1954, vol. V

Carter, Captain Herbert Augustine, 1874–1916, vol. II

Carter, Herbert James, 1858–1940, vol. III (A), vol. IV

Carter, Hester Marion, 1867–1944, vol. IV

Carter, Howard, 1873–1939, vol. III

Carter, Hugh Hoyles, died 1919, vol. II

Carter, Humphrey G.; see Gilbert-Carter.

Carter, Huntly, died 1942, vol. IV

Carter, Ian Malcolm B.; see Bonham-Carter.

Carter, Rev. John, 1861–1944, vol. IV

Carter, John Corrie, 1839–1927, vol. II

Carter, Lt-Col John Fillis Carré, 1882–1944, vol. IV

Carter, John Hilton, died 1926, vol. II

Carter, John Ridgely, 1865–1944, vol. IV

Carter, John Somers, 1901–1989, vol. VIII

Carter, Maj. Gen. Sir John Thomas, 1855–1939, vol. III

Carter, John Waynflete, 1905–1975, vol. VII

Carter, Malcolm Ogilvy, 1898–1982, vol. VIII

Carter, Sir Maurice B.; see Bonham-Carter.

Carter, Sir Morris; see Carter, Sir W. M.

Carter, Norman St Clair, 1875–1963, vol. VI

Carter, Air Cdre North, 1902–1984, vol. VIII

Carter, Octavius Cyril, 1893–1964, vol. VI

Carter, Peter Anthony, 1914–1983, vol. VIII

Carter, Reginald, 1868–1936, vol. III

Carter, Rei Alfred Deakin, 1856–1938, vol. III

Carter, Sir (Richard Henry) Archibald, 1887–1958, vol. V

Carter, Robert Brudenell, 1828–1918, vol. II

Carter, Lt-Col Robert Markham, 1875–1961, vol. VI

Carter, Adm. Sir Stuart Sumner B.; see Bonham-Carter.

Carter, Hon. Thomas Fortescue, 1855–1945, vol. IV

Carter, Vivian, 1878–1956, vol. V

Carter, W. Horsfall, 1900–1976, vol. VII

Carter, Walter, 1883–1964, vol. VI

Carter, Walter, 1873–1975, vol. VII

Carter, Sir Walker Kelly, 1899–1985, vol. VIII

Carter, Wilfred George, died 1969, vol. VI

Carter, William, 1836–1913, vol. I

Carter, Sir William, 1848–1932, vol. III

Carter, William, died 1932, vol. III

Carter, William, 1867–1940, vol. III

Carter, William Edward, 1885–1965, vol. VI

Carter, Col William Graydon, 1857–1938, vol. III

Carter, William Henry, 1868–1944, vol. IV

Carter, Most Rev. William Marlborough, 1850–1941, vol. IV

Carter, Sir (William) Morris, 1873–1960, vol. V

Carter, William Stovold, 1915–1985, vol. VIII

Carter-Campbell, Col George Tupper Campbell, 1869–1921, vol. II

Carter-Cotton, Francis, 1847–1919, vol. II

Carteret, Captain Charles Edward M. de; see Malet de Carteret.

Carteret, Lt-Col E. C. M. de; see Malet de Carteret.

Carteret, Reginald M. de; see Malet de Carteret.

Carthew, Lt-Col Thomas Walter Colby, 1880–1955, vol. V

Carthew-Yorstoun, Brig.-Gen. Archibald Morden, 1855–1925, vol. III

Cartier De Marchienne, Baron de, 1871–1946, vol. IV

Cartland, J. Ronald H., 1907–1940, vol. III

Cartland, Major John Howard, 1849–1940, vol. III

Cartledge, Jack Pickering, 1900–1966, vol. VI

Cartmel, Lt-Col Alfred Edward, 1893–1974, vol. VII

Cartmel-Robinson, Sir Harold Francis, 1889–1957, vol. V

Cartmell, Sir Harry, died 1923, vol. II

Cartmell, James Austen-, 1862–1921, vol. II

Carton, Richard Claude, 1856–1928, vol. II

Carton, Richard Paul, 1836–1907, vol. I

Carton, Ronald Lewis, 1888–1960, vol. V

Carton de Wiart, Lt-Gen. Sir Adrian, 1880–1963, vol. VI

Carton de Wiart, Count Edmund, 1876–1959, vol. V (A), vol. VI (AI)

Carton de Wiart, Comte Henry, 1869–1951, vol. V

Carton de Wiart, Léon Constant Ghislain, 1854–1915, vol. I
Carton de Wiart, Rt Rev. Mgr Maurice E., 1872–1935, vol. III
Cartwright, Albert, 1868–1956, vol. V
Cartwright, (Aubrey) Ralph Thomas, 1880–1936, vol. III
Cartwright, Beatrice, died 1947, vol. IV
Cartwright, Charles Frederic, 1846–1929, vol. III
Cartwright, Sir Charles Henry, 1865–1959, vol. V
Cartwright, Col Charles Marling, 1862–1946, vol. IV
Cartwright, Sir Chauncy, 1853–1933, vol. III
Cartwright, Rt Hon. Sir Fairfax Leighton, 1857–1928, vol. II
Cartwright, Lt-Col Francis Lennox, 1874–1957, vol. V
Cartwright, Brig.-Gen. Garnier Norton, 1868–1924, vol. II
Cartwright, Brig.-Gen. George Strachan, 1866–1959, vol. V
Cartwright, Col Henry Antrobus, 1887–1957, col. V
Cartwright, Lt-Col Henry Aubrey, 1858–1945, vol. IV
Cartwright, Sir Henry Edmund, 1821–1899, vol. I
Cartwright, J. R., died 1919, vol. II
Cartwright, Rev. Canon James Lawrence, 1889–1978, vol. VII
Cartwright, Rt Hon. John Robert, 1895–1979, vol. VII (AII)
Cartwright, Lt-Col John Rogers, 1882–1942, vol. IV
Cartwright, Julia; see Ady, J.
Cartwright, Ralph Thomas; see Cartwright, A. R. T.
Cartwright, Rt Hon. Sir Richard John, 1835–1912, vol. I
Cartwright, Lt-Col Robert, 1860–1942, vol. IV
Cartwright, Thomas Robert Brook Leslie-Melville, 1830–1921, vol. II
Cartwright, Sir William Bramwell, 1876–1958, vol. V
Cartwright, William Cornwallis, 1826–1915, vol. I
Cartwright-Taylor, Gen. Sir Malcolm Cartwright, 1911–1969, vol. VI
Caruana, Col Alfred Joseph, 1865–1953, vol. V
Caruana, Most Rev. Maurus, 1867–1943, vol. IV
Carus, Dr Paul, 1852–1919, vol. II
Carus-Wilson, Mrs C. Ashley, (Mary Louisa Georgina), died 1935, vol. III
Carus-Wilson, Charles Ashley, 1860–1942, vol. IV
Carus-Wilson, Eleanora Mary, 1897–1977, vol. VII
Caruso, Enrico, 1873–1921, vol. II
Carvell, John Eric Maclean, 1894–1978, vol. VII
Carver, Rev. Alfred James, 1826–1909, vol. I
Carver, David Dove, 1903–1974, vol. VII
Carver, Captain Edmund Clifton, 1873–1942, vol. IV
Carver, Rev. George Albert, 1862–1930, vol. III
Carver, Sir Stanley Roy, 1897–1967, vol. VI
Carver, Sydney Ralph Pitts, died 1940, vol. III
Carver, Thomas Gilbert, 1848–1906, vol. I
Carver, Col William Henton, 1868–1961, vol. VI
Carvill, Patrick George Hamilton, 1839–1924, vol. II
Carwardine, Thomas, died 1947, vol. IV
Cary, (Arthur) Joyce (Lunel), 1888–1957, vol. V
Cary, Sir (Arthur Lucius) Michael, 1914–1976, vol. VII
Cary, Joyce; see Cary, A. J. L.

Cary, Max, 1881–1958, vol. V
Cary, Sir Michael; see Cary, Sir A. L. M.
Cary, Hon. Philip Plantagenet, 1895–1968, vol. VI
Cary, Sir Robert Archibald, 1st Bt, 1898–1979, vol. VII
Cary, Maj.-Gen. Rupert Tristram Oliver, 1896–1980, vol. VII
Cary-Barnard, Brig.-Gen. Cyril Darcy Vivien, 1876–1933, vol. III
Cary-Elwes, Rt Rev. Dudley Charles, 1868–1932, vol. III
Cary-Elwes, Gervase Henry; see Elwes.
Cary-Elwes, Valentine Dudley Henry; see Elwes.
Caryll, Ivan, died 1921, vol. II
Carysfort, 5th Earl of, 1836–1909, vol. I
Casadesus, Robert, 1899–1972, vol. VII
Casalis, Jeanne de, 1898–1966, vol. VI
Casals, Pablo, 1876–1973, vol. VII
Casartelli, Rt Rev. Louis Charles, 1852–1925, vol. II
Casault, Hon. Sir Louis Edelmar Napoleon, 1822–1908, vol. I
Case, Air Vice-Marshal Albert Avion, 1916–1990, vol. VIII
Case, Air Vice-Marshal Avion; see Case, Air Vice-Marshal Albert A.
Case, Col Horace Akroyd, 1879–1968, vol. VI
Case, Robert Hope, 1857–1944, vol. IV
Case, Thomas, 1844–1925, vol. II
Casella, Alfredo, 1883–1947, vol. IV
Casement, Maj.-Gen. Francis, 1881–1967, vol. VI
Casement, Adm. John Moore, 1877–1952, vol. V
Casey, Baron (Life Peer); Richard Gardiner Casey, 1890–1976, vol. VII
Casey, Captain Denis Arthur, 1889–1968, vol. VI
Casey, Hon. James Joseph, 1831–1913, vol. I
Casey, Rt Rev. Patrick, 1873–1940, vol. III
Casey, Terence Anthony, 1920–1987, vol. VIII
Casey, Thomas Worrall, 1869–1949, vol. IV
Casey, Most Rev. Timothy, 1862–1931, vol. III
Casey, William Francis, 1884–1957, vol. V
Casgrain, Alexandre Chase-, 1879–1941, vol. IV
Casgrain, Hon. Col Hon. Joseph Philippe Baby-, born 1856, vol. III
Casgrain, Rev. Philippe Henri Duperron, 1864–1942, vol. IV
Casgrain, Rt Hon. Thomas Chase, 1852–1916, vol. II
Cash, J. Theodore, 1854–1936, vol. III
Cash, Col Sir Reginald John, 1892–1959, vol. V
Cash, Sir Thomas James, 1888–1978, vol. VII
Cash, Sir William, 1891–1964, vol. VI
Cash, Rt Rev. William Wilson, 1880–1955, vol. V
Cash-Reed, Bellamy Alexander, 1888–1965, vol. VI
Cashin, Hon. Sir Michael Patrick, 1864–1926, vol. II
Cashman, Rt Rev. David John, 1912–1971, vol. VII
Cashmore, Herbert Maurice, 1882–1972, vol. VII
Cashmore, Rt Rev. Thomas Herbert, 1892–1984, vol. VIII
Casimir-Perier, Jean Paul Pierre, 1847–1907, vol. I
Caslon, Vice-Adm. Clifford, 1896–1973, vol. VII
Caspersz, Charles P., 1855–1951, vol. V
Cass, Major Charles Herbert Davis, 1858–1929, vol. II
Cass, Brig. Edward Earnshaw Eden, 1898–1968, vol. VI

Cass, Rev. Gilbert Henning, 1873–1931, vol. III
Cass, Sir John, 1832–1898, vol. I
Cass, Col Walter Edmund Hutchinson, 1876–1931, vol. III
Cassal, Col Charles Edward, 1858–1921, vol. II
Cassar De Sain, 9th Marquess, 1880–1927, vol. II
Cassar De Sain, 10th Marquess, 1907–1958, vol. V
Cassatt, Alexander Johnston, 1839–1906, vol. I
Cassel, Rt Hon. Sir Ernest Joseph, 1852–1921, vol. II
Cassel, Rt Hon. Sir Felix, 1st Bt, 1869–1953, vol. V
Cassel, Sir Francis Edward, 2nd Bt, 1912–1969, vol. VI
Cassel, Gustav, 1866–1945, vol. IV
Cassells, Alexander, 1883–1967, vol. VI
Cassells, Hugh Hutchison, 1886–1950, vol. IV
Cassells, Thomas, 1902–1944, vol. IV
Cassels, Francis Henry, 1910–1987, vol. VIII
Cassels, Brig. George Hamilton, 1882–1944, vol. IV
Cassels, Brig.-Gen. Gilbert Robert, 1870–1951, vol. V
Cassels, Sir James Dale, 1877–1972, vol. VII
Cassels, Gen. Sir Robert Archibald, 1876–1959, vol. V
Cassels, Hon. Sir Walter, 1845–1923, vol. II
Cassels, Walter Richard, 1826–1907, vol. I
Cassels, Walter Seton, 1873–1932, vol. III
Cassels, Rt Rev. William Wharton, 1858–1925, vol. II
Casserly, Col Gordon, died 1947, vol. IV
Cassia, Francis Joseph Nicholas Paul S.; see Sant-Cassia.
Cassidy, David Mackay, 1846–1936, vol. III
Cassidy, Sir Jack Evelyn, 1894–1975, vol. VII
Cassidy, John, 1860–1939, vol. III
Cassidy, Sir Maurice Alan, 1880–1949, vol. IV
Cassie, Arnold Blatchford David, 1905–1982, vol. VIII
Cassie, W(illiam) Fisher, 1905–1985, vol. VIII
Cassie, William Riach, 1861–1908, vol. I
Cassin, René, 1887–1976, vol. VII
Casson, Elizabeth, 1881–1954, vol. V
Casson, Herbert Alexander, 1867–1952, vol. V
Casson, Brig.-Gen. Hugh Gilbert, 1866–1951, vol. V
Casson, Rev. Canon John, 1869–1955, vol. V
Casson, Sir Lewis, 1875–1969, vol. VI
Casson, Stanley, 1889–1944, vol. IV
Casson, Dame Sybil; see Thorndike, Dame Sybil.
Casswell, Joshua David, died 1963, vol. VI
Castaing, Jacques C. de; see Chastenet de Castaing.
Castéja, Marie Emmanuel Alvar de Biaudos-Scarisbrick, the Marquis de, 1849–1911, vol. I
Castellani, Marchese Count Aldo, 1877–1971, vol. VII
Castenskiold, H. Grevenkop, 1862–1921, vol. II
Casteret, Norbert, 1897–1987, vol. VIII
Castillejo, José, 1877–1945, vol. IV
Castle, Baron (Life Peer); Edward Cyril Castle, 1907–1979, vol. VII
Castle, Agnes, died 1922, vol. II
Castle, Edgar Bradshaw, 1897–1973, vol. VII
Castle, Egerton, 1858–1920, vol. II
Castle, Frances; see Blackburn, E. B.
Castle, Marcellus Purnell, 1849–1917, vol. II

Castle, Norman Henry, 1913–1988, vol. VIII
Castle, Lt-Col Reginald Wingfield, 1874–1952, vol. V
Castle, Walter Frances Raphael, 1892–1926, vol. II
Castle, William, 1833–1911, vol. I
Castle-Miller, Rudolph Valdemar Thor, 1905–1987, vol. VIII
Castle Stewart (styled Castlestewart), 5th Earl, 1837–1914, vol. I
Castle Stewart (styled Castlestewart), 6th Earl, 1841–1921, vol. II
Castle Stewart, 7th Earl, 1889–1961, vol. VI
Castlemaine, 5th Baron, 1863–1937, vol. III
Castlemaine, 6th Baron, 1864–1954, vol. V
Castlemaine, 7th Baron, 1904–1973, vol. VII
Castleman-Smith, Col Edward Castleman, died 1943, vol. IV
Castletown, 2nd Baron, 1849–1937, vol. III
Catarinich, John, 1882–1974, vol. VII
Catchpool, Egerton St John Pettifor, 1890–1971, vol. VII
Cater, Sir (Alexander) Norman (Ley), 1880–1957, vol. V
Cater, Sir John James, 1885–1962, vol. VI
Cater, Sir Norman; see Cater, Sir A. N. L.
Cates, Arthur, 1829–1901, vol. I
Cathcart, 3rd Earl, 1828–1905, vol. I
Cathcart, 4th Earl, 1856–1911, vol. I
Cathcart, 5th Earl, 1862–1927, vol. II
Cathcart, Col Hon. Augustus Murray, 1830–1914, vol. I
Cathcart, Charles Walker, 1853–1932, vol. III
Cathcart, Edward Provan, 1877–1954, vol. V
Cathcart, George Clark, died 1951, vol. V
Cathcart, Sir Reginald Archibald Edward, 6th Bt, 1838–1916, vol. II
Cathcart, Robert, died 1907, vol. I
Cathcart, William Taylor, 1859–1940, vol. III
Cathels, Rt Rev. David, 1853–1925, vol. II
Cather, Willa Sibert, 1876–1947, vol. IV
Cathery, Edmund, 1852–1925, vol. III
Cathie, Ian Aysgarth Bewley, 1908–1989, vol. VIII
Catledge, Turner, 1901–1983, vol. VIII
Catlin, Sir George Edward Gordon, 1896–1979, vol. VII
Catling, Thomas, 1838–1920, vol. II
Catlow, Sir John William, died 1947, vol. IV
Catnach, Agnes, 1891–1979, vol. VII
Caton, Richard, died 1926, vol. II
Caton-Jones, Col Frederick William, 1860–1944, vol. IV
Caton-Thompson, Gertrude, 1888–1985, vol. VIII
Cator, Maj.-Gen. Albemarle Bertie Edward, 1877–1932, vol. III
Cator, Sir Geoffrey Edmund, 1884–1973, vol. VII
Cator, Lt-Col Henry John, 1897–1965, vol. VI
Cator, John, 1862–1944, vol. IV
Cator, Lt-Col Philip James, 1901–1944, vol. IV
Cator, Sir Ralph Bertie Peter, 1861–1945, vol. IV
Cator, Rev. William Lumley Bertie, died 1918, vol. II
Catroux, Gén. Georges Albert Julian, 1877–1969, vol. VI
Cattanach, William, 1863–1932, vol. III
Catterall, Arthur, 1884–1943, vol. IV
Catterall, Sir Robert, 1880–1962, vol. VI

Catterns, Basil Gage, 1886–1969, vol. VI
Catterson-Smith, John Keats, 1882–1945, vol. IV
Cattley, M. H., *died* 1958, vol. V
Catto, 1st Baron, 1879–1959, vol. V
Catton, Bruce, 1899–1978, vol. VII
Catty, Col Thomas Claude, 1879–1967, vol. VI
Caulcutt, Sir John, 1876–1943, vol. IV
Caulfeild, Major Algernon Montgomerie, 1858–1915, vol. I
Caulfeild, Algernon Thomas St George, 1869–1933, vol. III
Caulfeild, Brig.-Gen. Charles Trevor, 1863–1947, vol. IV
Caulfeild, Francis St George, 1852–1933, vol. III
Caulfeild, Vice-Adm. Francis Wade, 1872–1947, vol. IV
Caulfeild, Brig.-Gen. Francis William John, 1859–1938, vol. III
Caulfeild, Col Gordon Napier, 1862–1922, vol. II
Caulfeild, Brig.-Gen. James Edward Wilmot Smyth, 1850–1925, vol. II
Caulfeild, Captain James Montgomerie, 1855–1946, vol. IV
Caulfield, Sidney Burgoyne Kitchener, *died* 1964, vol. VI
Caullery, Maurice, 1868–1958, vol. V
Caulton, Rt Rev. Sidney Gething, 1895–1976, vol. VII
Caumont, Rt Rev. Mgr Fortunatus Henry, 1871–1930, vol. III
Caunt, Ven. Frederic, *died* 1933, vol. III
Caunter, Brig. Alan; *see* Caunter, Brig. J. A. L.
Caunter, Brig.-Gen. James Eales, 1859–1937, vol. III
Caunter, Brig. John Alan Lyde, 1889–1981, vol. VIII
Causer, William Sidney, *died* 1958, vol. V
Causton, Rev. Francis Jervoise, *died* 1932, vol. III
Cauthery, Harold William, 1914–1987, vol. VIII
Cautley, 1st Baron, 1863–1946, vol. IV
Cautley, Edmund, *died* 1944, vol. IV
Cauty, Sir Arthur Belcher, 1870–1954, vol. V
Cavalcanti, Alberto de Almeida, 1897–1982, vol. VIII
Cavalieri, Lina, 1874–1944, vol. IV
Cavan, 9th Earl of, 1839–1900, vol. I
Cavan, 10th Earl of, 1865–1946, vol. IV
Cavan, 11th Earl of, 1878–1950, vol. IV
Cavan, 12th Earl of, 1911–1988, vol. VIII
Cavanagh, Captain John Duncan Macaulay, 1881–1957, vol. V
Cavaye, Maj.-Gen. William Frederick, *died* 1926, vol. II
Cave, 1st Viscount, 1856–1928, vol. II
Cave of Richmond, Countess; (1st in line), *died* 1938, vol. III
Cave, Rev. Alfred, 1847–1900, vol. I
Cave, Arthur Wilson, *died* 1930, vol. III
Cave, Sir Basil Shillito, 1865–1931, vol. III
Cave, Sir Charles Daniel, 1st Bt (*cr* 1896), 1832–1922, vol. II
Cave, Sir Charles Henry, 2nd Bt (*cr* 1896), 1861–1932, vol. III
Cave, Charles John Philip, 1871–1950, vol. IV
Cave, Edmund, 1859–1946, vol. IV
Cave, Sir Edward Charles, 3rd Bt (*cr* 1896), 1893–1946, vol. IV

Cave, Edward Watkins, *died* 1948, vol. IV
Cave, Captain George Ellis, 1867–1938, vol. III
Cave, Air Vice-Marshal Henry Meyrick C.-B.; *see* Cave-Browne-Cave.
Cave, Adm. John Halliday, 1827–1913, vol. I
Cave, Hon. Sir Lewis William, 1832–1897, vol. I
Cave, Sir Mylles Cave-Browne-, 11th Bt (*cr* 1641), 1822–1907, vol. I
Cave, Sir Richard Guy, 1920–1986, vol. VIII
Cave, Sir Richard Philip, 1912–1988, vol. VIII
Cave, Rev. Sydney, 1883–1953, vol. V
Cave, Sir Thomas C.-B.; *see* Cave-Browne-Cave.
Cave, Wing Comdr Thomas Reginald C.-B.; *see* Cave-Browne-Cave.
Cave, Sir Thomas Sturmy, 1846–1936, vol. III
Cave, Walter F., *died* 1939, vol. III
Cave-Browne, Edward Raban, 1835–1907, vol. I
Cave-Browne, Maj.-Gen. William, 1884–1967, vol. VI
Cave-Browne-Cave, Sir Clement Charles, 15th Bt (*cr* 1641), 1896–1945, vol. IV
Cave-Browne-Cave, Rev. Sir Genille, 12th Bt (*cr* 1641), 1869–1929, vol. III
Cave-Browne-Cave, Air Vice-Marshal Henry Meyrick, 1887–1965, vol. VI
Cave-Browne-Cave, Sir Mylles; *see* Cave.
Cave-Browne-Cave, Captain Sir Reginald Ambrose, 13th Bt (*cr* 1641), 1860–1930, vol. III
Cave-Browne-Cave, Sir Rowland Henry, 14th Bt (*cr* 1641), 1865–1943, vol. IV
Cave-Browne-Cave, Sir Thomas, 1835–1924, vol. II
Cave-Browne-Cave, Wing Comdr Thomas Reginald, 1885–1969, vol. VI
Caven, Rev. Principal, 1830–1904, vol. I
Caven, Robert Martin, 1870–1934, vol. III
Cavenagh, Prof. Francis Alexander, 1884–1946, vol. IV
Cavendish; *see* Jones, Henry.
Cavendish, Brig.-Gen. Alfred Edward John, 1859–1943, vol. IV
Cavendish, Lord Charles A. F., 1905–1944, vol. IV
Cavendish, Major Frederick George, 1891–1936, vol. III
Cavendish, Brig.-Gen. Frederick William Lawrence Sheppard Hart, 1878–1931, vol. III
Cavendish, Captain Lord John Spencer, 1875–1914, vol. I
Cavendish, Col Ralph Henry Voltelin, 1887–1968, vol. VI
Cavendish, Richard Charles Alexander, 1885–1941, vol. IV
Cavendish, Rt Hon. Lord Richard Frederick, 1871–1946, vol. IV
Cavendish, Brig.-Gen. Hon. William Edwin, 1862–1931, vol. III
Cavendish-Acheson, Hon. Patrick George Edward; *see* Acheson.
Cavendish-Bentinck, Lt-Col Lord Charles, 1868–1956, vol. V
Cavendish-Bentinck, Frederick; *see* Bentinck.
Cavendish-Bentinck, Lord William Augustus; *see* Bentinck.
Caverhill, William Melville; *see* Melville, Alan.
Cavill, William Victor, *died* 1959, vol. V
Caw, Sir James Lewis, 1864–1950, vol. IV

Cawadias, Alexander Pocnagioti, *died* 1971, vol. VII
Cawdor, 2nd Earl, 1817–1898, vol. I
Cawdor, 3rd Earl, 1847–1911, vol. I
Cawdor, 4th Earl, 1870–1914, vol. I
Cawdor, 5th Earl, 1900–1970, vol. VI
Cawley, 1st Baron, 1850–1937, vol. III
Cawley, 2nd Baron, 1877–1954, vol. V
Cawley, Rev. Frederick, 1884–1978, vol. VII
Cawley, George, 1848–1927, vol. II
Cawley, Harold Thomas, 1878–1915, vol. I
Cawley, Hon. Oswald, 1882–1918, vol. II
Cawood, Herbert Harry, 1890–1957, vol. V
Cawood, Sir Walter, 1907–1967, vol. VI
Cawston, (Edwin) Richard, 1923–1986, vol. VIII
Cawston, Sir John Westerman, 1859–1927, vol. II
Cawston, Richard; *see* Cawston, E. R.
Cawthorn, Maj.-Gen. Sir Walter Joseph, 1896–1970, vol. VI (AII)
Cawthorne, Sir Terence Edward, 1902–1970, vol. VI
Cawthra-Elliot, Maj.-Gen. Harry Macintire, 1867–1949, vol. IV
Cay, Armistead, 1872–1957, vol. V
Cayley, Hon. Maj.-Gen. Douglas Edward, 1870–1951, vol. V
Cayley, Adm. George Cuthbert, 1866–1944, vol. IV
Cayley, Sir George Everard Arthur, 9th Bt, 1861–1917, vol. II
Cayley, Captain Harry Francis, 1873–1954, vol. V
Cayley, Dep. Surg.-Gen. Henry, 1834–1904, vol. I
Cayley, Sir Kenelm Henry Ernest, 10th Bt, 1896–1967, vol. VI
Cayley, Sir Richard, 1833–1908, vol. I
Cayley, Maj.-Gen. Sir Walter de Sausmarez, 1863–1952, vol. V
Cayley, William, 1836–1916, vol. II
Cayley-Robinson, Frederic; *see* Robinson.
Cayzer, Hon. Anthony; *see* Cayzer, Hon. M. A. R.
Cayzer, Sir August Bernard Tellefsen, 1st Bt (*cr* 1921), 1876–1943, vol. IV
Cayzer, Sir Charles, 1st Bt (*cr* 1904), 1843–1916, vol. II
Cayzer, Sir Charles William, 2nd Bt (*cr* 1904), 1869–1917, vol. II
Cayzer, Sir Charles William, 3rd Bt (*cr* 1904), 1896–1940, vol. III
Cayzer, Major Harold Stanley, 1882–1948, vol. IV
Cayzer, Major John Sanders, 1871–1908, vol. I
Cayzer, Hon. (Michael) Anthony (Rathborne), 1920–1990, vol. VIII
Cayzer, Sir Nigel John, 4th Bt (*cr* 1904), 1920–1943, vol. IV
Cazalet, Edward Alexander, *died* 1923, vol. II
Cazalet, Vice-Adm. Sir Peter Grenville Lyon, 1899–1982, vol. VIII
Cazalet, Peter Victor Ferdinand, 1907–1973, vol. VII
Cazalet, Lt-Col Victor Alexander, 1896–1943, vol. IV
Cazalet, William Marshall, 1865–1932, vol. III
Cazalet-Keir, Thelma, 1899–1989, vol. VIII
Cazamian, Louis, 1877–1965, vol. VI
Cazenove, Brig. Arnold de Lerisson, *died* 1969, vol. VI
Cazenove, Philip Henry de Lerisson, 1901–1978, vol. VII
Cecil of Chelwood, 1st Viscount, 1864–1958, vol. V

Cecil, Algernon, 1879–1953, vol. V
Cecil, Lord Arthur, 1851–1913, vol. I
Cecil, Lord David; *see* Cecil, Lord E. C. D. G.
Cecil, Ean Francis, 1880–1942, vol. IV
Cecil, Lord (Edward Christian) David (Gascoyne), 1902–1986, vol. VIII
Cecil, Col Lord Edward Herbert, 1867–1918, vol. II
Cecil, Lord Eustace Brownlow Henry, 1834–1921, vol. II
Cecil, Henry; *see* Leon, H. C.
Cecil, Lord John Pakenham Joicey-, 1867–1942, vol. IV
Cecil, Rev. Philip Henry, 1918–1977, vol. VII
Cecil, Victor Alexander G.; *see* Gascoyne-Cecil.
Cecil, Lord William, 1854–1943, vol. IV
Cecil, Hon. William Amherst, 1886–1914, vol. I
Cecil, Rt Rev. Lord William Gascoyne-, 1863–1936, vol. III
Cecil-Williams, Sir John Lias Cecil, 1892–1964, vol. VI
Cecil-Wright, Air Cdre John Allan Cecil, 1886–1982, vol. VIII
Cederström, Baron Rolf, *died* 1947, vol. IV
Cederström, Baroness Rolf, *see* Patti, Mme Adelina.
Céitinn, Seán; *see* Keating, John.
Cellier, Jacobus Stephanus, *born* 1878, vol. III
Cemlyn-Jones, Sir E. Wynne, 1888–1966, vol. VI
Cenez, Rt Rev. Jules Joseph, 1865–1944, vol. IV
Centlivres, Hon. Albert van de Sandt, 1887–1966, vol. VI
Ceram, C. W.; *see* Marek, K. W.
Cerf, Bennett, 1898–1971, vol. VII
Cerny, Jaroslav, 1898–1970, vol. VI
Cerretti, His Eminence Cardinal Bonaventura, 1872–1933, vol. III
Cerutty, Charles John, 1870–1941, vol. IV
Cervera, Adm. Pascual Cervera y Topete, 1839–1909, vol. I
Chadburn, George Haworthe, 1870–1950, vol. IV
Chadburn, Maud Mary, *died* 1957, vol. V
Chads, Adm. Sir Henry, 1819–1906, vol. I
Chads, Maj.-Gen. William John, 1830–1915, vol. I
Chadwell, Rt Rev. Arthur Ernest, 1892–1967, vol. VI
Chadwick, Sir Albert Edward, 1897–1983, vol. VIII
Chadwick, Brig. Cecil Arthur Harrop, 1901–1970, vol. VI
Chadwick, Rev. Charles Egerton, 1880–1958, vol. V
Chadwick, Sir David Thomas, 1876–1954, vol. V
Chadwick, Edward Marion, 1840–1921, vol. II
Chadwick, Rt Rev. George Alexander, 1840–1923, vol. II
Chadwick, Hector Munro, 1870–1947, vol. IV
Chadwick, Sir James, 1891–1974, vol. VII
Chadwick, John Courtenay Chasman, 1846–1932, vol. III
Chadwick, Sir John Edward, 1911–1987, vol. VIII
Chadwick, Nora Kershaw, 1891–1972, vol. VII
Chadwick, Osbert, 1844–1913, vol. I
Chadwick, Sir Peter B.; *see* Burton-Chadwick, Sir R.
Chadwick, Rev. Canon Robert, *died* 1927, vol. II
Chadwick, Sir Robert B.; *see* Burton-Chadwick.
Chadwick, Roy, 1893–1947, vol. IV
Chadwick, Rev. Samuel, 1860–1932, vol. III
Chadwick, Sir Thomas, 1888–1969, vol. VI

Chadwick, Rev. William Edward, *died* 1934, vol. III
Chadwyck-Healey, Sir Charles Arthur, 4th Bt, 1910–1986, vol. VIII
Chadwyck-Healey, Sir Charles Edward Heley, 1st Bt, 1845–1919, vol. II
Chadwyck-Healey, Sir Edward Randal, 3rd Bt, 1898–1979, vol. VII
Chadwyck-Healey, Sir Gerald Edward, 2nd Bt, 1873–1955, vol. V
Chadwyck-Healey, Oliver Nowell, 1886–1960, vol. V
Chaffey, Hon. Frank A., 1888–1940, vol. III
Chaffey, Col Ralph Anderson, 1856–1925, vol. II
Chagall, Marc, 1887–1985, vol. VIII
Chagla, Shri Mohomedali Currim, 1900–1981, vol. VIII
Chain, Sir Ernst Boris, 1906–1979, vol. VII
Chaine, Lt-Col William, 1838–1916, vol. II
Chaliapin, Fedor Ivanovitch, 1873–1938, vol. III
Chalkley, Alfred Philip, 1886–1959, vol. V
Chalkley, Sir (Harry) Owen, 1882–1958, vol. V
Chalkley, Sir Owen; *see* Chalkley, Sir H. O.
Challacombe, Rev. William Allen, *died* 1951, vol. V
Challans, Mary; *see* Renault, M.
Challe, Général d'Armée Aérienne Maurice, 1905–1979, vol. VII
Challen, Charles, 1894–1960, vol. V
Challenger, Frederick, 1887–1983, vol. VIII
Challenor, Brig.-Gen. Edward Lacy, 1873–1935, vol. III
Challinor, William Francis, 1882–1967, vol. VI
Challis, John Humphrey Thornton, 1896–1958, vol. V
Chalmer, Col Francis George, 1884–1951, vol. V
Chalmer, Col Reginald, 1844–1911, vol. I
Chalmers, 1st Baron, 1858–1938, vol. III
Chalmers, Albert John, 1870–1920, vol. II
Chalmers, Sir Alfred John George, 1845–1937, vol. III
Chalmers, Archibald Kerr, 1856–1942, vol. IV
Chalmers, Archibald MacDonald, 1883–1977, vol. VII
Chalmers, Arthur Morison, 1862–1949, vol. IV
Chalmers, Sir Charles, 1861–1924, vol. II
Chalmers, Sir David Patrick, *died* 1899, vol. I
Chalmers, Lt-Col Frederick Roydon, 1881–1943, vol. IV
Chalmers, George Buchanan, 1929–1989, vol. VIII
Chalmers, John, 1915–1983, vol. VIII
Chalmers, Sir Mackenzie Dalzell, 1847–1927, vol. II
Chalmers, P. MacGregor, 1859–1922, vol. II
Chalmers, Patrick Reginald, *died* 1942, vol. IV
Chalmers, Rev. Reginald, 1893–1974, vol. VII
Chalmers, Thomas Andrew, *died* 1944, vol. IV
Chalmers, William John, 1914–1986, vol. VIII
Chalmers, Rear-Adm. William Scott, 1888–1971, vol. VII
Chamba, Raja of, 1869–1919, vol. II
Chamberlain, Arthur, *died* 1913, vol. I
Chamberlain, Rt Hon. (Arthur) Neville, 1869–1940, vol. III
Chamberlain, Rt Hon. Sir Austen; *see* Chamberlain, Rt Hon. Sir J. A.
Chamberlain, Basil Hall, 1850–1935, vol. III

Chamberlain, Gen. Sir Crawford Trotter, 1821–1902, vol. I
Chamberlain, Digby, 1896–1962, vol. VI
Chamberlain, Fernley John, 1879–1958, vol. V
Chamberlain, Francis Walter, 1892–1970, vol. VI
Chamberlain, Rt Rev. (Frank) Noel, 1900–1975, vol. VII
Chamberlain, Sir Henry Hamilton Erroll, 4th Bt, 1857–1936, vol. III
Chamberlain, Henry Richardson, 1859–1911, vol. I
Chamberlain, Sir Henry Wilmot, 5th Bt, 1899–1980, vol. VII (AII)
Chamberlain, Houston Stewart, 1855–1927, vol. II
Chamberlain, Ivy Muriel, (Lady Chamberlain), *died* 1941, vol. IV
Chamberlain, Rt Hon. Joseph, 1836–1914, vol. I
Chamberlain, Rt Hon. Sir (Joseph) Austen, 1863–1937, vol. III
Chamberlain, Rt Hon. Neville; *see* Chamberlain, Rt Hon. A. N.
Chamberlain, Field Marshal Sir Nevile Bowles, 1820–1902, vol. I
Chamberlain, Col Sir Neville Francis Fitzgerald, 1856–1944, vol. IV
Chamberlain, Rt Rev. Noel; *see* Chamberlain, Rt Rev. F. N.
Chamberlain, Ronald, 1901–1987, vol. VIII
Chamberlain, Ven. Thomas, *born* 1854, vol. II
Chamberlain, Sir William, 1877–1944, vol. IV
Chamberlayne, Air Cdre Paul Richard Tankerville James Michael Isidore Camille, 1898–1972, vol. VII
Chamberlayne, Tankerville, 1843–1924, vol. II
Chamberlayne, Gen. William John, 1821–1910, vol. I
Chamberlin, Arthur George, *died* 1925, vol. II
Chamberlin, Edson J., *died* 1924, vol. II
Chamberlin, Frederick, 1870–1943, vol. IV
Chamberlin, Sir George, 1846–1928, vol. II
Chamberlin, Sir Michael, 1891–1972, vol. VII
Chamberlin, Peter Hugh Girard, 1919–1978, vol. VII
Chambers, Rev. Arthur, *died* 1918, vol. II
Chambers, Adm. Bertram Mordaunt, 1866–1945, vol. IV
Chambers, Maj.-Gen. Brooke Rynd, 1834–1915, vol. I
Chambers, Charles Edward Stuart, 1859–1936, vol. III
Chambers, Charles Haddon, 1860–1921, vol. II
Chambers, Sir Cornelius, 1862–1941, vol. IV
Chambers, Sir Edmund Kerchever, 1866–1954, vol. V
Chambers, Rev. Frederick Charles, 1860–1933, vol. III
Chambers, Rt Rev. George Alexander, *died* 1963, vol. VI
Chambers, George Frederick, 1841–1915, vol. I
Chambers, Sir George Henry, 1816–1903, vol. I
Chambers, George Lawson, 1852–1934, vol. III
Chambers, Helen, *died* 1935, vol. III
Chambers, James, 1863–1917, vol. II
Chambers, John Ferguson, 1894–1941, vol. IV
Chambers, Major John Reginald, 1882–1953, vol. V
Chambers, Jonathan David, 1898–1970, vol. VI
Chambers, Surg. Vice-Adm. Sir Joseph, 1864–1935, vol. III

Chambers, Lt-Col Joseph Charles, 1857–1940, vol. III (A), vol. IV

Chambers, Julius, 1850–1920, vol. II

Chambers, Lloyd Eld, 1863–1930, vol. III

Chambers, Sir Newman Pitts-, *died* 1922, vol. II

Chambers, Sir Paul; *see* Chambers, Sir S. P.

Chambers, Raymond Wilson, 1874–1942, vol. IV

Chambers, Rev. Robert Halley, 1853–1934, vol. III

Chambers, Maj.-Gen. Robert Macdonald, 1833–1924, vol. II

Chambers, Robert Sharp Borgnis H.; *see* Hammond-Chambers.

Chambers, Robert William, 1865–1933, vol. III

Chambers, Sir (Stanley) Paul, 1904–1981, vol. VIII

Chambers, Sir Theodore Gervase, 1871–1957, vol. V

Chambers, William Walker, 1913–1985, vol. VIII

Chamier, Sir Edward Maynard Des Champs, 1866–1945, vol. IV

Chamier, Maj.-Gen. Francis Edward Archibald, 1833–1923, vol. II

Chamier, Brig.-Gen. George Daniel, 1860–1920, vol. II

Chamier, Air Cdre Sir John Adrian, 1883–1974, vol. VII

Chamier, Lt-Col Richard Outram, 1888–1980, vol. VII

Chamier, Lt-Gen. Stephen, 1834–1910, vol. I

Chaminade, Cécile, *died* 1944, vol. IV

Chamney, Lt-Col Henry, 1861–1947, vol. IV

Champain, Brig.-Gen. Hugh Frederick B.; *see* Bateman-Champain.

Champain, Rt Rev. John Norman B.; *see* Bateman-Champain.

Champion, Baron (Life Peer); Arthur Joseph Champion, 1897–1985, vol. VIII

Champion, Arthur Mortimer, 1885–1950, vol. IV

Champion, Frank Clive, 1907–1976, vol. VII

Champion, Sir Harry George, 1891–1979, vol. VII

Champion, Henry Hyde, 1859–1928, vol. II

Champion, Captain John Pelham, 1883–1955, vol. V

Champion, Pierre, 1880–1942, vol. IV

Champion, Rev. Sir Reginald Stuart, 1895–1982, vol. VIII

Champion de Crespigny, Captain Claude, 1873–1910, vol. I

Champion de Crespigny, Sir Claude, 4th Bt, 1847–1935, vol. III

Champion de Crespigny, Brig.-Gen. Sir Claude Raul, 5th Bt, 1878–1941, vol. IV

Champion-de Crespigny, Col Sir (Constantine) Trent, 1882–1952, vol. V

Champion de Crespigny, Comdr Sir Frederick Philip, 7th Bt, 1884–1947, vol. IV

Champion de Crespigny, Lt-Col George Harrison, 1863–1945, vol. IV

Champion de Crespigny, Sir Henry, 6th Bt, 1882–1946, vol. IV

Champion de Crespigny, Air Vice-Marshal Hugh Vivian, 1897–1969, vol. VI

Champion de Crespigny, Rose, (Mrs Philip Champion de Crespigny), *died* 1935, vol. III

Champion-de Crespigny, Col Sir Trent; *see* Champion-de Crespigny, Col Sir C. T.

Champion de Crespigny, Sir Vivian Tyrell, 8th Bt, 1907–1952, vol. V

Champness, Captain Charles Henry, 1889–1963, vol. VI

Champness, Henry Robert, 1852–1923, vol. II

Champness, Major Sir William Henry, 1873–1956, vol. V

Champneys, Basil, 1842–1935, vol. III

Champneys, Sir Francis Henry, 1848–1930, vol. III

Champneys, Rev. Francis Weldon, *died* 1929, vol. III

Champneys, Captain Sir Weldon D.; *see* Dalrymple-Champneys.

Champtaloup, Sydney Taylor, 1880–1921, vol. II

Chamson, André, 1900–1983, vol. VIII

Chance, Sir Arthur, 1859–1928, vol. II

Chance, Frederick Selby, 1886–1946, vol. IV

Chance, Sir Frederick William, 1852–1932, vol. III

Chance, Maj. Geoffrey Henry Barrington, 1893–1987, vol. VIII

Chance, George Ferguson, 1854–1933, vol. III

Chance, Sir Hugh; *see* Chance, Sir W. H. S.

Chance, Ivan Oswald, 1910–1984, vol. VIII

Chance, James Frederick, 1856–1938, vol. III

Chance, Sir James Timmins, 1st Bt, 1814–1902, vol. I

Chance, Kenneth Macomb, 1879–1966, vol. VI

Chance, Kenneth Miles, 1893–1980, vol. VII

Chance, Miles; *see* Chance, K. M.

Chance, Brig.-Gen. Oswald Kesteven, 1880–1935, vol. III

Chance, Percival Vincent, 1888–1970, vol. VI

Chance, Sir Robert Christopher, 1883–1960, vol. V

Chance, Sir Roger James Ferguson, 3rd Bt, 1893–1987, vol. VIII

Chance, Thomas Williams, 1872–1954, vol. V

Chance, Walter Lucas, 1880–1963, vol. VI

Chance, Sir William, 2nd Bt, 1853–1935, vol. III

Chance, Sir (William) Hugh (Stobart), 1896–1981, vol. VIII

Chancellor, Alexander Richard, 1869–1959, vol. V

Chancellor, Sir Christopher John, 1904–1989, vol. VIII

Chancellor, Edwin Beresford, 1868–1937, vol. III

Chancellor, Henry George, 1863–1945, vol. IV

Chancellor, Lt-Col Sir John Robert, 1870–1952, vol. V

Chand, Masheerud-dowal Rai Bahadur N.; *see* Nanak Chand.

Chandavarkar, Sir Narayen Ganesh, 1855–1923, vol. II

Chandavarkar, Sir Vithal Narayan, 1887–1959, vol. V

Chandler, Alfred, 1853–1923, vol. II

Chandler, Rt Rev. Arthur, 1860–1939, vol. III

Chandler, Frederick George, *died* 1942, vol. IV

Chandler, Hon. Sir Gilbert Lawrence, 1903–1974, vol. VII

Chandler, Sir John Beals, 1887–1962, vol. VI

Chandler, Sir John DeLisle, 1889–1967, vol. VI

Chandler, Louise; *see* Moulton, Mrs.

Chandler, Pretor Whitty, 1858–1941, vol. IV

Chandler, Raymond Thornton, 1888–1959, vol. V

Chandler, Sir William Kellman, 1857–1940, vol. III

Chandos, 1st Viscount, 1893–1972, vol. VII

Chandos, 2nd Viscount, 1920–1980, vol. VII

Chandos-Pole, Brig.-Gen. Harry Anthony, *died* 1934, vol. III

Chandy, Ven. Jacob, *born* 1852, vol. III

Chaney, Henry James, 1842–1906, vol. I

Chaney, Maj.-Gen. James E., 1885–1967, vol. VI

Channell, Rt Hon. Sir Arthur Moseley, 1838–1928, vol. II

Channer, Col Bernard, 1846–1916, vol. II

Channer, Frederick Francis Ralph, 1875–1950, vol. IV

Channer, Gen. George Nicholas, 1843–1905, vol. I

Channer, Maj.-Gen. George Osborne De Renzy, 1890–1969, vol. VI

Channing of Wellingborough, 1st Baron, 1841–1926, vol. II

Channing, Edward, 1856–1931, vol. III

Channing Williams, Maj.-Gen. John William, 1908–1990, vol. VIII

Channon, Harold John, 1897–1979, vol. VII

Channon, Sir Henry, 1897–1958, vol. V

Chant, Clarence Augustus, 1865–1956, vol. V

Chant, Mrs Laura Ormiston, 1848–1923, vol. II

Chanter, Hon. John Moore, 1845–1931, vol. III

Chantler, Philip, 1911–1988, vol. VIII

Chapais, Hon. Sir Thomas, 1858–1946, vol. IV

Chapel, Sir William, 1870–1950, vol. IV (A)

Chapin, Harold, 1886–1915, vol. I

Chapin, Captain Sidney H., 1875–1918, vol. II

Chapleau, Hon. Sir Joseph Adolphe, 1840–1898, vol. I

Chapleau, Samuel Edmour St Onge, 1839–1921, vol. II

Chaplin, 1st Viscount, 1840–1923, vol. II (A)

Chaplin, 2nd Viscount, 1877–1949, vol. IV

Chaplin, 3rd Viscount, 1906–1981, vol. VIII

Chaplin, Alan Geoffrey Tunstal, 1908–1967, vol. VI

Chaplin, Arnold; *see* Chaplin, T. H. A.

Chaplin, Sir Charles Spencer, 1889–1977, vol. VII

Chaplin, Sir Drummond Percy; *see* Chaplin, Sir F. D. P.

Chaplin, Sir (Francis) Drummond Percy, 1866–1933, vol. III

Chaplin, Frederick Leslie, 1905–1977, vol. VII

Chaplin, Sir George Frederick, 1900–1975, vol. VII

Chaplin, Brig.-Gen. James Graham, 1873–1956, vol. V

Chaplin, Col John Worthy, 1840–1920, vol. II

Chaplin, (T. H.) Arnold, 1864–1944, vol. IV

Chaplin, Rev. W. Knight, 1863–1951, vol. V

Chaplin, William Robert, 1888–1974, vol. VII

Chapling, Norman Charles, 1903–1986, vol. VIII

Chapman, Abel, 1851–1929, vol. III

Chapman, Captain Alexander Colin, 1897–1970, vol. VI

Chapman, Alfred Chaston, 1869–1932, vol. III

Chapman, Allan, 1897–1966, vol. VI

Chapman, (Anthony) Colin (Bruce), 1928–1982, vol. VIII

Chapman, Brig.-Gen. Archibald John, 1862–1950, vol. IV

Chapman, Sir Arthur, 1851–1918, vol. II

Chapman, Sir Arthur Wakefield, 1849–1926, vol. II

Chapman, Hon. Sir Austin, 1864–1926, vol. II

Chapman, Sir Benjamin Rupert, 6th Bt, 1865–1914, vol. I

Chapman, Brian, 1923–1981, vol. VIII

Chapman, Rev. C., 1828–1922, vol. II

Chapman, Cecil Maurice, 1852–1938, vol. III

Chapman, Charles Williams, 1843–1941, vol. IV

Chapman, Very Rev. Clifford Thomas, 1913–1982, vol. VIII

Chapman, Colin; *see* Chapman, A. C. B.

Chapman, Rear-Adm. Cuthbert Godfrey, 1862–1931, vol. III

Chapman, David Leonard, 1869–1958, vol. V

Chapman, Col David Phelips, 1855–1939, vol. III

Chapman, Dorothy, 1878–1967, vol. VI

Chapman, Edmund Pelly, 1867–1923, vol. II

Chapman, Edward, *died* 1906, vol. I

Chapman, Gen. Sir Edward Francis, 1840–1926, vol. II

Chapman, Edward Henry, 1874–1933, vol. III

Chapman, Rev. Edward William, 1841–1919, vol. II

Chapman, Captain Ernest John Collis, 1876–1958, vol. V

Chapman, Fitzroy Tozer, 1880–1976, vol. VII

Chapman, Frank M., 1864–1945, vol. IV

Chapman, Ven. Frank Robert, *died* 1924, vol. II

Chapman, Col Frederic Hamilton, 1863–1925, vol. II

Chapman, Frederick, 1864–1943, vol. II

Chapman, Sir Frederick Revans, 1849–1936, vol. III

Chapman, Lt-Col Frederick S.; *see* Spencer Chapman.

Chapman, Guy Patterson, 1889–1972, vol. VII

Chapman, Maj.-Gen. Hamilton, 1835–1926, vol. II

Chapman, Harold Thomas, 1896–1985, vol. VIII

Chapman, Henry, *died* 1908, vol. I

Chapman, Sir Henry, *died* 1947, vol. IV

Chapman, Henry George, 1879–1934, vol. III

Chapman, Rt Rev. Henry Palmer, 1865–1933, vol. III

Chapman, Col Herbert Alexander, 1858–1939, vol. III

Chapman, Mrs Hester Wolferstan, (Mrs R. L. Griffin), 1899–1976, vol. VII

Chapman, Air Vice-Marshal Hubert Huntlea, 1910–1972, vol. VII

Chapman, Rev. Hugh Boswell, *died* 1933, vol. III

Chapman, Rev. James, 1849–1913, vol. I

Chapman, James Ernest, *died* 1941, vol. IV

Chapman, Rt Rev. John; *see* Chapman, Rt Rev. H. P.

Chapman, Maj.-Gen. John Austin, 1896–1963, vol. VI

Chapman, Kenneth Herbert, 1908–1989, vol. VIII

Chapman, Brig.-Gen. Lawrence Joseph, 1867–1930, vol. III

Chapman, Lewis, 1890–1963, vol. VI

Chapman, Martin, 1846–1924, vol. II

Chapman, Sir Montagu Richard, 5th Bt (*cr* 1782), 1853–1907, vol. I

Chapman, Mrs Murray, (Olive Chapman), *died* 1977, vol. VII

Chapman, Olive; *see* Chapman, Mrs Murray.

Chapman, Oscar Littleton, 1896–1978, vol. VII

Chapman, Rev. Percy Hugh, 1866–1953, vol. V

Chapman, Col Philip Francis, 1870–1956, vol. V

Chapman, Col Sir Robert, 1st Bt (*cr* 1958), 1880–1963, vol. VI

Chapman, Robert Barclay, 1829–1909, vol. I
Chapman, Robert Hall, 1890–1953, vol. V
Chapman, Sir Robert William, 1866–1942, vol. IV
Chapman, Robert William, 1881–1960, vol. V
Chapman, Sir Robin (Robert Macgowan), 2nd Bt, 1911–1987, vol. VIII
Chapman, Air Chief Marshal Sir Ronald I.; see Ivelaw-Chapman.
Chapman, Sir Samuel, 1859–1947, vol. IV
Chapman, Sydney, 1888–1970, vol. VI
Chapman, Sir Sydney John, 1871–1951, vol. V
Chapman, Rt Rev. Thomas Alfred, 1867–1949, vol. IV
Chapman, Thomas Algernon, 1842–1921, vol. II
Chapman, Sir Thomas Robert Tighe, 7th Bt (cr 1782), 1846–1919, vol. II
Chapman, William Arthur, 1849–1917, vol. II
Chapman, Major William P.; see Percy-Chapman.
Chapman-Andrews, Sir Edwin Arthur, 1903–1980, vol. VII
Chapman-Huston, Major Desmond Wellesley William Desmond Mountjoy, died 1952, vol. V
Chapman-Mortimer, William Charles, 1907–1988, vol. VIII
Chappel, Rev. William Haighton, 1860–1922, vol. II
Chappell, Sir Ernest, 1864–1943, vol. IV
Chappell, Robert Kingsley, 1884–1937, vol. III
Chappell, T. Stanley, died 1933, vol. III
Chapple, Charles Roberts, 1874–1965, vol. VI
Chapple, Frederic, 1845–1924, vol. II
Chapple, Harold, 1881–1945, vol. IV
Chapple, Paymaster Rear-Adm. Sir John Henry George, 1859–1925, vol. II
Chapple, Stanley, 1900–1987, vol. VIII
Chapple, William Allan, 1864–1936, vol. III
Chapuis, Mgr Marie Auguste, 1869–1930, vol. III
Chaput de Saintonge, Rev. Rolland Alfred Aimé, 1912–1989, vol. VIII
Charbonneau, Most Rev. Joseph, died 1959, vol. V
Charbonneau, Napoleon, 1853–1916, vol. II
Charcot, Dr Jean Baptiste Etienne Auguste, 1867–1936, vol. III
Chari, P. N., vol. III
Charkhari, HH Maharaja Dhiraj Sipah-Darul-Mulk Sir Malkhan Sinh Ju Dev Bahadur, 1872–1908, vol. I
Charkhari State, HH Maharaja-Dhiraja Sipahdar-ul-Mulk Arimardan Singh Ju Deo Bahadur, 1903–1941, vol. IV
Charlemont, 7th Viscount, 1830–1913, vol. I
Charlemont, 8th Viscount, 1880–1949, vol. IV
Charlemont, 9th Viscount, 1887–1964, vol. VI
Charlemont, 10th Viscount, 1881–1967, vol. VI
Charlemont, 11th Viscount, 1884–1971, vol. VII
Charlemont, 12th Viscount, 1887–1979, vol. VII
Charlemont, 13th Viscount (Ireland), 1899–1985, vol. VIII
Charles, Captain Sir Allen Aitchison Havelock, 2nd Bt, 1887–1936, vol. III
Charles, Anthony Harold, 1908–1990, vol. VIII
Charles, Rt Hon. Sir Arthur, 1839–1921, vol. II
Charles, Sir Arthur Eber Sydney, 1910–1965, vol. VI
Charles, Enid, 1894–1972, vol. VII

Charles, Brig. Eric Montagu Seton, 1878–1964, vol. VI
Charles, Sir Ernest Bruce, 1871–1950, vol. IV
Charles, Rev. George B., 1862–1936, vol. III
Charles, Rt Rev. Harold John, 1914–1987, vol. VIII
Charles, Rev. James Hamilton, 1854–1939, vol. III
Charles, Lt-Gen. Sir (James) Ronald (Edmondston), 1875–1955, vol. V
Charles, Cdre Sir James Thomas Walter, 1865–1928, vol. II
Charles, Sir John Alexander, died 1971, vol. VII
Charles, John James, 1845–1912, vol. I
Charles, Sir John Pendrill, 1914–1984, vol. VIII
Charles, John Roger, 1872–1962, vol. VI
Charles, Sir Noel Hughes Havelock, 3rd Bt, 1891–1975, vol. VII
Charles, Maj.-Gen. Sir Richard Havelock, 1st Bt, 1858–1934, vol. III
Charles, Ven. Robert Henry, 1855–1931, vol. III
Charles, Robert Henry, 1882–1951, vol. V
Charles, Robert Lonsdale, 1916–1977, vol. VII
Charles, Lt-Gen. Sir Ronald; see Charles, Lt-Gen. Sir J. R. E.
Charles, Rev. Canon Sebastian, 1932–1989, vol. VIII
Charles, Captain Ulick de Burgh, 1884–1947, vol. IV
Charles, William Travers, 1908–1990, vol. VIII
Charles-Edwards, Rt Rev. Lewis Mervyn, 1902–1983, vol. VIII
Charles-Roux, François, 1879–1961, vol. VI
Charleson, Ian, 1949–1990, vol. VIII
Charlesworth, Albany Hawke, 1854–1914, vol. I
Charlesworth, Col Henry, 1851–1926, vol. II
Charlesworth, John, 1893–1957, vol. V
Charlesworth, John Kaye, 1889–1972, vol. VII
Charlesworth, Lilian E., died 1970, vol. VI
Charlesworth, Rev. Martin Percival, 1895–1950, vol. IV
Charleton, Henry Charles, 1870–1959, vol. V
Charley, Col Harold Richard, 1875–1956, vol. V
Charley, Sir Philip Belmont, 1893–1976, vol. VII
Charley, Sir William Thomas, 1833–1904, vol. I
Charlot, André Eugene Maurice, 1882–1956, vol. V
Charlton, Archibald Campbell, 1877–1952, vol. V
Charlton, Brig.-Gen. Claud Edward Charles Graham, died 1961, vol. VI
Charlton, Adm. Sir Edward Francis Benedict, 1865–1937, vol. III
Charlton, George, 1899–1979, vol. VII
Charlton, Henry Buckley, 1890–1961, vol. VI
Charlton, Hon. John, 1829–1910, vol. I
Charlton, John, died 1917, vol. II
Charlton, Air Cdre Lionel Evelyn Oswald, 1879–1958, vol. V
Charlton, Matthew, 1866–1948, vol. IV
Charlton, Sir William Arthur, 1893–1983, vol. VIII
Charlton, Captain William Henry, 1876–1950, vol. IV
Charlton-Meyrick, Col Sir Thomas, 1st Bt, 1837–1921, vol. II
Charmes, Francis, 1848–1916, vol. II
Charnley, Sir John, 1911–1982, vol. VIII
Charnock, George Frederick, 1860–1929, vol. III
Charnwood, 1st Baron, 1864–1945, vol. IV
Charnwood, 2nd Baron, 1901–1955, vol. V
Charoux, Siegfried Joseph, 1896–1967, vol. VI

Charpentier, Gustave, 1860–1956, vol. V
Charques, Mrs Dorothy, (Mrs S. A. G. Emms), 1899–1976, vol. VII
Charrington, Captain Eric, 1872–1927, vol. II
Charrington, Lt-Col Francis, 1858–1921, vol. II
Charrington, Frederick Nicholas, 1850–1936, vol. III
Charrington, John, 1856–1939, vol. III
Charrington, Sir John, 1886–1977, vol. VII
Charrington, John Arthur Pepys, 1905–1979, vol. VII
Charrington, Spencer, 1818–1904, vol. I
Charrington, Lt-Col Sydney Herbert, 1878–1954, vol. V
Charry, Sir Vembakkam C. D.; see Desika-Charry.
Chart, Edwin, 1848–1926, vol. II
Charteris, Very Rev. Archibald Hamilton, 1835–1908, vol. I
Charteris, Archibald Hamilton, 1874–1940, vol. III
Charteris, Hon. Sir Evan, 1864–1940, vol. III
Charteris, Francis James, 1875–1964, vol. VI
Charteris, Hon. Guy Lawrence, 1886–1967, vol. VI
Charteris, Hugo Francis Guy, 1922–1970, vol. VI
Charteris, Brig.-Gen. John, 1877–1946, vol. IV
Charteris, Col Nigel Keppel, 1878–1967, vol. VI
Charters, Col Alexander Burnet, 1876–1948, vol. IV
Chase, Anya Seton; see Seton, A.
Chase, Beatrice; see Parr, Olive Katharine.
Chase, Rev. Drummond Percy, 1820–1902, vol. I
Chase, Rt Rev. Frederic Henry, 1853–1925, vol. II
Chase, Rt Rev. George Armitage, 1886–1971, vol. VII
Chase, Lewis, 1873–1937, vol. III (A), vol. IV
Chase, Marian Emma, 1844–1905, vol. I
Chase, Mary Ellen, 1887–1973, vol. VII
Chase, Stuart, 1888–1985, vol. VIII
Chase, William Henry, 1880–1965, vol. VI
Chase, Col William St Lucian, 1856–1908, vol. I
Chase-Casgrain, Alexandre; see Casgrain.
Chastel De Boinville, Rev. Basil William, died 1943, vol. IV
Chastenet de Castaing, Jacques, 1893–1978, vol. VII
Chasteney, Howard Everson, 1888–1947, vol. IV
Chatelain, Henri Louis, 1877–1915, vol. I
Chater, Maj.-Gen. Arthur Reginald, 1896–1979, vol. VII
Chater, Sir Catchick Paul, 1846–1926, vol. II
Chater, Daniel, 1870–1959, vol. V
Chater, Col Vernor, 1842–1923, vol. II
Chatfeild-Clarke, Sir Edgar, 1863–1925, vol. II
Chatfield, 1st Baron, 1873–1967, vol. VI
Chatfield, Adm. Alfred John, 1831–1910, vol. I
Chatfield, George Ernle, 1875–1930, vol. III
Chatfield-Taylor, Hobart Chatfield, 1865–1945, vol. IV
Chatham, William, 1859–1940, vol. III
Chattaway, Edward, 1873–1956, vol. V
Chattaway, Frederick Daniel, died 1944, vol. IV
Chatterjee, Sir Atul Chandra, 1874–1955, vol. V
Chatterjee, Gopal Chunder, 1873–1953, vol. V
Chatterji, Sir Nalini Ranjan, died 1942, vol. IV
Chatterji, Sir Protul Chandra, 1848–1917, vol. II
Chatterton, Sir Alfred, 1866–1958, vol. V
Chatterton, Edward Keble, 1878–1944, vol. IV
Chatterton, Rt Rev. Eyre, 1863–1950, vol. IV

Chatterton, Col Frank Beauchamp Macaulay, 1873–1934, vol. III
Chatterton, Col Frank William, 1839–1924, vol. II
Chatterton, Frederick, died 1934, vol. III
Chatterton, Rev. Sir Percy, 1898–1984, vol. VIII
Chattisham, 1st Baron, 1886–1945, vol. IV
Chattock, Arthur Prince, 1860–1934, vol. III
Chatwin, Bruce; see Chatwin, C. B.
Chatwin, (Charles) Bruce, 1940–1989, vol. VIII
Chau, Hon. Sir Sik-Nin, born 1903, vol. VIII
Chau Tsun-Nin, Sir, 1893–1971, vol. VII
Chaubal, Sir Mahadev Bhaskar, 1857–1933, vol. III
Chaudhuri, Asutosh, 1860–1924, vol. II
Chaumeix, André, 1874–1955, vol. V
Chauncy, Col Charles Henry Kemble, died 1945, vol. IV
Chauncy, Maj. Frederick Charles Leslie, 1904–1986, vol. VIII
Chauvel, Gen. Sir Henry George, 1865–1945, vol. IV
Chauvel, Jean Michel Henri, 1897–1979, vol. VII
Chauvel, Ven. John Henry Allan, 1895–1946, vol. IV
Chavan, Yeshwantrao Balvantrao, 1913–1984, vol. VIII
Chavasse, Rt Rev. Christopher Maude, 1884–1962, vol. VI
Chavasse, Rt Rev. Francis James, 1846–1928, vol. II
Chavasse, Michael Louis Maude, 1923–1983, vol. VIII
Chavasse, Sir Thomas Frederick, 1854–1913, vol. I
Chave, Captain Sir Benjamin, 1870–1954, vol. V
Chave, Elmer Hargreaves, 1891–1957, vol. V
Chawner, William, 1848–1911, vol. I
Chaworth-Musters, Col John Nevile, 1890–1970, vol. VI
Chaytor, Alfred Henry, 1869–1931, vol. III
Chaytor, Lt-Col Clervaux Alexander, died 1941, vol. IV
Chaytor, Col D'Arcy, 1873–1960, vol. V
Chaytor, Sir Edmund Hugh, 6th Bt, 1876–1935, vol. III
Chaytor, Maj.-Gen. Sir Edward Walter Clervaux, 1868–1939, vol. III
Chaytor, Rev. Henry John, 1871–1954, vol. V
Chaytor, Lt-Col John Clervaux, 1888–1964, vol. VI
Chaytor, Sir Walter Clervaux, 5th Bt, 1874–1913, vol. I
Chaytor, Sir William Henry Clervaux, 7th Bt, 1914–1976, vol. VII
Chaytor, Sir William Henry Edward, 4th Bt, 1867–1908, vol. I
Cheadle, Walter Butler, 1835–1910, vol. I
Cheape, Brig.-Gen. (George) Ronald (Hamilton), 1881–1957, vol. V
Cheape, Lt-Col Hugh Annesley Gray-, 1878–1918, vol. II
Cheape, James, 1853–1943, vol. IV
Cheape, Brig.-Gen. Ronald; see Cheape, Brig.-Gen. G. R. H.
Cheatle, Arthur Henry, 1866–1929, vol. III
Cheatle, Sir (George) Lenthal, 1865–1951, vol. V
Cheatle, Sir Lenthal; see Cheatle, Sir G. L.
Checkland, Sydney George, 1916–1986, vol. VIII
Checkley, Frank S., died 1918, vol. II
Cheeseman, A. K. A.; see Wymark, Patrick Carl.

Cheeseman, Eric Arthur, 1912–1987, vol. VIII
Cheeseman, Harold Ambrose Robinson, 1889–1961, vol. VI
Cheeseman, Lt-Col William Joseph Robert, 1894–1938, vol. III
Cheesewright, William Frederick, *died* 1934, vol. III
Cheesman, Rev. Alfred Hunter, 1864–1941, vol. IV
Cheesman, Evelyn; *see* Cheesman, L. E.
Cheesman, (Lucy) Evelyn, 1881–1969, vol. VI
Cheesman, Col Robert Ernest, 1878–1962, vol. VI
Cheetham, Rev. Canon Frederic Philip, 1890–1970, vol. VI
Cheetham, Maj.-Gen. Geoffrey, 1891–1962, vol. VI
Cheetham, Rt Rev. Henry, 1827–1899, vol. I
Cheetham, Rt Hon. John Frederick, 1835–1916, vol. II
Cheetham, Sir Milne, 1869–1938, vol. III
Cheetham, Ven. Samuel, 1827–1908, vol. I
Cheever, John, 1912–1982, vol. VIII
Chegwidden, Sir Thomas Sidney, 1895–1986, vol. VIII
Cheiro; *see* Hamon, Count Louis
Cheke, Sir Marcus John, 1906–1960, vol. V
Chelmick, William George Hamar, 1882–1969, vol. VI
Chelmsford, 1st Viscount, 1868–1933, vol. III
Chelmsford, 2nd Viscount, 1903–1970, vol. VI
Chelmsford, Viscountess; (Frances Charlotte), 1869–1957, vol. V
Chelmsford, 2nd Baron, 1827–1905, vol. I
Chelsea, Viscount; Edward George Humphry John Cadogan, 1903–1910, vol. I
Chelsea, Viscount; Henry Arthur Cadogan, 1868–1908, vol. I
Chelwood, Baron (Life Peer); Tufton Victor Hamilton Beamish, 1917–1989, vol. VIII
Chenevix-Trench, Anthony, 1919–1979, vol. VII
Chenevix-Trench, Col Arthur Henry, 1884–1968, vol. VI
Chenevix-Trench, Charles Godfrey, 1877–1964, vol. VI
Chenevix-Trench, Lt-Col George Frederick, 1859–1937, vol. III
Chenevix-Trench, Col Lawrence, 1883–1958, vol. V
Chenevix-Trench, Brig. Ralph, 1885–1974, vol. VII
Chenevix-Trench, Lt-Col Sir Richard Henry, 1876–1954, vol. V
Cheney, Christopher Robert, 1906–1987, vol. VIII
Cheney, E. John, 1862–1921, vol. II
Cheng, F. T.; *see* Cheng, Tien-Hsi.
Cheng, Tien-Hsi, (F. T. Cheng), 1884–1970, vol. VI
Chéret, Jules, 1836–1932, vol. III
Chermside, Lt-Gen. Sir Herbert Charles, 1850–1929, vol. III
Cherniavsky, Mischel, 1893–1982, vol. VIII
Cherrington, Rt Rev. Cecil Arthur, *died* 1950, vol. IV
Cherry, Sir Benjamin Lennard, 1869–1932, vol. III
Cherry, Colin; *see* Cherry, E. C.
Cherry, (Edward) Colin, 1914–1979, vol. VII
Cherry, Sir John Arnold, 1879–1950, vol. IV
Cherry, Rt Hon. Richard Robert, 1859–1923, vol. II
Cherry, Sir Thomas MacFarland, 1898–1966, vol. VI
Cherry-Garrard, Maj.-Gen. Apsley, 1832–1907, vol. I

Cherry-Garrard, Apsley George Benet, 1886–1959, vol. V
Cherwell, 1st Viscount, 1886–1957, vol. V
Chesebrough, Robert Augustus, 1837–1933, vol. III
Chesham, 3rd Baron, 1850–1907, vol. I
Chesham, 4th Baron, 1894–1952, vol. V
Chesham, 5th Baron, 1916–1989, vol. VIII
Cheshire, Frederic John, 1860–1939, vol. III
Cheshire, Geoffrey Chevalier, 1886–1978, vol. VII
Cheshire, Rt Rev. Joseph Blount, 1850–1932, vol. III
Cheshire, Comdt Dame Mary Kathleen, 1902–1972, vol. VII
Cheshire, Air Chief Marshal Sir Walter Graemes, 1907–1978, vol. VII
Chesney, Col Alexander George, 1858–1939, vol. III
Chesney, Lt-Col Clement Hope Rawdon, 1883–1962, vol. VI
Chesney, Col Harold Frank, 1859–1920, vol. II
Chesney, Kathleen, 1899–1976, vol. VII
Chesser, Elizabeth Sloan, *died* 1940, vol. III
Chesser, Eustace, 1902–1973, vol. VII
Chesshire, Rev. Reginald Stanley Pargeter, 1869–1940, vol. III
Chesson, Nora; *see* Hopper, N.
Chester, Cecil Harry, 1900–1964, vol. VI
Chester, Sir (Daniel) Norman, 1907–1986, vol. VIII
Chester, Sir George, 1886–1949, vol. IV
Chester, Col Heneage Charles B.; *see* Bagot-Chester.
Chester, Sir Norman; *see* Chester, Sir D. N.
Chester-Master, Rev. Harold, 1889–1948, vol. IV
Chester-Master, Lt-Col Richard, 1870–1917, vol. II
Chester-Master, Thomas William Chester, 1841–1914, vol. I
Chester-Master, Col William Alfred, 1903–1963, vol. VI
Chesterfield, 10th Earl of, 1854–1933, vol. III
Chesterfield, 11th Earl of, 1855–1935, vol. III
Chesterfield, 12th Earl of, 1889–1952, vol. V
Chesterman, Sir Clement Clapton, 1894–1983, vol. VIII
Chesterton, Ada Elizabeth, (Mrs Cecil Chesterton), *died* 1962, vol. VI
Chesterton, Cecil Edward, 1879–1918, vol. II
Chesterton, Gilbert Keith, 1874–1936, vol. III
Cheston, Charles Sidney, *died* 1960, vol. V
Cheston, Evelyn, *died* 1929, vol. III
Chetham-Strode, Edward David, 1871–1958, vol. V
Chetham-Strode, Warren, 1896–1974, vol. VII
Chettiar, Rajah Sir Annamalai Chettiar of Chettinad, 1881–1948, vol. IV
Chettiar, Sir M. C. T. M.; *see* Muthiah Chettiar.
Chettiar, Sir Ramanatha A.; *see* Alagappa Chettiar.
Chettle, Major Henry Francis, 1882–1958, vol. V
Chettur, Govinda Krishna, 1898–1936, vol. III (A)
Chetty, Amatyasiromani Sir Bernard T. T.; *see* Thumboo Chetty.
Chetty, Sir Krishnarajapur Palligondé P.; *see* Puttanna Chetty.
Chetty, Sir Shanmukham, 1892–1953, vol. V
Chetwode, 1st Baron, 1869–1950, vol. IV
Chetwode, Adm. Sir George Knightley, 1877–1957, vol. V
Chetwynd, 7th Viscount, 1823–1911, vol. I
Chetwynd, 8th Viscount, 1863–1936, vol. III

Chetwynd, 9th Viscount, 1904–1965, vol. VI

Chetwynd, Sir (Arthur Henry) Talbot, 7th Bt, 1887–1972, vol. VII

Chetwynd, Lady Florence Cecilia; see Hastings, Marchioness of

Chetwynd, Sir George, 4th Bt, 1849–1917, vol. II

Chetwynd, Sir (George) Guy, 5th Bt, 1874–1935, vol. III

Chetwynd, Sir George Roland, 1916–1982, vol. VIII

Chetwynd, Sir Guy; see Chetwynd, Sir George G.

Chetwynd, Henry Goulburn Willoughby, 1858–1909, vol. I

Chetwynd, Hon. Richard Walter, 1859–1908, vol. I

Chetwynd, Sir Talbot; see Chetwynd, Sir A. H. T.

Chetwynd, Sir Victor James Guy, 6th Bt, 1902–1938, vol. III

Chetwynd-Stapylton, Col Bryan Henry, died 1958, vol. V

Chetwynd-Stapylton, Granville Brian, 1887–1964, vol. VI

Chetwynd-Stapylton, Lt-Gen. Granville George, 1823–1915, vol. I

Chetwynd-Stapylton, Rev. William, 1825–1919, vol. II

Chevalier, Albert, 1861–1923, vol. II

Chevalier, Maurice, 1888–1972, vol. VII

Chevallier, Captain Barrington Henry, 1851–1930, vol. III

Chevassût, Rev. Frederick George, died 1932, vol. III

Chevassût, Rev. Canon Frederick George, 1889–1974, vol. VII

Chevis, Sir William, 1864–1939, vol. III

Chevrier, Hon. Lionel, 1903–1987, vol. VIII

Chevrillon, André, 1864–1957, vol. V

Chew, Frederic Robert Gansel, 1907–1970, vol. VI

Cheylesmore, 2nd Baron, 1843–1902, vol. I

Cheylesmore, 3rd Baron, 1848–1925, vol. II

Cheylesmore, 4th Baron, 1893–1974, vol. VII

Cheyne, Brig. Douglas Gordon, 1889–1966, vol. VI

Cheyne, James, 1894–1973, vol. VII

Cheyne, Sir John, 1841–1907, vol. I

Cheyne, Col Sir Joseph Lister, 2nd Bt, 1888–1957, vol. V

Cheyne, Rev. Thomas Kelly, 1841–1915, vol. I

Cheyne, Sir Watson; see Cheyne, Sir William W.

Cheyne, Sir (William) Watson, 1st Bt, 1852–1932, vol. III

Cheyney, Peter, (Major Reginald Evelyn Peter Southouse-Cheyney), 1896–1951, vol. V

Cheyney, Major Reginald Evelyn Peter Southouse-; see Cheyney, Peter.

Chhajju Ram Chowdhry, Sir, born 1865, vol. V

Chhatarpur, Sir Maharaja of, 1866–1932, vol. III

Chhotu Ram, Rao Bahadur Chaudhri Sir, died 1945, vol. IV

Chhota Udepur, Maharawal Shri Natwarsinhji Fatehsinhji, Raja of, 1906–1946, vol. IV

Chiang, Yee, 1903–1977, vol. VII

Chiang Kai-Shek, Generalissimo, 1887–1975, vol. VII

Chiasson, Rt Rev. Patrice Alexandre, 1867–1942, vol. IV

Chiazzari, Comdr Nicholas William, 1868–1929, vol. III

Chibnall, Albert Charles, 1894–1988, vol. VIII

Chichele-Plowden, Sir Trevor John Chichele, 1846–1905, vol. I

Chichester, 4th Earl of, 1838–1902, vol. I

Chichester, 5th Earl of, 1844–1905, vol. I

Chichester, 6th Earl of, 1871–1926, vol. II

Chichester, 7th Earl of, 1905–1926, vol. II

Chichester, 8th Earl of, 1912–1944, vol. IV

Chichester, Lt-Col Alan, died 1947, vol. IV

Chichester, Maj.-Gen. Sir Arlington Augustus, 1863–1948, vol. IV

Chichester, Sir Arthur, 8th Bt, 1822-1898, vol. I

Chichester, Lt-Col Arthur O'Neill Cubitt, 1889–1972, vol. VII

Chichester, Most Rev. Aston, 1879–1962, vol. VI

Chichester, Rear-Adm. Sir Edward, 9th Bt, 1849–1906, vol. I

Chichester, Rev. Edward Arthur, 1849–1925, vol. II

Chichester, Sir Edward George, 10th Bt, 1888–1940, vol. III

Chichester, Sir Francis, 1901–1972, vol. VII

Chichester, Hon. Sir Gerald Henry Crofton, 1886–1939, vol. III

Chichester, Lord Henry Fitzwarine, 1834–1928, vol. II

Chichester, Maj.-Gen. Robert Bruce, 1825–1902, vol. I

Chichester, Col Robert Peel Dawson Spencer, 1873–1921, vol. II

Chichester-Clark, Captain James Lenox, 1884–1933, vol. III

Chichester-Constable, Brig. Raleigh Charles Joseph, 1890–1963, vol. VI

Chichester-Constable, Walter George Raleigh, 1863–1942, vol. IV

Chichester Smith, Charles Henry, 1897–1966, vol. VI

Chick, Sir (Alfred) Louis, 1904–1972, vol. VII

Chick, Dame Harriette, 1875–1977, vol. VII

Chick, Herbert George, 1882–1951, vol. V

Chick, Sir Louis; see Chick, Sir A. L.

Chiene, George Lyall, 1873–1951, vol. V

Chiene, John, 1843–1923, vol. II

Chiesman, Sir Walter Eric, 1900–1973, vol. VII

Chifley, Rt Hon. Joseph Benedict, 1885–1951, vol. V

Chignell, Rev. Hugh Scott, died 1950, vol. IV

Chilcott, Rear-Adm. Ronald Evered, 1876–1935, vol. III

Chilcott, Lt-Comdr Sir Warden Stanley, 1871–1942, vol. IV

Chilcott, William Winsland, 1848–1915, vol. I

Child, Arthur, 1852–1902, vol. I

Child, Sir Coles, 1st Bt (cr 1919), 1862–1929, vol. III

Child, Major Sir (Coles) John, 2nd Bt (cr 1919), 1906–1971, vol. VII

Child, Harold Hannyngton, 1869–1945, vol. IV

Child, Lieut Herbert Alexander, died 1914, vol. I

Child, Brig.-Gen. Sir Hill; see Child, Brig.-Gen. Sir S. H.

Child, Major Sir John; see Child, Major Sir C. J.

Child, Ven. Kenneth, 1916–1983, vol. VIII

Child, Rev. Robert Leonard, 1891–1971, vol. VII

Child, Brig.-Gen. Sir (Smith) Hill, 2nd Bt (cr 1868), 1880–1958, vol. V

Childe, Rev. Christopher Venn, died 1937, vol. III

Childe, Col Ralph Bromfield Willington F.; *see* Fisher-Childe.

Childe, V. Gordon, 1892–1957, vol. V

Childe, Wilfred Rowland Mary, 1890–1952, vol. V

Childe-Pemberton, William Shakespear, 1859–1924, vol. II

Childers, Charles Edward Eardley, 1851–1931, vol. III

Childers, Col Edmund Spencer Eardley, 1854–1919, vol. II

Childers, Lt-Comdr Erskine; *see* Childers, Lt-Comdr R. E.

Childers, Erskine Hamilton, 1905–1974, vol. VII

Childers, Lt-Col Hugh Francis Eardley, 1886–1941, vol. IV

Childers, Lt-Comdr (Robert) Erskine, 1870–1922, vol. II

Childs, Maj.-Gen. Sir (Borlase Elward) Wyndham, 1876–1946, vol. IV

Childs, Most Rev. Derrick Greenslade, 1918–1987, vol. VIII

Childs, Hubert, 1905–1983, vol. VIII

Childs, Leonard, 1897–1982, vol. VIII

Childs, William Macbride, 1869–1939, vol. III

Childs, Maj.-Gen. Sir Wyndham; *see* Childs, Maj.-Gen. Sir B. E. W.

Childs-Clarke, Col Charles, 1861–1934, vol. III

Childs-Clarke, Rev. Septimus John, 1876–1964, vol. VI

Chilston, 1st Viscount, 1851–1926, vol. II

Chilston, 2nd Viscount, 1876–1947, vol. IV

Chilston, 3rd Viscount, 1910–1982, vol. VIII

Chilton, Rev. Arthur, 1864–1947, vol. IV

Chilton, Charles, 1860–1926, vol. III

Chilton, Donovan, 1909–1978, vol. VII

Chilton, Vice-Adm. Francis George Gillilan, 1879–1964, vol. VI

Chilton, Sir Henry Getty, 1877–1954, vol. V

Chilton, Lt-Gen. Sir Maurice Somerville, 1898–1956, vol. V

Chilver, Guy Edward Farquhar, 1910–1982, vol. VIII

Chilver, Richard Clementson, 1912–1985, vol. VIII

Chilvers, Rev. H. Tydeman, 1872–1963, vol. VI

Chimay, Lt-Col Prince Alphonse de, 1899–1973, vol. VII

China, William Edward, 1895–1979, vol. VII

Chinda, Count Sutemi, 1856–1929, vol. III

Chinn, Wilfred Henry, 1901–1970, vol. VI

Chinnery, E. W. Pearson, 1887–1972, vol. VII

Chinnery-Haldane, James Brodrick, 1868–1941, vol. IV

Chinnery-Haldane, Rt Rev. James Robert Alexander, 1842–1906, vol. I

Chinoy, Hon. Fazulbhoy Meherally, *died* 1915, vol. I

Chinoy, Sir Rahimtoola Meherally, 1882–1957, vol. V

Chinoy, Sir Sultan Meherally, 1885–1968, vol. VI

Chintamani, Sir Chirravoori Yajneswara, 1880–1941, vol. IV

Chipman, Warwick Fielding, 1880–1967, vol. VI

Chippindall, Lt-Gen. Edward, 1827–1902, vol. I

Chippindall, Sir Giles Tatlock, 1893–1969, vol. VI

Chirgwin, Rev. Arthur Mitchell, 1885–1966, vol. VI

Chirico, Giorgio de, 1888–1978, vol. VII

Chirnside, Captain John Percy, 1856–1944, vol. IV

Chirol, Sir Valentine, 1852–1929, vol. III

Chisholm, Rt Rev. Aeneas, 1836–1918, vol. II

Chisholm, Sir (Albert) Roderick, 1897–1967, vol. VI

Chisholm, Ven. Alexander, 1887–1975, vol. VII

Chisholm, Alexander Hugh, 1890–1977, vol. VII

Chisholm, Dame Alice, 1856–1954, vol. V

Chisholm, Brock; *see* Chisholm, G. B.

Chisholm, Catherine, 1878–1952, vol. V

Chisholm, Hon. Christopher P., 1854–1934, vol. III

Chisholm, (George) Brock, 1896–1971, vol. VII

Chisholm, George Goudie, 1850–1930, vol. III

Chisholm, Sir Henry, 1900–1981, vol. VIII

Chisholm, Hugh, 1866–1924, vol. II

Chisholm, Col Hugh Alexander, 1883–1940, vol. III (A), vol. IV

Chisholm, John, 1857–1929, vol. III

Chisholm, Most Rev. John Wallace, 1922–1975, vol. VII

Chisholm, Hon. Sir Joseph Andrew, 1863–1950, vol. IV

Chisholm, Dr Murdoch, *died* 1929, vol. III

Chisholm, Sir Roderick; *see* Chisholm, Sir A. R.

Chisholm, Roderick William, 1925–1979, vol. VII

Chisholm, Ronald George, 1910–1972, vol. VII

Chisholm, Sir Samuel, 1st Bt, 1836–1923, vol. II

Chisholm, William Wilson, 1854–1935, vol. III

Chitham, Sir Charles Carter, 1886–1972, vol. VII

Chitnavis, Sir Gangadhar Madhav, 1863–1929, vol. III

Chitnavis, Sir Shankar Madhavi, 1863–1931, vol. III

Chitral, Major HH Muhammad Sir Nasir-ul-Mulk, Mehtar of, 1898–1943, vol. IV

Chittenden, Frederick James, 1873–1950, vol. IV

Chittenden, Russell Henry, 1856–1943, vol. IV

Chitty, Anthony Merlott, 1907–1976, vol. VII

Chitty, Sir Arthur, 1864–1948, vol. IV

Chitty, Arthur Whatley, 1824–1905, vol. I

Chitty, Sir Charles William, 1859–1932, vol. III

Chitty, Sir Henry Willes; *see* Chitty, Sir T. H. W.

Chitty, Sir Joseph Henry Pollock, 1861–1942, vol. IV

Chitty, Rt Hon. Sir Joseph William, 1828–1899, vol. I

Chitty, Letitia, 1897–1982, vol. VIII

Chitty, Sir (Thomas) Henry Willes, 2nd Bt, 1891–1955, vol. V

Chitty, Sir Thomas Willes, 1st Bt, 1855–1930, vol. III

Chitty, Rev. Walter Henry, 1867–1940, vol. III

Chitty, Col Walter Willis, 1866–1933, vol. III

Chivers, Edgar Warren, 1906–1979, vol. VII

Chivers, Stephen Oswald, 1899–1975, vol. VII

Chlapowska, Helena M.; *see* Modjeska-Chlapowska.

Chloros, Alexander George, 1926–1982, vol. VIII

Choate, Joseph Hodges, 1832–1917, vol. II

Chodat, Robert, 1865–1934, vol. III

Choksy, Khan Bahadur Sir Nasarvanji Hormasji, 1861–1939, vol. III

Cholmeley, Francis William Alfred F.; *see* Fairfax-Cholmeley.

Cholmeley, Sir Hugh Arthur Henry, 3rd Bt (*cr* 1806), 1839–1904, vol. I

Cholmeley, Major Sir Hugh John Francis Sibthorp, 5th Bt (*cr* 1806), 1906–1964, vol. VI

Cholmeley, Sir Montague Aubrey Rowley, 4th Bt (*cr* 1806), 1876–1914, vol. I

Cholmeley, Norman Goodford, 1863–1947, vol. IV
Cholmeley, Robert Francis, 1862–1947, vol. IV
Cholmondeley, 4th Marquess of, 1858–1923, vol. II
Cholmondeley, 5th Marquess of, 1883–1968, vol. VI
Cholmondeley, 6th Marquess of, 1919–1990, vol. VIII
Cholmondeley, Lord George Hugo, 1887–1958, vol. V
Cholmondeley, Rev. Hon. Henry Pitt, 1820–1905, vol. I
Cholmondeley, Brig.-Gen. Hugh Cecil, 1852–1941, vol. IV
Cholmondeley, Mary, 1859–1925, vol. II
Cholmondeley-Pennell, Henry; *see* Pennell.
Chomley, Arthur Wolfe, 1837–1914, vol. I
Chomley, Charles Henry, 1868–1942, vol. IV
Chope, Brig. Arthur John Herbert, 1884–1942, vol. IV
Chope, Robert Charles, 1913–1988, vol. VIII
Chopping, Col Arthur, 1871–1951, vol. V
Chopra, Iqbal Chand, 1896–1976, vol. VII
Choquette, Rt Rev. Mgr Charles Philippe, *died* 1947, vol. IV
Choquette, Hon. Philippe Auguste, *born* 1854, vol. III
Chorley, 1st Baron, 1895–1978, vol. VII
Chorley, (Charles) Harold, 1912–1990, vol. VIII
Chorley, Harold; *see* Chorley, C. H.
Chorlton, Alan Ernest Leofric, 1874–1946, vol. IV
Chorlton, Rev. Samuel, *died* 1911, vol. I
Chotzner, Alfred James, 1873–1958, vol. V
Chou En-Lai, 1898–1976, vol. VII
Chouinard, Honore Julien Jean Baptiste, 1850–1928, vol. II
Chow, Sir Shou-Son, 1861–1959, vol. V
Chowdhury, Abu Sayeed, 1921–1987, vol. VIII
Chowdhury, Maharaja Sir Manmatha Nath Ray, *died* 1939, vol. III
Chown, Maj.-Gen. Ernest Edward, 1864–1922, vol. II
Chown, John, *died* 1922, vol. II
Choyce, Charles Coley, 1875–1937, vol. III
Chree, Charles, 1860–1928, vol. II
Chree, Sir William, 1858–1936, vol. III
Chrimes, Sir Bertram; *see* Chrimes, Sir W. B.
Chrimes, Stanley Bertram, 1907–1984, vol. VIII
Chrimes, Sir (William) Bertram, 1883–1972, vol. VII
Chris, A. Lauri; *see* Christensen, A. L.
Christ, George Elgie, 1904–1972, vol. VII
Christelow, Allan, 1911–1975, vol. VII
Christensen, Arent Lauri, (A. Lauri Chris), 1893–1982, vol. VIII
Christensen, Christian Neils, 1901–1982, vol. VIII
Christensen, Elsa, (Mrs Adolph Christensen); *see* Stralia, E.
Christian, Adm. Arthur Henry, 1863–1926, vol. II
Christian, Bertram, *died* 1953, vol. V
Christian, Rear-Adm. Charles Arbuthnot, 1862–1937, vol. III
Christian, Edmund Brown Viney, 1864–1938, vol. III
Christian, Brig.-Gen. Gerard, 1867–1930, vol. III
Christian, Adm. Henry, 1828–1916, vol. II
Christian, Henry A., 1876–1951, vol. V
Christian, Brig.-Gen. Sydney Ernest, 1867–1931, vol. III
Christian, Lt-Col William Francis, 1879–1954, vol. V
Christiansen, Arthur, 1904–1963, vol. VI
Christiansen, Michael Robin, 1927–1984, vol. VIII

Christie, Dame Agatha Mary Clarissa, 1890–1976, vol. VII
Christie, Alexander Wishart, 1871–1955, vol. V
Christie, Col Archibald, 1889–1962, vol. VI
Christie, Augustus Langham, 1857–1930, vol. III
Christie, Maj.-Gen. Campbell Manning, 1893–1963, vol. VI
Christie, Daniel Hall, 1881–1965, vol. VI
Christie, Dugald, 1855–1936, vol. III
Christie, Harold Alfred Hunter, 1884–1960, vol. V
Christie, Hon. Sir Harold George, 1896–1973, vol. VII
Christie, Herbert Bertram, 1863–1916, vol. II
Christie, Brig.-Gen. Herbert Willie Andrew, 1868–1946, vol. IV
Christie, James, *died* 1960, vol. V (A)
Christie, James Archibald, 1873–1958, vol. V
Christie, James Roberton, 1866–1932, vol. III
Christie, John, 1882–1962, vol. VI
Christie, John Denham, *died* 1950, vol. IV
Christie, John Traill, 1899–1980, vol. VII
Christie, Joseph MacNaughtan, 1871–1936, vol. III
Christie, Gp-Captain Malcolm Grahame, 1881–1971, vol. VII
Christie, Richard Copley, 1830–1901, vol. I
Christie, Ronald Victor, 1902–1986, vol. VIII
Christie, Walter Henry John, 1905–1983, vol. VIII
Christie, Sir William, 1896–1983, vol. VIII
Christie, Sir William Henry Mahoney, 1845–1922, vol. II
Christie, William Langham, 1830–1913, vol. I
Christie, Very Rev. William Leslie, 1858–1931, vol. III
Christie, William Lorenzo, 1858–1962, vol. VI
Christie-Miller, Col. Sir Geoffry, 1881–1969, vol. VI
Christie-Miller, Samuel Vandeleur, 1911–1968, vol. VI
Christie-Miller, Sydney Richardson, 1874–1931, vol. III
Christison, Sir Alexander, 2nd Bt, 1828–1918, vol. II
Christison, Sir Robert Alexander, 3rd Bt, 1870–1945, vol. IV
Christmas, E. W., *died* 1918, vol. II
Christoffelsz, Arthur Eric, *born* 1890, vol. VII
Christoffelsz, William Sperling, 1846–1937, vol. III
Christopher, Rev. Alfred Millard William, 1820–1913, vol. I
Christopher, Col Charles de Lona, 1885–1942, vol. IV
Christopher, Eleanor Caroline, 1873–1959, vol. V
Christopher, Sir George Perrin, 1890–1977, vol. VII
Christopher, Maj.-Gen. Leonard William, 1848–1927, vol. II
Christophers, Bt Col Sir Richard; *see* Christophers, Bt Col Sir S. R.
Christophers, Bt Col Sir (Samuel) Rickard, 1873–1978, vol. VII
Christopherson, Douglas, 1869–1944, vol. IV
Christopherson, John Brian, 1868–1955, vol. V
Christopherson, Very Rev. Noel Charles, *died* 1968, vol. VI
Christopherson, Stanley, *died* 1949, vol. IV
Christy, Cuthbert, 1863–1932, vol. III
Christy, Ronald Kington, 1905–1987, vol. VIII
Christy, Stephen Henry, 1879–1914, vol. I

Chrystal, George, 1851–1911, vol. I
Chrystal, Sir George William, 1880–1944, vol. IV
Chrystall, Brig. John Inglis, 1887–1960, vol. V
Chubb, Sir Cecil Herbert Edward, 1st Bt, 1876–1934, vol. III
Chubb, Hon. Charles Edward, 1845–1930, vol. III
Chubb, Gilbert Charles, died 1966, vol. VI
Chubb, Harry Emory, 1880–1960, vol. V
Chubb, Sir John Corbin, 2nd Bt, 1904–1957, vol. V
Chubb, Sir Lawrence Wensley, 1873–1948, vol. IV
Chudoba, František, 1878–1941, vol. IV
Chula-Chakrabongse of Thailand, HRH Prince, 1908–1963, vol. VI
Chulaparambil, Rt Rev. Alexander, 1877–1951, vol. V
Chunilal Bose, Rai Bahadur, 1861–1930, vol. III
Church, Rev. Alfred John, 1829–1912, vol. I
Church, Major Archibald George, 1886–1954, vol. V
Church, Arthur Frederick, 1868–1939, vol. III
Church, Arthur Harry, died 1937, vol. III
Church, Sir Arthur Herbert, 1834–1915, vol. I
Church, Col Arthur John Bromley, 1869–1954, vol. V
Church, Rev. Charles Marcus, died 1915, vol. I
Church, Eric Edmund Raitt, 1907–1972, vol. VII
Church, Brig. Sir Geoffrey Selby, 2nd Bt, 1887–1979, vol. VII
Church, Col George Earl, 1835–1910, vol. I
Church, Col George Ross Marryat, 1868–1940, vol. III
Church, Rev. Leslie Frederic, 1886–1961, vol. VI
Church, Richard Thomas, 1893–1972, vol. VII
Church, Robert William, 1882–1923, vol. II
Church, Samuel Harden, 1858–1943, vol. IV
Church, Maj.-Gen. Thomas Ross, 1831–1926, vol. II
Church, Vice-Adm. William Drummond, died 1937, vol. III
Church, Sir William Selby, 1st Bt, 1837–1928, vol. II
Churcher, Col Sir Arthur, 1871–1951, vol. V
Churchill, 1st Viscount, 1864–1934, vol. III
Churchill, 2nd Viscount, 1890–1973, vol. VII
Churchill, Surg.-Gen. Alexander Ferrier, 1839–1928, vol. II
Churchill, Col Arthur Gillespie, 1860–1940, vol. III
Churchill, Clementine Ogilvy S.; see Baroness Spencer-Churchill.
Churchill, Captain Edward George Spencer-, 1876–1964, vol. VI
Churchill, Lord Edward Spencer-, 1853–1911, vol. I
Churchill, George Percy, 1877–1973, vol. VII
Churchill, Hon. Gordon, 1898–1985, vol. VIII
Churchill, Harry Lionel, 1860–1924, vol. II
Churchill, Lord Ivor Charles Spencer, 1898–1956, vol. V
Churchill, Jennie Spencer; see Churchill, Lady Randolph Spencer.
Churchill, Brig. John Atherton, 1887–1965, vol. VI
Churchill, Very Rev. John Howard, 1920–1990, vol. VIII
Churchill, John Strange Spencer, 1880–1947, vol. IV
Churchill, Peter Morland, 1909–1972, vol. VII
Churchill, Hon. Randolph Frederick Edward Spencer, 1911–1968, vol. VI
Churchill, Lady Randolph Spencer, 1854–1921, vol. II

Churchill, Rev. Robert Reginald, 1890–1970, vol. VI
Churchill, Lt-Col Seton, died 1933, vol. III
Churchill, Sidney John Alexander, 1862–1921, vol. II
Churchill, Stella, died 1954, vol. V
Churchill, Maj.-Gen. Thomas Bell Lindsay, 1907–1990, vol. VIII
Churchill, William, 1859–1920, vol. II (A), vol. III
Churchill, William Foster Norton, 1898–1963, vol. VI
Churchill, Winston, 1871–1947, vol. IV
Churchill, Rt Hon. Sir Winston Leonard Spencer, 1874–1965, vol. VI
Churchman, Air Cdre Allan Robert, 1896–1970, vol. VI
Churchman, Sir William Alfred, 1st Bt, 1863–1947, vol. IV
Churchward, Captain Alaric Watts, 1845–1929, vol. III
Churchward, George Jackson, died 1933, vol. III
Churchward, Rev. Marcus Wellesley, 1860–1940, vol. III
Churchward, Col Paul Rycaut Stanbury, 1858–1935, vol. III
Churchward, Percy Albert, 1862–1924, vol. II
Churchward, William Brown, 1844–1920, vol. II
Churston, 2nd Baron, 1846–1910, vol. I
Churston, 3rd Baron, 1873–1930, vol. III
Churton, Rt Rev. Edward Townson, 1841–1912, vol. I
Churton, Rt Rev. Henry Norris, 1843–1904, vol. I
Churton, Ven. Theodore Townson, 1853–1915, vol. I
Churton, Lt-Col William Arthur Vere, 1876–1949, vol. IV
Chute, Ven. Anthony William, 1884–1958, vol. V
Chute, Sir Charles Lennard, 1st Bt, 1879–1956, vol. V
Chute, Ven. John Chaloner, 1881–1961, vol. VI
Chuter-Ede, Baron (Life-Peer); James Chuter Chuter-Ede, 1882–1965, vol. VI
Chwatt, Prof. Leonard Jan B.; see Bruce-Chwatt.
Ciano, Conte Cortellazzo, Galeazzo, 1903–1944, vol. IV
Cilcennin, 1st Viscount, 1903–1960, vol. V
Cilea, Francesco, 1866–1950, vol. IV
Cilento, Sir Raphael West, 1893–1985, vol. VIII
Cippico, Count Antonio, 1877–1935, vol. III
Citrine, 1st Baron, 1887–1983, vol. VIII
Civil, Alan, 1928–1989, vol. VIII
Clague, Ven. Arthur Ashford, 1915–1983, vol. VIII
Clague, Col Sir Douglas; see Clague, Col Sir J. D.
Clague, Sir John, 1882–1958, vol. V
Clague, Col Sir (John) Douglas, 1917–1981, vol. VIII
Clair, René, 1898–1981, vol. VIII
Clampett, Ven. Albert Wyndham, 1860–1953, vol. V
Clancarty, 5th Earl of, 1868–1929, vol. III
Clancarty, 6th Earl of, 1891–1971, vol. VII
Clancarty, 7th Earl of, 1902–1975, vol. VII
Clancey, John Charles, 1854–1932, vol. III
Clancy, Rt Rev. John, 1856–1912, vol. I
Clancy, John Joseph, 1847–1928, vol. II
Clancy, Sir John Sydney James, 1895–1970, vol. VI (AII)
Clanmorris, 5th Baron, 1852–1916, vol. II
Clanmorris, 6th Baron, 1879–1960, vol. V
Clanmorris, 7th Baron, 1908–1988, vol. VIII
Clanricarde, 2nd Marquis of, 1832–1916, vol. II

Clanwilliam, 4th Earl of, 1832–1907, vol. I
Clanwilliam, 5th Earl of, 1873–1953, vol. V
Clanwilliam, 6th Earl of; John Charles Edmund Carson Meade, 1914–1989, vol. VIII
Clapham, Sir Alfred William, 1883–1950, vol. IV
Clapham, Arthur Roy, 1904–1990, vol. VIII
Clapham, Edward William, *died* 1943, vol. IV
Clapham, Sir John Harold, 1873–1946, vol. IV
Clapin, Adolphus Philip, 1828–1914, vol. I
Clapp, Sir Harold Winthrop, 1875–1952, vol. V
Clappen, Air Cdre Donald William, 1895–1978, vol. VII
Clapperton, Alan Ernest, *died* 1931, vol. III
Clapperton, T. J., 1879–1962, vol. VI
Clarabut, Maj.-Gen. Reginald Blaxland, 1893–1977, vol. VII
Clare, Captain Chapman James, 1853–1940, vol. III
Clare, Sir Harcourt Everard, 1854–1922, vol. II
Clare, Henry Lewis, 1858–1920, vol. II
Clare, Mary, (Mrs L. Mawhood), 1892–1970, vol. VI
Clare, Octavius Leigh, 1841–1912, vol. I
Clare, Lt-Col Oliver Cecil, 1881–1933, vol. III
Clarendon, 5th Earl of, 1846–1915, vol. I
Clarendon, 6th Earl of, 1877–1955, vol. V
Clarendon, Very Rev. Thomas William, 1855–1934, vol. III
Claretie, Jules Arsène Arnaud, 1840–1913, vol. I
Clarina, 4th Baron, 1830–1897, vol. I
Clarina, 5th Baron, 1837–1922, vol. II
Clarina, 6th Baron, 1880–1952, vol. V
Claringbull, Sir Frank; *see* Claringbull, Sir G. F.
Claringbull, Sir (Gordon) Frank, 1911–1990, vol. VIII
Clark, Baron (Life Peer); Kenneth Mackenzie Clark, 1903–1983, vol. VIII
Clark, Adrian, 1889–1944, vol. IV
Clark, Albert Curtis, 1859–1937, vol. III
Clark, Alec Fulton Charles, 1898–1979, vol. VII
Clark, Alfred, 1873–1950, vol. IV
Clark, Alfred Alexander G.; *see* Gordon Clark.
Clark, Alfred Joseph, 1885–1941, vol. IV
Clark, Sir Allen George, 1898–1962, vol. VI
Clark, Andrew, *died* 1913, vol. I
Clark, Sir Andrew Edmund James, 3rd Bt (*cr* 1883), 1898–1979, vol. VII
Clark, Andrew Rutherfurd Clark, 1828–1899, vol. I
Clark, Sir Arthur; *see* Clark, Sir W. A. W.
Clark, Arthur Campbell S.; *see* Stuart-Clark.
Clark, Arthur L., 1873–1956, vol. V
Clark of Herriotshall, Arthur Melville, 1895–1990, vol. VIII
Clark, Sir Beresford; *see* Clark, Sir J. B.
Clark, Rt Rev. Bernard T., *died* 1916, vol. II
Clark, Vice-Adm. Sir Bouverie Francis, 1842–1922, vol. II
Clark, Brig. Cecil Horace, 1880–1958, vol. V
Clark, Charles Alexander, 1860–1939, vol. III
Clark, Rear-Adm. Charles Carr, 1902–1965, vol. VI
Clark, Charles Heber; *see* Adeler, M.
Clark, Lt-Col Charles Watson, *died* 1944, vol. IV
Clark, Col Charles Willoughby, 1888–1988, vol. VIII
Clark, Christopher, 1875–1942, vol. IV
Clark, Colin Grant, 1905–1989, vol. VIII
Clark, Cosmo; *see* Clark, J. C.

Clark, Lt-Col Craufurd Alexander G.; *see* Gordon-Clark.
Clark, Col D'Arcy Melville, *died* 1964, vol. VI
Clark, David Allen Richard, 1905–1986, vol. VIII
Clark, Donald George, 1868–1935, vol. III
Clark, Edmund Graham, 1889–1954, vol. V
Clark, Edwin Charles, 1835–1917, vol. II
Clark, Lt-Col Edwin Kitson, 1866–1943, vol. IV
Clark, Elisabeth; *see* Lutyens, E.
Clark, Sir Ernest, 1864–1951, vol. V
Clark, Sir Fife; *see* Clark, Sir T. F.
Clark, Francis, 1864–1940, vol. III
Clark, Rev. Francis E., *died* 1927, vol. II
Clark, Rev. Francis Storer, 1836–1909, vol. I
Clark, Rt Rev. (Frederick) Patrick, 1908–1954, vol. V
Clark, Gavin Brown, 1846–1930, vol. III
Clark, George Albert, 1894–1963, vol. VI
Clark, George Ernest, *died* 1919, vol. II
Clark, Sir George Ernest, 2nd Bt (*cr* 1917), 1882–1950, vol. IV
Clark, Sir George Norman, 1890–1979, vol. VII
Clark, Brig. George Philip, 1901–1977, vol. VII
Clark, George Sidney Roberts K.; *see* Kitson Clark.
Clark, Sir George Smith, 1st Bt (*cr* 1917), 1861–1935, vol. III
Clark, Sir (Gordon Colvin) Lindesay, 1896–1986, vol. VIII
Clark, Gowan Cresswell Strange, 1856–1929, vol. III
Clark, Harold Frederick, *died* 1957, vol. V
Clark, Henry, 1829–1900, vol. I
Clark, Henry Herbert G.; *see* Gordon Clark.
Clark, Sir Henry Laurence U.; *see* Urling Clark.
Clark, Rev. Henry W., 1869–1949, vol. IV
Clark, Captain Henry William Alfred, *died* 1935, vol. III
Clark, Most Rev. Howard Hewlett, 1903–1983, vol. VIII
Clark, James, 1859–1915, vol. I
Clark, James, *died* 1935, vol. III
Clark, James, *died* 1943, vol. IV
Clark, James, (Jim Clark), 1936–1968, vol. VI
Clark, James John, 1870–1936, vol. III
Clark, Captain James Lenox C.; *see* Chichester-Clark.
Clark, James Oscar Max, 1877–1958, vol. V
Clark, Col Sir James Richardson Andrew, 2nd Bt (*cr* 1883), 1852–1948, vol. IV
Clark, James Robert, 1844–1919, vol. II
Clark, James T.; *see* Towers-Clark.
Clark, James Walker, 1858–1936, vol. III
Clark, James William, 1851–1921, vol. II
Clark, John, *died* 1931, vol. III
Clark, John, 1903–1977, vol. VII
Clark, John Anthony, 1908–1985, vol. VIII
Clark, Brig.-Gen. John Arthur, *died* 1976, vol. VII
Clark, Sir (John) Beresford, 1902–1968, vol. VI
Clark, John Brown, 1861–1947, vol. IV
Clark, (John) Cosmo, 1897–1967, vol. VI
Clark, Sir John Forbes, 2nd Bt (*cr* 1837), 1821–1910, vol. I
Clark, Lt-Gen. John George Walters, 1892–1948, vol. IV
Clark, Sir John Maurice, 2nd Bt (*cr* 1886), 1859–1924, vol. II

Clark, John Maurice, 1884–1963, vol. VI

Clark, John Murray, 1860–1929, vol. III

Clark, Sir John S.; *see* Stewart-Clark.

Clark, John William, 1851–1929, vol. III

Clark, John Willis, 1833–1910, vol. I

Clark, Joseph, 1834–1926, vol. II

Clark, Col Joseph Arthur Myles Ariel, 1872–1935, vol. III

Clark, (Josiah) Latimer, 1822–1898, vol. I

Clark, Kenneth MacKenzie, 1868–1932, vol. III

Clark, Latimer; *see* Clark, J. L.

Clark, Leonard, 1905–1981, vol. VIII

Clark, Sir Lindesay; *see* Clark, Sir G. C. L.

Clark, Sir Marcus; *see* Clark, Sir R. M.

Clark, Mrs Margaret; *see* Storm, Lesley.

Clark, Marjorie, (Georgia Rivers), *died* 1989, vol. VIII

Clark, Gen. Mark Wayne, 1896–1984, vol. VIII

Clark, Michael Lindsey, 1918–1990, vol. VIII

Clark, Rt Rev. Patrick; *see* Clark, Rt Rev. F. P.

Clark, Percy, 1917–1985, vol. VIII

Clark, Col Percy William, 1888–1943, vol. IV

Clark, Philip Lindsey, 1889–1977, vol. VII

Clark, Reginald, 1895–1981, vol. VIII

Clark, Sir (Reginald) Marcus, 1883–1953, vol. V

Clark, Col Robert, 1859–1940, vol. III (A), vol. IV

Clark, Sir Stewart S.; *see* Stewart-Clark.

Clark, Stuart Ellis, *born* 1899, vol. VIII

Clark, Rev. Canon Stuart Harrington, 1869–1947, vol. IV

Clark, Sir Thomas, 1st Bt (*cr* 1886), 1823–1900, vol. I

Clark, Sir Thomas, 3rd Bt (*cr* 1886), 1886–1977, vol. VII

Clark, Thomas Archibald B.; *see* Bennet-Clark.

Clark, Thomas Campbell, (Tom C. Clark), 1899–1977, vol. VII

Clark, Sir (Thomas) Fife, 1907–1985, vol. VIII

Clark, Sir Wilfrid Edward Le Gros, 1895–1971, vol. VII

Clark, William Andrews, 1839–1925, vol. II

Clark, Sir (William) Arthur (Weir), 1908–1967, vol. VI

Clark, William Clifford, 1889–1952, vol. V

Clark, William Donaldson, 1916–1985, vol. VIII

Clark, Brig. William Ellis, 1877–1969, vol. VI

Clark, Hon. William George, 1865–1948, vol. IV

Clark, Rev. William Gilchrist; *see* Clark-Maxwell.

Clark, Sir William Henry, 1876–1952, vol. V

Clark, Sir William Mortimer, 1836–1917, vol. II

Clark, Sir William Ovens, 1849–1937, vol. III

Clark, Rt Rev. William Reid, *died* 1925, vol. II

Clark, Rev. William Robinson, *died* 1912, vol. I

Clark-Hall, Air Marshal Sir Robert Hamilton, 1883–1964, vol. VI

Clark-Kennedy, Archibald Edmund, 1893–1985, vol. VIII

Clark-Kennedy, John William James; *see* Kennedy.

Clark-Kennedy of Knockgray, Lt-Col William Hew; *see* Kennedy of Knockgray.

Clark-Maxwell, Rev. William Gilchrist, 1865–1935, vol. III

Clarke, Lt-Col Albert Edward Stanley, 1879–1926, vol. II

Clarke, Col Alexander Ross, 1828–1914, vol. I

Clarke, Alfred Henry, 1860–1942, vol. IV

Clarke, Hon. Sir Andrew, 1824–1902, vol. I

Clarke, Andrew B., *died* 1940, vol. III

Clarke, Vice-Adm. Arthur Calvert, 1848–1926, vol. II

Clarke, Brig. Arthur Christopher Lancelot S.; *see* Stanley-Clarke.

Clarke, Rev. Arthur Frederic, 1848–1932, vol. III

Clarke, Col Arthur Lionel Crisp, 1874–1935, vol. III

Clarke, Captain Sir Arthur Wellesley, 1857–1932, vol. III

Clarke, Captain Arthur Wellesley, 1898–1985, vol. VIII

Clarke, Astley Vavasour, 1870–1945, vol. IV

Clarke, Austin, 1896–1974, vol. VII

Clarke, Sir Basil, 1879–1947, vol. IV

Clarke, Rev. Basil Fulford Lowther, 1903–1978, vol. VII

Clarke, Brig. Bowcher Campbell Senhouse, 1882–1969, vol. VI

Clarke, Sir Campbell, 1835–1902, vol. I

Clarke, Maj.-Gen. Sir Campbell; *see* Clarke, Maj.-Gen. Sir E. M. C.

Clarke, Sir Caspar Purdon, 1846–1911, vol. I

Clarke, Rev. Sir Charles, 2nd Bt (*cr* 1831), 1812–1899, vol. I

Clarke, Charles Agacy, 1872–1939, vol. III

Clarke, Charles Allen, 1863–1935, vol. III

Clarke, Charles Baron, 1832–1906, vol. I

Clarke, Col Charles C.; *see* Childs-Clarke.

Clarke, Charles Cyril, 1882–1968, vol. VI

Clarke, Charles Edward, 1912–1981, vol. VIII

Clarke, Charles Goddard, 1849–1908, vol. I

Clarke, Bt-Col (Charles Henry Geoffrey) Mansfield, 1873–1919, vol. II

Clarke, Charles Kirk, 1857–1924, vol. II

Clarke, Gen. Sir Charles Mansfield, 3rd Bt (*cr* 1831), 1839–1932, vol. III

Clarke, Sir Charles Noble A.; *see* Arden-Clark.

Clarke, Rear-Adm. Sir (Charles) Philip, 1898–1966, vol. VI

Clarke, Ven. Charles Philip Stewart, 1871–1947, vol. IV

Clarke, Hon. Sir Charles Pitcher, 1857–1926, vol. II

Clarke, Very Rev. Charles William B.; *see* Barnett-Clarke.

Clarke, Comdr Courtney; *see* Clarke, Comdr H. C. C.

Clarke, Dennis Robert, 1902–1967, vol. VI

Clarke, Denzil Robert Noble, 1908–1985, vol. VIII

Clarke, Maj.-Gen. Desmond Alexander Bruce, 1912–1986, vol. VIII

Clarke, Sir Douglas, 1901–1969, vol. VI

Clarke, Brig. Dudley Wrangel, 1899–1974, vol. VII

Clarke, Sir Edgar C.; *see* Chatfeild-Clarke.

Clarke, Edith, 1844–1926, vol. II

Clarke, Edward, 1908–1989, vol. VIII

Clarke, Edward Ashley Walrond, 1860–1913, vol. I

Clarke, Edward de Courcy, 1880–1958, vol. V

Clarke, Captain Edward Denman, 1898–1966, vol. VI

Clarke, Rt Hon. Sir Edward George, 1841–1931, vol. III

Clarke, Lt-Col Sir Edward Henry St Lawrence, 4th Bt (*cr* 1804), 1857–1926, vol. II

Clarke, Edward Henry Scamander, 1856–1947, vol. IV

Clarke, Major Edward John Arundell, 1868–1932, vol. III

Clarke, Edward Lionel Alexander, 1837–1917, vol. II

Clarke, Maj.-Gen. Sir (Edward Montagu) Campbell, 1885–1971, vol. VII

Clarke, Sir Ernest, 1856–1923, vol. II

Clarke, Ernest, *died* 1932, vol. III

Clarke, (Ernest) Meredyth H.; *see* Hyde-Clarke.

Clarke, Sir Ernest Michael, 1868–1956, vol. V

Clarke, Hon.Sir Fielding, 1851–1928, vol. II

Clarke, Hon. Sir Francis Grenville, 1879–1955, vol. V

Clarke, Frank Edward, 1886–1938, vol. III

Clarke, Frank Wigglesworth, 1847–1931, vol. III

Clarke, Sir Fred, 1880–1952, vol. V

Clarke, Brig. Frederick Arthur Stanley, 1892–1972, vol. VII

Clarke, Ven. Frederick James, 1858–1937, vol. III

Clarke, Hon. Sir Frederick James, 1859–1944, vol. IV

Clarke, Sir Frederick Joseph, 1912–1980, vol. VII (AII)

Clarke, Frederick Seymour, 1855–1932, vol. III

Clarke, Sir Frederick William Alfred, 1857–1927, vol. II

Clarke, Sir Geoffrey, *died* 1950, vol. IV

Clarke, George, 1878–1944, vol. IV

Clarke, Gen. George Calvert, 1814–1900, vol. I

Clarke, George Johnson, *died* 1917, vol. II

Clarke, Gerald Bryan, 1909–1981, vol. VIII

Clarke, Brig.-Gen. Goland Vanhalt, 1875–1944, vol. IV

Clarke, Very Rev. Harold George Michael, 1898–1978, vol. VII

Clarke, Henry, 1854–1936, vol. III

Clarke, Brig.-Gen. Henry Calvert Stanley, 1872–1943, vol. IV

Clarke, Comdr H(enry) C(ecil) Courtney, 1890–1968, vol. VI

Clarke, Adm. Henry James Langford, 1866–1944, vol. IV

Clarke, Most Rev. Henry Lowther, 1850–1926, vol. II

Clarke, Sir Henry O.; *see* Osmond-Clarke.

Clarke, Herbert, 1863–1925, vol. II

Clarke, Ven. Herbert Lovell, 1881–1962, vol. VI

Clarke, Sir Horace William, 1883–1963, vol. VI

Clarke, Sir Humphrey Orme, 5th Bt (*cr* 1831), 1906–1973, vol. VII

Clarke, Isabel Constance, *died* 1951, vol. V

Clarke, Col J. de W. L.; *see* Lardner-Clarke.

Clarke, J. Jackson, *died* 1940, vol. III (A), vol. IV

Clarke, James Greville, 1854–1901, vol. I

Clarke, Rev. John, *died* 1923, vol. II

Clarke, John, *died* 1939, vol. III

Clarke, John Courtenay, 1880–1939, vol. III

Clarke, Rev. John Erskine, 1827–1920, vol. II

Clarke, John Henry, 1852–1931, vol. III

Clarke, John Joseph, 1879–1969, vol. VI

Clarke, Brig.-Gen. John Louis Justice, 1870–1944, vol. IV

Clarke, John Mason, 1857–1925, vol. II

Clarke, John Smith, 1885–1959, vol. V

Clarke, Col John Thomas, 1870–1947, vol. IV (A)

Clarke, Joseph Percival, 1862–1930, vol. III

Clarke, Col Lancelot Fox, 1858–1925, vol. II

Clarke, Captain Lionel Altham G.; *see* Graham-Clarke.

Clarke, Hon. Lionel H., 1859–1922, vol. II

Clarke, Loftus Otway, 1871–1954, vol. V

Clarke, Louis Colville Gray, 1881–1960, vol. V, vol. VI

Clarke, Bt-Col Mansfield; *see* Clarke, Bt-Col C. H. G. M.

Clarke, Lt-Col Sir Marshal James, 1841–1909, vol. I

Clarke, Adm. Sir Marshal Llewelyn, 1887–1959, vol. V

Clarke, Mary Gavin, 1881–1976, vol. VII

Clarke, Mrs Mary Victoria Cowden, 1809–1898, vol. I

Clarke, Lt-Col Matthew John, 1895–1954, vol. V

Clarke, Maude Violet, 1892–1935, vol. III

Clarke, Meredyth H.; *see* Hyde-Clarke, E. M.

Clarke, Rear-Adm. Noel Edward Harwood, 1904–1980, vol. VII

Clarke, Rt Rev. Norman Harry, 1892–1974, vol. VII

Clarke, Sir Orme Bigland, 4th Bt (*cr* 1831), 1880–1949, vol. IV

Clarke, Paul Henry Francis, 1921–1989, vol. VIII

Clarke, Sir Percival, 1872–1936, vol. III

Clarke, Rear-Adm. Sir Philip; *see* Clarke, Rear-Adm. Sir C. P.

Clarke, Sir Philip Haughton, 11th Bt (*cr* 1617), 1819-1898, vol. I

Clarke, Col Sir Ralph Stephenson, 1892–1970, vol. VI

Clarke, Sir Reginald, 1876–1956, vol. V

Clarke, Reginald Arnold, 1921–1989, vol. VIII

Clarke, Col Reginald Graham, 1879–1959, vol. V

Clarke, Sir Richard William Barnes, 1910–1975, vol. VII

Clarke, Robert Coningsby, 1879–1934, vol. III

Clarke, Col Robert Ffoulke Noel, 1853–1904, vol. I

Clarke, Lt-Col Robert Joyce, 1874–1949, vol. IV

Clarke, Roger Simon Woodchurch, 1903–1988, vol. VIII

Clarke, Sir Rupert Turner Havelock, 2nd Bt (*cr* 1882), 1865–1926, vol. II

Clarke, Sir Selwyn S.; *see* Selwyn-Clarke.

Clarke, Rev. Septimus John C.; *see* Childs-Clarke.

Clarke, Rev. Sidney Lampard, 1871–1945, vol. IV

Clarke, Somers, 1841–1926, vol. II

Clarke, Lt-Gen. Somerset Molyneux W.; *see* Wiseman-Clarke.

Clarke, Maj.-Gen. Sir Stanley de Astel Calvert, 1837–1911, vol. I

Clarke, Stephenson Robert, 1862–1948, vol. IV

Clarke, Rev. Sydney Herbert, 1894–1974, vol. VII

Clarke, Ven. Thomas, 1907–1965, vol. VI

Clarke, Col Thomas Cecil Arthur, 1898–1979, vol. VII

Clarke, Thomas Ernest Bennett, 1907–1989, vol. VIII

Clarke, Col Thomas Henry Matthews, 1869–1941, vol. IV

Clarke, Tom, 1884–1957, vol. V

Clarke, Lt-Gen. Sir Travers Edwards, 1871–1962, vol. VI

Clarke, William, 1842–1918, vol. II

Clarke, William Bruce, *died* 1914, vol. I

Clarke, William Eagle, 1853–1938, vol. III

Clarke, Sir William Henry, *died* 1930, vol. III

Clarke, Sir William Henry, 1847–1930, vol. III

Clarke, Sir William John, 1st Bt (*cr* 1882), 1831–1897, vol. I

Clarke, William John, 1857–1951, vol. V

Clarke, Rev. William Kemp Lowther, 1879–1968, vol. VI

Clarke, Hon. William Lionel Russell, 1876–1954, vol. V

Clarke, Brig. William Stanhope, 1899–1973, vol. VII

Clarke, Maj.-Gen. Willoughby Charles Stanley, 1833–1909, vol. I

Clarke Hall, Edna (Lady Clarke Hall), 1879–1979, vol. VII

Clarke-Jervoise, Sir Arthur Henry; *see* Jervoise.

Clarke-Jervoise, Sir Dudley Alan Lestock; *see* Jervoise.

Clarke Taylor, Air Vice-Marshal James; *see* Taylor.

Clarke-Thornhill, Thomas Bryan, 1857–1934, vol. III

Clarke-Travers, Sir Guy Francis Travers; *see* Travers.

Clarkson, Anthony; *see* Clarkson, G. W. A.

Clarkson, Lt-Col Bertie St John, 1868–1954, vol. V

Clarkson, (George Wensley) Anthony, 1912–1977, vol. VII

Clarkson, Rt Rev. George William, 1897–1977, vol. VII

Clarkson, Mabel, *died* 1950, vol. IV

Clarkson, Patrick Wensley, 1911–1969, vol. VI

Clarkson, Rev. Peter, 1871–1936, vol. III

Clarkson, Randolph Norman Macgregor, 1889–1967, vol. VI

Clarkson, Engr-Vice-Adm. Sir William, 1859–1934, vol. III

Clarry, Sir Reginald, 1882–1945, vol. IV

Clasen, Andrew Joseph, 1906–1984, vol. VIII

Claude, Albert, 1898–1983, vol. VIII

Claudel, Paul, 1868–1955, vol. V

Claughton, Sir Gilbert Henry, 1st Bt, 1856–1921, vol. II

Claughton, Sir Harold, 1882–1969, vol. VI

Claus, Emile, 1849–1924, vol. II

Clause, William Lionel, 1887–1946, vol. IV

Clausen, Sir George, 1852–1944, vol. IV

Clausen, Raymond John, *died* 1966, vol. VI

Clauson, 1st Baron, 1870–1946, vol. IV

Clauson, Sir Gerard Leslie Makins, 1891–1974, vol. VII

Clauson, Major Sir John Eugene, 1866–1918, vol. II

Clavering, Sir Albert, 1887–1972, vol. VII

Clavering, Col Charles Warren N.; *see* Napier-Clavering.

Clavering, Maj.-Gen. Noel Warren N.; *see* Napier-Clavering.

Claxton, Hon. Brooke, 1898–1960, vol. V

Claxton, Thomas Folkes, 1874–1952, vol. V

Clay, Sir Arthur Temple Felix, 4th Bt, 1842–1928, vol. II

Clay, Brig.-Gen. Bertie Gordon, 1874–1937, vol. III

Clay, Charles Felix, 1861–1947, vol. IV

Clay, Charles John Jervis, 1910–1988, vol. VIII

Clay, Sir Charles Travis, 1885–1978, vol. VII

Clay, Lt-Col Ernest Charles, 1872–1955, vol. V

Clay, Sir Felix, 5th Bt, 1871–1941, vol. IV

Clay, Sir Geoffrey Fletcher, 1895–1969, vol. VI

Clay, Col Henry, 1872–1945, vol. IV

Clay, Sir Henry, 1883–1954, vol. V

Clay, Sir Henry Felix, 6th Bt, 1909–1985, vol. VIII

Clay, Lt-Col Rt Hon. Herbert Henry S.; *see* Spender-Clay.

Clay, Col John, *died* 1962, vol. VI

Clay, Rev. John Harden, *died* 1923, vol. II

Clay, Sir Joseph Miles, 1881–1949, vol. IV

Clay, Gen. Lucius DuBignon, 1897–1978, vol. VII

Clay, Reginald S., *died* 1954, vol. V

Clay, William Henry, 1841–1921, vol. II

Clay, Rev. William Leslie, 1863–1928, vol. II

Clayden, Arthur William, 1855–1944, vol. IV

Clayden, Rt Hon. Sir (Henry) John, 1904–1986, vol. VIII

Clayden, Rt Hon. Sir John; *see* Clayden, Rt Hon. Sir H. J.

Clayden, Peter William, 1827–1902, vol. I

Claydon, Rev. Canon Ernest Henry Beales, 1863–1930, vol. III

Claye, Sir Andrew Moynihan, 1896–1977, vol. VII

Claye, Rev. Canon Arthur Needham, 1863–1956, vol. V

Clayhills, George, 1877–1914, vol. I

Clayson, Sir Eric Maurice, 1908–1989, vol. VIII

Clayson, Rev. Canon Jesse Alec Maynard, 1905–1971, vol. VII

Clayton, Rev. Albert, *died* 1907, vol. I

Clayton, Sir Arthur Harold, 11th Bt, 1903–1985, vol. VIII

Clayton, Arthur Ross, 1876–1963, vol. VI

Clayton, Sir Christopher; *see* Clayton, Sir G. C.

Clayton, Colin, 1895–1975, vol. VII

Clayton, Edward, 1856–1938, vol. III

Clayton, Edward Chapman, 1837–1935, vol. III

Clayton, Major Edward Francis, 1864–1922, vol. II

Clayton, Major Sir Edward Gilbert, 1841–1917, vol. II

Clayton, Maj.-Gen. Edward Hadrill, 1899–1962, vol. VI

Clayton, Col Edward Robert, 1877–1957, vol. V

Clayton, Edwin, 1887–1973, vol. VII

Clayton, Col Sir Fitz-Roy Augustus Talbot, 1834–1913, vol. I

Clayton, Col Forrester, 1878–1942, vol. IV

Clayton, Sir Francis Hare, 1869–1956, vol. V

Clayton, Frederick, 1872–1932, vol. III

Clayton, Lt-Gen. Sir Frederick Thomas, 1855-1933, vol. III

Clayton, Most Rev. Geoffrey Hare, 1884–1957, vol. V

Clayton, Sir (George) Christopher, 1869–1945, vol. IV

Clayton, Brig.-Gen. Sir Gilbert Falkingham, 1875–1929, vol. III

Clayton, Harold, 1874–1963, vol. VI

Clayton, Sir Harold Dudley, 10th Bt (*cr* 1732), 1877–1951, vol. V

Clayton, Col Hon. Sir Hector Joseph Richard, 1885–1975, vol. VII

Clayton, Rev. Horace Evelyn, 1853–1916, vol. II

Clayton, Sir Hugh Byard, 1877–1947, vol. IV

Clayton, Brig. Sir Iltyd Nicholl, 1886–1955, vol. V

Clayton, Rev. John Francis, 1883–1947, vol. IV

Clayton, Rear-Adm. John Wittewronge, 1888–1952, vol. V

Clayton, Joseph, 1868–1943, vol. IV

Clayton, Rt Rev. Lewis, 1838–1917, vol. II

Clayton, Lt-Col Muirhead Collins, 1892–1957, vol. V

Clayton, Col Patrick Andrew, 1896–1962, vol. VI

Clayton, Rev. Philip Thomas Byard, 1885–1972, vol. VII

Clayton, Reginald John Byard, 1875–1962, vol. VI

Clayton, Adm. Sir Richard Pilkington, 1925–1984, vol. VIII

Clayton, Hon. Brig.-Gen. Robert Clayton B.; *see* Browne Clayton.

Clayton, Sir Stanley George, 1911–1986, vol. VIII

Clayton, Lt-Col William Kitson, *died* 1937, vol. III

Clayton, William Lockhart, 1880–1966, vol. VI

Clayton, Sir William Robert, 6th Bt (*cr* 1732), 1842–1914, vol. I

Clayton-East, Sir George Frederick Lancelot, 8th Bt and 4th Bt; *see* East.

Clayton East, Sir Gilbert Augustus Clayton, 7th Bt and 3rd Bt; *see* East.

Clayton East Clayton, Sir Robert Alan, 9th Bt (*cr* 1732), and 5th Bt (*cr* 1838), 1908–1932, vol. III

Clayton-Greene, William Henry, *died* 1926, vol. II

Cleall, Ven. Aubrey Victor George, 1898–1982, vol. VIII

Cleary, Frederick Ernest, 1905–1984, vol. VIII

Cleary, Rt Rev. Henry William, 1859–1929, vol. III

Cleary, Ven. Robert, *died* 1919, vol. II

Cleary, Hon. Sir Timothy Patrick, 1900–1962, vol. VI

Cleary, Sir William Castle, 1886–1971, vol. VII

Cleather, Edward Gordon, 1872–1967, vol. VI

Cleaton, John Davies, *died* 1901, vol. I

Cleave, John, 1837–1928, vol. II

Cleave, John Kyrie Frederick, 1861–1947, vol. IV

Cleaver, Sir Frederick, 1875–1936, vol. III

Cleaver, Col Frederick Holden, 1875–1944, vol. IV

Cleaver, Reginald; *see* Cleaver, T. R.

Cleaver, (Thomas) Reginald, *died* 1954, vol. V

Clee, Sir Charles Beaupré Bell, 1893–1980, vol. VII

Cleeve, Brig. Francis Charles Frederick, 1896–1975, vol. VII

Cleeve, Lt-Col Herbert, 1870–1948, vol. IV

Cleeve, Lucas, (Mrs Howard Kingscote), *died* 1908, vol. I

Cleeve, Col Stewart Dalrymple, 1856–1939, vol. III

Cleeve, Sir Thomas Henry, 1844–1908, vol. I

Cleeve, Maj.-Gen. William Frederick, 1853–1922, vol. II

Clegg, Sir Alec, (Alexander Bradshaw Clegg), 1909–1986, vol. VIII

Clegg, Sir (Alfred) Rowland, 1872–1957, vol. V

Clegg, Sir Cuthbert Barwick, 1904–1986, vol. VIII

Clegg, Hugh Anthony, 1900–1983, vol. VIII

Clegg, Sir James Travis T.; *see* Travis-Clegg.

Clegg, Rev. James Whitehead, *died* 1930, vol. III

Clegg, Sir John Charles, 1850–1937, vol. III

Clegg, Rear-Adm. John Harry Kay, 1884–1962, vol. VI

Clegg, Sir Robert Bailey, 1865–1929, vol. III

Clegg, Sir Rowland; *see* Clegg, Sir A. R.

Clegg, Sir William Edwin, 1852–1932, vol. III

Clegg, William Henry, *died* 1945, vol. IV

Cleghorn, Isabel, *died* 1922, vol. II

Cleghorn, Surg.-Gen. James, 1841–1920, vol. II

Cleland, Sir Charles, 1867–1941, vol. IV

Cleland, Brig. Sir Donald Mackinnon, 1901–1975, vol. VII

Cleland, Edward Erskine, 1869–1943, vol. IV (A)

Cleland, James William, 1874–1914, vol. I

Cleland, John, 1835–1924, vol. II

Cleland, Sir John Burton, 1878–1971, vol. VII

Clemenceau, Georges, 1841–1929, vol. III

Clemens, Benjamin, *died* 1957, vol. V

Clemens, Samuel Langhorne; *see* Twain, Mark.

Clemens, Sir William James, 1873–1941, vol. IV

Clement, Sir Anchitel Piers A.; *see* Ashburnham-Clement.

Clement, Ernest Wilson, 1860–1941, vol. IV

Clement, Sir Thomas, *died* 1956, vol. V

Clementi, Sir Cecil, 1875–1947, vol. IV

Clementi, Air Vice-Marshal Cresswell Montagu, 1918–1981, vol. VIII

Clements, Arthur; *see* Baker, Andrew Clement.

Clements, Arthur Frederick, 1877–1968, vol. VI

Clements, Bernard; *see* Clements, W. D. B.

Clements, Clyde Edwin, 1897–1983, vol. VIII

Clements, Rev. Jacob, 1820–1898, vol. I

Clements, Sir John Selby, 1910–1988, vol. VIII

Clements, Kay, (Dorothy Katharine), (Lady Clements); *see* Hammond, Kay.

Clements, Maj.-Gen. Ralph Arthur Penrhyn, 1855–1909, vol. I

Clements, Col Robert William, *died* 1941, vol. IV

Clements, (William Dudley) Bernard, 1880–1942, vol. IV

Clemesha, Lt-Col William Wesley, 1871–1958, vol. V

Cleminson, Frederick John, 1878–1943, vol. IV

Cleminson, Henry Millican, 1885–1970, vol. VI

Clemitson, Rear-Adm. Francis Edward, 1899–1981, vol. VIII

Clemmey, Sir William Henry, 1846–1933, vol. III

Clemo, George Roger, 1889–1983, vol. VIII

Clemow, Frank Gerard, *died* 1939, vol. III

Clemson, Brig.-Gen. William Fletcher, 1866–1946, vol. IV

Clerici, Charles John Emil, *died* 1938, vol. III

Clerk, Sir Dugald, 1854–1932, vol. III

Clerk, Sir George Douglas, 8th Bt, 1852–1911, vol. I

Clerk, Sir George James Robert, 9th Bt, 1876–1943, vol. IV

Clerk, Rt Hon. Sir George Russell, 1874–1951, vol. V

Clerk, Gen. Sir Godfrey, 1835–1908, vol. I

Clerk, Maj.-Gen. Henry, 1821–1913, vol. I

Clerk, Hugh Edward, 1859–1942, vol. IV

Clerk, Col John, *died* 1919, vol. II

Clerk-Rattray, Lt-Gen. Sir James, 1832–1910, vol. I

Clerke, Agnes Mary, 1842–1907, vol. I

Clerke, Major Augustus Basil Holt, 1871–1949, vol. IV

Clerke, Ellen Mary, 1840–1906, vol. I

Clerke, Sir William Francis, 11th Bt, 1856–1930, vol. III

Clermont-Ganneau, Charles Simon, *born* 1846, vol. II

Clery, Arthur Edward, *died* 1932, vol. III

Clery, Maj.-Gen. Carleton Buckley Laming, 1869–1937, vol. III

Clery, Lt-Gen. Sir Francis, 1838–1926, vol. II

Clery, Surg.-Gen. James Albert, 1846–1920, vol. II

Cleugh, Eric Arthur, 1894–1964, vol. VI

Cleveland, Duchess of; (Catherine Lucy Wilhelmina), 1819–1901, vol. I

Cleveland, Sir Charles Raitt, 1866–1929, vol. III

Cleveland, Grover, 1837–1908, vol. I

Cleveland, Adm. Henry Forster, 1834–1924, vol. II

Cleveland, Col Henry Francis, 1863–1938, vol. III

Cleveland, Sydney Dyson, 1898–1975, vol. VII

Cleveland-Stevens, William, 1881–1957, vol. V

Cleverdon, Douglas; *see* Cleverdon, T. D. J.

Cleverdon, (Thomas) Douglas (James), 1903–1987, vol. VIII

Cleverly, Charles F. M., *died* 1921, vol. II

Cleverly, Sir Osmund Somers, 1891–1966, vol. VI

Clewer, Maj.-Gen. Donald, 1892–1945, vol. IV

Clewes, Howard Charles Vivian, 1912–1988, vol. VIII

Clewes, Winston, 1906–1957, vol. V

Cleworth, Ralph, 1896–1975, vol. VII

Cleworth, Rev. Thomas Ebenezer, 1854–1909, vol. I

Clibborn, Col John, 1847–1938, vol. III

Clifden, 5th Viscount, 1829–1899, vol. I

Clifden, 6th Viscount, 1844–1930, vol. III

Clifden, 7th Viscount, 1883–1966, vol. VI

Clifden, 8th Viscount, 1887–1974, vol. VII

Cliff, Eric Francis, 1884–1969, vol. VI

Cliffe, Anthony Loftus, 1861–1922, vol. II

Cliffe, Michael, 1904–1964, vol. VI

Clifford of Chudleigh, 9th Baron, 1851–1916, vol. II

Clifford of Chudleigh, 10th Baron, 1858–1943, vol. IV

Clifford of Chudleigh, 11th Baron, 1887–1962, vol. VI

Clifford of Chudleigh, 12th Baron, 1889–1964, vol. VI

Clifford of Chudleigh, 13th Baron, 1916–1988, vol. VIII

Clifford, Rt Rev. Alfred, 1849–1931, vol. III

Clifford, Captain Hon. Sir Bede Edmund Hugh, 1890–1969, vol. VI

Clifford, Sir Charles, *died* 1936, vol. III

Clifford, Sir Charles Lewis, 3rd Bt, 1885–1938, vol. III

Clifford, Edward C., *died* 1910, vol. I

Clifford, Elizabeth Lydia Rosabelle, (Lady Clifford), (Mrs Henry de la Pasture), *died* 1945, vol. IV

Clifford, Vice-Adm. Sir Eric George Anderson, 1900–1964, vol. VI

Clifford, Col Esmond Humphrey Miller, 1895–1970, vol. VI

Clifford, Ethel, *died* 1959, vol. V

Clifford, Frederick, 1828–1904, vol. I

Clifford, Sir (Geoffrey) Miles, 1897–1986, vol. VIII

Clifford, Sir George Hugh Charles, 2nd Bt, 1847–1930, vol. III

Clifford, Graham Douglas, 1913–1989, vol. VIII

Clifford, Henry Charles, 1861–1947, vol. IV

Clifford, Brig.-Gen. Henry Frederick Hugh, 1867–1916, vol. II

Clifford, Sir Hugh, 1866–1941, vol. IV

Clifford, James Lowry, 1901–1978, vol. VII

Clifford, Rev. John, 1836–1923, vol. II

Clifford, Julian, 1877–1921, vol. II

Clifford, Rev. Sir Lewis Arthur Joseph, 5th Bt, 1896–1970, vol. VI

Clifford, Sir Miles; *see* Clifford, Sir G. M.

Clifford, Maj.-Gen. Richard Melville, 1841–1915, vol. I

Clifford, Lt-Gen. Robert Cecil Richard, 1839–1930, vol. III

Clifford, Rev. Robert Rowntree, 1867–1943, vol. IV

Clifford, Sir Roger Charles Joseph Gerrard, 6th Bt, 1910–1982, vol. VIII

Clifford, Sir Walter Lovelace, 4th Bt, 1852–1944, vol. IV

Clifford, Brig.-Gen. Walter Rees, 1866–1947, vol. IV

Clifford, Major Wigram, 1876–1917, vol. II

Clifford, Mrs William Kingdom, (Lucy Clifford), *died* 1929, vol. III

Clift, Hon. James Augustus, 1857–1923, vol. II

Clift, Col Sir Sidney William, 1885–1951, vol. V

Clifton, Baroness (17th in line), 1900–1937, vol. III

Clifton, Augustus Wykeham, 1829–1915, vol. I

Clifton, John Talbot, 1868–1928, vol. II

Clifton, Leon James Thomas, 1912–1978, vol. VII

Clifton, Lt-Col Percy Robert, 1872–1944, vol. IV

Clifton, Robert Bellamy, 1836–1921, vol. II

Clifton, Robert Cecil, 1854–1931, vol. III

Clifton, Violet Mary, (Mrs Talbot Clifton), 1883–1961, vol. VI

Clifton-Brown, Anthony George, 1903–1984, vol. VIII

Clifton Brown, Cedric, 1887–1968, vol. VI

Clifton-Brown, Edward Clifton, 1870–1944, vol. IV

Clifton-Brown, Lt-Col Geoffrey Benedict, 1899–1983, vol. VIII

Clifton-Taylor, Alec, 1907–1985, vol. VIII

Climie, Robert, 1868–1929, vol. III

Climo, Lt-Gen. Sir Skipton Hill, 1868–1937, vol. III

Clinch, George, 1860–1921, vol. II

Clinton, 20th Baron, 1834–1904, vol. I

Clinton, 21st Baron, 1863–1957, vol. V

Clinton, David Osbert F.; *see* Fynes-Clinton.

Clinton, Lord Edward William Pelham-, 1836–1907, vol. I

Clinton, (Francis) Gordon, 1912–1988, vol. VIII

Clinton, Gordon; *see* Clinton, F. G.

Clinton, Rev. Henry Joy F.; *see* Fynes-Clinton.

Clinton, Michael Denys Arthur, 1918–1976, vol. VII

Clinton, Osbert Henry F.; *see* Fynes-Clinton.

Clinton, Ven. Thomas William, *died* 1926, vol. II

Clinton-Baddeley, Madeline Angela, (Angela Baddeley), 1904–1976, vol. VII

Clinton-Baker, Henry William, 1865–1935, vol. III

Clinton-Baker, Adm. Sir Lewis, 1866–1939, vol. III

Clinton-Thomas, Robert Antony, 1913–1981, vol. VIII

Clipperton, Sir Charles Bell Child, 1864–1927, vol. II

Clissitt, William Cyrus, 1898–1977, vol. VII

Clissold, Major Harry, *died* 1917, vol. II

Clitheroe, 1st Baron, 1901–1984, vol. VIII

Clitherow, Lt-Col John Bourchier S.; *see* Stracey-Clitherow.

Clitherow, Richard, 1902–1947, vol. IV

Clitherow, Rt Rev. Richard George, 1909–1984, vol. VIII

Clive, Viscount; Mervyn Horatio Herbert, 1904–1943, vol. IV

Clive, Viscount; Percy Robert Herbert, 1892–1916, vol. II

Clive, Gen. Edward Henry, 1837–1916, vol. II

Clive, Lt-Col Hon. George Herbert Windsor W.; *see* Windsor-Clive.

Clive, Lt-Gen. Sir (George) Sidney, 1874–1959, vol. V

Clive, Lt-Col George W.; *se* Windsor-Clive.

Clive, Col Harry, 1880–1963, vol. VI

Clive, Captain Percy Archer, 1873–1918, vol. II

Clive, Rt Hon. Sir Robert Henry, 1877–1948, vol. IV

Clive, Lt-Gen. Sir Sidney; *see* Clive, Lt-Gen. Sir G. S.

Cloake, Philip Cyril, 1890–1969, vol. VI

Clodd, Edward, 1840–1930, vol. III

Clode, Sir Walter Baker, 1856–1937, vol. III

Cloete, (Edward Fairly) Stuart (Graham), 1897–1976, vol. VII

Cloete, Col Evelyn, 1863–1943, vol. IV

Cloete, Hendrik, 1851–1920, vol. II

Cloete, Lt-Gen. Josias Gordon, 1840–1907, vol. I

Cloete, Stuart; *see* Cloete, E. F. S. G.

Cloete, William Broderick, 1851–1915, vol. I

Clogg, Rev. Bertram; *see* Clogg, Rev. F. B.

Clogg, Rev. (Frank) Bertram, 1884–1955, vol. V

Clogg, Herbert Sherwell, *died* 1932, vol. III

Clogstoun, Herbert Cunningham, 1857–1936, vol. III

Clonbrock, 4th Baron, 1834–1917, vol. II

Clonbrock, 5th Baron, 1869–1926, vol. II

Cloncurry, 4th Baron, 1840–1928, vol. II

Cloncurry, 5th Baron, 1847–1929, vol. III

Clonmell, 6th Earl of, 1847–1898, vol. I

Clonmell, 7th Earl of, 1877–1928, vol. II

Clonmell, 8th Earl of, 1853–1935, vol. III

Cloran, Hon. Henry Joseph, 1855–1928, vol. II

Clore, Sir Charles, 1904–1979, vol. VII

Close, Col Sir Charles Frederick A.; *see* Arden-Close.

Close, Etta, *died* 1945, vol. IV

Close, Adm. Francis Arden, 1829–1918, vol. II

Close, Brig.-Gen. Geoffrey Dominic, 1866–1942, vol. IV

Close, Harold Arden, 1863–1932, vol. III

Close, Col Lewis Henry, 1869–1924, vol. II

Close, Major Maxwell Archibald, 1853–1935, vol. III

Close, Ralph William, 1867–1945, vol. IV

Close, S. P., vol. II

Close-Smith, Charles Nugent, 1911–1988, vol. VIII

Closs, August, 1898–1990, vol. VIII

Clothier, Henry Williamson, 1878–1958, vol. V

Clothier, Wilfrid, 1887–1967, vol. VI

Clotworthy, Stanley Edward, 1902–1983, vol. VIII

Cloudesley-Brereton, Maud Adeline; *see* Brereton.

Clough, Lt-Col Alfred Herrick Butler, 1856–1935, vol. III

Clough, Arthur Harold, 1897–1967, vol. VI

Clough, Blanche Athena, 1861–1960, vol. V

Clough, (Ernest Marshall) Owen, 1873–1964, vol. VI

Clough, Frederic Horton, 1878–1957, vol. V

Clough, Howard James Butler, 1890–1967, vol. VI

Clough, Sir John, 1836–1922, vol. II

Clough, Owen; *see* Clough, E. M. O.

Clough, Sir Robert, 1873–1965, vol. VI

Clough, Tom, 1867–1943, vol. IV

Clough, Walter Owen, 1846–1922, vol. II

Clough, William, 1862–1937, vol. III

Clouston, Air Cdre Arthur Edmond, 1908–1984, vol. VIII

Clouston, David, 1872–1948, vol. IV

Clouston, Sir Edward Seaborne, 1st Bt, 1849–1912, vol. I

Clouston, J. Storer, 1870–1944, vol. IV

Clouston, Sir Thomas Smith, 1840–1915, vol. I

Cloutier, Rt Rev. Francis Xavier, 1848–1933, vol. III

Cloutman, Sir Brett Mackay, 1891–1971, vol. VII

Clover, Maj.-Gen. Frederick Sherwood, 1894–1962, vol. VI

Clow, Sir Andrew Gourlay, 1890–1957, vol. V

Clow, Paymaster Rear-Adm. George James, *died* 1932, vol. III

Clow, Lt-Col William, 1863–1934, vol. III

Clow, William McCallum, 1853–1930, vol. III

Clowes, Lt-Gen. Cyril Albert, 1892–1968, vol. VI

Clowes, Frank, 1848–1923, vol. II

Clowes, Geoffrey Swinford Laird, 1883–1937, vol. III

Clowes, Col George Charles Knight, 1882–1941, vol. IV

Clowes, Sir Harold, 1903–1968, vol. VI

Clowes, Maj.-Gen. Norman, 1893–1980, vol. VII

Clowes, Lt-Col Peter Legh, 1853–1925, vol. II

Clowes, Samuel, 1864–1928, vol. II

Clowes, William Archibald, 1866–1937, vol. III

Clowes, Sir William Laird, 1856–1905, vol. I

Clubb, Hon. William Reid, 1884–1962, vol. VI

Clubbe, Sir Charles Percy Barlee, *died* 1932, vol. III

Clucas, Sir Frederick; *see* Clucas, Sir G. F.

Clucas, Sir (George) Frederick, 1870–1937, vol. III

Cluer, Albert Rowland, 1852–1942, vol. IV

Clune, Most Rev. Patrick Joseph, 1864–1935, vol. III

Clunes, Alec Sheriff de Moro, 1912–1970, vol. VI

Clunie, James, 1889–1974, vol. VII

Clunies-Ross, Sir Ian, 1899–1959, vol. V

Cluny Macpherson; *see* Macpherson, A. C.

Cluny Macpherson; *see* Macpherson, Brig. A. D.

Cluny Macpherson, *see* Macpherson, Brig.-Gen. E. H. D.

Cluse, William Sampson, 1875–1955, vol. V

Clute, Hon. Roger Conger, 1848–1921, vol. II

Clutsam, George H., 1866–1951, vol. V

Clutterbuck, Sir Alexander; *see* Clutterbuck, Sir P. A.

Clutterbuck, Sir (Peter) Alexander, 1897–1975, vol. VII

Clutterbuck, Sir Peter Henry, 1868–1951, vol. V

Clutterbuck, Maj.-Gen. Walter Edmond, 1894–1987, vol. VIII

Clutton, Sir George Lisle, 1909–1970, vol. VI

Clutton, Henry Hugh, 1850–1909, vol. I

Clutton-Brock, Alan Francis, *died* 1976, vol. VII

Clutton-Brock, Arthur, 1868–1924, vol. II

144

Cluver, Eustace Henry, 1894–1982, vol. VIII
Clwyd, 1st Baron, 1863–1955, vol. V
Clwyd, 2nd Baron, 1900–1987, vol. VIII
Clyde, Rt Hon. Lord; Rt Hon. James Avon Clyde, 1863–1944, vol. IV
Clyde, Rt Hon. Lord; Rt Hon. James Latham McDiarmid Clyde, 1898–1975, vol. VII
Clyde, Col Sir David, 1894–1966, vol. VI
Clyde, Rt Hon. James Avon; *see* Clyde, Rt Hon. Lord.
Clyde, Rt Hon. James Latham McDiarmid; *see* Clyde, Rt Hon. Lord.
Clyde, William McCallum, 1901–1972, vol. VII
Clydesmuir, 1st Baron, 1894–1954, vol. V
Clyne, Hon. Sir Thomas Stuart, 1887–1967, vol. VI
Clynes, Rt Hon. John Robert, 1869–1949, vol. IV
Coad, Maj.-Gen. Aubrey; *see* Coad, Maj.-Gen. B. A.
Coad, Maj.-Gen. Basil Aubrey, 1906–1980, vol. VII
Coad, Rev. Canon William Samuel, 1882–1965, vol. VI
Coade, Thorold Francis, 1896–1963, vol. VI
Coaker, Maj.-Gen. Ronald Edward, 1917–1983, vol. VIII
Coaker, Hon. Sir William Ford, 1871–1938, vol. III
Coakes, Ven. E. Lloyd, 1853–1930, vol. III
Coape-Arnold, Henry Fraser James; *see* Arnold.
Coape-Smith, Maj.-Gen. Henry, 1829–1921, vol. II
Coast, James Percy Chatterton, 1880–1962, vol. VI
Coatalen, Louis Hervé, 1879–1962, vol. VI
Coate, Rev. Harry, *died* 1939, vol. III
Coate, Maj.-Gen. Sir Raymond Douglas, 1908–1983, vol. VIII
Coaten, Arthur Wells, 1879–1939, vol. III (A), vol. IV
Coates, Abraham George, 1861–1928, vol. II
Coates, Albert, 1882–1953, vol. V
Coates, Sir Albert Ernest, 1895–1977, vol. VII
Coates, Captain Sir Clive Milnes-, 2nd Bt (*cr* 1911), 1879–1971, vol. VII
Coates, David Wilson, 1886–1968, vol. VI
Coates, Dora; *see* Meeson, D.
Coates, Edith, 1908–1983, vol. VIII
Coates, Major Sir Edward Feetham, 1st Bt (*cr* 1911), 1853–1921, vol. II
Coates, Eric, 1886–1957, vol. V
Coates, Sir Eric Thomas, 1897–1968, vol. VI
Coates, Florence Earle, *died* 1927, vol. II
Coates, George James, 1869–1930, vol. III
Coates, Henry, 1880–1963, vol. VI
Coates, Sir James Hugh Buchanan, 1851–1935, vol. III
Coates, John, 1865–1941, vol. IV
Coates, Rev. John Rider, 1879–1956, vol. V
Coates, Joseph Edward, 1883–1973, vol. VII
Coates, Rt Hon. Joseph Gordon, 1878–1943, vol. IV
Coates, Sir Leonard James, 1883–1944, vol. IV
Coates, Patrick Devereux, 1916–1990, vol. VIII
Coates, Rev. Percy, 1855–1925, vol. II
Coates, Brig.-Gen. Reginald Carlyon, 1869–1958, vol. V
Coates, Sir Robert Edward James Clive M.; *see* Milnes Coates.
Coates, Maj.-Gen. Thomas Seymour, 1879–1954, vol. V
Coates, Wells Wintemute, 1895–1958, vol. V

Coates, Col Sir William, 1860–1962, vol. VI
Coates, Sir William Frederick, 1st Bt (*cr* 1921), 1866–1932, vol. III
Coates, Sir William Henry, 1882–1963, vol. VI
Coath, Howell Lang L.; *see* Lang-Coath.
Coatman, John, 1889–1963, vol. VI
Coats, Major Andrew, 1862–1930, vol. III
Coats, George, 1876–1915, vol. I
Coats, Col George Henry Brook, 1852–1919, vol. II
Coats, Sir James, 1st Bt (*cr* 1905), 1834–1913, vol. I
Coats, Sir James Stuart, 3rd Bt (*cr* 1905), 1894–1966, vol. VI
Coats, Rev. Jervis, 1844–1921, vol. II
Coats, Joseph, 1846–1899, vol. I
Coats, Robert Hamilton, 1874–1960, vol. V
Coats, Rev. Robert Hay, 1873–1956, vol. V
Coats, Air Cdre Rowland, 1904–1974, vol. VII
Coats, Sir Stuart Auchincloss, 2nd Bt (*cr* 1905), 1868–1959, vol. V
Coats, Sir Thomas Coats Glen Glen-, 2nd Bt (*cr* 1894), 1878–1954, vol. V
Coats, Sir Thomas Glen G., 1st Bt; *see* Glen-Coats.
Coats, Rev. Walter William, 1856–1941, vol. IV
Coats, William Hodge, 1866–1928, vol. II
Coatsworth, Emerson, 1854–1943, vol. IV
Cobb, Lt-Col Charles, 1884–1947, vol. IV
Cobb, Sir Cyril Stephen, 1861–1938, vol. III
Cobb, Captain Edward Charles, 1891–1957, vol. V
Cobb, Maj.-Gen. Edwyn Harland Wolstenholme, 1902–1955, vol. V
Cobb, Frederick Arthur, 1901–1950, vol. IV
Cobb, Geoffry Edward Wheatly, 1858–1931, vol. III
Cobb, Gerard Francis, 1838–1904, vol. I
Cobb, Col Henry Frederick, 1881–1939, vol. III
Cobb, Henry Venn, 1864–1949, vol. IV
Cobb, Ivo Geikie-, 1887–1953, vol. V
Cobb, Sir John Francis Scott, 1922–1977, vol. VII
Cobb, John Leslie, 1923–1977, vol. VII
Cobb, John Rhodes, 1899–1952, vol. V
Cobb, John William, 1873–1950, vol. IV
Cobb, Rear-Adm. Robert Harborne, 1900–1978, vol. VII
Cobb, Thomas, 1854–1932, vol. III
Cobb, Rev. William Frederick G.; *see* Geikie-Cobb.
Cobban, Alfred, 1901–1968, vol. VI
Cobban, James MacLaren, 1849–1903, vol. I
Cobbe, Gen. Sir Alexander Stanhope, 1870–1931, vol. III
Cobbe, Frances Power, 1822–1904, vol. I
Cobbe, Col Henry Hercules, 1869–1939, vol. III
Cobbe, Hon. John George, *died* 1944, vol. IV
Cobbett, Louis, 1862–1947, vol. IV
Cobbett, Pitt, *died* 1919, vol. II
Cobbett, Sir Walter Palmer, 1871–1955, vol. V
Cobbett, Walter Willson, 1847–1937, vol. III
Cobbett, Sir William, 1846–1926, vol. II
Cobbold, 1st Baron, 1904–1987, vol. VIII
Cobbold, Lt-Col Ernest Cazenove, 1866–1932, vol. III
Cobbold, Lady Evelyn, *died* 1963, vol. VI
Cobbold, Felix Thornley, 1841–1909, vol. I
Cobbold, Herbert St George, *died* 1944, vol. IV
Cobbold, John Dupuis, 1861–1929, vol. III
Cobbold, Lt-Col John Murray, 1897–1944, vol. IV

Cobden, Lt-Col George Gough, 1878–1949, vol. IV
Cobden-Ramsay, Louis Eveleigh Bawtree, 1873–1962, vol. VI
Cobham, 8th Viscount, 1842–1922, vol. II
Cobham, 9th Viscount, 1881–1949, vol. IV
Cobham, 10th Viscount, 1909–1977, vol. VII
Cobham, 15th Baron, 1880–1933, vol. III
Cobham, 16th Baron, 1885–1951, vol. V
Cobham, Sir Alan John, 1894–1973, vol. VII
Cobham, Claude Delaval, 1842–1915, vol. I
Cobham, Brig.-Gen. Horace Walter, *died* 1958, vol. V
Cobham, Ven. John Lawrence, 1873–1960, vol. V, vol. VI
Cobham, Ven. John Oldcastle, 1899–1987, vol. VIII
Cobley, Walter Henry, 1850–1938, vol. III
Coborn, Charles, (Colin Whitton McCallum), 1852–1945, vol. IV
Coburn, Sir (Marmaduke) Robert, 1885–1966, vol. VI
Coburn, Sir Robert; *see* Coburn, Sir M. R.
Cochin, Rajah of, *died* 1932, vol. III
Cochin, Maharaja of, 1861–1941, vol. IV
Cochin, Maharaja of, *died* 1943, vol. IV
Cochin, Henry Denys Benoit Marie, 1854–1922, vol. II
Cochran, Alexander, *died* 1961, vol. VI
Cochran, Sir Charles Blake, 1872–1951, vol. V
Cochran, Vice-Adm. Charles Home, 1850–1930, vol. III
Cochran-Patrick, Major Charles Kennedy; *see* Patrick.
Cochran-Patrick, Sir Neil James Kennedy, 1866–1958, vol. V
Cochrane of Cults, 1st Baron, 1857–1951, vol. V
Cochrane of Cults, 2nd Baron, 1883–1968, vol. VI
Cochrane of Cults, 3rd Baron, 1922–1990, vol. VIII
Cochrane, Alfred, 1865–1948, vol. IV
Cochrane, Dame Anne Annette Minnie, *died* 1943, vol. IV
Cochrane, Rear-Adm. Archibald, 1874–1952, vol. V
Cochrane, Captain Hon. Sir Archibald Douglas, 1885–1958, vol. V
Cochrane, Hon. Sir Arthur Auckland Leopold Pedro, 1824–1905, vol. I
Cochrane, Sir Arthur William Steuart, 1872–1954, vol. V
Cochrane, Vice-Adm. Basil Edward, 1841–1922, vol. II
Cochrane, Sir Cecil Algernon, 1869–1960, vol. V
Cochrane, Mrs Catherine, 1849–1934, vol. III
Cochrane, Charles Walter Hamilton, 1876–1932, vol. III
Cochrane, Sir Desmond Oriel Alastair George Weston, 3rd Bt (*cr* 1903), 1918–1979, vol. VII
Cochrane, Rev. Canon Edmund Lewis, 1876–1955, vol. V
Cochrane, Rear-Adm. Sir Edward Owen, 1881–1972, vol. VII
Cochrane, Captain Sir Ernest Cecil, 2nd Bt (*cr* 1903), 1873–1952, vol. V
Cochrane, Captain Hon. Ernest Grey Lambton, 1834–1911, vol. I
Cochrane, Hon. Francis, 1852–1919, vol. II
Cochrane, Helen Lavinia, *died* 1946, vol. IV

Cochrane, Sir Henry, 1st Bt (*cr* 1903), *died* 1904, vol. I
Cochrane, Brig.-Gen. James Kilvington, 1873–1948, vol. IV
Cochrane, Maj.-Gen. James Rupert, 1904–1978, vol. VII
Cochrane, Col John Ernest Charles James, 1870–1938, vol. III
Cochrane, Julia Dorothy, (Hon. Lady Cochrane), 1888–1971, vol. VII
Cochrane, Lt-Col R. C., 1871–1925, vol. III
Cochrane, Air Chief Marshal Hon. Sir Ralph Alexander, 1895–1977, vol. VII
Cochrane, Robert Greenhill, 1899–1985, vol. VIII
Cochrane, Sir Stanley Herbert, 1st Bt (*cr* 1915), 1877–1949, vol. IV
Cochrane, Col Thomas Henry, 1867–1950, vol. IV
Cochrane, Col William Francis Dundonald, 1847–1928, vol. II
Cock, Rev. Albert A., 1883–1953, vol. V
Cock, F. William, 1858–1943, vol. IV
Cock, Gerald, 1887–1973, vol. VII
Cock, Henry, 1842–1922, vol. II
Cock, Julia, *died* 1914, vol. I
Cockayne, Edward Alfred, 1880–1956, vol. V
Cockayne, Dame Elizabeth, 1894–1988, vol. VIII
Cockayne, Leonard, 1855–1934, vol. III
Cockbill, Ven. Charles Shipley, 1888–1965, vol. VI
Cockburn, Archibald William, 1887–1969, vol. VI
Cockburn, Col Charles Douglas L.; *see* Learoyd-Cockburn.
Cockburn, Claud, 1904–1981, vol. VIII
Cockburn, Sir Edward Cludde, 8th Bt, 1834–1903, vol. I
Cockburn, Major Ernest Radcliffe, 1875–1955, vol. V
Cockburn, Col George, 1856–1925, vol. II
Cockburn, Sir George Jack, 1848–1927, vol. II
Cockburn, Major H. Z. C., *died* 1913, vol. I
Cockburn, Henry, 1859–1927, vol. II
Cockburn, Gen. Henry Alexander, 1831–1922, vol. II
Cockburn, Very Rev. James Hutchison, 1882–1973, vol. VII
Cockburn, Sir James Stanhope, 10th Bt, 1867–1947, vol. IV
Cockburn, Hon. Sir John Alexander, 1850–1929, vol. III
Cockburn, Lt-Col Sir John Brydges, 11th Bt, 1870–1949, vol. IV
Cockburn, Nathaniel Clayton, 1866–1924, vol. II
Cockburn, Sir Robert, 9th Bt, 1861–1938, vol. III
Cockburn, Captain William, 1893–1970, vol. VI
Cockburn, Sir William Robert Marshall, 1891–1957, vol. V
Cockburn-Campbell, Sir Alexander Thomas; *see* Campbell.
Cockcraft, Lt-Col Louis William la Trobe, 1880–1963, vol. VI
Cockcroft, Sir John Douglas, 1897–1967, vol. VI
Cocke, Sir Hugh, *died* 1958, vol. V
Cockell, Seton F.; *see* Forbes-Cockell.
Cocker, Ralph, 1908–1986, vol. VIII
Cocker, William Hollis, 1896–1962, vol. VI
Cocker, Sir William Wiggins, 1896–1982, vol. VIII
Cockeram, William Henry, 1857–1946, vol. IV
Cockerell, Douglas Bennett, 1870–1945, vol. IV

Cockerell, Horace Abel, 1832–1908, vol. I

Cockerell, Sir Sydney Carlyle, 1867–1962, vol. VI

Cockerell, Sydney Morris, 1906–1987, vol. VIII

Cockerill, Brig.-Gen. Sir George Kynaston, 1867–1957, vol. V

Cockerline, Sir Walter Herbert, 1856–1941, vol. IV

Cockey, Air Cdre Leonard Herbert, 1893–1978, vol. VII

Cockin, Rt Rev. Frederic Arthur, 1888–1969, vol. VI

Cockin, Ven John Irwin Browne, 1850–1924, vol. II

Cocking, John Martin, 1914–1986, vol. VIII

Cocking, William Trusting, 1862–1912, vol. I

Cockram, Ben, 1903–1981, vol. VIII

Cockram, George, 1861–1950, vol. IV

Cockran, William Bourke, 1854–1923, vol. II

Cocks, Hon. Sir Arthur Alfred Clement, 1862–1943, vol. IV

Cocks, Sir Barnett; *see* Cocks, Sir T. G. B.

Cocks, Charles Sebastian Somers, 1870–1951, vol. V

Cocks, Frederick Seymour, 1882–1953, vol. V

Cocks, George Arthur, *died* 1933, vol. III

Cocks, Rev. Henry Lawrence S.; *see* Somers-Cocks.

Cocks, John Sebastian S.; *see* Somers Cocks.

Cocks, Philip Alphonso Somers, 1862–1940, vol. III

Cocks, Sir (Thomas George) Barnett, 1907–1989, vol. VIII

Cockshutt, Col Hon. Henry, 1868–1944, vol. IV

Cocoto, Spiridon Gerge, 1843–1916, vol. II

Cocteau, Jean, 1889–1963, vol. VI

Codd, Rt Rev. William, 1864–1938, vol. III

Coddington, Fitzherbert John Osbourne, 1881–1956, vol. V

Coddington, Col Herbert Adolphe, 1864–1939, vol. III

Coddington, Sir William, 1st Bt, 1830–1918, vol. II

Code, Rev. Canon George Brereton, 1886–1946, vol. IV

Code Holland, Robert Henry; *see* Holland.

Coderre, Louis, 1865–1935, vol. III

Codling, Sir William Richard, 1879–1947, vol. IV

Codner, Maurice Frederick, 1888–1958, vol. V

Codrington, Lt-Gen. Sir Alfred Edward, 1854–1945, vol. IV

Codrington, Sir Christopher William Gerald Henry, 2nd Bt (*cr* 1876), 1894–1979, vol. VII

Codrington, Engr-Comdr Claude Alexander, 1877–1955, vol. V

Codrington, Col Sir Geoffrey Ronald, 1888–1973, vol. VII

Codrington, Sir Gerald William Henry, 1st Bt (*cr* 1876), 1850–1929, vol. III

Codrington, Brig.-Gen. Hubert Walter, 1864–1940, vol. III

Codrington, Kenneth de Burgh, 1899–1986, vol. VIII

Codrington, Robert Edward, 1869–1908, vol. I

Codrington, Rev. Robert Henry, 1830–1922, vol. II

Codrington, Sir William Mary Joseph, 5th Bt (*cr* 1721), 1829–1904, vol. I

Codrington, William Melville, 1892–1963, vol. VI

Codrington, Sir William Richard, 7th Bt (*cr* 1721), 1904–1961, vol. VI

Codrington, Lt-Col Sir William Robert, 6th Bt (*cr* 1721), 1867–1932, vol. III

Cody, Rev. Henry John, 1868–1951, vol. V

Coe, Captain; *see* Mitchell, Edward Card.

Coe, Peter Leonard, 1929–1987, vol. VIII

Coen, Sir Terence Bernard C.; *see* Creagh Coen.

Coffey, Christopher, 1902–1976, vol. VII

Coffey, Denis Joseph, *died* 1945, vol. V

Coffey, George, 1857–1916, vol. II

Coffey, Rt Rev. John, *died* 1904, vol. I

Coffey, John Nimmo, 1929–1981, vol. VIII

Coffey, Rev. Peter, 1876–1943, vol. IV

Coffey, Hon. Thomas, 1843–1914, vol. I

Coffey, Thomas Malo, 1894–1968, vol. VI

Coffin, Col Campbell, 1867–1952, vol. V

Coffin, Charles Hayden, 1862–1935, vol. III

Coffin, Maj.-Gen. Clifford, 1870–1959, vol. V

Coffin, Rev. Henry Sloane, 1877–1954, vol. V

Coffin, Major John Edward P.; *see* Pine-Coffin.

Coffin, Gen. Roger P.; *see* Pine-Coffin.

Coffin, Walter Harris, 1853–1916, vol. II

Cofman-Nicoresti, Carol Adolph, 1881–1938, vol. III (A), vol. IV

Cogan, Rev. Horace Barbut, *died* 1933, vol. III

Coghill, Col Charles Edward, 1861–1948, vol. IV

Coghill, Douglas Harry, 1855–1928, vol. II

Coghill, Sir Egerton Bushe, 5th Bt, 1853–1921, vol. II

Coghill, Rev. Canon Ernest Arthur, 1859–1941, vol. IV

Coghill, Sir John Joscelyn, 4th Bt, 1826–1905, vol. I

Coghill, John Percival, 1902–1984, vol. VIII

Coghill, Sir Joscelyn Ambrose Cramer, 7th Bt, 1902–1983, vol. VIII

Coghill, Col Kendal Josiah William, 1832–1919, vol. II

Coghill, Sir (Marmaduke Nevill) Patrick (Somerville), 6th Bt, 1896–1981, vol. VIII

Coghill, Nevill Henry Kendal Aylmer, 1899–1980, vol. VII

Coghill, Sir Patrick; *see* Coghill, Sir M. N. P. S.

Coghlan, Col Charles, 1852–1921, vol. II

Coghlan, Hon. Sir Charles Patrick John, 1863–1927, vol. II

Coghlan, Rt Rev. Mgr John, 1887–1963, vol. VI

Coghlan, Hon. Sir Timothy Augustine, 1857–1926, vol. II

Cogswell, Mark James, *died* 1934, vol. III

Cogswell, Rev. Canon William, 1845–1917, vol. II

Cohalan, Most Rev. Daniel, 1858–1952, vol. V

Cohalan, Most Rev. Daniel, 1884–1965, vol. VI

Cohan, George Michael, 1878–1942, vol. IV

Cohen, Baron (Life Peer); Lionel Leonard Cohen, 1888–1973, vol. VII

Cohen of Birkenhead, 1st Baron, 1900–1977, vol. VII

Cohen of Brighton, Baron (Life Peer); Lewis Coleman Cohen, 1897–1966, vol. VI

Cohen, Sir Andrew Benjamin, 1909–1968, vol. VI

Cohen, Rt Hon. Arthur, 1830–1914, vol. I

Cohen, Arthur S.; *see* Sefton-Cohen.

Cohen, Augustus, *died* 1903, vol. I

Cohen, Sir Benjamin Arthur, 1862–1942, vol. IV

Cohen, Sir Benjamin Louis, 1st Bt, 1844–1909, vol. I

Cohen, Major Sir Brunel; *see* Cohen, Major Sir J. B. B.

Cohen, Lt-Col Charles Waley, 1879–1963, vol. VI

Cohen, Clifford Theodore, 1906–1972, vol. VII

Cohen, Sir Edgar Abraham, 1908–1973, vol. VII

Cohen, Rabbi Francis Lyon, 1862–1934, vol. III

Cohen, Hannah F., *died* 1946, vol. IV
Cohen, Brig. Hon. Harold Edward, 1881–1946, vol. IV
Cohen, Harriet, 1895–1967, vol. VI
Cohen, Harry F.; *see* Freeman-Cohen.
Cohen, Hon. Henry Emanuel, 1840–1912, vol. I
Cohen, Hon. Henry Isaac, 1872–1942, vol. IV
Cohen, Sir Herbert Benjamin, 2nd Bt, 1874–1968, vol. VI
Cohen, Isaac Michael, 1884–1951, vol. V
Cohen, Israel, 1879–1961, vol. VI
Cohen, Sir Jack, 1896–1982, vol. VIII
Cohen, Major Sir (Jack Benn) Brunel, 1886–1965, vol. VI
Cohen, Col Jacob Waley, 1874–1948, vol. IV
Cohen, Sir John Edward, 1898–1979, vol. VII
Cohen, John, 1911–1985, vol. VIII
Cohen, John Michael, 1903–1989, vol. VIII
Cohen, Joseph L., *died* 1940, vol. III
Cohen, Julius Berend, 1859–1935, vol. III
Cohen, Sir Karl Cyril, *died* 1973, vol. VII
Cohen, Comdr Kenneth H. S., 1900–1984, vol. VIII
Cohen, Sir Leonard Lionel, 1858–1938, vol. III
Cohen, Sir Lewis, 1849–1933, vol. III
Cohen, Marcel, 1884–1974, vol. VII
Cohen, Mary Gwendolen, (Mrs Arthur M. Cohen), 1893–1962, vol. VI
Cohen, Nat, 1905–1988, vol. VIII
Cohen, Mrs Nathaniel Louis, *died* 1917, vol. II
Cohen, Percy, 1891–1987, vol. VIII
Cohen, Reuben, 1880–1958, vol. V
Cohen, Reuben K.; *see* Kelf-Cohen.
Cohen, Sir Rex Arthur Louis, 1906–1988, vol. VIII
Cohen, Sir Robert Waley, 1877–1952, vol. V
Cohen, Sir Samuel Sydney, 1869–1948, vol. IV
Cohn, Jefferson Davis, 1881–1951, vol. V
Coia, Jack Antonio, 1898–1981, vol. VIII
Coit, Stanton, 1857–1944, vol. IV
Cokayne, George Edward, 1825–1911, vol. I
Coke, Adm. Sir Charles Henry, 1854–1945, vol. IV
Coke, Charlotte, (Mrs Talbot Coke), 1843–1922, vol. II
Coke, Captain Desmond, 1879–1931, vol. III
Coke, Dorothy Josephine, 1897–1979, vol. VII (AII)
Coke, Brig.-Gen. Edward Beresford, 1850–1924, vol. II
Coke, Brig.-Gen. Edward Sacheverell D'Ewes, 1872–1941, vol. IV
Coke, Gerald Edward, 1907–1990, vol. VIII
Coke, Hon. Henry John, 1827–1916, vol. II
Coke, Col Jacynth d'Ewes FitzErcald, 1879–1963, vol. VI
Coke, Sir John, 1807–1897, vol. I
Coke, Captain John Gilbert de Odingsells, 1874–1937, vol. III
Coke, Major Hon. Sir John Spencer, 1880–1957, vol. V
Coke, Maj.-Gen. John Talbot, 1841–1912, vol. I
Coke, Captain Hon. Reginald, 1883–1969, vol. VI
Coke, Major Hon. Richard, 1876–1964, vol. VI
Coke, Comdr Hon. Roger, 1886–1960, vol. V
Coke, Mrs Talbot; *see* Coke, Charlotte.
Coke, Lt-Col Wenman Clarence Walpole, 1828–1907, vol. I

Coke Wallis, Leonard George, 1900–1974, vol. VII
Coker, Col Edmund Rogers, 1844–1914, vol. I
Coker, Dame Elizabeth, 1915–1988, vol. VIII
Coker, Ernest George, 1869–1946, vol. IV
Coker, Sir Salako Ambrosius B.; *see* Benka-Coker.
Colahan, Nicholas Whistler, *died* 1930, vol. III
Colam, Sir Harold Nugent, 1882–1956, vol. V
Colam, Robert Frederick, *died* 1942, vol. IV
Colban, Erik Andreas, 1876–1956, vol. V
Colbeck, Edmund Henry, 1865–1942, vol. IV
Colbert, John Patrick, 1898–1975, vol. VII
Colborne, Col Hon. Francis Lionel Lydstone, 1855–1924, vol. II
Colborne, Surg. Rear-Adm. William John, 1865–1945, vol. IV
Colborne, Surg. Rear-Adm. William John, *died* 1971, vol. VII
Colburn, Oscar Henry, 1925–1990, vol. VIII
Colby, Col Cecil John Herbert S.; *see* Spence-Colby.
Colby, Charles W., 1867–1955, vol. V
Colby, Sir Geoffrey Francis Taylor, 1901–1958, vol. V
Colchester, 3rd Baron, 1842–1919, vol. II
Colchester-Wemyss, Sir Francis, 1872–1954, vol. V
Colchester-Wemyss, Maynard Willoughby, 1846–1930, vol. III
Colclough, Rear-Adm. (S) Beauchamp Urquhart, 1867–1949, vol. IV
Coldrick, William, 1896–1975, vol. VII
Coldridge, Ward, 1864–1926, vol. II
Coldstream, Sir John, 1877–1954, vol. V
Coldstream, John Phillips, 1842–1909, vol. I
Coldstream, Col William Menzies, 1869–1943, vol. IV
Coldstream, Sir William Menzies, 1908–1987, vol. VIII
Coldwell, Hon. George Robson, 1858–1924, vol. II
Coldwell-Smith, Lt-Col Frederick Lawrence, 1895–1967, vol. VI (AII)
Cole, Viscount; Michael Galbraith Lowry Cole, 1921–1956, vol. V
Cole, Baron (Life Peer); George James Cole, 1906–1979, vol. VII
Cole, Air Vice-Marshal Adrian Trevor, 1895–1966, vol. VI
Cole, Alan Summerly, 1846–1934, vol. III
Cole, Alfred Clayton, 1854–1920, vol. II
Cole, Vice-Adm. Sir Antony Bartholomew, 1909–1967, vol. VI
Cole, Brig.-Gen. Arthur Willoughby George Lowry, 1860–1915, vol. I
Cole, Major Aubrey du Plat Thorold, 1877–1939, vol. III
Cole, Madame Belle, *died* 1904, vol. I
Cole, Charles Woolsey, 1906–1978, vol. VII
Cole, Col Sir Edward Hearle, 1863–1949, vol. IV
Cole, Edward Nicholas, 1909–1977, vol. VII
Cole, Rev. Edward Pattinson, *died* 1926, vol. II
Cole, Eric Kirkham, 1901–1966, vol. VI
Cole, Francis Joseph, 1872–1959, vol. V
Cole, George, *died* 1913, vol. I
Cole, George Douglas Howard, 1889–1959, vol. V
Cole, Lt-Gen. Sir George Sinclair, 1911–1973, vol. VII

Cole, Maj.-Gen. George Wynne, 1836–1908, vol. I
Cole, Grenville Arthur James, 1859–1924, vol. II
Cole, Harold William, 1884–1959, vol. V
Cole, Lt-Col Henry W.; see Wells-Cole.
Cole, Lt-Col Sir Henry Walter George, died 1932, vol. III
Cole, Herbert Aubrey, 1911–1984, vol. VIII
Cole, Maj.-Gen. Sir Herbert Covington, died 1959, vol. V
Cole, John, 1903–1975, vol. VII
Cole, Rev. John Francis, died 1921, vol. II
Cole, John Sydney Richard, 1907–1989, vol. VIII
Cole, Leslie Barrett, 1898–1983, vol. VIII
Cole, Dame Margaret Isabel, 1893–1980, vol. VII
Cole, Sir Noel, 1892–1975, vol. VII
Cole, Norman John, 1909–1979, vol. VII
Cole, Percival Pasley, died 1948, vol. IV
Cole, Percy Frederick, 1882–1968, vol. VI
Cole, Reginald John Vicat; see Cole, John.
Cole, Rex Vicat, 1870–1940, vol. III
Cole, Gp Captain Robert Arthur Alexander, 1901–1949, vol. IV
Cole, Rev. Robert Eden George, died 1921, vol. II
Cole, Robert Henry, 1866–1926, vol. II
Cole, Ven. Robert Henry, died 1934, vol. III
Cole, Robert Langton, 1858–1928, vol. II
Cole, Robin John, 1935–1988, vol. VIII
Cole, Sophie, 1862–1947, vol. IV
Cole, Lt-Col Stanley James, 1884–1949, vol. IV
Cole, Rev. Theodore Edward Fortescue, died 1944, vol. IV
Cole, Thomas Loftus, died 1961, vol. VI
Cole, Walton Adamson, 1912–1963, vol. VI
Cole, Rev. William John, died 1933, vol. III
Cole-Deacon, Gerald John, 1890–1968, vol. VI
Cole-Hamilton, Lt-Col Claud George; see Hamilton.
Cole-Hamilton, Air Vice-Marshal John Beresford, 1894–1945, vol. IV
Colebatch, Hon. Sir Hal Pateshall, 1872–1953, vol. V
Colebrook, Edward Hilder, 1898–1977, vol. VII
Colebrook, Leonard, 1883–1967, vol. VI
Colebrooke, 1st Baron, 1861–1939, vol. III
Colefax, Sir Arthur, died 1936, vol. III
Colegate, Sir Arthur, died 1956, vol. V
Coleman, Arthur Philemon, 1852–1939, vol. III
Coleman, Lt-Gen. Sir Charles; see Coleman, Lt-Gen. Sir C. F. C.
Coleman, Charles James, died 1908, vol. I
Coleman, Lt-Gen. Sir (Cyril Frederick) Charles, died 1974, vol. VII
Coleman, D'Alton Corry, 1879–1956, vol. V
Coleman, Ephraim Herbert, 1890–1961, vol. VI
Coleman, Frank, 1876–1962, vol. VI
Coleman, Lt-Col George Burdett, died 1923, vol. II
Coleman, Herbert Cecil, 1893–1965, vol. V
Coleman, Rev. James, 1831–1913, vol. I
Coleman, Rt Rev. John Aloysius, 1887–1947, vol. IV, vol. V
Coleman, Laurence Vail, 1893–1982, vol. VIII
Coleman, Leslie Charles, died 1954, vol. V
Coleman, Rt Rev. Michael Edward, 1902–1969, vol. VI
Coleman, Rev. Canon Noel Dolben, 1891–1948, vol. IV

Colenbrander, Col Johann William, 1859–1918, vol. II
Coleraine, 1st Baron, 1901–1980, vol. VII
Coleridge, 2nd Baron, 1851–1927, vol. II
Coleridge, 3rd Baron, 1877–1955, vol. V
Coleridge, 4th Baron, 1905–1984, vol. VIII
Coleridge, Christabel Rose, 1843–1921, vol. II
Coleridge, Ernest Hartley, 1846–1920, vol. II
Coleridge, Hon. Gilbert James Duke, 1859–1953, vol. V
Coleridge, Lt-Col Hugh Fortescue, 1859–1928, vol. II
Coleridge, Gen. Sir John Francis Stanhope Duke, 1878–1951, vol. V
Coleridge, Miss Mary Elizabeth, 1861–1907, vol. I
Coleridge, Hon. Stephen, 1854–1936, vol. III
Coleridge, Wilfrid Duke, 1889–1956, vol. V
Coleridge-Taylor, Samuel, 1875–1912, vol. I
Coles, Captain Arthur Edward, 1902–1982, vol. VIII
Coles, Col Arthur Horsman, 1856–1931, vol. III
Coles, Sir Arthur William, 1892–1982, vol. VIII
Coles, Charles, 1853–1926, vol. II
Coles, Charles, 1878–1947, vol. IV
Coles, Sir Edgar Barton, 1899–1981, vol. VIII
Coles, Edward Horsman, 1865–1948, vol. IV
Coles, Sir George James, 1885–1977, vol. VII
Coles, Gordon Robert, 1913–1975, vol. VII
Coles, Hon. Sir Jenkin, 1842–1911, vol. I
Coles, John, died 1919, vol. II
Coles, Sir Kenneth Frank, 1896–1985, vol. VIII
Coles, Col Morton Calverley, 1863–1943, vol. IV
Coles, Sir Norman Cameron, 1907–1989, vol. VIII
Coles, Sir Richard James, 1862–1935, vol. III
Coles, Sherard Osborn C.; see Cowper-Coles.
Coles, Rev. Vincent Stuckey Stratton, 1845–1929, vol. III
Coles, Air Marshal Sir William Edward, 1913–1979, vol. VII
Coles, Major William Hewett, 1882–1955, vol. V
Colette, 1873–1954, vol. V
Coley, Frederic Collins, died 1928, vol. II
Coley, (Howard William) Maitland, 1910–1981, vol. VIII
Coley, Maitland; see Coley, H. W. M.
Colfox, Lt-Col Sir Philip; see Colfox, Lt-Col Sir W. P.
Colfox, Lt-Col Sir (William) Philip, 1st Bt, 1888–1966, vol. VI
Colgan, Most Rev. Joseph, 1824–1911, vol. I
Colgate, Dennis Harvey, 1922–1990, vol. VIII
Colgrain, 1st Baron, 1866–1954, vol. V
Colgrain, 2nd Baron, 1891–1973, vol. VII
Colijn, Hendrikus, 1869–1944, vol. IV
Colivet, Michael Patrick, 1884–1955, vol. V
Coll, Sir Anthony Michael, 1861–1931, vol. III
Collar, (Arthur) Roderick, 1908–1986, vol. VIII
Collar, Roderick; see Collar, A. R.
Collard, Maj.-Gen. Albert Sydney, 1876–1938, vol. III (A), vol. IV
Collard, Col Alexander Arthur Lysons, 1871–1947, vol. IV
Collard, Major Alfred Stephen, 1865–1941, vol. IV
Collard, Allan Ovenden, 1861–1928, vol. II
Collard, Vice-Adm. Bernard St G., 1876–1962, vol. VI
Collard, Lt-Col Charles Edwin, died 1942, vol. IV

Collard, Sir George, 1840–1921, vol. II

Collard, Patrick John, 1920–1989, vol. VIII

Collard, Gp Captain Richard Charles Marler, 1911–1962, vol. VI

Collcutt, Thomas Edward, 1840–1924, vol. II

Colledge, Lionel, 1883–1948, vol. IV

Collen, Lt-Col Edwin Henry Ethelbert, 1875–1943, vol. IV

Collen, Lt-Gen. Sir Edwin Henry Hayter, 1843–1911, vol. I

Collens, John Antony, 1930–1988, vol. VIII

Coller, Frank Herbert, 1866–1938, vol. III

Colles, Comdr Sir Dudley; *see* Colles, Comdr Sir E. D. G.

Colles, Comdr Sir (Ernest) Dudley (Gordon), 1889–1976, vol. VII

Colles, Henry Cope, 1879–1943, vol. IV

Colles, Ramsay, 1862–1919, vol. II

Colles, William Morris, *died* 1926, vol. II

Collet, Clara E., 1860–1948, vol. IV

Collet, Sir Mark Edlmann, 2nd Bt, 1864–1944, vol. IV

Collet, Sir Mark Wilks, 1st Bt, 1816–1905, vol. I

Collet, Sir Wilfred, 1856–1929, vol. III

Colleton, Sir Robert Augustus William, 9th Bt, 1854–1938, vol. III

Collett, Charles Benjamin, 1871–1952, vol. V

Collett, Sir Charles Henry, 1st Bt, 1864–1938, vol. III

Collett, Rear-Adm. George Kempthorne, 1907–1982, vol. VIII

Collett, Sir Henry, 1836–1901, vol. I

Collett, Sir Henry Seymour, 2nd Bt, 1893–1971, vol. VII

Collett, Col Hon. Herbert Brayley, 1877–1947, vol. IV

Collett, Col John Henry, 1876–1942, vol. IV

Collett, Sir Kingsley; *see* Collett, Sir T. K.

Collett, Rt Rev. Dom Martin, 1879–1948, vol. IV

Collett, Sir (Thomas) Kingsley, 1906–1987, vol. VIII

Collette, Charles, 1842–1924, vol. II

Colley, David Isherwood, 1916–1975, vol. VII

Colley, Richard, 1893–1964, vol. VI

Colley, Robert D.; *see* Davies-Colley.

Colley, Thomas, 1894–1983, vol. VIII

Collick, Percy Henry, 1899–1984, vol. VIII

Collie, J. Norman, 1859–1942, vol. IV

Collie, Sir John, 1860–1935, vol. III

Collie, Ruth, *died* 1936, vol. III

Collier, Air Vice-Marshal Sir (Alfred) Conrad, 1895–1986, vol. VIII

Collier, Maj.-Gen. Angus Lyell, 1893–1971, vol. VII

Collier, Charles Saint John, 1880–1944, vol. IV

Collier, Air Vice-Marshal Sir Conrad; *see* Collier, Air Vice-Marshal, Sir A. C.

Collier, Constance, 1880–1955, vol. V

Collier, Dorothy Josephine, 1894–1972, vol. VII

Collier, Lt-Col Ernest Victor, 1878–1964, vol. VI

Collier, Frank Simon, 1900–1964, vol. VI

Collier, Frederick William, 1851–1925, vol. II

Collier, Sir George Herman, 1856–1941, vol. IV

Collier, Horace Stansfield, *died* 1930, vol. III

Collier, James, 1846–1925, vol. II (A), vol. III

Collier, James, 1870–1935, vol. III

Collier, Hon. John, 1850–1934, vol. III

Collier, John Francis, 1829–1913, vol. I

Collier, Joseph, *died* 1967, vol. VI

Collier, Air Cdre Kenneth Dowsett Gould, 1892–1971, vol. VII

Collier, Sir Laurence, 1890–1976, vol. VII

Collier, Hon. Margaret Isabella; *see* Galletti di Cadilhac, Countess.

Collier, Marie Elizabeth, 1927–1971, vol. VII

Collier, Mayo, 1857–1931, vol. III

Collier, Most Rev. Patrick, 1880–1964, vol. VI

Collier, Peter Fenelon, 1849–1909, vol. I

Collier, Hon. Philip, 1874–1948, vol. IV

Collier, Rev. Samuel Francis, 1855–1921, vol. II

Collier, Rev. Thomas Grey, 1844–1933, vol. III

Collier, William, 1856–1935, vol. III

Collier, William Adrian Larry, 1913–1984, vol. VIII

Collier, William Douglas, 1894–1953, vol. V

Collin, Annie Rosalie, 1852–1957, vol. V

Collindridge, Frank, *died* 1951, vol. V

Colling, Rev. James, *died* 1929, vol. III

Collinge, Walter E., *died* 1947, vol. IV

Collingridge, George Rooke, 1867–1944, vol. IV

Collingridge, William, 1854–1927, vol. II

Collings, Albert Henry, *died* 1947, vol. IV

Collings, Col Alfred Henry, 1847–1933, vol. III

Collings, Col Godfrey Disney, 1855–1941, vol. IV

Collings, Rt Hon. Jesse, 1831–1920, vol. II

Collings, Maj.-Gen. Wilfred d'Auvergne, 1893–1984, vol. VIII

Collingwood, Adrian Redman, 1910–1987, vol. VIII

Collingwood, Arthur, 1879–1952, vol. V

Collingwood, Bertram James, *died* 1934, vol. III

Collingwood, Sir Charles Arthur, 1887–1964, vol. VI

Collingwood, Brig.-Gen. Clennell William, 1873–1960, vol. V

Collingwood, Cuthbert, 1826–1908, vol. I

Collingwood, Rt Rev. Mgr Canon Cuthbert, 1908–1980, vol. VII

Collingwood, Col Cuthbert George, 1848–1933, vol. III

Collingwood, Sir Edward Foyle, 1900–1970, vol. VI

Collingwood, Lt-Gen. Sir George; *see* Collingwood, Lt-Gen. Sir R. G.

Collingwood, Rear-Adm. George Trevor, 1863–1922, vol. II

Collingwood, Harry; *see* Lancaster, W. J. C.

Collingwood, Lawrance Arthur, 1887–1982, vol. VIII

Collingwood, Lt-Gen. Sir (Richard) George, 1903–1986, vol. VIII

Collingwood, Robin George, 1889–1943, vol. IV

Collingwood, Brig. Sydney, 1892–1986, vol. VIII

Collingwood, Sir William, 1855–1928, vol. II

Collingwood, William Gershom, 1854–1932, vol. III

Collins, Baron (Life Peer); Richard Henn Collins, 1842–1911, vol. I

Collins, Alfred Tenison, 1852–1945, vol. IV

Collins, Sir Archibald John, 1890–1955, vol. V

Collins, Lt-Col Arthur, 1845–1911, vol. I

Collins, Arthur, 1880–1952, vol. V

Collins, Arthur Ernest, 1871–1926, vol. II

Collins, Brig. Arthur Francis St Clair, 1892–1980, vol. VII

Collins, Arthur Jefferies, 1893–1976, vol. VII

Collins, Sir Arthur John Hammond, 1834–1915, vol. I
Collins, Arthur Pelham, 1863–1932, vol. III
Collins, Bernard Abdy, 1880–1951, vol. V
Collins, Bernard John, 1909–1989, vol. VIII
Collins, Charles, *died* 1921, vol. II
Collins, Maj.-Gen. Charles Edward E.; *see* Edward-Collins.
Collins, Sir Charles Henry, 1887–1983, vol. VIII
Collins, Cyril George, 1880–1947, vol. IV
Collins, Dale, 1897–1956, vol. V
Collins, Sir D(aniel) George, 1869–1959, vol. V
Collins, Sir David Charles, 1908–1983, vol. VIII
Collins, Maj.-Gen. Dennis Joseph, *died* 1939, vol. III
Collins, Douglas, 1912–1972, vol. VII
Collins, Douglas Henry, 1907–1964, vol. VI
Collins, Maj.-Gen. Sir Dudley Stuart, 1881–1959, vol. V
Collins, Edward Treacher, 1862–1932, vol. III
Collins, Adm. Sir Frederick (Basset) E.; *see* Edward-Collins.
Collins, Sir Geoffrey Abdy, 1888–1986, vol. VIII
Collins, Sir George, *see* Collins, Sir D. G.
Collins, George Edward, 1880–1968, vol. VI
Collins, Adm. Sir (George) Frederick (Basset) E.; *see* Edward-Collins.
Collins, Hon. George Thomas, 1839–1926, vol. II
Collins, Brig. Gerald E.; *see* Edward-Collins.
Collins, Sir Godfrey Ferdinando Stratford, 1888–1952, vol. V
Collins, Rt Hon. Sir Godfrey P., 1875–1936, vol. III
Collins, Herbert Frederick, 1890–1967, vol. VI
Collins, Herbert Jeffery, 1907–1968, vol. VI
Collins, Horatio John, 1894–1963, vol. VI
Collins, Sir James Patrick, 1891–1964, vol. VI
Collins, James Richard, 1869–1934, vol. III
Collins, Rev. Canon John; *see* Collins, Rev. Canon L. J.
Collins, Vice-Adm. Sir John Augustine, 1899–1989, vol. VIII
Collins, John Churton, 1848–1908, vol. I
Collins, John Henry, 1880–1952, vol. V
Collins, Rt Rev. John J., 1857–1934, vol. III
Collins, John Philip, *died* 1954, vol. V
Collins, John Rupert, *died* 1965, vol. VI
Collins, Maj.-Gen. John Stratford, 1851–1908, vol. I
Collins, Gen. J(oseph) Lawton, 1896–1987, vol. VIII
Collins, Joseph Thomas, 1863–1938, vol. III
Collins, Rear-Adm. Kenneth St Barbe, 1904–1982, vol. VIII
Collins, Rev. Canon Lewis John, 1905–1982, vol. VIII
Collins, Brig. Lionel Peter, 1878–1957, vol. V
Collins, Mabel; *see* Cook, Mrs M.
Collins, Mark, vol. III
Collins, Michael, 1890–1922, vol. II
Collins, Norman Richard, 1907–1982, vol. VIII
Collins, Patrick, 1859–1943, vol. IV
Collins, Rev. Percy Herbert, *died* 1941, vol. IV
Collins, Rear-Adm. Ralph, 1877–1957, vol. VI
Collins, Rev. Reginald Francis, 1851–1933, vol. III
Collins, Rt Rev. Richard, 1857–1924, vol. II
Collins, Lt-Col Hon. Richard Henn, 1873–1952, vol. V

Collins, Sir Robert Hawthorn, 1841–1908, vol. I
Collins, Maj.-Gen. Robert John, 1880–1950, vol. IV
Collins, Col Robert Joseph, 1848–1924, vol. II
Collins, Sir Robert Muirhead, 1852–1927, vol. II
Collins, Seymour John, 1906–1970, vol. VI
Collins, Sir Stephen, 1847–1925, vol. II
Collins, Hon. Sir Stephen Ogle H.; *see* Henn-Collins.
Collins, Sir Thomas, 1860–1944, vol. IV
Collins, Most Rev. Thomas Gibson George, 1873–1927, vol. II
Collins, Victor John; *see* Baron Stonham.
Collins, Rt Rev. W. E., 1867–1911, vol. I
Collins, Lt-Col William Alexander, 1873–1945, vol. IV
Collins, Sir William Alexander Roy, 1900–1976, vol. VII
Collins, Col Hon. William Edward, 1853–1934, vol. III
Collins, Sir William Henry, *died* 1947, vol. IV
Collins, Sir William Job, 1859–1946, vol. IV
Collins, Col Comdt Hon. William Richard, 1876–1944, vol. IV
Collins, William Wiehe, 1862–1951, vol. V
Collinson, Alfred Howe, 1866–1927, vol. II
Collinson, Col Harold, 1876–1945, vol. IV
Collinson, Lt-Col John, 1859–1901, vol. I
Collinson, Joseph, 1871–1952, vol. V
Collinson, Richard Jeffreys Hampton, 1924–1983, vol. VIII
Collinson, Thomas Henry, 1858–1928, vol. II
Collinson, William Edward, 1889–1969, vol. VI
Collip, James Bertram, 1892–1965, vol. VI
Collis, Edgar Leigh, 1870–1957, vol. V
Collis, Maj.-Gen. Francis William, 1839–1905, vol. I
Collis, Maj.-Gen. Sir James Norman C.; *see* Cooke-Collis.
Collis, John Stewart, 1900–1984, vol. VIII
Collis, Maurice, 1889–1973, vol. VII
Collis, Very Rev. Maurice Henry Fitzgerald, 1859–1947, vol. IV
Collis, Lt-Col Robert Henry, 1874–1930, vol. III
Collis, Col William C.; *see* Cooke-Collis.
Collis, William Robert FitzGerald, 1900–1975, vol. VII
Collishaw, Air Vice-Marshal Raymond, 1893–1976, vol. VII
Collison, Bt Col Charles Sydney, 1871–1935, vol. III
Collison, Levi, 1875–1965, vol. VI (AII)
Collison, Lewis Herbert, 1908–1988, vol. VIII
Collison, Ven. William Henry, 1847–1922, vol. II
Collisson, Rev. William Alexander Houston, 1865–1920, vol. II
Collister, Sir Harold James, 1885–1950, vol. IV
Colls, John Howard, *died* 1910, vol. I
Collyer, Ven. Daniel, 1848–1924, vol. II
Collyer, Maj.-Gen. John Johnston, 1870–1941, vol. IV
Collyer, Robert, 1823–1912, vol. I
Collyer, William Robert, 1842–1928, vol. II
Collymore, Sir Allan; *see* Collymore, Sir E. A.
Collymore, Sir (Ernest) Allan, 1893–1962, vol. VI
Colman, Cecil, 1878–1954, vol. V
Colman, Lt-Col Frederick Gordon Dalziel, *died* 1969, vol. VI

Colman, Sir (George) Stanley, *died* 1966, vol. VI

Colman, Grace Mary, 1892–1971, vol. VII

Colman, Sir Jeremiah, 1st Bt (*cr* 1907), 1859–1942, vol. IV

Colman, Sir Jeremiah, 2nd Bt (*cr* 1907), 1886–1961, vol. VI

Colman, Sir Nigel Claudian Dalziel, 1st Bt (*cr* 1952), *died* 1966, vol. VI

Colman, Col Percy Edward, 1875–1951, vol. V

Colman, Ronald, 1891–1958, vol. V

Colman, Russell James, 1861–1946, vol. IV

Colman, Sir Stanley; *see* Colman, Sir G. S.

Colmer, Joseph Grose, 1856–1937, vol. III

Colmore, G.; *see* Weaver, Mrs Baillie.

Colmore, Wing-Comdr Reginald Blayney Bulteel, 1888–1930, vol. III

Colmore, Thomas Milnes, 1845–1916, vol. II

Colnaghi, Sir Dominic Ellis, 1834–1908, vol. I

Colomb, Brig.-Gen. George Henry Cooper, 1862–1934, vol. III

Colomb, Vice-Adm. Philip Howard, 1831–1899, vol. I

Colomb, Adm. Philip Howard, 1867–1958, vol. V

Colomb, Rupert Palmer, 1869–1955, vol. V

Colombos, C(onstantine) John, *died* 1968, vol. VI

Colonne, Edouard, 1838–1910, vol. I

Colquhoun, Col Sir Alan John, 6th Bt *cr* 1786 (styled 13th Bt, *cr* 1625), 1838–1910, vol. I

Colquhoun, Archibald Ross, 1848–1914, vol. I

Colquhoun, Brian; *see* Colquhoun, C. B. H.

Colquhoun, (Cecil) Brian (Hugh), 1902–1977, vol. VII

Colquhoun, Ethel M., (Mrs Tawse Jollie), *died* 1950, vol. IV (A), vol. V

Colquhoun, Sir Iain, 7th Bt (*cr* 1786), 1887–1948, vol. IV

Colquhoun, Sir James, 5th Bt *cr* 1786 (styled 12th Bt, *cr* 1625), 1844–1907, vol. I

Colquhoun, Major Julian Campbell, 1870–1937, vol. III

Colquhoun, Col Malcolm Alexander, 1870–1950, vol. IV

Colquhoun, Robert, 1914–1962, vol. VI

Colquhoun, Ven. William, *died* 1920, vol. II

Colquhoun, William Erskine C.; *see* Campbell-Colquhoun.

Colquhoun, Comdr William Jarvie, 1859–1908, vol. I

Colson, Charles, 1839–1915, vol. I

Colson, Charles Henry, 1864–1939, vol. III

Colson, Francis Henry, 1857–1943, vol. IV

Colson, Rev. Francis Tovey, 1858–1929, vol. III

Colson, Surg. Vice-Adm. Sir Henry St Clair, 1887–1968, vol. VI

Colson, Lionel Hewitt, 1887–1943, vol. IV

Colson, Percy, 1873–1952, vol. V

Colson, Phyllis Constance, 1904–1972, vol. VII

Colston, Sir Charles Blampied, 1891–1969, vol. VI

Colston-Baynes, Dorothy Julia, *died* 1973, vol. VII

Colt, Rev. Sir Edward Harry Dutton, 8th Bt, 1850–1931, vol. III

Colt, George Frederick Russell, 1837–1909, vol. I

Colt, Sir Henry Archer, 9th Bt, 1882–1951, vol. V

Coltart, Captain Cyril George Bucknill, 1889–1964, vol. VI

Coltart, James Milne, 1903–1986, vol. VIII

Colthurst, Sir George Oliver, 7th Bt, 1882–1951, vol. V

Colthurst, Sir George St John, 6th Bt, 1850–1925, vol. II

Colthurst, Captain Sir Richard St John Jefferyes, 8th Bt, 1887–1955, vol. V

Colthurst-Vesey, Captain Charles Nicholas, 1860–1915, vol. I

Coltman-Rogers, Muriel Augusta Gillian, *died* 1952, vol. V

Colton, Cyril Hadlow, 1902–1988, vol. VIII

Colton, Gladys, 1909–1986, vol. VIII

Colton, Hon. Sir John, 1823–1902, vol. I

Colton, William Robert, 1867–1921, vol. II

Colum, Padraic, 1881–1972, vol. VII

Colvile, Ernest Frederick, 1879–1967, vol. VI

Colvile, Lt-Gen. Sir Fiennes Middleton, 1832–1917, vol. II

Colvile, Brig.-Gen. George Northcote, 1867–1940, vol. III

Colvile, Lancelot Edward, 1876–1947, vol. IV

Colvile, Comdr Mansel Brabazon Fiennes, 1887–1942, vol. IV

Colvill, Lt-Col David Chaigneau, 1898–1979, vol. VII

Colvill, Robert Frederick Stewart, 1860–1936, vol. III

Colville of Culross, 1st Viscount, 1818–1903, vol. I

Colville of Culross, 2nd Viscount, 1854–1928, vol. II

Colville of Culross, 3rd Viscount, 1888–1945, vol. IV

Colville, Brig.-Gen. Arthur Edward William, 1857–1942, vol. IV

Colville, Sir Cecil; *see* Colville, Sir H. C.

Colville, Lady Cynthia; *see* Colville, Lady H. C.

Colville, Maj.-Gen. Edward Charles, 1905–1982, vol. VIII

Colville, Hon. George Charles, 1867–1943, vol. IV

Colville, Lady (Helen) Cynthia, 1884–1968, vol. VI

Colville, Sir (Henry) Cecil, 1891–1984, vol. VIII

Colville, Maj.-Gen. Sir Henry Edward, 1852–1907, vol. I

Colville, Rev. James, *died* 1953, vol. V

Colville, John, 1852–1901, vol. I

Colville, Lt-Col John Ross, 1878–1935, vol. III

Colville, Sir John Rupert, 1915–1987, vol. VIII

Colville, Norman Robert, 1893–1974, vol. VII

Colville, Comdr Sir Richard, 1907–1975, vol. VII

Colville, Adm. Hon. Sir Stanley Cecil James, 1861–1939, vol. III

Colville, Col Hon. Sir William James, 1827–1903, vol. I

Colvin, Arthur Edmund, 1884–1966, vol. VI (AII)

Colvin, Sir Auckland, 1838–1908, vol. I

Colvin, Sir C. Preston, 1879–1950, vol. IV

Colvin, Col Cecil Hodgson, 1858–1938, vol. III

Colvin, Sir Elliot Graham, 1861–1940, vol. III

Colvin, Lt-Col Elliot James Dowell, 1885–1950, vol. IV

Colvin, Lt-Col Forrester Farnell, 1860–1936, vol. III

Colvin, Sir George Lethbridge, 1878–1962, vol. VI

Colvin, Major Hugh, 1887–1962, vol. VI

Colvin, Ian Duncan, 1877–1938, vol. III

Colvin, Col J. M. C., 1870–1945, vol. IV

Colvin, Brig. Dame Mary Katherine Rosamond, 1907–1988, vol. VIII

Colvin, Sir Preston; *see* Colvin, Sir C. P.

Colvin, Adm. Sir Ragnar Musgrave, 1882–1954, vol. V

Colvin, Brig.-Gen. Sir Richard Beale, 1856–1936, vol. III

Colvin, Sir Sidney, 1845–1927, vol. II

Colvin, Thomas, 1863–1940, vol. III (A), vol. IV

Colvin, Sir Walter Mytton, 1847–1908, vol. I

Colvin, Very Rev. William Evans, *died* 1949, vol. IV

Colvin-Smith, Surg.-Gen. Sir Colvin, 1829–1913, vol. I

Colwell, Gen. George Harrie Thorn, 1841–1913, vol. I

Colwell, Hector Alfred, 1875–1946, vol. IV

Colwell, Rev. James, 1860–1930, vol. III

Colwyn, 1st Baron, 1859–1946, vol. IV

Colwyn, 2nd Baron, 1914–1966, vol. VI

Colyer, Air Marshal Douglas, 1893–1978, vol. VII

Colyer, Sir Frank, 1866–1954, vol. V

Colyer-Fergusson, Sir Thomas Colyer, 3rd Bt, 1865–1951, vol. V

Comay, Michael, 1908–1987, vol. VIII

Combe, Maj.-Gen. Boyce Albert, 1841–1920, vol. II

Combe, Charles, 1836–1920, vol. II

Combe, Charles Harvey, 1863–1935, vol. III

Combe, Captain Christian, 1858–1940, vol. III

Combe, George Alexander, 1877–1933, vol. III

Combe, Air Vice-Marshal Gerard, 1902–1979, vol. VII

Combe, Harvey Trewythen Brabazon, 1852–1923, vol. II

Combe, Lt-Col Herbert, 1878–1931, vol. III

Combe, Maj.-Gen. John Frederick Boyce, 1895–1967, vol. VI

Combe, Brig.-Gen. Lionel, 1861–1950, vol. IV

Combe, Sir Ralph Molyneux, 1872–1946, vol. IV

Combe, Richard Henry, 1829–1900, vol. I

Combe, Simon Harvey, 1903–1965, vol. VI

Comben, Robert Stone, 1868–1957, vol. V

Comber, Henry Gordon, 1869–1935, vol. III

Comber, Norman Mederson, 1888–1953, vol. V

Combermere, 4th Viscount, 1887–1969, vol. VI

Combes, Emile, 1839–1921, vol. II

Combridge, Annie, 1862–1949, vol. IV

Comerford, Lt-Col Augustine Ambrose, 1886–1944, vol. IV

Comfort, Mrs Bessie; *see* Marchant, Bessie.

Comino, Demetrius, 1902–1988, vol. VIII

Comins, Ven. Richard Blundell, *died* 1919, vol. II

Commerell, Sir John Edmund, 1829–1901, vol. I

Commings, Maj.-Gen. Percy Ryan Conway, 1880–1958, vol. V

Commins, Andrew, 1829–1916, vol. II

Common, Sir Andrew; *see* Common, Sir L. A.

Common, Andrew Ainslie, 1841–1903, vol. I

Common, Frank Breadon, 1891–1969, vol. VI

Common, Sir (Lawrence) Andrew, 1889–1953, vol. V

Commons, John Rogers, 1862–1945, vol. IV

Commy, Rt Rev. John, 1843–1911, vol. I

Comparetti, Domenico, 1835–1927, vol. II

Comper, Sir (John) Ninian, 1864–1960, vol. V, vol. VI

Comper, Sir Ninian; *see* Comper, Sir J. N.

Compston, Rev. Herbert Fuller Bright, 1866–1931, vol. III

Compston, John Albert, *died* 1930, vol. III

Compston, Nigel Dean, 1918–1986, vol. VIII

Compton, Rt Rev. Lord Alwyne, 1825–1906, vol. I

Compton, Lord Alwyne Frederick, 1855–1911, vol. I

Compton, Arthur Holly, 1892–1962, vol. VI

Compton, Brig.-Gen. Charles William, 1869–1933, vol. III

Compton, Col. Lord Douglas James Cecil, 1865–1944, vol. IV

Compton, Edward Robert Francis, 1891–1977, vol. VII

Compton, Eric Henry, 1902–1982, vol. VIII

Compton, Fay, 1894–1978, vol. VII

Compton, Henry Francis, 1872–1943, vol. IV

Compton, Herbert Eastwick, 1853–1906, vol. I

Compton, Joseph, 1881–1937, vol. III

Compton, Joseph, 1891–1964, vol. VI

Compton, Karl Taylor, 1887–1954, vol. V

Compton, Maurice, 1908–1974, vol. VII

Compton, Robert Herbert K.; *see* Keppel-Compton.

Compton, Captain Walter Burge, *died* 1932, vol. III

Compton, Rev. William Cookworthy, 1854–1936, vol. III

Compton, Air Vice-Marshal William Vernon C.; *see* Crawford-Compton.

Compton-Burnett, Dame Ivy, 1884–1969, vol. VI

Compton Mackenzie, Faith; *see* Mackenzie, Lady.

Compton-Rickett, Arthur, 1869–1937, vol. III

Compton-Rickett, Rt Hon. Sir Joseph, 1847–1919, vol. II

Compton-Thornhill, Sir Anthony John; *see* Thornhill.

Comrie, John Dixon, 1875–1939, vol. III

Comrie, Leslie John, 1893–1950, vol. IV

Comyn, Lt-Col Edward Walter, 1868–1949, vol. IV

Comyn, Henry Ernest Fitzwilliam, 1854–1941, vol. IV

Comyn, Col Lewis James, 1878–1961, vol. VI

Comyn, Michael, 1877–1952, vol. V

Comyn-Platt, Sir Thomas Walter; *see* Platt.

Comyns, Henry Joseph, 1868–1943, vol. IV

Comyns, Louis, *died* 1962, vol. VI

Comyns Carr, Sir Arthur Strettell, 1882–1965, vol. VI

Conacher, Hamilton, 1881–1939, vol. III

Conacher, Mungo, 1901–1977, vol. VII

Conan Doyle, Adrian Malcolm, 1910–1970, vol. VI

Conant, James Bryant, 1893–1978, vol. VII

Conant, Sir Roger John Edward, 1st Bt, 1899–1973, vol. VII

Concanon, Col Henry, 1861–1926, vol. II

Concannon, Terence Patrick, 1932–1990, vol. VIII

Conde, Harold Graydon, *died* 1959, vol. V

Conder, Charles, 1868–1909, vol. I

Conder, Claude Reignier, 1848–1910, vol. I

Conder, Rev. Canon Edward Baines, 1872–1936, vol. III

Condliffe, John Bell, 1891–1981, vol. VIII

Condon, Edward Uhler, 1902–1974, vol. VII

Conerney, Very Rev. John Pirrie, *died* 1940, vol. III (A), vol. IV

Conesford, 1st Baron, 1892–1974, vol. VII

Coney, Rev. Canon Harold Robert Harvey, 1889–1982, vol. VIII

Coneybeer, Hon. Frederick William, 1859–1950, vol. IV

Congdon, Col Arthur Edward Osmond, *died* 1924, vol. II

Conger, Edwin H., 1843–1907, vol. I

Congleton, 4th Baron, 1839–1906, vol. I

Congleton, 5th Baron, 1890–1914, vol. I

Congleton, 6th Baron, 1892–1932, vol. III

Congleton, 7th Baron, 1925–1967, vol. VI

Congreve, Cecil Ralph Townshend, 1876–1952, vol. V

Congreve, Comdr Sir Geoffrey, 1st Bt, *died* 1941, vol. IV

Congreve, John, 1872–1957, vol. V

Congreve, Gen. Sir Walter Norris, 1862–1927, vol. II

Coningham, Air Marshal Sir Arthur, 1895–1948, vol. IV

Coningham, Maj.-Gen. Frank Evelyn, 1870–1934, vol. III

Coningham, Captain Herbert John, 1867–1936, vol. III

Coningsby, Eric Alfred, 1909–1955, vol. V

Conklin, Edwin Grant, 1863–1952, vol. V

Conlay, William Lance, 1869–1927, vol. II

Connal, Benjamin Michael, 1861–1944, vol. IV

Connal, Col Kenneth Hugh Munro, 1870–1949, vol. IV

Connally, Thomas Terry; *see* Connally, Tom.

Conally, Tom, (Thomas Terry Connally), 1877–1963, vol. VI

Connard, Philip, 1875–1958, vol. V

Connaught, Prince Arthur of, 1883–1938, vol. III

Connaught, HRH Princess Arthur of; *see* Fife, Duchess of.

Connaught and Strathearn, 2nd Duke of, 1914–1943, vol. IV

Connel, John Arthur, 1903–1961, vol. VI

Connell, Rev. Alexander, 1866–1920, vol. II

Connell, Sir Charles, 1900–1972, vol. VII

Connell, Sir Charles Gibson, 1899–1985, vol. VIII

Connell, Major Hugh John, 1884–1934, vol. III

Connell, Sir Isaac, 1858–1935, vol. III

Connell, James MacLuckie, 1867–1947, vol. IV

Connell, Jim, *died* 1929, vol. III

Connell, John, (John Henry Robertson), 1909–1965, vol. VI

Connell, Rev. Robert, 1852–1936, vol. III

Connell, Sir Robert Lowden, 1867–1936, vol. III

Connell, Walter Thomas, 1873–1964, vol. VI

Connellan, Joseph, *died* 1967, vol. VI (AII)

Connelly, Sir Francis Raymond, 1895–1949, vol. IV

Connelly, Marc, 1890–1980, vol. VII

Connely, Willard, 1888–1967, vol. VI

Connemara, 1st Baron, 1827–1901, vol. I

Conner, Cyril, 1900–1981, vol. VIII

Conner, Henry Daniel, 1859–1925, vol. II

Conner, Lewis Atterbury, 1867–1950, vol. IV (A), vol. V

Connibere, Sir Charles Wellington, *died* 1941, vol. IV

Connolly, Col Benjamin Bloomfield, 1845–1924, vol. II

Connolly, Cyril Vernon, 1903–1974, vol. VII

Connolly, Air Cdre Hugh Patrick, 1915–1968, vol. VI

Connolly, Hon. Sir James Daniel, 1869–1962, vol. VI

Connolly, Martin, 1874–1945, vol. IV

Connolly, Richard Joseph, 1873–1948, vol. IV

Connolly, Thomas James D.; *see* Doull-Connolly.

Connolly, William Patrick Joseph, *died* 1935, vol. III

Connolly, Sir Willis Henry, 1901–1981, vol. VIII

Connor, Dame (Annie) Jean, 1899–1968, vol. VI

Connor, Comdr Edward Richard, *died* 1903, vol. I

Connor, Francis Richard, 1870–1956, vol. V

Connor, Maj.-Gen. Sir Frank Powell, *died* 1954, vol. V

Connor, Captain Harry George A.; *see* Adams-Connor.

Connor, Dame Jean; *see* Connor, Dame A. J.

Connor, Col John Colpoys, 1867–1936, vol. III

Connor, Rev. Muirhead Mitchell, *died* 1930, vol. III

Connor, Ralph, (Rev. Charles W. Gordon), 1860–1937, vol. III

Connor, Sir William Neil, 1909–1967, vol. VI

Conolly, Major Edward Michael, 1874–1956, vol. V

Conolly, Brig. John James Pollock, 1896–1950, vol. IV

Conor, William, 1881–1968, vol. VI

Conrad, Joseph, 1857–1924, vol. II

Conran, (George) Loraine, 1912–1986, vol. VIII

Conran, Loraine; *see* Conran, G. L.

Conran-Smith, Sir Eric Conran, 1890–1960, vol. V

Conroy, Charles O'Neill, 1871–1946, vol. IV

Conroy, Sir Diarmaid William, 1913–1978, vol. VII

Conroy, J. G., *died* 1915, vol. I

Conroy, Sir John, 3rd Bt, 1845–1900, vol. I

Conry, Major James Lionel Joyce, 1873–1914, vol. I

Conry, Brig. John de Lisle, 1882–1971, vol. VII

Consett, Rear-Adm. Montagu William Warcop Peter, 1871–1945, vol. IV

Considine, Sir Heffernan James Fritz, 1846–1912, vol. I

Constable, Hon. Lord; Andrew Henderson Briggs Constable, 1865–1928, vol. II

Constable, Andrew Henderson Briggs; *see* Constable, Hon. Lord.

Constable, Frank Challice, 1846–1937, vol. III

Constable, Sir Henry Marmaduke S.; *see* Strickland-Constable.

Constable, Brig. Raleigh Charles Joseph C.; *see* Chichester-Constable.

Constable, Walter George Raleigh C.; *see* Chichester-Constable.

Constable, William George, 1887–1976, vol. VII

Constable-Maxwell-Scott, Mary Monica; *see* Scott, Hon. Mrs Maxwell.

Constanduros, Mabel, *died* 1957, vol. V

Constant, Hayne, 1904–1968, vol. VI

Constant, Jean Joseph B.; *see* Benjamin-Constant.

Constantine, Baron (Life Peer); Learie Nicholas Constantine, 1901–1971, vol. VII

Constantine, Maj.-Gen. Charles Francis, *died* 1953, vol. V

Constantine, Sir George Baxandall, 1902–1969, vol. VI

Constantine, Tom, 1926–1981, vol. VIII

Constantinides, Most Rev. Michael, 1892–1958, vol. V

Constandin, Fernand Joseph Désiré; *see* Fernandel.

Conti, Italia, *died* 1946, vol. IV

Converse, Frederick Shepherd, 1871–1940, vol. III (A), vol. IV

Conway of Allington, 1st Baron, 1856–1937, vol. III
Conway, Brig. Albert Edward, 1891–1974, vol. VII
Conway, Arthur William, 1875–1950, vol. IV (A)
Conway, Conway Joseph, *died* 1953, vol. V
Conway, Edward Joseph, 1894–1968, vol. VI
Conway, Essie Ruth, *died* 1934, vol. III
Conway, Hugh Graham, 1914–1989, vol. VIII
Conway, James, 1915–1974, vol. VII
Conway, Lt-Col John Marcus Hobson, *died* 1940, vol. III
Conway, Marmaduke Percy, 1885–1961, vol. VI
Conway, Moncure Daniel, 1832–1907, vol. I
Conway, Robert Russ, 1863–1950, vol. IV
Conway, Prof. Robert Seymour, 1864–1933, vol. III
Conway, His Eminence Cardinal William, 1913–1977, vol. VII
Conway-Gordon, Col Esme Cosmo William, 1875–1962, vol. VI
Conway-Gordon, Col Gwynnedd, 1868–1936, vol. III
Conway-Gordon, Lt-Gen. Lewis, 1863–1933, vol. III
Conwy, Rear-Adm. Rafe Grenville Rowley-, 1875–1951, vol. V
Conybeare, Alfred Edward, 1875–1952, vol. V
Conybeare, Charles Augustus Vansittart, 1853–1919, vol. II
Conybeare, Charles Frederick Pringle, 1860–1927, vol. II
Conybeare, Rear-Adm. Crawford James Markland, 1854–1937, vol. III
Conybeare, Frederick Cornwallis, 1856–1924, vol. II
Conybeare, Sir John Josias, 1888–1967, vol. VI
Conybeare, John William Edward, 1843–1931, vol. III
Conybeare, Very Rev. William James, 1871–1955, vol. V
Conyers, Dorothea, 1873–1949, vol. IV
Conyers, Evelyn Augusta, *died* 1944, vol. IV
Conyers, Sir James Reginald, 1879–1948, vol. IV
Conyngham, 4th Marquess, 1857–1897, vol. I
Conyngham, 5th Marquess, 1883–1906, vol. I
Conyngham, 6th Marquess, 1890–1974, vol. VII
Conyngham, Col Sir Gerald Ponsonby L.; *see* Lenox-Conyngham.
Conyngham, Sir William Fitzwilliam L.; *see* Lenox-Conyngham.
Cooch, Col Charles, 1829–1917, vol. II
Cooch Behar, Col Maharajah Sir Nripendra Narayan Bhup Bahadur of, 1862–1911, vol. I
Cooch Behar, Maharaja of, *died* 1913, vol. I
Cooch Behar, Maharaja Bhup Bahadur of, 1886–1922, vol. II
Coode, Sir Bernard Henry, 1887–1962, vol. VI
Coode, Rear-Adm. Charles Penrose Rushton, 1870–1939, vol. III
Coode, Captain Percival, *died* 1902, vol. I
Coode-Adams, Sir John; *see* Adams.
Coo-ee; *see* Walker, William Sylvester.
Cook, Air Vice-Marshal Albert Frederick, 1901–1980, vol. VII
Cook, Sir Albert Ruskin, 1870–1951, vol. V
Cook, Albert Stanburrough, 1853–1927, vol. II
Cook, Alexander Edward, 1906–1984, vol. VIII
Cook, Arthur Bernard, 1868–1952, vol. V
Cook, Arthur Herbert, 1911–1988, vol. VIII

Cook, Arthur James, 1885–1931, vol. III
Cook, Arthur Kemball, 1851–1928, vol. II
Cook, Rev. Canon Arthur Malcolm, 1883–1964, vol. VI
Cook, Arthur Willsteed, *died* 1930, vol. III
Cook, Sir Basil (Alfred) Kemball-, 1876–1949, vol. IV
Cook, Bernard Christopher Allen, 1906–1985, vol. VIII
Cook, Sir Charles Archer, 1849–1934, vol. III
Cook, Col Charles Chesney, 1866–1937, vol. III
Cook, Charles Henry; *see* Bickerdyke, John.
Cook, Edgar T., 1880–1953, vol. IV
Cook, Sir Edmund Ralph, *died* 1942, vol. IV
Cook, Sir Edward Mitchener, 1881–1955, vol. V
Cook, Sir Edward Tyas, 1857–1919, vol. II
Cook, Ven. Edwin Arthur, 1888–1972, vol. VII
Cook, Lt-Col Edwin Berkeley, 1869–1914, vol. I
Cook, Elsie, (Mrs E. Thornton Cook), *died* 1960, vol. V
Cook, Air Vice-Marshal Eric, 1920–1985, vol. VIII
Cook, Eric William, 1920–1990, vol. VIII
Cook, Vice-Adm. Eric William L.; *see* Longley-Cook.
Cook, Ernest Benjamin, 1879–1952, vol. V
Cook, Sir Ernest Henry, 1855–1945, vol. IV
Cook, Sir Francis, 1st Bt, 1817–1901, vol. I
Cook, Sir Francis Ferdinand Maurice, 4th Bt, 1907–1978, vol. VII
Cook, Frank, 1888–1972, vol. VII
Cook, Frank Allan Grafton, 1902–1973, vol. VII
Cook, Sir Frederick Charles, 1875–1947, vol. IV
Cook, Sir Frederick Lucas, 2nd Bt, 1844–1920, vol. II
Cook, Lt-Col George Trevor-Roper, 1877–1918, vol. II
Cook, Gilbert, 1885–1951, vol. V
Cook, Sir Halford; *see* Cook, Sir P. H.
Cook, Sir Henry, 1848–1928, vol. II
Cook, Henry Caldwell, 1886–1939, vol. III
Cook, Ven. Henry Lucas, *died* 1928, vol. II
Cook, Brig.-Gen. Henry Rex, 1863–1950, vol. IV
Cook, Sir Herbert Frederick, 3rd Bt, 1868–1939, vol. III
Cook, Herbert George Graham, 1864–1939, vol. III
Cook, Maj.-Gen. James, 1844–1928, vol. II
Cook, James Allan, 1858–1933, vol. III
Cook, Hon. James H.; *see* Hume-Cook.
Cook, Sir James Wilfred, 1900–1975, vol. VII
Cook, John Gilbert, 1911–1979, vol. VII
Cook, John Irvine, 1892–1952, vol. V
Cook, Rt Hon. Sir Joseph, 1860–1947, vol. IV
Cook, Mrs Keningale, (Mabel Collins), 1851–1927, vol. II
Cook, Percival Robert, 1867–1939, vol. III
Cook, Sir (Philip) Halford, 1912–1990, vol. VIII
Cook, Stanley Arthur, 1873–1949, vol. IV
Cook, Stanley Smith, 1875–1952, vol. V
Cook, Hon. Sir Tasker Keech, 1867–1937, vol. III
Cook, Sir Theodore Andrea, 1867–1928, vol. II
Cook, Thomas Fotheringham, 1908–1952, vol. V
Cook, Thomas Reginald Hague, 1866–1925, vol. II
Cook, Lt-Col Thomas Russell Albert Mason, 1902–1970, vol. VI
Cook, Rt Rev. Thomas William, 1866–1928, vol. II
Cook, Sir William, 1834–1908, vol. I

Cook, Sir William Richard Joseph, 1905–1987, vol. VIII

Cooke, Col Alfred Fothergill, 1871–1946, vol. IV

Cooke, Rev. Alfred Hands, *died* 1937, vol. III

Cooke, Amos John, 1885–1961, vol. VI

Cooke, Lt-Gen. Anthony Charles, 1826–1905, vol. I

Cooke, Arthur Hafford, 1912–1987, vol. VIII

Cooke, Lt-Col Aubrey St John, 1872–1935, vol. III

Cooke, Brig.-Gen. Bertram Hewett Hunter, 1874–1946, vol. IV

Cooke, Brian K.; *see* Kennedy-Cooke.

Cooke, Sir Charles Arthur John, 11th Bt, 1905–1978, vol. VII

Cooke, Rev. Canon Charles Edward, 1860–1939, vol. III

Cooke, Charles John Bowen, 1859–1920, vol. II

Cooke, Charles Wallwyn Radcliffe-, *died* 1911, vol. I

Cooke, Christopher Herbert, 1899–1979, vol. VII

Cooke, Sir Clement K.; *see* Kinloch-Cooke.

Cooke, Conrad William, 1843–1926, vol. II

Cooke, Air Marshal Sir Cyril Bertram, 1895–1972, vol. VII

Cooke, Deryck Victor, 1919–1976, vol. VII

Cooke, Sir Douglas; *see* Cooke, Sir J. D.

Cooke, Sir (Edward) Marriott, 1852–1931, vol. III

Cooke, Rev. George Albert, 1865–1939, vol. III

Cooke, Rev. Canon Greville Vaughan Turner, 1894–1989, vol. VIII

Cooke, Henry Arthur, 1862–1946, vol. IV

Cooke, Sir Henry Frank, 1900–1973, vol. VII

Cooke, Sir Henry P.; *see* Paget-Cooke.

Cooke, Lt-Gen. Sir Herbert Fothergill, 1871–1936, vol. III

Cooke, Isaac, 1846–1922, vol. II

Cooke, Sir (James) Douglas, *died* 1949, vol. IV

Cooke, Rear-Adm. John Ernest, 1899–1980, vol. VII

Cooke, Sir John F.; *see* Fletcher-Cooke.

Cooke, John Fitzpatrick, *died* 1930, vol. III

Cooke, Rear-Adm. John Gervaise Beresford, 1911–1976, vol. VII

Cooke, John Hunt, 1828–1908, vol. I

Cooke, John Sholto Fitzpatrick, 1906–1975, vol. VII

Cooke, Sir Leonard, 1901–1976, vol. VII

Cooke, Rev. Leslie Edward, 1908–1967, vol. VI

Cooke, Lewis Henry, *died* 1929, vol. III

Cooke, Sir Marriott; *see* Cooke, Sir E. M.

Cooke, Michael Joseph, 1881–1960, vol. V

Cooke, Mordecai Cubitt, 1825–1913, vol. I

Cooke, Oliver Dayrell Paget P.; *see* Paget-Cooke.

Cooke, Col Philip Ralph D.; *see* Davies-Cooke.

Cooke, Philip Tatton Davies-, 1863–1946, vol. IV

Cooke, Sir Robert Gordon, 1930–1987, vol. VIII

Cooke, Rev. Canon Robert Herbert Michael, 1864–1939, vol. III

Cooke, Brig. Robert Thomas, 1897–1984, vol. VIII

Cooke, Robert Victor, 1902–1978, vol. VII

Cooke, Roger Gresham, 1907–1970, vol. VI

Cooke, Maj.-Gen. Ronald Basil Bowen Bancroft, 1899–1971, vol. VII

Cooke, Rupert C.; *see* Croft-Cooke.

Cooke, Hon. Sir Samuel Burgess Ridgway, 1912–1978, vol. VII

Cooke, Maj.-Gen. Sidney Arthur, 1903–1977, vol. VII

Cooke, Sir Stenson, 1874–1942, vol. IV

Cooke, Temple, 1851–1925, vol. II

Cooke, Theodore, 1836–1910, vol. I

Cooke, Tom Harry, 1923–1987, vol. VIII

Cooke, William Charles Cyril, 1881–1966, vol. VI

Cooke, William Cubitt, 1866–1951, vol. V

Cooke, William Ernest, 1863–1947, vol. IV

Cooke, William Henry, 1843–1921, vol. II

Cooke, Sir William Henry Charles Wemyss, 10th Bt, 1872–1964, vol. VI

Cooke-Collis, Maj.-Gen. Sir James; *see* Cooke-Collis, Maj.-Gen. Sir W. J. N.

Cooke-Collis, Col William, 1847–1933, vol. III

Cooke-Collis, Maj.-Gen. Sir (William) James Norman, 1876–1941, vol. IV

Cooke-Hurle, Col Edward Forbes; *see* Hurle.

Cooke-Hurle, John A.; *see* Hurle.

Cooke-Taylor, Richard Whately, 1842–1918, vol. II

Cooke-Yarborough, George Eustace, 1876–1938, vol. III

Cooke-Yarborough, Rev. John James; *see* Yarborough.

Cookman, Anthony Victor, 1894–1962, vol. VI

Cookson, Sir Charles Alfred, 1829–1906, vol. I

Cookson, Charles Lisle Stirling, 1855–1919, vol. II

Cookson, Christopher, *died* 1948, vol. IV

Cookson, Captain Claude Edward, 1879–1963, vol. VI

Cookson, Clive, 1879–1971, vol. VII

Cookson, Maj.-Gen. George Arthur, 1860–1929, vol. III

Cookson, Henry Anstey, 1886–1949, vol. IV

Cookson, John Blencowe, 1843–1910, vol. I

Cookson, Lt-Col John Cookson F.; *see* Fife-Cookson.

Cookson, Col Philip Blencowe, 1871–1928, vol. II

Cookson, Sydney Spencer S.; *see* Sawrey-Cookson.

Coolidge, Archibald Cary, 1866–1928, vol. II

Coolidge, Calvin, 1872–1933, vol. III

Coolidge, William Augustus Brevoort, 1850–1926, vol. II

Coolidge, William David, 1873–1975, vol. VII

Cools-Lartigue, Alexander Raphael, 1899–1973, vol. VII

Coomaraswamy, Ananda K., 1877–1947, vol. IV

Coomaraswamy, Sir Velupillai, 1892–1972, vol. VII

Coombe, Sir Thomas Melrose, 1877–1959, vol. V

Coomber, John Edward, 1901–1963, vol. VI

Coombes, Very Rev. George Frederick, 1856–1922, vol. II

Coombs, Carey Franklin, 1879–1932, vol. III

Coombs, Captain Thomas Edward, 1884–1953, vol. V

Coombs, William Harry, 1893–1969, vol. VI

Coombs, William Heron, 1851–1931, vol. III

Coombs, Rev. Canon William Joseph Mundy, 1871–1966, vol. VI

Coop, Hubert, 1872–1953, vol. V

Coop, Rev. James Ogden, 1869–1928, vol. II

Coope, Edward Jesser, 1849–1918, vol. II

Cooper of Culross, 1st Baron, 1892–1955, vol. V

Cooper of Stockton Heath, Baron (Life Peer); John Cooper, 1908–1988, vol. VIII

Cooper, Sqdn Ldr Albert Edward, 1910–1986, vol. VIII

Cooper, Sir Alfred, 1838–1908, vol. I

Cooper, Sir Alfred, 1846–1916, vol. II

Cooper, Alfred B., 1863–1936, vol. III

Cooper, Rt Rev. Alfred Cecil, *died* 1964, vol. VI

Cooper, Alfred Heaton, *died* 1929, vol. III

Cooper, Rev. Alfred William Francis, *died* 1920, vol. II

Cooper, Alice J., *died* 1917, vol. II

Cooper, Captain Archibald Frederick, 1885–1975, vol. VII

Cooper, Archibald Samuel, 1871–1942, vol. IV

Cooper, Col Arthur; *see* Aglionby, Col A.

Cooper, Rev. Arthur Nevile, 1850–1943, vol. IV

Cooper, (Arthur William) Douglas, 1911–1984, vol. VIII

Cooper, Sir Astley Paston P.; *see* Paston-Cooper.

Cooper, Austin Edwin, 1869–1954, vol. V

Cooper, Bryan Ricco, 1884–1930, vol. III

Cooper, Very Rev. Cecil Henry Hamilton, 1871–1942, vol. IV

Cooper, Charles Alfred, 1829–1916, vol. II

Cooper, Maj.-Gen. Charles Duncan, 1849–1929, vol. III

Cooper, Sir Charles Eric Daniel, 5th Bt (*cr* 1863), 1906–1984, vol. VIII

Cooper, Col Charles James, *died* 1931, vol. III

Cooper, Sir Charles Naunton Paston P., 4th Bt (*cr* 1821); *see* Paston-Cooper.

Cooper, Sir Clive F.; *see* Forster-Cooper.

Cooper, Major Colin, 1892–1938, vol. III

Cooper, Sir Daniel, 1st Bt (*cr* 1863), 1821–1902, vol. I

Cooper, Sir Daniel, 2nd Bt (*cr* 1863), 1848–1909, vol. I

Cooper, Sir Daniel; *see* Cooper, Sir W. G. D.

Cooper, David, 1855–1940, vol. III

Cooper, Sir Dhanjishah Bomanjee, *died* 1947, vol. IV

Cooper, Lady Diana, (Diana, Viscountess Norwich), 1892–1986, vol. VIII

Cooper, Douglas; *see* Cooper, A. W. D.

Cooper, Sir Edward Ernest, 1st Bt (*cr* 1920), 1848–1922, vol. II

Cooper, Rt Hon. Edward Henry, 1827–1902, vol. I

Cooper, Edward Herbert, 1867–1910, vol. I

Cooper, Maj.-Gen. Edward Joshua, 1858–1945, vol. IV

Cooper, Sir Edwin, 1874–1942, vol. IV

Cooper, Sir Ernest Herbert, 1877–1962, vol. VI

Cooper, Francis Alfred, 1860–1933, vol. III

Cooper, Sir Francis Ashmole, (Sir Frank), 4th Bt, 1905–1987, vol. VIII

Cooper, Sir Francis D'Arcy, 1st Bt (*cr* 1941), 1882–1941, vol. IV

Cooper, Hon. Frank Arthur, 1872–1949, vol. IV

Cooper, Col Frank Sandiford, 1873–1936, vol. III

Cooper, Frank Shewell, 1864–1949, vol. IV

Cooper, Frank Towers, 1863–1915, vol. I

Cooper, Rev. Frederic Wilson, 1860–1941, vol. IV

Cooper, Gary Frank James, 1901–1961, vol. V

Cooper, Sir George Alexander, 1st Bt (*cr* 1905, of Hursley), 1856–1940, vol. III

Cooper, Captain Sir George James Robertson, 2nd Bt (*cr* 1905, of Hursley), 1890–1961, vol. VI

Cooper, George Joseph, *died* 1909, vol. I

Cooper, Gerald Melbourne, 1892–1947, vol. IV

Cooper, Sir Gilbert Alexander, 1903–1989, vol. VIII

Cooper, Giles Stannus, 1918–1966, vol. VI

Cooper, Dame Gladys Constance, 1888–1971, vol. VII

Cooper, Sir Guy; *see* Cooper, Sir H. G.

Cooper, Harold H.; *see* Hinton-Cooper.

Cooper, Sir (Harold) Stanford, 1889–1976, vol. VII

Cooper, Col Harry, 1847–1928, vol. II

Cooper, Sir Henry, 1873–1962, vol. VI

Cooper, Sir Henry; *see* Cooper, Sir W. H.

Cooper, Henry, 1877–1947, vol. IV

Cooper, Rt Rev. Henry Edward, 1845–1916, vol. II

Cooper, Sir (Henry) Guy, 1890–1975, vol. VII

Cooper, Sir Henry Lovick, 5th Bt (*cr* 1821), 1875–1959, vol. V

Cooper, Henry St John, 1869–1926, vol. II

Cooper, Very Rev. James, 1846–1922, vol. II

Cooper, James, 1882–1949, vol. IV

Cooper, Sir James Alexander, *died* 1936, vol. III

Cooper, Rev. James Hughes, *died* 1909, vol. I

Cooper, James Lees, 1907–1980, vol. VII

Cooper, Rev. Canon James Sidmouth, 1869–1961, vol. VI

Cooper, John Paul, *died* 1933, vol. III

Cooper, Joshua Edward Synge, 1901–1981, vol. VIII

Cooper, Maj.-Gen. Kenneth Christie, 1905–1981, vol. VIII

Cooper, Lance Harries, 1890–1972, vol. VII

Cooper, Leslie Hugh Norman, 1905–1985, vol. VIII

Cooper, Col Lyall Newcomen, *died* 1929, vol. III

Cooper, Malcolm Edward, 1907–1977, vol. VII

Cooper, Prof. Malcolm McGregor, 1910–1989, vol. VIII

Cooper, Margaret, *died* 1922, vol. II

Cooper, Martin Du Pré, 1910–1986, vol. VIII

Cooper, Sir Patrick Ashley, 1887–1961, vol. VI

Cooper, Percival Martin, 1887–1951, vol. V

Cooper, Hon. Sir Pope Alexander, 1848–1923, vol. II

Cooper, Sir Richard Ashmole, 2nd Bt (*cr* 1905, of Shenstone Court), 1874–1946, vol. IV

Cooper, Brig.-Gen. Richard Joshua, 1860–1938, vol. III

Cooper, Sir Richard Powell, 1st Bt (*cr* 1905, of Shenstone Court), 1847–1913, vol. I

Cooper, Sir Robert Elliott-, 1845–1942, vol. IV

Cooper, Robert Higham, 1878–1944, vol. IV

Cooper, Robert William, 1877–1970, vol. VI

Cooper, Sir Stanford; *see* Cooper, Sir H. S.

Cooper, Rev. Canon Sydney, 1862–1942, vol. IV

Cooper, Hon. Sir Theo, 1850–1925, vol. II

Cooper, Thomas Edwin; *see* Utley, T. E.

Cooper, Rev. Thomas John, 1837–1911, vol. I

Cooper, Thomas Sidney, 1803–1902, vol. I

Cooper, Rev. Vincent King, 1849–1922, vol. II

Cooper, Hon. Sir Walter Jackson, 1892–1973, vol. VII

Cooper, Wilbraham Villiers, 1876–1955, vol. V

Cooper, Wilfred Edward S.; *see* Shewell-Cooper.

Cooper, Sir William Charles, 3rd Bt (*cr* 1863), 1851–1925, vol. II

Cooper, William Edward Deck, 1877–1962, vol. VI

Cooper, Lt-Col Sir William Earnshaw, 1843–1924, vol. II

Cooper, Sir (William George) Daniel, 4th Bt (cr 1863), 1877–1954, vol. V

Cooper, Sir (William) Henry, 1909–1990, vol. VIII

Cooper, Sir William Herbert, 3rd Bt (cr 1905, of Shenstone Court), 1901–1970, vol. VI

Cooper, William Ranson, 1868–1926, vol. II

Cooper, Lt-Col William Weldon H.; see Herring-Cooper.

Cooper-Key, Major Sir Aston, 1861–1930, vol. III

Cooper-Key, Captain Edmund Moore Cooper, 1862–1933, vol. III

Cooper-Key, Sir Neill, 1907–1981, vol. VIII

Coopland, George William, 1875–1975, vol. VII

Cooray, Edmund Joseph, 1907–1979, vol. VII

Cooray, His Eminence Thomas Benjamin, Cardinal, 1901–1988, vol. VIII

Coote, Rev. Sir Algernon, 11th Bt, 1817–1899, vol. I

Coote, Sir Algernon Charles Plumptre, 12th Bt, 1847–1920, vol. II

Coote, Captain Sir Colin Reith, 1893–1979, vol. VII

Coote, Sir Eyre, 1857–1925, vol. II

Coote, Rt Rev. Mgr Canon George, 1881–1961, vol. VI

Coote, Howard, 1865–1943, vol. IV

Coote, Rear-Adm. Sir John Ralph, 14th Bt, 1905–1978, vol. VII

Coote, Sir Ralph Algernon, 13th Bt, 1874–1941, vol. IV

Coote, William, 1863–1924, vol. II

Coote, William Alexander, 1842–1919, vol. II

Cope, 1st Baron, 1870–1946, vol. IV

Cope, Sir Alfred, died 1954, vol. V

Cope, Sir Anthony, 13th Bt (cr 1611), 1842–1932, vol. III

Cope, Sir Anthony Mohun Leckonby, 15th Bt (cr 1611), 1927–1966, vol. VI

Cope, Sir Arthur Stockdale, 1857–1940, vol. III

Cope, Charles Elvey, died 1943, vol. IV

Cope, Captain Sir Denzil, 14th Bt (cr 1611), 1873–1940, vol. III

Cope, John Hautenville, died 1942, vol. IV

Cope, John Wigley, 1907–1987, vol. VIII

Cope, Sir Mordaunt Leckonby, 16th Bt (cr 1611), 1878–1972, vol. VII

Cope, Sir Ralph, 1862–1949, vol. IV

Cope, Sir Thomas, 1st Bt (cr 1918), 1840–1924, vol. II

Cope, Brig.-Gen. Sir Thomas George, 2nd Bt (cr 1918), 1884–1966, vol. VI

Cope, Sir (Vincent) Zachary, 1881–1974, vol. VII

Cope, Sir Zachary; see Cope, Sir V. Z.

Copeau, Jacques, 1879–1949, vol. IV

Copeland, Edwin Bingham, 1873–1964, vol. VI

Copeland, Hon. Henry, 1839–1904, vol. I

Copeland, Ida, (Mrs Ronald Copeland), died 1964, vol. VI

Copeland, Ralph, 1837–1905, vol. I

Copeland, (Richard) Ronald (John), died 1958, vol. V

Copeland, Ronald; see Copeland, Richard R. J.

Copeland, Theodore Benfey, 1878–1952, vol. V

Copeman, Col Charles Edward Fraser, died 1949, vol. IV

Copeman, Constance Gertrude, 1864–1953, vol. V (A), vol. VI

Copeman, Lt-Col Hugh Charles, 1862–1955, vol. V

Copeman, Vice-Adm. Sir Nicholas Alfred, 1906–1969, vol. VI

Copeman, Sydney A. Monckton, 1862–1947, vol. IV

Copeman, William Sydney Charles, 1900–1970, vol. VI

Copestake, Barry; see Copestake, T. B.

Copestake, Thomas Barry, 1930–1989, vol. VIII

Copinger, Walter Arthur, 1847–1910, vol. I

Copland, Aaron, 1900–1990, vol. VIII

Copland, Col Alexander, 1833–1908, vol. I

Copland, Sir Douglas Berry, 1894–1971, vol. VII

Copland, Harold W.; see Wallace-Copland.

Copland, Sir William Robertson, 1838–1907, vol. I

Copland, William Wallace, 1853–1922, vol. II

Copland-Griffiths, Brig. Felix Alexander Vincent, 1894–1967, vol. VI

Copland Simmons, Rev. Frederic Pearson; see Simmons.

Copland-Sparkes, Rear-Adm. Robert, 1851–1924, vol. II

Coplans, Major Myer, died 1961, vol. VI

Copleston, Rt Rev. Ernest Arthur, died 1933, vol. III

Copleston, Frederick Selwyn, 1850–1935, vol. III

Copleston, Most Rev. Reginald Stephen, 1845–1925, vol. II

Copleston, Waters Edward, died 1949, vol. IV

Coplestone, Frederick, 1850–1932, vol. III

Copley, Ethel Leontine; see Gabain, E. L.

Copley, John, 1875–1950, vol. IV

Copley, Mrs John; see Gabain, Ethel Leontine.

Copley, Very Rev. John Robert, died 1923, vol. II

Copley, Brig.-Gen. Sir Robert Calverley Alington Bewicke B.; see Bewicke-Copley.

Copley, Samuel William, 1859–1937, vol. III

Copnall, Bainbridge; see Copnall, E. B.

Copnall, (Edward) Bainbridge, 1903–1973, vol. VII

Coppard, Alfred Edgar, 1878–1957, vol. V

Coppee, François Edouard Joachim, 1842–1908, vol. I

Coppel, Elias Godfrey, 1896–1978, vol. VII

Coppel, Rt Rev. Francis Stephen, 1867–1933, vol. III

Coppin, Hon. George, 1820–1906, vol. I

Copping, Arthur E., 1865–1941, vol. IV

Copping, Harold, died 1932, vol. III

Coppinger, Rear-Adm. Robert Henry, 1877–1967, vol. VI

Coppinger, Maj.-Gen. Walter Valentine, 1875–1957, vol. V

Coppleson, Sir Lionel Wolfe, 1901–1980, vol. VII (AII)

Coppleson, Sir Victor Marcus, 1893–1965, vol. VI

Copplestone, Bennet; see Kitchin, F. H.

Coppock, Sir Richard, 1885–1971, vol. VII

Copson, Edward Thomas, 1901–1980, vol. VII

Copus, George Frederick, 1868–1949, vol. IV

Coquelin, Benoit Constant, (Coquelin aîné), 1841–1909, vol. I

Coquelin, Ernest Alexandre Honoré, (Coquelin cadet), 1848–1909, vol. I

Corah, Sir John Harold, 1884–1978, vol. VII

Corbally, Elias, 1868–1933, vol. III

Corban, Maj.-Gen. William Watts, 1829–1916, vol. II

Corbet, Maj.-Gen. Arthur Domville, 1847–1918, vol. II

Corbet, Eustace Kynaston, 1854–1920, vol. II

Corbet, Hon. Frederick Hugh Mackenzie, 1862–1916, vol. II

Corbet, Sir Gerald Vincent, 6th Bt, 1868–1955, vol. V

Corbet, Hon. Mrs (Katherine), 1861–1950, vol. IV

Corbet, Air Vice-Marshal Lancelot Miller, 1898–1990, vol. VIII

Corbet, Reginald, 1857–1945, vol. IV

Corbet, Sir Roland James, 5th Bt, 1892–1915, vol. I

Corbet, Sir Walter Orlando, 4th Bt, 1856–1910, vol. I

Corbet, William Joseph, 1824–1909, vol. I

Corbett, Adm. Charles Frederick, 1867–1955, vol. V

Corbett, Charles Henry Joseph, 1853–1935, vol. III

Corbett, Edward, 1843–1918, vol. II

Corbett, (Edward) James, (Jim Corbett), 1875–1955, vol. V

Corbett, Sir Francis Edmund George A.; *see* Astley-Corbett.

Corbett, Sir (Francis) Henry (Rivers) A.; *see* Astley-Corbett.

Corbett, Rev. Frederick St John, 1862–1919, vol. II

Corbett, Sir Geoffrey Latham, 1881–1937, vol. III

Corbett, Captain Godfrey Edwin, 1871–1929, vol. III

Corbett, Harvey Wiley, 1873–1954, vol. V

Corbett, J. Soden, 1871–1935, vol. III

Corbett, James; *see* Corbett, E. J.

Corbett, Rt Rev. James Francis, 1840–1912, vol. I

Corbett, Jim; *see* Corbett, E. J.

Corbett, John, 1817–1901, vol. I

Corbett, Rev. John Reginald, 1844–1920, vol. II

Corbett, Sir Julian Stafford, 1854–1922, vol. II

Corbett, Col Robert de la Cour, 1844–1904, vol. I

Corbett, Captain Roland, 1881–1938, vol. III

Corbett, Rupert Shelton, 1893–1985, vol. VIII

Corbett, Thomas Lorimer, 1854–1910, vol. I

Corbett, Lt-Gen. Thomas William, 1888–1981, vol. VIII

Corbett, Captain Sir Vincent Edwin Henry, 1861–1936, vol. III

Corbett, William John, *died* 1941, vol. IV

Corbett Ashby, Dame Margery Irene, 1882–1981, vol. VIII

Corbett-Smith, Arthur, 1879–1945, vol. IV

Corbett-Winder, Col John Lyon, 1911–1990, vol. VIII

Corbett-Winder, Major William John, 1875–1950, vol. IV

Corbin, (André) Charles, 1881–1970, vol. VI

Corbin, Charles; *see* Corbin, A. C.

Corbin, John, 1870–1959, vol. V

Corbishley, Rev. Thomas, 1903–1976, vol. VII

Corby, Henry, *died* 1917, vol. II

Corbyn, Ernest Nugent, 1881–1961, vol. VI

Corcoran, Sir John A., 1862–1932, vol. III

Corcoran, Percy John, 1920–1984, vol. VIII

Corcoran, Rev. Timothy, 1872–1943, vol. IV

Cordeaux, Captain Edward Cawdron, 1894–1963, vol. VI

Cordeaux, Col Edward Kyme, 1866–1946, vol. IV

Cordeaux, Major Sir Harry Edward Spiller, 1870–1943, vol. IV

Cordeaux, Lt-Col John Kyme, 1902–1982, vol. VIII

Cordellis, Mrs M.; *see* Groom, Gladys Laurence.

Corder, Lt-Col Arthur Annerley, *died* 1923, vol. II

Corder, Frederick, 1852–1932, vol. III

Corder, Paul Walford, 1879–1942, vol. IV

Corder, Philip, 1891–1961, vol. VI

Cordes, Thomas, 1826–1901, vol. I

Cordier, Andrew Wellington, 1901–1975, vol. VII

Cordiner, George Ritchie Mather, *died* 1957, vol. V

Cordiner, Thomas Smith, 1902–1965, vol. VI

Cordingley, Charles, 1862–1914, vol. I

Cordingley, Air Vice-Marshal Sir John Walter, 1890–1977, vol. VII

Cordingley, Reginald Annandale, 1896–1962, vol. VI

Cordingly, Rt Rev. Eric William Bradley, 1911–1976, vol. VII

Cordon, Cecil Gilbert William, *died* 1952, vol. V

Core, Thomas Hamilton, 1836–1910, vol. I

Corea, Sir Claude; *see* Corea, Sir G. C. S.

Corea, Sir (George) Claude (Stanley), 1894–1962, vol. VI

Corelli, Marie, 1855–1924, vol. II

Corfe, Rt Rev. Charles John, 1843–1921, vol. II

Corfiato, Hector Othon, *died* 1963, vol. VI

Corfield, Rt Rev. Bernard Conyngham, 1890–1965, vol. VI

Corfield, Rev. Claud Evelyn Lacey, *died* 1926, vol. II

Corfield, Sir Conrad Laurence, 1893–1980, vol. VII

Corfield, Col Frederick Alleyne, 1884–1939, vol. III

Corfield, Gerald Frederick Conyngham, 1886–1961, vol. VI

Corfield, William Henry, 1843–1903, vol. I

Cori, Carl Ferdinand, 1896–1984, vol. VIII

Cori, Gerty Theresa, 1896–1957, vol. V

Corish, Brendan, 1918–1990, vol. VIII

Cork and Orrery, 9th Earl of, 1829–1904, vol. I

Cork and Orrery, 10th Earl of, 1861–1925, vol. II

Cork and Orrery, 11th Earl of, 1864–1934, vol. III

Cork and Orrery, 12th Earl of, 1873–1967, vol. VI

Cork, Philip Clark, 1854–1936, vol. III (A), vol. IV

Corke, Sir John Henry, *died* 1927, vol. II

Corker, Maj.-Gen. Thomas Martin, 1856–1937, vol. III

Corkery, Daniel, 1878–1964, vol. VI

Corkey, Very Rev. Rt Hon. Robert, 1881–1966, vol. VI

Corkhill, Percy Fullerton, *died* 1959, vol. V

Corkill, Norman Lace, 1898–1966, vol. VI

Corkill, Thomas Frederick, 1893–1965, vol. VI

Corkran, Alice, *died* 1916, vol. II

Corkran, Maj.-Gen. Sir Charles Edward, 1872–1939, vol. III

Corkran, Sir Victor Seymour, 1873–1934, vol. III

Corless, Richard, 1884–1967, vol. VI

Corlett, John, 1841–1915, vol. I

Corlette, Major Hubert Christian, 1869–1956, vol. V

Corlette, Brig. James Montagu Christian, 1880–1969, vol. VI (AII)

Cormack, Benjamin George, 1866–1936, vol. III

Cormack, James Maxwell Ross, 1909–1975, vol. VII

Cormack, John Dewar, 1870–1935, vol. III

Cormie, David; *see* Cormie, J. D.

Cormie, (John) David, 1930–1983, vol. VIII

Cornaby, Rev. William Arthur, 1860–1921, vol. II

Cornelius, Percival, 1874–1960, vol. V
Cornell, Katharine, 1898–1974, vol. VII
Corner, Edred Moss, 1873–1950, vol. IV
Corner, George, 1869–1947, vol. IV
Corner, George Washington, 1889–1981, vol. VIII
Corner, Engr Rear-Adm. John Thomas, 1849–1912, vol. I
Cornewall, Sir Geoffrey, 6th Bt, 1869–1951, vol. V
Cornewall, Rev. Sir George Henry, 5th Bt, 1833–1908, vol. I
Cornewall, Sir William Francis, 7th Bt, 1871–1962, vol. VI
Corney, Bolton Glanvill, 1851–1924, vol. II
Corney, Leonard George, 1886–1955, vol. V
Cornford, Frances Crofts, 1886–1960, vol. V
Cornford, Francis Macdonald, 1874–1943, vol. IV
Cornford, Leslie Cope, died 1927, vol. II
Cornil, Georges, 1863–1944, vol. IV
Cornish, Rt Rev. Charles Edward, 1842–1936, vol. III
Cornish, Charles John, 1859–1906, vol. I
Cornish, Rev. Ebenezer Darrel, 1849–1922, vol. II
Cornish, Francis Warre, 1839–1916, vol. II
Cornish, George Augustus, 1874–1960, vol. V
Cornish, Rt Rev. George Kestell K.; see Kestell-Cornish.
Cornish, Henry Dauncey, 1877–1948, vol. IV
Cornish, Herbert, 1862–1945, vol. IV
Cornish, Hubert Warre, 1872–1934, vol. III
Cornish, Rt Rev. John Rundle, 1837–1918, vol. II
Cornish, Rt Rev. (John) Vernon (Kestell), 1931–1982, vol. VIII
Cornish, Josiah Easton, 1841–1912, vol. I
Cornish, Rt Rev. Robert Kestell K.; see Kestell-Cornish.
Cornish, Ronald James, 1898–1986, vol. VIII
Cornish, Vaughan, 1862–1948, vol. IV
Cornish, Rt Rev. Vernon; see Cornish, Rt Rev. J. V. K.
Cornish-Bowden, Col James Hubert Thomas, 1870–1938, vol. III
Cornwall, Ven. Alan Whitmore, 1858–1932, vol. III
Cornwall, Rt Hon. Sir Edwin, 1st Bt, 1863–1953, vol. V
Cornwall, Ernest, 1875–1966, vol. VI
Cornwall, Gen. Sir James Handyside M.; see Marshall-Cornwall.
Cornwall, Lt-Col John Wolfran, 1870–1947, vol. IV
Cornwall, Rt Rev. Nigel Edmund, 1903–1984, vol. VIII
Cornwall, Sir Reginald Edwin, 2nd Bt, 1887–1962, vol. VI
Cornwall, Maj.-Gen. Richard Frank, 1902–1967, vol. VI
Cornwall-Jones, Brig. Arthur Thomas, 1900–1980, vol. VII
Cornwallis, 1st Baron, 1864–1935, vol. III
Cornwallis, 2nd Baron, 1892–1982, vol, VIII
Cornwallis, Sir Kinahan, 1883–1959, vol. V
Cornwallis-West, Major George F. M., 1874–1951, vol. V
Cornwallis-West, William Cornwallis; see West.
Cornwell, Ven. Leonard Cyril, 1893–1971, vol. VII
Corrance, Frederick Snowden, died 1906, vol. I
Corrie, Major Alfred Wynne, 1856–1919, vol. II

Corrie, Sir Owen Cecil Kirkpatrick, 1882–1965, vol. VI
Corrie, Maj.-Gen. William Taylor, 1838–1931, vol. III
Corrigan, Most Rev. Michael Augustine, 1839–1902, vol. I
Corrigan, Rev. Terence Edward, 1915–1975, vol. VII
Corry, Adm. Hon. Armar L.; see Lowry-Corry.
Corry, Lt-Col Sir Henry Charles L.; see Lowry-Corry.
Corry, Col Hon. Henry William L.; see Lowry-Corry.
Corry, Sir James Perowne Ivo Myles, 3rd Bt, 1892–1987, vol. VIII
Corry, Major John Beaumont, 1874–1914, vol. I
Corry, Brig.-Gen. Noel Armar L.; see Lowry-Corry.
Corry, Sir William, 2nd Bt, 1859–1926, vol. II
Corsan, Brig. Reginald Arthur, 1893–1942, vol. IV
Corser, Captain Charles Huskisson, 1886–1962, vol. VI
Corser, Haden, 1845–1906, vol. I
Corson, Rear-Adm. Eric Reid, 1887–1972, vol. VII
Corstorphine, George Steuart, 1868–1919, vol. II
Cortelyou, George Bruce, 1862–1940, vol. III
Cortie, Rev. Father Aloysius Laurence, 1859–1925, vol. II
Cortis-Stanford, Gp Captain C. E., 1874–1933, vol. III
Cortissoz, Royal, 1869–1948, vol. IV
Cortlandt, Lyn, 1926–1979, vol. VII
Cortot, Alfred, 1877–1962, vol. VI
Corwin, Edward Samuel, 1878–1963, vol. VI
Cory, Ven. Alexander, 1890–1973, vol. VII
Cory, Ven. Charles Page, 1859–1942, vol. IV
Cory, Sir Clifford John, 1st Bt (cr 1907), 1859–1941, vol. IV
Cory, Elizabeth Cansh, (Lady Cory), died 1956, vol. V
Cory, Lt-Col Evan James Trevor, 1863–1957, vol. V
Cory, Sir George Edward, 1862–1935, vol. III
Cory, Lt-Gen. Sir George Norton, 1874–1968, vol. VI
Cory, Sir Herbert; see Cory, Sir J. H.
Cory, Sir Herbert George Donald, 2nd Bt (cr 1919), 1879–1935, vol. III
Cory, Sir (James) Herbert, 1st Bt (cr 1919), 1857–1933, vol. III
Cory, John, 1828–1910, vol. I
Cory, John Herbert, 1889–1939, vol. III
Cory, Percy Albert, 1870–1936, vol. III
Cory, Richard, 1830–1914, vol. I
Cory, Surg. Rear-Adm. Robert Francis Preston, 1885–1961, vol. VI
Cory, Mrs Theodore; see Graham, W.
Cory, Sir Vyvyan Donald, 3rd Bt (cr 1919), 1906–1941, vol. IV
Cory, William Wallace, 1865–1943, vol. IV
Cory, Winifred; see Graham, W.
Cory-Wright, Sir Arthur Cory, 2nd Bt, 1869–1951, vol. V
Cory-Wright, Sir Cory Francis, 1st Bt, 1839–1909, vol. I
Cory-Wright, Sir Geoffrey, 3rd Bt, 1892–1969, vol. VI
Coryndon, Sir Robert Thorne, 1870–1925, vol. II

Coryton, Air Chief Marshal Sir Alec; *see* Coryton, Air Chief Marshal Sir W. A.

Coryton, Frederick, 1850–1924, vol. II

Coryton, William, 1847–1919, vol. II

Coryton, Air Chief Marshal Sir (William) Alec, 1895–1981, vol. VIII

Cosby, Dudley Sydney Ashworth, 1862–1923, vol. II

Cosby, Brig. Noel Robert Charles, 1890–1981, vol. VIII

Cosby, Col Robert Ashworth Godolphin, 1837–1920, vol. II

Cosgrave, Rev. Francis Herbert, 1880–1971, vol. VII

Cosgrave, Col L. Moore, 1890–1971, vol. VII

Cosgrave, MacDowel, *died* 1925, vol. II

Cosgrave, Mary Josephine, *died* 1941, vol. IV

Cosgrave, Sir William Alexander, 1879–1952, vol. V

Cosgrave, Rev. William Frederick, 1857–1936, vol. III

Cosgrave, William Thomas, 1880–1965, vol. VI

Cosgrove, Dame Gertrude Ann, 1882–1962, vol. VI

Cosgrove, Hon. Sir Robert, 1884–1969, vol. VI

Coslett, Air Marshal Sir Norman; *see* Air Marshal Sir T. N.

Coslett, Air Marshal Sir (Thomas) Norman, 1909–1987, vol. VIII

Cossar, George Carter, 1880–1942, vol. IV

Cossimbazar, Maharaja Srischandra Nandy, 1897–1952, vol. V

Cosslett, Ellis; *see* Cosslett, V. E.

Cosslett, (Vernon) Ellis, 1908–1990, vol. VIII

Costain, Sir Albert Percy, 1910–1987, vol. VIII

Costain, Rev. Alfred James, 1881–1963, vol. VI

Costain, Sir Richard Rylandes, 1902–1966, vol. VI

Costain, Thomas Bertram, 1885–1965, vol. VI

Costaki, Anthopoulos Pasha, 1838–1902, vol. I

Coste, John Henry, 1871–1949, vol. IV

Costeker, Captain John Henry Dives, 1879–1915, vol. I

Costello, Desmond Patrick, 1912–1964, vol. VI

Costello, Brig.-Gen. Edmund W., 1873–1949, vol. IV

Costello, John Aloysius, 1891–1976, vol. VII

Costello, Sir Leonard Wilfred James, 1881–1972, vol. VII

Coster, Howard, (Howard Sydney Musgrave Coster), *died* 1959, vol. V

Costigan, Captain Charles Telford, *died* 1917, vol. II

Costigan, Hon. John, 1835–1916, vol. II

Costigan, Rev. John, 1916–1978, vol. VII

Costin, Maj.-Gen. Eric Boyd, 1889–1971, vol. VII

Costin, William Conrad, 1893–1970, vol. VI

Costley-White, Cyril Grove, 1913–1979, vol. VII

Costley-White, Very Rev. Harold, 1878–1966, vol. VI

Cotes, Lt-Col Charles James, 1847–1913, vol. I

Cotes, Mrs Everard; *see* Cotes, S. J.

Cotes, Everard, 1862–1944, vol. IV

Cotes, Sara Jeanette, (Mrs Everard Cotes), 1861–1922, vol. II

Cotes, Sir Merton Russell, 1835–1921, vol. II

Cotes-Preedy, Digby, 1875–1942, vol. IV

Cotman, Frederic George, 1850–1920, vol. II

Cotsworth, Moses B., 1859–1943, vol. IV

Cott, Hugh Bamford, 1900–1987, vol. VIII

Cottam, Rev. Maj.-Gen. Algernon Edward, 1893–1964, vol. VI

Cottell, Col Reginald James Cope, 1858–1924, vol. II

Cottenham, 4th Earl of, 1874–1919, vol. II

Cottenham, 5th Earl of, 1901–1922, vol. II

Cottenham, 6th Earl of, 1903–1943, vol. IV

Cottenham, 7th Earl of, 1907–1968, vol. VI

Cotter, Col Edward, 1892–1961, vol. VI

Cotter, Maj.-Gen. Francis Gibson, 1857–1928, vol. II

Cotter, Lt-Col Harry John, 1871–1921, vol. II

Cotter, Sir James Laurence, 5th Bt, 1887–1924, vol. II

Cotter, Most Rev. William Timothy, 1866–1940, vol. III

Cotterell, Cecil Bernard, 1875–1957, vol. V

Cotterell, Sir Geers Henry, 3rd Bt, 1834–1900, vol. I

Cotterell, Gilbert Thorp, 1891–1963, vol. VI

Cotterell, Sir John Richard Geers, 4th Bt, 1866–1937, vol. III

Cotterell, Mabel, *died* 1968, vol. VI

Cotterell, Lt-Col Sir Richard Charles Geers, 5th Bt, 1907–1978, vol. VII

Cotterill, James Henry, 1836–1922, vol. II

Cotterill, Sir (Joseph) Montagu, 1851–1933, vol. III

Cotterill, Sir Montagu; *see* Cotterill, Sir J. M.

Cottesloe, 2nd Baron, 1830–1918, vol. II

Cottesloe, 3rd Baron, 1862–1956, vol. V

Cottet, Charles, *died* 1925, vol. II

Cottier, Sir Charles Edward, 1869–1928, vol. II

Cottingham, Lt-Col Edward Roden, 1866–1930, vol. III

Cottingham, Dame Margaret; *see* Teyte, Dame Maggie.

Cottington-Taylor, Dorothy Daisy, *died* 1944, vol. IV

Cottle, Adela, 1861–1940, vol. III

Cotton, Lt-Col Arthur Egerton, 1876–1922, vol. II

Cotton, Brig.-Gen. Arthur Stedman, 1873–1952, vol. V

Cotton, Sir Arthur Thomas, 1803–1899, vol. I

Cotton, Baron Francis C.; *see* Carter-Cotton.

Cotton, Charles, 1856–1939, vol. III

Cotton, Sir Charles Andrew, 1885–1970, vol. VI (AII)

Cotton, Charles William Egerton, *died* 1931, vol. III

Cotton, Sir Evan; *see* Cotton, Sir H. E. A.

Cotton, Maj.-Gen. Frederic Conyers, 1807–1901, vol. I

Cotton, Sir George, 1842–1905, vol. I

Cotton, Sir George Frederick, 1877–1943, vol. IV

Cotton, Harry, 1889–1985, vol. VIII

Cotton, Sir (Harry) Evan Auguste, 1868–1939, vol. III

Cotton, Henry; *see* Cotton, T. H.

Cotton, Rev. Henry Aldrich, 1835–1927, vol. II

Cotton, Sir Henry John Stedman, 1845–1915, vol. I

Cotton, Jack, 1903–1964, vol. VI

Cotton, Rev. (James) Stapleton, 1849–1932, vol. III

Cotton, James Sutherland, 1847–1918, vol. II

Cotton, Sir James Temple, 1879–1965, vol. VI

Cotton, Leo Arthur, 1883–1963, vol. VI

Cotton, Michael James, 1920–1981, vol. VIII

Cotton, Montagu Arthur Finch, 1885–1915, vol. I

Cotton, Percy Horace Gordon P.; *see* Powell-Cotton.

Cotton, Adm. Richard Greville Arthur Wellington S.; *see* Stapleton-Cotton.

Cotton, Col Hon. Richard Southwell George S.; *see* Stapleton-Cotton.

Cotton, Lt-Col Ronald Egerton, 1876–1932, vol. III

Cotton, Rev. Stapleton; *see* Cotton, Rev. J. S.
Cotton, Captain Stapleton Charles, 1831–1908, vol. I
Cotton, Thomas Forrest, *died* 1965, vol. VI
Cotton, (Thomas) Henry, 1907–1987, vol. VIII
Cotton, Lt-Col Vere Egerton, 1888–1970, vol. VI
Cotton, William Francis, 1847–1917, vol. II
Cotton, Sir William James Richmond, 1822–1902, vol. I
Cotton-Jodrell, Col Sir Edward Thomas Davenant, 1847–1917, vol. II
Cottrell, Brig. Arthur Foulkes Baglietto, 1891–1962, vol. VI
Cottrell, Sir Edward Baglietto, 1896–1976, vol. VII
Cottrell, Leonard, 1913–1974, vol. VII
Cottrell, Lt-Col Reginald Foulkes, 1885–1924, vol. II
Cottrell, Tom Leadbetter, 1923–1973, vol. VII
Cottrell, William Henry, 1863–1926, vol. II
Cottrell-Dormer, Charles Walter, 1860–1945, vol. IV
Cottrell-Hill, Maj.-Gen. Robert Charles, 1903–1965, vol. VI
Cotts, Sir Campbell Mitchell; *see* Cotts, Sir W. C. M.
Cotts, Sir (William) Campbell Mitchell-, 2nd Bt, 1902–1964, vol. VI
Cotts, Sir William Dingwall Mitchell, 1st Bt, 1871–1932, vol. III
Coty, René, 1882–1962, vol. VI
Coubertin, Pierre de Fredi, Baron de, 1863–1937, vol. III
Coubrough, Anthony Cathcart, 1877–1963, vol. VI
Couch, Sir Arthur Thomas Q.; *see* Quiller-Couch.
Couch, Rt Hon. Sir Richard, 1817–1905, vol. I
Couch, William Charles Milford, 1894–1975, vol. VII
Couchman, Dame Elizabeth May Ramsay, 1878–1982, vol. VIII
Couchman, Sir Francis Dundas, 1864–1948, vol. IV
Couchman, Col George Henry Holbeche, 1859–1936, vol. III
Couchman, Brig. Sir Harold John, 1882–1956, vol. V
Couchman, Malcolm Edward, 1869–1938, vol. III
Couchman, Rev. Reginald Henry, 1874–1948, vol. IV
Couchman, Adm. Sir Walter Thomas, 1905–1981, vol. VIII
Coudenhove-Kalergi, Richard N., 1894–1972, vol. VII
Coudert, Most Rev. Antony, 1861–1929, vol. III
Coudurier de Chassaigne, Joseph, 1878–1961, vol. VI
Coué, Emile, *died* 1926, vol. II
Coughlan, Cornelius, 1828–1915, vol. I
Coughtrie, Thomas, 1895–1985, vol. VIII
Coulcher, Mary Caroline, 1852–1925, vol. II
Couldrey, Robert Charles, 1890–1974, vol. VII
Couling, Samuel, 1859–1922, vol. II
Coull, Hon. William, 1857–1918, vol. II
Coulshaw, Rev. Leonard, 1896–1988, vol. VIII
Coulson, Charles Alfred, 1910–1974, vol. VII
Coulson, Lt-Col Frank Morris, 1880–1953, vol. V
Coulson, Frederick Raymond, 1864–1922, vol. II
Coulson, Lt-Col John, 1873–1929, vol. III
Coulson, John Metcalfe, 1910–1990, vol. VIII
Coulson, Noel James, 1928–1986, vol. VIII
Coulson, Maj.-Gen. Samuel M.; *see* Moore-Coulson.
Coulson, William Lisle B., 1840–1911, vol. I
Coultas, Frederick George, 1888–1961, vol. VI
Coultas, William Whitham, 1890–1973, vol. VII
Coulter, Very Rev. Isaac, 1851–1934, vol. III

Coulter, Ven. J. W., 1867–1956, vol. V
Coulter, Robert, 1914–1987, vol. VIII
Coulter, Robert Millar, 1857–1927, vol. II
Coulthard, Rev. Canon Hugh Robert, 1860–1939, vol. III
Coulthard, Alan George Weall, 1924–1988, vol. VIII
Coulton, George Gordon, 1858–1947, vol. IV
Counsell, John William, 1905–1987, vol. VIII
Couper, Sir George Ebenezer Wilson, 2nd Bt, 1824–1908, vol. I
Couper, Major Sir George Robert Cecil, 5th Bt, 1898–1975, vol. VII
Couper, Sir Guy, 4th Bt, 1889–1973, vol. VII
Couper, James Brown, *died* 1946, vol. IV
Couper, John, *died* 1918, vol. II
Couper, Sir John C., 1867–1937, vol. III
Couper, John Duncan Campbell, 1876–1962, vol. VI
Couper, Leslie, 1871–1929, vol. III
Couper, Sir Ramsay George Henry, 3rd Bt, 1855–1949, vol. IV
Couper, Sir Thomas, 1878–1954, vol. V
Couper, Maj.-Gen. Sir Victor Arthur, 1859–1938, vol. III
Couperus, Louis, 1863–1923, vol. II
Coupland, Sir Reginald, 1884–1952, vol. V
Coupland, Sidney, 1849–1930, vol. III
Coupland, William Chatterton, 1838–1915, vol. I
Courage, Brig.-Gen. Anthony, 1875–1944, vol. IV
Courage, Edward Raymond, 1906–1982, vol. VIII
Courage, James Francis, 1903–1963, vol. VI
Courage, Lt-Col John Hubert, 1891–1967, vol. VI
Courage, John Michell, 1868–1931, vol. III
Courage, Comdr Rafe Edward, 1902–1960, vol. V
Couratin, Rev. Canon Arthur Hubert, 1902–1988, vol. VIII
Courchesne, Most Rev. Georges, 1880–1950, vol IV (A), vol. V
Courlander, Alphonse, 1881–1914, vol. I
Cournand, André Frédéric, 1895–1988, vol. VIII
Cournos, John, 1881–1966, vol. VI
Courroux, George Augustus, 1852–1923, vol. II
Court, Emily, *died* 1957, vol. V
Court, Sir Josiah, 1841–1938, vol. III
Court, William Henry Bassano, 1904–1971, vol. VII
Courtauld, Augustine, 1904–1959, vol. VI
Courtauld, Major John Sewell, 1880–1942, vol. IV
Courtauld, Samuel, 1876–1947, vol. IV
Courtauld, Samuel Augustine, 1865–1953, vol. V
Courtauld, Sir Stephen Lewis, 1883–1967, vol. VI
Courtauld, Sir William Julien, 1st Bt, 1870–1940, vol. III
Courtauld Thomson, 1st Baron, 1865–1954, vol. V
Courtenay, Lord; Henry Reginald Courtenay, 1836–1898, vol. I
Courtenay, Col Arthur Henry, 1852–1927, vol. II
Courtenay, Brig.-Gen. Edward Reginald, 1853–1919, vol. II
Courtenay, Hon. Sir Harrison; *see* Courtenay, Hon. Sir W. H.
Courtenay, Henry, *died* 1921, vol. II
Courtenay, Sir Irving; *see* Courtenay, Sir J. I.
Courtenay, Sir (John) Irving, 1837–1912, vol. I
Courtenay, Rt Rev. Reginald, 1813–1906, vol. I

Courtenay, Hon. Sir (Woldrich) Harrison, 1904–1982, vol. VIII

Courthope, 1st Baron, 1877–1955, vol. V

Courthope, William John, 1842–1917, vol. II

Courthope-Munroe, Sir Harry, 1860–1951, vol. V

Courtice, Col James George, *died* 1939, vol. III

Courtis, Sir John Wesley, 1859–1939, vol. III

Courtneidge, Dame Cicely; *see* Courtneidge, Dame E. C.

Courtneidge, Dame (Esmerelda) Cicely, 1893–1980, vol. VII

Courtney of Penwith, 1st Baron, 1832–1918, vol. II

Courtney, Comdr Anthony Tosswill, 1908–1988, vol. VIII

Courtney, Air Chief Marshal Sir Christopher Lloyd, 1890–1976, vol. VII

Courtney, Col Edward Arthur Waldegrave, 1868–1926, vol. II

Courtney, Maj.-Gen. Edward Henry, 1836–1913, vol. I

Courtney, Rt Rev. Frederick, 1837–1918, vol. II

Courtney, Lt-Col Frederick Harold, 1875–1937, vol. III

Courtney, Gp Captain Ivon Terence, 1885–1978, vol. VII

Courtney, Janet Elizabeth, 1865–1954, vol. V

Courtney, John Mortimer, 1838–1920, vol. II

Courtney, Dame Kathleen D'Olier, 1878–1974, vol. VII

Courtney, Col Richard Edmond, 1870–1919, vol. II

Courtney, Victor Desmond, 1894–1970, vol. VI (AII)

Courtney, William Leonard, 1850–1928, vol. II

Courtney, William Prideaux, 1845–1913, vol. I

Courtown, 5th Earl of, 1823–1914, vol. I

Courtown, 6th Earl of, 1853–1933, vol. III

Courtown, 7th Earl of, 1877–1957, vol. V

Courtown, 8th Earl of, 1908–1975, vol. VII

Coury, Captain Gabriel George, 1896–1956, vol. V

Cousens, Col Robert Baxter, 1880–1943, vol. IV

Cousin, David Ross, 1904–1984, vol. VIII

Cousins, Arthur George, 1882–1949, vol. IV

Cousins, Clarence W., *died* 1954, vol. V

Cousins, Donald, 1900–1964, vol. VI

Cousins, Edmund Richard John Ratcliffe, 1888–1955, vol. V

Cousins, Rt Hon. Frank, 1904–1986, vol. VIII

Cousins, Sir Harry, 1852–1935, vol. III

Cousins, Herbert H., 1869–1949, vol. IV

Cousins, John Ratcliffe, 1863–1928, vol. II

Cousins, Norman, 1915–1990, vol. VIII

Cousins, William Henry, 1833–1917, vol. II

Coussey, Sir James Henley, 1891–1958, vol. V

Coussirat, Rev. Daniel, 1841–1907, vol. I

Coussmaker, Col Lannoy John, 1883–1937, vol. III

Coutanche, Baron (Life Peer); Alexander Moncrieff Coutanche, 1892–1973, vol. VII

Coutts, Charles Ronald Vawdrey, 1876–1938, vol. III

Coutts, Francis James Henderson, 1865–1949, vol. IV

Coutts, Gen. Frederick, 1899–1986, vol. VIII

Coutts, James, 1852–1913, vol. I

Coutts, Sir Walter Fleming, 1912–1988, vol. VIII

Coutts, Rt Hon. William Lehman Ashmead Bartlett-B.; *see* Burdett-Coutts.

Coutts, William Strachan, 1873–1963, vol. VI

Coutts Donald, William, 1906–1974, vol. VII

Covell, Maj.-Gen. Sir Gordon, 1887–1975, vol. VII

Coverdale, Ralph, 1918–1975, vol. VII

Couvreur, Mme Jessie, *died* 1897, vol. I

Couzens, Sir George Edwin, 1851–1925, vol. II

Couzens, Sir Henry Herbert, *died* 1944, vol. IV

Cove, Captain George Edward, 1889–1967, vol. VI

Cove, William George, 1888–1963, vol. VI

Coventry, 9th Earl of, 1838–1930, vol. III

Coventry, 10th Earl of, 1900–1940, vol. III

Coventry, Bernard, 1859–1929, vol. III

Coventry, Col Hon. Charles John, 1867–1929, vol. III

Coventry, Henry Arthur, 1852–1925, vol. II

Coventry, Henry Robert Beauclerk, 1871–1953, vol. V

Coventry, Hon. Henry Thomas, 1868–1934, vol. III

Coventry, Rev. Henry William, *died* 1920, vol. II

Coventry, Millis, 1838–1930, vol. III

Coventry, R. M. G., *died* 1914, vol. I

Coventry, Hon. Sir Reginald, 1869–1940, vol. III

Covernton, Alfred Laurence, 1872–1961, vol. VI

Covernton, James Gargrave, 1868–1957, vol. V

Covington, Stenton, 1857–1935, vol. III

Covington, Walter George, *died* 1939, vol. III

Covington, Rev. William, *died* 1908, vol. I

Cowan, Sir Christopher (George) Armstrong, 1889–1979, vol. VII

Cowan, Sir Darcy Rivers Warren, 1885–1958, vol. V

Cowan, Rev. David Galloway, *died* 1921, vol. II

Cowan, Maj.-Gen. David Tennant, 1896–1983, vol. VIII

Cowan, Dugald M'Coig, 1865–1933, vol. III

Cowan, Rev. Henry, 1844–1932, vol. III

Cowan, Sir Henry, 1862–1932, vol. III

Cowan, Sir (Henry) Kenneth, 1900–1971, vol. VII

Cowan, Col Henry Vivian, 1854–1918, vol. II

Cowan, Ian Borthwick, 1932–1990, vol. VIII

Cowan, James, 1870–1943, vol. IV

Cowan, Col James Henry, 1856–1943, vol. IV

Cowan, James Macfarlane, 1912–1967, vol. VI

Cowan, Captain James William Alston, 1868–1899, vol. I

Cowan, Sir John, 1st Bt (*cr* 1894), 1814–1900, vol. I

Cowan, John, 1849–1926, vol. II

Cowan, Hon. John, 1847–1927, vol. II

Cowan, Sir John, 1844–1929, vol. III

Cowan, John, 1869–1935, vol. III

Cowan, John, 1870–1947, vol. IV

Cowan, Hon. Sir John, 1866–1953, vol. V

Cowan, Sir Kenneth; *see* Cowan, Sir H. K.

Cowan, Lt-Col Percy John, *died* 1954, vol. V

Cowan, Samuel, 1835–1914, vol. I

Cowan, Thomas William, 1840–1926, vol. II

Cowan, Adm. Sir Walter Henry, 1st Bt (*cr* 1921), 1871–1956, vol. V

Cowan, William Christie, 1878–1950, vol. IV (A)

Cowan-Douglas, Hugh, 1895–1960, vol. V

Cowans, Harry Lowes, 1932–1985, vol. VIII

Cowans, Gen. Sir John Steven, 1862–1921, vol. II

Coward, Sir Cecil Allen, 1845–1938, vol. III

Coward, Sir Henry, 1849–1944, vol. IV

Coward, Sir (John Charles) Lewis, 1852–1930, vol. III

Coward, Sir Noel, 1899–1973, vol. VII

Coward, Thomas Alfred, 1867–1933, vol. III

Cowderoy, Most Rev. Mgr Cyril Conrad, 1905–1976, vol. VII

Cowdray, 1st Viscount, 1856–1927, vol. II

Cowdray, 2nd Viscount, 1882–1933, vol. III

Cowdroy, Joan Alice, *died* 1946, vol. IV

Cowdry, Rt Rev. Roy Walter Frederick, 1915–1984, vol. VIII

Cowell, Maj.-Gen. Sir Ernest Marshall, 1886–1971, vol. VII

Cowell, Frank Richard, 1897–1978, vol. VII

Cowell, George, 1836–1927, vol. II

Cowell, Very Rev. George Young, 1838–1930, vol. III

Cowell, Hubert Russell, *died* 1967, vol. VI

Cowell, Rev. Maurice Byles, *died* 1919, vol. II

Cowell, Philip Herbert, *died* 1949, vol. IV

Cowell, Sibert Forrest, 1863–1949, vol. IV

Cowell, Stuart Jasper, 1891–1971, vol. VII

Cowell-Stepney, Sir Emile Algernon Arthur Keppel, 2nd Bt, 1834–1909, vol. I

Cowen, Alan Biddulph, 1896–1989, vol. VIII

Cowen, Sir Frederic Hyman, 1852–1935, vol. III

Cowen, John David, 1904–1981, vol. VIII

Cowen, John Edward, 1873–1938, vol. III

Cowen, Joseph, 1831–1899, vol. I

Cowen, Richard John, 1871–1928, vol. II

Cowern, Raymond Teague, 1913–1986, vol. VIII

Cowgill, John Vincent, 1888–1959, vol. V

Cowgill, Rt Rev. Joseph Robert, 1860–1936, vol. III

Cowham, Hilda, *died* 1964, vol. VI

Cowie, Brig.-Gen. Alexander Hugh, 1860–1933, vol. III

Cowie, Very Rev. Benjamin Morgan, *died* 1900, vol. I

Cowie, Maj.-Gen. Charles Henry, 1861–1941, vol. IV

Cowie, Col Henry Edward Colvin, 1872–1963, vol. VI

Cowie, Major Hugh Norman Ramsay, 1872–1915, vol. I

Cowie, Rev. James Ratchford de Wolfe, 1855–1935, vol. III

Cowie, Rt Rev. William Garden, 1831–1902, vol. I

Cowie, William Patrick, *died* 1924, vol. II

Cowland, Rear-Adm. Geoffrey; *see* Cowland, Rear-Adm. W. G.

Cowland, Bt Lt-Col Walter Storey, 1888–1942, vol. IV

Cowland, Rear-Adm. (William) Geoffrey, 1895–1966, vol. VI

Cowles, Virginia, 1910–1983, vol. VIII

Cowles-Voysey, Charles, 1889–1981, vol. VIII

Cowley, 3rd Earl, 1866–1919, vol. II

Cowley, 4th Earl, 1890–1962, vol. VI

Cowley, 5th Earl, 1921–1968, vol. VI

Cowley, 6th Earl, 1946–1975, vol. VII

Cowley, Hon. Sir Alfred Sandlings Cowley, 1848–1926, vol. II

Cowley, Sir Arthur Ernest, 1861–1931, vol. III

Cowley, Air Vice-Marshal Arthur Thomas Noel, 1888–1960, vol. V

Cowley, Denis Martin, 1919–1985, vol. VIII

Cowley, Herbert, 1885–1967, vol. VI

Cowley, John Duncan, 1897–1944, vol. IV

Cowley, Sir Percy; *see* Cowley, Sir W. P.

Cowley, Sir (William) Percy, 1886–1958, vol. V

Cowley-Brown, Rev. George James, 1832–1924, vol. II

Cowlin, Sir Francis Nicholas, 1868–1945, vol. IV

Cowling, Donald George, 1904–1975, vol. VII

Cowling, George H., 1881–1946, vol. IV

Cowling, Richard John, 1911–1987, vol. VIII

Cowling, Thomas George, 1906–1990, vol. VIII

Cowper, 7th Earl, 1834–1905, vol. I

Cowper, Brig. Anthony William, 1913–1983, vol. VIII

Cowper, Cecil, 1856–1916, vol. II

Cowper, Frank, 1849–1930, vol. III

Cowper, Frank Cadogan, 1877–1958, vol. V

Cowper, Henry Swainson, 1865–1941, vol. IV

Cowper, Maj.-Gen. Maitland, 1859–1932, vol. III

Cowper, Lt-Col Malcolm Gordon, 1877–1931, vol. III

Cowper, Sir Norman Lethbridge, 1896–1987, vol. VIII

Cowper, Sydney, 1854–1922, vol. II

Cowper-Coles, Sherard Osborn, *died* 1936, vol. III

Cowtan, Air Vice-Marshal Frank Cuninghame, 1888–1950, vol. IV

Cox, A. W., 1857–1919, vol. II

Cox, Adelaide, 1860–1945, vol. IV

Cox, Col Alexander Temple, 1836–1907, vol. I

Cox, Alfred, 1866–1954, vol. V

Cox, Alfred Innes, 1894–1970, vol. VI

Cox, Rev. Alfred Peachey, 1862–1930, vol. III

Cox, Arthur Frederick, 1849–1925, vol. II

Cox, Arthur Henry, 1888–1971, vol. VII

Cox, Arthur Hubert, 1884–1961, vol. VI

Cox, Arthur Sambell, 1876–1951, vol. V

Cox, Captain Bernard Thomas, 1884–1935, vol. III

Cox, Rt Rev. Charles, 1848–1936, vol. III

Cox, Maj.-Gen. Charles Frederick, 1863–1947, vol. IV

Cox, Lt-Col Sir (Charles) Henry (Fortnom), 1880–1953, vol. V

Cox, Charles Leslie, 1880–1963, vol. VI

Cox, Sir Charles Thomas, 1858–1933, vol. III

Cox, Maj.-Gen. Charles Vyvyan, 1819–1903, vol. I

Cox, Sir Christopher William Machell, 1899–1982, vol. VIII

Cox, Cuthbert Eustace Connop, 1885–1958, vol. V

Cox, Cuthbert Machell, 1881–1962, vol. VI

Cox, E. Albert, 1876–1955, vol. V

Cox, Col Edgar William, 1882–1918, vol. II

Cox, Edmund Charles, 1856–1935, vol. III

Cox, Bt-Col Sir (Edward) Geoffrey Hippisley, 1884–1954, vol. V

Cox, Lt-Col Edward Henry, 1863–1925, vol. II

Cox, Hon. Sir (Edward) Owen, 1866–1932, vol. III

Cox, Lt-Col Edwin Charles, 1868–1958, vol. V

Cox, Euan Hillhouse Methven, 1893–1977, vol. VII

Cox, Major Eustace R.; *see* Richardson-Cox.

Cox, Francis Albert, 1862–1920, vol. II

Cox, Bt-Col Sir Geoffrey Hippisley; *see* Cox, Bt Col Sir E. G. H.

Cox, Maj.-Gen. George, 1838–1909, vol. I

Cox, Hon. George Albertus, 1840–1914, vol. I

Cox, Rt Rev. George Bede, 1854–1938, vol. III

Cox, George Henry, 1848–1935, vol. III

Cox, George Lissant, 1879–1967, vol. VI

Cox, Rev. Sir George William, 14th Bt (*cr* 1706), 1827–1902, vol. I

Cox, Gen. Sir H. Vaughan, 1860–1923, vol. II

Cox, Major Harding, *died* 1944, vol. IV

Cox, Harold, 1859–1936, vol. III

Cox, Harry Bernard, 1906–1989, vol. VIII

Cox, Lt-Col Sir Henry; *see* Cox, Lt-Col Sir C. H. F.

Cox, Rev. Heraclitus Matthew, 1816–1938, vol. III

Cox, Sir Herbert Charles Fahie, 1893–1973, vol. VII

Cox, Hugh Bertram, 1861–1930, vol. III

Cox, Ian Herbert, 1910–1990, vol. VIII

Cox, Irwin Edward Bainbridge, 1838–1922, vol. II

Cox, Sir Ivor Richard, 1891–1964, vol. VI

Cox, Rev. James Taylor, 1865–1948, vol. IV

Cox, John Charles, 1843–1919, vol. II

Cox, John Hugh, 1870–1922, vol. II

Cox, John S.; *see* Snead-Cox.

Cox, Sir John William, 1821–1901, vol. I

Cox, Sir John William, 1900–1990, vol. VIII

Cox, Air Vice-Marshal Joseph, 1904–1986, vol. VIII

Cox, Leonard Bell, 1894–1976, vol. VII (AII)

Cox, Leslie Reginald, 1897–1965, vol. VI

Cox, Sir Lionel; *see* Cox, Sir W. H. L.

Cox, Rev. Lionel Edgar, 1868–1945, vol. IV

Cox, Maj.-Gen. Lionel Howard, 1893–1949, vol. IV

Cox, Louisa Belle, (Lady Cox), *died* 1956, vol. V

Cox, Dame Marjorie Sophie, 1893–1979, vol. VII

Cox, Brig. Sir Matthew Henry, 1892–1966, vol. VI

Cox, Maj.-Gen. Maurice L.; *see* Lea-Cox.

Cox, Rt Hon. Michael Francis, 1852–1926, vol. II

Cox, Sir Montagu Hounsel, 1873–1936, vol. III

Cox, Hon. Sir Owen; *see* Cox, Hon. Sir E. O.

Cox, Palmer, 1840–1924, vol. II

Cox, Percy Stuart, 1868–1929, vol. III

Cox, Maj.-Gen. Sir Percy Zachariah, 1864–1937, vol. III

Cox, Sir Reginald Henry, 1st Bt (*cr* 1921), *died* 1922, vol. II

Cox, Sir Reginald Kennedy K.; *see* Kennedy-Cox.

Cox, Robert, 1845–1899, vol. I

Cox, Sir Robert; *see* Cox, Sir W. R.

Cox, S. Herbert, *died* 1920, vol. II

Cox, Lt-Col St John Augustus, 1869–1936, vol. III

Cox, Stephen, 1870–1943, vol. IV

Cox, Thomas, 1865–1947, vol. IV

Cox, Thomas Richard Fisher, 1907–1986, vol. VIII

Cox, Sir Thomas S.; *see* Skewes-Cox.

Cox, William Edward, 1880–1960, vol. V

Cox, Sir (William Henry) Lionel, 1864–1921, vol. II

Cox, Ven. William Lang Paige, 1855–1934, vol. III

Cox, Maj.-Gen. William Reginald, 1905–1988, vol. VIII

Cox, Sir (William) Robert, 1922–1981, vol. VIII

Cox, Lt-Col Sir William Thomas, 1881–1939, vol. III

Cox-Davies, Rachael Annie, 1863–1944, vol. IV

Cox-Edwards, Rev. John Cox, *died* 1926, vol. II

Cox-Taylor, Col Herbert James; *see* Taylor.

Coxe, Henry Reynell Holled, 1863–1938, vol. III

Coxe, Rev. Seymour Richard, 1842–1922, vol. II

Coxen, Maj.-Gen. Walter Adams, 1870–1949, vol. IV

Coxen, Sir William George, 1st Bt, 1867–1946, vol. IV

Coxhead, Brig.-Gen. James Alfred, 1851–1929, vol. III

Coxhead, Lt-Col Thomas Langhorne, 1864–1939, vol. III

Coxwell, Charles Blake, 1889–1967, vol. VI

Coxwell-Rogers, Maj.-Gen. Norman Annesley, 1896–1985, vol. VIII

Coyajee, Sir Jahangir Cooverjee, 1875–1943, vol. IV (A), vol. V

Coyle, James Vincent, 1864–1948, vol. IV

Coyle, William Thomas, *died* 1951, vol. V

Cozens-Hardy, 1st Baron, 1838–1920, vol. II

Cozens-Hardy, 2nd Baron, 1868–1924, vol. II

Cozens-Hardy, 3rd Baron, 1873–1956, vol. V

Cozens-Hardy, 4th Baron, 1907–1975, vol. VII

Cozens-Hardy, Archibald, 1869–1957, vol. V

Cozens-Hardy, Edgar Wrigly, 1872–1945, vol. IV

Cozzens, James Gould, 1903–1978, vol. VII

Crabb, Edward, 1853–1914, vol. I

Crabbe, Sir Cecil Brooksby, 1898–1971, vol. VII

Crabbe, Brig.-Gen. Eyre Macdonnell Stewart, 1852–1905, vol. I

Crabbe, Herbert Ernest, 1867–1940, vol. III

Crabbe, Col Sir John Gordon, 1892–1961, vol. VI

Crabbe, Vice-Adm. Lewis Gonne Eyre, 1882–1951, vol. V

Crabbe, Rt Rev. Reginald Percy, 1883–1964, vol. VI

Crabtree, Harold, 1884–1956, vol. V

Crace, Adm. Sir John Gregory, 1887–1968, vol. VI

Crackanthorpe, Dayrell Montague, *died* 1950, vol. IV

Crackanthorpe, Montague Hughes, 1832–1913, vol. I

Cracknall, Walter Borthwick, 1850–1902, vol. I

Cracroft-Amcotts, Lt-Comdr John, *died* 1956, vol. V

Cracroft-Amcotts, Lt-Col Sir Weston, 1888–1975, vol. VII

Craddock, Col Alexander Bainbridge, 1893–1962, vol. VI

Craddock, Sir Beresford; *see* Craddock, Sir G. B.

Craddock, Charles Egbert; *see* Murfree, Mary Noailles.

Craddock, George, 1897–1974, vol. VII

Craddock, Sir (George) Beresford, 1898–1976, vol. VII

Craddock, Sir Reginald Henry, 1864–1937, vol. III

Craddock, Lt-Gen. Sir Richard Walter, 1910–1977, vol. VII

Craddock, Sir Walter Merry, 1883–1972, vol. VII

Cradock, Rear-Adm. Sir Christopher George Francis Maurice, 1862–1914, vol. I

Cradock, Lt-Col Montagu, 1859–1929, vol. III

Cradock, Major Sheldon William Keith, 1858–1922, vol. II

Cradock-Hartopp, Sir Charles Edward; *see* Hartopp.

Cradock-Hartopp, Sir Charles (William Everard); *see* Hartopp.

Cradock-Hartopp, Sir Frederick; *see* Hartopp.

Cradock-Hartopp, Sir George Francis Fleetwood; *see* Hartopp.

Cradock-Watson, Henry, 1864–1951, vol. V

Crafer, Rev. Thomas Wilfrid, 1870–1949, vol. IV

Craft, Percy Robert, *died* 1934, vol. III

Crafts, Wilbur Fisk, 1850–1922, vol. II

Cragg, Ven. Herbert Wallace, 1910–1980, vol. VII

Cragg, Major William Gilliat, 1883–1956, vol. V

Craggs, Sir John George, 1856–1928, vol. II

Craib, William Grant, 1882–1933, vol. III

Craies, William Feilden, 1854–1911, vol. I
Craig, Alexander, *died* 1935, vol. III
Craig, Major Sir Algernon Tudor T.; *see* Tudor-Craig.
Craig, Sir Archibald, *died* 1927, vol. II
Craig, Sir Archibald Charles G.; *see* Gibson-Craig.
Craig, Very Rev. Archibald Campbell, 1888–1985, vol. VIII
Craig, Maj.-Gen. Archibald Maxwell, 1895–1953, vol. V
Craig, Sir Arthur John Edward, 1886–1972, vol. VII
Craig, Barry; *see* Craig, F. B.
Craig, Captain Rt Hon. Charles Curtis, 1869–1960, vol. V
Craig, Clifford, 1896–1986, vol. VIII
Craig, Edward Gordon, 1872–1966, vol. VI
Craig, Edward Hubert Cunningham, 1874–1946, vol. IV
Craig, Edwin Stewart, 1865–1939, vol. III
Craig, Elizabeth Josephine, 1883–1980, vol. VII
Craig, Sir Ernest, 1st Bt, 1859–1933, vol. III
Craig, Sir (Ernest) Gordon, 1891–1966, vol. VI
Craig, Frank, 1874–1918, vol. II
Craig, Frank Barrington, (Barry Craig), 1902–1951, vol. V
Craig, George, 1873–1947, vol. IV
Craig, Sir Gilfrid Gordon, 1871–1953, vol. V
Craig, Sir Gordon; *see* Craig, Sir E. G.
Craig, Very Rev. Graham, *died* 1904, vol. I
Craig, Hamish M.; *see* Millar-Craig.
Craig, Herbert James, 1869–1934, vol. III
Craig, J. Humbert, *died* 1944, vol. IV
Craig, James, 1851–1931, vol. III
Craig, Lt-Col James, 1864–1931, vol. III
Craig, Sir James, 1861–1933, vol. III
Craig, James A., *died* 1958, vol. V
Craig, James Alfred, 1858–1942, vol. IV
Craig, James Douglas, 1882–1950, vol. IV
Craig, Sir James Henry G.; *see* Gibson-Craig.
Craig, James Ireland, 1868–1952, vol. V
Craig, Sir John, 1874–1957, vol. V
Craig, John, 1898–1977, vol. VII
Craig, John Douglas, 1887–1968, vol. VI
Craig, Col John Francis, 1856–1927, vol. II
Craig, Sir John Herbert McCutcheon, 1885–1977, vol. VII
Craig, John Manson, 1896–1970, vol. VI
Craig, Sir (John) Walker, 1847–1926, vol. II
Craig, Sir Marshall Millar, 1880–1957, vol. V
Craig, Sir Maurice, 1866–1935, vol. III
Craig, Col Noel Newman Lombard, *died* 1968, vol. VI
Craig, Lt-Comdr Norman Carlyle, 1868–1919, vol. II
Craig, Rev. Oswald, 1867–1935, vol. III
Craig, R. Hunter, 1839–1913, vol. I
Craig, Col Robert Annesley, 1869–1932, vol. III
Craig, Stuart E., *died* 1904, vol. I
Craig, Thomas Joseph Alexander, 1881–1970, vol. VI
Craig, Sir Walker; *see* Craig, Sir J. W.
Craig, Dep. Surg.-Gen. William Maxwell, 1859–1914, vol. I
Craig, William Stuart McRae, 1903–1975, vol. VII
Craig-Brown, Lt-Col Ernest, 1871–1966, vol. VI
Craig-Brown, Thomas, 1844–1922, vol. II

Craigavon, 1st Viscount, 1871–1940, vol. III
Craigavon, 2nd Viscount, 1906–1974, vol. VII
Craigavon, Viscountess; (Cecil Mary Nowell Dering), *died* 1960, vol. V
Craighead, Edwin Boone, 1861–1920, vol. II (A), vol. III
Craigie, Rev. Charles Edward, *died* 1922, vol. II
Craigie, James, 1899–1978, vol. VII
Craigie, John, 1857–1919, vol. II
Craigie, Major Patrick George, 1843–1930, vol. III
Craigie, Pearl Mary Teresa; *see* Hobbes, John Oliver.
Craigie, Rt Hon. Sir Robert Leslie, 1883–1959, vol. V
Craigie, Adm. Robert William, 1849–1911, vol. I
Craigie, Sir William A., 1867–1957, vol. V
Craigmyle, 1st Baron, 1850–1937, vol. III
Craigmyle, 2nd Baron, 1883–1944, vol. IV
Craik, Sir George Lillie, 2nd Bt, 1874–1929, vol. III
Craik, Rt Hon. Sir Henry, 1st Bt, 1846–1927, vol. II
Craik, Sir Henry Duffield, 3rd Bt, 1876–1955, vol. V
Craik, Lt-Col James, 1871–1942, vol. IV
Craik, Robert, 1829–1906, vol. I
Cram, Ralph Adams, 1863–1942, vol. IV
Cramb, Alexander Charles, 1874–1956, vol. V
Cramb, J. A., 1862–1913, vol. I
Cramer, Dame Mary Theresa, *died* 1984, vol. VIII
Cramer, William, 1878–1945, vol. IV
Cramer-Roberts, Major Marmaduke Torin; *see* Roberts.
Cramp, Charles Henry, 1828–1913, vol. I
Cramp, Concemore Thomas, 1876–1933, vol. III
Cramp, Karl Reginald, 1878–1956, vol. V
Cramp, William, 1876–1939, vol. III
Cramp, Sir William Dawkins, 1840–1927, vol. II
Crampton, Vice-Adm. Denis Burke, 1873–1936, vol. III
Crampton, Brig.-Gen. Fiennes Henry, 1862–1938, vol. III
Crampton, Harold Percy, 1878–1969, vol. VI
Crampton, Col Philip John Ribton, 1860–1932, vol. III
Cran, Marion, 1875–1942, vol. IV
Cranage, Very Rev. David Herbert Somerset, 1866–1957, vol. V
Cranbrook, 1st Earl of, 1814–1906, vol. I
Cranbrook, 2nd Earl of, 1839–1911, vol. I
Cranbrook, 3rd Earl of, 1870–1915, vol. I
Cranbrook, 4th Earl of, 1900–1978, vol. VII
Crane, Sir Alfred Victor, 1892–1955, vol. V
Crane, Lt-Col Charles Paston, *died* 1939, vol. III
Crane, Sir Edmund Frank, 1886–1957, vol. V
Crane, Sir Harry Walter Victor, 1903–1986, vol. VIII
Crane, Morley Benjamin, 1890–1983, vol. VIII
Crane, Robert Newton, 1848–1927, vol. II
Crane, Walter, 1845–1915, vol. I
Crane, Sir William, 1874–1959, vol. V
Crane, William Alfred James, 1925–1982, vol. VIII
Cranfield, Arthur Leslie, 1892–1957, vol. V
Cranko, John, 1927–1973, vol. VII
Crankshaw, Edward, 1909–1984, vol. VIII
Crankshaw, Lt-Col Sir Eric Norman Spencer, 1885–1966, vol. VI
Cranmer-Byng, L., 1872–1945, vol. IV
Cranston, Robert, *died* 1906, vol. I
Cranston, Brig.-Gen. Sir Robert, 1843–1923, vol. II

Cranston, William Patrick, 1913–1967, vol. VI
Cranstone, Bryan Allan Lefevre, 1918–1989, vol. VIII
Cranstoun, Lady; (Elizabeth), *died* 1899, vol. I
Cranstoun, Charles Joseph Edmondstoune-, 1877–1950, vol. IV
Cranstoun, James, *died* 1931, vol. III
Cranswick, Rt Rev. Geoffrey Franceys, 1894–1978, vol. VII
Cranswick, Rt Rev. George Harvard, 1882–1954, vol. V
Cranworth, 1st Baron, 1829–1902, vol. I
Cranworth, 2nd Baron, 1877–1964, vol. VI
Craske, A(rthur) H(ugh) Glenn, 1904–1967, vol. VI
Craske, Rt Rev. Frederick William Thomas, 1901–1971, vol. VII
Craske, Glenn; *see* Craske, A. H. G.
Craske, Lt-Col John, 1869–1936, vol. III
Craster, Sir Edmund; *see* Craster, Sir H. H. E.
Cra'ster, Lt-Col Edmund Henry Bertram, 1869–1942, vol. IV
Craster, Col George, 1878–1958, vol. V
Craster, Maj.-Gen. George Ayton, 1830–1912, vol. I
Craster, Sir (Herbert Henry) Edmund, 1879–1959, vol. V
Craster, Sir John Montagu, 1901–1975, vol. VII
Cra'ster, Col Shafto Longfield, 1862–1943, vol. IV
Craster, Thomas William, 1860–1938, vol. III
Crathorne, 1st Baron, 1897–1977, vol. VII
Craufurd, Rev. Alexander Henry, 1843–1917, vol. II
Craufurd, Sir Alexander John Fortescue, 7th Bt, 1876–1966, vol. VI
Craufurd, Sir Charles William Frederick, 4th Bt, 1847–1939, vol. III
Craufurd, Mrs Eleanor Louisa Houison, *died* 1950, vol. IV
Craufurd, Brig.-Gen. Sir (George) Standish (Gage), 5th Bt, 1872–1957, vol. V
Craufurd, Sir James Gregan, 8th Bt, 1886–1970, vol. VI
Craufurd, Brig.-Gen. John Archibald Houison, 1862–1933, vol. III
Craufurd, Sir Quentin Charles Alexander, 6th Bt, 1875–1957, vol. V
Craufurd, Col Robert Quentin, 1880–1943, vol. IV
Craufurd, Brig.-Gen. Sir Standish; *see* Craufurd, Brig.-Gen. Sir G. S. G.
Craufurd-Stuart, Lt-Col Charles Kennedy; *see* Stuart.
Cravath, Paul Drennan, 1861–1940, vol. III
Craven, 4th Earl of, 1868–1921, vol. II
Craven, 5th Earl of, 1897–1932, vol. III
Craven, 6th Earl of, 1917–1965, vol. VI
Craven, 7th Earl of, 1957–1983, vol. VIII
Craven, 8th Earl of, 1961–1990, vol. VIII
Craven, Brig.-Gen. Arthur Julius, 1867–1933, vol. III
Craven, Arthur Scott, (Captain Arthur Keedwell Harvey James), 1875–1917, vol. II
Craven, Avery O., 1886–1980, vol. VII
Craven, Comdr Sir Charles Worthington, 1st Bt, 1884–1944, vol. IV
Craven, Sir Derek Worthington Clunes, 2nd Bt, 1910–1946, vol. IV
Craven, Rt Rev. George L., 1884–1967, vol. VI
Craven, Ven. James Brown, 1850–1924, vol. II

Craven, Majorie Eadon, 1895–1983, vol. VIII
Craven, Hon. Osbert William, 1848–1923, vol. II
Craven, Sir Robert Martin, 1824–1903, vol. I
Craven, Major Hon. Rupert Cecil, 1870–1959, vol. V
Craven, Lt-Col Waldemar Sigismund Dacre, 1880–1928, vol. II
Craven, William George, 1835–1906, vol. I
Craven-Ellis, William, *died* 1959, vol. V
Craw, Sir Henry Hewat, 1882–1964, vol. VI
Crawford, 26th Earl of, **and Balcarres,** 9th Earl of, 1847–1913, vol. I
Crawford, 27th Earl of, **and Balcarres,** 10th Earl of, 1871–1940, vol. III
Crawford, 28th Earl of, **and Balcarres,** 11th Earl of, 1900–1975, vol. VII
Crawford, Brig. Alastair Wardrop Euing, 1896–1978, vol. VII
Crawford, Alexander W., 1866–1933, vol. III
Crawford, Andrew, 1871–1936, vol. III
Crawford, Archibald, 1882–1960, vol. V
Crawford, Sir (Archibald James) Dirom, 1899–1983, vol. VIII
Crawford, Arthur Muir, 1882–1962, vol. VI
Crawford, Arthur Travers, 1835–1911, vol. I
Crawford, Captain Charles Wispington Glover, *died* 1934, vol. III
Crawford, Colin Grant, 1890–1959, vol. V
Crawford, David Gordon, 1928–1981, vol. VIII
Crawford, Sir Dirom; *see* Crawford, Sir A. J. D.
Crawford, Donald, 1837–1919, vol. II
Crawford, Brig. Sir Douglas Inglis, 1904–1981, vol. VIII
Crawford, Very Rev. Edward Patrick, 1846–1912, vol. I
Crawford, Col Edward William, 1879–1961, vol. VI
Crawford, Mrs Emily, *died* 1915, vol. I
Crawford, Sir Ferguson; *see* Crawford, Sir W. F.
Crawford, Sir Francis Collum, 1862–1934, vol. III
Crawford, Francis Marion, 1854–1909, vol. I
Crawford, Sir Frederick, 1906–1978, vol. VII
Crawford, Lt-Col Frederick Hugh, 1861–1952, vol. V
Crawford, Col George Rainier, 1862–1915, vol. I
Crawford, Lt-Col Gilbert Stewart, 1868–1953, vol. V
Crawford, Henry Leighton, 1855–1931, vol. III
Crawford, Sir Homewood, 1850–1936, vol. III
Crawford, Hugh Adam, 1898–1982, vol. VIII
Crawford, James, 1896–1982, vol. VIII
Crawford, James Archibald, 1905–1953, vol. V
Crawford, Joan, *died* 1977, vol. VII
Crawford, Very Rev. John, *died* 1924, vol. II
Crawford, John Balfour, 1887–1962, vol. VI
Crawford, John Dawson, 1861–1946, vol. IV
Crawford, Sir John Grenfell, 1910–1984, vol. VIII
Crawford, Lt-Col John Halket, 1868–1936, vol. III
Crawford, Maj.-Gen. John Scott, 1889–1978, vol. VII
Crawford, Captain John Stuart, 1900–1985, vol. VIII
Crawford, Gen. Sir Kenneth Noel, 1895–1961, vol. VI
Crawford, Lawrence, 1867–1951, vol. V
Crawford, Captain Lawrence Hugh, *died* 1918, vol. II
Crawford, Osbert Guy Stanhope, 1886–1957, vol. V
Crawford, Col Raymund, 1858–1927, vol. II
Crawford, Sir Richard Frederick, 1863–1919, vol. II
Crawford, Col Richmond Irvine, 1839–1910, vol. I

Crawford, Robert, *died* 1946, vol. IV
Crawford, Col Robert Duncan, *died* 1936, vol. III
Crawford, Col Rt Hon. Robert Gordon S.; *see* Sharman-Crawford.
Crawford, Susan Fletcher, *died* 1919, vol. II
Crawford, Rev. Thomas, 1860–1937, vol. III
Crawford, Thomas Clark, 1886–1955, vol. V
Crawford, Col Vincent James, 1877–1932, vol. III
Crawford, Sir (Walter) Ferguson, 1894–1978, vol. VII
Crawford, Sir William, 1840–1922, vol. II
Crawford, Lt-Col William Loftus, 1868–1951, vol. V
Crawford, William Neil Kennedy Mellon, 1910–1978, vol. VII
Crawford, Sir William S., 1878–1950, vol. IV
Crawford-Compton, Air Vice-Marshal William Vernon, 1915–1988, vol. VIII
Crawfurd, Major Horace Evelyn, 1882–1958, vol. V
Crawfurd, Rt Rev. Lionel Payne, 1864–1934, vol. III
Crawfurd, Oswald John Frederick, 1834–1909, vol. I
Crawfurd, Sir Raymond Henry Payne, 1865–1938, vol. III
Crawfurd-Price, Walter Harrington, 1881–1967, vol. VI
Crawfurd-Stirling-Stuart, William, 1854–1938, vol. III
Crawhall, Joseph, *died* 1913, vol. I
Crawhall, Rev. Thomas Emerson, 1866–1934, vol. III
Crawley, Alfred Ernest, 1869–1924, vol. II
Crawley, Rev. Canon Arthur Stafford, 1876–1948, vol. IV
Crawley, Cecil, 1862–1931, vol. III
Crawley, Francis, 1853–1914, vol. I
Crawley, Frank C., 1871–1935, vol. III
Crawley, Major Sir Philip Arthur Sambrooke, 1869–1933, vol. III
Crawley, Col Richard Parry, 1876–1933, vol. III
Crawley, Virginia, (Mrs Aidan Crawley); *see* Cowles, V.
Crawley, William John Chetwode, 1844–1916, vol. II
Crawley-Boevey, Sir Francis Hyde; *see* Boevey.
Crawley-Boevey, Sir Lance, (Launcelot Valentine Hyde), 7th Bt, 1900–1968, vol. VI
Crawshaw, 1st Baron, 1825–1908, vol. I
Crawshaw, 2nd Baron, 1853–1929, vol. III
Crawshaw, 3rd Baron, 1884–1946, vol. IV
Crawshaw of Aintree, Baron (Life Peer); Lt-Col Richard Crawshaw, 1917–1986, vol. VIII
Crawshaw, Lionel Townsend, *died* 1949, vol. IV
Crawshaw, Philip, 1912–1984, vol. VIII
Crawshay, Lt-Col Codrington Howard Rees, 1882–1937, vol. III
Crawshay, Captain Geoffrey Cartland Hugh, 1892–1954, vol. V
Crawshay-Williams, Lt-Col Eliot, 1879–1962, vol. VI
Craxton, Harold, 1885–1971, vol. VII
Cray, Rev. Canon Frank Maynard, 1898–1967, vol. VI
Creagh, Maj.-Gen. Arthur Gethin, 1855–1941, vol. IV
Creagh, Col Arthur Henry Dopping, 1866–1941, vol. IV
Creagh, Charles Vandeleur, 1842–1917, vol. II
Creagh, Maj.-Gen. Edward Philip Nagle, 1896–1981, vol. VIII

Creagh, Col George Washington B.; *see* Brazier-Creagh.
Creagh, Rear-Adm. James Vandeleur, 1883–1956, vol. V
Creagh, Maj.-Gen. Sir Michael O'Moore, 1892–1970, vol. VI
Creagh, Gen. Sir O'Moore, 1848–1923, vol. II
Creagh, Lt-Col Peter H., 1882–1933, vol. III
Creagh Coen, Sir Terence Bernard, 1903–1970, vol. VI
Creagh-Osborne, Captain F.; *see* Osborne.
Creak, Captain Ettrick William, 1835–1920, vol. II
Crealock, Major John Mansfield, *died* 1959, vol. V
Creamer, Amos Albert, 1917–1978, vol. VII
Crean, Sir Bernard Arthur, 1881–1956, vol. V
Crean, Eugene, 1856–1939, vol. III
Crean, Major Thomas Joseph, 1873–1923, vol. II
Crease, Hon. Sir Henry Pering Pellew, 1823–1905, vol. I
Crease, Maj.-Gen. Sir John Frederick, *died* 1907, vol. I
Crease, Captain Thomas Evans, 1875–1942, vol. IV
Creasey, Gordon Leonard, 1873–1943, vol. IV
Creasey, John, 1908–1973, vol. VII
Creasey, Gen. Sir Timothy May, 1923–1986, vol. VIII
Creasy, Adm. of the Fleet Sir George Elvey, 1895–1972, vol. VII
Creasy, Sir Gerald Hallen, 1897–1983, vol. VIII
Creasy, Harold Thomas, 1873–1950, vol. IV
Creasy, Leonard, 1854–1922, vol. II
Cree, Maj.-Gen. Gerald, 1862–1932, vol. III
Cree, Kate; *see* Rorke, K.
Creed, Albert Lowry, 1909–1987, vol. VIII
Creed, Clarence James, 1894–1955, vol. V
Creed, Edward ffolliott, 1893–1947, vol. IV
Creed, Rev. John Martin, 1889–1940, vol. III
Creed, Hon. John Mildred, 1842–1930, vol. III
Creed, Richard Stephen, 1898–1964, vol. VI
Creed, Sir Thomas Percival, 1897–1969, vol. VI
Creedy, Sir Herbert James, 1878–1973, vol. VII
Creelman, James, 1859–1915, vol. I
Creelman, Col John Jennings, 1882–1949, vol. IV
Crees, James Harold Edward, 1882–1941, vol. IV
Cregan, Rev. James, 1857–1935, vol. III
Creighton, Charles, 1847–1927, vol. II
Creighton, Rev. Cuthbert, 1876–1963, vol. VI
Creighton, Donald Grant, 1902–1979, vol. VII
Creighton, James George Aylwin, 1850–1930, vol. III
Creighton, Rear-Adm. Sir Kenelm Everard Lane, 1883–1963, vol. VI
Creighton, Mrs Louise, 1850–1936, vol. III
Creighton, Rt Hon. and Rt Rev. Mandell, 1843–1901, vol. I
Cremer, Herbert William, 1893–1970, vol. VI
Cremer, Robert Wyndham K.; *see* Ketton-Cremer.
Cremer, Sir William Randal, 1838–1908, vol. I
Cremieu-Javal, Paul, 1857–1927, vol. II
Cremin, Cornelius Christopher, 1908–1987, vol. VIII
Crerar, Gen. Henry Duncan Graham, 1888–1965, vol. VI
Crerar, Sir James, 1877–1960, vol. V
Crerar, Hon. Thomas Alexander, 1876–1975, vol. VII

Cresswell, Rev. Cyril Leonard, 1890–1974, vol. VII

Cresswell, Col George Francis Addison, 1852–1926, vol. II

Cresswell, Herbert Osborn, 1860–1919, vol. II

Cresswell, Col Pearson Robert, 1834–1905, vol. I

Cresswell, Stuart Cornwallis, *died* 1959, vol. V

Cresswell, William Foy, 1895–1981, vol. VIII

Cressy-Marcks, Violet Olivia, (Mrs Francis Fisher), *died* 1970, vol. VI

Creston, Dormer; *see* Colston-Baynes, D. J.

Creswell, Sir Archibald; *see* Creswell, Sir K. A. C.

Creswell, Col Edmund Fraser, 1876–1941, vol. IV

Creswell, Lt-Col Hon. Frederic Hugh Page, 1866–1948, vol. IV

Creswell, Rear-Adm. George Hector, 1889–1967, vol. VI

Creswell, Harry Bulkeley, 1869–1960, vol. V

Creswell, John Edwards, 1864–1928, vol. II

Creswell, Sir (Keppel) Archibald (Cameron), 1879–1974, vol. VII

Creswell, Margaret Susan, *died* 1936, vol. III

Creswell, Sir Michael Justin, 1909–1986, vol. VIII

Creswell, Vice-Adm. Sir William Rooke, 1852–1933, vol. III

Creswell, William Thomas, 1872–1946, vol. IV

Creswick, Sir Alexander Reid, (Sir Alec Creswick), 1912–1983, vol. VIII

Creswick, Harry Richardson, 1902–1988, vol. VIII

Creswick, Col Sir Nathaniel, 1831–1917, vol. II

Creswick, Paul, 1866–1947, vol. IV

Cretney, Sir Godfrey; *see* Cretney, Sir W. G.

Cretney, Sir (William) Godfrey, 1912–1971, vol. VII

Crew, Albert, *died* 1942, vol. IV

Crew, Francis Albert Eley, 1886–1973, vol. VII

Crewdson, Bernard Francis, 1887–1966, vol. VI

Crewdson, Rev. George, 1840–1920, vol. II

Crewdson, Bt-Col William Dillworth, 1897–1972, vol. VII

Crewdson, Wilson, 1856–1918, vol. II

Crewe, 1st Marquess of, 1858–1945, vol. IV

Crewe, Marchioness of; (Margaret Etrenne Hannah), *died* 1967, vol. VI

Crewe, Bertie Gibson, 1884–1971, vol. VII

Crewe, Brig.-Gen. Hon. Sir Charles Preston, 1858–1936, vol. III

Crewe, Major James Hugh Hamilton D.; *see* Dodds Crewe.

Crewe, Sir Vauncey Harpur, 10th Bt, 1846–1924, vol. II

Crewe-Read, Col Randulph Offley, *died* 1932, vol. III

Creyke, Ralph, 1849–1908, vol. I

Cribbett, Sir George; *see* Cribbett, Sir W. C. G.

Cribbett, Sir (Wilfrid Charles) George, 1897–1964, vol. VI

Crichton, Hon. Arthur Owen, 1876–1970, vol. VI

Crichton, Lt-Col Hon. Charles Frederick, 1841–1918, vol. II

Crichton, Lady Emma, *died* 1936, vol. III

Crichton, Col Hon. Sir George Arthur Charles, 1874–1952, vol. IV

Crichton, Lt-Col Gerald Charles Lawrence, 1900–1969, vol. VI

Crichton, Brig. Henry Coventry Maitland-Makgill-, 1880–1953, vol. V

Crichton, Col Hon. Sir Henry George Louis, 1844–1922, vol. II

Crichton, Air Cdre Henry Lumsden, 1890–1952, vol. V

Crichton, Captain Hon. James Archibald, 1877–1956, vol. V

Crichton, Sir (John) Robertson (Dunn), 1912–1985, vol. VIII

Crichton, Engr Captain Peter Thomson, 1863–1935, vol. III

Crichton, Lt-Col Richmond Trevor, 1865–1934, vol. III

Crichton, Sir Robert, 1881–1950, vol. IV

Crichton, Sir Robertson; *see* Crichton, Sir J. R. D.

Crichton, Col Walter Hugh, 1896–1984, vol. VIII

Crichton-Browne, Col Harold William Alexander Francis, 1866–1937, vol. III

Crichton-Browne, Sir James, 1840–1938, vol. III

Crichton-Maitland, Maj.-Gen. David M.; *see* Makgill-Crichton-Maitland.

Crichton-Miller, Hugh, 1877–1959, vol. V

Crichton-Stuart, Lord Colum Edmund, 1886–1957, vol. V

Crichton-Stuart, Lord Ninian Edward, 1883–1915, vol. I

Crick, Rt Rev. Douglas Henry, *died* 1973, vol. VII

Crick, Rt Rev. Philip Charles Thurlow, 1882–1937, vol. III

Crick, Very Rev. Thomas, 1885–1970, vol. VI

Crick, Hon. William P., *died* 1908, vol. I

Cridland, Charles Elliot Tapscott, 1900–1983, vol. VIII

Cridland, Frank, 1873–1954, vol. V

Crilly, Daniel, 1857–1923, vol. II

Crimmin, Col John, 1859–1945, vol. IV

Cripps, Col Arthur William, 1862–1945, vol. IV

Cripps, Sir Cyril Thomas, 1892–1979, vol. VII

Cripps, Sir Edward Stewart, 1885–1955, vol. V

Cripps, Major Sir Frederick William Beresford, 1873–1959, vol. V

Cripps, Henry William, *died* 1899, vol. I

Cripps, Dame Isobel, 1891–1979, vol. VII

Cripps, Major Hon. Leonard Harrison, *died* 1959, vol. V

Cripps, Hon. Lionel, 1863–1950, vol. IV

Cripps, Rt Hon. Sir (Richard) Stafford, 1889–1952, vol. V

Cripps, Rt Hon. Sir Stafford; *see* Cripps, Rt Hon. Sir R. S.

Cripps, W. Harrison, *died* 1923, vol. II

Cripps, William Parry, 1903–1972, vol. VII

Crisham, Air Vice-Marshal William Joseph, 1906–1987, vol. VIII

Crisp, Col Rev. Alan Percy, 1889–1972, vol. VII

Crisp, Sir Frank, 1st Bt, 1843–1919, vol. II

Crisp, Sir Frank Morris, 2nd Bt, 1872–1938, vol. III

Crisp, Frederick Arthur, 1851–1922, vol. II

Crisp, Sir Harold, 1874–1942, vol. IV

Crisp, Dennis John, 1916–1990, vol. VIII

Crisp, Sir John Wilson, 3rd Bt, 1873–1950, vol. IV

Crisp, Leslie Finlay, 1917–1984, vol. VIII

Crisp, Sir (Malcolm) Peter, 1912–1984, vol. VIII

Crisp, Sir Peter; *see* Crisp, Sir M. P.

Crispe, Thomas Edward, *died* 1911, vol. I

Crispi, Francesco, 1819–1901, vol. I

Crispin, Edward Smyth, 1874–1958, vol. V

Crispin, Geoffrey Hollis, 1905–1976, vol. VII

Critchell, James Troubridge, 1850–1917, vol. II

Critchett, Sir George Anderson, 1st Bt, died 1925, vol. II

Critchett, Sir (George) Montague, 2nd Bt, 1884–1941, vol. IV

Critchett, Sir Montague; see Critchett, Sir G. M.

Critchley, Alexander, 1893–1974, vol. VII

Critchley, Brig.-Gen. Alfred Cecil, 1890–1963, vol. VI

Critchley-Waring, Captain Arthur Cunliffe Bernard, 1886–1930, vol. III

Crittall, Francis Henry, died 1935, vol. III

Croal, John P., 1852–1932, vol. III

Croce, Benedetto, 1866–1952, vol. V

Crockatt, James Laird, 1876–1936, vol. III

Crockatt, Brig. Norman Richard, 1894–1956, vol. V

Crocker, George, 1846–1923, vol. II

Crocker, Antony James Gulliford, 1918–1988, vol. VIII

Crocker, Brig.-Gen. George Delamain, died 1938, vol. III

Crocker, Henry Radcliffe, 1845--1909, vol. I

Crocker, Lt-Col Herbert Edmund, 1877–1962, vol. VI

Crocker, Gen. Sir John Tredinnick, 1896–1963, vol. VI

Crocker, Brig.-Gen. Sydney Francis, 1864–1952, vol. V

Crocker, Sir William Charles, 1886–1973, vol. VII

Crocker, Rear-Adm. (S) William Ernest, died 1951, vol. V

Crocket, Henry Edgar, died 1926, vol. II

Crocket, James, 1878–1944, vol. IV

Crocket, Oswald Smith, 1868–1945, vol. IV

Crockett, Sir James Henry Clifden, 1848–1931, vol. III

Crockett, Samuel Rutherford, 1860–1914, vol. I

Crockett, Rev. William Shillinglaw, 1866–1945, vol. IV

Crocombe, Leonard Cecil, 1890–1968, vol. VI

Croft, 1st Baron, 1881–1947, vol. IV

Croft, Sir Alfred Woodley, 1841–1925, vol. II

Croft, Sir Arthur, 1886–1961, vol. VI

Croft, Sir Bernard Hugh Denman, 13th Bt (cr 1671), 1903–1984, vol. VIII

Croft, Sir Frederick Leigh, 3rd Bt (cr 1818), 1860–1930, vol. III

Croft, Henry Herbert Stephen, 1842–1923, vol. II

Croft, Sir Herbert Archer, 10th Bt (cr 1671), 1868–1915, vol. I

Croft, Sir Herbert George Denman, 9th Bt (cr 1671), 1838–1902, vol. I

Croft, Sir Hugh Matthew Fiennes, 12th Bt (cr 1671), 1874–1954, vol. V

Croft, Sir James Herbert, 11th Bt (cr 1671), 1907–1941, vol. IV

Croft, Major Sir John Archibald Radcliffe, 5th Bt, 1910–1990, vol. VIII

Croft, Sir John Frederick, 2nd Bt (cr 1818), 1828–1904, vol. I

Croft, (John) Michael, 1922–1986, vol. VIII

Croft, Sir John William Graham, 4th Bt (cr 1818), 1910–1979, vol. VII

Croft, Michael; see Croft, J. M.

Croft, Major Owen George Scudamore, 1880–1956, vol. V

Croft, Richard Benyon, 1843–1912, vol. I

Croft, Sir William Dawson, 1892–1964, vol. VI

Croft, Brig.-Gen. William Denman, 1879–1968, vol. VI

Croft-Cooke, Rupert, 1903–1979, vol. VII

Croft-Murray, Edward, 1907–1980, vol. VII

Crofton, 3rd Baron, 1834–1911, vol. I

Crofton, 4th Baron, 1866–1942, vol. IV

Crofton, 5th Baron, 1926–1974, vol. VII

Crofton, 6th Baron, 1949–1989, vol. VIII

Crofton, Brig.-Gen. Cyril Randell, 1867–1941, vol. IV

Crofton, Vice-Adm. Edward George L.; see Lowther-Crofton.

Crofton, Major Sir Henry; see Crofton, Major Sir M. R. H.

Crofton, Sir Hugh Denis, 5th Bt (cr 1801), 1878–1902, vol. I

Crofton, Lt-Gen. James, 1826–1908, vol. I

Crofton, Sir Malby, 3rd Bt (cr 1838), 1857–1926, vol. II

Crofton, Major Sir (Malby Richard) Henry, 4th Bt (cr 1838), 1881–1962, vol. VI

Crofton, Col Morgan, 1850–1916, vol. II

Crofton, Sir Morgan George, 4th Bt (cr 1801), 1850–1900, vol. I

Crofton, Sir Morgan George, 6th Bt (cr 1801), 1879–1958, vol. V

Crofton, Morgan William, 1826–1915, vol. I

Crofton, Sir Patrick Simon, 7th Bt, 1936–1987, vol. VIII

Crofton, Sir Richard Marsh, 1891–1955, vol. V

Crofton, Brig. Roger, 1888–1972, vol. VII

Crofton, Rt Hon. Sir Walter Frederic, 1815–1897, vol. I

Crofts, Surg.-Gen. Aylmer Martin, 1854–1915, vol. I

Crofts, Ernest, 1847–1911, vol. I

Crofts, Freeman Wills, 1879–1957, vol. V

Crofts, John Ernest Victor, 1887–1972, vol. VII

Crofts, Lt-Col Leonard Markham, 1867–1942, vol. IV

Crofts, Major Richard, 1859–1916, vol. II

Crofts, Thomas Robert Norman, 1874–1949, vol. IV

Crofts, Rev. William John H.; see Humble-Crofts.

Croiset, Alfred, 1845–1923, vol. II

Croisset, Francis de, 1885–1937, vol. III

Croke, Air Cdre Lewis George Le Blount, 1894–1971, vol. VII

Croke, Most Rev. Thomas W., 1824–1902, vol. I

Croker, Bithia Mary, died 1920, vol. II

Croker, Engr Rear-Adm. Edward James O'Brien, 1881–1960, vol. V

Croker, Maj.-Gen. Sir Henry Leycester, 1864–1938, vol. III

Croker, Richard, 1841–1922, vol. II

Croker, Captain Thomas Joseph, 1876–1956, vol. V

Crole, Charles Stewart, died 1916, vol. II

Crole, Gerard Lake, 1855–1927, vol. II

Croll, David Gifford, 1885–1948, vol. IV

Croly, Very Rev. Daniel George Hayes, *died* 1916, vol. II

Cromartie, Countess of (3rd in line), 1878–1962, vol. VI

Cromartie, 4th Earl of, 1904–1989, vol. VIII

Cromartie, Ian; *see* Cromartie, R. I. T.

Cromartie, (Ronald) Ian (Talbot), 1929–1987, vol. VIII

Cromb, David Lyall, 1875–1961, vol. VI

Crombie, Alan Douglas, 1894–1958, vol. V

Crombie, Bde-Surg. Lt-Col Alexander, 1845–1906, vol. I

Crombie, Col David Campbell, 1877–1952, vol. V

Crombie, George Edmond, 1908–1972, vol. VII

Crombie, Sir James Ian Cormack, 1902–1969, vol. VI

Crombie, Rear-Adm. John Harvey Forbes, 1900–1972, vol. VII

Crombie, John William, 1858–1908, vol. I

Cromer, 1st Earl of, 1841–1917, vol. II

Cromer, 2nd Earl of, 1877–1953, vol. V

Cromie, Captain Charles Francis, 1858–1907, vol. I

Cromie, Comdr Francis Newton Allen, 1882–1918, vol. II

Cromie, Robert, 1856–1907, vol. I

Cromie, Rev. William Patrick, *died* 1927, vol. II

Crommelin, Andrew Claude de la Cherois, 1865–1939, vol. III

Crommelin, May de la Cherois, *died* 1930, vol. III

Crompton, James Shaw, 1853–1916, vol. II

Crompton, John Gilbert Frederic, 1869–1919, vol. II

Crompton, Richmal; *see* Lamburn, R. C.

Crompton, Robert, 1869–1958, vol. V

Crompton, Col Rookes Evelyn Bell, 1845–1940, vol. III

Crompton-Inglefield, Col Sir John Frederick, 1904–1988, vol. VIII

Crompton-Roberts, Lt-Col Henry Roger; *see* Roberts.

Cromwell, 5th Baron, 1893–1966, vol. VI

Cromwell, 6th Baron, 1929–1982, vol. VIII

Crone, Anne, 1915–1972, vol. VII

Crone, Col Desmond Roe, 1900–1974, vol. VII

Crone, John Smyth, 1858–1945, vol. IV

Cronin, Archibald Joseph, 1896–1981, vol. VIII

Cronin, Rt Rev. Mgr Francis, 1879–1939, vol. III

Cronin, Henry Francis, 1894–1977, vol. VII

Cronin, John Desmond, 1916–1986, vol. VIII

Cronin, John Walton, 1915–1990, vol. VIII

Cronin, Rt Rev. Mgr Michael, 1871–1943, vol. IV

Cronje, Gen. Piet A., 1835–1911, vol. I

Cronne, Henry Alfred, 1904–1990, vol. VIII

Cronshaw, Cecil John Turrell, 1889–1961, vol. VI

Cronshaw, Rev. Christopher, *died* 1921, vol. II

Cronshaw, Rev. George Bernard, *died* 1928, vol. II

Cronshaw, Rev. Herbert Priestley, 1863–1930, vol. III

Cronwright, Samuel Cron, 1863–1936, vol. III (A), vol. IV

Cronwright Schreiner, Mrs S. C.; *see* Schreiner, Olive.

Cronyn, Captain St John, 1901–1973, vol. VII

Crook, 1st Baron, 1901–1989, vol. VIII

Crook, Charles W., 1862–1926, vol. II

Crook, Eric Ashley, 1894–1984, vol. VIII

Crook, Thomas Mewburn, 1869–1949, vol. IV

Crook, William Montgomery, 1860–1945, vol. IV

Crooke, Lt-Col Charles Douglas Parry, 1870–1948, vol. IV

Crooke, Adm. Sir (Henry) Ralph, 1875–1952, vol. V

Crooke, Sir (John) Smedley, *died* 1951, vol. V

Crooke, Adm. Sir Ralph; *see* Crooke, Adm. Sir H. R.

Crooke, Sir Smedley; *see* Crooke, Sir J. S.

Crooke, William, 1848–1923, vol. II

Crooke-Lawless, Surg. Lt-Col Sir Warren Roland; *see* Lawless.

Crookenden, Col Arthur, 1877–1962, vol. VI

Crookenden, Harry Mitten, 1862–1947, vol. IV

Crookes, Sir William, 1832–1919, vol. II

Crookham, Rev. William Thomas Rupert, *died* 1945, vol. IV

Crooks, Sir James, 1858–1940, vol. III

Crooks, James, 1901–1980, vol. VII

Crooks, Captain Robert Crawford, 1894–1951, vol. V

Crooks, Very Rev. Samuel Bennett, 1920–1986, vol. VIII

Crooks, Rt Hon. William, 1852–1921, vol. II

Crookshank, 1st Viscount, 1893–1961, vol. VI

Crookshank, Col Chichester de Windt, *died* 1958, vol. V

Crookshank, Francis Graham, 1873–1933, vol. III

Crookshank, Harry Maule, 1849–1914, vol. I

Crookshank, Henry, 1893–1972, vol. VII

Crookshank, Maj.-Gen. Sir Sydney D'Aguilar, 1870–1941, vol. IV

Croom, Sir Halliday; *see* Croom, Sir J. H.

Croom, Sir (J.) Halliday, 1847–1923, vol. II

Croom, Sir John Halliday, 1909–1986, vol. VIII

Croom-Johnson, Hon. Sir Reginald Powell, *died* 1957, vol. V

Croome, Honor Renée Minturn, 1908–1960, vol. V

Croome, William Iveson, 1891–1967, vol. VI

Croot, Sir (Horace) John, 1907–1981, vol. VIII

Croot, Sir John; *see* Croot, Sir H. J.

Cropper, Anthony Charles, 1912–1967, vol. VI

Cropper, Charles James, 1852–1924, vol. II

Cropper, Rev. James, *died* 1938, vol. III

Cropper, James Winstanley, 1879–1956, vol. V

Crosbie, Lt-Gen. Adolphus Brett, *died* 1916, vol. II

Crosbie, George, 1864–1934, vol. III

Crosbie, Henry, 1852–1928, vol. II

Crosbie, Brig.-Gen. James Dayrolles, 1865–1947, vol. IV

Crosbie, Hon. Sir John Chalker, 1876–1932, vol. III

Crosbie, Robert Edward Harold, 1886–1950, vol. IV

Crosbie, Sir William Edward Douglas, 8th Bt, 1855–1936, vol. III

Crosby, Bing; *see* Crosby, H. L.

Crosby, Very Rev. Ernest Henry L.; *see* Lewis-Crosby.

Crosby, Fanny, 1820–1915, vol. I

Crosby, Harry Lillis, (Bing Crosby), 1904–1977, vol. VII

Crosby, John Michael, 1940–1988, vol. VIII

Crosby, Sir Josiah, 1880–1958, vol. V

Crosby, Sir Thomas Boor, 1830–1916, vol. II

Crosby, William, 1832–1910, vol. I

Crosfield, Sir Arthur Henry, 1st Bt, 1865–1938, vol. III

Crosfield, Bertram Fothergill, 1882–1951, vol. V

Crosfield, Domini, (Lady Crosfield), *died* 1963, vol. VI

Crosfield, Lt-Col George Rowlandson, 1877–1962, vol. VI

Crosland, Rt Hon. Anthony; *see* Crosland, Rt Hon. C. A. R.

Crosland, Rt Hon. (Charles) Anthony (Raven), 1918–1977, vol. VII

Crosland, Brig. Harold Powell, 1893–1973, vol. VII

Crosland, Sir Joseph, 1826–1904, vol. I

Crosland, Joseph Beardsell, 1874–1935, vol. III

Crosland, T. W. H., 1868–1924, vol. II

Crosland, Brig. Walter Hugh, 1894–1960, vol. V

Cross, 1st Viscount, 1823–1914, vol. I

Cross, 2nd Viscount, 1882–1932, vol. III

Cross of Chelsea, Baron (Life Peer); (Arthur) Geoffrey (Neale) Cross, 1904–1989, vol. VIII

Cross, Ada, (Mrs George Frederick Cross); *see* Cambridge, A.

Cross, Sir Alexander, 1st Bt (*cr* 1912), 1847–1914, vol. I

Cross, Sir Alexander, 3rd Bt (*cr* 1912), 1880–1963, vol. VI

Cross, Alexander George, 1858–1919, vol. II

Cross, Sir (Alfred) Rupert (Neale), 1912–1980, vol. VII

Cross, Alfred William Stephens, 1860–1932, vol. III

Cross, Arthur Lyon, 1873–1940, vol. III (A), vol. IV

Cross, Sir Cecil Lancelot Stewart, (Sir Lance Cross), 1912–1989, vol. VIII

Cross, Rev. Hon. Charles Francis, 1860–1937, vol. III

Cross, Charles Frederick, 1855–1935, vol. III

Cross, Adm. Charles Henry, *died* 1915, vol. I

Cross, Charles Wilson, *died* 1928, vol. II

Cross, Rt Rev. (David) Stewart, 1928–1989, vol. VIII

Cross, Sir Eugene, 1896–1981, vol. VIII

Cross, Francis John Kynaston, 1865–1950, vol. IV

Cross, Francis Richardson, *died* 1931, vol. III

Cross, Rev. Frank Leslie, 1900–1968, vol. VI

Cross, Frederick Victor, 1907–1981, vol. VIII

Cross, Herbert S.; *see* Shepherd-Cross.

Cross, Col James Albert, 1876–1952, vol. V

Cross, Hon. John Edward, 1858–1921, vol. II

Cross, Kenneth Mervyn Baskerville, 1890–1968, vol. VI

Cross, Kenneth William, 1916–1990, vol. VIII

Cross, Sir Lance; *see* Cross, Sir C. L. S.

Cross, Rev. Leslie Basil, 1895–1974, vol. VII

Cross, Brig. Lionel Lesley, 1899–1984, vol. VIII

Cross, Mark; *see* Pechey, Archibald T.

Cross, Richard Basil, 1881–1952, vol. V

Cross, Rev. Robert Nicol, 1883–1970, vol. VI

Cross, Rt Hon. Sir Ronald Hibbert, 1st Bt (*cr* 1941), 1896–1968, vol. VI

Cross, Sir Rupert; *see* Cross, Sir A. R. N.

Cross, Rt Rev. Stewart; *see* Cross, Rt Rev. D. S.

Cross, Rev. Thomas George, *died* 1932, vol. III

Cross, Sir William Coats, 2nd Bt (*cr* 1912), 1877–1947, vol. IV

Cross Brown, Lt-Col James, 1884–1969, vol. VI

Crosse, Ven. Arthur B., 1830–1909, vol. I

Crosse, Rev. Arthur John William, 1857–1948, vol. IV

Crosse, Lt-Col Charles Robert, 1851–1921, vol. II

Crosse, Ven. Edmond Francis, 1858–1941, vol. IV

Crosse, Rev. Canon Ernest Courtenay, 1887–1955, vol. V

Crosse, Rev. Frank Parker, 1897–1979, vol. VII

Crosse, Herbert D. H., 1863–1908, vol. I

Crossfield, Robert Sands, 1904–1978, vol. VII

Crossing, William, 1847–1928, vol. II

Crossley, Madame Ada, *died* 1929, vol. III

Crossley, Anthony Crommelin, 1903–1939, vol. III

Crossley, Arthur William, 1869–1927, vol. II

Crossley, Sir Christopher John, 3rd Bt, 1931–1989, vol. VIII

Crossley, Edward; *see* Crossley, J. E.

Crossley, Eric Lomax, 1903–1982, vol. VIII

Crossley, Lt-Col Henry Joseph, 1874–1936, vol. III

Crossley, (Joseph) Edward, 1908–1969, vol. VI

Crossley, Sir Julian Stanley, 1899–1971, vol. VII

Crossley, Sir Kenneth Irwin, 2nd Bt, 1877–1957, vol. V

Crossley, Wing-Comdr Michael Nicholson, 1912–1987, vol. VIII

Crossley, Rt Rev. Owen Thomas Lloyd, 1860–1926, vol. II

Crossley, Thomas Hastings Henry, 1846–1926, vol. II

Crossley, Sir William John, 1st Bt, 1844–1911, vol. I

Crossley-Holland, Frank William, 1878–1956, vol. V

Crossman, Hon. Sir (Charles) Stafford, 1870–1941, vol. IV

Crossman, Sir (Douglas) Peter, 1908–1989, vol. VIII

Crossman, Maj.-Gen. Francis Lindisfarne Morley, 1888–1947, vol. IV

Crossman, Col George Lytton, 1877–1947, vol. IV

Crossman, Percy, 1872–1929, vol. III

Crossman, Sir Peter; *see* Crossman, Sir D. P.

Crossman, Rt Hon. Richard Howard Stafford, 1907–1974, vol. VII

Crossman, Hon. Sir Stafford; *see* Crossman, Hon. Sir C. S.

Crossman, Sir William, 1830–1901, vol. I

Crossman, Sir William Smith, 1854–1929, vol. III

Crosswell, Noel Alfred, 1909–1964, vol. VI

Crosthwait, Col Herbert Leland, 1867–1940, vol. III

Crosthwaite, Arthur Tinley, 1880–1951, vol. V

Crosthwaite, Sir Bertram Maitland, 1880–1974, vol. VII

Crosthwaite, Cecil, 1909–1978, vol. VII

Crosthwaite, Lt-Col Charles Gilbert, 1878–1940, vol. III

Crosthwaite, Sir Charles Haukes Todd, 1835–1915, vol. I

Crosthwaite, Lt-Col Henry Robert, 1876–1956, vol. V

Crosthwaite, Sir Hugh Stuart, 1879–1952, vol. V

Crosthwaite, Sir Moore; *see* Crosthwaite, Sir P. M.

Crosthwaite, Sir (Ponsonby) Moore, 1907–1989, vol. VIII

Crosthwaite, Robert, 1868–1953, vol. V

Crosthwaite, Rt Rev. Robert Jarratt, 1837–1925, vol. II

Crosthwaite, Sir Robert Joseph, 1841–1917, vol. II

Crosthwaite, W. M., *died* 1956, vol. V

Crosthwaite, Sir William Henry, 1880–1968, vol. VI

Crosthwaite-Eyre, Sir Oliver Eyre, 1913–1978, vol. VII

Crotch, William Walter, 1874–1947, vol. IV

Crothers, Thomas Wilson, 1850–1921, vol. II

Crotty, Rt Rev. Horace, 1886–1952, vol. V

Crouch, Lt-Col Ernest George, 1875–1935, vol. III

Crouch, Henry Arthur, 1870–1955, vol. V

Crouch, Col Hon. Richard Armstrong, 1869–1949, vol. IV, vol. V

Crouch, Robert Fisher, 1904–1957, vol. V

Croudace, Rev. William Darnell, 1848–1942, vol. IV

Crousaz, Engr Rear-Adm. Augustus George, 1884–1977, vol. VII

Crouse, Russel, 1893–1966, vol. VI

Crout, Dame Mabel, 1890–1984, vol. VIII

Crow, Sir Alwyn Douglas, 1894–1965, vol. VI

Crow, Douglas Arthur, 1889–1945, vol. IV

Crow, Francis Edward, 1863–1939, vol. III

Crowden, Rev. Charles, 1836–1936, vol. III

Crowden, Guy Pascoe, 1894–1966, vol. VI

Crowder, Sir John Ellenborough, 1890–1961, vol. VI

Crowder, Michael, 1934–1988, vol. VIII

Crowdy, Edith Frances, *died* 1947, vol. IV

Crowdy, James Fuidge, 1876–1934, vol. III

Crowdy, Mary, *died* 1961, vol. VI

Crowdy, Dame Rachel Eleanor, (Dame Rachel Thornhill), 1884–1964, vol. VI

Crowe, Sir Colin Tradescant, 1913–1989, vol. VIII

Crowe, Sir Edward Thomas Frederick, 1877–1960, vol. V

Crowe, Eric Eyre, 1905–1952, vol. V

Crowe, Eyre, 1824–1910, vol. I

Crowe, Sir Eyre, 1864–1925, vol. II

Crowe, F. J. W., 1864–1931, vol. III

Crowe, Captain Fritz Hauch Eden, 1849–1904, vol. I

Crowe, Brig.-Gen. John Henry Verinder, 1862–1948, vol. IV

Crowe, Col Mordaunt Abingdon Carlisle, 1867–1939, vol. III

Crowe, Percy Robert, 1904–1979, vol. VII

Crowe, Philip Kingsland, 1908–1976, vol. VII

Crowe, Ralph Vernon, 1915–1990, vol. VIII

Crowe, Maj.-Gen. Thomas Carlisle, 1830–1917, vol. II

Crowe, William Henry, 1844–1925, vol. II

Crowest, Frederick J., 1860–1927, vol. II

Crowfoot, Rev. John Henchman, 1841–1926, vol. II

Crowfoot, John Winter, 1873–1959, vol. V

Crowley, Sir Brian Hurtle, 1896–1982, vol. VIII

Crowley, James, *died* 1946, vol. IV

Crowley, John, *died* 1934, vol. III

Crowley, Ralph Henry, 1869–1953, vol. V

Crowley, Rt Rev. Timothy, 1880–1946, vol. IV

Crowley, Dep. Insp.-Gen. Timothy Joseph, *died* 1912, vol. I

Crowley, Thomas Michael, 1917–1988, vol. VIII

Crowly, Joseph Patrick, 1859–1917, vol. II

Crown, Jennifer Brigit, (Mrs Leon Crown); *see* Vyvyan, J. B.

Crowther, Baron (Life Peer); Geoffrey Crowther, 1907–1972, vol. VII

Crowther, Charles, 1876–1964, vol. VI

Crowther, Edward, 1897–1979, vol. VII

Crowther, Francis Harold, 1914–1984, vol. VIII

Crowther, Henry, 1848–1937, vol. III

Crowther, James Arnold, 1883–1950, vol. IV

Crowther, Sir William Edward Lodewyk Hamilton, 1887–1981, vol. VIII

Crowther-Hunt, Baron (Life Peer); Norman Crowther Crowther-Hunt, 1920–1987, vol. VIII

Crowther-Smith, Vivian Francis, 1875–1961, vol. VI

Croxton, Arthur, *died* 1956, vol. V

Croysdale, Sir James, 1886–1971, vol. VII

Croysdill, Clifford William, 1874–1935, vol. III

Crozier, Maj.-Gen. Baptist Barton, 1878–1957, vol. V

Crozier, Douglas James Smyth, 1908–1976, vol. VII

Crozier, Rev. Edward Travers, *died* 1940, vol. III

Crozier, Brig.-Gen. Frank Percy, 1879–1937, vol. III

Crozier, George, *died* 1914, vol. I

Crozier, Most Rev. John Baptist, 1853–1920, vol. II

Crozier, John Beattie, 1849–1921, vol. II

Crozier, Rt Rev. John Winthrop, 1879–1966, vol. VI

Crozier, Major Sir Thomas Henry, *died* 1948, vol. IV

Crozier, William Percival, 1879–1944, vol. IV

Cru, Robert L., 1884–1944, vol. IV

Cruddas, Bt Col Bernard, 1882–1959, vol. V

Cruddas, Col Hamilton Maxwell, 1874–1955, vol. V

Cruddas, Lt-Col Hugh Wilson, 1868–1916, vol. II

Cruddas, Maj.-Gen. Ralph Cyril, 1900–1979, vol. VII

Cruddas, William Donaldson, 1831–1912, vol. I

Cruickshank, Alexander Walmsley, 1851–1925, vol. II

Cruickshank, Rev. Alfred Hamilton, 1862–1927, vol. II

Cruickshank, Andrew John Maxton, 1907–1988, vol. VIII

Cruickshank, Charles Greig, 1914–1989, vol. VIII

Cruickshank, Ernest William Henderson, 1888–1964, vol. VI

Cruickshank, Dame Joanna Margaret, *died* 1958, vol. V

Cruickshank, John, 1884–1966, vol. VI

Cruickshank, John Cecil, 1899–1956, vol. V

Cruickshank, Col Martin Melvin, 1888–1964, vol. VI

Cruickshank, Robert, 1899–1974, vol. VII

Cruickshank, Robert James, 1898–1956, vol. V

Cruickshank, Sir William Dickson, 1845–1929, vol. III

Cruikshank, John Merrill, 1901–1984, vol. VIII

Cruise, Sir Francis Richard, 1834–1912, vol. I

Cruise, Sir Richard Robert, *died* 1946, vol. IV

Crum, Rev. John Macleod Campbell, 1872–1958, vol. V

Crum, Maj.-Gen. Vernon Forbes E.; *see* Erskine Crum.

Crum, Sir Walter Erskine, 1874–1923, vol. II

Crum, Walter Ewing, 1865–1944, vol. IV

Crumly, Patrick, vol. II

Crump, Basil Woodward, 1866–1945, vol. IV

Crump, Charles George, 1862–1935, vol. III

Crump, Edwin Samuel, 1882–1961, vol. VI

Crump, Frederick Octavius, 1840–1900, vol. I

Crump, Sir Henry Ashbrooke, 1863–1941, vol. IV

Crump, Rev. John Herbert, 1849–1924, vol. II

Crump, Leslie Maurice, 1875–1929, vol. III

Crump, Sir Louis Charles, 1869–1960, vol. V

Crump, Norman Easedale, 1896–1964, vol. VI

Crump, Sir William John, 1850–1923, vol. II

Crundall, Sir William Henry, 1847–1934, vol. III

Cruse, Rt Rev. John Howard, 1908–1979, vol. VII

Crutchley, Arthur Felton, 1883–1966, vol. VI

Crutchley, Maj.-Gen. Sir Charles, 1856–1920, vol. II

Crutchley, Ernest Tristram, 1878–1940, vol. III

Crutchley, Percy Edward, 1855–1940, vol. III

Crutchley, Adm. Sir Victor Alexander Charles, 1893–1986, vol. VIII

Crutchley, William Caius, 1848–1923, vol. II

Crute, Robert, 1907–1967, vol. VI (AII)

Cruttwell, Charles Robert Mowbray Fraser, 1887–1941, vol. IV

Cruttwell, Rev. Charles Thomas, 1847–1911, vol. I

Cruz, Joao Carlos Lopes Cardoso de F.; *see* de Freitas-Cruz.

Crymble, Percival Templeton, 1880–1970, vol. VI

Cubbon, William, 1865–1955, vol. V

Cubitt, Sir Bertram Blakiston, 1862–1942, vol. IV

Cubitt, Hon. (Charles) Guy, 1903–1979, vol. VII

Cubitt, Edward George, 1860–1933, vol. III

Cubitt, Hon. Guy; *see* Cubitt, Hon. C. G.

Cubitt, James William Archibald, 1914–1983, vol. VIII

Cubitt, Thomas, 1870–1947, vol. IV

Cubitt, Gen. Sir Thomas Astley, 1871–1939, vol. III

Cubitt, Col William George, 1835–1903, vol. I

Cuckney, Air Vice-Marshal Ernest John, 1896–1965, vol. VI

Cudlip, Mrs Pender; *see* Thomas, Annie.

Cudlipp, Percy, 1905–1962, vol. VI

Cudmore, Sir Arthur Murray, 1870–1951, vol. V

Cudmore, Hon. Sir Collier Robert, 1885–1971, vol. VII

Cudmore, Derek George, 1923–1981, vol. VIII

Cuff, Maj.-Gen. Brian, 1889–1970, vol. VI

Cuffe, Sir Charles Frederick Denny Wheeler-, 2nd Bt, 1832–1915, vol. I

Cuffe, Surg.-Gen. Sir Charles M'Donough, 1842–1915, vol. I

Cuffe, Sir George Eustace, 1892–1962, vol. VI

Cuffe, Col James Aloysius Francis, 1876–1957, vol. V

Cuffe, Sir Otway Fortescue Luke Wheeler-, 3rd Bt, 1866–1934, vol. III

Cuffe, Hon. Otway Frederick Seymour, 1853–1912, vol. I

Cuke, Sir Hampden Archibald, 1892–1968, vol. VI

Culbertson, Ely, 1891–1955, vol. V

Cull, Vice-Adm. Sir Malcolm Giffard Stebbing, 1891–1962, vol. VI

Cullen, Hon. Lord; William James Cullen, 1859–1941, vol. IV

Cullen of Ashbourne, 1st Baron, 1864–1932, vol. III

Cullen, Mrs Alice, (Mrs William Reynolds), *died* 1969, vol. VI

Cullen, Rt Rev. Archibald Howard, 1887–1968, vol. VI

Cullen, Brian; *see* Cullen, J. B.

Cullen, Brig.-Gen. Ernest Henry Scott, 1869–1951, vol. V

Cullen, (James) Brian, 1905–1972, vol. VII

Cullen, Rev. John, 1836–1914, vol. I

Cullen, Kenneth Douglas, 1889–1956, vol. V

Cullen, Rt Rev. Matthew, 1864–1936, vol. III

Cullen, Comdr Percy, 1861–1918, vol. II

Cullen, William, 1867–1948, vol. IV

Cullen, William James; *see* Cullen, Hon. Lord.

Cullen, Hon. Sir William Portus, 1855–1935, vol. III

Culley, Rev. Arnold Duncan, 1867–1947, vol. IV

Culley, Gp Captain Stuart Douglas, 1895–1975, vol. VII

Cullinan, Edward Revill, 1901–1965, vol. VI

Cullinan, Sir Frederick Fitzjames, 1845–1913, vol. I

Cullinan, Sir Thomas Major, 1862–1936, vol. III

Cullinan, Paymaster-Rear-Adm. William Frederick, 1876–1937, vol. III

Culling, James William Henry, 1870–1949, vol. IV

Culling, Maj.-Gen. John Chislett, 1858–1938, vol. III

Cullingford, Rev. Cecil Howard Dunstan, 1904–1990, vol. VIII

Cullingworth, Charles James, 1841–1908, vol. I

Cullis, Charles Edgar, 1899–1964, vol. VI

Cullis, Carles Gilbert, 1871–1941, vol. IV

Cullis, Winifred Clara, 1875–1956, vol. V

Cullum, George Gery Milner-Gibson, 1857–1921, vol. II

Cullum, Ridgwell, 1867–1943, vol. IV

Cullwick, Ernest Geoffrey, 1903–1981, vol. VIII

Culme-Seymour, Sir Michael; *see* Seymour.

Culme-Seymour, Vice-Adm. Sir Michael; *see* Seymour.

Culpin, Ewart Gladstone, 1877–1946, vol. IV

Culpin, Millais, 1874–1952, vol. V

Culshaw, John Royds, 1924–1980, vol. VII

Culver, Roland Joseph, 1900–1984, vol. VIII

Culverwell, Cyril Tom, 1895–1963, vol. VI

Culverwell, Edward Parnall, 1855–1931, vol. III

Cumber, William John, 1878–1974, vol. VII

Cumberbatch, Arthur Noel, 1895–1982, vol. VIII

Cumberbatch, Elkin Percy, 1880–1939, vol. III

Cumberbatch, Henry Alfred, 1858–1918, vol. II

Cumberbatch, Sir Hugh Douglas, 1897–1951, vol. V

Cumberbatch, Isaac William, 1888–1971, vol. VII

Cumberland, Maj.-Gen. Charles Edward, 1830–1920, vol. II

Cumberland, Major Charles Sperling, 1847–1922, vol. II

Cumberland, Gerald, 1879–1926, vol. II

Cumberlege, Geoffrey Fenwick Jocelyn, 1891–1979, vol. VII

Cumbrae-Stewart, Francis William Sutton, 1865–1938, vol. III

Cumine, Alexander, *died* 1909, vol. I

Cuming, Sir Arthur Herbert, *died* 1941, vol. IV

Cuming, Edward William Dirom, 1862–1941, vol. IV

Cuming, Col Helier Brohier, 1867–1950, vol. IV (A)

Cuming, Mariannus Adrian, 1901–1988, vol. VIII

Cuming, Adm. Robert Stevenson Dalton, 1852–1940, vol. III

Cumings, Sir Charles Cecil George, 1904–1981, vol. VIII

Cumings, John Nathaniel, 1905–1974, vol. VII

Cumming, Alexander Neilson, *died* 1913, vol. I

Cumming, Major Sir Alexander Penrose G.; *see* Gordon-Cumming.

Cumming, Brig. Arthur Edward, 1896–1971, vol. VII

Cumming, Col Charles Chevin, 1875–1947, vol. IV

Cumming, Miss Constance Frederica G.; *see* Gordon-Cumming.

Cumming, Sir Duncan Cameron, 1903–1979, vol. VII

Cumming, Rev. James, *died* 1946, vol. IV

Cumming, Sir John Ghest, 1868–1958, vol. V

Cumming, Sir Kenneth William, 7th Bt, 1837–1915, vol. I

Cumming, Lt-Col Malcolm Edward Durant, 1907–1985, vol. VIII

Cumming, Captain Sir Mansfield, 1859–1923, vol. II

Cumming, Lt-Col Sir Ronald Stuart, 1900–1982, vol. VIII

Cumming, Ronald William, 1920–1986, vol. VIII

Cumming, Roualeyn Charles Rossiter, 1891–1981, vol. VIII

Cumming, Col William Gordon, 1842–1908, vol. I

Cumming, Sir William Gordon G.; *see* Gordon-Cumming.

Cumming, William Richard, 1911–1984, vol. VIII

Cummings, Arthur John, *died* 1957, vol. V

Cummings, David Charles, 1861–1942, vol. IV

Cummings, Edward Estlin, 1894–1962, vol. VI

Cummings, William Hayman, 1831–1915, vol. I

Cummins, Ashley; *see* Cummins, W. E. A.

Cummins, Geraldine Dorothy, 1890–1969, vol. VI

Cummins, Maj.-Gen. Harry Ashley Vane, 1870–1953, vol. V

Cummins, Major Henry Alfred, 1864–1938, vol. III

Cummins, Henry Ashley Travers, 1847–1926, vol. II

Cummins, Herbert Ashley Cunard, 1871–1943, vol. IV

Cummins, Maj.-Gen. James Turner, 1843–1912, vol. I

Cummins, Rt Rev. John Ildefonsus, 1850–1938, vol. III

Cummins, Col Stevenson Lyle, 1873–1949, vol. IV

Cummins, Walter Herbert, 1881–1953, vol. V

Cummins, (William Edward) Ashley, *died* 1923, vol. II

Cumont, Franz Valery Marie, 1868–1947, vol. IV

Cumpston, John Howard Lidgett, 1880–1954, vol. V

Cunard, Sir Bache, 3rd Bt, 1851–1925, vol. II

Cunard, Sir Edward, 5th Bt, 1891–1962, vol. VI

Cunard, Ernest Haliburton, 1862–1926, vol. II

Cunard, Sir Gordon, 4th Bt, 1857–1933, vol. III

Cunard, Major Sir Guy Alick, 7th Bt, 1911–1989, vol. VIII

Cunard, Sir Henry Palmes, 6th Bt, 1909–1973, vol. VII

Cundall, Charles, 1890–1971, vol. VII

Cundall, Frank, 1858–1937, vol. III

Cundall, Herbert Minton, 1848–1940, vol. III

Cundall, Joseph Leslie, 1906–1964, vol. VI

Cundell, Edric, 1893–1961, vol. VI

Cundiff, Major Frederick William, 1895–1982, vol. VIII

Cundiff, Sir William, 1861–1935, vol. III

Cuneo, Cyrus Cincinatto, *died* 1916, vol. II

Cuningham, Maj.-Gen. Charles Alexander, 1842–1925, vol. II

Cuningham, Granville Carlyle, 1847–1927, vol. II

Cuningham, Surg.-Gen. James Macnabb, 1829–1905, vol. I

Cuningham, Sir William John, 1848–1929, vol. III

Cuninghame, Sir Alfred Edward F., 12th Bt (*cr* 1630); *see* Fairlie-Cuninghame.

Cuninghame, Sir Charles Arthur F., 11th Bt (*cr* 1630); *see* Fairlie-Cuninghame.

Cuninghame, Lt-Col Edward William Montgomery, 1878–1935, vol. III

Cuninghame, Sir Hussey Burgh Fairlie-, 14th Bt (*cr* 1630), 1890–1939, vol. III

Cuninghame, Col John Anstruther Smith, 1852–1921, vol. II

Cuninghame, John Charles, 1851–1917, vol. II

Cuninghame, Sir Thomas Andrew Alexander Montgomery-, 10th Bt (*cr* 1672), 1877–1945, vol. IV

Cuninghame, Sir William Alan F.; *see* Fairlie-Cuninghame.

Cuninghame, Sir (William) Andrew Malcolm Martin Oliphant Montgomery-, 11th Bt (*cr* 1672), 1929–1959, vol. V

Cuninghame, Sir William Edward Fairlie-, 13th Bt (*cr* 1630), 1856–1929, vol. III

Cuninghame, Sir William James Montgomery-, 9th Bt (*cr* 1672), 1834–1897, vol. I

Cuninghame, Lt-Col William Wallace Smith, 1889–1959, vol. V

Cunliffe, 1st Baron, 1855–1920, vol. II

Cunliffe, 2nd Baron, 1899–1963, vol. VI

Cunliffe, Sir Cyril Henley, 8th Bt, 1901–1969, vol. VI

Cunliffe, Sir Ellis; *see* Cunliffe, Sir R. E.

Cunliffe, Sir Foster Hugh Egerton, 6th Bt, 1875–1916, vol. II

Cunliffe, Brig.-Gen. Frederick Hugh Gordon, 1861–1955, vol. V

Cunliffe, Hon. Geoffrey, 1903–1978, vol. VII

Cunliffe, Sir Herbert; *see* Cunliffe, Sir J. H.

Cunliffe, Sir John Robert Ellis, 1886–1967, vol. VI

Cunliffe, John William, 1865–1946, vol. IV

Cunliffe, Sir (Joseph) Herbert, 1867–1963, vol. VI

Cunliffe, Marcus Falkner, 1922–1990, vol. VIII

Cunliffe, Sir Robert Alfred, 5th Bt, 1839–1905, vol. I

Cunliffe, Sir (Robert) Ellis, 1858–1927, vol. II

Cunliffe, Capt. Robert Lionel Brooke, 1895–1990, vol. VIII

Cunliffe, Sir Robert Neville Henry, 7th Bt, 1884–1949, vol. IV

Cunliffe, Thomas, 1895–1966, vol. VI

Cunliffe-Owen, Brig.-Gen. Charles, 1863–1932, vol. III

Cunliffe-Owen, Sir Dudley Herbert, 2nd Bt, 1923–1983, vol. VIII

Cunliffe-Owen, Lt-Col F., *died* 1946, vol. IV

Cunliffe-Owen, Sir Hugo, 1st Bt, 1870–1947, vol. IV

Cunning, Joseph, 1872–1948, vol. IV

Cunningham of Hyndhope, 1st Viscount, 1883–1963, vol. VI

Cunningham, Gen. Sir Alan Gordon, 1887–1983, vol. VIII

Cunningham, Air Cdre Alexander Duncan, 1888–1981, vol. VIII

Cunningham, Sir (Alexander) Frederick (Douglas), 1852–1935, vol. III

Cunningham, Alfred, 1870–1918, vol. II

Cunningham, Alfred G., 1870–1951, vol. V

Cunningham, Lt-Col Aylmer Basil, 1879–1940, vol. III (A), vol. IV

Cunningham, Rev. Bertram Keir, 1871–1944, vol. IV

Cunningham, Brysson, 1868–1950, vol. IV

Cunningham, Sir Charles Banks, 1884–1967, vol. VI

Cunningham, Daniel John, 1850–1909, vol. I

Cunningham, Col David Douglas, 1843–1914, vol. I

Cunningham, E. Margaret, 1872–1940, vol. III

Cunningham, Ebenezer, 1881–1977, vol. VII

Cunningham, Edward Charles, 1872–1929, vol. III

Cunningham, Sir Edward Sheldon, 1859–1957, vol. V

Cunningham, Sir Frederick; *see* Cunningham, Sir A. F. D.

Cunningham, Sir George, 1888–1964, vol. VI

Cunningham, George Charles, 1883–1950, vol. IV

Cunningham, Brig.-Gen. George Glencairn, 1862–1943, vol. IV

Cunningham, Sir George M.; *see* Miller-Cunningham.

Cunningham, Gordon Herriot, 1892–1962, vol. VI

Cunningham, Sir Graham, 1892–1978, vol. VII

Cunningham, Sir Henry Stewart, 1832–1920, vol. II

Cunningham, Rt Rev. Jack, 1926–1978, vol. VII

Cunningham, Rt Rev. James, 1910–1974, vol. VII

Cunningham, Lt-Col John, *died* 1968, vol. VI

Cunningham, Engr-Rear-Adm. John Edward Greig, 1878–1954, vol. V

Cunningham, Rt Rev. John F., 1842–1919, vol. II (A), vol. III

Cunningham, John Francis, *died* 1932, vol. III

Cunningham, Adm. of the Fleet Sir John Henry Dacres, 1885–1962, vol. VI

Cunningham, John Jeffrey, 1907–1959, vol. V

Cunningham, Rev. Canon John Manstead, 1879–1947, vol. IV

Cunningham, John Richard, 1876–1942, vol. IV

Cunningham, Lt-Col John Sydney, 1876–1943, vol. IV

Cunningham, Joseph Thomas, 1859–1935, vol. III

Cunningham, Sir Knox; *see* Cunningham, Sir S. K.

Cunningham, Lallie S. C., *died* 1937, vol. III

Cunningham, Marta, *died* 1937, vol. III

Cunningham, Mary Elizabeth, *died* 1939, vol. III

Cunningham, Patrick, *died* 1960, vol. V

Cunningham, Rt Hon. Samuel, 1862–1946, vol. IV

Cunningham, Sir (Samuel) Knox, 1st Bt, 1909–1976, vol. VII

Cunningham, Wilfred Bertram, 1882–1960, vol. V

Cunningham, Ven. William, 1849–1919, vol. II

Cunningham, William Allison, *died* 1939, vol. III

Cunningham, Maj.-Gen. Sir William Henry, 1883–1959, vol. V

Cunningham, William Ross, 1890–1953, vol. V

Cunningham Craig, Edward Hubert; *see* Craig.

Cunningham-Reid, Captain Alec Stratford, *died* 1977, vol. VII

Cunninghame, Sir James Fraser, 1870–1952, vol. V

Cunninghame Graham of Gartmore, Adm. Sir Angus Edward Malise Bontine, 1893–1981, vol. VIII

Cunninghame Graham, Comdr Charles Elphinstone Fleeming, 1854–1917, vol. II

Cunninghame Graham, Robert Bontine, 1852–1936, vol. III

Cunnington, Cecil Willett, 1878–1961, vol. VI

Cunnington, Maud Edith, 1869–1951, vol. V

Cunnison, Sir Alexander, 1879–1959, vol. V

Cunnison, David Keith, 1881–1972, vol. VII

Cunyngham, Major Sir Colin Keith Dick-, 11th Bt, 1908–1941, vol. IV

Cunyngham, Maj.-Gen. James Keith D.; *see* Dick-Cunyngham.

Cunyngham of Lamburghtoun, Sir Robert Keith Alexander Dick-, 9th Bt, 1836–1897, vol. I

Cunyngham, Lt-Col William Henry Dick-, *died* 1900, vol. I

Cunyngham, Sir William Stewart-Dick-, 10th Bt, 1871–1922, vol. II

Cunynghame, Sir David; *see* Cunynghame, Sir H. D. St L. B. S.

Cunynghame, Sir Francis George Thurlow, 9th Bt, 1835–1900, vol. I

Cunynghame, Sir (Henry) David St Leger Brooke Selwyn, 11th Bt, 1905–1978, vol. VII

Cunynghame, Sir Henry Hardinge, 1848–1935, vol. III

Cunynghame, Sir James Ogilvy B.; *see* Blair-Cunynghame.

Cunynghame, Sir Percy, 10th Bt, 1867–1941, vol. IV

Curci, Amelita G.; *see* Galli-Curci.

Cure, Sir Edward Capel, 1866–1923, vol. II

Cure, Col Herbert Capel, 1859–1909, vol. I

Curgenven, Sir Arthur Joseph, 1876–1965, vol. VI

Curie, Jean F. J.; *see* Joliot-Curie.

Curie, Madame Marie, 1867–1934, vol. III

Curie, Pierre, 1859–1906, vol. I

Curle, Alexander Ormiston, 1866–1955, vol. V

Curle, James, 1862–1944, vol. IV

Curle, Richard Henry Parnell, 1883–1968, vol. VI

Curlewis, Sir Adrian Herbert, 1901–1985, vol. VIII

Curlewis, Ethel; *see* Turner, E.

Curlewis, Rt Hon. John Stephen, 1863–1940, vol. III

Curling, Brig.-Gen. Bryan James, 1877–1955, vol. V

Curling, Rev. Joseph James, 1844–1906, vol. I

Curling, Rev. Canon Thomas Higham, 1872–1944, vol. IV

Curnick, Captain Alfred James, 1865–1936, vol. III

Curnock, Rev. Nehemiah, 1840–1915, vol. I

Curnow, John, 1846–1902, vol. I

Curphey, Col Sir Aldington George, 1880–1958, vol. V

Curran, Charles, 1903–1972, vol. VII

Curran, Sir Charles John, 1921–1980, vol. VII

Curran, Desmond, 1903–1985, vol. VIII

Curran, Harry Gibson, 1901–1986, vol. VIII

Curran, John Adye, 1837–1919, vol. II

Curran, Rt Hon. Sir Lancelot Ernest, 1899–1984, vol. VIII

Curran, Pete, 1860–1910, vol. I

Curran, Thomas, *died* 1913, vol. I

Curran, Thomas Bartholomew, 1870–1929, vol. III

Curre, Augusta, (Lady Curre), *died* 1956, vol. V

Curre, John Mathew, 1859–1919, vol. II

Curre, Sir William Edward Carne, 1855–1930, vol. III

Currer Briggs, D. H.; *see* Briggs.

Currey, Adm. Bernard, *died* 1936, vol. III

Currey, Rear-Adm. Harry Philip, 1902–1979, vol. VII

Currey, Henry Latham, 1863–1945, vol. IV

Currey, Brig. Henry Percivall, 1886–1969, vol. VI

Currey, Rear-Adm. Hugh Schomberg, 1876–1955, vol. V

Currey, Ronald Fairbridge, 1894–1983, vol. VIII

Currie, 1st Baron, 1834–1906, vol. I

Currie, Agnes Jean, 1899–1968, vol. VI

Currie, Major Hon. Sir Alan; *see* Currie, Major Hon. Sir H. A.

Currie, Sir Alick Bradley, 6th Bt, 1904–1987, vol. VIII

Currie, Brig.-Gen. Arthur Cecil, *died* 1942, vol. IV

Currie, Gen. Sir Arthur William, 1875–1933, vol. III

Currie, Captain Bertram Francis George, 1899–1959, vol. V

Currie, David, 1870–1933, vol. III

Currie, Sir Donald, 1825–1909, vol. I

Currie, Brig. Douglas Hendrie, 1892–1966, vol. VI

Currie, Sir Edmund Hay, 1834–1913, vol. I

Currie, Very Rev. Edward Reid, 1844–1921, vol. II

Currie, Maj.-Gen. Fendall, 1841–1920, vol. II

Currie, Rev. Sir Frederick Larkins, 2nd Bt, 1823–1900, vol. I

Currie, Sir Frederick Reeve, 3rd Bt, 1851–1930, vol. III

Currie, Sir George Alexander, 1896–1984, vol. VIII

Currie, George Boyle Hanna, 1905–1978, vol. VII

Currie, Lt-Col George Selkirk, 1889–1975, vol. VII

Currie, George Welsh, 1870–1950, vol. IV

Currie, Harry Augustus Frederick, 1866–1912, vol. I

Currie, Major Hon. Sir (Henry) Alan, 1868–1942, vol. IV

Currie, Rev. Hugh Penton, 1854–1903, vol. I

Currie, Lt-Col Ivor Bertram Fendall, 1872–1924, vol. II

Currie, Sir James, 1868–1937, vol. III

Currie, Sir James, 1907–1983, vol. VIII

Currie, Sir James Thomson, 1868–1943, vol. IV

Currie, John Ronald, *died* 1949, vol. IV

Currie, Laurence, 1867–1934, vol. III

Currie, Mark Mainwaring Lee, 1882–1951, vol. V

Currie, Mary Montgomerie, (Lady Currie), 1843–1905, vol. I

Currie, Patrick, 1883–1949, vol. IV

Currie, Col Ryves Alexander Mark, 1875–1920, vol. II

Currie, Col Thomas, 1851–1931, vol. III

Currie, Sir Walter Louis Rackham, 4th Bt, 1856–1941, vol. IV

Currie, Sir Walter Mordaunt Cyril, 5th Bt, 1894–1978, vol. VII

Currie, Sir William Crawford, 1884–1961, vol. VI

Currie, Major William Leopold, 1856–1929, vol. III

Currie-Blyth, James Pattison, 1824–1908, vol. I

Currin, Richard William, 1872–1942, vol. IV

Curry, Aaron Charlton, 1887–1957, vol. V

Curry, Comdr Hugh Fortescue, 1890–1932, vol. III

Curry, Brig.-Gen. Montagu Crichton, *died* 1931, vol. III

Cursetjee, Maj.-Gen. Sir Heerajee Jehangir Manockjee, 1885–1964, vol. VI

Cursiter, Stanley, 1887–1976, vol. VII

Cursley, Norman Sharpe, 1898–1972, vol. VII

Curson, Bernard Robert, 1913–1988, vol. VIII

Curteis, Adm. Sir Alban Thomas Buckley, 1887–1961, vol. VI

Curteis, Col Cyril Samuel Sackville, 1874–1943, vol. IV

Curteis, Brig.-Gen. Francis Algernon, 1856–1928, vol. II

Curteis, Captain Sir Gerald, 1892–1972, vol. VII

Curteis, Maj.-Gen. Reginald Lawrence Herbert, 1843–1919, vol. II

Curthoys, Alfred, *died* 1969, vol. VI

Curthoys, Roy Lancaster, 1892–1971, vol. VII

Curtice, Harlow H., 1893–1962, vol. VI

Curtin, Rt Rev. Mgr Canon Jeremiah John, 1907–1988, vol. VIII

Curtin, Rt Hon. John, 1885–1945, vol. IV

Curtis, Maj.-Gen. Alfred Cyril, 1894–1971, vol. VII

Curtis, Amy, 1894–1970, vol. VI

Curtis, Sir Arthur Colin, 3rd Bt (*cr* 1794), 1858–1898, vol. I

Curtis, Sqdn Ldr Sir Arthur Randolph Wormeley, 1889–1966, vol. VI

Curtis, Vice-Adm. Berwick, 1876–1965, vol. VI

Curtis, Charles, 1860–1936, vol. III

Curtis, Cyrus Hermann Kotzschmar, 1850–1933, vol. III

Curtis, Sir (Edgar) Francis (Egerton), 5th Bt (*cr* 1802), 1875–1943, vol. IV

Curtis, Edmund, 1881–1943, vol. IV

Curtis, Edward Beaumont Cotton, 1863–1939, vol. III

Curtis, Col Edward George, 1868–1923, vol. II

Curtis, Edward Herbert, 1867–1937, vol. III

Curtis, Sir Francis; *see* Curtis, Sir E. F. E.

Curtis, Brig. Francis Cockburn, 1898–1986, vol. VIII

Curtis, Col Francis George Savage, 1836–1906, vol. I

Curtis, Very Rev. Canon George, 1861–1948, vol. IV

Curtis, George Byron, 1843–1907, vol. I

Curtis, Sir George Harold, 1902–1972, vol. VII

Curtis, Col George Reginald, 1892–1958, vol. V

Curtis, Sir George Seymour, 1867–1931, vol. III

Curtis, Henry, *died* 1944, vol. IV

Curtis, Maj.-Gen. Henry Osborne, 1888–1964, vol. VI

Curtis, Sir James, 1868–1942, vol. IV

Curtis, Rt Rev. John, 1880–1962, vol. VI

Curtis, John S.; *see* Sutton Curtis.

Curtis, Lionel George, 1872–1955, vol. V

Curtis, Dame Myra, 1886–1971, vol. VII

Curtis, Percy John, 1900–1985, vol. VIII

Curtis, Sir Peter, 6th Bt (*cr* 1802), 1907–1976, vol. VII

Curtis, Maj.-Gen. Sir Reginald Salmond, 1863–1922, vol. II

Curtis, Richard James Seymour, 1900–1985, vol. VIII

Curtis, Sir Roger Colin Molyneux, 4th Bt (*cr* 1794), 1886–1954, vol. V

Curtis, Air Vice-Marshal Walter John Brice, 1888–1973, vol. VII

Curtis, Air Marshal Wilfred Austin, 1893–1977, vol. VII

Curtis, Wilfred Harry, 1897–1988, vol. VIII

Curtis, Rev. William Alexander, 1876–1961, vol. VI

Curtis, William Edward, 1889–1969, vol. VI

Curtis, Sir William Michael, 4th Bt (*cr* 1802), 1859–1916, vol. II

Curtis-Bennett, Derek; *see* Curtis-Bennett, F. H.

Curtis-Bennett, Sir (Francis) Noel, 1882–1950, vol. IV

Curtis-Bennett, Frederick Henry, (Derek), 1904–1956, vol. V

Curtis-Bennett, Sir Henry Honywood, 1879–1936, vol. III

Curtis-Bennett, Sir Noel; *see* Curtis-Bennett, Sir F. N.

Curtis Brown, Spencer, 1906–1980, vol. VII

Curtis-Raleigh, Nigel Hugh, 1914–1986, vol. VIII

Curtis-Willson, William Thomas, 1888–1957, vol. V

Curtoys, Maj.-Gen. Charles Ernest Edward, 1863–1940, vol. III

Curwen, Alan de Lancy, 1869–1930, vol. III

Curwen, Dame (Anne) May, 1889–1973, vol. VII

Curwen, Annie J., 1845–1932, vol. III

Curwen, Rev. Edward Hasell, 1847–1929, vol. III

Curwen, Eldred Vincent Morris, 1842–1927, vol. II

Curwen, Harold Spedding, 1885–1949, vol. IV

Curwen, Henry, 1879–1946, vol. IV

Curwen, John Spencer, 1847–1916, vol. II

Curwen, Dame May; *see* Curwen, Dame A. M.

Curwood, James Oliver, 1879–1927, vol. II

Curzon of Kedleston, 1st Marquess, 1859–1925, vol. II

Curzon of Kedleston, Marchioness; (Grace Elvina), *died* 1958, vol. V

Curzon, Hon. Alfred Nathaniel, 1860–1920, vol. II

Curzon, Rt Rev. Charles Edward, *died* 1954, vol. V

Curzon, Sir Clifford Michael, 1907–1982, vol. VIII

Curzon, Mrs Edith Basset Penn, 1861–1943, vol. IV

Curzon, Hon. Francis Nathaniel, 1865–1941, vol. IV

Curzon, Frank, 1868–1927, vol. II

Curzon, Col George Augustus, 1836–1912, vol. I

Curzon, Harry Edward James, 1880–1935, vol. III

Curzon, Hon. Henry Dugdale, 1824–1910, vol. I

Curzon, Col Hon. Montagu, 1846–1907, vol. I

Curzon-Howe, Adm. Hon. Sir Assheton Gore, 1850–1911, vol. I

Curzon-Howe, Captain Leicester Charles Assheton St John, 1894–1941, vol. IV

Curzon-Siggers, Ven. William, 1860–1947, vol. IV

Cusack, John, 1867–1940, vol. III

Cusack, John Winder, 1907–1968, vol. VI

Cusack, Sir Ralph Smith, 1822–1910, vol. I

Cusack, Hon. Sir Ralph Vincent, 1916–1978, vol. VII

Cusack-Smith, Sir Berry, 5th Bt, 1859–1929, vol. III

Cusack-Smith, Sir Dermot; *see* Cusack-Smith, Sir W. R. D. J.

Cusack-Smith, Sir William, 4th Bt, 1822–1919, vol. II

Cusack-Smith, Sir (William Robert) Dermot (Joshua), 6th Bt, 1907–1970, vol. VI

Cuscaden, Maj.-Gen. Sir George, 1857–1933, vol. III

Cuscaden, William Andrew, 1853–1936, vol. III

Cusden, Victor Vincent, 1893–1980, vol. VII

Cushendun, 1st Baron, 1861–1936, vol. III

Cushing, Harvey Williams, 1869–1939, vol. III

Cushion, Air Vice-Marshal Sir William Boston, 1891–1978, vol. VII

Cushny, Arthur Robertson, 1866–1926, vol. II

Cusins, Col Albert George Teeling, 1871–1936, vol. III

Cussen, Edward James Patrick, 1904–1973, vol. VII

Cussen, Hon. Sir Leo Finn Bernard, 1859–1933, vol. III

Cust, Aleen Isabel, *died* 1937, vol. III

Cust, Col Sir Archer; *see* Cust, Col Sir L. G. A.

Cust, Very Rev. Arthur Perceval Purey-, 1828–1916, vol. II

Cust, Sir Charles Leopold, 3rd Bt, 1864–1931, vol. III

Cust, Mrs Henry, (Emmeline Mary Elizabeth), (Nina), *died* 1955, vol. V

Cust, Henry John Cockayne, 1861–1917, vol. II

Cust, Adm. Sir Herbert Edward Purey-, 1857–1938, vol. III

Cust, Col Sir (Lionel George) Archer, 1896–1962, vol. VI

Cust, Sir Lionel Henry, 1859–1929, vol. III

Cust, Nina; *see* Cust, Mrs Henry.

Cust, Sir Reginald John, 1828–1912, vol. I

Cust, Brig. Richard Brownlow P.; *see* Purey-Cust.

Cust, Robert Henry Hobart, 1861–1940, vol. III

Cust, Robert Needham, 1821–1909, vol. I

Cust, Rev. Canon William Arthur Purey, 1855–1938, vol. III

Custance, Col Frederic Hambleton, 1844–1925, vol. II

Custance, Adm. Sir Reginald Neville, 1847–1935, vol. III

Custance, Rear-Adm. Wilfred Neville, 1884–1939, vol. III

Custard, Reginald G.; *see* Goss-Custard.

Custard, Walter Henry Goss, 1871–1964, vol. VI

Cutbill, Col Reginald Heaton Locke, 1878–1956, vol. V

Cutforth, Sir Arthur Edwin, 1881–1958, vol. V

Cutforth, Maj.-Gen. Sir Lancelot Eric, 1899–1980, vol. VII

Cuthbert, Very Rev. Father, 1866–1939, vol. III

Cuthbert, David, 1866–1953, vol. V

Cuthbert, Maj.-Gen. Gerald James, 1861–1931, vol. III

Cuthbert, Harold David, 1909–1959, vol. V

Cuthbert, Hon. Sir Henry, 1829–1907, vol. I

Cuthbert, Captain James Harold, 1876–1915, vol. I

Cuthbert, Vice-Adm. Sir John Wilson, 1902–1987, vol. VIII

Cuthbert, Lt-Col Thomas Wilkinson, *died* 1936, vol. III

Cuthbert, William Moncrieff, 1936–1989, vol. VIII

Cuthbert, William Nicolson, *died* 1960, vol. V

Cuthbertson, Clive, 1863–1943, vol. IV

Cuthbertson, David, 1856–1935, vol. III

Cuthbertson, Sir David Paton, 1900–1989, vol. VIII

Cuthbertson, Brig.-Gen. Edward Boustead, 1880–1942, vol. IV

Cuthbertson, Henry, 1859–1903, vol. I

Cuthbertson, Sir John Neilson, 1829–1905, vol. I

Cuthbertson, Joseph William, 1901–1984, vol. VIII

Cutlack, Col William Philip, 1881–1965, vol. VI

Cutler, Edward, 1831–1916, vol. II

Cutler, Elliott Carr, 1888–1947, vol. IV

Cutler, John, 1839–1924, vol. II

Cutner, Solomon; *see* Solomon.

Cuttle, William Linsdell, 1896–1958, vol. V

Cuyler, Sir Charles, 4th Bt, 1867–1919, vol. II

Cuyler, Sir George Hallifax, 5th Bt, 1876–1947, vol. IV
Cuyler, Rev. Theodore Ledyard, *died* 1909, vol. I
Cynan; *see* Evans-Jones, Rev. Sir Albert.
Cyriax, James Henry, 1904–1985, vol. VIII
Czaplicka, Marie Antoinette, *died* 1921, vol. II

D

Dabbs, George Henry Roque, 1846–1913, vol. I
D'Abernon, 1st Viscount, 1857–1941, vol. IV
Dabholkar, Sir Vasantrao Anandrao, 1881–1933, vol. III
Dabney, Hon. Charles William, 1855–1945, vol. IV
d'Abo, Gerard Louis, 1884–1962, vol. VI
d'Abreu, Alphonso Liguori, 1906–1976, vol. VII
Dacca, Nawab Bahadur, Sir Khwaya Salimulla, *died* 1915, vol. I
D'Ache, Caran, (Emmanuel Poire), *died* 1909, vol. I
D'Costa, Sir Alfred Horace, 1873–1967, vol. VI
Da Costa, Brig.-Gen. Evan Campbell, 1871–1949, vol. IV
Da Costa, John, 1867–1931, vol. III
Dacre, Air Cdre George Bentley, 1891–1962, vol. VI
Dadabhoy, Sir Maneckji Byramji, 1865–1953, vol. V
Dadd, Frank, 1851–1929, vol. III
Daeniker, Armin, 1898–1983, vol. VIII
D'Aeth, Rear-Adm. Arthur Cloudesley Shovel H.; *see* Hughes D'Aeth.
D'Aeth, John, 1853–1922, vol. II
D'Aeth, Air Vice-Marshal Narborough Hughes, 1901–1986, vol. VIII
Da Fano, Corrado Donato, 1879–1927, vol. II
Da Fano, Dorothea, (Mrs C. D. Da Fano); *see* Landau, D.
Dafoe, Allan Roy, 1883–1943, vol. IV
Dafoe, John Wesley, 1866–1944, vol. IV
Daga, Sir Dewan Bahadur Kasturchand, 1855–1917, vol. II
Daga, Raja Rai Bahadur Sir Seth Bisesardass, 1877–1941, vol. IV (A), vol. V
Daggar, George, *died* 1950, vol. IV
Daggett, William Ingledew, 1900–1980, vol. VII
Daglish, Eric Fitch, 1892–1966, vol. VI
Daglish, Hon. Henry, 1866–1920, vol. II
Dagnan-Bouveret, Pascal Adolph Jean, 1852–1929, vol. III
D'Aguilar, Sir Charles Lawrence, 1821–1912, vol. I
Dahl, Knut, 1871–1953, vol. V
Dahl, Roald, 1916–1990, vol. VIII
Dahlgaard, Tyge, 1921–1985, vol. VIII
Dain, Charles Kenneth, 1879–1950, vol. IV (A)
Dain, George Rutherford, 1884–1954, vol. V
Dain, Sir Guy; *see* Dain, Sir H. G.
Dain, Sir (Harry) Guy, 1870–1966, vol. VI
Dain, Sir John Rutherford, 1883–1957, vol. V
Daines, Percy, *died* 1957, vol. V
Daintree, Captain John Dodson, 1864–1952, vol. V
Dakers, A. W., 1868–1947, vol. IV
Dakers, Jane, (Mrs Andrew Dakers); *see* Lane, J.
Dakin, Henry Drysdale, 1880–1952, vol. V

Dakin, William John, 1883–1950, vol. IV
Dakin, William Radford, 1860–1935, vol. III
Dakyns, George Doherty, 1856–1939, vol. III (A), vol. IV
Dakyns, Winifred, 1875–1960, vol. V
Daladier, Edouard, 1884–1970, vol. VI
Dalal, Sir Ardeshir Rustomji, 1884–1949, vol. IV
Dalal, Sirdar Sir Bamanjee Ardeshir, 1854–1932, vol. III
Dalal, Sir Barjor Jamshedji, 1871–1936, vol. III
Dalal, Sir Dadiba Merwanjee, 1870–1941, vol. IV
Dalal, Sir Ratanji Dinshaw, 1868–1957, vol. V
d'Albe, Edmund Edward F.; *see* Fournier d'Albe.
D'Albert, Eugen, 1864–1932, vol. III
D'Albiac, Air Marshal Sir John Henry, 1894–1963, vol. VI
Dalbiac, Philip Hugh, 1855–1927, vol. II
d'Albuquerque, Nino Pedroso, 1894–1969, vol. VI
Dalby, Rev. Francis Higgs, 1853–1933, vol. III
Dalby, Maj.-Gen. Thomas Gerald, 1880–1963, vol. VI
Dalby, W. Ernest, *died* 1936, vol. III
Dalby, Sir William Bartlett, 1840–1918, vol. II
Dalcroze, Emile J.; *see* Jaques-Dalcroze.
Daldry, Sir Leonard Charles, 1908–1988, vol. VIII
Daldy, Ven. Alfred Edward, 1865–1935, vol. III
Daldy, Frederick Francis, 1857–1928, vol. II
Dale, Adm. Alfred Taylor, 1840–1925, vol. II
Dale, Sir Alfred William Winterslow, 1855–1921, vol. II
Dale, Rt Rev. Basil Montague, 1903–1976, vol. VII
Dale, Benjamin James, 1885–1943, vol. IV
Dale, Charles Ernest, 1867–1956, vol. V
Dale, Major Claude Henry, 1882–1946, vol. IV
Dale, Darley; *see* Steele, F. M.
Dale, Sir Edgar Thorniley, 1886–1966, vol. VI
Dale, Francis Richard, 1883–1976, vol. VII
Dale, Frank Harry, 1871–1918, vol. II
Dale, Brig.-Gen. George Arthur, 1866–1940, vol. III
Dale, Harold Edward, 1875–1954, vol. V
Dale, Rev. Harold Montague, 1873–1951, vol. V
Dale, Henry Angley L.; *see* Lewis-Dale.
Dale, Sir Henry Hallett, 1875–1968, vol. VI
Dale, Henry Sheppard, 1852–1921, vol. II
Dale, James A., 1874–1951, vol. V
Dale, Sir James Backhouse, 2nd Bt, 1855–1932, vol. III
Dale, John Ainsworth, 1887–1938, vol. III
Dale, John Gilbert, 1869–1926, vol. II
Dale, Louise Mary, (Lady Mulleneux-Grayson), *died* 1954, vol. V
Dale, Ven. Canon Percy John, 1876–1957, vol. V
Dale, Rev. Thomas F., *died* 1923, vol. II
Dale, Rev. William, 1841–1924, vol. II
Dalen, Nils Gustaf, 1869–1937, vol. III
Daley, Sir Allen; *see* Daley, Sir W. A.
Daley, Sir Denis Leo, 1888–1965, vol. VI
Daley, Sir (William) Allen, 1887–1969, vol. VI
Dalgetty, James Simpson, 1907–1981, vol. VIII
Dalgety, Arthur William Hugh, 1899–1972, vol. VII
Dalgety, Col Edmund Henry, 1847–1914, vol. I
Dalgety, Major Frederick John, 1866–1926, vol. II
Dalgleish, Wing Comdr James William O.; *see* Ogilvy-Dalgleish.

Dalgleish, Oakley Hedley, 1910–1963, vol. VI

Dalgleish, Walter Scott, 1834–1897, vol. I

Dalgleish, Sir William Ogilvy, 1st Bt, 1832–1913, vol. I

Dalgliesh, Richard, 1844–1922, vol. II

Dalgliesh, Theodore Irving, *died* 1941, vol. IV

Dalglish, Rear-Adm. Robin Campsie, 1880–1934, vol. III

Dalhoff, Most Rev. T., *died* 1906, vol. I

Dalhousie, 14th Earl of, 1878–1928, vol. II

Dalhousie, 15th Earl of, 1904–1950, vol. IV

Dali, Salvador Felipe Jacinto, 1904–1989, vol. VIII

Dalison, Maj.-Gen. John Bernard, 1898–1964, vol. VI

Dalison, Rev. Canon Roger William H., 1860–1939, vol. III

Dallapiccola, Luigi, 1904–1975, vol. VII

Dallard, Berkeley Lionel Scudamore, 1889–1983, vol. VIII

Dallas, Lt-Col Alexander Egerton, 1869–1949, vol. IV

Dallas, Surg.-Gen. Alexander Morison, 1830–1912, vol. I

Dallas, Maj.-Gen. Alister Grant, 1866–1931, vol. III

Dallas, Lt-Col Charles Mowbray, 1861–1936, vol. III

Dallas, Hon. Francis Henry, 1865–1920, vol. II

Dallas, George, 1878–1961, vol. VI

Dallas, Sir George Edward, 3rd Bt, 1842–1918, vol. II

Dallin, Cyrus Edwin, 1861–1944, vol. IV

Dalling, Sir Thomas, 1892–1982, vol. VIII

Dallinger, Rev. William Henry, 1842–1909, vol. I

Dally, John Frederick Halls, *died* 1944, vol. IV

Dalmahoy, Maj.-Gen. Patrick Carfrae, 1840–1926, vol. II

Dalmahoy, Patrick Carfrae, 1872–1928, vol. II

Dalmahoy, Patrick James Edward, 1896–1963, vol. VI

Dalmeny, Lord; Archibald Ronald Primrose, 1910–1931, vol. III

Dalrymple, Rt Hon. Sir Charles, 1st Bt (*cr* 1887), 1839–1916, vol. II

Dalrymple, Sir (Charles) Mark, 3rd Bt (*cr* 1887), 1915–1971, vol. VII

Dalrymple, Sir David Charles Herbert, 2nd Bt (*cr* 1887), 1879–1932, vol. III

Dalrymple, Hon. David Hay, 1840–1912, vol. II

Dalrymple, Sir Edward Arthur E.; *see* Elphinstone-Dalrymple.

Dalrymple, Col Sir Francis Napier E.; *see* Elphinstone-Dalrymple.

Dalrymple, Sir Hew (Clifford) Hamilton-, 9th Bt (*cr* 1697), 1888–1959, vol. V

Dalrymple, Hon. Sir Hew Hamilton, 1857–1945, vol. IV

Dalrymple, Ian Murray, 1903–1989, vol. VIII

Dalrymple, James, 1859–1934, vol. III

Dalrymple, Joseph, 1869–1949, vol. IV

Dalrymple, Sir Mark; *see* Dalrymple, Sir C. M.

Dalrymple, Sir Robert Graeme E.; *see* Elphinstone-Dalrymple.

Dalrymple, Sir Walter Hamilton-, 8th Bt (*cr* 1697), 1854–1920, vol. II

Dalrymple, Col Sir William, 1864–1941, vol. IV

Dalrymple, Maj.-Gen. William Liston, 1845–1938, vol. III

Dalrymple-Champneys, Captain Sir Weldon, 2nd Bt, 1892–1980, vol. VII

Dalrymple-Hamilton, Adm. Sir Frederick Hew George, 1890–1974, vol. VII

Dalrymple-Hamilton, Col Hon. North de Coigny, 1853–1906, vol. I

Dalrymple-Hamilton, Col Sir North Victor Cecil, 1883–1953, vol. V

Dalrymple Hay, Sir Charles John, 5th Bt, 1865–1952, vol. V

Dalrymple-Hay, Sir Harley Hugh, 1861–1940, vol. III

Dalrymple-Horn-Elphinstone, Sir Græme Hepburn; *see* Elphinstone.

Dalrymple-Smith, Captain Hugh, 1901–1987, vol. VIII

Dalrymple-White, Lt-Col Sir Godfrey Dalrymple, 1st Bt, 1866–1954, vol. V

Dalton, Baron (Life Peer); Edward Hugh John Neale Dalton, 1887–1962, vol. VI

Dalton, Rev. Prebendary Arthur Edison, 1853–1938, vol. III

Dalton, Charles, 1850–1913, vol. I

Dalton, Hon. Charles, 1850–1933, vol. III

Dalton, Captain Charles G.; *see* Grant-Dalton.

Dalton, Maj.-Gen. Sir Charles James George, 1902–1989, vol. VIII

Dalton, Sir Cornelius Neale, 1842–1920, vol. II

Dalton, Lt-Col Duncan G.; *see* Grant-Dalton.

D'Alton, Rt Rev. Edward A., 1860–1941, vol. IV

Dalton, Emilie Hilda; *see* Dalton, Mrs John E.

Dalton, Surg.-Rear-Adm. Frederick James Abercrombie, 1868–1940, vol. III

Dalton, Frederick Thomas, 1855–1927, vol. II

Dalton, Sir Henry, 1891–1966, vol. VI

Dalton, Rev. Herbert Andrew, 1852–1928, vol. II

Dalton, Adm. Hubert G.; *see* Grant-Dalton.

Dalton, Maj.-Gen. James Cecil, 1848–1931, vol. III

D'Alton, His Eminence Cardinal John, *died* 1963, vol. VI

Dalton, Maj.-Gen. John Cecil D'Arcy, 1907–1981, vol. VIII

Dalton, Sir John Cornelius, *died* 1959, vol. V

Dalton, Mrs John E., (Emilie Hilda Dalton), 1886–1950, vol. IV

Dalton, Rev. John Neale, 1839–1931, vol. III

Dalton, John Patrick, 1886–1965, vol. VI

Dalton, Comdr (E) Lionel Sydney, 1902–1941, vol. IV

Dalton, Sir Llewelyn Chisholm, 1879–1945, vol. IV

Dalton, Norman, *died* 1923, vol. II

Dalton, Ormonde Maddock, 1866–1945, vol. IV

Dalton, Philip Neale, 1909–1989, vol. VIII

Dalton, Sir Robert William, 1882–1961, vol. VI

Dalton, Seymour Berkeley P.; *see* Portman-Dalton.

Dalton, Thomas Wilson Fox, 1886–1977, vol. VII

Dalton, William Bower, 1868–1965, vol. VI

Dalton-Morris, Air Marshal Sir Leslie, 1906–1976, vol. VII

D'Alvarez, Marguerite, 1886–1953, vol. V

D'Alviella, Count Goblet, 1846–1925, vol. II

Dalwood, Hubert, 1924–1976, vol. VII

Dalwood, Lt-Col John H.; *see* Hall-Dalwood.

Daly, Maj.-Gen. Arthur Crawford, 1871–1936, vol. III

Daly, Ashley Skeffington, 1882–1977, vol. VII
Daly, Augustin, 1838–1899, vol. I
Daly, Lt-Col Sir Clive Kirkpatrick, 1888–1966, vol. VI
Daly, Major Denis St George, 1862–1942, vol. IV
Daly, Lt-Col Francis Augustus Bonner, 1855–1946, vol. IV
Daly, Francis Charles, 1868–1945, vol. IV
Daly, Harry John, 1893–1980, vol. VII (AII)
Daly, Very Rev. Henry Edward, *died* 1949, vol. IV
Daly, Ven. Henry Varian, 1838–1925, vol. III
Daly, Lt-Col Sir Hugh, 1860–1939, vol. III
Daly, Ivan de Burgh, 1893–1974, vol. VII
Daly, John Archer Blake-, 1835–1917, vol. II (A), vol. III
Daly, Col Louis Dominic, 1885–1967, vol. VI
Daly, Lt-Col Ludger Jules Olivier G.; *see* Gingras-Daly.
Daly, Hon. Sir Malachy Bowes, 1836–1920, vol. II
Daly, Dame Mary Dora, *died* 1983, vol. VIII
Daly, Sir Oscar Bedford, 1880–1953, vol. V
Daly, Col Patrick Joseph, 1872–1931, vol. III
Daly, Col Thomas, *died* 1917, vol. II
Daly, Thomas Denis, 1890–1956, vol. V
Daly Lewis, Edward; *see* Lewis.
Dalyell of the Binns, Lt-Col Gordon, 1887–1953, vol. V
Dalyell, Major Sir James Bruce Wilkie-, 9th Bt, 1867–1935, vol. III
Dalyell, Lt-Gen. John Thomas, 1827–1919, vol. II
Dalyell, Ralph, 1834–1915, vol. I
Dalzell, Lord; Robert Hippisley Dalzell, 1877–1904, vol. I
Dalzell, Lt-Col John Norton, 1897–1957, vol. V
Dalzell, Reginald Alexander, 1865–1928, vol. II
Dalziel of Kirkcaldy, 1st Baron, 1868–1935, vol. III
Dalziel of Wooler, 1st Baron, 1854–1928, vol. II
Dalziel, Edward, 1817–1905, vol. I
Dalziel, George, 1815–1902, vol. I
Dalziel, Gilbert, 1853–1930, vol. III
Dalziel, Sir Kennedy, 1861–1924, vol. II
Dalziel, Walter Watson, 1900–1967, vol. VI
Dam, (Carl Peter) Henrik, 1895–1976, vol. VII
Dam, Henrik; *see* Dam, C. P. H.
D'Amade, Albert, 1856–1941, vol. IV
Damant, Lt-Col Frederick Hugh, 1864–1926, vol. II
Damant, Captain Guybon Chesney Castell, *died* 1963, vol. VI
d'Ambrumenil, Sir Philip, 1886–1974, vol. VII
Damiano, Most Rev. Celestine Joseph, *died* 1967, vol. VI
D'Amico Inguanez, Baroness Mary Frances Carmen Maria Teresa Sceberras Trigona, 1865–1947, vol. IV
Damle, Keshav Govind, 1868–1930, vol. III
Dampier, Adm. Cecil Frederick, 1868–1950, vol. IV
Dampier, Henry Lucius, 1828–1913, vol. I
Dampier, Sir William Cecil Dampier, 1867–1952, vol. V
Damrosch, Walter, 1862–1950, vol. IV
Dana, Charles L., 1852–1935, vol. III
Dana, John Cotton, 1856–1929, vol. III
Dana, Paul, 1852–1930, vol. III
Dana, Robert Washington, 1868–1956, vol. V

Danby, Vice-Adm. Sir Clinton Francis Samuel, 1882–1945, vol. IV
Danby, Frank, 1864–1916, vol. II
Danby, Rev. Herbert, 1889–1953, vol. V
Dance, Sir George, *died* 1932, vol. III
Dance, James, 1907–1971, vol. VII
Dancer, Sir Thomas Johnston, 7th Bt, 1852–1933, vol. III
Danckwerts, Rt Hon. Sir Harold Otto, 1888–1978, vol. VII
Danckwerts, Peter Victor, 1916–1984, vol. VIII
Danckwerts, Rear-Adm. Victor Hilary, *died* 1944, vol. IV
Danckwerts, William Otto Adolph Julius, 1853–1914, vol. I
Dandie, James Naughton, 1894–1976, vol. VII
Dando, Kenneth Walter, 1921–1980, vol. VII
Dandridge, Cecil Gerald Graham, 1890–1960, vol. V
Dandurand, Rt Hon. Raoul, 1861–1942, vol. IV
Dandy, Rev. Henry Edward, *died* 1930, vol. III
Dandy, James Edgar, 1903–1976, vol. VII
Dane, Clemence Winifred Ashton, *died* 1965, vol. VI
Dane, Hal; *see* Macfall, Haldane.
Dane, Lt-Col James Auchinleck, 1883–1927, vol. II
Dane, Sir Louis William, 1856–1946, vol. IV
Dane, Richard Martin, 1852–1903, vol. I
Dane, Sir Richard Morris, 1854–1940, vol. III
Dane, William Surrey, 1892–1978, vol. VII
Danesfort, 1st Baron, 1853–1935, vol. III
Dangar, Rev. James George, 1841–1917, vol. II
Danger, Frank Charles, 1873–1943, vol. IV
Dangerfield, Roland Edmund, 1897–1964, vol. VI
Dangin, François T.; *see* Thureau-Dangin.
Dangin, Paul Marie Pierre T.; *see* Thureau-Dangin.
Danglow, Rabbi Jacob, 1880–1962, vol. VI
Daniel, Sir Augustus Moore, 1866–1950, vol. IV
Daniel, Rev. Charles Henry Olive, 1836–1919, vol. II
Daniel, Lt-Col Charles James, 1861–1949, vol. IV
Daniel, Adm. Sir Charles Saumarez, 1894–1981, vol. VIII
Daniel, Lt-Col Edward Yorke, 1865–1941, vol. IV
Daniel, Rev. Canon Evan, 1837–1904, vol. I
Daniel, Glyn Edmund, 1914–1986, vol. VIII
Daniel, Henry Cave, 1896–1980, vol. VII
Daniel, Brig. James Alfred, 1893–1959, vol. V
Daniel, Sir John, 1870–1938, vol. III
Daniel, (John) Stuart, 1912–1977, vol. VII
Daniel, Hon. John Waterhouse, 1845–1933, vol. III
Daniel, Stuart; *see* Daniel, J. S.
Daniel, Thomas Ernest, 1898–1968, vol. VI
Daniel, Rev. Wilson Eustace, 1841–1924, vol. II
Daniel-Rops, Henry, 1901–1965, vol. VI
Daniell, Major Edward Henry Edwin, 1868–1914, vol. I
Daniell, Very Rev. Edward M., 1864–1952, vol. V
Daniell, Emily Hilda, (Mrs J. A. H. Daniell); *see* Young, E. H.
Daniell, Major Francis Edward Lloyd, 1874–1916, vol. II
Daniell, Brig.-Gen. Frederick Francis Williamson, 1866–1937, vol. III
Daniell, Rev. George William, 1853–1931, vol. III
Daniell, John, 1878–1963, vol. VI

Daniell, Maj.-Gen. Sir John Frederic, 1859–1943, vol. IV

Daniell, Percy John, 1889–1946, vol. IV

Daniell, Lt-Col William Augustus Bampfylde, 1875–1956, vol. V

Daniell-Bainbridge, Rev. Howard Gurney, *died* 1950, vol. IV

Danielli, James Frederic, 1911–1984, vol. VIII

Daniels, Charles Wilberforce, *died* 1927, vol. II

Daniels, David Kingsley, 1905–1986, vol. VIII

Daniels, George William, 1878–1937, vol. III

Daniels, Harold Griffith, 1874–1952, vol. V

Daniels, Lt-Col Harry, 1884–1953, vol. V

Daniels, Jeffery, 1932–1986, vol. VIII

Daniels, Sir Percy, 1875–1951, vol. V

Daniels, Sidney Reginald, 1873–1937, vol. III

Danielsen, Col Frederick Gustavus, 1874–1951, vol. V

Danks, Sir Aaron Turner, 1861–1928, vol. II

Danks, Ven. William, 1845–1916, vol. II

Dann, Alfred Clarence, 1893–1953, vol. V

Dann, Howard Ernest, 1914–1986, vol. VIII

Dann, Brig.-Gen. William Rowland Harris, 1876–1957, vol. V

Dannatt, Sir Cecil, 1896–1981, vol. VIII

Dannay, Frederic, 1905–1982, vol. VIII

Dannreuther, Edward, 1844–1905, vol. I

Dannreuther, Rear-Adm. Hubert Edward, 1880–1977, vol. VII

Dannreuther, Sir Sigmund, 1873–1965, vol. VI

D'Annunzio, Gabriele, 1864–1938, vol. III

Dansey, Lt-Col Sir Claude Edward Marjoribanks, 1876–1947, vol. IV

Dansey, Col Francis Henry, 1878–1953, vol. V

Dansey-Browning, Col George; *see* Browning.

Danson, Rt Rev. Ernest Denny Logie, 1880–1946, vol. IV

Danson, Sir Francis Chatillon, 1855–1926, vol. II

Danter, Harold Walter Phillips, 1886–1976, vol. VII

Danvers, Frederick Charles, 1833–1906, vol. I

Danvers, Sir Juland, 1826–1902, vol. I

d'Aranyi, Jelly, *died* 1966, vol. VI

Darbhanga, Maharajadhiraja of, 1907–1962, vol. VI

Darbishire, Charles William, 1875–1925, vol. II

Darbishire, David Harold, 1914–1986, vol. VIII

Darbishire, Helen, 1881–1961, vol. VI

Darbishire, Otto Vernon, 1870–1934, vol. III

Darboux, Jean Gaston, 1842–1917, vol. II

Darby, Very Rev. John Lionel, 1831–1919, vol. II

Darby, William Evans, 1844–1922, vol. II

Darbyshire, Most Rev. John Russell, 1880–1948, vol. IV

Darbyshire, Ruth Eveline, *died* 1946, vol. IV

Darbyshire, Taylor, 1875–1943, vol. IV

D'Arcy, Most Rev. Charles Frederick, 1859–1938, vol. III

D'Arcy, Dame Constance Elizabeth, *died* 1950, vol. IV

D'Arcy, Rev. George James Audomar, 1861–1941, vol. IV

D'Arcy, Lt-Gen. John Conyers, 1894–1966, vol. VI

D'Arcy, Very Rev. Martin Cyril, 1888–1976, vol. VII

D'Arcy, Surgeon Rear-Adm. Thomas Norman, 1896–1987, vol. VIII

D'Arcy, William Knox, 1849–1917, vol. II

Darcy de Knayth, Baroness (16th in line), 1865–1929, vol. III

Darcy de Knayth, 17th Baron; *see* Clive, Viscount, vol. IV

D'Arcy-Irvine, Rt Rev. Gerard Addington, 1862–1932, vol. III

D'Arcy-Irvine, Adm. Sir St George Caufield; *see* Irvine.

Dare, Adm. Sir Charles Holcombe, 1854–1924, vol. II

Dare, Edith Graham, 1883–1969, vol. VI

Dare, Robert Westley H.; *see* Hall-Dare.

Darell, Lt-Col Harry Francis, 1872–1934, vol. III

Darell, Sir Lionel Edward, 5th Bt, 1845–1919, vol. II

Darell, Sir Lionel Edward Hamilton Marmaduke, 6th Bt, 1876–1954, vol. V

Darell, Sir Oswald; *see* Darell, Sir W. O.

Darell, Brig.-Gen. William Harry Verelst, 1878–1954, vol. V

Darell, Sir (William) Oswald, 7th Bt, 1910–1959, vol. V

Daresbury, 1st Baron, 1867–1938, vol. III

Daresbury, 2nd Baron, 1902–1990, vol. VIII

Darewski, Herman, *died* 1947, vol. IV

Dargan, William J., *died* 1944, vol. IV

Dark, Sidney, 1874–1947, vol. IV

Darke, Harold Edwin, 1888–1976, vol. VII

Darke, Rear-Adm. Reginald Burnard, 1885–1962, vol. VI

Darkin, Maj.-Gen. Roy Bertram, 1916–1987, vol. VIII

Darlan, Admiral de la Flotte Jean François, 1881–1942, vol. IV

Darley, Sir Bernard D'Olier, 1880–1953, vol. V

Darley, Cecil West, 1842–1928, vol. II

Darley, Air Cdre Charles Curtis, 1890–1962, vol. VI

Darley, Rt Hon. Sir Frederick Matthew, 1830–1910, vol. I

Darley, Major Henry Read, 1865–1931, vol. III

Darley, J. F., *died* 1932, vol. III

Darley, Lt-Col James Russell, 1868–1951, vol. V

Darling, 1st Baron, 1849–1936, vol. III

Darling of Hillsborough, Baron (Life Peer); George Darling, 1905–1985, vol. VIII

Darling, Arthur Ivan, 1916–1987, vol. VIII

Darling, Rev. Charles Brian Auchinleck, 1905–1978, vol. VII

Darling, Col Charles Henry, 1852–1931, vol. III

Darling, Charles Robert, 1870–1942, vol. IV

Darling, Maj.-Gen. Douglas Lyall, 1914–1978, vol. VII

Darling, Rev. Canon Edward M.; *see* Moore Darling.

Darling, Frank, 1850–1923, vol. II

Darling, Sir Frank F.; *see* Fraser Darling.

Darling, Frederick, 1884–1953, vol. V

Darling, George Kenneth, 1879–1964, vol. VI

Darling, Ven. James George Reginald, 1868–1938, vol. III

Darling, Major Hon. John Clive, 1887–1933, vol. III

Darling, Major John Collier S.; *see* Stormonth-Darling.

Darling, John Ford, 1864–1938, vol. III

Darling, Major John May, 1878–1942, vol. IV

Darling, Hon. Joseph, 1870–1946, vol. IV

Darling, Sir Malcolm Lyall, 1880–1969, vol. VI

Darling, Moir Tod Stormonth; *see* Hon. Lord Stormonth-Darling.

Darling, Sir William Young, 1885–1962, vol. VI

Darlington, Cyril Dean, 1903–1981, vol. VIII

Darlington, Edwin, 1839–1928, vol. II

Darlington, Col Sir Henry Clayton, 1877–1959, vol. V

Darlington, Rt Rev. James Henry, 1856–1930, vol. III

Darlington, Rev. John, 1868–1947, vol. IV

Darlington, Rev. Joseph, 1850–1939, vol. III

Darlington, Reginald Ralph, 1903–1977, vol. VII

Darlington, William Aubrey, 1890–1979, vol. VII

Darlow, Rev. Thomas Herbert, 1858–1927, vol. II

Darnley, 7th Earl of, 1851–1900, vol. I

Darnley, 8th Earl of, 1859–1927, vol. II

Darnley, 9th Earl of, 1886–1955, vol. V

Darnley, 10th Earl of, 1915–1980, vol. VII

Darracott, Sir William, 1860–1947, vol. IV

Darrah, Henry Zouch, 1854–1909, vol. I

Darrell, Hon. Richard Darrell, 1827–1904, vol. I

Darroch, Alexander, 1862–1924, vol. II

Darrow, Clarence, 18547–1938, vol. III

Dart, Rt Rev. John, 1837–1910, vol. I

Dart, Rev. John Lovering Campbell, 1882–1961, vol. VI

Dart, Raymond Arthur, 1893–1988, vol. VIII

Dart, Thurston, 1921–1971, vol. VII

Dartmouth, 6th Earl of, 1851–1936, vol. III

Dartmouth, 7th Earl of, 1881–1958, vol. V

Dartmouth, 8th Earl of, 1888–1962, vol. VI

Dartnell, Maj.-Gen. Sir John George, 1838–1913, vol. I

Dartrey, 1st Earl of, 1817–1897, vol. I

Dartrey, 2nd Earl of, 1842–1920, vol. II

Dartrey, 3rd Earl of, 1855–1933, vol. III

Darvall, Frank Ongley, 1906–1987, vol. VIII

Darvall, Air Marshal Sir Lawrence, 1898–1968, vol. VI

Darvil-Smith, Major Percy George, 1880–1962, vol. VI

Darvill, Harold Edgar, 1908–1972, vol. VII

Darwall, Lt-Gen. Robert Henry, 1879–1956, vol. V

Darwen, 1st Baron, 1885–1950, vol. IV

Darwen, 2nd Baron, 1915–1988, vol. VIII

Darwin, Bernard, 1876–1961, vol. VI

Darwin, Sir Charles Galton, 1887–1962, vol. VI

Darwin, Squadron Leader Charles John Wharton, 1894–1941, vol. IV

Darwin, Col Charles Waring, 1855–1928, vol. II

Darwin, Sir Francis, 1848–1925, vol. II

Darwin, Sir George Howard, 1845–1912, vol. I

Darwin, Sir Horace, 1851–1928, vol. II

Darwin, John Henry, 1884–1962, vol. VI

Darwin, Major Leonard, 1850–1943, vol. IV

Darwin, Robert Vere; *see* Darwin, Sir Robin.

Darwin, Sir Robin, 1910–1974, vol. VII

Darwin, Ruth, *died* 1972, vol. VII

Darwood, Sir John William, 1873–1951, vol. V

Daryngton, 1st Baron, 1867–1949, vol. IV

Das, Sir Kedarnath; *see* Kedarnath Das.

Das, Hon. M. S., 1848–1934, vol. III

Das, Hon. Satish Ranjan, 1872–1928, vol. II

Das, Sudhi Ranjan, 1894–1977, vol. VII

Dasent, Arthur Irwin, *died* 1939, vol. III

Dasent, Sir John Roche, 1847–1914, vol. I

Dasgupta, Surendra Nath, 1887–1952, vol. V

Dash, Sir Arthur Jules, 1887–1974, vol. VII

Dash, Sir Roydon Englefield Ashford, 1888–1984, vol. VIII

Dashwood, Arthur George Frederick, 1860–1922, vol. II

Dashwood, Charles James, 1843–1919, vol. II

Dashwood, Col Edmund William, 1858–1946, vol. IV

Dashwood, Elizabeth Monica, 1890–1943, vol. IV

Dashwood, Sir George John Egerton, 6th Bt (*cr* 1684), 1851–1933, vol. III

Dashwood, Sir Henry George Massy, 8th Bt (*cr* 1684), 1908–1972, vol. VII

Dashwood, Sir Henry Thomas Alexander, 1878–1959, vol. V

Dashwood, Sir John Lindsay, 10th Bt (*cr* 1707), 1896–1966, vol. VI

Dashwood, Maj.-Gen. Richard Lewes, 1837–1905, vol. I

Dashwood, Major Sir Robert Henry Seymour, 7th Bt (*cr* 1684), 1876–1947, vol. IV

Dashwood, Sir Robert John, 9th Bt (*cr* 1707), 1859–1908, vol. I

Datar Singh, Sardar Bahadur Sir, *died* 1973, vol. VII

Datia, HH Maharajah Sir Govind Singh Bahadur, 1886–1951, vol. V

Datia, HH Maharajah Sir Lockindar Bhawani Singh Bahadur, 1846–1907, vol. I

Datta, Surendra Kumar, 1878–1942, vol. IV

Daubeney, Brig.-Gen. Edward Kaye, 1858–1932, vol. III

Daubeney, Gen. Sir Henry Charles Barnston, 1810–1903, vol. I

Daubeny, Sir Peter Lauderdale, 1921–1975, vol. VII

Daubeny, Col Reginald Ernest, 1877–1935, vol. III

Dauber, J. H., *died* 1915, vol. I

Daubney, Robert, 1891–1977, vol. VII

Daudet, Alphonse, 1840–1897, vol. I

Daudet, Léon, 1867–1942, vol. IV

Dauglish, Captain Edward Heath, 1882–1950, vol. IV

Dauglish, Rt Rev. John, 1879–1952, vol. V

Daukes, Lt-Col Sir Clendon Turberville, 1879–1947, vol. IV

Daukes, Rt Rev. Francis Whitfield, 1877–1954, vol. V

Daukes, Frederick Clendon, 1848–1915, vol. I

Daukes, Sidney Herbert, 1879–1947, vol. IV

Daunt, Very Rev. Ernest George, 1909–1966, vol. VI

Daunt, Lt-Col Richard Algernon Craigie, 1872–1928, vol. II

Daunt, Maj.-Gen. William, 1831–1899, vol. I

Daunt, Ven. William, 1841–1919, vol. II

Dauntesey, Lt-Col William Bathurst, 1864–1937, vol. III

Davar, Sir Dinsha Dhurjibhai, 1856–1916, vol. II

Daven-Thomas, Rev. Canon Dennis; *see* Thomas.

Davenport, Charles Benedict, 1866–1944, vol. IV

Davenport, Major Cyril James H., 1848–1941, vol. IV

Davenport, Rear-Adm. Dudley Leslie, 1919–1990, vol. VIII

Davenport, Frederic Richard, 1872–1952, vol. V

Davenport, Hon. Sir George Arthur, 1893–1970, vol. VI

Davenport, Harold, 1907–1969, vol. VI
Davenport, Sir Henry Edward, 1866–1941, vol. IV
Davenport, Major John Lewes, 1910–1964, vol. VI
Davenport, Dame Lilian Emily Isabel Jane B.; *see* Bromley-Davenport.
Davenport, Muriel Coomber B.; *see* Bromley-Davenport.
Davenport, Robert Cecil, 1893–1961, vol. VI
Davenport, Vice-Adm. Robert Clutterbuck, 1882–1965, vol. VI
Davenport, Sir Samuel, 1818–1906, vol. I
Davenport, Lt-Col Sir Walter Henry B.; *see* Bromley-Davenport.
Davenport, Brig.-Gen. Sir William B.; *see* Bromley-Davenport.
Daventry, 1st Viscountess, 1869–1962, vol. VI
Daventry, 2nd Viscount, 1893–1986, vol. VIII
Daverin, John, 1851–1922, vol. II
Davey, Baron (Life Peer); Horace Davey, 1833–1907, vol. I
Davey, Maj.-Gen. Basil Charles, 1897–1959, vol. V
Davey, Comdr Charles Henry, 1879–1940, vol. III
Davey, George, 1911–1959, vol. V
Davey, Henry, 1843–1928, vol. II
Davey, Herbert, 1871–1931, vol. III
Davey, Lt-Col Hon. Horace Scott, 1865–1935, vol. III
Davey, Lt-Col James Edgar, 1873–1969, vol. VI
Davey, Rev. J(ames) Ernest, 1890–1960, vol. V, vol. VI
Davey, Rev. James Penry, 1878–1939, vol. III
Davey, Rev. Thomas Arthur Edwards, *died* 1944, vol. IV
Davey, Thomas Herbert, 1899–1978, vol. VII
Davey, Very Rev. William Harrison, 1825–1917, vol. II
Davey, William Kendall, 1887–1968, vol. VI
David, Rt Rev. Albert Augustus, 1867–1950, vol. IV
David, Alexander Jones, 1851–1929, vol. III
David, Ven. Arthur Evan, 1861–1913, vol. I
David, Brian Guvney, 1926–1990, vol. VIII
David, Lt-Col Sir Edgeworth; *see* David, Lt-Col Sir T. W. E.
David, Sir Edgeworth Beresford, 1908–1965, vol. VI
David, Herman Francis, 1905–1974, vol. VI
David, Hon. Laurent Olivier, 1840–1926, vol. II
David, Sir Percival Victor, 2nd Bt, 1892–1964, vol. VI
David, Rev. Richard, *died* 1947, vol. IV (A)
David, Sir Sassoon, 1st Bt, 1849–1926, vol. II
David, Lt-Col Sir (Tannatt William) Edgeworth, 1858–1934, vol. III
David, Bt-Col Thomas Jenkins, 1881–1926, vol. II
David, W. T., *died* 1948, vol. IV
David-Weill, David, 1871–1952, vol. V
Davidge, Cecil William, 1863–1936, vol. III
Davidge, William Robert, *died* 1961, vol. VI
Davids, Caroline A. F. Rhys, *died* 1942, vol. IV
Davids, Thomas William Rhys, 1843–1922, vol. II
Davidson, 1st Viscount, 1889–1970, vol. VI
Davidson, Dowager Viscountess; Frances Joan Davidson; Baroness Northchurch (Life Peer), 1894–1985, vol. VIII
Davidson, 1st Baron, 1848–1930, vol. III
Davidson, Rev. Alan Munro, 1894–1959, vol. V

Davidson, Albert, 1869–1932, vol. III
Davidson, Maj.-Gen. Alexander Elliott, 1880–1962, vol. VI
Davidson, Air Vice-Marshal Sir Alexander Paul, 1894–1971, vol. VII
Davidson, Vice-Adm. Alexander Percy, 1868–1930, vol. III
Davidson, Sir Alfred Charles, 1882–1952, vol. V
Davidson, Allan Douglas, 1873–1932, vol. III
Davidson, Sir Andrew, 1892–1962, vol. VI
Davidson, Rev. Andrew Bruce, 1840–1902, vol. I
Davidson, Andrew Hope, 1895–1967, vol. VI
Davidson, Very Rev. (Andrew) Nevile, 1899–1976, vol. VII
Davidson, Col Sir Arthur, 1856–1922, vol. II
Davidson, Sir Charles, 1878–1927, vol. II
Davidson, Charles Findlay, 1911–1967, vol. VI
Davidson, Lt-Col Charles George Francis, 1884–1956, vol. V
Davidson, Col Charles John Lloyd, 1858–1941, vol. IV
Davidson, Sir Charles Peers, 1841–1929, vol. III
Davidson, Charles Rundle, 1875–1970, vol. VI
Davidson, Brig.-Gen. Charles Steer, 1866–1942, vol. IV
Davidson, Hon. Sir Charles William, 1897–1985, vol. VIII
Davidson, Sir Colin George Watt, 1878–1954, vol. V
Davidson, Sir Colin John, 1878–1930, vol. III
Davidson, Lt-Col Colin Keppel, 1895–1943, vol. IV
Davidson, Col Sir David, 1811–1900, vol. I
Davidson, Brig. Douglas Stewart, 1892–1958, vol. V
Davidson, Duncan, 1865–1917, vol. II
Davidson, Brig. Edmund, 1875–1945, vol. IV
Davidson, Sir Edward; *see* Davidson, Sir W. E.
Davidson, Lt-Col Edward Humphrey, 1886–1962, vol. VI
Davidson, Rt Rev. Edwin John, 1899–1958, vol. V
Davidson, Ethel Sarah, 1877–1939, vol. III
Davidson, Maj.-Gen. Francis Henry Norman, 1892–1973, vol. VII
Davidson, Frederick Lewis Maitland, *died* 1936, vol. III
Davidson, George, *died* 1928, vol. II
Davidson, Major George Harry, 1866–1927, vol. II
Davidson, Ven. Gilbert Farquhar, 1871–1930, vol. III
Davidson, Ian Douglas, 1901–1989, vol. VIII
Davidson, Col James, 1853–1932, vol. III
Davidson, Ven. James, *died* 1933, vol. III
Davidson, Lt-Col James, 1865–1933, vol. III
Davidson, James, 1885–1945, vol. IV
Davidson, James, 1875–1959, vol. V
Davidson, James, 1896–1985, vol. VIII
Davidson, James Leigh S.; *see* Strachan-Davidson.
Davidson, Sir James Inglis, 1852–1934, vol. III
Davidson, Sir James Mackenzie, 1856–1919, vol. II
Davidson, (James) Norman, 1911–1972, vol. VII
Davidson, James Walker, 1872–1939, vol. III
Davidson, James Wightman, 1915–1973, vol. VII
Davidson, Jo, 1883–1952, vol. V
Davidson, John, 1869–1905, vol. I
Davidson, John, 1857–1909, vol. I
Davidson, Col John, 1845–1917, vol. II
Davidson, John, 1878–1957, vol. V

Davidson, John, 1882–1960, vol. V
Davidson, Maj.-Gen. Sir John Humphrey, 1876–1954, vol. V
Davidson, John Wallace Ord, 1888–1973, vol. VII
Davidson, Col Sir Jonathan Roberts, 1874–1961, vol. VI
Davidson, Maj.-Gen. Kenneth Chisholm, 1897–1985, vol. VIII
Davidson, Major Leslie Evan Outram, 1882–1925, vol. II
Davidson, Sir Leybourne Francis Watson, 1859–1934, vol. III
Davidson, Sir (Leybourne) Stanley (Patrick), 1894–1981, vol. VIII
Davidson, Lindsay Gordon, 1893–1965, vol. VI
Davidson, Sir Lionel, 1868–1944, vol. IV
Davidson, Dame Margaret Agnes, 1871–1964, vol. VI
Davidson, Mark George, 1859–1933, vol. III
Davidson, Maurice, 1883–1967, vol. VI
Davidson, Very Rev. Nevile; see Davidson, Very Rev. A. N.
Davidson, Sir Nigel George, 1873–1961, vol. VI
Davidson, Norman; see Davidson, J. N.
Davidson, Lt-Col Peers, 1870–1920, vol. II
Davidson, Lt-Col Percival, 1874–1930, vol. III
Davidson, Randall George, 1874–1963, vol. VI
Davidson, Rev. Richard, 1876–1944, vol. IV
Davidson, Robert, 1831–1913, vol. I
Davidson, Robert, 1888–1952, vol. V
Davidson, Roger Alastair McLaren, 1900–1983, vol. VIII
Davidson, Sir Samuel C., died 1921, vol. II
Davidson, Maj.-Gen. Sisley Richard, 1869–1952, vol. V
Davidson, Col Stuart, 1859–1941, vol. IV
Davidson, Sir Stanley; see Davidson, Sir L. S. P.
Davidson, Thomas, 1856–1923, vol. II
Davidson, Sir Walter Edward, 1859–1923, vol. II
Davidson, William Bird, 1912–1990, vol. VIII
Davidson, Sir (William) Edward, 1853–1923, vol. II
Davidson, Col William Leslie, 1850–1915, vol. I
Davidson, William Leslie, 1848–1929, vol. III
Davidson, William Tennent Gairdner, 1889–1949, vol. IV
Davidson-Houston, Major Charles Elrington Duncan, 1873–1915, vol. I
Davidson-Houston, Lt-Col Wilfred Bennett, 1870–1960, vol. V
Davidson-Smith, Maj.-Gen. E.; see Smith.
Davie, Major Arthur Francis Ferguson-, 1867–1916, vol. II
Davie, Rev. Sir Arthur Patrick F.; see Ferguson Davie.
Davie, Cedric Thorpe, 1913–1983, vol. VIII
Davie, Rt Rev. Charles James F.; see Ferguson-Davie.
Davie, Sir Henry Augustus Ferguson-, 1865–1946, vol. IV
Davie, Sir John Davie Ferguson-, 2nd Bt, 1830–1907, vol. I
Davie, Sir Paul Christopher, 1901–1990, vol. VIII
Davie, Thomas Benjamin, 1895–1955, vol. V
Davie, Sir William Augustus Ferguson-, 3rd Bt, 1833–1915, vol. I

Davie, Major Sir William John F., 4th Bt; see Ferguson-Davie.
Davies, 1st Baron, 1880–1944, vol. IV
Davies, 2nd Baron, 1915–1944, vol. IV
Davies of Leek, Baron (Life Peer); Harold Davies, 1904–1985, vol. VIII
Davies, Aaron, 1830–1915, vol. I
Davies, Air Cdre Adolphus Dan, 1902–1984, vol. VIII
Davies, Alan B.; see Bowen-Davies.
Davies, Sir Alan Meredyth H.; see Hudson-Davies.
Davies, Albert Edward, 1900–1953, vol. V
Davies, Albert Emil, 1875–1950, vol. IV
Davies, Alfred, 1848–1907, vol. I
Davies, Sir Alfred Thomas, 1881–1941, vol. IV
Davies, Sir Alfred Thomas, 1861–1949, vol. IV
Davies, Alice Hollingdrake, 1878–1968, vol. VI
Davies, Alun Bennett O.; see Oldfield-Davies.
Davies, Rt Hon. Sir Arthian; see Davies, Rt Hon. Sir W. A.
Davies, Sir Arthur; see Davies, Sir D. A.
Davies, Arthur Cecil, 1889–1947, vol. IV
Davies, Arthur Charles F.; see Fox-Davies.
Davies, (Arthur Edward) Miles, 1903–1977, vol. VII
Davies, Adm. Sir Arthur John, died 1954, vol. V
Davies, Rev. Arthur Llywelyn, died 1957, vol. V
Davies, Lt-Gen. Arthur Matcham, 1832–1908, vol. I
Davies, Arthur Templer, 1858–1929, vol. III
Davies, Arthur Vernon, died 1942, vol. IV
Davies, Very Rev. Arthur Whitcliffe, died 1966, vol. VI
Davies, Arthur William 1878–1969, vol. VI
Davies, Ashton, 1874–1958, vol. V
Davies, Ben, 1858–1943, vol. IV
Davies, Rev. Canon Benjamin, 1880–1941, vol. IV
Davies, Bernard Nöel L.; see Langdon-Davies.
Davies, Brian H.; see Humphreys-Davies.
Davies, Carlton Griffith, 1895–1981, vol. VIII
Davies, Cecil Bertrand, 1876–1960, vol. VI
Davies, Sir Charles; see Davies, Sir R. C.
Davies, Rev. Charles Douglas Percy, died 1931, vol. III
Davies, Hon. Charles Ellis, 1848–1921, vol. II
Davies, Brig.-Gen. Charles Henry, 1867–1954, vol. V
Davies, Charles Llewelyn, 1860–1927, vol. II
Davies, Brig. Charles Stafford P.; see Price-Davies.
Davies, Lt-Col Charles Stewart, 1880–1946, vol. IV
Davies, Clara Novello, 1861–1943, vol. IV
Davies, Rt Hon. Clement, 1884–1962, vol. VI
Davies, Sir Colin R.; see Rees-Davies.
Davies, Cuthbert Collin, 1896–1974, vol. VII
Davies, Rt Rev. Daniel, 1863–1928, vol. II
Davies, Daniel James, 1880–1946, vol. IV
Davies, Sir Daniel Thomas, 1899–1966, vol. VI
Davies, Ven. David, 1858–1930, vol. III
Davies, David, 1862–1932, vol. III
Davies, Sir David, 1870–1958, vol. V
Davies, Sir David, 1889–1964, vol. VI
Davies, David, 1877–1966, vol. VI
Davies, David Alban, 1873–1951, vol. V
Davies, Sir (David) Arthur, 1913–1990, vol. VIII
Davies, Rt Rev. David E.; see Edwardes-Davies.
Davies, David F.; see Ffrangcon-Davies.

Davies, Rt Rev. David Henry S.; *see* Saunders-Davies.

Davies, Ven David John, 1879–1935, vol. III

Davies, David Lewis, *died* 1937, vol. III

Davies, David Lewis, 1911–1982, vol. VIII

Davies, David Percy, 1891–1946, vol. IV

Davies, David Richard Seaborne, 1904–1984, vol. VIII

Davies, David Samuel, *died* 1933, vol. III

Davies, Sir David Sanders, 1852–1934, vol. III

Davies, David Vaughan, 1911–1969, vol. VI

Davies, Derek George G.; *see* Gill-Davies.

Davies, Duncan Sheppey, 1921–1987, vol. VIII

Davies, Edward, *died* 1920, vol. II

Davies, Col Edward Campbell, *died* 1919, vol. II

Davies, Edward Gwynfryn, 1904–1980, vol. VII (AII)

Davies, Edward Harold, 1867–1947, vol. IV

Davies, Sir (Edward) John, 1898–1969, vol. VI

Davies, Ellis William, 1871–1939, vol. III

Davies, Elwyn, 1908–1986, vol. VIII

Davies, Emily; *see* Davies, S. E.

Davies, Eric John W.; *see* Warlow-Davies.

Davies, Ernest, 1873–1946, vol. IV

Davies, Ernest Herbert, *died* 1934, vol. III

Davies, Ernest James, 1875–1935, vol. III

Davies, Ernest S.; *see* Salter Davies.

Davies, Rev. Ernest William, 1901–1978, vol. VII

Davies, Eryl Oliver, 1922–1982, vol. VIII

Davies, Rev. Evan Thomas, *died* 1927, vol. II

Davies, Evan Thomas, 1878–1969, vol. VI

Davies, Evan Tom, 1904–1973, vol. VII

Davies, Fanny, 1861–1934, vol. III

Davies, Francis, 1897–1965, vol. VI

Davies, Gen. Sir Francis John, 1864–1948, vol. IV

Davies, Rev. (Francis Maurice) Russell, 1871–1956, vol. V

Davies, Rev. Francis Parry W.; *see* Watkin-Davies.

Davies, Rev. Frederick Charles, *died* 1929, vol. III

Davies, Frederick William Samuel, *died* 1919, vol. II

Davies, Rev. Canon George Colliss Boardman, 1912–1982, vol. VIII

Davies, Sir George Edmund, 1857–1932, vol. III

Davies, George Francis, 1911–1987, vol. VIII (A)

Davies, Major Sir George Frederick, 1875–1950, vol. IV

Davies, Maj.-Gen. George Freshfield, 1872–1936, vol. III

Davies, George Maitland Lloyd, 1880–1949, vol. IV

Davies, Ven. George Middlecott, 1858–1937, vol. III

Davies, Rev. Gerald Stanley, 1845–1927, vol. II

Davies, Rev. Gilbert Austin, 1868–1948, vol. IV

Davies, Gwendoline Elizabeth, *died* 1951, vol. V

Davies, Harold Haydn, 1897–1982, vol. VIII

Davies, Harold Whitridge, *died* 1946, vol. IV

Davies, Haydn, 1905–1976, vol. VII

Davies, Hector Leighton, 1894–1980, vol. VII

Davies, Lt-Col Henry, 1867–1923, vol. II

Davies, Sir Henry, 1856–1936, vol. III

Davies, Lt-Gen. Henry Fanshawe, 1837–1914, vol. I

Davies, Henry J.; *see* Jones-Davies.

Davies, Maj.-Gen. Henry Lowrie, 1898–1975, vol. VII

Davies, Henry Meirion, 1875–1950, vol. IV (A), vol. V

Davies, Maj.-Gen. Henry Rodolph, 1865–1950, vol. IV

Davies, Sir (Henry) Walford, 1869–1941, vol. IV

Davies, Col Sir Horatio David, 1842–1912, vol. I

Davies, Sir Howell; *see* Davies, Sir H. W.

Davies, Hubert Henry, *died* 1917, vol. II

Davies, Hugh Morriston, 1879–1965, vol. VI

Davies, Rev. Canon Hywel Islwyn, 1909–1981, vol. VIII

Davies, Ifor, 1910–1982, vol. VIII

Davies, Iforwyn Glyndwr, 1901–1984, vol. VIII

Davies, James Henry W.; *see* Wootton-Davies.

Davies, Jenkin A.; *see* Alban Davies.

Davies, Sir John; *see* Davies, Sir E. J.

Davies, John Bowen, 1876–1943, vol. IV

Davies, Sir John Cecil, 1864–1927, vol. II

Davies, John Cledwyn, *died* 1952, vol. V

Davies, John David Griffith, 1899–1953, vol. V

Davies, John Edward Henry, *died* 1939, vol. III

Davies, Rt Hon. John Emerson Harding, 1916–1979, vol. VII

Davies, Hon. Sir John George, 1846–1913, vol. I

Davies, Rev. John Gordon, 1919–1990, vol. VIII

Davies, John Humphreys, *died* 1926, vol. II

Davies, Rev. John J., 1863–1938, vol. III

Davies, John L.; *see* Langdon-Davies.

Davies, Rev. John Llewelyn, 1826–1916, vol. II

Davies, John Llewelyn, 1888–1959, vol. V

Davies, Hon. Sir John Mark, *died* 1919, vol. II

Davies, J(ohn) Prysor, 1900–1959, vol. V

Davies, John Robert, 1856–1934, vol. III

Davies, John Tasman, 1924–1987, vol. VIII

Davies, Sir John Thomas, 1881–1938, vol. III

Davies, Very Rev. John Thomas, 1881–1966, vol. VI

Davies, Rev. John Timothy, *died* 1931, vol. III

Davies, Rev. (John) Trevor, 1907–1974, vol. VII

Davies, Sir Joseph, 1866–1954, vol. V

Davies, Joseph Edward, 1876–1958, vol. V

Davies, Very Rev. Joseph Gwyn, 1890–1952, vol. V

Davies, Joshua David, 1889–1966, vol. VI

Davies, Kenneth; *see* Davies, S. K.

Davies, Sir Leonard Twiston, 1894–1953, vol. V

Davies, Lewis, 1886–1971, vol. VII

Davies, Maj.-Gen. Llewelyn Alberic Emilius P.; *see* Price-Davies.

Davies, Rt Hon. Sir Louis Henry, 1845–1924, vol. II

Davies, Margaret, (Lady Davies); *see* Kennedy, Margaret.

Davies, Sir Martin, 1908–1975, vol. VII

Davies, Mrs Mary, 1855–1930, vol. III

Davies, Hon. Sir Matthew Henry, 1850–1912, vol. I

Davies, Michael John, 1918–1984, vol. VIII

Davies, Miles; *see* Davies, A. E. M.

Davies, N. P.; *see* Prescott-Davies.

Davies, Oswald Vaughan L.; *see* Lloyd-Davies.

Davies, Owen Picton, 1872–1940, vol. III

Davies, Bt-Col Owen Stanley, *died* 1926, vol. II

Davies, Col Percy George, *died* 1947, vol. IV

Davies, Peter H.; *see* Humphreys-Davies.

Davies, Rev. Philip Latimer, 1864–1928, vol. II

Davies, Rev. R. W. F. S.; *see* Singers-Davies.

Davies, Rachael Annie C.; *see* Cox-Davies.

Davies, Randall Robert Henry, 1866–1946, vol. IV

Davies, Reginald, 1887–1971, vol. VII

Davies, Sir (Reginald) Charles, 1886–1958, vol. V
Davies, Rhisiart Morgan, 1903–1958, vol. V
Davies, Rhys, 1903–1978, vol. VII
Davies, Rhys John, 1877–1954, vol. V
Davies, Sir Richard, 1853–1939, vol. III
Davies, Vice-Adm. Richard Bell, died 1966, vol. VI
Davies, Richard Humphrey, 1872–1970, vol. VI
Davies, Col Richard Hutton, died 1918, vol. II
Davies, Robert Gwyneddon, 1870–1928, vol. II
Davies, Sir Robert Henry, 1824–1902, vol. I
Davies, Sir Robert John, 1900–1967, vol. VI
Davies, Robert Malcolm Deryck, 1918–1967, vol. VI
Davies, Rev. Robert Owen, 1857–1929, vol. III
Davies, Roy Dicker Salter, 1906–1984, vol. VIII
Davies, Rev. Russell; see Davies, Rev. F. M. R.
Davies, Ven. Samuel Morris, 1879–1963, vol. VI
Davies, (Sarah) Emily, 1830–1921, vol. II
Davies, Rev. Sidney Edmund, died 1918, vol. II
Davies, (Stanley) Kenneth, 1899–1987, vol. VIII
Davies, Rt Rev. Stephen Harris, 1883–1961, vol. VI
Davies, Stephen Owen, 1886–1972, vol. VII
Davies, Sydney John, 1891–1967, vol. VI
Davies, T. Witton, 1851–1923, vol. II
Davies, Sir Thomas, 1858–1939, vol. III
Davies, Thomas A.; see Anwyl-Davies.
Davies, Col Thomas Arthur Harkness, 1857–1942, vol. IV
Davies, Thomas H.; see Hart-Davies.
Davies, Thomas Walton, 1907–1948, vol. IV
Davies, Timothy, 1857–1951, vol. V
Davies, Rev. Trevor; see Davies, Rev. J. T.
Davies, Tudor, died 1958, vol. V
Davies, Sir Victor Caddy, died 1977, vol. VII (AII)
Davies, Sir Walford; see Davies, Sir H. W.
Davies, Walter, 1865–1939, vol. III
Davies, Hon. Brig.-Gen. Walter Percy Lionel, 1871–1952, vol. V
Davies, Col Warburton Edward, 1879–1956, vol. V
Davies, Rev. Canon Watkin, 1869–1943, vol. IV
Davies, Sir William, 1863–1935, vol. III
Davies, William, 1899–1968, vol. VI
Davies, Rt Hon. Sir (William) Arthian, 1901–1979, vol. VII
Davies, William Frank de Rolante, died 1942, vol. IV
Davies, Sir William George, 1828–1898, vol. I
Davies, William Henry, 1871–1940, vol. III
Davies, Sir (William) Howell, 1851–1932, vol. III
Davies, William John, 1848–1934, vol. IV
Davies, William John, 1891–1975, vol. VII
Davies, William John Abbott, 1890–1967, vol. VI
Davies, Sir William Llewelyn, 1887–1952, vol. V
Davies, Sir William Rees-, 1863–1939, vol. III
Davies, William Robert, 1870–1949, vol. IV
Davies, William Thomas Frederick, 1860–1947, vol. IV
Davies, William Tudor, died 1978, vol. VII
Davies, William Watkin, 1895–1973, vol. VII
Davies, Wyndham Matabele, 1893–1972, vol. VII
Davies, Wyndham Roy, 1926–1984, vol. VIII
Davies-Colley, Robert, died 1955, vol. V
Davies-Cooke, Col Philip Ralph, 1896–1974, vol. VII
Davies-Cooke, Philip Tatton; see Cooke.
Davies-Evans, Herbert, 1842–1928, vol. II

Davies-Gilbert, Mrs Grace Catherine Rose, died 1951, vol. V
d'Avigdor-Goldsmid, Major Sir Henry Joseph, 2nd Bt, 1909–1976, vol. VII
d'Avigdor-Goldsmid, Maj.-Gen. Sir James Arthur, 3rd Bt, 1912–1987, vol. VIII
d'Avigdor-Goldsmid, Sir Osmond Elim, 1st Bt, 1877–1940, vol. III
Davin, Daniel Marcus, (Dan Davin), 1913–1990, vol. VIII
Davin, Nicholas Flood, 1843–1901, vol. I
Daviot, Gordon, 1896–1952, vol. V
Davis, Alexander, 1861–1945, vol. IV
Davis, Sir Alfred George Fletcher H.; see Hall-Davis.
Davis, Anthony Tilton, 1931–1978, vol. VII
Davis, Archibald William, 1900–1979, vol. VII
Davis, Arthur Henry, 1886–1931, vol. III
Davis, Arthur J., 1878–1951, vol. V
Davis, Bette Ruth Elizabeth, 1908–1989, vol. VIII
Davis, Brian; see ffolkes, Michael.
Davis, Sir Charles, 1st Bt, 1878–1950, vol. IV
Davis, Ven. Charles Henderson, died 1915, vol. I
Davis, Sir Charles Henry, 1847–1938, vol. III
Davis, Charles Henry H.; see Hart-Davis.
Davis, Col Charles Herbert, 1872–1922, vol. II
Davis, Sir Charles Thomas, 1873–1938, vol. III
Davis, Brig. Cyril Elliott, 1892–1986, vol. VIII
Davis, David, 1877–1930, vol. III
Davis, Sir David, 1859–1938, vol. III
Davis, Ven. David Grimaldi, died 1936, vol. III
Davis, Dwight Filley, 1879–1945, vol. IV
Davis, Sir Edmund, died 1939, vol. III
Davis, Edward David Darelan, 1880–1976, vol. VII
Davis, Air Vice-Marshal Edward Derek, 1895–1955, vol. V
Davis, Adm. Edward Henry Meggs, 1846–1929, vol. III
Davis, Eliza Jeffries, 1875–1943, vol. IV
Davis, Elmer Holmes, 1890–1958, vol. V
Davis, Sir Ernest, 1872–1962, vol. VI
Davis, Very Rev. Evans, 1848–1918, vol. II
Davis, Col Evans Greenwood, 1885–1951, vol. V
Davis, F. W., died 1919, vol. II
Davis, Francis John, 1900–1980, vol. VII
Davis, Francis Robert Edward, 1887–1960, vol. V
Davis, Hon. Frank Roy, 1888–1948, vol. IV
Davis, Sir George Francis, 1883–1947, vol. IV
Davis, Col George M'Bride, 1846–1909, vol. I
Davis, Sir Gilbert, 2nd Bt, 1901–1973, vol. VII
Davis, Sir Godfrey, 1890–1968, vol. VI
Davis, Lt-Col Gronow John, 1869–1919, vol. II
Davis, H. Haldin; see Haldin-Davis.
Davis, Lt-Col Harold James Norman, 1882–1960, vol. V
Davis, Harold Sydney, 1908–1988, vol. VIII
Davis, Henry John B.; see Banks-Davis.
Davis, Henry William Banks, 1833–1914, vol. I
Davis, Henry William Carless, 1874–1928, vol. II
Davis, Sir Herbert, 1891–1972, vol. VII
Davis, Herbert John, 1893–1967, vol. VI
Davis, Captain Herbert Ludlow, 1887–1951, vol. V
Davis, James; see Hall, Owen.
Davis, James Corbett, 1870–1957, vol. V
Davis, James Richard A.; see Ainsworth-Davis.

Davis, Col John, 1834–1902, vol. I

Davis, John Creyghton A.; *see* Ainsworth-Davis.

Davis, Air Chief Marshal Sir John Gilbert, 1911–1989, vol. VIII

Davis, John King, 1884–1967, vol. VI

Davis, John Merle, 1875–1960, vol. V

Davis, John Samuel Champion, 1859–1926, vol. II

Davis, John William, 1873–1955, vol. V

Davis, Leslie John, 1899–1980, vol. VII

Davis, Lucien, 1860–1941, vol. IV

Davis, Dame Margaret; *see* Rutherford, Dame M.

Davis, Morris Cael, 1907–1987, vol. VIII

Davis, Sir Mortimer Barnett, 1866–1928, vol. II

Davis, Lt-Col Nathaniel N.; *see* Newnham-Davis.

Davis, Rt Rev. Nathaniel William Newnham, 1903–1966, vol. VI

Davis, Nicholas Darnell, 1846–1915, vol. I

Davis, Norman, 1913–1989, vol. VIII

Davis, Hon. Norman H., *died* 1944, vol. IV

Davis, R. Bramwell, 1849–1932, vol. II

Davis, Ralph, 1915–1978, vol. VII

Davis, Richard Harding, 1864–1916, vol. II

Davis, Sir Robert Henry, 1870–1965, vol. VI

Davis, Maj.-Gen. Ronald Albert B.; *see* Bramwell Davis.

Davis, Rushworth Kennard, 1883–1969, vol. VI

Davis, Sir Spencer; *see* Davis, Sir S. S.

Davis, Sir (Steuart) Spencer, 1875–1950, vol. IV

Davis, Hon. Thomas C., 1889–1960, vol. V

Davis, Thomas Frederick, 1891–1974, vol. VII

Davis, Rev. Canon Thomas Henry, 1867–1947, vol. IV

Davis, Val, 1854–1930, vol. III

Davis, Vernon Mansfield, 1855–1931, vol. III

Davis, Major William Hathaway, 1881–1928, vol. II (A), vol. III

Davis, William Morris, 1850–1934, vol. III

Davis, Most Rev. William Wallace, 1908–1987, vol. VIII

Davis, Adm. Sir William Wellclose, 1901–1987, vol. VIII

Davis-Goff, Sir Ernest William; *see* Goff.

Davis-Goff, Sir Herbert William; *see* Goff.

Davis-Goff, Sir William Goff; *see* Goff.

Davison, Archibald Thompson, 1883–1961, vol. VI

Davison, Charles, 1858–1940, vol. III

Davison, Charles Stewart, 1855–1942, vol. IV (A), vol. V

Davison, Major Douglas Stewart, 1888–1929, vol. III

Davison, Frederick Charles, 1851–1935, vol. III

Davison, Rev. Gilderoy, 1892–1954, vol. V

Davison, Mrs J. W.; *see* Goddard, Arabella.

Davison, Sir John Alec B.; *see* Biggs-Davison.

Davison, John Armstrong, 1906–1966, vol. VI

Davison, John Clarke, 1875–1946, vol. IV

Davison, John Emanuel, 1870–1927, vol. II

Davison, Rt Hon. Sir Joseph, 1868–1948, vol. IV

Davison, Maj.-Gen. Kenneth Stewart, 1856–1934, vol. III

Davison, Rev. Leslie, 1906–1972, vol. VII

Davison, Ralph, 1914–1977, vol. VII

Davison, Sir Ronald Conway, 1884–1958, vol. V

Davison, T. Raffles, 1853–1937, vol. III

Davison, Rev. Canon William Holmes, 1884–1955, vol. V

Davison, William Norris, 1919–1986, vol. VIII

Davison, William Theophilus, 1846–1935, vol. III

Davisson, Clinton Joseph, 1881–1958, vol. V

Davitt, Cahir, 1894–1986, vol. VIII

Davitt, Michael, 1846–1906, vol. I

Davray, Henry D., 1873–1944, vol. IV

Davson, Sir Charles Simon, 1857–1933, vol. III

Davson, Sir Edward, 1st Bt, *died* 1937, vol. III

Davson, Lt-Col Harry Miller, 1872–1961, vol. VI

Davson, Sir Henry Katz, 1830–1909, vol. I

Davson, Lt-Col Sir Ivan Buchanan, 1884–1947, vol. IV

Davy, Col Cecil William, 1868–1957, vol. V

Davy, Francis Herbert Mountjoy Nelson H.; *see* Humphrey-Davy.

Davy, Brig. George Mark Oswald, 1898–1983, vol. VIII

Davy, Georges Ambroise, 1883–1976, vol. VII

Davy, Sir Henry, 1855–1922, vol. II

Davy, Sir James Stewart, 1848–1915, vol. I

Davy, Joseph B.; *see* Burtt Davy.

Davy, Lila, 1873–1949, vol. IV

Davy, Maurice John Bernard, 1892–1950, vol. IV

Davy, Lt-Col Philip Claude Tresilian, 1877–1951, vol. V

Davy, Richard, 1838–1920, vol. II

Davy, Sir William, 1863–1939, vol. III

Davys, Rev. Owen William, *died* 1914, vol. I

Daw, Sir John Edward, 1866–1959, vol. V

Daw, Sydney Ernest Henry, 1897–1963, vol. VI

Daw, Sir William Herbert, 1859–1941, vol. IV

Dawbarn, Charles, 1871–1925, vol. II

Dawbarn, Graham Richards, 1893–1976, vol. VII

Dawber, Sir Guy, 1861–1938, vol. III

Dawe, Sir Arthur James, 1891–1950, vol. IV

Dawe, Carlton, *died* 1935, vol. III

Dawes, Sir (Albert) Cecil, 1890–1959, vol. V

Dawes, Sir Cecil; *see* Dawes, Sir A. C.

Dawes, Charles Ambrose William, 1919–1982, vol. VIII

Dawes, Brig.-Gen. Charles Gates, 1865–1951, vol. V

Dawes, Edgar Rowland, 1902–1973, vol. VII

Dawes, Sir Edwyn Sandys, 1838–1903, vol. I

Dawes, Lt-Col George William Patrick, 1880–1960, vol. V

Dawes, Brig. Hugh Frank, 1884–1965, vol. VI

Dawes, James Arthur, 1866–1921, vol. II

Dawes, Rt Rev. Nathaniel, 1843–1910, vol. I

Dawes, William Charles, 1865–1920, vol. II

Dawkins, Lady Bertha Mabel, 1866–1943, vol. IV

Dawkins, Charles John Massey, 1905–1975, vol. VII

Dawkins, Maj.-Gen. Sir Charles Tyrwhitt, 1858–1919, vol. II

Dawkins, Charles William, 1870–1948, vol. IV

Dawkins, Sir Clinton Edward, 1859–1905, vol. I

Dawkins, Brig.-Gen. Henry Stopford, 1856–1933, vol. III

Dawkins, Sir Horace Christian, 1867–1944, vol. IV

Dawkins, Col John Wyndham George, 1861–1913, vol. I

Dawkins, Richard MacGillivray, 1871–1955, vol. V

Dawkins, Sir William Boyd, 1837–1929, vol. III

Dawnay, Col Alan Geoffrey Charles, 1888–1938, vol. III
Dawnay, Sir Archibald Davis, *died* 1919, vol. II
Dawnay, Lt-Col Christopher Payan, 1909–1989, vol. VIII
Dawnay, Lt-Col Cuthbert Henry, 1891–1964, vol. VI
Dawnay, Maj.-Gen. Sir David, 1903–1971, vol. VII
Dawnay, Hon. Eustace Henry, 1850–1928, vol. II (A), vol. III
Dawnay, Hon. George William ffolkes, 1909–1990, vol. VIII
Dawnay, Maj.-Gen. Guy Payan, 1878–1952, vol. V
Dawnay, Major Hon. Hugh, 1875–1914, vol. I
Dawnay, Lt-Col Hon. Lewis Payn, 1846–1910, vol. I
Dawnay, Captain Oliver Payan, 1920–1988, vol. VIII
Dawnay, Vice-Adm. Sir Peter, 1904–1989, vol. VIII
Dawnay, Hon. William Frederick, 1851–1904, vol. I
Dawood, Khan Sahib Sir Adamjee Hajee, *died* 1948, vol. IV
Dawson of Penn, 1st Viscount, 1864–1945, vol. IV
Dawson, A. J., 1872–1951, vol. V
Dawson, Very Rev. Abraham Dawson, 1826–1905, vol. I
Dawson, Aimée Evelyn, (Lady Dawson), *died* 1946, vol. IV
Dawson, Albert, 1866–1930, vol. III
Dawson, Col Algernon Cecil, 1849–1934, vol. III
Dawson, Alistair Benedict, 1922–1978, vol. VII
Dawson, Sir Arthur James, 1859–1943, vol. IV
Dawson, Maj.-Gen. Arthur Peel, 1888–1958, vol. V
Dawson, Sir (Arthur) Trevor, 1st Bt (*cr* 1920), 1866–1931, vol. III
Dawson, Sir Benajmin, 1st Bt (*cr* 1929), 1878–1966, vol. VI
Dawson, Sir Bernard; *see* Dawson, Sir J. B.
Dawson, Christopher, 1889–1970, vol. VI
Dawson, Christopher William, 1896–1983, vol. VIII
Dawson, Coningsby, 1883–1959, vol. V
Dawson, Brig.-Gen. Sir Douglas Frederick Rawdon, 1854–1933, vol. III
Dawson, Hon. Edward Stanley, 1843–1919, vol. II
Dawson, Rev. Edwin Collas, *died* 1925, vol. II
Dawson, Gen. Francis, 1827–1911, vol. I
Dawson, Captain Francis Evelyn M.; *see* Massy-Dawson.
Dawson, Frank Harold, 1896–1972, vol. VII
Dawson, Lt-Col Frederick Stewart, *died* 1920, vol. II
Dawson, Geoffrey, 1874–1944, vol. IV
Dawson, George Mercer, 1849–1901, vol. I
Dawson, George W., 1868–1959, vol. V
Dawson, Air Vice-Marshal Grahame George, *died* 1944, vol. IV
Dawson, Col Harry Leonard, 1854–1920, vol. II
Dawson, Harry Medforth, 1875–1939, vol. III
Dawson, Lt-Col Henry King, 1871–1941, vol. IV
Dawson, Sir (Hugh Halliday) Trevor, 3rd Bt (*cr* 1920), 1931–1983, vol. VIII
Dawson, Comdr Sir Hugh Trevor, 2nd Bt (*cr* 1920), 1893–1976, vol. VII
Dawson, Hugh W., *died* 1939, vol. III
Dawson, James Alexander, 1880–1956, vol. V
Dawson, James Lawrence, 1924–1984, vol. VIII
Dawson, Rev. James Edward le Strange, 1853–1930, vol. III

Dawson, John Alexander, 1886–1985, vol. VIII
Dawson, John Miles, 1871–1948, vol. IV
Dawson, Sir John William, 1820–1899, vol. I
Dawson, Sir (Joseph) Bernard, 1883–1965, vol. VI
Dawson, (Sir) Lawrence Saville, 2nd Bt (*cr* 1929), 1908–1974, vol. VII
Dawson, Lucy, *died* 1958, vol. V
Dawson, M. Damer, 1875–1920, vol. II
Dawson, Nelson, *died* 1941, vol. IV
Dawson, Rear-Adm. Sir Oswald Henry, 1882–1950, vol. IV
Dawson, Peter, 1882–1961, vol. VI
Dawson, Sir Philip, *died* 1938, vol. III
Dawson, Richard Cecil, 1865–1955, vol. V
Dawson, Brig.-Gen. Robert, 1861–1930, vol. III
Dawson, Robert Arthur, *died* 1948, vol. IV
Dawson, Maj.-Gen. Robert Boyd, 1916–1977, vol. VII
Dawson, Robert MacGregor, 1895–1958, vol. V
Dawson, Col Rupert George, 1887–1975, vol. VII
Dawson, Sidney Stanley, *died* 1926, vol. II
Dawson, Lt-Col Thomas Henry, 1878–1956, vol. V
Dawson, Sir Trevor; *see* Dawson, Sir A. T.
Dawson, Sir Trevor; *see* Dawson, Sir H. H. T.
Dawson, Sir Vernon, 1881–1958, vol. V
Dawson, Maj.-Gen. Vesey John, 1853–1930, vol. III
Dawson, Warren Royal, 1888–1968, vol. VI
Dawson, Warrington, 1878–1962, vol. VI
Dawson, Wilfred, 1923–1984, vol. VIII
Dawson, Comdr William, 1831–1911, vol. I
Dawson, William Harbutt, 1860–1948, vol. IV
Dawson, Rev. William James, 1854–1928, vol. II
Dawson, William Richard, 1864–1950, vol. IV
Dawson, Major William Robert Aufrère, 1891–1918, vol. II
Dawson, Rev. Canon William Rodgers, 1871–1936, vol. III
Dawson, William Siegfried, 1891–1975, vol. VII
Dawson Scott, Catharine Amy, *died* 1934, vol. III
Dawson-Scott, Gen. Robert Nicholl, 1836–1922, vol. II
Dawson-Walker, Rev. Dawson, 1868–1934, vol. III
Day, Sir (Albert) Cecil, 1885–1963, vol. VI
Day, Sir Albert James Taylor, 1892–1972, vol. VII
Day, Rev. Alfred E. Bloxsome, 1873–1951, vol. V
Day, Vice-Adm. Sir Archibald, 1899–1970, vol. VI
Day, Bernard, *died* 1952, vol. V
Day, Sir Cecil; *see* Day, Sir A. C.
Day, Charles, 1868–1949, vol. IV
Day, Rev. Charles V. P., 1864–1922, vol. II
Day, Clive, 1871–1951, vol. V
Day, Edith, 1896–1971, vol. VII
Day, Edmund Ezra, 1883–1951, vol. V
Day, Rev. Edward Rouviere, 1867–1948, vol. IV
Day, Edward Victor Grace, 1896–1968, vol. VI
Day, Rev. Ernest Hermitage, 1866–1946, vol. IV
Day, Frank Parker, 1881–1950, vol. IV (A)
Day, Harold Benjamin, 1880–1959, vol. V
Day, Col Harry, 1880–1939, vol. III
Day, Rev. Henry, 1865–1951, vol. V
Day, Rt Rev. Mgr James, 1869–1946, vol. IV
Day, James Nathaniel Da' Russell, 1849–1933, vol. III
Day, James Roscoe, *died* 1923, vol. II

Day, James Wentworth, 1899–1983, vol. VIII
Day, John Adam, 1901–1966, vol. VI
Day, Rt Hon. Sir John Charles, 1826–1908, vol. I
Day, Rev. John Duncan, 1882–1954, vol. V
Day, Most Rev. John Godfrey Fitzmaurice, 1874–1938, vol. III
Day, Lewis Foreman, 1845–1910, vol. I
Day, Rev. Louis Ernest, 1866–1935, vol. III
Day, Margaret; *see* Lockwood, M. M.
Day, Rt Rev. Maurice, 1843–1923, vol. II
Day, Rt Rev. Maurice FitzGerald, 1816–1904, vol. I
Day, Col Maurice Fitzmaurice, *died* 1952, vol. V
Day, Very Rev. Maurice William, 1858–1916, vol. II
Day, Lt-Col Noel Arthur Lacy, 1882–1932, vol. III
Day, Samuel Henry, 1854–1944, vol. IV
Day, Captain Selwyn Mitchell, 1873–1938, vol. III
Day, Theodora, *died* 1976, vol. VII
Day, W. Cave, 1862–1924, vol. II
Day-Lewis, Cecil, 1904–1972, vol. VII
Daymond, Douglas Godfrey, 1917–1990, vol. VIII
Daynes, John Norman, 1884–1966, vol. VI
Dayrell, Elphinstone, 1869–1917, vol. II
Daysh, George Henry John, 1901–1987, vol. VIII
Deacon, Rev. Alfred Wranius Newport, 1847–1915, vol. I
Deacon, Lt-Col Edmund Henry, 1902–1982, vol. VIII
Deacon, Sir George Edward Raven, 1906–1984, vol. VIII
Deacon, George Frederick, 1843–1909, vol. I
Deacon, Gerald John C.; *see* Cole-Deacon.
Deacon, Sir Henry Wade, 1852–1932, vol. III
Deacon, John Francis William, 1859–1941, vol. IV
Deacon, Stuart, 1868–1947, vol. IV
Deacon, Walter, *died* 1955, vol. V
Deacon, Col William Thomas, 1850–1916, vol. II (A), vol. III
Deadman, H. E., 1843–1925, vol. II
Deadman, Ronald Thomas A., 1919–1988, vol. VIII
Deakin, Hon. Alfred, 1856–1919, vol. II
Deakin, Rt Hon. Arthur, 1890–1955, vol. V
Deakin, Ralph, 1888–1952, vol. V
Deakin, Rt Rev. Thomas Carlyle Joseph Robert Hamish, 1917–1985, vol. VIII
Dealtry, Lawrence Percival, 1896–1963, vol. VI
Dealy, Jane M.; *see* Lewis, Jane.
Dealy, Brig.-Gen. John Anderson, 1865–1935, vol. III
De Amicis, Edmondo, 1846–1908, vol. I
Dean, Arthur, 1903–1968, vol. VI
Dean, Hon. Sir Arthur, 1893–1970, vol. VI
Dean, Arthur Edis, 1883–1961, vol. VI
Dean, Arthur Wellesley, 1857–1929, vol. III
Dean, Sir Arthur William Henry, 1892–1976, vol. VII
Dean, Barbara Florence, 1924–1989, vol. VIII
Dean, Bashford, 1867–1928, vol. II
Dean, Basil, 1888–1978, vol. VII
Dean, Comdr Brian, 1895–1976, vol. VII
Dean, Col Donald John, 1897–1985, vol. VIII
Dean, Engr Rear-Adm. Francis Edward, 1881–1965, vol. VI
Dean, Frederic William Charles, 1867–1942, vol. IV
Dean, Frederick William, 1884–1959, vol. V
Dean, George, 1863–1914, vol. I
Dean, Brig.-Gen. George Henry, 1859–1953, vol. V

Dean, Gertrude Mary, 1878–1962, vol. VI
Dean, Gordon Evans, 1905–1958, vol. V
Dean, Henry Edwin, 1881–1973, vol. VII
Dean, Henry Percy, *died* 1931, vol. III
Dean, Henry Roy, 1879–1961, vol. VI
Dean, Herbert Samuel, 1870–1942, vol. IV
Dean, Sir John Norman, 1899–1988, vol. VIII
Dean, Sir Maurice Joseph, 1906–1978, vol. VII
Dean, Lt-Comdr Percy Thompson, 1877–1939, vol. III
Dean, Rt Rev. Ralph Stanley, 1913–1987, vol. VIII
Dean, William John Lyon, 1911–1990, vol. VIII
Dean, William Reginald, 1896–1973, vol. VII
Dean-Leslie, John, 1860–1946, vol. IV
Deane, Rev. Anthony Charles, 1870–1946, vol. IV
Deane, Rev. Canon Arthur Mackreth, 1837–1926, vol. II
Deane, Augustus Henry, 1851–1928, vol. II
Deane, Maj.-Gen. Sir Dennis, 1874–1953, vol. V
Deane, Major Donald Victor, 1902–1978, vol. VII
Deane, Edgar Ernest, 1860–1933, vol. III
Deane, Rt Rev. Frederic Llewellyn, 1868–1952, vol. V
Deane, Sir George Campbell, 1873–1948, vol. IV (A), vol. V
Deane, Col George Williams, 1850–1931, vol. III
Deane, Lt-Col Sir Harold Arthur, 1854–1908, vol. I
Deane, Sir Henry Bargrave, 1846–1919, vol. II
Deane, Hermann Frederick Williams, 1858–1921, vol. II
Deane, Major James, 1863–1942, vol. IV
Deane, Rt Hon. Sir James Parker, 1812–1902, vol. I
Deane, Nora Bryan, 1902–1973, vol. VII
Deane, Percy Edgar, 1890–1946, vol. IV
Deane, Captain Richard Burton, 1848–1930, vol. III
Deane, Col Richard Woodforde, 1859–1940, vol. III
Deane, Lt-Col Robert, 1879–1969, vol. VI
Deane, Col Thomas, 1841–1907, vol. I
Deane, Sir Thomas Manly, 1851–1933, vol. III
Deane, Sir Thomas Newenham, 1830–1899, vol. I
Deane, Walter Meredith, 1840–1906, vol. I
Deane, William, 1894–1972, vol. VII
Deanesly, Margaret, 1885–1977, vol. VII
Deans, Harris, 1886–1961, vol. VI
Deans, Richard Storry, *died* 1938, vol. III
Deans, Engr-Rear-Adm. William Jordan, *died* 1947, vol. IV
Dearbergh, Geoffrey Frederick, 1924–1979, vol. VII
Dearden, Harold, 1883–1962, vol. VI
Deare, Maj.-Gen. Benjamin Hobbs, 1867–1940, vol. III
Deare, Ronald Frank Robert, 1927–1989, vol. VIII
Dearing, George Edmund, 1911–1968, vol. VI
Dearlove, Rev. William John, 1869–1935, vol. III
Dearmer, Mabel, 1872–1915, vol. I
Dearmer, Rev. Percy, 1867–1936, vol. III
Dearnley, Gertrude, 1884–1982, vol. VIII
Deas, J. A. Charlton, 1874–1951, vol. V
Deas, (James) Stewart, 1903–1985, vol. VIII
Deas, Stewart; *see* Deas, J. S.
Dease, Edmund Gerald, 1829–1904, vol. I
Dease, Major Edmund J., 1861–1945, vol. IV
Dease, Col Sir Gerald Richard, 1831–1903, vol. I
Deasy, Major Henry Hugh Peter, 1866–1947, vol. IV

De'Ath, Lt-Col Ian Dudley, 1918–1960, vol. V

De Azcarate, Pablo; *see* Azcarate.

De Bathe, Sir Christopher Albert, 6th Bt, 1905–1941, vol. IV

De Bathe, Gen. Sir Henry Perceval, 4th Bt, 1823–1907, vol. I

De Bathe, Sir Hugo Gerald, 5th Bt, 1871–1940, vol. III

De Bathe, Patrick Wynne, 1876–1930, vol. III

de Bazus, Baroness; *see* Leslie, Mrs Frank.

de Beauvoir, Simone Lucie Ernestine Marie Bertrand; *see* Beauvoir.

de Beer, Esmond Samuel, 1895–1990, vol. VIII

de Beer, Sir Gavin Rylands, 1899–1972, vol. VII

de Belabre, Louis Fradin, Baron, 1862–1945, vol. IV

Debenham, Sir Ernest Ridley, 1st Bt, 1865–1952, vol. V

Debenham, Frank, 1883–1965, vol. VI

Debenham, Sir Piers Kenrick, 2nd Bt, 1904–1964, vol. VI

De Bernochi, Francesco, 1887–1962, vol. VI

de Berry, Brig.-Gen. Philip Patrick Evelyn, 1872–1938, vol. III

De Bildt, Baron, 1850–1931, vol. III

de Blank, Most Rev. Joost, 1908–1968, vol. VI

de Blaquiere, 6th Baron, 1856–1920, vol. II

de Blogue, Rev. Oswald William Charles, 1874–1959, vol. V

de Boer, Henry Speldewinde, 1889–1957, vol. V

De Boinville, Rev. Basil William C.; *see* Chastel De Boinville.

Debono, Massimiliano, 1852–1932, vol. III

De Boucherville, Hon. Sir Charles Eugene Boucher, 1822–1915, vol. I

de Brath, Lt-Gen. Sir Ernest, 1858–1933, vol. III

de Brett, Hon. Brig.-Gen. Harry Simonds, 1870–1965, vol. VI

De Brigard, Camilo, 1906–1972, vol. VII

de Broglie, 7th Duc, 1892–1987, vol. VIII

de Bruyne, Pieter Louis; *see* Bruyne.

De Bucy, 11th Marquess, 1864–1929, vol. III

de Bunsen, Sir Bernard, 1907–1990, vol. VIII

de Bunsen, Rt Hon. Sir Maurice William Ernest, 1st Bt, 1852–1932, vol. III

de Burgh, Captain Charles, 1886–1973, vol. VII

de Burgh, Gen. Sir Eric, 1881–1973, vol. VII

de Burgh, Lt-Col Thomas John, 1851–1931, vol. III

de Burgh, Col Ulick George Campbell, 1855–1922, vol. II

de Burgh, William George, 1866–1943, vol. IV

Debus, Heinrich, 1824–1915, vol. I

Debussy, Claude Achille, 1862–1918, vol. II

De Butts, Brig. Frederick Cromie, 1888–1977, vol. VII

Debye, Peter Joseph William, 1884–1966, vol. VI

de Candole, Eric Armar Vully, 1901–1989, vol. VIII

de Candole, Rt Rev. Henry Handley Vully, 1895–1971, vol. VII

de Candole, Very Rev. Henry Lawe Corry Vully, 1868–1933, vol. III

de Candolle, Maj.-Gen. Raymond, *died* 1935, vol. III

de Capell Brooke, Sir Edward Geoffrey, 6th Bt, 1880–1968, vol. VI

Decarie, Hon. Jeremie L., 1870–1927, vol. II

de Carteret, Rt Rev. George Frederick Cecil, 1886–1932, vol. III

de Carteret, Samuel Laurence, 1885–1956, vol. V

De Celles, Alfred Duclos, 1844–1925, vol. II

de Chair, Adm. Sir Dudley Rawson Stratford, 1864–1958, vol. V

de Chair, Rev. Frederick Blackett, 1888–1932, vol. III

Dechamps, Jules, 1888–1968, vol. VI

de Chazal, Hon. Pierre Edmond, 1837–1914, vol. I

Dechene, Hon. F. G. M., *died* 1902, vol. I

Decie, Brig.-Gen. Cyril Prescott-, 1865–1953, vol. V

Decies, 4th Baron, 1865–1910, vol. I

Decies, 5th Baron, 1866–1944, vol. IV

de Clifford, 25th Baron, 1884–1909, vol. I

de Clifford, 26th Baron, 1907–1982, vol. VIII

de Colyar, Henry Anselm, *died* 1925, vol. II

de Comarmond, Sir Joseph Henri Maxime, 1899–1957, vol. V

Decoppet, Camille, 1862–1925, vol. II

de Cordova, Rudolph, *died* 1941, vol. IV

de Courcy-Ireland, Lt-Col Gerald Blakeney, 1895–1986, vol. VIII

de Courcy-Perry, Sir Gerald Raoul, 1836–1903, vol. I

De Courville, Albert Pierre, (Albert Peter Hugh), 1887–1960, vol. V

de Crespigny, Captain Claude C.; *see* Champion de Crespigny.

de Crespigny, Sir Claude C.; *see* Champion de Crespigny.

de Crespigny, Brig.-Gen. Sir Claude Raul C.; *see* Champion de Crespigny.

de Crespigny, Col Sir (Constantine) Trent C.; *see* Champion-de Crespigny.

de Crespigny, Comdr Sir Frederick Philip C.; *see* Champion de Crespigny.

de Crespigny, Lt-Col George Harrison C.; *see* Champion de Crespigny.

de Crespigny, Sir Henry C.; *see* Champion de Crespigny.

de Crespigny, Air Vice-Marshal Hugh Vivian C.; *see* Champion de Crespigny.

de Crespigny, Rose C.; *see* Champion de Crespigny.

de Crespigny, Col Sir Trent C.; *see* Champion-de Crespigny.

de Crespigny, Sir Vivian Tyrell C.; *see* Champion de Crespigny.

De Curel, Viscomte François, 1854–1928, vol. II

Dedijer, Vladimir, 1914–1990, vol. VIII

Dee, Philip Ivor, 1904–1983, vol. VIII

Deed, Rev. Canon John George, 1842–1923, vol. II

Deedes, Rev. Arthur Gordon, 1861–1916, vol. II

Deedes, Ven. Brook, 1847–1922, vol. II

Deedes, Rev. Cecil, 1843–1920, vol. II

Deedes, Gen. Sir Charles Parker, 1879–1969, vol. VI

Deedes, John Gordon, 1892–1962, vol. VI

Deedes, Percy Gordon, 1899–1973, vol. VII

Deedes, Lt-Gen. Sir Ralph Bouverie, 1890–1954, vol. V

Deedes, Maj.-Gen. William Henry, 1839–1915, vol. I

Deedes, Brig.-Gen. Sir Wyndham Henry, 1883–1956, vol. V

Deeley, Sir Anthony Meyrick M.; *see* Mallaby-Deeley.

Deeley, Sir Guy Meyrick Mallaby M.; *see* Mallaby-Deeley.

Deeley, Sir Harry Mallaby M.; *see* Mallaby-Deeley.

Deeping, (George) Warwick, *died* 1950, vol. IV

Deeping, Warwick; *see* Deeping, G. W.

Deer, George, 1890–1974, vol. VI

Deer, Mrs Olive Gertrude, 1897–1983, vol. VIII

Deerhurst, Viscount; George William Coventry, 1865–1928, vol. II

Deering, William Henry, 1848–1925, vol. II

Deeves, Thomas William, 1893–1977, vol. VII

De Falbe, Brig. Gen. Vigant William, 1867–1940, vol. III

De Falla, Manuel, 1876–1946, vol. IV

de Ferranti, Basil Reginald Vincent Ziani, 1930–1988, vol. VIII

de Ferranti, Sebastian Ziani, 1864–1930, vol. III

de Ferranti, Sir Vincent Ziani, 1893–1980, vol. VII

De Ferrieres, 3rd Baron, 1823–1908, vol. I

Defferre, Gaston, 1910–1986, vol. VIII

De Filippi, Cav. Filippo, 1869–1938, vol. III

de Fischer-Reichenbach, Henry-Béat, 1901–1984, vol. VIII

de Fonblanque, Maj.-Gen. Edward Barrington, 1895–1981, vol. VIII

de Fonblanque, Maj.-Gen. Philip, 1885–1940, vol. III

De Fonseka, Sir (Deepal) Susanta, 1900–1963, vol. VI

De Fonseka, Sir Susanta; *see* De Fonseka, Sir D. S.

De Foville, Alfred, 1842–1913, vol. I

de Frece, Lady; *see* Tilley, Vesta.

de Frece, Sir Walter, 1870–1935, vol. III

De Freitas, Sir Anthony, 1869–1940, vol. III

de Freitas, Rt Hon. Sir Geoffrey Stanley, 1913–1982, vol. VIII

de Freitas-Cruz, Jono Carlos Lopes Cardoso, *born* 1925, vol. VIII

De Freycinet, C. L., 1828–1923, vol. II

De Freyne, 4th Baron, 1855–1913, vol. I

De Freyne, 5th Baron, 1879–1915, vol. I

De Freyne, 6th Baron, 1884–1935, vol. III

Degacher, Maj.-Gen. Henry James, 1835–1902, vol. I

de Gale, Hugh Otway, 1891–1966, vol. VI

de Gale, Sir Leo Victor, 1921–1986, vol. VIII

De Garston, Edward Mervyn, 1869–1939, vol. III

Degas, Hilaire Germain Edgard, 1834–1917, vol. II

De Gasperi, Alcide, 1881–1954, vol. V

de Gaulle, Gén. Charles André Joseph Marie, 1890–1970, vol. VI

De Geer, Baron Gerard, 1858–1943, vol. IV

De Gerlache De Gomery, Baron, 1866–1934, vol. III

de Gex, Col Francis John, 1861–1917, vol. II

de Gex, Maj.-Gen. George Francis, 1911–1986, vol. VIII

De Giberne, Agnes; *see* Giberne, Agnes.

De Glanville, Sir Oscar James Lardner, *died* 1942, vol. IV (A), vol. V

De Glehn, Wilfrid Gabriel, 1870–1951, vol. V

De Greef, Arthur, 1862–1940, vol. III (A), vol. IV

de Grey, Nigel, 1886–1951, vol. V

de Grunwald, Anatole, 1910–1967, vol. VI

De Gruyther, Leslie, *died* 1937, vol. III

de Guingand, Maj.-Gen. Sir Francis Wilfred, 1900–1979, vol. VII

de Guiringaud, Louis; *see* Guiringaud.

d'Egville, Major Alan Hervey, 1891–1951, vol. V

d'Egville, Sir Howard, *died* 1965, vol. VI

de Gylpyn, Very Rev. Edwin, 1821–1906, vol. I

de Haan, Edward Peter Nayler, 1919–1977, vol. VII

de Haas, Wander Johannes, 1878–1960, vol. V

Dehan, Richard; *see* Graves, Clotilde I. M.

de Havilland, Captain Sir Geoffrey, 1882–1965, vol. VI

de Havilland, Maj.-Gen. Peter Hugh, 1904–1989, vol. VIII

de Havilland, Col Thomas Lyttleton, 1872–1939, vol. III

Dehlavi, Sir Ali Mahomed Khan, 1871–1952, vol. V

Dehlavi, Samiulla Khan, 1913–1976, vol. VII

Dehn, Adolf Arthur, 1895–1968, vol. VI

Dehn, Paul Edward, 1912–1976, vol. VII

de Hochepied, 10th Baron, 1900–1945, vol. IV

de Hochepied Larpent, Maj.-Gen. Lionel Henry Planta, 1834–1907, vol. I

de Hoghton, Sir Anthony; *see* de Hoghton, Sir H. P. A. M.

de Hoghton, Sir Cuthbert, 12th Bt, 1880–1958, vol. V

de Hoghton, Sir (Henry Philip) Anthony (Mary), 13th Bt, 1919–1978, vol. VII

de Hoghton, Sir James, 11th Bt, 1851–1938, vol. III

de Horsey, Adm. Sir Algernon Frederick Rous, 1827–1922, vol. II

de Horsey, Adm. Spencer, 1863–1937, vol. III

De Horsey, Lt-Gen. William Henry Beaumont, 1826–1915, vol. I

Deichmann, Baron Adolph Wilhelm, 1831–1907, vol. I

Deighton, Frederick, 1854–1924, vol. II

de Jersey, Rear-Adm. Gilbert Carey, 1905–1974, vol. VII

de Jersey, Rt Rev. Norman Stewart, 1866–1934, vol. III

De Jersey, Col William Grant, 1853–1935, vol. III

de Joux, Lt-Col John Sedley Newton, 1876–1949, vol. IV

De Kalb, Courtenay, 1861–1931, vol. III

de Kantzow, Comdr Arthur Henry, *died* 1928, vol. II

de Kerillis, Henri, 1889–1958, vol. V

De Keyser, Sir Polydore, 1832–1897, vol. I

Dekobra, Maurice, 1885–1973, vol. VII

de la Bedoyere, Count Michael, 1900–1973, vol. VII

De la Bere, Henry D., 1861–1937, vol. III

De La Bere, Brig. Sir Ivan, 1893–1970, vol. VI

de la Bere, Captain Richard Norman, 1869–1922, vol. II

De la Bère, Sir Rupert, 1st Bt, 1893–1978, vol. VII

de la Bere, Stephen B.; *see* Baghot de la Bere.

de Labilliere, Rt Rev. Paul Fulcrand Delacour, 1879–1946, vol. IV

Delacombe, Lt-Col Addis, 1865–1941, vol. IV

Delacourt-Smith, Baron (Life Peer); Charles George Percy Smith, 1917–1972, vol. VII

de Lacretelle, Jacques, 1888–1985, vol. VIII

Delafaye, Sir Louis Victor, 1842–1920, vol. II

de la Ferte, Air Chief Marshal Sir Philip Bennet J.; *see* Joubert de la Ferte.

Delafield, E. M.; *see* Dashwood, Elizabeth M.

Delafield, Max Everard, 1886–1974, vol. VII

de Lafontaine, Lt-Col Henry Philip L. C.; *see* Cart de Lafontaine.

Delaforce, Brig.-Gen. Edwin Francis, 1870–1954, vol. V

de La Fosse, Sir Claude Fraser, 1868–1950, vol. IV

de La Fosse, Maj.-Gen. Henry George, 1835–1905, vol. I

Delage, Hon. Cyrille Fraser, 1869–1957, vol. V

Delage, Yves, 1854–1920, vol. II

De la Gorce, Pierre, 1846–1934, vol. III

Delahaye, Col James Viner, 1890–1948, vol. IV

de la Hey, Rev. Richard Willis, 1872–1942, vol. IV

Delalle, Rt Rev. Henry, 1869–1949, vol. IV

Delamain, Lt-Gen. Sir Walter Sinclair, 1862–1932, vol. III

de la Mare, Peter Bernard David, 1920–1989, vol. VIII

de la Mare, Richard Herbert Ingpen, 1901–1986, vol. VIII

De La Mare, Walter, 1873–1956, vol. V

Delamere, 3rd Baron, 1870–1931, vol. III

Delamere, 4th Baron, 1900–1979, vol. VII

De La Mothe, Sir Joseph Terence, 1876–1953, vol. V

Delamothe, Hon. Sir Peter Roylance, 1906–1973, vol. VII

De Lancey Forth, Lt-Col Nowell Barnard, 1879–1933, vol. III

Deland, Margaret, 1857–1945, vol. IV

Delaney, Colin John, 1897–1969, vol. VI (AII)

De Laney, Brig.-Gen. Matthew A., 1874–1936, vol. III

de Lange, Daniel, 1841–1918, vol. II

Delano, William Adams, 1874–1960, vol. V

Delano-Osborne, Maj.-Gen. Osborne Herbert, 1879–1958, vol. V

Delany, Mgr Patrick, 1853–1926, vol. II

Delany, Rev. William, 1835–1924, vol. II

Delany, William P., 1855–1916, vol. II

Delap, Rev. Alexander, *died* 1906, vol. I

Delap, Col George Goslett, 1873–1945, vol. IV

de la Pasture, Elizabeth Lydia Rosabelle, (Mrs Henry de la Pasture); *see* Clifford, E. L. R.

de la Poer, Edmond, 1841–1915, vol. I

de la Poer, John William Rivallon de Poher, 1882–1939, vol. III

De la Pryme, Ven. Alexander George, 1870–1935, vol. III

de Lara, Adelina, (Lottie Adelina de Lara Shipwright), 1872–1961, vol. VI

De Lara, Isidore, 1858–1935, vol. III

de la Ramée, Marie Louise; *see* Ouida.

Delarey, Gen. Hon. Jacobus Hendrik, 1848–1914, vol. I

Delargey, His Eminence Cardinal Reginald John, 1914–1979, vol. VII

de Largie, Hon. Hugh, 1859–1947, vol. IV

Delargy, Captain Hugh James, 1908–1976, vol. VII

de la Roche, Mazo, 1885–1961, vol. VI

de la Rue, Sir Eric Vincent, 3rd Bt, 1906–1989, vol. VIII

de la Rue, Sir Ernest, 1852–1929, vol. III

de la Rue, Sir Evelyn Andros, 2nd Bt, 1879–1950, vol. IV

de la Rue, Stuart Andros, 1883-1927, vol. II

de la Rue, Sir Thomas Andros, 1st Bt, 1849–1911, vol. I

de la Rue, Warren William, 1847–1921, vol. II

de Laszlo, Patrick David, 1909–1980, vol. VII

de Laszowska, (Jane) Emily; *see* Gerard, J. E.

de Lattre de Tassigny, Général d'Armée Jean Joseph Marie Gabriel, 1889–1952, vol. V

de Lavis-Trafford, Marcus Antonius Johnston, 1880–1960, vol. V

De la Voye, Brig.-Gen. Alexander Edwin, 1871–1940, vol. III

Delavoye, Col Alexander Marin, 1845–1917, vol. II

De La Warr, 8th Earl, 1869–1915, vol. I

De La Warr, 9th Earl, 1900–1976, vol. VII

De La Warr, 10th Earl, 1921–1988, vol. VIII

Delay, Jean, 1907–1987, vol. VIII

Delbridge, Rt Rev. Graham Richard, 1917–1980, vol. VII

Delbrück, Max, 1906–1981, vol. VIII

Delcasse, Théephile, 1852–1923, vol. II

Delderfield, Ronald Frederick, 1912–1972, vol. VII

Deledda, Grazia, 1875–1936, vol. III

De Lemos, Charles Herman, 1855–1928, vol. II (A), vol. III

Delepine, Sheridan, 1855–1921, vol. II

Delevingne, Sir Malcolm, 1868–1950, vol. IV

De L'Hôpital, René le Brun (Count), 1877–1929, vol. III

De L'Isle and Dudley, 2nd Baron, 1828–1898, vol. I

De L'Isle and Dudley, 3rd Baron, 1853–1922, vol. II

De L'Isle and Dudley, 4th Baron, 1854–1945, vol. IV

De L'Isle and Dudley, 5th Baron, 1859–1945, vol. IV

de Lisle, Gen. Sir Beauvoir, 1864–1955, vol. V

de Lisle, Edwin Joseph Lisle March Phillipps, 1852–1920, vol. II

de Lisle, Everard March Phillipps, *died* 1947, vol. IV

De Lisle, Brig.-Gen. George de Saumarez, 1862–1954, vol. V

De Lisle, Leopold Victor, 1826–1910, vol. I

de Lisser, Herbert George, 1878–1944, vol. IV

Delius, Frederick, 1862–1934, vol. III

Dell, Draycot Montagu, 1888–1940, vol. III

Dell, Ethel Mary, 1881–1939, vol. III

Della Taflia, Marchioness, *died* 1953, vol. V

Della Torre Alta, Il Marchese Albert Félix Schmitt, 1873–1954, vol. V

Deller, Alfred, 1912–1979, vol. VII

Deller, Sir Edwin, 1883–1936, vol. III

Deller, Captain Harold Arthur, 1897–1976, vol. VII

Delme-Radcliffe, Brig.-Gen. Sir Charles, 1864–1937, vol. III

Delme-Radcliffe, Sir Ralph Hubert John, 1877–1963, vol. VI

Delmege, Alfred Gideon, 1846–1923, vol. II

Delmer, (Denis) Sefton, 1904–1979, vol. VII

Delmer, Sefton; *see* Delmer, D. S.

de Longueuil, 8th Baron, 1856–1931, vol. III

de Longueuil, 9th Baron, 1861–1938, vol. III

De Lotbinière, Maj.-Gen. Alain Chartier Joly; *see* Joly De Lotbinière.

de Lotbinière, Brig.-Gen. Henri Gustave J.; *see* Joly de Lotbinière.

de Lotbinière, Hon. Sir Henry Gustave J.; *see* Joly de Lotbinière.

de Lotbinière, Seymour Joly, 1905–1984, vol. VIII
de Lotbiniere-Harwood, Charles Auguste; see Harwood.
de Loynes, John Barraclough, 1909–1969, vol. VI
Delpech, Reginald George Marius, 1881–1935, vol. III
Delprat, Guillaume Daniel, 1856–1937, vol. III
del Re, Cavaliere Arundel, 1892–1974, vol. VII
del Riego, Teresa, 1876–1968, vol. VI
del Tufo, Sir (Moroböe) Vincent, 1901–1961, vol. VI
Delury, Justin Sarsfield, 1884–1968, vol. VI
Delves, Robert Harvey Addington, 1873–1952, vol. V
Delysia, Alice, 1889–1979, vol. VII
de Manio, Jack, 1914–1988, vol. VIII
Demant, Rev. Vigo Auguste, 1893–1983, vol. VIII
de Marees-Van Swinderen, Jonkheer Rene; see Van Swinderen.
de Margerie, Emmanuel, 1862–1953, vol. V
de Margerie, Pierre, 1861–1942, vol. IV
de Margerie, Roland Jacquin, 1899–1990, vol. VIII
de Mauley, 3rd Baron, 1843–1918, vol. II
de Mauley, 4th Baron, 1846–1945, vol. IV
de Mauley, 5th Baron, 1878–1962, vol. VI
De Mel, Sir Henry Lawson, 1877–1936, vol. III
De Mel, Most Rev. (Hiyanirindu) Lakdasa Jacob, 1902–1976, vol. VII
De Mel, Most Rev. Lakdasa Jacob; see De Mel, Most Rev. H. L. J.
de Mendieta, Rev. Emmanuel Alexandre A.; see Amand de Mendieta.
de Meric, Rear-Adm. Martin John Coucher, 1887–1943, vol. IV
Demers, Marie Joseph, 1871–1940, vol. III (A), vol. IV
Demetriadi, Sir Stephen, 1880–1952, vol. V
deMille, Cecil Blount, 1881–1959, vol. V
de Miranda, Comtesse; see Nilsson, Mme Christine.
De Mole, Lancelot Eldin, 1880–1950, vol. IV
de Moleyns, Thomas, 1807–1900, vol. I
de Moleyns, Maj.-Gen. Townsend Aremberg, 1838–1926, vol. II
de Montalt, 1st Earl, 1817–1905, vol. I
de Monte, Frank Thomas, 1879–1950, vol. IV
de Montherlant, Henry; see Montherlant.
de Montmorency, Sir Angus; see de Montmorency, Sir H. A.
de Montmorency, Hon. Francis Raymond, 1835–1910, vol. I
de Montmorency, Sir Geoffrey Fitzhervey, 1876–1955, vol. V
de Montmorency, Sir (Hervey) Angus, 16th Bt, 1888–1959, vol. V
de Montmorency, Major Hervey Guy Francis Edward, 1868–1942, vol. IV
de Montmorency, James Edward Geoffrey, 1866–1934, vol. III
De Montmorency, Captain John Pratt, 1873–1960, vol. V
de Montmorency, Sir Miles Fletcher, 17th Bt, 1893–1963, vol. VI
de Montmorency, Hon. Raymond Hervey, 1867–1900, vol. I
de Montmorency, Sir Reginald D'Alton Lodge, 18th Bt, 1899–1979, vol. VII

de Montmorency, Reymond Hervey, 1871–1938, vol. III
de Montmorency, Ven. Waller, 1841–1924, vol. II
De Morgan, William Frend, 1839–1917, vol. II
de Morley, 21st Baron, 1844–1918, vol. II
de Mourgues, Odette Marie Hélène Louise, 1914–1988, vol. VIII
Dempsey, Sir Alexander, 1852–1920, vol. II
Dempsey, James, 1917–1982, vol. VIII
Dempsey, Gen. Sir Miles Christopher, 1896–1969, vol. VI
Dempster, Francis Erskine, 1858–1941, vol. IV
Dempster, Col Reginald Hawkins H.; see Hall-Dempster.
Denbigh, 9th Earl of, and Desmond, 8th Earl of, 1859–1939, vol. III
Denbigh, 10th Earl of, and Desmond, 9th Earl of, 1912–1966, vol. VI
Denby, Elizabeth Marian, died 1965, vol. VI
Denby, Sir Ellis, 1856–1939, vol. III
Denby, Sir Richard Kenneth, 1915–1986, vol. VIII
Dence, Ernest Martin, 1873–1937, vol. III
Dench, William George, 1888–1963, vol. VI
Dendy, Arthur, 1865–1925, vol. II
Dendy, Edward Evershed, 1861–1929, vol. III
Dendy, Mary, 1855–1933, vol. III
Dendy, Brig. Murray Heathfield, 1885–1951, vol. V
Dene, Col Arthur Pollard, died 1945, vol. IV
Deneke, Margaret Clara Adèle, 1882–1969, vol. VI
de Neuflize, Baron Jean, 1850–1928, vol. II
Deneys, Comdr James Godfrey Wood, 1897–1962, vol. VI
Denham, 1st Baron, 1886–1948, vol. IV
Denham, Algernon, died 1961, vol. VI
Denham, Hon. Digby Frank, 1859–1944, vol. IV
Denham, Sir Edward Brandis, 1876–1938, vol. III
Denham, Godfrey Charles, 1883–1956, vol. V
Denham, Harold Arthur, 1878–1921, vol. II
Denham, Henry George, 1880–1943, vol. IV
Denham, Humphrey John, 1893–1970, vol. VI
Denham, Sir James, died 1927, vol. II
Denham, William Smith, 1878–1964, vol. VI
Denham-White, Lt-Col Arthur; see White.
Denholm, John, 1853–1937, vol. III
Denholm, Sir John Carmichael, 1893–1981, vol. VIII
Denholm, Col Sir William Lang, 1901–1986, vol. VIII
Deniker, Joseph, 1852–1918, vol. III
Dening, Sir Esler; see Dening, Sir M. E.
Dening, Lt-Gen. Sir Lewis, 1848–1911, vol. I
Dening, Sir (Maberly) Esler, 1897–1977, vol. VII
Dening, Maj.-Gen. Roland, 1888–1978, vol. VII
Denis de Vitré, Col Percy Theodosius, 1870–1940, vol. III
Denison, Rear-Adm. Hon. Albert Denison Somerville, 1835–1903, vol. I
Denison, Captain Edward C., 1888–1960, vol. V
Denison, Col George Taylor, 1839–1925, vol. II
Denison, Hon. Harold Albert, 1856–1948, vol. IV
Denison, Captain Hon. Henry, 1849–1936, vol. III
Denison, Brig.-Gen. Henry, 1847–1938, vol. III
Denison, Rev. Henry Phipps, 1848–1940, vol. III
Denison, Sir Hugh Robert, 1865–1940, vol. III
Denison, Adm. John, 1853–1939, vol. III
Denison, Robert Beckett, 1879–1951, vol. V

Denison, Maj.-Gen. Septimus Julius Augustus, 1859–1937, vol. III

Denison, William Evelyn, 1843–1916, vol. II

Denison-Pender, Sir John Denison; *see* Pender.

de Niverville, Air Vice-Marshal Joseph Lionel Elphege Albert, 1897–1968, vol. VI (AII)

Denman, 3rd Baron, 1874–1954, vol. V

Denman, 4th Baron, 1905–1971, vol. VII

Denman, Lady; (Gertrude Mary), 1884–1954, vol. V

Denman, Sir Arthur, 1857–1931, vol. III

Denman, George Lewis, 1854–1929, vol. III

Denman, John Leopold, 1882–1975, vol. VII

Denman, Hon. Sir Richard Douglas, 1st Bt, 1876–1957, vol. V

Denne, Major William Henry, 1876–1917, vol. II

Dennehy, Sir Harold George, 1890–1956, vol. V

Dennehy, Maj.-Gen. Sir Thomas, 1829–1915, vol. I

Dennehy, William Francis, *died* 1918, vol. II (A), vol. III

Dennell, Ralph, 1907–1989, vol. VIII

Dennett, Richard Edward, 1857–1921, vol. II

Denney, Rev. James, 1856–1917, vol. II

Denning, Sir Howard, 1885–1943, vol. IV

Denning, Vice-Adm. Sir Norman Egbert, 1904–1979, vol. VII

Denning, Lt-Gen. Sir Reginald Francis Stewart, 1894–1990, vol. VIII

Denning, William Frederick, 1848–1931, vol. III

Dennis, Mrs A. E. Forbes; *see* Bottome, Phyllis.

Dennis, Sir Alfred Hull, 1858–1947, vol. IV

Dennis, Geoffrey Pomeroy, 1892–1963, vol. VI

Dennis, Sir (Herbert) Raymond, 1878–1939, vol. III

Dennis, Rev. Canon Herbert Wesley, *died* 1938, vol. III

Dennis, Rev. James Shepard, 1842–1914, vol. I

Dennis, Surg.-Rear-Adm. John Jeffreys, 1858–1958, vol. V

Dennis, Col John Stoughton, 1856–1938, vol. III

Dennis, John William, 1865–1949, vol. IV

Dennis, Maj.-Gen. Meade Edward, 1893–1965, vol. VI

Dennis, Col Meade James Crosbie, 1865–1945, vol. IV

Dennis, Nigel Forbes, 1912–1989, vol. VIII

Dennis, Sir Raymond; *see* Dennis, Sir H. R.

Dennis, Ven. Thomas John, 1869–1917, vol. II

Dennis, Trevor, 1882–1950, vol. IV

Dennis, Will; *see* Townesend, Stephen.

Dennis, William, 1856–1920, vol. II

Dennis Smith, Edgar; *see* Smith.

Dennison, Major Charles George, *born* 1844, vol. III

Dennison, Major Gilbert, 1883–1957, vol. V

Dennison, Robert, 1879–1951, vol. V

Dennison, Adm. Robert Lee, 1901–1980, vol. VII

Dennison, Thomas Andrews, 1906–1972, vol. VII

Denniss, Charles Sherwood, 1860–1917, vol. II

Denniss, Lt-Col Cyril Edmund Bartley B.; *see* Bartley-Denniss.

Denniss, Sir Edmund Robert Bartley B.; *see* Bartley-Denniss.

Denniss, George Hamson, 1854–1940, vol. III (A), vol. IV

Denniston, Alexander Guthrie Alistair, 1881–1961, vol. VI

Denniston, John Dewar, 1887–1949, vol. IV

Denniston, Hon. Sir John Edward, 1845–1919, vol. II

Denniston, Sir Robert, 1890–1946, vol. IV

Dennistoun, Lt-Col Ian Onslow, 1879–1938, vol. III

Dennistoun, Lt-Col James George, 1871–1939, vol. III

Dennistoun, Hon. Robert Maxwell, 1864–1952, vol. V

Denny, Sir Archibald, 1st Bt (*cr* 1913), 1860–1936, vol. III

Denny, Barbara Mary, (Mrs Edward Denny), 1880–1965, vol. VI

Denny, Captain Sir Cecil Edward, 6th Bt (*cr* 1782), 1850–1928, vol. II

Denny, Major Ernest Wriothesley, 1872–1949, vol. IV

Denny, Frederick Anthony, 1860–1941, vol. IV

Denny, Col Henry Cuthbert, 1858–1934, vol. III

Denny, Rev. Sir Henry Lyttelton Lyster, 7th Bt (*cr* 1782), 1878–1953, vol. V

Denny, Henry Samuel, *died* 1938, vol. III

Denny, Comdr Herbert Maynard, 1876–1957, vol. V

Denny, Surg. Rear-Adm. Herbert Reginald Harry, 1876–1943, vol. IV

Denny, James Runciman, 1908–1978, vol. VII

Denny, John M'Ausland, 1858–1922, vol. II

Denny, Sir J(onathan) Lionel P(ercy), 1897–1985, vol. VIII

Denny, Sir Lionel; *see* Denny, Sir J. L. P.

Denny, Sir Maurice Edward, 2nd Bt (*cr* 1913), 1886–1955, vol. V

Denny, Adm. Sir Michael Maynard, 1896–1972, vol. VII

Denny, Sir Robert Arthur, 5th Bt (*cr* 1782), 1838–1921, vol. II

Denny, Rev. William Henry, *died* 1907, vol. I

Denny, Hon. William Joseph, *died* 1946, vol. IV

Denny-Brown, Derek Ernest, 1901–1981, vol. VIII

Dennys, Col George William Patrick, 1857–1924, vol. II

Dennys, Lt-Col Sir Hector Travers, 1864–1922, vol. II

Dennys, Gen. Julius Bentall, 1822–1907, vol. I

de Normann, Sir Eric, 1893–1982, vol. VIII

Densham, Sir Harry Percival, 1866–1933, vol. III

Densmore, Emmet, 1837–1912, vol. I

Dent, Alan Holmes, 1905–1978, vol. VII

Dent, Sir Alfred, 1844–1927, vol. II

Dent, Brig.-Gen. Bertie Coore, 1872–1960, vol. V

Dent, Charles Enrique, 1911–1976, vol. VII

Dent, Clinton Thomas, 1850–1912, vol. I

Dent, Adm. Douglas Lionel, 1869–1959, vol. V

Dent, Edward Joseph, 1876–1957, vol. V

Dent, Sir Francis Henry, 1866–1955, vol. V

Dent, Frederick James, 1905–1973, vol. VII

Dent, George Irving, 1918–1976, vol. VII

Dent, Lt-Col Henry Francis, 1839–1916, vol. II

Dent, Rear-Adm. John, 1899–1973, vol. VII

Dent, John James, 1856–1936, vol. III

Dent, Lt-Col John Ralph Congreve, 1884–1969, vol. VI

Dent, Major John William, 1857–1943, vol. IV

Dent, Rev. Joseph Jonathan Dent, 1829–1907, vol. I

Dent, Major Joseph Leslie, 1889–1917, vol. II

Dent, Joseph Mallaby, 1849–1926, vol. II

Dent, Major Leonard Maurice Edward, 1888–1987, vol. VIII

Dent, Sir Robert Annesley Wilkinson, 1895–1983, vol. VIII

Dent, Maj.-Gen. Wilkinson, 1883–1934, vol. III

Dent-Brocklehurst, Major John Henry; *see* Brocklehurst.

Dent-Brocklehurst, Mary, 1902–1988, vol. VIII

Denton, Sir George Chardin, 1851–1928, vol. II

Denton, Mrs H. S., *died* 1953, vol. V

Denton, William, 1844–1915, vol. I

Denton-Thompson, Merrick Arnold Bardsley, 1888–1969, vol. VI

d'Entrèves, Alexander Passerin, 1902–1985, vol. VIII

Denville, Alfred, 1876–1955, vol. V

Denyer, Charles Leonard, 1887–1969, vol. VI

Denyer, Stanley Edward, 1869–1931, vol. III

Denys, Sir (Charles) Peter, 4th Bt (*cr* 1813), 1899–1960, vol. V

Denys, Sir Peter; *see* Denys, Sir C. P.

Denys-Burton, Sir Francis Charles Edward, 3rd Bt (*cr* 1913), 1849–1922, vol. II

Denza, Luigi, 1846–1922, vol. II

de Paravicini, Percy J., 1862–1921, vol. II

de Pass, Sir Eliot Arthur, 1851–1937, vol. III

de Pass, Col Guy Eliot, 1898–1985, vol. VIII

de Pauley, Rt Rev. William Cecil, 1893–1968, vol. VI

De Pencier, Most Rev. Adam Urias, 1866–1949, vol. IV

Depew, Chauncey Mitchell, 1834–1928, vol. II

de Peyer, Charles Hubert, 1905–1983, vol. VIII

d'Epinay, Charles Adrien Prosper; *see* Epinay.

de Polnay, Peter, 1906–1984, vol. VIII

de Pourtalès, Count Guy, 1881–1941, vol. IV

De Pree, Maj.-Gen. Hugo Douglas, 1870–1943, vol. IV

de Putron, Air Cdre Owen Washington, 1893–1980, vol. VII

Deramore, 3rd Baron, 1865–1936, vol. III

Deramore, 4th Baron, 1870–1943, vol. IV

Deramore, 5th Baron, 1903–1964, vol. VI

De Ramsey, 2nd Baron, 1848–1925, vol. II

Derby, 16th Earl of, 1841–1908, vol. I

Derby, 17th Earl of, 1865–1948, vol. IV

Derbyshire, Sir Harold, 1886–1972, vol. VII

Derbyshire, Job Nightingale, 1866–1954, vol. V

De Renzy, Sir Annesley Charles Castriot, 1829–1914, vol. I

De Renzy-Martin, Lt-Col Edward Cuthbert, 1883–1974, vol. VII

Derham, Sir David Plumley, 1920–1985, vol. VIII

Derham, Maj.-Gen. Frank Plumley, 1885–1957, vol. V

Derham, Brig.-Gen. Frank Seymour, 1858–1941, vol. IV

Derham, Hon. Frederick Thomas, 1844–1922, vol. II

de Rhé-Philipe, Maj.-Gen. Arthur Terence, 1905–1971, vol. VII

Dering, Sir Anthony Myles Cholmeley, 11th Bt, 1901–1958, vol. V

Dering, Comdr Claud Lacy Yea, 1885–1943, vol. IV

Dering, Sir Henry Edward, 10th Bt, 1866–1931, vol. III

Dering, Sir Henry Nevill, 9th Bt, 1839–1906, vol. I

Dering, Sir Herbert Guy, 1867–1933, vol. III

Dering, Lt-Col Rupert Anthony Yea, 12th Bt, 1915–1975, vol. VII

d'Erlanger, Baron Emile Beaumont, 1866–1939, vol. III

d'Erlanger, Baron Frederic A., 1868–1943, vol. IV

d'Erlanger, Sir Gerard John Regis Leo, 1906–1962, vol. VI

d'Erlanger, Leo Frederic Alfred, 1898–1978, vol. VII

de Robeck, 4th Baron, 1823–1904, vol. I

de Robeck, 5th Baron, 1859–1929, vol. III

de Robeck, 6th Baron, 1895–1965, vol. VI

de Robeck, Adm. of the Fleet Sir John Michael, 1st Bt, 1862–1928, vol. II

de Ros, 24th Baron, 1827–1907, vol. I

de Ros, Baroness (25th in line), 1854–1939, vol. III

de Ros, Baroness (26th in line), 1879–1956, vol. V

de Rothschild, Anthony Gustav; *see* Rothschild.

de Rougemont, Brig.-Gen. Cecil Henry, 1865–1951, vol. V

de Rougemont, Charles Irving, 1864–1939, vol. III

Deroulède, Paul, 1846–1914, vol. I

Derrick, Col George Alexander, 1860–1945, vol. IV

Derrick, Thomas, *died* 1954, vol. V

Derrig, Thomas; *see* O'Deirg, Tomás.

Derriman, Captain G. L., *died* 1915, vol. I

Derry, Cyril, 1895–1964, vol. VI

Derry, Henry B.; *see* Bromley-Derry.

Derry, Henry Forster H.; *see* Handley-Derry.

Derry, John, 1854–1937, vol. III

Derry, Ven. Percy A., 1859–1928, vol. II

Derry, Warren, 1899–1986, vol. VIII

de Ros, Baroness (27th in line), 1933–1983, vol. VIII

de Rutzen, Baron, John Frederick Foley, 1909–1944, vol. IV

de Rutzen, Sir Albert, 1831–1913, vol. I

Derviche-Jones, Lt-Col Arthur Daniel, 1873–1940, vol. III

Derville, Major Max T.; *see* Teichman-Derville.

Derwent, 1st Baron, 1829–1916, vol. II

Derwent, 2nd Baron, 1851–1929, vol. III

Derwent, 3rd Baron, 1899–1949, vol. IV

Derwent, 4th Baron, 1901–1986, vol. VIII

Derwent, William Raymond, 1883–1960, vol. V

de Sabata, Victor, 1892–1967, vol. VI

de Sales La Terrière, Col. Fenwick Bulmer, 1856–1925, vol. II

De Salis, Sir Cecil Fane, 1857–1948, vol. IV

De Salis, Rt Rev. Charles Fane, 1860–1942, vol. IV

De Salis, Lt-Col Edward Augustus Alfred, 1874–1943, vol. IV

De Salis, Rev. Henry Jerome, 1828–1915, vol. I

de Salis, Lt-Col John Eugene, 8th Count De Salis, 1891–1949, vol. IV

de Salis, John Francis Charles, Count de Salis, 1864–1939, vol. III

De Salis, Rodolph Fane, 1854–1931, vol. III

De Salis, Adm. Sir William Fane, 1858–1939, vol. III

de Saram, John Henricus, 1844–1920, vol. II

Desart, 4th Earl of, 1845–1898, vol. I

Desart, 5th Earl of, 1848–1934, vol. III

Desart, Ellen Odette, 1857–1933, vol. III

de Satgé, Lt-Col Sir Henry Valentine Bache, 1874–1964, vol. VI

De Saumarez, 4th Baron, 1843–1937, vol. III
De Saumarez, 5th Baron, 1889–1969, vol. VI
de Sausmarez, Annie Elizabeth, (Lady de Sausmarez), *died* 1947, vol. IV
De Sausmarez, Brig.-Gen. Cecil, 1870–1966, vol. VI
de Sausmarez, Sir Havilland Walter de; *see* Sausmarez.
de Sausmarez, (Lionel) Maurice, 1915–1969, vol. VI
de Sausmarez, Maurice; *see* de Sausmarez, L. M.
Desbarats, George Joseph, 1861–1944, vol. IV
Desborough, 1st Baron, 1855–1945, vol. IV
Desborough, Arthur Peregrine Henry, 1868–1949, vol. IV
Desborough, Maj.-Gen. John, 1824–1918, vol. II
Desborough, Vincent Robin d'Arba, 1914–1978, vol. VII
Descamps, Baron, *died* 1933, vol. III
Desch, Cecil Henry, 1874–1958, vol. V
Deschanel, Paul Eugène Louis, 1856–1922, vol. II
de Segonzac, A. D.; *see* Dunoyer de Segonzac.
de Selincourt, Anne Douglas, (Mrs Basil de Selincourt); *see* Sedgwick, A. D.
de Selincourt, Aubrey, 1894–1962, vol. VI
de Selincourt, Martin, 1864–1950, vol. IV
des Forges, Sir Charles Lee, 1879–1972, vol. VII
des Graz, Charles Geoffrey Maurice, 1893–1953, vol. V
Des Graz, Sir Charles Louis, 1860–1940, vol. III
Deshmukh, Sir Chintaman Dwarkanath, 1896–1982, vol. VIII
Deshon, Col Charles John, 1840–1929, vol. III
Deshon, Edward, 1836–1924, vol. II
Deshon, Lt-Gen. Frederick George Thomas, 1818–1913, vol. I
Deshon, H. F., 1858–1924, vol. II
Deshumbert, Marius, 1856–1943, vol. IV
De Sica, Vittorio, 1901–1974, vol. VII
Desika-Charry, Sir Vembakkam C., *born* 1861, vol. II
Desikachari, Diwan Bahadur Sir Tirumalai, 1868–1940, vol. III(A), vol. IV
de Silva, Sir Albert Ernest, 1887–1957, vol. V(A), vol. VI(AI)
de Silva, Sir Arthur Marcellus, 1879–1957, vol. V
de Silva, Rt Hon. Lucien Macull Dominic, 1893–1962, vol. VI
Desjardins, Hon. Alphonse, 1841–1912, vol. I
Deslandes, Sir Charles Frederick, 1884–1957, vol. V
Deslandes, Baronne M., vol. III
de Smidt, Lt-Col Errol Mervyn, 1877–1931, vol. III
de Smidt, Henry, 1845–1919, vol. II
de Smith, Stanley Alexander, 1922–1974, vol. VII
Desmond, Astra, (Lady Neame), 1893–1973, vol. VII
Desmond, John, *died* 1938, vol. III
Desmond, Shaw, 1877–1960, vol. V, vol. VI
de Soissons, Louis, 1890–1962, vol. VI
de Sola, Rev. Meldola, 1853–1918, vol. II
De Soveral, Marquess (Sir), *died* 1922, vol. II
de Soyres, Rev. John, 1849–1905, vol. I
de Soysa, Rt Rev. Charles Harold Wilfred, *died* 1971, vol. VII
de Soysa, Sir (Lambert) Wilfred (Alexander), 1884–1968, vol. VI
de Soysa, Sir Wilfred; *see* de Soysa, Sir L. W. A.
de Soyza, Gunasena, 1902–1961, vol. VI

Despard, Captain Herbert John, 1860–1937, vol. III
Despencer-Robertson, Lt-Col James Archibald St George Fitzwarenne, 1893–1942, vol. IV
d'Esperey, Franchet, 1856–1942, vol. IV
Dessaulles, Hon. George Casimir, 1827–1930, vol. III
de Stein, Sir Edward, 1887–1965, vol. VI
de Stacpoole, 4th Duke, 1860–1929, vol. III
de Stacpoole, 5th Duke, 1886–1965, vol. VI
d'Esterre, Elsa, *died* 1935, vol. III
Destinn, Emmy, 1878–1930, vol. III
D'Estournelles de Constant, Baron, 1852–1924, vol. II
Des Vœux, Sir Charles Champagné, 6th Bt, 1827–1914, vol. I
Des Vœux, Lt-Gen. Sir Charles Hamilton, 1853–1911, vol. I
Des Vœux, Sir Edward Alfred, 8th Bt, 1864–1941, vol. IV
Des Vœux, Sir Frederick, 7th Bt, 1857–1937, vol. III
Des Vœux, Sir George William, 1834–1909, vol. I
Des Vœux, Lt-Col Henry Bertram, 1868–1930, vol. III
Des Vœux, Lt-Col Henry J., 1876–1940, vol. III
Des Vœux, Lt-Col Herbert, 1864–1945, vol. IV
Des Vœux, Lt-Col Sir Richard de Bacquencourt; *see* Des Vœux, Lt-Col Sir W. R. de B.
Des Vœux, Sir William; *see* Des Vœux, Sir G. W.
Des Vœux, Lt-Col Sir (William) Richard de Bacquencourt, 9th Bt, 1911–1944, vol. IV
De Tabley, Lady; (Elizabeth), *died* 1915, vol. I
Detaille, Edouard, *died* 1912, vol. I
de Teissier, Baron Henry de Teissier, 1862–1931, vol. III
Deterding, Sir Henri Wilhelm August, 1866–1939, vol. III
de Thieusies, Vicomte Alain O.; *see* Obert de Thieusies.
Dethridge, George James, 1864–1938, vol. III
Dethridge, Hon. George Leo, 1903–1978, vol. VII
Detmold, Edward J., 1883–1957, vol. V
Detmold, Maurice, 1883–1908, vol. I
de Torrenté, Henry, 1893–1962, vol. VI
De Trafford, Lt Augustus Francis, 1879–1904, vol. I
De Trafford, (Charles) Edmund, 1864–1951, vol. V
De Trafford, Edmund; *see* De Trafford, C. E.
de Trafford, Captain Sir Humphrey Edmund, 4th Bt, 1891–1971, vol. VII
de Trafford, Sir Humphrey Francis, 3rd Bt, 1862–1929, vol. III
de Trafford, Sir Rudolph Edgar Francis, 5th Bt, 1894–1983, vol. VIII
de Trafford, Sigismund Cathcart, 1853–1936, vol. III
Dettmann, Herbert Stanley, 1875–1940, vol. III
Deuchar, William, 1849–1923, vol. II
Deutsch, John James, 1911–1976, vol. VII
Deutsch, Otto Erich, 1883–1967, vol. VI
Deutscher, Isaac, 1907–1967, vol. VI
Devadhar, Gopal Krishna, 1871–1935, vol. III
Devadoss, Sir David Muthiah, 1868–1955, vol. V
De Valera, Eamon, 1882–1975, vol. VII
Devals, Rt Rev. Adrian, 1882–1945, vol. IV
Devas, Anthony, 1911–1958, vol. V
Devas, Charles Stanton, 1848–1906, vol. I
Devas, Rev. Francis Charles, 1877–1951, vol. V
Devaux, J. Louis, 1884–1943, vol. IV

de Vaux, Father Roland, 1903–1971, vol. VII
de Veber, Hon. Leverett George, 1849–1925, vol. II
Devenish, Rev. Robert Cecil Silvester, 1888–1973, vol. VII
Devenish, Very Rev. Robert Jones Sylvester, *died* 1916, vol. II
Devenish-Meares, Maj.-Gen. William Lewis, 1832–1907, vol. I
Dever, Hon. James, 1825–1904, vol. I
de Vere, Aubrey Thomas, 1814–1902, vol. I
de Vere, Robert Stephen Vere, 1872–1936, vol. III
de Vere, Sir Stephen Edward, 4th Bt, 1812–1904, vol. I
Deverell, Field Marshal Sir Cyril John, 1874–1947, vol. IV
Devereux, Rev. Edward Robert Price, *died* 1941, vol. IV
Devereux, Sir Joseph, 1816–1903, vol. I
Devereux, Wallace Charles, 1893–1952, vol. V
Devers, Gen. Jacob Loucks, 1887–1979, vol. VII
de Versan, Raoul Couturier, 1848–1936, vol. III
De Vesci, 5th Viscount, 1881–1958, vol. V
de Vesci, 6th Viscount, 1919–1983, vol. VIII
de Veulle, Henry Marett, 1847–1930, vol. III
de Villiers, 1st Baron, 1842–1914, vol. I
de Villiers, 2nd Baron, 1871–1934, vol. III
de Villiers, Hon. Sir Etienne; *see* de Villiers, Hon. Sir J. E. R.
de Villiers, Sir (H.) Nicolas, 1902–1958, vol. V
de Villiers, Maj.-Gen. Isaac Pierre, 1891–1967, vol. VI
de Villiers, Jacob, 1868–1932, vol. III
de Villiers, Hon. Sir (Jean) Etienne (Reenen), 1875–1947, vol. IV
de Villiers, Sir John Abraham Jacob, 1863–1931, vol. III
Devine, Alexander, 1865–1930, vol. III
Devine, George Alexander Cassady, 1910–1966, vol. VI
Devine, Henry, 1879–1940, vol. III
Devine, Sir Hugh Berchmans, *died* 1959, vol. V
Devine, Major James Arthur, 1869–1939, vol. III
Devine, Rev. Minos, 1871–1937, vol. III
De Vinne, Theodore Low, 1828–1914, vol. I
Devitt, Sir Philip Henry, 1st Bt (*cr* 1931), 1876–1947, vol. IV
Devitt, Sir Thomas Lane, 1st Bt (*cr* 1916), 1839–1923, vol. II
Devlin, Hon. Charles Ramsay, 1858–1914, vol. I
Devlin, Emmanuel, 1872–1921, vol. II
Devlin, Joseph, 1872–1934, vol. III
Devlin, William, 1911–1987, vol. VIII
de Voil, Very Rev. Walter Harry, 1893–1964, vol. VI
Devon, 13th Earl of, 1811–1904, vol. I
Devon, 14th Earl of, 1870–1927, vol. II
Devon, 15th Earl of, 1872–1935, vol. III
Devon, 16th Earl of, 1875–1935, vol. III
Devon, James, 1866–1939, vol. III
Devonport, 1st Viscount, 1856–1934, vol. III
Devonport, 2nd Viscount, 1890–1973, vol. VII
Devons, Ely, 1913–1967, vol. VI
Devonshire, 9th Duke of, 1868–1938, vol. III
Devonshire, 10th Duke of, 1895–1950, vol. IV

Devonshire, Dowager Duchess of, (Mary Alice), 1895–1988, vol. VIII
Devonshire, Sir James Lyne, 1863–1946, vol. IV
DeVoto, Bernard Augustine, 1897–1955, vol. V
de Vries, Hugo, 1848–1935, vol. III
Dew, Col Sir Armine Brereton, 1867–1941, vol. IV
Dew, Armine Roderick, 1906–1945, vol. IV
Dew, Sir Harold Robert, 1891–1962, vol. VI
De Waal, Hon. Daniel, 1873–1938, vol. III
De Waal, Brig. Pieter, 1899–1977, vol. VII
Dewar, 1st Baron, 1864–1930, vol. III
Dewar, Hon. Lord; Arthur Dewar, *died* 1917, vol. II
Dewar, Rev. Alexander, 1864–1943, vol. IV
Dewar, Arthur; *see* Dewar, Hon. Lord.
Dewar, Douglas, 1875–1957, vol. V
Dewar, George A. B., 1862–1934, vol. III
Dewar, Sir James, 1842–1923, vol. II
Dewar, John, 1883–1964, vol. VI
Dewar, John Arthur, 1891–1954, vol. V
Dewar, Vice-Adm. Kenneth Gilbert Balmain, 1879–1964, vol. VI
Dewar, Rev. Canon Lindsay, 1891–1976, vol. VII
Dewar, Michael Bruce Urquhart, 1886–1950, vol. IV
Dewar, Brig. Michael Preston Douglas, 1906–1984, vol. VIII
Dewar, Robert, 1882–1956, vol. V
Dewar, Vice-Adm. Robert Gordon Douglas, *died* 1948, vol. IV
Dewar, Thomas Finlayson, 1866–1929, vol. III
Dewar, William McLachlan, 1905–1979, vol. VII
Dewas State, Maharaja Tukoji Rao Puar, 1888–1937, vol. III
de Watteville, Lt-Col Herman Gaston, 1875–1963, vol. VI
de Watteville, John Edward, 1892–1976, vol. VII
Dewdney, Rt Rev. Alfred Daniel Alexander, 1863–1945, vol. IV
Dewdney, Ven. Arthur John Bible, *died* 1946, vol. IV
de Wend-Fenton, West Fenton, 1881–1920, vol. II
Dewes, Sir Herbert John Salisbury, 1897–1988, vol. VIII
de Wesselow, Owen Lambert Vaughan, 1883–1959, vol. V
De Wet, Gen. Hon. Christian Rudolf, 1854–1922, vol. II
De Wet, Sir Jacobus Albertus, 1840–1911, vol. I
De Wet, Sir Jacobus Petrus, 1838–1900, vol. I
De Wet, Rt Hon. Nicolas Jacobus, 1873–1960, vol. V
de Wet, Captain Thomas Oloff, 1869–1940, vol. III
Dewey, (Alexander) Gordon, 1890–1953, vol. V
Dewey, Cyril Marston, 1907–1973, vol. VII
Dewey, Rt Rev. Mgr Edward, 1884–1965, vol. VI
Dewey, George, 1837–1917, vol. II
Dewey, Gordon; *see* Dewey, A. G.
Dewey, John, 1859–1952, vol. V
Dewey, Kenneth Thomas, 1902–1961, vol. VI
Dewey, Rev. Sir Stanley Daws, 2nd Bt, 1867–1948, vol. IV
Dewey, Sir Thomas Charles, 1st Bt, 1840–1926, vol. II
Dewey, Thomas Edmund, 1902–1971, vol. VII
Dewhurst, Captain Gerard Powys, 1872–1956, vol. V
Dewhurst, Lt-Comdr Harry, 1866–1931, vol. III
Dewhurst, Keith Ward, 1924–1984, vol. VIII

Dewhurst, Comdr Ronald Hugh, 1905–1990, vol. VIII

Dewhurst, Wynford, *died* 1941, vol. IV

Dewick, Rev. E. C., 1884–1958, vol. V

De Windt, Harry, 1856–1933, vol. III

Dewing, Maj.-Gen. Maurice Nelson, 1896–1976, vol. VII

Dewing, Maj.-Gen. Richard Henry, 1891–1981, vol. VIII

de Winton, Brig.-Gen. Charles, 1860–1943, vol. IV

de Winton, Charles Henry, 1856–1936, vol. III

de Winton, Sir Francis Walter, 1835–1901, vol. I

de Winton, Ven. Frederic Henry, 1852–1932, vol. III

de Winton, Walter Bernard, 1850–1944, vol. IV

de Winton, Wilfred Seymour, 1856–1929, vol. III

DeWitt, Norman Wentworth, 1876–1958, vol. V

Dewolfe, Rev. Henry Todd, 1867–1947, vol. IV

de Wolff, Brig. Charles Esmond, 1893–1986, vol. VIII

Dewrance, Sir John, 1858–1937, vol. III

Dewsnup, Ernest Ritson, 1874–1950, vol. IV

Dexter, John, 1925–1990, vol. VIII

Dexter, Keith, 1928–1989, vol. VIII

Dexter, Walter, 1877–1944, vol. IV

Dexter, Walter, 1876–1958, vol. V

Dey, George Goodair, 1876–1955, vol. V

Dey, Helen, 1888–1968, vol. VI

Deym, Count; Franz de Paula, 1838–1903, vol. I

d'Eyncourt, Edmund Charles T.; *see* Tennyson-d'Eyncourt.

d'Eyncourt, Adm. Edwin Clayton Tennyson, *died* 1903, vol. I

d'Eyncourt, Sir Eustace Henry William T.; *see* Tennyson-d'Eyncourt.

d'Eyncourt, Sir Gervais T.; *see* Tennyson d'Eyncourt, Sir E. G.

d'Eyncourt, Sir Giles Gervais T.; *see* Tennyson-d'Eyncourt.

d'Eyncourt, Sir Jeremy T.; *see* Tennyson-d'Eyncourt, Sir John J. E.

d'Eyncourt, Sir (John) Jeremy (Eustace) T.; *see* Tennyson-d'Eyncourt.

de Young, Michel Harry, 1849–1925, vol. II

de Zouche, Dorothy Eva, 1886–1969, vol. VI

De Zoysa, Sir Cyril, 1897–1978, vol. VII

de Zulueta, Sir Philip Francis; *see* Zulueta.

Dhar, Lt-Col HH Maharaja Sir Udaji Rao Puar Major, Bahadur, 1886–1926, vol. II

Dharampur, Maharana of, 1863–1921, vol. II

D'Harcourt, Robert, 1881–1965, vol. VI(AII)

d'Hardelot, Guy; *see* Rhodes, Mrs Helen.

d'Hautpoul, Marquis, 1859–1934, vol. III

D'Herelle, Felix H., 1873–1949, vol. IV

Dhingra, Sir Behari Lal, 1873–1936, vol. III

Dholpur, Maharaj Rana of, 1893–1954, vol. V

Dholpur, Captain HH, 1883–1911, vol. I

Dhondup, Rai Bahadur Norbhu, *died* 1943, vol. IV

Dhrangadhra, Maharaja Raj Saheb of, 1889–1942, vol. IV

Diack, Sir Alexander Henderson, 1862–1929, vol. III

Diaghileff, Serge de, 1872–1929, vol. III

Diamond, Arthur Sigismund, 1897–1978, vol. VII

Diamond, Charles, 1858–1934, vol. III

Diamond, George Clifford, 1902–1985, vol. VIII

Diamond, George le Boutillier, 1893–1964, vol. VI

Diamond, Jack, 1912–1990, vol. VIII

Diamond, Sir William Henry, 1865–1941, vol. IV

Diaz, Maresciallo d'Italia Armando, 1861–1928, vol. II

Diaz, Sir Porfirio, 1830–1915, vol. I

Dibben, Major Cecil Reginald, 1885–1965, vol. VI

Dibblee, George Binney, 1868–1952, vol. V

Dibbs, Alexander; *see* Dibbs, A. H. A.

Dibbs, (Arthur Henry) Alexander, 1918–1985, vol. VIII

Dibbs, Hon. Sir George Richard, 1834–1904, vol. I

Dibbs, Sir Thomas Allwright, 1832–1923, vol. II

Dibden, Edgar, 1888–1971, vol. VII

Dibdin, Aubrey, 1892–1958, vol. V

Dibdin, Charles, 1849–1910, vol. I

Dibdin, Edward Rimbault, 1853–1941, vol. IV

Dibdin, Sir Lewis Tonna, 1852–1938, vol. III

Dibdin, Sir Robert William, 1848–1933, vol. III

Dibdin, William Joseph, 1850–1925, vol. II

Dible, James Henry, *died* 1971, vol. VII

Dible, James Kenneth Victor, 1890–1976, vol. VII

Dible, William Cuthbert, 1886–1971, vol. VII

Dibley, Rear-Adm. Albert Kingsley, 1890–1958, vol. V

Dicconson, Hon. Robert Joseph Gerard-, 1857–1918, vol. II

Dicey, Albert Venn, 1835–1922, vol. II

Dicey, Edward, 1832–1911, vol. I

Dick, Bt Col Alan Macdonald, 1884–1970, vol. VI

Dick, Alick Sydney, 1916–1986, vol. VIII

Dick, Brig.-Gen. Archibald Campbell Douglas, 1847–1927, vol. II

Dick, Col Sir Arthur Robert, 1860–1943, vol. IV

Dick, Charles George Cotsford, 1846–1911, vol. I

Dick, Clare L.; *see* Lawson Dick.

Dick, Lt-Col Dighton Hay Abercromby, 1869–1941, vol. IV

Dick, George Paris, 1866–1941, vol. IV

Dick, Gladys; *see* Ripley, G.

Dick, Henry Charles, 1872–1946, vol. IV

Dick, Col James Adam, 1866–1942, vol. IV

Dick, Sir James Nicholas, 1832–1920, vol. II

Dick, John, 1902–1970, vol. VI

Dick, John Lawson, 1870–1944, vol. IV

Dick, Cdre John Mathew, 1899–1981, vol. VIII

Dick, Captain Quintin, 1847–1923, vol. II

Dick, Brig.-Gen. Robert Nicholas, 1879–1967, vol. VI

Dick, Sir W(illiam) R.; *see* Reid Dick.

Dick-Cunyngham, Major Sir Colin Keith; *see* Cunyngham.

Dick-Cunyngham, Maj.-Gen. James Keith, 1877–1935, vol. III

Dick-Cunyngham of Lamburghtoun, Sir Robert Keith Alexander; *see* Cunyngham.

Dick-Cunyngham, Lt-Col William Henry; *see* Cunyngham.

Dick-Lauder, Sir George Andrew; *see* Lauder.

Dick-Lauder, Sir George William Dalrymple; *see* Lauder.

Dick-Lauder, Lt-Col Sir John North Dalrymple; *see* Lauder.

Dick-Lauder, Sir Thomas North; *see* Lauder.

Dick-Read, Grantly; *see* Read.

Dicken, Adm. Charles Gauntlett, 1854–1937, vol.III

Dicken, Charles Shortt, 1841–1902, vol. I

Dicken, Charles Vernon, 1881–1955, vol. V

Dicken, Rear-Adm. Edward Bernard Cornish, 1888–1964, vol. VI

Dicken, Col William Popham, 1834–1912, vol. I

Dickens, Craven Hildesley, 1822–1900, vol. I

Dickens, Frank, 1899–1986, vol. VIII

Dickens, Adm. Sir Gerald Charles, 1879–1962, vol. VI

Dickens, Sir Henry Fielding, 1849–1933, vol. III

Dickens, Sir Louis Walter, 1903–1988, vol. VIII

Dickens, Mary Angela, *died* 1948, vol. IV

Dickens, Air Cdre Thomas Charles, 1906–1972, vol. VII

Dickenson, Lt-Col Edward Stanley Newton, *died* 1910, vol. I

Dickenson, Rev. Lenthall Greville T.; *see* Trotman-Dickenson.

Dickeson, Sir Richard, 1823–1900, vol. I

Dickey, Rev. Charles A., *died* 1910, vol. I

Dickey, Edward Montgomery O'Rorke, 1894–1977, vol. VII

Dickey, Robert H. F., 1856–1915, vol. I

Dickie, Archibald Campbell, 1868–1941, vol. IV

Dickie, Captain David, 1880–1930, vol. III

Dickie, Rev. James F., 1845–1933, vol. III

Dickie, Very Rev. John, 1875–1942, vol. IV

Dickie, Maj.-Gen. John Elford, 1856–1939, vol. III

Dickie, William, 1856–1919, vol. II

Dickin, Maria Elisabeth, 1870–1951, vol. V

Dickins, Aileen Marian, 1917–1987, vol. VIII

Dickins, Bruce, 1889–1978, vol. VII

Dickins, Brig. Frederick, 1879–1975, vol. VII

Dickins, Frederick Victor, 1838–1915, vol. I

Dickins, Rev. Henry Compton, 1838–1920, vol. II

Dickins, Col Spencer William Scrase-, 1862–1919, vol. II

Dickins, Rev. Thomas Bourne, 1832–1919, vol. II

Dickins, Col Vernon William Frank, 1867–1942, vol. IV

Dickins, Ven. William Arthur, *died* 1921, vol. II

Dickins, Maj.-Gen. William Drummond S.; *see* Scrase-Dickins.

Dickinson, 1st Baron, 1859–1943, vol. IV

Dickinson, Sir Alwin Robinson, 1873–1944, vol. IV

Dickinson, Anne Hepple, 1877–1959, vol. V

Dickinson, Arthur Harold, 1892–1978, vol. VII

Dickinson, Sir Arthur Lowes, 1859–1935, vol. III

Dickinson, Ven. Charles Henry, 1871–1930, vol. III

Dickinson, Croft; *see* Dickinson, W. C.

Dickinson, Maj.-Gen. Douglas Povah, 1886–1949, vol. IV

Dickinson, Frederic William, 1856–1922, vol. II

Dickinson, Gladys, 1895–1964, vol. VI

Dickinson, Goldsworthy Lowes, 1862–1932, vol. III

Dickinson, Henry Douglas, 1899–1969, vol. VI

Dickinson, Very Rev. Hercules Henry, 1827–1905, vol. I

Dickinson, James, *died* 1933, vol. III

Dickinson, Sir John, 1848–1933, vol. III

Dickinson, John Alfred Ernst, 1859–1933, vol. III

Dickinson, Major Neville Hope Campbell, 1862–1935, vol. III

Dickinson, Rear-Adm. Norman Vincent, 1901–1981, vol. VIII

Dickinson, Reginald Percy, 1914–1987, vol. VIII

Dickinson, Hon. Richard Sebastian Willoughby, 1897–1935, vol. III

Dickinson, Robert Edmund, 1862–1947, vol. IV

Dickinson, Robert Eric, 1905–1981, vol. VIII

Dickinson, Ronald Arthur, 1910–1986, vol. VIII

Dickinson, Ronald Sigismund Shepherd, 1906–1984, vol. VIII

Dickinson, Thomas Vincent, 1858–1941, vol. IV

Dickinson, Thorold Barron, 1903–1984, vol. VIII

Dickinson, Lt-Col William, 1831–1917, vol. II

Dickinson, W(illiam) Croft, 1897–1963, vol. VI

Dickinson, William Howship, 1832–1913, vol. I

Dickinson, Col William Vicris, 1856–1917, vol. II

Dicks, Captain Henry Leage, 1870–1942, vol. IV

Dicksee, Sir Francis Bernard, (Frank), 1853–1928, vol. II

Dicksee, Frank; *see* Dicksee, Sir F. B.

Dicksee, Herbert, 1862–1942, vol. IV

Dicksee, Lawrence Robert, 1864–1932, vol. III

Dickson, Rt Hon. Lord; Scott Dickson, 1850–1922, vol. II

Dickson, Bertram Thomas, 1886–1982, vol. VIII

Dickson, Bonner William Arthur, 1887–1976, vol. VII

Dickson, Charles Gordon, 1884–1963, vol. VI

Dickson, Gen. Sir Collingwood, 1817–1904, vol. I

Dickson, Rev. Canon Daniel Eccles Lucas, *died* 1924, vol. II

Dickson, David, 1908–1982, vol. VIII

Dickson, Air Vice-Marshal Edward Dalziel, 1895–1979, vol. VII

Dickson, Maj.-Gen. Edward Thompson, 1850–1938, vol. III

Dickson, Frank, 1862–1936, vol. III

Dickson, Lt-Col George Arthur Hamilton, 1863–1918, vol. II

Dickson, Lt-Col Harold Richard Patrick, 1881–1959, vol. V

Dickson, Rev. Henry Granville, 1844–1929, vol. III

Dickson, Henry Newton, 1866–1922, vol. II

Dickson, (Horatio Henry) Lovat, 1902–1987, vol. VIII

Dickson, Ian Anderson, 1905–1982, vol. VIII

Dickson, James, 1859–1941, vol. IV

Dickson, James Douglas Hamilton, 1849–1931, vol. III

Dickson, James Hill, 1863–1938, vol. III

Dickson, Hon. Sir James Robert, 1832–1901, vol. I

Dickson, Maj.-Gen. John Baillie Ballantyne, 1842–1925, vol. II

Dickson, John Harold, 1898–1967, vol. VI

Dickson, Col John Herbert, 1867–1938, vol. III

Dickson, John Robert, 1884–1937, vol. III

Dickson, Lovat; *see* Dickson, H. H. L.

Dickson, Lt-Col Maurice Rhynd, 1882–1940, vol. III

Dickson, Norman Bonnington, 1868–1944, vol. IV

Dickson, Rear-Adm. Robert Kirk, 1898–1952, vol. V

Dickson, Scott; *see* Dickson, Rt Hon. Lord.

Dickson, Spencer Stuart, 1873–1951, vol. V

Dickson, Thomas A.; *see* Ainsworth Dickson.

Dickson, Rt Hon. Thomas Alexander, 1833–1909, vol. I

Dickson, Rev. Thomas Knox Whitaker, *died* 1931, vol. III

Dickson, Thomas S., 1885–1935, vol. III

Dickson, Brig.-Gen. William Edmund Ritchie, 1871–1957, vol. V

Dickson, Rev. William Edward, 1823–1910, vol. I

Dickson, William Elliot Carnegie, 1878–1954, vol. V

Dickson, William Everard, *died* 1945, vol. IV

Dickson, Marshal of the Royal Air Force Sir William Forster, 1898–1987, vol. VIII

Dickson, William Kirk, 1860–1949, vol. IV

Dickson, Rev. William Purdle, 1823–1901, vol. I

Dickson, Lt-Gen. William Thomas, 1830–1909, vol. I

Dickson Wright, Arthur; *see* Wright.

Diddams, Harry John Charles, 1864–1929, vol. III

Didon, Very Rev. Fr Henri, 1840–1900, vol. I

Didsbury, Brian, 1926–1970, vol. VI

Dieckhoff, Hans Heinrich, 1884–1952, vol. V

Diederichs, Hon. Nicolaas, 1903–1978, vol. VII

Diefenbaker, Rt Hon. John George, 1895–1979, vol. VII

Diehl, Alice Mangold, *died* 1912, vol. I

Diels, Otto Paul Hermann, 1876–1954, vol. V

Diesel, Rudolf, 1858–1913, vol. I

Digan, Lt-Col Augustine J., 1878–1926, vol. II

Digby, 10th Baron, 1846–1920, vol. II

Digby, 11th Baron, 1894–1964, vol. VI

Digby, Comdr Edward Aylmer, 1883–1935, vol. III

Digby, Col Hon. Everard Charles, 1852–1914, vol. I

Digby, Col Frederick James Bosworth Digby Wingfield, 1885–1952, vol. V

Digby, George F. Wingfield, 1911–1989, vol. VIII

Digby, Hon. Gerald Fitzmaurice, 1858–1942, vol. IV

Digby, John Kenelm Digby Wingfield, 1859–1904, vol. I

Digby, Sir Kenelm Edward, 1836–1916, vol. II

Digby, Kenelm George, 1890–1944, vol. IV

Digby, Kenelm Hutchinson, 1884–1954, vol. V

Digby, Hon. Robert Henry, 1903–1959, vol. V

Digby, Samuel, *died* 1925, vol. II

Digby, Rev. Stephen Harold Wingfield, 1872–1942, vol. IV

Digby, William, 1849–1904, vol. I

Digby-Beste, Captain Sir Henry Aloysius Bruno 1883–1964, vol. VI

Diggines, Christopher Ewart, 1920–1990, vol. VIII

Diggines, Sir William Ewart, 1881–1952, vol. V

Diggle, F. Holt, 1886–1942, vol. IV

Diggle, Rt Rev. John William, 1847–1920, vol. II

Diggle, Joseph Robert, 1849–1917, vol. II

Diggle, Captain Neston William, 1880–1963, vol. VI

Diggle, Rev. Reginald Fraser, 1889–1975, vol. VII

Diggle, Wadham Neston, 1848–1934, vol. III

Dignan, Most Rev. John, *died* 1953, vol. V

Dike, Kenneth Onwuka, 1917–1983, vol. VIII

Dilhorne, 1st Viscount, 1905–1980, vol. VII

Dilke, Beaumont Albany F.; *see* Fetherstone-Dilke.

Dilke, Rt Hon. Sir Charles Wentworth, 2nd Bt, 1843–1911, vol. I

Dilke, Sir Charles Wentworth, 3rd Bt, 1874–1918, vol. II

Dilke, Emilia Francis, (Lady Dilke), 1840–1904, vol. I

Dilke, Sir Fisher Wentworth, 4th Bt, 1877–1944, vol. IV

Dill, Field-Marshal Sir John Greer, 1881–1944, vol. IV

Dill, Very Rev. S. Marcus, 1843–1924, vol. II

Dill, Sir Samuel, 1844–1924, vol. II

Dill-Russell, Patrick Wimberley, 1910–1977, vol. VII

Dilley, Sir Arthur George, 1854–1938, vol. III

Dilling, Walter James, 1886–1950, vol. IV

Dillingham, Cyril Claud, 1886–1943, vol. IV

Dillon, 17th Viscount, 1844–1932, vol. III

Dillon, 18th Viscount, 1875–1934, vol. III

Dillon, 19th Viscount, 1881–1946, vol. IV

Dillon, 20th Viscount, 1911–1979, vol. VII

Dillon, 21st Viscount, 1945–1982, vol. VIII

Dillon, Hon. Conrad Adderly, 1845–1901, vol. I

Dillon, Captain Constantine Theobold Francis, 1873–1920, vol. II

Dillon, Emile Joseph, 1854–1933, vol. III

Dillon, Frank, 1823–1909, vol. I

Dillon, Frederick, 1887–1965, vol. VI

Dillon, Lt-Col George Frederick Horace, 1859–1906, vol. I

Dillon, Hon. Harry Lee Stanton; L., *see* Lee-Dillon.

Dillon, Major Henry Mountford, 1881–1918, vol. II

Dillon, John, 1851–1927, vol. II

Dillon, Sir John Fox, 7th Bt, 1843–1925, vol. II

Dillon, Malcolm, 1859–1945, vol. IV

Dillon, Gen. Sir Martin Andrew, 1826–1913, vol. I

Dillon, Sir Robert William Charlier, 8th Bt, 1914–1982, vol. VIII

Dillon, Comdr Stafford Harry, 1887–1935, vol. III

Dillon, Thomas, 1884–1971, vol. VII

Dillwyn-Llewelyn, Sir John Talbot; *see* Llewelyn.

Dillwyn-Venables-Llewelyn, Sir Charles Leyshon; *see* Venables-Llewelyn.

Dillwyn-Venables-Llewelyn, Brig. Sir Michael; *see* Venables-Llewelyn, Brig. Sir C. M. D.

Dilnot, Frank, 1875–1946, vol. IV

Dilworth, W. J., 1863–1922, vol. II

Dilworth-Harrison, Ven. Talbot, 1886–1975, vol. VII

Di Maria, Most Rev. Pietro, 1865–1937, vol. III

Dimbleby, Richard, 1913–1965, vol. VI

Dimmer, Lt-Col John Henry Stephen, 1884–1918, vol. II

Dimmitt, Hon. James Albert, 1888–1957, vol. V

Dimnet, Very Rev. Abbè Ernest, 1866–1954, vol. V

Dimoline, Hon. Brig. Harry Kenneth, 1903–1972, vol. VII

Dimoline, Maj.-Gen. William Alfred, 1897–1965, vol. VI

Dimond, Maj.-Gen. William Elliot Randal, 1893–1960, vol. V

Dimont, Rev. Canon Charles Tunnacliff, 1872–1953, vol. V

Dimsdale, 6th Baron of the Russian Empire, 1828–1898, vol. I

Dimsdale, 7th Baron of the Russian Empire, 1856–1928, vol. II

Dimsdale, Mrs Helen Easdale, 1907–1977, vol. VII

Dimsdale, Sir John Holdsworth, 2nd Bt, 1874–1923, vol. II

Dimsdale, Sir John Holdsworth, 3rd Bt, 1901–1978, vol. VII

Dimsdale, Rt Hon. Sir Joseph Cockfield, 1st Bt, 1849–1912, vol. I

Dimsey, Surg. Rear-Adm. Edgar Ralph, 1861–1930, vol. III

Dinajpur, Bahadur of, 1860–1919, vol. II

D'Indy, (Paul Marie Théodore) Vincent, 1851–1931, vol. III

D'Indy, Vincent; *see* D'Indy, P. M. T. V.

Dineen, Rev. Canon Frederick George K.; *see* Kerr-Dineen.

Dines, Henry George, 1891–1964, vol. VI

Dines, William Henry, 1855–1927, vol. II

Dinesen, Isak, (Karen Blixen Finecke), 1885–1962, vol. VI

Dinesen, Thomas, 1892–1979, vol. VII

Dingle, Aylward Edward, *died* 1947, vol. IV

Dingle, Herbert, 1890–1978, vol. VII

Dingle, Percival Alfred, 1881–1963, vol. VI

Dingle, Sir Philip Burrington, 1906–1978, vol. VII

Dingley, Allen Roy, 1892–1978, vol. VII

Dingli, Sir Adriano, 1817–1900, vol. I

Dingwall, Eric John, 1890–1986, vol. VIII

Dingwall, Walter Spender, 1900–1990, vol. VIII

Dingwall-Fordyce, Alexander, 1875–1940, vol. III

Dinkel, Ernest Michael, 1894–1983, vol. VIII

Dinkel, Michael; *see* Dinkel, E. M.

Dinneen, Rev. Patrick Stephen, *died* 1934, vol. III

Dinshaw, Sir Hormusjee Cowasjee, 1857–1939, vol. III

Dinwiddie, Melville, 1892–1975, vol. VII

Dinwoody, Very Rev. Loefric Matthews H.; *see* Hay-Dinwoody.

Diogenes; *see* Brown, W. J.

Dionne, Narcisse-Eutrope, 1848–1917, vol. II

Dior, Christian Ernest, 1905–1957, vol. V

Diósy, Arthur, 1856–1923, vol. II

Diplock, Baron (Life Peer); (William John) Kenneth Diplock, 1907–1985, vol. VIII

Dippie, Herbert, 1885–1945, vol. IV

Dirac, Paul Adrien Maurice, 1902–1984, vol. VIII

Dircks, Rudolf, *died* 1936, vol. III

Dirksen, Herbert von, 1882–1955, vol. V

Disbrowe-Wise, Lt-Col Henry Edward Disbrowe; *see* Wise.

Disher, Maurice Willson, 1893–1969, vol. VI

Disney, Lt-Col Henry Anthony Patrick, 1893–1974, vol. VII

Disney, Henry William, 1858–1925, vol. II

Disney, Hon. Sir James, 1896–1952, vol. V

Disney, Walter E., 1901–1966, vol. VI

Disraeli, Coningsby Ralph, 1867–1936, vol. III

Distant, William Lucas, 1845–1922, vol. II

Disturnal, William Josiah, *died* 1923, vol. II

Ditchburn, Robert William, 1903–1987, vol. VIII

Ditchfield, Rt Rev. John Edwin.; *see* Watts-Ditchfield.

Ditchfield, Rev. Peter Hampson, 1854–1930, vol. III

Ditmars, Raymond Lee, 1876–1942, vol. IV

Ditmas, Lt-Col Francis Ivan Leslie, 1876–1969, vol. VI

Ditzen, Rudolf, 1893–1947, vol. IV

Dive, Lt-Col Gilbert Henry, 1882–1939, vol. III

Diver, Captain Cyril Roper Pollock, 1892–1969, vol. VI

Diver, (Katherine Helen) Maud, *died* 1945, vol. IV

Diver, Maud; *see* Diver, K. H. M.

Divers, Edward, 1837–1912, vol. I

Divers, Brig. Sydney Thomas, 1896–1979, vol. VII

Divine, Arthur Durham (David Divine), 1904–1987, vol. VIII

Divine, David; *see* Divine, A. D.

Dix, Comdr Charles Cabry, 1881–1951, vol. V

Dix, Dorothy Knight; *see* Waddy, D. K.

Dix, G. E. A., *see* Dix, Rev. Dom Gregory.

Dix, Rev. G. H., *died* 1932, vol. III

Dix, Rev. Dom Gregory, (G. E. A. Dix), 1901–1952, vol. V

Dixey, Arthur Carlyne Niven, 1889–1954, vol. V

Dixey, Charles Neville Douglas, 1881–1947, vol. IV

Dixey, Sir Frank, 1892–1982, vol. VIII

Dixey, Frederick Augustus, 1855–1935, vol. III

Dixey, Sir Harry Edward, 1853–1927, vol. II

Dixey, Marmaduke; *see* Howard, Geoffrey.

Dixie, Sir (Alexander Archibald Douglas) Wolstan, 13th Bt, 1910–1975, vol. VII

Dixie, Sir Alexander Beaumont Churchill, 11th Bt, 1851–1924, vol. II

Dixie, Sir Douglas; *see* Dixie, Sir G. D.

Dixie, Llady Florence, 1857–1905, vol. I

Dixie, Sir (George) Douglas, 12th Bt, 1876–1948, vol. IV

Dixie, Sir Wolstan; *see* Dixie, Sir A. A. D. W.

Dixon, Alfred Cardew, 1865–1936, vol. III

Dixon, Sir Alfred Herbert, 1st Bt (*cr* 1918), 1857–1920, vol. II

Dixon, Amzi Clarence, 1854–1925, vol. II

Dixon, Andrew Francis, *died* 1936, vol. III

Dixon, Arthur Frederic William, 1892–1948, vol. IV

Dixon, Arthur Lee, 1867–1955, vol. V

Dixon, Sir Arthur Lewis, 1881–1969, vol. VI

Dixon, Augustus Edward, 1860–1946, vol. IV

Dixon, Bernard, 1906–1983, vol. VIII

Dixon, Maj.-Gen. Bernard Edward Cooke, 1896–1973, vol. VII

Dixon, Campbell; *see* Dixon, G. C.

Dixon, Cecil Edith Mary, 1891–1979, vol. VII

Dixon, Charles, 1858–1926, vol. II

Dixon, Charles, 1872–1934, vol. III

Dixon, Charles Harvey, 1862–1923, vol. II

Dixon, Sir Charles William, 1888–1976, vol. VII

Dixon, Rt Hon. Sir Daniel, 1st Bt (*cr* 1903), 1844–1907, vol. I

Dixon, Maj.-Gen. Edward George, 1837–1918, vol. II

Dixon, Ella Nora Hepworth, *died* 1932, vol. III

Dixon, Sir Francis Netherwood, 1879–1968, vol. VI

Dixon, Air Vice-Marshal Sir (Francis Wilfred) Peter, 1907–1988, vol. VIII

Dixon, Lt-Col Frederick Alfred, 1880–1925, vol. II

Dixon, George, 1820–1898, vol. I

Dixon, Col Sir George, 1st Bt (*cr* 1919), 1842–1924, vol. II

Dixon, (George) Campbell, 1895–1960, vol. V

Dixon, Gertrude Caroline, 1886–1966, vol. VI

Dixon, Col Graham Patrick, 1873–1947, vol. IV

Dixon, Harold Baily, 1852–1930, vol. III

Dixon, Harry, 1861–1941, vol. IV

Dixon, Brig.-Gen. Sir Henry Grey, 1850–1933, vol. III

Dixon, Henry Horatio, 1869–1953, vol. V

Dixon, Henry Sydenham, 1848–1931, vol. III

Dixon, Ven. Henry Thomas, 1874–1939, vol. III

Dixon, Rt Rev. Horace Henry, 1869–1964, vol. VI

Dixon, Hubert John, 1895–1971, vol. VII

Dixon, Sir John, 2nd Bt (cr 1919), 1886–1976, vol. VII

Dixon, John Edwin F.; see Fowler-Dixon.

Dixon, Sir John George, 3rd Bt (cr 1919), 1911–1990, vol. VIII

Dixon, Most Rev. John Harkness, 1888–1972, vol. VII

Dixon, John Reginald, 1886–1972, vol. VII

Dixon, Kendal Cartwright, 1911–1990, vol. VIII

Dixon, Captain Kennet, died 1927, vol. II

Dixon, Kevin, 1902–1959, vol. V

Dixon, Leslie Charles G.; see Graham-Dixon.

Dixon, Malcolm, 1899–1985, vol. VIII

Dixon, Maj.-Gen. Matthew Charles, 1821–1905, vol. I

Dixon, Michael George, 1920–1990, vol. VIII

Dixon, Lt-Col Oscar, 1883–1966, vol. VI

Dixon, Rt Hon. Sir Owen, 1886–1972, vol. VII

Dixon, Air Vice-Marshal Sir Peter; see Dixon, Air Vice-Marshal Sir F. W. P.

Dixon, Sir Pierson John, 1904–1965, vol. VI

Dixon, Sir Raylton, 1838–1901, vol. I

Dixon, Engr-Vice-Adm. Sir Robert Bland, 1867–1939, vol. III

Dixon, Sir Samuel G.; see Gurney-Dixon.

Dixon, Stephen Mitchell, died 1940, vol. III

Dixon, Rev. Thomas Harold, died 1963, vol. VI

Dixon, Rt Hon. Sir Thomas James, 2nd Bt (cr 1903), 1868–1950, vol. IV

Dixon, Walter Ernest, 1870–1931, vol. III

Dixon, Lt-Col William, 1868–1958, vol. V

Dixon, William Gray, 1854–1928, vol. II

Dixon, William Macneile, 1866–1946, vol. IV

Dixon, Sir William Vibart, 1850–1930, vol. III

Dixon-Hartland, Sir Frederick Dixon, 1st Bt, 1832–1909, vol. I

Dixon-Nuttall, Major William Francis, 1885–1981, vol. VIII

Dixon-Spain, John Edward, died 1955, vol. V

Dixon-Wright, Rev. Henry Dixon, 1870–1916, vol. II

Dixson, Sir Hugh, 1841–1926, vol. II

Dixson, Sir William, 1870–1952, vol. V

Dixwell-Oxenden, Sir Percy Dixwell Nowell; see Oxenden.

Doak, Sir James, 1904–1975, vol. VII

Doane, Rt Rev. W. Crosswell, 1832–1913, vol. I

Dobb, Harry, 1867–1928, vol. II

Dobb, Maurice Herbert, 1900–1976, vol. VII

Dobbie, Edward David, 1857–1915, vol. I

Dobbie, Sir James Johnston, 1852–1924, vol. II

Dobbie, Sir Joseph, 1862–1943, vol. IV

Dobbie, Mitchell Macdonald, 1901–1982, vol. VIII

Dobbie, William, 1878–1950, vol. IV

Dobbie, Lt-Gen. Sir William George Sheddon, 1879–1964, vol. VI

Dobbie, William Herbert, 1851–1941, vol. IV

Dobbie, Brig.-Gen. William Hugh, 1859–1922, vol. II

Dobbie-Bateman, Rev. Arthur Fitzroy, 1897–1974, vol. VII

Dobbin, Sir Alfred Graham, 1853–1942, vol. IV

Dobbin, Gertrude; see Page, G.

Dobbin, Brig.-Gen. Herbert Thomas, 1878–1946, vol. IV

Dobbin, Lt-Col Leonard George William, 1871–1936, vol. III

Dobbin, Lt-Col William James Knowles, 1856–1926, vol. II

Dobbs, Cecil Moore, 1882–1969, vol. VI

Dobbs, Col Charles Fairlie, 1872–1936, vol. III

Dobbs, Sir Henry Robert Conway, 1871–1934, vol. III

Dobbs, Lt-Col Richard Conway, 1878–1957, vol. V

Dobbs, Richard Heyworth, 1905–1980, vol. VII

Dobell, Lt-Gen. Sir Charles Macpherson, 1869–1954, vol. V

Dobell, Clifford, 1886–1949, vol. IV

Dobell, Air Cdre Frederic Osborne Storey, 1912–1965, vol. VI

Dobell, Rev. Joseph, 1844–1908, vol. I

Dobell, Hon. Richard Reid, 1837–1902, vol. I

Dobell, Sir William, 1899–1970, vol. VI

Dobie, Very Rev. George Nelson, died 1933, vol. III

Dobie, Marryat Ross, 1888–1973, vol. VII

Dobie, William Jardine, 1892–1956, vol. V

Dobinson, Charles Henry, 1903–1980, vol. VII

Dobie, Rev. Gilbert Hunter, 1880–1945, vol. IV

Dobree, Alfred, 1864–1937, vol. III

Dobrée, Lt-Col Bonamy, 1891–1974, vol. VII

Dobree, Claude Hatherley, died 1960, vol. V, vol. VI

Dobree, George, 1873–1907, vol. I

Dobree, Rev. Osmond, 1832–1929, vol. III

Dobson, Alban Tabor Austin, 1885–1962, vol. VI

Dobson, Hon. Alfred, 1848–1908, vol. I

Dobson, Maj.-Gen. Anthony Henry George, 1911–1987, vol. VIII

Dobson, Sir Arthur Dudley, 1841–1934, vol. III

Dobson, Sir Benjamin Alfred, 1847–1898, vol. I

Dobson, Bernard Henry, 1881–1945, vol. IV

Dobson, Rear-Adm. Claude Congreve, 1885–1940, vol. III

Dobson, Cowan, died 1980, vol. VII

Dobson, Eric John, 1913–1984, vol. VIII

Dobson, Lt-Col Francis George, 1879–1941, vol. IV

Dobson, Frank, 1888–1963, vol. VI

Dobson, George, died 1938, vol. III

Dobson, Gordon Miller Bourne, 1889–1976, vol. VII

Dobson, Henry Austin, 1840–1921, vol. II

Dobson, Henry John, 1858–1928, vol. II

Dobson, John Frederic, 1875–1947, vol. IV

Dobson, Cdre John Petter, 1901–1985, vol. VIII

Dobson, Lt-Col Joseph Henry, 1878–1954, vol. V

Dobson, Mildred Eaton, died 1952, vol. V

Dobson, Raymond Francis Harvey, 1925–1980, vol. VII

Dobson, Richard Rhimes, 1877–1960, vol. V

Dobson, Sir Roy Hardy, 1891–1968, vol. VI

Dobson, Sydney George, 1883–1969, vol. VI

Dobson, Thomas William, 1853–1935, vol. III

Dobson, William Charles Thomas, 1817–1898, vol. I

Dobson, Sir William Lambert, 1833–1898, vol. I

Dobson, Col Sir William Warrington, 1861–1941, vol. IV

Docker, Sir Bernard Dudley Frank, 1896–1978, vol. VII

Docker, Frank Dudley, 1862–1944, vol. IV

Docker, Ludford Charles, 1860–1940, vol. III

Docker, Rev. Wilfrid Brougham, 1882–1956, vol. V

Dockrell, Benjamin Morgan, 1860–1920, vol. II

Dockrell, Sir Maurice Edward, 1850–1929, vol. III

Dockrill, Col Walter R., 1877–1942, vol. IV

Dod, Brig.-Gen. Owen Cadogan W.; *see* Wolley-Dod.

Dodd, Brig. Arthur Harvey Russell, 1883–1955, vol. V

Dodd, Catherine I., *died* 1932, vol. III

Dodd, Charles Edward Shuter, 1891–1974, vol. VII

Dodd, Rev. Charles Harold, 1884–1973, vol. VII

Dodd, Cyril, *died* 1913, vol. I

Dodd, Sir Edward James, 1909–1966, vol. VI

Dodd, Sir Edwin, *died* 1933, vol. III

Dodd, Francis, 1874–1949, vol. IV

Dodd, Frederick Henry, 1890–1950, vol. IV

Dodd, Major George, 1872–1914, vol. I

Dodd, Rev. Harold, 1899–1987, vol. VIII

Dodd, Henry Work, *died* 1921, vol. II

Dodd, James Munro, 1915–1986, vol. VIII

Dodd, Col John Richard, 1858–1930, vol. III

Dodd, Sir John Samuel, 1904–1973, vol. VII

Dodd, Norris Edward, 1879–1968, vol. VI

Dodd, Sir Robert John Sherwood, 1878–1950, vol. IV

Dodd, Stanley, *died* 1946, vol. IV

Dodd, Col Wilfrid T., *died* 1942, vol. IV

Dodd, Rev. William Harold Alfred; *see* Dodd, Rev. Harold.

Dodd, Rt Hon. William Huston, 1844–1930, vol. III

Dodds, Sir Charles; *see* Dodds, Sir E. C.

Dodds, Sir (Edward) Charles, 1st Bt, 1899–1973, vol. VII

Dodds, Eric Robertson, 1893–1979, vol. VII

Dodds, George Elliott, 1889–1977, vol. VII

Dodds, Gladys Helen, 1898–1982, vol. VIII

Dodds, Harold Willis, 1889–1980, vol. VII

Dodds, Jackson, 1881–1961, vol. VI

Dodds, Sir James Leishman, 1891–1972, vol. VII

Dodds, Sir James Miller, 1861–1935, vol. III

Dodds, Hon. Sir John Stokell, 1848–1914, vol. I

Dodds, Rev. Canon Matthew Archbold, 1864–1928, vol. II

Dodds, Norman Noel, 1903–1965, vol. VI

Dodds, Stephen Roxby, 1881–1943, vol. IV

Dodds, Maj.-Gen. Thomas Henry, 1873–1943, vol. IV

Dodds, Brig.-Gen. William Okell Holden, 1867–1934, vol. III

Dodds Crewe, Major James Hugh Hamilton, 1880–1956, vol. V

Dodge, Bayard, 1888–1972, vol. VII

Dodge, Grenville Mellen, 1831–1916, vol. II

Dodge, John Bigelow, 1894–1960, vol. V

Dodgson, Campbell, 1867–1948, vol. IV

Dodgson, Rev. Charles L.; *see* Carroll, Lewis.

Dodgson, Brig.-Gen. Golquhoun Scott, 1867–1947, vol. IV

Dodgson, Sir David Scott, 1821–1898, vol. I

Dodgson, Major Heathfield Butler, 1863–1937, vol. III

Dodgson, John Arthur, 1890–1969, vol. VI

Dodington, Brig.-Gen. Wilfred Marriott-, 1871–1931, vol. III

Dods, Alexander Waddell, *died* 1952, vol. V

Dods, Lt-Col Joseph Espie, 1874–1930, vol. III

Dods, Sir Lorimer Fenton, 1900–1981, vol. VIII

Dods, Marcus, 1834–1909, vol. I

Dods, Marcus, *died* 1935, vol. III

Dods-Withers, Isobelle, 1876–1939, vol. III

Dodson, Sir Gerald, 1884–1966, vol. VI

Dodson, John Michael, 1919–1977, vol. VII

Dodson, Rev. Canon Thomas Hatheway, 1862–1931, vol. III

Dodsworth, Sir Claude Matthew S., 7th Bt; *see* Smith-Dodsworth.

Dodsworth, Sir (Leonard) Lumley (Savage), 1890–1968, vol. VI

Dodsworth, Sir Lumley; *see* Dodsworth, Sir Leonard L. S.

Dodsworth, Sir Matthew Blayney Smith, 6th Bt, 1856–1931, vol. III

Dodwell, David William, 1898–1980, vol. VII

Dodwell, Henry Herbert, 1879–1946, vol. IV

Doel, James, 1804–1902, vol. I

Doggart, Arthur Robert, 1866–1932, vol. III

Doggart, James Hamilton, 1900–1989, vol. VIII

Doggett, Frank John, 1910–1988, vol. VIII

Doherty, Rt Hon. Charles Joseph, 1855–1931, vol. III

Doherty, F. C., *died* 1959, vol. V

Doherty, William David, 1893–1966, vol. VI

Doherty-Holwell, Captain Raymond Vernon; *see* Holwell.

Dohnányi Ernest, 1877–1960, vol. V

Doidge, Sir Frederick Widdowson, 1884–1954, vol. V

Doig, Henry Stuart, 1874–1931, vol. III

Doig, Sir James Nimmo Crawford, 1913–1984, vol. VIII

Doig, Peter, 1882–1952, vol. V

d'Oisly, (Emile) Maurice, 1882–1949, vol. IV

d'Oisly, Maurice; *see* d'Oisly, E. M.

Doisy, Edward A., 1893–1986, vol. VIII

Doke, Clement Martyn, 1893–1980, vol. VII

Dolamore, William Henry, *died* 1938, vol. III

Doland, Lt-Col George Frederick, 1872–1946, vol. IV

Dolbey, Robert Valentine, 1878–1937, vol. III

Dolby, Major Sir George Alexander, 1854–1939, vol. III

Dolgorouki, Prince Alexis, 1846–1915, vol. I

Dolgorouki, Princess Alexis, (Frances), *died* 1919, vol. II

Dolin, Sir Anton, 1904–1983, vol. VIII

Doll, William Alfred Millner, 1885–1977, vol. VII

Dollan, Sir Patrick Joseph, *died* 1963, vol. VI

Dollar, Jean Marguerite, 1900–1982, vol. VIII

Dolley, Michael, 1925–1983, vol. VIII

Dollfuss, Engelbert, 1892–1934, vol. III

Dollman, John Charles, 1851–1934, vol. III

Dolman, Eric Charles, 1903–1969, vol. VI

Dolman, Frederick, *born* 1867, vol. II

Dolmetsch, Arnold, 1858–1940, vol. III

Dolphin, Albert Edward, 1895–1972, vol. VII

Dolphin, Lt-Comdr Edgar H., *died* 1930, vol. III

Dolphin, Rear-Adm. George Verner Motley, 1902–1979, vol. VII
Dolphin, John Robert Vernon, 1905–1973, vol. VII
Dolton, David, *died* 1932, vol. III
Domagk, Gerhard, 1895–1964, vol. VI
Domenichetti, Richard, *died* 1901, vol. I
Dominguez, Florencio L., *died* 1910, vol. I
Dominguez, Don Vicente J., *died* 1916, vol. II
Dominy, Reginald Hugh, *died* 1953, vol. V
Domvile, Adm. Sir Barry Edward, 1878–1971, vol. VII
Domvile, Sir Compton Edward, 1842–1924, vol. II
Domvile, Sir Compton Meade, 4th Bt, 1857–1935, vol. III
Domvile, Sir Hugo Compton Domvile P.; *see* Pöe Domvile.
Domville, Rear-Adm. Sir Cecil; *see* Domville, Rear-Adm. Sir W. C. H.
Domville, Captain Sir Cecil Lionel, 6th Bt, 1892–1930, vol. III
Domville, Sir Gerald Guy, 7th Bt, 1896–1981, vol. VIII
Domville, Lt-Col Hon. James, 1842–1921, vol. II
Domville, Sir James Henry, 5th Bt, 1889–1919, vol. II
Domville, Rear-Adm. Sir (William) Cecil H., 4th Bt, 1849–1904, vol. I
Domville-Fife, Charles William, 1887–1960, vol. V (A)
Don, Rev. Alan Campbell, 1885–1966, vol. VI
Don, Charles Davidson, 1874–1959, vol. V
Don, Air Vice-Marshal Francis Percival, 1886–1964, vol. VI
Don, Kaye Ernest, 1891–1981, vol. VIII
Don, Sir William, 1861–1926, vol. II
Don, Surg.-Gen. William Gerard, 1836–1920, vol. II
Don-Wauchope, Sir John Douglas; *see* Wauchope.
Don-Wauchope, Sir Patrick George; *see* Wauchope.
Donachy, Frank, 1899–1970, vol. VI
Donald, Alexander Douglas, *died* 1948, vol. IV
Donald, Archibald, 1860–1937, vol. III
Donald, Charles, 1896–1955, vol. V
Donald, Maj.-Gen. Colin George, 1854–1939, vol. III
Donald, David William Alexander, 1915–1986, vol. VIII
Donald, Douglas, 1865–1953, vol. V
Donald, Douglas Alexander, *died* 1975, vol. VII
Donald, Air Marshal Sir Grahame, 1891–1976, vol. VII
Donald, Ian, 1910–1987, vol. VIII
Donald, Sir James, 1873–1957, vol. V
Donald, Sir James Bell, 1879–1971, vol. VII
Donald, Sir John Stewart, 1861–1948, vol. IV
Donald, Mary Jane; *see* Longstaff, M. J.
Donald, Maxwell Bruce, 1897–1978, vol. VII
Donald, Sir Robert, 1861–1933, vol. III
Donald, William C.; *see* Coutts Donald.
Donaldson, Rev. Canon Alexander Edward, 1878–1960, vol. V
Donaldson, Rev. Augustus Blair, 1841–1903, vol. I
Donaldson, Comdr Charles Edward McArthur, 1903–1964, vol. VI
Donaldson, Sir Dawson, 1903–1990, vol. VIII
Donaldson, Eion Pelly, 1896–1963, vol. VI
Donaldson, Rev. Frederic Lewis, 1860–1953, vol. V

Donaldson, Sir George, 1845–1925, vol. II
Donaldson, Sir Hey Frederick, 1856–1916, vol. II
Donaldson, Sir James, 1831–1915, vol. I
Donaldson, John Coote, 1895–1980, vol. VII
Donaldson, Adm. Leonard Andrew Boyd, 1875–1956, vol. V
Donaldson, Malcolm, 1884–1973, vol. VII
Donaldson, Mary Ethel Muir, 1876–1958, vol. V
Donaldson, Norman Patrick, 1878–1955, vol. V
Donaldson, Robert, *died* 1933, vol. III
Donaldson, Rt Rev. St Clair George, 1863–1935, vol. III
Donaldson, William, 1838–1924, vol. II
Donaldson-Hudson, Lt-Col Ralph Charles, 1874–1941, vol. IV
Donat, (Frederick) Robert, 1905–1958, vol. V
Donat, Robert; *see* Donat, F. R.
Doncaster, John Priestman, 1907–1981, vol. VIII
Doncaster, Leonard, 1877–1920, vol. II
Doncaster, Sir Robert, 1872–1955, vol. V
Done, Brig.-Gen. Herbert Richard, 1876–1950, vol. IV
Done, William Edward Pears, 1883–1976, vol. VII
Donegall, 5th Marquess of, 1822–1904, vol. I
Donegall, 6th Marquis of, 1903–1975, vol. VII
Donegan, Lt-Col James Francis, 1863–1934, vol. III
Donelan, Captain Anthony J., 1846–1924, vol. II
Donelan, James, *died* 1922, vol. II
Doneraile, 6th Viscount, 1866–1941, vol. IV
Doneraile, 7th Viscount, 1869–1956, vol. V
Doneraile, 8th Viscount, 1878–1957, vol. V
Doneraile, 9th Viscount, 1923–1983, vol. VIII
Dönges, Theophilus Ebenhaézer, 1898–1968, vol. VI
Donington, 3rd Baron, 1859–1927, vol. II
Donkin, Sir Bryan; *see* Donkin, Sir H. B.
Donkin, Bryan, 1835–1902, vol. I
Donkin, Sir (Horatio) Bryan, 1845–1927, vol. II
Donkin, Richard Sims, 1836–1919, vol. II
Donkin, Sydney Bryan, 1871–1952, vol. V
Donn-Byrne, Brian Oswald; *see* Byrne, Donn.
Donnan, Frederick George, 1870–1956, vol. V
Donnan, James, 1837–1915, vol. I
Donnay, Maurice, 1859–1945, vol. IV
Donne, Col Benjamin Donisthorpe Alsop, 1856–1907, vol. I
Donne, Col Henry Richard Beadon, 1860–1949, vol. IV
Donne, Thomas Edward, 1859–1945, vol. IV
Donne, Ven. William, 1845–1914, vol. I
Donnelly, Alex. E., *died* 1958, vol. V
Donnelly, Sir Arthur Telford, 1890–1954, vol. V
Donnelly, Desmond Louis, 1920–1974, vol. VII
Donnelly, Harry Hill, 1909–1969, vol. VI
Donnelly, Sir John Fretcheville Dykes, 1834–1902, vol. I
Donnelly, Rt Rev. Nicholas, 1837–1920, vol. II
Donnelly, Patrick, *died* 1947, vol. IV
Donner, Anna Maria, (Lady Donner), *died* 1935, vol. III
Donner, Sir Edward, 1st Bt, 1840–1934, vol. III
Donner, Frederic Garrett, 1902–1987, vol. VIII
Donner, Ossian, 1866–1957, vol. V
Donner, Sir Patrick William, 1904–1988, vol. VIII

Donnet of Balgay, Baron (Life Peer); Alexander Mitchell Donnet, 1916–1985, vol. VIII

Donnet, Sir James John Louis, 1816–1905, vol. I

Donnithorne, Rev. Vyvyan Henry, 1886–1968, vol. VI

Donoghue, Stephen, (Steve), 1884–1945, vol. IV

Donohoe, Martin Henry, 1869–1927, vol. II

Donohue, Col William Edward, 1861–1945, vol. IV

Donoughmore, 5th Earl of, 1848–1900, vol. I

Donoughmore, 6th Earl of, 1875–1948, vol. IV

Donoughmore, 7th Earl of, 1902–1981, vol. VIII

Donovan, Baron (Life Peer); Terence Norbert Donovan, 1898–1971, vol. VII

Donovan, Dame Florence May; *see* Hancock, Dame F. M.

Donovan, Francis Desmond, 1894–1948, vol. IV

Donovan, Hedley Williams, 1914–1990, vol. VIII

Donovan, John, 1891–1971, vol. VII

Donovan, John Thomas, 1878–1922, vol. II

Donovan, John Thomas, 1885–1973, vol. VII

Donovan, Robert, 1862–1934, vol. III

Donovan, Maj.-Gen. Sir William, 1850–1934, vol. III

Donovan, Maj.-Gen. William Joseph, 1883–1959, vol. V

Dontenwill, Most Rev. Augustin, 1857–1931, vol. III

Doodson, Arthur Thomas, 1890–1968, vol. VI

Doogan, P. C., *died* 1906, vol. I

Doolette, Sir George Philip, 1840–1924, vol. II

Doolin, William, 1887–1962, vol. VI

Dooner, Lt-Col William Dundas, 1876–1927, vol. II

Dooner, Col William Toke, *died* 1926, vol. II

Doorly, Sir Charles William, 1875–1942, vol. IV

Doorly, Most Rev. Edward, 1870–1950, vol. IV

Doorly, Rev. Canon Wiltshire Stokely, *died* 1932, vol. III

Dopping-Hepenstal, Major Lambert John, 1859–1928, vol. II

Dopping-Hepenstal, Col Maxwell Edward, 1872–1965, vol. VI

Doran, Alban Henry Griffiths, 1849–1927, vol. II

Doran, Maj.-Gen. Beauchamp John Colclough, 1860–1943, vol. IV

Doran, Edward, 1892–1945, vol. IV

Doran, Edward Anthony, *died* 1922, vol. II

Doran, Sir Henry Francis, 1856–1928, vol. II

Doran, Gen. Sir John, 1824–1903, vol. I

Doran, Brig. John Crampton Morton, 1880–1957, vol. V

Doran, Brig.-Gen. Walter Robert Butler, 1861–1945, vol. IV

Doráti, Antal, 1906–1988, vol. VIII

Dorchester, 4th Baron, 1822–1897, vol. I

Dorchester, Baroness (5th in line), 1846–1925, vol. II

Dorchester, 6th Baron, 1876–1963, vol VI

Dore, Gp Captain Alan Sydney Whitehorn, 1882–1953, vol. V

Dore, Ernest, *died* 1950, vol. IV

Doré, Victor, 1880–1954, vol. V

Dorey, Edgar Aleck, 1886–1976, vol. VII

Dorey, Stanley Fabes, 1891–1972, vol. VII

Dorez, Léon Louis Marie, 1864–1922, vol. II (A), vol. III

Dorington, Hubert, 1878–1935, vol. III

Dorington, Rt Hon. Sir John Edward, 1st Bt, 1832–1911, vol. I

Doris, William, 1860–1926, vol. II

Dorland, Arthur Garratt, 1887–1980, vol. VII

Dorling, Captain Henry Taprell, 1883–1968, vol. VI

Dorling, Vice-Adm. James Wilfred Sussex, 1889–1966, vol. VI

Dorling, Col Lionel, 1860–1925, vol. II

Dorman, Sir Arthur John, 1st Bt, 1848–1931, vol. III

Dorman, Sir Bedford Lockwood, 2nd Bt, *died* 1956, vol. V

Dorman, Brig. Edward Mungo, 1885–1967, vol. VI

Dorman, Surg.-Gen. John Cotter, 1852–1944, vol. IV

Dorman-Smith, Col Rt Hon. Sir Reginald Hugh, 1899–1977, vol. VII

Dormer, 12th Baron, 1830–1900, vol. I

Dormer, 13th Baron, 1862–1920, vol. II

Dormer, 14th Baron, 1864–1922, vol. II

Dormer, 15th Baron, 1903–1975, vol. VII

Dormer, Sir Cecil Francis Joseph, 1883–1979, vol. VII

Dormer, Charles Walter C.; *see* Cottrell-Dormer.

D'Ormesson, Count Wladimir Olivier Marie François de Paule Le Fèvre, 1888–1973, vol. VII

Dornhorst, Frederick, 1849–1927, vol. II

Dorrell, Bt Lt-Col George Thomas, *died* 1971, vol. VII

Dorrien, Gen. Sir Horace Lockwood S.; *see* Smith-Dorrien.

Dorrien, Lady (Olive Crofton) S.; *see* Smith-Dorrien.

Dorrien, Rev. Walter Montgomery S.; *see* Smith-Dorrien.

Dorrien-Smith, Major Edward Pendarves, 1879–1937, vol. III

Dorrien-Smith, Thomas Algernon, 1846–1918, vol. II

Dorrity, Rev. David, *died* 1926, vol. II

Dorté, Philip Hoghton, 1904–1970, vol. VI

Dorward, Alan James, 1889–1956, vol. V

Dorward, Maj.-Gen. Sir Arthur Robert Ford, 1848–1934, vol. III

Dorward, Ivor Gardiner Menzies Gordon, 1927–1983, vol. VIII

Dos Passos, John, 1896–1970, vol. VI

Dossor, Rear-Adm. Frederick, 1913–1990, vol. VIII

Dott, Norman McOmish, 1897–1973, vol. VII

Dottin, Henri Georges, 1863–1928, vol. II (A), vol. III

Dottridge, Edwin Thomas, 1876–1947, vol. IV

Doubleday, Rt Rev. Arthur, 1865–1951, vol. V

Doubleday, Frederic Nicklin, 1885–1971, vol. VII

Doubleday, John Gordon, 1920–1982, vol. VIII

Doubleday, Sir Leslie, 1887–1975, vol. VII

Doudney, Sarah, 1843–1926, vol. II

Dougal, Daniel, 1884–1948, vol. IV

Dougall, Lily, 1858–1923, vol. II

Dougan, James Lockhart, 1874–1941, vol. IV

Dougan, Thomas Wilson, *died* 1907, vol. I

Dougherty, HE Cardinal Denis J., *died* 1951, vol. V

Dougherty, Rt Hon. Sir James Brown, 1844–1934, vol. III

Doughty, Dame Adelaide Baillieu, 1908–1986, vol. VIII

Doughty, Sir Arthur, *died* 1936, vol. III

Doughty, Sir Charles, 1878–1956, vol. V

Doughty, Charles John Addison, 1902–1973, vol. VII

Doughty, Charles Montagu, 1843–1926, vol. II

Doughty, Sir George, 1854–1914, vol. I

Doughty, Rear-Adm. Henry Montagu, 1870–1921, vol. II

Doughty-Tichborne, Sir Anthony Joseph Henry Doughty; *see* Tichborne.

Doughty-Tichborne, Sir Henry Alfred Joseph; *see* Tichborne.

Doughty-Tichborne, Sir Joseph Henry Bernard; *see* Tichborne.

Doughty-Wylie, Major Charles Hotham Montagu; *see* Wylie.

Douglas of Barloch, 1st Baron, 1889–1980, vol. VII

Douglas of Kirtleside, 1st Baron, 1893–1969, vol. VI

Douglas, Hon. Sir Adyl, 1815–1906, vol. I

Douglas, Alexander Edgar, 1916–1981, vol. VIII

Douglas, Lord Alfred Bruce, 1870–1945, vol. IV

Douglas, Andrew, *died* 1935, vol. III

Douglas, Very Rev. Canon Lord Archibald, 1850–1938, vol. III

Douglas, Archibald Campbell, 1872–1943, vol. IV

Douglas, Adm. Sir Archibald Lucius, 1842–1913, vol. I

Douglas, Col Archibald Philip, 1867–1953, vol. V

Douglas, Lt-Col Archibald Vivian Campbell, 1902–1977, vol. VII

Douglas, Arthur, 1850–1920, vol. II

Douglas, Rt Rev. Hon. Arthur Gascoigne, 1827–1905, vol. I

Douglas, Arthur Henry Johnstone-, 1846–1923, vol. II

Douglas, Sir Arthur Percy, 5th Bt (*cr* 1777), 1845–1913, vol. I

Douglas, Campbell Mellis, *died* 1909, vol. I

Douglas, Carstairs Cumming, 1866–1940, vol. III

Douglas, Lord Cecil Charles, 1898–1981, vol. VIII

Douglas, Cecil George, 1854–1919, vol. II

Douglas, Lt-Col Charles Edward, 1855–1943, vol. IV

Douglas, Charles Mackinnon, 1865–1924, vol. II

Douglas, Gen. Sir Charles Whittingham Horsley, 1850–1914, vol. I

Douglas, Claude, 1852–1945, vol. IV

Douglas, Claude Gordon, 1882–1963, vol. VI

Douglas, Clifford Hugh, 1879–1952, vol. V

Douglas, David, 1823–1916, vol. II

Douglas, David Charles, 1898–1982, vol. VIII

Douglas, Donald Wills, 1892–1981, vol. VIII

Douglas, Brig.-Gen. Douglas Campbell, 1964–1927, vol. II

Douglas, Rt Rev. Edward, 1901–1967, vol. VI

Douglas, Hon. Edward Archibald, 1877–1947, vol. IV

Douglas, Rev. Evelyn Keith, 1959–1920, vol. II

Douglas, Francis John, 1858–1934, vol. III

Douglas, Sir George Brisbane, 5th Bt (*cr* 1786), 1856–1935, vol. III

Douglas, Rev. George Cunninghame Monteath, 1826–1904, vol. I

Douglas, Adm. Hon. George Henry, 1821–1905, vol. I

Douglas, Very Rev. George James Cosmo, *died* 1973, vol. VII

Douglas, (George) Keith, 1903–1949, vol. IV

Douglas, Lt-Col George Stuart, 1879–1947, vol IV

Douglas, Rt Rev. Gerald Wybergh, 1875–1934, vol. III

Douglas, Rev. Hon. Henry, 1822–1907, vol I

Douglas, Maj.-Gen. Henry Edward Manning, 1875–1939, vol. III

Douglas, Vice-Adm. Sir (Henry) Percy, 1876–1939, vol. III

Douglas, Horace James, 1866–1962, vol. VI

Douglas, Hugh C; *see* Cowan-Douglas

Douglas, Very Rev. Hugh Osborne, 1911–1986, vol. VIII

Douglas, Irvine; *see* Douglas, R. I.

Douglas, James, 1826–1904, vol. I

Douglas, James, 1837–1910, vol. I

Douglas, James, 1837–1918, vol. II

Douglas, James, 1867–1940, vol. III

Douglas, James Albert Sholto, 1913–1981, vol. VIII

Douglas, Maj.-Gen. James Archibald, 1862–1932, vol. III

Douglas, James Archibald, 1884–1978, vol. VII

Douglas, Sir James Boyd, 1893–1964, vol. VI

Douglas, James G., 1887–1954, vol. V

Douglas, Sir James Louis Fitzroy Scott, 6th Bt *cr* 1786), 1930–1969, vol. VI

Douglas, Hon. James Moffat, 1839–1921, vol. II

Douglas, James Sholto Cameron, 1879–1931, vol. III

Douglas, Major Sir James Stewart, 6th Bt (*cr* 1777), 1859–1940, vol. III

Douglas, Major James Wightman, 1873–1937, vol. III

Douglas, Hon. John, 1828–1904, vol. I

Douglas, Rev. Canon John Albert, *died* 1956, vol. V

Douglas, Maj.-Gen. John Primrose, 1908–1975, vol. VII

Douglas, Katharine Greenhill, 1908–1979, vol. VII

Douglas, Keith; *see* Douglas, G. K.

Douglas, Sir Kenneth, 4th Bt (*cr* 1831), 1868–1954, vol. V

Douglas, Lewis Williams, 1894–1974, vol. VII

Douglas, Lloyd C., 1877–1951, vol. V

Douglas, Lt-Col Montagu William, 1863–1957, vol. V

Douglas, Norman, 1868–1952, vol. V

Douglas, Col Norman, 1887–1968, vol. VI

Douglas, O.; *see* Buchan, Anna.

Douglas, Vice-Adm. Sir Percy; *see* Douglas, Vice-Adm. Sir H. P.

Douglas, Reginald Stair, 1877–1933, vol. III

Douglas, Lt-Col Robert Jeffray, 1869–1916, vol. II

Douglas, Sir Robert Kennaway, 1838–1913, vol. I

Douglas, Captain Robert Langton, 1864–1951, vol. V

Douglas, Rev. Robert Noel, 1868–1957, vol. V

Douglas, Major Robert Vaughan, 1881–1922, vol. II

Douglas, Col Roderick, 1898–1965, vol. VI

Douglas, (Ronald) Irvine, 1899–1973, vol. VII

Douglas, Adm. Sholto, 1833–1913, vol. I

Douglas, Sir Sholto (Courtenay Mackenzie), 5th Bt, 1890–1986, vol. VIII

Douglas, Captain Sholto Grant, 1867–1956, vol. V

Douglas, Major Sholto William, 1870–1959, vol. V

Douglas, Captain Stewart Ranken, 1871–1936, vol. III

Douglas, Maj.-Gen. Sir William, 1858–1920, vol. II

Douglas, Brig.-Gen. William Charles, 1862–1938, vol. III

Douglas, William Douglas Robinson-, 1851–1921, vol. II

Douglas, William Orville, 1898–1980, vol. VII

Douglas, Comdr William Ramsay Binny, *died* 1919, vol. II

Douglas, Sir William Scott, 1890–1953, vol. V

Douglas-Hamilton, Rev. Hamilton Anne, 1853–1929, vol. III

Douglas-Hamilton, Lord Malcolm Avendale, 1909–1964, vol. VI

Douglas-Hamilton, Percy Seymour, 1875–1940, vol. III

Douglas-Henry, Major James, 1881–1943, vol. IV

Douglas-Home, Charles Cospatrick, 1937–1985, vol. VIII

Douglas-Jones, Sir Crawford Douglas, 1874–1956, vol. V

Douglas-Pennant, Hon. Alan George Sholto, 1890–1915, vol. I

Douglas-Pennant, Hon. Charles, 1877–1914, vol. I

Douglas-Pennant, Adm. Hon. Sir Cyril Eustace, 1894–1961, vol. VI

Douglas-Pennant, Captain Hon. George Henry, 1876–1915, vol. I

Douglas-Pennant, Hon. Violet Blanche, *died* 1945, vol. IV

Douglas-Scott, Lord Charles Thomas Montagu; *see* Scott

Douglas-Scott-Montagu, Hon. Robert Henry, 1867–1916, vol. II

Douglass of Cleveland, Baron (Life Peer); Harry Douglass, 1902–1978, vol. VII

Douglass, Sir James Nicholas, 1826–1898, vol. I

Douglass, Walter John, 1863–1945, vol. IV

Douglass, William Tregarthen, *died* 1913, vol. I

Douie, Charles Oswald Gaskell, 1896–1953, vol. V

Douie, Col Francis McCrone, 1886–1935, vol. III

Douie, Sir James McCrone, 1854–1935, vol. III

Doull, Rt Rev. Alexander John, 1870–1937, vol. III

Doull, John, 1878–1969, vol. VI (AII)

Doull-Connolly, Thomas James, 1878–1949, vol. IV (A)

Doulton, Sir Henry, 1820–1897, vol. I

Doulton, Henry Lewis, 1853–1930, vol. III

Doumer, Paul, 1857–1932, vol. III

Doumergue, Emile, 1844–1937, vol. III

Doumergue, Gaston, 1863–1937, vol. III

Doumic, Rene, *died* 1937, vol. III

Douthwaite, Arthur Henry, 1896–1974, vol. VII

Douthwaite, James Lungley, 1877–1960, vol. V

Douty, Edward Henry, 1861–1911, vol. I

Dove, Maj.-Gen. Arthur Julian Hadfield, 1902–1985, vol. VIII

Dove, Sir Clifford Alfred, 1904–1988, vol. VIII

Dove, Dame Frances, 1847–1942, vol. IV

Dove-Edwin, George Frederick, 1896–1973, vol. VII

Dove-Wilson, Sir John Carnegie; *see* Wilson

Dovener, John Montague, 1923–1981, vol. VIII

Dover, Rev. Thomas Birkett, 1846–1926, vol. II

Dovercourt, 1st Baron, 1878–1961, vol. VI

Doverdale, 1st Baron, 1836–1925, vol. II

Doverdale, 2nd Baron, 1872–1935, vol. III

Doverdale, 3rd Baron, 1904–1949, vol. IV

Doveton, Frederick Bazett, 1841–1911, vol. I

Dow, Alexander Warren, 1873–1948, vol. IV

Dow, David Rutherford, 1887–1979, vol. VII

Dow, Sir Hugh, 1886–1978, vol. VII

Dow, James Findlay, 1911–1983, vol. VIII

Dow, R(onald) Graham, 1909–1983, vol. VIII

Dow, Samuel, 1908–1976, vol. VII

Dow, Thomas Millie, *died* 1919, vol. II

Dowbiggin, Sir Herbert Layard, 1880–1966, vol. VI

Dowd, (Eric) Ronald; *see* Dowd, R.

Dowd, Ronald, 1914–1990, vol. VIII

Dowdall, Hon. Mary Frances Harriet, 1876–1939, vol. III

Dowdall, Harold Chaloner, 1868–1955, vol. V

Dowdall, Sir Laurence Charles Edward Downing, 1851–1936, vol. III

Dowden, Major Charles Henry, 1880–1937, vol. III

Dowden, Edward, 1843–1913, vol. I

Dowden, Rt Rev. John, 1840–1910, vol. I

Dowden, John Wheeler, 1866–1936, vol. III

Dowding, 1st Baron, 1882–1970, vol. VI

Dowding, Vice-Adm. Sir Arthur Ninian, 1886–1966, vol. VI

Dowding, Cdre John Charles Keith, 1891–1965, vol. VI

Dowding, Gen. Townley Ward, 1847–1927, vol. II

Dowell, Brig.-Gen. Arthur John William, 1861–1943, vol. IV

Dowell, Col George Cecil, 1862–1949, vol. IV

Dowell, Bt Lt-Col George William, 1860–1940, vol. III

Dowell, Sir William Montagu, 1825–1912, vol. I

Dower, Col Alan Vincent Gandar, 1898–1980, vol. VII

Dower, Eric Leslie G.; *see* Gandar Dower.

Dowker, Gen. Howard Codrington, 1829–1912, vol. I

Dowler, Lt-Gen. Sir Arthur Arnhold Bullick, 1895–1963, vol. VI

Dowley, Francis Michael, 1885–1948, vol. IV

Dowling, Geoffrey Barrow, 1891–1976, vol. VII

Dowling, Sir Hallam Walter, 1909–1983, vol. VIII

Dowling, Most Rev. John Pius, 1860–1940, vol. III

Dowling, Vice-Adm. Sir Roy Russell, 1901–1969, vol. VI

Dowling, Rev. Theodore Edward, 1937–1921, vol. II

Dowling, Rt Rev. Thomas Joseph, 1840–1924, vol. II

Down, Lt-Comdr Sir Charles Edward, 1857–1927, vol. II

Down, Lt-Gen. Sir Ernest Edward, 1902–1980, vol. VII

Down, Air Cdre Harold Hunter, 1895–1974, vol. VII

Down, Norman Cecil Sommers, 1893–1984, vol. VIII

Down, Captain Richard Thornton, 1882–1944, vol. IV

Downe, 8th Viscount, 1844–1924, vol. II

Downe, 9th Viscount, 1872–1931, vol. III

Downe, 10th Viscount, 1903–1965, vol. VI

Downer, Hon. Sir Alexander Russell, 1910–1981, vol. VIII

Downer, Ven. George William, *died* 1912, vol. I

Downer, Sir Harold George, 1871–1935, vol. III

Downer, Hon. Sir John William, 1844–1915, vol. I

Downer, William James, 1851–1939, vol. III

Downes, Sir Arthur Henry, 1851–1938, vol. III

Downes, Commissary-Gen. Arthur William, 1827–1905, vol. I

Downes, Very Rev. Edmund Audley, 1877–1950, vol. IV

Downes, Sir Joseph, 1848–1925, vol. II

Downes, Maj.-Gen. Major Francis, 1834–1923 vol. II

Downes, Rev. Robert Percival, 1842–1924, vol. II

Downes, Ronald Geoffrey, 1916–1985, vol. VIII

Downes, Maj.-Gen. Rupert Major, 1885–1945, vol. IV

Downes, Col William Knox, 1855–1911, vol. I

Downes-Shaw, Sir (Archibald) Havergal, 1884–1961, vol. VI

Downes-Shaw, Sir Havergal; see Downes-Shaw, Sir A. H.

Downey, Edmund, died 1937, vol. III

Downey, Most Rev. Richard, 1881–1953, vol V

Downham, 1st Baron, 1853–1920, vol. II

Downham, Rev. Isaac, died 1923, vol. II

Downe, Major Fairbairn, 1880–1949, vol. IV

Downie, Allan Watt, 1901–1988, vol. VIII

Downie, Sir Harold Frederick, 1889–1966, vol. VI

Downie, Captain John, died 1921, vol. II

Downie, John P., died 1945, vol. IV

Downie, Hon. John Wallace, 1876–1940, vol. III

Downie, Walker, died 1921, vol. II

Downing, Arthur Matthew Weld, 1850–1917, vol. II

Downing, Col Cameron Macartney Harwood, 1845–1926, vol. II

Downing, Rev. Edward Andrew, died 1931, vol. III

Downing, George Henry, 1878–1940, vol. III (A), vol. IV

Downing, Henry Philip Burke, 1865–1947, vol. IV

Downing, Richard Ivan, 1915–1975, vol. VII

Downing, Sir Stanford Edwin, 1870–1933, vol. III

Downing, Rev. Thomas William, 1864–1932, vol. III

Downman, Charles Beaumont Benoy, 1916–1982, vol. VIII

Downs, Brian Westerdale, 1893–1984, vol. VIII

Downs, Edgar, died 1963, vol. VI

Downs, James, 1856–1941, vol. IV

Downshire, 6th Marquess of, 1871–1918, vol.II

Downshire, 7th Marquess of, 1894–1989, vol. VIII

Dowse, Rt Rev. Charles Benjamin, died 1934, vol. III

Dowse, Maj.-Gen. John Cecil Alexander, 1891–1964, vol. VI

Dowse, Rev. John Clarence, died 1930, vol. III

Dowse, Maj.-Gen. Sir Maurice Brian, 1899–1986, vol. VIII

Dowse, Very Rev. William, 1856–1939, vol.III

Dowsett, Col Ernest Blair, died 1951, vol. V

Dowson, Maj.-Gen. Arthur Henley, 1908–1989, vol. VIII

Dowson, Sir Ernest MacLeod, 1876–1950, vol. IV

Dowson, Sir Hubert Arthur, 1866–1946, vol. IV

Dowson, Joseph Emerson, 1844–1940, vol. III

Dowson, Sir Oscar Follett, 1879–1961, vol. VI

Dowty, Sir George Herbert, 1901–1975, vol. VII

Doxat, Major Alexis Charles, 1867–1942, vol. IV

Doxford, Sir William Theodore, 1841–1916, vol. II

Doxiadis, Constantinos Apostolos, 1913–1975, vol. VII

Doyen, E., 1859–1916, vol. II

Doyle, Adrian Malcolm C.; see Conan Doyle.

Doyle, Rear-Adm. Alec Broughton, 1888–1984, vol. VIII

Doyle, Sir Arthur Conan, 1859–1930, vol. III

Doyle, Col Sir Arthur Havelock James, 4th Bt, 1858–1948, vol. IV

Doyle, Charles Francis, 1866–1928, vol. II

Doyle, Edward, 1892–1965, vol. VI

Doyle, Lt-Col Eric Edward, 1886–1937, vol. III

Doyle, Sir Everard Hastings, 3rd Bt, 1852–1933, vol. III

Doyle, Hon. Henry Martin, died 1929, vol. III

Doyle, Major Ignatius Purcell, 1863–1923, vol. II

Doyle, John Andrew, 1844–1907, vol. I

Doyle, Lt-Col John Francis Innes Hay, 1873–1919, vol. II

Doyle, Sir John Francis Reginald William Hastings, 5th Bt, 1912–1987, vol. VIII

Doyle, Joseph, 1891–1974, vol. VII

Doyle, Lynn, (Leslie Alexander Montgomery), 1873–1961, vol. VI

Doyle, Sir Nicholas G.; see Grattan-Doyle.

Doyle, Rt Rev. Mgr Richard Barry-, 1878–1933, vol. III

Doyle, Brig. Richard Stanislaus, 1911–1982, vol. VIII

Doyle, Very Rev. Thomas, 1853–1926, vol. II

Doyle, William Patrick, 1927–1983, vol. VIII

Doyle-Jones, F. W., died 1938, vol. III

D'Oyly, Sir Charles Hastings, 12th Bt, 1898–1962, vol. VI

D'Oyly, Sir Charles Walters, 9th Bt, 1822–1900, vol. I

D'Oyly, Sir Hadley; see D'Oyly, Sir. H. H.

D'Oyly, Sir (Hastings) Hadley, 11th Bt, 1864–1948, vol. IV

D'Oyly, Sir John Rochfort, 13th Bt, 1900–1986, vol. VIII

D'Oyly, Sir Warren Hastings, 10th Bt, 1838–1921, vol. II

D'Oyly Carte, Dame Bridget, 1908–1985, vol. VIII

D'Oyly Carte, Rupert, 1876–1948, vol. IV

D'Oyly-Hughes, Captain Guy, 1891–1940, vol. III

Doyne, Charles Mervyn, 1839–1924, vol.II

Doyne, Dermot Henry, 1871–1942, vol. IV

Doyne, Philip Geoffry, 1886–1959, vol. V

Doyne, Robert Walter, 1857–1916, vol. II

Drabble, John Frederick, 1906–1982, vol. VIII

Drachmann, Holger, 1846–1908, vol. I

Drage, Sir Benjamin, died 1952, vol. V

Drage, Geoffrey, 1860–1955, vol. V

Drage, Lt-Col William Henry,1855–1915, vol. I

Drago, Luis Maria, 1859–1921, vol. II

Drake, Antony Elliot, 1907–1990, vol. VIII

Drake, Brig.-Gen. Bernard Francis, 1862–1954, vol. V

Drake, Bernard Harpur, 1876–1941, vol. IV

Drake, Donald Henry Charles, 1887–1974, vol. VII

Drake, Sir Eugen John Henry Vandersteqen M.; see Millington-Drake.

Drake, Rev. F. W., died 1930, vol. III

Drake, Sir Francis George Augustus Fuller-Eliott-, 2nd Bt, 1837–1916, vol. II

Drake, Lt-Col Francis Richard, 1862–1935, vol. III

Drake, Sir Garrard Tyrwhitt-; see Drake, Sir H. G. T.

Drake, Harold William, 1889–1973, vol. VII

Drake, Col Henry Dowrish, 1859–1931, vol. III
Drake, Sir (Hugh) Garrard Tyrwhitt-, 1881–1964, vol. VI
Drake, Sir James, 1907–1989, vol. VIII
Drake, Hon. James George, 1850–1941, vol. IV
Drake, James Mackay Henry M.; *see* Millington-Drake.
Drake, John Alexander, 1878–1952, vol. V
Drake, John Collard Bernard, 1884–1975, vol. VII
Drake, Maurice, 1875–1923, vol. II
Drake, Hon. Montague W. Tyrwhitt-, *died* 1908, vol. I
Drake, Lt-Col Reginald John, *died* 1948, vol. IV
Drake, Robert James, *died* 1916, vol. II
Drake, Samuel Bingham, *died* 1935, vol. III
Drake, Captain Thomas Oakley, 1863–1928, vol. II
Drake, Col William Hacche, 1873–1956, vol. V
Drake, William James, 1872–1919, vol. II
Drake, William Wyckham Tyrwhitt, 1851–1919, vol. II
Drake-Brockman, Brig.-Gen. David Henry, 1868–1960, vol. V
Drake-Brockman, Sir Digby Livingstone, 1877–1959, vol. V
Drake-Brockman, Maj.-Gen. Edmund Alfred, 1884–1949, vol. IV
Drake-Brockman, Sir Henry Vernon, 1865–1933, vol. III
Drake-Brockman, Lt-Col Ralph Evelyn, 1875–1952, vol. V
Drakeley, Thomas James, 1890–1981, vol. VIII
Drakoules, Platon Soterios, 1858–1942, vol. IV
Draper, Bernard Montagu, 1875–1950, vol. IV
Draper, Charles; *see* Draper, R. C.
Draper, Charles, 1869–1952, vol. V
Draper, Brig.-Gen. Denis Colbarn, 1873–1951, vol. V
Draper, Col Gerald Irving Anthony Dare, 1914–1989, vol. VIII
Draper, Herbert James, *died* 1920, vol. II
Draper, (Reginald) Charles, 1932–1983, vol. VIII
Draper, Ruth, 1884–1956, vol. V
Draper, Hon. Thomas Percy, 1864–1946, vol. IV
Draper, William Franklin, 1842–1910, vol. I
Draper, William H., Jr, 1894–1974, vol. VII
Draper, Rev. William Henry, 1855–1933, vol. III
Drawbell, James Wedgwood, 1899–1979, vol. VII
Drawbridge, Rev. Cyprian Leycester, 1868–1937, vol. III
Drax, Adm. Hon. Sir Reginald Aylmer Ranfurly P. E. E.; *see* Plunkett-Ernle-Erle-Drax.
Drayson, Rear-Adm. Edwin Howard, 1889–1977, vol. VII
Drayson, Brig. Fitz-Alan George, 1888–1964, vol. VI
Drayson, George Burnaby, 1913–1983, vol. VIII
Drayton, Edward Rawle, 1859–1927, vol. II
Drayton, Miss Gertrude Drayton Grimké, 1880–1941, vol. IV
Drayton, Harley; *see* Drayton, Harold Charles.
Drayton, Harold Charles, (Harley Drayton), *died* 1966, vol. VI
Drayton, Sir Henry Lumley, 1869–1950, vol. IV
Drayton, Sir Robert Harry, 1892–1963, vol. VI
Dreaper, Surg. Rear-Adm. George Albert, 1863–1927, vol. II

Dreaper, William Porter, 1868–1938, vol. III
Dredge, James, 1840–1906, vol. I
Dreiser, Theodore, 1871–1945, vol. IV
Drennan, Alexander Murray, 1884–1984, vol. VIII
Drennan, Basil St George, 1903–1976, vol. VII
Drennan, (C.) Max, 1870–1935, vol. III
Drennan, John Cherry, 1899–1982, vol. VIII
Drennan, Max; *see* Drennan, C. M.
Dreschfeld, Julius, 1846–1907, vol. I
Dresdel, Sonia, 1909–1976, vol. VII
Dressel, Dettmar, 1878–1961, vol. VI
Dressel, Otto, 1880–1941, vol. IV
Dresser, Henry Eeles, 1838–1915, vol I
Dresser, Horatio Willis, 1866–1954, vol. V
Drever, James, 1873–1950, vol. IV (A)
Drew, Brig.-Gen. Arthur Blanshard Hawley, 1865–1947, vol. IV
Drew, Air Cdre Bertie Clephane Hawley, 1880–1969, vol. VI
Drew, Brig. Cecil Francis, 1890–1987, vol. VIII
Drew, Charles Edwin, 1916–1987, vol. VIII
Drew, Clifford Luxmoore, *died* 1919, vol. II
Drew, Douglas, 1867–1931, vol. III
Drew, Sir Ferdinand Caire, 1895–1986, vol. VIII
Drew, Maj.-Gen. Francis Barry, 1825–1905, vol. I
Drew, Rt Rev. Mgr Count Francis Browning Drew B.; *see* Bickerstaffe-Drew.
Drew, Brig. Francis Greville, 1892–1962, vol. VI
Drew, Lt-Col Hon. George Alexander, 1894–1973, vol. VII
Drew, Lt-Col George Barry, 1868–1930, vol. III
Drew, Rev. Harry, *died* 1910, vol. I
Drew, Harry Edward, 1909–1988, vol. VIII
Drew, Gen. Henry Rawlins, 1822–1906, vol. I
Drew, Lt-Col Horace Robert Hawley, 1871–1936, vol. III
Drew, Maj.-Gen. Sir James Syme, 1883–1955, vol. V
Drew, Hon. John Michael, 1865–1947, vol. IV
Drew, Mary, 1847–1927, vol. II
Drew, Sir Thomas, 1838–1910, vol. I
Drew, Vice-Adm. Thomas Bernard, *died* 1960, vol. V
Drew, William Wilson, *died* 1923, vol. II
Drew-Wilkinson, Clennell Frank Massy, 1877–1956, vol. V
Drewe, Basil, 1894–1974, vol. VII
Drewe, Sir Cedric, 1896–1971, vol. VII
Drewe, Rev. Ernest, *died* 1935, vol. III
Drewe, Geoffrey Grabham, 1904–1986, vol. VIII
Drewitt, Frederic George Dawtrey, 1848–1942, vol. IV
Drewry, Arthur, 1891–1961, vol. VI
Drewry, Lt George Leslie, 1894–1918, vol. II
Dreyer, Adm. Sir Fredric Charles, 1878–1956, vol. V
Dreyer, Georges, 1873–1934, vol. III
Dreyer, John Louis Emil, 1852–1926, vol. II
Dreyer, Maj.-Gen. John Tuthill, 1876–1959, vol. V
Dreyfus, Henry, 1882–1944, vol. IV
Driberg, Thomas Edward Neil; *see* Baron Bradwell.
Driesch, Hans, 1867–1941, vol. IV
Dring, (Dennis) William, 1904–1990, vol. VIII
Dring, William; *see* Dring, D. W.
Dring Sir William Arthur, 1859–1912, vol. I
Drinkwater, Daisy; *see* Kennedy, D.
Drinkwater, George, 1852–1930, vol. III

Drinkwater, George Carr, 1880–1941, vol. IV
Drinkwater, John, 1882–1937, vol. III
Drinkwater, Sir William Leece, 1812–1909, vol. I
Driscoll, Lt-Col Daniel Patrick, 1862–1934, vol. III
Driscoll, Very Rev. James, 1870–1927, vol. II
Driver, Sir Arthur John, 1900–1990, vol. VIII
Driver, Major Arthur Robert, 1909–1981, vol. VIII
Driver, Sir Godfrey Rolles, 1892–1975, vol. VII
Driver, John Edmund, 1900–1965, vol. VI
Driver, Rev. Samuel Rolles, 1846–1914, vol. I
Driver, Thomas, 1912–1988, vol. VIII
Droch; *see* Bridges, Robert.
Drogheda, 9th Earl of, 1846–1908, vol. I
Drogheda, 10th Earl of, 1884–1957, vol. V
Drogheda, 11th Earl of, 1910–1989, vol. VIII
Dromgoole, Charles, *died* 1927, vol. II
Dron, Robert Wilson, 1869–1932, vol. III
Dronfield, John, 1898–1983, vol. VIII
Droop, John Percival, 1882–1963, vol. VI
Drought, Rev. Charles Edward, 1847–1917, vol. II
Drought, Charles W.; *see* Worster-Drought.
Drower, Sir Edwin Mortimer, 1880–1951, vol. V
Drower, Ethel May Stefana, (Lady Drower), 1879–1972, vol. VII
Drower, John Edmund, 1853–1945, vol. IV
Drowley, Air Vice-Marshal Thomas Edward, 1894–1985, vol. VIII
Drown, Thomas Messinger, 1842–1904, vol. I
Druce, George Claridge, 1850–1932, vol. III
Drucker, Adolphus, 1868–1903, vol. I
Drucquer, Sir Leonard, 1902–1975, vol. VII
Drucquer, Maurice Nathaniel, 1876–1970, vol. VI
Drughorn, Sir John Frederick, 1st Bt, 1862–1943, vol. IV
Druitt, Rt. Rev. Cecil Henry, 1874–1921, vol. II
Druitt, Sir Harvey; *see* Druitt, Sir W. A. H.
Druitt, Sir (William Arthur) Harvey, 1910–1973, vol. VII
Drum, Col Lorne, 1871–1933, vol. III
Drumalbyn, 1st Baron, 1908–1987, vol. VIII
Drummond, Lt-Gen. Sir Alexander; *see* Drummond, Lt-Gen. Sir W. A. D.
Drummond, Allan Harvey, 1845–1913, vol. I
Drummond, Andrew Cecil, 1865–1913, vol. I
Drummond, Arthur, 1871–1951, vol. V
Drummond, Rev. Arthur Hislop, 1843–1925, vol. II
Drummond, Arthur William Henry H; *see* Hay-Drummond.
Drummond, Col Hon. Charles Rowley H.; *see* Hay-Drummond.
Drummond, Cyril Augustus, 1873–1945, vol. IV
Drummond, Sir David, 1852–1932, vol. III
Drummond, Lady Edith, 1854–1937, vol. III
Drummond, Dame (Edith) Margaret, 1917–1987, vol. VIII
Drummond, Adm. Edmund Charles, 1841–1911, vol. I
Drummond, Vice-Adm. Hon. Edmund Rupert, 1884–1965, vol. VI
Drummond, Sir Francis Dudley Williams, 1863–1935, vol. III
Drummond, Maj.-Gen. Sir Francis Henry Rutherford, 1857–1919, vol. II
Drummond, Lt-Comdr Geoffrey Heneage, 1886–1941, vol. IV
Drummond, Hon. Sir George Alexander, 1829–1910, vol. I
Drummond, George Henry, 1883–1963, vol. VI
Drummond, Captain George Robinson Bridge, 1845–1917, vol. II
Drummond, Hon. Mrs Geraldine Margaret, *died* 1956, vol. V
Drummond, Hamilton, *died* 1935, vol. III
Drummond, Henry, 1851–1897, vol. I
Drummond, Lt-Col Henry Edward S. H.; *see* Stirling Home Drummond.
Drummond, Brig.-Gen. Sir Hugh Henry John, 1st Bt, 1859–1924, vol. II
Drummond, Isabella Martha, *died* 1949, vol. IV
Drummond, Sir Jack Cecil, 1891–1952, vol. V
Drummond, Rev. James, 1835–1918, vol. II
Drummond, James, 1869–1940, vol. III
Drummond, Sir James Hamlyn Williams-, 4th Bt, 1857–1913, vol. I
Drummond, Sir James Hamlyn Williams Williams-, 5th Bt, 1891–1970, vol. VI
Drummond, James Montagu Frank, 1881–1965, vol. VI
Drummond, Maj.-Gen. Laurence George, 1861–1946, vol. IV
Drummond, Lister Maurice, 1856–1916, vol. II
Drummond, Malcolm, 1856–1924, vol. II
Drummond, Captain Maldwin, 1872–1929, vol. III
Drummond, Dame Margaret; *see* Drummond, Dame E. M.
Drummond, Col Hon. Sir Maurice Charles Andrew, 1877–1957, vol. V
Drummond, Michael, 1850–1921, vol. II (A), vol. III
Drummond, Air Marshal Sir Peter Roy Maxwell, 1894–1945, vol. IV
Drummond, Rev. Robert J., 1858–1951, vol. V
Drummond, Rev. Robert Skiell, 1828–1911, vol. I
Drummond, Sir Victor Arthur Wellington, 1833–1907, vol. I
Drummond, Sir Walter James, 1891–1965, vol. VI
Drummond, Col William, 1880–1960, vol. V
Drummond, Lt-Gen. Sir (William) Alexander (Duncan), 1901–1988, vol. VIII
Drummond, Rev. William Hamilton, 1863–1945, vol. IV
Drummond, William Henry, 1854–1907, vol. I
Drummond, Sir William Hugh Dudley Williams-, 6th Bt, 1901–1976, vol. VII
Drummond-Hay, Francis Edward; *see* Hay.
Drummond-Hay, Sir Francis Ringler; *see* Hay.
Drummond-Willoughby, Brig.-Gen. Hon. Charles Strathavon Heathcote; *see* Willoughby.
Drummond-Wolff, Henry, 1899–1982, vol. VIII
Drury, Sir Alan Nigel, 1889–1980, vol. VII
Drury, Alfred, 1856–1944, vol. IV
Drury, (Alfred) Paul (Dalou), 1903–1987, vol. VIII
Drury, Amy Gertrude (Lady Drury), *died* 1953, vol. V
Drury, Adm. Sir Charles Carter, 1846–1914, vol. I
Drury, Maj.-Gen. Charles William, 1856–1913, vol. I
Drury, George Thorn-, 1860–1931, vol. III
Drury, Henry Cooke, 1860–1944, vol. IV

Drury, Henry George, 1839–1941, vol. IV

Drury, Rev. John Frederick William, 1858–1923, vol. II

Drury, Paul; *see* Drury, A. P. D.

Drury, Lt-Col Richard Frederick, 1866–1956, vol. V

Drury, Rev. Thomas William Ernest, *died* 1960, vol. V

Drury, Rt. Rev. Thomas Wortley, 1847–1926, vol. II

Drury, William D., 1857–1928, vol. II

Drury, Lt-Col William Price, 1861–1949, vol. IV

Drury-Lowe, Sir Drury Curzon, 1830–1908, vol. I

Drury-Lowe, Vice-Adm. Sidney Robert, 1871–1945, vol. IV

Druso; *see* Lumley, Lyulph.

Dryburgh, Edward Gelderd, 1909–1965, vol. VI

Dryden, Sir Alfred Erasmus, 5th and 8th Bt, 1821–1912, vol. I

Dryden, Sir Arthur, 6th and 9th Bt, 1852–1938, vol. III

Dryden, Sir Henry Edward Leigh, 4th and 7th Bt, 1818–1899, vol. I

Dryden, Hon. John, 1840–1909, vol. I

Dryden, Sir Noel Percy Hugh, 7th and 10th Bt, 1910–1970, vol. VI

Dryerre, Henry, 1881–1959, vol. V

Dryfoos, Orvil E., 1912–1963, vol. VI

Dryhurst, Frederick John, *died* 1931, vol. III

Dryland, Alfred, 1865–1946, vol. IV

Drysdale, Rev. A. H., 1837–1924, vol. II

Drysdale, Arthur, 1857–1922, vol. II

Drysdale, Charles Vickery, 1874–1961, vol. VI

Drysdale, Sir (George) Russell, 1912–1981, vol. VIII

Drysdale, Learmont, 1866–1909, vol. I

Drysdale, Sir Matthew Watt, 1892–1962, vol. VI

Drysdale, Sir Russell; *see* Drysdale, Sir G. R.

Drysdale, Sir William, 1819–1900, vol. I

Drysdale, Lt-Col William, 1876–1916, vol. II

D'Silva, John Leonard, 1910–1973, vol. VII

D'Souza, Most Rev. Albert V., 1904–1977, vol. VII

D'Souza, Frank, 1883–1960, vol. V

Dube, Bhugwandin, 1876–1938, vol. III

Dubilier, William, 1888–1969, vol. VI

Dubois, Paul, 1829–1905, vol. I

Dubois, Théodore, 1837–1924, vol. II

Du Bois, William Edward Burghardt, 1868–1963, vol. VI

Du Boisrouvray, Rt Rev. Bernard Jacquelot, 1877–1970, vol. VI (AII)

Dubose, William Porcher, 1836–1918, vol. II

Dubost, Antonin, 1844–1921, vol.II

Du Boulay, George Cornibert, 1883–1951, vol. V

Du Boulay, Ven. Henry Houssemayne, 1840–1925, vol.II

Du Boulay, Sir James Houssemayne, 1868–1945, vol. IV

Dubs, Homer H., 1892–1969, vol. VI

Dubuc, Arthur Edouard, 1880–1944, vol. IV

Dubuc, Sir Joseph, 1840–1914, vol. I

Dubuffet, Jean, 1901–1985, vol. VIII

Du Buisson, Very Rev. John Clement, 1871–1938, vol. III

Du Cane, Sir Edmund Frederick, 1830–1903, vol. I

Du Cane, Col Hubert John, 1859–1916, vol. II

Ducane, Gen. Sir John Philip, 1865–1947, vol. IV

Du Cane, Comdr Peter, 1901–1984, vol. VIII

Ducat, Col Charles Merewether, 1860–1934, vol. III

Ducat, David, 1904–1989, vol. VIII

Ducat, Ven. William Methven Gordon, *died* 1922, vol. II

Du Chaillu, Paul Belloni, 1835–1903, vol. I

Duchemin, Rt Rev. Mgr Charles L. H., 1886–1965, vol. VI

Duchemin, Henry Pope, *died* 1950, vol. IV

Duchesne, Jacques; *see* Saint-Denis, M. J.

Duchesne, Mgr Louis Marie Olivier, 1843–1922, vol. II

Ducie, 3rd Earl of, 1827–1921, vol. II

Ducie, 4th Earl of, 1834–1924, vol. II

Ducie, 5th Earl of, 1875–1952, vol. V

Duck, Vet. Col Sir Francis, 1845–1934, vol. III

Duck, Leslie, 1935–1989, vol. VIII

Duckett, Sir George Floyd, 3rd Bt, 1811–1902, vol. I

Duckett, Lt-Col John Steuart, 1876–1952, vol. V

Duckham, Alec Narraway, 1903–1988, vol. VIII

Duckham, Sir Arthur McDougall, 1879–1932, vol. III

Duckworth, Arthur; *see* Duckworth, G. A. V.

Duckworth, Sir Dyce, 1st Bt, 1840–1928, vol. II

Duckworth, Sir Edward Dyce, 2nd Bt, 1875–1945, vol. IV

Duckworth, Francis R. G., 1881–1964, vol. VI

Duckworth, Frederick Victor, 1901–1974, vol. VII

Duckworth, (George) Arthur (Victor), 1901–1986, vol. VIII

Duckworth, Sir George Herbert,1868–1934, vol. III

Duckworth, Sir James, 1840–1915, vol. I

Duckworth, James, 1869–1937, vol. III

Duckworth, John, 1863–1946, vol. IV

Duckworth, Captain Ralph Campbell Musbury, 1907–1983, vol. VIII

Duckworth, Rev. Robinson, 1834–1911, vol. I

Duckworth, Rev. William Arthur, 1829–1917, vol.II

Duckworth, William Rostron, 1879–1952, vol. V

Duckworth, Wynfrid Laurence Henry, 1870–1956, vol. V

Duckworth-King, Col Sir Dudley Gordon Alan, 5th Bt, 1851–1909, vol. I

Duckworth-King, Sir George Henry James, 6th Bt, 1891–1952, vol. V

Duckworth-King, Sir John Richard, 7th Bt, 1899–1972, vol. VII

Duclos, Arnold Willard, 1874–1947, vol. IV

Duclos, Hon. Joseph Adolphe, 1873–1933, vol. III

Du Cros, Alfred, 1868–1946, vol. IV

Du Cros, Sir Arthur Philip, 1st Bt, 1871–1955, vol. V

Du Cros, Sir (Harvey) Philip, 2nd Bt, 1898–1975, vol. VII

Du Cros, Sir Philip; *see* Du Cros, Sir H. P.

du Cros, William Harvey, 1846–1918, vol. II

Duddell, W., 1872–1917, vol. II

Dudden, Rev. Frederick Homes,1874–1955, vol. V

Dudding, Rear-Adm. Horatio Nelson, 1849–1917, vol. II

Dudding, Surg. Rear-Adm. John Scarbrough, 1877–1951, vol. V

Dudding, Sir John Scarbrough, 1915–1986, vol. VIII

Dudeney, Mrs Henry, *died* 1945, vol. IV

Dudeney, Henry Ernest, 1857–1930, vol. III

Dudgeon, Alastair; *see* Dudgeon, J. A.

Dudgeon, Major Cecil Randolph, 1885–1970, vol. VI
Dudgeon, Sir Charles John, 1855–1928, vol. II
Dudgeon, Maj.-Gen. Frederick Annesley, 1866–1943, vol. IV
Dudgeon, Gerald Cecil, 1867–1930, vol. III
Dudgeon, Henry Alexander, 1924–1984, vol. VIII
Dudgeon, (John) Alastair, 1916–1989, vol. VIII
Dudgeon, Leonard Stanley, 1876–1938, vol. III
Dudgeon, Lt-Col Robert Francis, 1851–1932, vol. III
Dudgeon, Brig.-Gen. Robert Maxwell, 1881–1962, vol. VI
Dudley, 2nd Earl of, 1867–1932, vol. III
Dudley, 3rd Earl of, 1894–1969, vol. VI
Dudley, 12th Baron, 1872–1936, vol. III
Dudley, 13th Baron, 1910–1972, vol. VII
Dudley, Sir Alan Alves, 1907–1971, vol. VII
Dudley, Donald Reynolds, 1910–1972, vol. VII
Dudley, Col George de Someri, 1874–1941, vol. IV
Dudley, Harold Ward, 1887–1935, vol. III
Dudley, Rev. Owen Francis, 1882–1952, vol. V
Dudley, Roland, 1879–1964, vol. VI
Dudley, Surg. Vice-Adm. Sir Sheldon Francis, 1884–1956, vol. V
Dudley, Sir Willem Edward, *died* 1938, vol. III
Dudley-Williams, Sir Rolf Dudley, 1st Bt, 1908–1987, vol. VIII
Dudman, George Edward, 1916–1984, vol. VIII
Dudman, Ven. Robert William, 1925–1984, vol. VIII
Dudok, Willem Marinus, 1884–1974, vol. VII
Duerden, J. E., *died* 1937, vol. III
Duesbury, Rt Rev. Charles Leonard T.; *see* Thornton-Duesbury.
Duesbery, Rev. Canon Julian Percy T.; *see* Thornton-Duesbery.
Duff, Major Adrian G.; *see* Grant-Duff.
Duff, Maj.-Gen. Alan Colquhoun, 1896–1973, vol. VII
Duff, Adm. Sir Alexander Ludovic, 1862–1933, vol. III
Duff, Archibald, 1845–1934, vol. III
Duff, Bt Lt-Col Arthur Abercromby S.; *see* Scott-Duff.
Duff, Adm. Sir Arthur Allan Morison, 1874–1952, vol. V
Duff, Sir Arthur Cuninghame G.; *see* Grant-Duff.
Duff, Gen. Sir Beauchamp, 1855–1918, vol. II
Duff, Lt-Col Benjamin Michael, 1840–1926, vol. II
Duff, Col Charles de Vertus, 1870–1950, vol. IV
Duff, Col Charles Edward, 1858–1936, vol. III
Duff, Sir (Charles) Michael (Robert Vivian), 3rd Bt, 1907–1980, vol. VII
Duff, Sir (Charles) Patrick, 1889–1972, vol. VII
Duff, Charles St Lawrence, 1894–1966, vol. VI
Duff, David, 1883–1959, vol. V
Duff, Edith Florence G.; *see* Grant-Duff.
Duff, Edward Gordon, 1863–1924, vol. II
Duff, Sir Evelyn G.; *see* Grant-Duff.
Duff, Francis Bluett, 1875–1947, vol. IV
Duff, Garden Alexander, 1853–1933, vol. III
Duff, Lt-Col Sir Garden Beauchamp, 1st Bt, 1879–1952, vol. V
Duff, Col George Mowat, 1862–1935, vol. III
Duff, Sir Hector Livingston, 1872–1954, vol. V
Duff, James Augustine, 1872–1943, vol. IV

Duff, Sir James Fitzjames, 1898–1970, vol. VI
Duff, Hon. James Stoddart, 1856–1916, vol. II
Duff, John, 1850–1921, vol. II
Duff, John Robert Keitley, 1862–1938, vol. III
Duff, John Wharton Wharton-, 1845–1935, vol. III
Duff, John Wight, 1866–1944, vol. IV
Duff, Rt. Hon. Sir Lyman Poore, 1865–1955, vol. V
Duff, Sir Michael; *see* Duff, Sir C. M. R. V.
Duff, Rt. Hon. Sir Mountstuart Elphinstone Grant, 1829–1906, vol. I
Duff, Sir Patrick; *see* Duff, Sir C. P.
Duff, Sir Robert George Vivian, (Sir Robin), 2nd Bt, 1876–1914, vol. I
Duff, Sir Robin; *see* Duff, Sir R. G. V.
Duff, Stanley Lewis, 1881–1943, vol. IV
Duff, Thomas Duff Gordon, 1848–1923, vol. II
Duff-Dunbar, Lt-Comdr Kenneth James; *see* Dunbar.
Duff Gordon, Sir Cosmo Edmund, 5th Bt; *see* Gordon.
Duff-Gordon, Sir Douglas Frederick, 7th Bt, 1892–1964, vol. VI
Duff-Gordon, Sir Henry William, 6th Bt, 1866–1953, vol. V
Duff-Sutherland-Dunbar, Sir George, 6th Bt; *see* Dunbar.
Duff-Sutherland-Dunbar, Sir George Cospatrick, 7th Bt, 1906–1963, vol. VI
Dufferin and Ava, 1st Marquess of, 1826–1902, vol. I
Dufferin and Ava, 2nd Marquess of, 1866–1918, vol. II
Dufferin and Ava, 3rd Marquess of, 1875–1930, vol. III
Dufferin and Ava, 4th Marquess of, 1909–1945, vol. IV
Dufferin and Ava, 5th Marquess of, 1938–1988, vol. VIII
Dufferin and Ava, Marchioness of; (Hariot), *died* 1936, vol. III
Duffes, Arthur Paterson, 1880–1968, vol. VI
Duffey, Sir George Frederick, 1843–1903, vol. I
Duffield, Anne, *died* 1976, vol. VII
Duffield, Mary Elizabeth, 1819–1914, vol. I
Duffield, William Bartleet, *died* 1918, vol. II
Duffus, Brig.-Gen. Edward John, 1866–1937, vol. III
Duffus, Col Francis Ferguson, 1870–1953, vol. V
Duffus, Sir William Algernon Holwell, 1911–1981, vol. VIII
Duffy, Hon. Sir Charles Gavan, 1816–1903, vol. I
Duffy, Charles Gavan, 1855–1932, vol. III
Duffy, Hon. Sir Charles Leonard G.; *see* Gavan-Duffy.
Duffy, Rt. Hon. Sir Frank Gavan, 1852–1936, vol. III
Duffy, George Gavan, 1882–1951, vol. V
Duffy, Hon. H. Thomas, *died* 1903, vol. I
Duffy, Hugh Herbert White, 1917–1983, vol. VIII
Duffy, Terence, 1922–1985, vol. VIII
Duffy, Thomas G.; *see* Gavan-Duffy.
Dufy, Raoul, 1877–1953, vol. V
Dugan of Victoria, 1st Baron, 1877–1951, vol. V
Dugas, Calixter Aimé, 1845–1918, vol. II
Dugas, François Octave, 1857–1918, vol. II (A), vol. III
Dugdale, Amy Katherine; *see* Browning, A. K.
Dugdale, Col Arthur, 1869–1941, vol. IV

Dugdale, Blanche Elizabeth Campbell; *see* Dugdale, Mrs Edgar Trevelyan Stratford.

Dugdale, Mrs Edgar Trevelyan Stratford, (Blanche Elizabeth Campbell Dugdale), *died* 1948, vol. IV

Dugdale, Col Frank, 1857–1925, vol. II

Dugdale, Frederick Brooks, *died* 1902, vol. I

Dugdale, James Broughton, 1855–1927, vol. II

Dugdale, Rt. Hon. John, 1905–1963, vol. VI

Dugdale, John Stratford, 1835–1920, vol. II

Dugdale, Rev. Sydney, *died* 1942, vol. IV

Dugdale, Thomas Cantrell, 1880–1952, vol. V

Dugdale, Sir William Francis Stratford, 1st Bt, 1872–1965, vol. VI

Dugdale, Major William Marshall, 1881–1952, vol. V

Duggan, Alfred Leo, 1903–1964, vol. VI

Duggan, Edmund John, *died* 1936, vol. III

Duggan, Rear-Adm. Eyre Sturdy, 1891–1956, vol. V

Duggan, George Chester, *died* 1969, vol. VI

Duggan, Major Harold Joseph, 1896–1942, vol. IV

Duggan, Hubert John, 1904–1943, vol. IV

Duggan, Col Sir Jamshedji, 1884–1957, vol. V

Dugmore, Arthur Radclyffe, 1870–1955, vol. V

Dugmore, Rev. Clifford William, 1909–1990, vol. VIII

Dugmore, Rev. Ernest Edward, 1843–1925, vol. II

Dugmore Lt-Col William Francis Brougham Radclyffe, 1868–1917, vol. II

Duguid, Charles, 1864–1923, vol. II

Duguid, Maj.-Gen. David Robertson, 1888–1973, vol. VII

Duguid, John Bright, 1895–1980, vol. VII

Duguid-McCombie, Col William McCombie, 1874–1970, vol. VI

Duhamel, Georges, 1884–1966, vol. VI

du Heaume, Sir (Francis) Herbert, 1897–1988, vol. VIII

du Heaume, Sir Herbert; *see* du Heaume, Sir F. H.

Duhig, Sir James, 1871–1965, vol. VI

Duhm, Bernhard Laward, 1847–1928, vol. II

Duigan, Maj.-Gen. Sir John Evelyn, 1882–1950, vol. IV

Dukas, Paul, 1865–1935, vol. III

Duke, Lt-Col Augustus Cecil Hare, *died* 1943, vol. IV

Duke, Brig. Cecil Leonard Basil, 1896–1963, vol. VI

Duke, Sir Charles Beresford, 1905–1978, vol. VII

Duke, Hon. Edgar Mortimer, 1895–1965, vol. VI

Duke, Rev. Edward St Arnaud, 1854–1939, vol. III

Duke, Sir (Frederick) William, 1863–1924, vol. II

Duke, Herbert Lyndhurst, 1883–1966, vol. VI

Duke, Sr James, 2nd Bt, 1865–1935, vol. III

Duke, James Buchanan, 1857–1925, vol. II

Duke, Brig. Jesse Pevensey, 1890–1980, vol. VII

Duke, Sir Norman; *see* Duke, Sir R. N.

Duke, Reginald Franklyn Hare, 1887–1929, vol. III

Duke, Sir (Robert) Norman, 1893–1969, vol. VI

Duke, Robin Antony Hare, 1916–1984, vol. VIII

Duke, Sir William; *see* Duke, Sir F. W.

Duke, Most Rev. William Mark, 1879–1971, vol. VII

Duke, Winifred, *died* 1962, vol. VI

Duke-Elder, Sir Stewart; *see* Duke-Elder, Sir W. S.

Duke-Elder, Sir (William) Stewart, 1898–1978, vol. VII

Dukes, Ashley, 1885–1959, vol. V

Dukes, Cuthbert Esquire, 1890–1977, vol. VII

Dukes, Dame Cyvia Myriam; *see* Rambert, Dame Marie.

Dukes, Dame Marie; *see* Rambert.

Dukes, Sir Paul, 1889–1967, vol. VI

Dukeston, 1st Baron, 1881–1948, vol. IV

Dulac, Edmund, 1882–1953, vol. V

Dulanty, John Whelan, *died* 1955, vol. V

Duleep Singh, Prince Frederick, 1868–1926, vol. II

Duleep Singh, Prince Victor Albert Jay, 1866–1918, vol. II

Dulles, Allen Welsh, 1893–1969, vol. VI

Dulles, John Foster, 1888–1959, vol. V

Dulverton, 1st Baron, 1880–1956, vol. V

Duly, Surg. Rear-Adm. (D) Philip Reginald John, 1925–1989, vol. VIII

Dumarchey, Pierre; *see* MacOrlan, Pierre.

Dumaresq, Rear-Adm. John Saumarez, 1873–1922, vol. II

Dumas, Hugh Charles Sowerby, 1865–1940, vol. III

Dumas, Sir Lloyd, 1891–1973, vol. VII

Dumas, Adm. Philip Wylie, 1868–1948, vol. IV

Dumas, Sir Russell John, 1887–1975, vol. VII

du Maurier, Dame Daphne, (Lady Browning), 1907–1989, vol. VIII

du Maurier, Sir Gerald, 1873–1934, vol. III

du Maurier, Lt-Col Guy Louis Busson, 1865–1915, vol. I

Dumayne, Sir Fredrick George, 1852–1930, vol. III

Dumbell, Sir Alured, 1835–1900, vol. I

Dumbell, Lt-Col Charles Harold, 1878–1935, vol. III

Dumbleton, Gen. Charles, 1824–1916, vol. II

Duminy, Jacobus Petrus, 1897–1980, vol. VII

Dummett, Robert Bryan, 1912–1977, vol. VII

Dummett, Sir Robert Ernest, 1872–1941, vol. IV

Du Moulin, Rt Rev. John Philip, 1834–1911, vol. I

Dumpleton, Cyril Walter, 1897–1966, vol. VI

Dumraon, Zamindar of, *died* 1933, vol. III

Dun, Robert Hay, 1870–1947, vol. IV

Dun, William Gibb, *died* 1927, vol. II

Dunalley, 4th Baron,1851–1927, vol. II

Dunalley, 5th Baron, 1877–1948, vol. IV

Dunbabin, Robert Leslie, 1869–1949, vol. IV

Dunbabin, Thomas, 1883–1973, vol. VII

Dunbabin, Thomas James, 1911–1955, vol. V

Dunbar of Mochrum, Sir Adrian Ivor, 12th Bt (*cr* 1694), 1893–1977, vol. VII

Dunbar, Sir Alexander, 1888–1955, vol. V

Dunbar, Sir Alexander James, 4th Bt (*cr* 1814), 1870–1900, vol. I

Dunbar, Alexander Robert, 1904–1980, vol. VII

Dunbar, Sir Archibald, 6th Bt (*cr* 1700), 1803–1898, vol. I

Dunbar, Sir (Archibald) Edward, 9th Bt (*cr* 1700), 1889–1969, vol. VI

Dunbar, Sir Archibald Hamilton, 7th Bt (*cr* 1700), 1828–1910, vol. I

Dunbar, Sir Basil Douglas H.; *see* Hope-Dunbar.

Dunbar, Paymaster Rear-Adm. Charles Augustus Royer Flood, 1849–1939, vol. III

Dunbar, Sir Charles Dunbar H.; *see* Hope-Dunbar.

Dunbar, Rev. Sir Charles Gordon-Cumming, 8th Bt (*cr* 1700), 1844–1916, vol. II

Dunbar, Maj.-Gen. Charles Whish, 1919–1981, vol. VIII

Dunbar, Maj.-Gen. Claude Ian Hurley, 1909–1971, vol. VII

Dunbar, Sir Drummond Miles, 7th Bt (*cr* 1697), 1845–1903, vol. I

Dunbar, Sir Edward; *see* Dunbar, Sir A. E.

Dunbar, Evelyn Mary, *died* 1960, vol. V

Dunbar, Sir Frederick George, 5th Bt (*cr* 1814), 1875–1937, vol. III

Dunbar, Sir George Alexander Drummond, 8th Bt (*cr* 1697), 1879–1949, vol. IV

Dunbar, Sir George Cospatrick D. S., 7th Bt; *see* Duff-Sutherland-Dunbar.

Dunbar Sir George Duff-Sutherland, 6th Bt, 1878–1962, vol. VI

Dunbar, Sir James George Hawker Rowland, 10th Bt (*cr* 1694), 1862–1953, vol. V

Dunbar, Sir John Greig, 1906–1978, vol. VII

Dunbar, Major John Telfer, *died* 1957, vol. V

Dunbar, Lt-Comdr Kenneth James Duff-, 1886–1916, vol. II

Dunbar, Sir Loraine Geddes, 1865–1943, vol. IV

Dunbar, Sir Richard Fredrick Roberts, 1900–1965, vol. VI

Dunbar, Sir Richard Sutherland, 11th Bt (*cr* 1694), 1873–1953, vol. V

Dunbar, Robert, 1895–1970, vol. VI

Dunbar, Robert Haig, *died* 1919, vol. II

Dunbar, Sir Uthred James Hay, 8th Bt (*cr* 1694), 1843–1904, vol. I

Dunbar, Sir William Cospatrick, 9th Bt (*cr* 1694), 1844–1931, vol. III

Dunbar-Buller, Charles William; *see* Buller.

Dunbar Kilburn, Bertram Edward, 1872–1948, vol. IV

Dunbar-Nasmith, Adm. Sir Martin Eric; *see* Nasmith.

Dunboyne, 24th Baron, 1839–1899, vol. I

Dunboyne, 25th Baron, 1844–1913, vol. I

Dunboyne, 26th Baron, 1874–1945, vol. IV

Duncalfe, Sir Roger, 1884–1961, vol. VI

Duncan, Col Sir Alan Gomme Gomme-, 1893–1963, vol. VI

Duncan, Alexander, *died* 1943, vol. IV

Duncan, Alexander Mitchell, 1888–1965, vol. VI

Duncan, Alexander Robert, 1844–1927, vol. II

Duncan, Alfred Charles, 1886–1979, vol. VII

Duncan, Andrew, *died* 1912, vol. I

Duncan, Rt. Hon. Sir Andrew Rae, 1884–1952, vol. V

Duncan, Sir Arthur Bryce, 1909–1984, vol. VIII

Duncan, Charles, 1865–1933, vol. III

Duncan, Sir (Charles Edgar) Oliver, 3rd Bt (*cr* 1905), 1892–1964, vol. VI

Duncan, Claude Woodruff, *died* 1945, vol. IV

Duncan, Colin; *see* Duncan, P. C.

Duncan, Sir David, *died* 1923, vol. II

Duncan, David, 1839–1923, vol. II

Duncan, Surg. Rear-Adm. David, 1900–1974, vol. VII

Duncan, Edmondstoune, 1866–1920, vol. II

Duncan, Ellen, vol. III

Duncan, Maj.-Gen. Francis John, *died* 1960, vol. V

Duncan, Sir Frederick William, 2nd Bt (*cr* 1905), 1859–1929, vol. III

Duncan, Captain George, 1863–1937, vol. III

Duncan, Rev. George, *died* 1932, vol. III

Duncan, George, *died* 1949, vol. IV

Duncan, George B., 1869–1941, vol. IV

Duncan, Very Rev. George Simpson, 1884–1965, vol. VI

Duncan, Sir Harold Handasyde, 1885–1962, vol. VI

Duncan, Sir Hastings; *see* Duncan, Sir J. H.

Duncan, Maj.-Gen. Henry Clare, 1876–1961, vol. VI

Duncan, Sir James, *died* 1926, vol. II

Duncan, Sir James Alexander Lawson, 1st Bt (*cr* 1957), 1899–1974, vol. VII

Duncan, James Archibald, 1858–1911, vol. I

Duncan, Lt-Col James Fergus, *died* 1941, vol. IV

Duncan, Sir (James) Hastings, 1855–1928, vol. II

Duncan, James Lindsay, 1905–1954, vol. V

Duncan, James Stuart, 1893–1986, vol. VIII

Duncan, Jane, 1910–1976, vol. VII

Duncan, Sir John, 1846–1914, vol. I

Duncan, John, *died* 1945, vol. IV

Duncan, Maj.-Gen. Sir John, 1872–1948, vol. IV

Duncan, Comdr John Alexander, 1878–1943, vol. IV

Duncan, John Douglas Grace, 1899–1969, vol. VI

Duncan, John Hudson E.; *see* Elder-Duncan.

Duncan, Hon. Sir John James, 1845–1913, vol. I

Duncan, John Murray, *died* 1922, vol. II

Duncan, Sir John Norman Valette; *see* Duncan, Sir Val.

Duncan, John Shiels, 1886–1949, vol. IV

Duncan, Rev. Joseph, 1843–1915, vol. I

Duncan, Joseph Forbes, 1879–1964, vol. VI

Duncan, Leland Lewis, 1862–1923, vol. II

Duncan, Col Macbeth Moir, 1866–1942, vol. IV

Duncan, Maj.-Gen. Nigel William, 1899–1987, vol. VIII

Duncan, Norman, 1871–1916, vol. II

Duncan, Sir Oliver; *see* Duncan, Sir C. E. O.

Duncan, Rt. Hon. Sir Patrick, 1870–1943, vol. IV

Duncan, (Peter) Colin, 1895–1979, vol. VII

Duncan, Lt-Col Ronald Cardew, 1886–1963, vol. VI

Duncan, Ronald Frederick Henry, 1914–1982, vol. VIII

Duncan, Sir Surr William, 1st Bt (*cr* 1905), 1834–1908, vol. I

Duncan, Sir Thomas Andrew, 1873–1960, vol. V

Duncan, Hon. Thomas Young, 1836–1914, vol. I

Duncan, Sir Val, (John Norman Valette), 1913–1975, vol. VII

Duncan, Hon. Sir Walter Gordon, 1885–1963, vol. VI

Duncan, Sir William Barr McKinnon, 1922–1984, vol. VIII

Duncan, Brig. William Edmonstone, 1890–1969, vol. VI

Duncan, William Jolly, 1894–1960, vol. V

Duncan-Hughes, Captain John Grant; *see* Hughes.

Duncan-Jones, Very Rev. Arthur Stuart, 1879–1955, vol. V

Duncan-Jones, Austin Ernest, 1908–1967, vol. VI

Duncan-Sandys, Baron (Life Peer); Duncan Edwin Duncan-Sandys, 1908–1987, vol. VIII

Duncanson, Sir John McLean, 1897–1963, vol. VI

Duncombe, Alfred Charles, 1843–1925, vol. II

Duncombe, Col (Charles) William (Ernest), 1862–1945, vol. IV

Duncombe, Maj.-Gen. Charles Wilmer, 1838–1911, vol. I

Duncombe, Sir Everard (Philip Digby) Pauncefort-, 3rd Bt (*cr* 1859), 1885–1971, vol. VII

Duncombe, Col Sir George Augustus, 1st Bt (*cr* 1919), 1848–1933, vol. III

Duncombe, Hon. Hubert Ernest Valentine, 1862–1918, vol. II

Duncombe, Walter Henry Octavius, 1846–1917, vol. II

Duncombe, Col William; *see* Duncombe, Col C. W. E.

Duncombe, Rev. William Duncombe Van der Horst, *died* 1925, vol. II

Dundas, Hon. Lord; David Dundas, 1854–1922, vol. II

Dundas of Dundas, Adam Duncan, 1903–1951, vol. V

Dundas, Sir Ambrose Dundas Flux, 1899–1973, vol. VII

Dundas of Dundas, Adm. Sir Charles, 1859–1924, vol. II

Dundas, Hon. Sir Charles Cecil Farquharson, 1884–1956, vol. V

Dundas, Sir Charles Henry, 4th Bt (*cr* 1821), 1851–1908, vol. I

Dundas, Rev. Charles Leslie, 1847–1932, vol. III

Dundas, David; *see* Dundas, Hon. Lord.

Dundas, Lt-Col Frederick Charles, 1868–1941, vol. IV

Dundas, Lord George Heneage Lawrence, 1882–1968, vol. VI

Dundas, George Smythe, 1842–1909, vol. I

Dundas, Sir George Whyte Melville, 5th Bt (*cr* 1821), 1856–1934, vol. III

Dundas, Sir Henry Herbert Philip, 3rd Bt (*cr* 1898), 1866–1930, vol. III

Dundas, Sir Henry Matthew, 5th Bt (*cr* 1898), 1937–1963, vol. VI

Dundas, Lt-Col James Colin, 1883–1966, vol. VI

Dundas, Sir James Durham, 6th Bt (*cr* 1898), 1905–1967, vol. VI

Dundas, Vice-Adm. John George Lawrence, 1893–1952, vol. V

Dundas, Hon. Kenneth Robert, 1882–1915, vol. I

Dundas, Major Laurance Charles, 1857–1908, vol. I

Dundas, Captain Lawrence Leopold, *died* 1939, vol. III

Dundas, Col Sir Lorenzo George, 1837–1917, vol. II

Dundas, Brig. Patrick Henry,1871–1936, vol. III

Dundas, Sir Philip, 4th Bt (*cr* 1898), 1899–1952, vol. V

Dundas, Sir Robert, 1st Bt (*cr* 1898) 1823–1909, vol. I

Dundas, Lt-Col Sir Robert, 2nd Bt (*cr* 1898), 1857–1910, vol. I

Dundas, Robert Giffen, 1909–1984, vol. VIII

Dundas, Robert Hamilton, 1884–1960, vol. V

Dundas, Rev. Robert J., 1832–1904, vol. I

Dundas, Robert Thomas, *died* 1948, vol. IV

Dundas, Sir Robert Whyte-Melville, 6th Bt (*cr* 1821), 1881–1981, vol. VIII

Dundas, Sir Sidney James, 3rd Bt (*cr* 1821), 1849–1904, vol. I

Dundas, Sir Thomas Calderwood, 7th Bt (*cr* 1898), 1906–1970, vol. VI

Dundas, William Charles Michael, 1873–1933, vol. III

Dundas, William John, 1848–1921, vol. II

Dundas-Grant, Sir James; *see* Grant.

Dundee, 11th Earl of, 1902–1983, vol. VIII

Dundee, Col William John Daniell, 1862–1940, vol. III

Dunderdale, Comdr Wilfred Albert, 1899–1990, vol. VIII

Dundon, John, *died* 1952, vol. V

Dundonald, 12th Earl of, 1852–1935, vol. III

Dundonald, 13th Earl of, 1886–1958, vol. V

Dundonald, 14th Earl of, 1918–1986, vol. VIII

Dunedin, 1st Viscount, 1849–1942, vol. IV

Dunedin, Viscountess; (Jean Elmslie), *died* 1944, vol. IV

Dunfee, Col Vickers, 1861–1927, vol. II

Dunfield, Sir Brian Edward Spencer, 1888–1968, vol. VI

Dunham, Cyril John, 1908–1986, vol. VIII

Dunham, E. K. 1860–1923, vol. II

Dunhill, Alfred, 1872–1959, vol. V

Dunhill, Thomas Frederick, 1877–1946, vol. IV

Dunhill, Sir Thomas Peel, 1876–1957, vol. V

Dunican, Peter Thomas, 1918–1989, vol. VIII

Dunk, Susan S.; *see* Spain-Dunk.

Dunk, Sir William Ernest, 1897–1984, vol. VIII

Dunkerley, Harvey John, 1902–1985, vol. VIII

Dunkerley, Ven. William Herbert Cecil, *died* 1922, vol. II

Dunkerly, John Samuel, 1881–1931, vol. III

Dunkin, Edwin, 1821–1898, vol. I

Dunkin, Major George William, 1886–1942, vol. IV

Dunkley, Rev. Charles, 1847–1936, vol. III

Dunkley, Sir Herbert Francis, 1886–1963, vol. VI (AII)

Dunkley, Philip Parker, 1922–1985, vol. VIII

Dunleath, 2nd Baron, 1854–1931, vol. III

Dunleath, 3rd Baron, 1886–1956, vol. V

Dunlop, Agnes Mary Robertson; *see* Kyle, Elisabeth.

Dunlop, Alexander Johnstone, 1848–1921, vol. II

Dunlop, Mrs Annie Isabella, 1897–1973, vol. VII

Dunlop, Charles Robertson, 1876–1932, vol. III

Dunlop, Major Colin Napier Buchanan, 1877–1915, vol. I

Dunlop, Rt Rev. David Colin, 1897–1968, vol. VI

Dunlop, Captain David Kennedy B.; *see* Buchanan-Dunlop.

Dunlop, Maj.-Gen. Dermott, 1898–1980, vol. VII

Dunlop, Sir Derrick Melville, 1902–1980, vol. VII

Dunlop, Douglas Morton, 1909–1987, vol. VIII

Dunlop, Ernest McMurchie, 1893–1969, vol. VI

Dunlop, Rev. Francis Wallace, 1875–1932, vol. III

Dunlop, Col Frank Passy, 1877–1940, vol. III

Dunlop, Col Henry Donald B.; *see* Buchanan-Dunlop.

Dunlop, Hugh Alexander, 1903–1954, vol. V

Dunlop, James Crauford, *died* 1944, vol. IV

Dunlop, James Marcus Muntz, *died* 1938, vol. III

Dunlop, James Matthew, 1867–1949, vol. IV

Dunlop, Col James William, 1854–1923, vol. II

Dunlop, Hon. John, 1837–1916, vol. II

Dunlop, Sir John Kinninmont, 1892–1974, vol. VII

Dunlop, Sir John Wallace, 1910–1983, vol. VIII

Dunlop, Louis Vandalle, 1878–1954, vol. V

Dunlop, Ven. Maxwell Tulloch, 1898–1964, vol. VI

Dunlop, Sir Nathaniel, 1830–1919, vol. II

Dunlop, Robert, *died* 1935, vol. III
Dunlop, Sir Robert William Layard, 1869–1962, vol. VI
Dunlop, Ronald Offory, 1894–1973, vol. VII
Dunlop, Roy Leslie, 1899–1981, vol. VIII
Dunlop, Col Samuel, 1838–1917, vol. II
Dunlop, Engr Rear-Adm. Samuel Harrison, 1884–1950, vol. IV
Dunlop, Sir Thomas, 1st Bt, 1855–1938, vol. III
Dunlop, Sir Thomas, 2nd Bt, 1881–1963, vol. VI
Dunlop, Bt Col Sir Thomas Charles, 1878–1960, vol. V
Dunlop, Sir Thomas Dacre, 1883–1963, vol. VI
Dunlop, Col William Bruce, 1877–1933, vol. III
Dunlop, Major William Hugh, 1857–1924, vol. II
Dunlop, William Louis Martial, 1882–1948, vol. IV
Dunlop, William Wallace, 1846–1930, vol. III
Dunmore, 7th Earl of, 1841–1907, vol. I
Dunmore, 8th Earl of, 1871–1962, vol. VI
Dunmore, 9th Earl of, 1939–1980, vol. VII
Dunmore, 10th Earl of, 1911–1981, vol. VIII
Dunn, Albert Edward, 1864–1937, vol. III
Dunn, Rt Rev. Andrew Hunter, 1839–1914, vol. I
Dunn, Captain Arthur Edward, 1876–1927, vol. II
Dunn, Charles William, 1877–1966, vol. VI
Dunn, Lt-Col Cuthbert Lindsay, 1875–1956, vol. V
Dunn, Edward, 1880–1945, vol. IV
Dunn, Most Rev. Edward Arthur, 1870–1955, vol. V
Dunn, Col Henry Nason, 1864–1952, vol. V
Dunn, Hugh Percy, 1854–1931, vol. III
Dunn, James Anthony, 1926–1985, vol. VIII
Dunn, James B., 1861–1930, vol. III
Dunn, Sir James Hamet, 1st Bt (*cr* 1921), 1875–1956, vol. V
Dunn, James Nicol, 1856–1919, vol. II
Dunn, James Stormont, 1879–1965, vol. VI
Dunn, John Freeman, 1874–1954, vol. V
Dunn, Sir John Henry, 2nd Bt (*cr* 1917), 1890–1971, vol. VII
Dunn, John Messenger, 1838–1904, vol. I
Dunn, John Shaw, 1883–1944, vol. IV
Dunn, Brig. Keith Frederick William, 1891–1985, vol. VIII
Dunn, John Thomas, 1858–1939, vol. III
Dunn, Louis Albert, 1858–1918, vol. II
Dunn, Naughton,1884–1939, vol. III
Dunn, Patrick Smith, 1848–1932, vol. III
Dunn, Peter Douglas Hay,1892–1965, vol. VI
Dunn, Sir Philip Gordon, 2nd Bt (*cr* 1921), 1905–1976, vol. VII
Dunn, Piers Duncan Williams, 1896–1957, vol. V
Dunn, Stanley Gerald, 1879–1964, vol. VI
Dunn, Rt Rev. Thomas, 1870–1931, vol. III
Dunn, Thomas Alexander, 1923–1988, vol. VIII
Dunn, Rev. Thomas Shelton, 1875–1949, vol. IV
Dunn, Thomas Smith, 1836–1916, vol. II
Dunn, Sir William, 1st Bt (*cr* 1895), 1833–1912, vol. I
Dunn, William, 1876–1949, vol. IV
Dunn, Sir William Henry, 1st Bt (*cr* 1917), 1856–1926, vol. II
Dunn, William Norman, 1873–1961, vol. VI
Dunne, Arthur Mountjoy, 1859–1947, vol. IV
Dunne, Lt-Col Edward Marten, 1864–1944, vol. IV
Dunne, Finley Peter, 1867–1936, vol. III

Dunne, Major Francis Plunkett Neville, 1872–1931, vol. III
Dunne, Irene Marie, 1898–1990, vol. VIII
Dunne, Rt Rev. Mgr James J., 1859–1934, vol. III
Dunne, Lt-Col James Stuart, 1877–1955, vol. V
Dunne, Sir John, 1825–1906, vol. I
Dunne, Rt Rev. John, 1846–1917, vol. II
Dunne, Gen. Sir John Hart, 1835–1924, vol. II
Dunne, Captain John J., 1837–1910, vol. I
Dunne, Rt Rev. John Mary, 1843–1919, vol. II
Dunne, John William *died* 1949, vol. IV
Dunne, Sir Laurence Rivers, 1893–1970, vol. VI
Dunne, Most Rev. Patrick, 1891–1988, vol. VIII
Dunne, Philip Russell Rendel, 1904–1965, vol. VI
Dunne, Col William, 1855–1932, vol. III
Dunnell, Sir Francis; *see* Dunnell, Sir R. F.
Dunnell, Sir (Robert) Francis, 1st Bt, 1868–1960, vol. V
Dunnett, Sir George Sangster, 1907–1984, vol. VIII
Dunnett, George Sinclair, 1906–1964, vol. VI
Dunnett, Sir James Macdonald, 1877–1953, vol. V
Dunnicliff, Rev. Canon Edward Frederick Holwell, 1901–1963, vol. VI
Dunnicliff, Horace Barratt, *died* 1958, vol. V
Dunnico, Rev. Sir Herbert,1876–1953, vol. V
Dunnill, W. F., *died* 1936, vol. III
Dunning, Albert Elijah, 1844–1923, vol. II
Dunning, Hon. Charles Avery, 1885–1958, vol. V
Dunning, Sir Edwin Harris, 1858–1923, vol. III
Dunning, J. Thomson, 1851–1931, vol. III
Dunning, James, 1873–1931, vol. III
Dunning, John Ray, 1907–1975, vol. VII
Dunning, Sir Leonard, 1st Bt, 1860–1941, vol. IV
Dunning, Rev. Thomas George, 1885–1975, vol. VII
Dunning, William Archibald, *died* 1922, vol. II
Dunning, Sir William Leonard, 2nd Bt, 1903–1961, vol. VI
Dunnington-Jefferson, Lt-Col Sir John Alexander, 1st Bt, 1884–1979, vol. VII
Dunoyer de Segonzac, André, 1884–1974, vol. VII
Dunphie, Sir Alfred Edwin, *died* 1938, vol. III
Dunphy, Rev. Thomas Patrick Joseph, 1913–1989, vol. VIII
Dunraven and Mount-Earl, 4th Earl of, 1841–1926, vol. II
Dunraven and Mount-Earl, 5th Earl of, 1857–1952, vol. V
Dunraven and Mount-Earl, 6th Earl of, 1887–1965, vol. VI
Dunrossil, 1st Viscount, 1893–1961, vol. VI
Duns, John, 1820–1909, vol. I
Dunsandle and Clan-Conal, 4th Baron, 1849–1911, vol. I
Dunsany, 17th Baron, 1853–1899, vol. I
Dunsany, 18th Baron, 1878–1957, vol. V
Dunsford, Brig.-Gen. Francis Pearson Shaw, 1866–1931, vol. III
Dunsheath, Percy, 1886–1979, vol. VII
Dunsmuir, Hon. James, 1851–1921, vol. II
Dunstaffnage, The Captain of, 1888–1958, vol. V
Dunstan, Hon. Sir Albert Arthur, *died* 1950, vol. IV
Dunstan, Albert Ernest, 1878–1964, vol. VI
Dunstan, Edgar Grieve, 1890–1963, vol. VI
Dunstan, Ven. Ephraim, *died* 1915, vol. I

Dunstan, Malcolm James Rowley, 1863–1938, vol. III
Dunstan, Victor Joseph, 1899–1970, vol. VI
Dunstan, William, 1895–1957, vol. V
Dunstan, Sir Wyndham Rowland, 1861–1949, vol. IV
Dunsterville, Col Arthur Bruce, 1859–1943, vol. IV
Dunsterville, Brig. Knightley Fletcher, 1883–1958, vol. V
Dunsterville, Col Knightley Stalker, 1857–1935, vol. III
Dunsterville, Maj.-Gen. Lionel Charles, 1865–1946, vol. IV
Dunsterville, Lt-Gen. Lionel D'Arcy, 1830–1912, vol. I
Dunton, Walter Theodore W.; *see* Watts-Dunton.
Duntze, Sir George Alexander, 4th Bt, 1839–1922, vol. II
Duntze, Sir George Edwin Douglas, 6th Bt, 1913–1985, vol. VIII
Duntze, Sir George Puxley, 5th Bt, 1873–1947, vol. IV
Duntze, Sir John Alexander, 7th Bt, 1909–1987, vol. VIII
Dunville, Lt-Col John, 1866–1929, vol. III
Dunville, Robert Grimshaw, 1838–1910, vol. I
Dunwoodie, Lallah Bessie, *died* 1950, vol. IV
Dunwoody, Robert Browne, 1879–1966, vol. VI
Duparc, Marie Eugene Henri, 1848–1933, vol. III
du Parcq, Baron (Life Peer); Herbert du Parcq, 1880–1949, vol. IV
Duperier, Maj.-Gen. Henry William, 1851–1940, vol. III
Du-Plat-Taylor, Francis Maurice Gustavus, 1878–1954, vol. V
du Plat-Taylor, Lt-Col St John Louis Hyde; *see* Taylor.
du Pont, Lammot, 1880–1952, vol. V
Dupont-Sommer, André, 1900–1983, vol. VIII
Du Port, Lt-Col Osmond Charteris, 1875–1929, vol. III
Dupplin, Viscount; Edmund Alfred Rollo George Hay, 1879–1903, vol. I
Duppuy, Rt Rev. Charles Ridley, *died* 1944, vol. IV
Dupré, August, 1835–1907, vol. I
du Pré, Jacqueline Mary, 1945–1987, vol. VIII
Dupré, Hon. Maurice, 1888–1941, vol. IV
Du Pre, William Baring, 1875–1946, vol. IV
Dupree, Sir Vernon, 3rd Bt, 1884–1971, vol. VII
Dupree, Sir Victor, 4th Bt, 1887–1976, vol. VII
Dupree, Col Sir William, 2nd Bt, 1882–1953, vol. V
Dupree, Col Sir William Thomas, 1st Bt, 1856–1933, vol. III
Dupuis, Charles George, 1886–1940, vol. III
Dupuis, Raymond, 1907–1970, vol. VI (AII)
Dupuis, Rev. Theodore Crane, 1830–1914, vol. I
Dupuy, Charles Alexander, 1851–1923, vol. II
Dupuy, Jean, *died* 1919, vol. II
Dupuy, Paul, *died* 1927, vol. II
Dupuy, Pierre, 1896–1969, vol. VI
Duran, Emile Auguste C.; *see* Carolus-Duran.
Durand, Brig. Sir Alan Algernon Marion, 3rd Bt, 1893–1971, vol. VII
Durand, Col Algernon George Arnold, 1854–1923, vol. II
Durand, Sir Edward Law, 1st Bt, 1845–1920, vol. II

Durand, Major Sir Edward Percy Marion, 2nd Bt, 1884–1955, vol. V
Durand, Rt Hon. Sir (Henry) Mortimer, 1850–1924, vol. II
Durand, Rt Hon. Sir Mortimer; *see* Durand, Rt Hon. Sir H. M.
Duranleau, Alfred, 1871–1951, vol. V
Durant, Rear-Adm. Bryan Cecil, 1910–1983, vol. VIII
Durant, Rt Rev. Henry Bickersteth, *died* 1932, vol. III
Durant, William James, 1885–1981, vol. VIII
Duranty, Walter, *died* 1957, vol. V
Durbhunga, Maharajadhiraj of, 1860–1929, vol. III
Durbin, Evan Frank Mottram, 1906–1948, vol. IV
Durden, James, *died* 1964, vol. VI
Duret, Rt Rev. Augustin, 1846–1920, vol. II
Durga Gati, Banerji, *died* 1903, vol. I
Durham, 3rd Earl of, 1855–1928, vol. II
Durham, 4th Earl of, 1855–1929, vol. III
Durham, 5th Earl of, 1884–1970, vol. VI
Durham, Frances Hermia, 1873–1948, vol. IV
Durham, Lt-Col Frank Rogers, *died* 1947, vol. IV
Durham, Herbert Edward, 1866–1945, vol. IV
Durham, Mary Edith, 1863–1944, vol. IV
Durham, Rev. Thomas Charles, 1825–1904, vol. I
Durham, Rev. William Edward, 1857–1921, vol. II
Durlacher, Sir Esmond Otho, 1901–1982, vol. VIII
Durlacher, Adm. Sir Laurence George, 1904–1986, vol. VIII
Durley, Richard John, 1868–1948, vol. IV
Durnford, Lt-Gen. Cyril Maton Periam, 1891–1965, vol. VI
Durnford, Hugh George Edmund, 1886–1965, vol. VI
Durnford, Adm. Sir John, 1849–1914, vol. I
Durnford, Vice-Adm. John Walter, 1891–1967, vol. VI
Durnford, Richard, 1843–1934, vol. III
Durnford, Robert Chichester, 1895–1918, vol. II
Durnford, Sir Walter, 1847–1926, vol. II
Durnford-Slater, Adm. Sir Robin Leonard Francis, 1902–1984, vol. VIII
Durning-Lawrence, Sir Edwin, 1st Bt, 1837–1914, vol. I
Durrant, Albert Arthur Molteno, 1898–1984, vol. VIII
Durrant, Sir Arthur Isaac, 1864–1939, vol. III
Durrant, Frederick Chester W.; *see* Wells-Durrant.
Durrant, Maj.-Gen. James Murdoch Archer, 1885–1963, vol. VI
Durrant, Maj.-Gen. James Thom, 1913–1990, vol. VIII
Durrant, Sir William Henry Estridge, 6th Bt, 1872–1953, vol. V
Durrant, Sir William Robert Estridge, 5th Bt, 1840–1912, vol. I
Durrant, William Scott, 1860–1932, vol. III
Durell, Col Arthur James Vavasor, 1871–1945, vol. IV
Durell, Henry E. Le Vavasseur dit, *died* 1921, vol. II
Durell, Rev. John Carlyon Vavasour, 1870–1946, vol. IV
Durrell, Lawrence George, 1912–1990, vol. VIII
Dürrenmatt, Friedrich, 1921–1990, vol. VIII
Durst, Alan Lydiat, 1883–1970, vol. VI

Durst, Rev. William, 1838–1922, vol. II
Durston, Air Marshal Sir Albert,1894–1959, vol. V
Durston, Sir Albert John, 1846–1917, vol. II
Durward, Archibald, 1902–1964, vol. VI
Durward, James, 1892–1971, vol. VII
Dury, Theodore Seton, 1854–1932, vol. III
Duse, Signora Eleonora, 1861–1924, vol. II
Duthie, George Ian, 1915–1967, vol. VI
Duthie, Sir John, 1858–1922, vol. II
Duthie, Sir William Smith, 1892–1980, vol. VII
du Toit, Alexander Logie, died 1948, vol. IV
du Toit, F. J., 1897–1961, vol. VI
du Toit, Very Rev. Lionel Meiring Spafford, 1903–1979, vol. VII
du Toit, P. J., 1888–1967, vol. VI
Dutoit, Rev. S. J., 1849–1911, vol. I
Dutt, Palme; see Dutt, R. P.
Dutt, (Rajani) Palme, 1896–1974, vol. VII
Dutt, Romesh Chunder, 1848–1909, vol. I
Dutt, William Alfred, 1870–1939, vol. III
Dutton, Alan Hart, 1913–1974, vol. VII
Dutton, Vice-Adm. Hon. Arthur Brandreth Scott, 1876–1932, vol. III
Dutton, Col Hon. Charles, 1842–1909, vol. I
Dutton, Eric Aldhelm Torlogh, 1895–1973, vol. VII
Dutton, Sir Ernest R.; see Rowe-Dutton.
Dutton, Sir Frederick, 1855–1930, vol. III
Dutton, Lt-Col Hugh Reginald, 1875–1950, vol. IV
Duval, Sir Francis John, 1909–1981, vol. VIII
Duval, Herbert Philip, died 1929, vol. III
Duveen, 1st Baron, 1869–1939, vol. III
Duveen, Claude Henry, 1903–1976, vol. VII
Duveen, Edward Joseph, died 1944, vol. IV
Duveen, Sir Geoffrey, 1883–1975, vol. VII
Duveen, Sir Joseph Joel, 1843–1908, vol. I
Du Vernet, Most Rev. Frederick Herbert, 1860–1924, vol. II
du Vigneaud, Vincent, 1901–1978, vol. VII
Dvorak, Pan Antonin, 1841–1904, vol. I
Dwelly, Very Rev. Frederick William, 1881–1957, vol. V
Dwight, Rev. Timothy, 1828–1916, vol. II
Dwyer, Edward, 1897–1916, vol. II
Dwyer, Lt-Col Ernest, 1880–1957, vol. V
Dwyer, Sir F. Conway, 1860–1935, vol. III
Dwyer, Most Rev. George Patrick, 1908–1987, vol. VIII
Dwyer, Sir John Patrick, 1880–1966, vol. VI
Dwyer, Rt Rev. Joseph Wilfred, 1869–1939, vol. III
Dwyer, Air Vice-Marshal Michael Harington, 1912–1989, vol. VIII
Dwyer, Rt Rev. Patrick Vincent, 1858–1931, vol. III
Dwyer, Hon. Sir Walter, 1875–1950, vol. IV, vol. V
Dwyer-Hampton, Lt-Col Bertie Cunynghame, 1872–1967, vol. VI
Dyall, Clarence George, 1858–1941, vol. IV
Dyall, Franklin, 1870–1950, vol. IV
Dyall, Valentine, 1908–1985, vol. VIII
Dyas, Col James Ridgeway, 1862–1933, vol. III
Dyball, Maj.-Gen. Antony John, 1919–1985, vol. VIII
Dyce, Col George Hugh Coles, 1846–1921, vol. II
Dyde, Samuel Walters, 1862–1947, vol. IV
Dye, Sidney, 1900–1958, vol. V

Dye, William David, 1887–1932, vol. III
Dyer, Sir Alfred, 1865–1947, vol. IV
Dyer, Ven. Alfred Saunders, 1853–1906, vol. I
Dyer, Arthur Reginald, 1877–1951, vol. V
Dyer, Bernard, 1856–1948, vol. IV
Dyer, Charles Edward, died 1937, vol. III
Dyer, Edward Jerome, died 1943, vol. IV
Dyer, Col George Nowers, died 1955, vol. V
Dyer, Maj.-Gen. Godfrey Maxwell, 1898–1979, vol. VII
Dyer, Henry, 1848–1918, vol. II
Dyer, Hugh Marshall, 1860–1938, vol. III
Dyer, James Ferguson, 1880–1940, vol. III
Dyer, Sir John Lodovick Swinnerton, 13th Bt, 1914–1940, vol. III
Dyer, Captain Sir John Swinnerton, 12th Bt, 1891–1917, vol. II
Dyer, Ven. Joseph Perry, 1855–1926, vol. II
Dyer, Sir Leonard Schroeder Swinnerton, 15th Bt, 1898–1975, vol. VII
Dyer, Sir Leonard Whitworth Swinnerton, 14th Bt, 1875–1947, vol. IV
Dyer, Brig.-Gen. Reginald Edward Harry, 1864–1927, vol. II
Dyer, Robert Morton, 1878–1936, vol. III
Dyer, Sidney Reginald, died 1934, vol. III
Dyer, Major Stewart Barton Bythesea, 1875–1917, vol. II
Dyer, Sir Thomas Swinnerton, 11th Bt, 1859–1907, vol. I
Dyer, Sir William Turner T.; see Thiselton-Dyer.
Dyett, Sir Gilbert Joseph Cullen, 1891–1964, vol. VI
Dyke, Sir Arthur James, 1872–1933, vol. III
Dyke, Sir Derek William H.; see Hart Dyke.
Dyke, Rev. Edwin Francis, 1842–1919, vol. II
Dyke, Lt-Col John Samuel, 1859–1927, vol. II
Dyke, Sir Oliver Hamilton Augustus Hart, 8th Bt, 1885–1969, vol. VI
Dyke, Sidney Campbell, 1886–1975, vol. VII
Dyke, Rt Hon. Sir William Hart, 7th Bt, 1837–1931, vol. III
Dykes, David Oswald, 1876–1942, vol. IV
Dykes, Frederick James, 1880–1957, vol. V
Dykes, Col Frescheville Hubert Ballantine-, 1881–1949, vol. IV
Dykes, Rev. James Oswald, 1835–1912, vol. I
Dykes, Brig. Vivian, 1898–1943, vol. IV
Dykes, William Rickatson, 1877–1926, vol. II
Dykes Bower, Sir John, 1905–1981, vol. VIII
Dykstra, John, 1898–1972, vol. VII
Dyment, Clifford Henry, 1914–1971, vol. VII
Dymoke, Frank Scaman, 1862–1946, vol. IV
Dymott, Rev. Sidney Edward, died 1924, vol. II
Dynes, Brig. Ernest, 1903–1968, vol. VI
Dynevor, 6th Baron, 1836–1911, vol. I
Dynevor, 7th Baron, 1873–1956, vol. V
Dynevor, 8th Baron, 1899–1962, vol. VI
Dynham, Edward, 1843–1914, vol. I
Dysart, 9th Earl of, 1859–1935, vol. III
Dysart, Countess of (10th in line), 1889–1975, vol. VII
Dyson, Sir (Charles) Frederick, 1854–1934, vol. III
Dyson, Sir Cyril Douglas, 1895–1976, vol. VII
Dyson, Edith Mary Beatrice, 1900–1986, vol. VIII

Dyson, Edward Trevor, 1886–1969, vol. VI
Dyson, Sir Frank Watson, 1868–1939, vol. III
Dyson, Fred, 1916–1987, vol. VIII
Dyson, Sir Frederick; *see* Dyson, Sir C. F.
Dyson, Sir George, 1883–1964, vol. VI
Dyson, Lt-Col Harry Hugo Bernard, 1869–1939, vol. III
Dyson, Herbert Kempton, 1880–1944, vol. IV
Dyson, James, 1914–1990, vol. VIII
Dyson, Richard George, 1909–1987, vol. VIII
Dyson, William, 1849–1928, vol. II
Dyson, William, 1871–1947, vol. IV
Dyson, William Henry, 1883–1938, vol. III

E

Eacott, Rev. Canon Henry James Theodore, 1882–1943, vol. IV
Eade, Charles Stanley, 1903–1964, vol. VI
Eade, Sir Peter, 1825–1915, vol. I
Eades, Sir Thomas, 1888–1971, vol. VII
Eadie, Dennis, 1875–1928, vol. II
Eadie, William Ewing, 1896–1976, vol. VII
Eady, Sir (Crawfurd) Wilfrid Griffin, 1890–1962, vol. VI
Eady, George Hathaway, *died* 1941, vol. IV
Eady, Sir Wilfrid; *see* Eady, Sir C. W. G.
Eagar, Waldo McGillycuddy, 1884–1966, vol. VI
Eager, Sir Clifden Henry Andrews, 1882–1969, vol. VI
Eagles, Rev. Charles Frederick, 1851–1931, vol. III
Eagles, Gen. Henry Cecil, 1855–1927, vol. II
Eaglesham, Eric John Ross, 1905–1988, vol. VIII
Eaglesome, Sir John, 1868–1950, vol. IV
Eagleston, Arthur John, 1870–1944, vol. IV
Eagleton, Guy Tryon, 1894–1988, vol. VIII
Eaker, Gen. Ira Clarence, 1896–1987, vol. VIII
Eakin, Rev. Thomas, 1871–1958, vol. V
Eales, Herbert, 1857–1927, vol. II
Eales, John Frederick, 1881–1936, vol. III
Eales, Shirley, 1883–1963, vol. VI
Eames, Alfred Edward, *died* 1924, vol. II
Eames, James Bromley, 1872–1916, vol. II
Eames, Sir William, 1821–1910, vol. I
Eames, Maj.-Gen. William L'Estrange, 1863–1956, vol. V
Eardley, Joan Kathleen Harding, 1921–1963, vol. VI
Eardley-Russell, Lt-Col Edmund Stuart Eardley Wilmot, 1869–1918, vol. II
Eardley-Wilmot, Col Arthur, 1856–1940, vol. III
Eardley-Wilmot, Captain Cecil F., 1855–1916, vol. II
Eardley-Wilmot, Rev. Ernest Augustus, 1848–1932, vol. III
Eardley-Wilmot, Hugh Eden, 1850–1926, vol. II
Eardley-Wilmot, Sir John, 4th Bt, 1882–1970, vol. VI
Eardley-Wilmot, May, 1883–1970, vol. VI
Eardley-Wilmot, Maj.-Gen. Revell, 1842–1922, vol. II
Eardley-Wilmot, Sir Sainthill, 1852–1929, vol. III
Eardley-Wilmot, Rear-Adm. Sir Sydney Marow, 1847–1929, vol. III

Earengey, William George, *died* 1961, vol. VI
Earl, Sir Austin, 1888–1958, vol. V
Earl, Frederick, 1857–1945, vol. IV
Earle, Rt Rev. Alfred, 1827–1918, vol. II
Earle, Air Chief Marshal Sir Alfred, 1907–1990, vol. VIII
Earle, Lt-Col Sir Algernon; *see* Earle, Lt-Col Sir T. A.
Earle, Sir Archdale, 1861–1934, vol. III
Earle, Arthur, 1838–1919, vol. II
Earle, Mrs C. W., (Maria Theresa Villiers), 1836–1925, vol. II
Earle, Lt-Col Charles, 1913–1989, vol. VIII
Earle, Charles Westwood, 1871–1950, vol. IV
Earle, Edward Mead, 1894–1954, vol. V
Earle, Brig. Eric Greville, 1893–1965, vol. VI
Earle, Sir George Foster, 1890–1965, vol. VI
Earle, Gerald Frederick, 1864–1944, vol. IV
Earle, Sir Hardman Alexander Mort, 5th Bt, 1902–1979, vol. VII
Earle, Lt-Col Sir Henry, 3rd Bt (*cr* 1869), 1854–1939, vol. III
Earle, Herbert Gastineau, 1882–1946, vol. IV
Earle, Rev. John, 1824–1903, vol. I
Earle, Hon. John, 1865–1932, vol. III
Earle, Gen. John March, 1825–1914, vol. I
Earle, Sir Lionel, 1866–1948, vol. IV
Earle, Col Maxwell, 1871–1953, vol. V
Earle, Rev. Canon Richard Cobden, 1867–1942, vol. IV
Earle, Col Robert Gilmour, 1874–1957, vol. V
Earle, Sir Thomas, 2nd Bt (*cr* 1869), 1820–1900, vol. I
Earle, Lt-Col Sir (Thomas) Algernon, 4th Bt (*cr* 1869), 1860–1945, vol. IV
Earle, Rev. Sir William, 11th Bt (*cr* 1629), *died* 1910, vol. I
Early, Stephen T., 1889–1951, vol. V
Earnshaw, Albert, 1865–1920, vol. II
Earnshaw, Mabel Lucie, (Mrs Harold Earnshaw); *see* Attwell, M. L.
Earp, Charles Anthony, 1871–1933, vol. III
Earp, Frank Russell, 1871–1955, vol. V
Earp, Hon. George Frederick, *died* 1933, vol. III
Earp, Thomas Wade, 1892–1958, vol. V
Eason, Sir Herbert Lightfoot, 1874–1949, vol. IV
Eason, John, 1874–1964, vol. VI
Eassie, Brig.-Gen. Fitzpatrick, 1864–1943, vol. IV
Eassie, Maj.-Gen. William James Fitzpatrick, 1899–1974, vol. VII
Easson, Rt Rev. Edward Frederick, 1905–1988, vol. VIII
Easson, Eric Craig, 1915–1983, vol. VIII
East, Sir Alfred, 1849–1913, vol. I
East, Gen. Sir Cecil James, 1837–1908, vol. I
East, Col Charles Conran, 1866–1942, vol. IV
East, Charles Frederick Terence, 1894–1967, vol. VI
East, Sir George Frederick Lancelot Clayton-, 8th Bt (*cr* 1732), and 4th Bt (*cr* 1838), 1872–1926, vol. II
East, Sir Gilbert Augustus Clayton, 7th Bt (*cr* 1732), and 3rd Bt (*cr* 1838), 1846–1925, vol. II
East, Hubert Frazer, 1893–1959, vol. V
East, Col Lionel William Pellew, 1866–1918, vol. II
East, Sir Norwood; *see* East, Sir W. N.
East, Sir (William) Norwood, 1872–1953, vol. V

Eastaugh, Rt Rev. Cyril, 1897–1988, vol. VIII

Eastaugh, Rt Rev. John Richard Gordon, 1920–1990, vol. VIII

Easten, Sir Stephen, *died* 1936, vol. III

Easter, Rev. Canon Arthur John Talbot, 1893–1969, vol. VI

Easter, Bertie Harry, 1893–1976, vol. VII (AII)

Easterbrook, James, 1851–1923, vol. II

Easterbrook, John Thomas, *died* 1934, vol. III

Easterbrook, William Thomas James, 1907–1985, vol. VIII

Easterfield, Sir Thomas Hill, 1866–1949, vol. IV

Eastes, Arthur Ernest, 1877–1948, vol. IV

Eastham, Leonard Ernest Sydney, 1893–1977, vol. VII

Eastham, Sir Tom, *died* 1967, vol. VI

Eastick, Brig. Sir Thomas Charles, 1900–1988, vol. VIII

Eastlake, Charles Locke, 1836–1906, vol.I

Eastman, George, 1854–1932, vol. III

Eastman, Gen. William Inglefield, 1856–1941, vol. IV

Easton, Brig.-Gen. Frederick Arthur, 1871–1949, vol. IV

Easton, Col George, 1868–1946, vol. IV

Easton, Hugh, *died* 1965, vol. VI

Easton, Admiral Sir Ian, 1917–1989, vol. VIII

Easton, Air Cdre Sir James (Alfred), 1908–1990, vol. VIII

Easton, John Murray,1889–1975, vol. VII

Easton, Lt-Col Philip George, 1878–1960, vol. V

Eastwood, Benjamin, 1863–1943, vol. IV

Eastwood, Charles, 1868–1940, vol. III

Eastwood, Christopher Gilbert, 1905–1983, vol. VIII

Eastwood, Sir Eric, 1910–1981, vol. VIII

Eastwood, Frank Sandford, 1895–1971, vol. VII

Eastwood, Major Sir Geoffrey Hugh, 1895–1983, vol. VIII

Eastwood, Harold, 1880–1941, vol. IV

Eastwood, Harold Edmund, 1889–1960, vol. V

Eastwood, Col Hugh de Crespigny, 1863–1934, vol. III

Eastwood, Col John Charles Basil, 1862–1934, vol. III

Eastwood, John Francis, 1887–1952, vol. V

Eastwood, Reginald Allen, 1893–1964, vol. VI

Eastwood, Lt-Gen. Sir T. Ralph, 1890–1959, vol. V

Eaton, Rev. Arthur Wentworth Hamilton, 1849–1937, vol. III

Eaton, Cecil; *see* Eaton, W. C.

Eaton, Cyrus Stephen, 1883–1979, vol. VII

Eaton, Sir Frederick Alexis, 1838–1913, vol. I

Eaton, Hon. Herbert Edward,1895–1962, vol. VI

Eaton, Sir John Craig, 1876–1922, vol. II

Eaton, Vice-Adm. Sir John Willson Musgrave, 1902–1981, vol. VIII

Eaton, Col Sir Richard William, 1876–1942, vol. IV

Eaton, (Walter) Cecil, 1875–1958, vol. V

Eayrs, Rev. George, 1864–1926, vol. II

Ebbels, Brig. Wilfred Austin, 1898–1976, vol. VII

Ebbisham, 1st Baron, 1868–1953, vol. V

Ebblewhite, Ernest Arthur, 1867–1947, vol. IV

Ebbs, William Alexander, 1890–1960, vol. V

Ebbutt, Norman, 1894–1968, vol. VI

Ebden, Mrs Agnes, *died* 1930, vol. III

Eberle, George Strachan John Fuller, 1881–1968, vol. VI

Ebers, Georg Maurice, 1837–1898, vol. I

Ebert, Carl Anton Charles, 1887–1980, vol. VII

Eberts, Hon. David MacEwen, 1850–1924, vol. II

Eberts, Edmond Melchior, 1873–1945, vol. IV

Eboo Pirbhai, Diwan Sir, 1905–1990, vol. VIII

Eborall, Sir Arthur; *see* Eborall, Sir E. A.

Eborall, Sir (Ernest) Arthur, 1878–1967, vol. VI

Ebrahim, Sir Currimbhoy; *see* Ebrahim, Sir H. C.

Ebrahim, Sir Currimbhoy, 1st Bt, 1840–1924, vol. II

Ebrahim, Sir Fazulbhoy Currimbhoy, 1873–1970, vol. VI (AII)

Ebrahim, Sir (Huseinali) Currimbhoy, 3rd Bt, 1903–1952, vol. V

Ebrahim, Sir Mahomedbhoy Currimbhoy, 2nd Bt, 1867–1928, vol. II

Ebrington, Viscount; Hugh Peter Fortescue, 1920–1942, vol. IV

Ebsworth, Brig. Wilfrid Algernon, 1897–1978, vol. VII

Ebury, 2nd Baron, 1834–1918, vol. II

Ebury, 3rd Baron, 1868–1921, vol.II

Ebury, 4th Baron, 1883–1932, vol. III

Ebury, 5th Baron, 1914–1957, vol. V

Eccles, Lt-Col Cuthbert John, 1870–1922, vol. II

Eccles, James Ronald, 1874–1956, vol. V

Eccles, Adm. Sir John Arthur Symons, 1898–1966, vol. VI

Eccles, Rev. Canon John Charles, *born* 1845, vol. II

Eccles, Sir Josiah, 1897–1967, vol. VI

Eccles, Launcelot William Gregory, 1890–1955, vol. V

Eccles, Miss O'C.; *see* O'Conor-Eccles, Miss.

Eccles, Maj.-Gen. Ronald Whalley, 1912–1975, vol. VII

Eccles, William Henry, 1875–1966, vol. VI

Eccles, William McAdam, *died* 1946, vol. IV

Eccleshare, Colin Forster, 1916–1989, vol. VIII

Echegaray, José, 1832–1916, vol. II

Echlin, Sir Henry Frederick, 8th Bt, 1846–1923, vol. II

Echlin, Sir John Frederick, 9th Bt, 1890–1932, vol. III

Echlin, Sir Thomas, 7th Bt, 1844–1906, vol. I

Eck, Rev. Herbert Vincent Shortgrave, *died* 1934, vol. III

Eckener, Hugo, 1868–1954, vol. V

Eckersley, Eva Mary, 1871–1944, vol. IV

Eckersley, Peter Pendleton, 1892–1963, vol. VI

Eckersley, Peter Thorp, 1904–1940, vol. III

Eckersley, Roger Huxley, 1885–1955, vol. V

Eckersley, Thomas Lydwell, 1886–1959, vol. V

Eckhoff, Nils Lovold Bjarne Victor, 1902–1969, vol. VI

Eckman, Samuel, Jr, *died* 1976, vol. VII

Eckstein, Captain Sir Bernard, 2nd Bt, 1894–1948, vol. IV

Eckstein, Sir Frederick, 1st Bt, 1857–1930, vol. III

Ecroyd, William Farrer, 1827–1915, vol. I

Edden, Vice-Adm. Sir Kaye; *see* Edden, Vice-Adm. Sir W. K.

Edden, Vice-Adm. Sir (William) Kaye, 1905–1990, vol. VIII

Eddie, Sir George Brand, 1893–1981, vol. VIII

Eddington, Sir Arthur Stanley, 1882–1944, vol. IV
Eddis, Sir Basil Eden Garth, *died* 1971, vol. VII
Eddis, Brig. Bruce Lindsay, 1883–1966, vol. VI
Eddison, Eric Rucker, 1882–1945, vol. IV
Eddison, John Edwin, 1842–1929, vol. III
Eddison, Rear-Adm. Talbot Leadam, 1908–1983, vol. VIII
Eddowes, Alfred, *died* 1946, vol. IV
Eddowes, Rev. Canon Edmund Edward, 1871–1963, vol. VI
Eddowes, Rev. John, 1826–1905, vol. I
Eddy, Sir (Edward) George, 1878–1967, vol. VI
Eddy, Sir George; *see* Eddy, Sir E. G.
Eddy, Sir (John) Montague, 1881–1949, vol. IV
Eddy, John Percy, 1881–1975, vol. VII
Eddy, Mary Baker Glover, 1821–1910, vol. VI
Eddy, Sir Montague; *see* Eddy, Sir J. M.
Ede, Comdr Lionel James Spencer, 1903–1956, vol. V
Ede, Very Rev. William Moore, *died* 1935, vol. III
Edelman, Maurice, 1911–1975, vol. VII
Edelsten, Col John Arthur, 1863–1931, vol. III
Edelsten, Adm. Sir John Hereward, 1891–1966, vol. VI
Edelston, Sir Thomas Dugald, 1878–1955, vol. V
Eden, Brig.-Gen. Archibald James Fergusson, 1872–1956, vol. V
Eden, Charles William Guy, 1874–1947, vol. IV
Eden, Denis, 1878–1949, vol. IV
Eden, Edward Norman, 1921–1990, vol. VIII
Eden, Rev. Frederick Nugent, 1857–1926, vol. II
Eden, Hon. George, 1861–1924, vol. II
Eden, Rt Rev. George Rodney, 1853–1940, vol. III
Eden, Guy E. Morton, *died* 1954, vol. V
Eden, Helen Parry, 1885–1960, vol. V
Eden, Rev. Robert Allan, 1839–1912, vol. I
Eden, Robert H. H., *died* 1932, vol. III
Eden, Col Schomberg Henley, 1873–1934, vol. III
Eden, Thomas Watts, 1863–1946, vol. IV
Eden, Sir Timothy Calvert, 8th Bt, 1893–1963, vol. VI
Eden, Sir William, 7th and 5th Bt, 1849–1915, vol. I
Eden, Brig.-Gen. William Rushbrooke, 1873–1920, vol. II
Edenborough, Eric John Horatio, 1893–1965, vol. VI
Eder, Montagu David, *died* 1936, vol. III
Edgar, Clifford Blackburn, 1857–1931, vol. III
Edgar, Sir Edward Mackay, 1st Bt, 1876–1934, vol. III
Edgar, Frederick Percy, 1884–1972, vol. VII
Edgar, George, 1877–1918, vol. II
Edgar, Gilbert Harold Samuel, 1898–1978, vol. VII
Edgar, Lt-Gen. Hector Geoffrey, 1903–1978, vol. VII
Edgar, Hon. Sir James David, 1841–1899, vol. I
Edgar, John, *died* 1922, vol. II
Edgar, Sir John Ware, 1839–1902, vol. I
Edgar, Pelham, 1871–1948, vol. IV
Edgar, William C., 1856–1932, vol. III
Edgar, Surg. Rear-Adm. William Harold, 1885–1959, vol. V
Edgcumbe, Aubrey Pearce; *see* Edgcumbe, J. A. P.
Edgcumbe, Sir (Edward) Robert Pearce, 1851–1929, vol. III
Edgcumbe, (John) Aubrey Pearce, 1886–1974, vol. VII

Edgcumbe, Maj.-Gen. Oliver Pearce, 1892–1956, vol. V
Edgcumbe, Richard John Frederick, 1843–1937, vol. III
Edgcumbe, Sir Robert Pearce; *see* Edgcumbe, Sir E. R. P.
Edge, Frederick, 1863–1937, vol. III
Edge, James Broughton, *died* 1926, vol. II
Edge, Rt Hon. Sir John, 1841–1926, vol. II
Edge, Maj.-Gen. John Dallas, 1848–1937, vol. III
Edge, John Henry, 1841–1916, vol. II
Edge, Sir Knowles, 1853–1931, vol. III
Edge, Sir Knowles, 2nd Bt, 1905–1984, vol. VIII
Edge, Samuel Rathbone, 1848–1936, vol. III
Edge, Selwyn Francis, 1868–1940, vol. III
Edge, Captain Sir William, 1st Bt, 1880–1948, vol. IV
Edge-Partington, Rev. Canon Ellis Foster, 1885–1957, vol. V
Edgedale, Samuel Richards, 1897–1966, vol. VI
Edgell, Beatrice, 1871–1948, vol. IV
Edgell, George Harold, 1887–1954, vol. V
Edgell, Vice-Adm. Sir John Augustine, 1880–1962, vol. VI
Edgerley, Catherine Mabel, *died* 1946, vol. IV
Edgerley, Sir Steyning William, 1857–1935, vol. III
Edgeworth, Francis H., 1864–1943, vol. IV
Edgeworth, Francis Ysidro, 1845–1926, vol. II
Edgeworth, Lt-Col Kenneth Essex, 1880–1972, vol. VII
Edgeworth-Johnstone, Maj.-Gen. Ralph, 1893–1990, vol. VIII
Edgeworth-Johnstone, Lt-Col Sir Walter, *died* 1936, vol. III
Edghill, Rev. John Cox, *died* 1917, vol. II
Edginton May, *died* 1957, vol. V
Edgley, Sir Norman George Armstrong, 1888–1960, vol. V
Edie, Arthur George, 1872–1937, vol. III
Edie, Rev. William, 1865–1936, vol.III
Edington, Alexander Robert, 1895–1964, vol. VI
Edington, George Henry, 1870–1943, vol. IV
Edington, James William, *died* 1939, vol. III
Edington, William Gerald, 1895–1968, vol. VI
Edis, Sir Robert William, 1839–1927, vol. II
Edison, Thomas Alva, 1847–1931, vol. III
Edkins, John Sydney, 1863–1940, vol. III
Edlin, Sir Peter Henry, 1819–1903, vol. I
Edlmann, Major Ernest Elliot, 1868–1915, vol. I
Edlmann, Col Francis Joseph Frederick, 1885–1950, vol. IV
Edman, Irwin, 1896–1954, vol. V
Edman, Pehr Victor, 1916–1977, vol. VII
Edmeades, Major Henry, 1875–1952, vol. V
Edmeades, Lt-Col James Frederick, 1843–1917, vol. II
Edmeades, Lt-Col William Allaire, 1880–1942, vol. IV
Edmond, Colin Alexander, 1888–1956, vol. V
Edmond, James, 1859–1933, vol. III
Edmond, John Philip, 1850–1906, vol. I
Edmondes, Ven. Frederic William, 1840–1918, vol. II
Edmonds, Cecil John, 1889–1979, vol. VII
Edmonds, Air Vice-Marshal Charles Humphrey Kingsman, 1891–1954, vol. V

Edmonds, Edward Alfred Jubal, 1907–1974, vol. VII
Edmonds, Edward Reginald, 1901–1979, vol. VII
Edmonds, Garnham, 1866–1946, vol. IV
Edmonds, Brig.-Gen. Sir James Edward, 1861–1956, vol. V
Edmonds, Rev. Walter John, 1834–1914, vol.I
Edmonds, William Stanley,1882–1969, vol. VI
Edmondson, George D'Arcy, 1904–1976, vol. VII
Edmondstoune-Cranstoun, Charles Joseph; see Cranstoun.
Edmonstone, Sir Archibald, 5th Bt, 1867–1954, vol. V
Edmonstone, Sir (Archibald) Charles, 6th Bt, 1898–1954, vol. V
Edmonstone, Sir Charles; see Edmonstone, Sir A. C.
Edmunds, Arthur, 1874–1945, vol. IV
Edmunds, Christopher Montague, 1899–1990, vol. VIII
Edmunds, Rev. Horace Vaughan, 1886–1958, vol. V
Edmunds, Humfrey Henry, 1890–1962, vol. VI
Edmunds, Lewis Humfrey, 1860–1941, vol. IV
Edmunds, Nellie M. Hepburn,died 1953, vol. V
Edmunds, Sir Percy James, 1890–1959, vol. V
Edmunds, Walter, died 1930, vol. III
Edmundson, Rev. George, 1848–1930, vol. III
Edridge, Col Frederick Lockwood, 1831–1913, vol. I
Edridge, Sir Frederick Thomas, 1843–1921, vol. II
Edridge-Green, Frederick William, 1864–1953, vol. V
Edsall, Rt Rev. Samuel Cook, 1860–1917, vol. II
Edser, Edwin, died 1932, vol. III
Edvina, Madame Marie Louise, died 1948, vol. IV
Edward, A. S., 1852–1915, vol. I
Edward-Collins, Maj.-Gen. Charles Edward, 1881–1967, vol. VI
Edward-Collins, Adm. Sir Frederick; see Edward-Collins, Adm. Sir G. F. B.
Edward-Collins, Adm. Sir (George) Frederick (Basset), 1883–1958, vol. V
Edward-Collins, Brig. Gerald 1885–1968, vol. VI
Edwardes, Lt-Col Alexander Coburn, 1873–1948, vol. IV
Edwardes, Arthur Henry Francis, 1885–1951, vol. V
Edwardes, Lt-Col Hon. Cuthbert Ellison, 1838–1911, vol. I
Edwardes, George, 1852–1915, vol. I
Edwardes, Sir Henry Hope, 10th Bt, 1829–1900, vol. I
Edwardes, Gen. Sir Stanley de Burgh, 1840–1918, vol. II
Edwardes, Col Stanley Malcolm, 1863–1937, vol. III
Edwardes, Stephen Meredyth, 1873–1927, vol. II
Edwardes, Tickner, 1865–1944, vol. IV
Edwardes-Davies, Rt Rev. David, 1897–1950, vol. IV
Edwardes Jones, Air Marshal Sir Humphrey; see Edwardes Jones, Sir J. H.
Edwardes Jones, Air Marshal Sir (John) Humphrey, 1905–1987, vol. VIII
Edwardes-Ker, Lt-Col Douglas Rous, 1886–1979, vol. VII
Edwards, Agustin, 1878–1941, vol. IV
Edwards, Alfred, 1888–1958, vol. V
Edwards, Most Rev. Alfred George, 1848–1937, vol. III
Edwards, Maj.-Gen. Sir Alfred Hamilton Mackenzie, 1862–1944, vol. IV
Edwards, Rev. Canon Allen, 1844–1917, vol. II

Edwards, (Allen) Clement, 1869–1938, vol. III
Edwards, Brig. Arthur Bertie Duncan, 1898–1990, vol. VIII
Edwards, Arthur James Howie, 1884–1944, vol. IV
Edwards, Arthur John Charles, 1883–1963, vol. VI
Edwards, (Arthur) Trystan, 1884–1973, vol. VII
Edwards, Arthur Tudor, died 1946, vol. IV
Edwards, Lt-Col Sir Bartle Mordaunt Marsham, 1891–1977, vol. VII
Edwards, Hon. Sir Bassett; see Edwards, Hon. Sir W. B.
Edwards, Mrs Bennett-, 1844–1936, vol. III
Edwards, Ven. Bickerton Cross, 1874–1949, vol. IV
Edwards, Brig. Brian Bingay, 1895–1947, vol. IV
Edwards, Carl Johannes, 1914–1985, vol. VIII
Edwards, Rt Hon. Sir Charles, 1867–1954, vol. V
Edwards, Charles Alfred, 1882–1960, vol. V
Edwards, Charles Lewis, 1865–1928, vol. II
Edwards, Lt-Comdr Charles Peter, 1885–1960, vol. V
Edwards, Brig.-Gen. Christopher Vaughan, 1875–1955, vol. V
Edwards, Clement; see Edwards, A. C.
Edwards, Corwin D., 1901–1979, vol. VII
Edwards, Lt-Col Cosmo Grant Niven, 1896–1964, vol. VI
Edwards, D., 1858–1916, vol. II
Edwards, Sir David, 1892–1966, vol. VI
Edwards, Rev. Father Douglas Allen, 1893–1953, vol. V
Edwards, Ebby, 1884–1961, vol. VI
Edwards, Rev. Canon Edgar Thomas, 1880–1935, vol. III
Edwards, Edward, 1865–1933, vol. III
Edwards, Edward John Rogers, 1891–1965, vol. VI
Edwards, Rev. Ellis, 1844–1915, vol. I
Edwards, Enoch, 1852–1912, vol. I
Edwards, Evangeline Dora, 1888–1957, vol. V
Edwards, Brig.-Gen. Fitz-James Maine, 1861–1929, vol. III
Edwards, Lt-Col Rt Hon. Sir Fleetwood Isham, 1842–1910, vol. I
Edwards, Sir Francis, 1st Bt (cr 1907), 1852–1927, vol. II
Edwards, Lt-Gen. Frederick Charles, 1870–1947, vol. IV
Edwards, Frederick Laurence, 1903–1962, vol. VI
Edwards, Frederick Swinford, 1853–1939, vol. III
Edwards, Frederick Wallace, 1888–1940, vol. III
Edwards, G. Spencer, died 1916, vol. II
Edwards, Geoffrey, 1917–1990, vol. VIII
Edwards, Geoffrey Richard, 1891–1961, vol. VI
Edwards, Sir George, 1850–1933, vol. III
Edwards, George, 1854–1946, vol. IV
Edwards, George, 1901–1989, vol. VIII
Edwards, Sir (George) Tristram, 1882–1960, vol. V
Edwards, Sir George William, 1818–1902, vol. I
Edwards, Gordon, 1899–1976, vol. VII
Edwards, Sir Goronwy; see Edwards, Sir J. G.
Edwards, Brig.-Gen. Graham Thomas George, 1864–1943, vol. IV
Edwards, Col Guy Janion, 1881–1962, vol. VI
Edwards, Gwilym Arthur, 1881–1963, vol. VI
Edwards, (H. C.) Ralph, 1894–1977, vol. VII

Edwards, Lt-Comdr Harington Douty, *died* 1916, vol. II

Edwards, Air Marshal Harold, 1892–1952, vol. V

Edwards, Harold Clifford, 1899–1989, vol. VIII

Edwards, Lt-Col Harold Walter, 1887–1973, vol. VII

Edwards, Sir Henry, 1820–1897, vol. I

Edwards, Sir Henry Charles Serrell Priestley, 4th Bt (*cr* 1866), 1893–1963, vol. VI

Edwards, Sir Henry Coster Lea, 2nd Bt (*cr* 1866), 1840–1896, vol. I

Edwards, Henry John, 1869–1923, vol. II

Edwards, Col Herbert Ivor Powell, 1884–1946, vol. IV

Edwards, Captain Hugh, 1873–1916, vol. II

Edwards, Air Cdre Sir Hughie Idwal, 1914–1982, vol. VIII

Edwards, Sir Ifan ab Owen, 1895–1970, vol. VI

Edwards, Very Rev. Irven David, 1907–1973, vol. VII

Edwards, Lt-Col Ivo Arthyr Exley, 1881–1947, vol. IV (A)

Edwards, Lt-Gen. Sir James Bevan, 1834–1922, vol. II

Edwards, James Keith O'Neill, 1920–1988, vol. VIII

Edwards, Rt Hon. John; *see* Edwards, Rt Hon. L. J.

Edwards, John, *died* 1954, vol. V

Edwards, John, 1882–1960, vol. V

Edwards, John, 1932–1989, vol. VIII

Edwards, Sir John Arthur, 1901–1983, vol. VIII

Edwards, John Braham Scott, 1928–1987, vol. VIII

Edwards, Sir John Bryn, 1st Bt (*cr* 1921), 1889–1922, vol. II

Edwards, Brig.-Gen. John Burnard, 1857–1937, vol. III

Edwards, Rev. John Cox C.; *see* Cox-Edwards.

Edwards, Vice-Adm. John Douglas, 1871–1952, vol. V

Edwards, John Francis H.; *see* Hall-Edwards.

Edwards, Sir (John) Goronwy, 1891–1976, vol. VII

Edwards, Sir John Henry Priestley Churchill, 3rd Bt (*cr* 1866), 1889–1942, vol. IV

Edwards, John Hugh, *died* 1945, vol. IV

Edwards, John Passmore, 1823–1911, vol. I

Edwards, Rev. John Rosindale W.; *see* Wynne-Edwards.

Edwards, Joseph, 1854–1931, vol. III

Edwards, Joshua Price, 1898–1966, vol. VI

Edwards, Kenneth Charles, 1904–1982, vol. VIII

Edwards, Laura Selina, (Lady Edwards), *died* 1919, vol. II

Edwards, Sir Lawrence, 1896–1968, vol. VI

Edwards, Rt Hon. (Lewis) John, 1904–1959, vol. V

Edwards, Rt Rev. Lewis Mervyn C.; *see* Charles-Edwards.

Edwards, Lionel D. R., 1878–1966, vol. VI

Edwards, Engr Rear-Adm. Macleod Gamul Arthur, 1884–1957, vol. V

Edwards, Rev. Maldwyn Lloyd, 1903–1974, vol. VII

Edwards, Sir Martin Llewellyn, 1909–1987, vol. VIII

Edwards, Matilda Betham-, *died* 1919, vol. II

Edwards, Rev. Maurice Henry, 1886–1961, vol. VII

Edwards, Rt Hon. Ness, 1897–1968, vol. VI

Edwards, Osman, 1864–1936, vol. III

Edwards, Sir Owen Morgan, 1858–1920, vol. II

Edwards, Ralph; *see* Edwards, H. C. R.

Edwards, Adm. Sir Ralph Alan Bevan, 1901–1963, vol. VI

Edwards, Brig.-Gen. Richard Fielding, 1866–1942, vol. IV

Edwards, Richard Lionel, 1907–1984, vol. VIII

Edwards, Robert, 1905–1990, vol. VIII

Edwards, Robert Hamilton, *born* 1872, vol. III

Edwards, Sir Robert Meredydd W.; *see* Wynne-Edwards.

Edwards, Captain Roderick Latimer Mackenzie 1900–1975, vol. VII

Edwards, Lt-Col Roderick Mackenzie, *died* 1940, vol. III

Edwards, Sir Ronald Stanley, 1910–1976, vol. VII

Edwards, Rev. Canon Rowland Alexander, 1890–1973, vol. VII

Edwards, Rev. Thomas, vol. II

Edwards, Rev. Thomas Charles, 1837–1900, vol. I

Edwards, Sir Tristram; *see* Edwards, Sir G. T.

Edwards, Trystan; *see* Edwards, A. T.

Edwards, Walter James, 1900–1964, vol. VI

Edwards, Lt-Col Walter Manoel, 1885–1971, vol. VII

Edwards, Wilbraham Tollemache Arthur, 1836–1929, vol. III

Edwards, Wilfred Norman, 1890–1956, vol. V

Edwards, William, 1851–1940, vol. III

Edwards, William, 1874–1969, vol. VI

Edwards, Lt-Col William Bickerton, 1870–1933, vol. III

Edwards, Hon. William Cameron, 1844–1921, vol. II

Edwards, Col William Egerton, 1875–1921, vol. II

Edwards, Brig.-Gen. William Frederick Savery, 1872–1941, vol. IV

Edwards, Rev. Canon William George, 1858–1942, vol. IV

Edwards, Rev. William Gilbert, 1846–1936, vol. III

Edwards, Major William Mordaunt Marsh, 1855–1912, vol. I

Edwards, William Powell, 1854–1935, vol. III

Edwards, Hon. Maj.-Gen. Sir William Rice, 1862–1923, vol. II

Edwards, William Stuart, 1880–1944, vol. IV

Edwards, Hon. Sir (Worley) Bassett, 1850–1927, vol. II

Edwards-Heathcote, Justinian Heathcote; *see* Heathcote.

Edwards-Moss, Sir John Edwards, 2nd Bt, 1850–1935, vol. III

Edwards-Moss, Sir John Herbert Theodore, 4th Bt, 1913–1988, vol. VIII

Edwards-Moss, Sir Thomas, 3rd Bt, 1874–1960, vol. V

Edwin, George Frederick D.; *see* Dove-Edwin.

Edye, Sir Benjamin Thomas, 1884–1962, vol. VI

Eeles, Francis Carolus, 1876–1954, vol. V

Eestermans, Fabian Anthony, 1858–1931, vol. III

Effingham, 3rd Earl of, 1837–1898, vol. I

Effingham, 4th Earl of, 1866–1927, vol. II

Effingham, 5th Earl of, 1873–1946, vol. IV

Egan, Harold, 1922–1984, vol. VIII

Egan, Sir Henry Kelly, 1848–1925, vol. II

Egan, Hon. Maurice Francis, 1852–1924, vol. II

Egan, Col Michael Henry, 1865–1940, vol. III

Egan, Rt Rev. T. Erkenwald, 1856–1939, vol. III

Egan, Major William, 1881–1929, vol. III
Egan, William Henry, 1869–1943, vol. IV
Egbert, Hon. William, 1857–1936, vol. III
Egerton, 1st Earl, 1832–1909, vol. I
Egerton of Tatton, 3rd Baron, 1845–1920, vol. II
Egerton of Tatton, 4th Baron, 1874–1958, vol. V
Egerton, Sir Alfred Charles Glyn, 1886–1959, vol. V
Egerton, Col Sir Alfred Mordaunt, 1843–1908, vol. I
Egerton, Lady Alice, 1923–1977, vol. VII
Egerton, Lt-Col Arthur Frederick, 1866–1942, vol. IV
Egerton, Sir Brian, 1857–1940, vol. III
Egerton, Rev. Sir Brooke de Malpas Grey-, 13th Bt, 1845–1945, vol. IV
Egerton, Charles Augustus, died 1912, vol. I
Egerton, Field-Marshal Sir Charles Comyn, 1848–1921, vol. II
Egerton, Charles William, 1862–1939, vol. III
Egerton, Rt Hon. Edwin Henry, 1841–1916, vol. II
Egerton, Rear-Adm. Frederick Wilbraham, 1838–1909, vol. I
Egerton, George, (Mrs Golding Bright), (Mary Chavelita), 1859–1945, vol. IV
Egerton, Adm. Sir George le Clerc, 1852–1940, vol. III
Egerton, Major George M. L., 1837–1898, vol. I
Egerton, Maj.-Gen. Granville George Algernon, 1859–1951, vol. V
Egerton, Vice-Adm. (Henry) Jack, 1892–1972, vol. VII
Egerton, Hugh Edward, 1855–1927, vol. II
Egerton, Comdr Hugh Sydney, 1890–1969, vol. VI
Egerton, Vice-Adm. Jack; see Egerton, Vice-Adm. H. J.
Egerton, Lady Mabelle, 1865–1927, vol. II
Egerton, Sir Philip Henry Brian Grey-, 12th Bt, 1864–1937, vol. III
Egerton, Sir Philip Reginald le Belward G.; see Grey Egerton.
Egerton, Lt-Gen. Sir Raleigh Gilbert, 1860–1931, vol. III
Egerton, Sir Reginald Arthur, 1850–1930, vol. III
Egerton, Sir Robert Eyles, 1857–1912, vol. I
Egerton, Hon. Thomas Henry Frederick, 1876–1953, vol. V
Egerton, Sir Walter, 1858–1947, vol. IV
Egerton, Rear-Adm. Wilfrid Allan, 1881–1931, vol. III
Egerton, William Francis, 1868–1949, vol. IV
Egerton, Rev. William Henry, 1811–1910, vol. I
Egerton, Vice-Adm. Wion De Malpas, 1879–1943, vol. IV
Egerton-Warburton, Geoffrey, 1888–1961, vol. VI
Egerton-Warburton, John, 1883–1915, vol. I
Egerton-Warburton, Piers, 1839–1914, vol. I
Eggar, Sir Arthur, 1877–1958, vol. V
Eggar, Sir Henry Cooper, 1851–1941, vol. IV
Eggar, James, 1880–1962, vol. VI
Eggeling, H. Julius, 1842–1918, vol. II
Eggers, Henry Howard, 1903–1980, vol. VII
Egginton, Wycliffe, 1875–1951, vol. V
Eggleston, Edward, 1837–1902, vol. I
Eggleston, Sir Frederic William, 1875–1954, vol. V
Eglington, Rev. Canon Arthur, 1871–1925, vol. II

Eglington, William, 1858–1933, vol. III
Eglinton and Winton, 15th Earl of, 1848–1919, vol. II
Eglinton and Winton, 16th Earl of, 1880–1945, vol. IV
Eglinton and Winton, 17th Earl of, 1914–1966, vol. VI
Egmont, 7th Earl of, 1845–1897, vol. I
Egmont, 8th Earl of, 1856–1910, vol. I
Egmont, 9th Earl of, 1858–1929, vol. III
Egmont, 10th Earl of, 1873–1932, vol. III
Egmont, Countess of; (Lucy), died 1932, vol. III
Egremont, 1st Baron, and Leconfield, 6th Baron, 1920–1972, vol. VII
Eha; see Aitken, E. H.
Ehrenburg, Ilya, 1891–1967, vol. VI
Ehrenberg, Victor Leopold, 1891–1976, vol. VII
Ehrhardt, Albert, 1862–1929, vol. III
Ehrlich, Georg, 1897–1966, vol. VI
Ehrlich, Paul, 1854–1915, vol. I
Eichholz, Alfred, 1869–1933, vol. III
Eiffel, Alexandre Gustave, 1832–1923, vol. II
Einaudi, Luigi, 1874–1961, vol. VI
Einstein, Albert, 1879–1955, vol. V
Einstein, Alfred, 1880–1952, vol. V
Einthoven, Willem, 1860–1927, vol. II
Einzig, Paul, 1897–1973, vol. VII
Eisdell, Hubert Mortimer, 1882–1948, vol. IV
Eisenberg, Maurice, 1902–1972, vol. VII
Eisenhower, Gen. Dwight David, 1890–1969, vol. VI
Eisenhower, Milton Stover, 1899–1985, vol. VIII
Eisenschitz, Robert Karl, 1898–1968, vol. VI
Ekin, Maj.-Gen. Roger Gillies, 1895–1990, vol. VIII
Eking, Maj.-Gen. Harold Cecil William, 1903–1978, vol. VII
Ekins, Emily Helen, 1879–1964, vol. VI
Ekwall, Bror Oscar Eilert, 1877–1964, vol. VI
Eland, John Shenton, 1872–1933, vol. III
Elatu, Eliahu, 1903–1990, vol. VIII
Elborne, Sydney Lipscomb, 1890–1986, vol. VIII
Elcho, Lord; Iain David Charteris, 1945–1954, vol. V
Elcock, William Dennis, 1910–1960, vol. III
Elder, Hugh, 1905–1986, vol. VIII
Elder, Sir James Alexander MacKenzie, 1869–1946, vol. IV
Elder, John Munro, 1860–1922, vol. II
Elder, John Rawson, 1880–1962, vol. VI
Elder, Sir Stewart D.; see Duke-Elder
Elder, William, 1864–1931, vol. III
Elder, William Alexander, 1881–1946, vol. IV(A)
Elder, Rear-Adm. William Leslie, 1874–1961, vol. VI
Elder, Sir (William) Stewart D.; see Duke-Elder.
Elder-Duncan, John Hudson, 1877–1938, vol. III
Elder-Jones, Thomas, 1904–1988, vol. VIII
Elderton, Ethel Mary, 1878–1954, vol. V
Elderton, Captain Ferdinand Halford, 1865–1942, vol. IV
Elderton, Sir Thomas Howard, 1886–1970, vol. VI
Elderton, Sir William Palin, 1877–1962, vol. VI
Eldin-Taylor, Kenneth Roy, 1902–1990, vol. VIII
Eldon, 3rd Earl of, 1845–1926, vol. II
Eldon, 4th Earl of, 1899–1976, vol. VII
Eldred, Paymaster-Captain Edward Henry, 1864–1929, vol. III
Eldridge, Captain George Bernard, died 1944, vol. IV
Eldridge, Lt-Gen. Sir John; see Eldridge, Lt-Gen. Sir W. J.

Eldridge, Lt-Col William James, 1917–1987, vol. VIII

Eldridge, Lt-Gen. Sir (William) John, 1898–1985, vol. VIII

Eley, Col Edward Henry, 1874–1949, vol. IV

Eley, Sir Frederick, 1st Bt, 1866–1951, vol. V

Eley, Sir Geoffrey Cecil Ryves, 1904–1990, vol. VIII

Eley, Rt Rev. Stanley Albert Hallam, 1899–1970, vol. VI

Elford, William Joseph, 1900–1952, vol. V

Elgar, Sir Edward, 1st Bt, 1857–1934, vol. III

Elgar, Francis, 1845–1909, vol. I

Elgee, Captain Cyril Hammond, 1871–1917, vol. II

Elgee, Frank, 1880–1944, vol. IV

Elger, Major Edward Gwyn, 1864–1929, vol. III

Elgin, 9th Earl of, **and Kincardine,** 13th Earl of, 1849–1917, vol. II

Elgin, 10th Earl of, **and Kincardine,** 14th Earl of, 1881–1968, vol. VI

Elgood, Sir Frank Minshull, 1865–1948, vol. IV

Elgood, George S., 1851–1943, vol. IV

Elgood, Captain Leonard Alsager, 1892–1987, vol. VIII

Elgood, Lt-Col Percival George, 1863–1941, vol. IV

Elhorst, Hendrik Jan, *born* 1861, vol. II

Elias, David Henry, 1882–1953, vol. V

Eliash, Mordecai, 1892–1950, vol. IV

Elibank, 1st Viscount, 1840–1927, vol. II

Elibank, 2nd Viscount, 1877–1951, vol. V

Elibank, 3rd Viscount, 1879–1962, vol. VI

Elibank, 13th Lord, 1902–1973, vol. VII

Eliot, Lord; Edward Henry John Cornwallis Elliot, 1885–1909, vol. I

Eliot, Hon. Arthur Ernest Henry, 1874–1936, vol. III

Eliot, Rt Hon. Sir Charles Norton Edgcumbe, 1862–1931, vol. III

Eliot, Charles William, 1834–1926, vol. II

Eliot, Edward Carlyon, *died* 1940, vol. III

Eliot, Ven. Edward Francis Whately, 1864–1943, vol. IV

Eliot, Sir John, 1839–1908, vol. I

Eliot, Laurence Stirling, 1845–1922, vol. II

Eliot, Lt-Col Nevill, 1880–1957, vol. V

Eliot, Very Rev. Philip Frank, 1835–1917, vol. II

Eliot, Rt Rev. Philip Herbert, 1862–1946, vol. IV

Eliot, Vice-Adm. Ralph, 1881–1958, vol. V

Eliot, Hon. Reginald Huyshe H.; *see* Huyshe-Eliot.

Eliot, Rev. Samuel Atkins, 1862–1950, vol. IV (A), vol. V

Eliot, Thomas Stearns, 1888–1965, vol. VI

Eliot, Rev. W., 1832–1910, vol. I

Eliot, Sir Whately, 1841–1927, vol. II

Eliott of Stobs, Sir Arthur Boswell, 9th Bt, 1856–1926, vol. II

Eliott, Lt-Col Francis Augustus Heathfield, 1867–1937, vol. III

Eliott, Lt-Col Francis Hardinge, 1862–1928, vol. II

Eliott of Stobs, Sir Arthur Francis Augustus Boswell, 11th Bt, 1915–1989, vol. VIII

Eliott of Stobs, Sir Gilbert Alexander Boswell, 10th Bt, 1885–1958, vol. V

Eliott of Stobs, Sir William Francis Augustus, 8th Bt, 1827–1910, vol. I

Eliott Lockhart, Sir Allan Robert, 1905–1977, vol. VII

Eliott-Lockhart, Lt-Col Percy Clare, 1867–1915, vol. I

Elkan, Benno, 1877–1960, vol. V

Elkan, Lt-Col Clarence John, 1877–1940, vol. III

Elkan, John, 1849–1927, vol. II

El'Kanemi, Alhaji Sir Umar Ibn Muhammed El'Amin, 1873–1967, vol. VI

Elkin, Adolphus Peter, 1891–1979, vol. VII (AII)

Elkington, Frederick Pellatt, 1874–1940, vol. III (A), vol. IV

Elkington, John St Clair, *died* 1963, vol. VI

Elkington, John Simeon, *born* 1841, vol. II

Elkington, Reginald Lawrence, 1898–1975, vol. VII

Elkington, Col Robert James Goodall, 1867–1939, vol. III

Elkins, Sir Anthony Joseph, 1904–1978, vol. VII

Elkins, Vice-Adm. Sir Robert Francis, 1903–1985, vol. VIII

Elkins, Stephen Benton, 1841–1911, vol. I

Elkins, Maj.-Gen. William Henry Pferinger, 1883–1964, vol. VI

Elkins, William Lukens, 1832–1903, vol. I

Elland, Percy, 1908–1960, vol. V

Ellenberger, Lt-Col Jules, 1871–1973, vol. VII

Ellenborough, 4th Baron, 1856–1902, vol. I

Ellenborough, 5th Baron, 1841–1915, vol. I

Ellenborough, 6th Baron, 1849–1931, vol. III

Ellenborough, 7th Baron, 1889–1945, vol. IV

Ellerman, Sir John Reeves, 1st Bt, 1862–1933, vol. III

Ellerman, Sir John Reeves, 2nd Bt, 1909–1973, vol. VII

Ellershaw, Brig.-Gen. Arthur, 1869–1929, vol. III

Ellershaw, Rev. Henry, 1863–1932, vol. III

Ellerton, Air Cdre Alban Spenser, 1894–1978, vol. VII

Ellerton, Rev. Arthur John Bicknell, 1865–1928, vol. II

Ellerton, Sir Cecil; *see* Ellerton, Sir F. C.

Ellerton, Sir (Frederick) Cecil, 1892–1962, vol. VI

Ellerton, Adm. Walter Maurice, 1870–1948, vol. IV

Ellery, Lt-Col Robert Lewis John, 1827–1908, vol. I

Elles, Lt-Gen. Sir Edmond Roche, 1848–1934, vol. III

Elles, Gen. Sir Hugh Jamieson, 1880–1945, vol. IV

Elles, Robin Jamieson, 1907–1987, vol. VIII

Ellesmere, 3rd Earl of, 1847–1914, vol. I

Ellesmere, 4th Earl of, 1872–1944, vol. IV

Ellice, Major Edward Charles, 1858–1934, vol. III

Ellicot, Rt Rev. Charles John, 1819–1905, vol. I

Ellicott, Arthur Becher, 1849–1931, vol. III

Ellicott, Langford Pannell, 1903–1972, vol. VII

Ellicott, Rosalind, *died* 1924, vol. II

Ellinger, Barnard, *died* 1947, vol. IV

Ellingford, Herbert Frederick, 1876–1966, vol. VI

Ellington, Duke; *see* Ellington, Hon. E. K.

Ellington, Hon. Edward Kennedy, (Duke), 1899–1974, vol. VII

Ellington, Marshal of the Royal Air Force Sir Edward Leonard, 1877–1967, vol. VI

Elliot, Maj.-Gen. Sir Alexander James Hardy, 1825–1909, vol. I

Elliot, Alison, 1891–1939, vol. III

Elliot, Hon. Arthur Ralph Douglas, 1846–1923, vol. II

Elliot, Sir Charles, 4th Bt, 1873–1911, vol. I
Elliot, Sir Duncan; see Elliot, Sir J. D.
Elliot, Major Sir Edmund Halbert, 1854–1926, vol. II
Elliot, Lt-Gen. Sir Edward Locke, 1850–1938, vol. III
Elliot, Sir Francis Edmund Hugh, 1851–1940, vol. III
Elliot, Frederick Augustus Hugh, 1847–1910, vol. I
Elliot, Frederick Barnard, 1877–1950, vol. IV
Elliot, Rev. Frederick Roberts, 1840–1918, vol. II
Elliot, Sir George, 1812–1901, vol. I
Elliot, Sir George, 3rd Bt, 1867–1904, vol. I
Elliot, Sir George, 1869–1956, vol. V
Elliot, Rev. Canon George Edward, 1851–1916, vol. II
Elliot, Maj.-Gen. Gilbert Minto, 1897–1969, vol. VI
Elliot, Brig.-Gen. Gilbert Sutherland McDowell, 1863–1937, vol. III
Elliot, Maj.-Gen. Harry Macintire C.; see Cawthra-Elliot.
Elliot, Rt Hon. Sir Henry George, 1817–1907, vol. I
Elliot, Sir Henry George, 1826–1912, vol. I
Elliot, Lt-Col Henry Hawes, 1891–1972, vol. VII
Elliot, Maj.-Gen. Henry Riversdale, 1836–1921, vol. II
Elliot, Hubert William Arthur, 1891–1967, vol. VI
Elliot, Hugh, 1881–1930, vol. III
Elliot, Hon. Hugh Frederick Hislop, 1848–1932, vol. III
Elliot, Sir (James) Duncan, 1862–1956, vol. V
Elliot, James Robert McDowell, 1896–1980, vol. VII
Elliot, Sir John, 1898–1988, vol. VIII
Elliot, Margaret, died 1901, vol. I
Elliot, Captain Mark F.; see Fogg Elliot.
Elliot, Maj.-Gen. Minto, 1833–1909, vol. I
Elliot, Robert H., 1837–1914, vol. I
Elliot, Lt-Col Robert Henry, died 1936, vol. III
Elliot, Captain Walter, 1910–1988, vol. VIII
Elliot, Rt Hon. Walter Elliot, 1888–1959, vol. V
Elliot, Walter Travers S.; see Scott-Elliot.
Elliot, Col William, 1861–1936, vol. III
Elliot, Air Chief Marshal Sir William, 1896–1971, vol. VII
Elliot, Col William Henry Wilson, 1864–1934, vol. III
Elliot, Lt-Col William Scott, 1873–1943, vol. IV
Elliott, Adshead, 1869–1922, vol. II
Elliott, Albert George, 1889–1975, vol. VII
Elliott, Lt-Col Alfred Charles, 1870–1952, vol. V
Elliott, Rt Rev. Alfred George, 1828–1915, vol. I
Elliott, Algernon, 1848–1934, vol. III
Elliott, Anthony; see Elliott, T. A. K.
Elliott, Rt Rev. Anthony Blacker, 1887–1970, vol. VI (AII)
Elliott, Archibald Campbell, 1861–1913, vol. I
Elliott, Sir Bignell George, 1857–1933, vol. III
Elliott, Sir Charles Alfred, 1835–1911, vol. I
Elliott, Sir Charles Bletterman, 1841–1911, vol. I
Elliott, Col Charles Hazell, 1882–1956, vol. V
Elliott, Charles Hugh Babington, 1852–1943, vol. IV
Elliott, Rev. Canon Charles Lister Boileau, 1864–1940, vol. III
Elliott, Christopher, 1849–1933, vol. III
Elliott, Clarence, 1881–1969, vol. VI
Elliott, Sir Claude Aurelius, 1888–1973, vol. VII
Elliott, (Colin) Fraser, 1888–1969, vol. VI
Elliott, David Lee L.; see Lee-Elliott.

Elliott, Edward Cassleton, 1881–1967, vol. VI
Elliott, Maj.-Gen. Edward Draper, 1838–1918, vol. II
Elliott, Edwin Bailey, 1851–1937, vol. III
Elliott, Ven. Francis William Thomas, died 1930, vol. III
Elliott, Frank Herbert, 1878–1966, vol. VI
Elliott, Frank Louis Dumbell, 1874–1939, vol. III
Elliott, Fraser; see Elliott, C. F.
Elliott, George, 1860–1916, vol. II
Elliott, Sir George Samuel, died 1925, vol. II
Elliott, Col Gilbert Charles Edward, 1872–1934, vol. III
Elliott, Maj.-Gen. Harold Edward, 1878–1931, vol. III
Elliott, Sir Hugh Francis Ivo, 3rd Bt, 1913–1989, vol. VIII
Elliott, Sir Ivo D'Oyly, 2nd Bt, 1882–1961, vol. VI
Elliott, Maj.-Gen. James Gordon, 1898–1990, vol. VIII
Elliott, Sir James Sands, 1880–1959, vol. V
Elliott, Mrs John; see Elliott, M. H.
Elliott, Col John, 1824–1911, vol. I
Elliott, Hon. John Campbell, 1872–1941, vol. IV
Elliott, Rev. John Robert Underwood, 1843–1936, vol. III
Elliott, John Wilson, 1886–1957, vol. V
Elliott, Maud Howe, (Mrs John Elliott), 1854–1948, vol. IV
Elliott, Vice-Adm. Sir Maurice Herbert, 1897–1972, vol. VII
Elliott, Michael Paul, 1931–1984, vol. VIII
Elliott, Ralph Edward, 1908–1981, vol. VIII
Elliott, Robert Charles Dunlop, 1886–1950, vol. IV
Elliott, Rt Rev. Robert Cyril Hamilton, 1890–1977, vol. VII
Elliott, Rowley, 1877–1944, vol. IV
Elliott, Rev. Canon Spencer Hayward, 1883–1967, vol. VI
Elliott, Sydney Robert, 1902–1987, vol. VIII
Elliott, (Thomas) Anthony (Keith), 1921–1976, vol. VII
Elliott, Sir Thomas Henry, 1st Bt, 1854–1926, vol. II
Elliott, Thomas Renton, 1877–1961, vol. VI
Elliott, Rev. Canon Wallace Harold, died 1957, vol. V
Elliott, Col William, 1879–1947, vol. IV
Elliott, William John, 1890–1940, vol. III
Elliott, Rev. William Thompson, 1880–1940, vol. III
Elliott-Binns, Edward Ussher Elliott, 1918–1990, vol. VIII
Elliott-Binns, Rev. Leonard Elliott; see Binns.
Elliott-Blake, Henry, 1902–1983, vol. VIII
Elliott-Cooper, Sir Robert; see Cooper.
Ellis, Sir Alan Edward, 1890–1960, vol. V
Ellis, Sir Albert Fuller, 1869–1951, vol. V
Ellis, Col Alfred Charles Samuel Burdon, 1876–1955, vol. V
Ellis, Annabel W.; see Williams-Ellis, M. A. N.
Ellis, Anthony Louis, died 1944, vol. IV
Ellis, Arthur, 1856–1918, vol. II
Ellis, Maj.-Gen. Sir Arthur Edward Augustus, 1837–1907, vol. I
Ellis, Arthur Isaac, 1883–1963, vol. VI
Ellis, Arthur Thomas, 1892–1964, vol. VI
Ellis, Sir Arthur William Mickle, died 1966, vol. VI

Ellis, Lt-Comdr Bernard Henry, 1885–1918, vol. II
Ellis, Sir (Bertram) Clough W.; *see* Williams-Ellis.
Ellis, Col Charles Conyngham, 1852–1921, vol. II
Ellis, Sir Charles Drummond, 1895–1980, vol. VII
Ellis, Sir Charles Edward, 1852–1937, vol. III
Ellis, Lt-Col Sir Charles Henry Brabazon H.; *see* Heaton-Ellis.
Ellis, Charles Howard, 1895–1975, vol. VII
Ellis, Col Clarence Isidore, 1871–1961, vol. VI
Ellis, Rear-Adm. (E.) Clement, *died* 1953, vol. V
Ellis, Colin Dare Bernard, 1895–1969, vol. VI
Ellis, Lt-Col Conyngham Richard Cecil, 1863–1938, vol. III
Ellis, David, 1874–1937, vol. III
Ellis, Rt Rev. Edward, 1899–1979, vol. VII
Ellis, Vice-Adm. Sir Edward Henry Fitzhardinge H.; *see* Heaton-Ellis.
Ellis, Engr Rear-Adm. Ernest Frank, 1855–1944, vol. IV
Ellis, Ernest Tetley, 1893–1953, vol. V
Ellis, Sir Evelyn Campbell, 1865–1920, vol. II
Ellis, Francis Newman, 1855–1934, vol. III
Ellis, Francis Robert, 1849–1915, vol. I
Ellis, Captain Frederick, 1826–1906, vol. I
Ellis, Sir Geoffrey; *see* Ellis, Sir R. G.
Ellis, Gerald Edward Harold, 1878–1967, vol. VI
Ellis, Harold Owen, 1906–1981, vol. VIII
Ellis, Rev. Canon Henry, 1909–1972, vol. VII
Ellis, Henry Arthur Augustus, *died* 1934, vol. III
Ellis, Henry Havelock, 1859–1939, vol. III
Ellis, Lt-Col Henry L.; *see* Leslie-Ellis.
Ellis, Col Herbert Charles, 1874–1952, vol. V
Ellis, Sir Herbert Mackay, 1851–1912, vol. I
Ellis, Sir Howard; *see* Ellis, Sir S. H.
Ellis, Rt Hon. John Edward, 1841–1910, vol. I
Ellis, J(ohn) Hugh, 1909–1959, vol. V
Ellis, Sir (John) Whittaker, 1st Bt (*cr* 1882), 1829–1912, vol. I
Ellis, Sir Joseph Baxter, *died* 1918, vol. II
Ellis, Hon. Sir Kevin, 1908–1975, vol. VII
Ellis, Major Lionel Frederic, 1885–1970, vol. VI
Ellis, Lyle Fullam, 1887–1951, vol. V
Ellis, Malcolm Henry, 1890–1969, vol. VI (AII)
Ellis, Mary Annabel Nassau W.; *see* Williams-Ellis.
Ellis, Mary Baxter, 1892–1968, vol. VI
Ellis, Mary Jenny Lake, 1921–1983, vol. VIII
Ellis, Maj.-Gen. Philip George Saxon G.; *see* Gregson-Ellis.
Ellis, Brig. Richard Stanley, 1884–1962, vol. VI
Ellis, Richard White Bernard, 1902–1966, vol. VI
Ellis, Sir (Robert) Geoffrey, 1st Bt (*cr* 1932), 1874–1956, vol. V
Ellis, Robert Powley, 1845–1918, vol. II
Ellis, Robinson, 1834–1913, vol. I
Ellis, Rt Rev. Rowland, 1841–1911, vol. I
Ellis, Sir (Samuel) Howard, 1889–1949, vol. IV
Ellis, Lt-Col Sherman Gordon Venn, 1880–1937, vol. III
Ellis, Stewart Marsh, *died* 1933, vol. III
Ellis, T. Mullett, 1850–1919, vol. II
Ellis, Thomas Edward, 1859–1899, vol. I
Ellis, Sir Thomas Hobart, 1894–1981, vol. VIII
Ellis, Thomas Iorwerth, 1899–1970, vol. VI
Ellis, Sir Thomas Ratcliffe R.; *see* Ratcliffe-Ellis.

Ellis, Tristram, 1844–1922, vol. II
Ellis, Valentine Herbert, *died* 1953, vol. V
Ellis, Very Rev. Vorley Spencer, 1882–1977, vol. VII
Ellis, Walter Devonshire, 1871–1957, vol. V
Ellis, Sir Whittaker; *see* Ellis, Sir J. W.
Ellis, Wilfred Desmond, 1914–1990, vol. VIII
Ellis, William, 1828–1916, vol. II
Ellis, William, 1868–1947, vol. IV
Ellis, William Barker, *died* 1934, vol. III
Ellis, William C.; *see* Craven-Ellis.
Ellis, Rev. Hon. William Charles, 1835–1923, vol. II
Ellis, Lt-Col W(illiam) Francis, 1878–1953, vol. V
Ellis, Sir William Henry, 1860–1945, vol. IV
Ellis, William Hodgson, 1845–1921, vol. II
Ellis, Col William Montague, 1862–1952, vol. V
Ellis-Fermor, Una Mary, 1894–1958, vol. V
Ellis-Griffith, Sir Elis Arundell; *see* Griffith, Sir E. A. E.
Ellis-Griffith, Rt Hon. Sir Ellis Jones; *see* Griffith.
Ellis-Rees, Sir Hugh, 1900–1974, vol. VII
Ellison, Rear-Adm. Alfred Astley, 1874–1932, vol. III
Ellison, Ven. Charles Ottley, 1898–1978, vol. VII
Ellison, Lt-Gen. Sir Gerald Francis, 1861–1947, vol. IV
Ellison, Grace Mary, *died* 1935, vol. III
Ellison, Rev. John Henry Joshua, 1855–1944, vol. IV
Ellison, Randall Erskine, 1904–1984, vol. VIII
Ellison, Captain Richard Todd, *died* 1932, vol. III
Ellison, William, 1911–1978, vol. VII
Ellison, William Augustine, 1855–1917, vol. II
Ellison, Rev. Canon William Frederick Archdall, 1864–1936, vol. III
Ellison-Macartney, John William; *see* Macartney.
Ellison-Macartney, Rt Hon. Sir William Grey; *see* Macartney.
Ellissen, Lt-Col Sir Herbert, 1876–1952, vol. V
Elliston, Col George Sampson, 1844–1921, vol. II
Elliston, Sir George Sampson, 1875–1954, vol. V
Elliston, Guy, 1872–1918, vol. II
Elliston, Julian Clement Peter, 1911–1970, vol. VI
Elliston, William Alfred, 1840–1908, vol. I
Elliston, William Rowley, 1869–1954, vol. V
Ellmann, Richard, 1918–1987, vol. VIII
Ellson, George, 1875–1949, vol. IV
Ellsworth, Lincoln, 1880–1951, vol. V
Ellwood, Bt Col Arthur Addison, 1886–1943, vol. IV
Ellwood, George Montague, 1875–1955, vol. V
Ellwood, Captain Michael Oliver Dundas, 1894–1984, vol. VIII
Elman, Mischa, 1891–1967, vol. VI
Elmhirst, Dorothy Whitney, 1887–1968, vol. VI
Elmhirst, Captain Edward Pennell, 1845–1916, vol. II
Elmhirst, Leonard Knight, *died* 1974, vol. VII
Elmhirst, Air Marshal Sir Thomas Walker, 1895–1982, vol. VIII
Elmitt, Lt-Col T. F., 1871–1938, vol. III
Elmsley, Maj.-Gen. James Harold, 1878–1954, vol. V
Elmslie, Christiana Deanes, 1869–1961, vol. VI
Elmslie, Brig.-Gen. Frederick Baumgardt, 1855–1916, vol. III
Elmslie, Noel, 1876–1956, vol. V
Elmslie, Reginald Cheyne, 1878–1940, vol. III
Elmslie, Rev. William Alexander Leslie, 1885–1965, vol. VI

Elnor, Rev. William George, *died* 1956, vol. V

Elphick, Ronald, 1918–1977, vol. VII

Elphinstone, 16th Lord, 1869–1955, vol. V

Elphinstone, 17th Lord, 1914–1975, vol. VII

Elphinstone of Glack, Sir Alexander Logie, 10th Bt (*cr* 1701), 1880–1970, vol. VI

Elphinstone, Archibald Howard L., 1865–1936, vol. III

Elphinstone, Sir Arthur Percy Archibald, 11th Bt (*cr* 1628), *born* 1863 (this entry was not transferred to Who was Who).

Elphinstone, Sir (George) Keith (Buller), 1865–1941, vol. IV

Elphinstone, Sir Græme Hepburn Dalrymple-Horn-, 4th Bt (*cr* 1828), 1841–1900, vol. I

Elphinstone, Sir Howard Graham, 4th Bt (*cr* 1816), 1898–1975, vol. VII

Elphinstone, Sir Howard Warburton, 3rd Bt (*cr* 1816), 1830–1917, vol. II

Elphinstone, Sir Keith; *see* Elphinstone, Sir G. K. B.

Elphinstone, Rev. Kenneth John Tristram, 1911–1980, vol. VII

Elphinstone, Kenneth Vaughan, 1878–1963, vol. VI

Elphinstone, Sir Lancelot Henry, 1879–1965, vol. VI

Elphinstone, Rev. Maurice Curteis, 1874–1969, vol. VI

Elphinstone, Hon. Mountstuart William, 1871–1957, vol. V

Elphinstone, Sir Nicholas, 10th Bt (*cr* 1628), 1825–1907, vol. I

Elphinstone-Dalrymple, Sir Edward Arthur, 6th Bt, 1877–1913, vol. I

Elphinstone-Dalrymple, Col Sir Francis Napier, 7th Bt, 1882–1956, vol. V

Elphinstone-Dalrymple, Sir Robert Graeme, 5th Bt, 1844–1908, vol. I

Elrington, Rev. Charles Andrew, 1856–1936, vol. III

Elrington, Gen. Frederick Robert, 1819–1904, vol. I

El-Sadat, Mohamed Anwar, 1918–1981, vol. VIII

Elsden, John Pascoe, 1887–1950, vol. IV

Else, Joseph, 1874–1955, vol. V

Elsee, Rev. Charles, *died* 1960, vol. V

Elsee, Rev. Henry John, *died* 1936, vol. III

Elsey, Rt Rev. William Edward, 1880–1966, vol. VI

Elsley, Rev. William James, 1870–1942, vol. IV

Elsmie, Maj.-Gen. Alexander Montagu Spears, 1869–1958, vol. V

Elsmie, George Robert, 1838–1909, vol. I

Elsmore, Geoffrey William, 1925–1985, vol. VIII

Elsner, Col Otto William Alexander, 1871–1953, vol. V

Elstob, Rev. John George, *died* 1926, vol. II

Elstob, Lt-Col Wilfrith, *died* 1918, vol. II

Elstub, Sir St John de Holt, 1915–1989, vol. VIII

Eltisley, 1st Baron, 1879–1942, vol. IV

Elton, 1st Baron, 1892–1973, vol. VII

Elton, Sir Ambrose, 9th Bt, 1869–1951, vol. V

Elton, Sir Arthur Hallam Rice, 10th Bt, 1906–1973, vol. VII

Elton, Charles Isaac, 1839–1900, vol. I

Elton, Sir Edmund Harry, 8th Bt, 1846–1920, vol. II

Elton, Col Frederick Coulthurst, 1836–1920, vol. II

Elton, Maj.-Gen. Henry Strachan, 1841–1934, vol. III

Elton, John Bullen, 1916–1983, vol. VIII

Elton, Oliver, 1861–1945, vol. IV

Elton, Lt-Col William M.; *see* Marwood-Elton.

Elton-Barratt, Major Stanley George Reeves, 1900–1973, vol. VII

Eltringham, Harry, 1873–1941, vol. IV

Elveden, Viscount; Arthur Onslow Edward Guinness, 1912–1945, vol. IV

Elverston, Sir Harold, 1866–1941, vol. IV

Elvey, Lewis Edgar, 1908–1974, vol. VII

Elvey, Maurice, 1887–1967, vol. VI

Elvin, Sir Arthur J., 1899–1957, vol. V

Elvin, Herbert Henry, 1874–1949, vol. IV

Elvin, Ven. John Elijah, 1900–1964, vol. VI

Elwell, Col Francis Edwin, 1858–1922, vol. II, vol. III

Elwell, Frederick William, 1870–1958, vol. V

Elwes, Arthur Henry Stuart, 1858–1908, vol. I

Elwes, Rt Rev. Dudley Charles Cary-; *see* Cary-Elwes.

Elwes, Ven. Edward Leighton, 1848–1930, vol. III

Elwes, Lt-Col Frederick Fenn, 1875–1962, vol. VI

Elwes, Gervase Henry Carey-, 1866–1921, vol. II

Elwes, Henry John, 1846–1922, vol. II

Elwes, Sir Richard Everard Augustine, 1901–1968, vol. VI

Elwes, Simon, 1902–1975, vol. VII

Elwes, Valentine Dudley Henry Cary-, 1832–1909, vol. I

Elwes, Ven. William Weston, *died* 1901, vol. I

Elwin, Rt Rev. Edmund Henry, 1871–1909, vol. I

Elwin, Verrier, 1902–1964, vol. VI

Elwood, Hon. Edward Lindsey, *born* 1868, vol. II

Elworthy-Jarman, Air Cdre Lance Michael, 1907–1986, vol. VIII

Elwyn-Jones, Baron (Life Peer); Frederick Elwyn-Jones, 1909–1989, vol. VIII

Ely, 5th Marquess of, 1851–1925, vol. II

Ely, 6th Marquess of, 1854–1935, vol. III

Ely, 7th Marquess of, 1903–1969, vol. VI

Ely, Paul, 1897–1975, vol. VII

Emanuel, Frank Lewis, 1865–1948, vol. IV

Emanuel, Joseph George, 1871–1958, vol. V

Emanuel, Samuel Henry, *died* 1925, vol. II

Emanuel, Walter, 1869–1915, vol. I

Emard, Most Rev. Mgr Joseph Medard, 1853–1927, vol. II

Emberton, John James, 1893–1976, vol. VII

Emberton, Lt-Col Sir (John) Wesley, 1896–1967, vol. VI

Emberton, Joseph, 1889–1956, vol. V

Emberton, Lt-Col Sir Wesley; *see* Emberton, Lt-Col Sir J. W.

Embleton, Dennis, 1881–1944, vol. IV

Embling, Air Vice-Marshal John Robert André, 1913–1959, vol. V

Embry, Air Chief Marshal Sir Basil Edward, 1902–1977, vol. VII

Embury, Brig.-Gen. Hon. John Fletcher Leopold, 1875–1943, vol. IV

Embury, Lt-Col P. Robinson, 1865–1952, vol. V

Emden, Alfred, 1849–1911, vol. I

Emden, Alfred Brotherston, 1888–1979, vol. VII

Emden, Walter, 1847–1913, vol. I

Emdin, Engr Rear-Adm. Archie Russell, 1865–1950, vol. IV

Emeleus, Karl George, 1901–1989, vol. VIII

Emerson, Hon. Charles H., 1864–1919, vol. II

Emerson, Hon. Sir Edward; *see* Emerson, Hon. Sir L. E.

Emerson, Ven. Edward Robert, 1838–1926, vol. II

Emerson, Edward Waldo, 1844–1930, vol. III

Emerson, Hon. George Henry, 1853–1916, vol. II

Emerson, Maj.-Gen. Henry Horace Andrews, 1881–1957, vol. V

Emerson, Sir Herbert William, 1881–1962, vol. VI

Emerson, Hon. Sir (Lewis) Edward, 1890–1949, vol. IV

Emerson, Very Rev. Norman David, 1900–1966, vol. VI

Emerson, Major Norman Zeal, 1872–1928, vol. II

Emerson, Sir Ralf Billing, 1897–1965, vol. VI

Emerson, Robert Jackson, *died* 1944, vol. IV

Emerson, Thomas, 1870–1956, vol. V

Emerson, Sir William, 1843–1924, vol. II

Emery, Rt Rev. Anthony Joseph, 1918–1988, vol. VIII

Emery, Douglas, 1915–1974, vol. VII

Emery, Sir Frederick; *see* Emery, Sir J. F.

Emery, George Edwin, 1859–1937, vol. III

Emery, Henry Crosby, 1872–1924, vol. II

Emery, Sir (James) Frederick, 1886–1983, vol. VIII

Emery, Walter Bryan, 1903–1971, vol. VII

Emery, Walter d'Este, *died* 1923, vol. II

Emery, Ven. William, 1825–1910, vol. I

Emery, Brig.-Gen. William Basil, 1871–1945, vol. IV

Emery, Winifred, (Isabel Winifred Maud Emery Maude), *died* 1924, vol. II

Emett, (Frederick) Rowland, 1906–1990, vol. VIII

Emett, Frederick William, 1865–1935, vol. III

Emett, Rowland; *see* Emett, F. R.

Emley, Herbert Barnes, 1891–1948, vol. IV

Emley, 2nd Baron, 1858–1932, vol. III

Emlyn-Jones, Hugh, 1902–1970, vol. VI

Emlyn-Jones, John Emlyn, 1889–1952, vol. V

Emlyn Williams, Arthur; *see* Williams.

Emmerson, Sir Harold Corti, 1896–1984, vol. VIII

Emmerson, Hon. Henry Robert, 1853–1914, vol. I

Emmerson, Thomas, 1909–1981, vol. VIII

Emmet of Amberley, Baroness (Life Peer); Evelyn Violet Elizabeth Emmet, 1899–1980, vol. VII

Emmet, Rev. Cyril William, 1875–1923, vol. II

Emminger, Otmar, 1911–1986, vol. VIII

Emmony, Harry Oliver, 1897–1956, vol. V

Emmott, 1st Baron, 1858–1926, vol. II

Emmott, Charles Ernest George Campbell, 1898–1953, vol. V

Emmott, George Henry, 1855–1916, vol. II

Emms, Mrs Dorothy, (Mrs S. A. G. Emms); *see* Charques, Mrs D.

Emms, John Frederick George, 1920–1990, vol. VIII

Empson, Sir Charles, 1898–1983, vol. VIII

Empson, Sir William, 1906–1984, vol. VIII

Emrys-Evans, John; *see* Evans.

Emrys-Evans, Paul Vychan, 1894–1967, vol. VI

Emrys-Roberts, Edward, 1878–1924, vol. II

Emslie, John William, 1901–1973, vol. VII

Emslie, Rosalie, 1891–1977, vol. VII

Emtage, William Thomas Allder, 1862–1942, vol. IV

Encombe, Viscount; John Scott, 1870–1900, vol. I

Enderl, Kurt H., 1913–1985, vol. VIII

Enders, John Franklin, 1897–1985, vol. VIII

Endicott, Very Rev. James, 1865–1954, vol. V

Endicott, William, 1865–1941, vol. IV

Energlyn, Baron (Life Peer); William David Evans, 1912–1985, vol. VIII

Enever, Sir Francis Alfred, 1893–1966, vol. VI

Enfield, Sir Ralph Roscoe, 1885–1973, vol. VII

Engelbach, Alfred H. H., 1850–1928, vol. II

Engelbach, Archibald Frank, 1881–1961, vol. VI

Engelbach, Mrs Florence, *died* 1951, vol. V

Engelbach, Lewis William, 1837–1908, vol. I

Engelbach, Reginald, 1888–1946, vol. IV

Engelhard, Charles William, 1917–1971, vol. VII

Engelmann, Franklin, 1908–1972, vol. VII

Engels, Johan Peter, 1908–1981, vol. VIII

Engholm, Sir Basil Charles, 1912–1990, vol. VIII

England, Col Abraham, 1867–1949, vol. IV

England, Rev. Arthur Creyke, 1872–1946, vol. IV

England, Maj.-Gen. Edward Lutwyche, 1839–1910, vol. I

England, Edwin Bourdieu, 1847–1936, vol. III

England, Edwin Thirlwall, *died* 1945, vol. IV

England, E(ric) C. Gordon, 1891–1976, vol. VII

England, Henry Barren, 1855–1942, vol. IV

England, Rear-Adm. Hugh Turnour, 1884–1978, vol. VII

England, Lt-Col Norman Ayrton, 1886–1939, vol. III

England, Peter Tiarks Ede, 1925–1978, vol. VII

England, Philip Remington, 1879–1959, vol. V

England, Sir Russell, *died* 1970, vol. VI

Engledow, Charles John, 1860–1933, vol. III (A), vol. IV

Engledow, Sir Frank Leonard, 1890–1985, vol. VIII

Engleheart, Lt-Col Evelyn Linzee, 1862–1943, vol. IV

Engleheart, Sir John Gardner Dillman, 1823–1923, vol. II

English, Alexander Emanuel, 1871–1962, vol. VI

English, Sir Crisp, *died* 1949, vol. IV

English, Douglas, 1870–1939, vol. III

English, Lt-Col Ernest Robert Maling, 1874–1941, vol. IV

English, Col Frederick Paul, 1859–1946, vol. IV

English, Sir John; *see* English, Sir W. J.

English, Joseph Sandys, 1890–1971, vol. VII

English, Comdr Reginald Wastell, 1894–1980, vol. VII

English, Lt-Col William John, 1882–1941, vol. IV

English, Sir (William) John, 1903–1973, vol. VII

Ennals, John Arthur Ford, 1918–1988, vol. VIII

Ennes Ulrich, Ruy, 1883–1966, vol. VI

Ennever, William Joseph, 1869–1947, vol. IV

Ennis, George Francis Macdaniel, 1868–1933, vol. III

Ennis, John Matthew, vol. II

Ennis, Lawrence, 1871–1938, vol. III

Ennisdale, 1st Baron, 1878–1963, vol. VI

Enniskillen, 4th Earl of, 1845–1924, vol. II

Enniskillen, 5th Earl of, 1876–1963, vol. VI

Enniskillen, 6th Earl of, 1918–1989, vol. VIII

Ennor, Sir Arnold Hughes, (Sir Hugh Ennor), 1912–1977, vol. VII

Ennor, Sir Hugh; *see* Ennor, Sir A. H.

Enock, Charles Reginald, 1868–1970, vol. VI

Enraght, Rev. Canon Hawtrey James, 1871–1938, vol. III

Enright, Adm. Sir Philip King, 1894–1960, vol. V

Enslin, Brig.-Gen. Barend Gotfried Leopold, 1879–1955, vol. V

Ensor, Alick Charles Davidson, (David), 1906–1987, vol. VIII

Ensor, Arthur Hinton, 1891–1977, vol. VII

Ensor, David; *see* Ensor, A. C. D.

Ensor, Maj.-Gen. Howard, 1874–1942, vol. IV

Ensor, Sir Robert Charles Kirkwood, 1877–1958, vol. V

Enters, Angna, 1907–1989, vol. VIII

Enthoven, Mrs (Augusta) Gabrielle (Eden), 1868–1950, vol. IV

Enthoven, Mrs Gabrielle; *see* Enthoven, Mrs A. G. E.

Enthoven, Reginald Edward, 1869–1952, vol. V

Enthoven, Roderick Eustace, 1900–1985, vol. VIII

Entrican, Lt-Col James, 1864–1935, vol. III

Entwisle, John Bertie Norreys, 1856–1945, vol. IV

Entwistle, Major Sir Cyril Fullard, 1887–1974, vol. VII

Entwistle, William James, *died* 1952, vol. V

Ephraim, Lee, *died* 1953, vol. V

Epinay, Charles Adrien Prosper d', 1836–1914, vol. I

Epps, Sir George Selby Washington, 1885–1951, vol. V

Eppstein, Rev. William Charles, 1864–1928, vol. II

Epstein, Sir Jacob, 1880–1959, vol. V

Epstein, Mortimer, *died* 1946, vol. IV

Erasmus, Hon. François Christiaan, 1896–1967, vol. VI

Erdelyi, Arthur, 1908–1977, vol. VII

Erhard, Ludwig, 1897–1977, vol. VII

Eriks, Sierd Sint, *died* 1966, vol. VI

Erith, Rev. Canon Lionel Edward Patrick, 1885–1939, vol. III

Erith, Raymond Charles, 1904–1973, vol. VII

Erlanger, E. Joseph, 1874–1965, vol. VI

Erle, Twynihoe William, 1828–1908, vol. I

Erne, 4th Earl of, 1839–1914, vol. I

Erne, 5th Earl of, 1907–1940, vol. III

Ernest, Maurice, 1872–1955, vol. V

Ernle, 1st Baron, 1851–1937, vol. III

Ernst, Harold Clarence, *died* 1922, vol. II

Ernst, Max, 1891–1976, vol. VII

Ernst, Morris Leopold, 1888–1976, vol. VII

Ernst, Noel Edward, 1891–1965, vol. VI

Ernst, Oswald Herbert, 1842–1926, vol. II

Ernst, William Gordon, 1897–1939, vol. III

Errington, Sir Eric, 1st Bt (*cr* 1963), 1900–1973, vol. VII

Errington, Lt-Col Francis Henry Launcelot, 1857–1942, vol. IV

Errington, Sir George, 1st Bt (*cr* 1885), 1839–1920, vol. II

Errington, Col Roger, 1887–1960, vol. V

Errock, Michael Warden, 1921–1970, vol. VI

Erroll, 20th Earl of, 1852–1927, vol. II

Erroll, 21st Earl of, 1876–1928, vol. II

Erroll, 22nd Earl of, 1901–1941, vol. IV

Erroll, Countess of (23rd in line), 1926–1978, vol. VII

Erskine, 5th Baron, 1841–1913, vol. I

Erskine, 6th Baron, 1865–1957, vol. V

Erskine of Rerrick, 1st Baron, 1893–1980, vol. VII

Erskine, Lord; John Francis Ashley Erskine, 1895–1953, vol. V

Erskine, Col Sir Arthur Edward, 1881–1963, vol. VI

Erskine, David, *died* 1922, vol. II

Erskine, Sir Derek Quicke, 1905–1977, vol. VII

Erskine, Major Esmé Nourse, 1885–1962, vol. VI

Erskine, Sir ffolliott Williams, 3rd Bt, 1850–1912, vol. I

Erskine, Hon. Francis Walter, 1899–1972, vol. VII

Erskine, Sir George; *see* Erskine, Sir R. G.

Erskine, Maj.-Gen. George Elphinstone, 1841–1912, vol. I

Erskine, George Oswald Harry Erskine Biber, 1857–1931, vol. III

Erskine, Gen. Sir George Watkin Eben James, 1899–1965, vol. VI

Erskine, Col Henry Adeane, 1857–1953, vol. V

Erskine, Sir Henry David, 1838–1921, vol. II

Erskine, Maj.-Gen. (Hon.) Ian David, 1898–1973, vol. VII

Erskine, James; *see* Rosslyn, 5th Earl of.

Erskine, Adm. of the Fleet Sir James Elphinstone, 1838–1911, vol. I

Erskine, Brig.-Gen. James Francis, 1862–1936, vol. III

Erskine, Sir James Malcolm Monteith, 1863–1944, vol. IV

Erskine, John, 1879–1951, vol. V

Erskine, Lt-Col Keith David, 1863–1914, vol. I

Erskine, Keith David, 1907–1974, vol. VII

Erskine, Robert, 1874–1933, vol. III

Erskine, Sir (Robert) George, 1896–1984, vol. VIII

Erskine, Hon. Ruaraidh, 1869–1960, vol. V

Erskine, Adm. Seymour Elphinstone, 1863–1945, vol. IV

Erskine, Mrs Steuart, *died* 1948, vol. IV

Erskine, Sir Thomas, 2nd Bt, 1824–1902, vol. I

Erskine, Col Thomas Harry, 1860–1924, vol. II

Erskine, Sir Thomas Wilfred Hargreaves John, 4th Bt, 1880–1944, vol. IV

Erskine, Walter Hugh, 1870–1948, vol. IV

Erskine, Rt Hon. Sir William Augustus Forbes, 1871–1952, vol. V

Erskine-Bolst, Captain Clifford Charles Alan Lawrence, 1878–1946, vol. IV

Erskine Crum, Maj.-Gen. Vernon Forbes, 1918–1971, vol. VII

Erskine-Hill, Sir Alexander Galloway, 1st Bt, 1894–1947, vol. IV

Erskine-Hill, Sir Robert, 2nd Bt, 1917–1989, vol. VIII

Erskine-Lindop, Audrey Beatrice Noël, 1920–1986, vol. VIII

Erskine-Murray, Lt-Col Arthur, 1877–1948, vol. IV

Erskine-Wyse, Marjorie Anne, (Mrs Michael Erskine-Wyse), 1914–1976, vol. VII

Ertz, Edward, 1862–1954, vol. V

Ertz, Susan, (Mrs J. R. McCrindle), 1887–1985, vol. VIII

Ervine, St John Greer, 1888–1971, vol. VII

Escombe, Captain Harold, *died* 1933, vol. III

Escombe, Rt Hon. Harry, 1838–1899, vol. I

Escombe, Captain William Malcolm Lingard, 1891–1973, vol. VII

Escott, Sir (Ernest) Bichkam S.; *see* Sweet-Escott.

Escott, Thomas Hay Sweet, *died* 1924, vol. II

Escreet, Ven. Charles Ernest, 1852–1919, vol. II

Escritt, (Charles) Ewart, 1905–1990, vol. VIII

Escritt, Ewart; *see* Escritt, C. E.

Escritt, Leonard Bushby, 1902–1973, vol. VII

Esdaile, Arundell James Kennedy, 1880–1956, vol. V

Esdaile, Katharine Ada, 1881–1950, vol. IV

Esdaile, Philippa Chichele, 1888–1989, vol. VIII

Eshelby, John Douglas, 1916–1981, vol. VIII

Esher, 1st Viscount, 1815–1899, vol. I

Esher, 2nd Viscount, 1852–1930, vol. III

Esher, 3rd Viscount, 1881–1963, vol. VI

Esler, Erminda Rentoul, *died* 1924, vol. II

Esmarch, Johannes Friedrich August von, 1823–1908, vol. I

Esmond, Eva; *see* Moore, E.

Esmond, Henry V., *died* 1922, vol. II

Esmonde, Sir Anthony Charles, 15th Bt, 1899–1981, vol. VIII

Esmonde, John, 1862–1915, vol. I

Esmonde, Sir John Henry Grattan, 16th Bt, 1928–1987, vol. VIII

Esmonde, Captain Sir John Lymbrick, 14th Bt, 1893–1958, vol. V

Esmonde, Lt-Col Sir Laurence Grattan, 13th Bt, 1863–1943, vol. IV

Esmonde, Sir Osmond Thomas Grattan, 12th Bt, 1896–1936, vol. III

Esmonde, Sir Thomas Henry Grattan, 11th Bt, 1862–1935, vol. III

Espin, Rev. John, 1836–1905, vol. I

Espin, Rev. Thomas Espinell, *died* 1912, vol. I

Espin, Rev. Thomas Henry Espinell Compton, 1858–1934, vol. III

Espinas, Alfred, 1844–1922, vol. II

'Espinasse, Paul Gilbert, 1900–1975, vol. VII

Espitalier-Noel, Andre; *see* Noel.

Esplen, Sir John, 1st Bt, 1863–1930, vol. III

Esplen, Sir William Graham, 2nd Bt, 1899–1989, vol. VIII

Espley, Arthur James, *died* 1971, vol. VII

Esposito, Michele, 1855–1929, vol. III

Essame, Maj.-Gen. Hubert, 1896–1976, vol. VII

Essell, Col Frederick Knight, 1864–1951, vol. V

Essendon, 1st Baron, 1870–1944, vol. IV

Essendon, 2nd Baron, 1903–1978, vol. VII

Essenhigh, Reginald Clare, 1890–1955, vol. V

Essery, William Joseph, 1860–1955, vol. V

Essex, 7th Earl of, 1857–1916, vol. II

Essex, 8th Earl of, 1884–1966, vol. VI

Essex, 9th Earl of, 1906–1981, vol. VIII

Essex, Air Vice-Marshal Bertram Edward, 1897–1959, vol. V

Essex, Mary; *see* Bloom, Ursula.

Essex, Sir (Richard) Walter, 1857–1941, vol. IV

Essex, Rosamund Sibyl, 1900–1985, vol. VIII

Essex, Sir Walter; *see* Essex, Sir R. W.

Esslemont, George Birnie, 1860–1917, vol. II

Esslemont, Mary, 1891–1984, vol. VIII

Esson, Col James Jacob, 1869–1940, vol. III

Esson, William, 1838–1916, vol. II

Estall, Thomas, 1848–1920, vol. II

Estaunie, Édouard, 1862–1942, vol. IV

Estcourt, 1st Baron, 1839–1915, vol. I

Estcourt, Rev. Edmund Walter S.; *see* Sotheron-Estcourt.

Estcourt, Maj.-Gen. Edward Noel Keith, 1905–1982, vol. VIII

Estcourt, Captain Thomas Edmund S.; *see* Sotheron-Estcourt.

Estell, Hon. John, 1861–1928, vol. II

Estes, Elliott M(arantette), 1916–1988, vol. VIII

Estey, James Wilfred, 1889–1956, vol. V

Etchells, Ernest Fiander, 1876–1927, vol. II

Etchells, Frederick, *died* 1973, vol. VII

Etches, Major Charles Edward, 1872–1944, vol. IV

Eteson, Surg.-Gen. Alfred, *died* 1910, vol. I

Eteson, Col Harold Carleton Wetherall, 1863–1947, vol. IV

Ethe, C. Hermann, 184–1917, vol. II

Etheridge, Col Cecil de Courcy, 1860–1940, vol. III

Etheridge, Rt Rev. Edward Harold, 1872–1954, vol. V

Etheridge, Robert, 1819–1903, vol. I

Etherington, Col Frederick, 1878–1955, vol. V

Etherington-Smith, John Henry, 1841–1923, vol. II

Etherton, Sir George Hammond, 1876–1949, vol. IV

Etherton, Col P. T., 1879–1963, vol. VI

Etherton, Ralph Humphrey, 1904–1987, vol. VIII

Eton, Robert; *see* Meynell, L. W.

Ettles, William James M'Culloch, 1869–1918, vol. II

Ettlinger, Leopold David, 1913–1989, vol. VIII

Etzdorf, Hasso von, 1900–1989, vol. VIII

Etzel, Franz, 1902–1970, vol. VI (AII)

Euan-Smith, Col Sir Charles Bean; *see* Smith.

Eucken, Rudolf Christoph, 1846–1926, vol. II

Eugenie, Empress, 1826–1920, vol. II

Eugster, Gen. Sir Basil Oscar Paul, 1914–1984, vol. VIII

Eugster, Lt-Col Oscar Lewis, 1880–1930, vol. III

Eumorfopoulos, George, 1863–1939, vol. III

Eurich, Frederick William, 1867–1945, vol. IV

Eustace, Maj.-Gen. Alexander Henry, 1863–1939, vol. III

Eustace, Major Charles Legge Eustace R.; *see* Robertson-Eustace.

Eustace, Edward Arthur Rawlins, 1899–1972, vol. VII

Eustace, Maj.-Gen. Sir Francis John William, 1849–1925, vol. II

Eustace, Lt-Col Henry Montague, 1863–1926, vol. II

Eustace, Adm. John Bridges, 1861–1947, vol. IV

Eustace, John Curtis Wernher, 1906–1972, vol. VII

Eustace, Mrs Marjory Edith R.; *see* Robertson-Eustace.

Eustace, Robert William Barrington R.; *see* Robertson-Eustace.

Eustace-Jameson, Lt-Col John; *see* Jameson.

Eustice, John, 1864–1943, vol. IV

Euston, Earl of; Henry James Fitzroy, 1848–1912, vol. I

Euwe, Machgielis, 1901–1981, vol. VIII

Evan-Jones, Cecil Artimus, 1912–1978, vol. VII

Evan-Jones, Rev. Canon Richard, 1849–1925, vol. II

Evan-Thomas, Adm. Sir Hugh, 1862–1928, vol. II

Evan-Thomas, Llewelyn, 1859–1947, vol. IV

Evang, Karl, 1902–1981, vol. VIII

Evans, 1st Baron, 1903–1963, vol. VI

Evans of Hungershall, Baron (Life Peer); Benjamin Ifor Evans, 1899–1982, vol. VIII

Evans, Alan Frederick Reginald, 1891–1960, vol. V

Evans, Albert, 1903–1988, vol. VIII

Evans, Ven. Albert Owen, 1864–1937, vol. III

Evans, Vice-Adm. Sir Alfred Englefield, 1884–1944, vol. IV

Evans, Sir Alfred Henry, 1847–1938, vol. III

Evans, Alfred Thomas, (Fred Evans), 1914–1987, vol. VIII

Evans, Annie Lloyd-, died 1938, vol. III

Evans, Arthur; see Evans, H. A.

Evans, Sir Arthur, 1851–1941, vol. IV

Evans, Col Sir Arthur, 1898–1958, vol. V

Evans, Rev. Canon Arthur Fitz-Gerald, 1854–1933, vol. III

Evans, Arthur Henry, died 1950, vol. IV

Evans, Rev. Arthur Norman, 1900–1975, vol. VII

Evans, Rev. Arthur Robertson, died 1923, vol. II

Evans, Sir Arthur Trevor, 1895–1983, vol. VIII

Evans, Rev. Arthur Wade W.; see Wade-Evans.

Evans, Sir Athol Donald, 1904–1988, vol. VIII

Evans, Sir Bernard, 1905–1981, vol. VIII

Evans, Bernard Walter, 1843–1922, vol. II

Evans, Captain Bertram Sutton, 1872–1919, vol. II

Evans, Brig. Brian P.; see Pennefather-Evans.

Evans, Caradoc, died 1945, vol. IV

Evans, Cecil Herbert, 1898–1957, vol. V

Evans, Charles; see Evans, W. C.

Evans, Sir Charles Arthur Lovatt, died 1968, vol. VI

Evans, Charles Barnard, died 1920, vol. II

Evans, Charles Glyn, 1883–1961, vol. VI

Evans, Maj.-Gen. Charles Harford B.; see Bowle-Evans.

Evans, Vice-Adm. Sir Charles Leo Glandore, 1908–1981, vol. VIII

Evans, Col Charles Robert, 1873–1956, vol. V

Evans, Charles Seddon, 1883–1944, vol. IV

Evans, Charles Tunstall, 1903–1980, vol. VII

Evans, Col Charles William Henry, 1851–1909, vol. I

Evans, Collis William, 1895–1984, vol. VIII

Evans, Brig.-Gen. Cuthbert, 1871–1934, vol. III

Evans, Rt Rev. Daniel Ivor, 1900–1962, vol. VI

Evans, Rev. Daniel Silvan, 1818–1903, vol. I

Evans, Sir David, 1849–1907, vol. I

Evans, Ven. David, died 1910, vol. I

Evans, David, 1874–1948, vol. IV

Evans, David Carey Rees Jones, 1899–1982, vol. VIII

Evans, David Charles Exton, 1878–1938, vol. III

Evans, David Eifion Puleston, 1902–1984, vol. VIII

Evans, Sir (David) Emrys, 1891–1966, vol. VI

Evans, Sir David Gwynne, 1909–1984, vol. VIII

Evans, Sir David Lewis, 1893–1987, vol. VIII

Evans, David M.; see Monle-Evans.

Evans, (David) Meurig, 1906–1983, vol. VIII

Evans, David Morgan, 1892–1977, vol. VII

Evans, David Owen, 1876–1945, vol. IV

Evans, Sir (David) Rowland, died 1953, vol. V

Evans, Maj.-Gen. David Sydney Carlyon, 1893–1955, vol. V

Evans, Sir David William, 1866–1926, vol. II

Evans, Dennis Frederick, 1928–1990, vol. VIII

Evans, Air Chief Marshal Sir Donald Randell, 1912–1975, vol. VII

Evans, Rev. E. Gwyn, 1898–1958, vol. V

Evans, Sir E. Vincent, died 1934, vol. III

Evans, Dame Edith, (Dame Edith Mary Booth), 1888–1976, vol. VII

Evans, Sir Edward, 1846–1917, vol. II

Evans, Maj.-Gen. Sir Edward, 1872–1949, vol. IV

Evans, Edward, 1883–1960, vol. V

Evans, Edward Francis Herbert, 1873–1958, vol. V

Evans, Col Edward Stokes, 1855–1926, vol. II

Evans, Edward Victor, 1882–1964, vol. VI

Evans, Edward Walter, 1890–1985, vol. VIII

Evans, Sir Edwin, died 1928, vol. II

Evans, Edwin, 1874–1945, vol. IV

Evans, Einion, 1896–1969, vol. VI

Evans, Ellen, 1891–1953, vol. V

Evans, Emily, died 1958, vol. V

Evans, Emlyn Hugh Garner, 1911–1963, vol. VI

Evans, Sir Emrys; see Evans, Sir D. E.

Evans, (Emyr) Estyn, 1905–1989, vol. VIII

Evans, Ven. Eric Herbert, 1902–1977, vol. VII

Evans, Ernest, 1885–1965, vol. VI

Evans, Estyn; see Evans, Emyr E.

Evans, Sir Evan Gwynne G.; see Gwynne-Evans.

Evans, Evan Jenkin, 1882–1944, vol. IV

Evans, Evan Laming, 1871–1945, vol. IV

Evans, Evan Stanley, 1904–1982, vol. VIII

Evans, Evan William, 1860–1925, vol. II

Evans, Sir Evelyn Ward, 3rd Bt (cr 1902), 1883–1970, vol. VI

Evans, Major Fisher Henry Freke, 1868–1961, vol. VI

Evans, Sir Francis Edward, 1897–1983, vol. VIII

Evans, Sir Francis Henry, 1st Bt (cr 1902), 1840–1907, vol. I

Evans, Frank Dudley, 1883–1941, vol. IV

Evans, Frankis Tilney, 1900–1974, vol. VII

Evans, Fred; see Evans, Alfred T.

Evans, Captain Frederic James, 1867–1945, vol. IV

Evans, Rev. Canon Frederic James, died 1946, vol. IV

Evans, Rev. Frederic Rawlins, 1842–1927, vol. II

Evans, Sir Frederick, 1849–1939, vol. III

Evans, Frederick Buisson, 1874–1952, vol. V

Evans, Sir Geoffrey, 1883–1963, vol. VI

Evans, Geoffrey A., 1886–1951, vol. V

Evans, Lt-Gen. Sir Geoffrey Charles, 1901–1987, vol. VIII

Evans, George Ewart, 1909–1988, vol. VIII

Evans, Rear-Adm. George Hammond, 1917–1980, vol. VII

Evans, Col George Henry, 1863–1948, vol. IV

Evans, Rev. George Simon T.; see Tudor-Evans.

Evans, Rev. George William, 1867–1938, vol. III

Evans, Lt-Col Granville P.; see Pennefather-Evans.

Evans, Griffith, 1835–1935, vol. III

Evans, Griffith Conrad, 1887–1973, vol. VII

Evans, Sir Griffith Humphrey Pugh, 1840–1902, vol. I

Evans, Griffith Ivor, 1889–1966, vol. VI

Evans, Sir Guildhaume M.; see Myrddin-Evans.

Evans, Sir Harold, 1st Bt, 1911–1983, vol. VIII

Evans, Harold Muir, 1866–1947, vol. IV

Evans, Lt-Col Harrie Smalley, 1887–1971, vol. VII

Evans, (Harry) Lindley, 1895–1982, vol. VIII
Evans, Rev. Henry, *died* 1924, vol. II
Evans, (Henry) Arthur, 1903–1965, vol. VI
Evans, Henry Farrington, 1845–1931, vol. III
Evans, Maj.-Gen. Henry Holland, 1914–1987, vol. VIII
Evans, Rt Rev. Henry St John Tomlinson, 1905–1956, vol. V
Evans, Major Herbert, 1868–1931, vol. III
Evans, Herbert D.; *see* Davies-Evans.
Evans, Herbert Edgar, 1884–1970, vol. VI (AII)
Evans, Herbert McLean, 1882–1971, vol. VII
Evans, Herbert Walter Lloyd, 1877–1956, vol. V
Evans, Gen. Sir Horace Moule, 1841–1923, vol. II
Evans, Brig.-Gen. Horatio James, 1850–1932, vol. III
Evans, Howard, 1839–1915, vol. I
Evans, Hubert John Filmer, 1904–1989, vol. VIII
Evans, Sir Hywel Wynn, 1920–1988, vol. VIII
Evans, Sir Ian William G.; *see* Gwynne-Evans.
Evans, Ifor Leslie, 1897–1952, vol. V
Evans, Illtyd Buller P.; *see* Pole-Evans.
Evans, Ioan Lyonel, 1927–1984, vol. VIII
Evans, Rev. J. T., 1878–1950, vol. IV
Evans, Major James John Pugh, 1885–1974, vol. VII
Evans, Dame Joan, *died* 1977, vol. VII
Evans, Sir John, 1823–1908, vol. I
Evans, Lt-Col John, *died* 1930, vol. III
Evans, Col John, 1868–1942, vol. IV
Evans, John, 1875–1961, vol. VI
Evans, John Cayo, 1879–1958, vol. V
Evans, Rev. John David, *died* 1912, vol. I
Evans, John Emrys-, 1853–1931, vol. III
Evans, John Gwenogvryn, 1852–1930, vol. III
Evans, Sir John Harold, 1904–1973, vol. VII
Evans, John Howell, 1870–1962, vol. VI
Evans, John Jameson, 1871–1941, vol. IV
Evans, John Owain, 1875–1943, vol. IV
Evans, Rev. John Thomas, 1869–1940, vol. III
Evans, John William, *died* 1930, vol. III
Evans, Hon. Sir John William, 1855–1943, vol. IV
Evans, Rev. John Young, 1865–1941, vol. IV
Evans, Rev. Joseph David Samuel P.; *see* Parry-Evans.
Evans, Rt Rev. Kenneth Charles, 1903–1970, vol. VI
Evans, Rt Hon. Sir Laming W.; *see* Worthington-Evans.
Evans, L(eonard) G(lyde) Lavington, 1888–1976, vol. VII
Evans, Rev. Leonard Hugh, 1863–1939, vol. III
Evans, Maj.-Gen. Leopold Exxel, 1837–1916, vol. II
Evans, Lewis, 1853–1930, vol. III
Evans, Rev. Lewis Herbert, 1870–1942, vol. IV
Evans, Lewis Noel Vincent, 1886–1967, vol. VI
Evans, Brig.-Gen. Lewis Pugh, 1881–1962, vol. VI
Evans, Sir Lincoln, 1889–1970, vol. VI
Evans, Lindley; *see* Evans, H. L.
Evans, Mgr Canon Lionel Ella, 1882–1942, vol. IV
Evans, Lt-Col Llewelyn, *died* 1963, vol. VI
Evans, Luther Harris, 1902–1981, vol. VIII
Evans, Maurice Hubert, 1901–1989, vol. VIII
Evans, Maurice Smethurst, 1854–1920, vol. II, vol. III
Evans, Meredith Gwynne, 1904–1952, vol. V
Evans, Merlyn Oliver, 1910–1973, vol. VII

Evans, Meurig; *see* Evans, D. M.
Evans, Rev. Sir Murland de Grasse, 2nd Bt (*cr* 1902), 1874–1946, vol. IV
Evans, Nevil Norton, 1865–1948, vol. IV
Evans, Lady Olwen Elizabeth C.; *see* Carey Evans.
Evans, Ven. Owen, *died* 1914, vol. I
Evans, Patrick Fleming, 1851–1902, vol. I
Evans, Paul Vychan E.; *see* Emrys-Evans.
Evans, Col Percy, 1868–1945, vol. IV
Evans, Percy William, 1882–1951, vol. V
Evans, Peter MacIntyre, 1859–1944, vol. IV
Evans, Philip Rainsford, 1910–1990, vol. VIII
Evans, Phyllis Mary Carlyon, 1913–1990, vol. VIII
Evans, Very Rev. Raymond Ellis, 1908–1983, vol. VIII
Evans, Dame Regina Margaret, 1885–1969, vol. VI
Evans, (Richard) Stanley, 1883–1949, vol. IV
Evans, Richard Thomas, 1890–1946, vol. IV
Evans, Richardson, 1846–1928, vol. II
Evans, Sir Robert Charles, 1878–1961, vol. VI
Evans, Maj.-Gen. Roger, 1886–1968, vol. VI
Evans, Sir Rowland; *see* Evans, Sir D. R.
Evans, Samuel T. G., 1829–1904, vol. I
Evans, Rt Hon. Sir Samuel Thomas, 1859–1918, vol. II
Evans, Very Rev. Seiriol John Arthur, 1894–1984, vol. VIII
Evans, Sir Shirley W.; *see* Worthington-Evans, Sir W. S. W.
Evans, Sir (Sidney) Harold; *see* Evans, Sir Harold.
Evans, Stanley; *see* Evans, E. S.
Evans, Stanley; *see* Evans, R. S.
Evans, Rev. Canon Stanley George, 1912–1965, vol. VI
Evans, Stanley Norman, 1898–1970, vol. VI
Evans, Very Rev. Sydney Hall, 1915–1988, vol. VIII
Evans, T. Hopkin, 1879–1940, vol. III
Evans, Thomas, *died* 1943, vol. IV
Evans, Col Thomas Dixon Byron, 1860–1908, vol. I
Evans, Very Rev. Thomas Frye Lewis, 1845–1920, vol. II
Evans, Major Sir Thomas John Carey, 1884–1947, vol. IV
Evans, Rev. Thomas Jones, 1856–1921, vol. II
Evans, Maj.-Gen. Thomas Julian Penrhys, 1854–1921, vol. II
Evans, Timothy, 1875–1945, vol. IV
Evans, Trefor Ellis, 1913–1974, vol. VII
Evans, Sir Trevor Maldwyn, 1902–1981, vol. VIII
Evans, Ulick Richardson, 1889–1980, vol. VII
Evans, Brig.-Gen. Usher Williamson, 1864–1946, vol. IV
Evans, Sir Walter, 1855–1935, vol. III
Evans, Sir Walter Harry, 1st Bt (*cr* 1920), 1872–1954, vol. V
Evans, Walter Jenkin, 1856–1927, vol. II
Evans, Walter John, 1864–1939, vol. III
Evans, Webster; *see* Evans, W. E. W.
Evans, Brig.-Gen. Wilfrid Keith, 1878–1934, vol. III
Evans, William, 1847–1918, vol. II
Evans, William, 1841–1919, vol. II
Evans, William, *died* 1936, vol. III
Evans, Brig.-Gen. William, 1871–1944, vol. IV
Evans, William, 1895–1988, vol. VIII

Evans, William B.; *see* Bulkeley-Evans.
Evans, William Campbell, 1916–1990, vol. VIII
Evans, (William) Charles, 1911–1988, vol. VIII
Evans, William David; *see* Baron Energlyn.
Evans, William Edis Webster, 1908–1982, vol. VIII
Evans, William Ewart, 1899–1990, vol. VIII
Evans, Sir William G.; *see* Gwynne-Evans.
Evans, William H., 1873–1934, vol. III
Evans, Brig. William Harry, 1876–1956, vol. V
Evans, William James, 1861–1944, vol. IV
Evans, William John, 1899–1983, vol. VIII
Evans, William Percival, 1864–1959, vol. V
Evans, Sir (William) Shirley (Worthington) W.; *see* Worthington-Evans.
Evans, Willmott Henderson, *died* 1938, vol. III
Evans Bevan, Sir David Martyn, 1st Bt, 1902–1973, vol. VII
Evans-Freke, Hon. Ralfe, 1897–1969, vol. VI
Evans-Gordon, Col Kenmure Alick Garth, 1885–1960, vol. V
Evans-Gwynne, Brig. Alfred Howel, 1882–1949, vol. IV
Evans-Jones, Rev. Sir Albert, 1895–1970, vol. VI
Evans-Lombe, Vice-Adm. Sir Edward Malcolm, 1901–1974, vol. VII
Evans-Pritchard, Sir Edward Evan, 1902–1973, vol. VII
Evanson, Maj.-Gen. Arthur Charles Tarver, 1895–1957, vol. V
Evatt, Maj.-Gen. Sir George Joseph Hamilton, 1843–1921, vol. II
Evatt, Rt Hon. Herbert Vere, 1894–1965, vol. VI
Evatt, Brig.-Gen. John Thorold, 1861–1949, vol. IV
Eve, Arthur Stewart, 1862–1948, vol. IV
Eve, Frank Cecil, *died* 1952, vol. V
Eve, Sir Frederic Samuel, *died* 1916, vol. II
Eve, George W., *died* 1914, vol. I
Eve, Rt Hon. Sir Harry Trelawney, 1856–1940, vol. III
Eve, Sir Herbert Trustram, 1865–1936, vol. III
Evelegh, Maj.-Gen. Vyvyan, 1898–1958, vol. V
Eveling, Walter Raphael Taylor, 1908–1987, vol. VIII
Evelyn, John Harcourt Chichester, 1876–1922, vol. II
Evelyn, William John, 1822–1908, vol. I
Even, Col George Eusebe, 1855–1924, vol. II
Evennett, Henry Outram, 1901–1964, vol. VI
Everall, John Harold, 1908–1984, vol. VIII
Everard, Captain Andrew Robert Guy, 1830–1925, vol. II, vol. III
Everard, Bernard, 1879–1963, vol. VI
Everard, Edward Everard Earle W.; *see* Welby-Everard.
Everard, Sir Lindsay; *see* Everard, Sir W. L.
Everard, Lt-Col Sir Nugent Henry, 3rd Bt, 1905–1984, vol. VIII
Everard, Col Sir Nugent Talbot, 1st Bt, 1849–1929, vol. III
Everard, Major Sir Richard William, 2nd Bt, 1874–1929, vol. III
Everard, Sir (William) Lindsay, *died* 1949, vol. IV
Everest, Arthur Ernest, 1888–1983, vol. VIII
Everett, Adm. Sir Allan Frederic, 1868–1938, vol. III
Everett, Rev. Bernard Charles Spencer, 1874–1943, vol. IV

Everett, Dorothy, 1894–1953, vol. V
Everett, Rear-Adm. Douglas Henry, 1900–1986, vol. VIII
Everett, Col Edward, 1837–1920, vol. II
Everett, Harry Poore, 1862–1955, vol. V
Everett, Maj.-Gen. Sir Henry Joseph, 1866–1951, vol. V
Everett, Joseph David, 1831–1904, vol. I
Everett, Sir Percy Winn, 1870–1952, vol. V
Everett, Richard Marven Hale, 1909–1978, vol. VII
Everett, Robert Lacey, 1833–1916, vol. II
Everett, Col Sir William, 1844–1908, vol. I
Everett-Green, Evelyn, 1856–1932, vol. III
Everidge, John, *died* 1955, vol. V
Everingham, Ven. William, 1856–1919, vol. II
Everington, Geoffrey Devas, 1915–1982, vol. VIII
Everitt, Sir Clement, 1873–1934, vol. III
Everitt, Major Sydney George, 1860–1932, vol. III
Evers, Claude Ronald, 1908–1988, vol. VIII
Evers, H(enry) Harvey, 1893–1979, vol. VII
Evershed, 1st Baron, 1899–1966, vol. VI
Evershed, Arthur, 1836–1919, vol. II
Evershed, John, 1864–1956, vol. V
Evershed, Sydney, 1825–1903, vol. I
Evershed, Sir Sydney Herbert, 1861–1937, vol. III
Evershed, Rear-Adm. Walter, 1907–1969, vol. VI
Eversley, 1st Baron, 1831–1928, vol. II
Eversley, William Pinder, 1850–1918, vol. II
Every, Rt Rev. Edward Francis, 1862–1941, vol. IV
Every, Sir Edward Oswald, 11th Bt, 1886–1959, vol. V
Every, Sir John Simon, 12th Bt, 1914–1988, vol. VIII
Eves, Sir Charles, 1864–1936, vol. III
Eves, Charles Washington, 1838–1899, vol. I
Eves, Sir Hubert Heath, 1883–1961, vol. VI
Eves, Reginald Grenville, 1876–1941, vol. IV
Evetts, Sir George, 1882–1958, vol. V
Evetts, Lt-Gen. Sir John Fullerton, 1891–1988, vol. VIII
Evill, Lt-Col Charles Ariel, 1874–1954, vol. V
Evill, Air Chief Marshal Sir Douglas Claude Strathern, 1892–1971, vol. VII
Evington, Rt Rev. Henry, 1848–1912, vol. I
Evoe; *see* Knox, E. G. V.
Ewald, Paul P., 1888–1985, vol. VIII
Ewan, Col Thomas George, 1856–1937, vol. III
Ewart, Alfred James, 1872–1937, vol. III
Ewart, Adm. Arthur Wartensleben, 1862–1922, vol. II
Ewart, Lt-Gen. Charles Brisbane, 1827–1903, vol. I
Ewart, David, 1841–1921, vol. II
Ewart, David Shanks, 1901–1965, vol. VI
Ewart, Lt-Col Ernest Andrew; *see* Cable, Boyd.
Ewart, Captain Frank Rowland, 1874–1906, vol. I
Ewart, George Arthur, 1886–1942, vol. IV
Ewart, Maj.-Gen. Sir Henry Peter, 1st Bt, 1838–1928, vol. II
Ewart, James Cossar, 1851–1933, vol. III
Ewart, Gen. Sir John Alexander, 1821–1904, vol. I
Ewart, Sir John Murray, 1884–1939, vol. III
Ewart, John S., 1849–1933, vol. III
Ewart, Lt-Gen. Sir John Spencer, 1861–1930, vol. III
Ewart, Sir Joseph, 1831–1906, vol. I

Ewart, Sir Lavens Mathewson Algernon, 4th Bt, 1885–1939, did not have an entry in Who's Who.

Ewart, Richard, 1904–1953, vol. V

Ewart, Maj.-Gen. Sir Richard Henry, 1864–1928, vol. II

Ewart, Sir Robert Heard, 3rd Bt, 1879–1939, vol. III

Ewart, Sir Talbot, 5th Bt, 1878–1959, vol. V

Ewart, William, 1848–1929, vol. III

Ewart, William Herbert Lee, 1881–1953, vol. V

Ewart, Sir William Quartus, 2nd Bt, 1844–1919, vol. II

Ewart-Biggs, Christopher Thomas Ewart, 1921–1976, vol. VII

Ewart James, William Henry, 1910–1988, vol. VIII

Ewbank, Sir Robert Benson, 1883–1967, vol. VI

Ewbank, Maj.-Gen. Sir Robert Withers, 1907–1981, vol. VIII

Ewbank, Brig.-Gen. William, 1865–1930, vol. III

Ewen, Sir David Alexander, 1884–1957, vol. V

Ewen, Hon. Guy Seymour, 1871–1936, vol. III

Ewer, Col George Guy, 1883–1965, vol. VI

Ewert, Alfred, 1891–1969, vol. VI

Ewing, Sir Alexander William Gordon, 1896–1980, vol. VII

Ewing, Sir Alfred; *see* Ewing, Sir J. A.

Ewing, Alfred Cyril, 1899–1973, vol. VII

Ewing, Sir Archibald Ernest O.; *see* Orr-Ewing.

Ewing, Charles Lindsay O.; *see* Orr-Ewing.

Ewing, Sir Ian Leslie O.; *see* Orr Ewing.

Ewing, James, 1884–1975, vol. VII

Ewing, Major James Alexander O.; *see* Orr-Ewing.

Ewing, Sir (James) Alfred, 1855–1935, vol. III

Ewing, Rev. James Carruthers Rhea, 1854–1925, vol. II

Ewing, Rev. John William, 1864–1951, vol. V

Ewing, Brig.-Gen. Sir Norman Archibald O.; *see* Orr Ewing.

Ewing, Hon. Norman Kirkwood, 1870–1928, vol. II

Ewing, Peter Dewar, *died* 1932, vol. III

Ewing, Rev. Robert, 1847–1908, vol. I

Ewing, Robert, 1871–1957, vol. V

Ewing, Hon. Sir Thomas Thomson, 1856–1920, vol. II

Ewing, Air Vice-Marshal Vyvyan Stewart, 1898–1981, vol. VIII

Ewing, Rev. William, 1857–1932, vol. III

Ewing, Sir William O.; *see* Orr-Ewing.

Ewins, Arthur James, 1882–1957, vol. V

Exeter, 4th Marquess of, 1849–1898, vol. I

Exeter, 5th Marquess of, 1876–1956, vol. V

Exeter, 6th Marquess of, 1905–1981, vol. VIII

Exeter, 7th Marquess of, 1909–1988, vol. VIII

Exham, Lt-Col Harold, 1884–1950, vol. IV

Exham, Maj.-Gen. Kenneth Godfrey, 1903–1974, vol. VII

Exham, Col Richard, 1848–1915, vol. I

Exham, Maj.-Gen. Robert Kenah, 1907–1985, vol. VIII

Exham, Col Simeon Hardy,. 1850–1926, vol. II

Exley, J. R. Granville, 1878–1967, vol. VI

Exmouth, 4th Viscount, 1861–1899, vol. I

Exmouth, 5th Viscount, 1890–1922, vol. II

Exmouth, 6th Viscount, 1828–1923, vol. II

Exmouth, 7th Viscount, 1863–1945, vol. IV

Exmouth, 8th Viscount, 1868–1951, vol. V

Exmouth, 9th Viscount, 1908–1970, vol. VI

Exon, Charles, 1862–1962, vol. VI

Exton-Smith, Arthur Norman, 1920–1990, vol. VIII

Eyles, Sir Alfred, 1856–1945, vol. IV

Eyles, Sir George Lancelot, 1849–1919, vol. II

Eyles, Leonora; *see* Eyles, M. L.

Eyles, (Margaret) Leonora, 1889–1960, vol. V

Eyre, Rev. Alfred Collet, 1851–1929, vol. III

Eyre, Most Rev. Charles, 1817–1902, vol. I

Eyre, Ven. Christopher Benson, 1849–1928, vol. II

Eyre, Col. Edmund Henry, 1838–1919, vol. II

Eyre, Edward John, 1815–1901, vol. I

Eyre, Rev. Edward Vincent, 1851–1925, vol. II

Eyre, Col Henry, 1834–1904, vol. I

Eyre, Col Henry Robert, 1842–1904, vol. I

Eyre, John, *died* 1927, vol. II

Eyre, Ven. John Rashdall, *died* 1912, vol. I

Eyre, John William Henry, 1869–1944, vol. IV

Eyre, Sir Oliver Eyre C.; *see* Crosthwaite-Eyre.

Eyre-Brook, Rev. Canon Alfred; *see* Brook.

Eyre-Matcham, Col William Eyre, 1865–1938, vol. III

Eyre-Todd, George, 1862–1937, vol. III

Eyres, Adm. Cresswell John, 1862–1949, vol. IV

Eyres, Sir Harry Charles Augustus, 1856–1944, vol. IV

Eyres, Harry Maurice, 1898–1962, vol. VI

Eyston, Charles Turbervile, 1868–1938, vol. III

Eyston, Captain George Edward Thomas, 1897–1979, vol. VII

Eyston, John Joseph, 1867–1916, vol. II

Eyston, Thomas More, 1902–1940, vol. III

Eyton, Alan John F. W.; *see* Fairbairn-Wynne-Eyton.

Eyton, Lt-Col Charles Reginald M.; *see* Morris-Eyton.

Eyton, Mrs Frances W.; *see* Wynne-Eyton, Mrs. S. F.

Eyton, Frank, 1894–1962, vol. VI

Eyton, Lt-Col Robert Charles Gilfrid M.; *see* Morris-Eyton.

Eyton, Mrs Selena Frances W.; *see* Wynne-Eyton.

Ezard, Bernard John Bycroft, 1900–1976, vol. VII

Ezard, Clarence Norbury, 1896–1986, vol. VIII

Ezechiel, Sir Percy Hubert, 1875–1950, vol. IV

Ezra, Sir Alwyn, 1900–1974, vol. VII

Ezra, Sir David, 1871–1947, vol. IV

F

Faber, 1st Baron, 1847–1920, vol. II

Faber, Sir Geoffrey Cust, 1889–1961, vol. VI

Faber, George Henry, 1839–1910, vol. I

Faber, Knud, 1862–1956, vol. V

Faber, Oscar, 1886–1956, vol. V

Faber, Lt-Col Walter Vavasour, 1857–1928, vol. II

Fabre, Hon. Hector, 1834–1910, vol. I

Fabre, Jean Henri, 1823–1915, vol. I

Fachiri, Adila Adrienne Adalbertina Marina, *died* 1962, vol. VI

Fadden, Rt Hon. Sir Arthur William, 1895–1973, vol. VII

Faed, John, 1819–1902, vol. I
Faed, Thomas, 1826–1900, vol. I
Fagan, Lt-Col Bernard Joseph, 1874–1939, vol. III
Fagan, Betty Maud Christian, *died* 1932, vol. III
Fagan, Brian Walter, 1893–1971, vol. VII
Fagan, Charles Edward, 1855–1921, vol. II
Fagan, Lt-Col Christopher George Forbes, 1856–1943, vol. IV
Fagan, Maj.-Gen. Sir Edward Arthur, 1871–1955, vol. V
Fagan, Hon. Henry Allan, 1889–1963, vol. VI
Fagan, James Bernard, 1873–1933, vol. III
Fagan, Maj.-Gen. James Lawtie, 1843–1919, vol. II
Fagan, Sir John, 1843–1930, vol. III
Fagan, Hon. Mark, 1873–1947, vol. IV
Fagan, Sir Patrick James, 1865–1942, vol. IV
Fagan, William Bateman, *died* 1948, vol. IV
Fagg, Bernard Evelyn Buller, 1915–1987, vol. VIII
Fage, Arthur, 1890–1977, vol. VII
Fagge, Charles Herbert, 1873–1939, vol. III
Fagge, Sir John Charles, 9th Bt, 1866–1930, vol. III
Fagge, Sir John Harry Lee, 10th Bt, 1868–1940, vol. III
Fagge, Sir John William Charles, 8th Bt, 1830–1909, vol. I
Faguet, Emile, 1847–1916, vol. II
Fahey, Edward Henry, *died* 1907, vol. I
Fahey, Rt Rev. Mgr Jerome, 1843–1920, vol. II
Fahie, Sen. Comdr Pauline Mary de Peauly, *died* 1947, vol. IV
Fahy, Francis Patrick, 1880–1953, vol. V
Faichnie, Col Douglas Charles, *died* 1938, vol. III
Fair, Hon. Sir Arthur, 1885–1970, vol. VI (AII)
Fair, Lt-Col Frederick Kendall, 1868–1953, vol. V
Fair, Lt-Col James George, 1864–1946, vol. IV
Fairbairn, Sir Andrew, 1828–1901, vol. I
Fairbairn, Andrew Martin, 1838–1912, vol. I
Fairbairn, Sir Arthur Henderson, 3rd Bt, 1852–1915, vol. I
Fairbairn, Vice-Adm. Bernard William Murray, 1880–1960, vol. V
Fairbairn, Douglas Chisholm, 1904–1987, vol. VIII
Fairbairn, Sir George, 1855–1943, vol. IV
Fairbairn, James, *died* 1950, vol. IV
Fairbairn, Hon. James Valentine, 1897–1940, vol. III
Fairbairn, John Shields, 1868–1944, vol. IV
Fairbairn, Richard Robert, 1867–1941, vol. IV
Fairbairn, Sir Robert Duncan, 1910–1988, vol. VIII
Fairbairn, Stephen, (Steve), 1862–1938, vol. III
Fairbairn, Thomas Charles, 1874–1978, vol. VII
Fairbairn, Sir Thomas Gordon, 4th Bt, 1854–1931, vol. III
Fairbairn, Sir William Albert, 5th Bt, 1902–1972, vol. VII
Fairbairn, William Ronald Dodds, 1889–1964, vol. VI
Fairbairn-Wynne-Eyton, Alan John, *died* 1960, vol. V
Fairbank, Alfred John, 1895–1982, vol. VIII
Fairbank, Sir (Harold Arthur) Thomas, 1876–1961, vol. VI
Fairbank, Sir Thomas; *see* Fairbank, Sir H. A. T.
Fairbank, Sir William, 1850–1929, vol. III
Fairbanks, Maj.-Gen. Cecil Benfield, 1903–1982, vol. VIII

Fairbanks, Charles Warren, 1852–1918, vol. II
Fairbanks, Douglas, 1883–1939, vol. III
Fairbrother, Ven. Rupert, *died* 1947, vol. IV
Fairbrother, William Henry, 1859–1927, vol. II
Fairbrother, Col William Tomes, 1856–1924, vol. II
Fairburn, Charles Edward, 1887–1945, vol. IV
Fairburn, Harold, 1884–1973, vol. VII
Fairchild, Rev. John, *died* 1942, vol. IV
Fairclough, Col Brereton, 1870–1945, vol. IV
Fairclough, Henry Rushton, 1862–1938, vol. III
Faire, Sir Arthur William, 1854–1933, vol. III
Faire, Sir Samuel, 1849–1931, vol. III
Fairey, Sir (Charles) Richard, 1887–1956, vol. V
Fairey, Sir Richard; *see* Fairey, Sir C. R.
Fairfax, 11th Lord, 1830–1900, vol. I
Fairfax of Cameron, 12th Lord, 1870–1939, vol. III
Fairfax of Cameron, 13th Lord, 1923–1964, vol. VI
Fairfax, Col Bryan Charles, 1873–1950, vol. IV
Fairfax, Hon. Charles Edmund, 1876–1939, vol. III (A), vol. IV
Fairfax, Guy Thomas, 1870–1934, vol. III
Fairfax, James Griffyth, 1886–1976, vol. VII
Fairfax, Sir James Oswald, 1863–1928, vol. II
Fairfax, Sir James Reading, 1834–1919, vol. II
Fairfax, Sir Warwick Oswald, 1901–1987, vol. VIII
Fairfax, Comdr William George Astell R.; *see* Ramsay-Fairfax
Fairfax, Sir William George Herbert Taylor Ramsay-, 2nd Bt, 1831–1902, vol. I
Fairfax-Cholmeley, Francis William Alfred, 1904–1983, vol. VIII
Fairfax-Lucy, Major Sir Brian Fulke Cameron-Ramsay-, 5th Bt, 1898–1974, vol. VII
Fairfax-Lucy, Captain Sir (Henry) Montgomerie (Ramsay), 4th Bt, 1896–1965, vol. VI
Fairfax-Lucy, Sir Henry William Cameron-Ramsay-, 3rd Bt, 1870–1944, vol. IV
Fairfax-Lucy, Captain Sir Montgomerie; *see* Fairfax-Lucy, Captain Sir H. M. R.
Fairfield, 1st Baron, 1863–1945, vol. IV
Fairfield, (Josephine) Letitia Denny, 1885–1978, vol. VII
Fairfield, Letitia; *see* Fairfield, J. L. D.
Fairfield, Sir Ronald McLeod, 1911–1978, vol. VII
Fairgrieve, James, 1870–1953, vol. V
Fairhaven, 1st Baron, 1896–1966, vol. VI
Fairhaven, 2nd Baron, 1900–1973, vol. VII
Fairholme, Edward George, *died* 1956, vol. V
Fairholme, George Frederick, 1858–1940, vol. III
Fairholme, Brig.-Gen. William Ernest, 1860–1920, vol. II
Fairhurst, Frank, 1892–1953, vol. V
Fairhurst, James Ashton, 1867–1944, vol. IV
Fairhurst, William Albert, 1903–1982, vol. VIII
Fairless, Benjamin F., 1890–1962, vol. VI
Fairless, Margaret, *died* 1968, vol. VI
Fairley, Alan Brand, *died* 1987, vol. VIII
Fairley, Sir Andrew Walker, *died* 1965, vol. VI
Fairley, Barker, 1887–1986, vol. VIII
Fairley, Sir Neil Hamilton, 1891–1966, vol. VI
Fairlie, James Ogilvy Reginald, 1848–1916, vol. II
Fairlie, Margaret, *died* 1963, vol. VI
Fairlie, Reginald Francis Joseph, 1883–1952, vol. V

Fairlie-Cuninghame, Sir Alfred Edward, 12th Bt, 1852–1901, vol. I

Fairlie-Cuninghame, Sir Charles Arthur, 11th Bt, 1846–1897, vol. I

Fairlie-Cuninghame, Sir Hussey Burgh; *see* Cuninghame.

Fairlie-Cuninghame, Sir William Alan, 15th Bt, 1893–1981, vol. VIII

Fairlie-Cuninghame, Sir William Edward; *see* Cuninghame.

Fairman, Herbert Walter, 1907–1982, vol. VIII

Fairn, Duncan; *see* Fairn, R. D.

Fairn, (Richard) Duncan, 1906–1986, vol. VIII

Fairtlough, Major Edward Charles D'Heillemer, 1869–1925, vol. II

Fairtlough, Maj.-Gen. Eric Victor Howard, 1887–1944, vol. IV

Fairtlough, Col Frederick Howard, 1860–1915, vol. I

Fairway, Sidney; *see* Daukes, S. H.

Fairweather, Sir Charles Edward Stuart, 1889–1963, vol. VI

Fairweather, Lt-Col James McIntyre, 1876–1917, vol. II

Fairweather, Sir Wallace, 1853–1939, vol. III

Faisal, King; *see* Saudi Arabia, HM the King of.

Faisandier, Rt Rev. Augustin, 1853–1935, vol. III

Faithfull, Lilian Mary, 1865–1952, vol. V

Faiyaz Ali Khan, Nawab, Sir Mumtazud-Dowlah, 1851–1922, vol. II

Falb, Rudolph, 1838–1903, vol. I

Falcon, Michael, 1888–1976, vol. VII

Falcon, Thomas Adolphus, 1872–1944, vol. IV

Falconbridge, Hon. Sir Glenholme, 1846–1920, vol. II

Falconbridge, John Delatre, 1875–1968, vol. VI

Falconer, Alexander Frederick, *died* 1987, vol. VIII

Falconer, Lt-Col Alexander Robertson, 1874–1955, vol. V

Falconer, Arthur Wellesley, *died* 1954, vol. V

Falconer, Lt-Col Sir George Arthur, 1894–1981, vol. VIII

Falconer, James, 1856–1931, vol. III

Falconer, John B., *died* 1924, vol. II

Falconer, John Downie, 1876–1947, vol. IV

Falconer, Sir John Ireland, 1879–1954, vol. V

Falconer, Lanoe; *see* Hawker, M. E.

Falconer, Murray Alexander, 1910–1977, vol. VII

Falconer, Sir Robert Alexander, 1867–1943, vol. IV

Falconer Jameson, Mrs; *see* Buckrose, J. E.

Falconio, HE Cardinal Diomed, 1842–1917, vol. II

Falk, Bernard, 1882–1960, vol. V

Falk, Oswald Toynbee, 1879–1972, vol. VII

Falke, Otto von, 1862–1943, vol. IV

Falkiner, Rt Hon. Sir Frederick Richard, 1831–1908, vol. I (A)

Falkiner, Sir Leslie Edmond Percy Riggs, 7th Bt, 1866–1917, vol. II

Falkiner, Lt-Col Sir Terence Edmond Patrick, 8th Bt, 1903–1987, vol. VIII

Falkland, 12th Viscount, 1845–1922, vol. II

Falkland, 13th Viscount, 1880–1961, vol. VI

Falkland, 14th Viscount, 1905–1984, vol. VIII

Falkner, Brig. Eric Felton, 1880–1956, vol. V

Falkner, John Meade, 1858–1932, vol. III

Falkner, Rev. Thomas Felton, 1847–1924, vol. II

Fall, Captain Ernest Matson, 1883–1955, vol. V

Falla, Norris Stephen, 1883–1945, vol. IV

Falla, Sir Robert Alexander, 1901–1979, vol. VII

Fallada, Hans; *see* Ditzen, Rudolf.

Fallas, Carl, 1885–1962, vol. VI

Falle, Lt-Col Philip Vernon Le Geyt, 1885–1936, vol. III

Falle, Very Rev. Samuel, 1854–1937, vol. III

Fallieres, Armand, 1841–1931, vol. III

Fallis, Lt-Col Rev. George Oliver, 1885–1952, vol. V

Fallon, Rt Rev. Michael Francis, 1867–1931, vol. III

Falloon, C. H., 1875–1959, vol. V

Fallows, Rt Rev. Gordon; *see* Fallows, Rt Rev. W. G.

Fallows, Rt Rev. (William) Gordon, 1913–1979, vol. VII

Falls, Major Sir Charles Fausset, 1860–1936, vol. III

Falls, Captain Cyril Bentham, 1888–1971, vol. VII

Falls, Lt-Col Horace Edward, 1874–1937, vol. III

Falmouth, 7th Viscount, 1847–1918, vol. II

Falmouth, 8th Viscount, 1887–1962, vol. VI

Falshaw, Sir Donald James, 1905–1984, vol. VIII

Falvey, Sir John Neil, 1918–1990, vol. VIII

Falwasser, Arthur Thomas, 1873–1959, vol. V

Fancourt, Col St John Fancourt Michell, 1847–1917, vol. II

Fancourt, Ven. Thomas, 1840–1919, vol. II

Fane, Lady Augusta, *died* 1950, vol. IV

Fane, Col Cecil, 1875–1960, vol. V

Fane, Cecil Francis William, 1856–1914, vol. I

Fane, Adm. Sir Charles George, 1837–1909, vol. I

Fane, Sir Edmund Douglas Veitch, 1837–1900, vol. I

Fane, Frederick William, 1857–1933, vol. III

Fane, Lenox; *see* Clifton, Baroness.

Fane, Major Hon. Mountjoy John Charles, Wedderburn, 1900–1963, vol. VI

Fane, Captain Octavius Edward, 1886–1918, vol. II

Fane, Rt Hon. Sir Spencer Cecil Brabazon P.; *see* Ponsonby-Fane.

Fane, Sydney Algernon, 1867–1929, vol. III

Fane, Maj.-Gen. Sir Vere Bonamy, 1863–1924, vol. II

Fane, Violet; *see* Currie, Mary Montgomerie, Lady.

Fane De Salis, Sir Cecil; *see* De Salis.

Fane De Salis, Rt Rev. Charles; *see* De Salis.

Fane De Salis, Rodolph; *see* De Salis.

Fane De Salis, Adm. Sir William; *see* De Salis.

Faning, Joseph Eaton, 1850–1927, vol. II

Fanner, John Lewis, 1921–1975, vol. VII

Fanning, Frederick William B.; *see* Burton-Fanning.

Fanning, Sir Roland Francis Nichol, 1829–1919, vol. I

Fanshawe, Sir Arthur Dalrymple, 1847–1936, vol. III

Fanshawe, Sir Arthur Upton, 1848–1931, vol. III

Fanshawe, Vice-Adm. Basil Hew, 1868–1929, vol. III

Fanshawe, Lt-Gen. Sir Edward Arthur, 1859–1952, vol. V

Fanshawe, Sir Edward Gennys, 1814–1906, vol. I

Fanshawe, Maj.-Gen. Sir Evelyn Dalrymple, 1895–1979, vol. VII

Fanshawe, Rev. Gerald Charles, 1870–1924, vol. II

Fanshawe, Captain Guy Dalrymple, *died* 1962, vol. VI

Fanshawe, Herbert Charles, 1852–1923, vol. II

Fanshawe, Lt-Gen. Sir Hew Dalrymple, 1860–1957, vol. V

Fanshawe, Brig. Lionel Arthur, 1874–1962, vol. VI
Fanshawe, Col Reginald Winnington, 1871–1932, vol. III
Fanshawe, Maj.-Gen. Sir Robert, 1863–1946, vol. IV
Fantham, Annie; see Porter, A.
Fantham, Harold Benjamin, died 1937, vol. III
Faraday, Wilfred Barnard, 1874–1953, vol. V
Fardell, Sir George; see Fardell, Sir T. G.
Fardell, Sir (Thomas) George, 1833–1917, vol. II
Fareed, Sir Razik, 1895–1984, vol. VIII
Farewell, Captain Michael Warren, 1868–1953, vol. V
Farey-Jones, Frederick William, 1904–1974, vol. VII
Farfan, Brig. Arthur Joseph Thomas, 1882–1953, vol. V
Fargher, John Adrian, 1901–1977, vol. VII
Fargus, Brig.-Gen. Harold, 1873–1962, vol. VI
Fargus, Lt-Col Nigel Harry Skinner, 1881–1962, vol. VI
Faridkot, Ruler of, 1915–1989, vol. VIII
Faridoonji Jamshedji, Nawab Sir Faridoon Jung, 1849–1928, vol. II
Farie, Rear-Adm. James Uchtred, died 1957, vol. V
Faringdon, 1st Baron, 1850–1934, vol. III
Faringdon, 2nd Baron, 1902–1977, vol. VII
Faris, Desmond William George, 1901–1957, vol. V
Farjeon, Benjamin Leopold, 1838–1903, vol. I
Farjeon, Eleanor, 1881–1965, vol. VI
Farjeon, Herbert, 1887–1945, vol. IV
Farjeon, Joseph Jefferson, 1883–1955, vol. V
Farleigh, John, 1900–1965, vol. VI
Farley, Albert Henry, 1887–1954, vol. V
Farley, Brig. Edward Lionel, 1889–1968, vol. VI
Farley, Sir Edwin Wood Thorp, 1864–1939, vol. III
Farley, HE Cardinal John, 1842–1918, vol. II
Farlow, Sir Sydney Nettleton K.; see King-Farlow.
Farman, Air Vice-Marshal Edward Crisp, 1897–1966, vol. VI
Farman, Henry, 1874–1958, vol. V
Farmar, Maj.-Gen. George Jasper, 1872–1958, vol. V
Farmar, Col Harold Mynors, 1878–1961, vol. VI
Farmar, Hugh William, 1908–1987, vol. VIII
Farmer, Charles Edward, 1847–1935, vol. III
Farmer, Emily, 1826–1905, vol. I
Farmer, Ernest Harold, died 1952, vol. V
Farmer, Sir Francis Mark, died 1922, vol. II
Farmer, Col George Devey, 1866–1928, vol. II
Farmer, Henry George, 1882–1965, vol. VI
Farmer, Rev. Herbert Henry, 1892–1981, vol. VIII
Farmer, John, 1835–1901, vol. I
Farmer, Sir John Bretland, 1865–1944, vol. IV
Farmer, John Cotton, 1886–1952, vol. V
Farmer, Norman William, 1901–1971, vol. VII
Farmer, Sir William, 1831–1908, vol. I
Farmer-Atkinson, Henry John; see Atkinson.
Farmiloe, Ven. William Thomas, 1863–1946, vol. IV
Farnall, Edmund Waterton, 1855–1918, vol. II
Farnall, Harry de la Rosa Burrard, 1852–1929, vol. III
Farnan, R. P., died 1962, vol. VI
Farnborough, Louisa Johanna, (Lady Farnborough), died 1901, vol. I
Farncomb, Rear-Adm. Harold Bruce, 1899–1971, vol. VII

Farndale, Joseph, 1865–1954, vol. V
Farndale, Rev. William Edward, 1881–1966, vol. VI
Farnell, Lewis Richard, 1856–1934, vol. III
Farnham, 10th Baron, 1849–1900, vol. I
Farnham, 11th Baron, 1879–1957, vol. V
Farnhill, Rear-Adm. Kenneth Haydn, 1913–1983, vol. VIII
Farnol, Jeffery; see Farnol, John J.
Farnol, (John) Jeffery, 1878–1952, vol. V
Farnsworth, John Windsor, 1912–1987, vol. VIII
Farnsworth, William Charles, 1892–1964, vol. VI
Farquhar, 1st Earl, 1844–1923, vol. II
Farquhar, Alfred, 1852–1928, vol. II
Farquhar, Sir Arthur, 1815–1908, vol. I
Farquhar, Adm. Sir Arthur Murray, 1855–1937, vol. III
Farquhar, Major Francis Douglas, 1874–1915, vol. I
Farquhar, George Neil, 1896–1948, vol. IV
Farquhar, Very Rev. George Taylor Shillito, died 1927, vol. II
Farquhar, Gilbert, 1850–1920, vol. II
Farquhar, Sir Harold Lister, 1894–1953, vol. V
Farquhar, Sir Henry Thomas, 4th Bt, 1838–1916, vol. II
Farquhar, John Nicol, 1861–1929, vol. III
Farquhar, Joseph, 1854–1929, vol. III
Farquhar, Lt-Col Sir Peter Walter, 6th Bt, 1904–1986, vol. VIII
Farquhar, Adm. Richard Bowles, 1859–1948, vol. IV
Farquhar, Sir Robert Townsend-, 6th Bt, 1841–1924, vol. II
Farquhar, Sir Walter Randolph Fitzroy, 5th Bt, 1878–1918, vol. II
Farquhar, Sir Walter Rockcliffe, 3rd Bt, 1810–1900, vol. I
Farquharson, Alexander Charles, 1864–1951, vol. V
Farquharson, Alexander Haldane, 1867–1936, vol. III
Farquharson, Bt Lt-Col Arthur Spenser Loat, died 1942, vol. IV
Farquharson, Sir Arthur Wildman, died 1947, vol. IV
Farquharson, Lt-Col David Lorraine Wilson-, 1862–1938, vol. III
Farquharson, Eric Leslie, 1905–1970, vol. VI
Farquharson, Lt-Gen. Henry Douglas, 1868–1947, vol. IV
Farquharson, James Miller, 1825–1906, vol. I
Farquharson, Col Sir John, 1839–1905, vol. I
Farquharson, John Malcolm, 1864–1936, vol. III
Farquharson, Joseph, 1846–1935, vol. III
Farquharson, Mrs Ogilvie-, died 1912, vol. I
Farquharson, Rt Hon. Robert, 1836–1918, vol. II
Farquharson-Lang, William Marshall, 1908–1988, vol. VIII
Farr, Clinton Coleridge, 1866–1943, vol. IV
Farr, Captain John, 1882–1951, vol. V
Farr, William Edward, 1872–1923, vol. II
Farran, Sir Charles Frederick, 1840–1898, vol. I
Farran, Major George Lambert, died 1925, vol. II
Farrand, Livingston, 1867–1939, vol. III
Farrant, Sir Geoffrey Upcott, 1881–1964, vol. VI
Farrant, Henry Gatchell, 1864–1946, vol. IV
Farrant, Maj.-Gen. Ralph Henry, 1909–1988, vol. VIII
Farrant, Reginald Douglas, 1877–1952, vol. V

Farrant, Sir Richard, 1835–1906, vol. I
Farrar, Rev. Adam Story, 1826–1905, vol. I
Farrar, Rev. Charles Frederick, *died* 1931, vol. III
Farrar, Hon. Ernest Henry, 1879–1952, vol. V
Farrar, Very Rev. Frederic William, 1831–1903, vol. I
Farrar, Sir George Herbert, 1st Bt, 1859–1915, vol. I
Farrar, Geraldine, 1882–1967, vol. VI
Farrar, Captain John Percy, 1857–1929, vol. III
Farrar, Rev. Piercy Austin, 1873–1947, vol. IV
Farrar, Rt Rev. Walter, 1865–1916, vol. II
Farrell, Arthur Acheson, 1898–1983, vol. VIII
Farrell, Arthur Denis, 1906–1990, vol. VIII
Farrell, Hon. Edward Matthew, 1854–1931, vol. III
Farrell, Frank James, 1877–1937, vol. III
Farrell, James A., 1863–1943, vol. IV
Farrell, James Gordon, 1935–1979, vol. VII
Farrell, James Patrick, 1865–1921, vol. II
Farrell, James T., 1904–1979, vol. VII
Farrell, Jerome; *see* Farrell, W. J.
Farrell, Joseph Jessop, 1866–1949, vol. IV
Farrell, Michael James, 1926–1975, vol. VII
Farrell, Robert Hamilton, 1895–1959, vol. V
Farrell, Sir Thomas, 1828–1900, vol. I
Farrell, (Wilfrid) Jerome, 1882–1960, vol. V
Farren, Most Rev. Neil, 1893–1980, vol. VII (AII)
Farren, Sir Richard Thomas, 1817–1909, vol. I
Farren, William, 1853–1937, vol. III
Farren, Sir William Scott, 1892–1970, vol. VI
Farrer, 1st Baron, 1819–1899, vol. I
Farrer, 2nd Baron, 1859–1940, vol. III
Farrer, 3rd Baron, 1893–1948, vol. IV
Farrer, 4th Baron, 1904–1954, vol. V
Farrer, 5th Baron, 1910–1964, vol. VI
Farrer, Augustine John Daniel, 1872–1954, vol. V
Farrer, Rev. Austin Marsden, 1904–1968, vol. VI
Farrer, Bryan, 1858–1944, vol. IV
Farrer, Claude St Aubyn, *died* 1940, vol. III
Farrer, Edmund Hugh, 1876–1955, vol. V
Farrer, Hon. Dame Frances Margaret, 1895–1977, vol. VII
Farrer, Harold Marson, 1882–1943, vol. IV
Farrer, Rev. Canon Henry Richard William, 1859–1933, vol. III
Farrer, Sir Leslie; *see* Farrer, Sir W. L.
Farrer, Hon. Noel Maitland, 1867–1929, vol. III
Farrer, Philip Tonstall, 1877–1966, vol. VI
Farrer, Reginald, 1880–1920, vol. II
Farrer, Roland John, 1873–1956, vol. V
Farrer, Ven. Walter, 1862–1934, vol. III
Farrer, Sir (Walter) Leslie, 1900–1984, vol. VIII
Farrer, Sir William James, 1822–1911, vol. I
Farrère, Claude, (Frédéric Charles Bargone), 1876–1957, vol. V
Farrington, Vice-Adm. Alexander, 1869–1933, vol. III
Farrington, Benjamin, 1891–1974, vol. VII
Farrington, Sir Henry Anthony, 6th Bt, 1871–1944, vol. IV
Farrington, Col Malcolm Charles, 1835–1925, vol. II
Farrington, Sir William Hicks, 5th Bt, 1838–1901, vol. I
Farris, Hon. John Lauchlan, 1911–1986, vol. VIII
Farris, Hon. John Wallace de Beque, 1878–1970, vol. VI

Farrow, G. Martin, 1896–1969, vol. VI(AII)
Farrow, Leslie William, 1888–1978, vol. VII
Farson, Negley, 1890–1960, vol. V
Farthing, Rt Rev. John Cragg, 1861–1947, vol. IV
Farthing, Walter John, 1889–1954, vol. V
Farwell, Sir Christopher John Wickens, 1877–1943, vol. IV
Farwell, Eveline Louisa Michell; *see* Forbes, Hon. Mrs Walter.
Farwell, Rt Hon. Sir George, 1845–1915, vol. I
Farwell, Rt Rev. Gerard Victor, 1913–1988, vol. VIII
Fasken, Maj.-Gen. Charles Grant Mansell, 1855–1928, vol. II
Fasken, Brig.-Gen. William Henry, 1863–1943, vol. IV
Fass, Sir Ernest; *see* Fass, Sir H. E.
Fass, Sir (Herbert) Ernest, *died* 1969, vol. VI
Fassbinder, Rainer Werner, 1946–1982, vol. VIII
Fasson, Brig.-Gen. Disney John Menzies, 1864–1931, vol. III
Fateh Ali Khan, Hon. Sir Hajee, Nawab Kizilbash, 1862–1923, vol. II
Fathers, Henry, 1860–1937, vol. III
Faucit, Helen, (Lady Martin), 1820–1898, vol. I
Fauconberg and Conyers, Baroness (13th in line), (Countess of Yarborough), 1863–1926, vol. II
Faudel-Phillips, Sir Benjamin Samuel, 2nd Bt, 1871–1927, vol. II
Faudel-Phillips, Sir George Faudel, 1st Bt, 1840–1922, vol. II
Faudel-Phillips, Sir Lionel Lawson Faudel, 3rd Bt, 1877–1941, vol. IV
Faught, Surg.-Maj.-Gen. John George, 1832–1910, vol. I
Faulds, Archibald Galbraith, 1860–1940, vol. III
Faulkner, Sir Alfred Edward, 1882–1963, vol. VI
Faulkner, Rt Hon. (Arthur) Brian (Deane), 1921–1977, vol. VII
Faulkner, Hon. Arthur James, 1921–1985, vol. VIII
Faulkner, Rt Hon. Brian; *see* Faulkner, Rt Hon. A. B. D.
Faulkner, Major George Aubrey, *died* 1930, vol. III
Faulkner, Hon. George Everett, 1855–1931, vol. III
Faulkner, Captain George Haines, 1893–1983, vol. VIII
Faulkner, Harry, 1892–1971, vol. VII
Faulkner, Rear-Adm. Hugh Webb, 1900–1969, vol. VI
Faulkner, Hon. James Albert, 1877–1944, vol. IV
Faulkner, John, 1871–1958, vol. V
Faulkner, Odin T., 1890–1958, vol. V
Faulkner, Sir Percy, 1907–1990, vol. VIII
Faulkner, Vincent Clements, 1888–1975, vol. VII
Faulkner, William Harrison, 1897–1962, vol. VI
Faulks, Hon. Sir Neville Major Ginner, 1908–1985, vol. VIII
Faull, Joseph Horace, 1870–1961, vol. VI
Faunce, Brig. Bonham, 1872–1961, vol. VI
Faunce, William Herbert Perry, 1859–1930, vol. III
Faunthorpe, Lt-Col John Champion, 1872–1929, vol. III
Faunthorpe, Rev. John Pincher, 1839–1924, vol. II
Faure, Edgar Jean, 1908–1988, vol. VIII
Fauré, Gabriel, 1845–1924, vol. II

Faure, Hon. Sir Pieter Hendrik, 1848–1914, vol. I

Fausset, Rev. Andrew Robert, 1821–1910, vol. I

Fausset, Hugh I'Anson, 1895–1965, vol. VI

Fausset, Rev. William Yorke, *died* 1914, vol. I

Faussett, Captain Sir Bryan Godfrey G.; *see* Godfrey-Faussett.

Faussett, Brig. Bryan Trevor G.; *see* Godfrey-Faussett.

Faussett, Brig.-Gen. Edmund Godfrey G.; *see* Godfrey-Faussett.

Faussett, Lt-Col Owen Godfrey G.; *see* Godfrey Faussett.

Fauteux, Rt Hon. Gérald; *see* Fauteux, Rt Hon. J. H. G.

Fauteux, Rt Hon. (Joseph Honoré) Gérald, 1900–1980, vol. VII(AII)

Faux, Col Edward, 1857–1937, vol. III

Favell, Richard, *died* 1918, vol. II

Faviell, Captain Douglas, 1884–1947, vol. IV

Faviell, Lt-Col William Frederick Oliver, 1882–1950, vol. IV

Faville, Air Vice-Marshal Roy, 1908–1980, vol. VII

Fawcett, Charles Bungay, 1883–1952, vol. V

Fawcett, Sir Charles Gordon Hill, 1869–1952, vol. V

Fawcett, Douglas; *see* Fawcett, E. D.

Fawcett, Edgar, 1847–1904, vol I

Fawcett, Edmund Alderson Sandford, 1868–1938, vol. III

Fawcett, Edward, 1867–1942, vol. IV

Fawcett, (Edward) Douglas, 1866–1960, vol. V

Fawcett, Edward Pinder, 1874–1954, vol. V

Fawcett, Sir Henry; *see* Fawcett, Sir J. H.

Fawcett, Henry Heath, 1863–1925, vol. II

Fawcett, John, 1866–1944, vol. IV

Fawcett, Sir (John) Henry, 1831–1898, vol. I

Fawcett, Sir Luke, 1881–1960, vol. V

Fawcett, Dame Millicent, 1847–1929, vol. III

Fawcett, Lt-Col Percy Harrison, 1867–1925, vol. II, vol. III

Fawcett, Philippa Garrett, *died* 1948, vol. IV

Fawcett, William, *died* 1941, vol. IV

Fawcett, Sir William Claude, 1868–1935, vol. III

Fawcett, Maj.-Gen. William James, 1848–1943, vol. IV

Fawcett, William Milner, 1832–1908, vol. I

Fawcus, Lt-Col Arthur, 1886–1936, vol. III

Fawcus, George Ernest, 1885–1958, vol. V

Fawcus, Lt-Gen. Sir Harold Ben, 1876–1947, vol. IV

Fawcus, Louis Reginald, 1887–1971, vol. VII

Fawdry, Reginald Charles, 1873–1965, vol. VI

Fawdry, Air Cdre Thomas, 1891–1968, vol. VI

Fawke, Sir Ernest John, *died* 1928, vol. II

Fawkes, Archibald Walter, 1855–1941, vol. IV

Fawkes, Frederick Hawksworth, 1870–1936, vol. III

Fawkes, Rear-Adm. George Barney Hamley, 1903–1967, vol. VI

Fawkes, Rowland Beattie, 1894–1965, vol. VI

Fawkes, Rupert Edward Francis, 1879–1967, vol. VI

Fawkes, Adm. Sir Wilmot Hawksworth, 1846–1926, vol. II

Fawsitt, Charles Edward, 1878–1960, vol. V(A)

Fay, Charles Ernest, 1846–1931, vol. III

Fay, Charles Ryle, 1884–1961, vol. VI

Fay, Rt Rev. Cyril Damian, 1903–1975, vol. VII

Fay, Sir Sam, 1856–1953, vol. V

Fay, Sidney Bradshaw, 1876–1967, vol. VI

Fayle, Lindley Robert Edmundson, 1903–1972, vol. VII

Fayolle, Emile, 1852–1928, vol. II

Fayrer, Sir Joseph, 1st Bt, 1824–1907, vol. I

Fayrer, Sir Joseph, 2nd Bt, 1859–1937, vol. III

Fayrer, Sir Joseph Herbert Spens, 3rd Bt, 1899–1976, vol. VII

Fazan, Sidney Herbert, 1888–1979, vol. VII

Fea, Allan, 1860–1956, vol. V

Fearfield, Joseph, 1883–1941, vol. IV

Fearnley, John Thorn, 1921–1986, vol. VIII

Fearnley, Thomas, 1880–1961, vol. VI

Fearnley Scarr, J. G.; *see* Scarr.

Fearnley-Whittingstall, Francis Herbert, 1894–1945, vol. IV

Fearnley-Whittingstall, William Arthur, 1903–1959, vol. V

Fearnsides, Edwin Greaves, 1883–1919, vol. II

Fearnsides, William George, 1879–1968, vol. VI

Fearon, Daniel Robert, 1835–1919, vol. II

Fearon, John Francis, 1867–1940, vol. III

Fearon, Percy Hutton (Poy), 1874–1948, vol. IV

Fearon, Rev. William Andrewes, 1841–1924, vol. II

Fearon, William Robert, 1892–1959, vol. V

Feather, Baron (Life Peer); Victor Grayson Hardie Feather, 1908–1976, vol. VII

Feather, Norman, 1904–1978, vol. VII

Featherstone, Eric Kellett, 1896–1965, vol. VI

Featherstone, Henry Walter, 1894–1967, vol. VI

Featherstone, Col Patrick Davies; *see* Featherstone, Col W. P. D.

Featherstone, Col (William) Patrick Davies, 1919–1983, vol. VIII

Feavearyear, Sir Albert Edgar, 1896–1953, vol. V

Fechteler, Adm. William Morrow, 1896–1967, vol. VI

Fedden, Sir (Alfred Hubert) Roy, 1885–1973, vol. VII

Fedden, (Henry) Robin Romilly, 1908–1977, vol. VII

Fedden, Katharine Waldo Douglas, *died* 1939, vol. III

Fedden, Robin Romilly; *see* Fedden, H. R. R.

Fedden, Romilly, *died* 1939, vol. III

Fedden, Sir Roy; *see* Fedden, Sir A. H. R.

Fedden, Walter Fedde, *died* 1952, vol. V

Feetham, Brig.-Gen. Edward, 1863–1918, vol. II

Feetham, Rt Rev. John Oliver, 1873–1947, vol. IV

Feetham, Hon. Richard, 1874–1965, vol. VI

Fegen, Rear-Adm. Frederick Fogarty, 1855–1911, vol. I

Fegen, Col Magrath Fogarty, 1858–1935, vol. III

Fehily, Rt Rev. Mgr Canon Thomas Francis, 1917–1987, vol. VIII

Fehr, Frank Emil, 1874–1948, vol. IV

Fehr, Henry Charles, *died* 1940, vol. III

Fehrenbacher, Rt Rev. Bruno, 1895–1965, vol. VI

Feilden, Cecil William Montague, 1863–1902, vol. I

Feilden, Major Granville Cholmondeley, 1863–1939, vol. III

Feilden, Major Guy; *see* Fielden, Major P. H. G.

Feilden, Maj.-Gen. Sir Henry Broome, 1834–1926, vol. II

Feilden, Col Henry Wemyss, 1838–1921, vol. II

Feilden, Major (Percy Henry) Guy, 1870–1944, vol. IV

Feilden, Maj.-Gen. Sir Randle Guy, 1904–1981, vol. VIII

Feilden, Lt-Col Randle Montague, 1871–1965, vol. VI

Feilden, Theodore John Valentine, 1863–1955, vol. V

Feilden, Col Wemyss Gawne Cunningham, 1870–1943, vol. IV

Feilden, Sir William Henry, 4th Bt, 1866–1946, vol. IV

Feilden, Rev. William Leyland, *died* 1907, vol. I

Feilden, Sir William Leyland, 3rd Bt, 1835–1912, vol. I

Feilden, Sir William Morton Buller, 5th Bt, 1893–1976, vol. VII

Feilding, Viscount; Lt-Col Rudolph Edmund Aloysius Feilding, 1885–1937, vol. III

Feilding, Maj.-Gen. Sir Geoffrey Percy Thynne, 1866–1932, vol. III

Feilding, Hon. Sir Percy Robert Basil, 1827–1904, vol. I

Feilding, Lt-Col Rowland Charles, *died* 1945, vol. IV

Feiling, Anthony, 1885–1975, vol. VII

Feiling, Sir Keith Grahame, 1884–1977, vol. VII

Feisal, King, *died* 1933, vol. III

Felberman, Louis, 1861–1927, vol. II

Feldman, Rev. Dayan Asher, 1873–1950, vol. IV

Feldman, William Moses, *died* 1939, vol. III

Felgate, Air Vice-Marshal Frank Westerman, 1901–1974, vol. VII

Felix, Arthur, 1887–1956, vol. V

Felkin, Mrs A. L.; *see* Fowler, Hon. Ellen Thorneycroft.

Felkin, Alfred Laurence, 1856–1942, vol. IV

Fell, Sir Arthur, 1850–1934, vol. III

Fell, Aubrey Llewellyn Coventry, 1869–1948, vol. IV

Fell, Sir Bryan Hugh, 1869–1955, vol. V

Fell, Charles Percival, 1894–1989, vol. VIII

Fell, Eleanor, *died* 1946, vol. IV

Fell, Sir Godfrey Butler Hunter, 1872–1955, vol. V

Fell, Herbert Granville, 1872–1951, vol. V

Fell, Dame Honor Bridget, 1900–1986, vol. VIII

Fell, John Robert Massey, 1890–1969, vol. VI

Fell, Lt-Gen. Sir Matthew Henry Gregson, 1872–1959, vol. V

Fell, Vice-Adm. Sir Michael Frampton, 1918–1976, vol. VII

Fell, Brig.-Gen. Robert Black, 1859–1934, vol. III

Fell, Sheila Mary, 1931–1979, vol. VII

Fell, Thomas Edward, 1873–1926, vol. II

Fell, Captain William Richmond, 1897–1981, vol. VIII

Fell-Smith, Charlotte, *died* 1937, vol. III

Felling, Sir Christian Ludolph Neethling, 1880–1928, vol. II

Fellowes, Hon. Coulson Churchill, 1883–1915, vol. I

Fellowes, Daisy, (Hon. Mrs Reginald Fellowes), *died* 1962, vol. VI

Fellowes, Rev. Edmund Horace, 1870–1951, vol. V

Fellowes, Sir Edward Abdy, 1895–1970, vol. VI

Fellowes, Maj.-Gen. Halford David, 1906–1985, vol. VIII

Fellowes, Vice-Adm. Sir John, 1843–1912, vol. I

Fellowes, Air Cdre Peregrine Forbes Morant, 1883–1955, vol. V

Fellowes, Brig. Reginald William Lyon, 1895–1982, vol. VIII

Fellowes, Rear-Adm. Sir Thomas Hounsom Butler, 1827–1923, vol. II

Fellowes, Sir William Albemarle, 1899–1986, vol. VIII

Fellows, Brig.-Gen. Bertram Charles, 1877–1956, vol. V

Fellows, Col Bruce; *see* Fellows, Col R. B.

Fellows, Col (Robert) Bruce, 1830–1922, vol. II

Fells, John Manger, 1858–1925, vol. II

Fels, Willi, 1858–1946, vol. IV(A)

Feltham, John Alric Percy, 1862–1929, vol. III

Feltin, HE Cardinal Maurice, 1883–1975, vol. VII

Felton, Sir John Robinson, 1880–1962, vol. VI

Felton, Mrs Monica, 1906–1970, vol. VI

Felton, Samuel Morse, 1853–1930, vol. III

Fenby, Charles, 1905–1974, vol. VII

Fenby, Thomas Davis, 1875–1956, vol. V

Fendall, Brig.-Gen. Charles Pears, 1860–1933, vol. III

Fendall, Percy Paul Wentworth, 1879–1910, vol. I

Fender, Percy George Herbert, 1892–1985, vol. VIII

Fendick, Rev. George Harold, 1883–1962, vol. VI

Fenn, Col Ernest Harrold, 1850–1916, vol. II

Fenn, Frederick, 1868–1924, vol. II

Fenn, George Manville, 1831–1909, vol. I

Fenn, Harold Robert Backwell, 1894–1974, vol. VII

Fenn, John Cyril Douglas, 1879–1927, vol. II

Fenn, William Wallace, 1862–1932, vol. III

Fennelly, Sir Daniel; *see* Fennelly, Sir R. D.

Fennelly, Sir (Reginald) Daniel, 1890–1969, vol. VI

Fennelly, Most Rev. Thomas, 1845–1927, vol. II

Fenner, Tan Sri Sir Claude Harry, 1916–1978, vol. VII

Fenning, Captain Edward George, 1878–1932, vol. III

Fenning, Frederick William, 1919–1988, vol. VIII

Fenton, Brig.-Gen. Alexander Bulstrode, 1856–1942, vol. IV

Fenton, Charles; *see* Fenton, T. C.

Fenton, Ferrar, 1832–1911, vol. I

Fenton, Henry John Horstman, 1854–1929, vol. III

Fenton, James, 1884–1962, vol. VI

Fenton, Hon. James Edward, 1864–1950, vol. IV

Fenton, James Stevenson, 1891–1975, vol. VII

Fenton, Sir John Charles, 1880–1951, vol. V

Fenton, Sir Michael William, 1862–1941, vol. IV

Fenton, Sir Myles, 1830–1918, vol. II

Fenton, Rt Rev. Patrick, 1837–1918, vol. II

Fenton, Richard, 1899–1959, vol. V

Fenton, Roy Pentelow, 1918–1979, vol. VII

Fenton, (Thomas) Charles, *died* 1927, vol. II

Fenton, West Fenton de W.; *see* de Wend-Fenton.

Fenton, Wilfrid David Drysdale, 1908–1985, vol. VIII

Fenton, Col Sir William Charles, 1891–1976, vol. VII

Fenton, William Hugh, 1854–1928, vol. II

Fenton, William James, 1868–1957, vol. V

Fenwick, Bedford, 1855–1939, vol. III

Fenwick, Mrs Bedford; *see* Fenwick, Ethel Gordon.

Fenwick, Rt Hon. Charles, 1850–1918, vol. II

Fenwick, Maj.-Gen. Charles Philip, 1891–1954, vol. V

Fenwick, Christian Bedford, 1888–1969, vol. VI

Fenwick, E. Hurry, 1856–1944, vol. IV

Fenwick, Edward Nicholas Fenwick-, 1847–1908, vol. I

Fenwick, Major Ernest Guy, 1867–1937, vol. III

Fenwick, Ethel Gordon, (Mrs Bedford Fenwick), 1857–1947, vol. IV

Fenwick, Sir George, 1847–1929, vol. III

Fenwick, Hon. Sir (George) Townsend, 1846–1927, vol. II

Fenwick, Lt-Col Gerard, 1868–1935, vol. III

Fenwick, Col Henry Thomas, 1863–1939, vol. III

Fenwick, Col Percival Clennell, 1870–1958, vol. V

Fenwick, Robert George, 1913–1987, vol. VIII

Fenwick, Thomas FitzRoy Phillipps, 1856–1938, vol. III

Fenwick, Hon. Sir Townsend; see Fenwick, Hon. Sir G. T.

Fenwick-Fenwick, Edward Nicholas; see Fenwick.

Fenwick-Palmer, Lt-Col Roderick George, 1892–1968, vol. VI

Fenwicke, William Soltau, died 1944, vol. IV

Ferard, Arthur George, 1858–1943, vol. IV

Ferard, Henry Cecil, 1864–1936, vol. III

Ferard, John Edward, 1869–1944, vol. IV

Ferard, Reginald Herbert, 1866–1934, vol. III

Ferber, Edna, 1885–1968, vol. VI

Ferens, Rt Hon. Thomas Robinson, 1847–1930, vol. III

Ferens, Rev. Canon William, 1859–1935, vol. III

Fergus, Andrew Freeland, 1858–1932, vol. III

Fergus, Most Rev. James, 1895–1989, vol. VIII

Fergus, John F., 1865–1943, vol. IV

Fergus, Hon. Thomas, 1851–1914, vol. I

Ferguson, Alexander Stewart, 1883–1958, vol. V

Ferguson, Brig.-Gen. Algernon Francis Holford, 1867–1943, vol. IV

Ferguson, Allan, 1880–1951, vol. V

Ferguson, Lt-Col Sir Arthur George, 1862–1935, vol. III

Ferguson, Maj.-Gen. Augustus Klingner, 1898–1965, vol. VI

Ferguson, Charles Edward Hamilton, died 1958, vol. V

Ferguson, Hon. Sir David Gilbert, 1861–1941, vol. IV

Ferguson, Sir David Gordon, 1895–1969, vol. VI

Ferguson, Hon. Donald, 1839–1909, vol. I

Ferguson, Sir Edward Alexander James J.; see Johnson-Ferguson.

Ferguson, Sir Edward Brown, 1892–1967, vol. VI

Ferguson, Erne Cecil, 1911–1968, vol. VI

Ferguson, Fergus James, 1878–1948, vol. IV

Ferguson, Frederic Sutherland, 1878–1967, vol. VI

Ferguson, Col George Andrew, 1872–1933, vol. III

Ferguson, Lt-Col George Arthur, 1835–1924, vol. II

Ferguson, Hon. (George) Howard, 1870–1946, vol. IV

Ferguson, Sir Gordon; see Ferguson, Sir D. G.

Ferguson, Harry George, 1884–1960, vol. V

Ferguson, Sir (Henry) Lindo, 1858–1948, vol. IV

Ferguson, Herbert, 1874–1953, vol. V

Ferguson, Hon. Howard; see Ferguson, Hon. G. H.

Ferguson, Sir (Jabez) Edward J.; see Johnson-Ferguson.

Ferguson of Kinmundy, James, 1857–1917, vol. II

Ferguson, James, 1879–1949, vol. IV

Ferguson, James Haig, 1862–1934, vol. III

Ferguson, Very Rev. John, died 1902, vol. I

Ferguson, John, 1842–1913, vol. I

Ferguson, John, 1854–1916, vol. II

Ferguson, Sir John, 1870–1932, vol. III

Ferguson, John, 1854–1939, vol. III

Ferguson, John, 1921–1989, vol. VIII

Ferguson, Hon. Sir John Alexander, 1882–1969, vol. VI

Ferguson, John Calvin, 1866–1945, vol. IV

Ferguson, Col John David, 1866–1961, vol. VI

Ferguson, Major Sir John Frederick, 1891–1975, vol. VII

Ferguson, John Macrae, 1849–1919, vol. II

Ferguson, Joshua, 1870–1951, vol. V

Ferguson, Sir Lindo; see Ferguson, Sir H. L.

Ferguson, Col Nicholas Charles, 1862–1930, vol. III

Ferguson, Rachel, 1893–1957, vol. V

Ferguson, Richard Saul, 1837–1900, vol. I

Ferguson, Samuel Fergus, 1897–1971, vol. VII

Ferguson, Engr Rear-Adm. Samuel Pringle, 1871–1938, vol. III

Ferguson, Thomas, 1900–1977, vol. VII

Ferguson, William Alexander, 1902–1973, vol. VII

Ferguson, William Bates, 1853–1937, vol. III

Ferguson, Rev. Canon William Harold, 1874–1950, vol. IV

Ferguson, William Nassau, 1869–1928, vol. II, vol. III

Ferguson-Davie, Major Arthur Francis, see Davie.

Ferguson Davie, Rev. Sir Arthur Patrick, 5th Bt, 1909–1988, vol. VIII

Ferguson-Davie, Rt Rev. Charles James, 1872–1963, vol. VI

Ferguson-Davie, Sir Henry Augustus; see Davie.

Ferguson-Davie, Sir John Davie; see Davie.

Ferguson-Davie, Sir William Augustus; see Davie.

Ferguson-Davie, Major Sir William John, 4th Bt, 1863–1947, vol. IV

Ferguson Jones, Hugh; see Jones.

Fergusson, Col Arthur Charles, 1871–1958, vol. V

Fergusson, Bernard Edward; see Baron Ballantrae.

Fergusson, Gen. Sir Charles, 7th Bt (cr 1703), 1865–1951, vol. V

Fergusson, Sir Donald; see Fergusson, Sir J. D. B.

Fergusson, Sir Ewen MacGregor Field, 1897–1974, vol. VII

Fergusson, Lt-Col Herbert Chaworth, 1865–1939, vol. III

Fergusson, Ian Victor Lyon, 1901–1990, vol. VIII

Fergusson, Rt Hon. Sir James, 6th Bt (cr 1703), 1832–1907, vol. I

Fergusson of Kilkerran, Sir James, 8th Bt (cr 1703), 1904–1973, vol. VII

Fergusson, Adm. Sir James Andrew, 1871–1942, vol. IV

Fergusson, Surg. Rear-Adm. James Herbert, 1874–1948, vol. IV

Fergusson, Sir James Ranken, 2nd Bt (cr 1866), 1835–1924, vol. II

Fergusson, John, 1835–1912, vol. I

Fergusson, Sir (John) Donald (Balfour), 1891–1963, vol. VI

Fergusson, John Douglas, 1909–1979, vol. VII

Fergusson, Rev. John Moore, 1863–1944, vol. IV

Fergusson, Sir Louis Forbes, 1878–1962, vol. VI

Fergusson, Sir Thomas Colyer C., 3rd Bt (*cr* 1866); *see* Colyer-Fergusson.

Fergusson, Lt-Col Vivian Moffatt, 1878–1926, vol. II

Fergusson, Col William James Smyth, 1864–1934, vol. III

Fergusson Hannay, Doris, (Lady Fergusson Hannay); *see* Leslie, D.

Fermi, Enrico, 1901–1954, vol. V

Fermor, Sir Lewis Leigh, 1880–1954, vol. V

Fermor, Una Mary E.; *see* Ellis-Fermor.

Fermor-Hesketh, Sir Thomas George; *see* Hesketh.

Fermoy, 2nd Baron, 1850–1920, vol. II

Fermoy, 3rd Baron, 1852–1920, vol. II

Fermoy, 4th Baron, 1885–1955, vol. V

Fermoy, 5th Baron, 1939–1984, vol. VIII

Fernald, Chester Bailey, 1869–1938, vol. III

Fernald, John Bailey, 1905–1985, vol. VIII

Fernandel, (Fernand Joseph Désiré Contandin), 1903–1971, vol. VII

Fernando, Sir Ernest Peter Arnold, 1904–1956, vol. V

Fernando, Sir Hilarion Marcus, 1864–1935, vol. III

Fernando, Hugh Norman Gregory, 1910–1976, vol. VII

Fernow, Bernhard Eduard, *born* 1851, vol. II

Fernyhough, Col Hugh Clifford, 1872–1947, vol. IV

Fernyhough, Brig. Hugh Edward, 1904–1982, vol. VIII

Ferraby, H. C., 1884–1942, vol. IV

Ferrall, John C.; *see* Carmichael-Ferrall.

Ferrand, Major James Brian Patrick, 1895–1934, vol. III

Ferranti, Sir Vincent Ziani de; *see* de Ferranti.

Ferrar, Lt-Col Henry Minchin 1863–1949, vol. IV

Ferrar, Lt-Col Michael Lloyd, 1876–1971, vol. VII

Ferrar, William Leonard, 1893–1990, vol. VIII

Ferrari, Enzo, 1898–1988, vol. VIII

Ferrari, Ermanno W.; *see* Wolf-Ferrari.

Ferraro, Rev. Preb. Francis William, 1888–1963, vol. VI

Ferraro, Vincenzo Consolato Antonino, 1907–1974, vol. VII

Ferrero, Gen. Annibale, 1839–1902, vol. I

Ferrero, Baron Augusto, vol. II

Ferrero, Guglielmo, 1871–1942, vol. IV

Ferrers, 10th Earl, 1847–1912, vol. I

Ferrers, 11th Earl, 1864–1937, vol. III

Ferrers, 12th Earl, 1894–1954, vol. V

Ferrers, Rev. Norman Macleod, 1829–1903, vol. I

Ferri, Enrico, 1856–1929, vol. III

Ferrier, Sir David, 1843–1928, vol. II

Ferrier, Sir Grant; *see* Ferrier, Sir H. G.

Ferrier, Sir (Harold) Grant, 1905–1976, vol. VII

Ferrier, Maj.-Gen. James Archibald, 1854–1934, vol. III

Ferrier, Kathleen, 1912–1953, vol. V

Ferrier, Thomas Archibald, 1877–1968, vol. VI

Ferris, Hon. Rt Rev. Mgr Francis, 1860–1931, vol. III

Ferris, Rev. Thomas Boys Barraclough, 1845–1931, vol. III

Ferris, Rev. William Bridger, *died* 1931, vol. III

Ferryman, Lt-Col Augustus Ferryman M.; *see* Mockler-Ferryman.

Ferryman, Col Eric Edward M.; *see* Mockler-Ferryman.

Fessenden, Clementina, *died* 1918, vol. II

Festetics de Tolna, Prince, 1850–1933, vol. III

Festing, Major Arthur Hoskyns-, 1870–1915, vol. I

Festing, Maj.-Gen. Edward Robert, 1839–1912, vol. I

Festing, Brig.-Gen. Francis Leycester, 1877–1948, vol. IV

Festing, Field Marshal Sir Francis Wogan, 1902–1976, vol. VII

Festing, Gabrielle, *died* 1924, vol. II

Festing, Major Harold England, 1886–1923, vol. II

Festing, Rt Rev. John Wogan, 1837–1902, vol. I

Fethers, Hon. Col Wilfrid Kent, 1885–1976, vol. VII

Fetherston, Rev. Sir George Ralph, 6th Bt, 1852–1923, vol. II

Fetherston-Dilke, Beaumont Albany, 1875–1968, vol. VI

Fetherston-Godley, Brig. Sir Francis William Crewe, 1893–1976, vol. VII

Fetherstonhaugh, Lt-Col Edward Phillips, 1879–1959, vol. V

Fetherstonhaugh, Frederick Barnard, 1864–1945, vol. IV

Fetherstonhaugh, Godfrey, 1858–1928, vol. II

Fetherstonhaugh, Captain Herbert Howard, *died* 1937, vol. III

Fetherstonhaugh, Adm. Hon. Sir Herbert M.; *see* Meade-Fetherstonhaugh.

Fetherstonhaugh, Hon. Keith Turnour-, 1848–1930, vol. III

Fetherstonhaugh, Lt-Col Timothy, 1869–1945, vol. IV

Fetherstonhaugh, Lt-Col Sir Timothy, 1899–1969, vol. VI

Fetherstonhaugh, Brig. William Albany, 1876–1947, vol. IV

Fetherstonhaugh-Whitney, Henry Ernest William, 1847–1921, vol. II

Fetterolf, Adam H., 1841–1912, vol. I

Feuchtwanger, Lion, 1884–1958, vol. V

Feversham, 1st Earl of, 1829–1915, vol. I

Feversham, 2nd Earl of, 1879–1916, vol. II

Feversham, 3rd Earl of, 1906–1963, vol. VI

Few, Bt Col Robert Jebb, 1876–1965, vol. VI

Fewtrell, Maj.-Gen. Albert Cecil, 1885–1950, vol. IV

Feynman, Richard Phillips, 1918–1988, vol. VIII

ffarington, Henry Nowell, 1868–1947, vol. IV

ffennell, Raymond William, 1871–1944, vol. IV

Ffinch, Benjamin Traill, 1840–1910, vol. I

Ffinch, Captain Matthew Benjamin Dipnall, *died* 1951, vol. V

Ffinch, Rev. Matthew Mortimer, 1838–1920, vol. II

ffolkes, Captain Sir (Edward John) Patrick (Boschetti), 6th Bt, 1899–1960, vol. V

Ffolkes, Sir Everard; *see* Ffolkes, Sir W. E. B.

Ffolkes, Rev. Sir Francis Arthur Stanley, 5th Bt, 1863–1938, vol. III

ffolkes, Michael, (Brian Davis), 1925–1988, vol. VIII

ffolkes, Captain Sir Patrick; *see* ffolkes, Captain Sir E. J. P. B.

Ffolkes, Sir (William) Everard Browne, 4th Bt, 1861–1930, vol. III

Ffolkes, Sir William Hovell Browne, 3rd Bt, 1847–1912, vol. I

fforde, Sir Arthur Frederic Brownlow, 1900–1985, vol. VIII

Fforde, Sir Cecil Robert, *died* 1951, vol. V

ffoulkes, Charles John, 1868–1947, vol. IV

ffoulkes, Captain Edmund Andrew, 1867–1949, vol. IV

Ffoulkes, William Wynne, *died* 1903, vol. I

Ffrangcon-Davies, David, 1850–1918, vol. II

ffrench, 6th Baron, 1868–1955, vol. V

ffrench, 7th Baron, 1926–1986, vol. VIII

ffrench, Rev. James Frederick Metge, *died* 1914, vol. I

ffrench, Hon. John Martin Valentine, 1872–1946, vol. IV

Ffrench, Peter, 1844–1929, vol. III

Ffrench-Blake, Lt-Col Arthur O'Brien; *see* Blake.

Ffrench-Mullen, Lt-Col John Lawrence William, 1868–1951, vol. V

Fiaschi, Col Thomas Henry, 1853–1927, vol. II

Ficklin, Maj.-Gen. Horatio Pettus Mackintosh B.; *see* Berney-Ficklin.

Fiddament, Air Vice-Marshal Arthur Leonard, 1896–1976, vol. VII

Fiddes, Edward, 1864–1942, vol. IV

Fiddes, Sir George Vandeleur, 1858–1936, vol. III

Fiddes, Sir James Raffan, 1883–1961, vol. VI

Fidge, Sir (Harold) Roy, 1904–1981, vol. VIII

Fidge, Sir Roy; *see* Fidge, Sir H. R.

Fidler, Alwyn Gwilym S.; *see* Sheppard Fidler.

Fidler, Henry, *died* 1912, vol. I

Fidler, Michael M., 1916–1989, vol. VIII

Fiedler, Hermann George, 1862–1945, vol. IV

Field, 1st Baron, 1813–1907, vol. I

Field, Allan Bertram, 1875–1962, vol. VI

Field, Adm. Sir (Arthur) Mostyn, 1855–1950, vol. IV

Field, Bradda, *died* 1957, vol. V

Field, Lt-Col Sir Donald Moyle, 1881–1956, vol. V

Field, Adm. Edward, 1828–1912, vol. I

Field, Edward, 1898–1978, vol. VII

Field, Sir Ernest Wensley Lapthorn, 1889–1974, vol. VII

Field, Frank Meade, 1863–1943, vol. IV

Field, Adm. of the Fleet Sir Frederick Laurence, 1871–1945, vol. IV

Field, Frederick William, 1884–1960, vol. V

Field, George David, 1887–1975, vol. VII

Field, Guy Cromwell, 1887–1955, vol. V

Field, Henry St John, 1883–1949, vol. IV

Field, Gen. Sir John, 1821–1899, vol. I

Field, Sir John Osbaldiston, 1913–1985, vol. VIII

Field, John William, 1899–1981, vol. VIII

Field, Major Kenneth Douglas, *born* 1880, vol. II

Field, Brig. Leonard Frank, 1898–1978, vol. VII

Field, Marshall, 1893–1956, vol. V

Field, Mary, (Mrs Agnes Mary Hankin), 1896–1968, vol. VI

Field, Michael, *died* 1914, vol. I

Field, Adm. Sir Mostyn; *see* Field, Adm. Sir A. M.

Field, Gp Captain Roger Martin, 1890–1974, vol. VII

Field, Roland Alfred Reginald, *died* 1969, vol. VI

Field, Sid, (Sidney Arthur Field), 1904–1950, vol. IV

Field, Stanley Alfred, 1913–1986, vol. VIII

Field, Rev. Thomas, 1855–1936, vol. III

Field, Walter, *died* 1902, vol. I

Field, William, 1848–1935, vol. III

Field, Hon. Winston Joseph, 1904–1969, vol. VI

Fielden, Lt-Col Edward Anthony, 1886–1972, vol. VII

Fielden, Edward Brocklehurst, *died* 1942, vol. IV

Fielden, Air Vice-Marshal Sir Edward Hedley, 1903–1976, vol. VII

Fielden, Captain Harold, 1868–1937, vol. III

Fielden, Lionel, 1896–1974, vol. VII

Fielden, Thomas, 1854–1897, vol. I

Fielden, Thomas Perceval, *died* 1974, vol. VII

Fielden, Victor George Leopold, 1867–1946, vol. IV

Fieldgate, Alan Frederic Edmond, *born* 1889, vol. VIII

Fieldhouse, Arnold; *see* Fieldhouse, R. A.

Fieldhouse, (Richard) Arnold, 1916–1990, vol. VIII

Fieldhouse, William, 1932–1988, vol. VIII

Fieldhouse, William John, 1858–1928, vol. II

Fielding, Sir Charles William, 1863–1941, vol. IV

Fielding, Frank Stanley, 1918–1990, vol. VIII

Fielding, Gabriel, (Alan Gabriel Barnsley), 1916–1986, vol. VIII

Fielding, Ven. Harold Ormandy, 1912–1987, vol. VIII

Fielding, Marjorie, 1892–1956, vol. V

Fielding, Col Thomas Evelyn, 1873–1937, vol. III

Fielding, Rt Hon. William Stevens, 1848–1929, vol. III

Fielding-Hall, Harold, 1859–1917, vol. II

Fielding-Ould, Robert, 1872–1951, vol. V

Fields, Dame Gracie, 1898–1979, vol. VII

Fields, John Charles, 1863–1932, vol. III

Fienburgh, Wilfred, 1919–1958, vol. V

Fiennes, Hon. Sir Eustace Edward, 1st Bt, 1864–1943, vol. IV

Fiennes, Gerard Francis Gisborne T. W.; *see* Twisleton-Wykeham-Fiennes.

Fiennes, Gerard Yorke Twisleton-Wykeham, 1864–1926, vol. II

Fiennes, Lt-Col Sir Ranulph Twisleton-Wykeham-, 2nd Bt, 1902–1943, vol. IV

Fife, Duchess of (2nd in line), 1891–1959, vol. V

Fife, Col Sir Aubone, 1846–1920, vol. II

Fife, Charles Morrison, 1903–1982, vol. VIII

Fife, Charles William D.; *see* Domville-Fife.

Fife, Herbert Legard, *died* 1941, vol. IV

Fife, Ian Braham, 1911–1990, vol. VIII

Fife, Lt-Col Ronald D'Arcy, 1868–1946, vol. IV

Fife-Cookson, Lt-Col John Cookson, 1844–1911, vol. I

Fifoot, Cecil Herbert Stuart, 1899–1975, vol. VII

Figg, Sir Clifford, 1890–1947, vol. IV

Figg, Captain Donald Whitly, 1886–1917, vol. II

Figgins, James Hugh Blair, 1893–1956, vol. V

Figgis, Rev. J. B., *died* 1916, vol. I

Figgis, Rev. John Neville, 1866–1919, vol. II

Figgures, Sir Frank Edward, 1910–1990, vol. VIII

Fihelly, Hon. John Arthur, 1883–1945, vol. IV

Fildes, Sir Henry, 1870–1948, vol. IV

Fildes, Sir Luke; *see* Fildes, Sir S. L.
Fildes, Sir Paul, 1882–1971, vol. VII
Fildes, Sir (Samuel) Luke, 1843–1927, vol. II
Filene, Edward A., *died* 1937, vol. III
Filer, Albert Jack, 1898–1989, vol. VIII
Filgate, John Victor Opynschae M.; *see* Macartney-Filgate.
Filgate, Captain Richard Alexander Baillie, 1877–1967, vol. VI
Filgate, Lt-Col Townley Richard, 1854–1931, vol. III
Filgate, William de Salis, 1834–1916, vol. II
Filliter, Douglas Freeland Shute, 1884–1968, vol. VI
Filliter, Freeland, 1814–1902, vol. I
Filmer, Sir Robert Marcus, 10th Bt, 1878–1916, vol. II
Filomena; *see* Miller, Florence Fenwick.
Filon, Louis Napoleon George, 1875–1937, vol. III
Filose, Lt-Col Clement, 1853–1938, vol. III
Filose, Lt-Col Sir Michael, 1836–1925, vol. II
Filson, Alexander Warnock Andrew, 1913–1986, vol. VIII
Finberg, Alexander Joseph, 1866–1939, vol. III
Finberg, Herbert Patrick Reginald, 1900–1974, vol. VII
Finburgh, Samuel, 1867–1935, vol. III
Fincastle, Viscount; Edward David Murray, 1908–1940, vol. III
Finch, Charles Hugh, 1866–1954, vol. V
Finch, Sir Ernest Frederick, 1884–1960, vol. V, vol. VI
Finch, Surg. Rear-Adm. Ernest James, 1868–1934, vol. III
Finch, Ven. Geoffrey Grenville, 1923–1984, vol. VIII
Finch, Rt Hon. George Henry, 1835–1907, vol. I
Finch, George Ingle, 1888–1970, vol. VI
Finch, Lt-Col Hamilton Walter Edward, 1868–1935, vol. III
Finch, Sir Harold Josiah, 1898–1979, vol. VII (AII)
Finch, Col John Charles W.; *see* Wynne Finch.
Finch, Major John Philip Gordon, 1898–1965, vol. VI
Finch, Maj.-Gen. Lionel Hugh Knightley, 1888–1982, vol. VIII
Finch, Peter, (Peter Ingle-Finch), 1916–1977, vol. VII
Finch, Wilfred Henry Montgomery, 1883–1939, vol. III
Finch, Col Sir William Heneage W.; *see* Wynne Finch.
Finch, Rev. William Robert W.; *see* Wykes-Finch.
Finch Hatton, Brig.-Gen. Edward Heneage, 1868–1940, vol. III
Finch-Hatton, Hon. Harold Heneage, 1856–1904, vol. I
Finck, Henry T., 1854–1926, vol. II
Finck, Herman, 1872–1939, vol. III
Findlater, Alexander, *died* 1931, vol. III
Findlater, Jane Helen, *died* 1946, vol. IV
Findlater, Mary, 1865–1963, vol. VI
Findlater, Richard, (Kenneth Bruce Findlater Bain), 1921–1985, vol. VIII
Findlater, Sir William Huffington, 1824–1906, vol. I
Findlay, Adam Fyfe, 1869–1962, vol. VI
Findlay, Alexander, 1874–1921, vol. II
Findlay, Alexander, 1874–1966, vol. VI

Findlay, Alexander, 1926–1990, vol. VIII
Findlay, Alexander John, 1886–1976, vol. VII
Findlay, Sir Charles Stewart, 1874–1951, vol. V
Findlay, Sir Edmund; *see* Findlay, Sir J. E. R.
Findlay, Col George de Cardonnel Elmsall, 1889–1967, vol. VI
Findlay, Rev. George Gillanders, 1849–1919, vol. II
Findlay, George Hugo, 1888–1966, vol. VI
Findlay, George William Marshall, 1893–1952, vol. V
Findlay, Col Harold, 1875–1939, vol. III
Findlay, Harriet, (Lady Findlay), *died* 1954, vol. V
Findlay, Comdr James Buchanan, 1895–1983, vol. VIII
Findlay, James Thomas, 1875–1927, vol. II
Findlay, Surg.-Maj. John, 1851–1920, vol. II
Findlay, Col John, 1869–1946, vol. IV
Findlay, Sir (John) Edmund (Ritchie), 2nd Bt, 1902–1962, vol. VI
Findlay, Hon. Sir John George, 1862–1929, vol. III
Findlay, John Niemeyer, 1903–1987, vol. VIII
Findlay, John Ritchie, 1824–1898, vol. I
Findlay, Sir John Ritchie, 1st Bt, 1866–1930, vol. III
Findlay, Joseph John, 1860–1940, vol. III
Findlay, Leonard, 1878–1947, vol. IV
Findlay, Sir Mansfeldt de Cardonnel, 1861–1932, vol. III
Findlay, Brig.-Gen. Neil Douglas, 1859–1914, vol. I
Findlay, Lt-Col Sir Roland Lewis, 3rd Bt, 1903–1979, vol. VII
Findlay, William, 1880–1953, vol. V
Findlay, Lt-Col William Henri de la Tour d'Auvergne, 1864–1941, vol. IV
Findlay-Hamilton, George Douglas, 1861–1941, vol. IV
Findon, Benjamin William, 1859–1943, vol. IV
Finegan, Most Rev. Patrick, 1858–1937, vol. III
Finer, Herman, 1898–1969, vol. VI
Finer, Sir Morris, 1917–1974, vol. VII
Fingall, 11th Earl of, 1859–1929, vol. III
Fingall, 12th Earl of, 1896–1984, vol. VIII
Fink, Hon. Theodore, 1855–1942, vol. IV
Finlaison, Alexander John, 1840–1900, vol. I
Finlaison, Brig. Alexander Montagu, 1904–1989, vol. VIII
Finlaison, Maj.-Gen. John Bruce, 1870–1950, vol. IV
Finlay, 1st Viscount, 1842–1929, vol III
Finlay, 2nd Viscount, 1875–1945, vol IV
Finlay, Bernard, 1913–1980, vol. VII(AII)
Finlay, Sir (Campbell) Kirkman, 1875–1937, vol. III
Finlay, David White, *died* 1923, vol. II
Finlay, Sir George Panton, 1886–1970, vol. VI (AII)
Finlay, Sir Graeme Bell, 1st Bt, 1917–1987, vol. VIII
Finlay, Ian Archibald, 1878–1925, vol. II
Finlay, James Fairbairn, *died,* 1930, vol. III
Finlay, Jane Little (Sheena), 1917–1985, vol. VIII
Finlay, Major John, 1833–1912, vol. I
Finlay, Very Rev. John, 1842–1921, vol. II
Finlay, John Alexander Robertson, 1917–1989, vol. VIII
Finlay, John Euston Bell, 1908–1982, vol. VIII
Finlay, Sir Kirkman, *see* Finlay, Sir C. K.
Finlay, Rev. Peter, 1851–1929, vol. III
Finlay, Sheena; *see* Finlay, J. L.
Finlay, Rev. Thomas A., 1848–1940, vol. III

Finlay, Thomas Victor William, 1899–1980, vol. VII
Finlay-Freundlich, Erwin, 1885–1964, vol. VI
Finlayson, Maj.-Gen. Forbes; *see* Finlayson, Maj.-Gen. W. F.
Finlayson, George Daniel, 1882–1955, vol. V
Finlayson, Surg. Captain Henry William, 1864–1944, vol. IV
Finlayson, Horace Courtenay Forbes, 1885–1969, vol. VI
Finlayson, Air Vice-Marshal James Richmond G.; *see* Gordon-Finlayson.
Finlayson, John Rankine, *died* 1935, vol. III
Finlayson, Lt-Col Robert Alexander, 1857–1940, vol. III
Finlayson, General Sir Robert G.; *see* Gordon-Finlayson.
Finlayson, Lt-Col Walter Taylor, 1877–1928, vol. II
Finlayson, Maj.-Gen. (William) Forbes, 1911–1989, vol. VIII
Finletter, Hon. Thomas Knight, 1893–1980, vol. VII
Finley, David Edward, 1890–1977, vol. VII
Finley, Frederick Gault, 1861–1940, vol. III
Finley, John Huston, 1863–1940, vol. III
Finley, Sir Moses, 1912–1986, vol. VIII
Finlow, Robert Steel, 1877–1953, vol. V
Finn, Alexander, 1847–1919, vol. II
Finn, Donovan Bartley, 1900–1982, vol. VIII
Finn, Frank, 1868–1932, vol. III
Finn, Brig.-Gen. Harry, 1852–1924, vol. II
Finnegan, Thomas, 1901–1964, vol. VI
Finnemore, Sir Donald Leslie, 1889–1974, vol. VII
Finnemore, Joseph, 1860–1939, vol. III
Finnemore, Robert Isaac, 1842–1906, vol. I
Finney, Samuel, 1857–1935, vol. III
Finney, Sir Stephen, 1852–1924, vol. II
Finney, Victor Harold, *died* 1970, vol. VI
Finnigan, Surg. Rear-Adm. Charles Joseph, 1901–1967, vol. VI
Finnis, Adm. Frank, 1851–1918, vol. II
Finnis, Col Frank Alexander, 1880–1941, vol. IV
Finnis, Col Henry, 1853–1929, vol. III
Finnis, Gen. Sir Henry, 1890–1945, vol. IV
Finnis, Rev. Herbert Robert, 1854–1936, vol. III
Finnis, Sidney Alexander, 1908–1969, vol. VI
Finny, Maj.-Gen. Charles Morgan, 1886–1955, vol. V
Finny, John Magee, 1841–1922, vol. II
Finot, Jean, 1856–1922, vol. II
Finsen, Niels Ryberg, 1860–1904, vol. I
Finucane, John, 1843–1902, vol. I
Finucane, Rt Hon. Michael, *died* 1911, vol. I
Finzi, Gerald, 1901–1956, vol. V
Finzi, Neville Samuel, 1881–1968, vol. VI
Firbank, (Arthur Annesley) Ronald, 1886–1926, vol. II
Firbank, Maj.-Gen. Cecil Llewellyn, 1903–1985, vol. VIII
Firbank, Sir Joseph Thomas, 1850–1910, vol. I
Firbank, Ronald; *see* Firbank, A. A. R.
Firebrace, Comdr Sir Aylmer Newton George, 1886–1972, vol. VII
Firman, Lt-Col Robert Bertram, 1859–1936, vol. III
Firminger, Ven. Walter K., 1870–1940, vol. III
Firth, Sir Algernon Freeman, 2nd Bt, 1856–1936, vol. III

Firth, Arthur Charles Douglas, *died* 1948, vol. IV
Firth, Arthur Percival, 1928–1987, vol. VIII
Firth, Sir Charles Harding, 1857–1936, vol. III
Firth, Col Sir Charles Henry, 1836–1910, vol. I
Firth, Rev. Edward Harding, 1863–1936, vol. III
Firth, Sir Harriss, 1876–1950, vol. IV
Firth, James Brierley, 1888–1966, vol. VI
Firth, John B., 1868–1943, vol. IV
Firth, Rev. Canon John D'Ewes Evelyn, 1900–1957, vol. V
Firth, Joseph, *died* 1931, vol. III
Firth, Col Sir Robert Hammill, 1858–1931, vol. III
Firth, Sir Thomas Freeman, 1st Bt, 1825–1909, vol. I
Firth, Sir William John, 1881–1957, vol. V
Fischer, Rt Hon. Abraham, 1850–1913, vol. I
Fischer, Edwin, 1886–1960, vol. V
Fischer, Elsa; *see* Stralia, E.
Fischer, Ernst Kuno Berthold, 1824–1907, vol. I
Fischer, Hans, 1881–1945, vol. IV
Fischer, Harry Robert, 1903–1977, vol. VII
Fischer, John, 1910–1978, vol. VII
Fischer, Louis, 1896–1970, vol. VI
Fischer, Percy Ulrich, 1878–1957, vol. V
Fischer, Thomas Halhed, 1830–1914, vol. I
Fiset, Maj.-Gen. Hon. Sir Eugene Marie Joseph, 1874–1951, vol. V
Fiset, Jean Baptiste Romuald, 1843–1917, vol. II, vol. III
Fish, Anne Harriet, (Mrs Walter Sefton), *died* 1964, vol. VI
Fish, Elizabeth, *died* 1944, vol. IV
Fish, Sir (Eric) Wilfred, 1894–1974, vol. VII
Fish, Ven. Lancelot John, 1861–1924, vol. II
Fish, Stuyvesant, 1851–1923, vol. II
Fish, Wallace Wilfrid B.; *see* Blair-Fish.
Fish, Walter George, 1874–1947, vol. IV
Fish, Sir Wilfred; *see* Fish, Sir E. W.
Fishenden, Margaret White, *died* 1977, vol. VII
Fishenden, Richard Bertie, 1880–1956, vol. V
Fisher, 1st Baron, 1841–1920, vol. II
Fisher, 2nd Baron, 1868–1955, vol. V
Fisher of Camden, Baron (Life Peer); Samuel Fisher, 1905–1979, vol. VII
Fisher of Lambeth, Baron (Life Peer); Most Rev. and Rt Hon. Geoffrey Francis Fisher, 1887–1972, vol. VII
Fisher, A. Hugh, 1867–1945, vol. IV
Fisher, Mrs A. O.; *see* Peterson, Margaret.
Fisher, Alan Wainwright, 1922–1988, vol. VIII
Fisher, Alfred George Timbrell, *died* 1967, vol. VI
Fisher, Allan George Barnard, 1895–1976, vol. VII
Fisher, Rt Hon. Andrew, 1862–1928, vol. II
Fisher, Mrs Arabella B., 1840–1929, vol. III
Fisher, Arthur Bedford K., *see* Knapp-Fisher.
Fisher, Brig. Arthur Francis, 1899–1972, vol. VII
Fisher, Ben, *died* 1939, vol. III
Fisher, Rev. Canon Bernard Horatio Parry, 1875–1953, vol. V
Fisher, Lt-Gen. Sir Bertie Drew, 1878–1972, vol. VII
Fisher, Rev. Cecil Edward, 1838–1925, vol. II
Fisher, Col Cecil James, 1890–1961, vol. VI
Fisher, Brig. Charles Alexander, 1872–1934, vol. III
Fisher, Charles Alfred, 1916–1982, vol. VIII
Fisher, Charles Browning, *died* 1929, vol. III

Fisher, Hon. Charles Douglas, 1921–1978, vol. VII

Fisher, Major (Hon.) Charles Howard Kerridge, 1895–1987, vol. VIII

Fisher, Maj.-Gen. Donald Rutherford Dacre, 1890–1962, vol. VI

Fisher, Dorothea Frances Canfield; see Canfield, Dorothy.

Fisher, Adm. Sir Douglas Blake, 1890–1963, vol. VI

Fisher, Sir Edward Francis K.; see Knapp-Fisher.

Fisher, Lt-Gen. Edward Henry, 1822–1910, vol. I

Fisher, Edwin, 1883–1947, vol. IV

Fisher, Hon. Francis Forman, 1919–1986, vol. VIII

Fisher, Francis Marion Bates, 1877–1960, vol. V

Fisher, Col Francis Torriano, 1863–1938, vol. III

Fisher, Frank Lindsay, died 1947, vol. IV

Fisher, Frederic Henry, 1849–1926, vol. II

Fisher, Rev. Frederic Horatio, 1837–1915, vol. I

Fisher, Adm. Sir Frederic William, 1851–1943, vol. IV

Fisher, Vice-Adm. Frederick Charles, 1877–1958, vol. V

Fisher, Frederick Jack, 1908–1988, vol. VIII

Fisher, Frederick Victor, 1870–1954, vol. V

Fisher, Rt Rev. George Carnac, 1844–1921, vol. II

Fisher, George Park, 1827–1909, vol. I

Fisher, Brig. Sir Gerald Thomas, 1887–1965, vol. VI

Fisher, Sir Godfrey Arthur, 1885–1969, vol. VI

Fisher, Captain Harold, 1877–1914, vol. I

Fisher, Rt Hon. Herbert Albert Laurens, 1865–1940, vol. III

Fisher, Irving, 1867–1947, vol. IV

Fisher, James Maxwell McConnell, 1912–1970, vol. VI

Fisher, Inspector-Gen. James W., died 1919, vol. II

Fisher, Rev. John, 1862–1930, vol. III

Fisher, Brig.-Gen. John, 1862–1942, vol. IV

Fisher, Sir John, 1892–1983, vol. VIII

Fisher, John Campbell, 1880–1943, vol. IV

Fisher, John Cartwright Braddon, 1911–1968, vol. VI

Fisher, Maj.-Gen. John Frederick Lane, 1832–1917, vol. II

Fisher, John Henry, 1856–1937, vol. III

Fisher, John Herbert, 1867–1933, vol. III

Fisher, John Lenox, 1899–1976, vol. VII

Fisher, Brig. John Malcolm, 1890–1943, vol. IV

Fisher, Rev. John Martyn, 1873–1939, vol. III

Fisher, Joseph R., 1855–1939, vol. III

Fisher, Lt-Col Julian Lawrence, 1877–1953, vol. V

Fisher, Kenneth, 1882–1945, vol. IV

Fisher, Rt Rev. Leonard Noel, 1881–1963, vol. VI

Fisher, Ven. Leslie Gravatt, 1906–1988, vol. VIII

Fisher, Mark, 1841–1923, vol. II

Fisher, Matthew George, 1888–1965, vol. VI

Fisher, Sir (Norman Fenwick) Warren, 1879–1948, vol. IV

Fisher, Norman George, 1910–1972, vol. VII

Fisher, Rev. Philip John, 1883–1961, vol. VI

Fisher, Rear-Adm. Ralph Lindsay, 1903–1988, vol. VIII

Fisher, Reginald Brettauer, 1907–1986, vol. VIII

Fisher, Rev. Robert, 1848–1933, vol. III

Fisher, Rev. Robert, 1855–1938, vol. III

Fisher, Rev. Robert Howie, 1861–1934, vol. III

Fisher, Sir Ronald Aylmer, 1890–1962, vol. VI

Fisher, S. Melton, 1860–1939, vol. III

Fisher, Sophie Florence Lothrop; see Wavertree, Lady.

Fisher, Sir Stanley, 1867–1949, vol. IV

Fisher, Col Stanley Howe, 1891–1967, vol VI

Fisher, Hon. Sydney Arthur, 1850–1921, vol. II

Fisher, Sydney Humbert, 1887–1980, vol. VII

Fisher, Theodore, 1863–1949, vol. IV

Fisher, Comdr Sir Thomas, 1883–1925, vol. II

Fisher, Rt Rev. Thomas Cathrew, 1871–1929, vol. III

Fisher, Vardis, 1895–1968, vol. VI(AII)

Fisher, Violet Olivia; see Cressy-Marcks, V. O.

Fisher, W. R., 1846–1910, vol. I

Fisher, Rev. Walter Henry, died 1931, vol. III

Fisher, Sir Walter Newton, 1844–1932, vol. III

Fisher, Sir Warren; see Fisher, Sir N. F. W.

Fisher, William Bayne, 1916–1984, vol. VIII

Fisher, Adm. William Blake, 1853–1926, vol. II

Fisher, William James, died 1924, vol. II

Fisher, Adm. Sir William Wordsworth, 1875–1937, vol. III

Fisher, Sir Woolf, 1912–1975, vol. VII

Fisher-Childe, Col Ralph Bromfield Willington, 1854–1936, vol. III

Fisher Prout, Margaret, died 1963, vol. VI

Fisher-Rowe, Edward Rowe, 1832–1909, vol. I

Fisher-Rowe, Col Herbert Mayow, 1870–1938, vol. III

Fisher-Smith, Sir George Henry, 1846–1931, vol. III

Fishwick, Lt-Col Henry, 1835–1914, vol. I

Fisk, Sir Ernest Thomas, 1886–1965, vol. VI

Fisk, James Brown, 1910–1981, vol. VIII

Fiske, Baron (Life Peer); William Geoffrey Fiske, 1905–1975, vol. VII

Fiske, Rear-Adm. Bradley Allen, 1854–1942, vol. IV

Fiske, Rt Rev. Charles, 1868–1942, vol. IV

Fiske, John, 1842–1901, vol. I

Fisken, Archibald Clyde Wanliss, 1897–1970, vol. VI(AII)

Fison, Alfred Henry, 1857–1923, vol. II

Fison, Sir Clavering; see Fison, Sir F. G. C.

Fison, Captain Sir (Francis) Geoffrey, 2nd Bt, 1873–1948, vol. IV

Fison, Sir (Frank Guy) Clavering, 1892–1985, vol. VIII

Fison, Sir Frederick William, 1st Bt, 1847–1927, vol. II

Fison, Captain Sir Geoffrey; see Fison, Captain Sir F. G.

Fison, Sir Guy; see Fison, Sir W. G.

Fison, Rt Rev. Joseph Edward, 1906–1972, vol. VII

Fison, Sir (William) Guy, 3rd Bt, 1890–1964, vol. VI

Fitch, Alan; see Fitch, E. A.

Fitch, Sir Cecil Edwin, 1870–1940, vol. III

Fitch, Charles Francis, 1860–1947, vol. IV

Fitch, Clyde, 1865–1909, vol. I

Fitch, Ven. Edward Arnold, died 1965, vol. VI

Fitch, (Ernest) Alan, 1915–1985, vol. VIII

Fitch, Sir Joshua Girling, 1824–1903, vol. I

Fitchett, Very Rev. Alfred Robertson, died 1929, vol. III

Fitchett, Frederick, 1851–1930, vol. III

Fitchett, Rt Rev. William Alfred Robertson, 1872–1952, vol. V

Fitchett, Rev. William Henry, died 1928, vol. II

Fithian, Sir Edward William, 1845–1936, vol. III
Fitt, Mary; see Freeman, Kathleen.
Fitton, Col Sir Charles Vernon, 1894–1967, vol. VI
Fitton, Col Guy William, 1862–1939, vol. III
Fitton, Hedley, 1857–1929, vol. III
Fitton, Col Hugh Gregory, 1863–1916, vol. II
Fitton, James, 1864–1952, vol. V
Fitton, James, 1899–1982, vol. VIII
Fitts, Sir Clive Hamilton, 1900–1984, vol. VIII
FitzAlan of Derwent, 1st Viscount, 1855–1947, vol. IV
FitzAlan of Derwent, 2nd Viscount, 1883–1962, vol. VI
FitzClarence, Lt-Col Charles, 1865–1914, vol. I
FitzClarence, Hon. Harold Edward, 1870–1926, vol. II
Fitze, Sir Kenneth Samuel, 1887–1960, vol. V
FitzGeorge, Rear-Adm. Sir Adolphus Augustus Frederick, 1846–1922, vol. II
Fitzgeorge, Col Sir Augustus Charles Frederick, 1847–1933, vol. III
Fitzgerald, Sir (Adolf) Alexander, 1890–1969, vol. VI(AII)
Fitzgerald, Sir Alexander; see Fitzgerald, Sir A. A.
FitzGerald, Sir Arthur Henry Brinsley, 4th Bt (cr 1880), 1885–1967, vol. VI
Fitzgerald, Brian Percy Seymour V.; see Vesey-Fitzgerald.
Fitzgerald, Lt-Col Brinsley, 1859–1931, vol. III
Fitzgerald, Adm. Charles Cooper Penrose, 1841–1921, vol. II
FitzGerald, Charles Edward, 1843–1916, vol. II
FitzGerald, Col Sir Charles John Oswald, 1840–1912, vol. I
FitzGerald, Hon. David, 1847–1920, vol. II
Fitzgerald, Denis P., 1871–1947, vol. IV
FitzGerald, Captain Lord Desmond, 1888–1916, vol. II
Fitzgerald, Desmond, died 1947, vol. IV
Fitzgerald, Desmond Fitzjohn Lloyd, 1862–1936, vol. III
Fitz-Gerald, Desmond Windham Otho, 1901–1949, vol. IV
Fitzgerald, Sir Edward, 1st Bt (cr 1903), 1846–1927, vol. II
Fitzgerald, Edward, 1874–1969, vol. VI(AII)
Fitzgerald, Major Edward Arthur, 1871–1931, vol. III
Fitzgerald, Rev. (Sir) Edward Thomas, 3rd Bt, 1912–1988, vol. VIII
Fitz-Gerald, Hon. Evelyn Charles Joseph, died 1946, vol. IV
Fitzgerald, Maj.-Gen. Fitzgerald Gabbett, died 1954, vol. V
Fitzgerald, Francis John, 1864–1939, vol. III
FitzGerald, Lt-Col Lord Frederick, 1857–1924, vol. II
Fitzgerald, Garrett Ernest, 1894–1970, vol. VI
FitzGerald, Col George Alfred, 1868–1959, vol. V
Fitzgerald, Sir George Cumming, 5th Bt (cr 1822), 1823–1908, vol. I
Fitzgerald, George Francis, 1851–1901, vol. I
FitzGerald, Hon. George Parker, 1843–1917, vol. II
Fitzgerald, Sir Gerald; see Fitzgerald, Sir W. G. S. V.
Fitzgerald, Hon. Gerald, 1849–1925, vol. II

FitzGerald, Gerald A. R., 1844–1925, vol. II
Fitzgerald, Lt-Col Gerald James, 1869–1944, vol. IV
FitzGerald, Maj.-Gen. Gerald Michael, 1889–1957, vol. V
Fitzgerald, Sir Gerald Seymour Vesey; see Fitz-gerald, Sir W. G. S. V.
FitzGerald, Brig.-Gen. Herbert Swayne, 1856–1924, vol. II
Fitzgerald, James, died 1909, vol. I
Fitzgerald, James Foster-Vesey-, 1846–1907, vol. I
Fitzgerald, Sir John, 1857–1930, vol. III
FitzGerald, Hon. John Donohoe, 1848–1918, vol. II
FitzGerald, John Foster V.; see Vesey-FitzGerald.
Fitzgerald, John Gerald, 1882–1940, vol. III(A), vol. IV
Fitzgerald, Sir John Joseph, 2nd Bt (cr 1903), 1876–1957, vol. V(A)
Fitzgerald, Sir John Peter Gerald Maurice, 3rd Bt (cr 1880), 1884–1957, vol. V
Fitzgerald, Rear-Adm. John Uniacke Penrose, 1888–1940, vol. III
FitzGerald, John Vesey V.; see Vesey-FitzGerald.
FitzGerald, Marion; see FitzGerald, Mrs Robert.
FitzGerald, Lord Maurice, 1852–1901, vol. I
FitzGerald, Sir Maurice, 2nd Bt (cr 1880), 1844–1916, vol. II
FitzGerald, Maurice F., died 1927, vol. II
Fitzgerald, Rev. Canon Maurice Henry, 1877–1963, vol. VI
Fitzgerald, Maurice Pembroke, died 1952, vol. V
Fitzgerald, Michael, 1851–1918, vol. II
Fitzgerald, Lt-Col Oswald Arthur Gerald, 1875–1916, vol. II
Fitz-Gerald, Sir Patrick Herbert, 1899–1978, vol. VII
Fitzgerald, Brig.-Gen. Percy Desmond, 1875–1933, vol. III
FitzGerald, Percy Seymour Vesey, died 1924, vol. II
Fitzgerald, Sir Raymond; see Fitzgerald, Sir W. R.
FitzGerald, Richard Charles, 1905–1959, vol. V
Fitzgerald, Rt Rev. Richard Joseph, 1881–1956, vol. V
FitzGerald, Mrs Robert, (Marion), 1860–1928, vol. II
Fitzgerald, Sir Robert Uniacke-Penrose-, 1st Bt (cr 1896), 1839–1919, vol. II
FitzGerald, Hon. Rowan Robert, born 1847, vol. II
Fitzgerald, Seymour Gonne V.; see Vesey-Fitzgerald.
Fitz-Gerald, Shafto Justin Adair, 1859–1925, vol. II
FitzGerald, Terence, 1919–1985, vol. VIII
Fitzgerald, Thomas, 1879–1959, vol. V
Fitzgerald, Sir Thomas Naghten, 1838–1908, vol. I
FitzGerald, Lord Walter, 1858–1923, vol. II
Fitzgerald, Walter, 1898–1949, vol. IV
Fitzgerald, Walter, (Walter Fitzgerald Bond), 1896–1976, vol. VII
Fitzgerald, Sir (William) Gerald Seymour Vesey, 1841–1910, vol. I
FitzGerald, Sir William James, 1894–1989, vol. VIII
Fitzgerald, Most Rev. William Michael, 1906–1971, vol. VII
Fitzgerald, Sir (William) Raymond, 1890–1964, vol. VI
Fitzgerald, William Walter Augustine, died 1936, vol. III
Fitzgerald-Kenney, James C., 1878–1956, vol. V

FitzGibbon, Constantine; see FitzGibbon, R. L. C. L-D.

Fitzgibbon, Edmond Gerald, 1825–1905, vol. I

FitzGibbon, Brig. Francis, 1883–1964, vol. VI

Fitzgibbon, Rt Hon. Gerald, 1837–1909, vol. I

Fitzgibbon, Gerald, died 1942, vol. IV

FitzGibbon, Gibbon, 1877–1952, vol. V

Fitzgibbon, Henry, 1824–1909, vol. I

Fitzgibbon, Henry Macaulay, 1855–1942, vol. IV

FitzGibbon, John, 1849–1919, vol. II

FitzGibbon, (Robert Louis) Constantine (Lee-Dillon), 1919–1983, vol. VIII

Fitz-Hardinge, 2nd Baron, 1826–1896, vol. I

Fitzhardinge, 3rd Baron, 1830–1916, vol. II

Fitzherbert, Basil Thomas, 1836–1919, vol. II

Fitzherbert, Cuthbert, 1899–1986, vol. VIII

Fitzherbert, Maj.-Gen. Edward Herbert, 1885–1979, vol. VII

FitzHerbert, Ven. Henry Edward, 1882–1958, vol. V

Fitzherbert, Adm. Sir Herbert, 1885–1958, vol. V

Fitzherbert, Sir Hugo Meynell, 6th Bt, 1872–1934, vol. III

FitzHerbert, Sir John Richard Frederick, 8th Bt, 1913–1989, vol. VIII

Fitz Herbert, Lt-Col Norman, 1858–1943, vol. IV

Fitzherbert, Rev. Sir Richard, 5th Bt, 1846–1906, vol. I

Fitzherbert, Sir William, 7th Bt, 1874–1963, vol. VI

Fitzherbert-Brockholes, John William, 1889–1963, vol. VI

Fitzherbert-Brockholes, William Joseph, 1851–1924, vol. II

Fitzhugh, Maj.-Gen. Alfred, 1837–1929, vol. III

FitzHugh, James, 1917–1989, vol. VIII

Fitzhugh, Captain Terrick Charles, 1876–1939, vol. III

Fitzmaurice, 1st Baron, 1846–1935, vol. III

Fitzmaurice, Sir Gerald Gray, 1901–1982, vol. VIII

Fitzmaurice, Gerald Henry, 1865–1939, vol. III

Fitzmaurice, Rev. Sir Henry, 1886–1952, vol. V

Fitzmaurice, Sir Maurice, 1861–1924, vol. II

Fitz Maurice, Vice-Adm. Sir Maurice Swynfen, 1870–1927, vol. II

Fitzmaurice, Nicholas, 1887–1960, vol. V

Fitzmaurice, Vice-Adm. Sir Raymond, 1878–1943, vol. IV

Fitzmaurice, Brig.-Gen. Robert, 1866–1952, vol. V

Fitzpatrick, Rt Rev. Mgr Bartholomew, 1847–1925, vol. II

Fitzpatrick, Rt Hon. Sir Charles, 1851–1942, vol. IV

Fitzpatrick, Sir Dennis, 1837–1920, vol. II

Fitzpatrick, Brig.-Gen. Sir (Ernest) Richard, 1878–1949, vol. IV

FitzPatrick, Lt-Col Geoffrey Henry Julian, 1873–1939, vol. III

Fitz Patrick, Herbert Lindsay, 1868–1949, vol. IV

Fitz-Patrick, Horace James, 1894–1967, vol. VI

Fitzpatrick, Sir James Alexander Ossory, 1879–1937, vol. III

Fitzpatrick, Sir (James) Percy, 1862–1931, vol. III

Fitzpatrick, Brig. Noel Trew, 1888–1938, vol. III

Fitzpatrick, Sir Percy; see Fitzpatrick, Sir J. P.

Fitzpatrick, Brig.-Gen. Sir Richard; see Fitzpatrick, Brig.-Gen. Sir E. R.

Fitzpatrick, Rev. Thomas Cecil, 1861–1931, vol. III

Fitzpatrick, Thomas William, died 1965, vol. VI

Fitzpatrick, William Francis Joseph, 1854–1940, vol. III

Fitzroy, Sir Almeric William, 1851–1935, vol. III

FitzRoy, Charles, 1904–1989, vol. VIII

Fitzroy, Rev. Lord Charles Edward, 1857–1911, vol. I

FitzRoy, Sir Charles Edward, 1876–1954, vol. V

Fitzroy, Captain Rt Hon. Edward Algernon, 1869–1943, vol. IV

FitzRoy, Lord Frederick John, 1823–1919, vol. II

Fitzsimmons, William J., 1845–1913, vol. I

Fitzsimons, Frederick William, 1875–1951, vol. V

Fitzsimons, Robert Allen, 1892–1978, vol. VII

Fitzwalter, 20th Baron, 1860–1932, vol. III

Fitzwilliam, 6th Earl, 1815–1902, vol. I

Fitzwilliam, 7th Earl, 1872–1943, vol. IV

Fitzwilliam, 8th Earl, 1910–1948, vol. IV

Fitzwilliam, 9th Earl, 1883–1952, vol. V

Fitzwilliam, 10th Earl, 1904–1979, vol. VII

Fitzwilliam, Captain Hon. Sir Charles Wentworth-; see Fitzwilliam, Captain Hon. Sir W. C. W.

Fitzwilliam, George Charles Wentworth-, died 1935, vol. III

Fitzwilliam, Captain Hon. Sir (William) Charles Wentworth-, 1848–1925, vol. II

Fitzwilliam, Hon. William Henry Wentworth-, 1840–1920, vol. II

Fitzwilliams, Duncan Campbell Lloyd, 1878–1954, vol. V

Fitzwilliams, Col Edward Crawford Lloyd, 1872–1936, vol. III

Fitzwygram, Sir Frederick Loftus Francis, 5th Bt, 1884–1920, vol. II

Fitzwygram, Sir Frederick Wellington John, 4th Bt, 1823–1904, vol. I

Flack, Harvey, 1912–1966, vol. VI

Flack, Martin, 1882–1931, vol. III

Fladgate, Maj.-Gen. Courtenay William, 1890–1958, vol. V

Fladgate, Sir Francis; see Fladgate, Sir W. F.

Fladgate, Sir (William) Francis, 1853–1937, vol. III

Flagstad, Kirsten, 1895–1962, vol. VI

Flaherty, Robert Joseph, 1884–1951, vol. V

Flahiff, His Eminence Cardinal George Bernard, 1905–1989, vol. VIII

Flammarion, Camille, 1842–1925, vol. II

Flanagan, Lt-Col Edward Martyn Woulfe, 1870–1954, vol. V

Flanagan, Rev. J., 1851–1918, vol. II

Flanagan, William Henry, 1871–1944, vol. IV

Flanders, Allan David, 1910–1973, vol. VII

Flanders, Michael Henry, 1922–1975, vol. VII

Flandin, Pierre Etienne, 1889–1958, vol. V

Flannery, Sir Harold Fortescue, 2nd Bt, 1883–1959, vol. V

Flannery, Sir James F.; see Fortescue-Flannery.

Flather, James Henry, 1853–1928, vol. II

Flatt, Leslie Neeve, 1889–1957, vol. V

Flavelle, Sir Ellsworth; see Flavelle, Sir J. E.

Flavelle, Sir (Joseph) Ellsworth, 2nd Bt, 1892–1977, vol. VII

Flavelle, Sir Joseph Wesley, 1st Bt, 1858–1939, vol. III

Flavin, Michael Joseph, 1861–1944, vol. IV

Flaxman, Brig. Sir Hubert James Marlowe, 1893–1976, vol. VII

Fleck, 1st Baron, 1889–1968, vol. VI

Flecker, H. L. O., 1896–1958, vol. V

Flecker, Rev. William Herman, 1859–1941, vol. IV

Fleet, Rear-Adm. Ernest James, 1850–1935, vol. III

Fleet, George Rutland B., *see* Barrington-Fleet.

Fleet, Vice-Adm. Henry Louis, 1850–1923, vol. II

Fleet, John Faithfull, 1847–1917, vol. II

Fleetwood-Hesketh, Charles Hesketh; *see* Hesketh.

Fleetwood-Hesketh, Peter; *see* Hesketh.

Fleetwood-Walker, Bernard, 1893–1965, vol. VI

Fleischmann, Louis, 1868–1954, vol. V

Fleming, Hon. Lord; David Pinkerton Fleming, 1877–1944, vol. IV

Fleming, Sir Alexander, 1881–1955, vol. V

Fleming, Sir Ambrose; *see* Fleming, Sir J. A.

Fleming, Amy Margaret, *died* 1981, vol. VIII

Fleming, Sir Andrew Fleming Hudleston le, 8th Bt, 1855–1925, vol. II

Fleming, Rev. Archibald, 1863–1941, vol. IV

Fleming, Rt Rev. Archibald Lang, 1883–1953, vol. V

Fleming, Col Archibald Nicol, 1870–1948, vol. IV

Fleming, Sir Arthur Percy Morris, 1881–1960, vol. V

Fleming, Dame Celia; *see* Johnson.

Fleming, Sir Charles Alexander, 1916–1987, vol. VIII

Fleming, Major Charles Christie, 1864–1917, vol. II

Fleming, Charles James, 1839–1904, vol. I

Fleming, Charles Mann, 1904–1985, vol. VIII

Fleming, Rev. David, *died* 1920, vol. II

Fleming, David Hay, 1849–1931, vol. III

Fleming, David Pinkerton; *see* Fleming, Hon. Lord.

Fleming, Hon. Donald Methuen, 1905–1986, vol. VIII

Fleming, Dorothy Leigh; *see* Sayers, D. L.

Fleming, Edward G.; *see* Gibson Fleming.

Fleming, Edward Lascelles, *died* 1950, vol. IV

Fleming, Edward Vandermere, 1869–1947, vol. IV

Fleming, Sir Francis, 1842–1922, vol. II

Fleming, Col Frank, 1876–1964, vol. VI

Fleming, Frederick, vol. II

Fleming, Geoffrey Balmanno, 1882–1952, vol. V

Fleming, George; *see* Fletcher, Constance.

Fleming, George, 1833–1901, vol. I

Fleming, Maj.-Gen. George, 1879–1957, vol. V

Fleming, Rev. Herbert James, 1873–1926, vol. II

Fleming, Horace, 1872–1941, vol. IV

Fleming, Very Rev. Horace Townsend, *died* 1909, vol. I

Fleming, Ian Lancaster, 1908–1964, vol. VI

Fleming, Rev. James, *died* 1908, vol. I

Fleming, James, 1841–1922, vol. II

Fleming, James Alexander, 1855–1926, vol. II

Fleming, Rev. James George Grant, 1895–1978, vol. VII

Fleming, Sir John, 1847–1925, vol. II

Fleming, Sir (John) Ambrose, 1849–1945, vol. IV

Fleming, Rev. John Dick, *died* 1938, vol. III

Fleming, Col John Gibson, 1880–1936, vol. III

Fleming, Lt-Col John Kenneth Sprot, 1874–1944, vol. IV

Fleming, John Marcus, 1911–1976, vol. VII

Fleming, Rev. John Robert, 1858–1937, vol. III

Fleming, Rt Rev. Launcelot; *see* Fleming, Rt Rev. W. L. S.

Fleming, Marston Greig, 1913–1982, vol. VIII

Fleming, Maxwell, 1871–1935, vol. III

Fleming, Patrick D., *died* 1928, vol. II

Fleming, Patrick Lyons, 1905–1985, vol. VIII

Fleming, Peter; *see* Fleming, R. P.

Fleming, Major Philip, 1889–1971, vol. VII

Fleming, Richard Evelyn, 1911–1977, vol. VII

Fleming, Robert, 1845–1933, vol. III

Fleming, Robert Alexander, 1862–1947, vol. IV

Fleming, (Robert) Peter, 1907–1971, vol. VII

Fleming, Lt-Col Samuel, 1865–1925, vol. II

Fleming, Sir Sandford, 1827–1915, vol. I

Fleming, Sir Thomas Henry, 1863–1933, vol. III

Fleming, Valentine, 1882–1917, vol. II

Fleming, Wilfrid Louis Remi, 1869–1944, vol. IV

Fleming, William Arnot, 1879–1970, vol. VI

Fleming, Rt Rev. (William) Launcelot (Scott), 1906–1990, vol. VIII

Fleming-Bernard, Andrew Milroy, 1871–1953, vol. V

Fleming-Sandes, Alfred James Terence, 1894–1961, vol. VI

Flemming, Cecil Wood, 1902–1981, vol. VIII

Flemming, Sir Gilbert Nicolson, 1897–1981, vol. VIII

Flemming, Hon. James Kidd, 1868–1927, vol. II

Flemming, Percy, *died* 1941, vol. IV

Flemwell, George Jackson, 1865–1928, vol. II

Flenley, Ralph, 1886–1969, vol. VI

Flers, Marquis de, (Robert de Flers), 1872–1927, vol. II

Fletcher, Baron (Life Peer); Eric George Molyneux Fletcher, 1903–1990, vol. VIII

Fletcher, Air Cdre Albert, *died* 1956, vol. V

Fletcher, Sir Alexander MacPherson, (Sir Alex Fletcher), 1929–1989, vol. VIII

Fletcher, Alfred Ewen, 1841–1915, vol. I

Fletcher, Sir Angus Somerville, 1883–1960, vol. V

Fletcher, Sir (Arthur George) Murchison, 1878–1954, vol. V

Fletcher, Banister, 1833–1899, vol. I

Fletcher, Sir Banister Flight, *died* 1953, vol. V

Fletcher, Basil Alais, 1900–1983, vol. VIII

Fletcher, Benton; *see* Fletcher, G. H. B.

Fletcher, Sir Carteret Ernest, 1868–1934, vol. III

Fletcher, Charles Brunsdon, 1859–1946, vol. IV

Fletcher, Charles John, 1843–1914, vol. I

Fletcher, Charles Robert Leslie, 1857–1934, vol. III

Fletcher, Clarence George Eugene, 1875–1929, vol. III

Fletcher, Constance, 1858–1938, vol. III

Fletcher, Rev. Canon Denis, 1881–1942, vol. IV

Fletcher, Hon. Edward Ernest, vol. II

Fletcher, Surg. Rear-Adm. Edward Ernest, 1886–1968, vol. VI

Fletcher, Edward Joseph, 1911–1983, vol. VIII

Fletcher, Sir (Edward) Lionel, 1876–1968, vol. VI

Fletcher, Lt-Col Edward Walter, 1899–1958, vol. V

Fletcher, Sir Ernest Edward, 1869–1940, vol. III

Fletcher, Ernest Tertius Decimus, 1891–1961, vol. VI

Fletcher, Sir Frank, 1870–1954, vol. V

Fletcher, Frank, 1867–1956, vol. V

Fletcher, Frank Morley, 1866–1949, vol. IV

Fletcher, Frank Thomas Herbert, 1898–1977, vol. VII

Fletcher, George Hamilton, 1860–1930, vol. III

Fletcher, (George Henry) Benton, *died* 1944, vol. IV

Fletcher, Hanslip, 1874–1955, vol. V

Fletcher, Harold Roy, 1907–1978, vol. VII

Fletcher, Lt-Col Sir Henry Arthur, 1843–1925, vol. II

Fletcher, Rt Hon. Sir Henry Aubrey-, 4th Bt, 1835–1910, vol. I

Fletcher, Major Sir Henry Lancelot A.; *see* Aubrey-Fletcher.

Fletcher, Henry Prather, 1873–1959, vol. V

Fletcher, Herbert Morley, *died* 1950, vol. IV

Fletcher, Herbert Phillips, 1872–1917, vol. II

Fletcher, J. K.; *see* Kebty-Fletcher.

Fletcher, J. S., 1863–1935, vol. III

Fletcher, Sir James, 1886–1974, vol. VII

Fletcher, James Douglas, 1857–1927, vol. II

Fletcher, Rev. James Michael John, 1852–1940, vol. III

Fletcher, James Thomas, 1898–1990, vol. VIII

Fletcher, Lt-Col John, 1815–1902, vol. I

Fletcher, John, 1827–1903, vol. I

Fletcher, Rev. John Charles Ballett, *died* 1926, vol. II

Fletcher, John Gould, 1886–1950, vol. IV(A), vol. V

Fletcher, Sir John Samuel, 1st Bt, 1841–1924, vol. II

Fletcher, Sir Lancelot A.; *see* Aubrey-Fletcher.

Fletcher, Sir Lazarus, 1854–1921, vol. II

Fletcher, Leonard Ralph, 1917–1974, vol. VII

Fletcher, Sir Lionel; *see* Fletcher, Sir E. L.

Fletcher, Michael Scott, 1868–1947, vol. IV

Fletcher, Sir Murchison; *see* Fletcher, Sir A. G. M.

Fletcher, Sir Norman Seymour, 1905–1986, vol. VIII

Fletcher, Hon. Sir Patrick Bisset, 1901–1981, vol. VIII

Fletcher, Rev. Philip, 1848–1928, vol. II

Fletcher, Rev. Reginald James, 1865–1932, vol. III

Fletcher, Richard Cawthorne, 1916–1986, vol. VIII

Fletcher, Rev. Robert, *died* 1921, vol. II

Fletcher, Ven. Robert Crompton, 1850–1917, vol. II

Fletcher, Sir Walter, 1892–1956, vol. V

Fletcher, Sir Walter Morley, 1873–1933, vol. III

Fletcher, Surg.-Maj. William, 1863–1933, vol. III

Fletcher, Major William Alfred Littledale, 1869–1919, vol. II

Fletcher, William Charles, 1865–1959, vol. V

Fletcher, Rev. Canon William Dudley Saul, 1863–1948, vol. IV

Fletcher, Ven. William Henry, *died* 1926, vol. II

Fletcher, William Younger, 1830–1913, vol. I

Fletcher-Cooke, Sir John, 1911–1989, vol. VIII

Fletcher-Twemlow, George Fletcher; *see* Twemlow.

Fletcher-Watson, P., 1842–1907, vol. I

Flett, Sir John Smith, 1869–1947, vol. IV

Flett, Sir Martin Teall, 1911–1982, vol. VIII

Fleure, Herbert John, 1877–1969, vol. VI

Fleuriau, Aimé Joseph de, 1870–1938, vol. III

Flew, John Douglas Score, 1902–1972, vol. VII

Flew, Rev. Robert Newton, 1886–1962, vol. VI

Flewett, Rt Rev. William Edward, 1861–1938, vol. III

Flexner, Abraham, 1866–1959, vol. V

Flexner, Simon, 1863–1946, vol. IV

Flick, Brig.-Gen. Ccharles Leonard, 1869–1948, vol. IV

Flight, Claude, 1881–1955, vol. V

Flinn, D. Edgar, 1850–1926, vol. II

Flinn, Major William Henry, 1895–1973, vol. VII

Flint, Abraham John, 1903–1971, vol. VII

Flint, Alexander, 1877–1932, vol. III

Flint, Austin, 1836–1915, vol. I

Flint, Charles Ranlett, 1850–1934, vol. III

Flint, Ethelbert Rest, 1880–1956, vol. V

Flint, Henry Thomas, 1890–1971, vol. VII

Flint, Joseph, 1855–1925, vol. III

Flint, Percy Sydney George, (Pip), 1921–1990, vol. VIII

Flint, Pip; *see* Flint, Percy S. G.

Flint, Rev. Robert, 1838–1910, vol. I

Flint, Robert Purves, 1883–1947, vol. IV

Flint, Ven. Stamford R. R.; *see* Raffles-Flint.

Flint, Thomas Barnard, 1847–1919, vol. II

Flint, Sir William Russell, 1880–1969, vol. VI

Flintoff, Lt-Col Thomas, 1851–1907, vol. I

Flitcroft, Sir Thomas Evans, 1861–1938, vol. III

Floersheim, Cecil L. F., 1871–1936, vol. III

Flood, Maj.-Gen. Arthur S.; *see* Solly-Flood.

Flood, Maj.-Gen. Sir Frederick Richard S.; *see* Solly-Flood.

Flood, John Ernest William, 1886–1940, vol. III

Flood, Brig.-Gen. Richard Elles S.; *see* Solly-Flood.

Flood, Chevalier William Henry Grattan, 1859–1928, vol. II

Florence, Lt-Col Henry Louis, 1843–1916, vol. II

Florence, Mary S.; *see* Sargant-Florence.

Florence, Philip Sargant, 1890–1982, vol. VIII

Florey, Baron (Life Peer); Howard Walter Florey, 1898–1968, vol. VI

Flory, Paul John, 1910–1985, vol. VIII

Floud, Bernard Francis Castle, 1915–1967, vol. VI

Floud, Sir Francis Lewis Castle, 1875–1965, vol. VI

Floud, Peter Castle, 1911–1960, vol. V

Flower, Sir Archibald Dennis, *died* 1950, vol. IV

Flower, Group Capt. Arthur Hyde, 1892–1987, vol. VIII

Flower, Benjamin Orange, 1858–1918, vol. II

Flower, Sir Cyril Thomas, 1879–1961, vol. VI

Flower, Sir Ernest Francis Swan, 1865–1926, vol. II

Flower, Lt-Col Sir Fordham, 1904–1966, vol. VI

Flower, Major Horace John, 1883–1919, vol. II

Flower, Sir Newman; *see* Flower, Sir W. N.

Flower, Robin Ernest William, 1881–1946, vol. IV

Flower, Major Victor Augustine, 1875–1917, vol. II

Flower, Rev. Walker, *died* 1910, vol. I

Flower, Sir (Walter) Newman, 1879–1964, vol. VI

Flower, Sir William Henry, 1831–1899, vol. I

Flowerdew, Herbert, 1866–1917, vol. II

Flowerdew, Richard Edward, 1886–1971, vol. VII

Flowerdew, Spencer Pelham, 1881–1959, vol. V

Flowers, Hon. Frederick, 1864–1928, vol. II

Floyd, Alfred Ernest, 1877–1974, vol. VII

Floyd, Charles Murray, 1905–1971, vol. VII

Floyd, Brig. Sir Henry Robert Kincaid, 5th Bt, 1899–1968, vol. VI

Floyd, Captain Sir Henry Robert Peel, 4th Bt, 1855–1915, vol. I

Floyd, Major Sir John, 3rd Bt, 1823–1909, vol. I

Floyd, Sir John Duckett, 6th Bt, 1903–1975, vol. VII
Floyer-Acland, Lt-Gen. Arthur Nugent, 1885–1980, vol. VII
Fludyer, Sir Arthur John, 5th Bt, 1844–1922, vol. II
Fludyer, Col Henry, 1847–1920, vol. II
Flugel, John Carl, 1884–1955, vol. V
Flux, Sir Alfred William, 1867–1942, vol. IV
Flynn, Alfred Axen Leonard, *died* 1943, vol. IV
Flynn, Sir Charles Joseph, 1884–1938, vol. III
Flynn, Hon. Edmund James, 1847–1927, vol. II
Flynn, Sir J. Albert; *see* Flynn, Sir J(oshua) Albert.
Flynn, James Christopher, 1852–1922, vol. II
Flynn, Sir J(oshua) Albert, 1863–1933, vol. III
Flynn, Theodore Thomson, *died* 1968, vol. VI
Flynn, Rt Rev. Thomas Edward, 1880–1961, vol. VI
Foad, Roland Walter, 1908–1978, vol. VII
Foakes-Jackson, Rev. Frederick John, 1855–1941, vol. IV
Foch, Field-Marshal Ferdinand, 1851–1929, vol. III
Foden, Air Vice-Marshal Arthur, 1914–1990, vol. VIII
Foden, William Bertram, 1892–1981, vol. VIII
Fogarty, Air Chief Marshal Sir Francis, 1899–1973, vol. VII
Fogarty, Most Rev. Michael, 1859–1955, vol. V
Fogarty, Rt Rev. Nelson Wellesley, 1871–1933, vol. III
Fogarty, Sir Reginald Francis Graham, 1892–1967, vol. VI
Fogarty, Susan Winthrop, 1930–1983, vol. VIII
Fogazzaro, Antonio, 1842–1911, vol. I
Fogerty, Elsie, *died* 1945, vol. IV
Fogg, Albert, 1909–1989, vol. VIII
Fogg, Charles William Eric, 1903–1939, vol. III
Fogg, Ven. Peter Parry, 1832–1920, vol. II
Fogg Elliot, Captain Mark, 1898–1950, vol. IV
Foggie, David, 1878–1948, vol. IV
Foggin, Lancelot Middleton, 1876–1968, vol. VI
Foggin, Myers; *see* Foggin, W. M.
Foggin, (Wilhelm) Myers, 1908–1986, vol. VIII
Foggitt, Mrs T. J.; *see* Bacon, Gertrude.
Fogh, Torkel W.; *see* Weis-Fogh.
Fokker, A. H. G., 1890–1939, vol. III
Foletta, George Gotardo, 1892–1973, vol. VII
Foley, 5th Baron, 1850–1905, vol. I
Foley, 6th Baron, 1852–1918, vol. II
Foley, 7th Baron, 1898–1927, vol. II
Foley, Blanchard, 1869–1950, vol. IV
Foley, Most Rev. Daniel, 1865–1941, vol. IV
Foley, Sir (Ernest) Julian, 1881–1966, vol. VI
Foley, Major Francis Edward, 1884–1958, vol. V
Foley, Rear-Adm. Francis John, 1855–1911, vol. I
Foley, Col Frank Wigram, 1865–1949, vol. IV
Foley, Guy Francis, 1896–1970, vol. VI
Foley, Rt Rev. Mgr John, *died* 1937, vol. III
Foley, Sir Julian; *see* Foley, Sir E. J.
Foley, Rt Rev. Patrick, 1858–1926, vol. II
Foley, Paul Henry, 1857–1928, vol. II
Foley, Hon. Sir St George Gerald, 1814–1897, vol. I
Foley-Phillipps, Sir Richard Foley, 4th Bt, 1920–1962, vol. VI
Folger, Henry C., 1857–1930, vol. III
Folger, Col Karl Creighton, *died* 1941, vol. IV
Foligno, Cesare, 1878–1863, vol. VI

Foljambe, Rt Hon. Francis John Savile, 1830–1917, vol. II
Foljambe, George Savile, 1856–1920, vol. II
Folkard, Charles James, 1878–1963, vol. VI
Folkard, Henry Coleman, *died* 1914, vol. I
Folker, Horace S.; *see* Shepherd-Folker.
Foll, Hon. Hattil Spencer, 1890–1977, vol. VII
Follett, Cathleen; *see* Mann, C.
Follett, Sir Charles John, 1838–1921, vol. II
Follett, Sir David Henry, 1907–1982, vol. VIII
Follett, Lt-Col Gilbert Burrell Spencer, 1878–1918, vol. II
Follett, Lt-Col Henry Spencer, 1866–1940, vol. III
Follett, Lt-Col Robert Spencer, 1882–1941, vol. IV
Follett, Col Robert William Webb, 1844–1921, vol. II
Follett, Samuel Frank, 1904–1988, vol. VIII
Folley, Sydney John, 1906–1970, vol. VI
Follick, Mont, 1887–1958, vol. V
Follows, Sir (Charles) Geoffry (Shield), 1896–1983, vol. VIII
Follows, Sir Denis, 1908–1983, vol. VIII
Follows, Sir Geoffry; *see* Follows, Sir C. G. S.
Follows, Lt-Col John Henry, 1869–1938, vol. III
Fonda, Henry, 1905–1982, vol. VIII
Fontanne, Lynn, 1887–1983, vol. VIII
Fooks, Sir Raymond Hatherell, 1888–1978, vol. VII
Foord, Francis Layton, 1874–1942, vol. IV
Foord, Rev. James, *died* 1932, vol. III
Foord-Kelcey, Air Vice-Marshal Alick, 1913–1973, vol. VII
Foot, Arthur Edward, 1901–1968, vol. VI
Foot, Adm. Cunningham Robert de Clare, 1864–1940, vol. III
Foot, Rt Hon. Sir Dingle Mackintosh, 1905–1978, vol. VII
Foot, Hugh Mackintosh; *see* Baron Caradon.
Foot, Rt Hon. Isaac, 1880–1960, vol. V
Foot, Brig.-Gen. Richard Mildmay, 1865–1933, vol. III
Foot, Robert William, 1889–1973, vol. VII
Foot, Stephen Henry, 1887–1966, vol. VI
Foot, Maj.-Gen. William, 1889–1971, vol. VII
Foote, Col F. Onslow Barrington, 1850–1911, vol. I
Foote, John Alderson, 1848–1922, vol. II
Foote, Rev. John Weir, 1904–1988, vol. VIII
Foote, Adm. Sir Randolph Frank Olive, 1853–1931, vol. III
Footman, David John, 1895–1983, vol. VIII
Footner, Col Foster Lake, 1881–1953, vol. V
Foott, Col Cecil Henry, 1876–1942, vol. IV
Foottet, Frederick Francis, *died* 1935, vol. III
Forain, Jean Louis, 1852–1931, vol. III
Forber, Sir Edward Rodolph, 1878–1960, vol. V
Forber, Janet Elizabeth, (Lady Forber), 1877–1967, vol. VI
Forbes, 19th Lord, 1829–1914, vol. I
Forbes, 20th (styled 21st) Lord, 1841–1916, vol. II
Forbes, 21st (styled 22nd) Lord, 1882–1953, vol. V
Forbes, Alexander, 1860–1942, vol. IV
Forbes, Archibald, 1838–1900, vol. I
Forbes, Sir Archibald Finlayson, 1903–1989, vol. VIII
Forbes, Archibald Jones, 1873–1901, vol. I
Forbes, Arthur, 1843–1919, vol. II

Forbes, Maj.-Gen. Arthur, 1869–1930, vol. III

Forbes, Arthur C., 1866–1950, vol. IV

Forbes, Arthur Harold, 1885–1967, vol. VI

Forbes, Hon. Brig.-Gen. Sir Arthur William, 1858–1935, vol. III

Forbes, Athol; see Phillips, Rev. Forbes Alexander.

Forbes, Lt-Col Atholl Murray Hay, 1870–1942, vol. IV

Forbes, Lt-Col Hon. Bertram Aloysius, 1882–1960, vol. V

Forbes of Pitsligo, Sir Charles Edward Stuart-, 12th Bt, 1903–1985, vol. VIII

Forbes, Charles Harington Gordon, 1896–1982, vol. VIII

Forbes of Pitsligo, Sir Charles Hay Hepburn Stuart-, 10th Bt (cr 1626), 1871–1927, vol. II

Forbes, Admiral of the Fleet Sir Charles Morton, 1880–1960, vol. V

Forbes, Sir Charles Stewart, 5th Bt (cr 1823), 1867–1927, vol. II

Forbes of Callendar, Charles William, 1871–1948, vol. IV

Forbes, Sir Courtenay; see Forbes, Sir V. C. W.

Forbes, Daniel, born 1853, vol. II

Forbes, Bt Col Hon. Donald Alexander, 1880–1938, vol. III

Forbes, Sir Douglas Stuart, 1890–1973, vol. VII

Forbes, Rev. Edward Archibald, 1869–1929, vol. III

Forbes, Elizabeth Adela, 1859–1912, vol. I

Forbes, Esther, died 1967, vol. VI

Forbes, Lt-Col Frederick William Dempster, 1883–1957, vol. V

Forbes, George, 1849–1936, vol. III

Forbes, Sir George Arthur D. Ogilvie-, 1891–1954, vol. V

Forbes, Sir George Stuart, 1849–1940, vol. III

Forbes, Lt-Gen. George Wentworth, 1820–1907, vol. I

Forbes, Rt Hon. George William, 1869–1947, vol. IV

Forbes, Gilbert, 1908–1986, vol. VIII

Forbes, Gordon Stewart Drummond, 1868–1915, vol. I

Forbes, Most Rev. Mgr Guillaume, 1865–1940, vol. III

Forbes, Harry, 1866–1937, vol. III

Forbes, Lady Helen Emily, 1874–1926, vol. II

Forbes, Henry Ogg, 1851–1932, vol. III

Forbes, Hon. Sir Hugh Harry Valentine, 1917–1985, vol. VIII

Forbes of Pitsligo, Sir Hugh Stuart-, 11th Bt (cr 1626), 1896–1937, vol. III

Forbes, Ian Alexander, 1915–1986, vol. VIII

Forbes, Col Ian Rose-Innes Joseph, 1875–1957, vol. V

Forbes, James, 1862–1919, vol. II

Forbes, James Graham, 1873–1941, vol. IV

Forbes, James Wright, 1866–1947, vol. IV

Forbes, (Joan) Rosita, (Mrs Arthur T. McGrath), died 1967, vol. VI

Forbes, John, 1838–1904, vol. I

Forbes, Gen. Sir John, 1817–1906, vol. I

Forbes, John Colin, 1846–1925, vol. II

Forbes, Lt-Col John Foster, 1835–1914, vol. I

Forbes, Col John Greenlaw, 1837–1910, vol. I

Forbes, Lt-Comdr John Hay, 1906–1940, vol. III(A), vol. IV

Forbes, John Houblon, 1852–1935, vol. III

Forbes, Col Sir John Stewart, 6th Bt, 1901–1984, vol. VIII

Forbes, Rev. John T., 1857–1936, vol. III

Forbes, Air Chief Comdt Dame Katherine Jane Trefusis; see Watson-Watt, Air Chief Comdt Dame K. J. T.

Forbes, Mansfield Duval, 1889–1936, vol. III

Forbes, Nevil, 1883–1929, vol. III

Forbes, Captain Hon. Reginald George Benedict, 1877–1908, vol. I

Forbes, Robert Brown, 1912–1989, vol. VIII

Forbes, Robert Jaffrey, 1878–1958, vol. V

Forbes, Col Ronald Foster, 1881–1936, vol. III

Forbes, Rosita; see Forbes, J. R.

Forbes, Stanhope Alexander, 1857–1947, vol. IV

Forbes, Sir (Victor) Courtenay (Walter), 1889–1958, vol. V

Forbes, Hon. Mrs Walter (Eveline Louisa Michell), 1866–1924, vol. II

Forbes, William, 1833–1914, vol. I

Forbes, Sir William, 1856–1936, vol. III

Forbes, William Alfred Beaumont, 1927–1981, vol. VIII

Forbes of Pitsligo, Sir William Stuart, 9th Bt (cr 1626), 1835–1906, vol. I

Forbes, Brig.-Gen. Willoughby Edward Gordon, 1851–1926, vol. II

Forbes-Cockell, Seton, 1927–1971, vol. VII

Forbes-Leith of Fyvie, Col Sir Charles Rosdew, 1st Bt, 1859–1930, vol. III

Forbes-Leith of Fyvie, Sir Ian; see Forbes-Leith of Fyvie, Sir R. I. A.

Forbes-Leith of Fyvie, Sir (Robert) Ian (Algernon), 2nd Bt, 1902–1973, vol. VII

Forbes-Robertson, Col James, 1884–1955, vol. V

Forbes-Robertson, Jean, 1905–1962, vol. VI

Forbes-Robertson, John, 1822–1903, vol. I

Forbes-Robertson, Sir Johnston, 1853–1937, vol. III

Forbes-Sempill, Major Hon. Douglas, 1865–1908, vol. I

Forbes-Trefusis, Hon. Henry Walter Hepburn-Stuart-; see Trefusis.

Forbes-Trefusis, Major Hon. John Frederick Hepburn-Stuart-; see Trefusis.

Ford, Ven. A. Lockett, 1853–1945, vol. IV

Ford, Col Arthur, 1834–1913, vol. I

Ford, Arthur Clow, died 1952, vol. V

Ford, Maj.-Gen. Barnett, died 1907, vol. I

Ford, Col Sir Bertram, 1869–1955, vol. V

Ford, Charles, 1844–1927, vol. II

Ford, Lt-Col Charles Hopewell, 1864–1950, vol. IV

Ford, Cdre Charles Musgrave, 1887–1974, vol. VII

Ford, Rt Hon. Sir Clare; see Ford, Rt Hon. Sir F. C.

Ford, Vice-Adm. Sir Denys Chester, 1890–1967, vol. VI

Ford, Edmund Brisco, 1901–1988, vol. VIII

Ford, Sir Edward, 1902–1986, vol. VIII

Ford, Edward Onslow, 1852–1901, vol. I

Ford, Ernest A. C., 1858–1919, vol. II

Ford, Rev. Ernest Robert, 1863–1942, vol. IV

Ford, Ford Madox, 1873–1939, vol. III

Ford, Sir (Francis Charles) Rupert, 5th Bt, 1877–1948, vol. IV

Ford, Rt Hon. Sir (Francis) Clare, 1830–1899, vol. I

Ford, Hon. Frank, 1873–1965, vol. VI

Ford, Ven. Frank Edward, 1902–1976, vol. VII

Ford, Col Frederick Samuel Lampson, 1869–1944, vol. IV

Ford, Rev. Gabriel Estwick, vol. II

Ford, Brig. Geoffrey Noel, 1883–1964, vol. VI

Ford, Ven. George Adam, *died* 1930, vol. III

Ford, Rev. George Paget, 1883–1950, vol. IV

Ford, Henry, 1863–1947, vol. IV

Ford, Henry, II, 1917–1987, vol. VIII

Ford, Henry Justice, 1860–1941, vol. IV

Ford, Sir Henry Russell, 2nd Bt, 1911–1989, vol. VIII

Ford, Air Vice-Marshal Howard, 1905–1986, vol. VIII

Ford, Hugh Alexander, 1885–1966, vol. VI

Ford, Isaac N., 1848–1912, vol. I

Ford, Sir James, 1863–1943, vol. IV

Ford, Jeremiah Denis Matthias, 1873–1958, vol. V

Ford, John, *died* 1917, vol. II

Ford, John, (Sean O'Feeney), 1895–1973, vol. VII

Ford, Maj.-Gen. John Randle Minshull-, 1881–1948, vol. IV

Ford, Sir Leslie Ewart, 1897–1981, vol. VIII

Ford, Very Rev. Lionel George Bridges Justice, 1865–1932, vol. III

Ford, Sir Patrick Johnstone, 1st Bt, 1880–1945, vol. IV

Ford, Paul Leicester, 1865–1902, vol. I

Ford, Percy, 1894–1983, vol. VIII

Ford, Maj.-Gen. Sir Peter St C.; *see* St Clair-Ford.

Ford, Maj.-Gen. Sir Reginald, 1868–1951, vol. V

Ford, Gen. Sir Richard Vernon Tredinnick, 1878–1949, vol. IV

Ford, Surg.-Gen. Sir Richard William, 1857–1925, vol. II

Ford, Sir Rupert; *see* Ford, Sir F. C. R.

Ford, Sir Sidney William George, 1909–1983, vol. VIII

Ford, Sir Theodore Thomas, 1829–1920, vol. II

Ford, Brig. Vincent Tennyson Randle, 1885–1957, vol. V

Ford, Walter Armitage Justice, 1861–1938, vol. III

Ford, Adm. Sir Wilbraham Tennyson Randle, 1880–1964, vol. VI

Ford, William, 1821–1905, vol. I

Ford, William Justice, 1853–1904, vol. I

Ford, Worthington Chauncey, 1858–1941, vol. IV

Ford-Hutchinson, Lt-Col George Higginson, 1863–1933, vol. III

Forde, Lt-Col Bernard, 1865–1939, vol. III

Forde, Daryll, 1902–1973, vol. VII

Forde, Rt Hon. Francis Michael, 1890–1983, vol. VIII

Forde, Sir Henry J., 1863–1929, vol. III

Forde, Rev. Hugh, *died* 1929, vol. III

Forde, Col Lionel, 1860–1926, vol. II

Forde, Rt Hon. William Brownlow, 1823–1902, vol I

Forder, Rev. Frank George, 1883–1930, vol. III

Forder, Henry George, 1889–1981, vol. VIII

Fordham, Sir (Alfred) Stanley, 1907–1981, vol. VIII

Fordham, Edward Snow, 1858–1919, vol. II

Fordham, Sir George; *see* Fordham, Sir H. G.

Fordham, Sir (Herbert) George, 1854–1929, vol. III

Fordham, Montague Edward, 1864–1948, vol. IV

Fordham, Lt-Col Reginald Sydney Walter, 1897–1976, vol. VII

Fordham, Sir Stanley; *see* Fordham, Sir A. S.

Fordham, Wilfrid Gurney, 1902–1988, vol. VIII

Fordham, Brig. William Marshall, 1875–1959, vol. V

Fordyce, Alexander D.; *see* Dingwall-Fordyce.

Fordyce, Catherine Mary, 1898–1983, vol. VIII

Fordyce, Christian James, 1901–1974, vol. VII

Forecast, Kenneth George, 1925–1988, vol. VIII

Foreman, Carl, 1914–1984, vol. VIII

Foreman, Sir Henry, 1852–1924, vol. II

Foreman, James Kenneth, 1928–1980, vol. VII

Forest Smith, John, *died* 1973, vol. VII

Forester, 5th Baron, 1842–1917, vol. II

Forester, 6th Baron, 1867–1932, vol. III

Forester, 7th Baron, 1899–1977, vol. VII

Forester, Cecil Scott, 1899–1966, vol. VI

Forester, Hon. Charles Cecil Orlando Weld-, 1869–1937, vol. III

Forester, Major Hon. Edric Alfred Cecil Weld-, 1880–1963, vol. VI

Forester, Francis William, 1860–1942, vol. IV

Forester, Lt-Comdr Wolstan Beaumont Charles W.; *see* Weld-Forester.

Forestier, Amédée, *died* 1930, vol. III

Forestier-Walker, Sir (Charles) Leolin, 1st Bt, 1866–1934, vol. III

Forestier-Walker, Lt-Col Claude Edward; *see* Walker.

Forestier-Walker, Sir Clive Radzivill; *see* Walker.

Forestier-Walker, Gen. Sir Frederick William Edward Forestier; *see* Walker.

Forestier-Walker, Sir George Ferdinand; *see* Walker.

Forestier-Walker, Major Sir George Ferdinand; *see* Walker.

Forestier-Walker, Maj.-Gen. Sir George Townshend; *see* Walker.

Forestier-Walker, Sir Leolin; *see* Forestier-Walker, Sir C. L.

Forestier-Walker, Bt-Col Roland Stuart; *see* Walker.

Forgan, Very Rev. James Rae, 1876–1966, vol. VI

Forgan, Robert, 1891–1976, vol. VII

Forget, Sir Guy Joseph, 1902–1972, vol. VII

Forget, Sir (Joseph David) Rodolphe, 1861–1919, vol. II

Forget, Sir Rodolphe; *see* Forget, Sir J. D. R.

Forman, Rev. Adam, 1876–1977, vol. VII

Forman, Brig.-Gen. Arthur Baron, 1873–1951, vol. V

Forman, Lt-Col Douglas Evans, 1872–1949, vol. IV

Forman, E. Baxter, *died* 1925, vol. II

Forman, Harry Buxton, 1842–1917, vol. II

Forman, Brig. James Francis Robert, 1899–1969, vol. VI

Forman, John Calder, 1884–1975, vol. VII

Forman, Justus Miles, 1875–1915, vol. I

Forman, Louis, 1901–1988, vol. VIII

Forman, Rev. Thomas Pears Gordon, 1885–1965, vol. VI

Forman Hardy, Col Thomas Eben, 1919–1989, vol. VIII

Formby, George, 1904–1961, vol. VI

Formilli, Cesare T. G., *died* 1942, vol. IV
Formosa, Mgr Canon John, 1869–1941, vol. IV
Forneret, Ven. George Augustus, *died* 1927, vol. II, vol. III
Forrer, Ludwig, 1845–1921, vol. II
Forres, 1st Baron, 1860–1931, vol. III
Forres, 2nd Baron, 1888–1954, vol. V
Forres, 3rd Baron, 1922–1978, vol. VII
Forrest, 1st Baron, 1847–1918, vol. II
Forrest, Andrew Bryson, 1884–1951, vol. V
Forrest, Archibald Stevenson, 1869–1963, vol. VI
Forrest, Sir Charles, 5th Bt, 1857–1928, vol. II
Forrest, Major Charles Evelyn, 1876–1915, vol. I
Forrest, Rev. David William, *died* 1918, vol. II
Forrest, George, 1922–1968, vol. VI
Forrest, Col George Atherley William, 1846–1904, vol. I
Forrest, George Topham, *died* 1945, vol. IV
Forrest, Sir George William, 1846–1926, vol. II
Forrest, Gilbert Alexander, 1912–1977, vol. VII
Forrest, Sir James, 4th Bt, 1853–1899, vol. I
Forrest, Lt-Col James, 1859–1939, vol. III
Forrest, Col John Vincent, 1873–1953, vol. V
Forrest, Sir John William, 1867–1951, vol. V
Forrest, Richard Haddow, 1908–1977, vol. VII
Forrest, Robert Edward Treston, *died* 1914, vol. I
Forrest, Very Rev. Robert William, *died* 1908, vol. I
Forrest, Sir Walter, 1869–1939, vol. III
Forrest, Lt-Col William, 1868–1921, vol. II
Forrest, Rev. William, 1867–1936, vol. III
Forrest, Gen. William Charles, 1819–1902, vol. I
Forrest, Sir William Croft, *died* 1928, vol. II
Forrestal, James, 1892–1949, vol. IV
Forrester, Charles, 1895–1980, vol. VII
Forrester, Rev. Canon John Charles, 1874–1933, vol. III
Forrester, Joseph, 1871–1967, vol. VI
Forrester, Peter, 1864–1941, vol. IV
Forrester, Rev. William Roxburgh, 1892–1984, vol. VIII
Forrester-Brown, Maud Frances, *died* 1970, vol. VI
Forrow, Air Cdre Henry Edward, *died* 1959, vol. V
Forsdyke, Sir (Edgar) John, 1883–1979, vol. VII
Forsdyke, Sir John; *see* Forsdyke, Sir E. J.
Forsey, Charles Benjamin, 1819–1908, vol. I
Forsey, George Frank, 1889–1974, vol. VII
Forsey, Sir John, 1856–1915, vol. I
Forshaw, John Henry, 1895–1973, vol. VII
Forshaw, Thomas, 1888–1976, vol. VII
Forson, A. J., 1872–1950, vol. IV(A)
Forssmann, Werner Theodor Otto, 1904–1979, vol. VII
Forster, 1st Baron, 1866–1936, vol. III
Forster, Lady; (Rachel Cecily), 1868–1962, vol. VI
Forster of Harraby, 1st Baron, 1888–1972, vol. VII
Forster, Lt-Gen. Alfred Leonard, *died* 1963, vol. VI
Forster, Arnold John, 1885–1968, vol. VI
Forster, Very Rev. Arthur Newburgh H.; *see* Haire-Forster.
Forster, Lt-Gen. Bowes Lennox, 1837–1919, vol. II
Forster, Sir Charles, 2nd Bt (*cr* 1874), 1841–1914, vol. I
Forster, Brig. David, 1878–1959, vol. V
Forster, Edward Morgan, 1879–1970, vol. VI
Forster, Edward Seymour, 1879–1950, vol. IV
Forster, Rear-Adm. Forster Delafield A.; *see* Arnold-Forster.
Forster, Major Francis Anson A.; *see* Arnold-Forster.
Forster, Sir (Francis) Villiers, 3rd Bt (*cr* 1874), 1850–1930, vol. III
Forster, Lt-Col George Norman Bowes, 1872–1918, vol. II
Forster, Rear-Adm. Herbert Acheson, *died* 1975, vol. VII
Forster, Comdr Hugh Christopher A.; *see* Arnold-Forster.
Forster, Rt Hon. Hugh Oakeley A.; *see* Arnold-Forster.
Forster, Maj.-Gen. John Burton, 1855–1938, vol. III
Forster, John Wycliffe Lowes, *died* 1938, vol. III
Forster, Lancelot, 1882–1968, vol. VI
Forster, Sir Martin Onslow, 1872–1945, vol. IV
Forster, Lady Mary Louise Elizabeth; *see* Hamilton and Brandon, Duchess of.
Förster, Max Theodor Wilhelm, 1869–1954, vol. V
Forster, Sir Ralph Collingwood, 1st Bt (*cr* 1912), 1850–1930, vol. III
Forster, Ralph George Elliott, 1865–1931, vol. III
Forster, Sir Robert, 4th Bt (*cr* 1794), 1827–1904, vol. I
Forster, Robert Henry, 1867–1923, vol. II
Forster, Sir Sadler; *see* Forster, Sir S. A. S.
Forster, Sir (Samuel Alexander) Sadler, 1900–1973, vol. VII
Forster, Sir Samuel John, 1873–1940, vol. III
Forster, Sir Thomas Edwards, 1859–1939, vol. III
Forster, Sir Villiers; *see* Forster, Sir F. V.
Forster, Walter Leslie, 1903–1985, vol. VIII
Forster, Maj.-Gen. William Charles Hughan, 1874–1939, vol. III
Forster, Rev. William Thomlinson, *died* 1929, vol. III
Forster-Cooper, Sir Clive, 1880–1947, vol. IV
Forsyth, Andrew Russell, 1858–1942, vol. IV
Forsyth, Ven. David, 1845–1933, vol. III
Forsyth, David, 1877–1941, vol. IV
Forsyth, Lt-Col Frederick Richard Gerrard, 1882–1962, vol. VI
Forsyth, Gordon M., 1879–1952, vol. V
Forsyth, Ian McMillan, 1892–1969, vol. VI
Forsyth, James Alexander, 1921–1968, vol. VI
Forsyth, Lt-Col James Archibald Charteris, 1877–1922, vol. II
Forsyth, John Andrew Cairns, 1876–1935, vol. III
Forsyth, Maj.-Gen. John Keatly, 1867–1928, vol. II
Forsyth, Neil, 1866–1915, vol. I
Forsyth, Rev. Peter Taylor, 1848–1921, vol. II
Forsyth, Robert Sutherland, 1880–1942, vol. IV
Forsyth, Thomas Miller, 1871–1958, vol. V
Forsyth, William, 1812–1899, vol. I
Forsyth, Major William Henry, 1882–1929, vol. III
Forsyth-Thompson, Aubrey Denzil, 1897–1982, vol. VIII
Fort, George Seymour, 1858–1951, vol. V
Fort, Sir Hugh, 1862–1919, vol. II
Fort, Richard, 1856–1918, vol. II
Fort, Richard, 1907–1959, vol. V

Forte, Major Herbert Augustus Nourse, 1868–1938, vol. III

Forter, Alexis Kougoulsky, 1925–1983, vol. VIII

Fortes, Meyer, 1906–1983, vol. VIII

Fortescue, 3rd Earl, 1818–1905, vol. I

Fortescue, 4th Earl, 1854–1932, vol. III

Fortescue, 5th Earl, 1888–1958, vol. V

Fortescue, 6th Earl, 1893–1977, vol. VII

Fortescue, Rev. Adrian, 1874–1923, vol. II

Fortescue, Col Archer I.; see Irvine-Fortescue.

Fortescue, Cecil Lewis, 1881–1949, vol. IV

Fortescue, Brig.-Gen. Hon. Charles Granville, 1861–1951, vol. V

Fortescue, Hon. Dudley Francis, 1820–1909, vol. I

Fortescue, Brig.-Gen. Francis Alexander, 1858–1942, vol. IV

Fortescue, George Knottesford, 1847–1912, vol. I

Fortescue, John Bevill, 1850–1938, vol. III

Fortescue, Hon. Sir John William, 1859–1933, vol. III

Fortescue, Laurence Knottesford-, 1845–1924, vol. II

Fortescue, Captain Hon. Sir Seymour John, 1856–1942, vol. IV

Fortescue, Rev. Vincent, 1849–1932, vol. III

Fortescue, Hon. Lady; (Winifred), 1888–1951, vol. V

Fortescue-Brickdale, Sir Charles, 1857–1944, vol. IV

Fortescue-Brickdale, Eleanor, died 1945, vol. IV

Fortescue-Brickdale, John Matthew, died 1921, vol. II

Fortescue-Flannery, Sir James, 1st Bt, 1851–1943, vol. IV

Forteviot, 1st Baron, 1856–1929, vol. III

Forteviot, 2nd Baron, 1885–1947, vol. IV

Forth, Francis Charles, died 1919, vol. II

Forth, Lt-Col Nowell Barnard De Lancey; see De Lancey Forth.

Fortin, Ven. Octave, 1842–1927, vol. II

Fortington, Harold Augustus, 1890–1944, vol. IV

Fortnum, Charles Drury Edward, 1820–1899, vol. I

Fortune, Allan Stewart, 1895–1975, vol. VII

Fortune, Maj.-Gen. Sir Victor Morven, 1883–1949, vol. IV

Forty, Francis John, 1900–1990, vol. VIII

Forward, Ernest Alfred, 1877–1959, vol. V

Forwood, Rt Hon. Sir Arthur Bower, 1st Bt, 1836–1898, vol. I

Forwood, Sir Dudley Baines, 2nd Bt, 1875–1961, vol. VI

Forwood, Sir William Bower, 1840–1928, vol. II

Fosbery, Hon. Edmund Walcott, 1834–1919, vol. II

Fosbery, Lt-Col George Vincent, died 1907, vol. I

Fosbery, Major Widenham Francis Widenham, 1869–1935, vol. III

Fosbrooke, Ven. Henry Leonard, died 1950, vol. IV

Fosdick, Rev. Harry Emerson, 1878–1969, vol. VI

Fosdick, Raymond Blaine, 1883–1969, vol. VI

Foskett, Rt Rev. Reginald, 1909–1973, vol. VII

Foss, Brig. Charles Calveley, 1885–1953, vol. V

Foss, Hubert James, 1899–1953, vol. V

Foss, Rt Rev. Hugh James, 1848–1932, vol. III

Foster, Sir (Albert) Ridgeby, 1907–1973, vol. VII

Foster, Alfred Edye Manning, died 1939, vol. III

Foster, Col Alfred James, 1864–1959, vol. V

Foster, Captain Alwyn, 1874–1953, vol. V

Foster, Rev. Arthur Austin, 1869–1942, vol. IV

Foster, Lt-Col Arthur Wellesley, 1855–1929, vol. III

Foster, Sir Augustus Vere, 4th Bt (cr 1831), 1873–1947, vol. IV

Foster, Sir Berkeley; see Foster, Sir H. W. B.

Foster, Birket, 1825–1899, vol. I

Foster, Rev. Canon Charles, 1907–1972, vol. VII

Foster, Rev. Charles Wilmer, 1866–1935, vol. III

Foster, Sir Clement Le Neve, 1841–1904, vol. I

Foster, Captain Sir Edward, 1881–1958, vol. V

Foster, Edward William Perceval, 1850–1932, vol. III

Foster, Ernest, died 1919, vol. II

Foster, Very Rev. Ernest, 1867–1925, vol. II

Foster, E(rnest) Marshall, 1907–1970, vol. VI

Foster, F(ermian) Le Neve, 1888–1972, vol. VII

Foster, Francis; see Foster, Major R. F.

Foster, Sir Frank Savin, 1879–1964, vol. VI

Foster, Geoffrey Norman, 1884–1971, vol. VII

Foster, George Carey, 1835–1919, vol. II

Foster, Rt Hon. Sir George Eulas, 1847–1931, vol. III

Foster, Hon. George G., 1860–1931, vol. III

Foster, George Ralph Cunliffe, 1869–1936, vol. III

Foster, Gilbert, 1855–1906, vol. I

Foster, Maj.-Gen. Gilbert Lafayette, 1874–1940, vol. III

Foster, Gordon Bentley, 1885–1963, vol. VI

Foster, Sir Gregory; see Foster, Sir T. G.

Foster, Lt-Col Harold William Alexander, died 1960, vol. V

Foster, Rt Hon. Sir Harry Braustyn Hylton H.; see Hylton-Foster.

Foster, Sir Harry Seymour, 1855–1938, vol. III

Foster, Maj.-Gen. Henry Nedham, 1878–1951, vol. V

Foster, Sir (Henry William) Berkeley, 4th Bt (cr 1838), 1892–1960, vol. V

Foster, Herbert Anderton, 1853–1930, vol. III

Foster, Rev. Herbert Charles, died 1926, vol. II

Foster, Rev. Canon Herbert Henry, 1864–1927, vol. II

Foster, Sir Hugh Matheson, 1886–1955, vol. V

Foster, Sir Idris Llewelyn, 1911–1984, vol. VIII

Foster, Ivor, 1870–1959, vol. V

Foster, Rev. James, died 1926, vol. II

Foster, John, 1832–1910, vol. I

Foster, Rev. John, 1898–1973, vol. VII

Foster, John Frederick, 1903–1975, vol. VII

Foster, Sir John Galway, 1904–1982, vol. VIII

Foster, Maj.-Gen. John Hulbert, 1925–1980, vol. VII

Foster, (John) Kenneth, died 1930, vol. III

Foster, John Stuart, 1890–1964, vol. VI

Foster, John Watson, 1836–1917, vol. II

Foster, Joseph, 1844–1905, vol. I

Foster, Joshua James, died 1923, vol. II

Foster, Kenneth; see Foster, J. K.

Foster, Leslie Thomas, 1905–1979, vol. VII

Foster, Sir Michael, 1836–1907, vol. I

Foster, Michael George, 1864–1934, vol. III

Foster, Major Montagu Amos, 1861–1940, vol. III

Foster, Sir Montagu Richard William, died 1935, vol. III

Foster, Muriel, died 1937, vol. III

Foster, Sir Norris Tildasley, 1855–1925, vol. II

Foster, Major Percy John, 1873–1969, vol. VI

Foster, Sir Peter Harry Batson Woodroffe, 1912–1985, vol. VIII

Foster, Philip Stanley, 1885–1965, vol. VI

Foster, Philip Staveley, 1865–1933, vol. III
Foster, Major Reginald Francis, 1896–1975, vol. VII
Foster, Gen. Sir Richard Foster Carter, 1879–1965, vol. VI
Foster, Hon. Richard Witty, 1856–1932, vol. III
Foster, Sir Ridgeby; see Foster, Sir A. R.
Foster, Robert, 1898–1989, vol. VIII
Foster, Robert Frederick, 1853–1945, vol. IV
Foster, Robert John, 1850–1925, vol. II
Foster, Air Chief Marshal Sir Robert Mordaunt, 1898–1973, vol. VII
Foster, Robert Spence, 1891–1947, vol. IV
Foster, Sidney, 1885–1958, vol. V
Foster, Brig. Thomas Francis Vere, 1885–1967, vol. VI
Foster, Sir (Thomas) Gregory, 1st Bt (cr 1930), died 1931, vol. III
Foster, Thomas Henry, 1888–1970, vol. VI
Foster, Sir Thomas Saxby Gregory, 2nd Bt (cr 1930), 1899–1957, vol. V
Foster, Sir Tom Scott, 1845–1918, vol. II
Foster, Brig.-Gen. Turville Douglas, 1865–1915, vol. I
Foster, Vere Henry Lewis, 1819–1900, vol. I
Foster, Major Wilfrid Lionel, 1874–1958, vol. V
Foster, Sir William, 2nd Bt (cr 1838), 1825–1911, vol. I
Foster, William, 1887–1947, vol. IV
Foster, Sir William, 1863–1951, vol. V
Foster, Sir William Edward, 1846–1921, vol. II
Foster, Air Vice-Marshal William Foster Mac-Neece, 1889–1978, vol. VII
Foster, Col William Henry, 1848–1908, vol. I
Foster, William Henry, 1846–1924, vol. II
Foster, Bt-Col William James, 1881–1927, vol. II
Foster, Maj.-Gen. William Wasbrough, died 1954, vol. V
Foster, Sir William Yorke, 3rd Bt (cr 1838), 1860–1948, vol. IV
Foster Pegg, Rev. Canon Henry, 1857–1940, vol. III
Foster-Skeffington, Hon. Oriel John Clotworthy Whyte-Melville; see Skeffington.
Foster-Vesey-Fitzgerald, James; see Fitzgerald.
Fothergill, (Arthur) Brian, 1921–1990, vol. VIII
Fothergill, Brian; see Fothergill, A. B.
Fothergill, (Charles) Philip, 1906–1959, vol. V
Fothergill, John Rowland, 1876–1957, vol. V
Fothergill, Philip; see Fothergill, C. P.
Fothergill, William Edward, 1865–1926, vol. II
Fotheringham, Rev. David Ross, 1872–1939, vol. III
Fotheringham, John Knight, 1874–1936, vol. III
Fotheringham, John Taylor, 1860–1940, vol. III(A), vol. IV
Fothringham, Walter Thomas James S.; see Scrymsoure-Steuart-Fothringham.
Fottrell, Sir George, 1849–1925, vol. II
Fouché, Jacobus Johannes, 1898–1980, vol. VII
Fouché, Leo, 1880–1949, vol. IV
Fougasse, see Bird, C. K.
Fouhy, David Emmet, 1891–1967, vol. VI
Foulds, John H., died 1939, vol. III
Foulds, Linton Harry, 1897–1952, vol. V
Foulerton, Alexander Grant Russell, 1863–1931, vol. III

Foulger, Robert Edward, 1899–1969, vol. VI
Foulis, Sir Archibald Charles Liston, 12th Bt, 1903–1961, vol. VI
Foulis, Sir Charles Liston, 11th Bt, 1873–1936, vol. III
Foulis, Douglas Ainslie, 1885–1969, vol. VI
Foulis, Sir William Liston-, 10th Bt, 1869–1918, vol. II
Foulkes, Gen. Charles, 1903–1969, vol. VI
Foulkes, Maj.-Gen. Charles Howard, 1875–1969, vol. VI
Foulkes, Hedworth; see Foulkes, P. H.
Foulkes, P. Hedworth, 1871–1965, vol. VI
Foulkes, Maj.-Gen. Thomas Herbert Fisher, 1908–1986, vol. VIII
Foulsham, Sir Charles Sidney, 1892–1955, vol. V
Fountain, Sir Henry, 1870–1957, vol. V
Fountaine, Vice-Adm. Charles Andrew, 1879–1946, vol. IV
Fournier, Pierre, 1906–1986, vol. VIII
Fournier d'Albe, Edmund Edward, 1868–1933, vol. III
Foweraker, A. Moulton, 1873–1942, vol. IV
Fowke, Frank Rede, 1847–1927, vol. II, vol. III
Fowke, Sir Frederick Ferrers Conant, 3rd Bt, 1879–1948, vol. IV
Fowke, Sir Frederick Thomas, 2nd Bt, 1816–1897, vol. I
Fowke, Sir Frederick Woollaston Rawdon, 4th Bt, 1910–1987, vol. VIII
Fowke, Lt-Gen. Sir George Henry, 1864–1936, vol. III
Fowke, Villiers Loftus Philip, 1887–1940, vol. III
Fowkes, Maj.-Gen. Charles Christopher, 1894–1966, vol. VI
Fowlds, Hon. Sir George, 1860–1934, vol. III
Fowle, Brig. Francis Ernlé, 1893–1969, vol. VI
Fowle, Col Frederick Trenchard Thomas, 1853–1914, vol. I
Fowle, Col Sir (Henry) Walter Hamilton, 1871–1954, vol. V
Fowle, Col John, 1862–1923, vol. II
Fowle, Brig. John Le Clerc, 1893–1978, vol. VII
Fowle, Col Thomas Ernlé, 1862–1932, vol. III
Fowle, Sir Trenchard Craven William, 1884–1940, vol. III
Fowle, Col Sir Walter Hamilton; see Fowle, Col Sir H. W. H.
Fowler, Alfred, 1868–1940, vol. III
Fowler, Maj.-Gen. Charles Astley, 1865–1940, vol. III
Fowler, Lt Charles Wilson, 1859–1907, vol. I
Fowler, Adm. Cole Cortlandt, died 1936, vol. III
Fowler, Lt-Col Edward Gardiner, 1879–1953, vol. V
Fowler, Hon. Ellen Thorneycroft, died 1929, vol. III
Fowler, Maj.-Gen. Francis John, 1864–1939, vol. III
Fowler, Frank James, 1911–1981, vol. VIII
Fowler, George Herbert, 1861–1940, vol. III
Fowler, Sir George Jefford, 1858–1937, vol. III
Fowler, George Merrick, 1852–1935, vol. III
Fowler, Harold North, 1859–1955, vol. V
Fowler, Sir Henry, 1870–1938, vol. III
Fowler, Henry Watson, 1858–1933, vol. III
Fowler, Sir James Kingston, 1852–1934, vol. III

Fowler, James Stewart, 1870–1925, vol. II
Fowler, Sir John, 1st Bt (cr 1890), 1817–1898, vol. I
Fowler, Sir John Arthur, 2nd Bt (cr 1890), 1854–1899, vol. I
Fowler, Sir John Edward, 3rd Bt (cr 1890), 1885–1915, vol. I
Fowler, Lt-Gen. Sir John Sharman, 1864–1939, vol. III
Fowler, Rev. Joseph Thomas, 1833–1924, vol. II
Fowler, Matthew, 1845–1898, vol. I
Fowler, Rev. Sir Montague, 4th Bt (cr 1890), 1858–1933, vol. III
Fowler, Sir Ralph Howard, 1889–1944, vol. IV
Fowler, Rees John, 1894–1974, vol. VII
Fowler, Robert, died 1926, vol. II
Fowler, Robert MacLaren, 1906–1980, vol. VII
Fowler, Sir Robert William Doughty, 1914–1985, vol. VIII
Fowler, Sir Thomas, 2nd Bt (cr 1885), 1868–1902, vol. I
Fowler, Rev. Thomas, 1832–1904, vol. I
Fowler, Walter B.; see Burroughs-Fowler.
Fowler, William, 1828–1905, vol. I
Fowler, William Hope, 1876–1933, vol. III
Fowler, William Warde, 1847–1921, vol. II
Fowler, Rev. William Weekes, 1849–1923, vol. II
Fowler-Butler, Lt-Col Richard, 1865–1931, vol. III
Fowler-Butler, Maj.-Gen. Robert Henry, 1838–1919, vol. II
Fowler-Dixon, John Edwin, 1850–1943, vol. IV
Fowweather, Frank Scott, 1892–1980, vol. VII
Fox, Rev. Canon Adam, 1883–1977, vol. VII
Fox, Lt-Col Arthur Claude, 1868–1917, vol. II
Fox, Arthur Wilson, 1861–1909, vol. I
Fox, Ven. (Benjamin) George (Burton), 1913–1978, vol. VII
Fox, Bernard Joshua, 1885–1977, vol. VII
Fox, Major Brabazon Hubert Maine, 1868–1940, vol. III
Fox, Rear-Adm. Cecil Henry, 1873–1963, vol. VI
Fox, Captain Charles, 1890–1977, vol. VII
Fox, Sir (Charles) Douglas, 1840–1921, vol. II
Fox, Sir Charles Edmund, 1854–1918, vol. II
Fox, Lt-Col Charles J., 1857–1930, vol. III
Fox, Major Charles Vincent, 1877–1928, vol. II
Fox, Sir Cyril Fred, 1882–1967, vol. VI
Fox, Sir Cyril Sankey, 1886–1951, vol. V
Fox, Sir David S.; see Scott Fox, Sir R. D. J.
Fox, Sir Douglas; see Fox, Sir C. D.
Fox, Douglas Gerard Arthur, 1893–1978, vol. VII
Fox, Hon. Mrs Eleanor Birch W.; see Wilson-Fox.
Fox, Dame Evelyn Emily Marion, 1874–1955, vol. V
Fox, Felicity L.; see Lane-Fox.
Fox, Sir Francis, 1844–1927, vol. II
Fox, Col Francis Gordon Ward L.; see Lane Fox.
Fox, Sir Frank, 1874–1960, vol. V
Fox, Ven. George; see Fox, Ven. B. G. B.
Fox, Rev. George, died 1911, vol. I
Fox, Sir Gifford Wheaton Grey, 2nd Bt, 1903–1959, vol. V
Fox, Sir Gilbert Wheaton, 1st Bt, 1863–1925, vol. II
Fox, H. B. Earle, died 1920, vol. II
Fox, Harold Munro, 1889–1967, vol. VI
Fox, Sir Harry Halton, 1872–1936, vol. III

Fox, Henry Benedict, 1875–1944, vol. IV
Fox, Rev. Henry Elliott, 1841–1926, vol. II
Fox, Henry Wilson-, 1863–1921, vol. II
Fox, Sir John, 1882–1970, vol. VI
Fox, Sir John Charles, 1855–1943, vol. IV
Fox, Major John Charles Ker, 1851–1929, vol. III
Fox, John Howard, 1864–1951, vol. V
Fox, Sir John Jacob, 1874–1944, vol. IV
Fox, John Junior, 1863–1919, vol. II
Fox, Major Sir John St Vigor, 1879–1968, vol. VI
Fox, John Scott, 1852–1918, vol. II
Fox, John Shirley S.; see Shirley-Fox.
Fox, Joscelyn Plunket B.; see Bushe-Fox.
Fox, Sir Lionel Wray, 1895–1961, vol. VI
Fox, Loftus Henry Kendal B.; see Bushe-Fox.
Fox, Col Sir Malcolm, 1843–1918, vol. II
Fox, Patrick Loftus B.; see Bushe-Fox.
Fox, R. Fortescue, died 1940, vol. III
Fox, Richard Hodding, 1876–1966, vol. VI
Fox, Robert Barclay, 1873–1934, vol. III
Fox, Sir (Robert) David (John) S.; see Scott Fox.
Fox, Sir Robert Eyes, 1861–1924, vol. II
Fox, Brig.-Gen. Robert Fanshawe, 1862–1939, vol. III
Fox, Sir Sidney Joseph, died 1962, vol. VI
Fox, Terence Robert Corelli, 1912–1962, vol. VI
Fox, Sir Theodore Fortescue, 1899–1989, vol. VIII
Fox, Thomas Colcott, 1849–1916, vol. II
Fox, Rt Rev. Thomas Martin, 1893–1967, vol. VI(AII)
Fox, Surg.-Gen. Thomas William, 1830–1908, vol. I
Fox, Uffa, 1898–1972, vol. VII
Fox, Wilfrid S., died 1962, vol. VI
Fox, William Sherwood, 1878–1967, vol. VI
Fox-Andrews, Norman Roy, 1894–1971, vol. VII
Fox-Davies, Arthur Charles, 1871–1928, vol. II
Fox-Pitt, Douglas, died 1922, vol. II
Fox-Pitt, Maj.-Gen. William Augustus Fitzgerald Lane, 1896–1988, vol. VIII
Fox-Pitt-Rivers, Augustus Henry Lane, 1820–1900, vol. I
Fox-Strangways, Maurice Walter, 1862–1938, vol. III
Fox-Symons, Sir Robert, 1870–1932, vol. III
Fox-Williams, Jack, 1893–1970, vol. VI
Foxcroft, Captain Charles Talbot, died 1929, vol. III
Foxcroft, Frederick Walter, 1858–1916, vol. II
Foxcroft, Miss H. C., died 1950, vol. IV
Foxell, Rev. Maurice Frederic, 1888–1981, vol. VIII
Foxell, Rev. William James, 1857–1933, vol. III
Foxlee, Richard William, 1885–1961, vol. VI
Foxley, Barbara, died 1958, vol. V
Foxon, George Eric Howard, 1908–1982, vol. VIII
Foxton, Col Hon. Justin Fox Greenlaw, 1849–1916, vol. I, vol. II
Foxwell, Arthur, 1853–1909, vol. I
Foxwell, Herbert Somerton, 1849–1936, vol. III
Foy, Ernest Rudolph, died 1951, vol. V
Foy, Hon. James Joseph, 1847–1916, vol. II
Foy, Sir Thomas Arthur Wyness, 1895–1971, vol. VII
Foylan, Rt Rev. Michael, 1907–1976, vol. VII
Foyle, Gilbert Samuel, 1886–1971, vol. VII
Foyle, William Alfred, 1885–1963, vol. VI
Fraenkel, Eduard, 1888–1970, vol. VI
Fraenkel, Heinrich, 1897–1986, vol. VIII

Frames, Col Percival R.; *see* Ross-Frames.

Frampton, Algernon de Kewer, 1904–1974, vol. VII

Frampton, E. Reginald, *died* 1923, vol. II

Frampton, Sir George James, 1860–1928, vol. II

Frampton, Henry James, 1897–1980, vol. VII

Frampton, Meredith, 1894–1984, vol. VIII

Frampton, Rev. Samuel, 1862–1943, vol. IV

Frampton, Walter, 1871–1939, vol. III

Frampton, Walter Bennett, 1903–1981, vol. VIII

France, Anatole, (Jacques Anatole François Thibault), 1844–1924, vol. II

France, Captain George Frederick Hayhurst H.; *see* Hayhurst-France.

France, Gerald Ashburner, 1870–1935, vol. III

France, Rev. Canon Walter Frederick, 1887–1963, vol. VI

France-Hayhurst, William Hosken; *see* Hayhurst.

Francia, Col. John Lewis, 1864–1934, vol. III

Francillon, Robert Edward, 1841–1919, vol. II

Francis, (Alan) David, 1900–1987, vol. VIII

Francis, Alfred Edwin, 1909–1985, vol. VIII

Francis, Arthur Gordon, 1880–1958, vol. V

Francis, Augustus Lawrence, 1848–1925, vol. II

Francis, Sir Brooke; *see* Francis, Sir C. G. B.

Francis, Lt-Col Charles John Henry Watson, 1879–1959, vol. V

Francis, Charles King, 1851–1925, vol. II

Francis, Sir (Cyril Gerard) Brooke, 1883–1971, vol. VII

Francis, David; *see* Francis, A. D.

Francis, Francis, *died* 1941, vol. IV

Francis, Sir Frank Chalton, 1901–1988, vol. VIII

Francis, Grant Richardson, 1868–1940, vol. III(A), vol. IV

Francis, Very Rev. Henry, *died* 1924, vol. II

Francis, Herbert William Sidney, 1880–1968, vol. VI

Francis, Hugh Elvet, 1907–1986, vol. VIII

Francis, James Schreiber, 1843–1915, vol. I

Francis, Sir John, 1864–1937, vol. III

Francis, Major John, 1879–1960, vol. V

Francis, Lt-Col John Clement Wolstan, 1888–1978, vol. VII

Francis, John Collins, 1838–1916, vol. II

Francis, John Gordon Loveband, 1907–1976, vol. VII

Francis, Rt Rev. Joseph Marshall, 1862–1939, vol. III

Francis, Hon. Sir Josiah, 1890–1964, vol. VI

Francis, M. E.; *see* Blundell, Mrs F.

Francis, Major Norton, 1871–1939, vol. III

Francis, Richard Henry, 1897–1961, vol. VI

Francis, Brig.-Gen. Sidney Goodall, 1874–1955, vol. V

Francis-Williams, Baron (Life Peer); Edward Francis Williams, 1903–1970, vol. VI

Francis-Williams, William St John, 1871–1930, vol. III

Franck, Harry Alverson, 1881–1962, vol. VI

Franck, James, 1882–1964, vol. VI

Franck, Sir Louis, 1868–1937, vol. III

Francke, Paul Mortimer, 1866–1929, vol. III

Franckenstein, Sir George, 1878–1953, vol. V

Francklin, John Liell, 1844–1915, vol. I

Francklin, Captain Philip, 1874–1914, vol. I

Franco Bahamonde, General Don Francisco, 1892–1975, vol. VII

François-Poncet, André, 1887–1978, vol. VII

Franey, John Sharman, 1864–1947, vol. IV

Frangulis, A. F., 1888–1975, vol. VII

Frank, Bruno, 1887–1945, vol. IV

Frank, Glenn, 1887–1940, vol. III

Frank, Sir Howard, 1st Bt, 1871–1932, vol. III

Frank, Sir Howard Frederick, 2nd Bt, 1923–1944, vol. IV

Frank, Ilya Mikhailovich, 1908–1990, vol. VIII

Frank, Leonhard, 1882–1961, vol. VI

Frank, Sir Peirson; *see* Frank, Sir T. P.

Frank, Phyllis Margaret Duncan, (Mrs Alan Frank); *see* Tate, P. M. D.

Frank, Sir Robert John, 3rd Bt, 1925–1987, vol. VIII

Frank, Tenney, 1876–1939, vol. III

Frank, Sir (Thomas) Peirson, 1881–1951, vol. V

Frankau, Sir Claude Howard Stanley, 1883–1967, vol. VI

Frankau, Captain Gilbert, 1884–1952, vol. V

Frankau, Mrs Julia; *see* Danby, Frank.

Frankau, Pamela, 1908–1967, vol. VI

Frankel, Benjamin, 1906–1973, vol. VII

Frankel, Dan, 1900–1988, vol. VIII

Frankel, Joseph, 1913–1989, vol. VIII

Franken, Rose Dorothy, 1895–1988, vol. VIII

Frankenburg, John Beeching, 1921–1981, vol. VIII

Frankfort de Montmorency, 3rd Viscount, 1835–1902, vol. I

Frankfort de Montmorency, 4th Viscount, 1868–1917, vol. II

Frankfort, Henri, 1897–1954, vol. V

Frankfurter, Felix, 1882–1965, vol. VI

Frankland, Cecil J., 1884–1942, vol. IV

Frankland, Sir Edward, 1825–1899, vol. I

Frankland, Edward Percy, 1884–1958, vol. V

Frankland, Sir Frederick William Francis George, 10th Bt, 1868–1937, vol. III

Frankland, Grace C., (Mrs Percy Frankland), 1858–1946, vol. IV

Frankland, Percy Faraday, 1858–1946, vol. IV

Frankland, Major Hon. Sir Thomas William Assheton, 11th Bt, 1902–1944, vol. IV

Frankland-Payne-Gallwey, Sir John; *see* Gallwey.

Frankland-Russell-Astley, Bertram Frankland; *see* Astley.

Frankland-Russell-Astley, Henry Jacob Delaval; *see* Astley.

Franklen, Sir Thomas Mansel, 1840–1928, vol. II

Franklin, Alfred White, 1905–1984, vol. VIII

Franklin, Arthur Ellis, 1857–1938, vol. III

Franklin, Surg.-Gen. Sir Benjamin, 1844–1917, vol. II

Franklin, David, 1908–1973, vol. VII

Franklin, Ernest Louis, 1859–1950, vol. IV

Franklin, Fabian, *died* 1939, vol. III

Franklin, Sir George, 1853–1916, vol. II

Franklin, George Cooper, 1846–1919, vol. II

Franklin, Bt-Col George Dennne, 1877–1946, vol. IV

Franklin, George Frederic, 1897–1987, vol. VIII

Franklin, Brig.-Gen. Harold Scott Erskine, 1878–1948, vol. IV

Franklin, Hon. Mrs Henrietta, 1866–1964, vol. VI

Franklin, Henry William Fernehough, 1901–1985, vol. VIII

Franklin, Hon. James Thomas, 1854–1940, vol. III

Franklin, John Lewis, 1904–1972, vol. VII

Franklin, Kenneth James, 1897–1966, vol. VI

Franklin, Sir Leonard, 1862–1944, vol. IV

Franklin, Norman Laurence, 1924–1986, vol. VIII

Franklin, Olga Heather, 1895–1987, vol. VIII

Franklin, Philip, *died* 1951, vol. V

Franklin, Sir Reginald Hector, 1893–1957, vol. V

Franklin, Richard Penrose, 1884–1942, vol. IV

Franklin, Col Will Hodgson, 1871–1941, vol. IV

Frankling, Herbert George, 1876–1962, vol. VI

Franklyn, Charles Aubrey Hamilton, 1896–1982, vol. VIII

Franklyn, Brig. Geoffrey Ernest Warren, 1889–1967, vol. VI

Franklyn, Gen. Harold Edmund, 1885–1963, vol. VI

Franklyn, Lt-Gen. Sir William Edmund, 1856–1914, vol. I

Franks, Sir Augustus Wollaston, 1826–1897, vol. I

Franks, Lt-Col George Despard, *died* 1918, vol. II

Franks, Maj.-Gen. Sir George McKenzie, 1868–1958, vol. V

Franks, Sir John Hamilton, 1848–1915, vol. I

Franks, Sir Kendal, 1851–1920, vol. II

Franks, Col Kendal Fergusson, 1886–1944, vol. IV

Franks, Captain Norman, 1843–1923, vol. II

Franks, Rev. Robert Sleightholme, 1871–1964, vol. VI

Franks, Maj.-Gen. William Astell, 1838–1929, vol. III

Franks, William Temple, 1863–1926, vol. II

Franqueville, Amable Charles Franquet, Comte de, 1840–1919, vol. II

Fransella, Albert, *died* 1935, vol. III

Franzos, Carl Emile, 1848–1904, vol. I

Fraser of Allander, 1st Baron, 1903–1966, vol. VI

Fraser of Lonsdale, Baron (Life Peer); William Jocelyn Ian Fraser, 1897–1974, vol. VII

Fraser of North Cape, 1st Baron, 1888–1981, vol. VIII

Fraser of Tullybelton, Baron (Life Peer); Walter Ian Reid Fraser, 1911–1989, vol. VIII

Fraser, Agnes Frances MacNab, 1859–1944, vol. IV

Fraser, Major Hon. Alastair Thomas Joseph, 1877–1949, vol. IV

Fraser, Alexander Brodie, 1871–1936, vol. III

Fraser, Alexander Campbell, 1819–1914, vol. I

Fraser, Maj.-Gen. Alexander Donald, 1884–1960, vol. V

Fraser, Rev. Alexander Garden, 1873–1962, vol. VI

Fraser, Sir Andrew Henderson Leith, 1848–1919, vol. II

Fraser, Mrs Angela Zelia, (Alice Spinner), *died* 1925, vol. II

Fraser, Sir Angus, 1909–1963, vol. VI

Fraser, Major Arthur Ion, 1879–1917, vol. II

Fraser, Sir (Arthur) Ronald, 1888–1974, vol. VII

Fraser, Lt-Col Cecil, 1885–1951, vol. V

Fraser, Sir Charles Frederick, 1850–1925, vol. II

Fraser, Charles Ian, 1903–1963, vol. VI

Fraser, Sir Colin, 1875–1944, vol. IV

Fraser, Colin Neil, 1905–1979, vol. VII

Fraser, Hon. Sir David MacDowall, 1825–1906, vol. I

Fraser, Lt-Col Sir Denholm de Montalt Stuart, 1889–1956, vol. V

Fraser, Very Rev. Donald, 1870–1933, vol. III

Fraser, Sir Douglas Were, 1899–1988, vol. VIII (A)

Fraser, Sir Drummond Drummond, 1867–1929, vol. III

Fraser, Rev. Duncan, 1814–1912, vol. I

Fraser, Duncan, 1880–1966, vol. VI

Fraser, Very Rev. Duncan, 1903–1977, vol. VII

Fraser, Surg.-Maj.-Gen. Duncan Alexander Campbell, 1831–1912, vol. I

Fraser, Sir Edward Cleather, 1853–1927, vol. II

Fraser, Sir Edward Henry, 1851–1921, vol. II

Fraser, Eric Malcolm, 1896–1960, vol. V, vol. VI

Fraser, Sir Everard Duncan Home, 1859–1922, vol. II

Fraser, Francis Charles, 1903–1978, vol. VII

Fraser, Sir Francis Richard, 1885–1964, vol. VI

Fraser, Frederick William, 1870–1936, vol. III

Fraser, Galloway, *died* 1925, vol. II

Fraser, Rear-Adm. Hon. George, 1887–1970, vol. VI

Fraser, Col George Ireland, 1876–1929, vol. III

Fraser, George M., 1862–1938, vol. III

Fraser, Gilbert, *born* 1848, vol. II

Fraser, Sir Gordon, 1873–1934, vol. III

Fraser, Captain Gordon Colquhoun, 1866–1952, vol. V

Fraser, Hanson Werry, 1850–1929, vol. III

Fraser, Col Henry Francis, 1872–1949, vol. IV

Fraser, Henry Lumsden Forbes, 1877–1951, vol. V

Fraser, Henry Ralph, 1896–1963, vol. VI

Fraser, Col Herbert Cecil, *died* 1943, vol. IV

Fraser, Col Howard Alan Denholm, 1867–1948, vol. IV

Fraser, Hon. Sir Hugh, *died* 1927, vol. II

Fraser, Mrs Hugh, (Mary), 1815–1922, vol. II, vol. III

Fraser, Sir Hugh, 2nd Bt, 1936–1987, vol. VIII

Fraser, Rt Hon. Sir Hugh Charles Patrick Joseph, 1918–1984, vol. VIII

Fraser, Air Vice-Marshal Hugh Henry Macleod, 1895–1962, vol. VI

Fraser, Sir Hugh Stein, 1863–1944, vol. IV

Fraser, Ian George Inglis, 1923–1980, vol. VII

Fraser, Captain Ian Mackenzie, 1854–1922, vol. II

Fraser, Ian Montagu, 1916–1987, vol. VIII

Fraser, Rev. James, 1842–1913, vol. I

Fraser, James, 1861–1936, vol. III

Fraser, Rev. James, 1883–1966, vol. VI

Fraser, James Alexander L.; *see* Lovat-Fraser.

Fraser, Col James Douglas, 1914–1981, vol. VIII

Fraser, James Duncan, 1915–1965, vol. VI

Fraser, Lt-Col James Johnson, 1876–1939, vol. III

Fraser, Lt-Col James Wilson, 1862–1943, vol. IV

Fraser, John, 1820–1911, vol. I

Fraser, John, *born* 1852, vol. II

Fraser, John, *died* 1925, vol. II

Fraser, John, 1882–1945, vol. IV

Fraser, Sir John, 1st Bt (*cr* 1943), 1885–1947, vol. IV

Fraser, Very Rev. John Annand, 1894–1985, vol. VIII

Fraser, Lt-Col John Edward, 1877–1934, vol. III

Fraser, Sir John Foster, 1868–1936, vol. III
Fraser, Sir John George, 1840–1927, vol. II
Fraser, Sir John George, 1864–1941, vol. IV
Fraser, John Henry Pearson, 1874–1949, vol. IV
Fraser, Sir John Hugh Ronald, 1878–1943, vol. IV
Fraser, Sir (John) Malcolm, 1st Bt (cr 1921), 1878–1949, vol. IV
Fraser, Rear-Adm. John Stewart Gordon, 1883–1973, vol. VII
Fraser, Kate, 1877–1957, vol. V
Fraser, Major Sir Keith Alexander, 5th Bt (cr 1806), 1867–1935, vol. III
Fraser, Sir Keith Charles Adolphus, 6th Bt (cr 1806), 1911–1979, vol. VII
Fraser, Kenneth, 1874–1941, vol. IV
Fraser, Sir Kenneth Barron, 1897–1969, vol. VI
Fraser, Kenneth Wharton, 1905–1981, vol. VIII
Fraser, Leon, 1889–1945, vol. IV
Fraser, Lindley Macnaghten, 1904–1963, vol. VI
Fraser, Louis Nathaniel B.; see Blache-Fraser.
Fraser, Lovat, 1871–1926, vol. II
Fraser, Brig.-Gen. Lyons David, 1868–1926, vol. II
Fraser, Sir Malcolm; see Fraser, Sir J. M.
Fraser, Hon. Sir Malcolm, 1834–1900, vol. I
Fraser, Malcolm, 1873–1949, vol. IV
Fraser, Marjory Kennedy, died 1930, vol. III
Fraser, Mary; see Fraser, Mrs Hugh
Fraser, Mary, died 1940, vol. III
Fraser, Sir Matthew Pollock, died 1937, vol. III
Fraser, Captain Norman, 1879–1914, vol. I
Fraser, Rt Hon. Peter, 1884–1950, vol. IV
Fraser, Rt Rev. Robert, 1858–1914, vol. I
Fraser, Sir Robert; see Fraser, Sir W. R.
Fraser, Sir Robert Brown, 1904–1985, vol. VIII
Fraser, Ronald; see Fraser, Sir A. R.
Fraser, Hon. Sir Simon, 1832–1919, vol. II
Fraser, Sir Stuart Mitford, 1864–1963, vol. VI
Fraser, Maj.-Gen. Sir Theodore, 1865–1953, vol. V
Fraser, Maj.-Gen. Sir Thomas, 1840–1922, vol. II
Fraser, Col Thomas, 1872–1951, vol. V
Fraser, Rt Hon. Thomas, 1911–1988, vol. VIII
Fraser, Thomas Cameron, 1909–1982, vol. VIII
Fraser, Sir Thomas Richard, 1841–1920, vol. II
Fraser, Sir William, 1816–1898, vol. I
Fraser, Rev. William, 1851–1919, vol. II
Fraser, Hon. Sir William, 1840–1923, vol. II
Fraser, Brig. Hon. William, 1890–1964, vol. VI
Fraser, William, 1911–1990, vol. VIII
Fraser, William Alexander, died 1933, vol. III
Fraser, Maj.-Gen. William Archibald Kenneth, 1886–1969, vol. VI
Fraser, Sir William Augustus, 4th Bt (cr 1806), 1826–1898, vol. I
Fraser, William Donald, 1890–1941, vol. IV
Fraser, William Henry, 1853–1916, vol. II
Fraser, William Henry, died 1966, vol. VI
Fraser, W(illiam) Lionel, died 1965, vol. VI
Fraser, Sir (William) Robert, 1891–1985, vol. VIII
Fraser, William Stuart, 1876–1954, vol. V
Fraser Darling, Sir Frank, 1903–1979, vol. VII
Fraser-Harris, David Fraser, 1867–1937, vol. III
Fraser Roberts, John Alexander; see Roberts.
Fraser-Simson, Harold, 1878–1944, vol. IV
Fraser-Tytler, Edward Grant, 1856–1918, vol. II

Fraser-Tytler, Gen. Sir James Macleod Bannatyne, 1821–1914, vol. I
Fraser-Tytler, Bt Col Neil, 1889–1937, vol. III
Fraser-Tytler, Lt-Col Sir William Kerr, 1886–1963, vol. VI
Frayling, Frederick George, born 1846, vol. II
Frazer, Alastair Campbell, 1909–1969, vol. VI
Frazer, Hon. Charles Edward, 1880–1913, vol. I
Frazer, Hon. Sir Francis Vernon, 1880–1948, vol. IV
Frazer, Col George Stanley, 1865–1950, vol. IV(A), vol. V
Frazer, Sir James George, 1854–1941, vol. IV
Frazer, John Ernest Sullivan, 1870–1946, vol. IV
Frazer, Robert, 1878–1947, vol. IV
Frazer, Robert Alexander, 1891–1959, vol. V
Frazer, Robert Watson, 1854–1921, vol. II
Frazer, Sir Thomas, 1884–1969, vol. VI
Frazer, William Miller, 1864–1961, vol. VI
Frazer, William Mowll, 1888–1958, vol. V
Freake, Sir Charles Arland Maitland, 4th Bt, 1904–1951, vol. V
Freake, Sir Frederick Charles Maitland, 3rd Bt, 1876–1950, vol. IV
Freake, Sir Thomas George, 2nd Bt, 1848–1920, vol. II
Fream, William, died 1906, vol. I
Frears, John Newton, 1906–1981, vol. VIII
Fréchette, Achille, 1847–1927, vol. II
Fréchette, Louis, 1839–1908, vol. I
Frecheville, William, 1854–1940, vol. III
Frederic, Harold, 1856–1898, vol. I
Frederick, Lt-Col Sir Charles Arthur Andrew, 1861–1913, vol. I
Frederick, Sir Charles Edward, 7th Bt (cr 1723), 1843–1913, vol. I
Frederick, Sir Charles Edward St John, 8th Bt, 1876–1938, vol. III
Frederick, Lt-Col Sir Edward Boscawen, 9th Bt, 1880–1956, vol. V
Frederick, Captain George Charles, 1855–1951, vol. V
Freedman, Barnett, 1901–1958, vol. V
Freedman, Maurice, 1920–1975, vol. VII
Freeland, Maj.-Gen. Sir Henry Francis Edward, 1870–1946, vol. IV
Freeland, Lt-Gen. Sir Ian Henry, 1912–1979, vol. VII
Freeland, Col John Cavendish, 1877–1944, vol. IV
Freeling, Sir Charles Edward Luard, 9th Bt, 1858–1941, vol. III
Freeling, Sir Clayton Pennington, 8th Bt, 1857–1927, vol. II
Freeling, Sir Harry, 6th Bt, 1852–1914, vol. I
Freeling, Rev. Sir James Robert, 7th Bt, 1825–1916, vol. II
Freeman, Anthony Mallows; see Freeman, P. A. M.
Freeman, Sir Bernard; see Freeman, Sir N. B.
Freeman, Edward Bothamley, 1838–1921, vol. II
Freeman, Col Ernest Carrick, 1860–1932, vol. III
Freeman, Comdr Frederick Arthur Peere W.; see Williams-Freeman.
Freeman, George Mallows, 1850–1934, vol. III
Freeman, George Robert, 1875–1972, vol. VII
Freeman, George Sydney, 1879–1938, vol. III
Freeman, Harry, 1888–1959, vol. V

Freeman, Rev. Herbert Bentley, 1855–1950, vol. IV
Freeman, Ifan Charles Harold, 1910–1990, vol. VIII
Freeman, James E., 1871–1929, vol. III
Freeman, Rt Rev. James Edward, 1866–1943, vol. IV
Freeman, John, 1880–1929, vol. III
Freeman, John, 1877–1962, vol. VI
Freeman, John Joseph, 1851–1937, vol. III
Freeman, Sir (John) Keith (Noel), 2nd Bt, 1923–1981, vol. VIII
Freeman, Kathleen, 1897–1959, vol. V
Freeman, Sir Keith; see Freeman, Sir J. K. N.
Freeman, Sir (Nathaniel) Bernard, 1896–1982, vol. VIII
Freeman, Nicholas Hall, 1939–1989, vol. VIII
Freeman, Patrick, 1919–1978, vol. VII
Freeman, Percy Tom, 1891–1956, vol. V
Freeman, Peter, 1888–1956, vol. V
Freeman, (Philip) Anthony Mallows, 1892–1971, vol. VII
Freeman, Sir Philip Horace, 1878–1933, vol. III
Freeman, Sir Ralph, 1880–1950, vol. IV
Freeman, Richard Austin, 1862–1943, vol. IV
Freeman, Captain Spencer, 1892–1982, vol. VIII
Freeman, Sterry Baines, 1875–1953, vol. V
Freeman, Air Chief Marshal Sir Wilfrid Rhodes, 1st Bt, 1888–1953, vol. V
Freeman, William Marshall, 1868–1953, vol. V
Freeman-Attwood, Harold Augustus, 1897–1963, vol. VI
Freeman-Cohen, Harry, died 1904, vol. I
Freeman-Mitford, Hon. Clement Bertram Ogilvy, 1876–1915, vol. I
Freeman-Mitford, Major Hon. Thomas David F.; see Mitford.
Freer, A. M. G.; see Goodrich-Freer.
Freer, Charles L., 1854–1919, vol. II
Freer, Ven. T. Henry, 1833–1904, vol. I
Freer Smith, Sir Hamilton Pym, 1845–1929, vol. III
Freese-Pennefather, Harold Wilfrid Armine, 1907–1967, vol. VI
Freeston, Sir Brian; see Freeston, Sir L. B.
Freeston, Charles Lincoln, 1865–1942, vol. IV
Freeston, Sir (Leslie) Brian, 1892–1958, vol. V
Freestun, Col William Humphrey May, 1878–1964, vol. VI
Freeth, Sir Evelyn, 1846–1911, vol. I
Freeth, Francis Arthur, 1884–1970, vol. VI
Freeth, Maj.-Gen. George Henry Basil, 1872–1949, vol. IV
Freeth, H. Andrew, 1912–1986, vol. VIII
Freeth, Rt Rev. Robert Evelyn, 1886–1979, vol. VII
Freke, Cecil George, 1887–1974, vol. VII
Freke, Hon. Ralfe E.; see Evans-Freke.
Fremantle, Gen. Sir Arthur James Lyon, 1835–1901, vol. I
Fremantle, Charles Albert, 1878–1952, vol. V
Fremantle, Hon. Sir Charles William, 1834–1914, vol. I
Fremantle, Adm. Hon. Sir Edmund Robert, 1836–1929, vol. III
Fremantle, Francis David Eardley, 1906–1968, vol. VI
Fremantle, Sir Francis Edward, 1872–1943, vol. IV

Fremantle, Henry Eardley Stephen, 1874–1931, vol. III
Fremantle, John Morton, 1876–1936, vol. III
Fremantle, Sir Selwyn Howe, 1869–1942, vol. IV
Fremantle, Adm. Sir Sydney Robert, 1867–1958, vol. V
Fremantle, Very Rev. Hon. William Henry, 1831–1916, vol. II
Frémiet, Emmanuel, 1824–1910, vol. I
French, Alice Octave Thanet, 1850–1934, vol. III
French, Gen. Arthur, 1840–1928, vol. II
French, Major Arthur Cecil, 1896–1974, vol. VII
French, Col Arthur Harwood, 1876–1939, vol. III
French, Hon. Charles, 1851–1925, vol. II
French, Brig. Charles Newenham, 1875–1959, vol. V
French, Daniel Chester, 1850–1931, vol. III
French, Daniel O'Connell, 1843–1902, vol. I
French, Lt-Col Hon. (Edward) Gerald, 1883–1970, vol. VI
French, Edward Henry, 1850–1935, vol. III
French, Sir Edward Lee, 1857–1916, vol. II
French, Francis Coope, 1868–1940, vol. III
French, Rev. Francis Laurence, 1868–1936, vol. III
French, Captain Sir Frederick Edward, 1882–1947, vol. IV
French, Frederick George, 1889–1963, vol. VI
French, Maj.-Gen. Sir George Arthur, 1841–1921, vol. II
French, Col George Arthur, 1865–1950, vol. IV
French, Lt-Col Hon. Gerald; see French, Lt-Col Hon. E. G.
French, Sir Henry Leon, 1883–1966, vol. VI
French, Herbert Stanley, 1875–1951, vol. V
French, Captain Sir Houston, 1853–1932, vol. III
French, Sir James Weir, 1876–1953, vol. V
French, Maj.-Gen. John, 1906–1978, vol. VII
French, John Gay, died 1951, vol. V
French, Brig. John Linnaeus, 1896–1953, vol. V
French, Sir John Russell, 1847–1921, vol. II
French, Lewis, 1873–1945, vol. IV
French, Percy, 1854–1920, vol. II
French, Rev. Reginald, 1883–1961, vol. VI
French, Reginald Thomas George, 1881–1965, vol. VI
French, Sir Somerset Richard, 1848–1929, vol. III
French, Adm. Sir Wilfred Frankland, 1880–1958, vol. V
French, William Innes, 1910–1971, vol. VII
Frend, Charles Herbert, 1909–1977, vol. VII
Frend, Col George, 1857–1923, vol. II
Frere, Alexander Stewart, 1892–1984, vol. VIII
Frere, Sir Bartle Compton Arthur, 1854–1933, vol. III
Frere, Sir Bartle Henry Temple, 1862–1953, vol. V
Frere, Rev. Hugh Corrie, 1857–1938, vol. III
Frere, Brig. Jasper Gray, 1894–1974, vol. VII
Frere, John Tudor, 1843–1918, vol. II
Frere, Noel Gray, 1885–1955, vol. V
Frere, Rt Rev. Walter Howard, 1863–1938, vol. III
Frere, William Edward, 1840–1900, vol. I
Freshfield, Douglas William, 1845–1934, vol. III
Freshwater, Douglas Hope, died 1945, vol. IV
Fresnay, Pierre, (Pierre Laudenbach), 1897–1975, vol. VII

Fressanges, Air Marshal Sir Francis J., 1902–1975, vol. VII

Freud, Anna, 1895–1982, vol. VIII

Freud, Sigmund, 1856–1939, vol. III

Freund, Sir Otto K.; *see* Kahn-Freund.

Freundlich, Erwin F.; *see* Finlay-Freundlich.

Freundlich, Herbert Max Finlay, 1880–1941, vol. IV

Frew, Rev. Dr, 1813–1910, vol. I

Frew, Sir John Lewtas, 1912–1985, vol. VIII

Frew, Air Vice-Marshal Sir Matthew Brown, 1895–1974, vol. VII

Frew, Engr Rear-Adm. Sir Sidney Oswell, *died* 1972, vol. VII

Frewen, Col Edward, 1850–1919, vol. II

Frewen, Adm. Sir John Byng, 1911–1975, vol. VII

Frewen, Moreton, 1853–1924, vol. II

Frewen-Laton, Col Stephen, 1857–1933, vol. III

Frewer, Rev. George Ernest, 1852–1935, vol. III

Frewer, Rt Rev. John, 1883–1974, vol. VII

Freyberg, 1st Baron, 1889–1963, vol. VI

Freyberg, Lady; (Barbara), *died* 1973, vol. VII

Freyberg, Captain Geoffrey Herbert, 1881–1966, vol. VI

Freyer, Sir Peter J., *died* 1921, vol. II

Freyer, Lt-Col Samuel Forster, 1858–1947, vol. IV

Frick, Henry Clay, 1849–1919, vol. II

Fricker, Edward T., *died* 1917, vol. II

Fricker, Peter Racine, 1920–1990, vol. VIII

Friederichs, Hulda, *died* 1927, vol. II

Friedlander, Max J., 1867–1958, vol. V

Friedlander, Michael, *died* 1910, vol. I

Friedman, Ignaz, 1882–1948, vol. IV

Friend, Maj.-Gen. Arthur Leslie Irvine, 1886–1961, vol. IV

Friend, John Albert Newton, 1881–1966, vol. VI

Friend, Maj.-Gen. Rt Hon. Sir Lovick Bransby, 1856–1944, vol. IV

Frigon, Augustin, 1888–1952, vol. V

Friml, Rudolf, 1879–1972, vol. VII

Fripp, Sir Alfred Downing, 1865–1930, vol. III

Fripp, Alfred Ernest, 1866–1938, vol. III

Fripp, Charles E., 1854–1906, vol. I

Frisby, Major Cyril Hubert, 1885–1961, vol. VI

Frisby, Lt-Col Lionel Claud, 1889–1936, vol. III

Frisby, Maj.-Gen. Richard George Fellowes, 1911–1982, vol. VIII

Frisch, Otto Robert, 1904–1979, vol. VII

Frisch, Ragnar Anton Kittil, 1895–1973, vol. VII

Friswell, Sir Charles Hain, 1871–1926, vol. II

Frith, Col Cyril Halsted, 1877–1946, vol. IV

Frith, Brig. Sir Eric Herbert Cokayne, 1897–1984, vol. VIII

Frith, Brig.-Gen. Gilbert Robertson, 1873–1958, vol. V

Frith, Col Herbert Cokayne, 1861–1942, vol. IV

Frith, W. S., *died* 1924, vol. II

Frith, Walter, *died* 1941, vol. IV

Frith, William Powell, 1819–1909, vol. I

Fritsch, Felix Eugen, 1879–1954, vol. V

Frizell, Rev. Charles William, *died* 1920, vol. II

Frizell, Brig.-Gen. Charles William, 1888–1951, vol. V

Frizelle, Sir Joseph, 1841–1921, vol. II

Frizzell, Edward, 1918–1987, vol. VIII

Frodsham, Rt Rev. George Horsfall, 1863–1937, vol. III

Frohawk, Frederick William, 1861–1946, vol. IV

Frohman, Charles, 1860–1915, vol. I

Frome, Sir Norman Frederick, 1899–1982, vol. VIII

Frood, Hester, 1882–1971, vol. VII

Froom, Sir Arthur Henry, 1873–1964, vol. VI

Frossard, Rev. Canon Edward Louis, 1887–1968, vol. VI

Frost, Edward Granville Gordon, 1886–1971, vol. VII

Frost, Edward Purkis, 1842–1922, vol. II

Frost, Brig.-Gen. Frank Dutton, *died* 1968, vol. VI

Frost, Hon. Sir John, 1828–1918, vol. II

Frost, Lt-Col John Meadows, 1885–1923, vol. II

Frost, Sir John Meadows, 1856–1935, vol. III

Frost, Mark Edwin Pescott, 1859–1953, vol. V

Frost, Captain Meadows, 1875–1954, vol. V

Frost, Norman, 1899–1985, vol. VIII

Frost, Percival, 1817–1898, vol. I

Frost, Robert, 1874–1963, vol. VI

Frost, Sir Thomas Gibbons, 1820–1904, vol. I

Frostick, James Arthur, 1857–1931, vol. III

Froude, Ashley Anthony, 1863–1949, vol. IV

Froude, Robert Edmund, 1846–1924, vol. II

Frowde, Henry, 1841–1927, vol. II

Frowen, Brig. John Harold, 1898–1980, vol. VII

Frumkin, Gad, 1887–1960, vol. VI

Fry, (Anna) Ruth, 1878–1962, vol. VI

Fry, Col Arthur Brownfield, 1873–1954, vol. V

Fry, Augustine Sargood, 1890–1962, vol. VI

Fry, Cecil Roderick, 1890–1952, vol. V

Fry, Charles Burgess, 1872–1956, vol. V

Fry, Rev. Canon Charles Edward Middleton, 1882–1950, vol. IV

Fry, Maj.-Gen. Charles Irwin, 1858–1931, vol. III

Fry, Dennis Butler, 1907–1983, vol. VIII

Fry, Rt Hon. Sir Edward, 1827–1918, vol. II

Fry, E(dwin) Maxwell, 1899–1987, vol. VIII

Fry, Francis Gibson, 1864–1914, vol. I

Fry, Francis James, 1835–1918, vol. II

Fry, Sir (Francis) Wilfrid, 5th Bt, 1904–1987, vol. VIII

Fry, Sir Frederick Morris, 1851–1943, vol. IV

Fry, Sir Geoffrey Storrs, 1st Bt (*cr* 1929), 1888–1960, vol. V

Fry, George Samuel, 1853–1938, vol. III

Fry, Sir Henry James Wakely, 1849–1920, vol. II

Fry, Henry Kenneth, 1886–1959, vol. V(A), vol. VI(AI)

Fry, Sir John Nicholas Pease, 4th Bt, 1897–1985, vol. VIII

Fry, Sir John Pease, 2nd Bt (*cr* 1894), 1864–1957, vol. V

Fry, Major Sir Leslie Alfred Charles, 1908–1976, vol. VII

Fry, Rt Hon. Lewis, 1832–1921, vol. II

Fry, Lewis G., 1860–1933, vol. III

Fry, Margery; *see* Fry, S. M.

Fry, Matthew Wyatt Joseph, *died* 1943, vol. IV

Fry, Oliver Armstrong, 1855–1931, vol. III

Fry, Sir Penrose; *see* Fry, Sir T. P.

Fry, Peter George, 1875–1925, vol. II

Fry, Roger E., 1866–1934, vol. III

Fry, Ruth; see Fry, A. R.
Fry, (Sara) Margery, 1874–1958, vol. V
Fry, Sir Theodore, 1st Bt (cr 1894), 1836–1912, vol. I
Fry, Sir (Theodore) Penrose, 3rd Bt (cr 1894), 1892–1971, vol. VII
Fry, Theodore Wilfrid, 1868–1947, vol. IV
Fry, Thomas, 1889–1958, vol. V
Fry, Very Rev. Thomas Charles, 1846–1930, vol. III
Fry, Sir Wilfrid; see Fry, Sir F. W.
Fry, Maj.-Gen. Sir William, 1858–1934, vol. III
Fry, Sir William, 1853–1939, vol. III
Fry, Sir William Kelsey, 1889–1963, vol. VI
Fry, Windsor, died 1947, vol. IV
Fryar, Samuel, 1863–1938, vol. III
Fryars, Sir Robert Furness, 1887–1978, vol. VII(AII)
Frye, Frederick Robert, 1851–1942, vol. IV
Frye, Jack, 1914–1975, vol. VII
Fryer, Sir Charles Edward, 1850–1920, vol. II
Fryer, Edward Harpur, 1879–1948, vol. IV
Fryer, Sir Frederic William Richards, 1845–1922, vol. II
Fryer, Herbert, 1877–1957, vol. V
Fryer, James, 1930–1981, vol. VIII
Fryer, Lt-Gen. Sir John, 1838–1917, vol. II
Fryer, Sir John Claud Fortescue, 1886–1948, vol. IV
Fryer, Walter John, 1871–1933, vol. III
Fuad, Mustafa Ziai, Bey, 1888–1968, vol. VI
Fuchs, Carl, 1865–1951, vol. V
Fuchs, Emile, 1866–1929, vol. III
Fudge, Edward George, 1888–1961, vol. VI
Fukushima, Gen. Baron, 1853–1919, vol. II
Fulford, Dame Catherine, 1881–1960, vol. V
Fulford, Francis, 1861–1926, vol. II
Fulford, Rev. Frederick John, 1860–1927, vol. II
Fulford, Henry English, 1859–1929, vol. III
Fulford, Sir Roger Thomas Baldwin, 1902–1983, vol. VIII
Fullagar, Sir Wilfred Kelsham, 1892–1961, vol. VI
Fullard, George, 1923–1973, vol. VII
Fullbrook-Leggatt, Maj.-Gen. Charles St Quentin Outen; see Leggatt.
Fuller, Lt-Col Albert George Hubert, died 1969, vol. VI
Fuller, Maj.-Gen. Algernon Clement, 1885–1970, vol. VI
Fuller, Rev. Arthur Rose, 1874–1959, vol. V
Fuller, Sir Bampfylde; see Fuller, Sir J. B.
Fuller, Sir Benjamin John, 1875–1952, vol. V
Fuller, Maj.-Gen. Cuthbert Graham, 1874–1960, vol. V
Fuller, Adm. Sir Cyril Thomas Moulden, 1874–1942, vol. IV
Fuller, Sir Francis Charles, 1866–1944, vol. IV
Fuller, Brig.-Gen. Francis George, 1869–1961, vol. VI
Fuller, Francis Matthew, 1899–1963, vol. VI
Fuller, George Pargiter, 1833–1927, vol. II
Fuller, Hon. Sir George Warburton, 1861–1940, vol. III
Fuller, Major Sir Gerard; see Fuller, Major Sir J. G. H. F.
Fuller, Henry Roxburgh, died 1929, vol. III
Fuller, Air Cdre Herbert Francis, 1893–1967, vol. VI
Fuller, James Franklin, 1835–1924, vol. II

Fuller, Gen. John Augustus, 1828–1902, vol. I
Fuller, Maj.-Gen. John Frederick Charles, 1878–1966, vol. VI
Fuller, Major Sir (John) Gerard (Henry Fleetwood), 2nd Bt, 1906–1981, vol. VIII
Fuller, Rt Rev. John Latimer, 1870–1950, vol. IV
Fuller, Sir John Michael Fleetwood, 1st Bt, 1864–1915, vol. I
Fuller, Sir (Joseph) Bampfylde, 1854–1935, vol. III
Fuller, Leonard J., 1891–1973, vol. VII
Fuller, Melville Weston, 1833–1910, vol. I
Fuller, Richard Buckminster, 1895–1983, vol. VIII
Fuller, Brig.-Gen. Richard Woodfield, 1861–1938, vol. III
Fuller, Sir Thomas Ekins, 1831–1910, vol. I
Fuller, Walter Everard, 1879–1942, vol. IV
Fuller, William Fleetwood, 1865–1947, vol. IV
Fuller-Eliott-Drake, Sir Francis George Augustus; see Drake.
Fuller-Good, Air Vice-Marshal James Laurence Fuller, 1903–1983, vol. VIII
Fuller-Maitland, J. A., 1856–1936, vol. III
Fuller-Maitland, William, 1844–1932, vol. III
Fullerton, Andrew, died 1934, vol. III
Fullerton, Adm. Sir Eric John Arthur, died 1962, vol. VI
Fullerton, Harold Williams, 1905–1970, vol. VI
Fullerton, Hugh, 1851–1922, vol. II
Fullerton, Brig. John Parke, 1894–1977, vol. VII
Fullerton, Adm. Sir John Reginald Thomas, 1840–1918, vol. II
Fullerton, John Skipwith Herbert, 1865–1940, vol. III
Fullerton, Rev. William Young, 1857–1932, vol. III
Fulleylove, John, 1847–1908, vol. I
Fullwood, John, died 1931, vol. III
Fülop-Miller, René, 1891–1963, vol. VI
Fulton, Baron (Life Peer); John Scott Fulton, 1902–1986, vol. VIII
Fulton, Alexander Strathern, 1888–1976, vol. VII
Fulton, Sir Edmund McGilldowny Hope, 1848–1913, vol. I
Fulton, Eustace Cecil, 1880–1954, vol. V
Fulton, Sir Forrest, 1846–1925, vol. II
Fulton, Forrest, 1913–1971, vol. VII
Fulton, Frederick John, 1862–1936, vol. III
Fulton, Lt-Col Harry Townsend, 1869–1918, vol. II
Fulton, Lt-Col J. D. B., 1876–1915, vol. I
Fulton, John Farquhar, 1899–1960, vol. V
Fulton, Robert Burwell, 1849–1918, vol. II
Fulton, Sir Robert Fulton, 1844–1927, vol. II
Fulton, Thomas Alexander Wemyss, 1855–1929, vol. III
Fulton, Rev. William, 1876–1952, vol. V
Funch, Christian Holger, 1865–1915, vol. I
Funk, Isaac Kaufman, 1839–1912, vol. I
Funsten, Rt Rev. James Bowen, died 1918, vol. II
Funston, Brig.-Gen. Frederick, 1865–1917, vol. II
Furber, Lt-Col Cecil Tidswell, 1883–1943, vol. IV
Furber, Douglas, 1885–1961, vol. VI
Furber, Edward Price, 1864–1940, vol. III
Furkert, Frederick William, 1876–1949, vol. IV
Furley, Sir John, 1836–1919, vol. II
Furley, John Talfourd, 1878–1956, vol. V
Furlong, Hon. L. O'Brien, 1856–1908, vol. I

Furlong, Robert O'Brien, 1842–1917, vol. II
Furlonge, Sir Geoffrey Warren, 1903–1984, vol. VIII
Furneaux, Rev. Henry, 1829–1900, vol. I
Furneaux, Rev. William Mordaunt, 1848–1928, vol. II
Furness, 1st Baron, 1852–1912, vol. I
Furness, 1st Viscount, 1883–1940, vol. III
Furness, Sir Christopher, 2nd Bt, 1900–1974, vol. VII
Furness, George James, 1868–1936, vol. III
Furness, George James Barnard, 1900–1962, vol. VI
Furness, Horace Howard, 1833–1912, vol. I
Furness, Reginald Albert, *died* 1951, vol. V
Furness, Sir Robert Allason, 1883–1954, vol. V
Furness, Sir Robert Howard, 1880–1959, vol. V
Furness, Stephen Noel, 1902–1974, vol. VII
Furness, Sir Stephen Wilson, 1st Bt, 1872–1914, vol. I
Furness-Smith, Sir Cecil, 1890–1971, vol. VII
Furney, Brig. John Leared, 1872–1936, vol. III
Furniss, Harry, 1854–1925, vol. II
Furniss, John Mawdsley, 1877–1956, vol. V
Furnivall, Baroness (19th in line), 1900–1968, vol. VI
Furnivall, Lt-Col Charles Hilton, 1873–1946, vol. IV
Furnivall, Frederick James, 1825–1910, vol. I
Furnivall, Maj.-Gen. Lewis Trevor, 1907–1986, vol. VIII
Furnivall, Percy, 1868–1938, vol. III
Furse, Ven. Charles Wellington, 1821–1900, vol. I
Furse, Charles Wellington, 1868–1904, vol. I
Furse, Rear-Adm. (John) Paul (Wellington), 1904–1978, vol. VII
Furse, Dame Katharine, 1875–1952, vol. V
Furse, Rt Rev. Michael Bolton, 1870–1955, vol. V
Furse, Rear-Adm. Paul; *see* Furse, Rear-Adm. J. P. W.
Furse, Major Ralph Dolignon, 1887–1973, vol. VII
Furse, Roger Kemble, 1903–1972, vol. VII
Furse, Lt-Gen. Sir William T., 1865–1953, vol. V
Furst, Herbert Ernest Augustus, 1874–1945, vol. IV
Furtwängler, Wilhelm, 1886–1954, vol. V
Fussell, Edward Coldham, 1901–1978, vol. VII
Fust, Herbert J.; *see* Jenner-Fust.
Fyers, FitzRoy Hubert, 1899–1981, vol. VIII
Fyers, Major Hubert Alcock Nepean, 1862–1951, vol. V
Fyfe, Sir Cleveland, 1888–1959, vol. V
Fyfe, David Theodore, 1875–1945, vol. IV
Fyfe, H. Hamilton, 1869–1951, vol. V
Fyfe, Thomas Alexander, 1852–1928, vol. II
Fyfe, Sir William Hamilton, 1878–1965, vol. VI
Fyffe, Rev. David, 1866–1929, vol. III
Fyffe, Lt-Gen. Sir Richard Alan, 1912–1972, vol. VII
Fyffe, Rt Rev. Rollestone Sterritt, 1868–1964, vol. VI
Fyleman, Rose, *died* 1957, vol. V
Fyler, Maj.-Gen. Arthur Roderic, 1911–1980, vol. VII
Fyler, Adm. Herbert Arthur Stevenson, 1864–1934, vol. III
Fynes-Clinton, David Osbert, 1909–1978, vol. VII
Fynes-Clinton, Rev. Henry Joy, 1875–1959, vol. V
Fynes-Clinton, Osbert Henry, *died* 1941, vol. IV
Fynn, Sir Basil Mortimer L.; *see* Lindsay-Fynn.
Fynn, Hon. Sir Percival Donald Leslie, 1872–1940, vol. III
Fynne, Robert John, *died* 1953, vol. V
Fysh, Sir Hudson; *see* Fysh, Sir W. H.

Fysh, Hon. Sir Philip Oakley, 1835–1919, vol. II
Fysh, Sir (Wilmot) Hudson, 1895–1974, vol. VII
Fyson, Rt Rev. Philip Kemball, 1846–1928, vol. II
Fyvie, Isabella; *see* Mayo, Isabella, (Mrs John R. Mayo).

G

Gabain, Ethel Leontine, (Mrs John Copley), *died* 1950, vol. IV
Gabbatt, John Percy, 1880–1956, vol. V
Gabin, Jean, (Alexis Jean Montgorge), 1904–1976, vol. VII
Gable, Clark, 1901–1960, vol. V
Gabor, Dennis, 1900–1979, vol. VII
Gabriel, Lt-Col Cecil Hamilton, 1879–1947, vol. IV
Gabriel, Col Sir (Edmund) Vivian, 1875–1950, vol. IV
Gabriel, Col Sir Vivian; *see* Gabriel, Col Sir E. V.
Gabriel, William Bashall, *died* 1975, vol. VII
Gadd, Maj.-Gen. Alfred Lockwood, (David), 1912–1986, vol. VIII
Gadd, Cyril John, 1893–1969, vol. VI
Gadd, Maj.-Gen. David; *see* Gadd, Maj.-Gen. A. L.
Gaddum, Arthur Graham, 1874–1948, vol. IV
Gaddum, Sir John Henry, 1900–1965, vol. VI
Gaddum, Captain Walter Frederick, 1888–1956, vol. V
Gadie, Lt-Col Sir Anthony, *died* 1948, vol. IV
Gadow, Hans Friedrich, 1855–1928, vol. II
Gadsby, Henry, 1842–1907, vol. I
Gadsby, John, 1884–1970, vol. VI
Gadsby, W. H., *died* 1924, vol. II
Gadsden, Cecil Holroyd, 1887–1957, vol. V
Gadsden, Edward Holroyd, 1859–1920, vol. II
Gadsdon, Sir Laurence Percival, 1897–1967, vol. VI(AII)
Gaekwad, Lt-Col Fatesinghrao P., 1930–1988, vol. VIII
Gaffney, Maj.-Gen. Edward Sebastian B.; *see* Burke-Gaffney.
Gaffney, Thomas Burke, 1839–1927, vol. II
Gagarin, Col Yuri Alexeyevich, 1934–1968, vol. VI
Gage, 5th Viscount, 1854–1912, vol. I
Gage, 6th Viscount, 1895–1982, vol. VIII
Gage, Col Aella Molyneux Berkeley, 1863–1937, vol. III
Gage, Andrew Thomas, 1871–1945, vol. IV
Gage, Conolly Hugh, 1905–1984, vol. VIII
Gage, Hon. Lyman Judson, 1836–1927, vol. II
Gage, Brig.-Gen. Moreton Foley, 1873–1953, vol. V
Gage, Thomas Robert Baillie-, 1842–1914, vol. I
Gage, Sir William James, 1849–1921, vol. II
Gaggero, Sir George, 1897–1978, vol. VII
Gagnon, Rt Rev. Mgr Cyrille, *died* 1945, vol. IV
Gahan, Charles Joseph, 1862–1939, vol. III
Gahan, Frank, 1890–1971, vol. VII
Gaiger, Sydney Herbert, 1884–1934, vol. III
Gailey, James Hamilton, 1869–1938, vol. III
Gailey, Thomas William Hamilton, 1906–1986, vol. VIII

Gailor, Rt Rev. Thomas Frank, 1856–1935, vol. III
Gaimes, John Austin, 1886–1921, vol. II
Gainer, Sir Donald St Clair, 1891–1966, vol. VI
Gainer, Rev. Canon Harry, 1858–1920, vol. II
Gainford, 1st Baron, 1860–1943, vol. IV
Gainford, 2nd Baron, 1889–1971, vol. VII
Gainsborough, 3rd Earl of, 1850–1926, vol. II
Gainsborough, 4th Earl of, 1884–1927, vol. II
Gainsborough, Hugh, 1893–1980, vol. VII
Gair, Col Sinclair, 1856–1939, vol. III
Gair, Walter Burgh, 1854–1951, vol. V
Gairdner, Arthur Charles Dalrymple, 1872–1950, vol. IV
Gairdner, Gen. Sir Charles Henry, 1898–1983, vol. VIII
Gairdner, Eric Dalrymple, 1878–1933, vol. III
Gairdner, James, 1828–1912, vol. I
Gairdner, Rev. Canon W. H. Temple, 1873–1928, vol. II
Gairdner, Sir William Tennant, 1824–1907, vol. I
Gairns, James Mather, 1880–1935, vol. III
Gaisford, Hugh William, 1874–1954, vol. V
Gaisford, Lt-Col Sir Philip, 1891–1973, vol. VII
Gaisford, Brig.-Gen. Richard Boileau, 1854–1924, vol. II
Gaisford, Wilfrid Fletcher, 1902–1988, vol. VIII
Gaisford-St Lawrence, Julian Charles, 1862–1932, vol. III
Gait, Sir Edward Albert, 1863–1950, vol. IV
Gaither, H. Rowan, Jr, 1909–1961, vol. VI
Gaitskell, Baroness (Life Peer); Anna Dora Gaitskell, 1901–1989, vol. VIII
Gaitskell, Sir Arthur, 1900–1985, vol. VIII
Gaitskell, Maj.-Gen. Frederick, 1806–1901, vol. I
Gaitskell, Rt Hon. Hugh Todd Naylor, 1906–1963, vol. VI
Gajjumal, Rai Sahib Lala, born 1857, vol. II
Galabin, Alfred Lewis, 1843–1913, vol. I
Galbraith, Angus, 1846–1915, vol. I
Galbraith, Very Rev. George, 1829–1911, vol. I
Galbraith, James Francis Wallace, 1872–1945, vol. IV
Galbraith, Lt-Col James Ponsonby, 1881–1950, vol. IV
Galbraith, Samuel, 1853–1936, vol. III
Galbraith, Hon. Sir Thomas Galloway Dunlop, 1917–1982, vol. VIII
Galbraith, Vivian Hunter, 1889–1976, vol. VII
Galbraith, Walter, 1839–1906, vol. I
Galbraith, Maj.-Gen. Sir William, 1837–1906, vol. I
Galbraith, Col William Campbell, 1870–1946, vol. IV
Galdos, Benito Perez, 1845–1920, vol. II
Gale, Anthony Eugene Myddelton, 1901–1959, vol. V
Gale, Arthur James Victor, 1895–1978, vol. VII
Gale, Rev. Canon Courtenay James Randolph, 1857–1937, vol. III
Gale, George Stafford, 1927–1990, vol. VIII
Gale, Brig. Henry John Gordon, 1883–1944, vol. IV
Gale, Brig.-Gen. Henry Richmond, 1866–1930, vol. III
Gale, Lt-Gen. Sir Humfrey Myddelton, 1890–1971, vol. VII
Gale, Rev. Isaac Sadler, died 1915, vol. I
Gale, James, 1833–1907, vol. I

Gale, Kenneth Frederick, 1914–1969, vol. VI
Gale, Sir Laurence George, 1905–1969, vol. VI
Gale, Malcolm Ruthven, 1909–1990, vol. VIII
Gale, Norman, died 1942, vol. IV
Gale, Gen. Sir Richard Nelson, 1896–1982, vol. VIII
Gale, Lt-Col Robert, 1887–1937, vol. III
Gale, Walter Frederick, 1865–1945, vol. IV
Gale, Zona, 1874–1939, vol. III
Galea, Robert V., 1882–1962, vol. VI (AII)
Galer, Sir Bertram; see Galer, Sir F. B.
Galer, Sir (Frederic) Bertram, 1873–1968, vol. VI
Galer, John Maxcey, 1839–1919, vol. II
Gales, Sir Robert Richard, 1864–1948, vol. IV
Gales, Wilfred Appleby, 1860–1937, vol. III
Galipeault, Hon. Antonin, 1879–1971, vol. VII
Gall, William James, 1867–1938, vol. III
Gallacher, William, 1876–1951, vol. V
Gallacher, William, 1881–1965, vol. VI
Gallagher, Lt-Col Albert Ernest, 1872–1940, vol. III
Gallagher, Sir James Michael, 1860–1926, vol. II
Gallagher, Rt Rev. John, 1846–1923, vol. II
Gallagher, John Andrew, 1919–1980, vol. VII
Gallagher, Sir William, 1851–1933, vol. III
Gallaher, Major Alexander, died 1938, vol. III
Gallaher, Patrick Edmund, 1917–1988, vol. VIII
Gallaher, Thomas, 1840–1927, vol. II
Gallannaugh, Bertram William Leonard, 1900–1957, vol. V
Gallarati Scotti, Tommaso, 1878–1966, vol. VI
Gallardo, Angel, 1867–1934, vol. III
Galleghan, Brig. Sir Frederick Gallagher, 1897–1971, vol. VII
Galletti di Cadilhac, Countess, (Hon. Margaret Isabella Collier), 1846–1928, vol. II
Galli-Curci, Amelita, 1882–1963, vol. VI
Gallichan, Walter M., died 1946, vol. IV
Gallico, Paul William, 1897–1976, vol. VII
Gallie, Maj.-Gen. James Stuart, 1870–1943, vol. IV
Gallieni, Joseph, 1849–1916, vol. II
Gallienne, Wilfred Hansford, 1897–1956, vol. V
Gallier, William Henry, 1855–1946, vol. IV
Galliffet, Marquis de; Gaston Alexandre Auguste, 1830–1909, vol. I
Galliher, Hon. William Alfred, 1860–1934, vol. III
Gallon, Tom, 1866–1914, vol. I
Gallon, William Anthony, 1898–1962, vol. VI
Gallop, Constantine, died 1967, vol. VI
Gallop, Rev. Edward Jordan, 1850–1928, vol. II
Gallop, Rodney Alexander, 1901–1948, vol. IV
Galloway, 10th Earl of, 1835–1901, vol. I
Galloway, 11th Earl of, 1836–1920, vol. II
Galloway, 12th Earl of, 1892–1978, vol. VII
Galloway, Countess of; (Mary Arabella Arthur Cecil), died 1903, vol. I
Galloway, Alexander, 1901–1965, vol. VI
Galloway, Lt-Gen. Sir Alexander, 1895–1977, vol. VII
Galloway, Lt-Col Arnold Crawshaw, 1901–1988, vol. VIII
Galloway, Adm. Arthur Archibald Campbell, 1855–1918, vol. II
Galloway, Sir David, 1858–1943, vol. IV
Galloway, Col Frank Lennox, 1869–1949, vol. IV
Galloway, George, died 1933, vol. III

Galloway, Sir James, 1862–1922, vol. II
Galloway, Maj.-Gen. John Mawby Clossey, 1840–1916, vol. II
Galloway, Maj.-Gen. Rudolf William, 1891–1976, vol. VII
Galloway, Sir William, 1840–1927, vol. II
Galloway, William Johnson, 1866–1931, vol. III
Gallwey, Col Edmond Joseph, 1850–1927, vol. II
Gallwey, Sir John Frankland-Payne-, 4th Bt, 1889–1955, vol. V
Gallwey, Hon. Sir Michael Henry, 1826–1912, vol. I
Gallwey, Sir Ralph William Frankland Payne-, 3rd Bt, 1843–1916, vol. II
Gallwey, Sir Reginald Frankland Payne-, 5th Bt, 1889–1964, vol. VI
Gallwey, Maj.-Gen. Sir Thomas Joseph, 1852–1933, vol. III
Gallwey, Sir Thomas Lionel, 1821–1906, vol. I
Gallwey, Captain William Thomas Frankland Payne-, 1881–1914, vol. I (A), vol. II
Galpin, Sir Albert James, 1903–1984, vol. VIII
Galpin, Rev. Arthur John, 1861–1926, vol. II
Galpin, Rev. Francis William, 1858–1945, vol. IV
Galsworthy, Sir Arthur Norman, 1916–1986, vol. VIII
Galsworthy, Sir Edwin Henry, 1831–1920, vol. II
Galsworthy, John, 1867–1933, vol. III
Galt, Alexander, 1854–1938, vol. III
Galt, Alexander Casimir, 1853–1936, vol. III
Galt, Sir Thomas, 1815–1901, vol. I
Galton, Rt Rev. Compton Theodore, 1855–1931, vol. III
Galton, Sir Douglas, 1822–1899, vol. I
Galton, Sir Francis, 1822–1911, vol. I
Galton, Frank Wallis, 1867–1952, vol. V
Galtrey, Albert Sidney, died 1935, vol. III
Galway, 7th Viscount, 1844–1931, vol. III
Galway, 8th Viscount, 1882–1943, vol. IV
Galway, 9th Viscount, 1929–1971, vol. VII
Galway, 10th Viscount, 1894–1977, vol. VII
Galway, 11th Viscount, 1900–1980, vol. VII
Galway, Lt-Col Sir Henry Lionel, 1859–1949, vol. IV
Gamage, Albert Walter, 1855–1930, vol. III
Gamage, Sir Leslie, 1887–1972, vol. VII
Gambier, Kenyon; see Lathrop, L. A.
Gambier-Parry, Major Ernest, 1853–1936, vol. III
Gambier-Parry, Maj.-Gen. Michael Denman, 1891–1976, vol. VII
Gambier-Parry, Brig. Sir Richard, 1894–1965, vol. VI
Gambier-Parry, Thomas Robert, 1883–1935, vol. III
Gamble, Rev. Arthur Mellor, 1899–1975, vol. VII
Gamble, Sir David, 1st Bt, 1823–1907, vol. I
Gamble, Sir David, 3rd Bt, 1876–1943, vol. IV
Gamble, Sir David, 5th Bt, 1933–1984, vol. VIII
Gamble, Sir David Arthur Josias, 4th Bt, 1907–1982, vol. VIII
Gamble, Adm. Sir Douglas Austin, 1856–1934, vol. III
Gamble, Sir (Frederick) Herbert, 1907–1983, vol. VIII
Gamble, Frederick William, 1869–1926, vol. II
Gamble, Brig. Geoffrey Massey, 1896–1970, vol. VI

Gamble, Very Rev. Henry Reginald, died 1931, vol. III
Gamble, Sir Herbert; see Gamble, Sir F. H.
Gamble, James Sykes, 1847–1925, vol. II
Gamble, Rev. John, 1859–1929, vol. III
Gamble, Sir Josias Christopher, 2nd Bt, 1848–1908, vol. I
Gamble, Sir Reginald Arthur, 1862–1930, vol. III
Gamble, Brig.-Gen. Richard Narrien, 1860–1937, vol. III
Gamble, Robert Edward, 1922–1975, vol. VII
Gamble, Victor Felix, 1886–1952, vol. V
Gamblin, Sir George Henry, 1870–1930, vol. III
Game, Henry Clement, died 1966, vol. VI
Game, Air Vice-Marshal Sir Philip Woolcott, 1876–1961, vol. VI
Gamelin, Général Maurice Gustave, 1872–1958, vol. V
Games, Ven. Joshua H.; see Hughes-Games.
Gamgee, Arthur, 1841–1909, vol. I
Gamlen, John Charles Blagdon, 1885–1952, vol. V
Gamley, Henry Snell, 1865–1928, vol. II
Gamlin, Lionel James, 1903–1967, vol. VI
Gammans, Ann Muriel, (Lady Gammans), 1898–1989, vol. VIII
Gammans, Sir David; see Gammans, Sir L. D.
Gammans, Sir (Leonard) David, 1st Bt, 1895–1957, vol. V
Gammell, Lt-Gen. Sir James Andrew Harcourt, 1892–1975, vol. VII
Gammell, Sir Sydney James, 1867–1946, vol. IV
Gammie, John, 1896–1968, vol. VI
Gammon, John Charles, 1887–1973, vol. VII
Gamon, Hugh Reece Percival, 1880–1953, vol. V
Gamow, George, 1904–1968, vol. VI
Gandar Dower, Eric Leslie, 1894–1987, vol. VIII
Gandell, Sir Alan Thomas, 1904–1988, vol. VIII
Gandell, Captain Wilfred Pearse, 1886–1986, vol. VIII
Gander, L(eonard) Marsland, 1902–1986, vol. VIII
Gandhi, Mrs Indira (Nehru), 1917–1984, vol. VIII
Gandhi, Mohandas Karamchand, 1869–1948, vol. IV
Gandhi, Nagardas P., 1886–1960, vol. V (A), vol. VI (AI)
Gandier, Rev. Alfred, 1861–1932, vol. III
Gandolfi, Duke, 1846–1906, vol. I
Gandolfi, Duke, 1899–1937, vol. III
Gandy, Eric Worsley, 1879–1958, vol. V
Gandy, Henry Garnett, 1860–1939, vol. III
Gane, Sir Irving Blanchard, 1892–1972, vol. VII
Gane, Richard Howard, 1912–1988, vol. VIII
Ganesh Datta Shastri, born 1861, vol. III
Ganga Ram, Rai Bahadur Sir Lala, 1851–1927, vol. II
Gange, Edwin Stanley, 1871–1944, vol. IV
Gangulee, Nagendra Nath, 1889–1954, vol. V
Ganguly, Most Rev. Theotonius A., 1920–1977, vol. VII
Ganley, Mrs Caroline Selina, 1879–1966, vol. VI
Gann, Thomas William Francis, died 1938, vol. III
Ganneau, Charles Simon C.; see Clermont-Ganneau.
Gannon, Brig. Jack Rose Compton, 1882–1980, vol. VIII
Gannon, Hon. James Conley, 1860–1924, vol. II
Gannon Rev. Patrick Joseph, 1879–1953, vol. V

Gant, Hon. Tetley, 1856–1928, vol. II
Ganz, Wilhelm, 1833–1914, vol. I
Garbe, Louis Richard, *died* 1957, vol. V
Garbett, Sir Colin Campbell, 1881–1972, vol. VII
Garbett, Most Rev. and Rt Hon. Cyril Forster, 1875–1955, vol. V
Garbett, Lt-Col Hubert Champion, 1873–1939, vol. III
Garbett, Captain Leonard Gillilan, 1879–1974, vol. VII
Garbo, Greta, (Greta Lovisa Gustafsson), 1905–1990, vol. VIII
Garcia, Manuel, 1805–1906, vol. I
Garcke, Emile, 1856–1930, vol. III
Garcke, Sidney, 1885–1948, vol. IV
Garçon, Maurice, 1889–1967, vol. VI
Gard, William Henry, 1854–1936, vol. III
Garde, Engr Captain Robert Boles, 1863–1921, vol. II
Garden, Mary, 1874–1967, vol. VI
Gardener, Sir (Alfred) John, 1897–1985, vol. VIII
Gardener, Sir John; *see* Gardener, Sir A. J.
Gardham, Arthur John, 1899–1983, vol. VIII
Gardiner, Baron (Life Peer); Gerald Austin Gardiner, 1900–1990, vol. VIII
Gardiner, Sir Alan Henderson, 1879–1963, vol. VI
Gardiner, Alfred G., 1865–1946, vol. IV
Gardiner, Col Bernard Calwoodley, 1879–1932, vol. III
Gardiner, Sir Chittampalam Abraham, 1899–1960, vol. V
Gardiner, Lt-Col Christopher John, 1907–1986, vol. VIII
Gardiner, Edward Rawson, 1859–1929, vol. III
Gardiner, Ernest David, 1909–1988, vol. VIII
Gardiner, Rev. Frederic Evelyn, *died* 1928, vol. II
Gardiner, Sir Frederick Crombie, 1855–1937, vol. III
Gardiner, Hon. Frederick George, 1874–1935, vol. III
Gardiner, Frederick Keith, 1904–1989, vol. VIII
Gardiner, Frederick William, 1849–1918, vol. II
Gardiner, Gp Captain George Cecil, 1892–1940, vol. III
Gardiner, Col Henry Lawrence, 1860–1946, vol. IV
Gardiner, Gen. Sir (Henry) Lynedoch, 1820–1897, vol. I
Gardiner, Henry Rolf, 1902–1971, vol. VII
Gardiner, James, 1860–1924, vol. II
Gardiner, Rt Hon. James Garfield, 1883–1962, vol. VI
Gardiner, John, 1852–1932, vol. III
Gardiner, John Stanley, 1872–1946, vol. IV
Gardiner, Keith; *see* Gardiner, F. K.
Gardiner, Linda, *died* 1941, vol. IV
Gardiner, Gen. Sir Lynedoch; *see* Gardiner, Gen. Sir H. L.
Gardiner, Brig. Richard, 1874–1957, vol. V
Gardiner, Brig. Richard, 1900–1989, vol. VIII
Gardiner, Sir Robert Septimus, 1856–1939, vol. III
Gardiner, Robert Strachan, 1874–1950, vol. IV
Gardiner, Samuel Rawson, 1829–1902, vol. I
Gardiner, Sir Thomas Robert, 1883–1964, vol. VI
Gardiner, Rev. Thory Gage, 1857–1941, vol. IV
Gardiner, Walter, 1859–1941, vol. IV

Gardiner, Rev. Canon William, 1848–1925, vol. II
Gardiner, William Dundas, 1830–1900, vol. I
Gardiner-Hill, Harold, 1891–1982, vol. VIII
Gardner, Hon. Mrs Alan, (Nora Beatrice), *died* 1944, vol. IV
Gardner, Col Alan Coulstoun, 1846–1907, vol. I
Gardner, Alice, 1854–1927, vol. II
Gardner, Arthur Duncan, 1884–1978, vol. VII
Gardner, Benjamin, 1896–1956, vol. V
Gardner, Benjamin Walter, 1865–1948, vol. IV
Gardner, Sir Charles B.; *see* Bruce-Gardner.
Gardner, Lt-Col Charles James Hookham, 1875–1962, vol. VI
Gardner, Christopher Thomas, 1842–1914, vol. I
Gardner, Edmund, 1874–1960, vol. V
Gardner, Edmund Garratt, 1869–1935, vol. III
Gardner, Eric Stanley, 1889–1970, vol. VI
Gardner, Sir Ernest, 1846–1925, vol. II
Gardner, Ernest Arthur, 1862–1939, vol. III
Gardner, Major Fitzroy, 1856–1936, vol. III
Gardner, Dame Frances Violet, 1913–1989, vol. VIII
Gardner, Francis William, 1891–1976, vol. VII
Gardner, Frank Matthias, 1908–1980, vol. VII (AII)
Gardner, Ven. George Lawrence Harter, *died* 1925, vol. II
Gardner, Sir George William Hoggan, 1903–1975, vol. VII
Gardner, Dame Helen Louise, 1908–1986, vol. VIII
Gardner, Henry Willoughby, 1861–1948, vol. IV
Gardner, Hugh, 1910–1986, vol. VIII
Gardner, J. Starkie, 1844–1930, vol. III
Gardner, James Clark Molesworth, 1894–1970, vol. VI
Gardner, James Patrick, 1883–1937, vol. III
Gardner, Rt Hon. Sir James Tynte Agg, 1846–1928, vol. II
Gardner, John Addyman, 1867–1946, vol. IV
Gardner, John Dunn, 1811–1903, vol. I
Gardner, Hon. Mrs Nora Beatrice; *see* Gardner, Hon. Mrs Alan.
Gardner, Percy, 1846–1937, vol. III
Gardner, Sir Robert, 1838–1920, vol. II
Gardner, Robert Cotton Bruce, 1889–1964, vol. VI
Gardner, W(alter) Frank, 1900–1983, vol. VIII
Gardner, Walter Myers, 1861–1939, vol. III
Gardner, William, 1845–1926, vol. II
Gardner, William Henry, 1895–1977, vol. VII
Gardner, Air Commodore William Steven, 1909–1983, vol. VIII
Gardner-Brown, Anthony Geoffrey Hopwood, 1913–1978, vol. VII
Gardyne, Lt-Col Charles G.; *see* Greenhill-Gardyne.
Gardyne, John, (Jock), B.; *see* Baron Bruce-Gardyne.
Garfit, William, 1840–1920, vol. II
Garforth, Rear-Adm. Edmund St John, 1836–1920, vol. II
Garforth, Captain Francis Edmund Musgrave, 1874–1953, vol. V
Garforth, Sir William Edward, 1845–1921, vol. II
Garforth, William Henry, 1856–1931, vol. III
Garioch, Lord, (Master of Mar); David Charles of Mar, 1944–1967, vol. VI
Garlake, Maj.-Gen. Storr, 1904–1983, vol. VIII

Garland, Ailsa Mary, (Mrs John Rollit Mason), *died* 1982, vol. VIII
Garland, Sir Archibald, 1867–1937, vol. III
Garland, Charles Alexander Spencer, 1861–1914, vol. I
Garland, Charles Samuel, 1887–1960, vol. V
Garland, Charles Tuller, *died* 1921, vol. II
Garland, Rev. David John, 1864–1939, vol. III
Garland, Col Ernest Alfred Crowder, 1857–1938, vol. III
Garland, Hamlin, 1860–1940, vol. III
Garland, Henry Burnard, 1907–1981, vol. VIII
Garland, Hon. John, 1863–1921, vol. II
Garland, Lester, V. L.; *see* Lester-Garland.
Garland, Patrick Joseph, 1867–1929, vol. III
Garlick, Rev. Canon Wilfred, 1910–1982, vol. VIII
Garmonsway, George Norman, 1898–1967, vol. VI
Garmoyle, Viscount; Hugh Wilfrid John Cairns, 1907–1942, vol. IV
Garnar, Sir James Wilson, 1871–1957, vol. V
Garneau, Sir George; *see* Garneau, Sir J. G.
Garneau, Sir (John) George, 1864–1944, vol. IV
Garneau, Hon. Némèse, 1847–1937, vol. III
Garner, Baron (Life Peer); (Joseph John) Saville Garner, 1908–1983, vol. VIII
Garner, Col Cathcart, 1861–1928, vol. II
Garner, Frank Harold, 1904–1990, vol. VIII
Garner, Frederic Horace, 1893–1964, vol. VI
Garner, Sir Harry Mason, 1891–1977, vol. VII
Garner, John Nance, 1868–1967, vol. VI
Garner, Robert Livingston, 1894–1975, vol. VII
Garner, Walter Wesley, 1864–1938, vol. III
Garner, William, 1870–1953, vol. V
Garner, William Edward, 1889–1960, vol. V
Garnett, Bernard John, 1913–1977, vol. VII
Garnett, David, 1892–1981, vol. VIII
Garnett, Edward, 1868–1937, vol. III
Garnett, Frank Walls, 1867–1922, vol. II
Garnett, Sir George, 1871–1955, vol. V
Garnett, Rear-Adm. Herbert Neville, 1875–1960, vol. V
Garnett, (James Clerk) Maxwell, 1880–1958, vol. V
Garnett, Lucy M. J., *died* 1934, vol. III
Garnett, Martha, 1869–1946, vol. IV
Garnett, Maxwell; *see* Garnett, J. C. M.
Garnett, Col Reginald, 1844–1910, vol. I
Garnett, Richard, 1835–1906, vol. I
Garnett, Robert Singleton, *died* 1932, vol. III
Garnett, Walter James, 1889–1958, vol. V
Garnett, William, 1850–1932, vol. III
Garnett, Lt-Col William Brooksbank, 1875–1946, vol. IV
Garnett, William James, 1878–1965, vol. VI
Garnier, Col Alan Parry, 1886–1963, vol. VI
Garnier, Rev. Edward Southwell, 1850–1938, vol. III
Garnier, John C.; *see* Carpenter-Garnier.
Garnier, Rt Rev. Mark Rodolph C.; *see* Carpenter-Garnier.
Garnier, Lt-Col Walter Keppel, 1882–1969, vol. VI
Garnons Williams, Captain Nevill Glennie, 1899–1983, vol. VIII
Garnsey, Sir Gilbert Francis, 1883–1932, vol. III
Garnsworthy, Baron (Life Peer); Charles James Garnsworthy, 1906–1974, vol. VII

Garnsworthy, Most Rev. Lewis Samuel, 1922–1990, vol. VIII
Garofalo, Baron Raffaele, 1851–1934, vol. III
Garran, Hon. Andrew, 1825–1901, vol. I
Garran, Sir Robert Randolph, 1867–1957, vol. V
Garrard, Maj.-Gen. Apsley C.; *see* Cherry-Garrard.
Garrard, Apsley George Benet C.; *see* Cherry-Garrard.
Garrard, Henry John, 1912–1990, vol. VIII
Garrard, Hon. Jacob, 1846–1931, vol. III
Garratt, Brig.-Gen. Sir Francis Sudlow, 1859–1928, vol. II
Garratt, Geoffrey Theodore, 1888–1942, vol. IV
Garratt, Gerald Reginald Mansel, 1906–1989, vol. VIII
Garratt, Lt-Col John Arthur Thomas, 1842–1919, vol. II
Garratt, Rev. Samuel, 1817–1906, vol. I
Garraway, Sir Edward Charles Frederick, 1865–1932, vol. III
Garrett, Alexander Adnett, 1886–1986, vol. VIII
Garrett, Lt-Gen. Sir (Alwyn) Ragnar, 1900–1977, vol. VII
Garrett, Col Arthur Newson Bruff, 1868–1942, vol. IV
Garrett, Sir (Arthur) Wilfrid, 1880–1967, vol. VI
Garrett, Rev. Charles, 1823–1900, vol. I
Garrett, Sir Douglas Thornbury, 1883–1949, vol. IV
Garrett, Col Edmund, 1840–1914, vol. I
Garrett, Edmund William, 1850–1936, vol. III
Garrett, Edward; *see* Mayo, Isabella
Garrett, F. Edmund, 1865–1907, vol. I
Garrett, Lt-Col Sir Frank, 1869–1952, vol. V
Garrett, Rev. George Henry St Patrick, 1855–1937, vol. III
Garrett, George Mursell, 1834–1897, vol. I
Garrett, Herbert Leonard Offley, 1881–1941, vol. IV
Garrett, Sir Hugh; *see* Garrett, Sir J. H.
Garrett, John Walter Percy, 1902–1966, vol. VI
Garrett, Sir (Joseph) Hugh, 1880–1978, vol. VII
Garrett, Captain Peter Bruff, 1866–1950, vol. IV
Garrett, Philip Leslie, 1888–1978, vol. VII
Garrett, R. W., 1853–1925, vol. II
Garrett, Lt-Gen. Sir Ragnar; *see* Garrett, Lt-Gen. Sir A. R.
Garrett, Sir Ronald Thornbury, 1888–1972, vol. VII
Garrett, Samuel, 1850–1923, vol. II
Garrett, Stephen Denis, 1906–1989, vol. VIII
Garrett, Sir Wilfrid; *see* Garrett, Sir A. W.
Garrett, William, 1890–1967, vol. VI
Garrett, Sir William Herbert, 1900–1977, vol. VII
Garrick, Hon. Sir James Francis, 1836–1907, vol. I
Garrick, Rev. James Percy, *died* 1919, vol. II
Garrison, Lindley Miller, 1864–1932, vol. III
Garrod, Sir Alfred Baring, 1819–1907, vol. I
Garrod, Air Chief Marshal Sir (Alfred) Guy (Roland), 1891–1965, vol. VI
Garrod, Sir Archibald Edward, 1856–1936, vol. III
Garrod, Dorothy Annie Elizabeth, 1892–1968, vol. VI
Garrod, Geoffrey, 1886–1974, vol. VII
Garrod, Rev. Canon George Watts, 1857–1936, vol. III

Garrod, Air Chief Marshal Sir Guy; *see* Garrod, Air Chief Marshal Sir A. G. R.

Garrod, Heathcote William, 1878–1960, vol. V

Garrod, Lawrence Paul, 1895–1979, vol. VII

Garrod, William Henry Edward, 1892–1967, vol. VI

Garrow, Alexander, 1923–1966, vol. VI

Garrow, Hon. James Thompson, 1843–1916, vol. II

Garrow, Sir Nicholas, 1895–1982, vol. VIII

Garrow, Col Robert G., 1876–1932, vol. III

Garsia, Lt-Col Herbert George Anderson, 1871–1965, vol. VI

Garsia, Lt-Col Michael Clare, 1838–1903, vol. I

Garsia, Lt-Col Willoughby Clive, 1881–1961, vol. VI

Garside, Captain Frederick Rodney, 1897–1940, vol. III

Garside, Kenneth, 1913–1983, vol. VIII

Garside, Air Vice-Marshal Kenneth Vernon, 1913–1986, vol. VIII

Garside, Oswald,1869–1942, vol. IV

Garson, Alexander Denis, 1904–1968, vol. VI

Garstang, Cecil, 1904–1979, vol. VII

Garstang, John, 1876–1956, vol. V

Garstang, Walter, 1868–1949, vol. IV

Garsten, John Henry, 1838–1903, vol. I

Garstin, Brig.-Gen. Alfred Allan, 1850–1937, vol. III

Garstin, Charles Fortescue, 1880–1969, vol. VI

Garstin, Crosbie Alfred Norman, 1887–1930, vol. III

Garstin, John Ribton, 1836–1917, vol. II, vol. III

Garstin, Lt-Col William Arthur MacDonell, 1882–1975, vol. VII

Garstin, Sir William Edmund, 1849–1925, vol. II

Garth, Rt Hon. Sir Richard, 1820–1903, vol. I

Garth, Thomas Colleton, 1822–1907, vol. I

Garth, Sir William, 1854–1923, vol. II

Garthwaite, Brig. Clive Charlton, 1909–1979, vol. VII

Garthwaite, Sir William, 1st Bt, 1874–1956, vol. V

Gartlan, Maj.-Gen. Gerald Ion, 1889–1975, vol. VII

Garton, Lt-Col James Archibald, 1891–1969, vol. VI

Garton, John William 1895–1971, vol. VII

Garton, Sir Richard Charles, 1857–1934, vol. III

Gartrell, Rt Rev. Frederick Roy, 1914–1987, vol. VIII

Gartside-Tipping, Col Robert Francis, 1852–1926, vol. II

Garvagh, 3rd Baron, 1852–1915, vol. I

Garvagh, 4th Baron, 1878–1956, vol. V

Garvan, Sir John Joseph, 1873–1927, vol. II

Garvey, Sir Terence Willcocks, 1915–1986, vol. VIII

Garvice, Charles, *died* 1920, vol. II

Garvice, Major Chudleigh, 1875–1921, vol. II

Garvie, Rev. Alfred Ernest, 1861–1945, vol. IV

Garvin, James Louis, *died* 1947, vol. IV

Garvin, Thomas, 1843–1922, vol. II

Garvin, Sir Thomas Forrest, 1881–1940, vol. III

Garwood, Edmund Johnston, 1864–1949, vol. IV

Garwood, Lt-Col Henry Percy, 1882–1956, vol. V

Garwood, Engr-Rear-Adm. Hugh Sydney, 1872–1948, vol. IV

Garwood, Lt-Col John Reginald, 1873–1948, vol. IV

Gary, Elbert Henry, *died* 1927, vol. II

Gary, Romain, 1914–1980, vol. VII

Gascoigne, Sir Alvary Douglas Frederick, 1893–1970, vol. VI

Gascoigne, Lt-Col Cecil Claud Hugh Orby, 1877–1929, vol. III

Gascoigne, Brig.-Gen. Sir (Ernest) Frederick (Orby), 1873–1944, vol. IV

Gascoigne, Col Frederic Richard Thomas Trench, 1851–1937, vol. III

Gascoigne, Brig.-Gen. Sir Frederick; *see* Gascoigne, Brig.-Gen. Sir E. F. O.

Gascoigne, Hubert Claude Victor, *died* 1959, vol. V

Gascoigne, John Henry, 1856–1928, vol. II

Gascoigne, Maj.-Gen. Sir Julian Alvery, 1903–1990, vol. VIII

Gascoigne, Laura Gwendolen, *died* 1949, vol. IV

Gascoigne, Maj.-Gen. Sir William Julius Gascoigne, 1844–1926, vol. II

Gascoyne-Cecil, Victor Alexander, 1891–1977, vol. VII

Gascoyne-Cecil, Rt Rev. Lord William; *see* Cecil.

Gaselee, Gen. Sir Alfred, 1844–1918, vol. II

Gaselee, Sir Stephen, 1882–1943, vol. III

Gash, Robert Walker, 1926–1986, vol. VIII

Gask, George Ernest, 1875–1951, vol. V

Gask, Rear-Adm. (S) Walter, 1870–1949, vol. IV

Gaskain, John Stuart Hinton, 1910–1971, vol. VII

Gaskell, Ven. Albert Fisher, 1874–1950, vol. IV

Gaskell, Surg. Vice-Adm. Sir Arthur, 1871–1952, vol. V

Gaskell, Rt Hon. Charles George Milnes, 1842–1919, vol. II

Gaskell, Lady Constance M.; *see* Milnes Gaskell.

Gaskell, Evelyn Milnes, 1877–1931, vol. III

Gaskell, George Percival, 1868–1934, vol. III

Gaskell, Helen Mary, *died* 1940, vol. III

Gaskell, Henry Melville, 1879–1954, vol. V

Gaskell, Maj.-Gen. Herbert Stuart, 1882–1957, vol. V

Gaskell, Sir Holbrook, 1878–1951, vol. V

Gaskell, Col Joseph, 1849–1930, vol. III

Gaskell, Col Joseph Gerald, 1885–1959, vol. V

Gaskell, Walter Holbrook, 1847–1914, vol. I

Gaskell, William, 1874–1954, vol. V

Gaskin, Arthur J., 1862–1928, vol. II

Gasking, Mrs Ella Hudson, *died* 1966, vol. VI

Gaskoin, Charles Jacinth Bellairs, *died* 1955, vol. V

Gasquet, His Eminence Cardinal Francis Aidan, 1846–1929, vol. III

Gass, John Bradshaw, 1855–1939, vol. III

Gass, Sir Michael David Irving, 1916–1983, vol. VIII

Gass, Sir Neville Archibald, 1893–1965, vol. VI

Gasser, Herbert Spencer, 1888–1963, vol. VI

Gasson, Sir Lionel Bell, 1889–1977, vol. VII

Gastambide, Philippe, 1905–1984, vol. VIII

Gaster, Moses, 1856–1939, vol. III

Gastrell, Lt-Col Everard Huddleston, 1898–1960, vol. V

Gastrell, Sir William Houghton-, 1852–1935, vol. III

Gastrell, William Shaw Harriss, 1862–1948, vol. IV

Gasyonga II, Sir Charles Godfrey, 1910–1982, vol. VIII

Gatacre, Rear-Adm. Galfry George Ormond, 1907–1983, vol. VIII

Gatacre, Maj.-Gen. Sir John, 1841–1932, vol. III

Gatacre, Maj.-Gen. Sir William Forbes, 1843–1906, vol. I

Gatehouse, Maj.-Gen. Alexander Hugh, 1895–1964, vol. VI

Gatenby, James Brontë, 1892–1960, vol. V

Gater, Sir George Henry, 1886–1963, vol. VI

Gates, Caleb Frank, 1857–1946, vol. IV

Gates, Edward, *died* 1965, vol. VI

Gates, Ernest Everard, 1903–1984, vol. VIII

Gates, Sir Frank Campbell, 1862–1947, vol. IV

Gates, Horace Frederick Alfred, 1903–1962, vol. VI

Gates, Lewis Edwards, 1860–1924, vol. II

Gates, Percy, *died* 1940, vol. III

Gates, R(eginald) Ruggles, 1882–1962, vol. VI

Gates, Sidney Barrington, 1893–1973, vol. VII

Gates, Sylvester Govett, 1901–1972, vol. VII

Gates, Thomas Sovereign, Jr, 1906–1983, vol. VIII

Gates, Walter George, *died* 1936, vol. III

Gates, William Thomas George, 1908–1990, vol. VIII

Gatey, Joseph, 1855–1912, vol. I

Gathorne-Hardy, Hon. Alfred Erskine, 1845–1918, vol. II

Gathorne-Hardy, Col Hon. Charles Gathorne, 1841–1919, vol. II

Gathorne-Hardy, Gen. Hon. Sir Francis; *see* Gathorne-Hardy, Gen. Hon. Sir J. F.

Gathorne-Hardy, Geoffrey Malcolm, 1878–1972, vol. VII

Gathorne-Hardy, Lady Isobel, 1875–1963, vol. VI

Gathorne-Hardy, Gen. Hon. Sir (John) Francis, 1874–1949, vol. IV

Gathorne-Hardy, Hon. Robert, 1902–1973, vol. VII

Gati, Benerji D.; *see* Durga Gati.

Gatley, Clement Carpenter, 1881–1936, vol. III

Gatley, John, 1845–1934, vol. III

Gatliff, Gen. Albert Farrar, 1857–1927, vol. II

Gatling, Richard Jordan, 1818–1903, vol. I

Gatt, Hon. Camillo, vol. II

Gatt, Hon. Lorenzo, 1857–1938, vol. III

Gatti, Sir John M., 1872–1929, vol. III

Gattie, Alfred Warwick, 1856–1925, vol. II

Gattie, Maj.-Gen. Kenneth Francis Drake, 1890–1982, vol. VIII

Gattie, Vernon Rodney Montagu, 1885–1966, vol. VI

Gatty, Rev. Alfred, 1813–1903, vol. I

Gatty, Sir Alfred Scott S.; *see* Scott-Gatty.

Gatty, Nicholas Comyn, 1874–1946, vol. IV

Gatty, Sir Stephen Herbert, 1849–1922, vol. II

Gaudet, Col Frederick Mondelet, 1867–1947, vol. IV

Gaudin, Engr-Rear-Adm. Edouard, *died* 1945, vol. IV

Gaughran, Rt Rev. Laurence, 1842–1928, vol. II

Gaughren, Rt Rev. Matthew, 1843–1914, vol. I

Gaul, Walter Miller, 1867–1938, vol. III

Gaul, Rt Rev. William Thomas, *died* 1928, vol. II

Gauld, David, *died* 1936, vol. III

Gault, Brig. A(ndrew) Hamilton, 1882–1958, vol. V

Gault, James, 1850–1927, vol. II

Gault, Brig. Sir James Frederick 1902–1977, vol. VII

Gaumont, Léon Ernest, 1864–1946, vol. IV

Gaunt, Lt-Col Cecil Robert, 1863–1938, vol. III

Gaunt, Sir Edwin, 1818–1903, vol. I

Gaunt, Adm. Sir Ernest Frederick Augustus, 1865–1940, vol. III

Gaunt, Adm. Sir Guy Reginald Archer, 1870–1953, vol. V

Gaunt, Rev. Canon Howard Charles Adie, (Tom Gaunt), 1902–1983, vol. VIII

Gaunt, Mary, *died* 1942, vol. IV

Gaunt, Percy Reginald, 1875–1926, vol. II

Gaunt, Rev. Canon Tom; *see* Gaunt, Rev. Canon H. C. A.

Gaunt, Walter Henry, 1874–1951, vol. V

Gaunt, William, 1900–1980, vol. VII

Gauntlett, Major Eric Gerald, 1885–1972, vol. VII

Gauntlett, Sir Frederic; *see* Gauntlett, Sir M. F.

Gauntlett, Sir (Mager) Frederic, 1873–1964, vol. VI

Gaussen, Maj.-Gen. Charles de Lisle, 1896–1971, vol. VII

Gaussen, Brig.-Gen. James Robert, 1871–1959, vol. V

Gaussen, Perceval David Campbell, 1862–1928, vol. II

Gauthier, Most Rev. Charles Hugh, 1843–1922, vol. II

Gauthier, Rt Rev. George, 1871–1940, vol. III

Gauthier-Villars, Henry, 1859–1931, vol. III

Gautier, C. Lucien, 1850–1924, vol. II

Gautier, Judith, *died* 1917, vol. II

Gauvain, (Catherine Joan) Suzette, (Mrs R. O. Murray), *died* 1980, vol. VII

Gauvain, Sir Henry, 1878–1945, vol. IV

Gauvain, Suzette; *see* Gauvain, C. J. S.

Gauvain, W., *died* 1910, vol. I

Gavan-Duffy, Hon. Sir Charles Leonard, 1882–1961, vol. VI

Gavan-Duffy, Thomas, 1867–1932, vol. III

Gavey, Clarence John, 1911–1982, vol. VIII

Gavey, Sir John, 1842–1923, vol. II

Gavin, Ethel, *died* 1918, vol. II

Gavin, Malcolm Ross, 1908–1989, vol. VIII

Gavin, Michael, 1843–1919, vol. II

Gavin, Sir William, 1886–1968, vol. VI

Gavin, William Aloysius, *died* 1948, vol. IV

Gavito, Vicente S.; *see* Sanchez-Gavito.

Gawan Taylor, Henry, 1855–1928, vol. II

Gawne, Ewan Moore, 1889–1978, vol. VII

Gawsworth, John, 1912–1970, vol. VI

Gawthorpe, Brig. John Bernard, 1891–1979, vol. VII

Gay, Maj.-Gen. Sir Arthur William, 1863–1944, vol. IV

Gay, Edwin Francis, 1867–1946, vol. IV

Gay, Maisie, 1883–1945, vol. IV

Gayda, Virginio, 1885–1944, vol. IV

Gaye, Sir Arthur Stretton, 1881–1960, vol. V

Gaye, Rev. Herbert Charles, *died* 1931, vol. III

Gayer, Arthur David, 1903–1951, vol. V

Gayer-Anderson, Major Robert Grenville, 1881–1945, vol. IV

Gayer-Anderson, Col Thomas Gayer, 1881–1960, vol. V

Gayford, Air Cdre Oswald Robert, 1893–1945, vol. IV

Gayley, Charles Mills, 1858–1932, vol. III

Gaze, Alfred Harold, 1885–1954, vol. V

Geach, William Foster, 1859–1940, vol. III (A), vol. IV

Geake, Charles, 1867–1919, vol. II

Geake, Maj.-Gen. Clifford Henry, 1894–1982, vol. VIII

Geard, John Reginald, 1861–1934, vol. III

Geary, Major Benjamin Handley, 1891–1976, vol. VII

Geary, Lt-Col Hon. George Reginald, 1874–1954, vol. V

Geary, Lt-Gen. Sir Henry Le Guay, 1837–1918, vol. II

Geary, Sir William Nevill Montgomerie, 5th Bt, 1859–1944, vol. IV

Gebbie, Sir Frederick St John, 1871–1939, vol. III

Geddes, 1st Baron, 1879–1954, vol. V

Geddes, 2nd Baron, 1907–1975, vol. VII

Geddes of Epsom, Baron (Life Peer); Charles John Geddes, 1897–1983, vol. VIII

Geddes, Air Cdre Andrew James Wray, 1906–1988, vol. VIII

Geddes, Rt Hon. Sir Eric Campbell, 1875–1937, vol. III

Geddes, Ewan, died 1935, vol. III

Geddes, Lt-Col George Hessing, 1864–1933, vol. III

Geddes, Irvine Campbell, 1882–1962, vol. VI

Geddes, Brig.-Gen. John Gordon, 1863–1919, vol. II

Geddes, Norman Bel, 1893–1958, vol. V

Geddes, Sir Patrick, 1854–1932, vol. III

Geddes, Col Robert James, 1858–1928, vol. II

Geddes, Rt Rev. William Archibald, 1894–1947, vol. IV

Geddes, Sir William Duguid, 1828–1900, vol. I

Geddie, John, 1848–1937, vol. III

Geddie, John Liddell, 1881–1969, vol. VI

Geddis, Sir William Duncan, 1896–1971, vol. VII

Geden, Alfred Shenington, 1857–1936, vol. III

Gedge, Rev. Edward Lionel, 1861–1932, vol. III

Gedge, Rev. Hugh Somerville, 1844–1923, vol. II

Gedge, Montagu Lathom, 1899–1958, vol. V

Gedge, Sydney, 1829–1923, vol. II

Gedye, George Eric Rowe, 1890–1970, vol. VI

Gedye, Nicholas George, 1874–1947, vol. IV

Gee, Col Ernest Edward, 1888–1959, vol. V

Gee, Lt-Col Frederick William, 1863–1930, vol. III

Gee, Harry Percy, 1874–1962, vol. VI

Gee, Very Rev. Henry, died 1938, vol. III

Gee, Hubert George, 1909–1959, vol. V

Gee, Rev. Richard, 1817–1902, vol. I

Gee, Captain Robert, 1876–1960, vol. V

Gee, Samuel Jones, 1839–1911, vol. I

Gee, William Winson Haldane, 1857–1928, vol. II

Geen, Burnard, 1882–1966, vol. VI

Geen, Harry, died 1939, vol. III

Geer, Ven. George Thomas, 1844–1918, vol. II

Geffen, John Lionel Henry, 1925–1975, vol. VII

Geijer, Eric Neville, died 1941, vol. IV

Geikie, Sir Archibald, 1835–1924, vol. II

Geikie, Rev. Cunningham, 1824–1906, vol. I

Geikie, James, 1839–1915, vol. I

Geikie-Cobb, Ivo; see Cobb.

Geikie-Cobb, Rev. William Frederick, 1857–1941, vol. IV

Geil, William Edgar, died 1925, vol. II

Geldart, Rev. Ernest, 1848–1929, vol. III

Geldart, Rev. James William, 1837–1914, vol. I

Geldart, William Martin, 1870–1922, vol. II

Gelder, Sir Alfred; see Gelder, Sir W. A.

Gelder, Sir (William) Alfred, 1855–1941, vol. IV

Gell, Hon. Mrs Edith Mary, 1860–1944, vol. IV

Gell, Rt Rev. Frederick, died 1902, vol. I

Gell, Herbert George, 1856–1931, vol. III

Gell, Sir James, 1823–1905, vol. I

Gell, Philip Lyttelton, 1852–1926, vol. II

Gell, Rev. Canon William, 1859–1939, vol. III

Gell, William Charles Coleman, 1888–1969, vol. VI

Gell, William John, 1893–1961, vol. VI

Gellert, Leon, 1892–1977, vol. VII

Gellibrand, Maj.-Gen. Sir John, 1872–1945, vol. IV

Gelsthorpe, Rt Rev. (Alfred) Morris, 1892–1968, vol. VI

Gelsthorpe, Rt Rev. Morris; see Gelsthorpe, Rt Rev. A. M.

Gem, Rev. Hubert Arnold, died 1936, vol. III

Gemmell, Alan Robertson, 1913–1986, vol. VIII

Gemmell, Sir Arthur Alexander, 1892–1960, vol. V

Gemmell, George Harrison, 1860–1941, vol. IV

Gemmell, Samson, died 1913, vol. I

Gemmell, Lt-Col William Alexander Stewart, 1874–1932, vol. III

Gemmill, James Fairlie, died 1926, vol. II

Gemmill, Lt-Col William, 1878–1918, vol. II

Genée-Isitt, Dame Adeline, 1878–1970, vol. VI

Genese, Robert William, 1848–1928, vol. II

Genevoix, Maurice Charles Louis, 1890–1980, vol. VII

Genn, Leo John, 1905–1978, vol. VII

Genn, Captain Otto Hermann H.; see Hawke-Genn.

Gennadius, Joannes, 1844–1932, vol. III

Gennings, John Frederick, 1885–1955, vol. V

Genochio, Henry, 1862–1933, vol. III

Gent, Sir Edward; see Gent, Sir G. E. J.

Gent, Sir (Gerard) Edward (James), 1895–1948, vol. IV

Gent, John, 1844–1927, vol. II

Gentele, (Claes-) Göran Herman Arvid, 1920–1972, vol. VII

Gentele, Göran; see Gentele, C.-G. H. A.

Gentili, Most Rev. Charles, 1842–1917, vol. II

Gentle, Francis Steward, 1894–1962, vol. VI

Gentle, Sir Frederick William, 1892–1966, vol. VI

Gentle, Sir William Benjamin, 1864–1948, vol. IV

Gentles, Thomas A., 1867–1943, vol. IV

Gentner, Wolfgang, 1906–1980, vol. VII (AII)

Gentry, Jack Sydney Bates, 1899–1978, vol. VII

Geoffrey-Lloyd, Baron (Life Peer); Geoffrey William Geoffrey-Lloyd, 1902–1984, vol. VIII

Geoffrion, Aimé, 1872–1946, vol. IV

Geoffrion, Victor, 1851–1923, vol. II

Geoghegan, Col Francis Edward, 1869–1945, vol. IV

Geoghegan, Hon. James, died 1951, vol. V

Geoghegan, Joseph, 1888–1948, vol. IV

Geoghegan, Col Norman Meredith, 1876–1962, vol. VI

Geoghegan, Brig.-Gen. Stannus, 1866–1929, vol. III

George, Sir Anthony Hastings, 1886–1944, vol. IV

George, Ven. Christopher Owen, 1891–1977, vol. VII

George, Daniel, 1890–1967, vol. VI

George, Edward Claudius Scotney, 1865–1936, vol. III

George, Sir Edward James, died 1950, vol. IV

George, Sir Ernest, 1839–1922, vol. II

George, Frank Bernard, 1899–1974, vol. VII

George, Rev. Canon George Frank, 1873–1942, vol. IV

George, Herbert Horace, 1890–1982, vol. VIII

George, Hereford B., 1838–1910, vol. I

George, Hugh Shaw, 1892–1967, vol. VI

George, Sir John Clarke, 1901–1972, vol. VII

George, Mary Dorothy, *died* 1971, vol. VII

George, Lady Megan L.; *see* Lloyd George.

George, Air Vice-Marshal Sir Robert Allingham, 1896–1967, vol. VI

George, Rt Rev. Mgr Thomas, 1872–1943, vol. IV

George, Thomas Neville, 1904–1980, vol. VII

George, W. L., 1882–1926, vol. II

George, Senator Walter Franklin, 1878–1957, vol. V

George, Hon. William James, 1853–1931, vol. III

George, William R., 1866–1936, vol. III

George-Brown, Baron (Life Peer); George Alfred George-Brown, 1914–1985, vol. VIII

Georges, Sir (James) Olva, 1890–1976, vol. VII

Georges, Sir Olva; *see* Georges, Sir J. O.

Georges-Picot, Jacques Marie Charles, 1900–1987, vol. VIII

Gepp, Maj.-Gen. Sir Cyril; *see* Gepp, Maj.-Gen. Sir E. C.

Gepp, Maj.-Gen. Sir (Ernest) Cyril, 1879–1964, vol. VI

Gepp, Sir Herbert William, 1877–1954, vol. V

Gepp, Rev. Nicolas Parker, *died* 1921, vol. II

Geraghty, Sir William, 1917–1977, vol. VII

Gerahty, Sir Charles Cyril, 1888–1978, vol. VII

Gerald, William John, 1850–1923, vol. II

Gerard, 2nd Baron, 1851–1902, vol. I

Gerard, 3rd Baron, 1883–1953, vol. V

Gerard, Amelia Louise, 1878–1970, vol. VI

Gerard, Bt Col Charles Robert Tolver Michael, 1894–1971, vol. VII

Gerard, Dorothea; *see* Longard de Longgarde, D.

Gerard, Rt Rev. George Vincent, 1898–1984, vol. VIII

Gerard, Hon. James Watson, 1867–1951, vol. V

Gerard, (Jane) Emily, (Madame de Laszowska), 1849–1905, vol. I

Gerard, Father John, 1840–1912, vol. I

Gerard, Gen. Sir Montagu Gilbert, 1843–1905, vol. 1

Gerard-Dicconson, Hon. Robert Joseph; *see* Dicconson.

Gerardy, Jean, 1877–1929, vol. III

Géraud, Charles Joseph André, 1882–1974, vol. VII

Gerbrandy, Pieter S., 1885–1961, vol. VI

Gere, Charles March, 1869–1957, vol. V

Gerhard, Roberto Juan René, 1896–1970, vol. VI

Gerhardie, William Alexander, 1895–1977, vol. VII

Gerhardt, Elena, 1883–1961, vol. VI

Gericke van Herwijnen, Baron, *died* 1930, vol. III

Gérin, Winifred Eveleen, (Mrs John Lock), 1901–1981, vol. VIII

Germaine, Robert Arthur, *died* 1905, vol. I

German, Sir Edward, 1862–1936, vol. III

German, Major Sir James, 1879–1958, vol. V

German, Sir Ronald Ernest, 1905–1983, vol. VIII

German, William Manley, 1851–1933, vol. III

Germanos, Strenopoulos, 1872–1951, vol. V

Gerome, Jean Leon, 1824–1904, vol. I

Gerothwohl, Maurice Alfred, 1877–1941, vol. IV

Gerrans, Henry Tresawna, 1858–1921, vol. II

Gerrard, Sir (Albert) Denis, 1903–1965, vol. VI

Gerrard, Charles Robert, *died* 1964, vol. VI

Gerrard, Sir Denis; *see* Gerrard, Sir A. D.

Gerrard, Air Cdre Eugene Louis, 1881–1963, vol. VI

Gerrard, Major Frederick Wernham, 1887–1974, vol. VII

Gerrard, Maj.-Gen. John Joseph, 1867–1938, vol. III

Gerry, Hon. Elbridge Thomas, 1837–1927, vol. II

Gershwin, George, 1898–1937, vol. III

Gertler, Mark, 1892–1939, vol. III

Gerty, Paymaster Captain Francis Hamilton, 1876–1955, vol. V

Gervais, Hon. Honoré Hippolyte Achille, 1864–1915, vol. I, vol. III

Gervers, Brig. Francis Richard Soutter, 1873–1971, vol. VII

Gervis, Henry, 1837–1924, vol. II

Gervis, Henry, 1863–1941, vol. IV

Gervis-Meyrick, Sir George Augustus Eliott Tapps; *see* Meyrick.

Gery, Henry Theodore W.; *see* Wade-Gery.

Gesell, Arnold, 1880–1961, vol. VI

Gethin, Sir Richard Charles Percy, 7th Bt, 1847–1921, vol. II

Gethin, Lt-Col Sir Richard Patrick St Lawrence, 9th Bt, 1911–1988, vol. VIII

Gethin, Col Sir Richard Walter St Lawrence, 8th Bt, 1878–1946, vol. IV

Gettins, Lt-Col Joseph Holmes, 1873–1954, vol. V

Getty, J(ean) Paul, 1892–1976, vol. VII

Geyer, Albertus Lourens, 1894–1969, vol. VI

Geyl, Pieter, 1887–1966, vol. VI

Ghislain, Léon; *see* Carton de Wiart, L. C. G.

Ghormley, Vice-Adm. Robert Lee, 1883–1958, vol. V

Ghosal, Mrs Srimati Svarna Kumari Devi, 1857–1932, vol. III

Ghose, Sir Bipin Behary, 1868–1934, vol. III

Ghose, Sir Charu Chunder, 1874–1934, vol. III

Ghose, Sir Chunder Madhub, 1838–1918, vol. II

Ghose, Hemendra Prasad, 1876–1962, vol. VI

Ghose, Sir Rashbehary, 1845–1921, vol. II

Ghose, Sir Sarat Kumar, 1879–1963, vol. VI

Ghosh, Sir Jnan Chandra, 1894–1959, vol. V

Ghulam Mohammed, 1895–1956, vol. V

Ghuznavi, Hon. Alhadj Nawab Bahadur Sir Abdelkerim Abu Ahmed Kahan of Dilduar, 1872–1939, vol. III

Giacometti, Alberto, 1901–1966, vol. VI

Giamatti, (Angelo) Bartlett, 1938–1989, vol. VIII

Giamatti, Bartlett; *see* Giamatti, A. B.

Giannini, Amadeo Peter, 1870–1949, vol. IV

Giauque, William Francis, 1895–1982, vol. VIII

Gib, Gen. Sir William Anthony, 1827–1915, vol. I

Gibb, Sir Alexander, 1872–1958, vol. V

Gibb, Alistair Monteith, 1901–1955, vol. V

Gibb, Andrew Dewar, *died* 1974, vol. VII

Gibb, Sir Claude Dixon, 1898–1959, vol. V

Gibb, Maj.-Gen. Sir Evan, 1877–1947, vol. IV

Gibb, George Dutton, 1920–1986, vol. VIII

Gibb, Sir George Stegmann, 1850–1925, vol. II

Gibb, Sir Hamilton Alexander Rosskeen, 1895–1971, vol. VII

Gibb, James, 1844–1910, vol. I

Gibb, Rev. James, 1857–1935, vol. III
Gibb, James A. T., 1842–1922, vol. II
Gibb, James Rattray, 1844–1946, vol. IV
Gibb, Rev. John, 1835–1915, vol. I
Gibb, Col John Hassard Stewart 1859–1933, vol. III
Gibb, Malcolm Couper, 1861–1938, vol. III
Gibb, Maurice Sylvester, 1878–1950, vol. IV
Gibb, Robert, 1845–1932, vol. III
Gibb, Robertson Fyffe, 1868–1944, vol. IV
Gibb, Lt-Col Ronald Charles, 1873–1946, vol. IV
Gibb, Thomas George, 1915–1980, vol. VII
Gibb, William Elphinstone, 1943–1988, vol. VIII
Gibbard, George, 1886–1960, vol. V
Gibbard, Maj.-Gen. Thomas Wykes, 1865–1957, vol. V
Gibbens, Brian; *see* Gibbens, E. B.
Gibbens, (Edward) Brian, 1912–1985, vol. VIII
Gibbens, Frank Edward Hilary George, 1913–1987, vol. VIII
Gibbens, Trevor Charles Noel, 1912–1983, vol. VIII
Gibberd, Sir Frederick, 1908–1984, vol. VIII
Gibberd, George Frederick, *died* 1976, vol. VII
Gibbes, Cuthbert Chapman, 1850–1927, vol. II
Gibbes, Sir Edward Osborne-, 3rd Bt, 1850–1931, vol. III
Gibbes, Sir Philip Arthur Osborne-, 4th Bt, 1884–1940, vol. III
Gibbes, Reginald Prescott, 1867–1933, vol. III
Gibbings, Robert John, 1889–1958, vol. V
Gibbins, Frederick William, 1861–1937, vol. III
Gibbins, Rev. Henry de Beltgens, 1865–1907, vol. I
Gibbins, Joseph, 1888–1965, vol. VI
Gibbins, Theodore, 1876–1952, vol. V
Gibbon, Col Charles Monk, 1877–1937, vol. III
Gibbon, Sir Douglas Stuart, 1882–1960, vol. V
Gibbon, Sir Gwilym; *see* Gibbon, Sir. I. G.
Gibbon, Sir (Ioan) Gwilym, 1874–1948, vol. IV
Gibbon, Brig.-Gen. James Aubrey, 1864–1947, vol. IV
Gibbon, Rev. James Morgan, *died* 1932, vol. III
Gibbon, Brig. John Houghton, 1878–1960, vol. V
Gibbon, Monk; *see* Gibbon, W. M.
Gibbon, Perceval, 1879–1926, vol. II
Gibbon, Thomas Mitchell, *died* 1921, vol. II
Gibbon, Sir William Duff, 1837–1919, vol. II
Gibbon, Lt-Col William Duff, 1880–1955, vol. V
Gibbon, (William) Monk, 1896–1987, vol. VIII
Gibbons, Major Sir Alexander Doran, 7th Bt, 1873–1956, vol. V
Gibbons, Sir Charles, 6th Bt, 1828–1909, vol. I
Gibbons, Brig. Edward John, 1906–1990, vol. VIII
Gibbons, Major Edward Stephen, 1883–1918, vol. II
Gibbons, Cdre George, *died* 1959, vol. V
Gibbons, Sir George Christie, 1848–1918, vol. II
Gibbons, His Eminence Cardinal James, 1834–1921, vol. II
Gibbons, James Francis, 1890–1957, vol. V
Gibbons, James Samuel, 1850–1914, vol. I
Gibbons, Sir John Edward, 8th Bt, 1914–1982, vol. VIII
Gibbons, John Lloyd, 1837–1919, vol. II
Gibbons, Stella Dorothea, (Mrs A. B. Webb), 1902–1989, vol. VIII

Gibbons, Sir Thomas Clarke Pilling, 1868–1934, vol. III
Gibbons, Lt-Col Sir Walter, 1871–1933, vol. III
Gibbons, Sir William, 1841–1930, vol. III
Gibbons, Col William Ernest, 1898–1976, vol. VII
Gibbons, Sir William Kenrick, 1876–1957, vol. V
Gibbs, Dame Anstice Rosa, 1905–1978, vol. VII
Gibbs, Antony, 1842–1907, vol. I
Gibbs, Major Arthur Hamilton, *died* 1964, vol. VI
Gibbs, Cecil Armstrong, 1889–1960, vol. V
Gibbs, Charles, *died* 1943, vol. IV
Gibbs, Sir Charles Henry, 1854–1924, vol. II
Gibbs, Dennis Raleigh, 1922–1985, vol. VIII
Gibbs, Edward Mitchel, 1847–1935, vol. III
Gibbs, Sir Frank Stannard, 1895–1983, vol. VIII
Gibbs, Hon. Sir Geoffrey Cokayne, 1901–1975, vol. VII
Gibbs, George Howard, 1889–1969, vol. VI
Gibbs, Captain George Louis Downall, 1882–1956, vol. V
Gibbs, Hon. Henry Lloyd, 1861–1907, vol. I
Gibbs, Rt Hon. Sir Humphrey Vicary, 1902–1990, vol. VIII
Gibbs, Col James Alec Charles, 1867–1930, vol. III
Gibbs, John Herbert, 1872–1962, vol. VI
Gibbs, Ven. Hon. Kenneth Francis, 1856–1935, vol. III
Gibbs, Brig. Lancelot Merivale, 1889–1966, vol. VI
Gibbs, Very Rev. Michael McCausland, 1900–1962, vol. VI
Gibbs, Hon. Michael Patrick, 1870–1943, vol. IV
Gibbs, Norman Henry, 1910–1990, vol. VIII
Gibbs, Sir Philip, 1877–1962, vol. VI
Gibbs, Rev. Thomas Crook, *died* 1914, vol. I
Gibbs, Hon. Vicary, 1853–1932, vol. III
Gibbs, Walter George, 1872–1929, vol. III
Gibbs, Lt-Col William, 1877–1963, vol. VI
Gibbs, William Edward, 1889–1934, vol. III
Gibbs-Smith, Charles Harvard, 1909–1981, vol. VIII
Gibbs-Smith, Very Rev. Oswin Harvard, 1901–1969, vol. VI
Giberne, Agnes, 1845–1939, vol. III
Giblin, Major Lyndhurst Falkiner, 1872–1951, vol. V
Giblin, Col Wilfrid Wanostrocht, 1872–1951, vol. V
Gibney, James, 1847–1908, vol. I (A), vol. III
Gibney, Rt Rev. Matthew, 1838–1925, vol. II
Gibson, Hon. Lord; Robert Gibson, 1886–1965, vol. VI
Gibson, Sir Ackroyd Herbert, 3rd Bt (*cr* 1926), 1893–1975, vol. VII
Gibson, Alan Frank, 1923–1988, vol. VIII
Gibson, Rt Rev. Alan George Sumner, 1856–1922, vol. II
Gibson, Alexander Boyce, 1900–1972, vol. VII
Gibson, Alexander George, 1875–1950, vol. IV
Gibson, Alexander James, 1876–1960, vol. V (A), vol. VI (AI)
Gibson, Andrew, 1864–1933, vol. III
Gibson, Arnold Hartley, 1878–1959, vol. V
Gibson, Arnold Mackenzie, *died* 1956, vol. V
Gibson, Sir Basil; *see* Gibson, Sir E. B.
Gibson, Charles Dana, 1867–1944, vol. IV
Gibson, Sir Charles Granville, 1880–1948, vol. IV
Gibson, Charles R., 1870–1931, vol. III

Gibson, Charles Stanley, 1884–1950, vol. IV
Gibson, Charles William, 1889–1977, vol. VII
Gibson, Sir Christopher Herbert, 2nd Bt (*cr* 1931), 1897–1962, vol. VI
Gibson, Clement William Osmund, 1878–1963, vol. VI
Gibson, Rear-Adm. Cuthbert Walter Sumner, 1890–1971, vol. VII
Gibson, Rt Rev. Edgar Charles Sumner, 1848–1924, vol. II
Gibson, Sir Edmund Currey, 1886–1974, vol. VII
Gibson, Hon. Edward Graves Mayne, 1873–1928, vol. II
Gibson, Elizabeth, 1869–1931, vol. III
Gibson, Sir (Ernest) Basil, 1877–1962, vol. VI
Gibson, Hon. Sir Frank Ernest, 1879–1965, vol. VI
Gibson, George, 1885–1953, vol. V
Gibson, George Alexander, 1854–1913, vol. I
Gibson, George Alexander, 1858–1930, vol. III
Gibson, George Herbert Rae, 1881–1932, vol. III
Gibson, Wing Comdr Guy Penrose, 1918–1944, vol. IV
Gibson, Harold, 1884–1961, vol. VI
Gibson, Harold Charles Lehrs, 1897–1960, vol. V
Gibson, Harry Frederick C.; *see* Carew-Gibson.
Gibson, Harvey Dow, 1882–1950, vol. IV
Gibson, Sir Henry James, 1860–1950, vol. IV
Gibson, Sir Herbert, 1st Bt (*cr* 1926), 1851–1932, vol. III
Gibson, Sir Herbert, 1st Bt (*cr* 1931), 1863–1934, vol. III
Gibson, Herbert Mellor, 1896–1954, vol. V
Gibson, Hope, 1859–1928, vol. II
Gibson, Sir (Horace) Stephen, 1897–1963, vol. VI
Gibson, Rear-Adm. Isham Worsley, 1882–1950, vol. IV
Gibson, James, 1864–1943, vol. IV
Gibson, Rt Rev. James Byers, 1881–1952, vol. V
Gibson, Sir James Puckering, 1st Bt (*cr* 1909), 1849–1912, vol. I
Gibson, John Ashley, 1885–1948, vol. IV
Gibson, Rev. John Campbell, *died* 1919, vol. II
Gibson, John Constant, 1861–1939, vol. III
Gibson, Rt Hon. John George, 1846–1923, vol. II
Gibson, Rev. John George, 1859–1927, vol. II
Gibson, John Gibson, 1889–1970, vol. VI
Gibson, Sir John Hinshelwood, 1907–1985, vol. VIII
Gibson, Rev. John Monro, 1838–1921, vol. II
Gibson, Maj.-Gen. Sir John Mortson, 1842–1929, vol. III
Gibson, Rev. John Paul S. R., *died* 1964, vol. VI
Gibson, Sir John Watson, 1885–1947, vol. IV
Gibson, Sir Kenneth Lloyd, 2nd Bt (*cr* 1926), 1888–1967, vol. VI
Gibson, Sir Leslie Bertram, 1896–1952, vol. V
Gibson, Major Lewis, 1880–1935, vol. III
Gibson, Hon. Sir Marcus George, 1898–1987, vol. VIII
Gibson, Margaret Dunlop, *died* 1920, vol. II
Gibson, Very Rev. Matthew Sayer, *died* 1971, vol. VII
Gibson, Rt Hon. Sir Maurice White, 1913–1987, vol. VIII
Gibson, Michael Joseph, 1876–1953, vol. V
Gibson, Myra Macindoe, 1886–1966, vol. VI

Gibson, Rt Rev. Percival William, 1893–1970, vol. VI
Gibson, Maj.-Gen. Ralph Burgess, 1894–1962, vol. VI
Gibson, Raymond Evelyn, 1878–1969, vol. VI
Gibson, Rev. Richard Hudson, *died* 1904, vol. I
Gibson, Robert; *see* Gibson, Hon. Lord.
Gibson, Sir Robert, 1864–1934, vol. III
Gibson, Rt Rev. Robert Atkinson, 1846–1919, vol. II
Gibson, Robert Clarence, 1892–1959, vol. V
Gibson, Robert John H.; *see* Harvey-Gibson.
Gibson, Sir Ronald George, 1909–1989, vol. VIII
Gibson, Sir Stephen; *see* Gibson, Sir H. S.
Gibson, Strickland, 1877–1958, vol. V
Gibson, Rt Rev. Theodore Sumner, 1885–1953, vol. V
Gibson, Thomas, 1875–1925, vol. II
Gibson, Very Rev. Thomas B., 1847–1927, vol. II
Gibson, Walcot, 1864–1941, vol. IV
Gibson, Sir Walter Matthew, 1856–1940, vol. III
Gibson, Wilfrid, 1878–1962, vol. VI
Gibson, Hon. William, 1849–1914, vol. I
Gibson, Lt-Col William, 1887–1969, vol. VI
Gibson, William John, 1865–1944, vol. IV
Gibson, Air Vice-Marshal William Norman, 1915–1982, vol. VIII
Gibson, William Pettigrew, 1902–1960, vol. V
Gibson, William Ralph Boyce, 1869–1935, vol. III
Gibson, William Sumner, 1876–1946, vol. IV
Gibson, William Victor Halliday, 1884–1954, vol. V
Gibson, Sir William Waymouth, 1873–1971, vol. VII
Gibson-Carmichael, John Murray, 1860–1923, vol. II
Gibson-Craig, Sir Archibald Charles, 4th Bt, 1883–1914, vol. I
Gibson-Craig, Sir James Henry, 3rd Bt, 1841–1908, vol. I
Gibson-Craig-Carmichael, Sir (Archibald Henry) William, 14th Bt (and 7th Bt), 1917–1969, vol. VI
Gibson-Craig-Carmichael, Sir Eardley Charles William, 13th Bt (and 6th Bt), 1887–1939, vol. III
Gibson-Craig-Carmichael, Captain Sir Henry Thomas, 5th Bt (and 12th Bt), 1885–1926, vol. II
Gibson-Craig-Carmichael, Sir William; *see* Gibson-Craig-Carmichael, Sir A. H. W.
Gibson Fleming, Edward, 1885–1962, vol. VI
Gibsone, Maj.-Gen. William Waring Primrose, 1872–1957, vol. V
Gick, Sir William John, 1877–1948, vol. IV
Giddens, George, 1855–1920, vol. II
Giddings, Franklin Henry, 1855–1931, vol. III
Giddings, William John Peter, 1861–1938, vol. III (A), vol. IV
Giddy, Harry Douglas, 1887–1959, vol. V
Gide, André Paul Guillaume, 1869–1951, vol. V
Gide, Prof. Charles, 1847–1932, vol. III
Gideon, Col James Henry, 1862–1958, vol. V
Gidhour, Maharaja Bahadur Chandra Mauleshvar Prasad Singh, 1890–1937, vol. III
Gidhour, Maharajah Sir Ravneswar Prasad Singh, Bahadur of, 1860–1923, vol. II
Gidney, Sir Claude Henry, 1887–1968, vol. VI
Gidney, Lt-Col Sir Henry Albert John, 1873–1942, vol. IV
Gie, S. F. N., 1884–1945, vol. IV
Gielgud, Lt-Col Lewis Evelyn, 1894–1953, vol. V

Gielgud, Val Henry, 1900–1981, vol. VIII

Gieseking, Walter Wilhelm, 1895–1956, vol. V

Giffard, Very Rev. Agnew Walter Giles, 1869–1947, vol. IV

Giffard, Adm. George Augustus, 1849–1925, vol. II

Giffard, George Campbell, 1853–1932, vol. III

Giffard, Gen. Sir George James, 1886–1964, vol. VI

Giffard, Maj.-Gen. Sir Gerald Godfray, 1867–1926, vol. II

Giffard, Hardinge Frank, died 1908, vol. I

Giffard, Sir Henry Alexander, 1838–1927, vol. II

Giffard, Walter Thomas Courtenay, 1839–1926, vol. II

Giffard, Col William Carter, 1859–1921, vol. II

Giffen, Edmund, 1902–1963, vol. VI

Giffen, Sir Robert, 1837–1910, vol. I

Gifford, 3rd Baron, 1849–1911, vol. I

Gifford, 4th Baron, 1857–1937, vol. III

Gifford, 5th Baron, 1899–1961, vol. VI

Gifford, Charles Edwin, 1843–1922, vol. II

Gifford, Ven. Edwin Hamilton, 1820–1905, vol. I

Gifford, (James) Maurice, 1922–1987, vol. VIII

Gifford, Maurice; see Gifford, J. M.

Gifford, Hon. Maurice Raymond, 1859–1910, vol. I

Gifford, Walter Sherman, 1885–1966, vol. VI

Gift, Theo.; see Boulger, D. H.

Gigli, Beniamino, 1890–1957, vol. V

Gilbert, Albert, died 1927, vol. II

Gilbert, Sir Alfred, 1854–1934, vol. III

Gilbert, Brig.-Gen. Arthur Robert, 1863–1937, vol. III

Gilbert, Sir Bernard William, 1891–1957, vol. V

Gilbert, Carew Davies, died 1913, vol. I

Gilbert, Carl Joyce, 1906–1983, vol. VIII

Gilbert, Cass, 1859–1934, vol. III

Gilbert, Charles E. L., died 1937, vol. III

Gilbert, Rev. Charles Robert, 1851–1919, vol. II

Gilbert, Charles W.; see Web-Gilbert.

Gilbert, Edmund William, 1900–1973, vol. VII

Gilbert, Frederick, 1899–1989, vol. VIII

Gilbert, Mrs Grace Catherine Rose D.; see Davies-Gilbert.

Gilbert, Sir Henry; see Gilbert, Sir J. H.

Gilbert, Sir Ian Anderson J.; see Johnson-Gilbert.

Gilbert, James Daniel, 1864–1941, vol. IV

Gilbert, Jean, died 1942, vol. IV

Gilbert, Sir John, 1817–1897, vol. I

Gilbert, Sir John Thomas, 1829–1898, vol. I

Gilbert, Sir John William, 1871–1934, vol. III

Gilbert, Sir (Joseph) Henry, 1817–1901, vol. I

Gilbert, Sir (Joseph) Trounsell, 1888–1975, vol. VII

Gilbert, Keith Reginald, 1914–1973, vol. VII

Gilbert, Brig. Leonard, 1889–1966, vol. VI

Gilbert, Lt-Col Leonard Erskine, 1874–1946, vol. IV

Gilbert, Rosa, (Lady Gilbert), (Rosa Mulholland), 1841–1921, vol. II

Gilbert, Hon. S. Parker, 1892–1938, vol. III

Gilbert, Adm. Thomas Drummond, 1870–1962, vol. VI

Gilbert, Rev. Thomas Morrell, died 1928, vol. II

Gilbert, Sir Trounsell; see Gilbert, Sir J. T.

Gilbert, Walter, 1871–1946, vol. IV

Gilbert, William Gladstone, 1877–1964, vol. VI

Gilbert, Brig. Sir William Herbert Ellery, 1916–1987, vol. VIII

Gilbert, Sir William Schwenck, 1836–1911, vol. I

Gilbert-Carter, Sir Gilbert Thomas, 1848–1927, vol. II

Gilbert-Carter, Humphrey, 1884–1969, vol. VI

Gilbertson, Rev. Canon Arthur Deane, 1883–1964, vol. VI

Gilbertson, Rev. Lewis, 1857–1928, vol. II

Gilbey, Lt-Col Alfred, 1859–1927, vol. II

Gilbey, Sir (Henry) Walter, 2nd Bt, 1859–1945, vol. IV

Gilbey, Tresham, 1862–1947, vol. IV

Gilbey, Sir Walter, 1st Bt, 1831–1914, vol. I

Gilbey, Sir Walter; see Gilbey, Sir H. W.

Gilchrist, Alexander Fitzmaurice, 1878–1956, vol. V

Gilchrist, Archibald, 1877–1932, vol. III

Gilchrist, Archibald Daniel, 1877–1964, vol. VI

Gilchrist, Douglas Alston, died 1927, vol. II

Gilchrist, Sir Finlay; see Gilchrist, Sir J. F. E.

Gilchrist, Sir James Albert, 1884–1965, vol. VI

Gilchrist, Sir (James) Finlay (Elder), 1903–1987, vol. VIII

Gilchrist, John, 1929–1982, vol. VIII

Gilchrist, John Dow Fisher, 1866–1926, vol. II

Gilchrist, Percy Carlyle, 1851–1935, vol. III

Gilchrist, Philip Thomson, 1865–1956, vol. V

Gilchrist, Captain Robert Allister, 1921–1973, vol. VII

Gilchrist, Robert Murray, 1868–1917, vol. II

Gilchrist, Robert Niven, 1888–1972, vol. VII

Gilchrist, Lt-Col Walter Fellowes Cowan, 1879–1943, vol. IV

Gilchrist, William James, 1879–1955, vol. V

Gilchrist-Clark, Rev. William; see Clark-Maxwell, Rev. W. G.

Gildea, Col Sir James, 1838–1920, vol. II

Gildea, Rev. William, 1833–1925, vol. II

Gilder, Jeannette Leonard, 1849–1916, vol. II

Gilder, Joseph B., 1858–1936, vol. III (A), vol. IV

Gilder, Richard Watson, 1844–1909, vol. I

Gildersleeve, Basil Lanneau, 1831–1924, vol. II

Gildersleeve, Virginia Crocheron, 1877–1965, vol. VI

Gilding, Henry Percy, 1895–1973, vol. VII

Giles, Rev. Alan Stanley, 1902–1975, vol. VII

Giles, Sir Alexander Falconer, 1915–1989, vol. VIII

Giles, Sub-Lt Alfred Edward Boscawen, died 1917, vol. II

Giles, Arthur Edward, 1864–1935, vol. III

Giles, Bertram, 1874–1928, vol. II

Giles, Carl P.; see Prausnitz Giles.

Giles, Sir Charles Tyrrell, 1850–1940, vol. III

Giles, Edward, 1849–1938, vol. III

Giles, Maj.-Gen. Edward Douglas, 1879–1966, vol. VI

Giles, Col Frank Lucas Netlam, 1879–1930, vol. III

Giles, G. C. T., died 1976, vol. VII

Giles, George Henry, 1904–1965, vol. VI

Giles, Major Godfrey Douglas, 1857–1941, vol. IV

Giles, Sir (Henry) Norman, 1905–1983, vol. VIII

Giles, Herbert Allen, 1845–1935, vol. III

Giles, John Laurent, 1901–1969, vol. VI

Giles, Lancelot, 1878–1934, vol. III

Giles, Lionel, 1875–1958, vol. V

Giles, Margaret M.; *see* Jenkin, Mrs Bernard.
Giles, Sir Norman; *see* Giles, Sir H. N.
Giles, Lt-Col Sir Oswald Bissill, 1888–1970, vol. VI
Giles, Peter, 1860–1935, vol. III
Giles, Peter Broome, 1850–1928, vol. II
Giles, Robert, 1846–1928, vol. II
Giles, Sir Robert Sidney, 1865–1944, vol. IV
Gilford, Hastings, 1861–1941, vol. IV
Gilham, Harold Sidney, 1897–1982, vol. VIII
Gilhooly, James Peter, 1847–1916, vol. II
Gilkes, Antony Newcombe, 1900–1977, vol. VII
Gilkes, Rev. Arthur Herman, *died* 1922, vol. II
Gilkes, Christopher Herman, 1898–1953, vol. V
Gilks, John Langton, 1880–1971, vol. VII
Gill, Alfred Henry, 1856–1914, vol. I
Gill, Allen, *died* 1933, vol. III
Gill, Andrew John Mitchell-, 1847–1921, vol. II
Gill, Sir Archibald Joseph, 1889–1976, vol. VII
Gill, Arthur Edmund, 1864–1932, vol. III
Gill, Austin, 1906–1990, vol. VIII
Gill, Sir Charles Frederick, 1851–1923, vol. II
Gill, Rt Rev. Charles Hope, 1861–1946, vol. IV
Gill, Colin Unwin, 1892–1940, vol. III
Gill, Conrad, 1883–1968, vol. VI
Gill, Cyril James, 1907–1990, vol. VIII
Gill, Sir David, 1843–1914, vol. I
Gill, Col Douglas Howard, 1877–1949, vol. IV
Gill, Eric, 1882–1940, vol. III
Gill, Rev. Ernest Compton, 1854–1912, vol. I
Gill, Ernest Walter Brudenell, 1883–1959, vol. V
Gill, Evan William Thistle, 1902–1990, vol. VIII
Gill, Air Cdre Hon. Frank; *see* Gill, Air Cdre Hon. T. F.
Gill, Sir Frank, 1866–1950, vol. IV
Gill, Frank Maxey, 1919–1990, vol. VIII
Gill, Frederick Gordon, 1881–1940, vol. III
Gill, Col Gordon Harry, 1882–1962, vol. VI
Gill, Sir Harry; *see* Gill, Sir. T. H.
Gill, Hubert Alexander, 1881–1954, vol. V
Gill, Ven. Hugh Stowell, 1830–1912, vol. I
Gill, Major James Herbert Wainwright, 1876–1951, vol. V
Gill, James Lester Willis, 1871–1939, vol. III
Gill, Maj.-Gen. John Galbraith, 1889–1981, vol. VIII
Gill, L. Upcott, 1846–1919, vol. II
Gill, MacDonald, 1884–1947, vol. IV
Gill, Air Cdre Napier John, 1890–1948, vol. IV
Gill, Robert Carey Chapple, 1875–1960, vol. V (A), vol. VI (AI)
Gill, Major Robert Harwar, 1877–1938, vol. III
Gill, Cdre Sir Roy, 1887–1967, vol. VI
Gill, Stanley, 1926–1975, vol. VII
Gill, Thomas, 1849–1923, vol. II
Gill, Air Cdre Hon. Thomas Francis, (Frank), 1917–1982, vol. VIII
Gill, Sir (Thomas) Harry, 1885–1955, vol. V
Gill, Thomas Patrick, 1858–1931, vol. III
Gill, Col William Smith, 1865–1957, vol. V
Gill-Carey, Chapple, 1897–1981, vol. VIII
Gill-Davies, Derek George, 1913–1974, vol. VII
Gillam, Brig.-Gen. Reynold Alexander, 1872–1942, vol. IV
Gillam, Major William Albert, 1870–1938, vol. III
Gillan, Sir Angus; *see* Gillan, Sir J. A.
Gillan, Lt-Col Sir George V. B., 1890–1974, vol. VII

Gillan, Sir (James) Angus, 1885–1981, vol. VIII
Gillan, Sir Robert Woodburn, 1867–1943, vol. IV
Gillanders, Jeannie Kathleen, 1896–1971, vol. VII
Gillanders, Hon. John Gordon, 1895–1946, vol. IV
Gillard, Hon. Sir Oliver James, 1906–1984, vol. VIII
Gillatt, Lt-Col John Maxwell, *died* 1937, vol. III
Gillen, Francis James, 1856–1912, vol. I
Gillen, Stanley James, 1911–1978, vol. VII
Gillespie, A. Lockhart, 1865–1904, vol. I
Gillespie, Charles Melville, 1866–1955, vol. V
Gillespie, Brig.-Gen. Ernest Carden Freeth, 1871–1942, vol. IV
Gillespie, Brig. Dame Helen Shiels, 1898–1974, vol. VII
Gillespie, Very Rev. Henry J., 1851–1936, vol. III
Gillespie, Ven. Henry Richard Butler, 1880–1943, vol. IV
Gillespie, Sir John, 1822–1901, vol. I
Gillespie, Very Rev. John, 1836–1912, vol. I
Gillespie, Peter, 1873–1929, vol. III
Gillespie, Sir Robert, *died* 1901, vol. I
Gillespie, Robert, 1897–1986, vol. VIII
Gillespie, Robert Alexander, 1848–1917, vol. II
Gillespie, Robert Dick, 1897–1945, vol. IV
Gillespie, Sir Robert Winton, *died* 1945, vol. IV
Gillespie, Col Rollo St John, 1872–1952, vol. V
Gillespie, Thomas Haining, 1876–1967, vol. VI
Gillespie, Maj.-Gen. William John, 1840–1931, vol. III
Gillespy, Rev. Francis Roebuck, 1880–1962, vol. VI
Gillett, Col Sir Alan; *see* Gillett, Col Sir W. A.
Gillett, Rev. Canon Charles Scott, 1880–1957, vol. V
Gillett, Charles William, 1901–1968, vol. VI
Gillett, Sir Edward Bailey, 1888–1978, vol. VII
Gillett, Lt-Col Edward Scott, 1877–1952, vol. V
Gillett, Eric, 1920–1987, vol. VIII
Gillett, Eric Walkey, 1893–1978, vol. VII
Gillett, Frederick Huntington, 1851–1935, vol. III
Gillett, Sir George Masterman, 1870–1939, vol. III
Gillett, Rev. Gresham F., 1867–1940, vol. III
Gillett, Sir Harold; *see* Gillett, Sir. S. H.
Gillett, Sir Michael Cavenagh, 1907–1971, vol. VII
Gillett, Adm. Owen Francis, 1863–1938, vol. III
Gillett, Maj.-Gen. Sir Peter Bernard, 1913–1989, vol. VIII
Gillett, Sir Stuart, 1903–1971, vol. VII
Gillett, Sir (Sydney) Harold, 1st Bt, 1890–1976, vol. VII
Gillett, Major William, 1839–1925, vol. II
Gillett, Col Sir (William) Alan, 1879–1959, vol. V
Gillette, William, 1857–1937, vol. III
Gillford, Lord; Richard Charles Meade, 1868–1905, vol. I
Gilliam, Laurence Duval, 1907–1964, vol. VI
Gilliat, Algernon Earle, 1884–1970, vol. VI
Gilliat, Rev. E., 1841–1915, vol. I
Gilliat, John Saunders, 1829–1912, vol. I
Gilliat-Smith, Bernard Joseph, 1883–1973, vol. VII
Gilliat-Smith, Guy Basil, 1885–1933, vol. III
Gilliatt, Sir William, 1884–1956, vol. V
Gillibrand, Brig. Albert, 1884–1942, vol. IV
Gillick, Ernest George, *died* 1951, vol. V
Gillick, Mary, *died* 1965, vol. VI

Gillie, Dame Annis Calder, (Dame Annis Smith), 1900–1985, vol. VIII

Gillie, Blaise; *see* Gillie, F. B.

Gillie, (Francis) Blaise, 1908–1981, vol. VIII

Gillie, Rev. Robert Calder, 1865–1941, vol. IV

Gillies, Alexander, 1907–1977, vol. VII

Gillies, Sir Alexander, 1891–1982, vol. VIII

Gillies, Arthur Hunter Denholm, 1890–1953, vol. V

Gillies, Brig. Frederick George, 1881–1955, vol. V

Gillies, Sir Harold Delf, 1882–1960, vol. V

Gillies, Hugh, 1903–1978, vol. VII

Gillies, Captain James, 1873–1938, vol. III

Gillies, Rev. James Robertson, 1855–1938, vol. III

Gillies, John, 1895–1976, vol. VII

Gillies, Marshall Macdonald, 1901–1976, vol. VII

Gillies, Sir William George, 1898–1973, vol. VII

Gillies, William King, 1875–1952, vol. V

Gillies, Hon. William Neal, 1868–1928, vol. II

Gilligan, Albert, 1874–1939, vol. III

Gilligan, Arthur Edward Robert, 1894–1976, vol. VII

Gilligan, Frank William, 1893–1960, vol. V

Gilliglan, Major Edward Gibson, 1880–1947, vol. IV

Gillingham, Rev. Canon Frank Hay, 1875–1953, vol. V

Gillis, Hon. Duncan, 1834–1903, vol. I

Gillis, William, 1859–1929, vol. III

Gillitt, Lt-Col William, 1879–1962, vol. VI

Gillman, Clement, 1882–1946, vol. IV

Gillman, Herbert Francis Webb, *died* 1918, vol. II

Gillman, Russell Davis, *died* 1910, vol. I

Gillman, Gen. Sir Webb, 1870–1933, vol. III

Gillmor, Rev. Fitzwilliam, 1867–1934, vol. III

Gillmore, Ven. Charles Albert, *died* 1939, vol. III

Gillon, Stair Agnew, 1877–1954, vol. V

Gillot, E. Louis, *born* 1867, vol. II

Gillot, Hon. Sir Samuel, 1838–1913, vol. I

Gillson, Brig.-Gen. Godfrey, 1867–1937, vol. III

Gillson, Lt-Col Robert Moore Thacker, 1878–1939, vol. III

Gillson, Thomas Huntington, 1917–1984, vol. VIII

Gilman, Sir Charles Rackham, 1833–1911, vol. I

Gilman, Charlotte Perkins, 1860–1935, vol. III

Gilman, Daniel Coit, 1831–1909, vol. I

Gilman, Edward Wilmot Francis, 1876–1955, vol. V

Gilman, Harold John Wilde, 1878–1919, vol. II

Gilman, Horace James, 1907–1976, vol. VII

Gilmartin, Most Rev. Thomas P., 1861–1939, vol. III

Gilmer, Dame Elizabeth May, 1880–1960, vol. V

Gilmore, Hon. George Crosby, 1859–1937, vol. III

Gilmore, Dame Mary, 1865–1962, vol. VI

Gilmour, Andrew, 1898–1988, vol. VIII

Gilmour, David, *died* 1946, vol. IV

Gilmour, James Pinkerton, 1860–1941, vol. IV

Gilmour, Sir John, 1st Bt (*cr* 1897), 1845–1920, vol. II

Gilmour, Lt-Col Rt Hon. Sir John, 2nd Bt (*cr* 1897), 1876–1940, vol. III

Gilmour, Major John, 1884–1943, vol. IV

Gilmour, Sir John Little, 2nd Bt (*cr* 1926), 1899–1977, vol. VII

Gilmour, John Scott Lennox, 1906–1986, vol. VIII

Gilmour, Michael Hugh Barrie, 1904–1982, vol. VIII

Gilmour, Brig.-Gen. Sir Robert Gordon, 1st Bt (*cr* 1926), 1857–1939, vol. III

Gilmour, Lady Susan, 1870–1962, vol. VI

Gilmour, Thomas Lennox, 1859–1936, vol. III

Gilmour, William Ewing, 1854–1924, vol. II

Gilmour, William Henry, 1869–1942, vol. IV

Gilpin, Archibald, 1906–1959, vol. V

Gilpin, Sir Edmund Henry; *see* Gilpin, Sir Harry.

Gilpin, Brig.-Gen. Frederic Charles Almon, 1860–1950, vol. IV

Gilpin, Sir Harry, (Edmund Henry), 1876–1950, vol. IV

Gilpin, John, 1930–1983, vol. VIII

Gilpin, Peter Valentine, 1858–1928, vol. II

Gilpin, Rt Rev. William Percy, 1902–1988, vol. VIII

Gilpin-Brown, Adm. Frederick Dundas, 1866–1934, vol. III

Gilray, Colin Macdonald, 1885–1974, vol. VII

Gilray, Thomas, 1851–1920, vol. II

Gilroy, Rev. James, 1859–1931, vol. III

Gilroy, John T. Y., 1898–1985, vol. VIII

Gilroy, His Eminence Cardinal Sir Norman Thomas, 1896–1977, vol. VII

Gilruth, John Anderson, 1871–1937, vol. III

Gilson, Lt-Col Charles Hugh, 1870–1930, vol. III

Gilson, Major Charles J. L. 1878–1943, vol. IV

Gilson, Etienne Henry, 1884–1978, vol. VII

Gilson, John Cary, 1912–1989, vol. VIII

Gilson, Julius Parnell, 1868–1929, vol. III

Gilson, Paul, 1865–1942, vol. IV

Gilson, Robert Cary, 1863–1939, vol. III

Gilstrap, Lt-Col John MacR.; *see* MacRae-Gilstrap.

Gilzean, Andrew, 1877–1957, vol. V

Gilzean-Reid, Sir Hugh; *see* Reid.

Gimblett, Charles Leonard, 1890–1957, vol. V

Gimlette, Lt-Col George Hart Desmond, 1855–1930, vol. III

Gimlette, Surg. Rear-Adm. Sir Thomas Desmond, 1857–1943, vol. IV

Gimson, Arthur Clive Stanford, 1919–1982, vol. VIII

Gimson, Christopher, 1886–1975, vol. VII

Gimson, Sir Franklin Charles, 1890–1975, vol. VII

Gimson, Col Thomas William, 1904–1979, vol. VII

Gingell, Overy Francis, 1916–1966, vol. VI

Gingold, Hermione, 1897–1987, vol. VIII

Gingras-Daly, Lt-Col Ludger Jules Olivier, 1876–1919, vol. II

Ginnell, Laurence, 1854–1923, vol. II

Ginner, Charles, 1878–1952, vol. V

Ginnett, Louis, *died* 1946, vol. IV

Ginsberg, Morris, 1889–1970, vol. VI

Ginsburg, Benedict William, 1859–1933, vol. III

Ginsburg, Christian David, 1831–1914, vol. I

Ginwala, Sir Padamji Pestonji, 1875–1962, vol. VI

Giolitti, Giovanni, 1842–1928, vol. II

Giordano, Umberto, 1867–1948, vol. IV

Giovanetti, Constantine William, 1868–1940, vol. III

Gipps, Sir Reginald Ramsay, 1831–1908, vol. I

Gipson, Lawrence Henry, 1880–1971, vol. VII

Girard, Robert George, 1859–1921, vol. II

Giraud, Surg.-Maj.-Gen. Charles Herve, *died* 1918, vol. II

Giraud, Gen. Henri Honoré, 1879–1949, vol. IV

Girault, Charles Louis, 1851–1932, vol. III

Girdlestone, Cuthbert Morton, 1895–1975, vol. VII

Girdlestone, Gathorne Robert, *died* 1950, vol. IV

Girdlestone, Rev. Robert Baker, 1836–1923, vol. II

Girdwood, Brig.-Gen. Austin Claude, 1875–1951, vol. V

Girdwood, Maj.-Gen. Sir Eric Stanley, 1876–1963, vol. VI

Girdwood, Gilbert P., 1832–1917, vol. II

Girdwood, John Graham, 1890–1981, vol. VIII

Giri, Varahagiri Venkata, 1894–1980, vol. VII

Giri de Teremala di Fogliano, Count Piero Mariano, 1885–1962, vol. VI

Girling, James Lawrence, 1901–1969, vol. VI

Girling, John Henry, *died* 1948, vol. IV

Girling, William Henry, 1872–1958, vol. V

Girouard, Hon. Désiré, 1836–1911, vol. I

Girouard, Col Sir (Edouard) Percy Cranwill, 1867–1932, vol. III

Girouard, Hon. Jean, 1856–1940, vol. III (A), vol. IV

Girouard, Col Sir Percy; *see* Girouard, Col Sir E. P. C.

Girtin, Thomas, 1874–1960, vol. V

Gisborne, Henry Paterson, 1888–1953, vol. V

Gisborne, Lt-Col Lionel Guy, 1866–1928, vol. II

Gisborough, 1st Baron, 1856–1938, vol. III

Gisborough, 2nd Baron, 1889–1951, vol. V

Gishford, Anthony Joseph, 1908–1975, vol. VII

Gissing, Algernon, 1860–1937, vol. III

Gissing, George, 1857–1903, vol. I

Gittins, Henry, 1858–1937, vol. III

Gittins, Robert John, 1895–1934, vol. III

Giuffrida-Ruggeri, Vincenzo, *born* 1872, vol. II

Given, Ernest Cranstoun, 1870–1961, vol. VI

Given, Rear-Adm. John Garnett Cranston, 1902–1988, vol. VIII

Given, Brig. Thomas Frederick, 1894–1952, vol. V

Givens, Hon. Thomas, 1864–1928, vol. II

Gjellerup, Karl Adolf, 1859–1919, vol. II

Gladding, Donald, 1888–1971, vol. VII

Gladstone, 1st Viscount, 1854–1930, vol. III

Gladstone of Hawarden, 1st Baron, 1852–1935, vol. III

Gladstone of Hawarden, Lady; (Maud Ernestine), *died* 1941, vol. IV

Gladstone, Sir Albert Charles, 5th Bt, 1886–1967, vol. VI

Gladstone, Charles Andrew, (6th Bt, but did not use the title), 1888–1968, vol. VI

Gladstone, Adm. Sir Gerald Vaughan, 1901–1978, vol. VII

Gladstone, Helen, 1849–1925, vol. II

Gladstone, Sir Hugh Steuart, 1877–1949, vol. IV

Gladstone, Sir John Evelyn, 4th Bt, 1855–1945, vol. IV

Gladstone, John Hall, 1827–1902, vol. I

Gladstone, Sir John Robert, 3rd Bt, 1852–1926, vol. II

Gladstone, Reginald John, 1865–1947, vol. IV

Gladstone, Robert, 1833–1919, vol. II

Gladstone, Samuel Steuart, 1837–1909, vol. I

Gladstone, Rev. Stephen Edward, 1844–1920, vol. II

Gladstone, Rt Hon. William Ewart, 1809–1898, vol. I

Gladstone, William Glynne Charles, 1885–1915, vol. I

Glaisher, James Whitbread Lee, 1848–1928, vol. II

Glaister, John, 1856–1932, vol. III

Glaister, John, 1892–1971, vol. VII

Glaister, Rev. William, *died* 1919, vol. II

Glancey, Rt Rev. Mgr Michael Francis, 1854–1925, vol. II

Glancy, Sir Bertrand James, 1882–1953, vol. V

Glancy, James Edward McAlinney, 1914–1980, vol. VII (AII)

Glancy, Sir Reginald Isidore Robert, 1874–1939, vol. III

Glanely, 1st Baron, 1868–1942, vol. IV

Glanfield, Sir Robert, 1862–1924, vol. II

Glantawe, 1st Baron, 1835–1915, vol. I

Glanusk, 1st Baron, 1858–1906, vol. I

Glanusk, 2nd Baron, 1864–1928, vol. II

Glanusk, 3rd Baron, 1891–1948, vol. IV

Glanville, Mrs Edythe Mary, 1876–1959, vol. V

Glanville, Brig.-Gen. Francis, 1862–1938, vol. III

Glanville, Harold James, 1854–1930, vol. III

Glanville, Harold James Abbott, 1884–1966, vol. VI

Glanville, James Edward, 1891–1958, vol. V

Glanville, Stephen Ranulph Kingdon, 1900–1956, vol. V

Glanville, Sir William Henry, 1900–1976, vol. VII

Glascock, Lancelot Colin Bradford, 1875–1931, vol. III

Glascott, John Richard Donovan, 1877–1938, vol. III

Glaser, Dorothy, (Mrs O. C. Glaser); *see* Wrinch, D.

Glasfurd, Col Alexander Inglis Robertson, 1870–1942, vol. IV

Glasgow, 7th Earl of, 1833–1915, vol. I

Glasgow, 8th Earl of, 1874–1963, vol. VI

Glasgow, 9th Earl of, 1910–1984, vol. VIII

Glasgow, Brig.-Gen. Alfred Edgar, 1870–1950, vol. IV

Glasgow, Edwin, 1874–1955, vol. V

Glasgow, Ellen, 1874–1945, vol. IV

Glasgow, George, 1891–1958, vol. V

Glasgow, Mary Cecilia, 1905–1983, vol. VIII

Glasgow, Raymond Charles R.; *see* Robertson-Glasgow.

Glasgow, Maj.-Gen. Hon. Sir (Thomas) William, 1876–1955, vol. V

Glasgow, Maj.-Gen. Hon. Sir William; *see* Glasgow, Maj.-Gen. Hon. Sir T. W.

Glasgow, Brig.-Gen. William James Theodore, 1862–1944, vol. IV

Glasier, Major Frank Bedford, 1872–1940, vol. III

Glaspell, Susan, 1882–1948, vol. IV

Glass, David Victor, 1911–1978, vol. VII

Glass, Frederick James, 1881–1930, vol. III

Glass, George William, 1877–1967, vol. VI

Glass, James George Henry, 1843–1911, vol. I

Glass, Sir Leslie Charles, 1911–1988, vol. VIII

Glass, Ruth, 1912–1990, vol. VIII

Glass, William Mervyn, 1885–1965, vol. VI

Glasse, Alfred Onslow, 1889–1977, vol. VII

Glasse, John, 1848–1918, vol. II

Glassey, Alec Ewart, 1887–1970, vol. VI

Glassington, Charles William, 1857–1922, vol. II

Glauert, Hermann, 1892–1934, vol. III

Glazebrook, Francis Kirkland, 1903–1988, vol. VIII

Glazebrook, Hugh de T., 1855–1937, vol. III

Glazebrook, Rev. Michael George, 1853–1926, vol. II

Glazebrook, Philip Kirkland, 1880–1918, vol. II

Glazebrook, Reginald Field, 1899–1986, vol. VIII

Glazebrook, Sir Richard Tetley, 1854–1935, vol. III
Glazebrook, William Rimington, 1864–1954, vol. V
Glazier, Edward Victor Denis, 1912–1972, vol. VII
Glazounow, Alexander Constantinovich, 1865–1936, vol. III
Gleadell, Maj.-Gen. Paul, 1910–1988, vol. VIII
Gleadowe, George Edward Yorke, 1856–1903, vol. I
Gleadowe, Reginald Morier Yorke, 1888–1944, vol. IV
Gleadowe-Newcomen, Col Arthur Hills, 1853–1928, vol. II
Gleave, Ruth Marjory, 1926–1986, vol. VIII
Gledhill, Alan, 1895–1983, vol. VIII
Gledhill, Gilbert, 1889–1946, vol. IV
Gledstanes, Elsie, 1891–1982, vol. VIII
Gleed, Sir John Wilson, 1865–1946, vol. IV
Gleeson, Most Rev. Edmund, 1869–1956, vol. V
Glegg, Sir Alexander, 1848–1933, vol. III
Glegg, Edward Maxwell, 1849–1927, vol. II
Gleichen, Maj.-Gen. Lord (Albert) Edward Wilfred, 1863–1937, vol. III
Gleichen, Maj.-Gen. Lord Edward; *see* Gleichen, Maj.-Gen. Lord A. E. W.
Gleichen, Lady Feodora, 1861–1922, vol. II
Gleichen, Lady Helena, *died* 1947, vol. IV
Glen, Alexander, 1850–1913, vol. I
Glen, Sir Alexander, 1893–1972, vol. VII
Glen, John Mackenzie, 1885–1976, vol. VII
Glen, Randolph Alexander, *died* 1934, vol. III
Glen-Coats, Sir Thomas Coats Glen, 2nd Bt; *see* Coats.
Glen-Coats, Sir Thomas Glen, 1st Bt, 1846–1922, vol. II
Glenarthur, 1st Baron, 1852–1928, vol. II
Glenarthur, 2nd Baron, 1883–1942, vol. IV
Glenarthur, 3rd Baron, 1909–1976, vol. VII
Glenavy, 1st Baron, 1851–1931, vol. III
Glenavy, 2nd Baron, 1885–1963, vol. VI
Glenavy, 3rd Baron, 1913–1980, vol. VII
Glenavy, 4th Baron, 1924–1984, vol. VIII
Glenconner, 1st Baron, 1859–1920, vol. II
Glenconner, 2nd Baron, 1899–1983, vol. VIII
Glenday, Dorothea Nonita, 1899–1982, vol. VIII
Glenday, Nonita; *see* Glenday, D. N.
Glenday, Roy Goncalves, 1889–1957, vol. V
Glenday, Sir Vincent Goncalves, 1891–1970, vol. VI
Glendenning, Raymond Carl, 1907–1974, vol. VII
Glendinning, Edward Green, 1922–1984, vol. VIII
Glendinning, Henry, 1863–1938, vol. III
Glendinning, John Clements, 1866–1949, vol. IV
Glendinning, Rt Hon. Robert Graham, 1844–1928, vol. II
Glendyne, 1st Baron, 1849–1930, vol. III
Glendyne, 2nd Baron, 1878–1967, vol. VI
Glenesk, 1st Baron, 1830–1908, vol. I
Glenkinglas, Baron (Life Peer); Michael Antony Cristobal Noble, 1913–1984, vol. VIII
Glenn, Very Rev. Henry Patterson, 1858–1923, vol. II
Glenn, Robert George, 1844–1900, vol. I
Glenn, Air Vice-Marshal Robert William Lowry, 1901–1970, vol. VI
Glenn, William James, 1911–1984, vol. VIII
Glennie, Alan Forbes Bourne, 1903–1984, vol. VIII
Glennie, Brig. Edward Aubrey, 1889–1980, vol. VII

Glennie, Rev. Herbert John, 1860–1926, vol. II
Glennie, Adm. Sir Irvine Gordon, 1892–1980, vol. VII
Glennie, Vice-Adm. Robert Woodyear, 1868–1930, vol. III
Glenny, Alexander Thomas, 1882–1965, vol. VI
Glenny, William James, 1873–1963, vol. VI
Glenravel, 1st Baron, 1858–1937, vol. III
Glentanar, 1st Baron, 1849–1918, vol. II
Glentanar, 2nd Baron, 1894–1971, vol. VII
Glentoran, 1st Baron, 1880–1950, vol. IV
Glentworth, Viscount; Edmond William Claude Gerard de Vere, 1894–1918, vol. II
Glin, 28th Knight of; *see* Fitz-Gerald, Desmond Windham Otho.
Glindoni, Henry Gillard, *died* 1913, vol. I
Gloag, Lt-Gen. Archibald Robertson, 1831–1914, vol. I
Gloag, John Edwards, 1896–1981, vol. VIII
Gloag, Paton James, 1823–1906, vol. I
Gloag, William Ellis; *see* Kincairney, Hon. Lord.
Gloag, William Murray, 1865–1934, vol. III
Glossop, Clifford William Hudson, 1901–1975, vol. VII
Glossop, Rev. George Henry Pownall, 1858–1925, vol. II
Glossop, Vice-Adm. John Collings-Taswell, 1871–1934, vol. III
Gloster, Brig.-Gen. Gerald Meade, 1864–1928, vol. II
Glover, Derek Harding, 1916–1981, vol. VIII
Glover, Sir Douglas, 1908–1982, vol. VIII
Glover, Sir (Edward) Otho, 1876–1956, vol. V
Glover, Elizabeth Rosetta, (Lady Glover), *died* 1927, vol. II
Glover, Sir Ernest William, 1st Bt, 1864–1934, vol. III
Glover, George Wright, 1884–1918, vol. II
Glover, Sir Gerald Alfred, 1908–1986, vol. VIII
Glover, Maj.-Gen. Sir Guy de Courcy, 1887–1967, vol. IV
Glover, Halcott, *died* 1949, vol. IV
Glover, Harold, 1917–1988, vol. VIII
Glover, Sir Harold Matthew, 1885–1961, vol. VI
Glover, Henry Percy, *died* 1938, vol. III
Glover, James Alison, 1876–1963, vol. VI
Glover, James Grey, *died* 1908, vol. I
Glover, James Mackey, 1861–1931, vol. III
Glover, Sir John, 1829–1920, vol. II
Glover, Maj.-Gen. Malcolm, 1897–1970, vol. VI
Glover, Sir Otho; *see* Glover, Sir E. O.
Glover, Richard, 1837–1919, vol. II
Glover, Ronald Everett, *died* 1975, vol. VII
Glover, Terrot Reaveley, 1869–1943, vol. IV
Glover, Thomas, 1862–1942, vol. IV
Glover, Col William Reid, 1882–1959, vol. V
Glubb, Maj.-Gen. Sir Frederic Manley, 1857–1938, vol. III
Glubb, Lt-Gen. Sir John Bagot, 1897–1986, vol. VIII
Gluckman, Max, 1911–1975, vol. VII
Gluckmann, Grigory, 1898–1973, vol. VII
Gluckstein, Isidore Montague, 1890–1975, vol. VII
Gluckstein, Sir Louis Halle, 1897–1979, vol. VII
Gluckstein, Montague,1854–1922, vol. II
Gluckstein, Major Montague, 1886–1958, vol. V
Gluckstein, Sir Samuel, 1880–1958, vol. V

Glueckauf, Eugen, 1906–1981, vol. VIII
Glunicke, Maj.-Gen. R. C. A., 1886–1963, vol. VI
Glyn, 1st Baron, 1885–1960, vol. V
Glyn, Hon. Alice Coralie, *died* 1928, vol. II
Glyn, Sir Arthur Robert, 7th Bt (*cr* 1759), 1870–1942, vol. IV
Glyn, Mrs Clayton, (Elinor), *died* 1943, vol. IV
Glyn, Rt Rev. Hon. Edward Carr, 1843–1928, vol. II
Glyn, Elinor; *see* Glyn, Mrs Clayton.
Glyn, Sir Francis Maurice Grosvenor, 1901–1969, vol. VI
Glyn, Rev. Frederick Ware, *died* 1918, vol. II
Glyn, Col Geoffrey Carr, 1864–1933, vol. III
Glyn, Hon. George Edward Dudley Carr, 1896–1930, vol. III
Glyn, Sir Gervas Powell, 6th Bt (*cr* 1759), 1862–1921, vol. II
Glyn, Lt-Gen. Sir John Plumptre Carr, 1837–1912, vol. I
Glyn, Sir Julius Richard, 1824–1905, vol. I
Glyn, Lewis Edmund, 1849–1919, vol. II
Glyn, Maurice George Carr, 1872–1920, vol. II
Glyn, Hon. Pascoe Charles, 1833–1904, vol. I
Glyn, Sir Richard Fitzgerald, 4th Bt (*cr* 1800) and 8th Bt (*cr* 1759), 1875–1960, vol. V
Glyn, Sir Richard George, 3rd Bt (*cr* 1800), 1831–1918, vol. II
Glyn, Col Sir Richard Hamilton, 5th Bt and 9th Bt, 1907–1980, vol. VII
Glyn, Lt-Gen. Richard Thomas, 1831–1900, vol. I
Glyn, Hon. Sidney Carr, 1835–1916, vol. II
Glyn Hughes, Hugh Llewelyn; *see* Hughes.
Glyn-Jones, Sir Hildreth, 1895–1980, vol. VII
Glyn-Jones, Sir William Samuel, 1869–1927, vol. II
Glynn, Air Cdre Arthur Samuel, 1885–1967, vol. VI
Glynn, Ernest E., *died* 1929, vol. III
Glynn, Sir Joseph Aloysius, 1869–1951, vol. V
Glynn, Hon. Patrick M'Mahon, 1855–1931, vol. III
Glynn, Prudence Loveday, (The Lady Windlesham), 1935–1986, vol. VIII
Glynn, Lt-Col Thomas George Powell, 1863–1949, vol. IV
Glynn, Thomas Robinson, *died* 1931, vol. III
Glynn Grylls, Rosalie; *see* Mander, Lady (Rosalie).
Glynton, Col Gerard Maxwell, *died* 1942, vol. IV
Gnien Is-Sultan, Paul Nicholas Apap-Pace-Bologna, 5th Marquis of, 1880–1955, vol. V
Goad, Harold Elsdale, 1878–1956, vol. V
Goad, Col Howard, 1857–1923, vol. II
Goadby, Hector Kenneth, 1902–1990, vol. VIII
Goadby, Sir Kenneth Weldon, 1873–1958, vol. V
Gobbi, Tito, 1915–1984, vol. VIII
Gobeil, Antoine, *born* 1854, vol. II
Goble, Leslie Herbert, 1901–1969, vol. VI
Goble, Air Vice-Marshal Stanley James, 1891–1948, vol. IV
Goble, Warwick, *died* 1943, vol. IV
Godber, 1st Baron, 1888–1976, vol. VII
Godber of Willington, Baron (Life Peer); Joseph Bradshaw Godber, 1914–1980, vol. VII
Godbout, Hon. Joseph, 1851–1923, vol. III
Godbout, Hon. Joseph Adélard, 1892–1956, vol. V
Godby, Col Charles, 1863–1956, vol. V

Goddard, Baron (Life Peer); Rayner Goddard, 1877–1971, vol. VII
Goddard, Alexander, 1867–1956, vol. V
Goddard, Arabella, (Mrs Davison), 1836–1922, vol. II
Goddard, Arthur, 1853–1920, vol. II
Goddard, Rt Hon. Sir Daniel Ford, 1850–1922, vol. II
Goddard, Ernest Hope, 1879–1939, vol. III
Goddard, Lt-Col Gerald Hamilton, 1873–1948, vol. IV
Goddard, Brig.-Gen. Henry Arthur, 1871–1955, vol. V
Goddard, Sir Holland; *see* Goddard, Sir. J. H.
Goddard, Maj.-Gen. John Desmond, 1919–1990, vol. VIII
Goddard, Sir (Joseph) Holland, *died* 1958, vol. V
Goddard, Air Marshal, Sir (Robert) Victor, 1897–1987, vol. VIII
Goddard, Thomas Herbert, 1885–1967, vol. VI
Goddard, Air Marshal Sir Victor; *see* Goddard, Air Marshal Sir R. V.
Godding, Insp.-Gen. Charles Cane, *died* 1939, vol. III
Gödel, Kurt, 1906–1978, vol. VII
Godfray, Col Sir James, 1816–1897, vol. I
Godfray, Brig.-Gen. John William, 1850–1921, vol. II
Godfrey, Brig. Arthur Harry Langham, 1896–1942, vol. IV
Godfrey, Captain Charles, *died* 1903, vol. I
Godfrey, Charles, 1873–1924, vol. II
Godfrey, Sir Dan, 1868–1939, vol. III
Godfrey, Derrick Edward Reid, 1918–1989, vol. VIII
Godfrey, Ernest Henry, 1862–1952, vol. V
Godfrey, Sir George Cochrane, 1871–1945, vol. IV
Godfrey, Vice-Adm. Harry Rowlandson, 1875–1947, vol. IV
Godfrey, Sir John Albert, 1889–1973, vol. VII
Godfrey, Sir John Ernest, 6th Bt, 1864–1935, vol. III
Godfrey, Sir John Fermor, 4th Bt, 1828–1900, vol. I
Godfrey, Adm. John Henry, 1888–1971, vol. VII
Godfrey, Hon. John M., 1871–1943, vol. IV
Godfrey, John Thomas, 1857–1911, vol. I
Godfrey, Sir Joseph Edward, 1858–1938, vol. III
Godfrey, Air Cdre Kenneth Walter, 1907–1979, vol. VII
Godfrey, Percy, 1859–1945, vol. IV
Godfrey, Robert Samuel, 1876–1953, vol. V
Godfrey, Lt-Col Stuart Hill, 1861–1941, vol. IV
Godfrey, Sir Walter, 1907–1976, vol. VII
Godfrey, Walter Hindes, 1881–1961, vol. VI
Godfrey, His Eminence Cardinal William, 1889–1963, vol. VI
Godfrey, Sir William Cecil, 5th Bt, 1857–1926, vol. II
Godfrey, Sir William Maurice, 7th Bt, 1909–1971, vol. VII
Godfrey, General Sir William Wellington, 1880–1952, vol. V
Godfrey-Faussett, Captain Sir Bryan Godfrey, 1863–1945, vol. IV
Godfrey-Faussett, Brig. Bryan Trevor, 1896–1970, vol. VI
Godfrey-Faussett, Brig.-Gen. Edmund Godfrey, 1868–1942, vol. IV

Godfrey Faussett, Lt-Col Owen Godfrey, 1866–1915, vol. I

Godkin, Edwin Lawrence, 1831–1902, vol. I

Godlee, Sir Rickman John, 1st Bt, 1849–1925, vol. II

Godley, Gen. Sir Alexander John, 1867–1957, vol. V

Godley, Alfred Denis, 1856–1925, vol. II

Godley, Hon. Eveline Charlotte, *died* 1951, vol. V

Godley, Brig.-Gen. Francis Clements, 1858–1941, vol. IV

Godley, Brig. Sir Francis William Crewe F.; *see* Fetherston-Godley.

Godley, Lt-Col Godfrey Archibald, 1871–1935, vol. III

Godley, Major Harry Crewe, 1861–1907, vol. I

Godley, John Cornwallis, 1861–1946, vol. IV

Godman, Dame Alice Mary, 1868–1944, vol. IV

Godman, Col Arthur Fitzpatrick, 1842–1930, vol. III

Godman, Air Cdre Arthur Lowthian, 1877–1956, vol. V

Godman, Col Charles Bulkeley, 1849–1941, vol. IV

Godman, Frederick Du Cane, 1834–1919, vol. II

Godman, Col John, 1886–1978, vol. VII

Godman, Major Laurence, 1880–1917, vol. II

Godman, Maj.-Gen. Richard Temple, 1832–1912, vol. I

Godman, Col Sherard Haughton, 1865–1938, vol. III

Godowsky, Leopold, 1870–1938, vol. III

Godsall, Walter Douglas, 1901–1964, vol. VI

Godsell, Sir William, 1838–1924, vol. II

Godson, Sir Augustus Frederick, 1835–1906, vol. I

Godson, Clement, 1845–1913, vol. I

Godwin, Sir Arthur, 1852–1921, vol. II

Godwin, Lt-Gen. Sir Charles Alexander Campbell, 1873–1951, vol. V

Godwin, Sir Harry, 1901–1985, vol. VIII

Godwin-Austen, Gen. Sir Alfred Reade, 1889–1963, vol. VI

Godwin-Austen, Henry Haversham, 1834–1923, vol. II

Goe, Rt Rev. Field Flowers, 1832–1910, vol. I

Goehr, Walter, 1903–1960, vol. V

Goenka, Rai Bahadur Sir Badridas, 1883–1973, vol. VII

Goenka, Rai Bahadur Sir Hariram, 1862–1935, vol. III

Goeppert Mayer, Maria; *see* Mayer.

Goethals, George Washington, 1858–1928, vol. II

Goetze, Sigismund Christian Hubert,1866–1939, vol. III

Goff, Col Algernon Hamilton Stannus, 1863–1936, vol. III

Goff, Major Cecil Willie Trevor Thomas, 1860–1907, vol. I

Goff, Eric Noel Porter, 1902–1981, vol. VIII

Goff, Sir Ernest William Davis-, 3rd Bt, 1904–1980, vol. VII

Goff, Sir Herbert William Davis-, 2nd Bt, 1870–1923, vol. II

Goff, Sir Park, 1st Bt, 1871–1939, vol. III

Goff, Captain Reginald Stannus, 1882–1965, vol. VI

Goff, Rt Hon. Sir Reginald William, 1907–1980, vol. VII

Goff, Col Robert Charles, *died* 1922, vol. II

Goff, Thomas Clarence Edward, 1867–1949, vol. IV

Goff, Sir William Goff Davis-, 1st Bt, 1838–1917, vol. II

Goffe, Sir Herbert, 1870–1939, vol. III

Goffin, Comr Sir Dean; *see* Goffin, Comr Sir J. D.

Goffin, Comr Sir (John) Dean, 1916–1984, vol. VIII

Gogarty, Col Henry Edward, 1868–1955, vol. V

Gogarty, Oliver St John, 1878–1957, vol. V

Goitein, Hugh, 1896–1976, vol. VII

Gokhale, Hon. Gopal Krishna, 1866–1915, vol. I

Gold, Major Sir Archibald Gilbey, 1870–1935, vol. III

Gold, Sir Charles, 1837–1924, vol. II

Gold, Ernest, 1881–1976, vol. VII

Gold, Sir Harcourt Gilbey, 1876–1952, vol. V

Gold, Henry, 1835–1900, vol. I

Gold, James Herbert, 1885–1974, vol. VII

Gold, Victor, 1922–1985, vol. VIII

Goldberg, Arthur Joseph, 1908–1990, vol. VIII

Golden, Lt-Col Harold Arthur, 1896–1976, vol. VII

Goldfinch, Sir Arthur Horne, 1866–1945, vol. IV

Goldfinch, Sir Philip Henry Macarthur, 1884–1943, vol. IV

Goldfinger, Ernö, 1902–1987, vol. VIII

Goldfrap, Brig. Harold Wyn, 1884–1940, vol. III

Goldhawk, Rev. Ira G., *died* 1967, vol. VI

Goldie, Archibald Hayman Robertson, 1888–1964, vol. VI

Goldie, Barré Algernon Highmore, 1870–1949, vol. IV

Goldie, Rt Rev. Frederick, 1914–1980, vol. VII

Goldie, Rt Hon. Sir George Dashwood Taubman, 1846–1925, vol. II

Goldie, Major Kenneth Oswald, 1882–1938, vol. III

Goldie, Captain Mark Leigh, 1875–1915, vol. I

Goldie, Sir Noel Barré, 1882–1964, vol. VI

Goldie, Robert George, 1893–1971, vol. VII

Goldie-Taubman, Sir John Senhouse, 1838–1898, vol. I

Golding, Frank Yeates, 1867–1938, vol. III

Golding, F(rederick) Campbell, 1901–1984, vol. VIII

Golding, Rev. Harry, 1889–1969, vol. VI

Golding, Captain John, 1871–1943, vol. IV

Golding, Louis, 1895–1958, vol. V

Golding, Captain Thomas, 1860–1937, vol. III

Golding-Bird, Cuthbert Hilton, 1848–1939, vol. III

Golding-Bird, Rt Rev. Cyril Henry, 1876–1955, vol. V

Goldman, Charles Sydney, 1868–1958, vol. V

Goldman, Peter, 1925–1987, vol. VIII

Goldmann, Edwin E., 1862–1913, vol. I

Goldmann, Nahum, 1895–1982, vol. VIII

Goldmark, Karl, 1832–1915, vol. I

Goldney, Maj.-Gen. Claude Le Bas, 1887–1978, vol. VII

Goldney, Francis B.; *see* Bennett-Goldney.

Goldney, Sir Frederick Hastings, 3rd Bt, 1845–1940, vol. III

Goldney, Sir Gabriel, 1st Bt, 1813–1900, vol. I

Goldney, Col George Francis Bennett, 1879–1953, vol. V

Goldney, Sir Henry Hastings, 4th Bt, 1886–1974, vol. VII

Goldney, Hon. Sir John Tankerville, 1846–1920, vol. II

Goldney, Sir Prior, 2nd Bt, 1843–1925, vol. II

Goldney, Col Thomas Holbrow, 1847–1915, vol. I

Goldring, Douglas, 1887–1960, vol. V

Goldsbrough, George Ridsdale, 1881–1963, vol. VI

Goldsbrough, Giles Forward, *died* 1933, vol. III

Goldschmidt, Otto, 1829–1907, vol. I

Goldschmidt, Lt-Col Sidney George, 1869–1949, vol. IV

Goldsmid, Col Albert Edward Williamson, 1846–1904, vol. I

Goldsmid, Sir Frederic John, 1818–1908, vol. I

Goldsmid, Major Sir Henry Joseph d'A.; *see* d'Avigdor-Goldsmid.

Goldsmid, Maj.-Gen. Sir James Arthur d'A.; *see* d'Avigdor-Goldsmid.

Goldsmid, Sir Osmond Elim d'A.; *see* d'Avigdor-Goldsmid.

Goldsmid, Sidney Hoffnung, 1863–1930, vol. III

Goldsmid-Montefiore, Claude Joseph; *see* Montefiore.

Goldsmid-Stern-Salomons, Sir David Lionel; *see* Salomons.

Goldsmith, Sir Allen John Bridson, 1909–1976, vol. VII

Goldsmith, Edward, 1868–1951, vol. V

Goldsmith, Francis, 1874–1940, vol. III

Goldsmith, Frank, 1878–1967, vol. VI

Goldsmith, Rt Rev. Frederick, 1853–1932, vol. III

Goldsmith, Col George Mills, 1876–1937, vol. III

Goldsmith, Col Harry Dundas, 1878–1955, vol. V

Goldsmith, Herbert Symonds, 1873–1945, vol. IV

Goldsmith, John Herman Thorburn, 1903–1987, vol. VIII

Goldsmith, John Mills, 1845–1912, vol. I

Goldsmith, Mac, 1902–1983, vol. VIII

Goldsmith, Rev. Malcolm George, 1849–1940, vol. III

Goldsmith, Vice-Adm. Sir Malcolm Lennon, 1880–1955, vol. V

Goldsmith, Col Perry Gladstone, 1874–1951, vol. V

Goldsmith, Rev. Sidney Willmer, 1869–1939, vol. III

Goldsmith, Captain Sir William Burgess, 1837–1912, vol. I

Goldsmith, William Noel, 1893–1975, vol. VII

Goldstein, Sydney, 1903–1989, vol. VIII

Goldstein, Baron W. van, 1831–1901, vol. I

Goldstone, Sir Frank Walter, 1870–1955, vol. V

Goldsworthy, Captain Ivan Ernest Goodman, 1894–1970, vol. VI

Goldsworthy, Walter Tuckfield, 1837–1911, vol. I

Goldwyn, Samuel, 1882–1974, vol. VII

Goligher, Hugh Garvin, 1873–1958, vol. V

Goligher, William Alexander, 1870–1941, vol. IV

Golightly, Col Robert Edmund, 1856–1935, vol. III

Golla, Frederick Lucian, 1878–1968, vol. VI

Gollan, Sir Alexander, *died* 1902, vol. I

Gollan, Eliza Margaret; *see* Rita.

Gollan, Sir Henry Cowper, 1868–1949, vol. IV

Gollan, Herbert Roy, 1892–1968, vol. VI

Gollan, Spencer Herbert, 1860–1934, vol. III

Gollancz, Rev. Sir Hermann, 1852–1930, vol. III

Gollancz, Sir Israel, 1863–1930, vol. III

Gollancz, Sir Victor, 1893–1967, vol. VI

Gollin, Alfred, 1861–1946, vol. IV

Golsworthy, Arnold, 1865–1939, vol. III

Gomes, Sir Stanley Eugene, 1901–1985, vol. VIII

Gomez, Alice, *died* 1922, vol. II

Gomm, Francis Culling C.; *see* Carr-Gomm.

Gomm, Hubert William Culling C.; *see* Carr-Gomm.

Gomme, Arnold Wycombe, 1886–1959, vol. V

Gomme, Sir (George) Laurence, 1853–1916, vol. II

Gomme, Sir Laurence; *see* Gomme, Sir G. L.

Gomme-Duncan, Col Sir Alan Gomme; *see* Duncan.

Gompers, Samuel, 1850–1924, vol. II

Gompertz, Frank Priestly V.; *see* Vincent-Gompertz.

Gompertz, Sir Henry Hessey Johnston, 1867–1930, vol. III

Gompertz, Brig. Martin Louis Alan, 1886–1951, vol. V

Gonard, Samuel Alexandre, 1896–1975, vol. VII

Gondal, HH Maharaja of, 1865–1944, vol. IV

Gonner, Sir Edward Carter Kersey, 1862–1922, vol. II

Gonner, Rev. Eric Peter, *died* 1930, vol. III

Gonthier, George, 1869–1943, vol. IV

Gonzalez-Llubera, Ignacio Miguel, 1893–1962, vol. VI

Gonzi, Most Rev. Michael, 1885–1984, vol. VIII

Gooch, Sir Alfred Sherlock, 9th Bt (*cr* 1746), 1851–1899, vol. I

Gooch, Brian Sherlock, 1904–1968, vol. VI

Gooch, Charles Edmund, 1870–1937, vol. III

Gooch, Sir Daniel Fulthorpe, 3rd Bt (*cr* 1866), 1869–1926, vol. II

Gooch, Edwin George, 1889–1964, vol. VI

Gooch, George Gordon, 1893–1967, vol. VI (AII)

Gooch, George Peabody, 1873–1968, vol. VI

Gooch, Sir Henry Cubitt, 1871–1959, vol. V

Gooch, Sir Henry Daniel, 2nd Bt (*cr* 1866), 1841–1897, vol. I

Gooch, Henry Martyn, 1874–1957, vol. V

Gooch, Brig. Richard Frank Sherlock, 1906–1973, vol. VII

Gooch, Sir Robert Douglas, 4th Bt, 1905–1989, vol. VIII

Gooch, Col Sir Robert Eric Sherlock, 11th Bt (*cr* 1746), 1903–1978, vol. VII

Gooch, Sir Thomas Vere Sherlock, 10th Bt (*cr* 1746), 1881–1946, vol. IV

Good, Alan Paul, 1906–1953, vol. V

Good, Christopher Frank, *died* 1949, vol. IV

Good, Air Vice-Marshal James Laurence Fuller F.; *see* Fuller-Good.

Good, James Winder, 1877–1930, vol. III

Good, Percy, *died* 1950, vol. IV

Goodacre, Hugh George, 1865–1952, vol. V

Goodale, Sir Ernest William, 1896–1984, vol. VIII

Goodall, Alexander, 1876–1941, vol. IV

Goodall, Edward A., 1819–1908, vol. I

Goodall, Edward Basil Herbert, 1885–1936, vol. III

Goodall, Lt-Col Edwin, 1863–1944, vol. IV

Goodall, Frederick, 1822–1904, vol. I

Goodall, Rev. John William, *died* 1932, vol. III

Goodall, Joseph Strickland, 1874–1934, vol. III

Goodall, Rev. Norman, 1896–1985, vol. VIII

Goodall, Sir Reginald, 1901–1990, vol. VIII

Goodall, Rev. Canon Robert William, 1862–1938, vol. III

Goodall, Sir Stanley Vernon, 1883–1965, vol. VI

Gooday, John Francis Sykes, *died* 1915, vol. I

Goodbody, Col Cecil Maurice, 1874–1936, vol. III

Goodbody, Francis Woodcock, 1870–1938, vol. III

Goodbody, Gen. Sir Richard Wakefield, 1903–1981, vol. VIII

Goodchild, George, 1888–1969, vol. VI

Goodchild, George Frederick, 1871–1956, vol. V

Goodchild, Norman Walter, 1901–1970, vol. VI

Goodchild, Sir William Alfred Cecil, 1885–1940, vol. III

Goodden, Abington, 1901–1978, vol. VII

Goodden, Rev. Edward Wyndham, 1847–1924, vol. II

Goodden, Col John Bernhard Harbin, 1876–1951, vol. V

Goode, Sir Charles Henry, 1827–1922, vol. II

Goode, Sir Richard Allmond Jeffrey, 1873–1953, vol. V

Goode, Samuel Walter, 1878–1935, vol. III

Goode, Sir William Allmond Codrington, 1907–1986, vol. VIII

Goode, Sir William Athelstane Meredith, *died* 1944, vol. IV

Gooden, Rev. Malcolm Cecil Whitridge, 1894–1969, vol. VI

Gooden, Stephen, 1892–1955, vol. V

Goodenough, Ethel Mary, *died* 1946, vol. IV

Goodenough, Sir Francis William, 1872–1940, vol. III

Goodenough, Frederick Cranfurd, 1866–1934, vol. III

Goodenough, Kenneth Mackenzie, 1891–1985, vol. VIII

Goodenough, Rear-Adm. Michael Grant, 1904–1955, vol. V

Goodenough, Samuel Kenneth Henry, 1930–1983, vol. VIII

Goodenough, Adm. Sir William Edmund, 1867–1945, vol. IV

Goodenough, Lt-Gen. Sir William Howley, 1833–1898, vol. I

Goodenough, Sir William Macnamara, 1st Bt, 1899–1951, vol. V

Gooderham, Col Sir Albert, 1861–1935, vol. III

Gooderham, Very Rev. Hector Bransby, 1901–1977, vol. VII

Gooderson, Richard Norman, 1915–1981, vol. VIII

Goodeve, Mrs Arthur, (Florence Everilda), *died* 1916, vol. II

Goodeve, Hon. Arthur Samuel, 1860–1920, vol. II

Goodeve, Sir Charles Frederick, 1904–1980, vol. VII

Goodeve, Florence Everilda; *see* Goodeve, Mrs Arthur.

Goodey, Tom, 1885–1953, vol. V

Goodfellow, Lt-Gen. Charles Augustus, 1836–1915, vol. I

Goodfellow, Maj.-Gen. Howard Courtney, 1898–1983, vol. VIII

Goodfellow, Keith Frank, 1926–1977, vol. VII

Goodfellow, Col Napier George Barras, 1878–1963, vol. VI

Goodfellow, Thomas Ashton, *died* 1937, vol. III

Goodfellow, Gen. W. W., 1833–1901, vol. I

Goodfellow, Sir William, 1880–1974, vol. VII

Goodhart, Arthur Lehman, 1891–1978, vol. VII

Goodhart, Sir Ernest Frederic, 2nd Bt, 1880–1961, vol. VI

Goodhart, Comdr Francis Herbert Heveningham, 1884–1917, vol. II

Goodhart, Gordon Wilkinson, 1882–1948, vol. IV

Goodhart, Sir James Frederic, 1st Bt, 1845–1916, vol. II

Goodhart, Sir John Gordon, 3rd Bt, 1916–1979, vol. VII

Goodhart, Leander McC.; *see* McCormick-Goodhart.

Goodhart-Rendel, Harry Stuart, 1887–1959, vol. V

Goodier, Most Rev. Alban, 1869–1939, vol. III

Goodier, Rev. Joseph Hulme, *died* 1920, vol. II

Goodland, Col Herbert Tom, 1874–1956, vol. V

Goodlet, Brian Laidlaw, 1903–1961, vol. VI

Goodliffe, Francis Foster, *died* 1925, vol. II

Goodman, Col Albert William, 1880–1937, vol. III

Goodman, Rev. Arthur Worthington, 1871–1951, vol. V

Goodman, Bruce Wilfred, 1906–1974, vol. VII

Goodman, Cyril, *died* 1938, vol. III

Goodman, Rev. George, 1821–1908, vol. I

Goodman, Hon. Sir Gerald Aubrey, 1862–1921, vol. II

Goodman, Brig.-Gen. Sir Godfrey Davenport, 1868–1957, vol. V

Goodman, Lt-Col Harry Russell, 1875–1936, vol. III

Goodman, John, 1862–1935, vol. III

Goodman, Maude, *died* 1938, vol. III

Goodman, Neville Marriott, 1898–1980, vol. VII

Goodman, Paul, 1875–1949, vol. IV

Goodman, Reginald Ernest, 1886–1968, vol. VI

Goodman, Robert Gwelo, *died* 1939, vol. III

Goodman, Sydney Charles Nichols, 1868–1936, vol. III

Goodman, Sir Victor Martin Reeves, 1899–1967, vol. VI

Goodman, Vyvian Edwin, 1889–1961, vol. VI

Goodman, Maj.-Gen. Walter Rutherfoord, 1899–1976, vol. VII

Goodman, Sir William George Toop, 1872–1961, vol. VI

Goodman, Hon. Sir William Meigh, 1847–1928, vol. II

Goodrich, Rev. A., 1840–1919, vol. II

Goodrich, Carter, 1897–1971, vol. VII

Goodrich, Edwin Stephen, 1868–1946, vol. IV

Goodrich, Henry E., 1887–1961, vol. VI

Goodrich, Adm. Sir James Edward Clifford, 1851–1925, vol. II

Goodrich, Dame Matilda, *died* 1972, vol. VII

Goodrich-Freer, A. M., *died* 1931, vol. III

Goodridge, Major Edwin, 1903–1969, vol. VI

Goodridge, Rear-Adm. Walter Somerville, 1849–1929, vol. III

Goodsall, David Henry, *died* 1906, vol. I

Goodsell, Sir John William, 1906–1981, vol. VIII

Goodship, Harold Edwin, 1877–1951, vol. V

Goodson, Alan, 1927–1990, vol. VIII

Goodson, Sir Alfred Lassam, 1st Bt, 1867–1940, vol. III

Goodson, Lt-Col Sir Alfred Lassam, 2nd Bt, 1893–1986, vol. VIII

Goodson, Arthur, 1913–1975, vol. VII

Goodson, Katharine, *died* 1958, vol. V

Goodstein, Reuben Louis, 1912–1985, vol. VIII
Goodwin, Albert, *died* 1932, vol. III
Goodwin, Aubrey, 1889–1964, vol. VI
Goodwin, Col Frank, 1857–1943, vol. IV
Goodwin, Engr-Rear-Adm. Frank Rheuben, 1875–1966, vol. VI
Goodwin, Major George Alfred, 1857–1945, vol. IV
Goodwin, Engr Vice-Adm. Sir George Goodwin, 1862–1945, vol. IV
Goodwin, Harvey, 1850–1917, vol. II
Goodwin, Lt-Gen. Sir John; *see* Goodwin, Lt-Gen. Sir T. H. J. C.
Goodwin, Michael Felix James, 1916–1988, vol. VIII
Goodwin, Nathaniel Carl, 1857–1919, vol. II
Goodwin, Sir Reginald Eustace, 1908–1986, vol. VIII
Goodwin, Lt-Gen. Sir Richard Elton, 1908–1986, vol. VIII
Goodwin, Shirley, 1880–1927, vol. II
Goodwin, Sir Stuart Coldwell, 1886–1969, vol. VI
Goodwin, Lt-Col Thomas Frederick, 1904–1965, vol. VI
Goodwin, Lt-Gen. Sir (Thomas Herbert) John (Chapman), 1871–1960, vol. V
Goodwin, William, 1873–1953, vol. V
Goodwin, William Lawton, 1856–1941, vol. IV
Goodwin, Lt-Col William Richard, 1882–1930, vol. III
Goodwin, Col William Richard Power,1875–1958, vol. V
Goodwin, Sir William V. S. Gradwell, 1865–1942, vol. IV
Goodwin-Tomkinson, Joseph; *see* Tomkinson.
Goodwyn, Rev. Canon Frederick Wildman, 1850–1931, vol. III
Goodwyn, Major Henry Edward, 1855–1929, vol. III
Goodwyn, Lt-Col Norton James, 1861–1906, vol. I
Goodyear, Francis Richard David, 1936–1987, vol. VIII
Goodyear, Robert Arthur Hanson, 1877–1948, vol. IV
Goodyear, William Henry, 1846–1923, vol. II
Goold, Sir George Ignatius, 6th Bt, 1903–1967, vol. VI
Goold, Sir (George) Patrick, 5th Bt, 1878–1954, vol. V (A)
Goold, Sir James Stephen, 4th Bt, 1848–1926, vol. II
Goold-Adams, Major Sir Hamilton John, 1858–1920, vol. II
Goold-Adams, Col Sir Henry Edward Fane, 1860–1935, vol. III
Goold-Adams, Ven. John Michael, 1850–1922, vol. II
Goolden, Barbara, 1900–1990, vol. VIII
Goolden, Rear-Adm. Francis Hugh Walter, 1885–1950, vol. IV
Goolden, Richard Percy Herbert, 1895–1981, vol. VIII
Goonetilleke, Sir Oliver Ernest, 1892–1978, vol. VII
Goosman, Hon. Sir Stanley; *see* Goosman, Hon. Sir W. S.
Goosman, Hon. Sir (William) Stanley, 1890–1969, vol. VI
Goossens, Sir Eugene, 1893–1962, vol. VI
Goossens, Léon Jean, 1897–1988, vol. VIII

Gopathi Narayanaswami Chetty, Diwan Bahadur Sir, 1881–1945, vol. IV
Gopallawa, William, 1897–1981, vol. VIII
Gordon, Lord Adam Granville, 1909–1984, vol. VIII
Gordon, Lt-Col Adrian Charles, 1889–1917, vol. II
Gordon, Alban Goodwin, 1890–1947, vol. IV
Gordon, Alec Knyvet, 1870–1951, vol. V
Gordon, Hon. Sir Alexander, 1858–1942, vol. IV
Gordon, Alexander, 1886–1965, vol. VI
Gordon, Lt-Gen. Sir Alexander Hamilton, 1859–1939, vol. III
Gordon, Alexander Morison, 1846–1913, vol. I
Gordon, Rev. Alexander Reid, 1872–1930, vol. III
Gordon, Lt-Col Rt Hon. Sir Alexander Robert Gisborne, 1882–1967, vol. VI
Gordon, Brig.-Gen. Alister Fraser, 1872–1917, vol. II
Gordon, Major Archibald Alexander, 1867–1949, vol. IV
Gordon, Sir (Archibald) Douglas, 1888–1966, vol. VI
Gordon, Sir Archibald McDonald, 1892–1974, vol. VII
Gordon, Rev. Hon. Arthur, 1854–1919, vol. II
Gordon of Ellon, Arthur John Lewis, 1847–1918, vol. II
Gordon, Brig. Barbara Masson, 1913–1980, vol. VII
Gordon, Lt-Gen. Sir Benjamin Lumsden, 1833–1916, vol. II
Gordon, Surg.-Gen. Sir Charles Alexander, 1821–1899, vol. I
Gordon, Sir Charles Blair, 1867–1939, vol. III
Gordon, Sir Charles Edward, 7th Bt (*cr* 1706), 1835–1910, vol. I
Gordon, Rev. Charles W.; *see* Connor, Ralph.
Gordon, Christie Wilson, 1911–1979, vol. VII
Gordon, Christopher Martin P.; *see* Pirie-Gordon.
Gordon, Major Colin Lindsay, *died* 1940, vol. III
Gordon, Cora Josephine, *died* 1950, vol. IV
Gordon, Sir Cosmo (Edmund) Duff, 5th Bt (*cr* 1813), 1862–1931, vol. III
Gordon, Crawford, 1914–1967, vol. VI
Gordon, Very Rev. Daniel Miner, 1845–1925, vol. II
Gordon, Hon. Sir David John, 1865–1946, vol. IV
Gordon, Donald, 1901–1969, vol. VI
Gordon, Donald James, 1915–1977, vol. VII
Gordon, Donald McDonald, 1921–1985, vol. VIII
Gordon, Sir Douglas; *see* Gordon, Sir A. D.
Gordon, Douglas; *see* Gordon, G. C. D.
Gordon, Sir Douglas Frederick D.; *see* Duff-Gordon.
Gordon, Hon. and Rev. Douglas H.; *see* Hamilton-Gordon.
Gordon, Douglas John, 1900–1959, vol. V
Gordon, Major Duncan Forbes, *born* 1849, vol. II
Gordon, Lt-Col Edward Hyde Hamilton-, *died* 1955, vol. V
Gordon, Eric V., 1896–1938, vol. III
Gordon, Col Esme Cosmo William C.; *see* Conway-Gordon.
Gordon, Lt-Col Evelyn Boscawen, 1877–1963, vol. VI
Gordon, Sir Eyre, 1884–1972, vol. VII
Gordon, Francis Frederick, 1866–1922, vol. II
Gordon, Lt-Col Francis Lewis, 1878–1920, vol. II
Gordon, Maj.-Gen. Hon. Sir Frederick, 1861–1927, vol. II
Gordon, Sir Garnet Hamilton, 1904–1975, vol. VII

Gordon, George, *died* 1914, vol. I
Gordon, George Angier, 1853–1929, vol. III
Gordon, Col George Grant, 1836–1912, vol. I
Gordon, Col George Grant, 1863–1926, vol. II
Gordon, Col George Hamilton, 1875–1961, vol. VI
Gordon, George Stuart, 1881–1942, vol. IV
Gordon, Lord Granville Armyne, 1856–1907, vol. I
Gordon, (Granville Cecil) Douglas, 1883–1930, vol. III
Gordon, Col Gwynnedd C.; *see* Conway-Gordon.
Gordon, Hampden Charles, *died* 1960, vol. V
Gordon, Harry Panmure, 1837–1902, vol. I
Gordon, Henry Erskine, 1849–1929, vol. III
Gordon, Captain Sir Henry Robert, 1886–1969, vol. VI
Gordon, Henry W.; *see* Wolrige-Gordon.
Gordon, Sir Henry William D., 6th Bt; *see* Duff-Gordon.
Gordon, Brig.-Gen. Herbert, 1869–1951, vol. V
Gordon, Herbert Ford, 1882–1963, vol. VI
Gordon, Sir Home Seton, 11th Bt (*cr* 1631), 1845–1906, vol. I
Gordon, Sir Home Seton Charles Montagu, 12th Bt (*cr* 1631), 1871–1956, vol. V
Gordon, Hugh Walker, 1897–1987, vol. VIII
Gordon, James Charles Maitland-, 1850–1915, vol. I
Gordon, Rt Rev. James Geoffrey, 1881–1938, vol. III
Gordon, Maj.-Gen. James Leslie, 1909–1985, vol. VIII
Gordon, James Scott, 1867–1946, vol. IV
Gordon, Jan, 1882–1944, vol. IV
Gordon, Rt Hon. John, 1849–1922, vol. III
Gordon, Lt-Col John, 1870–1938, vol. III
Gordon, Sir John Charles, 9th Bt, 1901–1982, vol. VIII
Gordon, Col John Charles Frederick, 1849–1923, vol. II
Gordon, Lt-Col John de la Hay, 1887–1959, vol. V
Gordon, Hon. John Edward, 1850–1915, vol. I
Gordon, Brig. John Evison, 1901–1977, vol. VII
Gordon, Rt Hon. John Fawcett, 1879–1965, vol. VI
Gordon, Col John Gordon W.; *see* Wolrige-Gordon.
Gordon, Hon. Sir John Hannah, 1850–1923, vol. II
Gordon, Gen. Sir John James Hood, 1832–1908, vol. I
Gordon, Brig. John Keily, 1883–1976, vol. VII
Gordon, Brig.-Gen. John Lewis Randolph, 1867–1953, vol. V
Gordon, John Rutherford, 1890–1974, vol. VII
Gordon, John William, 1853–1936, vol. III
Gordon, Maj.-Gen. Joseph Maria, 1856–1929, vol. III
Gordon, Kathleen Olivia, 1898–1985, vol. VIII
Gordon, Col Kenmure Alick Garth E.; *see* Evans-Gordon.
Gordon, Kenneth, 1897–1955, vol. V
Gordon, Brig.-Gen. Laurence George Frank, 1864–1943, vol. IV
Gordon, Captain Lewis, 1883–1915, vol. I
Gordon, Lewis, *died* 1935, vol. III
Gordon, Lt-Gen. Lewis C.; *see* Conway-Gordon.
Gordon, Sir Lionel Eldred Pottinger S. (3rd Bt); *see* Smith-Gordon.
Gordon, Sir Lionel Eldred Pottinger S. (4th Bt); *see* Smith-Gordon.

Gordon, Sir Lionel Eldred S.; *see* Smith-Gordon.
Gordon, Maj.-Gen. Lochinvar Alexander Charles, 1864–1927, vol. II
Gordon, Col Louis Augustus, 1857–1935, vol. III
Gordon, Dame Maria M. O.; *see* Ogilvie Gordon.
Gordon, Mervyn Henry, 1872–1953, vol. V
Gordon, Captain Oliver Loudon, 1896–1973, vol. VII
Gordon, Percival Hector, 1884–1975, vol. VII
Gordon, Col Philip Cecil Harcourt, 1864–1920, vol. II
Gordon, Lt-Col Ramsay Frederick Clayton, 1864–1943, vol. IV
Gordon, Reginald Hugh Lyall, 1863–1924, vol. II
Gordon, Richard J., 1881–1966, vol. VI
Gordon, Air Cdre Robert, 1882–1954, vol. V
Gordon, Robert Abercromby, *died* 1954, vol. V
Gordon, Sir Robert Charles, 8th Bt (*cr* 1706), 1862–1939, vol. III
Gordon, Sir Robert Glendonwyn, 9th Bt (*cr* 1625), 1824–1908, vol. I
Gordon, Captain Robert W.; *see* Wolrige Gordon.
Gordon, Captain Roderick Cosmo, 1902–1975, vol. VII
Gordon, Roland Graham, 1880–1958, vol. V
Gordon, Ronald Grey, 1889–1950, vol. IV
Gordon, Rupert Montgomery, 1893–1961, vol. VI
Gordon, Seton, 1886–1977, vol. VII
Gordon, Col Stannus Verner, 1846–1933, vol. III
Gordon, Strathearn, 1902–1983, vol. VIII
Gordon, Thomas Eagleson, *died* 1929, vol. III
Gordon, Gen. Sir Thomas Edward, 1832–1914, vol. I
Gordon, Sir Thomas Steward, 1882–1949, vol. IV
Gordon, Victor, 1884–1928, vol. II
Gordon, Vivian; *see* Bowden, V. G.
Gordon, Walter Maxwell, *died* 1951, vol. V
Gordon, Webster Boyle, 1859–1943, vol. IV
Gordon, Hon. Wesley Ashton, 1884–1943, vol. IV
Gordon, Sir William, 6th Bt (*cr* 1706), 1830–1906, vol. I
Gordon, Maj.-Gen. William, 1831–1909, vol. I
Gordon, Gen. William, 1824–1917, vol. II
Gordon, William, 1863–1929, vol. III
Gordon, Col William Alexander, 1869–1936, vol. III
Gordon, Col William Eagleson, 1866–1941, vol. IV
Gordon, Major Sir William Eden Evans, 1857–1913, vol. I
Gordon, Adm. William Everard Alphonso, 1817–1906, vol. I
Gordon, Col William Fanshawe Loudon, 1872–1931, vol. III
Gordon, William Smith, 1902–1967, vol. VI
Gordon, William Thomas, 1884–1950, vol. IV
Gordon Clark, Alfred Alexander, 1900–1958, vol. V
Gordon-Clark, Lt-Col Craufurd Alexander, 1864–1950, vol. IV
Gordon Clark, Henry Herbert, 1861–1951, vol. V
Gordon-Cumming, Major Sir Alexander Penrose, 5th Bt, 1893–1939, vol. III
Gordon-Cumming, Miss Constance Frederica, 1837–1924, vol. II
Gordon-Cumming, Sir William Gordon, 4th Bt, 1848–1930, vol. III
Gordon-Finlayson, Air Vice-Marshal James Richmond, 1914–1990, vol. VIII

Gordon-Finlayson, Gen. Sir Robert, 1881–1956, vol. V

Gordon-Hall, Maj.-Gen. Frederick William, 1902–1990, vol. VIII

Gordon-Hall, Col Frederick William George, 1861–1942, vol. IV

Gordon-Hall, Lt-Col Gordon Charles William, 1875–1940, vol. III

Gordon-Ives, Col Gordon Maynard, 1837–1907, vol. I

Gordon Lennox, Rear-Adm. Sir Alexander Henry Charles, 1911–1987, vol. VIII

Gordon-Lennox, Col Lord Algernon Charles, 1847–1921, vol. II

Gordon-Lennox, Lady Algernon, (Blanche), *died* 1945, vol. IV

Gordon-Lennox, Lord Bernard Charles, 1878–1914, vol. I

Gordon-Lennox, Cosmo Charles, 1869–1921, vol. II

Gordon-Lennox, Lord Esme Charles, 1875–1949, vol. IV

Gordon Lennox, Lieut-Gen. Sir George Charles, 1908–1988, vol. VIII

Gordon-Lennox, Rt Hon. Lord Walter Charles, 1865–1922, vol. II

Gordon-Luhrs, Lt-Col Henry; *see* Luhrs.

Gordon-Smith, Sir Allan Gordon, 1881–1951, vol. V

Gordon-Smith, Frederic, 1886–1967, vol. VI

Gordon-Smith, Richard, 1858–1918, vol. II

Gordon-Stables, William, 1840–1910, vol. I

Gordon-Taylor, Sir Gordon, *died* 1960, vol. V

Gordon-Walker, Baron (Life Peer); Patrick Chrestien Gordon Walker, 1907–1980, vol. VII

Gordon-Watson, Maj.-Gen. Sir Charles Gordon, 1874–1949, vol. IV

Gordon Watson, Hugh; *see* Watson.

Gore, Surg.-Gen. Albert H., 1839–1901, vol. I

Gore, Rev. Arthur, 1829–1913, vol. I

Gore, Col Arthur Francis Gore P. K.; *see* Pery-Knox-Gore.

Gore, Arthur (William Charles) Wentworth, 1868–1928, vol. II

Gore, Rt Rev. Charles, 1853–1932, vol. III

Gore, Col Charles Clitherow, 1839–1926, vol. II

Gore, Charles Henry, 1862–1945, vol. IV

Gore, Lt-Gen. Edward Arthur, 1839–1912, vol. I

Gore, Sir Francis Charles, 1846–1940, vol. III

Gore, Lt-Col Francis William George, 1855–1938, vol. III

Gore, Lt-Col Frederic Lawrence, 1884–1952, vol. V

Gore, George, 1826–1908, vol. I

Gore, Lt-Col J. C., 1852–1926, vol. II

Gore, John Ellard, 1845–1910, vol. I

Gore, John Francis, 1885–1983, vol. VIII

Gore, John Kearns, 1924–1980, vol. VII

Gore, Sir Ralph; *see* Gore, Sir St G. R.

Gore, Lt-Col Sir Ralph St George Brian, 11th Bt, 1908–1973, vol. VII

Gore, Sir Ralph St George Claude, 10th Bt, 1877–1961, vol. VI

Gore, Col Robert Clements, 1867–1918, vol. II

Gore, Sir (St George) Ralph, 12th Bt, 1914–1973, vol. VII

Gore, Col Sir St John Corbet, 1859–1949, vol. IV

Gore, Hon. Seymour Fitzroy O.; *see* Ormsby-Gore.

Gore-Booth, Baron (Life Peer); Paul Henry Gore-Booth, 1909–1984, vol. VIII

Gore-Booth, Eva Selina, *died* 1926, vol. II

Gore-Booth, Sir Henry William; *see* Booth.

Gore-Booth, Sir Josslyn Augustus Richard; *see* Booth.

Gore-Booth, Sir Michael Savile, 7th Bt, 1908–1987, vol. VIII

Gore-Browne, Col Sir Eric, 1885–1964, vol. VI

Gore-Browne, Sir Francis, 1860–1922, vol. II

Gore-Browne, Comdr Godfrey, 1863–1900, vol. I

Gore-Browne, Henry George, 1830–1912, vol. I

Gore-Browne, Lt-Col Sir Stewart, 1883–1967, vol. VI

Gore-Browne, Sir Thomas Anthony, 1918–1988, vol. VIII

Gore-Browne, Rt Rev. Wilfred, *died* 1928, vol. II

Gore-Langton, Hon. Chandos Graham T.; *see* Temple-Gore-Langton.

Gore-Langton, Comdr Hon. Evelyn Arthur Grenville T.; *see* Temple-Gore-Langton.

Gore-Langton, Major Gerald Wentworth, *died* 1937, vol. III

Gore-Langton, Hon. Henry Powell, 1854–1913, vol. I

Gorell, 1st Baron, 1848–1913, vol. I

Gorell, 2nd Baron, 1882–1917, vol. II

Gorell, 3rd Baron, 1884–1963, vol. VI

Gorell Barnes, Sir William Lethbridge, 1909–1987, vol. VIII

Gorer, Peter Alfred, 1907–1961, vol. VI

Gorgas, William Crawford, 1854–1920, vol. II

Gorges, Sir (Edmond) Howard (Lacam), 1872–1924, vol. II

Gorges, Brig.-Gen. Edmund Howard, 1868–1949, vol. IV

Gorges, Sir Howard; *see* Gorges, Sir E. H. L.

Gorham, Maurice Anthony Coneys, 1902–1975, vol. VII

Goring, Sir Craven Charles, 10th Bt, 1841–1897, vol. I

Goring, Captain Sir Forster Gurney, 12th Bt, 1876–1956, vol. V

Goring, Sir Harry Yelverton, 11th Bt, 1840–1911, vol. I

Göring, Field-Marshal Hermann Wilhelm, 1893–1946, vol. IV

Goring-Jones, Lt-Col Michael Durwas; *see* Jones.

Goring-Morris, Rex, 1926–1988, vol. VIII

Gorky, Maxim, (Alexei Maximovitch Pieshkov), 1868–1936, vol. III

Gorle, Major Harry Vaughan, 1868–1937, vol. III

Gorman, Albert, 1883–1959, vol. V

Gorman, Arthur Pue, 1839–1906, vol. I

Gorman, Sir Eugene, 1891–1973, vol. VII

Gorman, Sir William, *died* 1964, vol. VI

Gorman, Ven. William Charles, 1826–1916, vol. II

Gormanston, 14th Viscount, 1837–1907, vol. I

Gormanston, 15th Viscount, 1879–1925, vol. II

Gormanston, 16th Viscount, 1914–1940, vol. III (A), vol. IV

Goronwy-Roberts, Baron (Life Peer); Goronwy Owen Goronwy-Roberts, 1913–1981, vol. VIII

Gorringe, Lt-Gen. Sir George F., 1868–1945, vol. IV

Gorringe, Rev. Reginald Ernest Pennington, 1871–1959, vol. V
Gorst, Sir Eldon, 1861–1911, vol. I
Gorst, Elliot Marcet, 1885–1973, vol. VII
Gorst, Rev. Ernest Freeland, 1871–1942, vol. IV
Gorst, Mrs Harold, (Nina Cecilia Francesca), 1869–1926, vol. II
Gorst, Harold E., 1868–1950, vol. IV
Gorst, Rt Hon. Sir John Eldon, 1835–1916, vol. II
Gorst, Nina Cecilia Francesca; see Gorst, Mrs Harold.
Gort, 4th Viscount, 1819–1900, vol. I
Gort, 5th Viscount, 1849–1902, vol. I
Gort, 6th Viscount, 1886–1946, vol. IV
Gort, 7th Viscount, 1888–1975, vol. VII
Gorton, Rt Rev. Neville Vincent, 1888–1955, vol. V
Gorton, Brig.-Gen. Reginald St George, 1866–1944, vol. IV
Gorvin, John Henry, 1886–1960, vol. V
Gos, Charles, 1885–1949, vol. IV
Goschen, 1st Viscount, 1831–1907, vol. I
Goschen, 2nd Viscount, 1866–1952, vol. V
Goschen, 3rd Viscount, 1906–1977, vol. VII
Goschen, Maj.-Gen. Arthur Alec, 1880–1975, vol. VII
Goschen, Charles Hermann, 1839–1915, vol. I
Goschen, Sir Edward Henry, 2nd Bt, 1876–1933, vol. III
Goschen, Hon. George Joachim, 1893–1916, vol. II
Goschen, Sir Harry, (William Henry Neville), 1865–1945, vol. IV
Goschen, Kenneth, 1882–1939, vol. III
Goschen, Rt Hon. Sir William Edward, 1st Bt, 1847–1924, vol. II
Goschen, Hon. Sir William Henry, 1870–1943, vol. IV
Goschen, Sir William Henry Neville; see Goschen, Sir Harry.
Gosford, 4th Earl of, 1841–1922, vol. II
Gosford, 5th Earl of, 1877–1954, vol. V
Gosford, 6th Earl of, 1911–1966, vol. VI
Gosling, Sir Arthur Hulin, 1901–1982, vol. VIII
Gosling, Sir Audley Charles, 1836–1913, vol. I
Gosling, Cecil, 1870–1944, vol. IV
Gosling, Col Charles, 1868–1917, vol. II
Gosling, Frederick; see Hamlyn, F.
Gosling, Col George, 1842–1915, vol. I
Gosling, Major George Edward, 1889–1938, vol. III
Gosling, Harry, 1861–1930, vol. III
Gosling, Herbert, 1841–1929, vol. III
Gosling, John Thomas, 1868–1933, vol. III
Gosling, Reginald George, 1899–1958, vol. V
Gosling, Richard Henry, 1853–1930, vol. III
Gosling, Major William Richard, 1891–1968, vol. VI
Gosnay, Maxwell, 1923–1986, vol. VIII
Goss, Alan; see Goss, W. A. B.
Goss, John, 1894–1953, vol. V
Goss, Leonard Cecil, 1925–1984, vol. VIII
Goss, Brig. Leonard George, 1895–1988, vol. VIII
Goss, (William) Alan (Belcher), 1908–1963, vol. VI
Goss-Custard, Reginald, 1877–1956, vol. V
Gossage, Alfred Milne, died 1948, vol. IV
Gossage, Air Marshal Sir Leslie, 1891–1949, vol. IV
Gosse, Alfred Hope, 1882–1956, vol. V
Gosse, Sir Edmund, 1849–1928, vol. II

Gosse, Sir James Hay, 1876–1952, vol. V
Gosse, Laura Sylvia, 1881–1968, vol. VI
Gosse, Philip, 1879–1959, vol. V
Gosselin, Rt Rev. Mgr Amédée, 1863–1941, vol. IV
Gosselin, L. L. T.; see Lenotre, G.
Gosselin, Sir Martin le Marchant Hadsley, 1847–1905, vol. I
Gosselin, Major Sir Nicholas, 1839–1917, vol. II
Gosselin-Grimshawe, Hellier Robert Hadsley, 1849–1924, vol. II
Gosset, Lt-Col Allen Butler, 1868–1948, vol. IV
Gosset, Ven. Charles Hilgrove, died 1923, vol. II
Gosset, Francis Russell, 1849–1930, vol. III
Gosset, Col Francis William, 1876–1931, vol. III
Gosset, Maj.-Gen. Sir Matthew William Edward, 1839–1909, vol. I
Gossip, Alex, 1862–1952, vol. V
Gossip, Rev. Arthur John, 1873–1954, vol. V
Gossling, Archibald George, 1878–1950, vol. IV
Gostling, Col Ernest Victor, 1872–1922, vol. II
Gostling, Maj.-Gen. Philip Le Marchant Stonhouse S.; see Stonhouse-Gostling.
Gotch, Francis, 1853–1913, vol. I
Gotch, John Alfred, 1852–1942, vol. IV
Gotch, Thomas Cooper, 1854–1931, vol. III
Gothard, Sir Clifford Frederic, 1893–1979, vol. VII
Gotley, George Rainald H.; see Henniker-Gotley.
Gotley, Roger Alwyn H.; see Henniker-Gotley.
Gott, Sir Benjamin S., died 1933, vol. III
Gott, Sir Charles Henry, 1866–1965, vol. VI
Gott, Rt Rev. John, 1830–1906, vol. I
Gott, Lt-Gen. William Henry Ewart, 1897–1942, vol. IV
Gotto, Basil, 1866–1954, vol. V
Gotto, Brig. Christopher Hugh, 1888–1959, vol. V
Götz, Sir Frank Léon Aroha, 1892–1970, vol. VI (AII)
Goudeket, Mme Maurice; see Colette.
Goudge, Elizabeth de Beauchamp, 1900–1984, vol. VIII
Goudge, Rev. Henry Leighton, 1866–1939, vol. III
Goudge, James Alfred, 1862–1955, vol. V
Goudie, Hon. Sir George Louis, 1866–1949, vol. IV
Goudie, William John, 1868–1945, vol. IV
Goudy, Henry, 1848–1921, vol. II
Gouge, Sir Arthur, 1890–1962, vol. VI
Gough, 3rd Viscount, 1849–1919, vol. II
Gough, 4th Viscount, 1892–1951, vol. V
Gough, Col Alan Percy George, 1863–1930, vol. III
Gough, Rev. Preb. Alfred William, 1862–1931, vol. III
Gough, Sir (Arthur) Ernest, 1878–1974, vol. VII
Gough, Col (Charles) Frederick (Howard), 1901–1977, vol. VII
Gough, Sir Charles John Stanley, 1832–1912, vol. I
Gough, Rev. Edwin Spencer, 1845–1927, vol. II
Gough, Sir Ernest; see Gough, Sir A. E.
Gough, Frederic Harrison, born 1863, vol. II
Gough, Col Frederick; see Gough, Col C. F. H.
Gough, Adm. Frederick William, 1824–1908, vol. I
Gough, Brig. Guy Francis, 1893–1988, vol. VIII
Gough, Harold Robert, 1889–1975, vol. VII
Gough, Lt-Col Henry Worsley Worsley-, 1874–1957, vol. V

Gough, Herbert John, 1890–1965, vol. VI

Gough, Gen. Sir Hubert de la Poer, 1870–1963, vol. VI

Gough, Lt-Col Hugh Augustus Keppel, 1871–1950, vol. IV

Gough, Gen. Sir Hugh Henry, 1833–1909, vol. I

Gough, Maj.-Gen. Hugh Sutlej, 1848–1920, vol. II

Gough, Jethro, 1903–1979, vol. VII (AII)

Gough, Brig.-Gen. John Edmond, 1871–1915, vol. I

Gough, William, 1876–1947, vol. IV

Gough-Calthorpe, Hon. Frederick Somerset; *see* Calthorpe.

Gough-Calthorpe, Admiral of the Fleet Hon. Sir Somerset Arthur; *see* Calthorpe.

Gouin, Hon. Sir Lomer, 1861–1929, vol. III

Goulburn, Brig.-Gen. Cuthbert Edward, 1860–1944, vol. IV

Goulburn, Maj.-Gen. Edward Henry, 1903–1980, vol. VII

Goulburn, Very Rev. Edward Meyrick, 1818–1897, vol. I

Gould, Hon. Sir Albert John, 1847–1936, vol. III

Gould, Alec Carruthers, 1870–1948, vol. IV

Gould, Sir Alfred Pearce, 1852–1922, vol. II

Gould, Barbara Ayrton, *died* 1950, vol. IV

Gould, Sir Basil John, 1883–1956, vol. V

Gould, Charles, *died* 1909, vol. I

Gould, Edward, 1837–1922, vol. II

Gould, Edward Blencowe, 1847–1916, vol. II

Gould, Edwin, 1866–1933, vol. III

Gould, Eric Lush Pearce, 1886–1940, vol. III

Gould, Sir Francis Carruthers, 1844–1925, vol. II

Gould, Frederick, 1879–1971, vol. VII

Gould, Frederick James, 1855–1938, vol. III

Gould, George Jay, 1864–1923, vol. II

Gould, Rev. George Pearce, 1848–1921, vol. II

Gould, Gerald, 1885–1936, vol. III

Gould, Ven. Henry George, 1851–1914, vol. I

Gould, Herbert Ross, 1887–1954, vol. V

Gould, Howard Gould, 1871–1959, vol. V

Gould, James Childs, 1882–1944, vol. IV

Gould, James Nutcombe, *died* 1899, vol. I

Gould, Nathaniel, 1857–1919, vol. II

Gould, Col Philip, 1870–1942, vol. IV

Gould, R(alph) Blair, 1904–1984, vol. VIII

Gould, Rev. Reginald Freestone, 1860–1939, vol. III

Gould, Sir Robert Macdonald, *died* 1971, vol. VII

Gould, Sir Ronald, 1904–1986, vol. VIII

Gould, Lt-Comdr Rupert Thomas, 1890–1948, vol. IV

Gould, Sabine B.; *see* Baring-Gould.

Gould, Sir Trevor Jack, 1906–1984, vol. VIII

Goulden, Charles Bernard, 1879–1953, vol. V

Goulden, Gontran Iceton, 1912–1986, vol. VIII

Goulden, Mark, *died* 1980, vol. VII

Goulden, Richard Reginald, *died* 1932, vol. III

Goulder, George Frederick, 1863–1942, vol. IV

Goulding, Sir Basil; *see* Goulding, Sir W. B.

Goulding, Henry Raynor, 1859–1934, vol. III

Goulding, Captain Sir Lingard; *see* Goulding, Captain Sir W. L. A.

Goulding, Lt-Col Terence Leslie Crawford P.; *see* Pierce-Goulding.

Goulding, Sir (William) Basil, 3rd Bt, 1909–1982, vol. VIII

Goulding, Rt Hon. Sir William Joshua, 1st Bt, 1856–1925, vol. II

Goulding, Captain Sir (William) Lingard Amphlett, 2nd Bt, 1883–1935, vol. III

Gouldsmith, Edmund, 1852–1932, vol. III

Gouldsmith, Rev. Herbert, *died* 1940, vol. III

Goument, Charles Ernest Vear, 1857–1941, vol. IV

Gour, Sir Hari Singh, 1866–1949, vol. IV

Gouraud, Gen. Henri, 1867–1946, vol. IV

Gourielli, Princess; *see* Rubinstein, Helena.

Gourlay, Charles, *died* 1926, vol. II

Gourlay, Harry Philp Heggie, 1916–1987, vol. VIII

Gourlay, Brig. Kenneth Ian, 1891–1970, vol. VI

Gourlay, William Robert, 1874–1938, vol. III

Gourley, Sir Edward Temperley, 1828–1902, vol. I

Govan, Raymond Eustace Grant, 1891–1940, vol. III

Gover, Brig. Charles Rhodes, 1881–1942, vol. IV

Gover, John Mahan, *died* 1947, vol. IV

Govett, Ven. Decimus Storry, 1827–1912, vol. I

Govett, Ven. Henry, 1819–1903, vol. I

Govett, John Romaine, 1897–1956, vol. V

Govindan Nair, Diwan Bahadur Chettur, 1881–1945, vol. IV (A), vol. V

Gow, Alexander, 1869–1955, vol. V

Gow, Alexander Edward, 1884–1952, vol. V

Gow, Andrew Carrick, 1848–1920, vol. II

Gow, Andrew Sydenham Farrar, 1886–1978, vol. VII

Gow, Charles, 1846–1929, vol. III

Gow, Rev. Henry, 1861–1938, vol. III

Gow, Ian Reginald Edward, 1937–1990, vol. VIII

Gow, Rev. James, 1854–1923, vol. II

Gow, Brig. John Wesley Harper, 1898–1986, vol. VIII

Gow, Leonard, 1859–1936, vol. III

Gow, Lt-Col Peter Fleming, 1885–1949, vol. IV

Gow, William, 1853–1919, vol. II

Gow, William John, 1863–1933, vol. III

Gowan, Miss E. M., *died* 1934, vol. III

Gowan, Sir Hyde Clarendon, 1878–1938, vol. III

Gowan, Hon. Sir James Robert, 1815–1909, vol. I

Gowans, Surg. Rear-Adm. Francis Jollie, 1880–1952, vol. V

Gowans, Hon. Lt-Col James, 1872–1936, vol. III (A), vol. IV

Gowen, Rev. Herbert H., *died* 1960, vol. V (A), vol. VI (AI)

Gower, Major Lord Alistair St Clair Sutherland L.; *see* Leveson Gower.

Gower, Arthur Francis Gresham L.; *see* Leveson Gower.

Gower, Col Charles Cameron L.; *see* Leveson-Gower.

Gower, Frederick Neville Sutherland L.; *see* Leveson-Gower.

Gower, Sir George Granville L.; *see* Leveson Gower.

Gower, Granville Charles Gresham L.; *see* Leveson Gower.

Gower, Sir Henry Dudley Gresham L.; *see* Leveson Gower.

Gower, Sir (Herbert) Raymond, 1916–1989, vol. VIII

Gower, Ivon Llewellyn Owen, 1874–1955, vol. V

Gower, Sir Patrick; *see* Gower, Sir R. P. M.

Gower, Col Philip L.; *see* Leveson Gower.

Gower, Sir Raymond; *see* Gower, Sir H. R.

Gower, Sir (Robert) Patrick (Malcolm), 1887–1964, vol. VI

Gower, Sir Robert Vaughan, 1880–1953, vol. V

Gower, Lord Ronald Sutherland-, 1845–1916, vol. II

Gower-Jones, Ven. Geoffrey, 1910–1982, vol. VIII

Gowers, Sir Ernest Arthur, 1880–1966, vol. VI

Gowers, Sir William Frederick, 1875–1954, vol. V

Gowers, Sir William Richard, 1845–1915, vol. I

Gowing, Ven. Ellis Norman, 1883–1960, vol. V

Gowing, Rt Rev. Eric Austin, 1913–1981, vol. VIII

Gowing, Lionel Francis, 1859–1925, vol. II

Gowing, Richard, 1831–1899, vol. I

Gowland, William, 1842–1922, vol. II

Gowlland, Lt-Col Edward Lake, 1876–1942, vol. IV

Gowrie, 1st Earl of, 1872–1955, vol. V

Graaff, Sir David Pieter de Villiers, 1st Bt, 1859–1931, vol. III

Graaff, Sir Jacobus Arnoldus Combrinck, *died* 1927, vol. II

Grabham, George Walter, 1882–1955, vol. V

Grabham, Michael Comport, 1840–1935, vol. III

Grace, David Mabe, 1945–1988, vol. VIII

Grace, Sir Gilbert; *see* Grace, Sir O. G.

Grace, Rev. Canon Harold Myers, 1888–1967, vol. VI

Grace, Harvey, 1874–1944, vol. IV

Grace, Adm. Henry Edgar, 1876–1937, vol. III

Grace, James E., 1850–1908, vol. I

Grace, John, 1886–1972, vol. VII

Grace, Sir John Te Herekiekie, 1905–1985, vol. VIII

Grace, Leo Bernard Aloysius, 1903–1969, vol. VI

Grace, Michael Anthony, 1920–1988, vol. VIII

Grace, Hon. Morgan Stanislaus, *died* 1903, vol. I

Grace, Sir (Oliver) Gilbert, 1896–1968, vol. VI

Grace, Sir Percy Raymond, 4th Bt, 1831–1903, vol. I

Grace, Sir Raymond Eustace, 6th Bt, 1903–1977, vol. VII

Grace, Col Sheffield Hamilton-, 1834–1915, vol. I

Grace, Ven. Thomas Samuel, 1850–1918, vol. II

Grace, Sir Valentine Raymond, 5th Bt, 1877–1945, vol. IV

Grace, Rear-Adm. Walter Keir Campbell, 1890–1964, vol. VI

Grace, Wilfrid Arnold, 1895–1964, vol. VI

Grace, William Gilbert, 1848–1915, vol. I

Gracey, Gen. Sir Douglas David, 1894–1964, vol. VI

Gracey, Captain George Frederick Handel, 1878–1958, vol. V

Gracey, Hugh Kirkwood, 1868–1929, vol. III

Gracey, Col Thomas, 1843–1921, vol. II

Gracias, HE Cardinal Valerian, 1900–1978, vol. VII

Gracie, Alan James, 1904–1973, vol. VII

Gracie, Sir Alexander, 1860–1930, vol. III

Gracie, George Handel H.; *see* Heath-Gracie.

Gracie, Captain Henry Stewart, 1901–1979, vol. VII

Gradwell, Leo Joseph Anthony, 1899–1969, vol. VI

Gradwell, Robert Bernard George Ashhurst, 1858–1935, vol. III

Grady, John William, 1915–1982, vol. VIII

Graeme, Bruce, (Graham Montague Jeffries), 1900–1982, vol. VIII

Graeme, Sir Egerton Hood Murray H.; *see* Hamond-Graeme.

Graeme, Sir Graham Eden William H.; *see* Hamond-Graeme.

Græme, Patrick Neale Sutherland, 1877–1958, vol. V

Græme-Sutherland, Alexander Malcolm, 1845–1908, vol. I

Graff, Stephen John, 1842–1940, vol. III

Grafftey-Smith, Sir Anthony Paul, 1903–1960, vol. V

Grafftey-Smith, Sir Laurence Barton, 1892–1989, vol. VIII

Grafton, 7th Duke of, 1821–1918, vol. II

Grafton, 8th Duke of, 1850–1930, vol. III

Grafton, 9th Duke of, 1914–1936, vol. III

Grafton, 10th Duke of, 1892–1970, vol. VI

Graham, Captain Alan Crosland, 1896–1964, vol. VI

Graham, Captain Lord Alastair Mungo, 1886–1976, vol. VII

Graham, Alexander, 1861–1941, vol. IV

Graham, Allan James, *died* 1941, vol. IV

Graham, Andrew Guillemard, 1913–1981, vol. VIII

Graham, Angus, 1892–1979, vol. VII

Graham, Adm. Sir Angus Edward Malise Bontine C.; *see* Cunninghame Graham.

Graham, Anthony George M.; *see* Maxtone-Graham.

Graham, Sir Aubrey Gregor, 1867–1947, vol. IV

Graham, Sir Cecil William Noble, 1872–1945, vol. IV

Graham, Comdr Charles Elphinstone Fleeming C.; *see* Cunninghame Graham.

Graham, Rt Rev. Charles Morice, 1834–1912, vol. I

Graham, Lt-Col Charles Percy, 1881–1961, vol. VI

Graham, Flt-Lt Charles Walter, 1893–1916, vol. II

Graham, Sir Clarence Johnston, 1st Bt (*cr* 1964), 1900–1966, vol. VI

Graham, Sir Claverhouse Frederick Charles, *died* 1924, vol. II

Graham, Constantine, 1882–1934, vol. III

Graham, Rear-Adm. Cosmo Moray, *died* 1946, vol. IV

Graham, Sir Crosland; *see* Graham, Sir J. C.

Graham, Brig.-Gen. Cuthbert Aubrey Lionel, 1882–1957, vol. V

Graham, Lt-Col David James, 1871–1929, vol. III

Graham, Donald, 1844–1901, vol. I

Graham, Maj.-Gen. Douglas Alexander Henry, 1893–1971, vol. VII

Graham, Brig. Lord (Douglas) Malise, 1883–1974, vol. VII

Graham, Douglas William, 1866–1936, vol. III

Graham, Duncan MacGregor, 1867–1942, vol. IV

Graham, Edward John, *died* 1918, vol. II

Graham, Maj.-Gen. Sir Edward Ritchie Coryton, 1858–1951, vol. V

Graham, Ennis; *see* Molesworth, Mary Louisa.

Graham, Rt Rev. Eric, 1888–1964, vol. VI

Graham, Sir Fergus; *see* Graham, Sir Frederick F.

Graham, Captain Francis, 1894–1918, vol. II

Graham, Sir Frederick, 1848–1923, vol. II

Graham, Maj.-Gen. Frederick Clarence Campbell, 1908–1988, vol. VIII

Graham, Sir (Frederick) Fergus, 5th Bt (*cr* 1783), 1893–1978, vol. VII

Graham, George, *born* 1838, vol. II

Graham, George, 1881–1949, vol. IV

Graham, George, 1882–1971, vol. VII

Graham, Very Rev. George Frederick, 1877–1962, vol. VI

Graham, Sir George Goldie, 1892–1974, vol. VII

Graham, Rt Hon. George Perry, 1859–1943, vol. IV

Graham, Rev. George R., 1850–1927, vol. II

Graham, Sir Gerald, 1831–1899, vol. I

Graham, Gerald Sandford, 1903–1988, vol. VIII

Graham, Gilbert Maxwell Adair, 1883–1960, vol. V

Graham, (Godfrey) Michael, 1898–1972, vol. VII

Graham, Major Sir Guy; see Graham, Major Sir R. G.

Graham, H. E.; see Hamilton, Col E. G.

Graham, Hamilton Maurice H.; see Howgrave-Graham.

Graham, Lt-Gen. Hamilton Maximillian Christian Williams, 1866–1934, vol. III

Graham, Harold, 1889–1963, vol. VI

Graham, Captain Harry J. C., 1874–1936, vol. III

Graham, Harry Robert, 1850–1933, vol. III

Graham, Captain Harry S. C., 1874–1936, vol. III

Graham, Lady Helen Violet, 1879–1945, vol. IV

Graham, Major Henry Archibald Roger, 1892–1970, vol. VI

Graham, Rev. Henry Burrans, 1909–1963, vol. VI

Graham, Rev. Henry Grey, 1843–1906, vol. I

Graham, Rt Rev. Henry Grey, 1874–1959, vol. V

Graham, Sir Henry John Lowndes, 1842–1930, vol. III

Graham, Air Vice-Marshal Henry Rudolph, 1910–1987, vol. VIII

Graham, Col Herman Witsius-Gore, 1859–1932, vol. III

Graham, Lt-Col Howard Boyd, 1891–1965, vol. VI (AII)

Graham, Lt-Gen. Howard Douglas, 1898–1986, vol. VIII

Graham, Hugh, died 1975, vol. VII

Graham, Sir James, 1856–1913, vol. I

Graham, Gen. Sir James; see Graham, Gen. Sir S. J.

Graham, James, 1870–1961, vol. VI

Graham, Maj.-Gen. Sir James Drummond, 1875–1958, vol. V

Graham, James Edward, died 1929, vol. III

Graham, James M.; see Maxtone Graham.

Graham, John, 1844–1918, vol. II

Graham, John, 1879–1958, vol. V

Graham, Rev. John; see Graham, Rev. Jonathan J. D.

Graham, Very Rev. John Anderson, 1861–1942, vol. IV

Graham, John Cameron, died 1929, vol. III

Graham, Sir John Frederick Noble, 2nd Bt (cr 1906), 1864–1936, vol. III

Graham, John Fuller, 1872–1946, vol. IV

Graham, Sir John Gibson, 1896–1964, vol. VI

Graham, Maj.-Gen. John Gordon, 1833–1911, vol. I

Graham, Sir John Hatt Noble, 1st Bt (cr 1906), 1837–1926, vol. II

Graham, Captain John Irvine, 1862–1947, vol. IV

Graham, Sir John James, 1847–1928, vol. II

Graham, John Macdonald, 1908–1982, vol. VIII

Graham, Ven. John Malcolm Alexander, died 1931, vol. III

Graham, Sir (John) Reginald (Noble), 3rd Bt (cr 1906), 1892–1980, vol. VII

Graham, John William, 1859–1932, vol. III

Graham, Rev. (Jonathan) John Drummond, died 1965, vol. VI

Graham, Joseph, 1828–1902, vol. I

Graham, Sir (Joseph) Crosland, 1866–1946, vol. IV

Graham, Col Lancelot, 1864–1932, vol. III

Graham, Sir Lancelot, 1880–1958, vol. V

Graham, Brig. Lancelot Cecil Torbock, 1890–1962, vol. VI

Graham, Col Malcolm David, 1865–1941, vol. IV

Graham, Brig. Lord Malise; see Graham, Brig. Lord D. M.

Graham, Col Malise, 1884–1929, vol. III

Graham, Michael; see Graham, G. M.

Graham, Michael, 1847–1925, vol. II

Graham, Maj.-Gen. Sir Miles William Arthur Peel, 1895–1976, vol. VII

Graham, Sir Montrose Stuart, 11th Bt (cr 1629), 1875–1939, vol. III

Graham, Sir Montrose Stuart, 12th Bt (cr 1629), 1904–1975, vol. VII

Graham, Norval Bantock, 1870–1944, vol. IV

Graham, P. Anderson, died 1925, vol. II

Graham, Peter, 1836–1921, vol. II

Graham, Sir Ralph Wolfe, 13th Bt, 1908–1988, vol. VIII

Graham, Sir Reginald; see Graham, Sir J. R. N.

Graham, Major Sir (Reginald) Guy, 9th Bt (cr 1662), 1878–1940, vol. III

Graham, Sir Reginald Henry, 8th Bt (cr 1662), 1835–1920, vol. II

Graham, Sir Richard Bellingham, 10th Bt, 1912–1982, vol. VIII

Graham, Richard Brockbank, 1893–1957, vol. V

Graham, Sir Richard James, 4th Bt (cr 1783), 1859–1932, vol. III

Graham, Sir Robert, 1846–1929, vol. III

Graham, Sir Robert, 1876–1947, vol. IV

Graham, Robert Arthur, 1870–1940, vol. III

Graham, Col Robert Blackall, 1874–1944, vol. IV

Graham, Robert Bontine C.; see Cunninghame Graham.

Graham, Robert Henry, 1870–1956, vol. V

Graham, Robert James Douglas, died 1950, vol. IV (A)

Graham, Sir Robert James Stuart, 10th Bt (cr 1629), 1845–1917, vol. II

Graham, Col Robert M.; see Mould-Graham.

Graham, Air Vice-Marshal Ronald, 1896–1967, vol. VI

Graham, Rt Hon. Sir Ronald William, 1870–1949, vol. IV

Graham, Rose, 1875–1963, vol. VI

Graham, Gen. Sir (S.) James, 1837–1917, vol. II

Graham, Stanley Galbraith, 1895–1975, vol. VII

Graham, Stephen, 1884–1975, vol. VII

Graham, Sydney, 1879–1966, vol. VI

Graham, Maj.-Gen. Sir Thomas, 1842–1925, vol. II

Graham, Thomas Alexander Ferguson, 1840–1906, vol. I

Graham, Hon. Sir Thomas Lynedoch, 1860–1940, vol. III

Graham, Thomas Ottiwell, 1883–1966, vol. VI

Graham, Tom; *see* Graham, T. A. F.

Graham, Sir Wallace, 1848–1917, vol. II

Graham, Walter Armstrong, 1868–1949, vol. IV

Graham, Adm. Walter Hodgson Bevan, 1849–1931, vol. III

Graham, Sir William, 1825–1907, vol. I

Graham, William, *died* 1911, vol. I

Graham, Sir William, 1861–1932, vol. III

Graham, Rt Hon. William, 1887–1932, vol. III

Graham, William, 1862–1943, vol. IV

Graham, William, 1896–1955, vol. V

Graham, William, 1894–1981, vol. VIII

Graham, Col William James, 1890–1971, vol. VII

Graham, William Murray, 1884–1956, vol. V

Graham, William Perceval Gore, 1861–1918, vol. II

Graham, Winifred, (Mrs Theodore Cory), *died* 1950, vol. IV

Graham Brown, Rt Rev. George Francis, 1891–1942, vol. IV

Graham Brown, Thomas, *died* 1965, vol. VI

Graham-Campbell, Rt Rev. Archibald Rollo, 1903–1978, vol. VII

Graham-Campbell, Sir Rollo Frederick, 1868–1946, vol. IV

Graham-Clarke, Captain Lionel Altham, 1867–1914, vol. I

Graham-Dixon, Charles; *see* Graham-Dixon, L. C.

Graham-Dixon, Leslie Charles, 1901–1986, vol. VIII

Graham Dow, Ronald; *see* Dow.

Graham-Green, Major Graham John, 1906–1985, vol. VIII

Graham-Harrison, Sir William Montagu, 1871–1949, vol. IV

Graham-Hodgson, Sir Harold Kingston; *see* Hodgson.

Graham-Little, Sir Ernest Gordon; *see* Little.

Graham-Montgomery, Sir Basil Templer; *see* Montgomery.

Graham-Montgomery, Rev. Sir Charles Percy; *see* Montgomery.

Graham-Moon, Sir Wilfred; *see* Moon.

Graham-Smith, George Stuart, *died* 1950, vol. IV

Graham Smith, Stanley, 1896–1989, vol. VIII

Graham-Stewart, Alexander, 1879–1944, vol. IV

Graham-Vivian, Preston; *see* Graham-Vivian, R. P.

Graham-Vivian, (Richard) Preston, 1896–1979, vol. VII

Grahame, Rt Hon. Sir George Dixon, 1873–1940, vol. III

Grahame, Lt-Col John Crum, 1870–1952, vol. V

Grahame, Kenneth, 1859–1932, vol. III

Grahame, Thomas George, 1861–1922, vol. II

Grahame-Thomson, Leslie; *see* MacDougall, L. G.

Grahame-White, Claude, 1879–1959, vol. V

Grain, Sir Peter, 1864–1947, vol. IV

Grainer, Ron, 1932–1981, vol. VIII

Grainger, Francis Edward; *see* Hill, Headon.

Grainger, (George) Percy Aldridge, 1882–1961, vol. VI

Grainger, Surg.-Gen. Thomas, 1862–1931, vol. III

Grainger-Stewart, Brig. Thomas, 1896–1979, vol. VII

Gramigna, Rt Rev. Fr Petronius, 1844–1917, vol. II

Granard, 8th Earl of, 1874–1948, vol. IV

Grand, Keith Walter Chamberlain, 1900–1983, vol. VIII

Grand, Maj.-Gen. Laurence Douglas, 1898–1975, vol. VII

Grand, Sarah, *died* 1943, vol. IV

Grand' Combe, Félix de; *see* Boillot, Félix.

Grande, Julian, 1874–1946, vol. IV

Grandi, Count (di Mordano), Dino, 1895–1988, vol. VIII

Grane, Rev. William Leighton, 1855–1952, vol. V

Graner, Most Rev. Lawrence L., 1901–1982, vol. VIII

Granet, Col Edward John, 1858–1918, vol. II

Granet, Sir Guy; *see* Granet, Sir W. G.

Granet, Sir (William) Guy, 1867–1943, vol. IV

Grange-Bennett, Rev. Canon Ronald du Pré, 1901–1972, vol. VII

Granger, Frank Stephen, 1864–1936, vol. III

Granger, Sir (Hugh) Rupert, 1890–1959, vol. V

Granger, Sir Rupert; *see* Granger, Sir H. R.

Granger, Col Thomas Arthur, *died* 1942, vol. IV

Granger, Sir Thomas Colpitts, 1852–1927, vol. II

Grannum, Sir Edward Allan, 1869–1956, vol. V

Grannum, Edward Thomas, 1843–1922, vol. II

Grannum, Reginald Clifton, 1872–1946, vol. IV

Gransden, Sir Robert, 1893–1972, vol. VII

Grant, Rt Hon. Lord; William Grant, 1909–1972, vol. VII

Grant, Sir (Albert) William, 1891–1965, vol. VI

Grant, Sir Alexander, 1st Bt (*cr* 1924), 1864–1937, vol. III

Grant, Alexander, 1866–1941, vol. IV

Grant, Captain Alexander, 1872–1961, vol. VI

Grant, Col Alexander Brown, 1840–1921, vol. II

Grant, Alexander Ludovic, 1901–1986, vol. VIII

Grant, Alexander Thomas Kingdom, 1906–1988, vol. VIII

Grant, Adm. Alfred Ernest Albert, 1861–1933, vol. III

Grant, Sir (Alfred) Hamilton, 12th Bt (*cr* 1688), 1872–1937, vol. III

Grant, Sir Allan John, 1875–1955, vol. V

Grant, Air Marshal Sir Andrew, 1890–1967, vol. VI

Grant, Col Sir Arthur, 10th Bt (*cr* 1705), 1879–1931, vol. III

Grant, Sir Arthur Henry, 9th Bt (*cr* 1705), 1849–1917, vol. II

Grant, Arthur James, 1862–1948, vol. IV

Grant, Major Sir Arthur Lindsay, 11th Bt (*cr* 1705), 1911–1944, vol. IV

Grant, Engr Rear-Adm. Arthur Robert, 1870–1952, vol. V

Grant, Rev. (Arthur) Rowland (Harry), 1882–1961, vol. VI

Grant, Cary, 1904–1986, vol. VIII

Grant, Rev. Cecil, 1870–1946, vol. IV

Grant, Sir Charles, 1836–1903, vol. I

Grant, Rt Rev. Charles Alexander, 1906–1989, vol. VIII

Grant, Charles Frederick, 1878–1966, vol. VI

Grant, Charles Graham, *died* 1935, vol. III

Grant, Col Charles James William, *died* 1932, vol. III

Grant, Gen. Sir Charles John Cecil, 1877–1950, vol. IV

Grant, Colin King, 1924–1981, vol. VIII
Grant, Corrie, 1850–1924, vol. II
Grant, Rev. Cyril Fletcher, *died* 1916, vol. II
Grant, Douglas; *see* Grant, W. D. B.
Grant, Lt.-Gen. Douglas Gordon Seafield St John, 1829–1907, vol. I
Grant, Comdr Duncan, 1882–1955, vol. V
Grant, Sir Duncan Alexander, 13th Bt (*cr* 1688), 1928–1961, vol. VI
Grant, Duncan James Corrowr, 1885–1978, vol. VII
Grant, Adm. Sir (Edmund) Percy (Fenwick George), 1867–1952, vol. V
Grant, Lt-Col Edward James, 1854–1928, vol. II
Grant, Sir Ewan George M.; *see* Macpherson-Grant.
Grant, Sir Francis Cullen, 12th Bt (*cr* 1705), 1914–1966, vol. VI
Grant, Francis Henry Symons, 1883–1963, vol. VI
Grant, Sir Francis James, 1863–1953, vol. V
Grant, Frank, 1890–1986, vol. VIII
Grant, Frederick, 1890–1954, vol. V
Grant, Captain George Bertram M.; *see* Macpherson-Grant.
Grant, Sir George M.; *see* Macpherson-Grant.
Grant, Very Rev. George Monro, 1835–1902, vol. I
Grant, Gordon, 1907–1979, vol. VII
Grant, Sir Hamilton; *see* Grant, Sir A. H.
Grant, Lt.-Gen. Harold George, 1884–1950, vol. IV
Grant, Adm. Sir Heathcoat Salusbury, 1864–1938, vol. III
Grant, Henry Eugene Walter, 1855–1934, vol. III
Grant, Gen. Sir Henry Fane, 1848–1919, vol. II
Grant, Adm. Henry William, 1870–1949, vol. IV
Grant, Col Hugh Gough, 1845–1922, vol. II
Grant, Maj.-Gen. Ian Cameron, 1891–1955, vol. V
Grant, Ian Dingwall, 1891–1962, vol. VI
Grant, Isabel Frances, 1887–1983, vol. VIII
Grant, Sir James Alexander, 1831–1920, vol. II
Grant, Sir James Augustus, 1st Bt (*cr* 1926), 1867–1932, vol. III
Grant, James Currie, 1914–1988, vol. VIII
Grant, Sir James Dundas-, 1854–1944, vol. IV
Grant, Sir James Monteith, 1903–1981, vol. VIII
Grant, James William Hamilton, 1876–1934, vol. III
Grant, Joan, (Mrs Denys Kelsey), 1907–1989, vol. VIII
Grant, Col John Duncan, 1877–1967, vol. VI
Grant, John Leslie, 1890–1975, vol. VII
Grant, Sir John M.; *see* Macpherson-Grant.
Grant, Captain John Moreau, 1895–1986, vol. VIII
Grant, John Peter, 1860–1927, vol. II
Grant, John Peter, 1885–1963, vol. VI
Grant, John Sharp, 1909–1974, vol. VII
Grant, Rt Rev. Kenneth, 1900–1959, vol. V
Grant, Sir (Kenneth) Lindsay, 1899–1989, vol. VIII
Grant, Sir Kerr, 1878–1967, vol. VI
Grant, Leonard Bishopp, 1882–1974, vol. VII
Grant, Sir Lindsay; *see* Grant, Sir K. L.
Grant, Adm. Sir Lowther; *see* Grant, Adm. Sir W. L.
Grant, Sir Ludovic James, 11th Bt (*cr* 1688), 1862–1936, vol. III
Grant, Hon. MacCallum, *died* 1928, vol. II
Grant, Col Maurice Harold, *died* 1962, vol. VI
Grant, Neil Forbes, 1882–1970, vol. VI
Grant, Rear-Adm. Noel, 1868–1920, vol. II

Grant, Adm. Sir Percy; *see* Grant, Adm. Sir E. P. F. G.
Grant, Peter Forbes, 1921–1974, vol. VII
Grant, Maj.-Gen. Sir Philip Gordon, 1869–1943, vol. IV
Grant, Lt-Gen. Sir Robert, 1837–1904, vol. I
Grant, Robert, 1842–1910, vol. I
Grant, Robert, 1852–1940, vol. III (A), vol. IV
Grant, Major Robert Francis Sidney, 1877–1927, vol. II
Grant, Sir Robert McVitie, 2nd Bt (*cr* 1924), 1894–1947, vol. IV
Grant, Sir Robert William L.; *see* Lyall Grant.
Grant, Brig.-Gen. Ronald Chas., 1864–1951, vol. V
Grant, Ronald Thomson, 1892–1989, vol. VIII
Grant, Rev. Rowland; *see* Grant, Rev. A. R. H.
Grant, Col Samuel Charles Norton, 1854–1939, vol. III
Grant, Lt-Gen. Seafield Falkland Murray Treasure, 1834–1910, vol. I
Grant, Air Vice Marshal Stanley Bernard, 1919–1987, vol. VIII
Grant, Lady Sybil, *died* 1955, vol. V
Grant, William; *see* Grant, Rt Hon. Lord.
Grant, Sir William; *see* Grant, Sir A. W.
Grant, William, 1863–1919, vol. II
Grant, Brig.-Gen. William, 1870–1939, vol. III
Grant, William, 1863–1946, vol. IV
Grant, Rt Hon. William, *died* 1949, vol. IV
Grant, (William) Douglas (Beattie), 1921–1969, vol. VI
Grant, William Lawson, 1872–1935, vol. III
Grant, Adm. Sir (William) Lowther, 1864–1929, vol. III
Grant, William Robert O.; *see* Ogilvie-Grant.
Grant, Willis, 1907–1981, vol. VIII
Grant-Dalton, Captain Charles, 1884–1952, vol. V
Grant-Dalton, Lt-Col Duncan, 1881–1969, vol. VI
Grant-Dalton, Adm. Hubert, 1862–1934, vol. III
Grant-Duff, Major Adrian, 1869–1914, vol. I
Grant-Duff, Sir Arthur Cuninghame, 1861–1948, vol. IV
Grant-Duff, Edith Florence, (Lady Grant-Duff), *died* 1937, vol. III
Grant-Duff, Sir Evelyn, 1863–1926, vol. II
Grant-Lawson, Col Sir Peter; *see* Lawson.
Grant-Sturgis, Sir Mark Beresford Russell, 1884–1949, vol. IV
Grant-Suttie, Sir George; *see* Suttie.
Grant-Suttie, Col Hubert Francis; *see* Suttie.
Grant Watson, Herbert Adolphus, 1881–1971, vol. VII
Grant-Wilson, Sir Wemyss, 1870–1953, vol. V
Grantchester, 1st Baron, 1893–1976, vol. VII
Grantham, Sir Alexander William George Herder, 1899–1978, vol. VII
Grantham, Vincent Alpe, 1889–1968, vol. VI
Grantham, Mrs Violet Hardisty, 1893–1983, vol. VIII
Grantham, Sir William, 1835–1911, vol. I
Grantham, William Wilson, 1866–1942, vol. IV
Grantley, 5th Baron, 1855–1943, vol. IV
Grantley, 6th Baron, 1892–1954, vol. V
Granville, 3rd Earl, 1872–1939, vol. III
Granville, 4th Earl, 1880–1953, vol. V

Granville, Countess; (Rose Constance), 1890–1967, vol. VI

Granville, Alexander, 1874–1929, vol. III

Granville, Col Bernard, *died* 1933, vol. III

Granville, Captain Dennis, 1863–1929, vol. III

Granville, Sir Keith, 1910–1990, vol. VIII

Granville, Rev. Roger, 1848–1911, vol. I

Granville-Barker, Harley Granville, 1877–1946, vol. IV

Granville-Barker, Helen, *died* 1950, vol. IV

Granville-Sharp, Gilbert; *see* Sharp.

Granville-Smith, Stuart Hayne, 1901–1977, vol. VII

Granville-West, Baron (Life Peer); Daniel Granville-West, 1904–1984, vol. VIII

Gras, Norman Scott Brien, 1884–1956, vol. V

Grasar, Rt Rev. William Eric, 1913–1982, vol. VIII

Grasett, Lt-Gen. Sir (Arthur) Edward, 1888–1971, vol. VII

Grasett, Lt-Gen. Sir Edward; *see* Grasett, Lt-Gen. Sir A. E.

Grasett, Col Henry James, 1847–1930, vol. III

Gratiaen, Edward Frederick Noel, 1904–1973, vol. VII

Grattan, Col Henry William, 1872–1952, vol. V

Grattan, John Henry Grafton, 1878–1951, vol. V

Grattan, Col O'Donnel Colley, 1855–1929, vol. III

Grattan-Bellew, Sir Arthur John, 1903–1985, vol. VIII

Grattan-Bellew, Lt-Col Sir Charles Christopher, 4th Bt, 1887–1948, vol. IV

Grattan-Bellew, Sir Henry Christopher, 3rd Bt, 1860–1942, vol. IV

Grattan-Doyle, Sir Nicholas, 1862–1941, vol. IV

Grattidge, Captain Harry, 1890–1979, vol. VII

Gratton, Norman Murray Gladstone, 1886–1965, vol. VI

Gratwicke, George Frederick, 1850–1912, vol. I

Grau, Maurice, 1849–1907, vol. I

Grauer, Albert Edward, 1906–1961, vol. VI

Graul, Isidore, 1894–1962, vol. VI

Graumann, Sir Harry, 1868–1938, vol. III

Gravely, Sir Walter B.; *see* Booth-Gravely.

Graves, 4th Baron, 1847–1904, vol. I

Graves, 5th Baron, 1847–1914, vol. I

Graves, 6th Baron, 1871–1937, vol. III

Graves, 7th Baron, 1877–1963, vol. VI

Graves, Alfred Perceval, 1846–1931, vol. III

Graves, Arnold F., 1847–1930, vol. III

Graves, Col Benjamin Chamney, 1845–1905, vol. I

Graves, Captain Sir Cecil George, 1892–1957, vol. V

Graves, Rt Rev. Charles, 1812–1899, vol. I

Graves, Rev. Charles Edward, 1839–1920, vol. II

Graves, Charles L., 1856–1944, vol. IV

Graves, Charles Patrick Ranke, 1899–1971, vol. VII

Graves, Clotilde Inez Mary, 1863–1932, vol. III

Graves, Rt Rev. Frederick Rogers, 1858–1940, vol. III (A), vol. IV

Graves, George, 1876–1949, vol. IV

Graves, Sir Hubert Ashton, 1894–1972, vol. VII

Graves, John George, 1865–1945, vol. IV

Graves, Marjorie, *died* 1961, vol. VI

Graves, Rev. Michael, 1855–1931, vol. III

Graves, Philip Perceval, 1876–1953, vol. V

Graves, Richard Massie, 1880–1960, vol. V

Graves, Robert Ernest, 1866–1922, vol. II

Graves, Robert Ranke, 1895–1985, vol. VIII

Graves, Sir Robert Windham, 1858–1934, vol. III

Graves, Rev. Walter Eccleston, *died* 1922, vol. II

Graves-Sawle, Sir Charles John; *see* Sawle.

Gravina, Conte Manfredi, 1883–1932, vol. III

Gray, Lady, (19th in line), 1841–1918, vol. II

Gray, 20th Lord, 1864–1919, vol. II

Gray, Lady (21st in line, shown as 22nd), 1866–1946, vol. IV

Gray, Master of; Hon. Lindsay Stuart Campbell-Gray, 1894–1945, vol. IV

Gray, Alan, 1855–1935, vol. III

Gray, Sir Albert, 1850–1928, vol. II

Gray, Albert Alexander, 1868–1936, vol. III

Gray, Sir Alexander, *died* 1933, vol. III

Gray, Sir Alexander, 1882–1968, vol. VI

Gray, Air Vice-Marshal Alexander, 1896–1980, vol. VII

Gray, Sir Alexander George, 1884–1968, vol. VI

Gray, Andrew, 1847–1925, vol. II

Gray, Sir Archibald Montague Henry, 1880–1967, vol. VI

Gray, Arthur, 1852–1940, vol. III

Gray, Col Arthur Claypon Horner, 1878–1963, vol. VI

Gray, A(rthur) Herbert, 1868–1956, vol. V

Gray, Arthur Wellesley, 1876–1944, vol. IV

Gray, Basil, 1904–1989, vol. VIII

Gray, Charles Herbert, *died* 1982, vol. VIII

Gray, Lt-Col Clive Osric Vere, 1882–1945, vol. IV

Gray, David, 1906–1976, vol. VII

Gray, David, 1927–1983, vol. VIII

Gray, Donald, 1893–1943, vol. IV

Gray, Douglas S., 1890–1959, vol. V

Gray, Rev. Edward Dundas McQueen, 1854–1932, vol. III

Gray, Edward Francis, 1871–1960, vol. V

Gray, Rev. Edward Ker, 1842–1903, vol. I

Gray, Sir Ernest, 1857–1932, vol. III

Gray, Ethel, *died* 1962, vol. VI

Gray, Frances Ralph, *died* 1935, vol. III

Gray, Frank, 1880–1935, vol. III

Gray, Brig.-Gen. Frederick William Barton, 1867–1931, vol. III

Gray, George Buchanan, 1865–1922, vol. II

Gray, George Charles, 1897–1981, vol. VIII

Gray, Lt-Col George Douglas, *died* 1946, vol. IV

Gray, George Kruger, 1880–1943, vol. IV

Gray, Sir George Mervyn, 1910–1973, vol. VII

Gray, Hon. George Wilkie, 1844–1924, vol. II

Gray, Gordon, 1909–1982, vol. VIII

Gray, Harold St George, 1872–1963, vol. VI

Gray, Sir Harold William Stannus, 1867–1951, vol. V

Gray, Rt Rev. Henry Allen, *died* 1939, vol. III

Gray, Sir Henry McIlree Williamson, 1870–1938, vol. III

Gray, Rev. Herbert Branston, 1851–1929, vol. III

Gray, Rev. Horace, 1874–1938, vol. III

Gray, Howard Alexander, 1870–1942, vol. IV

Gray, Ian, 1926–1983, vol. VIII

Gray, James, 1877–1968, vol. VI

Gray, Sir James, 1891–1975, vol. VII

Gray, James Andrew, 1890–1966, vol. VI

Gray, James Cooke, 1847–1902, vol. I
Gray, James Gordon, *died* 1934, vol. III
Gray, James Hugo, 1909–1941, vol. IV
Gray, James Hunter, 1867–1925, vol. II
Gray, James Neville, *died* 1959, vol. V
Gray, Lt-Col John Anselm Samuel, 1874–1950, vol. IV
Gray, Air Vice-Marshal John Astley, 1899–1987, vol. VIII
Gray, Sir John Milner, 1889–1970, vol. VI
Gray, Very Rev. John Rodger, 1913–1984, vol. VIII
Gray, Joseph Alexander, 1884–1966, vol. VI
Gray, Rev. Joseph Henry, 1856–1932, vol. III
Gray, Leonard Thomas Miller, 1893–1969, vol. VI
Gray, Louis Harold, 1905–1965, vol. VI
Gray, Mary Elizabeth, 1903–1983, vol. VIII
Gray, Maxwell, (Mary Gleed Tuttiett), 1847–1923, vol. II
Gray, Milner, 1871–1943, vol. IV
Gray, Nicol; *see* Gray, W. N.
Gray, Norah Neilson-, *died* 1931, vol. III
Gray, Sir Reginald, 1851–1935, vol. III
Gray, Robert Whytlaw W.; *see* Whytlaw-Gray.
Gray, Ronald, 1868–1951, vol. V
Gray, Sir Samuel Brownlow, 1823–1910, vol. I
Gray, Stephen Alexander Reith, 1926–1982, vol. VIII
Gray, Theodore Grant, 1884–1964, vol. VI
Gray, Thomas, 1869–1932, vol. III
Gray, Trevor Robert, 1919–1985, vol. VIII
Gray, Vernon Foxwell, 1882–1978, vol. VII
Gray, Lt-Col Sir Vivian Beaconsfield, 1885–1948, vol. IV
Gray, Sir Walter, 1848–1918, vol. II
Gray, Sir William, 1823–1898, vol. I
Gray, Sir William, 2nd Bt, 1895–1978, vol. VII
Gray, Lt-Col William A.; *see* Anstruther-Gray.
Gray, Major William Bain, 1886–1949, vol. IV
Gray, Major William Birrell-, 1872–1940, vol. III
Gray, Rt Rev. William Crane, 1835–1919, vol. II
Gray, Sir William Cresswell, 1st Bt, 1867–1924, vol. II
Gray, Maj.-Gen. William du Gard, 1856–1932, vol. III
Gray, William Forbes, 1874–1950, vol. IV
Gray, Very Rev. William Henry, 1825–1908, vol. I
Gray, Ven. William James, 1874–1960, vol. V
Gray, William John, 1911–1985, vol. VIII
Gray, William John A.; *see* Anstruther-Gray.
Gray, Col William Lewis, 1864–1924, vol. II
Gray, William Macfarlane, 1910–1984, vol. VIII
Gray, (William) Nicol, 1908–1988, vol. VIII
Gray-Cheape, Lt-Col Hugh Annesley; *see* Cheape.
Gray Horton, Lt-Col W(illiam); *see* Horton.
Gray-Smith, James Maclaren, 1832–1900, vol. I
Grayburn, Sir Vandeleur Molyneux, 1881–1943, vol. IV
Graydon, Newenham Arthur Eustace, *died* 1914, vol. I
Grayfoot, Col Blenman Buhot, *died* 1916, vol. II
Grayson, Sir Denys Henry Harrington, 2nd Bt, 1892–1955, vol. V
Grayson, Lt-Col Sir Henry Mulleneux, 1st Bt, 1865–1951, vol. V

Grayson, Sir Ronald Henry Rudyard, 3rd Bt, 1916–1987, vol. VIII
Grazebrook, Brig. George Charles, 1873–1930, vol. III
Grazebrook, Henry Broome Durley, 1884–1969, vol. VI
Grazebrook, Brig. Tom Neville, 1904–1967, vol. VI
Grazebrook, William, *died* 1955, vol. V
Greany, Surg.-Gen. John Philip, 1851–1919, vol. II
Greany, Captain John Wingate, 1892–1916, vol. II
Greatbatch, Sir Bruce, 1917–1989, vol. VIII
Greathed, Rear-Adm. Bernard Wilberforce, 1891–1961, vol. VI
Greatorex, Adm. Clement, 1869–1937, vol. III
Greaves, Rt Rev. Arthur Ivan, 1873–1959, vol. V
Greaves, Maj.-Gen. Bill; *see* Greaves, Maj.-Gen. C. G. B.
Greaves, Maj.-Gen. Charles Granville Barry, 1900–1982, vol. VIII
Greaves, Sir Ewart; *see* Greaves, Sir W. E.
Greaves, Gen. Sir George Richards, 1831–1922, vol. II
Greaves, Harold Richard Goring, 1907–1981, vol. VIII
Greaves, Sir John Bewley, 1890–1977, vol. VII
Greaves, Sir John Brownson, 1900–1965, vol. VI
Greaves, John Ernest, 1847–1945, vol. IV
Greaves, Robert William, 1909–1979, vol. VII
Greaves, Ronald Ivan Norreys, 1908–1990, vol. VIII
Greaves, Sir Western; *see* Greaves, Sir W. W.
Greaves, Sir (William) Ewart, 1869–1956, vol. V
Greaves, Sir William Herbert, 1857–1936, vol. III
Greaves, William Michael Herbert, 1897–1955, vol. V
Greaves, Sir (William) Western, 1905–1982, vol. VIII
Greaves-Lord, Sir Walter, 1878–1942, vol. IV
Grech, Herbert Felix, 1899–1982, vol. VIII
Grech-Biancardi, Lt-Col Nicola, 1850–1913, vol. I
Greely, Maj.-Gen. Adolphus Washington, 1844–1935, vol. III
Green, Sir Alan Michael, 1885–1958, vol. V
Green, Albert, 1874–1941, vol. IV
Green, Hon. Albert Ernest, 1869–1940, vol. III
Green, Alice Sophia Amelia, *died* 1929, vol. III
Green, Anna Katharine; *see* Rohlfs, Mrs Charles.
Green, Major Arthur Dowson, 1874–1914, vol. I
Green, Arthur Eatough, 1892–1984, vol. VIII
Green, Brig.-Gen. Arthur Frank Umfreville, 1878–1964, vol. VI
Green, Arthur George, 1864–1941, vol. IV
Green, Rt Rev. Arthur Vincent, 1857–1944, vol. IV
Green, Col Bernard Charles, 1866–1925, vol. II
Green, Cecil Alfred, 1908–1980, vol. VII
Green, Rt Rev. Charles Alfred Howell, 1864–1944, vol. IV
Green, Charles Edward, 1866–1920, vol. II
Green, Rev. Charles Edward Maddison, *died* 1911, vol. I
Green, Charles L.; *see* Leedham-Green.
Green, David, *died* 1918, vol. II
Green, Engr Rear-Adm. Sir (Donald) Percy, 1866–1950, vol. IV
Green, Brig.-Gen. Edgar Walter Butler, 1869–1938, vol. III
Green, Rev. Edmund Tyrrell-, 1864–1937, vol. III

Green, Sir Edward, 1st Bt (*cr* 1886), 1831–1923, vol. II

Green, Col Sir Edward Arthur Lycett, 3rd Bt (*cr* 1886), 1886–1941, vol. IV

Green, Sir (Edward) Lycett, 2nd Bt (*cr* 1886), 1860–1940, vol. III

Green, Ernest, 1885–1977, vol. VII

Green, Col Ernest Edward, 1878–1956, vol. V

Green, Miss Evelyn E.; *see* Everett-Green.

Green, Everard, 1844–1926, vol. II

Green, Sir Francis Haydn, 2nd Bt (*cr* 1901), 1871–1956, vol. V

Green, Francis Henry Knethell, 1900–1977, vol. VII

Green, Sir Frank, 1st Bt (*cr* 1901), 1835–1902, vol. I

Green, Sir Frederick, 1845–1927, vol. II

Green, Frederick Charles, 1891–1964, vol. VI

Green, Sir Frederick Daniel, 1869–1932, vol. III

Green, Frederick Ernest, 1867–1922, vol. II

Green, Frederick Lawrence, 1902–1953, vol. V

Green, Rev. Frederick Wastie, 1884–1953, vol. V

Green, Frederick William E.; *see* Edridge-Green.

Green, Geoffrey, 1918–1978, vol. VII

Green, Sir George, 1843–1916, vol. III

Green, George Alfred Lawrence, *died* 1949, vol. IV

Green, Sir George Arthur Haydn, 4th Bt (*cr* 1901), 1884–1959, vol. V

Green, George Comerford, *died* 1940, vol. III

Green, George Conrad, 1897–1976, vol. VII

Green, Sir George Ernest, 1892–1982, vol. VIII

Green, George Henry, 1881–1956, vol. V

Green, George Norman, 1906–1968, vol. VI

Green, Major Graham John G.; *see* Graham-Green.

Green, Lt-Col Harold Philip, 1877–1944, vol. IV

Green, Harry Norman, 1903–1967, vol. VI

Green, Henry, 1905–1973, vol. VII

Green, Brig.-Gen. Henry Clifford Rodes, 1872–1935, vol. III

Green, Henry Rupert, 1900–1988, vol. VIII

Green, Mrs Hetty Howland Robinson, 1835–1916, vol. II

Green, Hon. Howard Charles, 1895–1989, vol. VIII

Green, Rev. James, 1868–1948, vol. IV

Green, (James) Maurice (Spurgeon), 1906–1987, vol. VIII

Green, Rev. James Paul Weston, *born* 1876, vol. III

Green, John Alfred, 1867–1922, vol. II

Green, Adm. Sir John Frederick Ernest, 1866–1948, vol. IV

Green, Sir John Little, 1862–1953, vol. V

Green, Joseph Frederick, 1855–1932, vol. III

Green, Joseph Reynolds, *died* 1914, vol. I

Green, Kathleen (Mary) Haydn, *died* 1944, vol. IV

Green, Hon. Sir Kenneth; *see* Green, Hon. Sir R. K.

Green, Maj.-Gen. Kenneth David, 1917–1987, vol. VIII

Green, Leonard, 1890–1963, vol. VI

Green, Captain Leonard Henry, 1885–1966, vol. VI

Green, Rev. Sir Leonard Henry Haydn, 3rd Bt (*cr* 1901), 1879–1958, vol. V

Green, Leslie William, 1912–1983, vol. VIII

Green, Sir Lycett; *see* Green, Sir E. L.

Green, Col Malcolm Scrimshire, 1824–1906, vol. I

Green, Maurice; *see* Green, J. M. S.

Green, Max Sullivan, 1864–1922, vol. II

Green, Brig. Michael Arthur, 1891–1971, vol. VII

Green, Paul Eliot, 1894–1981, vol. VIII

Green, Engr Rear-Adm. Sir Percy; *see* Green, Engr Rear-Adm. Sir D. P.

Green, Rev. Canon Peter, 1871–1961, vol. VI

Green, P(hilip) M(arion) Kirby, 1905–1969, vol. VI

Green, Hon. Sir (Richard) Kenneth, 1907–1961, vol. VI

Green, Hon. Robert Francis, 1861–1946, vol. IV

Green, Roger Gilbert Lancelyn, 1918–1987, vol. VIII

Green, Roger James N.; *see* Northcote-Green.

Green, Roland, 1895–1972, vol. VII

Green, Ronald Bramble, 1895–1973, vol. VII

Green, Ronald Frank, 1905–1971, vol. VII

Green, Rev. Samuel Walter, 1853–1926, vol. II

Green, Maj.-Gen. Sebert Francis St David's, 1868–1930, vol. III

Green, Thomas Ernest, 1872–1937, vol. III

Green, Thomas Farrimond, 1899–1966, vol. VI

Green, Vincent, *died* 1958, vol. V

Green, Walford Davis, 1869–1941, vol. IV

Green, Walter Henry, 1878–1958, vol. V

Green, Brig.-Gen. Wilfrith Gerald Key, 1872–1937, vol. III

Green, Sir William, 1836–1897, vol. I

Green, Maj.-Gen. William, 1882–1947, vol. IV

Green, William, 1873–1952, vol. V

Green, William Allan McInnes, 1896–1972, vol. VII

Green, Rev. William Charles, 1832–1914, vol. I

Green, William Curtis, 1875–1960, vol. V

Green, Maj.-Gen. Sir William Henry Rodes, 1823–1912, vol. I

Green, William Kirby, 1876–1945, vol. IV

Green, Rev. William Spotswood, 1847–1919, vol. II

Green, Lt-Gen. Sir (William) Wyndham, 1887–1979, vol. VII

Green, Lt-Gen. Sir Wyndham; *see* Green, Lt-Gen. Sir W. W.

Green-Armytage, Lt-Col Vivian Bartley, 1882–1961, vol. VI

Green-Price, Sir John, 4th Bt, 1908–1964, vol. VI

Green-Price, Sir Richard Dansey, 2nd Bt, 1838–1909, vol. I

Green-Price, Major Sir Robert Henry, 3rd Bt, 1872–1962, vol. VI

Green-Wilkinson, Most Rev. Francis Oliver, 1913–1970, vol. VI

Green-Wilkinson, Lt-Gen. Frederick, 1825–1913, vol. I

Green-Wilkinson, Brig.-Gen. Lewis Frederic, 1865–1950, vol. IV

Greenacre, Sir Benjamin Wesley, 1832–1911, vol. I

Greenacre, Brig. Walter Douglas Campbell, 1900–1978, vol. VII

Greenall, Cyril Edward, *died* 1939, vol. III

Greenall, Thomas, 1857–1937, vol. III

Greenaway, Sir Percy Walter, 1st Bt, 1874–1956, vol. V

Greenaway, Sir Thomas Moore, 1902–1980, vol. VII (AII)

Greenbank, Percy, 1878–1968, vol. VI

Greenberg, Leopold, 1885–1964, vol. VI

Greenberg, Leopold J., *died* 1931, vol. III

Greene, 1st Baron, 1883–1952, vol. V

Greene, Benjamin Buck, 1808–1902, vol. I
Greene, Charles Henry, 1865–1942, vol. IV
Greene, (Charles) Raymond, 1901–1982, vol. VIII
Greene, Rt Hon. Sir Conyngham, 1854–1934, vol. III
Greene, Sir Edward Allan, 3rd Bt, 1882–1966, vol. VI
Greene, Col Hon. Edward Mackenzie, 1857–1944, vol. IV
Greene, Edward Reginald, 1904–1990, vol. VIII
Greene, Sir (Edward) Walter, 1st Bt, 1842–1920, vol. II
Greene, Eric Gordon, 1904–1966, vol. VI
Greene, Felix, 1909–1985, vol. VIII
Greene, Gen. Francis Vinton, *died* 1921, vol. II
Greene, Geoffrey Philip, 1868–1930, vol. III
Greene, George Arthur, 1853–1921, vol. II
Greene, George Ball, 1872–1945, vol. IV
Greene, Rev. Godfrey George, 1860–1929, vol. III
Greene, Sir Graham; *see* Greene, Sir W. G.
Greene, H. Barrett, 1861–1927, vol. II
Greene, Harry Plunket, 1865–1936, vol. III
Greene, Henry David, 1843–1915, vol. I
Greene, Sir Hugh Carleton, 1910–1987, vol. VIII
Greene, Jerome Davis, 1874–1959, vol. V
Greene, Brig.-Gen. John, 1878–1956, vol. V
Greene, John Arch, *died* 1934, vol. III
Greene, John Arthur, 1879–1945, vol. IV
Greene, Maurice Cherry, 1881–1959, vol. V
Greene, Raymond; *see* Greene, C. R.
Greene, Sir Raymond; *see* Greene, Sir W. R.
Greene, W. H. C.; *see* Clayton-Greene.
Greene, Sir Walter; *see* Greene, Sir E. W.
Greene, Hon. Sir Walter M.; *see* Massy-Greene.
Greene, Sir (Walter) Raymond, 2nd Bt, 1869–1947, vol. IV
Greene, Very Rev. William Conyngham, *died* 1910, vol. I
Greene, Sir (William) Graham, 1857–1950, vol. IV
Greene, William Pomeroy Crawford, 1884–1959, vol. V
Greene Kelly, Sir Henry, 1865–1934, vol. III
Greener, Lt-Col Herbert, 1862–1943, vol. IV
Greenfield, Sir Cornelius Ewen MacLean, 1906–1980, vol. VII
Greenfield, Sir Harry, 1898–1981, vol. VIII
Greenfield, Brig. Hector Robert Hume, 1893–1975, vol. VII
Greenfield, Sir Henry Challen, 1885–1967, vol. VI
Greenfield, Herbert, 1869–1949, vol. IV (A), vol. V
Greenfield, Brig.-Gen. Richard Menteith, 1856–1916, vol. II
Greenfield, Stanley Samuel, 1873–1956, vol. V
Greenfield, William Smith, 1846–1919, vol. II
Greenhalgh, Mrs Stobart; *see* Stobart, Mrs St Clair.
Greenham, Alfred Howard, 1895–1966, vol. VI
Greenham, Robert Duckworth, 1906–1976, vol. VII
Greenhill, 1st Baron, 1887–1967, vol. VI
Greenhill, 2nd Baron, 1917–1989, vol. VIII
Greenhill, Sir George, 1847–1927, vol. II
Greenhill-Gardyne, Lt-Col Charles, 1831–1923, vol. II
Greenhough, Col Frederick Harry, 1871–1953, vol. V
Greenhow, William Thomas, 1831–1921, vol. II
Greenidge, Charles Wilton Wood, 1889–1972, vol. VII

Greenish, Henry George, 1855–1933, vol. III
Greenland, Rev. William Kingscote, 1868–1957, vol. V
Greenleaves, Herbert Leslie, 1897–1975, vol. VII
Greenlees, Ian Gordon, 1913–1988, vol. VIII
Greenlees, James Robertson Campbell, 1878–1951, vol. V
Greenley, William Alfred, 1884–1949, vol. IV
Greenly, Edward, 1861–1951, vol. V
Greenly, Edward Howorth, 1837–1926, vol. II
Greenly, Lt-Col Sir John Henry Maitland, 1885–1950, vol. IV
Greenly, Maj.-Gen. Walter Howorth, 1875–1955, vol. V
Greenshields, James Naismith, 1853–1937, vol. III
Greenshields, R. A. E., *died* 1942, vol. IV
Greenslade, Brig. Cyrus, 1892–1985, vol. VIII
Greenslade, David Rex Willman, 1916–1977, vol. VII
Greenslade, Rev. Stanley Lawrence, 1905–1977, vol. VII
Greenstreet, Reginald Hawkins, 1858–1930, vol. III
Greenstreet, William John, 1861–1930, vol. III
Greenup, Rev. Albert William, 1866–1952, vol. V
Greenway, 1st Baron, 1857–1934, vol. III
Greenway, 2nd Baron, 1888–1963, vol. VI
Greenway, 3rd Baron, 1917–1975, vol. VII
Greenway, Maj.-Gen. Charles William, 1900–1968, vol. VI
Greenway, John Dee, 1896–1967, vol. VI
Greenwell, Allan, 1860–1944, vol. IV
Greenwell, Sir Bernard Eyre, 2nd Bt, 1874–1939, vol. III
Greenwell, Sir Francis, 1852–1931, vol. III
Greenwell, Captain Sir Peter McClintock, 3rd Bt, 1914–1978, vol. VII
Greenwell, Col Thomas George, 1894–1967, vol. VI
Greenwell, Sir Walpole Lloyd, 1st Bt, 1847–1919, vol. II
Greenwell, Rev. William, 1820–1918, vol. II
Greenwell, Col William Basil, 1881–1964, vol. VI
Greenwood, 1st Viscount, 1870–1948, vol. IV
Greenwood, Viscountess; (Marjery), 1886–1968, vol. VI
Greenwood of Rossendale, Baron (Life Peer); Arthur William James Greenwood, (Anthony Greenwood), 1911–1982, vol. VIII
Greenwood, Rt Hon. Arthur, 1880–1954, vol. V
Greenwood, Col Charles Francis Hill, 1871–1944, vol. IV
Greenwood, Frederick, 1830–1909, vol. I
Greenwood, George David, 1881–1953, vol. V
Greenwood, Sir (Granville) George, 1850–1928, vol. II
Greenwood, Brig. Harold Gustave Francis, 1894–1978, vol. VII
Greenwood, Col Harry, 1881–1948, vol. IV
Greenwood, Henry Harold, 1873–1962, vol. VI
Greenwood, Hubert John, 1867–1932, vol. III
Greenwood, Jack Neville, 1922–1989, vol. VIII
Greenwood, Sir James Mantle, 1902–1969, vol. VI
Greenwood, Joan, 1921–1987, vol. VIII
Greenwood, John Eric, 1891–1975, vol. VII
Greenwood, John Frederic, 1885–1954, vol. V
Greenwood, John French, 1904–1968, vol. VI

Greenwood, John Neill, 1894–1981, vol. VIII
Greenwood, Major, 1880–1949, vol. IV
Greenwood, Ranolf Nelson, 1889–1977, vol. VII
Greenwood, Robert, 1897–1981, vol. VIII
Greenwood, Robert Morrell, died 1947, vol. IV
Greenwood, Rev. Sydney, died 1926, vol. II
Greenwood, Thomas, 1851–1908, vol. I
Greenwood, Rt Rev. Tom, 1903–1974, vol. VII
Greenwood, Walter, 1903–1974, vol. VII
Greenwood, William, 1875–1925, vol. II
Greenwood, William Frederick, 1861–1933, vol. III
Greenwood Wilson, John; see Wilson.
Greer, Rt Rev. David Hummell, 1844–1919, vol. II
Greer, Sir (Edmund) Wyly, 1862–1957, vol. V
Greer, Sir Francis Nugent, 1869–1925, vol. II
Greer, Brig.-Gen. Frederick Augustus, 1871–1958, vol. V
Greer, Rev. George Samuel, died 1921, vol. II
Greer, Sir Harry, 1876–1947, vol. IV
Greer, Sir Henry, 1855–1934, vol. III
Greer, Joseph, 1854–1922, vol. II
Greer, Richard Townsend, 1854–1942, vol. IV
Greer, Thomas Macgregor, 1853–1928, vol. II
Greer, Rt Rev. William Derrick Lindsay, 1902–1972, vol. VII
Greer, Sir Wyly; see Greer, Sir E. W.
Greeson, Surgeon Vice-Adm. Sir (Clarence) Edward, 1888–1979, vol. VII
Greeson, Surg. Vice-Adm. Sir Edward; see Greeson, Surg. Vice-Adm. Sir C. E.
Greet, Sir Philip Ben, 1857–1936, vol. III
Greeves, Rev. Frederic, 1903–1985, vol. VIII
Greeves, John Ernest, 1910–1987, vol. VIII
Greeves, R(eginald) Affleck, 1878–1966, vol. VI
Greeves, Maj.-Gen. Sir Stuart, 1897–1989, vol. VIII
Greffulhe, Comtesse, died 1952, vol. V
Greg, Lt-Col Alexander, 1867–1952, vol. V
Greg, Barbara, 1900–1983, vol. VIII
Greg, Col Ernest William, 1862–1934, vol. III
Greg, John Ronald, 1866–1950, vol. IV
Greg, Lionel Hyde, 1879–1945, vol. IV
Greg, Sir Robert Hyde, 1876–1953, vol. V
Greg, Sir Walter Wilson, 1875–1959, vol. V
Gregg, Miss; see Grier, Sydney C.
Gregg, Sir Cornelius Joseph, died 1959, vol. V
Gregg, Edward Andrew, 1881–1969, vol. VI
Gregg, Sir Henry, 1859–1928, vol. II
Gregg, Humphrey P.; see Procter-Gregg.
Gregg, Very Rev. James Fitzgerald, died 1905, vol. I
Gregg, James Reali, 1899–1978, vol. VII
Gregg, Most Rev. John Allen Fitzgerald, 1873–1961, vol. VI
Gregg, John Frank, 1912–1960, vol. V
Gregg, Milton Fowler, 1892–1978, vol. VII
Gregg, Sir Norman McAlister, died 1966, vol. VI
Gregge-Hopwood, Major Edward Byng George, 1880–1917, vol. II
Gregge-Hopwood, Edward Robert, 1846–1942, vol. IV
Grego, Joseph, 1843–1908, vol. I
Gregor, James Wyllie, 1900–1980, vol. VII (AII)
Gregorie, Maj.-Gen. Charles Frederick, 1834–1918, vol. II
Gregorowski, Hon. Reinhold, 1856–1922, vol. II

Gregory, Hon. Alexander Frederick, 1843–1927, vol. II
Gregory, Arnold, 1924–1976, vol. VII
Gregory, Augusta, (Lady Gregory), died 1932, vol. III
Gregory, Hon. Sir Augustus Charles, 1819–1905, vol. I
Gregory, Rev. Benjamin, 1875–1950, vol. IV
Gregory, Charles, died 1920, vol. II
Gregory, Sir Charles Hutton, 1817–1898, vol. I
Gregory, Maj.-Gen. Charles Levinge, 1870–1944, vol. IV
Gregory, Vice-Adm. Sir David; see Gregory, Vice-Adm. Sir G. D. A.
Gregory, Rev. Edmund Ironside, 1835–1912, vol. I
Gregory, Edward John, 1850–1909, vol. I
Gregory, Eric Craven, 1887–1959, vol. V
Gregory, Captain Ernest Foster, 1873–1940, vol. III
Gregory, Rt Rev. Francis Ambrose, 1848–1927, vol. II
Gregory, Lt-Col Francis Brooke, 1862–1936, vol. III
Gregory, Frederick, 1831–1919, vol. II
Gregory, Frederick Gugenheim, 1893–1961, vol. VI
Gregory, Captain George, 1872–1929, vol. III
Gregory, Vice-Adm. Sir (George) David (Archibald), 1909–1975, vol. VII
Gregory, George Frederick, born 1839, vol. II
Gregory, Hon. Henry, 1860–1940, vol. III
Gregory, Sir Henry Stanley, 1890–1959, vol. V
Gregory, Sir Holman, 1864–1947, vol. IV
Gregory, Jackson, 1882–1943, vol. IV
Gregory, John Duncan, 1878–1951, vol. V
Gregory, Sir (John) Roger Burrow, 1861–1938, vol. III
Gregory, John Water, 1864–1932, vol. III
Gregory, Joshua C., 1875–1964, vol. VI
Gregory, Padraic, 1886–1962, vol. VI
Gregory, Philip Herries, 1907–1986, vol. VIII
Gregory, Sir Philip Spencer, 1851–1918, vol. II
Gregory, Reginald Philip, 1879–1918, vol. II
Gregory, Sir Richard Arman, 1st Bt, 1864–1952, vol. V
Gregory, Very Rev. Robert, 1819–1911, vol. I
Gregory, Roderic Alfred, 1913–1990, vol. VIII
Gregory, Sir Roger; see Gregory, Sir J. R. B.
Gregory, Sir Theodore, 1890–1970, vol. VI
Gregory, Theophilus Stephen, 1897–1975, vol. VII
Gregory, Thomas Sherwin P.; see Pearson-Gregory.
Gregory, William King, 1876–1970, vol. VI (AII)
Gregory Smith, George, 1865–1932, vol. III
Gregson, Edward Gelson, 1877–1942, vol. IV
Gregson, Ven. Francis Sitwell Knight, died 1926, vol. II
Gregson, Maj.-Gen. Guy Patrick, 1906–1988, vol. VIII
Gregson, Col Henry Guy Fulljames Savage, 1872–1949, vol. IV
Gregson-Ellis, Maj.-Gen. Philip George Saxon, 1898–1956, vol. V
Greiffenhagen, Maurice, 1862–1931, vol. III
Greig, Sir Alexander, 1878–1950, vol. IV
Greig, Alexander Rodger, 1872–1947, vol. IV
Greig, Charles Alexis, 1880–1958, vol. V
Greig, David Middleton, died 1936, vol. III

Greig, Lt-Col Edward David Wilson, 1874–1950, vol. IV

Greig, Edward Hagerup, 1843–1907, vol. I

Greig, Col Frederick James, 1863–1931, vol. III

Greig, Sir James, *died* 1934, vol. III

Greig, James, 1861–1941, vol. IV

Greig, Rev. Lt-Col John Glennie, 1871–1958, vol. V

Greig, Rt Rev. John Harold, 1865–1938, vol. III

Greig, John Russell, 1889–1963, vol. VI

Greig, John Young Thomson, 1891–1963, vol. VI

Greig, Gp Captain Sir Louis, 1880–1953, vol. V

Greig, Maysie, (Mrs Jan Sopoushek), *died* 1971, vol. VII

Greig, Rear-Adm. Morice Gordon, 1914–1980, vol. VII

Greig, Sir Robert Blyth, 1874–1947, vol. IV

Greig, Captain Ronald Henry, 1876–1916, vol. II

Grein, J. T., 1862–1935, vol. III

Grenfell, 1st Baron, 1841–1925, vol. II

Grenfell, 2nd Baron, 1905–1976, vol. VII

Grenfell, Bernard Pyne, 1869–1926, vol. II

Grenfell, Lt-Col Cecil Alfred, 1864–1924, vol. II

Grenfell, Charles Seymour, 1839–1924, vol. II

Grenfell, Rt Hon. David Rhys, 1881–1968, vol. VI

Grenfell, Rev. George, 1849–1906, vol. I

Grenfell, Col Harold Maxwell, 1870–1929, vol. III

Grenfell, Vice-Adm. Harry Tremenheere, 1845–1906, vol. I

Grenfell, Henry Riversdale, 1824–1902, vol. I

Grenfell, Joyce Irene, 1910–1979, vol. VII

Grenfell, Hon. Julian Henry Francis, 1888–1915, vol. I

Grenfell, Sir Wilfred Thomason, 1865–1940, vol. III

Grenier, Gerard, *died* 1917, vol. II

Grenier, Gustave, *born* 1847, vol. II

Grenier, Joseph Richard, 1852–1926, vol. II

Grenside, Rev. William Bent, 1821–1913, vol. I

Grensted, Rev. Frederic Finnis, 1857–1919, vol. II

Grensted, Rev. Canon Laurence William, 1884–1964, vol. VI

Grente, HE Cardinal George, 1872–1959, vol. V

Grenville, Lt-Col Hon. Thomas George Breadalbane M.; *see* Morgan-Grenville.

Gresford Jones, Rt Rev. Edward Michael, 1901–1982, vol. VIII

Gresford Jones, Rt Rev. Michael; *see* Gresford Jones, Rt Rev. E. M.

Gresley, Sir Herbert Nigel, 1876–1941, vol. IV

Gresley, Sir Nigel, 12th Bt, 1894–1974, vol. VII

Gresley, Rear-Adm. Richard Nigel, 1850–1928, vol. II

Gresley, Sir Robert, 11th Bt, 1866–1936, vol. III

Gresley, Rev. Roger St John, *died* 1935, vol. III

Gresley, Sir William Frances, 13th Bt, 1897–1976, vol. VII

Gresson, Rt Hon. Sir Kenneth Macfarlane, 1891–1974, vol. VII

Gresson, Lt-Col Thomas Tinning, 1870–1921, vol. II

Gresson, William Jardine, *died* 1934, vol. III

Gresty, Hugh, 1899–1958, vol. V

Greswell, Richard Egerton, 1916–1979, vol. VII

Greswell, Rev. William Henry Parr, *died* 1923, vol. II

Greswolde-Williams, Francis Wigley Greswolde, 1873–1931, vol. III

Gretton, 1st Baron, 1867–1947, vol. IV

Gretton, 2nd Baron, 1902–1982, vol. VIII

Gretton, 3rd Baron, 1941–1989, vol. VIII

Gretton, Major Frederic, *died* 1928, vol. II

Gretton, Brig. John Cunliffe, 1880–1953, vol. V

Gretton, Mary Sturge, *died* 1961, vol. VI

Greville, 2nd Baron, 1841–1910, vol. I

Greville, 3rd Baron, 1871–1952, vol. V

Greville, 4th Baron, 1912–1987, vol. VIII

Greville, Col Hon. Alwyn Henry Fulke, 1854–1929, vol. III

Greville, Major Charles Henry, 1889–1931, vol. III

Greville, Sir George, 1851–1937, vol. III

Greville, Hon. Louis George, 1856–1941, vol. IV

Greville, Dame Margaret Helen Anderson, (Hon. Mrs Ronald Greville), *died* 1942, vol. IV

Greville, Hon. Maynard, 1898–1960, vol. V

Greville, Hon. Mrs Ronald; *see* Greville, Dame M. H. A.

Greville, Hon. Ronald Henry Fulke, 1864–1908, vol. I

Greville, Hon. Sir Sidney Robert, 1866–1927, vol. II

Grew, Major Benjamin Dixon, 1892–1977, vol. VII

Grew, Edwin Sharpe, 1866–1950, vol. IV

Grew, Joseph Clark, 1880–1965, vol. VI

Grey, 4th Earl, 1851–1917, vol. II

Grey, 5th Earl, 1879–1963, vol. VI

Grey of Fallodon, 1st Viscount, 1862–1933, vol. III

Grey of Fallodon, Viscountess; (Pamela Adelaide Geneviève), 1871–1928, vol. II

Grey de Ruthyn, 23rd (shown as 24th) Baron, 1858–1912, vol. I

Grey de Ruthyn, 24th Baron, 1862–1934, vol. III

Grey de Ruthyn, 25th Baron, 1883–1963, vol. VI

Grey, Annie, vol. III

Grey, Arthur, 1840–1911, vol. I

Grey, Col Arthur, 1855–1924, vol. II

Grey, Charles Frederick, 1903–1984, vol. VIII

Grey, Sir Charles George, 4th Bt (*cr* 1814), 1880–1957, vol. V

Grey, Charles Grey, 1875–1953, vol. V

Grey, Clifford, 1887–1941, vol. IV

Grey, Egerton Spenser, 1863–1950, vol. IV

Grey, Francis Temple, 1886–1941, vol. IV

Grey, Col Geoffrey Bridgman, 1911–1983, vol. VIII

Grey, Rt Hon. Sir George, 1812–1898, vol. I

Grey, Captain George Charles, 1918–1944, vol. IV

Grey, Sir George Duncan, 1868–1937, vol. III

Grey, Rev. Harry George, 1851–1925, vol. II

Grey, Sir (Harry) Martin, 5th Bt (*cr* 1814), 1882–1960, vol. V

Grey, Sir Henry Foley, 7th Bt (*cr* 1710), 1861–1914, vol. I

Grey, Sir John Foley, 8th Bt (*cr* 1710), 1893–1938, vol. III

Grey, Sir John Howarth, 1875–1960, vol. V

Grey, Col Leopold John Herbert, 1840–1921, vol. II

Grey, Sir Martin; *see* Grey, Sir H. M.

Grey, (Patrick) Ronald, 1927–1985, vol. VIII

Grey, Sir Paul Francis, 1908–1990, vol. VIII

Grey, Lt-Col Sir Raleigh, 1860–1936, vol. III

Grey, Major Robin, 1874–1922, vol. II

Grey, Sir Robin Edward Dysart, 6th Bt (*cr* 1814), 1886–1974, vol. VII

Grey, Ronald; *see* Grey, P. R.

Grey, Rowland; *see* Brown, Lilian Kate Rowland.

Grey, Samuel John, 1878–1942, vol. IV

Grey, Comdr Spenser Douglas Adair, 1889–1937, vol. III

Grey, Lt-Col William George, 1866–1953, vol. V

Grey, Maj.-Gen. Wulff Henry, *died* 1961, vol. VI

Grey, Zane, 1875–1939, vol. III

Grey-Egerton, Rev. Sir Brooke de Malpas; *see* Egerton.

Grey-Egerton, Sir Philip Henry Brian; *see* Egerton.

Grey-Egerton, Sir Philip Reginald le Belward, 14th Bt, 1885–1962, vol. VI

Grey-Smith, Sir Ross, 1901–1973, vol. VII

Grey-Turner, Elston, 1916–1984, vol. VIII

Grey Walter, William; *see* Walter.

Grey-Wilson, Sir William, 1852–1926, vol. II

Gribble, Bernard Finegan, 1872–1962, vol. VI

Gribble, Francis Henry, 1862–1946, vol. IV

Gribble, George James, 1846–1927, vol. II

Gribble, Col (Hon.) Howard Charles, 1886–1956, vol. V

Gribble, Leonard Reginald, 1908–1985, vol. VIII

Gribbon, Brig. Walter Harold, 1881–1944, vol. IV

Grice, Sir John, 1850–1935, vol. III

Grice, Col Walter Thomas, 1868–1926, vol. II

Grice-Hutchinson, George William, 1848–1906, vol. I

Gridley, 1st Baron, 1878–1965, vol. VI

Gridley, John Crandon, 1904–1968, vol. VI

Grier, Anthony MacGregor, 1911–1989, vol. VIII

Grier, Brig.-Gen. Harry Dixon, 1863–1942, vol. IV

Grier, John Arthur Bolton, 1882–1946, vol. IV

Grier, Louis Monro, 1864–1920, vol. II

Grier, Lynda, 1880–1967, vol. VI

Grier, Very Rev. Roy Macgregor, 1877–1940, vol. III

Grier, Sir Selwyn Macgregor, 1878–1946, vol. IV

Grier, Sydney C., 1868–1933, vol. III

Grierson, Sir Alexander Davidson, 9th Bt, 1858–1912, vol. I

Grierson, Sir Andrew, *died* 1936, vol. III

Grierson, Charles MacIver, 1864–1939, vol. III (A), vol. IV

Grierson, Rt Rev. Charles Thornton Primrose, 1857–1935, vol. III

Grierson, Edgar, 1884–1959, vol. V

Grierson, Francis, 1848–1927, vol. II

Grierson, Sir George Abraham, 1851–1941, vol. IV

Grierson, Sir Herbert John Clifford, 1866–1960, vol. V

Grierson, James Cullen, 1863–1919, vol. II

Grierson, Lt-Gen. Sir James Moncrieff, 1859–1914, vol. I

Grierson, John, 1898–1964, vol. VI

Grierson, John, 1898–1972, vol. VII

Grierson, Philip Francis H.; *see* Hamilton-Grierson.

Grierson, Sir Philip James Hamilton-, 1851–1927, vol. II

Grierson, Sir Richard Douglas, 11th Bt, 1912–1987, vol. VIII

Grierson, Sir Robert Gilbert White, 10th Bt, 1883–1957, vol. V

Grierson, William Wylie, *died* 1935, vol. III

Griesbach, Charles Ludolf, 1847–1907, vol. I

Griesbach, Maj.-Gen. Hon. William Antrobus, 1878–1945, vol. IV

Grieve, Rev. Alexander James, 1874–1952, vol. V

Grieve, Lt-Col Angus Alexander M.; *see* Macfarlane-Grieve.

Grieve, Christopher Murray, 1892–1978, vol. VII

Grieve, Captain Edward Leonard, 1880–1936, vol. III

Grieve, Edward William Lawrence, 1902–1960, vol. V (A)

Grieve, Sir (Herbert) Ronald (Robinson), 1896–1982, vol. VIII

Grieve, Rev. Canon James Gavin, 1880–1937, vol. III

Grieve, Robert, 1839–1906, vol. I

Grieve, Robert G., 1881–1952, vol. V

Grieve, Sir Ronald; *see* Grieve, Sir H. R. R.

Grieve, Thomas Robert, 1909–1987, vol. VIII

Grieve, Hon. Walter Baine, 1850–1921, vol. II

Grieve, Walter Graham, *died* 1937, vol. III

Grieve, William, 1885–1967, vol. VI

Grieve, William Alexander M.; *see* Macfarlane-Grieve.

Grieves, Joseph Arthur, 1907–1976, vol. VII

Griffin, Alan Francis Rathbone, 1911–1965, vol. VI

Griffin, Alexander, 1883–1966, vol. VI

Griffin, Sir Arthur Cecil, 1888–1970, vol. VI

Griffin, Lt-Col Atholl Edwin, 1877–1956, vol. V

Griffin, His Eminence Cardinal Bernard W., 1899–1956, vol. V

Griffin, Sir Cecil; *see* Griffin, Sir L. C. L.

Griffin, Lt-Col Cecil Pender Griffith, 1864–1922, vol. II

Griffin, Sir Charles James, 1875–1962, vol. VI

Griffin, Air Vice-Marshal Charles Robert, 1919–1979, vol. VII

Griffin, Charles Thomas, *died* 1923, vol. II

Griffin, Brig.-Gen. Christopher Joseph, 1874–1957, vol. V

Griffin, Lt-Gen. Edward Christian, 1836–1917, vol. II

Griffin, Sir Elton Reginald, 1906–1975, vol. VII

Griffin, Ernest Harrison, 1877–1936, vol. III

Griffin, Sir Francis Frederick, 1904–1982, vol. VIII

Griffin, Sir Henry Daly, 1864–1936, vol. III

Griffin, Major Henry Lysaght, 1866–1930, vol. III

Griffin, Sir Herbert John Gordon, 1889–1969, vol. VI

Griffin, Hester Wolferstan, (Mrs R. L. Griffin); *see* Chapman, Mrs H. W.

Griffin, Irene Marie, (Mrs F. D. Griffin); *see* Dunne, I. M.

Griffin, Maj.-Gen. John Arnold Atkinson, 1891–1972, vol. VII

Griffin, Sir (Lancelot) Cecil Lepel, 1900–1964, vol. VI

Griffin, Sir Lepel Henry, 1840–1908, vol. I

Griffin, Martin Joseph, 1847–1921, vol. II

Griffin, William Vincent, 1886–1958, vol. V

Griffis, Rev. William Elliot, 1843–1928, vol. II

Griffith, Alan Arnold, 1893–1963, vol. VI

Griffith, Arthur, 1872–1922, vol. II

Griffith, Hon. Arthur, *died* 1946, vol. IV

Griffith, Arthur Donald, 1882–1944, vol. IV

Griffith, Hon. Sir Arthur Frederick, 1913–1982, vol. VIII

Griffith, Major Arthur Lefroy Pritchard, 1886–1932, vol. III

Griffith, Arthur Stanley, 1875–1941, vol. IV

Griffith, Very Rev. Charles Edward Thomas, 1857–1934, vol. III

Griffith, Brig.-Gen. Charles Richard Jebb, 1867–1948, vol. IV

Griffith, Cyril Cobham, 1891–1972, vol. VII

Griffith, Rev. David, vol. II

Griffith, Lt-Col Edward Hugh, 1858–1936, vol. III

Griffith, Lt-Col Edward Waldegrave, 1871–1937, vol. III

Griffith, Sir Elis Arundell Ellis-, 2nd Bt (*cr* 1918), 1896–1934, vol. III

Griffith, Ven. Ellis Hughes, *died* 1938, vol. III

Griffith, Rt Hon. Sir Ellis Jones Ellis-, 1st Bt (*cr* 1918), 1860–1926, vol. III

Griffith, Brig. Eric Llewellyn Griffith G.; *see* Griffith-Williams.

Griffith, Sir Francis Charles, 1878–1942, vol. IV

Griffith, Francis Llewellyn, 1862–1934, vol. III

Griffith, Frank Kingsley, 1889–1962, vol. VI

Griffith, George Chetwynd, *died* 1906, vol. I

Griffith, George Herbert, 1877–1947, vol. IV

Griffith, Lt-Col George Richard, 1857–1920, vol. II

Griffith, Grosvenor Talbot, 1899–1981, vol. VIII

Griffith, Guy Thompson, 1908–1985, vol. VIII

Griffith, Rev. Henry Allday, 1875–1942, vol. IV

Griffith, Ven. Henry Wager, 1850–1932, vol. III

Griffith, Horace Major Brandford, 1863–1909, vol. I

Griffith, Hubert Freeling, 1896–1953, vol. V

Griffith, Hugh Emrys, 1912–1980, vol. VII

Griffith, Rev. James Shaw, 1875–1939, vol. III

Griffith, John Eaton, 1894–1985, vol. VIII

Griffith, Sir John Purser, 1848–1938, vol. III

Griffith, (Llewelyn) Wyn, 1890–1977, vol. VII

Griffith, Patrick Waldron Cobham, 1925–1980, vol. VII

Griffith, Lt-Col Sir Ralph Edwin Hotchkin, 1882–1963, vol. VI

Griffith, Ralph Thomas Hotchkin, 1826–1906, vol. I

Griffith, Sir Richard (John) Waldie-, 3rd Bt (*cr* 1858), 1850–1933, vol. III

Griffith, Rt Hon. Sir Samuel Walker, 1845–1920, vol. II

Griffith, Thomas Wardrop, *died* 1946, vol. IV

Griffith, W. St Bodfan, 1876–1941, vol. IV

Griffith, Walter Spencer Anderson, 1854–1946, vol. IV

Griffith, William, 1868–1953, vol. V

Griffith, Sir William Brandford, 1858–1939, vol. III

Griffith, William Downes, *died* 1908, vol. I

Griffith, William L., 1864–1934, vol. III

Griffith, Wyn; *see* Griffith, L. W.

Griffith-Boscawen Rt Hon. Sir Arthur Sackville Trevor, 1865–1946, vol. IV

Griffith-Jones, Ebenezer, 1860–1942, vol. IV

Griffith-Jones, Sir Eric Newton, 1913–1979, vol. VII

Griffith-Jones, (John) Mervyn (Guthrie), 1909–1979, vol. VII

Griffith-Jones, Mervyn; *see* Griffith-Jones, J. M. G.

Griffith-Jones, Morgan Phillips, 1876–1939, vol. III

Griffith-Jones, Rev. William, 1895–1961, vol. VI

Griffith-Williams, Brig. Eric Llewellyn Griffith, 1894–1987, vol. VIII

Griffiths, Albert Edward, 1908–1970, vol. VI

Griffiths, Rev. Charles, 1847–1924, vol. II

Griffiths, Major Charles Du Plat R.; *see* Richardson-Griffiths.

Griffiths, Lt-Col Cyril Tracy, 1873–1934, vol. III

Griffiths, Surg. Rear-Adm. Cyril Verity, 1883–1959, vol. V

Griffiths, David, 1896–1977, vol. VII

Griffiths, Sir David Edward, *died* 1957, vol. V

Griffiths, Ven. David Henry, 1864–1926, vol. II

Griffiths, David Nathaniel, *died* 1961, vol. VI

Griffiths, Ernest Howard, 1851–1932, vol. III

Griffiths, Ezer, 1888–1962, vol. VI

Griffiths, Brig. Felix Alexander Vincent C.; *see* Copland-Griffiths.

Griffiths, Lt-Gen. Francis Home, 1877–1961, vol. VI

Griffiths, George Arthur, 1880–1945, vol. IV

Griffiths, Lt-Col George Cruickshank, 1884–1949, vol. IV

Griffiths, George Hollier, 1839–1911, vol. I

Griffiths, Gilbert, 1901–1979, vol. VII

Griffiths, Captain Hubert Penry, 1894–1983, vol. VIII

Griffiths, Sir Hugh Ernest, 1891–1961, vol. VI

Griffiths, Rt Hon. James, 1890–1975, vol. VII

Griffiths, James Howard Eagle, 1908–1981, vol. VIII

Griffiths, Ven. John, *died* 1897, vol. I

Griffiths, John, *died* 1947, vol. IV

Griffiths, John G., 1845–1922, vol. II

Griffiths, Lt-Col Sir John Norton-, 1st Bt, 1871–1930, vol. III

Griffiths, John Samuel, *died* 1933, vol. III

Griffiths, Air Cdre John Swire, 1894–1969, vol. VI

Griffiths, Col Joseph, *died* 1945, vol. IV

Griffiths, Engr Comdr Percy Frederick, 1873–1960, vol. V

Griffiths, Sir Peter N.; *see* Norton-Griffiths.

Griffiths, Richard Cerdin, 1915–1985, vol. VIII

Griffiths, Brig.-Gen. Thomas, 1865–1947, vol. IV

Griffiths, Thomas, 1867–1955, vol. V

Griffiths, Vincent, 1831–1917, vol. II

Griffiths, Ward David, 1915–1988, vol. VIII

Griffiths, William, 1912–1973, vol. VII

Griffiths, William Russell, 1845–1910, vol. I

Griffiths, Sir William Thomas, 1895–1952, vol. V

Grigg, Rt Hon. Sir James; *see* Grigg, Rt Hon. Sir P. J.

Grigg, Rt Hon. Sir (Percy) James, 1890–1964, vol. VI

Grigg-Smith, Rev. Canon Thomas, *died* 1971, vol. VII

Griggs, Clare H., *died* 1950, vol. IV

Griggs, Frederick Landseer Maur, 1876–1938, vol. III

Griggs, Hon. John William, 1849–1927, vol. II, vol. III

Griggs, Sir Peter; *see* Griggs, Sir W. P.

Griggs, Sir (William) Peter, 1854–1920, vol. II

Grignard, (François Auguste) Victor, 1871–1935, vol. III

Grignard, Victor; *see* Grignard, F. A. V.

Grigorov, Mitko, 1920–1987, vol. VIII

Grigson, Geoffrey Edward Harvey, 1905–1985, vol. VIII

Grigson, (Heather Mabel) Jane, 1928–1990, vol. VIII

Grigson, Jane; *see* Grigson, H. M. J.

Grigson, Air Cdre John William Boldero, 1893–1943, vol. IV

Grigson, Sir Wilfrid Vernon, 1896–1948, vol. IV

Grigson, Rev. William Shuckforth, 1845–1930, vol. III

Grille, Sir Frederick Louis, 1889–1958, vol. V

Grillo, Ernesto N. G., 1877–1946, vol. IV

Grimble, Sir Arthur Francis, 1888–1956, vol. V

Grimble, Augustus, 1840–1925, vol. II

Grime, Arthur, *died* 1938, vol. III

Grime, Sir Harold Riley, 1896–1984, vol. VIII

Grimes, Ven. (Cecil) John, 1881–1976, vol. VII

Grimes, Ven. John; *see* Grimes, Ven. C. J.

Grimes, Mary Katharine, 1861–1921, vol. II

Grimes, William Francis, 1905–1988, vol. VIII

Grimley, Bertram Griffiths, 1867–1952, vol. V

Grimm, Stanley, 1891–1966, vol. VI

Grimmer, Hon. W. C. Hazen, 1858–1945, vol. IV

Grimsdale, Harold Barr, 1866–1942, vol. IV

Grimsditch, Herbert Borthwick, 1898–1971, vol. VII

Grimshaw, Beatrice, *died* 1953, vol. V

Grimshaw, Captain Cecil Thomas Wrigley, 1875–1915, vol. I

Grimshaw, Most Rev. Francis Joseph, 1901–1965, vol. VI

Grimshaw, Thomas Wrigley, 1839–1900, vol. I

Grimshaw, Sir William Josiah, 1886–1958, vol. V

Grimshawe, Hellier Robert Hadsley G.; *see* Gosselin-Grimshawe.

Grimston of Westbury, 1st Baron, 1897–1979, vol. VII

Grimston, Col Lionel Augustus, 1868–1943, vol. IV

Grimston, Rev. Hon. Robert, 1860–1927, vol. V

Grimston, Brig.-Gen. Sir Rollo Estouteville, 1861–1916, vol. II

Grimston, Brig.-Gen. Sylvester Bertram, 1864–1924, vol. II

Grimston, William Hunter; *see* Kendal, W. H.

Grimthorpe, 1st Baron, 1816–1905, vol. I

Grimthorpe, 2nd Baron, 1856–1917, vol. II

Grimthorpe, 3rd Baron, 1891–1963, vol. VI

Grimwade, Hon. Frederick Sheppard, 1840–1910, vol. I

Grimwade, Geoffrey Holt, 1902–1961, vol. VI

Grimwade, Maj.-Gen. Harold William, 1869–1949, vol. IV

Grimwade, Sir Russell; *see* Grimwade, Sir W. R.

Grimwade, Sir (Wilfrid) Russell, 1879–1955, vol. V

Grimwood, Frank Southgate, 1904–1990, vol. VIII

Grimwood, Lt-Col James, 1873–1934, vol. III

Grindell-Matthews, Harry, 1880–1941, vol. IV

Grindle, Bernard Richard Theodore, 1879–1955, vol. V

Grindle, Sir Gilbert Edmund Augustine, 1869–1934, vol. III

Grinke, Frederick Otto, 1911–1987, vol. VIII

Grinling, Charles Herbert, 1870–1906, vol. I

Grinling, Brig. Edward Johns, 1889–1963, vol. VI

Grinlinton, Frederick Henry, 1853–1938, vol. III

Grinlinton, Sir John Joseph, 1828–1912, vol. I

Grinsted, Harold, 1889–1955, vol. V

Gripenberg, Georg Achates, 1890–1975, vol. VII

Gripper, Col Hugh Thomas, 1867–1956, vol. V

Griscom, Sir Lloyd C., 1872–1959, vol. V

Grisdale, Rt Rev. John, *born* 1845, vol. II

Grisewood, Frederick Henry, 1888–1972, vol. VII

Grissell, Hartwell de la Garde, 1839–1907, vol. I

Grist, Frederic Edwin, 1883–1951, vol. V

Griswold, A(lfred) Whitney, 1906–1963, vol. VI

Griswold, Rev. H. D., 1860–1945, vol. IV

Griswold, Rt Rev. Sheldon M., 1861–1930, vol. III

Gritten, William George Howard, *died* 1943, vol. IV

Grobecker, Ven. Geoffrey Frank, 1922–1989, vol. VIII

Groener, Maria, 1883–1937, vol. III

Grogan, Brig.-Gen. Edward George, 1851–1944, vol. IV

Grogan, Col Sir Edward Ion Beresford, 2nd Bt, 1873–1927, vol. II

Grogan, Lt-Col George Meredyth, *died* 1942, vol. IV

Grogan, Brig.-Gen. George William St George, 1875–1962, vol. VI

Grogan, William Edward, 1863–1937, vol. III

Grohman, Vice-Adm. Harold Tom B.; *see* Baillie-Grohman.

Grohman, William A. B.; *see* Baillie-Grohman.

Gromyko, Andrei Andreevich, 1909–1989, vol. VIII

Gronchi, Giovanni, 1887–1978, vol. VII

Gronow, Albert George, 1878–1950, vol. IV

Gronow, Alun Gwilym, 1931–1989, vol. VIII

Groom, Gladys Laurence, (Mrs M. Cordellis), *died* 1948, vol. IV (A)

Groom, Hon. Sir Littleton Ernest, 1867–1936, vol. III

Groom, Percy, 1865–1931, vol. III

Groom, Sir Reginald; *see* Groom, Sir T. R.

Groom, Sir (Thomas) Reginald, 1906–1987, vol. VIII

Groom, Air Marshal Sir Victor Emmanuel, 1898–1990, vol. VIII

Groome, Francis Hindes, 1851–1902, vol. I

Groome, Adm. Robert Leonard, 1848–1917, vol. II

Gropius, Walter, 1883–1969, vol. VI

Gropper, William, 1897–1977, vol. VII

Grose, Frank Samuel, 1881–1941, vol. IV

Grose, Sir James Trevilly, 1872–1944, vol. IV

Grose-Hodge, Humfrey, 1891–1962, vol. VI

Gross, Anthony Imre Alexander, 1905–1984, vol. VIII

Gross, Edward John, 1844–1923, vol. II

Gross, Richard Oliver, 1882–1964, vol. VI

Grossmith, Caryll Archibald, 1895–1964, vol. VI

Grossmith, George, 1847–1912, vol. I

Grossmith, George, 1874–1934, vol. III

Grossmith, (Walter) Weedon, 1854–1919, vol. II

Grossmith, Weedon; *see* Grossmith, Walter W.

Grosvenor, Earl; Edward George Hugh Grosvenor, 1904–1909, vol. I

Grosvenor, Countess; (Sibell Mary), 1855–1929, vol. III

Grosvenor, Lord Arthur Hugh, 1860–1929, vol. III

Grosvenor, Mrs Beatrice Elizabeth Katherine, 1915–1985, vol. VIII

Grosvenor, Caroline, *died* 1940, vol. III

Grosvenor, Lord Edward Arthur, 1892–1929, vol. III

Grosvenor, Lord Gerald Richard, 1874–1940, vol. III

Grosvenor, Hon. Gilbert, 1881–1939, vol. III

Grosvenor, Gilbert Hovey, 1875–1966, vol. VI

Grosvenor, Lady Henry, (Rosamund Angharad), *died* 1941, vol. IV

Grosvenor, Lord Henry George, 1861–1914, vol. I

Grosvenor, Captain Lord Hugh William, 1884–1914, vol. II

Grosvenor, John Ernest, 1887–1963, vol. VI
Grosvenor, Hon. Richard Cecil, 1848–1919, vol. II
Grosvenor, Captain Robert Arthur, 1895–1953, vol. V
Grosvenor, Rosamund Angharad; *see* Grosvenor, Lady Henry.
Grosvenor, Vernon William, 1889–1961, vol. VI
Grotrian, Frederick Brent, *died* 1905, vol. I
Grotrian, Sir Herbert Brent, 1st Bt, 1870–1951, vol. V
Grotrian, Sir John Appelbe Brent, 2nd Bt, 1904–1984, vol. VIII
Grouard, Rt Rev. Mgr Emile, 1840–1931, vol. III
Grounds, George Ambrose, 1886–1983, vol. VIII
Grounds, Sir Roy Burman, 1905–1981, vol. VIII
Grousset, René, 1885–1952, vol. V
Grout, Rev. George W. G., 1837–1917, vol. II
Grout, Reginald George, 1901–1963, vol. VI
Grove, Agnes, (Lady Grove), 1864–1926, vol. II
Grove, Alfred John, 1888–1962, vol. VI
Grove, Archibald; *see* Grove, T. N. A.
Grove, Maj.-Gen. Sir Coleridge, 1839–1920, vol. II
Grove, Brig.-Gen. Edward Aickin William Stewart, 1852–1932, vol. III
Grove, Lt-Col Ernest William, 1870–1939, vol. III
Grove, Sir George, 1820–1900, vol. I
Grove, George Alexander, 1908–1971, vol. VII
Grove, Sir Gerald, 3rd Bt, 1886–1962, vol. VI
Grove, Henry Montgomery, 1867–1942, vol. IV
Grove, Col Reginald Parker, 1859–1942, vol. IV
Grove, (Thomas Newcomen) Archibald, *died* 1920, vol. II
Grove, Col Thomas Thackeray, 1879–1965, vol. VI
Grove, Sir Walter Felipe Philip, 4th Bt, 1927–1974, vol. VII
Grove, Sir Walter John, 2nd Bt, 1852–1932, vol. III
Grove-Hills, Col Edmond Herbert, 1864–1922, vol. II
Grove-White, Col James, 1852–1938, vol. III
Grove-White, Lt-Gen. Sir Maurice Fitzgibbon, 1887–1965, vol. VI
Grover, Sir Anthony Charles, 1907–1981, vol. VIII
Grover, Maj.-Gen. John Malcolm Lawrence, 1897–1979, vol. VII
Grover, Gen. Sir Malcolm Henry Stanley, 1858–1945, vol. IV
Grover, Montague Macgregor, 1870–1943, vol. IV
Groves, Charles Nixon, 1871–1950, vol. IV
Groves, Ernest William Hey, 1872–1944, vol. IV
Groves, Herbert Austen, 1880–1943, vol. IV
Groves, James Grimble, 1854–1914, vol. I
Groves, Sir John, 1828–1905, vol. I
Groves, Col John Edward Grimble, 1863–1948, vol. IV
Groves, Brig.-Gen. Percy Robert Clifford, *died* 1959, vol. V
Groves, Thomas Edward, 1884–1958, vol. V
Groves-Raines, Lt-Col Ralph Gore Devereux; *see* Raines.
Grozier, Edwin Atkins, 1859–1924, vol. II
Grubb, Col Alexander Henry Watkins, 1873–1933, vol. III
Grubb, Edward, 1854–1939, vol. III
Grubb, Lt-Col Herbert Watkins, 1875–1934, vol. III
Grubb, Sir Howard, 1844–1931, vol. III
Grubb, Sir Kenneth George, 1900–1980, vol. VII

Grubb, Violet Margaret, 1898–1985, vol. VIII
Grubbe, Adm. Sir Walter James H.; *see* Hunt-Grubbe.
Grubbe, Walter John, *died* 1926, vol. II
Gruber, Rudolph, 1868–1945, vol. IV
Grueber, Herbert Appold, 1846–1927, vol. II
Gruenther, Gen. Alfred Maximilian, 1899–1983, vol. VIII
Gruer, Harold George, 1886–1956, vol. V
Gruffydd, William John, 1881–1954, vol. V
Grumell, Ernest Sydney, 1885–1962, vol. VI
Grummitt, John Halliday, 1901–1974, vol. VII
Grundy, Cecil Reginald, 1870–1944, vol. IV
Grundy, Sir Claude Herbert, 1891–1967, vol. VI
Grundy, Sir Cuthbert Cartwright, 1846–1946, vol. IV
Grundy, Air Marshal Sir Edouard Michael FitzFrederick, 1908–1987, vol. VIII
Grundy, Eustace Beardoe, 1849–1938, vol. III
Grundy, Francis, 1882–1953, vol. V
Grundy, Fred, 1905–1989, vol. VIII
Grundy, George Beardoe, *died* 1948, vol. IV
Grundy, John Brownsdon Clowes, 1902–1987, vol. VIII
Grundy, Rupert Francis Brooks, 1903–1988, vol. VIII
Grundy, Sydney, 1848–1914, vol. I
Grundy, Thomas Walter, 1864–1942, vol. IV
Grundy, Wilfred Walker, 1884–1936, vol. III
Grundy, William Mitchell, *died* 1960, vol. V
Grüneberg, Hans, 1907–1982, vol. VIII
Gruning, John Frederick, 1870–1922, vol. II
Grutschnig, Karl, 1888–1965, vol. VI (AII)
Grylls, Charles John Tench Bedford, 1874–1946, vol. IV
Grylls, Rear-Adm. Henry John Bedford, 1903–1978, vol. VII
Grylls, Rosalie Glynn; *see* Mander, Lady (Rosalie).
Gsell, Most Rev. Francis Xavier, 1872–1960, vol. V
Guard, Lt-Col Frederic Henry Wickham, *died* 1927, vol. II
Gubbay, Henri Abraham, 1883–1940, vol. III
Gubbay, Moses Mordecai Simeon, 1876–1947, vol. IV
Gubbins, Sir Charles O'Grady, *died* 1911, vol. I
Gubbins, Maj.-Gen. Sir Colin McVean, 1896–1976, vol. VII
Gubbins, Frederick Bebb, 1818–1902, vol. I
Gubbins, John Harington, 1852–1929, vol. III
Gubbins, John R., 1839–1906, vol. I
Gubbins, Nathaniel; *see* Mott, Edward Spencer.
Gubbins, Lt-Col Richard Rolls, 1868–1918, vol. II
Gubbins, Lt-Col Stamer, 1882–1940, vol. III
Gubbins, Lt-Gen. Sir W. Launcelotte, 1849–1925, vol. II
Gubbins, Major William John Mounsey, 1907–1979, vol. VII
Gudenian, Haig, 1918–1985, vol. VIII
Gudgeon, Stanley Herbert, 1896–1966, vol. VI
Guébhard, Madame; *see* Severine, Madame.
Guedalla, Philip, 1889–1944, vol. IV
Guedella, Mrs Herbert; *see* Hanbury, Lily.
Guerbel, Countess de; *see* Ward, Dame Genevieve.
Guerin, Hon. Edmund, 1858–1934, vol. III
Guerin, Hon. James John, 1856–1932, vol. III

Guérisse, Count Albert Marie Edmond, 1911–1989, vol. VIII

Gueritz, Edward Peregrine, 1855–1938, vol. III

Guernsey, Lord; Heneage Greville Finch, 1883–1914, vol. I

Guess, George A., 1873–1954, vol. V

Guest, Baron (Life Peer); Christopher William Graham Guest, 1901–1984, vol. VIII

Guest, Air Marshal Sir Charles Edward Neville, 1900–1977, vol. VII

Guest, Lt-Col Hon. (Christian) Henry (Charles), 1874–1957, vol. V

Guest, Col Hon. Sir Ernest Lucas, 1882–1972, vol. VII

Guest, Captain Rt Hon. Frederick Edward, 1875–1937, vol. III

Guest, Lt-Col Hon. Henry; see Guest, Lt-Col Hon. C. H. C.

Guest, John, 1867–1931, vol. III

Guest, Hon. Lionel George William, 1880–1935, vol. III

Guest, Montagu, 1839–1909, vol. I

Guest, Hon. Oscar Montague, 1888–1958, vol. V

Guest, Thomas Merthyr, 1838–1904, vol. I

Guest, William Campbell, 1864–1932, vol. III

Guest Williams, Rev. Samuel Blackwell, 1851–1920, vol. II

Gueterbock, Col Sir Paul Gottlieb Julius, 1886–1954, vol. V

Guggenheim, Edward Armand, 1901–1970, vol. VI

Guggisberg, Decima (Lady Guggisberg); see Moore Guggisberg.

Guggisberg, Brig.-Gen. Sir (Frederick) Gordon, 1869–1930, vol. III

Guggisberg, Brig.-Gen. Sir Gordon; see Guggisberg, Brig.-Gen. Sir F. G.

Gui, Vittorio, 1885–1975, vol. VII

Guibault, Joseph Alexandre, 1870–1940, vol. III (A), vol. IV

Guichard, Beatrice Catherine, (Beatrice Baskerville), 1878–1955, vol. V

Guider, James Adolphus, 1862–1943, vol. IV

Guidotti, Gastone, 1901–1982, vol. VIII

Guilbert, Yvette, 1865–1944, vol. IV

Guild David Alexander, 1884–1961, vol. VI

Guild, Surgeon Captain William John Forbes, 1908–1982, vol. VIII

Guilford, 8th Earl of, 1876–1949, vol. IV

Guilford, Rev. Edward, 1853–1937, vol. III

Guillamore, 5th Viscount, 1841–1918, vol. II

Guillamore, 6th Viscount, 1847–1927, vol. II

Guillamore, 7th Viscount, 1860–1930, vol. III

Guillamore, 8th Viscount, 1867–1943, vol. IV

Guillamore, 9th Viscount, 1869–1955, vol. V

Guilland, Antoine, 1861–1938, vol. III

Guillaume, Rev. Alfred, 1888–1965, vol. VI

Guillaume, Charles Edouard, 1861–1938, vol. III

Guillebaud, Claude William, 1890–1971, vol. VII

Guillebaud, Walter Henry, 1890–1973, vol. VII

Guillemard, Francis Henry Hill, 1852–1933, vol. III

Guillemard, Hugh W.; see Wilkinson-Guillemard, W. H. J.

Guillemard, Sir Laurence Nunns, 1862–1951, vol. V

Guillum Scott, Sir John Arthur, 1910–1983, vol. VIII

Guiney, John, 1868–1931, vol. III

Guiney, Louise Imogen, died 1920, vol. II

Guiney, Patrick, 1862–1913, vol. I

Guinness, Sir Algernon Arthur St Lawrence Lee, 3rd Bt, 1883–1954, vol. V

Guinness, Hon. (Arthur) Ernest, 1876–1949, vol. IV

Guinness, Arthur Eustace Seymour, 1867–1955, vol. V

Guinness, Hon. Sir Arthur Robert, 1846–1913, vol. I

Guinness, Sir Arthur Rundell, 1895–1951, vol. V

Guinness, Benjamin Lee, 1842–1900, vol. I

Guinness, Benjamin Seymour, 1868–1947, vol. IV

Guinness, Lt Eric Cecil, 1894–1920, vol. II

Guinness, Hon. Ernest; see Guinness, Hon. A. E.

Guinness, Rev. Henry Grattan, 1835–1910, vol. I

Guinness, Henry Samuel Howard, 1888–1975, vol. VII

Guinness, Henry Seymour, 1858–1945, vol. IV

Guinness, Col Henry William Newton, 1854–1925, vol. II

Guinness, Loel; see Guinness, T. L. E. B.

Guinness, Sir Reginald Robert Bruce, 1842–1909, vol. I

Guinness, Robert Darley, 1858–1938, vol. III

Guinness Thomas Loel Evelyn Bulkeley, 1906–1988, vol. VIII

Guiringaud, Louis de, 1911–1982, vol. VIII

Guise, Sir Anselm William Edward, 6th Bt, 1888–1970, vol. VI

Guise, Sir William Francis George, 5th Bt, 1851–1920, vol. II

Guise-Moores, Col Charles Frederick; see Moores.

Guise-Moores, Maj.-Gen. Sir Guise, 1863–1942, vol. IV

Guitry, Lucien, 1860–1925, vol. II

Guitry, Sacha, 1885–1957, vol. V

Gulbenkian, Calouste Sarkis, 1869–1955, vol. V

Gulbenkian, Nubar Sarkis, 1896–1972, vol. VII

Gull, Sir Cameron; see Gull, Sir W. C.

Gull, Cyril Arthur Edward Ranger, 1876–1923, vol. II

Gull, Sir Michael Swinnerton Cameron, 4th Bt, 1919–1989, vol. VIII

Gull, Captain Sir Richard Cameron, 3rd Bt, 1894–1960, vol. V

Gull, Sir (William) Cameron, 2nd Bt, 1860–1922, vol. II

Gullan, Marjorie Isabel Morton, died 1959, vol. V

Gulland, George Lovell, 1862–1941, vol. IV

Gulland, John Alan, 1926–1990, vol. VIII

Gulland, John Masson, 1898–1947, vol. IV

Gulland, Rt Hon. John William, 1864–1920, vol. II

Gullett, Hon. Sir Henry Somer, 1878–1940, vol. III

Gullick, Joseph William, died 1909, vol. I

Gullstrand, Allvar, 1862–1930, vol. III

Gully, Hon. Edward Walford Karslake, 1870–1931, vol. III

Gumbleton, Rt Rev. Maxwell Homfray M.; see Maxwell-Gumbleton.

Gumbley, Douglas William Mew, 1880–1973, vol. VII

Gumley, Sir Louis Stewart, 1872–1941, vol. IV

Gun, William Townsend Jackson, 1876–1946, vol. IV

Gundelach, Finn Olav, 1925–1981, vol. VIII

Gundry, Rev. Canon Dudley William, 1916–1990, vol. VIII

Gundry, Philip George, 1877–1929, vol. III

Gundry, Richard Simpson, 1838–1924, vol. II

Gunesekera, Sir Frank Arnold, 1887–1952, vol. V

Gunlake, John Henry, 1905–1990, vol. VIII

Gunn, Major Alistair Dudley, 1884–1943, vol. IV

Gunn, Alistair Livingston, 1903–1970, vol. VI

Gunn, Battiscombe George, 1883–1950, vol. IV

Gunn, Air Marshal Sir George Roy, 1910–1974, vol. VII

Gunn, Herbert Smith, 1904–1962, vol. VI

Gunn, Hugh, 1870–1931, vol. III

Gunn, Sir James, 1893–1964, vol. VI

Gunn, James Andrew, 1882–1958, vol. V

Gunn, Sir John, 1837–1918, vol. II

Gunn, Col John Alexander, 1878–1960, vol. VI (AI)

Gunn, Maj.-Gen. John Alexander, 1873–1966, vol. V (A), vol. VI

Gunn, John William Cormack, 1889–1941, vol. IV

Gunn, Neil M., 1891–1973, vol. VII

Gunn, Robert Marcus, 1850–1909, vol. I

Gunnarsson, Gunnar, 1889–1975, vol. VII

Gunning, Brig.-Gen. Sir Charles Vere, 7th Bt, 1859–1950, vol. IV

Gunning, Sir Frederick Digby, 6th Bt, 1853–1906, vol. I

Gunning, Col George Hamilton, 1876–1936, vol. III

Gunning, Sir George William, 5th Bt, 1828–1903, vol. I

Gunning, Col Orlando George, 1867–1917, vol. II

Gunning, Sir (Orlando) Peter, 1908–1964, vol. VI

Gunning, Sir Peter; see Gunning, Sir O. P.

Gunning, Sir Robert Charles, 8th Bt, 1901–1989, vol. VIII

Gunsaulus, Frank Wakeley, 1856–1921, vol. II

Gunsbourg, Raoul, 1859–1955, vol. V

Gunson, Sir James Henry, 1877–1963, vol. VI

Gunston, Major Sir Derrick Wellesley, 1st Bt, 1891–1985, vol. VIII

Gunter, Archibald Clavering, 1847–1907, vol. I

Gunter, Eustace Edward, 1873–1935, vol. III

Gunter, Lt-Col Francis Ernest, 1869–1936, vol. III

Gunter, Sir Geoffrey Campbell, 1879–1961, vol. VI

Gunter, Maj.-Gen. James, 1833–1908, vol. I

Gunter, Rt Hon. Raymond Jones, 1909–1977, vol. VII

Gunter, Sir Robert, 1st Bt, 1831–1905, vol. I

Gunter, Col Sir Robert Benyon Nevill, 2nd Bt, 1871–1917, vol. II

Gunter, Sir Ronald Vernon, 3rd Bt, 1904–1980, vol. VII

Günther, Albert Charles Lewis Gotthilf, 1830–1914, vol. I

Gunther, Charles Eugene, 1863–1931, vol. III

Gunther, Eustace Rolfe, 1902–1940, vol. III

Gunther, John, 1901–1970, vol. VI

Gunther, Sir John Thomson, 1910–1984, vol. VIII

Gunther, Robert Theodore, 1869–1940, vol. III

Gunther, Ven. William James, 1839–1918, vol. II

Guppy, Henry, 1861–1948, vol. IV

Guppy, Henry Brougham, 1854–1926, vol. II

Guppy, Ronald James, 1916–1977, vol. VII

Gupta, Bihari Lal, 1849–1916, vol. II

Gupta, J. N., 1870–1947, vol. IV (A), vol. V

Gupta, Sir Krishna Govinda, 1851–1926, vol. II

Gupta, Satyendra Nath, 1895–1956, vol. V

Gurd, Surg. Rear-Adm. Dudley Plunket, 1910–1987, vol. VIII

Gurden, Sir Harold Edward, 1903–1989, vol. VIII

Gurdon, Lt-Col Bertrand Evelyn Mellish, 1867–1949, vol. IV

Gurdon, Charles, 1855–1931, vol. III

Gurdon, Maj.-Gen. Edward Temple Leigh, 1896–1959, vol. V

Gurdon, Maj.-Gen. Evelyn Pulteney, 1833–1921, vol. II

Gurdon, Rt Rev. Francis, 1861–1929, vol. III

Gurdon, Lt-Col Philip Richard Thornhagh, 1863–1942, vol. IV

Gurdon, Rt Hon. Sir William Brampton, 1840–1910, vol. I

Gurion, David B.; see Ben-Gurion.

Gurnell, Engr Rear-Adm. Thompson, 1878–1965, vol. VI

Gurner, Sir (Cyril) Walter, 1888–1960, vol. V

Gurner, Henry Edward, 1853–1915, vol. I

Gurner, John Augustus, 1854–1937, vol. III

Gurner, Stanley Ronald Kershaw, 1890–1939, vol. III

Gurner, Vice-Adm. Victor Gallafent, 1869–1950, vol. IV

Gurner, Sir Walter; see Gurner, Sir C. W.

Gurney, (Ernest) Russell, 1879–1958, vol. V

Gurney, Sir Eustace, 1876–1927, vol. II

Gurney, Sir Henry Lovell Goldsworthy, 1898–1951, vol. V

Gurney, Rev. Henry Palin, 1847–1904, vol. I

Gurney, Sir Hugh, 1878–1968, vol. VI

Gurney, John Henry, 1848–1922, vol. II

Gurney, Martyn Pierre Cecil, 1861–1930, vol. III

Gurney, Norman William, 1880–1973, vol. VII

Gurney, Quintin Edward, 1883–1968, vol. VI

Gurney, Russell; see Gurney, E. R.

Gurney, Maj.-Gen. Russell, 1890–1947, vol. IV

Gurney, Sir Somerville Arthur, 1835–1917, vol. II

Gurney, Sir Walter Edwin, died 1924, vol. II

Gurney-Dixon, Sir Samuel, 1878–1970, vol. VI

Gurney-Salter, Emma, 1875–1967, vol. VI

Gurnhill, Rev. James, died 1928, vol. II

Gurowski, Major Count Dudley Beaumont, 1865–1939, vol. III

Gustafsson, Greta Lovisa; see Garbo, G.

Gutch, Sir John, 1905–1988, vol. VIII

Guthrie, Hon. Lord; Charles John Guthrie, 1849–1920, vol. II

Guthrie, Hon. Lord; Henry Wallace Guthrie, 1903–1970, vol. VI

Guthrie, Charles, died 1953, vol. V

Guthrie, Charles John; see Guthrie, Hon. Lord.

Guthrie, Captain Sir Connop, 1st Bt, 1882–1945, vol. IV

Guthrie, David Charles, 1861–1918, vol. II

Guthrie, Douglas James, 1885–1975, vol. VII

Guthrie, Sir Giles Connop McEacharn, 2nd Bt, 1916–1979, vol. VII

Guthrie, Henry Wallace; see Guthrie, Hon. Lord.

Guthrie, Hon. Hugh, 1866–1939, vol. III

Guthrie, Sir James, 1859–1930, vol. III

Guthrie, John Douglas Maude, 1856–1928, vol. II
Guthrie, Leonard George, 1858–1918, vol. II
Guthrie, Malcolm, 1903–1972, vol. VII
Guthrie, Mrs Murray, *died* 1945, vol. IV
Guthrie, Ramsay; *see* Bowran, Rev. J. G.
Guthrie, Robert Lyall, 1867–1937, vol. III
Guthrie, Robin Craig, 1902–1971, vol. VII
Guthrie, Hon. Sir Rutherford Campbell, 1899–1990, vol. VIII
Guthrie, Thomas Anstey, 1856–1934, vol. III
Guthrie, Thomas Maule, *died* 1943, vol. IV
Guthrie, Sir Tyrone; *see* Guthrie, Sir W. T.
Guthrie, Walter Murray, 1869–1911, vol. I
Guthrie, William, 1835–1908, vol. I
Guthrie, William Keith Chambers, 1906–1981, vol. VIII
Guthrie, Sir (William) Tyrone, 1900–1971, vol. VII
Guthrie-James, David, 1919–1986, vol. VIII
Guthrie-Smith, William Herbert, 1861–1940, vol. III
Gutierrez-Ponce, Don Ignacio, *died* 1942, vol. IV
Gutt, Camille, 1884–1971, vol. VII
Gutteridge, Harold Cooke, 1876–1953, vol. V
Guttery, Rev. Arthur Thomas, 1862–1920, vol. II
Guttery, Sir Norman Arthur, 1889–1962, vol. VI
Guttmann, Sir Ludwig, 1899–1980, vol. VII
Guttridge, George Herbert, 1898–1969, vol. VI
Guy, Comdr Basil John Douglas, 1882–1956, vol. V
Guy, Rt Rev. Basil Tudor, 1910–1975, vol. VII
Guy, Ven. Cuthbert Arnold, 1884–1954, vol. V
Guy, Rev. Douglas Sherwood, 1885–1934, vol. III
Guy, Sir Henry Lewis, 1887–1956, vol. V
Guy, Hon. James Allan, 1890–1980, vol. VII
Guy, John Crawford, 1861–1928, vol. II
Guy, Oswald Vernon, 1890–1973, vol. VII
Guy, Lt-Col Philip Langstaffe Ord, 1885–1952, vol. V
Guy, Lt-Col Robert Francis, 1878–1927, vol. II
Guy, Sydney Slater, 1884–1971, vol. VII
Guy, William, 1859–1950, vol. IV
Guy, William Henry, *died* 1968, vol. VI
Guymer, Maurice Juniper, 1914–1985, vol. VIII
Guymer, Robert, 1908–1981, vol. VIII
Guyomard, Rt Rev. John Alfred, 1884–1956, vol. V
Guyot, Y.; *see* Yves-Guyot.
Gwalior, HH Maharajah Sindhia of, 1876–1925, vol. II
Gwalior, Ruler of, 1916–1961, vol. VI
Gwatkin, Frank Trelawny Arthur A.; *see* Ashton-Gwatkin.
Gwatkin, Maj.-Gen. Sir Frederick, 1885–1969, vol. VI
Gwatkin, Col Frederick Stapleton, 1849–1940, vol. III
Gwatkin, Rev. Henry Melvill, *died* 1916, vol. II
Gwatkin, Brig. Sir Norman Wilmshurst, 1899–1971, vol. VII
Gwatkin, Rev. Walter Henry Trelawny Ashton-, 1861–1945, vol. IV
Gwatkin, Maj.-Gen. Sir Willoughby Garnons, 1859–1925, vol. II
Gwatkin-Williams, Captain Rupert Stanley, *died* 1949, vol. IV

Gwenn, Edmund, 1877–1959, vol. V
Gwillim, Calvert Merton, *died* 1972, vol. VII
Gwillim, John Cole, *died* 1920, vol. II
Gwilt, Richard Lloyd, 1901–1972, vol. VII
Gwydyr, 4th Baron, 1810–1909, vol. I
Gwydyr, 5th Baron, 1841–1915, vol. I
Gwyer, Barbara Elizabeth, *died* 1974, vol. VII
Gwyer, Rt Rev. Herbert Linford, *died* 1960, vol. V
Gwyer, Sir Maurice Linford, 1878–1952, vol. V
Gwyn, Tatham, 1839–1915, vol. I
Gwyn-Thomas, Brig.-Gen. Gwyn, 1871–1946, vol. IV
Gwynn, Maj.-Gen. Sir Charles William, 1870–1963, vol. VI
Gwynn, Denis Rolleston, 1893–1971, vol. VII
Gwynn, Edward John, 1868–1941, vol. IV
Gwynn, Rev. John, 1827–1917, vol. II, vol. III
Gwynn, John Tudor, 1881–1956, vol. V
Gwynn, Rev. Robert Malcolm, 1877–1962, vol. VI
Gwynn, Stephen Lucius, 1864–1950, vol. IV
Gwynn, Col William Purnell, *died* 1940, vol. III
Gwynne, Comdr Alban Lewis, 1880–1942, vol. IV
Gwynne, Brig. Alfred Howel E.; *see* Evans-Gwynne.
Gwynne, Clement Wansbrough, 1883–1939, vol. III
Gwynne, H. A., 1865–1950, vol. IV
Gwynne, Hon. J. W., *died* 1902, vol. I
Gwynne, Rt Rev. Llewellyn Henry, 1863–1957, vol. V
Gwynne, Maj.-Gen. Nadolig Ximenes, 1832–1920, vol. II
Gwynne, Nevile Gwyn, 1868–1951, vol. V
Gwynne, Paul; *see* Slater, Ernest.
Gwynne, Brig.-Gen. Reginald John, 1863–1942, vol. IV
Gwynne, Lt-Col Sir Roland Vaughan, *died* 1971, vol. VII
Gwynne, Rupert Sackville, 1873–1924, vol. II
Gwynne-Evans, Sir Evan Gwynne, 2nd Bt, 1877–1959, vol. V
Gwynne-Evans, Sir Ian William, 3rd Bt, 1909–1985, vol. VIII
Gwynne-Evans, Sir William, 1st Bt, 1845–1927, vol. II
Gwynne-Hughes, John Williams; *see* Hughes.
Gwynne-James, Sir Arthur Gwynne; *see* James.
Gwynne-Jones, Allan, 1892–1982, vol. VIII
Gwynne-Jones, Howell, 1890–1946, vol. IV
Gwynne-Vaughan, David Thomas, 1871–1915, vol. I
Gwynne-Vaughan, Dame Helen Charlotte Isabella, 1879–1967, vol. VI
Gwyther, Ven. Arthur, *died* 1921, vol. II
Gwyther, Frank Edwin, *died* 1918, vol. II
Gwyther, Lt-Col Graham Howard, 1872–1934, vol. III
Gwyther, Reginald Duncan, 1887–1965, vol. VI
Gwyther, Very Rev. William Clements, 1866–1940, vol. III
Gye, Ernest Frederick, 1879–1955, vol. V
Gye, Percy, 1845–1916, vol. II
Gye, William Ewart, 1884–1952, vol. V
Gyee, Sir Maung, 1886–1971, vol. VII
Gyi, Sir Joseph Augustus Maung, 1872–1955, vol. V

Györgi, Albert S.; *see* Szent-Györgyi.

Gyp, Sybille Gabrielle Marie Antoinette de Riquetti de Mirabeau, Comtesse de Martel, *died* 1932, vol. III

Gzowski, Sir Casimir Stanislas, 1813–1898, vol. I

H

Haag, Carl, 1820–1915, vol. I
Haag, Norman C., 1871–1950, vol. IV
Haagner, Alwin Karl, 1880–1962, vol. VI
Haarhoff, T. J., 1892–1971, vol. VII
Haas, Paul, 1877–1960, vol. V
Habberton, John, 1842–1921, vol. II
Habdank-Woynicz; *see* Voynich, Wilfrid Michael.
Häberlin, Henry, 1868–1947, vol. IV
Habershon, Samuel Herbert, 1857–1915, vol. I
Hackenley, Most Rev. John, 1877–1943, vol. IV
Hacker, Arthur, 1858–1919, vol. II
Hacker, Louis Morton, 1899–1987, vol. VIII
Hacket-Thompson, Brig.-Gen. Frederick; *see* Thompson.
Hackett, Most Rev. Bernard, *died* 1932, vol. III
Hackett, Felix E. W., 1882–1970, vol. VI (AII)
Hackett, Francis, 1883–1962, vol. VI
Hackett, Very Rev. Henry Monck Mason, 1849–1933, vol. III
Hackett, Hon. Sir John Winthrop, 1848–1916, vol. II
Hackett, Sir Maurice Frederick, 1905–1980, vol. VII
Hackett, Col Robert Isaac Dalby, 1857–1925, vol. II
Hackett, Very Rev. T. Aylmer P., 1854–1928, vol. II
Hackett, Walter, 1876–1944, vol. IV
Hackett, Walter William, 1874–1964, vol. VI
Hackett, William Henry, 1853–1926, vol. II
Hackforth, Edgar, *died* 1952, vol. V
Hackforth, Reginald, 1887–1957, vol. V
Hacking, 1st Baron, 1884–1950, vol. IV
Hacking, 2nd Baron, 1910–1971, vol. VII
Hacking, Ven. Egbert, 1854–1936, vol. III
Hacking, Sir James, 1850–1929, vol. III
Hacking, Sir John, 1888–1969, vol. VI
Hackney, Rev. Walter, 1852–1938, vol. III
Hadath, Gunby, *died* 1954, vol. V
Hadcock, Sir (Albert) George, 1861–1936, vol. III
Hadcock, Sir George; *see* Hadcock, Sir A. G.
Hadden, Sir Charles Frederick, 1854–1924, vol. II
Hadden, J. Cuthbert, 1816–1914, vol. I
Hadden, Rev. Robert Henry, 1854–1909, vol. I
Haddington, 11th Earl of, 1827–1917, vol. II
Haddington, 12th Earl of, 1894–1986, vol. VIII
Haddock, Edgar Augustus, 1859–1926, vol. II
Haddock, George Bahr, 1863–1930, vol. III
Haddock, Captain Herbert James, 1861–1946, vol. IV
Haddock, Rev. Jeremiah William, *died* 1913, vol. I
Haddock, Maurice Robert, 1909–1974, vol. VII
Haddon, Alfred Cort, 1855–1940, vol. III
Haddon, Archibald, *died* 1942, vol. IV
Haddon, Eric Edwin, 1908–1984, vol. VIII
Haddon, Frederick William, 1839–1906, vol. I
Haddon, Sir Richard Walker, 1893–1967, vol. VI
Haddon, Trevor, *died* 1941, vol. IV

Haddon-Smith, Sir George Basil, 1861–1931, vol. III
Haddow, Sir Alexander, 1907–1976, vol. VII
Haddow, Alexander John, 1912–1978, vol. VII
Haddow, Sir Douglas; *see* Haddow, Sir T. D.
Haddow, Sir Renwick; *see* Haddow, Sir R. R.
Haddow, Sir (Robert) Renwick, 1891–1946, vol. IV
Haddow, Sir (Thomas) Douglas, 1913–1986, vol. VIII
Haddrill, Harry Victor, 1914–1983, vol. VIII
Haddy, Engr Rear-Adm. Frederick George, 1875–1950, vol. IV
Haden, Sir Francis Seymour, 1818–1910, vol. I
Haden, Francis Seymour, 1850–1918, vol. II
Haden-Guest, 1st Baron, 1877–1960, vol. V
Haden-Guest, 2nd Baron, 1902–1974, vol. VII
Haden-Guest, 3rd Baron, 1904–1987, vol. VIII
Hadfield, Maj.-Gen. Charles Arthur, 1852–1938, vol. III
Hadfield, Charles Frederick, 1875–1965, vol. VI
Hadfield, Sir Ernest, 1873–1947, vol. IV
Hadfield, Geoffrey, 1889–1968, vol. VI
Hadfield, James Arthur, 1882–1967, vol. VI
Hadfield, Rt Rev. Octavius, *died* 1904, vol. I
Hadfield, Sir Robert A., 1st Bt, 1858–1940, vol. III
Hadfield, Walton John, *died* 1944, vol. IV
Hadland, Rev. Richard Phipps, *died* 1934, vol. III
Hadley, Arthur Edward, 1870–1954, vol. V
Hadley, Arthur Twining, 1856–1930, vol. III
Hadley, George Dickinson, 1908–1984, vol. VIII
Hadley, Patrick Arthur Sheldon, 1899–1973, vol. VII
Hadley, Wilfred James, 1862–1944, vol. IV
Hadley, William Sheldon, 1859–1927, vol. II
Hadley, William Waite *died* 1960, vol. V
Hadow, Lt-Col Arthur Lovell, 1877–1968, vol. VI
Hadow, Sir Austen; *see* Hadow, Sir F. A.
Hadow, Sir (Frederick) Austen, 1873–1932, vol. III
Hadow, Maj.-Gen. Frederick Edward, 1836–1915, vol. I
Hadow, Grace Eleanor, 1875–1940, vol. III
Hadow, Sir Henry; *see* Hadow, Sir W. H.
Hadow, Sir Raymond Patrick, 1879–1962, vol. VI
Hadow, Col Reginald Campbell, 1851–1919, vol. II
Hadow, Sir Robert Henry, 1895–1963, vol. VI
Hadow, Sir (William) Henry, 1859–1937, vol. III
Hadrill, John Michael W.; *see* Wallace-Hadrill.
Hadwen, Walter Robert, 1854–1932, vol. III
Hadwick, Sir William, 1891–1951, vol. V
Haffenden, Maj.-Gen. Donald James W.; *see* Wilson-Haffenden.
Haffkine, Waldemar Mordecai Wolff, 1860–1930, vol. III
Hagan, Very Rev. Edward J., 1879–1956, vol. V
Hagan, Rt Rev. Mgr John, *died* 1930, vol. III
Hagart-Speirs, Alexander Archibald; *see* Speirs.
Hagarty, Hon. Sir John Hawkins, 1816–1900, vol. I
Hagarty, Parker, 1859–1934, vol. III
Hagen, John Peter, 1908–1990, vol. VIII
Hagenbeck, Carl, 1844–1913, vol. I
Hagerty, James Campbell, (Jim Hagerty), 1909–1981, vol. VIII
Hagestadt, Leonard, 1907–1974, vol. VII
Haggard, Lt-Col Andrew Charles Parker, 1854–1923, vol. II
Haggard, Lt-Col Claude Mason, *died* 1909, vol. I
Haggard, Major Edward Arthur, 1860–1925, vol. II

Haggard, Sir Godfrey Digby Napier, 1884–1969, vol. VI

Haggard, Sir (Henry) Rider, 1856–1925, vol. II

Haggard, Lilias Margitson Rider, 1892–1968, vol. VI

Haggard, Sir Rider; *see* Haggard, Sir H. R.

Haggard, Adm. Sir Vernon Harry Stuart, 1874–1960, vol. V

Haggard, Sir William Henry Doveton, 1846–1926, vol. II

Haggas, Sir James Ellison, 1849–1939, vol. III

Haggerston of Haggerston, Captain Sir Carnaby de Marie; *see* Haggerston of Haggerston, Captain Sir H. C. de M.

Haggerston of Haggerston, Sir Edward Charlton de Marie, 10th Bt, 1857–1925, vol. II

Haggerston of Haggerston, Captain Sir (Hugh) Carnaby de Marie, 11th Bt, 1906–1971, vol. VII

Haggerston of Haggerston, Sir John de Marie, 9th Bt, 1852–1918, vol. II

Haggerston, Sir Ralph Raphael Stanley de Marie, 12th Bt, 1912–1972, vol. VII

Haggitt, Very Rev. Percy Bolton, 1878–1957, vol. V

Hague, Anderson, *died* 1916, vol. II

Hague, Arnold, 1840–1918, vol. II

Hague, Bernard, 1893–1960, vol. V(A), vol. VI(AI)

Hague, Sir (Charles) Kenneth (Felix), 1901–1974, vol. VII

Hague, Rev. Dyson, *died* 1935, vol. III

Hague, Sir Harry, *died* 1960, vol. V

Hague, Harry, *born* 1922, vol. VIII

Hague, Sir Kenneth; *see* Hague, Sir C. K. F.

Hahn, Kurt Matthias Robert Martin, 1886–1974, vol. VII

Hahn, Otto, 1879–1968, vol. VI

Haider, Michael Lawrence, 1904–1986, vol. VIII

Haig, 1st Earl, 1861–1928, vol. II

Haig, Lt-Col Alan Gordon, 1877–1951, vol. V

Haig, Alexander, 1853–1924, vol. II

Haig, Captain Alexander Price, *died* 1940, vol. III

Haig, Lt-Col Arthur Balfour, 1840–1925, vol. II

Haig, Gen. Sir (Arthur) Brodie, 1886–1957, vol. V

Haig, Axel Herman, 1835–1921, vol. II

Haig, Gen. Sir Brodie; *see* Haig, Gen. Sir A. B.

Haig, Maj.-Gen. Charles Thomas, 1834–1907, vol. I

Haig, Col Claude Henry, 1874–1955, vol. V

Haig, Sir Harry Graham, 1881–1956, vol. V

Haig, Brig.-Gen. Neil Wolseley, 1868–1926, vol. II

Haig, Lt-Col Patrick Balfour, 1866–1949, vol. IV

Haig, Brig.-Gen. Roland Charles, 1873–1953, vol. V

Haig, Lt-Col Sir (Thomas) Wolseley, 1865–1938, vol. III

Haig, Lt-Col Sir Wolseley; *see* Haig, Lt-Col Sir T. W.

Haig, Lt-Col Wolseley de Haga, 1884–1960, vol. V

Haig-Brown, Rev. William, 1823–1907, vol. I

Haigh, Anthony; *see* Haigh, A. A. F.

Haigh, Arthur Elam, 1855–1905, vol. I

Haigh, (Austin) Anthony (Francis), 1907–1989, vol. VIII

Haigh, Hon. Col Bernard, 1876–1939, vol. III

Haigh, Bernard Parker, 1884–1941, vol. IV

Haigh, Charles, *died* 1913, vol. I

Haigh, Ernest Varley-, *died* 1948, vol. IV

Haigh, Engr Captain Francis Evans Percy, 1873–1934, vol. III

Haigh, Frank Fraser, 1891–1970, vol. VI

Haigh, Sir Fred, 1889–1954, vol. V

Haigh, Ven. Henry, 1837–1906, vol. I

Haigh, Rev. Henry, 1853–1917, vol. II

Haigh, Rt Rev. Mervyn George, 1887–1962, vol. VI

Haigh, Rev. William E., 1850–1932, vol. III

Haight, Gordon Sherman, 1901–1985, vol. VIII

Haile Sellassie, 1892–1975, vol. VII

Hailes, 1st Baron, 1901–1974, vol. VII

Hailes, Clements David Grierson, 1860–1929, vol. III

Hailey, 1st Baron, 1872–1969, vol. VI

Hailey, Hammett Reginald Clode, *died* 1960, vol. V

Hailsham, 1st Viscount, 1872–1950, vol. IV

Hailstone, Bernard, 1910–1987, vol. VIII

Hailwood, Augustine, 1875–1939, vol. III

Hain, Sir Edward, 1851–1917, vol. II

Hain, Henry William Theodore, 1899–1972, vol. VII

Haine, Paymaster-Comdr Alec Ernest, 1885–1953, vol. V

Haine, Reginald Leonard, 1896–1982, vol. VIII

Haines, Sir Cyril Henry, 1895–1988, vol. VIII

Haines, F(rederick) Merlin, 1898–1963, vol. VI

Haines, Field-Marshal Sir Frederick Paul, 1819–1909, vol. I

Haines, Geoffrey Colton, 1899–1981, vol. VIII

Haines, Air Cdre Harold Alfred, 1899–1955, vol. V

Haines, Henry Haselfoot, *died* 1945, vol. IV

Haines, James, 1868–1936, vol. III

Haines, Maj.-Gen. James Laurence Piggott, 1896–1974, vol. VII

Haining, Gen. Sir Robert Hadden, 1882–1959, vol. V

Hains, Charles Brazier, 1882–1962, vol. VI

Hair, Gilbert, 1899–1965, vol. VI

Haire of Whiteabbey, Baron (Life Peer); John Edwin Haire, 1908–1966, vol. VI

Haire, Very Rev. James, *died* 1959, vol. V

Haire, Norman, 1892–1952, vol. V

Haire, Rev. William John, *died* 1932, vol. III

Haire-Forster, Very Rev. Arthur Newburgh, *died* 1932, vol. III

Haite, George Charles, 1855–1924, vol. II

Hajibhoy, Sir Mahomedbhoy, *died* 1926, vol. II

Hajihafiz Hidayet Hosain, Khan Bahadur, 1881–1935, vol. III

Hake, Guy Donne Gordon, 1887–1964, vol. VI

Hake, Sir Henry M., 1892–1951, vol. V

Hake, Henry Wilson, 1851–1930, vol. III

Hake, Herbert Denys, 1894–1975, vol. VII

Hake, William Augustus Gordon, 1811–1914, vol. I

Hakewill Smith, Maj.-Gen. Sir Edmund, 1896–1986, vol. VIII

Haking, Gen. Sir Richard Cyril Byrne, 1862–1945, vol. IV

Halahan, Air Vice-Marshal Frederick Crosby, *died* 1965, vol. VI

Halahan, Very Rev. John, *died* 1920, vol. II

Halahan, Gp Captain John Crosby, 1878–1967, vol. VI

Halcrow, Sir William Thomson, 1883–1958, vol. V

Haldane, 1st Viscount, 1856–1928, vol. II

Haldane, Archibald Richard Burdon, 1900–1982, vol. VIII

Haldane, Lt-Col Charles Levenax, 1866–1934, vol. III

Haldane, Elizabeth Sanderson, 1862–1937, vol. III
Haldane, Henry Chicheley, 1872–1957, vol. V
Haldane, Gen. Sir J. Aylmer L., 1862–1950, vol. IV
Haldane, James Brodrick C.; *see* Chinnery-Haldane.
Haldane, Rt Rev. James Robert Alexander C.; *see* Chinnery-Haldane.
Haldane, Very Rev. John Bernard, 1881–1938, vol. III
Haldane, John Burdon Sanderson, 1892–1964, vol. VI
Haldane, John Rodger, 1882–1967, vol. VI
Haldane, John Scott, 1860–1936, vol. III
Haldane, Sir William Stowell, 1864–1951, vol. V
Haldar, Hiralal, 1865–1942, vol. IV
Haldeman, Donald Carmichael, 1860–1930, vol. III
Haldin, Henry Hyman, 1863–1931, vol. III
Haldin, Sir Philip Edward, 1880–1953, vol. V
Haldin-Davis, H., *died* 1949, vol. IV
Haldon, 2nd Baron, 1846–1903, vol. I
Haldon, 3rd Baron, 1869–1933, vol. III
Haldon, 4th Baron, 1896–1938, vol. III
Haldon, 5th Baron, 1854–1939, vol. III (A), vol. IV
Hale, Baron (Life Peer); (Charles) Leslie Hale, 1902–1985, vol. VIII
Hale, Arthur James, 1877–1970, vol. VI
Hale, Col Charles Henry, 1863–1921, vol. II
Hale, Col E. Matthew, *died* 1924, vol. II
Hale, Sir Edward, 1895–1978, vol. VII
Hale, Rev. Edward Everett, *died* 1909, vol. I
Hale, Frederick Marten, 1864–1931, vol. III
Hale, George Ellery, 1868–1938, vol. III
Hale, Lt-Col George Ernest, 1861–1933, vol. III
Hale, Herbert Edward John, 1927–1978, vol. VII
Hale, John Howard, 1863–1955, vol. V
Hale, Comdr John William, 1907–1985, vol. VIII
Hale, Joseph, 1913–1985, vol. VIII
Hale, Kathleen; *see* Burke, K.
Hale, Lionel Ramsay, 1909–1977, vol. VII
Hale, Col Sir Lonsdale Augustus, 1834–1914, vol. I
Hale, Maj.-Gen. Robert, 1834–1907, vol. I
Hale, Sarah J., *died* 1920, vol. II
Hale, Major Thomas Egerton, 1832–1909, vol. I
Hale, Brig.-Gen. Thomas Wyatt, 1864–1937, vol. III
Hale, W. Matthew, *died* 1929, vol. III
Hale, Sir William Edward, 1883–1967, vol. VI
Hale-White, Sir William, 1857–1949, vol. IV
Hales, A. G., 1870–1936, vol. III
Hales, Rev. Canon G. T. B.; *see* Brunwin-Hales.
Hales, Harold Keates, 1868–1942, vol. IV
Hales, Ven. John Percy, 1870–1952, vol. V
Hales, John Wesley, 1836–1914, vol. I
Halevy, Elie, 1870–1937, vol. III
Halevy, Ludovic, 1834–1908, vol. I
Haley, Francis Raymond, 1862–1931, vol. III
Haley, Philip William Raymond Chatterton, 1917–1987, vol. VIII
Haley, Sir William John, 1901–1987, vol. VIII
Halford, Frank Bernard, 1894–1955, vol. V
Halford, Frederic Michael, 1844–1914, vol. I
Halford, Rt Rev. George Dowglas, 1865–1948, vol. IV
Halford, Jeannette, *died* 1950, vol. IV
Halford, Rev. Sir John Frederick, 4th Bt, 1830–1897, vol. I

Haliburton, 1st Baron, 1832–1907, vol. I
Haliburton, Hugh; *see* Robertson, J. L.
Halifax, 1st Earl of, 1881–1959, vol. V
Halifax, 2nd Earl of, 1912–1980, vol. VII
Halifax, Dowager Countess of; (Dorothy Evelyn Augusta), 1885–1976, vol. VII
Halifax, 2nd Viscount, 1839–1934, vol. III
Halkett, Baron; Hugh Colin Gustave George, 1861–1904, vol. I
Halkett, George Roland, 1855–1918, vol. II
Halkett, Brig.-Gen. Hugh Marjoribanks Craigie, 1880–1952, vol. V
Halkett, Lt-Col John Cornelius Craigie, 1830–1912, vol. I
Halkett, John Gilbert Hay, 1863–1937, vol. III
Halkett, Sir Peter Arthur, 8th Bt, 1834–1904, vol. I
Halkyard, Col Alfred, 1892–1964, vol. VI
Hall, 1st Viscount, 1881–1965, vol. VI
Hall, 2nd Viscount, 1913–1985, vol. VIII
Hall, Rev. Abraham Richard, 1851–1942, vol. IV
Hall, Alexander Cross, 1869–1920, vol. II
Hall, Alexander William, 1838–1919, vol. II
Hall, Alfred, 1873–1958, vol. V
Hall, Sir (Alfred) Daniel, 1864–1942, vol. IV
Hall, Rev. Alleyne Hall, 1845–1937, vol. III
Hall, Col Sir Angus William, 1834–1907, vol. I
Hall, Anmer; *see* Horne, A. B.
Hall, Rt Rev. Arthur Crawshay Alliston, 1847–1930, vol. III
Hall, Instr Rear-Adm. Sir Arthur Edward, 1885–1959, vol. V
Hall, Arthur Henderson, 1906–1983, vol. VIII
Hall, Arthur Henry, 1876–1949, vol. IV
Hall, Sir Arthur John, 1866–1951, vol. V
Hall, Arthur Lewis, 1872–1955, vol. V
Hall, Surg. Vice-Adm. Sir Basil; *see* Hall, Surg. Vice-Adm. Sir R. W. B.
Hall, Sir Basil Francis, 7th Bt (*cr* 1687), 1832–1909, vol. I
Hall, Benjamin Tom, 1864–1931, vol. III
Hall, Cecil Charles, 1907–1987, vol. VIII
Hall, Rt Hon. Sir Charles, 1843–1900, vol. I
Hall, Rev. Charles Albert, 1872–1965, vol. VI
Hall, Sir Daniel; *see* Hall, Sir A. D.
Hall, Daniel George Edward, 1891–1979, vol. VII
Hall, Hon. David Robert, 1874–1945, vol. IV
Hall, Rt Rev. Denis Bartlett, 1899–1983, vol. VIII
Hall, Sir Douglas Bernard, 1st Bt (*cr* 1919), 1866–1923, vol. II
Hall, Maj.-Gen. Douglas Keith Elphinstone, 1869–1929, vol. III
Hall, Lt-Col Sir Douglas Montgomery Bernard, 2nd Bt (*cr* 1919), 1891–1962, vol. VI
Hall, Ven. Edgar Francis, 1888–1987, vol. VIII
Hall, Edna, (Lady Hall); *see* Clarke Hall, Edna.
Hall, Col Edward, 1872–1941, vol. IV
Hall, Brig. Edward George, 1882–1968, vol. VI
Hall, Edward Laret, 1864–1947, vol. IV
Hall, Sir Edward M.; *see* Marshall-Hall.
Hall, Edwin Geoffrey S.; *see* Sarsfield-Hall.
Hall, Edwin Stanley, 1881–1940, vol. III
Hall, Edwin Thomas, 1851–1923, vol. II
Hall, Col Ernest Frederic, 1856–1942, vol. IV
Hall, Ernest Thomas, 1871–1954, vol. V

Hall, Francis de Havilland, 1847–1929, vol. III
Hall, Brig.-Gen. Francis Henry, 1852–1919, vol. II
Hall, Francis J., 1857–1932, vol. III
Hall, Fred, 1855–1933, vol. III
Hall, Lt-Col Sir Frederick, 1st Bt (*cr* 1923), 1864–1932, vol. III
Hall, Frederick, 1860–1948, vol. IV
Hall, Sir Frederick Henry, 2nd Bt (*cr* 1923), 1899–1949, vol. IV
Hall, Frederick Thomas Duncan, 1902–1988, vol. VIII
Hall, Frederick William, *died* 1933, vol. III
Hall, Maj.-Gen. Frederick William G.; *see* Gordon-Hall.
Hall, Col Frederick William George G.; *see* Gordon-Hall.
Hall, G. W. L. M.; *see* Marshall-Hall.
Hall, Captain Geoffrey Fowler, 1888–1970, vol. VI
Hall, Geoffrey William, 1906–1974, vol. VII
Hall, George, 1879–1955, vol. V
Hall, George A., *died* 1945, vol. IV
Hall, Lt-Col George Clifford Miller, 1872–1930, vol. III
Hall, George Derek Gordon, 1924–1975, vol. VII
Hall, George Edmund, 1925–1980, vol. VII
Hall, Adm. Sir George Fowler K.; *see* King-Hall.
Hall, Rt Rev. (George) Noel (Lankester), 1891–1962, vol. VI
Hall, George Thompson, 1865–1948, vol. IV
Hall, Lt-Col Gordon Charles William G.; *see* Gordon-Hall.
Hall, Grahame; *see* Muncaster, Claude.
Hall, Granville Stanley, 1846–1924, vol. II
Hall, Hammond, 1857–1940, vol. III
Hall, Harold F.; *see* Fielding-Hall.
Hall, (Harold) Peter, 1916–1986, vol. VIII
Hall, Major Harold Wesley, 1888–1964, vol. VI
Hall, Harry Reginald Holland, 1873–1930, vol. III
Hall, Sir Henry, *died* 1928, vol. II
Hall, Sir Henry, 1845–1936, vol. III
Hall, Ven. Henry Armstrong, 1853–1921, vol. II
Hall, Sir Henry John, 8th Bt (*cr* 1687), 1835–1913, vol. I
Hall, Henry Noble, 1872–1949, vol. IV
Hall, Col Henry Samuel, *died* 1923, vol. II
Hall, Henry Sinclair, 1848–1934, vol. III
Hall, Rev. Herbert, 1845–1921, vol. II
Hall, Herbert Austen, 1881–1968, vol. VI
Hall, Adm. Sir Herbert Goodenough K.; *see* King-Hall.
Hall, Sir Herbert Hall, 1879–1964, vol. VI
Hall, Rt Rev. Herbert William, 1889–1955, vol. V
Hall, Hubert, 1857–1944, vol. IV
Hall, Sir Hugh, 1848–1940, vol. III
Hall, Paymaster Rear-Adm. Hugh Seymour, 1869–1940, vol. III
Hall, I. Walker, 1868–1953, vol. V
Hall, James Henry, 1877–1942, vol. IV
Hall, Hon. Sir John, 1824–1907, vol. I
Hall, John, 1915–1966, vol. VI
Hall, Sir John, 1911–1978, vol. VII
Hall, John Basil, 1866–1926, vol. II
Hall, John Carey, 1844–1921, vol. II
Hall, John Edward Beauchamp, 1905–1989, vol. VIII

Hall, Surg. Rear-Adm. John Falconer, 1872–1946, vol. IV
Hall, Sir John Frederick, 1882–1959, vol. V
Hall, Brig.-Gen. John Hamilton, 1871–1953, vol. V
Hall, Sir John Hathorn, 1894–1979, vol. VII
Hall, Col Sir John Richard, 9th Bt (*cr* 1687), 1865–1928, vol. II
Hall, Rear-Adm. John Talbot Savignac, 1896–1964, vol. VI
Hall, John Thomas, 1896–1955, vol. V
Hall, Joseph, 1854–1927, vol. II
Hall, Joseph Compton, 1863–1937, vol. III
Hall, Lt-Gen. Julian, 1837–1911, vol. I
Hall, Julian Dudley, 1887–1961, vol. VI
Hall, Sir Julian Henry, 11th Bt (*cr* 1687), 1907–1974, vol. VII
Hall, Maj.-Gen. Kenneth, 1916–1987, vol. VIII
Hall, Kenneth Lambert, 1887–1979, vol. VII
Hall, Kenneth Ronald Lambert, 1917–1965, vol. VI
Hall, Captain Leonard Joseph, 1879–1953, vol. V
Hall, Brig.-Gen. Lewis Montgomery Murray, 1855–1928, vol. II
Hall, Lindsay Bernard, 1859–1935, vol. III
Hall, Sir Lionel Reid, 12th Bt (*cr* 1687), 1898–1975, vol. VII
Hall, Magdalen K.; *see* King-Hall.
Hall, Marie, 1884–1956, vol. V
Hall, Sir Martin Julian, 10th Bt (*cr* 1687), 1874–1958, vol. V
Hall, Lt-Col Montagu Heath, 1856–1928, vol. II
Hall, Sir Neville Reynolds, 13th Bt (*cr* 1687), 1900–1978, vol. VII
Hall, Rev. Newman, 1816–1902, vol. I
Hall, Rt Rev. Noel; *see* Hall, Rt Rev. G. N. L.
Hall, Sir Noel Frederick, 1902–1983, vol. VIII
Hall, Oliver, 1869–1957, vol. V
Hall, Owen, *died* 1907, vol. I
Hall, Percival Stanhope, 1879–1972, vol. VII
Hall, Percy, 1882–1955, vol. V
Hall, Peter; *see* Hall, H. P.
Hall, Philip, 1904–1982, vol. VIII
Hall, Col Philip de Havilland, 1885–1972, vol. VII
Hall, Miss Radclyffe, 1886–1943, vol. IV
Hall, Col Ralph Ellis Carr-, 1873–1963, vol. VI
Hall, Adm. Sir Reginald; *see* Hall, Adm. Sir W. R.
Hall, Richard James, *died* 1930, vol. III
Hall, Richard Nicklin, 1853–1914, vol. I
Hall, Robert, 1867–1949, vol. IV
Hall, Air Marshal Sir Robert Hamilton C.; *see* Clark-Hall.
Hall, Hon. Robert Newton, 1836–1917, vol. I
Hall, Surg. Vice-Adm. Sir (Robert William) Basil, 1876–1951, vol. V
Hall, Sir Roger Evans, 1883–1969, vol. VI
Hall, Roger Wilby, 1907–1973, vol. VII
Hall, Ronald, 1900–1975, vol. VII
Hall, Ronald Acott, 1892–1966, vol. VI
Hall, Rt Rev. Ronald Owen, *died* 1975, vol. VII
Hall, Sir Samuel, 1841–1907, vol. I
Hall, Stewart S.; *see* Scott Hall.
Hall, Sydney Prior, 1842–1922, vol. II
Hall, Adm. Sydney Stewart, 1872–1955, vol. V
Hall, T. Walter, 1862–1953, vol. V
Hall, Thomas Donald Horn, 1885–1970, vol. VI

Hall, Thomas Sergeant, *died* 1915, vol. I
Hall, Lt-Col Walter D'Arcy, 1891–1980, vol. VII
Hall, Wilfrid John, 1892–1965, vol. VI
Hall, William Carby, 1864–1938, vol. III
Hall, Sir William Clarke, 1866–1932, vol. III
Hall, William Codrington Briggs, 1845–1914, vol. I
Hall, Rt Hon. William Glenvil, 1887–1962, vol. VI
Hall, Hon. William Lorimer, 1876–1958, vol. V
Hall, William M.; *see* Macalister-Hall.
Hall, Adm. Sir (William) Reginald, 1870–1943, vol. IV
Hall, William Telford, 1895–1985, vol. VIII
Hall, William Thomas, 1855–1938, vol. III
Hall Caine, Gordon Ralph, 1884–1962, vol. VI
Hall-Dalwood, Lt-Col John, *died* 1954, vol. V
Hall-Dare, Robert Westley, 1866–1939, vol. III
Hall-Davis, Sir Alfred George Fletcher, 1924–1979, vol. VII
Hall-Dempster, Col Reginald Hawkins, 1854–1922, vol. II
Hall-Edwards, John Francis, 1858–1926, vol. II
Hall-Jones, Hon. Sir William, 1851–1936, vol. III
Hall-Patch, Sir Edmund Leo, 1896–1975, vol. VII
Hall-Thompson, Adm. Percival Henry, 1874–1950, vol. IV
Hall-Thompson, Lt-Col Rt Hon. S. H., 1885–1954, vol. V
Hallam, (Arthur) Rupert, 1877–1955, vol. V
Hallam, Sir Clement Thornton, *died* 1965, vol. VI
Hallam, Rupert; *see* Hallam, A. R.
Hallam, Rt Rev. William Thomas Thompson, 1878–1956, vol. V
Halland, Col Gordon Herbert Ramsay, 1888–1981, vol. VIII
Hallaran, Ven. Thomas Tuckey, *died* 1915, vol. I
Hallas, Eldred, 1870–1926, vol. II
Hallé, Charles E., 1846–1919, vol. II
Hallé, Wilma Maria Francisca, (Lady Hallé; Madame Norman Neruda), 1839–1911, vol. I
Hallen, Vet. Lt-Col James Herbert Brockencote, 1829–1901, vol. I
Hallett, Vice Adm. Sir Charles H.; *see* Hughes Hallett.
Hallett, Rev. Canon Cyril, 1864–1942, vol. IV
Hallett, Sir Frederic G., 1860–1933, vol. III
Hallett, Harold Foster, 1886–1966, vol. VI
Hallett, Holt S., *died* 1911, vol. I
Hallett, Sir Hugh Imbert Periam, 1886–1967, vol. VI
Hallett, Col James Wyndham H.; *see* Hughes-Hallett.
Hallett, Vice-Adm. John H.; *see* Hughes-Hallett.
Hallett, Leslie Charles H.; *see* Hughes-Hallett.
Hallett, Sir Maurice Garnier, 1883–1969, vol. VI
Hallett, Rt Rev. Mgr Philip Edward, 1884–1948, vol. IV
Hallett, Vice-Adm. Sir Theodore John, 1878–1957, vol. V
Hallewell, Lt-Col Henry Lonsdale, 1852–1908, vol. I
Halliburton, Richard, 1900–1939, vol. III
Halliburton, William Dobinson, 1860–1931, vol. III
Halliday, Edward Irvine, 1902–1984, vol. VIII
Halliday, Gen. Francis Edward, 1834–1911, vol. I
Halliday, Frank Ernest, 1903–1982, vol. VIII
Halliday, Sir Frederick James, 1806–1901, vol. I

Halliday, Sir Frederick Loch, 1864–1937, vol. III
Halliday, Sir George Clifton, 1901–1987, vol. VIII
Halliday, Lt-Gen. George Thomas, 1841–1922, vol. II
Halliday, J., *died* 1962, vol. VI
Halliday, James; *see* Symington, David.
Halliday, Gen. John Gustavus, 1822–1917, vol. II
Halliday, Gen. Sir Lewis Stratford Tollemache, 1870–1966, vol. VI
Halliday, Sir William Reginald, 1886–1966, vol. VI
Hallifax, Charles Joseph, *died* 1946, vol. IV
Hallifax, Edwin Richard, 1874–1950, vol. IV
Hallifax, Rear-Adm. Guy Waterhouse, 1884–1941, vol. IV
Hallifax, Mrs Joanne Mary, 1900–1972, vol. VII
Hallifax, Vice-Adm. Ronald Hamilton Curzon, 1885–1943, vol. IV
Hallilay, Lt-Col Herbert, *died* 1940, vol. III
Hallinan, Sir Charles Stuart, 1895–1981, vol. VIII
Hallinan, Most Rev. Denis, 1849–1923, vol. II
Hallinan, Sir Eric, 1900–1985, vol. VIII
Hallinan, Major Thomas John, 1886–1960, vol. V
Halliwell, Leslie, 1929–1989, vol. VIII
Hallowes, Basil John Knight, 1884–1973, vol. VII
Hallowes, Col Francis William, 1866–1942, vol. IV
Hallowes, Frederick, 1907–1968, vol. VI
Hallowes, Maj.-Gen. Henry Jardine, 1838–1926, vol. II
Hallows, Ralph Ingham, 1913–1990, vol. VIII
Hallows, Tim; *see* Hallows, R. I.
Hallpike, Charles Skinner, 1900–1979, vol. VII
Halls, Arthur Norman, (Michael), 1915–1970, vol. VI
Halls, Michael; *see* Halls, Arthur Norman.
Halls, Walter, 1871–1953, vol. V
Hallstein, Walter, 1901–1982, vol. VIII
Hallstrom, Sir Edward John Leeds, 1886–1970, vol. VI
Hallsworth, H. M., 1876–1953, vol. V
Hallsworth, Sir Joseph, 1884–1974, vol. VII
Hallward, Rev. Lancelot William, 1867–1951, vol. V
Hallward, Reginald, 1858–1948, vol. IV
Hallworth, Albert, 1898–1962, vol. VI
Halmos, Paul, 1911–1977, vol. VII
Halnon, Frederick James, 1881–1958, vol. V
Halpin, James, 1843–1909, vol. I
Halsall, Rt Rev. Joseph Formby, 1902–1958, vol. V
Halsbury, 1st Earl of, 1823–1921, vol. II
Halsbury, 2nd Earl of, 1880–1943, vol. IV
Halse, Most Rev. Reginald Charles, 1881–1962, vol. VI
Halse, Col Stanley Clarence, 1872–1961, vol. VI
Halsey, Captain Arthur, 1869–1957, vol. V
Halsey, Rt Hon. Sir Frederick; *see* Halsey, Rt Hon. Sir T. F.
Halsey, Sir Laurence Edward, 1871–1945, vol. IV
Halsey, Adm. Sir Lionel, 1872–1949, vol. IV
Halsey, Reginald John, 1902–1982, vol. VIII
Halsey, Captain Sir Thomas Edgar, 3rd Bt, 1898–1970, vol. VI
Halsey, Rt Hon. Sir (Thomas) Frederick, 1st Bt, 1839–1927, vol. II
Halsey, Lt-Col Sir Walter Johnston, 2nd Bt, 1868–1950, vol. IV

Halsey-Bircham, Sir Bernard Edward, 1869–1945, vol. IV

Halstead, Albert, 1867–1949, vol. IV (A)

Halstead, Major David, 1861–1937, vol. III

Halsted, Maj.-Gen. John Gregson, 1890–1980, vol. VII

Halton, Herbert Welch, 1863–1919, vol. II

Halward, Rt Rev. (Nelson) Victor, 1897–1953, vol. V

Halward, Rt Rev. Victor; *see* Halward, Rt Rev. N. V.

Haly, Maj.-Gen. Richard Hebden O'G.; *see* O'Grady-Haly.

Ham, Very Rev. Herbert, *died* 1964, vol. VI

Ham, Engr-Rear-Adm. John William, 1863–1931, vol. III

Ham, Wilbur Lincoln, 1883–1948, vol. IV

Hamber, Col Hon. Eric W., 1879–1960, vol. V

Hambidge, Jay, 1867–1924, vol. II

Hambleden, Viscountess (1st in line), 1828–1913, vol. I

Hambleden, 2nd Viscount, 1868–1928, vol. II

Hambleden, 3rd Viscount, 1903–1948, vol. IV

Hambling, Captain Sir Guy; *see* Hambling, Captain Sir H. G. M.

Hambling, Sir Herbert, 1st Bt, 1857–1932, vol. III

Hambling, Captain Sir (Herbert) Guy (Musgrave), 2nd Bt, 1883–1966, vol. VI

Hambly, Wilfrid Dyson, 1886–1962, vol. VI

Hambourg, Mark, 1879–1960, vol. V

Hambro, Captain Angus Valdemar, 1883–1957, vol. V

Hambro, Sir Charles Jocelyn, 1897–1963, vol. VI

Hambro, Sir Eric, 1872–1947, vol. IV

Hambro, Sir Everard Alexander, 1842–1925, vol. II

Hambro, Lt-Col Harold Everard, 1876–1952, vol. V

Hambro, John Henry, 1904–1965, vol. VI

Hambro, Maj.-Gen. Sir Percy, 1870–1931, vol. III

Hambro, Ronald Olaf, 1885–1961, vol. VI

Hamburger, H. J., 1859–1924, vol. II

Hamel, Auguste-Charles, 1854–1923, vol. II

Hamel, Gustav, 1861–1922, vol. II

Hamer, Rev. Charles John, 1856–1943, vol. IV

Hamer, Sir George Frederick, 1885–1965, vol. VI

Hamer, Jean; *see* Rhys, J.

Hamer, John, 1910–1990, vol. VIII

Hamer, Captain Richard Lloyd, 1884–1951, vol. V

Hamer, Sam Hield, *died* 1941, vol. IV

Hamer, Sir William Heaton, *died* 1936, vol. III

Hamersley, Alfred St George, 1848–1929, vol. III

Hamerton, Bt Col Albert Ernest, 1873–1955, vol. V

Hames, Sir George Colvile H.; *see* Hayter Hames.

Hames, Jack Hamawi, 1920–1988, vol. VIII

Hamid, Khan Bahadur Dewan Sir Abdul, 1881–1973, vol. VII (AII)

Hamill, John Molyneux, 1880–1960, vol. V

Hamill, Rev. Thomas Macafee, *died* 1919, vol. II

Hamilton, 13th Duke of, **and Brandon,** 10th Duke of, 1862–1940, vol. III

Hamilton, 14th Duke of, **and Brandon,** 11th Duke of, 1903–1973, vol. VII

Hamilton and Brandon, Duchess of; (Mary Louise Elizabeth), 1854–1934, vol. III

Hamilton, Marquess of; Captain James Albert Edward Hamilton, 1869–1913, vol. I

Hamilton of Dalzell, 1st Baron, 1829–1900, vol. I

Hamilton of Dalzell, 2nd Baron, 1872–1952, vol. V

Hamilton of Dalzell, 3rd Baron, 1911–1990, vol. VIII

Hamilton, Hon. Adam, 1880–1952, vol. V

Hamilton, Hon. Brig.-Gen. Alexander Beamish, 1860–1918, vol. II

Hamilton, Alexander Michell, 1872–1959, vol. V

Hamilton, Allan M'Lane, *died* 1919, vol. II

Hamilton, Allister McNicoll, 1895–1973, vol. VII

Hamilton, Andrew, 1862–1934, vol. III

Hamilton, Col Andrew Lorne, 1871–1951, vol. V

Hamilton, (Anthony Walter) Patrick, 1904–1962, vol. VI

Hamilton, Sir Archibald; *see* Hamilton, Sir C. E. A. W.

Hamilton, Archibald, 1895–1974, vol. VII

Hamilton, (Arthur Douglas) Bruce, 1900–1974, vol. VII

Hamilton, Lt-Col Arthur Francis, 1880–1965, vol. VI

Hamilton, Arthur Plumptre Faunce, 1895–1977, vol. VII

Hamilton, Bruce; *see* Hamilton, A. D. B.

Hamilton, Gen. Sir Bruce Meade, 1857–1936, vol. III

Hamilton, Sir Bruce S.; *see* Stirling-Hamilton.

Hamilton, Charles Boughton, 1850–1927, vol. II

Hamilton, Sir (Charles) Denis, 1918–1988, vol. VIII

Hamilton, Sir Charles Edward, 1st Bt (*cr* 1892), 1845–1928, vol. II

Hamilton, Sir (Charles Edward) Archibald Watkin, 5th Bt (*cr* 1776) and 3rd Bt (*cr* 1819), 1876–1939, vol. III

Hamilton, Charles Gipps, 1857–1955, vol. V

Hamilton, Charles Harold St John; *see* Richards, Frank.

Hamilton, Rev. Charles James, 1840–1917, vol. II

Hamilton, Charles Keith Johnstone, 1890–1978, vol. VII

Hamilton, Hon. Charles William B.; *see* Baillie-Hamilton.

Hamilton, Sir (Charles) William (Feilden), 1899–1978, vol. VII

Hamilton, Cicely, 1872–1952, vol. V

Hamilton, Rev. Clarence Haselwood, 1877–1940, vol. III

Hamilton, Lt-Col Claud George Cole-, 1869–1957, vol. V

Hamilton, Rt Hon. Lord Claud John, 1843–1925, vol. II

Hamilton, Col Claud Lorn Campbell, 1874–1954, vol. V

Hamilton, Captain Lord Claud Nigel, 1889–1975, vol. VII

Hamilton, Col Claude de Courcy, 1861–1910, vol. I

Hamilton, Cosmo, *died* 1942, vol. IV

Hamilton, Cyril Robert Parke, 1903–1990, vol. VIII

Hamilton, Sir Daniel Mackinnon, 1860–1939, vol. III

Hamilton, David James, 1849–1909, vol. I

Hamilton, Captain David Monteith, 1874–1942, vol. IV

Hamilton, Sir Denis; *see* Hamilton, Sir C. D.

Hamilton, Col Douglas James; *see* Proby, Col D. J.

Hamilton, Sir Edward Archibald, 4th Bt (*cr* 1776) and 2nd Bt (*cr* 1819), 1843–1915, vol. I

Hamilton, Maj.-Gen. Sir Edward Owen Fisher, 1854–1944, vol. IV

Hamilton, Sir Edward Walter, 1847–1908, vol. I
Hamilton, Edwin, *died* 1919, vol. II
Hamilton, Edwin J., 1852–1946, vol. IV
Hamilton, Emily Moore, *died* 1972, vol. VII
Hamilton, Rt Rev. Eric Knightley Chetwode, 1890–1962, vol. VI
Hamilton, Eric Ronald, 1893–1967, vol. VI
Hamilton, Col Ernest Graham, *died* 1950, vol. IV
Hamilton, Lord Ernest William, 1858–1939, vol. III
Hamilton, Eugene L.; *see* Lee-Hamilton.
Hamilton, Rev. Francis Cole Lowry, *died* 1936, vol. III
Hamilton, Sir Frederic Harding Anson, 7th Bt (*cr* 1647), 1836–1919, vol. II
Hamilton, Lord Frederic Spencer, 1856–1928, vol. II
Hamilton, Sir Frederic Howard, 1865–1956, vol. V
Hamilton, Adm. Sir Frederick Hew George D.; *see* Dalrymple-Hamilton.
Hamilton, Adm. Sir Frederick Tower, 1856–1917, vol. II
Hamilton, G. E., vol. II
Hamilton, Gavin Macaulay, 1880–1941, vol. IV
Hamilton, Brig. Gawaine Basil R.; *see* Rowan-Hamilton.
Hamilton, Col Gawin William Rowan-, 1844–1930, vol. III
Hamilton, Sir George Clements, 1st Bt (*cr* 1937), 1877–1947, vol. IV
Hamilton, George Douglas F.; *see* Findlay-Hamilton.
Hamilton, Rt Hon. Lord George Francis, 1845–1927, vol. II
Hamilton, Ven. George Hans, *died* 1905, vol. I
Hamilton, Sir George Rostrevor, 1888–1967, vol. VI
Hamilton, Lt-Col George Vaughan, 1851–1911, vol. I
Hamilton, Col Gilbert Claud, 1879–1943, vol. IV
Hamilton, Col Gilbert Henry Claude, 1853–1933, vol. III
Hamilton, Maj.-Gen. Godfrey John, 1912–1985, vol. VIII
Hamilton, Rev. Hamilton Anne D.; *see* Douglas-Hamilton.
Hamilton, Hamish, 1900–1988, vol. VIII
Hamilton, Rt Rev. Heber James, 1862–1952, vol. V
Hamilton, Henry, *died* 1918, vol. II
Hamilton, Surg.-Gen. Sir Henry, 1851–1932, vol. III
Hamilton, Henry, 1896–1964, vol. VI
Hamilton, Col Henry Best Hans, 1850–1935, vol. III
Hamilton, Col Henry Blackburne, 1841–1920, vol. II
Hamilton, Rev. Herbert Alfred, 1897–1977, vol. VII
Hamilton, Sir Horace Perkins, 1880–1971, vol. VII
Hamilton, Maj.-Gen. Hubert Ion Wetherall, 1861–1914, vol. I
Hamilton, Hugh Brown, 1892–1960, vol. V
Hamilton, Rear-Adm. Hugh Dundas, 1882–1963, vol. VI
Hamilton, Brig. Hugh William Roberts, 1892–1959, vol. V
Hamilton, Gen. Sir Ian Standish Monteith, 1853–1947, vol. IV
Hamilton, Iain Bertram, 1920–1986, vol. VIII
Hamilton, Rev. J. M'Curdy, 1834–1915, vol. I
Hamilton, Very Rev. James, *died* 1925, vol. II
Hamilton, Sir James, 1857–1935, vol. III

Hamilton, Surg. Rear-Adm. James, 1899–1964, vol. VI
Hamilton, Rear-Adm. James de Courcy, 1860–1936, vol. III
Hamilton, James Fetherstonhaugh, 1850–1915, vol. I
Hamilton, James Gilbert Murdoch, 1907–1972, vol. VII
Hamilton, Brig. James Melvill, 1886–1972, vol. VII
Hamilton, Lt-Col James S.; *see* Stevenson-Hamilton.
Hamilton, James Whitelaw, 1860–1932, vol. III
Hamilton, James Winterbottom, 1849–1899, vol. I
Hamilton, John, 1851–1939, vol. III
Hamilton, John Almeric de Courcy, 1896–1973, vol. VII
Hamilton, John Angus Lushington Moore, *died* 1913, vol. I
Hamilton, Col John Archibald, 1869–1931, vol. III
Hamilton, Air Vice-Marshal John Beresford C.; *see* Cole-Hamilton.
Hamilton, John Gardiner, 1859–1912, vol. I
Hamilton, Brig.-Gen. John George Harry, 1869–1945, vol. IV
Hamilton, John McLure, 1853–1936, vol. III
Hamilton, Maj.-Gen. John Robert Crosse, 1906–1985, vol. VIII
Hamilton, Captain Keith Randolph, 1871–1918, vol. II
Hamilton, Kismet Leland Brewer, 1883–1966, vol. VI
Hamilton, Hon. Leslie d'Henin, 1873–1914, vol. I
Hamilton, Lillias, *died* 1925, vol. II
Hamilton, Adm. Sir Louis Henry Keppel, 1890–1957, vol. V
Hamilton, Lord Malcolm Avendale D.; *see* Douglas-Hamilton.
Hamilton, Mary Agnes, *died* 1966, vol. VI
Hamilton, Col Hon. North de Coigny D.; *see* Dalrymple-Hamilton.
Hamilton, Col Sir North Victor Cecil D.; *see* Dalrymple-Hamilton.
Hamilton, Sir Orme R.; *see* Rowan-Hamilton.
Hamilton, Patrick; *see* Hamilton, A. W. P.
Hamilton, Patrick John Sinclair, 1934–1988, vol. VIII
Hamilton, Brig.-Gen. Percy Douglas, 1867–1936, vol. III
Hamilton, Percy Seymour D.; *see* Douglas-Hamilton.
Hamilton, Pryce Bowman, 1844–1918, vol. II
Hamilton, Adm. Sir Richard Vesey, 1829–1912, vol. I
Hamilton, Sir Robert Caradoc, 8th Bt (*cr* 1647), 1877–1959, vol. V
Hamilton, Very Rev. Robert James S.; *see* Shaw-Hamilton.
Hamilton, Very Rev. Robert Smyly Greer, 1861–1928, vol. II
Hamilton, Brig. Robert Sydney, 1871–1945, vol. IV
Hamilton, Sir Robert William, 1867–1944, vol. IV
Hamilton, Captain Sir Robert William Stirling-, 12th Bt, 1903–1982, vol. VIII
Hamilton, Lt-Col Roland, 1886–1953, vol. V
Hamilton, Sir Sydney; *see* Hamilton, Sir T. S. P.
Hamilton, Rt Hon. and Rev. Thomas, 1842–1925, vol. II
Hamilton, Maj.-Gen. Thomas de Courcy, 1825–1908, vol. I

Hamilton, Sir (Thomas) Sydney (Percival), 6th Bt (*cr* 1776) and 4th Bt (*cr* 1819), 1881–1966, vol. VI

Hamilton, Col Thomas William O'Hara, 1860–1918, vol. II

Hamilton, Walter, 1844–1899, vol. I

Hamilton, Walter, 1908–1988, vol. VIII

Hamilton, Sir William; *see* Hamilton, Sir C. W. F.

Hamilton, William Aitken Brown, 1909–1982, vol. VIII

Hamilton, Sir William Alexander B.; *see* Baillie-Hamilton.

Hamilton, Rear-Adm. William Des Vœux, 1852–1907, vol. I

Hamilton, William Frederick, 1848–1922, vol. II

Hamilton, Brig.-Gen. William George, 1860–1940, vol. III

Hamilton, Rev. William Hamilton, 1886–1958, vol. V

Hamilton, Maj.-Gen. William Haywood, *died* 1955, vol. V

Hamilton, William James, 1903–1975, vol. VII

Hamilton, Maj.-Gen. William Ralston Duncan, 1895–1969, vol. VI

Hamilton, Sir William Stirling, 10th Bt (*cr* 1673), 1830–1913, vol. I

Hamilton, Sir William Stirling-, 11th Bt (*cr* 1673), 1868–1946, vol. IV

Hamilton-Dalrymple, Sir Hew Clifford; *see* Dalrymple.

Hamilton-Dalrymple, Sir Walter; *see* Dalrymple.

Hamilton-Gordon, Hon. and Rev. Douglas, 1824–1901, vol. I

Hamilton-Gordon, Lt-Col Edward Hyde; *see* Gordon.

Hamilton-Grace, Col Sheffield; *see* Grace.

Hamilton-Grierson, Philip Francis, 1883–1963, vol. VI

Hamilton-Grierson, Sir Philip James; *see* Grierson.

Hamilton Harding, George Trevor, 1895–1967, vol. VI

Hamilton-Hoare, Henry William, 1844–1931, vol. III

Hamilton-King, Mrs Grace M., *died* 1980, vol. VII

Hamilton-Montgomery, Sir Basil Purvis-Russell; *see* Montgomery.

Hamilton-Russell, Hon. Claud Eustace, 1871–1948, vol. IV

Hamilton-Russell, Hon. Frederick Gustavus, 1867–1941, vol. IV

Hamilton-Russell, Hon. Gustavus Lascelles, 1907–1940, vol. III

Hamilton-Spencer-Smith, Sir Drummond Cospatric; *see* Spencer-Smith.

Hamilton-Spencer-Smith, Sir Thomas Cospatric; *see* Spencer-Smith.

Hamilton Stubber, Lt-Col John Henry, 1921–1986, vol. VIII

Hamley, Edmund Gilbert, 1818–1902, vol. I

Hamley, Col Francis Gilbert, 1851–1918, vol. II

Hamley, Herbert Russell, 1883–1949, vol. IV

Hamley, Joseph Osbertus, 1820–1911, vol. I

Hamling, William, 1912–1975, vol. VII

Hamlyn, Mrs Christine Louisa, 1855–1936, vol. III

Hamlyn, Frederick, 1846–1904, vol. I

Hamlyn, Rt Rev. N. Temple, 1864–1929, vol. III

Hamman, Lt-Col Jacob L., 1876–1948, vol. IV

Hammarskjöld, Dag Hjalmar Agne Carl, 1905–1961, vol. VI

Hammer, Armand, 1898–1990, vol. VIII

Hammersley, Maj.-Gen. Frederick, 1858–1924, vol. II

Hammersley, Samuel Schofield, 1892–1965, vol. VI

Hammersley-Smith, Ralph Henry, 1880–1964, vol. VI

Hammerstein, Oscar, 1847–1919, vol. II

Hammerstein, Oscar, 2nd, 1895–1960, vol. V

Hammerton, Col George Herbert Leonard, 1875–1961, vol. VI

Hammerton, Sir John Alexander, 1871–1949, vol. IV

Hammet, Rear-Adm. James Lacon, 1849–1905, vol. I

Hammett, Dashiell; *see* Hammett, S. D.

Hammett, Richard C., 1880–1952, vol. V

Hammett, (Samuel) Dashiell, 1894–1961, vol. VI

Hammick, Dalziel Llewellyn, 1887–1966, vol. VI

Hammick, Ven. Ernest Austen, 1850–1920, vol. II

Hammick, Sir George Frederick, 4th Bt, 1885–1964, vol. VI

Hammick, Sir Murray, 1854–1936, vol. III

Hammick, Vice-Adm. Robert Frederick, 1843–1922, vol. II

Hammick, Brig. Robert Townsend, 1882–1947, vol. IV

Hammick, Sir St Vincent Alexander, 3rd Bt, 1839–1927, vol. II

Hammill, Captain Charles Ford, 1891–1980, vol. VII

Hammill, Captain John Schomberg, 1890–1959, vol. V

Hammond, Col Sir Arthur George, 1843–1919, vol. II

Hammond, Arthur Henry K.; *see* Knighton-Hammond.

Hammond, Maj.-Gen. Arthur Verney, 1892–1982, vol. VIII

Hammond, Aubrey Lindsay, 1893–1940, vol. III

Hammond, Basil Edward, 1842–1916, vol. II

Hammond, Rev. Charles Edward, 1837–1914, vol. I

Hammond, Chris, *died* 1900, vol. I

Hammond, Brig.-Gen. Dayrell Talbot, 1856–1942, vol. IV

Hammond, Dennis, 1913–1969, vol. VI

Hammond, Sir (Egbert) Laurie Lucas, 1873–1939, vol. III

Hammond, Brig.-Gen. Frederick Dawson, 1881–1952, vol. V

Hammond, Gertrude Demain, *died* 1952, vol. V

Hammond, John, *died* 1907, vol. I

Hammond, Sir John, 1889–1964, vol. VI

Hammond, John Harold, *died* 1932, vol. III

Hammond, John Hays, 1855–1936, vol. III

Hammond, John Lawrence Le Breton, 1872–1949, vol. IV

Hammond, Rev. Joseph, 1839–1912, vol. I

Hammond, Kay, (Dorothy Katharine), 1909–1980, vol. VII

Hammond, Sir Laurie; *see* Hammond, Sir E. L. L.

Hammond, Rt Rev. Lempriere Durell, 1881–1965, vol. VI

Hammond, Captain Leslie Jennings Lucas, 1877–1943, vol. IV

Hammond, Lucy Barbara, 1873–1961, vol. VI

Hammond, Col Peter Henry, 1848–1933, vol. III

Hammond, Stanley Alfred Andrew, 1898–1981, vol. VIII

Hammond, Ven. Thomas Chatterton, 1877–1961, vol. VI

Hammond, Thomas Edwin, 1888–1943, vol. IV

Hammond, Walter R., 1903–1965, vol. VI

Hammond, Rev. William A., 1853–1931, vol. III

Hammond-Chambers, Robert Sharp Borgnis, 1855–1907, vol. I

Hammonds, Rev. Edwin, *died* 1933, vol. III

Hamnett, Baron (Life Peer); Cyril Hamnett, 1906–1980, vol. VII

Hamnett, George, 1826–1904, vol. I

Hamon, Count Louis, 1866–1936, vol. III

Hamond, Sir Charles Frederick, 1817–1905, vol. I

Hamond-Graeme, Sir Egerton Hood Murray, 5th Bt, 1877–1969, vol. VI

Hamond-Graeme, Sir Graham Eden William, 4th Bt, 1845–1920, vol. II

Hamp, Arthur Edward, 1886–1951, vol. V

Hampden, 2nd Viscount, 1841–1906, vol. I

Hampden, 3rd Viscount, 1869–1958, vol. V

Hampden, 4th Viscount, 1900–1965, vol. VI

Hampden, 5th Viscount, 1902–1975, vol. VII

Hampden, Hon. Charles Edward H.; *see* Hobart-Hampden.

Hampden, Ernest Miles H.; *see* Hobart-Hampden.

Hampden, John, 1898–1974, vol. VII

Hamper, Rev. Richard John, 1928–1986, vol. VIII

Hampshire, Charles Herbert, 1885–1955, vol. V

Hampshire, Dugan Homfray, *died* 1942, vol. IV

Hampshire, Frederick William, 1863–1941, vol. IV

Hampshire, Sir (George) Peter, 1912–1981, vol. VIII

Hampshire, Sir Peter; *see* Hampshire, Sir G. P.

Hampson, Arthur Cecil, 1894–1972, vol. VII

Hampson, Sir Cyril Aubrey Charles, 12th Bt, 1909–1969, vol. VI

Hampson, Sir Dennys Francis, 11th Bt, 1897–1939, vol. III

Hampson, Sir George Francis, 10th Bt, 1860–1936, vol. III

Hampson, Sir Robert Alfred, 1852–1919, vol. II

Hampson, William, *died* 1926, vol. II

Hampton, 3rd Baron, 1848–1906, vol. I

Hampton, 4th Baron, 1883–1962, vol. VI

Hampton, 5th Baron, 1888–1974, vol. VII

Hampton, Lt-Col Bertie Cunynghame D.; *see* Dwyer-Hampton.

Hampton, Frederick, 1889–1958, vol. V

Hampton, Herbert, 1862–1929, vol. III

Hamson, Charles John, 1905–1987, vol. VIII

Hamson, Vincent Everard, 1888–1975, vol. VII

Hamsun, Knut, 1859–1952, vol. V

Hanafin, Lt-Col John Berchmans, 1882–1970, vol. VI

Hanauer, Rev. Canon James Edward, 1850–1938, vol. III

Hanbury, Rev. Hon. Arthur Allen B.; *see* Bateman-Hanbury.

Hanbury, Sir Cecil, 1871–1937, vol. III

Hanbury, Captain Hon. Charles Stanhope Melville B.; *see* Bateman-Hanbury.

Hanbury, Daniel, 1876–1948, vol. IV

Hanbury, Major Edward Reginald B.; *see* Bateman-Hanbury.

Hanbury, Evan, 1854–1918, vol. II

Hanbury, Frederick Janson, 1851–1938, vol. III

Hanbury, Sir James Arthur, 1832–1908, vol. I

Hanbury, Lily, *died* 1908, vol. I

Hanbury, Lt-Col Lionel Henry, 1864–1954, vol. V

Hanbury, Noel, 1881–1935, vol. III

Hanbury, Brig.-Gen. Philip Lewis, 1879–1966, vol. VI

Hanbury, Brig. Richard Nigel, 1911–1971, vol. VII

Hanbury, Rt Hon. Robert William, 1845–1903, vol. I

Hanbury, Sir Thomas, 1832–1907, vol. I

Hanbury Tenison, Marika, 1938–1982, vol. VIII

Hanbury-Tracy, Major Hon. Algernon Henry Charles, 1871–1915, vol. I

Hanbury-Tracy, Hon. Frederick Stephen Archibald, 1848–1906, vol. I

Hanbury-Williams, Maj.-Gen. Sir John, 1859–1946, vol. IV

Hanbury-Williams, Sir John Coldbrook, 1892–1965, vol. VI

Hance, Lt-Gen. Sir Bennett; *see* Hance, Lt-Gen. Sir J. B.

Hance, Lt-Gen. Sir (James) Bennett, 1887–1958, vol. V

Hancock, Anthony Ilbert, 1906–1955, vol. V

Hancock, Anthony John, (Tony Hancock), 1924–1968, vol. VI

Hancock, Lt-Col Sir Cyril Percy, 1896–1990, vol. VIII

Hancock, Ernest, 1887–1950, vol. IV

Hancock, Ernest Legassicke, 1862–1932, vol. III

Hancock, Dame Florence May, 1893–1974, vol. VII

Hancock, Rev. Frederick, 1848–1920, vol. II

Hancock, George Charles, 1868–1938, vol. III

Hancock, Sir Henry Drummond, 1895–1965, vol. VI

Hancock, Sir Henry Tom, 1877–1957, vol. V

Hancock, John George, 1857–1940, vol. III

Hancock, Sir Keith; *see* Hancock, Sir W. K.

Hancock, Kingsley Montague, 1899–1969, vol. VI

Hancock, Col Mortimer Pawson, 1870–1939, vol. III

Hancock, Sir Patrick Francis, 1914–1980, vol. VII

Hancock, Comdr Reginald L., 1880–1919, vol. II

Hancock, Tony; *see* Hancock, A. J.

Hancock, Rev. William Edward, *died* 1927, vol. II

Hancock, William Ilbert, 1873–1910, vol. I

Hancock, Sir (William) Keith, 1898–1988, vol. VIII

Hancox, Leslie Pascoe, 1906–1975, vol. VII

Hand, Rt Rev. George Sumner, *died* 1945, vol. IV

Hand, John Pierce, 1883–1933, vol. III

Hand, Hon. Learned, 1872–1961, vol. VI

Handfield-Jones, Montagu, 1855–1920, vol. II

Handfield-Jones, Ranald Montagu, 1892–1978, vol. VII

Handford, Sir John James William, 1881–1959, vol. V

Handford, Stanley Alexander, 1898–1978, vol. VII

Handley, Lt-Col Arthur, 1861–1927, vol. II

Handley, Richard Sampson, 1909–1984, vol. VIII

Handley, Tommy, 1896–1949, vol. IV

Handley, William Sampson, *died* 1962, vol. VI

Handley-Derry, Henry Forster, 1879–1966, vol. VI

Handley Page, Sir Frederick; *see* Page, Sir F. H.

Handley-Read, Edward Harry, *died* 1935, vol. III

Handman, Frederick William Adolph, 1876–1948, vol. IV

Handover, Lt-Col Sir Harry George, 1868–1948, vol. IV

Hands, C. E., *died* 1937, vol. III

Hands, Sir Harry, 1860–1948, vol. IV

Hands, Rev. John Compton, 1842–1928, vol. II, vol. III

Hands, Rev. Thomas, 1856–1926, vol. II

Hands, William Joseph, *died* 1947, vol. IV

Handy, Gen. Thomas Troy, 1892–1982, vol. VIII

Handyside, Surg. Rear-Adm. Sir Patrick Brodie, 1860–1939, vol. III

Hanes, Charles Samuel, 1903–1990, vol. VIII

Hanford, Col John Compton, 1849–1911, vol. I

Hanforth, Thomas William, 1867–1948, vol. IV

Hanger, Sir Mostyn, 1908–1980, vol. VII

Hanham, Sir Henry Phelips, 11th Bt, 1901–1973, vol. VII

Hanham, Sir John Alexander, 9th Bt, 1854–1911, vol. I

Hanham, John Castleman S.; *see* Swinburne-Hanham.

Hanham, Sir John Ludlow, 10th Bt, 1898–1955, vol. V

Hanington, Rev. Edward A. W., *died* 1917, vol. II

Hanitsch, Karl Richard, 1860–1940, vol. III

Hankey, 1st Baron, 1877–1963, vol. VI

Hankey, Basil Howard Alers, *died* 1948, vol. IV

Hankey, Lt-Col Cyril, *died* 1945, vol. IV

Hankey, Very Rev. Cyril Patrick, 1886–1973, vol. VII

Hankey, Brig.-Gen. Edward Barnard, 1875–1959, vol. V

Hankey, Col George Trevor, 1900–1987, vol. VIII

Hankey, Mabel, *died* 1943, vol. IV

Hankey, Richard Lyons A.; *see* Alers Hankey.

Hankey, W. L.; *see* Lee-Hankey.

Hankin, Mrs Agnes Mary; *see* Field, M.

Hankin, Arthur Crommelin, 1859–1930, vol. III

Hankin, Arthur Maxwell, 1905–1972, vol. VII

Hankin, Ernest Hanbury, 1865–1939, vol. III

Hankin, Gen. George Crommelin, 1826–1902, vol. I

Hankin, St John, 1869–1909, vol. I

Hankins, George Alexander, 1895–1950, vol. IV

Hankinson, Charles James; *see* Holland, Clive.

Hankinson, Cyril Francis James, 1895–1984, vol. VIII

Hankinson, Sir Walter Crossfield, 1894–1984, vol. VIII

Hanley, Allan Hastings, 1863–1921, vol. II

Hanley, Denis Augustine, 1903–1980, vol. VII

Hanley, James, 1901–1985, vol. VIII

Hanley, James Alec, 1886–1960, vol. V

Hanlon, Rt Rev. Henry, 1862–1937, vol. III

Hanlon, John Austin Thomas, 1905–1983, vol. VIII

Hanlon, Air Vice-Marshal Thomas James, 1916–1977, vol. VII

Hanmer, Lt-Col Sir Edward; *see* Hanmer, Lt-Col Sir G. W. E.

Hanmer, Lt-Col Sir (Griffin Wyndham) Edward, 7th Bt, 1893–1977, vol. VII

Hanmer, Adm. John Graham Job, 1836–1919, vol. II

Hanmer, Marguerite Frances, 1895–1975, vol. VII

Hanmer, Sir Wyndham Charles Henry, 6th Bt, 1867–1922, vol. II

Hann, Edmund Lawrence, 1881–1968, vol. VI

Hanna, George Boyle, 1877–1938, vol. III

Hanna, Hon. Henry, 1871–1946, vol. IV

Hanna, Marcus Alonzo, 1837–1904, vol. I

Hanna, Very Rev. Robert K., 1872–1947, vol. IV

Hanna, Hon. William John, 1862–1919, vol. II

Hannaford, Charles Arthur, 1887–1972, vol. VII

Hannaford, Charles E., 1863–1955, vol. V

Hannaford, Guy George, 1901–1976, vol. VII

Hannah, Air Marshal Sir Colin Thomas, 1914–1978, vol. VII

Hannah, Ian Campbell, 1874–1944, vol. IV

Hannah, Flt-Sgt John, 1921–1947, vol. IV

Hannah, Very Rev. John Julius, 1843–1931, vol. III

Hannah, Rev. Joseph Addison, 1867–1928, vol. II

Hannah, William George, 1868–1945, vol. IV

Hannan, Albert James, 1887–1965, vol. VI

Hannan, William, 1906–1987, vol. VIII

Hannay, Alexander Howard, 1889–1955, vol. V

Hannay, David, 1853–1934, vol. III

Hannay, Doris F., (Lady Fergusson Hannay); *see* Leslie, D.

Hannay, Brig.-Gen. Frederick R.; *see* Rainsford-Hannay.

Hannay, Col Frederick R.; *see* Rainsford-Hannay.

Hannay, Sir Hugh Augustus Macnish, 1878–1962, vol. VI

Hannay, James, 1842–1910, vol. I

Hannay, James Lennox, 1826–1903, vol. I

Hannay, Rev. James Owen, 1865–1950, vol. IV

Hannay, Mrs Jane Ewing, 1868–1938, vol. III

Hannay, Col Ramsay William R.; *see* Rainsford-Hannay

Hannay, Robert Kerr, 1867–1940, vol. III

Hannay, Maj.-Gen. Robert Strickland, 1871–1948, vol. IV

Hannay, Samuel Beveridge A.; *see* Armour-Hannay.

Hannay, Rt Rev. Thomas, 1887–1970, vol. VI

Hannay, Sir Walter Fergusson Leisrinck, 1904–1961, vol. VI

Hannay, Captain Walter Maxwell, 1873–1952, vol. V

Hannays, Sir Courtenay; *see* Hannays, Sir L. C.

Hannays, Sir (Leonard) Courtenay, 1892–1964, vol. VI

Hannen, Athene, (Mrs Nicholas Hannen); *see* Seyler, A.

Hannen, Lancelot, 1866–1942, vol. IV

Hannen, Nicholas James, 1881–1972, vol. VII

Hannen, Sir Nicholas John, 1842–1900, vol. I

Hannon, Ven. Arthur Gordon, 1891–1978, vol. VII

Hannon, Rt Rev. Daniel Joseph, 1884–1946, vol. IV

Hannon, Sir Patrick Joseph Henry, *died* 1963, vol. VI

Hannyngton, Col John Arthur, 1868–1918, vol. II

Hanotaux, Gabriel, 1853–1944, vol. IV

Hansard, Col Arthur Clifton, 1855–1927, vol. II

Hansell, Rev. Arthur Lloyd, 1865–1948, vol. IV

Hansell, Sir (Edward) William, 1856–1937, vol. III

Hansell, Henry Peter, 1863–1935, vol. III

Hansell, Sir William; *see* Hansell, Sir E. W.

Hansen, Alvin H., 1887–1975, vol. VII

Hansen, David Ernest, 1884–1972, vol. VII

Hansen, Hans, *died* 1947, vol. IV

Hansen, Harry, 1884–1977, vol. VII

Hansen, Brig. Percy Howard, 1890–1951, vol. V

Hansen, Sir Sven Wohlford, 1st Bt, 1876–1958, vol. V

Hansford, Col Sir Benjamin, 1863–1954, vol. V

Hansford, S(idney) Howard, 1899–1973, vol. VII
Hansford Johnson, Pamela; *see* Johnson, P. H.
Hansi, (Jacques Walz), *died* 1951, vol. V
Hanson, Albert Henry, 1913–1971, vol. VII
Hanson, Sir Charles Augustin, 1st Bt (*cr* 1918), 1846–1922, vol. II
Hanson, Major Sir Charles Edwin Bourne, 2nd Bt (*cr* 1918), 1874–1958, vol. V
Hanson, Daniel, 1892–1953, vol. V
Hanson, (Emmeline) Jean, 1919–1973, vol. VII
Hanson, Sir Francis Stanhope, 1868–1910, vol. I
Hanson, Frederick Horowhenua Melrose, 1896–1979, vol. VII
Hanson, Sir Gerald Stanhope, 2nd Bt (*cr* 1887), 1867–1946, vol. IV
Hanson, Lt-Col Harry Ernest, 1873–1934, vol. III
Hanson, Jean; *see* Hanson, E. J.
Hanson, Sir Philip, 1871–1955, vol. V
Hanson, Sir Reginald, 1st Bt (*cr* 1887), 1840–1905, vol. I
Hanson, Rev. Preb. Richard, 1880–1963, vol. VI
Hanson, Hon. Richard Burpee, 1879–1948, vol. IV
Hanson, Sir Richard Leslie Reginald, 3rd Bt (*cr* 1887), 1905–1951, vol. V
Hanson, Rt Rev. Richard Patrick Crosland, 1916–1988, vol. VIII
Hanson, Rev. Robert Edward Vernon, 1866–1947, vol. IV
Hanson, Rupert Willoughby, 1873–1936, vol. III
Hanworth, 1st Viscount, 1861–1936, vol. III
Hapgood, Henry James, 1855–1931, vol. III
Hapgood, Norman, 1868–1937, vol. III
Happell, Sir Alexander John, 1887–1968, vol. VI
Happell, Sir Arthur Comyn, 1891–1975, vol. VII
Happell, Brig. William Horatio, 1890–1971, vol. VII
Happold, Frederick Crossfield, 1893–1971, vol. VII
Harada, Rev. Tasuku, 1863–1940, vol. III
Haran, James Augustine, *died* 1940, vol. III (A), vol. IV
Haran, Timotheus, *died* 1904, vol. I
Harari, Sir Victor Pasha, 1857–1945, vol. IV
Harbach, Otto A., 1873–1963, vol. VI
Harben, Guy Philip, 1881–1949, vol. IV
Harben, Sir Henry, 1823–1911, vol. I
Harben, William Nathaniel, 1858–1919, vol. II
Harberton, 6th Viscount, 1836–1912, vol. I
Harberton, 7th Viscount, 1867–1944, vol. IV
Harberton, 8th Viscount, 1869–1956, vol. V
Harberton, 9th Viscount, 1908–1980, vol. VII
Harbison, Thomas James Stanislaus, 1864–1930, vol. III
Harbord, Sir Arthur, 1865–1941, vol. IV
Harbord, Rev. and Hon. (Charles) Derek (Gardner), 1902–1987, vol. VIII
Harbord, Brig.-Gen. Cyril Rodney, 1873–1958, vol. V
Harbord, Rev. and Hon. Derek; *see* Harbord, Rev. and Hon. C. D. G.
Harbord, Captain Eric Walter, 1879–1952, vol. V
Harbord, Frank William, *died* 1942, vol. IV
Harbord, Captain Maurice Assheton, 1874–1954, vol. V
Harbottle, Col Colin Clark, 1875–1933, vol. III
Harbottle, Frank, 1872–1923, vol. II
Harbottle, Sir John George, 1858–1920, vol. II

Harbour, Brian Hugo, 1899–1974, vol. VII
Harby, Sir Frank Neville, 1888–1952, vol. V
Harcourt, 1st Viscount, 1863–1922, vol. II
Harcourt, 2nd Viscount, 1908–1979, vol. VII
Harcourt, Alfred, 1881–1954, vol. V
Harcourt, Aubrey, 1852–1904, vol. I
Harcourt, Augustus George V.; *see* Vernon Harcourt.
Harcourt, Adm. Sir Cecil Halliday Jepson, 1892–1959, vol. V
Harcourt, Evelyn, (Lady Harcourt); *see* Suart, Evelyn.
Harcourt, George, 1868–1947, vol. IV
Harcourt, Captain Guy Elliot, 1869–1936, vol. III
Harcourt, Henry, 1873–1933, vol. III
Harcourt, Sir John; *see* Harcourt, Sir R. J. R.
Harcourt, Leveson Francis V.; *see* Vernon-Harcourt.
Harcourt, Hon. Richard, 1849–1932, vol. III
Harcourt, Sir (Robert) John (Rolston), *died* 1969, vol. VI
Harcourt, Robert Vernon, 1878–1962, vol. VI
Harcourt, Rt Hon. Sir William George Granville Venables Vernon-, 1827–1904, vol. I
Harcourt-Smith, Sir Cecil; *see* Smith.
Harcourt-Smith, Air Vice-Marshal Gilbert, 1901–1968, vol. VI
Harcourt Williams, E. G.; *see* Williams.
Harcus, Rev. A(ndrew) Drummond, 1885–1964, vol. VI
Hardaker, Alan, 1912–1980, vol. VII
Hardaker, Benjamin Rigby, 1890–1961, vol. VI
Hardcastle, Captain Alexander, 1872–1933, vol. III
Hardcastle, Edward, 1826–1905, vol. I
Hardcastle, Ven. Edward Hoare, 1862–1945, vol. IV
Hardcastle, Joseph Alfred, 1868–1917, vol. II
Hardcastle, Mary, 1901–1964, vol. VI
Hardcastle, Monica Alice, 1904–1966, vol. VI
Hardcastle, Engr-Captain Sydney Undercliffe, 1875–1960, vol. V
Harden, Sir Arthur, 1865–1940, vol. III
Harden, Rt Rev. John Mason, *died* 1931, vol. III
Hardie, Agnes; *see* Hardie, Mrs G. D.
Hardie, Archibald William, 1911–1980, vol. VII
Hardie, Charles Martin, 1858–1916, vol. II
Hardie, David, *died* 1939, vol. III
Hardie, Sir David, 1856–1945, vol. IV
Hardie, Frank; *see* Hardie, W. F. R.
Hardie, Mrs George Downie, (Agnes Hardie), *died* 1951, vol. V
Hardie, George Downie Blyth Crookston, *died* 1937, vol. III
Hardie, James Keir, 1856–1915, vol. I
Hardie, Maj.-Gen. John Leslie, 1882–1956, vol. V
Hardie, John William Somerville, 1912–1987, vol. VIII
Hardie, Martin, 1875–1952, vol. V
Hardie, Captain Maurice Linton, 1909–1972, vol. VII
Hardie, Robert Purves, 1864–1942, vol. IV
Hardie, Steven James Lindsay, 1885–1969, vol. VI
Hardie, Rt Rev. William Auchterlonie, 1904–1980, vol. VII
Hardie, William Francis Ross, 1902–1990, vol. VIII
Hardie, Most Rev. William George, 1878–1950, vol. IV

Hardie, William Ross, 1862–1916, vol. II
Hardie Neil, James, 1875–1955, vol. V
Hardiman, Alfred Frank, 1891–1949, vol. IV
Hardiman, John Percy, 1874–1964, vol. VI
Harding of Petherton, 1st Baron, 1896–1989, vol. VIII
Harding, Rt Rev. Alfred, 1852–1923, vol. II
Harding, Sir (Alfred) John, 1878–1953, vol. V
Harding, Ann, 1902–1981, vol. VIII
Harding, Sir Charles O'Brien, 1859–1929, vol. III
Harding, Col Colin, 1863–1939, vol. III
Harding, Edward Archibald Fraser, 1903–1953, vol. V
Harding, Sir Edward John, 1880–1954, vol. V
Harding, Rev. Edwin Elmer, died 1909, vol. I
Harding, Francis Egerton, 1856–1937, vol. III
Harding, George Frederick Morris, 1874–1964, vol. VI
Harding, George Richardson, 1884–1976, vol. VII
Harding, George Trevor H.; see Hamilton Harding.
Harding, Gerald William Lankester, 1901–1979, vol. VII
Harding, Gilbert Charles, 1907–1960, vol. V
Harding, Harold Ivan, 1883–1943, vol. IV
Harding, Sir Harold John Boyer, 1900–1986, vol. VIII
Harding, Sir John; see Harding, Sir A. J.
Harding, Rev. John Taylor, 1835–1928, vol. II
Harding, Most Rev. Malcolm Taylor McAdam, died 1949, vol. IV
Harding, Lt-Col Maynard Ffolliott, died 1961, vol. VI
Harding, Maj.-Gen. Reginald Peregrine, 1905–1981, vol. VIII
Harding, Rosamond Evelyn Mary, 1898–1982, vol. VIII
Harding, Sidnie M.; see Manton, S. M.
Harding, Walter; see Harding, T. W.
Harding, Col Thomas Walter, 1843–1927, vol. II
Harding, Walter Ambrose Heath, 1870–1942, vol. IV
Harding, Warren Gamaliel, 1865–1923, vol. II
Harding, Lt-Col William, died 1945, vol. IV
Harding-Newman, Brig.-Gen. Edward; see Newman.
Harding-Newman, Maj.-Gen. John Cartwright, 1874–1935, vol. III
Hardinge, 3rd Viscount, 1857–1924, vol. II
Hardinge, 4th Viscount, 1905–1979, vol. VII
Hardinge, 5th Viscount, 1929–1984, vol. VIII
Hardinge of Penshurst, 1st Baron, 1858–1944, vol. IV
Hardinge of Penshurst, 2nd Baron, 1894–1960, vol. V
Hardinge, Rt Hon. Sir Arthur Henry, 1859–1933, vol. III
Hardinge, Sir Charles Edmund, 5th Bt, 1878–1968, vol. VI
Hardinge, Sir Edmund Stracey, 4th Bt, 1833–1924, vol. II
Hardinge, Hon. Henry Ralph, 1895–1915, vol. I
Hardinge, Sir Robert, 6th Bt, 1887–1973, vol. VII
Hardisty, Charles William, 1893–1973, vol. VII
Hardman, Amy Elizabeth, 1909–1990, vol. VIII
Hardman, David Rennie, 1901–1989, vol. VIII
Hardman, Air Chief Marshal Sir Donald Innes; see Hardman, Air Chief Marshal Sir J. D. I.

Hardman, Air Chief Marshal Sir (James) Donald Innes, 1899–1982, vol. VIII
Hardman, Rev. Oscar, 1880–1964, vol. VI
Hardman, Lt-Col Reginald Stanley, 1870–1936, vol. III
Hardman-Jones, Vice-Adm. Everard John, 1881–1962, vol. VI
Hardwick, Charles Aubrey, 1885–1984, vol. VIII
Hardwick, Donald Ross, 1895–1977, vol. VII
Hardwick, Francis William, 1861–1934, vol. III
Hardwick, Rev. John Charlton, 1885–1953, vol. V
Hardwick, John Jessop, 1831–1917, vol. II
Hardwick, Lt-Col Philip Edward, 1875–1919, vol. II
Hardwicke, 5th Earl of, 1836–1897, vol. I
Hardwicke, 6th Earl of, 1867–1904, vol. I
Hardwicke, 7th Earl of, 1840–1909, vol. I
Hardwicke, 8th Earl of, 1869–1936, vol. III
Hardwicke, 9th Earl of, 1906–1974, vol. VII
Hardwicke, Sir Cedric Webster, 1893–1964, vol. VI
Hardwicke, Herbert Junius, died 1921, vol. II
Hardy, Hon. Alfred Erskine G.; see Gathorne-Hardy.
Hardy, Sir Alister Clavering, 1896–1985, vol. VIII
Hardy, Hon. Arthur Charles, 1872–1962, vol. VI
Hardy, Rev. Arthur Octavius, 1838–1910, vol. I
Hardy, Arthur Sherburne, 1847–1930, vol. III
Hardy, Rev. Canon Basil Augustus, 1901–1973, vol. VII
Hardy, Major Sir Bertram, 3rd Bt, 1877–1953, vol. V
Hardy, Gen. Sir Campbell Richard, 1906–1984, vol. VIII
Hardy, Charles, 1874–1940, vol. III
Hardy, Col Hon. Charles Gathorne G.; see Gathorne-Hardy.
Hardy, Charles Stewart, 1842–1914, vol. I
Hardy, Vice-Adm. Charles Talbot, 1877–1935, vol. III
Hardy, Dudley, 1867–1922, vol. II
Hardy, Rev. E. J., 1849–1920, vol. II
Hardy, Edgar Wrigley C.; see Cozens-Hardy.
Hardy, Sir Edward, 1887–1975, vol. VII
Hardy, Edward Arthur, 1884–1960, vol. V
Hardy, Col Edwin Greenwood, 1867–1944, vol. IV
Hardy, Major Eric John, 1884–1965, vol. VI
Hardy, Ernest George, 1852–1925, vol. II
Hardy, Evan A., 1890–1963, vol. VI
Hardy, Lt-Col Francis, 1875–1929, vol. III
Hardy, Francis, 1879–1977, vol. VII
Hardy, Maj.-Gen. Frederick, 1830–1916, vol. II
Hardy, Geoffrey Malcolm G.; see Gathorne-Hardy.
Hardy, George Alexander, 1851–1920, vol. II
Hardy, Brig. George Alfred, 1923–1990, vol. VIII
Hardy, Sir George Francis, died 1914, vol. I
Hardy, Gerald Holbech, 1852–1929, vol. III
Hardy, Godfrey Harold, 1877–1947, vol. IV
Hardy, Gordon Sidey, 1884–1936, vol. III
Hardy, Sir Harry, 1896–1984, vol. VIII
Hardy, Henry Harrison, 1882–1958, vol. V
Hardy, Herbert Ronald, 1900–1954, vol. V
Hardy, Lady Isobel G.; see Gathorne-Hardy.
Hardy, Iza Duffus, died 1922, vol. II
Hardy, Sir James Douglas, 1915–1986, vol. VIII
Hardy, Major Jocelyn Lee, 1894–1958, vol. V

Hardy, Sir (John) Francis G.; *see* Gathorne-Hardy.
Hardy, Rt Hon. Laurence, 1854–1933, vol. III
Hardy, Lt-Col Leonard Henry, 1882–1954, vol. V
Hardy, Oswald Henry, *died* 1940, vol. III
Hardy, Sir Reginald, 2nd Bt, 1848–1938, vol. III
Hardy, Richard Gillies, 1852–1923, vol. II
Hardy, Hon. Robert G.; *see* Gathorne-Hardy.
Hardy, Air Cdre Stephen Haistwell, 1905–1945, vol. IV
Hardy, Rev. Theodore Bayley, 1866–1918, vol. II
Hardy, Thomas, 1840–1928, vol. II
Hardy, Co. Thomas Eben F.; *see* Forman Hardy.
Hardy, Maj.-Gen. Thomas Henry, 1863–1938, vol. III
Hardy, Thomas Lionel, 1887–1969, vol. VI
Hardy, Lt-Gen. William, 1822–1901, vol. I
Hardy, Sir William Bate, 1864–1934, vol. III
Hardy, William John, 1857–1919, vol. II
Hare, Alfred Thomas, 1855–1945, vol. IV
Hare, Amy, *died* 1939, vol. III
Hare, Augustus John Cuthbert, 1834–1903, vol. I
Hare, Bt Lt-Col Charles Tristram Melville, 1879–1950, vol. IV
Hare, Christopher, *died* 1929, vol. III
Hare, Cyril; *see* Gordon Clark, Alfred Alexander.
Hare, Dorothy Christian, *died* 1967, vol. VI
Hare, Edgar James, 1884–1969, vol. VI
Hare, Francis, 1858–1928, vol. II, vol. III
Hare, Col Frederick Stephen Christian, 1857–1931, vol. III
Hare, Geoffrey, 1940–1988, vol. VIII
Hare, Brig. George Ambrose, 1880–1948, vol. IV
Hare, Sir (George) Ralph Leigh, 3rd Bt (*cr* 1818), 1866–1933, vol. III
Hare, George Thompson, 1863–1906, vol. I
Hare, Henry Thomas, *died* 1921, vol. II
Hare, Rev. Hugh James, 1829–1909, vol. I
Hare, Maj.-Gen. James Francis, 1897–1970, vol. VI
Hare, Sir John, 1844–1921, vol. II
Hare, John Gilbert, 1869–1951, vol. V
Hare, John Hugh Montague, *died* 1935, vol. III
Hare, Rt Rev. John Tyrrell Holmes, 1912–1976, vol. VII
Hare, Julius, 1859–1932, vol. III
Hare, Kenneth, 1888–1962, vol. VI
Hare, Sir Lancelot, 1851–1922, vol. II
Hare, Patrick James, 1920–1982, vol. VIII
Hare, Sir Ralph; *see* Hare, Sir G. R. L.
Hare, Major Sir Ralph Leigh, 4th Bt (*cr* 1818), 1903–1976, vol. VII
Hare, Reginald Charles, *died* 1933, vol. III
Hare, Rear-Adm. Hon. Richard, 1836–1903, vol. I
Hare, Col Richard Charles, 1844–1917, vol. II
Hare, Hon. Richard Gilbert, 1907–1966, vol. VI
Hare, Robert Douglas, 1848–1929, vol. III
Hare, Brig.-Gen. Robert Hugh, 1867–1950, vol. IV
Hare, Brig.-Gen. Robert William, 1872–1953, vol. V
Hare, Robertson, 1891–1979, vol. VII
Hare, Ronald, 1899–1986, vol. VIII
Hare, St George, 1857–1933, vol. III
Hare, Maj.-Gen. Sir Steuart Welwood, 1867–1952, vol. V
Hare, Theodore Julius, 1839–1907, vol. I

Hare, Sir Thomas Leigh, 1st Bt (*cr* 1905), 1859–1941, vol. IV
Hare, Thomas Leman, *died* 1935, vol. III
Hare, Tom, 1895–1959, vol. V
Hare, William Loftus, 1868–1943, vol. IV
Hares, Ven. Archdeacon Walter P., 1877–1962, vol. VI
Harewood, 5th Earl of, 1846–1929, vol. III
Harewood, 6th Earl of, 1882–1947, vol. IV
Harford, Sir Arthur; *see* Harford, Sir G. A.
Harford, Charles Forbes, *died* 1925, vol. II
Harford, Rev. Edward John, *died* 1917, vol. II
Harford, Frederic Dundas, 1862–1931, vol. III
Harford, Rev. George, 1860–1921, vol. II
Harford, Sir (George) Arthur, 2nd Bt, 1897–1967, vol. VI
Harford, Col Henry Charles, 1850–1937, vol. III
Harford, Rev. John Battersby, 1857–1937, vol. III
Harford, Major Sir John Charles, 1st Bt, 1860–1934, vol. III
Hargest, Brig. James, 1891–1944, vol. IV
Hargrave, John Gordon, 1894–1982, vol. VIII
Hargreaves, Alfred, 1899–1978, vol. VII (AII)
Hargreaves, Anthony Dalzell, 1904–1959, vol. V
Hargreaves, Eric Lyde, 1898–1984, vol. VIII
Hargreaves, George Ronald, 1908–1962, vol. VI
Hargreaves, Sir Gerald de la Pryme, *died* 1972, vol. VII
Hargreaves, John, 1864–1926, vol. II
Hargreaves, John Henry, 1856–1934, vol. III
Hargreaves, Brig. Kenneth, 1903–1990, vol. VIII
Hargreaves, Lionel Stanley, 1882–1954, vol. V
Hargreaves, Sir Thomas, 1889–1966, vol. VI
Hargreaves, Sir Walter Ernest, 1865–1954, vol. V
Hargrove, Rev. Joseph, 1843–1914, vol. I
Hari Kishan Kaul, Raja Pandit, 1869–1942, vol. IV
Hari Singhji Raja, Rao Bahadur, 1877–1933, vol. III
Harington, Gen. Sir Charles Harington, 1872–1940, vol. III
Harington, Sir Charles Robert, 1897–1972, vol. VII
Harington, Edward, 1863–1937, vol. III
Harington, Brig.-Gen. John, 1873–1943, vol. IV
Harington, Maj.-Gen. John, 1912–1989, vol. VIII
Harington, John Charles Dundas, 1903–1980, vol. VII
Harington, Sir Richard, 11th Bt, 1835–1911, vol. I
Harington, Sir Richard, 12th Bt, 1861–1931, vol. III
Harington, Sir Richard Dundas, 13th Bt, 1900–1981, vol. VIII
Harington Hawes, Derrick Gordon, 1907–1986, vol. VIII
Harisinghji, Lt-Gen. Shri Sir, 1895–1961, vol. VI
Harker, Alfred, 1859–1939, vol. III
Harker, Mrs Allen, (Lizzie Harker), *died* 1933, vol. III
Harker, Brig. Arthur William Allen, 1890–1960, vol. V
Harker, Ven. Ernest Gardner, *died* 1928, vol. II
Harker, Gordon, 1885–1967, vol. VI
Harker, John Allen, 1870–1923, vol. II
Harker, Joseph Cunningham, 1855–1927, vol. II
Harker, Lizzie; *see* Harker, Mrs A.
Harker, Rowand, 1879–1946, vol. IV

Harkness, Sir Douglas Alexander Earsman, 1902–1980, vol. VII

Harkness, Edward Burns, 1874–1957, vol. V

Harkness, Rev. Canon Edward Law, 1874–1931, vol. III

Harkness, Edward S., 1874–1940, vol. III

Harkness, Col Henry D'Alton, 1859–1934, vol. III

Harkness, James, 1864–1923, vol. II

Harkness, Sir Joseph Welsh Park, 1890–1962, vol. VI

Harkness, Captain Kenneth Lanyan, 1900–1990, vol. VIII

Harlan, John M., 1899–1971, vol. VII

Harland, Albert, 1869–1957, vol. V

Harland, Henry, 1861–1905, vol. I

Harland, Henry Peirson, 1876–1945, vol. IV

Harland, Ven. Lawrence Winston, 1905–1977, vol. VII

Harland, Rt Rev. Maurice Henry, 1896–1986, vol. VIII

Harland, Sydney Cross, 1891–1982, vol. VIII

Harland, William Arthur, 1926–1985, vol. VIII

Harlech, 2nd Baron, 1819–1904, vol. I

Harlech, 3rd Baron, 1855–1938, vol. III

Harlech, 4th Baron, 1885–1964, vol. VI

Harlech, 5th Baron, 1918–1985, vol. VIII

Harlech, Lady; (Beatrice Mildred Edith), 1891–1980, vol. VII

Harley, Alexander Hamilton, 1882–1951, vol. V

Harley, Rev. Alfred W. M., 1862–1941, vol. IV

Harley, Col George Ernest, 1844–1907, vol. I

Harley, Sir Harry, (Herbert Henry), 1877–1951, vol. V

Harley, Lt-Col Henry Kellett, 1868–1920, vol. II

Harley, Sir Herbert Henry; *see* Harley, Sir Harry.

Harley, John Hunter, 1865–1947, vol. IV

Harley, John Laker, 1911–1990, vol. VIII

Harley, Rev. Robert, 1828–1910, vol. I

Harley, Sir Stanley Jaffa, 1905–1979, vol. VII

Harley, Lt-Col Thomas William, 1876–1950, vol. IV

Harley, Vaughan, 1863–1923, vol. II

Harlock, Maj.-Gen. Hugh George Frederick, 1900–1981, vol. VIII

Harlow, Christopher Millward, 1889–1972, vol. VII

Harlow, Frederick James, *died* 1965, vol. VI

Harlow, Vincent Todd, 1898–1961, vol. VI

Harman, Brig.-Gen. Alexander Ramsay, 1877–1954, vol. V

Harman, Lt-Gen. Sir (Antony Ernest) Wentworth, 1872–1961, vol. VI

Harman, Sir Cecil William Francis S. K.; *see* Stafford-King-Harman.

Harman, Sir Charles Anthony K.; *see* King-Harman.

Harman, Rt Hon. Sir Charles Eustace, 1894–1970, vol. VI

Harman, Sir (Clement) James, 1894–1975, vol. VII

Harman, Captain Douglas K.; *see* King-Harman.

Harman, Edward George, 1862–1921, vol. II

Harman, Ernest Henry, 1908–1989, vol. VIII

Harman, Major George Malcolm Nixon, 1872–1914, vol. I

Harman, Sir James; *see* Harman, Sir C. J.

Harman, N. Bishop, 1869–1945, vol. IV

Harman, Lt-Col Richard, 1864–1905, vol. I

Harman, Captain (Robert) Douglas K.; *see* King-Harman.

Harman, Lt-Gen. Sir Wentworth; *see* Harman, Lt-Gen. Sir A. E. W.

Harman, Col Wentworth Henry K.; *see* King-Harman.

Harmar, Fairlie, *died* 1945, vol. IV

Harmer, Cyril Henry Carrington, 1903–1986, vol. VIII

Harmer, Florence Elizabeth, *died* 1967, vol. VI

Harmer, Frederic William, 1835–1923, vol. II

Harmer, Rt Rev. John Reginald, 1857–1944, vol. IV

Harmer, Lewis Charles, 1902–1975, vol. VII

Harmer, Sir Sidney Frederic, 1862–1950, vol. IV

Harmer, William Douglas, 1873–1962, vol. VI

Harmood-Banner, Sir George Knowles, 3rd Bt, 1918–1990, vol. VIII

Harmood-Banner, Major Sir Harmood, 2nd Bt, 1876–1950, vol. IV

Harmood-Banner, Sir John Sutherland, 1st Bt, 1847–1929, vol. II

Harmsworth, 1st Baron, 1869–1948, vol. IV

Harmsworth, 2nd Baron, 1903–1990, vol. VIII

Harmsworth, Sir Alfred Leicester St Barbe, 2nd Bt (*cr* 1918), 1892–1962, vol. VI

Harmsworth, Anthony; *see* Harmsworth, P. A. T. H.

Harmsworth, Sir (Arthur) Geoffrey (Annesley), 3rd Bt (*cr* 1918), 1904–1980, vol. VII

Harmsworth, Sir Geoffrey; *see* Harmsworth, Sir A. G. A.

Harmsworth, Sir Harold Cecil Aubrey, 1897–1952, vol. V

Harmsworth, Sir Hildebrand Alfred Beresford, 2nd Bt (*cr* 1922), 1901–1977, vol. VII

Harmsworth, Sir Hildebrand Aubrey, 1st Bt (*cr* 1922), *died* 1929, vol. III

Harmsworth, Sir Leicester; *see* Harmsworth, Sir R. L.

Harmsworth, (Perceval) Anthony (Thomas Hildebrand), 1907–1968, vol. VI

Harmsworth, Sir (Robert) Leicester, 1st Bt (*cr* 1918), 1870–1937, vol. III

Harmsworth, Vyvyan George, 1881–1957, vol. V

Harnack, Adolf von, 1851–1930, vol. III

Harnam Singh, Hon. Raja Sir, 1851–1930, vol. III

Harness, Maj.-Gen. Arthur, 1838–1927, vol. II

Harnett, Air Cdre Edward St Clair, 1881–1964, vol. VI

Harnett, Walter Lidwell, 1879–1957, vol. V

Harnett, Rev. William Lee, 1864–1937, vol. III

Harney, Edward Augustine St Aubyn, *died* 1929, vol. III

Harold, Bt Lt-Col Charles Henry Hasler, 1885–1938, vol. III

Harold, Eileen, 1909–1974, vol. VII

Harold, John, *died* 1916, vol. II

Haroon, Seth Haji Sir Abdoola, 1872–1942, vol. IV

Harper, Sir Arthur Grant, 1898–1982, vol. VIII

Harper, Bill; *see* Harper, F. A.

Harper, Charles G., 1863–1943, vol. IV

Harper, Sir Charles Henry, 1876–1950, vol. IV

Harper, Sir Edgar, 1860–1934, vol. III

Harper, Frank Appleby (Bill), 1920–1983, vol. VIII

Harper, Sir George, 1843–1937, vol. III

Harper, George Clifford, 1900–1986, vol. VIII

Harper, George MacGowan, 1899–1976, vol. VII
Harper, George McLean, 1863–1947, vol. IV
Harper, George Milne, 1882–1943, vol. IV
Harper, Lt-Gen. Sir George Montague, 1865–1922, vol. II
Harper, Gerald, *died* 1929, vol. III
Harper, Harry, 1880–1960, vol. V
Harper, Ven. Henry William, *died* 1922, vol. II
Harper, Very Rev. James Walker, 1859–1938, vol. III
Harper, Vice-Adm. John Ernest Troyte, 1874–1949, vol. IV
Harper, Lt-Col John Robinson, 1867–1947, vol. IV
Harper, Joseph, 1914–1978, vol. VII
Harper, Sir Kenneth Brand, 1891–1961, vol. VI
Harper, Norman, 1904–1967, vol. VI
Harper, Norman Adamson, 1913–1982, vol. VIII
Harper, Lt-Col Reginald Tristram, 1876–1958, vol. V
Harper, Sir Richard Stephenson, 1902–1973, vol. VII
Harper, Very Rev. Walter, 1848–1930, vol. III
Harper, William Rainey, 1856–1906, vol. I
Harpignies, Henri Joseph, 1819–1916, vol. II
Harpole, James; *see* Abraham, J. J.
Harraden, Beatrice, 1864–1936, vol. III
Harragin, Alfred Ernest Albert, 1877–1941, vol. IV
Harragin, Sir Walter, 1890–1966, vol. VI
Harrap, George Godfrey, 1867–1938, vol. III
Harrap, (George) Paull (Munro), 1917–1985, vol. VIII
Harrap, Paull; *see* Harrap, G. P. M.
Harrap, Walter Godfrey, 1894–1967, vol. VI
Harrel, Rt Hon. Sir David, 1841–1939, vol. III
Harrel, William Vesey, 1866–1956, vol. V
Harrey, Cyril Ogden W.; *se* Wakefield-Harrey.
Harries, Arthur John, 1856–1922, vol. II
Harries, Sir Arthur Trevor, 1892–1959, vol. V
Harries, Rear-Adm. David Hugh, 1903–1980, vol. VII
Harries, Air Vice-Marshal Sir Douglas, 1893–1972, vol. VII
Harries, Frederick James, *died* 1934, vol. III
Harries, Robert Henry, 1859–1918, vol. II
Harries, Victor Percy, 1907–1977, vol. VII
Harriman, Averell; *see* Harriman, W. A.
Harriman, Edward Henry, *died* 1909, vol. I
Harriman, Sir George, *died* 1973, vol. VII
Harriman, (William) Averell, 1891–1986, vol. VIII
Harrington, 8th Earl of, 1844–1917, vol. II
Harrington, 9th Earl of, 1859–1928, vol. II
Harrington, 10th Earl of, 1887–1929, vol. III
Harrington, Charles, *died* 1943, vol. IV
Harrington, Ernest John, 1864–1944, vol. IV
Harrington, Col Hon. Gordon Sidney, 1883–1943, vol. IV
Harrington, Vice-Adm. Sir Hastings; *see* Harrington, Vice-Adm. Sir W. H.
Harrington, Sir John Lane, 1865–1927, vol. II
Harrington, Rt Hon. Sir Stanley, 1856–1949, vol. IV
Harrington, Thomas Joseph, 1875–1953, vol. V
Harrington, Timothy Charles, 1851–1910, vol. I
Harrington, Vice-Adm. Sir (Wilfred) Hastings, 1906–1965, vol. VI
Harriott, George Moss, 1858–1943, vol. IV
Harris, 4th Baron, 1851–1932, vol. III
Harris, 5th Baron, 1889–1984, vol. VIII

Harris, Hon. Addison C., 1840–1916, vol. II
Harris, Albert Henry, 1885–1945, vol. IV
Harris, Sir Alexander; *see* Harris, Sir C. A.
Harris, Lt-Col Alexander Sutherland S.; *see* Sutherland-Harris.
Harris, Sir Archibald, 1883–1971, vol. VII
Harris, Sir Arthur Ambrose Hall, 1854–1939, vol. III
Harris, Marshal of the Royal Air Force, Sir Arthur Travers, Bt, 1892–1984, vol. VIII
Harris, Sir Austin Edward, 1870–1958, vol. V
Harris, Ven. Charles, *died* 1934, vol. III
Harris, Rev. Charles, 1865–1936, vol. III
Harris, Sir Charles, 1864–1943, vol. IV
Harris, Sir (Charles) Alexander, 1855–1947, vol. IV
Harris, Lt-Col Charles Beresford Maule, 1866–1932, vol. III
Harris, Sir Charles Felix, 1900–1974, vol. VII
Harris, Rear-Adm. Charles Frederick, 1887–1957, vol. V
Harris, Sir Charles Joseph William, 1901–1986, vol. VIII
Harris, Charles Reginald Schiller, 1896–1979, vol. VII
Harris, Col Sir David, 1852–1942, vol. IV
Harris, David Fraser F.; *see* Fraser-Harris.
Harris, David R., *died* 1958, vol. V
Harris, Sir Douglas Gordon, 1883–1967, vol. VI
Harris, Edward, 1849–1933, vol. III
Harris, (Emanuel) Vincent, 1876–1971, vol. VII
Harris, Evan Cadogan, 1906–1988, vol. VIII
Harris, Frank, 1856–1931, vol. III
Harris, Captain Hon. Frank Ernest, 1877–1951, vol. V
Harris, Frederic Walter, 1915–1979, vol. VII
Harris, Lt-Gen. Sir Frederick, 1891–1976, vol. VII
Harris, Rt Hon. Frederick Leverton, 1864–1926, vol. II
Harris, Frederick Rutherfoord, 1856–1920, vol. II
Harris, Frederick William, 1833–1917, vol. II
Harris, Geoffrey Wingfield, 1913–1971, vol. VII
Harris, George, 1844–1922, vol. II
Harris, Major George Arthur, 1879–1935, vol. III
Harris, Sir George David, 1827–1920, vol. I
Harris, Maj.-Gen. George Francis Angelo, 1856–1931, vol. III
Harris, Rev. Canon George Herbert, 1885–1968, vol. VI
Harris, George Montagu, 1868–1951, vol. V
Harris, Col Gerald Noel Anstice, 1866–1952, vol. V
Harris, Henry, *died* 1950, vol. IV
Harris, Henry Albert, 1886–1968, vol. VI
Harris, Sir Henry Percy, 1856–1941, vol. IV
Harris, (Henry) Wilson, 1883–1955, vol. V
Harris, Rev. Preb. Herbert, 1884–1971, vol. VII
Harris, Col Herbert Sextus, 1884–1932, vol. III
Harris, Sir Jack Alexander S.; *see* Sutherland-Harris.
Harris, Air Vice-Marshal Jack Harris, 1903–1963, vol. VI
Harris, Sir James Charles, 1831–1904, vol. I
Harris, James Rendel, 1852–1941, vol. IV
Harris, Maj.-Gen. James Thomas, *died* 1914, vol. I
Harris, Joel Chandler, 1848–1908, vol. I
Harris, John Edward, 1910–1968, vol. VI
Harris, Sir John H., 1874–1940, vol. III

Harris, John Henry, 1875–1962, vol. VI
Harris, John Mitchell, 1856–1927, vol. II
Harris, John Redford Oberlin, 1877–1960, vol. V (A), vol. VI (AI)
Harris, Hon. Sir John Richards, 1868–1946, vol. IV
Harris, Hon. John William, 1849–1932, vol. III
Harris, Kenneth Edwin, 1900–1981, vol. VIII
Harris, Brig. Lawrence Anstie, 1896–1970, vol. VI
Harris, Leonard Charles, 1873–1953, vol. V
Harris, Leonard Tatham, died 1960, vol. V
Harris, Leslie J., 1898–1973, vol. VII
Harris, Sir Lewis Edward, 1900–1983, vol. VIII
Harris, Brig. Sir Lionel Herbert, 1897–1971, vol. VII
Harris, Lloyd, 1867–1925, vol. II
Harris, Mary Kathleen, 1885–1968, vol. VI
Harris, Sir Matthew, 1840–1917, vol. II
Harris, Noel Gordon, 1897–1963, vol. VI
Harris, Norman Charles, 1887–1963, vol. VI
Harris, Rt Hon. Sir Percy Alfred, 1st Bt, 1876–1952, vol. V
Harris, Percy Graham, 1894–1945, vol. IV
Harris, Sir Percy W.; see Wyn-Harris.
Harris, Gen. Philip Henry Farrell, 1833–1913, vol. I
Harris, Reader, 1847–1909, vol. I
Harris, Richard, died 1906, vol. I
Harris, Richard Hancock William Henry, 1851–1927, vol. II
Harris, Sir Richard Olver, 1894–1955, vol. V
Harris, Robert, died 1919, vol. II
Harris, Adm. Sir Robert Hastings, 1843–1926, vol. II
Harris, Robert John Cecil, 1922–1980, vol. VII
Harris, Robert Thornhill, 1865–1934, vol. III
Harris, Rev. Samuel Collard, 1869–1940, vol. III (A), vol. IV
Harris, Sidney, 1903–1976, vol. VII
Harris, Sir Sidney West, 1876–1962, vol. VI
Harris, Thomas Emlyn, 1894–1955, vol. V
Harris, Thomas Maxwell, 1903–1983, vol. VIII
Harris, Vincent; see Harris, E. V.
Harris, Walter B., 1866–1933, vol. III
Harris, Sir Walter Henry, 1851–1922, vol. II
Harris, Wilfred John, 1869–1960, vol. V
Harris, William, 1864–1923, vol. II
Harris, Sir William Henry, 1883–1973, vol. VII
Harris, William James, 1835–1911, vol. I
Harris, Ven. William Stuart, died 1935, vol. III
Harris, Sir William Woolf, 1910–1988, vol. VIII
Harris, Wilson; see Harris, H. W.
Harris-Burland, John Burland, 1870–1926, vol. II
Harrison, Albert John, 1862–1941, vol. IV
Harrison, Alexander, 1890–1988, vol. VIII
Harrison, Alfred Bayford, 1845–1918, vol. II
Harrison, Alick Robin Walsham, 1900–1969, vol. VI
Harrison, Sir Archibald Frederick, 1894–1976, vol. VII
Harrison, Archibald Walter, 1882–1946, vol. IV
Harrison, Brig.-Gen. Arthur Howarth Pryce, 1871–1949, vol. IV
Harrison, Arthur Neville John, 1881–1973, vol. VII
Harrison, Austin, 1873–1928, vol. II
Harrison, Beatrice, died 1965, vol. VI
Harrison, Benjamin, 1833–1901, vol. I
Harrison, Sir (Bernard) Guy, 1885–1978, vol. VII
Harrison, Rev. Cecil Marriott, 1911–1986, vol. VIII

Harrison, Major Cecil Pryce, 1880–1938, vol. III
Harrison, Sir Cecil Reeves, 1856–1940, vol. III
Harrison, Cecil Stanley, 1902–1962, vol. VI
Harrison, Charles, 1835–1897, vol. I
Harrison, Charles, died 1943, vol. IV
Harrison, Charles Custis, 1844–1929, vol. III
Harrison, Col Charles Edward, 1852–1944, vol. IV
Harrison, Sir Charlton Scott Cholmeley, 1881–1951, vol. V
Harrison, Col Cholmeley Edward Carl Branfill, 1857–1937, vol. III
Harrison, Constance Cary, died 1920, vol. II
Harrison, Sir Cyril Ernest, 1901–1980, vol. VII
Harrison, Maj.-Gen. Desmond, 1896–1984, vol. VIII
Harrison, Very Rev. Douglas Ernest William, 1903–1974, vol. VII
Harrison, Lt-Col Edgar Garston, 1863–1947, vol. IV
Harrison, Sir Edward Richard, 1872–1960, vol. V
Harrison, Ven. Edward Stanley, 1889–1948, vol. IV
Harrison, Maj.-Gen. Eric George William Warde, 1893–1987, vol. VIII
Harrison, Rt Hon. Sir Eric John, 1892–1974, vol. VII
Harrison, Ernest, 1877–1943, vol. IV
Harrison, Ernest, 1886–1981, vol. VIII
Harrison, Major Esme Stuart Erskine, 1864–1902, vol. I
Harrison, Sir Fowler; see Harrison, Sir J. F.
Harrison, Francis Capel, 1863–1938, vol. III
Harrison, Francis Llewelyn, 1905–1987, vol. VIII
Harrison, Fred, 1865–1954, vol. V
Harrison, Frederic, 1831–1923, vol. II
Harrison, Frederic James, died 1915, vol. I
Harrison, Lt-Col Sir Frederick, 1844–1914, vol. I
Harrison, Frederick, died 1926, vol. II
Harrison, Rev. Frederick, 1884–1958, vol. V
Harrison, Gabriel Harold, 1921–1974, vol. VII
Harrison, Sir Geoffrey Wedgwood, 1908–1990, vol. VIII
Harrison, Major George, 1885–1961, vol. VI
Harrison, Major George Arthur, 1876–1939, vol. III
Harrison, Brig.-Gen. George Hyde, 1877–1965, vol. VI
Harrison, George Leslie, 1887–1958, vol. V
Harrison, Gerald Joseph Cuthbert, 1895–1954, vol. V
Harrison, Brig.-Gen. Gilbert Harwood, 1866–1930, vol. III
Harrison, Sir Guy; see Harrison, Sir B. G.
Harrison, Brig. Harold Cecil, died 1940, vol. III
Harrison, Sir Harwood; see Harrison, Sir J. H.
Harrison, Sir Heath, 1st Bt (cr 1917), 1857–1934, vol. III
Harrison, Henry, 1867–1954, vol. V
Harrison, Captain Henry Neville Baskcomb-, 1879–1915, vol. I
Harrison, Rear-Adm. Hubert Southwood, 1898–1985, vol. VIII
Harrison, James, 1899–1959, vol. V
Harrison, James Fraser, 1890–1971, vol. VII
Harrison, Sir (James) Harwood, 1st Bt (cr 1961), 1907–1980, vol. VII
Harrison, Sir James Humphreys, 1848–1933, vol. III
Harrison, James Jonathan, 1858–1923, vol. II
Harrison, Maj.-Gen. James Murray Robert, 1880–1957, vol. V

Harrison, Maj.-Gen. Sir James William, 1912–1971, vol. VII

Harrison, Jane Ellen, 1850–1928, vol. II

Harrison, John, 1847–1922, vol. II

Harrison, Sir John, 1st Bt (*cr* 1922), 1856–1936, vol. III

Harrison, Sir John, 1866–1944, vol. IV

Harrison, Sir John Burchmore, 1856–1926, vol. II

Harrison, Sir (John) Fowler, 2nd Bt (*cr* 1922), 1899–1947, vol. IV

Harrison, Maj.-Gen. John Martin Donald W.; *see* Ward-Harrison.

Harrison, John Vernon, 1892–1972, vol. VII

Harrison, John William H.; *see* Heslop-Harrison.

Harrison, Sir (John) Wyndham, 3rd Bt (*cr* 1922), 1933–1955, vol. V

Harrison, Joseph Richard, 1888–1957, vol. V

Harrison, Julius Allan Greenway, 1885–1963, vol. VI

Harrison, Laurence, 1897–1982, vol. VIII

Harrison, Lawrence Alexander, *died* 1937, vol. III

Harrison, Col Lawrence Whitaker, 1876–1964, vol. VI

Harrison, Lloyd Adnitt, 1911–1985, vol. VIII

Harrison, Bt Col Louis Kenneth, 1871–1951, vol. V

Harrison, Mary St Leger, 1852–1931, vol. III

Harrison, May, *died* 1959, vol. V

Harrison, Michael, 1876–1935, vol. III

Harrison, Lt-Col Norman, *died* 1949, vol. IV

Harrison, Philip, *died* 1933, vol. III

Harrison, Reginald, 1837–1908, vol. I

Harrison, Sir Reginald Carey, (Sir Rex), 1908–1990, vol. VIII

Harrison, Sir Rex; *see* Harrison, Sir Reginald C.

Harrison, Gen. Sir Richard, 1837–1931, vol. III

Harrison, Air Vice-Marshal Richard, 1893–1974, vol. VII

Harrison, Rev. Robert, 1841–1927, vol. II

Harrison, Brig.-Gen. Robert Arthur Gwynne, 1855–1943, vol. IV

Harrison, Robert Francis, 1858–1927, vol. II

Harrison, Robert Hichens Camden, *died* 1924, vol. II

Harrison, Robert Tullis, 1876–1950, vol. IV

Harrison, Ronald George, 1921–1982, vol. VIII

Harrison, Rosamond Mary, *died* 1948, vol. IV

Harrison, Ross G., 1870–1959, vol. V

Harrison, Ven. Talbot D.; *see* Dilworth-Harrison.

Harrison, Col Thomas Aylet, 1865–1935, vol. III

Harrison, Brig. Thomas Carleton, 1896–1962, vol. VI

Harrison, Sir Thomas Dalkin, 1885–1954, vol. V

Harrison, Lt-Col Thomas Elliot, 1862–1939, vol. III

Harrison, Thomas Fenwick, 1852–1916, vol. II

Harrison, Captain Walter Gordon, 1888–1951, vol. V

Harrison, Lt-Col Walter Lewis, *died* 1938, vol. III

Harrison, Wilfrid, 1909–1980, vol. VII

Harrison, William, *died* 1940, vol. III

Harrison, William English, *died* 1933, vol. III

Harrison, William Henry, 1880–1955, vol. V

Harrison, William Herbert, 1909–1975, vol. VII

Harrison, William Jerome, 1845–1909, vol. I

Harrison, William John, *died* 1943, vol. IV

Harrison, Sir William Montagu G.; *see* Graham-Harrison.

Harrison, Rt Rev. William Thomas, 1837–1920, vol. II

Harrison, Sir Wyndham; *see* Harrison, Sir J. W.

Harrison-Broadley, Henry Broadley; *see* Broadley.

Harrison-Smith, Sir Francis, *died* 1927, vol. II

Harrison-Topham, Lt-Col Thomas, 1864–1939, vol. III

Harrison-Wallace, Captain Henry Steuart Macnaghten, *died* 1963, vol. VI

Harriss, Charles Albert Edwin, 1862–1929, vol. III

Harrisson, Damer, 1852–1918, vol. II

Harrisson, Geoffry Harnett, *died* 1939, vol. III

Harrisson, Sydney Thirlwall, 1865–1953, vol. V

Harrisson, Tom, 1911–1976, vol. VII

Harrod, Frances M. D., 1866–1956, vol. V

Harrod, Sir Roy Forbes, 1900–1978, vol. VII

Harrop, Angus John, 1900–1963, vol. VI

Harrop, Wilfrid Orrell, 1893–1969, vol. VI

Harrop, William Edward Montagu H.; *see* Hulton-Harrop.

Harrop, Maj.-Gen. William Harrington H.; *see* Hulton-Harrop.

Harrowby, 3rd Earl of, 1831–1900, vol. I

Harrowby, 4th Earl of, 1836–1900, vol. I

Harrowby, 5th Earl of, 1864–1956, vol. V

Harrowby, 6th Earl of, 1892–1987, vol. VIII

Harrower, John, 1857–1933, vol. III

Harrower, John Gordon, 1890–1936, vol. III

Harrowing, Sir John H., 1859–1937, vol. III

Harrowing, Lt-Col Wilkinson Wilberforce, 1898–1967, vol. VI

Harry, Philip A., *died* 1953, vol. V

Harry, Ralph Gordon, 1908–1984, vol. VIII

Harsant, Maj.-Gen. Arnold Guy, 1893–1977, vol. VII

Harston, Major Sir Ernest Sirdefield, 1891–1975, vol. VII

Hart, Albert Bushnell, 1854–1943, vol. IV

Hart, Alfred H., *died* 1953, vol. V

Hart, Arthur W.; *see* Woolley-Hart.

Hart, Sir Basil Henry L.; *see* Liddell Hart.

Hart, Bernard, 1879–1966, vol. VI

Hart, Bernard John W.; *see* Wilden-Hart.

Hart, Sir Bruce; *see* Hart, Sir E. B.

Hart, Sir Byrne, 1895–1989, vol. VIII

Hart, Cecil Augustus, 1902–1970, vol. VI

Hart, Charles Henry, 1847–1917, vol. II

Hart, Col Charles Joseph, 1851–1925, vol. II

Hart, Sir (Edgar) Bruce, 2nd Bt, 1873–1963, vol. VI

Hart, Lt-Col Eric George, 1878–1946, vol. IV

Hart, Ernest Abraham, 1836–1898, vol. I

Hart, Sir Ernest Sidney Walter, 1870–1957, vol. V

Hart, Frank, 1878–1959, vol. V

Hart, Sir George Charles, 1901–1981, vol. VIII

Hart, Sir George Sankey, 1866–1937, vol. III

Hart, George Vaughan, 1841–1912, vol. I

Hart, Heber Leonidas, *died* 1948, vol. IV

Hart, Henry George, 1843–1921, vol. II

Hart, Lt-Col Henry Travers, *died* 1948, vol. IV

Hart, Brig.-Gen. Sir Herbert Ernest, 1882–1968, vol. VI

Hart, Sir Israel, 1835–1911, vol. I

Hart, Ivor Blashka, 1889–1962, vol. VI

Hart, Rt Rev. John Stephen, 1866–1952, vol. V

Hart, Moss, 1904–1961, vol. VI

Hart, Air Marshal Sir Raymund George, 1899–1960, vol. V

Hart, Gen. Sir Reginald Clare, 1848–1931, vol. III
Hart, Sir Robert, 1st Bt, 1835–1911, vol. I
Hart, Sir Robert, 3rd Bt, 1918–1970, vol. VI
Hart, Siriol; *see* Hugh-Jones, S. M. A.
Hart, Thomas Wheeler, 1875–1958, vol. V
Hart, Vincent, 1881–1939, vol. III
Hart, Sir William Edward, 1866–1942, vol. IV
Hart, Sir William Ogden, 1903–1977, vol. VII
Hart, Rev. William Roland R.; *see* Raven-Hart.
Hart-Davies, Thomas, 1849–1920, vol. II
Hart-Davis, Charles Henry, 1874–1958, vol. V
Hart Dyke, Sir Derek William, 9th Bt, 1924–1987, vol. VIII
Hart-Synnot, Maj.-Gen. Arthur FitzRoy, 1884–1910, vol. I
Hart-Synnot, Brig.-Gen. Arthur Henry Seton, 1870–1942, vol. IV
Hart-Synnot, Ronald Victor Okes, 1879–1976, vol. VII
Harte, Bret; *see* Harte, F. B.
Harte, (Francis) Bret, 1839–1902, vol. I
Harte, Walter James, 1866–1954, vol. V
Harte, Wilma, 1916–1976, vol. VII
Harter, Maj.-Gen. James Francis, 1888–1960, vol. V
Harter, James Francis Hatfeild, 1854–1910, vol. I
Hartert, Ernst, 1859–1933, vol. III
Hartfall, Stanley Jack, 1899–1982, vol. VIII
Hartford, Captain George Bibby, 1883–1941, vol. IV
Hartford, Rev. Canon Richard Randall, 1904–1962, vol. VI
Hartgill, Maj.-Gen. William Clavering, 1888–1968, vol. VI
Hartigan, Lt-Gen. Sir James Andrew, 1876–1962, vol. VI
Hartill, Ven. Percy, 1892–1964, vol. VI
Harting, James Edmund, 1841–1928, vol. II
Harting, Pieter, 1892–1970, vol. VI
Hartington, Marquess of; William John Robert Cavendish, 1917–1944, vol. IV
Hartland, Edwin Sidney, 1848–1927, vol. II
Hartland, Sir Frederick Dixon D.; *see* Dixon-Hartland.
Hartland, George Albert, 1884–1944, vol. IV
Hartland, William John, 1909–1972, vol. VII
Hartland-Swann, Louis Herbert, 1878–1947, vol. IV
Hartley, Gen. Sir Alan Fleming, 1882–1954, vol. V
Hartley, Alfred, 1855–1933, vol. III
Hartley, Arthur Clifford, 1889–1960, vol. V
Hartley, Col Bernard Charles, 1879–1960, vol. V
Hartley, C. Gasquoine, (Mrs Arthur D. Lewis), 1869–1928, vol. II
Hartley, Sir Charles Augustus, 1825–1915, vol. I
Hartley, Christiana, *died* 1948, vol. IV
Hartley, Lt-Col Donald Reginald Cavendish, 1893–1970, vol. VI
Hartley, Edmund Baron, 1847–1919, vol. II
Hartley, Frederic St Aubyn, 1896–1969, vol. VI
Hartley, Brig.-Gen. Sir Harold, 1878–1972, vol. VII
Hartley, Harold T., 1851–1943, vol. IV
Hartley, Rev. John Thorneycroft, 1849–1935, vol. III
Hartley, Leslie Poles, 1895–1972, vol. VII
Hartley, Lewis Wynne, 1867–1931, vol. III
Hartley, Rev. Marshall, 1846–1928, vol. II
Hartley, Sir Percival, 1881–1957, vol. V

Hartley, Sir Percival Horton-Smith-, 1867–1952, vol. V
Hartley, Percival Hubert Graham Horton-Smith, 1896–1977, vol. VII
Hartley, Sir Walter Noel, 1846–1913, vol. I
Hartley, Sir William Pickles, 1846–1922, vol. II
Hartline, Haldan Keffer, 1903–1983, vol. VIII
Hartmann, Karl Robert Eduard von, 1842–1906, vol. I
Hartmann, William, 1844–1926, vol. II
Hartnell, Air Vice-Marshal Geoffrey Clark, 1916–1981, vol. VIII
Hartnell, Sir Norman, 1901–1979, vol. VII
Hartnett, Sir Laurence John, 1898–1986, vol. VIII
Hartnoll, Comdr Henry James, 1890–1940, vol. III
Hartnoll, Sir Henry Sulivan, 1862–1935, vol. III
Hartog, Marcus, *died* 1923, vol. II
Hartog, Sir Philip Joseph, 1864–1947, vol. IV
Harton, Very Rev. Frederic Percy, 1889–1958, vol. V
Hartopp, Sir Charles Edward Cradock-, 5th Bt, 1858–1929, vol. III
Hartopp, Sir Charles (William Everard) Cradock-, 6th Bt, 1893–1930, vol. III
Hartopp, Sir Frederick Cradock-, 7th Bt, 1869–1937, vol. III
Hartopp, Sir George Francis Fleetwood Cradock-, 8th Bt, 1870–1949, vol. IV
Hartree, Douglas Rayner, 1897–1958, vol. V
Hartrick, Archibald Standish, 1864–1950, vol. IV
Hartridge, Gustavus, *died* 1923, vol. II
Hartridge, Hamilton, 1886–1976, vol. VII
Hartshorn, Rt Hon. Vernon, 1872–1931, vol. III
Hartshorne, Albert, 1839–1910, vol. I
Hartung, Ernst Johannes, 1893–1979, vol. VII
Hartvigson, Frits, 1841–1919, vol. II
Hartwell, Lady; Pamela Margaret Elizabeth Berry, 1914–1982, vol. VIII
Hartwell, Sir Brodrick Cecil Denham Arkwright, 4th Bt, 1876–1948, vol. IV
Hartwell, Sir Charles Herbert, 1904–1982, vol. VIII
Hartwell, Charles Leonard, 1873–1951, vol. V
Hartwell, Sir Francis Houlton, 3rd Bt, 1835–1900, vol. I
Hartwell, Maj.-Gen. John Redmond, 1887–1970, vol. VI
Harty, Agnes Helen, (Lady Harty), 1877–1959, vol. V
Harty, Maj.-Gen. Arthur Henry, 1890–1977, vol. VII
Harty, (Fredric) Russell, 1934–1988, vol. VIII
Harty, Sir Hamilton; *see* Harty, Sir Herbert H.
Harty, Sir Henry Lockington, 3rd Bt, 1826–1913, vol. I
Harty, Sir (Herbert) Hamilton, 1880–1941, vol. IV
Harty, Most Rev. J. M., 1867–1946, vol. IV
Harty, Sir Lionel Lockington, 4th Bt, 1864–1939, vol. III
Harty, Sir Robert, 2nd Bt, 1815–1902, vol. I
Harty, Russell; *see* Harty, F. R.
Harty, Hon. William, *died* 1929, vol. III
Hartzell, Joseph Crane, 1842–1928, vol. II
Harvatt, Thomas, 1901–1984, vol. VIII
Harvey of Tasburgh, 1st Baron, 1893–1968, vol. VI
Harvey, Alexander, 1904–1987, vol. VIII
Harvey, Alexander Gordon Cummins, 1858–1922, vol. II

Harvey, Maj.-Gen. Alexander William Montgomery, 1881–1942, vol. IV

Harvey, Lt-Col Cecil Walter Lewery, 1897–1958, vol. V

Harvey, Sir Charles, 2nd Bt (*cr* 1868, of Crown Point), 1849–1928, vol. II

Harvey, Lt-Col Charles Darley, 1881–1929, vol. III

Harvey, Sir (Charles) Malcolm B.; *see* Barclay-Harvey.

Harvey, Maj.-Gen. Sir Charles Offley, 1888–1969, vol. VI

Harvey, Sir Charles Robert Lambart Edward, 3rd Bt (*cr* 1868, of Crown Point), 1871–1954, vol. V

Harvey, Rev. Clement Fox, 1847–1917, vol. II

Harvey, Conway, 1880–1943, vol. IV

Harvey, Cyril Pearce, 1900–1968, vol. VI

Harvey, Maj.-Gen. David, 1871–1958, vol. V

Harvey, Captain Edward M.; *see* Murray-Harvey.

Harvey, Sir Ernest Maes, 1872–1926, vol. II

Harvey, Sir Ernest Musgrave, 1st Bt (*cr* 1933), 1867–1955, vol. V

Harvey, Rev. Francis Clyde, *died* 1922, vol. II

Harvey, Col Francis George, 1872–1944, vol. IV

Harvey, Lt-Col Francis Henry, 1878–1960, vol. V

Harvey, Ven. Francis William, 1930–1986, vol. VIII

Harvey, Frederick William, *died* 1915, vol. I

Harvey, Col George, 1864–1928, vol. II

Harvey, Sir George, 1870–1939, vol. III

Harvey, Maj.-Gen. George Alfred Duncan, *died* 1957, vol. V

Harvey, Air Vice-Marshal Sir George David, 1905–1969, vol. VI

Harvey, Col Sir George Samuel Abercrombie, 1854–1930, vol. III

Harvey, Harold, *died* 1941, vol. IV

Harvey, Rear-Adm. Harold Lane, 1884–1960, vol. V

Harvey, Henry, 1899–1965, vol. VI

Harvey, Sir (Henry) Paul, 1869–1948, vol. IV

Harvey, Herbert Frost, 1875–1959, vol. V

Harvey, Hildebrand Wolfe, 1887–1970, vol. VI

Harvey, Hon. Horace, 1863–1949, vol. IV

Harvey, Ian Douglas, 1914–1987, vol. VIII

Harvey, Rev. James, 1859–1950, vol. IV

Harvey, James Graham, 1869–1950, vol. IV (A), vol. V

Harvey, John, 1841–1915, vol. I

Harvey, John Edmund Audley, 1851–1927, vol. II

Harvey, Sir John Martin-, 1863–1944, vol. IV

Harvey, Hon. Sir John Musgrave, 1865–1940, vol. III

Harvey, Lt-Col John Robert, 1861–1921, vol. II

Harvey, John Wilfred, 1889–1967, vol. VI

Harvey, Laurence, (Larushka Mischa Skikne), 1929–1973, vol. VII

Harvey, Leslie Arthur, 1903–1986, vol. VIII

Harvey, Air Marshal Sir Leslie Gordon, 1896–1972, vol. VII

Harvey, Rev. Moses, 1820–1901, vol. I

Harvey, Sir Paul; *see* Harvey, Sir H. P.

Harvey, Sir Percy Norman, 1887–1946, vol. IV

Harvey, Rachel; *see* Bloom, Ursula.

Harvey, Ven. Richard Charles Musgrave, 1864–1944, vol. IV

Harvey, Richard Jon Stanley, 1917–1986, vol. VIII

Harvey, Sir Richard Musgrave, 2nd Bt (*cr* 1933), 1898–1978, vol. VII

Harvey, Surg.-Gen. Robert, 1842–1901, vol. I

Harvey, Sir Robert, 1847–1930, vol. III

Harvey, Sir Robert Grenville, 2nd Bt (*cr* 1868, of Langley Park), 1856–1931, vol. III

Harvey, Sir Robert James Paterson, 1904–1965, vol. VI

Harvey, Maj.-Gen. Robert Napier, 1868–1937, vol. III

Harvey, Major Sir Samuel Emile, 1885–1959, vol. V

Harvey, Thomas, 1864–1940, vol. III

Harvey, Rt Rev. Thomas Arnold, 1878–1966, vol. VI

Harvey, Thomas Edmund, 1875–1955, vol. V

Harvey, Rev. Canon Treffry, 1853–1932, vol. III

Harvey, Lt-Col Valentine Vivyan, 1885–1930, vol. III

Harvey, Wilfred John, 1895–1971, vol. VII

Harvey, William, 1859–1927, vol. II

Harvey, William, 1874–1936, vol. III

Harvey, William Alfred, 1883–1946, vol. IV

Harvey, William Edwin, 1852–1914, vol. I

Harvey, Lt-Col William Frederick, 1873–1948, vol. IV

Harvey, William Leathem, *died* 1910, vol. I

Harvey, Lt-Col William Lueg, 1858–1937, vol. III

Harvey Evers, Henry; *see* Evers.

Harvey-Gibson, Robert John, 1860–1929, vol. III

Harvey-Kelly, Captain Hubert Dunsterville; *see* Kelly.

Harvie Anderson, Margaret Betty; *see* Baroness Skrimshire.

Harvie-Brown, John A., 1844–1916, vol. II

Harvie-Watt, Sir George Steven, 1st Bt, 1903–1989, vol. VIII

Harward, Col Arthur John Netherton, 1867–1938, vol. III

Harward, Charles Cuthbert, 1866–1933, vol. III

Harward, Lt-Gen. Thomas Netherton, 1829–1908, vol. I

Harwood, Antony; *see* Harwood, B. A.

Harwood, Basil, 1859–1949, vol. IV

Harwood, (Basil) Antony, 1903–1990, vol. VIII

Harwood, Charles Auguste de Lotbinière-, 1869–1954, vol. V

Harwood, Sir Edmund George, *died* 1964, vol. VI

Harwood, Elizabeth Jean, (Mrs J. A. C. Royle), 1938–1990, vol. VIII

Harwood, George, 1845–1912, vol. I

Harwood, Harold Marsh, *died* 1959, vol. V

Harwood, Henry Cecil, 1893–1964, vol. VI

Harwood, Adm. Sir Henry Harwood, 1888–1950, vol. IV

Harwood, Henry William Forsyth, 1856–1923, vol. II

Harwood, John Augustus, 1845–1929, vol. III

Harwood, Sir John James, 1832–1906, vol. I

Harwood, Sir Ralph Endersby, 1883–1951, vol. V

Hasan, Saiyid Ahmad, 1873–1936, vol. III

Haselden, Edward Christopher, 1903–1988, vol. VIII

Haselden, Rev. John, 1854–1937, vol. III

Haselden, William Kerridge, 1872–1953, vol. V

Haselfoot, Captain Francis Edmund Blechynden, 1885–1938, vol. III

Hasell, Edward William, 1888–1972, vol. VII

Hasell, Rev. George Edmund, 1847–1932, vol. III

Haseltine, Herbert, 1877–1962, vol. VI

Haskard, Brig.-Gen. John McDougall, 1877–1967, vol. VI

Haskell, Arnold Lionel, 1903–1980, vol. VII

Haskell, Harold Noad, 1887–1955, vol. V

Haskell, Jacob Silas, 1857–1939, vol. III

Haskett-Smith, W. P.; see Smith.

Haskins, Charles Homer, 1870–1937, vol. III

Haskins, M. Louise, 1875–1957, vol. V

Haslam, Sir Alfred Seale, 1844–1927, vol. II

Haslam, Henry Cobden, 1870–1948, vol. IV

Haslam, Hon. Lt-Col Sir Humphrey; see Haslam, Hon. Lt-Col Sir R. H.

Haslam, J., 1842–1913, vol. I

Haslam, James, died 1937, vol. III

Haslam, Sir John, 1878–1940, vol. III

Haslam, John Fearby Campbell, 1888–1955, vol. V

Haslam, Lewis, 1856–1922, vol. II

Haslam, Robert Heywood, 1878–1954, vol. V

Haslam, Hon. Lt-Col Sir (Robert) Humphrey, 1882–1962, vol. VI

Haslam, Rev. Samuel Holker, died 1922, vol. II

Haslam, William Frederick, died 1932, vol. III

Haslegrave, Lt-Col Henry John, 1871–1956, vol. V

Haslegrave, John Ramsden, 1913–1980, vol. VII

Haslehust, Ernest William, died 1949, vol. IV

Haslett, Dame Caroline, died 1957, vol. V

Haslett, Sir James Horner, 1832–1905, vol. I

Haslett, Very Rev. Thomas, died 1947, vol. IV

Haslett, Sir William John Handfield, 1866–1954, vol. V

Hasluck, Paul Nooncree, 1854–1931, vol. III

Hassall, Arthur, 1853–1930, vol. III

Hassall, Christopher Vernon, 1912–1963, vol. VI

Hassall, Joan, 1906–1988, vol. VIII

Hassall, John, 1868–1948, vol. IV

Hassam, Childe, 1859–1935, vol. III

Hassanein, Sir Ahmed Mohamed Pasha, 1889–1946, vol. IV

Hassard, Sir John, 1831–1900, vol. I

Hassard, Rev. Richard Samuel, 1848–1921, vol. II

Hassard-Short, Adrian Hugh, 1879–1956, vol. V

Hassard-Short, Rev. Canon Frederick Winning, 1873–1953, vol. V

Hassé, Henry Ronald, 1884–1955, vol. V

Hassel, Odd, 1897–1981, vol. VIII

Hasselkus, John William, 1874–1951, vol. V

Hasted, Col Arthur Walter, 1864–1937, vol. III

Hasted, Lt-Col John Ord Cobbold, 1890–1942, vol. IV

Hasted, Maj.-Gen. William Freke, 1897–1977, vol. VII

Hastie, Edward, 1876–1947, vol. IV

Hastie, William, 1842–1903, vol. I

Hastilow, Cyril Alexander Frederick, 1895–1975, vol. VII

Hastings, 20th Baron, 1857–1904, vol. I

Hastings, 21st Baron, 1882–1956, vol. V

Hastings, Marchioness of; (Florence Cecilia), 1842–1907, vol. I

Hastings, Adm. Alexander Plantagenet, 1843–1925, vol. II

Hastings, Anne Wilson, died 1975, vol. VII

Hastings, Hon. Anthea, (Esther), 1924–1981, vol. VIII

Hastings, Basil Macdonald, 1881–1928, vol. II

Hastings, Bernard Ratcliffe, 1930–1989, vol. VIII

Hastings, Charles Godolphin William, 1854–1920, vol. II

Hastings, Rev. Edward, 1890–1980, vol. VII

Hastings, Maj.-Gen. Edward Spence, 1856–1932, vol. III

Hastings, Maj.-Gen. Francis Eddowes, 1843–1915, vol. I

Hastings, Lt-Gen. Francis William, 1825–1914, vol. I

Hastings, Frank, 1869–1940, vol. III (A), vol. IV

Hastings, Rev. Frederick, 1838–1937, vol. III

Hastings, Col Sir George, 1853–1943, vol. IV

Hastings, Graham, 1830–1922, vol. II

Hastings, Hubert De Cronin, 1902–1986, vol. VIII

Hastings, Rev. James, 1852–1922, vol. II

Hastings, Col John Henry, 1858–1940, vol. III

Hastings, Hon. Osmond William Toone Westenra, 1873–1933, vol. III

Hastings, Sir Patrick, 1880–1952, vol. V

Hastings, Paulyn Charles James Reginald Rawdon-, 1889–1915, vol. I

Hastings, Hon. Paulyn Francis Cuthbert R.; see Rawdon-Hastings.

Hastings, Lt-Col Robin Hood William Stewart, 1917–1990, vol. VIII

Hastings, Somerville, 1878–1967, vol. VI

Hastings, Thomas, 1860–1929, vol. III

Hastings, Lt-Col Wilfred Charles Norrington, 1873–1925, vol. II

Hastings, Col William Holland, 1884–1930, vol. III

Haston, Dougal, 1940–1977, vol. VII

Haswell, Brig. Chetwynd Henry, 1879–1956, vol. V

Haswell, Col John Francis, 1864–1949, vol. IV

Haswell, William A., 1854–1925, vol. II

Haszard, Col Gerald Fenwick, 1894–1967, vol. VI

Hatch, Sir Ernest Frederick George, 1st Bt, 1859–1927, vol. II

Hatch, Frederick Henry, 1864–1932, vol. III

Hatch, Lt-Col George Pelham, 1855–1923, vol. II

Hatch, George Washington, 1872–1963, vol. VI

Hatchard, Caroline, (Caroline Langford), 1883–1970, vol. VI

Hatchell, Maj.-Gen. George, 1838–1912, vol. I

Hatchell, Col Henry Melville, 1852–1933, vol. III

Hatchell, John, 1825–1902, vol. I

Hatcher, Captain James Olden, 1867–1936, vol. III

Hatfield, Rev. Cyril Northcote, 1882–1940, vol. III

Hatfield, Henry, 1854–1926, vol. II

Hatfield, William Herbert, 1882–1943, vol. IV

Hathaway, Frank John, died 1942, vol. IV

Hathaway, Maj.-Gen. Harold George, 1860–1942, vol. IV

Hathaway, Dame Sibyl Mary, 1884–1974, vol. VII

Hatherell, William, 1855–1928, vol. II

Hatherton, 3rd Baron, 1842–1930, vol. III

Hatherton, 4th Baron, 1868–1944, vol. IV

Hatherton, 5th Baron, 1900–1969, vol. VI

Hatherton, 6th Baron, 1906–1973, vol. VII

Hatherton, 7th Baron, 1907–1985, vol. VIII

Hatt, Sir Harry Thomas, 1858–1934, vol. III

Hatten, Rev. Preb. John Charles Le Pelley, 1875–1943, vol. IV

Hattersley, Alan Frederick, 1893–1976, vol. VII

Hatton, Brig.-Gen. Edward Heneage F.; *see* Finch Hatton.

Hatton, Edwin Fullarton, 1858–1940, vol. III

Hatton, Frank, 1921–1978, vol. VII

Hatton, George, 1849–1933, vol. III

Hatton, Maj.-Gen. George Seton, 1899–1974, vol. VII

Hatton, Hon. Harold F.; *see* Finch-Hatton.

Hatton, John Leigh Smeathman, 1865–1933, vol. III

Hatton, Joseph, 1841–1907, vol. I

Hatton, Richard George, 1864–1926, vol. II

Hatton, Sir Ronald George, 1886–1965, vol. VI

Hatton, Thomas Fielding, 1931–1989, vol. VIII

Hatton, Maj.-Gen. Villiers, 1852–1914, vol. I

Hatzfeldt, Prince Francis (Edmond Joseph Gabriel Vit), 1853–1910, vol. I

Hatzfeldt-Wildenburg, Count Paul von, 1831–1901, vol. I

Hauff, Mrs Janet Alderson, 1913–1973, vol. VII

Haugh, Hon. Kevin O'Hanrahan, 1901–1969, vol. VI

Haughton, Benjamin, 1865–1924, vol. II

Haughton, Daniel Jeremiah, 1911–1987, vol. VIII

Haughton, Maj.-Gen. Henry Lawrence, 1883–1955, vol. V

Haughton, Lt-Col Henry Wilfred, 1862–1931, vol. III

Haughton, Col Samuel George Steele, 1883–1956, vol. V

Haughton, Col Samuel Gillmor, 1889–1959, vol. V

Haughton, Sidney Henry, 1888–1982, vol. VIII

Haulfryn Williams, John; *see* Williams.

Haultain, Hon. Sir Frederick William Gordon, 1857–1942, vol. IV

Haultain, Herbert Edward Terrick, 1869–1961, vol. VI

Haupt, Paul, 1858–1926, vol. II

Hauptmann, Gerhart Johann Robert, 1862–1946, vol. IV

Haussonville, Othenin Bernard Gabrielle de Cleron, Comte d', *died* 1924, vol. II

Havard, Sir Godfrey Thomas, 1885–1952, vol. V

Havard, Rt Rev. William Thomas, 1889–1956, vol. V

Havell, Ernest B., 1861–1934, vol. III

Havelock, Sir Arthur Elibank, 1844–1908, vol. I

Havelock, Eric Henry Edwardes, 1891–1974, vol. IV

Havelock, Sir Thomas Henry, 1877–1968, vol. VI

Havelock-Allan, Sir Henry Marshman, 1st Bt, 1830–1897, vol. I

Havelock-Allan, Sir Henry Ralph Moreton, 3rd Bt, 1899–1975, vol. VII

Havelock-Allan, Sir Henry Spencer Moreton, 2nd Bt, 1872–1953, vol. V

Havenga, Hon. Nicolaas Christiaan, *died* 1957, vol. V

Haverfield, Francis John, 1860–1919, vol. II

Havergal, Henry MacLeod, 1902–1989, vol. VIII

Havers, Sir Cecil Robert, 1889–1977, vol. VII

Havers, Air Vice-Marshal Sir E. William, 1887–1979, vol. VII

Havers, Air Vice-Marshal Sir William; *see* Havers, Air Vice-Marshal Sir E. W.

Haversham, 1st Baron, 1835–1917, vol. II

Haviland, Rev. Edmund Arthur, 1874–1966, vol. VI

Haviland, Ven. Francis Ernest, *died* 1945, vol. IV

Havinden, Ashley Eldrid, 1903–1973, vol. VII

Haward, Edwin, 1884–1961, vol. VI

Haward, Sir Harry Edwin, 1863–1953, vol. V

Haward, J. Warrington, 1841–1921, vol. II

Haward, Lawrence, 1878–1957, vol. V

Haward, Sir Walter, 1882–1959, vol. V

Hawarden, 5th Viscount, 1842–1908, vol. I

Hawarden, 6th Viscount, 1890–1914, vol. I

Hawarden, 7th Viscount, 1877–1958, vol. V

Haweis, Rev. Hugh Reginald, 1838–1901, vol. I

Hawes, Albert G. S., *died* 1897, vol. I

Hawes, Alexander Travers, 1851–1924, vol. II

Hawes, Col Benjamin Reddie, 1854–1941, vol. IV

Hawes, Charles George, 1890–1963, vol. VI

Hawes, Derrick Gordon H.; *see* Harington Hawes.

Hawes, Maj.-Gen. Leonard Arthur, 1892–1986, vol. VIII

Hawes, Sir Richard Brunel, 1893–1964, vol. VI

Hawes, Sir Ronald N.; *see* Nesbitt-Hawes.

Hawgood, John Arkas, 1905–1971, vol. VII

Hawk, William, 1851–1944, vol. IV

Hawke, 7th Baron, 1860–1938, vol. III

Hawke, 8th Baron, 1873–1939, vol. III

Hawke, 9th Baron, 1901–1985, vol. VIII

Hawke, Sir Anthony; *see* Hawke, Sir E. A.

Hawke, Sir Anthony; *see* Hawke, Sir J. A.

Hawke, Sir (Edward) Anthony, 1895–1964, vol. VI

Hawke, John, 1846–1932, vol. III

Hawke, Sir (John) Anthony, 1869–1941, vol. IV

Hawke, Adm. Hon. Stanhope, 1863–1936, vol. III

Hawke-Genn, Captain Otto Hermann, 1875–1955, vol. V

Hawken, Rev. Charles Sydney, 1862–1930, vol. III

Hawken, Roger William Hercules, 1878–1947, vol. IV

Hawker, Brig.-Gen. Claude Julian, 1867–1936, vol. III

Hawker, Sqdn Comdr Lanoe George, 1890–1916, vol. II

Hawker, Mary Elizabeth, 1848–1908, vol. I

Hawker, Sir Richard George, 1907–1982, vol. VIII

Hawkes, Arthur John, 1885–1952, vol. V

Hawkes, Charles John, 1880–1953, vol. V

Hawkes, Lt-Col Charles Pascoe, 1877–1956, vol. V

Hawkes, Lt-Col Corlis St Leger Gillman, 1871–1963, vol. VI

Hawkes, Frederic Clare, 1892–1974, vol. VII

Hawkes, Rt Rev. Frederick Ochterloney Taylor, 1878–1966, vol. VI

Hawkes, Maj.-Gen. Sir Henry Montague Pakington, 1855–1946, vol. IV

Hawkes, Lt-Gen. Henry Philip, 1834–1900, vol. I

Hawkes, Leonard, 1891–1981, vol. VIII

Hawkes, Ven. Leonard Stephen, 1907–1969, vol. VI

Hawkes, Captain William Arthur, 1881–1962, vol. VI

Hawkesworth, Sir (Edward) Gerald, *died* 1949, vol. IV

Hawkesworth, Geoffrey, 1904–1969, vol. VI

Hawkesworth, Sir Gerald; *see* Hawkesworth, Sir E. G.

Hawkesworth, Lt-Gen. Sir John Ledlie Inglis, 1893–1945, vol. IV

Hawkesworth, Rear-Adm. Richard Arthur, 1890–1968, vol. VI

Hawkey, Sir (Alfred) James, 1st Bt, 1877–1952, vol. V

Hawkey, Sir James; see Hawkey, Sir A. J.

Hawkey, Sir Roger Pryce, 2nd Bt, 1905–1975, vol. VII

Hawkings, Sir (Francis) Geoffrey, 1913–1990, vol. VIII

Hawkings, Sir Geoffrey; see Hawkings, Sir F. G.

Hawkins, Maj.-Gen. Alexander Caesar, 1823–1916, vol. II

Hawkins, Sir Anthony Hope, 1863–1933, vol. III

Hawkins, Arthur Vernon, died 1933, vol. III

Hawkins, Sir Benjamin, 1867–1930, vol. III

Hawkins, Brian Charles Keith, 1900–1962, vol. VI

Hawkins, Charles Caesar, 1864–1938, vol. III

Hawkins, (Clive) David B.; see Black-Hawkins.

Hawkins, David B.; see Black-Hawkins, C. D.

Hawkins, Maj.-Gen. Edward Brian Barkley, died 1966, vol. VI

Hawkins, Rev. Edwards Comerford, 1872–1906, vol. I

Hawkins, Francis Henry, 1863–1936, vol. III

Hawkins, Adm. Sir Geoffrey Alan Brooke, 1895–1980, vol. VII

Hawkins, Maj.-Gen. George Ledsam Seymour, 1898–1978, vol. VII

Hawkins, Major Henry, 1876–1930, vol. III

Hawkins, Herbert Leader, 1887–1968, vol. VI

Hawkins, Herbert Pennell, 1859–1940, vol. III

Hawkins, Jack, 1910–1973, vol. VII

Hawkins, Rev. Sir John Caesar, 4th Bt, 1837–1929, vol. III

Hawkins, Sir John Scott Caesar, 5th Bt, 1875–1939, vol. III

Hawkins, Ven. John Stanley, 1903–1965, vol. VI

Hawkins, Leonard Cecil, 1897–1974, vol. VII

Hawkins, Sir Michael Babington Charles, 1914–1977, vol. VII

Hawkins, Percy, 1870–1949, vol. IV

Hawkins, Rt Rev. Ralph Gordon, 1911–1987, vol. VIII

Hawkins, Vice-Adm. Sir Raymond Shayle, 1909–1987, vol. VIII

Hawkins, Reginald Thomas, 1888–1978, vol. VII

Hawkins, Rev. Robert Henry, 1892–1989, vol. VIII

Hawkins, Col Thomas Henry, 1873–1944, vol. IV

Hawkins, Sir Villiers Geoffry Caesar, 6th Bt, 1890–1955, vol. V

Hawkins, Col Walter Francis, 1856–1936, vol. III

Hawkins, Lt-Col William, 1861–1932, vol. III

Hawkins, William Francis Spencer, 1896–1979, vol. VII

Hawks, Ellison, 1889–1971, vol. VII

Hawkshaw, John Clarke, 1841–1921, vol. II

Hawksley, Dorothy Webster, 1884–1970, vol. VI

Hawksley, Ernest B., died 1931, vol. III

Hawksley, Vice-Adm. James Rose Price, died 1955, vol. V

Hawksley, Brig.-Gen. Randal Plunkett Taylor, 1870–1961, vol. VI

Hawksley, Richard Walter Benson, 1915–1976, vol. VII

Hawksworth, Frederick William, 1884–1976, vol. VII

Hawksworth, William Thomas Martin, died 1935, vol. III

Hawley, Arthur, 1870–1952, vol. V

Hawley, Rev. Charles Cusac, 1851–1914, vol. I

Hawley, Major Sir David Henry, 7th Bt, 1913–1988, vol. VIII

Hawley, Sir Henry Cusack Wingfield, 6th Bt, 1876–1923, vol. II

Hawley, Sir Henry James, 4th Bt, 1815–1898, vol. I

Hawley, Sir Henry Michael, 5th Bt, 1848–1909, vol. I

Hawley, Maj.-Gen. William Hanbury, 1829–1917, vol. II

Hawley, Willis Chatman, 1864–1941, vol. IV

Haworth, Sir Arthur Adlington, 1st Bt, 1865–1944, vol. IV

Haworth, Sir (Arthur) Geoffrey, 2nd Bt, 1896–1987, vol. VIII

Haworth, Sir Geoffrey; see Haworth, Sir A. G.

Haworth, Rev. James, 1853–1942, vol. IV

Haworth, James, 1896–1976, vol. VII

Haworth, Very Rev. Kenneth William, 1903–1988, vol. VIII

Haworth, Lt-Col Sir Lionel Berkeley Holt, 1873–1951, vol. V

Haworth, Sir Norman; see Haworth, Sir W. N.

Haworth, Peter, 1891–1956, vol. V

Haworth, Robert Downs, 1898–1990, vol. VIII

Haworth, Sir (Walter) Norman, 1883–1950, vol. IV

Haworth, Very Rev. William, 1880–1960, vol. V

Haworth, Hon. Sir William Crawford, 1905–1984, vol. VIII

Haworth-Booth, Rear-Adm. Sir Francis Fitzgerald, 1864–1935, vol. III

Hawser, (Cyril) Lewis, 1916–1990, vol. VIII

Hawser, Lewis; see Hawser, C. L.

Hawtayne, George Hammond, 1832–1902, vol. I

Hawtayne, Lionel Edward, died 1920, vol. II

Hawthorn, Maj.-Gen. Douglas Cyril, 1897–1974, vol. VII

Hawthorn, Bt-Col Frank, died 1931, vol. III

Hawthorn, Brig.-Gen. George Montague Philip, 1873–1945, vol. IV

Hawthorne, Julian, 1846–1934, vol. III

Hawton, Sir John Malcolm Kenneth, 1904–1982, vol. VIII

Hawtrey, Sir Charles, 1858–1923, vol. II

Hawtrey, Brig. Henry Courtenay, 1882–1961, vol. VI

Hawtrey, Air Vice-Marshal John Gosset, 1901–1954, vol. V

Hawtrey, Sir Ralph George, 1879–1975, vol. VII

Hawtrey, Stephen Charles, 1907–1990, vol. VIII

Hay, Sir (Alan) Philip, 1918–1986, vol. VIII

Hay, Col (Alexander S.) Leith, 1818–1900, vol. I

Hay, Alfred, 1866–1932, vol. III

Hay, Hon. Alistair George, 1861–1929, vol. III

Hay, Major Hon. Arthur, 1855–1932, vol. III

Hay, Maj.-Gen. Arthur Kenneth, died 1949, vol. IV

Hay, Lt-Col Arthur Sidney, 1879–1940, vol. III

Hay, Athole S., 1861–1933, vol. III

Hay, Sir Bache McEvers Athole, 11th Bt (cr 1635), 1892–1966, vol. VI

Hay, Charles Edward Norman L.; see Leith-Hay.

Hay, Maj.-Gen. Charles John Bruce, 1877–1940, vol. III

Hay, Sir Charles John D.; *see* Dalrymple Hay.
Hay, Hon. Claude George Drummond, 1862–1920, vol. II
Hay, Clifford Henderson, 1878–1949, vol. IV
Hay, Sir David Allan, 1878–1957, vol. V
Hay, Douglas, *died* 1949, vol. IV
Hay, Sir Duncan Edwyn, 10th Bt (*cr* 1635), 1882–1965, vol. VI
Hay, Ven. Edgar, 1863–1949, vol. IV
Hay, Lord Edward Douglas John, 1888–1944, vol. IV
Hay, Sir Edward Hamilton, 9th Bt (*cr* 1703), 1870–1936, did not prove his succession or use the title, and did not have an entry in Who's Who.
Hay, Maj.-Gen. Edward Owen, 1846–1946, vol. IV
Hay, Francis Edward Drummond-, 1868–1943, vol. IV
Hay, Sir Francis Ringler Drummond-, 1830–1905, vol. I
Hay, Francis Stuart, 1863–1928, vol. II
Hay, Sir Frederick Baden-Powell, 10th Bt, 1900–1985, vol. VIII
Hay, George, *died* 1912, vol. I
Hay, Col Sir George Jackson, 1840–1921, vol. II
Hay, Col George Lennox, 1873–1946, vol. IV
Hay, Sir Harley Hugh D.; *see* Dalrymple-Hay.
Hay, Sir Hector Maclean, 7th Bt (*cr* 1703), 1821–1916, vol. II
Hay, Henry Hanby, 1849–1940, vol. III
Hay, Ian; *see* Beith, Maj.-Gen. J. H.
Hay, Col James, 1842–1915, vol. I
Hay, Col James Adam Gordon Richardson-Drummond-, 1863–1928, vol. II
Hay, Col James Charles Edward, 1889–1975, vol. VII
Hay, Sir James Lawrence, 1888–1971, vol. VII
Hay, James Paterson, 1863–1925, vol. II
Hay, Brig.-Gen. James Reginald Maitland Dalrymple, 1858–1924, vol. II
Hay, Sir James Shaw, 1839–1924, vol. II
Hay, Hon. Col John, 1838–1905, vol. I
Hay, Rt Hon. Lord John, 1827–1916, vol. II
Hay, John, 1873–1959, vol. V
Hay, John Arthur Machray, 1887–1960, vol. V
Hay, John Binny, 1870–1939, vol. III
Hay, Rt Hon. Sir John Charles Dalrymple, 3rd Bt (*cr* 1798), 1821–1912, vol. I
Hay, Sir John George, 1883–1964, vol. VI
Hay, Captain John Primrose, 1878–1949, vol. IV
Hay, Paymaster Rear-Adm. Kenneth Sydney, 1872–1932, vol. III
Hay, Col Leith; *see* Hay, Col A. S. L.
Hay, Sir Lewis John Erroll, 9th Bt (*cr* 1663), 1866–1923, vol. II
Hay of Seaton, Major Malcolm Vivian, 1881–1962, vol. VI
Hay, Lady Margaret Katharine, 1918–1975, vol. VII
Hay, Marie, 1873–1938, vol. III
Hay, Mrs Mary Verena Campbell, 1875–1940, vol. III
Hay, Matthew, 1855–1932, vol. III
Hay, Noel Grant, 1910–1974, vol. VII
Hay, Peter Alexander, 1866–1952, vol. V
Hay, Sir Philip; *see* Hay, Sir A. P.
Hay, Lt-Gen. Sir Robert, 1889–1980, vol. VII
Hay, Robert Edwin, (Roy), 1910–1989, vol. VIII

Hay, Sir Robert Hay-Drummond-, 1846–1926, vol. II
Hay, Lt-Gen. Sir Robert John, 1828–1910, vol. I
Hay, Rt Rev. Robert Milton, 1884–1973, vol. VII
Hay, Rt Rev. Robert Snowdon, 1867–1943, vol. IV
Hay, Brig. Ronald Bruce, 1887–1961, vol. VI
Hay, Sir Ronald Nelson, 11th Bt, 1910–1988, vol. VIII
Hay, Roy; *see* Hay, Robert E.
Hay, Lt-Col Sir Rupert; *see* Hay, Lt-Col Sir W. R.
Hay, Stephen Moffatt, 1857–1943, vol. IV
Hay, Thomas, *died* 1953, vol. V
Hay, Lt-Col Thomas William, 1882–1956, vol. V
Hay, Col Westwood Norman, 1871–1946, vol. IV
Hay, Will, 1888–1949, vol. IV
Hay, Sir William Archibald Dalrymple, 4th Bt (*cr* 1798), 1851–1929, vol. III
Hay, William Gosse, 1875–1945, vol. IV
Hay, Sir William Henry, 8th Bt (*cr* 1703), 1867–1927, vol. II, vol. IV
Hay, Lt-Col Sir (William) Rupert, 1893–1962, vol. VI
Hay-Dinwoody, Very Rev. Leofric Matthews, 1868–1936, vol. III
Hay-Drummond, Arthur William Henry, 1862–1953, vol. V
Hay-Drummond, Col Hon. Charles Rowley, 1836–1918, vol. II
Hay-Drummond-Hay, Sir Robert; *see* Hay.
Hay-Newton, Francis John Stuart, 1843–1913, vol. I
Hayashi, Gonsuke, 1861–1939, vol. III
Hayashi, Count Tadasu, 1850–1913, vol. I
Haycock, Alexander Wilkinson, 1882–1970, vol. VI
Haycock, Rev. Trevitt Reginald H.; *see* Hine-Haycock.
Haycock, Col Vaughan Randolph H.; *see* Hine-Haycock.
Haycocks, Norman, 1907–1982, vol. VIII
Haycraft, John Berry, *died* 1922, vol. II
Haycraft, John Berry, 1888–1969, vol. VI
Haycraft, Sir Thomas Wagstaffe, *died* 1936, vol. III
Hayday, Arthur, 1869–1956, vol. V
Hayday, Sir Frederick, 1912–1990, vol. VIII
Hayden, Arthur, 1868–1946, vol. IV
Hayden, Sir Henry Hubert, 1869–1923, vol. II
Hayden, John Patrick, 1863–1954, vol. V
Hayden, Luke Patrick, 1850–1897, vol. I
Hayden, Mary Teresa, *died* 1942, vol. IV
Hayden, Most Rev. William, 1868–1936, vol. III
Haydn Williams, Benjamin, 1902–1965, vol. VI
Haydon, Dame Anne, 1892–1966, vol. VI
Haydon, Arthur Lincoln, 1872–1954, vol. V
Haydon, Denis Arthur, 1930–1988, vol. VIII
Haydon, Maj.-Gen. Joseph Charles, 1899–1970, vol. VI
Haydon, Thomas Edmett, *died* 1952, vol. V
Haydon-Lewis, Jack; *see* Lewis.
Hayes, Alfred, 1857–1936, vol. III
Hayes, Rev. Arthur Herbert, 1850–1933, vol. III
Hayes, Surg.-Lt-Col Aylmer Ellis, 1850–1900, vol. I
Hayes, Cdre Sir Bertram Fox, 1864–1941, vol. IV
Hayes, Carlton Joseph Huntley, 1882–1964, vol. VI
Hayes, Claude, 1852–1922, vol. II
Hayes, Sir Edmund Francis, 5th Bt, 1850–1912, vol. I
Hayes, Edwin, 1819–1904, vol. I

Hayes, Lt-Col Edwin Charles, 1868–1942, vol. IV
Hayes, Maj.-Gen. Eric Charles, 1896–1951, vol. V
Hayes, Rev. Francis Carlile, died 1931, vol. III
Hayes, Frederick William, 1848–1914, vol. II
Hayes, Gerald Ravenscourt, 1889–1955, vol. V
Hayes, Gertrude, (Mrs E. M. Betts), 1872–1956, vol. V
Hayes, Hugh, died 1928, vol. II, vol. III
Hayes, Rt Rev. James Thomas, 1847–1904, vol. I
Hayes, John, vol. II
Hayes, Hon. John Blyth, 1868–1956, vol. V
Hayes, John Henry, 1889–1941, vol. IV
Hayes, Lt-Col Joseph, 1864–1944, vol. IV
Hayes, Maurice Richard Joseph, died 1930, vol. III
Hayes, Michael, 1889–1976, vol. VII
Hayes, His Eminence Patrick Cardinal, 1867–1938, vol. III
Hayes, Very Rev. Richard, 1854–1938, vol. III
Hayes, Robert Edward, 1869–1931, vol. III
Hayes, Lt-Col Robert Hall, 1867–1946, vol. IV
Hayes, Rt Rev. Romuald, 1892–1945, vol. IV
Hayes, Sir Samuel Hercules, 1840–1901, vol. I
Hayes, Thomas Crawford, died 1909, vol. I
Hayes, Thomas William Henry, 1912–1989, vol. VIII
Hayes, Brig.-Gen. Wade Hampton, 1879–1956, vol. V
Hayes, Captain William, 1891–1918, vol. II
Hayes, William, 1855–1940, vol. III
Hayford, John Fillmore, 1868–1925, vol. II, vol. III
Haygarth, Col Sir Joseph Henry, 1892–1969, vol. VI
Haygarth Jackson, Harold; see Jackson.
Hayhurst, William Hosken France-, 1873–1947, vol. IV
Hayhurst-France, Captain George Frederick Hayhurst, 1895–1940, vol. III
Hayler, Guy, 1850–1943, vol. IV
Hayley, Frederic Austin, 1881–1968, vol. VI
Hayman, Sir (Cecil George) Graham, 1893–1966, vol. VI
Hayman, Frank Harold, 1894–1966, vol. VI
Hayman, Sir Graham; see Hayman, Sir C. G. G.
Hayman, Rev. Henry, 1823–1904, vol. I
Hayman, Rev. Canon Henry Telford, 1853–1941, vol. IV
Hayman, Perceval Mills Cobham, 1883–1974, vol. VII
Hayman, Ven. Reginald John Edward, 1861–1927, vol. II
Hayman-Joyce, Maj.-Gen. Hayman John, 1897–1958, vol. V
Haymes, Lt-Col Robert Leycester, 1870–1942, vol. IV
Hayne, Louis Brightwell, 1869–1926, vol. II
Haynes, Col Alleyne, 1859–1938, vol. III
Haynes, Alwyn Sidney, 1878–1963, vol. VI
Haynes, Col Charles Edward, 1855–1935, vol. III
Haynes, Edmund Sidney Pollock, 1877–1949, vol. IV
Haynes, Sir George Ernest, 1902–1983, vol. VIII
Haynes, Brig.-Gen. Kenneth Edward, 1871–1944, vol. IV
Haynes, Richard Septimus, 1857–1922, vol. II
Haynes, Robert, 1920–1976, vol. VII
Haynes, Hon. Samuel Johnson, 1852–1932, vol. III

Haynes, Rear-Adm. William Allen, 1913–1985, vol. VIII
Haynes-Rudge, Mrs Florence, died 1934, vol. III
Haynes-Williams, John, died 1908, vol. I
Hays, Arthur Garfield, 1881–1954, vol. V
Hays, Very Rev. Francis, 1870–1943, vol. IV
Hays, Sir Marshall, 1872–1948, vol. IV
Hays, Will H., 1879–1954, vol. V
Haysom, Sir George, 1862–1924, vol. II
Hayter, 1st Baron, 1848–1946, vol. IV
Hayter, 2nd Baron, 1871–1967, vol. VI
Hayter, Harrison, 1825–1898, vol. I
Hayter, Rev. Harrison Goodenough, 1855–1934, vol. III
Hayter, Brig. Ross John Finnis, 1875–1929, vol. III
Hayter, Stanley William, 1901–1988, vol. VIII
Hayter, Sir William Goodenough, 1869–1924, vol. II
Hayter, Rev. William Thomas Baring, 1858–1935, vol. III
Hayter Hames, Sir George Colvile, 1898–1968, vol. VI
Haythornthwaite, Rev. John Parker, 1862–1928, vol. II
Hayward, Sir Alfred, 1896–1988, vol. VIII
Hayward, Alfred Robert, 1875–1971, vol. VII
Hayward, Arthur Canler, 1870–1945, vol. IV
Hayward, Arthur Lawrence, 1885–1967, vol. VI
Hayward, Sir Charles William, 1892–1983, vol. VIII
Hayward, Rev. Edward, 1884–1974, vol. VII
Hayward, Sir Edward Waterfield, 1903–1983, vol. VIII
Hayward, Sir Edwin James, 1868–1929, vol. III
Hayward, Lt-Col Edwyn Walton, died 1933, vol. III
Hayward, Evan, 1876–1958, vol. V
Hayward, Sir Fred, 1876–1944, vol. IV
Hayward, Frederick Edward Godfrey, 1893–1961, vol. VI
Hayward, Graham William, 1911–1976, vol. VII
Hayward, Maj.-Gen. Henry Blakeney, 1838–1930, vol. III
Hayward, Ven. Henry Rudge, died 1912, vol. I
Hayward, Ian Dudley, 1899–1964, vol. VI
Hayward, Sir Isaac James, 1884–1976, vol. VII
Hayward, John Davy, 1905–1965, vol. VI
Hayward, Marjorie Olive, 1885–1953, vol. V
Hayward, Sir Maurice Henry Weston, 1868–1964, vol. VI
Hayward, Lt-Col Reginald Frederick Johnson, died 1970, vol. VI
Hayward, Richard Frederick, 1879–1962, vol. VI
Hayward, Robert Baldwin, 1829–1903, vol. I
Hayward, Sidney Pascoe, 1896–1961, vol. VI
Hayward, Tom Christopher, 1904–1975, vol. VII
Hayward, William Thornborough, 1854–1928, vol. II
Hayward, Sir William Webb, 1818–1899, vol. I
Haywood, Col Austin Hubert Wightwick, died 1965, vol. VI
Haywood, Horace Mason, died 1942, vol. IV
Hazan, Hon. Sir John Boris Roderick, 1926–1988, vol VIII
Hazel, Alfred Ernest William, died 1944, vol. IV
Hazeldine, Evelyn Lilian; see Martinengo-Cesaresco, Countess.
Hazell, W. Howard, 1869–1929, vol. III

Hazell, Walter, 1843–1919, vol. II
Hazell, Captain William, 1857–1927, vol. II
Hazeltine, Harold Dexter, 1871–1960, vol. V
Hazelton, Maj.-Gen. Percy Orr, 1871–1952, vol. V
Hazen, Hon. Sir Douglas; *see* Hazen, Hon. Sir J. D.
Hazen, Hon. Sir (John) Douglas, 1860–1937, vol. III
Hazlehurst, Rev. George Arthur, 1873–1940, vol. III
Hazlehurst, Thomas Francis, *died* 1918, vol. II
Hazlerigg, 1st Baron, 1878–1949, vol. IV
Hazlerigg, Lt-Col Thomas, 1877–1935, vol. III
Hazlerigg, Maj.-Gen. Thomas Maynard, 1840–1915, vol. I
Hazleton, Richard, 1880–1943, vol. IV
Hazlitt, William Carew, 1834–1913, vol. I
Head, 1st Viscount, 1906–1983, vol. VIII
Head, Lt-Col Alfred Searle, 1874–1952, vol. V
Head, Alice Maud, 1886–1981, vol. VIII
Head, Lt-Col Arthur Edward Maxwell, 1876–1921, vol. II
Head, Barclay Vincent, 1844–1914, vol. I
Head, Lt-Col Charles Octavius, 1869–1952, vol. V
Head, Ernest, 1871–1923, vol. II
Head, Francis Somerville Cameron C.; *see* Cameron-Head.
Head, Most Rev. Frederick Waldegrave, 1874–1941, vol. IV
Head, Rev. Canon George Frederick, 1836–1912, vol. I
Head, George Herbert, *died* 1927, vol. II
Head, Sir Henry, 1861–1940, vol. III
Head, James C.; *see* Cameron-Head.
Head, John Joshua, 1838–1925, vol. II
Head, Leslie Charles B.; *see* Broughton-Head.
Head, Robert, *died* 1957, vol. V
Head, Sir Robert Garnett, 3rd Bt, 1845–1907, vol. I
Head, Sir (Robert Pollock) Somerville, 4th Bt, 1884–1924, vol. II
Head, Sir Somerville; *see* Head, Sir R. P. S.
Headfort, 4th Marquess of, 1878–1943, vol. IV
Headfort, 5th Marquess of, 1902–1960, vol. V
Heading, Sir James Alfred, 1884–1969, vol. VI (AII)
Headington, Arthur Hutton, 1878–1917, vol. II
Headington, Kenneth George John, 1898–1960, vol. V
Headlam, Rt Rev. Arthur Cayley, 1862–1947, vol. IV
Headlam, Rev. Arthur William, 1826–1909, vol. I
Headlam, Cecil, 1872–1934, vol. III
Headlam, Lt-Col Rt Hon. Sir Cuthbert Morley, 1st Bt, 1876–1964, vol. VI
Headlam, Captain Sir Edward James, 1873–1943, vol. IV
Headlam, Francis John, 1829–1908, vol. I
Headlam, Air Vice-Marshal Frank, 1914–1976, vol. VII
Headlam, Gerald Erskine, 1877–1954, vol. V
Headlam, Brig.-Gen. Hugh Roger, 1877–1955, vol. V
Headlam, Maj.-Gen. Sir John Emerson Wharton, 1864–1946, vol. IV
Headlam, Maurice Francis, 1873–1956, vol. V
Headlam, Rev. Canon Morley Lewis Caulfield, 1868–1953, vol. V
Headlam, Rev. Stewart Duckworth, *died* 1924, vol. II
Headlam, Walter George, 1866–1908, vol. I
Headlam-Morley, Agnes, 1902–1986, vol. VIII

Headlam-Morley, Sir James Wycliffe, 1863–1929, vol. III
Headlam-Morley, Kenneth Arthur Sonntag, 1901–1982, vol. VIII
Headland, Isaac Taylor, 1859–1942, vol. IV
Headland, John, 1840–1927, vol. II
Headley, 4th Baron, 1845–1913, vol. I
Headley, 5th Baron, 1855–1935, vol. III
Headley, 6th Baron, 1901–1969, vol. VI
Headley, Ven. Charles Theophilus, 1870–1930, vol. III
Headridge, David, 1869–1938, vol. III
Heaf, Frederick Roland George, 1894–1973, vol. VII
Heakes, Air Vice-Marshal Francis Vernon, 1894–1989, vol. VIII
Heal, Sir Ambrose, 1872–1959, vol. V
Heald, Sir Benjamin Herbert, 1874–1940, vol. III
Heald, Charles Brehmer, 1882–1974, vol. VII
Heald, Edith Shackleton, *died* 1976, vol. VII
Heald, Henry Townley, 1904–1975, vol. VII
Heald, Rt Hon. Sir Lionel Frederick, 1897–1981, vol. VIII
Heald, Nora Shackleton, *died* 1961, vol. VI
Heald, William, 1910–1980, vol. VII
Heale, Lt-Col Robert John Wingfield, 1876–1962, vol. VI
Healey, Col. Charles, 1856–1939, vol. III
Healey, Sir Charles Arthur C.; *see* Chadwyck-Healey.
Healey, Sir Charles Edward Heley C.; *see* Chadwyck-Healey.
Healey, Col Coryndon William Rutherford, 1864–1953, vol. V
Healey, Donald Mitchell, 1898–1988, vol. VIII
Healey, Sir Edward Randal C.; *see* Chadwyck-Healey.
Healey, Sir Gerald Edward C.; *see* Chadwyck-Healey.
Healey, Rt Rev. Kenneth, 1899–1985, vol. VIII
Healey, Oliver Nowell C.; *see* Chadwyck-Healey.
Healey-Kay, Patrick; *see* Dolin, Sir Anton.
Healy, Cahir, 1877–1970, vol. VI
Healy, Daniel, 1884–1962, vol. VI
Healy, Rev. George White, *died* 1943, vol. IV
Healy, Most Rev. John, 1841–1918, vol. II
Healy, Ven. John, 1850–1942, vol. IV
Healy, John Edward, *died* 1934, vol. III
Healy, Rt Rev. John F., 1900–1973, vol. VII
Healy, Maurice, 1859–1923, vol. II
Healy, Maurice, 1887–1943, vol. IV
Healy, Thomas Joseph, 1854–1925, vol. II
Healy, Timothy Michael, 1855–1931, vol. III
Hean, Hon. Alexander, 1859–1927, vol. II
Heane, Brig.-Gen. James, 1874–1954, vol. V
Heaney, Brig. George Frederick, 1897–1983, vol. VIII
Heape, Walter, 1855–1929, vol. III
Heape, William Leslie, 1896–1972, vol. VII
Heard, Gerald; *see* Heard, H. F. G.
Heard, Henry Fitz Gerald, 1889–1971, vol. VII
Heard, Rev. Henry James, 1856–1931, vol. III
Heard, Adm. Hugh Lindsay Patrick, 1869–1954, vol. V
Heard, Brig. Leonard Ferguson, 1903–1976, vol. VII

Heard, Maj.-Gen. Richard, 1870–1950, vol. IV

Heard, Rev. Richard Grenville, *died* 1952, vol. V

Heard, Rev. William Augustus, 1847–1921, vol. II

Heard, His Eminence Cardinal William Theodore, 1884–1973, vol. VII

Hearle, Col Arthur Basset, 1884–1935, vol. III

Hearle, Francis Trounson, 1886–1965, vol. VI

Hearn, Sir Arthur Charles, 1877–1952, vol. V

Hearn, Col George William Richard, 1893–1973, vol. VII

Hearn, Col Sir Gordon Risley, 1871–1953, vol. V

Hearn, John Whitcombe, 1885–1968, vol. VI

Hearn, Lafcadio, 1850–1904, vol. I

Hearn, Rt Rev. Robert Thomas, *died* 1952, vol. V

Hearn, Sir Walter Risley, 1853–1930, vol. III

Hearne, Sir Hector, 1892–1962, vol. VI

Hearnshaw, Fossey John Cobb, 1869–1946, vol. IV

Hearson, Air Cdre John Glanville, 1883–1964, vol. VI

Hearst, Hon. Sir William Howard, 1864–1941, vol. IV

Hearst, William Randolph, 1863–1951, vol. V

Heartz, Hon. Frank Richard, 1871–1955, vol. V

Heaslett, Rt Rev. Samuel, 1875–1947, vol. IV

Heath, Albert Edward, 1887–1956, vol. V

Heath, Ambrose, 1891–1969, vol. VI

Heath, Archie Edward, 1887–1961, vol. VI

Heath, Arthur Douglas, *died* 1937, vol. III

Heath, Arthur Howard, 1856–1930, vol. III

Heath, Arthur Raymond, *died* 1943, vol. IV

Heath, Sir Barrie, 1916–1988, vol. VIII

Heath, Maj.-Gen. Sir Charles Ernest, 1854–1936, vol. III

Heath, Charles Joseph, 1856–1934, vol. III

Heath, Christopher, 1835–1905, vol. I

Heath, Cuthbert Eden, *died* 1939, vol. III

Heath, Col Edward, 1854–1927, vol. II

Heath, Col Edward Charles, 1873–1946, vol. IV

Heath, Francis George, 1843–1913, vol. I

Heath, Lt-Col Francis William, 1865–1936, vol. III

Heath, Sir Frank; *see* Heath, Sir H. F.

Heath, Col George Noah, 1881–1967, vol. VI

Heath, Maj.-Gen. Sir Gerard Moore, 1863–1929, vol. III

Heath, Maj.-Gen. Gerard William Egerton, 1897–1980, vol. VII

Heath, Harry Cecil, 1898–1972, vol. VII

Heath, Col Harry Heptinstall Rose, 1850–1922, vol. II

Heath, Sir (Henry) Frank, 1863–1946, vol. IV

Heath, Maj.-Gen. Henry Newport Charles, 1860–1915, vol. I

Heath, Adm. Sir Herbert Leopold, 1861–1954, vol. V

Heath, Sir James, 1st Bt, 1852–1942, vol. IV

Heath, Lt-Col John Macclesfield, 1843–1911, vol. I

Heath, Adm. Sir Leopold George, 1817–1907, vol. I

Heath, Lt-Gen. Sir Lewis Macclesfield, 1885–1954, vol. V

Heath, Robert Samuel, 1858–1931, vol. III

Heath, Brig.-Gen. Ronald Macclesfield, 1876–1942, vol. IV

Heath, Sir Thomas Little, 1861–1940, vol. III

Heath, Rear-Adm. William Andrew James, 1820–1903, vol. I

Heath-Caldwell, Maj.-Gen. Frederick Crofton, 1858–1945, vol. IV

Heath-Gracie, George Handel, 1892–1987, vol. VIII

Heath-Jones, Edgar, *died* 1949, vol. IV

Heathcoat-Amory, Sir Ian Murray Heathcoat, 2nd Bt; *see* Amory.

Heathcoat-Amory, Major Sir John, 3rd Bt; *see* Amory.

Heathcoat-Amory, Sir John Heathcoat, 1st Bt, 1829–1914, vol. I

Heathcoat-Amory, Sir William, 5th Bt, 1901–1982, vol. VIII

Heathcote, Lt Alfred Spencer, *died* 1912, vol. I

Heathcote, Brig.-Gen. Charles Edensor, 1875–1947, vol. IV

Heathcote, Rt Rev. Sir Francis Cooke Caulfeild, 9th Bt, 1868–1961, vol. VI

Heathcote, Lt-Col Sir Gilbert Redvers, 8th Bt, 1854–1937, vol. III

Heathcote, John Norman, 1863–1946, vol. IV

Heathcote, Justinian Heathcote Edwards-, 1843–1928, vol. II

Heathcote, Sir Leonard Vyvyan, 10th Bt, 1885–1963, vol. VI

Heathcote, Reginald St Alban, 1888–1951, vol. V

Heathcote, Robert Evelyn Manners, 1884–1970, vol. VI

Heathcote, Rev. Sir William Arthur, 7th Bt, 1853–1924, vol. II

Heathcote, Sir William Perceval, 6th Bt, 1826–1903, vol. I

Heathcote-Drummond-Willoughby, Brig.-Gen. Hon. Charles Strathavon; *see* Willoughby.

Heathcote-Smith, Sir Clifford Edward, 1883–1963, vol. VI

Heathcote-Williams, Harold, 1896–1964, vol. VI

Heather, Very Rev. George Abraham, *died* 1907, vol. I

Heather, Henry James Shedlock, 1863–1939, vol. III(A), vol. IV

Heathershaw, James Thomas, 1871–1943, vol. IV

Heatley, David Playfair, 1867–1944, vol. IV

Heatly-Spencer, Col John, 1880–1946, vol. IV

Heaton, Sir Frederick; *see* Heaton, Sir J. F.

Heaton, Gwenllian Margaret, 1897–1979, vol. VII

Heaton, Herbert, 1890–1973, vol. VII

Heaton, Sir Herbert Henniker, 1880–1961, vol. VI

Heaton, Sir (John) Frederick, 1880–1949, vol. IV

Heaton, Sir John Henniker, 1st Bt, 1848–1914, vol. I

Heaton, Sir John Henniker, 2nd Bt, 1877–1963, vol. VI

Heaton, Sir (John Victor) Peregrine Henniker-, 3rd Bt, 1903–1971, vol. VII

Heaton, Sir Joseph John, 1860–1934, vol. III

Heaton, Joseph Rowland, 1881–1951, vol. V

Heaton, Sir Peregrine Henniker; *see* Heaton, Sir J. V. P. H.

Heaton, Raymond H.; *see* Henniker-Heaton.

Heaton, Rose Henniker, (Mrs Adrian Porter), 1884–1975, vol. VII

Heaton, Trevor Braby, 1886–1972, vol. VII

Heaton, William Haslam, *died* 1941, vol. IV

Heaton-Armstrong, Sir John Dunamace, 1888–1967, vol. VI

Heaton-Armstrong, William Charles, 1853–1917, vol. II

Heaton-Ellis, Lt-Col Sir Charles Henry Brabazon, 1864–1945, vol. IV

Heaton-Ellis, Vice-Adm. Sir Edward Henry Fitzhardinge, 1868–1943, vol. IV

Heaven, Rev. Hudson Grosett, 1826–1916, vol. II

Heaven, Joseph Robert, 1840–1911, vol. I

Heaviside, Arthur West, 1844–1923, vol. II

Heaviside, Oliver, 1850–1925, vol. II

Heawood, Edward, 1863–1949, vol. IV

Heawood, Geoffrey Leonard, 1893–1982, vol. VIII

Heawood, Percy John, 1861–1955, vol. V

Hebb, Donald Olding, 1904–1985, vol. VIII

Hebb, Rev. Harry Arthur, 1850–1934, vol. III

Hebb, Sir John Harry, 1878–1942, vol. IV

Hebb, R. G., died 1918, vol. II

Hebblethwaite, Percival, 1849–1922, vol. II

Hebblethwaite, Sidney Horace, 1914–1987, vol. VIII

Hebden, George Brentnall, 1886–1968, vol. VI

Hebel, John William, 1891–1934, vol. III

Heber-Percy, Algernon; see Percy.

Heberden, Charles Buller, 1849–1921, vol. II

Heberden, Surg. Captain George Alfred, 1860–1916, vol. II

Heberden, William Buller, 1838–1922, vol. II

Hebert, Godfrey Taunton, died 1957, vol. V

Hebert, Louis Philippe, 1850–1917, vol. II

Hebrard, Emile A., 1862–1927, vol. II

Hechle, James Herbert, 1864–1935, vol. III

Hecker, William Rundle, 1899–1983, vol. VIII

Heckle, Arnold, 1906–1982, vol. VIII

Heckstall-Smith, Major Brooke, 1869–1944, vol. IV

Heckstall-Smith, Hugh William, 1896–1973, vol. VII

Hector, Annie, (Mrs Alexander), 1825–1902, vol. I

Hector, Sir James, 1834–1907, vol. I

Hedderwick, Arthur Stuart, 1885–1939, vol. III

Hedderwick, Edwin Charles, 1850–1935, vol. III

Hedderwick, Thomas Charles Hunter, 1850–1918, vol. II

Heddle, (Bentley) John, 1941–1989, vol. VIII

Heddle, John; see Heddle, B. J.

Hedgcock, Frank Arthur, 1875–1954, vol. V

Hedgcock, Walter W., died 1932, vol. III

Hedgeland, Rev. Philip, 1825–1911, vol. I

Hedges, Alfred Paget, 1867–1929, vol. III

Hedges, Frederick Albert M.; see Mitchell-Hedges.

Hedges, John, 1847–1934, vol. III

Hedges, Sir John Francis, 1917–1983, vol. VIII

Hedges, Killingworth, died 1945, vol. IV

Hedges, Brig. Killingworth Michael Fentham, 1890–1969, vol. VI

Hedges, Robert Yorke, 1903–1963, vol. VI

Hedges, Sidney George, 1897–1974, vol. VII

Hedin, Sven Anders, 1865–1952, vol. V

Hedley, Col Sir Coote; see Hedley, Col Sir W. C.

Hedley, Hilda Mabel, 1918–1988, vol. VIII

Hedley, John, 1834–1916, vol. II

Hedley, Rt Rev. John Cuthbert, 1837–1915, vol. I

Hedley, John Prescott, 1876–1957, vol. V

Hedley, Lt-Col John Ralph, 1871–1917, vol. II

Hedley, Ralph, 1851–1913, vol. I

Hedley, Maj.-Gen. Robert Cecil Osborne, 1900–1973, vol. VII

Hedley, Walter, 1879–1951, vol. V

Hedley, Col Sir (Walter) Coote, 1865–1937, vol. III

Hedley-Whyte, Angus, 1897–1971, vol. VII

Hedstrom, Sir (John) Maynard, 1872–1951, vol. V

Hedstrom, Sir (John) Maynard, 1908–1983, vol. VIII

Hedstrom, Sir Maynard; see Hedstrom, Sir J. M.

Hedworth, Rev. Thomas, died 1950, vol. IV

Heelis, Frederick, 1868–1930, vol. III

Heenan, His Eminence Cardinal John Carmel, 1905–1975, vol. VII

Heenan, Sir Joseph William Allan, 1888–1951, vol. V

Heenan, Hon. Peter, 1875–1948, vol. IV

Heeney, Arnold Danford Patrick, 1902–1970, vol. VI

Heffernan, Sir John Harold, 1834–1921, vol. II

Heffernan, Col Nesbitt Breillat, 1861–1930, vol. III

Hegan, Col Edward, 1855–1922, vol. II

Hegarty, Sir Daniel, 1849–1914, vol. I

Hegedus, Ferencz, 1881–1944, vol. IV

Heger, Paul, 1846–1925, vol. II

Heger, Robert, 1886–1978, vol. VII

Heggs, Gordon Barrett M.; see Mitchell-Heggs.

Hehir, Maj.-Gen. Sir Patrick, 1859–1937, vol. III

Heidegger, Martin, 1889–1976, vol. VII

Heidenstam, Karl Gustaf Verner von, 1859–1940, vol. III

Heifetz, Jascha, 1901–1987, vol. VIII

Heilbron, Sir Ian, 1886–1959, vol. V

Heilbronn, Hans Arnold, 1908–1975, vol. VII

Heilbuth, George Henry, died 1942, vol. IV

Heilgers, Lt-Col Frank Frederick Alexander, 1892–1944, vol. IV

Heilpern, Godfrey, 1911–1973, vol. VII

Hein, Sir (Charles Henri) Raymond, 1901–1983, vol. VIII

Hein, Sir Raymond; see Hein, Sir C. H. R.

Heinemann, William, 1863–1920, vol. II

Heinz, Henry John, II, 1908–1987, vol. VIII

Heinz, Howard, 1877–1941, vol. IV

Heinze, Sir Bernard Thomas, 1894–1982, vol. VIII

Heisenberg, Werner Karl, 1901–1976, vol. VII

Heiser, Rev. Canon F. B., died 1952, vol. V

Heiser, Victor George, 1873–1972, vol. VII

Heitland, M. (Margaret), 1860–1938, vol. III

Heitler, Walter Heinrich, 1904–1981, vol. VIII

Heitner, H. Jesse, 1893–1965, vol. VI

Hektoen, Ludvig, 1863–1951, vol. V

Helbert, Lt-Col Geoffrey Gladstone, died 1934, vol. III

Helder, Augustus, 1827–1906, vol. I

Hele, Thomas Shirley, 1881–1953, vol. V

Hele-Shaw, Henry Selby, 1854–1941, vol. IV

Helfrich, Adm. Conrad Emile Lambert, 1886–1962, vol. VI

Hellard, Frederick, 1850–1925, vol. II

Hellard, Col Robert Charles, 1851–1929, vol. III

Heller, Hans, 1905–1974, vol. VII

Heller, J. H. S.; see Heller, Hans.

Helleu, Paul-César, 1859–1927, vol. II

Hellier, John Banjamin, died 1924, vol. II

Hellings, Gen. Sir Peter William Cradock, 1916–1990, vol. VIII

Hellings, Robert Bailey, 1863–1947, vol. IV

Hellins, Rev. Edgar William James, 1872–1946, vol. IV

Helliwell, Maj.-Gen. John Percival, 1884–1948, vol. IV

Hellman, Lillian, 1907–1984, vol. VIII

Hellmuth, Rt Rev. Isaac, 1820–1901, vol. I

Helm, Sir (Alexander) Knox, 1893–1964, vol. VI

Helm, Rev. George Francis, 1882–1958, vol. V

Helm, Henry James, 1839–1918, vol. II

Helm, Sir Knox; see Helm, Sir A. K.

Helm, William Henry, 1860–1936, vol. III

Helme, Sir Norval Watson, 1849–1932, vol. III

Helmer, Col Richard Alexis, 1864–1920, vol. II

Helmore, Sir James Reginald Carroll, 1906–1972, vol. VII

Helmore, Hon. Air Cdre William, 1894–1964, vol. VI

Helmsley, Viscountess; (Muriel Frances Talbot), died 1925, vol. II

Helpmann, Sir Robert Murray, 1909–1986, vol. VIII

Helps, Rev. Canon Arthur Leonard, 1872–1960, vol. V

Helsby, Baron (Life Peer); Laurence Norman Helsby, 1908–1978, vol. VII

Helsham, Rev. Edward, 1891–1955, vol. V

Hely, Brig. Alfred Francis, 1902–1990, vol. VIII

Hely, Air Vice-Marshal William Lloyd, 1909–1970, vol. VI (AII)

Hely-Hutchinson, Christopher Douglas, 1885–1958, vol. V

Hely-Hutchinson, Maurice Robert, 1887–1961, vol. VI

Hely-Hutchinson, May, (Hon. Lady Hely-Hutchinson), died 1938, vol. III

Hely-Hutchinson, Victor, 1901–1947, vol. IV

Hely-Hutchinson, Rt Hon. Sir Walter Francis, 1849–1913, vol. I

Helyar, Brig.-Gen. Arthur Beaumont, 1858–1933, vol. III

Helyar, Lt-Comdr Kenneth Cary, 1887–1941, vol. IV

Hembry, Henry William McQuitty, 1903–1961, vol. VI

Hemeon, Clarence Reid, 1897–1953, vol. V

Heming, George Booth, 1858–1938, vol. III

Heming, Captain Thomas Henry, 1856–1932, vol. III

Hemingford, 1st Baron, 1869–1947, vol. IV

Hemingford, 2nd Baron, 1904–1982, vol. VIII

Hemingway, Charles Robert, 1860–1947, vol. IV

Hemingway, Ernest Miller, 1898–1961, vol. VI

Hemingway, Sir William, 1880–1967, vol. VI

Hemmant, George, 1880–1964, vol. VI

Hemmerde, Edward George, 1871–1948, vol. IV

Hemming, (Arthur) Francis, 1893–1964, vol. VI

Hemming, Sir Augustus William Lawson, 1841–1907, vol. I

Hemming, Gen. Edward Hughes, 1860–1943, vol. IV

Hemming, Francis; see Hemming, A. F.

Hemming, Maj.-Gen. Frederick Wilson, 1850–1934, vol. III

Hemming, George Wirgman, 1821–1905, vol. I

Hemming, Rev. George, 1859–1931, vol. III

Hemming, Lt-Col Henry Harold, 1893–1976, vol. VII

Hemming, Col Norman Mackenzie, 1868–1950, vol. IV

Hemming, Maj.-Gen. William Edward Gordon, 1899–1953, vol. V

Hempel, Frieda, died 1955, vol. V

Hemphill, 1st Baron, 1821–1908, vol. I

Hemphill, 2nd Baron, 1853–1919, vol. II

Hemphill, 3rd Baron, 1860–1930, vol. III

Hemphill, 4th Baron, 1901–1957, vol. V

Hemphill, Major Robert, 1888–1935, vol. III

Hemphill, Ven. Samuel, 1859–1927, vol. II

Hemsley, William, 1817–1906, vol. I

Hemsley, William Bottin, 1843–1924, vol. II

Hemsted, Captain John Rustat, 1881–1953, vol. V

Hemsted, Rupert William, 1876–1952, vol. V

Hemy, Charles Napier, 1841–1917, vol. II

Henare, Sir James Clendon Tau, 1911–1989, vol. VIII

Hench, Philip Showalter, 1896–1965, vol. VI

Henchley, Lt-Col Albert Richard, died 1938, vol. III

Henchmen, Hereward Humfry, 1874–1939, vol. III

Hendel, Charles William, 1890–1982, vol. VIII

Henderson, 1st Baron, 1891–1984, vol. VIII

Henderson of Ardwick, 1st Baron, died 1950, vol. IV

Henderson, Acheson Thompson, died 1909, vol. I

Henderson, Sir Alan Gerald Russell, 1886–1963, vol. VI

Henderson, Rev. Alexander, died 1937, vol. III

Henderson, Alexander, 1914–1954, vol. V

Henderson, Alexander Edward, 1844–1906, vol. I

Henderson, Rev. Alexander Roy, 1862–1950, vol. IV

Henderson, Amos, 1864–1922, vol. II

Henderson, Col Andrew, 1867–1951, vol. V

Henderson, Andrew Graham, 1882–1963, vol. VI

Henderson, Ann, 1921–1976, vol. VII

Henderson, Rev. Archibald, 1837–1927, vol. II

Henderson, Archibald, 1886–1962, vol. VI

Henderson, Archibald, 1877–1963, vol. III

Henderson, Arthur; see Baron Rowley.

Henderson, Rt Hon. Arthur, 1863–1935, vol. III

Henderson, Arthur Edward, 1870–1956, vol. V

Henderson, Bernard William, 1871–1929, vol. III

Henderson, Brig.-Gen. Sir Brodie Haldane, 1869–1936, vol. III

Henderson, Charles Alexander, 1882–1956, vol. V

Henderson, Sir Charles James, 1882–1974, vol. VII

Henderson, Charles Lamond, 1896–1966, vol. VI

Henderson, Lt-Gen. Sir David, 1862–1921, vol. II

Henderson, Sir David Kennedy, 1884–1965, vol. VI

Henderson, David Patrick, 1865–1931, vol. III

Henderson, David Willis Wilson, 1903–1968, vol. VI

Henderson, Duncan, 1870–1934, vol. III

Henderson, Rt Rev. Edward Barry, 1910–1986, vol. VIII

Henderson, Very Rev. Edward Lowry, 1873–1947, vol. IV

Henderson, Effie; see Albanesi, Mme.

Henderson, Hon. Eric Brand B.; see Butler-Henderson.

Henderson, Eugénie Jane Andrina, 1914–1989, vol. VIII

Henderson, Comdr Francis Barkley, 1859–1934, vol. III

Henderson, Vice-Adm. Frank Hannam, 1850–1918, vol. II

Henderson, Frank Young, 1894–1966, vol. VI

Henderson, Sir Frederick Ness, 1862–1944, vol. IV

Henderson, Rear-Adm. Geoffrey Archer, 1913–1985, vol. VIII

Henderson, Col George Burton, 1890–1940, vol. III

Henderson, George Cockburn, 1870–1944, vol. IV

Henderson, Very Rev. George David, 1888–1957, vol. V

Henderson, Col George Francis Robert, *died* 1903, vol. I

Henderson, George Gerald, 1862–1942, vol. IV

Henderson, Sir George Henry, 1889–1958, vol. V

Henderson, George Hugh, 1892–1949, vol. IV

Henderson, Adm. George Morris, 1851–1915, vol. I

Henderson, George William, 1854–1934, vol. III

Henderson, Sir Guy Wilmot McLintock, 1897–1987, vol. VIII

Henderson, Lt-Col Hon. Harold Greenwood, 1875–1922, vol. II

Henderson, Col Harry Dalton, 1858–1945, vol. IV

Henderson, Hector Bruce, 1895–1962, vol. VI

Henderson, Dame Henrietta Caroline, (Lady Henderson), *died* 1959, vol. V

Henderson, Lt-Col Henry Cockcroft P.; *see* Page-Henderson.

Henderson, Henry Ludwig, 1880–1963, vol. VI

Henderson, Herbert Stephen, 1870–1942, vol. IV

Henderson, Sir Hubert Douglas, 1890–1952, vol. V

Henderson, Rev. Ian, 1910–1969, vol. VI

Henderson, Sir Ian Leslie, 1901–1971, vol. VII

Henderson, Sir James, 1848–1914, vol. I

Henderson, Ven. James, 1840–1935, vol. III

Henderson, James, 1868–1945, vol. IV

Henderson, James, 1889–1963, vol. VI

Henderson, Sir James, 1882–1967, vol. VI

Henderson, James Bell, 1883–1975, vol. VII

Henderson, Sir James Blacklock, 1871–1950, vol. IV

Henderson, John, 1862–1938, vol. III

Henderson, John, 1876–1949, vol. IV

Henderson, John, 1883–1965, vol. VI

Henderson, Sir John, 1888–1975, vol. VII

Henderson, John Cochrane, 1881–1946, vol. IV

Henderson, Sir John Craik, 1890–1971, vol. VII

Henderson, John Louis, 1907–1985, vol. VIII

Henderson, John M'Donald, 1846–1922, vol. II

Henderson, John Robertson, 1863–1925, vol. II

Henderson, John Scott, 1895–1964, vol. VI

Henderson, Joseph Morris, 1863–1936, vol. III

Henderson, Keith, 1883–1982, vol. VIII

Henderson, Kenneth David Druitt, 1903–1988, vol. VIII

Henderson, Maj.-Gen. Kennett Gregg, 1836–1902, vol. I

Henderson, Kingsley Anketell, 1883–1942, vol. IV

Henderson, Lt-Col Malcolm, *died* 1923, vol. II

Henderson, Air Vice-Marshal Malcolm, 1891–1978, vol. VII

Henderson, Sir Malcolm Siborne, 1905–1981, vol. VIII

Henderson, Rt Hon. Sir Nevile Meyrick, *died* 1942, vol. IV

Henderson, Sir Neville Vicars, 1899–1986, vol. VIII

Henderson, Comdr Oscar, 1891–1969, vol. VI

Henderson, Rev. Patrick Arkley W.; *see* Wright-Henderson.

Henderson, Maj.-Gen. Patrick Hagart, 1876–1968, vol. VI

Henderson, Peter, 1904–1983, vol. VIII

Henderson, Maj.-Gen. Philip Durham, 1840–1918, vol. II

Henderson, Philip Prichard, 1906–1977, vol. VII

Henderson, R. B., 1880–1958, vol. V

Henderson, Ralph, 1897–1979, vol. VII

Henderson, Adm. Sir Reginald Friend Hannam, 1846–1932, vol. III

Henderson, Adm. Sir Reginald Guy Hannam, 1881–1939, vol. III

Henderson, Richard, 1854–1945, vol. IV

Henderson, Richard McNeil, 1886–1972, vol. VII

Henderson, Robert, 1842–1925, vol. II

Henderson, Robert Candlish, 1874–1964, vol. VI

Henderson, Sir Robert Herriot, *died* 1932, vol. III

Henderson, Hon. Robert Hugh, 1862–1956, vol. V

Henderson, Captain Robert Ronald, 1876–1932, vol. III

Henderson, Maj.-Gen. Sir Robert Samuel Findlay, 1858–1924, vol. II

Henderson, Rupert Albert Geary, 1896–1986, vol. VIII

Henderson, T. F., 1844–1923, vol. II

Henderson, Thomas, 1870–1945, vol. IV

Henderson, Sir Thomas, 1874–1951, vol. V

Henderson, Thomas, 1867–1960, vol. V

Henderson, Captain Thomas Maxwell Stuart M.; *see* Milne-Henderson.

Henderson, Thomson, *died* 1960, vol. V

Henderson, Sir Trevor, 1862–1930, vol. III

Henderson, Velyien Ewart, 1877–1945, vol. IV

Henderson, Lt-Col Sir Vivian Leonard, 1884–1965, vol. VI

Henderson, Rev. W. J., 1843–1929, vol. III

Henderson, Vice-Adm. Wilfred, 1873–1930, vol. III

Henderson, Sir William, 1826–1904, vol. I

Henderson, Sir William, 1863–1940, vol. III

Henderson, Brig. William Alexander, 1882–1949, vol. IV, vol. V

Henderson, William Craig, 1873–1959, vol. V

Henderson, Very Rev. William George, 1819–1905, vol. I

Henderson, Adm. Sir William Hannam, 1845–1931, vol. III

Henderson, William James, 1855–1937, vol. III

Henderson, William Walker, 1886–1960, vol. V

Henderson-Begg, Rev. Canon William, 1877–1934, vol. III

Henderson-Howat, Very Rev. Rudolph, 1896–1957, vol. V

Henderson-Scott, Lt-Col Archibald Malcolm, 1882–1967, vol. VI

Henderson-Smith, Mrs; *see* Klickmann, F.

Henderson-Stewart, Sir James, 1st Bt, 1897–1961, vol. VI

Hendley, Brig.-Gen. Charles Edward, 1863–1920, vol. II

Hendley, Maj.-Gen. Harold, 1861–1932, vol. III

Hendley, Col Thomas Holbein, 1847–1917, vol. II

Hendrey, Eiluned, (Mrs Graeme Hendrey); *see* Lewis Eiluned.

Hendrick, James, 1867–1949, vol. IV

Hendrie, Donald Stewart, 1909–1965, vol. VI

Hendrie, Herbert, 1887–1946, vol. IV

Hendrie, Col Sir John Strathearn, 1857–1923, vol. II

Hendriks, Sir Charles, (C. A. C. J. Hendriks), 1883–1960, vol. V

Hendry, Sir Alexander, 1867–1932, vol. III

Hendry, (Alexander) Forbes, 1908–1980, vol. VII

Hendry, Charles, 1870–1952, vol. V

Hendry, Forbes; *see* Hendry, A. F.

Hendry, James, 1885–1945, vol. IV

Hendry, Brig.-Gen. Patrick William, 1861–1952, vol. V

Hendry, Robert, 1876–1951, vol. V

Hendry, William Edward Russell, 1911–1965, vol. VI

Hendy, Arthur, 1874–1953, vol. V

Hendy, Frederick James Roberts, 1858–1933, vol. III

Hendy, Sir Philip, 1900–1980, vol. VII

Hendy, Roy, 1890–1959, vol. V

Heneage, 1st Baron, 1840–1922, vol. II

Heneage, 2nd Baron, 1866–1954, vol. V

Heneage, 3rd Baron, 1877–1967, vol. VI

Heneage, Sir Algernon Charles Fiesché, 1834–1915, vol. I

Heneage, Lt-Col Sir Arthur Pelham, 1881–1971, vol. VII

Heneage, Major Godfrey Clement Walker, 1868–1939, vol. III

Heneage, Lt-Col Hon. Henry Granville, 1868–1947, vol. IV

Henegan, Lt-Col John, 1865–1920, vol. II

Heneker, Gen. Sir William Charles Giffard, 1867–1939, vol. III

Heney, Thomas William, 1862–1928, vol. II

Henig, Sir Mark, 1911–1979, vol. VII

Henley, 3rd Baron, 1825–1899, vol. I

Henley, 4th Baron, 1849–1923, vol. II

Henley, 5th Baron, 1858–1925, vol. II

Henley, 6th Baron, 1877–1962, vol. VI

Henley, 7th Baron, 1914–1977, vol. VII

Henley, Brig.-Gen. Hon. Anthony Morton, *died* 1925, vol. II

Henley, Col Frank Le Leu, 1888–1941, vol. IV

Henley, Herbert James, 1882–1937, vol. III

Henley, Vice-Adm. Joseph Charles Walrond, 1879–1968, vol. VI

Henley, Joseph John, 1821–1910, vol. I

Henley, Sir Thomas, 1860–1935, vol. III

Henley, William Ernest, 1849–1903, vol. I

Henman, Philip Sydney, 1900–1986, vol. VIII

Henn, Rt Rev. Henry, 1858–1931, vol. III

Henn, Sir Sydney Herbert Holcroft, 1861–1936, vol. III

Henn, Thomas Rice, 1814–1901, vol. I

Henn, Thomas Rice, 1901–1974, vol. VII

Henn, Col William Francis, 1892–1964, vol. VI

Henn-Collins, Hon. Sir Stephen Ogle, *died* 1958, vol. V

Hennell, Col Sir Reginald, 1844–1925, vol. II

Henner, Jean Jacques, 1829–1905, vol. I

Hennessey, John Baboneau Nicklerlien, 1829–1910, vol. I

Hennessey, Robert Samuel Fleming, 1905–1989, vol. VIII

Hennessy, Hon. Sir Alfred Theodore, 1875–1963, vol. VI

Hennessy, Rt Hon. Sir David Valentine, 1855–1923, vol. II

Hennessy, Denis William, 1912–1990, vol. VIII

Hennessy, Maj.-Gen. Sir George Robertson, 1837–1905, vol. I

Hennessy, James P.; *see* Pope-Hennessy.

Hennessy, Lt-Col John, 1867–1954, vol. V

Hennessy, Col John Patrick Cumberlege, 1867–1933, vol. III

Hennessy, Maj.-Gen. Ladislaus Herbert Richard P.; *see* Pope-Hennessy.

Hennessy, Sir Patrick, 1898–1981, vol. VIII

Hennessy, Captain Richard, 1876–1953, vol. V

Hennessy, Richard M., 1854–1926, vol. II

Hennessy, Dame Una P.; *see* Pope-Hennessy.

Hennessy, William John, vol. II

Henniker, 5th Baron, 1842–1902, vol. I

Henniker, 6th Baron, 1872–1956, vol. V

Henniker, 7th Baron, 1883–1980, vol. VII

Henniker, Col Alan Major, 1870–1949, vol. IV

Henniker, Hon. Mrs Arthur, (Hon. Florence Ellen Hungerford Henniker-Major), 1885–1923, vol. II

Henniker, Adm. Sir Arthur John, 6th Bt; *see* Henniker-Hughan.

Henniker, Sir Brydges Powell, 4th Bt, 1835–1906, vol. I

Henniker, Sir Frederick Brydges Major, 5th Bt, 1862–1908, vol. I

Henniker, Lt-Col Sir Robert John Aldborough, 7th Bt, 1888–1958, vol. V

Henniker-Gotley, George Rainald, 1893–1974, vol. VII

Henniker-Gotley, Roger Alwyn, 1898–1985, vol. VIII

Henniker-Heaton, Sir (John Victor) Peregrine; *see* Heaton.

Henniker-Heaton, Raymond, 1874–1963, vol. VI

Henniker-Hughan, Adm. Sir Arthur John, 6th Bt, 1866–1925, vol. II

Henniker-Major, Maj.-Gen. Hon. Arthur Henry, 1855–1912, vol. I

Henniker-Major, Hon. Edward Minet, 1848–1924, vol. II

Henniker-Major, Hon. Florence Ellen Hungerford; *see* Henniker, Hon. Mrs Arthur.

Henniker-Major, Hon. Gerald Arthur George, 1872–1955, vol. V

Henning, Basil Duke, 1910–1990, vol. VIII

Henning, Walter Bruno, 1908–1967, vol. VI

Hennings, John Dunn, 1922–1985, vol. VIII

Henri, Robert, 1865–1929, vol. III

Henrici, Olaus M. F. E., 1840–1918, vol. II

Henrion, Frederic Henri Kay, 1914–1990, vol. VIII

Henriot, Emile, 1889–1961, vol. VI

Henriques, Sir Basil L. Q., 1890–1961, vol. VI

Henriques, Sir Cyril George Xavier, 1908–1982, vol. VIII

Henriques, Henry Straus Quixano, 1866–1925, vol. II

Henriques, Louis Fernando, 1916–1976, vol. VII

Henriques, Sir Philip Gutterez, 1867–1950, vol. IV

Henriques, Col Robert David Quixano, 1905–1967, vol. VI

Henry, Hon. Albert Royle, 1907–1981, vol. VIII

Henry, Alexander, *died* 1904, vol. I

Henry, Augustine, 1857–1930, vol. III

Henry, Sir Charles Solomon, 1st Bt (*cr* 1911), 1860–1919, vol. II

Henry, Cyril Bowdler, (C. Bowdler-Henry), 1893–1981, vol. VIII
Henry, Sir David, 1888–1963, vol. IV
Henry, Rt Hon. Sir Denis Stanislaus, 1st Bt (cr 1922), 1864–1925, vol. II
Henry, Sir Edward Richard, 1st Bt (cr 1918), 1850–1931, vol. III
Henry, (Ernest James) Gordon, 1919–1989, vol. VIII
Henry, Lt-Gen. George, 1846–1922, vol. II
Henry, George, 1858–1943, vol. IV
Henry, Hon. George Stewart, 1871–1958, vol. V
Henry, Gordon; see Henry, E. J. G.
Henry, Rt Rev. Henry, died 1908, vol. I
Henry, Rev. J. Edgar, 1841–1911, vol. I
Henry, Major James D.; see Douglas-Henry.
Henry, James Macintyre, 1852–1929, vol. III
Henry, Sir John, 1858–1930, vol. III
Henry, Mitchell, 1826–1910, vol. I
Henry, Paul, died 1958, vol. V
Henry, Robert Francis Jack, 1902–1970, vol. VI
Henry, Robert Mitchell, 1873–1950, vol. IV
Henry, Maj.-Gen. St George Charles Henry, 1860–1909, vol. I
Henry, Seaghan P.; see Mac Enri, Seaghan P.
Henry, Col Vivian, 1868–1929, vol. III
Henry, William Alexander, 1863–1927, vol. II
Henry, Sir William Daniel, 1855–1934, vol. III
Hensby, Frederick Charles, 1919–1982, vol. VIII
Henschel, Sir George, 1850–1934, vol. III
Henshall, John Henry, 1856–1928, vol. II
Henshaw, Rt Rev. Thomas, 1873–1938, vol. III
Hensley, Rev. Lewis, 1824–1905, vol. I
Hensley, Sir Robert Mitton, 1840–1912, vol. I
Henslow, Rev. George, 1835–1925, vol. II
Hensman, Col Henry Frank, 1839–1911, vol. I
Hensman, Howard, died 1916, vol. II
Henson, Rt Rev. Herbert Hensley, 1863–1947, vol. IV
Henson, John, 1879–1969, vol. VI
Henson, John James, 1868–1948, vol. IV
Henson, Leslie Lincoln, 1891–1957, vol. V
Hentschel, Christopher Carl, 1899–1986, vol. VIII
Hentschel, Carl, 1864–1930, vol. III
Henty, Hon. Sir Denham; see Henly, Hon. Sir N. H. D.
Henty, George Alfred, 1832–1902, vol. I
Henty, Hon. Sir (Norman Henry) Denham, 1903–1978, vol. VII
Henvey, Col Ralph, 1876–1945, vol. IV
Hepburn, Sir Archibald B.; see Buchan-Hepburn.
Hepburn, Col Bernard Richard, 1876–1939, vol. III
Hepburn, Lt-Col David, died 1931, vol. III
Hepburn, Sir Harry Frankland, 1867–1931, vol. III
Hepburn, Sir John Karslake Thomas B.; see Buchan-Hepburn.
Hepburn, Malcolm Langton, 1866–1942, vol. IV
Hepburn, Hon. Mitchell F., 1896–1953, vol. V
Hepburn, Sir Thomas Henry, 1840–1917, vol. II
Hepburn, Thomas Nicoll Gabriel Setoun, 1861–1930, vol. III
Hepburn, William Andrew Hardie, 1898–1965, vol. VI
Hepburn-Stuart-Forbes-Trefusis, Hon. Henry Walter; see Trefusis.

Hepburn-Stuart-Forbes-Trefusis, Major Hon. John Frederick; see Trefusis.
Hepburne-Scott, Hon. Henry Robert, 1847–1914, vol. I
Hepburne-Scott, James Cospatrick; see Scott.
Hepenstal, Major Lambert John D.; see Dopping-Hepenstal.
Hepenstal, Col Maxwell Edward D.; see Dopping-Hepenstal.
Hepher, Rev. Canon Cyril, 1872–1931, vol. III
Heppel, Richard Purdon, 1913–1986, vol. VIII
Heppell, Ralph Gordon, 1910–1976, vol. VII
Heppenstall, (John) Rayner, 1911–1981, vol. VIII
Heppenstall, Rayner; see Heppenstall, J. R.
Hepper, Col Albert James, 1839–1915, vol. I
Hepper, Sir Lawless, 1870–1935, vol. III
Hepple, Anne; see Dickinson, A. H.
Hepworth, Dame Barbara; see Hepworth, Dame J. B.
Hepworth, Dame (Jocelyn) Barbara, 1903–1975, vol. VII
Hepworth, Joseph, died 1945, vol. IV
Hepworth, Captain Melville Willis Campbell, 1849–1919, vol. II
Herapath, Lt-Col Edgar, 1853–1933, vol. III
Herapath, Col Lionel, 1880–1934, vol. III
Herbage, Julian Livingston-, 1904–1976, vol. VII
Herbert, Agnes, died 1960, vol. V
Herbert, Sir Alan Patrick, 1890–1971, vol. VII
Herbert, Hon. Alan Percy Harty Molyneux, died 1907, vol. I
Herbert, Sir Alfred, 1866–1957, vol. V
Herbert, Arnold; see Herbert, T. A.
Herbert, Sir Arthur James, 1820–1897, vol. I
Herbert, Sir Arthur James, 1855–1921, vol. II
Herbert, Hon. Auberon Edward William Molyneux, 1838–1906, vol. I
Herbert, Hon. Aubrey Nigel Henry Molyneux, 1880–1923, vol. II
Herbert, Lt-Col Charles, 1854–1919, vol. II
Herbert, Sir Charles Gordon, 1893–1970, vol. VI
Herbert, Christopher Alfred, 1913–1988, vol. VIII
Herbert, Lt-Col Claude, 1862–1937, vol. III
Herbert, Desmond Andrew, 1898–1976, vol. VII
Herbert, Brig.-Gen. Edmund Arthur, 1866–1946, vol. IV
Herbert, Sir Edward Dave Asher, 1892–1963, vol. VI
Herbert, Edward Maxwell K.; see Kenney-Herbert.
Herbert, Brig.-Gen. Edward Sidney, 1866–1936, vol. III
Herbert, Col. Edward William, 1855–1924, vol. II
Herbert, Lieut-Gen. Sir (Edwin) Otway, 1901–1984, vol. VIII
Herbert, Edwin Savory; see Baron Tangley.
Herbert of Lea, Lady; (Elizabeth), died 1911, vol. I
Herbert, Maj. George, 1892–1982, vol. VIII
Herbert, Col Hon. Sir George Sidney, 1st Bt (cr 1937), 1886–1942, vol. IV
Herbert, Lt-Col Herbert, 1865–1942, vol. IV
Herbert, Hilary A., died 1919, vol. II, vol. III
Herbert, Sir Jesse, 1851–1916, vol. II
Herbert, Jesse Basil, 1899–1972, vol. VII
Herbert, John Alexander, 1862–1948, vol. IV
Herbert, Lt-Col Sir John Arthur, 1895–1943, vol. IV
Herbert, Maj.-Gen. Lionel, 1860–1929, vol. III

Herbert, Hon. Mervyn Robert Howard Molyneux, 1882–1929, vol. III

Herbert, Hon. Sir Michael Henry, 1857–1903, vol. I

Herbert, Lieut-Gen. Sir Otway; *see* Herbert, Lieut-Gen. Sir E. O.

Herbert, Brig.-Gen. Otway Charles, 1877–1955, vol. V

Herbert, Rt Rev. Percy Mark, 1885–1968, vol. VI

Herbert, Air Cdre Philip Lee William, 1882–1936, vol. III

Herbert, Rt Hon. Sir Robert George Wyndham, 1831–1905, vol. I

Herbert, Roscoe, 1895–1975, vol. VII

Herbert, Captain Sir Sidney, 1st Bt (*cr* 1936), 1890–1939, vol. III

Herbert, Solomon, 1874–1940, vol. III

Herbert, Sydney, 1886–1967, vol. VI

Herbert, (Thomas) Arnold, *died* 1940, vol. III

Herbert, Violet Ida Evelyn; *see* Baroness Darcy de Knayth.

Herbert, Walter Elmes, 1902–1980, vol. VII

Herbert, William de Bracy, 1872–1928, vol. II

Herbert, Maj.-Gen. Hon. William Henry, 1834–1909, vol. I

Herbert, Maj.-Gen. William Norman, 1880–1949, vol. IV

Herbert-Smith, Charles, 1862–1944, vol. IV

Herbertson, Andrew John, *died* 1914, vol. I

Herbertson, James John William, 1883–1974, vol. VII

Herbst, Major John Frederick, 1873–1961, vol. VI

Herchenroder, Sir Francis; *see* Herchenroder, Sir M. J. B. F.

Herchenroder, Sir Furcy Alfred, 1865–1932, vol. III

Herchenroder, (Marie Ferdinand) Philippe, 1893–1968, vol. VI

Herchenroder, Sir (Marie Joseph Barnabe) Francis, 1896–1982, vol. VIII

Herchenroder, Philippe; *see* Herchenroder, M. F. P.

Hercus, Sir Charles Ernest, 1888–1971, vol. VII

Hercy, Sir Francis Hugh George, 1868–1947, vol. IV

Herd, Harold, 1893–1976, vol. VII

Herdman, Hon. Sir Alexander Lawrence, 1869–1953, vol. V

Herdman, Major Sir Emerson Crawford, 1869–1949, vol. IV

Herdman, Sir Ernest; *see* Herdman, Sir R. E.

Herdman, Sir (Robert) Ernest, 1857–1952, vol. V

Herdman, Robert Duddingstone, 1863–1922, vol. II

Herdman, Sir William Abbott, 1858–1924, vol. II

Herdon, Maj.-Gen. Hugh Edward, *died* 1958, vol. V

Herdt, Louis A., 1872–1926, vol. II

Hereford, 16th Viscount, 1843–1930, vol. III

Hereford, 17th Viscount, 1865–1952, vol. IV

Herford, Charles Harold, *died* 1931, vol. III

Herford, Ethilda B. Meakin, 1872–1956, vol. V

Hergesheimer, Joseph, 1880–1954, vol. V

Heriot, Maj.-Gen. Mackay A. H. J., 1839–1918, vol. II

Heriot, Sir William M.; *see* Maitland-Heriot.

Heriot-Maitland, Brig.-Gen. James Dalgleish, 1814–1958, vol. V.

Heriot-Maitland, Maj.-Gen. Sir James Makgill; *see* Maitland.

Heritage, Brig. Francis Bede, 1877–1934, vol. III

Heritage, James Edgar, 1880–1957, vol. V

Heritage, Stanley James, *died* 1980, vol. VII

Heriz, Captain Reginald Yorke, 1851–1910, vol. I

Herkless, Very Rev. Sir John, 1855–1920, vol. II

Herklots, Geoffrey Alton Craig, 1902–1986, vol. VIII

Herklots, Rev. Hugh Gerard Gibson, 1903–1971, vol. VII

Herkomer, Sir Hubert von, 1849–1914, vol. I

Herman, E., (Mrs M. Herman), *died* 1923, vol. II

Herman, George Ernest, 1849–1914, vol. I

Herman-Hodge, Rear-Adm. Hon. Claude Preston, 1888–1952, vol. V

Hermes, Gertrude Anna Bertha, 1901–1983, vol. VIII

Hermon-Hodge, Major Hon. Robert Edward Udny, 1882–1937, vol. III

Hern, William, *died* 1939, vol. III

Hernaman-Johnson, Francis, 1879–1949, vol. IV

Herne-Soame, Sir Charles Buckworth; *see* Soame.

Herne-Soame, Sir Charles Burnett Buckworth-; *see* Soame.

Heron, Hon. Col Alexander Robert, 1888–1949, vol. IV

Heron, (Cuthbert) George, 1911–1979, vol. VII

Heron, Lt-Col Davis, 1878–1941, vol. IV

Heron, Edward Thomas, 1867–1949, vol. IV

Heron, George; *see* Heron, C. G.

Heron, George Allan, 1845–1915, vol. I

Heron, Col Sir George Wykeham, 1880–1963, vol. VI

Heron, Rev. James, 1836–1918, vol. II

Heron, Brig.-Gen. Sir Thomas, 1857–1931, vol. III

Heron-Allen, Edward, 1861–1943, vol. IV

Heron-Maxwell, Mrs Beatrice Maude Emilia, *died* 1927, vol. II

Heron-Maxwell, Captain Sir Ivor Walter, 8th Bt, 1871–1928, vol. II

Heron-Maxwell, Sir John Robert, 7th Bt, 1836–1910, vol. I

Heron-Maxwell, Sir Patrick Ivor, 9th Bt, 1916–1982, vol. VIII

Heron-Maxwell, Robert Charles, 1848–1938, vol. III

Herrera, Senator Luis Alberto de, 1873–1959, vol. V

Herreshoff, Nathanael Greene, 1848–1938, vol. III

Herrick, Frederick Charles, 1887–1970, vol. VI

Herrick, Col Henry, 1872–1928, vol. II

Herrick, Myron T., 1854–1929, vol. III

Herrick, Very Rev. Richard William, 1913–1981, vol. VIII

Herrick, Robert, 1868–1938, vol. III

Herrick, Major Robert Lysle Warren, 1895–1936, vol. III

Herridge, Major Hon. William Duncan, 1888–1961, vol. VI

Herries, 11th Lord, 1837–1908, vol. I

Herries, Lady (12th in line), 1877–1945, vol. IV

Herries, Edward, 1821–1911, vol. I

Herries, Hon. Sir William Herbert, 1859–1923, vol. II

Herring, Major Alfred Cecil, 1888–1966, vol. VI

Herring, Lt-Gen. Hon. Sir Edmund Francis, 1892–1982, vol. VIII

Herring, George, 1832–1906, vol. I

Herring, Dame Mary Ranken, 1895–1981, vol. VIII

Herring, Percy Theodore, 1872–1967, vol. VI

Herring, Robert, 1903–1975, vol. VII

Herring, Brig.-Gen. Sydney Charles Edgar, 1882–1951, vol. V

Herring, Lt-Col William, 1839–1917, vol. II

Herring-Cooper, Lt-Col William Weldon, 1873–1953, vol. V

Herringham, Sir Wilmot Parker, 1855–1936, vol. III

Herrington, Hugh Geoffrey, 1900–1980, vol. VII

Herriot, Edonard, 1872–1957, vol. V

Herriotts, John, *died* 1935, vol. III

Herron, Very Rev. David Craig, 1882–1955, vol. V

Herron, Hon. Sir Leslie James, 1902–1973, vol. VII

Herron, Sir Robert, 1836–1900, vol. I, vol. III

Herron, Shaun, 1912–1989, vol. VIII

Herschel, Alexander Stewart, 1836–1907, vol. I

Herschel, Col John, 1837–1921, vol. II

Herschel, Rev. Sir John Charles William, 3rd Bt, 1869–1950, vol. IV

Herschel, Sir William James, 2nd Bt, 1833–1917, vol. II

Herschell, 1st Baron, 1837–1899, vol. I

Herschell, 2nd Baron, 1878–1929, vol. III

Herschell, Charles Richard, 1877–1962, vol. VI

Herschell, George, 1856–1914, vol. I

Herter, Christian Archibald, 1895–1966, vol. VI

Hertford, 7th Marquess of, 1871–1940, vol. III

Hertslet, Sir Cecil, 1850–1934, vol. III

Hertslet, Sir Edward, 1824–1902, vol. I

Hertslet, Rev. Canon Edward Lewis Augustine, 1878–1936, vol. III

Hertslet, George Thomas, 1822–1906, vol. I

Hertslet, Harry Lester, 1856–1925, vol. II

Hertz, Alfred, 1872–1942, vol. IV

Hertz, Henry Felix, 1863–1932, vol. III

Hertz, Very Rev. Joseph Herman, 1872–1946, vol. IV

Hertz, William Axel, 1859–1950, vol. IV

Hertzberg, Maj.-Gen. Charles Sumner Lund, 1886–1944, vol. IV

Hertzberg, Maj.-Gen. Halfdan Fenton Harbo, 1884–1959, vol. V

Hertzog, Gen. Hon. James Barry Munnik, 1866–1942, vol. IV

Hervey, Arthur, 1855–1922, vol. II

Hervey, Gen. Charles Robert West, 1818–1903, vol. I

Hervey, Dudley Francis Amelius, 1849–1911, vol. I

Hervey, Lord Francis, 1846–1931, vol. III

Hervey, Rev. Frederick Alfred John, 1846–1910, vol. I

Hervey, Sir George William, 1845–1915, vol. I

Hervey, Henry Arthur William, 1832–1908, vol. I

Hervey, Lord Walter John, 1865–1948, vol. IV

Hervey-Bathurst, Major Sir Frederick Edward William; *see* Bathurst.

Hervieu, Paul Ernest, 1857–1915, vol. I

Herzfeld, Ernst Emil, 1879–1948, vol. IV

Herzfeld, Gertrude Marianne Amalia, 1890–1981, vol. VIII

Herzog, Rt Rev. Edward, 1841–1924, vol. II

Herzog, Frederick Joseph, 1890–1987, vol. VIII

Herzog, Chief Rabbi Isaac, 1888–1959, vol. V

Heseltine, Lt-Col Christopher, 1869–1944, vol. III

Heseltine, Major Godfrey, 1871–1932, vol. III

Heseltine, Harry Nelson, *died* 1935, vol. III

Heseltine, John Postle, 1843–1929, vol. III

Heseltine, Michael, 1886–1952, vol. V

Hesilrige, Arthur George Maynard, 1863–1953, vol. V

Hesketh, 1st Baron, 1881–1944, vol. IV

Hesketh, 2nd Baron, 1916–1955, vol. V

Hesketh, Air Vice-Marshal Allan, *died* 1973, vol. VII

Hesketh, Charles Hesketh Fleetwood-, 1871–1947, vol. IV

Hesketh, (Charles) Peter (Fleetwood) Fleetwood-, 1905–1985, vol. VIII

Hesketh, Lt-Col George, 1878–1929, vol. III

Hesketh, Lt-Col James Arthur, 1863–1923, vol. II

Hesketh, Col Rawdon John Isherwood, 1872–1959, vol. V

Hesketh, Roger Fleetwood, 1902–1987, vol. VIII

Hesketh, Sir Thomas George Fermor-, 7th Bt, 1849–1924, vol. II

Heslop, Major Alfred Herbert, 1880–1929, vol. III

Heslop, Air Vice-Marshal Herbert William, 1898–1976, vol. VII

Heslop, Richard Oliver, 1842–1916, vol. II

Heslop, Major Thomas Bernard, 1891–1938, vol. III

Heslop-Harrison, John William, 1881–1967, vol. VI

Hespeler, Hon. Wilhelm, *born* 1850, vol. II

Hess, Dame Myra, 1890–1965, vol. VI

Hess, Victor Francis, 1883–1964, vol. VI

Hess, Walter Rudolf, 1881–1973, vol. VII

Hess, Willy, 1859–1939, vol. III

Hesse, Hermann, 1877–1962, vol. VI

Hessey, Rev. Robert Falkner, 1826–1911, vol. I

Hessey, Brig.-Gen. William Francis, 1868–1939, vol. III

Hetherington, Arthur Lonsdale, 1881–1960, vol. V

Hetherington, Sir Hector James Wright, 1888–1965, vol. VI

Hetherington, Ivystan, *died* 1917, vol. II

Hetherington, Sir Roger Gaskell, 1876–1952, vol. V

Hetherington, Roger le Geyt, 1908–1990, vol. VIII

Hetherington, Gp Captain Thomas Gerard, 1886–1951, vol. V

Hetherington, William Lonsdale, 1845–1911, vol. I

Hetherwick, Rev. Alexander, 1860–1939, vol. III

Hett, Major Francis Paget, *died* 1966, vol. VI

Hett, Geoffrey Seccombe, 1878–1949, vol. IV

Hett, Walter Stanley, 1882–1948, vol. IV

Heugh, Comdr John George, 1856–1915, vol. I

Heuston, Lt-Col Frederick Samuel, 1857–1914, vol. I

Heuvel, Frederick V.; *see* Vanden Heuvel.

Hevesy, George Charles de, 1885–1966, vol. VI

Hewan, Gethyn Elliot, 1916–1988, vol. VIII

Heward, Leslie Hays, 1897–1943, vol. IV

Hewart, 1st Viscount, 1870–1943, vol. IV

Hewart, 2nd Viscount, 1896–1964, vol. VI

Hewat, Aubrey Middleton, 1884–1976, vol. VII

Hewat, Air Cdre Harry Aitken, 1888–1970, vol. VI

Hewat, Col Sir John, 1863–1928, vol. II

Hewby, Louis John, 1871–1925, vol. II

Hewby, William Petch, 1866–1946, vol. IV

Hewer, Christopher Langton, 1897–1986, vol. VIII

Hewer, Humphrey Robert, 1903–1974, vol. VII

Hewer, Maj.-Gen. Reginald Kingscote, 1892–1970, vol. VII

Hewetson, John T., 1872–1936, vol. III

Hewett, Edbert Ansgar, 1860–1915, vol. I

Hewett, Edward Osborne, 1835–1897, vol. I

Hewett, Lt-Col Edward Vincent Osborne, 1867–1953, vol. V
Hewett, Sir (Frederick) Stanley, 1880–1954, vol. V
Hewett, Rear-Adm. George Hayley, 1855–1930, vol. III
Hewett, Captain George Stuart, 1863–1937, vol. III
Hewett, Captain Gilbert George Pearse, 1880–1966, vol. VI
Hewett, Sir Harold George, 4th Bt, 1858–1949, vol. IV
Hewett, Sir John George, 5th Bt, 1895–1990, vol. VIII
Hewett, Sir John Prescott, 1854–1941, vol. IV
Hewett, Col Murray Selwood, 1881–1939, vol. III
Hewett, Captain Robert Roy Scott, 1886–1967, vol. VI
Hewett, Sir Stanley; see Hewett, Sir F. S.
Hewins, Harold Preece, 1877–1956, vol. V
Hewins, Maurice Gravenor, 1897–1953, vol. V
Hewins, William Albert Samuel, 1865–1931, vol. III
Hewison, Robert, 1876–1959, vol. V
Hewit, Forrest, died 1956, vol. V
Hewitson, Captain Mark, 1897–1973, vol. VII
Hewitson, Rev. William, died 1932, vol. III
Hewitt, Abram S., 1822–1903, vol. I
Hewitt, Surg. Rear-Adm. Alfred James, died 1947, vol. IV
Hewitt, Captain Hon. Archibald Rodney, 1883–1915, vol. 1
Hewitt, Brig. Charles Caulfield, 1883–1949, vol. IV
Hewitt, Surg.-Rear-Adm. David Walker, 1870–1940, vol. III
Hewitt, Lt-Col Dudley Riddiford, 1877–1971, vol. VII
Hewitt, Edgar Percy, died 1928, vol. II
Hewitt, Air Chief Marshal Sir Edgar Rainey L.; see Ludlow-Hewitt.
Hewitt, Hon. Edward, 1848–1931, vol. III
Hewitt, Sir Frederic William, 1857–1916, vol. II
Hewitt, Adm. Henry Kent, 1887–1972, vol. VII
Hewitt, Sir John Francis, 1910–1979, vol. VII
Hewitt, John Theodore, died 1954, vol. V
Hewitt, Lt-Col Sir Joseph, 1st Bt, 1865–1923, vol. II
Hewitt, Sir Joseph, 2nd Bt, 1907–1973, vol. VII
Hewitt, Air Vice-Marshal, Joseph Eric, 1901–1985, vol. VIII
Hewitt, Sir Thomas, died 1923, vol. II
Hewitt, William Graily, 1864–1952, vol. V
Hewlett, Baron (Life Peer); Thomas Clyde Hewlett, 1923–1979, vol. VII
Hewlett, Brig.-Gen. Ernest, 1879–1965, vol. VI
Hewlett, Paymaster Captain Graham, 1864–1937, vol. III
Hewlett, Maurice Henry, 1861–1923, vol. II
Hewlett, Sir Meyrick; see Hewlett, Sir W. M.
Hewlett, Richard Tanner, 1865–1940, vol. III
Hewlett, Thomas Henry, 1882–1956, vol. V
Hewlett, Sir (William) Meyrick, died 1944, vol. IV
Hewlett, William Oxenham, 1845–1912, vol. I
Hews, (Gordon) Rodney (Donald), 1917–1988, vol. VIII
Hews, Rodney; see Hews, G. R. D.
Hewson, Hon. Mrs Anne Elizabeth Mary Llywelyn, 1902–1963, vol. VI

Hewson, Sir Bushby; see Hewson, Sir J. B.
Hewson, George Henry Phillips, 1881–1972, vol. VII
Hewson, Sir (Joseph) Bushby, 1902–1976, vol. VII
Hext, Maj.-Gen. Frederick Maurice, 1901–1987, vol. VIII
Hext, Rear-Adm. Sir John, 1842–1924, vol. II
Hext, Brig.-Gen. Lyonel John, 1871–1934, vol. III
Hey, Donald Holroyde, 1904–1987, vol. VIII
Heycock, Baron (Life Peer); Llewelyn Heycock, 1905–1990, vol. VIII
Heycock, Charles Thomas, 1858–1931, vol. III
Heycock, Air Cdre George Francis Wheaton, 1909–1983, vol. VIII
Heydeman, Maj.-Gen. C. A., 1889–1967, vol. VI
Heydon, Charles Gilbert, 1845–1932, vol. III
Heydon, Hon. Louis Francis, 1848–1918, vol. II
Heydon, Sir Peter Richard, 1913–1971, vol. VII
Heyer, Georgette, 1902–1974, vol. VII
Heyes, Morris, died 1940, vol. III
Heyes, Sir Tasman Hudson Eastwood, 1896–1980, vol. VII (AII)
Heygate, Rev. Ambrose, 1852–1941, vol. IV
Heygate, Arthur Conolly Gage, 1862–1935, vol. III
Heygate, Sir Frederick Gage, 3rd Bt, 1854–1940, vol. III
Heygate, Sir John Edward Nourse, 4th Bt, 1903–1976, vol. VII
Heygate, Captain Richard Lionel, 1859–1926, vol. II
Heygate, Col Robert Henry Gage, 1859–1923, vol. II
Heygate, Rev. William Augustine, 1847–1941, vol. IV
Heygate, William Unwin, 1825–1902, vol. I
Heyman, Lt-Col Arthur Augustus Inglis, 1864–1931, vol. III
Heyman, Maj.-Gen. George Douglas Gordon Dufferin, 1905–1965, vol. VI
Heyman, Lt-Col Sir (Herman) Melville, 1859–1938, vol. III
Heyman, Lt-Col Sir Melville; see Heyman, Lt-Col Sir H. M.
Heymanson, Sir Randal; see Heymanson, Sir S. H. R.
Heymanson, Sir (Sydney Henry) Randal, 1903–1984, vol. VIII
Heyner, Herbert, 1881–1954, vol. V
Heyrovský, Jaroslav, 1890–1967, vol. VI
Heys, Derek Isaac, 1911–1984, vol. VIII
Heys, John, 1899–1963, vol. VI
Heyse, Paul Johann Ludwig, 1830–1914, vol. I
Heysen, Sir Hans, 1877–1968, vol. VI
Heytesbury, 3rd Baron, 1862–1903, vol. I
Heytesbury, 4th Baron, 1863–1949, vol. IV
Heytesbury, 5th Baron, 1906–1971, vol. VII
Heyward, DuBose, 1885–1940, vol. III (A), vol. IV
Heywood, Sir Arthur Percival, 3rd Bt, 1849–1916, vol. II
Heywood, Rt Rev. Bernard O. F., 1871–1960, vol. V
Heywood, Bertram Charles Percival, 1864–1914, vol. II
Heywood, Maj.-Gen. Cecil Percival, 1880–1936, vol. III
Heywood, Charles Christopher, 1865–1948, vol IV
Heywood, Geoffrey Henry, 1903–1986, vol. VIII
Heywood, Sir (Graham) Percival, 4th Bt, 1878–1946, vol. IV

Heywood, Very Rev. Hugh Christopher Lempriere, 1896–1987, vol. VIII

Heywood, James Barnes, *died* 1924, vol. II

Heywood, Sir Percival; *see* Heywood, Sir G. P.

Heywood, Rt Rev. Richard Stanley, 1867–1955, vol. V

Heywood, Maj.-Gen. Thomas George Gordon, 1886–1943, vol. IV

Heywood, Sir Thomas Percival, 2nd Bt, 1823–1897, vol. I

Heywood, Valentine, 1891–1963, vol. VI

Heywood, Wilfred Lanceley, 1900–1977, vol. VII

Heywood-Lonsdale, Lt-Col Arthur, 1900–1976, vol. VII

Heywood-Lonsdale, Arthur Pemberton, 1835–1897, vol. I

Heywood-Lonsdale, Lt-Col Henry Heywood, 1864–1930, vol. III

Heywood-Lonsdale, John Pemberton Heywood, 1869–1944, vol. IV

Heyworth, 1st Baron, 1894–1974, vol. VII

Heyworth, Brig.-Gen. Frederic James, 1863–1916, vol. II

Hezlet, Lt-Col Charles Owen, 1891–1965, vol. VI

Hezlet, Maj.-Gen. Robert Knox, 1879–1963, vol. VI

Hezlett, James, 1875–1963, vol. VI

Hiam, Sir Frederick, 1871–1938, vol. III

Hibbard, Howard, 1928–1984, vol. VIII

Hibben, John Grier, 1861–1933, vol. III

Hibberd, (Andrew) Stuard, 1893–1983, vol. VIII

Hibberd, Charles M.; *see* Maxwell-Hibberd.

Hibberd, Sir Donald James, 1916–1982, vol. VIII

Hibberd, George, 1901–1989, vol. VIII

Hibberd, Stuart; *see* Hibberd, A. S.

Hibbert, Denys Heseltine, 1905–1977, vol. VII

Hibbert, Rev. Preb. Francis Aidan, 1866–1933, vol. III

Hibbert, Francis Dennis, 1906–1975, vol. VII

Hibbert, Col Godfrey Leicester, 1864–1924, vol. II

Hibbert, Sir Henry Flemming, 1st Bt, 1850–1927, vol. II

Hibbert, Maj.-Gen. Hugh Brownlow, 1893–1988, vol. VIII

Hibbert, Adm. Hugh Thomas, 1863–1951, vol. V

Hibbert, John Geoffrey, 1890–1968, vol. VI

Hibbert, Rt Hon. Sir John Tomlinson, 1824–1908, vol. I

Hibbert, Brig. Oswald Yates, 1882–1966, vol. VI

Hibbert, Paul Edgar Tichborne, 1846–1929, vol. III

Hibbert, Walter, 1852–1935, vol. III

Hibbert, Hon. Wilfrid H.; *see* Holland-Hibbert.

Hibbert, William Nembhard, 1873–1936, vol. III

Hichens, Rev. Frederick Harrison, 1836–1921, vol. II

Hichens, John Knill Jope, 1836–1908, vol. I

Hichens, Lionel; *see* Hichens, W. L.

Hichens, Mrs Mary Hermione, 1894–1985, vol. VIII

Hichens, Robert Smythe, 1864–1950, vol. IV

Hichens, Rev. Thomas Sikes, *died* 1916, vol. II

Hichens, (William) Lionel, 1874–1940, vol. III

Hickes, Maj.-Gen. Lancelot Daryl, 1884–1965, vol. VI

Hickey, Captain Daniel, 1851–1935, vol. III

Hickey, Emily Henrietta, 1845–1924, vol. II

Hickey, Nancy Maureen, 1924–1986, vol. VIII

Hickford, Lawrence David, 1904–1978, vol. VII

Hickie, Brig.-Gen. Carlos Joseph, *died* 1959, vol. V

Hickie, Brig. George William Clement, 1897–1972, vol. VII

Hickie, Maj.-Gen. Sir William Bernard, 1865–1950, vol. IV

Hickin, Rev. Canon Henry Arthur, 1859–1938, vol. III

Hickin, Welton, 1876–1968, vol. VI

Hickinbotham, Rev. James Peter, 1914–1990, vol. VIII

Hickinbotham, Sir Tom, 1903–1983, vol. VIII

Hicking, Sir William Norton, 1st Bt, 1865–1947, vol. IV

Hickley, Adm. Cecil Spencer, 1865–1941, vol. IV

Hickley, Victor North, 1858–1923, vol. II

Hickling, Charles Frederick, 1902–1977, vol. VII

Hickling, Vice-Adm. Harold, 1892–1969, vol. VI

Hickling, Henry George Albert, 1883–1954, vol. V

Hickling, Lt-Col Horace Cyril Benjamin, 1879–1948, vol. IV

Hickman, Hon. Albert Edgar, 1875–1943, vol. IV

Hickman, Sir Alfred, 1st Bt, 1830–1910, vol. I

Hickman, Major Sir Alfred Edward, 2nd Bt, 1885–1947, vol. IV

Hickman, Sir (Alfred) Howard (Whitby), 3rd Bt, 1920–1979, vol. VII

Hickman, Captain Charlie Steward, 1868–1941, vol. IV

Hickman, Brig.-Gen. Harry Otho Devereux, 1860–1946, vol. IV

Hickman, Maj.-Gen. Henry Temple Devereux, 1888–1960, vol. V

Hickman, Sir Howard; *see* Hickman, Sir A. H. W.

Hickman, Maj.-Gen. Hugh Palliser, 1856–1930, vol. III

Hickman, Robert St John, 1867–1947, vol. IV

Hickman, Brig.-Gen. Thomas Edgecumbe, 1859–1930, vol. III

Hicks, Beatrice Janie, (Mrs Philip Hicks); *see* Whitby, B. J.

Hicks, Brig. Sir (Cedric) Stanton, 1892–1976, vol. VII

Hicks, Col Sir Denys Theodore, 1908–1987, vol. VIII

Hicks, Donald, 1902–1986, vol. VIII

Hicks, Rev. Canon Edward Barry, 1858–1939, vol. III

Hicks, Rt Rev. Edward Lee, 1843–1919, vol. II

Hicks, Sir (Edward) Seymour, 1871–1949, vol. IV

· **Hicks,** Sir Edwin William, 1910–1984, vol. VIII

Hicks, (Ernest) George, 1879–1954, vol. V

Hicks, Rt Rev. (Frederick Cyril) Nugent, 1872–1942, vol. IV

Hicks, George; *see* Hicks, E. G.

Hicks, Rt Rev. George Bruno, 1878–1954, vol. V

Hicks, George Dawes, 1862–1941, vol. IV

Hicks, Henry, 1837–1899, vol. I

Hicks, Brig.-Gen. Henry T.; *see* Tempest-Hicks.

Hicks, Rev. Herbert S., *died* 1928, vol. II

Hicks, Howard Arthur, 1914–1989, vol. VIII

Hicks, Lt-Col James Hamilton, 1909–1985, vol. VIII

Hicks, John Donald, 1890–1972, vol. VII

Hicks, Sir John Richard, 1904–1989, vol. VIII

Hicks, Rt Rev. John Wale, 1840–1899, vol. I

Hicks, Lt-Col Sir Maxwell, 1878–1959, vol. V

Hicks, Rt Rev. Nugent; *see* Hicks, Rt Rev. F. C. N.

Hicks, Brig. Philip Hugh Whitby, 1895–1967, vol. VI

Hicks, Reginald Jack, 1922–1980, vol. VII

Hicks, Robert Drew, 1850–1929, vol. III

Hicks, Sir Seymour; *see* Hicks, Sir E. S.

Hicks, Shadrach, *died* 1936, vol. III

Hicks, Brig. Sir Stanton; *see* Hicks, Brig. Sir C. S.

Hicks, Ursula Kathleen, (Lady Hicks), 1896–1985, vol. VIII

Hicks, Rev. Walter, 1868–1937, vol. III

Hicks, William Edward, 1852–1921, vol. II

Hicks, William Mitchinson, 1850–1934, vol. III

Hicks-Beach, Lady Victoria Alexandrina, 1879–1963, vol. VI

Hicks Beach, William Frederick, 1841–1923, vol. II

Hicks Beach, Major William Whitehead, 1907–1975, vol. VII

Hicks-Beach, Rt Hon. William Wither Bramston, 1826–1901, vol. I

Hickson, Geoffrey Fletcher, 1900–1978, vol. VII

Hickson, Lt-Gen. Sir Gerald Robert Stedall, 1879–1957, vol. V

Hickson, Sir Joseph, 1830–1897, vol. I

Hickson, Joseph William Andrew, *died* 1956, vol. V

Hickson, Mrs Murray; *see* Kitcat, M.

Hickson, Oswald Squire, 1877–1944, vol. IV

Hickson, Brig.-Gen. Robert Albert, 1848–1934, vol. III

Hickson, Robert Rowan Purdon, 1842–1923, vol. II

Hickson, Maj.-Gen. Sir Samuel, 1859–1928, vol. II

Hickson, Hon. Brig.-Gen. Samuel Arthur Einem, 1853–1932, vol. III

Hickson, Sydney John, 1859–1940, vol. III

Hidayat Hosain, M., 1887–1941, vol. IV

Hidayatallah, Hon. Khan Bahadur Shaikh (Sir) Ghulam Husain, *died* 1948, vol. IV

Hide, Percy, 1874–1938, vol. III

Hieger, Izrael, 1901–1986, vol. VIII

Hiern, William Philip, 1839–1925, vol. II

Higgens, Charles, *died* 1920, vol. II

Higgin, Walter Wynnefield, 1889–1971, vol. VII

Higginbottom, Frederick James, 1859–1943, vol. IV

Higginbottom, S. W., *died* 1902, vol. I

Higgins, A., *died* 1903, vol. I

Higgins, Alexander Pearce, 1865–1935, vol. III

Higgins, Brig.-Gen. Charles Graeme, 1879–1961, vol. VI

Higgins, Clement, 1844–1916, vol. II

Higgins, Edward John, 1864–1947, vol. IV

Higgins, Ellen C., *died* 1951, vol. V

Higgins, Frederick P.; *see* Platt-Higgins.

Higgins, Frederick Robert, 1896–1941, vol. IV

Higgins, Sir George; *see* Higgins, Sir S. G.

Higgins, George Herbert, 1878–1937, vol. III

Higgins, Maj.-Gen. Harold John, 1894–1951, vol. V

Higgins, Hon. Henry Bournes, *died* 1929, vol. III

Higgins, Henry Vincent, 1855–1928, vol. II

Higgins, John Comyn, 1882–1952, vol. V

Higgins, Rev. Canon John Denis P.; *see* Pearce-Higgins.

Higgins, Air Marshal Sir John Frederick Andrews, 1875–1948, vol. IV

Higgins, Sir John Michael, 1862–1937, vol. III

Higgins, Rt Rev. Joseph, 1838–1915, vol. I

Higgins, Rt Rev. Michael, 1863–1918, vol. II

Higgins, Reginald Edward, 1877–1933, vol. III

Higgins, Sir (Sydney) George, 1867–1947, vol. IV

Higgins, Air Cdre Thomas Charles Reginald, 1880–1953, vol. V

Higgins, Thomas Twistington, 1887–1966, vol. VI

Higgins, Rev. Canon Walter Norman, 1880–1957, vol. V

Higgins Bernard, Lt-Col Francis Tyringham, *died* 1935, vol. III

Higginson, Captain Archibald Bertram Watson, *died* 1950, vol. IV

Higginson, Brig.-Gen. Cecil Pickford, 1866–1951, vol. V

Higginson, Charles James, 1871–1964, vol. VI

Higginson, Brig. Sir Frank, 1890–1958, vol. V

Higginson, Gen. Sir George Wentworth Alexander, 1826–1927, vol. II

Higginson, Maj.-Gen. Harold Whitla, 1873–1954, vol. V

Higginson, Col Theophilus, 1839–1903, vol. I

Higginson, Thomas Wentworth, 1823–1911, vol. I

Higgon, Col Laurence Hugh, 1884–1987, vol. VIII

Higgs, Col Frederick William, 1881–1924, vol. II

Higgs, Godfrey Walter, 1907–1986, vol. VIII

Higgs, Henry, 1864–1940, vol. III

Higgs, Sir John Walter Yeoman, 1923–1986, vol. VIII

Higgs, Captain Michael Arnold, 1927–1978, vol. VII

Higgs, Sydney Limbrey, 1892–1977, vol. VII

Higgs, Walter Frank, 1886–1961, vol. VI

Higgs, Hon. William Guy, 1862–1951, vol. V

Higgs-Walker, James Arthur, 1892–1979, vol. VII

High, Sir William, 1857–1934, vol. III

Higham, Anthony Richard Charles, 1907–1975, vol. VII

Higham, Lt-Col Bernard, 1880–1944, vol. IV

Higham, Charles Daniel, 1849–1935, vol. III

Higham, Sir Charles Frederick, 1876–1938, vol. III

Higham, John Sharp, 1857–1932, vol. III

Higham, Sir Thomas, 1847–1910, vol. I

Higham, Sir Thomas, 1866–1947, vol. IV

Higham, Thomas Farrant, 1890–1975, vol. VII

Highet, Gilbert Arthur, 1906–1978, vol. VII

Highet, Hugh Campbell, 1868–1929, vol. III

Highet, Sir Robert Swan, 1859–1934, vol. III

Highfield, John Somerville, 1871–1945, vol. IV

Highmore, Sir Nathaniel Joseph, 1844–1924, vol. II

Hight, Sir James, 1870–1958, vol. V

Highton, Rear-Adm. Jack Kenneth, 1904–1988, vol. VIII

Highton, John Elborn, 1884–1937, vol. III

Highton, Mark Edward, 1888–1966, vol. VI

Higinbotham, Major George Mowat, 1866–1915, vol. I

Hignell, Harold, 1879–1943, vol. IV

Hignell, Sidney Robert, 1873–1939, vol. III

Hignett, Mrs Dorothy Eleanor Augusta, *died* 1946, vol. IV

Hilbers, Ven. George Christopher, *died* 1918, vol. II

Hilbery, Rt Hon. Sir Malcolm, 1883–1965, vol. VI

Hilborne, Rev. Frederick Wilfred, 1901–1980, vol. VII

Hildebrand, Brig.-Gen. Arthur Blois Ross, 1870–1937, vol. III

Hildebrand, Arthur Hedding, 1843–1918, vol. II

Hilder, Lt-Col Frank, 1864–1951, vol. V

Hilder, Rev. Geoffrey Frank, 1906–1988, vol. VIII

Hildesley, Alfred, 1873–1958, vol. V

Hilditch, Clarence Clifford, 1912–1974, vol. VII

Hilditch, Thomas Percy, 1886–1965, vol. VI

Hildred, Sir William Percival, 1893–1986, vol. VIII

Hildreth, Lt-Col Harold Crossley, 1876–1937, vol. III

Hildyard, Rev. Christopher, 1901–1987, vol. VIII

Hildyard, Gerard Moresby Thoroton, 1874–1956, vol. V

Hildyard, Brig.-Gen. Harold Charles Thoroton, 1872–1956, vol. V

Hildyard, Gen. Sir Henry John Thoroton, 1846–1916, vol. II

Hildyard, John Arundell, 1861–1935, vol. III

Hildyard, Gen. Sir Reginald John Thoroton, 1876–1965, vol. VI

Hiles, Sir Herbert, 1881–1968, vol. VI

Hiley, Sir (Ernest) Haviland, *died* 1943, vol. IV

Hiley, Sir Ernest Varvill, 1868–1949, vol. IV

Hiley, Sir Haviland; *see* Hiley, Sir E. H.

Hiley, Joseph, 1902–1989, vol. VIII

Hilgendorf, Sir Charles, 1908–1990, vol. VIII

Hilken, Captain Thomas John Norman, 1901–1969, vol. VI

Hill, 4th Viscount, 1863–1923, vol. II

Hill, 5th Viscount, 1866–1924, vol. II

Hill, 6th Viscount, 1876–1957, vol. V

Hill, 7th Viscount, 1904–1974, vol. VII

Hill of Luton, Baron (Life Peer); Charles Hill, 1904–1989, vol. VIII

Hill of Wivenhoe, Baron (Life Peer); Edward James Hill, 1899–1969, vol. VI

Hill, Adrian Keith Graham, 1895–1977, vol. VII

Hill, Sir Albert, 2nd Bt (*cr* 1917), 1877–1946, vol. IV

Hill, Alex, 1856–1929, vol. III

Hill, Rev. Alexander Currie, 1906–1983, vol. VIII

Hill, Sir Alexander Galloway E.; *see* Erskine-Hill.

Hill, Rt Hon. Alexander Staveley, 1825–1905, vol. I

Hill, Alfred, *died* 1945, vol. IV

Hill, Alfred Bostock, 1854–1932, vol. III

Hill, Alfred Francis, 1870–1960, vol. V

Hill, Alfred John, 1862–1927, vol. II

Hill, Rt Rev. Alfred Thomas, 1901–1969, vol. VI

Hill, Annie; *see* Hill, Lady Arthur.

Hill, Rev. Canon Archdall, *died* 1936, vol. III

Hill, Archibald Vivian, 1886–1977, vol. VII

Hill, Captain Arthur, 1873–1913, vol. I

Hill, Arthur, 1854–1927, vol. II

Hill, Arthur, 1858–1927, vol. II

Hill, Lady Arthur, (Annie), *died* 1944, vol. IV

Hill, Captain Arthur Blundell George Sandys, 1837–1923, vol. II

Hill, Lord (Arthur) Francis (Henry), 1895–1953, vol. V

Hill, Arthur George, 1857–1923, vol. II

Hill, Lt-Col Arthur Hardie, 1887–1963, vol. VI

Hill, Sir Arthur Norman, 1st Bt (*cr* 1919), 1863–1944, vol. IV

Hill, Rt Hon. Lord Arthur William, 1846–1931, vol. III

Hill, Sir Arthur William, 1875–1941, vol. IV

Hill, Ven. Arundel Charles, 1845–1921, vol. II

Hill, Brig.-Gen. Augustus West, 1853–1922, vol. II

Hill, Maj.-Gen. Sir Basil Alexander, 1880–1960, vol. V

Hill, Brig.-Gen. Cecil, 1861–1942, vol. IV

Hill, Charles Alexander, 1874–1948, vol. IV

Hill, Major Charles Glencairn, 1872–1915, vol. I

Hill, Charles Loraine, 1891–1976, vol. VII

Hill, Rev. Charles N.; *see* Noel-Hill.

Hill, Christopher Pascoe, 1903–1983, vol. VIII

Hill, Sir Claude Hamilton Archer, 1866–1934, vol. III

Hill, Sir Clement Lloyd, 1845–1913, vol. I

Hill, Clifford Francis, 1930–1979, vol. VII

Hill, Colin de Neufville, 1917–1989, vol. VIII

Hill, Constance, *died* 1929, vol. III

Hill, Sir Cyril Rowley; *see* Hill, Sir G. C. R.

Hill, Hon. David Jayne, 1850–1932, vol. III

Hill, Col David John Jackson, 1874–1938, vol. III

Hill, Sir Denis; *see* Hill, Sir J. D. N.

Hill, Rev. Canon Douglas George, 1912–1980, vol. VII

Hill, Douglas Rowland Holdsworth, 1904–1966, vol. VI

Hill, Douglas William, 1904–1985, vol. VIII

Hill, Captain Duncan C., 1900–1977, vol. VII

Hill, Edward Bernard Lewin, 1834–1915, vol. I

Hill, Rev. Edward F., 1858–1931, vol. III

Hill, Edward John, 1897–1965, vol. VI

Hill, Sir Edward Stock, 1834–1902, vol. I

Hill, Rev. Canon Edwin, 1843–1933, vol. III

Hill, Sir Enoch, 1865–1942, vol. IV

Hill, Brig. Ernest Frederick John, 1879–1962, vol. VI

Hill, Ernest George, 1872–1917, vol. II

Hill, Ernest Saphir, 1891–1967, vol. VI

Hill, Col Eustace, 1869–1946, vol. IV

Hill, Eveline, (Mrs J. S. Hill), 1898–1973, vol. VII

Hill, Brig.-Gen. Felix Frederic, 1860–1940, vol. III

Hill, Lord Francis; *see* Hill, Lord A. F. H.

Hill, Sir Francis; *see* Hill, Sir J. W. F.

Hill, (Francis) John, 1915–1984, vol. VIII

Hill, Lt-Col Francis Robert, 1873–1956, vol. V

Hill, Major Francis Rowley, 1872–1939, vol. III

Hill, Lt-Col Frank William Rowland, 1875–1942, vol. IV

Hill, Brig.-Gen. Frederic William, 1866–1954, vol. V

Hill, Frederick George, 1865–1936, vol. III

Hill, Sir G. Rowland, 1855–1928, vol. II

Hill, Sir George Alfred Rowley, 9th Bt, 1899–1985, vol. VIII

Hill, George Birkbeck Norman, 1835–1903, vol. I

Hill, Sir (George) Cyril Rowley, 8th Bt (*cr* 1779), 1890–1980, vol. VII

Hill, Sir George Francis, 1867–1948, vol. IV

Hill, Sir George Rowley, 7th Bt (*cr* 1779), 1864–1954, vol. V

Hill, Col Gerald Victor Wilmot, 1887–1958, vol. V

Hill, Gerard Robert, 1872–1946, vol. IV

Hill, Grace Livingston, (Mrs Thomas Franklin Hill), 1865–1947, vol. IV

Hill, Graham, 1929–1975, vol. VII

Hill, H. Lancelot H., 1883–1944, vol. IV

Hill, Harold G.; *see* Gardiner-Hill.

Hill, Headon, (F. Grainger), *died* 1927, vol. II

Hill, Sir Henry Blyth, 6th Bt (*cr* 1779), 1867–1929, vol. III
Hill, Col Henry Cecil de la Montague, 1864–1931, vol. III
Hill, Rev. Henry Erskine, 1864–1939, vol. III
Hill, Henry Staveley S.; *see* Staveley-Hill.
Hill, Col Henry Warburton, 1877–1951, vol. V
Hill, Henry William, 1850–1926, vol. II
Hill, Lt-Col Hugh, 1875–1916, vol. II
Hill, Sir Ian George Wilson, 1904–1982, vol. VIII
Hill, J. Arthur, 1872–1951, vol. V
Hill, J. Smith, 1866–1944, vol. IV
Hill, Sir James, 1st Bt (*cr* 1917), 1849–1936, vol. III
Hill, Sir James, 3rd Bt (*cr* 1917), 1905–1976, vol. VII
Hill, James Bastian, 1861–1927, vol. II
Hill, James J., 1838–1916, vol. II
Hill, James Meechan, 1899–1966, vol. VI
Hill, James Peter, 1873–1954, vol. V
Hill, James Stevens, 1854–1921, vol. II
Hill, Sir (James William) Francis, 1899–1980, vol. VII
Hill, John; *see* Hill, F. J.
Hill, Maj.-Gen. John, 1866–1935, vol. III
Hill, Rt Rev. John Charles, 1862–1943, vol. IV
Hill, Sir (John) Denis (Nelson), 1913–1982, vol. VIII
Hill, Sir John Edward Gray, 1839–1914, vol. I
Hill, John Gibson, 1910–1975, vol. VII
Hill, Mrs John Stanley; *see* Hill, Eveline.
Hill, Col Joseph, 1850–1918, vol. II
Hill, Joseph, 1888–1947, vol. IV
Hill, Kenneth Robson, 1911–1973, vol. VII
Hill, Laurence Carr, 1890–1959, vol. V
Hill, Sir Leonard Erskine, 1866–1952, vol. V
Hill, Leonard R.; *see* Raven-Hill.
Hill, Maj.-Gen. Leslie Rowley, 1884–1975, vol. VII
Hill, Levi Clement, 1883–1961, vol. VI
Hill, Martin; *see* Hill, W. M.
Hill, Martin Spencer, 1893–1968, vol. VI
Hill, Matthew Davenport, 1872–1958, vol. V
Hill, Maurice; *see* Hill, P. M.
Hill, Sir Maurice, 1862–1934, vol. III
Hill, Maurice Neville, 1919–1966, vol. VI
Hill, Micaiah John Muller, 1856–1929, vol. III
Hill, Montague, *died* 1929, vol. III
Hill, Lt-Col Sir Norman Gray, 2nd Bt (*cr* 1919), 1894–1944, vol. IV
Hill, Norman Hammond, 1893–1984, vol. VIII
Hill, Octavia, 1838–1912, vol. I
Hill, Oliver, 1887–1968, vol. VI
Hill, Osman; *see* Hill, W. C. O.
Hill, Col Peter Edward, 1834–1919, vol. II
Hill, Philip Ernest, *died* 1944, vol. IV
Hill, (Philip) Maurice, 1892–1952, vol. V
Hill, Sir Quintin; *see* Hill, Sir T. St Q.
Hill, Ralph William, 1893–1966, vol. VI
Hill, Reginald Duke, 1866–1922, vol. II
Hill, Reginald Dykers Richardson, 1902–1973, vol. VII
Hill, Reginald Harrison, 1894–1976, vol. VII
Hill, Sir Reginald Herbert, 1888–1971, vol. VII
Hill, Reginald John James, 1905–1977, vol. VII
Hill, Vice-Adm. Hon. Sir Richard A. S., 1880–1954, vol. V
Hill, Surg. Vice-Adm. Sir Robert, 1865–1938, vol. III

Hill, Maj.-Gen. Robert Charles C.; *see* Cottrell-Hill.
Hill, Sir Robert E.; *see* Erskine-Hill.
Hill, Robert Hughes, 1892–1963, vol. VI
Hill, Lt-Col Robert Montagu, 1872–1934, vol. III
Hill, Air Chief Marshal Sir Roderic Maxwell, 1894–1954, vol. V
Hill, Rowland, 1883–1962, vol. VI
Hill, Brig. Rowland Clement Ridley, 1879–1967, vol. VI
Hill, Gen. Sir Rowley Sale S.; *see* Sale-Hill.
Hill, Sir Sidney Pearson, 1900–1968, vol. VI
Hill, Sydney, 1902–1968, vol. VI
Hill, Thomas Arthur, 1854–1931, vol. III
Hill, Sir Thomas Eustace, *died* 1931, vol. III
Hill, Thomas George, 1876–1954, vol. V
Hill, Major Thomas Henry, 1844–1930, vol. III
Hill, Thomas Rowland, 1903–1967, vol. VI
Hill, Sir (Thomas St) Quintin, 1889–1963, vol. VI
Hill, Thomas William, 1866–1953, vol. V
Hill, Thomson; *see* Hill, W. T.
Hill, Victor Archibald Lord, 1905–1988, vol. VIII
Hill, Vincent Walker, *died* 1913, vol. I
Hill, Lt-Col Walter de Marchot, 1877–1927, vol. II
Hill, Maj.-Gen. Walter Pitts Hendy, 1877–1942, vol. IV
Hill, Engr Rear-Adm. Walter S.; *see* Scott-Hill.
Hill, Maj.-Gen. William, 1846–1903, vol. I
Hill, William, *died* 1928, vol. II
Hill, Col Sir William Alexander, 1846–1931, vol. III
Hill, Hon. William Caldwell, 1866–1939, vol. III
Hill, William Charles Osman, 1901–1975, vol. VII
Hill, William George John, 1876–1933, vol. III
Hill, William Henry, 1872–1957, vol. V
Hill, William Kirkpatrick, 1862–1944, vol. IV
Hill, (William) Martin, 1905–1976, vol. VII
Hill, (William) Thomson, 1875–1959, vol. V
Hill, William Wills, 1881–1974, vol. VII
Hill-Trevor, Hon. George Edwyn; *see* Trevor.
Hill-Walker, Major Alan Richard, 1859–1944, vol. IV
Hill Watson, Hon. Lord; Laurence Hill Watson, 1895–1957, vol. V
Hill Watson, Laurence; *see* Hill Watson, Hon. Lord.
Hill-Wood, Captain Sir Basil Samuel Hill, 2nd Bt, 1900–1954, vol. V
Hill-Wood, Major Sir Samuel Hill, 1st Bt, 1872–1949, vol. IV
Hill-Wood, Sir Wilfred William Hill, 1901–1980, vol. VII
Hillard, Rev. Albert Ernest, 1865–1935, vol. III
Hillard, Frederick Arthur, 1868–1937, vol. III
Hillard, Ronald Johnstone, 1903–1971, vol. VII
Hillary, Albert Ernest, 1868–1954, vol. V
Hillary, Michael, 1886–1976, vol. VII
Hiller, George François, 1916–1972, vol. VII
Hillgarth, Captain Alan Hugh, 1899–1978, vol. VII
Hillhouse, Percy Archibald, 1869–1942, vol. IV
Hillhouse, William, 1850–1910, vol. I
Hilliam, Maj.-Gen. Edward, 1863–1949, vol. IV
Hilliar, Harry William, *died* 1941, vol. IV
Hilliard, Christopher Richard, 1930–1985, vol. VIII
Hilliard, Edward, 1867–1940, vol. III
Hilliard, Harvey, *died* 1956, vol. V
Hilliard, Captain Maurice Alfred, 1863–1907, vol. I

Hilliard, Rt Rev. William George, *died* 1960, vol. V

Hillier, Alfred Peter, 1858–1911, vol. I

Hillier, Arthur, 1895–1986, vol. VIII

Hillier, Edward Guy, 1857–1924, vol. II

Hillier, Frank Norton, 1894–1959, vol. V

Hillier, Frederick James, 1869–1920, vol. II

Hillier, George Lacy, 1856–1941, vol. IV

Hillier, Sir Harold George, 1905–1985, vol. VIII

Hillier, Joseph Hillier, vol. II

Hillier, Tristram Paul, 1905–1983, vol. VIII

Hillier, Sir Walter Caine, 1849–1927, vol. II

Hillingdon, 1st Baron, 1830–1898, vol. I

Hillingdon, 2nd Baron, 1855–1919, vol. II

Hillingdon, 3rd Baron, 1891–1952, vol. V

Hillingdon, 4th Baron, 1922–1978, vol. VII

Hillingdon, 5th Baron, 1906–1982, vol. VIII

Hillis, Rev. Newell Dwight, 1858–1929, vol. III

Hillman, G. B., 1867–1932, vol. III

Hills, Adam, 1880–1941, vol. IV

Hills, Sir Andrew Ashton Waller, 1st Bt, 1933–1955, vol. V

Hills, Col Edmond Herbert G.; *see* Grove-Hills.

Hills, Edwin Sherbon, 1906–1986, vol. VIII

Hills, Eustace Gilbert, *died* 1934, vol. III

Hills, Maj.-Gen. Sir John, 1834–1902, vol. I

Hills, Lt-Col John David, 1895–1975, vol. VII

Hills, Rt Hon. John Waller, 1867–1938, vol. III

Hills, Lawrence Donegan, 1911–1990, vol. VIII

Hills, Sir Reginald Playfair, 1877–1967, vol. VI

Hills-Johnes, Lt-Gen. Sir James, 1833–1919, vol. II

Hillyard, Comdr George Whiteside, 1864–1943, vol. IV

Hilston, Sir Duncan, 1837–1913, vol. I

Hilton of Upton, Baron (Life Peer); Albert Victor Hilton, 1908–1977, vol. VII

Hilton, Cecil, 1884–1931, vol. III

Hilton, Conrad Nicholson, 1887–1979, vol. VII

Hilton, Sir Derek Percy, 1908–1986, vol. VIII

Hilton, Gwen, 1898–1971, vol. VII

Hilton, Harold Horsfall, 1869–1942, vol. IV

Hilton, James, 1900–1954, vol. V

Hilton, John, 1880–1943, vol. IV

Hilton, Reginald, 1895–1969, vol. VI

Hilton, Maj.-Gen. Richard, 1894–1978, vol. VII

Hilton, Sir Robert Stuart, 1870–1943, vol. IV

Hilton, Roger, 1911–1975, vol. VII

Hilton-Sergeant, Maj.-Gen. Frederick Cavendish, 1898–1978, vol. VII

Hilton-Simpson, Melville William, 1881–1938, vol. III

Him, George, 1900–1982, vol. VIII

Himbury, Sir William Henry, *died* 1955, vol. V

Hime, Lt-Col Rt Hon. Sir Albert Henry, 1842–1919, vol. II

Hime, Maj.-Gen. Henry Charles Rupert, 1877–1945, vol. IV

Hime, Lt-Col Henry William Lovett, 1840–1929, vol. III

Himmelweit, Hildegard Therese, (Hilde), 1918–1989, vol. VIII

Hinchcliff, William Fryer, *died* 1931, vol. III

Hinchcliffe, Hon. Albert, 1860–1935, vol. III

Hinchcliffe, Sir (George) Raymond, 1900–1973, vol. VII

Hinchcliffe, Brig. John William, 1893–1975, vol. VII

Hinchcliffe, Sir Raymond; *see* Hinchcliffe, Sir G. R.

Hinchcliffe, Richard George, *died* 1942, vol. IV

Hinchey, Herbert John, 1908–1988, vol. VIII

Hinchley, John William, 1871–1931, vol. III

Hinchliffe, Sir (Albert) Henry (Stanley), 1893–1980, vol. VII

Hinchliffe, (Frank) Philip (Rideal), 1923–1976, vol. VII

Hinchliffe, Sir Henry; *see* Hinchliffe, Sir A. H. S.

Hinchliffe, Sir James Peace, 1861–1933, vol. III

Hinchliffe, Philip; *see* Hinchliffe, F. P. R.

Hinchliffe, William Algernon S.; *see* Simpson-Hinchliffe.

Hincks, Hon. Sir Cecil Stephen, 1894–1963, vol. VI

Hincks, Rev. Thomas, 1818–1899, vol. I

Hind, Arthur Mayger, 1880–1957, vol. V

Hind, C. Lewis, 1862–1927, vol. II

Hind, Sir Jesse William, 1866–1946, vol. IV

Hind, Rt Rev. John, 1879–1958, vol. V

Hind, Maj.-Gen. Neville Godfray, 1892–1973, vol. VII

Hind, Richard Dacre A.; *see* Archer-Hind.

Hinde, Brig.-Gen. Alan, 1876–1950, vol. IV

Hinde, George Jennings, *died* 1918, vol. II

Hinde, George Langford, 1832–1910, vol. I

Hinde, Brig. Harold Montague, 1895–1965, vol. VI

Hinde, Rev. Herbert William, 1877–1955, vol. V

Hinde, Col John Henry Edward, 1847–1931, vol. III

Hinde, Lt-Col Reginald Graham, 1887–1971, vol. VII

Hinde, Maj.-Gen. Sir Robert; *see* Hinde, Maj.-Gen. Sir W. R. N.

Hinde, Sidney Langford, 1863–1930, vol. III

Hinde, Maj.-Gen. (Hon.) Sir (William) Robert (Norris), 1900–1981, vol. VIII

Hindemith, Paul, 1895–1963, vol. VI

Hindenburg, Frau Herbert von; *see* Hay, Marie.

Hindenburg, Field-Marshal Paul von Beneckendorff und von, 1847–1934, vol. III

Hinderks, Hermann Ernst, *born* 1907, vol. VIII

Hindle, Edward, 1886–1973, vol. VII

Hindle, Sir Frederick, 1877–1953, vol. V

Hindle, Frederick George, 1848–1925, vol. II

Hindle, Wilfrid Hope, 1903–1967, vol. VI

Hindley, Sir Clement D. M., 1874–1944, vol. IV

Hindley, Brig. Geoffrey Bernard Sylvester, 1902–1980, vol. VII

Hindley, Henry Oliver Rait, 1906–1988, vol. VIII

Hindley, Ven. William George, *died* 1936, vol. III

Hindley-Smith, James Dury, 1894–1974, vol. VII

Hindlip, 2nd Baron, 1842–1897, vol. I

Hindlip, 3rd Baron, 1877–1931, vol. III

Hindlip, 4th Baron, 1906–1966, vol. VI

Hindmarsh, W(illiam) Russell, 1929–1973, vol. VII

Hinds, Benjamin, 1882–1952, vol. V

Hinds, John, 1862–1928, vol. II

Hindus, Maurice Gerschon, 1891–1969, vol. VI

Hine, George T., 1841–1916, vol. II

Hine, Harry, 1845–1941, vol. IV

Hine, Rt Rev. John Edward, 1857–1934, vol. III

Hine, Montague Leonard, 1883–1967, vol. VI

Hine, Reginald Leslie, 1883–1949, vol. IV

Hine-Haycock, Rev. Trevitt Reginald, 1861–1953, vol. V

Hine-Haycock, Col Vaughan Randolph, 1871–1937, vol. III

Hines, Gerald; *see* Hines, V. G.

Hines, Robert Henry, 1931–1982, vol. VIII

Hines, (Vivian) Gerald, 1912–1987, vol. VIII

Hinge, Maj.-Gen. Harry Alexander, 1868–1948, vol. IV

Hingeston-Randolph, Rev. Francis Charles, 1833–1910, vol. I

Hingley, Anthony Capper Moore, 1908–1983, vol. VIII

Hingley, Sir Benjamin, 1st Bt, 1830–1905, vol. I

Hingley, Sir George Benjamin, 2nd Bt, 1850–1918, vol. II

Hingston, Lt-Col Clayton Alexander Francis, 1877–1969, vol. VI

Hingston, George, *died* 1925, vol. II

Hingston, Major Richard William George, 1887–1966, vol. VI

Hingston, Hon. Sir William Hales, 1829–1907, vol. I

Hingston, Surg. Captain William Percival, 1879–1950, vol. IV

Hinks, Arthur Robert, 1873–1945, vol. IV

Hinkson, Henry Albert, 1865–1919, vol. II

Hinkson, Mrs Katharine Tynan; *see* Tynan, Katharine.

Hinkson, Pamela, *died* 1982, vol. VIII

Hinshelwood, Sir Cyril Norman, 1897–1967, vol. VI

Hinsley, His Eminence Cardinal Arthur, 1865–1943, vol. IV

Hinsley, Frederick Baden, 1900–1988, vol. VIII

Hinton of Bankside, Baron (Life Peer); Christopher Hinton, 1901–1983, vol. VIII

Hinton, A. Horsley, 1863–1908, vol. I

Hinton, Arthur, 1869–1941, vol. IV

Hinton, Mrs Arthur; *see* Goodson, K.

Hinton, Captain Eric Perceval, 1902–1970, vol. VI

Hinton, Geoffrey Thomas Searle, 1918–1980, vol. VII

Hinton, Lt-Col Godfrey Bingham, 1871–1918, vol. II

Hinton, Howard Everest, 1912–1977, vol. VII

Hinton, Martin Alister Campbell, 1883–1961, vol. VI

Hinton, Wilfred John, 1887–1949, vol. IV

Hinton-Cooper, Harold, 1891–1980, vol. VII

Hintz, Orton Sutherland, 1907–1985, vol. VIII

Hinwood, George Yorke, 1894–1960, vol. V

Hinxman, Lionel Wordsworth, 1855–1936, vol. III

Hiorns, Frederick Robert, 1876–1961, vol. VI

Hipkins, Alfred James, 1826–1903, vol. I

Hippisley, John, *died* 1898, vol. I

Hippisley, Richard John Bayntun, *died* 1956, vol. V

Hippisley, Col Richard Lionel, 1853–1936, vol. III

Hipwell, Col Alfred George, 1853–1939, vol. III

Hipwell, Ven. Richard Senior, 1881–1962, vol. VI

Hipwood, Sir Charles, 1869–1946, vol. IV

Hirachand, Walchand, 1882–1953, vol. V

Hird, Rev. Arthur, 1883–1932, vol. III

Hird, Norman Leslie, 1886–1946, vol. IV

Hirohito, Emperor of Japan, (Emperor Showa), 1901–1989, vol. VIII

Hirsch, Maj.-Gen. Charles Ernest Rickards, 1903–1975, vol. VII

Hirsch, Emil G., 1851–1923, vol. II

Hirsch, Kurt August, 1906–1986, vol. VIII

Hirsch, Lt-Col Leonard, 1879–1942, vol. IV

Hirsch, Paul Adolf, 1881–1951, vol. V

Hirst, 1st Baron, 1863–1943, vol. IV

Hirst, Sir Amos Brook, 1878–1955, vol. V

Hirst, Sir Edmund Langley, 1898–1975, vol. VII

Hirst, Col Edward Audus, 1872–1937, vol. III

Hirst, Francis W., 1873–1953, vol. V

Hirst, Sir (Frank) Wyndham, *died* 1972, vol. VII

Hirst, Geoffrey Audus Nicholson, 1904–1984, vol. VIII

Hirst, George Henry, 1869–1933, vol. III

Hirst, George S. S., 1871–1912, vol. I

Hirst, Reginald John, 1880–1959, vol. V

Hirst, William, 1873–1946, vol. IV

Hirst, William Alfred, 1870–1948, vol. IV

Hirst, Sir Wyndham; *see* Hirst, Sir F. W.

Hirtzel, Sir Arthur, 1870–1937, vol. III

Hiscock, Alfred James, *died* 1930, vol. III

Hiscocks, Edward Stanley, 1903–1973, vol. VII

Hiscox, Ralph, 1907–1970, vol. VI

Hislop, James, 1870–1932, vol. III

Hislop, Joseph, *died* 1977, vol. VII

Hislop, Margaret Ross, 1894–1972, vol. VII

Hislop, Thomas Charles Atkinson, 1888–1965, vol. VI

Hislop, Hon. Thomas William, 1850–1925, vol. II

Hissey, James John, *died* 1921, vol. II

Hitch, Frederick Brook, 1877–1957, vol. V

Hitchcock, Sir Alfred Joseph, 1899–1980, vol. VII

Hitchcock, Lt-Gen. Sir Basil Ferguson Burnett-, 1877–1938, vol. III

Hitchcock, Sir Eldred Frederick, 1887–1959, vol. V

Hitchcock, Ethan Allen, 1835–1909, vol. I

Hitchcock, Rev. Francis Ryan Montgomery, 1867–1951, vol. V

Hitchcock, Geoffrey Lionel Henry, 1915–1987, vol. VIII

Hitchcock, Rev. George Edward, 1862–1939, vol. III

Hitchcock, Henry-Russell, 1903–1987, vol. VIII

Hitchcock, Howard, 1866–1932, vol. III

Hitchcock, Rev. William Maunder, 1835–1921, vol. II

Hitchen, Rt Rev. Anthony, 1930–1988, vol. VIII

Hitchens, Harry Butler, 1910–1963, vol. VI

Hitchens, Ivon; *see* Hitchens, S. I.

Hitchens, (Sydney) Ivon, 1893–1979, vol. VII

Hitching, Sir Thomas Henry B.; *see* Brooke-Hitching.

Hitching, Gp Captain John Phelp, 1899–1979, vol. VII

Hitchins, Col Charles Faunce, *died* 1959, vol. V

Hitchins, Col Charles Henry Macintire, 1860–1931, vol. III

Hitchins, Brig. Edward Norman Fortescue, 1884–1959, vol. V

Hitchins, Francis Eric, 1891–1983, vol. VIII

Hitchins, Captain Henry Luxmoore, 1885–1961, vol. VI

Hitchman, Sir Alan; *see* Hitchman, Sir E. A.

Hitchman, Sir (Edwin) Alan, 1903–1980, vol. VII

Hitler, Adolph, 1889–1945, vol. IV

Hives, 1st Baron, 1886–1965, vol. VI

Hives, Rt Rev. Harry Ernest, 1901–1974, vol. VII

Hjelt, Edvard Immanuel, 1855–1921, vol. II

Hjort, Johan, 1869–1948, vol. IV

Ho Tung, Sir Robert, 1862–1956, vol. V

Hoad, Maj.-Gen. Sir John Charles, 1856–1911, vol. I
Hoadley, Charles Archibald, 1887–1947, vol. IV
Hoadley, Jane, died 1946, vol. IV
Hoar, Arthur Stanley George, 1903–1972, vol. VII
Hoar, Hon. Ernest Knight, 1898–1979, vol. VII
Hoar, George F., 1826–1904, vol. I
Hoare, Alfred, 1850–1938, vol. III
Hoare, Sir Archer, 1876–1973, vol. VII
Hoare, Lt-Col Arthur Fanshawe, 1854–1925, vol. II
Hoare, Arthur Hervey, 1877–1953, vol. V
Hoare, Cecil Arthur, 1892–1984, vol. VIII
Hoare, Charles Richard, 1868–1933, vol. III
Hoare, Christopher Gurney, 1882–1973, vol. VII
Hoare, Brig.-Gen. Cuthbert Gurney, 1883–1969, vol. VI
Hoare, Rear-Adm. Dennis John, 1891–1979, vol. VII
Hoare, Rear-Adm. Desmond John, 1910–1988, vol. VIII
Hoare, Douglas, 1875–1947, vol. IV
Hoare, Edward Brodie, 1841–1911, vol. I
Hoare, Sir Edward O'Bryen, 7th Bt (cr 1784), 1898–1969, vol. VI
Hoare, Edward Ralphe Douro, 1894–1936, vol. III
Hoare, Edward Wallis, 1863–1920, vol. II, vol. III
Hoare, Maj.-Gen. Francis Richard Gurney, 1879–1959, vol. V
Hoare, Sir Frederick Alfred, 1st Bt, 1913–1986, vol. VIII
Hoare, Lt-Col Geoffrey Lennard, 1879–1960, vol. V
Hoare, Henry, 1866–1956, vol. V
Hoare, Sir Henry Hugh Arthur, 6th Bt (cr 1786), 1865–1947, vol. IV
Hoare, Henry Noel, 1877–1962, vol. VI
Hoare, Henry William H.; see Hamilton-Hoare.
Hoare, Hugh Edward, 1854–1929, vol. III
Hoare, Rev. John Gurney, 1847–1923, vol. II
Hoare, Rt Rev. Joseph, 1842–1927, vol. II
Hoare, Rt Rev. Joseph Charles, 1851–1906, vol. I
Hoare, Sir Joseph Wallis O'Bryen, 5th Bt (cr 1784), 1828–1904, vol. I
Hoare, Maj.-Gen. Lionel Lennard, 1881–1975, vol. VII
Hoare, Michael Richard, 1903–1970, vol. VI
Hoare, Oliver Vaughan Gurney, 1882–1957, vol. V
Hoare, Peter Arthur Marsham, 1869–1939, vol. III
Hoare, Sir Peter William, 7th Bt (cr 1786), 1898–1973, vol. VII
Hoare, Brig.-Gen. Reginald, 1865–1947, vol. IV
Hoare, Sir Reginald Hervey, died 1954, vol. V
Hoare, Rev. Richard Whitehead, 1840–1924, vol. II
Hoare, Major Robert Basil, 1870–1931, vol. III
Hoare, Col Robert Rawdon, 1897–1977, vol. VII
Hoare, Sir Samuel, 1st Bt (cr 1899), 1841–1915, vol. I
Hoare, Sir Samuel, 1896–1976, vol. VII
Hoare, Sir Sydney James O'Bryen, 6th Bt (cr 1784), 1860–1933, vol. III
Hoare, William Douro, 1862–1928, vol. II
Hobart, Lt-Col Sir (Claud) Vere Cavendish, 2nd Bt, 1870–1949, vol. IV
Hobart, Henry Metcalf, 1868–1946, vol. IV
Hobart, Brig. James Wilfred Lang Stanley, 1890–1970, vol. VI
Hobart, Maj.-Gen. Patrick Robert Chamier, 1917–1986, vol. VIII

Hobart, Maj.-Gen. Sir Percy Cleghorn Stanley, 1885–1957, vol. V
Hobart, Robert Charles Arthur Stanley, 1881–1955, vol. V
Hobart, Lt-Cmdr Sir Robert Hampden, 3rd Bt, 1915–1988, vol. VIII
Hobart, Sir Robert Henry, 1st Bt, 1836–1928, vol. II
Hobart, Lt-Col Sir Vere; see Hobart, Sir C. V. C.
Hobart-Hampden, Hon. Charles Edward, 1825–1913, vol. I
Hobart-Hampden, Ernest Miles, 1864–1949, vol. IV
Hobbes, John Oliver, 1867–1906, vol. I
Hobbins, Robert, died 1922, vol. II
Hobbins, Thomas Phillips, 1877–1959, vol. V
Hobbs, Lt-Col George Radley, 1853–1907, vol. I
Hobbs, Harold William, 1903–1976, vol. VII
Hobbs, Captain Horace Edwin, 1896–1935, vol. III
Hobbs, Jack; see Hobbs, Sir John B.
Hobbs, Sir John (Berry), (Jack), 1882–1963, vol. VI
Hobbs, Lt-Gen. Sir (Joseph John) Talbot, 1864–1938, vol. III
Hobbs, Maj.-Gen. Percy Eyre Francis, 1865–1939, vol. III
Hobbs, Brig.-Gen. Reginald Francis Arthur, 1878–1953, vol. V
Hobbs, Maj.-Gen. Reginald Geoffrey Stirling, 1908–1977, vol. VII
Hobbs, Lt-Gen. Sir Talbot; see Hobbs, Lt-Gen. Sir J. J. T.
Hobbs, William Alfred, 1912–1984, vol. VIII
Hobday, Alfred, 1870–1942, vol. IV
Hobday, Col Edmund Arthur Ponsonby, 1859–1931, vol. III
Hobday, Sir Frederick T. G., died 1939, vol. III
Hobday, Maj.-Gen. Thomas Francis, 1847–1938, vol. III
Hobhouse, 1st Baron, 1819–1904, vol. I
Hobhouse, Sir Arthur Lawrence, 1886–1965, vol. VI
Hobhouse, Rt Hon. Sir Charles Edward Henry, 4th Bt, 1862–1941, vol. IV
Hobhouse, Sir Charles Parry, 3rd Bt, 1825–1916, vol. II
Hobhouse, Rt Rev. Edmund, 1817–1904, vol. I
Hobhouse, Edmund, 1860–1933, vol. III
Hobhouse, Edmund W. Neill, 1888–1973, vol. VII
Hobhouse, Rt Hon. Henry, 1854–1937, vol. III
Hobhouse, Sir John Richard, 1893–1961, vol. VI
Hobhouse, Leonard Trelawney, 1864–1929, vol. III
Hobhouse, Sir Reginald Arthur, 5th Bt, 1878–1947, vol. IV
Hobhouse, Rev. Walter, 1862–1928, vol. II
Hobkirk, Brig.-Gen. Clarence John, 1869–1949, vol. IV
Hobkirk, Col Elspeth Isabel Weatherley, 1903–1990, vol. VIII
Hobley, Charles William, 1867–1947, vol. IV
Hobman, Joseph Burton, 1872–1953, vol. V
Hobson, Baron (Life Peer); Charles Rider Hobson, 1904–1966, vol. VI
Hobson, Sir Albert John, died 1923, vol. II
Hobson, Alec, 1899–1986, vol. VIII
Hobson, Alfred Dennis, 1901–1974, vol. VII
Hobson, Alice Mary, 1860–1954, vol. V
Hobson, Clement, 1877–1952, vol. V

Hobson, Ven. Edward Waller, 1851–1924, vol. II
Hobson, Rev. Edwin, 1847–1936, vol. III
Hobson, Ernest William, 1856–1933, vol. III
Hobson, Maj.-Gen. Frederic Taylor, 1840–1909, vol. I
Hobson, Frederick Greig, died 1961, vol. VI
Hobson, Geoffrey Dudley, 1882–1949, vol. IV
Hobson, Lt-Col Gerald Walton, 1873–1962, vol. VI
Hobson, Harold, 1891–1973, vol. VII
Hobson, Harry Roy, died 1965, vol. VI
Hobson, Sir Henry Arthur, 1893–1968, vol. VI
Hobson, John Atkinson, 1858–1940, vol. III
Hobson, (John) Basil, 1905–1985, vol. VIII
Hobson, Rt Hon. Sir John Gardiner Sumner, 1912–1967, vol. VI
Hobson, John Lombard, died 1932, vol. III
Hobson, Neville, 1886–1975, vol. VII
Hobson, Sir Oscar Rudolf, 1886–1961, vol. VI
Hobson, Sir Patrick, 1909–1970, vol. VI
Hobson, Rev. R., died 1914, vol. I
Hobson, Robert Lockhart, 1872–1941, vol. IV
Hobson, Sidney, 1887–1970, vol. VI
Hobson, William, 1911–1982, vol. VIII
Hoby, Major John Charles James, died 1938, vol. III
Hochoy, Sir Solomon, 1905–1983, vol. VIII
Hockaday, William Thomas, 1858–1933, vol. III
Hocken, Col Charles Augustus Frederick, 1870–1958, vol. V
Hocken, Hon. Horatio Clarence, 1857–1937, vol. III
Hocking, Sir Henry Hicks, 1842–1907, vol. I
Hocking, Joseph, died 1937, vol. III
Hocking, Silas Kitto, 1850–1935, vol. III
Hocking, William John, 1864–1953, vol. V
Hockley, Ven. Guy Wittenoom, 1869–1946, vol. IV
Hockliffe, Ernest, 1863–1944, vol. IV
Hodd, Ven. Henry Norman, 1905–1973, vol. VII
Hodder, Lt-Col Andrew Edward, died 1938, vol. III
Hodder, Edwin, 1837–1904, vol. I
Hodder-Williams, Sir Ernest; see Hodder-Williams, Sir J. E.
Hodder-Williams, Sir (John) Ernest, 1876–1927, vol. II
Hodder-Williams, Ralph Wilfred, 1890–1961, vol. VI
Hodder-Williams, Robert Percy, 1880–1958, vol. V
Hodding, Col John, 1854–1919, vol. II
Hodge, Alan, 1915–1979, vol. VII
Hodge, Albert H., 1875–1918, vol. II
Hodge, Rear-Adm. Hon. Claude Preston H.; see Herman-Hodge.
Hodge, Rev. Canon Edward Grose, died 1928, vol. II
Hodge, Lt-Col Edward Humfrey Vere, 1883–1968, vol. VI
Hodge, Francis Edwin, 1883–1949, vol. IV
Hodge, Frederick Webb, 1864–1956, vol. V
Hodge, Harold, 1862–1937, vol. III
Hodge, Harry, 1872–1947, vol. IV
Hodge, Horace Emerton, 1940–1958, vol. V
Hodge, Humfrey G.; see Grose-Hodge.
Hodge, Lt-Col James Philip, 1879–1946, vol. IV
Hodge, Rt Hon. John, 1855–1937, vol. III
Hodge, John Douglass Vere, 1887–1973, vol. VII
Hodge, John Ernest, 1911–1989, vol. VIII
Hodge, Merton; see Hodge, H. E.

Hodge, Major Hon. Robert Edward Udny H.; see Hermon-Hodge.
Hodge, Sir Rowland Frederic William, 1st Bt, 1859–1950, vol. IV
Hodge, Stephen Oswald Vere, 1891–1979, vol. VII
Hodge, Sir William Vallance Douglas, 1903–1975, vol. VII
Hodgen, Maj.-Gen. Gordon West, 1894–1968, vol. VI
Hodges, Rev. Alfred, 1853–1909, vol. I
Hodges, Arthur Harris, 1884–1941, vol. IV
Hodges, Lt-Col Aubrey Dallas Percival, 1861–1946, vol. IV
Hodges, Barbara K., 1893–1949, vol. IV
Hodges, Rt Rev. Edward Noel, 1849–1928, vol. II
Hodges, Rt Rev. Evelyn Charles, 1887–1980, vol. VII
Hodges, Frank, 1887–1947, vol. IV
Hodges, Ven. George, 1851–1922, vol. II
Hodges, Hon. Sir Henry Edward Agincourt, 1844–1919, vol. II
Hodges, Herbert Arthur, 1905–1976, vol. VII
Hodges, Kenneth Henry, 1915–1961, vol. VI
Hodges, Captain Michael, 1904–1977, vol. VII
Hodges, Adm. Sir Michael Henry, 1874–1951, vol. V
Hodges, Sir Reginald John, 1889–1973, vol. VII
Hodges, Rev. William Herbert, 1873–1948, vol. IV
Hodgett, Rev. Richard, 1884–1927, vol. II
Hodgetts, Charles Alfred, 1859–1952, vol. V
Hodgetts, Edward Arthur Brayley, 1859–1932, vol. III
Hodgins, Frank Egerton, died 1932, vol. III
Hodgins, Lt-Col Frederick Owen, 1887–1924, vol. II
Hodgins, Rev. Joseph Rogerson Edmond Cotter, died 1919, vol. II
Hodgins, Thomas, 1828–1910, vol. I
Hodgins, Maj.-Gen. William Egerton, 1850–1930, vol. III
Hodgkin, (Curwen) Eliot, 1905–1987, vol. VIII
Hodgkin, Eliot; see Hodgkin, C. E.
Hodgkin, Lt-Col Harry Sidney, 1879–1943, vol. IV
Hodgkin, Henry Theodore, 1877–1933, vol. III
Hodgkin, Jonathan Edward, 1875–1953, vol. V
Hodgkin, Lucy Violet (Mrs John Holdsworth), 1869–1954, vol. V
Hodgkin, Robert Howard, 1877–1951, vol. V
Hodgkin, Thomas, 1831–1913, vol. I
Hodgkin, Thomas Lionel, 1910–1982, vol. VIII
Hodgkins, T., died 1909, vol. I
Hodgkinson, Col Charles, 1870–1939, vol. III
Hodgkinson, Rev. George Langton, 1837–1915, vol. I
Hodgkinson, Comdr Guy Beauchamp, 1903–1981, vol. VIII
Hodgkinson, Jonathan, 1886–1940, vol. III
Hodgkinson, William Richard, 1851–1935, vol. III
Hodgson, Sir Arthur, 1818–1902, vol. I
Hodgson, Arthur John, 1887–1971, vol. VII
Hodgson, Lt-Col Barnard Thornton, 1863–1939, vol. III
Hodgson, Sir Edward Highton, 1880–1955, vol. V
Hodgson, Sir Edward Matthew, 1820–1904, vol. I
Hodgson, Ernest Atkinson, 1886–1975, vol. VII
Hodgson, Rev. Francis Greaves, 1840–1920, vol. II
Hodgson, Rev. Francis Henry, 1848–1930, vol. III
Hodgson, Francis Henry Birkett, 1879–1935, vol. III

Hodgson, Rev. Francis Roger, *died* 1920, vol. II
Hodgson, Sir Frederic Mitchell, 1851–1925, vol. II
Hodgson, George Bryan, 1863–1926, vol. II
Hodgson, Sir Gerald Hassall, 1891–1971, vol. VII
Hodgson, Geraldine E., 1865–1937, vol. III
Hodgson, Lt-Col Greenwood, 1875–1950, vol. IV
Hodgson, Sir Harold (Kingston) Graham-, *died* 1960, vol. V
Hodgson, Rt Rev. Henry Bernard, 1856–1921, vol. II
Hodgson, Maj.-Gen. Sir Henry West, 1868–1930, vol. III
Hodgson, Herbert Henry, 1883–1967, vol. VI
Hodgson, Rev. James Muscutt, *died* 1923, vol. II
Hodgson, Rear-Adm. John Coombe, 1881–1936, vol. III
Hodgson, (John) Stuart, 1877–1950, vol. IV
Hodgson, Rev. Leonard, 1889–1969, vol. VI
Hodgson, Sir Mark, 1880–1967, vol. VI
Hodgson, Norman, 1891–1963, vol. VI
Hodgson, Patrick Kirkman, 1884–1963, vol. VI
Hodgson, Ralph, 1871–1962, vol. VI
Hodgson, Ven. Robert, 1844–1917, vol. II
Hodgson, Robert Kirkman, 1850–1924, vol. II
Hodgson, Sir Robert MacLeod, 1874–1956, vol. V
Hodgson, Shadworth Hollway, 1832–1912, vol. I
Hodgson, Stuart; *see* Hodgson, J. S.
Hodgson, Ven. Thomas, *died* 1921, vol. II
Hodgson, Thomas Charles Birkett, 1907–1986, vol. VIII
Hodgson, Thomas Edward Highton, 1907–1985, vol. VIII
Hodgson, Brig. Walter Thornton, 1880–1957, vol. V
Hodgson, Rev. William, *died* 1919, vol. II
Hodgson, Sir William, 1854–1940, vol. III
Hodgson, Sir William, *died* 1945, vol. IV
Hodgson, William Archer, 1887–1965, vol. VI
Hodgson, William Earl, *died* 1910, vol. I
Hodgson, William Hope, 1877–1918, vol. II
Hodgson, Lt-Col William Roy, 1892–1958, vol. V
Hodgson, Mrs Willoughby, *died* 1949, vol. IV
Hodsdon, Sir James William Beeman, 1858–1928, vol. II
Hodsoll, Wing Comdr Sir (Eric) John, 1894–1971, vol. VII
Hodsoll, Wing Comdr Sir John; *see* Hodsoll, Wing Comdr Sir E. J.
Hodson, Baron (Life Peer); Francis Lord Charlton Hodson, 1895–1984, vol. VIII
Hodson, Sir Arnold Wienholt, 1881–1944, vol. IV
Hodson, Rt Rev. Augustine John, 1879–1961, vol. VI
Hodson, Cecil John, 1915–1985, vol. VIII
Hodson, Charles William, *died* 1910, vol. I
Hodson, Donald Manly, 1913–1988, vol. VIII
Hodson, Major Sir Edmond Adair, 5th Bt, 1893–1972, vol. VII
Hodson, Col Frederic Arthur, 1866–1925, vol. II
Hodson, Col George Benjamin, 1863–1916, vol. II
Hodson, Air Vice-Marshal George Stacey, 1899–1976, vol. VII
Hodson, James Lansdale, 1891–1956, vol. V
Hodson, Joseph John, 1912–1983, vol. VIII
Hodson, Leslie Manfred Noel, 1902–1985, vol. VIII
Hodson, Rt Rev. Mark Allin, 1907–1985, vol. VIII
Hodson, Sir Robert Adair, 4th Bt, 1853–1921, vol. II

Hodson, Rt Rev. Robert Leighton, 1885–1960, vol. V
Hodson, Samuel John, *died* 1908, vol. I
Hodson, Thomas Callan, *died* 1953, vol. V
Hoehne, Most Rev. John, 1910–1978, vol. VII
Hoenig, Rose, *died* 1966, vol. VI
Hoerne, Augustus Frederic Rudolf, 1841–1918, vol. II
Hoernlé, R. F. Alfred, *died* 1943, vol. IV
Hoesch, Leopold Gustav Alexander von, 1881–1936, vol. III
Hoey, Frances Sarah, (Mrs Cashel Hoey), 1830–1908, vol. I
Hoey, Robert Alexander, 1883–1965, vol. VI
Hoey, William, 1849–1919, vol. II
Hoffding, Harold, 1843–1931, vol. III
Hoffe, Monckton, 1881–1951, vol. V
Hoffert, Hermann H., *born* 1860, vol. II
Hoffman, Anna Rosenberg, 1902–1983, vol. VIII
Hoffman, Paul Gray, 1891–1974, vol. VII
Hoffman, Philip Christopher, 1878–1959, vol. V
Hoffman, Prof.; *see* Lewis, Angelo.
Hoffmeister, William, 1843–1910, vol. I
Hoffnung, Gerard, 1925–1959, vol. V
Hofmann, Josef, 1876–1957, vol. V
Hofmeyr, George Morgan, 1867–1928, vol. II, vol. III
Hofmeyr, Hon. Gysbert Reitz, 1871–1942, vol. IV
Hofmeyr, Hon. Jan Hendrik, 1845–1909, vol. I
Hofmeyr, Rt Hon. Jan Hendrik, 1894–1948, vol. IV
Hofstadter, Richard, 1916–1970, vol. VI
Hofstadter, Robert, 1915–1990, vol. VIII
Hog, Major Roger Thomas Alexander, 1893–1979, vol. VII
Hog, Steuart Bayley, 1864–1944, vol. IV
Hogan, Hon. Edmond John, 1884–1964, vol. VI
Hogan, Lt-Col Edward Vincent, 1874–1933, vol. III
Hogan, Henry Charles, 1860–1924, vol. II
Hogan, James Francis, 1855–1924, vol. II
Hogan, James H., 1883–1948, vol. IV
Hogan, Rt Rev. Mgr John F., 1858–1918, vol. II
Hogan, Hon. Sir Michael Joseph Patrick, 1908–1986, vol. VIII
Hogan, Patrick, 1891–1936, vol. III
Hogarth, Alfred Moore, 1876–1947, vol. IV
Hogarth, David George, 1862–1927, vol. II
Hogarth, Maj.-Gen. Donald Macdonald, 1879–1950, vol. IV (A), vol. V
Hogarth, Margaret Cameron, 1885–1980, vol. VII
Hogarth, Mary H. U., *died* 1935, vol. III
Hogarth, Robert George, 1868–1953, vol. V
Hogarth, William David, 1901–1965, vol. VI
Hogben, George, 1853–1920, vol. II
Hogben, Herbert Edward, 1905–1984, vol. VIII
Hogben, Lancelot, 1895–1975, vol. VII
Hogbin, Ven. George Henry, 1869–1937, vol. III
Hogbin, Henry Cairn, 1880–1966, vol. VI
Hogg, Lt-Gen. Sir Adam George Forbes, 1836–1908, vol. I
Hogg, Adam Spencer, 1870–1937, vol. III
Hogg, Hon. Alan, *died* 1934, vol. III
Hogg, Alexander Hubert Arthur, 1908–1989, vol. VIII
Hogg, Rev. Andrew Albert Victor, 1867–1927, vol. II
Hogg, Sir Anthony Henry L.; *see* Lindsay-Hogg.

Hogg, Sir Cecil; *see* Hogg, Sir J. C.
Hogg, Col Conrad Charles Henry, 1875–1950, vol. IV
Hogg, Cuthbert Stuart, 1911–1973, vol. VII
Hogg, David C., 1840–1914, vol. I
Hogg, Maj.-Gen. Douglas MacArthur, 1888–1965, vol. VI
Hogg, Edward Gascoigne, 1882–1971, vol. VII
Hogg, Sir Frederick Russell, 1836–1923, vol. II
Hogg, Maj.-Gen. George Crawford, 1842–1921, vol. II
Hogg, George Robert Disraeli, 1894–1977, vol. VII
Hogg, Sir Gilbert Pitcairn, 1884–1950, vol. IV
Hogg, Guy Weir, 1861–1943, vol. IV
Hogg, Wing Comdr Henry Robert William, 1886–1942, vol. IV
Hogg, Hope W., 1863–1912, vol. I
Hogg, Lt-Col Ian Graham, 1875–1914, vol. I
Hogg, Jabez, 1817–1899, vol. I
Hogg, Sir (James) Cecil, 1900–1973, vol. VII
Hogg, John Drummond, 1886–1937, vol. III
Hogg, Rt Hon. Jonathan, 1847–1930, vol. III
Hogg, Sir Kenneth Weir, 6th Bt, 1894–1985, vol. VIII
Hogg, Sir Lindsay L.; *see* Lindsay-Hogg.
Hogg, Sir Malcolm Nicholson, 1883–1948, vol. IV
Hogg, Margaret, 1877–1975, vol. VII
Hogg, Norman, 1907–1975, vol. VII
Hogg, Brig. Oliver Frederick Gillilan, 1887–1979, vol. VII
Hogg, Percy Herbertson, 1898–1978, vol. VII
Hogg, Quintin, 1845–1903, vol. I
Hogg, Robert Henry, *died* 1949, vol. IV
Hogg, Brig.-Gen. Rudolph Edward Trower, 1877–1955, vol. V
Hogg, Sir Stuart Saunders, 1833–1921, vol. II
Hogg, William Edward, 1880–1968, vol. VI
Hogg, Sir William Lindsay L.; *see* Lindsay-Hogg.
Hogg, Lt-Col Willoughby Lugard, 1881–1969, vol. VI
Hoggan, Maj.-Gen. John William, 1833–1900, vol. I
Hoggarth, Arthur Henry Graham, 1882–1964, vol. VI
Hoggatt, William, 1880–1961, vol. VI
Hogge, Col Charles, 1851–1911, vol. I
Hogge, James Myles, 1873–1928, vol. II
Hogge, Col John William, 1852–1910, vol. I
Hogger, Rear-Adm. Henry Charles, 1907–1982, vol. VIII
Hogshaw, Brig. John Harold, 1896–1968, vol. VI
Hogue, Hon. James Alexander, 1846–1920, vol. II
Hogue, Oliver Alfred John, 1910–1987, vol. VIII
Hohenlohe-Langenburg, Prince of; Ernest William Frederic Charles Maximilian, *died* 1913, vol. I
Hohler, Sir Gerald Fitzroy, 1862–1934, vol. III
Hohler, Henry Booth, 1835–1916, vol. II
Hohler, Sir Thomas Beaumont, 1871–1946, vol. IV
Hohler, Thomas Sidney A.; *see* Astell Hohler.
Holbech, Rev. Charles William, 1816–1901, vol. I
Holbech, Lt-Col Laurence, 1888–1963, vol. V
Holbech, Ronald Herbert Acland, 1887–1956, vol. V
Holbech, Rt Rev. William Arthur, 1850–1930, vol. III
Holbeche, Brian Harry, 1920–1982, vol. VIII
Holbein, Arthur Montague, 1897–1970, vol. VI
Holberton, Sir Edgar Joseph, 1874–1949, vol. IV

Holborow, Col William Hillier, 1841–1917, vol. II, vol. III
Holbrook, Col Sir Arthur Richard, 1850–1946, vol. IV
Holbrook, Col Sir Claude Vivian, 1886–1979, vol. VII
Holbrook, Rear-Adm. Leonard Stanley, 1882–1974, vol. VII
Holbrook, Comdr Norman Douglas, 1888–1976, vol. VII
Holbrooke, Josef, 1878–1958, vol. V
Holbrooke, Maj.-Gen. Philip Lancelot, 1872–1958, vol. V
Holburn, James, 1900–1988, vol. VIII
Holburn, John Goundry, 1843–1899, vol. I
Holcroft, Sir Charles, 1st Bt (*cr* 1905), 1831–1917, vol. II
Holcroft, Sir George Harry, 1st Bt (*cr* 1921), 1856–1951, vol. V
Holcroft, Sir Reginald Culcheth, 2nd Bt (*cr* 1921), 1899–1978, vol. VII
Holden, 1st Baron, 1833–1912, vol. I
Holden, 2nd Baron, 1867–1937, vol. III
Holden, 3rd Baron, 1898–1951, vol. V
Holden, Rev. Albert Thomas, 1866–1935, vol. III
Holden, Arthur, 1881–1964, vol. VI
Holden, Brig.-Gen. Sir Capel Lofft; *see* Holden, Brig.-Gen. Sir H. C. L.
Holden, Charles, 1875–1960, vol. V
Holden, Col Charles Walter, *died* 1939, vol. III
Holden, Captain Edward Charles Shuttleworth, 1865–1916, vol. II
Holden, Sir Edward Hopkinson, 1st Bt (*cr* 1909), 1848–1919, vol. II
Holden, Sir Edward Thomas, 1831–1926, vol. II
Holden, Hon. Sir Edward Wheewall, 1885–1947, vol. IV
Holden, Sir George, 2nd Bt (*cr* 1919), 1890–1937, vol. III
Holden, Sir George, 3rd Bt (*cr* 1919), 1914–1976, vol. VII
Holden, Harold Henry, 1885–1977, vol. VII
Holden, Sir Harry Cassie, 2nd Bt (*cr* 1909), 1877–1965, vol. VI
Holden, Rev. Henry, 1814–1909, vol. I
Holden, Brig.-Gen. Sir (Henry) Capel Lofft, 1856–1937, vol. III
Holden, Henry Smith, 1887–1963, vol. VI
Holden, Sir Isaac, 1st Bt (*cr* 1893), 1807–1897, vol. I
Holden, Sir Isaac Holden, 5th Bt (*cr* 1893), 1867–1962, vol. VI
Holden, Sir James Robert, 1903–1977, vol. VII
Holden, Rt Rev. John, 1882–1949, vol. IV
Holden, Sir John Henry, 1st Bt (*cr* 1919), 1862–1926, vol. II
Holden, Rev. John Stuart, *died* 1934, vol. III
Holden, Kenneth Graham, 1910–1990, vol. VIII
Holden, Luther, 1815–1905, vol. I
Holden, Sir Michael Herbert Frank, 1913–1982, vol. VIII
Holden, Norman Edward, 1879–1946, vol. IV
Holden, Philip Edward, 1905–1987, vol. VIII
Holden, Rev. Robert, 1853–1926, vol. II
Holden, Maj.-Gen. William Corson, 1893–1955, vol. V

Holder, Douglas William, 1923–1977, vol. VII
Holder, Sir Frank Wilfred, 1897–1967, vol. VI
Holder, Hon. Sir Frederick William, 1850–1909, vol. I
Holder, Sir Henry Charles, 2nd Bt, 1874–1945, vol. IV
Holder, Rear-Adm. Henry Lowe, 1832–1924, vol. II
Holder, Sir John Charles, 1st Bt, 1838–1923, vol. II
Holder, Sir Eric Duncan, 3rd Bt, 1899–1986, vol. VIII
Holder, Rt Rev. Mgr Joseph, 1845–1917, vol. II
Holderness, Sir Ernest William Elsmie, 2nd Bt, 1890–1968, vol. VI
Holderness, Rt Rev. George Edward, 1913–1987, vol. VIII
Holderness Sir Thomas William, 1st Bt, 1849–1924, vol. II
Holdgate, Rev. William Wyatt, 1872–1949, vol. IV
Holdich, Gen. Sir Edward Alan, 1822–1909, vol. I
Holdich, Lt-Col Godfrey William Vanrennen, 1882–1921, vol. II
Holdich, Brig.-Gen. Harold Adrian, 1874–1964, vol. VI
Holdich, Col Sir Thomas Hungerford, 1843–1929, vol. III
Holding, Edgar Thomas, 1870–1952, vol. V
Holdsworth, Hon. Col Albert Amrytage, *died* 1932, vol. III
Holdsworth, Benjamin George, 1892–1943, vol. IV
Holdsworth, Sir Charles, 1863–1935, vol. III
Holdsworth, David, 1918–1978, vol. VII
Holdsworth, Sir Frank Wild, 1904–1969, vol. VI
Holdsworth, Brig.-Gen. George Lewis, 1862–1942, vol. IV
Holdsworth, Sir Herbert, 1890–1949, vol. IV
Holdsworth, Lt-Col John Joseph, 1844–1920, vol. II
Holdsworth, Lucy Violet; *see* Hodgkin, L. V.
Holdsworth, Mary, 1908–1978, vol. VII
Holdsworth, Max Ernest, 1895–1982, vol. VIII
Holdsworth, Sir William Searle, 1871–1944, vol. IV
Hole, Edwyn Cecil, *died* 1976, vol. VII
Hole, Francis George, 1904–1973, vol. VII
Hole, George Vincer, 1910–1988, vol. VIII
Hole, Lt-Col Hugh Marshall, 1865–1941, vol. IV
Hole, Robert Selby, 1875–1938, vol. III
Hole, S. Hugh F., 1862–1948, vol. IV
Hole, Very Rev. Samuel Reynolds, 1819–1904, vol. I
Hole, Tahu Ronald Charles Pearce, 1908–1985, vol. VIII
Hole, William, 1846–1917, vol. II
Holford, Baron (Life Peer); William Graham Holford, 1907–1975, vol. VII
Holford, Lt-Col Cecil Francis Lovell, 1900–1963, vol. VI
Holford, Lt-Col Sir George Lindsay, 1860–1926, vol. II
Holford, Mrs Gwynne, (Mary Eleanor), *died* 1947, vol. IV
Holford, Lt-Col James Henry Edward, 1873–1936, vol. III
Holford, James Price William Gwynne, 1833–1916, vol. II
Holford, Mary Eleanor; *see* Holford, Mrs Gwynne.
Holiday, Sir Frederick Charles, 1843–1930, vol. III
Holiday, Henry, 1839–1927, vol. II

Hollams, Frederick William, 1848–1941, vol. IV
Hollams, Sir John, 1820–1910, vol. I
Holland, Alfred, 1900–1936, vol. III
Holland, Sir Alfred Herbert, 1878–1968, vol. VI
Holland, Sir Arthur, 1842–1928, vol. II
Holland, Lt-Gen. Sir Arthur Edward Aveling, 1862–1927, vol. II
Holland, Bernard Henry, 1856–1926, vol. II
Holland, Vice-Adm. Cedric Swinton, 1889–1950, vol. IV
Holland, Charles Thurstan, *died* 1941, vol. IV
Holland, Clive, (Charles James Hankinson), 1866–1959, vol. V
Holland, Sir Eardley Lancelot, 1879–1967, vol. VI
Holland, Edgar William, 1899–1973, vol. VII
Holland, Sir Edward John, 1865–1939, vol. III
Holland, Sir (Edward) Milner, 1902–1969, vol. VI
Holland, Sir Erskine; *see* Holland, Sir T. E.
Holland, Fanny, (Mrs William Arthur Law), 1847–1931, vol. III
Holland, Rev. Francis James, 1828–1907, vol. I
Holland, Frank, 1899–1972, vol. VII
Holland, Frank William C.; *see* Crossley-Holland.
Holland, Sir George William Frederick, 1897–1962, vol. VI
Holland, Comdr Gerald Edward, 1860–1917, vol. II
Holland, Lt-Col Guy Lushington, *born* 1861, vol. II
Holland, Henry, 1859–1944, vol. IV
Holland, Henry Edmund, 1868–1933, vol. III
Holland, Rev. Henry Scott, 1847–1918, vol. II
Holland, Sir Henry Tristram, 1875–1965, vol. VI
Holland, Maj.-Gen. Henry William, 1825–1920, vol. II
Holland, Captain Herbert Christian, 1858–1916, vol. II
Holland, Rt Rev. Herbert St Barbe, 1882–1966, vol. VI
Holland, Hetty L.; *see* Lee-Holland.
Holland, Instr Captain Horace Herbert, *died* 1952, vol. V
Holland, Rear-Adm. Hubert Henry, 1873–1957, vol. V
Holland, Major Hugh, 1884–1922, vol. II
Holland, Sir Jim Sothern, 2nd Bt, 1911–1981, vol. VIII
Holland, Maj.-Gen. John Charles Francis, 1897–1956, vol. V
Holland, Rt Rev. John Tristram, 1912–1990, vol. VIII
Holland, Major John Vincent, 1889–1975, vol. VII
Holland, Col Lancelot, 1876–1943, vol. IV
Holland, Vice-Adm. Lancelot Ernest, 1887–1941, vol. IV
Holland, Leonard Duncan, 1874–1964, vol. VI
Holland, Hon. Lionel Raleigh, 1865–1936, vol. III
Holland, Sir Milner; *see* Holland, Sir E. M.
Holland, Sir (Reginald) Sothern, 1st Bt, 1876–1948, vol. IV
Holland, Richard, *died* 1942, vol. IV
Holland, Sir Robert Erskine, 1873–1965, vol. VI
Holland, Robert Henry Code, 1904–1974, vol. VII
Holland, Robert Wolstenholme, 1880–1962, vol. VI
Holland, Rt Hon. Sir Sidney George, 1893–1961, vol. VI

Holland, Sir Sothern; *see* Holland, Sir R. S.
Holland, Adm. Swinton Colthurst, 1844–1922, vol. II
Holland, Theodore, 1878–1947, vol. IV
Holland, Sir (Thomas) Erskine, 1835–1926, vol. II
Holland, Sir Thomas Henry, 1868–1947, vol. IV
Holland, Col Trevenen James, 1836–1910, vol. I
Holland, Vyvyan Beresford, 1886–1967, vol. VI
Holland, Rev. Preb. William Edward Sladen, 1873–1951, vol. V
Holland, William Jacob, 1848–1932, vol. III
Holland, Rev. William Lyall, 1846–1934, vol. III
Holland-Hibbert, Hon. Wilfrid, 1893–1961, vol. VI
Holland-Martin, Christopher John, 1910–1960, vol. V
Holland-Martin, Adm. Sir Deric Douglas Eric, 1906–1977, vol. VII
Holland-Martin, Edward, 1900–1981, vol. VIII
Holland-Pryor, Maj.-Gen. Sir Pomeroy; *see* Pryor.
Hollander, Bernard, 1864–1934, vol. III
Hollely, Sir Arthur Newton, *died* 1961, vol. VI
Hollenden, 1st Baron, 1845–1929, vol. III
Hollenden, 2nd Baron, 1885–1977, vol. VII
Holley, Maj.-Gen. Edmund Hunt, 1842–1919, vol. II
Holliday, Clifford, 1897–1960, vol. V
Holliday, Gilbert Leonard Gibson, 1910–1980, vol. VII
Holliday, Major Lionel Brook, 1880–1965, vol. VI
Holliman, John William, 1861–1937, vol. III
Hollingdrake, Sir Henry, 1872–1923, vol. II
Hollinghurst, Air Chief Marshal Sir Leslie Norman, 1895–1971, vol. VII
Hollings, Herbert John Butler, 1855–1922, vol. II
Hollingshead, John, 1827–1904, vol. I
Hollingsworth, Howard, 1871–1938, vol. III
Hollingsworth, John Ernest, 1916–1963, vol. VI
Hollington, Alfred Jordan, 1845–1926, vol. II
Hollingworth, Rev. Henry, 1841–1930, vol. III
Hollingworth, John, 1885–1976, vol. VII
Hollingworth, Sydney Ewart, 1899–1966, vol. VI
Hollins, Alfred, 1865–1942, vol. IV
Hollins, Arthur, 1876–1962, vol. VI
Hollins, Sir (Arthur) Meyrick, 2nd Bt, 1876–1938, vol. III
Hollins, Lt-Col Charles Ernest, 1875–1939, vol. III
Hollins, Sir Frank, 1st Bt, 1843–1924, vol. II
Hollins, Frank, 1907–1967, vol. VI
Hollins, Sir Frank Hubert, 3rd Bt, 1877–1963, vol. VI
Hollins, James Henry, *died* 1954, vol. V
Hollins, Sir Meyrick; *see* Hollins, Sir A. M.
Hollins, Samuel Thomas, 1881–1965, vol. VI
Hollinshead-Blundell, Henry B.; *see* Blundell-Hollinshead-Blundell.
Hollinshead-Blundell, Maj.-Gen. Richard B.; *see* Blundell-Hollinshead-Blundell.
Hollis, Sir (Alfred) Claud, 1874–1961, vol. VI
Hollis, Rt Rev. (Arthur) Michael, 1899–1986, vol. VIII
Hollis Christopher; *see* Hollis, M. C.
Hollis, Sir Claud; *see* Hollis, Sir A. C.
Hollis, Rt Rev. Francis Septimus, 1884–1955, vol. V
Hollis, Rt Rev. George Arthur, 1868–1944, vol. IV
Hollis, Henry Park, 1858–1939, vol. III
Hollis, Hugh, 1910–1986, vol. VIII
Hollis, Sir Leslie Chasemore, 1897–1963, vol. VI

Hollis, (Maurice) Christopher, 1902–1977, vol. VII
Hollis, Sir Roger Henry, 1905–1973, vol. VII
Hollis, William Ainslie, 1839–1922, vol. II
Hollond, Henry Arthur, 1884–1974, vol. VII
Hollond, Maj.-Gen. Spencer Edmund, 1874–1950, vol. IV
Holloway, Baliol, 1883–1967, vol. VI
Holloway, Basil Edward, *died* 1947, vol. IV
Holloway, Maj.-Gen. Benjamin, 1861–1922, vol. II
Holloway, Rt Hon. Edward James, 1880–1967, vol. VI
Holloway, Sir Ernest, 1887–1961, vol. VI
Holloway, Frederick William, 1873–1954, vol. V
Holloway, Gwendoline Elizabeth, 1893–1981, vol. VIII
Holloway, Sir Henry, 1857–1923, vol. II
Holloway, Sir Henry Thomas, 1876–1951, vol. V
Holloway, Rev. John Ernest, 1881–1945, vol. IV
Holloway, Leonard Cloudesley, 1885–1966, vol. VI
Holloway, Stanley, 1890–1982, vol. VIII
Hollowood, Albert Bernard, 1910–1981, vol. VIII
Holm, Alexander, 1878–1943, vol. IV
Holman, Sir Adrian, 1895–1974, vol. VII
Holman, Arthur Treve, 1893–1959, vol. V
Holman, Bernard Welpton, *died* 1964, vol. VI
Holman, Sir Constantine, 1829–1910, vol. I
Holman, Lt-Gen. Sir Herbert Campbell, 1869–1949, vol. IV
Holman, James Frederick, 1916–1974, vol. VII
Holman, Percy, 1891–1978, vol. VII
Holman, Portia Grenfell, 1903–1983, vol. VIII
Holman, Col Richard Charles, 1861–1933, vol. III
Holman, Hon. William Arthur, 1871–1934, vol. III
Holman-Hunt, Hilary Lushington Holman, 1879–1949, vol. IV
Holman-Hunt, William, 1827–1910, vol. I
Holmden, Major Frank Alfred Amphlett, 1861–1935, vol. III
Holmden, Sir Osborn George, 1869–1945, vol. IV
Holme, Alan Thomas, 1872–1931, vol. III
Holme, Charles, 1848–1923, vol. II
Holme, C(harles) Geoffrey, 1887–1954, vol. V
Holme, Charles Henry, 1853–1928, vol. II
Holme, Constance, (Mrs Punchard), 1880–1955, vol. V
Holme, Ernest Rudolph, *died* 1952, vol. V
Holme, George A., 1848–1917, vol. II
Holme, Major Harold L., 1879–1931, vol. III
Holme, Sir Randle Fynes Wilson, 1864–1957, vol. V
Holme-Sumner, Captain Berkeley, 1872–1943, vol. IV
Holmes, Albert Edward, *died* 1953, vol. V
Holmes, Arthur, 1890–1965, vol. VI
Holmes, Arthur Bromley, 1849–1927, vol. II
Holmes, Sir Arthur William, 1877–1960, vol. V
Holmes, Ven. Bernard Edgar, 1860–1928, vol. II
Holmes, Burton, 1870–1958, vol. V
Holmes, Rev. Cecil Frederick Joy, 1877–1938, vol. III
Holmes, Sir Charles John, 1868–1936, vol. III
Holmes, Daniel Turner, 1863–1955, vol. V
Holmes, Sir (David) Ronald, 1913–1981, vol. VIII
Holmes, Doris Livesey, (Mrs Arthur Holmes; *see* Reynolds, D. L.
Holmes, Edmond Gore Alexander, 1850–1936, vol. III

Holmes, Edward Morell, 1843–1930, vol. III

Holmes, Eric Gordon, 1897–1972, vol. VII

Holmes, Eric Montagu Price, 1909–1983, vol. VIII

Holmes, Ven. Ernest Edward, 1854–1931, vol. III

Holmes, Ernest Hamilton, 1876–1957, vol. V

Holmes, Florence Mary, (Lady Holmes); see Rivington, Mme Hill.

Holmes, Rt Rev. George, 1858–1912, vol. I

Holmes, George Augustus, 1861–1943, vol. IV

Holmes, Sir George Charles Vincent, 1848–1926, vol. II

Holmes, Rev. Canon George Edward Wilmot, 1869–1937, vol. III

Holmes, Ven. George Hedley, 1883–1972, vol. VII

Holmes, George John, 1874–1937, vol. III

Holmes, Comdr Gerard Robert Addison, 1881–1963, vol. VI

Holmes, Sir Gordon Morgan, died 1965, vol. VI

Holmes, Brig.-Gen. Hardress Gilbert, 1862–1922, vol. II

Holmes, Harold Kennard, 1875–1942, vol. IV

Holmes, Haywood Temple, 1865–1959, vol. V

Holmes, Lt-Col Henry, 1863–1933, vol. III

Holmes, Rev. Henry Comber, died 1920, vol. II

Holmes, Sir Henry Nicholas, 1868–1940, vol. III

Holmes, Sir Horace Edwin, 1888–1971, vol. VII

Holmes, Rt Hon. Hugh, 1840–1916, vol. II

Holmes, Sir Hugh Oliver, 1886–1955, vol. V

Holmes, James Macdonald, 1896–1966, vol. VI

Holmes, Paymaster Rear-Adm. John Dickonson, 1875–1947, vol. IV

Holmes, Rt Rev. John Garraway, died 1904, vol. I

Holmes, Rev. John Haynes, 1879–1964, vol. VI

Holmes, Rev. Joseph, 1820–1911, vol. I

Holmes, Hon. Julius Cecil, 1899–1968, vol. VI

Holmes, Brig. Leonard Geoffrey, 1899–1985, vol. VIII

Holmes, Sir Leonard Stanistreet, 1884–1961, vol. VI

Holmes, Sir Maurice Gerald, 1885–1964, vol. VI

Holmes, Maj.-Gen. Sir Noel Galway, 1891–1982, vol. VIII

Holmes, Hon. Oliver Wendell, 1841–1935, vol. III

Holmes, Air Vice-Marshal Peter Hamilton, 1912–1977, vol. VII

Holmes, Sir Richard Rivington, 1835–1911, vol. I

Holmes, Robert, 1861–1930, vol. III

Holmes, Col Robert Heuston, 1870–1952, vol. V

Holmes, Sir Robert William Arbuthnot, 1843–1910, vol. I

Holmes, Sir Ronald; see Holmes, Sir D. R.

Holmes, Sir Stanley, 1912–1987, vol. VIII

Holmes, Sir Stephen Lewis, 1896–1980, vol. VII

Holmes, Thomas, 1846–1918, vol. II

Holmes, Thomas Rice Edward, 1855–1933, vol. III

Holmes, Rev. Thomas Scott, 1852–1918, vol. II

Holmes, Sir Valentine, 1888–1956, vol. V

Holmes, Col William, 1862–1917, vol. II

Holmes, Lt-Gen. Sir William George, 1892–1969, vol. VI

Holmes, Rt Rev. William Hardy, 1873–1951, vol. V

Holmes-à-Court, Hon. Edward Alexander, 1845–1923, vol. II

Holmes à Court, Vice-Adm. Hon. Herbert Edward, 1869–1934, vol. III

Holmes à Court, (Michael) Robert (Hamilton), 1937–1990, vol. VIII

Holmes à Court, Robert; see Holmes à Court, M. R. H.

Holmes à Court, Col Rupert Edward, 1882–1958, vol. V

Holmes Sellors, Sir Thomas; see Sellors.

Holm-Patrick, 1st Baron, 1839–1898, vol. I

Holmpatrick, 2nd Baron, 1886–1942, vol. IV

Holms, John Mitchell, 1863–1948, vol. IV

Holms, William Frederick, 1866–1950, vol. IV

Holmwood, Sir Herbert, 1856–1930, vol. III

Holmyard, Eric John, 1891–1959, vol. V

Holness, Col Harold James, 1882–1941, vol. IV

Holroyd, Sir Charles, 1861–1917, vol. II

Holroyd, Hon. Sir Edward Dundas, 1828–1916, vol. II

Holroyd, Michael, 1892–1953, vol. V

Holroyd, Sir Ronald, 1904–1973, vol. VII

Holroyd Pearce, Edward; see Baron Pearce.

Holroyd-Reece, John, 1897–1969, vol. VI

Holst, Axel, 1860–1931, vol. III

Holst, Gustav, 1874–1934, vol. III

Holst, Imogen Clare, 1907–1984, vol. VIII

Holt, Lt-Col Alwyn Vesey, 1887–1956, vol. V

Holt, Charles, 1899–1966, vol. VI

Holt, Sir Edward, 1st Bt (cr 1916), 1849–1928, vol. II

Holt, Sir Edward, 2nd Bt (cr 1916), 1883–1968, vol. VI

Holt, Very Rev. Edward John, 1867–1948, vol. IV (A), vol. V

Holt, Ernest James Henry, 1883–1972, vol. VII

Holt, Air Vice-Marshal Felton Vesey, 1886–1931, vol. III

Holt, Sir Follett, 1865–1944, vol. IV

Holt, Rt Hon. Harold Edward, 1908–1968, vol. VI

Holt, Harold Edward Sherwin, 1862–1932, vol. III

Holt, Henry, 1840–1926, vol. II

Holt, Sir Henry Gisborne, 1864–1944, vol. IV

Holt, Herbert, 1894–1978, vol. VII

Holt, Major Herbert Paton, 1890–1971, vol. VII

Holt, Sir Herbert S., 1856–1941, vol. IV

Holt, James, 1899–1965, vol. VI

Holt, Sir James Arthur, 1899–1982, vol. VIII

Holt, James Maden, 1829–1911, vol. I

Holt, Sir James Richard, 1912–1990, vol. VIII

Holt, John Alphonse, 1906–1968, vol. VI

Holt, L. Emmett, died 1924, vol. II

Holt, Lawrence During, 1882–1961, vol. VI

Holt, Martin Drummond Vesey, died 1956, vol. V

Holt, Maj.-Gen. Sir Maurice Percy Cue, 1862–1954, vol. V

Holt, Rev. Raymond Vincent, 1885–1957, vol. V

Holt, Vice-Adm. Reginald Vesey, 1884–1957, vol. V

Holt, Sir Richard Durning, 1st Bt (cr 1935), 1868–1941, vol. IV

Holt, Sir Stanley Silverwood, 1892–1973, vol. VII

Holt, Sir Vesey George Mackenzie, 1854–1923, vol. II

Holt, Sir Vyvyan, 1896–1960, vol. V

Holt, Col William John, 1839–1913, vol. I

Holt, William R., born 1870, vol. II

Holt-Thomas, George, 1869–1929, vol. III

Holt-Wilson, Brig. Sir Eric Edward Boketon, 1875–1950, vol. IV

Holtby, Winifred, 1898–1935, vol. III
Holthouse, Edwin Hermus, 1855–1949, vol. IV
Holttum, Eric; see Holttum, R. E.
Holttum, Richard Eric, 1895–1990, vol. VIII
Holtz, Alfred Christian Carlsen, 1874–1948, vol. IV
Holtze, Maurice, 1840–1923, vol. II
Holwell, Captain Raymond Vernon Doherty-, 1882–1917, vol. II
Holyman, Sir Ivan Nello, 1896–1957, vol. V
Holyoake, George Jacob, 1817–1906, vol. I
Holyoake, Rt Hon. Sir Keith Jacka, 1904–1983, vol. VIII
Holyoake, Dame Norma Janet, 1909–1984, vol. VIII
Holzmann, Sir Maurice, 1835–1909, vol. I
Homan, Philip John Lindsay, 1916–1988, vol. VIII
Hombersley, Ven. Arthur, 1855–1941, vol. IV
Homburg, Robert, 1848–1912, vol. I
Home, 12th Earl of, 1834–1918, vol. II
Home, 13th Earl of, 1873–1951, vol. V
Home, Sir Anthony Dickson, 1826–1914, vol. I
Home, Brig.-Gen. Sir Archibald Fraser, 1874–1953, vol. V
Home, Charles Cospatrick D.; see Douglas-Home.
Home, David William M.; see Milne-Home.
Home, Ethel, died 1954, vol. V
Home, Col Frederick Jervis, 1839–1919, vol. II
Home, Lt-Col George, 1870–1956, vol. V
Home, Major George John Ninian L.; see Logan-Home.
Home, Gordon Cochrane, 1878–1969, vol. VI
Home, Sir James, 11th Bt, 1861–1931, vol. III
Home, Hon. James Archibald, 1837–1909, vol. I
Home, Col James Murray, 1866–1946, vol. IV
Home, Sir John, 12th Bt, 1872–1938, vol. III
Home, Sir John Hepburn Milne, 1876–1963, vol. VI
Home, Col Robert Elton, 1869–1943, vol. IV
Home, Walter, 1855–1936, vol. III
Home, Maj.-Gen. Hon. William Sholto, 1842–1916, vol. II
Home Drummond, Lt-Col Henry Edward S.; see Stirling Home Drummond.
Homer, John Twigg, 1865–1934, vol. III
Homer, Louise, died 1947, vol. IV
Homer, Sidney, 1864–1953, vol. V
Homer, Winslow, 1836–1910, vol. I
Homewood, William Dennis, 1920–1989, vol. VIII
Homfray, Herbert Richards, 1864–1940, vol. III
Homfray, Captain John Glynne Richards, 1861–1934, vol. III
Homfray, Lt-Col John Robert Henry, 1868–1944, vol. IV
Homolle, Jean Théophile, 1848–1925, vol. II
Hone, Sir Brian William, 1907–1978, vol. VII
Hone, Rt Rev. Campbell Richard, 1873–1967, vol. VI
Hone, Sir Evelyn Dennison, 1911–1979, vol. VII
Hone, Elvie S., 1894–1955, vol. V
Hone, Frank Sandland, died 1951, vol. V
Hone, Joseph Maunsell, 1882–1959, vol. V
Hone, Nathaniel, died 1917, vol. II
Hone, Lt-Col Percy Frederick, 1878–1940, vol. III
Honegger, Arthur, 1892–1955, vol. V
Honey, Sir de Symons Montagu George, 1872–1945, vol. IV
Honey, John William, 1862–1932, vol. III

Honey, William Bowyer, 1889–1956, vol. V
Honeyball, Mrs Olympia Lœtitia, 1876–1956, vol. V
Honeyman, Alexander Mackie, 1907–1988, vol. VIII
Honeyman, Sir George Gordon, 1898–1972, vol. VII
Honeyman, John, 1831–1914, vol. I
Honeyman, Tom John, 1891–1971, vol. VII
Honner, Joseph, 1859–1940, vol. III
Honoré, Bertha; see Palmer, Mrs Poter.
Honour, Benjamin, 1888–1961, vol. VI
Honyman, Sir William Macdonald, 5th Bt, 1820–1911, vol. I
Honywood, Constance Mary, (Lady Honywood), died 1956, vol. V
Honywood, Sir Courtenay John, 9th Bt, 1880–1944, vol. IV
Honywood, Sir John William, 8th Bt, 1857–1907, vol. I
Honywood, Col Sir William Wynne, 10th Bt, 1891–1982, vol. VIII
Hood, 4th Viscount, 1838–1907, vol. I
Hood, 5th Viscount, 1868–1933, vol. III
Hood, 6th Viscount, 1910–1981, vol. VIII
Hood of Avalon, 1st Baron, 1824–1901, vol. I
Hood, Lt-Gen. Sir Alexander, 1888–1980, vol. VII
Hood, Sir (Alexander) Jarvie, 1860–1934, vol. III
Hood, Hon. Sir Alexander Nelson, 1854–1937, vol. III
Hood, Rev. Canon (Archibald) Frederic, 1895–1975, vol. VII
Hood, Captain Basil, 1864–1917, vol. II
Hood, Paymaster-Captain Basil Frederick, 1886–1941, vol. IV
Hood, Clifford Firoved, 1894–1978, vol. VII
Hood, David Wilson, 1874–1924, vol. II
Hood, Donald William Charles, 1847–1924, vol. II
Hood, Hon. Dorothy Violet, 1877–1965, vol. VI
Hood, Douglas; see Hood, J. D.
Hood, Maj.-Gen. Ernest Lionel Ouseley, 1915–1982, vol. VIII
Hood, Francis Campbell, 1895–1971, vol. VII
Hood, Rev. Canon Frederic; see Hood, Rev. Canon A. F.
Hood, George Percy J.; see Jacomb-Hood.
Hood, Rear-Adm. Hon. Horace Lambert Alexander, 1870–1916, vol. II
Hood, Sir Hugh Meggison, 1885–1952, vol. V
Hood, (James) Douglas, 1905–1981, vol. VIII
Hood, James Reaney, 1888–1968, vol. VI
Hood, Sir Jarvie; see Hood, Sir A. J.
Hood, Rev. John Charles Fulton, 1884–1964, vol. VI
Hood, Gen. John Cockburn, died 1901, vol. I
Hood, Sir Joseph, 1st Bt, 1863–1931, vol. III
Hood, Hon. Sir Joseph Henry, 1846–1922, vol. II
Hood, Hon. Maurice Henry Nelson, 1881–1915, vol. I
Hood, Lt-Col Hon. Neville Albert, 1872–1948, vol. IV
Hood, Rev. Norman Arthur, 1924–1990, vol. VIII
Hood, Sydney Walter, 1886–1960, vol. V
Hood, Col Sir Tom Fielden, 1904–1986, vol. VIII
Hood, Thomas, 1870–1949, vol. IV
Hood, Hon. Victor Albert Nelson, 1862–1929, vol. III
Hood, William Francis, 1902–1980, vol. VII

Hooft, Willem Adolf V.; *see* Visser't Hooft.
Hook, Rt Rev. Cecil, 1844–1938, vol. III
Hook, Frederick Arthur, 1864–1935, vol. III
Hook, Henry, *died* 1905, vol. I
Hook, James Clarke, 1819–1907, vol. I
Hook, Very Rev. Norman, 1898–1976, vol. VII
Hook, Sidney, 1902–1989, vol. VIII
Hooke, Rev. Daniel Burford, 1847–1933, vol. III
Hooke, Sir Lionel George Alfred, 1895–1974, vol. VII
Hooke, Samuel Henry, *died* 1968, vol. VI
Hooker, Sir Joseph Dalton, 1817–1911, vol. I
Hooker, Sir Leslie Joseph, 1901–1976, vol. VII
Hooker, Sir Stanley George, 1907–1984, vol. VIII
Hookey, James, 1839–1903, vol. I
Hookins, Rev. William, 1845–1917, vol. II
Hookway, Reginald John Samuel, 1920–1982, vol. VIII
Hoole, Lt-Col James, 1850–1917, vol. II
Hooley, Maj.-Gen. St John Cutler, 1902–1985, vol. VIII
Hooley, Samuel Cutler, 1848–1929, vol. III
Hooley, Lt-Col Vernon Vavasour, 1862–1952, vol. V
Hooper, Sir Anthony Robin Maurice, 2nd Bt, 1918–1987, vol. VIII
Hooper, Arthur George, 1857–1940, vol. III
Hooper, Col Arthur Winsmore, 1869–1945, vol. IV
Hooper, Barrington, 1885–1960, vol. V
Hooper, Charles Arthur, 1889–1960, vol. V
Hooper, Cyril Noel, 1884–1952, vol. V
Hooper, David, 1858–1947, vol. IV
Hooper, Edmund Huntly, 1845–1931, vol. III
Hooper, Sir Frederic Collins, 1st Bt, 1892–1963, vol. VI
Hooper, Rev. George, *born* 1866, vol. III
Hooper, Lt-Col Harry Uppington, *died* 1940, vol. III
Hooper, Howard Owen, 1911–1980, vol. VII
Hooper, Ian Mackay, 1902–1958, vol. V
Hooper, John, *died* 1907, vol. I
Hooper, John Robert Thomas, 1914–1975, vol. VII
Hooper, Reginald Stewart, 1889–1945, vol. IV
Hooper, Major Richard Grenside, 1873–1940, vol. III
Hooper, Sir Robin William John, 1914–1989, vol. VIII
Hooper, Lt-Col Stuart Huntly, 1867–1915, vol. I
Hooper, Sydney Ernest, 1880–1966, vol. VI
Hooper, Rev. William, 1837–1922, vol. II
Hooper, William Henry, 1876–1946, vol. IV
Hooper, Col Sir William Roe, 1837–1921, vol. II
Hooper, Wynnard, 1853–1935, vol. III
Hoops, Albert Launcelot, 1876–1940, vol. III (A), vol. IV
Hooson, Tom Ellis, 1933–1985, vol. VIII
Hooton, Maj.-Gen. Alfred, 1870–1967, vol. VI
Hooton, John Charles, 1912–1980, vol. VII
Hoover, Calvin Bryce, 1897–1974, vol. VII
Hoover, Herbert, 1874–1964, vol. VI
Hoover, Herbert Clark, Jr, 1903–1969, vol. VI
Hoover, John Edgar, 1895–1972, vol. VII
Hope, Adrian Elias, 1845–1919, vol. II
Hope, Adrian James Robert, 1874–1963, vol. VI
Hope, Col Adrian Victor Webley, 1873–1960, vol. V
Hope, Sir Alexander, 15th Bt (*cr* 1628), 1824–1918, vol. II

Hope, Anthony; *see* Hawkins, Sir A. H.
Hope, Sir Archibald Philip, 17th Bt, 1912–1987, vol. VIII
Hope, Ascott R.; *see* Moncrieff, Robert Hope.
Hope, Col Charles, 1850–1930, vol. III
Hope, Lord Charles Melbourne, 1892–1962, vol. VI
Hope, Collingwood, 1858–1949, vol. IV
Hope, Sir Edward Stanley, 1846–1921, vol. II
Hope, Edward William, 1854–1950, vol. IV
Hope, George Everard, 1886–1917, vol. II
Hope, Adm. Sir George Price Webley, 1869–1959, vol. V
Hope, Graham, *died* 1920, vol. II
Hope, Sir Harry, 1st Bt (*cr* 1932), 1865–1959, vol. V
Hope, Henry Walter, 1839–1913, vol. I
Hope, Sir Herbert James, 1851–1930, vol. III
Hope, Adm. Herbert Willes Webley, 1878–1968, vol. VI
Hope, Sir James, 2nd Bt (*cr* 1932), 1898–1979, vol. VII
Hope, James Kenneth, 1896–1983, vol. VIII
Hope, Jasper Edward, 1852–1917, vol. II
Hope, Captain John, 1843–1915, vol. I
Hope, Col John Andrew, 1890–1954, vol. V
Hope, Lt-Col Sir John Augustus, 16th Bt (*cr* 1628), 1869–1924, vol. II
Hope, John Deans, 1860–1949, vol. IV
Hope, Brig.-Gen. John Frederic Roundell, 1883–1970, vol. VI
Hope, John Owen Webley, 1875–1927, vol. II
Hope, Lt-Col John William, 1876–1942, vol. IV
Hope, John Wilson, 1856–1938, vol. III
Hope, Laura Elizabeth Rachel, *died* 1929, vol. III
Hope, Captain Laurence Nugent, 1890–1973, vol. VII
Hope, Col Lewis Anstruther, 1855–1929, vol. III
Hope, Lt-Col Sir Percy Mirehouse, 1886–1972, vol. VII
Hope, Hon. Richard Frederick, 1901–1964, vol. VI
Hope, Robert, *died* 1936, vol. III
Hope, Robert Charles, 1855–1926, vol. II
Hope, Sydney, 1905–1959, vol. V
Hope, Sir Theodore Cracraft, 1831–1915, vol. I
Hope, Col Thomas, 1848–1925, vol. II
Hope, Sir William, 14th Bt (*cr* 1628), 1819–1898, vol. I
Hope, Sir William Henry St John, 1854–1919, vol. II
Hope, Lt-Col William Henry Webley, 1871–1919, vol. II
Hope-Dunbar, Sir Basil Douglas, 7th Bt, 1907–1961, vol. VI
Hope-Dunbar, Sir Charles Dunbar, 6th Bt, 1873–1958, vol. V
Hope Gill, Cecil Gervase, 1894–1984, vol. VIII
Hope-Johnstone, John James, 1842–1912, vol. I
Hope-Jones, Sir Arthur, 1911–1984, vol. VIII
Hope-Morley, Captain Hon. Claude Hope, 1887–1968, vol. VI
Hope-Vere, James Charles, 1858–1933, vol. III
Hope-Wallace, Philip Adrian, 191–1979, vol. VII
Hopewell, Alan Francis John, 1892–1957, vol. V
Hopewell-Ash, Edwin Lancelot; *see* Ash.
Hopewell-Smith, Arthur, 1865–1931, vol. III
Hopkin, Major Daniel, 1886–1951, vol. V

Hopkin-James, Rev. Lemuel John, 1874–1937, vol. III

Hopkins, Major Adrian Edmund, 1894–1967, vol. VI

Hopkins, Arthur, 1848–1930, vol. III

Hopkins, Arthur Antwis, 1855–1916, vol. II

Hopkins, Rev. Charles, 1834–1908, vol. I

Hopkins, Charles James William, 1887–1954, vol. V

Hopkins, Paymaster-in-Chief David Bertie Lyndsay, 1862–1925, vol. II

Hopkins, Edward John, 1818–1901, vol. I

Hopkins, Everard, 1860–1928, vol. II

Hopkins, Adm. Sir Frank Henry Edward, 1910–1990, vol. VIII

Hopkins, Rt Rev. Frederick C., 1844–1923, vol. II

Hopkins, Sir Frederick Gowland, 1861–1947, vol. IV

Hopkins, Gerard Walter Sturgis, 1892–1961, vol. VI

Hopkins, Col Harold Leslie, 1897–1981, vol. VIII

Hopkins, Harry Geoffrey, 1918–1982, vol. VIII

Hopkins, Harry L., 1890–1946, vol. IV

Hopkins, Harry Sinclair, 1870–1953, vol. V

Hopkins, Henry Mayne Reid, 1867–1956, vol. V

Hopkins, John Castell, 1864–1923, vol. II

Hopkins, John Collier Frederick, 1898–1981, vol. VIII

Hopkins, Sir John Ommanney, 1834–1916, vol. II

Hopkins, Sir John Wells Wainwright, 1st Bt, 1863–1946, vol. IV

Hopkins, Rev. Canon Leslie Freeman, 1914–1987, vol. VIII

Hopkins, Lt-Col Lewis Egerton, 1873–1945, vol. IV

Hopkins, Lionel Charles, 1854–1952, vol. V

Hopkins, Livingston, 1846–1927, vol. II

Hopkins, Very Rev. Noel Thomas, 1892–1969, vol. VI

Hopkins, Reginald Haydn, 1891–1965, vol. VI

Hopkins, Rt Hon. Sir Richard Valentine Nind, 1880–1955, vol. V

Hopkins, Robert Thurston, *died* 1958, vol. V

Hopkins, Maj.-Gen. Ronald Nicholas Lamond, 1897–1990, vol. VIII

Hopkins, Tighe, 1856–1919, vol. II

Hopkins, William Joseph, 1863–1927, vol. II

Hopkinson, Sir Alfred, 1851–1939, vol. III

Hopkinson, Rev. Arthur John, 1894–1953, vol. V

Hopkinson, Austin, 1879–1962, vol. VI

Hopkinson, Bertram, 1874–1918, vol. II

Hopkinson, Edward, 1859–1922, vol. II

Hopkinson, Emilius, 1869–1951, vol. V

Hopkinson, Sir Frederick Thomas, 1863–1947, vol. IV

Hopkinson, Maj.-Gen. Gerald Charles, 1910–1989, vol. VIII

Hopkinson, Gen. Henry, 1820–1899, vol. I

Hopkinson, Col Henry Charles Barwick Pasha, 1867–1946, vol. IV

Hopkinson, Sir Henry L., 1855–1936, vol. III

Hopkinson, Col (Henry) Somerset (Parnell), 1899–1988, vol. VIII

Hopkinson, Sir (Henry) Thomas, 1905–1990, vol. VIII

Hopkinson, John, 1849–1898, vol. I

Hopkinson, John, 1844–1919, vol. II

Hopkinson, Rev. John Henry, *died* 1957, vol. V

Hopkinson, Col Somerset; *see* Hopkinson, Col H. S. P.

Hopkinson, Sir Thomas; *see* Hopkinson, Sir H. T.

Hopley, Ven. Arthur, 1906–1981, vol. VIII

Hopley, Hon. William Musgrove, 1853–1919, vol. II

Hoppé, E. O., 1878–1972, vol. VII

Hopper, Nora, 1871–1906, vol. I

Hopper, Robert John, 1910–1987, vol. VIII

Hopps, Air Vice-Marshal Frank Linden, *died* 1976, vol. VII

Hopps, John Page, 1834–1911, vol. I

Hopson, Sir Donald Charles, 1915–1974, vol. VII

Hopton, Ven. Charles Ernest, 1861–1946, vol. IV

Hopton, Lt-Gen. Sir Edward, 1837–1912, vol. I

Hopton, Col John Dutton, 1858–1934, vol. III

Hopton, Rev. Preb. Michael, 1838–1928, vol. II

Hopwood, Brig. Alfred Henry, *died* 1956, vol. V

Hopwood, Aubrey, 1863–1917, vol. II

Hopwood, Avery, *died* 1928, vol. II

Hopwood, Charles Augustus, 1847–1922, vol. II

Hopwood, Major Edward Byng George G.; *see* Gregge-Hopwood.

Hopwood, Edward Robert G.; *see* Gregge-Hopwood.

Hopwood, Frank Lloyd, 1884–1954, vol. V

Hopwood, Vice-Adm. Geoffrey, 1877–1947, vol. IV

Hopwood, Henry Silkstone, 1860–1914, vol. I

Hopwood, Brig.-Gen. Herbert Reginald, 1871–1938, vol. III

Hopwood, Brig. John Adam, 1910–1987, vol. VIII

Hopwood, Adm. Ronald Arthur, 1868–1949, vol. IV

Hopwood, Sir William, 1862–1936, vol. III

Horabin, Thomas Lewis, 1896–1956, vol. V

Horan, Rev. Charles Trevor, 1863–1932, vol. III

Horan, Gerald, 1879–1949, vol. IV

Horan, Henry Edward, 1890–1961, vol. VI

Horder, 1st Baron, 1871–1955, vol. V

Hordern, Anthony, 1889–1970, vol. VI (AII)

Hordern, Sir Archibald Frederick, 1889–1950, vol. IV

Hordern, Rev. Arthur Venables Calveley, 1866–1946, vol. IV

Hordern, Captain Edward Joseph Calveley, 1867–1944, vol. IV

Hordern, Brig.-Gen. Gwyn Venables, 1870–1945, vol. IV

Hordern, Rt Rev. Hugh Maudslay, 1868–1949, vol. IV

Hordern, Sir Samuel, 1876–1956, vol. V

Hordern, Samuel, 1909–1960, vol. V

Hore, Sir Adair; *see* Hore, Sir C. F. A.

Hore, Sir (Charles Fraser) Adair, 1874–1950, vol. IV

Hore, Col Charles Owen, 1860–1916, vol. II

Hore, Engr-Rear-Adm. Fred, 1863–1932, vol. III

Hore, Maj.-Gen. Walter Stuart, 1843–1918, vol. II

Hore-Belisha, 1st Baron, 1893–1957, vol. V

Hore-Ruthven, Col Hon. Malise; *see* Ruthven.

Horenstein, Jascha, 1899–1973, vol. VII

Horgan, John Joseph, 1881–1967, vol. VI

Horler, Sydney, 1888–1954, vol. V

Horlick, Sir Ernest Burford, 2nd Bt, 1880–1934, vol. III

Horlick, Sir James, 1st Bt, 1884–1921, vol. II

Horlick, Lt-Col Sir James Nockells, 4th Bt, 1886–1972, vol. VII

Horlick, Sir Peter James Cunliffe, 3rd Bt, 1908–1958, vol. V

Hormasji Bhiwandiwalla, Khan Bahadur Sir Dosabhai, *died* 1940, vol. III (A), vol. IV

Horn, Sir Arthur Edwin, *died* 1943, vol. IV

Horn, David Bayne, 1851–1927, vol. II

Horn, David Bayne, 1901–1969, vol. VI

Horn, Gunnar, 1894–1946, vol. IV

Horn, Brig. Robert Victor Galbraith, 1886–1959, vol. V

Horn, William Austin, 1841–1922, vol. II

Horn-Elphinstone, Sir Graeme Hepburn D.; *see* Elphinstone.

Hornabrook, Ven. Charles Soward, *died* 1922, vol. II

Hornabrook, Rev. John, 1848–1937, vol. III

Hornaday, William Temple, 1854–1937, vol. III

Hornby, Maj.-Gen. Alan Hugh, 1894–1958, vol. V

Hornby, Albert Neilson, 1847–1925, vol. II

Hornby, C. H. St John, 1867–1946, vol. IV

Hornby, Charles Windham Leycester P.; *see* Penrhyn-Hornby.

Hornby, Brig.-Gen. Edmund John Phipps, 1857–1947, vol. IV

Hornby, Frank, 1863–1936, vol. III

Hornby, Frank Robert, 1911–1987, vol. VIII

Hornby, Sir Henry; *see* Hornby, Sir W. H.

Hornby, Sir (Henry) Russell, 2nd Bt, 1888–1971, vol. VI

Hornby, Rt Rev. Hugh Leycester, 1888–1965, vol. VI

Hornby, Rev. James John, 1826–1909, vol. I

Hornby, James William, 1924–1984, vol. VIII

Hornby, Michael Charles St John, 1899–1987, vol. VIII

Hornby, Brig.-Gen. Montague Leyland, 1870–1948, vol. IV

Hornby, Ven. Phipps John, 1853–1936, vol. III

Hornby, Adm. Robert Stewart Phipps, 1866–1956, vol. V

Hornby, Sir (Roger) Antony, 1904–1987, vol. VIII

Hornby, Sir Russell; *see* Hornby, Sir H. R.

Hornby, Rt Hon. Wilfrid Bird, 1851–1935, vol. III

Hornby, Ven. William, 1810–1899, vol. I

Hornby, Sir (William) Henry, 1st Bt, 1841–1928, vol. II

Hornby, Sir Windham, 1812–1899, vol. I

Horncastle, Walter Radcliffe, 1850–1908, vol. I

Horndon, David, 1863–1938, vol. III

Horne, 1st Baron, 1861–1929, vol. III

Horne of Slamannan, 1st Viscount, 1871–1940, vol. III

Horne, Sir Alan Edgar, 2nd Bt, 1889–1984, vol. VIII

Horne, Alderson Burrell, 1863–1953, vol. V

Horne, Sir Allan; *see* Horne, Sir J. A.

Horne, Sir Andrew John, 1856–1924, vol. II

Horne, Rev. C. Silvester, 1865–1914, vol. I

Horne, (Charles) Kenneth, 1907–1969, vol. VI

Horne, Sir Edgar; *see* Horne, Sir W. E.

Horne, Edward Butler, 1881–1947, vol. IV

Horne, Col Edward William, 1857–1941, vol. IV

Horne, Frank Robert, 1904–1975, vol. VII

Horne, Frederic, 1863–1927, vol. II

Horne, Frederick Newman, 1863–1946, vol. IV

Horne, Maj.-Gen. Gerald Tom Warlters, 1898–1978, vol. VII

Horne, Herbert P., *died* 1916, vol. II

Horne, Sir (James) Allan, 1876–1944, vol. IV

Horne, Jobson; *see* Horne, W. J.

Horne, John, 1848–1928, vol. II

Horne, Kenneth; *see* Horne, C. K.

Horne, Lancelot Worthy, 1875–1924, vol. II

Horne, Leonard Thomas, 1860–1934, vol. III

Horne, Maynard, 1870–1944, vol. IV

Horne, (Walter) Jobson, 1865–1953, vol. V

Horne, Sir (William) Edgar, 1st Bt, 1856–1941, vol. IV

Horne, Major William Guy, 1889–1974, vol. VII

Horne, Sir William Kenneth, 1883–1959, vol. V

Horne, William Ogilvie, *died* 1943, vol. IV

Hornel, Edward Atkinson, 1864–1933, vol. III

Hornell, Vice-Adm. Sir Robert Arthur, 1877–1949, vol. IV

Hornell, Sir William Woodward, 1878–1950, vol. IV

Horner, Andrew L., 1863–1916, vol. II

Horner, Arthur Lewis, 1894–1968, vol. VI

Horner, Rev. Bernard, 1873–1960, vol. V

Horner, Egbert Foster, 1864–1928, vol. II

Horner, Hallam; *see* Horner, L. J. H.

Horner, Sir John Francis Fortescue, 1842–1927, vol. II

Horner, (Lawrence John) Hallam, 1907–1989, vol. VIII

Horner, Norman Gerald, 1882–1954, vol. V

Horner, Mrs Sibyl Gertrude, 1895–1978, vol. VII

Horniblow, Brig.-Gen. Frank Herbert, 1860–1931, vol. III

Horniblow, Col Frederick, 1862–1945, vol. IV

Hornibrook, Sir Manuel Richard, 1893–1970, vol. VI (AII)

Horniman, Annie Elizabeth Fredericka, 1860–1937, vol. III

Horniman, Benjamin Guy, 1873–1948, vol. IV

Horniman, Emslie John, 1863–1932, vol. III

Horniman, Frederick John, 1835–1906, vol. I

Horniman, Rear-Adm. Henry, *died* 1956, vol. V

Horniman, Laurence Ivan, 1893–1963, vol. VI

Horniman, Roy, *died* 1930, vol. III

Horning, Eric Stephen Gurney, 1900–1959, vol. V

Horning, Lewis Emerson, 1858–1925, vol. II

Hornsby, Sir Bertram, *died* 1943, vol. IV

Hornsby, Frederick Middleton, 1874–1931, vol. III

Hornsby, Harker William, 1912–1971, vol. VII

Hornsby, Harry Reginald, 1907–1983, vol. VIII

Hornsby, Captain James Arthur, 1891–1972, vol. VII

Hornsby-Smith, Baroness (Life Peer); Margaret Patricia Hornsby-Smith, 1914–1985, vol. VIII

Hornsby-Wright, Lt-Col Guy Jefferys, 1872–1941, vol. IV

Hornung, Ernest William, 1866–1921, vol. II

Hornung, Lt-Col Sir John Derek, 1915–1978, vol. VII

Hornung, John Peter, 1861–1940, vol. III

Hornyold-Strickland, Henry, 1890–1975, vol. VII

Hornyold-Strickland, Hon. Mary Constance Elizabeth Christina, 1896–1970, vol. VI

Horobin, Sir Ian Macdonald, 1899–1976, vol. VII

Horobin, Norah Maud, 1898–1976, vol. VII

Horonitz, Vladimir, 1904–1989, vol. VIII

Horrabin, James Francis, 1884–1962, vol. VI

Horridge, John, 1893–1951, vol. V

Horridge, Sir Thomas Gardner, 1857–1938, vol. III
Horrobin, Walter, 1894–1967, vol. VI (AII)
Horrocks, Lt-Gen. Sir Brian Gwynne, 1895–1985, vol. VIII
Horrocks, Peter, *died* 1909, vol. I
Horrocks, Walter James Hodgson, 1897–1946, vol. IV
Horrocks, Col Sir William Heaton, 1859–1941, vol. IV
Horrox, Lewis, 1898–1975, vol. VII
Horsbrugh, Baroness (Life Peer); Florence Gertrude Horsbrugh, 1889–1969, vol. VI
Horsbrugh-Porter, Sir Andrew Marshall, 3rd Bt, 1907–1986, vol. VIII
Horsbrugh-Porter, Sir John Scott; *see* Porter.
Horsburgh, Benjamin, 1868–1935, vol. III (A), vol. IV
Horsefield, Rev. Frederic John, 1859–1933, vol. III
Horsey, Captain Frank Lankester, 1884–1956, vol. V
Horsfall, Sir Donald; *see* Horsfall, Sir J. D.
Horsfall, Geoffrey Jonas, 1905–1985, vol. VIII
Horsfall, Jeremiah Garnett, 1840–1920, vol. II
Horsfall, Sir John Cousin, 1st Bt, 1846–1920, vol. II
Horsfall, Sir (John) Donald, 2nd Bt, 1891–1975, vol. VII
Horsfall, Thomas Coglan, 1841–1932, vol. III
Horsfall Turner, Harold, 1909–1981, vol. VIII
Horsfield, George, 1882–1956, vol. V
Horsfield, Brig. Herbert Eric, 1895–1981, vol. VIII
Horsfield, Lt-Col Richard Marshall, *died* 1940, vol. III
Horsford, Cyril Arthur Bennett, 1876–1953, vol. V
Horsley, Major Bernard Hill, *died* 1940, vol. III
Horsley, Rt Rev. Cecil Douglas, 1903–1953, vol. V
Horsley, Gerald Callcott, 1862–1917, vol. II
Horsley, John Callcott, 1817–1903, vol. I
Horsley, Rev. John William, 1845–1921, vol. II
Horsley, Reginald Ernest, 1863–1926, vol. II
Horsley, Terence Beresford, 1904–1949, vol. IV
Horsley, Sir Victor Alexander Haden, 1857–1916, vol. II
Horsley, Col Walter Charles, 1855–1934, vol. III
Horsman, Sir Henry, 1887–1966, vol. VI
Horsnell, Horace, 1882–1949, vol. IV
Horstead, Rt Rev. Cecil; *see* Horstead, Rt Rev. J. L. C.
Horstead, Rt Rev. James Lawrence Cecil, 1898–1989, vol. VIII
Hort, Sir Arthur Fenton, 6th Bt, 1864–1935, vol. III
Hort, Edward Collett, 1868–1922, vol. II
Hort, Sir Fenton George, 7th Bt, 1896–1960, vol. V
Hort, Sir Fenton Josiah, 5th Bt, 1836–1902, vol. I
Hort, Greta, 1903–1967, vol. VI
Horthy de Nagybanya, Adm. Nicholas Vitéz, 1868–1957, vol. V
Horton, Frank, 1878–1957, vol. V
Horton, Maj.-Gen. Frank Cyril, 1907–1989, vol. VIII
Horton, Sir Henry, 1870–1943, vol. IV
Horton, Major James, 1845–1925, vol. II
Horton, Lt-Col James H., 1871–1917, vol. II
Horton, Adm. Sir Max Kennedy, 1883–1951, vol. V
Horton, Percy Frederick, 1897–1970, vol. VI
Horton, Ralph Albert, 1885–1969, vol. VI
Horton, Rev. Reginald, 1852–1914, vol. I
Horton, Rev. Robert Forman, 1855–1934, vol. III

Horton, William, 1854–1944, vol. IV
Horton, Brig.-Gen. William Edward, 1868–1935, vol. III
Horton, Lt-Col W(illiam) Gray, 1897–1974, vol. VII
Horton-Smith, Lionel Graham Horton, 1871–1953, vol. V
Horton-Smith, Richard Horton, 1831–1919, vol. II
Horton-Smith-Hartley, Sir Percival; *see* Hartley.
Horton-Smith-Hartley, Percival Hubert Graham; *see* Hartley.
Horton-Starkie, Rev. Preb. Le Gendre George, 1859–1943, vol. IV
Horwill, Herbert William, 1864–1952, vol. V
Horwill, Sir Lionel Clifford, 1890–1972, vol. VII
Horwood, Hon. Sir William Henry, 1862–1945, vol. IV
Horwood, Brig.-Gen. Sir William Thomas Francis, 1868–1943, vol. IV
Hose, Charles, 1863–1929, vol. III
Hose, Edward Shaw, 1871–1946, vol. IV
Hose, Rt Rev. George Frederick, 1838–1922, vol. II
Hose, Sir (John) Walter, 1865–1958, vol. V
Hose, Robert John, 1863–1935, vol. III
Hose, Sir Walter; *see* Hose, Sir J. W.
Hosegood, Philip James, 1920–1987, vol. VIII
Hosie, Sir Alexander, 1853–1925, vol. II
Hosie, Lt-Col Andrew, 1860–1931, vol. III
Hosie, Dorothea, (Lady Hosie), 1885–1959, vol. V
Hosie, Ian, 1905–1970, vol. VI
Hosier, Arthur Julius, 1877–1963, vol. VI
Hosken, Clifford; *see* Keverne, Richard.
Hosken, Ernest Charles Heath, *died* 1934, vol. III
Hosker, Sir James Atkinson, 1857–1929, vol. III
Hoskin, Alan Simson, 1886–1945, vol. IV
Hoskin, John, 1836–1921, vol. II
Hoskin, Theo. Jenner Hooper, 1888–1954, vol. V
Hosking, Ethelbert Bernard, 1890–1960, vol. V
Hosking, Hon. Sir John Henry, 1854–1928, vol. II
Hosking, Paymaster Rear-Adm. Richard Bosustow, 1869–1962, vol. VI
Hoskins, Sir Anthony Hiley, 1828–1901, vol. I
Hoskins, Maj.-Gen. Sir (Arthur) Reginald, 1871–1942, vol. IV
Hoskins, Sir Cecil Harold, 1899–1971, vol. VII
Hoskins, Maj.-Gen. Sir Reginald; *see* Hoskins, Maj.-Gen. Sir A. R.
Hoskins, William, *died* 1928, vol. II
Hoskyn, Col John Cunningham Moore, 1875–1941, vol. IV
Hoskyns, Ven. Benedict George, 1856–1935, vol. III
Hoskyns, Col Sir Chandos, 10th Bt, 1848–1914, vol. I
Hoskyns, Sir Chandos Wren, 14th Bt, 1923–1945, vol. IV
Hoskyns, Rt Rev. Sir Edwyn, 12th Bt, 1851–1925, vol. II
Hoskyns, Rev. Canon Sir Edwyn Clement, 13th Bt, 1884–1937, vol. III
Hoskyns, Sir John Chevallier, 15th Bt, 1926–1956, vol. V
Hoskyns, Rev. Sir John Leigh, 9th Bt, 1817–1911, vol. I
Hoskyns, Sir Leigh, 11th Bt, 1850–1923, vol. II
Hoskyns, Rear-Adm. Peyton, 1852–1919, vol. II

Hoskyns-Abrahall, Rt Rev. Anthony Leigh Egerton, 1903–1982, vol. VIII

Hoskyns-Abrahall, Bennet, 1858–1951, vol. V

Hoskyns-Abrahall, Sir Chandos; *see* Hoskyns-Abrahall, Sir T. C.

Hoskyns-Abrahall, Sir (Theo) Chandos, 1896–1975, vol. VII

Hoskyns-Festing, Major Arthur; *see* Festing.

Hosmer, James Kendall, 1834–1927, vol. II

Hossie, Major David Neil, 1890–1962, vol. VI

Hoste, Maj.-Gen. Dixon Edward, 1827–1905, vol. I

Hoste, Dixon Edward, 1861–1946, vol. IV

Hoste, Sir William Graham, 4th Bt, 1895–1915, vol. II

Hoste, Sir William Henry Charles, 3rd Bt, 1860–1902, vol. I

Hoster, Mrs Albert, 1864–1939, vol. III

Hotblack, Maj.-Gen. Frederick Elliot, 1887–1979, vol. VII

Hotblack, George Finch, 1883–1951, vol. V

Hotchin, Sir Claude, 1898–1977, vol. VII

Hotchkin, Stafford Vere, 1876–1953, vol. V

Hotham, 5th Baron, 1838–1907, vol. I

Hotham, 6th Baron, 1863–1923, vol. II

Hotham, 7th Baron, 1899–1967, vol. VI

Hotham, Adm. Sir Alan Geoffrey, 1876–1965, vol. VI

Hotham, Sir Charles Frederick, 1843–1925, vol. II

Hotham, Captain Henry Edward, 1855–1912, vol. I

Hotham, Brig.-Gen. John, 1851–1932, vol. III

Hotham, Rev. John Hallett, 1811–1901, vol. I

Hothfield, 1st Baron, 1844–1926, vol. II

Hothfield, 2nd Baron 1873–1952, vol. V

Hothfield, 3rd Baron, 1897–1961, vol. VI

Hothfield, 4th Baron, 1916–1986, vol. VIII

Hotine, Brig. Martin, 1898–1968, vol. VI

Hotson, Sir Ernest; *see* Hotson, Sir J. E. B.

Hotson, Sir (John) Ernest (Buttery), 1877–1944, vol. IV

Houblon, Mrs Doreen A.; *see* Archer Houblon.

Houblon, Col George Bramston Archer-, 1843–1913, vol. I

Houblon, Rev. Thomas Henry Archer, 1849–1933, vol. III

Houchen, Harry Owen, 1907–1981, vol. VIII

Houde, Camillien, 1889–1958, vol. V

Houfton, Sir John Plowright, 1857–1929, vol. III

Hough, Edwin Leadam, 1852–1928, vol. II

Hough, Graham Goulder, 1908–1990, vol. VIII

Hough, James Fisher, 1878–1960, vol. V

Hough, John Stanley, 1856–1928, vol. II

Hough, Rev. Lynn Harold, 1877–1971, vol. VII

Hough, Sydney Samuel, 1870–1923, vol. II

Hough, William, 1884–1962, vol. VI

Hough, Rt Rev. William Woodcock, 1859–1934, vol. III

Houghton, Alanson Bigelow, 1863–1941, vol. IV

Houghton, Albert Morley, 1914–1987, vol. VIII

Houghton, Arthur Amory, Jr, 1906–1990, vol. VIII

Houghton, Charles Thomas, 1892–1975, vol. VII

Houghton, Claude; *see* Oldfield, C. H.

Houghton, Rev. Edward James, 1838–1919, vol. II

Houghton, Rev. Edward John Walford, 1867–1955, vol. V

Houghton, Rt Rev. Frank, *died* 1972, vol. VII

Houghton, Sir William Frederick, 1909–1971, vol. VII

Houghton, Rev. Canon William Reginald, 1910–1989, vol. VIII

Houghton, William Stanley, 1881–1913, vol. I

Houghton-Gastrell, Sir William; *see* Gastrell.

Houlden, George Houldsworth, 1902–1972, vol. VII

Houlder, Howard, 1858–1932, vol. III

Houldsworth, Sir Basil; *see* Houldsworth, Sir H. B.

Houldsworth, Sir (Harold) Basil, 2nd Bt (*cr* 1956), 1922–1990, vol. VIII

Houldsworth, Sir Henry Hamilton, 2nd Bt (*cr* 1887), 1867–1947, vol. IV

Houldsworth, Brig. Sir Henry Walter, 1896–1963, vol. VI

Houldsworth, Sir Hubert Stanley, 1st Bt (*cr* 1956), 1889–1956, vol. V

Houldsworth, J. H., *died* 1910, vol. I

Houldsworth, J. Hamilton, 1867–1941, vol. IV

Houldsworth, Sir Reginald Douglas Henry, 4th Bt, 1903–1989, vol. VIII

Houldsworth, Sir William Henry, 1st Bt (*cr* 1887), 1834–1917, vol. II

Houldsworth, Col Sir William Thomas Reginald, 3rd Bt (*cr* 1887), 1874–1960, vol. V

Hoult, (Eleanor) Norah, *died* 1984, vol. VIII

Hoult, Joseph, 1847–1917, vol. II

Houlton, Charlotte Leighton, 1882–1956, vol. V

Houlton, Sir Edward Victor Lewis, 1823–1899, vol. I

Houlton, Sir John Wardle, 1892–1973, vol. VII

Houndle, Henry Charles Herman Hawker, 1851–1919, vol. II

Hounsell, Maj.-Gen. Harold Arthur, 1897–1970, vol. VI

Hourigan, Thomas, 1904–1975, vol. VII

House, (Arthur) Humphry, 1908–1955, vol. V

House, Edward Mandell, 1858–1938, vol. III

House, George, 1892–1949, vol. IV

House, Harry Wilfred, 1895–1987, vol. VIII

House, Humphry; *see* House, A. H.

House, John William, 1919–1984, vol. VIII

Household, Geoffrey Edward West, 1900–1988, vol. VIII

Housman, Alfred Edward, 1859–1936, vol. III

Housman, Laurence, 1865–1959, vol. V

Houssay, Bernardo Alberto, 1887–1971, vol. VII

Houssaye, Henry, 1848–1911, vol. I

Houssemayne Du Boulay, Brig.-Gen. Noel Wilmot, 1861–1949, vol. IV

Houston, Sir Alexander Cruikshank, 1865–1933, vol. III

Houston, Arthur, 1833–1914, vol. I

Houston, Major Charles B.; *see* Blakiston-Houston.

Houston, Major Charles Elrington Duncan D.; *see* Davidson-Houston.

Houston, Dame Fanny Lucy, 1857–1936, vol. III

Houston, George, *died* 1947, vol. IV

Houston, John B.; *see* Blakiston-Houston.

Houston, Maj.-Gen. John B.; *see* Blakiston-Houston.

Houston, John R., 1856–1932, vol. III

Houston, Sir Robert Paterson, 1st Bt, 1853–1926, vol. II

Houston, Sir Thomas, *died* 1949, vol. IV

Houston, Lt-Col Wilfred Bennett D.; *see* Davidson-Houston.

Houston, William, 1846–1932, vol. III

Houston-Boswall-Preston, Thomas Alford, 1850–1918, vol. II

Houstoun, Robert Alexander, 1883–1975, vol. VII

Houstoun-Boswall, Sir George Lauderdale, 3rd Bt, 1847–1908, vol. I

Houstoun-Boswall, Sir George Reginald, 4th Bt, 1877–1915, vol. I

Houstoun-Boswall, Major Sir Gordon, 6th Bt, 1887–1961, vol. VI

Houstoun-Boswall, Sir Randolph; *see* Houstoun-Boswall, Sir T. R.

Houstoun-Boswall, Sir Thomas, 7th Bt, 1919–1982, vol. VIII

Houstoun-Boswall, Sir (Thomas) Randolph, 5th Bt, 1882–1953, vol. V

Houstoun-Boswall, Sir William Evelyn, 1892–1960, vol. V

Houthuesen, Albert Antony John, 1903–1979, vol. VII

Hovde, Frederick Lawson, 1908–1983, vol. VIII

Hovell, Very Rev. De Berdt, 1850–1905, vol. I

Hovell, Lt-Col Hugh De Berdt, 1863–1923, vol. II

Hovell, T. Mark, *died* 1925, vol. II

Hovil, Major Richard, *died* 1931, vol. III

How, Sir Friston Charles, 1897–1990, vol. VIII

How, Ven. Henry Walsham, 1856–1923, vol. II

How, Rt Rev. John Charles Halland, *died* 1961, vol. VI

How, Rev. John Hall, 1871–1938, vol. III

How, Walter Wybergh, 1861–1932, vol. III

How, Rt Rev. William Walsham, 1823–1897, vol. I

Howard de Walden, 7th Baron, 1830–1899, vol. I

Howard de Walden, 8th Baron, 1880–1946, vol. IV

Howard of Glossop, 2nd Baron, 1859–1924, vol. II

Howard of Glossop, 3rd Baron, 1885–1972, vol. VII

Howard of Glossop, Lady; (Winifred), *died* 1909, vol. I

Howard of Henderskelfe, Baron (Life Peer); George Anthony Geoffrey Howard, 1920–1984, vol. VIII

Howard of Penrith, 1st Baron, 1863–1939, vol. III

Howard, Captain Alan Frederic William, 1883–1971, vol. VII

Howard, Sir Albert, 1873–1947, vol. IV

Howard, Sir Algar Henry Stafford, 1880–1970, vol. VI

Howard, Andrée, 1910–1968, vol. VI

Howard, Sir (Andrew) Charles, *died* 1909, vol. I

Howard, Hon. Sir Arthur Jared Palmer, 1896–1971, vol. VII

Howard, Bronson, 1842–1908, vol. I

Howard, Sir Charles; *see* Howard, Sir A. C.

Howard, Brig. Sir Charles Alfred, 1878–1958, vol. V

Howard, Sir Douglas Frederick, 1897–1987, vol. VIII

Howard, Sir Ebenezer, 1850–1928, vol. II

Howard, Major Edmund, 1881–1960, vol. V

Howard, Sir (Edward) Stafford, 1851–1916, vol. II

Howard, Edwin Johnston, 1901–1971, vol. VII

Howard, Maj.-Gen. Sir Francis, 1848–1930, vol. III

Howard, Francis, 1874–1954, vol. V

Howard, Col Francis James Leigh, 1870–1942, vol. IV

Howard, Major Frederic George, 1872–1915, vol. I

Howard, Sir Frederick, 1827–1915, vol. I

Howard, Frederick Richard, 1894–1977, vol. VII

Howard, Geoffrey, 1889–1973, vol. VII

Howard, Lt-Gen. Sir Geoffrey Weston, 1876–1966, vol. VI

Howard, Hon. Geoffrey William Algernon, 1877–1935, vol. III

Howard, Captain George Augustus Hotham, 1853–1931, vol. III

Howard, G(eorge) Wren, 1893–1968, vol. VI

Howard, Sir Gerald; *see* Howard, Sir S. G.

Howard, Maj.-Gen. Gordon Byron, 1895–1976, vol. VII

Howard, Lt Comdr Hon. Greville Reginald, 1909–1987, vol. VIII

Howard, Captain Guy Robert, 1886–1918, vol. II

Howard, Sir (Harold Walter) Seymour, 1st Bt, 1888–1967, vol. VI

Howard, Sir Harry, (Henry Rudolph Howard), 1890–1970, vol. VI

Howard, Sir Henry, 1843–1921, vol. II

Howard, Rev. Henry, 1859–1933, vol. III

Howard, Lt-Col Hon. Henry Anthony Camillo, 1913–1977, vol. VII

Howard, Col Henry Cecil Lloyd, 1882–1950, vol. IV

Howard, Henry Charles, 1850–1914, vol. I

Howard, Sir Henry Francis, 1809–1898, vol. I

Howard, Sir Henry Fraser, 1874–1943, vol. IV

Howard, Major Sir Henry George, 1883–1968, vol. VI

Howard, Henry Newman, 1861–1929, vol. III

Howard, Col Henry Richard Lloyd, 1853–1922, vol. II

Howard, Henry Rudolph; *see* Howard, Sir Harry.

Howard, Sir Herbert; *see* Howard, Sir S. H.

Howard, Hon. Hugh Melville, 1883–1919, vol. II

Howard, John, *died* 1911, vol. I

Howard, John, *died* 1929, vol. III

Howard, Sir John Alfred Golding, 1901–1986, vol. VIII

Howard, Sir John Curtois, 1887–1970, vol. VI

Howard, John Melbourne, 1913–1982, vol. VIII

Howard, Joseph, 1834–1923, vol. II

Howard, Keble; *see* Bell, John Keble.

Howard, Leon Alexander L.; *see* Lee Howard.

Howard, Leslie, 1893–1943, vol. IV

Howard, Lady Mabel, 1878–1942, vol. IV

Howard, Hon. Mabel Bowden, *died* 1972, vol. VII

Howard, Marghanita; *see* Laski, M.

Howard, Hon. Oliver, 1875–1908, vol. I

Howard, Peter D., 1908–1965, vol. VI

Howard, Philip John Canning, 1853–1934, vol. III

Howard, Sir Richard Nicholas, 1832–1905, vol. I

Howard, Very Rev. Richard Thomas, 1884–1981, vol. VIII

Howard, Robert Jared Bliss, *died* 1921, vol. II

Howard, Robert Mowbray, 1854–1928, vol. II

Howard, Rev. Robert Wilmot, 1887–1960, vol. V

Howard, Robin Jarel Stanley, 1924–1989, vol. VIII

Howard, Roy Wilson, 1883–1964, vol. VI

Howard, Russell John, 1875–1942, vol. IV

Howard, Lt-Col Samuel Lloyd, 1827–1901, vol. I

Howard, Sir Seymour; *see* Howard, Sir H. W. S.

Howard, Sir Stafford; *see* Howard, Sir E. S.
Howard, Sir (Stanley) Herbert, 1888–1968, vol. VI
Howard, Sir (Stephen) Gerald, 1896–1973, vol. VII
Howard, Major Stephen Goodwin, 1867–1934, vol. III
Howard, T. Henry, 1849–1923, vol. II
Howard, Rev. Thomas Henry, *died* 1931, vol. III
Howard, Brig.-Gen. Thomas Nairne Scott Moncrieff, *died* 1960, vol. V
Howard, Tom Forrest, 1888–1953, vol. V
Howard, Trevor Wallace, 1913–1988, vol. VIII
Howard, Walter, 1866–1922, vol. II
Howard, Rev. Wilbert Francis, 1880–1952, vol. V
Howard, Captain William Gilbert, 1877–1960, vol. V
Howard, William McLaren, 1921–1990, vol. VIII
Howard, William Reginald, 1879–1966, vol. VI
Howard, Captain William Van Sittart, 1859–1937, vol. III
Howard-Brooke, Col Richard Edward Frederic, 1847–1918, vol. II
Howard-Jones, Maj.-Gen. Leonard Hamilton, 1905–1987, vol. VIII
Howard-Smith, Trevor Wallace; *see* Howard.
Howard-Vyse, Lt-Gen. Edward, 1826–1909, vol. I
Howard-Vyse, Howard Henry, 1858–1927, vol. II
Howard-Vyse, Maj.-Gen. Sir Richard Granville Hylton, 1883–1962, vol. VI
Howard-Williams, W., 1879–1962, vol. VI
Howarth, Sir Alfred, 1867–1937, vol. III
Howarth, Sir Edward, *died* 1953, vol. V
Howarth, Elijah, *died* 1938, vol. III
Howarth, Harry, 1916–1969, vol. VI
Howarth, Herbert Lomax, 1900–1974, vol. VII
Howarth, Osbert John Radclyffe, 1877–1954, vol. V
Howarth, Thomas Edward Brodie, 1914–1988, vol. VIII
Howarth, Walter Goldie, 1879–1962, vol. VI
Howarth, William James, *died* 1928, vol. II
Howat, Very Rev. Rudolph H.; *see* Henderson-Howat.
Howden, Charles Robert Andrew, 1862–1936, vol. III
Howden, Captain Harry Leslie, 1896–1969, vol. VI
Howden, Robert, 1856–1940, vol. III
Howe, 3rd Earl, 1822–1900, vol. I
Howe, 4th Earl, 1861–1929, vol. III
Howe, 5th Earl, 1884–1964, vol. VI
Howe, 6th Earl, 1908–1984, vol. VIII
Howe, Adm. Hon. Sir Assheton Gore C.; *see* Curzon-Howe.
Howe, Rt Hon. Clarence Decatur, 1886–1960, vol. V
Howe, George Frederick, 1856–1937, vol. III
Howe, George William Osborn, 1875–1960, vol. V
Howe, Sir Gerard Lewis, 1899–1955, vol. V
Howe, Hon. James Henderson, 1839–1920, vol. II
Howe, John Allen, 1869–1952, vol. V
Howe, Julia Ward, 1819–1910, vol. I
Howe, Captain Leicester Charles Assheton St John C.; *see* Curzon-Howe.
Howe, Col Randall Charles Annesley, 1858–1930, vol. III
Howe, Sir Robert George, 1893–1981, vol. VIII
Howe, Sir Ronald Martin, 1896–1977, vol. VII
Howe, Air Cdre Thomas Edward Barham, 1886–1970, vol. VI

Howel-Jones, Lt-Col Walter, 1868–1948, vol. IV
Howell, Col Arthur Anthony, 1862–1918, vol. II
Howell, Charles Alfred, 1905–1974, vol. VII
Howell, Hon. Clark, 1863–1936, vol. III
Howell, Conrad Meredyth Hinds, 1877–1960, vol. V
Howell, Very Rev. David, 1831–1903, vol. I
Howell, David Arnold, 1890–1953, vol. V
Howell, Dorothy, 1898–1982, vol. VIII
Howell, Sir Evelyn Berkeley, 1877–1971, vol. VII
Howell, Maj.-Gen. Frederick Duke Gwynne, 1881–1967, vol. VI
Howell, Rev. G., *died* 1918, vol. II
Howell, Lt-Col Geoffrey Llewellyn Hinds, 1875–1948, vol. IV
Howell, Col Harry Arthur Leonard, 1867–1937, vol. III
Howell, Hon. Hector Mansfield, 1842–1918, vol. II
Howell, Lt-Col Herbert Gwynne, 1879–1925, vol. II
Howell, John, 1871–1945, vol. IV
Howell, John Aldersey, 1888–1928, vol. II
Howell, Mortimer Sloper, 1841–1925, vol. II
Howell, Brig.-Gen. Philip, 1877–1916, vol. II
Howell, Sir Walter Jack, 1854–1913, vol. I
Howell, Col Wilfrid Russell, 1865–1930, vol. III
Howell, William Gough, 1922–1974, vol. VII
Howell, William Gruffydd Rhys, 1904–1956, vol. V
Howell, William H., 1860–1945, vol. IV
Howell, Rev. Canon Willoughby John, *died* 1938, vol. III
Howell-Jones, Col John Hyndman, 1877–1941, vol. IV
Howell-Price, Lt-Col Owen Glendower, vol. II
Howells, Rt Rev. Adelakun Williamson, 1905–1963, vol. VI
Howells, Rt Rev. Adolphus Williamson, 1866–1938, vol. III
Howells, Christopher John, 1933–1984, vol. VIII
Howells, Derek William, 1928–1987, vol. VIII
Howells, George, 1871–1955, vol. V
Howells, Gilbert Haywood, 1897–1982, vol. VIII
Howells, Herbert Norman, 1892–1983, vol. VIII
Howells, William Dean, 1837–1920, vol. II
Howes, Lt-Gen. Albert Joseph, 1837–1914, vol. I
Howes, Arthur Burnaby, 1879–1963, vol. VI
Howes, Bobby, 1895–1972, vol. VII
Howes, Ernest James, 1895–1974, vol. VII
Howes, Frank Stewart, 1891–1974, vol. VII
Howes, George Bond, 1853–1905, vol. I
Howes, Henry William, 1896–1978, vol. VII
Howes, Rear-Adm. Peter Norris, 1916–1983, vol. VIII
Howes, Brig. Sidney Gerald, *died* 1961, vol. VI
Howey, Maj.-Gen. William, 1838–1924, vol. II
Howgill, Richard John Frederick, 1895–1975, vol. VII
Howgrave-Graham, Hamilton Maurice, 1882–1963, vol. VI
Howick of Glendale, 1st Baron, 1903–1973, vol. VII
Howie, Hon. Sir Archibald, 1879–1943, vol. IV
Howie, Rev. Robert, 1836–1918, vol. II
Howie, Thomas McIntyre, 1926–1986, vol. VIII
Howison, George Holmes, 1834–1916, vol. II
Howitt, Sir Alfred Bakewell, 1879–1954, vol. V
Howitt, Alfred William, 1830–1908, vol. I

Howitt, Cecil; *see* Howitt, T. C.
Howitt, Charles Roberts, 1894–1969, vol. VI
Howitt, Frank Dutch, 1894–1954, vol. V
Howitt, Sir Harold Gibson, 1886–1969, vol. VI
Howitt, (Thomas) Cecil, 1889–1968, vol. VI
Howkins, Col Cyril Henry, 1876–1947, vol. IV
Howland, Hewitt Hanson, 1863–1944, vol. IV
Howland, Oliver Aiken, 1847–1904, vol. I
Howland, Robert Leslie, 1905–1986, vol. VIII
Howland, William Bailey, 1849–1917, vol. II
Howland, Hon. Sir William Pierce, 1811–1907, vol. I
Howles, Leonard, 1896–1957, vol. V
Howlett, Charles Edgar, 1854–1939, vol. III
Howlett, Edmund Henry, 1854–1930, vol. III
Howlett, Rt Rev. Mgr Martin, 1863–1949, vol. IV
Howlett, Brig. Reginald, 1882–1942, vol. IV
Howlett, Reginald, 1908–1969, vol. VI
Howlett, Richard, 1841–1917, vol. II
Howley, Major Jasper Joseph, 1868–1915, vol. I
Howley, John F. W., 1866–1941, vol. IV
Howley, Most Rev. Michael Francis, 1843–1914, vol. I
Howley, Richard Joseph, *died* 1955, vol. V
Howley, William John Joseph, 1865–1948, vol. IV
Howley, William Richard, 1875–1941, vol. IV
Howman, Brig. Ross Cosens, 1899–1976, vol. VII
Howorth, Col Henry Godfrey, 1870–1947, vol. IV
Howorth, Sir Henry Hoyle, 1842–1923, vol. II
Howorth, Sir Rupert Beswicke, 1880–1964, vol. VI
Howsam, Air Vice-Marshal George Roberts, 1895–1988, vol. VIII
Howse, Francis, 1851–1925, vol. II
Howse, Sir Henry Greenway, 1841–1914, vol. I
Howse, Maj.-Gen. Hon. Sir Neville Reginald, 1863–1930, vol. III
Howson, G. W. S., *died* 1919, vol. II
Howson, Brig. Geoffrey, 1883–1961, vol. VI
Howson, Ven. George John, 1854–1943, vol. IV
Howson, Ven. James Francis, 1856–1934, vol. III
Howson, Hon. Comdr John, 1829–1907, vol. I
Howson, Captain John, 1871–1948, vol. IV
Howson, Captain John Montagu, 1893–1959, vol. V
Howth, 4th Earl of, 1827–1909, vol. I
Hoy, Baron (Life Peer); James Hutchison Hoy, 1909–1976, vol. VII
Hoy, Col Sir William Wilson, 1868–1930, vol. III
Hoyer-Millar, Dame (Evelyn Louisa) Elizabeth, 1910–1984, vol. VIII
Hoyland, Harold Allan Dilke, 1885–1959, vol. V
Hoyland, John S., 1887–1957, vol. V
Hoyle, Arthur, *born* 1857, vol. III
Hoyle, Lt-Col Sir Emmanuel, 1st Bt, 1866–1939, vol. III
Hoyle, George, 1900–1979, vol. VII
Hoyle, Hon. Henry Clement, 1852–1926, vol. II
Hoyle, J. Rossiter, 1856–1926, vol. II
Hoyle, John Clifford, 1901–1976, vol. VII
Hoyle, William Evans, *died* 1926, vol. II
Hoyles, Newman Wright, 1844–1928, vol. II
Hoysted, Col Desmond Murree Fitzgerald, 1874–1945, vol. IV
Hozier, Col Sir Henry Montague, 1838–1907, vol. I
Hozumi, Baron Nobushige, 1855–1926, vol. II, vol. III

Hrdlicka, Aleš, 1869–1943, vol. IV
Hsu Chen-Ping, Rt Rev. Francis, 1920–1974, vol. VII
Huban, Maj.-Gen. John Patrick, 1891–1957, vol. V
Hubback, Brig.-Gen. Arthur Benison, 1871–1948, vol. IV
Hubback, Vice-Adm. Sir (Arthur) Gordon Voules, 1902–1970, vol. VI
Hubback, Mrs Eva M., 1886–1949, vol. IV
Hubback, Most Rev. George Clay, 1882–1955, vol. V
Hubback, Vice-Adm. Sir Gordon Voules; *see* Hubback, Vice-Adm. Sir A. G. V.
Hubback, Sir John Austen, 1878–1968, vol. VI
Hubbard, Charles Edward, 1900–1980, vol. VII
Hubbard, Elbert, 1859–1915, vol. I
Hubbard, (Eric) Hesketh, 1892–1957, vol. V
Hubbard, Hon. Evelyn, 1852–1934, vol. III
Hubbard, George, 1859–1936, vol. III
Hubbard, George William, 1870–1939, vol. III
Hubbard, Rt Rev. Harold Evelyn, 1883–1953, vol. V
Hubbard, Hesketh; *see* Hubbard, E. H.
Hubbard, Cdre Lancelot Fortescue; *see* Hubbard, Cdre R. L. F.
Hubbard, Louisa Maria, 1836–1906, vol. I
Hubbard, Percival Cyril, 1902–1961, vol. VI
Hubbard, Cdre (Robert) Lancelot Fortescue, 1887–1972, vol. VII
Hubbard, Bey Robert Richard, 1843–1926, vol. II, vol. III
Hubbard, Thomas Frederick, 1898–1961, vol. VI
Hubbard, William Egerton, *died* 1918, vol. II
Hubble, Sir Douglas Vernon, 1900–1981, vol. VIII
Hubble, Edwin Powell, 1889–1953, vol. V
Huberman, Bronislaw, 1882–1947, vol. IV
Hubrecht, J. B., 1883–1978, vol. VII
Hucker, Ernest George, 1908–1986, vol. VIII
Huckin, Victor Henry St John, 1880–1943, vol. IV
Hudd, Hon. Sir Herbert Sydney, 1881–1948, vol. IV
Hudd, Walter, 1898–1963, vol. VI
Huddleston, Sir Arthur James Croft, 1880–1948, vol. IV
Huddleston, Lady Diana De Vere, *died* 1905, vol. I
Huddleston, Captain Sir Ernest Whiteside, 1874–1959, vol. V
Huddleston, George, 1862–1944, vol. IV
Huddleston, Maj.-Gen. Sir Hubert Jervoise, 1880–1950, vol. IV
Huddleston, Sisley, 1883–1952, vol. V
Huddleston, Tristram Frederick Croft, 1848–1936, vol. III
Huddleston, Captain Willoughby Baynes, 1866–1953, vol. V
Hudleston, Ven. Cuthbert, *died* 1944, vol. IV
Hudleston, Lt-Gen. John Wallace, 1880–1961, vol. VI
Hudleston, Wilfred H., 1828–1909, vol. I
Hudleston, Col Wilfrid Edward, 1872–1952, vol. V
Hudon, Lt-Col Joseph Alfred George, 1858–1918, vol. II, vol. III
Hudson, 1st Viscount, 1886–1957, vol. V
Hudson, 2nd Viscount, 1924–1963 (this entry was not transferred to Who was Who).
Hudson, Albert Blellock, 1875–1947, vol. IV
Hudson, Alfred Arthur, *died* 1930, vol. III
Hudson, Arthur, 1861–1948, vol. IV
Hudson, Arthur Cyril, 1875–1962, vol. VI

Hudson, Col Arthur Ross, 1876–1963, vol. VI
Hudson, Rt Rev. Arthur William Goodwin, 1906–1985, vol. VIII
Hudson, Sir Austin Uvedale Morgan, 1st Bt, 1897–1956, vol. V
Hudson, Bernard, 1877–1957, vol. V
Hudson, Brig. Charles Edward, 1892–1959, vol. V
Hudson, Charles Thomas, 1828–1903, vol. I
Hudson, Lt-Col Charles Tilson, 1865–1948, vol. IV
Hudson, Maj.-Gen. Corrie, 1874–1958, vol. V
Hudson, Rev. Canon Cyril Edward, 1888–1960, vol. V
Hudson, Sir Edmund Peder, 1903–1978, vol. VII
Hudson, Edward, died 1936, vol. III
Hudson, Sir Edward Herbert, 1898–1966, vol. VI
Hudson, Eric Hamilton, 1902–1990, vol. VIII
Hudson, Sir Frank; see Hudson, Sir W. F.
Hudson, George Bickersteth, 1845–1912, vol. I
Hudson, Engr Rear-Adm. George William, 1861–1941, vol. IV
Hudson, H. Lindsay, (Harry Lindsay), died 1926, vol. II
Hudson, Harry Kynoch, 1867–1958, vol. V
Hudson, Gen. Sir Havelock, 1862–1944, vol. IV
Hudson, Lt-Col Henry Cecil Harland, 1885–1929, vol. III
Hudson, James Frank, 1872–1949, vol. IV
Hudson, James Hindle, 1881–1962, vol. VI
Hudson, Rev. Joseph, 1834–1919, vol. II
Hudson, Sir Leslie S., 1872–1946, vol. IV
Hudson, Manley Ottmer, 1886–1960, vol. V
Hudson, Mary Elizabeth, (Lady Hudson), 1867–1963, vol. VI
Hudson, Rt Rev. Noel Baring, 1893–1970, vol. VI
Hudson, Col Percy, 1876–1955, vol. V
Hudson, Lt-Col Ralph Charles D.; see Donaldson-Hudson.
Hudson, Ralph Milbanke, 1849–1938, vol. III
Hudson, Rev. Robert, 1862–1936, vol. III
Hudson, Major Robert Arthur, 1880–1917, vol. II
Hudson, Sir Robert Arundell, 1864–1927, vol. II
Hudson, Robert George Spencer, 1895–1965, vol. VI
Hudson, Hon. Sir Robert James, 1885–1963, vol. VI
Hudson, Rowland Skeffington, 1900–1980, vol. VII
Hudson, R(upert) Vaughan, 1895–1967, vol. VI
Hudson, Sidney Rowland, 1897–1966, vol. VI
Hudson, Brig. Stanley Grey, 1902–1960, vol. V
Hudson, Stephen, died 1944, vol. IV
Hudson, Brig.-Gen. Thomas Roe Christopher, 1866–1940, vol. III
Hudson, Rev. Thomas William, 1861–1929, vol. III
Hudson, Sir William Brereton, 1843–1914, vol. I
Hudson, William Henry, 1841–1922, vol. II
Hudson, Walter, 1852–1935, vol. III
Hudson, Sir (Walter) Frank, 1875–1958, vol. V
Hudson, Walter Richard Austen, 1894–1970, vol. VI
Hudson, Rt Rev. Wilfrid John, 1904–1981, vol. VIII
Hudson, Lt-Col William, 1880–1967, vol. VI
Hudson, Sir William, 1896–1978, vol. VII
Hudson, William Henry, 1862–1918, vol. II
Hudson, William Henry Hoar, 1838–1915, vol. I
Hudson-Davies, Sir Alan Meredyth, 1901–1975, vol. VII
Hudson-Kinahan, Sir Edward Hudson; see Kinahan.

Hudson-Kinahan, Lt-Col George Frederick, 1879–1939, vol. III
Hudson-Kinahan, Sir Robert Henry; see Kinahan.
Hudson-Williams, Thomas, 1873–1961, vol. VI
Hudspeth, Major Henry Moore, 1886–1971, vol. VII
Hueffer, Oliver Madox, died 1931, vol. III
Huffam, Major James Palmer, 1897–1968, vol. VI
Hufton, Philip Arthur, 1911–1974, vol. VII
Hügel, Anatole, Baron von, 1854–1928, vol. II
Hügel, Friedrich, Baron von, 1852–1925, vol. II
Hugessen, Adrian Norton K.; see Knatchbull-Hugessen.
Hugessen, Herbert Thomas K.; see Knatchbull-Hugessen.
Hugessen, Sir Hughe Montgomery K.; see Knatchbull-Hugessen.
Huggard, Sir Walter Clarence, died 1957, vol. V
Huggett, Arthur St George Joseph McCarthy, 1897–1968, vol. VI
Huggett, Esther Margaret; see Killick, E. M.
Huggill, Henry Percy, 1886–1957, vol. V
Huggins, Brig.-Gen. Alfred, 1884–1959, vol. V
Huggins, Sir George Frederick, died 1941, vol. IV
Huggins, Lt-Col Henry William, 1891–1965, vol. VI
Huggins, Sir John, 1891–1971, vol. VII
Huggins, Margaret Lindsay, (Lady Huggins), 1849–1915, vol. I
Huggins, Lt-Col Ponsonby Glenn, 1857–1925, vol. II
Huggins, Sir William, 1824–1910, vol. I
Hugh-Jones, Evan Bonnor, 1890–1978, vol. VII
Hugh-Jones, Llewelyn Arthur, 1888–1970, vol. VI
Hugh-Jones, Siriol (Mary Aprille), (Siriol Hart), 1924–1964, vol. VI
Hughan, Adm. Sir Arthur John H.; see Henniker-Hughan.
Hughes, Rt Rev. Albert Edward, 1878–1954, vol. V
Hughes, Albert Henry, 1917–1985, vol. VIII
Hughes, Sir Alfred, 9th Bt (cr 1773), 1825–1898, vol. I
Hughes, Alfred, 1860–1940, vol. III
Hughes, Alfred James, died 1947, vol. IV
Hughes, Col Arbuthnott James, 1856–1945, vol. IV
Hughes, Brig. Archibald Cecil, 1886–1961, vol. VI
Hughes, Captain Arthur Beckett, 1873–1925, vol. II
Hughes, Arthur John, 1843–1910, vol. I
Hughes, Maj. Arthur John, 1914–1984, vol. VIII
Hughes, Arthur Montague D'Urban, 1873–1974, vol. VII
Hughes, Major Basil, 1878–1953, vol. V
Hughes, Maj.-Gen. Basil Perronet, 1903–1989, vol. VIII
Hughes, Brodie; see Hughes, E. B. C.
Hughes, Cecil Hugh Myddleton, died 1960, vol. V
Hughes, Charles Evans, 1862–1948, vol. IV
Hughes, Maj.-Gen. Charles Frederick, 1844–1932, vol. III
Hughes, Sir Collingwood, 10th Bt (cr 1773), 1854–1932, vol. III
Hughes, Collingwood, 1872–1963, vol. VI
Hughes, Col Cyril E., 1890–1958, vol. V
Hughes, David Arthur, 1905–1968, vol. VI
Hughes, David Edward, 1831–1900, vol. I
Hughes, David Leslie, 1912–1990, vol. VIII
Hughes, Donald Wynn, 1911–1967, vol. VI
Hughes, Col Edmund Locock, 1880–1945, vol. IV

Hughes, Rev. Edward, *died* 1910, vol. I
Hughes, Edward, 1899–1965, vol. VI
Hughes, Edward David, 1906–1963, vol. VI
Hughes, Captain Edward Glyn de Styrap J.; *see* Jukes Hughes.
Hughes, Captain Edward Llewellyn, 1875–1955, vol. V
Hughes, Edward R., *died* 1908, vol. I
Hughes, Col Edward Talfourd, 1855–1943, vol. IV (A), vol. V
Hughes, Col Sir Edwin, 1832–1904, vol. I
Hughes, Elizabeth Phillipps, 1851–1925, vol. II
Hughes, Col Emilius, 1844–1926, vol. II
Hughes, Emmet John, 1920–1982, vol. VIII
Hughes, Emrys, 1894–1969, vol. VI
Hughes, (Ernest) Brodie (Cobbett), 1913–1989, vol. VIII
Hughes, Rev. Ernest Richard, 1883–1956, vol. V
Hughes, Rev. Ernest Selwyn, 1860–1942, vol. IV
Hughes, Evan, 1882–1951, vol. V
Hughes, Maj.-Gen. Frederick Godfrey, 1857–1944, vol. IV
Hughes, Very Rev. Frederick Llewelyn, 1894–1967, vol. VI
Hughes, G. Bernard, *died* 1975, vol. VII
Hughes, Maj.-Gen. Garnet Burk, 1880–1937, vol. III
Hughes, Col George Arthur, 1851–1926, vol. II
Hughes, Hon. George Edward, 1854–1937, vol. III
Hughes, George Lewis Hollingsworth, 1876–1932, vol. III
Hughes, George Ravensworth, 1888–1983, vol. VIII
Hughes, Brig. Gerald Birdwood V.; *see* Vaughan-Hughes.
Hughes, Gerald Stephen, 1878–1959, vol. V
Hughes, Captain Guy D'O.; *see* D'Oyly-Hughes.
Hughes, Guy Erskine, 1904–1980, vol. VII
Hughes, Rev. Harold, 1884–1950, vol. IV
Hughes, Hector, *died* 1970, vol. VI
Hughes, Maj.-Gen. Henry Bernard Wylde, 1887–1953, vol. V
Hughes, Henry Harold, *died* 1940, vol. III
Hughes, Rear-Adm. Henry Hugh, 1911–1986, vol. VIII
Hughes, Rev. Henry Maldwyn, 1875–1940, vol. III
Hughes, Brig.-Gen. Henry Thoresby, 1873–1947, vol. IV
Hughes, Rev. H(enry) Trevor, 1910–1988, vol. VIII
Hughes, Herbert, 1853–1917, vol. II
Hughes, Major Herbert Francis, *died* 1939, vol. III
Hughes, H(ugh) L(lewelyn) Glyn, 1892–1973, vol. VII
Hughes, Rev. Hugh Price, 1847–1902, vol. I
Hughes, Hugh Robert, 1827–1911, vol. I
Hughes, Maj.-Gen. Ivor Thomas Percival, 1897–1962, vol. VI
Hughes, James John, 1874–1952, vol. V
Hughes, John, 1850–1932, vol. III
Hughes, Col John Arthur, 1860–1938, vol. III
Hughes, John David Ivor, 1885–1969, vol. VI
Hughes, Col John Gethin, 1866–1954, vol. V
Hughes, Captain John Grant Duncan-, 1882–1962, vol. VI
Hughes, Rt Rev. John Richard Worthington P.; *see* Poole Hughes.

Hughes, John Rowland, 1856–1937, vol. III
Hughes, John Turnbull, 1919–1977, vol. VII
Hughes, John William Gwynne-, 1858–1917, vol. II
Hughes, Joseph John, 1928–1976, vol. VII
Hughes, Rt Rev. Joshua Pritchard, 1847–1938, vol. III
Hughes, Katherine, *died* 1931, vol. III
Hughes, Rev. Levi Gethin, 1885–1953, vol. V
Hughes, Rev. Llewelyn Robert, *died* 1925, vol. II
Hughes, Dame Mary Ethel, *died* 1958, vol. V
Hughes, Mary Katherine H. P.; *see* Price Hughes.
Hughes, Myra Kathleen, *died* 1918, vol. II
Hughes, Rev. Nathaniel Thomas, 1834–1913, vol. I
Hughes, Paul Grant, 1928–1985, vol. VIII
Hughes, Sir Reginald Johnasson, 11th Bt (*cr* 1773), 1882–1945, vol. IV
Hughes, Reginald Richard M.; *see* Meyric Hughes.
Hughes, Ven. Richard, 1881–1962, vol. VI
Hughes, Richard Arthur Warren, 1900–1976, vol. VII
Hughes, Sir Richard Edgar, 13th Bt (*cr* 1773), 1897–1970, vol. VI
Hughes, Captain Robert Herbert Wilfrid, 1872–1936, vol. III
Hughes, Sir Robert Heywood, 12th Bt (*cr* 1773), 1865–1951, vol. V
Hughes, Sir Robert John, 1822–1904, vol. I
Hughes, Ronw Moelwyn, 1897–1955, vol. V
Hughes, Hon. Lt-Gen. Hon. Sir Sam, 1853–1921, vol. II
Hughes, Rev. Samuel William, 1874–1954, vol. V
Hughes, Sean Francis, 1946–1990, vol. VIII
Hughes, Spencer Leigh, 1858–1920, vol. II
Hughes, Sydney Herbert George, 1879–1962, vol. VI
Hughes, Talbot, 1869–1942, vol. IV
Hughes, Sir Thomas, 1838–1923, vol. II
Hughes, Hon. Sir Thomas, 1863–1930, vol. III
Hughes, Sir Thomas, 1863–1942, vol. IV
Hughes, Thomas Cann, 1860–1948, vol. IV
Hughes, Mrs Thomas H. R., *died* 1930, vol. III
Hughes, Sir Thomas Harrison, 1st Bt (*cr* 1942), 1881–1958, vol. V
Hughes, Thomas Lewis, 1897–1980, vol. VII
Hughes, Thomas M'Kenny, *died* 1917, vol. II
Hughes, Rt Rev. Thomas Maurice, 1895–1981, vol. VIII
Hughes, Sir Thomas Raffles, 1856–1938, vol. III
Hughes, Rev. W. Worthington P.; *see* Poole-Hughes.
Hughes, Sir Walter Charleton, 1850–1922, vol. II
Hughes, Rev. Walter Octavius Marsh, *died* 1931, vol. III
Hughes, Walter Tatham, 1849–1917, vol. II
Hughes, Hon. Sir Wilfrid (Selwyn) Kent, 1895–1970, vol. VI
Hughes, William Henry, 1915–1990, vol. VIII
Hughes, Bt Col William Hesketh, 1872–1940, vol. III
Hughes, Rt Rev. William James, *died* 1979, vol. VII
Hughes, Rt Hon. William Morris, 1864–1952, vol. V
Hughes, William Reginald Noel, 1913–1990, vol. VIII
Hughes, Sir William Templer, 1822–1897, vol. I
Hughes-Buller, Ralph Buller, 1871–1949, vol. IV
Hughes D'Aeth, Rear-Adm. Arthur Cloudesley Shovel, 1875–1956, vol. V
Hughes-Games, Ven. Joshua, 1831–1904, vol. I

Hughes Hallett, Vice Adm. Sir (Cecil) Charles, 1898–1985, vol. VIII

Hughes Hallett, Vice Adm. Sir Charles; *see* Hughes Hallett, Sir Cecil C.

Hughes-Hallett, Col James Wyndham, 1852–1927, vol. II

Hughes-Hallett, Vice-Adm. John, 1901–1972, vol. VII

Hughes-Hallett, Leslie Charles, 1887–1966, vol. VI

Hughes-Hunter, Sir Charles, 1st Bt (*cr* 1906), 1844–1907, did not have an entry in Who's Who.

Hughes-Hunter, Sir William Bulkeley Hughes, 2nd Bt, 1880–1951, vol. V

Hughes-Morgan, Major Sir David, 1st Bt; *see* Morgan.

Hughes-Morgan, Sir John Vernon, 2nd Bt, 1900–1969, vol. VI

Hughes-Onslow, Sir Geoffrey Henry, 1893–1971, vol. VII

Hughes-Onslow, Henry, 1871–1932, vol. III

Hughes-Parry, Robert, 1895–1986, vol. VIII

Hughes-Roberts, John Gwyndeg, 1894–1949, vol. IV

Hughes-Stanton, Blair Rowlands, 1902–1981, vol. VIII

Hughes-Stanton, Sir Herbert, 1870–1937, vol. III

Hughman, Sir (Ernest) Montague, 1876–1956, vol. V

Hughman, Sir Montague; *see* Hughman, Sir E. M.

Hugill, Rear-Adm. Réné Charles, 1883–1962, vol. VI

Hugo, Lt-Col Edward Victor, 1865–1951, vol. V

Hugo, Lt-Col James Henry, 1870–1943, vol. IV

Huguenet, A. P., *died* 1910, vol. I

Huish, Marcus Bourne, *died* 1921, vol. II

Huish, Sir Raymond Douglas, 1898–1970, vol. VI

Hulbert, Sir Charles, *died* 1932, vol. III

Hulbert, Rev. Charles Augustus, 1838–1919, vol. II

Hulbert, Dame Cicely; *see* Courtneidge, Dame Cicely.

Hulbert, Claude Noel, 1900–1964, vol. VI

Hulbert, Jack; *see* Hulbert, J. N.

Hulbert, John Norman, (Jack), 1892–1978, vol. VII

Hulbert, Wing Comdr Sir Norman John, 1903–1972, vol. VII

Hulett, Hon. Sir (James) Liege, 1838–1928, vol. II

Hulett, Hon. Sir Liege; *see* Hulett, Hon. Sir J. L.

Hulin de Loo, Georges Charles Nicolas Marie, 1862–1946, vol. IV

Hull, Arthur Eaglefield, 1876–1928, vol. II

Hull, Maj.-Gen. Sir Charles Patrick Amyatt, 1865–1920, vol. II

Hull, Cordell, 1871–1955, vol. V

Hull, Edward, 1829–1917, vol. II

Hull, Eleanor H., 1860–1935, vol. III

Hull, Hon. Henry Charles, 1860–1932, vol. III

Hull, Henry Mitchell, 1861–1946, vol. IV

Hull, Surg. Rear-Adm. Herbert Richard Barnes, 1886–1970, vol. VI

Hull, Sir Hubert, 1887–1976, vol. VII

Hull, Lt-Col Hubert Charles Edward, 1891–1939, vol. III

Hull, Sir Percy Clarke, *died* 1968, vol. VI

Hull, Field Marshal Sir Richard Amyatt, 1907–1989, vol. VIII

Hull, Comdr Thomas A., *died* 1904, vol. I

Hullah, John, 1876–1955, vol. V

Hullah-Brown, J., 1875–1973, vol. VII

Hulme, Hon. Sir Alan Shallcross, 1907–1989, vol. VIII

Hulme, Alfred Clive, 1911–1982, vol. VIII

Hulme, Edward Maslin, 1869–1951, vol. V

Hulme, Frederick Edward, 1841–1909, vol. I

Hulme, Rev. Thomas Ferrier, 1856–1942, vol. IV

Hulme-Moir, Rt Rev. Francis Oag, 1910–1979, vol. VII

Hulme Taylor, Col Jack, 1894–1970, vol. VI

Hulse, Sir Edward, 5th Bt, 1809–1899, vol. I

Hulse, Sir Edward Hamilton Westrow, 7th Bt, 1889–1915, vol. I

Hulse, Sir Edward Henry, 6th Bt, 1859–1903, vol. I

Hulse, Sir Hamilton, 8th Bt, 1864–1931, vol. III

Hulton, Sir Edward, 1st Bt (*cr* 1921), 1869–1925, vol. II

Hulton, Sir Edward George Warris, 1906–1988, vol. VIII

Hulton, Col Frederick Courtenay Longuet, 1864–1940, vol. III (A), vol. IV

Hulton, Rev. Henry Edward, 1839–1922, vol. II

Hulton, Lt-Col Henry Horne, 1882–1941, vol. IV

Hulton, Col John Meredith, 1882–1942, vol. IV

Hulton, Sir Roger Braddyll, 3rd Bt (*cr* 1905), 1891–1956, vol. V

Hulton, Sir William Rothwell, 2nd Bt (*cr* 1905), 1868–1943, vol. IV

Hulton, Sir William Wilbraham Blethyn, 1st Bt (*cr* 1905), 1844–1907, vol. I

Hulton-Harrop, William Edward Montagu, 1848–1916, vol. II

Hulton-Harrop, Maj.-Gen. William Harrington, 1906–1979, vol. VII

Humble, Joseph Graeme, 1913–1980, vol. VII

Humble-Burkitt, Col Bernard Maynard, 1864–1945, vol. IV

Humble-Crofts, Rev. William John, 1846–1924, vol. II

Humby, Lt-Col James Frederick, 1860–1943, vol. IV

Hume, Alexander Williamson, 1850–1925, vol. II, vol. III

Hume, Allan Octavian, 1829–1912, vol. I

Hume, Basil; *see* Hume, J. B.

Hume, Col Charles Vernon, 1860–1915, vol. I

Hume, Major Charles Westley, 1886–1981, vol. VIII

Hume, Fergus, 1859–1932, vol. III

Hume, George Alexander, 1860–1905, vol. I

Hume, George Haliburton, 1845–1923, vol. II

Hume, Sir George Hopwood, 1866–1946, vol. IV

Hume, Sir (Hubert) Nutcombe, 1893–1967, vol. VI

Hume, James Gibson, 1860–1949, vol. IV, vol. V

Hume, John Basil, 1893–1974, vol. VII

Hume, Col John Edward, 1866–1939, vol. III

Hume, Brig.-Gen. John James Francis, 1858–1935, vol. III

Hume, Maj.-Gen. John Richard, 1831–1906, vol. I

Hume, Major Martin Andrew Sharp, 1847–1910, vol. I

Hume, Sir Nutcombe; *see* Hume, Sir H. N.

Hume, Brig. Reginald Vernon, 1898–1960, vol. V

Hume, Sir Robert, 1828–1909, vol. I

Hume, Sir William Errington, 1879–1960, vol. V

Hume, William Fraser, 1867–1949, vol. IV

Hume, Lt-Col William James Parke, 1866–1952, vol. V

Hume-Campbell, Sir John Home-Purves; *see* Campbell.

Hume-Cook, Hon. James, 1866–1942, vol. IV

Hume-Rothery, William, 1899–1968, vol. VI

Hume-Spry, Lt-Col Leighton; *see* Spry.

Hume-Williams, Rt Hon. Sir Ellis, 1st Bt, 1863–1947, vol. IV

Hume-Williams, Sir Roy Ellis, 2nd Bt, 1887–1980, vol. VII

Humfrey, Rev. John B.; *see* Blake-Humfrey.

Humfrey, Lt-Col Richard Edmond, 1881–1962, vol. VI

Hummel, Rt Rev. Francis Ignatius, 1870–1924, vol. II

Humphery, Lt-Col Sir John, 1872–1938, vol. III

Humphery, John Edward, 1873–1946, vol. IV

Humphery, Sir William Henry, 1st Bt, 1827–1909, vol. I

Humphrey, Marshal of the Royal Air Force Sir Andrew Henry, 1921–1977, vol. VII

Humphrey, Douglas, 1880–1945, vol. IV

Humphrey, George, 1889–1966, vol. VI

Humphrey, George Magoffin, 1890–1970, vol. VI

Humphrey, Herbert Alfred, 1868–1951, vol. V

Humphrey, Hubert Horatio, Jr, 1911–1978, vol. VII

Humphrey, John, 1862–1933, vol. III

Humphrey, John, 1879–1956, vol. V

Humphrey, Rev. John Henry, 1860–1934, vol. III

Humphrey, John Herbert, 1915–1987, vol. VIII

Humphrey-Davy, Francis Herbert Mountjoy Nelson, *died* 1953, vol. V

Humphreys, Rev. Alfred Edward, 1843–1922, vol. II

Humphreys, Arthur L., 1865–1946, vol. IV

Humphreys, Arthur Raleigh, 1911–1988, vol. VIII

Humphreys, Cecil Lee Howard, 1893–1941, vol. IV

Humphreys, His Honour Christmas; *see* Humphreys, His Honour T. C.

Humphreys, Major Dashwood William Harrington, 1872–1917, vol. II

Humphreys, Lt-Gen. Sir (Edward) Thomas, 1878–1955, vol. V

Humphreys, Brig.-Gen. Gardiner, 1865–1942, vol. IV

Humphreys, George Alfred, *died* 1948, vol. IV

Humphreys, Sir George William, 1863–1945, vol. IV

Humphreys, Gordon Noel, *died* 1966, vol. VI

Humphreys, Engr Rear-Adm. Sir Henry, *died* 1924, vol. II

Humphreys, Hubert, 1878–1967, vol. VI

Humphreys, Humphrey Francis, 1885–1977, vol. VII

Humphreys, John Lisseter, *died* 1929, vol. III

Humphreys, Captain Kenneth Noel, 1881–1955, vol. V

Humphreys, Sir Kenneth Owens, 1918–1981, vol. VIII

Humphreys, Noel Algernon, 1837–1923, vol. II

Humphreys, Very Rev. Robert, *died* 1917, vol. II

Humphreys, Lt-Gen. Sir Thomas; *see* Humphreys, Lt-Gen. Sir E. T.

Humphreys, Rt Hon. Sir Travers, 1867–1956, vol. V

Humphreys, His Honour (Travers) Christmas, 1901–1983, vol. VIII

Humphreys, Mrs W. Desmond; *see* Rita.

Humphreys-Davies, Brian, 1917–1971, vol. VII

Humphreys-Davies, (George) Peter, 1909–1985, vol. VIII

Humphreys-Davies, Peter; *see* Humphreys-Davies, G. P.

Humphreys-Owen, Arthur Charles, 1836–1905, vol. I

Humphries, Albert, 1872–1951, vol. V

Humphries, Sir Albert Edward, *died* 1935, vol. III

Humphries, George James, 1900–1981, vol. VIII

Humphries, Sir Herbert Henry, *died* 1938, vol. III

Humphries, Rev. Canon James Henry, 1890–1962, vol. VI

Humphries, Sir Sidney Richard White, 1857–1941, vol. IV

Humphries, Sydney S.; *see* Sidney-Humphries.

Humphris, Francis Howard, 1866–1947, vol. IV

Humphry, Alfred Paget, 1850–1916, vol. II

Humphry, Mrs C. E., *died* 1925, vol. II

Humphry, Laurence, 1856–1920, vol. II

Humphry, Maj.-Gen. Lawrence, 1875–1931, vol. III

Humphrys, Brig.-Gen. Charles Vesey, 1862–1944, vol. IV

Humphrys, Lt-Col Sir Francis Henry, 1879–1971, vol. VII

Humpidge, Kenneth Palmer, 1902–1987, vol. VIII

Huneker, James Gibbons, 1860–1921, vol. II

Hungarton, 1st Baron, 1890–1966, vol. VI

Hungerford, Sir (Alexander) Wilson, *died* 1969, vol. VI

Hungerford, Margaret Wolfe, *died* 1897, vol. I

Hungerford, Samuel James, 1872–1955, vol. V

Hungerford, Sir Wilson; *see* Hungerford, Sir A. W.

Hunkin, Rt Rev. Joseph Wellington, 1887–1950, vol. IV

Hunloke, Henry Philip, 1906–1978, vol. VII

Hunloke, Major Sir Philip, 1868–1947, vol. IV

Hunn, Major Sydney Arthur, 1889–1942, vol. IV

Hunnings, Gordon, 1926–1986, vol. VIII

Hunsdon of Hunsdon, 1st Baron, 1854–1935, vol. III

Hunsdon of Hunsdon, 2nd Baron; *see* Aldenham, 4th Baron.

Hunt of Fawley, Baron (Life Peer); John Henderson Hunt, 1905–1987, vol. VIII

Hunt, Dame Agnes Gwendoline, 1866–1948, vol. IV

Hunt, Alan Henderson, 1908–1970, vol. VI

Hunt, Albert, 1863–1957, vol. V

Hunt, Rev. Canon Alfred, 1862–1937, vol. III

Hunt, Adm. Sir (Allen) Thomas, 1866–1943, vol. IV

Hunt, Arthur Surridge, 1871–1934, vol. III

Hunt, Atlee Arthur, 1864–1935, vol. III

Hunt, Cecil Arthur, 1873–1965, vol. VI

Hunt, Rev. David J. Stather, 1856–1929, vol. III

Hunt, Edmund Langley, 1868–1925, vol. II

Hunt, Major Edwin Watkin, 1869–1945, vol. IV

Hunt, Frank William, 1870–1955, vol. V

Hunt, Surg. Rear-Adm. Frederick George, 1894–1975, vol. VII

Hunt, Sir Frederick Seager, 1st Bt, 1837–1904, vol. I

Hunt, Brig. Frederick Welsley, 1871–1944, vol. IV

Hunt, Rear-Adm. Geoffrey Harry C.; *see* Carew Hunt.

Hunt, George Henry, 1853–1940, vol. III

Hunt, Captain George Percy Edward, *died* 1917, vol. II

Hunt, Col (George) Vivian, 1905–1979, vol. VII

Hunt, Major Gerald Ponsonby Sneyd, 1877–1918, vol. II
Hunt, Gerard L.; see Leigh-Hunt.
Hunt, Rev. H. G. Bonavia, 1847–1917, vol. II
Hunt, Henry Ambrose, 1866–1946, vol. IV
Hunt, Rev. Henry de Vere, 1856–1919, vol. II
Hunt, Herbert James, 1899–1973, vol. VII
Hunt, Hilary Lushington Holman H.; see Holman-Hunt.
Hunt, Hubert Walter, 1865–1945, vol. IV
Hunt, (Jack) Naylor, 1917–1986, vol. VIII
Hunt, Sir John, 1859–1945, vol. IV
Hunt, John Francis, 1906–1979, vol. VII
Hunt, Sir John Joseph, died 1933, vol. III
Hunt, John Middlemass, 1858–1932, vol. III
Hunt, Lt-Col John Patrick, 1875–1938, vol. III
Hunt, Col John Philip, 1907–1970, vol. VI
Hunt, Joseph, 1854–1936, vol. III
Hunt, Sir Joseph Anthony, 1905–1982, vol. VIII
Hunt, Margaret, 1831–1912, vol. I
Hunt, Martita, 1900–1969, vol. VI
Hunt, Gen. Sir Peter Mervyn, 1916–1988, vol. VIII
Hunt, Ralph Holmes V.; see Vernon-Hunt.
Hunt, Reginald Heber, 1891–1982, vol. VIII
Hunt, Lt-Col Reginald Seager, 1874–1942, vol. IV
Hunt, Sir Reuben James, 1888–1970, vol. VI
Hunt, Richard William, 1908–1979, vol. VII
Hunt, Maj.-Gen. Robert Augustus Carew, 1838–1935, vol. III
Hunt, Comdr Robert Gregory Maze Durrant, 1886–1937, vol. III
Hunt, Captain Roland Cecil C.; see Carew Hunt.
Hunt, Rowland, 1858–1943, vol. IV
Hunt, Stanley Herbert, died 1934, vol. III
Hunt, Adm. Sir Thomas; see Hunt, Adm. Sir A. T.
Hunt, Thomas, 1854–1929, vol. III
Hunt, Thomas Cecil, 1901–1980, vol. VII
Hunt, Lt-Col Thomas Edward C.; see Carew-Hunt.
Hunt, Rev. Thomas Hankey, 1842–1921, vol. II
Hunt, Rev. Thomas Henry, 1865–1941, vol. IV
Hunt, Vernon Arthur Moore, 1912–1983, vol. VIII
Hunt, Violet, died 1942, vol. IV
Hunt, Violet B.; see Brooke-Hunt.
Hunt, Col Vivian; see Hunt, Col G. V.
Hunt, Rev. William, 1842–1931, vol. III
Hunt, Sir William Duffus, 1867–1939, vol. III
Hunt, Sir William Edgar, 1883–1969, vol. VI
Hunt, William Field, 1900–1981, vol. VIII
Hunt, William H.; see Holman-Hunt.
Hunt, Major William Morgan, 1881–1925, vol. II
Hunt-Grubbe, Adm. Sir Walter James, 1833–1922, vol. II
Hunter, Hon. Lord; William Hunter, 1865–1957, vol. V
Hunter, Maj.-Gen. Sir Alan John, 1881–1942, vol. IV
Hunter, Alastair; see Hunter, M. I. A.
Hunter, Albert Edward, 1900–1969, vol. VI
Hunter, Andrew, 1876–1969, vol. VI
Hunter, Rev. Andrew Johnston, 1844–1914, vol. I
Hunter, Rev. Archer George, 1850–1939, vol. III
Hunter, Gen. Sir Archibald, 1856–1936, vol. III
Hunter, Sir Bernard; see Hunter, Sir W. B.
Hunter, Lt-Col Cecil Stuart, 1882–1935, vol. III

Hunter, Brig.-Gen. Charles George Woodburn, 1871–1932, vol. III
Hunter, Sir Charles Roderick, 3rd Bt, 1858–1924, vol. II
Hunter, Colin, 1841–1904, vol. I
Hunter, Adm. Cuthbert, 1866–1952, vol. V
Hunter, Sir David, 1841–1914, vol. I
Hunter, Donald, 1898–1978, vol. VII
Hunter, Captain Douglas William, died 1918, vol. II
Hunter, Sir Ellis, 1892–1961, vol. VI
Hunter, Sir (Ernest) John, 1912–1983, vol. VIII
Hunter, Col Evan Austin, 1887–1954, vol. V
Hunter, G(eorge) Sherwood, 1882–1920, vol. II
Hunter, Sir George, 1860–1930, vol. III
Hunter, Sir George Burton, 1845–1937, vol. III
Hunter, Maj.-Gen. George Douglas, 1860–1922, vol. II
Hunter, Brig.-Gen. George Gillett, 1864–1930, vol. III
Hunter, Gordon, 1863–1929, vol. III
Hunter, Hamilton, 1845–1923, vol. II
Hunter, Henry Charles Vicars, 1861–1934, vol. III
Hunter, Henry Hamilton, 1875–1944, vol. IV
Hunter, Air Cdre Henry John Francis, 1893–1966, vol. VI
Hunter, Brig. Henry Noel Alexander, 1881–1964, vol. VI
Hunter, Sir Herbert; see Hunter, Sir J. H.
Hunter, Col Sir Herbert Patrick, 1880–1968, vol. VI
Hunter, Ian Basil, 1900–1975, vol. VII
Hunter, James de Graaff, 1881–1967, vol. VI
Hunter, Captain James Edward, 1834–1932, vol. III
Hunter, Sir John; see Hunter, Sir E. J.
Hunter, John, 1833–1914, vol. I
Hunter, Rev. John, 1849–1917, vol. II
Hunter, Sir John, 1863–1936, vol. III
Hunter, Rt Rev. John, 1897–1965, vol. VI
Hunter, Sir John Adams, 1890–1962, vol. VI
Hunter, John B., 1890–1951, vol. V
Hunter, John George, 1888–1964, vol. VI
Hunter, Maj.-Gen. John Gunning, 1859–1926, vol. II
Hunter, Sir (John) Herbert, 1864–1930, vol. III
Hunter, Hon. John McEwan, 1863–1940, vol. III (A), vol. IV
Hunter, Sir (John) Mark (Somers), 1865–1932, vol. III
Hunter, Lt-Col John Muir, 1844–1920, vol. II
Hunter, Joseph, 1875–1935, vol. III
Hunter, Maj. Joseph Charles, 1894–1983, vol. VIII
Hunter, Rt Rev. Leslie Stannard, 1890–1983, vol. VIII
Hunter, Louis, 1899–1986, vol. VIII
Hunter, Louis Lucien, 1889–1959, vol. V
Hunter, Sir Mark; see Hunter, Sir J. M. S.
Hunter, (Mark Ian) Alastair, 1909–1983, vol. VIII
Hunter, Matthew, died 1941, vol. IV
Hunter, Captain Michael John, 1891–1951, vol. V
Hunter, Norman Charles, 1908–1971, vol. VII
Hunter, Rev. Peter Hay, 1854–1909, vol. I
Hunter, Peter Sinclair, 1883–1954, vol. V
Hunter, Philip Vassar, 1883–1956, vol. V
Hunter, Sir Robert, 1844–1913, vol. I
Hunter, Robert Lewin, 1852–1942, vol. IV
Hunter, Samuel Robert, 1877–1948, vol. IV

Hunter, Summers, 1856–1940, vol. III
Hunter, Sir Summers, 1890–1963, vol. VI
Hunter, Sir Thomas, 1850–1919, vol. II
Hunter, Sir Thomas, 1872–1953, vol. V
Hunter, Lt-Col Thomas, 1873–1965, vol. VI
Hunter, Sir Thomas Alexander, 1876–1953, vol. V
Hunter, Sir Thomas Anderson, died 1958, vol. V
Hunter, Thomas Briggs, died 1957, vol. V
Hunter, Trevor Havard, died 1960, vol. V
Hunter, Walter King, 1867–1947, vol. IV
Hunter, William; see Hunter, Hon. Lord.
Hunter, William, 1861–1937, vol. III
Hunter, William, died 1967, vol. VI
Hunter, William Alexander, 1844–1898, vol. I
Hunter, Sir (William) Bernard, 1868–1924, vol. II
Hunter, Sir William Bulkeley Hughes H.; see
Hughes-Hunter.
Hunter, William George, 1869–1950, vol. IV (A)
Hunter, Sir William Guyer, 1829–1902, vol. I
Hunter, Sir William Henry, 1849–1917, vol. II
Hunter, Sir William Wilson, 1840–1900, vol. I
Hunter-Blair, Rt Rev. Sir David, 5th Bt, 1853–1939,
vol. III
Hunter-Blair, Captain Sir Edward, 6th Bt,
1858–1945, vol. IV
Hunter Blair, Sir James, 7th Bt, 1889–1985, vol. VIII
Hunter Blair, Peter, 1912–1982, vol. VIII
Hunter-Blair, Maj.-Gen. Walter Charles, 1860–1938,
vol. III
Hunter-Rodwell, Sir Cecil; see Rodwell.
Hunter-Weston, Lt-Gen. Sir Aylmer, 1864–1940,
vol. III
Hunter-Weston, Lt-Col Gould, 1823–1904, vol. I
Hunting, (Gerald) Lindsay, 1891–1966, vol. VI
Hunting, Lindsay; see Hunting, G. L.
Hunting, Sir Percy Llewellyn, 1885–1973, vol. VII
Hunting, Richard Haigh, 1927–1988, vol. VIII
Huntingdon, 14th Earl of, 1868–1939, vol. III
Huntingdon, 15th Earl of, 1901–1990, vol. VIII
Huntingfield, 3rd Baron, 1818–1897, vol. I
Huntingfield, 4th Baron, 1842–1915, vol. I
Huntingfield, 5th Baron, 1883–1969, vol. VI
Huntingford, Lt-Col Walter Legh, 1882–1933, vol. III
Huntington, Archer Milton, 1870–1955, vol. V
Huntington, Major Arthur William, 1871–1933,
vol. III
Huntington, Sir Charles Philip, 1st Bt, 1833–1906,
vol. I
Huntington, Sir Charles Philip, 3rd Bt, 1888–1928,
vol. II
Huntington, Emily Mabel, died 1948, vol. IV
Huntington, Henry Edwards, 1850–1927, vol. II
Huntington, Sir Henry Leslie, 2nd Bt, 1885–1907,
vol. I
Huntington-Whiteley, Sir Herbert; see Whiteley.
Huntington-Whiteley, Captain Sir (Herbert) Maurice,
2nd Bt, 1896–1975, vol. VII
Huntington-Whiteley, Captain Sir Maurice; see
Huntington-Whiteley, Captain Sir H. M.
Huntley, Arthur Geoffrey, 1897–1980, vol. VII (AII)
Huntly, 11th Marquess of, 1847–1937, vol. III
Huntly, 12th Marquess of, 1908–1987, vol. VIII
Huntly, Frances E.; see Mayne, Ethel Colburn.
Hunton, Sidney W., died 1941, vol. IV

Hunton, Gen. Sir Thomas Lionel, 1885–1970, vol. VI
Hurcomb, 1st Baron, 1883–1975, vol. VII
Hurd, Baron (Life Peer); Anthony Richard Hurd,
1901–1966, vol. VI
Hurd, Sir Archibald, died 1959, vol. V
Hurd, Derrick Guy Edmund, 1928–1986, vol. VIII
Hurd, Sir Percy Angier, died 1950, vol. IV
Hurdon, Elizabeth, died 1941, vol. IV
Hurlbatt, Ethel, died 1934, vol. III
Hurle, Col Edward Forbes Cooke-, 1866–1923,
vol. II
Hurle, John A. Cooke-, 1863–1941, vol. IV
Hurley, Ven. Alfred Vincent, 1896–1986, vol. VIII
Hurley, Captain Frank, (James Francis Hurley),
1890–1962, vol. VI
Hurley, Sir Hugh; see Hurley, Sir W. H.
Hurley, James Francis; see Hurley, Captain Frank.
Hurley, Sir John Garling, 1906–1990, vol. VIII
Hurley, Col Lionel James, 1879–1955, vol. V
Hurley, Sir (Thomas Ernest) Victor, 1888–1958,
vol. V
Hurley, Sir Victor; see Hurley, Sir T. E. V.
Hurley, Sir (Wilfred) Hugh, 1910–1984, vol. VIII
Hurndall, Brig. Frank Brereton, 1883–1968, vol. VI
Hurok, Sol, 1888–1974, vol. VII
Hurrell, Col Geoffrey Taylor, 1900–1989, vol. VIII
Hurrell, Ian Murray, 1914–1989, vol. VIII
Hurrell, Ven. William Philip, 1860–1952, vol. V
Hurren, Samuel, 1875–1953, vol. V
Hurry, Jamieson Boyd, 1857–1930, vol. III
Hurry, Leslie, 1909–1978, vol. VII
Hurst, Sir Alfred William, 1884–1975, vol. VII
Hurst, Sir Arthur Frederick, 1879–1944, vol. IV
Hurst, Bertram Lawrance, 1875–1943, vol. IV
Hurst, Sir Cecil James Barrington, 1870–1963,
vol. VI
Hurst, Charles Chamberlain, 1870–1947, vol. IV
Hurst, Christopher Salkeld, 1886–1963, vol. VI
Hurst, Sir Donald; see Hurst, Sir J. H. D.
Hurst, Edward Weston, 1900–1980, vol. VII
Hurst, Fannie, died 1968, vol. VI
Hurst, Frank Arnold, 1883–1967, vol. VI
Hurst, Sir Gerald Berkeley, 1877–1957, vol. V
Hurst, Gilbert Harrison John, 1872–1930, vol. III
Hurst, Hal, 1865–1938, vol. III
Hurst, Harold Edwin, 1880–1978, vol. VII
Hurst, Col Herbert Clarence, 1884–1951, vol. V
Hurst, James Edgar, 1893–1959, vol. V
Hurst, Sir (James Henry) Donald, 1895–1980,
vol. VII
Hurst, John Gibbard, died 1931, vol. III
Hurst, Leonard Henry, 1889–1981, vol. VIII
Hurst, Margery, 1913–1989, vol. VIII
Hurst, Robert H., died 1905, vol. I
Hurst, William M.; see Martin-Hurst.
Hurstfield, Joel, 1911–1980, vol. VII
Hurt, Francis Cecil Albert, 1878–1930, vol. III
Hurt, Captain Henry Albert le Fowne, 1881–1969,
vol. IV
Hurth, Peter Joseph, 1857–1935, vol. III
Hurwitz, Alter Max, 1899–1970, vol. VI
Husain, Hon. Mian Sir, Fazl-i-, 1877–1936, vol. III
Husain, Zakir, 1897–1969, vol. VI
Husband, Sir Charles; see Husband, Sir H. C.

Husband, Sir (Henry) Charles, 1908–1983, vol. VIII
Husband, Rev. John, 1841–1909, vol. I
Husband, Thomas Fair, 1862–1921, vol. II
Huskinson, Edward, 1877–1941, vol. IV
Huskinson, Air Cdre Patrick, 1897–1966, vol. VI
Huskinson, Richard King; see King, Richard.
Huskisson, Major Alfred, 1892–1984, vol. VIII
Huskisson, Col Samuel George, 1837–1911, vol. I
Huskisson, Maj.-Gen. William, 1859–1946, vol. IV
Huskisson, Lt-Col William Gordon, 1877–1949, vol. IV
Huson, Thomas, 1844–1920, vol. II
Hussain, Wajahat, 1894–1945, vol. IV
Hussein bin Onn, Datuk, 1922–1990, vol. VIII
Hussey, Col Arthur Herbert, 1863–1923, vol. II
Hussey, Christopher Edward Clive, 1899–1970, vol. VI
Hussey, Dyneley, 1893–1972, vol. VII
Hussey, Edward Windsor, 1855–1952, vol. V
Hussey, Eric Robert James, 1885–1958, vol. V
Hussey, Sir George Alfred Ernest, 1864–1950, vol. IV
Hussey, Very Rev. (John) Walter (Atherton), 1909–1985, vol. VIII
Hussey, Captain Thomas Edgar Cyril, 1884–1958, vol. V
Hussey, Very Rev. Walter; see Hussey, Very Rev. J. W. A.
Hussey, Major William Clive, died 1929, vol. III
Hussey-Walsh, Valentine John; see Walsh.
Hussey-Walsh, Lt-Col William, 1863–1925, vol. II
Huston, Major Desmond Wellesley William Desmond Mountjoy C.; see Chapman-Huston.
Huston, Maj.-Gen. John, 1901–1969, vol. VI
Huston, John, 1906–1987, vol. VIII
Hutber, Patrick, 1928–1980, vol. VII
Hutchen, Frank, 1870–1942, vol. IV
Hutchen, Lt-Col James William, 1880–1943, vol. IV
Hutcheon, Sir Alexander Byres, 1891–1956, vol. V
Hutcheson, Captain Bellenden Seymour, 1883–1954, vol. V
Hutcheson, John, 1870–1959, vol. V
Hutchings, Sir Alan, 1880–1951, vol. V
Hutchings, Arthur James Bramwell, 1906–1989, vol. VIII
Hutchings, Charles Henry, 1869–1946, vol. IV
Hutchings, Geoffrey Balfour, 1904–1982, vol. VIII
Hutchings, Harold Varlo, 1885–1948, vol. IV
Hutchings, Hugh Houston, 1869–1937, vol. III
Hutchings, Captain John Fenwick, 1885–1968, vol. VI
Hutchings, Norman Edwin, 1899–1960, vol. V
Hutchings, Sir Robert Howell, 1897–1976, vol. VII
Hutchings, Ven. William Henry, 1835–1912, vol. I
Hutchins, Sir David Ernest, 1850–1920, vol. II
Hutchins, Frank Ernest, 1922–1988, vol. VIII
Hutchins, George D'Oyly, 1866–1949, vol. IV
Hutchins, Ven. George Francis, 1909–1977, vol. VII
Hutchins, Harry Burns, 1847–1930, vol. III
Hutchins, Horace Albert, died 1923, vol. III
Hutchins, Sir Philip Perceval, 1838–1928, vol. II
Hutchins, Robert Maynard, 1899–1977, vol. VII
Hutchinson, Brig. Alan George Caldwell, 1879–1947, vol. IV

Hutchinson, Rev. Canon Archibald Campbell, 1883–1981, vol. VIII
Hutchinson, Arthur, 1866–1937, vol. III
Hutchinson, Arthur Cyril William, 1889–1969, vol. VI
Hutchinson, Arthur Stuart Menteth, 1879–1971, vol. VII
Hutchinson, Sir Arthur Sydney, 1896–1981, vol. VIII
Hutchinson, Col Charles Alexander Robert, 1872–1928, vol. II
Hutchinson, Sir Charles Fred., 1850–1907, vol. I
Hutchinson, Maj.-Gen. Charles Scrope, 1826–1912, vol. I
Hutchinson, Rev. Christopher Blick, 1828–1910, vol. I
Hutchinson, Christopher Clarke, 1854–1914, vol. I
Hutchinson, Christopher Douglas H.; see Hely-Hutchinson.
Hutchinson, Rear-Adm. Christopher Haynes, 1906–1990, vol. VIII
Hutchinson, Claude Mackenzie, 1869–1941, vol. IV
Hutchinson, Rev. Canon Deryck Reeves, 1911–1971, vol. VII
Hutchinson, Col Edward Douglas B. S.; see Browne-Synge-Hutchinson.
Hutchinson, Sir Edward Synge-, 4th Bt, 1830–1906, vol. I
Hutchinson, Rev. Francis Ernest, 1871–1947, vol. IV
Hutchinson, Maj.-Gen. Francis Hope Grant, 1870–1931, vol. III
Hutchinson, Col Francis Patrick, 1858–1944, vol. IV
Hutchinson, Frederick Heap, 1892–1975, vol. VII
Hutchinson, Rev. Canon Frederick William, 1870–1964, vol. VI
Hutchinson, Geoffrey Clegg; see Baron Ilford.
Hutchinson, Lt-Col George Higginson F.; see Ford-Hutchinson.
Hutchinson, George Thomas, 1880–1948, vol. IV
Hutchinson, Sir George Thompson, 1857–1931, vol. III
Hutchinson, George William G.; see Grice-Hutchinson.
Hutchinson, Lt-Gen. Henry Doveton, 1847–1924, vol. II
Hutchinson, Rev. Henry Neville, 1856–1927, vol. II
Hutchinson, Sir Herbert John, 1889–1971, vol. VII
Hutchinson, Horatio Gordon, 1859–1932, vol. III
Hutchinson, Lt-Col Hugh Moore, 1874–1924, vol. II
Hutchinson, Col James Bird, 1844–1921, vol. II
Hutchinson, John, died 1916, vol. II
Hutchinson, John, 1884–1972, vol. VII
Hutchinson, Sir Jonathan, 1828–1913, vol. I
Hutchinson, Jonathan, 1859–1933, vol. III
Hutchinson, Sir Joseph Burtt, 1902–1988, vol. VIII
Hutchinson, Hon. Sir Joseph Turner, 1850–1924, vol. II
Hutchinson, Sir Lewis Bede, 1899–1975, vol. VII
Hutchinson, Maurice Robert H.; see Hely-Hutchinson.
Hutchinson, May H., (Hon. Lady Hutchinson); see Hely-Hutchinson.
Hutchinson, Ormond, 1896–1979, vol. VII
Hutchinson, Ray Coryton, 1907–1975, vol. VII
Hutchinson, St John, 1884–1942, vol. IV

Hutchinson, Sir Sydney Hutton Cooper, 1852–1929, vol. III

Hutchinson, Teasdale H., 1837–1928, vol. II

Hutchinson, Col Thomas Massie, 1877–1952, vol. V

Hutchinson, Vere Stuart Menteth, 1891–1932, vol. III

Hutchinson, Victor H.; *see* Hely-Hutchinson.

Hutchinson, Rt Hon. Sir Walter Francis H.; *see* Hely-Hutchinson.

Hutchinson, Walter Victor, 1887–1950, vol. IV

Hutchinson, Maj.-Gen. William Francis Moore, 1841–1917, vol. II

Hutchinson, William H., *died* 1965, vol. VI

Hutchinson, William James, 1919–1985, vol. VIII

Hutchinson, Rev. William P. H., 1810–1910, vol. I

Hutchison of Montrose, 1st Baron, 1873–1950, vol. IV

Hutchison, Gen. Sir Alexander Richard Hamilton, 1871–1930, vol. III

Hutchison, Lt-Gen. Sir Balfour Oliphant, 1889–1967, vol. VI

Hutchison, Brig. Colin Ross Marshall, 1893–1943, vol. IV

Hutchison, Hon. Sir Douglas; *see* Hutchison, Sir J. D.

Hutchison, Brig. Sir Eric Alexander Ogilvy, 2nd Bt (*cr* 1923), 1897–1972, vol. VII

Hutchison, Sir George Aitken Clark, 1873–1928, vol. II

Hutchison, George Andrew, 1841–1913, vol. I

Hutchison, George William, 1882–1947, vol. IV

Hutchison, Lt-Col Graham Seton, 1890–1946, vol. IV

Hutchison, Col Henry Oliphant, 1883–1935, vol. III

Hutchison, Isobel Wylie, *died* 1982, vol. VIII

Hutchison, Sir James, 1867–1946, vol. IV

Hutchison, Hon. Sir (James) Douglas, 1894–1981, vol. VIII

Hutchison, James Holmes, 1912–1987, vol. VIII

Hutchison, Sir James Riley Holt, 1st Bt (*cr* 1956), 1893–1979, vol. VII

Hutchison, James Seller, 1904–1986, vol. VIII

Hutchison, John, *died* 1910, vol. I

Hutchison, Sir John Colville, 1890–1965, vol. VI

Hutchison, Adm. John de Mestre, 1862–1932, vol. III

Hutchison, Sir Kenneth; *see* Hutchison, Sir W. K.

Hutchison, Very Rev. Michael Balfour, *born* 1844, vol. II

Hutchison, Sir Robert, 1st Bt (*cr* 1939), 1871–1960, vol. V

Hutchison, Robert Gemmell, *died* 1936, vol. III

Hutchison, Sir Thomas, 1st Bt (*cr* 1923), 1866–1925, vol. II

Hutchison, William, *died* 1924, vol. II

Hutchison, William, 1926–1976, vol. VII

Hutchison, William Gordon Douglas, 1904–1975, vol. VII

Hutchison, Sir (William) Kenneth, 1903–1989, vol. VIII

Hutchison, Sir William Oliphant, 1889–1970, vol. VI

Huth, Alfred Henry, 1850–1910, vol. I

Huth, Edward, 1847–1935, vol. III

Hutch, Louis, 1821–1905, vol. I

Hutin, Marcel, 1869–1950, vol. IV

Hutson, Most Rev. Edward, *died* 1936, vol. III

Hutson, Ven. Eyre, *born* 1830, vol. II

Hutson, Sir Eyre, 1864–1936, vol. III

Hutson, Sir John, 1859–1950, vol. IV

Hutson, Thomas, 1896–1952, vol. V

Hutt, Sir (Alexander McDonald) Bruce, 1904–1978, vol. VII

Hutt, Sir Bruce; *see* Hutt, Sir A. McD. B.

Hutt, Rev. Henry Robert Mackenzie, 1870–1933, vol. III

Hutt, William Harold, 1899–1988, vol. VIII

Hutten, Baroness von, 1874–1957, vol. V

Hutton, Captain Alfred, 1840–1910, vol. I

Hutton, Alfred Eddison, 1865–1947, vol. IV

Hutton, Air Vice-Marshal Arthur Francis, 1900–1979, vol. VII

Hutton, Arthur Hill, 1859–1922, vol. II

Hutton, Rev. Arthur Wollaston, 1848–1912, vol. I

Hutton, (David) Graham, 1904–1988, vol. VIII

Hutton, Edward, 1875–1969, vol. VI

Hutton, Lt-Gen. Sir Edward Thomas Henry, 1848–1923, vol. II

Hutton, Rear-Adm. FitzRoy Evelyn Patrick, 1894–1975, vol. VII

Hutton, Captain Frederick Wollaston, 1836–1905, vol. I

Hutton, Rev. George Clark, 1825–1908, vol. I

Hutton, George Morland, *died* 1901, vol. I

Hutton, Major Gilbert Montgomerie, 1865–1911, vol. I

Hutton, Graham; *see* Hutton, D. G.

Hutton, Rev. Henry Wollaston, 1835–1916, vol. I

Hutton, Isabel Emslie, (Lady Hutton), *died* 1960, vol. V

Hutton, James Arthur, 1862–1955, vol. V

Hutton, Sir John, 1842–1903, vol. I

Hutton, John, 1847–1921, vol. II

Hutton, Rev. John Alexander, 1868–1947, vol. IV

Hutton, John Campbell, 1906–1978, vol. VII

Hutton, John Henry, 1885–1968, vol. VI

Hutton, Sir Leonard, 1916–1990, vol. VIII

Hutton, Maurice, 1856–1940, vol. III

Hutton, Maurice, 1914–1986, vol. VIII

Hutton, Sir Maurice Inglis, 1904–1970, vol. VI

Hutton, Sir Noël Kilpatrick, 1907–1984, vol. VIII

Hutton, Maj.-Gen. Reginald Antony, 1899–1983, vol. VIII

Hutton, Rear-Adm. Reginald Maurice James, 1899–1973, vol. VII

Hutton, Richard Holt, 1826–1897, vol. I

Hutton, Robert Crompton, 1897–1978, vol. VII

Hutton, Robert Salmon, 1876–1970, vol. VI

Hutton, Samuel King, 1877–1961, vol. VI

Hutton, Stamford, 1866–1941, vol. IV

Hutton, Lt-Gen. Sir Thomas Jacomb, 1890–1981, vol. VII

Hutton, Thomas Winter, 1887–1973, vol. VII

Hutton, William, 1871–1933, vol. III

Hutton, William, 1902–1983, vol. VIII

Hutton, Very Rev. William Holden, 1860–1930, vol. III

Hutton, William Kilpatrick, 1870–1937, vol. III

Hutton-Wilson, Col Arthur Harry, 1873–1955, vol. V

Hutty, Sir Fred Harvey, 1903–1974, vol. VII

Huxham, Harold James, 1889–1961, vol. VI

Huxham, Henry William Walter, 1908–1982, vol. VIII

Huxham, Hon. John, *died* 1949, vol. IV

Huxley, Aldous Leonard, 1894–1963, vol. VI
Huxley, Gervas, 1894–1971, vol. VII
Huxley, Sir Julian Sorell, 1887–1975, vol. VII
Huxley, Leonard, 1860–1933, vol. III
Huxley, Sir Leonard George Holden, 1902–1988, vol. VIII
Huxley, Mrs Lindsey Kathleen, 1894–1945, vol. IV
Huxley, Michael Heathorn, 1899–1979, vol. VII
Huxtable, Rev. John; see Huxtable, Rev. W. J. F.
Huxtable, Lt-Col Robert Beveridge, 1867–1920, vol. II
Huxtable, Rev. (William) John (Fairchild), 1912–1990, vol. VIII
Huybers, Jessie; see Couvreur, Mme Jessie.
Huyshe-Eliot, Hon. Reginald Hyshe, 1868–1920, vol. II
Huysmans, Joris Karl, 1848–1907, vol. I
Hyams, Edward, 1910–1975, vol. VII
Hyamson, Albert Montefiore, 1875–1954, vol. V
Hyamson, Derek Joseph, 1914–1971, vol. VII
Hyamson, Moses, 1862–1949, vol. IV
Hyat-Khan, Hon. Lt-Col Sirdar Sir Sikander, 1892–1942, vol. IV
Hyatt, Stanley Portal, 1877–1914, vol. I
Hyatt-Woolf, Charles, 1863–1938, vol. III
Hydari, Rt Hon. Sir Akbar, 1869–1942, vol. IV
Hydari, Sir Muhammad Saleh Akbar, 1894–1948, vol. IV
Hyde, Lord; George Herbert Arthur Edward Hyde Villiers, 1906–1935, vol. III
Hyde, Lady; (Marion Féoderovna Louise), 1900–1970, vol. VI
Hyde, Sir Charles, 1st Bt, 1876–1942, vol. IV
Hyde, Sir Clarendon Golding, 1858–1934, vol. III
Hyde, Lt-Col Dermot Owen, 1877–1928, vol. II
Hyde, Donald Frizell, 1909–1966, vol. VI
Hyde, Douglas, 1860–1949, vol. IV
Hyde, Edward Wyllys, 1843–1930, vol. III
Hyde, Adm. Sir Francis; see Hyde, Adm. Sir G. F.
Hyde, Francis Edwin, 1908–1978, vol. VII
Hyde, Frederick, 1870–1939, vol. III
Hyde, Adm. Sir (George) Francis, 1877–1937, vol. III
Hyde, H(arford) Montgomery, 1907–1989, vol. VIII
Hyde, Sir Harry, died 1957, vol. V
Hyde, Henry Armroid, 1885–1976, vol. VII
Hyde, Rev. Henry Barry, 1854–1932, vol. III
Hyde, Rev. Canon Henry Edward, 1884–1941, vol. IV
Hyde, James Hazen, 1876–1959, vol. V (A), vol. VI (AI)
Hyde, James Wilson, 1841–1918, vol. II
Hyde, John Bean, 1928–1985, vol. VIII
Hyde, Lt-Col John Irvine L.; see Lang-Hyde.
Hyde, Vice-Adm. Richard, 1872–1931, vol. III
Hyde, Sir Robert Robertson, 1878–1967, vol. VI
Hyde, Walter, died 1951, vol. V
Hyde, Walter Henry, 1864–1953, vol. V
Hyde, William, 1889–1945, vol. IV
Hyde, William De Witt, 1858–1917, vol. II
Hyde-Clarke, (Ernest) Meredyth, 1950–1972, vol. VI
Hyde-Clarke, Meredyth; see Hyde-Clarke, E. M.
Hyde-Lees, Rev. Harold Montagu, 1890–1963, vol. VI

Hyde-Page, Lt-Gen. George, 1823–1908, vol. I
Hyde Parker, Sir William Stephen; see Parker.
Hyderabad (Deccan), HH the Nizam of, 1866–1911, vol. I
Hyderabad, Nizam of, 1886–1967, vol. VI
Hyett, Sir Francis Adams, 1844–1941, vol. IV
Hyett, John Edward, died 1936, vol. III
Hyland, Maj.-Gen. Frederick Gordon, 1888–1962, vol. VI
Hyland, Hon. Sir Herbert John Thornhill, died 1970, vol. VI
Hylton, 2nd Baron, 1829–1899, vol. I
Hylton, 3rd Baron, 1862–1945, vol. IV
Hylton, 4th Baron, 1898–1967, vol. VI
Hylton, Jack, 1892–1965, vol. VI
Hylton-Foster, Rt Hon. Sir Harry Braustyn Hylton, 1905–1965, vol. VI
Hyman, Hon. Charles Smith, 1854–1926, vol. II
Hymans, Paul, 1865–1941, vol. IV
Hynard, Sir William George, 1881–1953, vol. V
Hynd, Henry, 1900–1985, vol. VIII
Hynd, John Burns, 1902–1971, vol. VII
Hyndley, 1st Viscount, 1883–1963, vol. VI
Hyndman, Henry Mayers, 1842–1921, vol. II
Hyndman-Jones, Sir William Henry, 1847–1926, vol. II
Hyne, Engr-Rear-Adm. Arthur Edward, 1874–1956, vol. V
Hyne, Charles John Cutcliffe Wright, 1865–1944, vol. IV
Hyne, Sir Ragnar, 1893–1966, vol. VI
Hynes, Arthur Cecil, 1873–1940, vol. III
Hynes, Group Captain George Bayard, 1887–1938, vol. III
Hynes, John William, died 1930, vol. III
Hynes, Sir Lincoln Carruthers, 1912–1977, vol. VII
Hynes, Captain William Bayard, 1889–1968, vol. VI
Hyslop, Rev. Archibald Richard Frith, 1866–1926, vol. II
Hyslop, Lt-Col Francis, died 1944, vol. IV
Hyslop, Brig.-Gen. Henry Hugh Gordon, 1873–1932, vol. III
Hyslop, Col James, 1856–1917, vol. II
Hyslop, James Morton, 1908–1984, vol. VIII
Hyslop, Sir Murray; see Hyslop, Sir R. M.
Hyslop, Sir (Robert) Murray, died 1935, vol. III
Hyslop, Theo Bulkeley, died 1933, vol. III
Hyslop, Sir Thomas, 1859–1919, vol. II
Hyslop, Lt-Col William Campbell, 1860–1915, vol. I
Hytten, Torleiv, 1890–1980, vol. VII

I

Iago-Trelawny, Maj.-Gen. John, died 1909, vol. I
Ibañez, Vicente Blasco, 1867–1928, vol. II
Ibberson, Dora, 1890–1962, vol. VI
Ibbetson, Hon. Sir Denzil Charles Jelf, 1847–1908, vol. I
Ibbotson, Sir William, 1886–1956, vol. V
Ibert, Jacques, 1890–1962, vol. VI
Ibsen, Henrik, 1828–1906, vol. I

Idar, Maharaja of, *died* 1931, vol. III
Iddesleigh, 2nd Earl of, 1845–1927, vol. II
Iddesleigh, 3rd Earl of, 1901–1970, vol. VI
Idelson, Vladimir Robert, *died* 1954, vol. V
Idington, Hon. John, 1840–1928, vol. II
Idris; *see* Mee, Arthur.
Idris, Thomas Howell Williams, 1842–1925, vol. II
Idun, Sir Samuel Okai Q.; *see* Quashie-Idun.
Ievers, Maj.-Gen. Osburne, *died* 1963, vol. VI
Ievers, Robert Wilson, *died* 1905, vol. I
Ife, HH Aderemi I, The Oni of Ife; Sir Titus Martins Adesoji Tadeniawo Aderemi, 1889–1980, vol. VII
Iftikhar-Ud-Din, Fakir Sayad, *died* 1914, vol. II
Igglesden, Sir Charles, 1861–1949, vol. IV
Iggulden, Sir Douglas Percy, 1907–1977, vol. VII
Iggulden, Brig.-Gen. Herbert Augustus, 1861–1937, vol. III
Ignatieff, George, 1913–1989, vol. VIII
Ignatius, Father, (Joseph Leycester Lyne), 1837–1908, vol. I
Ikin, Rutherford Graham, 1903–1989, vol. VIII
Ikramullah, Mohammad, 1903–1963, vol. VI
Ilbert, Sir Courtenay Peregrine, 1841–1924, vol. II
Ilchester, 5th Earl of, 1847–1905, vol. I
Ilchester, 6th Earl of, 1874–1959, vol. V
Ilchester, 7th Earl of, 1905–1964, vol. VI
Ilchester, 8th Earl of, 1887–1970, vol. VI
Ilderton, Col Charles Edward, 1841–1905, vol. I
Iles, Col Frederic Arthur, 1874–1966, vol. VI
Iles, John Henry, *died* 1951, vol. V
Iles, Air Vice-Marshal Leslie Millington, 1894–1974, vol. VII
Ilford, Baron (Life Peer); Geoffrey Clegg Hutchinson, 1893–1974, vol. VII
Iliff, Rt Rev. Geoffrey Durnford, 1867–1946, vol. IV
Iliff, Neil Atkinson, 1916–1973, vol. VII
Iliff, Sir William Angus Boyd, 1898–1972, vol. VII
Iliffe, 1st Baron, 1877–1960, vol. V
Iliffe, Frederick, 1847–1928, vol. II
Ilkeston, 1st Baron, 1840–1913, vol. I
Ilkeston, 2nd Baron, 1867–1952, vol. V
Illing, Vincent C., *died* 1969, vol. VI
Illingworth, 1st Baron, 1865–1942, vol. IV
Illingworth, Alfred, 1827–1907, vol. I
Illingworth, Captain Sir (Cyril) Gordon, *died* 1959, vol. V
Illingworth, Dudley Holden, 1876–1958, vol. V
Illingworth, Captain Sir Gordon; *see* Illingworth, Captain Sir C. G.
Illingworth, Rev. John Richardson, *died* 1915, vol. I
Illingworth, Leslie Gilbert, 1902–1979, vol. VII
Illingworth, Percy Holden, 1869–1915, vol. I
Illingworth, Rear Adm. Philip Holden Crothers, 1916–1987, vol. VIII
Illingworth, Ronald Stanley, 1909–1990, vol. VIII
Ilott, Sir John Moody Albert, 1884–1973, vol. VII
Ilsley, Most Rev. Edward, 1838–1926, vol. II
Ilsley, Rt Hon. James Lorimer, 1894–1967, vol. VI
Ilyushin, Sergei Vladimirovich, 1894–1977, vol. VII
Image, Selwyn, 1849–1930, vol. III
Imam, Bahksh Khan, Mazari Sir, Mir Nawab, *died* 1903, vol. I
Imbert-Terry, Sir Andrew Henry Bouhier, 4th Bt, 1945–1985, vol. VIII

Imbert-Terry, Lt-Col Claude Henry Maxwell, 1880–1942, vol. IV
Imbert-Terry, Major Sir Edward Henry Bouhier, 3rd Bt, 1920–1978, vol. VII
Imbert-Terry, Captain Frederic Bouhier; *see* Terry.
Imbert-Terry, Lt-Col Sir Henry Bouhier, 2nd Bt, 1885–1962, vol. VI
Imbert-Terry, Sir Henry Machu, 1st Bt, 1854–1938, vol. III
Imms, Augustus Daniel, 1880–1949, vol. IV
Imperiali, Marquis Guglielmo, 1858–1944, vol. IV
Impey, Col Eugene Clutterbuck, 1830–1904, vol. I
Impey, Lt-Col Lawrence, 1862–1944, vol. IV
Impey, William Henry Lockington, 1856–1905, vol. I
Imrie, Lt-Col Hew Francis Blair, 1873–1942, vol. IV
Imrie, Sir John Dunlop, 1891–1981, vol. VIII
im Thurn, Sir Everard, 1852–1932, vol. III
Im Thurn, Vice-Adm. John Knowles, 1881–1956, vol. V
Inayat-Khan, Pir-o-Murshid, 1882–1927, vol. II
Inayat Masih, Rt Rev.; *see* Masih.
Ince, Brig. Cecil Edward Ronald, 1897–1988, vol. VIII
Ince, Charles Percy, 1875–1952, vol. V
Ince, Edward Lindsay, 1891–1941, vol. IV
Ince, Captain Edward Watkins W.; *see* Whittington-Ince.
Ince, Evelyn Grace, *died* 1941, vol. IV
Ince, Sir Godfrey Herbert, 1891–1960, vol. V (A), vol. VI (AI)
Ince, Rev. William, 1825–1910, vol. I
Inch, Rev. Alex. S., 1863–1932, vol. III
Inchcape, 1st Earl of, 1852–1932, vol. III
Inchcape, 2nd Earl of, 1887–1939, vol. III
Inches, Cyrus Fiske, 1883–1956, vol. V
Inches, Lt-Col Edward James, 1877–1934, vol. III
Inches, Sir Robert Kirk, 1840–1918, vol. II
Inchiquin, 14th Baron, 1839–1900, vol. I
Inchiquin, 15th Baron, 1864–1929, vol. III
Inchiquin, 16th Baron, 1897–1968, vol. VI
Inchiquin, 17th Baron of, 1900–1982, vol. VIII
Inchyra, 1st Baron, 1900–1989, vol. VIII
Incledon-Webber, Brig.-Gen. Adrian Beare, 1876–1946, vol. IV
Incledon-Webber, Lt-Col Godfrey Sturdy, 1904–1986, vol. VIII
Incze, Jenö, 1901–1969, vol. VI
Ind, Charles Francis, 1905–1940, vol. III
Ind, Edward Murray, 1853–1915, vol. I
Inderwick, Frederic Andrew, 1836–1904, vol. I
Indore, HH Maharaj-dhiraj Sir Shivaji Rao Holkar Bahadur, 1860–1908, vol. I
Indore, Maj.-Gen. HH Maharaja of, 1908–1961, vol. VI
Indore, Ex-Maharaja of; HH Tukoji Rao Holkar, 1890–1978, vol. VII
Infield, Henry John, *died* 1921, vol. II
Ing, Col George Harold Absell, 1880–1957, vol. V
Ing, Harry Raymond, 1899–1974, vol. VII
Ingall, Douglas Heber, 1891–1968, vol. VI
Ingalls, John James, 1833–1900, vol. I
Inge, Mary Caroline, (Mrs W. F. Inge), *died* 1961, vol. VI
Inge, Mrs W. F.; *see* Inge, Mary Caroline.

Inge, William, 1829–1903, vol. I

Inge, Very Rev. William Ralph, 1860–1954, vol. V

Ingelow, Jean, 1820–1897, vol. I

Ingersoll, Ralph McAllister, 1900–1985, vol. VIII

Ingestre, Viscount; Charles John Alton Chetwynd Chetwynd-Talbot, 1882–1915, vol. I

Ingham, Albert Edward, 1900–1967, vol. VI

Ingham, Brig.-Gen. Charles St Maur, *died* 1936, vol. III

Ingham, Rt Rev. Ernest Graham, 1851–1926, vol. II

Ingham, Robert Wood, 1846–1928, vol. II

Ingham, Major Samuel, 1893–1950, vol. IV

Ingilby, Sir Henry Day, 2nd Bt, 1826–1911, vol. I

Ingilby, Sir Joslan William Vivian, 5th Bt, 1907–1974, vol. VII

Ingilby, Sir William, 3rd Bt, 1829–1918, vol. II

Ingilby, Sir William Henry, 4th Bt, 1874–1950, vol. IV

Ingle, Charles Fiennes, 1908–1983, vol. VIII

Ingle, Rt Rev. George Ernest, 1895–1964, vol. VI

Ingle-Finch, Peter; *see* Finch.

Ingleby, 1st Viscount, 1897–1966, vol. VI

Ingleby, Holcombe, 1854–1926, vol. II

Ingleby Mackenzie, Surg. Vice-Adm. Sir Alexander; *see* Ingleby Mackenzie, Surg. Vice-Adm. Sir K. A.

Ingleby Mackenzie, Surg. Vice-Adm. Sir (Kenneth) Alexander, 1892–1961, vol. VI

Inglefield, Rear-Adm. Sir Edward Fitzmaurice, 1861–1945, vol. IV

Inglefield, Maj.-Gen. Francis Seymour, 1855–1930, vol. III

Inglefield, Adm. Sir Frederick Samuel, 1854–1921, vol. II

Inglefield, Col Sir John Frederick C.; *see* Crompton-Inglefield.

Inglefield, Brig. Lionel Dalton, 1881–1953, vol. V

Inglefield, Brig.-Gen. Norman Bruce, 1855–1912, vol. I

Inglefield-Watson, Captain Sir Derrick William Inglefield; *see* Watson.

Ingles, Ven. Charles Leycester, 1856–1930, vol. III

Ingles, Rev. Charles William Chamberlayne, 1869–1954, vol. V

Ingles, Rev. David, 1836–1921, vol. II

Ingles, Brig.-Gen. John Darnley, 1872–1957, vol. V

Ingleson, Philip, 1892–1985, vol. VIII

Inglewood, 1st Baron; William Morgan Fletcher-Vane, 1909–1989, vol. VIII

Inglis, Sir (Albemarle) Percy, 1841–1932, vol. III

Inglis, Allan, 1906–1984, vol. VIII

Inglis, Captain Arthur McCulloch, 1884–1919, vol. II

Inglis, Sir Charles Edward, 1875–1952, vol. V

Inglis, Lt-Col Charles Elliot, 1878–1936, vol. III

Inglis, Sir Claude Cavendish, 1883–1974, vol. VII

Inglis, Maj.-Gen. Sir Drummond; *see* Inglis, Maj.-Gen. Sir J. D.

Inglis, Air Vice-Marshal Francis Frederic, 1899–1969, vol. VI

Inglis, Maj.-Gen. George Henry, 1902–1979, vol. VII

Inglis, Rev. George John, 1900–1965, vol. VI

Inglis, Col Henry Alves, 1859–1924, vol. II

Inglis, Sir Hugh Arbuthnot, 1890–1948, vol. IV

Inglis, Hon. James, 1845–1908, vol. I

Inglis, Sir James Charles, 1851–1911, vol. I

Inglis, Rev. James W., 1861–1943, vol. IV

Inglis, Lt-Col John, 1882–1967, vol. VI

Inglis, John Alexander, 1873–1941, vol. IV

Inglis, Maj.-Gen. Sir (John) Drummond, 1895–1985, vol. VIII

Inglis, Vice-Adm. Sir John Gilchrist Thesiger, 1906–1972, vol. VII

Inglis, John Kenneth Harold, 1877–1935, vol. III

Inglis, Lindsay Merritt, 1894–1966, vol. VI

Inglis of Glencorse, Sir Maxwell Ian Hector, 9th Bt, 1903–1974, vol. VII

Inglis, Sir Percy; *see* Inglis, Sir A. P.

Inglis, Sir Robert John Mathison, 1881–1962, vol. VI

Inglis, Lt-Col Sir Robert William, 1843–1923, vol. II

Inglis, Col Russell Tracy-, 1875–1937, vol. III

Inglis, William Arbuthnot, 1853–1936, vol. III

Ingold, Sir Christopher Kelk, 1893–1970, vol. VI

Ingoldby, Eric, 1892–1986, vol. VIII

Ingpen, Arthur Robert, *died* 1917, vol. II

Ingpen, Lt-Col Percy Leigh, 1874–1930, vol. III

Ingpen, Roger, *died* 1936, vol. III

Ingram, Captain Alexander Gordon, 1883–1929, vol. III

Ingram, Archibald Kenneth, 1882–1965, vol. VI

Ingram, Rt Rev. and Rt Hon. Arthur Foley Winnington, 1858–1946, vol. IV

Ingram, Rev. Arthur John, *died* 1931, vol. III

Ingram, Ven. Arthur John W.; *see* Winnington-Ingram.

Ingram, Sir Bruce Stirling, 1877–1963, vol. VI

Ingram, Rev. Edward Henry Winnington-, 1849–1930, vol. III

Ingram, Edward Maurice Berkeley, 1890–1941, vol. IV

Ingram, Sir Herbert, 2nd Bt, 1875–1958, vol. V

Ingram, Sir Herbert, 3rd Bt, 1912–1980, vol. VII

Ingram, John H., 1849–1916, vol. II

Ingram, John Kells, 1823–1907, vol. I

Ingram, Lt-Col John O'Donnell, 1870–1939, vol. III

Ingram, John Thornton, 1899–1972, vol. VII

Ingram, Hon. Mrs Meynell, (Emily Charlotte), 1840–1904, vol. I

Ingram, Thomas Allan, 1870–1922, vol. II

Ingram, Captain Thomas Lewis, 1875–1916, vol. II

Ingram, W. Ayerst, 1855–1913, vol. I

Ingram, William, 1865–1943, vol. IV

Ingram, Very Rev. William Clavell, 1834–1901, vol. I

Ingram, Sir William James, 1st Bt, 1847–1924, vol. II

Ingram-Johnson, Rev. Rowland Theodore, 1877–1964, vol. VI

Ingrams, Leonard St Clair, 1900–1953, vol. V

Ingrams, William Harold, 1897–1973, vol. VII

Ingrem, Rev. Charles, 1854–1937, vol. III

Inigo-Jones, Captain Henry Richmund, 1899–1978, vol. VII

Inkson, Col Edgar Thomas, 1872–1947, vol. IV

Inman, 1st Baron, 1892–1979, vol. VII

Inman, Arnold, 1867–1951, vol. V

Inman, Arthur Conyers, 1879–1926, vol. II

Inman, Rev. Canon Edward, *died* 1924, vol. II

Inman, Peter Donald, 1916–1987, vol. VIII

Inman, Rt Rev. Thomas George Vernon, 1904–1989, vol. VII

Innes, Alexander Taylor, 1833–1912, vol. I

Innes, Alfred M.; *see* Mitchell-Innes.
Innes, Sir Andrew Lockhart, 1898–1960, vol. V
Innes, Arthur Donald, *died* 1938, vol. III
Innes, Lt-Col Sir Berowald; *see* Innes, Lt-Col Sir R. G. B.
Innes, Captain Cecil M; *see* Mitchell-Innes.
Innes, Sir Charles Alexander, 1874–1959, vol. V
Innes, Sir Charles Alexander, 1902–1963, vol. VI
Innes of Coxton, Sir Charles Kenneth Gordon, 11th Bt, 1910–1990, vol. VIII
Innes, Donald Esme, 1888–1961, vol. VI
Innes, Edward Alfred M.; *see* Mitchell-Innes.
Innes, Guy Edward Mitchell, 1882–1953, vol. V
Innes, Sir James, 13th Bt, 1846–1919, vol. II
Innes, Lt-Col James Archibald, 1875–1948, vol. IV
Innes, Sir James Bourchier, 14th Bt, 1883–1950, vol. IV
Innes, James John M'Leod, 1830–1907, vol. I
Innes, Rt Hon. Sir James R.; *see* Rose-Innes.
Innes, Captain James William Guy, 1873–1939, vol. III
Innes, Sir John, 12th Bt, 1840–1912, vol. I
Innes, John, 1888–1961, vol. VI
Innes, Surg.-Gen. Sir John Harry Ker, 1820–1907, vol. I
Innes, John Robert, 1863–1948, vol. IV
Innes, Sir Patrick R.; *see* Rose-Innes.
Innes, Sir Peter David, 1881–1961, vol. VI
Innes, Hon. Reginald Heath L.; *se* Long Innes.
Innes, Rev. Reginald John Simpson M.; *see* Mitchell-Innes.
Innes, Robert T. A., 1861–1933, vol. III
Innes, Lt-Col Sir (Ronald Gordon) Berowald, 16th Bt, 1907–1988, vol. VIII
Innes of Learney, Col. Thomas, 1814–1912, vol. I
Innes of Learney, Sir Thomas, 1893–1971, vol. VII
Innes, Sir Walter James, 15th Bt, 1903–1978, vol. VII
Innes, William Arnold, 1902–1973, vol. VI
Innes-Ker, Lord Alastair Robert, 1880–1936, vol. III
Innes-Ker, Major Lord Robert Edward, 1885–1958, vol. V
Innes-Noad, Sidney Reginald, *died* 1931, vol. III
Innes-Wilson, Col. Campbell Aubrey Kenneth, 1905–1978, vol. VII
Inness, George, 1854–1926, vol. II
Inness, Air Cdre William Innes Cosmo, 1916–1986, vol. VIII
Inness, William James Deacon, 1877–1948, vol. IV
Innis, Harold Adams, 1894–1952, vol. V
Inonu, Gen. Ismet, 1884–1973, vol. VII
Inouyé, Marquis Kaoru, 1835–1915, vol. I
Inouyé, Marquis Katsunoske, 1861–1929, vol. III
Insall, Gp Captain Gilbert Stuart Martin, 1894–1972, vol. VII
Insh, George Pratt, 1883–1956, vol. V (A), vol. VI (AI)
Inskip, Sir Arthur Cecil, 1894–1951, vol. V
Inskip, J. Henry, *died* 1947, vol. IV
Inskip, Rt Rev. James Theodore, 1868–1949, vol. IV
Inskip, Sir John Hampden, 1879–1960, vol. V
Inskip, Rev. Oliver Digby, *died* 1934, vol. III
Inskip, Maj.-Gen. Roland Debenham, 1885–1971, vol. VII
Instone, Sir Samuel, 1878–1937, vol. III

Insull, Samuel, 1859–1938, vol. III
Inverchapel, 1st Baron, 1882–1951, vol. V
Inverclyde, 1st Baron, 1829–1901, vol. I
Inverclyde, 2nd Baron, 1861–1905, vol. I
Inverclyde, 3rd Baron, 1864–1919, vol. II
Inverclyde, 4th Baron, 1897–1957, vol. V
Inverforth, 1st Baron, 1865–1955, vol. V
Inverforth, 2nd Baron, 1897–1975, vol. VII
Inverforth, 3rd Baron, 1932–1982, vol. VIII
Invernairn, 1st Baron, 1856–1936, vol. III
Inverurie, Lord; Ian Douglas Montagu Keith Falconer, 1877–1897, vol. I
Inwards, Richard, 1840–1937, vol. III
Ionides, Basil, 1884–1950, vol. IV
Ipswich, Viscount; William Henry Alfred Fitzroy, 1884–1918, vol. II
Irby, Hon. Cecil Saumarez, 1862–1935, vol. III
Iredell, Air Vice-Marshal Sir Alfred William, 1879–1967, vol. VI
Iredell, Charles Edward, 1877–1961, vol. VI
Iredell, Lt-Gen. Francis Shrubb, 1837–1924, vol. II
Ireland, Alleyne; *see* Ireland, W. A.
Ireland, Arthur Joseph, 1874–1931, vol. III
Ireland, Frank, 1909–1983, vol. VIII
Ireland, Lt-Col Gerald Blakeney de C.; *see* de Courcy-Ireland.
Ireland, Most Rev. John, 1838–1918, vol. II
Ireland, John, 1879–1962, vol. VI
Ireland, Col Sir Robert Megaw, 1849–1919, vol. II
Ireland, (Walter) Alleyne, *died* 1951, vol. V
Iremonger, Col Edgar Assheton, 1862–1953, vol. V
Iremonger, Very Rev. Frederic Athelwold, 1878–1952, vol. V
Iremonger, Major Harold Edward William, *died* 1937, vol. III
Irgens, Johannes, 1869–1939, vol. III
Iron, Air Cdre Douglas, 1893–1983, vol. VIII
Ironmonger, Sir (Charles) Ronald, 1914–1984, vol. VIII
Ironmonger, Sir Ronald; *see* Ironmonger, Sir C. R.
Irons, Ralph; *see* Schreiner, Olive.
Ironside, 1st Baron, 1880–1959, vol. V
Ironside, Sir Henry George Outram B.; *see* Bax-Ironside.
Ironside, Redvers Nowell, 1899–1968, vol. VI
Ironside, Robin, 1912–1965, vol. VI
Irvin, Sir John Hannell, 1874–1952, vol. V
Irvin, Captain William Dion, 1870–1965, vol. V
Irvine, Lt-Col Acheson Gosford, *born* 1837, vol. II
Irvine, Alexander, 1863–1941, vol. IV
Irvine, Alexander Forbes, 1881–1922, vol. II
Irvine, Brig.-Gen. Alfred Ernest, 1876–1962, vol. VI
Irvine, Lt-Col Andrew Alexander, 1871–1939, vol. III
Irvine, Rt Hon. Sir Arthur James, 1909–1978, vol. VII
Irvine, Captain Charles Alexander Lindsay, 1876–1965, vol. VI
Irvine, Col Francis Stephen, 1873–1962, vol. VI
Irvine, Rt Rev. Gerard Addington D'A; *see* D'Arcy-Irvine.
Irvine, Lt-Col Gerard Beatty, 1863–1947, vol. IV
Irvine, Sir James Colquhoun, 1877–1952, vol. V
Irvine, James Mercer, *died* 1945, vol. IV

Irvine, Lt-Col Richard Abercrombie, *died* 1946, vol. IV

Irvine, Adm. Sir St George Caufield D'Arcy-, 1883–1916, vol. II

Irvine, Rev. Thomas Thurstan, 1913–1985, vol. VIII

Irvine, William Fergusson, 1869–1962, vol. VI

Irvine, Hon. Sir William Hill, 1858–1943, vol. IV

Irvine, William Tait, 1925–1980, vol. VII

Irvine-Fortescue, Col Archer, 1880–1959, vol. V

Irvine-Jones, Douglas Vivian, 1904–1974, vol. VII

Irvine Smith, Thomas, 1908–1985, vol. VIII

Irving of Dartford, Baron (Life Peer); Sydney Irving, 1918–1989, vol. VIII

Irving, Sir Æmilius, 1823–1913, vol. I

Irving, Lt-Col Andrew B.; *see* Bell-Irving.

Irving, Captain Charles Edward, 1871–1955, vol. V

Irving, Charles John, 1831–1917, vol. II

Irving, David Blair, 1903–1986, vol. VIII

Irving, David Daniel, 1854–1924, vol. II

Irving, David Jarvis M.; *see* Mill Irving.

Irving, Dorothea, (Mrs Henry Irving), *died* 1933, vol. III

Irving, Rear-Adm. Sir Edmund George, 1910–1990, vol. VIII

Irving, Ven. Edward Arthur, 1850–1943, vol. IV

Irving, Mrs H. B.; *see* Irving, Dorothea.

Irving, Sir Henry, 1838–1905, vol. I

Irving, Henry Brodribb, 1870–1919, vol. II

Irving, Sir Henry Turner, 1833–1923, vol. II

Irving, Herbert Cavan, 1854–1930, vol. III

Irving, James Jardine B.; *see* Bell-Irving.

Irving, John B.; *see* Bell-Irving.

Irving, Kelville Ernest, 1877–1953, vol. V

Irving, Laurence Henry Forster, 1897–1988, vol. VIII

Irving, Laurence Sydney Brodribb, 1871–1914, vol. I

Irving, Martin Howy, 1831–1912, vol. I

Irving, Sir Miles, 1876–1962, vol. VI

Irving, Hon. Paulus Æmilius, 1857–1916, vol. II

Irving, Rev. Robert, 1840–1922, vol. II

Irving, Captain Sir Robert Beaufin, 1877–1954, vol. V

Irving, Robert Lock Graham, 1877–1969, vol. VI

Irving, Sir Stanley Gordon, 1886–1970, vol. VI

Irving, Rev. Thomas Henry, 1856–1926, vol. II

Irving, William John, 1892–1967, vol. VI

Irwin, Alfred, 1865–1951, vol. V

Irwin, Sir Alfred Macdonald Bulteel, 1853–1921, vol. II

Irwin, Ven. Charles King, 1837–1915, vol. I

Irwin, Rt Rev. Charles King, 1874–1960, vol. V

Irwin, Rev. Clarke Huston, 1858–1934, vol. III

Irwin, Cyril James, 1881–1962, vol. VI

Irwin, Col De la Cherois Thomas, 1843–1928, vol. II

Irwin, Francis Charles, 1928–1990, vol. VIII

Irwin, Sir George, 1832–1899, vol. I

Irwin, George Robert, 1855–1933, vol. III

Irwin, Henry, 1841–1922, vol. II

Irwin, Henry Raikes Alexander, 1858–1937, vol. III

Irwin, Sir James Campbell, 1906–1990, vol. VIII

Irwin, Col Sir (James) Murray, 1858–1938, vol. III

Irwin, Sir John, 1857–1935, vol. III

Irwin, Rev. John, *died* 1932, vol. III

Irwin, Lt-Gen. John Staples, 1846–1917, vol. II

Irwin, Joseph Boyd, 1895–1968, vol. VI

Irwin, Leighton Francis, 1892–1962, vol. VI

Irwin, Margaret, *died* 1967, vol. VI

Irwin, Margaret Hardinge, *died* 1940, vol. III

Irwin, Col Sir Murray; *see* Irwin, Col. Sir J. M.

Irwin, Lt-Gen. Noel Mackintosh Stuart, 1892–1972, vol. VII

Irwin, Raymond, 1902–1976, vol. VII

Irwin, Robert, *died* 1941, vol. IV

Irwin, Robert Christopher, 1865–1937, vol. III

Irwin, Ven. Ronald John Beresford, 1880–1930, vol. III

Irwin, Sir Samuel Thompson, 1877–1961, vol. VI

Irwin, Maj.-Gen. Stephen Fenemore, 1895–1964, vol. VI

Irwin, Thomas Lennox, 1846–1918, vol. II

Irwin, William Henry, 1907–1974, vol. VII

Irwin, William Knox, 1883–1973, vol. VII

Isaac, Very Rev. Abraham, *died* 1906, vol. I

Isaac, Charles Leonard, *died* 1944, vol. IV

Isaac, Rev. Gerald Moore, *died* 1940, vol. III

Isaac, Joseph Charles, 1859–1939, vol. III

Isaac, Sir Neil, 1915–1987, vol. VIII

Isaac, Lt-Col Thomas William Talbot, 1880–1930, vol. III

Isaacs, Alick, 1921–1967, vol. VI

Isaacs, Edward Maurice, 1881–1953, vol. V

Isaacs, Evelyn M.; *see* Lawrence, E. M.

Isaacs, Rev. Frederick Walter, 1858–1935, vol. III

Isaacs, Rt Hon. George Alfred, 1883–1979, vol. VII

Isaacs, Godfrey Charles, *died* 1925, vol. II

Isaacs, Sir Henry Aaron, 1830–1909, vol. I

Isaacs, Rt Hon. Sir Isaac Alfred, 1855–1948, vol. IV

Isaacs, Jacob, 1896–1973, vol. VII

Isaacs, Susan Sutherland, 1885–1948, vol. IV

Isaacson, Frederick Wootton, 1836–1898, vol. I

Isaacson, Sir Robert Spencer, 1907–1972, vol. VII

Isacke, Maj.-Gen. Hubert, 1872–1943, vol. IV

Isbister, William James, 1866–1950, vol. IV

Iselin, Charles Oliver, *died* 1932, vol. III

Isemonger, Frederick Charles, 1876–1960, vol. V

Isham, Sir Charles Edmund, 10th Bt, 1819–1903, vol. I

Isham, Sir Gyles, 12th Bt, 1903–1976, vol. VII

Isham, Lt-Col Ralph Heyward, 1890–1955, vol. V

Isham, Sir Vere, 11th Bt, 1862–1941, vol. IV

Isherwood, Albert Arthur Mangnall, 1889–1957, vol. V

Isherwood, Col Charles Edward Ramsbottom, 1849–1934, vol. III

Isherwood, Christopher William Bradshaw-, 1904–1986, vol. VIII

Isherwood, Rt Rev. Harold, 1907–1989, vol. VIII

Isherwood, Lt-Col James, *died* 1929, vol. III

Isherwood, John Henry Bradshaw-, 1841–1924, vol. II

Isherwood, Sir Joseph William, 1st Bt, 1870–1937, vol. III

Isherwood, Sir William, 2nd Bt, 1898–1946, vol. IV

Ishibashi, Kazunori, *died* 1928, vol. II

Isitt, Dame Adeline G.; *see* Genée-Isitt.

Isitt, Air Vice-Marshal Sir Leonard Monk, 1891–1976, vol. VII

Isle, William Herbert Mosley, 1896–1973, vol. VII

Isles, Keith Sydney, 1902–1977, vol. VII

Islington, 1st Baron, 1866–1936, vol. III

Ismail, Sir Miras M., 1883–1959, vol. V
Ismail Sait, Khan Bahadur Fukhr-ut-tujjar Sir Hajee, 1859–1934, vol. III
Ismay, 1st Baron, 1887–1965, vol. VI
Ismay, Sir George, 1891–1984, vol. VIII
Ismay, James Hainsworth, 1867–1930, vol. III
Ismay, Joseph Bruce, 1862–1937, vol. III
Ismay, Sir Stanley, 1848–1914, vol. I
Ismay, Thomas Henry, 1837–1899, vol. I
Ismay, Rev. William, 1846–192, vol. II
Isola; see Teeling, Mrs Bartle.
Ispahani, Mirza Abol Hassan, 1902–1981, vol. VIII
Israel, John William, 1850–1926, vol. II
Israels, Joseph, 1824–1911, vol. I
Israr, Hon. Sir Maulvi Mohammad Israr Hasan Khan, 1865–1934, vol. III
Isserlis, Alexander Reginald, 1922–1986, vol. VIII
Isserstedt, Hans S.; see Schmidt-Isserstedt.
Issigonis, Sir Alec Arnold Constantine, 1906–1988, vol. VIII
Ithel Jones, Rev. John; see Jones.
Ito, Prince Hirobumi, 1838–1909, vol. I
Ito, Admiral of the Fleet Count Yuko, 1843–1914, vol. I
Iturbi, José, 1895–1980, vol. VII
Ivatt, Henry George, 1886–1972, vol. VII
Iveagh, 1st Earl of, 1847–1927, vol. II
Iveagh, 2nd Earl of, 1874–1967, vol. VI
Iveagh, Countess of; (Gwendolen), died 1966, vol. VI
Ivelaw-Chapman, Air Chief Marshal Sir Ronald, 1899–1978, vol. VII
Ivens, Rev. Charles Llewelyn, 1854–1931, vol. III
Ivens, Richard, died 1931, vol. III
Ivens, Rev. William Edmunds, 1845–1910, vol. I
Iverach, Rev. James, 1839–1922, vol. II
Iversen, Johannes, 1904–1971, vol. VII
Ives, George Cecil, 1867–1950, vol. IV
Ives, Col Gordon Maynard G.; see Gordon-Ives.
Ives, Harry William Maclean, 1867–1941, vol. IV
Ives, Robert, 1906–1985, vol. VIII
Ivimey, John William, 1868–1961, vol. VI
Ivimey, Julia B., (Mrs Fairfax Ivimey); see Matthews, J. B.
Ivins, Derek; see Ivins, J. D.
Ivins, John Derek, 1923–1986, vol. VIII
Iwi, Edward Frank, 1904–1966, vol. VI
Iyengar, S. Kasturi Ranga, 1859–1923, vol. II
Izard, Ven. Herbert Crawford, 1869–1934, vol. III
Izat, Alexander, 1844–1920, vol. II
Izat, Sir (James) Rennie, 1886–1962, vol. VI
Izat, John, 1879–1966, vol. VI
Izat, Sir Rennie; see Izat, Sir J. R.
Izycki de Notto, Sir Matthew, 1899–1952, vol. V

J

Jack, Adolphus Alfred, 1868–1946, vol. IV
Jack, Alexander G. Mackenzie, 1851–1927, vol. II
Jack, Brig.-Gen. Archibald, 1874–1939, vol. III
Jack, Sir Daniel Thomson, 1901–1984, vol. VIII
Jack, Brig. Evan Maclean, 1873–1951, vol. V

Jack, Col Herbert Rowett Henry, 1863–1932, vol. III
Jack, James, 1910–1987, vol. VIII
Jack, Brig.-Gen. James Lochhead, 1880–1962, vol. VI
Jack, John Louttit, 1878–1954, vol. V
Jack, Mackenzie; see Jack, A. G. M.
Jack, Richard, 1866–1952, vol. V
Jack, Sir Robert Ernest, died 1962, vol. VI
Jack, Robert Logan, 1845–1921, vol. II
Jack, Hon. Sir Roy Emile, 1914–1977, vol. VII
Jack, William, 1834–1924, vol. II
Jack, William Robert, 1866–1927, vol. II
Jacklin Air Vice-Marshal Edward Ward Seymour, 1917–1969, vol. VI
Jackling, Sir Roger William, 1913–1986, vol. VIII
Jackman, Mgr Canon Arthur, 1878–1945, vol. IV
Jackman, Frank Downer, 1901–1981, vol. VIII
Jackman, William T., 1871–1951, vol. V
Jacks, Graham Vernon, 1901–1977, vol. VII
Jacks, Lawrence Pearsall, 1860–1955, vol. V
Jacks, Maurice Leonard, 1894–1964, vol. VI
Jacks, Thomas Lavington, 1884–1966, vol. VI
Jacks, William, 1841–1907, vol. I
Jackson, 1st Baron, 1893–1954, vol. V
Jackson of Burnley, Baron (Life Peer); Willis Jackson, 1904–1970, vol. VI
Jackson of Lodsworth, Baroness (Life Peer); Barbara Mary Jackson, 1914–1981, vol. VIII
Jackson, Abraham Valentine Williams, 1862–1937, vol. III
Jackson, Albert Edward, 1865–1930, vol. III
Jackson, Alexander Young, 1882–1974, vol. VII
Jackson, Sir Anthony Henry Mather M.; see Mather-Jackson.
Jackson, Col Arnold Nugent Strode S.; see Strode-Jackson.
Jackson, Arthur, 1853–1938, vol. III
Jackson, Sir Arthur, died 1940, vol. III
Jackson, Maj.-Gen. Arthur James, 1923–1987, vol. VIII
Jackson, B. Leslie, born 1866, vol. III
Jackson, Sir Barry Vincent, 1879–1961, vol. VI
Jackson, Lt-Col Basil A.; see Archer-Jackson.
Jackson, Basil Rawdon, 1892–1957, vol. V
Jackson, Benjamin Daydon, 1846–1927, vol. II
Jackson, Rev. Blomfield, 1839–1905, vol. I
Jackson, Rev. Brice Lee, 1864–1941, vol. IV
Jackson, Hon. Cecil Gower, 1872–1920, vol. II
Jackson, Brig. Cecil Vivian Staveley, 1887–1964, vol. VI
Jackson, Charles d'Orville Pilkington, 1887–1973, vol. VII
Jackson, Sir Charles James, 1849–1923, vol. II
Jackson, Major Charles Lionel Atkins W.; see Ward-Jackson.
Jackson, Sir Christopher Mather M., 5th Bt (cr 1869); see Mather-Jackson, Sir G. C. M.
Jackson, Colin; see Jackson, G. C.
Jackson, Sir Cyril, 1863–1924, vol. II
Jackson, Rev. Canon Cyril, 1897–1969, vol. VI
Jackson, Daniel, 1858–1931, vol. III
Jackson, Derek Ainslie, 1906–1982, vol. VIII
Jackson, Sir Donald Edward, 1892–1981, vol. VIII

Jackson, Sir Edward Arthur Mather-, 4th Bt (*cr* 1869), 1899–1956, vol. V

Jackson, Edward Francis, 1915–1989, vol. VIII

Jackson, Sir Edward St John, 1886–1961, vol. VI

Jackson, Rev. Canon Edwin B.; *see* Brook-Jackson.

Jackson, Egbert Joseph William, *died* 1975, vol. VII

Jackson, Sir Ernest; *see* Jackson, Sir J. E.

Jackson, Lt-Col Ernest Somerville, 1872–1943, vol. IV

Jackson, F. Ernest, *died* 1945, vol. IV

Jackson, Rt Rev. Fabian Menteath Elliot, 1902–1978, vol. VII

Jackson, Rev. Forbes, *died* 1913, vol. I

Jackson, Col Sir Francis (James) Gidlow, 1889–1979, vol. VII

Jackson, Rt Hon. Sir (Francis) Stanley, 1870–1947, vol. IV

Jackson, Major Sir Francis Walter Fitton, 1881–1936, vol. III

Jackson, Rev. Canon Frank Hilton, 1870–1960, vol. V

Jackson, Col Frank Lawson John, 1919–1976, vol. VII

Jackson, Frank Stather, 1853–1922, vol. II

Jackson, Major Frank Whitford, 1886–1955, vol. V

Jackson, Most Rev. Frederic; *see* Jackson, Most Rev. G. F. C.

Jackson, Major Frederick George, *died* 1938, vol. III

Jackson, Frederick Hamilton, 1848–1923, vol. II

Jackson, Rt Hon. Frederick Huth, 1863–1921, vol. II

Jackson, Sir Frederick John, 1860–1929, vol. III

Jackson, Frederick John F.; *see* Foakes-Jackson.

Jackson, Sir Geoffrey Holt Seymour, 1915–1987, vol. VIII

Jackson, Brig.-Gen. Geoffrey Meinertzhagen, 1869–1946, vol. IV

Jackson, George, 1843–1931, vol. III

Jackson, Rev. George, 1864–1945, vol. IV

Jackson, (George) Colin, 1921–1981, vol. VIII

Jackson, Most Rev. George Frederic Clarence, 1907–1990, vol. VIII

Jackson, Maj.-Gen. George Hanbury, 1876–1958, vol. V

Jackson, Major Sir George Julius, 3rd Bt (*cr* 1902), 1883–1956, vol. V

Jackson, Lt-Col George Scott, *died* 1946, vol. IV

Jackson, Sir Gilbert Hollinshead Blomfield, 1875–1956, vol. V

Jackson, Gordon Cameron, 1923–1990, vol. VIII

Jackson, Lt-Col Guy, 1903–1960, vol. V

Jackson, Harold Gordon, 1888–1950, vol. IV

Jackson, Captain Harold Gordon, *died* 1950, vol. IV

Jackson, H(arold) Haygarth, 1896–1972, vol. VII

Jackson, Sir Harold Warters, 1883–1972, vol. VII

Jackson, Harry, 1892–1976, vol. VII

Jackson, Harry W., 1855–1930, vol. III

Jackson, Harvey, 1900–1982, vol. VIII

Jackson, Henry, 1839–1921, vol. II

Jackson, Sir Henry, 1st Bt (*cr* 1935), 1875–1937, vol. III

Jackson, Admiral of the Fleet Sir Henry Bradwardine, 1855–1929, vol. III

Jackson, Gen. Sir Henry Cholmondeley, 1879–1972, vol. VII

Jackson, Rev. Henry Latimer, 1851–1926, vol. II

Jackson, Captain Henry Leigh, 1886–1956, vol. V

Jackson, Captain Henry Mather-, 1894–1928, vol. II

Jackson, Sir Henry Mather-, 3rd Bt (*cr* 1869), 1855–1942, vol. IV

Jackson, Sir Henry Moore, 1849–1908, vol. I

Jackson, Sir Herbert, 1863–1936, vol. III

Jackson, Herbert, 1909–1989, vol. VIII

Jackson, Brig.-Gen. Herbert Kendall, 1859–1938, vol. III

Jackson, Maj.-Gen. Sir Herbert William, 1861–1931, vol. III

Jackson, Maj.-Gen. Herbert William, 1872–1940, vol. III

Jackson, Holbrook, 1874–1948, vol. IV

Jackson, Hugh Marrison Gower, 1870–1934, vol. III

Jackson, Col Hugh Milbourne, 1858–1940, vol. III

Jackson, Sir Hugh Nicholas, 2nd Bt (*cr* 1913), 1881–1979, vol. VII

Jackson, Maj.-Gen. James, 1866–1957, vol. V

Jackson, James Barry; *see* Barry, Michael.

Jackson, Ven. James M'Creight, 1841–1913, vol. I

Jackson, Sir John, 1851–1919, vol. II

Jackson, Sir John, 1865–1933, vol. III

Jackson, John, 1887–1958, vol. V

Jackson, John Arthur, 1862–1937, vol. III

Jackson, John Brinckerhoff, 1862–1920, vol. II

Jackson, Sir (John) Ernest, 1876–1941, vol. IV

Jackson, John Hughlings, 1835–1911, vol. I

Jackson, Sir John Montrésor, 6th Bt (*cr* 1815), 1914–1980, vol. VII

Jackson, Sir John Peter Todd, 1868–1945, vol. IV

Jackson, John Wharton, 1902–1986, vol. VIII

Jackson, John Whitfield-, 1847–1910, vol. I

Jackson, Joseph, 1924–1987, vol. VIII

Jackson, Joseph Cooksey, 1879–1938, vol. III

Jackson, Sir Keith George, 4th Bt (*cr* 1815), 1842–1916, vol. II

Jackson, Col Lambert Cameron, 1875–1953, vol. V

Jackson, Lawrence Colvile, *died* 1905, vol. I

Jackson, Brig.-Gen. Lionel Warren de Vere S.; *see* Sadleir-Jackson.

Jackson, Maj.-Gen. Sir Louis Charles, 1856–1946, vol. IV

Jackson, Maunsell Bowers, *died* 1922, vol. II

Jackson, Morton Strode, 1848–1913, vol. I

Jackson, Nicholas L.; *see* Lane-Jackson.

Jackson, Rev. Percival, 1845–1929, vol. III

Jackson, Sir Percy Richard, 1869–1941, vol. IV

Jackson, Sir Ralph, 1872–1943, vol. IV

Jackson, Reginald Nevill, 1887–1937, vol. III

Jackson, Sir Richard Hoyle, 1869–1944, vol. IV

Jackson, Col Richard John Laurence, 1908–1989, vol. VIII

Jackson, Sir Richard Leofric, 1902–1975, vol. VII

Jackson, Richard Meredith, 1903–1986, vol. VIII

Jackson, Lt-Col Richard Rolt Brash, 1874–1943, vol. IV

Jackson, Richard Stephens, 1850–1938, vol. III

Jackson, Maj.-Gen. Robert Edward, 1886–1948, vol. IV

Jackson, Robert Edwin, 1826–1909, vol. I

Jackson, Robert Frederick, 1880–1951, vol. V

Jackson, Robert H., 1892–1954, vol. V

Jackson, Sir Robert Montrésor, 5th Bt (*cr* 1815), 1876–1940, vol. III
Jackson, Col Sir Robert Whyte Melville, 1860–1928, vol. II
Jackson, Sir Robert William, 1826–1921, vol. II
Jackson, Rt Rev. Robert Wyse, 1908–1976, vol. VII
Jackson, Sir Russell; *see* Jackson, Sir W. D. R.
Jackson, Col Samuel, 1845–1911, vol. I
Jackson, Samuel Macauley, 1851–1912, vol. I
Jackson, Samuel Phillips, 1830–1904, vol. I
Jackson, Rt Hon. Sir Stanley; *see* Jackson, Sir F. S.
Jackson, Col Sydney Charles Fishburn, 1863–1928, vol. II
Jackson, Sir Thomas, 1st Bt (*cr* 1902), 1841–1915, vol. I
Jackson, Adm. Sir Thomas, 1868–1945, vol. IV
Jackson, Brig.-Gen. Sir Thomas Daare, 2nd Bt (*cr* 1902), 1876–1954, vol. V
Jackson, Sir Thomas Graham, 1st Bt (*cr* 1913), 1835–1924, vol. II
Jackson, Adm. Sir Thomas Sturges, 1842–1934, vol. III
Jackson, Thomas Vincent, *died* 1901, vol. I
Jackson, Rt Rev. Vibert, 1874–1963, vol. VI
Jackson, Lt-Col Vivian Archer, 1882–1943, vol. IV
Jackson, Sir (Walter David) Russell, 4th Bt (*cr* 1902), 1890–1956, vol. V
Jackson, Sir Wilfrid Edward Francis, 1883–1971, vol. VII
Jackson, Maj.-Gen. William, 1830–1912, vol. I
Jackson, William Alexander, 1905–1964, vol. VI
Jackson, William Henry, *died* 1920, vol. II
Jackson, Rear-Adm. William Lindsay, 1889–1962, vol. VI
Jackson, Sir William M.; *see* Mather-Jackson.
Jackson, Rev. William V.; *see* Vincent-Jackson.
Jackson, Rev. William Walrond, 1838–1931, vol. III
Jacob, Albert Edward, 1858–1929, vol. III
Jacob, Mrs Arthur, (Violet Jacob), *died* 1946, vol. IV
Jacob, Maj.-Gen. Arthur Le Grand, 1867–1942, vol. IV
Jacob, Lt-Col Arthur Leslie, 1870–1944, vol. IV
Jacob, Field-Marshal Sir Claud William, 1863–1948, vol. IV
Jacob, Rt Rev. Edgar, 1844–1920, vol. II
Jacob, Edward Fountaine, 1852–1912, vol. I
Jacob, Ernest Fraser, 1894–1971, vol. VII
Jacob, Sir George Harold L.; *see* Lloyd-Jacob.
Jacob, Gordon Percival Septimus, 1895–1984, vol. VIII
Jacob, Lt-Col Harold Fenton, 1866–1936, vol. III
Jacob, John Hier, 1884–1964, vol. VI
Jacob, Sir Lionel Montague, 1853–1934, vol. III
Jacob, Naomi, 1884–1964, vol. VI
Jacob, Rhoda Hannah, 1900–1979, vol. VII
Jacob, Sir (Samuel) Swinton, 1841–1917, vol. II
Jacob, Sir Swinton; *see* Jacob, Sir S. S.
Jacob, Col Sydney Long, 1845–1911, vol. I
Jacob, Violet; *see* Jacob, Mrs Arthur.
Jacob, Lt-Col Walter Henry Bell, 1871–1925, vol. II
Jacob, Maj.-Gen. William, 1837–1917, vol. II
Jacob, Rev. William, *died* 1940, vol. III
Jacob, Very Rev. William Ungoed, 1910–1990, vol. VIII

Jacobi, Georges, 1840–1906, vol. I
Jacobs, Brig. John Conrad S.; *see* Saunders-Jacobs.
Jacobs, Joseph, 1854–1916, vol. II
Jacobs, Sir Roland Ellis, 1891–1981, vol. VIII
Jacobs, William Wymark, 1863–1943, vol. IV
Jacobs-Bond, Carrie; *see* Bond.
Jacobs-Larkcom, Eric Herbert Larkcom, 1895–1982, vol. VIII
Jacobsen, Arne, 1902–1971, vol. VII
Jacobsen, Thomas Owen, 1864–1941, vol. IV
Jacobson, Baron (Life Peer); Sydney Jacobson, 1908–1988, vol. VIII
Jacobson, Ernest Nathaniel Joseph, 1877–1947, vol. IV
Jacobsson, Per, 1894–1963, vol. VI
Jacobsthal, Paul Ferdinand, 1880–1957, vol. V
Jacoby, Felix, 1876–1959, vol. V
Jacoby, Sir James Alfred, 1852–1909, vol. I
Jacomb, Rear-Adm. Humphrey Benson, 1891–1969, vol. VI
Jacomb-Hood, George Percy, 1857–1929, vol. III
Jacques, Rev. Kinton, 1837–1915, vol. I
Jacques, Brig. Leslie Innes, 1897–1959, vol. V
Jacques, Reginald; *see* Jacques, T. R.
Jacques, (Thomas) Reginald, 1894–1969, vol. VI
Jacquot, Général d'Armée Pierre Elie, 1902–1984, vol. VIII
Jacson, Rev. Owen Fitzherbert, 1861–1935, vol. III
Jadunath Mazoomdar, Rai Bahadur, Vedanta Bachaspati, 1859–1932, vol. III
Jaeger, John Conrad, 1907–1979, vol. VII
Jaeger, Werner W., 1888–1961, vol. VI
Jafar, Rafa Sir Saiyid Abu, *died* 1927, vol. II
Ja'far El Askeri, General, 1885–1936, vol. III
Jaffe, Sir Otto, 1846–1929, vol. III
Jaffer, Sir Ebrahim Haroon, 1881–1930, vol. III
Jaffray, Sir John, 1st Bt, 1818–1901, vol. I
Jaffray, Sir John Henry, 3rd Bt, 1893–1916, vol. II
Jaffray, Hon. Robert, 1832–1914, vol. I
Jaffray, Sir William, 2nd Bt, 1852–1914, vol. I
Jaffray, Sir William Edmund, 4th Bt, 1895–1953, vol. V
Jaffray, Rev. William Stevenson, 1867–1941, vol. IV
Jaffrey, Francis, 1861–1919, vol. II
Jaffrey, Sir Thomas, 1st Bt, 1861–1953, vol. V
Jagatsingh, Hon. Sir Keharsingh, (Hon. Sir Kher), 1931–1985, vol. VIII
Jagatsingh, Hon. Sir Kher; *see* Jagatsingh, Hon. Sir Keharsingh.
Jaggard, Captain William, *died* 1947, vol. IV
Jagger, Charles Sargeant, 1885–1934, vol. III
Jagger, David, *died* 1958, vol. V
Jagger, Rev. James Edwin, *died* 1937, vol. III
Jagger, John, 1872–1942, vol. IV
Jago, Thomas Sampson, 1835–1915, vol. I
Jago, William, 1854–1938, vol. III
Jagoe, Rt Rev. John Arthur, 1889–1962, vol. VI
Jahn, Gunnar, 1883–1971, vol. VII
Jahn, Hermann Arthur, 1907–1979, vol. VII
Jaipur, Maharaja of, 1861–1922, vol. II
Jaipur, Maharaja of, 1911–1970, vol. VI
Jaisalmer, Maharajahdhiraj of, 1882–1949, vol. IV (A), vol. V
Jakobson, Roman, 1896–1982, vol. VIII

Jalland, Arthur Edgar, 1889–1958, vol. V

Jalland, Rev. Trevor Gervase, 1896–1975, vol. VII

Jamal Sir Abdul Karim Abdul Shakur, 1862–1924, vol. II

Jamer, Herman Watson, 1904–1972, vol. VII

James of Hereford, 1st Baron, 1828–1911, vol. I

James, Abraham Thomas, 1883–1940, vol. III

James, Alexander, 1850–1932, vol. III

James, Alfred Henry, 1868–1941, vol. IV

James, Brig.-Gen. Alfred Henry Cotes, 1873–1947, vol. IV

James, Antony B.; *see* Brett-James, E. A.

James, Wing Comdr Sir Archibald William Henry, 1893–1980, vol. VII

James, Arthur, 1871–1959, vol. V

James, Rev. Canon Arthur Dyfrig, 1902–1980, vol. VII

James, Rt Hon. Sir Arthur Evan, 1916–1976, vol. VII

James, Arthur Godfrey, 1876–1959, vol. V

James, Sir Arthur Gwynne Gwynne-, 1885–1936, vol. III

James, Captain Arthur Keedwell Harvey; *see* Craven, Arthur Scott.

James, Arthur L.; *see* Lloyd James.

James, Rev. Arthur Oswel, 1849–1932, vol. III

James, Maj.-Gen. Sir Bernard; *see* James, Maj.-Gen. Sir W. B.

James, Col Bernard Ramsden, 1864–1938, vol. III

James, Lt-Col Boucher Charlewood, 1882–1930, vol. III

James, Col Cecil Polglase, 1879–1943, vol. IV

James, Charles Ashworth, *died* 1937, vol. III

James, Charles Canniff, 1863–1916, vol. II

James, Lt-Col Charles Henry, 1863–1944, vol. IV

James, Charles Holloway, 1893–1953, vol. V

James, Engr Rear-Adm. Charles John, 1862–1943, vol. IV

James, Hon. Sir Claude Ernest Weymouth, *died* 1961, vol. VI

James, Lt-Col Hon. Cuthbert, 1872–1930, vol. III

James, Brig.-Gen. Cyril Henry Leigh, *died* 1946, vol. IV

James, David G.; *see* Guthrie-James.

James, David Gwilym, 1905–1968, vol. VI

James, Sir David John, 1887–1967, vol. VI

James, David Pelham; *see* Guthrie-James, D.

James, Ven. Denis, 1895–1965, vol. VI

James, Lt-Col Edmund Henry Salt, 1874–1952, vol. V

James, Edmund Janes, 1855–1925, vol. II

James, Rev. Edward, 1828–1913, vol. I

James, Edward, 1885–1971, vol. VII

James, Sir Edward Albert, 5th Bt, 1862–1942, vol. IV

James, Sir Edward Burnet, 1857–1927, vol. II

James, Rev. Edwin Oliver, 1888–1972, vol. VII

James, (Eliot) Antony B.; *see* Brett-James.

James, Florence, 1857–1929, vol. III

James, Sir Francis; *see* James, Sir J. F. W.

James, Francis Edward, *died* 1920, vol. II

James, F(rank) Cyril, 1903–1973, vol. VII

James, Sir Frederick Ernest, 1891–1971, vol. VII

James, Sir Frederick Seton, 1870–1934, vol. III

James, Captain Sir Fullarton, 6th Bt, 1864–1955, vol. V

James, Sir Gavin Fullarton, 4th Bt, 1859–1937, vol. III

James, George William Blomfield, *died* 1968, vol. VI

James, Mrs Helena Constance R.; *see* Romanne-James.

James, Henry, 1843–1916, vol. II

James, Sir Henry Evan Murchison, 1846–1923, vol. II

James, Very Rev. Henry Lewis, 1864–1949, vol. IV

James, Henry Rosher, 1862–1931, vol. III

James, Col Herbert, 1859–1943, vol. IV

James, Rev. Herbert Armitage, 1844–1931, vol. III

James, Lt-Col Herbert Ellison Rhodes, *died* 1939, vol. III

James, Lt-Col Herbert Lionel, 1863–1946, vol. IV

James, Ivor Benjamin Hugh, 1882–1963, vol. VI

James, Sir Jack; *see* James, Sir John H.

James, Gen. Sir John, 1832–1901, vol. I

James, John Arthur, 1853–1917, vol. II

James, Ven. John D., 1862–1938, vol. III

James, John Egbert, 1876–1965, vol. VI

James, Sir John Ernest, *died* 1963, vol. VI

James, Sir (John) Francis (William), 1879–1950, vol. IV

James, Very Rev. John Gwynno, 1912–1967, vol. VI

James, Sir John Hastings, (Sir Jack), 1906–1980, vol. VII

James, Sir John Kingston Fullarton, 3rd Bt, 1852–1933, vol. III

James, John Morrice Cairns; *see* Baron Saint Brides.

James, John Richings, 1912–1980, vol. VII

James, John William, 1907–1975, vol. VII

James, John Wynford George, 1911–1990, vol. VIII

James, Rev. Lemuel John H.; *see* Hopkin-James.

James, Lewis Cairns, 1865–1946, vol. IV

James, Lionel, 1868–1948, vol. IV

James, Col Lionel, 1871–1955, vol. V

James, Brig. Manley Angell, 1896–1975, vol. VII

James, Rt Rev. Melville Charles, 1877–1957, vol. V

James, Montague Rhodes, 1862–1936, vol. III

James, Col Murray Ray de Bruyne, 1870–1939, vol. III

James, Norah C., 1901–1979, vol. VII

James, Philip Brutton, 1901–1974, vol. VII

James, Philip Gaved, 1904–1978, vol. VII

James, Lt-Col Ralph Ernest Haweis, 1875–1964, vol. VI

James, Reginald Hugh Lloyd L.; *see* Langford-James.

James, Reginald William, 1891–1964, vol. VI

James, Richard Bush, 1889–1970, vol. VI

James, Richard Lewis Malcolm, 1897–1972, vol. VII

James, Hon. Robert, 1873–1960, vol. V

James, Robert Leoline, 1905–1982, vol. VIII

James, Rolfe Arnold S.; *see* Scott-James.

James, Lt-Col Sydney Price, *died* 1946, vol. IV

James, Ven. Sydney Rhodes, 1855–1934, vol. III

James, Thomas David, 1871–1955, vol. V

James, Thomas Maurice, 1890–1962, vol. VI

James, Vice-Adm. Thomas Norman, 1878–1965, vol. VI

James, Thurstan Trewartha, 1903–1975, vol. VII

James, Lt-Col Tristram Bernard Wordsworth, 1883–1939, vol. III

James, Hon. Sir Walter Hartwell, 1863–1943, vol. IV
James, Lt-Col Walter Haweis, 1847–1927, vol. II
James, Rev. Walter Hill, 1828–1910, vol. I
James, William, 1842–1910, vol. I
James, Maj.-Gen. Sir (William) Bernard, 1865–1940, vol. III
James, William Dodge, 1854–1912, vol. I
James, William Garnet, 1895–1977, vol. VII
James, William Henry E.; *see* Ewart James.
James, Adm. Sir William Milbourne, 1881–1973, vol. VII
James, William Owen, 1900–1978, vol. VII
James, Col William Reginald Wallwyn, 1860–1925, vol. II
James, William Thomas, 1892–1982, vol. VIII
James, William Warwick, 1874–1965, vol. VI
James, Winifred Lewellin, (Mrs Henry de Jan), *died* 1941, vol. IV
Jameson, Adam, 1860–1907, vol. I
Jameson, Alexander Hope, 1874–1952, vol. V
Jameson, Rt Hon. Andrew, 1855–1941, vol. IV
Jameson, Andrew; *see* Ardwall, Hon. Lord.
Jameson, Cecil Stuart, *born* 1883, vol. VI
Jameson, Ven. Francis Bernard, 1889–1960, vol. V (A), vol. VI (AI)
Jameson, Brig. Frank Robert Wordsworth, 1893–1965, vol. VI
Jameson, Surgeon-Gen. James, 1837–1904, vol. I
Jameson, James Alexander, 1885–1961, vol. VI
Jameson, John, *died* 1920, vol. II
Jameson, Lt-Col John Bland, *died* 1954, vol. V
Jameson, Lt-Col John Eustace-, 1853–1919, vol. II
Jameson, John Franklin, 1859–1937, vol. III
Jameson, John Gordon, 1878–1955, vol. V
Jameson, Rt Hon. Sir Leander Starr, 1st Bt, 1853–1917, vol. II
Jameson, (Margaret) Storm, 1891–1986, vol. VIII
Jameson, Noel Rutherford, 1892–1971, vol. VII
Jameson, Surg.-Captain Robert Dundonald, 1869–1938, vol. III
Jameson, Storm; *see* Jameson, M. S.
Jameson, Maj.-Gen. Thomas Henry, 1894–1985, vol. VIII
Jameson, William George, 1851–1939, vol. III
Jameson, Rear-Adm. Sir William Scarlett, 1899–1966, vol. VI
Jameson, Sir (William) Wilson, 1885–1962, vol. VI
Jameson, Sir Wilson; *see* Jameson, Sir W. W.
Jamiat Rai, Diwan, Rai Bahadur, Diwan Bahadur, 1861–1941, vol. IV
Jamieson, Rt Hon. Lord; Douglas Jamieson, 1880–1952, vol. V
Jamieson, Alexander, 1873–1937, vol. III
Jamieson, Sir Archibald Auldjo, 1884–1959, vol. V
Jamieson, Hon. Donald Campbell, 1921–1986, vol. VIII
Jamieson, Douglas; *see* Jamieson, Rt Hon. Lord.
Jamieson, Vice-Adm. Douglas Y.; *see* Young-Jamieson.
Jamieson, Edgar George, 1882–1958, vol. V
Jamieson, George, 1843–1920, vol. II
Jamieson, Sir James William, 1867–1946, vol. IV
Jamieson, John Kay, 1873–1948, vol. IV
Jamieson, R. Kirkland, 1881–1950, vol. IV

Jamieson, Stanley Wyndham, 1885–1970, vol. VI
Jamieson, William Allan, 1839–1916, vol. II
Jamison, Evelyn Mary, 1877–1972, vol. VII
Jan, Winifred Lewellin de; *see* James, W. L.
Jane, Frank William, 1901–1963, vol. VI
Jane, Fred. T., 1870–1916, vol. II
Janes, Emily, *died* 1928, vol. II
Janes, Sir Herbert Charles, 1884–1977, vol. VII
Janes, Rev. Maxwell Osborne, 1902–1981, vol. VIII
Janes, Norman Thomas, 1892–1980, vol. VII
Janet, Pierre, 1859–1947, vol. IV
Janion, Edwin Manifold, 1863–1952, vol. V
Janisch, Noel, *died* 1930, vol. III
Janjira, HH Nawab, 1862–1922, vol. II
Jannaris, Anthony, 1852–1909, vol. I
Janner, Baron (Life Peer); Barnett Janner, 1892–1982, vol. VIII
Jansen, Ernest George, 1881–1959, vol. V
Janson, Stanley Eric, 1908–1974, vol. VII
Jansz, Sir Eric; *see* Jansz, Sir H. E.
Jansz, Sir (Herbert) Eric, 1890–1976, vol. VII
Janvrin, Rev. William Langston Benest, 1853–1927, vol. II
Jaora State, Lt-Col HH Fakhr-ud-Daulah Nawab Sir Mohammad Iftikhar Ali Khan Bahadur Saulat Jang, 1883–1947, vol. IV
Japp, Francis Robert, 1848–1925, vol. II
Japp, Sir Henry, 1869–1939, vol. III
Jaques-Dalcroze, Emile, 1865–1950, vol. IV
Jaquet, Sir Robert Glover, 1856–1937, vol. III
Jardine, Sir Alexander, 10th Bt (*cr* 1672), 1868–1942, vol. IV
Jardine, Brig. Christian West B.; *see* Bayne-Jardine.
Jardine, Christopher Willoughby, 1911–1982, vol. VIII
Jardine, Maj.-Gen. Sir Colin Arthur, 3rd Bt (*cr* 1916), 1892–1957, vol. V
Jardine, David Jardine, 1847–1922, vol. II
Jardine, Sir Douglas James, 1888–1946, vol. IV
Jardine, Douglas Robert, 1900–1958, vol. V
Jardine, Sir Ernest, 1st Bt (*cr* 1919), 1859–1947, vol. IV
Jardine, Brig. Sir Ian Liddell, 4th Bt, 1923–1982, vol. VIII
Jardine, James, 1846–1909, vol. I
Jardine, Brig.-Gen. James Bruce, 1870–1955, vol. V
Jardine, James Willoughby, 1879–1945, vol. IV
Jardine, Sir John, 1st Bt (*cr* 1916), 1844–1919, vol. II
Jardine, Sir John, 2nd Bt (*cr* 1919), 1884–1965, vol. VI
Jardine, John, 1881–1974, vol. VII
Jardine, Major Sir John Eric Birdwood, 2nd Bt (*cr* 1916), 1890–1924, vol. II
Jardine, John Frederick James, 1926–1990, vol. VIII
Jardine, Captain Sir John William Buchanan-, 3rd Bt (*cr* 1885), 1900–1969, vol. VI
Jardine, Lionel Westropp, 1895–1980, vol. VII
Jardine, Malcolm Robert, 1869–1947, vol. IV
Jardine, Michael James, 1915–1988, vol. VIII
Jardine, Sir Robert, 1st Bt (*cr* 1885), 1825–1905, vol. I
Jardine, Robert, 1862–1932, vol. III
Jardine, Robert Frier, 1894–1982, vol. VIII

Jardine, Sir Robert William Buchanan, 2nd Bt (*cr* 1885), 1868–1927, vol. II

Jardine, Sir William, 9th Bt (*cr* 1672), 1865–1915, vol. I

Jardine of Applegirth, Col Sir William Edward, 11th Bt, 1917–1986, vol. VIII

Jardine, William Ellis, 1867–1944, vol. IV

Jardine-Brown, Robert, 1905–1972, vol. VII

Jardine Paterson, Lt Col Arthur James, 1918–1988, vol. VIII

Jarman, Charles, 1893–1947, vol. IV

Jarman, Rev. Canon Cyril Edgar, 1892–1978, vol. VII

Jarman, John Robert, 1844–1922, vol. II

Jarman, Air Cdre Lance Michael E.; *see* Elworthy-Jarman.

Jarmay, Sir John Gustav, 1856–1944, vol. IV

Jarrad, Sir Vivian Everard Donne, *died* 1938, vol. III

Jarratt, Sir Arthur William, 1894–1958, vol. V

Jarratt, Sir William Smith, 1871–1966, vol. VI

Jarrell, Randall, 1914–1965, vol. VI

Jarrett, Sir Francis Moncreiff K.; *see* Kerr-Jarrett.

Jarrett, George William Symonds, 1880–1960, vol. V

Jarrett, Col Henry Sullivan, 1839–1919, vol. II

Jarrett, James Henry, 1895–1943, vol. IV

Jarrett, Norman Rowlstone, 1889–1982, vol. VIII

Jarrold, (Herbert) John, 1906–1979, vol. VII

Jarrold, John; *see* Jarrold, H. J.

Jarvie, John Gibson, 1883–1964, vol. VI

Jarvis, Sir Adrian; *see* Jarvis, Sir A. A.

Jarvis, Alan Hepburn, 1915–1972, vol. VII

Jarvis, Very Rev. Alfred Charles Eustace, 1876–1957, vol. V

Jarvis, Ven. Alfred Clifford, 1908–1981, vol. VIII

Jarvis, Sir (Arnold) Adrian, 2nd Bt, 1904–1965, vol. VI

Jarvis, Lt-Col Arthur Leonard Fitzgerald, 1852–1927, vol. II

Jarvis, Lt-Col Arthur Murray, 1863–1930, vol. III

Jarvis, Lt-Col Charles Francis Cracroft, *died* 1957, vol. V

Jarvis, Major Claude Scudamore, 1879–1953, vol. V

Jarvis, Mrs Doris Annie, *born* 1912, vol. VIII

Jarvis, Edward Blackwell, 1873–1950, vol. IV

Jarvis, Hon. Eric William George, 1907–1987, vol. VIII

Jarvis, Very Rev. Ernest David, 1888–1964, vol. VI

Jarvis, Rev. Francis Amcotts, *died* 1937, vol. III

Jarvis, Sir John, 1st Bt, 1876–1950, vol. IV

Jarvis, Sir John Layton, 1887–1968, vol. VI

Jarvis, Maj.-Gen. Samuel Peters, 1820–1905, vol. I

Jarvis, Col Sir Weston, 1855–1939, vol. III

Jarvis, William Rose, 1885–1943, vol. IV

Jaspar, Henri, 1870–1939, vol. III

Jasper, Cyril Charles, 1923–1987, vol. VIII

Jasper, Very Rev. Ronald Claud Dudley, 1917–1990, vol. VIII

Jaspers, Karl, 1883–1969, vol. VI

Jast, L. Stanley, 1868–1944, vol. IV

Jastrow, Morris, Jr, 1861–1921, vol. II

Jatia, Sir Onkar Mull, 1882–1938, vol. III

Jaujard, Jacques, 1895–1967, vol. VI (AII)

Jaurès, Jean Léon, 1859–1914, vol. I

Javal, Paul C.; *see* Cremieu-Javal.

Jawahir Singh, Sardar Bahadur Sir Sardar, *died* 1947, vol. IV

Jay, Major Charles Douglas, *died* 1941, vol. IV

Jay, Edith Katharine Spicer; *see* Prescott, E. Livingston.

Jay, Rev. Canon Eric George, 1907–1989, vol. VIII

Jay, Harriett, 1863–1932, vol. III

Jay, Thomas, 1887–1962, vol. VI

Jay, William Samuel, *died* 1933, vol. III

Jayakar, Rt Hon. Mukund R., *died* 1959, vol. V

Jayasundera, Sir Ukwatte, 1896–1962, vol. VI

Jayatilaka, Sir Don Baron, 1868–1944, vol. IV

Jayetileke, Sir Edward George Perera, 1888–1975, vol. VII

Jayewardene, E. W., *died* 1932, vol. III

Jayne, Col Arthur Alfred, 1878–1934, vol. III

Jayne, Rt Rev. Francis John, 1845–1921, vol. II

Jayne, Ronald Garland, 1877–1951, vol. V

Jays, Tom, 1868–1947, vol. IV

Jeaffreson, John Cordy, 1831–1901, vol. I

Jeakes, Rev. James, 1829–1915, vol. I

Jeanneret, Charles-Edouard; *see* Le Corbusier.

Jeanneret, François Charles Archile, 1890–1967, vol. VI

Jeanniot, Pierre Georges, 1848–1934, vol. III

Jeans, Sir Alexander Grigor, 1849–1924, vol. II

Jeans, Sir Alick, (Alexander Grigor), 1912–1972, vol. VII

Jeans, Allan, 1877–1961, vol. VI

Jeans, Hon. Maj.-Gen. Charles Gilchrist, 1854–1920, vol. II

Jeans, Frank, 1878–1933, vol. III

Jeans, Isabel, 1891–1985, vol. VIII

Jeans, J. Stephen, 1846–1913, vol. I

Jeans, Sir James Hopwood, 1877–1946, vol. IV

Jeans, Sir Richard Walter, 1846–1924, vol. II

Jeans, Ronald, *died* 1973, vol. VII

Jeans, Major Thomas Kilvington, 1885–1962, vol. VI

Jeans, Surg. Rear-Adm. Thomas Tendron, *died* 1938, vol. III

Jeans, Ursula, *died* 1973, vol. VII

Jeans, William, *died* 1916, vol. II

Jebb, Eglantyne Mary, 1889–1978, vol. VII

Jebb, Geraldine Emma May, *died* 1959, vol. V

Jebb, Brig.-Gen. Gladwyn Dundas, 1877–1947, vol. IV

Jebb, Col (Joshua Henry) Miles, 1875–1935, vol. III

Jebb, Col Miles; *see* Jebb, Col J. H. M.

Jebb, Richard, 1874–1953, vol. V

Jebb, Sir Richard Claverhouse, 1841–1905, vol. I

Jeckell, George Allen, 1880–1950, vol. IV (A), vol. V

Jedlizka, Marie; *see* Jeritza, M.

Jee, Joseph, *died* 1899, vol. I

Jeejeebhoy, Sir Byramjee, 1881–1946, vol. IV

Jeeves, William John, *died* 1932, vol. III

Jeffcoat, Col Algernon Cautley, 1877–1963, vol. VI

Jeffcoat, Captain Henry Jamieson Powell, *died* 1901, vol. I

Jeffcott, Henry Homan, *died* 1937, vol. III

Jefferis, Maj.-Gen. Sir Millis Rowland, 1899–1963, vol. VI

Jeffers, Le Roy, 1878–1926, vol. II

Jeffers, William Martin, 1876–1953, vol. V

Jefferson, Frederick Thomas, 1854–1920, vol. II

Jefferson, Sir Geoffrey, 1886–1961, vol. VI
Jefferson, Captain Henry, 1865–1937, vol. III
Jefferson, Lt-Col Sir John Alexander D.; *see* Dunnington-Jefferson.
Jefferson, Joseph, 1829–1905, vol. I
Jefferson, Rt Rev. Robert, 1881–1968, vol. VI
Jefferson, Wood G., *died* 1912, vol. I
Jeffery, Cecil Albert, 1888–1970, vol. VI (AII)
Jeffery, Edward Turner, 1843–1927, vol. II, vol. III
Jeffery, George Barker, 1891–1957, vol. V
Jeffery, George H. Everett, *died* 1935, vol. III
Jeffery, George Henry Padget, 1907–1987, vol. VIII
Jeffery, Lilian Hamilton, 1915–1986, vol. VIII
Jeffery, Rev. Samuel, *died* 1934, vol. III
Jeffery, Walter, 1861–1922, vol. II
Jeffery, Col Walter Hugh, 1878–1957, vol. V
Jefferys, Charles William, 1869–1951, vol. V
Jeffes, Maurice, *died* 1954, vol. V
Jefford, Vice-Adm. James Wilfred, 1901–1980, vol. VII
Jeffrey, Very Rev. George Johnstone, 1881–1961, vol. VI
Jeffrey, Maj.-Gen. Hugh Crozier, 1914–1976, vol. VII
Jeffrey, Sir John, 1871–1947, vol. IV
Jeffrey, Rev. Norman Stuart, *died* 1919, vol. II
Jeffrey, Robert, 1884–1956, vol. V
Jeffrey, William, 1896–1946, vol. IV
Jeffrey-Waddell, John, 1876–1941, vol. IV
Jeffreys, 1st Baron, 1878–1960, vol. V
Jeffreys, 2nd Baron, 1932–1986, vol. VIII
Jeffreys, Anthony Henry, 1896–1984, vol. VIII
Jeffreys, Rt Hon. Arthur Frederick, 1848–1906, vol. I
Jeffreys, Adm. Edmund Frederick, 1846–1925, vol. II
Jeffreys, Sir Harold, 1891–1989, vol. VIII
Jeffreys, Maj.-Gen. Henry Byron, 1854–1949, vol. IV
Jeffreys, Montagu Vaughan Castelman, 1900–1985, vol. VIII
Jeffreys, Brig.-Gen. Patrick Douglas, 1848–1922, vol. II
Jeffreys, Rev. Tom Reginald Frederic, 1871–1938, vol. III
Jeffreys, W. Rees, 1871–1954, vol. V
Jeffreys Jones, David; *see* Jones.
Jeffries, Charles H., 1864–1936, vol. III
Jeffries, Sir Charles Joseph, 1895–1972, vol. VII
Jeffries, Graham Montague; *see* Graeme, Bruce.
Jeffries, Hon. Sir Shirley Williams, 1886–1963, vol. VI
Jeffries, Brig. William Francis, 1891–1969, vol. VI
Jeffs, Ernest Harry, 1885–1973, vol. VII
Jeffs, Harry, 1860–1938, vol. III
Jeger, George, 1903–1971, vol. VII
Jeger, Santo Wayburn, 1898–1953, vol. V
Jehanghir, Sir Cowasjee, 1st Bt, 1853–1934, vol. III
Jehanghir, Sir Cowasjee, 2nd Bt, 1879–1962, vol. VI
Jehangir, Vakil Hon. Khan Bahadur Sardar Sir Rustom, *died* 1933, vol. III
Jehu, Ivor Stewart, 1908–1960, vol. V
Jehu, Thomas John, 1871–1943, vol. IV
Jejeebhoy, Sir Jamsetjee, (Manockjee Cursetjee), 3rd Bt, 1851–1898, vol. I
Jejeebhoy, Sir Jamsetjee, (Cowasjee Cursetjee), 4th Bt, 1852–1908, vol. I

Jejeebhoy, Sir Jamsetjee, 6th Bt, 1909–1968, vol. VI
Jejeebhoy, Sir Jamsetjee; *see* Jejeebhoy, Sir R. C. C. J.
Jejeebhoy, Sir (Rustomjee Cowasjee Cursetjee) Jamsetjee, 5th Bt, 1878–1931, vol. III
Jekyll, Agnes, (Lady Jekyll), 1861–1937, vol. III
Jekyll, Gertrude, 1843–1932, vol. III
Jekyll, Col Sir Herbert, 1846–1932, vol. III
Jelf, Sir Arthur Richard, 1837–1917, vol. II
Jelf, Sir Arthur Selborne, 1876–1947, vol. IV
Jelf, Sir Ernest Arthur, 1868–1949, vol. IV
Jelf, Rev. George Edward, 1834–1908, vol. I
Jelf, Herbert William, 1882–1943, vol. IV
Jelf, Col Richard Henry, 1844–1913, vol. I
Jelf, Brig.-Gen. Rudolf George, 1873–1958, vol. V
Jelf, Col Wilfrid Wykeham, 1880–1933, vol. III
Jellett, Very Rev. Henry, *died* 1901, vol. I
Jellett, Henry, 1872–1948, vol. IV
Jellett, Col John Hewitt, 1859–1938, vol. III
Jellett, John Holmes, 1905–1971, vol. VII
Jellett, William Morgan, *died* 1936, vol. III
Jellicoe, 1st Earl, 1859–1935, vol. III
Jellicoe, Rear-Adm. Christopher Theodore, 1903–1977, vol. VII
Jellicoe, Brig.-Gen. Richard Carey, 1875–1962, vol. VI
Jellicorse, Rev. William, *died* 1920, vol. II
Jellinek, Lionel, 1898–1979, vol. VII
Jencken, Maj.-Gen. Francis John, 1858–1943, vol. IV
Jenkin, Mrs Bernard, (Margaret M. Giles), 1868–1949, vol. IV
Jenkin, Charles Frewen, 1865–1940, vol. III
Jenkin, Henry Archibald Tregarthen, 1886–1951, vol. V
Jenkin, Engr Rear-Adm. John Harry, 1866–1933, vol. III
Jenkin, Mary Elizabeth, 1892–1979, vol. VII
Jenkin, Thomas James, 1885–1965, vol. VI
Jenkin, Sir William Norman Prentice, 1899–1983, vol. VIII
Jenkin-Jones, Charles Mark, 1885–1971, vol. VII
Jenkin Pugh, Rev. Canon Thomas; *see* Pugh.
Jenkings, Adm. Albert Baldwin, 1846–1942, vol. IV
Jenkins, Baron (Life Peer); David Llewelyn Jenkins, 1899–1969, vol. VI
Jenkins, Rev. Canon Alfred Thomas, 1893–1960, vol. V
Jenkins, Arthur, *died* 1946, vol. IV
Jenkins, A(rthur) Robert, 1908–1989, vol. VIII
Jenkins, Charles Elliott Edward, 1859–1946, vol. IV
Jenkins, Rev. Canon Claude, 1877–1959, vol. V
Jenkins, David, 1848–1915, vol. I
Jenkins, Rev. David, *died* 1926, vol. II
Jenkins, Ven. David, 1876–1960, vol. V
Jenkins, Rev. David Erwyd, *died* 1937, vol. III
Jenkins, Douglas, 1880–1961, vol. VI
Jenkins, Edward, 1838–1910, vol. I
Jenkins, Sir (Edward) Enoch, 1895–1960, vol. V
Jenkins, Major Edward Vaughan, 1879–1941, vol. IV
Jenkins, Sir Enoch; *see* Jenkins, Sir E. E.
Jenkins, Evan David Thomas, 1882–1960, vol. V
Jenkins, Sir Evan Meredith, 1896–1985, vol. VIII
Jenkins, Lt-Col Francis, 1877–1927, vol. II
Jenkins, Brig.-Gen. Francis Conway, 1888–1933, vol. III

Jenkins, Col Sir Francis Howell, 1832–1906, vol. I
Jenkins, Frank L.; *see* Lynn-Jenkins.
Jenkins, Sir George Frederick, 1878–1957, vol. V
Jenkins, Sir George Henry, 1843–1911, vol. I
Jenkins, George Kirkhouse, *died* 1957, vol. V
Jenkins, Gilbert Henry, 1875–1957, vol. V
Jenkins, Sir Gilmour; *see* Jenkins, Sir T. G.
Jenkins, Herbert, *died* 1923, vol. II
Jenkins, Lt-Col Herbert Harold, 1877–1932, vol. III
Jenkins, Herbert Riches, 1880–1944, vol. IV
Jenkins, Huntly E., *died* 1923, vol. II
Jenkins, Mrs Inez Mary Mackay, 1895–1981, vol. VIII
Jenkins, Sir James, 1818–1912, vol. I
Jenkins, John, *born* 1852, vol. III
Jenkins, Hon. John Greeley, 1851–1923, vol. II
Jenkins, John Lewis, 1857–1912, vol. I
Jenkins, Ven. (John) Owen, 1906–1988, vol. VIII
Jenkins, Joseph Barclay, 1870–1950, vol. IV
Jenkins, Rt Hon. Sir Lawrence Hugh, 1858–1928, vol. II
Jenkins, Leslie Augustus Westover, 1910–1978, vol. VII
Jenkins, Brig.-Gen. Noble Fleming, 1860–1927, vol. II
Jenkins, Ven. Owen; *see* Jenkins, Ven. J. O.
Jenkins, Robert Christmas Dewar, 1900–1978, vol. VII
Jenkins, Robert Thomas, 1881–1969, vol. VI
Jenkins, Romilly James Heald, 1907–1969, vol. VI
Jenkins, Sir (Thomas) Gilmour, 1894–1981, vol. VIII
Jenkins, Walter Allen, 1891–1958, vol. V
Jenkins, Sir Walter St David, 1874–1951, vol. V
Jenkins, Sir William, 1871–1944, vol. IV
Jenkins, Sir William, 1904–1983, vol. VIII
Jenkins, Sir William Albert, *died* 1968, vol. VI
Jenkins, William Frank, 1889–1980, vol. VII
Jenkins, William Henry Philips, 1842–1916, vol. II
Jenkins, Sir William John, 1892–1957, vol. V
Jenkins, Rev. William Owen, 1863–1919, vol. II
Jenkinson, Sir Anthony Banks, 13th Bt, 1912–1989, vol. VIII
Jenkinson, Sir (Charles) Hilary, *died* 1961, vol. VI
Jenkinson, Sir Edward George, 1835–1919, vol. II
Jenkinson, Francis Broxholm Grey, 1846–1902, vol. I
Jenkinson, Francis John Henry, 1853–1923, vol. II
Jenkinson, Sir George Banks, 12th Bt, 1851–1915, vol. I
Jenkinson, Major George Seymour Charles, 1858–1907, vol. I
Jenkinson, Sir Hilary; *see* Jenkinson, Sir C. H.
Jenkinson, John Edward, 1858–1937, vol. III (A), vol. IV
Jenkinson, Sir Mark Webster, *died* 1935, vol. III
Jenks, Clarence Wilfred, 1909–1973, vol. VII
Jenks, Rev. David, 1866–1935, vol. III
Jenks, Edward, 1861–1939, vol. III
Jenks, Sir Maurice, 1st Bt, 1872–1946, vol. IV
Jenks, Very Rev. Walter, 1864–1935, vol. III
Jenkyns, Sir Henry, 1838–1899, vol. I
Jenner, Lt-Col Sir Albert Victor, 3rd Bt, 1862–1954, vol. V
Jenner, George Francis Birt, *born* 1840, vol. II
Jenner, Rt Rev. Henry Lascelles, 1820–1898, vol. I

Jenner, Katherine Lee, *died* 1936, vol. III
Jenner, Lt-Col Leopold Christian Duncan, 1869–1953, vol. V
Jenner, Sir Walter Kentish William, 2nd Bt, 1860–1948, vol. IV
Jenner, Sir William, 1st Bt, 1815–1898, vol. I
Jenner-Fust, Herbert, 1806–1904, vol. I
Jenney, Col Archibald Offley, 1864–1946, vol. IV
Jenney, Brig. Reginald Charles Napier, 1906–1960, vol. V
Jennings, Antony; *see* Jennings, B. A.
Jennings, Sir Arthur Oldham, 1855–1934, vol. III
Jennings, Arthur Seymour, *born* 1860, vol. II
Jennings, (Bernard) Antony, 1939–1990, vol. VIII
Jennings, Christopher; *see* Jennings, R. E. C.
Jennings, (Edgar) Owen, 1899–1985, vol. VIII
Jennings, Edward Charles, 1877–1955, vol. V
Jennings, Col Edward Lawrence Frederick, 1850–1931, vol. III
Jennings, Rev. Edward Linck, *died* 1940, vol. III
Jennings, Gertrude E., *died* 1958, vol. V
Jennings, Henry Cecil, 1908–1983, vol. VIII
Jennings, Brig.-Gen. Herbert Alexander Kaye, 1862–1921, vol. II
Jennings, Herbert Spencer, 1868–1947, vol. IV
Jennings, Sir Ivor; *see* Jennings, Sir W. I.
Jennings, James George, 1866–1921, vol. III
Jennings, James George, 1866–1941, vol. IV
Jennings, Lt-Col James Willes, 1866–1954, vol. V
Jennings, Rev. Canon John Andrew, 1855–1923, vol. II
Jennings, John Charles, 1903–1990, vol. VIII
Jennings, Sir John Rogers, 1820–1897, vol. I
Jennings, Leonard, *died* 1956, vol. V
Jennings, Owen; *see* Jennings, E. O.
Jennings, Hon. Sir Patrick Alfred, 1831–1897, vol. I
Jennings, Paul Francis, 1918–1989, vol. VIII
Jennings, Col Richard, 1856–1935, vol. III
Jennings, (Richard Edward) Christopher, 1911–1982, vol. VIII
Jennings, Col Robert Henry, 1852–1918, vol. II
Jennings, Gen. Sir Robert Melvill, 1841–1922, vol. II
Jennings, Sir Roland, 1894–1968, vol. VI
Jennings, Sir (William) Ivor, 1903–1965, vol. VI
Jennings, William Thomas, 1854–1923, vol. II
Jenour, Brig.-Gen. Arthur Stawell, 1867–1938, vol. III
Jensen, Ernest T., 1873–1950, vol. IV
Jensen, Johannes Hans Daniel, 1906–1973, vol. VII
Jensen, Sir John Klunder, 1884–1970, vol. VI
Jephcott, Alfred Roger, 1853–1932, vol. III
Jephcott, Hon. Sir Bruce Reginald, 1929–1987, vol. VIII
Jephcott, Sir Harry, 1st Bt, 1891–1978, vol. VII
Jephson, Sir Alfred, 1841–1900, vol. I
Jephson, Arthur Jermy Mounteney, 1858–1908, vol. I
Jephson, Rev. Arthur W., 1853–1935, vol. III
Jephson, Harriet Julia, (Lady Jephson), *died* 1930, vol. III
Jephson, Brig. Maurice Denham, 1890–1968, vol. VI
Jephson, Sir Stanhope William, 4th Bt, 1810–1900, vol. I
Jephson-Jones, Brig. Robert Llewellyn, 1905–1985, vol. VIII

Jeppe, Sir Julius, 1859–1929, vol. III

Jepson, Edgar, 1863–1938, vol. III

Jepson, Richard Pomfret, 1918–1980, vol. VII

Jepson, Captain Rowland Walter, 1888–1954, vol. V

Jepson, Selwyn, 1899–1989, vol. VIII

Jepson, Stanley, 1894–1976, vol. VII

Jerdan, Rev. Charles, 1843–1926, vol. II

Jerichow, Herbert Peter Andreas, 1889–1967, vol. VI

Jeritza, Maria, 1887–1982, vol. VIII

Jermyn, Sir Alfred, 1845–1921, vol. II

Jermyn, Rt Rev. Hugh Willoughby, 1820–1903, vol. I

Jerningham, Charles Edward Wynne, 1854–1921, vol. II

Jerningham, Sir Henry William Stafford, 11th Bt, 1867–1935, vol. III

Jerningham, Sir Hubert Edward Henry, 1842–1914, vol. I

Jerome, Maj.-Gen. Henry Edward, 1830–1901, vol. I

Jerome, Col Henry Joseph Walker, 1854–1943, vol. IV

Jerome, Jerome Klapka, 1859–1927, vol. II

Jerome, Lucien Joseph, 1870–1943, vol. IV

Jerome, Thomas Stroud, *died* 1917, vol. II

Jerome, William J. Smith, 1839–1929, vol. III

Jerram, Rev. Arnold Escombe, *died* 1934, vol. III

Jerram, Sir Bertrand; *see* Jerram, Sir C. B.

Jerram, Sir (Cecil) Bertrand, 1891–1971, vol. VII

Jerram, Lt-Col Charles Frederic, 1882–1969, vol. VI

Jerram, Adm. Sir Martyn; *see* Jerram, Adm. Sir T. H. M.

Jerram, Maurice William, 1922–1981, vol. VIII

Jerram, Rear-Adm. Sir Rowland Christopher, 1890–1981, vol. VIII

Jerram, Brig. Roy Martyn, 1895–1974, vol. VII

Jerram, Adm. Sir (Thomas Henry) Martyn, 1858–1933, vol. III

Jerrard, Brig. Charles Ian, 1900–1977, vol. VII

Jerred, Sir Walter Tapper, 1864–1918, vol. II

Jerrold, Douglas, 1893–1964, vol. VI

Jerrold, Laurence, 1873–1918, vol. II

Jerrold, Mary, 1877–1955, vol. V

Jerrold, Walter Copeland, 1865–1929, vol. III

Jersey, 7th Earl of, 1845–1915, vol. I

Jersey, 8th Earl of, 1873–1923, vol. II

Jersey, Dowager Countess of; (Margaret Elizabeth), 1849–1945, vol. IV

Jervis, Charles Walter Lionel, 1914–1989, vol. VIII

Jervis, Sir Henry (Felix) Jervis-White-, 5th Bt, 1859–1947, vol. IV

Jervis, Col Herbert Swynfen, 1878–1965, vol. VI

Jervis, Captain Hon. John Cyril Carnegie, 1898–1929, vol. III

Jervis, Col Sir John Henry Jervis-White-, 4th Bt, 1857–1943, vol. IV

Jervis, John Johnstone, 1882–1969, vol. VI

Jervis, Col Nicholas Gordon Mainwaring, 1881–1943, vol. IV

Jervis, Lt-Col Hon. St Leger Henry, 1863–1952, vol. V

Jervis, Hon. William Monk, 1827–1909, vol. I

Jervis, Lt-Col William Swynfen Whitehall P.; *see* Parker-Jervis.

Jervis Read, Simon Holcombe; *see* Read.

Jervis-Smith, Rev. Frederick J., 1848–1911, vol. I

Jervis-White-Jervis, Sir Henry; *see* Jervis, Sir H. F. J. W.

Jervis-White-Jervis, Col Sir John Henry; *see* Jervis.

Jervois, Sir William Francis Drummond, 1821–1897, vol. I

Jervoise, Sir Arthur Henry Clarke-, 3rd Bt, 1856–1902, vol. I

Jervoise, Sir Dudley Alan Lestock Clarke-, 7th Bt, 1876–1933, vol. III

Jervoise, Rear-Adm. Edmund Purefoy Ellis, 1861–1950, vol. IV

Jervoise, Sir Eustace James Clarke, 6th Bt, 1870–1916, vol. II

Jervoise, Francis Henry Tristram, 1872–1959, vol. V

Jervoise, Sir Harry Samuel Cumming Clarke, 5th Bt, 1832–1911, vol. I

Jervoise, Sir Henry Clarke, 4th Bt, 1831–1908, vol. I

Jerwood, Rev. Thomas Frederick, *died* 1926, vol. II

Jesper, Col Norman McKay, 1896–1968, vol. VI

Jesperson, Otto, 1860–1943, vol. IV

Jess, Lt-Gen. Sir Carl Herman, 1884–1948, vol. IV

Jesse, F. Tennyson, *died* 1958, vol. V

Jesse, Col John Leonard, 1876–1944, vol. IV

Jesse, Richard Henry, 1853–1921, vol. II, vol. III

Jesse, William, 1870–1945, vol. IV

Jessel, 1st Baron, 1866–1950, vol. IV

Jessel, 2nd Baron, 1904–1990, vol. VIII

Jessel, Albert Henry, 1864–1917, vol. VII

Jessel, Sir Charles James, 1st Bt, 1860–1928, vol. II

Jessel, David Charles George, 1924–1985, vol. VIII

Jessel, Sir George, 2nd Bt, 1891–1977, vol. VII

Jessel, Sir Richard Hugh, 1896–1979, vol. VII

Jesson, Charles, *born* 1862, vol. II

Jesson, Major Thomas Edward, 1883–1958, vol. V

Jessop, Col Charles Thorp, 1858–1915, vol. I

Jessop, Frederic Hubert, 1882–1969, vol. VI

Jessop, Gilbert Laird, 1874–1955, vol. V

Jessop, Lt-Comdr John de Burgh, 1885–1924, vol. II

Jessop, Joseph Chasser, 1892–1972, vol. VII

Jessop, Thomas Edmund, 1896–1980, vol. VII

Jessop, Thomas Richard, 1837–1903, vol. I

Jessop, Walter Hamilton Hylton, 1853–1917, vol. II

Jessopp, Rev. Augustus, 1823–1914, vol. I

Jessup, Frank William, 1909–1990, vol. VIII

Jessup, Philip Caryl, 1897–1986, vol. VIII

Jette, Sir Louis Amable, 1836–1920, vol. II

Jeudwine, Rev. George Wynne, 1849–1933, vol. III

Jeudwine, Lt-Gen. Sir Hugh Sandham, 1862–1942, vol. IV

Jeudwine, Lt-Col Wilfrid Wynne, 1877–1943, vol. IV

Jeune, Rt Hon. Sir Francis Henry; *see* St Helier, Baron.

Jeune, John Frederic Symons-, 1849–1925, vol. II

Jevons, Frank Byron, 1858–1936, vol. III

Jevons, Herbert Stanley, 1875–1955, vol. V

Jevons, Shirley Byron, *died* 1928, vol. II

Jewell, Maurice Frederick Stewart, 1885–1978, vol. VII

Jewesbury, Reginald Charles, 1878–1971, vol. VII

Jewett, Sarah Orne, 1849–1909, vol. I

Jewkes, John, 1902–1988, vol. VIII

Jewson, Dorothy, 1884–1964, vol. VI

Jewson, Percy William, 1881–1962, vol. VI

Jex-Blake, Arthur John, *died* 1957, vol. V

Jex-Blake, Henrietta, *died* 1953, vol. V
Jex-Blake, Katharine, 1860–1951, vol. V
Jex-Blake, Sophia Louisa, 1840–1912, vol. I
Jex-Blake, Very Rev. Thomas William, 1832–1915, vol. I
Jeyes, Samuel Henry, *died* 1911, vol. I
Jeypore, Samasthanam, Maharaja Sri Sri Sri Ramachendra Deo of, 1893–1931, vol. III
Jha, Sir Mahamahopadhyaya Ganganath, *born* 1871, vol. V
Jhalawar, HH Maharaj Rana Sir Bhawani Singh Bahadur of, 1874–1929, vol. III
Jhalawar, Lieut HH Maharaj Rana Sir Shri Rajendra Singh Ji Dev Bahadur of, 1900–1943, vol. IV
Jibowu, Hon. Sir Olumuyiwa, 1899–1959, vol. V
Jillett, Raymond Leslie, 1925–1983, vol. VIII
Jiménez (Mantacon), Juan Ramón, 1881–1958, vol. V
Jind, Brig. HH Farzand-i-Dilband Rasikh-ul-Itikad Daulat-i-Inglishia, Raja-i-Rajgan Maharaja Sir Ranbir Singh Rajendra Bahadur, 1879–1948, vol. IV
Jinkin, Paymaster Rear-Adm. Robert Alfred, 1876–1944, vol. IV
Jinks, John Leonard, 1929–1987, vol. VIII
Jinnah, Mahomed Ali, 1876–1948, vol. IV
Jivanjee, Sir Yusufali Alibhal Karimjee, 1882–1966, vol. VI
Joachim, Harold Henry, 1868–1938, vol. III
Joachim, Joseph, 1831–1907, vol. I
Joad, Cyril Edwin Mitchinson, 1891–1953, vol. V
Job, William Carson, 1864–1943, vol. IV
Jobberns, Very Rev. Joseph Brewer, 1868–1936, vol. III
Jobling, Geoffrey Lionel, 1889–1965, vol. VI
Jobson, Brig.-Gen. Alexander, 1875–1933, vol. III
Jocelyn, Ada Maria; *see* Roden, Dowager Countess of.
Jocelyn, Captain Arthur Cecil, 1880–1959, vol. V
Jocelyn, Col Julian Robert John, 1852–1929, vol. III
Jödahl, Ole Erik, 1910–1982, vol. VIII
Jodhpur, Maharaja of, 1880–1911, vol. I
Jodhpur, Maharaja of, 1898–1918, vol. II
Jodhpur, Maharaja of, 1903–1947, vol. IV
Jodhpur, Maharaja of, 1923–1952, vol. V
Jodl, Friedrich, 1849–1914, vol. I
Jodrell, Sir Alfred, 4th Bt, 1847–1929, vol. III
Jodrell, Dorothy Lynch R.; *see* Ramsden-Jodrell.
Jodrell, Col Sir Edward Thomas Davenant C.; *see* Cotton-Jodrell.
Jodrell, Lt-Col Henry Ramsden, *died* 1950, vol. IV
Jodrell, Sir Neville Paul, 1858–1932, vol. III
Joel, Dudley Jack Barnato, 1904–1941, vol. IV
Joel, Jack Barnato, 1862–1940, vol. III
Joel, Lt-Col Solomon Barnato, *died* 1931, vol. III
Joel, Woolf, *died* 1898, vol. I
Joelson, Ferdinand Stephen, 1893–1979, vol. VII
Joffre, Marshal Joseph Jacques Césaire, 1852–1931, vol. III
Jogendra Singh, Sir Sardar, 1877–1946, vol. IV
Joglekar, Rao Bahadur Ramchandra Narayan, 1858–1928, vol. II, vol. III
Johannson, Arwid, 1862–1935, vol. III
John XXIII, His Holiness Pope, (Angelo Giuseppe Roncalli), 1881–1963, vol. VI

John, Augustus Edwin, 1878–1961, vol. VI
John, Brynmor Thomas, 1934–1988, vol. VIII
John, Adm. of the Fleet Sir Caspar, 1903–1984, vol. VIII
John, De Witt, 1915–1985, vol. VIII
John, Edward Thomas, 1857–1931, vol. III
John, Sir Edwin, 1856–1935, vol. III
John, Sir Goscombe; *see* John, Sir W. G.
John, Rev. Griffith, 1831–1912, vol. I
John, Robert Michael, 1924–1980, vol. VII
John, Rt Rev. Thomas Charles, 1871–1936, vol. III
John, William, 1878–1955, vol. V
John, Sir (William) Goscombe, 1860–1952, vol. V
John O'London; *see* Whitten, Wilfred.
John Paul I, His Holiness Pope, (Albino Luciani), 1912–1978, vol. VII
Johnes, Herbert Johnes L.; *see* Lloyd-Johnes.
Johnes, Lt-Gen. Sir James H.; *see* Hills-Johnes.
Johns, Alun Morris, *died* 1990, vol. VIII
Johns, Sir Arthur William, 1873–1937, vol. III
Johns, Charles Rowland, 1882–1961, vol. VI
Johns, Rev. Claude Hermann Walter, 1857–1920, vol. II
Johns, Fred, 1868–1932, vol. III
Johns, Horace John, 1890–1961, vol. VI
Johns, John Francis, 1885–1967, vol. VI
Johns, Peter Magrath, 1914–1983, vol. VIII
Johns, Richard Henry, 1878–1960, vol. V
Johns, Rev. Thomas, *died* 1915, vol. I
Johns, Lt-Col Whitfield Glanville, 1877–1941, vol. IV
Johns, Col Sir William Arthur, 1858–1918, vol. II
Johns, Captain William Earl, 1893–1968, vol. VI
Johnson, Alan Woodworth, 1917–1982, vol. VIII
Johnson, Alexander, *died* 1913, vol. I
Johnson, Alice Neville Vowe, *died* 1938, vol. III
Johnson, Gen. Sir Allen Bayard, 1829–1907, vol. I
Johnson, Col Allen Victor, 1871–1939, vol. III
Johnson, Alvin Saunders, 1874–1971, vol. VII
Johnson, Amy, *died* 1941, vol. IV
Johnson, (Arthur) Basil (Noel), 1861–1950, vol. IV
Johnson, Rev. Arthur Henry, 1845–1927, vol. II
Johnson, Col Arthur Morrell, 1887–1946, vol. IV
Johnson, Sir Arthur Palmer, 1865–1944, vol. IV
Johnson, Rev. Aubrey Rodway, 1901–1985, vol. VIII
Johnson, B. S., (Bryan Stanley William Johnson), 1933–1973, vol. VIII
Johnson, Basil; *see* Johnson, A. B. N.
Johnson, Sir Benjamin Sands, 1865–1937, vol. III
Johnson, Bernard, 1868–1935, vol. III
Johnson, Bernard Richard Millar, 1905–1959, vol. V
Johnson, Bertha Jane, 1846–1927, vol. II
Johnson, Borough; *see* Johnson, E. B.
Johnson, Bryan Stanley William; *see* Johnson, B. S.
Johnson, Cecil W.; *see* Webb-Johnson.
Johnson, Dame Celia, (Dame Celia Fleming), 1908–1982, vol. VIII
Johnson, Ven. Charles, 1850–1927, vol. II
Johnson, Charles, 1870–1961, vol. VI
Johnson, Gen. Sir Charles Cooper, 1827–1905, vol. I
Johnson, Adm. Charles Duncan, 1869–1930, vol. III
Johnson, Charles Edward, 1832–1913, vol. I
Johnson, Charles Plumptre, 1853–1938, vol. III
Johnson, Brig. Charles Reginald, 1876–1953, vol. V

Johnson, Charles William Heaton, 1896–1964, vol. VI

Johnson, Christopher Hollis, 1904–1978, vol. VII

Johnson, Claude Goodman, 1864–1926, vol. II

Johnson, Maj.-Gen. Cyril Maxwell R.; *see* Ross-Johnson.

Johnson, Rear-Adm. (S) Cyril Sheldon, 1882–1954, vol. V

Johnson, Cyrus, 1848–1925, vol. II

Johnson, Daniel Cowan, 1915–1969, vol. VI

Johnson, Dennis R.; *see* Ross-Johnson.

Johnson, Donald McIntosh, 1903–1978, vol. VII

Johnson, Hon. Dame Doris Louise, 1921–1983, vol. VIII

Johnson, Dorothy, 1890–1977, vol. VII

Johnson, Maj.-Gen. Dudley Graham, 1884–1975, vol. VII

Johnson, Sir (Edward) Gordon, 5th Bt (*cr* 1755), 1867–1957, vol. V

Johnson, Rt Rev. Edward Ralph, *died* 1911, vol. I

Johnson, Hon. Sir Elliot; *see* Johnson, Hon. Sir W. E.

Johnson, Eric Seymour Thewlis, 1897–1978, vol. VII

Johnson, Eric Townsend, 1875–1942, vol. IV

Johnson, (Ernest) Borough, *died* 1949, vol. IV

Johnson, Sir Ernest James, 1881–1962, vol. VI

Johnson, Eyvind, 1900–1976, vol. VII

Johnson, Francis H.; *see* Hernaman-Johnson.

Johnson, Rev. Frank, *died* 1927, vol. II

Johnson, Maj.-Gen. Frank Ernest, 1861–1945, vol. IV

Johnson, Lt-Col Sir Frank William Frederick, 1866–1943, vol. IV

Johnson, Sir Frederic Charles, 1890–1972, vol. VII

Johnson, Lt-Col Frederic L.; *see* Luttman-Johnson.

Johnson, Major Frederick Colpoys Ormsby, 1858–1932, vol. III

Johnson, Maj.-Gen. Frederick Francis, 1852–1931, vol. III

Johnson, Major Frederick Henry, 1890–1917, vol. II

Johnson, Very Rev. Frederick Wells, vol. III

Johnson, Sir George, 1867–1947, vol. IV

Johnson, George Arthur, 1903–1972, vol. VII

Johnson, Maj.-Gen. Sir George Frederick, 1903–1980, vol. VII

Johnson, George H., *died* 1933, vol. III

Johnson, Hon. Sir George H., 1872–1936, vol. III

Johnson, George Lindsay, 1853–1943, vol. IV

Johnson, George Macness, 1853–1935, vol. III

Johnson, Air Marshal George Owen, 1896–1980, vol. VII

Johnson, George William, 1857–1926, vol. II

Johnson, Sir Gordon; *see* Johnson, Sir E. G.

Johnson, Sir Gordon; *see* Johnson, Sir J. N. G.

Johnson, Brig. Guy Allen Colpoys Ormsby, 1886–1957, vol. V

Johnson, Guy Francis, *died* 1969, vol. VI

Johnson, H. C. Brooke, 1873–1949, vol. IV

Johnson, Harold Cottam, 1903–1973, vol. VII

Johnson, Harold Daintree, 1910–1980, vol. VII

Johnson, Captain Harry Cecil, 1877–1915, vol. I

Johnson, Harry Gordon, 1923–1977, vol. VII

Johnson, Col Harry Hall, 1892–1973, vol. VII

Johnson, Engr Rear-Adm. Harry Herbert, 1875–1961, vol. VI

Johnson, Sir Henry Allen Beaumont, 5th Bt (*cr* 1818), 1887–1965, vol. VI

Johnson, Brig.-Gen. Sir Henry Allen William, 4th Bt (*cr* 1818), 1855–1944, vol. IV

Johnson, Sir Henry Cecil, 1906–1988, vol. VIII

Johnson, Rt Rev. Henry Frank, 1834–1908, vol. I

Johnson, Henry Harrold, 1869–1940, vol. III (A), vol. IV

Johnson, Sir Henry James, 1851–1917, vol. II

Johnson, Henry Langhorne, 1874–1945, vol. IV

Johnson, Herbert, 1856–1949, vol. IV

Johnson, Herschel V., 1894–1966, vol. VI

Johnson, Very Rev. Hewlett, 1874–1966, vol. VI

Johnson, Hiram Warren, 1866–1945, vol. IV

Johnson, Major Hugh Spencer, *died* 1962, vol. VI

Johnson, Rev. James, *died* 1911, vol. I

Johnson, Rt Rev. James, *died* 1917, vol. II

Johnson, John, 1850–1910, vol. I

Johnson, John, 1882–1956, vol. V

Johnson, John Charles S.; *see* Sperrin-Johnson.

Johnson, Sir John Henry, 1826–1909, vol. I

Johnson, Sir (John Nesbitt) Gordon, 1885–1955, vol. V

Johnson, Sir John Paley, 6th Bt (*cr* 1755), 1907–1975, vol. VII

Johnson, Hon. John W. Fordham, 1866–1938, vol. III

Johnson, Rt Rev. Joseph Horsfall, 1847–1928, vol. II, vol. III

Johnson, Lionel Pigot, 1867–1902, vol. I

Johnson, Louis Arthur, 1891–1966, vol. VI

Johnson, Sir (Louis) Stanley, 1869–1937, vol. III

Johnson, Lyndon Baines, 1908–1973, vol. VII

Johnson, Most Rev. Martin Michael, 1899–1975, vol. VII

Johnson, Lt-Col Maurice Eustace Stanley, 1879–1937, vol. III

Johnson, Sir Nelson King, 1892–1954, vol. V

Johnson, Owen, 1878–1952, vol. V

Johnson, Pamela Hansford, (Lady Snow), 1912–1981, vol. VIII

Johnson, Lt-Col Pelham; *see* Johnson, Lt-Col T. P.

Johnson, Sir Philip Bulmer, 1887–1964, vol. VI

Johnson, R. Brimley, 1867–1932, vol. III

Johnson, Raymond, *died* 1944, vol. IV

Johnson, Hon. Sir Reginald Powell C.; *see* Croom-Johnson.

Johnson, Brig.-Gen. Richard Francis, 1852–1938, vol. III

Johnson, Richard Stringer, 1907–1981, vol. VIII

Johnson, Sir Robert Arthur, 1874–1938, vol. III

Johnson, Sir Robert Stewart, 1872–1951, vol. V

Johnson, Robert Underwood, 1853–1937, vol. III

Johnson, Brig.-Gen. Ronald Marr, 1873–1925, vol. II

Johnson, Rev. Rowland Theodore I.; *see* Ingram-Johnson.

Johnson, Sir Samuel George, 1831–1909, vol. I

Johnson, Samuel Waite, *died* 1912, vol. I

Johnson, Seymour Shepherd, 1875–1962, vol. VI

Johnson, Sir Sidney Midlane, 1885–1960, vol. V

Johnson, Sir Stanley; *see* Johnson, Sir L. S.

Johnson, Stanley W.; *see* Webb-Johnson.

Johnson, Stephen Keymer, 1899–1936, vol. III

Johnson, Lt-Col T. Pelham, 1871–1918, vol. II

Johnson, Thomas, 1863–1954, vol. V
Johnson, Thomas Frank, *died* 1972, vol. VII
Johnson, Lt-Col Thomas Gordon Blois-, 1867–1918, vol. II
Johnson, Rt Rev. Thomas Sylvester Claudius, 1873–1955, vol. V
Johnson, Tom Loftin, 1854–1911, vol. I
Johnson, Tom Richard, *died* 1935, vol. III
Johnson, Sir Victor Philipse Hill, 6th Bt, 1905–1986, vol. VIII
Johnson, Sir Walter, 1845–1912, vol. I
Johnson, Sir Walter Burford, 1885–1951, vol. V
Johnson, Lt-Col Walter R.; *see* Russell-Johnson.
Johnson, Wilfrid A.; *see* Athelstan-Johnson.
Johnson, Rev. Wilfrid Harry Cowper, 1879–1967, vol. VI
Johnson, William, 1849–1919, vol. II
Johnson, Rt Rev. William Anthony, 1832–1909, vol. I
Johnson, Sir William Clarence, 1899–1982, vol. VIII
Johnson, Rev. William Cowper, *died* 1916, vol. II
Johnson, Hon. William Dartnell, 1872–1948, vol. IV
Johnson, Hon. Sir (William) Elliot, 1862–1932, vol. III
Johnson, William Evelyn Patrick, 1902–1976, vol. VII
Johnson, Sir William George, 4th Bt (*cr* 1755), 1830–1908, vol. I
Johnson, Rt Rev. William Herbert, 1889–1960, vol. V
Johnson, William Joseph, 1892–1971, vol. VII
Johnson, Rt Hon. Sir William Moore, 1st Bt (*cr* 1909), 1828–1918, vol. II
Johnson, Ven. William Percival, *died* 1928, vol. II
Johnson-Ferguson, Sir Edward; *see* Johnson-Ferguson, Sir J. E.
Johnson-Ferguson, Sir Edward Alexander James, 2nd Bt, 1875–1953, vol. V
Johnson-Ferguson, Sir (Jabez) Edward, 1st Bt, 1849–1929, vol. III
Johnson-Gilbert, Sir Ian Anderson, 1891–1974, vol. VII
Johnson-Marshall, Sir Stirrat Andrew William, 1912–1981, vol. VIII
Johnson-Walsh, Sir Hunt Henry Allen; *see* Walsh.
Johnston, Hon. Lord; Henry Johnston, 1844–1931, vol. III
Johnston, Alexander, 1867–1951, vol. V
Johnston, Alice Crawford, 1902–1976, vol. VII
Johnston, Andrew, 1835–1922, vol. II
Johnston, A(nthony) G(ordon) Knox, 1909–1972, vol. VII
Johnston, Archibald Gilchrist, 1931–1985, vol. VIII
Johnston, Carruthers Melvill, 1909–1970, vol. VI
Johnston, Sir Charles, 1st Bt (*cr* 1916), 1848–1933, vol. III
Johnston, Col Charles Arthur, 1867–1926, vol. II
Johnston, Lt-Col Charles Evelyn, 1878–1922, vol. II
Johnston, Ven. Charles Francis Harding, 1842–1925, vol. II
Johnston, Charles Hampton, 1919–1981, vol. VIII
Johnston, Sir Charles Hepburn, 1912–1986, vol. VIII
Johnston, Christopher Nicholson; *see* Sands, Hon. Lord.
Johnston, David, 1836–1899, vol. I
Johnston, Col David Seton, 1886–1960, vol. V
Johnston, Denis; *see* Johnston, W. D.

Johnston, Hon. Lord; Douglas Harold Johnston, 1907–1985, vol. VIII
Johnston, Col Sir Duncan Alexander, 1847–1931, vol. III
Johnston, Edward, 1872–1944, vol. IV
Johnston, Edward Hamilton, 1885–1942, vol. IV
Johnston, Wing Comdr Ernest Henry, 1885–1938, vol. III
Johnston, Francis Alexander, 1864–1958, vol. V
Johnston, Brig.-Gen. Francis Earl, 1871–1917, vol. II
Johnston, Rt Rev. Francis Featherstonhaugh, 1891–1963, vol. VI
Johnston, Lt-Col Francis Gawen Dillon, 1875–1945, vol. IV
Johnston, Frederick, 1859–1937, vol. III
Johnston, Frederick Mair, 1903–1973, vol. VII
Johnston, Sir Frederick William, 1872–1947, vol. IV
Johnston, Frederick William, 1899–1981, vol. VIII
Johnston, Sir Gaston, 1874–1965, vol. VI (AII)
Johnston, Sir George, 10th Bt, 1845–1921, vol. II
Johnston, George Alexander, 1888–1983, vol. VIII
Johnston, George Douglas, 1886–1971, vol. VII
Johnston, George Francis, 1860–1943, vol. IV
Johnston, George Jameson, 1866–1926, vol. II
Johnston, Maj.-Gen. George Jameson, 1868–1949, vol. IV
Johnston, Brig.-Gen. George Napier, 1867–1947, vol. IV
Johnston, Grace L. Keith, *died* 1929, vol. III
Johnston, Sir Harold Featherston, 1875–1959, vol. V
Johnston, Sir Harry Hamilton, 1858–1927, vol. II
Johnston, Henry; *see* Johnston, Hon. Lord.
Johnston, Col Henry Halcro, 1856–1939, vol. III
Johnston, Henry Joseph, 1858–1906, vol. I
Johnston, Hugh Anthony Stephen, 1913–1967, vol. VI
Johnston, Rev. Hugh William, *died* 1918, vol. II
Johnston, Rt Hon. Sir James, 1849–1924, vol. II
Johnston, Maj.-Gen. James Alexander Deans, 1911–1988, vol. VIII
Johnston, Rev. James B., 1862–1953, vol. V
Johnston, James Osborne, 1921–1978, vol. VII
Johnston, Rt Rev. James Steptoe, 1843–1924, vol. II, vol. III
Johnston, Maj.-Gen. James Thomason, 1860–1938, vol. III
Johnston, James Wellwood, 1900–1958, vol. V
Johnston, Sir John, 1873–1952, vol. V
Johnston, John Alexander Hope, 1871–1938, vol. III
Johnston, Major John Alexander Weir, 1879–1957, vol. V
Johnston, Sir John Barr, 1843–1919, vol. II
Johnston, John Lawson, 1839–1900, vol. I
Johnston, Rev. John Octavius, 1852–1923, vol. II
Johnston, Joseph, 1890–1972, vol. VII
Johnston, Joseph Wilson-, 1876–1933, vol. III
Johnston, Malcolm Campbell-; *see* Campbell-Johnston.
Johnston, Mary, 1870–1936, vol. III
Johnston, Ninian Rutherford Jamieson, 1912–1990, vol. VIII
Johnston, Col Osmond Moncreiff, 1848–1934, vol. III
Johnston, Patrick Murdoch, 1911–1981, vol. VIII
Johnston, Col Percy Herbert, 1851–1932, vol. III

Johnston, Peter Hope, 1915–1982, vol. VIII
Johnston, Philip Mainwaring, 1865–1936, vol. III
Johnston, R. M'Kenzie, 1856–1930, vol. III
Johnston, Reginald Eden, 1847–1922, vol. II
Johnston, Sir Reginald Fleming, 1874–1938, vol. III
Johnston, Major Robert, 1872–1950, vol. IV
Johnston, Brig. Robert, 1879–1956, vol. V
Johnston, Major Robert Douglas, 1882–1959, vol. V
Johnston, Robert Mackenzie, *died* 1918, vol. II
Johnston, Robert Matteson, 1867–1920, vol. II
Johnston, Ronald Carlyle, 1907–1990, vol. VIII
Johnston, Samuel, *born* 1835, vol. II
Johnston, Rev. Samuel Alfred, 1864–1940, vol. III
Johnston, Rt Hon. Thomas, 1881–1965, vol. VI
Johnston, Sir Thomas Alexander, 11th Bt, 1857–1950, vol. IV
Johnston, Sir Thomas Alexander, 12th Bt, 1888–1959, vol. V
Johnston, Sir Thomas Alexander, 13th Bt, 1916–1984, vol. VIII
Johnston, Thomas Baillie, 1883–1960, vol. V
Johnston, Thomas Harvey, 1881–1951, vol. V
Johnston, Brig.-Gen. Thomas Kelly Evans, 1860–1936, vol. III
Johnston, Thomas Kenneth, 1878–1953, vol. V
Johnston, Maj.-Gen. Walter Edward Wilson-, 1878–1948, vol. IV
Johnston, William, 1829–1902, vol. I
Johnston, Col William, 1843–1914, vol. I
Johnston, Sir William, 9th Bt, 1849–1917, vol. II
Johnston, William, 1890–1976, vol. VII
Johnston, Rt Rev. William, 1914–1986, vol. VIII
Johnston, Sir William Campbell, 1860–1938, vol. III
Johnston, (William) Denis, 1901–1984, vol. VIII
Johnston, Sir William Ernest George, 1884–1951, vol. V
Johnston, Lt-Col William Hamilton Hall, *died* 1952, vol. V
Johnston, Lt-Col William James, 1870–1937, vol. III
Johnston, William John, 1869–1940, vol. III (A), vol. IV
Johnston, Rev. William Murdoch, 1847–1905, vol. I
Johnston, Sir William Wallace Stewart, 1887–1962, vol. VI
Johnston-Saint, Captain Peter Johnston, *died* 1974, vol. VII
Johnston-Stewart of Physgill, Adm. Robert Hathorn, 1858–1940, vol. III
Johnstone, Alan Stewart, 1905–1990, vol. VIII
Johnstone, Hon. Sir Alan Vanden-Bempde-, 1858–1932, vol. III
Johnstone, Sir Alexander Howat, 1876–1956, vol. V
Johnstone, Alfred; *see* Johnstone, J. A.
Johnstone, Lt-Col Bede, 1877–1942, vol. IV
Johnstone, Vice-Adm. Charles, 1843–1927, vol. II
Johnstone, Major David Patrick, 1876–1951, vol. V
Johnstone, Sir Donald Campbell, 1857–1920, vol. II
Johnstone, Mrs Dorothy Christian Liddle, 1915–1981, vol. VIII
Johnstone, Brig.-Gen. Francis Buchanan, 1863–1947, vol. IV
Johnstone, Sir Frederic John William, 8th Bt, 1841–1913, vol. I
Johnstone, Frederick John, 1841–1934, vol. III

Johnstone, Rev. George Alexander, 1868–1932, vol. III
Johnstone, Lt-Col George Charles Keppel, 1841–1912, vol. I
Johnstone, Sir George Frederic Thomas Tankerville, 9th Bt, 1876–1952, vol. V
Johnstone, Gerald Ewart, 1906–1973, vol. VII
Johnstone, Rt Hon. Harcourt, 1895–1945, vol. IV
Johnstone, Hilda, 1882–1961, vol. VI
Johnstone, Col Hope, 1868–1939, vol. III
Johnstone, J. Alfred, 1861–1941, vol. IV
Johnstone, James Arthur, 1913–1989, vol. VIII
Johnstone, Major James Henry L'Estrange, 1865–1906, vol. I
Johnstone, Maj.-Gen. James Robert, 1859–1932, vol. III
Johnstone, James William Douglas, 1855–1925, vol. II
Johnstone, Lt John Andrew, 1893–1915, vol. II
Johnstone, John Heywood, 1850–1904, vol. I
Johnstone, John James H.; *see* Hope-Johnstone.
Johnstone, Joseph, 1860–1931, vol. III
Johnstone, Kenneth Roy, 1902–1978, vol. VII
Johnstone, Lewis Martin, 1870–1960, vol. V
Johnstone, Col Montague George, 1848–1928, vol. II
Johnstone, Morris Mackintosh O.; *see* Ord Johnstone.
Johnstone, Maj.-Gen. Ralph E.; *see* Edgeworth-Johnstone.
Johnstone, Ralph William, *died* 1915, vol. I
Johnstone, Maj.-Gen. Reginald Forster, 1904–1976, vol. VII
Johnstone, Robert, 1861–1944, vol. IV
Johnstone, Rev. Robert Cuthbert, 1857–1934, vol. III
Johnstone, Sir Robert J., 1872–1938, vol. III
Johnstone, Maj.-Gen. Robert Maxwell, 1914–1990, vol. VIII
Johnstone, Sir Robert Stewart, 1855–1936, vol. III
Johnstone, Robert William, 1879–1969, vol. VI
Johnstone, Very Rev. Thomas McGimpsey, 1876–1961, vol. VI
Johnstone, Thomas Muir, 1924–1983, vol. VIII
Johnstone, Lt-Col Sir Walter E.; *see* Edgeworth-Johnstone.
Johnstone-Burt, Charles Kingsley, 1891–1973, vol. VII
Johnstone-Douglas, Arthur Henry; *see* Douglas.
Johnstone-Wallace, Denis Bowes, 1894–1960, vol. V
Johore, Sultan of, 1873–1959, vol. V
Johore, Sultan of, 1894–1981, vol. VIII
Joicey, 1st Baron, 1846–1936, vol. III
Joicey, 2nd Baron, 1880–1940, vol. III
Joicey, 3rd Baron, 1881–1966, vol. VI
Joicey, Major James, 1836–1912, vol. I
Joicey, James John, 1870–1932, vol. III
Joicey-Cecil, Lord John Packenham; *see* Cecil.
Joint, Sir (Edgar) James, 1902–1981, vol. VIII
Joint, Sir James; *see* Joint, Sir E. J.
Jokai, Maurus, 1825–1904, vol. I
Joliot-Curie, Jean Frédéric, 1900–1958, vol. V
Joll, Cecil Augustus, *died* 1945, vol. IV
Jolley, Maj.-Gen. Norman Kempe, 1894–1951, vol. V
Jollie, Ethel M.; *see* Colquhoun, E. M.

Jollie, Mrs Tawse; *see* Colquhoun, Ethel M.
Jolliffe, Arthur Ernest, 1871–1944, vol. IV
Jolliffe, John Edward Austin, 1891–1964, vol. VI
Jolliffe, John William, 1924–1985, vol. VIII
Jolliffe, Richard Orlando, 1876–1932, vol. III
Jolliffe, Lt-Col Thomas William, 1873–1944, vol. IV
Jolliffe, Captain Hon. William Sydney Hylton, 1841–1912, vol. I
Jolly, Gen. Sir Alan, 1910–1977, vol. VII
Jolly, Lt-Gen. Sir Gordon Gray, *died* 1962, vol. VI
Jolly, Hugh Reginald, 1918–1986, vol. VIII
Jolly, James, 1902–1968, vol. VI
Jolly, James Hornby, 1887–1972, vol. VII
Jolly, John Catterall, 1887–1950, vol. IV
Jolly, Rev. Canon Reginald Bradley, 1885–1972, vol. VII
Jolly, Thomas Riley, 1849–1929, vol. III
Jolly, William Adam, *died* 1939, vol. III
Jolly, William Alfred, *died* 1955, vol. V
Jolly, Rear-Adm. Sir William E. H., 1887–1961, vol. VI
Jolowicz, Herbert Felix, 1890–1954, vol. V
Joly, Charles Jasper, 1864–1906, vol. I
Joly, John, *died* 1933, vol. III
Joly, John Swift, *died* 1943, vol. IV
Joly de Lotbinière, Maj.-Gen. Alain Chartier, 1862–1944, vol. IV
Joly de Lotbinière, Hon. Sir Henry Gustave, 1829–1908, vol. I
Joly de Lotbinière, Brig.-Gen. Henri Gustave, 1868–1960, vol. V
Joly de Lotbinière, Seymour; *see* de Lotbinière.
Jon, Montague; *see* Dovener, J. M.
Jonas, Harry Marshall, 1866–1939, vol. III
Jones, Abel John, *died* 1949, vol. IV
Jones, Captain Adrian, 1845–1938, vol. III
Jones, Brig. Alan Harvey, 1910–1975, vol. VII
Jones, Alan Trevor, 1901–1979, vol. VII
Jones, Rev. Sir Albert E.; *see* Evans-Jones.
Jones, Rt Hon. Alec; *see* Jones, Rt Hon. T. A.
Jones, Alfred; *see* Jones, E. A.
Jones, (Alfred) Ernest, *died* 1958, vol. V
Jones, Alfred Gilpin, 1824–1906, vol. I
Jones, Sir Alfred Lewis, 1846–1909, vol. I
Jones, Lt-Col Alfred Stowell, 1832–1920, vol. II
Jones, Allan G.; *see* Gwynne-Jones.
Jones, Sir Andrew; *see* Jones, Sir W. J. A.
Jones, Arnold Hugh Martin, 1904–1970, vol. VI
Jones, Rt Hon. Arthur Creech, 1891–1964, vol. VI
Jones, Lt-Col Arthur Daniel D.; *see* Derviche-Jones.
Jones, Arthur Davies, 1897–1980, vol. VII
Jones, Arthur Griffith M.; *see* Maitland-Jones.
Jones, Sir Arthur Probyn P.; *see* Probyn-Jones.
Jones, Arthur R.; *see* Rocyn-Jones.
Jones, Very Rev. Arthur Stuart D.; *see* Duncan-Jones.
Jones, Brig. Arthur Thomas C.; *see* Cornwall-Jones.
Jones, Hon. Sir Austin Ellis Lloyd, 1884–1967, vol. VI
Jones, Austin Ernest D.; *see* Duncan-Jones.
Jones, Sir Barry; *see* Jones, Sir T. B.
Jones, Rev. Basil M., *died* 1925, vol. II
Jones, Rev. Canon Benjamin, 1865–1955, vol. V
Jones, Benjamin George, 1914–1989, vol. VIII

Jones, Captain Benjamin Henry, *died* 1949, vol. IV
Jones, Benjamin Howell, *died* 1913, vol. I
Jones, Benjamin Rowland R.; *see* Rice-Jones.
Jones, Sir (Bennett) Melvill, 1887–1975, vol. VII
Jones, Bernard Mouat, 1882–1953, vol. V
Jones, Sir Bertram Hyde, 1879–1961, vol. VI
Jones, Bobby; *see* Jones, Robert Tyre.
Jones, Major Bryan John, 1874–1918, vol. II
Jones, Sir Brynmor, 1903–1989, vol. VIII
Jones, Rev. Bulkeley Owen, 1824–1914, vol. I
Jones, Sir Cadwaladr Bryner, 1872–1954, vol. V
Jones, Cecil Artimus E.; *see* Evan-Jones.
Jones, Cecil Charles, 1872–1943, vol. IV
Jones, Chapman; *see* Jones, H. C.
Jones, Charles Alfred, 1848–1934, vol. III
Jones, Charles Edward, 1852–1932, vol. III
Jones, Charles Edward Irvine, 1899–1951, vol. V
Jones, Sir Charles Ernest, 1892–1953, vol. V
Jones, Charles Evan William, 1879–1951, vol. V
Jones, Charles Henry, 1857–1936, vol. III
Jones, Lt-Col Charles Herbert, 1865–1953, vol. V
Jones, Charles Hugh LePailleur, *died* 1949, vol. IV
Jones, Charles Jerome, 1847–1929, vol. III
Jones, Major Charles Llewelyn W.; *see* Wynne-Jones.
Jones, Sir Charles Lloyd, 1878–1958, vol. V
Jones, Charles Mark J.; *see* Jenkin-Jones.
Jones, Gen. Sir Charles Phibbs, 1906–1988, vol. VIII
Jones, Sir (Charles) Sydney, 1872–1947, vol. IV
Jones, Rev. Canon Cheslyn Peter Montague, 1918–1987, vol. VIII
Jones, Chester, 1854–1922, vol. II
Jones, Sir Clement Wakefield, 1880–1963, vol. VI
Jones, Clifford T., 1873–1948, vol. IV
Jones, Clinton; *see* Jones, J. C.
Jones, Constance; *see* Jones, E. E. C.
Jones, Col Conwyn M.; *see* Mansel-Jones.
Jones, Sir Crawford Douglas D.; *see* Douglas-Jones.
Jones, Sir Cyril Edgar, 1891–1970, vol. VI
Jones, Rev Cyril L.; *see* Leslie-Jones.
Jones, Lt-Col Sir Cyril Vivian, 1882–1961, vol. VI
Jones, Cyril Walter L.; *see* Lloyd Jones.
Jones, Rev. Daniel, *died* 1934, vol. III
Jones, Daniel, 1881–1967, vol. VI
Jones, Daniel, 1908–1985, vol. VIII
Jones, Rev. David, 1848–1909, vol. I
Jones, David, 1895–1974, vol. VII
Jones, Rev. Canon David A.; *see* Akrill-Jones.
Jones, Rt Hon. Sir David Brynmor, 1852–1921, vol. II
Jones, Sir (David) Fletcher, 1895–1977, vol. VII
Jones, David Jeffreys, 1909–1981, vol. VIII
Jones, Very Rev. David John, 1870–1949, vol. IV
Jones, David Lewis, 1889–1953, vol. V
Jones, Ven. David Morgan, 1874–1950, vol. IV
Jones, D(avid) Prys, 1913–1982, vol. VIII
Jones, David Thomas, 1866–1931, vol. III
Jones, David Thomas, *died* 1963, vol. VI
Jones, Sir David Thomas R.; *see* Rocyn-Jones.
Jones, Rev. Donald, 1857–1925, vol. II
Jones, Douglas Vivian I.; *see* Irvine-Jones.
Jones, Dudley William Carmalt, 1874–1957, vol. V
Jones, E. Alfred, 1872–1943, vol. IV
Jones, E. E. Constance, *died* 1922, vol. II
Jones, Sir E. Wynne C.; *see* Cemlyn-Jones.

Jones, Ebenezer G.; *see* Griffith-Jones.
Jones, Edgar H.; *see* Heath-Jones.
Jones, Edgar Montague, 1866–1938, vol. III
Jones, Sir Edgar Rees, 1878–1962, vol. VI
Jones, Edmund Angus, 1903–1983, vol. VIII
Jones, Sir Edmund Britten, 1888–1953, vol. V
Jones, Rev. Edmund Osborne, 1858–1931, vol. III
Jones, Sir Edward Coley B.; *see* Burne-Jones.
Jones, Rt Rev. Edward Michael G.; *see* Gresford Jones.
Jones, Edward Norton, 1902–1983, vol. VIII
Jones, Col Sir Edward P.; *see* Pryce-Jones.
Jones, Rear-Adm. Edward Pitcairn, 1850–1908, vol. I
Jones, Sir Edward R.; *see* Redmayne-Jones.
Jones, Edward Taylor, 1872–1961, vol. VI
Jones, Edward William M.; *see* Milner-Jones.
Jones, Edwin, 1841–1900, vol. I
Jones, Elfryn, 1913–1983, vol. VIII
Jones, Eli Stanley, 1884–1973, vol. VII
Jones, Elwyn; *see* Baron Elwyn-Jones.
Jones, Sir Elwyn; *see* Jones, Sir W. E. E.
Jones, Enid, (Lady Jones); *see* Bagnold, E.
Jones, Eric Kyffin, 1896–1977, vol. VII
Jones, Sir Eric Malcolm, 1907–1986, vol. VIII
Jones, Sir Eric Newton G.; *see* Griffith-Jones.
Jones, Ernest; *see* Jones, A. E.
Jones, Ernest; *see* Jones, W. E.
Jones, Ernest L.; *see* Lancaster-Jones.
Jones, Ernest Turner, 1897–1981, vol. VIII
Jones, Ernest W.; *see* Whitley-Jones.
Jones, Captain Sir Evan, *died* 1949, vol. IV
Jones, Evan Bonnor H.; *see* Hugh-Jones.
Jones, Evan Bowen, 1869–1940, vol. III
Jones, Evan David, 1903–1987, vol. VIII
Jones, Sir Evan Davies, 1st Bt (*cr* 1917), 1859–1949, vol. IV
Jones, Major Evan Rowland, 1840–1920, vol. II
Jones, Vice-Adm. Everard John H.; *see* Hardman-Jones.
Jones, F. W. D.; *see* Doyle-Jones.
Jones, Sir Felix E. A.; *see* Aylmer-Jones.
Jones, Sir Fletcher; *see* Jones, Sir D. F.
Jones, Francis, 1845–1925, vol. II
Jones, Sir Francis Adolphus, 1861–1947, vol. IV
Jones, Francis Edgar, 1914–1988, vol. VIII
Jones, Frank, 1873–1961, vol. VI
Jones, Lt-Col Frank Aubrey, 1873–1916, vol. II
Jones, Ven. Frank Emlyn, *died* 1935, vol. III
Jones, Frank Ernest, *died* 1974, vol. VII
Jones, Rt Rev. Frank Melville, 1866–1941, vol. IV
Jones, Frank Newling, *died* 1942, vol. IV
Jones, (Frederic) Wood, 1879–1954, vol. V
Jones, Hon. Frederick, 1884–1966, vol. VI
Jones, Frederick Archibald L.; *see* Leslie-Jones.
Jones, Frederick Elwyn; *see* Baron Elwyn-Jones.
Jones, Frederick Herbert P.; *see* Page-Jones.
Jones, Frederick James, 1874–1943, vol. IV
Jones, Sir Frederick John, 1st Bt (*cr* 1919), 1854–1936, vol. III
Jones, Frederick L.; *see* Llewellyn-Jones.
Jones, Frederick Theodore, 1885–1968, vol. VI
Jones, Col Frederick William C.; *see* Caton-Jones.
Jones, Frederick William F.; *see* Farey-Jones.
Jones, Ven. Geoffrey G.; *see* Gower-Jones.

Jones, George, 1844–1921, vol. II
Jones, George Arthur, 1889–1962, vol. VI
Jones, George Basil Harris, 1896–1946, vol. IV
Jones, Sir (George) Basil T.; *see* Todd-Jones.
Jones, Vice-Adm. George Clarence, 1895–1946, vol. IV
Jones, Sir George L.; *see* Legh-Jones.
Jones, George Lewis, 1907–1971, vol. VII
Jones, George Mallory, 1873–1940, vol. III
Jones, George Morgan Edwardes, 1858–1936, vol. III
Jones, George William, 1860–1942, vol. IV
Jones, Sir George William Henry, *died* 1956, vol. V
Jones, Cdre Gerald N., 1885–1958, vol. V
Jones, Rev. Gilbert Basil, 1894–1958, vol. V (A), vol. VI (AI)
Jones, Rev. Gustavus John, 1848–1929, vol. III
Jones, Maj.-Gen. Guy Carleton, 1864–1950, vol. IV
Jones, Maj.-Gen. Sir Guy S.; *see* Salisbury-Jones.
Jones, Gwilym Arthur, 1887–1957, vol. V
Jones, Gwilym Peredur, 1892–1975, vol. VII
Jones, G(wyneth) Ceris, 1906–1987, vol. VIII
Jones, H. Chapman, 1854–1932, vol. III
Jones, Sir Harold Spencer, 1890–1960, vol. V
Jones, Harry, 1866–1925, vol. II
Jones, Harry, 1905–1986, vol. VIII
Jones, Col Harry Balfour, 1866–1952, vol. V
Jones, Harry Davies Campbell, 1863–1935, vol. III
Jones, Harry O.; *see* Orton-Jones.
Jones, Henry, (Cavendish), 1831–1899, vol. I
Jones, Sir Henry, 1852–1922, vol. II
Jones, Sir Henry, 1862–1926, vol. II
Jones, Henry Albert, *died* 1945, vol. IV
Jones, Lt-Gen. Henry Albert H., *died* 1944, vol. IV
Jones, Henry Arthur, 1851–1929, vol. III
Jones, Rev. Henry David, 1842–1925, vol. II
Jones, Very Rev. Henry Donald Maurice S.; *see* Spence-Jones.
Jones, Henry Festing, 1851–1928, vol. II
Jones, Sir Henry Frank Harding, 1906–1987, vol. VIII
Jones, Sir Henry Haydn, 1863–1950, vol. IV
Jones, Ven. Henry James Church, 1870–1941, vol. IV
Jones, Henry Lewis, 1857–1915, vol. I
Jones, Henry M.; *see* Macnaughton-Jones.
Jones, Sir Henry M.; *see* Morris-Jones, Sir J. H.
Jones, Captain Henry Michael, *died* 1916, vol. II
Jones, Bt Col Henry Morris P.; *see* Pryce-Jones.
Jones, Captain Henry Richmund I.; *see* Inigo-Jones.
Jones, Sir Henry S.; *see* Stuart-Jones.
Jones, Brig.-Gen. Herbert Arthur, *died* 1955, vol. V
Jones, Very Rev. Herbert Arthur, *died* 1969, vol. VI
Jones, Rt Rev. Herbert Edward, 1861–1920, vol. II
Jones, Air Cdre Herbert George, 1884–1979, vol. VII
Jones, Rt Rev. Herbert Gresford, 1870–1958, vol. V
Jones, Herbert Lee Jackson, 1870–1936, vol. III
Jones, Herbert Riversdale M.; *see* Mansel-Jones.
Jones, Sir Hildreth G.; *see* Glyn-Jones.
Jones, Howard Parker, 1863–1924, vol. II
Jones, Gen. Sir Howard Sutton, 1835–1912, vol. I
Jones, Rev. Howard W.; *see* Watkin-Jones.
Jones, Howell G.; *see* Gwynne-Jones.
Jones, Ven. Hugh, 1815–1897, vol. I
Jones, Hugh E.; *see* Emlyn-Jones.
Jones, Hugh Ferguson, 1913–1979, vol. VII

Jones, Air Marshal Sir Humphrey E.; *see* Edwardes Jones.

Jones, Humphrey Lloyd, 1910–1983, vol. VIII

Jones, Humphrey Stanley Herbert, *died* 1902, vol. I

Jones, Ven. Humphrey Tudor Morrey, *died* 1936, vol. III

Jones, Huw M.; *see* Morris-Jones.

Jones, Idris Deane, 1899–1947, vol. IV

Jones, Ifano, 1865–1955, vol. V

Jones, Maj.-Gen. Inigo Richmund, 1848–1914, vol. I

Jones, Isaac, 1883–1968, vol. VI

Jones, Ivan Ellis, 1903–1984, vol. VIII

Jones, J. Clinton, 1848–1936, vol. III

Jones, J. Morgan, 1873–1946, vol. IV

Jones, Jack, 1884–1970, vol. VI

Jones, Sir James, 1895–1962, vol. VI

Jones, James, 1921–1977, vol. VII

Jones, James Edmund, 1866–1939, vol. III

Jones, Sir James Edward, 1843–1922, vol. II

Jones, James Idwal, 1900–1982, vol. VIII

Jones, James Ilston, 1911–1976, vol. VII

Jones, Gp Captain James Ira Thomas, 1896–1960, vol. V

Jones, Lt-Col James Walker, 1887–1933, vol. III

Jones, Ven. James William Percy, 1881–1980, vol. VII

Jones, James William W.; *see* Webb-Jones.

Jones, John Arthur, 1867–1939, vol. III

Jones, Sir John Bowen Bowen-, 1st Bt (*cr* 1911), 1840–1925, vol. II

Jones, Rt Rev. John Charles, 1904–1956, vol. V

Jones, John Cyril, 1899–1990, vol. VIII

Jones, Rev. John Daniel, 1865–1942, vol. IV

Jones, John David Rheinallt, 1884–1953, vol. V

Jones, Paymaster Rear-Adm. John Edward, 1866–1948, vol. IV

Jones, Sir John Edward L.; *see* Lennard-Jones.

Jones, John Emlyn E.; *see* Emlyn-Jones.

Jones, John Harry, 1881–1973, vol. VII

Jones, John Henry, 1894–1962, vol. VI

Jones, Sir (John) Henry M.; *see* Morris-Jones.

Jones, Rev. John Hugh Watkins, 1862–1937, vol. III

Jones, Col John Hyndman H.; *see* Howell-Jones.

Jones, John Iorwerth, *born* 1901, vol. VIII

Jones, Rev. J(ohn) Ithel, 1911–1980, vol. VII (AII)

Jones, Rev. John James, *died* 1934, vol. III

Jones, Col Sir John James, 1845–1938, vol. III

Jones, John Joseph, 1873–1941, vol. IV

Jones, John Joseph Casimer, 1839–1929, vol. III

Jones, John Kenyon Netherton, 1912–1977, vol. VII

Jones, John L.; *see* Lees-Jones.

Jones, Ven. John Lloyd-, 1848–1934, vol. III

Jones, (John) Mervyn (Guthrie) G.; *see* Griffith-Jones.

Jones, John Morgan, 1903–1989, vol. VIII

Jones, Sir John Morris-, 1864–1929, vol. III

Jones, Sir John P.; *see* Prichard-Jones.

Jones, John Richard, 1881–1955, vol. V

Jones, (John) Share, *died* 1950, vol. IV

Jones, John Viriamu, 1856–1901, vol. I

Jones, John Walter, 1892–1973, vol. VII

Jones, Air Chief Marshal Sir John Whitworth, 1896–1981, vol. VIII

Jones, Joseph, *died* 1948, vol. IV

Jones, Joseph, 1890–1979, vol. VII

Jones, Rev. Josiah Towyn, 1858–1925, vol. II

Jones, Dame Katharine Henrietta, 1888–1967, vol. VI

Jones, Keith M.; *see* Miller Jones.

Jones, Kennedy; *see* Jones, N. K.

Jones, Captain Kingsmill Williams, 1875–1918, vol. II

Jones, Lawrence, *died* 1949, vol. IV

Jones, Sir Lawrence Evelyn, 5th Bt (*cr* 1831), 1885–1969, vol. VI

Jones, Sir Lawrence John, 4th Bt (*cr* 1831), 1857–1954, vol. V

Jones, Leonard Ivan S.; *see* Stranger-Jones.

Jones, Maj.-Gen. Leslie Cockburn, 1870–1960, vol. V

Jones, Rev. Lewis, 1842–1928, vol. II

Jones, Maj.-Gen. Lewis, 1862–1935, vol. III

Jones, Sir Lewis, 1884–1968, vol. VI

Jones, Lewis; *see* Jones, G. L.

Jones, Lewis; *see* Jones, W. L.

Jones, Leycester Hudson L.; *see* Leslie-Jones.

Jones, Lionel P.; *see* Powys-Jones.

Jones, Rt Rev. Llewellyn, 1840–1918, vol. II

Jones, Llewellyn Archer A.; *see* Atherley-Jones.

Jones, Col Llewellyn Murray, 1871–1946, vol. IV

Jones, Llewellyn Rodwell, 1881–1947, vol. IV

Jones, Llewelyn Arthur H.; *see* Hugh-Jones.

Jones, Maj.-Gen. Llewelyn W.; *see* Wansbrough-Jones.

Jones, Very Rev. Llewelyn W.; *see* Wynne-Jones.

Jones, Rev. Lloyd Timothy, *died* 1920, vol. II

Jones, Brig.-Gen. Lumley Owen Williames, 1876–1918, vol. II

Jones, Sir Lyman Melvin, 1843–1917, vol. II

Jones, Mrs Mabel Mary Cheveley; *see* Rayner, M. M. C.

Jones, Martin, 1897–1979, vol. VII

Jones, Marvin, *died* 1976, vol. VII

Jones, Dame Mary Latchford Kingsmill, *died* 1968, vol. VI

Jones, Rev. Maurice, 1863–1957, vol. V

Jones, Maurice; *see* Jones, S. M.

Jones, Sir Melvill; *see* Jones, Sir B. M.

Jones, Mervyn; *see* Jones, T. M.

Jones, Lt-Col Michael Durwas Goring-, 1866–1919, vol. II

Jones, Rt Rev. Michael G.; *see* Gresford Jones, Rt Rev. E. M.

Jones, Montagu H.; *see* Handfield-Jones.

Jones, Brig.-Gen. Morey Q.; *see* Quayle-Jones.

Jones, Morgan, 1885–1939, vol. III

Jones, Morgan; *see* Jones, J. M.

Jones, Morgan Philips G.; *see* Griffith-Jones.

Jones, Norman Edward, 1904–1972, vol. VII

Jones, Rt Rev. Norman Sherwood, 1911–1951, vol. V

Jones, Captain Oscar Philip, 1898–1980, vol. VII

Jones, Captain Owen, 1866–1941, vol. IV

Jones, Owen Daniel, 1861–1951, vol. V

Jones, Sir Owen Haddon W.; *see* Wansbrough-Jones.

Jones, Owen Thomas, 1878–1967, vol. VI

Jones, Parry William John, 1891–1963, vol. VI

Jones, Patrick Nicholas Hill, 1864–1934, vol. III

Jones, Sir Pendrill Charles V.; *see* Varrier-Jones.

Jones, Penrhyn Grant, 1878–1945, vol. IV

Jones, Major Percy Arnold Lloyd-, 1876–1916, vol. II

Jones, Maj.-Gen. Percy George C.; *see* Calvert-Jones.

Jones, Rev. Percy Herbert, 1864–1941, vol. IV

Jones, Percy Mansell, 1889–1968, vol. VI

Jones, Hon. Percy Sydney T.; *see* Twentyman-Jones.

Jones, Sir Peter (Fawcett) Benton, 3rd Bt (*cr* 1919), 1911–1972, vol. VII

Jones, Peter Howard, 1911–1975, vol. VII

Jones, Philip Asterley, 1914–1978, vol. VII

Jones, Sir Philip B.; *see* Burne-Jones.

Jones, Sir Philip Frederick, 1912–1983, vol. VIII

Jones, Col Philip Reginald B.; *see* Bence-Jones.

Jones, Sir Philip Sydney, 1836–1918, vol. II

Jones, Sir Pryce P.; *see* Pryce-Jones.

Jones, Sir Pryce Victor P.; *see* Pryce-Jones.

Jones, Ranald Montagu H.; *see* Handfield-Jones.

Jones, Raymond R.; *see* Ray-Jones.

Jones, Reginald Trevor, 1888–1974, vol. VII

Jones, Sir Reginald W.; *see* Watson-Jones.

Jones, Rev. Richard Charles Stuart, *died* 1941, vol. IV

Jones, Rev. Canon Richard E.; *see* Evan-Jones.

Jones, Richard Francis L.; *see* Lloyd Jones.

Jones, Lt-Col Richard Godfrey, 1855–1934, vol. III

Jones, Rev. Richard Thomas, *died* 1917, vol. II

Jones, Rt Rev. Richard William, *died* 1953, vol. V

Jones, Sir Robert, 1st Bt (*cr* 1926), 1858–1933, vol. III

Jones, Sir Robert Armstrong-, 1857–1943, vol. IV

Jones, Robert Edmond, 1887–1954, vol. V

Jones, Brig. Robert Llewellyn J.; *see* Jephson-Jones.

Jones, Robert Noble, 1864–1942, vol. IV

Jones, Maj.-Gen. Robert Owen, 1837–1926, vol. II

Jones, Air Marshal Sir R(obert) Owen, 1901–1972, vol. VII

Jones, Robert Thomas, *died* 1940, vol. III

Jones, Robert Tyre, (Bobby), 1902–1971, vol. VII

Jones, Robert Walter, 1890–1951, vol. V

Jones, Sir Roderick, 1877–1962, vol. VI

Jones, Maj.-Gen. Roderick Idrisyn, 1895–1970, vol. VI

Jones, Comdr Ronald L.; *see* Langton-Jones.

Jones, Ronald Owen Lloyd A.; *see* Armstrong-Jones.

Jones, Royston Oscar, 1925–1974, vol. VII

Jones, Rufus M., 1863–1948, vol. IV

Jones, Rev. S. M.; *see* Martin-Jones.

Jones, S. Maurice, *died* 1932, vol. III

Jones, Sir Samuel Bankole-, 1911–1981, vol. VIII

Jones, Sir Samuel Owen, 1905–1985, vol. VIII

Jones, Share; *see* Jones, J. S.

Jones, Siriol (Mary Aprille) H.; *see* Hugh-Jones.

Jones, Rev. Spencer John, 1857–1943, vol. IV

Jones, Stanley Wilson, 1888–1962, vol. VI

Jones, Sir Sydney; *see* Jones, Sir C. S.

Jones, Sydney, 1911–1990, vol. VIII

Jones, Hon. Sydney Twentyman, 1849–1913, vol. I

Jones, Sir (Tom) Barry, 2nd Bt (*cr* 1917), 1888–1952, vol. V

Jones, Col Theophilus Percy, 1866–1934, vol. III

Jones, Rev. Canon Thomas, 1839–1927, vol. II

Jones, Sir Thomas, 1870–1945, vol. IV

Jones, Thomas, 1870–1955, vol. V

Jones, Captain Thomas Alban, 1869–1945, vol. IV

Jones, Sir Thomas Artemus, *died* 1943, vol. IV

Jones, Thomas Boughton B.; *see* Bovell-Jones.

Jones, Thomas E.; *see* Elder-Jones.

Jones, Rt Rev. Thomas Edward, 1903–1972, vol. VII

Jones, Sir Thomas George, 1881–1948, vol. IV

Jones, Thomas Gwynn, 1871–1949, vol. IV

Jones, Thomas Isaac M.; *see* Mardy Jones.

Jones, Rev. Thomas Jesse, *died* 1930, vol. III

Jones, Sir Thomas M.; *see* Miller-Jones.

Jones, (Thomas) Mervyn, 1910–1989, vol. VIII

Jones, Thomas Rees, 1863–1938, vol. III

Jones, Thomas Ridge, 1840–1924, vol. II

Jones, Thomas Rupert, 1819–1911, vol. I

Jones, Rt Rev. Thomas Sherwood, 1872–1972, vol. VII

Jones, Thomas William; *see* Baron Maelor.

Jones, Tom, 1908–1985, vol. VIII

Jones, Tom, 1908–1990, vol. VIII

Jones, Tom Neville W.; *see* Wynne-Jones.

Jones, Sir Tracy French Gavin, 1872–1953, vol. V

Jones, Rt Hon. (Trevor) Alec, 1924–1983, vol. VIII

Jones, Vernon Stanley V.; *see* Vernon-Jones.

Jones, Sir Vincent L.; *see* Lloyd-Jones.

Jones, Sir Vincent Strickland, 1874–1967, vol. VI

Jones, W. Lewis, 1866–1922, vol. II

Jones, Walter, 1846–1924, vol. II

Jones, Sir Walter Benton, 2nd Bt (*cr* 1919), 1880–1967, vol. VI

Jones, Lt-Col Walter Dally, 1855–1926, vol. II

Jones, Lt-Col Walter H.; *see* Howel-Jones.

Jones, Captain Walter Henry Clulee, 1899–1932, vol. III

Jones, W(alter) Idris, 1900–1971, vol. VII

Jones, Walter L.; *see* Lindley-Jones.

Jones, Lt-Col Walter Thomas Cresswell, 1874–1923, vol. II

Jones, Wendell Phillips, 1866–1944, vol. IV

Jones, William, *died* 1915, vol. I

Jones, Sir William, 1888–1961, vol. VI

Jones, William Brittain, 1834–1912, vol. I

Jones, Rev. William David, 1909–1976, vol. VII

Jones, Very Rev. William Edward, 1897–1974, vol. VII

Jones, Sir (William) Elwyn (Edwards), 1904–1989, vol. VIII

Jones, William Ernest, 1867–1957, vol. V (A)

Jones, (William) Ernest, 1895–1973, vol. VII

Jones, William Everard Tyldesley, 1874–1938, vol. III

Jones, Rev. William G.; *see* Griffith-Jones.

Jones, William Garmon, 1884–1937, vol. III

Jones, Hon. Sir William H.; *see* Hall-Jones.

Jones, William Henry, 1873–1944, vol. IV

Jones, Sir William Henry H.; *see* Hyndman-Jones.

Jones, William Henry Samuel, 1876–1963, vol. VI

Jones, Sir William Hollingworth Quayle, 1854–1925, vol. II

Jones, Rev. William Hudson M.; *see* Macnaughton-Jones.

Jones, William Hugh, 1866–1960, vol. V

Jones, William Jenkyn, 1867–1934, vol. III

Jones, Sir William John, 1866–1938, vol. III

Jones, Sir (William John) Andrew, 1889–1971, vol. VII

Jones, (William) Kennedy, 1865–1921, vol. II
Jones, William Llewellyn, 1881–1950, vol. IV
Jones, William Morris, 1889–1963, vol. VI
Jones, Lt-Col William Nathaniel, 1858–1934, vol. III
Jones, William Neilson, 1883–1974, vol. VII
Jones, William Richard, 1880–1970, vol. VI
Jones, William Ronald Rees; see Rhys, Keidrych.
Jones, Rt Rev. William S.; see Stanton-Jones.
Jones, Sir William Samuel G.; see Glyn-Jones.
Jones, William Stephen, 1913–1981, vol. VIII
Jones, William Sydney, 1888–1959, vol. V
Jones, William Thorpe, 1864–1932, vol. III
Jones, William Tinnion, 1927–1981, vol. VIII
Jones, William Tudor, 1865–1946, vol. IV
Jones, Most Rev. William West, 1838–1908, vol. I
Jones, Rt Rev. William Wynn, 1900–1950, vol. IV
Jones, Sir William Y.; see Yarworth-Jones.
Jones, Wood; see Jones, F. W.
Jones-Davies, Henry, 1870–1955, vol. V
Jones Mitton, Col George, 1860–1949, vol. IV
Jones-Parry, Rear-Adm. John Parry, 1829–1920, vol. II
Jones-Roberts, Kate Winifred, 1889–1971, vol. VII
Jones-Vaughan, Maj.-Gen. Hugh Thomas, 1841–1916, vol. II
Jonnart, Celestin Auguste, 1857–1927, vol. II
Jonsson, Einar, 1874–1954, vol. V
Jooste, Gerhardus Petrus, 1904–1990, vol. VIII
Jopling, Louise, 1843–1933, vol. III
Jopling-Rowe, Louise; see Jopling, Louise.
Jopp, Col John, 1940–1923, vol. II
Jopson, Sir Keith; see Jopson, Sir R. K.
Jopson, Norman Brooke, 1890–1969, vol. VI
Jopson, Sir (Reginald) Keith, 1898–1957, vol. V
Jordan, Alfred Charles, 1872–1956, vol. V
Jordan, Most Rev. Anthony, 1901–1982, vol. VIII
Jordan, David Starr, 1851–1931, vol. III
Jordan, Edwin Oakes, 1866–1926, vol. II, vol. III
Jordan, Elizabeth, died 1947, vol. IV
Jordan, Sir Frederick Richard, 1881–1949, vol. IV
Jordan, Rev. George, 1876–1936, vol. III
Jordan, Heinrich Ernst Karl, 1861–1959, vol. V
Jordan, Helen; see Ashton, H.
Jordan, Herbert William, 1874–1947, vol. IV
Jordon, Rev. Preb. Hugh, 1906–1984, vol. VIII
Jordan, Humfrey Robertson, 1885–1963, vol. VI
Jordan, Rev. Canon James Henry, 1882–1959, vol. V
Jordan, Jeremiah, died 1911, vol. I
Jordan, Rt Hon. Sir John Newell, 1852–1925, vol. II
Jordan, Maj.-Gen. Joseph, 1826–1899, vol. I
Jordan, Karl; see Jordan, H. E. K.
Jordan, Louis Arnold, 1892–1964, vol. VI
Jordan, Rev. Louis Henry, 1855–1923, vol. II
Jordan, Philip Furneaux, 1902–1951, vol. V
Jordan, Lt-Col Richard Price, 1869–1963, vol. VI
Jordan, Sara M., (Mrs Penfield Mower), 1884–1959, vol. V
Jordan, Rev. W. G., 1852–1939, vol. III
Jordan, Wilbur Kitchener, 1902–1980, vol. VII
Jordan, William Edward, 1869–1938, vol. III
Jordan, William George, 1864–1928, vol. II
Jordan, Rt Hon. Sir William Joseph, died 1959, vol. V
Jordan Lloyd, Dorothy, 1889–1946, vol. IV
Jordan Malkin, Harold; see Malkin.

Jorden, John M., died 1907, vol. I
Jorisch, Norah; see Lofts, N.
Jory, Norman Adams, 1896–1965, vol. VI
Jory, Philip John, 1892–1973, vol. VII
Josa, Ven. Fortunato Pietro Luigi, 1851–1922, vol. II
Joscelyne, Rt Rev. Albert Ernest, 1866–1945, vol. IV
Jose, Captain Arthur Wilberforce, 1863–1934, vol. III
Jose, Very Rev. George Herbert, 1868–1956, vol. V
Jose, Sir Ivan Bede, 1893–1969, vol. VI (AII)
Joseph, Delissa, 1859–1927, vol. II
Joseph, Sir Francis L'Estrange, 1st Bt, 1870–1951, vol. V
Joseph, Horace William Brindley, 1867–1943, vol. IV
Joseph, Sir Maxwell, 1910–1982, vol. VIII
Joseph, Michael, 1897–1958, vol. V
Joseph, Hon. Mrs Michael; see Hastings, Hon. Anthea.
Joseph, Rev. Morris, 1848–1930, vol. III
Joseph, Sir Norman; see Joseph, Sir S. N.
Joseph, Sir Samuel George, 1888–1944, vol. IV
Joseph, Sir (Samuel) Norman, 1908–1974, vol. VII
Joshi, Rev. Canon D. L., 1864–1923, vol. II
Joshi, Narayan Malhar, 1879–1955, vol. V
Joske, Hon. Sir Percy Ernest, 1895–1981, vol. VIII
Joslin, David Maelgwyn, 1925–1970, vol. VI
Joslin, Ivy Collin, 1900–1986, vol. VIII
Joslin, Maj.-Gen. Stanley William, 1899–1982, vol. VIII
Josselyn, Col John, 1872–1943, vol. IV
Joubert de la Ferte, Air Chief Marshal Sir Philip Bennet, died 1965, vol. V
Jouhaux, Léon, 1879–1954, vol. V
Joulain, Rt Rev. Henry, 1852–1919, vol. II
Joules, Horace, 1902–1977, vol. VII
Jourdain, Lt-Col Charles Edward Arthur, 1869–1918, vol. II
Jourdain, Eleanor Frances, died 1924, vol. II
Jourdain, Rev. Francis C. R., died 1940, vol. III
Jourdain, Lt-Col Henry Francis Newdigate, 1872–1968, vol. VI
Jourdain, Sir Henry John, 1835–1901, vol. I
Jourdan, Rev. George Viviliers, died 1955, vol. V
Jowers, Reginald Francis, 1861–1934, vol. III
Jowett, Edmund, 1858–1936, vol. III
Jowett, Rt Hon. Frederick William, 1864–1944, vol. IV
Jowett, Rev. John Henry, 1864–1923, vol. II
Jowett, Percy Hague, 1882–1955, vol. V
Jowett, Ronald Edward, 1901–1986, vol. VIII
Jowitt, 1st Earl, 1885–1957, vol. V
Jowitt, Frederick McCulloch, 1868–1919, vol. II
Jowitt, Harold, 1893–1963, vol. VI
Jowsey, Col Thomas, 1853–1934, vol. III
Joy, Albert B.; see Bruce-Joy.
Joy, David, died 1903, vol. I
Joy, Edith Katharine Spicer; see Prescott, E. Livingston.
Joy, Sir George Andrew, 1896–1974, vol. VII
Joy, George William, 1844–1925, vol. II
Joy, Henry Holmes, died 1934, vol. III
Joyce, Alec Houghton, 1894–1982, vol. VIII
Joyce, Archibald, 1873–1963, vol. VI
Joyce, Rt Rev. Edward Michael, 1907–1964, vol. VI

Joyce, Rev. Frederick Wayland, 1852–1934, vol. III
Joyce, Rt Rev. Gilbert Cunningham, 1866–1942, vol. IV
Joyce, Maj.-Gen. Hayman John H.; *see* Hayman-Joyce.
Joyce, James, 1882–1941, vol. IV
Joyce, Rev. James Barclay, *died* 1934, vol. III
Joyce, John Hall, 1906–1982, vol. VIII
Joyce, Rt Hon. Sir Matthew Ingle, 1839–1930, vol. III
Joyce, Patrick Weston, 1827–1914, vol. I
Joyce, Lt-Col Pierce Charles, *died* 1965, vol. VI
Joyce, Rt Rev. Mgr T. J., *died* 1947, vol. IV
Joyce, Thomas Athol, 1878–1942, vol. IV
Joyce, Thomas Heath, 1850–1925, vol. II
Joyner, Robert Batson, 1844–1919, vol. II
Joynt, John William, 1852–1933, vol. III
Joynt, Rev. Robert Charles, 1856–1938, vol. III
Jubb, Edwin Charles, 1883–1978, vol. VII
Juda, Hans Peter, 1904–1975, vol. VII
Judd, Alfred, *died* 1932, vol. III
Judd, Charles Wilfred, 1896–1974, vol. VII
Judd, Sir George, 1840–1909, vol. I
Judd, George William, *born* 1854, vol. II
Judd, Harold Godfrey, 1878–1961, vol. VI
Judd, John Basil Thomas, 1909–1983, vol. VIII
Judd, John Wesley, 1840–1916, vol. II
Judd, Thomas Langley, 1880–1945, vol. IV
Judd, Walter Albert, 1861–1931, vol. III
Jude, Sir Norman Lane, 1905–1975, vol. VII
Judge, Mark Hayler, 1847–1927, vol. II
Judge, Captain Spencer Francis, 1861–1911, vol. I
Judges, Arthur Valentine, 1898–1973, vol. VII
Judkins, Rev. Eimer, 1855–1940, vol. III
Judson, Harry Pratt, 1849–1927, vol. II
Jugmohandas Varjivandas, Sir, 1869–1934, vol. III
Juin, Alphonse Pierre, 1888–1967, vol. VI
Jukes, E(rnest) Martin, 1909–1982, vol. VIII
Jukes, John Edwin Clapham, 1878–1955, vol. V
Jukes, Richard Starr, 1906–1987, vol. VIII
Jukes-Browne, Alfred John, 1851–1914, vol. I
Jukes Hughes, Captain Edward Glyn de Styrap, 1883–1966, vol. VI
Juler, Frank Anderson, 1880–1962, vol. VI
Juler, Henry Edward, *died* 1921, vol. II
Julian, Ernest Laurence, *died* 1915, vol. I
Julian, Sir Ivor; *see* Julian, Sir K. I.
Julian, Rev. John, 1839–1913, vol. I
Julian, Sir (Kenneth) Ivor, 1895–1971, vol. VII
Julian, Maj.-Gen. Sir Oliver Richard Archer, 1863–1925, vol. II
Julius, Most Rev. Churchill, 1847–1938, vol. III
Julius, Sir George Alfred, 1873–1946, vol. IV
Julius, Very Rev. John Awdry, 1874–1956, vol. V
Jullian, Camille, 1859–1933, vol. III
Julyan, Sir Penrose Goodchild, 1816–1907, vol. I
Julyan, Lt-Col William Leopold, 1888–1972, vol. VII
Juma, Sa'ad, *born* 1916
Junagadh, Nawab Saheb of, 1900–1959, vol. V
Junagarh, HH Sir Rasul Khanji Muhabat Khanji, Nawab of, *died* 1911, vol. I
Jung, Carl Gustav, 1875–1961, vol. VI
Jungwirth, Sir John; *see* Jungwirth, Sir W. J.
Jungwirth, Sir (William) John, 1897–1981, vol. VIII

Jupp, Rev. Canon, *died* 1911, vol. I
Jupp, Clifford Norman, 1919–1989, vol. VIII
Jury, Col Edward Cotton, 1881–1966, vol. VI
Jury, Sir William Frederick, 1870–1944, vol. IV
Jusserand, Jean Adrien Antoine Jules, 1855–1932, vol. III
Just, Sir Hartmann, 1854–1929, vol. III
Justice, Maj.-Gen. Henry Annesley, 1832–1908, vol. I
Justice, James Norval Harald R.; *see* Robertson-Justice.
Justice, Maj.-Gen. William Clive, 1835–1908, vol. I
Juta, Sir Henry Hubert, 1857–1930, vol. III

K

Kadoorie, Sir Ellis, 1865–1922, vol. II
Kadoorie, Sir Elly, 1867–1944, vol. IV
Kagwa, Sir Apolo, *died* 1927, vol. II
Kahle, Paul Ernest, 1875–1964, vol. VI
Kahn, Baron (Life Peer), Richard Ferdinand Kahn, 1905–1989, vol. VIII
Kahn-Freund, Sir Otto, 1900–1979, vol. VII
Khan, Otto Hermann, 1867–1934, vol. III
Kaine, Hon. John Charles, 1854–1921, vol. II
Kaiser, Henry J., 1882–1967, vol. VI
Kaiser Shamsher Jang Bahadur Rana, HH Commanding-Gen. Sir, 1892–1964, vol. VI
Kalat, Wali of, *died* 1931, vol. III
Kalat, HH Sir Beglar Begi Nawab Bahadur Mir Azam Jan, *died* 1933, vol. III
Kaldor, Baron (Life Peer); Nicholas Kaldor, 1908–1986, vol. VIII
Kalergi, Richard N. C.; *see* Coudenhove-Kalergi.
Kalinin, Mikhail Ivanovich, 1875–1946, vol. IV
Kalisch, Alfred, 1863–1933, vol. III
Kallas, Madame Aino Julia Maria, *died* 1956, vol. V
Kallas, Oskar Philipp, 1868–1946, vol. IV
Kalmus, Herbert Thomas, 1881–1963, vol. VI
Kamâl, Gazi Mustafa; *see* Atatürk, K.
Kamal-ud-Din, Khwaja, 1870–1932, vol. III
Kamat, B. S., 1871–1945, vol. IV
Kambal, Miralai (Col) Beshir Bey, 1855–1919, vol. II
Kamphausen, Adolf Hermann Heinrich, 1829–1909, vol. I
Kandathil, Most Rev. Augustine, 1874–1956, vol. V
Kandel, Isaac Leon, 1881–1965, vol. VI
Kane, Albert Edmond, 1867–1949, vol. IV
Kane, Edward William, *died* 1934, vol. III
Kane, Adm. Sir Henry Coey, 1843–1917, vol. II
Kane, Robert Romney, 1842–1902, vol. I
Kane, Captain Robert Romney Godred, 1888–1918, vol. II
Kane, William Francis de Vismes, 1840–1918, vol. II
Kania, Hon. Sir Harilal Jekisundas, 1890–1951, vol. V
Kanika, Raja of, 1881–1948, vol. IV
Kantaraj Urs, Sir Mysore, 1870–1923, vol. II
Kanthack, Alfred Antunes, 1863–1898, vol. I
Kanthack, Francis Edgar, 1872–1961, vol. VI
Kantorovich, Leonid Vitaljevich, 1912–1986, vol. VIII

Kantorowicz, Hermann, 1877–1940, vol. III
Kapadia, Shaporji Aspaniarji, 1857–1941, vol. IV
Kapitza, Peter Leonidovich, 1894–1984, vol. VIII
Kapp Edmond X., 1890–1978, vol. VII
Kapp, Gisbert, died 1922, vol. II
Kapp, Helen, 1907–1978, vol. VII
Kapp, Reginald Otto, 1885–1966, vol. VI
Kapurthala, HH Maharajah Raja-i-Rajgan of, 1872–1949, vol. IV
Karajan, Herbert von; see von Karajan.
Karasek, Franz, 1924–1986, vol. VIII
Karanjia, Sir Behram Narosji, 1876–1957, vol. V
Karauli, HH Maharaja Dhiraj Sir Bhanwar Pal, Deo Bahadur, Yadukul Chandra Bhal, 1864–1927, vol. II
Karauli, Maharaja of, HH Maharaja Sir Bhom Pal Deo Bahadur Yadukul Chandra Bhal, 1866–1947, vol. IV
Karimjee, Sir Tayabali Hassanali Alibhoy, 1897–1987, vol. VIII
Karkaria, R. P., 1869–1919, vol. II
Karloff, Boris (William Henry Pratt), 1887–1969, vol. VI
Karmel, David, 1907–1982, vol. VIII
Karminski, Rt Hon. Sir Seymour Edward, 1902–1974, vol. VII
Karn, Frederick James, 1862–1940, vol. III
Karney, Rt Rev. Arthur Baillie Lumsdaine, 1874–1963, vol. VI
Karr, Sir Henry S.; see Seton-Karr.
Karr, Heywood Walter S.; see Seton-Karr.
Karrer, Paul, 1889–1971, vol. VII
Karsavina, Tamara, (Mrs H. J. Bruce), 1885–1978, vol. VII
Karslake, Lt-Gen. Sir Henry, 1879–1942, vol. IV
Karslake, Lt-Col John Burgess Preston, 1868–1942, vol. IV
Karslake, Sir William Wollaston, 1834–1913, vol. I
Karve, Dattatreya Gopal, 1898–1967, vol. VI
Kashmir and Jammu, Lt-Gen. HH Maharaja of, 1850–1925, vol. II
Kasimbazar, Maharaja of, 1860–1929, vol. III
Kassanis, Basil, 1911–1985, vol. VIII
Kastler, Alfred, 1902–1984, vol. VIII
Kästner, Erich, 1899–1974, vol. VII
Kastner, L. E., died 1940, vol. III
Katchen, Julius, 1926–1969, vol. VI
Katenga, Bridger Winston, 1926–1975, vol. VII
Kater, Sir Gregory Blaxland, 1912–1978, vol. VII
Kater, Hon. Sir Norman William, 1874–1965, vol. VI
Kato, Viscount Takaaki, 1860–1926, vol. II
Kato, Adm. Baron Tomosaburo, 1859–1923, vol. II
Katrak, Khan Bahadur Sir Kavasji Hormusji, died 1946, vol. IV
Katsina, Emir of; see Nagogo, Alhaji Hon. Sir Usuman.
Katsura, Gen. Marquess Taro, 1847–1913, vol. I
Katz, Mindru, 1925–1978, vol. VII
Katzin, Olga, 1896–1987, vol. VIII
Kauffer, Edward McKnight, died 1954, vol. V
Kaufman, George Simon, 1889–1961, vol. VII
Kaufmann, Rev. Moritz, 1839–1920, vol. II
Kaula, Sir Ganga, 1877–1970, vol. VI
Kaulbach, Ven. James Albert, 1839–1913, vol. II

Kauntze, William Henry, 1887–1947, vol. IV
Kautsky, Karl, 1854–1938, vol. III
Kavan, Anna, died 1968, vol. VI
Kavanagh, Lt-Gen. Sir Charles Toler McMurrough, 1864–1950, vol. IV
Kavanagh, Col Sir Dermot M.; see McMorrough Kavanagh.
Kavanagh, Lt-Col Edward James, 1881–1940, vol. III
Kavanagh, Patrick, 1905–1967, vol. VI
Kavanagh, Rt Hon. Walter MacMurrough, 1856–1922, vol. II
Kawamata, Katsuji, 1905–1986, vol. VIII
Kay, Archibald, 1860–1935, vol. III
Kay, Arthur, died 1939, vol. III
Kay, Arthur William, 1904–1970, vol. VI
Kay, Sir Brook, 4th Bt, 1820–1907, vol. I
Kay, Rev. D. Miller, died 1930, vol. III
Kay, Rt Hon. Sir Edward Ebenezer, 1822–1897, vol. I
Kay, Harold Isherwood, 1893–1938, vol. III
Kay, Sir Herbert, 1879–1957, vol. V
Kay, Herbert Davenport, 1893–1976, vol. VII
Kay, James, 1858–1942, vol. IV
Kay, Sir James Reid, 1885–1965, vol. VI
Kay, Sir Joseph Aspden, 1884–1958, vol. V
Kay, Katharine Cameron, died 1965, vol. VI
Kay, Ven. Kenneth, 1902–1958, vol. V
Kay, Patrick Healey-; see Dolin, Sir Anton.
Kay, Sir Robert Newbald, 1869–1947, vol. IV
Kay, Sydney Entwisle, 1888–1978, vol. VII
Kay, Thomas, died 1938, vol. III
Kay, Sir William, 1868–1955, vol. V
Kay, Very Rev. William, 1894–1980, vol. VII
Kay, Sir William Algernon, 5th Bt, 1837–1914, vol. I
Kay, Lt-Col Sir William Algernon Ireland, 6th Bt, 1876–1918, vol. II
Kay, Maj.-Gen. William Heape, 1871–1929, vol. III
Kay, Col William Martin, 1871–1948, vol. IV (A), vol. V
Kay-Mouat, John Richard, 1881–1952, vol. V
Kay-Shuttleworth, Edward James, 1890–1917, vol. II
Kay-Shuttleworth, Hon. Lawrence Ughtred, 1887–1917, vol. II
Kaye, Lt-Col Sir Cecil, 1868–1935, vol. III
Kaye, Sir Cecil Edmund L.; see Lister-Kaye.
Kaye, Cecil William, 1865–1941, vol. IV
Kaye, Danny, (Daniel Kominski), 1913–1987, vol. VIII
Kaye, George William Clarkson, 1880–1941, vol. IV
Kaye, Captain and Flt Comdr Sir Henry Gordon, 2nd Bt, 1889–1965, vol. V
Kaye, Lt-Col James Levett, 1861–1917, vol. II
Kaye, Sir John Christopher Lister L.; see Lister-Kaye.
Kaye, Sir John Pepys L.; see Lister-Kaye.
Kaye, Sir Joseph H., 1st Bt, 1856–1923, vol. II
Kaye, Sir Kenelm Arthur L.; see Lister-Kaye.
Kaye, Levett Mackenzie, 1869–1941, vol. IV
Kaye, Sir Lister L.; see Lister-Kaye.
Kaye, Ven. Martin, 1919–1977, vol. VII
Kaye, Col Ralph Arthur, 1863–1933, vol. III
Kaye, Robert Walter, 1871–1957, vol. V
Kaye, Sir Stephen Henry Gordon, 3rd Bt, 1917–1983, vol. VIII
Kaye, Ven. William Frederick John, died 1913, vol. I

Kaye, Sir William Squire Barker, 1831–1901, vol. I
Kaye-Smith, Sheila, *died* 1956, vol. V
Kays, Brig.-Gen. Horace Francis, 1861–1945, vol. IV
Kays, Brig.-Gen. Walpole Swinton, 1858–1941, vol. IV
Kayser, Charles William, 1870–1947, vol. IV
Kazanjian, Varaztad Hovhannes, 1879–1974, vol. VII
Keable, Robert, 1887–1927, vol. II
Kealy, Sir (Edward) Herbert, 1873–1953, vol. V
Kealy, Sir Herbert; *see* Kealy, Sir E. H.
Kean, Captain Abraham, 1855–1945, vol. IV
Kean, Oscar, 1875–1961, vol. VI
Kean, Thomas Alban, 1894–1968, vol. VI (AII)
Keane, Augustus Henry, 1833–1912, vol. I
Keane, Charles Alexander, *died* 1931, vol. III
Keane, Most Rev. David, 1871–1945, vol. IV
Keane, Major Gerald Joseph, 1880–1943, vol. IV
Keane, Lt-Col Sir John, 5th Bt, 1873–1956, vol. V
Keane, John Fryer Thomas, 1854–1937, vol. III
Keane, Sir Michael, 1874–1937, vol. III
Keane, Lt-Col Richard Henry, 1881–1925, vol. II
Kearney, Very Rev. Alexander Major, *died* 1912, vol. I
Kearney, Count Cecil; *see* Kearney, R. C. J. P.
Kearney, Elfric Wells Chalmers, 1881–1966, vol. VI
Kearney, Sir Francis Edgar, 1870–1938, vol. III
Kearney, Robert Cecil Joseph Patrick, (Count Cecil-Kearney), *died* 1911, vol. I
Kearns, Sir Frederick Matthias, 1921–1983, vol. VIII
Kearns, Sir (Henry Ward) Lionel, 1891–1962, vol. VI
Kearns, Howard George Henry, 1902–1986, vol. VIII
Kearns, Sir Lionel; *see* Kearns, Sir H. W. L.
Kearns, Rev. John Willis, *died* 1962, vol. VI
Kearns, Major Reginald Arthur Ernest Holmes, *died* 1918, vol. II
Kearns, Col Thomas Joseph, 1861–1920, vol. II
Kearon, Air Cdre Norman Walter, 1913–1981, vol. VIII
Kearsley, Brig.-Gen. Sir Harvey; *see* Kearsley, Brig.-Gen. Sir R. H.
Kearsley, Brig.-Gen. Sir (Robert) Harvey, 1880–1956, vol. V
Kearton, Cherry, 1871–1940, vol. III
Kearton, Richard, 1862–1928, vol. II
Kearton, William Johnston, 1893–1978, vol. VII
Keary, Charles Francis, *died* 1917, vol. II
Keary, Lt-Gen. Sir Henry D'Urban, 1857–1937, vol. III
Keary, Peter, 1865–1915, vol. I
Keating, Most Rev. Frederick William, 1859–1928, vol. II
Keating, Brig. Harold John Buckler, 1893–1970, vol. VI (AII)
Keating, John, (Seán Céitinn), 1889–1977, vol. VII
Keating, Rev. John Fitzstephen, 1850–1911, vol. I
Keating, Hon. John Henry, 1872–1940, vol. III
Keating, Joseph, 1871–1934, vol. III
Keating, Rev. Joseph Ignatius, 1865–1939, vol. III
Keating, Matthew, 1869–1937, vol. III
Keating, Paul John Geoffrey, 1924–1980, vol. VII
Keatinge, Gerald Francis, 1872–1965, vol. VI
Keatinge, Henry Pottinger, 1860–1928, vol. II
Keatinge, Maurice Walter, 1868–1935, vol. III
Keatinge, Gen. Richard Harte, 1825–1904, vol. I

Keatinge, Richard Herbert, 1911–1968, vol. VI
Keatinge, Rt Rev. William Lewis, 1869–1934, vol. III
Keay, Herbert O., 1875–1958, vol. V
Keay, James Donald, *died* 1933, vol. III
Keay, Lt-Col John, *died* 1943, vol. IV
Keay, Sir John, 1894–1964, vol. VI
Keay, John Seymour, 1839–1909, vol. I
Keay, Sir Lancelot Herman, 1883–1974, vol. VII
Keble, Col Alfred Ernest Conquer, 1869–1940, vol. III
Kebty-Fletcher, John Robert, 1868–1918, vol. II
Keck, Thomas Charles Leycester P.; *see* Powys-Keck.
Kedarnath Das, Sir, 1867–1936, vol. III
Keddie, Henrietta, (Sarah Tytler), 1827–1914, vol. I
Keddie, Col Herbert William Graham, 1873–1943, vol. IV
Kedward, Rev. Roderick Morris, 1881–1937, vol. III
Keeble, Sir Frederick William, 1870–1952, vol. V
Keeble, Lillah, (Lady Keeble); *see* McCarthy, L.
Keefe, Sir Ronald Barry, 1901–1967, vol. VI
Keefer, Thomas Coltrin, 1821–1915, vol. I
Keegan, Lt-Col Herbert Leo, 1888–1937, vol. III
Keel, James Frederick, 1871–1954, vol. V
Keel, Jonathan Edgar, 1895–1979, vol. VII
Keelan, Percival Stanley, 1875–1950, vol. IV (A)
Keele, Cyril Arthur, 1905–1987, vol. VIII
Keeley, Thomas Clews, 1894–1988, vol. VIII
Keeling, (Cyril) Desmond (Evans), 1921–1979, vol. VII
Keeling, Desmond; *see* Keeling, C. D. E.
Keeling, Edward Allis, 1885–1975, vol. VII
Keeling, Sir Edward Herbert, *died* 1954, vol. V
Keeling, Sir Hugh Trowbridge, *died* 1955, vol. V
Keeling, Sir John Henry, 1895–1978, vol. VII
Keeling, Thomas, 1882–1963, vol. VI
Keeling, Rev. William Hulton, 1840–1916, vol. II
Keeling, Rev. William Theodore, 1871–1946, vol. IV
Keely, Eric Philipps, 1899–1988, vol. VIII
Keen, Archibald, 1860–1932, vol. III
Keen, Arthur, *died* 1915, vol. I
Keen, Austin, *died* 1922, vol. II
Keen, Sir Bernard Augustus, 1890–1981, vol. VIII
Keen, Frank Noel, 1869–1957, vol. V
Keen, Frederick Grinham; *see* Kerr, Frederick.
Keen, Col Sir Frederick John, 1834–1902, vol. I
Keen, Col Frederick Stewart, 1874–1949, vol. IV
Keen, Gregory Bernard, 1844–1930, vol. III
Keen, Col John Fred, 1881–1949, vol. IV
Keen, Brig. Patrick Houston, 1877–1954, vol. V
Keen, Patrick John, 1911–1983, vol. VIII
Keen, Col. Sidney, 1868–1941, vol. IV
Keen, Lt-Col William John, *died* 1958, vol. V
Keen, William Williams, 1837–1932, vol. III
Keenan, Margaret Helen, 1869–1939, vol. III
Keenan, Hon. Sir Norbert, 1866–1954, vol. V
Keenan, William, *died* 1955, vol. V
Keene, Air Vice-Marshal Allan Lancelot Addison P.; *see* Perry-Keene.
Keene, Col Alfred, 1855–1918, vol. II
Keene, Charles James, 1850–1917, vol. II
Keene, Sir Charles Robert, 1891–1977, vol. VII
Keene, Henry George, 1825–1915, vol. I
Keene, Most Rev. James Bennett, 1849–1919, vol. II
Keene, James Robert, 1838–1913, vol. I

Keene, Mary Frances Lucas, *died* 1977, vol. VII
Keene, Vice-Adm. Philip R.; *see* Ruck Keene.
Keene, William, 1851–1920, vol. II
Keene, Adm. William George Elmhirst Ruck, 1867–1935, vol. III
Keenlyside, Francis Hugh, 1911–1990, vol. VIII
Keens, Philip Francis, 1903–1989, vol. VIII
Keens, Sir Thomas, 1870–1953, vol. V
Keep, Arthur Corrie, 1861–1940, vol. III
Keeping, Charles William James, 1924–1988, vol. VIII
Keesey, Walter Monckton, 1887–1970, vol. VI
Keesing, Felix Maxwell, 1902–1961, vol. VI
Keetley, Charles Robert Bell, *died* 1909, vol. I
Keeton, George Haydn, 1878–1949, vol. IV
Keeton, George Williams, 1902–1989, vol. VIII
Keeton, Haydn, 1847–1921, vol. II
Keevil, Col Sir Ambrose, 1893–1973, vol. VII
Kefauver, Estes, 1903–1963, vol. VI
Keflegzi, Gabre-Mascal, 1917–1969, vol. VI
Keggin, Air Vice-Marshal Harold, 1909–1989, vol. VIII
Kegie, James, 1913–1984, vol. VIII
Kehoe, Miles, *died* 1907, vol. I
Keighley, Col Charles Marsh, 1847–1911, vol. I
Keighley, Frank, 1900–1981, vol. VIII
Keighley, Lt-Col Vernon Aubrey Scott, 1874–1939, vol. III
Keighly-Peach, Adm. Charles William, 1865–1943, vol. IV
Keightley, Gen. Sir Charles Frederic, 1901–1974, vol. VII
Keightley, Sir Samuel Robert, 1859–1949, vol. IV
Keigwin, Richard Prescott, 1883–1972, vol. VII
Keilin, David, *died* 1963, vol. VI
Keiller, Brian Edwin, 1901–1977, vol. VII
Keily, Maj.-Gen. Frederick Peter Charles, 1870–1938, vol. III
Keily, Rt Rev. John, 1854–1928, vol. II
Keir, Sir David Lindsay, 1895–1973, vol. VII
Keir, Lt-Gen. Sir John Lindesay, 1856–1937, vol. III
Keir, Thelma C.; *see* Cazalet-Keir.
Keir, Surg. Rear-Adm. William Wallace, 1876–1949, vol. IV
Keirstead, Burton Seely, 1907–1973, vol. VII
Keirstead, Wilfred Currier, 1871–1944, vol. IV
Keith of Avonholm, Baron (Life Peer); James Keith, 1886–1964, vol. VIII
Keith, Alexander Milne, 1886–1967, vol. VI
Keith, Rev. Canon Archibald Leslie, 1871–1956, vol. V
Keith, Sir Arthur, 1866–1955, vol. V
Keith, Arthur Berriedale, 1879–1944, vol. IV
Keith, Edward John, 1908–1968, vol. VI
Keith, George Skene, 1819–1910, vol. I
Keith, Sir Henry Shanks, 1852–1944, vol. IV
Keith, Col James, 1842–1919, vol. II
Keith, James, 1879–1953, vol. V
Keith, John Lucien, 1895–1988, vol. VIII
Keith, Leslie; *see* Johnston, Grace L. Keith.
Keith, Robert Farquharson, 1912–1988, vol. VIII
Keith, Skene, 1858–1919, vol. II
Keith, Trevor, 1921–1988, vol. VIII
Keith, Sir William John, 1873–1937, vol. III

Keith-Roach, Edward, 1885–1954, vol. V
Kekewich, Rt Hon. Sir Arthur, 1832–1907, vol. I
Kekewich, Sir George William, 1841–1921, vol. II
Kekewich, Rear-Adm. Piers Keane, 1889–1967, vol. VI
Kekewich, Maj.-Gen. Robert George, 1854–1914, vol. I
Kekewich, Sir Trehawke Herbert, 1st Bt, 1851–1932, vol. III
Kekwick, Alan, 1909–1974, vol. VII
Kelcey, Air Vice-Marshal Alick F.; *see* Foord-Kelcey.
Kelf-Cohen, Reuben, 1895–1981, vol. VIII
Kelham, Brig.-Gen. Henry Robert, 1853–1931, vol. III
Kelk, Sir John William, 2nd Bt, 1851–1923, vol. II
Kell, Maj.-Gen. Sir Vernon George Waldegrave, 1873–1942, vol. IV
Kelland, Sir John; *see* Kelland, Sir P. J. L.
Kelland, Sir (Percy) John (Luxton), *died* 1958, vol. V
Kellar, Robert James, *died* 1980, vol. VII
Kellas, A. M., *died* 1921, vol. II
Kellaway, Charles Halliley, 1889–1952, vol. V
Kellaway, Rt Hon. Frederick George, 1870–1933, vol. III
Kelleher, Stephen B., 1875–1917, vol. II
Keller, Adolf, 1872–1963, vol. VI
Keller, Helen Adams, 1880–1968, vol. VI
Keller, Hon. John; *see* Keller, Hon. L. J. W.
Keller, Hon. (Laurence) John Walter, 1885–1959, vol. V
Keller, Maj.-Gen. Rodney Frederick Leopold, 1900–1954, vol. V
Kellett, Adelaide Maud, *died* 1945, vol. IV
Kellett, Lt-Col Edward Orlando, 1902–1943, vol. IV
Kellett, Ernest Edward, 1864–1950, vol. IV
Kellett, Maj.-Gen. Gerald, 1905–1973, vol. VII
Kellett, Sir Henry de Castres, 3rd Bt, 1851–1924, vol. II
Kellett, Sir Henry de Castres, 4th Bt, 1882–1966, vol. VI
Kellett, Sir Henry de Castres, 5th Bt, 1914–1966, vol. VI
Kellett, Col John Philip, 1890–1959, vol. V
Kellett, Maj.-Gen. Richard Orlando, 1864–1931, vol. III
Kellett, Sir Stanley Everard, 6th Bt, 1911–1983, vol. VIII
Kelley, Major Sir Frederic Arthur, 1863–1926, vol. II
Kelley, Howard G., 1858–1928, vol. II
Kelley, Richard, 1904–1984, vol. VIII
Kellie, Lawrence, 1862–1932, vol. III
Kellock, Hon. Roy Lindsay, 1893–1975, vol. VII
Kellock, Thomas Herbert, 1863–1922, vol. II
Kellogg, Frank Billings, 1856–1937, vol. III
Kellor, Alexander James, 1905–1982, vol. VIII
Kelly, Annie Elizabeth, *died* 1946, vol. IV
Kelly, Major Arthur Dillon Denis, The O'Kelly, 1853–1936, vol. III
Kelly, Brig.-Gen. Arthur James, 1857–1930, vol. III
Kelly, Sir Arthur John, 1898–1983, vol. VIII
Kelly, Charles, 1815–1905, vol. I
Kelly, Rev. Charles H., 1833–1911, vol. I
Kelly, Col Courtenay Russell, 1872–1945, vol. IV

Kelly, Sir Dalziel; *see* Kelly, Sir G. D.

Kelly, Sir David Victor, 1891–1959, vol. V

Kelly, Rt Rev. Denis, 1852–1924, vol. II

Kelly, Denis; *see* Kelly, R. D. L.

Kelly, Edward Festus, 1854–1939, vol. III

Kelly, Brig. Edward Henry, 1883–1963, vol. VI

Kelly, Dame Elisabeth Hariott, 1878–1962, vol. VI

Kelly, Francis, 1868–1939, vol. III

Kelly, Maj.-Gen. Francis Henry, 1859–1937, vol. III

Kelly, Francis Michael, 1879–1945, vol. IV

Kelly, Frederick Septimus, 1881–1916, vol. II

Kelly, Brig. George Alexander, 1888–1973, vol. VII

Kelly, Maj.-Gen. George Charles, 1880–1938, vol. III

Kelly, Sir (George) Dalziel, 1891–1953, vol. V

Kelly, Sir Gerald Festus, 1879–1972, vol. VII

Kelly, Major Henry, *died* 1960, vol. V

Kelly, Brig.-Gen. Henry Edward Theodore, 1870–1932, vol. III

Kelly, Sir Henry G.; *see* Greene Kelly.

Kelly, Rev. Herbert Hamilton, 1860–1950, vol. IV

Kelly, Adm. Sir Howard; *see* Kelly, Adm. Sir W. A. H.

Kelly, Howard Atwood, 1858–1943, vol. IV

Kelly, Captain Hubert Dunsterville Harvey-, 1891–1917, vol. II

Kelly, Hon. Hugh Thomas, 1858–1945, vol. IV

Kelly, Captain James Alphonse Mari Joseph Patrick, 1875–1909, vol. I

Kelly, Most Rev. James Butler Knill, *born* 1832.

Kelly, Rev. James Davenport, 1828–1912, vol. I

Kelly, James Gerald, 1897–1942, vol. IV

Kelly, Col James Graves, 1843–1923, vol. II

Kelly, John, vol. II

Kelly, Admiral of the Fleet Sir John Donald, 1871–1936, vol. III

Kelly, Lt-Col John Sherwood-, 1880–1931, vol. III

Kelly, Major John Upton, 1882–1943, vol. IV

Kelly, John William, 1885–1966, vol. VI

Kelly, Kenneth Linden, 1913–1985, vol. VIII

Kelly, Sir Malachy, 1850–1916, vol. II

Kelly, Mark Jamestown, 1848–1916, vol. II

Kelly, Mervin J., 1894–1971, vol. VII

Kelly, Most Rev. Michael, 1850–1940, vol. III

Kelly, Sir Patrick Aloysius, 1880–1966, vol. VI

Kelly, Lt-Surg. Peter Burrowes, 1888–1920, vol. II

Kelly, Brig.-Gen. Philip James Vandeleur, *died* 1948, vol. IV

Kelly, Hon. Sir Raymond; *see* Kelly, Hon. Sir W. R.

Kelly, Richard Barrett Talbot, 1896–1971, vol. VII

Kelly, Sir Richard Denis, (The O'Kelly Mor), 1815–1897, vol. I

Kelly, Richard Denis Lucien, 1916–1990, vol. VIII

Kelly, Richard John, *died* 1931, vol. III

Kelly, Brig.-Gen. Richard Makdougall Brisbane Francis, 1857–1915, vol. I

Kelly, R. Talbot, 1861–1934, vol. III

Kelly, Robert Alsop, 1881–1950, vol. IV

Kelly, Sir Robert Ernest, 1879–1944, vol. IV

Kelly, Sir Robert McErlean, 1902–1971, vol. VII

Kelly, Sir Samuel, *died* 1937, vol. III

Kelly, Sir Stanley Anthony Hill, 1869–1949, vol. IV

Kelly, Rev. Thomas, *died* 1926, vol. II

Kelly, Sir Thomas, 1862–1947, vol. IV

Kelly, Thomas Dwyer, 1880–1949, vol. IV

Kelly, Lt-Col Thomas Francis Henry, 1899–1940, vol. III

Kelly, Air Vice-Marshal Thomas James, 1890–1967, vol. VI

Kelly, Col Tom, 1869–1965, vol. VI

Kelly, William, *died* 1944, vol. IV

Kelly, Adm. Sir (William Archibald) Howard, 1873–1952, vol. V

Kelly, Rt Rev. William Bernard, 1855–1921, vol. II

Kelly, Lt-Gen. Sir William Freeman, 1847–1914, vol. I

Kelly, Captain William Henry, 1873–1941, vol. IV

Kelly, Hon. Sir (William) Raymond, 1898–1956, vol. V

Kelly, William Thomas, 1874–1944, vol. IV

Kelly-Kenny, Gen. Sir Thomas, 1840–1914, vol. I

Kelman, Rev. John, 1864–1929, vol. III

Kelsey, Emanuel, 1905–1985, vol. VIII

Kelsey, Joan; *see* Grant, J.

Kelsey, Vice-Adm. Marcel Harcourt Attwood, 1894–1964, vol. VI

Kelso, Maj.-Gen. John Edward U.; *see* Utterson-Kelso.

Kelson, William Henry, 1862–1940, vol. III

Keltie, Sir John Scott, 1840–1927, vol. II

Kelvin, 1st Baron, 1824–1907, vol. I

Kelway, Albert Clifton, 1865–1952, vol. V

Kelway, Col George Trevor, 1899–1990, vol. VIII

Kelynack, Theo N., 1866–1944, vol. IV

Kem, 1906–1988, vol. VIII

Kemball, Gen. Sir Arnold Burrowes, 1820–1908, vol. I

Kemball, Col Arnold Henry Grant, 1861–1917, vol. II

Kemball, Lt-Col Charles Arnold, 1860–1943, vol. IV

Kemball, Christopher Gurdon, 1899–1969, vol. VI

Kemball, Maj.-Gen. Sir George Vero, 1859–1941, vol. IV

Kemball-Cook, Sir Basil Alfred; *see* Cook.

Kemmis, Lt-Col William, 1861–1932, vol. III

Kemmis Betty, Vice-Adm. Arthur, 1877–1961, vol. VI

Kemmis Betty, Lt-Col Paget, 1876–1948, vol. IV

Kemnal, Sir James, 1864–1927, vol. II

Kemp, Hon. Sir (Albert) Edward, 1858–1929, vol. III

Kemp, Charles, 1897–1983, vol. VIII

Kemp, Charles Edward, 1901–1986, vol. VIII

Kemp, Dixon, 1839–1899, vol. I

Kemp, Hon. Sir Edward; *see* Kemp, Hon. Sir A. E.

Kemp, Sir Ernest, 1870–1938, vol. III

Kemp, Rev. Frederick James, 1885–1943, vol. IV

Kemp, Brig.-Gen. Geoffrey Chicheley, 1868–1936, vol. III

Kemp, Maj.-Gen. Geoffrey Chicheley, 1890–1976, vol. VII

Kemp, Henry Thomas, 1852–1943, vol. IV

Kemp, Sir John, 1883–1955, vol. V

Kemp, Sir Joseph Horsford, 1874–1950, vol. IV

Kemp, Sir Kenneth Hagar, 12th Bt, 1853–1936, vol. III

Kemp, Sir Kenneth McIntrye, 1883–1949, vol. IV

Kemp, Sir Leslie Charles, 1890–1988, vol. VIII

Kemp, Sir Norman Wright, *died* 1937, vol. III

Kemp, Stanley Wells, 1882–1945, vol. IV

Kemp, Stephen, 1849–1918, vol. II

Kemp, Thomas R., 1836–1905, vol. I
Kemp, Adm. Thomas Webster, 1866–1928, vol. II
Kemp-Welch, Lucy Elizabeth, died 1958, vol. V
Kemp-Welch, Margaret, died 1968, vol. VI
Kemp-Welch, Brig.-Gen. Martin, 1885–1951, vol. V
Kempe, Sir Alfred Bray, 1849–1922, vol. II
Kempe, Charles Eamer, 1837–1907, vol. I
Kempe, Rev. Edward Wood, 1844–1918, vol. II
Kempe, Lt-Col Frederick Hawke, died 1954, vol. V
Kempe, Harry Robert, 1852–1935, vol. III
Kempe, Sir John Arrow, 1846–1928, vol. II
Kempe, Rev. John Edward, 1810–1907, vol. I
Kempe, Rudolf, 1910–1976, vol. VII
Kempling, William Bailey, died 1941, vol. IV
Kempson, Rt Rev. Edwin Hone, 1862–1931, vol. III
Kempson, Eric William Edward, died 1948, vol. IV
Kempster, Christopher Richard, 1869–1948, vol. IV
Kempster, Col Francis James, 1855–1925, vol. II
Kempster, Lt-Col Herbert William, died 1944, vol. IV
Kempster, John Westbeech, 1864–1947, vol. IV
Kempthorne, Lt-Col Gerard Ainslie, 1876–1939, vol. III
Kempthorne, Rt Rev. John Augustine, 1864–1946, vol. IV
Kempthorne, Rt Rev. Leonard Stanley, 1886–1963, vol. VI
Kempton, Charles Leslie, died 1965, vol. VI
Kemsley, 1st Viscount, 1883–1968, vol. VI
Kemsley, Col Sir Alfred Newcombe, 1896–1987, vol. VIII (A)
Kemsley, Col Sir Colin Norman T.; see Thornton-Kemsley.
Kenchington, Brig. Arthur George, 1890–1966, vol. VI
Kendal, Dame Madge Grimston, 1849–1935, vol. III
Kendal, Sir Norman, 1880–1966, vol. VI
Kendal, William Hunter, 1843–1917, vol. II
Kendall, Anthony Colin, 1898–1967, vol. VI
Kendall, Arthur Wallis, 1904–1975, vol. VII
Kendall, Sir Charles Henry Bayley, 1878–1935, vol. III
Kendall, Captain Charles James Cope, 1864–1943, vol. IV
Kendall, Edward Calvin, 1886–1972, vol. VII
Kendall, Col Ernest Arthur, 1876–1938, vol. III
Kendall, Guy, 1876–1960, vol. V
Kendall, H. Bickerstaffe, 1844–1919, vol. II
Kendall, Henry, 1897–1962, vol. VI
Kendall, Rev. Henry Ewing, 1888–1963, vol. VI
Kendall, James, 1889–1978, vol. VII
Kendall, John David, 1893–1936, vol. III
Kendall, Rev. John Francis, 1862–1931, vol. III
Kendall, Major John Kaye, died 1952, vol. V
Kendall, Katherine Githa; see Sowerby, K. G.
Kendall, Sir Maurice George, 1907–1983, vol. VIII
Kendall, Percy Fry, 1856–1936, vol. III
Kendall, Maj.-Gen. Roy, 1897–1963, vol. VI
Kendall, Lt-Col Sydney Robert Gordon, 1879–1959, vol. V
Kendall, William Henry, died 1951, vol. V
Kendall-Carpenter, John MacGregor Kendall, 1925–1990, vol. VIII
Kenderdine, Sir Charles Halstaff, 1866–1936, vol. III
Kendon, Donald Henry, 1895–1985, vol. VIII

Kendon, Frank, 1893–1959, vol. V
Kendrew, Maj.-Gen. Sir Douglas Anthony, 1910–1989, vol. VIII
Kendrew, Hubert, 1894–1966, vol. VI
Kendrew, Wilfrid George, died 1962, vol. VI
Kendrick, Albert Frank, 1872–1954, vol. V
Kendrick, Sydney Percy, 1874–1955, vol. V
Kendrick, Sir Thomas Downing, 1895–1979, vol. VII
Kenealy, Alexander, 1864–1915, vol. I
Kenealy, Most Rev. Anselm E. J., 1864–1943, vol. IV
Kenealy, Arabella, died 1938, vol. III
Kenealy, Noel Byron, died 1918, vol. II
Kenilworth, 1st Baron, 1866–1953, vol. V
Kenilworth, 2nd Baron, 1894–1971, vol. VII
Kenilworth, 3rd Baron; see Siddeley, J. T. D.
Kenmare, 4th Earl of, 1825–1905, vol. I
Kenmare, 5th Earl of, 1860–1941, vol. IV
Kenmare, 6th Earl of, 1891–1943, vol. IV
Kenmare, 7th Earl of, 1896–1952, vol. V
Kenna, Col Paul Aloysius, 1862–1915, vol. I
Kennan, George, 1845–1924, vol. II
Kennan, John Melville, 1904–1960, vol. V
Kennan, Thomas Brereton, 1891–1965, vol. VI
Kennard, Adam Steinmetz, 1833–1915, vol. I
Kennard, Major Arthur Molloy, 1867–1917, vol. II
Kennard, Rt Rev. Mgr Charles H., 1840–1920, vol. II
Kennard, Sir Coleridge Arthur Fitzroy, 1st Bt, 1885–1948, vol. IV
Kennard, Col Edmund Hegan, died 1912, vol. I
Kennard, Col Henry Gerard, died 1946, vol. IV
Kennard, Sir Howard William, 1878–1955, vol. V
Kennard, Sir Lawrence Ury Charles, 2nd Bt, 1912–1967, vol. VI
Kennard, Martyn Thomas, 1859–1920, vol. II
Kennard, Captain Willoughby Arthur, 1881–1918, vol. II
Kennaway, Sir Ernest Laurence, 1881–1958, vol. V
Kennaway, Sir John, 4th Bt, 1879–1956, vol. V
Kennaway, Rt Hon. Sir John Henry, 3rd Bt, 1837–1919, vol. II
Kennaway, Sir Walter, 1835–1920, vol. II
Kennedy, Hon. Lord; Neil J. D. Kennedy, 1855–1918, vol. II
Kennedy, Alex. Mills, died 1960, vol. V
Kennedy, Alexander, 1909–1960, vol. V
Kennedy, Sir Alexander Blackie William, 1847–1928, vol. II
Kennedy, Sir Alexander McAusland, 1860–1939, vol. III
Kennedy, Maj.-Gen. Alfred Alexander, 1870–1926, vol. II
Kennedy, Alfred Ravenscroft, 1879–1943, vol. IV
Kennedy, Lt-Col Andrew Campbell, 1872–1941, vol. IV
Kennedy, Rev. Archibald Cowan, 1892–1966, vol. VI
Kennedy, Archibald Edmund C.; see Clark-Kennedy.
Kennedy, Brig. Archibald Gordon M.; see Mackenzie-Kennedy.
Kennedy, Rev. Archibald Robert Stirling, 1859–1938, vol. III
Kennedy, Aubrey Leo, 1885–1965, vol. VI
Kennedy, Bart, 1861–1930, vol. III
Kennedy, Brig.-Gen. Charles Henry, 1860–1916, vol. II

Kennedy, Sir Charles Malcolm, 1831–1908, vol. I
Kennedy, Charles Rann, 1871–1950, vol. IV
Kennedy, Daisy, 1893–1981, vol. VIII
Kennedy, Sir Derrick Edward de Vere, 6th Bt, 1904–1976, vol. VII
Kennedy, Sir Donald; see Mackenzie-Kennedy, Sir H. C. D. C.
Kennedy, Douglas Neil, 1893–1988, vol. VIII
Kennedy, Maj.-Gen. Sir Edward Charles William M.; see Mackenzie-Kennedy.
Kennedy, Major Francis Malcolm Evory, 1869–1945, vol. IV
Kennedy, Adm. Francis William, 1862–1939, vol. III
Kennedy, Frank Robert, 1895–1971, vol. VII
Kennedy, Frederick Charles, 1849–1916, vol. II
Kennedy, Rev. Geoffrey Anketell Studdert, died 1929, vol. III
Kennedy, George, 1838–1916, vol. II, vol. III
Kennedy, Lt-Col Sir (George) Ronald (Derrick), 7th Bt, 1927–1988, vol. VIII
Kennedy, Gilbert George, 1844–1909, vol. I
Kennedy, Rev. Harry Angus Alexander, 1866–1934, vol. III
Kennedy, Hartley, 1852–1938, vol. III
Kennedy, Henry Albert, 1877–1965, vol. VI
Kennedy, Brig.-Gen. Henry Brewster Percy Lion, died 1953, vol. V
Kennedy, Sir (Henry Charles) Donald (Cleveland) M.; see Mackenzie-Kennedy.
Kennedy, Very Rev. Herbert Brownlow, 1863–1939, vol. III
Kennedy, Howard Angus, 1861–1938, vol. III
Kennedy, Brig.-Gen. Hugh, 1864–1930, vol. III
Kennedy, Hugh, 1879–1936, vol. III
Kennedy, Hon. Sir James Arthur, 1882–1954, vol. V
Kennedy, James Cowie, 1914–1989, vol. VIII
Kennedy, Col James Crawford, 1879–1944, vol. IV
Kennedy, Sir James Edward, 5th Bt, 1898–1974, vol. VII
Kennedy, Rev. James Houghton, died 1924, vol. II
Kennedy, Rev. John, 1813–1900, vol. I
Kennedy, Brig.-Gen. John, 1878–1921, vol. II
Kennedy, Rev. John, died 1931, vol. III
Kennedy, Maj.-Gen. Sir John, 1878–1948, vol. IV
Kennedy, Sir John Charles, 3rd Bt, 1856–1923, vol. II
Kennedy, John Fitzgerald, 1917–1963, vol. VI
Kennedy, Sir John Gordon, 1836–1912, vol. I
Kennedy, Rev. John Joseph, born 1882, vol. III
Kennedy, Sir John Macfarlane, 1879–1954, vol. V
Kennedy, Col John Murray, 1841–1928, vol. II
Kennedy, Maj.-Gen. Sir John Noble, 1893–1970, vol. VI
Kennedy, John Norman, 1927–1985, vol. VIII
Kennedy, Sir John Ralph Bayly, 4th Bt, 1896–1968, vol. VI
Kennedy, John Robert, 1871–1956, vol. V
Kennedy, Lt-Col John Ross, 1905–1942, vol. IV
Kennedy, John William James Clark-, 1875–1939, vol. III
Kennedy, Joseph Patrick, 1888–1969, vol. VI
Kennedy, Rt Rev. Kenneth William Stewart, died 1943, vol. IV
Kennedy, Captain Macdougall Ralston, 1878–1924, vol. II

Kennedy, Margaret, (Lady Davies), died 1967, vol. VI
Kennedy, Michael, 1859–1932, vol. III
Kennedy, Sir Michael Kavanagh, 1824–1898, vol. I
Kennedy, Milward; see Burge, M. R. K.
Kennedy, Rev. Mortimer Egerton, 1853–1929, vol. III
Kennedy, Myles, 1862–1928, vol. II
Kennedy, Captain Myles Arthur Claude, 1885–1918, vol. II
Kennedy, Myles Burton, 1861–1914, vol. I
Kennedy, Myles Storr Nigel, 1889–1964, vol. VI
Kennedy, Neil J. D.; see Kennedy, Hon. Lord.
Kennedy, Bt-Col Norman, 1881–1960, vol. V
Kennedy, Patrick James, 1864–1947, vol. IV
Kennedy, Robert, 1865–1913, vol. I
Kennedy, Robert, 1865–1924, vol. II
Kennedy, Hon. Sir Robert, 1887–1974, vol. VII
Kennedy, Robert Francis, 1925–1968, vol. VI
Kennedy, Robert Gregg, 1851–1920, vol. II
Kennedy, Sir Robert John, 1851–1936, vol. III
Kennedy, Lt-Col Sir Ronald; see Kennedy, Lt-Col Sir G. R. D.
Kennedy, Vice-Adm. Theobald Walter, 1871–1934, vol. III
Kennedy, Rev. Thomas, 1828–1913, vol. I
Kennedy, Rt Hon. Thomas, 1876–1954, vol. V
Kennedy, Lt-Col Thomas Francis Archibald W.; see Watson-Kennedy.
Kennedy, Sir Thomas Sinclair, 1884–1951, vol. V
Kennedy, Vincent, 1876–1943, vol. IV
Kennedy, William, 1866–1936, vol. III
Kennedy of Knockgray, Lt-Col William Hew Clark-, 1879–1961, vol. VI
Kennedy, Lt-Col William Magill, 1868–1923, vol. II
Kennedy, William Paul McClure, 1879–1963, vol. VI
Kennedy, William Quarrier, 1903–1979, vol. VII
Kennedy, Rt Hon. Sir William Rann, 1846–1915, vol. I
Kennedy, Adm. Sir William Robert, 1838–1916, vol. II
Kennedy, Lt-Col Willoughby Pitcairn, 1850–1928, vol. II
Kennedy-Cooke, Brian, 1894–1963, vol. VI
Kennedy-Cox, Sir Reginald Kennedy, died 1966, vol. VI
Kennedy-Craufurd-Stuart, Lt-Col Charles; see Stuart.
Kennedy-Purvis, Adm. Sir Charles Edward, died 1946, vol. IV
Kenner, George Wallace, 1922–1978, vol. VII
Kenner, James, 1885–1974, vol. VII
Kennet, 1st Baron, 1879–1960, vol. V
Kennet, Lady; (Kathleen), died 1947, vol. IV
Kennett, Lt-Col Brackley Herbert Barrington B.; see Barrington-Kennett.
Kennett, Rev. Robert Hatch, 1864–1932, vol. III
Kennett-Barrington, Sir Vincent Hunter Barrington, 1844–1903, vol. I
Kenney, Col Arthur Herbert, 1855–1923, vol. II
Kenney, James C. F.; see Fitzgerald-Kenney.
Kenney, Reginald, 1912–1986, vol. VIII
Kenney-Herbert, Edward Maxwell, 1845–1916, vol. II
Kenning, Sir George, 1880–1956, vol. V
Kennington, Eric Henri, died 1960, vol. V
Kennington, T. B., died 1916, vol. II

Kennion, Rt Rev. George Wyndham, 1845–1922, vol. II

Kennion, Lt-Col Roger Lloyd, 1866–1942, vol. IV

Kenny, Augustus Leo, 1863–1946, vol. IV

Kenny, Courtney Stanhope, 1847–1930, vol. III

Kenny, Elizabeth, 1886–1952, vol. V

Kenny, Joseph Edward, 1845–1900, vol. I

Kenny, Matthew J., 1861–1942, vol. IV

Kenny, Sir Patrick John, 1914–1987, vol. VIII

Kenny, Sean, 1932–1973, vol. VII

Kenny, Gen. Sir Thomas K.; *see* Kelly-Kenny.

Kenny, Brig. Vincent Raymond, 1882–1966, vol. VI

Kenny, Rt Hon. William, 1846–1921, vol. II

Kenny, Maj.-Gen. William Wallace, 1854–1929, vol. III

Kenrick, Frank Boteler, 1874–1951, vol. V

Kenrick, Sir George Cranmer, 1863–1939, vol. III

Kenrick, Brig.-Gen. George Edmund Reginald, 1871–1935, vol. III

Kenrick, Sir George Hamilton, 1850–1939, vol. III

Kenrick, George Harry Blair, *died* 1952, vol. V

Kenrick, Brig. Harry Selwyn, 1898–1979, vol. VII

Kenrick, John Arthur, 1829–1926, vol. II

Kenrick, Rt Hon. William, 1831–1919, vol. II

Kensington, 5th Baron, 1863–1900, vol. I

Kensington, 6th Baron, 1873–1938, vol. III

Kensington, 7th Baron, 1904–1981, vol. VIII

Kensington, Sir Alfred, 1855–1918, vol. II

Kensington, Brig. Edgar Claude, 1879–1967, vol. VI

Kensington, William Charles, 1845–1922, vol. II

Kenswood, 1st Baron, 1887–1963, vol. VI

Kent, Albert Frank Stanley, 1863–1958, vol. V

Kent, Charles; *see* Kent, W. C. M.

Kent, Rev. Charles, 1857–1929, vol. III

Kent, Charles Kenneth Stafford, 1892–1963, vol. VI

Kent, Charles Weller, 1864–1952, vol. V

Kent, Chris Shotter, 1887–1954, vol. V

Kent, Rear-Adm. Derrick George, 1920–1983, vol. VIII

Kent, Dorothy Miriam, 1920–1988, vol. VIII

Kent, Rev. Harry Arnold, 1880–1962, vol. VI

Kent, Lt-Gen. Henry, 1825–1921, vol. II

Kent, Col Herbert Vaughan, 1863–1944, vol. IV

Kent, Hon. James M., 1872–1939, vol. III

Kent, Col Sir John; *see* Kent, Col Sir W. J.

Kent, Keneth; *see* Kent, C. K. S.

Kent, Sir Percy Edward, (Sir Peter Kent), 1913–1986, vol. VIII

Kent, Percy Horace Braund, 1876–1963, vol. VI

Kent, Sir Peter; *see* Kent, Sir Percy E.

Kent, Rockwell, 1882–1971, vol. VII

Kent, Sir Stephenson Hamilton, 1873–1954, vol. V

Kent, Thomas Parkes, *died* 1923, vol. II

Kent, Sir Walter George, 1858–1938, vol. III

Kent, (William) Charles (Monk), 1823–1902, vol. I

Kent, Col Sir (William) John, 1877–1960, vol. V

Kent, William Richard Gladstone, 1884–1963, vol. VI

Kent-Lemon, Brig. Arthur Leslie, 1889–1970, vol. VI

Kentish, Brig.-Gen. Reginald John, 1876–1956, vol. V

Kentner, Louis Philip, 1905–1987, vol. VIII

Kenward, Rev. Herbert, *died* 1954, vol. V

Kenwood, Lt-Col Henry Richard, 1862–1945, vol. IV

Kenworthy, John Dalzell, 1858–1954, vol. V

Kenyatta, Hon. Mzee Jomo, 1889–1978, vol. VII

Kenyon, 4th Baron, 1864–1927, vol. II

Kenyon, Alec Hindle, 1905–1982, vol. VIII

Kenyon, Arthur William, *died* 1969, vol. VI

Kenyon, Barnet, 1853–1930, vol. III

Kenyon, Sir Bernard, 1940–1977, vol. VII

Kenyon, Edith C., *died* 1925, vol. II

Kenyon, Maj.-Gen. Edward Ranulph, 1854–1937, vol. III

Kenyon, Sir Frederic George, 1863–1952, vol. V

Kenyon, Hon. George Thomas, 1840–1908, vol. I

Kenyon, Sir Harold Vaughan, 1875–1959, vol. V

Kenyon, Hugh, 1910–1981, vol. VIII

Kenyon, James, 1846–1924, vol. II

Kenyon, John George, 1843–1914, vol. I

Kenyon, Joseph, 1885–1961, vol. VI

Kenyon, Dame Kathleen Mary, 1906–1978, vol. VII

Kenyon, Maj.-Gen. Lionel Richard, 1867–1952, vol. V

Kenyon, Myles Noel, 1886–1960, vol. V

Kenyon, Sir Norris Vaughan, 1903–1958, vol. V

Kenyon, Robert Lloyd, 1848–1931, vol. III

Kenyon, Hon. and Rev. William Trevor, 1847–1930, vol. III

Kenyon-Slaney, Col Francis Gerald, 1858–1938, vol. III

Kenyon-Slaney, Major Philip Percy, 1896–1928, vol. II

Kenyon-Slaney, Major Robert Orlando Rodolph, 1892–1965, vol. VI

Kenyon-Slaney, Sybil Agnes, 1888–1970, vol. VI

Kenyon-Slaney, Maj.-Gen. Walter Rupert, 1851–1936, vol. III

Kenyon-Slaney, Rt Hon. William Slaney, 1847–1908, vol. I

Keogh, Lt-Gen. Sir Alfred, 1857–1936, vol. III

Keogh, Col James Blair, 1871–1944, vol. IV

Keogh, Joseph Wiseman, *died* 1947, vol. IV

Keogh, Martin Jerome, 1855–1928, vol. II, vol. III

Keogh, Michael Frederick, 1866–1940, vol. III

Keogh, Most Rev. Thomas, 1884–1969, vol. VI

Keown, Anna Gordon, *died* 1957, vol. V

Keown, Eric Oliver Dilworth, 1904–1963, vol. VI

Keown-Boyd, Sir Alexander William, 1884–1954, vol. V

Keppel, Adm. Sir Colin Richard, 1862–1947, vol. IV

Keppel, Hon. Sir Derek, 1863–1944, vol. IV

Keppel, Col Edward George, 1847–1934, vol. III

Keppel, Frederick Paul, 1875–1943, vol. IV

Keppel, Lt-Col Hon. George, 1865–1947, vol. IV

Keppel, Sir George Roos-, 1866–1921, vol. II

Keppel, Hon. Sir Henry, 1809–1904, vol. I

Keppel, Rear-Adm. Leicester Chantrey, *died* 1917, vol. II

Keppel, Captain Hon. Rupert Oswald Derek, 1886–1964, vol. VI

Keppel-Compton, Robert Herbert, 1900–1989, vol. VIII

Keppie, John, 1862–1945, vol. IV

Ker, Lord Alastair Robert I.; *see* Innes-Ker.

Ker, Major Allan Ebenezer, *died* 1958, vol. V

Ker, Sir Arthur Milford, 1853–1915, vol. I

Ker, Charles, 1860–1940, vol. III

Ker, Maj.-Gen. Charles Arthur, 1875–1962, vol. VI

Ker, Lt-Col Douglas Rous E.; *see* Edwardes-Ker.
Ker, Frederick Innes, *died* 1977, vol. VII
Ker, James Campbell, 1878–1961, vol. VI
Ker, James Inglis, *died* 1936, vol. III
Ker, Ven. John, 1848–1913, vol. I
Ker, Hon. John Errington, 1860–1918, vol. II
Ker, K(eith) R(eginald) Welbore, 1913–1984, vol. VIII
Ker, Neil Ripley, 1908–1982, vol. VIII
Ker, Mrs Phyllis de Burgh; *see* Lett, Phyllis.
Ker, Richard William Blackwood, 1850–1942, vol. IV
Ker, Major Lord Robert Edward I.; *see* Innes-Ker.
Ker, William Paton, 1855–1923, vol. II
Ker, William Pollock, 1864–1945, vol. IV
Kerans, Comdr John Simon, 1915–1985, vol. VIII
Kerby, Air Vice-Marshal Harold Spencer, 1893–1963, vol. VI
Kerby, Captain Henry Briton, 1914–1971, vol. VII
Kerensky, Oleg Alexander, 1905–1984, vol. VIII
Kerin, Col Michael William, 1856–1912, vol. I
Kerley, Sir Peter James, 1900–1979, vol. VII
Kerly, Sir Duncan Mackenzie, 1863–1938, vol. III
Kermack, Stuart Grace, 1888–1981, vol. VIII
Kermack, William Ogilvy, 1898–1970, vol. VI
Kermode, Air Vice-Marshal Alfred Cotterill, 1897–1973, vol. VII
Kermode, Rev. Sir Derwent William, 1898–1960, vol. V
Kern, Jerome, 1885–1945, vol. IV
Kernahan, Coulson, 1858–1943, vol. IV
Kernahan, Mrs Coulson, *died* 1941, vol. IV
Kernoff, Harry, 1900–1974, vol. VII
Kernot, W. C., 1845–1909, vol. I
Kerouac, Jack, (Jean-Louis), 1922–1969, vol. VI
Kerr, Col Alex. Ferrier K.; *see* Kidston-Kerr.
Kerr, Mrs Anne Patricia, (Mrs R. W. Kerr), 1925–1973, vol. VII
Kerr, Archibald Brown, 1907–1990, vol. VIII
Kerr, Douglas James Acworth, 1894–1960, vol. V
Kerr, Rev. F. W., 1881–1945, vol. IV
Kerr, Captain Frank Robison, 1889–1977, vol. VII
Kerr, Col Frederic Walter, 1867–1914, vol. I
Kerr, Frederick, 1858–1933, vol. III
Kerr, Sir Hamilton William, 1st Bt, 1903–1974, vol. VII
Kerr, Maj.-Gen. Sir (Harold) Reginald, 1897–1974, vol. VII
Kerr, Henry W., 1857–1936, vol. III
Kerr, Lt-Col Sir Howard; *see* Kerr, Lt-Col Sir L. W. H.
Kerr, James, *died* 1941, vol. IV
Kerr, Hon. James Kirkpatrick, 1841–1916, vol. II
Kerr, James Lennox, 1899–1963, vol. VI
Kerr, James Rutherford, 1878–1942, vol. IV
Kerr, Rev. John, *died* 1907, vol. I
Kerr, John, 1830–1916, vol. II
Kerr, John, *born* 1852, vol. II
Kerr, Rev. John, 1852–1920, vol. II
Kerr, Sir John Graham, 1869–1957, vol. V
Kerr, Sir John Henry, 1871–1934, vol. III
Kerr, (John Martin) Munro, 1868–1960, vol. V
Kerr, Lt-Col Sir (Louis William) Howard, 1894–1977, vol. VII
Kerr, Lt-Col Mark Ancrum, 1859–1941, vol. IV

Kerr, Adm. Mark Edward Frederic, 1864–1944, vol. IV
Kerr, Gen. Lord Mark Ralph George, 1817–1900, vol. I
Kerr, Munro; *see* Kerr, J. M. M.
Kerr, Philip Walter, *died* 1941, vol. IV
Kerr, Lord Ralph Drury, 1837–1916, vol. II
Kerr, Rev. Ralph Francis, 1874–1932, vol. III
Kerr, Maj.-Gen. Sir Reginald; *see* Kerr, Maj.-Gen. Sir H. R.
Kerr, Robert, 1823–1904, vol. I
Kerr, Robert Bird, 1867–1951, vol. V
Kerr, Robert Malcolm, 1821–1902, vol. I
Kerr, Brig.-Gen. Robert S.; *see* Scott-Kerr.
Kerr, Col Rowan Scrope R.; *see* Rait Kerr.
Kerr, Sir Russell James, 1863–1952, vol. V
Kerr, Russell Whiston, 1921–1983, vol. VIII
Kerr, Thomas, 1818–1907, vol. I
Kerr, Admiral of the Fleet Lord Walter Talbot, 1839–1927, vol. II
Kerr, Captain William, 1877–1918, vol. II
Kerr, Sir William, 1895–1959, vol. V
Kerr, Captain William Alexander, *died* 1919, vol. II
Kerr, Rev. William Goodwin, 1862–1934, vol. III
Kerr, Adm. Sir William Munro, 1876–1959, vol. V
Kerr, William Richard, 1853–1943, vol. IV
Kerr, Rt Rev. William Shaw, 1873–1960, vol. V
Kerr, William Warren, 1864–1949, vol. IV
Kerr-Dineen, Rev. Canon Frederick George, 1915–1988, vol. VIII
Kerr-Jarrett, Sir Francis Moncreiff, 1885–1968, vol. VI
Kerr-Muir, Ronald John, 1910–1974, vol. VII
Kerr-Pearse, Major Beauchamp Albert Thomas, 1871–1934, vol. III
Kerr-Smiley, Peter Kerr, 1879–1943, vol. IV
Kerrich, Lt-Col Walter Edmund, 1860–1938, vol. III
Kerridge, Sir Robert James, 1901–1979, vol. VII
Kerrigan, Daniel Patrick, 1909–1971, vol. VII
Kerrin, Very Rev. Richard Elual, 1898–1988, vol. VIII
Kerrison, Lt-Col Edmund Roger Allday, 1855–1944, vol. IV
Kerrison, Roger, 1842–1924, vol. II
Kerry, Earl of; Henry Maurice John Petty-Fitzmaurice, 1913–1933, vol. III
Kersey, Major Henry Maitland, 1859–1941, vol. IV
Kersh, Gerald, 1911–1968, vol. VI
Kershaw, 1st Baron, 1881–1961, vol. VI
Kershaw, 2nd Baron, 1904–1961, vol. VI
Kershaw, 3rd Baron, 1906–1962, vol. VI
Kershaw, Harold Slaney, 1882–1969, vol. VI
Kershaw, John Felix, 1873–1927, vol. II
Kershaw, Rev. John Frederick, 1853–1935, vol. III
Kershaw, Sir Leonard William, 1864–1949, vol. IV
Kershaw, Sir Lewis Addin, 1845–1899, vol. I
Kershaw, Sir Louis James, 1869–1947, vol. IV
Kershaw, Sir Noel Thomas, 1863–1930, vol. III
Kershaw, Philip Charles Stones, 1910–1986, vol. VIII
Kershaw, Raymond Newton, 1898–1981, vol. VIII
Kershaw, S. Wayland, *died* 1914, vol. I
Kershaw, Thomas Herbert, 1851–1913, vol. I
Kertesz, Istvan, 1929–1973, vol. VII
Kerwin, Hon. Patrick, 1899–1963, vol. VI

Kessel, Lipmann, 1914–1986, vol. VIII
Kessell, Ernest, 1868–1948, vol. IV
Kestell-Cornish, Rt Rev. George Kestell, 1856–1925, vol. II
Kestell-Cornish, Rt Rev. Robert Kestell, 1824–1909, vol. I
Kesteven, 2nd Baron, 1851–1915, vol. I
Kesteven, 3rd Baron, 1891–1915, vol. I
Kesteven, Sir Charles Henry, *died* 1923, vol. II
Keswick, David Johnston, 1901–1976, vol. VII
Keswick, Major Henry, 1870–1928, vol. II
Keswick, Sir John Henry, 1906–1982, vol. VIII
Keswick, William, 1835–1912, vol. I
Keswick, Sir William Johnston, 1903–1990, vol. VIII
Ketchen, Maj.-Gen. Huntly Douglas Brodie, 1872–1959, vol. V
Ketchen, Maj.-Gen. Isaac, 1839–1920, vol. II
Ketchum, Philip A. C., 1899–1964, vol. VI
Kethley, Andrew Horace Victor P.; *see* Pitt-Kethley.
Kettering, Charles Franklin, 1876–1958, vol. V
Kettle, Edgar Hartley, 1882–1936, vol. III
Kettle, Marguerite Henrietta, 1887–1939, vol. III
Kettle, Rupert Edward Cooke, 1854–1908, vol. I
Kettle, Sir Russell, 1887–1968, vol. VI
Kettle, Thomas Michael, 1880–1916, vol. II
Kettlewell, Arthur Bradley, 1871–1945, vol. IV
Kettlewell, Bernard; *see* Kettlewell, H. B. D.
Kettlewell, (Henry) Bernard (Davis), 1907–1979, vol. VII
Kettlewell, Rev. Percy W. H., 1868–1950, vol. IV
Ketton-Cremer, Robert Wyndham, 1906–1969, vol. VI
Kevenhoerster, Most Rev. John Bernard, 1869–1949, vol. IV
Keverne, Richard, 1882–1950, vol. IV
Kewish, John Douglas, 1907–1989, vol. VIII
Kewley, Rev. James William, 1846–1935, vol. III
Kewley, Ven. John, 1860–1941, vol. IV
Key, Major Sir Aston C.; *see* Cooper-Key.
Key, Maj.-Gen. Berthold Wells, 1895–1986, vol. VIII
Key, Rt Rev. Bransby Lewis, 1838–1901, vol. I
Key, Carl Axel Helmer, 1864–1938, vol. III (A), vol. IV
Key, Sir Charles Edward, 1900–1978, vol. VII
Key, Rt Hon. Charles William, *died* 1964, vol. VI
Key, Captain Edmund Moore Cooper C.; *see* Cooper-Key.
Key, Edward Emmerson, 1917–1976, vol. VII
Key, Ellen, 1849–1926, vol. II
Key, Rev. Sir John Kingsmill Causton, 3rd Bt, 1853–1926, vol. II
Key, Rt Rev. John Maurice, 1905–1984, vol. VIII
Key, Sir Kingsmill Grove, 2nd Bt, 1815–1899, vol. I
Key, Sir Kingsmill James, 4th Bt, 1864–1932, vol. III
Key, Sir Neill C.; *see* Cooper-Key.
Keyes, 1st Baron, 1872–1945, vol. IV
Keyes, Comdr Adrian St Vincent, 1882–1926, vol. II
Keyes, Frances Parkinson, (Mrs Henry Wilder Keyes), 1885–1970, vol. VI
Keyes, Brig.-Gen. Sir Terence Humphrey, 1877–1939, vol. III
Keymer, Sir Daniel Thomas, 1857–1933, vol. III
Keymer, Rev. Nathaniel, 1844–1922, vol. II
Keynes, 1st Baron, 1883–1946, vol. IV

Keynes, Lady; (Lydia Lopokova), 1892–1981, vol. VIII
Keynes, Sir Geoffrey Langdon, 1887–1982, vol. VIII
Keynes, John Neville, 1852–1949, vol. IV
Keys, David Reid, 1856–1939, vol. III
Keys, Rear-Adm. (S) John Anthony, 1863–1955, vol. V
Keys, William Herbert, 1923–1990, vol. VIII
Keyser, Agnes, (Sister Agnes), *died* 1941, vol. IV
Keyser, Arthur Louis, *died* 1924, vol. II
Keyser, Charles Edward, 1847–1929, vol. III
Keyser, Col Frederick Charles, 1841–1920, vol. II
Keyser, Lionel Edward, 1878–1955, vol. V
Keyserling, Count Hermann, 1880–1946, vol. IV
Khachaturyan, Aram Ilych, 1903–1978, vol. VII
Khairpur, HH Mir Sir Faiz Mohammad Khan Talpur, Mir of, *died* 1909, vol. I
Khairpur State, HH Mir Imam Baksh Khan, Ruler of, *died* 1921, vol. II
Khairpur State, HH Mir Ali Nawaz Khan, Ruler of, *died* 1935, vol. III
Khalil, Mohammed Bey, 1895–1950, vol. IV (A), vol. V
Khama, Sir Seretse M., 1921–1980, vol. VII
Khan, Vice-Adm. Afzal Rahman, 1921–1983, vol. VIII
Khan, Gen. Agha Muhammad Y.; *see* Yahya Khan.
Khan, Hon. Chaudin Sir Muhammad Z.; *see* Zafrulla Khan.
Khan, Brig. Fazalur Rahman, 1914–1980, vol. VII
Khan, Ghaanfar Ali, 1875–1959, vol. V
Khan, Major Sir Khan Hashmatullah, *died* 1936, vol. III (A), vol. IV
Khan, Nawab Sir Khan-i-Zaman, *died* 1936, vol. III
Khan, Liaquat Ali, 1895–1951, vol. V
Khan, Field-Marshal Mohammad Ayub, *died* 1974, vol. VII
Khan, Sir Mohammed Y.; *see* Yamin Khan.
Khan, Raja Sir Muhammud Nazim, *died* 1938, vol. III
Khan, Pir-o-Murshid I.; *see* Inayat-Khan.
Khan, Sir Shafa'at Ahmad, 1893–1947, vol. IV
Kher, Shri Bal Gangadhar, 1888–1957, vol. V
Khrushchev, Nikita Sergeyevich, 1894–1971, vol. VII
Khundkar, Sir Nurul Azeem, 1890–1947, vol. IV
Khurshid Jah, Bahadur Sir, Nawab, *died* 1902, vol. I
Kibblewhite, Ebenezer Job, 1846–1924, vol. II
Kidd, Beatrice Ethel, 1867–1958, vol. V
Kidd, Benjamin, 1858–1916, vol. II
Kidd, Rev. Beresford James, 1864–1948, vol. IV
Kidd, Lt-Col Bertram Graham Balfour, 1875–1943, vol. IV
Kidd, Frank S., 1878–1934, vol. III
Kidd, Franklin, 1890–1974, vol. VII
Kidd, Frederic William, 1890–1971, vol. VII
Kidd, Henry, 1862–1923, vol. II
Kidd, James, 1872–1928, vol. II
Kidd, John, 1821–1910, vol. I
Kidd, Lt-Col John Franklin, *died* 1933, vol. III
Kidd, Rt Rev. John Thomas, 1868–1950, vol. IV (A), vol. V
Kidd, Rev. Joseph Henry, 1877–1930, vol. III
Kidd, Dame Margaret Henderson; *see* Macdonald, Dame M. H.

Kidd, Percy M., 1851–1942, vol. IV
Kiddle, Adm. Sir Edward Buxton, 1866–1933, vol. III
Kiddle, Col Frederick, 1871–1936, vol. III
Kiddle, Captain Kerrison, 1876–1949, vol. IV
Kiddy, Arthur William, 1868–1950, vol. IV
Kidman, Sir Sidney, 1857–1935, vol. III
Kidner, Brig. William Elworthy, 1884–1969, vol. VI
Kidron, Abraham, 1919–1982, vol. VIII
Kidson, Edward, 1882–1939, vol. III
Kidson, Fenn, 1874–1965, vol. VI
Kidson, Harold Percy, 1887–1971, vol. VII
Kidston, George Jardine, 1873–1954, vol. V
Kidston, Robert, died 1924, vol. II
Kidston, Hon. William, 1849–1919, vol. II
Kidston-Kerr, Col Alex. Ferrier, 1840–1926, vol. II
Kiek, Rev. Edward S., 1883–1959, vol. V
Kielberg, Sir Michael K.; see Kroyer-Kielberg.
Kielhorn, Franz, 1840–1908, vol. I
Kier, Olaf, 1899–1986, vol. VIII
Kierkels, Most Rev. Leo Peter, 1882–1957, vol. V
Kiesinger, Kurt Georg, 1904–1988, vol. VIII
Kiggell, Lt-Gen. Sir Launcelot Edward, 1862–1954, vol. V
Kikuchi, Baron Dairoku, 1855–1917, vol. II
Kilbracken, 1st Baron, 1847–1932, vol. III
Kilbracken, 2nd Baron, 1877–1950, vol. IV
Kilbrandon, Baron (Life Peer); Charles James Dalrymple Shaw, 1906–1989, vol. VIII
Kilbride, Dennis, 1848–1924, vol. II
Kilburn, Bertram Edward D.; see Dunbar Kilburn.
Kilburn, John Maurice, 1885–1965, vol. VI
Kilburne, George Goodwin, 1839–1924, vol. II
Kilby, Reginald George, died 1949, vol. IV
Kiley, James Daniel, 1865–1953, vol. V
Kilgour, Rev. Robert, 1867–1942, vol. IV
Kilham Roberts, Denys, 1903–1976, vol. VII
Kilkelly, Surg.-Lt-Col Charles Randolph, 1861–1953, vol. V
Killam, Albert Clements, 1849–1908, vol. I
Killanin, 1st Baron; see Morris and Killanin.
Killanin, 2nd Baron, 1867–1927, vol. II
Killby, Leonard Gibbs, 1883–1975, vol. VII
Killearn, 1st Baron, 1880–1964, vol. VI
Killen, Rev. William Dool, 1806–1902, vol. I
Killey, Homer Charles, 1915–1976, vol. VII
Killian, Most Rev. Andrew, 1872–1939, vol. III
Killian, James Rhyne, Jr, 1904–1988, vol. VIII
Killick, Brig. Sir Alexander Herbert, 1894–1975, vol. VII
Killick, Sir Anthony Bernard, 1901–1966, vol. VI
Killick, Esther Margaret, (Mrs A. St G. Huggett), 1902–1960, vol. V
Killick, John Spencer, 1878–1952, vol. V
Killik, Sir Stephen Henry Molyneux, 1861–1938, vol. III
Killin, Robert, 1870–1943, vol. IV
Kilmaine, 4th Baron, 1843–1907, vol. I
Kilmaine, 5th Baron, 1878–1946, vol. IV
Kilmaine, 6th Baron, 1902–1978, vol. VII
Kilmany, Baron (Life Peer); William John St Clair Anstruther-Gray, 1905–1985, vol. VIII
Kilmarnock, 6th Baron, 1903–1975, vol. VII
Kilmorey, 3rd Earl of, 1842–1915, vol. I
Kilmorey, 4th Earl of, 1883–1961, vol. VI

Kilmorey, 5th Earl of, 1915–1977, vol. VII
Kilmuir, 1st Earl of, 1900–1967, vol. VI
Kilner, Group Captain Cecil Francis, 1883–1925, vol. II
Kilner, Lt-Col Charles Harold, 1864–1936, vol. III
Kilner, Cyril, 1910–1985, vol. VIII
Kilner, Rt Rev. Francis Charles, died 1921, vol. II
Kilner, Major Sir Hew Ross, 1892–1953, vol. V
Kilner, T(homas) Pomfret, 1890–1964, vol. VI
Kilpatrick, Florence Antoinette, died 1968, vol. VI
Kilpatrick, Rev. George Dunbar, 1910–1989, vol. VIII
Kilpatrick, George Gordon Dinwiddie, 1888–1975, vol. VII
Kilpatrick, Sir James MacConnell, 1902–1960, vol. V
Kilpatrick, Sir William John, 1906–1985, vol. VIII
Kilpin, Sir Ernest Fuller, 1854–1931, vol. III
Kilvert, Sir Harry Vernon, 1862–1924, vol. II
Kim, Tan Jiak, died 1917, vol. II
Kimalel, Shadrack Kiptenai, 1930–1980, vol. VII
Kimball, Katharine, 1866–1949, vol. IV
Kimball, Major Lawrence, 1900–1971, vol. VII
Kimball, LeRoy Elwood, 1888–1962, vol. VI
Kimbell, Rev. Ralph Raymond, 1884–1964, vol. VI
Kimber, Augustus Charles Edmund, died 1930, vol. III
Kimber, Lt-Col Edmund Gibbs, 1870–1954, vol. V
Kimber, Gurth, 1906–1978, vol. VII
Kimber, Sir Henry, 1st Bt, 1834–1923, vol. II
Kimber, Sir Henry Dixon, 2nd Bt, 1862–1950, vol. IV
Kimber, Sir Sidney Guy, 1873–1949, vol. IV
Kimberley, 1st Earl of, 1826–1902, vol. I
Kimberley, 2nd Earl of, 1848–1932, vol. III
Kimberley, 3rd Earl of, 1883–1941, vol. IV
Kimberley, Paul, died 1964, vol. VI
Kimens, Richard Edward, 1872–1950, vol. IV
Kimmins, Captain Anthony Martin, 1901–1964, vol. VI
Kimmins, Lt-Gen. Sir Brian Charles Hannam, 1899–1979, vol. VII
Kimmins, Charles William, died 1948, vol. IV
Kimmins, Dame Grace Thyrza, died 1954, vol. V
Kimpton, Lawrence Alpheus, 1910–1977, vol. VII
Kinahan, Sir Edward Hudson Hudson-, 2nd Bt, 1865–1938, vol. III
Kinahan, Lt-Col George Frederick H.; see Hudson-Kinahan.
Kinahan, Adm. Sir Harold Richard George, 1893–1980, vol. VII
Kinahan, Sir Robert Henry Hudson-, 3rd Bt, 1872–1949, vol. IV
Kinane, Most Rev. Jeremiah, 1884–1959, vol. V
Kincaid, Charles Augustus, 1870–1954, vol. V
Kincaid, Maj.-Gen. William, 1831–1909, vol. I
Kincaid, Col William Francis Henry Style, 1861–1945, vol. IV
Kincaid-Lennox, Charles Spencer Bateman-Hanbury, 1827–1912, vol. I
Kincaid-Smith, Brig.-Gen. Kenneth John, 1871–1949, vol. IV
Kincaid-Smith, Lt-Col Malcolm, 1874–1938, vol. III
Kincairney, Hon. Lord; William Ellis Gloag, 1828–1909, vol. I
Kinch, Edward, 1848–1920, vol. II

Kinder, Claude William, 1852–1936, vol. III

Kindersley, 1st Baron, 1871–1954, vol. V

Kindersley, 2nd Baron, 1899–1976, vol. VII

Kindersley, Lt-Col Archibald Ogilvie Lyttelton, 1869–1955, vol. V

Kindersley, Rt Rev. George Aelred, 1860–1934, vol. III

Kindersley, Major Guy Molesworth, 1877–1956, vol. V

Kindersley, Major James Benjamin, 1893–1939, vol. III

King, Maj.-Gen. Augustus Henry, 1831–1899, vol. I

King, Very Rev. Albert Edward, 1865–1938, vol. III

King, Albert Theodore, 1885–1939, vol. III

King, Sir Alexander Boyne, 1888–1973, vol. VII

King, Sir Alexander Freeman, 1851–1942, vol. IV

King, Lt-Col Alexander James, 1863–1943, vol. IV

King, Sir Alexander William, 6th Bt (cr 1815), 1892–1969, vol. VI

King, Alfred Hazell, 1896–1956, vol. V

King, Alfred John, 1859–1920, vol. II

King, Brig.-Gen. Algernon D'Aguilar, 1862–1945, vol. IV

King, Sir Anthony Highmore, 1890–1977, vol. VII

King, Sir Archibald John, 1887–1961, vol. VI

King, Sir (Arthur) Henry (William), 1889–1966, vol. VI

King, Arthur Thomas, 1845–1922, vol. II

King, Basil Charles, 1915–1985, vol. VIII

King, Sir Carleton Moss, 1878–1954, vol. V

King, Cecil, 1881–1942, vol. IV

King, Cecil Edward, 1912–1981, vol. VIII

King, Cecil Harmsworth, 1901–1987, vol. VIII

King, Maj.-Gen. Charles, 1844–1933, vol. III

King, Charles A., died 1936, vol. III

King, Sir Charles Albert, 1853–1922, vol. II

King, Col Charles Dickson, 1860–1933, vol. III

King, Major Charles Edward Stuart, 1869–1934, vol. III

King, Lt-Gen. Sir Charles John Stuart, 1890–1967, vol. VI

King, Charles Macintosh, 1836–1920, vol. II

King, Charles Montague, 1872–1956, vol. V

King, Sir Charles Simeon, 3rd Bt (cr 1821), 1840–1921, vol. II

King, Charles Thomas, died 1932, vol. III

King, Brig.-Gen. Sir Charles Wallis, 1861–1943, vol. IV

King, Sir (Clifford) Robertson, 1895–1976, vol. VII

King, Colin Henry Harmsworth, 1931–1977, vol. VII

King, Rev. Cuthbert, 1889–1981, vol. VIII

King, Cyril Lander, died 1972, vol. VII

King, David Wylie, died 1945, vol. IV

King, Col Sir Dudley Gordon Alan D.; see Duckworth-King.

King, Earl Judson, 1901–1962, vol. VI

King, Rt Rev. Edward, 1829–1910, vol. I

King, E(dward) J(ohn) Boswell, died 1975, vol. VII

King, Adm. Edward Leigh Stuart, 1889–1971, vol. VII

King, Col Sir Edwin James, 1877–1952, vol. V

King, Ernest Gerald, died 1955, vol. V

King, Fleet Admiral Ernest Joseph, 1878–1956, vol. V

King, Dame Ethel Locke, 1864–1956, vol. V

King, Frank Gordon, 1915–1988, vol. VIII

King, Engr Rear-Adm. Frank Victor, 1889–1961, vol. VI

King, Frederic, 1853–1933, vol. III

King, Sir (Frederic) Truby, 1858–1938, vol. III

King, Sir Geoffrey Stuart, 1894–1981, vol. VIII

King, Lt-Col Sir George, 1840–1909, vol. I

King, Mrs George, (Sister Janet Wells); see King, Janet.

King, George, died 1922, vol. II

King, Sir George Adolphus, 5th Bt (cr 1815), 1864–1954, vol. V

King, Sir George Anthony, 1858–1928, vol. II

King, George Edward Fenton, 1887–1962, vol. VI

King, George Falconer, died 1929, vol. III

King, Sir George Henry James D.; see Duckworth-King.

King, George Kemp, 1880–1920, vol. II

King, Rt Rev. George Lanchester, 1860–1941, vol. IV

King, Major Gerald Hartley, 1882–1940, vol. III

King, Lt-Col Giffard Hamilton Macarthur, 1885–1956, vol. V (A), vol. VI (AI)

King, Sir Gilbert, 4th Bt (cr 1815), 1846–1920, vol. II

King, Gilbert Walter, 1871–1937, vol. III

King, Mrs Grace M. H.; see Hamilton-King.

King, Harold, 1887–1956, vol. V

King, Maj.-Gen. Harold Francis Sylvester, 1895–1974, vol. VII

King, Lt-Col Harold Holmes, 1884–1961, vol. VI

King, Mrs Harriet Eleanor Baillie Hamilton, died 1920, vol. II

King, Haynes, 1831–1904, vol. I

King, Sir Henry; see King, Sir A. H. W.

King, Sir Henry Clark, 1857–1920, vol. II

King, Cdre Rt Hon. Henry Douglas, 1877–1930, vol. III

King, Rev. Henry Hugh, 1869–1918, vol. II

King, Sir (Henry) Seymour, 1st Bt (cr 1932), 1852–1933, vol. III

King, Hubert John, 1915–1988, vol. VIII

King, Hugh Charles, 1872–1937, vol. III

King, Humphrey Hastings, 1880–1950, vol. IV

King, Ivor Edward, 1889–1983, vol. VIII

King, Rev. J. Harper, died 1933, vol. III

King, Sir James, 1st Bt (cr 1888), 1830–1911, vol. I

King, James Edward, died 1933, vol. III

King, James Foster, 1862–1947, vol. IV

King, Sir James Granville Le Neve, 3rd Bt, 1898–1989, vol. VIII

King, Brig.-Gen. James Gurwood K.; see King-King.

King, James H., 1873–1955, vol. V

King, Janet, (Mrs George King), died 1911, vol. I

King, John Baragwanath, died 1939, vol. III

King, John Charles, 1847–1918, vol. II

King, John Hampden, 1865–1945, vol. IV

King, Most Rev. John Henry, 1880–1965, vol. VI

King, Rev. John Richard, 1835–1907, vol. I

King, Sir John Richard D.; see Duckworth-King.

King, Sir John Westall, 2nd Bt (cr 1888), 1863–1940, vol. III

King, Joseph, 1860–1943, vol. IV

King, Sir Kelso, 1853–1943, vol. IV

King, Kenneth Charles, 1911–1970, vol. VI

King, Lt-Col Lancelot Noel Friedrick Irving, 1878–1947, vol. IV

King, Laurence Edward, 1907–1981, vol. VIII

King, Leonard William, 1869–1919, vol. II

King, Sir Louis, 1904–1972, vol. VII

King, Louis Vessot, 1886–1956, vol. V

King, Sir Lucas White, 1856–1925, vol. II

King, Martin Luther, Jr, 1929–1968, vol. VI

King, Maurice John, 1880–1952, vol. V

King, Merton, died 1939, vol. III

King, Sir Norman, 1880–1963, vol. VI

King, Bt Col Norman Carew, 1871–1953, vol. V

King, Oliver, 1855–1923, vol. II, vol. III

King, Sir Peter Alexander, 7th Bt (cr 1815), 1928–1973, vol. VII

King, Philip, 1904–1979, vol. VII

King, Preston, 1862–1943, vol. IV

King, Richard, (Richard King Huskinson), 1879–1947, vol. IV

King, Richard Ashe, 1839–1932, vol. III

King, Very Rev. Richard George Salmon, died 1958, vol. V

King, Rear-Adm. Richard Matthew, 1883–1969, vol. VI

King, Maj.-Gen. Robert Charles Moss, 1904–1983, vol. VIII

King, Sir Robertson; see King, Sir C. R.

King, Sir Seymour; see King, Sir H. S.

King, Thomas, 1842–1903, vol. I

King, Thomas Mulhall, 1842–1914, vol. I

King, Thomas William, 1881–1936, vol. III

King, Sir Truby; see King, Sir F. T.

King, Col Walter Gawen, 1851–1935, vol. III

King, Sir Wilfred Creyke, died 1943, vol. IV

King, William Benjamin Basil, 1859–1928, vol. II

King, William Bernard Robinson, 1889–1963, vol. VI

King, Maj.-Gen. William Birchall Macaulay, 1878–1950, vol. III

King, William Charles Holland, 1884–1973, vol. VII

King, William Cyril Campbell, 1891–1963, vol. VI

King, William Frederick, 1854–1916, vol. II

King, William Joseph Harding, 1869–1933, vol. III

King, Rt Hon. W(illiam) L(yon) Mackenzie, 1874–1950, vol. IV

King, Sir William Oliver Evelyn M.; see Meade-King.

King, Rev. William Templeton, 1849–1933, vol. III

King, Yeend, 1855–1924, vol. II

King-Farlow, Sir Sydney Nettleton, 1864–1957, vol. V

King-Hall, Baron (Life Peer); William Stephen Richard King-Hall, 1893–1966, vol. VI

King-Hall, Adm. Sir George Fowler, 1850–1939, vol. III

King-Hall, Adm. Sir Herbert Goodenough, 1862–1936, vol. III

King-Hall, Magdalen, (Mrs Patrick Perceval-Maxwell), 1904–1971, vol. VII

King-Harman, Sir Charles Anthony, 1851–1939, vol. III

King-Harman, Captain (Robert) Douglas, 1891–1978, vol. VII

King-Harman, Col Wentworth Henry, 1840–1919, vol. II

King-King, Brig.-Gen. James Gurwood, 1863–1939, vol. III

King-Wood, William, 1867–1921, vol. II

Kingan, William Sinclair, 1876–1946, vol. IV

Kingcome, Engr Vice-Adm. Sir John, 1890–1950, vol. IV

Kingdom, Thomas, 1881–1957, vol. V

Kingdom, Thomas Doyle, 1910–1990, vol. VIII

Kingdon, Sir Donald, 1883–1961, vol. VI

Kingdon, Rt Rev. Hollingworth Tully, 1835–1907, vol. I

Kingdon-Ward, F., 1885–1958, vol. V

Kingham, Sir Robert Dixon, 1883–1966, vol. VI

Kinghorn, Col Harry Jackson, 1867–1947, vol. IV

Kinglake, Robert Alexander, 1843–1915, vol. I

Kingsale, 33rd Baron, 1855–1931, vol. III

Kingsale, 34th Baron, 1882–1969, vol. VI

Kingsburgh, Rt Hon. Lord, 1836–1919, vol. II

Kingsbury, Allan Neave, 1888–1965, vol. VI

Kingscote, Lady Emily Marie, 1836–1910, vol. I

Kingscote, Mrs Howard; see Cleeve, Lucas.

Kingscote, Col Sir Robert Nigel FitzHardinge, 1830–1908, vol. I

Kingscote, Thomas Arthur Fitzhardinge, 1845–1935, vol. III

Kingsford, A. Beresford, died 1944, vol. IV

Kingsford, Charles Lethbridge, 1862–1926, vol. II

Kingsford, Adm. Henry Coare, 1858–1941, vol. IV

Kingsford, Reginald John Lethbridge, 1900–1978, vol. VII

Kingsford-Smith, Air Cdre Sir Charles Edward, 1897–1935, vol. III

Kingsley, Brig. Harold Evelyn William Bell, 1885–1970, vol. VI

Kingsley, Hyman Herbert, 1897–1956, vol. V

Kingsley, J(ohn) Donald, 1908–1972, vol. VII

Kingsley, Col William Henry Bell, 1835–1901, vol. I

Kingsmill, Lt-Col Andrew de Portal, 1881–1956, vol. V

Kingsmill, Adm. Sir Charles Edmund, 1855–1935, vol. III

Kingsmill, Hugh, (Hugh Kingsmill Lunn), 1889–1949, vol. IV

Kingsmill, Sir Walter, 1864–1935, vol. III

Kingsmill, Lt-Col Walter B., 1876–1957, vol. V

Kingsmill, Lt-Col William Henry, 1905–1971, vol. VII

Kingsnorth, Engr Rear-Adm. Sir Arthur Frederick, 1864–1947, vol. IV

Kingston, 9th Earl of, 1874–1946, vol. IV

Kingston, 10th Earl of, 1897–1948, vol. IV

Kingston, Rt Hon. Charles Cameron, 1850–1908, vol. I

Kingston, Most Rev. George Frederick, 1889–1950, vol. IV

Kingston, George Henry, 1866–1933, vol. III

Kingston, Gertrude, died 1937, vol. III

Kingston-McCloughry, Air Vice-Marshal Edgar James, 1896–1972, vol. VII

Kingstone, Arthur Courtney, 1874–1938, vol. III

Kingstone, Brig. James Joseph, died 1966, vol. VI

Kington, Captain William Miles, 1876–1914, vol. I

Kington-Blair-Oliphant, Lt-Col Philip Lawrence, 1867–1918, vol. II

Kingzett, Charles Thomas, 1852–1935, vol. III

Kininmonth, Sir William Hardie, 1904–1988, vol. VIII

Kinkead, Richard John, *died* 1928, vol. II
Kinley, John, *died* 1957, vol. V
Kinloch, Sir Alexander, 10th Bt (*cr* 1686), 1830–1912, vol. I
Kinloch, Maj.-Gen. Alexander Angus Airlie, 1838–1919, vol. II
Kinloch, Sir Alexander Davenport, 12th Bt, 1902–1982, vol. VIII
Kinloch, Brig.-Gen. Sir David Alexander, 11th Bt (*cr* 1686), 1856–1944, vol. IV
Kinloch, Sir George, 3rd Bt (*cr* 1873), 1880–1948, vol. IV
Kinloch, J. Parlane, *died* 1932, vol. III
Kinloch, James Laird, 1878–1952, vol. V
Kinloch, Sir John George Smyth, 2nd Bt (*cr* 1873), 1849–1910, vol. I
Kinloch-Cooke, Sir Clement, 1st Bt, *died* 1944, vol. IV
Kinloss, Baroness (11th in line, styled 8th), 1852–1944, vol. IV
Kinloss, Master of; Rev. Hon. Luis Chandos Francis Temple Morgan-Grenville, 1889–1944, vol. IV
Kinmonth, John Bernard, 1916–1982, vol. VIII
Kinnaird, 11th Lord, 1847–1923, vol. II
Kinnaird, 12th Lord, 1880–1972, vol. VII
Kinnaird, Master of; Hon. Douglas Arthur Kinnaird, 1879–1914, vol. I
Kinnaird, Hon. Emily, *died* 1947, vol. IV
Kinnaird, Hon. Patrick, 1898–1948, vol. IV
Kinnear, 1st Baron, 1833–1917, vol. II
Kinnear, Alfred, *died* 1912, vol. I
Kinnear, Hon. Helen Alice, 1894–1970, vol. VI
Kinnear, John Boyd, 1828–1920, vol. II
Kinnear, Sir Norman Boyd, 1882–1957, vol. V
Kinnear, Sir Walter Samuel, 1872–1953, vol. V
Kinnell, Rev. Gordon, 1891–1971, vol. VII
Kinnoull, 13th (shown as 12th) Earl of, 1855–1916, vol. II
Kinnoull, 14th Earl of, 1902–1938, vol. III
Kino, Major Algernon Roderick, 1880–1924, vol. II
Kinross, 1st Baron, 1837–1905, vol. I
Kinross, 2nd Baron, 1870–1939, vol. III
Kinross, 3rd Baron, 1904–1976, vol. VII
Kinross, 4th Baron, 1906–1985, vol. VIII
Kinross, Albert, 1870–1929, vol. III
Kinross, John, *died* 1931, vol. III
Kinross, John Blythe, 1904–1989, vol. VIII
Kinsey, Sir Joseph James, 1852–1936, vol. III
Kinsey, Joseph Ronald, 1921–1983, vol. VIII
Kinsley, Albert, 1852–1945, vol. IV
Kinsley, Rev. James, 1922–1984, vol. VIII
Kinsman, Frederick Joseph, 1868–1944, vol. IV
Kinsman, Col Gerald Richard Vivian, 1876–1963, vol. VI
Kintore, 9th Earl of, (incorrectly shown as 10th), 1852–1930, vol. III
Kintore, 10th Earl of, (incorrectly shown as 11th), 1879–1966, vol. VI
Kintore, Countess of (11th in line), 1874–1974, vol. VII
Kintore, 12th Earl of, 1908–1989, vol. VIII
Kinvig, Robert Henry, 1893–1969, vol. VI
Kipling, John Lockwood, 1837–1911, vol. I
Kipling, (Joseph) Rudyard, 1865–1936, vol. III
Kipling, Rudyard; *see* Kipling, J. R.

Kippen, William James, *died* 1928, vol. II
Kippenberger, Maj.-Gen. Sir Howard Karl, 1897–1957, vol. V
Kipping, Frederic Stanley, 1863–1949, vol. IV
Kipping, Sir Norman Victor, 1901–1979, vol. VII
Kipps, William John, 1866–1938, vol. III
Kiralfy, Imre, *died* 1919, vol. II
Kirby, Sir Alfred, 1840–1900, vol. I
Kirby, Brig.-Gen. Arthur Durham, 1867–1948, vol. IV
Kirby, Sir Arthur Frank, 1899–1983, vol. VIII
Kirby, Bertie Victor, 1887–1953, vol. V
Kirby, Adm. Francis George, 1854–1951, vol. V
Kirby, Gp Captain Frank Howard, 1871–1956, vol. V
Kirby, George, 1845–1937, vol. III
Kirby, Sir (Horace) Woodburn, 1853–1932, vol. III
Kirby, Jack Howard, 1913–1989, vol. VIII
Kirby, Sir James Norman, 1899–1971, vol. VII
Kirby, Air Cdre John Lawrence, 1899–1980, vol. VII
Kirby, Col Norbone, 1863–1922, vol. II
Kirby, Maj.-Gen. Stanley Woodburn, 1895–1968, vol. VI
Kirby, Brig.-Gen. Stuart Rodger, 1873–1959, vol. V
Kirby, Walter, 1891–1981, vol. VIII
Kirby, William Forsell, 1844–1912, vol. I
Kirby, Sir Woodburn; *see* Kirby, Sir H. W.
Kirchhoffer, Hon. John Nesbitt, 1848–1914, vol. I
Kirchner, Bernard Joseph, 1894–1982, vol. VIII
Kirk, Adam Kennedy, 1893–1975, vol. VII
Kirk, Adm. Alan Goodrich, 1888–1963, vol. VI
Kirk, Alexander Comstock, 1888–1979, vol. VII
Kirk, Sir Amos Child, 1856–1928, vol. II
Kirk, Geoffrey William, 1907–1975, vol. VII
Kirk, Harry B., *died* 1948, vol. IV
Kirk, Sir Henry Alexander, 1847–1929, vol. III
Kirk, James Balfour, 1893–1984, vol. VIII
Kirk, Sir John, 1832–1922, vol. II
Kirk, Sir John, 1847–1922, vol. II
Kirk, John, 1881–1959, vol. V
Kirk, Rt Rev. Kenneth Escott, 1886–1954, vol. V
Kirk, Lucy Phoebe, 1890–1961, vol. VI
Kirk, Rt Hon. Norman Eric, 1923–1974, vol. VII
Kirk, Rev. Paul Thomas Radford-Rowe, *died* 1962, vol. VI
Kirk, Sir Peter Michael, 1928–1977, vol. VII
Kirk, Thomas Sinclair, 1869–1940, vol. III
Kirkaldy, Adam Willis, 1867–1931, vol. III
Kirkaldy, Harold Stewart, 1902–1976, vol. VII
Kirkaldy, John Francis, 1908–1990, vol. VIII
Kirkbride, Sir Alec Seath, 1897–1978, vol. VII
Kirkby, Lt-Col Henry McKenzie, 1877–1952, vol. V
Kirkby, Rt Rev. Sydney James, 1879–1935, vol. III
Kirkconnell, Watson, 1895–1977, vol. VII
Kirke, Claud Cecil Augustus, 1875–1959, vol. V
Kirke, Henry, 1842–1925, vol. II
Kirke, Percy St George, *died* 1966, vol. VI
Kirke, Gen. Sir Walter Mervyn St George, 1877–1949, vol. IV
Kirkhope, Lt-Col Kenneth Macleay, 1877–1950, vol. IV
Kirkland, Edward Chase, 1894–1975, vol. VII
Kirkland, James Hampton, 1859–1939, vol. III
Kirkland, Rev. Canon Thomas James, 1884–1965, vol. VI

Kirkley, 1st Baron, 1863–1935, vol. III
Kirkley, Sir (Howard) Leslie, 1911–1989, vol. VIII
Kirkley, Sir Leslie; *see* Kirkley, Sir H. L.
Kirkman, Frederick Bernulf Beever, 1869–1945, vol. IV
Kirkman, Maj.-Gen. John Mather, 1898–1964, vol. VI
Kirkman, Gen. Sir Sidney Chevalier, 1895–1982, vol. VIII
Kirkman, Hon. Thomas, 1843–1919, vol. II
Kirkness, Lewis Hawker, 1881–1950, vol. IV
Kirkpatrick, Very Rev. Alexander Francis, 1849–1940, vol. III
Kirkpatrick, Lt-Col Alexander Ronald Yvone, 1868–1950, vol. IV
Kirkpatrick, Hon. Andrew Alexander, 1848–1928, vol. II
Kirkpatrick, Maj.-Gen. Charles, 1879–1955, vol. V
Kirkpatrick, Sir Charles Sharpe, 9th Bt, 1874–1937, vol. III
Kirkpatrick, Sir Cyril Reginald Sutton, 1872–1957, vol. V
Kirkpatrick, Francis, 1840–1921, vol. II
Kirkpatrick, Frederick Alex., 1861–1953, vol. V
Kirkpatrick, Hon. Sir George Airey, 1841–1899, vol. I
Kirkpatrick, Gen. Sir George Macaulay, 1866–1950, vol. IV
Kirkpatrick, Lt-Col Henry, 1871–1958, vol. V
Kirkpatrick, Lt-Col Henry Pownall, 1862–1919, vol. II
Kirkpatrick, Rev. Canon Herbert Francis, 1888–1971, vol. VII
Kirkpatrick, Air Vice-Marshal Herbert James, 1910–1977, vol. VII
Kirkpatrick, Col Ivone, 1860–1936, vol. III
Kirkpatrick, Sir Ivone Augustine, *died* 1964, vol. VI
Kirkpatrick, Sir James, 8th Bt, 1841–1899, vol. I
Kirkpatrick, Sir James Alexander, 10th Bt, 1918–1954, vol. V
Kirkpatrick, John, 1835–1926, vol. II
Kirkpatrick, Col Roger, 1859–1933, vol. III
Kirkpatrick, T. Percy C., 1869–1954, vol. V
Kirkpatrick, Major William, 1863–1941, vol. IV
Kirkpatrick, William, 1886–1947, vol. IV
Kirkpatrick, William MacColin, 1878–1953, vol. V
Kirkpatrick, Brig.-Gen. William Johnston, 1851–1931, vol. III
Kirkpatrick-Caldecot, Ivone, 1867–1951, vol. V
Kirkup, Brig. Philip, 1893–1959, vol. V
Kirkup, Thomas, 1844–1912, vol. I
Kirkup, Thomas Henry, 1864–1951, vol. V
Kirkwood, 1st Baron, 1872–1955, vol. V
Kirkwood, 2nd Baron, 1903–1970, vol. VI
Kirkwood, Col Carleton Hooper Morrison, 1860–1937, vol. III
Kirkwood, Lt-Col James George, 1872–1955, vol. V
Kirkwood, Major John Hendley Morrison, 1877–1924, vol. II
Kirkwood, Sir Robert Lucien Morrison, 1904–1984, vol. VIII
Kirkwood, Sir Walter Guy Coffin, 1856–1935, vol. III
Kirkwood, William Montague Hammett, 1850–1926, vol. II

Kirton, Robert James, 1901–1988, vol. VIII
Kirwan, Lt-Gen. Sir Bertram Richard, 1871–1960, vol. V
Kirwan, Rev. Ernest Cecil, 1867–1936, vol. III
Kirwan, Lt-Col Ernest William O'Gorman, 1887–1965, vol. VI
Kirwan, Geoffrey Dugdale, 1896–1970, vol. VI
Kirwan, Hon. Sir John Waters, 1866–1949, vol. IV
Kirwan, Lionel M.; *see* Maitland-Kirwan.
Kirwan-Taylor, Harold George, 1895–1981, vol. VIII
Kisch, Barthold Schlesinger, 1882–1961, vol. VI
Kisch, Sir Cecil Hermann, 1884–1961, vol. VI
Kisch, Brig. Frederick Hermann, 1888–1943, vol. IV
Kisch, Harold, *died* 1959, vol. V
Kisch, Hermann Michael, 1850–1942, vol. IV
Kishangarh, Lt-Col HH Umdai Rajhae Buland Makan Maharajadhiraj Maharaj Sir Madan Singh Bahadur, 1884–1926, vol. II
Kishun Pershad, Raja-i-Rajayan Maharajah Bahadur, Yamin-us-Saltanat, Sir, 1864–1940, vol. III
Kissan, Edgar Duguid, *died* 1932, vol. III
Kissen, Hon. Lord; Manuel Kissen, 1912–1981, vol. VIII
Kissen, Manuel; *see* Kissen, Hon. Lord.
Kistiakowsky, George Bogdan, 1900–1982, vol. VIII
Kitcat, Mabel, (Mrs S. A. P. Kitcat), *died* 1922, vol. II
Kitchen, Sir Geoffrey, 1906–1978, vol. VII
Kitchen, Percy Inman, 1883–1963, vol. VI
Kitchener of Khartoum, 1st Earl, 1850–1916, vol. II
Kitchener of Khartoum, 2nd Earl, 1846–1937, vol. III
Kitchener, Francis Elliott, 1838–1915, vol. I
Kitchener, Lt-Gen. Sir Frederick Walter, 1858–1912, vol. I
Kitchin, Ven. Arthur, 1855–1928, vol. II
Kitchin, Arthur James Warburton, 1870–1957, vol. V
Kitchin, Clifford Henry Benn, 1895–1967, vol. VI
Kitchin, Darcy Butterworth, 1863–1939, vol. III
Kitchin, Finlay Lorimer, *died* 1934, vol. III
Kitchin, Frederick Harcourt, 1867–1932, vol. III
Kitchin, Very Rev. George William, 1827–1912, vol. I
Kitchin, John, 1869–1951, vol. V
Kitchin, John Leslie Harlow, 1924–1982, vol. VIII
Kitchin, Shepherd Braithwaite, *died* 1944, vol. IV
Kitching, Rt Rev. Arthur Leonard, 1875–1960, vol. V
Kitching, Elsie, 1870–1955, vol. V
Kitching, Theodore Hopkins, 1866–1930, vol. III
Kitching, Wilfred, 1893–1977, vol. VII
Kite, Frederick William, 1856–1940, vol. III
Kite, Rev. Joseph Bertram, 1857–1939, vol. III
Kitiyakara, Prince Nakkhatra Mangala, 1898–1953, vol. V
Kitson, Sir Albert Ernest, 1868–1937, vol. III
Kitson, Col Charles Edward, 1874–1928, vol. II
Kitson, Charles Herbert, 1874–1944, vol. IV
Kitson, Geoffrey Herbert, 1896–1974, vol. VII
Kitson, Sir George Vernon, 1899–1980, vol. VII
Kitson, Maj.-Gen. Sir Gerald Charles, 1856–1950, vol. IV
Kitson, Vice-Adm. Sir Henry Karslake, 1877–1952, vol. V
Kitson, Captain James Buller, 1883–1976, vol. VII
Kitson, Hon. James Clifford, 1864–1942, vol. IV
Kitson, Col James Edward, 1848–1912, vol. I

Kitson, Sydney Decimus, 1871–1937, vol. III
Kitson, William Henry, 1886–1952, vol. V
Kitson Clark, George Sidney Roberts, 1900–1975, vol. VII
Kittermaster, F. R., 1899–1972, vol. VII
Kittermaster, Sir Harold Baxter, 1879–1939, vol. III
Kitto, Humphrey Davy Findley, 1897–1982, vol. VIII
Kitto, John Vivian, 1875–1953, vol. V
Kittoe, Lt-Col Montagu Francis Markham Sloane, *died* 1967, vol. VI
Kitton, Frederic George, 1856–1904, vol. I
Kitts, Sir Francis Joseph, 1914–1979, vol. VII
Kittson, Rev. Henry, 1848–1925, vol. II, vol. III
Klaestad, Helge, 1885–1965, vol. VI
Klecki, Paul; *see* Kletzi, P.
Kleczkowski, Alfred Alexander Peter, 1908–1970, vol. VI
Kleffens, Eelco Nicolaas van, 1894–1983, vol. VIII
Kleiber, Erich, 1890–1956, vol. V
Klein, Edward Emanuel, 1844–1925, vol. II
Klein, Abbé Felix, 1862–1954, vol. V
Klein, Herman, 1856–1934, vol. III
Klein, Sydney Turner, 1853–1934, vol. III
Kleinwort, Sir Alexander Drake, 1st Bt, 1858–1935, vol. III
Kleinwort, Sir Alexander Santiago, 2nd Bt, 1892–1983, vol. VIII
Kleinwort, Sir Cyril Hugh, 1905–1980, vol. VII
Kleinwort, Ernest Greverus, 1901–1977, vol. VII
Kleinwort, Herman Greverus, 1856–1942, vol. IV
Klemperer, Otto, 1885–1973, vol. VII
Kletzi, Paul, (Paul Klecki), 1900–1973, vol. VII
Klickmann, Flora, (Mrs Henderson-Smith), *died* 1958, vol. V
Klijnstra, Gerrit Dirk Ale, 1912–1976, vol. VII
Klinck, Leonard Sylvanus, 1877–1969, vol. VI
Klinghoffer, Clara, 1900–1970, vol. VI
Klopsch, Louis, *died* 1910, vol. I
Klotz, Otto, 1852–1923, vol. II
Klugh, Ven. Leonard, 1859–1943, vol. IV
Klyne, William, 1913–1977, vol. VII
Knaggs, Col Henry Thomas, 1863–1946, vol. IV
Knaggs, Col Morton Herbert, 1871–1948, vol. IV
Knaggs, Robert Lawford, *died* 1945, vol. IV
Knaggs, Sir Samuel William, 1856–1924, vol. II
Knapp, Sir Arthur Rowland, *died* 1954, vol. V
Knapp, Charles Welbourne, 1848–1916, vol. II
Knapp, Brig.-Gen. Kempster Kenmure, 1866–1948, vol. IV
Knapp, Marion Domville, 1870–1963, vol. VI
Knapp, Valentine, 1861–1935, vol. III
Knapp, William Ireland, 1835–1908, vol. I
Knapp-Fisher, Arthur Bedford, 1888–1965, vol. VI
Knapp-Fisher, Sir Edward Francis, 1864–1940, vol. III
Knaresborough, 1st Baron, 1845–1929, vol. III
Knatchbull, Brig.-Gen. George Wyndham Chichester, 1862–1943, vol. IV
Knatchbull, Major Reginald Norton, 1872–1917, vol. II
Knatchbull, Sir Wyndham, 12th Bt, 1844–1917, vol. II
Knatchbull-Hugessen, Hon. Adrian Norton, 1891–1976, vol. VII

Knatchbull-Hugessen, Herbert Thomas, 1835–1922, vol. II
Knatchbull-Hugessen, Sir Hughe Montgomery, 1886–1971, vol. VII
Kneale, Sydney James, 1895–1975, vol. VII
Kneale, William Calvert, 1906–1990, vol. VIII
Knebworth, Viscount; Edward Anthony James Lytton, 1903–1933, vol. III
Knebworth, Viscount; Alexander Edward John Lytton, 1910–1942, vol. IV
Knecht, Edmund, 1861–1925, vol. II
Kneeland, Abner W., 1853–1928, vol. II
Kneen, John Joseph, 1873–1938, vol. III
Kneen, Thomas, *died* 1916, vol. II
Kneen, William, 1862–1921, vol. II
Knell, Rt Rev. Eric Henry, 1903–1987, vol. VIII
Knibbs, Sir George Handley, 1858–1929, vol. III
Knight, A. Charles, *died* 1958, vol. V
Knight, Most Rev. Alan John, 1902–1979, vol. VII
Knight, Rt Rev. Albion Williamson, 1859–1936, vol. III
Knight, Alfred Ernest, 1861–1934, vol. III
Knight, Rev. Angus Clifton, 1873–1931, vol. III
Knight, Archibald Patterson, *died* 1935, vol. III
Knight, Arthur Harold John, 1903–1963, vol. VI
Knight, Rt Rev. Arthur Mesac, 1964–1939, vol. III
Knight, (Arthur) Rex, 1903–1963, vol. VI
Knight, Bert Cyril James Gabriel, 1904–1981, vol. VIII
Knight, Charles, 1863–1941, vol. IV
Knight, Charles, 1901–1990, vol. VIII
Knight, Charles Andrew R. B.; *see* Rouse-Boughton-Knight.
Knight, Charles Joseph, 1863–1950, vol. IV
Knight, Captain Charles William Robert, 1884–1957, vol. V
Knight, Clara Millicent, *died* 1950, vol. IV
Knight, Clifford, 1909–1959, vol. V
Knight, Edward Frederick, 1852–1925, vol. II
Knight, Eric, 1897–1943, vol. IV
Knight, Eric Ayshford, 1863–1944, vol. IV
Knight, Eric John Percy Crawford L; *see* Lombard Knight.
Knight, Esmond Pennington, 1906–1987, vol. VIII
Knight, Sir Frederic Winn, 1812–1897, vol. I
Knight, Sir George, 1874–1951, vol. V
Knight, (George Richard) Wilson, 1897–1985, vol. VIII
Knight, Gerald Hocken, 1908–1979, vol. VII
Knight, Gilfred Norman, 1891–1978, vol. VII
Knight, Air Vice-Marshal Glen Albyn Martin, 1903–1990, vol. VIII
Knight, Harold, 1874–1961, vol. VI
Knight, Sir Henry Edmund, 1833–1917, vol. II
Knight, Sir Henry Foley, 1886–1960, vol. V
Knight, Rt Rev. Henry Joseph Corbett, *died* 1920, vol. II
Knight, Brig.-Gen. Henry Lewkenor, 1874–1945, vol. IV
Knight, Henry Lougher, 1907–1986, vol. VIII
Knight, Rev. Herbert Theodore, 1869–1934, vol. III
Knight, Holford, 1877–1936, vol. III
Knight, Jasper Frederick, 1909–1972, vol. VII
Knight, John Broughton, 1863–1937, vol. III

Knight, John Buxton, 1842–1908, vol. I
Knight, Captain John Peake, 1890–1916, vol. II
Knight, Jonathan; *see* Knight, B. C. J. G.
Knight, Joseph, 1829–1907, vol. I
Knight, Joseph, 1838–1909, vol. I
Knight, Dame Laura, 1877–1970, vol. VI
Knight, Rt Rev. Leslie Albert, 1890–1950, vol. IV (A), vol. V
Knight, Very Rev. Marcus, 1903–1988, vol. VIII
Knight, Nicholas, 1861–1942, vol. IV
Knight, Percy, 1891–1968, vol. VI
Knight, Rex; *see* Knight, A. R.
Knight, Rt Rev. Samuel Kirshbaum, 1868–1932, vol. III
Knight, Chief Engr T. H., *died* 1918, vol. II
Knight, William Anderson, 1861–1915, vol. I, vol. III
Knight, William Angus, 1836–1916, vol. II
Knight, William Francis Jackson, 1895–1964, vol. VI
Knight, William George, *died* 1938, vol. III
Knight, William George, 1858–1943, vol. IV
Knight, William Lowry Craig, 1889–1955, vol. V
Knight, William Stanley Macbean, 1869–1950, vol. IV
Knight, Wilson; *see* Knight, G. R. W.
Knight, Maj.-Gen. Sir Wyndham Charles, 1863–1942, vol. IV
Knight-Adkin, Harry Kenrick, 1851–1927, vol. II
Knight-Adkin, Rev. Walter Kenrick, 1880–1957, vol. V
Knight Dix, Dorothy; *see* Waddy, D. K.
Knightley, Lady; (Louisa Mary), 1842–1913, vol. I
Knightley, Sir Charles Valentine, 5th Bt, 1853–1932, vol. III
Knightley, Rev. Sir Henry Francis, 6th Bt, 1854–1938, vol. III
Knightley, Captain Percy Frank, 1874–1942, vol. IV
Knightley, Rev. Sir Valentine, 4th Bt, 1812–1898, vol. I
Knighton, William, *died* 1900, vol. I
Knighton-Hammond, Arthur Henry, 1875–1970, vol. VI
Knights, Henry Newton, *died* 1959, vol. V
Knights, Maj.-Gen. Robert William, 1912–1975, vol. VII
Knill, Sir Ian S.; *see* Stuart-Knill.
Knill, Sir John, 2nd Bt, 1856–1934, vol. III
Knill, Sir Stuart, 1st Bt, 1824–1898, vol. I
Knittel, John Herman Emanuel, 1891–1970, vol. VI
Knobel, Edward Ball, 1841–1930, vol. III
Knoblock, Edward, 1874–1945, vol. IV
Knocker, Sir Edward Wollaston Nadir, 1838–1907, vol. I
Knollys, 1st Viscount, 1837–1924, vol. II
Knollys, 2nd Viscount, 1895–1966, vol. VI
Knollys, Rev. Archibald A., 1851–1940, vol. III
Knollys, Hon. Charlotte; *see* Knollys, Hon. E. C.
Knollys, Sir Courtenay (Clement), 1849–1905, vol. I
Knollys, Sir Courtney; *see* Knollys, Sir C. C.
Knollys, Hon. (Elizabeth) Charlotte, 1835–1930, vol. III
Knollys, Rev. Erskine William, 1842–1923, vol. II
Knollys, Col Sir Henry, 1840–1930, vol. III
Knollys, Major Louis Frederic, 1847–1922, vol. II
Knollys, William Edward, 1843–1910, vol. I

Knoop, Douglas, 1883–1948, vol. IV
Knopf, Alfred A., 1892–1984, vol. VIII
Knott, Rev. Alfred Ernest, 1869–1951, vol. V
Knott, Cargill Gilston, 1856–1922, vol. II
Knott, Frank Alexander, 1889–1962, vol. VI
Knott, Lt-Gen. Sir Harold Edwin, 1903–1974, vol. VII
Knott, Sir James, 1st Bt, 1855–1934, vol. III
Knott, John, 1853–1921, vol. II
Knott, John Espenett, *died* 1959, vol. V
Knott, Ralph, 1878–1929, vol. III
Knott, Stratton Collings, 1856–1904, vol. I
Knott, Sir Thomas Garbutt, 2nd Bt, 1879–1949, vol. IV
Knottesford-Fortescue, Laurence; *see* Fortescue.
Knowland, William Fife, 1908–1974, vol. VII
Knowles, Arthur, 1858–1929, vol. III
Knowles, Arthur Richard, 1899–1960, vol. V
Knowles, Maj.-Gen. Sir Charles Benjamin, 1835–1924, vol. II
Knowles, Sir Charles George Frederick, 4th Bt, 1832–1918, vol. II
Knowles, Rev. David; *see* Knowles, Rev. Michael Clive.
Knowles, Rt Rev. Donald Rowland, 1898–1977, vol. VII
Knowles, Air Vice-Marshal Edgar, 1907–1977, vol. VII
Knowles, Rt Rev. Edwin Hubert, 1874–1962, vol. VI
Knowles, Frances Ivens; *see* Knowles, M. H. F. I.
Knowles, Rev. Francis, 1830–1916, vol. II
Knowles, Sir Francis Gerald William, 6th Bt, 1915–1974, vol. VII
Knowles, Sir Francis Howe Seymour, 5th Bt, 1886–1953, vol. V
Knowles, Frank, 1865–1934, vol. III
Knowles, Frederick Arthur, 1872–1922, vol. II
Knowles, Rear-Adm. George Herbert, 1881–1961, vol. VI
Knowles, Sir George Shaw, 1882–1947, vol. IV
Knowles, George Sheridan, 1863–1931, vol. III
Knowles, John, 1898–1977, vol. VII
Knowles, Lt-Col John George, *died* 1919, vol. II
Knowles, Joshua Kenneth, 1903–1974, vol. VII
Knowles, Ven. Kenneth Davenport, 1874–1944, vol. IV
Knowles, Sir Lees, 1st Bt (*cr* 1903), 1857–1928, vol. II
Knowles, Lilian Charlotte Anne, *died* 1926, vol. II
Knowles, Mabel Winifred, (May Wynne), 1875–1949, vol. IV
Knowles, (Mary Hannah) Frances Ivens, *died* 1944, vol. IV
Knowles, Maurice Baxendale, 1893–1988, vol. VIII
Knowles, Rev. Michael Clive, (Rev. David Knowles), 1896–1974, vol. VII
Knowles, Lt-Col Robert, 1883–1936, vol. III
Knowles, Robert Millington, 1843–1924, vol. II
Knowles, William Henry, 1857–1943, vol. IV
Knowling, Hon. George, 1841–1923, vol. II
Knowling, Rev. Richard John, 1851–1919, vol. II
Knowlson, Thomas Sharper, 1867–1947, vol. IV
Knox, Rt Hon. Sir Adrian, 1863–1932, vol. III
Knox, Alfred Dilwyn, *died* 1943, vol. IV

Knox, Maj.-Gen. Sir Alfred William Fortescue, 1870–1964, vol. VI
Knox, Rev. Andrew, 1849–1915, vol. I
Knox, Col Arthur Francis Gore P. K. G.; see Pery-Knox-Gore.
Knox, Major Arthur Rice, 1863–1917, vol. II
Knox, Lt-Gen. Sir Charles Edmond, 1846–1938, vol. III
Knox, Collie, died 1977, vol. VII
Knox, Rt Rev. Edmund Arbuthnott, 1847–1937, vol. III
Knox, (Edmund Francis) Vesey, 1865–1921, vol. II
Knox, Edmund George Valpy, 1881–1971, vol. VII
Knox, Sir Edward, 1819–1901, vol. I
Knox, Sir Edward Ritchie, 1889–1973, vol. VII
Knox, Brig. Sir Errol Galbraith, 1889–1949, vol. IV
Knox, Sir Geoffrey George, 1884–1958, vol. V
Knox, Sir George Edward, 1845–1922, vol. II
Knox, Brig. Hon. Sir George Hodges, 1885–1960, vol. V
Knox, Lt-Col George Stuart, 1871–1945, vol. IV
Knox, Lt-Col Sir Hamish James Stuart, died 1940, vol. III
Knox, Gen. Sir Harry Hugh Sidney, 1873–1971, vol. VII
Knox, Henry Murray Owen, 1909–1986, vol. VIII
Knox, Brig.-Gen. Henry Owen, 1874–1955, vol. V
Knox, Sir James, 1850–1926, vol. II
Knox, Sir James, 1862–1938, vol. III
Knox, His Eminence Cardinal James Robert, 1914–1983, vol. VIII
Knox, John Crawford, 1891–1964, vol. VI
Knox, Joseph Alan Cruden, 1911–1984, vol. VIII
Knox, Sir Malcolm; see Knox, Sir T. M.
Knox, Rt Hon. Sir Ralph Henry, 1836–1913, vol. I
Knox, Lt-Col Richard, 1848–1918, vol. II
Knox, Robert, died 1928, vol. II
Knox, Sir Robert Uchtred Eyre, 1889–1965, vol. VI
Knox, Sir Robert Wilson, 1890–1973, vol. VII
Knox, Rt Rev. Mgr Ronald Arbuthnott, 1888–1957, vol. V
Knox, Lt-Col Stuart George, 1869–1956, vol. V
Knox, Sir (Thomas) Malcolm, 1900–1980, vol. VII
Knox, Vesey; see Knox, E. F. V.
Knox, Walter Ernest, 1894–1970, vol. VI
Knox, Rev. Wilfred Lawrence, died 1950, vol. IV
Knox, Hon. William, 1850–1913, vol. I
Knox, Maj.-Gen. Sir William George, 1847–1916, vol. II
Knox Johnston, Anthony Gordon; see Johnston.
Knox Little, Rev. William John, 1839–1918, vol. II
Knox-Shaw, Charles Thomas, 1854–1939, vol. III
Knox-Shaw, Harold, 1885–1970, vol. VI
Knox-Shaw, Thomas, 1886–1972, vol. VII
Knubley, Rev. Edward Ponsonby, 1850–1931, vol. III
Knudsen, Sir Karl Fredrik, 1872–1937, vol. III
Knudsen, Martin, 1871–1949, vol. IV
Knuthsen, Sir Louis Francis Roebuck, died 1957, vol. V
Knutsford, 1st Viscount, 1825–1914, vol. I
Knutsford, 2nd Viscount, 1855–1931, vol. III
Knutsford, 3rd Viscount, 1855–1935, vol. III
Knutsford, 4th Viscount, 1888–1976, vol. VII
Knutsford, 5th Viscount, 1920–1986, vol. VIII

Knyvett, Alexander Vansittart, 1848–1911, vol. I
Knyvett, Rt Rev. Carey Frederick, 1885–1967, vol. VI
Knyvett, Seymour Henry, 1849–1915, vol. I
Koch, Lauge, 1892–1964, vol. VI
Koch, Ludwig, 1881–1974, vol. VII
Koch, Robert, 1843–1910, vol. I
Kodàly, Zoltán, 1882–1967, vol. VI
Kodama, Lt-Gen. Baron Gentaro, 1855–1906, vol. I
Kodicek, Egon Hynek, 1908–1982, vol. VIII
Koe, Maj.-Gen. Frederick William Brooke, 1862–1935, vol. III
Koe, Brig.-Gen. Lancelot Charles, died 1941, vol. IV
Koebel, Major Frederick Ernest, 1881–1940, vol. III
Koebel, W. H., 1872–1923, vol. II
Koechlin, Raymond, 1860–1931, vol. III
Koelle, Vice-Adm. Sir Harry Philpot, 1901–1980, vol. VII
Koenig, Gén. d'Armée Marie-Pierre, 1898–1970, vol. VI
Koenigsberger, Franz, 1907–1979, vol. VII
Koeppler, Sir Henry, (Sir Heinz), 1912–1979, vol. VII
Koestler, Arthur, 1905–1983, vol. VIII
Kohan, Major Charles Mendel, 1884–1974, vol. VII
Kohan, Robert Mendel, 1883–1967, vol. VI
Kohler, Joy David, 1908–1990, vol. VIII
Kohler, Kaufmann, 1843–1926, vol. II
Kohlsaat, Herman H., 1853–1924, vol. II, vol. III
Koizumi, Yakumo; see Hearn, L.
Kokkinakis, Theodoros G.; see Athenagoras, T.
Kokoschka, Oskar, 1886–1980, vol. VII
Kolbuszewski, Janusz, 1915–1984, vol. VIII
Kole, Nene Sir Emmanuel Mate, 1860–1939, vol. III
Kolhapur, Maharaja of, 1874–1922, vol. II
Kolhapur, Maharaja of, 1897–1940, vol. III
Kolhapur, Maharaja of, 1910–1983, vol. VIII
Kollengode, Raja Sir Vengarad of, 1873–1940, vol. III
Koller, Pius Charles, 1904–1979, vol. VII
Kominski, Daniel; see Kaye, Danny.
Komisarjevsky, Theodore, died 1954, vol. V
Komura, Marquis Jutaro, 1855–1911, vol. I
Kon, George Armand Robert, 1892–1951, vol. V
Konig, Frederick Adolphus, 1867–1940, vol. III
Konody, Paul G., 1872–1933, vol. III
Konovalov, Sergey, 1899–1982, vol. VIII
Konstam, Edwin Max., 1870–1956, vol. V
Konstam, Geoffrey Lawrence Samuel, 1899–1962, vol. VI
Koo, Vi Kyuin Wellington, 1888–1985, vol. VIII
Koop, Albert James, 1877–1945, vol. IV
Koopmans, Tjalling Charles, 1910–1985, vol. VIII
Koppel, Percy Alexander, 1876–1932, vol. III
Korda, Sir Alexander, 1893–1956, vol. V
Korngold, Erich Wolfgang, 1897–1957, vol. V
Korsah, Sir Arku; see Korsah, Sir K. A.
Korsah, Sir (Kobina) Arku, 1894–1967, vol. VI
Kortright, Sir Cornelius Hendrichsen, 1817–1897, vol. I
Kortright, Henry Somers, 1870–1942, vol. IV
Kossuth, Francis, 1841–1914, vol. I
Kostelanetz, André, 1901–1980, vol. VII
Kosygin, Alexei Nikolaevich, 1904–1980, vol. VII
Kotah, Lt-Col HH Maharajahdiraj Maharaj Mahimahendra Maharaorajaji Shri Sir Umed Singh Bahadur, 1873–1941, vol. IV

Kotelawala, Col Rt Hon. Sir John Lionel, 1897–1980, vol. VII

Kotewall, Sir Robert Hormus, 1880–1949, vol. IV

Kothari, Sir Jehangir Hormasji, *died* 1934, vol. III

Kothavala, Tehmasp Tehmul, 1893–1977, vol. VII

Kotval, Peshotan Sohrabji, 1868–1949, vol. IV (A)

Kotze, Sir John Gilbert, 1849–1940, vol. III

Kotzé, Sir Robert Nelson, 1870–1953, vol. V

Kouropatkin, Alexei Nicholaevitch, 1848–1921, vol. II

Koussevitzky, Serge, 1874–1951, vol. V

Kozygin, Alexei Nikolaevich; *see* Kosygin, A. N.

Kraay, Colin Mackennal, 1918–1982, vol. VIII

Krabbé, Col Clarence Brehmer, 1886–1985, vol. VIII

Krabbé, Paymaster-Rear-Adm. Frederick James, 1860–1933, vol. III

Kratovil, Bohuslav G., 1901–1972, vol. VII

Kraus, Adolf, 1849–1928, vol. II, vol. III

Kraus, Otakar, 1909–1980, vol. VII

Krause, Frederick Edward Traugott, 1868–1959, vol. V

Krause, Lotte, (Madame Otto Krause); *see* Lehmann, Lotte.

Krausse, Alexis Sidney, 1859–1904, vol. I

Krebs, Sir Hans Adolf, 1900–1981, vol. VIII

Kreisler, Fritz, 1875–1962, vol. VI

Kremer, Michael, 1907–1988, vol. VIII

Kretser, Edward de, 1854–1925, vol. II

Kreuger, Ivar, 1880–1932, vol. III

Kreyer, Brig. Hubert Stanley, 1890–1949, vol. IV

Krips, Josef, 1902–1974, vol. VII

Krishna, Sri, 1896–1984, vol. VIII

Krishna Menon, Vengalil Krishnan, 1896–1974, vol. VII

Krishna Rau, Sir Mysore Nanjundiah, 1877–1958, vol. V

Krishna Shumshere, Jung Bahadur Rana, General, 1900–1977, vol. VII

Krishnama Chariar, Sir Vangal Thiruvenkatachari, 1881–1964, vol. VI

Krishnamurti, Jiddu, 1895–1986, vol. VIII

Krishnan, Cheruvari, 1868–1927, vol. II

Krishnan, Sir Kariamanikkam Srinivasa, 1898–1961, vol. VI

Krishnan Nair, Dewan Bahadur Sir M., 1870–1938, vol. III

Krishnaswami Ayyar, Diwan Bahadur Sir Alladi, 1883–1953, vol. V

Kristensen, Thorkil, 1899–1989, vol. VIII

Krogh, August, 1874–1949, vol. IV

Kroll, Wilhelm, 1869–1939, vol. III

Kronberger, Hans, 1920–1970, vol. VI

Kropotkin, Prince Peter Alexeieivitch, 1842–1921, vol. II

Kroyer-Kielberg, Sir (F.) Michael, 1882–1958, vol. V

Krug, Julius A., 1907–1970, vol. VI

Kruger, Stephen J. Paul, 1825–1904, vol. I

Kubelik, Jan, 1880–1940, vol. III

Küchemann, Dietrich, 1911–1976, vol. VII

Kuenen, Johannes Petrus, 1866–1922, vol. II

Kuhe, William, 1823–1912, vol. I

Kuhn, Richard, 1900–1967, vol. VI

Kuiper, Gerard Peter, 1905–1973, vol. VII

Kukday, Col Sir Krishnaji Vishnoo, 1870–1958, vol. V (A), vol. VI (AI)

Kuklos; *see* Wray, W. Fitzwater.

Kuprin, Aleksandr Ivonovich, 1870–1938, vol. III

Kuroki, General Count, 1844–1923, vol. II

Kurz, Otto, 1908–1975, vol. VII

Kusel, Baron de, 1848–1917, vol. II

Küssner, Amalia, *died* 1932, vol. III

Kutch, Maharao of; Lt-Col HH Maharaja Dhiraj Mirza Maharao Shri Sir Vijayaraji, Savai Bahadur, 1885–1948, vol. IV

Kutch, HH Maharaja Dhiraj Mirzan Maharao Shri Khengarji Sawai Bahadur Maharao of, 1866–1942, vol. IV

Kutlehr, Raja Ram Pal of, 1849–1927, vol. II, vol. III

Kuwait, Emir of, 1895–1965, vol. VI

Kuyper, A., 1837–1920, vol. II

Kuypers, Henricus Gerardus Jacobus Maria, 1925–1989, vol. VIII

Kuznets, Simon, 1901–1985, vol. VIII

Kwan, Sir Cho-Yiu, 1907–1971, vol. VII

Kwan Sai Kheong, 1920–1981, vol. VIII

Kyd, Sir David Hope, 1862–1933, vol. III

Kyd, James Gray, 1882–1968, vol. VI

Kyd, John Normansell, 1864–1931, vol. III

Kydd, Ronald Robertson, 1920–1972, vol. VII

Kyffin-Taylor, Brig.-Gen. Gerald; *see* Taylor.

Kyle, Elizabeth, (Agnes Mary Robertson Dunlop), *died* 1982, vol. VIII

Kyle, Emily Escher, *died* 1958, vol. V

Kyle, Henry Greville, *died* 1956, vol. V

Kyle, Lt-Col Robert, 1862–1942, vol. IV

Kyle, Air Chief Marshal Sir Wallace Hart, 1910–1988, vol. VIII

Kyle, William Galloway, 1875–1967, vol. VI

Kyllachy, Hon. Lord; William Mackintosh, 1842–1918, vol. II

Kylsant, 1st Baron, 1863–1937, vol. III

Kynaston, George Henry, 1850–1906, vol. I

Kynaston, Rev. Herbert, 1835–1910, vol. I

Kynaston, Walter Roger Owen, 1874–1935, vol. III

Kynch, George James, 1915–1987, vol. VIII

Kyne, Most Rev. John Anthony, 1904–1966, vol. VI

Kynnaird, Viscount; Sigismondo Maria Giuseppe Rospigliosi, 1886–1918, vol. II

Kynnersley, Charles Walter Sneyd-, 1849–1904, vol. I

Kynoch, John Alexander, *died* 1931, vol. III

Kynoch, Sir John Wheen, 1878–1946, vol. IV

Kynsey, Sir William Raymond, 1840–1904, vol. I

Kyrke, Lt-Col Henry Vernon Venables, 1881–1933, vol. III

Kyrle, Ven. Rowland Tracy Ashe M.; *see* Money-Kyrle.

Kyte, George William, 1864–1940, vol. III (A), vol. IV

L

Labarthe, André, 1902–1967, vol. VI

Labia, Princess Ida, *died* 1961, vol. VI

La Billois, Hon. Charles H., 1856–1928, vol. II

Laborde, Edward Daniel, 1863–1928, vol. II

Labori, Fernand, 1860–1917, vol. II
Labouchere, Rt Hon. Henry Du Pré, 1831–1912, vol. I
Labouisse, Henry Richardson, 1904–1987, vol. VIII
La Brooy, Justin Theodore, 1857–1944, vol. IV
Laby, Thomas Howell, 1880–1946, vol. IV
Lacaita, Charles Carmichael, 1853–1933, vol. III
Lace, John Henry, died 1918, vol. II
Lacey, Alfred Travers, 1892–1966, vol. VI
Lacey, Daniel; see Lacey, W. D.
Lacey, Sir Francis Eden, 1859–1946, vol. IV
Lacey, Gerald, 1887–1979, vol. VII
Lacey, Janet, 1903–1988, vol. VIII
Lacey, Sir Ralph Wilfred, 1900–1965, vol. VI
Lacey, Rev. Thomas Alexander, 1853–1931, vol. III
Lacey, Walter Graham, 1894–1974, vol. VII
Lacey, (William) Daniel, 1923–1985, vol. VIII
Lachaise, Gaston, 1882–1935, vol. III
Lachance, Arthur, 1868–1945, vol. IV
Lachman, Harry, 1886–1975, vol. VII
Lack, David, 1910–1973, vol. VII
Lack, Harry Lambert, 1867–1943, vol. IV
Lack, Henry Martyn, 1909–1979, vol. VII
Lack, Sir Henry Reader, 1832–1908, vol. I
Lack, Victor John Frederick, 1893–1988, vol. VIII
Lackey, Hon. Sir John, 1830–1903, vol. I
Lackie, William Walter, 1869–1945, vol. IV
Lacon, Sir Edmund Beecroft Francis Heathcote, 5th Bt, 1878–1911, vol. I
Lacon, Sir Edmund Broughton Knowles, 4th Bt, 1842–1899, vol. I
Lacon, Sir George Haworth Ussher, 6th Bt, 1881–1950, vol. IV
Lacon, Sir George Vere Francis, 7th Bt, 1909–1980, vol. VII
Lacon, Captain Henry Edmund, 1849–1924, vol. II
Lacoste, Hon. Sir Alexandre, 1842–1923, vol. II
La Cour, Leonard Francis, 1907–1984, vol. VIII
Lacy, Captain Ernest Edward, 1865–1946, vol. IV
Lacy, Francis Brandon, 1872–1954, vol. V
Lacy, Frederick St John, 1862–1935, vol. III
Lacy, Sir Maurice John Pierce, 2nd Bt, 1900–1965, vol. VI
Lacy, Sir Pierce Thomas, 1st Bt, 1872–1956, vol. V
Lacy, Rt Rev. Richard, 1841–1929, vol. III
Ladd, George Trumbull, 1842–1921, vol. II
Lade, Hon. Henry Augustus M.; see Milles-Lade.
La Dell, Edwin, 1914–1970, vol. VI
Laemmle, Carl, 1867–1939, vol. III
La Fárge, John, 1835–1910, vol. I
La Farge, Oliver, 1901–1963, vol. VI
Laferla, Albert Victor, 1887–1943, vol. IV
Laferté, Hon. Hector, 1885–1971, vol. VII
Laffan, Bertha Jane; see Laffan, Mrs Robert Stuart de Courcy.
Laffan, Col Henry David, 1858–1931, vol. III
Laffan, Robert George Dalrymple, 1887–1972, vol. VII
Laffan, Mrs Robert Stuart de Courcy, (Bertha Jane Laffan), died 1912, vol. I
Laffan, Rev. Robert Stuart de Courcy, 1853–1927, vol. II
Laffan, William M., 1848–1909, vol. I
Lafleche, Maj.-Gen. Léo-Richer, died 1956, vol. V

Lafleur, Paul Theodore, died 1924, vol. II
La Follette, Robert M., jun., 1895–1953, vol. V
La Follette, Robert Marion, 1855–1925, vol. II
Lafone, Rear-Adm. Albert Sumner, 1863–1933, vol. III
Lafone, Alfred, 1821–1911, vol. I
Lafone, Major Edgar Mortimore, died 1938, vol. III
Lafone, Harold Carlisle, 1879–1938, vol. III
Lafone, Ven. Henry Pownall Malins, 1867–1955, vol. V
Lafont, Rev. Eugène, 1837–1908, vol. I
Lafontaine, Henri Marie, 1854–1943, vol. IV
La Fontaine, Lt-Col Sydney Hubert, 1885–1964, vol. VI
La Force, Auguste de Caumont, Duc de, 1878–1961, vol. VI
Lagden, Godfrey William, 1906–1989, vol. VIII
Lagden, Sir Godfrey Yeatman, 1851–1934, vol. III
Lagerkvist, Pär Fabian, 1891–1974, vol. VII
Lagerlof, Selma, 1858–1940, vol. III
Lagos, Oba of, died 1964, vol. VI
LaGuardia, Fiorello Henry, 1882–1947, vol. IV
Lahej, Sultan of, Sir Abdul Karim Fadthli Bin Ali, died 1947, vol. IV
Laidlaw, Sir George, 1883–1969, vol. VI
Laidlaw, James, 1847–1913, vol. I
Laidlaw, Rev. John, 1832–1906, vol. I
Laidlaw, Sir Patrick Playfair, 1881–1940, vol. III
Laidlaw, Sir Robert, 1856–1915, vol. I
Laidlaw, Robert, 1897–1964, vol. VI
Laidlaw, Rt Hon. Thomas Kennedy, 1864–1943, vol. IV
Laidlaw, William Allison, 1898–1983, vol. VIII
Laidlay, William James, 1846–1912, vol. I
Lailey, Barnard, died 1944, vol. II
Lailey, Guy Patrick Barnard, 1888–1946, vol. IV
Lailey, John Raymond N.; see Nicholson-Lailey.
Laine, Sir Abraham James, 1876–1948, vol. IV
Laing, Alfred Martin, 1875–1949, vol. IV
Laing, Andrew, died 1931, vol. III
Laing, Bertram Mitchell, died 1960, vol. V
Laing, Frederick Ninian Robert, 1856–1931, vol. III
Laing, Air Vice-Marshal Sir George, 1884–1956, vol. V
Laing, Sir James, 1823–1901, vol. I
Laing, Sir John William, 1879–1978, vol. VII
Laing, Malcolm Alfred, 1846–1917, vol. II
Laing, Malcolm Buchanan, 1890–1974, vol. VII
Laing, Percy Lyndon, 1909–1979, vol. VII
Laing, Ronald David, 1927–1989, vol. VIII
Laing, Samuel, 1812–1897, vol. I
Laing, Col Stanley van Buren, 1884–1962, vol. VI
Lainson, Major Alexander John, 1869–1931, vol. III
Laird, David, 1833–1914, vol. I
Laird, John, 1887–1946, vol. IV
Laird, Brig. Kenneth Macgregor, 1880–1954, vol. V
Laird, Sir Patrick Ramsay, 1888–1967, vol. VI
Laird, Thomas Patrick, 1860–1927, vol. II
Laird, Sir William, died 1901, vol. I
Laird, William, 1881–1962, vol. VI
Laistner, Max Ludwig Wolfram, 1890–1959, vol. V
Laithwaite, Sir Gilbert; see Laithwaite, Sir J. G.
Laithwaite, Sir (John) Gilbert, 1894–1986, vol. VIII

Lake, Sir Arthur Johnstone, 8th Bt, 1849–1924, vol. II

Lake, Captain Sir Atwell Henry, 9th Bt, 1891–1972, vol. VII

Lake, Sir Atwell King, 6th Bt, 1834–1897, vol. I

Lake, Adm. Atwell Peregrine Macleod, 1842–1915, vol. I

Lake, Col Ernest Atwell Winter, 1886–1945, vol. IV

Lake, Col Harry William, *died* 1940, vol. III

Lake, Rev. Henry Ashton, 1847–1929, vol. III

Lake, Kirsopp, 1872–1946, vol. IV

Lake, Lt-Col Morice Challoner, 1885–1943, vol. IV

Lake, Brig.-Gen. Noel Montagu, 1852–1932, vol. III

Lake, Norman C., 1888–1966, vol. VI

Lake, Lt-Gen. Sir Percy Henry Noel, 1855–1940, vol. III

Lake, Richard, 1861–1949, vol. IV

Lake, Sir Richard Stuart, 1860–1950, vol. IV

Lake, Sir St Vincent Atwell, 7th Bt, 1862–1916, vol. II

Laker, Albert, 1875–1948, vol. IV

Lakin, Charles Ernest, 1878–1972, vol. VII

Lakin, Cyril Harry Alfred, 1893–1948, vol. IV

Lakin, Sir Henry, 3rd Bt, 1904–1979, vol. VII

Lakin, John Edmund Douglas, 1920–1977, vol. VII

Lakin, Maj.-Gen. John Henry Foster, 1878–1943, vol. IV

Lakin, Sir Michael Henry, 1st Bt, 1846–1931, vol. III

Lakin, Sir Richard, 2nd Bt, 1873–1955, vol. V

Laking, Sir Francis Henry, 1st Bt, 1847–1914, vol. I

Laking, Sir Guy Francis, 2nd Bt, 1875–1919, vol. II

Laking, Sir Guy Francis William, 3rd Bt, 1904–1930, vol. III

Lal, Kanhaiya Lal, 1866–1945, vol. IV

Lal, Shavax Ardeshir, 1899–1987, vol. VIII

Lalaing, Count de, 1856–1919, vol. II

Lalique, René, 1860–1945, vol. IV (A), vol. V

Lall, I. C., 1863–1922, vol. II

Lall, Panna; *see* Panna Lall.

Lall, Sir Shankar, 1901–1951, vol. V

Lally, Miss Gwen, *died* 1963, vol. VI

Lamarche, Rt Rev. Charles, 1870–1940, vol. III

Lamarque, Walter Geoffrey, 1913–1979, vol. VII

Lamb, Major Algernon Joseph Rutherfurd, 1891–1941, vol. IV

Lamb, Sir Archibald, 3rd Bt, 1845–1921, vol. II

Lamb, Arthur Moore, 1873–1946, vol. IV

Lamb, Rev. Benjamin, *died* 1925, vol. II

Lamb, Col Sir Charles Anthony, 4th Bt, 1857–1948, vol. IV

Lamb, David C., 1866–1951, vol. V

Lamb, Col David Ogilvy Wight, 1885–1942, vol. IV

Lamb, Edmund, 1863–1925, vol. II

Lamb, Ernest Horace, 1878–1946, vol. IV

Lamb, Frank de Villiers, 1880–1962, vol. VI

Lamb, Sir Harry Harling, 1857–1948, vol. IV

Lamb, Henry, 1883–1960, vol. V

Lamb, Sir Horace, 1849–1934, vol. III

Lamb, Sir John, 1871–1952, vol. V

Lamb, Rev. John, 1886–1974, vol. VII

Lamb, Sir John Cameron, 1845–1915, vol. I

Lamb, Sir John Edward Stewart, 1892–1954, vol. V

Lamb, Sir Joseph Quinton, 1873–1949, vol. IV

Lamb, Lynton Harold, 1907–1977, vol. VII

Lamb, Percy, 1896–1973, vol. VII

Lamb, Sir Richard Amphlett, 1858–1923, vol. II

Lamb, Lt-Col Roger Montague Radcliffe, 1881–1937, vol. III

Lamb, Sir Thomas, *died* 1943, vol. IV

Lamb, Sir Walter Rangeley Maitland, 1882–1961, vol. VI

Lambarde, Brig.-Gen. Francis Fane, 1868–1948, vol. IV

Lambart, Brig.-Gen. Edgar Alan, 1857–1930, vol. III

Lambart, Lt-Col Sir Gustavus Francis, 1st Bt, 1848–1926, vol. II

Lambart, Julian Harold Legge, 1893–1982, vol. VIII

Lambart, Hon. Lionel John Olive, 1873–1940, vol. III

Lambart, Sir Oliver Francis, 2nd Bt, 1913–1986, vol. VIII

Lambart, Richard, 1875–1924, vol. II

Lambe, Adm. of the Fleet Sir Charles Edward, 1900–1960, vol. V

Lambe, Air Vice-Marshal Sir Charles Laverock, *died* 1953, vol. V

Lambe, Philip Agnew, 1897–1968, vol. VI

Lambert, 1st Viscount, 1866–1958, vol. V

Lambert, 2nd Viscount, 1909–1989, vol. VIII

Lambert, Agnes, *died* 1917, vol. II

Lambert, Alfred Uvedale Miller, *died* 1928, vol. II

Lambert, Arthur Bradley, 1858–1929, vol. III

Lambert, Sir Arthur William, 1876–1948, vol. IV

Lambert, Bertram, 1881–1963, vol. VI

Lambert, Rev. Brooke, 1834–1901, vol. I

Lambert, Adm. Sir Cecil Foley, 1864–1928, vol. II

Lambert, Ven. Charles Edmund, 1872–1954, vol. V

Lambert, Charles Ernest, 1900–1974, vol. VII

Lambert, Ven. Charles Henry, 1894–1983, vol. VIII

Lambert, Engr. Rear-Adm. Charles William, 1891–1961, vol. VI

Lambert, Constant, 1905–1951, vol. V

Lambert, Rear-Adm. Sir David Sidney, 1885–1966, vol. VI

Lambert, Brig.-Gen. Edward Parry, 1865–1932, vol. III

Lambert, Ernest, 1874–1951, vol. V

Lambert, Dame Florence Barrie, 1871–1957, vol. V

Lambert, Francis Henry, 1867–1929, vol. III

Lambert, Francis L., 1838–1925, vol. II

Lambert, Frank, 1884–1973, vol. VII

Lambert, Rev. Frederick Fox, *died* 1920, vol. II

Lambert, Sir George Bancroft, 1873–1945, vol. IV

Lambert, Sir George Thomas, 1837–1918, vol. II

Lambert, George Washington, 1873–1930, vol. III

Lambert, Sir Greville Foley, 9th Bt, 1900–1988, vol. VIII

Lambert, Col Guy Lenox B.; *see* Bence-Lambert.

Lambert, Guy William, 1889–1983, vol. VIII

Lambert, Maj.-Gen. Harold Roger, 1896–1980, vol. VII

Lambert, Sir Henry Charles Miller, 1868–1935, vol. III

Lambert, Jack Walter, 1917–1986, vol. VIII

Lambert, Vet.-Col James Drummond, 1835–1905, vol. I

Lambert, Sir John, 1838–1916, vol. II

Lambert, Ven. Joseph Malet, 1853–1931, vol. III

Lambert, Maurice, 1901–1964, vol. VI

Lambert, Richard Cornthwaite, *died* 1939, vol. III
Lambert, Richard Stanton, 1894–1981, vol. VIII
Lambert, Robert, 1908–1971, vol. VII
Lambert, Rear-Adm. Robert Cathcart Kemble, 1874–1950, vol. IV
Lambert, Surgeon Vice-Adm. Roger John William, 1928–1984, vol. VIII
Lambert, Royston James, 1932–1982, vol. VIII
Lambert, Col Thomas Stanton, 1871–1921, vol. II
Lambert, Victor Albert George, 1897–1971, vol. VII
Lambert, Victor Francis, 1899–1981, vol. VIII
Lambert, Brig.-Gen. Walter John, 1876–1944, vol. IV
Lambert, Lt-Col Walter Miller, 1843–1924, vol. II
Lambert, Maj.-Gen. William, 1836–1907, vol. I
Lambert, Maj.-Gen. William Harold, 1905–1978, vol. VII
Lambert, Rev. William Henry, 1833–1924, vol. II
Lambie, Charles George, 1891–1961, vol. VI
Lambkin, Col Francis, 1858–1912, vol. I
Lamble, Ven. George Edwin, 1877–1939, vol. III
Lambooy, Maj.-Gen. Albert Percy, 1899–1976, vol. VII
Lamborn, Edmund Arnold Greening, 1877–1950, vol. IV
Lamborn, Harry George, 1915–1982, vol. VIII
Lambotte, Paul, 1862–1939, vol. III
Lambourne, 1st Baron, 1847–1928, vol. II
Lambrick, Hugh Trevor, 1904–1982, vol. VIII
Lambton, Viscount; John Roderick Geoffrey Francis Edward Lambton, 1920–1941, vol. IV
Lambton, Lt-Gen. Arthur, 1836–1908, vol. I
Lambton, Arthur, 1869–1935, vol. III
Lambton, Brig.-Gen. Hon. Charles, 1857–1949, vol. IV
Lambton, Lt-Col Francis W., 1834–1921, vol. II
Lambton, Hon. George, 1860–1945, vol. IV
Lambton, Lt-Col George Charles, 1872–1927, vol. II
Lambton, Maj.-Gen. Hon. Sir William, 1863–1936, vol. III
Lamburn, Richmal Crompton, 1890–1969, vol. VI
Lambury, 1st Baron, 1896–1967, vol. VI
Lamert, Sidney Streatfield, 1875–1963, vol. VI
Laming, Rev. Canon Frank Fairbairn, 1908–1989, vol. VIII
Laming, Major Henry Thornton, 1863–1934, vol. III
Laming, Richard Valentine, 1887–1959, vol. V
Lamington, 2nd Baron, 1860–1940, vol. III
Lamington, 3rd Baron, 1896–1951, vol. V
Lammie, Col George, 1891–1946, vol. IV
Lamonby, Isaac Wannop, 1886–1938, vol. III
Lamond, Frederic, 1868–1948, vol. IV
Lamond, Henry, 1869–1934, vol. III
Lamond, Sir William, 1887–1974, vol. VII
Lamont, Very Rev. Daniel, *died* 1950, vol. IV
Lamont, Daniel Scott, 1851–1905, vol. I
Lamont, Sir James, 1st Bt, 1828–1913, vol. I
Lamont, Lt-Col John Charles, 1864–1945, vol. IV
Lamont, Hon. John Henderson, 1865–1936, vol. III
Lamont, Brig.-Gen. John William Fraser, 1872–1956, vol. V
Lamont, Sir Norman, 2nd Bt, 1869–1949, vol. IV
Lamont, Thomas William, 1870–1948, vol. IV
Lamont, William Dawson, 1901–1982, vol. VIII
La Mothe, Frederick Malcolm, 1864–1947, vol. IV

Lamotte, Brig.-Gen. Frank Grimshaw Lagier, 1864–1938, vol. III
Lamotte, Major George Moorsom Lagier, 1869–1935, vol. III
Lampard-Vachell, Benjamin Garnet, 1892–1965, vol. VI
Lampe, Rev. Geoffrey William Hugo, 1912–1980, vol. VII
Lampen, Rev. Charles Dudley, 1859–1943, vol. IV
Lampen, Graham Dudley, 1899–1960, vol. V
Lampen, Rev. Canon Herbert Dudley, 1868–1941, vol. IV
Lampen, Lt-Gen. Lewis Charles, 1878–1946, vol. IV
Lampitt, Leslie Herbert, 1887–1957, vol. V
Lamplough, Augustus Osborne, 1877–1930, vol. III
Lamplough, Maj.-Gen. Charles Robert Wharram, 1896–1981, vol. VIII
Lamplugh, George William, 1859–1926, vol. II
Lamplugh, Rt Rev. Kenneth Edward Norman, 1901–1979, vol. VII
Lamplugh, Maj.-Gen. Stephen, 1900–1983, vol. VIII
Lampson, Sir Curtis George, 3rd Bt, 1890–1971, vol. VII
Lampson, Curtis Walter, 1875–1952, vol. V
Lampson, Sir George Curtis, 2nd Bt, 1833–1899, vol. I
Lampson, Rt Hon. Godfrey Lampson Tennyson L.; *see* Locker-Lampson.
Lampson, Jane L.; *see* Locker-Lampson.
Lampson, Comdr Oliver Stillingfleet L.; *see* Locker-Lampson.
Lamrock, Brig.-Gen. John, 1859–1935, vol. III
Lamsdorff, Count Wladimir, 1844–1907, vol. I
Lamy, Etienne Marie Victor, 1845–1919, vol. II
Lancashire, George Herbert, 1866–1945, vol. IV
Lancaster, Col Claude Granville, 1899–1977, vol. VII
Lancaster, Brig. Edmund Henry, 1881–1975, vol. VII
Lancaster, John Roy, 1871–1951, vol. V
Lancaster, Joseph Torry, 1892–1966, vol. VI
Lancaster, Sir Osbert, 1908–1986, vol. VIII
Lancaster, Percy, 1878–1950, vol. IV
Lancaster, Sir Robert Fisher, 1885–1945, vol. IV
Lancaster, Sir William John, 1841–1929, vol. III
Lancaster, William Joseph Cosens, 1851–1922, vol. II
Lancaster-Jones, Ernest, 1891–1945, vol. IV
Lancaster-Ranking, Maj.-Gen. Robert Philip; *see* Ranking.
Lancastre, Countess of; (Adeline Louise Maria); *see* Cardigan and Lancastre.
Lance, Rev. Edwin Mildred, 1862–1935, vol. III
Lance, Lt-Gen. Sir Frederick, 1837–1913, vol. I
Lancelot, Rev. John Bennett, 1864–1944, vol. IV
Lanchester, Elsa, 1902–1986, vol. VIII
Lanchester, Frank, 1870–1960, vol. V
Lanchester, Frederick William, 1868–1946, vol. IV
Lanchester, Henry Vaughan, 1863–1953, vol. V
Lanciani, Commendatore Rodolfo, 1846–1929, vol. III
Lanctot, Charles, 1863–1946, vol. IV
Land, Frank William, 1911–1990, vol. VIII
Land, Roger Burton, 1940–1988, vol. VIII
Landale, David, 1868–1935, vol. III
Landale, David Fortune, 1905–1970, vol. VI
Landale, Russell Talbot, 1911–1984, vol. VIII

Landau, Dorothea, (Mrs C. Da Fano), *died* 1941, vol. IV

Landau, Lev Davidovich, 1908–1968, vol. VI

Landau, Muriel Elsie, (Mrs Samuel Sacks), 1895–1972, vol. VII

Landau, Rom, 1899–1974, vol. VII

Lander, Cecil Howard, 1881–1949, vol. IV

Lander, Frank Patrick Lee, 1906–1981, vol. VIII

Lander, Rt Rev. Gerard Heath, 1861–1934, vol. III

Lander, Rt Rev. Richard Brook, *died* 1937, vol. III

Landey, Very Rev. Theophilus Patrick, *died* 1935, vol. III

Landis, James McCauley, 1899–1964, vol. VI

Landon, Alfred Mossman, 1887–1987, vol. VIII

Landon, Lt-Col Charles Richard Henry Palmer, 1879–1940, vol. III

Landon, Maj.-Gen. Sir Frederick William Bainbridge, 1860–1937, vol. III

Landon, Maj.-Gen. Herman James Shelley, 1859–1948, vol. IV

Landon, Col James William Bainbridge, 1890–1966, vol. VI

Landon, Gp Captain Joseph Herbert Arthur, *died* 1935, vol. III

Landon, Perceval, 1869–1927, vol. II

Landon, Philip Aislabie, 1888–1961, vol. VI

Landor, A. Henry Savage, *died* 1924, vol. II

Landouzy, Louis Joseph, *died* 1917, vol. II

Landowski, Paul, 1875–1961, vol. VI

Landry, Col Hon. Auguste Charles Philippe Robert, 1846–1919, vol. II

Landry, Hon. David V., 1866–1929, vol. III

Landry, Maj.-Gen. Joseph Phillippe, 1870–1926, vol. II

Landry, Hon. Sir Pierre Armand, 1846–1916, vol. II

Landsteiner, Karl, 1868–1943, vol. IV

Lane, Sir Allen Lane Williams, 1902–1970, vol. VI

Lane, Annie E.; *see* Lane, Mrs John.

Lane, Sir Arbuthnot; *see* Lane, Sir W. A.

Lane, Charles Macdonald, 1882–1956, vol. V

Lane, Maj.-Gen. Sir Charles Reginald Cambridge, 1890–1964, vol. VI

Lane, Maj.-Gen. Charles Stuart, 1831–1913, vol. I

Lane, Sir Charlton Adelbert Gustavus, 1890–1962, vol. VI

Lane, Col Clayton Turner, 1842–1920, vol. II

Lane, Edward Arthur, 1909–1963, vol. VI

Lane, Dame Elizabeth Kathleen, 1905–1988, vol. VIII

Lane, Very Rev. Ernald, 1836–1913, vol. I

Lane, Ernest Frederick Cambridge, 1882–1958, vol. V

Lane, Ernest Olaf, 1916–1976, vol. VII

Lane, Brig. Frank, 1888–1963, vol. VI

Lane, Col George Howard M.; *see* Moore-Lane.

Lane, Harry George, 1881–1957, vol. V

Lane, Sir Harry Philip Parnell, 1870–1927, vol. II

Lane, Brig.-Gen. Henry Arthur, 1868–1930, vol. III

Lane, Rear-Adm. Henry Gerald Elliot, 1875–1946, vol. IV

Lane, H(enry) J(errold) Randall, 1898–1975, vol. VII

Lane, Henry Murray, 1833–1913, vol. I

Lane, Rev. Henry Tydd, 1846–1939, vol. III

Lane, Herbert Allardyce, 1883–1959, vol. V

Lane, Brig.-Gen. Herbert Edward Bruce, 1862–1950, vol. IV

Lane, Sir Hugh Percy, 1875–1915, vol. I

Lane, Brig. Hugh Robert Charles, 1885–1953, vol. V

Lane, James Ernest, *died* 1926, vol. II

Lane, Jane, (Mrs Andrew Dakers), *died* 1978, vol. VII

Lane, John, 1854–1925, vol. II

Lane, Mrs John, (Annie E. Lane), *died* 1927, vol. II

Lane, John Henry Hervey Vincent, 1867–1917, vol. II

Lane, John Macdonald, 1840–1927, vol. II

Lane, Lupino, 1892–1959, vol. V

Lane, Col Maitland Moore-, 1841–1915, vol. I

Lane, Rhona Arbuthnot, *died* 1953, vol. V

Lane, Richard Ouseley Blake, 1842–1914, vol. I

Lane, Maj.-Gen. Sir Ronald Bertram, 1847–1937, vol. III

Lane, Col Samuel Willington, 1860–1948, vol. IV

Lane, Rear-Adm. Walter Frederick Boyt, 1909–1988, vol. VIII

Lane, Sir (William) Arbuthnot, 1st Bt, 1856–1943, vol. IV

Lane, Sir William Arbuthnot, 2nd Bt, 1897–1972, vol. VII

Lane, Lt-Col William Byam, 1866–1945, vol. IV

Lane-Fox, Baroness (Life Peer); Felicity Lane-Fox, 1918–1988, vol. VIII

Lane-Fox, Col Francis Gordon Ward, 1899–1989, vol. VIII

Lane-Jackson, Nicholas, 1849–1937, vol. III

Lane-Notter, Col J.; *see* Notter.

Lane Poole, Charles Edward, 1885–1970, vol. VI (AII)

Lane-Poole, Vice-Adm. Sir Richard Hayden Owen, 1883–1971, vol. VII

Lane-Poole, Stanley, 1854–1931, vol. III

Lane-Roberts, Cedric Sydney, *died* 1959, vol. V

Lanesborough, 6th Earl of, 1839–1905, vol. I

Lanesborough, 7th Earl of, 1865–1929, vol. III

Lanesborough, 8th Earl of, 1868–1950, vol. IV

Lang of Lambeth, 1st Baron, 1864–1945, vol. IV

Lang, Air Vice-Marshal Albert Frank, 1895–1977, vol. VII

Lang, Alexander, 1848–1930, vol. III

Lang, (Alexander) Matheson, *died* 1948, vol. IV

Lang, Andrew, 1844–1912, vol. I

Lang, Archibald Orr, 1880–1957, vol. V

Lang, Col Arthur Moffatt, 1832–1916, vol. II

Lang, Col Bertram John, 1878–1975, vol. VII

Lang, Charles Dowson, 1845–1930, vol. III

Lang, Charles Russell, 1862–1940, vol. III

Lang, Col Elliott Brownlow, 1862–1955, vol. V

Lang, Hon. Sir Frederic William, 1852–1937, vol. III

Lang, Lt-Col Godfrey George, 1867–1923, vol. II

Lang, Rev. Gordon, 1893–1981, vol. VIII

Lang, Sir John Gerald, 1896–1984, vol. VIII

Lang, Very Rev. John Marshall, 1834–1909, vol. I

Lang, Hon. John Thomas, 1876–1975, vol. VII

Lang, Rt Rev. Leslie Hamilton, 1889–1974, vol. VII

Lang, Lt-Col Lionel Edward, 1885–1956, vol. V

Lang, Very Rev. Marshall B., 1868–1954, vol. V

Lang, Matheson; *see* Lang, A. M.

Lang, Rt Rev. Norman Macleod, 1875–1956, vol. V

Lang, Patrick Keith, 1863–1961, vol. VI

Lang, Sir Peter Redford Scott, 1850–1926, vol. II

Lang, Robert Buntin, 1906–1970, vol. VI
Lang, Sir Robert Hamilton, 1836–1913, vol. I
Lang, William, 1852–1937, vol. III
Lang, Sir William Biggart, 1868–1942, vol. IV
Lang, William Dickson, 1878–1966, vol. VI
Lang, William Henry, *died* 1960, vol. V
Lang, William Lindsay Holmes, 1888–1928, vol. II
Lang, William Marshall F.; *see* Farquharson-Lang.
Lang, Col William Robert, *died* 1925, vol. II
Lang-Coath, Howell Lang, 1878–1949, vol. IV
Lang-Hyde, Lt-Col John Irvine, 1859–1940, vol. III
Langbridge, Rev. Frederick, 1849–1922, vol. II
Langbridge, Rosamond Grant, *died* 1964, vol. VI
Langdale, Henry Joseph, *died* 1923, vol. II
Langdale, Lt-Col Philip Joseph, *died* 1950, vol. IV
Langdon, Adolph Max, *died* 1949, vol. IV
Langdon, Rev. Alfred, *died* 1925, vol. II
Langdon, Alfred Gordon, 1915–1988, vol. VIII
Langdon, George, 1867–1957, vol. V
Langdon, Col Harry, 1855–1925, vol. II
Langdon, Stephen Herbert, 1876–1937, vol. III
Langdon, Hon. Thomas, 1832–1914, vol. I
Langdon, Air Cdre William Frederick, 1898–1976, vol. VII
Langdon-Brown, Sir Walter, 1870–1946, vol. IV
Langdon-Davies, Bernard Noël, 1876–1952, vol. V
Langdon-Davies, John, 1897–1971, vol. VII
Lange, Christian Lous, 1869–1938, vol. III
Langelier, Hon. Charles, 1852–1920, vol. II
Langelier, Sir François Charles Stanislas, 1838–1915, vol. I
Langerman, Sir Jan Willem Stuckeris, 1853–1931, vol. III
Langevin, Hon. Sir Hector Louis, 1826–1906, vol. I
Langevin, Most Rev. Louis Philip Adelard, 1855–1915, vol. I
Langford, 4th Baron, 1848–1919, vol. II
Langford, 5th Baron, 1894–1922, vol. II
Langford, 6th Baron, 1849–1931, vol. III
Langford, 7th Baron, 1885–1952, vol. V
Langford, 8th Baron, 1870–1953, vol. V
Langford, Caroline; *see* Hatchard, C.
Langford, John Alfred, 1823–1903, vol. I
Langford, Surgeon Martyn Henry, *died* 1918, vol. II
Langford-James, Reginald Hugh Lloyd, 1876–1961, vol. VI
Langford-Sainsbury, Air Vice-Marshal Thomas Audley, 1897–1972, vol. VII
Langham, Sir Charles Arthur; *see* Langham, Sir H. C. A.
Langham, Sir Cyril Leigh Macrae, 1885–1950, vol. IV
Langham, Col Frederick George, 1863–1946, vol. IV
Langham, Sir (Herbert) Charles Arthur, 13th Bt, 1870–1951, vol. V
Langham, Sir Herbert Hay, 12th Bt, 1840–1909, vol. I
Langham, Sir John Charles Patrick, 14th Bt, 1894–1972, vol. VII
Langhorne, Maj.-Gen. Algernon Philip Yorke, 1882–1945, vol. IV
Langhorne, Brig.-Gen. Harold Stephen, 1866–1932, vol. III
Langhorne, Brig. James Archibald Dunboyne, 1879–1950, vol. IV
Langker, Sir Erik, 1899–1982, vol. VIII

Langler, Sir Alfred, 1865–1928, vol. II
Langley, Alexander, 1871–1952, vol. V
Langley, Comdr Arthur Sydney, 1881–1964, vol. VI
Langley, Batty, 1834–1914, vol. I
Langley, Beatrice, (Mrs Basil Tozer), 1872–1958, vol. V
Langley, Sir Carleton George, 1885–1963, vol. VI
Langley, Brig. Charles Ardagh, 1897–1987, vol. VIII
Langley, Frederick Oswald, 1883–1947, vol. IV
Langley, Brig. George Furner, 1891–1971, vol. VII
Langley, George Harry, 1881–1951, vol. V
Langley, Adm. Gerald Charles, 1848–1914, vol. I
Langley, Vice-Adm. Gerald Maxwell Bradshaw, 1895–1971, vol. VII
Langley, Rt Rev. Henry Archdall, *died* 1906, vol. I
Langley, Very Rev. Henry Thomas, 1877–1968, vol. VI
Langley, Rt Rev. John Douse, 1836–1930, vol. III
Langley, John Newport, 1852–1925, vol. II
Langley, Col John Penrice, 1860–1933, vol. III
Langley, Noel A., 1911–1980, vol. VII
Langley, Samuel Pierpont, 1834–1906, vol. I
Langley, Walter, 1852–1922, vol. II, vol. III
Langley, Sir Walter Louis Frederick Goltz, 1855–1918, vol. II
Langley, William Henry, *died* 1913, vol. I
Langley, William Kenneth Macaulay, 1883–1965, vol. VI
Langley Moore, Doris; *see* Moore, D. L.
Langley-Taylor, Sir George, 1888–1968, vol. VI
Langlois, Hippolyte, 1839–1912, vol. I
Langlois, Most Rev. Mgr J. Alfred, 1876–1966, vol. VI
Langmaid, Lt-Comdr Rowland John Robb, 1897–1956, vol. V
Langmaid, Brig. Thomas John Robert, 1887–1965, vol. VI
Langman, Sir Archibald Lawrence, 2nd Bt, 1872–1949, vol. IV
Langman, Sir John Lawrence, 1st Bt, 1846–1928, vol. II
Langman, Sir John Lyell, 3rd Bt, 1912–1985, vol. VIII
Langman, Thomas Witheridge, 1882–1960, vol. V
Langmead, Frederick, 1879–1969, vol. VI
Langmore, Col Edward Ham, 1828–1913, vol. I
Langmuir, Irving, 1881–1957, vol. V
Langrishe, Comdr Sir Hercules Robert, 5th Bt, 1859–1943, vol. IV
Langrishe, Sir James, 4th Bt, 1823–1910, vol. I
Langrishe, Captain Sir Terence Hume, 6th Bt, 1895–1973, vol. VII
Langton, Bennet, 1870–1955, vol. V
Langton, Bernard Sydney, 1914–1982, vol. VIII
Langton, Hon. Chandos Graham T. G.; *see* Temple-Gore-Langton.
Langton, Comdr Hon. Evelyn Arthur Grenville T. G.; *see* Temple-Gore-Langton.
Langton, Sir George Philip, 1881–1942, vol. IV
Langton, Major Gerald Wentworth G.; *see* Gore-Langton.
Langton, Hon. Henry Powell G.; *see* Gore-Langton.
Langton, John, *died* 1910, vol. I
Langton, Joseph L., 1877–1961, vol. VI

Langton, Thomas Bennett, 1917–1986, vol. VIII
Langton-Jones, Comdr Ronald, 1884–1967, vol. VI
Lankester, Edward Forbes, 1855–1934, vol. III
Lankester, Sir Edwin Ray, 1847–1929, vol. III
Lankester, Herbert, 1862–1947, vol. IV
Lanktree, Col Charles Joseph Dane, 1895–1951, vol. V
Lanman, Charles Rockwell, 1850–1941, vol. IV
Lannowe, Brig.-Gen. Edmund Byam Mathew-, 1875–1940, vol. III
Lansbury, Rt Hon. George, 1859–1940, vol. III
Lansdell, Rev. Henry, 1841–1919, vol. II
Lansdowne, 5th Marquess of, 1845–1927, vol. II
Lansdowne, 6th Marquess of, 1872–1936, vol. III
Lansdowne, 7th Marquess of, 1917–1944, vol. IV
Lansell, Col Hon. Sir George Victor, 1883–1959, vol. V
Lansing, Robert, 1864–1928, vol. II
Lanson, Gustave, 1857–1934, vol. III
Lanteri, Edward, died 1917, vol. II
Lanyon, (George) Peter, 1918–1964, vol. VI
Lanyon, Peter; see Lanyon, G. P.
Lapage, Charles Paget, 1879–1947, vol. IV
Lapointe, Rt Hon. Ernest, 1876–1941, vol. IV
Lapointe, Col Hon. Hugues, 1911–1982, vol. VIII
Laporte, Hon. Sir Hormisdas, 1850–1934, vol. III
Laprimaudaye, Comdr Clement, died 1910, vol. I
Lapworth, Arthur, died 1941, vol. IV
Lapworth, Charles, 1842–1920, vol. II
Larcom, Arthur, 1847–1924, vol. II
Larcom, Sir Philip, 4th Bt, 1887–1967, vol. VI
Larcom, Sir Thomas Perceval, 3rd Bt, 1882–1950, vol. IV
Larcombe, Dudley Thomas Reynolds, 1879–1944, vol. IV
Larcombe, Thomas, 1842–1916, vol. II
Lardinois, Petrus Josephus, 1924–1987, vol. VIII
Lardner, James Carrige Rushe, 1879–1925, vol. II
Lardner-Clarke, Col J. de W., 1858–1951, vol. V
Large, Captain Edwin Ryder, 1878–1928, vol. II
Large, Stanley Dermott, 1889–1965, vol. VI
Large, Tennyson J. D., 1879–1959, vol. V
Larivière, Hon. Alphonse Alfred Clément, 1842–1925, vol. II, vol. III
Lark, Rev. William Blake, 1838–1913, vol. I
Larkcom, Eric Herbert Larkcom J.; see Jacobs-Larkcom.
Larke, Sir William James, died 1959, vol. V
Larken, Lt-Col Edmund, 1876–1951, vol. V
Larken, Rear-Adm. Edmund Thomas, 1907–1965, vol. VI
Larken, Adm. Sir Frank, 1875–1953, vol. V
Larken, Rev. Preb. Hubert, died 1964, vol. VI
Larkin, Alfred Sloane, 1894–1982, vol. VIII
Larkin, Herbert Benjamin George, 1872–1944, vol. IV
Larkin, Hon. Peter Charles, 1856–1930, vol. III
Larkin, Philip Arthur, 1922–1985, vol. VIII
Larking, Captain Albert, 1857–1932, vol. III
Larking, Lt-Col Sir (Charles) Gordon, 1893–1978, vol. VII
Larking, Col Cuthbert, 1842–1910, vol. I
Larking, Captain Dennis Augustus Hugo, 1876–1970, vol. VI

Larking, Lt-Col Sir Gordon; see Larking, Lt-Col Sir C. G.
Larking, Sir John, 1857–1931, vol. III
Larking, Lt-Col Reginald Nesbitt Wingfield, 1868–1943, vol. IV
Larkins, Laurence Brouncker Southey, 1891–1953, vol. V
Larkworthy, Falconer, 1833–1928, vol. II
Larminie, Margaret Rivers, (Mrs M. R. Tragett), 1885–1964, vol. VI
Larmor, Alexander, died 1936, vol. III
Larmor, Sir Graham; see Larmor, Sir J. G.
Larmor, Sir (John) Graham, 1897–1968, vol. VI
Larmor, Sir Joseph, 1857–1942, vol. IV
Larnach, James Walker, 1849–1919, vol. II
Larnder, Col Eugene William, 1864–1941, vol. IV
La Rochelle, Michael Gautron, 1868–1934, vol. III
La Rocque, Rt Rev. Paul, 1846–1926, vol. II
Larpent, Sir George Albert de Hochepied, 3rd Bt, 1846–1899, vol. I
Larpent, Maj.-Gen. Lionel Henry Planta de H.; see de Hochepied Larpent.
Larsen, Roy Edward, 1899–1979, vol. VII
Lartigue, Alexander Raphael C.; see Cools-Lartigue.
Larue, Rt Rev. Stephen, 1865–1935, vol. III
Larymore, Major Henry Douglas, 1867–1946, vol. IV
Lasbrey, Rt Rev. Bertram, died 1976, vol. VII
Lascelles, Rt Hon. Sir Alan Frederick, 1887–1981, vol. VIII
Lascelles, Sir Alfred George, 1857–1952, vol. V
Lascelles, Daniel Richard, 1908–1985, vol. VIII
Lascelles, Sir Daniel William, 1902–1967, vol. VI
Lascelles, Bt Major Hon. Edward Cecil, 1887–1935, vol. III
Lascelles, Edward Charles Ponsonby, 1884–1956, vol. V
Lascelles, Lt-Col Edward ffrancis Ward, died 1959, vol. V
Lascelles, Sir Francis William, 1890–1979, vol. VII
Lascelles, Frank, died 1934, vol. III
Lascelles, Rt Hon. Sir Frank Cavendish, 1841–1920, vol. II
Lascelles, Hon. Frederick Canning, 1848–1928, vol. II
Lascelles, Hon. George Edwin, 1826–1911, vol. I
Lascelles, Lt-Col George Reginald, 1864–1939, vol. III
Lascelles, Hon. Gerald William, 1849–1928, vol. II
Lascelles, Rev. Hon. James Walter, 1831–1901, vol. I
Lascelles, Rev. Maurice G., 1860–1940, vol. III
Lascelles, Captain Walter Charles, 1867–1911, vol. I
Lash, Zebulun Aiton, 1846–1920, vol. II
Lash, Rt Rev. William Quinlan, 1905–1986, vol. VIII
Lashmore, Engr Rear-Adm. Harry, 1868–1945, vol. IV
Lasker, Emanuel, 1868–1941, vol. IV
Laskey, Sir Denis Seward, 1916–1987, vol. VIII
Laskey, Francis Seward, 1886–1972, vol. VII
Laski, Harold J., 1893–1950, vol. IV
Laski, Marghanita, (Mrs J. E. Howard), 1915–1988, vol. VIII
Laski, Nathan, 1863–1941, vol. IV
Laski, Neville Jonas, 1890–1969, vol. VI
Laskin, Rt Hon. Bora, 1912–1984, vol. VIII

Lasky, Jesse L., 1880–1958, vol. V
Laslett, Henry James, 1844–1914, vol. I
Lassalle, Jean Louis, 1847–1909, vol. I
Lassetter, Brig.-Gen. Harry Beauchamp, 1860–1926, vol. II
Last, Hugh Macilwain, died 1957, vol. V
Last, William Isaac, 1857–1911, vol. I
Laszlo de Lombos, Philip Alexius, 1869–1937, vol. III
Latchford, Francis Robert, 1854–1938, vol. III
Latey, John, 1842–1902, vol. I
Latey, William, 1885–1976, vol. VII
Latham, 1st Baron, 1888–1970, vol. VI
Latham, Albert George, 1864–1940, vol. III
Latham, Alexander Mere, 1862–1934, vol. III
Latham, Charles, 1868–1917, vol. II
Latham, Hon. Sir Charles George, 1882–1968, vol. VI
Latham, Edward Bryan, 1895–1980, vol. VII
Latham, Brig. Francis, 1883–1958, vol. V
Latham, Gustavus Henry, 1888–1975, vol. VII
Latham, Rev. Henry, 1821–1902, vol. I
Latham, Sir (Herbert) Paul, 2nd Bt, 1905–1955, vol. V
Latham, Ven. James King, 1847–1932, vol. III
Latham, Rt Hon. Sir John Greig, 1877–1964, vol. VI
Latham, Sir Joseph, 1905–1988, vol. VIII
Latham, Sir Paul; see Latham, Sir H. P.
Latham, Peter Wallwork, 1832–1923, vol. II
Latham, Russell, 1896–1964, vol. VI
Latham, Sir Thomas Paul, 1st Bt, 1855–1931, vol. III
Latham, William, died 1915, vol. I
Lathan, George, 1875–1942, vol. IV
La Thangue, H. H., died 1929, vol. III
Lathbury, Daniel Conner, 1831–1922, vol. II
Lathbury, Gen. Sir Gerald William, 1906–1978, vol. VII
Lathlain, Sir William Francis, 1862–1936, vol. III
Lathom, 1st Earl of, 1837–1898, vol. I
Lathom, 2nd Earl of, 1864–1910, vol. I
Lathom, 3rd Earl of, 1895–1930, vol. III
Lathrop, Lorin Andrews, died 1929, vol. III
Lathrop, Mother Mary Alphonsa; see Lathrop, R. H.
Lathrop, Rose Hawthorne, (Mother Mary Alphonsa Lathrop), 1851–1926, vol. II, vol. III
Latifi, Almá, 1879–1959, vol. V
Latimer, Sir Courtenay, 1880–1944, vol. IV
Latimer, Frederick William, 1845–1910, vol. I
Latimer, Rev. William Thomas, died 1919, vol. II
Laton, Col Stephen F.; see Frewen-Laton.
La Touche, Sir James John Digges, 1844–1921, vol. II
Latouche, John; see Crawfurd, Oswald.
La Touche, Robert Percy O'Connor, 1846–1921, vol. II
Latourette, Kenneth Scott, 1884–1968, vol. VI
Latrobe, William Sanderson, 1870–1943, vol. IV
La Trobe-Bateman, Rev. William Fairbairn; see Bateman.
Latta, Sir Andrew Gibson, died 1953, vol. V
Latta, Sir John, 1st Bt, 1867–1946, vol. IV
Latta, Robert, 1865–1932, vol. III
Latta, Hon. Samuel John, 1866–1946, vol. IV
Latter, Algernon, 1870–1944, vol. IV
Latter, Arthur Malcolm, 1875–1961, vol. VI
Latter, Maj.-Gen. John Cecil, 1896–1972, vol. VII

Latter, Oswald Hawkins, 1864–1948, vol. IV
Lattey, Rev. Cuthbert Charles, 1877–1954, vol. V
Lattimer, Robert Binney, 1863–1929, vol. III
Lattimore, Owen, 1900–1989, vol. VIII
Lattin, Francis Joseph, 1905–1986, vol. VIII
Latulipe, Rt Rev. E. A., 1859–1922, vol. II
Latymer, 5th Baron, 1852–1923, vol. II
Latymer, 6th Baron, 1876–1949, vol. IV
Latymer, 7th Baron, 1901–1987, vol. VIII
Laudenbach, Pierre; see Fresnay, P.
Lauder, Charles James, died 1920, vol. II
Lauder, Sir George Andrew Dick-, 12th Bt, 1917–1981, vol. VIII
Lauder, Sir George William Dalrymple Dick-, 10th Bt, 1852–1936, vol. III
Lauder, Sir Harry MacLennan, 1870–1950, vol. IV
Lauder, Major James La Fayette, 1889–1934, vol. III
Lauder, Lt-Col Sir John North Dalrymple Dick-, 11th Bt, 1883–1958, vol. V
Lauder, Sir Thomas North Dick-, 9th Bt, 1846–1919, vol. II
Lauderdale, 13th Earl of, 1840–1924, vol. II
Lauderdale, 14th Earl of, 1868–1931, vol. III
Lauderdale, 15th Earl of, 1891–1953, vol. V
Lauderdale, 16th Earl of, 1904–1968, vol. VI
Laughlin, Irwin, 1871–1941, vol. IV
Laughton, Col Arthur Frederick, 1840–1915, vol. I
Laughton, Charles, 1899–1962, vol. VI
Laughton, Eric, 1911–1988, vol. VIII
Laughton, Lt-Gen. George Arnold, 1830–1912, vol. I
Laughton, George Christian, 1887–1952, vol. V
Laughton, Very Rev. John George, 1891–1965, vol. VI
Laughton, Sir John Knox, 1830–1915, vol. I
Laughton, Major Joseph Vinters, 1862–1948, vol. IV
Laughton-Scott, Edward Hey, 1926–1978, vol. VII
Laurence, Frederick Andrew, 1843–1912, vol. I
Laurence, Adm. Sir Noel Frank, died 1970, vol. VI
Laurence, Sir Perceval Maitland, 1854–1930, vol. III
Laurence, Reginald Vere, 1876–1934, vol. III
Laurie, Rev. Albert Ernest, 1866–1937, vol. III
Laurie, Arthur Pillans, 1861–1949, vol. IV
Laurie, Col Sir Claude Villiers Emilius, 4th Bt (cr 1834), 1855–1930, vol. III
Laurie, Rev. Sir Emilius; see Laurie, Rev. Sir J. R. L. E.
Laurie, Lt-Col George Halliburton Foster Peel V.; see Vere-Laurie.
Laurie, James Stuart, 1831–1904, vol. I
Laurie, John B., 1865–1934, vol. III
Laurie, Lt-Col Sir John Dawson, 1st Bt (cr 1942), 1872–1954, vol. V
Laurie, Maj.-Gen. Sir John Emilius, 6th Bt, 1892–1983, vol. VIII
Laurie, Rev. Sir (John Robert Laurie) Emilius, 3rd Bt (cr 1834), 1823–1917, vol. II
Laurie, Lt-Gen. John Wimburn, 1835–1912, vol. I
Laurie, Malcolm Vyvyan, 1901–1973, vol. VII
Laurie, Brig. Sir Percy Robert, 1880–1962, vol. VI
Laurie, Ranald Macdonald, 1869–1927, vol. II
Laurie, Robert Douglas, 1874–1953, vol. V
Laurie, Col Robert Peter, 1835–1905, vol. I
Laurie, Maj.-Gen. Rufus Henry, 1892–1961, vol. VI
Laurie, Simon Somerville, 1829–1909, vol. I

Laurie, Col Vernon Stewart, 1896–1981, vol. VIII

Laurie, Sir Wilfrid Emilius, 5th Bt (*cr* 1834), 1859–1936, vol. III

Laurier, Rt Hon. Sir Wilfrid, 1841–1919, vol. II

Laurvig, Count Preben Ferdinand A.; *see* Ahlefeldt-Laurvig.

Lauterpacht, Sir Hersch, 1897–1960, vol. V

Lauwerys, Joseph Albert, 1902–1981, vol. VIII

Laval, Pierre, 1883–1945, vol. IV

Lavarack, Lt-Gen. Sir John Dudley, 1885–1957, vol. V

Lavedan, Henri, 1859–1940, vol. III

Lavelle, Rev. Canon Alexander Bannerman, 1899–1964, vol. VI

Laver, James, 1899–1975, vol. VII

Laver, William Adolphus, 1866–1940, vol. III (A), vol. IV

Laver, William Scott, 1909–1988, vol. VIII

Laverack, Frederick Joseph, 1871–1928, vol. II

Lavergne, Joseph, 1847–1922, vol. II

Lavergne, Hon. Louis, 1845–1931, vol. III

Lavers, Sydney Charles Robert, 1898–1972, vol. VII

Lavery, Cecil, 1894–1967, vol. VI

Lavery, Sir John, 1856–1941, vol. IV

Lavington, Cyril Michael, 1912–1990, vol. VIII

Lavington, Michael; *see* Lavington, C. M.

Lavington Evans, Leonard Glyde; *see* Evans.

Lavis, Rt Rev. Sidney Warren, *died* 1965, vol. VI

Lavisse, Ernest, 1842–1922, vol. II

Lavoipierre, Jacques Joseph Maurice, 1909–1987, vol. VIII

Lavrin, Janko John, 1887–1986, vol. VIII

Law, Albert, 1872–1956, vol. V

Law, Lt-Col Alfred, 1871–1928, vol. II

Law, Sir Alfred Joseph, 1860–1939, vol. III

Law, Alfred Noel, *born* 1895, vol. VIII

Law, Sir Algernon, 1856–1943, vol. IV

Law, Anastasia, (Mrs Nigel Law), 1886–1976, vol. VII

Law, Rt Hon. Andrew Bonar, 1858–1923, vol. II

Law, Sir Archibald Fitzgerald, 1853–1921, vol. II

Law, Arthur, 1876–1933, vol. III

Law, Sir Charles Ewan, 1884–1974, vol. VII

Law, Edward, 1853–1930, vol. III

Law, Major Sir Edward FitzGerald, 1846–1908, vol. I

Law, Sir Eric John Ewan, 1913–1988, vol. VIII

Law, Ernest, 1854–1930, vol. III

Law, Francis Towry Adeane, 1835–1901, vol. I

Law, Frank William, 1898–1987, vol. VIII

Law, Harry Davis, 1930–1990, vol. VIII

Law, Henry Duncan Graves, 1883–1964, vol. VI

Law, Herbert Henry, 1862–1943, vol. IV

Law, Hugh Alexander, *died* 1943, vol. IV

Law, Col Hugh Francis d'Assisi Stuart, 1897–1984, vol. VIII

Law, Margaret Dorothy, *died* 1980, vol. VII

Law, Mary, 1889–1919, vol. II

Law, Ralph Hamilton, 1915–1967, vol. VI

Law, Raja Reshee Case, 1852–1935, vol. III

Law, Rev. Robert, 1860–1919, vol. II

Law, Brig.-Gen. Robert Theophilus Hewitt, 1855–1949, vol. IV

Law, Samuel Horace, 1873–1940, vol. III (A), vol. IV

Law, Sir Sydney, 1861–1949, vol. IV

Law, Rev. Thomas, 1854–1910, vol. I

Law, Thomas Pakenham, 1834–1905, vol. I

Law, Maj.-Gen. Victor Edward, 1842–1910, vol. I

Law, William Arthur, 1844–1913, vol. I

Law, Mrs William Arthur; *see* Holland, Fanny.

Law, Rev. William Smalley, 1865–1937, vol. III

Lawder, Rear-Adm. Keith Macleod, 1893–1986, vol. VIII

Lawes, Edward Thornton Hill, 1869–1921, vol. II

Lawes, Sir John Bennet, 1st Bt, 1814–1899, vol. I

Lawes, Sir John Claud Bennet, 4th Bt, 1898–1979, vol. VII

Lawes Wittewronge, Sir Charles Bennet, 2nd Bt, 1843–1911, vol. I

Lawes-Wittewronge, Sir John Bennet, 3rd Bt, 1872–1931, vol. III

Lawford, John Bowring, 1858–1934, vol. III

Lawford, Lt-Gen. Sir Sydney Turing Barlow, 1865–1953, vol. V

Lawford, Captain (S) Vincent Adrian, 1871–1959, vol. V

Lawler, Wallace Leslie, 1912–1972, vol. VII

Lawless, Col Hon. Edward, 1841–1921, vol. II

Lawless, Hon. Emily, *died* 1913, vol. I

Lawless, Henry Hamilton, *died* 1913, vol. I

Lawless, Surg. Lt-Col Sir Warren Roland Crooke-, 1863–1931, vol. III

Lawley, Hon. Alethea Jane Wiel, *died* 1929, vol. III

Lawley, Edgar Ernest, *died* 1977, vol. VII

Lawlor, Very Rev. Hugh Jackson, 1860–1938, vol. III

Lawlor, John, 1906–1975, vol. VII

Lawn, James Gunson, 1868–1952, vol. V

Lawrance, Major Sir Arthur Salisbury, 1880–1965, vol. VI

Lawrance, Rt Hon. Sir John Compton, 1832–1912, vol. I

Lawrance, Very Rev. Walter John, 1840–1914, vol. I

Lawrance, William Thomas, *died* 1932, vol. III

Lawrence, 2nd Baron, 1846–1913, vol. I

Lawrence, 3rd Baron, 1878–1947, vol. IV

Lawrence, 4th Baron, 1908–1968, vol. VI

Lawrence of Kingsgate, 1st Baron, 1855–1927, vol. II

Lawrence, Albert, 1893–1961, vol. VI

Lawrence, Alexander John, 1837–1905, vol. I

Lawrence, Sir Alexander Waldemar, 4th Bt (*cr* 1858), 1874–1939, vol. III

Lawrence, Hon. (Alfred) Clive, 1876–1926, vol. II

Lawrence, Alfred Kingsley, *died* 1975, vol. VII

Lawrence, (Arabella) Susan, 1871–1947, vol. IV

Lawrence, Rev. Arthur Evelyn B.; *see* Barnes-Lawrence.

Lawrence, Aubrey Trevor, 1875–1930, vol. III

Lawrence, Bernard Edwin, 1901–1988, vol. VIII

Lawrence, Lt-Col Bryan Turner Tom, 1873–1949, vol. IV

Lawrence, C. E., 1870–1940, vol. III

Lawrence, Ven. Charles D'Aguilar, 1847–1935, vol. III

Lawrence, Hon. Clive; *see* Lawrence, Hon. A. C.

Lawrence, David Herbert, 1885–1930, vol. III

Lawrence, Sir Edward, 1825–1909, vol. I

Lawrence, Sir Edwin D.; *see* Durning-Lawrence.

Lawrence, Ernest Orlando, 1901–1958, vol. V

Lawrence, Evelyn M., (Mrs Nathan Isaacs), 1892–1987, vol. VIII
Lawrence, Sir Frederick, 1889–1981, vol. VIII
Lawrence, Sir (Frederick) Geoffrey, 1902–1967, vol. VI
Lawrence, Major Freeling Ross, 1872–1914, vol. I
Lawrence, Sir Geoffrey; see Lawrence, Sir F. G.
Lawrence, Lt-Col George Henniker, 1868–1932, vol. III
Lawrence, Gertrude, (Mrs Richard Stoddard Aldrich), 1898–1952, vol. V
Lawrence, Sir Henry Eustace Waldemar, 5th Bt (cr 1858), 1905–1967, vol. VI
Lawrence, Sir Henry Hayes, 2nd Bt (cr 1858), 1864–1898, vol. I
Lawrence, Lt-Col Henry Rundle, 1878–1949, vol. IV
Lawrence, Sir Henry Staveley, 1870–1949, vol. IV
Lawrence, Sir Henry Waldemar, 3rd Bt (cr 1858), 1845–1908, vol. I
Lawrence, Captain Henry Walter Neville, 1891–1959, vol. V
Lawrence, Gen. Hon. Sir Herbert Alexander, 1861–1943, vol. IV
Lawrence, Herbert Cecil B.; see Barnes-Lawrence.
Lawrence, Col Hugh Duncan, 1862–1946, vol. IV
Lawrence, Sir James Clarke, 1st Bt (cr 1869), 1820–1897, vol. I
Lawrence, Sir James John Trevor, 2nd Bt (cr 1867), 1831–1913, vol. I
Lawrence, Sir (James) Taylor, 1888–1944, vol. IV
Lawrence, Sir Joseph, 1st Bt (cr 1918), 1848–1919, vol. II
Lawrence, Margery, (Mrs Arthur Towle), died 1969, vol. VI
Lawrence, Marjorie Florence, died 1979, vol. VII
Lawrence, Hon. Dame Maude Agnes, 1864–1933, vol. III
Lawrence, Rt Hon. Sir Paul Ogden, 1861–1952, vol. V
Lawrence, Penelope, died 1932, vol. III
Lawrence, Lt-Col Sir (Percy) Roland (Bradford), 2nd Bt (cr 1906), 1886–1950, vol. IV
Lawrence, Peter Frederick, 1937–1976, vol. VII
Lawrence, Lt-Col Richard Travers, 1890–1973, vol. VII
Lawrence, Robert Daniel, 1892–1968, vol. VI
Lawrence, Sir Robert Leslie Edward, 1915–1984, vol. VIII
Lawrence, Roger Bernard, died 1925, vol. II
Lawrence, Lt-Col Sir Roland; see Lawrence, Lt-Col Sir P. R. B.
Lawrence, Sir Russell; see Lawrence, Sir W. R.
Lawrence, Samuel Chave, 1894–1980, vol. VII
Lawrence, Susan; see Lawrence, A. S.
Lawrence, Sydney, 1905–1976, vol. VII
Lawrence, Sydney Boyle, died 1951, vol. V
Lawrence, Sir Taylor; see Lawrence, Sir J. T.
Lawrence, Thomas Edward; see Shaw, T. E.
Lawrence, Rev. Thomas Joseph, 1849–1919, vol. II
Lawrence, Vernon, 1899–1971, vol. VII
Lawrence, Sir Walter, 1872–1939, vol. III
Lawrence, Sir Walter Roper, 1st Bt (cr 1906), 1857–1940, vol. III
Lawrence, Sir William, 1818–1897, vol. I
Lawrence, Rt Rev. William, 1850–1941, vol. IV
Lawrence, Sir William, 4th Bt, 1913–1986, vol. VIII
Lawrence, Maj.-Gen. William Alexander, 1843–1924, vol. II
Lawrence, William Frederic, 1844–1935, vol. III
Lawrence, William John, 1862–1940, vol. III
Lawrence, Sir William Matthew Trevor, 3rd Bt (cr 1867), 1870–1934, vol. III
Lawrence, Sir (William) Russell, 1903–1976, vol. VII
Lawrence-Archer, Col James Henry, 1871–1948, vol. IV
Lawrence-Wilson, Harry Lawrence, 1920–1986, vol. VIII
Lawrie, Allan James, 1873–1926, vol. II
Lawrie, Sir Archibald Campbell, 1837–1914, vol. I
Lawrie, Maj.-Gen. Charles Edward, 1864–1953, vol. V
Lawrie, Captain Edward McConnell Wyndham, 1882–1933, vol. III
Lawrie, James Haldane, 1907–1979, vol. VII
Lawrie, John, 1861–1935, vol. III
Laws, Bernard Courtney, died 1947, vol. IV
Laws, Gp Captain Frederick Charles Victor, 1887–1975, vol. VII
Laws, Rev. George Edward, died 1923, vol. II
Laws, Lt-Col Henry William, 1876–1954, vol. V
Laws, Robert, 1851–1934, vol. III
Laws, Samuel Charles, 1879–1963, vol. VI
Lawson, 1st Baron, 1881–1965, vol. VI
Lawson, Abercrombie Anstruther, died 1927, vol. II
Lawson, Alexander, 1852–1921, vol. II
Lawson, Brig.-Gen. Algernon, 1869–1929, vol. III
Lawson, Andrew Sherlock, 1855–1914, vol. I
Lawson, Sir Arnold, 1867–1947, vol. IV
Lawson, Arthur Ernest, 1863–1933, vol. III
Lawson, Sir Arthur Tredgold, 1st Bt (cr 1900), 1844–1915, vol. I
Lawson, Charles, 1916–1989, vol. VIII
Lawson, Sir Charles Allen, 1838–1915, vol. I
Lawson, Sir Digby, 2nd Bt (cr 1900), 1880–1959, vol. V
Lawson, Frederick Henry, 1897–1983, vol. VIII
Lawson, Rev. Frederick Pike, died 1920, vol. II
Lawson, Major Frederick Washington, 1869–1924, vol. II
Lawson, Sir George, 1838–1898, vol. I
Lawson, George McArthur, 1906–1978, vol. VII
Lawson, H. S., 1876–1918, vol. II
Lawson, Lt-Col Harold Andrew Balvaird, 1899–1985, vol. VIII
Lawson, Sir Harry Sutherland Wightman, 1875–1952, vol. V
Lawson, Sir Henry Brailsford, 1898–1978, vol. VII
Lawson, Henry Hertzberg, 1867–1922, vol. II
Lawson, Sir Henry Joseph, 3rd Bt (cr 1841), 1877–1947, vol. IV
Lawson, Lt-Gen. Sir Henry Merrick, 1859–1933, vol. III
Lawson, Major Sir Hilton, 4th Bt (cr 1831), 1895–1959, vol. V
Lawson, Hon. James Earl, 1891–1950, vol. IV
Lawson, Sir John, 2nd Bt (cr 1841), 1829–1910, vol. I
Lawson, John, 1893–1977, vol. VII

Lawson, Sir John Grant, 1st Bt (*cr* 1905), 1856–1919, vol. II

Lawson, Col Sir Peter Grant, 2nd Bt (*cr* 1905), 1903–1973, vol. VII

Lawson, Sir Ralph Henry, 4th Bt (*cr* 1841), 1905–1975, vol. VII

Lawson, Rear-Adm. Robert Neale, 1873–1945, vol. IV

Lawson, Thomas William, 1857–1925, vol. II

Lawson, Victor F., 1850–1925, vol. II

Lawson, Sir Wilfrid, 2nd Bt (*cr* 1831), 1829–1906, vol. I

Lawson, Sir Wilfrid, 3rd Bt (*cr* 1831), 1862–1937, vol. III

Lawson, Sir William Halford, 1899–1971, vol. VII

Lawson, Sir William Howard, 5th Bt, 1907–1990, vol. VIII

Lawson, William Norton, 1830–1911, vol. I

Lawson, Rev. William Thomas, *died* 1937, vol. III

Lawson, Dick Clare, 1913–1987, vol. VIII

Lawson-Tancred, Major Sir Thomas Selby, 9th Bt, 1870–1945, vol. IV

Lawther, Barry Charles Alfred, 1888–1974, vol. VII

Lawther, Sir William, 1889–1976, vol. VII

Lawton, Frank, 1904–1969, vol. VI

Lawton, Frank Dickinson, 1915–1983, vol. VIII

Lawton, Frank Warburton, 1881–1966, vol. VI

Lawton, Kenneth Keith Fullerton, 1924–1985, vol. VIII

Lay, Arthur Hyde, 1865–1934, vol. III

Lay, Brig. William Oswald, 1892–1952, vol. V

Layard, Austen Havelock, 1895–1956, vol. V

Layard, Sir Charles Peter, 1849–1915, vol. I

Layard, Edgar Leopold, 1824–1900, vol. I

Layard, George Somes, 1857–1925, vol. II

Layard, Raymond de Burgh Money, 1859–1941, vol. IV

Laybourne, Rear-Adm. Alan Watson, 1898–1977, vol. VII

Laybourne-Smith, Louis, 1880–1965, vol. VI

Laycock, Brig.-Gen. Sir Joseph Frederick, 1867–1952, vol. V

Laycock, Sir Leslie Ernest, 1903–1981, vol. VIII

Laycock, Maj.-Gen. Sir Robert Edward, 1907–1968, vol. VI

Laye, Maj.-Gen. Joseph Henry, 1849–1938, vol. III

Layh, Lt-Col Herbert Thomas Christoph, 1885–1964, vol. VI

Layland-Barratt, Sir Francis; *see* Barratt.

Layland-Barratt, Captain Sir Francis Henry Godolphin, 2nd Bt, 1896–1968, vol. VI

Layman, Captain Herbert Francis Hope, 1899–1989, vol. VIII

Layng, Rev. Thomas Malcolm, 1892–1958, vol. V

Layng, Rev. William Wright, 1845–1936, vol. III

Layton, 1st Baron, 1884–1966, vol. VI

Layton, Major Edward, 1857–1913, vol. I

Layton, 2nd Baron, 1912–1989, vol. VIII

Layton, Lt-Col Basil Douglas Bailey, 1907–1986, vol. VIII

Layton, Edwin J., 1850–1929, vol. III

Layton, Adm. Sir Geoffrey, 1884–1964, vol. VI

Layton, Paul Henry, 1905–1989, vol. VIII

Layton, Captain Perceval Norman, 1872–1943, vol. IV

Layton, Thomas Arthur, 1910–1988, vol. VIII

Layton, Thomas Bramley, 1882–1964, vol. VI

Layton, William Grazebrook, 1868–1949, vol. IV

Lazarovich-Hrebelianovich, HH Princess, (Eleanor Calhoun), *died* 1957, vol. V

Lazarus, Ruth, (Mrs David V. Glass); *see* Glass, R.

Lazarus-Barlow, Walter Sydney, *died* 1950, vol. IV

Lazell, Henry George Leslie, 1903–1982, vol. VIII

Lazenby, Frederick George, 1876–1943, vol. VIII

Lazier, Stephen Franklin, 1841–1916, vol. II

Lea, Arthur Sheridan, *died* 1915, vol. I

Lea, Edward Thomas, 1852–1938, vol. III

Lea, Frederick Charles, *died* 1952, vol. V

Lea, Sir Frederick Measham, 1900–1984, vol. VIII

Lea, George Harris, 1843–1915, vol. I

Lea, Lt-Gen. Sir George Harris, 1912–1990, vol. VIII

Lea, Lt-Col Harold Futvoye, 1867–1940, vol. III

Lea, Henry Charles, 1852–1909, vol. I

Lea, Hugh Cecil, 1869–1926, vol. II

Lea, John, 1871–1958, vol. V

Lea, Sir Julian; *see* Lea, Sir T. J.

Lea, Measham, 1869–1963, vol. VI

Lea, Lt-Col Percy Gerald Parker, 1875–1945, vol. IV

Lea, Col Samuel Job, 1851–1919, vol. II

Lea, Sir Sydney; *see* Lea, Sir T. S.

Lea, Sir Thomas, 1st Bt, 1841–1902, vol. I

Lea, Sir Thomas Claude Harris, 3rd Bt, 1901–1985, vol. VIII

Lea, Sir (Thomas) Julian, 4th Bt, 1934–1990, vol. VIII

Lea, Sir (Thomas) Sydney, 2nd Bt, 1867–1946, vol. IV

Lea-Cox, Maj.-Gen. Maurice, 1898–1974, vol. VII

Leach, Rt Hon. Sir (Alfred Henry) Lionel, 1883–1960, vol. V

Leach, Archibald A.; *see* Grant, Cary.

Leach, Arthur Francis, 1851–1915, vol. I

Leach, Arthur Gordon, 1885–1978, vol. VII

Leach, Bernard Howell, 1887–1979, vol. VII

Leach, Charles, 1847–1919, vol. II

Leach, Charles Harold, 1901–1975, vol. VII

Leach, Maj.-Gen. Sir Edmund, 1836–1923, vol. II

Leach, Rev. Edmund Foxcroft, 1851–1939, vol. III

Leach, Sir Edmund Ronald, 1910–1989, vol. VIII

Leach, Gen. Sir Edward Pemberton, 1847–1913, vol. I

Leach, Frank Burton, 1881–1961, vol. VI

Leach, Frederick, 1843–1916, vol. II

Leach, Lt-Col Sir George Archibald, 1820–1913, vol. I

Leach, Brig.-Gen. Harold Pemberton, 1851–1930, vol. III

Leach, Rev. Henry, *died* 1921, vol. II

Leach, Henry, 1874–1942, vol. IV

Leach, Brig.-Gen. Henry Edmund Burleigh, 1870–1936, vol. III

Leach, Sir John, 1848–1927, vol. II

Leach, Captain John Catterall, 1894–1941, vol. IV

Leach, Rt Hon. Sir Lionel; *see* Leach, Rt Hon. Sir A. H. L.

Leach, Col Reginald Pemberton, 1855–1929, vol. III

Leach, Rear-Adm. Robert Owen, 1832–1920, vol. II

Leach, Thomas Stephen, 1896–1973, vol. VII
Leach, William, 1870–1949, vol. IV
Leachman, Col Gerard Evelyn, 1880–1920, vol. II
Leacock, Sir Dudley Gordon, 1880–1954, vol. V
Leacock, Stephen Butler, 1869–1944, vol. IV
Lead, Major Sir William Chollerton, *died* 1942, vol. IV
Leadam, Isaac Saunders, *died* 1913, vol. I
Leadbetter, James Stevenson, 1867–1939, vol. III
Leadbitter, Sir Eric Cyril Egerton, 1891–1971, vol. VII
Leadbitter, Jasper Michael, 1912–1989, vol. VIII
Leader, Barbara; *see* Blackburn, E. B.
Leader, Maj.-Gen. Henry Peregrine, 1865–1934, vol. III
Leader, William Nicholas, 1851–1931, vol. III
Leaf, Cecil Huntington, 1864–1910, vol. I
Leaf, Major Henry Meredith, 1862–1931, vol. III
Leaf, Walter, 1852–1927, vol. II
Leah, Samuel Dawson, 1844–1916, vol. II
Leahy, Arthur Herbert, 1857–1928, vol. II
Leahy, Engr Rear-Adm. James Palmer, 1871–1940, vol. III
Leahy, Lt-Col John Patrick Daunt, 1869–1935, vol. III
Leahy, Brig. Thomas Bernard Arthur, 1878–1947, vol. IV
Leahy, Major Thomas Joseph Carroll, 1889–1942, vol. IV
Leahy, Fleet Adm. William Daniel, 1875–1959, vol. V
Leak, Hector, 1887–1976, vol. VII
Leake, Lt-Col Arthur Martin-, 1874–1953, vol. V
Leake, Vice-Adm. Francis M.; *see* Martin-Leake.
Leake, George, 1856–1902, vol. I
Leake, Henry Dashwood Stucley, 1876–1970, vol. VI
Leake, Hugh Martin-, 1878–1977, vol. VII
Leake, Col Jonas William, 1873–1934, vol. III
Leake, Percy Dewe, *died* 1949, vol. IV
Leake, Sidney Henry, 1892–1973, vol. VII
Leakey, Louis Seymour Bazett, 1903–1972, vol. VII
Leale, Rev. Sir John, 1892–1969, vol. VI
Leamy, Edmund, 1848–1904, vol. I
Lean, Air Vice-Marshal Daniel Alexander Ronald, 1927–1982, vol. VIII
Lean, (Edward) Tangye, 1911–1974, vol. VII
Lean, Florence; *see* Marryat, F.
Lean, Captain John Trevor, 1903–1961, vol. VI
Lean, Maj.-Gen. Kenneth Edward, 1859–1921, vol. II
Lean, Tangye; *see* Lean, E. T.
Leane, Col Edwin Thomas, 1867–1928, vol. II
Leane, Brig.-Gen. Sir Raymond Lionel, 1878–1962, vol. VI
Lear, Cyril James, 1911–1987, vol. VIII
Lear, Ven. Francis, 1823–1914, vol. I
Learmont, Captain Percy Hewitt, 1894–1983, vol. VIII
Learmonth, Agnes Moore L.; *see* Livingstone-Learmonth.
Learmonth, Lt-Col (Francis) Leger (Christian) Livingstone-, 1875–1930, vol. III
Learmonth, Adm. Sir Frederick Charles, 1866–1941, vol. IV

Learmonth, Frederick Valiant Cotton L.; *see* Livingstone-Learmonth.
Learmonth, Sir James Rögnvald, 1895–1967, vol. VI
Learmonth, Brig.-Gen. John Eric Christian L.; *see* Livingstone-Learmonth.
Learmonth, Lt-Col Leger Livingstone-; *see* Learmonth, Lt-Col F. L. C. L.
Learoyd-Cockburn, Col Charles Douglas, 1859–1946, vol. IV
Leary, Leonard Poulter, 1891–1990, vol. VIII
Leask, George Alfred, 1878–1950, vol. IV (A)
Leask, Air Vice-Marshal Kenneth Malise St Clair Graeme, 1896–1974, vol. VII
Leatham, Major Bertram Henry, 1881–1915, vol. I
Leatham, Vice-Adm. Eustace La Trobe, 1870–1935, vol. III
Leatham, Adm. Sir Ralph, 1886–1954, vol. V
Leathem, John Gaston, 1906–1984, vol. VIII
Leathem, Walter Henry, 1894–1967, vol. VI
Leather, Col Francis Holdsworth, 1864–1929, vol. III
Leather, John Walter, 1860–1934, vol. III
Leather, Lt-Col Kenneth John Walters, 1878–1963, vol. VI
Leathers, 1st Viscount, 1883–1965, vol. VI
Leathes, John Beresford, 1864–1956, vol. V
Leathes, Maj.-Gen. Reginald Carteret de Mussenden, 1909–1987, vol. VIII
Leathes, Rev. Stanley, 1830–1900, vol. I
Leathes, Sir Stanley Mordaunt, 1861–1938, vol. III
Leaver, Noel Harry, 1889–1951, vol. V
Leavis, Frank Raymond, 1895–1978, vol. VII
Le Bargy, Charles Gustave, 1858–1936, vol. III
Le Bas, Edward, 1904–1966, vol. VI
Le Bas, Sir Hedley Francis, 1868–1926, vol. II
Le Bas, Air Vice-Marshal Michael Henry, 1916–1988, vol. VIII
Le Blanc, Rt Rev. Edouard, 1870–1935, vol. III
Le Blanc, Sir Pierre Evariste, 1854–1918, vol. II
Le Blond, Elizabeth Alice Frances, (Mrs Aubrey Le Blond), *died* 1934, vol. III
Lebour, George Alexander Louis, 1847–1918, vol. II
Le Braz, Anatole, 1859–1926, vol. II
Le Breton, Clement Martin, 1852–1927, vol. II
Le Breton, Col Sir Edward Philip, 1883–1961, vol. VI
Le Breton-Simmons, Col George Francis Henry, 1864–1930, vol. III
Lebrun, Albert, 1871–1950, vol. IV
Le Brun, Paymaster Captain William Henry, *died* 1942, vol. IV
Leburn, Gilmour; *see* Leburn, W. G.
Leburn, (William) Gilmour, 1913–1963, vol. VI
Lebus, Sir Herman Andrew Harris, 1884–1957, vol. V
Le Chatelier, Henry Louis, 1850–1936, vol. III
Leche, Sir John Hurleston, 1889–1960, vol. V
Lechmere, Sir Edmund Arthur, 4th Bt, 1865–1937, vol. III
Lechmere, Captain Sir Ronald Berwick Hungerford, 5th Bt, 1886–1965, vol. VI
Leck, David Calder, 1857–1927, vol. II
Leckie, Col John Edwards, 1872–1950, vol. IV
Leckie, Joseph Alexander, 1866–1938, vol. III
Leckie, Joseph Hannay, 1865–1935, vol. III
Leckie, Air Marshal Robert, 1890–1975, vol. VII
Leckonby, William Douglas, 1907–1989, vol. VIII

Lecky, Captain Arthur Macaulay, 1881–1933, vol. III

Lecky, Col Frederick Beauchamp, 1858–1928, vol. II

Lecky, Captain Halton Stirling, 1878–1940, vol. III

Lecky, Maj.-Gen. Robert St Clair, 1863–1940, vol. III

Lecky, Sir Thomas, 1828–1907, vol. I

Lecky, Rt Hon. William Edward Hartpole, 1838–1903, vol. I

Leclerc, Maj.-Gen. Pierre Edouard, 1893–1982, vol. VIII

Leclercq, Auguste B.; *see* Bouche-Leclercq.

Leclézio, Sir Eugène Pierre Jules, 1832–1915, vol. II

Leclezio, Hon. Sir Henry, *died* 1929, vol. III

Leclézio, Sir Jules, 1877–1951, vol. V

Lecocq, Charles, 1832–1918, vol. II

Lecomte, Georges, 1867–1958, vol. V

Leconfield, 2nd Baron, 1830–1901, vol. I

Leconfield, 3rd Baron, 1872–1952, voi. V

Leconfield, 4th Baron, 1877–1963, vol. VI

Leconfield, 5th Baron, 1883–1967, vol. VI

Le Corbusier, (Charles-Edouard Jeanneret), 1887–1965, vol. VI

Le Cornu, Col Charles Philip, 1829–1911, vol. I

le Couteur, Frank, *died* 1950, vol. IV

Ledeboer, John Henry, 1853–1930, vol. III

Ledgard, Sir Henry, 1853–1946, vol. IV

Ledgard, Rev. Ralph Gilbert, *died* 1939, vol. III

Ledgard, Reginald Armitage, 1883–1949, vol. IV

Ledger, Air Vice-Marshal Arthur Percy, 1897–1970, vol. VI

Ledger, Claude Kirwood, 1888–1974, vol. VII

Ledger, Edward, *died* 1921, vol. II

Ledingham, Col George Alexander, 1890–1978, vol. VII

Ledingham, Sir John Charles Grant, 1875–1944, vol. IV

Ledingham, Mrs Una Christina, 1900–1965, vol. VI

Ledlie, James Crawford, 1860–1928, vol. II

Ledlie, Reginald Cyril Bell, 1898–1966, vol. VI

Ledóchowski, Wlodimir Halka, Count, 1866–1942, vol. IV

Leduc, Paul, 1889–1971, vol. VII

Ledward, Gilbert, 1888–1960, vol. V

Ledward, Richard Thomas Davenport, 1915–1963, vol. VI

Lee of Asheridge, Baroness (Life Peer); Janet Bevan, (Jennie Lee), 1904–1988, vol. VIII

Lee of Fareham, 1st Viscount, 1868–1947, vol. IV

Lee of Newton, Baron (Life Peer); Frederick Lee, 1906–1984, vol. VIII

Lee, Rev. Albert, 1852–1935, vol. III

Lee, Lt-Col Sir (Albert) George, 1879–1967, vol. VI

Lee, Maj.-Gen. Alec Wilfred, 1896–1973, vol. VII

Lee, Alfred Morgan, 1901–1975, vol. VII

Lee, Arthur Michael, 1913–1983, vol. VIII

Lee, Lt-Col Arthur Neale, 1877–1954, vol. V

Lee, Air Vice-Marshal Arthur Stanley Gould, 1894–1975, vol. VII

Lee, Col Arthur Vaughan Hanning V.; *see* Vaughan-Lee.

Lee, Mrs Asher; *see* Lee, Mollie Carpenter.

Lee, Auriol, 1880–1941, vol. IV

Lee, Bremner Patrick, 1864–1937, vol. III

Lee, Hon. Charles Alfred, 1842–1926, vol. II

Lee, Charles Guy V.; *see* Vaughan-Lee.

Lee, Adm. Sir Charles Lionel V.; *see* Vaughan-Lee.

Lee, Rev. Donald Rathbone, 1911–1988, vol. VIII

Lee, Edgar, 1851–1908, vol. I

Lee, Sir Edward, 1833–1909, vol. I

Lee, Edward Owen, 1891–1950, vol. IV

Lee, Rev. Canon Edwin Maywood O'Hara, 1859–1942, vol. IV

Lee, Ernest Markham, 1874–1956, vol. V

Lee, Fitzhugh, *died* 1905, vol. I

Lee, Brig.-Gen. Francis, 1866–1932, vol. III

Lee, Frank, 1867–1941, vol. IV

Lee, Rt Hon. Sir Frank Godbould, 1903–1971, vol. VII

Lee, Frank Herbert, *born* 1869, vol. V

Lee, Rev. Frederick George, 1832–1902, vol. I

Lee, Lt-Col Sir George; *see* Lee, Lt-Col Sir A. G.

Lee, Lt-Gen. George Leonard, 1860–1939, vol. III

Lee, Sir (George) Wilton, 1904–1986, vol. VIII

Lee, Gordon Ambrose de Lisle, 1864–1927, vol. II

Lee, Lt-Col H. R.; *see* Romer-Lee.

Lee, Harry Wilmot, 1848–1914, vol. I

Lee, Sir Henry Austin, 1847–1918, vol. II

Lee, Col Tun Sir Henry Hau Shik, 1901–1988, vol. VIII

Lee, Maj.-Gen. Henry Herbert, 1838–1920, vol. II

Lee, Henry William, 1865–1932, vol. III

Lee, Herbert William, 1865–1940, vol. III

Lee, Ivy Ledbetter, 1877–1934, vol. III

Lee, James Paris, 1831–1904, vol. I

Lee, Rev. James Wideman, 1849–1919, vol. II

Lee, John, 1867–1928, vol. II

Lee, Joseph Johnston, 1876–1954, vol. V (A)

Lee, Sir Kenneth, 1st Bt, *died* 1967, vol. VI

Lee, Lawford Y.; *see* Yate-Lee.

Lee, Lennox B., 1864–1949, vol. IV

Lee, Manfred B., *died* 1971, vol. VII

Lee, May B.; *see* Stott, May, (Lady Stott).

Lee, Mollie Carpenter, (Mrs Asher Lee), *died* 1973, vol. VII

Lee, Col Reginald Tilson, 1878–1940, vol. III

Lee, Rev. Richard, *died* 1922, vol. II

Lee, Richard Henry, *died* 1923, vol. II

Lee, Maj.-Gen. Sir Richard Phillips, 1865–1953, vol. V

Lee, Robert Warden, 1868–1958, vol. V

Lee, Roger Malcolm, 1902–1972, vol. VII

Lee, S. Richmond, (Mrs John W. Richmond Lee); *see* Yorke, Curtis.

Lee, Sir Sidney, 1859–1926, vol. II

Lee, Brig. Stanlake Swinton, 1890–1952, vol. V

Lee, Sydney, 1866–1949, vol. IV

Lee, Vernon; *see* Paget, Violet.

Lee, Hon. Sir Walter Henry, 1874–1963, vol. VI

Lee, Rt Rev. William, 1875–1948, vol. IV

Lee, William Alexander, 1886–1971, vol. VII

Lee, William Frederick, 1857–1930, vol. III

Lee, William Stevens, 1871–1965, vol. VI

Lee, Rev. William Walker, 1909–1979, vol. VII

Lee, Sir Wilton; *see* Lee, Sir G. W.

Lee-Dillon, Hon. Harry Lee Stanton, 1874–1923, vol. II

Lee-Elliott, David Lee, 1869–1956, vol. V

Lee-Hamilton, Eugene Jacob, 1845–1907, vol. I
Lee-Hankey, W., 1869–1952, vol. V
Lee-Holland, Hetty, *died* 1954, vol. V
Lee-Howard, Leon Alexander, 1914–1978, vol. VII
Lee Lander, Frank Patrick; *see* Lander.
Lee Potter, Air Marshal Sir Patrick Brunton, 1904–1982, vol. VIII
Lee Steere, Sir Ernest Augustus, 1866–1957, vol. V
Lee-Warner, Lt-Col Harry Granville, 1883–1932, vol. III
Lee Warner, Philip Henry, 1877–1925, vol. II
Lee-Warner, Sir William, 1846–1914, vol. I
Leebody, John R., 1840–1927, vol. II
Leece, Rev. Charles Henry, *died* 1930, vol. III
Leech, Arthur John, 1873–1940, vol. III
Leech, Sir Bosdin Thomas, 1836–1912, vol. I
Leech, Clifford, 1909–1977, vol. VII
Leech, Ernest Bosdin, 1875–1950, vol. IV
Leech, George William, 1894–1966, vol. VI
Leech, Henry Brougham, 1843–1921, vol. II
Leech, John, 1857–1942, vol. IV
Leech, Sir Joseph William, 1865–1940, vol. III
Leech, Priestley, *died* 1936, vol. III
Leech, Samuel Chetwynd, 1872–1931, vol. III
Leech, Sir Stephen, 1864–1925, vol. II
Leech, (Sir) William Charles, 1900–1990, vol. VIII
Leech, William John, 1881–1968, vol. VI
Leech, William Thomas, 1869–1953, vol. V
Leech-Porter, Maj.-Gen. John Edmund, 1896–1979, vol. VII
Leechman, Hon. Lord; James Graham Leechman, 1906–1986, vol. VIII
Leechman, Barclay, 1901–1984, vol. VIII
Leeder, S. H., *died* 1930, vol. III
Leedham, Air Cdre Hugh, 1889–1947, vol. IV
Leedham-Green, Charles, *died* 1931, vol. III
Leeds, 10th Duke of, 1862–1927, vol. II
Leeds, 11th Duke of, 1901–1963, vol. VI
Leeds, 12th Duke of, 1884–1964, vol. VI
Leeds, Duchess of; (Katherine), *died* 1952, vol. V
Leeds, Sir Edward Templer, 5th Bt, 1859–1924, vol. II
Leeds, Edward Thurlow, 1877–1955, vol. V
Leeds, Sir George Graham Mortimer, 7th Bt, 1927–1983, vol. VIII
Leeds, Comdr Sir Reginald Arthur St John, 6th Bt, 1899–1970, vol. VI
Leeds, Lt-Col Thomas Louis, 1869–1926, vol. II
Leeds, William Henry Arthur St John, 1864–1917, vol. II
Leefe, Gen. John Beckwith, 1849–1922, vol. II
Leek, James, 1892–1978, vol. VII
Leeke, Rev. Edward Tucker, 1841–1925, vol. II
Leeke, George, *died* 1939, vol. III
Leeke, Rt Rev. John Cox, 1843–1919, vol. II
Leeke, Col Ralph, 1849–1943, vol. IV
Leeke, Ven. Thomas Newton, 1854–1933, vol. III
Leeland, John Roger, 1930–1990, vol. VIII
Leen, Very Rev. Edward, 1885–1944, vol. IV
Leen, Rt Rev. James, 1888–1949, vol. IV
Leeper, Alexander, 1848–1934, vol. III
Leeper, Alexander Wigram Allen, 1887–1935, vol. III
Leeper, Rev. Canon Arthur Lindsay, 1883–1942, vol. IV

Leeper, Sir Reginald Wildig Allen, 1888–1968, vol. VI
Leeper, Richard Kevin, 1894–1987, vol. VIII
Lees, Air Marshal Sir Alan, 1895–1973, vol. VII
Lees, Sir Arthur Henry James, 5th Bt (*cr* 1804), 1863–1949, vol. IV
Lees, Arthur John, 1867–1956, vol. V
Lees, Mrs Charles; *see* Lees, Sarah Anne.
Lees, Charles Archibald, 1869–1943, vol. IV
Lees, Sir Charles Archibald Edward Ivor, 7th Bt (*cr* 1804), 1902–1963, vol. VI
Lees, Sir Charles Cameron, 1837–1898, vol. I
Lees, Col Charles Henry Brownlow, 1871–1941, vol. IV
Lees, Charles Herbert, 1864–1952, vol. V
Lees, Sir Clare; *see* Lees, Sir W. C.
Lees, David, *died* 1934, vol. III
Lees, David, 1910–1986, vol. VIII
Lees, David Bridge, *died* 1915, vol. I
Lees, Rear-Adm. Dennis Marescaux, 1900–1973, vol. VII
Lees, Donald Hector, *died* 1953, vol. V
Lees, Edith Mabel Lucy, 1878–1956, vol. V
Lees, Sir Elliott, 1st Bt (*cr* 1897), 1860–1908, vol. I
Lees, George Martin, 1898–1955, vol. V
Lees, Rev. George Robinson, 1860–1944, vol. IV
Lees, Sir Harcourt James, 4th Bt (*cr* 1804), 1840–1917, vol. II
Lees, Rev. Harold Montagu H.; *see* Hyde-Lees.
Lees, Most Rev. Harrington Clare, 1870–1929, vol. III
Lees, Sir Hereward; *see* Lees, Sir W. H. C.
Lees, Jack, *died* 1941, vol. IV
Lees, Very Rev. Sir James Cameron, 1834–1913, vol. I
Lees, James Ferguson, 1872–1935, vol. III
Lees, Sir Jean Marie Ivor, 6th Bt (*cr* 1804), 1875–1957, vol. V
Lees, Sir John M'Kie, 1843–1926, vol. II
Lees, Col Sir John Victor Elliott, 3rd Bt (*cr* 1897), 1887–1955, vol. V
Lees, Lt-Col Lawrence Werner Wyld, 1887–1976, vol. VII
Lees, Oswald Campbell, 1857–1945, vol. IV
Lees, Col Roderick Livingstone, 1864–1936, vol. III
Lees, Roland James, 1917–1985, vol. VIII
Lees, Samuel, 1885–1940, vol. III
Lees, Sarah Anne, 1842–1935, vol. III
Lees, Stanley Lawrence, 1911–1980, vol. VII
Lees, Sir Thomas Evans Keith, 2nd Bt (*cr* 1897), 1886–1915, vol. I
Lees, Thomas Orde Hastings, 1846–1924, vol. II
Lees, Walter Kinnear P.; *see* Pyke-Lees.
Lees, Sir (William) Clare, 1st Bt (*cr* 1937), 1874–1951, vol. V
Lees, Sir (William) Hereward (Clare), 2nd Bt (*cr* 1937), 1904–1976, vol. VII
Lees-Jones, John, 1887–1966, vol. VI
Lees Read, Bertie, 1903–1960, vol. V
Lees-Smith, Rt Hon. Hastings Bertrand, 1878–1941, vol. IV
Leese, Sir Alexander William, 4th Bt, 1909–1979, vol. VII
Leese, Charles William, 1876–1969, vol. VI

Leese, Sir Joseph Francis, 1st Bt, 1845–1914, vol. I

Leese, Lt-Gen. Sir Oliver William Hargreaves, 3rd Bt, 1894–1978, vol. VII

Leese, Sir William Hargreaves, 2nd Bt, 1868–1937, vol. III

Leeson, Rt Rev. Spencer, 1892–1956, vol. V

Leeson-Marshall, Markham Richard, 1859–1939, vol. III

Leete, Alfred Chew, 1882–1933, vol. III

Leete, Frederick Alexander, *died* 1941, vol. IV

Leete, Leslie William Thomas, 1909–1976, vol. VII

Leetham, Lt-Col Sir Arthur, 1859–1933, vol. III

Le Fanu, George Ernest Hugh, 1874–1965, vol. VI

Le Fanu, Most Rev. Henry Frewen, 1870–1946, vol. IV

Le Fanu, Adm. Sir Michael, 1913–1970, vol. VI

Le Fanu, Thomas Philip, 1858–1945, vol. IV

Le Fanu, William Richard, 1861–1925, vol. II

Lefeaux, Leslie, 1886–1962, vol. VI

Le Feuvre, Amy, *died* 1929, vol. III

Le Fèvre, Raymond James Wood, 1905–1986, vol. VIII

Leffingwell, Russell Cornell, 1878–1960, vol. V

Leffler, Gösta M.; *see* Mittag-Leffler.

le Fleming, Sir Andrew Fleming Hudleston; *see* Fleming.

Le Fleming, Sir (Ernest) Kaye, 1872–1946, vol. IV

le Fleming, Sir Frank Thomas, 10th Bt, 1887–1971, vol. VII

Le Fleming, Sir Kaye; *see* Le Fleming, Sir E. K.

Le Fleming, Maj.-Gen. Roger Eustace, 1895–1962, vol. VI

Le Fleming, Stanley Hughes, 1855–1939, vol. III

Le Fleming, Sir William Hudleston, 9th Bt, 1861–1945, vol. IV

le Fleming, Sir William Kelland, 11th Bt, 1922–1988, vol. VIII

Lefroy, A. H. F., 1852–1919, vol. II

Lefroy, Sir Anthony Langlois Bruce, 1881–1958, vol. V

Lefroy, Bt Major Bertram Perceval, 1878–1915, vol. I

Lefroy, Captain Cecil Maxwell-, 1876–1931, vol. III

Lefroy, Rev. Charles Edward Cotterell, *died* 1940, vol. III

Lefroy, Sir Edward Henry Bruce, 1887–1966, vol. VI

Lefroy, Rev. Frederick Anthony, 1846–1920, vol. II

Lefroy, Rt Rev. George Alfred, 1854–1919, vol. II

Lefroy, Major H., *died* 1935, vol. III

Lefroy, Harold Maxwell-, 1877–1925, vol. II

Lefroy, Hon. Sir Henry Bruce, 1854–1930, vol. III

Lefroy, Walter John Magrath, 1870–1955, vol. V

Lefroy, Very Rev. William, 1836–1909, vol. I

Lefroy, William Chambers, 1849–1915, vol. I

Lefschetz, Solomon, 1884–1972, vol. VII

Le Gallais, Sir Richard Lyle, 1916–1983, vol. VIII

Le Gallais, Theodore, 1852–1903, vol. I

Le Gallienne, Richard, 1866–1947, vol. IV

Legard, Albert George, 1845–1922, vol. II

Legard, Bt-Col Alfred Digby, 1878–1939, vol. III

Legard, Sir Algernon Willoughby, 12th Bt, 1842–1923, vol. II

Legard, Rev. Cecil Henry, 1843–1918, vol. II

Legard, Sir Charles, 11th Bt, 1846–1901, vol. I

Legard, Brig.-Gen. D'Arcy, 1873–1953, vol. V

Legard, Sir Digby Algernon Hall, 13th Bt, 1876–1961, vol. VI

Legard, Col Sir James Digby, 1846–1935, vol. III

Legard, Captain Sir Thomas Digby, 14th Bt, 1905–1984, vol. VIII

Legat, Charles Edward, 1876–1966, vol. VI

Legat, Harold, *died* 1960, vol. V

Legentilhomme, Général Paul Louis, 1884–1975, vol. VII

Léger, Alexis; *see* Léger, M.-R. A. A. St-L.

Léger, Rt Hon. Jules, 1913–1980, vol. VII

Léger, (Marie-René Auguste) Alexis Saint-Léger, 1887–1975, vol. VII

Le Geyt, Maj.-Gen. Philip Harrison, 1834–1922, vol. II

Legg, Captain Sir George Edward Wickham, 1870–1927, vol. II

Legg, John Wickham, 1843–1921, vol. II

Legg, Leopold George Wickham, 1877–1962, vol. VI

Legg, Ven. Richard Wickham, 1867–1952, vol. V

Legg, Thomas Percy, 1872–1930, vol. III

Leggate, John Mortimer, 1904–1985, vol. VIII

Leggate, Hon. William Muter, 1879–1955, vol. V

Leggatt, Charles Ashley Scott, 1861–1935, vol. III

Leggatt, Maj.-Gen. Charles St Quentin Outen Fullbrook-, 1889–1972, vol. VII

Leggatt, Captain Charles William Stares, 1864–1954, vol. V

Leggatt, Col Hon. Sir William Watt, 1894–1968, vol. VI

Legge, Rt Rev. Hon. Augustus, 1839–1913, vol. I

Legge, Hon. Charles Gounter, 1842–1907, vol. I

Legge, Dominica; *see* Legge, M. D.

Legge, Francis Cecil, 1873–1940, vol. III

Legge, Col Hon. Sir Harry Charles, 1852–1924, vol. II

Legge, Col Hon. Heneage, 1845–1911, vol. I

Legge, Rev. James, 1815–1897, vol. I

Legge, Lt-Gen. James Gordon, 1863–1947, vol. IV

Legge, James Granville, 1861–1940, vol. III

Legge, (Mary) Dominica, 1905–1986, vol. VIII

Legge, Rear-Adm. Montague George Bentinck, 1883–1951, vol. V

Legge, Lt-Col Norton, 1860–1900, vol. I

Legge, Brig.-Gen. Reginald Francis, *died* 1955, vol. V

Legge, Robin Humphrey, 1862–1933, vol. III

Legge, Maj.-Gen. Stanley Ferguson, 1900–1977, vol. VII

Legge, Sir Thomas Morison, 1863–1932, vol. III

Legge, Brig.-Gen. William Kaye, 1869–1946, vol. IV

Legge-Bourke, Major Sir (Edward Alexander) Henry, (Sir Harry), 1914–1973, vol. VII

Legge-Bourke, Major Sir Harry; *see* Legge-Bourke, Major Sir E. A. H.

Leggett, Col Archibald Herbert, 1877–1936, vol. III

Leggett, B. J., 1890–1968, vol. VI (AII)

Leggett, Major Sir Edward Humphrey Manisty, 1871–1947, vol. IV

Leggett, Major Eric Henry Goodwin, 1880–1916, vol. II

Leggett, Sir Frederick William, 1884–1983, vol. VIII

Leggett, Henry Aufrere, 1874–1950, vol. IV

Leggett, Vice-Adm. Oliver Elles, 1876–1946, vol. IV

Leggo, Sir Jack Frederick, 1916–1983, vol. VIII

Legh, Edmund Willoughby, 1874–1943, vol. IV
Legh, Maj. Hon. Sir Francis Michael, 1919–1984, vol. VIII
Legh, Major Hon. Gilbert, 1858–1939, vol. III
Legh, Col Harry Shuldham S.; see Shuldham-Legh.
Legh, Lt-Col Hon. Sir Piers Walter, 1890–1955, vol. V
Legh-Jones, Sir George, 1890–1960, vol. V
Legouis, Emile, 1861–1937, vol. III
Le Grand, Gen. Frederick Gasper, 1836–1905, vol. I
Legrand, Rt Rev. Joseph, 1853–1937, vol. III
Le Grave, Rev. William, 1843–1922, vol. II
Le Grice, Charles Henry, 1870–1942, vol. IV
Legris, Hon. Joseph Hormidas, 1850–1932, vol. III
Legros, Alphonse, 1837–1911, vol. I
Lehar, Franz, 1870–1948, vol. IV
Lehfeldt, Robert Alfred, 1868–1927, vol. II
Lehman, Hon. Herbert H., 1878–1963, vol. VI
Lehmann, Adolf Ludwig Ferdinand, 1863–1937, vol. III
Lehmann, Beatrix, 1903–1979, vol. VII
Lehmann, Hermann, 1910–1985, vol. VIII
Lehmann, John Frederick, 1907–1987, vol. VIII
Lehmann, Liza, (Elizabeth Nina Mary Frederika), (Mrs Herbert Bedford), 1862–1918, vol. II
Lehmann, Lotte, 1888–1976, vol. VII
Lehmann, Rosamond Nina, 1901–1990, vol. VIII
Lehmann, Rudolf, 1819–1905, vol. I
Lehmann, Rudolf Chambers, 1856–1929, vol. III
Le Hunte, Sir George Ruthven, 1852–1925, vol. II
Lei Wang-Kee, Most Rev. Peter, 1922–1974, vol. VII
Leicester, 2nd Earl of, 1822–1909, vol. I
Leicester, 3rd Earl of, 1848–1941, vol. IV
Leicester, 4th Earl of, 1880–1949, vol. IV
Leicester, 5th Earl of, 1908–1976, vol. VII
Leicester, Sir Charles Byrne Warren, 9th Bt, 1896–1968, vol. VI
Leicester, James, 1915–1976, vol. VII
Leicester, Lt-Col John Cyril Holdich, 1872–1949, vol. IV
Leicester, Sir Peter Fleming Frederic, 8th Bt, 1863–1945, vol. IV
Leicester-Warren, Cuthbert, 1877–1954, vol. V
Leicester-Warren, Lt-Col John Leighton Byrne, 1907–1975, vol. VII
Leigh, 2nd Baron, 1824–1905, vol. I
Leigh, 3rd Baron, 1855–1938, vol. III
Leigh, 4th Baron, 1908–1979, vol. VII
Leigh, Alan de Verd, 1891–1961, vol. VI
Leigh, Arthur George, 1909–1968, vol. VI
Leigh, Major Chandos, 1873–1915, vol. I
Leigh, Charles Edward A.; see Austen-Leigh.
Leigh, Christopher Thomas Bowes, 1905–1971, vol. VII
Leigh, Hon. Sir Edward Chandos, 1832–1915, vol. I
Leigh, Egerton, 1843–1928, vol. II
Leigh, Lt-Col Henry Percy Poingdestre, 1851–1928, vol. II
Leigh, Hon. and Very Rev. James Wentworth, 1838–1923, vol. II
Leigh, Sir John, 1st Bt, 1884–1959, vol. V
Leigh, John Blundell, 1858–1931, vol. III
Leigh, Lt-Col John Cecil Gerard, 1889–1965, vol. VI
Leigh, Sir Joseph, 1841–1908, vol. I

Leigh, Rev. Neville Egerton, 1852–1929, vol. III
Leigh, Col Oswald Mosley, 1864–1949, vol. IV
Leigh, Ralph Alexander, 1915–1987, vol. VIII
Leigh, Reginald Gerard, 1880–1962, vol. VI
Leigh, Richard Arthur A., see Austen-Leigh.
Leigh, Roger, 1840–1924, vol. II
Leigh, Hon. Rupert, 1856–1919, vol. II
Leigh, Thomas Bowes, 1867–1947, vol. IV
Leigh, Vivien, 1913–1967, vol. VI
Leigh-Bennett, Henry Currie, 1852–1903, vol. I
Leigh-Bennett, Percy Raymond, 1887–1964, vol. VI
Leigh-Hunt, Gerard, 1873–1945, vol. IV
Leigh-Mallory, Rev. Herbert Leigh, 1856–1943, vol. IV
Leigh-Mallory, Air Chief Marshal Sir Trafford Leigh, 1892–1944, vol. IV
Leigh-Pemberton, Sir Edward, 1823–1910, vol. I
Leigh-Wood, Lt-Col Sir James, died 1949, vol. IV
Leigh-Wood, Roger, 1906–1987, vol. VIII
Leighton of St Mellons, 1st Baron, 1896–1963, vol. VI
Leighton, Arthur Edgar, 1873–1961, vol. VI
Leighton, Major Bertie Edward Parker, 1875–1952, vol. V
Leighton, Major Sir Bryan Baldwin Mawddwy, 9th Bt, 1868–1919, vol. II
Leighton, Clare, 1899–1989, vol. VIII
Leighton, Edmund Blair, 1853–1922, vol. II
Leighton, Gerald, 1868–1953, vol. V
Leighton, John, 1822–1912, vol. I
Leighton, Captain John Albert, 1881–1945, vol. IV
Leighton, Kenneth, 1929–1988, vol. VIII
Leighton, Margaret, 1922–1976, vol. VII
Leighton, Marie Connor, died 1941, vol. IV
Leighton, Bt Col Sir Richard Tihel, 10th Bt, 1893–1957, vol. V
Leighton, Robert, died 1934, vol. III
Leighton, Sir Robert, 1884–1959, vol. V
Leighton, Stanley, 1837–1901, vol. I
Leighton-Boyce, Guy Gilbert, 1920–1989, vol. VIII
Leiningen, HSH Prince Ernest Leopold Victor Charles Auguste Joseph Emich, 1830–1904, vol. I
Leinster, 6th Duke of, 1887–1922, vol. II
Leinster, 7th Duke of, 1892–1976, vol. VII
Leiper, Robert Thomson, 1881–1969, vol. VI
Leiper, William, 1839–1916, vol. II
Leir, Rear-Adm. Ernest W., 1883–1971, vol. VII
Leir-Carleton, Maj.-Gen. Richard Langford, 1841–1933, vol. III
Leishman, Alan Ross, died 1937, vol. III
Leishman, Sir James, died 1939, vol. III
Leishman, James Blair, 1902–1963, vol. VI
Leishman, John G. A., 1857–1924, vol. II
Leishman, Maj.-Gen. John Thomas, 1835–1920, vol. II
Leishman, Rev. Thomas, 1825–1904, vol. I
Leishman, Lt-Gen. Sir William Boog, 1865–1926, vol. II
Leisk, James Rankine, 1876–1948, vol. IV
Leitch, Archibald, 1878–1931, vol. III
Leitch, Isabella, 1890–1980, vol. VII (AII)
Leitch, Hon. James, born 1850, vol. II
Leitch, Lt-Col John Wilson, 1873–1935, vol. III
Leitch, Rev. Matthew, died 1922, vol. II
Leitch, Sir Walter, 1867–1945, vol. IV

Leitch, Sir William, 1880–1965, vol. VI
Leiter, Joseph, 1868–1932, vol. III
Leiter, Levi Zeigler, 1834–1904, vol. I
Leith of Fyvie, 1st Baron, 1847–1925, vol. II
Leith, Lt-Col Sir Alexander, 1st Bt, 1869–1956, vol. V
Leith, Captain George Piercy, 1877–1945, vol. IV
Leith, Gordon, 1879–1941, vol. IV
Leith of Fyvie, Sir Ian F.; see Forbes-Leith of Fyvie, Sir R. I. A.
Leith, Captain Lockhart, 1876–1940, vol. III
Leith, Robert Fraser Calder, 1854–1936, vol. III
Leith, Major Thomas, 1830–1920, vol. II
Leith-Buchanan, Sir Alexander Wellesley George Thomas, 5th Bt, 1866–1925, vol. II
Leith-Buchanan, Sir George Hector, 4th Bt, 1833–1903, vol. I
Leith-Buchanan, Sir George Hector Macdonald, 6th Bt, 1889–1973, vol. VII
Leith-Hay, Charles Edward Norman, 1858–1939, vol. III
Leith-Ross, Sir Frederick William, 1887–1968, vol. VI
Leitrim, 5th Earl of, 1879–1952, vol. V
Lejeune, Caroline Alice, (Mrs E. Roffe Thompson), 1897–1973, vol. VII
Lejeune, Maj.-Gen. Francis St David Benwell, 1899–1984, vol. VIII
Le Jeune, Henry, 1819–1904, vol. I
Leland, Charles Godfrey, 1824–1903, vol. I
Leland, Col Francis William George, 1877–1943, vol. IV
Leland, Captain Herbert John Collett, 1873–1931, vol. III
Lelean, Percy Samuel, 1871–1956, vol. V
Leleux, Sydney Wallis, 1862–1941, vol. IV
Leloir, Luis Federico, 1906–1987, vol. VIII
Lelong, Lucien, 1889–1958, vol. V
Lely, Sir Frederic Styles Philpin, 1846–1934, vol. III
Lely, John Mountney, 1839–1907, vol. I
Lemaire, Ernest Joseph, 1874–1945, vol. IV
Lemaire, Most Rev. Ishmael Samuel Mills, died 1984, vol. VIII
Le Maistre, Charles, died 1953, vol. V
Le Maitre, Sir Alfred Sutherland, 1896–1959, vol. V
Le Maitre, Ella Katharine Irving, 1896–1960, vol. V
Lemaitre, François Elie Jules, 1853–1915, vol. I
Leman, Count Georges, 1851–1920, vol. II
Le Marchant, Sir Denis, 3rd Bt, 1870–1922, vol. II
Le Marchant, Sir Denis, 5th Bt, 1906–1987, vol. VIII
Le Marchant, Brig.-Gen. Sir Edward Thomas, 4th Bt, 1871–1953, vol. V
Le Marchant, Adm. Evelyn Robert, died 1949, vol. IV
Le Marchant, Sir Henry Denis, 2nd Bt, 1839–1915, vol. I
Le Marchant, Lt-Col Louis St Gratien, 1866–1914, vol. I
Le Marchant, Sir Spencer, 1931–1986, vol. VIII
Lemare, Edwin H., 1866–1934, vol. III
Le Marinel, Very Rev. Matthew, 1883–1963, vol. VI
Lemass, Edwin Stephen, 1890–1970, vol. VI
Lemass, Peter Edmund, 1850–1928, vol. II, vol. III
Lemass, Seán Francis, 1899–1971, vol. VII
le May, Reginald Stuart, 1885–1972, vol. VII

Le May, Gp Captain William Kent, 1911–1978, vol. VII
Lemberg, (Max) Rudolf, 1896–1975, vol. VII
Lemberg, Rudolf; see Lemberg, M. R.
Le Messurier, Col Augustus, 1837–1916, vol. II
Le Messurier, Henry William, 1848–1931, vol. III
Le Mesurier, Col Cecil Brooke, 1831–1913, vol. I
Le Mesurier, Captain Charles Edward, died 1917, vol. II
Le Mesurier, Captain Edward Kirby, 1903–1980, vol. VII
Le Mesurier, Wing Comdr Eric Clive, 1915–1943, vol. IV
Le Mesurier, Col Frederick Augustus, 1839–1926, vol. II
Le Mesurier, Sir Havilland, 1866–1931, vol. III
Le Mesurier, Lt-Col Herbert Grenville, 1873–1940, vol. III
Lemieux, Auguste, 1874–1956, vol. V
Lemieux, Sir François Xavier, 1851–1933, vol. III
Lemieux, Louis Joseph, born 1870, vol. IV
Lemieux, Rodolphe, 1866–1937, vol. III
Lemmon, Col Sir Thomas Warne, 1838–1928, vol. II
Lemnitzer, Gen. Lyman Louis, 1899–1988, vol. VIII
Le Moine, Jucherean de St Denis, 1850–1922, vol. II
Le Moine, Sir James MacPherson, 1825–1912, vol. I
Lemon, Arthur Henry, 1864–1933, vol. III
Lemon, Brig. Arthur Leslie K.; see Kent-Lemon.
Lemon, Sir Ernest John Hutchings, 1884–1954, vol. V
Lemon, Lt-Col Frederick Joseph, 1879–1952, vol. V
Lemon, Sir James, 1833–1923, vol. II
Lemonius, Lt-Col Gerard Maclean, died 1950, vol. IV
Lemonnier, Adm. André Georges, 1896–1963, vol. VI
Lempfert, Rudolph Gustave Karl, 1875–1957, vol. V
Lempriere, Lt-Col Henry Anderson, 1867–1914, vol. I
Lempriere, Rev. Philip Charles, 1890–1949, vol. IV (A), vol. V
Lempriere, Reginald Raoul, 1851–1931, vol. III
Lenanton, Carola Mary Anima, (Lady Lenanton); see Oman, C. M. A.
Lenanton, Sir Gerald, 1896–1952, vol. V
Lenbach, T. von, died 1904, vol. I
Lendon, Alfred Austin, 1856–1935, vol. III
Lendon, Penry Bruce, 1882–1914, vol. I
Le Neve Foster, Fermian; see Foster.
Lenfestey, Giffard Hocart, 1872–1943, vol. IV
Lenfestey, Col Leopold d'Estreville, 1875–1948, vol. IV
Leng, Christopher David, 1861–1921, vol. II
Leng, Sir Hilary Howard, 1862–1936, vol. III
Leng, Sir John, 1828–1906, vol. I
Leng, Sir William Christopher, 1825–1902, vol. I
Lenglen, Suzanne, died 1938, vol. III
Lenman, Rt Rev. Thomas, 1883–1959, vol. V
Lenn, Paymaster Captain Frank, 1868–1932, vol. III
Lennard, Sir Fiennes B.; see Barrett-Lennard.
Lennard, Lt-Col Sir Henry Arthur Hallam Farnaby, 2nd Bt (cr 1880), 1859–1928, vol. II
Lennard, Lt-Col John B.; see Barrett-Lennard.
Lennard, Sir John Farnaby, 1st Bt (cr 1880), 1816–1899, vol. I
Lennard, Reginald Vivian, 1885–1967, vol. VI

Lennard, Sir Richard Barrett-; *see* Lennard, Sir T. R. F. B.

Lennard, Sir Richard Fiennes Barrett-, 4th Bt (*cr* 1801), 1861–1934, vol. III

Lennard, Lt-Col Sir Stephen Arthur Hallam Farnaby, 3rd Bt (*cr* 1880), 1899–1980, vol. VII

Lennard, Sir Thomas Barrett-, 2nd Bt (*cr* 1801), 1826–1919, vol. II

Lennard, Sir Thomas Barrett-, 3rd Bt (*cr* 1801), 1853–1923, vol. II

Lennard, Sir Thomas J., 1861–1938, vol. III

Lennard, Sir (Thomas) Richard (Fiennes) Barrett-, 5th Bt (*cr* 1801), 1898–1977, vol. VII

Lennard-Jones, Sir John Edward, 1894–1954, vol. V

Lennie, Robert Aim, 1889–1961, vol. VI

Lennon, Most Rev. James Gerard, 1923–1989, vol. VIII

Lennon, Most Rev. Patrick, 1914–1990, vol. VIII

Lennon, Hon. William, 1849–1938, vol. III

Lennox, Rear Adm. Sir Alexander Henry Charles G.; *see* Gordon Lennox.

Lennox, Col Lord Algernon Charles G.; *see* Gordon-Lennox.

Lennox, Lady Algernon G.; *see* Gordon-Lennox.

Lennox, Lord Bernard Charles G.; *see* Gordon-Lennox.

Lennox, Charles Spencer Bateman-Hanbury K.; *see* Kincaid-Lennox.

Lennox, Cosmo Charles G.; *see* Gordon-Lennox.

Lennox, Lord Esme Charles G.; *see* Gordon-Lennox.

Lennox, Lt-Gen. Sir George Charles G.; *see* Gordon Lennox.

Lennox, Rt Hon. Lord Walter Charles G.; *see* Gordon-Lennox.

Lennox, Sir Wilbraham Oates, 1830–1897, vol. I

Lenny, Most Rev. Francis, 1928–1978, vol. VII (AII)

Lenotre, G., 1857–1935, vol. III

Lenox-Conyngham, Col Sir Gerald Ponsonby, 1866–1956, vol. V

Lenox-Conyngham, Sir William Fitzwilliam, 1824–1906, vol. I

Lenski, Lois, 1893–1974, vol. VII

Lentaigne, Sir John, *died* 1915, vol. I

Lentaigne, Maj.-Gen. Walter David Alexander, 1899–1955, vol. II

Lenton, Rev. Charles H., 1873–1951, vol. V

Lenton, Jessie; *see* Pope, J.

Leny, Bt Lt-Col R. L. Macalpine-, 1870–1941, vol. IV

Leo XIII, His Holiness Pope, (Vincent Joachim Pecci), 1810–1903, vol. I

Leon, Sir George Edward, 2nd Bt, 1875–1947, vol. IV

Leon, Henri Marcel, 1855–1932, vol. III

Leon, Henry Cecil, 1902–1976, vol. VII

Leon, Sir Herbert Samuel, 1st Bt, 1850–1926, vol. II

Leon, Paul, 1874–1962, vol. VI

Leon, Philip, 1895–1974, vol. VII

Leon, Sir Ronald George, 3rd Bt, 1902–1964, vol. VI

Leon, Samuel, 1848–1933, vol. III

Leonard, Baron (Life Peer); John Denis Leonard, 1909–1983, vol. VIII

Leonard, George Hare, 1863–1941, vol. IV

Leonard, James W., *died* 1909, vol. I

Leonard, John William, *died* 1910, vol. I

Leonard, Rt Rev. Martin Patrick Grainge, 1889–1963, vol. VI

Leonard, Patrick Marcellinus, 1821–1901, vol. I

Leonard, Sir Reginald Byron, 1907–1986, vol. VIII

Leonard, Lt-Col Reuben Wells, 1860–1930, vol. III

Leonard, Robert Galloway Louis, 1878–1957, vol. V

Leonard, Samuel Henry, 1854–1929, vol. III

Leonard, Sir Walter McEllister, 1915–1985, vol. VIII

Leonard, William, 1887–1969, vol. VI

Leonard, Rt Rev. William Andrew, 1848–1930, vol. III

Leonard, Col William Hugh, 1876–1960, vol. V

Leoncavallo, Ruggiero, 1858–1919, vol. II

Leoni, Franco, 1864–1949, vol. IV

Le Page, Engr-Rear-Adm. George Wilfred, 1883–1940, vol. III

Lepailleur, Rt Rev. Alfred, 1886–1952, vol. V

le Patourel, Herbert Augustus, 1875–1934, vol. III

Le Patourel, Brig. Herbert Wallace, 1916–1979, vol. VII

Le Patourel, John Herbert, 1909–1981, vol. VIII

Le Pelley, Lt-Col Edward Carey, 1870–1942, vol. IV

Lepicier, Cardinal Alexis Henry Marie, 1863–1936, vol. III

Lepine, Louis, 1846–1933, vol. III

Le Poer Trench, Hon. Frederick, 1835–1913, vol. I

Le Poer Trench, Lt-Col Frederick Amelius, 1857–1942, vol. IV

Le-Poer-Trench, Col Hon. William, 1837–1920, vol. II

Le Quesne, Charles Thomas, 1885–1954, vol. V

Le Quesne, Ferdinand Simeon, 1863–1950, vol. IV

Le Queux, William Tufnell, 1864–1927, vol. II

Leray, Mgr Joseph M. M., 1854–1929, vol. III

Lermon, Norman, 1915–1989, vol. VIII

Lerner, Alan Jay, 1918–1986, vol. VIII

Le Rossignol, Col Alfred Ernest, 1869–1951, vol. V

Le Rossignol, James Edward, 1866–1959, vol. V

Le Rossignol, Walter Aubin, *died* 1945, vol. IV

Le Rougetel, Sir John Helier, 1894–1975, vol. VII

Le Roy, Édouard Louis Emmanuel Julien, 1870–1954, vol. V

Le Roy-Lewis, Col Herman, 1860–1931, vol. III

Le Sage, Sir John Merry, 1837–1926, vol. II

Lescaze, William, 1896–1969, vol. VI

Lescher, Joseph Francis, 1842–1923, vol. II

Lescher, Thomas Edward, 1877–1938, vol. III

Leschititzky, Theodore, 1830–1915, vol. I

Leslie, Lt-Col Archibald Stewart, 1873–1928, vol. II

Leslie, Col Archibald Young, *died* 1913, vol. I

Leslie, Sir Bradford, 1831–1926, vol. II

Leslie, Lt-Col Sir Bradford, 1867–1936, vol. III

Leslie, Lt-Col Charles, *died* 1930, vol. III

Leslie, Sir Charles Henry, 7th Bt (*cr* 1625), 1848–1905, vol. I

Leslie, Doris, (Lady Fergusson Hannay), 1891–1982, vol. VIII

Leslie, Edward Henry John, 1880–1966, vol. VI

Leslie, Sir Francis Galloway, 1902–1971, vol. VII

Leslie, Frank, (Miriam Florence Folline, Baroness de Bazus), 1851–1914, vol. I

Leslie, Maj.-Gen. George Arthur James, 1867–1936, vol. III

Leslie, Rear-Adm. George Cunningham, 1920–1988, vol. VIII

Leslie, George Dunlop, 1835–1921, vol. II

Leslie, Hon. George Waldegrave-, 1825–1904, vol. I

Leslie, Harald Robert; see Birsay, Hon. Lord.

Leslie, Henrietta, (Mrs Harrie Schütze), died 1946, vol. IV

Leslie, Sir (Henry John) Lindores, 9th Bt (cr 1625), 1920–1967, vol. VI

Leslie, Ian William Murray, 1905–1987, vol VIII

Leslie, James Campbell, died 1974, vol. VII

Leslie, Rt Hon. James Graham, 1868–1949, vol. IV

Leslie, Sir John, 1st Bt (cr 1876), 1822–1916, vol. II

Leslie, Col Sir John, 2nd Bt (cr 1876), 1857–1944, vol. IV

Leslie, Lt-Col John, 1888–1965, vol. VI

Leslie, John D.; see Dean-Leslie.

Leslie, Lt-Col John Henry, 1858–1943, vol. IV

Leslie, Very Rev. John Herbert, 1867–1934, vol. III

Leslie, Sir (John Randolph) Shane, 3rd Bt (cr 1876), 1885–1971, vol. VII

Leslie, John Robert, 1873–1955, vol. V

Leslie, Col John Robert Sloan, 1871–1943, vol. IV

Leslie, Lt-Col John Tasman Waddell, 1861–1911, vol. I

Leslie, John William St Lawrance, died 1934, vol. III

Leslie, Sir Lindores; see Leslie, Sir H. J. L.

Leslie, Miriam Florence Folline; see Leslie, Frank.

Leslie, Sir Norman Alexander, 1870–1945, vol. IV

Leslie, Wing Comdr Sir Norman Roderick Alexander David, 8th Bt (cr 1625), 1889–1937, vol. III

Leslie, Robert, 1885–1951, vol. V

Leslie, Robert Murray, 1866–1921, vol. II

Leslie, Maj.-Gen. Robert Walter Dickson, 1883–1957, vol. V

Leslie, Samuel Clement, 1898–1980, vol. VII

Leslie, Seymour Argent Sandford, 1902–1953, vol. V

Leslie, Sir Shane; see Leslie, Sir J. R. S.

Leslie, Gen. Sir Walter Stewart, 1876–1947, vol. IV

Leslie of Warthill, William A.; see Arbuthnot-Leslie.

Leslie-Ellis, Lt-Col Henry, 1852–1919, vol. II

Leslie-Jones, Rev. Cyril, 1873–1932, vol. III

Leslie-Jones, Frederick Archibald, 1874–1946, vol. IV

Leslie-Jones, Leycester Hudson, died 1935, vol. III

Leslie Melville, Lt-Col Hon. Ian, 1894–1967, vol. VI

Leslie-Roberts, H(ugh); see Roberts.

Le Souef, Albert Sherbourne, 1877–1951, vol. V

Le Souëf, W. H. Dudley, died 1924, vol. II

Lessard, Maj.-Gen. François Louis, 1860–1927, vol. II

Lesser, Henry, died 1966, vol. VI

Lesser, Most Rev. Norman Alfred, 1902–1985, vol. VIII

Lessing, Edward Albert, 1890–1964, vol. VI

Lessing, Rudolf, 1878–1964, vol. VI

Lesslie, Brig.-Gen. William Breck, 1868–1942, vol. IV

Lessore, Frederick, 1879–1951, vol. V

Lessore, Thérèse, died 1945, vol. IV

Lester, Engr-Rear-Adm. Arthur Ellis, 1878–1956, vol. V

Lester, Rev. Henry Arthur, died 1922, vol. II

Lester, Sean, 1888–1959, vol. V

Lester, Rev. T. Major, died 1903, vol. I

Lester-Garland, Lester V., died 1944, vol. IV

Lestrade, Gérard Paul, 1897–1962, vol. VI

Le Strange, Charles Alfred, 1892–1933, vol. III

L'Estrange, Constance; see Collier, C.

Le Strange, Guy, 1854–1933, vol. III

Le Strange, Hamon, 1840–1918, vol. II

L'Estrange, Lawrence Percy Farrer, 1912–1990, vol. VIII

Le Strange, Roland, 1869–1919, vol. II

Lesueur, Daniel, died 1921, vol. II

Letch, Sir Robert, 1899–1962, vol. VI

Letchworth, Rev. Arnold, 1840–1923, vol. II

Letchworth, Sir Edward, 1833–1917, vol. II

Letchworth, Rev. Henry Howard, 1836–1921, vol. II

Letchworth, Thomas Edwin, 1906–1973, vol. VII

Lethaby, William Richard, 1857–1931, vol. III

Letham, James, 1907–1972, vol. VII

Lethbridge, Alan Bourchier, 1878–1923, vol. II

Lethbridge, Col Alfred, 1884–1968, vol. VI

Lethbridge, Lt-Col Sir Alfred Swaine, 1844–1917, vol. II

Lethbridge, Col Ernest Astley Edmund, 1864–1943, vol. IV

Lethbridge, Lt-Col Francis Washington, 1867–1939, vol. II

Lethbridge, Captain Sir Hector Wroth, 6th Bt, 1898–1978, vol. VII

Lethbridge, Maj.-Gen. John Sydney, 1897–1961, vol. VI

Lethbridge, Marion Eva, 1879–1959, vol. V

Lethbridge, Sir Roper, 1840–1919, vol. II

Lethbridge, Thomas Charles, 1901–1971, vol. VII

Lethbridge, Sir Wroth Acland, 4th Bt, 1831–1902, vol. I

Lethbridge, Sir Wroth Periam Christopher, 5th Bt, 1863–1950, vol. IV

Lethem, Sir Gordon James, 1886–1962, vol. VI

Letourneau, Séverin, 1871–1949, vol. IV

Lett, Eva, died 1945, vol. IV

Lett, Rev. Henry William, 1838–1920, vol. II

Lett, Sir Hugh, 1st Bt, 1876–1964, vol. VI

Lett, Phyllis, (Mrs Phyllis de Burgh Ker), died 1962, vol. VI

Letton, Charles Thomas, 1878–1949, vol. IV

Letts, Edmund Albert, 1852–1918, vol. II

Letts, Malcolm Henry Ikin, 1882–1957, vol. V

Letts, Rev. Reginald, 1857–1940, vol. III

Letts, Sir William Malesbury, 1873–1957, vol. V

Letts, Winifred M., 1882–1972, vol. VII

Leuba, James Henri, 1868–1946, vol. IV

Leuchars, Col Hon. Sir George, 1868–1924, vol. II

Leudesdorf, Charles, 1853–1924, vol. II

Leuty, Thomas Richmond, 1853–1911, vol. I

Levame, Mgr Albert, 1881–1958, vol. V

Levander, F. W., died 1916, vol. II

Leveen, Jacob, 1891–1980, vol. VII

Leven, 11th Earl of, and Melville, 10th Earl of, 1835–1906, vol. I

Leven, 12th Earl of, and Melville, 11th Earl of, 1886–1913, vol. I

Leven, 13th Earl of, and Melville, 12th Earl of, 1890–1947, vol. IV

Lever, Baron (Life Peer); Leslie Maurice Lever, 1905–1977, vol. VII

Lever, Col Sir Arthur Levy, 1st Bt (*cr* 1911), 1860–1924, vol. II

Lever, Sir Ernest Harry, 1890–1970, vol. VI

Lever, Sir Hardman; *see* Lever, Sir S. H.

Lever, Richard Hayley, 1876–1958, vol. V(A), vol. VI (AI)

Lever, Sir (Samuel) Hardman, 1st Bt (*cr* 1920), 1869–1947, vol. IV

Lever, Sir Tresham Joseph Philip, 2nd Bt (*cr* 1911), 1900–1975, vol. VII

Leverhulme, 1st Viscount, 1851–1925, vol. II

Leverhulme, 2nd Viscount, 1888–1949, vol. IV

Leverson, Col George Francis, *died* 1938, vol. III

Leverson, Lt-Col George Riland Francis, 1886–1936, vol. III

Leverson, Col Julian John, 1853–1941, vol. IV

Levertoff, Rev. Paul Philip, 1878–1954, vol. V

Leveson, Adm. Sir Arthur Cavenagh, 1868–1929, vol. III

Leveson Gower, Major Lord Alastair St Clair Sutherland-, 1890–1921, vol. II

Leveson Gower, Arthur Francis Gresham, 1851–1922, vol. II

Leveson-Gower, Col Charles Cameron, 1866–1951, vol. V

Leveson Gower, Frederick Neville Sutherland, 1874–1959, vol. V

Leveson Gower, Sir George Granville, 1858–1951, vol. V

Leveson Gower, Granville Charles Gresham, 1865–1948, vol. IV

Leveson Gower, Sir Henry Dudley Gresham, 1873–1954, vol. V

Leveson Gower, Col Philip, *died* 1939, vol. III

Lévesque, Hon. René, 1922–1987, vol. VIII

Levett, Major Berkeley John Talbot, 1863–1941, vol. IV

Levett, Ernest Laurence, *died* 1916, vol. II

Levett, Theophilus Basil Percy, 1856–1929, vol. III

Levett-Yeats, Gerald Aylmer, 1863–1938, vol. III

Levey, Charles Joseph, 1846–1920, vol. II

Levey, George Collins, 1835–1919, vol. II

Levi, Sylvain, 1863–1935, vol. III

Levi, T. Arthur, 1874–1954, vol. V

Levick, Claude Blaxland, 1896–1953, vol. V

Levick, Surg.-Comdr G. Murray, *died* 1956, vol. V

Levick, Sir Hugh Gwynne, 1870–1937, vol. III

Levick, Thomas Henry Carlton, 1867–1957, vol. V

Levien, Jerome William John, 1893–1961, vol. VI

Levien, John Mewburn, 1863–1953, vol. V

Levin, Nyman, 1906–1965, vol. VI

Levine, Abraham, 1870–1949, vol. IV

Levinge, Sir Edward Vere, 1867–1954, vol. V

Levinge, Major Sir Richard Vere Henry, 1911–1984, vol. VIII

Levinge, Sir Richard William, 10th Bt, 1878–1914, vol. I

Levinstein, Herbert, *died* 1956, vol. V

Lévis Mirepoix, Antoine, Duc de, 1884–1981, vol. VIII

Levison, Sir Leon, 1881–1936, vol. III

Levita, Lt-Col Sir Cecil Bingham, 1867–1953, vol. V

Levitt, Walter Montague, 1900–1983, vol. VIII

Levy, Aaron Harold, *died* 1977, vol. VII

Levy, Sir Albert, *died* 1937, vol. III

Levy, Sir Arthur, 1855–1938, vol. III

Levy, Benn Wolfe, 1900–1973, vol. VII

Levy, Sir Bruce; *see* Levy, Sir E. B.

Levy, Hon. Sir Daniel, 1873–1937, vol. III

Levy, Sir (Enoch) Bruce, 1892–1985, vol. VIII

Levy, Hermann, 1881–1949, vol. IV

Levy, Hyman, 1889–1975, vol. VII

Levy, J. Langley, 1870–1945, vol. IV

Levy, Joseph Hiam, 1838–1913, vol. I

Levy, Joshua Moses, 1854–1922, vol. II

Levy, Sir Maurice, 1st Bt, 1859–1933, vol. III

Levy, Reuben, 1891–1966, vol. VI

Levy, Richard Francis, 1892–1968, vol. VI

Levy, Stanley Isaac, 1890–1968, vol. VI

Levy, Thomas, *died* 1953, vol. V

Levy, Major Walter Henry, 1876–1923, vol. II

Lewanika III, Sir Mwanawina; *see* Barotseland, Litunga of.

Lewenhaupt, Count Carl, 1835–1906, vol. I

Lewer, Ethel, 1861–1946, vol. IV

Lewer, Surg.-Maj.-Gen. Robert, *died* 1914, vol. I

Lewers, Arthur Hamilton Nicholson, *died* 1934, vol. III

Lewes, Earl of; Henry John Montacute Nevill, 1948–1965, vol. VI

Lewes, Brig.-Gen. Charles George, 1869–1938, vol. III

Lewes, Maj.-Gen. H. C., 1838–1907, vol. I

Lewes, Col Price Kinnear, 1870–1943, vol. IV

Lewes, Captain Price Vaughan, 1865–1914, vol. I

Lewes, Sir Samuel William Sayer, 1824–1907, vol. I

Lewes, Captain Thomas Powell, 1860–1940, vol. III

Lewes, Vivian Byam, 1852–1915, vol. I

Lewey, Sir Arthur Werner, 1894–1973, vol. VII

Lewin, Brig.-Gen. Arthur Corrie, 1874–1952, vol. V

Lewin, Captain Duncan; *see* Lewin, Captain E. D. G.

Lewin, Captain (Edgar) Duncan (Goodenough), 1912–1983, vol. VIII

Lewin, Maj.-Gen. Ernest Ord, 1879–1950, vol. IV

Lewin, George Arthur, 1867–1941, vol. IV

Lewin, Rev. George Harrison R.; *see* Ross-Lewin.

Lewin, (George) Ronald, 1914–1984, vol. VIII

Lewin, Brig.-Gen. Henry Frederick Elliott, 1872–1946, vol. IV

Lewin, Octavia Margaret Sophia, *died* 1955, vol. V

Lewin, Percy Evans, 1876–1955, vol. V

Lewin, Ven. Richard S. R.; *see* Ross-Lewin.

Lewin, Rev. Robert O'Donelan R.; *see* Ross-Lewin.

Lewin, Ronald; *see* Lewin, G. R.

Lewin, Lt-Col Thomas Herbert, 1839–1916, vol. II

Lewin, Walpole Sinclair, 1915–1980, vol. VII

Lewin, William Charles James; *see* Terriss, William.

Lewis, Ada Travers, *died* 1931, vol. III

Lewis, Mrs Agnes Smith, 1843–1926, vol. II

Lewis, Sir Alfred Edward, 1868–1940, vol. III

Lewis, A(lfred) Neville; *see* Lewis, Neville.

Lewis, Sir Andrew Jopp Williams, 1875–1952, vol. V

Lewis, Angelo, 1839–1919, vol. II

Lewis, Sir Anthony Carey, 1915–1983, vol. VIII

Lewis, Arthur Cyril Wentworth, 1885–1928, vol. II

Lewis, Lt-Col Arthur Francis O.; *see* Owen-Lewis.

Lewis, Arthur Griffith Poyer, 1848–1909, vol. I
Lewis, Arthur Hornby, 1843–1926, vol. II
Lewis, Arthur King, 1867–1954, vol. V
Lewis, Sir Aubrey Julian, 1900–1975, vol. VII
Lewis, B. Roland, 1884–1959, vol. V
Lewis, Barnet, *died* 1929, vol. III
Lewis, Brig.-Gen. Bridges George, 1857–1925, vol. II
Lewis, Bunnell, 1824–1908, vol. I
Lewis, C. Gasquoine; *see* Hartley, C. G.
Lewis, Cecil D.; *see* Day-Lewis.
Lewis, Ven. Charles Gerwyn Rice, *died* 1964, vol. VI
Lewis, Ven. Christopher Gwynne, 1895–1963, vol. VI
Lewis, Brig. Sir Clinton Gresham, 1885–1978, vol. VII
Lewis, Clive Staples, 1898–1963, vol. VI
Lewis, Cyril Alexander O.; *see* Owen-Lewis.
Lewis, Cyril Arthur Liddon, 1873–1943, vol. IV
Lewis, D. Morgan, 1851–1937, vol. III
Lewis, David, 1849–1897, vol. I
Lewis, Col David Francis, 1855–1927, vol. II
Lewis, David John, 1893–1982, vol. VIII
Lewis, Dominic Bevan Wyndham, *died* 1969, vol. VI
Lewis, Lt Donald Swain, 1886–1916, vol. II
Lewis, Mrs Dorothy; *see* Lewis, Mrs M. D.
Lewis, Sir Duncan O.; *see* Orr-Lewis.
Lewis, Edgar Samuel, 1853–1922, vol. II
Lewis, E(dward) Daly, 1908–1977, vol. VII
Lewis, Rev. Edward Lincoln, 1865–1939, vol. III
Lewis, Maj.-Gen. Edward Mann, 1863–1949, vol. IV
Lewis, Sir Edward Roberts, 1900–1980, vol. VII
Lewis, Eiluned, *died* 1979, vol. VII
Lewis, Hon. Sir Elliott; *see* Lewis, Hon. Sir N. E.
Lewis, Emily Catherine, *died* 1965, vol. VI
Lewis, Eric William Charles, 1914–1981, vol. VIII
Lewis, Major Ernest Albert, 1873–1937, vol. III
Lewis, Ernest Harry, 1877–1951, vol. V
Lewis, Essington, 1881–1961, vol. VI
Lewis, Very Rev. Evan, 1818–1901, vol. I
Lewis, Francis John, 1875–1955, vol. V
Lewis, Rev. Frank Ernest, *died* 1929, vol. III
Lewis, Frederic Henry, 1865–1940, vol. III
Lewis, Brig.-Gen. Frederick Gustav, 1873–1967, vol. VI
Lewis, Sir Frederick Orr O.; *see* Orr-Lewis.
Lewis, Lt-Col George Alfred, 1869–1961, vol. VI
Lewis, Sir George Henry, 1st Bt, 1833–1911, vol. I
Lewis, Sir George James Ernest, 3rd Bt, 1910–1945, vol. IV
Lewis, Sir George James Graham, 2nd Bt, 1868–1927, vol. II
Lewis, George P.; *see* Pitt-Lewis.
Lewis, Gerald Champion, 1863–1939, vol. III
Lewis, Gilbert Newton, 1875–1946, vol. IV
Lewis, Harold, 1856–1924, vol. II
Lewis, Maj.-Gen. Harold Victor, 1887–1945, vol. IV
Lewis, (Harry) Sinclair, 1885–1951, vol. V
Lewis, Sir Hawthorne; *see* Lewis, Sir W. H.
Lewis, Rev. Henry, 1857–1914, vol. I
Lewis, Sir Henry, 1847–1923, vol. II
Lewis, Col Henry, 1847–1925, vol. II
Lewis, Henry, 1889–1968, vol. VI
Lewis, Maj.-Gen. Henry Augustus, 1879–1966, vol. VI
Lewis, Henry David, 1875–1936, vol. III

Lewis, Captain Henry Edward, 1889–1979, vol. VII
Lewis, Henry Gethin, 1899–1986, vol. VIII
Lewis, Rt Hon. Sir Herbert; *see* Lewis, Rt Hon. Sir J. H.
Lewis, Sir Herbert David William, 1872–1931, vol. III
Lewis, Col Herman Le R.; *see* Le Roy-Lewis.
Lewis, Howell Elvet, 1860–1953, vol. V
Lewis, Hugh, *died* 1937, vol. III
Lewis, Sir Ian Malcolm, 1925–1990, vol. VIII
Lewis, Isaac, 1849–1927, vol. II
Lewis, Ivor Evan Gerwyn, 1904–1977, vol. VII
Lewis, J(ack) Haydon, 1904–1971, vol. VII
Lewis, Rev. Canon James Abraham, 1874–1946, vol. IV
Lewis, Brig. James Charles W.; *see* Windsor Lewis.
Lewis, Rev. James Dawson, 1845–1905, vol. I
Lewis, James Hamilton, *died* 1939, vol. III
Lewis, James Henry, 1856–1924, vol. II
Lewis, Jane, (Lady Lewis), *died* 1939, vol. III
Lewis, Hon. John, 1842–1923, vol. II
Lewis, Lt-Col John, 1859–1937, vol. III
Lewis, John, 1851–1943, vol. IV
Lewis, John, 1912–1969, vol. VI
Lewis, John Christopher, 1842–1918, vol. II
Lewis, Sir (John) Duncan O.; *see* Orr-Lewis.
Lewis, John F., 1876–1963, vol. VI
Lewis, John Hardwicke, 1840–1927, vol. II
Lewis, Rt Hon. Sir (John) Herbert, 1858–1933, vol. III
Lewis, John Llewellyn, 1880–1969, vol. VI
Lewis, John Penry, 1854–1923, vol. II
Lewis, Rev. John Price, 1857–1930, vol. III
Lewis, John Spedan, 1885–1963, vol. VI
Lewis, Sir John Todd, 1901–1977, vol. VII
Lewis, Most Rev. John Travers, 1825–1901, vol. I
Lewis, Ven. John Wilfred, 1909–1984, vol. VIII
Lewis, Very Rev. Julius, *died* 1920, vol. III
Lewis, Rt Rev. Lewis, 1821–1905, vol. I
Lewis, Lucas Reginald, 1883–1931, vol. III
Lewis, Mabel Terry, (Mrs R. C. Batley), *died* 1957, vol. V
Lewis, Malcolm Meredith, 1891–1955, vol. V
Lewis, Mary; *see* Milne, Mrs Leslie.
Lewis, Mrs (Mary) Dorothy, 1894–1975, vol. VII
Lewis, Mary W.; *see* Wolseley-Lewis.
Lewis, Michael Arthur, 1890–1970, vol. VI
Lewis, Morris Michael, 1898–1971, vol. VII
Lewis, Hon. Sir (Neil) Elliott, 1858–1935, vol. III
Lewis, Neville, 1895–1972, vol. VII
Lewis, Norman Bache, 1896–1988, vol. VIII
Lewis, Oswald, 1887–1966, vol. VI
Lewis, Percival Cecil, 1912–1983, vol. VIII
Lewis, Percy G., 1862–1935, vol. III
Lewis, Col Percy John Tonson, 1861–1910, vol. I
Lewis, (Percy) Wyndham, 1884–1957, vol. V
Lewis, Peter Edwin, 1912–1976, vol. VII
Lewis, Richard, 1914–1990, vol. VIII
Lewis, Lt-Col Richard Charles, *died* 1914, vol. I
Lewis, Maj.-Gen. Sir Richard George, 1895–1965, vol. VI
Lewis, Maj.-Gen. Robert Stedman, 1898–1987, vol. VIII
Lewis, Ronald Howard, 1909–1990, vol. VIII

Lewis, Sir Samuel, 1843–1903, vol. I
Lewis, Saunders, 1893–1983, vol. VIII
Lewis, Sinclair; see Lewis, H. S.
Lewis, Col Somers Reginald, 1843–1931, vol. III
Lewis, Stanley Radcliffe, 1878–1964, vol. VI
Lewis, Thomas, died 1928, vol. II
Lewis, Sir Thomas, 1881–1945, vol. IV
Lewis, Thomas, 1868–1953, vol. V
Lewis, Thomas, 1873–1962, vol. VI
Lewis, Thomas Arthur, 1881–1923, vol. II
Lewis, Col Thomas Lewis Hampton, 1834–1912, vol. I
Lewis, Sir Thomas Williams, 1852–1926, vol. II
Lewis, Vernon Arthur, died 1950, vol. IV
Lewis, Sir Walter Llewellyn, 1849–1930, vol. III
Lewis, Walter Samuel, 1894–1962, vol. VI
Lewis, Wilfrid Bennett, 1908–1987, vol. VIII
Lewis, Sir Wilfrid Hubert Poyer, 1881–1950, vol. IV
Lewis, Rev. Canon William, died 1922, vol. II
Lewis, William B.; see Bevan-Lewis.
Lewis, William Cudmore McCullagh, died 1956, vol. V
Lewis, William Edmund Ames, 1912–1988, vol. VIII
Lewis, William George, 1844–1926, vol. II
Lewis, Sir (William) Hawthorne, 1888–1970, vol. VI
Lewis, William Henry, 1866–1948, vol. IV
Lewis, William Henry, 1869–1963, vol. VI
Lewis, William James, 1847–1926, vol. II
Lewis, William Waller; see Waller, Lewis.
Lewis, Sir Willmott Harsant, 1877–1950, vol. IV
Lewis, Wilmarth Sheldon, 1895–1979, vol. VII
Lewis, Wyndham; see Lewis, P. W.
Lewis-Crosby, Very Rev. Ernest Henry, died 1961, vol. VI
Lewis-Dale, Henry Angley, 1876–1938, vol. III
Lewisham, Viscount; William Legge, 1913–1942, vol. IV
Lewisohn, Frederick, 1878–1951, vol. V
Lewtas, Lt-Col John, died 1920, vol. II
Lewthwaite, Raymond, 1894–1972, vol. VII
Lewthwaite, Sir William, 1st Bt, 1853–1927, vol. II
Lewthwaite, Sir William, 2nd Bt, 1882–1933, vol. III
Lewton-Brian, Lawrence, 1879–1922, vol. II
Ley, Arthur Herbert, 1879–1938, vol. III
Ley, Sir Francis, 1st Bt, 1846–1916, vol. II
Ley, Sir Gerald Gordon, 3rd Bt, 1902–1980, vol. VII
Ley, Sir Gordon; see Ley, Sir H. G.
Ley, Henry George, 1887–1962, vol. VI
Ley, Sir (Henry) Gordon, 2nd Bt, 1874–1944, vol. IV
Ley, Adm. James Clement, 1869–1946, vol. IV
Ley, James William Thomas, died 1943, vol. IV
Ley, William Henry, 1847–1919, vol. II
Leyborne-Popham, Francis William, 1862–1907, vol. I
Leycester, William Hamilton, 1864–1925, vol. II
Leyds, Willem Johannes, 1859–1940, vol. III
Leyel, Mrs C. F., (Hilda Winifred), died 1957, vol. V
Leyland, Christopher John, 1849–1926, vol. II
Leyland, Sir Edward N.; see Naylor-Leyland.
Leyland, Captain Sir Herbert Scarisbrick N.; see Naylor-Leyland.
Leyland, John, died 1924, vol. II
Leyland, Norman Harrison, 1921–1981, vol. VIII
Leyland, Peter; see Pyke-Lees, W. K.

Leyland, Sir Vivyan Edward N.; see Naylor-Leyland.
Leys, Sir Cecil; see Leys, Sir W. C.
Leys, John Kirkwood, 1847–1909, vol. I
Leys, Sir (William) Cecil, 1877–1950, vol. IV
Leyton, Albert Sidney Frankau, 1869–1921, vol. II
Leyton, Nevil; see Leyton, R. N. A.
Leyton, Otto, 1873–1938, vol. III
Leyton, (Robert) Nevil (Arthur), born 1910, vol. VIII
Li Ching Fong, 1854–1934, vol. III
Liakat Ali, Sir Syed, 1878–1947, vol. IV
Liaqat Hyat Khan, Nawab Sir, 1887–1948, vol. IV
Liardet, Maj-Gen. Sir Claude Francis, 1881–1966, vol. VI
Lias, Rev. John James, 1834–1923, vol. II
Lias, William John, died 1941, vol. IV
Libbert, Laurence Joseph, 1933–1985, vol. VIII
Libby, Willard Frank, 1908–1980, vol. VII
Liberty, Sir Arthur Lasenby, 1843–1917, vol. II
Liberty, Captain Ivor Stewart-, 1887–1952, vol. V
Lichfield, 3rd Earl of, 1856–1918, vol. II
Lichfield, 4th Earl of, 1883–1960, vol. V
Lichine, David, 1910–1972, vol. VII
Lichnowsky, Princess Mechtilde, 1879–1958, vol. V
Lichtenberger, Rt Rev. Arthur Carl, 1900–1968, vol. VI
Lichtenburg, Captain John Wills, 1872–1912, vol. I
Lidbury, Sir Charles, 1880–1978, vol. VII
Lidbury, Sir David John, 1884–1973, vol. VII
Lidbury, Ernest Alan, 1862–1948, vol. IV
Liddall, Sir Walter Sydney, 1884–1963, vol. VI
Liddell, Adolphus George Charles, 1846–1920, vol. II
Liddell, Lt-Col Arthur Robert, 1872–1966, vol. VI
Liddell, Charles, 1856–1922, vol. II
Liddell, Gen. Sir Clive Gerard, 1883–1956, vol. V
Liddell, Colin, 1862–1916, vol. II, vol. III
Liddell, Rev. Edward, died 1914, vol. I
Liddell, Edward George Tandy, 1895–1981, vol. VIII
Liddell, Sir Frederick Francis, 1865–1950, vol. IV
Liddell, Guy Maynard, 1892–1958, vol. V
Liddell, Harry, died 1931, vol. III
Liddell, Very Rev. Henry George, 1811–1898, vol. I
Liddell, Major John Stewart, died 1934, vol. III
Liddell, Laurence Ernest, 1916–1985, vol. VIII
Liddell, Lionel Charles, 1868–1942, vol. IV
Liddell, Mark Harvey, 1866–1936, vol. III
Liddell, Maximilian Friedrich, 1887–1968, vol. VI
Liddell, Peter John, 1921–1979, vol. VII
Liddell, Sir Robert Morris, 1870–1928, vol. III
Liddell, T. Hodgson, 1860–1925, vol. II
Liddell, Maj.-Gen. Sir William Andrew, 1865–1949, vol. IV
Liddell Hart, Sir Basil Henry, 1895–1970, vol. VI
Lidderdale, Rt Hon. William, 1832–1902, vol. I
Liddiard, Mabel, 1882–1962, vol. VI
Liddle, Sir Donald Ross, 1906–1989, vol. VIII
Liddle, Henry Weddell, 1885–1956, vol. V
Liddle, Robert W., 1864–1917, vol. II
Lidgett, Rev. John Scott, 1854–1953, vol. V
Lidiard, Sir Herbert, 1864–1941, vol. IV
Lidstone, George James, 1870–1952, vol. V
Lie, Jonas, 1833–1908, vol. I
Lie, Trygve Halvdan, 1896–1968, vol. VI
Lieber, B. Franklin, died 1915, vol. I
Liebling, George, died 1946, vol. IV

Lienhop, Sir John Henry, 1898–1967, vol. VI (AII)
Liesching, Sir Percivale, 1895–1973, vol. VII
Lifar, Serge, 1905–1986, vol. VIII
Lifford, 5th Viscount, 1837–1913, vol. I
Lifford, 6th Viscount, 1844–1925, vol. II
Lifford, 7th Viscount, 1880–1954, vol. V
Lifford, 8th Viscount, 1900–1987, vol. VIII
Ligertwood, Sir George Coutts, 1888–1967, vol. VI
Light, Sir Edgar William, 1885–1969, vol. VI
Lightbody, Philip Frazer, 1880–1936, vol. III
Lightbody, William Paterson Hay, 1893–1962, vol. VI
Lightbound, Rt Rev. Aloysius Anselm, *died* 1973, vol. VII
Lightfoot, Ben, 1888–1966, vol. VI
Lightfoot, Rev. John, 1853–1917, vol. II
Lightfoot, Rev. John Alfred, 1861–1928, vol. II
Lightfoot, Nicholas Morpeth Hutchinson, 1902–1962, vol. VI
Lightfoot, Ven. Reginald Prideaux, 1836–1906, vol. I
Lightfoot, Robert Henry, 1883–1953, vol. V
Lightfoot, Ven. Thomas Fothergill, 1831–1904, vol. I
Lightfoot Boston, Sir Henry Josiah; *see* Boston.
Lighthall, William Douw, 1857–1954, vol. V
Lightley, Rev. John W., 1867–1948, vol. IV
Lighton, Sir (Christopher) Robert, 7th Bt, 1848–1929, vol. III
Lighton, Sir Robert; *see* Lighton, Sir C. R.
Lightstone, Herbert, 1878–1942, vol. IV
Lightwood, Reginald, 1898–1985, vol. VIII
Liley, Sir (Albert) William, 1929–1983, vol. VIII
Liley, Sir William; *see* Liley, Sir A. W.
Lilford, 5th Baron, 1863–1945, vol. IV
Lilford, 6th Baron, 1869–1949, vol. IV
Lilienthal, David Eli, 1899–1981, vol. VIII
Lilley, Rev. Canon Alfred Leslie, 1860–1948, vol. IV
Lilley, Cecil William, 1878–1953, vol. V
Lilley, Sir Charles, 1830–1897, vol. I
Lilley, Ernest Lewis, 1876–1948, vol. IV
Lilley, Francis James Patrick, 1907–1971, vol. VII
Lilley, Captain James Lindsay, 1871–1923, vol. II
Lilley, Thomas, 1902–1959, vol. V
Lillico, Hon. Sir Alexander, 1872–1966, vol. VI
Lillico, William Lionel James, 1880–1948, vol. IV
Lillicrap, Sir Charles Swift, 1887–1966, vol. VI
Lillie, Beatrice Gladys, (Lady Peel), 1894–1989, vol. VIII
Lillie, Rev. Handley William Russell, 1902–1967, vol. VI
Lillie, Very Rev. Henry Alexander, 1911–1986, vol. VIII
Lillie, John Adam, 1884–1983, vol. VIII
Lillingston, Rev. Canon Arthur Blackwell Goulburn, 1864–1943, vol. IV
Lilly, Walter Elsworthy, 1867–1940, vol. III
Lilly, William Samuel, 1840–1919, vol. II
Lima, Sir Bertram Lewis, 1883–1919, vol. II
Lima, Most Rev. Mgr Joaquim Rodriques, 1875–1936, vol. III
Limbdi, Thakore Saheb Shri Daulatsinhji Jaswantsinhji Bahadur, 1868–1940, vol. III
Limbert, Roy, *died* 1954, vol. V
Limentani, Prof. Uberto, 1913–1989, vol. VIII
Limerick, 4th Earl of, 1863–1929, vol. III
Limerick, 5th Earl of, 1888–1967, vol. VI

Limerick, Countess of; (Mary Imelda Josephine), *died* 1943, vol. IV
Limerick, Dowager Countess of; (Angela Olivia Pery), 1897–1981, vol. VIII
Limpenny, Engr-Rear-Adm. Charles Joseph, 1881–1952, vol. V
Limpus, Adm. Sir Arthur Henry, 1863–1931, vol. III
Limri, Thakur Saheb Sir, 1859–1907, vol. I
Lin Yutang, 1895–1976, vol. VII
Lincoln, Joseph, 1870–1944, vol. IV
Lincoln, Air Cdre Philip Lionel, 1892–1981, vol. VIII
Lincolnshire, 1st Marquess of, 1843–1928, vol. II
Lind, Hon. Sir Albert Eli, 1878–1964, vol. VI
Lind-af-Hageby, Emelie Augusta Louise, 1878–1963, vol. VI
Lind-Smith, Gerard Gustave, 1903–1982, vol. VIII
Lindbergh, Col Charles Augustus, 1902–1974, vol. VII
Lindell, John Henry Stockton, 1908–1973, vol. VII
Lindemann, Lt-Col Charles Lionel, 1885–1970, vol. VI
Lindgren, Baron (Life Peer); George Samuel Lindgren, 1900–1971, vol. VII
Lindley, Baron (Life Peer); Nathaniel Lindley, 1828–1921, vol. II
Lindley, Charles Gustaf, 1865–1957, vol. V
Lindley, Rt Hon. Sir Francis Oswald, 1872–1950, vol. IV
Lindley, Sir Frank; *see* Lindley, Sir M. F.
Lindley, Rear-Adm. George Robert, 1850–1918, vol. II
Lindley, James Bryant, 1851–1940, vol. III
Lindley, Maj.-Gen. Hon. John Edward, 1860–1925, vol. II
Lindley, Sir (Mark) Frank, 1881–1951, vol. V
Lindley, Hon. Walter Barry, 1861–1944, vol. IV
Lindley, Sir William Heerlein, 1853–1917, vol. II
Lindley-Jones, Walter, 1863–1930, vol. III
Lindner, Doris Lexey Margaret, 1896–1979, vol. VII
Lindner, Ingram Joseph, *died* 1959, vol. V
Lindner, Peter Moffat, 1852–1949, vol. IV
Lindo, Sir (Henry) Laurence, 1911–1980, vol. VII
Lindo, Sir Laurence; *see* Lindo, Sir H. L.
Lindon, John Benjamin, 1884–1960, vol. V
Lindon, Sir Leonard Charles Edward, 1896–1978, vol. VII
Lindop, Audrey Beatrice Noël E.; *see* Erskine-Lindop.
Lindop, Col Carl Arthur Boys, 1899–1968, vol. VI
Lindow, Lt-Col Isaac William B.; *see* Burns-Lindow.
Lindrum, Walter, 1898–1960, vol. V
Lindsay, 11th Earl of, 1832–1917, vol. II
Lindsay, 12th Earl of, 1867–1939, vol. III
Lindsay, 13th Earl of, 1872–1943, vol. IV
Lindsay, 14th Earl of, 1901–1985, vol. VIII
Lindsay, 15th Earl of, 1926–1989, vol. VIII
Lindsay of Birker, 1st Baron, 1879–1952, vol. V
Lindsay, Alexander Martin, 1844–1906, vol. I
Lindsay, Sir Benjamin, *died* 1939, vol. III
Lindsay, Caroline Blanche Elizabeth, (Lady Lindsay), *died* 1912, vol. I
Lindsay, Sir Charles William, 1856–1939, vol. III
Lindsay, Sir Coutts, 2nd Bt, 1824–1913, vol. I

Lindsay, Col Creighton Hutchinson, 1877–1941, vol. IV
Lindsay, Sir Darcy, 1865–1941, vol. IV
Lindsay, Sir Daryl; *see* Lindsay, Sir E. D.
Lindsay, David, 1856–1922, vol. II
Lindsay, Maj.-Gen. Edward Stewart, 1905–1990, vol. VIII
Lindsay, Ernest Charles, 1883–1943, vol. IV
Lindsay, Sir (Ernest) Daryl, 1889–1976, vol. VII
Lindsay, Maj.-Gen. George Mackintosh, 1880–1956, vol. V
Lindsay, Harry; *see* Hudson, H. Lindsay.
Lindsay, Sir Harry Alexander Fanshawe, 1881–1963, vol. VI
Lindsay, Col Henry Arthur Peyton, 1868–1926, vol. II
Lindsay, Col Henry Edzell Morgan, 1857–1935, vol. III
Lindsay, Lt-Col Henry Gore, 1830–1914, vol. I
Lindsay, Howard, 1889–1968, vol. VI
Lindsay, Major Sir Humphrey B.; *see* Broun Lindsay.
Lindsay, Ian Gordon, 1906–1966, vol. VI
Lindsay, Jack, 1900–1990, vol. VIII
Lindsay, Rev. James, *died* 1923, vol. II
Lindsay, James Alexander, 1856–1931, vol. III
Lindsay, Lt-Col James Howard, *died* 1940, vol. III
Lindsay, Sir John, 1860–1927, vol. II
Lindsay, John Allan, 1865–1942, vol. IV
Lindsay, Leonard Cecil Colin, 1857–1941, vol. IV
Lindsay, Lionel Arthur, 1861–1945, vol. IV
Lindsay, Sir Lionel Arthur, 1874–1961, vol. VI
Lindsay of Dowhill, Sir Martin Alexander, 1st Bt, 1905–1981, vol. VIII
Lindsay, Nicholas Vachel; *see* Lindsay, Vachel.
Lindsay, Norman Alfred William, 1879–1969, vol. VI
Lindsay, Maj.-Gen. Peter; *see* Lindsay, Maj.-Gen. E. S.
Lindsay, Philip, 1906–1958, vol. V
Lindsay, Rt Hon. Sir Ronald Charles, 1877–1945, vol. IV
Lindsay, Ven. Thomas Enraght, *died* 1947, vol. IV
Lindsay, Thomas Martin, 1843–1914, vol. I
Lindsay, Ven. Thomas Somerville, 1854–1933, vol. III
Lindsay, Vachel, 1879–1931, vol. III
Lindsay, Wallace M., 1858–1937, vol. III
Lindsay, Walter Charles, 1866–1929, vol. III
Lindsay, Maj.-Gen. Sir Walter Fullerton Lodovic, 1855–1930, vol. III
Lindsay, Sir William, 1907–1986, vol. VIII
Lindsay, William Alexander, 1846–1926, vol. II
Lindsay, William Arthur, 1866–1936, vol. III
Lindsay, Maj.-Gen. William Bethune, 1880–1933, vol. III
Lindsay, Sir William O'Brien, 1909–1975, vol. VII
Lindsay-Fynn, Sir Basil Mortimer, 1901–1988, vol. VIII
Lindsay-Hogg, Sir Anthony Henry, 2nd Bt, 1908–1968, vol. VI
Lindsay-Hogg, Sir Lindsay, 1st Bt, 1853–1923, vol. II
Lindsay-Hogg, Sir William Lindsay, 3rd Bt, 1930–1987, vol. VIII
Lindsay-Rea, Robert; *see* Rea.
Lindsell, Henry Martin, 1846–1925, vol. II
Lindsell, Herbert George, 1903–1973, vol. VII

Lindsell, Col Robert Frederick, 1856–1914, vol. I
Lindsell, Lt-Gen. Sir Wilfrid Gordon, 1884–1973, vol. VII
Lindsey, 11th Earl of, 1815–1899, vol. I
Lindsey, 12th Earl of, 1861–1938, vol. III
Lindsey, 13th Earl of, and **Abingdon,** 8th Earl of, 1887–1963, vol. VI
Line, Ven. Henry, *died* 1938, vol. III
Lineham, Joseph, 1869–1952, vol. V
Linehan, John, 1865–1935, vol. III
Linehan, Patrick Aloysius, 1904–1973, vol. VII
Linehan, William, 1892–1955, vol. V
Lines, Albert Walter, 1914–1976, vol. VII
Lines, Rt Rev. Edwin S., 1845–1927, vol. II
Lines, Vincent, 1909–1968, vol. VI
Lines, Walter, 1882–1972, vol. VII
Linfield, Sir Arthur George, *died* 1974, vol. VII (AII)
Linfield, Frederick Caesar, *died* 1939, vol. III
Linfoot, Edward Hubert, 1905–1982, vol. VIII
Ling, Arthur Robert, 1861–1937, vol. III
Ling, Brig. Christopher George, 1880–1953, vol. V
Ling, George Herbert, 1874–1942, vol. IV
Lingeman, Eric Ralph, 1898–1966, vol. VI
Lingen, 1st Baron, 1819–1905, vol. I
Lingham, Brig. John, 1897–1976, vol. VII
Link, Edwin Albert, 1904–1981, vol. VIII
Linklater, Eric, 1899–1974, vol. VII
Linklater, John Edmund, 1848–1917, vol. II
Linklater, Rev. Robert, 1839–1915, vol. I
Linlithgow, 1st Marquess of, 1860–1908, vol. I
Linlithgow, 2nd Marquess of, 1887–1952, vol. V
Linlithgow, 3rd Marquess of, 1912–1987, vol. VIII
Linnell, Air Marshal Sir Francis John, 1892–1944, vol. IV
Linnell, John Wycliffe, 1878–1967, vol. VI
Linnell, Wilfred Herbert, 1894–1983, vol. VIII
Linnett, John Wilfrid, 1913–1975, vol. VII
Linsley, Ven. Stanley Frederick, 1903–1974, vol. VII
Linstead, Sir Hugh Nicholas, 1901–1987, vol. VIII
Linstead, Sir Patrick; *see* Linstead, Sir R. P.
Linstead, Sir (Reginald) Patrick, 1902–1966, vol. VI
Lintern, Bernard Francis, 1908–1979, vol. VII
Lintern, Reep, 1902–1967, vol. VI
Linthorne, Sir Richard Roope, 1864–1935, vol. III
Linton, Sir Andrew, 1893–1971, vol. VII
Linton, David Leslie, 1906–1971, vol. VII
Linton, Elizabeth Lynn, 1822–1898, vol. I
Linton, Sir James Dromgole, 1840–1916, vol. II
Linton, Rt Rev. James Henry, 1879–1958, vol. V
Linton, Ralph, 1893–1953, vol. V
Linton, Sir Richard, 1879–1959, vol. V
Linton, Robert George, 1882–1960, vol. V
Lintott, Major Alfred Lord, *died* 1940, vol. III
Lintott, Henry John, 1877–1965, vol. VI
Linzee, Captain Robert Gordon Hood, 1900–1973, vol. VII
Lion, Flora, *died* 1958, vol. V
Lion, Leon M., 1879–1947, vol. IV
Lipatti, Dinu, 1917–1950, vol. IV
Lipinsky, Sigmund, 1873–1940, vol. III
Lipman, Vivian David, 1921–1990, vol. VIII
Lipmann, Fritz Albert, 1899–1986, vol. VIII
Lippincott, Craige, 1846–1911, vol. I
Lippmann, Walter, 1889–1974, vol. VII

Lipscomb, Maj.-Gen. Christopher Godfrey, 1907–1982, vol. VIII
Lipsett, Maj.-Gen. Louis James, 1874–1918, vol. II
Lipson, Daniel Leopold, 1886–1963, vol. VI
Lipson, Ephraim, 1888–1960, vol. V
Lipton, Marcus, 1900–1978, vol. VII
Lipton, Sir Thomas Johnstone, 1st Bt, 1850–1931, vol. III
Lisburne, 6th Earl of, 1862–1899, vol. I
Lisburne, 7th Earl of, 1892–1965, vol. VI
Lish, Joseph J., *died* 1923, vol. II
Lisle, 5th Baron, 1811–1898, vol. I
Lisle, 6th Baron, 1840–1919, vol. II
Lisle, Aubrey Edwin O.; *see* Orchard-Lisle.
Lismer, Arthur, 1885–1969, vol. VI
Lismore, 2nd Viscount, 1815–1898, vol. I
Lissack, Victor Jack, 1930–1981, vol. VIII
Lister, 1st Baron, 1827–1912, vol. I
Lister, Arthur, 1905–1975, vol. VII
Lister, Sir Ashton, 1845–1929, vol. III
Lister, Hon. Charles Alfred, 1887–1915, vol. I
Lister, Charles Ashton, 1871–1965, vol. VI
Lister, Sir (Charles) Percy, 1897–1983, vol. VIII
Lister, Sir Frederick; *see* Lister, Sir T. F.
Lister, Lt-Col Frederick Hamilton, 1880–1971, vol. VII
Lister, Sir (Frederick) Spencer, 1876–1939, vol. III
Lister, Lt-Col Harry Laidman, 1902–1982, vol. VIII
Lister, Col James Fraser, *died* 1944, vol. IV
Lister, John, 1931–1989, vol. VIII
Lister, Joseph Jackson, *died* 1927, vol. II
Lister, Laurier, 1907–1986, vol. VIII
Lister, Sir Percy; *see* Lister, Sir C. P.
Lister, Hon. Sir Reginald, 1865–1912, vol. I
Lister, Sir Spencer; *see* Lister, Sir F. S.
Lister, Hon. Thomas, 1878–1904, vol. I
Lister, Thomas, 1892–1967, vol. VI
Lister, Thomas David, 1869–1924, vol. II
Lister, Sir (Thomas) Frederick, *died* 1966, vol. VI
Lister, Thomas Liddell, 1922–1985, vol. VIII
Lister, Rev. Thomas Llewellyn, *died* 1926, vol. II
Lister, Sir Thomas Villiers, 1832–1902, vol. I
Lister, Tom, 1887–1945, vol. IV
Lister, Sir William Tindall, 1868–1944, vol. IV
Lister-Kaye, Sir Cecil Edmund, 4th Bt, 1854–1931, vol. III
Lister-Kaye, Sir John Christopher Lister, 7th Bt, 1913–1982, vol. VIII
Lister-Kaye, Sir John Pepys, 3rd Bt, 1853–1924, vol. II
Lister-Kaye, Sir Kenelm Arthur, 5th Bt, 1892–1955, vol. V
Lister-Kaye, Sir Lister, 6th Bt, 1873–1962, vol. VI
Liston, David Joel, 1914–1990, vol. VIII
Liston, Most Rev. James Michael, 1881–1976, vol. VII
Liston, Lt-Col William Glen, 1873–1950, vol. IV
Liston-Foulis, Sir Archibald Charles; *see* Foulis.
Liston-Foulis, Sir William; *see* Foulis.
Listowel, 3rd Earl of, 1833–1924, vol. II
Listowel, 4th Earl of, 1866–1931, vol. III
Litauer, Stefan, 1892–1959, vol. V
Litchfield, Captain F. Shirley; *see* Speer, Rear-Adm. F. Shirley L.

Litchfield, Frederick, 1850–1930, vol. III
Litchfield-Speer, Rear-Adm. F. Shirley; *see* Speer.
Lithgow, Sir James, 1st Bt, 1883–1952, vol. V
Lithgow, Michael John, 1920–1963, vol. VI
Lithgow, Samuel, 1860–1937, vol. III
Lithiby, Sir John, 1852–1936, vol. III
Litster, William James, 1869–1930, vol. III
Litten, Maurice Sidney, 1919–1979, vol. VII
Litterick, Thomas, 1929–1981, vol. VIII
Little, Alan Neville, 1934–1986, vol. VIII
Little, Sir Alexander; *see* Little, Sir R. A.
Little, Andrew George, 1863–1945, vol. IV
Little, Mrs Archibald, *died* 1926, vol. II
Little, Archibald John, 1838–1908, vol. I
Little, Gen. Arthur Greenway, 1875–1948, vol. IV
Little, Rev. Arthur Wentworth Roberts, 1880–1932, vol. III
Little, Col Charles Blakeway, 1859–1929, vol. III
Little, Adm. Sir Charles James Colebrooke, 1882–1973, vol. VII
Little, David, 1867–1947, vol. IV
Little, David John, *died* 1984, vol. VIII
Little, Hon. Sir Douglas Macfarlan, 1904–1990, vol. VIII
Little, Sir Ernest Gordon Graham-, *died* 1950, vol. IV
Little, Ernest Muirhead, 1854–1935, vol. III
Little, George Jerningham Knightley, 1886–1966, vol. VI
Little, George Leon, *died* 1941, vol. IV
Little, Lt-Gen. Henry Alexander, 1837–1908, vol. I
Little, Engr-Rear-Adm. Henry Augustus, 1883–1954, vol. V
Little, James, *died* 1916, vol. II
Little, Rev. James, 1868–1946, vol. IV
Little, James Stanley, 1856–1940, vol. III
Little, John Carruthers, 1874–1957, vol. V
Little, Sir Joseph Ignatius, *died* 1902, vol. I
Little, Brig-Gen. Malcolm Orme, 1857–1931, vol. III
Little, Robert, *died* 1944, vol. IV
Little, Sir (Rudolf) Alexander, 1895–1977, vol. VII
Little, Rev. William John K.; *see* Knox Little.
Little, William Morison, 1909–1984, vol. VIII
Littleboy, Col Charles Norman, 1894–1966, vol. VI
Littledale, Harold, 1853–1930, vol. III
Littlehailes, Richard, 1878–1950, vol. IV
Littlejohn, Harvey, *died* 1927, vol. II
Littlejohn, Sir Henry Duncan, 1828–1914, vol. I
Littlejohn, Robert, *died* 1920, vol. II
Littlejohn, William Still, 1859–1933, vol. III
Littlejohns, Captain Astle Scott, 1875–1939, vol. III
Littler, Captain Charles Augustus, *died* 1916, vol. II
Littler, Sir Emile, 1903–1985, vol. VIII
Littler, Rev. Harold Davies, 1887–1948, vol. IV
Littler, Prince, 1901–1973, vol. VII
Littler, Sir Ralph Daniel Makinson, 1835–1908, vol. I
Littleton, Alfred Henry, 1845–1914, vol. I
Littleton, Rev. Hon. Cecil James, 1850–1912, vol. I
Littleton, Hon. Charles Christopher Josceline, 1872–1950, vol. IV
Littlewood, Rear-Adm. Charles, 1902–1984, vol. VIII
Littlewood, Bt-Col Harry, 1861–1921, vol. II
Littlewood, James, 1885–1968, vol. VI
Littlewood, John Edensor, 1885–1977, vol. VII

Littlewood, Samuel Robinson, 1875–1963, vol. VI
Littlewood, Sir Sydney Charles Thomas, 1895–1967, vol. VI
Litvinov, Maxim, 1876–1951, vol. V
Liveing, Lt-Col Charles Hawker, 1872–1934, vol. III
Liveing, Edward, 1832–1919, vol. II
Liveing, Edward George Downing, 1895–1963, vol. VI
Liveing, George Downing, 1827–1924, vol. II
Liveing, Robert, 1834–1919, vol. II
Livens, Horace Mann, 1862–1936, vol. III
Livermore, Sir Harry, 1908–1989, vol. VIII
Liverpool, 1st Earl of (*cr* 1905, 2nd creation), 1846–1907, vol. I
Liverpool, 2nd Earl of, 1870–1941, vol. IV
Liverpool, 3rd Earl of, 1878–1962, vol. VI
Liverpool, 4th Earl of, 1887–1969, vol. VI
Liversidge, Archibald, 1847–1927, vol. II
Livesay, Brig.-Gen. Robert O'Hara, 1876–1946, vol. IV
Livesey, Sir Harry, 1860–1932, vol. III
Livesey, Rev. Herbert, 1892–1970, vol. VI
Livesey, James, 1831–1925, vol. II
Livesey, Roger, 1906–1976, vol. VII
Livingston, Charles, 1857–1937, vol. III
Livingston, Brig.-Gen. Guy, 1881–1950, vol. IV
Livingston, Henry Brockholst, 1895–1968, vol. VI
Livingston, Sir Noel Brooks, 1882–1954, vol. V
Livingston, Air Marshal Sir Philip Clermont, 1893–1982, vol. VIII
Livingston-Herbage, Julian; *see* Herbage.
Livingstone, Dame Adelaide Lord, *died* 1970, vol. VI
Livingstone, Sir Alexander Mackenzie, 1880–1950, vol. IV
Livingstone, Archibald Macdonald, *died* 1972, vol. VII
Livingstone, Ven. Arthur Guinness, 1840–1902, vol. I
Livingstone, Maj.-Gen. Sir Hubert Armine Anson, 1865–1940, vol. III
Livingstone, James Livingstone, 1900–1988, vol. VIII
Livingstone, Matthew, 1837–1917, vol. II
Livingstone, Rev. Richard John, 1828–1907, vol. I
Livingstone, Sir Richard Winn, 1880–1960, vol. V
Livingstone, Rev. Robert George, 1838–1935, vol. III
Livingstone, Stuart Moodie, *died* 1902, vol. I
Livingstone, William P., *died* 1950, vol. IV (A)
Livingstone-Learmonth, Agnes Moore, 1877–1936, vol. III
Livingstone-Learmonth, Lt-Col (Francis) Leger (Christian); *see* Learmonth.
Livingstone-Learmonth, Frederick Valiant Cotton, 1862–1945, vol. IV
Livingstone-Learmonth, Brig.-Gen. John Eric Christian, 1876–1936, vol. III
Ljungberg, Göta, *died* 1955, vol. V
Llandaff, 1st Viscount, 1826–1913, vol. I
Llangattock, 1st Baron, 1837–1912, vol. I
Llangattock, 2nd Baron, 1870–1916, vol. II
Llewellin, 1st Baron, 1893–1957, vol. V
Llewellin, George Herbert, 1871–1946, vol. IV
Llewellyn, Sir David Richard, 1st Bt, 1879–1940, vol. III
Llewellyn, Col Evan Henry, 1847–1914, vol. I

Llewellyn, Brig.-Gen. Evan Henry, 1871–1948, vol. IV
Llewellyn, Sir (Frederick) John, 1915–1988, vol. VIII
Llewellyn, Col Sir Godfrey; *see* Llewellyn, Col Sir R. G.
Llewellyn, Col Sir Hoel, 1871–1945, vol. IV
Llewellyn, Sir John; *see* Llewellyn, Sir F. J.
Llewellyn, John Charles, 1908–1990, vol. VIII
Llewellyn, Lt-Col John Malet, *died* 1945, vol. IV
Llewellyn, Captain Llewellyn Evan Hugh, 1879–1970, vol. VI
Llewellyn, Lt-Col Sir Rhys, 2nd Bt, 1910–1978, vol. VII
Llewellyn, Richard; *see* Lloyd, R. D. V. L.
Llewellyn, Richard Llewelyn Jones, *died* 1934, vol. III
Llewellyn, Col Sir (Robert) Godfrey, 1st Bt, 1893–1986, vol. VIII
Llewellyn, Robert William, 1848–1910, vol. I
Llewellyn, Sir (Samuel Henry) William, 1863–1941, vol. IV
Llewellyn, Sir William; *see* Llewellyn Sir S. H. W.
Llewellyn-Jones, Frederick, 1866–1941, vol. IV
Llewelyn, Sir John Talbot Dillwyn-, 1st Bt, 1836–1927, vol. II
Llewelyn, Sir Leonard Wilkinson, 1874–1924, vol. II
Llewelyn, Brig. Sir Michael Dillwyn-V.; *see* Venables-Llewelyn.
Llewelyn, Sir Robert Baxter, 1845–1919, vol. II
Llewelyn, W. Craven, *died* 1966, vol. VI
Llewelyn-Davies, Baron (Life Peer); Richard Llewelyn-Davies, 1912–1981, vol. VIII
Llewelyn-Williams, David, 1870–1949, vol. IV
Llewhellin, Col George Elliot, 1874–1940, vol. III
Lloyd, 1st Baron, 1879–1941, vol. IV
Lloyd, 2nd Baron, 1912–1985, vol. VIII
Lloyd, Sir Alan Hubert, 1883–1948, vol. IV
Lloyd, Rev. Albert Henry, *died* 1941, vol. IV
Lloyd, Arnold de Gorges; *see* Lloyd, W. A. de G.
Lloyd, Rev. Arthur, 1851–1911, vol. I
Lloyd, Captain Arthur Athelwold, 1864–1940, vol. III
Lloyd, Rev. Arthur Gittins, 1865–1931, vol. III
Lloyd, Brig.-Gen. Arthur Henry Orlando, 1864–1944, vol. IV
Lloyd, Rt Rev. Arthur Selden, 1857–1936, vol. III
Lloyd, Rt Rev. Arthur Thomas, *died* 1907, vol. I
Lloyd, Captain Arthur Wynell, 1883–1967, vol. VI
Lloyd, Bernard Dean, 1923–1987, vol. VIII
Lloyd, Bertram Arthur, 1884–1948, vol. IV
Lloyd, (Charles) Christopher, 1906–1986, vol. VIII
Lloyd, Charles Ellis, *died* 1939, vol. III
Lloyd, Lt-Col Charles Geoffrey, 1884–1953, vol. V
Lloyd, Charles Harford, 1849–1919, vol. II
Lloyd, Col Charles Robert, 1882–1930, vol. III
Lloyd, Christopher; *see* Lloyd, Charles C.
Lloyd, Maj.-Gen. Cyril, 1906–1989, vol. VIII
Lloyd, Cyril Edward, 1876–1963, vol. VI
Lloyd, Rt Rev. Daniel Lewis, 1843–1899, vol. I
Lloyd, David John, 1886–1951, vol. V
Lloyd, Dorothy J.; *see* Jordan Lloyd.
Lloyd, Edward, 1845–1927, vol. II
Lloyd, Edward Honoratus, 1860–1930, vol. III
Lloyd, Edward Mayow Hastings, 1889–1968, vol. VI
Lloyd, Col Edward Prince, 1887–1970, vol. VI

Lloyd, Comdr Edward William, 1855–1945, vol. IV
Lloyd, Eric Ivan, 1892–1954, vol. V
Lloyd, Major Sir (Ernest) Guy (Richard) 1st Bt, 1890–1987, vol. VIII
Lloyd, Ernest Sampson, 1870–1945, vol. IV
Lloyd, Lt-Col Fitzwarren, 1859–1923, vol. II
Lloyd, Lt-Gen. Sir Francis, 1853–1926, vol. II
Lloyd, Francis Ernest, 1868–1947, vol. IV
Lloyd, Francis Nelson, 1907–1974, vol. VII
Lloyd, Maj.-Gen. Francis Thomas, 1838–1912, vol. I
Lloyd, Col Frederic Percy L.; see Lousada Lloyd.
Lloyd, Brig.-Gen. Frederick Charles, 1860–1957, vol. V
Lloyd, Col Frederick Lindsay, 1866–1940, vol. III
Lloyd, Geoffrey William; see Baron Geoffrey-Lloyd.
Lloyd, Major Sir Guy; see Lloyd, Major Sir E. G. R.
Lloyd, George Butler, 1854–1930, vol. III
Lloyd, Col George Evan, 1855–1900, vol. I
Lloyd, Rt Rev. George Exton, 1861–1940, vol. III
Lloyd, George Whitelocke, 1830–1910, vol. I
Lloyd, Guy Vaughan, 1901–1975, vol. VII
Lloyd, Maj.-Gen. Herbert William, 1883–1957, vol. V
Lloyd, Dame Hilda Nora; see Rose, Dame H. N.
Lloyd, Brig.-Gen. Horace Giesler, 1872–1936, vol. III
Lloyd, Sir Horatio, 1829–1920, vol. II
Lloyd, Howard, 1837–1920, vol. II
Lloyd, Sir Howard Watson, 1868–1955, vol. V
Lloyd, Air Chief Marshal Sir Hugh Pughe, 1894–1981, vol. VIII
Lloyd, Captain Sir Humphrey Clifford, 1893–1966, vol. VI
Lloyd, Huw Ifor, 1893–1977, vol. VII
Lloyd, Sir Idwal Geoffrey, 1878–1946, vol. IV
Lloyd, Ifor Bowen, 1902–1990, vol. VIII
Lloyd, Rev. Iorwerth Grey, 1844–1920, vol. II
Lloyd, Air Cdre Ivor Thomas, 1896–1966, vol. VI
Lloyd, J. A. R., died 1956, vol. V
Lloyd, Rt Rev. John, 1847–1915, vol. I
Lloyd, Sir John Buck, 1874–1952, vol. V
Lloyd, Lt-Col Sir John Conway, 1878–1954, vol. V
Lloyd, John Davies Knatchbull, 1900–1978, vol. VII
Lloyd, Sir John Edward, 1861–1947, vol. IV
Lloyd, Col John Edward, 1894–1965, vol. VI
Lloyd, Sir John Hall S.; see Seymour-Lloyd.
Lloyd, Brig.-Gen. John Hardress, 1874–1952, vol. V
Lloyd, Brig.-Gen. John Henry, 1872–1941, vol. IV
Lloyd, John Owen, 1914–1982, vol. VIII
Lloyd, (John) Selwyn (Brooke); see Baron Selwyn-Lloyd.
Lloyd, Ven. John Walter, 1879–1951, vol. V
Lloyd, Jordan, died 1913, vol. I
Lloyd, Rev. Joseph, died 1938, vol. III
Lloyd, Air Vice-Marshal Kenneth Buchanan, 1897–1973, vol. VII
Lloyd, Col Langford Newman, 1873–1956, vol. V
Lloyd, Llewelyn Southworth, 1876–1956, vol. V
Lloyd, Sir Marteine Owen Mowbray, 2nd Bt, 1851–1933, vol. III
Lloyd, Martin, 1908–1989, vol. VIII
Lloyd, Col Sir Morgan George, 1843–1917, vol. II
Lloyd, Nathaniel, 1867–1933, vol. III
Lloyd, Norman, 1895–1983, vol. VIII

Lloyd, Maj.-Gen. Sir Owen Edward Pennefather, 1854–1941, vol. IV
Lloyd, Col Pen; see Lloyd, Col Philip H.
Lloyd, Col Philip Henry, (Pen), 1905–1979, vol. VII
Lloyd, Lt-Col Reginald Broughton, 1881–1975, vol. VII
Lloyd, Richard Dafydd Vivian Llewellyn, (Richard Llewellyn), 1906–1983, vol. VIII
Lloyd, Major Richard Ernest, 1875–1935, vol. III
Lloyd, Rickard William, 1859–1933, vol. III
Lloyd, Col Robert Oliver, 1849–1921, vol. II
Lloyd, Sir Robert Owen, 1894–1970, vol. VI
Lloyd, Adm. Rodney Maclaine, 1841–1911, vol. I
Lloyd, Rev. Canon Roger Bradshaigh, died 1966, vol. VI
Lloyd, Samuel Cook, 1854–1929, vol. III
Lloyd, Brig.-Gen. Samuel Eyre Massy, 1867–1952, vol. V
Lloyd, Selwyn; see Baron Selwyn-Lloyd.
Lloyd, Stuart, vol. III
Lloyd, T. Alwyn, 1881–1960, vol. V
Lloyd, Theodore Howard, 1872–1959, vol. V
Lloyd, Col Thomas, 1853–1916, vol. II
Lloyd, Rt Rev. Thomas, 1857–1935, vol. III
Lloyd, Col Thomas Edward John, 1856–1937, vol. III
Lloyd, Maj.-Gen. Thomas Francis, 1839–1921, vol. II
Lloyd, Brig. Thomas Ifan, 1903–1981, vol. VIII
Lloyd, Sir Thomas Ingram Kynaston, 1896–1968, vol. VI
Lloyd, Lt-Col Thomas Owen, 1866–1945, vol. IV
Lloyd, Tom, died 1910, vol. I
Lloyd, Col Wilford Neville, 1855–1935, vol. III
Lloyd, Maj.-Gen. Wilfrid Lewis, 1896–1944, vol. IV
Lloyd, William, 1874–1948, vol. IV
Lloyd, (William) Arnold de Gorges, 1904–1982, vol. VIII
Lloyd, William Ernest, died 1975, vol. VII
Lloyd, Rt Hon. Sir William Frederick, 1864–1937, vol. III
Lloyd, William Harris, 1836–1923, vol. II
Lloyd, Wilson, 1835–1908, vol. I
Lloyd, Wynne Llewelyn, 1910–1973, vol. VII
Lloyd-Anstruther, Lt-Col Robert Hamilton; see Anstruther.
Lloyd-Baker, Granville Edwin Lloyd, 1841–1924, vol. II
Lloyd-Baker, Olive Katherine Lloyd, 1902–1975, vol. VII
Lloyd-Blood, Lancelot Ivan Neptune; see Blood.
Lloyd-Davies, Oswald Vaughan, 1905–1987, vol. VIII
Lloyd-Evans, Annie; see Evans.
Lloyd George of Dwyfor, 1st Earl, 1863–1945, vol. IV
Lloyd George of Dwyfor, 2nd Earl, 1889–1968, vol. VI
Lloyd George of Dwyfor, Countess; (Frances Louise), 1888–1972, vol. VII
Lloyd George, Lady Megan Arvon, 1902–1966, vol. VI
Lloyd-Jacob, Sir George Harold, 1897–1969, vol. VI
Lloyd James, Arthur, 1884–1943, vol. IV
Lloyd-Johnes, Herbert Johnes, 1900–1983, vol. VIII
Lloyd Jones, Cyril Walter, 1881–1981, vol. VIII
Lloyd-Jones, Sir (Harry) Vincent, 1901–1986, vol. VIII

Lloyd-Jones, Ven. John; *see* Jones.

Lloyd-Jones, Major Percy Arnold; *see* Jones.

Lloyd Jones, Richard Francis, 1908–1975, vol. VII

Lloyd-Jones, Sir Vincent; *see* Lloyd-Jones, Sir H. V.

Lloyd-Mostyn, Hon. Henry Richard Howel, 1857–1938, vol. III

Lloyd-Mostyn, Maj.-Gen. Hon. Sir Savage, 1835–1914, vol. I

Lloyd Owen, David Charles, *died* 1925, vol. II

Lloyd Phillips, Ivan, 1910–1984, vol. VIII

Lloyd-Roberts, George Charles, 1918–1986, vol. VIII

Lloyd-Roberts, Sir Richard, 1885–1956, vol. V

Lloyd Webber, William Southcombe, 1914–1982, vol. VIII

Lloyd-Williams, Dorothy Sylvia, 1901–1977, vol. VII

Lloyd-Williams, Hugh, 1889–1968, vol. VI

Lloyd-Williams, Comdr Hugh, 1900–1977, vol. VII

Lloyd-Williams, Captain James Evan, 1888–1969, vol. VI

Lloyd-Williams, Katharine Georgina, 1896–1973, vol. VII

Llubera, Ignacio Miguel G.; *see* Gonzalez-Llubera.

Llucen; *see* Cullen, Rev. John.

Llwyd, Very Rev. John Plummer Derwent, 1861–1933, vol. III

Lo, Hon. Sir Man-kam, 1893–1959, vol. V

Lo Feng-Luh, Sir Chih Chen, 1850–1903, vol. I

Loane, Miss M., *died* 1922, vol. II

Lobb, John, 1840–1921, vol. II

Lobban, Charles Henry, 1881–1963, vol. VI

Lobjoit, Sir William George, 1859–1939, vol. III

Lobnitz, Sir Frederick, 1863–1932, vol. III

Loch, 1st Baron, 1827–1900, vol. I

Loch, 2nd Baron, 1873–1942, vol. IV

Loch, 3rd Baron, 1916–1982, vol. VIII

Loch, Sir Charles Stewart, 1849–1923, vol. II

Loch, Maj.-Gen. Granville George, 1870–1950, vol. IV

Loch, Lt-Col Granville Henry, 1859–1929, vol. III

Loch, Col John Carysfort, 1877–1974, vol. VII

Loch, Lt-Gen. Sir Kenneth Morley, 1890–1961, vol. VI

Loch, Maj.-Gen. Stewart Gordon, 1873–1952, vol. V

Loch, Lt-Col William, 1845–1912, vol. I

Lochee, 1st Baron, 1845–1911, vol. I

Lochhead, James, *died* 1940, vol. III

Lochhead, John, *died* 1921, vol. II

Lochhead, William, 1864–1927, vol. II

Lochore, Sir James, 1874–1953, vol. V

Lock, B. Fossett, 1847–1922, vol. II

Lock, Air Vice-Marshal Basil Goodhand, 1923–1989, vol. VIII

Lock, (Cecil) Max, 1909–1988, vol. VIII

Lock, Flt Lt Eric Stanley, 1919–1942, vol. IV

Lock, Brig.-Gen. Frederic Robert Edward, 1867–1945, vol. IV

Lock, Rev. John Bascombe, 1849–1921, vol. II

Lock, Max; *see* Lock, C. M.

Lock, Maj.-Gen. Sir Robert Ferguson, 1879–1957, vol. V

Lock, Robert Heath, 1879–1915, vol. I

Lock, Rev. Walter, 1846–1933, vol. III

Lock, Winifred; *see* Gérin, W.

Locke, Arthur, 1872–1932, vol. III

Locke, Arthur D'Arcy, (Bobby Locke), 1917–1987, vol. VIII

Locke, Bobby; *see* Locke, A. D'A.

Locke, Charles Holland, 1887–1980, vol. VII (AII)

Locke, George Herbert, 1870–1937, vol. III

Locke, George T., 1872–1968, vol. VI

Locke, William John, 1863–1930, vol. III

Locke King, Dame Ethel; *see* King, Dame E. L.

Locker, William Algernon, 1863–1930, vol. III

Locker-Lampson, Rt Hon. Godfrey Lampson Tennyson, 1875–1946, vol. IV

Locker-Lampson, (Hannah) Jane, *died* 1915, vol. I

Locker-Lampson, Jane; *see* Locker-Lampson, H. J.

Locker-Lampson, Comdr Oliver Stillingfleet, 1880–1954, vol. V

Lockett, Air Cdre Charles Edward Stuart, 1910–1966, vol. VI

Lockett, Richard Jeffery, 1907–1980, vol. VII

Lockhart, Sir Allan Robert E.; *see* Eliott Lockhart.

Lockhart, Sir Charles Ramsdale, 1892–1954, vol. V

Lockhart, Sir Graeme Alexander Sinclair, 10th Bt (*cr* 1636), 1820–1904, vol. I

Lockhart, Sir Graeme Duncan Power S.; *see* Sinclair-Lockhart.

Lockhart, Sir James Haldane Stewart, 1858–1937, vol. III

Lockhart, Sir John Beresford S.; *see* Sinclair-Lockhart.

Lockhart, John Gilbert, 1891–1960, vol. V

Lockhart, John Harold Bruce, 1889–1956, vol. V

Lockhart, John Macgregor B.; *see* Bruce Lockhart.

Lockhart, Maj.-Gen. Leslie Keith, 1897–1966, vol. VI

Lockhart, Sir Muir Edward S.; *see* Sinclair-Lockhart.

Lockhart, Lt-Col Percy Clare E.; *see* Eliott-Lockhart.

Lockhart, Rab Brougham B.; *see* Bruce Lockhart.

Lockhart, Gen. Sir Rob MacGregor Macdonald, 1893–1981, vol. VIII

Lockhart, Sir Robert Cook, 1861–1943, vol. IV

Lockhart, Robert Douglas, 1894–1987, vol. VIII

Lockhart, Sir Robert Duncan S.; *see* Sinclair-Lockhart.

Lockhart, Sir Robert Hamilton B.; *see* Bruce Lockhart.

Lockhart, Sidney Alexander, 1914–1969, vol. VI

Lockhart, Sir Simon Macdonald, 5th Bt (*cr* 1806), 1849–1919, vol. II

Lockhart, Stephen Alexander, 1905–1989, vol. VIII

Lockhart, William Ewart, 1846–1900, vol. I

Lockhart-Mummery, Sir Hugh Evelyn, 1918–1988, vol. VIII

Lockhart-Mummery, John Percy, 1875–1957, vol. V

Lockie, John, 1863–1906, vol. I

Lockitt, Charles Henry, 1877–1964, vol. VI

Lockroy, Edouard, 1838–1913, vol. I

Lockroy, Etienne Auguste Edouard Simon; *see* Lockroy, Edouard.

Lockspeiser, Sir Ben, 1891–1990, vol. VIII

Lockton, Charles Langton, 1856–1932, vol. III

Lockwood, Charles Barrett, *died* 1914, vol. I

Lockwood, Sir Francis, 1847–1897, vol. I

Lockwood, Francis William, 1908–1955, vol. V

Lockwood, James Horace, 1888–1972, vol. VII

Lockwood, Lt-Col John Cutts, 1890–1983, vol. VIII

Lockwood, Sir John Francis, 1903–1965, vol. VI

Lockwood, Margaret Mary, 1916–1990, vol. VIII

Lockwood, Walter Sydney Douglas, 1895–1989, vol. VIII

Lockyer, Air Vice-Marshal Clarence Edward Williams, 1892–1963, vol. VI

Lockyer, Cuthbert H. J., 1867–1957, vol. V

Lockyer, Captain Hughes Campbell, 1866–1941, vol. IV

Lockyer, Sir (Joseph) Norman, 1836–1920, vol. II

Lockyer, Sir Nicholas Colston, 1855–1933, vol. III

Lockyer, Sir Norman; *see* Lockyer, Sir J. N.

Lockyer, William James Stewart, 1868–1936, vol. III

Locmaria, Marquis du P.; *see* Parc-Locmaria.

Locock, Sir Charles Bird, 3rd Bt, 1878–1965, vol. VI

Locock, Sir Guy Harold, 1883–1958, vol. V

Locock, Col Herbert, 1847–1910, vol. I

Loder, Sir Edmund Giles, 2nd Bt, 1849–1920, vol. II

Loder, Major Eustace, 1867–1914, vol. I

Loder, Lt-Col Giles Harold, 1884–1966, vol. VI

Loder, Sir Louis Francis, 1896–1972, vol. VII

Loder, Reginald Bernhard, 1864–1931, vol. III

Loder-Symonds, Captain F. C.; *see* Symonds.

Loder-Symonds, Vice-Adm. Frederick Parland; *see* Symonds.

Lodge, Alfred, 1854–1937, vol. III

Lodge, Alfred, 1893–1957, vol. V

Lodge, Eleanor Constance, 1869–1936, vol. III

Lodge, Lt-Col Francis Cecil, 1868–1951, vol. V

Lodge, Frank Adrian, 1861–1947, vol. IV

Lodge, Henry Cabot, 1850–1924, vol. II

Lodge, Henry Cabot, 1902–1985, vol. VIII

Lodge, John, 1890–1954, vol. V

Lodge, Sir Oliver Joseph, 1851–1940, vol. III

Lodge, Oliver William Foster, 1878–1955, vol. V

Lodge, Sir Richard, 1855–1936, vol. III

Lodge, Sir Ronald Francis, 1889–1960, vol. V

Lodge, Rupert Clendon, 1886–1961, vol. VI

Lodge, Thomas, 1882–1958, vol. V

Lodge, Thomas Arthur, 1888–1967, vol. VI

Lodge, Tom Stewart, 1909–1987, vol. VIII

Lodwick, John Alan Patrick, 1916–1959, vol. V

Lodwick, Captain John Thornton, 1882–1915, vol. I

Loeb, Jacques, 1859–1924, vol. II

Loeb, James, 1867–1933, vol. III

Loewe, Frederick, 1901–1988, vol. VIII

Loewe, Herbert Martin James, 1882–1940, vol. III

Loewen, Gen. Sir Charles Falkland, 1900–1986, vol. VIII

Loewenstein-Wertheim, HSH Princess, 1866–1927, vol. II

Loewenstein-Wertheim-Freudenberg, Hubertus Friedrich, Prince of, 1906–1984, vol. VIII

Loewenthal, Sir John, 1914–1979, vol. VII

Loewi, Otto, 1873–1961, vol. VI

Loewy, Raymond Fernand, 1893–1986, vol. VIII

Lofthouse, Rt Rev. Joseph, 1855–1933, vol. III

Lofthouse, Rt Rev. Joseph, 1880–1962, vol. VI

Lofthouse, Samuel Hill Smith, 1843–1915, vol. I

Lofthouse, Rev. William Frederick, 1871–1965, vol. VI

Loftie, Rev. Arthur Gershom, 1843–1922, vol. II

Loftie, Rev. William John, 1839–1911, vol. I

Lofting, Hugh John, 1886–1947, vol. IV

Lofts, Norah, (Mrs Robert Jorisch), 1904–1983, vol. VIII

Loftus, Rt Hon. Lord Augustus William Frederick Spencer, 1817–1904, vol. I

Loftus, Cissie; *see* M'Carthy, Marie Cecilia.

Loftus, Col Ernest Achey, 1884–1987, vol. VIII

Loftus, Montague Egerton, 1860–1934, vol. III

Loftus, Pierse Creagh, 1877–1956, vol V

Logan, Sir Charles Bowman, 1837–1907, vol. I

Logan, Brig.-Gen. David Finlay Hosken, 1862–1923, vol. II

Logan, David Gilbert, 1871–1964, vol. VI

Logan, Sir Douglas William, 1910–1987, vol. VIII

Logan, Lt-Col Edward Townshend, *died* 1915, vol. I

Logan, Sir Ewen Reginald, 1868–1945, vol. IV

Logan, Brig.-Gen. Francis Douglas, 1875–1947, vol. IV

Logan, Hon. Hance James, 1869–1944, vol. IV

Logan, Lt-Col Harry Tremaine, 1887–1971, vol. VII

Logan, Lt-Col John, 1907–1987, vol VIII

Logan, John William, 1845–1925, vol. II

Logan, Col Robert, 1863–1935, vol. III

Logan, Thomas Moffat, 1904–1981, vol. VIII

Logan, Sir William Marston, 1889–1968, vol. VI

Logan-Home, Major George John Ninian, 1855–1936, vol. III

Loggin, George Nicholas, 1882–1955, vol. V

Logie, William Alexander, 1866–1933, vol. III

Login, Rear-Adm. Spencer Henry Metcalfe Login, 1851–1909, vol. I

Logsdail, William, 1859–1944, vol. IV

Logsdon, Geoffrey Edward, 1914–1982, vol. VIII

Logue, Lionel, 1880–1953, vol. V

Logue, His Eminence Cardinal Michael, 1840–1924, vol. II

Loharu, Hon. Nawab Sir Amir-ud-Din Ahmed Khan Bahadur, 1860–1937, vol. III

Lohr, Hervey, 1856–1927, vol. II

Löhr, Marie, 1890–1975, vol. VII

Loisy, Alfred, 1857–1940, vol. III

Lomas, Surg.-Captain Ernest Courtney, 1864–1921, vol. II

Lomas, Ernest Gabriel, 1878–1947, vol. IV

Lomas, Harry, 1916–1980, vol. VII

Lomas, Herbert, 1887–1961, vol. VI

Lomas, John, 1846–1927, vol. II

Lomas, Sophie Crawford, *died* 1929, vol. III

Lomas-Walker, Sir G. Bernard, 1881–1960, vol. V

Lomax, Maj.-Gen. Cyril Ernest Napier, 1893–1973, vol. VII

Lomax, Sir John, 1864–1936, vol. III

Lomax, John A., 1857–1923, vol. II

Lomax, Sir John Garnett, 1896–1987, vol. VIII

Lomax, Michael Roger T.; *see* Trappes-Lomax

Lomax, Maj.-Gen. Samuel Holt, 1855–1915, vol. I

Lomax, Brig. Thomas Byrnand T.; *see* Trappes-Lomax.

Lombard Knight, Eric John Percy Crawford, 1907–1987, vol. VIII

Lombe, Vice-Adm. Sir Edward Malcolm E.; *see* Evans-Lombe.

Lombroso, Cesare, 1836–1909, vol. I

Londesborough, 1st Earl of, 1834–1900, vol. I

Londesborough, 2nd Earl of, 1864–1917, vol. II

Londesborough, 3rd Earl of, 1892–1920, vol. II
Londesborough, 4th Earl of, 1894–1937, vol. III
Londesborough, 6th Baron, 1876–1963, vol. VI
Londesborough, 7th Baron, 1885–1967, vol. VI
Londesborough, 8th Baron, 1901–1968, vol. VI
London, Sir (Edgar) Stanford, 1861–1943, vol. IV
London, Sir George Ernest, 1889–1957, vol. V
London, Heinz, 1907–1970, vol. VI
London, Hugh Stanford, 1884–1959, vol. V
London, Jack, 1876–1916, vol. II
London, Sir Stanford; *see* London, Sir E. S.
Londonderry, 6th Marquess of, 1852–1915, vol. I
Londonderry, 7th Marquess of, 1878–1949, vol. IV
Londonderry, 8th Marquess of, 1902–1955, vol. V
Londonderry, Dowager Marchioness of; (Edith Helen), 1879–1959, vol. V
Loney, Sidney Luxton, 1860–1939, vol. III
Long, 2nd Viscount, 1911–1944, vol. IV
Long, 3rd Viscount, 1892–1967, vol. VI
Long, (Adrian) Douglas, 1925–1990, vol. VIII
Long, Lt-Col Albert de Lande, 1880–1956, vol. V
Long, Alfred James, 1890–1952, vol. V
Long, Brig.-Gen. Sir Arthur, 1866–1941, vol. VI
Long, Arthur Tilney, 1871–1946, vol. IV
Long, Basil Kellett, 1878–1944, vol. IV
Long, Basil Somerset, 1881–1937, vol. III
Long, Sir Bertram, 1889–1975, vol. VII
Long, Charles Wigram, 1842–1911, vol. I
Long, Douglas; *see* Long, A. D.
Long, Edward Charles, 1860–1940, vol. III
Long, Edward Ernest, *died* 1956, vol. V
Long, Ernest, 1898–1982, vol. VIII
Long, Captain Eustace Ruffel Drake, 1883–1941, vol. IV
Long, Air Vice-Marshal Francis William, 1899–1983, vol. VIII
Long, Gabrielle; *see* Long, M. G.
Long, Gavin Merrick, 1901–1968, vol. VI
Long, George Bathurst, 1855–1917, vol. II
Long, Sir George Henry, 1818–1900, vol. I
Long, Rt Rev. George Merrick, 1874–1930, vol. III
Long, Sir James, 1862–1928, vol. II
Long, John Luther, 1861–1927, vol. II
Long, Kathleen Ida, 1896–1968, vol. VI
Long, (Margaret) Gabrielle, 1888–1952, vol. V
Long, Ven. Robert, *died* 1907, vol. I
Long, Robert Edward Crozier, 1872–1938, vol. III
Long, Sir Ronald, 1902–1987, vol. VIII
Long, Maj.-Gen. Sidney Selden, 1863–1940, vol. III
Long, Sydney, (Sid Long), 1878–1955, vol. V
Long, Sydney Herbert, 1870–1939, vol. III
Long, Lt-Col Walter, 1879–1917, vol. II
Long, Col Walter Edward Lionel, 1884–1960, vol. V
Long, Lt-Col Wilfred James, 1871–1954, vol. V
Long, Lt-Col William, 1843–1926, vol. II
Long, William Henry, 1900–1969, vol. VI
Long, Lt-Col William Hoare Bourchier, 1868–1943, vol. IV
Long, Rev. William Joseph, 1866–1952, vol. V
Long Innes, Hon. Reginald Heath, 1869–1947, vol. IV
Longard de Longgarde, Dorothea, 1855–1915, vol. I
Longbotham, Hugh Ashley, 1880–1938, vol. III
Longbotham, Samuel, 1908–1988, vol. VIII

Longbottom, Arthur William, 1883–1943, vol. IV
Longbottom, Sir Benjamin, 1876–1930, vol. III
Longbourne, Brig.-Gen. Francis Cecil M. M.; *see* More-Molyneux-Longbourne.
Longcroft, Air Vice-Marshal Sir Charles Alexander Holcombe, 1883–1958, vol. V
Longden, Major Alfred Appleby, *died* 1954, vol. V
Longden, Clifford; *see* Longden, H. C.
Longden, Fred, 1894–1952, vol. V
Longden, (Harry) Clifford, 1869–1953, vol. V
Longden, Maj.-Gen. Harry Leicester, 1900–1981, vol. VIII
Longden, Vice-Adm. Horace Walker, 1877–1953, vol. V
Longden, Robert Paton, 1903–1940, vol. III
Longe, Desmond Evelyn, 1914–1990, vol. VIII
Longe, Col Francis Bacon, 1856–1922, vol. II
Longfellow, Ernest Wadsworth, 1845–1921, vol. II
Longfield, Captain John Percival, 1885–1915, vol. I
Longford, 5th Earl of, 1864–1915, vol. I
Longford, 6th Earl of, 1902–1961, vol. VI
Longford, Joseph Henry, 1849–1925, vol. II
Longford, Rev. William Wingfield, 1882–1964, vol. VI
Longhurst, Col Arthur Lyster, 1872–1952, vol. V
Longhurst, Cyril, 1879–1948, vol. IV
Longhurst, Sir Henry Bell, 1835–1926, vol. II
Longhurst, Henry Carpenter, 1909–1978, vol. VII
Longhurst, Margaret Helen, 1882–1958, vol. V
Longhurst, Ven. William Belsey, 1847–1939, vol. III
Longhurst, William Henry, 1819–1904, vol. I
Longhurst, Rev. William Henry Roberts, 1838–1943, vol. IV
Longland, Austin Charles, 1888–1972, vol. VII
Longland, Sir David Walter, 1909–1988, vol. VIII
Longland, Rev. Sydney Ernest, 1873–1957, vol. V
Longley, Sir Henry, 1833–1899, vol. I
Longley, James Wilberforce, 1849–1922, vol. II
Longley, Maj.-Gen. Sir John Raynsford, 1867–1953, vol. V
Longley, Stanislaus Soutten, 1894–1966, vol. VI
Longley-Cook, Vice-Adm. Eric William, 1898–1983, vol. VIII
Longman, Charles James, 1852–1934, vol. III
Longman, Sir Hubert Harry, 1st Bt, 1856–1940, vol. III
Longman, Mark Frederic Kerr, 1916–1972, vol. VII
Longman, Thomas Norton, 1849–1930, vol. III
Longman, William, 1882–1967, vol. VI
Longmore, Air Chief Marshal Sir Arthur Murray, 1885–1970, vol. VI
Longmore, Col Sir Charles Elton, 1855–1930, vol. III
Longmore, Lt-Col Charles Moorsom, 1882–1933, vol. III
Longmore, Brig. John Alexander, 1899–1973, vol. VII
Longmore, Brig.-Gen. John Constantine Gordon, 1870–1958, vol. V
Longmore, Philip Elton, 1884–1954, vol. V
Longmore, William James Maitland, 1919–1988, vol. VIII
Longmuir, Very Rev. James Boyd, 1907–1973, vol. VII
Longmuir, Robert Findlay, 1864–1942, vol. IV
Longridge, Rev. George, 1857–1936, vol. III

Longridge, Lt-Col Theodore, 1860–1940, vol. III

Longrigg, Brig. Stephen Hemsley, 1893–1979, vol. VII

Longson, Edward Harold, 1872–1941, vol. IV

Longstaff, Cedric Llewellyn, 1876–1950, vol. IV

Longstaff, George Blundell, 1849–1921, vol. II

Longstaff, Mrs George Blundell; see Longstaff, M. J.

Longstaff, Gilbert Conrad, 1884–1964, vol. VI

Longstaff, Sir John, 1862–1941, vol. IV

Longstaff, Llewellyn Wood, 1841–1918, vol. II

Longstaff, Mary Jane, (Mrs George Longstaff), died 1935, vol. III

Longstaff, Tom George, 1875–1964, vol. VI

Longstaffe, Amyas Philip, 1868–1914, vol. I

Longstreth-Thompson, Francis, 1890–1973, vol. VII

Longueville, Thomas, 1844–1922, vol. II

Longworth, Francis Travers Dames, 1834–1898, vol. I

Longworth, Sir Fred, 1890–1973, vol. VII

Longworth, Nicholas, 1869–1931, vol. III

Longworth, Rt Rev. Tom, 1891–1977, vol. VII

Lonsdale, 5th Earl of, 1857–1944, vol. IV

Lonsdale, 6th Earl of, 1867–1953, vol. V

Lonsdale, Allister, 1926–1977, vol. VII

Lonsdale, Lt-Col Arthur H.; see Heywood-Lonsdale.

Lonsdale, Arthur Pemberton H.; see Heywood-Lonsdale.

Lonsdale, Frederick, 1881–1954, vol. V

Lonsdale, Rev. Henry, died 1926, vol. II

Lonsdale, Lt-Col Henry Heywood H.; see Heywood-Lonsdale.

Lonsdale, James Rolston, 1865–1921, vol. II

Lonsdale, Rev. John Gylby, 1818–1907, vol. I

Lonsdale, John Pemberton Heywood H.; see Heywood-Lonsdale.

Lonsdale, Dame Kathleen, 1903–1971, vol. VII

Looker, Herbert William, 1871–1951, vol. V

Loombe, Claude Evan, 1905–1978, vol. VII

Loomis, Maj.-Gen. Sir Frederick Oscar Warren, 1870–1937, vol. III

Loomis, Roger Sherman, 1887–1966, vol. VI

Lopes, George, 1857–1910, vol. I

Lopes, Sir Henry Yarde Buller, 4th Bt; see Roborough, 1st Baron.

Lopes, Rt Hon. Sir (Lopes) Massey, 3rd Bt, 1818–1908, vol. I

Lopes, Rt Hon. Sir Massey; see Lopes, Rt Hon. Sir L. M.

Lopokova, Lydia; see Keynes, Lady.

Loraine, John Alexander, 1924–1988, vol. VIII

Loraine, Sir Lambton, 11th Bt, 1838–1917, vol. II

Loraine, Rev. Nevison, died 1917, vol. II

Loraine, Rt Hon. Sir Percy Lyham, 12th Bt, 1880–1961, vol. VI

Loraine, Robert, 1876–1935, vol. III

Loram, Charles Templeman, 1879–1940, vol. III (A), vol. IV

Lord, Sir Ackland Archibald, 1901–1982, vol. VIII

Lord, Cyril, 1911–1984, vol. VIII

Lord, Sir Frank, 1894–1974, vol. VII

Lord, Rev. Fred Townley, 1893–1962, vol. VI

Lord, Herbert Owen, 1854–1928, vol. II

Lord, Col John Ernest Cecil, 1870–1949, vol. IV

Lord, John King, 1848–1926, vol. II

Lord, John Robert, 1874–1931, vol. III

Lord, Sir Percy, 1903–1968, vol. VI

Lord, Sir Riley, 1838–1920, vol. II

Lord, Captain S(ydney) Riley, 1884–1959, vol. V

Lord, Sir Walter G.; see Greaves-Lord.

Lord, Maj.-Gen. Wilfrid Austin, 1902–1982, vol. VIII

Lorden, Sir John William, 1862–1944, vol. IV

Loreburn, 1st Earl, 1846–1923, vol. II

Lorenz, Konrad Zacharias, 1903–1989, vol. VIII

Lorimer, Lt-Col David Lockhart Robertson, 1876–1962, vol. VI

Lorimer, Emily Overend, (Mrs D. L. R. Lorimer), 1881–1949, vol. IV

Lorimer, George Horace, 1868–1937, vol. III

Lorimer, Henry Dubs, 1879–1933, vol. III

Lorimer, John Campbell, died 1922, vol. II

Lorimer, John Gordon, 1870–1914, vol. I

Lorimer, John Henry, 1856–1936, vol. III

Lorimer, Norma, died 1948, vol. IV

Lorimer, Sir Robert Stodart, 1864–1929, vol. III

Lorimer, Sir William, 1844–1922, vol. II

Lorimer, William Laughton, 1885–1967, vol. VI

Loring, Andrew; see Lathrop, L. A.

Loring, Vice-Adm. Ernest Kindersley, 1869–1945, vol. IV

Loring, Frederick George, 1869–1951, vol. V

Loring, James Adrian, 1918–1990, vol. VIII

Loring, Sir (John) Nigel, 1896–1979, vol. VII

Loring, Sir Nigel; see Loring, Sir J. N.

Loring, William, 1865–1915, vol. I

Loring, Col William, 1872–1935, vol. III

Lorne, Marion, 1888–1968, vol. VI

Lornie, James, 1876–1959, vol. V

Lorrain, Rt Rev. Narcisse Zephyrin, 1842–1915, vol. I

Lort Phillips, Lt-Col John Frederick, 1854–1926, vol. II

Lort-Williams, Sir John Rolleston, 1881–1966, vol. VI

Lory, Frederic Burton Pendarves, 1875–1954, vol. V

Losey, Joseph, 1909–1984, vol. VIII

Loss, Joe; see Loss, Joshua A.

Loss, Joshua Alexander, (Joe Loss), 1909–1990, vol. VIII

Lote, Thomas Alfred, born 1863, vol. II

Loten, Harold Ivens, 1887–1980, vol. VII

Loth, David, born 1899, vol. VIII

Lothian, 9th Marquess of, 1833–1900, vol. I

Lothian, 10th Marquess of, 1874–1930, vol. III

Lothian, 11th Marquess of, 1882–1940, vol. III

Lothian, Sir Arthur Cunningham, 1887–1962, vol. VI

Loti, Pierre, 1850–1923, vol. II

Loton, Sir Ernest Thorley, 1895–1973, vol. VII

Loten, Sir William Thorley, 1839–1924, vol. II

Lott, Air Vice-Marshal Charles George, 1906–1989, vol. VIII

Lott, Frank Melville, 1896–1982, vol. VIII

Lott, Air Vice-Marshal George; see Lott, Air Vice-Marshal C. G.

Loubet, Émile François, 1838–1929, vol. III

Louch, Ven. Thomas, 1848–1927, vol. II

Loucks, Rev. Edwin, 1829–1919, vol. II

Loud, Arthur Bertram, 1863–1931, vol. III

Loudan, Mouat, 1868–1925, vol. II

Loudon, James, 1841–1916, vol. II
Loudon, Sir John, 1881–1948, vol. IV
Loudon, John, *died* 1966, vol. VI
Loudoun, 11th Earl of, 1855–1920, vol. II
Loudoun, Countess of (12th in line), 1883–1960, vol. V
Loudoun, Donaldson, 1909–1980, vol. VII
Lough, Brig. John Robertson Stewart, 1887–1970, vol. VI
Lough, Lt-Gen. Reginald Dawson Hopcraft, 1885–1958, vol. V
Lough, Rt Hon. Thomas, 1850–1922, vol. II
Loughborough, Lord; Francis Edward Scudamore St Clair Erskine, 1892–1929, vol. III
Loughborough, Maj.-Gen. Arthur Harold, 1883–1967, vol. VI
Lougheed, Hon. Sir James Alexander, 1854–1925, vol. II
Lougheed, Lt-Col Samuel Forster, 1860–1932, vol. III
Lougher, Sir Lewis, 1871–1955, vol. V
Loughlin, Dame Anne, 1894–1979, vol. VII
Loughnane, Farquhar McGillivray, 1885–1948, vol. IV
Loughnane, Norman Gerald, 1883–1955, vol. V
Louis, Sir Charles, 4th Bt, 1818–1900, vol. I
Louis, Sir Charles, 5th Bt, 1859–1949, vol. IV
Louis, Henry, 1855–1939, vol. III
Louisson, Hon. Charles, 1842–1924, vol. II
Lounsbury, Thomas Raynesford, 1838–1915, vol. I
Lousada, Duc de; Comdr Francis Clifford de Lousada, 1842–1916, vol. II
Lousada Lloyd, Col Frederic Percy, 1853–1930, vol. III
Louth, 14th Baron, 1868–1941, vol. IV
Louth, 15th Baron, 1892–1950, vol. IV
Louw, Hon. Eric Hendrik, 1890–1968, vol. VI
Louys, Pierre, 1870–1925, vol. II
Lovat, 14th Baron, 1871–1933, vol. III
Lovat-Fraser, James Alexander, 1868–1938, vol. III
Love, Augustus Edward Hough, 1863–1940, vol. III
Love, Sir Clifton; *see* Love, Sir J. C.
Love, Enid Rosamond, (Mrs G. C. F. Whitaker), 1911–1979, vol. VII
Love, James Kerr, 1858–1942, vol. IV
Love, Sir (Joseph) Clifton, 1868–1951, vol. V
Love, Richard Archibald, 1873–1941, vol. IV
Love, Robert, 1867–1934, vol. III
Love, Robert John McNeill, 1891–1974, vol. VII
Loveday, Alexander, 1888–1962, vol. VI
Loveday, Arthur Frederic, 1878–1968, vol. VI
Loveday, Rt Rev. David Goodwin, 1896–1985, vol. VIII
Loveday, Rev. Eric Stephen, 1904–1947, vol. IV
Loveday, George Arthur, 1909–1981, vol. VIII
Loveday, Thomas, 1875–1966, vol. VI
Lovegrove, Edwin William, 1868–1956, vol. V
Lovejoy, Arthur Oncken, 1873–1962, vol. VI
Lovel, Raymond William, 1912–1969, vol. VI
Lovelace, 2nd Earl of, 1839–1906, vol. I
Lovelace, 3rd Earl of, 1865–1929, vol. III
Lovelace, 4th Earl of, 1905–1964, vol. VI
Lovelace, Countess of; (Mary Caroline), *died* 1941, vol. IV

Lovelace, Lt-Col Alec, 1907–1981, vol. VIII
Loveland, Richard Loveland, 1841–1923, vol. II
Lovell, Arnold Henry, 1926–1990, vol. VIII
Lovell, Sir Francis Henry, 1844–1916, vol. II
Lovell, Henry Willoughby, 1866–1939, vol. III
Lovell, Mark; *see* Tollemache, David.
Lovell, Reginald, 1897–1972, vol. VII
Lovell, Stanley Hains, 1906–1985, vol. VIII
Lovell, William George, 1868–1944, vol. IV
Lovely, Percy Thomas, 1894–1975, vol. VII
Lovemore, Wing Comdr Robert Baillie, *died* 1978, vol. VII
Loveridge, Arthur John, 1904–1975, vol. VII
Loveridge, Charles William, 1869–1957, vol. V
Loveridge, Joan Mary, 1912–1987, vol. VIII
Loveridge, Walter David,1867–1940, vol. III (A), vol. IV
Loverseed, John Frederick 1881–1928, vol. II
Lovett, Col Alfred Crowdy, 1862–1919, vol. II
Lovett, Maj.-Gen. Beresford, 1839–1926, vol. II
Lovett, Rt Rev. Ernest Neville, 1869–1951, vol. V
Lovett, Sir (Harrington) Verney, 1864–1945, vol. IV
Lovett, Rev. Canon John Percival Willoughby, 1880–1968, vol. VI
Lovett, Maj.-Gen. Osmond de Turville, 1898–1982, vol. VIII
Lovett, Rev. Richard, 1851–1904, vol. I
Lovett, Robert Abercrombie, 1895–1986, vol. VIII
Lovett, Sir Verney; *see* Lovett, Sir H. V.
Lovett-Cameron, Rev. Charles Leslie, 1843–1927, vol. II
Loveys, Walter Harris, 1920–1969, vol. VI
Lovibond, Joseph Williams, 1833–1918, vol. II
Low, Hon. Lord; Alexander Low, 1845–1910, vol. I
Low, A. M., 1888–1956, vol. V
Low, Sir A. Maurice, 1860–1929, vol. III
Low, Gen. Alexander, 1817–1904, vol. I
Low, Alexander, 1868–1950, vol. II
Low, Alexander; *see* Low, Hon. Lord.
Low, Sir Austin; 1862–1956, vol. V
Low, Sir Charles Ernest, 1869–1941, vol. IV
Low, Charles Rathbone, 1837–1918, vol. II
Low, Sir David Alexander Cecil, 1891–1963, vol. VI
Low, David Allan, 1857–1937, vol. III
Low, David Morrice, 1890–1972, vol. VII
Low, Sir Francis, 1893–1972, vol. VII
Low, Frank Harrison, 1854–1912, vol. I
Low, Sir Frederick, 1856–1917, vol. II
Low, George Carmichael, 1872–1952, vol. V
Low, George Macritchie,1849–1922, vol. II
Low, Harold, 1863–1932, vol. III
Low, Sir Henry Telfer, 1880–1964, vol. VI
Low, Sir Hugh, 1824–1905, vol. I
Low, Sir James, 1st Bt, 1849–1923, vol. II
Low, John Laing, 1869–1929, vol. III
Low, Mabel Bruce, *died* 1972, vol. VII
Low, Lt-Col Robert Balmain, 1864–1927, vol. II
Low, Robert Bruce, 1846–1922, vol. II
Low, Robert Cranston, 1879–1949, vol. IV
Low, Gen. Sir Robert Cunliffe, 1838–1911, vol. I
Low, Hon. Seth, 1850–1916, vol. II
Low, Sir Sidney, 1857–1932, vol. III
Low, Sir Stephen Philpot, 1883–1955, vol. V
Low, Col Stuart, 1888–1942, vol. IV

Low, Vincent Warren, *died* 1942, vol. IV
Low, Sir Walter John Morrison-, 2nd Bt, 1899–1955, vol.V
Low, Ven. Walter Percival, 1876–1960, vol. V
Low, Will Hicok, 1853–1932, vol. III
Low, William Alexander, *died* 1970, vol. VI
Low, Rev. William Leslie, 1840–1929, vol. III
Low, William Malcolm, 1835–1923, vol. II
Low, William S.; *see* Stuart-Low.
Lowdon, Andrew Gilchrist Ross, 1911–1965, vol. VI
Lowdon, John, 1881–1963, vol. VI
Lowe, Sir (Albert) George, 1901–1967, vol. VI
Lowe, Alexander Francis, 1861–1929, vol. III
Lowe, Arthur, 1915–1982, vol. VIII
Lowe, Lt-Col Arthur Cecil, 1868–1917, vol. II
Lowe, Arthur Labron, 1861–1928, vol. II
Lowe, Charles, *died* 1931, vol. III
Lowe, Sir Charles John, 1880–1969, vol. VI
Lowe, Gp Captain Cyril Nelson, 1891–1983, vol. VIII
Lowe, David, 1868–1947, vol. IV
Lowe, Sir David, 1899–1980, vol. VII
Lowe, Douglas Gordon Arthur, 1902–1981, vol. VIII
Lowe, Sir Drury Curzon D., *see* Drury-Lowe.
Lowe, Rev. Edward Clarke, 1823–1912, vol. I
Lowe, Edward Cronin, 1880–1958, vol. V
Lowe, Edwin Ernest, 1877–1958, vol. V
Lowe, Elias Avery, 1879–1969, vol. VI
Lowe, Mrs Eveline M., *died* 1956, vol.V
Lowe, Sir (Francis) Gordon, 2nd Bt, 1884–1972, vol. VII
Lowe, Major Francis Manley, 1859–1934, vol. III
Lowe, Sir Francis Reginald Gordon, 3rd Bt, 1931–1986, vol. VIII
Lowe, Rt Hon. Sir Francis William, 1st Bt, 1852–1929, vol. III
Lowe, Sir George; *see* Lowe, Sir A. G.
Lowe, Sir Gordon; *see* Lowe, Sir F. G.
Lowe, Rev. Herbert Hampson, 1865–1945, vol. IV
Lowe, Herbert John, 1892–1960, vol. V
Lowe, Rear-Adm. John, 1838–1930, vol. III
Lowe, Rev. John, 1899–1960, vol. V
Lowe, Rev. Joseph, *died* 1920, vol. II
Lowe, Sir Lionel Harold Harvey, 1897–1960, vol. V
Lowe, Percy Roycroft, 1870–1948, vol. IV
Lowe, Rouxville Mark, 1881–1957, vol. V
Lowe, Ven. Sidney Edward, 1882–1968, vol. VI
Lowe, Vice-Adm. Sidney Robert D.; *see* Drury-Lowe.
Lowe, Lt-Col Thomas Alfred, 1888–1967, vol. VI
Lowe, Maj.-Gen. William Henry Muir, 1861–1944, vol. IV
Lowe, Very Rev. William James, 1853–1931, vol. III
Lowe-Brown, William Lowe, 1876–1956, vol. V
Lowell, Abbott Lawrence, 1856–1943, vol. IV
Lowell, Army, 1874–1925, vol. II
Lowell, Percival, 1855–1916, vol. II
Lowell, Robert Traill Spence, Jr, 1917–1977, vol. VII
Lowenfeld, Margaret Frances Jane, 1890–1973, vol. VII
Lowenthal, Charles Frederick, *died* 1933, vol. III
Lowery, Harry, 1896–1967, vol. VI
Lowes, John Livingston, 1867–1945, vol. IV
Loweth, Sidney Harold, 1893–1977, vol. VII
Loweth, Walter Ernest, 1892–1968, vol. VI

Lowinger, Victor Alexander, 1879–1957, vol. V
Lowinsky, Thomas Esmond, 1892–1947, vol. IV
Lowis, Cecil Champain, 1866–1948, vol. IV
Lowis, Frank Currie, 1872–1963, vol. VI
Lowis, Lt-Col Penton Shakspear, 1870–1931, vol. III
Lowles, Sir Geoffrey; *see* Lowles, Sir J. G. N.
Lowles, Sir (John) Geoffrey (Nelson), 1898–1962, vol. VI
Lowman, Rev. Canon Edward Sydney Charles, 1908–1974, vol. VI
Lowndes, Alan, 1921–1978, vol. VII
Lowndes, Frederic Sawrey Archibald, *died* 1940, vol. III
Lowndes, Rt Hon. Sir George Rivers, 1862–1943, vol. IV
Lowndes, Marie; *see* Belloc, Marie Adelaide.
Lowndes, Mary E., 1863–1947, vol. IV
Lowndes, Brig. Montacute William Worrall S.; *see* Selby-Lowndes.
Lowndes, Maj.-Gen. Thomas, *died* 1927, vol. II
Lowndes, William Selby-, 1836–1920, vol. II
Lowndes, Col William Selby-, 1871–1951, vol. V
Lowrey, Sir Joseph, 1859–1936, vol. III
Lowry, Rev. Walter, 1868–1959, vol. V
Lowry, Sir Arthur, 1868–1938, vol. III
Lowry, Charles, 1857–1922, vol. II
Lowry, Charles Gibson, 1880–1951, vol. V
Lowry, Henry Dawson, 1869–1906, vol. I
Lowry, Hugh Avant, 1913–1982, vol. VIII
Lowry, Col James, 1856–1937, vol. III
Lowry, Laurence Stephen, 1887–1976, vol. VII
Lowry, Adm. Sir Robert Swinburne, 1854–1920, vol. II
Lowry, Lt-Gen. Robert William, 1824–1905, vol. I
Lowry, Thomas Martin, 1874–1936, vol. III
Lowry, Rt Hon. William, *died* 1949, vol. IV
Lowry-Corry, Adm. Hon. Armar, 1836–1919, vol. II
Lowry-Corry, Lt-Col Sir Henry Charles, 1887–1973, vol. VII
Lowry-Corry, Col Hon. Henry William, 1845–1927, vol. II
Lowry-Corry, Brig.-Gen. Noel Armar, 1867–1935, vol. III
Lowsley, Col Herbert de Lisle P.; *see* Pollard-Lowsley.
Lowsley-Williams, George, 1869–1937, vol. III
Lowson, Sir Denys Colquhoun Flowerdew, 1st Bt, 1906–1975, vol. VII
Lowson, James Gray Flowerdew, 1860–1942, vol. IV
Lowth, Lt-Col Frank Robert, 1850–1931, vol. III
Lowth, Thomas, 1858–1931, vol. III
Lowther, Viscount; Anthony Edward Lowther, 1896–1949, vol. IV
Lowther, Captain Hon. Anthony George, 1925–1981, vol. VIII
Lowther, Maj.-Gen. Sir Cecil; *see* Lowther, Maj.-Gen. Sir H. C.
Lowther, Lt-Col Sir Charles Bingham, 4th Bt (*cr* 1824), 1880–1949, vol. IV
Lowther, Major Hon. Christopher William, 1887–1935, vol. III
Lowther, Claude, 1872–1929, vol. III
Lowther, Rt Hon. Sir Gerard Augustus, 1st Bt (*cr* 1914), 1858–1916, vol. II

Lowther, Maj.-Gen. Sir (Henry) Cecil, 1869–1940, vol. III

Lowther, Sir Henry Crofton, 1858–1939, vol. III

Lowther, Rt Hon. James, 1840–1904, vol. I

Lowther, John Arthur, 1910–1942, vol. IV

Lowther, Col John George, 1885–1977, vol. VII

Lowther, Hon. William, 1821–1912, vol. I

Lowther, Lt-Col Sir William Guy, 5th Bt, 1912–1982, vol. VIII

Lowther-Crofton, Vice-Adm. Edward George, 1873–1942, vol. IV

Lowthian, Caroline; see Prescott, C.

Lowthian, George Henry, 1908–1986, vol. VIII

Loyd, Archie Kirkman, 1847–1922, vol. II

Loyd, Arthur Thomas, 1882–1944, vol. IV

Loyd, Gen. Sir Charles; see Loyd, Gen. Sir H. C.

Loyd, Edward Henry, 1861–1938, vol. III

Loyd, Gen. Sir (Henry) Charles, 1891–1973, vol. VII

Loyd, Lewis Vivian, 1852–1908, vol. I

Loyd, Llewellyn Foster, 1861–1939, vol. III

Loyd, Lady Mary, died 1936, vol. III

Loyd, Rt Rev. Philip Henry, 1884–1952, vol. V

Luard, Maj.-Gen. Charles Camac, 1867–1947, vol. IV

Luard, Lt-Col Charles Eckford, 1869–1927, vol. II

Luard, Maj.-Gen. Charles Edward, 1939–1908, vol. I

Luard, Major Edward Bourryau, 1870–1916, vol. II

Luard, Adm. John Scott, 1865–1936, vol. III

Luard, Lowes Dalbiac, died 1944, vol. IV

Luard, Comdr William Blaine, 1897–1979, vol. VII

Luard, Adm. Sir William Garnham, 1820–1910, vol. I

Lubbock, Sir Alan, 1897–1990, vol. VIII

Lubbock, Arthur Nevile, 1869–1939, vol. III

Lubbock, Basil, 1876–1944, vol. IV

Lubbock, Cecil, 1872–1956, vol. V

Lubbock, Edgar, 1847–1907, vol. I

Lubbock, Frederic, 1844–1927, vol. II

Lubbock, Geoffrey, 1873–1932, vol. III

Lubbock, Brig.-Gen. Guy, 1870–1956, vol. V

Lubbock, Hon. Harold Fox-Pitt, 1888–1918, vol. II

Lubbock, Henry James, 1838–1910, vol. I

Lubbock, Hon. Maurice Fox Pitt, 1900–1957, vol. V

Lubbock, Montagu, 1842–1925, vol. II

Lubbock, Sir Nevile, 1839–1914, vol. I

Lubbock, Hon. Norman, 1861–1926, vol. II

Lubbock, Percy, 1879–1965, vol. VI

Lubbock, Roy, 1892–1985, vol. VIII

Lubbock, Samuel Gurney, died 1958, vol. V

Lubbock, Lady Sybil Marjorie, 1879–1943, vol. IV

Lubienski, Count Louis B.; see Bodenham-Lubienski.

Lubitsch, Ernst, 1892–1947, vol. IV

Lucan, 4th Earl of, 1830–1914, vol. I

Lucan, 5th Earl of, 1860–1949, vol. IV

Lucan, 6th Earl of, 1898–1964, vol. IV

Lucas of Chilworth, 1st Baron, 1896–1967, vol. VI

Lucas of Crudwell, 8th Baron, and Dingwall, 5th Lord, 1876–1916, vol. II

Lucas of Crudwell, Baroness (9th in line), and Dingwall, Lady (6th in line), 1880–1958, vol. V

Lucas, Col Alfred George, 1854–1941, vol. IV

Lucas, Captain Armytage Anthony, died 1950, vol. IV

Lucas, Rev. Arthur, 1851–1921, vol. II

Lucas, Sir Arthur, 1845–1922, vol. II

Lucas, Arthur, 1863–1932, vol. III

Lucas, Sir Arthur Charles, 2nd Bt, 1853–1915, vol. I

Lucas, Brig.-Gen. Cecil Courtenay, 1883–1957, vol. V

Lucas, Rear-Adm. Charles Davis, 1834–1914, vol. I

Lucas, Charles James, 1853–1928, vol. II

Lucas, Sir Charles Prestwood, 1853–1931, vol. III

Lucas, Claude Arthur, 1894–1974, vol. VII

Lucas, Colin Anderson, 1906–1984, vol. VIII

Lucas, Maj.-Gen. Cuthbert Henry Tindall, 1879–1958, vol. V

Lucas, Donald William, 1905–1985, vol. VIII

Lucas, Hon. Sir Edward, 1857–1950, vol. IV

Lucas, Sir Edward Lingard, 3rd Bt, 1860–1936, vol. III

Lucas, Edward Verrall, 1868–1938, vol. III

Lucas, Edward William, 1864–1940, vol. III

Lucas, Rev. Egbert de Grey, 1878–1958, vol. V

Lucas, Col Francis Alfred, 1850–1918, vol. II

Lucas, Francis Herman, 1878–1920, vol. II

Lucas, Hon. Frank Archibald William, 1881–1959, vol. V

Lucas, Frank Laurence, 1894–1967, vol. VI

Lucas, Brig.-Gen. Frederic George, 1866–1922, vol. II

Lucas, Maj.-Gen. Geoffrey, 1904–1982, vol. VIII

Lucas, Henry Frederick Lucas, died 1943, vol. IV

Lucas, Hon. Isaac Benson, 1867–1940, vol. III

Lucas, Rt Rev. James Richard, 1867–1938, vol. III

Lucas, Major Sir Jocelyn Morton, 4th Bt, 1889–1980, vol. VII

Lucas, John Seymour, 1849–1923, vol. II

Lucas, Keith, 1879–1916, vol. II

Lucas, Marie Elizabeth Seymour, 1855–1921, vol. II

Lucas, Brig. Reginald Hutchinson, 1888–1956, vol. V

Lucas, Reginald Jafray, 1865–1914, vol. I

Lucas, Richard Clement, died 1915, vol. I

Lucas, St John Welles, 1879–1934, vol. III

Lucas, Sir Thomas, 1st Bt, 1822–1902, vol. I

Lucas, Col Thomas John Rashleigh, 1858–1929, vol. III

Lucas, Wilfrid Irvine, 1905–1973, vol. VII

Lucas, William Henry, 1867–1937, vol. III

Lucas, Rt Rev. William Vincent, 1883–1945, vol. IV

Lucas-Shadwell, William, 1852–1915, vol. I

Lucas-Tooth, Sir (Archibald) Leonard (Lucas), 2nd Bt, 1884–1918, vol. II

Lucas-Tooth, Sir Leonard; see Lucas-Tooth, Sir A. L. L.

Lucas-Tooth, Sir Robert Lucas, 1st Bt, 1844–1915, vol. I

Lucceshi, Andrea Carlo, 1860–1925, vol. II

Luce, Rev. Arthur Aston, 1882–1977, vol. VII

Luce, Hon. Clare Boothe, 1903–1987, vol. VIII

Luce, Adm. Sir David; see Luce, Adm. Sir J. D.

Luce, Rev. Edward, 1851–1917, vol. II

Luce, Rev. Canon Harry Kenneth, 1897–1972, vol. VII

Luce, Henry Robinson, 1898–1967, vol. VI

Luce, Adm. John, 1870–1932, vol. III

Luce, Adm. Sir (John) David, 1906–1971, vol. VII

Luce, Morton, 1849–1943, vol. IV

Luce, Reginald William, 1893–1971, vol. VII

Luce, Maj.-Gen. Sir Richard Harman, 1867–1952, vol. V

Luce, Sir William Henry Tucker, 1907–1977, vol. VII

Lucet, Charles Ernest, 1910–1990, vol. VIII
Lucey, Most Rev. Cornelius, died 1982, vol. VIII
Lucey, Col Walter Francis, 1880–1962, vol. VI
Luciani, Albino; see John Paul I.
Lucie-Smith, Sir Alfred van W., 1854–1947, vol. IV
Lucie-Smith, Sir John Alfred, 1888–1969, vol. VI
Luck, Col Brian John Michael, 1874–1948, vol. IV
Luck, Captain Cyril Montagu, 1872–1944, vol. IV
Luck, Gen. Sir George, 1840–1916, vol. II
Luck, Richard, 1847–1920, vol. II
Lucker, Sydney Charles, 1897–1977, vol. VII
Luckes, Eva C. E., died 1919, vol. II
Luckham, Major Arthur Albert, 1883–1957, vol. V
Luckham, Ven. William Arthur Grant, 1857–1921, vol. II
Luckner, Felix, Count, 1881–1966, vol. VI
Luckock, Maj.-Gen. Russell Mortimer, 1877–1950, vol. IV
Lucraft, Frederick Hickman, 1894–1981, vol. VIII
Lucy, Major Sir Brian Fulke Cameron-Ramsay-F.; see Fairfax-Lucy.
Lucy, Sir Henry, 1845–1924, vol. II
Lucy, Sir Henry William Cameron-Ramsay-F.; see Fairfax-Lucy.
Lucy, Captain Sir Montgomerie F.; see Fairfax-Lucy, Captain Sir H. M. R.
Ludbrook, Samuel Lawrence, 1895–1976, vol. VII
Ludby, Max, 1858–1943, vol. IV
Luddington, James Little, 1853–1935, vol. III
Ludlow, 1st Baron, 1827–1899, vol. I
Ludlow, 2nd Baron, 1865–1922, vol. II
Ludlow, Lady; (Alice Sedgwick), died 1945, vol. IV
Ludlow, Brig.-Gen. Edmund Ranald Owen, 1864–1929, vol. III
Ludlow, Col Edmund Samuel, 1840–1906, vol. I
Ludlow, Sir Henry, 1834–1903, vol. I
Ludlow, John Malcolm, 1821–1911, vol. I
Ludlow, Sir Richard Robert, 1882–1956, vol. V
Ludlow, Brig.-Gen. Sir Walter Robert, 1857–1941, vol. IV
Ludlow-Hewitt, Air Chief Marshal Sir Edgar Rainey, 1886–1973, vol. VII
Ludovici, Captain Anthony M., 1882–1971, vol. VII
Ludwig, Emil, 1881–1948, vol. IV
Lueger, Karl, 1844–1910, vol. I
Luff, Arthur Pearson, 1855–1938, vol. III
Luff, Richard Edmund Reife, 1887–1969, vol. VI
Luft, Rev. Canon Hyam Mark, 1913–1986, vol. VIII
Luft, Rev. Canon Mark; see Luft, Rev. Canon H. M.
Lugard, 1st Baron, 1858–1945, vol. IV
Lugard, Lady; (Flora), died 1929, vol. III
Lugard, Rt Hon. Sir Edward, 1810–1898, vol. I
Lugard, Major Edward James, 1865–1957, vol. V
Lugard, Col Edward John, 1845–1911, vol. I
Lugg, Gp Captain Sidney, 1906–1972, vol. VII
Luhrs, Lt-Col Henry Gordon-, 1880–1954, vol. V
Luke, 1st Baron, 1873–1943, vol. IV
Luke, Sir Charles Manley, 1857–1941, vol. IV
Luke, Lt-Col Edward Vyvyan, 1861–1908, vol. I
Luke, Hon. Sir Emile Fashole, born 1895, vol. VII (AII)
Luke, Eric Howard Manley, 1894–1987, vol. VIII
Luke, Sir Harry Charles, 1884–1969, vol. VI
Luke, Sir John Pearce, 1858–1931, vol. III
Luke, Sir Kenneth George, 1898–1971, vol. VII

Luke, Sir Stephen Elliot Vyvyan, 1905–1988, vol. VIII
Luke, Stephen Paget Walter Vyvyan, 1845–1929, vol. III
Luke, Brig.-Gen. Thomas Mawe, 1872–1952, vol. V
Luke, William Edgell, 1909–1987, vol. VIII
Luke, William Joseph, 1862–1934, vol. III
Luker, Col Roland, 1878–1947, vol. IV
Lukin, Maj.-Gen. Sir Henry Timson, 1860–1925, vol. II
Lukin, Hon. Lionel Oscar, 1868–1944, vol. IV
Lukin, Brig.-Gen. Robert Clarence Wellesley, 1870–1955, vol. V
Lukis, Surg.-Gen. Hon. Sir Charles Pardey, 1857–1918, vol. II
Lukis, Maj.-Gen. Wilfrid Boyd Fellowes, 1896–1969, vol. VI
Luling, Sylvia; see Thompson, S.
Lumb, Sir Charles Frederick, 1846–1911, vol. I
Lumb, Col Frederick George Edward, 1877–1958, vol. V
Lumby, Lt-Col Arthur Friedrich Rawson, 1890–1943, vol. IV
Lumby, Sir Henry, 1909–1989, vol. VIII
Lumby, John Henry, died 1948, vol. IV
Lumholtz, Carl, 1851–1922, vol. II
Lumière, Louis, 1864–1948, vol. IV
Lumley, Sir Dudley Owen, 1895–1964, vol. VI
Lumley, Air Cdr Eric Alfred, 1891–1979, vol. VII
Lumley, Col Francis Douglas, 1857–1925, vol. II
Lumley, Lyulph, died 1944, vol. IV
Lumley, Brig.-Gen. Hon. Osbert Victor George Atheling, 1862–1923, vol. II
Lumley, Theodore, died 1922, vol. II
Lumley-Smith, Major Sir Thomas Gabriel Lumley, 1879–1961, vol. VI
Lumsdaine, Edwin Robert John S.; see Sandys-Lumsdaine.
Lumsden, Col Bruce John David, 1907–1965, vol. VI
Lumsden, Col Dugald M'Tavish, 1851–1915, vol. I
Lumsden, E. S., 1883–1948, vol. IV
Lumsden, Maj.-Gen. Herbert, 1897–1945, vol. IV
Lumsden, Sir James Robert, 1884–1970, vol. VI
Lumsden, Sir John, 1869–1944, vol. IV
Lumsden, Dame Louisa Innes, 1840–1935, vol. III
Lumsden, Gen. Sir Peter Stark, 1829–1918, vol. II
Lumsden, Thomas William, 1874–1953, vol. V
Lumsden, Rear-Adm. Walter, 1865–1947, vol. IV
Lunawada, Rajah of, 1860–1929, vol. III
Lund, Henrik, 1879–1935, vol. III
Lund, Niels M., 1863–1916, vol. II
Lund, Lt-Gen. Sir Otto Marling, 1891–1956, vol. V
Lund, Sir Thomas George, 1906–1981, vol. VIII
Lundgren, Captain Albert Edvin, 1878–1942, vol. IV
Lundon, Thomas, 1883–1951, vol. V
Lunham, Col Sir Ainslie, died 1930, vol. III
Lunn, Sir Arnold, 1888–1974, vol. VII
Lunn, Sir George, 1861–1939, vol. III
Lunn, Sir Henry Simpson, 1859–1939, vol. III
Lunn, Hugh Kingsmill; see Kingsmill, Hugh.
Lunn, Louise Kirkby, 1873–1930, vol. III
Lunn, William, 1872–1942, vol. IV
Lunt, Alfred, 1892–1977, vol. VII
Lunt, Rt Rev. Francis Evered, 1900–1982, vol. VIII

Lunt, Rt Rev. Geoffrey Charles Lester, *died* 1948, vol. IV

Lupton, Arnold, *died* 1930, vol. III

Lupton, Arthur Sinclair, 1877–1949, vol. IV

Lupton, Charles, 1855–1935, vol. III

Lupton, John, 1869–1946, vol. IV

Lurgan, 3rd Baron, 1858–1937, vol. III

Lurgan, 4th Baron, 1902–1984, vol. VIII

Luscombe, Sir John Henry, 1848–1937, vol. III

Luscombe, Norman Percival, 1902–1976, vol. VII

Luscombe, Ven. Popham Street, *died* 1927, vol. II

Lush, Sir Archibald James, 1900–1976, vol. VII

Lush, Rt Hon. Sir Charles Montague, 1853–1930, vol. III

Lush, Maurice Stanley, 1896–1990, vol. VIII

Lush-Wilson, Sir Herbert W., 1850–1941, vol. IV

Lushington, Alfred Wyndham, *died* 1920, vol. II

Lushington, Major Sir Arthur Patrick Douglas, 5th Bt, 1861–1937, vol. III

Lushington, Rev. Franklyn de Winton, 1868–1941, vol. IV

Lushington, Sir Godfrey, 1832–1907, vol. I

Lushington, Maj.-Gen. Godfrey Edward W.; *see* Wildman-Lushington.

Lushington, Sir Henry, 3rd Bt, 1802–1897, vol. I

Lushington, Sir Henry, 4th Bt, 1826–1898, vol. I

Lushington, Sir Henry Edmund Castleman, 7th Bt, 1909–1988, vol. VIII

Lushington, Sir Herbert Castleman, 6th Bt, 1879–1968, vol. VI

Lushington, Brig.-Gen. Stephen, 1864–1940, vol. III

Lushington, Sydney George, 1859–1909, vol. I

Lushington, Vernon, 1832–1912, vol. I

Lusk, Sir Andrew, 1st Bt, 1810–1909, vol. I

Lusk, William C., 1875–1944, vol. IV

Lustgarten, Edgar, 1907–1978, vol. VII

Luther, Col Anthony John, 1864–1937, vol. III

Luther, Rev. George Minchin, *died* 1911, vol. I

Luthuli, Albert John Mvumbi, 1899–1967, vol. VI

Lutoslawski, Wincenty, 1863–1955, vol. V

Luttig, Hendrik Gerhardus, 1907–1975, vol. VII

Luttman, Willie Lewis, 1874–1930, vol. III

Luttman-Johnson, Lt-Col Frederic, 1845–1917, vol. II

Luttrell, Alexander Fownes, 1855–1944, vol. IV

Luttrell, George Fownes, 1826–1910, vol. I

Luttrell, Hugh Courtenay Fownes, 1857–1918, vol. II

Lutwyche, Hudson Latham, 1856–1925, vol. II

Lutyens, (Agnes) Elisabeth, (Mrs Edward Clark), 1906–1983, vol. VIII

Lutyens, Sir Edwin Landseer, 1869–1944, vol. IV

Lutyens, Elisabeth; *see* Lutyens, A.

Lutyens, Lady Emily, 1874–1964, vol. VI

Lützow, Count, *died* 1916, vol. II

Luwum, Most Rev. Janani, 1924–1977, vol. VII

Luxford, Major Rev. John Aldred, *died* 1921, vol. II

Luxford, John Hector, 1890–1971, vol. VII

Luxmoore, Rt Hon. Sir (Arthur) Fairfax (Charles Coryndon), 1876–1944, vol. IV

Luxmoore, Rt Hon. Sir Fairfax; *see* Luxmoore, Rt Hon. Sir A. F. C. C.

Luxmoore, Henry Elford, *died* 1926, vol. II

Luxton, Brig. Daniel Aston, 1891–1960, vol. V (A)

Luxton, Rt Rev. George Nasmith, 1901–1970, vol. VI

Luxton, Sir Harold, 1888–1957, vol. V

Luzzatti, Luigi, 1841–1927, vol. II

Lyal, David Hume, 1892–1965, vol. VI

Lyall, Rt Hon. Sir Alfred Comyn, 1835–1911, vol. I

Lyall, Archibald Laurence, 1904–1964, vol. VI

Lyall, Dame Beatrix Margaret, *died* 1948, vol. IV

Lyall, Charles Elliott, 1877–1942, vol. IV

Lyall, Sir Charles James, 1845–1920, vol. II

Lyall, David Robert, 1841–1917, vol. II

Lyall, Edna; *see* Bayly, Ada Ellen.

Lyall, Major Edward, 1869–1929, vol. III

Lyall, Frank Frederick, 1872–1950, vol. IV

Lyall, George, 1883–1959, vol. V

Lyall, Col Graham Thomson, 1892–1941, vol. IV

Lyall, Sir James Broadwood, 1838–1916, vol. II

Lyall, Lt-Col Robert Adolphus, 1876–1948, vol. IV

Lyall Grant, Sir Robert William, 1875–1955, vol. V

Lyautey, Marshal Hubert, 1854–1934, vol. III

Lycett, Brig. Cyril Vernon Lechmere, 1894–1978, vol. VII

Lyddon, Vice-Adm. Sir Horace Collier, 1912–1968, vol. VI

Lyddon, Col William George, 1871–1944, vol. IV

Lyde, Lionel William, 1863–1947, vol. IV

Lydekker, Richard, 1849–1915, vol. I

Lydford, Air Marshal Sir Harold Thomas, 1898–1979, vol. VII

Lye, Lt-Col Robert Cobbe, 1865–1917, vol. II

Lyell, 1st Baron, 1850–1926, vol. II

Lyell, 2nd Baron, 1913–1943, vol. IV

Lyell, Hon. Charles Henry, 1875–1918, vol. II

Lyell, Col David, 1866–1940, vol. III

Lyell, Denis David, 1871–1946, vol. IV

Lyell, Sir Maurice Legat, 1901–1975, vol. VII

Lyell, William Darling, 1860–1925, vol. II

Lygon, Major Hon. Henry, 1884–1936, vol. III

Lygon, Lt-Col Hon. Robert, 1879–1952, vol. V

Lyle of Westbourne, 1st Baron, 1882–1954, vol. V

Lyle of Westbourne, 2nd Baron, 1905–1976, vol. VII

Lyle, Sir Alexander Park, 1st Bt (*cr* 1929), 1849–1933, vol. III

Lyle, Sir Archibald Moir Park, 2nd Bt (*cr* 1929), 1884–1946, vol. IV

Lyle, Charles, 1851–1929, vol. III

Lyle, Col George Samuel Bateson, 1865–1943, vol. IV (A)

Lyle, Sir Harold, 1873–1927, vol. II

Lyle, Henry Samuel, 1857–1916, vol. II

Lyle, Herbert Willoughby, *died* 1956, vol. V

Lyle, Col Hugh Thomas, 1858–1942, vol. IV

Lyle, Sir Ian D., 1907–1978, vol. VII

Lyle, James Duncan, 1887–1972, vol. VII

Lyle, John Cromie, 1862–1947, vol. IV

Lyle, Sir Oliver, 1890–1961, vol. VI

Lyle, Robert, 1905–1966, vol. VI

Lyle, Robert Charles, 1887–1943, vol. IV

Lyle, Sir Robert Park, 1st Bt (*cr* 1915), 1859–1923, vol. II

Lyle, Robert Patton Ranken, 1870–1950, vol. IV

Lyle, Samuel, *died* 1941, vol. IV

Lyle, Thomas Keith, 1903–1987, vol. VIII

Lyle, Thomas McElderry, 1886–1962, vol. VI

Lyle, Sir Thomas Ranken, 1860–1944, vol. IV

Lyle, William, 1871–1949, vol. IV

Lyle-Samuel, Alexander, 1883–1942, vol. IV
Lymer, Brig. Rymel Watts, 1909–1972, vol. VII
Lymington, Viscount; Oliver Kintzing Wallop, 1923–1984, vol. VIII
Lynam, Alfred Edmund, 1873–1956, vol. V
Lynam, Edward William O'Flaherty, died 1950, vol. IV
Lynam, Jocelyn Humphrey Rickman, 1902–1978, vol. VII
Lynch, Col Arthur 1861–1934, vol. III
Lynch, Col Charles Joseph, born 1878, vol. III
Lynch, Col David A., 1880–1944, vol. IV
Lynch, Finian, 1889–1966, vol. VI
Lynch, Francis Joseph, 1909–1980, vol. VII
Lynch, George, 1868–1928, vol. II
Lynch, George William Augustus, died 1940, vol. III
Lynch, G(erald) Roche, 1889–1957, vol. V
Lynch, Hannah, died 1904, vol. I
Lynch, Henry Finnis Blosse, 1862–1913, vol. I
Lynch, Sir Henry Joseph, 1878–1958, vol. V
Lynch, John Gilbret Bohun, 1884–1928, vol. II
Lynch, Sir John Patrick, 1858–1921, vol. II
Lynch, Patrick, died 1947, vol. IV
Lynch, Hon. Patrick Joseph, 1867–1944, vol. IV
Lynch, Rt Hon. Sir Phillip Reginald, 1933–1984, vol. VIII
Lynch, Richard Irwin,1850–1924, vol. II
Lynch, Captain Vincent James, 1892–1961, vol. VI
Lynch, William Joseph, 1853–1937, vol. III
Lynch-Blosse, Sir David Edward, 16th Bt, 1925–1971, vol. VII
Lynch-Blosse, Sir Henry, 15th Bt, 1884–1969, vol. VI
Lynch-Blosse, Sir Robert Cyril; see Blosse.
Lynch-Blosse, Sir Robert Geoffrey; see Blosse.
Lynch-Robinson, Sir Christopher Henry, 2nd Bt, 1884–1958, vol. V
Lynch-White, Lt-Col Robert, 1875–1940, vol. III
Lynd, Robert, 1879–1949, vol. IV
Lynd, Sylvia, 1888–1952, vol. V
Lynde, Carleton John, 1872–1971, vol. VII
Lynden-Bell, Maj.-Gen. Sir Arthur Lynden, 1867–1943, vol. IV
Lynden-Bell, Col Edward Horace Lynden, 1858–1922, vol. II
Lyndhurst, Lady; (Georgina), died 1901, vol. I
Lyne, Arthur W., 1884–1971, vol. VII
Lyne, Joseph Leycester; see Ignatius, Father.
Lyne, Rev. Leonard Augustus, died 1919, vol. II
Lyne, Maj.-Gen. Lewis Owne, 1899–1970, vol. VI
Lyne, Robert Francis, 1885–1957, vol. V
Lyne, Robert Nunez, 1864–1961, vol. VI
Lyne, Rear-Adm. Sir Thomas John Spence, 1870–1955, vol. V
Lyne, Hon. Sir William John, 1844–1913, vol. I
Lynen, Feodor Felix Konrad, 1911–1979, vol. VII
Lynes, Rear-Adm. Charles Edward, 1875–1977, vol. VII
Lynes, Rear-Adm. Hubert, 1874–1942, vol. IV
Lynham, John E. A., 1882–1946, vol. IV
Lynn, Col Graham Rigby, died 1966, vol. VI
Lynn, Rev. Joseph, 1887–1956, vol. V
Lynn, Ralph, 1882–1962, vol. VI
Lynn, Sir Robert, 1873–1945, vol. IV
Lynn, Stanley B.; see Balfour-Lynn.

Lynn, William H., died 1915, vol. I
Lynn-Jenkins, Frank, 1870–1927, vol. II
Lynn-Thomas, Sir John, 1861–1939, vol. III
Lynskey, Sir George Justin, 1888–1957, vol. V
Lynx, Larry; see Sarl, Arthur J.
Lyon, Sir Alexander, 1850–1927, vol. II
Lyon, Lt-Col Charles, 1865–1944, vol. IV
Lyon, Brig.-Gen. Charles Harry, 1878–1959, vol. V
Lyon, Brig. Cyril Arthur, 1880–1955, vol. V
Lyon, Hon. Sir David B.; see Bowes-Lyon.
Lyon, David Murray, 1888–1956, vol. V
Lyon, Brig.-Gen. Francis, 1867–1953, vol. V
Lyon, Hon. Francis B.; see Bowes-Lyon.
Lyon, Maj.-Gen. Sir Francis James Cecil B.; see Bowes-Lyon.
Lyon, Captain Geoffrey Francis B.; see Bowes-Lyon.
Lyon, Adm. Sir George Hamilton D'Oyly, 1883–1947, vol. IV
Lyon, Adm. Herbert, 1856–1919, vol. II
Lyon, Hugh; see Lyon, P. H. B.
Lyon, Brig. Surg. Lt-Col Isidore Bernadotte, 1839–1911, vol. I
Lyon, Kenneth, 1886–1956, vol. V
Lyon, Laurance, 1875–1932, vol. III
Lyon, Malcolm Douglas, 1898–1964, vol. VI
Lyon, Hon. Michael Claude Hamilton B.; see Bowes-Lyon.
Lyon, Percy Comyn, 1862–1952, vol. V
Lyon, (Percy) Hugh (Beverley), 1893–1986, vol. VIII
Lyo, Lt-Col Ralph Edward, 1865–1930, vol. III
Lyon, Rev. Ralph John, died 1914, vol. I
Lyon, Robert, 1894–1978, vol. VII
Lyon, Captain Ronald George B.; see Bowes Lyon.
Lyon, Thomas Glover, 1855–1915, vol. I
Lyon, Thomas Henry, 1825–1914, vol. I
Lyon, Thomas Stewart, 1866–1946, vol. IV
Lyon, Ursula Mary, died 1961, vol. VI
Lyon, Ven. William John, 1883–1961, vol. VI
Lyon Dean, William John; see Dean.
Lyons of Brighton, Baron (Life Peer); Braham Jack Dennis Lyons, 1918–1978, vol. VII
Lyons, A. Neil, 1880–1940, vol. III
Lyons, Abraham Montagu, 1894–1961, vol. VI
Lyons, Sir Algernon McLennan, 1833–1908, vol. I
Lyons, Hon. Dame Enid Muriel, 1897–1981, vol. VIII
Lyons, Eric Alfred, 1912–1980, vol. VII
Lyons, Francis Stewart Leland, 1923–1983, vol VIII
Lyons, Col Sir Henry George, 1864–1944, vol. IV
Lyons, James, 1887–1983, vol. VIII
Lyons, Most Rev. John, 1878–1958, vol. V
Lyons, Sir Joseph, died 1917, vol. II
Lyons, Rt Hon. Joseph Aloysius, 1879–1939, vol. III
Lyons, Mrs Miriam Isabel, 1880–1968, vol. VI
Lyons, Most Rev. Patrick, 1875–1949, vol. IV
Lyons, Most Rev. Patrick Francis, 1903–1967, vol. VI
Lyons, Brig. Richard Clarke, 1893–1981, vol. VIII
Lyons, Thomas, 1896–1985, vol. VIII
Lyons, Sir William, 1901–1985, vol. VIII
Lyons, Rt Hon. William Henry Holmes, 1843–1924, vol. II
Lyons-Montgomery, Col Hugh Frederick, 1856–1931, vol. III

Lys, Christian; *see* Brebner, P. J.
Lys, Rev. Francis John, 1863–1947, vol. IV
Lysaght, Desmond Royse, 1903–1970, vol. VI
Lysaght, Gerald Stuart, 1869–1951, vol. V
Lysaght, Hon. Horace George,1873–1918, vol. II
Lysaght, Sidney Royse, *died* 1941, vol. IV
Lysaght, William Royse, 1858–1945, vol. IV
Lysons, Sir Daniel, 1816–1898, vol. I
Lyster, Anthony St George, 1888–1971, vol. VII
Lyster, Adm. Sir (Arthur) Lumley (St George), 1888–1957, vol. V
Lyster, Cecil Rupert Chaworth, 1859–1920, vol. II
Lyster, Lt-Gen. Harry Hammon, 1830–1922, vol. II
Lyster, Very Rev. Henry Cameron, 1862–1932, vol. III
Lyster, Rt Rev. John,1850–1911, vol. I
Lyster, Adm. Sir Lumley; *see* Lyster, Adm. Sir A. L. St G.
Lyster, Robert Arthur, *died* 1955, vol. V
Lyster, Thomas William, 1855–1922, vol. II
Lyte, Sir Henry Churchill Maxwell-, 1848–1940, vol. III
Lythgoe, Sir James, 1891–1972, vol. VII
Lythgoe, Richard James, 1896–1940, vol. III
Lyttelton, Rt Hon. Alfred, 1857–1913, vol. I
Lyttelton, Hon. Mrs Alfred, (Dame Edith Lyttelton), *died* 1948, vol. IV
Lyttleton, Rt Rev. Hon. Arthur Temple, 1852–1903, vol. I
Lyttelton, Rev. Hon. Charles Frederick, 1887–1931, vol. III
Lyttelton, Dame Edith Sophie; *see* Lyttelton, Hon. Mrs Alfred.
Lyttelton, Rev. Hon. Edward, 1855–1942, vol. IV
Lyttelton, Hon. George William, 1883–1962, vol. VI
Lyttelton, Hon. George William Spencer, 1847–1913, vol. I
Lyttelton, Gen. Rt Hon. Sir Neville Gerald, 1845–1931, vol. III
Lyttelton, Hon. Robert Henry, 1854–1939, vol. III
Lyttelton, Comdr Stephen Clive, 1887–1959, vol. V
Lyttelton-Annesley, Lt-Gen. Sir Arthur Lyttelton, 1837–1926, vol. II
Lytton, 2nd Earl of, 1876–1947, vol. IV
Lytton, 3rd Earl of, 1879–1951, vol. V
Lytton, 4th Earl of, 1900–1985, vol. VIII
Lytton, Countess of; (Edith), 1841–1936, vol. III
Lytton, Lady Constance Georgina, 1869–1923, vol. II
Lytton, Sir Henry Alfred, 1867–1936, vol. III
Lytton Sells, Arthur Lytton,1895–1978, vol. VII
Lyveden, 2nd Baron, 1824–1900, vol. I
Lyveden, 3rd Baron, 1857–1926, vol. II
Lyveden, 4th Baron, 1892–1969, vol. VI
Lyveden, 5th Baron, 1888–1973, vol. VII
Lywood, Air Vice-Marshal Oswyn George William Gifford, 1895–1957, vol. V

M

Maartens, Maarten, 1858–1915, vol. I
Maas, Paul, 1880–1964, vol. VI

Maasdorp, Hon. Sir Andries Ferdinand Stockenström, 1847–1931, vol. III
Maasdorp, Christian George, 1848–1926, vol. II
Maass, Otto, 1890–1961, vol. VI
Mabane, 1st Baron, 1895–1969, vol. VI
Mabbott, John David, 1898–1988, vol. VIII
Maberly, Col Charles Evan, 1854–1920, vol. II
Mabie, Hamilton Wright, *died* 1917, vol. II
Mabson, Richard Rous, 1846–1933, vol. III
Maby, Sir Charles George, 1888–1967, vol. VI
Macadam, Sir Ivison Stevenson, 1894–1974, vol. VII
McAdam, Robert, 1906–1978, vol. VII
Macadam, Col Walter, 1865–1930, vol. III
M'Adam, Walter, 1866–1935, vol. III
McAdam, William, 1886–1952, vol. V
MacAdam, William, 1885–1976, vol. VII
McAdam, William Alexander, 1889–1961, vol. VI
McAdden, Sir Stephen James, 1907–1979, vol. VII
McAdoo, William Gibbs, 1863–1941, vol. IV
Macafee, Charles Horner Greer, 1898–1978, vol. VII
Macafee, Col John Leeper Anketell, 1915–1974, vol. VII
McAleer, Hugh K., *died* 1941, vol. IV
Macaleese, Daniel, 1840–1900, vol. I
MacAlevey, Maj.-Gen. Gerald Esmond, 1894–1969, vol. VI
Macalister, Alexander, 1844–1919, vol. II
Macalister, Charles John, *died* 1943, vol. IV
MacAlister, Sir Donald, 1st Bt, 1854–1934, vol. III
Macalister, George Hugh Kidd, 1879–1930, vol. III
MacAlister, Sir Ian, 1878–1957, vol. V
MacAlister, Sir John Young Walker, 1856–1925, vol. II
McAlister, Mary A., (Mrs J. Alexander McAlister), *died* 1976, vol. VII
Macalister, Robert Alexander Stewart, 1870–1950, vol. IV
Macalister, Sir Robert Lachlan,1890–1967, vol. VI
McAlister, Samuel, 1896–1971, vol. VII
McAlister, William James, 1877–1937, vol. III
Macalister-Hall, William, 1872–1938, vol. III
McAllen, Captain Thomas Wilfred, 1888–1957, vol. V
McAllister, Alister; *see* Wharton, Anthony.
McAllister, Gilbert, 1906–1964, vol. VI
McAllister, Sir Reginald Basil, *born* 1900, vol. VIII
Macallum, Archibald Byron, 1858–1934, vol. III
McAlpin, Malcolm Caird, 1876–1930, vol. III
McAlpine of Moffat, Baron (Life Peer); Robert Edwin McAlpine, 1907–1990, vol. VIII
McAlpine, Sir Alfred David, 1881–1944, vol. IV
McAlpine, Sir (Alfred) Robert, 3rd Bt, 1907–1968, vol. VI
McAlpine, Archibald Douglas; *see* McAlpine, D.
McAlpine, Douglas, 1890–1981, vol. VIII
MacAlpine, Sir George Watson, 1850–1920, vol. II
McAlpine, Hon. Sir John Kenneth, 1906–1984, vol. VIII
MacAlpine, J(ohn) Warren, *died* 1956, vol. V
McAlpine, Sir Malcolm; *see* McAlpine, Sir T. M.
McAlpine, Sir Robert; *see* McAlpine, Sir A. R.
McAlpine, Sir Robert, 1st Bt, 1847–1934, vol. III
McAlpine, Sir Robert, 2nd Bt, 1868–1934, vol. III

McAlpine, Sir Thomas George Bishop, 4th Bt, 1901–1983, vol. VIII

McAlpine, Sir (Thomas) Malcolm, 1877–1967, vol. VI

Malcalpine-Leny, Bt Lt-Col R. L.; *see* Leny.

Macan, Sir Arthur Vernon, 1843–1908, vol. I

Macan, Reginald Walter, 1848–1941, vol. IV

Macan, Col Thomas Townley, 1860–1934, vol. III

Macan-Markar, Hadji Sir Mohamed, 1879–1952, vol. V (A), vol. VI (AI)

McAnally, Rev. Charles Mortimer, 1854–1938, vol. III

McAnally, Sir Henry William Watson, 1870–1952, vol. V

Macandie, George Lionel, 1877–1968, vol. VI

MacAndrew, 1st Baron, 1888–1979, vol. VII

MacAndrew, 2nd Baron, 1919–1989, vol. VIII

Macandrew, Sir Henry Cockburn, 1832–1898, vol. I

Macandrew, Maj.-Gen. Henry John Milnes, 1866–1919, vol. II

MacAndrew, Lt-Col James Orr, 1899–1979, vol. VII

Macann, Lt-Col Arthur Ernest Henry, 1898–1944, vol. IV

Macara, Sir (Charles) Douglas, 3rd Bt, 1904–1982, vol. VIII

Macara, Sir Charles Wright, 1st Bt, 1845–1929, vol. III

Macara, Sir Douglas; *see* Macara, Sir C. D.

McAra, Sir Thomas W., 1864–1942, vol. IV

Macara, Sir William Cowper, 2nd Bt, 1875–1931, vol. III

M'Ardle, John Stephen, 1859–1928, vol. II

McArdle, Michael John Francis, 1909–1989, vol. VIII

McArdle, Sean; *see* McArdle, M. J. F.

Macardle, Sir Thomas Callan, 1856–1925, vol. II

M'Arthur, Alexander, 1814–1909, vol. I

M'Arthur, Charles, 1844–1910, vol. I

MacArthur, (David) Wilson, 1903–1981, vol. VIII

McArthur, Donald Neil, 1892–1965, vol. VI

MacArthur, General of the Army Douglas, 1880–1964, vol. VI

McArthur, Hon. Sir Gordon Stewart, 1896–1965, vol. VI

Macarthur, Sir Ian Hannay, 1906–1975, vol. VII

Macarthur, Rt Rev. James, 1848–1922, vol. II

McArthur, Col Sir Malcolm Hugh, 1912–1985, vol. VIII

MacArthur, Mary Reid, 1880–1921, vol. II

MacArthur, Neil, 1886–1973, vol. VII

MacArthur, Sir Oliphant; *see* MacArthur, Sir W. O.

McArthur, Hon. Sir Stewart; *see* McArthur, Hon. Sir W. G. S.

M'Arthur, William Alexander, 1857–1923, vol. II

McArthur, Hon. Sir (William Gilbert) Stewart, 1861–1935, vol. III

McArthur, William Lyon, 1870–1946, vol. IV

MacArthur, Sir (William) Oliphant, 1871–1953, vol. V

MacArthur, Lt-Gen. Sir William Porter, 1884–1964, vol. VI

MacArthur, Wilson; *see* MacArthur, D. W.

Macarthur-Onslow, Maj.-Gen. Sir Denzil, 1904–1984, vol. VIII

Macarthur Onslow, Brig.-Gen. George Macleay, 1875–1931, vol. III

Macarthur-Onslow, Maj.Gen. Hon. James William, 1867–1946, vol. IV

Macartney, Sir Alexander Miller, 5th Bt, 1869–1960, vol. V

Macartney, Carlile Aylmer, 1895–1978, vol. VII

Macartney, Sir Edward Henry, 1863–1956, vol. V

Macartney, Sir George, 1867–1945, vol. IV

Macartney, Sir Halliday; *see* Macartney, Sir S. H.

Macartney, Lt-Col Henry Dundas Keith, 1880–1932, vol. III

Macartney, Sir John, 3rd Bt, 1832–1911, vol. I

Macartney, John William Ellison-, 1818–1904, vol. I

Macartney, John William Merton, 1850–1925, vol. II

Macartney, Sir Mervyn Edmund, *died* 1932, vol. III

Macartney, Sir (Samuel) Halliday, 1833–1906, vol. I

Macartney, Rt Hon. Sir William Grey Ellison-, 1852–1924, vol. II

Macartney, Sir William Isaac, 4th Bt, 1867–1942, vol. IV

Macartney-Filgate, John Victor Opynschae, 1897–1964, vol. VI

Macaskie, Charles Frederick Cunningham, 1888–1969, vol. VI

Macaskie, Nicholas Lechmere Cunningham, 1881–1967, vol. VI

Macaskie, Stuart Cunningham, 1853–1903, vol. I

Macassey, Rev. Ernest Livingston, *died* 1947, vol. IV

Macassey, Sir Lynden Livingston, 1876–1963, vol. VI

M'Aulay, Alexander, 1863–1931, vol. III

Macaulay, Rev. Alexander Beith, 1871–1950, vol. IV

Macaulay, Sir Alfred Newton, 1864–1939, vol. III

McAulay, Allan; *see* Stewart, Charlotte.

Macaulay, Lt-Col Archibald Duncan Campbell, 1897–1982, vol. VIII

Macaulay, Dame (Emily) Rose, 1881–1958, vol. V

Macaulay, Francis Sowerby, 1862–1937, vol. III

Macaulay, Frederic Julius, 1830–1912, vol. I

Macaulay, Sir Hamilton, 1901–1986, vol. VIII

Macaulay, G. C., 1852–1915, vol. I

Macaulay, James, 1817–1902, vol. I

Macaulay, Very Rev. James J., 1870–1951, vol. V

Macaulay, James Morison, 1889–1955, vol. V

Macaulay, Rev. John Heyrick, *died* 1914, vol. I

McAulay, (John) Roy (Vincent), 1933–1987, vol. VIII

Macaulay, Hon. Leopold, 1887–1979, vol. VII

Macaulay, Dame Rose; *see* Macaulay, Dame E. R.

McAulay, Roy; *see* McAulay, J. R. V.

Macaulay, Thomas Bassett, 1860–1942, vol. IV

Macaulay, William Herrick, 1853–1936, vol. III

Macaulay, William J. B., 1892–1964, vol. VI

Macaulay-Owen, Peter, 1906–1962, vol. VI

Macauley, Brig. Gen. Sir George Bohun, 1869–1940, vol. III

McAuliffe, Gen. Anthony Clement, 1898–1975, vol. VII

McAuliffe, Sir Henry T., 1867–1951, vol. V

McAvity, Lt-Col Thomas Malcolm, 1889–1944, vol. IV

Macbain, Alexander, 1855–1907, vol. I

McBain, Alexander Richardson, 1887–1971, vol. VII

M'Bain, James Anderson Dickson, 1869–1938, vol. III

McBain, James William, 1882–1953, vol. V
McBain, Rev. John, 1871–1936, vol. III
McBarnet, Alexander Cockburn, 1867–1934, vol. III
M'Barnet, Lt-Col Alexander Edward, 1865–1932, vol. III
McBean, Col Alexander, 1854–1937, vol. III
McBean, Angus Rowland, 1904–1990, vol. VIII
Macbean, Maj.-Gen. Forbes, 1857–1919, vol. II
Macbean, Gen. George Scougal, died 1903, vol. I
Macbean, Captain John Albert Emmanuel, 1865–1900, vol. I
Macbean, Reginald Gambier, 1859–1942, vol. IV
Macbeath, Alexander,1888–1964, vol. VI
Macbeath, Rev. John, died 1967, vol. VI
McBeath, Rear-Adm. John Edwin Home, 1907–1982, vol. VIII
McBeath, Sir William George, 1865–1931, vol. III
McBee, Silas, 1853–1924, vol. III
Macbeth, Alexander Killen, 1889–1957, vol. V
Macbeth, Rev. John,1841–1924, vol. II
Macbeth, Percy, 1877–1938, vol. III
Macbeth, Robert Walker, 1848–1910, vol. I
Macbeth-Raeburn, Henry Raeburn; see Raeburn.
McBey, James, 1883–1959, vol. V
MacBride, Alexander, 1859–1955, vol. V
MacBride, Ernest William, 1866–1940, vol. III
MacBride, Geoffrey Ernest Derek, 1917–1975, vol. VII
McBride, Neil, 1910–1974, vol. VII
M'Bride, Hon. Sir Peter,1867–1923, vol. II
M'Bride, Peter, 1854–1946, vol. IV
McBride, Rt Hon. Sir Philip Albert Martin, 1892–1982, vol. VIII
M'Bride, Sir Richard, 1870–1917, vol. II
McBride, Robert, died 1934, vol. III
Macbride, Robert Knox, 1844–1905, vol. I
MacBridge, Seán, 1904–1988, vol. VIII
McBride, Wilbert George, 1879–1943, vol. IV
McBride, Vice-Adm. Sir William,1895–1959, vol. V
MacBrien, Maj.-Gen. Sir James Howden, 1878–1938, vol. III
McBryde, Hon. Duncan Elphinstone, 1853–1920, vol. II
McBurney, Charles Brian Montagu, 1914–1979, vol. VII
McCabe, Alasdair, died 1972, vol. VII
M'Cabe, Sir Daniel, 1852–1919, vol. II
MacCabe, Sir Francis Xavier Frederick, 1833–1914, vol. I
McCabe, Joseph, 1867–1955, vol. V
McCabe, Most Rev. Thomas, 1902–1983, vol. VIII
Maccaffrey, Rt Rev. Mgr James, 1875–1935, vol. III
McCahearty, Ven. Reginald George Henry, died 1966, vol. VI
McCall, Sir Alexander, died 1973, vol. VII
McCall, Charles James, 1907–1989, vol. VIII
McCall, Charles William Home, 1877–1958, vol. V
Maccall, Hon. Maj.-Gen. Henry Blackwood, 1845–1921, vol. II
McCall, Adm. Sir Henry William Urquhart, 1895–1980, vol. VII
McCall, Lt-Col Hugh William, 1878–1957, vol. V
M'Call, Hon. Sir John, 1860–1919, vol. II
M'Call, Brig.-Gen. John P.; see Pollok-M'Call.

McCall, Kenneth Murray, 1912–1987, vol. VIII
McCall, Sir Robert Alfred, 1849–1934, vol. III
McCall, Robert Clark, 1906–1970, vol. VI
McCall, Rt Rev. Theodore Bruce, 1911–1969, vol. VI
McCall, William, 1851–1929, vol. III
MacCallan, Arthur Ferguson, died 1955, vol. V
McCallum, Colin Whitton; see Coborn, Charles.
McCallum, Major Sir Duncan, 1888–1958, vol. V
McCallum, Brig. Frank, 1900–1983, vol. VIII
McCallum, Col Sir Henry Edward, 1852–1919, vol. II
MacCallum, James Dalgleish Kellie, 1845–1932, vol. III
McCallum, Rev. John Donaldson, 1856–1930, vol. III
McCallum, Major John Dunwoodie Martin, 1883–1967, vol. VI
M'Callum, Sir John Mills, 1847–1920, vol. II
MacCallum, Sir Mungo William, 1854–1942, vol. IV
MacCallum, Sir Peter, 1885–1975, vol. VII
McCallum, Ronald Buchanan, 1898–1973, vol. VII
McCallum, Sir William Alexander, 1883–1959, vol. V
MacCalman, Douglas Robert, 1903–1957, vol. V
M'Calmont, Col Barklie Cairns, 1860–1929, vol. III
M'Calmont, Harry Leslie Blundell, 1861–1902, vol. I
McCalmont, Maj.-Gen. Sir Hugh, 1845–1924, vol. II
M'Calmont, James Martin, 1847–1913, vol. I
McCalmont, Brig.-Gen. Sir Robert Chaine Alexander, 1881–1953, vol. V
M'Cammond, Sir William, 1831–1898, vol. I
McCance, Sir Andrew, 1889–1983, vol. VIII
McCandlish, Douglas, 1883–1954, vol. V
McCandlish, Maj.-Gen. John Edward Chalmers, 1901–1974, vol. VII
McCandlish, Lt-Col Patrick Dalmahoy, 1871–1942, vol. IV
McCann, Sir Charles Francis Gerald, 1880–1951, vol. V
McCann, Frederick John, died 1941, vol. IV
McCann, Hugh James, 1916–1986, vol. VIII
M'Cann, James, died 1904, vol. I
McCann, Most Rev. James, 1897–1983, vol. VIII
McCann, John, 1910–1972, vol. VII
McCann, Rt Rev. Philip Justin, 1882–1959, vol. V
McCann, Pierce, died 1919, vol. II
M'Cann, Thomas S., 1868–1942, vol. IV
McCannell, Otway, 1883–1969, vol. VI
McCardie, Sir Henry Alfred, 1869–1933, vol. III
McCarrison, Maj.-Gen. Sir Robert,1878–1960, vol. V
McCarroll, James Joseph, 1889–1937, vol. III
McCarroll, Col James Neil, 1873–1951, vol. V
McCarron, Edward Patrick, died 1970, vol. VI
M'Cartan, Michael, 1851–1902, vol. I
McCartan, Patrick, 1878–1963, vol. VII
MacCarthy, Sir Desmond, 1877–1952, vol. V
McCarthy, Adm. Sir Desmond; see McCarthy, Adm. Sir E. D. B.
McCarthy, Adm. Sir (Edward) Desmond (Bewley), 1893–1966, vol. VI
McCarthy, Most Rev. Edward Joseph, 1850–1931, vol. III
McCarthy, Sir Edwin, 1896–1980, vol. VII
McCarthy, Dame (Emma) Maud, 1858–1949, vol. IV
McCarthy, Sir Frank, died 1924, vol. II
M'Carthy, James Desmond, 1839–1923, vol. II

McCarthy, Rt Rev. James W., 1853–1943, vol. IV
M'Carthy, Jeremiah, *died* 1924, vol. II
M'Carthy, Most Rev. John, 1858–1950, vol. IV
McCarthy, John Haydon, 1914–1984, vol. VIII
McCarthy, John William, 1854–1935, vol. III
McCarthy, Joseph R., 1909–1957, vol. V
M'Carthy, Justin, 1830–1912, vol. I
M'Carthy, Justin Huntly, 1861–1936, vol. III
McCarthy, Hon. Leighton Goldie, 1869–1952, vol. V
McCarthy, Sir Leslie Ernest Vivian, 1885–1970, vol. VI
McCarthy, Lillah, (Lady Keeble), 1875–1960, vol. V
M'Carthy, Marie Cecilia, 1876–1943, vol. IV
McCarthy, Mary, (Mrs James West), 1912–1989, vol. VIII
McCarthy, Dame Maud; *see* McCarthy, Dame E. M.
McCarthy, Michael John Fitzgerald, *died* 1928, vol. II
MacCarthy, Brig.-Gen. Morgan John, 1867–1939, vol. III
McCarthy, Sir Mortimer Eugene, 1890–1967, vol. VI
McCarthy, Ralph, 1906–1976, vol. VII
M'Carthy, Robert Henry, *died* 1927, vol. II
McCarthy, Tim, *died* 1928, vol. II
McCarthy, Lt-Col W. H. Leslie, 1885–1962, vol. VI
Maccarthy, Rt Rev. Welbore, *died* 1925, vol. II
MacCarthy-Morrogh, Lt-Col Donald Florence, 1869–1932, vol. III
McCarthy-O'Leary, Brig. Heffernan William Denis; *see* O'Leary.
Maccartie, Lt-Col Frederick Fitzgerald, 1851–1916, vol. II
McCartney, James Elvins, 1891–1969, vol. VI
McCaughey, Sir (David) Roy, 1898–1971, vol. VII
M'Caughey, Sir Roy; *see* McCaughey, Sir D. R.
M'Caughey, Hon. Sir Samuel, *died* 1919, vol. II
McCaul, Ethel Rosalie Ferrier, 1867–1931, vol. III
McCauley, Ven. George James, *died* 1917, vol. II
McCauley, Air Marshal Sir John Patrick Joseph, 1899–1989, vol. VIII
M'Causland, Lt-Gen. Edwin Loftus, *died* 1923, vol. II
McCausland, Lucius Perronet T.; *see* Thompson-McCausland.
McCausland, Rt Hon. Maurice Marcus, 1872–1938, vol. III
M'Causland, Sir Richard Bolton, 1810–1900, vol. I
McCausland, Maj. Gen. William Henry, 1836–1916, vol. II
McCaw, George Tyrrell, 1870–1942, vol. IV
MacCaw, Sir Vivian, 1883–1936, vol. III
MacCaw, William John MacGeagh, *died* 1928, vol. II
McCawley, Thomas William, 1881–1925, vol. II
McCay, Lt-Col David, 1873–1948, vol. IV
M'Cay, Lt-Gen. Hon. Sir James Whiteside, 1864–1930, vol. III
McCay, Lt-Gen. (Hon.) Sir Ross Cairns, 1895–1969, vol. VI
McCheane, Col Montague William Hiley, 1872–1955, vol. V
MacChesney, Brig.-Gen. Nathan William, 1878–1954, vol. III
McClaughry, Air Vice-Marshal Wilfred Ashton, 1894–1943, vol. IV
McClean, (Donald Francis) Stuart, 1909–1960, vol. V

McClean, Sir Francis Kennedy, 1876–1955, vol. V
M'Clean, Frank, 1837–1904, vol. I
McClean, Rt Rev. Gerard; *see* McClean, Rt Rev. J. G.
McClean, Rt Rev. (John) Gerard, 1914–1978, vol. VII
McClean, Rev. Richard Arthur, 1862–1948, vol. IV
McClean, Stuart; *see* McClean, D. F. S.
McCleary, George Frederick, 1867–1962, vol. VI
McCleary, Robert, 1869–1936, vol. III
McCleery, Rt Hon. Sir William Victor, 1887–1957, vol. V
M'Clelan, Hon. Abner Reid, 1831–1917, vol. II
McClellan, Frank Campbell, 1871–1957, vol. V
McClellan, George B., 1865–1940, vol. III
M'Clellan, Rev. John B., *died* 1916, vol. II
McClellan, John William Tyndale, 1865–1948, vol. IV
McClelland, Rev. Henry Simpson, 1882–1961, vol. VI
McClelland, Hugh Charles, 1893–1966, vol. VI
M'Clelland, John Alexander, 1870–1920, vol. II
McClelland, Sir Peter Hannay, 1856–1924, vol. II
McClelland, William, 1889–1968 (this entry was not transferred to Who was Who).
McClelland, William, 1873–1971, vol. VII
McClemens, John Henry, 1905–1975, vol. VII
Macclement, William Thomas, 1861–1938, vol. III
McClenaghan, Ven. Henry St George, 1865–1950, vol. IV
McClenaghan, Herbert Eric St George, 1896–1955, vol. V
Macclesfield, 7th Earl of, 1888–1975, vol. VII
McClintic, Katharine, (Mrs Guthrie McClintic); *see* Cornell, K.
M'Clintock, Lt-Col Arthur George, 1878–1936, vol. III
M'Clintock, Arthur George Florence, 1856–1930, vol. III
M'Clintock, Major Augustus, 1866–1912, vol. I
McClintock, Very Rev. Francis George le Poer, *died* 1924, vol. II
M'Clintock, Sir Francis Leopold, 1819–1907, vol. I
McClintock, Bt Col John Knox, 1864–1936, vol. III
McClintock, Vice-Adm. John William Leopold, 1874–1929, vol. III
McClintock, Lt-Col Robert Lyle, 1874–1943, vol. IV
McClintock, Brig.-Gen. William Kerr, 1858–1940, vol. III
McCloughry, Air Vice-Marshal Edgar James K.; *see* Kingston-McCloughry.
McCloy, John Jay, 1895–1989, vol. VIII
McCloy, John Moorcroft, 1874–1943, vol. IV
M'Clure, Alexander Logan, 1860–1932, vol. III
M'Clure, Rev. Edmund, *died* 1922, vol. II
McClure, George Buchanan, 1887–1955, vol. V
McClure, Ivor Herbert, *died* 1981, vol. VIII
McClure, J. Campbell, 1873–1934, vol. III
M'Clure, James Gore King, 1848–1932, vol. III
McClure, Sir John David, 1860–1922, vol. II
McClure, Samuel S., 1857–1949, vol. IV
MacClure, Victor, 1887–1963, vol. VI
McClure, Sir William Kidston, 1877–1939, vol. III
McClure-Smith, Hugh Alexander, 1902–1961, vol. VI

McCluskey, Alexander, 1908–1959, vol. V

M'Clymont, Rt Rev. James A., 1848–1927, vol. II

McClymont, Lt-Col Robert Arthur, 1874–1949, vol. IV

MacColl, Sir Albert Edward, 1882–1951, vol. V

McColl, Sir Alexander Lowe, 1878–1962, vol. VI

McColl, Angus John, 1854–1902, vol. I

MacColl, Dugald Sutherland, 1859–1948, vol. IV

McColl, Col George Guthrie, 1858–1938, vol. III

MacColl, James Eugene, 1908–1971, vol. VII

M'Coll, Hon. James Hiers, 1844–1929, vol. III

MacColl, Rev. Malcolm, 1831–1907, vol. I

MacColl, Norman, 1843–1905, vol. I

MacColl, René, 1905–1971, vol. VII

McCollum, Elmer Verner, 1879–1967, vol. VI

McColvin, Lionel Roy, 1896–1976, vol. VII

McComas, Robert Bond, 1862–1938, vol. III

McComb, James Ellis, 1909–1982, vol. VIII

McComb, Col Robert Brophy, 1855–1925, vol. II, vol. III

McComb, Rev. Samuel, 1864–1938, vol. III

McCombe, Francis William Walker, 1894–1969, vol. VI

McCombe, Lt-Col Gault, 1885–1970, vol. VI (AII)

McCombe, Brig. John Smith, 1885–1959, vol. V

McCombie, Major Hamilton, 1880–1962, vol. VI

McCombie, Col William McCombie D.; *see* Duguid-McCombie.

McCombs, Hon. Sir Terence Henderson, 1905–1982, vol. VIII

McConachie, George William Grant, 1909–1965, vol. VI

M'Conaghey, Lt-Col Allen, 1864–1925, vol. II

McConaghy, Hugh, 1877–1943, vol. IV

McConaghy, Col John Gerald, 1879–1942, vol. IV

McConnach, James, 1896–1955, vol. V

McConnan, Sir Leslie James, 1887–1954, vol. V

McConnel, Maj.-Gen. Douglas Fitzgerald, 1893–1961, vol. VI

McConnel, John Wanklyn, 1855–1922, vol. II

McConnell, Adams Andrew, 1884–1973, vol. VII

McConnell, Gerard Hamilton, 1913–1982, vol. VIII

McConnell, Sir Joseph, 2nd Bt, 1877–1942, vol. IV

M'Connell, Robert, *died* 1942, vol. IV

M'Connell, Sir Robert John, 1st Bt, 1853–1927, vol. II

McConnell, Comdr Sir Robert Melville Terence, 3rd Bt, 1902–1987, vol. VIII

McConnell, Sir Thomas Edward, 1868–1938, vol. III

M'Connell, W. R., 1837–1906, vol. I

McConnell, William Samuel, 1904–1982, vol. VIII

McCorkell, Sir Dudley Evelyn Bruce, 1883–1960, vol. V

McCorkill, Hon. John Charles, 1854–1920, vol. II

MacCormac, Henry, *died* 1950, vol. IV

Mac Cormac, Sir William, 1st Bt, 1836–1901, vol. I

McCormack, Arthur John, 1866–1936, vol. III

MacCormack, Charles Joseph, 1861–1952, vol. V

Maccormack, Rt Rev. Francis Joseph, 1833–1909, vol. I

McCormack, John, Count, 1884–1945, vol. IV

McCormack, John William, 1891–1980, vol. VII

McCormack, Rt Rev. Joseph, 1887–1958, vol. V

McCormack, Percy Hicks, 1890–1980, vol. VII

McCormack, Robert John Murray, 1922–1981, vol. VIII

McCormack, Hon. William, 1879–1947, vol. IV

MacCormick, Sir Alexander, 1856–1947, vol. IV

McCormick, Lt-Col Andrew Louis Charles, 1869–1943, vol. IV

McCormick, Anne O'Hare, *died* 1954, vol. V

M'Cormick, Arthur David, 1860–1943, vol. IV

McCormick, Ven. George Fitzherbert, *died* 1935, vol. III

McCormick, Gerald Bernard, *died* 1966, vol. VI

McCormick, Rev. James, *died* 1921, vol. II

McCormick, Major James Hanna, 1875–1955, vol. V

MacCormick, John MacDonald, 1904–1961, vol. VI

McCormick, Rt Rev. John Newton, 1863–1939, vol. III (A), vol. IV

McCormick, Rev. Joseph, 1834–1914, vol. I

McCormick, Very Rev. Joseph Gough, 1874–1924, vol. II

MacCormick, Brig. Kenneth, 1891–1963, vol. VI

McCormick, Adm. Lynde Dupuy, 1895–1956, vol. V

M'Cormick, Robert, *died* 1919, vol. II

McCormick, Robert Rutherford, 1880–1955, vol. V

McCormick, Rev. William Patrick Glyn, 1877–1940, vol. III

M'Cormick, Sir William Symington, 1859–1930, vol. III

McCormick-Goodhart, Leander, 1884–1965, vol. VI

McCorquodale of Newton, 1st Baron, 1901–1971, vol. VII

McCosh, Andrew Kirkwood, 1880–1967, vol. VI

McCosh, Robert, 1885–1959, vol. VI

McCourt, Hon. William, *died* 1913, vol. I

McCourt, William Rupert, 1884–1947, vol. IV

McCowan, Sir David, 1st Bt, 1860–1937, vol. III

McCowan, Sir David James Cargill, 2nd Bt, 1897–1965, vol. VI

McCowan, Lt-Col William Hew, 1878–1958, vol. V

McCowen, Oliver Hill, 1870–1942, vol. IV

M'Coy, Sir Frederick, 1823–1899, vol. I

McCoy, Captain James Abernethy, 1900–1955, vol. V

Maccoy, Sir John, 1843–1935, vol. III

McCoy, William Frederick, *died* 1976, vol. VII

McCoy, William Taylor, 1866–1929, vol. III

McCracken, Esther Helen, 1902–1971, vol. VII

McCracken, Lt-Gen. Sir Frederick William Nicholas, 1859–1949, vol. IV

Maccracken, Henry Mitchell, 1840–1919, vol. II

MacCracken, Henry Noble, 1880–1970, vol. VI

McCracken, William, *died* 1948, vol. IV

M'Crae, Sir George, 1860–1928, vol. II

McCraith, Sir Douglas, 1878–1952, vol. V

McCraith, Sir James William, 1853–1928, vol. II

M'Craith, Sir John Tom, 1847–1919, vol. II

McCraken, Sir Robert, 1846–1924, vol. II

McCray, Sir Lionel Joseph, 1908–1984, vol. VIII

McCrea, Rev. Alexander, 1879–1963, vol. VI

McCrea, Brig.-Gen. Alfred Coryton, 1864–1942, vol. IV

McCrea, Charles, 1877–1952, vol. V

McCrea, Major Frederick Bradford, 1833–1914, vol. I

McCrea, Hugh Moreland, *died* 1941, vol. IV

McCready, Hugh Latimer, 1876–1950, vol. IV

McCreery, Gen. Sir Richard Loudon,1898–1967, vol. VI

M'Crie, Charles Greig, 1836–1910, vol. I

McCrie, John Gibb, 1902–1977, vol. VII

McCrindle, Major John Ronald, 1894–1977, vol. VII

McCrone, Robert Watson, 1893–1982, vol. VIII

McCrossan, Mary, died 1934, vol. III

McCrostie, Hugh Cecil, 1897–1970, vol. VI

McCuaig, Maj.-Gen. George Eric, 1885–1958, vol. V

McCubbin, Frederick, 1855–1917, vol. II

McCubbin, Lt-Col Thomas, died 1925, vol. II, vol. III

McCullagh, Rt Hon. Sir Crawford, 1st Bt, 1868–1948, vol. IV

McCullagh, Sir Crawford; see McCullagh, Sir J. C.

M'Cullagh, Francis, 1874–1956, vol. V

MacCullagh, Sir James Acheson, 1854–1918, vol. II

McCullagh, Sir (Joseph) Crawford, 2nd Bt, 1907–1974, vol. VII

McCullagh, McKim; see McCullagh, W.McK. H.

McCullagh, (William) McKim (Herbert), 1889–1964, vol. VI

McCullers, Carson, (Mrs Carson Smith McCullers), 1917–1967, vol. VI

McCulloch, Allan Riverstone, 1885–1925, vol. II

McCulloch, Maj.-Gen. Sir Andrew Jameson, 1876–1960, vol. V

McCulloch, Derek Ivor Breashur, 1897–1967, vol. VI

M'Culloch, George, 1848–1907, vol. I

M'Culloch, Rev. James Duff, 1836–1926, vol. II

MacCulloch, Rev. Canon John Arnott, 1868–1950, vol. IV

McCulloch, Joseph, 1893–1961, vol. VI

McCulloch, Sir Malcolm McLeod, 1894–1969, vol. VI

McCulloch, Norman George, 1882–1965, vol. VI

McCulloch, Brig.-Gen. Robert Henry Frederick, 1869–1946, vol. IV

M'Culloch, Hon. William, died 1909, vol. I

McCulloch, William Edward, 1896–1963, vol. VI

McCullough, Donald; see McCullough, W. D. H.

McCullough, Thomas Warburton, 1901–1989, vol. VIII

McCullough, (William) Donald (Hamilton), 1901–1978, vol. VII

MacCunn, Captain Fergus, 1890–1941, vol. IV

MacCunn, Hamish, 1868–1916, vol. II

McCunn, Major James, 1894–1967, vol. VI

MacCunn, John, 1846–1929, vol. III

McCurdy, Rt Hon. Charles Albert, 1870–1941, vol. IV

MacCurdy, Edward Alexander Coles, 1871–1957, vol. V

McCurdy, Hon. Fleming Blanchard, 1875–1952, vol. V

M'Curdy, J. F., 1847–1935, vol. III

MacCurdy, John Thomson, 1886–1947, vol. IV

McCusker, Harold; see McCusker, J. H.

McCusker, (James) Harold, 1940–1990, vol. VIII

M'Cutcheon, George Barr, 1866–1928, vol. II

McCutcheon, Katharine Howard, 1875–1956, vol. V

McCutcheon, Hon. (Malcolm) Wallace, 1906–1969, vol. VI

McCutcheon, Sir Osborn; see McCutcheon, Sir W. O.

McCutcheon, Hon. Wallace; see McCutcheon, Hon. M. W.

McCutcheon, Sir (Walter) Osborn, 1899–1983, vol. VIII

McDavid, Sir Edwin Frank, 1895–1980, vol. VII

McDavid, Sir Herbert Gladstone, 1898–1966, vol. VI

McDavid, James Wallace, 1887–1964, vol. VI

MacDermot, The, (Charles Edward), 1862–1947, vol. IV

MacDermot, The, (Charles John), 1899–1979, vol. VII

MacDermot, The, (Sir Dermot MacDermot), 1906–1989, vol. VIII

MacDermot, The, (Rt Hon. Hugh Hyacinth O'Rorke), 1834–1904, vol. I

MacDermot, Charles Edward; see MacDermot, The.

MacDermot, Charles John; see MacDermot, The.

MacDermot, Sir Dermot; see MacDermot, The.

MacDermot, Captain Ffrench, died 1917, vol. II

MacDermot, Rev. Henry Myles Fleetwood, 1837–1918, vol. II

MacDermot, Rt Hon. Hugh Hyacinth O'Rorke; see MacDermot, The.

MacDermot, Terence W. L., 1896–1966, vol. VI

MacDermot-Roe, The; see MacDermot, Captain Ffrench.

MacDermott, Baron (Life Peer); John Clarke MacDermott, 1896–1979, vol. VII

M'Dermott, Edward R., 1847–1932, vol. III

McDermott, Geoffrey Lyster, 1912–1978, vol. VII

Mac Dermott, Rev. George Martius, 1863–1939, vol. III

McDermott, John Frederick, 1906–1958, vol. V

Macdermott, Patrick, 1859–1942, vol. IV

M'Dermott, Peter Joseph, 1858–1922, vol. II

Macdiarmid, Sir Allan Campbell, 1880–1945, vol. IV

Macdiarmid, Duncan Stewart, 1873–1954, vol. V

Macdiarmid, Hon. Finlay George, 1869–1933, vol. III

McDiarmid, Hugh; see Grieve, C. M.

Macdiarmid, Niall Campbell, 1919–1978, vol. VII

Macdona, Brian Fraser,1901–1971, vol. VII

Macdona, John Cumming, 1836–1907, vol. I

McDonagh, James Eustace Radclyffe, 1881–1965, vol. VI

Macdonagh, Michael, 1860–1946, vol. IV

Macdonald, 6th Baron, 1853–1947, vol. IV

Macdonald, 7th Baron, 1909–1970, vol. VI

Macdonald of Earnscliffe, Baroness (1st in line), 1836–1920, vol. II

Macdonald of Gwaenysgor, 1st Baron, 1888–1966, vol. VI

Macdonald, Adam Davidson, 1895–1978, vol. VII

Macdonald, Lt-Gen. Alastair M'Ian, 1830–1910, vol. I

Macdonald, Alexander, died 1921, vol. II

Macdonald, Alexander, 1878–1939, vol. III

Macdonald, Most Rev. Alexander, 1858–1941, vol. IV

MacDonald, Alexander, 1894–1954, vol. V

McDonald, Alexander, 1903–1968, vol. VI

McDonald, Sir Alexander Forbes, 1911–1981, vol. VIII

McDonald, Alexander Hugh, 1908–1979, vol. VII

Macdonald of Sleat, Sir (Alexander) Somerled (Angus Bosville), 16th Bt (*cr* 1625), 1917–1958, vol. V

Macdonald of the Isles, Sir Alexander Wentworth Macdonald Bosville, 14th Bt (*cr* 1625), 1865–1933, vol. III

Macdonald, Rev. Allan John Macdonald, 1887–1959, vol. V

Macdonald, Allan Ronald, 1906–1984, vol. VIII

M'Donald, Sir Andrew, 1836–1919, vol. II

Macdonald, Hon. Andrew Archibald, 1829–1912, vol. I

Macdonald, Most Rev. Andrew Joseph, 1871–1950, vol. IV

Macdonald, Most Rev. Angus, 1844–1900, vol. I

Macdonald, Angus Alexander, 1904–1965, vol. VI

Macdonald, Hon. Angus Lewis, *died* 1954, vol. V

Macdonald, Angus Roderick, 1858–1944, vol. IV

McDonald, Air Comdt Ann Smith, 1914–1972, vol. VII

Macdonald, Anne, *died* 1958, vol. V

MacDonald, Anne Elizabeth Campbell Bard, (Betty MacDonald), 1908–1958, vol. V

Macdonald, Archibald James Florence, 1904–1983, vol. VIII

Macdonald, Sir Archibald John, 4th Bt (*cr* 1813), 1871–1919, vol. II

Macdonald, Sir Archibald Keppel, 3rd Bt (*cr* 1813), 1820–1901, vol. I

Macdonald, Col Archibald William, 1869–1939, vol. III

Macdonald, Sir Arthur, 1887–1953, vol. V

Macdonald, Lt-Col Arthur Cameron, *died* 1940, vol. III

Macdonald, Augustine Colin, 1837–1919, vol. II

MacDonald, Betty; *see* MacDonald, A. E. C. B.

McDonald, Bouverie Francis Primrose, 1861–1931, vol. III

Macdonald of Sleat, Miss Celia Violet Bosville, 1889–1976, vol. VII

M'Donald, Hon. Charles, *died* 1925, vol. II

Macdonald, Charles Blair, 1855–1939, vol. III

McDonald, Sir Charles George, 1892–1970, vol. VI

Macdonald, Charles James Black, 1864–1930, vol. III

MacDonald, Col Charles Joseph, 1862–1947, vol. IV

Macdonald, Lt-Col Charles Leslie, 1881–1939, vol. III

Macdonald, Col Clarence Reginald, 1876–1962, vol. VI

Macdonald, Rt Hon. Sir Claude Maxwell, 1852–1915, vol. I

Macdonald, Coll, 1924–1983, vol. VIII

Macdonald, Daniel Alexander, 1858–1937, vol. III

MacDonald, David Keith Chalmers, 1920–1963, vol. VI

Macdonald, Adm. David R.; *see* Robertson-Macdonald.

Macdonald, Donald, *died* 1932, vol. III

McDonald, Sir Donald, 1849–1934, vol. III

McDonald, Hon. Donald, *born* 1865, vol. III

Macdonald, Maj.-Gen. Sir Donald Alexander, 1845–1920, vol. II

Macdonald, Rev. Donald Bruce, 1872–1962, vol. VI

Macdonald, Donald Farquhar, 1906–1988, vol. VIII

Macdonald, Donald Hardman, 1908–1990, vol. VIII

Macdonald, Air Vice-Marshal Donald Malcolm Thomas, 1909–1988, vol. VIII

Macdonald, Major Donald R., 1884–1934, vol. III

MacDonald, Douglas George, 1930–1989, vol. VIII

MacDonald, Rev. Duncan, 1885–1941, vol. IV

Macdonald, Rev. Duncan Black, 1863–1943, vol. IV

Macdonald, Edward Mortimer, 1865–1940, vol. III

Macdonald, Dame Ethel, *died* 1941, vol. IV

Macdonald, Rev. Frederic William, 1842–1928, vol. II

Macdonald, Rev. Frederick Charles, *died* 1936, vol. III

Macdonald, Rev. Frederick William, 1848–1928, vol. II

Macdonald, George, 1824–1905, vol. I

Macdonald, Sir George, 1862–1940, vol. III

Macdonald, George, 1903–1967, vol. VI

MacDonald, George Alan, 1909–1985, vol. VIII

Macdonald, Hon. Godfrey Evan Hugh, 1879–1915, vol. I

Macdonald of the Isles, Sir Godfrey Middleton Bosville, 15th Bt (*cr* 1625), 1887–1951, vol. V

MacDonald, Greville, 1856–1944, vol. IV

McDonald, Brig.-Gen. Harold French, 1885–1943, vol. IV

Macdonald, Maj.-Gen. Harry, 1886–1976, vol. VII

Macdonald, Maj.-Gen. Sir Hector Archibald, 1853–1903, vol. I

Macdonald, Hector Munro, 1865–1935, vol. III

Macdonald, Hugh, 1885–1958, vol. V

M'Donald, Hugh Campbell, 1869–1921, vol. II

Macdonald, Hon. Sir Hugh John, 1850–1929, vol. III

Macdonald, Ian Wilson, 1907–1989, vol. VIII

Macdonald, Ishbel Allan; *see* Peterkin, I. A.

Macdonald, James, 1852–1913, vol. I

Macdonald, James, 1877–1954, vol. V

Macdonald, James, 1898–1963, vol. VI

McDonald, Sir James, 1899–1989, vol. VIII

Macdonald, James Alexander, 1862–1923, vol. II

Macdonald, Hon. James Alexaner, 1858–1939, vol. III (A), vol. IV

Macdonald, Maj.-Gen. James Balfour, 1898–1959, vol. V

MacDonald, James E. H., *died* 1932, vol. III

McDonald, Sir James Gordon, 1867–1942, vol. IV

Macdonald, James Harold, 1878–1955, vol. V

MacDonald, Rt Hon. James Ramsay, 1866–1937, vol. III

Macdonald, Maj.-Gen. Sir James Ronald Leslie, 1862–1927, vol. II

Macdonald, James Smith, 1873–1923, vol. II

MacDonald, James Stuart, 1878–1952, vol. V

MacDonald, John, 1843–1928, vol. II

Macdonald, John, *died* 1940, vol. III

McDonald, Sir John, 1874–1964, vol. VI

Macdonald, Col John Andrew, 1837–1916, vol. II

Macdonald, Rt Hon. John Archibald Murray, 1854–1939, vol. III

Macdonald, John Blake, 1829–1902, vol. I

Macdonald, Sir John Denis, 1826–1908, vol. I

Macdonald, Maj.-Gen. John Frederick Matheson, 1907–1979, vol. VII

McDonald, Hon. Sir John Gladstone Black, 1898–1977, vol. VII

Macdonald, Rt Hon. Sir John Hay Athole; *see* Kingsburgh, Rt Hon. Lord.

MacDonald, Most Rev. John Hugh, 1881–1965, vol. VI

Macdonald, John Robert, 1879–1965, vol. VI

Macdonald, John Ronald Moreton, 1873–1921, vol. II

Macdonald, John Smyth, 1867–1941, vol. IV

Macdonald, Rev. John Somerled, 1871–1956, vol. V

Macdonald, John William, 1882–1934, vol. III

Macdonald, Lt-Col Kenneth Lachlan, 1867–1938, vol. III

MacDonald, Sir Kenneth Mackenzie, 1879–1954, vol. V

Macdonald, Mrs L. M., (L. M. Montgomery), 1874–1942, vol. IV

MacDonald, Rt Hon. Malcolm John, 1901–1981, vol. VIII

Macdonald, Dame Margaret Henderson, (Dame Margaret Kidd), 1900–1989, vol. VIII

Macdonald, Sir Murdoch, 1866–1957, vol. V

McDonald, Niel, 1886–1968, vol. VI

Macdonald, Col Norman, 1890–1948, vol. IV

Macdonald, Patrick Donald, 1909–1987, vol. VIII

Macdonald, Sir Percy, *died* 1957, vol. V

Macdonald, Percy Stuart, 1890–1945, vol. IV

Macdonald, Captain Sir Peter Drummond, 1895–1961, vol. VI

Macdonald, Sir Peter George, 1898–1983, vol. VIII

MacDonald, Pirie, 1867–1942, vol. IV

MacDonald, Ranald, 1868–1931, vol. III

Macdonald, Ranald Mackintosh, 1860–1928, vol. II

Macdonald, Sir Reginald John, 1820–1899, vol. I

MacDonald, Lt-Col Reginald Percy, *born* 1856, vol. II

MacDonald, Robert, *died* 1971, vol. VII

McDonald, Sir (Robert) Ross, 1888–1964, vol. VI

Macdonald, Lt-Col Roderick William, 1881–1959, vol. V

MacDonald, Ronald, 1860–1933, vol. III

McDonald, Sir Ross; *see* McDonald, Sir Robert R.

McDonald, Samuel, 1877–1957, vol. V

Macdonald of Sleat, Sir Somerled; *see* Macdonald of Sleat, Sir A. S. A. B.

Macdonald, Air Vice-Marshal Somerled Douglas, 1899–1979, vol. VII

Macdonald, Maj.-Gen. Stuart, 1861–1939, vol. III

MacDonald, Sydney Gray, 1879–1946, vol. IV

MacDonald, Hon. Sir Thomas Lachlan, 1898–1980, vol. VII

McDonald, Thomas Pringle, 1901–1969, vol. VI

M'Donald, Rev. Walter, 1854–1920, vol. II

McDonald, Sir Warren D'Arcy, 1901–1965, vol. VI

Macdonald, William, 1875–1935, vol. III

Macdonald, Captain William Balfour, 1870–1937, vol. III

Macdonald, Sir William Christopher, 1831–1917, vol. II

MacDonald, Air Chief Marshal Sir William Laurence Mary, 1908–1984, vol. VIII

Macdonald, William Marshall, 1872–1956, vol. V

Macdonald, William Rae, 1843–1923, vol. II

Macdonald-Buchanan, Major Sir Reginald Narcissus, 1898–1981, vol. VIII

Macdonald-Tyler, Sir Henry Hewey Francis, 1877–1962, vol. VI

McDonell, Æneas Ranald, 1875–1941, vol. IV

Macdonell, Angus Claude, 1861–1924, vol. II

Macdonell, Lt-Gen. Sir Archibald Cameron, 1864–1941, vol. IV

Macdonell, Archibald Gordon, 1895–1941, vol. IV

Macdonell, Maj.Gen. Hon. Archibald Hayes, 1868–1939, vol. III

Macdonell, Arthur Anthony, 1854–1930, vol. III

MacDonell, Edgar Errol Napier, 1874–1928, vol. II

Macdonell, Rt Hon. Sir Hugh Guion, 1832–1904, vol. I

Macdonell, Sir John, 1846–1921, vol. II

Macdonell, Rt Hon. Sir Philip James, 1873–1940, vol. III

Macdonnell, 1st Baron, 1844–1925, vol. II

McDonnell, Col Hon. Angus, 1881–1966, vol. VI

M'Donnell, Col Francis, 1828–1904, vol. I

Macdonnell, Henry, 1839–1922, vol. II

McDonnell, Col John, 1851–1928, vol. II

Macdonnell, Very Rev. John Cotter, *died* 1902, vol. I

MacDonnell, John de Courcy, 1869–1915, vol. I

MacDonnell, Mark Antony, 1854–1906, vol. I

MacDonnell, Mervyn Sorley, 1880–1949, vol. IV

McDonnell, Sir Michael Francis Joseph, 1882–1956, vol. V

Macdonnell, Hon. Norman Scarth, 1886–1938, vol. III

M'Donnell, Richard Grant Peter Purcell, *died* 1927, vol. II

McDonnell, Hon Sir Schomberg Kerr, 1861–1915, vol. I

Macdonnell, Col William, 1831–1919, vol. II, vol. III

Macdonnell, Rt Rev. William Andrew, 1853–1920, vol. II

Macdonogh, Lt-Gen. Sir George Mark Watson, 1865–1942, vol. IV

McDouall, John Crichton, 1912–1979, vol. VII

McDouall, Brig.-Gen. Robert, 1871–1941, vol. IV

M'Douall, William, 1855–1924, vol. II

M'Douall, Thomas William Houldsworth, 1885–1931, vol. III

M'Dougald, John, 1848–1919, vol. II

Macdougall, Maj.-Gen. Alastair Ian, 1888–1972, vol. VII

MacDougall, Brig.-Gen. Alexander, 1878–1927, vol. II

MacDougall, Alexander James, 1872–1953, vol. V

MacDougall, Sir Alexander Maclean, 1878–1953, vol. V

McDougall, Alexander Patrick, *died* 1959, vol. V

McDougall, Archibald, 1903–1984, vol. VIII

MacDougall of MacDougall, Madam; (Coline Helen Elizabeth), 1904–1990, vol. VIII

McDougall, Dugald Gordon, 1867–1944, vol. IV

M'Dougall, Ernest Hugh, 1877–1908, vol. I

McDougall, Frank Lidgett, 1884–1958, vol. V

Macdougall, Gordon Walters, *died* 1947, vol. IV

MacDougall, Air Cdre Ian Neil, 1920–1987, vol. VIII

MacDougall, Maj.-Gen. James Charles, 1863–1927, vol. II

McDougall, James Currie, 1890–1957, vol. V
MacDougall, Sir James Patten, 1849–1919, vol. II
M'Dougall, Sir John, 1844–1917, vol. II
McDougall, John Bowes, 1890–1967, vol. VI
McDougall, John Henry Gordon, 1889–1969, vol. VI
M'Dougall, John Lorn, 1838–1909, vol. I
MacDougall, Leslie Grahame, 1896–1974, vol. VII
McDougall, Sir Malcolm, 1899–1970, vol. VI
Macdougall, Margaret, died 1943, vol. IV
MacDougall, Sir Raibeart MacIntyre, 1892–1949, vol. IV
McDougall, Richard Sedgwick, 1904–1983, vol. VIII
McDougall, Sir Robert, 1871–1938, vol. III
McDowall, Robert John Stewart, 1892–1990, vol. VIII
Macdougall, Robert Stewart, 1862–1947, vol. IV
MacDougall, Lt-Col Stewart, 1854–1916, vol. II
Macdougall, Hon. William, 1822–1905, vol. I
McDougall, William, 1871–1938, vol. III
Macdougall, William Brown, died 1936, vol. III
M'Dowall, Rev. Charles Robert Loraine, 1872–1950, vol. IV
McDowall, Robert William, 1914–1987, vol. VIII
McDowall, Roger Gordon, 1886–1972, vol. VII
McDowall, Rev. Stewart Andrew, 1882–1935, vol. III
M'Dowall, Thomas William, died 1936, vol. III
McDowell, Lt-Col Arnott Edward Connell, 1883–1944, vol. IV
MacDowell, Col Charles Carlyle, died 1959, vol. V
McDowell, Donald Keith, 1867–1940, vol. III
M'Dowell, Surg.-Col Edmund Greswold, 1831–1907, vol. I
Macdowell, Edward, 1861–1908, vol. I
McDowell, Sir Frank Schofield, 1889–1982, vol. VIII
McDowell, John, 1874–1936, vol. III
MacDowell, Lt-Col Thain Wendell, 1890–1960, vol. V
McDowell, William Fraser, 1858–1937, vol. III
MacDuff, John Levy, 1905–1963, vol. VI
Mace, Cecil Alec, 1894–1971, vol. VII
Mace, Comdr Frederick William, 1872–1960, vol I
MacEacharn, Hon. Sir Malcolm Donald, 1852–1910, vol. I
McEachern, Malcolm, died 1945, vol. IV
M'Eachran, Duncan, 1841–1926, vol. II, vol. III
M'Elderry, Robert Knox, 1869–1949, vol. IV
McElderry, Samuel Burnside Boyd, 1885–1984, vol. VIII
McEleney, Most Rev. John, 1895–1986, vol. VIII
McElheran, Robert Benjamin, died 1939, vol. III
McElhone, Frank, 1929–1982, vol. VIII
McElligott, Edward John, died 1946, vol. IV
McElligott, James, 1893–1974, vol. VII
McElligott, Neil Martin, 1915–1989, vol. VIII
McElroy, Neil H., 1904–1972, vol. VII
McElroy, Robert, 1872–1959, vol. V
McElwaine, Sir Percy Alexander, 1884–1969, vol. VI
Mac Enri, (Henry), Seaghan P., died 1930, vol. III
McEntee, 1st Baron, 1871–1953, vol. V
MacEntee, Seán, 1889–1984, vol. VIII
McEntegart, Air Vice-Marshal Bernard, 1891–1954, vol. V
MacEoin, Lt-Gen. Seán, 1893–1973, vol. VII
M'Evay, Most Rev. Fergus Patrick, 1852–1911, vol. I

MacEvilly, Most Rev. John, 1817–1902, vol. I
McEvoy, Ambrose, 1878–1927, vol. II
M'Evoy, Charles, 1879–1929, vol. III
McEvoy, John Alexander, 1882–1935, vol. III
MacEwan, David, 1830–1910, vol. I
MacEwan, David, 1846–1927, vol. II
MacEwan, Very Rev. James, died 1911, vol. I
MacEwan, Peter, 1856–1917, vol. II
M'Ewan, Rt Hon. William, 1827–1913, vol. I
MacEwen, Sir Alexander Malcolm, 1875–1941, vol. IV
MacEwen, Alexander R., 1851–1916, vol. II
MacEwen, Alexander Robert, 1894–1946, vol. IV
MacEwen, Brig.-Gen. Douglas Lilburn, 1867–1941, vol. IV
McEwen, Sir James Francis Lindley, 4th Bt, 1960–1983, vol. VIII
McEwen, Sir James Napier Finnie, 2nd Bt, 1924–1971, vol. VII
McEwen, Rt Hon. Sir John, 1900–1980, vol. VII
MacEwen, John A. C., died 1944, vol. IV
McEwen, Sir John Blackwood, 1868–1948, vol. IV
McEwen, Sir John Helias Finnie, 1st Bt, 1894–1962, vol. VI
MacEwen, Brig.-Gen. Maurice Lilburn, 1869–1943, vol. IV
Macewen, Air Vice-Marshal Sir Norman Duckworth Kerr, 1881–1953, vol. V
McEwen, Robert Finnis, 1861–1926, vol. II
McEwen, Sir Robert Lindley, 3rd Bt, 1926–1980, vol. VII
MacEwen, Sir William, 1848–1924, vol. II
McEwin, Hon. Sir (Alexander) Lyell, 1897–1988, vol. VIII
McEwin, Hon. Sir Lyell; see McEwin, Hon. Sir A. L.
Macey, John Percival, 1906–1987, vol. VIII
MacFadden, Arthur William James, 1869–1933, vol. III
McFadden, Hon. David Henry, 1856–1935, vol. III
M'Fadden, Edward, 1862–1922, vol. II
McFadden, Gertrude Violet, died 1963, vol. VI
McFadyean, Sir Andrew, 1887–1974, vol. VII
McFadyean, Sir John, 1853–1941, vol. IV
Macfadyen, Allan, 1860–1907, vol. I
Macfadyen, Air Marshal Sir Douglas, 1902–1968, vol. VI
Macfadyen, Rev. Dugald, 1867–1936, vol. III
Macfadyen, Sir Eric, 1879–1966, vol. VI
M'Fadyen, John Edgar, 1870–1933, vol. III
Macfadyen, William Allison, 1865–1924, vol. II
McFall, David Bernard, 1919–1988, vol. VIII
Macfall, Haldane, 1860–1928, vol. II
Macfall, John Edward Whitley, 1873–1938, vol. III
Macfarlan, Brig.-Gen. Frederic Alexander, 1866–1954, vol. V
Macfarlan, Hon. Sir James Ross, 1872–1955, vol. V
McFarland, Arthur, 1893–1966, vol. VI
McFarland, Sir Basil Alexander Talbot, 2nd Bt, 1898–1986, vol. VIII
McFarland, Bryan Leslie, 1900–1963, vol. VI
MacFarland, Sir John Henry, 1851–1935, vol. III
MacFarland, Robert Arthur Henry, died 1922, vol. II
Macfarlane, Rt Rev. Angus, 1843–1912, vol. I
McFarlane, Sir Charles Stuart, 1895–1958, vol. V

458

Macfarlane, Col David Mason, 1862–1930, vol. III
Macfarlane, Donald, 1882–1946, vol. IV
Macfarlane, Sir Donald Horne, 1830–1904, vol. I
Macfarlane, Very Rev. Dugald, 1869–1956, vol. V
Macfarlane, Brig.-Gen. Duncan Alwyn, 1857–1941, vol. IV
MacFarlane, Lt-Gen. Sir (Frank) Noel Mason-, 1889–1953, vol. V
Macfarlane, George James, 1855–1933, vol. III
Macfarlane, George Lewis; *see* Ormidale, Hon. Lord.
Macfarlane, Hon. James, 1844–1914, vol. I
Macfarlane, Sir James, 1857–1944, vol. IV
Macfarlane, James Waddell, 1877–1952, vol. V
Macfarlane, Janet Alston, *died* 1980, vol. VII
Macfarlane, Lt-Gen. Sir Noel Mason-; *see* Macfarlane, Lt-Gen. Sir F. N. M.
McFarlane, Brig. Percy Muir, 1880–1946, vol. IV
Macfarlane, Robert Campbell, 1892–1963, vol. VI
Macfarlane, Robert Gwyn, 1907–1987, vol. VIII
Macfarlane, Hon. Sir Robert Mafeking, 1901–1981, vol. VIII
McFarlane, Major Ronald, 1860–1915, vol. I
McFarlane, Stuart Gordon, 1885–1970, vol. VI
Macfarlane, Thomas, 1834–1907, vol. I
Macfarlane, William Dove, *died* 1932, vol. III
Macfarlane-Grieve, Lt-Col Angus Alexander, 1891–1970, vol. VI
Macfarlane-Grieve, William Alexander, 1844–1917, vol. II
MacFarquhar, Sir Alexander, 1903–1987, vol. VIII
Macfarren, Walter Cecil, 1826–1905, vol. I
McFee, William, 1881–1966, vol. VI
MacFeely, Most Rev. Anthony C., 1909–1986, vol. VIII
McFerran, Lt-Col Edwin Millar Gilliland, 1873–1962, vol. VI
McFetrich, Cecil, 1911–1988, vol. VIII
Macfetridge, Ven. Charles, *died* 1920, vol. II
Macfetridge, William C., 1878–1957, vol. V
Macfie, Alec Lawrence, 1898–1980, vol. VII
Macfie, Brig.-Gen. Andrew Laurie, 1860–1936, vol. III
Macfie, Maj.-Gen. John Mandeville, 1891–1985, vol. VIII
Macfie, John William Scott, 1879–1948, vol. IV
Macfie, Ronald Campbell, *died* 1931, vol. III
Macfie, Col William, 1840–1912, vol. I
McGann, Lt-Col H. H., *died* 1943, vol. IV
McGarry, Hon. Thomas William, 1871–1935, vol. III
McGarvey, Daniel, 1919–1977, vol. VII
McGavin, Maj.-Gen. Sir Donald Johnstone, 1876–1960, vol. V
McGavin, Lawrie Hugh, 1868–1932, vol. III
McGaw, Andrew Kidd, 1873–1956, vol. V
McGaw, Rev. Joseph Thoburn, 1836–1905, vol. I
McGaw, William Rankin, 1900–1974, vol. VII
MacGeagh, Col Sir Henry Davies Foster, 1883–1962, vol. VII
McGee, James Dwyer, 1903–1987, vol. VIII
McGee, Rt Rev. Joseph, 1904–1983, vol. VIII
McGeer, Gerald Grattan, 1888–1947, vol. IV
Macgeorge, Col Henry King, 1865–1940, vol. III
Macgeorge, W. S. *died* 1931, vol. III
McGeough, Most Rev. Joseph F., 1903–1970, vol. VI

Macgeough Bond, Sir Walter Adrian, 1857–1945, vol. IV
McGhee, Henry George, 1898–1959, vol. V
McGhie, Maj.-Gen. John, 1914–1985, vol. VIII
MacGibbon, Rev. James, 1865–1922, vol. II
McGibbon, John E. G., *died* 1959, vol. V
M'Giffert, Arthur Cushman, 1861–1933, vol. III
McGill, Maj.-Gen. Allan, 1914–1989, vol. VIII
MacGill, Major Campbell Gerald Hertslet, 1876–1922, vol. II
McGill, Air Vice-Marshal Frank Scholes, 1894–1980, vol. VII (AII)
MacGill, Adm. Thomas, 1850–1926, vol. II
MacGillivray, Hon. Angus, 1842–1918, vol. II
MacGillivray of MacGillivray, Angus, 1865–1947, vol. IV
MacGillivray of MacGillivray, Angus Robertson, 1892–1955, vol. V
MacGillivray, Charles Watson, 1851–1932, vol. III
MacGillivray, Donald, 1862–1931, vol. III
MacGillivray, Sir Donald Charles, 1906–1966, vol. VI
MacGillivray, Evan James, 1873–1955, vol. V
Macgillivray, James Pittendrigh, 1856–1938, vol. III
Macgillivray, John, 1855–1930, vol. III
Macgillivray, John Walker, 1884–1961, vol. VI
MacGillivray, William, 1823–1917, vol. II
McGillivray, Hon. William Alexander, 1918–1984, vol. VIII
McGillycuddy, Denis Donough Charles, (The McGillycuddy of the Reeks), 1852–1921, vol. II
McGillycuddy, John Patrick, (The McGillycuddy of the Reeks), 1909–1959, vol. V
McGillycuddy, Lt-Col Ross Kinloch, (The McGillycuddy of the Reeks), 1882–1950, vol. IV
M'Gilp, Major Clyde, 1885–1918, vol. II
McGilvray, Sir William, 1887–1956, vol. V
M'Ginness, Brig-Gen. John R., 1840–1918, vol. II
McGinnety, Frank Edward, 1907–1973, vol. VII
McGirr, John Joseph Gregory, 1879–1949, vol. IV
McGivern, Cecil, 1907–1963, vol. VI
Macgivern, Rt Rev. Thomas, *died* 1900, vol. I
McGlashan, Rear-Adm. Sir Alexander Davidson, 1901–1976, vol. VII
McGlashan, Archibald A., 1888–1980, vol. VII
McGlashan, Sir George Tait, 1885–1968, vol. VI
MacGlashan, John, 1874–1948, vol. IV
McGlinn, Brig.-Gen. John Patrick, 1869–1946, vol. IV
McGonigal, Rt Hon. Sir Ambrose Joseph, 1917–1979, vol. VII
McGonigal, John, 1870–1943, vol. IV
MacGonigal, Maurice, 1900–1979, vol. VII
M'Gonigle, Rev. William Alexander, 1849–1939, vol. III
McGougan, Malcolm, 1905–1976, vol. VII
M'Goun, Archibald, 1853–1921, vol. II
McGovern, John, 1887–1968, vol. VI
McGovern, Sir Patrick Silvesta, 1895–1975, vol. VII
M'Govern, Thomas, *died* 1904, vol. I
McGovern, William Montgomery, 1897–1964, vol. VI
McGowan, 1st Baron, 1874–1961, vol. VI
McGowan, 2nd Baron, 1906–1966, vol. VI

459

McGowan, Ven. Frank, 1895–1968, vol. VI
Macgowan, Gault, 1894–1970, vol. VI
McGowan, Rt Rev. Henry, 1891–1948, vol. IV
Macgowan, Rev. William Stuart, 1864–1939, vol. III
McGowen, Hon. James Sinclair Taylor, 1855–1922, vol. II
MacGranahan, Very Rev. James, 1855–1940, vol. III(A), vol. IV
McGrath, Sir Charles; see McGrath, Sir J. C.
McGrath, Sir Charles Gullan, 1910–1984, vol. VIII
McGrath, John Cornelius, 1905–1985, vol. VIII
M'Grath, Sir Joseph, 1858–1923, vol. II
McGrath, Sir (Joseph) Charles, 1875–1951, vol. V
McGrath, Most Rev. Michael Joseph, 1882–1961, vol. VI
McGrath, Hon. Sir Patrick Thomas, 1868–1929, vol. III
McGrath, Peter William, 1931–1990, vol. VIII
McGrath, Raymond, 1903–1977, vol. VII
McGrath, Rosita, (Mrs Arthur T. McGrath); see Forbes, Joan R.
McGrath, Captain William, 1917–1942, vol. IV
M'Grath, William Martin, died 1912, vol. I
McGraw, Curtis Whittlesey, 1895–1953, vol. V
MacGregor, Alasdair Alpin, 1899–1970, vol. VI
MacGregor, Sir (Alasdair Duncan) Atholl, 1883–1945, vol. IV
Macgregor, Alastair Goold, 1919–1972, vol. VII
Macgregor, Alexander Brittan, 1909–1965, vol. VI
McGregor, Hon. Alexander John, 1864–1946, vol. IV
Macgregor, Sir Alexander S. M., 1881–1967, vol. VI
MacGregor, Alexander Stewart, 1848–1906, vol. I
MacGregor, Air Vice-Marshal Andrew, 1897–1983, vol. VIII
MacGregor, Sir Atholl; see MacGregor, Sir Alasdair D. A.
Macgregor, Col Charles Reginald, 1847–1902, vol. I(A)
MacGregor, Sir Colin Malcolm, 1901–1982, vol. VIII
Macgregor, Sir Cyril Patrick M'Connell, 5th Bt (cr 1828), 1887–1958, vol. V
Macgregor, David Hutchison, 1877–1953, vol. V
MacGregor, David Sliman, 1864–1952, vol. V
MacGregor, Duncan, 1892–1984, vol. VIII
Macgregor, Rev. Duncan Campbell, 1858–1943, vol. IV
MacGregor, Edward Ian Roy, 1911–1989, vol. VIII
MacGregor, Eric Dickson, 1886–1950, vol. IV
MacGregor, Sir Evan, 1842–1926, vol. II
Macgregor, Rev. George Hogarth Carnaby, 1892–1963, vol. VI
McGregor, Sir George Innes, 1899–1976, vol. VII
M'Gregor, Hon. Gregor, 1848–1913, vol. I
MacGregor, Gregor, 1869–1919, vol. II
MacGregor of MacGregor, Gylla Constance Susan, (Hon. Lady MacGregor of MacGregor), died 1980, vol. VII
McGregor, Air Marshal Sir Hector Douglas, 1910–1973, vol. VII
MacGregor, Col Henry Grey, 1838–1925, vol. II
MacGregor, Very Rev. James, 1832–1910, vol. I
M'Gregor, Rt Rev. Mgr James, 1860–1928, vol. II
Macgregor, James, 1889–1953, vol. V

Macgregor, James Cochran Stevenson, 1897–1949, vol. IV
Macgregor, Sir James Comyn, 1861–1935, vol. III
McGregor, James Drummond, 1838–1919, vol. II
McGregor, Hon. James Duncan, 1860–1935, vol. III
MacGregor, James Gordon, 1852–1913, vol. I
McGregor, James Reid, 1896–1984, vol. VIII
McGregor, Sir James Robert, 1889–1973, vol. VII
MacGregor, Lt-Col John, died 1932, vol. III
Macgregor, John, died 1967, vol. VI
Macgregor, John Julius, 1869–1948, vol. IV
MacGregor, John Marshall, 1879–1936, vol. III
McGregor, Kenneth, 1903–1984, vol. VIII
Macgregor, Lewis Richard, 1886–1973, vol. VII
MacGregor of MacGregor, Sir Malcolm, 5th Bt (cr 1795), 1873–1958, vol. V
MacGregor, Malcolm Evan, 1889–1933, vol. III
Macgregor, Maj.-Gen. Malcolm John Robert, 1840–1914, vol. I
Macgregor, Lt-Col Philip Arthur, 1877–1934, vol. III
Macgregor, Robert, 1847–1922, vol. II
MacGregor, Robert Anderson, 1888–1953, vol. V
MacGregor, Robert Barr, 1896–1979, vol. VII
MacGregor, Lt-Col Robert Forrester Douglas, 1885–1960, vol. V
Macgregor, Sir Robert James McConnell, 6th Bt (cr 1828), 1890–1963, vol. VI
MacGregor, Hon. Robert Malcolm, 1876–1924, vol. II
MacGregor, Robert Menzies, 1882–1946, vol. IV
MacGregor, Robert Roy, 1847–1922, vol. II
Macgregor, W. Y., 1855–1923, vol. II
MacGregor, Rt Hon. Sir William, 1847–1919, vol. II
MacGregor, William Cunningham, 1862–1934, vol. III
MacGregor, William Duncan, 1878–1974, vol. VII
Macgregor, Sir William Gordon, 4th Bt (cr 1828), 1846–1905, vol. I
Macgregor, Very Rev. William Malcolm, 1861–1944, vol. IV
Macgregor Mitchell, Hon. Lord; Robert Macgregor Mitchell, died 1938, vol. III
Macgregor-Morris, John Turner, 1872–1959, vol. V
McGrigor, Lt-Col Sir Charles Colquhoun, 4th Bt, 1893–1946, vol. IV
M'Grigor, Brig.Gen. Charles Roderic Robert, 1860–1927, vol. II
M'Grigor, Captain Sir James Rhoderick Duff, 3rd Bt, 1857–1924, vol. II
McGrigor, Adm. of the Fleet Sir Rhoderick Robert, 1893–1959, vol. V
M'Guckin, Barton, 1853–1913, vol. I
MacGuckin, Charles John Graham, died 1934, vol. III
McGuffie, Kenneth Cunningham, 1913–1972, vol. VII
McGuffin, Samuel, 1863–1952, vol. V
McGuigan, His Eminence Cardinal James Charles, 1894–1974, vol. VII
M'Guinness, Bingham, vol. III
McGuinness, Brig. Edward, 1883–1958, vol. V
McGuinness, James Henry, 1912–1987, vol. VIII
McGuinness, Joseph, died 1922, vol. II
McGuinness, Norah Allison, died 1980, vol. VII (AII)

McGuire, (Dominic) Paul, 1903–1978, vol. VII (AII)
McGuire, Paul; *see* McGuire, D. P.
McGuire, Most Rev. Terence Bernard, 1881–1957, vol. V
McGuire, Thomas Horace, 1849–1923, vol. II
McGusty, Victor William Tighe, 1887–1981, vol. VIII
MccGwire, Maj.-Gen. Edward Thomas St Lawrance, 1830–1917, vol. II
MccGwire, Lt-Col John Edward, *died* 1950, vol. IV
Machain, Monsieur, 1839–1910, vol. I
McHardy, Maj.-Gen. Alexander Anderson, 1868–1958, vol. V
McHardy, Lt-Col Sir Alexander Burness, 1842–1917, vol. II
McHardy, Rev. Archibald, 1890–1973, vol. VII
M'Hardy, Malcolm Macdonald, 1852–1913, vol. I
Macharg, Sir Andrew Simpson, 1871–1959, vol. V
Machell, James Octavius, 1837–1902, vol. I
Machell, Percy Wilfrid, 1862–1916, vol. II
Machell, Lady Valda, 1868–1951, vol. V
Machen, Arthur, 1863–1947, vol. IV
Machin, George, 1922–1989, vol. VIII
Machin, Sir Stanley, 1861–1939, vol. III
Machray, Most Rev. Robert, 1831–1904, vol. I
Machray, Robert, 1857–1946, vol. IV
Machray, Robert, 1906–1968, vol. VI
Machtig, Sir Eric Gustav, 1889–1973, vol. VII
Machugh, Rt Rev. Charles, 1855–1926, vol. II
M'Hugh, Edward, *died* 1900, vol. I
M'Hugh, Patrick Aloysius, 1858–1909, vol. I
Machugh, Lt-Col Robert Joseph, *died* 1925, vol. II
McIllree, John Henry, 1849–1925, vol. II
McIlquham, Sir Gilbert, 1863–1953, vol. V
MacIlreith, R. T., *died* 1943, vol. IV
McIlroy, Dame (Anne) Louise, 1878–1968, vol. VI
McIlroy, Dame Louise; *see* McIlroy, Dame A. L.
McIlroy, Robert, *died* 1911, vol. I
McIlroy, William Ewart Clarke, 1893–1963, vol. VI
McIlveen, Brig. Sir Arthur William, *died* 1979, vol. VII (AII)
McIlwain, Charles Howard, 1871–1968, vol. VI(AII)
MacIlwaine, Alexander Gillilan Johnson, 1887–1942, vol. IV
MacIlwaine, John Bedell Stanford, 1857–1945, vol. IV
MacIlwaine, John Elder, 1874–1930, vol. III
McIlwaine, Hon. Sir Robert, 1871–1943, vol. IV
M'Ilwraith, Jean H., *died* 1938, vol. III
McIlwraith, Sir Malcolm, 1865–1941, vol. IV
M'Ilwraith, Hon. Sir Thomas, 1835–1900, vol. I
McIlwraith, William, 1924–1968, vol. VI
McIndoe, Sir Archibald Hector, 1900–1960, vol. V
Macinerney, Michael Chartres, 1850–1929, vol. III
McInerney, Hon. Sir Murray Vincent, 1911–1988, vol. VIII
M'Inerney, Lt-Col Timothy Marcus, 1869–1929, vol. III
MacInnes, Rev. Alexander M. F., 1866–1934, vol. III
MacInnes, Rt Rev. Angus Campbell, 1901–1977, vol. VII
MacInnes, Charles Malcolm, 1891–1971, vol. VII
MacInnes, Charles Stephen, 1872–1952, vol. V
MacInnes, Colin, 1914–1976, vol. VII
MacInnes, Rt Rev. Duncan, *died* 1970, vol. VI

Macinnes, Lt-Col Duncan Sayre, 1870–1918, vol. II
MacInnes, Helen Clark, 1907–1985, vol. VIII
McInnes, James, 1901–1974, vol. VII
MacInnes, Miles, 1830–1909, vol. I
MacInnes, Rt Rev. Rennie, 1870–1931, vol. III
MacInnes, Robert Ian Aonas, 1902–1972, vol. VII
MacInnes, William Alexander, 1892–1977, vol. VII
MacInnes Shaw, Sir Douglas; *see* Shaw, Sir A. D. M.
McInnis, Lt-Col Edward Bowater, 1846–1927, vol. II
M'Inroy, Col Charles, 1838–1919, vol. II
McIntosh, Alastair James, 1913–1973, vol. VII
McIntosh, Alexander Morrison, 1877–1944, vol. IV
McIntosh, Sir Alister Donald, 1906–1978, vol. VII
McIntosh, Annie, 1871–1951, vol. V
McIntosh, Arthur Johnston, 1890–1956, vol. V
Macintosh, Douglas Clyde, 1877–1948, vol. IV(A), vol. V
MacIntosh, Duncan William, 1904–1966, vol. VI
Macintosh, Edward Hyde, 1895–1970, vol. VI
McIntosh, George, 1889–1949, vol. IV
McIntosh, Hon. Hugh Donald, 1876–1942, vol. IV
McIntosh, Ian Donald, 1908–1975, vol. VII
Macintosh, John Macintosh, *died* 1913, vol. I
McIntosh, Hon. Sir Malcolm, 1888–1960, vol. V
McIntosh, Robert, 1894–1972, vol. VII
Macintosh, Sir Robert Reynolds, 1897–1989, vol. VIII
Macintosh, Sir William, 1863–1929, vol. III
M'Intosh, William Carmichael, 1838–1931, vol. III
MacIntyre, Sir Alexander, 1879–1952, vol. V
MacIntyre, David Lowe, 1895–1967, vol. VI
McIntyre, Rev. David Martin, 1859–1938, vol. III
Macintyre, Maj.-Gen. Donald, 1831–1903, vol. I
McIntyre, Donald, 1891–1954, vol. V
Macintyre, Sir Donald, 1891–1978, vol. VII
Macintyre, Maj.-Gen. Donald Charles Frederick, 1859–1938, vol. III
McIntyre, F(rederick) Donald (Livingstone), 1905–1981, vol. VIII
MacIntyre, Ian, 1869–1946, vol. IV
Macintyre, Captain Ian Agnew Patteson, 1893–1967, vol. VI
McIntyre, Rev. Canon James, 1888–1978, vol. VII
McIntyre, Cardinal James Francis Aloysius, 1886–1979, vol. VII
McIntyre, James Gordon; *see* Sarn, Hon. Lord.
M'Intyre, Hon. Sir John, 1832–1904, vol. I
Macintyre, John, 1859–1928, vol. II
M'Intyre, Most Rev. John, 1855–1934, vol. III
McIntyre, Air Vice-Marshal Sir John, *died* 1950, vol. IV.
M'Intyre, John M'Intyre, 1842–1930, vol. III
McIntyre, Air Commodore Kenneth John, 1908–1989, vol. VIII
McIntyre, Sir Laurence Rupert, 1912–1981, vol. VIII
Macintyre, Margaret, *died* 1943, vol. IV
McIntyre, Raymond, *died* 1933, vol. III
Macintyre, Very Rev. Ronald George, 1863–1954, vol. V
McIntyre, Stuart Charles, 1912–1989, vol. VIII
McIntyre, William Keverall, 1882–1969, vol. VI
McIntyre, Surgeon Rear-Adm. William Percival Edwin, 1903–1986, vol. VIII
MacIver, Alan Squarey, 1894–1975, vol. VII

MacIver, Arthur Milne, 1905–1972, vol. VII
MacIver, Major Sir Charles, 1866–1935, vol. III
MacIver, David, 1840–1907, vol. I
MacIver, David R.; *see* Randall-MacIver.
M'Iver, Sir Lewis, 1st Bt, 1846–1920, vol. II
MacIver, Robert Morrison, 1882–1970, vol. VI
McIver, William, 1871–1930, vol. III
Mack, Alan Frederick, 1920–1989, vol. VIII
Mack, Rear-Adm. Frederick Robert Joseph, 1897–1959, vol. V
Mack, Sir Henry; *see* Mack, Sir W. H. B.
Mack, Sir Hugh, 1832–1920, vol. II
Mack, Hon. Jason Miller, 1843–1927, vol. II
Mack, John David, *died* 1957, vol. V
Mack, Rear-Adm. Philip John, 1892–1943, vol. IV
Mack, Hon. Sir Ronald William, 1904–1968, vol. VI
Mack, Sir William George, 1904–1979, vol. VII
Mack, Sir (William) Henry (Bradshaw), 1894–1974, vol. VII
McKaig, Col Sir John Bickerton, 1883–1962, vol. VI
Mackail, Denis George, 1892–1971, vol. VII
Mackail, John William, 1859–1945, vol. IV
Mackain of Ardnamurchan, Rev. William James, 1854–1936, vol. III
Mackarness, Ven. Charles Coleridge, 1850–1918, vol. II
Mackarness, Cuthbert George Milford, 1890–1962, vol. VI
Mackarness, Frederic Coleridge, 1854–1920, vol. II
Mackawee, Khan Bahadur Sir Mohamed Abdul Kader, 1875–1954, vol. V(A)
Mackay, Hon. Lord; Alexander Morrice Mackay, 1875–1955, vol. V
Mackay, Æneas James George, 1839–1911, vol. I
McKay, Sir Alex, (Sir Alick Benson McKay), 1909–1983, vol. VIII
Mackay, Alexander Grant, 1860–1920, vol. II
Mackay, Hon. Col Alexander Howard, 1848–1929, vol. III
Mackay, Alexander Morrice; *see* Mackay, Hon. Lord.
McKay, Sir Alick Benson; *see* McKay, Sir Alex.
McKay, Andrew Foggo, 1923–1979, vol. VII
McKay, Sir Charles Holly, 1896–1972, vol. VII
MacKay, Donald G., 1870–1958, vol. V
MacKay, Donald MacCrimmon, 1922–1987, vol. VIII
McKay, Hon. Sir Donald Norman, 1908–1988, vol. VIII
MacKay, Ebenezer, 1864–1920, vol. II
Mackay, Edward Fairbairn, 1868–1953, vol. V
Mackay, Eric, 1851–1898, vol. I
Mackay, Ernest John Henry, 1880–1943, vol. IV
Mackay, George, *died* 1949, vol. IV
Mackay, Hon. George Hugh, 1872–1961, vol. VI
McKay, Sir George Mills, 1869–1937, vol. III
Mackay, Gillian Helen, (Mrs Walter Tallis), 1923–1984, vol. VIII
Mackay, Helen M. M., 1891–1965, vol. VI
Mackay, Rev. Henry Falconar Barclay, *died* 1936, vol. III
McKay, Col Henry Kellock, 1850–1930, vol. III
Mackay, Henry Martyn, 1868–1930, vol. III
Mackay, Ian Keith, 1909–1985, vol. VIII

MacKay, Ira Allen, 1875–1934, vol. III
Mackay, Lt-Gen. Sir Iven Giffard, 1882–1966, vol. VI
M'Kay, James, 1862–1931, vol. III
Mackay, Maj.-Gen. Hon. James Alexander Kenneth, 1859–1935, vol. III
Mackay, James Francis, 1855–1933, vol. III
Mackay, Sir James Mackerron, 1907–1985, vol. VIII
Mackay, Jessie, 1864–1938, vol. III
Mackay, John, 1839–1914, vol. I
Mackay, Rev. John, *died* 1938, vol. III
McKay, Ven. John, 1870–1942, vol. IV
McKay, John, *died* 1964, vol. VI
Mackay, Ven. John Alexander, 1838–1923, vol. II
Mackay, John Alexander, 1889–1983, vol. VIII
Mackay, Lt-Col John F., *died* 1930, vol. III
Mackay, Hon. John Keiller, 1888–1970, vol. VI
Mackay, John Martin, 1899–1970, vol. VI
Mackay, Rev. John Robertson, 1865–1939, vol. III
Mackay, John Sturgeon, 1843–1914, vol. I
Mackay, John William, 1831–1902, vol. I
McKay, John William, 1883–1936, vol. III
Mackay, John Yule, 1860–1930, vol. III
Mackay, Brig. Kenneth, 1901–1974, vol. VII
Mackay, Rev. Canon Malcolm, 1873–1953, vol. V
Mackay, Mary; *see* Corelli, Marie.
Mackay, Hon. Robert, 1840–1916, vol. II
Mackay, Robert John, 1859–1935, vol. III
Mackay, Very Rev. Roderick John, 1874–1956, vol. V
Mackay, Ronald William Gordon, 1902–1960, vol. V
M'Kay, Hon. Thomas, 1839–1912, vol. I
Mackay, William Æneas, 1871–1929, vol. III
Mackay, Lt-Col William Bertie, 1863–1938, vol. III
Mackay, Sir William Calder, 1896–1990, vol. VIII
M'Kay, William D., 1844–1924, vol. II
Mackay-Tallack, Sir Hugh, 1912–1989, vol. VIII
McKeag, Major William, 1897–1972, vol. VII
M'Kean, Col Alexander Chalmers, 1895–1933, vol. III
M'Kean, Captain George Burdon, 1890–1926, vol. II
McKean, Air Vice-Marshal Sir Lionel Douglas Dalzell, 1886–1963, vol. VI
Mackean, Rev. Canon William Herbert, 1877–1960, vol. V
M'Kechnie, Alexander Balfour, 1860–1930, vol. III
M'Kechnie, Dugald, 1845–1912, vol. I
McKechnie, Hector, 1899–1966, vol. VI
McKechnie, Sir James, *died* 1931, vol. III
McKechnie, James, 1911–1964, vol. VI
McKechnie, William Sharp, 1863–1930, vol. III
McKechnie, Sir William Wallace, *died* 1947, vol. IV
McKee, Air Marshal Sir Andrew, 1901–1988, vol. VIII
McKee, Sir Dermot St Oswald, 1904–1980, vol. VII
McKee, Major Hugh Kennedy, 1896–1957, vol. V
McKee, Captain James, 1886–1934, vol. III
McKee, J(ohn) Ritchie, 1900–1964, vol. VI
McKee, Rev. Robert Alexander, 1847–1926, vol. II
McKee, Col Samuel Hanford, 1875–1942, vol. IV
McKee, William Desmond, 1926–1982, vol. VIII
McKee, William Henry, 1881–1956, vol. V
McKeefry, His Eminence Cardinal Peter Thomas Bertram, 1899–1973, vol. VII

Mackeen, Hon. David, 1839–1916, vol. II
McKeever, Ronald Fraser, 1914–1981, vol. VIII
Mackeith, Malcolm Henry, 1895–1942, vol. IV
Mac Keith, Ronald Charles, 1908–1977, vol. VII
McKell, Rt Hon. Sir William John, 1891–1985, vol. VIII
Mackellar, Hon. Sir Charles Kinnaird, 1844–1926, vol. II
McKelvey, Sir John Lawrance, 1881–1939, vol. III
MacKelvie, Col Maxwell, 1877–1933, vol. III
Mackelvie, Col Thomas, 1867–1952, vol. V
Macken, Frederic Raymond, 1903–1987, vol. VIII
McKendrick, Archibald, 1876–1960, vol. V (A), vol. VI (AI)
M'Kendrick, John Gray, 1841–1926, vol. II
MacKenna, Sir Bernard Joseph Maxwell, (Sir Brian), 1905–1989, vol. VIII
MacKenna, Sir Brian; see MacKenna, Sir Bernard J. M.
McKenna, Harold, 1879–1946, vol. IV
MacKenna, Sir James, 1872–1940, vol. III
McKenna, Brig. James Charles, 1879–1943, vol. IV
M'Kenna, Sir Joseph Neale, 1819–1906, vol. I
McKenna, Rt Rev. Patrick, 1869–1942, vol. IV
McKenna, Rt Hon. Reginald, 1863–1943, vol. IV
MacKenna, Robert Merttins Bird, 1903–1984, vol. VIII
Mackenna, Robert William, 1874–1930, vol. III
McKenna, Siobhán, 1923–1986, vol. VIII
McKenna, Stephen, 1888–1967, vol. VI
Mackennal, Rev. Alexander, 1835–1904, vol. I
Mackennal, Sir Bertram, 1863–1931, vol. III
Mackennal, Ven. William Leavers, 1881–1947, vol. IV
Mackenzie, Hon. Lord; Charles Kincaid Mackenzie, 1857–1938, vol. III
Mackenzie, Agnes Mure, 1891–1955, vol. V
MacKenzie, Alasdair Francis, 1910–1971, vol. VII
Mackenzie, Alasdair Roderick, 1903–1970, vol. VI
Mackenzie, Alastair Oswald Morison, 1858–1949, vol. IV
Mackenzie, Alastair Stewart, (Sandy), 1930–1986, vol. VIII
McKenzie, Alex., 1869–1951, vol. V
Mackenzie, Sir Alexander, 1842–1902, vol. I
Mackenzie, Sir Alexander, 1860–1943, vol. IV
Mackenzie, Alexander, 1915–1982, vol. VIII
Mackenzie, Sir Alexander Campbell, 1847–1935, vol. III
Mackenzie, Lt-Col Alexander Dalziel; see Mackenzie, Lt-Col D. W. A. D.
Mackenzie, Col Alexander Francis, 1861–1935, vol. III
Mackenzie, Alexander George Robertson, 1879–1963, vol. VI
Mackenzie, Alexander Herbert, 1867–1952, vol. V
Mackenzie, Sir Alexander M.; see Muir-Mackenzie.
Mackenzie, Alexander Marshall, 1848–1933, vol. III
Mackenzie, Col Sir Alfred Robert Davidson, 1835–1921, vol. II
Mackenzie, Sir Allan Russell, 2nd Bt (cr 1890), 1850–1906, vol. I
M'Kenzie, Lt-Col Archibald Ernest Graham, 1878–1918, vol. II

Mackenzie, Sir Arthur George Ramsay, 11th Bt (cr 1673), 1865–1935, vol. III
Mackenzie, Arthur Henderson, 1880–1936, vol. III
Mackenzie, Arthur Stanley, 1865–1938, vol. III
Mackenzie, Austin, 1856–1935, vol. III
Mackenzie, Captain Cecil James Granville, 1889–1959, vol. V
Mackenzie, Chalmers Jack, 1888–1984, vol. VIII
Mackenzie, Lt-Col Charles, 1869–1953, vol. V
Mackenzie, Major Charles Fraser, died 1955, vol. V
Mackenzie, Charles Kincaid; see Mackenzie, Hon. Lord.
Mackenzie, Sir Clutha Nantes, 1895–1966, vol. VI
MacKenzie, Sir Colin, 1877–1938, vol. III
Mackenzie, Rear-Adm. Colin, 1872–1968, vol. VI
Mackenzie, Colin Hercules, 1898–1986, vol. VIII
Mackenzie, Maj.-Gen. Sir Colin John, 1861–1956, vol. V
Mackenzie, Sir Compton, 1883–1972, vol. VII
M'Kenzie, Dan, died 1935, vol. III
MacKenzie, David Alexander, 1922–1989, vol. VIII
Mackenzie, Brig. David Alexander Laurance, 1897–1976, vol. VII
Mackenzie, David James, 1855–1925, vol. II
Mackenzie, Donald Alexander, 1873–1936, vol. III
M'Kenzie, Donald Duncan, 1859–1927, vol. II
Mackenzie, Lt-Col (Douglas William) Alexander Dalziel, 1889–1955, vol. V
Mackenzie, Brig-Gen. Sir Duncan, 1859–1932, vol. III
Mackenzie, Sir Duncan George, 1883–1965, vol. VI
Mackenzie, Col Edward Leslie, 1870–1947, vol. IV
Mackenzie, Sir Edward Montague Compton; see Mackenzie, Sir C.
Mackenzie, Col Edward Philippe, 1842–1929, vol. III
Mackenzie, Col Eric Dighton, 1891–1972, vol. VII
Mackenzie, Faith Compton, (Lady Mackenzie), died 1960, vol. V
Mackenzie, Col Sir Felix Calvert, 1826–1902, vol. I
Mackenzie, Rev. Francis Scott, 1884–1970, vol. VI
MacKenzie, Fraser, 1905–1978, vol. VII
Mackenzie, Frederick A., 1869–1931, vol. III
Mackenzie, Lt-Col Frederick Finch, 1849–1934, vol. III
Mackenzie, Ven. Gaden Crawford, died 1920, vol. II
Mackenzie, George, 1881–1950, vol. IV
Mackenzie, Brig.- Gen. George Birnie, 1872–1952, vol. V
Mackenzie, Col George Frederick Campbell, 1855–1909, vol. I
Mackenzie, Sir George Sutherland, 1844–1910, vol. I
Mackenzie, H. Millicent, 1863–1942, vol. IV
Mackenzie, Col Harry Malcolm, died 1947, vol. IV
M'Kenzie, Rev. Harry Ward, 1850–1941, vol. IV
Mackenzie, Sir Hector David, 8th Bt (cr 1703, of Gairloch), 1893–1958, vol. V
Mackenzie, Lt-Col Hector G. Gordon, 1869–1930, vol. III
Mackenzie, Sir Hector William Gavin, 1856–1929, vol III
Mackenzie, Helen Margaret, died 1966, vol. VI
Mackenzie, Lt-Col Herbert John, 1878–1941, vol. IV
Mackenzie, Hugh, 1861–1940, vol. III
M'Kenzie, Hon. Hugh, 1853–1942, vol. IV

Mackenzie, Sir Hugh, 1888–1959, vol. V
Mackenzie, Rt Hon. Ian Alistair, 1890–1949, vol. IV
Mackenzie, J. Hamilton, 1875–1926, vol. II
Mackenzie, J. J., 1865–1922, vol. II
Mackenzie, Sir James, 1853–1925, vol. II
Mackenzie, Rev. James Cameron, *died* 1931, vol. III
Mackenzie, Sir James Dixon, 7th Bt (*cr* 1703, of Scatwell), 1830–1900, vol. I
MacKenzie, Brig. James Dunbar, 1889–1947, vol. IV
Mackenzie, Sir (James) Kenneth Douglas, 8th Bt (*cr* 1703, of Scatwell), 1859–1930, vol. III
Mackenzie, Sir (James) Moir, 1886–1963, vol. VI
Mackenzie, James Young, 1914–1971, vol. VII
Mackenzie, Lt-Col John, 1876–1949, vol.IV
McKenzie, Very Rev. John, 1883–1955, vol. V
McKenzie, John, 1915–1986, vol. VIII
MacKenzie, Lt-Col John Alexander, 1881–1960, vol. V
Mackenzie, John Alexander S.; *see* Shaw-Mackenzie.
McKenzie, John Grant, 1882–1963, vol. VI
Mackenzie, John Gurney, 1907–1975, vol. VII
Mackenzie, Col John Hugh, 1876–1963, vol. VI
Mackenzie, John Moncrieff Ord, 1911–1985, vol. VIII
Mackenzie, Maj.-Gen. John Percival, 1884–1961, vol. VI
McKenzie, Sir John Robert, 1876–1955, vol. V
Mackenzie, John Stuart, 1860–1935, vol. III
Mackenzie, Sir John William Pitt M.; *see* Muir-Mackenzie.
Mackenzie, Keith Roderick Turing, 1921–1990, vol. VIII
Mackenzie, Rt Rev. Kenneth, 1863–1945, vol. IV
Mackenzie, Surg. Vice-Adm. Sir (Kenneth) Alexander I.; *see* Ingleby Mackenzie.
Mackenzie, Rt Rev. Kenneth Donald, 1876–1966, vol. VI
Mackenzie, Sir Kenneth Douglas; *see* Mackenzie, Sir J. K. D.
Mackenzie, Rear-Adm. Kenneth Harry Litton, 1889–1970, vol. VI
Mackenzie, Kenneth James Joseph, 1867–1924, vol. II
Mackenzie, Col Kenneth James Loch, *died* 1903, vol. I
Mackenzie, Kenneth James M.; *see* Muir Mackenzie.
Mackenzie, Sir Kenneth John, 7th Bt (*cr* 1703, of Gairloch), 1861–1929, vol. III
Mackenzie, Sir Kenneth Smith, 6th Bt (*cr* 1703, of Gairloch), 1832–1900, vol. I
Mackenzie, Sir Leslie, 1862–1935, vol. III
Mackenzie, Sir (Lewis) Roderick Kenneth, 9th Bt (*cr* 1703, of Scatwell), 1902–1972, vol. VII
McKenzie, Malcolm George, 1917–1979, vol. VII
McKenzie, Marian, *died* 1927, vol. II
Mackenzie, Melville Douglas, 1889–1972, vol. VII
Mackenzie, Michael Alexander, 1866–1949, vol. IV
Mackenzie, Sir Moir; *see* Mackenzie, Sir J. M.
Mackenzie, Montague M.; *see* Muir-Mackenzie.
MacKenzie, Nicol Finlayson, 1857–1943, vol. IV
MacKenzie, Norman Archibald MacRae, 1894–1986, vol. VIII
MacKenzie, Peter Alexander Cameron; *see* Serra Largo, Count de.

Mackenzie, Col Sir Robert Campbell, 1856–1945, vol. IV
Mackenzie, Sir Robert Cecil M.; *see* Muir-Mackenzie.
McKenzie, Hon. Robert Donald, 1865–1928, vol. II, vol. III
Mackenzie, Sir Robert Evelyn, 12th Bt, 1906–1990, vol. VIII
Mackenzie, Sir Robert Henry M.; *see* Muir Mackenzie
Mackenzie, Col Robert Holden, vol. II
Mackenzie, Robert Jameson, 1857–1912, vol. I
Mackenzie, Lt-Col Sir Robert Smythe M.; *see* Muir-Mackenzie.
McKenzie, (Robert) Tait, 1867–1938, vol. III
McKenzie, Robert Trelford, 1917–1981, vol. VIII
Mackenzie, Maj.-Gen. Roderick, 1830–1916, vol. II
Mackenzie, Sir Roderick; *see* Mackenzie, Sir L. R. K.
Mackenzie, Sir Roderick Campbell, 10th Bt, 1954–1981, vol. VIII
Mackenzie, Captain Sir Roderick Edward François McQuhae, 11th Bt, 1894–1986, vol. VIII
Mackenzie, Ronald Pierson, 1864–1930, vol. III
Mackenzie, Sandy; *see* Mackenzie, A. S.
McKenzie, Tait; *see* McKenzie, R. T.
Mackenzie, Hon. Sir Thomas, 1854–1930, vol. III
McKenzie, Thomas, 1891–1954, vol. V
Mackenzie, Thomas William, 1875–1939, vol. III
Mackenzie, Col Sir Victor Audley Falconer, 3rd Bt (*cr* 1890), 1882–1944, vol. IV
Mackenzie, W. G., vol. II
Mackenzie, Sir William, 1849–1923, vol. II
Mackenzie, William Andrew, 1870–1942, vol. IV
Mackenzie, William Cook, 1862–1952, vol. V
Mackenzie, William Dalziel, 1840–1928, vol. II
Mackenzie, William Douglas, 1859–1936, vol. III
MacKenzie, William Forbes, 1907–1980, vol. VII
Mackenzie, William Lyon, *died* 1938, vol. III
Mackenzie, William Mackay, 1871–1952, vol. V
Mackenzie, Major William Roderick Dalziel, 1864–1952, vol. V
Mackenzie, Lt-Col William Scobie, *died* 1926, vol. II
Mackenzie, Col William Shand, 1876–1944, vol. IV
Mackenzie-Kennedy, Brig. Archibald Gordon, 1904–1987, vol. VIII
Mackenzie-Kennedy, Sir Donald; *see* Mackenzie-Kennedy, Sir H. C. D. C.
Mackenzie-Kennedy, Maj.-Gen. Sir Edward Charles William, *died* 1932, vol. III
Mackenzie-Kennedy, Sir (Henry Charles) Donald (Cleveland), 1889–1965, vol. VI
Mackenzie King, Rt Hon. William Lyon; *see* King.
Mackenzie-Rogan, Lt-Col John, 1855–1932, vol. III
M'Keown, Hon. Harrison Andrew, 1863–1932, vol. III
Mackeown, John Ainslie, 1902–1984, vol. VIII
McKeown, Robert John, 1869–1925, vol. II
McKeown, Thomas, 1912–1988, vol. VIII
McKeown, Walter, 1866–1925, vol. II
McKercher, Sir William Gourley, *died* 1937, vol. III
MacKereth, Sir Gilbert, 1893–1962, vol. VI
McKergow, Lt-Col Robert Wilson, 1866–1947, vol. IV
McKerihan, Sir (Clarence) Roy, 1896–1969, vol. VI

McKerihan, Sir Roy; *see* McKerihan, Sir C. R.
M'Kerlie, Sir John Graham, 1814–1900, vol. I
McKerral, Andrew, 1876–1967, vol. VI
McKerrell, Brig-Comdr Augustus de Ségur, 1863–1916, vol. II
McKerron, Sir Patrick Alexander Bruce, 1896–1964, vol. VI
McKerron, Robert Gordon, 1862–1937, vol. III
McKerron, Robert Gordon, 1900–1973, vol. VII
McKerrow, Ronald Brunlees, 1872–1940, vol. III
Mackeson, Brig. Sir Harry Ripley, 1st Bt, 1905–1964, vol. VI
Mackessack, George Ross, 1851–1935, vol. III
Mackessack, Lt-Col Kenneth, 1902–1982, vol. VIII
Mackesy, Col Charles Ernest Randolph, 1861–1925, vol. II
Mackesy, Maj.-Gen. Pierse Joseph, 1883–1956, vol. V
Mackesy, Lt-Gen. William Henry, 1837–1914, vol. I
Mackeurtan, Harold Graham, 1884–1942, vol. IV
McKew, Rev. Robert, *died* 1944, vol. IV
Mackey, Archibald John, 1844–1936, vol. III
Mackey, Brig.-Gen. Hugh James Alexander, 1876–1927, vol. II
Mackey, Hon. Sir John Emanuel, 1865–1924, vol. II
Mackey, William Arthur, 1906–1990, vol. VIII
McKibbin, Col Alan John, 1892–1958, vol. V
McKibbin, Major Thomas, 1879–1943, vol. IV
Mackichan, Rev. D., 1851–1932, vol. III
Mackie, Alexander, 1876–1955, vol. V
Mackie, Alfred William White, 1877–1951, vol. V
Mackie, Brig. Andrew Hugh, 1897–1968, vol. VI
Mackie, Charles, *died* 1940, vol. III(A), vol. IV
Mackie, Charles H., 1862–1920, vol. II
McKie, Douglas, 1896–1967, vol. VI
Mackie, Edwin Gordon, 1896–1980, vol. VII
Mackie, Bt Col F. Percival, 1875–1944, vol. IV
Mackie, Rev. George M., 1854–1922, vol. II
McKie, Helen Madeleine, *died* 1957, vol. V
Mackie, Sir Horatio George Arthur, 1868–1940, vol. III
Mackie, Sir James, 1838–1898, vol. I
Mackie, James Richard, 1896–1981, vol. VIII
McKie, Lt-Col John, 1857–1934, vol. III
Mackie, John, 1862–1939, vol. III
Mackie, John Beveridge, 1848–1919, vol. II
Mackie, John Duncan, 1887–1978, vol. VII
Mackie, John Hamilton, 1898–1958, vol. V
Mackie, John Leslie, 1917–1981, vol. VIII
Mackie, John Lindsay, 1864–1956, vol. V
Mackie, Sir Peter Jeffrey, 1st Bt, 1855–1924, vol. II
Mackie, Peter Robert McLeod, *died* 1959, vol. V
Mackie, Sir Richard, 1851–1923, vol. II
Mackie, Thomas Jones, 1888–1955, vol. V
Mackie, Col Tom Darke, 1883–1941, vol. IV
McKie, William Murray, 1866–1932, vol. III
McKie, Sir William Neil, 1901–1984, vol. VIII
McKie Reid, Col Andrew; *see* Reid.
Mackilligin, Robert Springett, 1890–1972, vol. VII
MacKillop, Douglas, 1891–1959, vol. V
McKillop, Edgar Ravenswood, 1895–1987, vol. VIII
McKillop, James, 1844–1913, vol. I
M'Killop, William, *died* 1909, vol. I
McKim, Ven. Charles W., 1867–1934, vol. III

McKim, Rt Rev. John, 1852–1936, vol. III
Mackinder, Rt Hon. Sir Halford John, 1861–1947, vol. IV
Mackinder, William, 1880–1930, vol. III
McKinlay, Adam Storey, *died* 1950, vol. IV
Mackinlay, Antoinette, (Mrs John Mackinlay); *see* Sterling, A.
Mackinlay, Lt-Col George, 1847–1928, vol. II
Mackinlay, Sir George Mason, 1906–1973, vol. VII
Mackinlay, Jean Sterling, *died* 1958, vol. V
Mackinlay, Malcolm Sterling, 1876–1952, vol. V
M'Kinley, William, 1842–1901, vol. I
McKinnell, James Jesse, 1869–1950, vol. IV
Mackinney, Frederick Walker, 1871–1950, vol. IV
McKinney, Sir William, 1897–1979, vol. VII
Mackinnon, Rev. Albert Glenthorne Tait, 1871–1939, vol. III
Mackinnon, Lt-Col Alexander Charles Broughton, 1878–1942, vol. IV
Mackinnon, Angus, 1911–1987, vol. VIII
Mackinnon, Archibald Donald, 1864–1937, vol. III
Mackinnon of Mackinnon, Comdr Arthur Avalon, 1893–1964, vol. VI
Mackinnon, Donald, *died* 1914, vol. I
Mackinnon, Hon. Donald, 1859–1932, vol. III
Mackinnon, Hon. Donald Alexander, 1863–1928, vol. II
Mackinnon, Doris Livingston, *died* 1956, vol. V
Mackinnon, Duncan, 1909–1984, vol. VIII
Mackinnon, Rear-Adm. Edmund Julius Gordon, 1880–1940, vol. III
MacKinnon of MacKinnon, Francis Alexander, 1848–1947, vol. IV
MacKinnon, Rt Hon. Sir Frank Douglas, 1871–1946, vol. IV
MacKinnon, Gena; *see* MacKinnon, Georgina R. D.
MacKinnon, Georgina Russell Davidson, (Gena MacKinnon), 1885–1973, vol. VII
McKinnon, Hector Brown, 1890–1981, vol. VIII
MacKinnon, Gen. Sir Henry; *see* MacKinnon, Gen. Sir W. H.
Mackinnon, Lt-Col Henry William Alexander, 1842–1905, vol. I
Mackinnon, James, 1860–1945, vol. IV
McKinnon, Sir James, 1894–1971, vol. VII
MacKinnon, James Alexander Rudolf, 1888–1955, vol. V
Mackinnon, John, 1886–1958, vol. V
Mackinnon, Kenneth Wulsten, 1906–1964, vol. VI
Mackinnon, Col Lachlan, 1886–1973, vol. VII
MacKinnon, Vice-Adm. Lachlan Donald Ian, 1882–1948, vol. IV
Mackinnon, Sir Lauchlan Charles, 1848–1925, vol. II
Mackinnon, Murdoch, 1865–1944, vol. IV
McKinnon, Neil Nairn, 1909–1988, vol. VIII
Mackinnon, Sir Percy Graham, 1872–1956, vol. V
M'Kinnon, Rev. W., 1843–1925, vol. II, vol. III
Mackinnon, Sir William Alexander, 1830–1897, vol. I
MacKinnon, Gen. Sir (William) Henry, 1852–1929, vol. III
Mackinnon, Lt-Col William Thomas Morris, *died* 1957, vol. V
McKinstry, Sir Archibald, 1877–1952, vol. V

McKinstry, Captain Edward Robert, 1861–1943, vol. IV

Mackintosh, Hon. Lord; Charles Machintosh, 1888–1978, vol. VII

Mackintosh of Halifax, 1st Viscount, 1891–1964, vol. VI

Mackintosh of Halifax, 2nd Viscount, 1921–1980, vol. VII

Mackintosh, The; Alfred Donald Mackintosh, 1851–1938, vol. III

Mackintosh, The; see Mackintosh of Mackintosh, Vice-Adm. L. D.

Mackintosh, Rt Rev. Mgr Alexander, 1854–1922, vol. II

Mackintosh, Sir Alexander, 1858–1948, vol. IV

Mackintosh, Alfred Donald; see Mackintosh, The.

MacKintosh, Sir Angus MacKay, 1915–1986, vol. VIII

Mackintosh, Sir Ashley Watson, 1868–1937, vol. III

Mackintosh, Charles; see Mackintosh, Hon. Lord.

Mackintosh, (Charles Ernest Whistler) Christopher, 1903–1974, vol. VII

Mackintosh, Charles Rennie, 1869–1928, vol. II

Mackintosh, Christopher; see Mackintosh, Charles E. W. C.

Mackintosh, David Forbes, 1900–1988, vol. VIII

Mackintosh, Most Rev. Donald, died 1943, vol. IV

Mackintosh, Most Rev. Donald A., 1845–1919, vol. II

Mackintosh, Donald James, 1862–1947, vol. IV

Mackintosh, Eric Donald, 1906–1978, vol. VII

Mackintosh, Col Ernest Elliot Buckland, 1880–1957, vol. V

Mackintosh, Col George, 1860–1954, vol. V

Mackintosh, Rev. Hugh Ross, 1870–1936, vol. III

Mackintosh, (Hugh) Stewart, 1903–1989, vol. VIII

Mackintosh, James, 1858–1944, vol. IV

Mackintosh, James M., 1891–1966, vol. VI

Mackintosh, John, 1833–1907, vol. I

Mackintosh, John Pitcairn, 1929–1978, vol. VII

Mackintosh, Captain Sir Kenneth Lachlan, 1902–1979, vol. VII

Mackintosh of Mackintosh, Vice-Adm. Lachlan Donald, (The Mackintosh), 1896–1957, vol. V

Mackintosh, Rev. Robert, 1858–1933, vol. III

Mackintosh, Stanley Hugh, 1883–1967, vol. VI

Mackintosh, Stewart; see Mackintosh, H. S.

Mackintosh, William; see Kyllachy, Hon. Lord.

Mackintosh, William Archibald, 1895–1970, vol. VI(AII)

Mackintosh, Rev. William Lachlan, 1858–1926, vol. II

McKisack, Sir Audley, 1903–1966, vol. VI

M'Kisack, Henry Lawrence, 1859–1928, vol. II

McKisack, May, 1900–1981, vol. VIII

McKittrick, Thomas Harrington, 1889–1970, vol. VI

Mackley, Garnet Hercules, 1883–1986, vol. VIII

Mackley, George Edward, 1900–1983, vol. VIII

Macklin, Sir (Albert) Noel (Campbell), died 1946, vol. IV

Macklin, Albert Romer, 1863–1921, vol. II

Macklin, Sir (Albert) Sortain (Romer), 1890–1976, vol. VII

Macklin, Sir James, 1864–1944, vol. IV

Macklin, Sir Noel; see Macklin, Sir A. N. C.

Macklin, Sir Sortain; see Macklin, Sir A. S. R.

Macklin, T. Eyre, 1867–1943, vol. IV

Mackness, Rev. George, 1834–1914, vol. I

Mackness, Lt-Comdr George John, 1892–1970, vol. VI

Mackness, William Robert, 1879–1963, vol. VI

Macknight, Dodge, 1860–1950, vol. IV(A)

Macknight, Lt-Col John James Thow, died 1965, vol. VI

Macknight, Thomas, 1829–1899, vol. I

Mackworth, Sir Arthur William, 6th Bt, 1842–1914, vol. I

Mackworth, Vice-Adm. Geoffrey, 1879–1952, vol. V

Mackworth, Col Sir Harry Llewellyn, 8th Bt, 1878–1952, vol. V

Mackworth, Sir Humphrey, 7th Bt, 1871–1948, vol. IV

Mackworth, John Dolben, 1887–1939, vol. III

Mackworth, Air Vice-Marshal Philip Herbert, 1897–1958, vol. V

Mackworth-Praed, Sir Herbert Bulkley; see Praed.

Mackworth-Young, Gerard; see Young.

Mackworth-Young, (Gerard) William, 1926–1984, vol. VIII

Maclachlan, Alan Bruce, 1874–1955, vol. V

Maclachlan, Lt-Col Alexander Fraser Campbell, 1875–1918, vol. II

McLachlan, Charles, 1931–1990, vol. VIII

Maclachlan, Adm. Crawford, 1867–1952, vol. V

McLachlan, Donald Harvey, 1908–1971, vol. VII

McLachlan, Duncan Clark, 1853–1929, vol. III

McLachlan, Herbert, 1876–1958, vol. V

McLachlan, Maj.-Gen. James Douglas, 1869–1937, vol. III

Maclachlan of Maclachlan, John, 1859–1942, vol. IV

M'Lachlan, Robert, 1837–1904, vol. I

MacLachlan, Robert Boyd, 1880–1975, vol. VII

Maclachlan, Brig.-Gen. Ronald Campbell, 1872–1917, vol. II

Maclachlan, Sir T. J. Leigh, 1864–1946, vol. IV

Maclachlan, Thomas Banks, died 1952, vol. V

Maclachlan, Thomas Kay, 1895–1972, vol. VII

Maclachlan, Col Thomas Robertson, 1870–1921, vol. II

McLagan, Archibald Gibson, 1853–1928, vol. II

Maclagan, Sir Douglas, 1812–1900, vol. I

Maclagan, Sir Edward Douglas, 1864–1952, vol. V

Maclagan, Sir Eric Robert Dalrymple, 1879–1951, vol. V

Maclagan, Maj.-Gen. Ewen George S.; see Sinclair-Maclagan.

Maclagan, John, 1846–1929, vol. III

Maclagan, Noel Francis, 1904–1987, vol. VIII

Maclagan, Col Robert Smeiton, 1860–1931, vol. III

Maclagan, Most Rev. William Dalrymple, 1826–1910, vol. I

Maclagan, William Gauld, 1903–1972, vol. VII

McLaggan, Sir Douglas; see McLaggan, Sir J. D.

McLaggan, Sir (John) Douglas, 1893–1967, vol. VI

McLaglen, Victor, 1886–1959, vol. V

Maclaine of Lochbuie, Kenneth Douglas Lorne, 1880–1935, vol. III

Maclaine of Lochbuie, Murdoch Gillian, 1845–1909, vol. I

M'Laren, Hon. Lord; John M'Laren, 1831–1910, vol. I

M'Laren, Rev. Alexander, 1826–1910, vol. I

MacLaren, Andrew, 1883–1975, vol. VII

Maclaren, Archibald Campbell, 1871–1944, vol. IV

MacLaren, Brig.-Gen. Charles Henry, 1878–1962, vol. VI

McLaren, Sir Charles Northrop, 1898–1955, vol. V

MacLaren of MacLaren, Donald, 1910–1966, vol VI

M'Laren, Rev. Douglas, 1866–1956, vol. V

M'Laren, Hon. Francis Walter Stafford, 1886–1917, vol. II

McLaren, Sir Hamish Duncan, 1898–1990, vol. VIII

McLaren, Henry, 1883–1943, vol. IV

McLaren, Hugh Cameron, 1913–1986, vol. VIII

Maclaren, Ian; *see* Watson, Rev. John.

McLaren, Ian; *see* McLaren, J. W.

McLaren, Jack, 1887–1954, vol. V

Maclaren, James Anderson, 1866–1926, vol. II

McLaren, Sir John, 1850–1920, vol. II

M'Laren, John; *see* M'Laren, Hon. Lord.

McLaren, Sir John Gilbert, 1871–1958, vol. V

Maclaren, John James, *died* 1926, vol. II

McLaren, John Watt, 1906–1982, vol. VIII

Maclaren, Major Kenneth, 1860–1924, vol. II

McLaren, Martin, 1914–1979, vol. VII

McLaren, Moray, 1901–1971, vol. VII

MacLaren, Col Murray, 1861–1942, vol. IV

McLaren, Robert, 1856–1940, vol. III

McLaren, Ross Scott, 1906–1975, vol. VII

M'Laren, Walter Stowe Bright, 1853–1912, vol. I

McLaren, Rev. William David, 1856–1921, vol. II

McLarty, Hon. Sir (Duncan) Ross, 1891–1962, vol. VI

McLarty, Hon. Norman Alexander, 1889–1945, vol. IV

McLarty, Hon. Sir Ross; *see* McLarty, Hon. Sir D. R.

Maclauchlan, Hugh Simon, *died* 1899, vol. I

McLaughlan, Roy James Philip, 1898–1982, vol. VIII

MacLaughlin, Lt-Col Alexander John Maunsell, 1854–1932, vol. III

M'Laughlin, Andrew Cunningham, 1861–1947, vol. IV

MacLaughlin, Col Arthur Maunsell, *died* 1954, vol. V

McLaughlin, Charles Redmond, 1909–1979, vol. VII

McLaughlin, George Vincent, 1922–1987, vol. VIII

McLaughlin, Sir Henry, 1876–1927, vol. II

M'Laughlin, Lt-Col Hubert James, 1860–1915, vol. I

McLaughlin, Rev. John Fletcher, 1863–1933, vol. III

McLaughlin, Rear-Adm. Patrick Vivian, 1901–1969, vol. VI

M'Laurin, Duncan, 1848–1921, vol. II

MacLaurin, Hon. Sir Henry Normand, 1835–1914, vol. I

McLaurin, Engr-Rear-Adm. John, *died* 1955, vol. V

Maclaurin, Richard Cockburn, 1870–1920, vol. II

Maclaverty, Edward Hyde East, 1847–1922, vol. II

Maclay, 1st Baron, 1857–1951, vol. V

Maclay, 2nd Baron, 1899–1969, vol. VI

Maclay, Hon. Walter Symington, 1901–1964, vol. VI

Maclean, Baron (Life Peer); Charles Hector Fitzroy Maclean, 1916–1990, vol. VIII

McLean, Major Sir Alan, 1875–1959, vol. V

Maclean, Alexander, 1867–1940, vol. III

Maclean, Surg. Rear-Adm. Alexander, 1868–1945, vol. IV

Maclean, Sir Alexander, 1872–1948, vol. IV

Maclean of Ardgour, Alexander John Hew, 1880–1930, vol. III

Maclean, Rev. Alexander Miller, 1865–1925, vol. II

Maclean, Alexander Morvaren, 1872–1936, vol. III

Maclean, Alick; *see* Maclean, Alexander Morvaren.

Maclean, Alistair, 1922–1987, vol. VIII

M'Lean, Hon. Allan, 1840–1911, vol. I

Maclean, Allan, 1858–1918, vol. II

McLean, Andrew Sinclair, 1919–1981, vol. VIII

MacLean, Angus, 1863–1948, vol. IV

Maclean, Angus Alexander, 1854–1943, vol. IV

MacLean, Col Archibald Campbell Holms, 1883–1970, vol. VI

Maclean, Most Rev. Arthur John, 1858–1943, vol. IV

McLean, Calvin Stowe, 1888–1970, vol. VI

Maclean, Catherine Macdonald, *died* 1960, vol. V

Maclean, Brig.-Gen. Charles Alexander Hugh, 1874–1947, vol. IV

MacLean, Col Charles Allan, 1892–1978, vol. VII

Maclean, Charles Donald, 1843–1916, vol. II

McLean, Lt-Col Charles Herbert, 1877–1940, vol. III(A), vol. IV

Maclean, Maj.-Gen. Charles Smith, 1836–1921, vol. II

McLean, Col Charles Wesley Weldon, 1882–1962, vol. VI

Maclean, Vice-Adm. Colin Kenneth, *died* 1935, vol. III

MacLean, Air Vice-Marshal Cuthbert Trelawder, 1886–1969, vol. VI

M'Lean, Donald, *died* 1915, vol. I

Maclean, Rt Hon. Sir Donald, 1864–1932, vol. III

Maclean, Captain Donald Charles Hugh, 1875–1909, vol. I

Maclean, Sir Douglas; *see* Maclean, Sir R. D. D.

McLean, Edward B., *died* 1941, vol. IV

Maclean, Sir Ewen John, *died* 1953, vol. V

Maclean, Sir Fitzroy Donald, 10th Bt, 1835–1936, vol. III

Maclean, Sir Francis William, 1844–1913, vol. I

Maclean, Frederick Gurr, 1848–1915, vol. I

M'Lean, Hon. Sir George, 1834–1917, vol. II

Maclean, George Edwin, 1850–1938, vol. III

Maclean, Brig. Gordon Forbes, 1897–1982, vol. VIII

Maclean, Gordon Thompson, 1884–1943, vol. IV

Maclean, Kaid, Gen. Sir Harry Aubrey deVere, 1848–1920, vol. II

Maclean, Lt-Col Henry Donald Neil, 1872–1926, vol. II

McLean, Lt-Col Henry John, 1868–1931, vol. III

MacLean, Hugh, 1879–1957, vol. V

McLean, Maj.-Gen. Hon. Hugh Havelock, 1854–1938, vol. III

Maclean, Ian Albert Druce, 1902–1986, vol. VIII

Maclean of Pennycross, Rear-Adm. Iain Gilleasbuig, 1902–1988, vol. VIII

MacLean, Ida Smedley, *died* 1944, vol. IV

MacLean, James A., 1868–1945, vol. IV
Maclean, James Borrowman, 1881–1940, vol. III
Maclean, James Mackenzie, 1835–1906, vol. I
McLean, Col James Reynolds, 1872–1921, vol. II
McLean, John, 1893–1978, vol. VII
Maclean, Lt-Col John Bayne, 1862–1950, vol. IV
Maclean, John Cassilis Birkmyre, 1849–1925, vol. II
MacLean, Hon. John Duncan, 1873–1948, vol. IV
Maclean, Col John Francis, 1901–1986, vol. VIII
Maclean, John Kennedy, 1874–1933, vol. III
McLean, John Reid, 1856–1935, vol. III
McLean, John Roll, 1848–1916, vol. II
McLean, Lt-Gen. Sir Kenneth Graeme, 1896–1987, vol. VIII
Maclean, Lachlan Frederick Copeland, 1885–1957, vol. V
Maclean, Magnus, died 1937, vol. III
McLean, Mary, died 1949, vol. IV
Maclean, Neil, died 1953, vol. V
MacLean, Neil Adam, 1885–1944, vol. IV
McLean, Lt-Col Neil Loudon Desmond, 1918–1986, vol. VIII
M'Lean, Norman, 1865–1947, vol. IV
Maclean, Very Rev. Norman, 1869–1952, vol. V
McLean, Sir Robert, 1884–1964, vol. VI
McLean, Robert Colquhoun, 1890–1981, vol. VIII
Maclean, Sir (Robert Donald) Douglas, 1852–1929, vol. III
M'Lean, Simon James, 1871–1946, vol. IV
Maclean, William Campbell, died 1898, vol. I
Maclean, William Findlay, 1854–1929, vol. III
McLean, Sir William Hannah, 1877–1967, vol. VI
McLean, Rev. Col William Richard James, 1858–1932, vol. III
McLean, Sir William Ross, 1901–1965, vol. VI
Macleane, Rev. Douglas, 1856–1925, vol. II
Maclear, Rev. George Frederick, 1833–1902, vol. I
Maclear, Lt-Col Harry, 1872–1916, vol. II
Maclear, Adm. John Pearse, 1838–1907, vol. I
McLearn, Sir William, 1837–1918, vol. II
McLeavy, Baron (Life Peer); Frank McLeavy, 1899–1976, vol. VII
Macleay, Col Alexander Caldcleugh, 1843–1907, vol. I
McLeay, Hon. George, 1892–1955, vol. V
Macleay, Sir (James William) Ronald, 1870–1943, vol. IV
McLeay, Hon. Sir John, 1893–1982, vol. VIII
Macleay, John Thomson, 1870–1955, vol. V
MacLeay, Oswell Searight, 1905–1982, vol. VIII
Macleay, Sir Ronald; see Macleay, Sir J. W. R.
Maclehose, James, 1857–1943, vol. IV
Maclehose, Norman M., 1859–1931, vol. III
MacLeish, Archibald, 1892–1982, vol. VIII
McLeish, Donald Alexander Stewart, 1893–1958, vol. V(A)
M'Leish, Col Duncan, 1851–1920, vol. II
M'Lellan, Alexander Matheson, 1872–1957, vol. V
MacLellan, Alexander Stephen, 1886–1966, vol. VI
M'Lellan, C. M. S., 1865–1916, vol. II
McLellan, David, 1904–1982, vol. VIII
McLellan, James Kidd, 1914–1981, vol. VIII
McLellan, Lt-Col William, died 1934, vol. III
MacLellan, William Turner, died 1945, vol. IV

MacLennan, Alexander, 1872–1953, vol. V
M'Lennan, Lt-Col Bartlett, 1868–1918, vol. II
Maclennan, Farquhar Stuart, died 1925, vol. II
MacLennan, Sir Hector, 1905–1978, vol. VII
MacLennan, Hugh; see McLennan, J. H.
Maclennan, Sir Ian Morrison Ross, 1909–1986, vol. VIII
M'Lennan, Sir John Cunningham, 1867–1935, vol. III
M'Lennan, John Ferguson, 1855–1917, vol. II
MacLennan, (John) Hugh, 1907–1990, vol. VIII
McLennan, John Stewart, 1853–1939, vol. III
Maclennan, Kenneth, 1872–1952, vol. V
MacLennan, Sir Robert Laing, 1888–1977, vol. VII
MacLennan of MacLennan, Ronald George, 1925–1989, vol. VIII
M'Lennan, William, 1856–1904, vol. I
McLeod, Sir Alan Cumbrae Rose, 1904–1981, vol. VIII
MacLeod, Alexander Cameron, 1899–1971, vol. VII
McLeod, Hon. Alexander Donald, 1872–1938, vol. III
Macleod, Allan, 1887–1955, vol. V
Macleod, Adm. Agnus, 1847–1920, vol. II
MacLeod, Cameron; see MacLeod, A. C.
McLeod, Sir Charles Campbell, 1st Bt (cr 1925), 1858–1936, vol. III
Macleod, Maj.-Gen. Charles William, 1881–1944, vol. IV
M'Leod, Clement Henry, died 1917, vol. II
Macleod, Very Rev. Donald, died 1916, vol. II
M'Leod, Hon. Donald, died 1918, vol. II, vol. III
M'Leod, Gen. Sir Donald James Sim, 1845–1922, vol. II
McLeod, Lt-Gen. Sir (Donald) Kenneth, 1885–1958, vol. V
MacLeod, Douglas Hamilton, 1901–1970, vol. VI
MacLeod, Duncan, 1876–1949, vol. IV
McLeod, Sir Ezekiel, 1840–1920, vol. II
Macleod, Fiona; see Sharp, William.
MacLeod of MacLeod, Dame Flora, 1878–1976, vol. VII
Macleod, Frederick Henry, died 1938, vol. III
MacLeod, Sir Frederick Larkins, 1858–1936, vol. III
McLeod, George William Buckham, 1868–1947, vol. IV
M'Leod, Hon. Harry Fulton, 1871–1920, vol. II
M'Leod, Herbert, 1841–1923, vol. II
Macleod, Rt Hon. Iain Norman, 1913–1970, vol. VI
MacLeod, Captain Sir Ian Francis Norman, 3rd Bt (cr 1924), 1921–1944, vol. IV
Macleod, James John, 1841–1919, vol. II
MacLeod, Sir James MacIver, 1866–1944, vol. IV
McLeod, (James) Walter, 1887–1978, vol. VII
Macleod, Rev. John, 1840–1898, vol. I
Macleod, John, 1839–1927, vol. II
Macleod, John, 1891–1969, vol. VI(AII)
MacLeod, Sir John, 1913–1984, vol. VIII
Macleod, John James Rickard, 1876–1935, vol. III
MacLeod, Sir John Lorne, 1873–1946, vol. IV
MacLeod, Sir John Mackintosh, 1st Bt (cr 1924), 1857–1934, vol. III
MacLeod, Sir (John Mackintosh) Norman, 2nd Bt (cr 1924), 1891–1939, vol. III

MacLeod, John MacLeod Hendrie, 1870–1954, vol. V

MacLeod, Col John Norman, 1865–1932, vol. III

Macleod, Joseph Todd Gordon, 1903–1984, vol. VIII

Macleod, Col Kenneth, 1840–1922, vol. II

McLeod, Lt-Gen. Sir Kenneth; see McLeod, Lt-Gen. Sir D. K.

Macleod, Lewis Rose, 1875–1941, vol. IV

MacLeod, Maj.-Gen. Malcolm Neynoe, 1882–1969, vol. VI

MacLeod, Maj.-Gen. Minden Whyte-Melville, 1896–1981, vol. VIII

McLeod, Sir Murdoch Campbell, 2nd Bt (cr 1925), 1893–1950, vol. IV

Macleod, Rev. Norman, 1838–1911, vol. I

Macleod, Lt-Col Norman, 1872–1960, vol. V

MacLeod, Sir Norman; see MacLeod, Sir J. M. N.

Macleod, Sir Norman Cranstoun, 1866–1945, vol. IV

M'Leod, Norman F., 1856–1921, vol. II

Macleod of Macleod, Norman Magnus, 1839–1929, vol. III

Macleod of Macleod, Sir Reginald, 1847–1935, vol. III

McLeod, Lt-Col Reginald George M'Queen, 1859–1910, vol. I

Macleod, Robert Duncan, died 1973, vol. VII

Macleod, Col Robert Lockhart Ross, 1863–1943, vol. IV

Macleod, Rev. Roderick Charles, 1852–1934, vol. III

Macleod, Col Roderick William, 1851–1932, vol. III

McLeod, Gen. Sir Roderick William, 1905–1980, vol. VII

Macleod, Roderick Willoughby, 1858–1931, vol. III

Macleod, Simon John Fraser, 1857–1938, vol III

McLeod, Walter; see McLeod, J. W.

Macleod, Inspector-Gen. William, died 1904, vol. I

Macleod, Very Rev. William Arthur, 1867–1932, vol. III

McLeod, Brig.-Gen. William Kelty, 1862–1928, vol. II

Macleod, Captain William Simon Fraser, 1888–1940, vol. III

McLetchie, James Leslie, 1909–1965, vol. VI

Mac Liammóir, Micheál, 1899–1978, vol. VII

McLintock, Sir Thomson, 2nd Bt, 1905–1953, vol. V

McLintock, Sir William, 1st Bt, 1873–1947, vol. IV

McLintock, William Francis Porter, 1887–1960, vol. V

McLintock, Sir William Traven, 3rd Bt, 1931–1987, vol. VIII

Macloone, James, died 1934, vol. III

McLoughlin, Edward Patrick, died 1956, vol. V

McLoughlin, Maj.-Gen. George Somers, 1867–1943, vol. IV

McLuhan, (Herbert) Marshall, 1911–1980, vol. VII

McLuhan, Marshall; see McLuhan, H. M.

Maclure, Lt-Col Alan Francis, 1873–1929, vol. III

Maclure, Very Rev. Edward Craig, 1833–1906, vol. I

Maclure, Sir John Edward Stanley, 2nd Bt, 1869–1938, vol. III

Maclure, Sir John William, 1st Bt, 1835–1901, vol. I

Maclure, Lt-Col Sir John William Spencer, 3rd Bt, 1899–1980, vol. VII

MacLysaght, Edward Anthony, 1887–1986, vol. VIII

McMahon, Col Sir (Arthur) Henry, 1862–1949, vol. IV

McMahon, Col Bernard William Lynedoch, 1865–1928, vol. II

McMahon, Gen. Charles Alexander, 1830–1904, vol. I

Macmahon, Cortlandt, died 1954, vol. V

MacMahon, Ella, died 1956, vol. V

McMahon, Gregan, 1874–1941, vol. IV

McMahon, Lt-Col Sir Eyre, 6th Bt, 1860–1935, vol. III

McMahon, Col Sir Henry; see McMahon, Col Sir A. H.

M'Mahon, Major Sir Horace Westropp, 5th Bt, 1863–1932, vol. III

Macmahon, Hugh, 1836–1911, vol. I

MacMahon, Maj.-Gen. Hugh Francis Edward, 1880–1939, vol. III

Macmahon, Rt Hon. James, 1865–1954, vol. V

McMahon, Rt Rev. Mgr John, 1844–1932, vol. III

M'Mahon, Sir Lionel, 4th Bt, 1856–1926, vol. II

McMahon, Lt-Col Norman Reginald, 1866–1914, vol. I

McMahon, Sir Patrick; see McMahon, Sir W. P.

Macmahon, Lt-Gen. Peadar, 1893–1975, vol. VII

MacMahon, Percy Alexander, 1854–1929, vol. III

McMahon, Rt Hon. Sir William, 1908–1988, vol. VIII

McMahon, Sir (William) Patrick, 7th Bt, 1900–1977, vol. VII

M'Mahon, Sir William Samuel, 3rd Bt, 1839–1905, vol. I

Macmanaway, Rt Rev. James, died 1947, vol. IV

MacManaway, Rev. James Godfrey, 1898–1951, vol. V

MacManus, Emily Elvira Primrose, 1886–1978, vol. VII

Macmanus, Joseph Edward, died 1921, vol. II

McManus, Maurice, 1906–1982, vol. VIII

MacManus, Seumas, died 1960, vol. V

McMaster, Hon. Andrew R., 1876–1937, vol. III

Macmaster, Sir Donald, 1st Bt, 1846–1922, vol. II

McMaster, Sir Fergus, 1879–1950, vol. IV(A), vol. V

McMaster, Sir Frederick Duncan, 1873–1954, vol. V

McMaster, Ian, 1898–1978, vol. VII

Macmaster, James, died 1933, vol. III

McMaster, John Bach, 1852–1932, vol. III

McMaster, Col John Maxwell, 1855–1937, vol. III

McMaster, Robert Maxwell, 1892–1936, vol. III

M'Means, Lt-Col Hon. Lendrum, 1859–1941, vol. IV(A), vol. V

MacMechan Archibald M'Kellar, 1862–1933, vol. III

McMeekan, Brig. Gilbert Reader, 1900–1982, vol. VIII

McMeekin, Lt-Gen. Sir Terence Douglas Herbert, 1918–1984, vol. VIII

McMenemey, William Henry, 1905–1977, vol. VII

MacMichael, Sir Harold Alfred, 1882–1969, vol. VI

Macmichael, Neil, 1871–1949, vol. III

MacMichael, Nicholas Hugh, 1933–1985, vol. VIII

McMichael, Robert Clark, 1878–1957, vol. V

M'Michael, Solon William, 1848–1923, vol. II

McMicking, Major Gilbert, 1862–1942, vol. IV

McMicking, Col Harry, 1867–1944, vol. IV

McMicking, Maj.-Gen. Neil, 1894–1963, vol. VI

Macmillan of Ovenden, Viscount; Maurice Victor Macmillan, 1921–1984, vol. VIII

Macmillan, Baron (Life Peer); Hugh Pattison Macmillan, 1873–1952, vol. V

McMillan, Alec, *died* 1919, vol. II

Macmillan, Lt-Col Alexander, 1871–1929, vol. III

Macmillan, Archibald Morven, 1880–1954, vol. V

McMillan, Rev. Charles D. H., *died* 1919, vol. II

Macmillan, Chrystal, *died* 1937, vol. III

Macmillan, Daniel, 1886–1965, vol. VI

McMillan, Sir Daniel Hunter, 1846–1933, vol. III

M'Millan, Hon. Donald, 1835–1914, vol. I

Macmillan, Rev. Donald, 1855–1927, vol. II

Macmillan, Donald, 1919–1982, vol. VIII

MacMillan, Donald Baxter, 1874–1970, vol. VI

Macmillan, Very Rev. Ebenezer, 1881–1944, vol. IV

MacMillan, Sir Ernest Campbell, 1893–1973, vol. VII

Macmillan, Sir Frederick, 1851–1936, vol. III

Macmillan, George A., 1855–1936, vol. III

MacMillan of MacMillan, Gen. Sir Gordon Holmes Alexander, 1897–1986, vol. VIII

MacMillan, Harvey Reginald, 1885–1976, vol. VII

Macmillan, Rev. Hugh, 1833–1903, vol. I

MacMillan, James, 1898–1985, vol. VIII

McMillan, James Athole, 1896–1977, vol. VII

Macmillan, Sir (James) Wilson, 1906–1989, vol. VIII

McMillan, John, 1873–1939, vol. III

Macmillan, Rt Rev. Mgr John, 1899–1957, vol. V

Macmillan, Rt Rev. John Victor, 1877–1956, vol. V

Macmillan, Malcolm K., 1913–1978, vol. VII

McMillan, Margaret, 1860–1931, vol. III

Macmillan, Maurice Crawford, 1853–1936, vol. III

Macmillan, Rt Hon. Maurice Victor; *see* Macmillan of Ovenden, Viscount.

Macmillan, Michael, 1853–1925, vol. II

Macmillan, Norman, 1892–1976, vol. VII

Macmillan, Rev. Robert Alexander Cameron, 1883–1917, vol. II

McMillan, Sir Robert Furse, 1858–1931, vol. III

McMillan, Thomas McLellan, 1919–1980, vol. VII

McMillan, W. H., *died* 1947, vol. IV

MacMillan, W. J. P., 1881–1957, vol. V

M'Millan, Hon. Sir William, 1850–1926, vol. II

McMillan, William, 1887–1977, vol. VII

McMillan, William Bentley, 1871–1922, vol. II

Macmillan, William Miller, 1885–1974, vol. VII

McMillan, Sir William Northrup, 1872–1925, vol. II

Macmillan, Sir Wilson; *see* Macmillan, Sir J. W.

MacMonnies, Frederick William, 1863–1937, vol. III

McMordie, Julia, *died* 1942, vol. IV

M'Mordie, Robert James, 1849–1914, vol. I.

M'Morine, Ven. John Ker, *died* 1912, vol. I

Macmorran, Alexander, 1852–1933, vol. III

McMorran, Donald Hanks, 1904–1965, vol. VI

McMorran, Helen Isabella, 1898–1985, vol. VIII

Macmorran, Kenneth Mead, 1883–1973, vol. VII

McMorrough Kavanagh, Col Sir Dermot, 1890–1958, vol. V

MacMullan, Charles W. Kirkpatrick, 1889–1973, vol. VII

McMullan, Henry Wallace, 1909–1988, vol. VIII

McMullan, Sir Thomas Wallace, 1864–1945, vol. IV

McMullen, Alexander Percy, 1875–1961, vol. VI

Macmullen, Gen. Sir (Cyril) Norman, 1877–1944, vol. IV

McMullen, Col Denis, 1902–1973, vol. VII

McMullen, Maj.-Gen. Sir Donald Jay, 1891–1967, vol. VI

MacMullen, Maj.-Gen. Hugh Tennent, 1892–1946, vol. IV

McMullen, Rear-Adm. Morrice Alexander, 1909–1990, vol. VIII

Macmullen, Gen. Sir Norman; *see* Macmullen, Gen. Sir C. N.

McMullen, Lt-Col Osmond Robert, *died* 1946, vol. IV

M'Mullen, William Halliburton, 1876–1958, vol. V

McMullin, Hon. Sir Alister Maxwell, 1900–1984, vol. VIII

MacMunn, Charles Alexander, 1852–1911, vol. I

MacMunn, Lt-Gen. Sir George Fletcher, 1869–1952, vol. V

McMunn, Maj.-Gen. James Robert, 1866–1945, vol. IV

MacMurchy, Helen, 1862–1953, vol. V

McMurdo, Captain Arthur Montagu, 1861–1914, vol. I

McMurray, Hon. Edward James, 1878–1969, vol. VI

McMurray, James Hamish, *died* 1950, vol. IV

Macmurray, John, 1891–1976, vol. VII

McMurray, Thomas Porter, 1887–1949, vol. IV

M'Murrich, James Playfair, 1859–1939, vol. III

McMurtrie, Francis Edwin, 1884–1949, vol. IV

M'Murtrie, Very Rev. John, 1831–1912, vol. I

Macnab, Col Allan James, 1864–1947, vol. IV

Macnab of Macnab, Archibald Corrie, 1886–1970, vol. VI

McNab, Hon. Archibald Peter, 1864–1945, vol. IV

Macnab, Brig.-Gen. Colin Lawrance, 1870–1918, vol. II

Macnab, George Henderson, 1904–1967, vol. VI

Macnab of Barachastlain, Iain, 1890–1967, vol. VI

Macnab, Brig. John Francis, 1906–1980, vol. VII

M'Nab, Hon. Robert, 1864–1917, vol. II

Macnab, William, 1858–1941, vol. IV

McNabb, Surg.-Rear-Adm. Sir Daniel Joseph Patrick, 1862–1937, vol. III

Macnabb, Sir Donald Campbell, 1832–1913, vol. I

Macnabb, Lt-Col Donald John Campbell, 1864–1936, vol. III

MacNachtan, Col Neil F., 1850–1928, vol. II

Macnaghten, Baron (Life Peer); Edward Macnaghten, 1830–1913, vol. I

Macnaghten, Sir Antony, 10th Bt, 1899–1972, vol. VII

Macnaghten, Sir Arthur Douglas, 7th Bt, 1897–1916, vol. II

Macnaghten, Col Charles Melville, 1879–1931, vol. III

Macnaghten, Hon. Sir Edward Charles, 5th Bt, 1859–1914, vol. I

Macnaghten, Sir Edward Henry, 6th Bt, 1896–1916, vol. II

Macnaghten, Brig.-Gen. Ernest Brander, 1872–1948, vol. IV

Macnaghten, Hon. Sir Francis Alexander, 8th Bt, 1863–1951, vol. V

Macnaghten, Rt Hon. Sir Francis Edmund Workman-, 3rd Bt, 1828–1911, vol. I

Macnaghten, Hon. Sir Frederic Fergus, 9th Bt, 1867–1955, vol. V

Macnaghten, Sir Henry, 1880–1949, vol. IV

Macnaghten, Rev. Henry Alexander, 1850–1928, vol. II

Macnaghten, Hugh Vibart, *died* 1929, vol. III

Macnaghten, Rt Hon. Sir Malcolm, 1869–1955, vol. V

Macnaghten, Sir Melville Leslie, 1853–1921, vol. II

Macnaghten, Steuart, 1873–1952, vol. V

Macnaghten, Terence Charles, 1872–1944, vol. IV

McNair, 1st Baron, 1885–1975, vol. VII

McNair, 2nd Baron, 1915–1989, vol. VIII

McNair, Arthur James, 1887–1964, vol. VI

McNair, Arthur Wyndham, 1872–1965, vol. VI

McNair, Sir Douglas; *see* McNair, Sir G. D.

M'Nair, Lt-Gen. Edward John, 1838–1921, vol. II

McNair, Captain Eric Archibald, *died* 1918, vol. II

McNair, Sir (George) Douglas, 1887–1967, vol. VI

McNair, Air Vice-Marshal James Jamieson, 1917–1990, vol. VIII

McNair, John, 1887–1968, vol. VI

M'Nair, Major John Frederick Adolphus, 1828–1910, vol. I

McNair, Brig. John Kirkland, 1893–1973, vol. VII

Macnair, Peter, 1868–1929, vol. III

Macnair, Sir Robert Hill, 1877–1959, vol. V

McNair, Sir William Lennox, 1892–1979, vol. VII

McNairn, Edward Somerville, 1907–1975, vol. VII

McNally, Most Rev. John Thomas, 1871–1952, vol. V

McNalty, Brig.-Gen. Arthur George Preston, 1871–1958, vol. V

MacNalty, Sir Arthur Salusbury, 1880–1969, vol. VI

M'Nalty, Lt-Col George William, 1837–1912, vol. I

Macnamara, Arthur, 1829–1906, vol. I

McNamara, Lt-Gen. Sir Arthur Edward, 1877–1949, vol. IV

MacNamara, Arthur James, 1885–1962, vol. VI

Macnamara, Eric Danvers, *died* 1934, vol. III

McNamara, Air Vice-Marshal Frank Hubert, 1894–1961, vol. VI

McNamara, George, 1881–1953, vol. V

Macnamara, Col John Robert Jermain, 1905–1944, vol. IV

McNamara, Most Rev. Kevin, 1926–1987, vol. VIII

Macnamara, N. C., *died* 1918, vol. II

Macnamara, Neil Cameron, 1891–1968, vol. VI

Macnamara, Rear-Adm. Sir Patrick, 1886–1957, vol. V

Macnamara, Rt Hon. Thomas James, 1861–1931, vol. III

Macnamara, Walter Henry, 1851–1920, vol. II

M'Namara, Surg.-Gen. William Henry, 1846–1915, vol. I

McNamara Ryan, Patrick John; *see* Ryan.

Mac-Namee, Rt Rev. James Joseph, 1876–1966, vol. VI

McNarney, Gen. Joseph Taggart, 1893–1972, vol. VII

M'Naught, W. G., 1849–1918, vol. II

McNaught, William, 1883–1953, vol. V

McNaught, William Kirkpatrick, 1845–1919, vol. II

Macnaughtan, S., *died* 1916, vol. II

Macnaughton, Allan Wight, 1859–1937, vol. III

McNaughton, Gen. Hon. Andrew George Latta, 1887–1966, vol. VI

McNaughton, Brig. Forbes Lankester, 1891–1959, vol. V

McNaughton, Sir George Matthew, *died* 1966, vol. VI

Macnaughton, Rev. John, 1858–1943, vol. IV

Macnaughton-Jones, Henry, *died* 1918, vol. II

Macnaughton-Jones, Rev. William Hudson, *died* 1941, vol. IV

Macneal, Sir Hector Murray, 1879–1966, vol. VI

McNee, Sir John William, 1887–1984, vol. VIII

MacNeece, Maj.-Gen. James Gaussen, 1856–1919, vol. II

MacNeece, William Foster; *see* Foster, Air Vice-Marshal W. F. MacN.

McNeely, Most Rev. William, 1888–1963, vol. VI

McNeice, Rt Rev. John Frederick, *died* 1942, vol. IV

Macneice, Louise, 1907–1963, vol. VI

McNeil, Anne, 1902–1984, vol. VIII

McNeil, Charles, 1881–1964, vol. VI

M'Neil, Daniel, 1853–1918, vol. II

McNeil, Rt Hon. Hector, 1907–1955, vol. V

McNeil, Sir Hector, 1904–1978, vol. VII

MacNeil, Hermon Atkins, 1866–1947, vol. IV(A)

McNeil, Kenneth Gordon, 1902–1970, vol. VI

M'Neil, Most Rev. Neil, 1851–1934, vol. III

McNeil, Engr Rear-Adm. Percival Edwin, 1883–1951, vol. V

Macneil of Barra, Robert Lister, (The Macneil of Barra), 1889–1970, vol. VI

M'Neile, Rev. Alan Hugh, 1871–1933, vol. III

McNeile, Lt-Col Cyril, 1888–1937, vol. III

McNeile, Robert Arbuthnot, 1913–1985, vol. VIII

McNeill, Maj.-Gen. Alister Argyll Campbell, 1884–1971, vol. VII

M'Neill, Brig.-Gen. Angus John, 1874–1950, vol. IV

McNeill, Sir David Bruce, 1922–1990, vol. VIII

Macneill, Eoin; *see* Macneill, John.

McNeill, Florence Marian, 1885–1973, vol. VII

McNeill, Sir Hector, 1892–1952, vol. V

McNeill, James, 1869–1938, vol. III

McNeill, Sir James Charles, 1916–1987, vol. VIII

MacNeill, Maj.-Gen. James Graham Robert Douglas, 1842–1904, vol. I

McNeill, Sir James McFadyen, 1892–1964, vol. VI

M'Neill, Rev. John, 1854–1933, vol. III

Macneill, Rev. John, 1874–1937, vol. III

Macneill, John, (Eoin Macneill), 1867–1945, vol. IV

M'Neill, Maj.-Gen. Sir John Carstairs, 1831–1904, vol. I

Macneill, John Gordon Swift, 1849–1926, vol. II

M'Neill, Captain Malcolm, 1866–1917, vol. II

McNeill, Sir Malcolm, 1839–1919, vol. II

Macneill, Murray, 1877–1951, vol. V

McNeill, Robert Norman, *died* 1956, vol. V

McNeill-Moss, Major Geoffrey, *died* 1954, vol. V

McNerney, Joshua William, 1872–1944, vol. IV

McNess, Sir Charles, 1853–1938, vol. III

Macnicol, Nicol, 1870–1952, vol. V

McNicoll, Vice-Adm. Sir Alan Wedel Ramsay, 1908–1987, vol. VIII

McNicoll, Brig.-Gen. Sir Walter Ramsay, 1877–1947, vol. IV

McNish, Col George, 1866–1943, vol. IV

McNulty, Rev. C. T. Bernard, 1875–1939, vol. III

McNulty, Rt Rev. John, 1879–1943, vol. IV

Macnutt, Ernest Augustus, 1876–1955, vol. V

Macnutt, Rev. Canon Frederick Brodie, 1873–1949, vol. IV

McNutt, Hon. Peter, 1834–1919, vol. II

MacNutt, Hon. Thomas, 1850–1927, vol. II

Maconachie, Sir Richard Roy, 1885–1962, vol. VI

Maconchy, Brig.-Gen. Ernest William Stuart King, 1860–1945, vol. IV

Maconchy, Captain Frederick Campbell, 1868–1943, vol. IV

Maconochie, A. White, 1855–1926, vol. II

Maconochie, Charles Cornelius, 1852–1930, vol. III

Maconochie, Sir Evan, 1868–1927, vol. II

Maconochie, Sir Robert Henry, 1883–1962, vol. VI

MacOrlan, Pierre, 1882–1970, vol. VI

Macoun, James Melville, 1862–1920, vol. II

Macoun, John, 1831–1921, vol. II

McOwan, George, 1894–1972, vol. VII

M'Owan, Islay, 1871–1948, vol. IV

MacOwan, Michael Charles Henry, 1906–1980, vol. VII

M'Peake, James Young, 1868–1924, vol. II

McPetrie, James Stuart, 1902–1990, vol. VIII

Macphail, Alexander, 1872–1938, vol. III

Macphail, Col Alexander, 1870–1949, vol. IV

Macphail, Sir Andrew, 1864–1938, vol. III

Macphail, Rev. Earle Monteith, 1861–1937, vol. III

Macphail, James Robert Nicolson, died 1933, vol. III

McPhail, Walter, died 1941, vol. IV

Macphail, Rev. William Merry, 1857–1916, vol. II

M'Phedran, Alexander, died 1934, vol. III

McPhee, Hon. Sir John Cameron, 1878–1952, vol. V

Macpherson of Drumochter, 1st Baron, 1888–1965, vol. VI

Macpherson, Alan, 1857–1930, vol. III

McPherson, Brig. Alan Bruce, 1887–1978, vol. VII

Macpherson, Brig. Alan David, (Cluny Macpherson), 1887–1969, vol. VI

Macpherson, Albert Cameron, (Cluny Macpherson), 1854–1932, vol. III

Macpherson, Brig.-Gen. Alexander Duncan, 1877–1944, vol. IV

Macpherson of Pitmain, Lt-Col Alexander Kilgour, 1888–1974, vol. VII

Macpherson, Lt-Col Archibald Duncan, 1872–1928, vol. II

Macpherson, Sir Arthur George, 1828–1921, vol. II

Macpherson, Arthur George Holdsworth, 1873–1942, vol. IV

Macpherson, Arthur Holte, 1867–1953, vol. V

Macpherson, Hon. Campbell Leonard, 1907–1973, vol. VII

Macpherson, Charles, 1870–1927, vol. II

Macpherson, Charles Gordon Welland, 1846–1910, vol. I

McPherson, Sir Clive, 1884–1958, vol. V

Macpherson, Lt-Col Cluny, 1879–1966, vol. VI

MacPherson, Rt Rev. Colin, 1917–1990, vol. VIII

Macpherson, Colin, 1927–1988, vol. VIII

Macpherson, Colin Francis, 1884–1970, vol. VI

McPherson, Col David William, 1869–1923, vol. II

MacPherson, Donald, 1894–1989, vol. VIII

McPherson, Donald George, 1914–1973, vol. VII

Macpherson, Sir Duncan James, 1855–1936, vol. III

Macpherson, Ewan Francis, died 1941, vol. IV

Macpherson, Ewen, 1872–1962, vol. VI

McPherson, Ewen Alexander, 1879–1954, vol. V

Macpherson, Rev. Ewen George Fitzroy, 1863–1926, vol. II

Macpherson, Brig.-Gen. Ewen Henry Davidson, (Cluny Macpherson), 1836–1900, vol. I

Macpherson, George, died 1924, vol. II

Macpherson, George Philip Stewart, 1903–1981, vol. VIII

Macpherson, Hector, died 1924, vol. II

Macpherson, Rev. Hector, 1888–1956, vol. V

McPherson, Henry Alexander, 1855–1939, vol. III

M'Pherson, Sir Hugh, 1870–1960, vol. V, vol. VI

Macpherson, Lt-Col James, 1876–1938, vol. III

McPherson, Bt Col James, 1876–1963, vol. VI

Macpherson, James, 1911–1982, vol. VIII

Macpherson, James Simpson, 1863–1935, vol. III

Macpherson, Sir John, 1857–1942, vol. IV

Macpherson, Sir John Molesworth, 1853–1914, vol. I

Macpherson, Sir John Stuart, 1898–1971, vol. VII

Macpherson, Rear-Adm. Kenneth Douglas Worsley, 1883–1962, vol. VI

MacPherson, Malcolm, 1904–1971, vol. VII

MacPherson, Major Hon. Murdoch Alexander, 1891–1966, vol. VI

Macpherson, Sir Norman Macgregor, died 1947, vol. IV

Macpherson, Stewart, died 1941, vol. IV

Macpherson, Sir Stewart; see Macpherson, Sir T. S.

McPherson, Sir Thomas, died 1947, vol. IV

Macpherson, Sir (Thomas) Stewart, 1876–1949, vol. IV

Macpherson, Rev. Thomas William, 1863–1936, vol. III

Macpherson, Sir William, 1836–1909, vol. I

Macpherson, William Charles, 1855–1936, vol. III

Macpherson, Maj.-Gen. Sir William Grant, 1858–1927, vol. II

McPherson, Hon. Sir William Murray, 1865–1932, vol. III

Macpherson, Very Rev. William Stuart, 1901–1978, vol. VII

Macpherson-Grant, Sir Ewan George, 6th Bt, 1907–1983, vol. VIII

Macpherson-Grant, Sir George, 5th Bt, 1890–1951, vol. V

Macpherson-Grant, Captain George Bertram, died 1932, vol. III

Macpherson-Grant, Sir John, 4th Bt, 1863–1914, vol. I

McPhillips, Captain Hon. Albert Edward, 1861–1938, vol. III

McQuade, John, 1912–1984, vol. VIII

McQuaid, Most Rev. John Charles, 1895–1973, vol. VII

Macquaker, Sir Thomas, 1851–1938, vol. III

MacQuarrie, Josiah H., 1897–1971, vol. VII

McQuarrie, William Garland, 1876–1943, vol. IV

Macqueen, James, 1853–1936, vol. III
MacQueen, Maj.-Gen. John Henry, 1893–1980, vol. VII
M'Queen, Lt-Gen. Sir John Withers, 1836–1909, vol. I
Macqueen-Pope, Walter James, 1888–1960, vol. V
McQuesten, Hon. Thomas Baker, 1882–1948, vol. IV
M'Quhae, Captain John Mackenzie, 1847–1901, vol. I
McQuibban, Lewis, 1866–1944, vol. IV
Macquisten, Frederick Alexander, 1870–1940, vol. III
Macquoid, Brig.-Gen. Charles Edward Every Francis Kirwan, 1869–1945, vol. IV
Macquoid, Gilbert Samuel, 1854–1940, vol. III
Macquoid, Katharine Sarah, 1824–1917, vol. II
Macquoid, Percy, *died* 1925, vol. II
Macquoid, Thomas Robert, 1820–1912, vol. I
Macrae, Maj.-Gen. Albert Edward, 1886–1958, vol. V
McRae, Maj.-Gen. Hon. Alexander Duncan, 1874–1946, vol. IV
Macrae, Col Alexander William, 1858–1920, vol. II
Macrae, Angus, 1893–1975, vol. VII
Macrae, Charles Colin, 1843–1922, vol. II
Macrae, Christopher, 1910–1990, vol. VIII
Macrae, Sir Colin George, 1844–1925, vol. II
MacRae of Feoirlinn, Col Sir Colin William, 1869–1952, vol. V
MacRae, Donald Mackenzie, 1869–1955, vol. V
McRae, Col Henry Napier, 1851–1915, vol. I
Macrae, Herbert Alexander, 1886–1967, vol. VI
Macrae, Hugh, 1880–1965, vol. VI
Macrae, Maj.-Gen. Ian Macpherson, 1882–1956, vol. V
Macrae, Col John Cecil, 1881–1940, vol. III
MacRae, Very Rev. John Eric, 1870–1947, vol. IV
Macrae, Robert Scarth Farquhar, 1877–1926, vol. II
Macrae, Col Roderick, 1850–1915, vol. I
Macrae, Russell Duncan, 1888–1956, vol. V
McRae, William, 1878–1952, vol. V
MacRae-Gilstrap, Lt-Col John, 1861–1937, vol. III
Macran, Henry Stewart, *died* 1937, vol. III
Macray, Rev. William Dunn, 1826–1916, vol. II
McRea, Sir Charles James Hugh, 1874–1951, vol. V
Macready, Gen. Rt Hon. Sir (Cecil Frederick) Nevil, 1st Bt, 1862–1946, vol. IV
Macready, Lt-Gen. Sir Gordon Nevil, 2nd Bt, 1891–1956, vol. V
Macready, Brig. John, 1887–1957, vol. V
Macready, Gen. Rt Hon. Sir Nevil; *see* Macready, Gen. Rt Hon. Sir C. F. N.
MacRedmond, Rt Rev. Thomas, 1838–1904, vol. I
MacRitchie, Farquhar, 1902–1988, vol. VIII
McRobert, Brig. Leslie Harrison, 1898–1981, vol. VIII
MacRitchie, David, 1851–1925, vol. II
MacRobert, Sir Alasdair Workman, 2nd Bt, 1912–1938, vol. III
M'Robert, Sir Alexander, 1st Bt, 1854–1922, vol. II
MacRobert, Rt Hon. Alexander Munro, 1873–1930, vol. III
McRobert, Sir George Reid, 1895–1976, vol. VII
MacRobert, Sir Iain Workman, 4th Bt, 1917–1941, vol. IV

MacRobert, Norman Murie, 1899–1972, vol. VII
MacRobert, Rachel W., (Lady MacRobert), *died* 1954, vol. V
MacRobert, Sir Roderic Alan, 3rd Bt, 1915–1941, vol. IV
MacRobert, Thomas Murray, 1884–1962, vol. VI
Macrorie, Vice-Adm. Arthur Kenneth, 1874–1947, vol. IV
Macrorie, Rt Rev. William Kenneth, 1831–1905, vol. I
Macrory, Edmund, *died* 1904, vol. I
MacRory, His Eminence Cardinal Joseph, 1861–1945, vol. IV
Macrossan, Hugh Denis, 1881–1940, vol. III
Macrossan, Hon. Neal William, 1889–1955, vol. V
McShane, John J., 1882–1972, vol. VII
McSheehy, Maj.-Gen. Oswald William, 1884–1975, vol. VII
Mac-Sherry, Most Rev. Hugh, 1852–1940, vol. III
McSparran, James, 1892–1970, vol. VI
MacSweeney, Rev. Patrick M., 1873–1935, vol. III
McSweeny, George, 1865–1923, vol. II, vol. III
McSwiney, Bryan Austin, 1894–1947, vol. IV
McSwiney, Col Edward Frederick Henry, 1858–1907, vol. I
McSwiney, Col Herbert Frederick Cyril, 1886–1963, vol. VI
MacSwiney, Terrence Joseph, 1880–1920, vol. II
MacTaggart, Sir Andrew McCormick, 1888–1978, vol. VII
Mactaggart, Col Charles, 1861–1930, vol. III
Mactaggart, Sir Ian Auld, 3rd Bt, 1923–1987, vol. VIII
Mactaggart, Sir John Auld, 1st Bt, 1867–1956, vol. V
Mactaggart, Sir John Auld, 2nd Bt, 1898–1960, vol. V
M'Taggart, John M'Taggart Ellis, 1866–1925, vol. II
McTaggart, Lt-Col Maxwell Fielding, 1874–1936, vol. III
McTaggart, Robert, 1945–1989, vol. VIII
McTaggart, Captain W. B., *died* 1919, vol. II
M'Taggart, William, 1835–1910, vol. I
MacTaggart, Sir William, 1903–1981, vol. VIII
MacTaggart-Stewart, Sir Edward Orde; *see* Stewart.
MacTier, Sir (Reginald) Stewart, 1905–1984, vol. VIII
MacTier, Sir Stewart; *see* MacTier, Sir R. S.
McTiernan, Rt Hon. Sir Edward Aloysius, 1892–1990, vol. VIII
M'Turk, Michael, 1843–1915, vol. I
M'Vail, Sir David Caldwell, 1845–1917, vol. II
McVail, John Christie, 1849–1926, vol. II
Macveagh, Jeremiah, 1870–1932, vol. III
M'Vean, Col Donald Archibald Dugald, 1870–1937, vol. III
McVeigh, Rt Hon. Sir Herbert Andrew, 1908–1977, vol. VII
McVey, Arthur Michael, 1879–1964, vol. VI
McVey, Sir Daniel, 1892–1972, vol. VII
MacVicar, Hon. John, 1859–1928, vol. II, vol. III
M'Vicker, Sir Robert, 1822–1897, vol. I
McVie, John, 1888–1967, vol. VI
M'Vittie, Surg.-Gen. Charles Edwin, *died* 1916, vol. II

McVittie, Lt-Col Charles Edwin, 1870–1933, vol. III
McVittie, Maj.-Gen. Charles Harold, 1908–1988, vol. VIII
McVittie, George Cunliffe, 1904–1988, vol. VIII
McVittie, Col Robert Henry, 1872–1949, vol. IV
McVittie, Wilfrid Wolters, 1906–1980, vol. VII
Macwatt, Maj.-Gen. Sir Charles; see Macwatt, Maj.-Gen. Sir R. C.
MacWatt, Hay, 1855–1920, vol. II
Macwatt, John, 1857–1938, vol. III
Macwatt, Maj.-Gen. Sir (Robert) Charles, 1865–1945, vol. IV
McWatters, Sir Arthur Cecil, 1880–1965, vol. VI
McWeeney, Edmond J., 1864–1925, vol. II, vol. III
McWeeney, Henry Charles, 1867–1935, vol. III
McWhae, Brig. Douglas Murray, 1884–1969, vol. VI
M'Whae, Hon. Sir John, 1858–1927, vol. II
McWhan, John, 1885–1943, vol. IV
McWhinnie, Donald, 1920–1987, vol. VIII
McWhinnie, Hugh, died 1923, vol. II
McWhirter, (Alan) Ross, 1925–1975, vol. VII
Macwhirter, Clara Elizabeth Littlewort, died 1971, vol. VII
MacWhirter, John, 1839–1911, vol. I
McWhirter, Ross; see McWhirter, A. R.
McWhirter, William Allan, 1888–1955, vol. V
MacWhite, Michael, 1883–1958, vol. V
M'William, Andrew, died 1922, vol. II
McWilliam, Sir John, 1910–1974, vol. VII
MacWilliam, John Alexander, 1857–1937, vol. III
McWilliam, William Nicholson, 1897–1987, vol. VIII
Macy, George, 1900–1956, vol. V
Madan, Falconer, 1851–1935, vol. III
Madan, Rev. Nigel, 1840–1915, vol. I
Madariaga, Don Salvador de, 1886–1978, vol. VII
Maddan, James Gracie, 1873–1966, vol. VI
Maddan, Martin, 1920–1973, vol. VII
Madden, Adm. Sir Alexander Cumming Gordon, 1895–1964, vol. VI
Madden, Archibald Maclean, 1864–1928, vol. II
Madden, Charles Dodgson, 1833–1910, vol. I
Madden, Admiral of the Fleet Sir Charles Edward, 1st Bt, 1862–1935, vol. III
Madden, Rt Hon. Dodgson Hamilton, 1840–1928, vol. II
Madden, Hon. Sir Frank, 1847–1921, vol. II
Madden, Frank Cole, 1873–1929, vol. III
Madden, Frederic William, 1839–1904, vol. I
Madden, Lt-Col George Colquhoun, 1856–1912, vol. I
Madden, Hon. Sir John, 1844–1918, vol. II
Madden, Lt-Col John Clements Waterhouse, 1870–1935, vol. III
Madden, Samuel Fitzgerald, 1878–1934, vol. III
Madden, Ven. T. J., 1853–1915, vol. I
Madden, Thomas More, 1844–1902, vol. I
Madden, Hon. Walter, 1848–1925, vol. II
Madden, William Thomas, 1877–1967, vol. VI
Madden, Wyndham D'Arcy, 1885–1968, vol. VI
Maddex, Sir George Henry, 1895–1982, vol. VIII
Maddick, Edmund Distin, died 1939, vol. III
Maddick, George John, 1849–1942, vol. IV
Maddison, Rev. Arthur Roland, 1843–1912, vol. I
Maddison, Fred, 1856–1937, vol. III

Maddison, Rev. William, 1853–1920, vol. II
Maddock, Rt Rev. David Rokeby, 1915–1984, vol. VIII
Maddock, Lt-Col Edward Cecil Gordon, 1876–1952, vol. V
Maddock, Sir Ieuan, 1917–1988, vol. VIII
Maddock, Sir Simon, 1869–1927, vol. II
Maddocks, George, 1896–1980, vol. VII
Maddocks, Sir Henry, 1871–1931, vol. III
Maddocks, Henry Hollingdrake, 1898–1969, vol. VI
Maddox, Ernest Edmund, 1860–1933, vol. III
Maddox, Sir (John) Kempson, 1901–1990, vol. VIII
Maddox, Sir Kempson; see Maddox, Sir J. K.
Maddox, Lt-Col Ralph Henry, 1864–1935, vol. III
Maddox, Samuel, 1930–1979, vol. VII
Maddox, Stuart Lockwood, 1866–1942, vol. IV
Maddrell, Rev. Thomas Fisher, 1861–1932, vol. III
Maddy, Rev. H. W., 1829–1909, vol. I
Madeley, Earl of; Richard George Archibald John Lucien Hungerford Crew-Milnes, 1911–1922, vol. II
Maden, Henry, 1892–1960, vol. V
Maden, Sir John Henry, 1862–1920, vol. II
Madgavkar, Sir Govind Dinanath, 1871–1948, vol. IV
Madge, Rev. Francis Thomas, 1849–1933, vol. III
Madge, Captain Sir Frank William, 2nd Bt, 1897–1962, vol. VI
Madge, Sidney Joseph, 1874–1961, vol. VI
Madge, Sir William Thomas, 1st Bt, 1845–1927, vol. II
Madgwick, Sir Robert Bowden, 1905–1979, vol. VII (AII)
Madhava, Rae, V. P., died 1934, vol. III(A), vol. IV
Madigan, Cecil Thomas, 1889–1947, vol. IV
Madill, Surg. Rear-Adm. Thomas, 1895–1962, vol. VI
Madoc, Lt-Col Henry William, died 1937, vol. III
Madoc, Maj.-Gen. Reginald William, 1907–1986, vol. VIII
Madocks, Brig.-Gen. William Robarts Napier, 1871–1946, vol. IV
Madrid, Duke of; see Carlos, Don.
Madsen, Sir John Percival Vissing, 1879–1969, vol. VI
Maegraith, Brian Gilmore, 1907–1989, vol. VIII
Maelor, Baron (Life Peer), Thomas William Jones, 1898–1984, vol. VIII
Maenan, 1st Baron, 1854–1951, vol. V
Maeterlinck, Count Maurice Polydore Marie Bernard, 1862–1949, vol. IV
Maflin, Major George Hamilton, vol. II
Magan, Lt-Col Arthur Tilson Shaen, 1880–1965, vol. VI
Magarey, Sir (James) Rupert, 1914–1990, vol. VIII
Magarey, Sir Rupert; see Magarey, Sir J. R.
Magauran, Wilfrid Henry Bertram, 1898–1964, vol. VI
Magee, Allan Angus, 1881–1961, vol. VI
Magee, Sir Cuthbert Gaulter, died 1963, vol. VI
Magee, Hon. James, born 1846, vol. III
Magee, Reginald Arthur Edward, 1914–1989, vol. VIII
Mageean, Most Rev. Daniel, 1882–1962, vol. VI

Magenis, Maj.-Gen. Henry Cole, 1838–1906, vol. I
Magennis, Rt Rev. Edward, *died* 1906, vol. I
Magennis, Edward, *died* 1938, vol. III
Magennis, William, 1869–1946, vol. IV
Mager, Sydney, 1877–1952, vol. V
Maggs, Joseph Herbert, 1875–1964, vol. VI
Magheramorne, 2nd Baron, 1861–1903, vol. I
Magheramorne, 3rd Baron, 1863–1946, vol. IV
Magheramorne, 4th Baron, 1865–1957, vol. V
Magian, Anthony John Capper, 1878–1956, vol. V
Magill, Andrew Philip, *died* 1941, vol. IV
Magill, Sir Ivan Whiteside, 1888–1986, vol. VIII
Magill, Col Sir James, 1850–1936, vol. III
Magill, Walter Alexander, 1879–1950, vol. IV
Maginess, Rt Hon. William Brian, 1901–1967, vol. VI
Maginness, Edmund John, 1857–1938, vol. III
Maginness, Sir Greville Simpson, 1888–1961, vol. VI
Maglione, His Eminence Cardinal Luigi, 1877–1944, vol. IV
Magnani, Anna, 1918–1973, vol. VII
Magnay, Brig. Arthur Douglas, 1893–1964, vol. VI
Magnay, Major Sir Christopher Boyd William, 3rd Bt, 1884–1960, vol. V
Magnay, Harold Swindale, 1904–1971, vol. VII
Magnay, Thomas, 1876–1949, vol. IV
Magnay, Sir William, 2nd Bt, 1855–1917, vol. II
Magner, Jeremiah John, 1891–1973, vol. VII
Magnes, Judah Leon, 1877–1948, vol. IV
Magniac, Brig.-Gen. Sir Charles Lane, 1873–1953, vol. V
Magniac, Major Hubert, *died* 1909, vol. I
Magniac, Oswald Cecil, *died* 1939, vol. III
Magnus, Henry Adolph, 1909–1967, vol. VI
Magnus, Hilary Barrow, 1909–1987, vol. VIII
Magnus, Katie, (Lady Magnus), 1844–1924, vol. II
Magnus, Laurie, 1872–1933, vol. III
Magnus, Sir Philip, 1st Bt, 1842–1933, vol. III
Magnus-Allcroft, Sir Philip, 2nd Bt, 1906–1988, vol. VIII
Magowan, Sir John Hall, 1893–1951, vol. V
Magowan, Joseph Irvine, 1901–1977, vol. VII
Magrane, Col John Plunkett, 1896–1963, vol. VI
Magrath, Maj.-Gen. Beauchamp Henry Whittingham, 1832–1920, vol. II
Magrath, Charles Alexander, 1860–1949, vol. IV
Magrath, Harry William, *died* 1969, vol. VI
Magrath, Rev. John Richard, 1839–1930, vol. III
Maguiness, Rev. John Thomas, *died* 1920, vol. II
Maguinness, William Stuart, 1903–1982, vol. VIII
Maguire, Sir Alexander Herbert, 1876–1947, vol. IV
Maguire, Conor A., 1889–1971, vol. VII
Maguire, Very Rev. Edward, 1822–1913, vol. I
Maguire, Frank; *see* Maguire, M. F.
Maguire, Maj.-Gen. Frederick Arthur, 1888–1953, vol. V(A)
Maguire, James Rochfort, 1855–1925, vol. II
Maguire, Most Rev. John A., 1851–1920, vol. II
Maguire, Meredith Francis, (Frank Maguire), 1929–1981, vol. VIII
Maguire, Robert, 1857–1915, vol. I
Maguire, William Joseph, *died* 1934, vol. III
Mahadeva, Sir Arunachalam, *born* 1885, vol. VI
Mahaffy, Alexander Francis, 1891–1962, vol. VI

Mahaffy, Arthur William, 1869–1919, vol. II
Mahaffy, Rev. Gilbert, *died* 1916, vol. II
Mahaffy, Sir John Pentland, 1839–1919, vol. II
Mahaffy, Robert Pentland, 1871–1943, vol. IV
Mahaim, Ernest A. J., 1865–1938, vol. III(A), vol. IV
Mahalanobis, Prasanta Chandra, 1893–1972, vol. VII
Mahalanobis, S. C., 1867–1953, vol. V
Mahan, Rear Adm. Alfred T., 1840–1914, vol. I
Mahdi Husain, Khan, Wahud-ud-Daula, Azod-ul-Mulk, Nawab Mirza, Khan Bahadur, *born* 1834, vol. II
Maher, Charles Ernest, 1896–1961, vol. VI
Maher, Maj.-Gen. Sir James, 1858–1928, vol. II
Maheshwari, Panchanan, 1904–1966, vol. VI
Maheu, René G., 1905–1975, vol. VII
Mahir, Thomas Edward, 1915–1970, vol. VI
Mahler, Kurt, 1903–1988, vol. VIII
Mahmudabad, Maharaja of, 1877–1931, vol. III
Mahon, Lt-Col Bryan MacMahon, 1890–1949, vol. IV
Mahon, Gen. Rt Hon. Sir Bryan Thomas, 1862–1930, vol. III
Mahon, Edward Elphinstone, 1851–1912, vol. I
Mahon, Sir George Edward John, 6th Bt, 1911–1987, vol. VIII
Mahon, Sir Gerald MacMahon, 1904–1982, vol. VIII
Mahon, Harold J. D., 1873–1938, vol. III
Mahon, Captain Henry P.; *see* Pakenham-Mahon.
Mahon, Hon. Hugh, 1858–1931, vol. III
Mahon, John FitzGerald, 1858–1942, vol. IV
Mahon, Ralph Bodkin, 1862–1943, vol. IV(A)
Mahon, Maj.-Gen. Reginald Henry, 1859–1929, vol. III
Mahon, Simon, 1914–1986, vol. VIII
Mahon, Sir William Henry, 5th Bt, 1856–1926, vol. II
Mahoney, Charles, 1903–1968, vol. VI
Mahoney, Sir John Andrew, 1883–1966, vol. VI
Mahoney, Merchant Michael, 1886–1946, vol. IV
Mahony, Lt-Col John Keefer, 1911–1990, vol. VIII
Mahony, Rt Rev. Mgr John Mathew, 1862–1918, vol. II
Mahony, Major Michael Joseph, *died* 1927, vol. II
Mahony, Peirce Gun, 1878–1914, vol. I
Mahood, James, 1876–1950, vol. IV
Mahtab, Maharajadhiraja Bahadur Sir Uday Chand, 1905–1984, vol. VIII
Maiden, Joseph Henry, 1859–1925, vol. II
Maidment, Kenneth John, 1910–1990, vol. VIII
Maillard, Staff Surgeon William J., *died* 1903, vol. I
Maillol, Aristide, 1861–1944, vol. IV
Main, Rev. Archibald, 1876–1947, vol. IV
Main, David, 1861–1941, vol. IV
Main, David Duncan, 1856–1934, vol. III
Main, Lt-Comdr Frank Morgan, *died* 1924, vol. II
Main, Henry, 1888–1949, vol. IV
Main, Brig. John Walter, 1900–1971, vol. VII
Main, Col Thomas Ryder, 1850–1934, vol. III
Maindron, Maurice Georges Rene, 1857–1911, vol. I
Mainds, Allan Douglass, 1881–1945, vol. IV
Maine, Rev. Basil Stephen, 1894–1972, vol. VII
Maine, Henry Cecil Sumner, 1886–1968, vol. VI
Maingot, Rodney Honor, 1893–1982, vol. VIII
Mainland, William Faulkner, 1905–1988, vol. VIII

Mainprise, Maj.-Gen. Cecil Wilmot, 1873–1951, vol. V

Mainprise, Captain William Thomas, *died* 1902, vol. I

Mainstone, Madeleine Françoise, 1925–1979, vol. VII

Mainwaring, Albert James, 1891–1941, vol. IV

Mainwaring, Charles Francis Kynaston, 1877–1949, vol. IV

Mainwaring, Col Charles Salusbury, 1845–1920, vol. II

Mainwaring, Brig. Guy Rowland, 1885–1956, vol. V

Mainwaring, Sir Harry Stapleton, 5th Bt, 1878–1934, vol. III

Mainwaring, Brig. Hugh Salusbury Kynaston, 1906–1976, vol. VII

Mainwaring, Sir Philip Tatton, 4th Bt, 1838–1906, vol. I

Mainwaring, Hon. Maj.-Gen. Rowland Broughton, 1850–1926, vol. II

Mainwaring, Col Sir Watkin Randle Kynaston, 1875–1944, vol. IV

Mainwaring, Hon. William Frederick Barton Massey-, 1845–1907, vol. I

Mainwaring, Gen. William George, 1823–1905, vol. I

Mainwaring, William Henry, 1884–1971, vol. VII

Mainwaring-Bowen, Arthur Charles, 1922–1980, vol. VII

Mair, Alexander, 1870–1927, vol. II

Mair, Alexander W., *died* 1928, vol. II

Mair, Charles, 1838–1927, vol. II

Mair, George Herbert, 1887–1926, vol. II

Mair, Brig.-Gen. George Tagore, 1873–1941, vol. IV

Mair, Rev. John, 1822–1902, vol. I

Mair, John Bagrie, 1857–1927, vol. II

Mair, Lucy Philip, 1901–1986, vol. VIII

Mair, Col Robert John Byford, 1868–1940, vol. III

Mair, Dame Sarah Elizabeth Siddons, 1846–1941, vol. IV

Mair, Very Rev. William, 1830–1920, vol. II

Mairet, Ethel, 1872–1952, vol. V

Mairis, Gen. Geoffrey, 1834–1917, vol. II

Mais, Stuart Petre Brodie, 1885–1975, vol. VII

Maisky, Ivan Mikhailovich, 1884–1975, vol. VII

Maistre, Le Roy de, (Roy de Maistre), 1894–1968, vol. VI

Maitland, Viscount; Ivor Colin James Maitland, 1915–1943, vol. IV

Maitland, Sir Adam, 1885–1949, vol. IV

Maitland, Rev. Adam Gray, *died* 1928, vol. II

Maitland, Agnes Catherine, 1849–1906, vol. I

Maitland, Sir Alexander, 1877–1965, vol. VI

Maitland, Sir Alexander Keith, 8th Bt, 1920–1963, vol. VI

Maitland, Rt Hon. Sir Arthur Herbert Drummond Ramsay S.; *see* Steel-Maitland.

Maitland, Dalrymple, 1848–1919, vol. II

Maitland, Maj.-Gen. David M. C.; *see* Makgill-Crichton-Maitland.

Maitland, Col Eardley, 1833–1911, vol. I

Maitland, Air-Cdre Edward Maitland, 1880–1921, vol. II

Maitland, Frederic William, 1850–1906, vol. I

Maitland, Lt-Col Sir (George) Ramsay, 7th Bt, 1882–1960, vol. V

Maitland, Lt-Col Hon. George Thomas, 1841–1910, vol. I

Maitland, Sir Herbert Lethington, 1868–1923, vol. II

Maitland, Hugh Bethune, 1895–1972, vol. VII

Maitland, J. A. F.; *see* Fuller-Maitland.

Maitland, Brig.-Gen. James Dalgleish H.; *see* Heriot-Maitland.

Maitland, Maj.-Gen. Sir James Makgill Heriot-, 1837–1902, vol. I

Maitland, Sir James S.; *see* Steel-Maitland.

Maitland, Sir John, 6th Bt, 1879–1949, vol. IV

Maitland, Comdr Sir John Francis Whitaker, 1903–1977, vol. VII

Maitland, Sir John Nisbet, 5th Bt, 1850–1936, vol. III

Maitland, Sir Keith Richard Felix Ramsay-Steel; *see* Steel-Maitland.

Maitland, Col Mark Edward Makgill Crichton, 1882–1972, vol. VII

Maitland, Maj.-Gen. Pelham James, 1847–1935, vol. III

Maitland, Air Vice-Marshal Percy Eric, 1895–1985, vol. VIII

Maitland, Lt-Col Sir Ramsay; *see* Maitland, Lt-Col Sir G. R.

Maitland, Lt-Col Reginald Charles Frederick, 1882–1939, vol. III

Maitland, Thomas Gwynne, *died* 1948, vol. IV

Maitland, Victor Kennard, 1897–1950, vol. IV

Maitland, William F.; *see* Fuller-Maitland.

Maitland, William James, 1847–1919, vol. II

Maitland, William Whitaker, 1864–1926, vol. II

Maitland-Gordon, James Charles; *see* Gordon.

Maitland-Heriot, Sir William, 1856–1939, vol. III

Maitland-Jones, Arthur Griffith, 1890–1957, vol. V

Maitland-Kirwan, Lionel, 1849–1927, vol. II

Maitland-Makgill-Crichton, Brig. Henry Coventry; *see* Crichton.

Maitland-Titterton, Major David Maitland, 1904–1988, vol. VIII

Maizels, Montague, 1899–1976, vol. VII

Majdalany, Fred, 1913–1967, vol. VI

Majendie, Brig.-Gen. Bernard J., 1875–1959, vol. V

Majendie, James Henry Alexander, 1871–1932, vol. III

Majendie, Sir Vivian Dering, 1836–1898, vol. I

Majendie, Maj.-Gen. Vivian Henry Bruce, 1886–1960, vol. V

Majendie, Rev. William Richard Stuart, 1869–1932, vol. III

Major, Albany Featherstonehaugh, 1858–1925, vol. II

Major, Sir Alfred, *died* 1907, vol. I

Major, Alfred George, 1879–1940, vol. III(A), vol. IV

Major, Maj.-Gen. Hon. Arthur Henry H.; *see* Henniker-Major.

Major, Charles, 1856–1913, vol. I

Major, Sir Charles Henry, 1860–1933, vol. III

Major, Charles Immanuel Forsyth, 1843–1923, vol. II

Major, Col Charles Thomas, 1869–1938, vol. III

Major, Edith Helen, 1867–1951, vol. V

Major, Hon. Edward Minet H.; *see* Henniker-Major.

Major, Ernest Harry, 1876–1941, vol. IV

Major, Francis William, 1863–1923, vol. II

Major, Hon. Gerald Arthur George H.; *see* Henniker-Major.

Major, Rev. Henry Dewsbury Alves, 1871–1961, vol. VI

Major, James Perrins, 1878–1964, vol. VI(AII)

Makarios III, Archbishop, 1913–1977, vol. VII

Makdougall, Hugh James Elibank S.; *see* Scott Makdougall.

Makgill, Sir George, 11th Bt, 1868–1926, vol. II

Makgill, Robert Haldane, 1870–1946, vol. IV

Makgill-Crichton-Maitland, Maj.-Gen. David, 1841–1907, vol. I

Makin, Frank, 1918–1984, vol. VIII

Makin, Hon. Norman John Oswald, 1889–1982, vol. VIII

Makino, Nobuaki, Count, 1861–1949, vol. IV

Makins, Sir (Alfred) John (Ware), 1894–1972, vol. VII

Makins, Brig.-Gen. Sir Ernest, 1869–1959, vol. V

Makins, Captain Geoffry, 1877–1915, vol. I

Makins, Sir George Henry, 1853–1933, vol. III

Makins, Sir John; *see* Makins, Sir A. J. W.

Makins, Sir Paul Augustine, 2nd Bt, 1871–1939, vol. III

Makins, Col Sir William Thomas, 1st Bt, 1840–1906, vol. I

Makins, Lt-Col Sir William Vivian, 3rd Bt, 1903–1969, vol. VI

Makinson, Joseph, 1836–1914, vol. I

Makower, Ernest Samuel, 1876–1946, vol. IV

Makower, Walter, 1879–1945, vol. IV

Malabari, Behramji Merwanji, 1854–1912, vol. I

Malalasekera, Gunapala Piyasena, 1899–1973, vol. VII

Malamud, Bernard, 1914–1986, vol. VIII

Malan, Gp Captain Adolph Gysbert, 1910–1963, vol. VI

Malan, Hon. Daniel François, 1874–1959, vol. V

Malan, Rt Hon. François Stephanus, 1871–1941, vol. IV

Malaviya, Pandit Madan Mohan, 1861–1946, vol. IV

Malbrán, Manuel E., 1876–1942, vol. IV

Malcolm of Poltalloch, 1st Baron, 1833–1902, vol. I

Malcolm, Angus Christian Edward, 1908–1971, vol. VII

Malcolm, Lt-Col Arthur William Alexander, 1903–1989, vol. VIII

Malcolm, Charles Adolf, 1879–1948, vol. IV

Malcolm, Sir Dougal Orme, 1877–1955, vol. V

Malcolm, Col Edward Donald, 1837–1930, vol. III

Malcolm, Sir George, 1818–1897, vol. I

Malcolm, George, 1876–1941, vol. IV

Malcolm, Col George Alexander, 1872–1933, vol. III

Malcolm of Poltalloch, Lt-Col George Ian, 1903–1976, vol. VII

Malcolm, Hon. George John Huntly, 1865–1930, vol. III

Malcolm, George William, 1870–1933, vol. III

Malcolm, Harcourt Gladstone, 1875–1936, vol. III

Malcolm, Brig.-Gen. Henry Huntly Leith, 1860–1938, vol. III

Malcolm, Sir Ian Zachary, 1868–1944, vol. IV

Malcolm, Sir James, 8th Bt, 1823–1901, vol. I

Malcolm, Hon. James, 1880–1935, vol. III

Malcolm, Sir James William, 9th Bt, 1862–1927, vol. II

Malcolm, John, 1873–1954, vol. V

Malcolm, John D., 1857–1937, vol. III

Malcolm, Kenneth Robert, 1908–1984, vol. VIII

Malcolm, Sir Michael Albert James, 1898–1976, vol. VII

Malcolm, Maj.-Gen. Sir Neill, 1869–1953, vol. V

Malcolm, Lt-Col Pulteney, 1861–1940, vol. III

Malcolm, Robert Carmichael, 1868–1941, vol. IV

Malcolm, Ronald, *died* 1949, vol. IV

Malcolmson, John Grant, *died* 1902, vol. I

Malcolmson, Maj.-Gen. John Henry Porter, 1832–1920, vol. II

Malcolmson, Vernon Austen, 1872–1947, vol. IV

Malden, Charles Edward, 1845–1926, vol. II

Malden, Edmund Claud, 1890–1962, vol. VI

Malden, Very Rev. Richard Henry, 1879–1951, vol. V

Male, Emile, 1862–1954, vol. V

Malenkov, Georgi Maximilianovich, 1902–1988, vol. VIII

Maler Kotla, Nawab of, 1881–1947, vol. IV

Malet, Sir Charles St Lo, 6th Bt, 1906–1918, vol. II

Malet, Rt Hon. Sir Edward Baldwin, 4th Bt, 1837–1908, vol. I

Malet, Sir Edward St Lo, 5th Bt, 1872–1909, vol. I

Malet, Col Sir Edward William St Lo, 8th Bt, 1908–1990, vol. VIII

Malet, Guilbert Edward Wyndham, 1839–1918, vol. II

Malet, Sir Harry Charles, 7th Bt, 1873–1931, vol. III

Malet, Sir Henry Charles Eden, 3rd Bt, 1835–1904, vol. I

Malet, John C., *died* 1901, vol. I

Malet, Lucas; *see* Harrison, Mary St Leger.

Malet de Carteret, Captain Charles Edward, *died* 1942, vol. IV

Malet de Carteret, Lt-Col Edouard Charles, 1838–1914, vol. I

Malet de Carteret, Reginald, 1865–1935, vol. III

Malherbe, Ernst G., 1895–1982, vol. VIII

Malik Khuda Bakhsh Khan Tiwana, Nawab Sir, *died* 1930, vol. III

Malik Mohammed Umar Hayat Khan (Tiwana), Maj.-Gen. Hon. Sir, 1874–1944, vol. IV

Malik, Sardar Bahadur Sir Teja Singh, *died* 1953, vol. V

Malik, Sardar Hardit Singh, 1894–1985, vol. VIII

Malik, Yakov Alexandrovich, 1906–1980, vol. VII

Malim, Comdr David Wentworth, 1914–1985, vol. VIII

Malim, Frederic Blagden, 1872–1966, vol. VI

Maling, George Allan, 1889–1929, vol. III

Maling, Captain Irwin Charles, 1841–1918, vol. II

Malinovsky, Marshal Rodion Yakovlevich, 1898–1967, vol. VI

Malinowski, Bronislaw, 1884–1942, vol. IV

Malins, Sir Edward, 1841–1922, vol. II

Malipiero, G. Francesco, 1882–1973, vol. VII

Malkin, Harold Jordan, 1898–1978, vol. VII

Malkin, Herbert Charles, 1836–1913, vol. I

Malkin, Sir (Herbert) William, 1883–1945, vol. IV

Malkin, Sir William; *see* Malkin, Sir H. W.

Malko, Nicolai, 1888–1961, vol. VI

Mallabar, Herbert John, 1871–1956, vol. V
Mallabar, Sir John Frederick, 1900–1988, vol. VIII
Mallaby, Col Aubertin Walter Sothern, 1899–1945, vol. IV
Mallaby, Sir George; *see* Mallaby, Sir H. G. C.
Mallaby, Sir (Howard) George (Charles), 1902–1978, vol. VII
Mallaby, Rev. John Jackson, *died* 1929, vol. III
Mallaby-Deeley, Sir Anthony Meyrick, 3rd Bt, 1923–1962, vol. VI
Mallaby-Deeley, Sir Guy Meyrick Mallaby, 2nd Bt, 1897–1946, vol. IV
Mallaby-Deeley, Sir Harry Mallaby, 1st Bt, 1863–1937, vol. III
Malladra, Alessandro, 1868–1944, vol. IV
Mallalieu, Sir Edward Lancelot, (Sir Lance), 1905–1979, vol. VII
Mallalieu, Frederick William, 1860–1932, vol. III
Mallalieu, Sir Joseph Percival William, 1908–1980, vol. VII
Mallalieu, Sir Lance; *see* Mallalieu, Sir E. L.
Mallalieu, Sir William; *see* Mallalieu, Sir J. P. W.
Mallam, Lt-Col Rev. George Leslie, 1895–1978, vol. VII
Mallarmé, Stéphane, 1842–1898, vol. I
Mallen, Sir Leonard Ross, 1902–1980, vol. VII (AII)
Malleson, Lady Constance, (Colette O'Niel), 1895–1975, vol. VII
Malleson, Col George Bruce, 1825–1898, vol. I
Malleson, Herbert Cecil, *died* 1935, vol. III
Malleson, Miles; *see* Malleson, W. M.
Malleson, Maj.-Gen. Sir Wilfrid, 1866–1946, vol. IV
Malleson, Comdr Wilfrid St Aubyn, *died* 1975, vol. VII
Malleson, (William) Miles, 1888–1969, vol. VI
Mallet, Sir Bernard, 1859–1932, vol. III
Mallet, Sir Charles Edward, 1862–1947, vol. IV
Mallet, Sir Claude Coventry, 1860–1941, vol. IV
Mallet, Hooper Pelgué, 1901–1985, vol. VIII
Mallet, Sir Ivo; *see* Mallet, Sir W. I.
Mallet, John William, 1832–1912, vol. I
Mallet, Rt Hon. Sir Louis du Pan, 1864–1936, vol. III
Mallet, Matilde de Obarrio, (Lady Mallet), 1872–1964, vol. VI
Mallet, Sir Victor Alexander Louis, 1893–1969, vol. VI
Mallet, Sir (William) Ivo, 1900–1988, vol. VIII
Mallett, Edward, 1888–1950, vol. IV
Mallett, Richard, 1910–1972, vol. VII
Mallett, Sir Rowland, 1869–1947, vol. IV
Malley, Cecil Patrick, 1902–1981, vol. VIII
Malley, William Bernard, 1889–1966, vol. VI
Mallik, Devendra Nath, 1866–1941, vol. IV
Mallik, Manmath C., *died* 1853, vol. III
Mallinson, Albert, 1870–1946, vol. IV
Mallinson, Sir Dyson, 1852–1929, vol. III
Mallinson, Lt-Col Henry, 1879–1940, vol. III
Mallinson, Sir Paul; *see* Mallinson, Sir W. P.
Mallinson, Col Sir Stuart Sidney, 1888–1981, vol. VIII
Mallinson, Sir William, 1st Bt, *died* 1936, vol. III
Mallinson, Sir William James, 2nd Bt, 1879–1944, vol. IV

Mallinson, Sir (William) Paul, 3rd Bt, 1909–1989, vol. VIII
Malloch, George Reston, *died* 1953, vol. V
Malloch, James, 1860–1932, vol. III
Mallock, Brig. Arthur Richard Ogilvie, 1885–1972, vol. VII
Mallock, Major Charles Herbert, 1878–1917, vol. II
Mallock, Henry Reginald A., *died* 1933, vol. III
Mallock, Richard, 1843–1900, vol. I
Mallock, Lt-Col Thomas Raymond, *died* 1934, vol. III
Mallock, William Hurrell, 1849–1923, vol. II
Mallon, James Joseph, 1875–1961, vol. VI
Mallory, Rev. Herbert Leigh L.; *see* Leigh-Mallory.
Mallory, Air Chief Marshal Sir Trafford Leigh L.; *see* Leigh-Mallory.
Mallowan, Dame Agatha; *see* Christie, Dame A. M. C.
Mallowan, Sir Max Edgar Lucien, 1904–1978, vol. VII
Malmesbury, 4th Earl of, 1842–1899, vol. I
Malmesbury, 5th Earl of, 1872–1950, vol. IV
Malone, Surg. Rear-Adm. Albert Edward, *died* 1970, vol. VI
Malone, Lt-Col Cecil L'Estrange, *died* 1965, vol. VI
Malone, Sir Clement, *died* 1967, vol. VI
Malone, Denis George Withers, 1906–1983, vol. VIII
Malone, Herbert, *died* 1962, vol. VI
Malone, Leah, (Mrs L'Estrange Malone), *died* 1951, vol. V
Malone, Major Sir Patrick Bernard, 1857–1939, vol. III
Malory, Shaun; *see* Russell, Reginald James Kingston.
Malouin, Arthur Cyrille Albert, 1857–1930, vol. III
Malraux, André, 1901–1976, vol. VII
Maltby, Maj.-Gen. (Christopher) Michael, 1891–1980, vol. VII
Maltby, Lt-Comdr Gerald Rivers, 1851–1922, vol. II
Maltby, Henry Francis, 1880–1963, vol. VI
Maltby, Maj.-Gen. Michael; *see* Maltby, Maj.-Gen. C. M.
Maltby, Air Vice-Marshal Sir Paul Copeland, 1892–1971, vol. VII
Maltby, Sir Thomas Karran, 1891–1976, vol. VII
Malthus, Col Sydenham, 1831–1916, vol. II
Maltwood, Katharine, *died* 1961, vol. VI
Malvern, 1st Viscount, 1883–1971, vol. VII
Malvern, 2nd Viscount, 1922–1978, vol. VII
Malvern, Harry Ladyman, 1908–1982, vol. VIII
Mamhead, 1st Baron, 1871–1945, vol. IV
Mamoulian, Rouben, 1897–1987, vol. VIII
Man, Maj.-Gen. Christopher Mark Morrice, 1914–1989, vol. VIII
Man, Edward Garnet, 1837–1920, vol. II
Man, Edward Horace, 1846–1929, vol. III
Man, Col Hubert William, *died* 1956, vol. V
Man, Col John Alexander; *see* Stuart, Col. J. A. M.
Man, Captain Joseph, 1867–1951, vol. V
Man, Morgan Charles Garnet, 1915–1986, vol. VIII
Man, Maj.-Gen. Patrick Holberton, 1913–1979, vol. VI
Manby, Sir Alan Reeve, 1848–1925, vol. II
Manby, Percy Alan Farrer, 1877–1940, vol. III

Mance, Brig.-Gen. Sir H. Osborne, 1875–1966, vol. VI

Mance, Sir Henry Christopher, 1840–1926, vol. II

Mance, Sir Henry Stenhouse, 1913–1981, vol. VIII

Manchester, 9th Duke of, 1877–1947, vol. IV

Manchester, 10th Duke of, 1902–1977, vol. VII

Manchester, 11th Duke of, 1929–1985, vol. VIII

Manchester, Sir William Edwin, 1869–1956, vol. V

Mancinelli, Luigi, 1848–1921, vol. II

Mancroft, 1st Baron, 1872–1942, vol. IV

Mancroft, 2nd Baron, 1914–1987, vol. VIII

Mander, Sir Charles Arthur, 2nd Bt, 1884–1951, vol. V

Mander, Sir Charles Tertius, 1st Bt, 1852–1929, vol. III

Mander, Sir Frederick, 1883–1964, vol. VI

Mander, Maj.-Gen. Frederick Day, 1842–1939, vol. III

Mander, Sir Geoffrey Le Mesurier, 1882–1962, vol. VI

Mander, Captain John Harold, 1869–1927, vol. II

Mander, Lionel Henry Miles, 1888–1946, vol. IV

Mander, Raymond Josiah Gale, 1911–1983, vol. VIII

Mander, Lady; (Rosalie), (R. Glynn Grylls), 1905–1988, vol. VIII

Manders, Horace Craigie, 1882–1963, vol. VI

Manders, Richard, 1854–1931, vol. III

Manderson, Maj.-Gen. George Rennie, 1834–1918, vol. II

Manderville, Rt Rev. Gay Lisle Griffith, 1894–1969, vol. VI

Mandi, Lt-Col Raja (Sir) Joginder Sen Bahadur of, 1904–1986, vol. VIII

Mandleberg, Sir G. Charles, 1860–1932, vol. III

Mandleberg, J. Harold, 1885–1973, vol. VII

Mandleberg, Brig. Lennard Charles, 1893–1975, vol. VII

Mandlik, Sir Narayan Vishvanath, 1870–1948, vol. IV

Manfield, Harry, died 1923, vol. II

Manfield, Sir Philip, 1819–1899, vol. I

Mangan, Rt Rev. John, 1852–1917, vol. II

Mangham, Sydney, 1886–1962, vol. VI

Mangiagalli, Riccardo P.; see Pick-Mangiagalli.

Mangin, Ven. Robert Rattray, 1863–1944, vol. IV

Mangin, Sir Thorleif Rattray Orde, 1896–1950, vol. IV

Mangles, Maj.-Gen. Cecil, 1842–1906, vol. I

Mangles, Brig.-Gen. Roland Henry, 1874–1948, vol. IV

Mangles, Ross Lowis, 1833–1905, vol. I

Mangles, Major Walter James, 1862–1929, vol. III

Manifold, Hon. Sir Chester; see Manifold, Hon. Sir T. C.

Manifold, Maj.-Gen. Sir Courtenay Clarke, 1864–1957, vol. V

Manifold, Maj.-Gen. Sir Graham; see Manifold, Maj.-Gen. Sir M. G. E. B.

Manifold, Maj.-Gen. John Alexander, 1884–1960, vol. V

Manifold, Lt-Col John Forster, 1857–1933, vol. III

Manifold, Maj.-Gen. Sir (Michael) Graham Egerton Bowman-, 1871–1940, vol. III

Manifold, Hon. Sir (Thomas) Chester, 1897–1979, vol. VII

Manifold, Hon. Sir Walter Synnot, 1849–1928, vol. II

Manion, Hon. Robert James, 1881–1943, vol. IV

Manipur, HH Sir Chura Chand Singh Maharajah of, 1886–1941, vol. IV

Manisty, Rear-Adm. Sir Eldon; see Manisty, Rear-Adm. Sir H. W. E.

Manisty, Rear-Adm. Sir (Henry Wilfred) Eldon, 1876–1960, vol. V

Manisty, Herbert Francis, 1853–1939, vol. III

Manktelow, Sir (Arthur) Richard, 1899–1977, vol. VII

Manktelow, Sir Richard; see Manktelow, Sir A. R.

Manley, Edgar Booth, 1897–1959, vol. V

Manley, Gordon, 1902–1980, vol. VII

Manley, Norman Washington, 1893–1969, vol. VI

Mann, Sir Alan Harbury, 1914–1970, vol. VI(AII)

Mann, Alexander, died 1908, vol. I

Mann, Arthur Henry, 1876–1972, vol. VII

Mann, Rt Rev. Cameron, 1851–1932, vol. III

Mann, Cathleen, (Mrs J. R. Follett), died 1959, vol. V

Mann, Sir Donald, 1853–1934, vol. III

Mann, Sir Duncombe; see Mann, Sir T. D.

Mann, Sir Edward, 1st Bt, 1854–1943, vol. IV

Mann, Sir (Edward) John, 2nd Bt, 1883–1971, vol. VII

Mann, Mrs Fairman; see Mann, Mary E.

Mann, Frederick George, 1897–1982, vol. VIII

Mann, Hon. Sir Frederick Wollaston, 1869–1958, vol. V

Mann, Rev. George Albert Douglas, 1914–1983, vol. VIII

Mann, Harold Hart, 1872–1961, vol. VI

Mann, Harrington, 1864–1937, vol. III

Mann, Heinrich, 1871–1950, vol. IV

Mann, Rt Rev. Mgr Horace K., 1859–1928, vol. II

Mann, Dame Ida Caroline, 1893–1983, vol. VIII

Mann, J. Dixon, died 1912, vol. I

Mann, Jacob, 1888–1940, vol. III(A), vol. IV

Mann, Sir James Gow, 1897–1962, vol. VI

Mann, Maj.-Gen. James Robert, 1823–1915, vol. I

Mann, James Scrimgeour, 1883–1946, vol. IV

Mann, Jean, died 1964, vol. VI

Mann, Sir John, 1863–1955, vol. VI

Mann, Sir John, died 1957, vol. V

Mann, Sir John; see Mann, Sir E. J.

Mann, Rt Rev. John Charles, 1880–1967, vol. VI

Mann, Julia de Lacy, 1891–1985, vol. VIII

Mann, Keith Cranston, 1903–1972, vol. VII

Mann, Ludovic MacLellan, died 1955, vol. V

Mann, Mary E., died 1929, vol. III

Mann, Ronald, 1908–1987, vol. VIII

Mann, Thomas, 1875–1955, vol. V

Mann, Sir (Thomas) Duncombe, 1857–1949, vol. IV

Mann, Tom, 1856–1941, vol. IV

Mann, Major William Edgar, 1885–1969, vol. VI

Mann, Air Cdre William Edward George, 1899–1966, vol. VI

Mann, William Somervell, 1924–1989, vol. VIII

Mannering, Rev. Ernest, 1882–1977, vol. VII

Mannering, Rev. Canon Leslie George, 1883–1974, vol. VII

Manners, 3rd Baron, 1852–1927, vol. II

Manners, 4th Baron, 1897–1972, vol. VII

Manners, Lord Cecil Reginald John, 1868–1945, vol. IV

Manners, Charles, 1857–1935, vol. III

Manners, Brig. Charles Molyneux Sandys, 1885–1954, vol. V

Manners, Lord Edward William John, 1864–1903, vol. I

Manners, Ernest John, 1877–1944, vol. IV

Manners, Rear-Adm. Sir Errol, 1883–1953, vol. V

Manners, Sir George Espec John, 1860–1939, vol. III

Manners, J. Hartley, 1870–1928, vol. II

Manners, Major Lord Robert William Orlando, 1870–1917, vol. II

Manners-Smith, Francis St George, *died* 1941, vol. IV

Manners-Sutton, Francis Henry Astley, 1869–1916, vol. II

Mannheim, Hermann, 1889–1974, vol. VII

Mannheim, Karl, 1893–1947, vol. IV

Mannheim, Lucie, 1905–1976, vol. VII

Mannin, Ethel, 1900–1984, vol. VIII

Manning, Miss, *died* 1905, vol. I

Manning, Bernard Lord, 1892–1941, vol. IV

Manning, Brian O'Donoghue, 1891–1964, vol. VI

Manning, Charles Anthony Woodward, 1894–1978, vol. VII

Manning, Cecil Aubrey Gwynne, 1892–1985, vol. VIII

Manning, Air Cdre Edye Rolleston, 1889–1957, vol. V

Manning, Dame (Elizabeth) Leah, 1886–1977, vol. VII

Manning, Frederick Edwin Alfred, 1897–1987, vol. VIII

Manning, Air Cdre Frederick John, 1912–1988, vol. VIII

Manning, Sir George, 1887–1976, vol. VII

Manning, Sir Henry Edward, 1877–1963, vol. VI

Manning, Sir (James) Kenneth, 1907–1976, vol. VII

Manning, John Westley, 1866–1954, vol. V

Manning, Sir Kenneth; *see* Manning, Sir J. K.

Manning, Dame Leah; *see* Manning, Dame E. L.

Manning, Olivia Mary, (Mrs R. D. Smith), 1915–1980, vol. VII

Manning, Richard Joseph, 1883–1979, vol. VII

Manning, W. Westley, *died* 1954, vol. V

Manning, Brig.-Gen. Sir William Henry, 1863–1932, vol. III

Manning, Sir William Patrick, 1845–1915, vol. I

Manning, Rt Rev. William Thomas, 1866–1949, vol. IV

Manningham-Buller, Lt-Col Sir Mervyn Edward, 3rd Bt, 1876–1956, vol. V

Manningham-Buller, Sir Morton Edward; *see* Buller.

Mannix, Most Rev. Daniel, 1864–1963, vol. VI

Mannooch, Geoffrey Herbert, 1890–1959, vol. V

Manns, Sir August, 1825–1907, vol. I

Manohar Lal, Hon. Sir, 1880–1949, vol. IV

Mansbridge, Albert, 1876–1952, vol. V

Mansbridge, Very Rev. Harold Chad, 1917–1980, vol. VII

Mansel, Col Alfred, 1852–1918, vol. II

Mansel, Sir Courtenay Cecil, 13th Bt (shown as 11th Bt), 1880–1933, vol. III (the 12th and 13th Bts are wrongly numbered in their entries).

Mansel, Sir Edward Berkeley, 12th Bt (shown as 10th Bt), 1839–1908, vol. I

Mansel, George, *died* 1914, vol. I

Mansel, Col George Clavell, 1861–1910, vol. I

Mansel, Sir John Philip Ferdinand, 14th Bt, 1910–1947, vol. IV

Mansel, Major Rhys Clavell, 1891–1969, vol. VI

Mansel-Jones, Col Conwyn, 1871–1942, vol. IV

Mansel-Jones, Herbert Riversdale, 1836–1907, vol. I

Mansel-Pleydell, Lt-Col Edmund Morton, 1850–1914, vol. I

Mansel-Pleydell, John Clavell, 1817–1902, vol. I

Mansel-Pleydell, Rev. John Colvile Morton, 1851–1938, vol. III

Mansell, Vice-Adm. Sir (George) Robert, 1868–1936, vol. III

Mansell, Lt-Col George William, 1904–1983, vol. VIII

Mansell, Lt-Col Sir John Herbert, 1864–1933, vol. III

Mansell, Air Vice-Marshal Reginald Baynes, 1896–1945, vol. IV

Mansell, Vice-Adm. Sir Robert; *see* Mansell, Vice-Adm. Sir G. R.

Mansell-Moullin, Charles William, 1851–1940, vol. III

Mansergh, Vice-Adm. Sir Aubrey; *see* Mansergh, Vice-Adm. Sir C. A. L.

Mansergh, Vice-Adm. Sir (Cecil) Aubrey (Lawson), 1898–1990, vol. VIII

Mansergh, Cornewall Lewis, 1863–1935, vol. III

Mansergh, Gen. Sir (E. C.) Robert, 1900–1970, vol. VI

Mansergh, Fanny; *see* Moody, F.

Mansergh, James, 1834–1905, vol. I

Mansergh, Adm. Sir Maurice James, 1896–1966, vol. VI

Mansergh, Gen. Sir Robert; *see* Mansergh, Gen. Sir E. C. R.

Mansergh, Southcote; *see* Manners, Charles.

Mansfield and Mansfield, 4th Earl of, 1806–1898, vol. I

Mansfield and Mansfield, 5th Earl of, 1860–1906, vol. I

Mansfield and Mansfield, 6th Earl of, 1864–1935, vol. III

Mansfield and Mansfield, 7th Earl of, 1900–1971, vol. VII

Mansfield, Hon. Sir Alan James, 1902–1980, vol. VII (AII)

Mansfield, Sir Alfred, 1870–1940, vol. III

Mansfield, Sir Charles Edward, 1828–1907, vol. I

Mansfield, Cyril James, *died* 1916, vol. II

Mansfield, F. J., 1872–1946, vol. IV

Mansfield, Henry, 1914–1979, vol. VII

Mansfield, Maj.-Gen. Sir Herbert, 1855–1939, vol. III

Mansfield, Horace Rendall, 1863–1914, vol. I

Mansfield, Vice-Adm. Sir John Maurice, 1893–1949, vol. IV

Mansfield, Orlando Augustine, 1863–1936, vol. III

Mansfield, Philip Theodore, 1892–1975, vol. VII

Mansfield, Purcell James, 1889–1968, vol. VI

Mansfield, Richard, 1857–1907, vol. I
Mansfield, Robert William, 1850–1911, vol. I
Mansfield, Walter, 1870–1916, vol. II
Mansfield, Wilfrid Stephen, 1894–1968, vol. VI
Mansfield, William Thomas, *died* 1939, vol. III(A), vol. IV
Manship, Paul, 1885–1966, vol. VI
Mansion, John Edmond, 1870–1942, vol. IV
Manson, Edward, 1849–1919, vol. II
Manson, Henry James, 1869–1952, vol. V
Manson, James Alexander, 1851–1921, vol. II
Manson, James Bolivar, 1879–1945, vol. IV
Manson, John, 1842–1923, vol. II
Manson, Sir Patrick, 1844–1922, vol. II
Manson, Robert George, 1893–1969, vol. VI
Manson, Rev. Thomas Walter, 1893–1958, vol. V
Manson, Rev. William, 1882–1958, vol. V
Manson-Bahr, Sir Philip, 1881–1966, vol. VI
Mant, Sir Cecil George, 1906–1990, vol. VIII
Mant, Sir Reginald Arthur, 1870–1942, vol. IV
Mantegazza, Paul, 1831–1910, vol. I
Mantell, Col Patrick Riners, 1862–1936, vol. III
Mantle, Lee, 1851–1934, vol. III
Mantle, Philip Jaques, 1901–1989, vol. VIII
Manton, 1st Baron (*cr* 1922), 1873–1922, vol. II
Manton, 2nd Baron, 1899–1968, vol. VI
Manton, G. Grenville, *died* 1932, vol. III
Manton, Sir Henry, 1835–1924, vol. II
Manton, Irene, 1904–1988, vol. VIII
Manton, Brig. Lionel, 1887–1961, vol. VI
Manton, Sidnie M., (Mrs J. P. Harding), 1902–1979, vol. VII
Mantoux, Paul Joseph, 1877–1956, vol. V
Manuel, Archibald Clark, 1901–1976, vol. VII
Manuel, Joseph Thomas, 1909–1990, vol. VIII
Manuel, Stephen, 1880–1954, vol. V
Manuwa, Chief Hon. Sir Samuel Layinka Ayodeji, 1903–1975, vol. VII
Manvell, Rev. Arnold Edward William, 1868–1927, vol. II
Manvell, (Arnold) Roger, 1909–1987, vol. VIII
Manvell, Roger; *see* Manvell, A. R.
Manvers, 3rd Earl, 1825–1900, vol. I
Manvers, 4th Earl, 1854–1926, vol. II
Manvers, 5th Earl, 1888–1940, vol. III
Manvers, 6th Earl, 1881–1955, vol. V
Manville, Sir Edward, 1862–1933, vol. III
Manwaring, George Ernest, 1882–1939, vol. III
Manzoni, Sir Herbert John Baptista, 1899–1972, vol. VII
Maori; *see* Inglis, Hon. J.
Maple, Sir John Blundell, 1st Bt, 1845–1903, vol. I
Maplesden, Rev. Arthur William, 1864–1932, vol. III
Mapleson, Henry, 1851–1927, vol. II
Maplestone, Philip Alan, *died* 1969, vol. VI
Mapother, Edward, 1881–1940, vol. III
Mapother, Edward Dillon, 1835–1908, vol. I
Mapp, Charles, 1903–1978, vol. VII
Mapp, Henry William, 1871–1955, vol. V
Mappin, Sir Charles Thomas Hewitt, 4th Bt, 1909–1941, vol. IV
Mappin, Sir Frank, 2nd Bt, 1846–1920, vol. II
Mappin, Sir Frank Crossley, 6th Bt, 1884–1975, vol. VII

Mappin, Sir Frederick Thorpe, 1st Bt, 1821–1910, vol. I
Mappin, Sir Samuel Wilson, 5th Bt, 1854–1942, vol. IV
Mappin, Sir Wilson, 3rd Bt, 1848–1925, vol. II
Mapson, Leslie William, 1907–1970, vol. VI
Mar, 27th (styled 33rd) Earl of, 1836–1930, vol. III
Mar, 28th (styled 34th) Earl of, 1868–1932, vol. III
Mar, 29th Earl of, 1891–1965, vol. VI
Mar, 30th Earl of, 1914–1975, vol. VII
Mar, Master of: *see* Garioch, Lord.
Mar, 12th Earl of, **and Kellie**, 14th Earl of, 1865–1955, vol. V
Mar, Helen, *died* 1940, vol. III(A), vol. IV
Marais, Colin B.; *see* Bain-Marais.
Marais, Rev. Johannes Izak, 1848–1919, vol. II
Maratib Ali, Sir Syed, 1883–1961, vol. VI
'Marc'; *see* Boxer, C. M. E.
Marcel, Gabriel, 1889–1973, vol. VII
Marcet, William, *died* 1900, vol. I
March, George Edward, 1834–1922, vol. II
March, George Frederick, 1893–1985, vol. VIII
March, Henry Arthur, 1905–1988, vol. VIII
March, Rt Rev. John, 1863–1940, vol. III
March, Gen. Peyton Conway, 1864–1955, vol. V
March, Samuel, 1861–1935, vol. III
Marchamley, 1st Baron, 1855–1925, vol. II
Marchamley, 2nd Baron, 1886–1949, vol. IV
Marchand, Geoffrey Isidore Charles, *died* 1965, vol. VI
Marchand, Gen. Jean Baptiste, 1863–1934, vol. III
Marchant, Maj.-Gen. Alfred Edmund, 1863–1924, vol. II
Marchant, Bessie, (Mrs J. A. Comfort), 1862–1941, vol. IV
Marchant, Edgar Cardew, 1864–1960, vol. V
Marchant, Edgar Walford, 1876–1962, vol. VI
Marchant, Ernest Cecil, 1902–1979, vol. VII
Marchant, Sir Herbert Stanley, 1906–1990, vol. VIII
Marchant, Sir James, 1867–1956, vol. V
Marchant, James Robert Vernam, 1853–1936, vol. III
Marchant, Sir Stanley, 1883–1949, vol. IV
Marchant, Brig.-Gen. Thomas Harry Saunders, 1875–1952, vol. V
Marchant, William Sydney, 1894–1953, vol. V
Marchbank, John, 1883–1946, vol. IV
Marchbanks, James, 1862–1947, vol. IV
Marchesi, Blanche, 1863–1940, vol. III
Marchesi, Mathilde, 1826–1913, vol. I
Marchmont, Arthur Williams, 1852–1923, vol. II
Marchwood, 1st Viscount, 1876–1955, vol. V
Marchwood, 2nd Viscount, 1912–1979, vol. VII
Marcil, Hon. Charles, 1860–1937, vol. III
Marcks, Violet Olivia C.; *see* Cressy-Marcks.
Marcon, Rev. Walter Hubert, *died* 1937, vol. III
Marconi, Marchese; Guglielmo Marconi, 1874–1937, vol. III
Marcosson, Isaac Frederick, 1876–1961, vol. VI
Marcotte, Rev. F. X., 1883–1967, vol. VI
Marcus, Michael, 1894–1960, vol. V(A), vol. VI(AI)
Marcuse, Herbert, 1898–1979, vol. VII
Marden, Orison Swett, 1850–1924, vol. II
Marden, Maj.-Gen. Sir Thomas Owen, 1866–1951, vol. V

Marder, Arthur Jacob, 1910–1980, vol. VII
Mardy Jones, Thomas Isaac, *died* 1970, vol. VI
Mare, Captain Philip Armitage, 1891–1951, vol. V
Marek, Kurt W., 1915–1972, vol. VII
Marengo, Kimon Evan; *see* Kem.
Marescaux, Captain Alfred Edward Hay, *died* 1942, vol. IV
Marescaux, Vice-Adm. Gerald Charles Adolphe, 1860–1920, vol. II
Marett, Sir Robert Hugh Kirk, 1907–1981, vol. VIII
Marett, Robert Ranulph, 1866–1943, vol. IV
Margai, Sir Albert Michael, 1910–1980, vol. VII
Margai, Rt Hon. Sir Milton Augustus Strieby, 1895–1964, vol. VI
Margerison, Sir Lawrence, 1872–1958, vol. V
Margesson, 1st Viscount, 1890–1965, vol. VI
Margesson, Col Evelyn William, 1865–1944, vol. IV
Margesson, Sir Mortimer R., 1861–1947, vol. IV
Margesson, Captain Wentworth Henry Davies, 1869–1950, vol. IV
Margesson, Lt-Col William George, 1821–1911, vol. I
Margetson, Alfred James, 1877–1944, vol. IV
Margetson, Maj. Sir Philip Reginald, 1894–1985, vol. VIII
Margetson, W. H., 1861–1940, vol. III
Margetson, Very Rev. William James, 1874–1946, vol. IV
Margetts, Frederick Chilton, 1905–1989, vol. VIII
Margoliouth, David Samuel, 1858–1940, vol. III
Margoliouth, Rev. G., 1853–1924, vol. II
Margoliouth, Herschel Maurice, 1887–1959, vol. V
Margrett, Charles Henry, 1863–1941, vol. IV
Marillier, Frank William, 1855–1928, vol. II
Marillier, Henry Currie, 1865–1951, vol. V
Marin, John C., 1870–1953, vol. V
Marindin, Maj.-Gen. Arthur Henry, 1868–1947, vol. IV
Marindin, Col Cecil Colvile, 1879–1932, vol. III
Marindin, Sir Francis Arthur, 1838–1900, vol. I
Marion, Léo Edmond, 1899–1979, vol. VII
Maris, Matthew, 1839–1917, vol. II
Maritain, Jacques, 1882–1973, vol. VII
Marix, Air Vice-Marshal Reginald Lennox George, 1889–1966, vol. VI
Marjolin, Robert Ernest, 1911–1986, vol. VIII
Marjoribanks, Hon. Coutts, 1860–1924, vol. II
Marjoribanks, Dudley Sinclair, 1858–1929, vol. III
Marjoribanks, Edward, 1900–1932, vol. III
Marjoribanks, Sir George John, 1856–1931, vol. III
Marjoribanks, Sir Norman Edward, 1872–1939, vol. III
Mark, J. M., *died* 1948, vol. IV
Mark, Sir John, 1832–1909, vol. I
Mark-Wardlaw, Rear-Adm. Alexander Livingston Penrose, 1891–1975, vol. VII
Mark-Wardlaw, Rear-Adm. William Penrose, 1887–1952, vol. V
Markar, Hadji Sir Mohamed M.; *see* Macan-Markar.
Markby, Sir William, 1829–1914, vol. I
Markelius, Sven Gottfrid, 1889–1972, vol. VII
Marker, Edwin Henry Simon, 1888–1973, vol. VII
Marker, Col Raymond John, 1867–1914, vol. I

Marker, Richard, 1835–1916, vol. II
Markham, Adm. Sir Albert Hastings, 1841–1918, vol. II
Markham, Rt Rev. Algernon A., 1869–1949, vol. IV
Markham, Sir Arthur Basil, 1st Bt, 1866–1916, vol. II
Markham, Rt Rev. Bernard, 1907–1984, vol. VIII
Markham, Sir Charles, 2nd Bt, 1899–1952, vol. V
Markham, Brig.-Gen. Charles John, 1862–1927, vol. II
Markham, Sir Clements Robert, 1830–1916, vol. II
Markham, Lt-Gen. Sir Edwin, 1833–1918, vol. II
Markham, Edwin, 1852–1940, vol. III
Markham, Sir Frank; *see* Markham, Sir S. F.
Markham, Sir Henry Vaughan, 1897–1946, vol. IV
Markham, Roy, 1916–1979, vol. VII
Markham, Sir (Sydney) Frank, 1897–1975, vol. VII
Markham, Violet Rosa, (Mrs J. Carruthers), *died* 1959, vol. V
Markievicz, Constance Georgine, *died* 1927, vol. II
Marklew, Ernest, 1874–1939, vol. III
Marks, 1st Baron, 1858–1938, vol. III
Marks of Broughton, 1st Baron, 1888–1964, vol. VI
Marks, Alexander Hammett, 1880–1954, vol. V
Marks, B. S., 1827–1916, vol. II
Marks, Major Claud Laurie, 1863–1910, vol. I
Marks, David Woolf, 1811–1909, vol. I
Marks, Derek John, 1921–1975, vol. VII
Marks, Eric Astor David; *see* Marshall, Eric.
Marks, Ernest Samuel, 1872–1947, vol. IV
Marks, Frederick William, 1886–1942, vol. IV
Marks, Geoffrey, 1864–1938, vol. III
Marks, Harry Hananel, 1855–1916, vol. II
Marks, Hon. Sir Henry, 1861–1938, vol. III
Marks, Henry Stacy, 1829–1898, vol. I
Marks, Sir John Hedley Douglas, 1916–1982, vol. VIII
Marks, Kenneth, 1920–1988, vol. VIII
Marks, Leslie, 1889–1956, vol. V
Marks, Oliver, 1866–1940, vol. III
Marks, Captain Percy D'Evelyn, 1883–1968, vol. VI
Markwick, Col Ernest Elliott, 1853–1925, vol. II
Marlar, Edward Alfred Geoffrey, 1901–1978, vol. VII
Marlay, Charles Brinsley, 1831–1912, vol. I
Marlborough, 9th Duke of, 1871–1934, vol. III
Marlborough, 10th Duke of, 1897–1972, vol. VII
Marler, Hon. Sir Herbert, 1876–1940, vol. III
Marler, Leslie Sydney, 1900–1981, vol. VIII
Marler, Sydney; *see* Marler, L. S.
Marler, William de Montmollin, 1849–1929, vol. III
Marley, 1st Baron, 1884–1952, vol. V
Marley, 2nd Baron, 1913–1990, vol. VIII
Marley, Brig. Cuthbert David, 1897–1960, vol. V
Marley, James, 1893–1954, vol. V
Marling, Sir Charles Murray, 1862–1933, vol. III
Marling, Lt-Col Sir John Stanley Vincent, 4th Bt, 1910–1977, vol. VII
Marling, Col Sir Percival Scrope, 3rd Bt, 1861–1936, vol. III
Marling, Sir William Henry, 2nd Bt, 1835–1919, vol. II
Marlow, Arthur Herbert, 1893–1964, vol. VI
Marlow, Col Benjamin William, 1863–1943, vol. IV
Marlow, Ewart, 1895–1965, vol. VI

Marlow, Frederick William, 1877–1936, vol. III
Marlow, Louis; see Wilkinson, L. U.
Marlow, Roger Douglas Frederick, 1912–1986, vol. VIII
Marlow, Roy George, 1931–1988, vol. VIII
Marlow, Sydney Raymond, 1896–1945, vol. IV
Marlowe, Anthony Alfred Harmsworth, 1904–1965, vol VI
Marlowe, Thomas, 1868–1935, vol. III
Marnan, John Fitzgerald, 1908–1990, vol. VIII
Marnham, Francis John, 1853–1941, vol. IV
Marnham, Harold, 1911–1987, vol. VIII
Marnham, John Ewart, 1916–1985, vol. VIII
Marnham, Sir Ralph, 1901–1984, vol. VIII
Marnoch, Col Sir John, 1867–1936, vol. III
Marochetti, Baron, 1894–1952, vol. V
Marples, Baron (Life Peer); Alfred Ernest Marples, 1907–1978, vol. VII
Marples, George, 1869–1939, vol. III
Marquand, Rt Hon. Hilary Adair, 1901–1972, vol. VII
Marquand, John Phillips, 1893–1960, vol. V
Marquand, Reginald, 1874–1931, vol. III
Marr, Alexander, 1876–1938, vol. III
Marr, Allan James, 1907–1989, vol. VIII
Marr, Sir Charles William Clanan, 1880–1960, vol. V
Marr, Francis Alleyne, 1894–1942, vol. IV
Marr, Hamilton Clelland, 1870–1936, vol. III
Marr, Sir James, 1st Bt, 1854–1932, vol. III
Marr, James William Slesser, 1902–1965, vol. VI
Marr, John Edward, 1857–1933, vol. III
Marr, Col John Lynn, 1877–1931, vol. III
Marrable, Brig.-Gen. Arthur George, 1863–1925, vol. II
Marrable, Mrs, died 1916, vol. II
Marrack, Rear-Adm. Hugh Richard, 1888–1972, vol. VII
Marrack, John Richardson, 1886–1976, vol. VII
Marre, Sir Alan Samuel, 1914–1990, vol. VIII
Marriage, Herbert James, 1872–1946, vol. IV
Marriage, John Goodbody, 1929–1984, vol. VIII
Marrian, Guy Frederic, 1904–1981, vol. VIII
Marrie, J. J.; see Creasey, John.
Marrinan, Patrick Aloysius, 1877–1940, vol. III
Marriner, Lt-Col Bryan Lister, 1888–1943, vol. IV
Marriott, Col Alfred Sinclair, 1876–1943, vol. IV
Marriott, Charles, 1869–1957, vol. V
Marriott, Charles Bertrand, 1868–1946, vol. IV
Marriott, Sir Charles Hayes, 1834–1910, vol. I
Marriott, Captain Charles John Bruce, 1861–1936, vol. III
Marriott, Cyril Herbert Alfred, 1897–1977, vol. VII
Marriott, Eric Llewellyn, 1888–1945, vol. IV
Marriott, Ernest, 1882–1918, vol. II
Marriott, Francis, 1876–1957, vol. V
Marriott, Frederick, 1860–1941, vol. IV
Marriott, Sir Hayes, 1873–1929, vol. III
Marriott, Ven. Henry, 1870–1952, vol. V
Marriott, Herbert, 1865–1935, vol. III
Marriott, Hugh Leslie, 1900–1983, vol. VIII
Marriott, Rev. Sir Hugh Randolph Cavendish S.; see Smith-Marriott.
Marriott, James William, 1884–1953, vol. V
Marriott, Brig.-Gen. John, 1861–1953, vol. V

Marriott, Sir John Arthur Ransome, 1859–1945, vol. IV
Marriott, Maj.-Gen. Sir John Charles Oakes, 1895–1978, vol. VII
Marriott, John Hayes, 1909–1982, vol. VIII
Marriott, Captain John Peter Ralph, 1879–1938, vol. III
Marriott, Sir John Richard Wyldbore S.; see Smith-Marriott.
Marriott, Very Rev. John Thomas, died 1924, vol. II
Marriott, Marjorie Jane; see Speed, M. J.
Marriott, Patrick Arthur, 1899–1980, vol. VII
Marriott, Sir Ralph George Cavendish S.; see Smith-Marriott.
Marriott, Major Reginald Adams, 1857–1930, vol. III
Marriott, Richard D'Arcy, 1911–1985, vol. VIII
Marriott, Major Richard George Armine, 1867–1924, vol. II
Marriott, Richard Michael Harris, 1926–1975, vol. VII
Marriott, Brig. Sir Robert Ecklin, 1887–1984, vol. VIII
Marriott, Rev. Stephen Jack, 1886–1964, vol. VI
Marriott, William, 1848–1916, vol. II
Marriott, Sir William Henry S.; see Smith-Marriott.
Marriott, Sir William John S.; see Smith-Marriott.
Marriott, William Mason, 1889–1960, vol. V
Marriott, Sir William S.; see Smith-Marriott.
Marriott, Rt Hon. Sir William Thackeray, 1834–1903, vol. I
Marriott-Dodington, Brig.-Gen. Wilfred; see Dodington.
Marris, Adam Denzil, 1906–1983, vol. VIII
Marris, Eric Denyer, 1891–1976, vol. VII
Marris, Rev. Nisbet Colquhoun, died 1937, vol. III
Marris, Sir William Sinclair, 1873–1945, vol. IV
Marrs, Robert, 1884–1951, vol. V
Marryat, Very Rev. Charles, 1827–1907, vol. I
Marryat, Florence, (Mrs Francis Lean), 1838–1899, vol. I
Marryshow, Hon. Theophilus Albert, 1887–1958, vol. V
Marsack, Sir Charles Croft, 1892–1987, vol. VIII
Marsden, Alexander Edwin, 1832–1902, vol. I
Marsden, Allen Gatenby, 1893–1988, vol. VIII
Marsden, Captain Arthur, 1883–1960, vol. V
Marsden, Ven. E(dwyn) Lisle, 1886–1960, vol. V
Marsden, Col Sir Ernest, 1889–1970, vol. VI
Marsden, Captain George, 1874–1916, vol. II
Marsden, Sir John Denton, 1st Bt, 1873–1944, vol. IV
Marsden, Sir John Denton, 2nd Bt, 1913–1985, vol. VIII
Marsden, Leslie Alfred, 1921–1987, vol. VIII
Marsden, Percy, 1888–1955, vol. V
Marsden, R. Sydney, 1856–1919, vol. II
Marsden, Rt Rev. Samuel Edward, 1832–1912, vol. I
Marsden, Terence Barclay, 1932–1981, vol. VIII
Marsden, Sir Thomas Rogerson, died 1927, vol. II
Marsden, Wilfred Alexander, 1878–1949, vol. IV
Marsden, Lt-Col William, 1841–1925, vol. II
Marsh, Col Cunliffe Hebbert, 1878–1938, vol. III
Marsh, David Charles, 1917–1983, vol. VIII
Marsh, Rt Rev. Donald Ben, 1903–1973, vol. VII

Marsh, Dame Edith Ngaio; *see* Marsh, Dame Ngaio.

Marsh, Maj.-Gen. Edward Bertram, 1890–1976, vol. VII

Marsh, Sir Edward Howard, 1872–1953, vol. V

Marsh, Col Frank, 1855–1943, vol. IV

Marsh, Frank Burr, 1880–1940, vol. III(A), vol. IV

Marsh, Brig.-Gen. Frank Graham, 1875–1957, vol. V

Marsh, Maj.-Gen. Frank Hale Berwick, 1841–1923, vol. II

Marsh, Rev. Fred Shipley, 1886–1953, vol. V

Marsh, George Fletcher Riley, 1895–1984, vol. VIII

Marsh, Henry, 1850–1939, vol. III

Marsh, Howard, 1839–1915, vol. I

Marsh, James Ernest, 1860–1938, vol. III

Marsh, Lt-Col Jeremy-Taylor, 1872–1944, vol. IV

Marsh, Margaret Munnerlyn Mitchell, (Mrs John Robert Marsh), *died* 1949, vol. IV

Marsh, Michael John Waller, 1921–1983, vol. VIII

Marsh, Dame Ngaio, 1899–1982, vol. VIII

Marsh, Othniel Charles, 1831–1899, vol. I

Marsh, Sir Percy William, 1881–1969, vol. VI

Marsh, Richard, *died* 1915, vol. I

Marsh, Richard, 1851–1933, vol. III

Marsh, Rev. Sidney Frank, 1860–1936, vol. III

Marsh, Thomas Robertson, 1847–1929, vol. III

Marsh, Sir William Henry, 1827–1906, vol. I

Marsh, William Thomas, 1897–1985, vol. VIII

Marsh, William Waller, 1877–1959, vol. V

Marsh Smith, Reginald Norman, 1891–1975, vol. VII

Marshall, 1st Baron, 1865–1936, vol. III

Marshall of Leeds, Baron (Life Peer); Frank Shaw Marshall, 1915–1990, vol. VIII

Marshall, Alfred, 1842–1924, vol. II

Marshall, Sir Anthony, 1826–1911, vol. I

Marshall, Archibald, 1866–1934, vol. III

Marshall, Archibald Cook, 1890–1959, vol. V

Marshall, Sir Archie Pellow, 1899–1966, vol. VI

Marshall, Arthur; *see* Marshall, C. A. B.

Marshall, Arthur, 1873–1968, vol. VI

Marshall, Sir Arthur Harold, 1870–1956, vol. V

Marshall, Col Sir Arthur Wellington, 1841–1918, vol. II

Marshall, Bruce, 1899–1987, vol. VIII

Marshall, (Charles) Arthur (Bertram), 1910–1989, vol. VIII

Marshall, Charles Devereux, 1867–1918, vol. II

Marshall, Charles Frederic, 1864–1940, vol. III

Marshall, Brig. Charles Frederick Keilk, 1888–1953, vol. V

Marshall, Charles Jennings, 1890–1954, vol. V

Marshall, Charles Robertshaw, 1869–1952, vol. V

Marshall, D. H., 1848–1932, vol. III

Marshall, (Davis) Edward, 1869–1933, vol. III

Marshall, Comdr Sir Douglas, 1906–1976, vol. VII

Marshall, Hon. Duncan M'Lean, 1872–1946, vol. IV

Marshall, Edward, *see* Marshall, D. E.

Marshall, Rev. Edward Thory, 1842–1933, vol. III

Marshall, Elizabeth Middleton O.; *see* Ord Marshall.

Marshall, Emma, 1828–1899, vol. I

Marshall, Eric, (Eric Astor David Marks), 1891–1961, vol. VI

Marshall, Eric Stewart, 1879–1963, vol. VI

Marshall, Frances; *see* St Aubyn, Alan.

Marshall, Francis Hugh Adam, 1878–1949, vol. IV

Marshall, Maj.-Gen. Francis James, 1876–1942, vol. IV

Marshall, Frank, 1886–1952, vol. V

Marshall, Frank James, 1877–1944, vol. IV

Marshall, Fred, 1883–1962, vol. VI

Marshall, Frederic, *died* 1910, vol. I

Marshall, Lt-Gen. Sir Frederick, 1829–1900, vol. I

Marshall, Frederick Henry, 1878–1955, vol. V

Marshall, Engr-Adm. Frederick William, 1870–1956, vol. V

Marshall, Sir Geoffrey, 1887–1982, vol. VIII

Marshall, George Balfour, 1863–1928, vol. II

Marshall, Hon. George Catlett, 1880–1959, vol. V

Marshall, Maj.-Gen. George Frederick Leycester, 1843–1934, vol. III

Marshall, Maj.-Gen. Sir George Henry, 1843–1909, vol. I

Marshall, George Leslie, *died* 1964, vol. VI

Marshall, George Wicks, 1916–1987, vol. VIII

Marshall, George William, 1839–1905, vol. I

Marshall, Major George William, 1867–1940, vol. III

Marshall, Rt Rev. Guy, 1909–1978, vol. VII

Marshall, Sir Guy Anstruther Knox, 1871–1959, vol. V

Marshall, Col Hannath Douglas, 1872–1944, vol. IV

Marshall, Hedley Herbert, 1909–1982, vol. VIII

Marshall, Henry D., *died* 1906, vol. I

Marshall, Major Henry Seymour, 1879–1937, vol. III

Marshall, Rt Rev. Henry Vincent, 1884–1955, vol. V

Marshall, Sir Herbert, 1851–1918, vol. II

Marshall, Herbert Brough Falcon, 1890–1966, vol. VI

Marshall, Herbert Menzies, 1841–1913, vol. I

Marshall, Horace, *died* 1944, vol. IV

Marshall, Howard Percival, 1900–1973, vol. VII

Marshall, Hugh, 1868–1913, vol. I

Marshall, Hugh John Cole, 1873–1947, vol. IV

Marshall, Brig.-Gen. Hugh John Miles, 1867–1946, vol. IV

Marshall, Sir Hugo Frank, 1905–1986, vol. VIII

Marshall, J. Fitz, 1859–1932, vol. III

Marshall, Sir James, 1894–1979, vol. VII

Marshall, Sir James Brown, 1853–1922, vol. II

Marshall, James Cole, 1876–1952, vol. V

Marshall, Rev. James M'Call, 1838–1926, vol. II

Marshall, James Rissik, 1886–1959, vol. V

Marshall, John, 1845–1915, vol. I

Marshall, John, 1860–1951, vol. V

Marshall, John, 1895–1970, vol. VI

Marshall, Captain John Dodds, 1878–1931, vol. III

Marshall, John Edwin, 1864–1937, vol. III

Marshall, John Frederick, 1874–1949, vol. IV

Marshall, Sir John Hubert, 1876–1958, vol. V

Marshall, John Robert Neil, 1922–1990, vol. VIII

Marshall, Rt Hon. Sir John Ross, 1912–1988, vol. VIII

Marshall, Maj.-Gen. John Stuart, 1883–1944, vol. IV

Marshall, Rev. John Turner, 1850–1923, vol. II

Marshall, Brig.-Gen. John Willoughby Astell, 1854–1921, vol. II

Marshall, John Wilson, *died* 1923, vol. II

Marshall, Rev. Joseph William, 1835–1915, vol. I

Marshall, Kenneth McLean, 1874–1954, vol. V

Marshall, Rev. Laurence Henry, 1882–1953, vol. V

Marshall, Lumley Arnold, 1852–1942, vol. IV
Marshall, Markham Richard L.; *see* Leeson-Marshall.
Marshall, Neil; *see* Marshall, J. R. N.
Marshall, Lt-Col Noel George Lambert, 1852–1926, vol. II
Marshall, Brig. Norman, 1886–1942, vol. IV
Marshall, Norman, 1901–1980, vol. VII
Marshall, Captain Oswald Percival, 1857–1939, vol. III
Marshall, Patrick, 1869–1950, vol. IV(A)
Marshall, Captain Robert, 1863–1910, vol. I
Marshall, Robert, 1889–1975, vol. VII
Marshall, Sir Robert C.; *see* Calder-Marshall.
Marshall, Robert Ian, 1899–1970, vol. VI
Marshall, Robert Smith, 1902–1976, vol. VII
Marshall, Maj.-Gen. Roy Stuart, 1917–1987, vol. VIII
Marshall, Septimus, 1876–1962, vol. VI
Marshall, Sheina Macalister, 1896–1977, vol. VII
Marshall, Sir Sidney, 1882–1973, vol. VII
Marshall, Sir Stirrat Andrew William J.; *see* Johnson-Marshall.
Marshall, Brig.-Gen. Thomas Edward, 1865–1946, vol. IV
Marshall, Col Sir Thomas Horatio, 1833–1917, vol. II
Marshall, Thomas Humphrey, 1893–1981, vol. VIII
Marshall, Thomas Riley, 1854–1925, vol. II
Marshall, Major W. R., *died* 1916, vol. II
Marshall, Cdre William, 1873–1930, vol. III
Marshall, Rev. William, 1875–1955, vol. V
Marshall, William Hibbert, 1866–1929, vol. III
Marshall, William Lawrence Wright, *died* 1939, vol. III
Marshall, Sir William Marchbank, 1875–1967, vol. VI
Marshall, Lt-Gen. Sir William Raine, 1865–1939, vol. III
Marshall, Lt-Col William Thomas, 1854–1920, vol. II
Marshall, William Thomas, 1907–1975, vol. VII
Marshall-Cornwall, Gen. Sir James Handyside, 1887–1985, vol. VIII
Marshall-Hall, Sir Edward, 1858–1927, vol. II
Marshall-Hall, G. W. L., 1862–1915, vol. I
Marshall-Reynolds, Clyde Albert, 1898–1977, vol. VII
Marsham, Brig. Francis William Bullock-, 1883–1971, vol. VII
Marsham, George, 1849–1927, vol. II
Marsham, Dame Joan; *see* Marsham, Hon. Mrs S.
Marsham, Rev. Hon. John, 1842–1926, vol. II
Marsham, Robert H. Bullock-, 1833–1913, vol. I
Marsham, Hon. Mrs Sydney, *died* 1972, vol. VII
Marsham, Thomas Nelson, 1923–1989, vol. VIII
Marsham-Townshend, Hon. Robert, 1834–1914, vol. I
Marsillac, Jacques J. B. de, 1879–1962, vol. VI
Marson, Air Vice-Marshal John, 1906–1988, vol. VIII
Marston, Archibald Daniel, 1891–1962, vol. VI
Marston, Sir Charles, 1867–1946, vol. IV
Marston, Edward, 1825–1914, vol. I
Marston, Freda, 1895–1949, vol. IV

Marston, Hedley Ralph, 1900–1965, vol. VI
Marston, Surg.-Gen. Jeffery Allen, 1831–1911, vol. I
Marston, Reginald St Clair, 1886–1943, vol. IV
Marston, Robert Bright, 1853–1927, vol. II
Martel, Comtesse de; *see* Gyp, Sybille.
Martel, Brig.-Gen. Sir Charles Philip, 1861–1945, vol. IV
Martel, Lt-Gen. Sir Giffard Le Quesne, 1889–1958, vol. V
Martelli, Ernest Wynne, *died* 1917, vol. II
Martelli, Maj.-Gen. Sir Horace de Courcy, 1877–1959, vol. V
Martello Tower; *see* Norman, Comdr F. M.
Marten, Hon. Sir Alfred George, 1839–1906, vol. I
Marten, Sir Amberson Barrington, 1870–1962, vol. VI
Marten, Sir (Clarence) Henry (Kennett), 1872–1948, vol. IV
Marten, Eric Charles, 1899–1948, vol. IV
Marten, Vice-Adm. Sir Francis Arthur, 1879–1950, vol. IV
Marten, Ven. George Henry, 1876–1966, vol. VI
Marten, Rt Hon. Sir (H.) Neil, 1916–1985, vol. VIII
Marten, Sir Henry; *see* Marten, Sir C. H. K.
Marten, John Thomas, 1872–1929, vol. III
Marti, Karl, 1855–1925, vol. II
Martin, Sir Albert, *died* 1943, vol. IV
Martin, Col Albert Edward, 1876–1936, vol. III
Martin, Sir Albert Victor, 1897–1968, vol. VI
Martin, Sir Alec, 1884–1971, vol. VII
Martin, Very Rev. Alexander, 1857–1946, vol. IV
Martin, Alfred James, 1875–1959, vol. V
Martin, Lt-Gen. Sir Alfred Robert, 1853–1926, vol. II
Martin, Andrew, 1906–1985, vol. VIII
Martin, Hon. Archer, 1865–1941, vol. IV
Martin, Arthur Anderson, *died* 1916, vol. II
Martin, Arthur Campbell, 1875–1963, vol. VI
Martin, Arthur John, 1883–1942, vol. IV
Martin, Arthur Patchett, 1851–1902, vol. I
Martin, (Basil) Kingsley, 1897–1969, vol. VI
Martin, Vice-Adm. Sir Benjamin Charles Stanley, 1891–1957, vol. V
Martin, Bradley, 1841–1913, vol. I
Martin, Sir Charles Carnegie, 1901–1969, vol. VI
Martin, Charles Emanuel, 1891–1977, vol. VII
Martin, Charles F., 1868–1953, vol. V
Martin, Sir Charles James, 1866–1955, vol. V
Martin, Chester, 1882–1958, vol. V
Martin, Christopher, 1866–1933, vol. III
Martin, Christopher John H.; *see* Holland-Martin.
Martin, Col Claude Buist, 1869–1950, vol. IV
Martin, Rt Rev. Clifford Arthur, 1895–1977, vol. VII
Martin, Cornwallis Philip Wykeham-, 1855–1924, vol. II
Martin, Col Cunliffe, 1834–1917, vol. II
Martin, Brig. Cyril Gordon, 1891–1980, vol. VII
Martin, Cyril Hubert, 1867–1940, vol. III(A), vol. IV
Martin, Daisy Maud, *died* 1964, vol. VI
Martin, Sir David Christie, 1914–1976, vol. VII
Martin, Rear-Adm. Sir David James, 1933–1990, vol. VIII
Martin, Adm. Sir Deric Douglas Eric H.; *see* Holland-Martin.

Martin, Rt Rev. Donald, 1873–1938, vol. III
Martin, Douglas Whitwell, 1906–1989, vol. VIII
Martin, Lt-Col Edward Cuthbert De R.; *see* De Renzy-Martin.
Martin, Brig.-Gen. Edward Fowell, 1875–1950, vol. IV
Martin, Edward H.; *see* Holland-Martin.
Martin, Captain Edward Harington, *died* 1921, vol. II
Martin, Edward Kenneth, 1883–1980, vol. VII
Martin, Edward Pritchard, 1844–1910, vol. I
Martin, Brig. Edwyn Sandys Dawes, 1894–1954, vol. V
Martin, Emma; *see* Marshall, E.
Martin, Sir Ernest, 1872–1957, vol. V
Martin, Col Ernest Edmund, 1869–1925, vol. II
Martin, Frank, 1890–1974, vol. VII
Martin, (Fred) Russell (Beauchamp), 1887–1981, vol. VIII
Martin, Frederick, 1882–1950, vol. IV
Martin, Frederick George Stephen, 1890–1981, vol. VIII
Martin, Frederick John, 1891–1964, vol. VI
Martin, Frederick Morris, 1923–1985, vol. VIII
Martin, Frederick Townsend, 1849–1914, vol. I
Martin, Col George Blake Napier, 1847–1917, vol. II
Martin, Sir George Clement, 1844–1916, vol. II
Martin, Rev. George Currie, 1865–1937, vol. III
Martin, George Peter, 1823–1910, vol. I
Martin, Sir George William, 1884–1976, vol. VII
Martin, Col Gerald Hamilton, 1879–1952, vol. V
Martin, Glenn Luther, 1886–1955, vol. V
Martin, Granville Edward B.; *see* Bromley-Martin.
Martin, Air Marshal Sir Harold Brownlow Morgan, 1918–1988, vol. VIII
Martin, Captain Harry Cutfield, 1852–1932, vol. III
Martin, Helen, (Lady Martin); *see* Faucit, H.
Martin, Rev. Henry, 1844–1919, vol. II
Martin, Rev. Henry, 1844–1923, vol. II
Martin, Henry, 1889–1964, vol. VI
Martin, Rt Rev. Henry David, 1889–1971, vol. VII
Martin, Col Henry Graham, 1872–1955, vol. V
Martin, Henry Robert Charles, 1889–1942, vol. IV
Martin, Brig.-Gen. Herbert, 1857–1931, vol. III
Martin, Howard, *died* 1924, vol. II
Martin, Hubert, *died* 1938, vol. III
Martin, Rev. Hugh, 1890–1964, vol. VI
Martin, Lt-Gen. Hugh Gray, 1887–1969, vol. VI
Martin, Humphrey Trice, *died* 1931, vol. III
Martin, Sir James, 1861–1935, vol. III
Martin, Sir James, 1893–1981, vol. VIII
Martin, Major James Evans Baillie, 1859–1931, vol. III
Martin, Maj.-Gen. James Fitzgerald, 1876–1958, vol. V
Martin, James Hamilton, 1841–1937, vol. III
Martin, Maj.-Gen. James Mansergh Wentworth, 1902–1986, vol. VIII
Martin, James Purdon, 1893–1984, vol. VIII
Martin, James Rea, 1877–1951, vol. V
Martin, John, 1847–1944, vol. IV
Martin, John, 1884–1949, vol. IV
Martin, Brig. John Crawford, 1896–1963, vol. VI
Martin, John Hanbury, 1892–1983, vol. VIII

Martin, Maj.-Gen. John Simson Stuart, 1888–1973, vol. VII
Martin, Hon. Joseph, 1852–1923, vol. II
Martin, Joseph Samuel, 1845–1911, vol. I
Martin, Maj.-Gen. Kevin John, 1890–1958, vol. V
Martin, Kingsley; *see* Martin, B. K.
Martin, Leonard Charles James, 1920–1987, vol. VIII
Martin, Leonard Cyril, 1886–1976, vol. VII
Martin, Sir Leslie Harold, 1900–1983, vol. VIII
Martin, Louis Claude, 1891–1981, vol. VIII
Martin, Hon. Maurice, 1872–1937, vol. III
Martin, Nicholas Henry, 1906–1981, vol. VIII
Martin, Hon. Sir Norman Angus, 1893–1978, vol. VII
Martin, Olaus Macleod, 1890–1981, vol. VIII
Martin, Olive F., 1887–1967, vol. VI
Martin, Percy F., 1861–1941, vol. IV
Martin, Rev. Philip Montague, 1913–1981, vol. VIII
Martin, Philippa Parry, 1897–1981, vol. VIII
Martin, Most Rev. Pierre, 1910–1987, vol. VIII
Martin, Reginald James, 1892–1970, vol. VI
Martin, Col Reginald Victor, 1889–1973, vol. VII
Martin, Rt Hon. Sir Richard, 1st Bt (*cr* 1885), 1831–1901, vol. I
Martin, Sir Richard, *died* 1922, vol. II
Martin, Rev. Richard, 1836–1927, vol. II
Martin, Sir Richard Biddulph, 1st Bt (*cr* 1905), 1838–1916, vol. II
Martin, Sir Richard Byam, 5th Bt, (*cr* 1791), 1841–1910, vol. I
Martin, Sir Richard Edward Rowley, 1847–1907, vol. I
Martin, Lt-Col Sir Robert Edmund, 1874–1961, vol. VI
Martin, Robert M. Holland, 1872–1944, vol. IV
Martin, Col Rowland Hill, 1848–1919, vol. II
Martin, Hon. Russell; *see* Martin, Hon. F. R. B.
Martin, Sidney, 1860–1927, vol. II
Martin, Stapleton, 1846–1922, vol. II
Martin, Sir T. Carlaw, *died* 1920, vol. II
Martin, Sir Theodore, 1816–1909, vol. I
Martin, Very Rev. Thomas, 1856–1942, vol. IV
Martin, Thomas, 1893–1971, vol. VII
Martin, Sir Thomas Acquin, 1850–1906, vol. I
Martin, Col Thomas Morgan, 1854–1928, vol. II
Martin, Thomas Shannon, 1891–1954, vol. V
Martin, Victoria Claflin Woodhull, 1838–1927, vol. II
Martin, Violet, 1862–1915, vol. I
Martin, W. A. P., 1827–1916, vol. II
Martin, Captain W. R., *died* 1913, vol. I
Martin, Willem, 1876–1954, vol. V
Martin, Sir William, 1856–1924, vol. II
Martin, Paymaster Rear-Adm. William Ernest Russell, 1867–1946, vol. IV
Martin, William Gregory W.; *see* Wood-Martin.
Martin, William Henry Blyth, 1862–1946, vol. IV
Martin, William Henry Porteous, 1886–1939, vol. III
Martin, Hon. William Lee, 1870–1950, vol. IV
Martin, William Pethebridge, 1859–1933, vol. III
Martin du Gard, Roger, 1881–1958, vol. V
Martin-Harvey, Sir John; *see* Harvey.
Martin-Hurst, William, 1876–1941, vol. IV
Martin-Jones, Rev. S., 1872–1941, vol. IV

Martin-Leake, Lt-Col Arthur; *see* Leake.
Martin-Leake, Vice-Adm. Francis, 1869–1928, vol. II
Martin-Leake, Hugh; *see* Leake.
Martindale, Sir Arthur Henry Temple, 1854–1942, vol. IV
Martindale, Col Benjamin Hay, 1824–1904, vol. I
Martindale, Rev. Cyril Charlie, 1879–1963, vol. VI
Martindale, Ven. Henry, 1879–1946, vol. IV
Martindale, Hilda, 1875–1952, vol. V
Martindale, Louisa, *died* 1966, vol. VI
Martindell, Herbert Edward West, 1866–1933, vol. III
Martineau, Alfred, *died* 1903, vol. I
Martineau, Edith, 1842–1909, vol. I
Martineau, Lt-Col Ernest, 1861–1951, vol. V
Martineau, George, 1835–1919, vol. II
Martineau, Rev. Canon George Edward, 1905–1969, vol. VI
Martineau, James, 1805–1900, vol. I
Martineau, Paul Gideon, 1858–1934, vol. III
Martineau, Sir Philip Hubert, 1862–1944, vol. IV
Martineau, Sir Wilfrid, 1889–1964, vol. VI
Martineau, Sir William, 1865–1950, vol. IV
Martinengo-Cesaresco, Countess; Evelyn Lilian Hazeldine, *died* 1931, vol. III
Martino, Commendatore Eduardo de, *died* 1912, vol. I
Martins, Armando; *see* Martins, V. A.
Martins, (Virgilio) Armando, 1914–1988, vol. VIII
Martinson, Rt Rev. Ezra Douglas, 1885–1968, vol. VI
Martinson, Harry Edmond, 1904–1978, vol. VII
Marton, Col George Blucher Heneage, 1839–1905, vol. I
Marton, Lt-Col Richard Oliver, 1872–1945, vol. IV
Martonmere, 1st Baron, 1907–1989, vol. VIII
Martyn, Col Anthony Wood, 1864–1955, vol. V
Martyn, Brig.-Gen. Arundel, 1868–1945, vol. IV
Martyn, Brig. Athelstan Markham, 1881–1956, vol. V
Martyn, David Forbes, 1906–1970, vol. VI
Martyn, Edward, 1859–1923, vol. II
Martyn, Sir Henry Linnington, 1888–1947, vol. IV
Martyn, Joan, 1899–1989, vol. VIII
Martyn, Rev. Richard James, 1846–1913, vol. I
Martyn, Selwyn Rawlings, 1892–1956, vol. V
Martyr, Lt-Col Cyril Godfrey, 1860–1936, vol. III
Martyr, (Joseph) Weston, 1885–1966, vol. VI
Martyr, Richard Edward, 1857–1940, vol. III
Marvin, Francis Sydney, 1863–1943, vol. IV
Marwick, Hugh, 1881–1965, vol. VI
Marwick, Sir James David, 1826–1908, vol. I
Marwood, Sidney Lionel, 1891–1981, vol. VIII
Marwood, Sir William Francis, 1863–1935, vol. III
Marwood-Elton, Lt-Col William, 1865–1931, vol. III
Marx, Adm. John Locke, 1852–1939, vol. III
Maryon, Herbert, 1874–1965, vol. VI
Maryon-Wilson, George Maryon; *see* Wilson.
Maryon-Wilson, Rev. Canon Sir (George) Percy (Maryon), 12th Bt, 1898–1965, vol. VI
Maryon-Wilson, Sir Hubert Guy Maryon, 13th Bt, 1888–1978, vol. VII
Maryon-Wilson, Rev. Canon Sir Percy; *see* Maryon-Wilson, Rev. Canon Sir G. P. M.

Maryon-Wilson, Sir Spencer Pocklington Maryon; *see* Wilson.
Marzban, Jehangier B., 1848–1928, vol. II
Marzban, Pherozeshah Jehangir, 1876–1933, vol. III
Marzials, Sir Frank Thomas, 1840–1912, vol. I
Masani, Sir Rustom Pestonji, 1876–1966, vol. VI
Masaryk, Jan Garrigue, 1886–1948, vol. IV
Masaryk, Thomas Garrigue, 1850–1937, vol. III
Mascagni, Pietro, 1863–1945, vol. IV
Mascall, Col Maurice Edward, 1882–1958, vol. V
Maschwitz, Eric, 1901–1969, vol. VI
Masefield, John, 1878–1967, vol. VI
Masefield, Col Robert Taylor, 1839–1922, vol. II
Masey, Albert, *died* 1910, vol. I
Masham, 1st Baron, 1815–1906, vol. I
Masham, 2nd Baron, 1857–1917, vol. II
Masham, 3rd Baron, 1867–1924, vol. II
Masham, William George, 1843–1916, vol. II
Mashiter, Col Sir George Coope, 1843–1927, vol. II
Masih, Rt Rev. Inayat, 1918–1980, vol. VII
Maskell, Alfred Ogle, *died* 1912, vol. I
Maskell, Ernest John, 1895–1958, vol. V
Maskelyne, John Nevil, 1839–1917, vol. II
Maskelyne, Mervyn Herbert Nevil Story, 1823–1911, vol. I
Maskew, Rev. Arthur Fairclough, 1854–1938, vol. III
Mason, Alan Kenneth, 1920–1990, vol. VIII
Mason, Alfred Edward Woodley, 1865–1948, vol. IV
Mason, Alfred John, 1853–1918, vol. II
Mason, Arnold Henry, 1885–1963, vol. VI
Mason, Rev. Arthur James, 1851–1928, vol. II
Mason, Sir Arthur Wier, 1860–1924, vol. II
Mason, Brewster, 1922–1987, vol. VIII
Mason, Charlotte Maria Shaw, 1842–1923, vol. II
Mason, Sir Dan Hurdis, 1911–1982, vol. VIII
Mason, Sir David, 1862–1940, vol. III
Mason, David Marshall, 1865–1945, vol. IV
Mason, Rev. Edmund Robert, *died* 1922, vol. II
Mason, Eudo Colecestra, 1901–1969, vol. VI
Mason, Vice-Adm. Sir Frank Trowbridge, 1900–1988, vol. VIII
Mason, Frank H., 1876–1965, vol. VI
Mason, Sir George Charles, 1855–1904, vol. I
Mason, Rev. George Edward, 1847–1928, vol. II
Mason, Maj.-Gen. Harry Macan, 1850–1929, vol. III
Mason, Rev. Henry Alfred, 1851–1939, vol. III
Mason, Hon. Henry Greathead Rex, 1885–1975, vol. VII
Mason, Col Hubert Oliver Browne B.; *see* Browne-Mason.
Mason, Rev. James, 1840–1912, vol. I
Mason, James, 1909–1984, vol. VIII
Mason, Lt-Col James Cooper, 1875–1923, vol. II
Mason, James Francis, 1861–1929, vol. III
Mason, John H., 1875–1951, vol. V
Mason, Joseph, 1866–1933, vol. III
Mason, Lt-Col Kenneth, 1887–1976, vol. VII
Mason, Ven. Lancelot, 1905–1990, vol. VIII
Mason, Sir Laurence, 1886–1970, vol. VI
Mason, Leonard Ralph, 1910–1974, vol. VII
Mason, Marianne Harriet, *died* 1932, vol. III
Mason, Michael; *see* Mason, R. M.
Mason, Michael Henry, 1900–1982, vol. VIII
Mason, Sir Paul, 1904–1978, vol. VII

Mason, Lt-Col Percival Lawrence, 1857–1938, vol. III

Mason, Major Philip Granville, 1872–1915, vol. I

Mason, (Richard) Michael, 1917–1977, vol. VII

Mason, Rev. Richard Swann S.; *see* Swann-Mason.

Mason, Robert, 1857–1927, vol. II

Mason, Robert Heath, 1918–1969, vol. VI

Mason, Robert Whyte, 1905–1984, vol. VIII

Mason, Brig. Searle Dwyer, 1892–1953, vol. V

Mason, Stewart Carlton, 1906–1983, vol. VIII

Mason, Sir Thomas, *died* 1924, vol. II

Mason, Thomas Godfrey, 1890–1959, vol. V(A)

Mason, Adm. Thomas Henry, 1811–1900, vol. I

Mason, Walt, 1862–1939, vol. III

Mason, Lt-Col Walter, 1863–1937, vol. III

Mason, William, 1872–1961, vol. VI

Mason-Macfarlane, Lt-Gen. Sir Noel; *see* Macfarlane.

Masood, Sir Syed Ross, 1889–1937, vol. III

Maspero, Sir Gaston Camille Charles, 1846–1916, vol. II

Massenet, Jules Emile Frédéric, 1842–1912, vol. I

Massereene, 11th Viscount, **and Ferrard,** 4th Viscount, 1842–1905, vol. I

Massereene, 12th Viscount, **and Ferrard,** 5th Viscount, 1873–1956, vol. V

Massey, Sir Arthur, 1894–1980, vol. VII

Massey, Dame Christina Allen, *died* 1932, vol. III

Massey, Rev. Edwyn Reynolds, 1847–1923, vol. II

Massey, Gerald, 1828–1907, vol. I

Massey, Gertrude, 1868–1957, vol. V

Massey, Sir Harrie Stewart Wilson, 1908–1983, vol. VIII

Massey, Rev. John Cooke, 1842–1928, vol. II

Massey, Raymond, 1896–1983, vol. VIII

Massey, Rt Hon. Vincent, 1887–1967, vol. VI

Massey, Rt Hon. William Ferguson, 1856–1925, vol. II

Massey, William Henry, *died* 1940, vol. III

Massey-Mainwaring, Hon. William Frederick Barton; *see* Mainwaring.

Massiah, Sir Grey; *see* Massiah, Sir H. G.

Massiah, Sir (Hallam) Grey, 1888–1972, vol. VII

Massie, Grant, 1896–1964, vol. VI

Massie, John, 1842–1925, vol. II

Massie, Major John Hamon, 1872–1914, vol. I

Massie, Lt-Col Robert Allwright, 1890–1966, vol. VI

Massie, Brig.-Gen. Roger Henry, 1869–1927, vol. II

Massie, Adm. Thomas Leeke, 1802–1898, vol. I

Massigli, René, 1888–1988, vol. VIII

Massine, Lénide, 1896–1979, vol. VII

Massingberd, Mrs, *died* 1897, vol. I

Massingberd, Field-Marshal Sir Archibald Armar M.; *see* Montgomery-Massingberd.

Massingberd, Stephen Langton, 1869–1925, vol. II

Massingham, Harold John, 1888–1952, vol. V

Massingham, Henry William, 1860–1924, vol. II

Masson, David, 1822–1907, vol. I

Masson, Sir David Orme, 1858–1937, vol. III

Masson, Hon. Col Sir David Parkes, 1847–1915, vol. I

Masson, Flora, *died* 1937, vol. III

Masson, Frederic, 1847–1923, vol. II

Masson, Sir Irvine; *see* Masson, Sir J. I. O.

Masson, Sir (James) Irvine (Orme), 1887–1862, vol. VI

Masson, John, *died* 1927, vol. II

Masson, Sir John Robertson, 1898–1965, vol. VI

Masson, Rosaline, *died* 1949, vol. IV

Massy, 6th Baron, 1835–1915, vol. I

Massy, 7th Baron, 1864–1926, vol. II

Massy, 8th Baron, 1894–1958, vol. V

Massy, Brig. Charles Walter, 1887–1973, vol. VII

Massy, Brig.-Gen. Edward Charles, 1868–1946, vol. IV

Massy, Col Godfrey, 1863–1944, vol. IV

Massy, Col Harry Stanley, 1855–1920, vol. II

Massy, Lt-Gen. Hugh Royds Stokes, 1884–1965, vol. VI

Massy, Col Percy Hugh Hamon, 1857–1939, vol. III

Massy, Col William George, 1857–1941, vol. IV

Massy, Lt-Gen. William Godfrey Dunham, 1838–1906, vol. I

Massy-Beresford, John George, 1856–1923, vol. II

Massy-Dawson, Captain Francis Evelyn, 1872–1939, vol. III

Massy-Greene, Hon. Sir Walter, 1874–1952, vol. V

Massy-Westropp, Col John, 1860–1951, vol. V

Master, Alfred, 1883–1978, vol. VII

Master, Lt-Col Arthur Gilbert, 1867–1942, vol. IV

Master, Captain Charles Edward Hoskins, 1878–1960, vol. V

Master, Charles Gilbert, *died* 1903, vol. I

Master, Rev. Harold C.; *see* Chester-Master.

Master, Lt-Col Richard C.; *see* Chester-Master.

Master, Thomas William Chester C; *see* Chester-Master.

Master, Col William Alfred C.; *see* Chester-Master.

Masterman, Arthur Thomas, 1869–1941, vol. IV

Masterman, Rt Hon. Charles Frederick Gurney, 1873–1927, vol. II

Masterman, Sir Christopher Hughes, 1889–1982, vol. VIII

Masterman, Air Cdre Edward Alexander Dimsdale, 1880–1957, vol. V

Masterman, Sir John Cecil, 1891–1977, vol. VII

Masterman, Rt Rev. John Howard Bertram, 1867–1933, vol. III

Masterman, William, 1846–1903, vol. I

Masters, Albert Edward Hefford, 1902–1968, vol. VI

Masters, Col Alexander, 1848–1936, vol. III

Masters, C. H., 1852–1931, vol. III

Masters, David, *died* 1965, vol. VI

Masters, Edgar Lee, 1869–1950, vol. IV

Masters, Sir Frederick, 1872–1947, vol. IV

Masters, Rev. Canon James Herbert, 1863–1942, vol. IV

Masters, Rev. James Hoare, *died* 1918, vol. II

Masters, John, 1914–1983, vol. VIII

Masters, Maxwell T., 1833–1907, vol. I

Masters, Hon. Robert, 1879–1967, vol. VI

Masters, Very Rev. Thomas Heywood, 1865–1939, vol. III

Masters, Rev. William Caldwall, 1843–1924, vol. II

Masterson, Major James Edward I., 1862–1935, vol. III

Masterson, Most Rev. Mgr Joseph, 1899–1953, vol. V

Masterton, William, 1913–1971, vol. VII

Masterton-Smith, Sir James Edward, 1878–1938, vol. III

Mastin, John, 1865–1932, vol. III

Maston, Charles James, 1912–1986, vol. VIII

Matania, Chevalier Fortunino, 1881–1963, vol. VI

Matcham, Col William Eyre E.; *see* Eyre-William.

Matchan, Leonard Joseph, 1911–1987, vol. VIII

Mather, Arthur Stanley, 1842–1929, vol. III

Mather, Rev. Frederic Vaughan, 1824–1914, vol. I

Mather, Rt Rev. Herbert, 1840–1922, vol. II

Mather, James Marshall, 1851–1916, vol. II

Mather, John Chadwick, 1904–1961, vol. VI

Mather, Sir Kenneth, 1911–1990, vol. VIII

Mather, Loris Emerson, 1886–1976, vol. VII

Mather, Richard, 1886–1964, vol. VI

Mather, Thomas, *died* 1937, vol. III

Mather, Rt Hon. Sir William, 1838–1920, vol. II

Mather, Col William, 1888–1966, vol. VI

Mather, William Allan, 1885–1961, vol. VI

Mather-Jackson, Sir Anthony Henry Mather, 6th Bt, 1899–1983, vol. VIII

Mather-Jackson, Sir Christopher; *see* Mather-Jackson, Sir G. C. M.

Mather-Jackson, Sir Edward Arthur; *see* Jackson.

Mather-Jackson, Sir (George) Christopher (Mather), 5th Bt, 1896–1976, vol. VII

Mather-Jackson, Sir Henry; *see* Jackson.

Mather-Jackson, Sir William, 7th Bt, 1902–1985, vol. VIII

Mathers, 1st Baron, 1886–1965, vol. VI

Mathers, Edward Peter, 1850–1924, vol. II

Mathers, Edward Powys, 1892–1939, vol. III

Mathers, Frederick Francis, 1871–1947, vol. IV

Mathers, Helen, 1853–1920, vol. II

Mathers, Thomas Graham, 1859–1927, vol. II

Matheson, Captain Alexander Francis, 1905–1976, vol. VII

Matheson, Sir Alexander Perceval, 3rd Bt, 1861–1929, vol. III

Matheson, Angus, 1912–1962, vol. VI

Matheson, Annie, 1853–1924, vol. II

Matheson, Lt-Col Archibald, 1876–1936, vol. III

Matheson, Arthur Alexander, 1919–1981, vol. VIII

Matheson, Lt-Col Hon. Arthur James, 1845–1913, vol. I

Matheson, Cdre Sir Charles George, 1876–1948, vol. IV

Matheson, Charles Louis, 1851–1921, vol. II

Matheson, Sir Donald, 1832–1901, vol. I

Matheson, Donald, *died* 1901, vol. I

Matheson, Donald Alexander, 1860–1935, vol. III

Matheson, Donald Capell, 1880–1948, vol. IV

Matheson, Donald Macleod, 1896–1979, vol. VII

Matheson, Lt-Col Duncan, 1850–1930, vol. III

Matheson, Very Rev. Frederick William, 1882–1942, vol. IV

Matheson, Rev. George, 1842–1906, vol. I

Matheson, John, 1873–1944, vol. IV

Matheson, Rt Rev. John A., 1901–1950, vol. IV

Matheson, Sir Kenneth James, 2nd Bt, 1854–1920, vol. II

Matheson, M. Cecile, *died* 1950, vol. IV

Matheson, Percy Ewing, 1859–1946, vol. IV

Matheson, Rt Hon. Sir Robert Edwin, 1845–1926, vol. II

Matheson, Sir Roderick Mackenzie Chisholm, 4th Bt, 1861–1944, vol. IV

Matheson, Most Rev. Samuel Pritchard, 1852–1942, vol. IV

Matheson, Gen. Sir Torquhil George, 5th Bt, 1871–1963, vol. VI

Mathew, Rev. Anthony Gervase, 1905–1976, vol. VII

Mathew, Sir Charles, 1903–1968, vol. VI

Mathew, Charles James, 1872–1923, vol. II

Mathew, Maj.-Gen. Sir Charles Massy, 1866–1932, vol. III

Mathew, Most Rev. David, 1902–1975, vol. VII

Mathew, Francis, 1907–1965, vol. VI

Mathew, Frank, 1865–1924, vol. II

Mathew, Lt-Gen. George, 1879–1958, vol. V

Mathew, George Felton, 1846–1931, vol. III

Mathew, Rt Hon. Sir James Charles, 1830–1908, vol. I

Mathew, Rev. John, *died* 1929, vol. III

Mathew, Robert, 1911–1966, vol. VI

Mathew, Theobald, 1866–1939, vol. III

Mathew, Sir Theobald, 1898–1964, vol. VI

Mathew-Lannowe, Brig.-Gen. Edmund Byam; *see* Lannowe.

Mathews, Basil Joseph, 1879–1951, vol. V

Mathews, Sir Charles Willie, 1st Bt, 1850–1920, vol. II

Mathews, Denis Owen, 1901–1984, vol. VIII

Mathews, Ernest, 1847–1930, vol. III

Mathews, George Ballard, 1861–1922, vol. II

Mathews, Gregory Macalister, 1876–1949, vol. IV

Mathews, Henry Edmund, 1868–1947, vol. IV

Mathews, Henry Mends, 1903–1982, vol. VIII

Mathews, Henry Montague Segundo, 1860–1941, vol. IV

Mathews, Sir Lloyd William, 1850–1901, vol. I

Mathews, Shailer, 1863–1941, vol. IV

Mathews, Dame Vera Elvira Sibyl Maria Laughton, 1888–1959, vol. V

Mathews, Rev. William Arnold, 1839–1925, vol. II

Mathewson, Sir Alexander Robert, 1907–1968, vol. VI

Mathias, Alfred Ernest, 1880–1963, vol. VI

Mathias, Charles Ronald, 1877–1949, vol. IV

Mathias, Col Henry Harding, 1850–1914, vol. I

Mathias, Brig. Leonard William Henry, 1890–1972, vol. VII

Mathias, Lewis James, 1864–1945, vol. IV

Mathias, Most Rev. Louis, 1887–1965, vol. VI

Mathias, Sir Richard, 1st Bt, 1863–1942, vol. IV

Mathias, Ronald Cavill, 1912–1968, vol. VI

Mathias, William Delamotte, 1877–1940, vol. III

Mathieson, Hon. John A., 1863–1947, vol. IV

Mathieson, William Gordon, 1902–1981, vol. VIII

Mathieson, William Law, 1868–1938, vol. III

Mathieu, Most Rev. Mgr Olivier Elzear, 1853–1929, vol. III

Mathieu-Perez, Sir Joseph Leon; *see* Perez.

Mathys, Sir (Herbert) Reginald, 1908–1977, vol. VII

Mathys, Sir Reginald; *see* Mathys, Sir H. R.

Matisse, Henri, 1869–1954, vol. V

Matley, Charles Alfred, 1866–1947, vol. IV

Matsudaira, Tsuneo, 1877–1949, vol. IV
Matsui, Rt Rev. Peter Yonetaro, 1869–1946, vol. IV
Matsumura, Jinzo, 1856–1928, vol. II, vol. III
Matt, Albert E., 1864–1941, vol. IV
Mattei, Marchese Alfred, 1853–1930, vol. III
Mattei, Tito, 1841–1914, vol. I
Matters, Sir Francis; *see* Matters, Sir R. F.
Matters, Leonard Warburton, 1881–1951, vol. V
Matters, Sir (Reginald) Francis, 1895–1975, vol. VII
Matthai, George, 1887–1947, vol. IV
Matthai, John, 1886–1959, vol. V
Matthay, Tobias, 1858–1945, vol. IV
Matthew, Edwin, *died* 1950, vol. IV
Matthew, Frederic David, 1838–1918, vol. II
Matthew, John Godfrey, 1881–1947, vol. IV
Matthew, Col John Smart, 1864–1935, vol. III
Matthew, Reginald Walter, 1879–1928, vol. II
Matthew, Sir Robert Hogg, 1906–1975, vol. VII
Matthew, Thomas Urquhart, 1909–1962, vol. VI
Matthews, Alfred Edward, 1869–1960, vol. V
Matthews, Sir (Alfred) Herbert (Henry), 1870–1958, vol. V
Matthews, Sir Arthur, 1886–1971, vol. VII
Matthews, Arthur Ratcliff, 1866–1932, vol. III
Matthews, Brander, 1852–1929, vol. III
Matthews, Sir Bromhead; *see* Matthews, Sir J. B.
Matthews, Sir Bryan Harold Cabot, 1906–1986, vol. VIII
Matthews, Ven. Cecil Lloyd, 1881–1962, vol. VI
Matthews, David, 1868–1960, vol. V
Matthews, Denis James, 1919–1988, vol. VIII
Matthews, Major Durham, 1876–1950, vol. IV
Matthews, Edith Marcia, 1883–1946, vol. IV
Matthews, Rev. Edward Walter, 1846–1933, vol. III
Matthews, Ernest Lewis, 1871–1941, vol. IV
Matthews, Ernest Romney, 1873–1930, vol. III
Matthews, Maj.-Gen. Francis Raymond Gage, 1903–1976, vol. VII
Matthews, Brig.-Gen. Frank Broadwood, 1857–1940, vol. III
Matthews, Frank Herbert, 1861–1909, vol. I
Matthews, Ven. Frederick Albert John, 1913–1985, vol. VIII
Matthews, Gilbert, *died* 1969, vol. VI
Matthews, Col Godfrey Estcourt, 1866–1917, vol. II
Matthews, Maj.-Gen. Harold Halford, 1877–1940, vol. III
Matthews, Sir (Harold Lancelot) Roy, 1901–1981, vol. VIII
Matthews, Harry G.; *see* Grindell-Matthews.
Matthews, Sir Herbert; *see* Matthews, Sir A. H. H.
Matthews, Ven. Hubert John, 1889–1971, vol. VII
Matthews, Sir James Henry John, 1887–1981, vol. VIII
Matthews, Rt Rev. James Joseph Edmund, 1871–1939, vol. III
Matthews, James Robert, 1889–1978, vol. VII
Matthews, Jessie, 1907–1981, vol. VIII
Matthews, Sir (John) Bromhead, 1864–1934, vol. III
Matthews, John Charles, 1872–1946, vol. IV
Matthews, Joseph Bridges, *died* 1928, vol. II
Matthews, Julia B., (Mrs Fairfax Ivimey), *died* 1948, vol. IV
Matthews, L(eonard) Harrison, 1901–1986, vol. VIII

Matthews, Norman Derek, 1922–1976, vol. VII
Matthews, Rev. Norman Gregory, 1904–1964, vol. VI
Matthews, Paul Taunton, 1919–1987, vol. VIII
Matthews, Percy John, 1895–1964, vol. VI
Matthews, Rt Rev. Ralph Vernon, 1928–1983, vol. VIII
Matthews, Hon. Robert Charles, 1871–1952, vol. V
Matthews, Robert Lee, 1876–1950, vol. IV
Matthews, Sir Ronald Wilfred, 1885–1959, vol. V
Matthews, Sir Roy; *see* Matthews, Sir H. L. R.
Matthews, Sir Russell, 1896–1987, vol. VIII
Matthews, Rt Rev. Seering John, 1900–1978, vol. VII
Matthews, Sir Thomas, 1849–1930, vol. III
Matthews, Sir Trevor Jocelyn, 1882–1954, vol. V
Matthews, Col Valentine, 1855–1921, vol. II
Matthews, Lt-Col Walter Hudson, 1864–1929, vol. III
Matthews, Very Rev. Walter Robert, 1881–1973, vol. VII
Matthews, Sir William, 1844–1922, vol. II
Matthews, William, 1905–1975, vol. VII
Matthews, William E., 1862–1938, vol. III
Matthews, William Kleesmann, 1901–1958, vol. V
Matthews, Sir William Thomas, 1888–1968, vol. VI
Matthey, Col Edward, 1836–1918, vol. II
Matthey, George, *died* 1913, vol. I
Matthiessen, Francis Otto, 1902–1950, vol. IV(A), vol. V
Mattingly, Garrett, 1900–1962, vol. VI
Mattingly, Harold, 1884–1964, vol. VI
Mattinson, Sir Miles, 1854–1944, vol. IV
Matturi, Sahr Thomas, 1925–1987, vol. VIII
Maturin, Father Basil William, 1847–1915, vol. I
Matz, Bertram Waldrom, 1865–1925, vol. II
Maubert, Louis, 1875–1949, vol. IV
Mauchline, Lord; Ian Huddleston Abney-Hastings, 1918–1944, vol. IV
Mauchline, Rev. John, 1902–1984, vol. VIII
Maud, Captain Charles Carus, 1875–1914, vol. I
Maud, Constance Elizabeth, *died* 1929, vol. III
Maud, Col Harry, 1867–1948, vol. IV
Maud, Rt Rev. John Primatt, 1860–1932, vol. III
Maud, Brig.-Gen. Philip, 1870–1947, vol. IV
Maud, W. T., *died* 1903, vol. I
Maud, Lt-Col William Hartley, 1868–1948, vol. IV
Maude, Col Alan Hamer, 1885–1979, vol. VII
Maude, Aylmer, 1858–1938, vol. III
Maude, Ven. Charles Bulmer, 1848–1927, vol. II
Maude, Charles John, 1847–1910, vol. I
Maude, Brig. Christian George, 1884–1971, vol. VII
Maude, Cyril, 1862–1951, vol. V
Maude, Edith Caroline, 1865–1922, vol. II
Maude, Evan Walter, 1919–1980, vol. VII
Maude, Sir (Evelyn) John, 1883–1963, vol. VI
Maude, Col Francis Cornwallis, 1828–1900, vol. I
Maude, Col Frederic Natusch, 1854–1933, vol. III
Maude, Sir Frederick Francis, 1821–1897, vol. I
Maude, Lt-Gen. Sir Frederick Stanley, 1864–1917, vol. II
Maude, Isabel Winifred Maud Emery; *see* Emery, Winifred.
Maude, Sir John; *see* Maude, Sir E. J.
Maude, John Cyril, 1901–1986, vol. VIII

Maude, Major Ralph Walter, 1873–1922, vol. II
Maude, Sir Walter, 1862–1943, vol. IV
Maude-Roxby, John Henry, 1919–1989, vol. VIII
Maudling, Rt Hon. Reginald, 1917–1979, vol. VII
Maudslay, Alfred Percival, 1850–1931, vol. III
Maudslay, Algernon, 1873–1948, vol. IV
Maudslay, Cecil Winton, 1880–1969, vol. VI
Maudslay, Major Sir (James) Rennie, 1915–1988, vol. VIII
Maudslay, Major Sir Rennie; see Maudslay, Major Sir J. R.
Maudslay, Walter Henry, 1844–1927, vol. II
Maudsley, Henry, 1835–1918, vol. II
Maudsley, Sir Henry Carr, 1859–1944, vol. IV
Maufe, Sir Edward Brantwood, 1883–1974, vol. VII
Maufe, Herbert Brantwood, 1879–1946, vol. IV
Maufe, Captain T. Harold Broadbent, 1898–1942, vol. IV
Mauger, Hon. Samuel, 1857–1936, vol. III
Maugham, 1st Viscount, 1866–1958, vol. V
Maugham, 2nd Viscount, 1916–1981, vol. VIII
Maugham, Reginald Charles Fulke, 1866–1956, vol. V
Maugham, Robin; see Maugham, 2nd Viscount
Maugham, Somerset; see Maugham, W. S.
Maugham, (William) Somerset, 1874–1965, vol. VI
Maughan, Sir David, 1873–1955, vol. V
Maughan, Janet Leith; see Story, J. L.
Maughan, Lt-Col Francis Gilfrid, died 1938, vol. III
Maul, Rev. John Frederic, 1849–1915, vol. I
Maula Bakhsh, Nawab Maula Bakhsh Khan Bahadur of Batala, 1862–1949, vol. IV
Maule, Col Henry Noel St John, 1873–1953, vol. V
Maule, Major Hugh Patrick Guarin, 1873–1940, vol. III
Maule, Sir Robert, 1852–1931, vol. III
Maulvi Haji, Rahim Bakhsh, died 1935, vol. III
Maund, Air Vice-Marshal Arthur Clinton, 1891–1942, vol. IV
Maund, Rear-Adm. Loben Edward Harold, 1892–1957, vol. V
Maunder, Annie Scott Dill, (Mrs Walter Maunder), 1868–1947, vol. IV
Maunder, Edward Walter, 1851–1928, vol. II
Maundrell, Captain Arthur Goodall, 1884–1972, vol. VII
Maung Kin, Hon. Sir, 1872–1924, vol. II
Maung Me, 1871–1952, vol. V
Maung Pe, 1858–1924, vol. II
Maunsell, Lt-Col Francis Richard, 1861–1936, vol. III
Maunsell, Brig.-Gen. Frederick Guy, 1864–1929, vol. III
Maunsell, Gen. Sir Frederick Richard, 1828–1916, vol. II
Maunsell, Col George William, 1859–1937, vol. III
Maunsell, Mark Stuart Ker, 1910–1980, vol. VII
Maunsell, Brig. Raymund John, 1903–1976, vol. VII
Maunsell, Richard Edward Lloyd, died 1944, vol. IV
Maunsell, Robert Charles Butler, 1872–1930, vol. III
Maunsell, Maj.-Gen. Sir Thomas, 1822–1908, vol. I
Maunsell, Surg.-Gen. Thomas, 1839–1937, vol. III
Mauny-Talvande, Countess de; (Lady Mary Elizabeth Agnes Byng), died 1946, vol. IV

Maurault, Rt Rev. Mgr Olivier, 1886–1968, vol. VI
Maurel, Victor, 1848–1923, vol. II
Mauriac, François, 1885–1970, vol. VI
Maurice, Lt-Col Albert Jafa, 1864–1943, vol. IV
Maurice, Lt-Col David Blake, 1866–1925, vol. II
Maurice, Maj.-Gen. Sir Frederick; see Maurice, Maj.-Gen. Sir J. F.
Maurice, Maj.-Gen. Sir Frederick Barton, 1871–1951, vol. V
Maurice, Col George Thelwall Kindersley, 1867–1950, vol. IV
Maurice, Col Godfrey Kindersley, 1887–1949, vol. IV
Maurice, Henry Gascoyen, 1874–1950, vol. IV
Maurice, Maj.-Gen. Sir (John) Frederick, 1841–1912, vol. I
Maurois, André, 1885–1967, vol. VI
Maurras, Charles, 1868–1952, vol. V
Maury, Amy-Gaston B.; see Bonet Maury.
Mavor, James, 1854–1925, vol. II
Mavor, O. H.; see Bridie, James.
Mavrogordato, John George, 1905–1987, vol. VIII
Mavrogordato, John Nicolas, 1882–1970, vol. VI
Maw, William Henry, 1838–1924, vol. II
Maw, William Nawton, 1869–1946, vol. IV
Mawbey, Adm. Henry Lancelot, 1870–1933, vol. III
Mawby, Sir Maurice Alan Edgar, 1904–1977, vol. VII
Mawby, Raymond Llewellyn, 1922–1990, vol. VIII
Mawer, Sir Allen, 1879–1942, vol. IV
Mawer, Air Cdre Allen Henry, 1921–1989, vol. VIII
Mawhinny, Col Robert John Watt, died 1953, vol. V
Mawhood, Mary; see Clare, M.
Mawson, Cecil Allerton Greville, 1876–1950, vol. IV
Mawson, Sir Douglas, 1882–1958, vol. V
Mawson, Thomas H., died 1933, vol. III
Max-Müller, Rt Hon. Friedrich, 1823–1900, vol. I
Max-Muller, Sir William Grenfell, 1867–1945, vol. IV
Maxim, Sir Hiram Stevens, 1840–1916, vol. II
Maxse, Ernest George Berkeley, 1863–1943, vol. IV
Maxse, Adm. Frederick Augustus, 1833–1900, vol. I
Maxse, Gen. Sir Ivor, 1862–1958, vol. V
Maxse, Leopold James, 1864–1932, vol. III
Maxse, Dame Marjorie, 1891–1975, vol. VII
Maxton, James, 1885–1946, vol. IV
Maxtone-Graham, Anthony George, 1854–1930, vol. III
Maxtone Graham, James, 1863–1940, vol. III
Maxwell, Sir Alexander, 1880–1963, vol. VI
Maxwell, Alexander Hyslop, 1864–1957, vol. V
Maxwell, Sir Alexander Hyslop, 1896–1971, vol. VII
Maxwell, Allan Victor, 1887–1975, vol. VII
Maxwell, Col Sir Arthur, 1875–1935, vol. III
Maxwell, Arthur Crawford, 1909–1964, vol. VI
Maxwell, Maj.-Gen. Sir Aymer, 1891–1971, vol. VII
Maxwell, Sir Aymer, 8th Bt, 1911–1987, vol. VIII
Maxwell, Beatrice H.; see Heron-Maxwell.
Maxwell, Hon. Bernard Constable, 1848–1938, vol. III
Maxwell, Bertram Wayburn, 1891–1972, vol. VII
Maxwell, Constantia Elizabeth, died 1962, vol. VI
Maxwell, Vice-Adm. Hon. Sir Denis Crichton, 1892–1970, vol. VI
Maxwell, Denis Oliver, 1906–1971, vol. VII

Maxwell, Donald, 1877–1936, vol. III
Maxwell, Douglas Rider, 1885–1967, vol. VI
Maxwell, Lt-Col F. D., 1862–1910, vol. I
Maxwell, Col Francis Aylmer, 1871–1917, vol. II
Maxwell, Sir Frederic Mackenzie, 1860–1931, vol. III
Maxwell, Gavin, 1914–1969, vol. VI
Maxwell, Col Geoffrey Archibald Prentice, 1885–1953, vol. V
Maxwell, Sir George; see Maxwell, Sir W. G.
Maxwell, George Arnot, died 1935, vol. III
Maxwell, Wing-Comdr Gerald Constable, 1895–1959, vol. V
Maxwell, Gerald Verner, 1877–1965, vol. VI
Maxwell, Hamilton, 1830–1923, vol. II
Maxwell, Rt Rev. Harold Alexander, 1897–1975, vol. VII
Maxwell, Col Hon. Henry Edward, 1857–1919, vol. II
Maxwell, Lt-Col Henry St Patrick, 1850–1928, vol. II
Maxwell, Rt Hon. Sir Herbert Eustace, 7th Bt (cr 1681), 1845–1937, vol. III
Maxwell, Herbert William, 1888–1979, vol. VII
Maxwell, Sir Ivor Walter H.; see Heron-Maxwell.
Maxwell, James, 1905–1956, vol. V
Maxwell, Major James Andrew Colvile W.; see Wedderburn-Maxwell.
Maxwell, Sir James Crawford, 1869–1932, vol. III
Maxwell, James Laidlaw, 1873–1951, vol. V
Maxwell, Brig.-Gen. James McCall, 1865–1945, vol. IV
Maxwell, James Robert, 1902–1970, vol. VI
Maxwell, Sir John, 1875–1946, vol. IV
Maxwell, John, 1905–1962, vol. VI
Maxwell, Sir John, 1882–1968, vol. VI
Maxwell, Gen. Rt Hon. Sir John Grenfell, 1859–1929, vol. III
Maxwell, Sir John Maxwell Stirling-, 10th Bt (cr 1682), 1866–1956, vol. V
Maxwell, Sir John Robert H.; see Heron-Maxwell.
Maxwell, Joseph, 1896–1967, vol. VI
Maxwell, Surgeon Rear-Adm. Joseph Archibald, 1890–1980, vol. VII
Maxwell, Brig.-Gen. Laurence Lockhart, 1868–1954, vol. V
Maxwell, Lawrence, 1853–1927, vol. II, vol. III
Maxwell, Magdalen Perceval, (Mrs Patrick Perceval-Maxwell); see King-Hall, M.
Maxwell, Mary Elizabeth; see Braddon, M. E.
Maxwell, Maurice William, 1910–1982, vol. VIII
Maxwell, Maxwell Hyslop, died 1937, vol. III
Maxwell, Sir Patrick Ivor H.; see Heron-Maxwell.
Maxwell, Perriton, died 1947, vol. IV(A)
Maxwell, Sir Reginald Maitland, 1882–1967, vol. VI
Maxwell, Brig. Richard Hobson, 1899–1965, vol. VI
Maxwell, Richard Ponsonby, 1853–1928, vol. II
Maxwell, Robert Charles H.; see Heron-Maxwell.
Maxwell, Col Rt Hon. Robert David Perceval, 1870–1932, vol. III
Maxwell, Lt-Gen. Sir Ronald Charles, 1852–1924, vol. II
Maxwell, Hon. Somerset Arthur, 1905–1942, vol. IV
Maxwell, Thomas Doveton, died 1946, vol. IV
Maxwell, Wellwood, 1857–1933, vol. III

Maxwell, Rear-Adm. Sir Wellwood George Courtenay, 1882–1965, vol. VI
Maxwell, Captain Sir William, died 1928, vol. II
Maxwell, Sir William, 1841–1929, vol. III
Maxwell, Sir William, 1870–1947, vol. IV
Maxwell, Sir William, died 1947, vol. IV
Maxwell, William, 1873–1957, vol. V
Maxwell, Captain William Babington, 1866–1938, vol. III
Maxwell, Sir William Edward, 1846–1897, vol. I
Maxwell, Lt-Col William Ernest, 1898–1951, vol. V
Maxwell, Sir William Francis, 4th Bt (cr (1804), 1844–1924, vol. II
Maxwell, Lt-Col William Frederick, 1878–1940, vol. III
Maxwell, Sir (William) George, 1871–1959, vol. V
Maxwell, Rev. William Gilchrist C.; see Clark-Maxwell.
Maxwell, Adm. William Henry, 1840–1920, vol. II
Maxwell, William Henry, 1852–1921, vol. II
Maxwell, William Jardine Herries, 1852–1933, vol. III
Maxwell, William Wayland, 1925–1986, vol. VIII
Maxwell-Anderson, Captain Sir Maxwell Hendry; see Anderson.
Maxwell-Carpendale, Major Frederic; see Carpendale.
Maxwell-Gumbleton, Rt Rev. Maxwell Homfray, 1872–1952, vol. V
Maxwell-Hibberd, Charles, 1853–1935, vol. III
Maxwell-Lefroy, Harold; see Lefroy.
Maxwell-Lyte, Sir Henry Church; see Lyte.
Maxwell-Scott, Rear-Adm. Malcolm; see Scott.
Maxwell Scott, Sir Michael Fergus, 13th Bt, 1921–1989, vol. VIII
Maxwell-Scott, Maj.-Gen. Sir Walter Joseph Constable, 1st Bt, 1875–1954, vol. V
Maxwell Stuart, Arthur Constable, 1845–1942, vol. IV
Maxwell-Stuart, Herbert Constable, 1842–1921, vol. II
Maxwell-Willshire, Sir Arthur Reginald Thomas; see Willshire.
Maxwell-Willshire, Sir Gerard Arthur; see Willshire.
May, 1st Baron, 1871–1946, vol. IV
May, 2nd Baron, 1904–1950, vol. IV
May, Rt Rev. Alston James Weller, 1869–1940, vol. III
May, Captain Arthur Dekewer Livius, 1875–1943, vol. IV
May, Sir Arthur William, 1854–1925, vol. II
May, Aylmer William, 1874–1950, vol. IV
May, Barry, 1869–1948, vol. IV
May, Bennett, 1846–1937, vol. III
May, Surgeon Vice-Adm. Sir Cyril; see May, Surgeon Vice-Adm. Sir R. C.
May, Edward Hooper, 1831–1914, vol. I
May, Maj.-Gen. Sir Edward Sinclair, 1856–1936, vol. III
May, Sir Francis Henry, 1860–1922, vol. II
May, Major Frederick, (Fred May), 1891–1976, vol. VII
May, Sir Gould, died 1944, vol. IV
May, Col Henry Allan Roughton, 1863–1930. vol. III

May, Rear-Adm. Henry John, 1853–1904, vol. I
May, Maj.-Gen. James, 1837–1903, vol. I
May, James Lewis, 1873–1961, vol. VI
May, John Cecil, 1890–1959, vol. V
May, Lt-Col John Cyril, 1874–1943, vol. IV
May, Otto, *died* 1946, vol. IV
May, Percy, 1886–1974, vol. VII
May, Phil, 1864–1903, vol. I
May, Gen. Sir Reginald Seaburne, 1879–1958, vol. V
May, Richard William Legerton, 1902–1967, vol. VI
May, Surgeon Vice-Adm. Sir (Robert) Cyril, 1897–1979, vol. VII
May, Rev. Thomas Henry, 1851–1932, vol. III
May, Major Thomas James, 1864–1952, vol. V
May, W. Charles, 1853–1931, vol. III
May, William, 1863–1932, vol. III
May, Col William Allan, 1850–1937, vol. III
May, Admiral of the Fleet Sir William Henry, 1849–1930, vol. III
May, Rt Hon. William Morrison, 1909–1962, vol. VI
May, Major William Southall Reid, 1864–1937, vol. III
Mayall, Robert Cecil, 1893–1962, vol. VI
Maybin, Sir Alexander, 1889–1941, vol. IV
Maybray-King, Baron (Life Peer); Horace Maybray Maybray-King, 1901–1986, vol. VIII
Maybrick, Michael, 1844–1913, vol. I
Maybury, Bernard Constable, 1888–1953, vol. V
Maybury, Brig.-Gen. Sir Henry Percy, 1864–1943, vol. IV
Maycock, Alan Lawson, 1898–1968, vol. VI
Maycock, Rev. Francis Hugh, 1903–1980, vol. VII
Maycock, Rev. Herbert William, 1863–1939, vol. III
Maycock, Sir William d'Auvergne, 1911–1987, vol. VIII
Maycock, Sir Willoughby Robert Dottin, 1849–1922, vol. II
Maydon, Hon. John George, 1857–1919, vol. II
Maydon, Lt-Comdr Stephen Lynch Conway, 1913–1971, vol. VII
Mayeda, Marquis Toshinari, 1885–1942, vol. IV
Mayer, Col Edward Rudolph, 1902–1973, vol. VII
Mayer, John, 1904–1967, vol. VI
Mayer, Maria Goeppert, 1906–1972, vol. VII
Mayer, René, 1895–1972, vol. VII
Mayer, Sir Robert, 1879–1985, vol. VIII
Mayer, Sylvain, 1863–1948, vol. IV
Mayers, Very Rev. George Samuel, *died* 1952, vol. V
Mayers, Norman, 1895–1986, vol. VIII
Mayers, Thomas Henry, 1907–1970, vol. VI
Mayes, William, 1874–1960, vol. V
Mayfield, Ven. Guy, 1905–1976, vol. VII
Maygar, Lt-Col Leslie Cecil, 1871–1917, vol. II
Mayhew, Rev. Arnold, 1873–1939, vol. III
Mayhew, Arthur Innes, 1878–1948, vol. IV
Mayhew, Sir Basil Edgar, 1883–1966, vol. VI
Mayhew, Captain George Henry, 1901–1973, vol. VII
Mayhew, Lt-Col Sir John, 1884–1954, vol. V
Mayle, Norman Leslie, 1899–1980, vol. VII
Maynard, Maj.-Gen. Sir Charles Clarkson Martin, 1870–1945, vol. IV
Maynard, Charles Gordon, 1889–1970, vol. VI
Maynard, Constance Louisa, 1849–1935, vol. III
Maynard, Dudley Christopher, 1874–1941, vol. IV

Maynard, Air Vice-Marshal Forster Herbert Martin, 1893–1976, vol. VII
Maynard, Brig.-Gen. Francis Herbert, 1881–1979, vol. VII
Maynard, Lt-Col Frederic P., *died* 1921, vol. II
Maynard, Harry Russell, 1873–1954, vol. V
Maynard, Rev. Henry Langston, 1865–1940, vol. III
Maynard, Sir (Herbert) John, 1865–1943, vol. IV
Maynard, Sir John; *see* Maynard, Sir H. J.
Maynard, John Percy Gordon, *died* 1918, vol. II
Maynard, Richard de Kirklevington, 1892–1969, vol. VI
Mayne, Arthur Brinley, 1893–1948, vol. IV
Mayne, Gen. Sir (Ashton Gerard Oswald) Mosley, 1889–1955, vol. V
Mayne, Brig.-Gen. Charles Robert Graham, 1874–1944, vol. IV
Mayne, Cuthbert Joseph, 1902–1972, vol. VII
Mayne, Ethel Colburn, *died* 1941, vol. IV
Mayne, Very Rev. Frank, *died* 1929, vol. III
Mayne, Lt-Col George Nisbet, 1854–1932, vol. III
Mayne, Gerald Outram, 1919–1980, vol. VII
Mayne, Horace Ardran, 1876–1958, vol. V
Mayne, Captain Jasper Graham, 1859–1936, vol. III
Mayne, Rev. Jonathan, 1838–1912, vol. I
Mayne, Jonathan Webster Coryton, 1868–1940, vol. III
Mayne, Ven. Joseph, 1843–1927, vol. II
Mayne, Gen. Sir Mosley; *see* Mayne, Gen. Sir A. G. O. M.
Mayne, Major Otway, 1855–1939, vol. III
Mayne, Col Richard Charles Graham, 1852–1939, vol. III
Mayne, Very Rev. William Cyril, 1877–1962, vol. VI
Mayneord, William Valentine, 1902–1988, vol. VIII
Mayo, 7th Earl of, 1851–1927, vol. II
Mayo, 8th Earl of, 1859–1939, vol. III
Mayo, 9th Earl of, 1890–1962, vol. VI
Mayo, Arthur, 1840–1920, vol. II
Mayo, Rev. Charles Herbert, 1845–1929, vol. III
Mayo, Charles Horace, 1865–1939, vol. III
Mayo, Charles William, 1898–1968, vol. VI
Mayo, Rev. Cuthbert Edward, 1860–1934, vol. III
Mayo, Sir Herbert, 1885–1972, vol. VII
Mayo, Isabella, (Mrs John Mayo), 1843–1914, vol. I
Mayo, Rev. John Augustus, *died* 1941, vol. IV
Mayo, Katherine, 1868–1940, vol. III
Mayo, Robert Hobart, 1890–1957, vol. V
Mayo, William James, 1861–1939, vol. III
Mayo-Robson, Sir Arthur William; *see* Robson.
Mayor, John Eyton Bickersteth, 1825–1910, vol. I
Mayor, Rev. Joseph Bickersteth, 1828–1916, vol. II
Mayor, Robert John Grote, 1869–1947, vol. IV
Mayou, M. Stephen, 1876–1934, vol. III
Mayrs, Edward Brice Cooper, 1891–1964, vol. VI
Mays, Raymond, 1899–1980, vol. VII (AII)
Mays-Smith, Sir Alfred, 1861–1931, vol. III
Mayston, Very Rev. Richard John Forrester, 1907–1963, vol. VI
Mayston, Engr Rear-Adm. Robert, 1851–1936, vol. III
Mayurbhanj, Maharaja of, *born* 1901, vol. VI
Maze, Sir Frederick William, *died* 1959, vol. V
Maze, Paul Lucien, 1887–1979, vol. VII

Mbanefo, Sir Louis Nwachukwu, 1911–1977, vol. VII
Mboya, Tom, (Thomas Joseph), 1930–1969, vol. VI
Meaby, Kenneth Tweedale, 1883–1965, vol. VI
Meachen, George Norman, 1876–1955, vol. V
Mead, Sir Cecil, 1900–1979, vol. VII
Mead, (Elsie) Stella, *died* 1981, vol. VIII
Mead, Frederick, 1847–1945, vol. IV
Mead, George Edward, 1849–1932, vol. III
Mead, George Robert Stow, 1863–1933, vol. III
Mead, John Phillips, 1886–1951, vol. V
Mead, Lloyd; *see* Mead, W. H. L.
Mead, Margaret, 1901–1978, vol. VII
Mead, Maj.-Gen. Owen Herbert, 1892–1942, vol. IV
Mead, Percy James, 1871–1923, vol. II
Mead, Rev. Richard Gawler, 1833–1909, vol. I
Mead, Stella; *see* Mead, E. S.
Mead, Brig. Stephen, 1882–1972, vol. VII
Mead, (William Howard) Lloyd, 1905–1987, vol. VIII
Meade, (Charles Alan) Gerald, 1905–1985, vol. VIII
Meade, Elizabeth Thomasina; *see* Meade, L. T.
Meade, Gerald; *see* Meade, C. A. G.
Meade, Major Harry Edward, 1884–1952, vol. V
Meade, Gen. John Michael de Courcy, 1831–1909, vol. I
Meade, Rt Hon. Joseph Michael, 1839–1900, vol. I
Meade, L. T., 1854–1914, vol. I
Meade, Lt-Col Malcolm John, 1854–1933, vol. III
Meade, Hon. Sir Robert Henry, 1835–1898, vol. I
Meade, Rev. Hon. Sidney, 1839–1917, vol. II
Meade, Rt Rev. William Edward, 1832–1912, vol. I
Meade-Fetherstonhaugh, Adm. Hon. Sir Herbert, 1875–1964, vol. VI
Meade-King, Sir William Oliver Evelyn, 1858–1940, vol. III
Meaden, Lt-Col Alban Anderson, 1876–1934, vol. III
Meaden, Surg.-Captain Edward Henry, 1864–1943, vol. IV
Meaden, Rt Rev. John Alfred, 1892–1987, vol. VIII
Meadon, Ernest John, 1911–1970, vol. VI
Meadon, Sir Percival Edward, 1878–1959, vol. V
Meadowcroft, Lancelot Vernon, 1884–1952, vol. V
Meadows, Alice Maud, *died* 1913, vol. I
Meadows, Surg.-Maj.-Gen. Robert Wyatt, 1832–1911, vol. I
Meadus, Engr-Captain Harry Howard, 1856–1934, vol. III
Meadus, Engr-Captain William Henry, 1862–1947, vol. IV
Meagher, Michael, 1846–1927, vol. II
Meagher, Hon. Nicholas Hogan, 1842–1932, vol. III
Meagher, Hon. Richard Denis, 1866–1931, vol. III
Meagher, Sir Thomas, 1902–1979, vol. VII
Meakin, Annette M. B., *died* 1959, vol. V
Meakin, Budgett, 1866–1906, vol. I
Meakin, Henry William, 1847–1939, vol. III
Meakin, Walter, 1878–1940, vol. III
Meakins, Brig. Jonathan Campbell, 1882–1959, vol. V
Meale, Arthur; *see* Meale, J. A.
Meale, (John) Arthur, 1880–1932, vol. III
Mealing, Sir Kenneth William, 1895–1968, vol. VI
Meany, George, 1894–1980, vol. VII

Meara, Rev. Henry George Jephson, *died* 1921, vol. II
Meares, John Willoughby, 1871–1946, vol. IV
Meares, Lt-Col Mervyn, 1880–1930, vol. III
Meares, Maj.-Gen. William Lewis D.; *see* Devenish-Meares.
Mearns, Andrew Daniel, 1857–1925, vol. II
Mears, Sir Frank Charles, 1880–1953, vol. V
Mears, Brig. Gerald Grimwood, 1896–1979, vol. VII
Mears, Sir Grimwood, 1869–1963, vol. VI
Mears, Margaret Mary, (Lady Mears); *see* Tempest, M. M.
Mears, Thomas Lambert, *died* 1918, vol. II, vol. III
Mears, Lt-Col Trevor Irvine Nevitt, 1875–1937, vol. III
Mease, Very Rev. Charles William O'Hara, 1856–1922, vol. II
Measham, Paymaster Rear-Adm. Herbert Stanley, 1875–1954, vol. V
Measham, Richard John Rupert, 1885–1976, vol. VII
Measom, Sir George Samuel, 1818–1901, vol. I
Measures, Wing Comdr Arthur Harold, 1882–1969, vol. VI
Measures, Harry Bell, 1862–1940, vol. III
Measures, Sir Philip Herbert, 1893–1961, vol. VI
Meath, 12th Earl of, 1841–1929, vol. III
Meath, 13th Earl of, 1869–1949, vol. IV
Mechan, Sir Henry, *died* 1943, vol. IV
Mecredy, Sir James, 1854–1938, vol. III
Mecredy, Richard James, 1861–1924, vol. II
Medawar, Sir Peter Brian, 1915–1987, vol. VIII
Medd, Rev. Peter Goldmsith, 1929–1908, vol. I
Medd, Wilfrid, 1877–1956, vol. V
Medforth, Marguerite Elizabeth, 1879–1966, vol. VI
Medhurst, Air Chief Marshal Sir Charles Edward Hastings, 1896–1954, vol. V
Medill, Brig. Percy Montomery, 1882–1963, vol. VI
Medland, Hubert Moses, 1881–1964, vol. VI
Medley, Charles Douglas, 1870–1963, vol. VI
Medley, Dudley Julius, 1861–1953, vol. V
Medley, Brig. Edgar J., 1893–1972, vol. VII
Medley, Sir John Dudley Gibbs, 1891–1962, vol. VI
Medlicott, Sir Frank, 1903–1972, vol. VII
Medlicott, Henry Benedict, 1829–1905, vol. I
Medlicott, Col Henry Edward, 1882–1948, vol. IV
Medlicott, Rev. Canon Robert Sumner, *died* 1941, vol. IV
Medlicott, William Norton, *died* 1923, vol. II
Medlicott, William Norton, 1900–1987, vol. VIII
Medlycott, Sir Edward Bradford, 4th Bt, 1832–1902, vol. I
Medlycott, Rev. Sir Hubert James, 6th Bt, 1841–1920, vol. II
Medlycott, Sir Hubert Mervyn, 7th Bt, 1874–1964, vol. VI
Medlycott, Sir (James) Christopher, 8th Bt, 1907–1986, vol. VIII
Medlycott, Sir Mervyn Bradford, 5th Bt, 1837–1908, vol. I
Medtner, Nicholas, 1879–1951, vol. V
Mee, Arthur, 1860–1926, vol. II
Mee, Arthur, 1875–1943, vol. IV
Mee, Ellen Catherine, 1894–1981, vol. VIII
Meech, Sir John Valentine, 1907–1971, vol. VII

Meech, Thomas Cox, *died* 1940, vol. III
Meecham, Bert, 1886–1964, vol. VI
Meehan, Francis Edward, 1868–1946, vol. IV
Meehan, Patrick Aloysius, 1852–1913, vol. I
Meek, Alexander, 1865–1949, vol. IV
Meek, Lt-Col Arthur Stanley, 1883–1955, vol. V
Meek, Charles Kingsley, 1885–1965, vol. VI
Meek, Sir David Burnett, 1885–1964, vol. VI
Meek, Col James, 1861–1939, vol. III
Meek, William Alfred, 1850–1929, vol. III
Meeking, Lt-Col Charles, 1839–1912, vol. I
Meeks, Hon. Sir Alfred William, 1849–1932, vol. III
Meenan, James Nahor, 1879–1950, vol. IV (A), vol. V
Meere, Sir Frank, (Francis Anthony), 1895–1985, vol. VIII
Meeres, Col Charles Stuart, 1861–1935, vol. III
Meers, James Blackader, 1850–1933, vol. III
Mees, Charles Edward Kenneth, 1882–1960, vol. V
Meeson, Dora, (Mrs George J. Coates), *died* 1955, vol. V
Meeson, Engr-Comdr Edward Hickman Tucker, 1877–1916, vol. II
Meff, Sir William, 1861–1935, vol. III
Megaw, Arthur Stanley, *died* 1961, vol. VI
Megaw, Maj.-Gen. Sir John Wallace Dick, 1874–1958, vol. V
Megaw, Robert Dick, *died* 1947, vol. IV
Meghnad Saha, 1893–1956, vol. V
Megrah, Maurice Henry, 1896–1985, vol. VIII
Mégroz, Rodolphe Louis, 1891–1968, vol. VI
Meharry, Rev. J. B., *died* 1916, vol. II
Mehta, Khan Bahadur, Sir Bezonji Dalabhoy, *died* 1927, vol. II
Mehta, Hon. Sir Homi, 1871–1948, vol. IV
Mehta, Jivraj Narayan, 1887–1978, vol. VII
Mehta, Sir Mangaldas Vijbhukandas, *died* 1945, vol. IV
Mehta, Sir Manubhai Nandshankar, 1868–1946, vol. IV
Mehta, Sir Phirozshah Merwanji, *died* 1915, vol. I
Mehta, Roostumjee Dhunjeebhoy, 1849–1930, vol. III
Mehta Shuja-ul-Mulk, Sir, *died* 1936, vol. III (A), vol. IV
Mehta, Sir Sorabji Bezonji, *died* 1938, vol. III
Meier, Frederic Alfred, 1887–1954, vol. V
Meiggs, Russell, 1902–1989, vol. VIII
Meighen, Rt Hon. Arthur, 1874–1960, vol. V
Meighen, Maj.-Gen. Frank Stephen, 1870–1946, vol. IV
Meikle, Alexander, 1905–1980, vol. VII
Meikle, Andrew, 1847–1922, vol. II
Meikle, Captain Archibald Robert, 1886–1958, vol. V
Meikle, Henry William, 1880–1958, vol. V
Meikle, Lt-Col James Hamilton, 1876–1941, vol. IV
Meiklejohn, Col John Forbes, 1889–1966, vol. VI
Meiklejohn, John Miller Dow, 1836–1902, vol. I
Meiklejohn, Major Matthew Fontaine Maury, 1870–1913, vol. I
Meiklejohn, Surg. Rear-Adm. Norman Sinclair, 1879–1961, vol. VI
Meiklejohn, Ven. Robert, 1889–1974, vol. VII
Meiklejohn, Sir Roderick Sinclair, 1876–1962, vol. VI

Meiklejohn, Maj.-Gen. Sir William Hope, 1845–1909, vol. I
Meiklereid, Sir (Ernest) William, 1899–1965, vol. VI
Meiklereid, Sir William; *see* Meiklereid, Sir E. W.
Meillet, Paul Jules Antoine, 1866–1936, vol. III
Mein, Major Desbrisay Blundell, 1889–1937, vol. III
Meinertzhagen, Sir Ernest Louis, 1854–1933, vol. III
Meinertzhagen, Col Richard, 1878–1967, vol. VI
Meir, Golda, 1898–1978, vol. VII
Meiss, Millard, 1904–1975, vol. VII
Meissas, Gaston, vol. II
Mekie, David Eric Cameron, 1902–1989, vol. VIII
Mekie, Eoin Cameron, 1906–1977, vol. VII
Melas, Michael Constantine, 1902–1967, vol. VI
Melba, Dame Nellie, 1861–1931, vol. III
Melcher, Frederic Gershom, 1879–1963, vol. VI
Melchett, 1st Baron, 1868–1930, vol. III
Melchett, 2nd Baron, 1898–1949, vol. IV
Melchett, 3rd Baron, 1925–1973, vol. VII
Melchett, Lady; (Violet), *died* 1945, vol. IV
Melchior, Lauritz L. H., 1890–1973, vol. VII
Meldola, Raphael, 1849–1915, vol. I
Meldon, Sir Albert, 1845–1924, vol. II
Meldon, Lt-Col James Austin, 1869–1931, vol. III
Meldon, Lt-Col Philip Albert, 1874–1942, vol. IV
Meldrum, Charles, 1821–1901, vol. I
Meldrum, David Storrar, 1864–1940, vol. III
Meldrum, Sir Peter Lowrie, 1910–1965, vol. VI
Meldrum, Brig.-Gen. William, 1865–1964, vol. VI
Melhado, Carlos, 1852–1922, vol. II
Melhuish, Sir Charles W., 1860–1946, vol. IV
Meline, Felix Jules, 1838–1925, vol. II
Melitus, Paul Gegory, 1858–1924, vol. II
Mellanby, Alexander Lawson, 1871–1951, vol. V
Mellanby, Sir Edward, 1884–1955, vol. V
Mellanby, John, 1878–1939, vol. III
Mellanby, May, (Lady Mellanby), 1882–1978, vol. VII
Mellanby, Molly, 1893–1962, vol. VI
Melland, Charles Herbert, 1872–1953, vol. V
Melland, Norman, 1865–1933, vol. III
Meller, Grahame Temple, 1905–1965, vol. VI
Meller, Sir Richard James, 1872–1940, vol. III
Mellersh, Arthur, 1857–1938, vol. III
Mellersh, Air Vice-Marshal Sir Francis John Williamson, 1898–1955, vol. V
Melles, Major William Eugene, 1883–1953, vol. V
Mellis, Rev. James, 1843–1925, vol. II
Mellis, Col William Andrew, *died* 1925, vol. II
Mellish, Rev. Edward Noel, 1880–1962, vol. VI
Mellish, Lt-Col Henry, 1856–1927, vol. II
Mellish, Humphrey, 1862–1937, vol. III
Mellish, Robert Walter, 1869–1938, vol. III
Melliss, Maj.-Gen. Sir Charles John, 1862–1936, vol. III
Melliss, Col Sir Howard, 1847–1921, vol. II
Mellon, Andrew William, 1855–1937, vol. III
Mellon, Rt Rev. William H., 1877–1952, vol. V
Mellone, Sydney Herbert, *died* 1956, vol. V
Mellor, Lt-Col Abel, 1880–1967, vol. VI
Mellor, Francis Hamilton, 1854–1925, vol. II
Mellor, Sir Frank, 1863–1941, vol. IV
Mellor, Sir George, *died* 1947, vol. IV
Mellor, Brig.-Gen. Sir Gilbert, 1872–1947, vol. IV

Mellor, Wing-Comdr Harry Manners, 1903–1941, vol. IV

Mellor, Sir James Robert, 1839–1926, vol. II

Mellor, John Edward, 1852–1925, vol. II

Mellor, Sir John Francis, 3rd Bt, 1925–1990, vol. VIII

Mellor, John James, 1830–1916, vol. II

Mellor, Sir John Paget, 1st Bt, 1862–1929, vol. III

Mellor, Sir John Serocold Paget, 2nd Bt, 1893–1986, vol. VIII

Mellor, Brig. John Seymour, 1883–1962, vol. VI

Mellor, Rt Hon. John William, 1835–1911, vol. I

Mellor, Joseph William, *died* 1938, vol. III

Mellor, Col Robert Ramsden, 1870–1951, vol. V

Mellor, Captain William, 1874–1928, vol. II

Mellor, William, 1888–1942, vol. IV

Mellowes, Liam; *see* Mellowes, W. J.

Mellowes, William Joseph (Liam), *died* 1922, vol. II

Melly, George Henry, 1860–1927, vol. II

Melrose, James, 1841–1922, vol. II

Melrose, James, 1828–1929, vol. III

Melrose, John, 1853–1927, vol. II

Melrose, Sir John, 1860–1938, vol. III

Melvill, Maj.-Gen. Charles William, 1878–1925, vol. II

Melvill, Philip Sandys, 1827–1906, vol. I

Melvill, Sir William Henry,1827–1911, vol. I

Melville, 5th Viscount, 1835–1904, vol. I

Melville, 6th Viscount, 1843–1926, vol. II

Melville, 7th Viscount, 1873–1935, vol. III

Melville, 8th Viscount, 1909–1971, vol. VII

Melville, Alan, 1910–1983, vol. VIII

Melville, Archibald Ralph, 1912–1982, vol. VIII

Melville, Arthur, 1855–1904, vol. I

Melville, Beresford Valentine, 1857–1931, vol. III

Melville, Col Charles Henderson, 1863–1943, vol. IV

Melville, Maj.-Gen. Charles William Francis, 1877–1949, vol. IV

Melville, Rev. David, 1813–1904, vol. I

Melville, Lt-Col Edward Patrick Alexander, 1880–1936, vol. III

Melville, Sir Eugene, 1911–1986, vol. VIII

Melville, Frances Helen, 1873–1962, vol. VI

Melville, Sir George, 1842–1924, vol. II

Melville, Lt-Col Harry George, 1869–1918, vol. II

Melville, Henry Edward, 1883–1976, vol. VII

Melville, Lt-Col Hon. Ian L.; *see* Leslie Melville.

Melville, James, 1908–1984, vol. VIII

Melville, Sir James Benjamin, 1885–1931, vol. III

Melville, Rev. Leslie, 1838–1908, vol. I

Melville, Leslie Melville B.; *see* Balfour-Melville.

Melville, Lewis; *see* Benjamin, L. S.

Melville, Robert Dundonald, 1872–1927, vol. II

Melville, William, 1852–1918, vol. II

Melville, Rev. William Gardner, 1863–1939, vol. III

Melvin, George Spencer, 1887–1949, vol. IV

Melvin, Air Cdre James Douglas, 1914–1987, vol. VIII

Melvin, Sir Martin John, 1st Bt, 1879–1952, vol. V

Menardos, Simos, 1872–1933, vol. III

Menary, Surg.-Captain John, 1865–1941, vol. IV

Menaul, Air Vice-Marshal Stewart William Blacker, 1915–1987, vol. VIII

Mencken, H. L., 1880–1956, vol. V

Mendel, William, 1854–1917, vol. II

Mendelsohn, Eric, 1887–1953, vol. V

Mendelson, John Jakob, 1917–1978, vol. VII

Mendelssohn, Kurt Alfred Georg, 1906–1980, vol. VII

Mendes, Catulle, 1841–1909, vol. I

Mendès France, Pierre, 1907–1982, vol. VIII

Mendl, Sir Charles, 1871–1958, vol. V

Mendl, Sir Sigismund Ferdinand, 1866–1945, vol. IV

Mends, Hon. Brig.-Gen. Horatio Reginald, 1851–1933, vol. III

Mends, Sir William Robert, 1812–1897, vol. I

Meneces, Maj.-Gen. Ambrose Neponucene Trelawny, 1904–1979, vol. VII

Menendez, Sir (Manuel) Raymond, 1864–1952, vol. V

Menéndez y Pelayo, Marcelino, 1856–1912, vol. I

Menendez, Sir Raymond; *see* Menendez, Sir M. R.

Mengelberg, Rudolf, 1892–1959, vol. V

Menges, Herbert, 1902–1972, vol. VII

Menges, Isolde, 1893–1976, vol. VII

Meninsky, Bernard, 1891–1950, vol. IV

Mennell, George Gillies, 1878–1959, vol. V

Mennell, James Beaver, 1880–1957, vol. V

Mennell, Peter, 1918–1981, vol. VIII

Mennell, Zebulon, 1876–1959, vol. V

Menninger, William C., 1899–1966, vol. VI

Menon, Sir Konkoth R.; *see* Ramunni Menon.

Menon, Rao Bahadur Vapal Pangunni, 1894–1966, vol. VI

Menon, Vengalil Krishnan K.; *see* Krishna Menon.

Menpes, Mortimer, *died* 1938, vol. III

Mensforth, Sir Holberry, 1871–1951, vol. V

Menson, Sir Charles William T.; *see* Tachie-Menson.

Menteth, Lt-Col Sir James Frederick Stuart-, 4th Bt, 1846–1926, vol. II

Menteth, Sir James Stuart-, 3rd Bt, 1841–1918, vol. II

Menteth, Sir William Frederick Stuart-, 5th Bt, 1874–1952, vol. V

Menzies, Alexander John Pople, 1863–1943, vol. IV

Menzies, Rev. Allan, 1845–1916, vol. II

Menzies, Captain Arthur John Alexander, *died* 1918, vol. II

Menzies, Col Charles T., 1858–1943, vol. IV

Menzies, Rt Hon. Sir Douglas Ian, 1907–1974, vol. VII

Menzies, Sir Frederick Norton Kay, 1875–1949, vol. IV

Menzies, George Kenneth, 1869–1954, vol. V

Menzies, James Acworth, *died* 1921, vol. II

Menzies, Sir Laurence James, 1906–1983, vol. VIII

Menzies, Marie Ney, 1895–1981, vol. VIII

Menzies, Sir Neil James, 8th Bt, 1855–1910, vol. I

Menzies, Sir Robert, 7th Bt, 1817–1903, vol. I

Menzies, Sir Robert, 1891–1967, vol. VI

Menzies, Rt Hon. Sir Robert Gordon, 1894–1978, vol. VII

Menzies of Menzies, Ronald Steuart, 1884–1961, vol. VI

Menzies, Maj.-Gen. Sir Stewart Graham, 1890–1968, vol. VI

Menzies, Maj.-Gen. Thomas, 1893–1969, vol. VI

Menzies, Thomas Graham, 1869–1958, vol. V

Menzies, Tom Alexander, 1877–1950, vol. IV (A)

Menzies, Sir Walter, 1856–1913, vol. I
Menzies, William George S.; *see* Steuart-Menzies.
Menzies, William Gladstone, 1879–1938, vol. III
Menzies Anderson, Sir Gilmour, 1914–1977, vol. VII
Menzler, Frederick August Andrew, 1888–1968, vol. VI
Mercadier, Elie, 1844–1916, vol. II
Mercer, Alexander Warren, 1871–1943, vol. IV
Mercer, Major Cecil William, 1885–1960, vol. V
Mercer, Maj-.Gen. Sir David, 1864–1920, vol. II
Mercer, David, 1928–1980, vol. VII
Mercer, Col Edward Gilbert, *died* 1926, vol. II
Mercer, Maj.-Gen. Sir Frederic; *see* Mercer, Maj.-Gen. Sir H. F.
Mercer, George Gibson, 1873–1964, vol. VI
Mercer, Maj.-Gen. Sir (Harvey) Frederic, 1858–1936, vol. III
Mercer, Col Herbert, 1862–1944, vol. IV
Mercer, Howard, 1896–1973, vol. VII
Mercer, James, 1883–1932, vol. III
Mercer, Rt Rev. John Edward, *died* 1922, vol. II
Mercer, John Swan, 1867–1947, vol. IV
Mercer, Laurence, 1863–1932, vol. III
Mercer, Rev. Samuel Alfred Browne, 1879–1969, vol. VI
Mercer, Stephen Pascal, 1891–1944, vol. IV
Mercer, Sir Walter, 1890–1971, vol. VII
Mercer, Sir William Hepworth, 1855–1932, vol. III
Mercer, Rev. William Marsden, 1858–1939, vol. III
Mercer-Nairne, Major Lord Charles George Francis, 1874–1914, vol. I
Merchant, Livingston Tallmadge, 1903–1976, vol. VII
Merchant, Vivien, 1929–1982, vol. VIII
Merchant, Wilfred, 1912–1965, vol. VI
Mercie, Jean Marius Antonin, 1845–1916, vol. II
Mercieca, Hon. Sir Arturo, 1878–1969, vol. VI
Mercier, Charles Arthur, 1852–1919, vol. II
Mercier, His Eminence Cardinal Desiré, 1851–1926, vol. II
Mercier, Hon. Honoré, 1875–1937, vol. III
Mercier, Winifred Louise, 1878–1934, vol. III
Meredith, Arthur, 1856–1915, vol. I
Meredith, Arthur C., *died* 1938, vol. III (A)
Meredith, Air Vice-Marshal Sir Charles Warburton, 1896–1977, vol. VII
Meredith, George, 1828–1909, vol. I
Meredith, George Patrick, 1904–1978, vol. VII
Meredith, George Thomas, 1907–1959, vol. V
Meredith, Sir Herbert Ribton, 1890–1959, vol. V
Meredith, Hubert Angelo, 1884–1965, vol. VI
Meredith, Hugh Owen, 1878–1964, vol. VI
Meredith, Sir James Creed, 1842–1912, vol. I
Meredith, James Creed, *died* 1942, vol. IV
Meredith, Leonard Arthur De Lacy, 1888–1971, vol. VII
Meredith, Rt Rev. Lewis Evan, 1900–1968, vol. VI
Meredith, Margaret, *died* 1964, vol. VI (AII)
Meredith, Rev. Canon Ralph Creed, 1887–1970, vol. VI
Meredith, Rev. Richard, *died* 1928, vol. II, vol. III
Meredith, Richard, 1867–1957, vol. V
Meredith, Rt Hon. Richard Edmund, 1855–1916, vol. II

Meredith, Richard Martin, 1847–1934, vol. III
Meredith, Sir Vincent, 1st Bt, 1850–1929, vol. III
Meredith, Sir Vincent Robert Sissons, 1877–1965, vol. VI
Meredith, William Appleton, 1848–1916, vol. II
Meredith, Rev. William Macdonald, 1848–1931, vol. III
Meredith, William Maxse, 1865–1937, vol. III
Meredith, Hon. Sir William Ralph, 1840–1923, vol. II
Meredith, Col William Rice, 1882–1964, vol. VI
Meredyth, Captain Arthur Gwynn Moreton, 1862–1955, vol. V
Meredyth, Paymaster Rear-Adm. Charles Edward Hughes, 1861–1949, vol. IV
Meredyth, Sir Edward Henry John, 10th Bt (*cr* 1660), 1828–1904, vol. I
Meredyth, Sir George Augustus Jérvis, 11th Bt (*cr* 1660), 1832–1907, vol. I
Meredyth, Sir Henry Bayly, 5th Bt (*cr* 1795), 1863–1923, vol. II
Merer, Air Vice-Marshal John William Frederick, 1899–1964, vol. VI
Merewether, Sir Edward Marsh, 1858–1938, vol. III
Merewether, Edward Rowland Alworth, 1892–1970, vol. VI
Merewether, Lt-Col John Walter Beresford, 1867–1942, vol. IV
Merewether, Rev. Wyndham Arthur Scinde, 1852–1928, vol. II
Merezhkovski, Dmitri Sergeievich, 1865–1941, vol. IV (A), vol. V
Meritt, Benjamin Dean, 1899–1989, vol. VIII
Merivale, Dame Gladys; *see* Cooper, Dame Gladys.
Merivale, Herman Charles, 1839–1906, vol. I
Merk, William Rudolph Henry, 1852–1925, vol. II
Mermagen, Patrick Hassell Frederick, 1911–1984, vol. VIII
Merrells, Thomas Ernest, 1891–1987, vol. VIII
Merrett, Sir Charles Edward, 1863–1948, vol. IV
Merrett, Sir Herbert, 1886–1959, vol. V
Merriam, John Campbell, 1869–1945, vol. IV
Merriam, Sir Laurence Pierce Brooke, 1894–1966, vol. VI
Merrick, Major George Charleton, 1872–1913, vol. I
Merrick, Sir John Edward-Siegfried, 1888–1968, vol. VI
Merrick, Leonard, 1864–1939, vol. III
Merricks, Frank, 1866–1936, vol. III
Merrifield, Leonard Stanford, 1880–1943, vol. IV
Merrill, Elmer Truesdell, 1860–1936, vol. III
Merriman, 1st Baron, 1880–1962, vol. VI
Merriman, Gen. Charles James, 1831–1906, vol. I
Merriman, Rev. Charles Victor, *died* 1931, vol. III
Merriman, Henry Seton, 1862–1903, vol. I
Merriman, Rt Hon. John Xavier, 1841–1926, vol. II
Merriman, P. J., 1877–1943, vol. IV
Merriman, Lt-Col Reginald Gordon, 1866–1938, vol. III
Merriman, Roger Bigelow, 1876–1945, vol. IV
Merriman, Sir Walter Thomas, 1882–1972, vol. VII
Merriman, Col William, 1838–1917, vol. II
Merrington, Rev. Ernest Northcroft, 1876–1953, vol. V
Merrison, Sir Alec; *see* Merrison, Sir Alexander W.

Merrison, Sir Alexander Walter, (Sir Alec Merrison), 1924–1989, vol. VIII

Merritt, Anna Lea, 1844–1930, vol. III

Merrivale, 1st Baron, 1855–1939, vol. III

Merrivale, 2nd Baron, 1883–1951, vol. V

Merry, Archibald William, *died* 1933, vol. III

Merry, Rev. William Walter, 1835–1918, vol. II

Merry del Val, Marquis de, 1864–1943, vol. IV

Merry del Val, His Eminence Cardinal Raphael, 1865–1930, vol. III

Mersey, 1st Viscount, 1840–1929, vol. III

Mersey, 2nd Viscount, 1872–1956, vol. V

Mersey, 3rd Viscount, 1906–1979, vol. VII

Merthyr, 1st Baron, 1837–1914, vol. I

Merthyr, 2nd Baron, 1866–1932, vol. III

Merthyr, 3rd Baron, 1901–1977, vol. VII

Merton, Sir Thomas Ralph, 1888–1969, vol. VI

Merton, Air Chief Marshal Sir Walter Hugh, 1905–1986, vol. VIII

Merz, Charles, 1893–1977, vol. VII

Merz, Charles Hesterman, 1874–1940, vol. III

Merz, John Theodore, 1840–1922, vol. II

Mess, Henry Adolphus, 1884–1944, vol. IV

Messager, André, 1853–1929, vol. III

Messager, Hope, (Mme André Messager); *see* Temple, Hope.

Messel, Oliver Hilary Sambourne, 1904–1978, vol. VII

Messel, Rudolph, 1848–1920, vol. II

Messent, Philip Glynn, 1862–1925, vol. II

Messent, Sir Philip Santo, 1895–1976, vol. VII

Messer, Adam Brunton, *died* 1919, vol. II

Messer, Allan Ernest, 1865–1954, vol. V

Messer, Lt-Col Arthur Albert, 1863–1934, vol. III

Messer, Sir Frederick, 1886–1971, vol. VII

Messer, Malcolm, 1901–1984, vol. VIII

Messervy, Albert, 1908–1985, vol. VIII

Messervy, Gen. Sir Frank Walter, 1893–1974, vol. VII

Messina, Count, Don Francesco (di Paola), *born* 1848, vol. III

Messiter, Lt-Col Charles Bayard, 1870–1940, vol. III

Meston, 1st Baron, 1865–1943, vol. IV

Meston, 2nd Baron, 1894–1984, vol. VIII

Meston, Rev. William, 1871–1933, vol. III

Mestrovic, Ivan, 1883–1962, vol. VI

Metalious, Grace, 1924–1964, vol. VI

Metaxa, Count Andrea, 1844–1921, vol. II

Metaxa, Vice-Adm. Count Frederick Cosmeto, 1847–1910, vol. I

Metaxas, Sir D. G., *died* 1928, vol. II

Metcalf, Maurice Rupert, 1905–1972, vol. VII

Metcalfe, Sir Aubrey; *see* Metcalfe, Sir H. A. F.

Metcalfe, Sir Charles Herbert Theophilus, 6th Bt, 1853–1928, vol. II

Metcalfe, Maj.-Gen. Charles Theophilus Evelyn, 1856–1912, vol. I

Metcalfe, Captain Christopher Powell, 1873–1935, vol. III

Metcalfe, Rev. Edmund Lionel, *died* 1941, vol. IV

Metcalfe, Major Edward Dudley, *died* 1957, vol. V

Metcalfe, Brig.-Gen. Francis Edward, 1878–1934, vol. III

Metcalfe, Sir Frederic William, 1886–1965, vol. VI

Metcalfe, Sir George, 1848–1931, vol. III

Metcalfe, Henry Wray, 1864–1937, vol. III

Metcalfe, Herbert, 1887–1940, vol. III

Metcalfe, Sir (Herbert) Aubrey (Francis), 1883–1957, vol. V

Metcalfe, Lt-Col Herbert Charles, 1864–1940, vol. III

Metcalfe, James, 1863–1930, vol. III

Metcalfe, Maj.-Gen. John Francis, 1908–1975, vol. VII

Metcalfe, Percy, 1895–1970, vol. VI

Metcalfe, Sir Ralph Ismay, 1896–1977, vol. VII

Metcalfe, Brig.-Gen. Sydney Fortescue, 1870–1948, vol. IV

Metcalfe, Sir Theophilus John, 8th Bt, 1916–1979, vol. VII

Metcalfe, Sir Theophilus John Massie, 7th Bt, 1866–1950, vol. IV

Metcalfe, Thomas Llewellyn, 1870–1922, vol. II

Metcalfe, Rev. W. M., 1840–1916, vol. II

Metcalfe-Smith, Lt-Col Bertram, 1863–1944, vol. IV

Metchnikoff, Élie, 1845–1916, vol. II

Metford, Col Sir Francis Killigrew Seymour, 1863–1946, vol. IV

Methold, Sir Henry Tindal, 1869–1952, vol. V

Methuen, 3rd Baron, 1845–1932, vol. III

Methuen, 4th Baron, 1886–1974, vol. VII

Methuen, 5th Baron, 1891–1975, vol. VII

Methuen, Sir Algernon Methuen Marshall, 1st Bt, 1856–1924, vol. II

Methven, Sir Harry Finlayson, 1886–1968, vol. VI

Methven, Sir John; *see* Methven, Sir M. J.

Methven, John Cecil Wilson, 1885–1968, vol. VI

Methven, Sir (Malcolm) John, 1926–1980, vol. VII

Metson, Gilbert Harold, 1907–1981, vol. VIII

Mettam, A. E., *died* 1917, vol. II

Meuleman, Most Rev. Brice, 1862–1924, vol. II

Meux, Admiral of the Fleet Hon. Sir Hedworth, 1856–1929, vol. III

Mewburn, Maj.-Gen. Hon. Sydney Chilton, 1863–1956, vol. V

Mews, Arthur, 1864–1947, vol. IV

Mexborough, 4th Earl of, 1810–1899, vol. I

Mexborough, 5th Earl of, 1843–1916, vol. II

Mexborough, 6th Earl of, 1868–1945, vol. IV

Mexborough, 7th Earl of, 1906–1980, vol. VII

Mexborough, Countess of; (Anne), *died* 1943, vol. IV

Meyendorff, Alexander, 1869–1964, vol. VI

Meyer, Alfred, 1895–1990, vol. VIII

Meyer, Arthur, 1845–1924, vol. II

Meyer, Sir Carl Ferdinand, 1st Bt, 1851–1922, vol. II

Meyer, Lt-Col Charles Hardwick Louw, 1859–1942, vol. IV

Meyer, Eugene, 1875–1959, vol. V

Meyer, Sir Frank Cecil, 2nd Bt, 1886–1935, vol. III

Meyer, Rev. Frederick Brotheron, 1847–1929, vol. III

Meyer, George von Lengerke, 1858–1918, vol. II

Meyer, Heinerich Carl, 1896–1972, vol. VII

Meyer, John Mount Montague, 1915–1979, vol. VII

Meyer, Kuno, 1859–1919, vol. II, vol. III

Meyer, Louis, 1871–1915, vol. I

Meyer, Sir Manasseh, 1831–1930, vol. III

Meyer, Sir Oscar Gwynne, 1910–1981, vol. VIII

Meyer, Paul, 1840–1917, vol. II
Meyer, Sir Robert, 1858–1935, vol. III
Meyer, Sir William Stevenson, 1860–1922, vol. II
Meyerheim, Robert Gustav, *died* 1920, vol. II
Meyerhof, Otto Fritz, 1884–1951, vol. V
Meyerstein, Edward Harry William, 1889–1952, vol. V
Meyerstein, Sir Edward William, 1863–1942, vol. IV
Meyjes, Anthony Cornelius, *died* 1929, vol. III
Meyler, Lt-Col Hugh Mowbray, 1875–1929, vol. III
Meynell, Alice Christiana Gertrude, 1847–1922, vol. II
Meynell, Edgar, 1859–1923, vol. II
Meynell, Edgar John, 1825–1901, vol. I
Meynell, Esther Hallam, (E. Hallam Moorhouse), *died* 1955, vol. V
Meynell, Everard, 1882–1926, vol. II
Meynell, Sir Everard Charles, 1885–1956, vol. V
Meynell, Sir Francis, 1891–1975, vol. VII
Meynell, Francis Hugo Lindley, 1880–1941, vol. IV
Meynell, Rev. Francis William, 1851–1932, vol. III
Meynell, Hon. Frederick George Lindley, 1846–1910, vol. I
Meynell, Brig.-Gen. Godfrey, 1870–1943, vol. IV
Meynell, Laurence Walter, 1899–1989, vol. VIII
Meynell, Viola, *died* 1956, vol. V
Meynell, Wilfrid, 1852–1948, vol. IV
Meyner, Robert Baumle, 1908–1990, vol. VIII
Meynink, John Fitzsimmons, 1887–1972, vol. VII
Meyric Hughes, Reginald Richard, 1915–1962, vol. VI
Meyrick, Edward, 1854–1938, vol. III
Meyrick, Brig.-Gen. Sir Frederick Charlton, 2nd Bt (*cr* 1880), 1862–1932, vol. III
Meyrick, Rev. Frederick J., 1871–1945, vol. IV
Meyrick, Sir George Augustus Eliott Tapps-Gervis-, 4th Bt (*cr* 1791), 1855–1928, vol. II
Meyrick, Lt-Col Sir George David Eliott Tapps Gervis-, 6th Bt, 1915–1988, vol. VIII
Meyrick, Major Sir George Llewelyn Tapps-Gervis-, 5th Bt (*cr* 1791), 1885–1960, vol. V
Meyrick, James Joseph, 1834–1925, vol. II
Meyrick, Adm. Sir Sidney Julius, 1879–1973, vol. VII
Meyrick, Col Sir Thomas C.; *see* Charlton-Meyrick.
Meyrick, Col Sir Thomas Frederick, 3rd Bt, 1899–1983, vol. VIII
Meyrick, Walter Henry, 1880–1950, vol. IV
Meysey-Thompson, Captain Sir Algar de Clifford Charles, 3rd Bt, 1885–1967, vol. VI
Meysey-Thompson, Captain Hon. Claude Henry, 1887–1915, vol. I
Meysey-Thompson, Ernest Claude, 1859–1944, vol. IV
Meysey-Thompson, Hubert Charles, 1883–1956, vol. V
Meysey-Thompson, Col Richard Frederick, 1847–1926, vol. II
Mézières, Alfred Jean François, *died* 1915, vol. I
Miall, Louis Compton, 1842–1921, vol. II
Micallef, Sir Richard, 1846–1933, vol. III
Michael, Albert Davidson, 1836–1927, vol. II
Michael, David Parry Martin, 1910–1986, vol. VIII
Michael, Rev. J. Hugh, 1878–1959, vol. V
Michael, Gen. James, 1828–1907, vol. I

Michaelis, Sir Archie, 1889–1975, vol. VII
Michaelis, Sir Maximillian, *died* 1932, vol. III
Michel, Louise, 1830–1905, vol. I
Michelham, 1st Baron, 1851–1919, vol. II
Michelham, 2nd Baron, 1900–1984, vol. VIII
Michelham, Lady; (Aimée Geraldine), *died* 1927, vol. II
Michelin, William Plunkett, 1872–1943, vol. IV
Michell, Alan, 1913–1985, vol. VIII
Michell, Anthony George Maldon, *died* 1959, vol. V
Michell, Rev. Francis Rodon, 1839–1920, vol. II
Michell, Francis Victor, 1908–1985, vol. VIII
Michell, George Babington, 1864–1936, vol. III
Michell, Rev. Gilbert Arthur, 1883–1960, vol. V
Michell, Harry Denis, 1923–1971, vol. VII
Michell, Humphrey, 1883–1970, vol. VI
Michell, John, 1836–1921, vol. III
Michell, John Henry, *died* 1940, vol. III
Michell, Comdr Kenneth, 1887–1967, vol. VI
Michell, Hon. Sir Lewis Loyd, 1842–1928, vol. II
Michell, Sir Robert Carminowe, 1876–1956, vol. V
Michell, Roland Lyons Nosworthy, 1847–1931, vol. III
Michell, Walter Cecil, 1864–1939, vol. III
Michelli, Sir James, 1853–1935, vol. III
Michelmore, Maj.-Gen. Sir Godwin; *see* Michelmore, Maj.-Gen. Sir W. G.
Michelmore, Sir Walter Harold Strachan, 1908–1988, vol. VIII
Michelmore, Maj.-Gen. Sir (William) Godwin, 1894–1982, vol. VIII
Michelson, Albert Abraham, 1852–1931, vol. III
Michelson, Christian, 1857–1925, vol. II
Michie, Alexander, 1833–1902, vol. I
Michie, Sir Archibald, 1810–1899, vol. I
Michie, Charles Watt, 1907–1982, vol. VIII
Michie, J. Coutts, 1861–1919, vol. II
Michie, James, 1867–1943, vol. IV
Michie, James Kilgour, 1887–1967, vol. VI
Michie, John, 1853–1934, vol. III
Michie, John Lundie, 1882–1946, vol. IV
Michie, Robert James, 1856–1928, vol. II
Micholls, E. Montefiore, 1852–1926, vol. II
Micklem, Major Charles, 1882–1955, vol. V
Micklem, Maj.-Gen. Edward, 1840–1934, vol. III
Micklem, Comdr Sir (Edward) Robert, 1891–1952, vol. V
Micklem, Col Henry Andrew, 1872–1963, vol. VI
Micklem, Brig.-Gen. John, 1889–1952, vol. V
Micklem, Nathaniel, 1853–1954, vol. V
Micklem, Rev. Nathaniel, 1888–1976, vol. VII
Micklem, Very Rev. Philip Arthur, 1876–1965, vol. VI
Micklem, Brig. Ralph, 1884–1977, vol. VII
Micklem, Comdr Sir Robert; *see* Micklem, Comdr Sir E. R.
Micklethwait, Frances Mary Gore, 1867–1950, vol. IV
Micklethwait, Hon. Ivy Mary, (Hon. Mrs Micklethwait), 1895–1967, vol. IV
Micklethwait, Rear-Adm. St John Aldrich, 1901–1977, vol. VII
Micklethwait, St John Gore, 1870–1951, vol. V
Micks, Sir Robert, 1825–1902, vol. I

Micks, Robert Henry, 1895–1970, vol. VI
Micks, William Lawson, 1851–1928, vol. II
Middlebro, William Sora, 1868–1948, vol. IV
Middlebrook, Sir Harold, 2nd Bt, 1887–1971, vol. VII
Middlebrook, Sir William, 1st Bt, 1851–1936, vol. III
Middlemas, Noel Allan, 1892–1967, vol. VI
Middlemiss, Charles Stewart, 1859–1945, vol. IV
Middlemiss, Sir Howard; see Middlemiss, Sir J. H.
Middlemiss, Sir (John) Howard, 1916–1983, vol. VIII
Middleditch, Edward, 1923–1987, vol. VIII
Middlemore, Sir John Throgmorton, 1st Bt, 1844–1925, vol. II
Middlemore, Sir William Hawkslow, 2nd Bt, 1908–1987, vol. VIII
Middleton, 9th Baron, 1844–1922, vol. II
Middleton, 10th Baron, 1847–1924, vol. II
Middleton, 11th Baron, 1887–1970, vol. VI
Middleton, A. Safroni, died 1950, vol. IV
Middleton, Sir Arthur Edward, 7th Bt, 1838–1933, vol. III
Middleton, Sir Arthur Edward, 1891–1953, vol. V
Middleton, Sir Charles Arthur, 8th Bt, 1873–1942, vol. IV
Middleton, Drew, 1914–1990, vol. VIII
Middleton, Edgar, 1894–1939, vol. III
Middleton, Sir Frederick Dobson, 1825–1898, vol. I
Middleton, Sir George, 1876–1938, vol. III
Middleton, Sir George Proctor, 1905–1987, vol. VIII
Middleton, George Walker, 1898–1971, vol. VII
Middleton, Adm. Gervase Boswell, 1893–1961, vol. VI
Middleton, Hubert Stanley, 1890–1959, vol. V
Middleton, Sir John, 1870–1954, vol. V
Middleton, Sir John Page, 1851–1954, vol. III
Middleton, Lambert William, 1877–1941, vol. IV
Middleton, Lucy Annie, 1894–1983, vol. VIII
Middleton, Noel, 1875–1955, vol. V
Middleton, Peggy Arline, 1916–1974, vol. VII
Middleton, Reginald Empson, 1844–1925, vol. II
Middleton, Richard William Evelyn, 1846–1905, vol. I
Middleton, Sir Thomas, 1863–1943, vol. IV
Middleton, William Aberdein, 1876–1940, vol. III
Midgley, Rt Hon. Harry, died 1957, vol. V
Midgley, Lt-Col Stephen, 1871–1954, vol. V
Midgley, Wilson, 1887–1954, vol. V
Midlane, Albert, 1825–1909, vol. I
Midleton, 1st Earl of, 1856–1942, vol. IV
Midleton, 2nd Earl of, 1888–1979, vol. VII
Midleton, 8th Viscount, 1830–1907, vol. I
Midleton, 11th Viscount, 1903–1988, vol. VIII
Midwinter, Captain Sir Edward Colpoys, 1872–1947, vol. IV
Midwood, Lt-Col Harrison, 1857–1944, vol. IV
Miers, Rear-Adm. Sir Anthony Cecil Capel, 1906–1985, vol. VIII
Miers, Sir Henry Alexander, 1858–1942, vol. IV
Mies van der Rohe, Ludwig, 1886–1969, vol. VI
Mieville, Arthur Leonard, 1879–1976, vol. VII
Mieville, Sir Eric Charles, 1896–1971, vol. VII
Miéville, Sir Walter Frederick, 1855–1929, vol. III
Mifflin, Lloyd, 1846–1921, vol. II
Mifsud, Edward Robert, 1875–1970, vol. VI
Mifsud, Hon. Sir Ugo Pasquale, 1889–1942, vol. IV

Migdale, Hon. Lord; James Frederick Gordon Thomson, 1897–1983, vol. VIII
Migeod, Frederick William Hugh, 1872–1952, vol. V
Mighell, Sir Norman Rupert, 1894–1955, vol. V
Mignault, Pierre Basile, 1854–1945, vol. IV
Mignot, Rev. Peter Thomas, 1863–1935, vol. III
Mijatovich, Chedomille, 1842–1932, vol. III
Mikes, George, 1912–1987, vol. VIII
Mikkelsen, Captain Ejnar, 1880–1971, vol. VII
Mikoyan, Anastas Ivanovich, 1895–1978, vol. VII
Milbank, Sir Frederick Acclom, 1st Bt, 1820–1898, vol. I
Milbank, Major Sir Frederick Richard Powlett, 3rd Bt, 1881–1964, vol. VI
Milbank, Maj. Sir Mark Vane, 4th Bt, 1907–1984, vol. VIII
Milbank, Sir Powlett Charles John, 2nd Bt, 1852–1918, vol. II
Milbanke, Sir John Charles Peniston, 11th Bt, 1902–1947, vol. IV
Milbanke, Sir John Peniston, 10th Bt, 1872–1915, vol. I
Milbanke, Sir Peniston, 9th Bt, 1847–1899, vol. I
Milbanke, Ralph, 1852–1903, vol. I
Milbanke, Sir Ralph Mark, 12th Bt, 1907–1949, vol. IV
Milborne-Swinnerton-Pilkington, Major Sir Arthur William; see Pilkington.
Milborne-Swinnerton-Pilkington, Sir Thomas Edward; see Pilkington.
Milburn, Captain Booker, 1888–1941, vol. IV
Milburn, Charles Henry, 1860–1948, vol. IV
Milburn, Sir Charles Stamp, 2nd Bt, 1878–1917, vol. II
Milburn, James Booth, 1860–1923, vol. II
Milburn, Sir John Davison, 1st Bt, 1851–1907, vol. I
Milburn, Sir John Nigel, 4th Bt, 1918–1985, vol. VIII
Milburn, Sir Leonard John, 3rd Bt, 1884–1957, vol. V
Mildmay of Flete, 1st Baron, 1861–1947, vol. IV
Mildmay of Flete, 2nd Baron, 1909–1950, vol. IV
Mildmay, Sir Anthony St John-, 8th Bt, 1894–1947, vol. IV
Mildmay, Rev. Sir (Aubrey) Neville St John-, 10th Bt, 1865–1955, vol. V
Mildmay, Sir Gerald Anthony Shaw-Lefevre St John-, 7th Bt, 1860–1929, vol. III
Mildmay, Sir Henry Bouverie Paulet St John-, 5th Bt, 1810–1902, vol. I
Mildmay, Sir Henry Gerald St John-, 9th Bt, 1926–1949, vol. IV
Mildmay, Major Sir Henry Paulet St John, 6th Bt, 1853–1916, vol. II
Mildmay, Lt-Col Herbert Alexander St John-, 1836–1922, vol. II
Mildmay, Rev. Sir Neville St John-; see Mildmay, Rev. Sir A. N. St J.
Mildmay, Major Wyndham Paulet St John-, 1855–1934, vol. III
Mildren, Col William Frederick, 1874–1948, vol. IV
Miles, Alexander, 1865–1953, vol. V
Miles, Alfred Henry, 1848–1929, vol. III
Miles, Alfred Henry, 1855–1933, vol. III
Miles, Sir (Arnold) Ashley, 1904–1988, vol. VIII
Miles, Major Arthur Tremayne, 1889–1934, vol. III

Miles, Sir Ashley; *see* Miles, Sir A. A.
Miles, Basil Raymond, 1906–1984, vol. VIII
Miles, Sir Cecil Leopold, 3rd Bt, 1873–1898, vol. I
Miles, Lt-Gen. Charles George Norman, 1884–1958, vol. V
Miles, Col Charles Napier, 1854–1918, vol. II
Miles, Sir Charles Watt, 1901–1970, vol. VI
Miles, Sir Charles William, 5th Bt, 1883–1966, vol. VI
Miles, Maj.-Gen. Eric Grant, 1891–1977, vol. VII
Miles, Eustace, 1868–1948, vol. IV
Miles, Rev. Frederic James, 1869–1962, vol. VI
Miles, Frederick George, 1903–1976, vol. VII
Miles, Adm. Sir Geoffrey John Audley, 1890–1986, vol. VIII
Miles, George Edward, 1852–1942, vol. IV
Miles, George Herbert, 1880–1955, vol. V
Miles, Gordon, 1891–1959, vol. V
Miles, Sir Henry Robert William, 4th Bt, 1843–1915, vol. I
Miles, Lt-Gen. Sir Herbert Scott Gould, 1850–1926, vol. II
Miles, Herbert William, 1898–1987, vol. VIII
Miles, Sir John Charles, 1870–1963, vol. VI
Miles, Rev. Joseph Henry, *died* 1935, vol. III
Miles, Maurice Edward, 1908–1985, vol. VIII
Miles, Maxine Frances Mary, 1901–1984, vol. VIII
Miles, Lt-Gen. Nelson Appleton, 1839–1925, vol. II
Miles, Brig.-Gen. Philip John, 1864–1948, vol. IV
Miles, Philip Napier, 1865–1935, vol. III
Miles, Brig. Reginald, 1892–1943, vol. IV
Miles, Richard, 1893–1976, vol. VII
Miles, Surgeon Rear-Adm. Stanley, 1911–1987, vol. VIII
Miles, Captain Wilfrid, 1885–1962, vol. VI
Miles, William Ernest, 1869–1947, vol. IV
Miley, Col James Aloysius, 1846–1919, vol. II
Milford, 1st Baron, 1874–1962, vol. VI
Milford, Rev. Canon Campbell Seymour, 1896–1981, vol. VIII
Milford, Maj.-Gen. Edward James, *died* 1972, vol. VII
Milford, Brig. Ernest William, 1898–1944, vol. IV
Milford, Sir Humphrey Sumner, 1877–1952, vol. V
Milford, Rev. Canon Theodore Richard, 1895–1987, vol. VIII
Milford Haven, 1st Marquess of, 1854–1921, vol. II
Milford Haven, 2nd Marquess of, 1892–1938, vol. III
Milford Haven, 3rd Marquess of, 1919–1970, vol. VI
Milhaud, Darius, 1892–1974, vol. VII
Mill, Rear-Adm. Ernest, 1906–1988, vol. VIII
Mill, Hugh Robert, 1861–1950, vol. IV
Mill, Laura Margaret Dorothea, 1897–1990, vol. VIII
Mill, Thomas, 1878–1941, vol. IV
Mill, William Allin, 1902–1968, vol. VI
Mill, William Claude Frederick V. B.; *see* Vaudrey-Barker-Mill.
Mill Irving, David Jarvis, 1904–1978, vol. VII
Millais, Sir Everett, 2nd Bt, 1856–1897, vol. I
Millais, Sir Geoffroy William, 4th Bt, 1863–1941, vol. IV
Millais, Sir John Everett, 3rd Bt, 1888–1920, vol. II
Millais, John Guille, 1865–1931, vol. III

Milland, Raymond Alton, 1907–1986, vol. VIII
Millar, A. H., 1847–1927, vol. II
Millar, Alexander, 1867–1944, vol. IV
Millar, Edric William Hoyer, 1880–1963, vol. VI
Millar, Eric George, 1887–1966, vol. VI
Millar, Dame (Evelyn Louisa) Elizabeth H.; *see* Hoyer-Millar.
Millar, Frederick Charles James, *died* 1899, vol. I
Millar, Henry James, 1878–1960, vol. V
Millar, Sir Jackson, 1888–1958, vol. V
Millar, Sir James Duncan, 1871–1932, vol. III
Millar, James Gardner, 1855–1917, vol. II
Millar, John, 1905–1978, vol. VII
Millar, John Alexander Stevenson, 1854–1938, vol. III
Millar, John Hepburn, 1864–1929, vol. III
Millar, Robert, 1850–1908, vol. I
Millar of Orton, Maj.-Gen. Robert Kirkpatrick, 1901–1981, vol. VIII
Millar-Craig, Hamish, 1918–1989, vol. VIII
Millard, Charles Killick, 1870–1952, vol. V
Millard, Ven. Ernest Norman, 1899–1969, vol. VI
Millard, Evelyn, *died* 1941, vol. IV
Millard, Col Reginald Jeffery, 1868–1943, vol. IV
Millard, Thomas, 1884–1935, vol. III
Millay, Edna St Vincent, 1892–1950, vol. IV
Millbourn, Rev. Arthur Russell, 1892–1973, vol. VII
Millbourn, Sir Eric; *see* Millbourn, Sir P. E.
Millbourn, Sir (Philip) Eric, 1902–1982, vol. VIII
Millbourn, Sir Ralph, 1862–1942, vol. IV
Miller, Sir Alastair George Lionel Joseph, 6th Bt (*cr* 1788), 1893–1964, vol. VI
Miller, Sir Alexander Edward, 1828–1903, vol. I
Miller, Alexander Gordon, 1843–1929, vol. III
Miller, Alexander James Nicol, 1911–1974, vol. VII
Miller, Alexander Thomas, 1875–1942, vol. IV
Miller, Brig.-Gen. Alfred Douglas, 1864–1933, vol. III
Miller, Rear-Adm. Andrew John, 1926–1986, vol. VIII
Miller, Archibald Elliot Haswell, 1887–1979, vol. VII
Miller, A(rthur) Austin, 1900–1968, vol. VI
Miller, Arthur Hallowes, 1880–1956, vol. V
Miller, Arthur William Kaye, 1849–1914, vol. I
Miller, Maj.-Gen. Austin T., 1888–1947, vol. IV
Miller, Charles A. Duff, 1854–1909, vol. I
Miller, Vice-Adm. Charles Blois, 1867–1926, vol. II
Miller, Lt-Col Charles Darley, 1868–1951, vol. V
Miller, Maj.-Gen. Charles Harvey, 1894–1974, vol. VII
Miller, Charles Hewitt, 1875–1939, vol. III
Miller, Sir (Charles John) Hubert, 8th Bt (*cr* 1705), 1858–1940, vol. III
Miller, Cincinnatus Heine; *see* Miller, Joaquin.
Miller, Brig.-Gen. David, 1857–1934, vol. III
Miller, Sir Dawson, 1867–1942, vol. IV
Miller, Sir Denison Samuel King, 1860–1923, vol. II
Miller, Desmond Campbell, 1914–1986, vol. VIII
Miller, Douglas Gordon, 1881–1956, vol. V
Miller, Edmund Morris, 1881–1964, vol. VI
Miller, Hon. Sir Edward, 1848–1932, vol. III
Miller, Lt-Col Edward Darley, 1865–1930, vol. III
Miller, Emanuel, 1894–1970, vol. VI
Miller, Sir Eric; *see* Miller, Sir H. E.

Miller, Sir Ernest, 1879–1939, vol. III

Miller, Sir Ernest Henry John, 10th Bt (*cr* 1705), 1897–1960, vol. V

Miller, Lt-Gen. Sir Euan Alfred Bews, 1897–1985, vol. III

Miller, Florence Fenwick, 1854–1935, vol. III

Miller, Rev. Francis Broughton Anson, 1855–1934, vol. III

Miller, Sir (Francis) Henry, 1865–1936, vol. III

Miller, Sir Francis N.; *see* Norie-Miller.

Miller, Adm. Francis Spurstow, 1863–1954, vol. V

Miller, Fred, 1863–1924, vol. II

Miller, Frederick Robert, *died* 1967, vol. VI

Miller, Col Sir Geoffry C.; *see* Christie-Miller.

Miller, George, 1833–1909, vol. I

Miller, George, 1842–1923, vol. II

Miller, Maj.-Gen. George Murray, 1829–1911, vol. I

Miller, Brig. George Patrick Rose-, 1897–1984, vol. VIII

Miller, George Waterston, 1874–1955, vol. V

Miller, Gerald Cedar, 1894–1982, vol. VIII

Miller, Gilbert Heron, 1884–1969, vol. VI

Miller, Sir Gordon William, 1844–1906, vol. I

Miller, Gray, 1885–1947, vol. IV

Miller, Captain Grenville Acton, *died* 1951, vol. V

Miller, Sir (Hans) Eric, 1882–1958, vol. V

Miller, Harold Tibbatts, 1873–1948, vol. IV

Miller, Henry, 1859–1927, vol. II

Miller, Sir Henry; *see* Miller, Sir F. H.

Miller, Henry George, 1913–1976, vol. VII

Miller, Sir Henry Holmes, 9th Bt (*cr* 1705), 1865–1952, vol. V

Miller, Hon. Sir Henry John, 1830–1918, vol. II

Miller, Henry Valentine, 1891–1980, vol. VII

Miller, Sir Holmes; *see* Miller, Sir J. H.

Miller, Sir Hubert; *see* Miller, Sir C. J. H.

Miller, Rear-Adm. Hugh, 1880–1972, vol. VII

Miller, Hugh C.; *see* Crichton-Miller.

Miller, Brig. Hugh de Burgh, 1874–1951, vol. V

Miller, Hugh Rodolph, 1875–1953, vol. V

Miller, Maj.-Gen. James, 1835–1929, vol. III

Miller, James, *died* 1947, vol. IV

Miller, James, 1875–1958, vol. V

Miller, Sir James, 1905–1977, vol. VII

Miller, James, 1893–1987, vol. VIII

Miller, James Gordon, 1874–1950, vol. IV

Miller, Bt Col Sir James MacBride, 1896–1977, vol. VII

Miller, Sir James Percy, 2nd Bt (*cr* 1874), 1864–1906, vol. I

Miller, Joaquin, 1842–1913, vol. I

Miller, John, 1911–1975, vol. VII

Miller, Sir John Alexander, 3rd Bt (*cr* 1874), 1867–1918, vol. II

Miller, John Duncan, 1902–1977, vol. VII

Miller, Very Rev. John Harry, 1869–1940, vol. III

Miller, Sir John Ontario, 1857–1943, vol. IV

Miller, Sir John Wilson Edington, 1894–1957, vol. V

Miller, Maj.-Gen. Joseph Esmond, 1914–1990, vol. VIII

Miller, Sir (Joseph) Holmes, 1919–1986, vol. VIII

Miller, Brig. Laurence Walter, 1882–1958, vol. V

Miller, Leonard; *see* Merrick, L.

Miller, Sir Leslie Creery, 1862–1925, vol. II

Miller, Dame Mabel, *died* 1978, vol. VII

Miller, Mrs Millie, 1923–1977, vol. VII

Miller, Rev. Norman, *died* 1980, vol. VII

Miller, Rev. Norman James, *died* 1932, vol. III

Miller, Rev. Peter Watters, 1890–1976, vol. VII

Miller, Philip Homan, *died* 1928, vol. II

Miller, Ralph William Richardson, 1892–1958, vol. V

Miller, Reginald Henry, *died* 1948, vol. IV

Miller, René F.; *see* Fülop-Miller.

Miller, Sir Richard Hope, 1904–1989, vol. VIII

Miller, Rt Rev. Robert, 1866–1931, vol. III

Miller, Robert Brown, 1905–1963, vol. VI

Miller, Robert Sydney, 1901–1980, vol. VII (AII)

Miller, Sir Roderick William, 1911–1971, vol. VII

Miller, Ronald, 1910–1990, vol. VIII

Miller, Rudolph Valdemar Thor C.; *see* Castle-Miller.

Miller, Samuel Vandeleur C.; *see* Christie-Miller.

Miller, Sinclair, 1885–1961, vol. VI

Miller, Sir Stanley N.; *see* Norie-Miller.

Miller, Stearnhall, 1813–1897, vol. I

Miller, Sydney Richardson C.; *see* Christie-Miller.

Miller, Thomas Butt, 1859–1915, vol. I

Miller, Willet G., *died* 1925, vol. II

Miller, Sir William, 1828–1900, vol. I

Miller, Rt Hon. William, 1834–1912, vol. I

Miller, Rev. William, 1838–1923, vol. II

Miller, William, 1864–1945, vol. IV

Miller, Major William Archibald, *died* 1925, vol. II

Miller, William Christopher, 1898–1976, vol. VII

Miller, Sir William Frederic, 5th Bt (*cr* 1788), 1868–1948, vol. IV

Miller, William Lash, 1866–1940, vol. III

Miller, Col William Miles, 1891–1946, vol. IV

Miller, William Thomas, 1865–1930, vol. III

Miller, William Thomas, 1880–1963, vol. VI

Miller-Cunningham, Sir George, 1867–1945, vol. IV

Miller Jones, Keith, 1899–1978, vol. VII

Miller-Jones, Sir Thomas, 1874–1944, vol. IV

Millerand, Alexandre, 1859–1943, vol. IV

Millers, Harold Cuthbert Townley, 1903–1968, vol. VI

Milles, Carl, 1875–1955, vol. V

Milles-Lade, Hon. Henry Augustus, 1867–1937, vol. III

Millet, Francis Davis, 1846–1912, vol. I

Millett, George Prideaux, 1863–1950, vol. IV

Millevoye, Lucien, 1850–1918, vol. II

Milligan, Lucien, 1850–1918, vol. II

Milligan, Rt Hon. Lord; William Rankine Milligan, 1898–1975, vol. VII

Milligan, Very Rev. George, 1860–1934, vol. III

Milligan, John Williamson, 1875–1965, vol. VI

Milligan, Patrick Ward, 1910–1978, vol. VII

Milligan, Samuel, 1874–1954, vol. V

Milligan, Lt-Col Stanley Lyndall, 1887–1968, vol. VI

Milligan, Sir William, 1864–1929, vol. III

Milligan, Rt Hon. William Rankine; *see* Milligan, Rt Hon. Lord.

Millikan, Robert Andrews, 1868–1953, vol. V

Milliken, Alexander, 1841–1914, vol. I

Milliken, Brig. Robert Cecil, 1883–1959, vol. V

Millin, Albert, 1893–1964, vol. VI

Millin, Sarah Gertrude, *died* 1968, vol. VI

Milling, Geoffrey, 1901–1983, vol. VIII
Millingen, Alexander van, 1840–1915, vol. I
Millington, Air Cdre Edward Geoffrey Lyall, 1914–1988, vol. VIII
Millington, Air Cdre Geoffrey; *see* Millington, Air Cdre E. G. L.
Millington, Powell; *see* Synge, Major Mark.
Millington-Drake, Sir Eugen John Henry Vanderstegen, 1889–1972, vol. VII
Millington-Drake, James Mackay Henry, 1928–1983, vol. VIII
Millis, Charles Howard Goulden, 1894–1984, vol. VIII
Millis, Sir Leonard William Francis, 1908–1986, vol. VIII
Milln, Rear-Adm. William Bryan Scott, 1915–1979, vol. VII
Millott, Norman, 1912–1990, vol. VIII
Mills, 1st Viscount, 1890–1968, vol. VI
Mills, 2nd Viscount, 1919–1988, vol. VIII
Mills, Hon. Algernon Henry, 1856–1922, vol. II
Mills, Arthur, 1887–1955, vol. V
Mills, Rev. Arthur Everard, 1863–1929, vol. III
Mills, Arthur John, 1868–1956, vol. V
Mills, Maj.-Gen. Sir Arthur Mordaunt, 1879–1964, vol. VI
Mills, Arthur Stewart Hunt, 1897–1968, vol. VI
Mills, Bertram Wagstaff, 1873–1938, vol. III
Mills, Charles A., vol. II
Mills, (Charles) Ernest, 1916–1983, vol. VIII
Mills, Hon. Charles Houghton, 1844–1923, vol. II
Mills, Darius Ogden, 1825–1910, vol. I
Mills, David, 1831–1903, vol. I
Mills, Lady Dorothy R. M., *died* 1959, vol. V
Mills, Edmund James, 1840–1921, vol. II
Mills, Edward, 1849–1933, vol. III
Mills, Eric, 1892–1961, vol. VI
Mills, Ernest; *see* Mills, C. E.
Mills, Sir Ernest Arnold, *died* 1949, vol. IV
Mills, Sir Frederick, 1st Bt, 1865–1953, vol. V
Mills, Major Sir (Frederick Leighton) Victor, 2nd Bt, 1893–1955, vol. V
Mills, Captain Hon. Geoffrey Edward, 1875–1917, vol. II
Mills, Brig.-Gen. George Arthur, 1855–1927, vol. II
Mills, Air Chief Marshal Sir George Holroyd, 1902–1971, vol. VII
Mills, George Percival, 1883–1952, vol. V
Mills, Harry Woosnam, 1873–1925, vol. II
Mills, Rev. Canon Henry Holroyd, 1860–1947, vol. IV
Mills, Herbert Horatio, 1917–1987, vol. VIII
Mills, Col Herbert James, 1836–1927, vol. II
Mills, J. Saxon, *died* 1929, vol. III
Mills, James, 1840–1924, vol. II
Mills, Sir James, 1847–1936, vol. III
Mills, Col James Edgar, 1878–1937, vol. III
Mills, James Philip, 1890–1960, vol. V
Mills, Col Sir John Digby, 1879–1972, vol. VII
Mills, John Edmund, *died* 1951, vol. V
Mills, John Frobisher, 1859–1929, vol. III
Mills, John Norton, 1914–1977, vol. VII
Mills, John Spencer, 1917–1976, vol. VII
Mills, (John) Vivian G., 1887–1987, vol. VIII

Mills, Joseph Trueman, 1836–1924, vol. II
Mills, Lawrence Heyworth, *born* 1837, vol. II
Mills, Hon. Ogden L., 1884–1937, vol. III
Mills, Maj.-Gen. Percy Strickland, *died* 1973, vol. VII
Mills, Air Vice-Marshal Reginald Percy, 1885–1968, vol. VI
Mills, Sir Richard, 1830–1906, vol. I
Mills, Richard Charles, 1886–1952, vol. V
Mills, Robert Watkin, 1856–1930, vol. III
Mills, Stephen, 1857–1948, vol. IV
Mills, Brig. Stephen Douglas, 1892–1984, vol. VIII
Mills, T. Wesley, *died* 1915, vol. I
Mills, Major Sir Victor; *see* Mills, Major Sir F. L. V.
Mills, Vivian G.; *see* Mills, J. V. G.
Mills, Rev. William, *died* 1922, vol. II
Mills, Sir William, 1856–1932, vol. III
Mills, William Haslam, 1874–1930, vol. III
Mills, William Hobson, 1873–1959, vol. V
Mills, Rt Rev. William Lennox, *died* 1917, vol. II
Mills-Owens, Richard Hugh, 1910–1987, vol. VIII
Mills-Roberts, Robert Herbert, 1862–1935, vol. III
Millspaugh, Arthur Chester, 1883–1955, vol. V
Millspaugh, Rt Rev. Frank Rosebrook, 1848–1916, vol. II
Milman, Archibald John Scott, *died* 1902, vol. I
Milman, Sir Dermot Lionel Kennedy, 8th Bt, 1912–1990, vol. VIII
Milman, Sir Francis, 5th Bt, 1872–1946, vol. IV
Milman, Sir Francis John, 4th Bt, 1842–1922, vol. II
Milman, Lt-Gen. Sir George Bryan, 1822–1915, vol. I
Milman, Brig.-Gen. Sir Lionel Charles Patrick, 7th Bt, 1877–1962, vol. VI
Milman, Lt-Col Octavius Rodney Everard, 1882–1971, vol. VII
Milman, Sir William Ernest, 6th Bt, 1875–1962, vol. VI
Milmo Sir Helenus Patrick Joseph, 1908–1988, vol. VIII
Miln, Mrs George Crichton, 1864–1933, vol. III
Miln, Louise Jordan; *see* Miln, Mrs George Crichton.
Milne, 1st Baron, 1866–1948, vol. IV
Milne, Alan Alexander, 1882–1956, vol. V
Milne, Alan Hay, 1869–1919, vol. II
Milne, Alexander, *died* 1903, vol. I
Milne, Alexander Boland, 1842–1904, vol. I
Milne, Alexander George, 1891–1981, vol. VIII
Milne, Rt Rev. Andrew Jamieson, 1831–1906, vol. I
Milne, Sir (Archibald) Berkeley, 2nd Bt, 1855–1938, vol. III
Milne, Archibald George, 1910–1980, vol. VII
Milne, Arthur; *see* Milne, E. A.
Milne, Arthur Dawson, 1867–1932, vol. III
Milne, Sir Berkeley; *see* Milne, Sir A. B.
Milne, Charles, *died* 1960, vol. V
Milne, Christian Hoyer Millar, 1870–1945, vol. IV
Milne, David, 1876–1954, vol. V
Milne, Sir David, 1896–1972, vol. VII
Milne, Rev. Edgar Astley, 1862–1945, vol. IV
Milne, (Edward) Arthur, 1896–1950, vol. IV
Milne, Edward James, 1915–1983, vol. VIII
Milne, Lt-Col George, 1857–1939, vol. III
Milne, George Torrance, 1862–1943, vol. IV
Milne, J. Maclauchlan, *died* 1957, vol. V
Milne, James, 1865–1951, vol. V

Milne, Sir James, 1883–1958, vol. V
Milne, James, 1921–1986, vol. VIII
Milne, Sir James Allan, 1896–1966, vol. VI
Milne, James Mathewson, 1883–1959, vol. V
Milne, John, 1850–1913, vol. I
Milne, John Alexander, 1872–1955, vol. V
Milne, Sir John Sydney W.; see Wardlaw-Milne.
Milne, Joseph Grafton, 1867–1951, vol. V
Milne, Kenneth John, 1880–1929, vol. III
Milne, Mrs Leslie, (Mary Lewis), 1860–1952, vol. V
Milne, Oswald Partridge, 1881–1968, vol. VI
Milne, Lt-Col Richard Lewis, 1832–1906, vol. I
Milne, Col Thomas, 1882–1959, vol. V
Milne, William Proctor, 1881–1967, vol. VI
Milne, Sir William Robertson, died 1959, vol. V
Milne-Bailey, Walter, died 1935, vol. III
Milne Henderson, Captain Thomas Maxwell Stuart, 1888–1968, vol. VI
Milne-Home, David William, 1873–1918, vol. II
Milne-Redhead, Lt-Col Richard Henry, 1862–1944, vol. IV
Milne-Thomson, Col Alexander, died 1944, vol. IV
Milne-Thomson, Louis Melville, 1891–1974, vol. VII
Milne-Watson, Sir David, 1st Bt, died 1945, vol. IV
Milne-Watson, Sir (David) Ronald, 2nd Bt, 1904–1982, vol. VIII
Milne-Watson, Sir Ronald; see Milne-Watson, Sir D. R.
Milner, 1st Viscount, 1854–1925, vol. II
Milner, Viscountess; (Violet Georgina), died 1958, vol. V
Milner of Leeds, 1st Baron, 1889–1967, vol. VI
Milner, Elizabeth Eleanor, died 1953, vol. V
Milner, Frank, 1875–1944, vol. IV
Milner, Frank Leopold, 1870–1946, vol. IV
Milner, Fred, died 1939, vol. III
Milner, Frederic, 1905–1957, vol. V
Milner, Rt Hon. Sir Frederick George, 7th Bt, 1849–1931, vol. III
Milner, George, 1829–1914, vol. I
Milner, George Andrew, 1927–1986, vol. VIII
Milner, Brig.-Gen. George Francis, 1862–1921, vol. II
Milner, James Donald, 1874–1927, vol. II
Milner, John Giddings, 1900–1985, vol. VIII
Milner, Engr-Rear-Adm. John William, died 1953, vol. V
Milner, Marcus Henry, 1864–1939, vol. III
Milner, Samuel Roslington, 1875–1958, vol. V
Milner, Thomas Stuart, 1909–1969, vol. VI
Milner, William Aldam, 1854–1931, vol. III
Milner, Sir William Frederick Victor Mordaunt, 8th Bt, 1893–1960, vol. V
Milner-Barry, E. L., died 1917, vol. II
Milner-Jones, Edward William, 1853–1942, vol. IV
Milner-White, Very Rev. Eric, 1884–1963, vol. VI
Milner-White, Sir Henry, 1854–1922, vol. II
Milnes, Alfred, 1849–1921, vol. II
Milnes, Nora, 1882–1972, vol. VII
Milnes, W. H., 1865–1957, vol. V
Milnes-Coates, Captain Sir Clive; see Coates.
Milnes Coates, Sir Robert Edward James Clive, 3rd Bt, 1907–1982, vol. VIII
Milnes Gaskell, Lady Constance, 1885–1964, vol. VI

Milnes Walker, Robert; see Walker, R. M.
Milroy, Hugh, 1840–1919, vol. II
Milroy, John Alexander, died 1934, vol. III
Milroy, Thomas Hugh, 1869–1950, vol. IV
Milsom, Hilda Maud, died 1972, vol. VII
Milson, Rev. Frederick William, 1912–1984, vol. VIII
Milthorpe, Frederick Leon, 1917–1985, vol. VIII
Milton, Ernest, 1890–1974, vol. VII
Milton, Sir Frank, 1906–1976, vol. VII
Milton, Sir William Henry, 1854–1930, vol. III
Milvain, Sir Thomas, 1844–1916, vol. II
Milverton, 1st Baron, 1885–1978, vol. VII
Milward, Sir Anthony Horace, 1905–1981, vol. VIII
Milward, Sir Christopher Annakin, 1834–1906, vol. I
Milward, Maj.-Gen. Sir Clement Arthur, 1877–1951, vol. V
Milward, John Frederic, 1908–1982, vol. VIII
Milward, Col Victor, died 1901, vol. I
Mimpriss, Trevor Walter, 1905–1989, vol. VIII
Minchin, Lt-Col Alfred Beckett, 1870–1939, vol. III
Minchin, Lt-Col Charles Frederick, 1862–1943, vol. IV
Minchin, Charles Owen, 1844–1930, vol. III
Minchin, E. A., 1866–1915, vol. I
Minchin, Maj.-Gen. Frederick Falkiner, 1860–1922, vol. II
Minchin, George M., died 1914, vol. I
Minchin, Harry Christopher, 1861–1941, vol. IV
Minchin, James George Cotton, died 1933, vol. III
Minchin, Col William Cyril, 1856–1924, vol. II
Mines, George Ralph, 1886–1914, vol. I
Minett, Francis Colin, 1890–1953, vol. V
Minford, Hugh, died 1950, vol. IV
Minford, Rt Hon. Nathaniel Owens, 1912–1975, vol. VII
Mingana, Alphonse, 1881–1937, vol. III
Minio-Paluello, Lorenzo, 1907–1986, vol. VIII
Minion, Stephen, 1908–1990, vol. VIII
Minney, Rubeigh James, 1895–1979, vol. VII
Minnis, Samuel Ellison, 1882–1971, vol. VII
Minns, Captain Allan Noel, 1891–1921, vol. II
Minns, Sir Ellis Hovell, 1874–1953, vol. V
Minogue, Hon. Sir John (Patrick), 1909–1989, vol. VIII
Minoprio, Frank Charles, 1870–1951, vol. V
Minor, Clark Haynes, 1878–1967, vol. VI
Minorsky, Vladimir, 1877–1966, vol. VI
Minot, Charles Sedgwick, 1852–1914, vol. I
Minot, George Richards, 1885–1950, vol. IV
Minshull-Ford, Maj.-Gen. John Randle; see Ford.
Minter, Sir Frederick Albert, 1887–1976, vol. VII
Minter, Percy, 1866–1955, vol. V
Minto, 4th Earl of, 1847–1914, vol. I
Minto, 5th Earl of, 1891–1975, vol. VII
Minto, John, 1863–1935, vol. III
Minton, (Francis) John, 1917–1957, vol. V
Minton, John; see Minton, F. J.
Miraj, (Junior), Chief of; Sir Shrimant Madhavrao Harihar, alias Baba Saheb Patwardhan, died 1950, vol. IV (A), vol. V
Mirbeau, Octave, 1850–1917, vol. II
Mirehouse, Lt-Col Richard Walter Byrd, 1849–1914, vol. I
Mirehouse, William Edward, 1844–1925, vol. II

Mirepoix, Antoine, Duc de L.; see Lévis Mirepoix.
Miró, Joan, 1893–1983, vol. VIII
Mirrielees, Sir Frederick James, 1851–1914, vol. I
Mirrlees, Maj.-Gen. William Henry Buchanan, 1892–1964, vol. VI
Mirza Ali Akbar Khan, 1880–1934, vol. III
Mirza, Maj.-Gen. Iskander, 1899–1969, vol. VI
Misa, Brig. Lawrence Edward, 1896–1968, vol. VI
Misra, Sir Lakshmipati, 1888–1964, vol. VI
Missen, Leslie Robert, 1897–1983, vol. VIII
Missenden, Sir Eustace James, 1886–1973, vol. VII
Mistinguett, (Jeanne Bourgeois), 1875–1956, vol V
Mistral, Frédéric, 1830–1914, vol. I
Mitchell, Alan Alexander McCaskill, 1882–1941, vol. IV
Mitchell, Alexander, 1871–1934, vol. III
Mitchell, Alexander Ferrier, 1822–1899, vol. I
Mitchell, Andrew, 1843–1915, vol. I
Mitchell, Andrew Park, 1894–1975, vol. VII
Mitchell, Sir Angus Sinclair, 1884–1961, vol. VI
Mitchell, Rt Rev. Anthony, 1868–1917, vol. II
Mitchell, Arnold, died 1944, vol. IV
Mitchell, Sir Arthur, 1826–1909, vol. I
Mitchell, Arthur Brownlow, 1865–1942, vol. IV
Mitchell, Arthur James, 1893–1967, vol. VI
Mitchell, Bertram, 1898–1978, vol. VII
Mitchell, Lt-Col Brian Granville Blayney, 1900–1983, vol. VIII
Mitchell, Charles, died 1957, vol. V
Mitchell, Charles Ainsworth, 1867–1948, vol. IV
Mitchell, Sir Charles Bullen Hugh, died 1899, vol. I
Mitchell, Brig.-Gen. Charles Hamilton, 1872–1941, vol. IV
Mitchell, Major Charles Johnstone, 1879–1918, vol. II
Mitchell, Hon. Charles Richmond, 1872–1942, vol. IV
Mitchell, Charles W., died 1903, vol. I
Mitchell, Craig, 1896–1975, vol. VII
Mitchell, Sir David George, 1879–1963, vol. VI
Mitchell, Edmund, 1861–1917, vol. II
Mitchell, Edward Card, 1853–1914, vol. I
Mitchell, Sir Edward Fancourt, 1855–1941, vol. IV
Mitchell, Edward Rosslyn, 1879–1965, vol. VI
Mitchell, Edwin Laurence, 1883–1960, vol. V
Mitchell, Adm. Francis Herbert, 1876–1946, vol. IV
Mitchell, Maj.-Gen. Francis Neville, 1904–1954, vol. V
Mitchell, Sir Frank Herbert, 1878–1951, vol. V
Mitchell, Frank William Drew, 1845–1936, vol. III
Mitchell, Air Vice-Marshal Frederick George Stewart, 1901–1974, vol. VII
Mitchell, Rt Rev. Frederick Julian, 1901–1979, vol. VII
Mitchell, George, 1867–1937, vol. III
Mitchell, Sir George Arthur, 1860–1948, vol. IV
Mitchell, George Hoole, 1902–1976, vol. VII
Mitchell, Sir George Irvine, 1911–1978, vol. VII
Mitchell, Mrs George J., (Maggie Richardson), died 1953, vol. V
Mitchell, George Winter, 1865–1935, vol. III
Mitchell, Gladys Maude Winifred, 1901–1983, vol. VIII
Mitchell, Sir Godfrey Way, 1891–1982, vol. VIII

Mitchell, Graham Russell, 1912–1984, vol. VIII
Mitchell, Sir Hamilton, 1910–1989, vol. VIII
Mitchell, Harold John, 1877–1941, vol. IV
Mitchell, Col Sir Harold Paton, 1st Bt, 1900–1983, vol. VIII
Mitchell, Rev. Harry, 1847–1933, vol. III
Mitchell, Helen Porter; see Melba, Dame Nellie.
Mitchell, Sir Henry, 1823–1898, vol. I
Mitchell, Henry McCormick, 1870–1935, vol. III
Mitchell, Henry Tai, 1877–1944, vol. IV
Mitchell, Henry Thomas, 1870–1946, vol. IV
Mitchell, Sir Herbert Edward, 1861–1936, vol. III
Mitchell, J. Campbell, 1865–1922, vol. II
Mitchell, Very Rev. James, 1830–1911, vol. I
Mitchell, James, 1865–1941, vol. IV
Mitchell, Hon. Sir James, 1866–1951, vol. V
Mitchell, Sir James, 1905–1968, vol. VI
Mitchell, James Alexander, 1849–1905, vol. I
Mitchell, James Alexander Hugh, 1939–1985, vol. VIII
Mitchell, James Leslie, 1901–1935, vol. III
Mitchell, Very Rev. James Robert Mitford, 1843–1914, vol. I
Mitchell, John, 1860–1923, vol. II
Mitchell, Sir John, died 1934, vol. III
Mitchell, John Ames, 1845–1918, vol. II
Mitchell, John David Bawden, 1917–1980, vol. VII
Mitchell, Lt-Col John Douglas, 1881–1955, vol. V
Mitchell, Sir John Edwin, 1865–1931, vol. III
Mitchell, John Fowler, 1886–1984, vol. VIII
Mitchell, John Malcolm, 1879–1940, vol. III
Mitchell, Rev. John Thomas, died 1947, vol. IV
Mitchell, Rt Rev. Joseph, 1859–1931, vol. III
Mitchell, Joseph Stanley, 1909–1987, vol. VIII
Mitchell, Sir Kenneth Grant, 1885–1966, vol. VI
Mitchell, Leslie Herbert, 1914–1989, vol. VIII
Mitchell, Margaret; see Marsh, Margaret Munnerlyn Mitchell.
Mitchell, Sir Mark Ledingham, 1902–1977, vol. VII
Mitchell, Sir Miles Ewart, 1875–1955, vol. V
Mitchell, Norman Frederick, 1900–1972, vol. VII
Mitchell, Oliver Worden, 1898–1963, vol. VI
Mitchell, Sir Peter Chalmers, 1864–1945, vol. IV
Mitchell, Maj.-Gen. Sir Philip Euen, 1890–1964, vol. VI
Mitchell, Philip George Mylne, 1875–1954, vol. V
Mitchell, Richard Arthur Henry, 1843–1905, vol. I
Mitchell, Major Robert, 1855–1933, vol. III
Mitchell, Major Robert, 1873–1939, vol. III
Mitchell, Very Rev. Robert Andrew, died 1949, vol. IV
Mitchell, Robert Lyell, 1910–1982, vol. VIII
Mitchell, Robert Macgregor; see Macgregor Mitchell, Hon. Lord.
Mitchell, Robert William Span, 1840–1909, vol. I
Mitchell, Sir (Seton) Steuart (Crichton), 1902–1990, vol. VIII
Mitchell, Silas Weir, 1829–1914, vol. I
Mitchell, Stephen, 1884–1951, vol. V
Mitchell, Sir Steuart; see Mitchell, Sir Seton S. C.
Mitchell, Sir Thomas, 1844–1919, vol. II
Mitchell, Col Thomas, 1839–1921, vol. II
Mitchell, Sir Thomas, 1869–1959, vol. V
Mitchell, Col Thomas John, 1882–1966, vol. VI

Mitchell, Thomas Walker, 1869–1944, vol. IV
Mitchell, Victor Evelyn, 1865–1932, vol. III
Mitchell, Col Wilfrid James, 1871–1953, vol. V
Mitchell, William, 1838–1914, vol. I
Mitchell, William, died 1937, vol. III
Mitchell, Sir William, 1861–1962, vol. VI
Mitchell, Captain William Edward Clifton, born 1875, vol. III
Mitchell, William Eric Marcus, 1897–1990, vol. VIII
Mitchell, Sir William Foot, 1859–1947, vol. IV
Mitchell, Air Chief Marshal Sir William Gore Sutherland, 1888–1944, vol. IV
Mitchell, William H., 1853–1929, vol. III
Mitchell, Sir William Lane, 1861–1940, vol. III
Mitchell, Sir William Wilson, 1840–1915, vol. I
Mitchell, Yvonne, 1925–1979, vol. VII
Mitchell-Cotts, Sir Campbell; see Cotts, Sir W. C. M.
Mitchell-Gill, Andrew John; see Gill.
Mitchell-Hedges, Frederick Albert, 1882–1959, vol. V
Mitchell-Heggs, Gordon Barrett, 1904–1975, vol. VII
Mitchell-Innes, Alfred, 1864–1950, vol. IV
Mitchell-Innes, Captain Cecil, 1866–1949, vol. IV
Mitchell-Innes, Edward Alfred, 1863–1932, vol. III
Mitchell-Innes, Rev. Reginald John Simpson, 1848–1930, vol. III
Mitchell-Thomson, Sir Mitchell, 1st Bt, 1846–1918, vol. II
Mitchelson, Sir Archibald, 1st Bt, 1878–1945, vol. IV
Mitchelson, Hon. Sir Edwin, 1846–1934, vol. III
Mitcheson, Sir George Gibson, 1883–1955, vol. V
Mitcheson, James Cecil, 1898–1979, vol. VII
Mitcheson, John Moncaster Ley, 1893–1966, vol. VI
Mitchiner, Philip Henry, 1888–1952, vol. V
Mitchinson, Rt Rev. John, 1833–1918, vol. II
Mitchison, Baron (Life Peer); Gilbert Richard Mitchison, 1890–1970, vol. VI
Mitchison, Rev. Richard Stovin, 1850–1936, vol. III
Mitford, Bertram, died 1914, vol. I
Mitford, Maj.-Gen. Bertram Reveley, 1863–1936, vol. III
Mitford, Hon. Clement Bertram Ogilvy F.; see Freeman-Mitford.
Mitford, Nancy, (Hon. Mrs Peter Rodd), 1904–1973, vol. VII
Mitford, Maj.-Gen. Reginald C. W. Reveley, 1839–1925, vol. II
Mitford, Captain Robert Osbaldeston-, 1846–1924, vol. II
Mitford, Robert Sidney, 1849–1931, vol. III
Mitford, Terence Bruce, 1905–1978, vol. VII
Mitford, Major Hon. Thomas David Freeman-, 1909–1945, vol. IV
Mitford, Col William Kenyon, 1857–1943, vol. IV
Mitford-Barberton, Ivan Graham; see Barberton.
Mitford-Slade, Col Cecil Townley, 1903–1986, vol. VIII
Mitha, Hon. Sardar Sir Suleman Cassum, vol. VII
Mitman, Frederick Snyder, 1900–1989, vol. VIII
Mitra, Sir Bhupendra Nath, 1875–1937, vol. III
Mitra, Sir Dhirendra Nath, 1891–1966, vol. VI
Mitra, S. M., 1856–1925, vol. II
Mitra, Sisir Kumar, 1890–1963, vol. VI
Mitrany, David, 1888–1975, vol VII
Mitropoulos, Dimitri, 1896–1960, vol. V

Mittag-Leffler, Gösta, 1846–1927, vol. II
Mittelholzer, Edgar Austin, 1909–1965, vol. VI
Mitter, Rt Hon. Sir Binof Chandra, 1872–1930, vol. III
Mitter, Sir Brojendra Lal, 1875–1950, vol. IV
Mitter, Sir Provash Chandra, 1875–1934, vol. III
Mitton, Geraldine Edith, (Lady Scott), died 1955, vol. V
Mitton, Col George J.; see Jones Mitton.
Mitton, H. Eustace, 1871–1946, vol. IV
Mitton, Rev. Henry Arthur, 1837–1918, vol. II
Mitton, Rev. Welbury Theodore, 1862–1933, vol. III
Mivart, Frederick St George, died 1925, vol. II
Mivart, St George Jackson, 1827–1900, vol. I
Mobbs, Sir (Arthur) Noel, 1880–1959, vol. V
Mobbs, Sir Noel; see Mobbs, Sir A. N.
Moberly, Brig. Archibald Henry, 1879–1960, vol. V
Moberly, Sir Arthur Norman, 1873–1934, vol. III
Moberly, Lt-Gen. Sir Bertrand Richard, 1877–1963, vol. VI
Moberly, Charles Noel, 1880–1969, vol. VI
Moberly, Charlotte Anne Elizabeth, 1846–1937, vol. III
Moberly, Brig.-Gen. Frederick James, 1867–1952, vol. V
Moberly, Brig. Hugh Stephenson, 1873–1947, vol. IV
Moberly, Rev. Robert Campbell, 1845–1903, vol. I
Moberly, Rt Rev. Robert Hamilton, 1884–1978, vol. VII
Moberly, Sir Walter Hamilton, 1881–1974, vol. VII
Moberly, Winifred Horsbrugh, 1875–1928, vol. II
Mocatta, Sir Alan Abraham, 1907–1990, vol. VIII
Mockett, Sir Vere, 1885–1977, vol. VII
Mockford, Julian, 1898–1950, vol. IV
Mockler, Col Percy Rice, 1860–1927, vol. II
Mockler-Ferryman, Lt-Col Augustus Ferryman, 1856–1930, vol. III
Mockler-Ferryman, Col Eric Edward, 1896–1978, vol. VII
Modi, Sir Jivanji Jamshedji, 1854–1933, vol. III
Modjeska-Chlapowska, Helena, 1844–1909, vol. I
Mody, Sir Homi Peroshaw, 1881–1969, vol. VI
Moe, Henry Allen, 1894–1975, vol. VII
Moens, Gen. Sir Arthur William Hamilton May, 1879–1939, vol. III
Moens, Hon. Lt-Col Seaburne Godfrey Arthur May, 1876–1956, vol. V
Moeran, Ernest John, 1894–1950, vol. IV
Moffat, Alfred, 1868–1950, vol. IV
Moffat, David H., 1839–1911, vol. I
Moffat, Graham, 1866–1951, vol. V
Moffat, Hon. Howard Unwin, 1869–1951, vol. V
Moffat, John, 1879–1966, vol. VI(AII), vol. VII
Moffat, John, 1891–1973, vol. VII
Moffat, Rev. John Smith, 1835–1918, vol. II
Moffat, Sir John Smith, 1905–1985, vol. VIII
Moffat, Rennie John, 1891–1978, vol. VII
Moffat, Robert Unwin, 1866–1947, vol. IV
Moffatt, Alexander, 1863–1921, vol. II
Moffatt, Rev. James, 1870–1944, vol. IV
Moffatt, Paul McGregor, died 1963, vol. VI
Moffet, Stanley Ormerod, 1886–1960, vol. V
Moffett, John Perry, 1909–1972, vol. VII
Moffett, Sir Thomas William, 1830–1908, vol. I

Mogg, Lt-Col Graham Beauchamp Coxeter R.; *see* Rees-Mogg.
Mogg, Rev. Henry Herbert, 1850–1929, vol. III
Mogg, Rev. Canon Joseph William, 1882–1970, vol. VI(AII)
Mogg, Engr Rear-Adm. William George, 1860–1929, vol. III
Moggridge, Adm. Arthur Yerbury, 1858–1946, vol. IV
Moggridge, Ernest Grant, 1863–1925, vol. II
Moggridge, Lt-Col Harry Weston, 1879–1960, vol. V
Mohamed, Hon. Sir Abdool Razack, 1906–1978, vol. VII
Mohamed Akbar Khan, Lt-Col Nawab Sir, 1885–1952, vol. V
Mohan Singh, Sardar Bahadur Sardar, 1897–1961, vol. VI
Mohsin-ul-Mulk, Nawab, 1837–1907, vol. I
Moinet, Rev. Charles, 1842–1913, vol. I
Moir, Brig.-Gen. Alan James Gordon, 1873–1940, vol. III
Moir, Alan John, 1903–1982, vol. VIII
Moir, Captain Sir Arrol, 2nd Bt, 1894–1957, vol. V
Moir, Byres, 1853–1928, vol. II
Moir, Vice-Adm. Dashwood Fowler, 1880–1942, vol. IV
Moir, Sir Ernest William, 1st Bt, 1862–1933, vol. III
Moir, Rt Rev. Francis Oag H.; *see* Hulme-Moir.
Moir, James, *died* 1915, vol. I
Moir, Col James Philip, 1872–1934, vol. III
Moir, James Reid, 1879–1944, vol. IV
Moir, John Chassar, 1900–1977, vol. VII
Moir, John William, *died* 1940, vol. III
Moir, Percival John, 1893–1980, vol. VII
Moir, Sir Thomas Eyebron, 1874–1932, vol. III
Moir, Rear-Adm. William Mitchell, 1873–1942, vol. IV
Moira, Gerald, *died* 1959, vol. V
Moiseiwitsch, Benno, 1890–1963, vol. VI
Mok, Rt Rev. Shau Tsang, 1866–1943, vol. IV
Molamure, Sir (Alexander) Francis, 1886–1951, vol. V
Molamure, Sir Francis; *see* Molamure, Sir A. F.
Mold, Brig. Gilbert Leslie, 1893–1963, vol. VI
Mole, Sir Charles Johns, 1886–1962, vol. VI
Mole, Brig. Gerard Herbert Leo, 1897–1944, vol. IV
Mole, Harold Frederic, 1866–1917, vol. II
Moles, Rt Hon. Thomas, 1871–1937, vol. III
Molesworth, 8th Viscount, 1829–1906, vol. I
Molesworth, 9th Viscount, 1867–1947, vol. IV
Molesworth, 10th Viscount, 1869–1961, vol. VI
Molesworth, Brig. Alec Lindsay Mortimer, 1881–1939, vol. III
Molesworth, Col Arthur Ludovic, 1860–1939, vol. III
Molesworth, Major Edward Algernon, *died* 1939, vol. III
Molesworth, Brig.-Gen. Edward Hogarth, 1854–1943, vol. III
Molesworth, Lt-Gen. George Noble, 1890–1968, vol. VI
Molesworth, Sir Guilford Lindsey, 1828–1925, vol. II
Molesworth, Hender Delves, 1907–1978, vol. VII
Molesworth, Col Herbert Ellicombe, 1872–1941, vol. IV

Molesworth, Hickman, 1842–1907, vol. I
Molesworth, Hugh Wilson, 1870–1959, vol. V
Molesworth, Sir Lewis William, 11th Bt, 1853–1912, vol. I
Molesworth, Mrs Mary Louisa, 1839–1921, vol. II
Molesworth, Col Richard Pigot, 1868–1946, vol. IV
Molesworth, Col William, 1865–1951, vol. V
Molesworth-St Aubyn, Sir Hugh, 13th Bt, 1865–1942, vol. IV
Molesworth-St Aubyn, Rev. Sir St A. Hender, 12th Bt, 1833–1913, vol. I
Molesworth-St Aubyn, Sir John, 14th Bt, 1899–1985, vol. VIII
Molin, C. Hjalmar V., 1868–1954, vol. V
Moline, Rev. Robert Percy, *died* 1935, vol. III
Moline, Most Rev. Robert William Haines, 1889–1979, vol. VII
Molineux, Rev. Arthur Ellison, *died* 1919, vol. II
Molineux, Rev. Charles Hurlock, *died* 1927, vol. II
Moll, Rev. William Edmund, 1856–1932, vol. III
Mollan, Maj.-Gen. Francis Robert Henry, 1893–1982, vol. VIII
Mollan, Lt-Col William Campbell, 1820–1910, vol. I
Moller, Marjorie, 1899–1981, vol. VIII
Mollett, Sir John, 1892–1952, vol. V
Mollison, James Alan, 1905–1959, vol. V
Mollison, James W., *died* 1927, vol. II
Mollison, William Loudon, 1851–1929, vol. III
Mollison, William Mayhew, 1878–1967, vol. VI
Mollo, Victor, 1909–1987, vol. VIII
Molloy, Bernard Charles, 1842–1916, vol. II
Molloy, Col Edward, 1842–1905, vol. I
Molloy, Rt Rev. Mgr Gerald, 1834–1906, vol. I
Molloy, Ven. John, *died* 1915, vol. I
Molloy, Joseph Fitzgerald, 1858–1908, vol. I
Molloy, Leonard Greenham Star, *died* 1937, vol. III
Molohan, Michael John Brew, 1906–1980, vol. VII
Moloney, Sir Cornelius Alfred, 1848–1913, vol. I
Moloney, Henry J., 1887–1965, vol. VI
Molony, Rev. Brian Charles, 1892–1963, vol. VI
Molony, Col Charles Mills, 1836–1901, vol. I
Molony, Edmund Alexander, 1866–1942, vol. IV
Molony, Rev. Henry William Eliott, *died* 1919, vol. II
Molony, Rt Rev. Herbert James, 1865–1939, vol. III
Molony, Sir Hugh Francis, 2nd Bt, 1900–1976, vol. VII
Molony, Sir Joseph Thomas, 1907–1978, vol. VII
Molony, Rt Hon. Sir Thomas Francis, 1st Bt, 1865–1949, vol. IV
Molotov, Vyacheslav Mikhailovich, 1890–1986, vol. VIII
Molson, Lt-Col Herbert, 1875–1938, vol. III
Molson, Major John Elsdale, 1863–1925, vol. II
Molteno, Hon. Sir James Tennant, 1865–1936, vol. III
Molteno, Percy Alport, 1861–1937, vol. III
Molteno, Vice-Adm. Vincent Barkly, 1872–1952, vol. V
Molyneux, Major Edward Mary Joseph, 1866–1913, vol. I
Molyneux, Sir Ernest, 10th Bt, 1865–1940, vol. III
Molyneux, Rt Rev. Frederick Merivale, 1885–1948, vol. IV

Molyneux, Maj.-Gen. George Hand M.; *see* More-Molyneux.

Molyneux, John Anthony, (Tony), 1923–1982, vol. VIII

Molyneux, Rev. Sir John Charles, 9th Bt, 1843–1928, vol. II

Molyneux, Sir John Harry, 1882–1968, vol. VI

Molyneux, Sir Percy, 1870–1937, vol. III

Molyneux, Major Philip Lucas, 1893–1939, vol. III

Molyneux, Major Hon. Sir Richard F., 1873–1954, vol. V

Molyneux, Adm. Sir Robert Henry M.; *see* More-Molyneaux.

Molyneux, Tony; *see* Molyneux, J. A.

Molyneux-Seel, Major Edward, 1862–1939, vol. III

Momber, Captain Edward Marie Felix, *died* 1917, vol. II

Momerie, Rev. Alfred Williams, 1848–1900, vol. I

Momigliano, Arnaldo Dante, 1908–1987, vol. VIII

Momin, Khan Bahadur Mohammad Abdul, 1876–1946, vol. IV

Mommsen, Theodor, 1817–1903, vol. I

Monaco, Prince of, Albert Honoré Charles, 1848–1922, vol. II

Monahan, Rt Rev. Alfred Edwin, 1877–1945, vol. IV

Monahan, George Henry, 1873–1944, vol. IV

Monahan, James Henry Francis, 1912–1985, vol. VIII

Monahan, Most Rev. Peter Joseph, 1882–1947, vol. IV

Monahan, Hon. Sir Robert Vincent, 1898–1975, vol. VII

Monash, Gen. Sir John, 1865–1931, vol. III

Moncheur, Ludovic, 2nd Baron, 1857–1940, vol. III

Monck, 5th Viscount, 1849–1927, vol. II

Monck, 6th Viscount, 1905–1982, vol. VIII

Monck, Hon. Charles Henry Stanley, 1876–1914, vol. I

Monck, Sir John Berkeley, 1883–1964, vol. VI

Monck, Nugent; *see* Monck, W. N. B.

Monck, Lt-Gen. Hon. Richard, 1829–1904, vol. V

Monck, (Walter) Nugent (Bligh), 1878–1958, vol. I

Monckton of Brenchley, 1st Viscount, 1891–1965, vol. VI

Monckton of Brenchley, Dowager Viscountess; *see* Ruthven of Freeland, Lady.

Monckton, Arthur, 1845–1917, vol. II

Monckton, Edward Philip, 1840–1916, vol. II

Monckton, Francis, 1844–1926, vol. II

Monckton, Col Hon. Horace Manners, 1824–1904, vol. I

Monckton, Sir John Braddick, 1832–1902, vol. I

Monckton, Lionel, 1862–1924, vol. II

Monckton, Reginald Francis Percy, 1896–1975, vol. VII

Moncreiff, 2nd Baron, 1840–1909, vol. I

Moncreiff, 3rd Baron, 1843–1913, vol. I

Moncreiff, 4th Baron, 1872–1942, vol. IV

Moncreiff, Rt Rev. Francis Hamilton, 1906–1984, vol. VIII

Moncreiff, Hon. Frederick Charles, 1847–1929, vol. III

Moncreiff, Hon. James William, 1845–1920, vol. II

Moncreiffe of that Ilk, Sir David Gerald, 10th Bt, 1922–1957, vol. V

Moncreiffe of that Ilk, Sir Iain; *see* Moncreiffe of that Ilk, Sir R. I. K.

Moncreiffe, Comdr Sir John Robert Guy, 9th Bt, 1884–1934, vol. III

Moncreiffe, Sir Robert Drummond, 8th Bt, 1856–1931, vol. III

Moncreiffe of that Ilk, Sir (Rupert) Iain (Kay), 11th Bt, 1919–1985, vol. VIII

Moncrief, Rev. Archibald, 1845–1938, vol. III

Moncrieff, Rt. Hon. Lord; Alexander Moncrieff, *died* 1949, vol. IV

Moncrieff, Sir Alan Aird, 1901–1971, vol. VII

Moncrieff, Adm. Sir Alan Kenneth S.; *see* Scott-Moncrieff.

Moncrieff, Col Sir Alexander, 1829–1906, vol. I

Moncrieff, Rt Hon. Alexander; *see* Moncrieff, Rt Hon. Lord.

Moncrieff, Alexander Bain, 1845–1928, vol. II

Moncrieff, Charles Kenneth S.; *see* Scott Moncrieff.

Moncrieff, Sir Colin Campbell S.; *see* Scott-Moncrieff.

Moncrieff, Lt-Gen. George Hay, 1836–1918, vol. II

Moncrieff, Maj.-Gen. Sir George Kenneth S.; *see* Scott-Moncrieff.

Moncrieff, Joanna Constance S.; *see* Scott-Moncrieff.

Moncrieff, Lt-Col John Mitchell, 1865–1931, vol. III

Moncrieff, Robert Hope, 1846–1927, vol. II

Moncrieff, William George S.; *see* Scott-Moncrieff.

Moncur, George, 1868–1946, vol. IV

Mond, Ludwig, 1839–1909, vol. I

Mond, Sir Robert Ludwig, 1867–1938, vol. III

Mondor, Henri Jean, 1885–1962, vol. VI

Monet, Claude, 1840–1926, vol. II

Monet, Dominique, 1865–1923, vol. II

Moneta, Ernesto Teodoro, 1833–1918, vol. II

Money, Sir Alonzo, *died* 1900, vol. I

Money, Maj.-Gen. Sir Arthur Wigram, 1866–1951, vol. V

Money, Vice-Adm. Brien Michael, 1880–1939, vol. III

Money, Col Charles Gilbert Colvin, 1852–1928, vol. II

Money, Brig.-Gen. Ernest Douglas, 1866–1952, vol. V

Money, Rev. Canon Frank Reginald, 1905–1968, vol. VI

Money, Brig.-Gen. Gordon Lorn Campbell, 1848–1929, vol. III

Money, Brig. Harold Douglas Kyrie, 1896–1965, vol. VI

Money, Maj.-Gen. Herbert Cecil, 1857–1939, vol. III

Money, Sir Leo (George) Chiozza, 1870–1944, vol. IV

Money, Brig.-Gen. Noel Ernest, 1867–1941, vol. IV

Money, Col Reginald Angel, 1897–1984, vol. VIII

Money, Col Robert Cotton, 1861–1954, vol. V

Money, Maj.-Gen. Robert Cotton, 1888–1985, vol. VIII

Money, Walter, 1836–1926, vol. II

Money, William James, *died* 1910, vol. I

Money-Kyrle, Ven. Rowland Tracy Ashe, *died* 1928, vol. II

Moneypenny, Frederick William, 1859–1912, vol. I

Moneypenny, Sir Frederick William, 1859–1932, vol. III

Monie, Rev. Peter William, 1877–1946, vol. IV

Monier-Williams, Clarence Faithfull, 1893–1974, vol. VII

Monier-Williams, Major Craufurd Victor, 1888–1922, vol. II

Monier-Williams, Sir Monier, 1819–1899, vol. I

Monier-Williams, Monier Faithfull, 1849–1928, vol. II

Monier-Williams, Montagu Sneade Faithfull, 1860–1931, vol. III

Moniz, Egas Antonio Caetano de Abren Freire, 1874–1955, vol. V

Moniz de Aragão, José Joaquim de Lima e Silva, 1887–1974, vol. VII (AII)

Monk, Albert Ernest, 1900–1975, vol. VII

Monk, Beatrice Marsh; see Monk, M. B. M.

Monk, Charles James, 1824–1900, vol. I

Monk, Hon. Frederick Debartzch, 1856–1914, vol. I

Monk, Mark James, 1858–1929, vol. III

Monk, (Mary) Beatrice Marsh, died 1962, vol. VI

Monk Bretton, 1st Baron, 1825–1897, vol. I

Monk Bretton, 2nd Baron, 1869–1933, vol. III

Monkhouse, Allan Noble, 1858–1936, vol. III

Monkhouse, Sir Edward Bertram, 1890–1959, vol. V

Monkhouse, Francis John, 1914–1975, vol. VII

Monkhouse, John Parry, 1899–1968, vol. VI

Monkhouse, Brig.-Gen. William Percival, 1871–1935, vol. III

Monks, Air Vice-Marshal Alfred Thomas, 1908–1972, vol. VII

Monks, Constance Mary, 1911–1989, vol. VIII

Monkswell, 2nd Baron, 1845–1909, vol. I

Monkswell, 3rd Baron, 1875–1964, vol. VI

Monnet, Jean Omer Marie Gabriel, 1888–1979, vol. VII

Mönnig, Hermann Otto, 1897–1978, vol. VII

Monnington, Sir Thomas; see Monnington, Sir W. T.

Monnington, Rev. Thomas Pateshall, died 1937, vol. III

Monnington, Sir (Walter) Thomas, 1902–1976, vol. VII

Monod, Gustave Jean Philippe, 1878–1932, vol. III

Monod, Jacques Lucien, 1910–1976, vol. VII

Monod, Théodore, 1836–1921, vol. II

Monod, Wilfred, 1867–1943, vol. IV

Monro, Alexander, 1847–1916, vol. II

Monro, Alexander, 1890–1953, vol. V

Monro, Alexander William, 1875–1960, vol. V

Monro, Gen. Sir Charles Carmichael, 1st Bt, 1860–1929, vol. III

Monro, David Binning, 1836–1905, vol. I

Monro, Maj.-Gen. David Carmichael, 1886–1960, vol. V, vol. VI

Monro, Edwin George, 1875–1954, vol. V

Monro, George, 1876–1951, vol. V

Monro, Harold Edward, 1879–1932, vol. III

Monro, Sir Horace Cecil, 1861–1949, vol. IV

Monro, James, 1838–1920, vol. II

Monro, Hon. Mary Caroline, (Hon. Lady Monro), 1879–1972, vol. VII

Monro, Col Seymour Charles Hale, 1856–1906, vol. I

Monro, Thomas Kirkpatrick, 1865–1958, vol. V

Monroe, Elizabeth, (Mrs Humphrey Neame), 1905–1986, vol. VIII

Monroe, Rev. Horace Granville, 1872–1933, vol. III

Monroe, Hubert Holmes, 1920–1982, vol. VIII

Monroe, Vice-Adm. Hubert Seeds, 1877–1966, vol. VI

Monroe, James Harvey, 1884–1944, vol. IV

Monroe, Rt Hon. John, 1839–1899, vol. I

Monroe, Paul, 1869–1947, vol. IV

Monroe, Hon. Walter S., 1871–1952, vol. V

Monroe, Will S., 1863–1939, vol. III(A), vol. IV

Monsarrat, Keith Waldergrave, 1872–1968, vol. VI

Monsarrat, Nicholas John Turney, 1910–1979, vol. VII

Monsell, 1st Viscount, 1881–1969, vol. VI

Monsey, Yvonne, (Mrs Derek Monsey); see Mitchell, Yvonne.

Monslow, Baron (Life Peer); Walter Monslow, 1895–1966, vol. VI

Monson, 8th Baron, 1830–1900, vol. I

Monson, 9th Baron, 1868–1940, vol. III

Monson, 10th Baron, 1907–1958, vol. V

Monson, Rt Hon. Sir Edmund John, 1st Bt, 1834–1909, vol. I

Monson, Sir Edmund St John Debonnaire John, 3rd Bt, 1883–1969, vol. VI

Monson, Sir George Louis Esmé John, 4th Bt, 1888–1969, vol. VI

Monson, Sir Maxwell William Edmund John, 2nd Bt, 1882–1936, vol. III

Montagu of Beaulieu, 1st Baron, 1832–1905, vol. I

Montagu of Beaulieu, 2nd Baron, 1866–1929, vol. III

Montagu, Ainsley Marshall Rendall, 1891–1977, vol. VII

Montagu, Lord Charles William Augustus, 1860–1939, vol. III

Montagu, Col Edward, 1861–1941, vol. IV

Montagu, Rt Hon. Edwin Samuel, 1879–1924, vol. II

Montagu, Sir Ernest William Sanders, 1862–1952, vol. V

Montagu, Hon. Ewen Edward Samuel, 1901–1985, vol. VIII

Montagu, Captain Frederick James Osbaldeston, 1878–1957, vol. V

Montagu, Gen. Sir Horace William, 1823–1916, vol. II

Montagu, (Hon.) Ivor (Goldsmid Samuel), 1904–1984, vol. VIII

Montagu, James Drogo, died 1958, vol. V

Montagu, Hon. Lilian Helen, 1873–1963, vol. VI

Montagu, Rt Hon. Lord Robert, 1825–1902, vol. I

Montagu, Hon. Robert Henry D. S.; see Douglas-Scott-Montagu.

Montagu, Rear-Adm. Hon. Victor Alexander, 1841–1915, vol. I

Montagu-Douglas-Scott, Lord Charles Thomas; see Scott.

Montagu-Douglas-Scott, Lt-Col Lord Francis George; see Scott.

Montagu-Douglas-Scott, Lord George William; see Scott.

Montagu-Douglas-Scott, Col Lord Henry Francis; see Scott.

Montagu-Douglas-Scott, Lord Herbert Andrew; *see* Scott.

Montagu-Douglas-Scott, Lt-Col Lord William Walter; *see* Scott.

Montagu-Pollock, Sir George Seymour; *see* Pollock.

Montagu-Pollock, Sir Montagu Frederick; *see* Pollock.

Montagu-Stuart-Wortley, Maj.-Gen. Hon. Edward James; *see* Stuart-Wortley.

Montagu-Stuart-Wortley, Lt-Gen. Hon. Sir Richard; *see* Stuart-Wortley.

Montague, Charles Edward, 1867–1928, vol. II

Montague, Francis Charles, 1858–1935, vol. III

Montague, Major Furry Ferguson, 1884–1950, vol. IV(A)

Montague, Leslie Clarence, 1901–1986, vol. VIII

Montague, Lt-Gen. Hon. Percival John, 1882–1966, vol. VI

Montague, Maj.-Gen. William Edward, 1838–1906, vol. I

Montague-Barlow, Rt Hon. Sir Anderson; *see* Montague-Barlow, Rt Hon. Sir C. A.

Montague-Barlow, Rt Hon. Sir (Clement) Anderson, 1868–1951, vol. V

Montague-Smith, Patrick Wykeham, 1920–1986, vol. VIII

Montalba, Clara, *died* 1929, vol. III

Montale, Eugenio, 1896–1981, vol. VIII

Montanaro, Col Arthur Forbes, 1862–1914, vol. I

Montanaro, Brig. Gerald Charles Stokes, 1916–1979, vol. VII

Montand, Simone Henriette Charlotte; *see* Signoret, S.

Monteagle of Brandon, 2nd Baron, 1849–1926, vol. II

Monteagle of Brandon, 3rd Baron, 1883–1934, vol. III

Monteagle of Brandon, 4th Baron, 1852–1937, vol. III

Monteagle of Brandon, 5th Baron, 1887–1946, vol. IV

Monteath, Alexander McLaurin, 1859–1933, vol. III

Monteath, Sir David Taylor, 1887–1961, vol. VI

Monteath, Harry Henderson, 1885–1962, vol. VI

Monteath, Sir James, 1847–1929, vol. III

Monteath, John, 1878–1955, vol. V

Monteath, Robert Campbell, 1907–1985, vol. VIII

Monteath, Sir Ruthven Grey, 1864–1949, vol. IV

Montefiore, Claude Joseph Goldsmid-, 1858–1938, vol. III

Montefiore, Edmund Sebag-, 1869–1929, vol. III

Montefiore, Sir Francis Abraham, 1st Bt, 1860–1935, vol. III

Montefiore, Sir Joseph Sebag-, 1822–1903, vol. I

Monteith, Col John, 1852–1928, vol. II

Monteith, Brig. John Cassels, 1915–1983, vol. VIII

Monteith, Jos. D., 1865–1934, vol. III

Monteith, Nelson, 1862–1949, vol. IV

Montessori, Maria, 1870–1952, vol. V

Monteux, Pierre, 1875–1964, vol. VI

Montford, Paul Raphael, 1868–1938, vol. III

Montgomerie, Lt-Col Alexander, 1882–1932, vol. III

Montgomerie, Alexander, 1879–1958, vol. V

Montgomerie, Harvey Hugh, 1888–1965, vol. VI

Montgomerie, James, 1873–1962, vol. VI

Montgomerie, Adm. John Eglinton, 1825–1902, vol. I

Montgomerie, Rear-Adm. Robert Archibald James, 1855–1908, vol. I

Montgomerie, Samuel Hynman, 1856–1915, vol. I

Montgomery of Alamein, 1st Viscount, 1887–1976, vol. VII

Montgomery, Sir Alexander, 5th Bt (*cr* 1808), 1859–1939, vol. III

Montgomery, Sir Basil Purvis-Russell Hamilton-, 8th Bt (*cr* 1801), 1884–1964, vol. VI

Montgomery, Sir Basil Templer Graham-, 5th Bt (*cr* 1801), 1852–1928, vol. II

Montgomery, Bo Gabriel de, Count, 1894–1969, vol. VI

Montgomery, Sir (Charles) Hubert, 1876–1942, vol. IV

Montgomery, Rev. Sir Charles Percy Graham-, 6th Bt (*cr* 1801), 1855–1930, vol. III

Montgomery, Brig. Ernest John, 1901–1972, vol. VII

Montgomery, Florence Sophia, 1843–1923, vol. II

Montgomery, Sir Frank Percival, 1892–1972, vol. VII

Montgomery, George Allison, 1898–1969, vol. VI

Montgomery, George H. A., 1874–1951, vol. V

Montgomery, Sir Graham Graham, 3rd Bt (*cr* 1801), 1823–1901, vol. I

Montgomery, Harold Robert, 1884–1958, vol. V

Montgomery, Henry Greville, 1864–1951, vol. V

Montgomery, Rt Rev. Henry Hutchinson, 1847–1932, vol. III

Montgomery, Sir Henry James Purvis-Russell-Hamilton, 7th Bt (*cr* 1801), 1859–1947, vol. IV

Montgomery, Lt-Col Henry Keith Purvis-Russell-, 1896–1954, vol. V

Montgomery, Sir Hubert; *see* Montgomery, Sir C. H.

Montgomery, Sir Hugh Conyngham Gaston, 4th Bt (*cr* 1808), 1847–1915, vol. I

Montgomery, Rt Hon. Hugh de Fellenberg, *died* 1924, vol. II

Montgomery, Col Hugh Frederick L.; *see* Lyons-Montgomery.

Montgomery, Maj.-Gen. Hugh Maude de Fellenberg, 1870–1954, vol. V

Montgomery, Ian, 1913–1971, vol. VII

Montgomery, Col James Alexander Lawrence, 1849–1940, vol. III

Montgomery, Sir James Gordon Henry Graham, 4th Bt (*cr* 1801), 1850–1902, vol. I

Montgomery, John, 1858–1937, vol. III

Montgomery, Col John Willoughby Verner, 1867–1968, vol. VI

Montgomery, K. L.; *see* Montgomery, Kathleen, and Montgomery, Letitia.

Montgomery, Kathleen, *died* 1960, vol. V

Montgomery, L. M.; *see* Macdonald, Mrs L. M.

Montgomery, Leslie Alexander; *see* Doyle, Lynn.

Montgomery, Letitia, *died* 1930, vol. III

Montgomery, Sir Matthew Walker, 1859–1933, vol. III

Montgomery of Blessingbourne, Captain Peter Stephen, 1909–1988, vol. VIII

Montgomery, Maj.-Gen. Robert Arthur, 1848–1931, vol. III

Montgomery, Maj.-Gen. Sir Robert Arundel Kerr, 1862–1951, vol. V

Montgomery, Robert Ernest, 1878–1962, vol. VI

Montgomery, Robert Eustace, 1880–1932, vol. III

Montgomery, Robert Mortimer, *died* 1948, vol. IV
Montgomery, Walter Basil Graham, 1881–1928, vol. II
Montgomery, Major William Alexander, *died* 1932, vol. III
Montgomery, William Barr, 1865–1936, vol. III
Montgomery, Maj.-Gen. William Edward, 1847–1927, vol. II
Montgomery, William Hugh, 1866–1958, vol. V
Montgomery Campbell, Rt Rev. and Rt Hon. Henry Colville, 1887–1970, vol. VI
Montgomery-Campbell, Brig-Gen. Herbert, 1861–1937, vol. III
Montgomery-Cuninghame, Sir Andrew; *see* Cuninghame, Sir W. A. M. M. O. M.
Montgomery-Cuninghame, Sir Thomas Andrew Alexander; *see* Cuninghame.
Montgomery-Cuninghame, Sir William James; *see* Cuninghame.
Montgomery-Massingberd, Field Marshal Sir Archibald Armar, 1871–1947, vol. IV
Montgomery-Moore, Gen. Sir Alexander George, 1833–1919, vol. II
Montgomery-Smith, Col Edwin Charles, 1869–1963, vol. VI
Montgomery White, Cyril; *see* White.
Montgorge, Alexis Jean; *see* Gabin, J.
Montherlant, Henry de, 1896–1972, vol. VII
Montini, Giovanni Battista; *see* Paul VI.
Montizambert, Frederick, 1843–1929, vol. III
Montresor, Miss F. F., *died* 1934, vol. III
Montrose, 5th Duke of, 1852–1925, vol. II
Montrose, 6th Duke of, 1878–1954, vol. V
Monty, Hon. Rodolphe, 1874–1928, vol. II
Moodie, Alexander Reid, 1886–1968, vol. VI
Moodie, Donald, 1892–1963, vol. VI
Moodie, William, 1886–1960, vol. V
Moody, Lt-Col Arthur Hatfield, 1875–1926, vol. II
Moody, Arthur Seymour, 1891–1976, vol. VII
Moody, Charles Harry, 1874–1965, vol. VI
Moody, Adm. Sir Clement, 1891–1960, vol. V
Moody, Madame Fanny, (Mrs Southcote Mansergh), 1866–1945, vol. IV
Moody, Sir George Edward James, 1859–1939, vol. III
Moody, Sir James Matthew, *died* 1915, vol. I
Moody, John C., 1884–1962, vol. VI
Moody, Maj.-Gen. Sir John Macdonald, 1839–1921, vol. II
Moody, Col Richard Stanley Hawks, 1854–1930, vol. III
Moody, Robert Ley, 1909–1970, vol. VI
Moody, Sydney, 1889–1979, vol. VII
Moody, Theodore William, 1907–1984, vol. VIII
Moody, William H., 1853–1917, vol. II
Moody-Stuart, Sir Alexander, 1899–1971, vol. VII
Mookerjee, Sir Asutosh, 1864–1924, vol. II
Mookerjee, Sir Rajendra Nath, 1854–1936, vol. III
Mookerji, Radha Kumud, 1884–1963, vol. VI
Moon, Maj.-Gen. Alan Neilson, 1906–1981, vol. VIII
Moon, Col Alfred, 1861–1943, vol. IV
Moon, Arthur, 1882–1961, vol. VI
Moon, Sir (Arthur) Wilfred Graham-, 4th Bt (*cr* 1855), 1905–1954, vol. V

Moon, Sir Cecil Ernest, 2nd Bt (*cr* 1887), 1867–1951, vol. V
Moon, Sir Edward, 5th Bt, 1911–1988, vol. VIII
Moon, Rev. Sir Edward Graham, 2nd Bt (*cr* 1855), 1825–1904, vol. I
Moon, Sir (Edward) Penderel, 1905–1987, vol. VIII
Moon, Edward Robert Pacy, 1858–1949, vol. IV
Moon, Sir Ernest Robert, 1854–1930, vol. III
Moon, Sir Francis Sidney Graham, 3rd Bt (cr 1855), 1855–1911, vol. I
Moon, George Washington, 1823–1909, vol. I
Moon, Harold Philip, 1910–1982, vol. VIII
Moon, Henry E., *died* 1920, vol. II
Moon, Sir John Arthur, 4th Bt (*cr* 1887), 1905–1979, vol. VII
Moon, Sir Penderel; *see* Moon, Sir E. P.
Moon, Sir Richard, 1st Bt (*cr* 1887), 1815–1899, vol. I
Moon, Sir Richard, 3rd Bt (*cr* 1887), 1901–1961, vol. VI
Moon, Robert Oswald, 1865–1953, vol. V
Moon, Lieut Rupert Vance, 1892–1986, vol. VIII
Moon, Walter, 1871–1954, vol. V
Moon, Sir Wilfred Graham-; *see* Moon, Sir A. W. G.
Mooney, His Eminence Cardinal Edward, 1882–1958, vol. V
Mooney, George Stuart, 1900–1965, vol. VI(AII)
Mooney, Herbert C., *died* 1948, vol. IV
Mooney, Herbert Francis, 1897–1964, vol. VI
Mooney, Sir John, 1874–1934, vol. III
Moor, Rev. Edward, 1880–1953, vol. V
Moor, Rt Hon. Sir Frederick Robert, 1853–1927, vol. II
Moor, George Raymond Dallas, *died* 1918, vol. II
Moor, Sir Ralph Denham Rayment, 1860–1909, vol. I
Moor, Samuel Albert, *died* 1944, vol. IV
Moorcroft, William, 1872–1945, vol. IV
Moore, Sir Alan Hilary, 2nd Bt (*cr* 1919), 1882–1959, vol. V
Moore, Ven. Alexander Duff, 1872–1942, vol. IV
Moore, Gen. Sir Alexander George M.; *see* Montgomery-Moore.
Moore, Rev. Alfred Edgar, *died* 1924, vol. II
Moore, Captain Alldin Usborne, 1878–1942, vol. IV
Moore, Adm. Sir Archibald Gordon Henry Wilson, 1862–1934, vol. III
Moore, Archie Murrell Acheson, 1904–1979, vol. VII
Moore, Arthur Collin, 1866–1952, vol. V
Moore, Ven. Arthur Crompton, *died* 1954, vol. V
Moore, Arthur Edward, 1872–1951, vol. V
Moore, Hon. Arthur Edward, 1876–1963, vol. VI
Moore, Count Arthur John, 1849–1904, vol. I
Moore, Rev. Arthur John, 1853–1919, vol. II
Moore, Maj.-Gen. Arthur Thomas, 1830–1913, vol. I
Moore, Col Arthur Trevelyan, *died* 1948, vol. IV
Moore, Arthur William, 1853–1909, vol. I
Moore, Adm. Sir Arthur William, 1847–1934, vol. III
Moore, Col Athelstan, 1879–1918, vol. II
Moore, Beatrice Esther, *died* 1953, vol. V
Moore, Benjamin, *died* 1922, vol. II
Moore, Maj.-Gen. Charles Alfred, 1839–1925, vol. II
Moore, Charles Gordon, 1884–1957, vol. V
Moore, Adm. Charles Henry Hodgson, 1858–1920, vol. II

Moore, Col Charles Hesketh Grant, 1868–1942, vol. IV

Moore, Sir Charles James S.; *see* Stevenson-Moore.

Moore, Charles Joseph Henry O'Hara, 1880–1965, vol. VI

Moore, Charles Thomas John, 1827–1900, vol. I

Moore, Clarence L., 1869–1953, vol. V

Moore, Maj.-Gen. Claude Douglas Hamilton, 1875–1928, vol. II

Moore, Rev. Mgr Clement Harington, 1845–1905, vol. I

Moore, Rev. Courtenay, 1840–1922, vol. II

Moore, Rev. Daniel, 1809–1899, vol. I

Moore, Rev. David Keys, 1854–1935, vol. III

Moore, Maj.-Gen. Denis Grattan, 1909–1987, vol. VIII

Moore, Doris Langley, 1903–1989, vol. VIII

Moore, Dorothea Mary, *died* 1933, vol. III

Moore, Rev. Edward, 1835–1916, vol. II

Moore, Rt Rev. Edward Alfred Livingstone, 1870–1944, vol. IV

Moore, Sir Edward Cecil, 1st Bt (*cr* 1923), 1851–1923, vol. II

Moore, Col Edward James, 1862–1925, vol. II

Moore, Ven. Edward Marsham, *died* 1921, vol. II

Moore, Eldon, 1901–1954, vol. V

Moore, Eric Olawolu, 1878–1944, vol. IV

Moore, Eva, (Mrs Henry V. Esmond), *died* 1955, vol. V

Moore, Evelyn, (Mrs Stuart Moore); *see* Underhill, E.

Moore, Rev. E(velyn) Garth, 1906–1990, vol. VIII

Moore, Col Francis, 1879–1938, vol. III

Moore, Lt-Col Francis Hamilton, 1876–1952, vol. V

Moore, Maj.-Gen. Francis Malcolm, 1897–1974, vol. VII

Moore, Francis William, 1849–1927, vol. II

Moore, Frank Frankfort, 1855–1931, vol. III

Moore, Sir Fred Denby, 1863–1951, vol. V

Moore, Frederick Craven, 1871–1943, vol. IV

Moore, Lt-Col Frederick Grattan, 1877–1955, vol. V

Moore, Frederick Thomas, 1913–1983, vol. VIII

Moore, Sir Frederick William, 1857–1949, vol. IV

Moore, Geoffrey Ernest, 1916–1989, vol. VIII

Moore, Col George A., 1869–1955, vol. V

Moore, George Arbuthnot, 1857–1923, vol. II

Moore, George Augustus, 1852–1933, vol. III

Moore, Rear-Adm. George Dunbar, 1893–1979, vol. VII

Moore, George Edward, 1873–1958, vol. V

Moore, George Foot, 1851–1931, vol. III

Moore, Lt-Col Sir George Montgomery John, 1844–1911, vol. I

Moore, Gerald, 1899–1987, vol. VIII

Moore, Grace; *see* Parera, G. M.

Moore, Brig. Guy Newton, 1893–1984, vol. VIII

Moore, Harold, 1878–1972, vol. VII

Moore, Col Harold Arthur, 1880–1945, vol. IV

Moore, Brig. Harold Edward, 1888–1968, vol. VI

Moore, Sir Harold John de Courcy, 1877–1976, vol. VII

Moore, Sir Harrison; *see* Moore, Sir W. H.

Moore, Harry, 1887–1960, vol. V

Moore, Harry Thornton, 1908–1981, vol. VIII

Moore, Captain Hartley Russell Gwennap, 1881–1953, vol. V

Moore, Lt-Gen. Sir Henry, 1829–1915, vol. I

Moore, Henry, 1898–1986, vol. VIII

Moore, Henry Charles, 1862–1933, vol. III

Moore, Rev. Henry Dodwell, 1838–1919, vol. II

Moore, Henry F., 1887–1954, vol. V

Moore, Henry Ian, 1905–1976, vol. VII

Moore, Henry John, 1872–1950, vol. V

Moore, Rev. Henry Kingsmill, *died* 1943, vol. IV

Moore, Sir Henry Monck-Mason, 1887–1964, vol. VI

Moore, Adm. Sir Henry Ruthven, 1886–1978, vol. VII

Moore, Rev. Herbert Augustine, *died* 1937, vol. III

Moore, Col Herbert Tregosse Gwennap, 1875–1958, vol. V

Moore, Rear-Adm. Humfrey John Bradley, 1898–1985, vol. VIII

Moore, James Lennox Irwin, 1866–1953, vol. V

Moore, James M., 1871–1932, vol. III

Moore, Gen. Sir (James Newton) Rodney, 1905–1985, vol. VIII

Moore, Jocelyn A. M., (Mrs David Symon), 1904–1979, vol. VII

Moore, Maj.-Gen. Sir John, 1864–1940, vol. III

Moore, John Bassett, 1860–1947, vol. IV

Moore, John Cecil, 1907–1967, vol. VI

Moore, Sir John Samuel, 1831–1916, vol. II

Moore, Sir John Voce, 1826–1904, vol. I

Moore, Rev. John Walter Barnwell, 1886–1969, vol. VI

Moore, Rev. John Walter Brady, *died* 1938, vol. III

Moore, Sir John William, 1845–1937, vol. III

Moore, Joseph Henry Hamilton, 1852–1933, vol. III

Moore, Kathleen Ella, 1874–1969, vol. VI

Moore, Kenneth Alfred Edgar, 1894–1976, vol. VII

Moore, Sir Leopold Frank, 1868–1945, vol. IV

Moore, Louis Herbert, 1860–1918, vol. II

Moore, Marianne Craig, 1887–1972, vol. VII

Moore, Mary, 1861–1931, vol. III

Moore, Mary Emily MacLeod; *see* Rees, Mrs Leonard.

Moore, Col Maurice George, 1854–1939, vol. III

Moore, Col Maxtone, 1876–1950, vol. IV

Moore, Major Montagu Seymour, 1896–1966, vol. VI

Moore, Maj.-Gen. Hon. Sir Newton James, 1870–1936, vol. III

Moore, Noel Temple, 1833–1903, vol. I

Moore, Sir Norman, 1st Bt (*cr* 1919), 1847–1922, vol. II

Moore, Rev. Obadiah, 1848–1923, vol. II

Moore, Percival, 1886–1964, vol. VI

Moore, Pierce Langrishe, 1873–1944, vol. IV

Moore, Ralph Westwood, 1906–1953, vol. V

Moore, Ramsey Bignall, 1880–1969, vol. VI

Moore, Reginald, 1910–1968, vol. VI

Moore, Sir Richard Greenslade, 1878–1966, vol. VI

Moore, Lt-Col Richard St Leger, 1848–1921, vol. II

Moore, Rev. Robert, 1863–1935, vol. III

Moore, Rev. and Rt Hon. Robert, 1886–1960, vol. V

Moore, Robert Ernest, 1863–1934, vol. III

Moore, Robert Foster, 1877–1963, vol. VI

Moore, Very Rev. Robert Henry, 1872–1964, vol. VI

Moore, Col Robert Reginald Heber, 1858–1942, vol. IV

Moore, Gen. Sir Rodney; *see* Moore, Gen. Sir. J. N. R.

Moore, Hon. Samuel Wilkinson, 1854–1935, vol. III

Moore, Stanford, 1913–1982, vol. VIII

Moore, Vice-Adm. Stephen St Leger, 1884–1955, vol. V

Moore, Thomas, 1858–1920, vol. II

Moore, Thomas, 1903–1983, vol. VIII

Moore, Lt-Col Sir Thomas Cecil Russell, 1st Bt (*cr* 1956), 1886–1971, vol. VII

Moore, Sir Thomas O'Connor, 11th Bt (*cr* 1681), 1845–1926, vol. II

Moore, Thomas Sturge, 1870–1944, vol. IV

Moore, Thomas Warren, 1872–1937, vol. III

Moore, Tom Sidney, 1881–1966, vol. VI

Moore, Vice-Adm. W. Usborne, 1849–1918, vol. II

Moore, Hon. William, 1817–1914, vol. II

Moore, Rev. Canon William, *died* 1943, vol. IV

Moore, Rt Hon. Sir William, 1st Bt (*cr* 1932), 1864–1944, vol. IV

Moore, Hon. William, 1817–1914, vol. I

Moore, W(illiam) Arthur, 1880–1962, vol. VI

Moore, Rev. William B.; *see* Bramley-Moore.

Moore, William H., 1848–1923, vol. II

Moore, Sir (William) Harrison, 1867–1935, vol. III

Moore, William Harvey, 1891–1961, vol. VI

Moore, William Monro, 1880–1936, vol. III

Moore, Rt Rev. William Richard, 1858–1930, vol. III

Moore, Sir William Samson, 2nd Bt (*cr* 1932), 1891–1978, vol. VII

Moore-Coulson, Maj.-Gen. Samuel, 1908–1983, vol. VIII

Moore Darling, Rev. Canon Edward, 1884–1968, vol. VI

Moore-Guggisberg, Decima, (Lady Moore-Guggisberg), *died* 1964, vol. VI

Moore-Lane, Col George Howard, 1844–1905, vol. I

Moore-Lane, Col Maitland; *see* Lane.

Moore-Park, Carton, 1877–1956, vol. V

Moorehead, Alan McCrae, 1910–1983, vol. VIII

Moores, Col Charles Frederick Guise-, 1873–1938, vol. III

Moores, Maj.-Gen. Sir Guise G.; *see* Guise-Moores.

Moorhead, Maj.-Gen. Charles Dawson, 1894–1965, vol. VI

Moorhead, Thomas Gillman, 1878–1960, vol. V

Moorhouse, E. Hallam; *see* Meynell, Esther H.

Moorhouse, Lt-Col Sir Harry Claude, 1872–1934, vol. III

Moorhouse, Rt Rev. James, 1826–1915, vol. I

Mooring, Sir (Arthur) George (Rixson), 1908–1969, vol. VI

Mooring, Sir George; *see* Mooring, Sir A. G. R.

Moorman, Frederic William, 1872–1919, vol. II

Moorman, Rt Rev. John Richard Humpidge, 1905–1989, vol. VIII

Moorshead, Engr-Rear-Adm. Herbert Brooks, 1870–1955, vol. V

Moorsom, Maj.-Gen. Charles John, 1837–1908, vol. I

Moorsom, Lt-Col Henry Martin, 1839–1921, vol. II

Moorsom, James Marshall, *died* 1918, vol. II

Moos, Sorab Nanabhoy, 1890–1974, vol. VII

Moran, 1st Baron, 1882–1977, vol. VII

Moran, Frances Elizabeth, 1893–1977, vol. VII

Moran, Joseph Michael, 1925–1978, vol. VII

Moran, Patrick Alfred Pierce, 1917–1988, vol. VIII

Moran, His Eminence Cardinal Patrick Francis, 1830–1911, vol. I

Moran, Thomas, 1899–1987, vol. VIII

Moran, Rev. Canon Walter Isidore, 1865–1958, vol. V

Morand, Paul, 1889–1975, vol. VII

Morant, Captain Edgar Robert, 1874–1931, vol. III

Morant, Adm. Sir George Digby, 1837–1921, vol. II

Morant, Brig.-Gen. Hubert Horatio Shirley, 1870–1946, vol. IV

Morant, Dame Mary Maud, (Sister Mary Regis), 1903–1985, vol. VIII

Morant, Sir Robert Laurie, 1863–1920, vol. II

Moraud, Hon. Lucien, *died* 1951, vol. V

Moravia, Alberto, 1907–1990, vol. VIII

Moray, 15th Earl of, 1840–1901, vol. I

Moray, 16th Earl of, 1842–1909, vol. I

Moray, 17th Earl of, 1855–1930, vol. III

Moray, 18th Earl of, 1892–1943, vol. IV

Moray, 19th Earl of, 1894–1974, vol. VII

Moray, Captain William Augustus Stirling Home Drummond, 1852–1939, vol. III

Moray Williams, Barbara, (Barbara Arnason), 1911–1975, vol. VII

Morcom, Lt-Col Reginald Keble, *died* 1961, vol. VI

Morcom, William Boase, 1846–1910, vol. I

Morcom, Sir William John, 1859–1934, vol. III

Mordaunt, Sir Charles, 10th Bt, 1836–1897, vol. I

Mordaunt, Elinor, *died* 1942, vol. IV

Mordaunt, Sir Henry, 12th Bt, 1867–1939, vol. III

Mordaunt, Lt-Col Sir Nigel John, 13th Bt, 1907–1979, vol. VII

Mordaunt, Sir Osbert L'Estrange, 11th Bt, 1884–1934, vol. III

Mordecai, Sir John Stanley, 1903–1986, vol. VIII

Mordell, Louis Joel, 1888–1972, vol. VII

Morden, Lt-Col Walter Grant, 1880–1932, vol. III

Mordey, William M., 1856–1938, vol. III

More, Lt-Col James Carmichael, 1883–1959, vol. V

More, Sir Jasper, 1907–1987, vol. VIII

More, John William, 1879–1959, vol. V

More, Kenneth Gilbert, 1914–1982, vol. VIII

More, Paul Elmer, 1864–1937, vol. III

More, Richard Edwardes, 1879–1936, vol. III

More, Brig.-Gen. Robert Henry, *died* 1951, vol. V

More, Robert Jasper, *died* 1903, vol. I

More-Molyneux, Maj.-Gen. George Hand, 1851–1903, vol. I

More-Molyneux, Adm. Sir Robert Henry, 1838–1904, vol. I

More-Molyneux-Longbourne, Brig.-Gen. Francis Cecil, 1883–1963, vol. VI

More-O'Ferrall, Dominic; *see* O'Ferrall.

Morecambe, Eric; *see* Bartholomew, J. E.

Moreau, Emile Edouard, 1856–1937, vol. III

Moreing, Adrian Charles, 1892–1940, vol. III

Moreing, Captain Algernon Henry, 1889–1974, vol. VII

Morel, Edmund Dene, 1873–1924, vol. II

Morel, Sir Thomas, 1847–1903, vol. I

Moreland, Rt Rev. William Hall, 1861–1946, vol. IV
Moreland, William Harrison, 1868–1938, vol. III
Morell, Sir Stephen Joseph, 1869–1944, vol. IV
Moresby, Adm. John, 1830–1922, vol. II
Moresby, Walter Halliday, *died* 1951, vol. V
Moreton, Lord; Henry Haughton Reynolds-Moreton, 1857–1920, vol. II
Moreton, Hon. Algernon Howard, 1880–1951, vol. V
Moreton, Rev. Arthur Cyprian, 1866–1936, vol. III
Moreton, Rev. Canon H. A. V., 1889–1966, vol. VI
Moreton, Hon. Sir Richard Charles, 1846–1928, vol. II
Morey, Very Rev. Dom Adrian, 1904–1989, vol. VIII
Morfee, Air Vice-Marshal Arthur Laurence, *born* 1897, vol. VIII
Morfill, William Richard, 1834–1909, vol. I
Morford, Maj.-Gen. Albert Clarence St C.; *see* St Clair-Morford.
Morford, Howard Frederick, 1894–1963, vol. VI
Morgan, Alexander, 1860–1946, vol. IV
Morgan, Col Alexander Braithwaite, 1866–1930, vol. III
Morgan, Col Sir Alexander Brooke, 1837–1911, vol. I
Morgan, Alfred Kedington, 1868–1928, vol. II
Morgan, Alun Michael, 1915–1981, vol. VIII
Morgan, Angela, *died* 1957, vol. V
Morgan, Lt-Col Anthony Hickman, 1858–1924, vol. II
Morgan, Hon. Sir Arthur, 1856–1916, vol. II
Morgan, Sir Arthur Croke, *died* 1955, vol. V
Morgan, Sir Arthur E., 1886–1956, vol. V
Morgan, Arthur Eustace, 1886–1972, vol. VII
Morgan, Sir Benjamin Howell, *died* 1937, vol. III
Morgan, Major Cecil Buckley, 1860–1918, vol. II
Morgan, Cecil Lloyd, 1882–1965, vol. VI
Morgan, Adm. Sir Charles Eric, 1889–1951, vol. V
Morgan, Sir Charles Langbridge, 1855–1940, vol. III
Morgan, Charles Langbridge, 1894–1958, vol. V
Morgan, Col Claude Kyd, 1871–1934, vol. III
Morgan, Clement Yorke, 1903–1960, vol. V
Morgan, Sir Clifford Naunton, 1901–1986, vol. VIII
Morgan, Conwy Lloyd, 1852–1936, vol. III
Morgan, D. J., 1844–1918, vol. II
Morgan, Major Sir David Hughes-, 1st Bt (*cr* 1925), 1871–1941, vol. IV
Morgan, David Loftus, 1904–1976, vol. VII
Morgan, Very Rev. David Watcyn, *died* 1940, vol. III
Morgan, Lt-Col David Watts, 1867–1933, vol. III
Morgan, Dennis, 1928–1987, vol. VIII
Morgan, Rt Rev. Edmund Robert, 1888–1979, vol. VII
Morgan, Hon. Sir Edward James Ranembe, 1900–1977, vol. VII
Morgan, Col Emmanuel Maria, 1853–1929, vol. III
Morgan, Col Farrar Robert Horton, 1893–1978, vol. VII
Morgan, Sir Frank William, 1887–1974, vol. VII
Morgan, Hon. Frederic Courtenay, 1834–1909, vol. I
Morgan, Lt-Gen. Sir Frederick Edgworth, 1894–1967, vol. VI
Morgan, Col Frederick James, 1862–1931, vol. III
Morgan, Rear-Adm. Frederick Robert William, 1861–1910, vol. I

Morgan, Captain Frederick Thomas de Mallet, 1889–1959, vol. V
Morgan, Rev. G. Campbell, 1863–1945, vol. IV
Morgan, Engr Rear-Adm. Geoffrey, 1889–1956, vol. V
Morgan, George, 1853–1943, vol. IV
Morgan, George, 1867–1957, vol. V
Morgan, George Ernest, 1861–1934, vol. III
Morgan, George Hay, 1866–1931, vol. III
Morgan, Rt Hon. Sir George Osborne, 1st Bt (*cr* 1892), 1826–1897, vol. I
Morgan, Sir Gilbert Thomas, 1872–1940, vol. III
Morgan, Gladys Mary, *died* 1957, vol. V
Morgan, Graham, 1903–1987, vol. VIII
Morgan, Guy Leslie Llewellyn, 1902–1987, vol. VIII
Morgan, Harington, *died* 1914, vol. I
Morgan, Maj.-Gen. Harold de Riemer, 1888–1964, vol. VI
Morgan, Rev. Harold Dunbar, *died* 1945, vol. IV
Morgan, Col Harrison Ross Lewin, 1842–1914, vol. I
Morgan, Ven. Harry J., 1871–1947, vol. IV
Morgan, Heaton Andrew Kenneth, 1889–1962, vol. VI
Morgan, Henry, 1875–1944, vol. IV
Morgan, Rev. Henry Arthur, 1830–1912, vol. I
Morgan, Henry James, 1842–1913, vol. I
Morgan, Sir Herbert Edward, 1880–1951, vol. V
Morgan, Hilda, (Mrs Charles Morgan); *see* Vaughan, H.
Morgan, Brig.-Gen. Sir Hill Godfrey, 1862–1923, vol. II
Morgan, Hopkin, 1849–1933, vol. III
Morgan, H(opkin) Trevor; *see* Morgan, Trevor.
Morgan, Captain Horace Leslie, 1888–1973, vol. VII
Morgan, Hugh Travers, 1919–1988, vol. VIII
Morgan, Hyacinth Bernard Wenceslaus, 1885–1956, vol. V
Morgan, Hywel Glyn, 1899–1966, vol. VI
Morgan, Irvonwy, 1907–1982, vol. VIII
Morgan, Very Rev. J., *died* 1904, vol. I
Morgan, James, 1882–1968, vol. VI
Morgan, James Conwy, 1910–1977, vol. VII
Morgan, Rev. John, *died* 1924, vol. II
Morgan, John, *died* 1938, vol. III
Morgan, John, 1892–1940, vol. III
Morgan, Most Rev. John, 1886–1957, vol. V
Morgan, Sir John David, 1874–1939, vol. III
Morgan, John Hammond, 1847–1924, vol. II
Morgan, Brig.-Gen. John Hartman, 1876–1955, vol. V
Morgan, John Lloyd, 1861–1944, vol. IV
Morgan, John Pierpont, 1837–1913, vol. I
Morgan, John Pierpont, 1867–1943, vol. IV
Morgan, John T., 1824–1907, vol. I
Morgan, Sir John Vernon H.; *see* Hughes-Morgan.
Morgan, Sir Kenyon Pascoe V.; *see* Vaughan-Morgan.
Morgan, Col Kevern Ivor, 1894–1971, vol. VII
Morgan, Leslie James Joseph, 1922–1988, vol. VIII
Morgan, Montagu Travers, 1889–1974, vol. VII
Morgan, Brig. Morgan Cyril, 1891–1960, vol. V
Morgan, Sir Morien Bedford, 1912–1978, vol. VII
Morgan, Oswald Gayer, 1889–1981, vol. VIII

Morgan, Rear-Adm. Sir Patrick John, 1917–1989, vol. VIII

Morgan, Paul Robert James, 1898–1974, vol. VII

Morgan, Lt-Gen. Reginald Hallward, 1871–1948, vol. IV

Morgan, Richard Cope, 1827–1908, vol. I

Morgan, Rev. Richard James Basil P.; *see* Paterson-Morgan.

Morgan, Robert Harry, 1880–1960, vol. V

Morgan, R(obert) Orlando, 1865–1956, vol. V

Morgan, Brig.-Gen. Rosslewin Westropp, 1879–1947, vol. IV

Morgan, Lt-Col Stuart Williams, 1867–1922, vol. II

Morgan, Sydney Cope, 1887–1967, vol. VI

Morgan, Thomas Hunt, 1866–1945, vol. IV

Morgan, Trevor, 1892–1976, vol. VII

Morgan, Adm. Sir Vaughan, 1891–1969, vol. VI

Morgan, Sir Walter, 1821–1906, vol. I

Morgan, Walter, 1886–1960, vol. V

Morgan, Walter J., *died* 1924, vol. II

Morgan, Sir Walter Vaughan, 1st Bt (*cr* 1906), 1831–1916, vol. II

Morgan, Air Cdre Wilfred W.; *see* Wynter-Morgan.

Morgan, Rev. William, 1862–1928, vol. II

Morgan, William, 1870–1945, vol. IV

Morgan, Gen. Sir William Duthie, 1891–1977, vol. VII

Morgan, Rev. Preb. William Edgar, 1888–1968, vol. VI

Morgan, Major William Henry, 1883–1966, vol. VI

Morgan, William Matheson, 1906–1972, vol. VII

Morgan, William Pritchard, 1844–1924, vol. II

Morgan, William Stanley, 1908–1986, vol. VIII

Morgan-Brown, Rev. Nigel Mackenzie, 1859–1932, vol. III

Morgan-Grenville, Lt-Col Hon. Thomas George Breadalbane, 1891–1965, vol. VI

Morgan Jones, John; *see* Jones.

Morgan-Owen, Maj.-Gen. Llewellyn Isaac Gethin, 1879–1960, vol. V

Morgan-Powell, Samuel, 1878–1962, vol. VI

Morgenthau, Henry, 1856–1946, vol. IV

Morgenthau, Henry, Jr, 1891–1967, vol. VI

Moriarty, Rt Rev. Ambrose James, 1870–1949, vol. IV

Moriarty, Cecil Charles Hudson, 1877–1958, vol. V

Moriarty, Captain Henry Augustus, 1815–1906, vol. I

Moriarty, Rt Hon. John Francis, *died* 1915, vol. I

Morice, Beaumont, *died* 1937, vol. III

Morice, Sir George, Pasha, *died* 1904, vol. I

Morin, Leopold Frédéric Germain, 1861–1946, vol. IV

Morine, Sir Alfred Bishop, 1857–1944, vol. IV

Morison, Rt Hon. Lord; Thomas Brash Morison, *died* 1945, vol. IV

Morison, Alexander Blackhall, 1850–1927, vol. II

Morison, Cecil Graham Traquair, 1881–1965, vol. VI

Morison, Donald, 1857–1924, vol. II

Morison, Hector, 1850–1939, vol. III

Morison, Sir John, 1893–1958, vol. V

Morison, Lt-Col John, 1879–1971, vol. VII

Morison, John Lyle, 1875–1952, vol. V

Morison, John Miller Woodburn, 1875–1951, vol. V

Morison, Engr-Rear-Adm. Richard Barns, 1871–1932, vol. III

Morison, Sir Ronald Peter, 1900–1976, vol. VII

Morison, Rutherford, 1853–1939, vol. III

Morison, Samuel Eliot, 1887–1976, vol. VII

Morison, Stanley, 1889–1967, vol. VI

Morison, Sir Theodore, 1863–1936, vol. III

Morison, Rt Hon. Thomas Brash; *see* Morison, Rt Hon. Lord.

Morison, Sir William Thomson, 1860–1931, vol. III

Moritz, Rudolph, 1878–1940, vol. III

Moritz, Siegmund, 1855–1932, vol. III

Morkill, William Lucius, 1858–1936, vol. III

Morland, Andrew John, 1896–1957, vol. V

Morland, Egbert Coleby, 1874–1955, vol. V

Morland, Captain Henry, 1876–1966, vol. VI (AII)

Morland, Sir Oscar Charles, 1904–1980, vol. VII

Morland, Gen. Sir Thomas Lethbridge Napier, 1865–1925, vol. II

Morland, William Vane, 1884–1962, vol. VI

Morle, Philip Bartlett, 1876–1956, vol. V

Morley, 3rd Earl of, 1843–1905, vol. I

Morley, 4th Earl of, 1877–1951, vol. V

Morley, 5th Earl of, 1878–1962, vol. VI

Morley of Blackburn, 1st Viscount, 1838–1923, vol. II

Morley, Agnes H.; *see* Headlam-Morley.

Morley, Sir Alexander Francis, 1908–1971, vol. VII

Morley, Rt Hon. Arnold, 1849–1916, vol. II

Morley, Arthur, 1881–1946, vol. IV

Morley, Arthur, 1876–1962, vol. VI

Morley, Austin, 1898–1970, vol. VI

Morley, Charles, *died* 1916, vol. II

Morley, Charles, 1847–1917, vol. II

Morley, Charles, 1885–1955, vol. V

Morley, Christopher, 1890–1957, vol. V

Morley, Captain Hon. Claude Hope H.; *see* Hope-Morley.

Morley, Edith Julia, 1875–1964, vol. VI

Morley, Edward Williams, 1838–1923, vol. II

Morley, Sir George, 1873–1942, vol. IV

Morley, Air Vice-Marshal George Henry, 1907–1971, vol. VII

Morley, Sir Godfrey William Rowland, 1909–1987, vol. VIII

Morley, Harry, 1881–1943, vol. IV

Morley, Henry Forster, 1855–1943, vol. IV

Morley, Henry Seaward, 1897–1960, vol. V

Morley, Sir James Wycliffe H.; *see* Headlam-Morley.

Morley, John, *died* 1974, vol. VII

Morley, Kenneth Arthur Sonntag H.; *see* Headlam-Morley.

Morley, Lt-Col Lyddon Charteris, 1877–1954, vol. V

Morley, Ralph, 1882–1955, vol. V

Morley, Robert, 1857–1941, vol. IV

Morley, Rt Rev. Samuel, 1841–1923, vol. II

Mornement, Bt Col Edward, 1867–1956, vol. V

Moro, Aldo, 1916–1978, vol. VII

Morony, Thomas Henry, *died* 1961, vol. VI

Morony, Gen. Sir Thomas Lovett, 1926–1989, vol. VIII

Morphett, Lt-Col George Charles, 1878–1968, vol. VI

Morphew, Col Edward Maudsley, 1867–1947, vol. IV

Morphy, Hugh Boulton, 1860–1932, vol. III

Morrah, Mrs Dermot; *see* Morrah, Ruth.

Morrah, Dermot Michael Macgregor, 1896–1974, vol. VII

Morrah, Herbert Arthur, *died* 1939, vol. III

Morrah, Ruth, (Mrs Dermot Morrah), 1899–1990, vol. VIII

Morrell, Rear-Adm. Arthur, *died* 1915, vol. I

Morrell, Arthur Claude, 1894–1978, vol. VII

Morrell, Captain Sir Arthur Routley Hutson, 1878–1968, vol. VI

Morrell, Charles, 1842–1913, vol. I

Morrell, Mrs G. Herbert, (Emily Alicia Morrell), *died* 1938, vol. III

Morrell, George Herbert, 1845–1906, vol. I

Morrell, Philip, 1870–1943, vol. IV

Morrell, R. M., *died* 1912, vol. I

Morrell, William Bowes, 1913–1981, vol. VIII

Morren, Sir William Booth Rennie, 1890–1972, vol. VII

Morrice, Humphrey Alan Walter, 1906–1959, vol. V

Morrice, Rev. James Cornelius, 1874–1953, vol. V

Morrice, Rev. John David, 1849–1938, vol. III

Morrice, Lt-Col Lewis Edward, 1862–1933, vol. III

Morrill, Thomas James, 1886–1969, vol. VI

Morris, 1st Baron, 1858–1935, vol. III

Morris, 2nd Baron, 1903–1975, vol. VII

Morris and Killanin, 1st Baron, 1827–1901, vol. I

Morris of Borth-y-Gest, Baron (Life Peer); John William Morris, 1896–1979, vol. VII

Morris of Grasmere, Baron (Life Peer); Charles Richard Morris, 1898–1990, vol. VIII

Morris of Kenwood, 1st Baron, 1893–1954, vol. V

Morris, Alfred, 1874–1945, vol. IV

Morris, Air Cdre Alfred Drummond W.; *see* Warrington-Morris.

Morris, Most Rev. (Alfred) Edwin, 1894–1971, vol. VII

Morris, Air Vice-Marshal Sir (Alfred) Samuel, 1889–1964, vol. VI

Morris, Brig. Arthur de Burgh, 1902–1978, vol. VII

Morris, Rt Rev. Arthur Harold, 1898–1977, vol. VII

Morris, Col Arthur Henry, 1861–1939, vol. III

Morris, Brig. Arthur Henry Musgrave, 1904–1972, vol. VII

Morris, Col Arthur Hugh, 1872–1941, vol. IV

Morris, Col Augustus William, 1845–1906, vol. I

Morris, Benjamin Stephen, 1910–1990, vol. VIII

Morris, C. J., *see* Morris, John.

Morris, Sir Cedric Lockwood, 9th Bt, 1889–1982, vol. VIII

Morris, Charles, *died* 1929, vol. III

Morris, Charles Alfred, 1898–1983, vol. VIII

Morris, Charles Arthur, *died* 1942, vol. IV

Morris, Lt-Col Charles Reade Monroe, 1882–1936, vol. III

Morris, Charles Sculthorpe, 1875–1949, vol. IV

Morris, Col Charles Temple, 1876–1956, vol. V

Morris, Colin John Owen Rhonabwy, 1910–1981, vol. VIII

Morris, Major Cyril Clarke Boville, 1882–1950, vol. IV

Morris, Sir Daniel, 1844–1933, vol. III

Morris, David Edward, 1915–1990, vol. VIII

Morris, Air Marshal Sir Douglas Griffith, 1908–1990, vol. VIII

Morris, Brig.-Gen. Edmund Merritt, 1868–1939, vol. III

Morris, Edmund Montague, 1871–1913, vol. I

Morris, Commissary-Gen. Sir Edward, 1833–1923, vol. II

Morris, Edward Ellis, 1843–1902, vol. I

Morris, Edward Gilbert, 1884–1943, vol. IV

Morris, Edward Robert, 1862–1934, vol. III

Morris, Most Rev. Edwin; *see* Morris, Most Rev. A. E.

Morris, Gen. Sir Edwin Logie, 1889–1970, vol. VI

Morris, Rev. Ernest Edwin, 1856–1924, vol. II

Morris, Sir Ernest William, *died* 1937, vol. III

Morris, Sir Francis, 1859–1944, vol. IV

Morris, Geoffrey Grant, 1888–1938, vol. III

Morris, Sir Geoffrey N.; *see* Newman-Morris.

Morris, Geoffrey O'C.; *see* O'Connor-Morris.

Morris, Sir George, 1833–1912, vol. I

Morris, Col George Abbott, 1879–1957, vol. V

Morris, Sir George Cecil, 6th Bt (*cr* 1806), 1852–1940, vol. IV

Morris, Lt-Col Hon. George Henry, 1872–1915, vol. I

Morris, Captain George Horace Guy, 1897–1979, vol. VII

Morris, Sir George Lockwood, 8th Bt (*cr* 1806), 1859–1947, vol. IV

Morris, Brig.-Gen. George Mortimer, 1868–1954, vol. V

Morris, Sir George Parker; *see* Morris, Sir Parker.

Morris, Greville, *died* 1922, vol. II

Morris, Guy Wilfrid, 1884–1956, vol. V

Morris, Sir Gwilym; *see* Morris, Sir T. G.

Morris, Gwilym Ivor, 1911–1965, vol. VI

Morris, Gwyn Rhyse Francis, 1910–1982, vol. VIII

Morris, Sir Harold Spencer, 1876–1967, vol. VI

Morris, Harrison Smith, 1856–1948, vol. IV

Morris, Harry Frank Grave, 1907–1982, vol. VIII

Morris, Sir Henry, 1st Bt (*cr* 1909), 1844–1926, vol. II

Morris, Sir Herbert Edward, 7th Bt (*cr* 1806), 1884–1947, vol. IV

Morris, Brig. Herbert Edwin Abrahall, 1894–1969, vol. VI

Morris, Herbert Picton, 1856–1946, vol. IV

Morris, Ira Nelson, *died* 1942, vol. IV

Morris, Rt Rev. James, 1876–1957, vol. V

Morris, James Archibald, 1857–1942, vol. IV

Morris, John, (C. J. Morris), 1895–1980, vol. VII

Morris, Rev. John C., 1870–1940, vol. III

Morris, John David, 1895–1972, vol. VII

Morris, Hon. Sir John Demetrius, 1902–1956, vol. V

Morris, Maj.-Gen. John Edward Longworth, 1909–1988, vol. VIII

Morris, Sir John Henry, 1828–1912, vol. I

Morris, John Humphrey Carlile, 1910–1984, vol. VIII

Morris, Maj.-Gen. John Ignatius, 1842–1902, vol. I

Morris, Rev. (John) Marcus (Harston), 1915–1989, vol. VIII

Morris, Sir John N.; *see* Newman-Morris.

Morris, Major John Patrick, 1894–1962, vol. VI

Morris, Brig. John Sidney, 1890–1961, vol. VI

Morris, John Turner M.; *see* Macgregor-Morris.

Morris, Sir Keith Douglas, 1908–1981, vol. VIII

Morris, Hon. Sir Kenneth James, 1903–1978, vol. VII
Morris, Lawrence Henry, 1902–1969, vol. VI
Morris, Air Marshal Sir Leslie D.; *see* Dalton-Morris.
Morris, Sir Lewis, 1833–1907, vol. I
Morris, Sir Malcolm Alexander, 1849–1924, vol. II
Morris, Malcolm John, 1913–1972, vol. VII
Morris, Rev. Marcus; *see* Morris, Rev. J. M. H.
Morris, May, *died* 1938, vol. III
Morris, Noah, *died* 1947, vol. IV
Morris, Sir Owen T.; *see* Temple-Morris.
Morris, Sir Parker, 1891–1972, vol. VII
Morris, Percy, 1893–1967, vol. VI
Morris, Philip Richard, 1833–1902, vol. I
Morris, Sir Philip Robert, 1901–1979, vol. VII
Morris, Quentin Mathew, 1930–1989, vol. VIII
Morris, Ralph Clarence, 1889–1959, vol. V
Morris, Reginald Owen, 1886–1948, vol. IV
Morris, Rex G.; *see* Goring-Morris.
Morris, Sir Rhys Hopkin, 1888–1956, vol. V
Morris, Rev. Richard, *died* 1923, vol. II
Morris, Richard John, 1860–1936, vol. III
Morris, Richard Murchison, 1898–1979, vol. VII
Morris, Maj.-Gen. Robert, 1840–1914, vol. I
Morris, Sir Robert Armine, 4th Bt (*cr* 1806), 1848–1927, vol. II
Morris, R(obert) Schofield, 1898–1964, vol. VI
Morris, Rev. Rupert Hugh, 1844–1918, vol. II
Morris, Samuel, 1846–1920, vol. II
Morris, Air Vice-Marshal Sir Samuel; *see* Morris, Air Vice-Marshal Sir A. S.
Morris, Sir Samuel Meeson, 1857–1937, vol. III
Morris, Rev. Silas, 1862–1923, vol. II
Morris, Captain Sir Tankerville Robert Armine, 5th Bt (*cr* 1806), 1892–1937, vol. III
Morris, Sir (Thomas) Gwilym, 1913–1982, vol. VIII
Morris, Lt-Col Thomas Henry, 1848–1927, vol. II
Morris, Thomas Joseph, 1876–1953, vol. V
Morris, Rev. Canon Walter Edmund Harston, 1872–1968, vol. VI
Morris, William Alexander, 1905–1979, vol. VII
Morris, William Alfred, 1912–1973, vol. VII
Morris, Col Sir William George, 1847–1935, vol. III
Morris, Sir William Gerard, 1909–1984, vol. VIII
Morris, William O'Connor, 1824–1904, vol. I
Morris, Col William P.; *see* Pollok Morris.
Morris, William Russell, 1853–1936, vol. III
Morris, Sir Willie, 1919–1982, vol. VIII
Morris-Airey, Harold, 1880–1927, vol. II
Morris-Eyton, Lt-Col Charles Reginald, 1890–1961, vol. VI
Morris-Eyton, Lt-Col Robert Charles Gilfrid, 1921–1990, vol. VIII
Morris Johns, Alun; *see* Johns.
Morris-Jones, Sir Henry; *see* Morris-Jones, Sir J. H.
Morris-Jones, Huw, 1912–1989, vol. VIII
Morris-Jones, Sir John; *see* Jones.
Morris-Jones, Sir (John) Henry, 1884–1972, vol. VII
Morrisby, Major Hon. Arthur, 1847–1925, vol. II
Morrish, Arthur Gabriel, 1869–1936, vol. III
Morrish, Rev. Francis, 1852–1937, vol. III
Morrish, Rear-Adm. William Douglas Travers, 1882–1958, vol. V
Morrison, 1st Baron, 1881–1953, vol. V

Morrison of Lambeth, Baron (Life Peer); Herbert Stanley Morrison, 1888–1965, vol. VI
Morrison, Agnes Brysson, 1867–1934, vol. III
Morrison, Maj.-Gen. Albert Edward, 1901–1989, vol. VIII
Morrison, Alexander, 1868–1941, vol. IV
Morrison, Alexander, 1917–1982, vol. VIII
Morrison, Alexander Thomas, 1886–1954, vol. V
Morrison, Archibald Cameron, 1870–1948, vol. IV
Morrison, Arthur, 1863–1945, vol. IV
Morrison, Arthur Andrew, 1858–1934, vol. III
Morrison, Arthur Cecil Lockwood, 1881–1960, vol. V
Morrison, Hon. Aulay MacAulay, 1863–1942, vol. IV
Morrison, Brig.-Gen. Colquhoun Grant, 1860–1916, vol. II
Morrison, David, *died* 1936, vol. III
Morrison, Maj.-Gen. Sir Edward Whipple Bancroft, 1867–1925, vol. II
Morrison, Col F. L., 1863–1917, vol. II
Morrison, Col Frank Stanley, 1881–1969, vol. VI
Morrison, George Alexander, 1869–1956, vol. V
Morrison, George Ernest, 1862–1920, vol. II
Morrison, Very Rev. George Herbert, 1866–1928, vol. II
Morrison, Herbert Needham, 1891–1963, vol. VI
Morrison, Hugh, 1868–1931, vol. III
Morrison, Hugh Smith, 1858–1929, vol. III
Morrison, Most Rev. James, 1861–1950, vol. IV
Morrison, James, 1900–1987, vol. VIII
Morrison, Major James Archibald, 1873–1934, vol. III
Morrison, Rt Rev. James Dow, 1844–1934, vol. III
Morrison, James Thomas Jackman, *died* 1933, vol. III
Morrison, James Victor, 1917–1990, vol. VIII
Morrison, Col John, *died* 1919, vol. II
Morrison, Joseph Albert Colquhoun, 1882–1964, vol. VI
Morrison, Julia Minnie, *died* 1942, vol. IV
Morrison, Sir Murray; *see* Morrison, Sir W. M.
Morrison, Sir Nicholas Godfrey, 1918–1981, vol. VIII
Morrison, R. E., *born* 1851, vol. II
Morrison, Rear-Adm. Thomas Kenneth, 1911–1983, vol. VIII
Morrison, Walter, 1836–1921, vol. II
Morrison, Sir William, 1877–1951, vol. V
Morrison, Rev. William Douglas, 1852–1943, vol. IV
Morrison, Sir (William) Murray, 1873–1948, vol. IV
Morrison-Bell, Sir (Arthur) Clive, 1st Bt (*cr* 1923), 1871–1956, vol. V
Morrison-Bell, Sir Charles Reginald Francis, 3rd Bt (*cr* 1905), 1915–1967, vol. VI
Morrison-Bell, Sir Charles William, 1st Bt (*cr* 1905), 1833–1914, vol. I
Morrison-Bell, Sir Claude William Hedley, 2nd Bt (*cr* 1905), 1867–1943, vol. IV
Morrison-Bell, Sir Clive; *see* Morrison-Bell, Sir A. C.
Morrison-Bell, Lt-Col Ernest FitzRoy, 1871–1960, vol. V
Morrison-Bell, Lt-Col Eustace Widdrington, 1874–1947, vol. IV
Morrison-Low, Sir Walter John; *see* Low.
Morrisroe, Rt Rev. Patrick, 1869–1946, vol. IV

Morrogh, Lt-Col Donald Florence MacC.; *see* MacCarthy-Morrogh.

Morrogh, Brig. Walter Francis, 1891–1954, vol. V

Morrogh Bernard, Rt Rev. Mgr Canon Eustace Anthony, 1893–1972, vol. VII

Morrow, Albert, 1863–1927, vol. II

Morrow, Sir (Arthur) William, 1903–1977, vol. VII

Morrow, Dwight Whitney, 1873–1931, vol. III

Morrow, Forbes St John, 1860–1949, vol. IV

Morrow, George, 1870–1955, vol. V

Morrow, Cdre James Cairns, 1905–1963, vol. VI

Morrow, Very Rev. John Love, *died* 1940, vol. III

Morrow, Sir William; *see* Morrow, Sir A. W.

Morrow, Very Rev. William Edward Reginald, 1869–1950, vol. IV

Morse, Vice-Adm. Sir Anthony; *see* Morse, Vice-Adm. Sir J. A. V.

Morse, Sir Arthur, 1892–1967, vol. VI

Morse, Charles, 1860–1945, vol. IV

Morse, David Abner, 1907–1990, vol. VIII

Morse, Sir George Henry, 1857–1931, vol. III

Morse, Hosea Ballou, 1855–1934, vol. III

Morse, Vice-Adm. Sir (John) Anthony (Vere), 1892–1960, vol. V

Morse, L. Lapper, 1853–1913, vol. I

Morse, Rev. Wallace Ransom, 1860–1932, vol. III

Morse, William Ewart, 1878–1952, vol. V

Morse, Withrow, 1880–1951, vol. V

Morse-Boycott, Rev. Desmond, 1892–1979, vol. VII

Morshead, Edmund Doidge Anderson, *died* 1912, vol. I

Morshead, Lt-Col Henry Treise, 1882–1931, vol. III

Morshead, Leonard Frederick, 1868–1936, vol. III

Morshead, Lt-Gen. Sir Leslie James, 1889–1959, vol. V

Morshead, Sir Owen Frederick, 1893–1977, vol. VII

Morshead, Lt-Col Rupert Henry A.; *see* Anderson-Morshead.

Morshead, Sir Warwick Charles, 3rd Bt, 1824–1905, vol. I

Morson, A(lbert) Clifford, 1881–1975, vol. VII

Morson, Walter Augustus Ormsby, 1851–1921, vol. II

Mort, David Llewellyn, 1888–1963, vol. VI

Morten, Edward, 1845–1929, vol. III

Morten, Frederick Joseph, 1888–1960, vol. V

Morten, Honnor, *died* 1913, vol. I

Mortensen, Theodor, 1868–1952, vol. V

Morter, Col Sidney Pelham, 1869–1933, vol. III

Mortimer, Chapman; *see* Chapman-Mortimer, W. C.

Mortimer, Sir Charles Edward, 1886–1974, vol. VII

Mortimer, Rev. Christian, *died* 1916, vol. II

Mortimer, Emile Samuel, 1853–1935, vol. III

Mortimer, Francis James, 1875–1944, vol. IV

Mortimer, George Frederick Lloyd, 1866–1928, vol. II

Mortimer, Lt-Col James, *died* 1916, vol. II

Mortimer, John Desmond, *died* 1942, vol. IV

Mortimer, Brig. Philip, 1882–1963, vol. VI

Mortimer, Sir Ralph George Elpinstone, 1869–1955, vol. V

Mortimer, Raymond, 1895–1980, vol. VII

Mortimer, Rt Rev. Robert Cecil, 1902–1976, vol. VII

Mortimer, William Charles C.; *see* Chapman-Mortimer.

Mortimer, William Egerton, 1878–1940, vol. III

Mortimer, Col Sir William Hugh, 1846–1921, vol. II

Mortimore, Lt-Col Claude Alick, 1875–1927, vol. II

Mortimore, Frederick William, 1858–1928, vol. II

Mortished, Ronald James Patrick, 1891–1957, vol. V

Mortlock, Rev. Canon Charles Bernard, 1888–1967, vol. VI

Mortlock, Rev. Canon E., 1859–1945, vol. IV

Morton, 20th Earl of, 1844–1935, vol. III

Morton, 21st Earl of, 1907–1976, vol. VII

Morton of Henryton, Baron (Life Peer); Fergus Dunlop Morton, 1887–1973, vol. VII

Morton, Sir Alpheus Cleophas, 1840–1923, vol. II

Morton, Anthony; *see* Creasey, John.

Morton, Arthur Henry Aylmer, 1836–1913, vol. I

Morton, Gen. Boyce William Dunlop, 1829–1919, vol. II

Morton, Charles, 1819–1904, vol. I

Morton, Charles Alexander, 1860–1929, vol. III

Morton, Sir Charles Henry, 1852–1939, vol. III

Morton, Lt-Col David Simson, *died* 1937, vol. III

Morton, Major Sir Desmond John Falkiner, 1891–1971, vol. VII

Morton, Digby; *see* Morton, H. D.

Morton, Edward, *died* 1922, vol. II

Morton, Brig.-Gen. Edward, 1871–1949, vol. IV

Morton, Edward John Chalmers, 1856–1902, vol. I

Morton, Edward Reginald, 1867–1944, vol. IV

Morton, Sir George, 1870–1953, vol. V

Morton, Sir George Bond, 1893–1954, vol. V

Morton, Lt-Gen. Sir Gerald de Courcy, 1845–1906, vol. I

Morton, George F., 1882–1975, vol. VII

Morton, Guy Mainwaring, 1896–1968, vol. VI

Morton, Major Harold Trestrail, 1894–1972, vol. VII

Morton, Rev. Harry Osborne, 1925–1988, vol. VIII

Morton, (Henry) Digby, 1906–1983, vol. VIII

Morton, Henry Vollam, 1892–1979, vol. VII

Morton, Hugh, 1883–1941, vol. IV

Morton, Col Hugh Murray, 1873–1946, vol. IV

Morton, J. B.; *see* Morton, J. C. A. B. M.

Morton, Sir James, 1867–1943, vol. IV

Morton, James Elliot Vowler, 1861–1924, vol. II

Morton, James H., 1881–1918, vol. II

Morton, John Cameron Andrieu Bingham Michael, (J. B. Morton), 1893–1979, vol. VII

Morton, John Percival, 1911–1985, vol. VIII

Morton, Levi Parsons, 1824–1920, vol. II

Morton, Michael, *died* 1931, vol. III

Morton, Sir Ralph John, 1896–1985, vol. VIII

Morton, Richard Alan, 1899–1977, vol. VII

Morton, Rev. Robert, 1847–1932, vol. III

Morton, Sir Stanley William Gibson, 1911–1975, vol. VII

Morton, Air Vice-Marshal Terence Charles St Clessie, 1893–1968, vol. VI

Morton, Thomas Corsan, 1859–1928, vol. II

Morton, Sir Wilfred; *see* Morton, Sir W. W.

Morton, William Blair, 1868–1949, vol. IV

Morton, William Cuthbert, 1875–1971, vol. VII

Morton, William Ernest, 1902–1981, vol. VIII

Morton, Sir (William) Wilfred, 1906–1981, vol. VIII

Morvi, HH Thakur Saheb Sir Waghji Ravaji, 1858–1922, vol. II

Morvi State, ex-Ruler of, 1876–1957, vol. V

Moscheles, Felix, 1833–1917, vol. II

Moseley, Charles Herbert Harley, 1857–1933, vol. III

Moseley, Geoffrey, 1882–1953, vol. V

Moseley, Herbert Harvey, 1873–1959, vol. V

Moseley, Sydney Alexander, 1888–1961, vol. VI

Mosely, Alfred, 1855–1917, vol. II

Mosely, Sir Archie Gerard, 1883–1951, vol. V

Moser, Oswald, 1874–1916, vol. II

Moser, Robert Oswald, *died* 1953, vol. V

Moses, Sir Charles Joseph Alfred, 1900–1988, vol. VIII

Moses, James J. H., 1873–1946, vol. IV

Moshier, H. H., 1889–1918, vol. II

Mosley, Sir Alexander, 1847–1927, vol. II

Mosley, Lady Cynthia Blanche, *died* 1933, vol. III

Mosley, Rt Rev. Henry, 1868–1948, vol. IV

Mosley, Brig. Henry Samuel, 1879–1975, vol. VII

Mosley, Sir Oswald, 4th Bt, 1848–1915, vol. I

Mosley, Sir Oswald, 5th Bt, 1873–1928, vol. II

Mosley, Sir Oswald Ernald, 6th Bt, 1896–1980, vol. VII

Moss, Abraham, 1899–1964, vol. VI

Moss, Alfred Allinson, 1912–1990, vol. VIII

Moss, Sir Charles, 1840–1912, vol. I

Moss, Charles Edward, 1872–1930, vol. III

Moss, Sir Edward; *see* Moss, Sir H. E.

Moss, Col Edward Lawton, 1880–1975, vol. VII

Moss, Sir Eric de Vere, 1896–1981, vol. VIII

Moss, Captain Ernest William, 1876–1915, vol. I

Moss, Geoffrey; *see* McNeill-Moss, Major G.

Moss, Sir George Sinclair, 1882–1959, vol. V

Moss, Rev. Henry Whitehead, 1841–1917, vol. II

Moss, Sir (Horace) Edward, *died* 1912, vol. I

Moss, John, 1890–1976, vol. VII

Moss, Sir John Edwards E.; *see* Edwards-Moss.

Moss, Sir John Herbert Theodore E.; *see* Edwards-Moss.

Moss, Kenneth Neville, 1891–1942, vol. IV

Moss, Lewis S., *died* 1903, vol. I

Moss, Brig.-Gen. Lionel Boyd B.; *see* Boyd-Moss.

Moss, Hon. Matthew Lewis, 1863–1946, vol. IV

Moss, Rev. Richard Waddy, 1850–1935, vol. III

Moss, Robert, *died* 1973, vol. VII

Moss, Rosalind Louisa Beaufort, 1890–1990, vol. VIII

Moss, Samuel, 1858–1918, vol. II

Moss, Sir Thomas E.; *see* Edwards-Moss.

Moss, Wilfred, 1867–1938, vol. III

Moss-Blundell, Lt-Col Bryan Seymour; *see* Blundell.

Moss-Blundell, Henry Seymour; *see* Blundell.

Mosscockle, Rita Francis, *died* 1943, vol. IV

Mosse, Lt-Col Arthur Henry Eyre, 1877–1943, vol. IV

Mosse, Charles Benjamin, 1830–1912, vol. I

Mosse, Robert Lee, 1877–1963, vol. VI

Mosse, Rev. William George, 1859–1929, vol. III

Mosses, William, 1858–1943, vol. IV

Mossman, Robert Cockburn, 1870–1940, vol. III

Mossop, Major Albert Isaac, *died* 1936, vol. III

Mossop, Sir Allan George, 1887–1965, vol. VI

Mossop, Joseph Upjohn, 1872–1928, vol. II, vol. III

Mossop, Leonard, 1869–1933, vol. III

Moston, Henry E., 1881–1962, vol. VI

Mostyn, 3rd Baron, 1856–1929, vol. III

Mostyn, 4th Baron, 1885–1965, vol. VI

Mostyn, Sir Basil Antony Trevor, 13th Bt, 1902–1956, vol. V

Mostyn, Most Rev. Francis, 1860–1939, vol. III

Mostyn, Hon. Henry Richard Howel L.; *see* Lloyd-Mostyn.

Mostyn, Rev. Hon. Hugh Wynne, 1838–1930, vol. III

Mostyn, Sir Jeremy John Anthony, 14th Bt, 1933–1988, vol. VIII

Mostyn, Sir Pyers Charles, 10th Bt, 1895–1917, vol. II

Mostyn, Sir Pyers Edward, 12th Bt, 1928–1955, vol. V

Mostyn, Captain Sir Pyers George Joseph, 11th Bt, 1893–1937, vol. III

Mostyn, Sir Pyers William, 9th Bt, 1846–1912, vol. I

Mostyn, Maj.-Gen. Hon. Sir Savage L.; *see* Lloyd-Mostyn.

Mostyn, Tom, 1864–1930, vol. III

Mostyn-Owen, Lt-Col Roger Arthur; *see* Owen.

Moten, Brig. Murray John, 1899–1953, vol. V

Motherwell, Hon. William Richard, 1860–1943, vol. IV

Moti Chand, Raja Sir, *died* 1934, vol. III

Motilal, Raja Bahadur Sir Bansilal, *died* 1935, vol. IV

Motion, Andrew Richard, 1857–1933, vol. III

Motion, Robert Russa, 1867–1940, vol. III (A), vol. IV

Motion, Major Thomas Augustus, *died* 1942, vol. IV

Mott, Sir Adrian Spear, 2nd Bt, 1889–1964, vol. VI

Mott, Sir Basil, 1st Bt, 1859–1938, vol. III

Mott, Edward Spencer, 1844–1910, vol. I

Mott, Sir Frederick Walker, 1853–1926, vol. II

Mott, John Raleigh, 1865–1955, vol. V

Mott, Norman Gilbert, 1910–1987, vol. VIII

Mott, Hon. Maj.-Gen. Stanley Fielder, 1873–1959, vol. V

Mottershead, Peter Michael Hall, 1926–1985, vol. VIII

Mottistone, 1st Baron, 1868–1947, vol. IV

Mottistone, 2nd Baron, 1899–1963, vol. VI

Mottistone, 3rd Baron, 1905–1966, vol. VI

Mottl, Felix, 1856–1911, vol. I

Motton, Paymaster-Rear-Adm. Frederick George, *died* 1935, vol. III

Mottram, James Cecil, 1880–1945, vol. IV

Mottram, Ralph Hale, 1883–1971, vol. VII

Mottram, Sir Richard, 1848–1914, vol. I

Mottram, Sir Thomas Harry, 1859–1937, vol. III

Mottram, Vernon Henry, 1882–1976, vol. VII

Mottram, Rev. William, 1836–1921, vol. II

Motz, Hans, 1909–1987, vol. VIII

Mouat, Sir James, 1815–1899, vol. I

Mouat, John Richard K.; *see* Kay-Mouat.

Moubray, John James, 1857–1928, vol. II

Mould, James, 1893–1958, vol. V

Mould, John, 1890–1964, vol. VI

Mould, Percy, *died* 1923, vol. II

Mould, Sam Carter, 1880–1963, vol. VI

Mould, Col William Thomas, 1865–1935, vol. III

Mould-Graham, Col Robert, 1895–1979, vol. VII

Moulden, Sir Frank Beaumont, 1876–1932, vol. III

Moule, Rev. Arthur Christopher, 1873–1957, vol. V
Moule, Ven. Arthur Evans, 1836–1918, vol. II
Moule, Charles Walter, 1834–1921, vol. II
Moule, Edward Christopher, 1902–1945, vol. IV
Moule, Rt Rev. George Evans, 1828–1912, vol. I
Moule, Rt Rev. Handley Carr Glyn, 1841–1920, vol. II
Moule, Horace Frederick D'Oyly, 1843–1925, vol. II
Moule, Ven. Walter Stephen, *died* 1949, vol. IV
Moule-Evans, David, 1905–1988, vol. VIII
Moullin, Charles William M.; *see* Mansell-Moullin.
Moullin, Eric Balliol, 1893–1963, vol. VI
Moulsdale, Rev. Stephen Richard Platt, 1872–1944, vol. IV
Moult, Thomas Moult, 1885–1974, vol. VII
Moulton, Baron (Life Peer); John Fletcher Moulton, 1844–1921, vol. II
Moulton, Hon. Hugh Fletcher, *died* 1962, vol. VI
Moulton, Rev. James Hope, 1863–1917, vol. II
Moulton, Louise Chandler, *died* 1908, vol. I
Moulton, Richard Green, 1849–1924, vol. II
Moulton, Rev. William Fiddian, 1835–1898, vol. I
Moulton-Barrett, Brig.-Gen. Edward Alfred, 1859–1932, vol. III
Mounet, Jean Sully, 1841–1916, vol. II
Mounsey, Sir George Augustus, 1879–1966, vol. VI
Mounsey, John Edward, 1879–1929, vol. III
Mounsey, John Little, 1852–1933, vol. III
Mounsey, Rt Rev. William Robert Rupert, 1867–1952, vol. V
Mount, Lt-Col Sir Alan Henry Lawrence, 1881–1955, vol. V
Mount, Ven. Francis John, 1831–1903, vol. I
Mount, Sir William Arthur, 1st Bt, 1866–1930, vol. III
Mount, William George, 1824–1906, vol. I
Mount Edgcumbe, 4th Earl of, 1832–1917, vol. II
Mount Edgcumbe, 5th Earl of, 1865–1944, vol. IV
Mount Edgcumbe, 6th Earl of, 1873–1965, vol. VI
Mount Edgcumbe, 7th Earl of, 1903–1982, vol. VIII
Mount Stephen, 1st Baron, 1829–1921, vol. II
Mount Stephen, Lady; (Gian), *died* 1933, vol. III
Mount Temple, 1st Baron, 1867–1939, vol. III
Mountain, Arthur Reginald, 1877–1940, vol. III
Mountain, Lt-Col Sir Brian Edward Stanley, 2nd Bt, 1899–1977, vol. VII
Mountain, Sir Edward Mortimer, 1st Bt, 1872–1948, vol. IV
Mountain, John Francis, 1895–1965, vol. VI
Mountain, Surgeon Rear-Adm. (D) William Leonard, 1908–1980, vol. VII
Mountbatten of Burma, 1st Earl, 1900–1979, vol. VII
Mountbatten of Burma, Countess; (Edwina Cynthia Annette), 1901–1960, vol. V
Mountbatten, Major Lord; Leopold Arthur Louis, 1889–1922, vol. II
Mountcashell, 5th Earl, 1826–1898, vol. I
Mountcashell, 6th Earl, 1829–1915, vol. I
Mountevans, 1st Baron, 1881–1957, vol. V
Mountevans, 2nd Baron, 1918–1974, vol. VII
Mountfield, Alexander Stuart, 1902–1984, vol. VIII
Mountfield, Stuart; *see* Mountfield, A. S.
Mountford, Edward William, 1855–1908, vol. I
Mountford, Sir James Frederick, 1897–1979, vol. VII

Mountford, Lewis James, 1871–1944, vol. IV
Mountgarret, 13th Viscount, 1816–1900, vol. I
Mountgarret, 14th Viscount, 1844–1912, vol. I
Mountgarret, 15th Viscount, 1875–1918, vol. II
Mountgarret, 16th Viscount, 1903–1966, vol. VI
Mountifield, Engr Rear-Adm. James, 1871–1957, vol. V
Mountmorres, 6th Viscount, 1872–1936, vol. III
Mountmorres, 7th Viscount, 1879–1951, vol. V
Mountstephen, Sir William H., 1868–1946, vol. IV
Mountseven, Col Francis Hender, 1844–1935, vol. III
Mousley, Edward Opotiki, 1886–1965, vol. VI
Mowat, Col Sir Alfred Law, 2nd Bt, 1890–1968, vol. VI
Mowat, Rev. Canon John Dickson, *died* 1955, vol. V
Mowat, Sir John Gunn, 1st Bt, 1859–1935, vol. III
Mowat, Brig.-Gen. Magnus, 1875–1953, vol. V
Mowat, Hon. Sir Oliver, 1820–1903, vol. I
Mowat, Robert Anderson, 1843–1925, vol. II
Mowat, Robert Balmain, 1883–1941, vol. IV
Mowatt, Lt-Col Charles Ryder John, 1872–1943, vol. IV
Mowatt, Rt Hon. Sir Francis, 1837–1919, vol. II
Mowbray, 24th Baron, Segrave, 25th Baron, and Stourton, 21st Baron, 1867–1936, vol. III
Mowbray, 25th Baron, Segrave, 26th Baron, and Stourton, 22nd Baron, 1895–1965, vol. VI
Mowbray, Rev. Sir Edmund George Lionel, 4th Bt, 1859–1919, vol. II
Mowbray, Sir George Robert, 5th Bt, 1899–1969, vol. VI
Mowbray, Major John Leslie, 1875–1916, vol. II
Mowbray, Rt Hon. Sir John Robert, 1st Bt, 1815–1899, vol. I
Mowbray, Sir Reginald Ambrose, 3rd Bt, 1852–1916, vol. II
Mowbray, Robert, 1877–1947, vol. IV
Mowbray, Sir Robert Gray Cornish, 2nd Bt, 1850–1916, vol. II
Mower, Sara M.; *see* Jordan, S. M.
Mowle, William Stewart, 1867–1935, vol. III
Mowlem, Rainsford, 1902–1986, vol. VIII
Mowll, Rt Rev. Edward Worsfold, 1881–1964, vol. VI
Mowll, Most Rev. Howard West Kilvinton, 1890–1958, vol. V
Mowrer, Edgar Ansel, 1892–1977, vol. VII
Moxham, Sir Harry Cuthbertson, *died* 1965, vol. VI
Moxon, Col Charles Carter, 1866–1924, vol. II
Moxon, Sir John, *died* 1943, vol. IV
Moxon, Rev. Canon Reginald Stewart, *died* 1950, vol. IV
Moxon, Ven. Robert Julius, vol. II
Moxon, Rev. Preb. Thomas Allen, 1877–1943, vol. IV
Moyer, L. Clare, 1887–1958, vol. V
Moyers, Sir George, 1836–1916, vol. II
Moyes, Rt Rev. John Stoward, 1884–1972, vol. VII
Moyes, William Henry, *died* 1926, vol. II
Moylan, Sir John Fitzgerald, 1882–1967, vol. VI
Moyle, Baron (Life Peer); Arthur Moyle, 1894–1974, vol. VII
Moynan, R. T., 1856–1906, vol. I
Moyne, 1st Baron, 1880–1944, vol. IV

Moynihan, 1st Baron, 1865–1936, vol. III
Moynihan, 2nd Baron, 1906–1965, vol. VI
Moynihan, Most Rev. Denis, 1885–1975, vol. VII
Moynihan, Rodrigo, 1910–1990, vol. VIII
Moyse, Charles E., 1852–1924, vol. II
Moysey, Maj.-Gen. Charles John, 1840–1922, vol. II
Moysey, Edward Luttrell, died 1970, vol. VI
Moysey, Henry Luttrell, 1849–1918, vol. II
Mozley, Lt-Col Edward Newman, 1875–1950, vol. IV
Mozley, Rev. John Kenneth, 1883–1946, vol. IV
Muchmore, Alfred, 1893–1962, vol. VI
Mucklow, Graham Fernie, 1894–1973, vol. VII
Mudaliar, Diwan Bahadur Sir Arcot Lakshmanaswami, 1887–1974, vol. VII
Mudaliar, Diwan Bahadur Sir Arcot Ramaswami, 1887–1976, vol. VII
Mudaliar, Dewan Bahadur V. Shanmuga, 1874–1953, vol. V
Mudaliyar, Rao Bahadur C. Jumbulingam, died 1906, vol. I
Muddiman, Sir Alexander Phillips, 1875–1928, vol. II
Muddock, J. E. Preston, died 1934, vol. III
Mudford, W. H., 1839–1916, vol. II
Mudge, Brig.-Gen. Arthur, 1871–1958, vol. V
Mudhol, Lt Meherban Raja Sir Malojirao Vyankatrao Raje Ghorpade, 1884–1937, vol. III
Mudholkar, Hon. Rao Bahadur Rangnath Narsinh, 1857–1921, vol. II
Mudie, Sir Francis; see Mudie, Sir R. F.
Mudie, Sir (Robert) Francis, 1890–1976, vol. VII
Mudie, Brig. Thomas Couper, 1880–1948, vol. IV
Mudie-Smith, Richard, 1877–1916, vol. II
Muecke, Francis Frederick, 1879–1945, vol. IV
Mueller, Sir Ferdinand von, 1825–1897, vol. I
Muggeridge, Douglas Thomas, 1928–1985, vol. VIII
Muggeridge, Henry Thomas, 1864–1942, vol. IV
Muggeridge, Malcolm; see Muggeridge, T. M.
Muggeridge, (Thomas) Malcolm, 1903–1990, vol. VIII
Mugliston, Francis Hugh, 1886–1932, vol. III
Muhammad, Valiyaveettil Abdulaziz Seyid, 1923–1985, vol. VIII
Muhammad Amir Hasan Khan, 1849–1903, vol. I
Muhammad Fakhr-ud-Din, Khan Bahadur Sir Saiyed, died 1933, vol. III
Muhammad Iqbal, Sheikh Sir, 1876–1938, vol. III
Muhammad Rafiq, Sir, died 1929, vol. III
Muhammed Aslam Khan, Hon. Col Nawab, died 1914, vol. I
Muhrman, Henry, 1854–1916, vol. II
Muil, Maj.-Gen. David John, 1898–1982, vol. VIII
Muir, Air Cdre Adam, 1908–1986, vol. VIII
Muir, Sir (Alexander) Kay, 2nd Bt, 1868–1951, vol. V
Muir, Col Archibald Huleatt Huntly, 1886–1948, vol. IV
Muir, Augustus; see Muir, C. A. C.
Muir, (Charles) Augustus (Carlow), 1892–1989, vol. VIII
Muir, Col Charles Wemyss, 1850–1920, vol. II
Muir, Sir David John, 1916–1986, vol. VIII
Muir, Sir Edward Francis, 1905–1979, vol. VII
Muir, Sir Edward Grainger, 1906–1973, vol. VII
Muir, Edwin, 1887–1959, vol. V
Muir, Ernest, 1880–1974, vol. VII

Muir, Gordon; see Muir, W. A. G.
Muir, James, 1875–1945, vol. IV
Muir, James, died 1960, vol. V
Muir, Sir John, 1st Bt, 1828–1903, vol. I
Muir, John, 1838–1914, vol. I
Muir, Lt-Col John Balderstone, died 1955, vol. V
Muir, John Cochran, 1902–1981, vol. VIII
Muir, John Gerald Grainger, 1918–1990, vol. VIII
Muir, John William, 1879–1931, vol. III
Muir, Sir Kay; see Muir, Sir A. K.
Muir, Matthew Moncrieff Pattison, 1848–1931, vol. III
Muir, Rt Rev. Pearson M'Adam, 1846–1924, vol. II
Muir, Percival Horace, 1894–1979, vol. VII
Muir, Ramsay, 1872–1941, vol. IV
Muir, Sir Richard David, 1857–1924, vol. II
Muir, Sir Robert, 1864–1959, vol. V
Muir, Ronald James Samuel, 1899–1960, vol. V
Muir, Ronald John K.; see Kerr-Muir.
Muir, Sir Thomas, 1844–1934, vol. III
Muir, Ward, 1878–1927, vol. II
Muir, Sir William, 1819–1905, vol. I
Muir, William, 1844–1929, vol. III
Muir, (William Archibald) Gordon, 1931–1981, vol. VIII
Muir, Lt-Col Wingate Wemyss, 1879–1966, vol. VI
Muir-Mackenzie, 1st Baron, 1845–1930, vol. III
Muir-Mackenzie, Sir Alexander, 3rd Bt, 1840–1909, vol. I
Muir-Mackenzie, Sir John William Pitt, 1854–1916, vol. II
Muir Mackenzie, Kenneth James, 1882–1932, vol. III
Muir-Mackenzie, Montague Johnstone, 1847–1919, vol. II
Muir-Mackenzie, Sir Robert Cecil, 5th Bt, 1891–1918, vol. II
Muir Mackenzie, Sir Robert Henry, 6th Bt, 1917–1970, vol. VI
Muir-Mackenzie, Lt-Col Sir Robert Smythe, 4th Bt, 1841–1918, vol. II
Muirhead, Alexander, died 1920, vol. II
Muirhead, Alexander, 1859–1935, vol. III
Muirhead, Lt-Col Anthony John, 1890–1939, vol. III
Muirhead, Charles Alexander, 1888–1967, vol. VI
Muirhead, David, died 1930, vol. III
Muirhead, Findlay, 1860–1935, vol. III
Muirhead, James Fullarton, 1853–1934, vol. III
Muirhead, Lt-Col James Ingram, 1893–1964, vol. VI
Muirhead, John, 1863–1927, vol. III
Muirhead, John Henry, 1855–1940, vol. III
Muirhead, Sir John Spencer, 1889–1972, vol. VII
Muirhead, (Litellus) Russell, 1896–1976, vol. VII
Muirhead, Peter Haig, died 1958, vol. V
Muirhead, Russell; see Muirhead, L. R.
Mukerjee, Most Rev. Arabinda Nath, 1892–1970, vol. VI (AII)
Mukerjee, Radhakamal, 1889–1968, vol. VI
Mukerjee, Air Marshal Subroto, 1911–1960, vol. V
Mukerji, Sir Lal Gopal, 1874–1942, vol. IV
Mukerji, Sir Manmatha Nath, 1874–1942, vol. IV
Mukerji, Rai Bahadur P. N., 1882–1965, vol. VI
Mukle, May, 1880–1963, vol. VI
Mulcahy, Hon. Edward, 1850–1927, vol. II

Mulcahy, Maj.-Gen. Sir Francis Edward, 1857–1940, vol. III

Mulcahy, Gen. Richard, 1886–1971, vol. VII

Muldoon, John, 1865–1938, vol. III

Mules, Sir Charles; *see* Mules, Sir H. C.

Mules, Rt Rev. Charles Oliver, 1837–1927, vol. II

Mules, Sir (Horace) Charles, 1856–1939, vol. III

Mulford, Clarence Edward, 1883–1956, vol. V

Mulhall, John Archibald, 1899–1971, vol. VII

Mulhall, Michael G., 1836–1900, vol. I

Mulhern, Most Rev. Edward C., 1863–1943, vol. IV

Mulholland, Hon. Alfred John, 1856–1938, vol. III

Mulholland, Hon. (Andrew) Edward (Somerset), 1882–1914, vol. I

Mulholland, Gp Captain Denis Osmond, 1891–1949, vol. IV

Mulholland, Hon. Edward; *see* Mulholland, Hon. A. E. S.

Mulholland, Hon. (Godfrey) John (Arthur Murray Lyle), 1892–1948, vol. IV

Mulholland, Rt Hon. Sir Henry George Hill, 1st Bt, 1888–1971, vol. VII

Mulholland, Hon. John; *see* Mulholland, Hon. G. J. A. M. L.

Mulholland, Hon. Mrs John, (Olivia Vernon), 1902–1984, vol. VIII

Mulholland, Hon. Olivia Vernon; *see* Mulholland, Hon. Mrs John.

Mulholland, Rosa; *see* Gilbert, Rosa, (Lady Gilbert).

Mulholland, W., 1843–1907, vol. I

Mulholland, Sir Walter; *see* Mulholland, Sir W. W.

Mulholland, Sir (William) Walter, 1887–1971, vol. VII

Mulji, Rao Sahib Sir Vasanji Trikamji, 1866–1925, vol. II, vol. III

Mulla, Rt Hon. Sir Dinshah Fardunji, 1868–1934, vol. III

Mullally, Gerald Thomas, 1887–1969, vol. VI

Mullaly, Maj.-Gen. Sir Herbert, 1860–1932, vol. III

Mullaly, Joseph John, 1853–1936, vol. III

Mullan, Charles Seymour, 1893–1969, vol. VI

Mullen, Benjamin Henry, 1862–1925, vol. II

Mullen, Lt-Col John Lawrence William F.; *see* Ffrench-Mullen.

Mullen, Lt-Col Leslie Miltiades, 1882–1943, vol. IV

Mulleneux, Captain Hugh Bowring, 1878–1947, vol. IV

Mulleneux-Grayson, Louise Mary, (Lady Mulleneux-Grayson); *see* Dale, Louise.

Mullens, Sir Harold Hill, 1900–1980, vol. VII

Mullens, Sir John Ashley, 1869–1937, vol. III

Mullens, Maj.-Gen. Richard Lucas, 1871–1952, vol. V

Mullens, Sir William John Herbert de Wette, 1909–1975, vol. VII

Müller, Rt Hon. Friedrich M.; *see* Max-Müller.

Muller, Col George Herbert, 1856–1932, vol. III

Muller, Hermann Joseph, 1890–1967, vol. VI

Muller, Hon. Hilgard, 1914–1985, vol. VIII

Müller, Hugo, *died* 1915, vol. I

Muller, J. P., 1866–1938, vol. III

Muller, Lt-Col John, 1883–1942, vol. IV

Muller, Oswald Valdemar, 1868–1900, vol. I

Müller, W. Max, 1862–1919, vol. II

Muller, Walter Angus, 1898–1970, vol. VI

Muller, Sir William Grenfell M.; *see* Max-Muller.

Mullick, Sir Basanta Kumar, 1868–1931, vol. III

Mulligan, Col Hugh Waddell, 1901–1982, vol. VIII

Mulligan, James, 1847–1937, vol. III

Mulliken, Robert Sanderson, 1896–1986, vol. VIII

Mullin, Daniel, *born* 1860, vol. III

Mulliner, Ven. Harold George, 1897–1946, vol. IV

Mullinger, James Bass, *died* 1917, vol. II

Mullings, Sir Clement Tudway, 1874–1962, vol. VI

Mullings, Frank Coningsby, 1881–1953, vol. V

Mullins, Arthur, 1895–1963, vol. VI

Mullins, Brian Percival, 1920–1990, vol. VIII

Mullins, Major Charles Herbert, *died* 1916, vol. II

Mullins, Claud, 1887–1968, vol. VI

Mullins, Gen. George James Herbert, *died* 1943, vol. IV

Mullins, Lt-Col George Lane, 1862–1918, vol. II

Mullins, Hon. John Lane, 1857–1939, vol. III

Mulock, Air Cdre Redford Henry, 1886–1961, vol. VI

Mulock, Rt Hon. Sir William, 1844–1944, vol. IV

Mulvany, Charles Mathew, 1867–1945, vol. IV

Mulvany, T. R., 1839–1907, vol. I

Mulvany, Most Rev. Thomas, *died* 1943, vol. IV

Mulvey, Anthony, 1882–1957, vol. V

Mulvey, Thomas, 1863–1935, vol. III

Mumford, A. Harold, 1864–1939, vol. III

Mumford, Sir Albert Henry, 1903–1989, vol. VIII

Mumford, Henry Plevy, 1862–1941, vol. IV

Mumford, L(awrence) Quincy, 1903–1982, vol. VIII

Mumford, Lewis, 1895–1990, vol. VIII

Mummery, Sir Hugh Evelyn L.; *see* Lockhart-Mummery.

Mummery, John Howard, 1847–1926, vol. II

Mummery, John Percy L.; *see* Lockhart-Mummery.

Mumtazud Dowlah Muhammad Faiyaz Ali Khan; *see* Faiyaz Ali Khan.

Mun, Adrien Albert Marie, Comte de, 1841–1914, vol. I

Munby, Alan Noel Latimer, 1913–1974, vol. VII

Munby, Lt-Col Aldwin Montgomery, 1882–1939, vol. III

Munby, Lt-Col Joseph Ernest, 1881–1962, vol. VI

Muncaster, 5th Baron, 1834–1917, vol. II

Muncaster, Claude, 1903–1974, vol. VII

Muncey, Rev. Edward Howard Parker, 1886–1954, vol. V

Munch, Charles, 1891–1968, vol. VI

Mundahl, Henry Smethurst, 1865–1938, vol. III

Munday, Charles Frederick, 1868–1948, vol. IV

Munday, John A., 1863–1932, vol. III

Munday, Luther, 1857–1922, vol. II

Munday, Maj.-Gen. Richard Cleveland, 1867–1952, vol. V

Munday, Sir William Luscombe, 1865–1952, vol. V

Mundelein, Cardinal George William, 1872–1939, vol. III

Mundella, Rt Hon. Anthony John, 1825–1897, vol. I

Mundy, Alfred Edward Miller, 1849–1920, vol. II

Mundy, Adm. Godfrey Harry Brydges, 1860–1928, vol. II

Mundy, John Cloudesley, 1900–1971, vol. VII

Mundy, Sir Otto, 1887–1958, vol. V

Mundy, Talbot, 1879–1940, vol. III
Munford, James, 1852–1932, vol. III
Muni, Paul, 1895–1967, vol. VI
Munir Bey, Sir Mehmed, 1890–1957, vol. V
Munn, Rt Rev. Eric George, 1903–1968, vol. VI
Munn, Mrs Marguerite; see Bryant, M.
Munn, Lt-Col Reginald George, died 1947, vol. IV
Munn, Rear-Adm. William James, 1911–1989, vol. VIII
Munnings, Sir Alfred J., 1878–1959, vol. V
Munro, Sir Alan Whiteside, 1898–1968, vol. VI
Munro, Maj.-Gen. Archibald Campbell, 1886–1961, vol. VI
Munro, Sir Arthur Herman, 14th Bt (cr 1634), 1893–1972, vol. VII
Munro, Sir Arthur Talbot, 13th Bt (cr 1634), 1866–1953, vol. V
Munro, Sir Campbell, 3rd Bt (cr 1825), 1823–1913, vol. I
Munro, C(harles) K.; see MacMullan, C. W. K.
Munro, Air Vice-Marshal Sir David, 1878–1952, vol. V
Munro, Lt-Col David Campbell Duncan, 1885–1974, vol. VII
Munro, Captain Donald John, 1865–1952, vol. V
Munro, Sir George Hamilton, 12th Bt (cr 1634), 1864–1945, vol. IV
Munro, Sir Gordon; see Munro, Sir R. G.
Munro, Lt-Gen. Gustavus Francis, 1835–1908, vol. I
Munro, Sir Hector, 11th Bt (cr 1634), 1849–1935, vol. III
Munro, Sir Henry, 1842–1921, vol. II
Munro, Sir Hugh Thomas, 4th Bt (cr 1825), 1856–1919, vol. II
Munro, John, died 1930, vol. III
Munro, John Arthur Ruskin, 1864–1944, vol. IV
Munro, Leo, 1878–1957, vol. V
Munro, Sir Leslie Knox, 1901–1974, vol. VII
Munro, Col Lewis, 1859–1927, vol. II
Munro, Neil, 1864–1930, vol. III
Munro, Patrick, 1883–1942, vol. IV
Munro, Sir (Richard) Gordon, 1895–1967, vol. VI
Munro, Robert, 1835–1920, vol. II
Munro, Robert Wilson, 1915–1985, vol. VIII
Munro, Sir Thomas, 2nd Bt (er 1825), 1819–1901, vol. I
Munro, Sir Thomas, 1866–1923, vol. II
Munro, Thomas Arthur Howard, 1905–1966, vol. VI
Munro, Sir (Thomas) Torquil (Alfonso), 5th Bt, 1901–1985, vol. VIII
Munro, Sir Torquil; see Munro, Sir T. T. A.
Munro, William Bennett, 1875–1957, vol. V
Munro, William Thow, 1884–1948, vol. IV
Munro-Lucas-Tooth, Sir Hugh Vere Huntly Duff, 1st Bt, 1903–1985, vol. VIII
Munroe, Sir Harry C.; see Courthope-Munroe.
Munroe, Lt-Col Hon. Hugh Edwin, 1879–1947, vol. IV
Munrow, David John, 1942–1976, vol. VII
Munrow, William Davis, 1903–1986, vol. VIII
Munsey, Frank Andrew, 1854–1925, vol. II
Munster, 2nd Earl of, 1824–1901, vol. I
Munster, 3rd Earl of, 1859–1902, vol. I
Munster, 4th Earl of, 1862–1928, vol. II

Munster, 5th Earl of, 1906–1975, vol. VII
Munster, 6th Earl of, 1899–1983, vol. VIII
Munster, Countess of; (Wilhelmina), 1830–1906, vol. I
Münster Derneburg, Prince, 1820–1902, vol. I
Münsterberg, Hugo, 1863–1916, vol. II
Munthe, Axel, 1857–1949, vol. IV
Muntz, Alan; see Muntz, F. A. I.
Muntz, (Frederick) Alan (Irving), 1899–1985, vol. VIII
Muntz, Frederick Ernest, 1845–1920, vol. II
Muntz, Sir Gerard Albert, 2nd Bt, 1864–1927, vol. II
Muntz, Sir Gerard Philip Graves, 3rd Bt, 1917–1940, vol. III (A), vol. IV
Muntz, Godric; see Muntz, T. G. A.
Muntz, Hope; see Muntz, I. H.
Muntz, (Isabelle) Hope, 1907–1981, vol. VIII
Muntz, Sir Philip Albert, 1st Bt, 1839–1908, vol. I
Muntz, Thomas Godric Aylett, 1906–1986, vol. VIII
Murchie, Lt-Gen. John Carl, 1895–1966, vol. VI
Murchison, Sir (Charles) Kenneth, 1872–1952, vol. V
Murchison, Sir Kenneth; see Murchison, Sir C. K.
Murchison, Very Rev. Thomas Moffat, 1907–1984, vol. VIII
Murdoch, Air Marshal Sir Alister Murray, 1912–1984, vol. VIII
Murdoch, Charles, 1902–1962, vol. VI (AII)
Murdoch, Charles, 1925–1979, vol. VII
Murdoch, Charles Stewart, 1838–1908, vol. I
Murdoch, Charles Townshend, 1837–1898, vol. I
Murdoch, Hector B.; see Burn-Murdoch.
Murdoch, James, 1856–1921, vol. II
Murdoch, Lt-Col Sir James Anderson, 1867–1939, vol. III
Murdoch, Rev. Canon James McGibbon B.; see Burn-Murdoch.
Murdoch, Maj.-Gen. Sir John Francis B.; see Burn-Murdoch.
Murdoch, John Smith, 1863–1945, vol. IV
Murdoch, Sir Keith Arthur, 1886–1952, vol. V
Murdoch, Richard Bernard, 1907–1990, vol. VIII
Murdoch, Hon. Thomas, 1868–1946, vol. IV
Murdoch, W. G. Blaikie, 1880–1934, vol. III
Murdoch, W. G. Burn; see Burn-Murdoch.
Murdoch, Sir Walter, 1874–1970, vol. VI
Murdoch, William, 1888–1942, vol. IV
Murdoch, William Lloyd, 1855–1911, vol. I
Murdock, Kenneth Ballard, 1895–1975, vol. VII
Mure, Geoffrey Reginald Gilchrist, 1893–1979, vol. VII
Mure, William, 1898–1977, vol. VII
Mure, William John, 1845–1924, vol. II
Murfree, Mary Noailles, died 1922, vol. II, vol. III
Murie, James, 1830–1925, vol. II
Muriel, Rev. Herbert Claude, 1867–1939, vol. III
Murison, Alexander Falconer, 1847–1934, vol. III
Murison, Alfred Ross, 1891–1968, vol. VI
Murison, Maj.-Gen. Charles Alexander Phipps, 1894–1981, vol. VIII
Murison, Sir (James) William, 1872–1945, vol. IV
Murison, Sir William; see Murison, Sir J. M.
Murland, William, died 1926, vol. II
Murless, Sir (Charles Francis) Noel, 1910–1987, vol. VIII

Murless, Sir Noel; *see* Sir C. F. N.

Murnaghan, Francis Dominic, 1893–1976, vol. VII

Murnaghan, George, 1847–1929, vol. III

Murnaghan, James Augustine, 1881–1973, vol. VII

Murphy, Sir Alexander Paterson, 1892–1976, vol. VII

Murphy, Alfred John, 1901–1980, vol. VII

Murphy, Hon. Charles, 1863–1935, vol. III

Murphy, Brig.-Gen. Cyril Francis de Sales, 1882–1961, vol. VI

Murphy, Hon. Denis, 1870–1947, vol. IV

Murphy, Sir Dermod Art Pelly, 1914–1975, vol. VII

Murphy, Rt Hon. Edward Sullivan, 1880–1945, vol. IV

Murphy, Sir Ellis; *see* Murphy, Sir O. E. J.

Murphy, Emily F., *died* 1933, vol. III

Murphy, Emmett Patrick, 1887–1960, vol. V

Murphy, Hon. Frank, 1890–1949, vol. IV

Murphy, Air Vice-Marshal Frederick John, 1892–1969, vol. VI

Murphy, George Fitzgerald, 1850–1920, vol. II

Murphy, Col George Francis, 1883–1962, vol. VI

Murphy, Sir George Francis, 2nd Bt (*cr* 1912), 1881–1963, vol. VI

Murphy, Col George Patterson, 1883–1938, vol. III

Murphy, Lt-Col Gerald Patrick, 1888–1978, vol. VII

Murphy, Harold Lawson, 1882–1942, vol. IV

Murphy, Most Rev. Henry, 1912–1973, vol. VII

Murphy, Rev. Hugh Davis, 1849–1927, vol. II

Murphy, Rt Hon. James, 1826–1901, vol. I

Murphy, James Francis, 1893–1949, vol. IV

Murphy, Sir James Joseph, 1st Bt (*cr* 1903), 1843–1922, vol. II

Murphy, James Keogh, 1869–1916, vol. II

Murphy, Very Rev. Jeremiah Matthias, *died* 1955, vol. V

Murphy, Very Rev. John, vol. II

Murphy, John, 1871–1930, vol. III (A), vol. IV

Murphy, Rev. John, 1876–1949, vol. IV

Murphy, Rt Rev. John Baptist Tuohill, 1854–1926, vol. II

Murphy, John Harvey, 1862–1924, vol. II

Murphy, John Patrick, 1831–1907, vol. I

Murphy, (John) Pelly, 1909–1979, vol. VII

Murphy, Lionel Keith, 1922–1986, vol. VIII

Murphy, Martin, 1832–1926, vol. II

Murphy, Martin Joseph, 1862–1919, vol. II

Murphy, Sir Michael, 1st Bt (*cr* 1912), 1845–1925, vol. II

Murphy, Neville Richard, 1890–1971, vol. VII

Murphy, Sir (Oswald) Ellis (Joseph), 1895–1980, vol. VII (AII)

Murphy, Patrick Charles, 1868–1925, vol. II

Murphy, Pelly; *see* Murphy, J. P.

Murphy, Maj.-Gen. Richard, 1896–1971, vol. VII

Murphy, Robert Daniel, 1894–1978, vol. VII

Murphy, Sir Shirley Forster, 1848–1923, vol. II

Murphy, Stephen Dunlop, 1921–1990, vol. VIII

Murphy, Sir Stephen James, *died* 1950, vol. IV

Murphy, Rev. William, 1872–1943, vol. IV

Murphy, Sir William Lindsay, 1887–1965, vol. VI

Murphy, William Lombard, *died* 1943, vol. IV

Murphy, William Martin, 1844–1919, vol. II

Murphy, William Parry, 1892–1987, vol. VIII

Murphy, Col William Reed, 1849–1927, vol. II

Murrant, Sir Ernest Henry, 1889–1974, vol. VII

Murray, Rt Hon. Lord; Charles David Murray, 1866–1936, vol. III

Murray of Elibank, 1st Baron, 1870–1920, vol. II

Murray of Gravesend, Baron (Life Peer); Albert James Murray, 1930–1980, vol. VII

Murray, Abijah, *died* 1912, vol. I

Murray, Adam George, 1893–1966, vol. VI

Murray, Alan James Ruthven-, 1900–1959, vol. V

Murray of Blackbarony, Sir Alan John Digby, 14th Bt (*cr* 1628), 1909–1978, vol. VII

Murray, Alastair Campbell, 1895–1957, vol. V

Murray, Albert E., 1849–1924, vol. II

Murray, Albert Victor, 1890–1967, vol. VI

Murray, Col Alexander, 1850–1910, vol. I

Murray, Alexander Davidson, 1840–1907, vol. I

Murray, Alexander Henry Hallam, 1854–1934, vol. III

Murray, Major Alexander Penrose, 1863–1926, vol. II

Murray, Sir Alexander Robertson, 1872–1956, vol. V

Murray, Alexander Stuart, 1841–1904, vol. I

Murray, Sir Alistair; *see* Murray, Sir R. A.

Murray, Alma, 1854–1945, vol. IV

Murray, Col Andrew, 1837–1915, vol. I

Murray, Hon. Andrew David, 1863–1901, vol. I

Murray, Sir Andrew Hunter Arbuthnot, 1903–1977, vol. VII

Murray, Angus, 1919–1982, vol. VIII

Murray, Sir Angus Johnston, *died* 1968, vol. VI

Murray, Maj.-Gen. Anthony Hepburn, 1840–1917, vol. II

Murray, Gen. Sir Archibald James, 1860–1945, vol. IV

Murray, Lt-Col Arthur Alexander W.; *see* Wolfe-Murray.

Murray, Lt-Col Arthur E.; *see* Erskine-Murray.

Murray, Adm. Arthur John Layard, 1886–1959, vol. V

Murray, Col Arthur Mordaunt, 1852–1920, vol. II

Murray, Catherine Joan Suzette; *see* Gauvain, C. J. S.

Murray, Charles, 1864–1941, vol. IV

Murray, Lt-Col Charles Crawford, 1863–1939, vol. III

Murray, Rt Hon. Charles David; *see* Murray, Rt Hon. Lord.

Murray, Charles de Bois, 1891–1974, vol. VII

Murray, Gp-Captain Charles Geoffrey, 1880–1962, vol. VI

Murray, Rt Rev. Charles Herbert, 1899–1950, vol. IV

Murray, Charles James, 1851–1929, vol. III

Murray, Charles Oliver, *died* 1924, vol. II

Murray, Charles Stewart, 1858–1903, vol. I

Murray, Charles Wadsworth, 1894–1945, vol. IV

Murray, Col Sir (Charles) Wyndham, 1844–1928, vol. II

Murray, Colin Alexander, 1847–1913, vol. I

Murray, Colin Robert Baillie, 1892–1979, vol. VII

Murray, Lt-Col Cyril Francis Tyrell, 1863–1929, vol. III

Murray, David, 1842–1928, vol. II

Murray, Sir David, 1849–1933, vol. III

Murray, David Christie, 1847–1907, vol. I

Murray, Col David Keith, 1865–1952, vol. V
Murray, David King; *see* Birnam, Hon. Lord.
Murray, David Leslie, 1888–1962, vol. VI
Murray of Blackbarony, Sir Digby, 11th Bt (*cr* 1628), 1829–1906, vol. I
Murray, Donald, 1862–1923, vol. II
Murray, Col Donald Norman Watson, 1876–1945, vol. IV
Murray, Rev. Canon Edmund Theodore, 1877–1969, vol. VI
Murray, Edward C.; *see* Croft-Murray.
Murray, Paymaster Rear-Adm. Edward F., 1877–1933, vol. III
Murray, Lt-Col Sir Edward Robert, 13th Bt (*cr* 1626), 1875–1958, vol. V
Murray, Sir Evelyn; *see* Murray, Sir G. E. P.
Murray, Everitt George Dunne, 1890–1964, vol. VI
Murray, Brig. Francis Mackenzie, 1880–1958, vol. V
Murray, Sir (Francis) Ralph (Hay), 1908–1983, vol. VIII
Murray, Col Frank, 1864–1917, vol. II
Murray, Ven. Frederic Richardson, 1845–1925, vol. II
Murray, Rev. Frederick William, *died* 1913, vol. I
Murray, Sir George, 1865–1942, vol. IV
Murray, Brig. Sir (George David) Keith, 1898–1965, vol. VI
Murray, Sir (George) Evelyn (Pemberton), 1880–1947, vol. IV
Murray, (George) Gilbert (Aimé), 1866–1957, vol. V
Murray, Hon. George Henry, 1861–1929, vol. III
Murray, Rt Hon. Sir George Herbert, 1849–1936, vol. III
Murray, Hon. Sir George John Robert, 1863–1942, vol. IV
Murray, George McIntosh, 1900–1970, vol. VI
Murray, George Redmayne, *died* 1939, vol. III
Murray, George Robert Milne, 1858–1911, vol. I
Murray, Sir George Sheppard, 1851–1928, vol. II
Murray, George William Welsh, 1885–1966, vol. VI
Murray, Most Rev. Gerald, *died* 1951, vol. V
Murray, Gilbert; *see* Murray, G. G. A.
Murray, Gladstone; *see* Murray, W. E. G.
Murray, Greig; *see* Murray, J. G.
Murray, Lt-Col Henry William, 1883–1966, vol. VI
Murray, Lt-Col Herbert Edward, 1889–1951, vol. V
Murray, Sir Herbert Harley, 1829–1904, vol. I
Murray, Herbert Leith, 1880–1932, vol. III
Murray, Rear-Adm. Herbert Patrick William George, 1880–1958, vol. V
Murray, Gen. Sir Horatius, 1903–1989, vol. VIII
Murray, Howard, 1859–1930, vol. III
Murray, Lt-Col Howard, 1876–1934, vol. III
Murray, Sir Hubert; *see* Murray, Sir J. H. P.
Murray, Hubert Leonard, 1886–1963, vol. VI
Murray, Hubert Montague, 1855–1907, vol. I
Murray, Sir Hugh, 1861–1941, vol. IV
Murray, Ian, 1899–1974, vol. VII
Murray, Sir (Jack) Keith, 1889–1979, vol. VII
Murray, Rt Rev. James, 1828–1909, vol. I
Murray, James, 1865–1914, vol. I
Murray, Sir James, 1850–1932, vol. III
Murray, James Alexander, 1873–1950, vol. IV

Murray, Sir James Augustus Henry, 1837–1915, vol. I
Murray, James Dalton, 1911–1984, vol. VIII
Murray, James Dixon, 1887–1965, vol. VI
Murray, James Greig, 1919–1987, vol. VIII
Murray, James Whiteford, *died* 1941, vol. IV
Murray, Lt-Gen. Sir James Wolfe, 1853–1919, vol. II
Murray, Captain James Wolfe, 1880–1930, vol. III
Murray, Sir John, 1841–1914, vol. I
Murray, Sir John, 1851–1928, vol. II
Murray, John, 1883–1937, vol. III
Murray, John, 1863–1943, vol. IV
Murray, John, 1871–1954, vol. V
Murray, John, 1879–1964, vol. VI
Murray, Sir John, 1884–1967, vol. VI
Murray, Engr Captain John Adam, 1860–1948, vol. IV
Murray of Blackbarony, Sir John Digby, 12th Bt (*cr* 1628), 1867–1938, vol. III
Murray, John George, 1864–1953, vol. V
Murray, Lt-Col John Hanna, *died* 1959, vol. V
Murray, Sir (John) Hubert (Plunkett), 1861–1940, vol. III
Murray, Gen. Sir John Irvine, 1826–1902, vol. I
Murray, Sir John Murray, 1888–1976, vol. VII
Murray, Rev. John Oswald, 1869–1943, vol. IV
Murray, Rev. John Owen Farquhar, 1858–1944, vol. IV
Murray, John Pears, 1866–1947, vol. IV (A), vol. V
Murray, Sir (John) Stanley, 1884–1971, vol. VII
Murray, Brig. Sir Keith; *see* Murray, Brig. Sir G. D. K.
Murray, Sir Keith; *see* Murray, Sir J. K.
Murray, Keith Day Pearce, 1892–1981, vol. VIII
Murray, Keith William, 1860–1922, vol. II
Murray of Blackbarony, Sir Kenelm Bold, 13th Bt (*cr* 1628), 1898–1959, vol. V
Murray, Col Kenelm Digby, 1839–1915, vol. I
Murray, Col Kenelm Digby Bold, 1879–1947, vol. IV
Murray, Sir Kenneth, 1891–1979, vol. III
Murray, Rear-Adm. Leonard Warren, 1896–1971, vol. VII
Murray, Lt-Col Sir Malcolm Donald, 1867–1938, vol. III
Murray, (Malcolm) Patrick, 1905–1979, vol. VII
Murray, Margaret Alice, 1863–1963, vol. VI
Murray, Margaret Mary Alberta, *died* 1974, vol. VII
Murray, Sir Norman McIver, *died* 1934, vol. III
Murray, Sir Oswyn Alexander Ruthven, 1873–1936, vol. III
Murray, Patrick; *see* Murray, M. P.
Murray, Sir Patrick Ian Keith, 10th Bt (*cr* 1673), 1904–1962, vol. VI
Murray, Sir Patrick Keith, 8th Bt (*cr* 1673), 1835–1921, vol. II
Murray, Philip, 1886–1952, vol. V
Murray, Sir Ralph; *see* Murray, Sir F. R. H.
Murray, Richard, 1865–1925, vol. II
Murray, Sir Robert, 1846–1924, vol. II
Murray, Robert, 1870–1950, vol. IV
Murray, Sir (Robert) Alistair, 1896–1973, vol. VII
Murray, Col Robert Davidson, 1851–1920, vol. II
Murray, Rev. Canon Robert Henry, *died* 1947, vol. IV
Murray, Robert Howson, 1882–1960, vol. V

Murray, Maj.-Gen. Robert Hunter, 1847–1925, vol. II

Murray, Rear-Adm. Ronald Gordon, 1898–1975, vol. VII

Murray, Major Hon. Ronald Thomas Graham, 1875–1934, vol. III

Murray, Col Shadwell John, 1867–1940, vol. III

Murray, Sir Stanley; see Murray, Sir J. S.

Murray, Lt-Col Stewart George Cromartie, 1884–1932, vol. III

Murray, T. C., 1873–1959, vol. V

Murray, T. Douglas, 1841–1911, vol. I

Murray, Brig. Terence Desmond, 1891–1961, vol. VI

Murray, Thomas J., 1880–1936, vol. III

Murray, Hon. Sir Thomas Keir, 1854–1936, vol. III

Murray, Brig.-Gen. Sir Valentine, 1867–1942, vol. IV

Murray, Violet Cecil, 1885–1961, vol. VI

Murray, Rev. W. Rigby, died 1914, vol. I

Murray, Walter Charles, 1866–1946, vol. IV

Murray, Lt-Col Walter Graham, 1868–1937, vol. III

Murray, Major William, 1865–1923, vol. II

Murray, William Alexander, 1889–1935, vol. III

Murray, Lt-Col William Atholl, 1879–1953, vol. V

Murray, (William Ewart) Gladstone, 1893–1970, vol. VI

Murray, Rev. William Hill, 1843–1911, vol. I

Murray, Brig.-Gen. William Hugh Eric, 1858–1915, vol. I

Murray, Sir William Keith, 9th Bt (cr 1673), 1872–1956, vol. V

Murray, Sir William Patrick Keith, 11th Bt (cr 1673), 1939–1977, vol. VII

Murray, Sir William Robert, 12th Bt (cr 1626), 1840–1904, vol. I

Murray, William Staite, 1881–1962, vol. VI

Murray, Col Sir Wyndham; see Murray, Col Sir C. W.

Murray-Aynsley, Sir Charles Murray, 1893–1967, vol. VI

Murray Baillie, Lt-Col Frederick David, 1862–1924, vol. II

Murray-Brown, Gilbert Alexander, 1893–1981, vol. VIII

Murray-Harvey, Captain Edward, 1886–1967, vol. VI

Murray-Philipson, Hylton Ralph; see Philipson.

Murray-Smith, Lt-Col Arthur, 1868–1943, vol. IV

Murray-Threipland, Col William, 1866–1942, vol. IV

Murray-White, Col Richard Stephen; see White.

Murrell, Frank Edric Joseph, 1874–1931, vol. III

Murrell, William, 1853–1912, vol. I

Murrell, William Lee, 1893–1971, vol. VII

Murrill, Herbert Henry John, 1909–1952, vol. V

Murrough, John Patrick, 1822–1901, vol. I

Murrow, Edward Roscoe, 1908–1965, vol. VI

Murry, John Middleton, 1889–1957, vol. V

Murshedabad, Nawab Bahadur of, 1846–1906, vol. I

Murshidabad, Nawab Bahadur of, 1875–1959, vol. V (A)

Murton, Sir Walter, 1836–1927, vol. II

Muscat, HH The Sultan of, died 1913, vol. I

Muschamp, Rt Rev. Cecil Emerson Barron, 1902–1984, vol. VIII

Muschamp, Sidney, died 1929, vol. III

Muscio, Bernard, 1887–1926, vol. II

Muselier, Vice-Am. d'Escadre Emile Henry, 1882–1965, vol. VI

Musgrave, Hon. Anthony, 1849–1912, vol. I

Musgrave, Brig.-Gen. Arthur David, 1874–1931, vol. III

Musgrave, Sir Charles, 14th Bt (cr 1611), 1913–1970, vol. VI

Musgrave, Charles Edwin, 1861–1923, vol. II

Musgrave, Sir Christopher George, 1855–1929, vol. III

Musgrave, Lt-Col Sir Christopher Norman, 6th Bt (cr 1782), 1892–1956, vol. V

Musgrave, Clifford, 1904–1982, vol. VIII

Musgrave, Sir Courtenay; see Musgrave, Sir N. C.

Musgrave, Sir Cyril; see Musgrave, Sir F. C.

Musgrave, Ernest Illingworth, 1901–1957, vol. V

Musgrave, Sir (Frank) Cyril, 1900–1986, vol. VIII

Musgrave, Major Herbert, 1876–1918, vol. II

Musgrave, Herbert Wenman W.; see Wykeham-Musgrave.

Musgrave, Sir James, 1st Bt (cr 1897), 1829–1904, vol. I

Musgrave, Sir (Nigel) Courtenay, 13th Bt (cr 1611), 1896–1957, vol. V

Musgrave, Noel Henry, 1903–1971, vol. VII

Musgrave, Sir Richard George, 12th Bt (cr 1611), 1872–1926, vol. III

Musgrave, Sir Richard John, 5th Bt (cr 1782), 1850–1930, vol. III

Musgrave, Rev. Vernon, died 1906, vol. I

Musgrove, James, 1862–1935, vol. III

Muskerry, 4th Baron, 1854–1929, vol. III

Muskerry, 5th Baron, 1874–1952, vol. V

Muskerry, 6th Baron, 1875–1954, vol. V

Muskerry, 7th Baron, 1874–1966, vol. VI

Muskerry, 8th Baron, 1907–1988, vol. VIII

Muskett, Arthur Edmund, 1900–1984, vol. VIII

Muspratt, Edmund Knowles, 1833–1923, vol. II

Muspratt, Brig.-Gen. Francis Clifton, 1864–1944, vol. IV

Muspratt, Sir Max, 1st Bt, 1872–1934, vol. III

Muspratt, Gen. Sir Sydney Frederick, 1878–1972, vol. VII

Muspratt-Williams, Lt-Col Charles Augustus, 1861–1925, vol. II

Musselwhite, Ven. William Ralph, 1887–1956, vol. V

Mussen, Sir Gerald, 1872–1960, vol. V

Mussen, Surgeon Rear-Adm. Robert Walsh, 1900–1985, vol. VIII

Mussenden, Maj.-Gen. William, 1836–1910, vol. I

Mussolini, Benito, 1883–1945, vol. IV

Musson, Maj.-Gen. Arthur Ingram, 1877–1961, vol. VI

Musson, Dame Ellen Mary, 1867–1960, vol. V

Musson, Francis William, 1894–1962, vol. VI

Musters, Col John Nevile C.; see Chaworth-Musters.

Musters, John Patricius Chaworth, 1860–1921, vol. II

Musto, Sir Arnold Albert, 1883–1977, vol. VII

Mustoe, Nelson Edwin, died 1976, vol. VII

Musurus Pasha, Stephen, 1841–1907, vol. I

Mutch, Air Cdre James Richard, 1905–1973, vol. VII

Mutch, Nathan, 1886–1982, vol. VIII

Muther, Richard, 1860–1909, vol. I

Muthiah Chettiar, Sir M. C. T., 1887–1929, vol. III
Mutter, Rev. Cecil G., 1876–1942, vol. IV
Muzammilullah Khan, Khan Bahadur Nawab Sir Muhammad, *died* 1938, vol. III
Mwendwa, Hon. Maluki Kitili, 1929–1985, vol. VIII
Myburgh, Brig. Philip Stafford, 1893–1963, vol. VI
Myddelton, Lt-Col Ririd, 1902–1988, vol. VIII
Myddelton, Robert Edward, 1866–1949, vol. IV
Myer, Lt-Col George Val., 1883–1959, vol. V
Myer, Horatio, 1850–1916, vol. II
Myer, Dame (Margery) Merlyn Baillieu, 1900–1982, vol. VIII
Myer, Dame Merlyn Baillieu; *see* Myer, Dame M. M. B.
Myer, Sir Norman, 1897–1956, vol. V
Myers, Hon. Sir Arthur, 1867–1926, vol. II
Myers, Arthur Wallis, 1878–1939, vol. III
Myers, Asher Isaac, 1848–1902, vol. I
Myers, Bernard, 1872–1957, vol. V
Myers, Rev. Canon Charles, 1856–1948, vol. IV
Myers, Charles Samuel, 1873–1946, vol. IV
Myers, Sir Dudley Borron, 1861–1944, vol. IV
Myers, Most Rev. Edward, 1875–1956, vol. V
Myers, Frederic W. H., 1843–1901, vol. I
Myers, Sir James Eckersley, 1890–1958, vol. V
Myers, Leo Hamilton, 1881–1944, vol. IV
Myers, Leonard William, *died* 1962, vol. VI
Myers, Mark, 1930–1990, vol. VIII
Myers, Rt Hon. Sir Michael, 1873–1950, vol. IV
Myers, Tom, 1872–1949, vol. IV
Myers, William Henry, 1854–1933, vol. III
Myerson, Aubrey Selwyn, 1926–1986, vol. VIII
Myint, Hla, 1920–1989, vol. VIII
Myles, Captain Edgar Kinghorn, 1894–1977, vol. VII
Myles, Sir Thomas, 1857–1937, vol. III
Myles, Surg.-Captain Thomas William, 1878–1933, vol. III
Mylks, Gordon Wright, 1874–1957, vol. V
Mylne, Rev. Alan Moultrie, 1886–1944, vol. IV
Mylne, Rt Rev. Louis George, 1843–1921, vol. II
Mynett, George Kenneth, 1913–1984, vol. VIII
Mynors, Rev. Aubrey Baskerville, 1865–1937, vol. III
Mynors, Sir Humphrey Charles Baskerville, 1st Bt, 1903–1989, vol. VIII
Mynors, Sir Roger Aubrey Baskerville, 1903–1989, vol. VIII
Myrander; *see* Stevenson, James Alexander.
Myrdal, Alva, 1902–1986, vol. VIII
Myrdal, Gunnar; *see* Myrdal, K. G.
Myrdal, (Karl) Gunnar, 1898–1987, vol. VIII
Myrddin-Evans, Sir Guildhaume, 1894–1964, vol. VI
Myres, Sir John Linton, 1869–1954, vol. V
Myres, John Nowell Linton, 1902–1989, vol. VIII
Myres, Nowell; *see* Myres, J. N. L.
Mysore, HH Maharaja of, 1884–1940, vol. III
Mysore, HH Maharaja of, 1919–1974, vol. VII
Mysore, Yuvaraja of, 1888–1940, vol. III
Mytton, Sir Thomas Henry, 1878–1966, vol. VI

N

Nabarro, David Nunes, 1874–1958, vol. V

Nabarro, Sir Gerald David Nunes, 1913–1973, vol. VII
Nabha, HH Rajah, 1843–1911, vol. I
Nabokov, Vladimir, 1899–1977, vol. VII
Nadia, Maharaja of, 1890–1928, vol. II
Naef, Sir Conrad James, 1871–1954, vol. V
Naegeli, Otto, *died* 1938, vol. III (A), vol. IV
Naesmith, Sir Andrew, 1888–1961, vol. VI
Naesmyth, Sir Douglas Arthur Bradley, 8th Bt, 1905–1928, vol. II
Naesmyth, Sir James Tolmé, 7th Bt, 1864–1922, vol. II
Naesmyth, Sir Michael George, 6th Bt, 1828–1907, vol. I
Nagar, Raja Sir Sikander Khan of, *died* 1940, vol. III
Nageon de Lestang, Sir Clement; *see* Nageon de Lestang, Sir M. C. E. C.
Nageon de Lestang, Sir (Marie Charles Emmanuel) Clement, 1910–1986, vol. VIII
Nagogo, Alhaji Hon. Sir Usuman, *died* 1981, vol. VIII
Nahum, Jack Messoud Eric di Victor, 1906–1959, vol. V
Naidu, Mme Sarojini, *died* 1949, vol. IV
Naipaul, Shivadhar Srinivasa, 1945–1985, vol. VIII
Nair, Rt Hon. Sir Chettur Madhavan, 1879–1970, vol. VI (AII)
Nair, Sir Chettur S.; *see* Sankaran Nair.
Nairac, Hon. Sir André Lawrence, 1905–1981, vol. VIII
Nairac, Sir Edouard; *see* Nairac, Sir G. E.
Nairac, Sir (George) Edouard, 1876–1960, vol. V (A), vol. VI (AI)
Nairn, Bryce James Miller, 1903–1978, vol. VII
Nairn, Sir Douglas Leslie Spencer-, 2nd Bt, 1906–1970, vol. VI
Nairn, Sir George; *see* Nairn, Sir M. G.
Nairn, George Alexander Stokes, 1889–1974, vol. VII
Nairn, Rev. John Arbuthnot, 1874–1957, vol. V
Nairn, Rt Rev. Louis George, 1843–1921, vol. II
Nairn, Sir Michael, 2nd Bt, 1874–1952, vol. V
Nairn, Sir Michael Barker, 1st Bt, 1838–1915, vol. I
Nairn, Sir (Michael) George, 3rd Bt, 1911–1984, vol. VIII
Nairn, Major Sir Robert S.; *see* Spencer-Nairn.
Nairn, Walter Maxwell, *died* 1958, vol. V
Nairne, Rev. Alexander, 1863–1936, vol. III
Nairne, Gen. Sir Charles Edward, 1836–1899, vol. I
Nairne, Major Lord Charles George Francis M.; *see* Mercer-Nairne.
Nairne, Brig.-Gen. Edward Spencer Hoare, 1869–1958, vol. V
Nairne, Sir Gordon; *see* Nairne, Sir J. G.
Nairne, Rev. John Domett, 1846–1929, vol. III
Nairne, Sir (John) Gordon, 1st Bt, 1861–1945, vol. IV
Nairne, Sir Perceval Alleyn, 1841–1921, vol. II
Naisby, John Vickers, 1894–1983, vol. VIII
Naish, Albert Ernest, 1871–1964, vol. VI
Naish, Rear-Adm. George Oswald, 1904–1960, vol. V
Naish, Lt-Comdr George Prideaux Brabant, 1909–1977, vol. VII
Naish, John Paull, *died* 1964, vol. VI
Naish, Redmond, *born* 1848, vol. II
Naismith, Lt-Col William John, 1847–1926, vol. II
Nalder, Leonard Fielding, 1888–1958, vol. V

Nalder, Maj.-Gen. Reginald Francis Heaton, 1895–1978, vol. VII

Naldrett, Edward James, *died* 1930, vol. III

Nall, J(ohn) Spencer, 1887–1970, vol. VI

Nall, Col Sir Joseph, 1st Bt, 1887–1958, vol. V

Nally, Will, 1914–1965, vol. VI

Namier, Sir Lewis Bernstein, 1888–1960, vol. V

Nan Kivell, Sir Rex de Charambac, 1899–1977, vol. VII

Nanak Chand, Masheerud-dowla Rai Bahadur, 1860–1920, vol. II, vol. III

Nanavati, Sir Manilal B., 1877–1967, vol. VI

Nanavatty, Col Sir Byramji Hormasji, 1861–1937, vol. III

Nance, Surg.-Captain Sir Arthur Stanley, 1860–1938, vol. III

Nance, Rev. James Trengove, 1852–1942, vol. IV

Nand Lal, Diwan Bahadur Pandit, 1857–1926, vol. II

Nandris, Grigore, 1895–1968, vol. VI

Nanjundayya, H. Velpanuru, 1860–1920, vol. II

NanKivell, Sir Rex de Charambac; *see* Nan Kivell.

Nannetti, Joseph Patrick, 1851–1915, vol. I

Nansen, Fridtjof, 1861–1930, vol. III

Nanson, Edward John, 1850–1936, vol. III

Nanson, Group Captain Eric Roper-Curzon, 1883–1960, vol. V

Nanson, Hon. John Leighton, 1863–1916, vol. II

Nantel, Hon. Wilfrid Bruno, 1857–1940, vol. III (A), vol. IV

Nanton, Sir Augustus Meredith, 1860–1925, vol. II

Nanton, Brig.-Gen. Herbert Colbourne, 1863–1935, vol. III

Naoroji, Dadabhai, 1825–1917, vol. II

Naper, Captain William Lenox, 1879–1942, vol. IV

Napier, 10th Lord, **and Ettrick,** 1st Baron, 1819–1898, vol. I

Napier, 11th Lord, **and Ettrick,** 2nd Baron, 1846–1913, vol. I

Napier, 12th Lord, **and Ettrick,** 3rd Baron, 1876–1941, vol. IV

Napier, 13th Lord, **and Ettrick,** 4th Baron, 1900–1954, vol. V

Napier of Magdala, 2nd Baron, 1845–1921, vol. II

Napier of Magdala, 3rd Baron, 1849–1935, vol. III

Napier of Magdala, 4th Baron, 1861–1948, vol. IV

Napier of Magdala, 5th Baron, 1904–1987, vol. VIII

Napier, Hon. Sir Albert Edward Alexander, 1881–1973, vol. VII

Napier, Albert Napier Williamson, 1894–1969, vol. VI

Napier, Col Alexander, 1851–1928, vol. II

Napier, Captain Sir Alexander Lennox Milliken, 11th Bt (*cr* 1627), 1882–1954, vol. V

Napier, Sir Archibald Lennox Milliken, 10th Bt (*cr* 1627), 1855–1907, vol. I

Napier, Arthur Sampson, 1853–1916, vol. II

Napier, Charles Frederick, 1862–1932, vol. III

Napier, Charles Goddard, 1889–1978, vol. VII

Napier, Adm. Charles Lionel, 1861–1934, vol. III

Napier, Col Charles Scott, 1899–1946, vol. IV

Napier, Major Egbert, 1867–1916, vol. II

Napier, Lt-Col Hon. George Campbell, 1845–1914, vol. I

Napier, Lt-Col Hon. Henry Dundas, 1864–1941, vol. IV

Napier, Ian Patrick Robert, 1895–1977, vol. VII

Napier, Brig. John Lenox Clavering, 1898–1966, vol. VI

Napier, Hon. Sir (John) Mellis, 1882–1976, vol. VII

Napier, Col Hon. John Scott, 1848–1938, vol. III

Napier, Sir Joseph William Lennox, 4th Bt, 1895–1986, vol. VIII

Napier, Lionel Everard, 1888–1957, vol. V

Napier, Hon. Mark Francis, 1852–1919, vol. II

Napier, Hon. Sir Mellis; *see* Napier, Hon. Sir J. M.

Napier, Sir Robert Archibald, 12th Bt (*cr* 1627), 1889–1965, vol. VI

Napier, Thomas Bateman, 1854–1933, vol. III

Napier, Vice-Adm. Sir Trevylyan Dacres Willes, 1867–1920, vol. II

Napier, Brig. Vernon Monro Colquhoun, 1881–1957, vol. V

Napier, Brig. Vivian John Lennox, 1898–1990, vol. VIII

Napier, Sir Walter John, 1857–1945, vol. IV

Napier, Col William, 1861–1920, vol. II, vol. III

Napier, Sir William Archibald, 13th Bt, 1915–1990, vol. VIII

Napier, William Heathcote Unwin, *died* 1959, vol. V

Napier, Maj.-Gen. William John, 1863–1925, vol. II

Napier, Sir William Lennox, 3rd Bt (*cr* 1867), 1867–1915, vol. I

Napier, Adm. William Rawdon, 1877–1951, vol. V

Napier-Clavering, Col Charles Warren, 1858–1931, vol. III

Napier-Clavering, Maj.-Gen. Noel Warren, 1888–1964, vol. VI

Napoleon, Prince Louis, 1864–1932, vol. III

Napoleon, HIH Prince (Victor Jerome Frederic), 1862–1926, vol. II

Napper, Jack Hollingworth, 1904–1978, vol. VII

Narang, Sir Gokul Chand, 1878–1970, vol. VI

Narasimha Gopalaswami Ayyangar, Sir, 1882–1953, vol. V

Narasimha Sarma, Rao Bahadur Sir Bayya, 1867–1932, vol. III

Naratomdas, Sir Harkisandas, 1849–1908, vol. I

Narayan Kissen Sen, 1861–1935, vol. III

Narbeth, John Harper, 1863–1944, vol. IV

Narborough, Rt Rev. Dudley Vaughan; *see* Narborough, Rt Rev. F. D. V.

Narborough, Rt Rev. (Frederick) Dudley Vaughan, 1895–1966, vol. VI

Narendra, Krishna, Sir, Maharaja Bahadur, 1822–1903, vol. I

Nares, Maj.-Gen. Eric Paytherus, 1892–1947, vol. IV

Nares, Sir George Strong, 1831–1915, vol. I

Nares, Vice-Adm. John Dodd, 1877–1957, vol. V

Nares, Owen Ramsay, *died* 1943, vol. IV

Nariman, Sir Temulji Bhicaji, 1848–1940, vol. III

Narracott, Arthur Henson, 1905–1967, vol. VI

Narsingarh, Sahib Bahadur of, 1887–1924, vol. II

Nash, Rev. Adam James Glendinning, *died* 1920, vol. II

Nash, Rev. Alexander, 1845–1924, vol. II

Nash, Alfred William, 1886–1942, vol. IV

Nash, Eveleigh, 1873–1956, vol. V

Nash, Captain Geoffrey Stewart Fleetwood, 1883–1936, vol. III
Nash, George Howard, 1881–1950, vol. IV
Nash, Gilbert John, 1905–1974, vol. VII
Nash, Rev. Glendinning, died 1915, vol. I
Nash, Brig.-Gen. Henry Edmund Palmer, 1869–1949, vol. IV
Nash, Rt Rev. James Okey, 1862–1943, vol. IV
Nash, Rev. James Palmer, 1842–1915, vol. I
Nash, John Brady, born 1857, vol. II
Nash, John Kevin Tyrie Llewellyn, 1922–1981, vol. VIII
Nash, John Northcote, 1893–1977, vol. VII
Nash, Joseph, died 1922, vol. II
Nash, Kenneth Twigg, 1918–1981, vol. VIII
Nash, Kevin; see Nash, J. K. T. L.
Nash, Col Llewellyn Thomas Manly, 1861–1928, vol. II
Nash, Norman E. Keown, 1885–1966, vol. VI
Nash, Ogden, 1902–1971, vol. VII
Nash, Paul, 1889–1946, vol. IV
Nash, Maj.-Gen. Sir Philip Arthur Manley, 1875–1936, vol. III
Nash, Rev. Robert Seymour, 1822–1904, vol. I
Nash, Vaughan, 1861–1932, vol. III
Nash, Sir Vincent, 1865–1942, vol. IV
Nash, Rt Hon. Sir Walter, 1882–1968, vol. VI
Nash, Major William Fleetwood, 1861–1915, vol. I
Nash, William Harry, 1848–1929, vol. III
Nash-Williams, Victor Erle, 1897–1955, vol. V
Nashimoto, Morimasa, Prince, 1874–1951, vol. V
Nasim Ali, Sir Syed, died 1946, vol. IV
Nasir, Rt Rev. Eric Samuel, 1916–1987, vol. VIII
Nasir-El-Mulk, Abdul Kassim Khan, 1858–1927, vol. II
Nasmith, Adm. Sir Martin Eric Dunbar-, died 1965, vol. VI
Nasmyth, Thomas Goodall, died 1937, vol. III
Nason, Col Fortescue John, 1859–1952, vol. V
Nason, Rev. George Stephen, 1901–1975, vol. VII
Nason, Lt-Col Henry Hyde Williamson, 1857–1929, vol. III
Nasser, Gamal Abdel, 1918–1970, vol. VI
Natali, Lorenzo, 1922–1989, vol. VIII
Nath, Rao Bahadur Bhagavatula V.; see Viswa Nath.
Nathan, 1st Baron, 1889–1963, vol. VI
Nathan, Lady; (Eleanor Joan Clara), 1892–1972, vol. VII
Nathan, Charles, 1891–1949, vol. IV
Nathan, Sir Charles Samuel, 1870–1936, vol. III
Nathan, Daniel; see Dannay, Frederic.
Nathan, Col Sir Frederic Lewis, 1861–1933, vol. III
Nathan, George Jean, 1882–1958, vol. V
Nathan, Sir Gustavus, 1835–1902, vol. I
Nathan, Kandiah Shanmuga, 1930–1990, vol. VIII
Nathan, Manfred, 1875–1945, vol. IV
Nathan, Lt-Col Rt Hon. Sir Matthew, 1862–1939, vol. III
Nathan, Sir Maurice Arnold, 1914–1982, vol. VIII
Nathan, Sir Nathaniel, 1843–1916, vol. II
Nathan, Sir Robert, 1866–1921, vol. II
Nathan, Major Walter Simeon, 1867–1940, vol. III
Nathubhai, Tribhovandas Mangaldas, 1856–1920, vol. II

Nation, Brig.-Gen. John James Henry, 1874–1946, vol. IV
Nation, Sir John Louis, 1825–1906, vol. I
Nation, William Hamilton Codrington, 1843–1914, vol. I
Natta, Giulio, 1903–1979, vol. VII
Nattrass, Frederick John, 1891–1979, vol. VII
Naughton, Most Rev. James, 1864–1950, vol. IV
Nauticus; see Clowes, Sir W. L.
Navarro, Mary Anderson de, 1859–1940, vol. III
Naville, Henri Edouard, 1844–1926, vol. II
Nawanagar, Maharaja Jamsaheb of, 1872–1933, vol. III
Nawanagar, Maharaja Jam Saheb of, 1895–1966, vol. VI
Naylor, Very Rev. Alfred Thomas Arthur, 1889–1966, vol. VI
Naylor, Arthur Holden, 1897–1983, vol. VIII
Naylor, Rev. Canon Basil; see Naylor, Rev. Canon C. B.
Naylor, Rev. Canon Charles Basil, 1911–1988, vol. VIII
Naylor, (Gordon) Keith, 1933–1990, vol. VIII
Naylor, Henry Darnley, 1872–1945, vol. IV
Naylor, James Richard, 1842–1922, vol. II
Naylor, Keith; see Naylor, G. K.
Naylor, Margaret Ailsa; see Naylor, Margot.
Naylor, Margot, (Margaret Ailsa), 1907–1972, vol. VII
Naylor, Maj.-Gen. Robert Francis Brydges, 1889–1971, vol. VII
Naylor, Thomas Ellis, 1868–1958, vol. V
Naylor, Thomas Humphrey, 1890–1966, vol. VI
Naylor, Ven. William Herbert, 1846–1918, vol. II
Naylor-Leyland, Sir (Albert) Edward (Herbert), 2nd Bt, 1890–1952, vol. V
Naylor-Leyland, Sir Edward; see Naylor-Leyland, Sir A. E. H.
Naylor-Leyland, Captain Sir Herbert Scarisbrick, 1st Bt, 1864–1899, vol. I
Naylor-Leyland, Sir Vivyan Edward, 3rd Bt, 1924–1987, vol. VIII
Naz, Sir Virgile, 1825–1901, vol. I
Nazimuddin, (Sir) Al-Haj Khwaja, 1894–1964, vol. VI
Neagle, Dame Anna, (Dame (Florence) Marjorie Wilcox), 1904–1986, vol. VIII
Neal, Arthur, 1862–1933, vol. III
Neal, Harold, 1897–1972, vol. VII
Neal, John, 1889–1962, vol. VI
Neal, Mary C. S., died 1944, vol. IV
Neal, Sir Phené; see Neal, Sir W. P.
Neal, Sir (William) Phené, 1st Bt, 1860–1942, vol. IV
Neale, Rev. Edgar, 1872–1937, vol. III
Neale, Edward A., 1858–1943, vol. IV
Neale, Folliott Sandford, 1901–1972, vol. VII
Neale, Lt-Col Sir Gordon; see Neale, Lt-Col Sir W. G.
Neale, Sir Henry James Vansittart-, 1842–1923, vol. II
Neale, Sir John Ernest, 1890–1975, vol. VII
Neale, Lt-Col Sir (Walter) Gordon, 1880–1966, vol. VI
Neales, Very Rev. Scovil, 1864–1936, vol. III

Neame, Lt-Col Arthur Laurence Cecil, 1883–1948, vol. IV

Neame, Captain Douglas Mortimer Lewes, 1901–1988, vol. VIII

Neame, Elizabeth; *see* Monroe, Elizabeth.

Neame, Gwendolyn Mary, (Lady Neame); *see* Desmond, Astra.

Neame, Humphrey, *died* 1968, vol. VI

Neame, Lawrence Elwin, *died* 1964, vol. VI

Neame, Lt-Gen. Sir Philip, 1888–1978, vol. VII

Neame, Sir Thomas, 1885–1973, vol. VII

Neat, Captain (S) Edward Hugh, 1864–1948, vol. IV

Neatby, Edwin Awdas, 1858–1933, vol. III

Neate, Horace Richard, 1891–1966, vol. VI

Neathercoat, Ernest Tom, 1880–1950, vol. IV

Neave, Airey Middleton Sheffield, 1916–1979, vol. VII

Neave, James Stephen, 1898–1970, vol. VI

Neave, Sheffield, 1853–1936, vol. III

Neave, Sheffield Airey, 1879–1961, vol. VI

Neave, Major Sir Thomas Lewis Hughes, 5th Bt, 1874–1940, vol. III

Neden, Sir Wilfred John, 1893–1978, vol. VII

Needham, Col Alfred Owen, 1883–1951, vol. V

Needham, Alicia Adelaide, *died* 1945, vol. IV

Needham, Col Charles, 1844–1934, vol. III

Needham, Sir Christopher Thomas, 1866–1944, vol. IV

Needham, Dorothy Mary Moyle, 1896–1987, vol. VIII

Needham, Major Hon. Francis Edward, 1886–1955, vol. V

Needham, Francis Jack, 1842–1924, vol. II

Needham, Sir Frederick, 1832–1924, vol. II

Needham, Sir George William, 1843–1928, vol. II

Needham, Maj.-Gen. Henry, 1876–1965, vol. VI

Needham, James Ernest, *died* 1937, vol. III

Needham, John, 1909–1990, vol. VIII

Needham, Comr John Edward Dunmore, 1917–1983, vol. VIII

Needham, Rev. Canon John Stafford, 1875–1942, vol. IV

Needham, Joseph, 1853–1920, vol. II

Needham, Col Joseph George, *died* 1939, vol. III

Needham, Sir Raymond Walter, 1877–1965, vol. VI

Needham, Bt Col Sir Richard Arthur, 1877–1949, vol. IV

Neef, Walter, 1857–1905, vol. I

Neel, Edmund, 1841–1933, vol. III

Neel, Louis Boyd, 1905–1981, vol VIII

Neelands, Abram Rupert, *died* 1971, vol. VII

Neeld, Sir Algernon William, 2nd Bt, 1846–1900, vol. I

Neeld, Lt-Col Sir Audley Dallas, 3rd Bt, 1849–1941, vol. IV

Neeld, Rear-Adm. Reginald Rundell, 1850–1939, vol. III

Neely, Major George Henry, 1885–1934, vol. III

Neely, Air Vice-Marshal John Conrad, 1901–1989, vol. VIII

Neep, Edward John Cecil, 1900–1980, vol. VII

Neerunjun, Sir Rampersad, 1906–1967, vol. VI

Neff, Erroll Aubrey, 1887–1942, vol. IV

Negus, Arthur George, 1903–1985, vol. VIII

Negus, Sir Victor Ewings, 1887–1974, vol. VII

Nehru, Shri Jawaharlal, 1889–1964, vol. VI

Nehru, Pandit Motilal, 1861–1931, vol. III

Neil, Albert Michael; *see* Lyons, A. Neil.

Neil, Edwin Lee, 1872–1934, vol. III

Neil, Eric, 1918–1990, vol. VIII

Neil, James H.; *see* Hardie Neil.

Neil, Rev. John, 1853–1928, vol. II

Neil, Robert Alexander, 1852–1901, vol. I

Neil, Rev. William, 1909–1979, vol. VII

Neilans, Alison R. N., 1884–1942, vol. IV

Neild, Rev. Canon Alfred, 1865–1941, vol. V

Neill, Alexander Sutherland, 1883–1973, vol. VII

Neill, Charles Ernest, 1873–1931, vol. III

Neill, Col Duncan Ferguson Dempster, 1868–1938, vol. III

Neill, Col Sir Frederick Austin, 1891–1967, vol. VI

Neill, James Scott, 1889–1958, vol. V

Neill, Col James William S.; *see* Smith-Neill.

Neill, Rt Rev. Stephen Charles, 1900–1984, vol. VIII

Neill, Sir Thomas, 1856–1937, vol. III

Neill, Sir William Frederick, 1889–1960, vol. V

Neilson, Alexander, 1868–1929, vol. III

Neilson, Francis, 1867–1961, vol. VI

Neilson, George, 1858–1923, vol. II

Neilson, Henry John, 1862–1949, vol. IV

Neilson, Col James, 1838–1903, vol. I

Neilson, Lt-Col John Beaumont, 1885–1957, vol. V

Neilson, Lt-Col John Fraser, 1884–1962, vol. VI

Neilson, John Shaw, 1872–1942, vol. IV

Neilson, Julia, (Mrs Fred Terry), *died* 1957, vol. V

Neilson, Richard Gillies, 1876–1956, vol. V

Neilson, Col Walter Gordon, 1876–1927, vol. II

Neilson, William Allan, 1869–1946, vol. IV

Neilson, Hon. William Arthur, 1925–1989, vol. VIII

Neilson-Gray, Norah; *see* Gray.

Neilson-Terry, Phyllis, 1892–1977, vol. VII

Neish, Arthur Charles, 1916–1973, vol. VII

Neish, Sir Charles Henry Lawrence, 1857–1934, vol. III

Neish, Edward William, *died* 1938, vol. III

Neitenstein, Frederick William, 1850–1921, vol. II

Neligan, Rt Rev. Moore Richard, *died* 1922, vol. II

Nelke, Paul, 1860–1925, vol. II

Nell, Sir Harry, 1882–1958, vol. V

Nelles, Brig.-Gen. Charles Macklem, 1863–1936, vol. III

Nelles, Adm. Percy Walker, 1892–1951, vol. V

Nelson, 3rd Earl, 1823–1913, vol. I

Nelson, 4th Earl, 1857–1947, vol. IV

Nelson, 5th Earl, 1860–1951, vol. V

Nelson, 6th Earl, 1890–1957, vol. V

Nelson, 7th Earl, 1894–1972, vol. VII

Nelson, 8th Earl, 1905–1981, vol. VIII

Nelson of Stafford, 1st Baron, 1887–1962, vol. VI

Nelson, Sir Amos, 1860–1947, vol. IV

Nelson, Sir Arthur Edward, 1875–1950, vol. IV

Nelson, Bertram, 1905–1984, vol. VIII

Nelson, Charles Gilbert, 1880–1962, vol. VI

Nelson, Rev. Canon Charles Moseley, 1843–1919, vol. II

Nelson, Rt Rev. Cleland Kinloch, 1852–1917, vol. II

Nelson, Lieut David, 1886–1918, vol. II

Nelson, Donald Marr, 1888–1959, vol. V

Nelson, Brig.-Gen. Edgar F., 1859–1933, vol. III
Nelson, Edward Milles, died 1938, vol. III
Nelson, Sir Edward Montague, 1841–1919, vol. II
Nelson, Sir Frank, 1883–1966, vol. VI
Nelson, Geoffrey Sheard, 1909–1984, vol. VIII
Nelson, Henry Ince, 1897–1981, vol. VIII
Nelson, Gp Captain Hugh, 1890–1948, vol. IV
Nelson, Rt Hon. Sir Hugh Muir, 1835–1906, vol. I
Nelson, Sir James Hope, 2nd Bt, 1883–1960, vol. V
Nelson, John Howard, 1925–1979, vol. VII
Nelson, Col John Joseph Harper, 1882–1961, vol. VI
Nelson, Major John Weddall, 1878–1935, vol. III
Nelson, Captain Maurice Henry Horatio, 1864–1942, vol. IV
Nelson, Rear-Adm. Hon. Maurice Horatio, 1832–1914, vol. I
Nelson, Col Percy Reginald, 1884–1939, vol. III
Nelson, Rt Rev. Richard Henry, 1859–1931, vol. III
Nelson, Rt Rev. Robert, 1913–1959, vol. V
Nelson, Robert Frederick William Robertson, 1888–1932, vol. III
Nelson, Sir William, 1st Bt, 1851–1922, vol. II
Nelson, William Henry, 1880–1948, vol. IV
Nelson-Ward, Adm. Philip, 1866–1937, vol. III
Nelthorpe, Col Oliver S.; see Sutton Nelthorpe.
Nelthorpe, Robert Nassau S.; see Sutton-Nelthorpe.
Nemon, Oscar, 1906–1985, vol. VIII
Nenk, David Moerel, 1916–1960, vol. V
Nepal, Maharaja Chandra Shum Shere Jung Bahadur Rana, 1863–1929, vol. III
Nepal, Maharaja Bhim Shum Shere Jung Bahadur Rana, 1865–1932, vol. III
Nepal, Ex-Maharaja of, 1875–1952, vol. V
Nepal, Maharaja Mohan Shamsher Jang Bahadur Rana, 1885–1967, vol. VI
Nepean, Sir Charles Evan Molyneux Yorke, 5th Bt, 1867–1953, vol. V
Nepean, Edith, died 1960, vol. V
Nepean, Sir Evan Colville, 1836–1908, vol. I
Nepean, Rev. Sir Evan Yorke, 4th Bt, 1825–1903, vol. I
Nepean, Col Herbert Dryden Home Yorke, 1893–1956, vol. V
Nepean, Brig.-Gen. Herbert Evan Charles, 1865–1951, vol. V
Nepean, Comdr St Vincent, 1844–1915, vol. I
Neruda, Pablo, 1904–1973, vol. VII
Nervi, Pier Luigi, 1891–1979, vol. VII
Nesbit, E(dith), (Mrs Hubert Bland), 1858–1924, vol. II
Nesbit, Paris, 1852–1927, vol. II
Nesbitt, Rev. Allan James, died 1918, vol. II
Nesbitt, Cathleen Mary, 1888–1982, vol. VIII
Nesbitt, Maj.-Gen. Frederick George B.; see Beaumont-Nesbitt.
Nesbitt, Major Randolph Cosby, 1867–1956, vol. V
Nesbitt, Lt-Col Richard Atholl, 1838–1905, vol. I
Nesbitt, Robert Chancellor, died 1944, vol. IV
Nesbitt, Hon. Wallace, 1858–1930, vol. III
Nesbitt-Hawes, Sir Ronald, 1895–1969, vol. VI
Ness, E. Wilhelmina; see Ness, Mrs P.
Ness, J. A., died 1931, vol. III
Ness, Mrs Patrick, (E. Wilhelmina Ness), died 1962, vol. VI

Ness, Robert Barclay, died 1954, vol. V
Nessi, Pio B.; see Baroja Nessi.
Nestle, (Christof) Eberhard, 1851–1913, vol. I
Nestle, Eberhard; see Nestle, C. E.
Nethersole, Lt-Col Frederick Ralph, died 1933, vol. III
Nethersole, Sir Michael, 1859–1920, vol. II
Nethersole, Sir Michael Henry Braddon, 1891–1965, vol. VI
Nethersole, Olga, 1870–1951, vol. V
Netherthorpe, 1st Baron, 1908–1980, vol. VII
Netherthorpe, 2nd Baron, 1936–1982, vol. VIII
Netherwood, A., died 1930, vol. III
Nettlefold, Sir Thomas Sydney, 1879–1956, vol. V
Nettleship, Edward, 1845–1913, vol. I
Nettleship, John Trivett, 1841–1902, vol. I
Nettleton, Wing Comdr John Dering, 1917–1943, vol. IV
Nettleton, Martin Barnes, 1911–1964, vol. VI
Neubauer, Adolf, 1832–1907, vol. I
Neumann, Sir Cecil Gustavus Jacques; see Newman.
Neumann, Sir Sigmund, 1st Bt, 1857–1916, vol. II
Nevada, Mignon, died 1971, vol. VII
Nevares, Celso, born 1850, vol. II
Neve, Arthur, 1858–1919, vol. II
Neve, Eric Read, 1887–1958, vol. V
Neve, Ernest Frederic, 1861–1946, vol. IV
Neven-Spence, Col Sir Basil Hamilton Hebden, 1888–1974, vol. VII
Nevile, Christopher, 1891–1962, vol. VI
Nevile, Sir Sydney Oswald, 1873–1969, vol. VI
Nevill, Air Vice-Marshal Sir Arthur de Terrotte, 1899–1985, vol. VIII
Nevill, Col Charles William, 1907–1973, vol. VII
Nevill, Lady Dorothy Fanny, died 1913, vol. I
Nevill, Edmund Neville, died 1940, vol. III
Nevill, Rev. Edmund Robert, 1862–1933, vol. III
Nevill, Lord George Montacute, 1856–1920, vol. II
Nevill, Ven. Henry Ralph, 1821–1900, vol. I
Nevill, Henry Rivers, 1876–1939, vol. III
Nevill, Captain Hugh Lewis, 1877–1915, vol. I
Nevill, Ralph Henry, 1865–1930, vol. III
Nevill, Hon. Ralph Pelham, 1832–1914, vol. I
Nevill, Lord Richard Plantagenet, 1864–1939, vol. III
Nevill, Lord Rupert Charles Montacute, 1923–1982, vol. VIII
Nevill, Most Rev. Samuel Tarratt, born 1837, vol. II
Nevill, Rev. Thomas Seymour, 1901–1980, vol. VII
Nevill, Rev. Valentine Paul, 1882–1954, vol. V
Nevill, Comdr Walter Howard, 1887–1956, vol. V
Nevill, Sir Walter Palmer, 1854–1929, vol. III
Neville, Brig. Alfred Geoffrey, 1891–1955, vol. V
Neville, Arthur William, 1884–1948, vol. IV
Neville, Bertie Aylmer Crampton, 1882–1973, vol. VII
Neville, Edith, 1874–1951, vol. V
Neville, Lt-Col Sir Edmund; see Neville, Lt-Col Sir J. E. H.
Neville, Eric Harold, 1889–1961, vol. VI
Neville, Francis Henry, 1847–1915, vol. I
Neville, Adm. Sir George, 1850–1923, vol. II
Neville, Rev. Hon. Grey, 1857–1920, vol. II
Neville, Henry; see Neville, T. H. G.
Neville, Henry Allen Dugdale, 1880–1952, vol. V

Neville, Lt-Col Sir (James) Edmund (Henderson), 2nd Bt, 1897–1982, vol. VIII

Neville, Kenneth Percival Rutherford, 1876–1957, vol. V

Neville, Nigel Charles Alfred, 1849–1923, vol. II

Neville, Captain Philip Lloyd, 1888–1976, vol. VII

Neville, Sir Ralph, 1848–1918, vol. II

Neville, Sir Reginald James Neville, 1st Bt, 1863–1950, vol. IV

Neville, Maj.-Gen. Sir Robert Arthur Ross, 1896–1987, vol. VIII

Neville, Thomas Henry Gartside, (Henry Neville), 1837–1910, vol. I

Neville, Col William Candler, 1859–1926, vol. II

Neville-Rolfe, Eustace, 1845–1908, vol. I

Nevin, Robert Wallace, 1907–1980, vol. VII

Nevin, Samuel, *died* 1979, vol. VII

Nevins, Allan, 1890–1971, vol. VII

Nevinson, Christopher Richard Wynne, 1889–1946, vol. IV

Nevinson, Henry Woodd, 1856–1941, vol. IV

Nevinson, Margaret Wynne, *died* 1932, vol. III

New, Charles George Morley, 1879–1957, vol. V

New, Edmund Hort, 1871–1931, vol. III

New, Sir Henry Francis, 1859–1931, vol. III

New, Rev. James Marr, 1855–1931, vol. III

Newall, 1st Baron, 1886–1963, vol. VI

Newall, Dame Bertha Surtees, 1877–1932, vol. III

Newall, Hugh Frank, 1857–1944, vol. IV

Newall, Norman Dakeyne, 1888–1952, vol. V

Newall, Col Stuart, 1843–1920, vol. II

Newark, Francis Headon, 1907–1976, vol. VII

Newberry, Percy Edward, 1869–1949, vol. IV

Newbery, Arthur, *died* 1930, vol. III

Newbery, Francis H., *died* 1946, vol. IV

Newbigging, Brig.-Gen. William Patrick Eric, 1871–1940, vol. III

Newbigin, Marion I., *died* 1934, vol. III

Newbold, Lt-Col Charles Joseph, *died* 1946, vol. IV

Newbold, Sir Douglas, 1894–1945, vol. IV

Newbold, John Turner Walton, 1888–1943, vol. IV

Newbolt, Captain (Arthur) Francis, 1893–1966, vol. VI

Newbolt, Captain Francis; *see* Newbolt, Captain A. F.

Newbolt, Sir Francis George, 1863–1940, vol. III

Newbolt, Sir Henry John, 1862–1938, vol. III

Newbolt, Rev. Michael Robert, 1874–1956, vol. V

Newbolt, Rev. William Charles Edmund, 1844–1930, vol. III

Newborough, 4th Baron, 1873–1916, vol. II

Newborough, 5th Baron, 1878–1957, vol. V

Newborough, 6th Baron, 1877–1965, vol. VI

Newbould, Alfred Ernest, 1873–1952, vol. V

Newbould, Sir (Babington) Bennett, 1867–1937, vol. III

Newbould, Sir Bennett; *see* Newbould, Sir Babington B.

Newboult, Sir Alexander Theodore, 1896–1964, vol. VI

Newburgh, 8th Earl of, 1818–1908, vol. I

Newburgh, 9th (shown as 10th) Earl of, 1862–1941, vol. IV

Newburgh, Countess of (10th in line), 1889–1977, vol. VII

Newburgh, 11th Earl of, 1907–1986, vol. VIII

Newcastle, 7th Duke of, 1864–1928, vol. II

Newcastle, 8th Duke of, 1866–1941, vol. IV

Newcastle, 9th Duke of, 1907–1988, vol. VIII

Newcastle, 10th Duke of, 1920–1988, vol. VIII

Newcastle, Duchess of; (Kathleen Florence May), *died* 1955, vol. V

Newcomb, Lt-Col Clive, 1882–1968, vol. VI

Newcomb, Simon, 1835–1909, vol. I

Newcomb, Wilfrid Davison, 1889–1971, vol. VII

Newcombe, Edmund Leslie, 1859–1931, vol. III

Newcombe, Major Edward Osborn Armstrong, 1874–1941, vol. IV

Newcombe, Maj.-Gen. Henry William, 1875–1963, vol. VI

Newcombe, Luxmoore, 1880–1952, vol. V

Newcombe, Col Stewart Francis, 1878–1956, vol. V

Newcomen, Col Arthur Hills G.; *see* Gleadowe-Newcomen.

Newcomen, Gleadowe Henry Turner, 1877–1932, vol. III

Newdegate, Anne Emily Newdigate-, (Lady Newdigate-Newdegate), *died* 1924, vol. II

Newdegate, Sir Edward Newdigate, 1825–1902, vol. I

Newdegate, Sir Francis Alexander Newdigate, 1862–1936, vol. III

Newdigate, Bernard Henry, 1869–1944, vol. IV

Newdigate, Lt-Gen. Sir Henry Richard Legge, 1832–1908, vol. I

Newdigate-Newdegate, A. E.; *see* Newdegate.

Newe, Rt Hon. Gerard Benedict, 1907–1982, vol. VIII

Newell, Arthur Franklin, 1885–1976, vol. VII

Newell, Gordon Ewart, 1908–1968, vol. VI

Newell, Harold, *died* 1937, vol. III

Newell, Lt-Col Herbert Andrews, 1869–1934, vol. III

Newell, Hugh Hamilton, 1878–1941, vol. IV

Newell, Rev. Canon John Philip Peter, 1911–1980, vol. VII

Newell, Kenneth Wyatt, 1925–1990, vol. VIII

Newell, Philip Staniforth, 1903–1990, vol. VIII

Newell, William Homan, 1819–1901, vol. I

Newenham, Brig.-Gen. Henry Edward Berkeley, 1866–1934, vol. III

Newham, Lt-Col Hugh Basil Greaves, 1874–1959, vol. V

Newhouse, Rev. Robert Perceval, *died* 1933, vol. III

Newill, Ven. Edward Joseph, 1877–1954, vol. V

Newitt, Dudley Maurice, 1894–1980, vol. VII

Newland, Col Edmund Walcott, 1858–1937, vol. III

Newland, Maj.-Gen. Sir Foster Reuss, 1862–1943, vol. IV

Newland, Captain H. Osman, *died* 1920, vol. II

Newland, Sir Henry Simpson, 1873–1969, vol. VI

Newland-Pedley, Frederick, *died* 1944, vol. IV

Newlands, 1st Baron, 1825–1906, vol. I

Newlands, 2nd Baron, 1851–1929, vol. III

Newlands, Alexander, 1870–1938, vol. III

Newlands, Harry Scott, 1884–1933, vol. III

Newlands, Hon. Sir John, 1864–1932, vol. III

Newlands, John, 1857–1937, vol. III

Newling, (Alfred) John, 1896–1957, vol. V

Newling, John; *see* Newling, A. J.
Newman, Albert Gordon, 1894–1956, vol. V
Newman, Lt-Col (Augustus) Charles, 1904–1972, vol. VII
Newman, Bernard, 1897–1968, vol. VI
Newman, Bertram, 1886–1962, vol. VI
Newman, Sir Cecil Gustavus Jacques, 2nd Bt (*cr* 1912), 1891–1955, vol. V
Newman, Lt-Col Charles; *see* Newman, Lt-Col A. C.
Newman, Charles Edward Kingsley, 1900–1989, vol. VIII
Newman, Maj.-Gen. Charles Richard, 1875–1954, vol. V
Newman, David, 1853–1924, vol. II
Newman, Edward, 1858–1946, vol. IV
Newman, Edward Braxton, 1842–1916, vol. II
Newman, Brig.-Gen. Edward Harding-, 1872–1955, vol. V
Newman, Captain Edward John Kendall, 1860–1941, vol. IV
Newman, Major Edward William Polson, 1887–1967, vol. VI
Newman, Ernest, 1868–1959, vol. V
Newman, Lt-Col Ernest Alan Robert, 1867–1943, vol. IV
Newman, Ven. Ernest Frederick, 1859–1928, vol. II
Newman, Francis William, 1805–1897, vol. I
Newman, Frank Herbert, 1875–1948, vol. IV
Newman, Sir George, 1870–1948, vol. IV
Newman, Sir Gerard Robert Henry Sigismund, 3rd Bt, 1927–1987, vol. VIII
Newman, Harold Lancelot, 1878–1949, vol. IV
Newman, Maj.-Gen. Hubert Thomas, 1895–1965, vol. VI
Newman, Maj.-Gen. John Cartwright H.; *see* Harding-Newman.
Newman, Sir John Robert Pretyman, 1871–1947, vol. IV
Newman, Maxwell Herman Alexander, 1897–1984, vol. VIII
Newman, Philip Harry, 1840–1927, vol. II
Newman, Sir Ralph Alured, 5th Bt (*cr* 1836), 1902–1968, vol. VI
Newman, Rev. Canon Richard, 1871–1961, vol. VI
Newman, Col Richard Ernest Upton, 1883–1956, vol. V
Newman, Robert Lydston, 1865–1937, vol. III
Newman, Ronald William, 1921–1987, vol. VIII
Newman, Sidney Thomas Mayow, 1906–1971, vol. VII
Newman, Thomas Prichard, 1846–1915, vol. I
Newman, Trevor Clyde, 1882–1955, vol. V
Newman, William Henry, 1865–1947, vol. IV
Newman-Morris, Sir Geoffrey, 1909–1981, vol. VIII
Newman-Morris, Sir John, 1879–1957, vol. V
Newmarch, Alexander, 1869–1935, vol. III
Newmarch, Bernard James, 1856–1929, vol. III
Newmarch, Francis Welles, 1853–1918, vol. II
Newmarch, Maj.-Gen. George, 1833–1912, vol. I
Newmarch, Sir Oliver Richardson, 1834–1920, vol. II
Newmarch, Rosa Harriet, 1857–1940, vol. III
Newnes, Sir Frank Hillyard, 2nd Bt, 1876–1955, vol. V
Newnes, Sir George, 1st Bt, 1851–1910, vol. I

Newnham, Ernest Percy, 1870–1943, vol. IV
Newnham, Hubert Ernest, 1886–1970, vol. VI
Newnham, Rt Rev. Jervois Arthur, 1852–1941, vol. IV
Newnham, Ven. Obadiah Samuel, 1848–1932, vol. III
Newnham, William Harry Christopher, 1859–1941, vol. IV
Newnham-Davis, Lt-Col Nathaniel, 1854–1917, vol. II
Newns, George Henry, 1908–1985, vol. VIII
Newport, Surg. Captain Alexander Charles William, 1874–1948, vol. IV
Newsam, Sir Frank Aubrey, 1893–1964, vol. VI
Newsam, Richard William, 1918–1983, vol. VIII
Newsholme, Sir Arthur, 1857–1943, vol. IV
Newsom, Col Augustus Charles, 1866–1936, vol. III
Newsom, Rev. George Ernest, 1871–1934, vol. III
Newsom, Rear-Adm. John Bertram, 1902–1971, vol. VII
Newsom, Sir John Hubert, 1910–1971, vol. VII
Newson, Sir Percy Wilson, 1st Bt, 1874–1950, vol. IV
Newson-Smith, Sir Frank Edwin, 1st Bt, 1879–1971, vol. VII
Newstead, Robert, 1859–1947, vol. IV
Newsum, Sir Clement Henry, 1865–1947, vol. IV
Newte, Horace Wykeham Can, *died* 1949, vol. IV
Newth, Brig. Arthur Leslie Walter, 1897–1978, vol. VII
Newth, David Richmond, 1921–1988, vol. VIII
Newton, 1st Baron, 1828–1898, vol. I
Newton, 2nd Baron, 1857–1942, vol. IV
Newton, 3rd Baron, 1888–1960, vol. V
Newton, Sir Alan, 1887–1949, vol. IV
Newton, Alfred, 1829–1907, vol. I
Newton, Sir Alfred James, 1st Bt (*cr* 1900), 1849–1921, vol. II
Newton, Algernon, 1880–1968, vol. VI
Newton, Arthur, 1858–1942, vol. IV
Newton, Arthur Percival, 1873–1942, vol. IV
Newton, Sir Basil Cochrane, 1889–1965, vol. VI
Newton, Bernard St John, 1890–1977, vol. VII
Newton, Charles Edmund, 1831–1908, vol. I
Newton, Sir Charles Henry, 1882–1973, vol. VII
Newton, Captain Denzil Onslow Cochrane, 1880–1915, vol. I
Newton, Sir Edgar Henry, 2nd Bt (*cr* 1924), 1893–1971, vol. VII
Newton, Sir Edward, 1832–1897, vol. I
Newton, Edwin Tulley, 1840–1930, vol. III
Newton, Eric, 1893–1965, vol. VI
Newton, Ernest, 1856–1922, vol. II
Newton, Sir Francis James, 1857–1948, vol. IV
Newton, Francis John Stuart H.; *see* Hay-Newton.
Newton, Lt-Col Frank Graham, 1877–1962, vol. VI
Newton, George Percival, 1868–1951, vol. V
Newton, Giles Fendall, 1891–1974, vol. VII
Newton, Sir Harry Kottingham, 2nd Bt (*cr* 1900), 1875–1951, vol. V
Newton, Rt Rev. Henry, 1866–1947, vol. IV
Newton, Lt-Col Henry, 1880–1959, vol. VI
Newton, Henry Chance, 1854–1931, vol. III
Newton, Sir Henry William, 1842–1914, vol. I
Newton, Sir Hibbert Alan Stephen; *see* Newton, Sir Alan.

Newton, Hibbert Henry, 1861–1927, vol. II
Newton, Rev. Horace, 1841–1920, vol. II
Newton, Sir Hubert, 1904–1989, vol. VIII
Newton, Ivor, 1892–1981, vol. VIII
Newton, John, 1864–1916, vol. II
Newton, John Mordaunt, 1913–1986, vol. VIII
Newton, Rev. Joseph Fort, 1880–1950, vol. IV
Newton, Lily, 1893–1981, vol. VIII
Newton, Col Sir Louis Arthur, 1st Bt (*cr* 1924), 1867–1945, vol. IV
Newton, Rev. Richard Heber, 1840–1914, vol. I
Newton, Robert, 1905–1956, vol. V
Newton, Robert, 1908–1983, vol. VIII
Newton, Robert Henry, 1864–1943, vol. IV
Newton, Robert Milnes, 1821–1900, vol. I
Newton, Maj.-Gen. Thomas Cochrane, 1885–1976, vol. VII
Newton, Sir Wilberforce Stephen, 1890–1956, vol. V
Newton, Sir William, *died* 1915, vol. I
Newton, William George, 1859–1920, vol. II
Newton, William Godfrey, 1885–1949, vol. IV
Newton, William Henry, 1904–1949, vol. IV
Newton, William James Oliver, 1884–1952, vol. V
Newton-Brady, Sir Andrew, 1849–1918, vol. II
Newton-Butler, Lord; John Brinsley Danvers, 1893–1912, vol. I
Newton-Robinson, Charles Edmund, 1853–1913, vol. I
Ney, Marie; *see* Menzies, M. N.
Neylan, Sir Daniel, 1866–1943, vol. IV
Neylan, Lt-Col John Nolan, *died* 1936, vol. III
Ngata, Hon. Sir Apirana Turupa, 1874–1950, vol. IV
Niblack, Rear-Adm. Albert P., 1859–1929, vol. III
Niblett, Adm. Harry Seawell Frank, 1852–1939, vol. III
Niblett, Robert Henry, 1859–1918, vol. II
Nichol, Col Charles Edward, 1859–1939, vol. III
Nichol, Robert, 1890–1925, vol. II
Nichol, Robert John, *died* 1946, vol. IV
Nichol, Hon. Walter Cameron, 1866–1928, vol. II
Nicholas, Sir Alfred James, 1900–1984, vol. VIII
Nicholas, Captain John, 1851–1920, vol. II
Nicholas, Montagu Richmond, 1905–1964, vol. VI
Nicholas, Reginald Owen Mercer, 1903–1981, vol. VIII
Nicholas, Col Stephen Henry Edmund, 1870–1948, vol. IV
Nicholas, Sir Walter Powell, 1868–1926, vol. II
Nicholas, Rev. William, 1838–1912, vol. I
Nicholetts, Air Marshal Sir Gilbert Edward, 1902–1983, vol. VIII
Nicholl, Sir Allan Hume, *died* 1941, vol. IV
Nicholl, Rear-Adm. Angus Dacres, 1896–1977, vol. VII
Nicholl, Maj.-Gen. Sir Christopher Rice Havard, 1836–1928, vol. II
Nicholl, Sir Edward, 1862–1939, vol. III
Nicholl, George Frederick, *died* 1913, vol. I
Nicholl, Air Vice-Marshal Sir Hazelton Robson, 1882–1956, vol. V
Nicholl, John Storer, 1888–1958, vol. V
Nicholls, Agnes; *see* Harty, A. H.
Nicholls, Albert George, 1870–1946, vol. IV
Nicholls, Arthur, 1880–1974, vol. VII

Nicholls, Rev. Arthur Bell, 1816–1906, vol. I
Nicholls, Bertram, 1883–1974, vol. VII
Nicholls, Pastor Sir Douglas Ralph, 1906–1988, vol. VIII
Nicholls, Frederick, 1871–1952, vol. V
Nicholls, George, 1864–1943, vol. IV
Nicholls, Rt Hon. George Heaton, 1876–1959, vol. V
Nicholls, Harry, 1852–1926, vol. II
Nicholls, Harry, 1915–1975, vol. VII
Nicholls, Hon. Sir Henry Alfred Alford, 1851–1926, vol. II
Nicholls, Hon. Sir Herbert, 1868–1940, vol. III
Nicholls, John Ralph, 1889–1970, vol. VI
Nicholls, Sir John Walter, 1909–1970, vol. VI
Nicholls, Maj.-Gen. Sir Leslie, (Burtonshaw), 1895–1975, vol. VII
Nicholls, Lucius, 1885–1969, vol. VI
Nicholls, Sir Marriott Fawckner, 1898–1969, vol. VI
Nicholls, Surg. Vice-Adm. Sir Percival Thomas, 1877–1959, vol. V
Nicholls, Richard Howell, 1868–1946, vol. IV
Nicholls, Sir Robert Dove, 1889–1970, vol. VI
Nicholls, Col Stephen Charles Phillips, 1883–1959, vol. V
Nicholls, William, 1882–1970, vol. VI
Nicholls, Lt-Col William Ashley, 1883–1941, vol. IV
Nicholls, Gen. Sir William Charles, 1854–1935, vol. III
Nicholls, Sir William Edgar, 1858–1932, vol. III
Nichols, Arthur Eastwood, 1891–1959, vol. V
Nichols, Beverley, 1898–1983, vol. VIII
Nichols, Catherine Maude, *died* 1923, vol. II
Nichols, Edward Leamington, 1854–1937, vol. III
Nichols, George Herbert Fosdike, *died* 1933, vol. III
Nichols, Herbert John, 1895–1959, vol. V
Nichols, Joseph Cowie, *died* 1954, vol. V
Nichols, Peter, 1928–1989, vol. VIII
Nichols, Sir Philip Bouverie Bowyer, 1894–1962, vol. VI
Nichols, Robert Malise Bowyer, 1893–1944, vol. IV
Nichols, Roy Franklin, 1896–1973, vol. VII
Nichols, Rt Rev. William Ford, 1849–1924, vol. II
Nicholson, 1st Baron, 1845–1918, vol. II
Nicholson, Sir Arthur, 1842–1929, vol. III
Nicholson, Bt Col Arthur Falkner, 1885–1954, vol. V
Nicholson, Arthur Pole, 1869–1940, vol. III
Nicholson, Sir Arthur William, 1852–1932, vol. III
Nicholson, Sir Arthur William, 1903–1981, vol. VIII
Nicholson, Ben, 1894–1982, vol. VIII
Nicholson, Bertram, 1875–1943, vol. IV
Nicholson, Captain Bertram William Lothian, 1879–1958, vol. V
Nicholson, Gen. Sir Cameron Gordon Graham, 1898–1979, vol. VII
Nicholson, Maj.-Gen. Sir Cecil Lothian, 1865–1933, vol. III
Nicholson, Sir Charles, 1st Bt (*cr* 1859), 1808–1903, vol. I
Nicholson, Sir Charles, 2nd Bt (*cr* 1859), 1867–1949, vol. IV
Nicholson, Charles Ernest, 1868–1954, vol. V
Nicholson, Rear-Adm. Charles Hepworth, 1891–1966, vol. VI

Nicholson, Sir Charles Norris, 1st Bt (*cr* 1912), 1857–1918, vol. II

Nicholson, Douglas; *see* Nicholson, F. D.

Nicholson, Adm. Sir Douglas Romilly Lothian, 1867–1946, vol. IV

Nicholson, Lt-Col Edmund James Houghton, 1870–1955, vol. V

Nicholson, Comdr Edward Hugh Meredith, 1876–1956, vol. V

Nicholson, Edward Williams Byron, 1849–1912, vol. I

Nicholson, Maj.-Gen. Francis Lothian, 1884–1953, vol. V

Nicholson, Sir Frank, 1875–1952, vol. V

Nicholson, Frank Carr, *died* 1962, vol. VI

Nicholson, (Frank) Douglas, 1905–1984, vol. VIII

Nicholson, Sir Frederick Augustus, 1846–1936, vol. III

Nicholson, Major Geoffrey, 1894–1976, vol. VII

Nicholson, George Crosfield Norris, 1884–1915, vol. I

Nicholson, George Gibb, 1875–1948, vol. IV

Nicholson, Brig.-Gen. George Harvey, 1862–1942, vol. IV

Nicholson, Brig.-Gen. Graham Henry Whalley, 1869–1946, vol. IV

Nicholson, Adm. Sir Gresham; *see* Nicholson, Adm. Sir R. S. G.

Nicholson, Harold, 1883–1949, vol. IV

Nicholson, Harry Oliphant, 1870–1941, vol. IV

Nicholson, Henry Alleyne, 1844–1899, vol. I

Nicholson, Adm. Sir Henry Frederick, 1835–1914, vol. I

Nicholson, Horace Watson, 1883–1935, vol. III

Nicholson, Major Hugh Blomfield, *died* 1957, vol. V

Nicholson, Ivor Percy, *died* 1937, vol. II

Nicholson, Sir John Charles, 3rd Bt, 1904–1986, vol. VIII

Nicholson, Brig. John Gerald, 1906–1979, vol. VII

Nicholson, Sir John Gibb, 1879–1959, vol. V

Nicholson, John Henry, 1889–1972, vol. VII

Nicholson, (John) Leonard, 1916–1990, vol. VIII

Nicholson, Rev. John Malcolm, 1908–1983, vol. VIII

Nicholson, Hon. John Paton, 1922–1985, vol. VIII

Nicholson, Sir John Rumney, 1866–1939, vol. III

Nicholson, Brig.-Gen. John Sanctuary, 1863–1924, vol. II

Nicholson, John Wilfred, 1893–1949, vol. IV

Nicholson, John William, *died* 1955, vol. V

Nicholson, Joseph Shield, 1850–1927, vol. II

Nicholson, Joseph Sinclair, 1882–1968, vol. VI

Nicholson, Leonard; *see* Nicholson, J. L.

Nicholson, Lt-Col Mark Alleyne, 1885–1952, vol. V

Nicholson, Meredith, 1866–1947, vol. IV

Nicholson, Norman Cornthwaite, 1914–1987, vol. VIII

Nicholson, Maj.-Gen. Octavius Henry Lothian, 1877–1938, vol. III

Nicholson, Otho William, 1891–1978, vol. VII

Nicholson, Rev. Ralph, 1856–1930, vol. III

Nicholson, Major Randolph, 1894–1928, vol. II

Nicholson, Adm. Sir (Randolph Stewart) Gresham, 1892–1975, vol. VII

Nicholson, Reginald, 1869–1946, vol. IV

Nicholson, Reginald Popham, 1874–1950, vol. IV

Nicholson, Reynold Alleyne, 1868–1945, vol. IV

Nicholson, Sir Richard, 1828–1913, vol. I

Nicholson, Captain Richard Lindsay, 1882–1940, vol. III

Nicholson, Adm. Stuart, 1865–1936, vol. III

Nicholson, Maj.-Gen. Stuart James, 1836–1917, vol. II

Nicholson, Sir Sydney Hugo, 1875–1947, vol. IV

Nicholson, Sir Walter Frederic, 1876–1946, vol. IV

Nicholson, Col Walter Norris, 1877–1964, vol. VI

Nicholson, Sir William, 1865–1944, vol. IV

Nicholson, Adm. Sir William Coldingham Masters, 1863–1932, vol. III

Nicholson, William Ewart, 1890–1983, vol. VIII

Nicholson, Rt Hon. William Graham, 1862–1942, vol. IV

Nicholson, Gen. Sir William Gustavus, 1845–1909, vol. I

Nicholson, Sir William Newzam Prior, 1872–1949, vol. IV

Nicholson, Adm. Wilmot Stuart, 1872–1947, vol. IV

Nicholson-Lailey, John Raymond, 1900–1979, vol. VII

Nickalls, Captain Guy, 1866–1935, vol. III

Nickalls, Guy Oliver, 1899–1974, vol. VII

Nickalls, Sir Patteson, 1836–1910, vol. I

Nickerson, Maj.-Gen. William Henry Snyder, 1875–1954, vol. V

Nicklin, Hon. Sir Francis; *see* Nicklin, Hon. Sir G. F. R.

Nicklin, Hon. Sir (George) Francis (Reuben), 1895–1978, vol. VII

Nicklin, Robert Shenstone, 1901–1975, vol. VII

Nickolls, Lewis Charles, 1899–1970, vol. VI

Nickson, Rt Rev. George, 1864–1949, vol. IV

Nickson, Col John Edgar, 1899–1969, vol. VI

Nicol, Rev. Anderson, 1906–1972, vol. VII

Nicol, Brig. Cameron Macdonald, 1891–1965, vol. VI

Nicol, Claude Scott, 1914–1984, vol. VIII

Nicol, Donald Ninian, 1843–1903, vol. I

Nicol, Erskine, 1825–1904, vol. I

Nicol, Henry, 1821–1905, vol. I

Nicol, Jacob, *died* 1958, vol. V

Nicol, James Lauder, 1889–1971, vol. VII

Nicol, John, 1838–1920, vol. II

Nicol, Hon. Brig.-Gen. Lewis Loyd, 1858–1935, vol. III

Nicol, Rev. Thomas, 1846–1916, vol. II

Nicol, Thomas, 1900–1983, vol. VIII

Nicol, Sir Thomas Drysdale, 1878–1961, vol. VI

Nicol, William Allardyce, 1909–1989, vol. VIII

Nicolas, Nicholas Harris, 1830–1905, vol. I

Nicolay, Col Bernard Underwood, 1873–1960, vol. V, vol. VI

Nicolet, Gabriel, 1856–1921, vol. II

Nicoll, Allardyce; *see* Nicoll, J. R. A.

Nicoll, Gordon, *died* 1959, vol. V

Nicoll, Gen. Henry, 1816–1907, vol. I

Nicoll, James Gibson, 1870–1949, vol. IV

Nicoll, James H., 1865–1921, vol. II

Nicoll, Sir John Fearns, 1899–1981, vol. VIII

Nicoll, John Ramsay Allardyce, 1894–1976, vol. VII

Nicoll, Maurice, 1884–1953, vol. V

Nicoll, Lt-Col Peter Strachan, 1864–1942, vol. IV

Nicoll, Sir William, 1860–1908, vol. I

Nicoll, Sir William Robertson, 1851–1923, vol. II
Nicolle, Edmund Toulmin, 1868–1929, vol. III
Nicolle, John Macarthur, 1885–1964, vol. VI
Nicolle, Maurice, 1862–1932, vol. III
Nicolls, Arthur Edward Jefferys, *died* 1963, vol. VI
Nicolls, Sir Basil Edward, 1893–1965, vol. VI
Nicolls, Brig.-Gen. Edmund Gustavus, 1858–1932, vol. III
Nicolls, Edward Hugh Dyneley, 1871–1963, vol. VI
Nicolls, Ven Gerald Edward, 1862–1937, vol. III
Nicolls, Maj.-Gen. Oliver Henry Atkins, 1834–1920, vol. II
Nicolson, Sir Arthur John Frederick William, 11th Bt (*cr* 1629), 1882–1952, vol. V
Nicolson, Sir Arthur Thomas Bennet Robert, 10th Bt (*cr* 1629), 1842–1917, vol. II
Nicolson, David, 1844–1932, vol. III
Nicolson, Wing Comdr Eric James Brindley, 1917–1945, vol. IV
Nicolson, Sir Frederick William Erskine, 10th Bt (*cr* 1637), 1815–1899, vol. I
Nicolson, Hon. Sir Harold George, 1886–1968, vol. VI
Nicolson, Sir (Harold) Stanley, 12th Bt, 1883–1961, vol. VI
Nicolson, Sir John William, 1895–1965, vol. VI
Nicolson, Sir Kenneth, 1891–1964, vol. VI
Nicolson, Lionel Benedict, 1914–1978, vol. VII
Nicolson, Lt-Gen. Malcolm Hassels, 1843–1904, vol. I
Nicolson, Sir Stanley; *see* Nicolson, Sir H. S.
Nicoresti, Carol Adolph C.; *see* Cofman-Nicoresti.
Nidditch, Peter Harold, 1928–1983, vol. VIII
Niebuhr, Reinhold, 1892–1971, vol. VII
Niecks, Frederick, 1845–1924, vol. II
Niehaus, Charles Henry, 1855–1935, vol. III
Nield, Rt Hon. Sir Herbert, 1862–1932, vol. III
Nielson, Hon. Niel, 1869–1930, vol. III
Niemeyer, Sir Otto Ernst, 1883–1971, vol. VII
Niemöller, Rev. (Friedrich Gustav Emil) Martin, 1892–1984, vol. VIII
Niemöller, Rev. Martin; *see* Niemöller, Rev. F. G. E. M.
Nietzsche, Friedrich Wilhelm, 1844–1900, vol. I
Nightingale, Sir Charles Athelstan, 16th Bt, 1902–1977, vol. VII
Nightingale, Sir Edward Manners, 14th Bt, 1888–1953, vol. V
Nightingale, Florence, 1820–1910, vol. I
Nightingale, Sir Geoffrey Slingsby, 15th Bt, 1904–1972, vol. VII
Nightingale, Sir Henry Dickonson, 13th (styled 9th) Bt, 1830–1911, vol. I
Nightingale, Maj.-Gen. Manners Ralph Willmot, 1871–1956, vol. V
Nightingale, Percy Herbert, 1907–1981, vol. VIII
Nightingale, Thomas Slingsby, 1866–1918, vol. II
Nihalsingh, Rev. Canon Solomon, 1852–1916, vol. II
Nihill, Sir Barclay; *see* Nihill, Sir J. H. B.
Nihill, Sir (John Harry) Barclay, 1892–1975, vol. VII
Nijland, Albertus Antonie, 1868–1936, vol. III
Niland, D'Arcy Francis, *died* 1967, vol. VI
Niles, Emory Hamilton, 1892–1976, vol. VII

Nilkanth, Rao Bahadur Sir Ramanbhai Mahipatram, *died* 1928, vol. II
Nilsson, Mme Christine, (Comtesse de Miranda), 1843–1921, vol. II
Nimitz, Fleet Adm. Chester William, 1885–1966, vol. VI
Nimmo, Sir Adam, *died* 1939, vol. III
Nimmo, Surg. Rear-Adm. Frank Hutton, 1872–1954, vol. V
Nimmo, Henry, 1885–1954, vol. V
Nimmo, Sir Robert, 1894–1979, vol. VII
Nimmo, Maj.-Gen. Thomas Rose, 1831–1904, vol. I
Nimptsch, Uli, 1897–1977, vol. VII
Nind, William Walker, 1882–1964, vol. VI
Ninis, Rev. Richard Duncan, 1867–1940, vol. III
Ninnes, Bernard, 1899–1971, vol. VII
Ninnis, Insp.-Gen. Belgrave, *died* 1922, vol. II
Nipher, Francis Eugene, 1847–1926, vol. II
Nisbet, Brig.-Gen. Francis Courtenay, 1869–1953, vol. V
Nisbet, Hugh Bryan, 1902–1969, vol. VI
Nisbet, Hume, *born* 1849, vol. II
Nisbet, James Wilkie, 1903–1974, vol. VII
Nisbet, John, 1853–1914, vol. I
Nisbet, John Ferguson, 1851–1899, vol. I
Nisbet, Rev. Matthew Alexander, 1838–1919, vol. II
Nisbet, Noel L., 1887–1956, vol. V
Nisbet, Pollok Sinclair, *born* 1848, vol. II
Nisbet, Robert Buchan, 1857–1942, vol. IV
Nisbet, Col Robert Parry, 1839–1916, vol. II
Nisbet, Col Thomas, 1882–1956, vol. V
Nisbet-Hamilton Ogilvy, Mrs; *see* Ogilvy.
Nisbett, Lt-Col George Dalrymple More, 1850–1922, vol. II
Nisbett, George Hinde, 1866–1940, vol. III
Nisse, Bertram Sydney, *died* 1946, vol. IV
Nissen, Lt-Col Peter Norman, 1871–1930, vol. III
Nissim, Charles, 1845–1918, vol. II
Nitch, Cyril Alfred Rankin, *died* 1969, vol. VI
Niven, Charles, *died* 1923, vol. II
Niven, David; *see* Niven, J. D. G.
Niven, Frederick John, 1878–1944, vol. IV
Niven, James, 1851–1925, vol. II
Niven, (James) David (Graham), 1910–1983, vol. VIII
Niven, Sir John, 1877–1947, vol. IV
Niven, Very Rev. T. B. W., 1834–1914, vol. I
Niven, Col Thomas Murray, 1900–1987, vol. VIII
Niven, William, *died* 1921, vol. II
Niven, Sir William Davidson, 1842–1917, vol. II
Niven, William Dickie, 1879–1965, vol. VI
Nixon, Alfred, 1858–1928, vol. III
Nixon, Maj.-Gen. Arundel James, 1849–1925, vol. II
Nixon, Sir (Charles) Norman, 1891–1978, vol. VII
Nixon, Sir Christopher John, 1st Bt, 1849–1914, vol. I
Nixon, Major Sir Christopher John Louis Joseph, 3rd Bt, 1918–1978, vol. VII
Nixon, Sir Christopher William, 2nd Bt, 1877–1945, vol. IV
Nixon, Sir Edwin Vandervord, 1876–1955, vol. V
Nixon, Sir Frank Horsfall, 1890–1966, vol. VI
Nixon, Ven. George Robinson, *died* 1963, vol. VI
Nixon, Rear-Adm. Harry Desmond, 1920–1986, vol. VIII

Nixon, Henry, 1874–1939, vol. III
Nixon, Rev. Howard, *died* 1936, vol. III
Nixon, Howard Millar, 1909–1983, vol. VIII
Nixon, Job, 1891–1938, vol. III
Nixon, John Alexander, 1874–1951, vol. V
Nixon, Sir John Carson, 1887–1958, vol. V
Nixon, Gen. Sir John Eccles, 1857–1921, vol. II
Nixon, John William, *died* 1949, vol. IV
Nixon, Rev. Leigh Hunter, 1871–1941, vol. IV
Nixon, Sir Norman; *see* Nixon, Sir C. N.
Nixon, Rev. Robin Ernest, 1931–1978, vol. VII
Nixon, Wilfrid Ernest, 1892–1970, vol. VI
Nixon, William Charles Wallace, 1903–1966, vol. VI
Nizamat Jung; *see* Ahmad, Maulvi Sir N.
Nkrumah, Kwame, 1909–1972, vol. VII
Noad, Lewis, 1865–1950, vol. IV
Noad, Sidney Reginald L.; *see* Innes-Noad.
Noakes, Ven. Edward Spencer, *died* 1944, vol. IV
Noakes, Col Geoffrey William, 1913–1989, vol. VIII
Noal, Comdr Richard John, 1870–1950, vol. IV
Nobbs, Percy Erskine, 1875–1966, vol. VI
Noble, Comdr Rt Hon. Sir Allan Herbert Percy, 1908–1982, vol. VIII
Noble, Sir Andrew, 1st Bt (*cr* 1902), 1831–1915, vol. I
Noble, Sir Andrew Napier, 2nd Bt, 1904–1987, vol. VIII
Noble, Col Sir Arthur, 1908–1982, vol. VIII
Noble, Dennis, 1898–1966, vol. VI
Noble, Edward, 1857–1941, vol. IV
Noble, Frederick Arnold W.; *see* Williamson-Noble.
Noble, Sir George John William, 2nd Bt (*cr* 1902), 1859–1937, vol. III
Noble, Sir Humphrey Brunel, 4th Bt (*cr* 1902), 1892–1968, vol. VI
Noble, J. Campbell, 1846–1913, vol. I
Noble, John, 1837–1898, vol. I
Noble, Sir John Henry Brunel, 1st Bt (*cr* 1923), 1865–1938, vol. III
Noble, Michael Alfred, 1935–1983, vol. VIII
Noble, Michael Antony Cristobal; *see* Baron Glenkinglas.
Noble, Adm. Sir Percy Lockhart Harnam, 1880–1955, vol. V
Noble, Sir Peter Scott, 1899–1987, vol. VIII
Noble, Philip Ernest, *died* 1931, vol. III
Noble, Robert, 1857–1917, vol. II
Noble, Robert More Hilary, 1909–1984, vol. VIII
Noble, Sir Saxton William Armstrong, 3rd Bt (*cr* 1902), 1863–1942, vol. IV
Noble, Thomas Tertius, 1867–1953, vol. V
Noble, Thomas Paterson, 1887–1959, vol. V
Noble, Rev. Walter James, 1879–1962, vol. VI
Noble, Sir William, 1861–1943, vol. IV
Noble, William James, 1855–1914, vol. I
Noble, Rev. William Mackreth, 1845–1929, vol. III
Noble, Wilson, 1854–1917, vol. II
Noblett, Bt Lt-Col Louis Hemington, 1869–1948, vol. IV
Nock, Arthur Darby, 1902–1963, vol. VI
Nock, Rt Rev. Frank Foley, 1916–1989, vol. VIII
Nock, Sir Norman Lindfield, 1899–1990, vol. VIII
Nockolds, Stephen Robert, 1909–1990, vol. VIII
Nodzu, Michitsura, Marshal Marquess, 1841–1908, vol. I

Noel, Andre Espitalier-, 1898–1950, vol. IV (A), vol. V
Noel, Lady Augusta, 1838–1902, vol. I
Noel, Hon. Charles Hubert Francis, 1885–1947, vol. IV
Noël, Sir Claude; *see* Noël, Sir M. E. C.
Noel, Rev. Conrad le Despenser Roden, 1869–1942, vol. IV
Noel, Lt-Col Hon. Edward, 1852–1917, vol. II
Noel, Ernest, 1831–1931, vol. III
Noel, Evan Baillie, 1879–1928, vol. II
Noel, Adm. Francis Charles Methuen, 1852–1925, vol. II
Noel, Admiral of the Fleet Sir Gerard Henry Uctred, 1845–1918, vol. II
Noel, Rt Hon. Gerard James, 1823–1911, vol. I
Noel, Bt Col Harold Ernest, 1884–1941, vol. IV
Noel, Rev. Canon John Monk, 1840–1921, vol. II
Noël, Sir (Martial Ernest) Claude, 1912–1985, vol. VIII
Noel-Baker, Baron (Life Peer); Philip John Noel-Baker, 1889–1982, vol. VIII
Noel-Buxton, 1st Baron, 1869–1948, vol. IV
Noel-Buxton, 2nd Baron, 1917–1980, vol. VII
Noel-Buxton, Lady; (Lucy Edith), *died* 1960, vol. V
Noel-Hill, Rev. Charles, 1848–1911, vol. I
Noel-Walker, Sir Edward; *see* Walker.
Noghi, Gen. Count Mare-Suke, 1849–1912, vol. I
Nokes, George Augustus; *see* Sekon, G. A.
Nokes, Gerald Dacre, 1899–1971, vol. VII
Nolan, Lt-Col Andrew Bellew, 1867–1932, vol. III
Nolan, Very Rev. Mgr Edmond, 1857–1931, vol. III
Nolan, James Joseph, 1869–1939, vol. III
Nolan, John J., 1888–1952, vol. V
Nolan, Col John Philip, *died* 1912, vol. I
Nolan, Michael James, 1859–1944, vol. IV
Nolan, Sir Robert Howard, *died* 1923, vol. II
Nöldeke, Theodor, 1836–1930, vol. III
Nolhac, Pierre de, 1859–1936, vol. III
Nollet, Edouard, 1865–1941, vol. IV
Nolloth, Rev. Charles Frederick, 1850–1932, vol. III
Nolloth, Rev. Henry Edward, 1846–1929, vol. III
Nonweiler, Maj.-Gen. Wilfrid Ivan, 1900–1953, vol. V
Noon, Firoz Khan, 1893–1970, vol. VI
Noon, Nawab Sir Malik Mohamed Hayat, 1875–1941, vol. IV
Noone, Paul, 1939–1989, vol. VIII
Noott, Col Cuthbert Cecil, 1870–1933, vol. III
Nops, Walter, 1850–1918, vol. II
Nops, Sir Wilfrid Walter, 1884–1948, vol. IV
Norbury, 4th Earl of, 1862–1943, vol. IV
Norbury, 5th Earl of, 1893–1955, vol. V
Norbury, Edwin Arthur, 1849–1918, vol. II
Norbury, Insp.-Gen. Sir Henry Frederick, 1839–1925, vol. II
Norbury, Sir Henry Frederick Oswald, 1880–1948, vol. IV
Norbury, Captain Herbert Reginald, 1876–1967, vol. VI
Norbury, Lionel Edward Close, 1882–1967, vol. VI
Norbury, Col Thomas Coningsby, 1829–1899, vol. I
Norcock, Vice-Adm. Charles James, 1847–1933, vol. III

Norcott, Col Charles Hawtrey Bruce, 1849–1931, vol. III

Nordau, Max Simon, 1849–1923, vol. II

Nordenskiold, Baron Adolphe Eric, 1832–1901, vol. I

Nordenskjöld, Otto, 1869–1928, vol. II

Nordhoff, Heinrich, 1899–1968, vol. VI

Nordica, Lillian, 1859–1914, vol. I

Nordmeyer, Hon. Sir Arnold Henry, 1901–1989, vol. VIII

Norfolk, 15th Duke of, 1847–1917, vol. II

Norfolk, 16th Duke of, 1908–1975, vol. VII

Norfolk, Rear-Adm. George Anthony Francis, 1907–1966, vol. VI

Norie, Maj.-Gen. Charles Edward Manley, 1866–1929, vol. III

Norie, Maj.-Gen. Evelyn Medows, 1833–1913, vol. I

Norie-Miller, Sir Francis, 1st Bt, 1859–1947, vol. IV

Norie-Miller, Sir Stanley, 2nd Bt, 1888–1973, vol. VII

Nörlund, Niels Erik, 1885–1981, vol. VIII

Norman, 1st Baron, 1871–1950, vol. IV

Norman, Vice-Adm. Alfred Headley, 1881–1973, vol. VII

Norman, Rev. Alfred Merle, 1831–1918, vol. II

Norman, Arthur William, 1850–1928, vol. II

Norman, Sir Charles, 1892–1976, vol. VII

Norman, Rev. Charles Frederick, 1829–1913, vol. I

Norman, Charles Kensit, 1857–1937, vol. III

Norman, Maj.-Gen. Charles Wake, 1891–1974, vol. VII

Norman, Brig.-Gen. Claude Lumsden, 1876–1967, vol. VI

Norman, Brig. Compton Cardew, 1877–1955, vol. V

Norman, Duncan Thomas, 1889–1972, vol. VII

Norman, Edward, 1847–1923, vol. II

Norman, Sir Edward James, 1900–1983, vol. VIII

Norman, Rt Rev. Edward Kinsella Norman, 1916–1987, vol. VIII

Norman, Comdr F. M., 1833–1918, vol. II

Norman, Sir Francis Booth, 1830–1901, vol. I

Norman, Sir Frederick, 1857–1936, vol. III

Norman, Frederick, 1897–1968, vol. VI

Norman, Col. Harold Hugh, 1875–1933, vol. III

Norman, Rt Hon. Sir Henry, 1st Bt, 1858–1939, vol. III

Norman, Henry Gordon, 1890–1967, vol. VI

Norman, Sir (Henry) Nigel St Valery, 2nd Bt, 1897–1943, vol. IV

Norman, Lt-Gen. Sir Henry Radford, 1818–1899, vol. I

Norman, Sir Henry Wylie, 1826–1904, vol. I

Norman, Herman Cameron, 1872–1955, vol. V

Norman, Brig. Hugh Ronald, 1905–1979, vol. VII

Norman, Sir Nigel; *see* Norman, Sir H. N. St V.

Norman, Philip, *died* 1931, vol. III

Norman, Ronald Collet, 1873–1963, vol. VI

Norman, Surg.-Vice-Adm. Sir William Henry, 1855–1934, vol. III

Norman, Col William Wylie, 1860–1935, vol. III

Norman Barnett, Lt-Col Henry, *died* 1952, vol. V

Norman-Walker, Sir Hugh Selby, 1916–1985, vol. VIII

Norman-Walker, Col John Norman, 1872–1951, vol. V

Normanbrook, 1st Baron, 1902–1967, vol. VI

Normanby, 3rd Marquess of, 1846–1932, vol. III

Normand, Baron (Life Peer); Wilfrid Guild Normand, 1884–1962, vol. VI

Normand, Alexander Robert, 1880–1958, vol. V

Normand, Sir Charles William Blyth, 1889–1982, vol. VIII

Normand, Mrs Ernest, (Henrietta Rae), 1859–1928, vol. II

Normand, Captain Patrick Hill, 1876–1943, vol. IV

Normand, Robert Casley, 1897–1962, vol. VI

Normanton, 4th Earl of, 1865–1933, vol. III

Normanton, 5th Earl of, 1910–1967, vol. VI

Normanton, Helena Florence, 1883–1957, vol. V

Norreys, Lord; Montagu Charles Francis Towneley-Bertie, 1860–1919, vol. II

Norrie, 1st Baron, 1893–1977, vol. VII

Norrie, Beatrice, *died* 1933, vol. III

Norrie, Col Edward Creer, 1885–1958, vol. V

Norrington, Sir Arthur Lionel Pugh, 1899–1982, vol. VIII

Norrington, Lt-Col Reginald Lewis, *died* 1960, vol. V

Norris, Dame Ada May, 1901–1989, vol. VIII

Norris, Alan Hedley, 1913–1981, vol. VIII

Norris, Sir Alfred Henry, 1894–1989, vol. VIII

Norris, Arthur Gilbert, 1889–1962, vol. VI

Norris, Arthur Herbert, 1875–1953, vol. V

Norris, Charles Arthur, 1874–1941, vol. IV

Norris, Vice-Adm. Sir Charles Fred Wivell, 1900–1989, vol. VIII

Norris, Charles Gilman, *died* 1945, vol. IV

Norris, Adm. David Thomas, 1875–1937, vol. III

Norris, Donald Craig, *died* 1968, vol. VI

Norris, Rev. Edward John, 1860–1940, vol. III

Norris, Edward Samuel, 1832–1908, vol. I

Norris, Francis Edward Boshear, *died* 1966, vol. VI

Norris, Rt Rev. Francis Lushington, 1864–1945, vol. IV

Norris, Maj.-Gen. Sir (Frank) Kingsley, 1893–1984, vol. VIII

Norris, George Michael, 1841–1922, vol. II

Norris, Henry, 1852–1954, vol. V

Norris, Col Henry Crawley, 1841–1914, vol. I

Norris, Lt-Col Henry Everard DuCane, 1869–1960, vol. V

Norris, Col Sir Henry George, 1865–1934, vol. III

Norris, Herbert, *died* 1950, vol. IV

Norris, Rt Rev. Ivor Arthur, 1901–1969, vol. VI

Norris, Very Rev. John, 1843–1911, vol. I

Norris, John Alexander, 1872–1962, vol. VI

Norris, John Freeman, 1842–1904, vol. I

Norris, Sir John Gerald, 1903–1990, vol. VIII

Norris, Kathleen, 1880–1966, vol. VI

Norris, Maj.-Gen. Sir Kingsley; *see* Norris, Maj.-Gen. Sir F. K.

Norris, Oswald Thomas, 1883–1973, vol. VII

Norris, Richard Hill, 1886–1970, vol. VI

Norris, Lt-Col Richard Joseph, 1854–1935, vol. III

Norris, Captain Stephen Hugh, 1903–1944, vol. IV

Norris, Rev. Canon Walter Edward, 1905–1971, vol. VII

Norris, William Edward, *died* 1925, vol. II

Norris, Very Rev. William Foxley, 1859–1937, vol. III

Norrish, Ronald George Wreyford, 1897–1978, vol. VII

Norritt, Sir James Henry, 1889–1963, vol. VI

Norstad, Gen. Lauris, 1907–1988, vol. VIII

North, 11th Baron, 1836–1932, vol. III

North, 12th Baron, 1860–1938, vol. III

North, 13th Baron, 1917–1941, vol. IV

North, Lord; Francis George North, 1902–1940, vol. III

North, Rt Hon. Sir Alfred Kingsley, 1900–1981, vol. VIII

North, Brig.-Gen. Bordrigge North, 1862–1936, vol. III

North, Rev. Christopher Richard, 1888–1975, vol. VII

North, Col Dudley, 1840–1917, vol. II

North, Adm. Sir Dudley Burton Napier, 1881–1961, vol. VI

North, Hon. Dudley William John, 1891–1936, vol. III

North, Col Edward, 1856–1927, vol. II

North, Lt-Col Edward Bunbury, 1869–1944, vol. IV

North, Major Edward Tempest Tunstall, 1900–1942, vol. IV

North, Rt Hon. Sir Ford, 1830–1913, vol. I

North, Brig. Francis Roger, 1894–1978, vol. VII

North, Frederic Dudley, 1866–1921, vol. II

North, Frederick Keppel, 1860–1948, vol. IV

North, Sir George Cecil, 1895–1971, vol. VII

North, Brig. Harold Napier, 1883–1957, vol. V

North, Sir Harry, 1866–1920, vol. II

North, Herbert L., 1871–1941, vol. IV

North, Major John, 1894–1973, vol. VII

North, John Dudley, 1893–1968, vol. VI

North, John W., *died* 1924, vol. II

North, Lt-Col Sir Jonathan, 1855–1939, vol. III

North, North, 1824–1910, vol. I

North, Roger, 1901–1985, vol. VIII

North, Roland Arthur Charles, 1889–1961, vol. VI

North, Walter Meyrick, *died* 1900, vol. I

North, William Albert, 1881–1946, vol. IV

Northam, Sir Reginald, *died* 1967, vol. VI

Northampton, 4th Marquess of, 1818–1897, vol. I

Northampton, 5th Marquess of, 1851–1913, vol. I

Northampton, 6th Marquess of, 1885–1978, vol. VII

Northbourne, 2nd Baron, 1846–1923, vol. II

Northbourne, 3rd Baron, 1869–1932, vol. III

Northbourne, 4th Baron, 1896–1982, vol. VIII

Northbrook, 1st Earl of, 1826–1904, vol. I

Northbrook, 2nd Earl of, 1850–1929, vol. III

Northbrook, Countess of; (Florence Anita Eyre), *died* 1946, vol. IV

Northbrook, 4th Baron, 1882–1947, vol. IV

Northbrook, 5th Baron, 1915–1990, vol. VIII

Northchurch, Baroness (Life Peer); *see* Davidson, Dowager Viscountess.

Northcliffe, 1st Viscount, 1865–1922, vol. II

Northcote, 1st Baron, 1846–1911, vol. I

Northcote, Lady; (Alice), *died* 1934, vol. III

Northcote, Rev. Hon. Arthur Francis, 1852–1943, vol. IV

Northcote, Sir Ernest Augustus, 1850–1915, vol. I

Northcote, Sir Geoffry Alexander Stafford, 1881–1948, vol. IV

Northcote, Rev. Hon. John Stafford, 1850–1920, vol. II

Northcote, Lady Rosalind Lucy Stafford, *died* 1950, vol. IV

Northcote-Green, Roger James, 1912–1990, vol. VIII

Northcott, Rev. Cecil; *see* Northcott, Rev. W. C.

Northcott, Gen. Sir John, 1890–1966, vol. VI

Northcott, Captain Ralph William Frank, 1907–1976, vol. VII

Northcott, Richard A., 1871–1931, vol. III

Northcott, Rev. William, 1854–1924, vol. II

Northcott, Rev. (William) Cecil, 1902–1987, vol. VIII

Northcroft, Sir Erima Harvey, 1884–1953, vol. V

Northcroft, Ernest George Drennan, 1896–1976, vol. VII

Northedge, Frederick Samuel, 1918–1985, vol. VIII

Northen, Lt-Col Arthur, 1873–1964, vol. VI

Northesk, 10th Earl of, 1865–1921, vol. II

Northesk, 11th Earl of, 1901–1963, vol. VI

Northesk, 12th Earl of, 1895–1975, vol. VII

Northey, Sir Armand Hunter Kennedy Wilbraham, 1897–1964, vol. VI

Northey, Maj.-Gen. Sir Edward, 1868–1953, vol. V

Northey, Lt-Col Herbert Hamilton, 1870–1938, vol. III

Northey, Captain William, 1876–1914, vol. I

Northfield, Douglas William Claridge, *died* 1976, vol. VII

Northland, Viscount; Thomas Uchter Caulfield Knox, 1882–1915, vol. I

Northmore, Sir John Alfred, 1865–1958, vol. V

Northrop, Cyrus, 1834–1922, vol. II

Northrop, John Howard, 1891–1987, vol. VIII

Northrup, William Barton, *died* 1925, vol. II

Northumberland, 6th Duke of, 1810–1899, vol. I

Northumberland, 7th Duke of, 1846–1918, vol. II

Northumberland, 8th Duke of, 1880–1930, vol. III

Northumberland, 9th Duke of, 1912–1940, vol. III

Northumberland, 10th Duke of, 1914–1988, vol. VIII

Northumberland, Duchess of; (Helen Magdalen), *died* 1965, vol. VI

Northwick, Lady; (Elizabeth Augusta), 1832–1912, vol. I

Norton, 1st Baron, 1814–1905, vol. I

Norton, 2nd Baron, 1846–1926, vol. II

Norton, 3rd Baron, 1872–1933, vol. III

Norton, 4th Baron, 1885–1944, vol. IV

Norton, 5th Baron, 1854–1945, vol. IV

Norton, 6th Baron, 1886–1961, vol. VI

Norton, Major Alfred Edward Marston, 1869–1922, vol. II

Norton, Arthur Trehern, 1841–1912, vol. I

Norton, Brig.-Gen. Cecil Burrington, 1868–1953, vol. V

Norton, Sir Charles; *see* Norton, Sir W. C.

Norton, Lt-Col Charles Edward, 1861–1931, vol. III

Norton, Charles Eliot, 1827–1908, vol. I

Norton, Brig.-Gen. Charles Ernest Graham, 1869–1953, vol. V

Norton, Charles William, 1870–1946, vol. IV

Norton, Sir Clifford John, 1891–1990, vol. VIII

Norton, Maj.-Gen. Cyril Henry, 1898–1983, vol. VIII

Norton, David, 1851–1929, vol. III

Norton, David Evans, 1863–1946, vol. IV

Norton, Edward, 1841–1923, vol. II
Norton, Lt-Gen. Edward Felix, 1884–1954, vol. V
Norton, Sir Evan Augustus, 1901–1967, vol. VI
Norton, George Frederic, *died* 1946, vol. IV
Norton, Col Gilbert Paul, 1882–1962, vol. VI
Norton, Ven. Hugh Ross, 1890–1969, vol. VI
Norton, Rt Rev. John F., 1891–1963, vol. VI
Norton, Ven. John George, 1840–1924, vol. II
Norton, Rt Rev. John Henry, 1855–1923, vol. II
Norton, Richard, 1872–1918, vol. II
Norton, Robert, 1838–1926, vol. II
Norton, Robert Frederick, 1854–1929, vol. III
Norton, Roger Edward, 1897–1978, vol. VII
Norton, Thomas, 1845–1935, vol. III
Norton, Sir (Walter) Charles, 1896–1974, vol. VII
Norton, Wilfrid, *died* 1973, vol. VII
Norton, William, *died* 1963, vol. VI
Norton-Griffiths, Lt-Col Sir John; *see* Griffiths.
Norton-Griffiths, Sir Peter, 2nd Bt, 1905–1983, vol. VIII
Norval, Sir James, 1862–1936, vol. III
Norway, Arthur Hamilton, 1859–1938, vol. III
Norway, Nevil Shute, 1899–1960, vol. V
Norwich, 1st Viscount, 1890–1954, vol. V
Norwood, Sir Charles John Boyd, 1871–1966, vol. VI
Norwood, Christopher Bonnewell Burton, 1932–1972, vol. VII
Norwood, Sir Cyril, 1875–1956, vol. V
Norwood, Rev. Frederick William, *died* 1958, vol. V
Norwood, Gilbert, 1880–1954, vol. V
Norwood, Captain John, 1876–1914, vol. I
Norwood, Rev. Reginald, 1874–1928, vol. II, vol. III
Norwood, William Stuart, *died* 1944, vol. IV
Noser, Most Rev. Adolf, 1900–1981, vol. VIII
Nosworthy, Lt-Gen. Sir Francis Poitiers, 1887–1971, vol. VII
Nosworthy, Sir John Reeve, 1915–1990, vol. VIII
Nosworthy, Richard, 1860–1946, vol. IV
Nosworthy, Sir Richard Lysle, 1885–1966, vol. VI
Nosworthy, Hon. Sir William, 1867–1946, vol. IV
Notcutt, Henry Clement, 1865–1935, vol. III
Notestein, Wallace, 1878–1969, vol. VI
Notley, Captain Sir Franke Bartlett Stuart, 1865–1939, vol. III
Nott, Frederic Trevor, 1885–1950, vol. IV
Nott, Comdr Sir James Grenvile P.; *see* Pyke-Nott.
Nott, Very Rev. Michael John, 1916–1988, vol. VIII
Nott-Bower, Sir Edmund Ernest, 1853–1933, vol. III
Nott-Bower, Sir Guy; *see* Nott-Bower, Sir W. G.
Nott-Bower, Sir John Reginald Hornby, 1892–1972, vol. VII
Nott-Bower, Captain Sir (John) William, 1849–1939, vol. III
Nott-Bower, Captain Sir William; *see* Nott-Bower, Captain Sir J. W.
Nott-Bower, Sir (William) Guy, 1890–1977, vol. VII
Notten-Pole, Sir Cecil Pery Van; *see* Pole.
Notter, Col J. Lane-, *died* 1923, vol. II
Nottidge, Sir William Rolfe, 1889–1966, vol. VI
Nottingham, Rev. Edward Emil, 1866–1921, vol. II
Nougués, Jean, *died* 1932, vol. III
Nourse, William John Chichele, *died* 1937, vol. III

Novar, 1st Viscount, 1860–1934, vol. III
Novar, Viscountess; (Helen Hermione), 1865–1941, vol. IV
Novello, Ivor, 1893–1951, vol. V
Novikoff, Mme Olga, 1848–1925, vol. II
Novy, Frederick G., 1864–1957, vol. V
Nowell, Arthur T., 1861–1940, vol. III
Nowell, Charles, 1890–1954, vol. V
Nowell, Air Cdre Henry Edward, 1903–1967, vol. VI
Nowell, Ralph Machattie, 1903–1973, vol. VII
Nowell, William, 1880–1968, vol. VI
Nowell, Rev. William Edward, *died* 1929, vol. III
Nowell-Rostron, Rev. Sydney, 1883–1948, vol. IV
Noxon, William Courtland, *died* 1943, vol. IV
Noyce, Sir Frank, 1878–1948, vol. IV
Noyes, Alfred, 1880–1958, vol. V
Noyes, Gen. Sir Cyril Dupré, 1885–1946, vol. IV
Nuffield, 1st Viscount, 1877–1963, vol. VI
Nugee, Rev. Francis Edward, *died* 1930, vol. III
Nugee, Francis John, 1891–1966, vol. VI
Nugent, 1st Baron, 1895–1973, vol. VII
Nugent, Albert Beauchamp, *died* 1938, vol. III
Nugent, Algernon John FitzRoy, 1865–1922, vol. II
Nugent, Sir Charles, 5th Bt (*cr* 1795), 1847–1927, vol. II
Nugent, Sir Charles Butler Peter Hodges, 1827–1899, vol. I
Nugent, Col Charles Hugh Hodges, 1868–1924, vol. II
Nugent of Bellême, David James Douglas, 1917–1988, vol. VIII
Nugent, Sir Edmund Charles, 3rd Bt (*cr* 1806), 1839–1928, vol. II
Nugent, Brig.-Gen. Frank B.; *see* Burnell-Nugent.
Nugent, Col George Colbourne, 1864–1915, vol. I
Nugent, Sir (George) Guy (Bulwer), 4th Bt (*cr* 1806), 1892–1970, vol. VI
Nugent, Sir Guy; *see* Nugent, Sir G. G. B.
Nugent of Clonlost, Guy Patrick Douglas John, 1915–1944, vol. IV
Nugent, Sir Horace Dickinson, 1858–1924, vol. II
Nugent, Sir Hugh Charles, 6th Bt, 1904–1983, vol. VIII
Nugent, Hon. John, 1843–1900, vol. I
Nugent, John Dillon, *died* 1940, vol. III
Nugent, Maj.-Gen. John Fagan Henslowe, 1889–1975, vol. VII
Nugent, Sir John Nugent, 3rd Bt (*cr* 1831 of Cloncoskoran), 1849–1929, vol. III
Nugent, Maj.-Gen. Sir Oliver Stewart Wood, 1860–1926, vol. II
Nugent, Vice-Adm. Raymond Andrew, 1870–1959, vol. V
Nugent, Hon. Richard Anthony, 1842–1912, vol. I
Nugent, Col Robert Arthur, 1853–1926, vol. II
Nugent, Rt Hon. Sir Roland Thomas, 1st Bt (*cr* 1961), 1886–1962, vol. VI
Nugent, Sir Walter Richard, 4th Bt (*cr* 1831 of Donore), 1865–1955, vol. V
Nugent, Col Walter Vyvian, 1880–1963, vol. VI

Nugent, Captain Hon. William Andrew, 1876–1915, vol. I

Nulty, Rt Rev. Thomas, *died* 1898, vol. I

Nunan, Sir Joseph, 1873–1934, vol. III

Nunan, William, 1880–1955, vol. V

Nunburnholme, 1st Baron, 1833–1907, vol. I

Nunburnholme, 2nd Baron, 1875–1924, vol. II

Nunburnholme, 3rd Baron, 1904–1974, vol. VII

Nunn, Rev. Henry Drury Cust, *died* 1922, vol. II

Nunn, Jean Josephine, 1916–1982, vol. VIII

Nunn, Col Joshua Arthur, 1853–1908, vol. I

Nunn, Sir Percy, 1870–1944, vol. IV

Nunn, Thomas William, 1825–1909, vol. I

Nunn, Vice-Adm. Wilfrid, *died* 1956, vol. V

Nunn, William, 1879–1971, vol. VII

Nunns, Hector Matthew, 1905–1979, vol. VII

Nurse, Ven. Charles Euston, 1909–1981, vol. VIII

Nurse, George Edward, 1873–1945, vol. IV

Nussey, Col Albert Henry Mortimer, 1880–1944, vol. IV

Nussey, Sir Thomas Moore, 2nd Bt, 1898–1971, vol. VII

Nussey, Sir Willans, 1st Bt, 1868–1947, vol. IV

Nuthall, Brig.-Gen. Charles Edwin, 1862–1943, vol. IV

Nuthall, Col Henry John, 1834–1914, vol. I

Nutt, Albert Boswell, 1898–1978, vol. VII

Nutt, Alfred Trübner, 1856–1910, vol. I

Nutt, Alfred Young, 1847–1924, vol. II

Nutt, Arthur Edgar W.; *see* Woodward-Nutt.

Nutt, Francis George, 1878–1954, vol. V

Nutt, Maj.-Gen. Harold Rothery, 1876–1953, vol. V

Nutt, Col Herbert John, 1861–1940, vol. III

Nutt, Col James Anson Francis, *died* 1924, vol. II

Nuttall, Sir Edmund, 1st Bt, 1870–1923, vol. II

Nuttall, Lt-Col Sir (Edmund) Keith, 2nd Bt, 1901–1941, vol. IV

Nuttall, Ellis, 1890–1951, vol. V

Nuttall, Most Rev. Enos, 1842–1916, vol. II

Nuttall, Rev. Frank, 1870–1943, vol. IV

Nuttall, George Henry Falkiner, 1862–1937, vol. III

Nuttall, Harry, 1849–1924, vol. II

Nuttall, Sir James, 1891–1962, vol. VI

Nuttall, Sir James Mansfield, 1827–1897, vol. I

Nuttall, Lt-Col Sir Keith; *see* Nuttall, Sir E. K.

Nuttall, Thomas Downham, 1877–1934, vol. III

Nuttall, Captain William Ewart, 1876–1939, vol. III

Nuttall, Major William Francis D.; *see* Dixon-Nuttall.

Nutting, Arthur Ronald Stansmore, 1888–1964, vol. VI

Nutting, Air Vice-Marshal Charles William, 1889–1964, vol. VI

Nutting, Sir Harold Stansmore, 2nd Bt, 1882–1972, vol. VII

Nutting, Sir John Gardiner, 1st Bt, 1852–1918, vol. II

Nye, Engr Captain Alfred John, 1855–1932, vol. III

Nye, Lt-Gen. Sir Archibald Edward, 1895–1967, vol. VI

Nye, Sir Geoffrey Walter, 1902–1976, vol. VII

Nygaardsvold, John, 1879–1952, vol. V

Nyholm, Sir Ronald Sydney, 1917–1971, vol. VII

Nys, Ernest, 1851–1920, vol. II

Nystrom, Anton, 1842–1931, vol. III

O

Oak-Rhind, Edwin Scoby, 1883–1963, vol. VI

Oakden, Sir Ralph, 1871–1953, vol. V

Oake, George Robert, 1903–1969, vol. VI

Oakeley, Sir Atholl; *see* Oakeley, Sir E. A.

Oakeley, Sir Charles John, 5th Bt, 1862–1938, vol. III

Oakeley, Sir Charles Richard Andrew, 6th Bt, 1900–1959, vol. V

Oakeley, Sir Charles William Atholl, 4th Bt, 1828–1915, vol. I

Oakeley, Sir (Edward) Atholl, 7th Bt, 1900–1987, vol. VIII

Oakeley, Sir Herbert Stanley, 1830–1903, vol. I

Oakeley, Hilda Diana, 1867–1950, vol. IV

Oakes, Sir Augustus Henry, 1839–1919, vol. II

Oakes, Sir Cecil, 1884–1959, vol. V

Oakes, Hon. Charles William, 1861–1928, vol. II

Oakes, Ven. George Spencer, 1855–1932, vol. III

Oakes, Sir Harry, 1st Bt (*cr* 1939), 1874–1943, vol. IV

Oakes, Sir Reginald Louis, 4th Bt (*cr* 1815), 1847–1927, vol. II

Oakes, Col Richard, 1876–1944, vol. IV

Oakes, Sir Sydney, 2nd Bt (*cr* 1939), 1927–1966, vol. VI

Oakeshott, Maj.-Gen. John Field Fraser, 1899–1957, vol. V

Oakeshott, Keith Robertson, 1920–1974, vol. VII

Oakeshott, Michael Joseph, 1901–1990, vol. VIII

Oakeshott, Sir Walter Fraser, 1903–1987, vol. VIII

Oakley, John Martin, 1888–1963, vol. VI

Oakley, Alfred James, 1880–1959, vol. V

Oakley, Rev. Austin, 1890–1977, vol. VII

Oakley, Cyril Leslie, 1907–1975, vol. VII

Oakley, Harry Ekermans, 1866–1943, vol. IV

Oakley, Sir Henry, 1823–1912, vol. I

Oakley, Lt-Col Henry John Percy, 1878–1942, vol. IV

Oakley, John, *died* 1945, vol. IV

Oakley, Sir John Hubert, 1867–1946, vol. IV

Oakley, Kenneth Page, 1911–1981, vol. VIII

Oakley, Philip Douglas, 1883–1958, vol. V

Oakley, Thomas, 1879–1936, vol. III

Oaksey, 1st Baron; *see under* Trevethin, 3rd Baron and Oaksey, 1st Baron.

Oakshott, Baron (Life Peer); Hendrie Dudley Oakshott, 1904–1975, vol. VII

Oaten, Edward Farley, 1884–1973, vol. VII

Oates, Francis Hamer, 1866–1923, vol. II

Oates, Frederick Arthur Harman, *died* 1928, vol. II

Oates, John Claud Trewinard, 1912–1990, vol. VIII

Oates, Lt-Col William Coape, 1862–1942, vol. IV

Oatley, Sir George Herbert, 1863–1950, vol. IV

Obaidulla Khan, Nowabzada Hafiz Mohamad Bahadur, 1878–1924, vol. II

O'Beirne, Hugh James, 1866–1916, vol. II
Oberg, Olof David August, 1893–1975, vol. VII
Oberon, Merle, (Estelle Merle O'Brien Thompson), 1911–1979, vol. VII
Obert de Thieusies, Vicomte Alain, 1888–1979, vol. VII
Obey, André, 1892–1975, vol. VII
Obeyesekere, Hon. Sir Christoffel; see Obeyesekere, Hon. Sir S. C.
Obeyesekere, Sir James Peter, 1879–1968, vol. VI
Obeyesekere, Hon. Sir (Solomon) Christoffel, 1848–1926, vol. II, vol. III
Obre, Henry, 1855–1922, vol. II
O'Briain, Art Patrick, 1872–1949, vol. IV
O'Briain, Hon. Barra, 1901–1988, vol. VIII
O'Brien, 1st Baron, 1842–1914, vol. I
O'Brien, Arthur John Rushton, 1883–1940, vol. III
O'Brien, Lt-Col Aubrey John, 1870–1930, vol. III
O'Brien, Brian, died 1973, vol. VII
O'Brien, Brig. Brian Palliser Tiegue, 1898–1966, vol. VI
O'Brien, Bryan Justin, 1902–1978, vol. VII
O'Brien, Lt-Col Sir Charles Richard Mackey, 1859–1935, vol. III
O'Brien, Christopher Michael, 1861–1935, vol. III
O'Brien, Most Rev. Cornelius, 1843–1906, vol. I
O'Brien, Daniel Joseph, died 1949, vol. IV
O'Brien, Sir David Edmond, 6th Bt, 1902–1982, vol. VIII
O'Brien, Dermod, 1865–1945, vol. IV
O'Brien, Hon. Donough, 1879–1953, vol. V
O'Brien, Brig.-Gen. Edmund Donough John, 1858–1945, vol. IV
O'Brien, Lt-Col Edward, 1872–1965, vol. VI
O'Brien, Edward Joseph Harrington, 1890–1941, vol. IV
O'Brien, Ernest Edward, 1869–1932, vol. III
O'Brien, Sir (Frederick) Lucius, 1896–1974, vol. VII
O'Brien, George, 1892–1973, vol. VII
O'Brien, Sir George Thomas Michael, 1844–1906, vol. I
O'Brien, Henry, born 1836, vol. III
O'Brien, Lt-Col Hon. Henry Barnaby, 1887–1969, vol. VI
O'Brien, James Francis Xavier, 1828–1905, vol. I
O'Brien, John, 1895–1947, vol. V
O'Brien, Sir John Edmond Noel, 5th Bt, 1899–1969, vol. VI
O'Brien, Sir John Terence Nicolls, 1830–1903, vol. I
O'Brien, Kate, 1897–1974, vol. VII
O'Brien, Kendal Edmund, 1849–1909, vol. I
O'Brien, Sir Lucius; see O'Brien, Sir F. L.
O'Brien, Very Rev. Lucius H., 1842–1913, vol. I
O'Brien, Most Rev. Michael, 1877–1952, vol. V
O'Brien, Michael, 1883–1958, vol. V
O'Brien, Rt Rev. Mgr Michael Joseph, 1913–1978, vol. VII
O'Brien, Lt-Col Hon. Murrough, 1866–1934, vol. III
O'Brien, Owen, 1920–1987, vol. VIII
O'Brien, Patrick, 1853–1917, vol. II
O'Brien, Patrick Joseph, died 1911, vol. I
O'Brien, Richard Alfred, 1878–1970, vol. VI
O'Brien, Richard Barry, 1847–1918, vol. II

O'Brien, Sir Robert Rollo Gillespie, 4th Bt, 1901–1952, vol. V
O'Brien, Sir Timothy Carew, 3rd Bt, 1861–1948, vol. IV
O'Brien, Sir Tom, 1900–1970, vol. VI
O'Brien, Rt Hon. William, 1832–1899, vol. I
O'Brien, William, 1852–1928, vol. II
O'Brien-Butler, Pierce Essex, 1858–1954, vol. V
O'Brien Twohig, Brig. Joseph Patrick, 1905–1973, vol. VII
O'Brien-Twohig, Col Michael Joseph, 1893–1971, vol. VII
O'Bryan, Sir Norman, 1894–1968, vol. VI
O'Byrne, Count John, 1834–1905, vol. I
O'Byrne, John, 1884–1954, vol. V
O'Callaghan, The; see O'Callaghan-Westropp, Col George.
O'Callaghan, Col Denis Moriarty, 1861–1926, vol. II
O'Callaghan, Maj.-Gen. Sir Desmond Dykes Tynte, 1843–1931, vol. III
O'Callaghan, Most Rev. Eugene, 1888–1973, vol. VII
O'Callaghan, Sir Francis Langford, 1839–1909, vol. I
O'Callaghan, Adm. George William Douglass, died 1900, vol. I
O'Callaghan, Adm. Michael Pelham, 1850–1937, vol. III
O'Callaghan, Robert Alexander, died 1903, vol. I
O'Callaghan, Most Rev. Thomas Alphonsus, 1839–1916, vol. II
O'Callaghan, Timothy Patrick Moriarty, 1886–1961, vol. VI
O'Callaghan-Westropp, Col George, (The O'Callaghan), 1864–1944, vol. IV
O'Carroll, Joseph Francis, 1855–1942, vol. IV
O'Carroll Scott, Maj.-Gen. Anthony Gerald; see Scott.
O'Casey, Sean, 1880–1964, vol. VI
Ochs, Adolph S., 1858–1935, vol. III
Ochterlony, Sir Charles Francis, 5th Bt, 1891–1964, vol. VI
Ochterlony, Sir David Ferguson, 3rd Bt, 1848–1931, vol. III
Ochterlony, Sir Matthew Montgomerie, 4th Bt, 1880–1946, vol. IV
O'Clery, Count, (The O'Clery), 1849–1913, vol. I
O'Collins, Most Rev. Sir James Patrick, 1892–1983, vol. VIII
O'Connell, Sir Bernard Thomas, 1909–1981, vol. VIII
O'Connell, Daniel Patrick, 1924–1979, vol. VII
O'Connell, Sir Daniel Ross, 3rd Bt, 1861–1905, vol. I
O'Connell, Captain Donal Bernard, 1893–1971, vol. VII
O'Connell, Rev. Frederick William, 1876–1929, vol. III
O'Connell, Captain James Ross, 1863–1925, vol. II
O'Connell, Rev. Sir John Robert, 1868–1943, vol. IV
O'Connell, Captain Sir Maurice James Arthur, 5th Bt, 1889–1949, vol. IV
O'Connell, Sir Morgan Donal Conail, 6th Bt, 1923–1989, vol. VIII
O'Connell, Sir Morgan Ross, 4th Bt, 1862–1919, vol. II
O'Connell, Sir Peter Reilly, died 1927, vol. II
O'Connell, Thomas J., 1882–1969, vol. VI

O'Connell, Hon. W. B., *died* 1903, vol. I
O'Connell, His Eminence Cardinal William Henry, 1859–1944, vol. IV
O'Connor, Arthur, 1844–1923, vol. II
O'Connor, Arthur John, 1888–1950, vol. IV (A), vol. V
O'Connor, Col Arthur Patrick, 1856–1920, vol. II
O'Connor, Rt Hon. Charles Andrew, 1854–1928, vol. II
O'Connor, Charles Gerald, 1890–1949, vol. IV (A)
O'Connor, Charles Yelverton, 1843–1902, vol. I
O'Connor, Most Rev. Denis, *died* 1911, vol. I
O'Connor, Lt-Gen. Sir Denis Stuart Scott, 1907–1988, vol. VIII
O'Connor, Rev. Edward Dominic, 1874–1954, vol. V
O'Connor, Frank, 1903–1966, vol. VI
O'Connor, Lt-Col Sir Frederick; *see* O'Connor, Lt-Col Sir W. F. T.
O'Connor, George Bligh, 1883–1957, vol. V
O'Connor, Col Henry Willis-, 1886–1957, vol. V
O'Connor, James, 1836–1910, vol. I
O'Connor, Rt Hon. Sir James, 1872–1931, vol. III
O'Connor, James Malachy, 1886–1974, vol. VII
O'Connor, John, 1850–1928, vol. II
O'Connor, Sir Kenneth Kennedy, 1896–1985, vol. VIII
O'Connor, Maj.-Gen. Sir Luke, 1832–1915, vol. I
O'Connor, Lt-Col Patrick Fenelon, 1850–1939, vol. III
O'Connor, Rt Rev. Patrick Joseph, *died* 1932, vol. III
O'Connor, Richard Edward, 1851–1912, vol. I
O'Connor, Gen. Sir Richard Nugent, 1889–1981, vol. VIII
O'Connor, Sir Terence James, 1891–1940, vol. III
O'Connor, Thomas Arthur Leslie S.; *see* Scott O'Connor.
O'Connor, Rt Hon. Thomas Power, 1848–1929, vol. III
O'Connor, Vincent Clarence Scott, *died* 1945, vol. IV
O'Connor, Lt-Col Sir (William) Frederick (Travers), 1870–1943, vol. IV
O'Connor-Morris, Geoffrey, 1886–1964, vol. VI
O'Conor, Rt Hon. Charles Owen, (The O'Conor Don), 1838–1906, vol. I
O'Conor, Rt Hon. Denis Charles Joseph, (The O'Conor Don), 1869–1917, vol. II
O'Conor, James Edward, 1843–1917, vol. II
O'Conor, Sir John, 1863–1927, vol. II
O'Conor, Norreys Jephson, 1885–1958, vol. V
O'Conor, Owen Phelim, (The O'Conor Don), 1870–1943, vol. IV
O'Conor Don, The; *see* O'Conor, Rt Hon. C. O.
O'Conor Don, The; *see* O'Conor, Rt Hon. D. C. J.
O'Conor Don, The; *see* O'Conor, O. P.
O'Conor-Eccles, Miss, *died* 1911, vol. I
Ó Dálaigh, Cearbhall, 1911–1978, vol. VII
Oddie, John William, *died* 1923, vol. II
Oddin-Taylor, Harry Willoughby, 1886–1967, vol. VI
Oddy, Sir John James, 1867–1921, vol. II
O'Dea, Rt Rev. Thomas, 1858–1923, vol. II
O'Dea, William, 1870–1936, vol. III (A), vol. V
O'Dea, William Thomas, 1905–1981, vol. VIII
O'Deirg, Tomás, (Thomas Derrig), 1897–1956, vol. V
O'Dell, Andrew Charles, 1909–1966, vol. VI

Odell, Noel Ewart, 1890–1987, vol. VIII
Odell, Thomas Alexander, 1847–1909, vol. I
Odets, Clifford, 1906–1963, vol. VI
Odey, George William, 1900–1985, vol. VIII
Odgers, Sir Charles Edwin, 1870–1964, vol. VI
Odgers, James Rowland, 1914–1985, vol. VIII
Odgers, Lindsey Noel Blake, 1892–1979, vol. VII
Odgers, Walter Blake, 1880–1969, vol. VI
Odgers, William Blake, 1849–1924, vol. II
Odhams, Ernest Lynch, 1880–1947, vol. IV
Odle, Dorothy M.; *see* Richardson, D. M.
Odling, Charles William, 1847–1932, vol. III
Odling, Thomas Francis, *died* 1906, vol. I
Odling, William, 1829–1921, vol. II
Odlum, Doris Maude, 1890–1985, vol. VIII
Odlum, Maj.-Gen. Victor Wentworth, 1880–1971, vol. VII
O'Dogherty, Engr-Rear-Adm. Francis Blake, *died* 1952, vol. V
O'Doherty, Most Rev. Eugene, 1896–1979, vol. VII
O'Doherty, Rt Rev. J. Keys, *died* 1907, vol. I
O'Doherty, Philip, 1871–1926, vol. II
O'Doherty, Rt Rev. Thomas, 1877–1936, vol. III
O'Doherty, William, 1868–1905, vol. I
Odom, Rev. William, 1846–1933, vol. III
O'Donnell, Charles James, 1850–1934, vol. III
O'Donnell, Elliott, *died* 1965, vol. VI
O'Donnell, Maj.-Gen. Eric Hugh, 1893–1950, vol. IV
O'Donnell, Frank Hugh Macdonald, 1848–1916, vol. II
O'Donnell, Maj.-Gen. Hugh, 1858–1917, vol. II
O'Donnell, Rev. Michael J., 1881–1944, vol. IV
O'Donnell, His Eminence Cardinal Patrick, 1856–1927, vol. II
O'Donnell, Most Rev. Patrick Mary, 1897–1980, vol. VII (AII)
O'Donnell, Peador, 1893–1986, vol. VIII
O'Donnell, Sir Samuel Perry, 1874–1946, vol. IV
O'Donnell, Thomas, 1872–1943, vol. IV
O'Donnell, Maj.-Gen. Sir Thomas Joseph, 1858–1947, vol. IV
O'Donoghue, Charles Henry, 1885–1961, vol. VI
O'Donoghue, David J., 1866–1917, vol. II, vol. III
O'Donoghue, Geoffrey Charles Patrick, (The O'Donoghue of the Glens), 1859–1935, vol. III
O'Donoghue, Geoffrey Charles Patrick Randal, (The O'Donoghue of the Glens), 1896–1974, vol. VII
O'Donoghue, John Kingston, 1894–1976, vol. VII
O'Donoghue, Col Montague Ernest, 1859–1943, vol. IV
O'Donoghue, Richard John Langford, 1889–1972, vol. VII
O'Donoghue, Thomas Henry, 1886–1957, vol. V
O'Donoghue of the Glens, The; *see* O'Donoghue, G. C. P.
O'Donoghue of the Glens, The; *see* O'Donoghue, G. C. P. R.
O'Donohoe, Sir James, *died* 1933, vol. III
O'Donovan, The; *see* O'Donovan, Brig. M. J. W.
O'Donovan, The; *see* O'Donovan, M. W.
O'Donovan, John, 1858–1927, vol. II
O'Donovan, Michael; *see* O'Connor, Frank.
O'Donovan, Brig. Morgan John Winthrop, (The O'Donovan), 1893–1969, vol. VI

O'Donovan, Morgan William, (The O'Donovan), 1861–1940, vol. III
O'Donovan, William James, *died* 1955, vol. V
O'Dowd, Sir James Cornelius, 1829–1903, vol. I
O'Dowda, Lt-Gen. Sir James Wilton, 1871–1961, vol. VI
O'Driscoll, Florence, *died* 1939, vol. III
O'Duffy, Eimar Ultan, 1893–1935, vol. III
O'Duffy, Gen. Eoin, 1892–1944, vol. IV
O'Dwyer, Rt Rev. Edward Thomas, 1842–1917, vol. II
O'Dwyer, Sir Michael Francis, 1864–1940, vol. III
O'Dwyer, Robert, 1862–1949, vol. IV
O'Dwyer, Surg.-Gen. Thomas Francis, *died* 1919, vol. II
O'Dwyer, Una, (Lady O'Dwyer), 1872–1956, vol. V
O'Dwyer, William, 1890–1964, vol. VI
Oehlers, Sir George Edward Noel, 1908–1968, vol. VI
Oelrichs, Hermann, 1850–1906, vol. I
Oelsner, Herman, 1871–1923, vol. II
Oesterley, Rev. William O. E., 1866–1950, vol. IV
O'Farrell, Sir Edward, 1856–1926, vol. II
O'Farrell, Sir George Plunkett, 1845–1911, vol. I
O'Farrell, Rt Rev. Michael, 1865–1928, vol. II
O'Feeney, Sean; *see* Ford, John.
O'Ferrall, Dominic More-, 1854–1942, vol. IV
O'Ferrall, Rt Rev. Ronald Stanhope More, 1890–1973, vol. VII
O'Fiaich, His Eminence Cardinal Tomás Séamus, 1923–1990, vol. VIII
Officer, Sir (Frank) Keith, 1889–1969, vol. VI
Officer, Sir Keith; *see* Officer, Sir F. K.
Officer, Maj.-Gen. William James, 1903–1989, vol. VIII
Officer Brown, Sir (Charles) James; *see* Brown, Sir C. J. O.
Offner, Richard, 1889–1965, vol. VI
Offor, Richard, 1882–1964, vol. VI
O'Flaherty, Liam, 1896–1984, vol. VIII
O'Flynn, Brig. Dennis John Edwin, 1907–1985, vol. VIII
O'Flynn, Surg. Rear-Adm. Joseph Aloysius, 1889–1976, vol. VII
Ogden, Sir Alwyne George Neville, 1889–1981, vol. VIII
Ogden, Charles Kay, 1889–1957, vol. V
Ogden, Frank Collinge, 1907–1989, vol. VIII
Ogden, Fred, 1871–1933, vol. III
Ogden, Sir George Chester, 1913–1983, vol. VIII
Ogden, George Washington, 1871–1966, vol. VI
Ogdon, John Andrew Howard, 1937–1989, vol. VIII
Ogg, David, 1887–1965, vol. VI
Ogg, Col George Sim, 1866–1935, vol. III
Ogg, Sir William Gammie, 1891–1979, vol. VII
Ogg, Col William Mortimer, 1873–1958, vol. V
Ogilby, Col Robert James Leslie, 1880–1964, vol. VI
Ogilvie, Alan Grant, 1887–1954, vol. V
Ogilvie, Hon. Albert George, 1891–1939, vol. III
Ogilvie, Alexander, 1882–1962, vol. VI
Ogilvie, Sir Andrew Muter John, 1858–1924, vol. II
Ogilvie, Sir Charles MacIvor Grant, 1891–1967, vol. VI
Ogilvie, Lt-Col Duncan, 1873–1941, vol. IV

Ogilvie, Col Edward Collingwood, 1867–1950, vol. IV
Ogilvie, Sir Francis Grant, 1858–1930, vol. III
Ogilvie, Sir Frederick Wolff, 1893–1949, vol. IV
Ogilvie, George, 1852–1918, vol. II
Ogilvie, Lt-Col Sir George Drummond, 1882–1966, vol. VI
Ogilvie, Glencairn Stuart, 1858–1932, vol. III
Ogilvie, Lt-Col Gordon, 1878–1958, vol. V
Ogilvie, Sir Heneage; *see* Ogilvie, Sir W. H.
Ogilvie, Rt Rev. James Nicoll, 1860–1926, vol. II
Ogilvie, Mary Helen, (Lady Ogilvie), 1900–1990, vol. VIII
Ogilvie, Robert Maxwell, 1932–1981, vol. VIII
Ogilvie, Lt-Col Sholto Stuart, 1884–1961, vol. VI
Ogilvie, Col Thomas, 1871–1944, vol. IV
Ogilvie, Maj.-Gen. Sir Walter Holland, 1869–1936, vol. III
Ogilvie, Sir (William) Heneage, 1887–1971, vol. VII
Ogilvie, William Henry, 1869–1963, vol. VI
Ogilvie-Farquharson, Mrs; *see* Farquharson.
Ogilvie-Forbes, Sir George Arthur D.; *see* Forbes.
Ogilvie Gordon, Dame Maria M., *died* 1939, vol. III
Ogilvie-Grant, William Robert, 1863–1924, vol. II
Ogilvy, Major Angus Howard Reginald, 1860–1906, vol. I
Ogilvy, Brig. David, 1881–1949, vol. IV
Ogilvy, Gilbert Francis Molyneux, 1868–1953, vol. V
Ogilvy, Sir Gilchrist Nevill, 11th Bt, 1892–1914, vol. I
Ogilvy, Henry Thomas Nisbet Hamilton, 1837–1909, vol. I
Ogilvy, Sir Herbert Kinnaird, 12th Bt, 1865–1956, vol. V
Ogilvy, Captain J. H. C., 1872–1901, vol. I
Ogilvy, Mary Georgiana Constance Nisbet-Hamilton; *see* Ogilvy, Mrs N.-H.
Ogilvy, Mrs Nisbet-Hamilton, (Mary Georgiana Constance), *died* 1920, vol. II
Ogilvy, Sir Reginald Howard Alexander, 10th Bt, 1832–1910, vol. I
Ogilvy, Col William Lewis Kinloch, 1840–1900, vol. I
Ogilvy-Dalgleish, Wing Comdr James William, 1888–1969, vol. VI
Ogilvy-Wedderburn, Sir John Andrew, 11th and 5th Bt, 1866–1956, vol. V
Ogilvy-Wedderburn, Comdr Sir (John) Peter, 12th and 6th Bt, 1917–1977, vol. VII
Ogilvy-Wedderburn, Comdr Sir Peter; *see* Ogilvy-Wedderburn, Comdr Sir J. P.
Oglander, Brig.-Gen. Cecil Faber A.; *see* Aspinall-Oglander.
Ogle, Col Sir Edmund Ashton, 8th Bt, 1857–1940, vol. III
Ogle, Lt-Col Edmund Chaloner, 1878–1935, vol. III
Ogle, Maj.-Gen. Frederic Amelius, 1841–1931, vol. III
Ogle, Sir Henry Asgill, 7th Bt, 1850–1921, vol. II
Ogle, Newton Charles, 1850–1912, vol. I
Ogle, William, 1827–1905, vol. I
Ogmore, 1st Baron, 1903–1976, vol. VII
O'Gorman, The; *see* O'Gorman, Col N. P.
O'Gorman, Col Charles John, 1872–1930, vol. III
O'Gorman, Rt Rev. John A., 1866–1935, vol. III
O'Gorman, Mervyn, 1871–1958, vol. V

O'Gorman, Col Nicholas Purcell, (The O'Gorman), 1845–1935, vol. III

O'Gorman, Lt-Col Patrick Wilkins, 1860–1950, vol. IV

O'Gowan, Maj.-Gen. Robert W.; *see* Wanless-O'Gowan.

O'Grady, The; *see* O'Grady, W. de R.

O'Grady, Donald de Courcy, 1881–1943, vol. IV

O'Grady, Guillamore, 1879–1952, vol. V

O'Grady, Brig.-Gen. Henry de Courcy, 1873–1949, vol. IV

O'Grady, Sir James, 1866–1934, vol. III

O'Grady, Lt-Col John de Courcy, 1856–1920, vol. II

O'Grady, Standish, 1846–1928, vol. II

O'Grady, Lt-Col Standish de Courcy, 1872–1920, vol. II

O'Grady, William de Rienzi, (The O'Grady), 1852–1932, vol. III

O'Grady, Rev. William Waller, 1844–1921, vol. II

O'Grady-Haly, Maj.-Gen. Richard Hebden, 1841–1911, vol. I

Ogston, Sir Alexander, 1844–1929, vol. III

Ogston, Brig.-Gen. Charles, 1877–1944, vol. IV

Ogston, Frank, 1846–1917, vol. II

Ogundipe, Brig. Babafemi Olatunde, 1924–1971, vol. VII

O'Hagan, 2nd Baron, 1878–1900, vol. I

O'Hagan, 3rd Baron, 1882–1961, vol. VI

O'Hagan, Thomas, 1855–1939, vol. III

O'Halloran, Cornelius Hawkins, 1890–1963, vol. VI

O'Halloran, George Finley, 1862–1937, vol. III

O'Halloran, Joseph Sylvester, 1842–1920, vol. II

O'Halloran, Rev. Richard, *died* 1925, vol. II

O'Hanlon, Rt Rev. Mgr James, 1840–1921, vol. II

O'Hara, Major Charles Kean, 1860–1947, vol. IV

O'Hara, Rear-Adm. Derek, 1927–1986, vol. VIII

O'Hara, Col Errill Robert, *died* 1956, vol. V

O'Hara, Francis Charles Trench, 1870–1954, vol. V

O'Hara, Frank, 1917–1985, vol. VIII

O'Hara, Most Rev. Gerald Patrick, 1895–1963, vol. VI

O'Hara, Rt Rev. Henry Stewart, 1843–1923, vol. II

O'Hara, Col James, 1865–1928, vol. II

O'Hara, John Bernard, 1862–1927, vol. II

O'Hara, John Henry, 1905–1970, vol. VI

O'Hara, Valentine J., 1875–1941, vol. IV

O'Hare, Patrick, 1849–1917, vol. II

O'Hare, Patrick Joseph, 1883–1961, vol. VI

O'Hegarty, Patrick Sarsfield, 1879–1955, vol. V

O'Higgins, Kevin Christopher, 1892–1927, vol. II

Ohlenschlager, Comdr Norman Albert Gustave, 1890–1938, vol. III

Ohlin, Bertil Gotthard, 1899–1979, vol. VII

Ohlson, Sir Erik, 1st Bt, 1873–1934, vol. III

Ohlson, Sir Eric James, 2nd Bt, 1911–1983, vol. VIII

Ohnet, Georges, 1848–1918, vol. II

Oistrakh, David Fyodorovich, 1908–1974, vol. VII

Ojukwu, Sir Odumegwu, 1909–1966, vol. VI

O'Kane, Rt Rev. Bernard, *died* 1939, vol. III

Oke, Harris Rendell, 1891–1940, vol. III

Okeden, Richard Godfrey Christian P.; *see* Parry-Okeden.

Okeden, William Edward P.; *see* Parry-Okeden.

O'Keefe, Hon. David John, 1864–1943, vol. IV

O'Keefe, Hon. Michael, 1865–1926, vol. II

O'Keeffe, Francis Arthur, 1856–1909, vol. I

O'Keeffe, Georgia, 1887–1986, vol. VIII

O'Keeffe, James George, *died* 1937, vol. III

O'Keeffe, Maj.-Gen. Sir Menus William, 1859–1944, vol. IV

O'Keeffe, Stephen Martin Lanigan, 1878–1948, vol. IV

Okell, Charles Cyril, 1888–1939, vol. III

Okell, Rt Rev. Frank Jackson, 1887–1950, vol. IV

O'Kelly, The; *see* Kelly, Major A. D. D.

O'Kelly, The; *see* Kelly, Sir R. D.

O'Kelly, Edward Peter, *died* 1914, vol. I

O'Kelly, James Joseph, 1845–1916, vol. II

O'Kelly, John Joseph, *died* 1957, vol. V

O'Kelly, Sean Thomas, 1882–1966, vol. VI

O'Kelly de Gallagh et Tycooly, Count Gerald Edward, 1890–1968, vol. VI

Okeover, Haughton Charles, 1825–1912, vol. I

Okeover, Col Sir Ian Peter Andrew Monro W.; *see* Walker-Okeover.

Okey, Thomas, 1852–1935, vol. III

O'Kinealy, Lt-Col Frederick, 1865–1940, vol. III

Okoro, Godfrey; *see* Benin, Oba of.

Oku, Field-Marshal Count Yasukata, 1845–1930, vol. III

Okuma, Prince Shigenobu, 1838–1922, vol. II

Okyar, Bay Fethi, *died* 1943, vol. IV

Olcott, Col Henry Steel, *died* 1907, vol. I

Oldcastle, John; *see* Meynell, Wilfred.

Oldershaw, John, 1850–1938, vol. III

Oldershaw, William James Norman, 1856–1926, vol. II

Oldfield, Col Arthur Radulphus, 1872–1940, vol. III

Oldfield, Rev. Charles, *died* 1908, vol. I

Oldfield, Col Christopher George, 1863–1944, vol. IV

Oldfield, Claude Houghton, *died* 1961, vol. VI

Oldfield, Sir Francis Du Pre, 1869–1928, vol. II

Oldfield, Rev. George Biscoe, 1840–1932, vol. III

Oldfield, Maj.-Gen. John Rawdon Hodge, *died* 1940, vol. III

Oldfield, Major John William, 1886–1955, vol. V

Oldfield, Josiah, *died* 1953, vol. V

Oldfield, Maj.-Gen. Sir Louis, 1872–1949, vol. IV

Oldfield, Sir Maurice, 1915–1981, vol. VIII

Oldfield, Sir Richard Charles, 1828–1918, vol. II

Oldfield, Richard Charles, 1909–1972, vol. VII

Oldfield, Bt Lt-Col Richard William, 1891–1933, vol. III

Oldfield, William Henry, *died* 1961, vol. VI

Oldfield, Rev. William John, 1857–1934, vol. III

Oldfield-Davies, Alun Bennett, 1905–1988, vol. VIII

Oldham, Alan Trevor, 1904–1971, vol. VII

Oldham, Ven. Algernon Langston, *died* 1916, vol. II

Oldham, Charles Evelyn Arbuthnot William, 1869–1949, vol. IV

Oldham, Charles H., *died* 1926, vol. II

Oldham, Sir Ernest Fitzjohn, 1870–1926, vol. II

Oldham, Col Sir Henry Hugh, 1840–1922, vol. II

Oldham, Henry Yule, 1862–1951, vol. V

Oldham, James Bagot, 1899–1977, vol. VII

Oldham, Joseph Houldsworth, 1874–1969, vol. VI

Oldham, Richard Dixon, 1858–1936, vol. III

Oldham, William Benjamin, 1845–1916, vol. II

Oldman, Cecil Bernard, 1894–1969, vol. VI
Oldman, Col Sir Hugh Richard Deare, 1914–1988, vol. VIII
Oldman, Maj.-Gen. Richard Deare Furley, 1877–1943, vol. IV
Oldmeadow, Ernest James, 1867–1949, vol. IV
Oldrieve, William Thomas, 1853–1922, vol. II
Oldroyd, George, 1886–1951, vol. V
Oldroyd, James Gardner, 1921–1982, vol. VIII
Oldroyd, Sir Mark, 1843–1927, vol. II
Olds, Irving Sands, 1887–1963, vol. VI
O'Leary, Daniel, 1878–1954, vol. V
O'Leary, Rev. De Lacy Evans, 1872–1957, vol. V
O'Leary, Brig. Heffernan William Denis McCarthy-, 1885–1948, vol. IV
O'Leary, Most Rev. Henry Joseph, 1879–1938, vol. III
O'Leary, Rt Hon. Sir Humphrey Francis, 1886–1953, vol. V
O'Leary, John, 1830–1907, vol. I
O'Leary, Rt Rev. Louis James, 1877–1930, vol. III
O'Leary, Major Michael J., 1888–1961, vol. VI
O'Leary, Patrick Albert; see Guérisse, Count A. M. E.
O'Leary, Brig.-Gen. Tom Evelyn, 1862–1924, vol. II
Oliphant, Ernest Henry Clark, 1862–1936, vol. III
Oliphant, Captain Henry Gerard Laurence, 1879–1955, vol. V
Oliphant, John Ninian, 1887–1960, vol. V
Oliphant, Sir Lancelot, 1881–1965, vol. VI
Oliphant, Mrs Laurence, 1846–1937, vol. III
Oliphant, Gen. Sir Laurence James, 1846–1914, vol. I
Oliphant, Margaret Oliphant Wilson, 1828–1897, vol. I
Oliphant, Patrick James, 1914–1979, vol. VII
Oliphant, Lt-Col Philip Lawrence; see Kington-Blair-Oliphant, P. L.
Oliphant, Rosamond; see Oliphant, Mrs Laurence.
Oliphant-Sheffield, Robert Stoney, 1864–1937, vol. III
Olive, George William, died 1963, vol. VI
Olive, Sir James William, 1856–1942, vol. IV
Oliveira, Mrs A. J. E.; see Tubb, Carrie.
Oliveira, Francisco Regis de, died 1916, vol. II
Oliver, Major Alfred Alexander, 1874–1965, vol. VI
Oliver, Sir Arthur Maule, 1871–1937, vol. III
Oliver, Rev. Arthur West, 1858–1941, vol. IV
Oliver, Dame Beryl, 1882–1972, vol. VII
Oliver, Charles A., 1861–1945, vol. IV
Oliver, Lt-Col Sir (Charles) Frederick, died 1939, vol. III
Oliver, Charles Nicholson Jewel, 1848–1920, vol. II, vol. III
Oliver, Charles Pye, 1861–1951, vol. V
Oliver, Daniel, 1830–1916, vol. II
Oliver, Wing-Comdr Douglas Austin, 1887–1939, vol. III
Oliver, Very Rev. Edmund Henry, 1882–1935, vol. III
Oliver, Edwin, died 1950, vol. IV
Oliver, Hon. Dame Florence C.; see Cardell-Oliver, Hon. Dame A. F. G.
Oliver, Francis Alfred, 1866–1944, vol. IV
Oliver, Francis Wall, 1864–1951, vol. V

Oliver, Hon. Frank, 1853–1933, vol. III
Oliver, Lt-Col Sir Frederick; see Oliver, Lt-Col Sir C. F.
Oliver, Frederick Scott, 1864–1934, vol. III
Oliver, Adm. Sir Geoffrey Nigel, 1898–1980, vol. VII
Oliver, George, 1841–1915, vol. I
Oliver, Rev. George, 1848–1920, vol. II
Oliver, George Harold, 1888–1984, vol. VIII
Oliver, Henry Alfred, 1854–1935, vol. III
Oliver, Admiral of the Fleet Sir Henry Francis, 1865–1965, vol. VI
Oliver, Henry John Callard, 1915–1978, vol. VII
Oliver, James, 1857–1941, vol. IV
Oliver, Brig. James Alexander, 1906–1990, vol. VIII
Oliver, John Orlando Hercules Norman, 1822–1901, vol. I
Oliver, John Rathbone, 1872–1943, vol. IV
Oliver, Maj.-Gen. John Ryder, 1834–1909, vol. I
Oliver, Sir John William Lambton, 1873–1952, vol. V
Oliver, Laurence Herbert, 1881–1962, vol. VI
Oliver, Leslie Claremont, 1909–1990, vol. VIII
Oliver, Col Lionel Grant, 1858–1936, vol. III
Oliver, Martin Hugh, 1916–1987, vol. VIII
Oliver, Mary Louise, (Lady Oliver), 1868–1950, vol. IV
Oliver, Matthew W. B., died 1926, vol. II
Oliver, Philip Milner, 1884–1954, vol. V
Oliver, Raymond, 1921–1976, vol. VII
Oliver, Rev. Richard John Deane, died 1942, vol. IV
Oliver, Vice-Adm. Robert Don, 1895–1980, vol. VII
Oliver, Sir Roland Giffard, 1882–1967, vol. VI
Oliver, Sir Thomas, 1853–1942, vol. IV
Oliver, Thomas, 1871–1946, vol. IV
Oliver, Victor, 1898–1964, vol. VI
Oliver, Walter Reginald Brook, 1883–1957, vol. V
Oliver, William, 1836–1917, vol. II
Oliver, William, died 1962, vol. VI
Oliver, Col William James, 1860–1937, vol. III
Oliver, Lt-Gen. Sir William Pasfield, 1901–1981, vol. VIII
Oliver-Bellasis, Captain Richard, 1900–1964, vol. VI
Olivey, Sir Walter Rice, 1831–1922, vol. II
Olivier, 1st Baron, 1859–1943, vol. IV
Olivier, Baron (Life Peer); Laurence Kerr Olivier, 1907–1989, vol. VIII
Olivier, C. F., died 1940, vol. III (A), vol. IV
Olivier, Rev. Dacres, 1831–1919, vol. II
Olivier, Edith, died 1948, vol. IV
Olivier, George B.; see Borg Olivier.
Olivier, Rev. Henry Eden, 1866–1936, vol. III
Olivier, Herbert Arnould, 1861–1952, vol. V
Olivier, Martin John, 1900–1959, vol. V
Olivier, Captain Sidney Richard, 1870–1932, vol. III
Ollard, Lt-Col John William Arthur, 1893–1961, vol. VI
Ollard, Rev. Sidney Leslie, 1875–1949, vol. IV
Ollerenshaw, Robert, 1882–1948, vol. IV
Ollivant, Alfred, 1874–1927, vol. II
Ollivant, Brig-Gen. Alfred Henry, 1871–1919, vol. II
Ollivant, Sir Charles; see Ollivant, Sir E. C. K.
Ollivant, Sir (Edward) Charles (Kyall), 1846–1928, vol. II
Ollivant, Col John Spencer, 1872–1937, vol. III
Ollivier, Olivier Emile, 1825–1913, vol. I

Olmsted, Rt Rev. Charles Sanford, 1853–1918, vol. II
Olmsted, Rt Rev. Charles Tyler, 1842–1924, vol. II
Olney, Hon. Sir Herbert Horace, 1875–1957, vol. V
Olney, Richard, 1835–1917, vol. II
O'Loghlen, Hon. Sir Bryan, 3rd Bt, 1928–1905, vol. I
O'Loghlen, Sir Charles Hugh Ross, 5th Bt, 1881–1951, vol. V
O'Loghlen, Sir Michael, 4th Bt, 1866–1934, vol. III
O'Loghlin, Hon. James Vincent, 1852–1925, vol. II
Olorenshaw, Leslie, 1912–1972, vol VII
O'Loughlin, Hon. Laurence, 1854–1927, vol. II
O'Loughlin, Very Rev. Robert Stuart, 1852–1925, vol. II
Olphert, Sir John, 1844–1917, vol. II
Olphert, Captain Wybrants, 1879–1938, vol. III
Olpherts, Sir William, 1822–1902, vol. I
Olsen, Björn Magnusson, 1850–1919, vol. II
Olson, Sven Olof, 1916–1977, vol. VII
Olsson, Julius, 1864–1942, vol. IV
Oluwasanmi, Hezekiah Adedunmola, 1919–1983, vol. VIII
Oluwole, Rt Rev. Isaac, died 1932, vol. III
Olver, Col Sir Arthur, 1875–1961, vol. VI
O'Mahony, The; see O'Mahony, P. C. de L.
O'Mahony, John, (Sean), died 1934, vol. III
O'Mahony, Pierce Charles de Lacy, (The O'Mahony), 1850–1930, vol. III
O'Máille, Tomás, died 1938, vol. III
O'Malley, Rt Hon. Brian Kevin, 1930–1976, vol. VII
O'Malley, Maj.-Gen. David Vincent, 1891–1955, vol. V
O'Malley, Sir Edward Loughlin, 1842–1932, vol. III
O'Malley, Hon. King, died 1953, vol. V
O'Malley, Lewis Sydney Steward, 1874–1941, vol. IV
O'Malley, Mary Dolling, (Lady O'Malley); see Bridge, Ann.
O'Malley, Sir Owen St Clair, 1887–1974, vol. VII
O'Malley, William, 1853–1939, vol. III
O'Malley, Col William Arthur D'Oyly, 1853–1925, vol. II
Oman, Carola Mary Anima, (Lady Lenanton), 1897–1978, vol. VII
Oman, Charles Chichele, 1901–1982, vol. VIII
Oman, Sir Charles William Chadwick, 1860–1946, vol. IV
Oman, John Campbell, 1841–1911, vol.I
Oman, John Wood, 1860–1939, vol. III
O'Mara, Joseph, died 1927, vol. II
O'Meagher, Col John Kevin, 1866–1946, vol. IV
O'Meara, Captain Bulkeley Ernest Adolphus, 1867–1916, vol. II
O'Meara, Lt-Col Charles Albert Edmond, 1868–1923, vol II
O'Meara, Rev. Daniel, 1877–1929, vol. III
O'Meara, Francis, 1886–1941, vol. IV
O'Meara, Maj.-Gen. Francis Joseph, 1900–1967, vol. VI
O'Meara, Stephen, 1854–1918, vol. II
O'Meara, Rev. Thomas Robert, 1864–1930, vol. III
O'Meara, Lt-Col Walter Alfred John, 1863–1939, vol. III
Ommanney, Brig.-Gen. Albert Edward, 1849–1930, vol. III
Ommanney, Charles Henry, 1852–1915, vol. I

Ommanney, Lt-Col Charles Vernon, 1872–1952, vol. V
Ommanney, Col Edward Lacon, 1834–1914, vol. I
Ommanney, Adm. Sir Erasmus, 1814–1904, vol. I
Ommanney, Francis Downes, 1903–1980, vol. VII
Ommanney, Sir Montague Frederick, 1842–1925, vol. II
Ommanney, Adm. Sir Nelson; see Ommanney, Adm. Sir R. N.
Ommanney, Adm. Sir (Robert) Nelson, 1854–1938, vol. III
Omolulu, Olumide Olusanya, 1925–1967, vol. VI
Omond, George William Thomson, 1846–1929, vol. III
Omond, Robert Traill, 1858–1914, vol. I
Omont, Henri, 1857–1940, vol. III (A), vol. IV
O'Morchoe, Captain Arthur Donel MacMurrogh, (The O'Morchoe), 1892–1966, vol. VI
O'Morchoe, Rev. Thomas Arthur, (The O'Morchoe), 1865–1921, vol. II
Onassis, Aristotle Socrates, 1906–1975, vol. VII
O'Neil, Bryan Hugh St John, 1905–1954, vol. V
O'Neil, Rt Rev. Henry, 1843–1915, vol. I
O'Neill, 2nd Baron, 1839–1928, vol. II
O'Neill, 3rd Baron, 1907–1944, vol. II
O'Neill of the Maine, Baron (Life Peer); Terence Marne O'Neill, 1914–1990, vol. VIII
O'Neill, Hon. Arthur Edward Bruce, 1876–1914, vol. I
O'Neill, Sir Arthur Eugene, 1877–1950, vol. IV
O'Neill, Charles, 1849–1918, vol. II
O'Neill, Hon. Sir Con Douglas Walter, 1912–1988, vol. VIII
O'Neill, Denis Edmund, 1908–1981, vol. VIII
O'Neill, Eugene Gladstone, 1888–1953, vol. V
O'Neill, Col Eugene Joseph, 1875–1962, vol. VI
O'Neill, Rev. George, 1863–1947, vol. IV
O'Neill, Herbert Charles, died 1953, vol. V
O'Neill, Most Rev. Hugh John, 1898–1955, vol. V
O'Neill, Rev. John, 1880–1947, vol. IV
O'Neill, Sir John; see O'Neill, Sir M. J.
O'Neill, Joseph, 1886–1953, vol. V
O'Neill, Sir (Matthew) John, 1914–1976, vol. VII
O'Neill, Michael, 1909–1976, vol. VII
O'Neill, Most Rev. Michael Cornelius, 1898–1983, vol. VIII
O'Neill, Norman, 1875–1934, vol. III
O'Neill, Patrick, died 1938, vol. III
O'Neill, Most Rev. Patrick, 1891–1958. vol. V
O'Neill, Col Patrick Laurence, 1876–1962, vol. VI
O'Neill, Rt Rev. Peter Austin, 1841–1911, vol. I
O'Neill, Hon. Robert Torrens, 1845–1910, vol. I
O'Neill, Col William Henry Slingsby, 1854–1931, vol. III
O'Nial, Surg.-Gen. John, 1827–1919, vol. II, vol. III
Onians, Richard Broxton, 1899–1986, vol. VIII
O'Niel, Colette; see Malleson, Lady Constance.
Onion, Francis Leo, 1903–1983, vol. VIII
Onions, Alfred, 1858–1921, vol. II
Onions, Berta, (Mrs Oliver Onions); see Ruck, B.
Onions, Charles Talbut, 1873–1965, vol. VI
Onions, Oliver, 1873–1961, vol. VI
Onkar Singh, Maj.-Gen. Sir Apji, 1872–1951, vol. V
Onnes, (Heike) Kamerlingh, 1853–1926, vol. II

Onnes, Kamerlingh; see Onnes, H. K.
Onraet, Rene Henry de S., 1887–1952, vol. V
Onsager, Lars, 1903–1976, vol. VII
Onslow, 4th Earl of, 1853–1911, vol. I
Onslow, 5th Earl of, 1876–1945, vol. IV
Onslow, 6th Earl of, 1913–1971, vol. VII
Onslow, Sir Alexander Campbell, 1842–1908, vol. I
Onslow, Brig.-Gen. Cranley Charlton, 1869–1940, vol. III
Onslow, Denzil Roberts, 1839–1908, vol. I
Onslow, Maj.-Gen. Sir Denzil M.; see Macarthur-Onslow.
Onslow, Sir Geoffrey Henry H.; see Hughes-Onslow.
Onslow, Brig.-Gen. George Macleay M.; see Macarthur Onslow.
Onslow, Maj.-Gen. George Thorp, 1858–1921, vol. II
Onslow, Henry H.; see Hughes-Onslow.
Onslow, Hon. Mrs Huia, died 1932, vol. III
Onslow, Maj.-Gen. Hon. James William M.; see Macarthur-Onslow.
Onslow, Muriel Wheldale; see Onslow, Hon. Mrs Huia.
Onslow, Captain Richard Francis John, died 1942, vol. IV
Onslow, Adm. Sir Richard George, 1904–1975, vol. VII
Onslow, Sir Richard Wilmot, 7th Bt, 1906–1963, vol. VI
Onslow, Sir Roger Warin Beaconsfield, 6th Bt, 1880–1931, vol. III
Onslow, Sibella Macarthur, 1871–1943, vol. IV
Onslow, William George, 1908–1983, vol. VIII
Onslow, Maj.-Gen. Sir William Henry, 1863–1929, vol. III
Onslow, Sir William Wallace Rhoderic, 5th Bt, 1845–1916, vol. II
Onyon, Engr-Captain William, 1862–1953, vol. V
Oonvala, Mancherahaw Framji, 1851–1914, vol. I
Openshaw, Sir James, 1871–1935, vol. III
Openshaw, Mary; see Binstead, Mary.
Openshaw, Thomas Horrocks, 1856–1929, vol. III
Openshaw, William Harrison, 1912–1981, vol. VIII
Opher, William David, 1903–1983, vol. VIII
Opie, Evelyn Arnold, 1905–1990, vol. VIII
Opie, Peter Mason, 1918–1982, vol. VIII
Opie, Redvers, 1900–1984, vol. VIII
Opie, Air Vice-Marshal William Alfred, 1901–1977, vol. VII
Oppé, Adolph Paul, 1878–1957, vol. V
Oppenheim, E(dward) Phillips, 1866–1946, vol. IV
Oppenheim, Ernest Ferdinand, 1875–1939, vol. III
Oppenheim, Henry, 1835–1912, vol. I
Oppenheim, Lassa Francis Lawrence, 1858–1919, vol. IV
Oppenheim, Lt-Col Lawrie Charles Frith, 1871–1923, vol. II
Oppenheimer, Albert Martin, 1872–1945, vol. IV
Oppenheimer, Sir Bernard, 1st Bt, 1866–1921, vol. II
Oppenheimer, Sir Charles, 1836–1900, vol. I
Oppenheimer, Charles, 1875–1961, vol. VI
Oppenheimer, Sir Ernest, 1880–1957, vol. V
Oppenheimer, Sir Francis Charles, 1870–1961, vol. VI
Oppenheimer, Joseph, born 1876, vol. VI
Oppenheimer, Julius Robert, 1904–1967, vol. VI

Oppenheimer, Sir Michael, 2nd Bt, 1892–1933, vol. III
Oppenheimer, Raymond Harry, 1905–1984, vol. VIII
Opper, Frederick Burr, 1857–1937, vol. III (A), vol. IV
Orage, Alfred Richard, 1873–1934, vol. III
Oram, Dame Elizabeth; see Oram, Dame S. E.
Oram, Engr Vice-Adm. Sir Henry John, 1858–1939, vol. III
Oram, Sir Matthew Henry, 1885–1969, vol. VI
Oram, Richard Edward Sprague, 1830–1909, vol. I
Oram, Dame (Sarah) Elizabeth, 1860–1946, vol. IV
Orange, Beatrice, died 1955, vol. V
Orange, George James, 1871–1925, vol. II
Orange, Sir Hugh William, 1866–1956, vol. V
Orange, William, 1833–1916, vol. II
Oranmore and Browne, 2nd Baron, 1819–1900, vol. I
Oranmore and Browne, 3rd Baron, 1861–1927, vol. II
Orbach, Maurice, 1902–1979, vol. VII
Orchard, Henry Ben, died 1937, vol. III
Orchard, Jonathan, 1853–1938, vol. III
Orchard, Hon. Richard Beaumont, 1871–1942, vol. IV
Orchard, W(illiam) Arundel, died 1961, vol. VI
Orchard, Rev. William Edwin, 1877–1955, vol. V
Orchard-Lisle, Aubrey Edwin, 1908–1989, vol. VIII
Orchardson, Sir William Quiller, 1835–1910, vol. I
Orchha, Maharaja, Sir Pratap Singh Bahadur, 1854–1930, vol. III
Orchin, Frederick Joseph, 1885–1971, vol. VII
Orczy, Baroness, (Mrs Montague Barstow), died 1947, vol. IV
Ord, Bernhard Boris, died 1961, vol. VI
Ord, Ven. Charles Edward B.; see Blackett Ord.
Ord, Col Frederick Cusac, 1851–1938, vol. III
Ord, William Miller, 1834–1902, vol. I
Ord Johnstone, Morris Mackintosh, 1907–1978, vol. VII
Ord Marshall, Elizabeth Middleton, died 1931, vol. III
Orde, Sir Arthur John Campbell-Orde, 4th Bt, 1865–1933, vol. III
Orde, Sir Charles William, 1884–1980, vol. VII
Orde, John Fosbery, 1870–1932, vol. III
Orde, Sir John William Powlett Campbell-, 3rd Bt, 1827–1897, vol. I
Orde, Sir Julian Walter, 1861–1929, vol. III
Orde, Sir Percy Lancelot, 1888–1975, vol. VII
Orde, Brig. Reginald John, 1893–1975, vol. VII
Orde, Roden Horace Powlett, 1867–1941, vol. IV
Orde, Major Sir Simon Arthur Campbell-, 5th Bt, 1907–1969, vol. VI
Orde Browne, Sir Granville St John, 1883–1947, vol. IV
Ordish, Thomas Fairman, 1855–1924, vol. II
O'Reilly, The; see O'Reilly, M. G.
O'Reilly, Rt Rev. James, 1856–1928, vol. II
O'Reilly, Sir Lennox Arthur Patrick, 1880–1949, vol. IV
O'Reilly, Myles George, (The O'Reilly), 1830–1911, vol. I
O'Reilly, William Edmund, 1873–1934, vol. III
O'Reily, Most Rev. John, 1846–1915, vol. I
O'Rell, Max, 1848–1903, vol. I

Orenstein, Maj.-Gen. Alexander Jeremiah, 1879–1972, vol. VII

Orford, 5th Earl of, 1854–1931, vol. III

Organe, Sir Geoffrey Stephen William, 1908–1989, vol. VIII

Orgill, Tyrrell Churton, 1884–1975, vol. VII

O'Riain, 'Liam P.; *see* Ryan, William Patrick.

Oriel, George Harold, 1894–1939, vol. III (A), vol. IV

Oriel, John Augustus, 1896–1968, vol. VI

Origo, Marchesa Iris, 1902–1988, vol. VIII

O'Riordan, Conal Holmes O'Connell, 1874–1948, vol. IV

O'Riordan, Rt Rev. Mgr Michael, 1857–1919, vol. II

Orkney, 7th Earl of, 1867–1951, vol. V

Orleans, Duc d'; Louis Philippe Robert, 1869–1926, vol. II

Orloff, Nicholas, *died* 1915, vol. I

Ormandy, Eugene, 1899–1985, vol. VIII

Ormandy, William Reginald, 1870–1941, vol. IV

Ormathwaite, 2nd Baron, 1827–1920, vol. II

Ormathwaite, 3rd Baron, 1859–1937, vol. III

Ormathwaite, 4th Baron, 1863–1943, vol. IV

Ormathwaite, 5th Baron, 1868–1944, vol. IV

Ormathwaite, 6th Baron, 1912–1984, vol. VIII

Orme, Edith Temple, *died* 1960, vol. V

Orme, Lt-Col Frank Leslie, 1898–1968, vol. VI

Orme, Frederick George, *died* 1954, vol. V

Orme, Gilbert Edward, 1874–1945, vol. IV

Orme, John Samuel, 1916–1984, vol. VIII

Orme, William Bryce, 1871–1962, vol. VI

Ormerod, Rt Hon. Sir Benjamin, 1890–1974, vol. VII

Ormerod, Major Sir Berkeley; *see* Ormerod, Major Sir C. B.

Ormerod, Major Sir (Cyril) Berkeley, 1897–1983, vol. VIII

Ormerod, Eleanor Anne, 1828–1901, vol. I

Ormerod, Frank Cunliffe, 1894–1967, vol. VI

Ormerod, George Milner, 1879–1936, vol. III

Ormerod, Henry Arderne, 1886–1964, vol. VI

Ormerod, Herbert Eliot, 1831–1911, vol. I

Ormerod, Joseph Arderne, 1848–1925, vol. II

Ormerod, Richard Caton, 1915–1981, vol. VIII

Ormidale, Hon. Lord; George Lewis Macfarlane, 1854–1941, vol. IV

Ormiston, Thomas, 1878–1937, vol. III

Ormiston, Lt-Col Thomas Lane, 1867–1954, vol. V

Ormond, Arthur William, 1871–1964, vol. VI

Ormond, Maj.-Gen. Daniel Mowat, 1885–1974, vol. VII

Ormond, E. W., 1863–1930, vol. III

Ormond, Ernest Charles, 1896–1962, vol. VI

Ormond, Sir Herbert John, 1867–1934, vol. III

Ormonde, 3rd Marquess of, 1844–1919, vol. II

Ormonde, 4th Marquess of, 1849–1943, vol. IV

Ormonde, 5th Marquess of, 1890–1949, vol. IV

Ormonde, 6th Marquess of, 1893–1971, vol. VII

Ormrod, Peter, 1869–1923, vol. II

Ormsby, Rev. Edwin Robert, 1845–1915, vol. I

Ormsby, Rt Rev. George Albert, 1843–1924, vol. II

Ormsby, Sir Lambert Hepenstal, 1850–1923, vol. II

Ormsby, Lt-Gen. Robert Daly, 1879–1946, vol. IV

Ormsby, Rev. Thomas, 1871–1942, vol. IV

Ormsby, Lt-Col Vincent Alexander, 1865–1917, vol. II

Ormsby-Gore, Hon. Seymour Fitzroy, 1863–1950, vol. IV

Ornstein, John Isidore Maurice, 1854–1919, vol. II

O'Rorke, Rev. Benjamin Garniss, 1875–1918, vol. II

O'Rorke, E. Brian, 1901–1974, vol. VII

O'Rorke, Lt-Col Frederick Charles, *died* 1976, vol. VII

O'Rorke, Lt-Col George Mackenzie, 1883–1958, vol. V

O'Rorke, Hon. Sir (George) Maurice, 1830–1916, vol. II

O'Rorke, Hon. Sir Maurice; *see* O'Rorke, Hon. Sir G. M.

O'Rorke, Rt Rev. Mowbray Stephen, 1869–1953, vol. V

Orowan, Egon, 1902–1989, vol. VIII

Orpen, R. Caulfeild, 1863–1938, vol. III

Orpen, Rt Rev. Raymond d'Audemar, 1837–1930, vol. III

Orpen, Major Redmond Newenham Morris, 1864–1940, vol. III (A), vol. IV

Orpen, Richard Theodore, 1869–1926, vol. II

Orpen, Major Sir William, 1878–1931, vol. III

Orpen-Palmer, Brig.-Gen. Harold Bland Herbert, 1876–1941, vol. IV

Orpen-Palmer, Col Reginald Arthur Herbert, 1877–1943, vol. IV

Orphoot, Burnett Napier Henderson, 1880–1964, vol. VI

Orr, Col Alexander Stewart, 1861–1914, vol. I

Orr, Arthur A., *died* 1949, vol. IV

Orr, Charles Roger, *died* 1938, vol. III

Orr, Sir Charles William James, 1870–1945, vol. IV

Orr, Christine Grant Millar, *died* 1963, vol. VI

Orr, Major Frank George, 1881–1945, vol. IV

Orr, Col Gerald Maxwell, 1876–1934, vol. III

Orr, James, 1844–1913, vol. I

Orr, James, 1841–1920, vol. II

Orr, James Peter, 1867–1949, vol. IV

Orr, Most Rev. John, 1874–1938, vol. III

Orr, John, 1885–1966, vol. VI

Orr, Major John Boyd, 1871–1915, vol. I

Orr, John Boyd; *see* Baron Boyd Orr.

Orr, John Charles, 1858–1941, vol. IV

Orr, John Washington, 1901–1984, vol. VIII

Orr, John Wellesley, 1878–1956, vol. V

Orr, Maj.-Gen. John William, 1829–1916, vol. II

Orr, Capt. Lawrence Percy Story, 1918–1990, vol. VIII

Orr, Major Michael Harrison, 1859–1926, vol. II

Orr, Robert Low, 1854–1944, vol. IV

Orr, Sir Samuel, 1886–1972, vol. VII

Orr, Thomas, 1857–1937, vol. III

Orr, William James, 1873–1963, vol. VI

Orr, William M'Fadden, 1866–1934, vol. III

Orr-Ewing, Sir Archibald Ernest, 3rd Bt, 1853–1919, vol. II

Orr-Ewing, Charles Lindsay, 1860–1903, vol. I

Orr Ewing, Sir Ian Leslie, 1893–1958, vol. V

Orr-Ewing, Major James Alexander, 1857–1900, vol. I

Orr Ewing, Brig.-Gen. Sir Norman Archibald, 4th Bt, 1880–1960, vol. V

Orr-Ewing, Sir William, 2nd Bt, 1848–1903, vol. I

Orr-Lewis, Sir Duncan; see Orr-Lewis, Sir J. D.

Orr-Lewis, Sir Frederick Orr, 1st Bt, 1866–1921, vol. II

Orr-Lewis, Sir (John) Duncan, 2nd Bt, 1898–1980, vol. VII

Orrin, Herbert Charles, 1878–1963, vol. VI

Orrock, James, 1829–1913, vol. I

Orsborn, Albert William Thomas, 1886–1967, vol. VI

Orsman, W. J., 1838–1923, vol. II

Ortcheson, Sir John, 1905–1977, vol. VII

Orton, Charles William P.; see Previté-Orton.

Orton, Maj.-Gen. Sir Ernest Frederick, 1874–1960, vol. V

Orton, George Harrison, 1873–1947, vol. IV

Orton, Harold, 1898–1975, vol. VII

Orton, James Herbert, 1884–1953, vol. V

Orton, Kennedy Joseph Previté, 1872–1930, vol. III

Orton, Brig. Sidney Bernard, 1881–1933, vol. III

Orton-Jones, Harry, 1894–1976, vol. VII

Orwell, George, (Eric Blair), died 1950, vol. IV

Orwin, Charles Stewart, 1876–1955, vol. V

Osbaldeston-Mitford, Captain Robert; see Mitford.

Osborn, Sir Algernon Kerr Butler, 7th Bt, 1870–1948, vol. IV

Osborn, Sir Danvers Lionel Rouse, 8th Bt, 1916–1983, vol. VIII

Osborn, E. B., died 1938, vol. III

Osborn, Sir Francis; see Osborn, Sir N. F. B.

Osborn, Sir Frederic James, 1885–1978, vol. VII

Osborn, Henry Fairfield, 1857–1935, vol. III

Osborn, Margaret, 1906–1985, vol. VIII

Osborn, Sir Melmoth, 1833–1899, vol. I

Osborn, Sir (N.) Francis (B.), 1872–1954, vol. V

Osborn, Major Philip Barlow, 1870–1909, vol. I

Osborn, Samuel, 1848–1936, vol. III

Osborn, Sir Samuel, 1864–1952, vol. V

Osborn, Theodore George Bentley, 1887–1973, vol. VII

Osborn, Brig.-Gen. William Lushington, 1871–1951, vol. V

Osborne, Col Arthur de Vere-W.; see Willoughby-Osborne.

Osborne, Sir Basil, 1907–1987, vol. VIII

Osborne, Rev. Charles Edward, 1856–1936, vol. III

Osborne, Sir Cyril, 1898–1969, vol. VI

Osborne, Lt-Gen. Edmund Archibald, 1885–1969, vol. VI

Osborne, Edward, 1861–1939, vol. III

Osborne, Vice-Adm. Edward Oliver Brudenell Seymour, 1883–1956, vol. V

Osborne, Rt Rev. Edward William, 1845–1926, vol. II

Osborne, Captain F. Creagh-, died 1943, vol. IV

Osborne, Sir Francis, 15th Bt, 1856–1948, vol. IV

Osborne, Lord Francis Granville Godolphin, 1864–1924, vol. II

Osborne, Sir George Francis, 16th Bt, 1894–1960, vol. V

Osborne, Col Henry Campbell, 1874–1949, vol. IV

Osborne, Rev. (Henry James) Reginald, died 1952, vol. V

Osborne, Rev. James Denham, 1854–1934, vol. III

Osborne, John, 1911–1984, vol. VIII

Osborne, Captain John Warde, 1851–1936, vol. III

Osborne, Surg. Rear-Adm. (D) Leslie Bartlet, 1900–1989, vol. VIII

Osborne, Lithgow, 1892–1980, vol. VII

Osborne, Malcolm, 1880–1963, vol. VI

Osborne, Maj.-Gen. Osborne Herbert D.; see Delano-Osborne.

Osborne, Rev. Reginald; see Osborne, Rev. H. J. R.

Osborne, Robert Ernest, 1861–1939, vol. III

Osborne, Rosabelle, died 1958, vol. V

Osborne, William Alexander, 1873–1967, vol. VI

Osborne-Gibbes, Sir Edward; see Gibbes.

Osborne-Gibbes, Sir Philip Arthur; see Gibbes.

Osbourne, Brig.-Gen. George Nowell Thomas S.; see Smyth-Osbourne.

Osbourne, Air Cdre Sir Henry Percy S.; see Smyth-Osbourne.

Osbourne, Lloyd, 1868–1947, vol. IV

Osburn, Lt-Col Arthur, died 1952, vol. V

Osburn, Comdr Francis, 1834–1917, vol. II

Osgood, Sir (Frederic) Stanley, 1872–1952, vol. V

Osgood, Sir Stanley; see Osgood, Sir F. S.

O'Shaughnessy, Patrick Joseph, 1872–1920, vol. II

O'Shaughnessy, Richard, 1842–1918, vol. II

O'Shaughnessy, Rt Hon. Sir Thomas Lopdell, 1850–1933, vol. III

O'Shea, Alexander Paterson, 1902–1990, vol. VIII

O'Shea, Sir Henry, 1858–1926, vol. II, vol. III

O'Shea, Henry George, 1838–1905, vol. I

O'Shea, Lucius Trant, died 1920, vol. II

O'Shea, Most Rev. Thomas, 1870–1954, vol. V

O'Shea, Lt-Col Timothy, 1856–1921, vol. II

O'Shee, James John, 1866–1946, vol. IV

O'Shee, Lt-Col Richard Alfred Poer, 1867–1942, vol. IV

Osler, Sir Edmund Boyd, 1845–1924, vol. II

Osler, Featherston, 1838–1924, vol. II

Osler, Col Stratton Harry, 1882–1930, vol. III

Osler, Sir William, 1st Bt, 1849–1919, vol. II

Osley, Arthur Sidney, 1917–1987, vol. VIII

Osmaston, Bertram Beresford, 1868–1961, vol. VI

Osmaston, Col Cecil Alvend FitzHerbert, 1866–1949, vol. IV

Osmond, Wing-Comdr Edward, 1890–1946, vol. IV

Osmond, Thomas Edward, 1884–1985, vol. VIII

Osmond, Brig. William Robert Fiddes, 1890–1952, vol. V

Osmond-Clarke, Sir Henry, 1905–1986, vol. VIII

Ossiannilsson, Karl Gustav, 1875–1970, vol. VI (AII)

Ossit; see Deslandes, Baronne M.

Ostberg, Ragnar, 1866–1945, vol. IV

Ostenso, Martha, 1900–1963, vol. VI

Ostler, Hon. Sir Henry Hubert, 1876–1944, vol. IV

Ostrer, Isidore, died 1975, vol. VII

Ostrorog, Count Leon, 1867–1932, vol. III

O'Sullevan, Col John Joseph, 1879–1936, vol. III

O'Sullivan, Most Rev. Charles, 1862–1927, vol. II

O'Sullivan, Cornelius, 1841–1907, vol. I

O'Sullivan, Col Daniel, 1853–1946, vol. IV (A)

O'Sullivan, Dennis Neil, 1899–1973, vol. VII

O'Sullivan, Hon. Edward William, 1846–1910, vol. I

O'Sullivan, Eugene, 1879–1942, vol. IV

O'Sullivan, Maj.-Gen. Hugh Dermod Evan, 1874–1958, vol. V

O'Sullivan, Rt Rev. James, 1834–1915, vol. I

O'Sullivan, John M., 1881–1948, vol. IV

O'Sullivan, Most Rev. Joseph Anthony, 1886–1972, vol. VII

O'Sullivan, Ven. Leopold, *died* 1919, vol. II

O'Sullivan, Sir Neil, 1900–1968, vol. VI

O'Sullivan, Richard, 1888–1963, vol. VI

O'Sullivan, Seumas, (James Sullivan Starkey), 1879–1958, vol. V

O'Sullivan, Hon. Thomas, 1856–1953, vol. V

O'Sullivan, Timothy, *died* 1950, vol. IV

O'Sullivan-Beare, Daniel Robert, 1865–1921, vol. II

Oswald, Arthur Louis, 1858–1931, vol. III

Oswald, Col Christopher Percy, 1875–1966, vol. VI

Oswald, Eugene, *died* 1912, vol. I

Oswald, Felix, 1866–1958, vol. V

Oswald, Henry Robert, *died* 1940, vol. III

Oswald, James Francis, 1838–1908, vol. I

Oswald, Brig.-Gen. Oswald Charles Williamson, 1863–1938, vol. III

Oswald, Richard Alexander, 1841–1921, vol. II

Oswald, Col St Clair, 1858–1938, vol. III

Oswald, Thomas, 1904–1990, vol. VIII

Oswald, William Digby, 1880–1916, vol. II

Ottaway, Christopher Wyndham, 1910–1978, vol. VII

Ottaway, Eric Carlton, 1904–1967, vol. VI

Otter, Rt Rev. Anthony, 1896–1986, vol. VIII

Otter, Sir John Lonsdale, 1852–1932, vol. III

Otter, Robert Edward, *died* 1932, vol. III

Otter, Gen. Sir William Dillon, 1843–1929, vol. III

Otter-Barry, Rt Rev. Hugh Van Lynden, 1887–1971, vol. VII

Otter-Barry, William Whitmore, 1878–1973, vol. VII

Otterson, Henry, 1846–1929, vol. III

Ottley, Agnes May, 1899–1990, vol. VIII

Ottley, Rear-Adm. Sir Charles Langdale, 1858–1932, vol. III

Ottley, Rev. Edward Bickersteth, 1853–1910, vol. I

Ottley, Rev. Feilding Hay, 1877–1958, vol. V

Ottley, Rev. Henry Bickersteth, *died* 1932, vol. III

Ottley, Col Sir John Walter, 1841–1931, vol. III

Ottley, Rev. Robert Lawrence, 1856–1933, vol. III

Ottley, Warner Herbert Taylor, 1889–1980, vol. VII (AII)

Otto, Rudolf, 1869–1937, vol. III

Otway, Rt Hon. Sir Arthur John, 3rd Bt, 1822–1912, vol. I

Oudendyk, Dame Margaret, 1876–1971, vol. VII

Oudendyk, William J., 1874–1953, vol. V

Ouida, 1839–1908, vol. I

Ouimet, Hon. Joseph Alderic, 1848–1916, vol. II, vol. III

Ould, Hermon, 1885–1951, vol. V

Ould, Robert F.; *see* Fielding-Ould.

Ouless, Walter William, 1848–1933, vol. III

Oulsnam, Sir Harrison; *see* Oulsnam, Sir S. H. Y.

Oulsnam, Sir (Samuel) Harrison (Yardley), 1898–1972, vol. VII

Oulton, George N., *died* 1928, vol. II

Oulton, Rev. John Ernest Leonard, 1886–1957, vol. V

Oulton, William Harold Stowe, 1869–1941, vol. IV

Oury, Libert, 1868–1939, vol. III

Ouseley, Brig.-Gen. Ralph Glynn, 1866–1931, vol. III

Outcault, Richard Felton, 1863–1928, vol. II

Outen, Roland Thomas, 1900–1957, vol. V

Outerbridge, Sir Joseph, 1843–1933, vol. III

Outerbridge, Col Hon. Sir Leonard Cecil, 1888–1986, vol. VIII

Outhwaite, Ernest, 1875–1931, vol. III

Outhwaite, R. L., 1868–1930, vol. III

Outram, Comdr Edmund, 1858–1937, vol. III

Outram, Sir Francis Boyd, 2nd Bt, 1836–1912, vol. I

Outram, Major Sir Francis Davidson, 4th Bt, 1867–1945, vol. IV

Outram, Lt-Col Harold William Sydney, *died* 1944, vol. IV

Outram, Sir James, 3rd Bt, 1864–1925, vol. II

Outtrim, Hon. Alfred Richard, 1845–1925, vol. II

Outtrim, Frank Leon, 1847–1917, vol. II

Ouvry, Ernest Carrington, 1866–1951, vol. V

Ovans, Major Hugh Lambert, 1881–1946, vol. IV

Ovenden, Very Rev. Charles T., 1846–1924, vol. II

Ovenden, Harry, 1876–1974, vol. VII

Ovens, Hon. Brig.-Gen. Gerald Hedley, 1856–1933, vol. III

Ovens, Col Robert Montgomery, 1868–1950, vol. IV

Overbury, Sir Robert Leslie, 1887–1955, vol. V

Overend, Douglas, 1914–1981, vol. VIII

Overend, Thomas George, 1846–1915, vol. I

Overend, Walker, *died* 1926, vol. II, vol. III

Overman, Henry Jacob, 1862–1933, vol. III

Overstreet, Harry Allen, 1875–1970, vol. VI

Overton, Sir Arnold Edersheim, 1893–1975, vol. VII

Overton, Charles Ernest, 1865–1933, vol. III

Overton, Rev. Frederick Arnold, 1862–1935, vol. III

Overton, George Leonard, 1875–1948, vol. IV

Overton, Rev. John Henry, 1835–1903, vol. I

Overton, Robert, 1859–1924, vol. II

Overtoun, 1st Baron, 1843–1908, vol. I

Overy, Sir Thomas Stuart, 1893–1973, vol. VII

Ovey, Sir Esmond, 1879–1963, vol. VI

Ovey, Lt-Col Richard Lockhart, 1878–1946, vol. IV

Owen, Sir Alfred George Beech, 1908–1975, vol. VII

Owen, Col Arthur Allen, 1842–1917, vol. II

Owen, Arthur Charles H.; *see* Humphreys-Owen.

Owen, Sir (Arthur) David Kemp, 1904–1970, vol. VI

Owen, Sir (Arthur) Douglas, 1904–1977, vol. VII

Owen, Col Arthur Lewis S.; *see* Scott-Owen.

Owen, Basil Wilberforce Longmore, *died* 1943, vol. IV

Owen, Sir Cecil; *see* Owen, Sir W. C.

Owen, Brig.-Gen. Charles C.; *see* Cunliffe-Owen.

Owen, Lt-Col Charles Harold Wells, 1872–1936, vol. III

Owen, Maj.-Gen. Charles Henry, 1830–1921, vol. II

Owen, Very Rev. Charles Mansfield, 1852–1940, vol. III

Owen, Col Charles Richard Blackstone, 1870–1954, vol. V

Owen, Brig.-Gen. Charles Samuel, 1879–1959, vol. V

Owen, Lt-Col Charles William, 1853–1922, vol. II

Owen, Collinson, 1882–1956, vol. V

Owen, David Charles L.; *see* Lloyd Owen.

Owen, David Elystan, 1912–1987, vol. VIII

Owen, Sir David John, 1874–1941, vol. IV
Owen, Sir David Kemp; see Owen, Sir A. D. K.
Owen, Most Rev. Derwyn Trevor, 1876–1947, vol. IV
Owen, Sir Douglas, 1850–1920, vol. II
Owen, Sir Douglas; see Owen, Sir A. D.
Owen, Sir Dudley Herbert C.; see Cunliffe-Owen.
Owen, Edmund, died 1915, vol. I
Owen, Edward Cunliffe, 1857–1918, vol. II
Owen, Rev. Edward Cunliffe, died 1937, vol. III
Owen, Edwin Augustine, 1887–1973, vol. VII
Owen, Eric Hamilton, 1903–1989, vol. VIII
Owen, Evan Roger, died 1930, vol. III
Owen, Lt-Col F. C.; see Cunliffe-Owen.
Owen, Frank, 1905–1979, vol. VII
Owen, Rev. G., died 1914, vol. I
Owen, George Douglas, 1887–1965, vol. VI
Owen, George Elmslie, 1899–1964, vol. VI
Owen, George Sherard, 1892–1976, vol. VII
Owen, Rev. George Vale, 1869–1931, vol. III
Owen, Lt-Col Sir Goronwy, 1881–1963, vol. VI
Owen, Grace, 1873–1965, vol. VI
Owen, Gwilym, 1880–1940, vol. III (A), vol. IV
Owen, Gwilym Ellis Lane, 1922–1982, vol. VIII
Owen, H. F.; see Owen, F.
Owen, Harold, 1872–1930, vol. III
Owen, Harrison, 1890–1966, vol. VI (AII)
Owen, Henry, died 1919, vol. II
Owen, Col Henry Mostyn, 1858–1927, vol. II
Owen, Captain Hilary Dorsett, 1894–1980, vol. VII
Owen, Sir Hugh, 1835–1916, vol. II
Owen, Sir Hugh Charles, 3rd Bt, 1826–1909, vol. I
Owen, Sir Hugo C.; see Cunliffe-Owen.
Owen, Sir Isambard, 1850–1927, vol. II
Owen, Rev. Ithel George, 1863–1941, vol. IV
Owen, Sir James George, 1869–1939, vol. III
Owen, Jean A., (Mrs Owen Visger), died 1922, vol. II
Owen, Rt Rev. John, 1854–1926, vol. II
Owen, John, died 1949, vol. IV
Owen, Sir John Arthur, 4th Bt, 1892–1973, vol. VII
Owen, Col John Edward, 1928–1989, vol. VIII
Owen, Gen. Sir John Fletcher, 1839–1924, vol. II
Owen, John Glendwr, 1914–1977, vol. VII
Owen, Rev. John Smith, died 1922, vol. II
Owen, Sir Langer Meade Loftus, 1862–1935, vol. III
Owen, Leonard, 1890–1965, vol. VI
Owen, Sir Leonard; see Owen, Sir W. L.
Owen, Leonard Victor Davies, 1888–1952, vol. V
Owen, Rt Rev. Leslie, 1886–1947, vol. IV
Owen, Lt-Col Lindsay Cunliffe, died 1941, vol. IV
Owen, Maj.-Gen. Llewellyn Isaac Gethin M.; see Morgan-Owen.
Owen, Lloyd, 1903–1966, vol. VI
Owen, Mary Alicia, 1858–1935, vol. III
Owen, O. Morgan, died 1930, vol. III
Owen, Owen William, 1863–1930, vol. III
Owen, Paul Robert, 1920–1990, vol. VIII
Owen, Col Percy Thomas, 1864–1936, vol. III
Owen, Peter Granville, 1918–1986, vol. VIII
Owen, Peter M.; see Macaulay-Owen.
Owen, Most Rev. Reginald Herbert, 1887–1961, vol. VI
Owen, Robert; see Owen, P. R.
Owen, Robert Davies, 1898–1988, vol. VIII
Owen, Lt-Col Robert Haylock, 1862–1927, vol. II

Owen, Lt-Col Roger Arthur Mostyn-, 1888–1947, vol. IV
Owen, Lt-Col Roger Carmichael Robert, 1866–1941, vol. IV
Owen, Ronald Allan, 1920–1982, vol. VIII
Owen, Sir Ronald Hugh, 1910–1988, vol. VIII
Owen, Rosamond Dale; see Oliphant, Mrs Laurence.
Owen, Sackville Herbert Edward Gregg, 1880–1960, vol. V
Owen, Sidney George, 1858–1940, vol. III
Owen, Sidney James, 1827–1912, vol. I
Owen, Lt-Col Sydney Lloyd, born 1872, vol. II
Owen, Thomas, 1840–1898, vol. I
Owen, Sir Thomas David, 1854–1921, vol. II
Owen, Thomas Joseph, 1903–1986, vol. VIII
Owen, Rev. Thomas M. Bulkeley B.; see Bulkeley-Owen.
Owen, Cdre Trevor Lewis, 1895–1980, vol. VII
Owen, Ven. Walter Edwin, 1879–1945, vol. IV
Owen, Will, 1869–1957, vol. V
Owen, Sir William, 1834–1912, vol. I
Owen, William, 1837–1918, vol. II
Owen, Sir (William) Cecil, 1872–1959, vol. V
Owen, Rt Hon. Sir William Francis Langer, 1899–1972, vol. VII
Owen, Captain William Henry, 1857–1931, vol. III
Owen, William Hugh, 1886–1957, vol. V
Owen, William James, 1901–1981, vol. VIII
Owen, Sir (William) Leonard, 1897–1971, vol. VII
Owen, William Stevenson, 1834–1909, vol. I
Owen-Lewis, Lt-Col Arthur Francis, 1868–1926, vol. II
Owen-Lewis, Cyril Alexander, 1871–1905, vol. I
Owen-Smyth, Charles Edward, 1851–1925, vol. II
Owens, Captain Sir Arthur Lewis, died 1967, vol. VI
Owens, Sir Charles John, 1845–1933, vol. III
Owens, Ernest Stanley, 1916–1983, vol. VIII
Owens, Most Rev. Richard, died 1909, vol. I
Owens, Richard Hugh M.; see Mills-Owens.
Owens, Col Robert Leonce, 1862–1937, vol. III
Owens, Tom Paterson, 1888–1968, vol. VI
Owens, Hon. William, 1840–1917, vol. II
Owles, Captain Garth Henry Fyson, 1896–1975, vol. VII
Owles, Thomas Arthur, 1890–1966, vol. VI
Owsley, John William, 1840–1929, vol. III
Owst, Gerald Robert, 1894–1962, vol. VI
Oxborrow, Brig. Claud Catton, 1898–1972, vol. VII
Oxenbridge, 1st Viscount, 1829–1898, vol. I
Oxenden, Sir Percy Dixwell Nowell Dixwell-, 10th Bt, 1838–1924, vol. II
Oxenham, Elsie Jeannette, died 1960, vol. V
Oxenham, John, died 1941, vol. IV
Oxford and Asquith, 1st Earl of, 1852–1928, vol. II
Oxford and Asquith, Countess of; (Emma Alice Margaret) (Margot), 1864–1945, vol. IV
Oxfuird, 12th Viscount, 1899–1986, vol. VIII
Oxland, Air Vice-Marshal Robert Dickinson, 1889–1959, vol. V
Oxley, Sir Alfred James R.; see Rice-Oxley.
Oxley, Adm. Charles Lister, 1841–1920, vol. II
Oxley, Douglas George R.; see Rice-Oxley.
Oxley, John Stewart, 1861–1935, vol. III

Oxley, Brig.-Gen. Reginald Stewart, 1863–1951, vol. V

Oxley, Maj.-Gen. Walter Hayes, 1891–1978, vol. VII

Oyama, Iwao, Field-Marshal Prince, 1842–1916, vol. II

Oyebode, Rt Rev. David Richard, 1898–1960, vol. V

Ozanne, Sir Edward Chepmell, 1852–1929, vol. III

Ozanne, James William, *died* 1931, vol. III

Ozanne, John Henry, 1850–1902, vol. I

Ozanne, Maj.-Gen. William Maingay, 1891–1966, vol. VI

P

Pace, Rev. Edward George, 1881–1953, vol. V

Pace, George Gaze, 1915–1975, vol. VII

Pace, Most Rev. Pietro, 1831–1914, vol. I

Pacelli, Eugene; *see* Pius XII.

Pachmann, Vladimir de, 1848–1933, vol. III

Pächt, Otto Ernest, 1902–1988, vol. VIII

Pack, Arthur Dennis Henry Heber R.; *see* Reynell-Pack.

Pack, Captain Stanley Walter Croucher, 1904–1977, vol VII

Pack-Beresford, Denis R., 1864–1942, vol. IV

Packard, Sir Edward, 1843–1932, vol. III

Packard, Lt-Col Henry Norrington, 1870–1916, vol. II

Packe, Sir Edward Hussey, 1878–1946, vol. IV

Packe, Lt-Col Frederick Edward, 1879–1953, vol. V

Packe, Hussey, 1846–1908, vol. I

Packer, Sir (Douglas) Frank (Hewson), 1906–1974, vol. VII

Packer, Sir Frank; *see* Packer, Sir D. F. H.

Packer, Col Harry Dixon, 1872–1947, vol. IV

Packer, Adm. Sir Herbert Annesley, 1894–1962, vol. VI

Packer, Joy, (Lady Packer), 1905–1977, vol. VII

Packman, Lt-Col Kenneth Chalmers, 1899–1969, vol.VI

Paddison, Sir George Frederick, *died* 1927, vol. II

Paddock, Rt Rev. Robert L., vol III

Paddon, Lt John Frederick, 1856–1913, vol. I

Paddon, Lt-Col Sir Stanley Somerset Wreford, 1881–1963, vol. VI

Paddon, Rev. William Francis Locke, *died* 1922, vol. II

Padel, Charles Frederick Christian, 1872–1958, vol. V

Paderewski, Ignace Jean, 1860–1941, vol. IV

Padfield, Rev. William Herbert Greenland, 1875–1936, vol. III

Padley, Walter Ernest, 1916–1984, vol. VIII

Padley, Wilfred, 1910–1968, vol. VI

Padwick, Francis Herbert, 1856–1945, vol. IV

Padwick, Surgeon-Captain Harold Boultbee, 1889–1972, vol. VII

Padwick, Philip Hugh, 1876–1958, vol. V

Pae, David, 1864–1948, vol. IV

Pagan, Brig.-Gen. Alexander William, 1878–1949, vol. IV

Pagan, Very Rev. John, 1830–1909, vol. I

Pagan, Brig. Sir John Ernest, 1914–1986, vol. VIII

Pagden, Arthur Sampson, 1858–1942, vol. IV

Page, Ven. Alfred Charles, 1912–1988, vol. VIII

Page, Col Alfred John, 1912–1987, vol. VIII

Page, Sir Archibald, 1875–1949, vol. IV

Page, Very Rev. Arnold Henry, 1851–1943, vol. IV

Page, Sir Arthur, 1876–1958, vol. V

Page, (Charles) James, 1925–1981, vol. VIII

Page, Sir (Charles) Max, 1882–1963, vol. VI

Page, Lt-Col Cuthbert Frederick Graham, 1880–1919, vol. II

Page, Sir Denys Lionel, 1908–1978, vol. VII

Page, Rt Hon. Sir Earle Christmas Grafton, 1880–1961, vol. VI

Page, Edward, 1877–1937, vol. III

Page, Ernest, 1848–1930, vol. III

Page, Lt-Col F., *died* 1917, vol. II

Page, Frederick, *died* 1919, vol. II

Page, Sir Frederick Handley, 1885–1962, vol. VI

Page, Lt-Gen. George H., *see* Hyde-Page.

Page, Gertrude, (Mrs Dobbin), *died* 1922, vol. II

Page, Rt Hon. Sir Graham; *see* Page, Rt Hon. Sir R. G.

Page, Major Harold Hillis, 1888–1942, vol. IV

Page, Harold James, 1890–1972, vol. VII

Page, Harry Marmaduke, 1860–1942, vol. IV

Page, Sir Harry Robertson, 1911–1985, vol. VIII

Page, Herbert William, 1845–1926, vol. II

Page, Hon. James, 1860–1921, vol. II

Page, James; *see* Page, C. J.

Page, John Lloyd Warden, 1858–1916, vol. II

Page, Sir Leo Francia, 1890–1951, vol. V

Page, Maj.-Gen. Lionel Frank, 1884–1944, vol. IV

Page, Sir Max; *see* Page, Sir C. M.

Page, Norman John, 1920–1985, vol. VIII

Page, Robert Palgrave, 1867–1947, vol. IV

Page, Rt Hon. Sir (Rodney) Graham, 1911–1981, vol. VIII

Page, Russell, 1906–1985, vol. VIII

Page, Sidney John, 1892–1973, vol. VII

Page, Lt-Col Stanley Hatch, 1874–1962, vol. VI

Page, Thomas Ethelbert, 1850–1936, vol. III

Page, Thomas Nelson, 1853–1922, vol. II

Page, Sir Thomas Spurgeon, 1879–1958, vol. V

Page, Thomas Walker, 1866–1937, vol. III

Page, Walter Hines, 1855–1918, vol. II

Page, William, 1861–1934, vol. III

Page, William Frank, 1894–1980, vol. VII

Page, William Morton, 1883–1950, vol. IV

Page, William Walter Keightly, 1878–1962, vol. VI

Page-Henderson, Lt-Col Henry Cockcroft, 1856–1942, vol. IV

Page-Jones, Frederick Herbert, 1903–1972, vol. VII

Page-Roberts, Very Rev. William; *see* Roberts.

Page Wood, Sir David John Hatherley, 7th Bt, 1921–1955, vol. V

Pagenstecher, Hermann, 1844–1932, vol. III

Paget of Northampton, Baron (Life Peer); Reginald Thomas Paget, 1908–1990, vol. VIII

Paget, Lt-Col Albert Edward Sydney Louis, 1879–1917, vol II

Paget, Adm. Sir Alfred Wyndham, 1852–1918, vol. II

Paget, Gen. Rt Hon. Sir Arthur Henry Fitzroy, 1851–1928, vol. II

Paget, Gen. Sir Bernard Charles Tolver, 1887–1961, vol. VI

Paget, Lt-Col Sir Cecil Walter, 2nd Bt (*cr* 1897), 1874–1936, vol. III

Paget, Major Eden Wilberforce, 1865–1955, vol. V

Paget, Very Rev. Edward Clarence, 1851–1927, vol. II

Paget, Most Rev. Edward Francis, 1886–1971, vol. VII

Paget, Sir Ernest; *see* Paget, Sir G. E.

Paget, Rt Rev. Francis, 1851–1911, vol. I

Paget, Sir (George) Ernest, 1st Bt (*cr* 1897), 1841–1923, vol. II

Paget, Major George Thomas Cavendish, 1853–1939, vol. III

Paget, Col Harold, 1849–1933, vol. III

Paget, Lt-Comdr Henry Edward Clarence, 1860–1940, vol. III

Paget, Rt Rev. Henry Luke, 1853–1937, vol. III

Paget, Henry Marriott, 1856–1936, vol. III

Paget, Captain J. Otho, 1860–1934, vol. III

Paget, Sir James, 1st Bt (*cr* 1871), 1814–1899, vol I

Paget, Captain Sir James Francis, 3rd Bt (*cr* 1871), 1890–1972, vol. VII

Paget, John, 1811–1898, vol. I

Paget, Sir John Rahere, 2nd Bt (*cr* 1871), 1848–1938, vol. III

Paget, Dame Leila; *see* Paget, Dame L. M. L. W.

Paget, Dame (Louise Margaret) Leila (Wemyss), 1881–1958, vol. V

Paget, Mary, (Lady Paget), *died* 1919, vol. II

Paget, Dame (Mary) Rosalind, 1855–1948, vol. IV

Paget, Paul Edward, 1901–1985, vol. VIII

Paget, Rt Hon. Sir Ralph Spencer, 1864–1940, vol. III

Paget, Sir Richard Arthur Surtees, 2nd Bt (*cr* 1886), 1869–1955, vol. V

Paget, Rt Hon. Sir Richard Horner, 1st Bt (*cr* 1886), 1832–1908, vol. I

Paget, Dame Rosalind; *see* Paget, Dame M. R.

Paget, Sidney Edward, 1860–1908, vol. I

Paget, Stephen, 1855–1926, vol. II

Paget, Major Thomas Guy Frederick, 1886–1952, vol. V

Paget, Lord Victor William, 1889–1952, vol. V

Paget, Violet, 1856–1935, vol. III

Paget, Walburga, (Lady Paget), 1839–1929, vol. III

Paget, Brig.-Gen. Wellesley Lynedoch Henry, 1858–1918, vol. II

Paget, William Edmund, 1879–1928, vol. II

Paget-Cooke, Sir Henry, 1861–1923, vol. II

Paget-Cooke, Oliver Dayrell Paget, 1891–1954, vol. V

Pagnol, Marcel, 1895–1974, vol. VII

Paice, Rev. Arthur, 1857–1923, vol. II

Paige, Lt-Col Cyril Penrose, 1882–1958, vol. V

Paige, Col Douglas, 1886–1958, vol. V

Pain, Arthur Bernard, 1904–1973, vol. VII

Pain, Rt Rev. Arthur Wellesley, 1841–1920, vol. II

Pain, Barry Eric Odell, 1864–1928, vol. II

Pain, Sir Charles John, 1873–1961, vol. VI

Pain, Brig.-Gen. Sir (George) William (Hacket), 1855–1924, vol. II

Pain, Sir William; *see* Pain, Sir G. W. H.

Paine, Lt-Col Albert Ingraham, 1874–1949, vol. IV

Paine, Brig. Douglas Duke, 1892–1960, vol. V (A)

Paine, Rear-Adm. Sir Godfrey Marshall, 1871–1932, vol. III

Paine, Sir (Herbert) Kingsley, 1883–1972, vol. VII

Paine, Hubert S.; *see* Scott-Paine.

Paine, Major James Henry, 1870–1918, vol. II

Paine, Brig.-Gen. John Jackson, 1864–1936, vol. III

Paine, Sir Kingsley; *see* Paine, Sir H. K.

Paine, Sir Thomas, 1822–1908, vol. I

Paine, William Worship, 1861–1946, vol. IV

Paine, Wyatt W.; *see* Wyatt-Paine.

Painleve, Paul, 1863–1933, vol. III

Painter, Brig.-Gen. Arnaud Clarke, 1863–1945, vol. IV

Painter, Sir Frederic George, 1844–1926, vol. II

Painter, Brig. Gordon Whistler Arnaud, 1893–1960, vol. V

Painter, Robert John, 1927–1972, vol. VII

Paish, Frank Walter, 1898–1988, vol. VIII

Paish, Sir George, 1867–1957, vol. V

Paisley, John Lawrence, 1909–1987, vol. VIII

Pakeman, Sir John, 1860–1946, vol. IV

Pakeman, Robert J., *died* 1906, vol. I

Pakenham, Hon. Sir Francis John, 1832–1905, vol. I

Pakenham, Col George de la Poer Beresford, 1875–1960, vol. V

Pakenham, Col Hercules Arthur, *died* 1937, vol. III

Pakenham, Lt-Gen. Thomas Henry, 1826–1913, vol. I

Pakenham, Adm. Sir William Christopher, 1861–1933, vol. III

Pakenham-Mahon, Captain Henry, 1851–1922, vol. II

Pakenham-Walsh, Ernst, 1875–1964, vol. VI

Pakenham-Walsh, Rt Rev. Herbert Pakenham, 1871–1959, vol. V (A)

Pakenham-Walsh, Maj.-Gen. Ridley P., 1888–1966, vol. VI

Pakes, Ernest John, 1899–1988, vol. VIII

Pal, Benjamin Peary, 1906–1989, vol. VIII

Palacio Valdés, Armando, 1853–1938, vol. III

Paladini, Carlo, 1864–1922, vol. II, vol. III

Palairet, Lionel Charles Hamilton, 1870–1933, vol. III

Palairet, Sir Michael, 1882–1956, vol. V

Palamountain, Edgar William Irwin, 1917–1990, vol. VIII

Palanpur, Nawab of, 1852–1918, vol. II

Palanpur, Nawab of, 1883–1957, vol. V

Paléologue, Maurice, 1859–1944, vol. IV

Paley, Col Alan Thomas, 1876–1950, vol. IV

Paley, Maj.-Gen. Sir (Alexander George) Victor, 1903–1976, vol. VII

Paley, Frederick John, 1859–1924, vol. II

Paley, Maj.-Gen. Sir Victor, *see* Paley, Maj.-Gen. Sir A. G. V.

Palfrey, William John Henry, 1906–1979, vol. VII

Palgrave, Francis Turner, 1824–1897, vol. I

Palgrave, Sir Reginald Francis Douce, 1829–1904, vol. I

Palgrave, Sir Robert Harry Inglis, 1827–1919, vol. II
Palin, Col Gilbert Walter, 1862–1946, vol. IV
Palin, John Henry, vol. III
Palin, Maj.-Gen. Sir Philip Charles, 1864–1937, vol. III
Palin, Lt-Col Randle Harry, 1873–1950, vol. IV
Palin, Ven. William, 1893–1967, vol. VI
Palin, William Mainwaring, 1862–1947, vol. IV
Paling, Gerald Richard, 1895–1966, vol. VI
Paling, Rt Hon. Wilfred, 1883–1971, vol. VII
Palit, Sir Tarak Nath, *died* 1914, vol. I
Palitana, Thakur Saheb Sir, Mansinghji Sursinghji, 1863–1905, vol. I
Palk, Major Hon. Lawrence Charles Walter, 1870–1916, vol. II
Palles, Rt Hon. Christopher, 1831–1920, vol. II
Pallin, Lt-Col Samuel Farrer Godfrey, 1878–1930, vol. III
Pallin, Col William Alfred, 1873–1956, vol. V
Pallis, Alex., 1851–1935, vol. III
Palliser, Adm. Sir Arthur Francis Eric, *died* 1956, vol. V
Palliser, Charles Frederick Wray Bury, 1854–1934, vol. III
Palliser, Adm. Henry St Leger Bury, 1839–1907, vol. I
Palliser, Herbert William, 1883–1963, vol. VI
Pallot, Rev. Elias George, 1876–1954, vol. VI
Palme, Olof; *see* Palme, S. O. J.
Palme, (Sven) Olof (Joachim), 1927–1986, vol. VIII
Palmella, 5th Duke of, 1897–1969, vol. VI
Palmer, 1st Baron, 1858–1948, vol. IV
Palmer, 2nd Baron, 1882–1950, vol. IV
Palmer, 3rd Baron, 1916–1990, vol. VIII
Palmer, Alan; *see* Palmer, C. A. S.
Palmer, Col Albert John, *died* 1940, vol. III
Palmer, Alexander Croydon, 1887–1963, vol. VI
Palmer, Captain Alexander Edward Guy, 1886–1926, vol. II
Palmer, Alexander Mitchell, 1872–1936, vol. III
Palmer, Col Aleyn Zouch, 1882–1934, vol. III
Palmer, Alfred, 1852–1936, vol. III
Palmer, Sir Alfred Molyneux, 3rd Bt (*cr* 1886), 1853–1935, vol. III
Palmer, Sir Anthony Frederick Mark, 4th Bt (*cr* 1886), 1914–1941, vol. IV
Palmer, Sir Archdale Robert, 4th Bt (*cr* 1791), 1838–1905, vol. I
Palmer, Arthur, 1841–1897, vol. I
Palmer, Sir Arthur Hunter, 1819–1898, vol. I
Palmer, Captain Arthur Percy, 1872–1915, vol. I
Palmer, Gen. Sir Arthur Power, 1840–1904, vol. I
Palmer, Charles, 1869–1920, vol. II
Palmer, Sir (Charles) Eric, *died* 1948, vol. IV
Palmer, Charles Felix, *died* 1919, vol. II
Palmer, Charles George, 1847–1940, vol. III
Palmer, Col Charles Henry Dayrell, 1872–1939, vol. III
Palmer, Ven. Charles Jasper, 1863–1931, vol. III
Palmer, Sir Charles Mark, 1st Bt (*cr* 1886), 1822–1907, vol. I
Palmer, Rev. Charles Samuel, 1830–1921, vol. II
Palmer, Lt-Col Claude Bowes, 1868–1949, vol. IV

Palmer, Clement Charlton, 1871–1944, vol. IV
Palmer, Brig.-Gen. Cyril Eustace, 1870–1939, vol. III
Palmer, Sir Edward Geoffrey Broadley, 10th Bt (*cr* 1660), 1864–1925, vol. II
Palmer, Edward Timothy, 1878–1947, vol. IV
Palmer, Rt Rev. Edwin James, 1869–1954, vol. V
Palmer, Sir Elwin Mitford, 1852–1906, vol. I
Palmer, Sir Eric; *see* Palmer, Sir C. E.
Palmer, Eustace Exall, 1878–1931, vol. III
Palmer, Sir Francis Beaufort, 1845–1917, vol. II
Palmer, Francis Noel, *died* 1961, vol. VI
Palmer, Sir Frederick, 1862–1934, vol. III
Palmer, Frederick, 1873–1958, vol. V
Palmer, Sir Frederick Archdale, 6th Bt (*cr* 1791), 1857–1933, vol. III
Palmer, Frederick Bernard, 1862–1947, vol. IV
Palmer, Lt-Col Frederick Carey Stuckley S.; *see* Sambourne-Palmer.
Palmer, Frederick Stephen, *died* 1926, vol. II
Palmer, Frederick William, 1891–1955, vol. V
Palmer, Lt-Col Sir Geoffrey Frederick Neill, 11th Bt (*cr* 1660), 1893–1951, vol. V
Palmer, Maj.-Gen. Geoffrey Woodroffe, 1891–1952, vol. V
Palmer, Rear-Adm. George, 1829–1917, vol. II
Palmer, Maj.-Gen. George Erroll P., *see* Prior-Palmer.
Palmer, George Henry, 1871–1945, vol. IV
Palmer, Rev. George Herbert, 1846–1926, vol. II
Palmer, Sir George Hudson, 5th Bt (*cr* 1791), 1841–1919, vol. II
Palmer, Brig.-Gen. George Llewellen, 1856–1932, vol. III
Palmer, Sir George Robson, 2nd Bt (*cr* 1886), 1849–1910, vol. I
Palmer, Rev. George Thomas, *died* 1908, vol. I
Palmer, Rt Hon. George William, 1851–1913, vol. I
Palmer, Gerald Eustace Howell, 1904–1984, vol. VIII
Palmer, Godfrey Mark, 1878–1933, vol. III
Palmer, Col Hon. Sir Gordon William Nottage, 1918–1989, vol. VIII
Palmer, Brig.-Gen. Harold Bland Herbert O.; *see* Orpen-Palmer.
Palmer, Rev. Henry, 1835–1931, vol. III
Palmer, Henry Alleyn, 1893–1965, vol. VI
Palmer, Col Henry Ingham Evered, 1862–1943, vol. IV
Palmer, Henry John, 1853–1903, vol. I
Palmer, Rev. Henry John, 1861–1936, vol. III
Palmer, Herbert Edward, 1880–1961, vol. VI
Palmer, Sir (Herbert) Richmond, 1877–1958, vol. V
Palmer, Horace Stanley, 1904–1968, vol. VI
Palmer, Howard; *see* Palmer, W. H.
Palmer, James L., *died* 1961, vol. VI
Palmer, James Lynwood, *died* 1941, vol. IV
Palmer, Rev. James Nelson, *died* 1908, vol. I
Palmer, Sir John Archdale, 7th Bt (*cr* 1791), 1894–1963, vol. VI
Palmer, John Leslie, 1885–1944, vol. IV
Palmer, Rev. Joseph Blades, 1849–1930, vol. III
Palmer, Ven. Joseph John Beauchamp, 1866–1942, vol. IV
Palmer, Leonard Robert, 1906–1984, vol. VIII
Palmer, Hon. Lewis; *see* Palmer, Hon. W. J. L.

Palmer, Rev. Sir Lewis Henry, 9th Bt (*cr* 1660), 1818–1909, vol. I
Palmer, Adm. Norman Craig, 1866–1926, vol. II
Palmer, Brig. Sir Otho Leslie P.; *see* Prior-Palmer.
Palmer, Maj.-Gen. Peter Garwood, 1914–1979, vol. VII
Palmer, Philip, 1867–1940, vol. III
Palmer, Mrs Potter, (Bertha Honoré), *died* 1918, vol. II
Palmer, Ralph Charlton, 1839–1923, vol. II
Palmer, Col Reginald Arthur Herbert O.; *see* Orpen-Palmer.
Palmer, Reginald Howard Reed, 1898–1970, vol. VI
Palmer, Sir Richmond; *see* Palmer, Sir H. R.
Palmer, Maj.-Gen. Robert John, 1891–1957, vol. V
Palmer, Lt-Col Roderick George F.; *see* Fenwick-Palmer.
Palmer, Sir Roger William Henry, 5th Bt (*cr* 1777), 1832–1910, vol. I
Palmer, Sutton, 1854–1933, vol. III
Palmer, Sir Sydney Bacon, 1890–1954, vol. V
Palmer, Sir Walter, 1st Bt (*cr* 1904), 1858–1910, vol. I
Palmer, Sir William, 1883–1964, vol. VI
Palmer, (William) Howard, 1865–1923, vol. II
Palmer, Hon. (William Jocelyn) Lewis, 1894–1971, vol. VII
Palmer, Lt-Col William Legh, 1868–1955, vol. V
Palmer, Col William Llewellen, 1883–1954, vol. V
Palmes, Rev. George, 1851–1927, vol. II
Palmes, Col Philip, 1856–1914, vol. I
Palmgren, Selim, 1878–1951, vol. V
Palmour, Sir Charles John Geoffrey, 1877–1948, vol. IV
Palmstierna, Baron Erik Kule, 1877–1959, vol. V
Paltridge, Sir Shane Dunne, 1910–1966, vol. VI
Paluello, Lorenzo M.; *see* Minio-Paluello.
Pam, Major Albert, 1875–1955, vol. V
Pamphlett, Engr Rear-Adm. William Frederic, *died* 1940, vol. III
Panagal, Rajah of, 1866–1928, vol. II
Panapa, Rt Rev. Wiremu Netana, 1898–1970, vol. VI
Panckridge, Sir Hugh Rahere, 1885–1942, vol. IV
Panckridge, Surg. Vice-Adm. Sir Robert; *see* Panckridge, Surg. Vice-Adm. Sir W. R. S.
Panckridge, Surg. Vice-Adm. Sir (William) Robert (Silvester), 1901–1990, vol. VIII
Pandit, Mrs Ranjit S.; *see* Pandit, V. L.
Pandit, Vijaya Lakshmi, (Mrs Ranjit S. Pandit), 1900–1990, vol. VIII
Pandya, Jagannath Bhavanishanker, 1891–1942, vol. IV
Panet, Brig.-Gen. Alphonse Eugene, 1867–1950, vol. IV
Panet, Maj.-Gen. Henri Alexandre, 1869–1951, vol. V
Panet, Brig. Henri de Lotbinière, 1896–1985, vol. VIII
Paneth, Friedrich Adolf, 1887–1958, vol. V
Panikkar, Kavalam Madhava, 1895–1963, vol. VI
Pank, Col Cecil Henry, 1876–1957, vol. V
Pank, Sir John Lovell, 1846–1922, vol. II
Pankhurst, Albert Stanley, 1897–1975, vol. VII
Pankhurst, Dame Christabel, 1880–1958, vol. V
Pankhurst, Emmeline, 1857–1928, vol. II

Pankhurst, (Estelle) Sylvia, 1882–1960, vol. V
Pankhurst, Sylvia; *see* Pankhurst, E. S.
Panna Lall, 1883–1967, vol. VI (AII)
Pannall, Major J. Charles, 1879–1960, vol. V
Pannell, Baron (Life Peer); Thomas Charles Pannell, 1902–1980, vol. VII
Pannell, Norman Alfred, 1901–1976, vol. VII
Pannett, Charles Aubrey, 1884–1969, vol. VI
Pannirselvam, Sir Arogyaswami Thamaraiselvam, Avargal, *died* 1940, vol. III
Panofsky, Erwin, 1892–1968, vol. VI
Pantcheff, Theodore Xenophon Henry, 1920–1989, vol. VIII
Panter, Air Vice-Marshal Arthur Edward, 1889–1969, vol. VI
Pantin, Carl Frederick Abel, 1899–1967, vol. VI
Pantin, William Abel, 1902–1973, vol. VII
Panton, Alexander Hugh, 1877–1951, vol. V
Panton, Edward Brooks Henderson, 1873–1929, vol. III
Panton, Mrs J. E., 1848–1923, vol. II
Panton, Col John Gerald, 1861–1915, vol. I
Panton, Sir Philip Noel, *died* 1950, vol. IV
Panzera, Lt-Col Francis William, 1851–1917, vol. II
Papalexopoulo, Rear-Adm. Dimitri, *died* 1959, vol. V
Pape, Archibald Gabriel, 1876–1927, vol. II
Pape, Sir George Augustus, 1903–1987, vol. VIII
Papillon, Lt-Col Pelham Rawstorn, 1864–1940, vol. III
Papillon, Rev. Thomas Leslie, 1841–1926, vol. II
Papini, Giovanni, 1881–1956, vol. V
Papprill, Rev. Frederick, 1859–1924, vol. II
Papworth, Rev. Sir Harold Charles, 1888–1967, vol. VI
Paradis, Hon. Philippe, 1868–1933, vol. III
Paramore, Richard Horace, 1876–1965, vol. VI
Paranjpye, Sir Raghunath Purushottam, 1876–1966, vol. VI
Parbury, George Mark, 1908–1988, vol. VIII
Parc-Locmaria, Marquis du, Alain, 1892–1973, vol. VII
Pardo-Bazan, Countess Emilia, 1852–1921, vol. II
Pardoe, Col Frank Lionel, 1880–1948, vol. IV
Pardoe, John George, 1871–1965, vol. VI
Pardoe-Thomas, Bertie, 1866–1937, vol. III
Pare, Rev. Canon Clive Frederick, 1908–1973, vol. VII
Parekh, Sir Gokuldas Kahandas, 1847–1925, vol. II
Parent, Most Rev. Charles Eugène, 1902–1982, vol. VIII
Parent, Hon. George, 1879–1942, vol. IV
Parent, Hon. Simon Napoleon, 1855–1920, vol. II
Pareparambil, Rt Rev. Aloysius, 1847–1919, vol. II
Parera, Grace Moore, *died* 1947, vol. IV
Pares, Surg. Lt-Col Basil, 1869–1943, vol. IV
Pares, Sir Bernard, 1867–1949, vol. IV
Pares, Rev. Canon Norman, 1857–1936, vol. III
Pares, Richard, 1902–1958, vol. V
Paret, Bishop William, 1826–1911, vol. I
Parfit, Rev. Joseph Thomas, 1870–1953, vol. V
Parfitt, James John, 1857–1926, vol. II
Parfitt, Rt Rev. Thomas Richards, 1911–1984, vol. VIII

Pargiter, Baron (Life Peer); George Albert Pargiter, 1897–1982, vol. VIII
Pargiter, Frederick Eden, 1852–1927, vol. II
Pargiter, Maj.-Gen. Robert Beverley, 1889–1984, vol. VIII
Parham, Rt Rev. Arthur Groom, 1883–1961, vol. VI
Parham, Hedley John, 1892–1978, vol. VII
Parham, Maj.-Gen. Hetman Jack, 1895–1974, vol. VII
Parikian, Manoug, 1920–1987, vol. VIII
Paris, Maj.-Gen. Sir Archibald, 1861–1937, vol. III
Paris, Sir Edward Talbot, 1889–1985, vol. VIII
Paris, Gaston Bruno Paulin, 1839–1903, vol. I
Paris, John, 1912–1985, vol. VIII
Pariser, Sir Maurice Philip, 1906–1968, vol. VI
Pariset, Georges, 1865–1927, vol. II
Parish, Alan Raymond, 1925–1985, vol. VIII
Parish, Arthur John, 1861–1942, vol. IV
Parish, Frank, 1824–1906, vol. I
Parish, Rev. John William, 1857–1937, vol. III
Parish, Ven. William Okes, 1859–1940, vol. III
Parish, Lt-Col Woodbine, 1862–1938, vol. III
Park, Alexander Dallas, 1882–1971, vol. VII
Park, Sir Archibald Richard, 1888–1959, vol. V
Park, Carton M,; see Moore-Park.
Park, Maj.-Gen. Cecil William, 1856–1913, vol. I
Park, James, 1857–1946, vol. IV
Park, Col James Smith, 1854–1921, vol. II
Park, John, died 1913, vol. I
Park, Air Chief Marshal Sir Keith Rodney, 1892–1975, vol. VII
Park, Sir Maitland Hall, 1862–1921, vol. II
Park, Rev. Philip Lees, 1860–1925, vol. II
Park, Rev. William, 1844–1925, vol. II
Park, William, 1909–1982, vol. VIII
Park, William H., 1863–1939, vol. III
Park, Rev. William Robert, 1880–1961, vol. VI
Park, Col William Urquart, 1846–1917, vol. II
Parke, Ernest, 1860–1944, vol. IV
Parke, Herbert William, 1903–1986, vol. VIII
Parke, Mary, 1908–1989, vol. VIII
Parke, Lt-Col Roger Kennedy, 1848–1911, vol. I
Parke, Sir William, 1822–1897, vol. I
Parker of Waddington, Baron (Life Peer); Robert John Parker, 1857–1918, vol. II
Parker of Waddington, Baron (Life Peer); Hubert Lister Parker, 1900–1972, vol. VII
Parker, Sir Alan; see Parker, Sir W. A.
Parker, Albert, 1892–1980, vol. VII
Parker, Alexander Augustine, 1908–1989, vol. VIII
Parker, Hon. Alexander Edward, 1864–1958, vol. V
Parker, Lt-Col Alfred Chevallier, 1874–1935, vol. III
Parker, Sir Alfred Livingston, 1875–1935, vol. III
Parker, Rear-Adm. (S) Alfred Ramsay, died 1951, vol. V
Parker, Alwyn, 1877–1951, vol. V
Parker, Dom Anselm Edward Stanislaus, 1880–1962, vol. VI
Parker, Brig.-Gen Arthur, 1867–1941, vol. IV
Parker, Bertie Patterson, 1871–1930, vol. III
Parker, Cecil, 1897–1971, vol. VII
Parker, Hon. Cecil Thomas, 1845–1931, vol. III
Parker, Charles Arthur, 1863–1938, vol. III
Parker, Charles Sandbach, 1864–1920, vol. II

Parker, Rt Hon. Charles Stuart, 1829–1910, vol. I
Parker, Charles Thomas, 1859–1944, vol. IV
Parker, Christopher John, 1859–1932, vol. III
Parker, Rt Rev. Clement George St Michael, 1900–1980, vol. VII
Parker, Rt Hon. Dame Dehra Kerr, died 1963, vol. VI
Parker, Dorothy, (Mrs Alan Campbell), 1893–1967, vol. VI
Parker, Sir Douglas William Leigh, 1900–1988, vol. VIII
Parker, Adm. Edmond Hyde, 1868–1951, vol. V
Parker, Sir Edmund; see Parker, Sir W. E.
Parker, Hon. Edmund William, 1857–1943, vol. IV
Parker, Edward Harper, 1849–1926, vol. II
Parker, Rt Rev. Edward Melville, 1855–1925, vol. II, vol. III
Parker, Eric; see Parker, R. E.
Parker, Eric, 1870–1955, vol. V
Parker, Rev. Ernest Julius, 1872–1942, vol. IV
Parker, Hon. Francis, 1851–1931, vol. III
Parker, Captain Francis Maitland Wyborn, 1876–1915, vol. I
Parker, Col Frederic James, 1861–1944, vol. IV
Parker, Geoffrey, 1917–1985, vol. VIII
Parker, Geoffrey Edward, 1902–1973, vol. VII
Parker, Adm. George, 1827–1904, vol. I
Parker, George, 1853–1937, vol. III
Parker, Sir George Arthur, 1843–1900, vol. I
Parker, George Howard, 1864–1955, vol. V
Parker, Sir George Phillips, 1863–1943, vol. IV
Parker, Rt Hon. Sir Gilbert, 1st Bt (cr 1915), 1862–1932, vol. III
Parker, Gordon; see Parker, H. G.
Parker, Hampton Wildman, 1897–1968, vol. VI
Parker, Col Harold, 1881–1939, vol. III
Parker, Harold, 1873–1962, vol. VI
Parker, Sir Harold, 1895–1980, vol. VII
Parker, Harper, 1864–1929, vol. III
Parker, Sir Henry; see Parker, Sir S. H.
Parker, (Henry) Gordon, 1892–1980, vol. VII
Parker, Henry Michael Denne, 1894–1971, vol. VII
Parker, Col Henry William Manwaring, died 1948, vol. IV
Parker, Adm. Henry Wise, 1875–1940, vol. III
Parker, Horatio William, 1863–1919, vol. II
Parker, Lt-Col Hon. Hubert Stanley Wyborn, 1883–1966, vol. VI
Parker, James, 1863–1948, vol. IV
Parker, James Gordon, 1869–1948, vol. IV
Parker, John, 1875–1952, vol. V
Parker, John, 1906–1987, vol. VIII
Parker, Sir John Edward, 1904–1985, vol. VIII
Parker, Hon. John Holford, 1886–1955, vol. V
Parker, Lt-Col John Oxley, 1886–1979, vol. VII
Parker, Col John William Robinson, 1857–1938, vol. III
Parker, John Williams, 1885–1961, vol. VI
Parker, Rev. Joseph, 1830–1902, vol. I
Parker, Joseph, 1831–1924, vol. II
Parker, Louis N., 1852–1944, vol. IV
Parker, Matthew Archibald, 1871–1953, vol. V
Parker, Sir Melville, 6th Bt (cr 1797), 1824–1903, vol. I

Parker, Rt Rev. Michael; *see* Parker, Rt Rev. C. G. St M.

Parker, Maj.-Gen. Neville Fraser, 1841–1916, vol. II

Parker, Owen, 1860–1936, vol. III

Parker, Vice-Adm. Patrick Edward, 1881–1941, vol. IV

Parker, Percy Livingstone, 1867–1925, vol. II

Parker, Hon. Reginald, 1854–1942, vol. IV

Parker, Captain Reginald Francis, 1871–1946, vol. IV

Parker, Richard Barry, *died* 1947, vol. IV

Parker, Col Richard Cecil Oxley, 1894–1959, vol. V

Parker, (Richard) Eric, 1925–1982, vol. VIII

Parker, Robert, 1847–1937, vol. III

Parker, Brig.-Gen. Robert Gabbett, 1875–1927, vol. II

Parker, Robert Lewis, 1862–1948, vol. IV

Parker, Rear-Adm. Robert William, 1902–1985, vol. VIII

Parker, Roger Henry, 1889–1973, vol. VII

Parker, Rushton, 1847–1932, vol. III

Parker, Brig.-Gen. St John William Topp, *died* 1943, vol. IV

Parker, Sir (Stephen) Henry, 1846–1927, vol. II

Parker, Rt Rev. Thomas Leo, 1887–1975, vol. VII

Parker, Rev. Thomas Maynard, 1906–1985, vol. VIII

Parker, Sir (Walter) Edmund, 1908–1981, vol. VIII

Parker, Captain Walter Henry, 1869–1935, vol. III

Parker, Brig.-Gen. Walter Mansel, 1875–1962, vol. VI

Parker, Wilfred Henry, 1888–1938, vol. III

Parker, Rt Rev. Wilfrid, 1883–1966, vol. VI

Parker, Rev. Canon William, 1871–1952, vol. V

Parker, Sir (William) Alan, 4th Bt, 1916–1990, vol. VIII

Parker, Rt Rev. William Alonzo, 1897–1982, vol. VIII

Parker, Sir William Biddulph, 2nd Bt (*cr* 1844), 1824–1902, vol. I

Parker, William Frye, *born* 1855, vol. II

Parker, Rev. William Hasell, *died* 1935, vol. III

Parker, Rev. Sir William Hyde, 10th Bt (*cr* 1681), 1863–1931, vol. III

Parker, Sir William Lorenzo, 3rd Bt (*cr* 1844), 1889–1971, vol. VII

Parker, William Newton, *died* 1923, vol. II

Parker, Engr-Captain William Ramsey, 1862–1943, vol. IV

Parker, Sir William Stephen Hyde, 11th Bt (*cr* 1681), 1892–1951, vol. V

Parker-Bowles, Dame Ann, 1918–1987, vol. VIII

Parker-Jervis, Lt-Col William Swynfen Whitehall, 1879–1936, vol. III

Parkes, Sir Alan Sterling, 1900–1990, vol. VIII

Parkes, Edward, 1890–1953, vol. V

Parkes, Sir Edward E., 1848–1919, vol. II

Parkes, Ernest William, 1873–1941, vol. IV

Parkes, Sir Fred, 1881–1962, vol. VI

Parkes, Geoffrey, 1902–1982, vol. VIII

Parkes, Major Harry Reeves, 1873–1949, vol. IV (A), vol. V

Parkes, Rev. James William, 1896–1981, vol. VIII

Parkes, Kineton, 1865–1938, vol. III

Parkes, Louis C., *died* 1942, vol. IV

Parkes, Oscar, 1885–1958, vol. V

Parkes, Sir Roderick Wallis, 1909–1972, vol. VII

Parkes, Sir Sydney, 1879–1961, vol. VI

Parkes, Col William Henry, 1864–1933, vol. III

Parkhill, Hon. Sir Archdale; *see* Parkhill, Hon. Sir R. A.

Parkhill, Hon. Sir (Robert) Archdale, 1879–1947, vol. IV

Parkin, Benjamin Theaker, 1906–1969, vol. VI

Parkin, Rev. George, 1846–1933, vol. III

Parkin, Sir George Robert, 1846–1922, vol. II

Parkin, Lt-Col Henry, 1858–1937, vol. III

Parkin, Sir Ian Stanley Colston, 1896–1971, vol. VII

Parkington, Sir John Roper, 1845–1924, vol. II

Parkington, Thomas Robert, 1866–1942, vol. IV

Parkinson, Sir (Albert) Lindsay, 1870–1936, vol. III

Parkinson, Sir (Arthur Charles) Cosmo, 1884–1967, vol. VI

Parkinson, Rev. Charles Meredith Octavius, 1852–1936, vol. III

Parkinson, Sir Cosmo; *see* Parkinson, Sir A. C. C.

Parkinson, Frank, 1887–1946, vol. IV

Parkinson, Brig. George Singleton, 1880–1953, vol. V

Parkinson, Maj.-Gen. Graham Beresford, 1896–1979, vol. VII

Parkinson, Hargreaves, 1896–1950, vol. IV

Parkinson, Sir Harold, 1894–1974, vol. VII

Parkinson, Rt Rev. Mgr Henry, 1852–1924, vol. II

Parkinson, John, 1872–1947, vol. IV

Parkinson, Sir John, 1885–1976, vol. VII

Parkinson, John Allen, 1870–1941, vol. IV

Parkinson, John Porter, 1863–1930, vol. III

Parkinson, John Wilson Henry, 1877–1923, vol. II

Parkinson, Joseph Ernest, 1883–1962, vol. VI

Parkinson, Sir Kenneth Wade, 1908–1981, vol. VIII

Parkinson, Sir Lindsay; *see* Parkinson, Sir A. L.

Parkinson, Dame Nancy Broadfield, 1904–1974, vol. VII

Parkinson, Norman, 1913–1990, vol. VIII

Parkinson, Sir Thomas Wright, 1863–1935, vol. III

Parkinson, Wilfrid, 1887–1965, vol. VI

Parkinson, William Edward, 1871–1927, vol. II

Parkinson Smith, Ronald; *see* Parkinson, N.

Parks, Sir Alan Guyatt, 1920–1982, vol. VIII

Parks, Elizabeth; *see* Robins, E.

Parks, Sir John, 1844–1919, vol. II

Parks, Rev. Leighton, 1852–1938, vol. III

Parks, William Arthur, 1868–1936, vol. III

Parkyn, Very Rev. Nathaniel Lindon, *died* 1931, vol. III

Parkyn, William Samuel, 1875–1949, vol. IV

Parkyns, Sir Thomas Mansfield Forbes, 7th Bt, 1853–1926, vol. II

Parlby, Joshua, 1889–1975, vol. VII

Parlett, Sir Harold George, 1869–1945, vol. IV

Parlett, Harry Edgar, *died* 1931, vol. III

Parmar, Rt Rev. Philip, 1909–1970, vol. VI

Parmelee, James Grannis, 1875–1953, vol. V

Parmelee, William Grannis, 1833–1921, vol. II

Parminter, Brig. Reginald Horace Roger, 1893–1967, vol. VI

Parmoor, 1st Baron, 1852–1941, vol. IV

Parmoor, 2nd Baron, 1882–1977, vol. VII

Parmoor, 3rd Baron, 1885–1977, vol. VII

Parnall, Robert Boyd Cochrane, 1912–1976, vol. VII

Parnall, Engr-Rear-Adm. Walter Rudolph, *died* 1954, vol. V

Parnell, Col Hon. Arthur, 1841–1914, vol. I

Parnell, Ven. Arthur Henry, *died* 1935, vol. III

Parnell, John Howard, 1843–1923, vol. II

Parnell, Lt-Gen. John William, 1860–1931, vol. III

Parnell, Valentine Charles, 1894–1972, vol. VII

Parnwell, Sidney Arthur, 1880–1944, vol. IV

Parodi, Ernest Victor, 1870–1944, vol. IV

Parr, Adm. Alfred Arthur Chase, 1849–1914, vol. I

Parr, Cecil Francis, 1847–1928, vol. II

Parr, Cecil William Chase, *died* 1943, vol. IV

Parr, Hon. Sir (Christopher) James, 1869–1941, vol. IV

Parr, Col Clements, 1865–1935, vol. III

Parr, George Herbert Edmeston, 1890–1969, vol. VI

Parr, Maj.-Gen. Sir Harington Owen, 1867–1928, vol. II

Parr, Maj.-Gen. Sir Henry Hallam, 1847–1914, vol. I

Parr, Hon. Sir James; *see* Parr, Hon. Sir C. J.

Parr, Rev. John, *died* 1935, vol. III

Parr, Joseph Charlton, 1837–1920, vol. II

Parr, Louisa, *died* 1903, vol. I

Parr, Martin Willoughby, 1892–1985, vol. VIII

Parr, Olive Katharine, (Beatrice Chase), 1874–1955, vol. V

Parr, Raymond Cecil, 1884–1965, vol. VI

Parr, Sir Robert, 1894–1979, vol. VII

Parr, Sir Robert John, 1862–1931, vol. III

Parr, Roger Charlton, 1874–1958, vol. V

Parr, Stanley, 1917–1985, vol. VIII

Parr, Thomas Henning, 1864–1937, vol. III

Parratt, Sir Walter, 1841–1924, vol. II

Parrington, Francis Rex, 1905–1981, vol. VIII

Parrington, Rex; *see* Parrington, F. R.

Parrish, Alfred Sherwen, 1931–1990, vol. VIII

Parrish, Anne, (Mrs Josiah Titzell), *died* 1957, vol. V

Parrish, Maxfield, 1870–1966, vol. VI

Parrock, Richard Arthur, 1869–1938, vol. III

Parrott, Sir Cecil Cuthbert, 1909–1984, vol. VIII

Parrott, Sir Edward; *see* Parrott, Sir J. E.

Parrott, Sir (James) Edward, 1863–1921, vol. II

Parrott, William, 1843–1905, vol. I

Parry, Very Rev. Albert William, *died* 1950, vol. IV

Parry, Rear-Adm. Cecil Ramsden Langworthy, 1901–1977, vol. VII

Parry, Charles de Courcy, 1869–1948, vol. IV

Parry, Sir (Charles) Hubert (Hastings), 1st Bt, 1848–1918, vol. II

Parry, Claude Frederick, 1896–1980, vol. VII

Parry, Clive, 1917–1982, vol. VIII

Parry, Captain Cuthbert Morris, 1907–1980, vol. VII

Parry, Sir David Hughes, 1893–1973, vol. VII

Parry, Adm. Sir Edward; *see* Parry, Adm. Sir W. E.

Parry, Sir Edward Abbott, 1863–1943, vol. IV

Parry, Most Rev. Edward Archibald, *died* 1943, vol. IV

Parry, Major Ernest G.; *see* Gambier-Parry.

Parry, Sir (Frederick) Sydney, 1861–1941, vol. IV

Parry, Lt-Col Henry Jules, 1867–1944, vol. IV

Parry, Hon. Sir Henry W.; *see* Wynn Parry.

Parry, Engr Rear-Adm. Herbert Lyell, 1875–1963, vol. VI

Parry, Ven. Herbert Thomas, 1869–1940, vol. III

Parry, Sir Hubert; *see* Parry, Sir C. H. H.

Parry, Adm. Sir John Franklin, 1863–1926, vol. II

Parry, John Horace, 1914–1982, vol. VIII

Parry, Rear-Adm. John Parry J.; *see* Jones-Parry.

Parry, Joseph, 1841–1903, vol. I

Parry, Rev. Kenneth Loyd, 1884–1962, vol. VI

Parry, Lt-Col Llewelyn England Sidney, 1856–1929, vol. III

Parry, Maj.-Gen. Michael Denman G.; *see* Gambier-Parry.

Parry, Rt Rev. Oswald Hutton, 1868–1936, vol. III

Parry, Rev. Reginald St John, 1858–1935, vol. III

Parry, Vice-Adm. Reginald St Pierre, 1879–1939, vol. III

Parry, Air Vice-Marshal Rey Griffith, 1889–1969, vol. VI

Parry, Brig. Sir Richard G.; *see* Gambier-Parry.

Parry, Robert H.; *see* Hughes-Parry.

Parry, Sir Sidney; *see* Parry, Sir F. S.

Parry, Sir Thomas, 1904–1985, vol. VIII

Parry, Lt-Col Thomas Henry, 1881–1939, vol. III

Parry, Thomas Robert G.; *see* Gambier-Parry.

Parry, Col William, 1867–1935, col. III

Parry, Hon. William Edward, 1878–1952, vol. V

Parry, Adm. Sir (William) Edward, 1893–1972, vol. VII

Parry, William John, 1842–1927, vol. II

Parry-Evans, Rev. Joseph David Samuel, 1876–1936, vol. III

Parry-Okeden, Richard Godfrey Christian, 1900–1978, vol. VII

Parry-Okeden, William Edward, 1840–1926, vol. II

Parry Pryce, Ven. Thomas, *died* 1953, vol. V

Parry-Williams, Sir Thomas Herbert, 1887–1975, vol. VII

Pars, Leopold Alexander, 1896–1985, vol. VIII

Parselle, Air Vice-Marshal Thomas Alford Boyd, 1911–1979, vol. VII

Parsey, Edward Moreland, 1900–1976, vol. VII

Parshall, Horace Field, 1865–1932, vol. III

Parshall, Horace Field, 1903–1986, vol. VIII

Parsloe, Charles Guy, 1900–1985, vol. VIII

Parsloe, Guy; *see* Parsloe, C. G.

Parson, Col George, 1879–1950, vol. IV (A)

Parsons, Sir Alan Lethbridge; *see* Parsons, Sir Alfred A. L.

Parsons, Albert, 1865–1938, vol. III

Parsons, Sir (Alfred) Alan Lethbridge, 1882–1964, vol. VI

Parsons, Alfred William, 1847–1920, vol. II

Parsons, Lt-Col Alfred Woodis, 1878–1954, vol. V

Parsons, Hon. Sir Angas; *see* Parsons, Hon. Sir H. A.

Parsons, Maj.-Gen. Sir Arthur Edward Broadbent, 1884–1966, vol. VI

Parsons, Beatrice, *died* 1955, vol. V

Parsons, Lt-Col Cecil, 1870–1935, vol. III

Parsons, Maj.-Gen. Sir Charles, 1855–1923, vol. II

Parsons, Hon. Sir Charles Algernon, 1854–1931, vol. III

Parsons, Mrs Clement, (Florence Mary Parsons), 1864–1934, vol. III

Parsons, Lt-Gen. Cunliffe McNeile, 1865–1923, vol. II

Parsons, Lt-Col Durie, 1872–1945, vol. IV
Parsons, Major Edward Howard Thornbrough, 1868–1946, vol. IV
Parsons, Rt Rev. Edward Lambe, 1868–1960, vol. V (A)
Parsons, Florence Mary; see Parsons, Mrs Clement.
Parsons, Frank Bett, 1902–1948, vol. IV
Parsons, Major Frederick George, 1856–1904, vol. I
Parsons, Col Frederick George, 1856–1933, vol. III
Parsons, Frederick Gymer, 1863–1943, vol. IV
Parsons, Hon. Geoffry Lawrence, 1874–1956, vol. V
Parsons, George Richard, 1898–1961, vol. VI
Parsons, Godfrey Valentine Hope, 1894–1948, vol. IV
Parsons, Maj.-Gen. Sir Harold Daniel Edmund, 1863–1925, vol. II
Parsons, Harold George, died 1905, vol. I
Parsons, Henry Franklin, 1846–1913, vol. I
Parsons, Hon. Sir (Herbert) Angas, 1872–1945, vol. IV
Parsons, Sir Herbert James Francis, 1st Bt, 1870–1940, vol. III
Parsons, Ian Macnaghten, 1906–1980, vol. VII
Parsons, J. W., 1859–1937, vol. III
Parsons, Col Sir John; see Parsons, Col Sir P. J.
Parsons, Sir John Herbert, died 1957, vol. V
Parsons, John Inglis, 1857–1928, vol. II
Parsons, John Randal, 1884–1967, vol. VI
Parsons, Brig. Johnston Lindsey Rowlett, 1876–1935, vol. III
Parsons, Rev. Canon Laurence Edmund, 1883–1972, vol. VII
Parsons, Lt-Gen. Sir Lawrence Worthington, 1850–1923, vol. II
Parsons, Sir Leonard Gregory, 1879–1950, vol. IV
Parsons, Sir Maurice Henry, 1910–1978, vol. VII
Parsons, Col Sir (Percy) John, 1881–1954, vol. V
Parsons, Philip Harry, died 1920, vol. II
Parsons, Rev. Hon. Randal, 1848–1936, vol. III
Parsons, Hon. Richard Clere, 1851–1923, vol. II
Parsons, Rev. Canon Richard Edward, 1888–1971, vol. VII
Parsons, Rt Rev. Richard Godfrey, 1882–1948, vol. IV
Parsons, William Barclay, 1859–1932, vol. III
Parsons, Col William Forster, 1879–1959, vol. V
Parsons, Engr Rear-Adm. William Roskilly, 1865–1954, vol. V
Parsons-Smith, Basil Thomas, 1882–1954, vol. V
Part, Sir Antony Alexander, 1916–1990, vol. VIII
Part, Lt-Col Sir Dealtry Charles, died 1961, vol. VI
Partabgarh, Maharawat of, 1857–1929, vol. III
Partington, Rev. Canon Ellis Foster E.; see Edge-Partington.
Partington, James Riddick, 1886–1965, vol. VI
Partington, Wilfred, 1888–1955, vol. V
Parton, Cyril John, 1880–1953, vol. V
Parton, Ernest, died 1933, vol. III
Partridge, Ann St John, died 1936, vol. III
Partridge, Sir Bernard, 1861–1945, vol. IV
Partridge, Sir Cecil, 1873–1937, vol. III
Partridge, Edward Hincks, 1901–1962, vol. VI
Partridge, Eric Honeywood, 1894–1979, vol. VII
Partridge, Ernest, 1895–1974, vol. VII

Partridge, Sir (Ernest) John, 1908–1982, vol. VIII
Partridge, Very Rev. Francis, 1846–1906, vol. I
Partridge, Rt Rev. Frank, 1877–1941, vol. IV
Partridge, Harry Cowderoy, 1925–1990, vol. VIII
Partridge, Sir John; see Partridge, Sir E. J.
Partridge, Maurice William, 1913–1973, vol. VII
Partridge, Col Sydney George, 1881–1957, vol. V
Partridge, William Ordway, 1861–1930, vol. III
Pascal, Rt Rev. Albert, 1848–1920, vol. II
Pascal, Gabriel, 1894–1954, vol. V
Pascal, Jean Louis, 1837–1920, vol. II, vol. III
Pascal, Roy, 1904–1980, vol. VII
Pascall, Charles, 1853–1931, vol. III
Paschalis, Neoptolemus, 1880–1946, vol. V
Pascoe, Sir Edwin Hall, 1878–1949, vol. IV
Pascoe, Sir (Frederick) John, 1893–1963, vol. VI
Pascoe, Sir John; see Pascoe, Sir F. J.
Pask, Edgar Alexander, 1912–1966, vol. VI
Paske-Smith, Montague Bentley Talbot, died 1946, vol. IV
Paskin, Sir (Jesse) John, 1892–1972, vol. VII
Paskin, Sir John; see Paskin, Sir J. J.
Pasley, Maj.-Gen. Gilbert James, 1834–1910, vol. I
Pasley, Maj.-Gen. Joseph Montagu Sabine, 1898–1978, vol. VII
Pasley, Sir Rodney Marshall Sabine, 4th Bt, 1899–1982, vol. VIII
Pasley, Major Sir Thomas Edward Sabine, 3rd Bt, 1863–1947, vol. IV
Pasley, Thomas Hamilton Sabine, 1861–1927, vol. II
Pasolini, Pierpaolo, 1922–1975, vol. VII
Pass, (Alfred) Douglas, 1885–1970, vol. VI
Pass, Douglas; see Pass, A. D.
Pass, Rev. Herman Leonard, 1875–1938, vol. III
Passant, Ernest James, 1890–1959, vol. V
Passey, Richard Douglas, 1888–1971, vol. VII
Passfield, 1st Baron, 1859–1947, vol. IV
Passfield, Lady; (Beatrice); see Webb, Mrs Sidney.
Passingham, Col Augustus Mervyn Owen A.; see Anwyl-Passingham.
Passmore, John Reginald Jutsum, 1878–1965, vol. VI
Passmore, Rt Rev. Nicholas Wilfrid, 1907–1976, vol. VII
Pasternak, Boris Leonidovich, 1890–1960, vol. V
Pasteur, Louis V.-R.; see Vallery-Radot Pasteur.
Pasteur, William, died 1943, vol. IV
Paston-Bedingfeld, Sir Henry Edward, 8th Bt, 1860–1941, vol. IV
Paston-Bedingfeld, Sir Henry George, 7th Bt, 1830–1902, vol. I
Paston-Cooper, Sir Astley Paston, 3rd Bt, 1824–1904, vol. I
Paston-Cooper, Sir Charles Naunton Paston, 4th Bt, 1867–1941, vol. IV
Pastor, Antonio Ricardo, 1894–1971, vol. VII
Pasture, 4th Marquis de la, 1836–1916, vol. II
Pasture, 5th Marquis de la, 1886–1962, vol. VI
Patch, Lt-Gen. Alexander McCarrell, 1889–1945, vol. IV
Patch, Sir Edmund Leo H.; see Hall-Patch.
Patch, Brig.-Gen. Francis Robert, 1868–1947, vol. IV
Patch, Air Chief Marshal Sir Hubert Leonard, 1904–1987, vol. VIII
Patch, Col Robert, 1842–1927, vol. II

Patchell, William Henry, 1862–1932, vol. III
Patchett, William, *died* 1915, vol. I
Pate, Henry Reginald, 1880–1942, vol. IV
Patel, Ambalal Bhailalbhai, 1898–1987, vol. VIII
Patel, Khan Bahadur Burjorji D., *died* 1931, vol. III
Patenaude, Esioff Léon, 1875–1963, vol. VI
Pater, John Edward, 1911–1989, vol. VIII
Paterson, A., 1865–1944, vol. IV
Paterson, Col Adrian Gordon, 1888–1940, vol. III
Paterson, Albert Rutherford, 1885–1959, vol. V
Paterson, Sir Alexander, 1884–1947, vol. IV
Paterson, Alexander Brown, 1917–1980, vol. VII
Paterson, Alexander Nisbet, 1862–1947, vol. IV
Paterson, Sir (Alexander) Swinton, 1893–1980, vol. VII
Paterson, Alfred Croom, 1875–1933, vol. III
Paterson, Andrew Barton, 1864–1941, vol. IV
Paterson, Andrew Melville, 1862–1919, vol. II
Paterson, Rev. Archibald, *died* 1932, vol. III
Paterson, Arthur Henry, 1862–1928, vol. II
Paterson, Lt Col Arthur James J.; *see* Jardine Paterson.
Paterson, Arthur Spencer, 1900–1983, vol. VIII
Paterson, Lt-Col Arthur William Sibbald, 1878–1937, vol. III
Paterson, Aylmer John Noel, 1902–1977, vol. VII
Paterson, Sir Clifford Copland, 1879–1948, vol. IV
Paterson, Donald Hugh, 1890–1968, vol. VI
Paterson, Emily Murray, *died* 1934, vol. III
Paterson, Brig.-Gen. Ewing, 1873–1950, vol. IV
Paterson, Col George Fredrick Joseph, 1885–1949, vol. IV
Paterson, George McLeod, 1891–1953, vol. V
Paterson, Graham, *died* 1938, vol. III
Paterson, Surg.-Maj.-Gen. Henry Foljambe, 1836–1920, vol. II
Paterson, Lt-Col Henry Francis William, 1880–1943, vol. IV
Paterson, Herbert John, 1868–1940, vol. III
Paterson, Maj.-Gen. Herbert MacGregor, 1898–1979, vol. VII
Paterson, James, 1854–1932, vol. III
Paterson, Rev. James Alexander, 1851–1915, vol. I
Paterson, James Ralston Kennedy, 1897–1981, vol. VIII
Paterson, James Veitch, 1866–1943, vol. IV
Paterson, John Sidney, 1899–1965, vol. VI
Paterson, John Waugh, 1869–1958, vol. V
Paterson, John Wilson, 1887–1970, vol. VI
Paterson, Marcus, 1870–1932, vol. III
Paterson, Mary Muirhead, *died* 1941, vol. IV
Paterson, Nicholas Julian, *died* 1934, vol. III
Paterson, Noel Kennedy, 1905–1984, vol. VIII
Paterson, Lt-Col Norman Fitzherbert, 1843–1925, vol. II
Paterson, Col Philip Joseph, 1874–1930, vol. III
Paterson, Captain Quentin Hunter, 1888–1975, vol. VII
Paterson, Ralston; *see* Paterson, J. R. K.
Paterson, Sir Reginald G. C., 1875–1939, vol. III
Paterson, Gen. Robert Ormiston, 1878–1941, vol. IV
Paterson, Brig.-Gen. Robert Walter, 1876–1936, vol. III
Paterson, Col Stanley, 1860–1950, vol. IV

Paterson, Stronach, 1886–1957, vol. V
Paterson, Sir Swinton; *see* Paterson, Sir A. S.
Paterson, Maj.-Gen. Thomas George Ferguson, 1876–1942, vol. IV
Paterson, Thomas Wilson, *born* 1851, vol. II
Paterson, William, 1815–1903, vol. I
Paterson, Sir William, 1874–1956, vol. V
Paterson, William Bromfield, *died* 1924, vol. II
Paterson, William G. R., 1878–1954, vol. V
Paterson, William James Macdonald, 1911–1976, vol. VII
Paterson, Very Rev. William Paterson, 1860–1939, vol. III
Paterson-Morgan, Rev. Richard James Basil, 1879–1966, vol. VI
Pateshall, Col Henry Evan Pateshall, 1879–1948, vol. IV
Patey, David Howard, 1899–1977, vol. VII
Patey, Adm. Sir George Edwin, 1859–1935, vol. III
Patiala, Lt-Gen. HH Maharaja Dhiraj of, 1891–1938, vol. III
Patiala, Lt-Gen. HH Maharajadhiraj of, 1913–1974, vol. VII
Patna, HH Maharaja of, 1912–1975, vol. VII
Paton, Alan Stewart, 1903–1988, vol. VIII
Paton, Col Alexander, 1897–1985, vol. VIII
Paton, Alexander Allan, *died* 1934, vol. III
Paton, Sir Alfred Vaughan, 1861–1930, vol. III
Paton, Brig. Charles Morgan, 1896–1979, vol. VII
Paton, Diarmid Noel, 1859–1928, vol. II
Paton, Florence Beatrice, *died* 1976, vol. VII
Paton, Frederick Noel, 1861–1914, vol. I
Paton, G., *died* 1906, vol. I
Paton, Maj.-Gen. George, 1841–1931, vol. III
Paton, George Campbell Henderson, 1905–1984, vol. VIII
Paton, George Pearson, 1882–1975, vol. VII
Paton, Sir George Whitecross, 1902–1985, vol. VIII
Paton, Sir George William, 1859–1934, vol. III
Paton, Harold William, 1900–1986, vol. VIII
Paton, Herbert James, 1887–1969, vol. VI
Paton, Hugh, 1853–1927, vol. II
Paton, James, 1843–1921, vol. II
Paton, James Bowie, *died* 1940, vol. III (A), vol. IV
Paton, Sir James Wallace, 1863–1948, vol. IV
Paton, Maj.-Gen. John, 1867–1943, vol. IV
Paton, John, 1886–1976, vol. VII
Paton, John Brown, 1830–1911, vol. I
Paton, John Gibson, 1824–1907, vol. I
Paton, John Lewis, 1863–1946, vol. IV
Paton, Sir Joseph Noël, 1821–1901, vol. I
Paton, Sir Leonard Cecil, 1892–1986, vol. VIII
Paton, Leslie, 1872–1943, vol. III
Paton, Rev. Lewis Bayles, 1864–1932, vol. III
Paton, Robert Thomson, 1856–1929, vol. III
Paton, Robert Young, 1894–1973, vol. VII
Paton, Sir Stuart Henry, 1900–1987, vol. VIII
Paton, Rev. William, 1886–1943, vol. IV
Paton, William Calder, 1886–1979, vol. VII
Paton, Vice-Adm. William Douglas, 1874–1952, vol. V
Patrick, Rt Hon. Lord; William Donald Patrick, 1889–1967, vol. VI
Patrick, Adam, 1883–1970, vol. VI

Patrick, Major Charles Kennedy Cochran-, 1896–1933, vol. III
Patrick, (Colin) Mark, 1893–1942, vol. IV
Patrick, David, 1849–1914, vol. I
Patrick, Rev. John, 1850–1933, vol. III
Patrick, Brig. John, 1898–1985, vol. VIII
Patrick, Mark; see Patrick, C. M.
Patrick, Mary Mills, 1850–1940, vol. III
Patrick, Sir Neil James Kennedy C.; see Cochran-Patrick.
Patrick, Nigel Dennis Wemyss, 1913–1981, vol. VIII
Patrick, Sir Paul Joseph, 1888–1975, vol. VII
Patrick, Rt Hon. William Donald; see Patrick, Rt Hon. Lord.
Patro Garu, Rao Bahadur Sir Annepu Parasuramadas, 1875–1946, vol. IV
Patron, Sir Joseph, 1896–1981, vol. VIII
Patron, Joseph Armand, 1856–1922, vol. II
Patry, Edward, died 1940, vol. III
Pattani, Sir Prabhashanker Dalpatram, 1862–1938, vol. III
Patten, Charles J., 1870–1948, vol. IV
Patten, Rev. John Alexander, 1883–1952, vol. V
Pattenson, Arthur Eric Tylden, 1888–1955, vol. V
Pattenson, Major Arthur Henry T.; see Tylden-Pattenson.
Pattenson, Lt-Col Edwin Cooke Tylden-, 1871–1940, vol. III
Patterson, Alexander Blakeley, 1842–1919, vol. II
Patterson, Rev. Alexander Hamilton, 1851–1943, vol. IV
Patterson, Annie W., died 1934, vol. III
Patterson, Daniel Wells, 1871–1932, vol. III
Patterson, David Clarke, 1879–1948, vol. IV
Patterson, Eric James, 1891–1972, vol. VII
Patterson, Geoffrey Crosbie, 1912–1984, vol. VIII
Patterson, George, 1846–1925, vol. II, vol. III
Patterson, Hon. James Colebrooke, 1839–1929, vol. III
Patterson, James Kennedy, 1833–1922, vol. II
Patterson, Rt Rev. James Laird, 1822–1902, vol. I
Patterson, Jocelyn, 1900–1965, vol. VI
Patterson, John Edward, died 1919, vol. II
Patterson, Sir John Robert, 1892–1976, vol. VII
Patterson, Rear-Adm. Julian Francis Chichester, 1884–1972, vol. VII
Patterson, Rev. Melville Watson, 1873–1944, vol. IV
Patterson, Norman, 1879–1909, vol. I
Patterson, Norman, 1877–1950, vol. IV
Patterson, Sir Reginald Stewart, 1878–1930, vol. III
Patterson, Sir Robert Lloyd, 1836–1906, vol. I
Patterson, Robert Porter, 1891–1952, vol. V
Patterson, Lt-Col Sir Stewart Blakeley Agnew, 1872–1942, vol. IV
Patterson, Thomas Redden, 1898–1972, vol. VII
Patterson, Thomas Stewart, 1872–1949, vol. IV
Patterson, Lt-Col Thomas W., 1844–1902, vol. I
Patterson, Adm. Sir Wilfrid Rupert, 1893–1954, vol. V
Patteson, John Coleridge, 1896–1954, vol. V
Patti, Mme Adelina, (Baroness Rolf Cederström), 1843–1919, vol. II
Pattinson, Arthur Edward, 1868–1939, vol. III
Pattinson, George Norman, 1887–1966, vol. VI

Pattinson, Rev. Canon Joseph Alfred, 1861–1919, vol. II
Pattinson, Air Marshal Sir Lawrence Arthur, 1890–1955, vol. V
Pattinson, Sir Robert, 1872–1954, vol. V
Pattinson, Samuel, 1870–1942, vol. IV
Pattison, Andrew Seth Pringle; see Seth, Andrew.
Pattison, Harold Arthur Langston, 1897–1966, vol. VI
Pattisson, Jacob Luard, 1841–1915, vol. I
Pattisson, Adm. John Robert Ebenezer, 1844–1928, vol. II
Patton, Arnold Gordon, 1892–1960, vol. V
Patton, Rev. Francis Landey, 1843–1932, vol. III
Patton, Gen. George Smith, Jr, 1885–1945, vol. IV
Patton, Col Henry Bethune, 1835–1915, vol. I
Patton, Rt Rev. Henry Edmund, 1867–1943, vol. IV
Patton, Walter Scott, 1876–1960, vol. V
Pattrick, Michael; see Pattrick, W. M. T.
Pattrick, (William) Michael (Thomas), 1913–1980, vol. VII
Pattullo, Hon. Thomas Dufferin, 1873–1956, vol. V
Pattullo, William Ogilvy, 1924–1975, vol. VII
Patwardhan, Baba Saheb; see Miraj (Junior), Chief of.
Pau, Gen. Paul Mary Cæsar Gerald, 1848–1932, vol. III
Pauer, Max, 1866–1945, vol. IV
Paul VI, His Holiness Pope, (Giovanni Battista Montini), 1897–1978, vol. VII
Paul, Alfred Wallis, 1847–1912, vol. I
Paul, Sir Aubrey Edward Henry Dean, 5th Bt (cr 1821), 1869–1961, vol. VI
Paul, Sir Brian Kenneth, 6th Bt (cr 1821), 1904–1972, vol. VII
Paul, Cedar, died 1972, vol. VII
Paul, Charles Kegan, 1828–1902, vol. I
Paul, Sir (Charles) Norman, 1883–1959, vol. V
Paul, Very Rev. David, 1845–1929, vol. III
Paul, Col Denis, 1865–1944, vol. IV
Paul, Elliot Harold, 1891–1958, vol. V
Paul, Eric Barlow, 1919–1968, vol. VI
Paul, Rev. F. J., died 1941, vol. IV
Paul, Francis Kinnier, 1911–1965, vol. VI
Paul, Frank Thomas, 1851–1941, vol. IV
Paul, Rev. G. W., 1820–1911, vol. I
Paul, Rt Rev. Geoffrey John, 1921–1983, vol. VIII
Paul, Sir (George) Graham, 1887–1960, vol. V
Paul, Sir George Morison, 1839–1926, vol. II
Paul, Brig.-Gen. Gerard Robert Clark, 1861–1913, vol. I
Paul, Sir Graham; see Paul, Sir George G.
Paul, Sir Gregory Charles, 1830–1900, vol. I
Paul, Sir Harisankar, 1888–1951, vol. V
Paul, Herbert Woodfield, 1853–1935, vol. III
Paul, Sir James Balfour, 1846–1931, vol. III
Paul, Rev. Sir Jeffrey; see Paul, Rev. Sir W. E. J.
Paul, Lt-Col John William Balfour, 1873–1957, vol. V
Paul, Leslie Allen, 1905–1985, vol. VIII
Paul, Leslie Douglas, 1903–1970, vol. VI
Paul, Maurice Eden, 1865–1944, vol. IV
Paul, Sir Norman; see Paul, Sir C. N.

Paul, Engr-Rear-Adm. Oliver Richard, 1868–1955, vol. V

Paul, Paul, 1865–1937, vol. III

Paul, Sir Robert Joshua, 3rd Bt (*cr* 1794), 1820–1898, vol. I

Paul, Captain Sir Robert Joshua, 5th Bt (*cr* 1794), 1883–1955, vol. V

Paul, Stuart, 1879–1961, vol. VI

Paul, Maj.-Gen. Walter Reginald, 1882–1953, vol. V

Paul, Rev. Sir (William Edmund) Jeffrey, 6th Bt (*cr* 1794), 1885–1961, vol. VI

Paul, Sir William Joshua, 4th Bt (*cr* 1794), 1851–1912, vol. I

Paul-Boncour, Joseph, 1873–1972, vol. VII

Paulet, Major Charles Standish, 1873–1953, vol. V

Paulin, Sir David, 1847–1930, vol. III

Paulin, George Henry, 1888–1962, vol. VI

Paulin, Sir William Thomas, 1848–1931, vol. III

Pauline, Sister; *see* Young, Hilda Beatrice.

Paull, Sir Gilbert James, 1896–1984, vol. VIII

Paull, Harry Major, 1854–1934, vol. III

Paull, Richard James, 1862–1937, vol. III

Paulson, Godfrey Martin Ellis, 1908–1990, vol. VIII

Paulton, James Mellor, 1857–1923, vol. II

Pauncefort-Duncombe, Sir Everard; *see* Duncombe, Sir E. P. D. P.

Pauncefote, 1st Baron, 1828–1902, vol. I

Paur, Emil, 1855–1932, vol. III

Paus, Christopher L., 1881–1963, vol. VI

Pavière, Sydney Herbert, 1891–1971, vol. VII

Pavitt, Laurence Anstice, 1914–1989, vol. VIII

Pavlides, Sir Paul George, 1897–1977, vol. VII

Pavlides, Stelios, 1892–1968, vol. VI (AII)

Pavry, Faredun Cursetji, 1877–1943, vol. IV

Pavy, Emily Dorothea, *died* 1967, vol. VI

Pavy, Frederick William, 1829–1911, vol. I

Pawan, Joseph Lennox, 1887–1957, vol. V

Pawel-Rammingen, Baron Luitbert Alexander George Lionel Alphons, 1843–1932, vol. III

Pawle, Brig. Hanbury, 1886–1972, vol. VII

Pawley, Ven. Bernard Clinton, 1911–1981, vol. VIII

Pawsey, Sir Charles Ridley, 1894–1972, vol. VII

Pawsey, Joseph Lade, 1908–1962, vol. VI

Pawson, Albert Guy, 1888–1986, vol. VIII

Pawson, Henry Cecil, 1897–1978, vol. VI

Pawson, Ven. Wilfrid Denys, 1905–1959, vol. V

Paxton, Air Vice-Marshal Sir Anthony Lauderdale, 1896–1957, vol. V

Paxton, Sir Thomas, 1st Bt, *died* 1930, vol. III

Payen-Payne, de Vincheles, 1866–1945, vol. IV

Payn, James, 1830–1898, vol. I

Payne, Col Alexander Vaughan, 1857–1943, vol. IV

Payne, Anson; *see* Payne, J. A.

Payne, Arthur Robert, 1926–1976, vol. VII

Payne, Ben Iden, 1881–1976, vol. VII

Payne, Charles, 1871–1948, vol. IV

Payne, Charles Frederick, 1875–1966, vol. VI

Payne, Charles Robert Salusbury, 1859–1942, vol. IV

Payne, Vice-Adm. Christopher Russell, 1874–1952, vol. V

Payne, Rev. David Bruce, 1827–1913, vol. I

Payne, de Vincheles P.; *see* Payen-Payne.

Payne, Col Edward Henry, 1868–1941, vol. IV

Payne, Edward John, 1844–1904, vol. I

Payne, Rev. Ernest Alexander, 1902–1980, vol. VII

Payne, Rev. Francis Reginald Chassereau, 1876–1961, vol. VI

Payne, Henry, 1871–1945, vol. IV

Payne, Henry A., 1868–1940, vol. III

Payne, Sir Henry Arthur, 1873–1931, vol. III

Payne, Col Herbert Chidgey Brine, 1862–1945, vol. IV

Payne, Hon. Herbert James Mockford, 1866–1944, vol. IV

Payne, Humfry Gilbert Garth, 1902–1936, vol. III

Payne, Jack Marsh, 1929–1988, vol. VIII

Payne, (John) Anson, 1917–1987, vol. VIII

Payne, John Bruce, *died* 1928, vol. II

Payne, John Horne, 1837–1920, vol. II

Payne, Joseph Frank, 1840–1910, vol. I

Payne, Lt-Col Leslie Herbert, 1888–1942, vol. IV

Payne, Sir Reginald Withers, 1904–1980, vol. VII

Payne, Maj.-Gen. Richard Lloyd, 1854–1921, vol. II

Payne, Sir Robert Frederick, 1908–1985, vol. VIII

Payne, Major Robert Leslie, 1880–1942, vol. IV

Payne, Sylvia May, 1880–1976, vol. VII

Payne, Walter, *died* 1949, vol. IV

Payne, Sir William Labatt, 1890–1962, vol. VI

Payne-Gallwey, Sir Ralph William Frankland; *see* Gallwey.

Payne-Gallwey, Sir Reginald Frankland; *see* Gallwey.

Payne-Gallwey, Captain William Thomas Frankland; *see* Gallwey.

Paynter, Col Camborne Haweis, 1864–1949, vol. IV

Paynter, Brig.-Gen. Sir George Camborne Beauclerk, 1880–1950, vol. IV

Paynter, (Thomas) William, 1903–1984, vol. VIII

Paynter, William; *see* Paynter, T. W.

Payton, Sir Charles Alfred, 1843–1926, vol. II

Payton, Rev. Wilfred Ernest Granville, 1913–1989, vol. VIII

Payton, Wilfrid Hugh, 1892–1965, vol. VI

Peabody, George Foster, 1852–1938, vol. III

Peace, Albert Lister, 1844–1912, vol. I

Peace, Captain Alfred Geoffrey, 1885–1940, vol. III

Peace, Sir Walter, 1840–1917, vol. II

Peacey, Rt Rev. Basil William, 1889–1969, vol. VI

Peacey, Rev. J. R., 1896–1971, vol. VII

Peach, Benjamin Neeve, 1842–1926, vol. II

Peach, Adm. Charles William K.; *see* Keighly-Peach.

Peach, Major Edmund, 1865–1902, vol. I

Peach, Lawrence du Garde, 1890–1974, vol. VII

Peachey, Captain Allan Thomas George Cumberland, 1896–1967, vol. VI

Peacock, Alexander David, *died* 1976, vol. VII

Peacock, Hon. Sir Alexander James, 1861–1933, vol. III

Peacock, Rev. Charles Alfred, 1868–1944, vol. IV

Peacock, David Henry, 1889–1978, vol. VII

Peacock, Edward Eden, 1850–1909, vol. I

Peacock, Sir Edward Robert, 1871–1962, vol. VI

Peacock, Major Ferdinand Mansel, 1861–1908, vol. I

Peacock, Frederick Hood, 1886–1969, vol. VI

Peacock, Major Frederick William, 1859–1924, vol. II

Peacock, (John) Roydon, 1902–1982, vol. VIII

Peacock, Sir Kenneth Swift, 1902–1968, vol VI

Peacock, Matthew Henry, 1856–1929, vol III
Peacock, Millie, (Lady Peacock), *died* 1948, vol. IV
Peacock, Sir Peter, 1872–1948, vol. IV
Peacock, Col Pryce, 1868–1956, vol. V
Peacock, Ralph, *died* 1946, vol. IV
Peacock, Sir Robert, 1859–1926, vol. II
Peacock, Roydon; *see* Peacock, J. R.
Peacock, Sir Thomas, *died* 1959, vol. V
Peacock, Rev. W. Arthur, 1905–1968, vol. VI
Peacock, Sir Walter, 1871–1956, vol. V
Peacock, Rev. Canon Wilfrid Morgan, 1890–1970, vol. VI
Peacock, William Henry, 1881–1946, vol. IV
Peacocke, Emilie Hawkes, 1883–1964, vol. VI
Peacocke, Most Rev. Joseph Ferguson, 1835–1916, vol. II
Peacocke, Rt Rev. Joseph Irvine, 1866–1962, vol. VI
Peacocke, Col Thomas George, 1865–1939, vol. III
Peacocke, Col William, 1848–1931, vol. III
Peake, Hon. Archibald Henry, 1859–1920, vol. II
Peake, Sir Arthur Copson, 1854–1934, vol. III
Peake, Arthur Samuel, 1865–1929, vol. III
Peake, Sir Charles Brinsley Pemberton, 1897–1958, vol. V
Peake, Brig. Edward Robert Luxmoore, 1894–1964, vol. VI
Peake, Sir Francis, 1889–1984, vol. VIII
Peake, Frederick Gerard, 1886–1970, vol. VI
Peake, George Herbert, 1859–1950, vol. IV
Peake, Sir Harald, 1899–1978, vol. VII
Peake, Harold John Edward, 1867–1946, vol. IV
Peake, Brig.-Gen. Malcolm, 1865–1917, vol. II
Peake, Mervyn, 1911–1968, vol. VI
Peake, Thomas, 1868–1945, vol. IV
Peaker, Alfred Pearson, 1896–1973, vol. VII
Peaker, Frederick, 1867–1942, vol. IV
Peal, Lt-Col Edward Raymond, 1884–1967, vol. VI
Pear, Tom Hatherley, 1886–1972, vol. VII
Pearce, Baron (Life Peer); Edward Holroyd Pearce, 1901–1990, vol. VIII
Pearce, C. Maresco, 1874–1964, vol. VI
Pearce, Charles E., *died* 1924, vol. II
Pearce, Sir (Charles) Frederick (Byrde), 1892–1964, vol. VI
Pearce, Charles William, 1856–1928, vol. II
Pearce, Clifford James, 1916–1985, vol. VIII
Pearce, Col Cyril Harvey, 1878–1943, vol. IV
Pearce, Rt Rev. Edmund Courtenay, 1870–1935, vol. III
Pearce, Sir Edward Charles, 1862–1928, vol. II
Pearce, E(dward) Ewart, 1898–1963, vol. VI
Pearce, Ernest Alfred John, 1868–1943, vol. IV
Pearce, Rt Rev. Ernest Harold, 1865–1930, vol. III
Pearce, Major Francis Barrow, 1866–1926, vol. II
Pearce, Sir Frank James, 1878–1946, vol. IV
Pearce, Sir Frederick; *see* Pearce, Sir C. F. B.
Pearce, Air Cdre Frederick Laurence, 1898–1975, vol. VII
Pearce, Sir George Alfred, 1894–1971, vol. VII
Pearce, Rt Hon. Sir George Foster, 1870–1952, vol. V
Pearce, Harold Seward, 1880–1961, vol. VI
Pearce, Henry, 1869–1925, vol. II

Pearce, Hon. James Edward Holroyd, 1934–1985, vol. VIII
Pearce, Kenneth Leslie, 1910–1988, vol. VIII
Pearce, Sir Leonard; *see* Pearce, Sir S. L.
Pearce, Malcolm Arthur Fraser, 1898–1979, vol. VII (AII)
Pearce, Hon. Richard Bruce Holroyd, 1930–1987, vol. VIII
Pearce, Sir Robert, 1840–1922, vol. II
Pearce, Rev. Robert John, 1841–1920, vol. II
Pearce, Seward, 1866–1951, vol. V
Pearce, Sir (Standen) Leonard, 1873–1947, vol. IV
Pearce, Thomas Ernest, 1883–1941, vol. IV
Pearce, Sir William, 1853–1932, vol. III
Pearce, Rev. William Fletcher, 1869–1935, vol. III
Pearce, Sir William George, 2nd Bt, 1861–1907, vol. I
Pearce, William Harvey, 1920–1982, vol. VIII
Pearce-Higgins, Rev. Canon John Denis, 1905–1985, vol. VIII
Pearce-Serocold, Brig.-Gen. Eric, 1870–1926, vol. II
Pearce-Serocold, Oswald, 1865–1951, vol. V
Peard, Frances Mary, *died* 1923, vol. II
Pearkes, Maj.-Gen. Hon. George Randolph, 1888–1984, vol. VIII
Pearl, Amy Lea, (Mrs F. Warren Pearl), 1880–1964, vol. VI
Pearl, Mrs F. Warren; *see* Pearl, Amy Lea.
Pearl, Raymond, 1879–1940, vol. III (A), vol. IV
Pearless, Brig.-Gen. Charles William, 1872–1940, vol. III
Pearman, Rev. Augustus John, *died* 1909, vol. I
Pearman-Smith, Sir William Joseph, 1863–1939, vol. III
Pears, Charles, 1873–1958, vol. V
Pears, Adm. Sir Edmund Radcliffe, 1862–1941, vol. IV
Pears, Sir Edwin, 1835–1919, vol. II
Pears, Harold Snowden, 1926–1982, vol. VIII
Pears, Major M. L., *died* 1916, vol. II
Pears, Sir Peter Neville Luard, 1910–1986, vol. VIII
Pears, Sidney John, 1900–1972, vol. VII
Pears, Rear-Adm. Steuart Arnold, 1894–1978, vol. VII
Pears, Sir Steuart Edmund, 1875–1931, vol. III
Pearsall, William Booth, 1845–1913, vol. I
Pearsall, William Harold, 1891–1964, vol. VI
Pearse, Albert William, 1857–1951, vol. V
Pearse, Captain Alfred, *died* 1933, vol. III
Pearse, Major Beauchamp Albert Thomas K.; *see* Kerr-Pearse.
Pearse, Gen. George Godfrey, 1827–1905, vol. I
Pearse, H. H. S., *died* 1905, vol. I
Pearse, Col Hugh Wodehouse, 1855–1919, vol. II
Pearse, James, 1871–1962, vol. VI
Pearse, Sir John Slocombe, 1870–1949, vol. IV
Pearse, Rev. Mark Guy, 1842–1930, vol. III
Pearse, Ronald Livian, 1880–1960, vol. V
Pearse, Lt-Col Sydney Arthur, *died* 1937, vol. III
Pearse, Thomas Lawrence S.; *see* Smith-Pearse.
Pearse, Rev. Thomas Northmore Hart S.; *see* Smith-Pearse.
Pearse, Brig.-Gen. Tom Harry Finch, 1864–1947, vol. IV

Pearson, Baron (Life Peer); Colin Hargreaves Pearson, 1899–1980, vol. VII

Pearson, Hon. Lord; Charles John Pearson, 1843–1910, vol. I

Pearson, Rt Rev. Alfred, 1848–1909, vol. I

Pearson, Gen. Sir Alfred Astley, 1850–1937, vol. III

Pearson, Alfred Chilton, 1861–1935, vol. III

Pearson, Rev. Andrew Forret Scott, 1886–1952, vol. V

Pearson, Andrew Russell; *see* Pearson, Drew.

Pearson, Sir Arthur; *see* Pearson, Sir C. A.

Pearson, Arthur, 1897–1980, vol. VII

Pearson, Arthur Ashley, 1847–1933, vol. III

Pearson, Aylmer Cavendish, 1876–1926, vol. II

Pearson, Hon. (Bernard) Clive, 1887–1965, vol. VI

Pearson, Bertram Lamb, 1893–1984, vol. VIII

Pearson, Burton, 1872–1937, vol. III

Pearson, Charles Child, 1875–1955, vol. V

Pearson, Charles John; *see* Pearson, Hon. Lord.

Pearson, Sir Charles Knight, 1834–1909, vol. I

Pearson, Charles Yelverton, 1857–1947, vol. IV

Pearson, Claude Edmund, 1903–1971, vol. VII

Pearson, Hon. Clive; *see* Pearson, Hon. B. C.

Pearson, Colin Bateman, 1889–1974, vol. VII

Pearson, Sir (Cyril) Arthur, 1st Bt, 1866–1921, vol. II

Pearson, David Morris, 1915–1985, vol. VIII

Pearson, Drew, (Andrew Russell Pearson), 1897–1969, vol. VI

Pearson, Sir Edward Ernest, 1874–1925, vol. II

Pearson, Egon Sharpe, 1895–1980, vol. VII

Pearson, Ethel Maud, (Lady Pearson), 1870–1959, vol. V

Pearson, Frederick John, 1866–1932, vol. III

Pearson, George Sherwin Hooke, 1875–1941, vol. IV

Pearson, Col George Thomson, 1876–1946, vol. IV

Pearson, Gerald Lionel, 1918–1978, vol. VII

Pearson, Sir Glen Gardner, 1907–1976, vol. VII

Pearson, Henry Harold Welch, 1870–1916, vol. II

Pearson, Sir Herbert Grayhurst, 1878–1958, vol. V

Pearson, Hesketh, 1887–1964, vol. VI

Pearson, Hugh Drummond, 1873–1922, vol. II

Pearson, Adm. Sir Hugo Lewis, 1843–1912, vol. I

Pearson, James Rae, 1871–1951, vol. V

Pearson, Sir (James) Reginald, 1897–1984, vol. VIII

Pearson, Vice-Adm. John Lewis, 1879–1965, vol. VI

Pearson, John Loughborough, 1817–1897, vol. I

Pearson, Joseph, 1881–1971, vol. VII

Pearson, Karl, 1857–1936, vol. III

Pearson, Rt Hon. Lester Bowles, 1897–1972, vol. VII

Pearson, Lionel Godfrey, 1879–1953, vol. V

Pearson, Sir Louis Frederick, 1863–1943, vol. IV

Pearson, Louise Kirkby; *see* Lunn, L. K.

Pearson, Rev. Marchant, 1871–1956, vol. V

Pearson, Col Michael Brown, 1840–1923, vol. II

Pearson, Sir Neville Arthur, 2nd Bt, 1898–1982, vol. VIII

Pearson, Lt-Col Noel Gervis, 1884–1958, vol. V

Pearson, Octavius Henry, 1839–1914, vol. I

Pearson, Sir Ralph Sneyd, 1874–1958, vol. V

Pearson, Sir Reginald; *see* Pearson, Sir J. R.

Pearson, Richard Francis Malachy, 1872–1956, vol. V

Pearson, Sir Robert Barclay, 1871–1954, vol. V

Pearson, Robert Hooper, 1866–1918, vol. II

Pearson, Rupert Samuel Bruce, 1904–1974, vol. VII

Pearson, Sidney Vere, 1875–1950, vol. IV

Pearson, Thomas Bailey, 1864–1927, vol. II

Pearson, Rt Rev. Thomas Bernard, 1907–1987, vol. VIII

Pearson, Thomas William, 1872–1957, vol. V

Pearson, Rt Rev. Thomas Wulstan, 1870–1938, vol. III

Pearson, Brig.-Gen. Vere Lorraine Nuttall, 1880–1939, vol. III

Pearson, Col Walter Bagot, 1872–1954, vol. V

Pearson, Major Wilfred John, 1884–1957, vol. V

Pearson, William, *died* 1907, vol. I

Pearson, William, 1882–1976, vol. VII

Pearson, William George, *died* 1963, vol. VI

Pearson, William Thomas Shipston, 1917–1990, vol. VIII

Pearson-Gregory, Thomas Sherwin, 1851–1935, vol. III

Peart, Baron (Life Peer); (Thomas) Frederick Peart, 1914–1988, vol. VIII

Peart, Col Charles Lubé, 1876–1957, vol. V

Peart, Donald Richard, 1909–1981, vol. VIII

Peart, Ernest Grafford, 1918–1982, vol. VIII

Peart, Joseph Norriss, 1900–1942, vol. IV

Peary, Robert Edwin, 1856–1920, vol. II

Pease, Sir Alfred Edward, 2nd Bt (*cr* 1882), 1857–1939, vol. III

Pease, Arthur, 1837–1898, vol. I

Pease, Sir Arthur Francis, 1st Bt (*cr* 1920), 1866–1927, vol. II

Pease, Sir Edward, 3rd Bt (*cr* 1882), 1880–1963, vol. VI

Pease, Edward R., 1857–1955, vol. V

Pease, Col Henry Thomas, 1862–1943, vol. IV

Pease, Joseph Gerald, 1863–1928, vol. II

Pease, Sir Joseph Whitwell, 1st Bt (*cr* 1882), 1828–1903, vol. I

Pease, Lt-Gen. Leonard Thales, 1857–1936, vol. III

Pease, Sir Richard Arthur, 2nd Bt (*cr* 1920), 1890–1969, vol. VI

Pease, Col Sir Thales, 1835–1919, vol. II

Pease, William Edwin, 1865–1926, vol. II

Peasgood, Osborne Harold, 1902–1962, vol. VI

Peat, Charles Urie, 1892–1979, vol. VII

Peat, Sir George, 1893–1945, vol. IV

Peat, Sir Harry William Henry, 1878–1959, vol. V

Peat, Lt-Comdr Percy Sutcliffe, 1889–1936, vol. III

Peat, Stanley, 1902–1969, vol. VI

Peat, Sir William Barclay, 1852–1936, vol. III

Peate, Iorwerth Cyfeiliog, 1901–1982, vol. VIII

Pecci, Vincent Joachim; *see* Leo XIII.

Pechell, Sir Alexander B., 7th Bt; *see* Brooke-Pechell, Sir Augustus A.

Pechell, Sir George Samuel Brooke-, 5th Bt, 1819–1897, vol. I

Pechell, Lt-Col Sir Paul, 8th Bt, 1889–1972, vol. VII

Pechell, Sir Ronald Horace, 9th Bt, 1918–1984, vol. VIII

Pechell, Sir Samuel George Brooke-, 6th Bt, 1852–1904, vol. I

Pechey, Archibald Thomas, 1876–1961, vol. VI

Peck, Vice-Adm. Ambrose Maynard, *died* 1963, vol. VI

Peck, Antony Dilwyn, 1914–1987, vol. VIII
Peck, Arthur Leslie, 1902–1974, vol. VII
Peck, Maj.-Gen. Arthur Wharton, 1869–1948, vol. IV
Peck, Col Cyrus Wesley, 1871–1956, vol. V
Peck, Lt-Col Edward George, died 1939, vol. III
Peck, Maj.-Gen. Henry Richardson, 1874–1965, vol. VI
Peck, Sir James Wallace, 1875–1964, vol. VI
Peck, Jasper Augustine, 1905–1980, vol. VII
Peck, Very Rev. Michael David Saville, 1914–1968, vol. VI
Peck, Air-Marshal Sir Richard Hallam, 1893–1952, vol. V
Peck, Maj.-Gen. Sydney Capel, 1871–1949, vol. IV
Peck, Sir William, 1862–1925, vol. II
Peck, Winifred Frances, (Lady Peck), died 1962, vol. VI
Peckitt, Reginald Godfrey, died 1937, vol. III
Peckover, 1st Baron, 1830–1919, vol. II
Pedder, John, 1850–1929, vol. III
Pedder, Sir John, 1869–1956, vol. V
Peddie, Baron (Life Peer); James Mortimer Peddie, 1907–1978, vol. VII
Peddie, Coventry Dick, 1863–1950, vol. IV
Peddie, Maj.-Gen. Graham, 1905–1987, vol. VIII
Peddie, John Ronald, 1887–1979, vol. VII
Peddie, John Taylor, 1879–1947, vol. IV
Peddie, Ronald, 1905–1986, vol. VIII
Peddie, William, 1861–1946, vol. IV
Peddie-Waddell, Alexander; see Waddell.
Peden, Hon. Sir John Beverley, 1871–1946, vol. IV
Pedersen, Charles John, 1904–1989, vol. VIII
Pedler, Sir Alexander, 1849–1918, vol. II
Pedler, Margaret, died 1948, vol. IV
Pedley, Arthur Charles, 1859–1943, vol. IV
Pedley, Frederick N.; see Newland-Pedley.
Pedley, John Edward, 1891–1972, vol. VII
Pedley, Richard Rodman, 1912–1973, vol. VII
Pedley, Robin, 1914–1988, vol. VIII
Pedley, Brig.-Gen. Stanhope Humphrey, 1865–1938, vol. III
Peebles, Allan Charles Chiappini, 1907–1974, vol. VII
Peebles, Lt-Col Arthur Stansfield, 1872–1933, vol. III
Peebles, Brig.-Gen. Evelyn Chiappini, 1865–1937, vol. III
Peebles, Major Herbert Walter, 1877–1955, vol. V
Peebles, James Ross, 1909–1967, vol. VI
Peech, James, 1878–1935, vol. III
Peek, Sir Cuthbert Edgar, 2nd Bt, 1855–1901, vol. I
Peek, Sir Henry William, 1st Bt, 1825–1898, vol. I
Peek, Sir Wilfrid, 3rd Bt, 1884–1927, vol. II
Peel, 1st Earl, 1867–1937, vol. III
Peel, 2nd Earl, 1901–1969, vol. VI
Peel, 1st Viscount, 1829–1913, vol. I
Peel, Lady Adelaide Margaret; see Peel, Lady Delia.
Peel, Rev. Albert, 1887–1949, vol. IV
Peel, Algernon Robert, died 1920, vol. II
Peel, Lt-Col Arthur, 1882–1938, vol. III
Peel, Hon. (Arthur) George (Villiers), 1868–1956, vol. V
Peel, Sir Arthur Robert, 1861–1952, vol. V
Peel, Lt-Col Basil Gerard, 1881–1954, vol. V

Peel, Beatrice Gladys, (Lady Peel); see Lillie, B. G.
Peel, Charles Lawrence Kinloch, 1883–1954, vol. V
Peel, Sir Charles Lennox, 1823–1899, vol. I
Peel, Mrs Charles S., died 1934, vol. III
Peel, Lady Delia, (Adelaide Margaret), 1889–1981, vol. VIII
Peel, Brig.-Gen. Edward John Russell, 1869–1939, vol. III
Peel, Sir Edward Townley, 1884–1961, vol. VI
Peel, Captain Sir (Francis Richard) Jonathan, 1897–1979, vol. VII
Peel, Rt Hon. Sir Frederick, 1823–1906, vol. I
Peel, Hon. George; see Peel, Hon. A. G. V.
Peel, (Gerald) Graham, 1877–1937, vol. III
Peel, Graham; see Peel, Gerald G.
Peel, Col Herbert Haworth, 1866–1956, vol. V
Peel, Horace, 1857–1940, vol. III
Peel, Major Hugh Edmund Ethelston, 1871–1950, vol. IV
Peel, James, 1811–1906, vol. I
Peel, Sir Jonathan; see Peel, Sir F. R. J.
Peel, Rev. Hon. Maurice Berkeley, 1873–1917, vol. II
Peel, Sir Mervyn Lloyd, 1856–1929, vol. III
Peel, Sir Robert, 4th Bt (cr 1800), 1867–1925, vol. II
Peel, Sir Robert, 5th Bt (cr 1800), 1898–1934, vol. III
Peel, Sir Robert, 6th Bt (cr 1800), 1920–1942, vol. IV
Peel, Robert, 1881–1969, vol. VI
Peel, Col Robert Francis, 1874–1924, vol. II
Peel, Roland Tennyson, 1892–1945, vol. IV
Peel, Ronald Francis Edward Waite, 1912–1985, vol. VIII
Peel, Col Hon. Sir Sidney Cornwallis, 1st Bt (cr 1936), 1870–1938, vol. III
Peel, Sir Theophilus, 1st Bt (cr 1897), 1837–1911, vol. I
Peel, Walter, 1868–1949, vol. IV
Peel, Sir William, 1875–1945, vol. IV
Peel, William Croughton, 1870–1957, vol. V
Peel, Rt Rev. William George, 1854–1916, vol. II
Peel Yates, Lt-Gen. Sir David, 1911–1978, vol. VII
Peers, Sir Charles Reed, 1868–1952, vol. V
Peers, Edgar Allison, died 1952, vol. V
Peers, Robert, 1888–1972, vol. VII
Peers, Roger Ernest, 1906–1968, vol. VI
Peet, Hubert William, 1886–1951, vol. V
Peet, Thomas Eric, 1882–1934, vol. III
Pegasus; see Lawrence, B. T. T.
Pegg, Arthur John, 1906–1978, vol. VII
Pegg, Rev. Canon Henry F.; see Foster Pegg.
Pegler, Louis Hemington, 1852–1927, vol. II
Pegram, A. Bertram, 1873–1941, vol. IV
Pegram, Vice-Adm. Frank Henderson, 1890–1944, vol. IV
Pegram, Frederick, 1870–1937, vol. III
Pegram, Henry, 1862–1937, vol. III
Peile, Rev. Arthur Lewis Babington, 1830–1911, vol. I
Peile, Henry, died 1935, vol. III
Peile, Sir James Braithwaite, 1833–1906, vol. I
Peile, Ven. James Hamilton Francis, 1863–1940, vol. III
Peile, John, 1838–1910, vol. I
Peile, Vice-Adm. Sir Lancelot Arthur Babington, 1905–1989, vol. VIII

Peile, Col Schofield Patten, 1859–1940, vol. III
Peile, Col Solomon Charles Frederick, 1855–1932, vol. III
Peirce, Lt-Col Harold Ernest, 1892–1979, vol. VII
Peiris, Hon. Sir James, 1856–1930, vol. III
Peiris, Mahapitage Velin Peter, 1898–1988, vol. VIII
Peirs, Hugh John Chevallier, 1886–1943, vol. IV
Peirse, Sir Henry Bernard de la Poer B.; see Beresford-Peirse.
Peirse, Sir Henry Campbell de la Poer B.; see Beresford-Peirse.
Peirse, Sir Henry Monson de la Poer B.; see Beresford-Peirse.
Peirse, Lt-Gen. Sir Noel Monson de la Poer B.; see Beresford-Peirse.
Peirse, Air Chief Marshal Sir Richard Edmund Charles, 1892–1970, vol. VI
Peirse, Adm. Sir Richard H., 1860–1940, vol. III
Peirse, Rev. Richard Windham de la Poer B.; see Beresford-Peirse.
Peirse, Rev. Canon Windham de la Poer B.; see Beresford-Peirse.
Peirson, David Edward Herbert, 1915–1976, vol. VII
Peirson, Garnet Frank, 1911–1963, vol. VI
Pelham, Sir Clinton; see Pelham, Sir G. C.
Pelham, Major Hon. Dudley Roger Hugh, 1872–1953, vol. V
Pelham, Sir (Edward) Henry, 1876–1949, vol. IV
Pelham, Adm. Frederick Sidney, 1854–1931, vol. III
Pelham, Sir (George) Clinton, 1898–1984, vol. VIII
Pelham, Sir Henry; see Pelham, Sir E. H.
Pelham, Henry Francis, 1846–1907, vol. I
Pelham, Rt Rev. Herbert S., 1881–1944, vol. IV
Pelham, James T.; see Thursby-Pelham.
Pelham, Rev. John Barrington, 1848–1941, vol. IV
Pelham, Rev. Sidney, 1849–1926, vol. II
Pelham, Hon. Thomas Henry William, 1847–1916, vol. II
Pelham Browne, Cynthia; see Stockley, C.
Pelham Burn, Brig.-Gen. Henry; see Burn.
Pelham-Clinton, Lord Edward William; see Clinton.
Pelham Welby, Charles Cornwallis Anderson, 1876–1959, vol. V
Pell, Albert, 1820–1907, vol. I
Pell, Major Albert Julian, 1863–1916, vol. II
Pell, Major Beauchamp Tyndall, 1866–1914, vol. I
Pellatt, Sir Henry Mill, 1860–1939, vol. III
Pelletier, Sir Charles Alphonse Pantaléon, 1837–1911, vol. I
Pelletier, Hector Rooney, 1911–1976, vol. VII
Pelletier, Lt-Col J. M. J. Pantaleon, 1860–1924, vol. II
Pelletier, Hon. Louis Philippe, 1857–1921, vol. II
Pelletier, Wilfrid, 1896–1982, vol. VIII
Pellew, Lancelot Vivian, 1899–1970, vol. VI
Pelliot, Paul, 1878–1945, vol. IV
Pellizzi, Camillo, 1896–1979, vol. VII (AII)
Pelloe, Rev. Canon John Parker, 1905–1983, vol. VIII
Pelly, Major Sir Alwyne; see Pelly, Major Sir H. A.
Pelly, Air Chief Marshal Sir Claude Bernard Raymond, 1902–1972, vol. VII
Pelly, Cornelius James, 1908–1985, vol. VIII
Pelly, Rev. Douglas Raymond, 1865–1943, vol. IV

Pelly, Lt-Col Edmund Godfrey, 1889–1939, vol. III
Pelly, Sir Harold, 4th Bt, 1863–1950, vol. IV
Pelly, Major Sir (Harold) Alwyne, 5th Bt, 1893–1981, vol. VIII
Pelly, Adm. Sir Henry Bertram, 1867–1942, vol. IV
Pelly, Captain John Noel, 1888–1945, vol. IV
Pelly, Lt-Col John Stannus, 1859–1938, vol. III
Pelly, Sir Kenneth Raymond, 1893–1973, vol. VII
Pelly, Rear-Adm. Peter Douglas Herbert Raymond, 1904–1980, vol. VII
Pelly, Rev. Raymond P., 1841–1911, vol. I
Pelly, Brig.-Gen. Raymond Theodore, 1881–1952, vol. V
Pelly, Rev. Canon Richard Lawrence, 1886–1976, vol. VII
Pember, Edward Henry, 1833–1911, vol. I
Pember, Francis William, 1862–1954, vol. V
Pemberton, Sir Edward Leigh; see Leigh-Pemberton, Sir E.
Pemberton, Horatio Nelson, 1902–1967, vol. VI
Pemberton, John Stapylton Grey, 1860–1940, vol. III
Pemberton, Sir Max, 1863–1950, vol. IV
Pemberton, Maj.-Gen. Robert Charles Boileau, 1934–1914, vol. I
Pemberton, T(homas) Edgar, 1849–1905, vol. I
Pemberton, Rev. Thomas Percy, died 1921, vol. II
Pemberton, William Shakespear C.; see Childe-Pemberton.
Pemberton, Maj.-Gen. Sir Wykeham Leigh, 1833–1918, vol. II
Pemberton-Pigott, Alan Desmond Frederick, 1916–1972, vol. VII
Pembleton, Edgar Stanley, 1888–1968, vol. VI
Pembrey, John Cripps, 1831–1918, vol. II
Pembrey, Marcus Seymour, 1868–1934, vol. III
Pembroke, 14th Earl of, and Montgomery, 11th Earl of, 1853–1913, vol. I
Pembroke, 15th Earl of, and Montgomery, 12th Earl of, 1880–1960, vol. V
Pembroke, 16th Earl of, and Montgomery, 13th Earl of, 1906–1969, vol. VI
Penberthy, John, 1858–1927, vol. II
Pendarves, William Cole, 1841–1929, vol. III
Pendavis, Ven. Whylock, died 1924, vol. II
Pendenys, Arthur; see Humphreys, Arthur L.
Pender, 1st Baron, 1882–1949, vol. IV
Pender, 2nd Baron, 1907–1965, vol. VI
Pender, Major Henry Denison Denison, 1884–1967, vol. VI
Pender, Sir James, 1st Bt, 1841–1921, vol. II
Pender, Major James, 1860–1936, vol. III
Pender, Sir John Denison Denison-, 1855–1929, vol. III
Pender, Bt Col William Stanhope, 1889–1948, vol. IV
Pendered, Mary Lucy, 1858–1940, vol. III (A), vol. IV
Penderel-Brodhurst, James George Joseph, 1859–1934, vol. III
Pendlebury, Charles, 1854–1941, vol. IV
Pendlebury, Herbert Stringfellow, 1870–1953, vol. V
Pendlebury, John Devitt Stringfellow, 1904–1941, vol. IV
Pendleton, Alan O'Bryan George William, 1837–1916, vol. II

Pendred, Air Marshal Sir Lawrence Fleming, 1899–1986, vol. VIII

Pendred, Loughnan St Lawrence, 1870–1953, vol. V

Penfield, Wilder Graves, 1891–1976, vol. VII

Penfold, Surg. Rear-Adm. Ernest Alfred, 1866–1956, vol. V

Penfold, Very Rev. John Brookes Vernon, 1864–1922, vol. II

Penfold, Captain Marchant Hubert, 1873–1961, vol. VI

Penfold, Lt-Col Sir Stephen, 1842–1925, vol. II

Pengelley, Gen. George Farquharson, 1843–1929, vol. III

Pengelly, Herbert Staddon, 1892–1963, vol. VI

Pengelly, William Lister, 1892–1983, vol. VIII

Pengilly, Sir Alexander, 1868–1965, vol. VI

Penhaligon, David Charles, 1944–1986, vol. VIII

Peniakoff, Lt-Col Vladimir, 1897–1951, vol. V

Penlake, Richard; *see* Salmon, Percy R.

Penley, Belville S., 1861–1940, vol. III

Penley, William Sydney, 1851–1912, vol. I

Penman, David, *died* 1961, vol. VI

Penman, Most Rev. David John, 1936–1989, vol. VIII

Penman, Gerard Giles, 1899–1982, vol. VIII

Penman, Howard Latimer, 1909–1984, vol. VIII

Penn, Sir Arthur Horace, 1886–1960, vol. V

Penn, John, 1848–1903, vol. I

Penn, Will C., *died* 1968, vol. VI

Pennant, Hon. Alan George Sholto D.; *see* Douglas-Pennant.

Pennant, Hon. Charles D.; *see* Douglas-Pennant.

Pennant, Adm. Hon. Sir Cyril Eustace D.; *see* Douglas-Pennant.

Pennant, Captain Hon. George Henry D.; *see* Douglas-Pennant.

Pennant, Hon. Violet Blanche D.; *see* Douglas-Pennant.

Pennefather, Sir (Alfred) Richard, 1845–1918, vol. II

Pennefather, Harold Wilfrid Armine F.; *see* Freese-Pennefather.

Pennefather, Sir John de Fonblanque, 1st Bt, 1856–1933, vol. III

Pennefather, Sir Richard; *see* Pennefather, Sir A. R.

Pennefather, Rev. Preb. Somerset Edward, 1848–1917, vol. II

Pennefather-Evans, Brig. Brian, 1897–1954, vol. V

Pennefather-Evans, Lt-Col Granville, *died* 1963, vol. VI

Pennell, Arthur, 1852–1926, vol. II

Pennell, Sir Charles Henry, 1805–1898, vol. I

Pennell, Charles Henry, *born* 1848, vol. III

Pennell, Elizabeth Robins, *died* 1936, vol. III

Pennell, Henry Cholmondeley-, 1837–1915, vol. I

Pennell, Captain Henry Singleton, 1874–1907, vol. I

Pennell, Joseph, *died* 1926, vol. II

Pennell, Kenneth Eustace Lee, 1890–1948, vol. IV

Pennell, Montague Mattinson, 1916–1981, vol. VIII

Pennell, Lt-Col Richard, 1885–1963, vol. VI

Pennell, Vernon Charles, 1889–1976, vol. VII

Pennethorne, Rev. Gregory Walton, 1837–1915, vol. I

Penney, Air Cdre Howard Wright, 1903–1970, vol. VI

Penney, José Campbell, 1893–1976, vol. VII

Penney, Maj.-Gen. Sir Ronald Campbell; *see* Penney, Maj.-Gen. Sir W. R. C.

Penney, Scott Moncrieff, 1857–1932, vol. III

Penney, Rev. William Campbell, *died* 1945, vol. IV

Penney, Maj.-Gen. Sir (William) Ronald Campbell, 1896–1964, vol. VI

Pennington, Hon. Alan Joseph, 1837–1913, vol. I

Pennington, Anne Elizabeth, 1934–1981, vol. VIII

Pennington, Brig.-Gen. Arthur Watson, 1867–1927, vol. II

Pennington, Lt-Gen. Sir Charles Richard, 1838–1910, vol. I

Pennington, Frederick, 1819–1914, vol. I

Pennington, Lt-Col Hubert Stanley Whitmore, *died* 1949, vol. IV

Pennington, Hon. John Warburton, 1870–1945, vol. IV

Pennington, Sydney Content Boeth, 1869–1937, vol. III

Pennington-Ramsden, Major Sir (Geoffrey) William, 7th Bt, 1904–1986, vol. VIII

Pennington-Ramsden, Sir William; *see* Pennington-Ramsden, Sir G. W.

Pennoyer, Richard Edmands, 1885–1968, vol. VI

Penny, Rev. Alfred, 1845–1935, vol. III

Penny, Major Arthur Taylor, 1871–1915, vol. I

Penny, Edmund, 1852–1919, vol. II

Penny, Fanny Emily, *died* 1939, vol. III

Penny, Col Frederick Septimus, 1869–1955, vol. V

Penny, Sir James Downing, 1886–1978, vol. VII

Pennybacker, Joseph Buford, 1907–1983, vol. VIII

Pennycuick, Hon. Alexander, 1844–1906, vol. I

Pennycuick, Charles Edward Ducat, *died* 1903, vol. I

Pennycuick, Brig. James Alexander Charles, 1890–1966, vol. VI

Pennycuick, Col John, 1841–1911, vol. I

Pennycuick, Rt Hon. Sir John, 1899–1982, vol. VIII

Pennyman, Rev. Preb. William Geoffrey, *died* 1942, vol. IV

Pennymore, Lt-Col Percy George, 1869–1940, vol. III (A), vol. IV

Penoyre, John, 1870–1954, vol. V

Penrhyn, 2nd Baron, 1836–1907, vol. I

Penrhyn, 3rd Baron, 1864–1927, vol. II

Penrhyn, 4th Baron, 1894–1949, vol. IV

Penrhyn, 5th Baron, 1865–1967, vol. VI

Penrhyn, Rev. Oswald Henry Leycester, 1828–1918, vol. II

Penrhyn-Hornby, Charles Windham Leycester, 1873–1966, vol. VI

Penrose, Brig.-Gen. Sir Cooper, 1855–1927, vol. II

Penrose, Dame Emily, 1858–1942, vol. IV

Penrose, Francis Cranmer, 1817–1903, vol. I

Penrose, Francis George, 1857–1932, vol. III

Penrose, J. Doyle, 1862–1932, vol. III

Penrose, James Edward, 1850–1936, vol. III

Penrose, Lionel Sharples, 1898–1972, vol. VII

Penrose, Sir Penrose Charles, 1822–1902, vol. I

Penrose, Sir Roland Algernon, 1900–1984, vol. VIII

Penrose-Welsted, Col Reginald Hugh, 1891–1966, vol. VI

Penruddock, Sir Clement Frederick, 1905–1988, vol. VIII

Penson, Sir Henry; *see* Penson, Sir T. H.

Penson, John Hubert, 1893–1979, vol. VII
Penson, Dame Lillian Margery, 1896–1963, vol. VI
Penson, Sir (Thomas) Henry, 1864–1955, vol. V
Penston, Norah Lillian, 1903–1974, vol. VII
Pentecost, Rev. George F., 1841–1920, vol. II
Pentin, Rev. Herbert, 1873–1965, vol. VI
Pentland, 1st Baron, 1860–1925, vol. II
Pentland, 2nd Baron, 1907–1984, vol. VIII
Pentland, Norman, 1912–1972, vol. VII
Pentney, Richard George, 1922–1990, vol. VIII
Penton, Maj.-Gen. Arthur Pole, 1854–1920, vol. II
Penton, Brig. Bertie Cyril, 1880–1962, vol. VI
Penton, Cyril Frederick, 1886–1960, vol. V
Penton, Sir Edward, 1875–1967, vol. VI
Penton, Frederick Thomas, 1851–1929, vol. III
Penton, Col Richard Hugh, 1863–1934, vol. III
Pentreath, Rev. Canon Arthur Godolphin Guy Carleton, 1902–1985, vol. VIII
Pentreath, Ven. Edwyn Sandys Wetmore, 1846–1913, vol. I
Penzance, 1st Baron, 1816–1899, vol. I
Penzer, Norman Mosley, 1892–1960, vol. V
Pepler, Sir George Lionel, 1882–1959, vol. V
Peploe, Rev. Hanmer William W.; *see* Webb-Peploe.
Peploe, Mrs J. R.; *see* Stevenson, D. E.
Peploe, S. J., *died* 1935, vol. III
Pepper, Augustus Joseph, *died* 1935, vol. III
Pepper, Claude Denson, 1900–1989, vol. VIII
Pepper, Brig. Ernest Cecil, 1899–1981, vol. VIII
Pepper, Sir Francis Henry, *died* 1936, vol. III
Pepper, George Wharton, 1867–1961, vol. VI
Peppercorn, Trevor Edward, 1904–1984, vol. VIII
Pepperell, Elizabeth Maud, (E. M. Brewin), 1914–1971, vol. VII
Peppiatt, Sir Kenneth Oswald, 1893–1983, vol. VIII
Peppiatt, Sir Leslie Ernest, 1891–1968, vol. VI
Pepys, Rev. Charles Sidney, 1875–1927, vol. II
Pepys, Rt Rev. George Christopher Cutts, 1914–1974, vol. VII
Pepys, George Digby, 1868–1957, vol. V
Pepys, Col Gerald Leslie, 1879–1936, vol. III
Pepys, Rev. Herbert George, 1830–1918, vol. II
Pepys, Walter Evelyn, 1885–1966, vol. VI
Perak, HH Sultan of, *died* 1916, vol. II
Perak, HH Sultan of, 1887–1948, vol. IV
Perceval, Col Charles C., 1866–1937, vol. III
Perceval, Col Christopher Peter Westby, 1890–1967, vol. VI
Perceval, Brig.-Gen. Claude John, 1864–1932, vol. III
Perceval, Maj.-Gen. Sir Edward Maxwell, 1861–1955, vol. V
Perceval, Sir Westby Brook, 1854–1928, vol. II
Perceval-Maxwell, Magdalen, (Mrs Patrick Perceval-Maxwell); *see* King-Hall, M.
Percival, Archibald Stanley, 1862–1935, vol. III
Percival, Lt-Gen. Arthur Ernest, 1887–1966, vol. VI
Percival, Major Arthur Jex-Blake, 1870–1914, vol. I
Percival, Edgar Wikner, 1897–1984, vol. VIII
Percival, Francis William, *died* 1929, vol. III
Percival, George Hector, 1901–1983, vol. VIII
Percival, Col Sir Harold Franz Passawer, 1876–1944, vol. IV
Percival, Harold Stanley, 1868–1914, vol. I

Percival, Rt Rev. John, 1834–1918, vol. II
Percival, John, *died* 1949, vol. IV
Percival, Sir John Hope, 1870–1954, vol. V
Percival, Rev. Preb. Launcelot Jefferson, 1869–1941, vol. IV
Percival, Philip Edward, 1872–1939, vol. III
Percival, Sir Tom, 1877–1933, vol. III
Percival, Rev. Wilfred Ernest Holtzendorff, 1861–1935, vol. III
Percy, Earl; Henry Algernon George, 1371–1909, vol. I
Percy of Newcastle, 1st Baron, 1887–1958, vol. V
Percy, Algernon Heber-, 1845–1911, vol. I
Percy, Lord Algernon Malcolm Arthur, 1851–1933, vol. III
Percy, Charles, *died* 1929, vol. III
Percy, Esmé; *see* Percy, S. E.
Percy, Sir James Campbell, 1869–1928, vol. II
Percy, Maj.-Gen. Sir Jocelyn, 1871–1952, vol. V
Percy, Lord Richard Charles, 1921–1989, vol. VIII
Percy, (Saville) Esmé, 1887–1957, vol. V
Percy, Col Lord William Richard, 1882–1963, vol. VI
Percy-Chapman, Major William, 1850–1932, vol. III
Perdue, Hon. William Egerton, 1850–1933, vol. III
Peregrine, Rev. David Wilkie, 1859–1940, vol. III
Pereira, Adeodato Anthony, 1889–1965, vol. VI
Pereira, Maj.-Gen. Sir Cecil Edward, 1869–1942, vol. IV
Pereira, Fredrick Linwood Clinton, 1880–1958, vol. V
Pereira, Brig.-Gen. George Edward, 1865–1923, vol. II
Pereira, Rt Rev. Henry Horace, 1845–1926, vol. II
Pereira, Sir Horace Alvarez de Courcy, 1879–1963, vol. VI
Pereira, Marguerite Scott, 1921–1987, vol. VIII
Pereira, Pedro T.; *see* Theotonio Pereira.
Pereira, Richard Lionel, 1880–1960, vol. V
Perelman, Sidney Joseph, 1904–1979, vol. VII
Peren, Sir Geoffrey Sylvester, 1892–1980, vol. VII
Perez, Sir Joseph Leon Mathieu-, 1896–1967, vol. VI
Perfect, Captain Herbert Mosley, 1867–1928, vol. II
Perham, Dame Margery, 1895–1982, vol. VIII
Perier, Jean Paul Pierre C.; *see* Casimir-Perier.
Peries, Sir Albert; *see* Peries, Sir P. P. A. F.
Peries, Sir (Pattiya Pathirannahalgae) Albert (Frederick), 1900–1967, vol. VI
Perini, Rt Rev. Paul, 1867–1932, vol. III
Peritz, Rev. Ismar J., 1863–1950, vol. IV (A), vol. V
Perkin, Arthur George, 1861–1937, vol. III
Perkin, Sir Athol; *see* Perkin, Sir E. A. O.
Perkin, (Edwin) Graham, 1929–1975, vol. VII
Perkin, Sir (Emil) Athol (Owen), 1889–1951, vol. V
Perkin, Frederick Mollwo, *died* 1928, vol. II
Perkin, Graham; *see* Perkin, E. G.
Perkin, Sir William Henry, 1838–1907, vol. I
Perkin, William Henry, 1860–1929, vol. III
Perkins, Gen. Sir Æneas, 1834–1901, vol. I
Perkins, Alan Hubert Banbury, 1898–1977, vol. VII
Perkins, Sir (Albert) Edward, 1908–1977, vol. VII
Perkins, Lt-Col Alfred Edward, *born* 1863, vol. II
Perkins, Col Alfred Thrale, 1843–1934, vol. III
Perkins, Major Alfred Thrale, 1869–1935, vol. III

Perkins, Brig.-Gen. Arthur Ernest John, *died* 1921, vol. II

Perkins, Dexter, 1889–1984, vol. VIII

Perkins, Dudley; *see* Perkins, G. D. G.

Perkins, Sir Edward; *see* Perkins, Sir A. E.

Perkins, Col Sir Edwin King, 1855–1937, vol. III

Perkins, Rev. E(rnest) Benson, 1881–1974, vol. VII

Perkins, Frances, *died* 1965, vol. VI

Perkins, Rev. Francis Leonard, 1865–1932, vol. III

Perkins, Sir Frederick, 1826–1902, vol. I

Perkins, Rev. Canon Frederick Howard, *died* 1977, vol. VII

Perkins, Frederick William, *died* 1938, vol. III

Perkins, George, *died* 1979, vol. VII

Perkins, (George) Dudley (Gwynne), 1911–1986, vol. VIII

Perkins, Col George Forder, 1884–1972, vol. VII

Perkins, George Walbridge, 1862–1920, vol. II

Perkins, Harry Innes, *died* 1924, vol. II

Perkins, J. H. Raymond R.; *see* Roze, Raymond.

Perkins, Rev. Jocelyn Henry Temple, 1870–1962, vol. VI

Perkins, John Bryan W.; *see* Ward-Perkins.

Perkins, Lt-Col John Charles Campbell, 1866–1916, vol. II

Perkins, Joseph John, *died* 1928, vol. II

Perkins, Air Vice-Marshal Maxwell Edmund Massy, 1907–1985, vol. VIII

Perkins, Norman Stuart, 1904–1972, vol. VII

Perkins, Sir Robert; *see* Perkins, Sir W. R. D.

Perkins, Surg.-Captain Robert Clerk, *died* 1916, vol. I, vol. II

Perkins, Robert Cyril Layton, 1866–1955, vol. V

Perkins, Robert George, 1850–1922, vol. II

Perkins, Thomas Luff, 1867–1940, vol. III

Perkins, Walter Frank, 1865–1946, vol. IV

Perkins, Sir (Walter) Robert (Dempster), 1903–1988, vol. VIII

Perkins, Rev. William, 1843–1922, vol. II

Perkins, William Jackson, *died* 1939, vol. III

Perkins, William Turner, *died* 1927, vol. II

Perks, Sir Malcolm; *see* Perks, Sir R. M. M.

Perks, Sir (Robert) Malcolm (Mewburn), 2nd Bt, 1892–1979, vol. VII

Perks, Sir Robert William, 1st Bt, 1849–1934, vol. III

Perks, Sydney, *died* 1944, vol. IV

Perley, Rt Hon. Sir George Halsey, 1857–1938, vol. III

Perlo, Rt Rev. G. O. Filippo, 1873–1948, vol. IV

Perlo, Rt Rev. P. G. Gabriele, 1879–1948, vol. IV

Pernet, George, 1861–1940, vol. III

Perodeau, Hon. Narcisse, 1851–1932, vol. III

Perowne, Rt Rev. Arthur William Thomson, 1867–1948, vol. IV

Perowne, Rev. Edward Henry, 1826–1906, vol. I

Perowne, Rt Rev. John James Stewart, 1823–1904, vol. I

Perowne, Sir John Victor Thomas Woolrych Tait, 1897–1951, vol. V

Perowne, Maj.-Gen. Lancelot Edgar Connop Mervyn, 1902–1982, vol. VIII

Perowne, Stewart Henry, 1901–1989, vol. VIII

Perowne, Ven. Thomas John, 1868–1954, vol. V

Perowne, Ven. Thomas Thomason, *died* 1913, vol. I

Perram, George James, 1848–1939, vol. III

Perrault, Hon. Joseph Edouard, 1874–1948, vol. IV

Perreau, Brig.-Gen. Arthur Montagu, 1870–1953, vol. V

Perreau, Col Charles Noel, 1874–1952, vol. V

Perree, Walter Francis, 1871–1950, vol. IV

Perren, Edward Arthur, 1900–1978, vol. VII

Perrier, Edmond, 1844–1921, vol. II

Perrin, Alice, 1867–1934, vol. III

Perrin, Harold Ernest, 1877–1948, vol. IV

Perrin, Harry Crane, 1865–1953, vol. V

Perrin, Sir Michael Willcox, 1905–1988, vol. VIII

Perrin, William Gordon, 1874–1931, vol. III

Perrin, Rt Rev. William Willcox, 1848–1934, vol. III

Perring, Engr Rear-Adm. Harold Hepworth, 1885–1949, vol. IV

Perring, Col Sir John, 1870–1948, vol. IV

Perring, Rev. Sir Philip, 4th Bt, 1828–1920, vol. II

Perring, Sir William, 1866–1937, vol. III

Perring, William George Arthur, 1898–1951, vol. V

Perrins, Charles William Dyson, 1864–1958, vol. V

Perrins, Wesley, 1905–1990, vol. VIII

Perris, Ernest A., *died* 1961, vol. VI

Perris, George Herbert, 1866–1920, vol. II

Perron, Hon. Joseph Léonide, 1872–1930, vol. III

Perrott, Arthur Finch, 1892–1969, vol. VI

Perrott, Sir Donald Cyril Vincent, 1902–1985, vol. VIII

Perrott, Sir Herbert Charles, 6th Bt, 1849–1922, vol. II

Perrott, Samuel Wright, 1870–1964, vol. VI

Perrott, Maj.-Gen. Sir Thomas, 1851–1919, vol. II

Perry, 1st Baron, 1878–1956, vol. V

Perry, Alan Cecil, 1892–1971, vol. VII

Perry, Hon. Sir (Alan) Clifford, 1907–1983, vol. VIII

Perry, Sir Allan, 1860–1929, vol. III

Perry, Rev. Arthur John, *died* 1926, vol. II

Perry, Maj.-Gen. Aylesworth Bowen, 1860–1956, vol. V

Perry, Bliss, 1860–1954, vol. V

Perry, Hon. Sir Clifford; *see* Perry, Hon. Sir A. C.

Perry, Sir Cooper; *see* Perry, Sir E. C.

Perry, Edward William, 1891–1971, vol. VII

Perry, Sir (Edwin) Cooper, 1856–1938, vol. III

Perry, Lt-Col Ernest Middleton, 1878–1963, vol. VI

Perry, Lt-Col Francis Frederic, 1854–1940, vol. III

Perry, Sir Frank Tennyson, 1887–1965, vol. VI

Perry, Ven. George Gresley, 1820–1897, vol. I

Perry, Rev. George Henry, 1854–1935, vol. III

Perry, Sir Gerald Raoul de C.; *see* de Courcy-Perry.

Perry, Maj.-Gen. Henry Marrian, 1884–1955, vol. V

Perry, Maj.-Gen. Sir Hugh Whitchurch, 1861–1938, vol. III

Perry, Rt Rev. James De Wolf, 1871–1947, vol. IV

Perry, John, 1850–1920, vol. II

Perry, Hon. John, 1845–1922, vol. II

Perry, Rear-Adm. John Laisné, *died* 1917, vol. II

Perry, John Tavenor, 1842–1915, vol. I

Perry, Kenneth Murray Allan, 1909–1984, vol. VIII

Perry, Rev. Nathaniel Irwin, 1867–1931, vol. III

Perry, Ralph Barton, 1876–1957, vol. V

Perry, Robert Grosvenor, 1873–1949, vol. IV

Perry, Lt-Col Robert Stanley Grosvenor, 1909–1987, vol. VIII

Perry, Samuel Frederick, 1877–1954, vol. V
Perry, Rev. Stephen Nugent, 1861–1941, vol. IV
Perry, Sir (Thomas) Wilfred, 1899–1979, vol. VII
Perry, Sir Wilfred; see Perry, Sir T. W.
Perry, Rev. William, died 1948, vol. IV
Perry, Sir William, 1863–1956, vol. V
Perry, Sir William, 1885–1968, vol. VI
Perry, William James, died 1949, vol. IV
Perry, Sir William Payne, 1858–1931, vol. III
Perry-Keene, Air Vice-Marshal Allan Lancelot Addison, 1898–1987, vol. VIII
Perse, St John; see Léger, M.-R. A. St-L.
Pershing, Gen. John Joseph, 1860–1948, vol. IV
Persse, Burton Walter, 1854–1935, vol. III
Pert, Maj.-Gen. Claude Ernest, 1898–1982, vol. VIII
Pertab Singhji, Gen. Sir, 1845–1922, vol. II
Perth, 14th Earl of, and Melfort, 6th Earl of, 1807–1902, vol. I
Perth, 15th Earl of, 1871–1937, vol. III
Perth, 16th Earl of, 1876–1951, vol. V
Pertinax; see Géraud, C. J. A.
Pertwee, Rev. Arthur, died 1919, vol. II
Pertwee, Captain Herbert Guy, 1893–1978, vol. VII
Pertwee, Roland, died 1963, vol. VI
Perugini, Charles Edward, died 1918, vol. II
Perugini, Kate, died 1929, vol. III
Perugini, Mark Edward, died 1948, vol. IV
Pery-Knox-Gore, Col Arthur Francis Gore, 1880–1954, vol. V
Peshall, Rev. Charles John Eyre, 1881–1957, vol. V
Peshall, Samuel Frederick, 1882–1977, vol. VII
Pestangi, Jehangir Khan Bahadur, died 1914, vol. I
Pétain, Philippe, 1856–1951, vol. V
Petavel, James William, 1870–1945, vol. IV
Petavel, Sir Joseph Ernest, 1873–1936, vol. III
Petch, Sir Louis, 1913–1981, vol. VIII
Peter, Bernard Hartley, 1885–1970, vol. VI
Peter, Sir John Charles, 1863–1939, vol. III
Peterkin, Col Alfred, 1854–1929, vol. III
Peterkin, Lt-Col Charles Duncan, 1887–1962, vol. VI
Peterkin, Rt Rev. George William, 1841–1916, vol. II
Peterkin, Ishbel Allan, 1903–1982, vol. VIII
Peters, Hon. Arthur, 1854–1908, vol. I
Peters, Arthur, died 1956, vol. V
Peters, Rev. Canon Arthur E. G., 1866–1943, vol. IV
Peters, Adm. Sir Arthur Malcolm, 1888–1979, vol. VII
Peters, Augustus Dudley, 1892–1973, vol. VII
Peters, Bernard George, 1903–1967, vol. VI
Peters, Sir Byron; see Peters, Sir L. B.
Peters, Edwin Arthur, died 1945, vol. IV
Peters, Captain Frederic Thornton, died 1942, vol. IV
Peters, Sir George Henry, 1853–1931, vol. III
Peters, John, 1929–1988, vol. VIII
Peters, Major John Weston Parsons, 1864–1924, vol. II, vol. III
Peters, Sir (Lindsley) Byron, 1867–1939, vol. III
Peters, Sir Rudolph Albert, 1889–1982, vol. VIII
Peters, Sidney John, 1885–1976, vol. VII
Peters, Sir William, 1889–1964, vol. VI
Peters, Maj.-Gen. William Henry Brooke, 1842–1913, vol. I
Petersen, Sir William, 1856–1925, vol. II

Peterson, Alexander Duncan Campbell, 1908–1988, vol. VIII
Peterson, Sir Arthur Frederick, 1859–1922, vol. II
Peterson, Sir Arthur William, 1916–1986, vol. VIII
Peterson, Brig.-Gen. Frederick Hopewell, 1864–1925, vol. II
Peterson, John Carlos Kennedy, 1876–1955, vol. V
Peterson, John Magnus, 1902–1978, vol. VII
Peterson, Margaret, 1883–1933, vol. III
Peterson, Sir Maurice Drummond, 1889–1952, vol. V
Peterson, Sir William, 1856–1921, vol. II
Peterson, Lt-Col William Gordon, 1888–1930, vol. III
Petfield, Sir Arthur Henry, 1912–1974, vol. VII
Pethebridge, Col Sir Samuel Augustus, 1862–1918, vol. II
Petheram, Sir William Comer, 1835–1922, vol. II
Petherick, Captain Cyril Hamley, 1893–1944, vol. IV
Petherick, Maurice, 1894–1985, vol. VIII
Pethick-Lawrence, 1st Baron, 1871–1961, vol. VI
Pethybridge, Frank, 1924–1989, vol. VIII
Petigara, Khan Bahadur Kavasji Jamshedji, 1877–1941, vol. IV
Petit, Sir Dinshaw Manockjee, 1st Bt, 1823–1901, vol. I
Petit, Sir Dinshaw Manockjee, 2nd Bt, 1873–1933, vol. III
Petit, Sir Dinshaw Manockjee, 3rd Bt, 1901–1983, vol. VIII
Petit, Rt Rev. John Edward, 1895–1973, vol. VII
Petit, Rev. Paul, 1856–1941, vol. IV
Petley, Eaton Wallace, 1850–1913, vol. I
Petman, Charles Earle Bevan, 1866–1939, vol. III
Peto, Sir Basil, 1st Bt (cr 1927), 1862–1945, vol. IV
Peto, Major (Basil Arthur) John, 1900–1954, vol. V
Peto, Brig. Sir Christopher Henry Maxwell, 3rd Bt (cr 1927), 1897–1980, vol. VII
Peto, Dorothy Olivia Georgiana, 1886–1974, vol. VII
Peto, Comdr Sir Francis; see Peto, Comdr Sir H. F. M.
Peto, Sir Geoffrey Kelsall, 1878–1956, vol. V
Peto, Gladys Emma, 1890–1977, vol. VII
Peto, Sir Henry, 2nd Bt (cr 1855), 1840–1938, vol. III
Peto, Comdr Sir (Henry) Francis (Morton), 3rd Bt (cr 1855), 1889–1978, vol. VII
Peto, Lt-Col Sir (James) Michael, 2nd Bt (cr 1927), 1894–1971, vol. VII
Peto, Major John; see Peto, Major B. A. J.
Peto, Mrs Mechtilde; see Lichnowsky, Princess Mechtilde.
Peto, Lt-Col Sir Michael; see Peto, Lt-Col Sir J. M.
Petre, 14th Baron, 1858–1908, vol. I
Petre, 15th Baron, 1864–1908, vol. I
Petre, 16th Baron, 1890–1914, vol. I
Petre, 17th Baron, 1914–1989, vol. VIII
Petre, Hon. Albert Henry, 1832–1917, vol. II
Petre, Major Edward Henry, 1881–1941, vol. IV
Petre, Edward Oswald Gabriel T.; see Turville-Petre.
Petre, Francis Loraine, 1852–1925, vol. II
Petre, Francis William, 1847–1918, vol. II
Petre, Sir George Glynn, 1822–1905, vol. I
Petre, Major Henry Aloysius, 1884–1962, vol. VI
Petre, Col Henry Cecil, 1861–1939, vol. III
Petre, Maud D. M., died 1942, vol. IV

Petre, Lt-Col Oswald Henry Philip T.; *see* Turville-Petre.

Petre, Maj.-Gen. Roderic Loraine, 1887–1971, vol. VII

Petre, Rear-Adm. Walter Reginald Glynn, 1873–1942, vol. IV

Petri, Egon, 1881–1962, vol. VI

Petrides, Sir Philip Bertie, 1881–1956, vol. V

Petrie, Ven. Alan Julian, 1888–1947, vol. IV

Petrie, Alfred Alexander Webster, 1884–1962, vol. VI

Petrie, Cecilia, (Lady Petrie), 1901–1987, vol. VIII

Petrie, Sir Charles, 1st Bt, 1853–1920, vol. II

Petrie, Sir Charles Alexander, 3rd Bt, 1895–1977, vol. VII

Petrie, Lt-Col Charles Louis Rowe, 1866–1922, vol. II

Petrie, Sir (Charles) Richard (Borthwick), 4th Bt, 1921–1988, vol. VIII

Petrie, Sir David, 1879–1961, vol. VI

Petrie, Edward James, 1907–1983, vol. VIII

Petrie, Sir Edward Lindsay Haddon, 2nd Bt, 1881–1927, vol. II

Petrie, Sir Flinders; *see* Petrie, Sir W. M. F.

Petrie, Ven. Frederick Herbert, 1875–1948, vol. IV

Petrie, Graham, 1859–1940, vol. III

Petrie, (Jessie) Cecilia, (Lady Petrie); *see* Petrie, C.

Petrie, Col Ricardo Dartnel, 1861–1925, vol. II

Petrie, Sir Richard; *see* Petrie, Sir C. R. B.

Petrie, Sir (William Matthew) Flinders, 1853–1942, vol. IV

Petter, Sir Ernest Willoughby, 1873–1954, vol. V

Petticrew, Rev. Francis, *died* 1909, vol. I

Pettigrew, Sir Andrew Hislop, 1857–1942, vol. IV

Pettigrew, James Bell, 1834–1908, vol. I

Pettingell, Sir William Walter, 1914–1987, vol. VIII

Petty, Hon. Sir Horace Rostill, 1904–1982, vol. VIII

Pevsner, Sir Nikolaus Bernhard Leon, 1902–1983, vol. VIII

Peyton, Sir Algernon, 7th Bt, 1889–1962, vol. VI

Peyton, Sir Algernon Francis, 6th Bt, 1855–1916, vol. II

Peyton, Francis, 1823–1905, vol. I

Peyton, Guy Wynne Alfred, 1862–1950, vol. IV

Peyton, Sidney Augustus, 1891–1982, vol. VIII

Peyton, Rev. Thomas Thornhill, 1856–1927, vol. II

Peyton, Gen. Sir William Eliot, 1866–1931, vol. III

Pfeiffer, Alois, 1924–1987, vol. VIII

Pfeiffer, Rudolf, 1889–1979, vol. VII

Pfeil, Leonard Bessemer, 1898–1969, vol. VI

Phair, Rev. Ernest Edward Maxwell, 1870–1915, vol. I

Phair, Rt Rev. John Percy, 1876–1967, vol. VI

Phalp, Geoffrey Anderson, 1915–1986, vol. VIII

Phayre, Lt-Gen. Sir Arthur, 1856–1940, vol. III

Phear, Arthur George, 1867–1959, vol. V

Phear, Sir John Budd, 1825–1905, vol. I

Phear, Rev. Samuel George, 1829–1918, vol. II

Phelan, Edward Joseph, 1888–1967, vol. VI

Phelan, Major Ernest Cyril, vol. II

Phelan, Maj.-Gen. Frederick Ross, 1885–1970, vol. VI (AII)

Phelan, Rt Rev. Patrick, 1860–1925, vol. II

Phelips, William Robert, 1846–1919, vol. II

Phelps, Lt-Gen. Arthur, 1837–1920, vol. II

Phelps, Brig.-Gen. Arthur, 1867–1940, vol. III

Phelps, Most Rev. Francis Robinson, 1863–1938, vol. III

Phelps, Rev. Lancelot Ridley, 1853–1936, vol. III

Phelps, William Lyon, 1865–1943, vol. IV

Phelps, William Peyton, 1865–1942, vol. IV

Phemister, James, 1893–1986, vol. VIII

Phemister, Thomas Crawford, 1902–1982, vol. VIII

Phibbs, Sir Charles, 1878–1964, vol. VI

Philbrick, Arthur James, 1866–1941, vol. IV

Philbrick, Frederick Adolphus, 1836–1910, vol. I

Philby, Harry St John Bridger, 1885–1960, vol. V

Philby, Captain Ralph Montague, 1884–1969, vol. VI

Philip, Very Rev. Adam, 1856–1945, vol. IV

Philip, Alexander, 1911–1979, vol. VII

Philip, Anne Glenday, 1878–1952, vol. V

Philip, Charles Lyall, 1881–1951, vol. V

Philip, James Charles, 1873–1941, vol. IV

Philip, Sir (James) Randall, 1900–1957, vol. V

Philip, Sir Randall; *see* Philip, Sir J. R.

Philip, Sir Robert William, 1857–1939, vol. III

Philip, William Marshall, 1872–1932, vol. III

Philip, Sir William Shearer, 1891–1975, vol. VII (AII)

Philipe, Maj.-Gen. Arthur Terence de R.; *see* de Rhé-Philipe.

Philipp, John, 1869–1938, vol. III (A), vol. IV

Philipps, Sir Charles Edward Gregg, 1st Bt (*cr* 1887), 1840–1928, vol. II

Philipps, Lt-Col Sir Grismond Picton, 1898–1967, vol. VI

Philipps, Captain Sir Henry Erasmus Edward, 2nd Bt (*cr* 1887), 1871–1938, vol. III

Philipps, Maj.-Gen. Sir Ivor, 1861–1940, vol. III

Philipps, Rev. Sir James Erasmus, 12th Bt (*cr* 1621), 1824–1912, vol. I

Philipps, Hon. James Perrott, 1905–1984, vol. VIII

Philipps, Sir John Erasmus Gwynne Alexander, 3rd Bt (*cr* 1887), 1915–1948, vol. IV

Philipps, Sir Richard Foley F., 4th Bt (*cr* 1887); *see* Foley-Philipps.

Philipps, Tracy, 1890–1959, vol. V

Philips, Austin; *see* Philips, J. A. D.

Philips, Lt-Col Burton Henry, 1858–1927, vol. II

Philips, F. C., 1849–1921, vol. II

Philips, John Austin Drury, 1875–1947, vol. IV

Philips, Lt-Col John Lionel, 1878–1975, vol. VII

Philips, Brig.-Gen. Lewis Francis, 1870–1935, vol. III

Philipson, Sir George Hare, 1836–1918, vol. II

Philipson, Hilton, 1892–1941, vol. IV

Philipson, Mrs Hilton, (Mabel Russell), 1887–1951, vol. V

Philipson, Hylton, 1866–1935, vol. III

Philipson, Hylton Ralph Murray-, 1902–1934, vol. III

Philipson, Oliphant James, 1905–1987, vol. VIII

Philipson, Robert, 1860–1916, vol. II

Philipson-Stow, Sir Edmond Cecil, 4th Bt, 1912–1982, vol. VIII

Philipson-Stow, Sir Elliot Philipson; *see* Stow.

Philipson-Stow, Sir Frederic Lawrence; *see* Stow.

Philipson-Stow, Sir Frederic Samuel; *see* Stow.

Philipson-Stow, Robert Frederic; *see* Stow.

Phillimore, 1st Baron, 1845–1929, vol. III

Phillimore, 2nd Baron, 1879–1947, vol. IV

Phillimore, 3rd Baron, 1939–1990, vol. VIII

Phillimore, Sir Augustus, 1822–1897, vol. I

Phillimore, Rt Hon. Sir Henry Josceline, 1910–1974, vol. VII

Phillimore, John Swinnerton, 1873–1926, vol. II

Phillimore, Col Reginald Henry, 1879–1964, vol. VI

Phillimore, Adm. Sir Richard Fortescue, 1864–1940, vol. III

Phillimore, Ven. Hon. Stephen Henry, 1881–1956, vol. V

Phillimore, Captain Valentine Egerton Bagot, 1875–1945, vol. IV

Phillimore, William P. W., 1853–1913, vol. I

Phillip, Colin Bent, 1855–1932, vol. III

Phillipps, Maj.-Gen. Henry Pye, 1836–1927, vol. II

Phillipps, Henry Vivian, died 1955, vol. V

Phillipps, Sir Herbert; see Phillipps, Sir W. H.

Phillipps, Lt-Gen. Picton, 1869–1928, vol. II

Phillipps, William Douglas, died 1932, vol. III

Phillipps, Sir (William) Herbert, 1847–1935, vol. III

Phillipps-Wolley, Sir Clive, 1854–1918, vol. II

Phillips, Col Alan Andrew, 1889–1972, vol. VII

Phillips, Alban William Housego, 1914–1975, vol. VII

Phillips, Alison; see Phillips, W. A.

Phillips, Sir Beaumont; see Phillips, Sir F. B.

Phillips, Sir Benjamin Samuel F.; see Faudel-Phillips.

Phillips, Rt Rev. Charles, 1847–1906, vol. I

Phillips, Sir Charles; see Phillips, Sir E. C.

Phillips, Maj.-Gen. Charles George, 1889–1982, vol. VIII

Phillips, Charles James, 1852–1930, vol. III

Phillips, Sir Claude, 1846–1924, vol. II

Phillips, Douglas Herbert Charles, 1924–1990, vol. VIII

Phillips, Maj.-Gen. Sir Edward, 1889–1973, vol. VII

Phillips, Sir (Edward) Charles, 1888–1974, vol. VII

Phillips, Major Edward Hawtin, 1876–1914, vol. I

Phillips, Eleanor Addison, 1874–1952, vol. V

Phillips, Col Eric Charles Malcolm, 1883–1957, vol. V

Phillips, Ernest, 1870–1956, vol. V

Phillips, Rear-Adm. Esmonde; see Phillips, Rear-Adm. P. E.

Phillips, Very Rev. Evan Owen, died 1897, vol. I

Phillips, Maj.-Gen. Sir Farndale, 1905–1961, vol. VI

Phillips, Rev. Forbes Alexander, 1866–1917, vol. II

Phillips, Francis, 1835–1925, vol. II

Phillips, Frank Coles, 1902–1982, vol. VIII

Phillips, Sir Frederick, 1884–1943, vol. IV

Phillips, Sir (Frederick) Beaumont, 1890–1957, vol. V

Phillips, Frederick William, 1879–1956, vol. V

Phillips, Col Geoffrey Francis, 1880–1968, vol. VI

Phillips, George, 1876–1948, vol. IV

Phillips, Surg. Rear-Adm. George, 1902–1980, vol. VII

Phillips, Major George Edward, died 1902, vol. I

Phillips, Sir George Faudel F.; see Faudel-Phillips.

Phillips, Brig.-Gen. George Fraser, 1863–1921, vol. II

Phillips, George Godfrey, 1900–1965, vol. VI

Phillips, Bt Lt-Col George Ingleton, 1866–1936, vol. III

Phillips, Rev. Godfrey Edward, 1878–1963, vol. VI

Phillips, Gordon, 1890–1952, vol. V

Phillips, Rev. Gordon Lewis, 1911–1982, vol. VIII

Phillips, Captain H. C. B., died 1906, vol. I

Phillips, Harold Ernest, 1877–1941, vol. IV

Phillips, Henry Bettesworth, 1866–1950, vol. IV

Phillips, Vice-Adm. Sir Henry Clarmont, died 1968, vol. VI

Phillips, Rev. Henry Frederick, died 1914, vol. I

Phillips, Major Henry Jacob Vaughan, died 1914, vol. I

Phillips, Sir Herbert, 1878–1957, vol. V

Phillips, Brig.-Gen. Herbert de Touffreville, 1862–1933, vol. III

Phillips, Herbert Moore, 1908–1987, vol. VIII

Phillips, Hubert, 1891–1964, vol. VI

Phillips, Hugh Richard, 1873–1932, vol. III

Phillips, Ven. Hugh Stowell, 1865–1940, vol. III

Phillips, Ivan L.; see Lloyd Phillips.

Phillips, J. S. Ragland, 1850–1919, vol. II

Phillips, James Falkner, died 1933, vol. III

Phillips, John, died 1917, vol. II

Phillips, Sir John, 1855–1928, vol. II

Phillips, Col John Alfred Steele, 1882–1960, vol. V

Phillips, Rev. Canon John Bertram, 1906–1982, vol. VIII

Phillips, Major John Charles S.; see Spencer-Phillips.

Phillips, Rev. John Francis, 1860–1934, vol. III

Phillips, Lt-Col John Frederick L.; see Lort Phillips.

Phillips, John George Crispin, 1938–1982, vol. VIII

Phillips, John George P.; see Porter-Phillips.

Phillips, Sir John Grant, 1911–1986, vol. VIII

Phillips, John Guest, 1933–1987, vol. VIII

Phillips, John Henry Hood, 1902–1977, vol. VII

Phillips, Rt Rev. John Henry Lawrence, 1910–1985, vol. VIII

Phillips, Very Rev. John Leoline, 1879–1947, vol. IV

Phillips, Sir John Randal, 1857–1945, vol. IV

Phillips, Sir (John) Raymond, 1915–1982, vol. VIII

Phillips, Rev. Lawrence Arthur, 1870–1949, vol. IV

Phillips, Lawrence Barnett, 1842–1922, vol. II

Phillips, Leonard George, 1890–1975, vol. VII

Phillips, Maj.-Gen. Sir Leslie Gordon, 1892–1966, vol. VI

Phillips, Sir Leslie Walter, 1894–1983, vol. VIII

Phillips, Sir Lionel, 1st Bt, 1855–1936, vol. III

Phillips, Captain Sir Lionel Francis, 2nd Bt, 1914–1944, vol. IV

Phillips, Sir Lionel Lawson Faudel F.; see Faudel-Phillips.

Phillips, Llewellyn Powell, 1871–1927, vol. II

Phillips, Mrs McGrigor, (Dorothy Una Ratcliffe), died 1967, vol. VI

Phillips, Mandeville Blackwood, 1848–1929, vol. III

Phillips, Air Cdre Manfred Norman, 1912–1986, vol. VIII

Phillips, Marion, 1881–1932, vol. III

Phillips, Montague Fawcett, 1885–1969, vol. VI

Phillips, Morgan Hector, 1885–1953, vol. V

Phillips, Morgan Walter, 1902–1963, vol. VI

Phillips, Lt-Col Noel Clive, 1883–1961, vol. VI

Phillips, Father Oliver Rodie V.; see Vassall-Phillips.

Phillips, Maj.-Gen. Owen Forbes, 1882–1966, vol. VI

Phillips, Owen Hood, 1907–1986, vol. VIII

Phillips, Patrick Edward, 1907–1976, vol. VII

Phillips, Patrick Laurence, 1912–1980, vol. VII

Phillips, Sir Percival, 1877–1937, vol. III

Phillips, Sir Philip David, 1897–1970, vol. VI
Phillips, Rear-Adm. (Philip) Esmonde, 1888–1960, vol. V
Phillips, Sir Raymond; *see* Phillips, Sir J. R.
Phillips, Reginald Arthur, 1913–1988, vol. VIII
Phillips, Reginald William, 1854–1926, vol. II
Phillips, Robert Randal, 1878–1967, vol. VI
Phillips, Air Cdre Ronald Lancelot, 1909–1956, vol. V
Phillips, Sir Rowland Ricketts, 1904–1976, vol. VII
Phillips, Rt Rev. Samuel Charles, 1881–1974, vol. VII
Phillips, Rev. Sidney, 1840–1917, vol. II
Phillips, Sidney, *died* 1951, vol. V
Phillips, Sidney Hill, 1882–1962, vol. VI
Phillips, Stephen, 1864–1915, vol. I
Phillips, Rev. Stephen, *died* 1919, vol. II
Phillips, Rev. Theodore Evelyn Reece, 1868–1942, vol. IV
Phillips, Maj.-Gen. Thomas, 1837–1913, vol. I
Phillips, Rev. Thomas, 1868–1936, vol. III
Phillips, Lt-Col Thomas Richmond, 1866–1963, vol. VI
Phillips, Rear-Adm. Thomas Tyacke, 1832–1920, vol. II
Phillips, Sir Thomas Williams, 1883–1966, vol. VI
Phillips, Ven. Thompson, *died* 1909, vol. I
Phillips, Adm. Sir Tom Spencer Vaughan, 1888–1941, vol. IV
Phillips, Wallace Banta, 1886–1952, vol. V
Phillips, (Walter) Alison, 1864–1950, vol. IV
Phillips, Bt-Col Walter Ernest, 1858–1911, vol. I
Phillips, Walter R., 1855–1930, vol. III
Phillips, William, 1867–1941, vol. IV
Phillips, William, 1878–1968, vol. VI
Phillips, Lt-Col William Eric, 1893–1964, vol. VI
Phillips, William James, *died* 1963, vol. VI
Phillips, William Lambert Collyer, 1858–1924, vol. II
Phillips, Sir William Watkin, 1870–1933, vol. III
Phillips Brocklehurst, Charles Douglas Fergusson, 1904–1977, vol. VII
Phillipson, Andrew Tindal, 1910–1977, vol. VII
Phillipson, Coleman, 1875–1958, vol. V
Phillipson, John Tindal, 1865–1929, vol. III
Phillipson, Sir Sydney, 1892–1966, vol. VI
Phillott, Constance, *died* 1931, vol. III
Phillott, Lt-Col Douglas Craven, 1860–1930, vol. III
Phillpotts, Arthur Stephens, 1844–1920, vol. II
Phillpotts, Dame Bertha Surtees; *see* Newall, Dame B. S.
Phillpotts, Christopher Louis George, 1915–1985, vol. VIII
Phillpotts, Eden, 1862–1960, vol. V
Phillpotts, Adm. Edward Montgomery, 1871–1952, vol. V
Phillpotts, James Surtees, 1839–1930, vol. III
Phillpotts, Lt-Col Louis Murray, 1870–1916, vol. II
Phillpotts, Owen Surtees, 1870–1932, vol. III
Phillpotts, Sir Ralegh Buller, 1871–1950, vol. IV
Philp, Hon. Sir Robert, 1851–1922, vol. II
Philp, Lt-Col Robert, 1896–1980, vol. VII
Philp Sir Roslyn Foster Bowie, 1895–1965, vol. VI
Philpot, Frederick Freeman, *died* 1916, vol. II
Philpot, Glyn Warren, 1884–1937, vol. III
Philpot, Joseph Henry, 1850–1939, vol. III

Philpot, Robert, 1849–1913, vol. I
Philpott, Rev. John Nigel, 1859–1932, vol. III
Philpott, Air Vice-Marshal Peter Theodore, 1915–1988, vol. VIII
Philps, (Alan) Seymour, 1906–1956, vol. V
Philps, Seymour; *see* Philps, A. S.
Phimister, Rev. Alexander, *died* 1921, vol. II
Phin, Sir John, 1881–1955, vol. V
Phippen, Hon. Frank Hedley, 1862–1932, vol. III
Phipps, Brig. Charles Constantine, 1889–1958, vol. V
Phipps, Lt-Col Charles Edward, 1864–1946, vol. IV
Phipps, Col Charles Foskett, 1871–1931, vol. III
Phipps, Charles Nicholas Paul, 1845–1913, vol. I
Phipps, Rev. Constantine Osborne, 1861–1921, vol. II
Phipps, Sir Edmund Bampfylde, 1869–1947, vol. IV
Phipps, Sir Edmund Constantine Henry, 1840–1911, vol. I
Phipps, Rt Hon. Sir Eric Clare Edmund, 1875–1945, vol. IV
Phipps, Rev. Frederick, 1858–1934, vol. III
Phipps, Gerald Hastings, 1882–1973, vol. VII
Phipps, Hon. Harriet Lepel, *died* 1922, vol. II
Phipps, Henry, 1839–1930, vol. III
Phipps, Maj.-Gen. Herbert Clive, 1898–1975, vol. VII
Phipps, Dame Jessie Wilton, 1855–1934, vol. III
Phipps, John Constantine, 1910–1986, vol. VIII
Phipps, Col John Hare, 1871–1936, vol. III
Phipps, Paul, 1880–1953, vol. V
Phipps, Vice-Adm. Sir Peter, 1909–1989, vol. VIII
Phipps, Ven. Richard, 1865–1934, vol. III
Phipps, Captain William Duncan, 1882–1967, vol. VI
Phipson, Col Edward Selby, 1884–1973, vol. VII
Phoenix, George, 1863–1935, vol. III
Phythian, John Ernest, 1858–1935, vol. III
Phythian-Adams, Rev. Canon William John Telia Phythian, 1888–1967, vol. VI
Piaget, Jean, 1896–1980, vol. VII
Piaggio, Henry Thomas Herbert, 1884–1967, vol. VI
Piatigorsky, Gregor, 1903–1976, vol. VII
Piatti, Alfredo, 1822–1901, vol. I
Pibworth, Charles James, 1878–1958, vol. V
Picard, Émile, 1856–1941, vol. IV
Picasso, Pablo Ruiz, 1881–1973, vol. VII
Piccard, Auguste Antoine, 1884–1962, vol. VI
Piccaver, Alfred, 1889–1958, vol. V
Picciotto, Cyril Moses, 1888–1940, vol. III
Pick, Surg. Rear.-Adm. Bryan Pickering, 1879–1959, vol. V
Pick, Frank, 1878–1941, vol. IV
Pick, Thomas Pickering, 1841–1919, vol. II
Pick-Mangiagalli, Riccardo, 1882–1949, vol. IV
Pickard, Alexander, 1897–1972, vol. VII
Pickard, Benjamin, 1842–1904, vol. I
Pickard, Lt-Col Jocelyn Arthur Adair, 1885–1962, vol. VI
Pickard, Gp Captain Percy Charles, 1915–1944, vol. IV
Pickard, Col Ransom, 1867–1953, vol. V
Pickard, Sir Robert Howson, 1874–1949, vol. IV
Pickard, Rt Rev. Stanley Chapman, 1910–1988, vol. VIII
Pickard-Cambridge, Sir Arthur Wallace, 1873–1952, vol. V

Pickard-Cambridge, Rev. Octavius, 1828–1917, vol. II

Pickard-Cambridge, William Adair, 1879–1957, vol. V

Picken, Andrew, 1886–1938, vol. III

Picken, David Kennedy, 1879–1956, vol. V

Picken, Ralph Montgomery Fullarton, 1884–1955, vol. V

Pickerill, Dame Cecily Mary Wise, *born* 1903, vol. VIII

Pickerill, Henry Percy, *died* 1956, vol. V

Pickering, Col Charles James, 1880–1951, vol. V

Pickering, Derek; *see* Pickering, F. D.

Pickering, Edward Charles, 1846–1919, vol. II

Pickering, Bt Col Emil William, 1882–1942, vol. IV

Pickering, Frederick Derwent, (Derek Pickering), 1909–1989, vol. VIII

Pickering, Frederick Pickering, 1909–1981, vol. VIII

Pickering, Sir George Hunter, 1877–1971, vol. VII

Pickering, Sir George White, 1904–1980, vol. VII

Pickering, Ian George Walker, 1915–1984, vol. VIII

Pickering, J. L., *died* 1912, vol. I

Pickering, Loring, 1888–1959, vol. V (A)

Pickering, Percival Spencer Umfreville, 1858–1920, vol. II

Pickering, Brig. Ralph Emerson, 1898–1962, vol. VI

Pickering, Wilfred Francis, 1915–1980, vol. VII

Pickering, Captain William, 1856–1933, vol. III

Pickering, William Alexander, 1840–1907, vol. I

Pickering, William Henry, 1858–1912, vol. I

Pickersgill, Frederick Richard, 1820–1900, vol. I

Pickersgill, William Clayton, 1846–1901, vol. I

Pickett, Rev. Henry John, *died* 1931, vol. III

Pickett, Jacob, 1835–1922, vol. II

Pickett, Rev. James, 1853–1918, vol. II

Pickford, Sir Alfred Donald, 1872–1947, vol. IV

Pickford, Sir Anthony Frederick Ingham, 1885–1970, vol. VI

Pickford, Frank, 1917–1984, vol. VIII

Pickford, Mary, 1893–1979, vol. VII

Pickford, Hon. Mary Ada, *died* 1934, vol. III

Pickford, Ralph William, 1903–1986, vol. VIII

Pickles, Edward Llewellyn, 1884–1949, vol. IV

Pickles, Sir John Sydney, 1898–1972, vol. VII

Pickles, Wilfred, 1904–1978, vol. VII

Pickles, William Norman, 1885–1969, vol. VI

Pickmere, Edward Ralph, *died* 1941, vol. IV

Pickop, Rev. James, 1847–1919, vol. II

Pickthall, Marmaduke William, 1875–1936, vol. III

Pickthall, Col Wallace Edward Colin, 1891–1948, vol. IV

Pickthorn, Rt Hon. Sir Kenneth William Murray, 1st Bt, 1892–1975, vol. VII

Pickup, Sir Arthur, 1878–1960, vol. V

Pickwoad, Col Edwin Hay, 1853–1932, vol. III

Pickworth, Sir Frederick, 1890–1959, vol. V

Picot, Francis Raymond, 1893–1971, vol. VII

Picot, Lt-Col Francis Slater, 1859–1939, vol. III

Picot, Lt-Col Henry Philip, 1857–1937, vol. III

Picot, Jacques Marie Charles G.; *see* Georges-Picot.

Picton, Ven. Arnold Stanley, 1899–1962, vol. VI

Picton, James Allanson, 1832–1910, vol. I

Picton, Col Reginald Ernest, 1863–1932, vol. III

Picton-Turbervill, Edith, *died* 1960, vol. V

Pidcock, Air Vice-Marshal Geoffrey Arthur Henzell, 1897–1976, vol. VII

Piddington, Albert Bathurst, 1862–1945, vol. IV

Pidduck, Frederick Bernard, 1885–1952, vol. V

Pidsley, Brig. Wilfrid Gould, 1892–1967, vol. VI

Pielou, Douglas Percival, 1887–1927, vol. II

Pienaar, Maj.-Gen. Daniel Hermanus, 1893–1942, vol. IV

Pierce, Bedford, 1861–1932, vol. III

Pierce, Rev. Charles Frederick, 1877–1936, vol. III

Pierce, Rev. Francis Dormer, *died* 1923, vol. II

Pierce, Sir John, 1863–1949, vol. IV

Pierce, Robert, 1884–1968, vol. VI

Pierce, Stephen Rowland, 1896–1966, vol. VI

Pierce-Goulding, Lt-Col Terence Leslie Crawford, 1918–1987, vol. VIII

Piercy, 1st Baron, 1886–1966, vol. VI

Piercy, 2nd Baron, 1918–1981, vol. VIII

Piercy, Benjamin Herbert, 1870–1941, vol. IV

Piercy, Norman Augustus Victor, 1891–1953, vol. V

Pieris, Sir Paulus Edward Deraniyagala, 1874–1959, vol. V

Pierpoint, Robert, 1845–1932, vol. III

Pierre, Hon. Charles Henry, 1878–1937, vol. III

Pierre, Sir Henry; *see* Pierre, Sir J. H.

Pierre, Sir (Joseph) Henry, 1904–1984, vol. VIII

Piers, Sir Charles Pigott, 9th Bt, 1870–1945, vol. IV

Piers, Sir Eustace Fitz-Maurice, 8th Bt, 1840–1913, vol. I

Pierse, Rev. Garrett, 1882–1932, vol. III

Pierson, Reginald Kirshaw, 1891–1948, vol. IV

Pierson, Warren Lee, 1896–1978, vol. VII

Pierssené, Sir Stephen Herbert, 1899–1966, vol. VI

Pieshkov, Alexei Maximovitch; *see* Gorky, Maxim.

Piggott, Maj.-Gen. Francis Stewart Gilderoy, 1883–1966, vol. VI

Piggott, Sir Francis Taylor, 1852–1925, vol. II

Piggott, Sir George Bettesworth, 1867–1952, vol. V

Piggott, Sir Henry Howard, 1871–1951, vol. V

Piggott, Col Joseph Clive, 1892–1975, vol. VII

Piggott, Julian Ito, 1888–1965, vol. VI

Piggott, Sir Theodore Caro, 1867–1944, vol. IV

Piggott, Rev. William Charter, *died* 1943, vol. IV

Pigot, Sir George, 5th Bt, 1850–1934, vol. III

Pigot, John H., 1863–1928, vol. II

Pigot, Brig.-Gen. Sir Robert, 6th Bt, 1882–1977, vol. VII

Pigot, Maj.-Gen. Sir Robert Anthony, 7th Bt, 1915–1986, vol. VIII

Pigot, Rev. William Melville, 1842–1916, vol. II

Pigott, Alan Desmond Frederick P.; *see* Pemberton-Pigott.

Pigott, Maj.-Gen. Alan John Keefe, 1892–1969, vol. VI

Pigott, Major Sir Berkeley, 4th Bt, 1894–1982, vol. VIII

Pigott, Sir Charles Robert, 3rd Bt, 1835–1911, vol. I

Pigott, Sir Digby; *see* Pigott, Sir T. D.

Pigott, Brig. Frank Borkman, 1894–1971, vol. VII

Pigott, Lt-Col Grenville Edmund, 1870–1942, vol. IV

Pigott, Rt Rev. Harold Grant, 1894–1979, vol. VII

Pigott, Harry, *died* 1974, vol. VII

Pigott, John Robert Wilson, 1850–1928, vol. II

Pigott, Gp Captain (Joseph) Ruscombe (Wadham) S.; see Smyth-Pigott.

Pigott, Air Vice-Marshal Michael Joseph, 1904–1990, vol. VIII

Pigott, Montague Horatio Mostyn Turtle, 1865–1927, vol. II

Pigott, Sir Paynton, 1840–1915, vol. I

Pigott, Richard, 1861–1931, vol. III

Pigott, Col Robert Edward Pemberton, 1866–1943, vol. IV

Pigott, Gp Captain Ruscombe S.; see Smyth-Pigott.

Pigott, Sir Stephen J., 1880–1955, vol. V

Pigott, Sir (Thomas) Digby, 1840–1927, vol. II

Pigott, William; see Wales, Hubert.

Pigott, Vice-Adm. William Harvey, 1848–1924, vol. II

Pigott-Brown, Captain Sir John Hargreaves, 2nd Bt, 1913–1942, vol. IV

Pigou, Arthur Cecil, 1877–1959, vol. V

Pigou, Very Rev. Francis, 1832–1916, vol. II

Pike, Andrew Hamilton, 1903–1984, vol. VIII

Pike, Cecil Frederick, 1898–1968, vol. VI

Pike, Lt-Col Cuthbert Joseph, 1868–1947, vol. IV

Pike, Douglas Henry, 1908–1974, vol. VII

Pike, Col Ebenezer John Lecky, 1884–1965, vol. VI

Pike, Edmund William, 1838–1910, vol. I

Pike, Vice-Adm. Frederick Owen, 1851–1921, vol. II

Pike, John Milton, 1872–1940, vol. III (A), vol. IV

Pike, Joseph, died 1929, vol. III

Pike, Leonard Henry, 1885–1961, vol. VI

Pike, Most Rev. Robert Bonsall, 1905–1973, vol. VII

Pike, Sir Theodore Ouseley, 1904–1987, vol. VIII

Pike, Marshal of the Royal Air Force Sir Thomas Geoffrey, 1906–1983, vol. VIII

Pike, Rt Rev. Victor Joseph, 1907–1986, vol. VIII

Pike, Maj.-Gen. Sir William Watson, 1860–1941, vol. IV

Pilcher, Lt-Col Alan Humphrey, 1898–1957, vol. V

Pilcher, Vice-Adm. Cecil Horace, 1877–1953, vol. V

Pilcher, Rt Rev. Charles Venn, 1879–1961, vol. VI

Pilcher, Maj.-Gen. Edgar Montagu, 1865–1947, vol. IV

Pilcher, George, 1882–1962, vol. VI

Pilcher, Sir Gonne St Clair, 1890–1966, vol. VI

Pilcher, Sir John Arthur, 1912–1990, vol. VIII

Pilcher, Robert Stuart, 1882–1961, vol. VI

Pilcher, Maj.-Gen. Thomas David, 1858–1928, vol. II

Pilditch, Sir Denys, 1891–1975, vol. VII

Pilditch, Sir Philip Edward, 1st Bt, 1861–1948, vol. IV

Pilditch, Sir Philip Harold, 2nd Bt, 1890–1949, vol. IV

Pilditch, Sir Philip John Frederick, 3rd Bt, 1919–1954, vol. V

Pile, Gen. Sir Frederick Alfred, 2nd Bt, 1884–1976, vol. VII

Pile, Sir George Clarke, 1821–1906, vol. I

Pile, Sir George Laurie, 1857–1948, vol. IV

Pile, Sir John Devereux, 1918–1982, vol. VIII

Pile, Sir Thomas Devereux, 1st Bt, 1856–1931, vol. III

Pilgrim, David; see Saunders, H. A. St G.

Pilgrim, Guy Ellcock, 1875–1943, vol. IV

Pilkington, Baron (Life Peer); Harry (William Henry) Pilkington, 1905–1983, vol. VIII

Pilkington, Major Sir Arthur William Milborne-Swinnerton-, 13th Bt, 1898–1952, vol. V

Pilkington, Lt-Col Charles Raymond, 1875–1938, vol. III

Pilkington, Charles Vere, 1905–1983, vol. VIII

Pilkington, Rev. Canon Evan Matthias, 1916–1987, vol. VIII

Pilkington, Sir George Augustus, 1848–1916, vol. II

Pilkington, Harry Seymour Hoyle, 1869–1954, vol. V

Pilkington, Major Sir Henry, 1849–1930, vol. III

Pilkington, Col Henry Lionel, 1857–1914, vol. I

Pilkington, Col Herbert Edward, 1877–1956, vol. V

Pilkington, Col Lionel Edward, died 1952, vol. V

Pilkington, Sir Lionel Milborne Swinnerton, 11th Bt, 1835–1901, vol. I

Pilkington, M. Evelyn, 1879–1955, vol. V

Pilkington, Margaret, 1891–1974, vol. VII

Pilkington, Captain Sir Richard Antony, 1908–1976, vol. VII

Pilkington, Robert Rivington, died 1942, vol. IV

Pilkington, Sir Thomas Edward Milborne-Swinnerton-, 12th Bt, 1857–1944, vol. IV

Pilkington, Sir William Handcock, 1859–1905, vol. I

Pilkington, Col William Norman, 1877–1935, vol. III

Pilkington Jackson, Charles d'Orville; see Jackson.

Pillans, Charles Eustace, 1850–1919, vol. II, vol. III

Pilleau, Maj.-Gen. Gerald Arthur, 1896–1964, vol. VI

Pilleau, Major Henry Charles, 1866–1914, vol. I

Pilley, Charles, 1885–1937, vol. III

Pilley, John Gustave, 1899–1968, vol. VI

Pilling, Sir Guy; see Pilling, Sir H. G.

Pilling, Sir (Henry) Guy, 1886–1953, vol. V

Pilling, Tom Sharpley, 1921–1977, vol. VII

Pillsbury, Harry N., 1872–1906, vol. I

Pilot, Rev. William, 1841–1913, vol. I

Pilson, Major Arthur Forde, 1865–1929, vol. III

Pilsudski, Joseph Clemens, 1867–1935, vol. III

Pilter, Sir John George, 1848–1935, vol. III

Pilter, Col William Frederick, 1831–1915, vol. I

Pim, Sir Alan William, died 1958, vol. V

Pim, Frederic William, 1839–1925, vol. II

Pim, Brig. George Adrien, 1888–1965, vol. VI

Pim, Howard, died 1934, vol. III

Pim, Rev. John, died 1932, vol. III

Pim, Rt Hon. Jonathan, 1858–1949, vol. IV

Pim, Captain Sir Richard Pike, 1900–1987, vol. VIII

Pimlott, John Alfred Ralph, 1909–1969, vol. VI

Pinault, Col Louis Felix, 1852–1906, vol. I

Pinchard, Rev. Arnold Theophilus Biddulph, died 1934, vol. III

Pinches, Theophilus Goldridge, 1856–1934, vol. III

Pinchin, Arthur John Scott, died 1936, vol. III

Pinchin, Ernest Alfred, 1874–1929, vol. III

Pinching, Sir Horace Henderson, 1857–1935, vol. III

Pinchot, Gifford, 1865–1946, vol. IV

Pinckard, George Henry, died 1950, vol. IV

Pinckney, Charles Percy, 1901–1982, vol. VIII

Pinckney, John Robert Hugh, 1876–1964, vol. VI

Pine, John Bradley, 1913–1989, vol. VIII

Pine, Leslie Gilbert, 1907–1987, vol. VIII

Pine-Coffin, Major John Edward, 1866–1919, vol. II

Pine-Coffin, Gen. Roger, 1847–1921, vol. II
Pinero, Sir Arthur Wing, 1855–1934, vol. III
Piney, Alfred, 1896–1965, vol. VI
Ping, Aubrey Charles, 1905–1978, vol. VII
Pinhey, Lt-Col Sir Alexander Fleetwood, 1861–1916, vol. II
Pinhorn, Col Henry Quinten, 1862–1929, vol. III
Pininfarina, Battista, 1895–1966, vol. VI
Pink, Col Francis John, 1857–1934, vol. III
Pink, Sir Harold Rufus, 1858–1952, vol. V
Pink, Ven Hubert Arthur Stanley, 1905–1976, vol. VII
Pink, Sir Ivor Thomas Montague, 1910–1966, vol. VI
Pink, Ralph Bonner, 1912–1984, vol. VIII
Pink, Air Cdre Richard Charles Montagu, 1888–1932, vol. III
Pink, Sir Thomas, 1855–1926, vol. II
Pink, Sir William, 1829–1906, vol. I
Pinker, Rev. Martin Wallis, 1893–1980, vol. VII (AII)
Pinkerton, John, 1845–1908, vol. I
Pinkerton, John Macpherson, 1941–1988, vol. VIII
Pinkerton, Robert Hamilton, 1855–1938, vol. III
Pinkham, Lt-Col Sir Charles, 1853–1938, vol. III
Pinkham, Rt Rev. William Cyprian, 1844–1928, vol. II
Pinkney, Col Edmund Walker Renny, 1876–1940, vol. III
Pinnell, Leonard George, 1896–1979, vol. VII
Pinney, Charles Robert, 1883–1945, vol. IV
Pinney, Maj.-Gen. Sir Reginald John, 1863–1943, vol. IV
Pinnock, Frank Frewin, 1902–1977, vol. VII
Pinsent, Dame Ellen Frances, 1866–1949, vol. IV
Pinsent, Gerald Hume Saverie, 1888–1976, vol. VII
Pinsent, Col John Ryland, 1888–1957, vol. V
Pinsent, Sir Richard Alfred, 1st Bt, 1852–1948, vol. IV
Pinsent, Sir Roy, 2nd Bt, 1883–1978, vol. VII
Pinto, Vivian de Sola, 1895–1969, vol. VI
Piper, Arthur William, 1865–1936, vol. III
Piper, Sir David Towry, 1918–1990, vol. VIII
Piper, Harold Bayard, 1894–1953, vol. V
Piper, Henry Mansell, 1890–1949, vol. IV
Piper, John Edwin, 1854–1938, vol. III
Piper, Stephen Harvey, 1887–1963, vol. VI
Piper, Air Marshal Sir Thomas William; see Piper, Air Marshal Sir Tim.
Piper, Air Marshal Sir Tim, (Thomas William), 1911–1978, vol. VII
Pipes, Hon. William Thomas, 1850–1908, vol. I
Pipon, Maj.-Gen. Henry, 1843–1924, vol. II
Pipon, Vice-Adm. Sir James Murray, 1882–1971, vol. VII
Pipon, John Pakenham, 1849–1899, vol. I
Pipon, Gen. Philip Gosset, 1824–1905, vol. I
Pipon, Philip James Griffiths, 1874–1960, vol. V
Pippard, Alfred John Sutton, 1891–1969, vol. VI
Pippett, Roger Samuel, 1895–1962, vol. VI
Pirandello, Luigi, 1867–1936, vol. III
Pirbhai, Diwan Sir E.; see Eboo Pirbhai.
Pirbright, 1st Baron, 1840–1903, vol. I
Pire, Rev. Père Dominique-Georges, 1910–1969, vol. VI

Pirenne, Henri, 1862–1935, vol. III
Pirie, Alexander Howard, 1875–1944, vol. IV
Pirie, Anne Gillespie, (Mrs J. H. Pirie); see Shaw, A. G.
Pirie, Major Arthur Murray, 1869–1917, vol. II
Pirie, Maj.-Gen. Charles Patrick William, 1859–1933, vol. III
Pirie, Duncan Vernon, 1858–1931, vol. III
Pirie, Rev. George, 1843–1904, vol. I
Pirie, Sir George, 1863–1946, vol. IV
Pirie, Air Chief Marshal Sir George Clark, 1896–1980, vol. VII
Pirie-Gordon of Buthlaw, Christopher Martin, 1911–1980, vol. VII
Pirow, Hon. Oswald, died 1959, vol. V
Pirquet, Clemens, Freiherr von, 1874–1929, vol. III
Pirrie, 1st Viscount, 1847–1924, vol. II
Pirrie, Viscountess; (Margaret), died 1935, vol. III
Pirrie, Col Francis William, 1867–1948, vol. IV
Pisani, Salvator Aloysius, 1828–1908, vol. I
Pissarro, Lucien, 1863–1944, vol. IV
Piston, Walter, 1894–1976, vol. VII
Pitcher; see Binstead, A. M.
Pitcher, Col Duncan George, born 1839, vol. II
Pitcher, Air Cdre Duncan le Geyt, 1877–1944, vol. IV
Pitcher, William J. C., 1858–1925, vol. II
Pitchford, Denys James W.; see Watkins-Pitchford.
Pitchford, Lt-Col Herbert W.; see Watkins-Pitchford.
Pitchforth, (Roland) Vivian, 1895–1982, vol. VIII
Pitchforth, Vivian; see Pitchforth, R. V.
Pite, Arthur Beresford, 1861–1934, vol. III
Pite, Arthur Goodhart, 1896–1938, vol. III
Pite, William Alfred, 1860–1949, vol. IV
Pithie, Michael, 1846–1915, vol. I
Pitkeathly, Sir James Scott, 1882–1949, vol. IV
Pitman, Hon. Lord; James Campbell Pitman, 1864–1941, vol. IV
Pitman, Alfred, 1862–1952, vol. V
Pitman, Charles Edward, 1845–1933, vol. III
Pitman, Charles Murray, 1872–1948, vol. IV
Pitman, Captain Charles Robert Senhouse, 1890–1975, vol. VII
Pitman, Clement Fothergill, 1894–1973, vol. VII
Pitman, Frederick Islay, 1863–1942, vol. IV
Pitman, Sir Henry Alfred, 1808–1908, vol. I
Pitman, Sir Hubert, 1901–1986, vol. VIII
Pitman, Sir (Isaac) James, 1901–1985, vol. VIII
Pitman, Sir James; see Pitman, Sir I. J.
Pitman, James Campbell; see Pitman, Hon. Lord.
Pitman, John Sitwell, 1860–1938, vol. III
Pitman, Captain Robert, 1836–1921, vol. II
Pitman, Maj.-Gen. Thomas Tait, 1868–1941, vol. IV
Pitt, Douglas F.; see Fox-Pitt.
Pitt, Dame Edith Maud, 1906–1966, vol. VI
Pitt, Frances, 1888–1964, vol. VI
Pitt, Captain Francis Joseph, 1840–1929, vol. III
Pitt, George Newton, 1853–1929, vol. III
Pitt, Henry Arthur, 1872–1955, vol. V
Pitt, Percy, 1870–1932, vol. III
Pitt, Col Robert Brindley, 1888–1974, vol. VII
Pitt, Captain Stanley Talbot Dean, 1853–1936, vol. III
Pitt, Terence John, 1937–1986, vol. VIII
Pitt, Col William, died 1933, vol. III

Pitt, Maj.-Gen. William Augustus Fitzgerald Lane F.; see Fox-Pitt.

Pitt-Kethley, Andrew Horace Victor, 1879–1955, vol. V

Pitt-Lewis, George, 1845–1906, vol. I

Pitt-Pitts, Ven. W. A., 1890–1940, vol. III

Pitt-Rivers, Augustus Henry Lane F.; see Fox-Pitt-Rivers.

Pitt-Rivers, George Henry Lane Fox, 1890–1966, vol. VI

Pitt-Rivers, Rosalind Venetia, 1907–1990, vol. VIII

Pitt-Taylor, Gen. Sir Walter William, 1878–1950, vol. IV

Pitt-Watson, Very Rev. James, 1893–1962, vol. VI

Pittar, Barry, 1880–1948, vol. IV

Pittar, Sir Thomas John, 1846–1924, vol. II

Pittendrigh, Rev. George, 1857–1930, vol. III

Pitti, Sir Thyagaraya Chetti Garum, Diwan Bahadur, died 1925, vol. II, vol. III

Pittman, Osmund, 1874–1958, vol. V

Pittom, L(ois) Audrey, 1918–1990, vol. VIII

Pitts, Arthur Thomas, 1881–1939, vol. III

Pitts, Hon. James Stewart, 1847–1914, vol. I

Pitts, Captain Percy, 1876–1937, vol. III

Pitts, Thomas, 1857–1919, vol. II

Pitts, Rev. Thomas, died 1929, vol. III

Pitts, Ven. W. A. P.; see Pitt-Pitts.

Pitts, William Ewart, 1900–1980, vol. VII

Pitts-Chambers, Sir Newman; see Chambers.

Pius X, His Holiness Pope, (Giuseppe Sarto), 1835–1914, vol. I

Pius XI, His Holiness Pope, (Achille Ambrogio Damiano Ratti), 1857–1939, vol. III

Piux XII, His Holiness Pope, (Eugene Pacelli), 1876–1958, vol. V

Pixley, Col Francis W., 1852–1933, vol. III

Place, Major (Charles) Godfrey (Morris), 1886–1931, vol. III

Place, Col Charles Otley, 1875–1955, vol. V

Place, Major Godfrey; see Place, Major C. G. M.

Placzek, Mrs A. K.; see Struther, Jan.

Plamenatz, John Petrov, 1912–1975, vol. VII

Planck, Max Karl Ernst Ludwig, 1858–1947, vol. IV

Plant, Baron (Life Peer); Cyril Thomas Howe Plant, 1910–1986, vol. VIII

Plant, Sir Arnold, 1898–1978, vol. VII

Plant, Edmund Carter, 1842–1902, vol. I

Plant, Maj.-Gen. Eric Clive Pegus, 1890–1950, vol. IV

Plant, George Frederick, 1877–1954, vol. V

Plant, Morton F., died 1918, vol. II

Plante, Mgr J. Omer, 1867–1948, vol. IV

Plarr, Victor Gustave, 1863–1929, vol. III

Plaskett, Harry Hemley, 1893–1980, vol. VII

Plaskett, John Stanley, 1865–1941, vol. IV

Platnauer, Maurice, 1887–1974, vol. VII

Platt, Baron (Life Peer); Robert Platt, 1900–1978, vol. VII

Platt, Benjamin Stanley, 1903–1969, vol. VI

Platt, Christopher; see Platt, D. C. M.

Platt, (Desmond) Christopher (Martin), 1934–1989, vol. VIII

Platt, Major Eric James Walter, 1871–1946, vol. IV

Platt, Comdr Francis Cuthbert, 1885–1941, vol. IV

Platt, Sir Frank, 1890–1955, vol. V

Platt, Rev. Frederic, 1859–1955, vol. V

Platt, Sir Harry, 1st Bt, 1886–1986, vol. VIII

Platt, Col Henry, 1842–1914, vol. I

Platt, J. Arthur, 1860–1925, vol. II

Platt, James Westlake, 1897–1972, vol. VII

Platt, Kenneth Harry, 1909–1985, vol. VIII

Platt, Samuel R., died 1902, vol. I

Platt, Sir Thomas Comyn-, 1875–1961, vol. VI

Platt, Gen. Sir William, 1885–1975, vol. VII

Platt-Higgins, Frederick, 1840–1910, vol. I

Platts, Frederick William, 1865–1941, vol. IV

Platts, Col Matthew George, 1886–1969, vol. VI

Platts, Thomas, 1843–1919, vol. II

Platts, W. Carter, 1864–1944, vol. IV

Platzer, Wilfried, 1909–1981, vol. VIII

Playfair, 1st Baron, 1818–1898, vol. I

Playfair, 2nd Baron, 1849–1939, vol. III

Playfair, Maj.-Gen. Archibald Lewis, 1838–1915, vol. I

Playfair, Arthur Lambert, died 1939, vol. III

Playfair, Arthur Wyndham, 1869–1918, vol. II

Playfair, George Macdonald Home, 1850–1917, vol. II

Playfair, Maj.-Gen. Ian Stanley Ord, 1894–1972, vol. VII

Playfair, Hon. Lyon George Henry Lyon, 1888–1915, vol. I

Playfair, Sir Nigel, 1874–1934, vol. III

Playfair, Sir Patrick, 1852–1915, vol. I

Playfair, Air Marshal Sir Patrick Henry Lyon, 1889–1974, vol. VII

Playfair, Rev. Patrick M., 1858–1924, vol. II

Playfair, Sir Robert Lambert, 1828–1899, vol. I

Playfair, William Smoult, 1835–1903, vol. I

Playford, Hon. Thomas, 1837–1915, vol. I

Playford, Hon. Sir Thomas, 1896–1981, vol. VIII

Playne, Air Cdre Basil Alfred, 1885–1944, vol. IV

Pleass, Sir Clement John, 1901–1988, vol. VIII

Pledge, Henry, died 1949, vol. IV (A), vol. V

Pledge, Humphrey Thomas, 1903–1960, vol. V, vol. VI

Plender, 1st Baron, 1861–1946, vol. IV

Plender, Lady; (Mabel Agnes), died 1970, vol. VI

Plenderleath, Captain Claude William Manners, 1863–1937, vol. III

Plenderleith, Air Vice-Marshal Brian William, 1927–1978, vol. VII

Pless, HSH Daisy, (Mary Theresa Olivia), Princess of, died 1943, vol. IV

Pleydell, Lt-Col Edmund Morton M.; see Mansel-Pleydell.

Pleydell, John Clavell M.; see Mansel-Pleydell.

Pleydell, Rev. John Colvile Morton M.; see Mansel-Pleydell.

Pleydell-Bouverie, Rev. Hon. Bertrand, 1845–1926, vol. II

Pleydell-Bouverie, Hon. Duncombe, 1842–1909, vol. I

Pleydell-Bouverie, Col Hon. Stuart, 1877–1947, vol. IV

Pleydell-Railston, Lt-Col Henry George Moreton, 1885–1936, vol. III

Plimmer, Sir Clifford Ulric, 1905–1988, vol. VIII

Plimmer, Henry George, *died* 1918, vol. II
Plimmer, Robert Henry Aders, 1877–1955, vol. V
Plimsoll, Sir James, 1917–1987, vol. VIII
Plomer, William Charles Franklyn, 1903–1973, vol. VII
Plomer, Col William Harry Percival, 1861–1937, vol. III
Plomley, (Francis) Roy, 1914–1985, vol. VIII
Plomley, Roy; *see* Plomley, F. R.
Plow, Maj.-Gen. Hon. Edward Chester, 1904–1988, vol. VIII
Plowden, Alfred Chichele, 1844–1914, vol. I
Plowden, Brig. Bryan Edward Chicheley, 1892–1965, vol. VI
Plowden, Cecil Ward Chicheley, 1864–1944, vol. IV
Plowden, Lt-Col Charles Terence Chichele, 1883–1956, vol. V
Plowden, Sir Henry Meredyth, 1840–1920, vol. II
Plowden, Rear-Adm. Richard Anthony Aston, *died* 1941, vol. IV
Plowden, Roger Edmund Joseph, 1879–1946, vol. IV
Plowden, Sir Trevor John Chichele C.; *see* Chichele-Plowden.
Plowden, Sir William Chichele, 1832–1915, vol. I
Plowden, William Francis, 1853–1914, vol. I
Plowden-Wardlaw, Rev. James Tait, 1873–1963, vol. VI
Plowman, Sir Claude, 1895–1954, vol. V
Plowman, Clifford Henry Fitzherbert, 1889–1948, vol. IV
Plowman, Sir George Thomas, 1858–1943, vol. IV
Plowman, Mark, (Max Plowman), 1883–1941, vol. IV
Plowman, Max; *see* Plowman, Mark.
Plucknett, Theodore Frank Thomas, 1897–1965, vol. VI
Plugge, Lt-Col Arthur, 1878–1934, vol. III
Plugge, Captain Leonard Frank, 1889–1981, vol. VIII
Plumb, Rt Rev. C. E., 1864–1930, vol. III
Plumbe, William John Conway, 1910–1979, vol. VII
Plume, William Thomas, 1869–1962, vol. VI
Plumer, 1st Viscount, 1857–1932, vol. III
Plumer, 2nd Viscount, 1890–1944, vol. IV
Plumer, Hon. Eleanor Mary, 1885–1967, vol. VI
Plummer, Baroness (Life Peer); Beatrice Plummer, 1903–1972, vol. VII
Plummer, Rev. Alfred, 1841–1926, vol. II
Plummer, Alfred, 1896–1978, vol. VII
Plummer, Rev. Charles, 1851–1927, vol. II
Plummer, Charles Henry Scott, 1859–1948, vol. IV
Plummer, Sir Edgar Stroud, 1873–1940, vol. III
Plummer, Rev. Francis Bowes, 1851–1932, vol. III
Plummer, Henry Crozier, 1875–1946, vol. IV
Plummer, John Archibald Temple, 1877–1943, vol. IV
Plummer, Sir Leslie Arthur, 1901–1963, vol. VI
Plummer, Norman Swift, 1907–1978, vol. VII
Plummer, Sir Walter Richard, 1858–1917, vol. II
Plummer, William Edward, 1849–1928, vol. II
Plumptre, Adelaide M., (Mrs H. P. Plumptre), *died* 1948, vol. IV
Plumptre, Mrs H. P.; *see* Plumptre, A. M.

Plumptre, Reginald Charles Edward, 1848–1929, vol. III
Plumtree, Air Vice-Marshal Eric, 1919–1990, vol. VIII
Plunket, 5th Baron, 1864–1920, vol. II
Plunket, 6th Baron, 1899–1938, vol. III
Plunket, 7th Baron, 1923–1975, vol. VII
Plunket, Hon. and Most Rev. Benjamin J., 1870–1947, vol. IV
Plunket, Hon. Emmeline Mary, 1835–1924, vol. II
Plunkett, Brig.-Gen. Edward Abadie, 1870–1926, vol. II
Plunkett, Rt Hon. Sir Francis Richard, 1835–1907, vol. I
Plunkett, George Noble, Count, 1851–1948, vol. IV
Plunkett, Lt-Col George Tindall, 1842–1922, vol. II
Plunkett, Rt Hon. Sir Horace Curzon, 1854–1932, vol. III
Plunkett, Brig. James Joseph, 1893–1990, vol. VIII
Plunkett-Ernle-Erle-Drax, Adm. Hon. Sir Reginald Aylmer Ranfurly, 1880–1967, vol. VI
Plurenden, Baron (Life Peer); Rudy Sternberg, 1917–1978, vol. VII
Plymen, Francis Joseph, 1879–1960, vol. V
Plymouth, 1st Earl of, 1857–1923, vol. II
Plymouth, 2nd Earl of, 1889–1943, vol. IV
Po, Sir San Crombie, 1870–1946, vol. IV
Poate, Sir Hugh Raymond Guy, 1884–1961, vol. VI
Pobedonosteff, Constantini Petrovitch, 1827–1907, vol. I
Pochin, Sir Edward Eric, 1909–1990, vol. VIII
Pochin, Horace Wilmer, 1903–1961, vol. VI
Pochin, Victor Robert, 1879–1972, vol. VII
Pochkhanawala, Sir Sorabji Nusserwanji, 1881–1937, vol. III
Pockley, Francis Antill, 1857–1941, vol. IV
Pocklington, Geoffrey Richard, 1879–1958, vol. V
Pocklington, Henry Cabourn, 1870–1952, vol. V
Pocock, Carmichael Charles Peter, (Michael Pocock), 1920–1979, vol. VII
Pocock, Sir Charles Guy Coventry, 4th Bt, 1863–1921, vol. II
Pocock, Childe, 1854–1934, vol. III
Pocock, Sir George Francis Coventry, 3rd Bt, 1830–1915, vol. I
Pocock, Guy Noël, 1880–1955, vol. V
Pocock, Col Herbert Innes, 1861–1947, vol. IV
Pocock, Hugh Shellshear, 1894–1987, vol. VIII
Pocock, Michael; *see* Pocock, C. C. P.
Pocock, Most Rev. Philip Francis, 1906–1984, vol. VIII
Pocock, Brig. Philip Frederick, 1871–1941, vol. IV
Pocock, Reginald Innes, 1863–1947, vol. IV
Pocock, Captain Roger, 1865–1941, vol. IV
Pocock, Sir Sidney Job, 1855–1931, vol. III
Pode, Sir (Edward) Julian, 1902–1968, vol. VI
Pode, Sir Julian; *see* Pode, Sir E. J.
Podmore, Edward Boyce, 1860–1928, vol. II
Podmore, Frank, 1856–1910, vol. I
Poe, Adm. Sir Edmund Samuel, 1849–1921, vol. II
Poe, Lt-Col Sir Hutcheson; *see* Poe, Lt-Col Sir W. H.
Poe, Col John, 1873–1941, vol. IV
Poe, Lt-Col Sir (William) Hutcheson, 1st Bt, 1848–1934, vol. III

Poë, Col William Skeffington, 1878–1958, vol. V
Poë Domvile, Sir Hugo Compton Domvile, 2nd Bt, 1889–1959, vol. V
Poel, William, 1852–1934, vol. III
Poett, Maj.-Gen. Joseph Howard, 1858–1929, vol. III
Pogany, Willy, (William Andrew), 1882–1955, vol. V
Poincaré, Jules Henri, 1854–1912, vol. I
Poincaré, Raymond, 1860–1934, vol. III
Pointer, Joseph, 1875–1914, vol. I
Poire, Emmanuel; see D'Ache, Caran.
Poiret, Paul, 1879–1944, vol. IV
Poirier, Hon. Pascal, 1852–1932, vol. III
Polack, Rudolph, 1842–1917, vol. II
Poland, Rear-Adm. Allan, 1888–1984, vol. VIII
Poland, Vice-Adm. Sir Albert Lawrence, 1895–1967, vol. VI
Poland, Sir Harry Bodkin, 1829–1928, vol. II
Poland, Vice-Adm. James Augustus, 1832–1918, vol. II
Poland, John, 1855–1937, vol. III
Poland, Comdr John Roberts, 1893–1961, vol. VI
Polanyi, Michael, 1891–1976, vol. VII
Pole, Alexander Edward, 1848–1909, vol. I
Pole, Sir Cecil Pery Van Notten-, 4th Bt (cr 1791), 1863–1948, vol. IV
Pole, Major David Graham, died 1952, vol. V
Pole, Sir Edmund Reginald Talbot de la, 10th Bt (cr 1628), 1844–1912, vol. I
Pole, Sir Felix John Clewett, 1877–1956, vol. V
Pole, Sir Frederick Arundell de la, 11th Bt (cr 1628), 1850–1926, vol. II
Pole, Brig.-Gen. Harry Anthony C.; see Chandos-Pole.
Pole, William, 1814–1900, vol. I
Pole-Evans, Illtyd Buller, 1879–1968, vol. VI
Poley, Thomas W.; see Weller-Poley.
Polhill, Rev. Arthur Twisleton, died 1935, vol. III
Polignano, 6th Duke of, died 1920, vol. II
Poling, Daniel Alfred, 1884–1968, vol. VI
Polk, Hon. Frank L., 1871–1943, vol. IV
Pollard, Alan Faraday Campbell, 1877–1948, vol. IV
Pollard, Albert Frederick, 1869–1948, vol. IV
Pollard, Captain Alfred Oliver, 1893–1960, vol. V (A), vol. VI (AI)
Pollard, Alfred William, 1859–1944, vol. IV
Pollard, Arthur Tempest, 1854–1934, vol. III
Pollard, Rt Rev. Benjamin, 1890–1967, vol. VI
Pollard, Bilton, 1855–1931, vol. III
Pollard, Lt-Gen. Charles, 1826–1911, vol. I
Pollard, Paymaster Rear-Adm. Sir Charles Fleetwood, 1868–1938, vol. III
Pollard, Sir (Charles) Herbert, 1898–1990, vol. VIII
Pollard, Claude, died 1957, vol. V
Pollaré, Rear-Adm. Edwin John, 1833–1909, vol. I
Pollard, Lt-Col George Chambers, died 1954, vol. V
Pollard, Sir George Herbert, 1864–1937, vol. III
Pollard, Rear-Adm. George Northmore Arthur, 1847–1920, vol. II
Pollard, Graham; see Pollard, H. G.
Pollard, (Henry) Graham, 1903–1976, vol. VII
Pollard, Sir Herbert; see Pollard, Sir C. H.
Pollard, Geoffrey Samuel, 1926–1985, vol. VIII
Pollard, Major Hugh B. C., died 1966, vol. VI

Pollard, Maj.-Gen. James Hawkins-Whitshed, 1866–1942, vol. IV
Pollard, Lt-Gen. Sir Reginald George, 1903–1978, vol. VII
Pollard-Lowsley, Col Herbert de Lisle, 1877–1936, vol. III
Pollard-Urquhart, Lt-Col Francis Edward Romulus, 1848–1915, vol. I
Pollen, Arthur Joseph Hungerford, 1866–1937, vol. III
Pollen, Captain Francis Gabriel Hungerford, 1862–1944, vol. IV
Pollen, Henry Court W.; see Willock-Pollen.
Pollen, John, 1848–1923, vol. II
Pollen, John Hungerford, 1820–1902, vol. I
Pollen, Rev. John Hungerford, 1858–1925, vol. II
Pollen, Sir John Launcelot Hungerford, 6th Bt, 1884–1959, vol. V
Pollen, Sir Richard, 5th Bt, 1878–1930, vol. III
Pollen, Sir Richard Hungerford, 4th Bt, 1846–1918, vol. II
Pollen, Lt-Col Stephen Hungerford, died 1935, vol. III
Pollen, Sir Walter Michael Hungerford, 1894–1968, vol. VI
Polley, Denis William, 1921–1983, vol. VIII
Pollitt, George Paton, 1878–1964, vol. VI
Pollitt, Gerald Paton, 1877–1943, vol. IV
Pollitt, Harry, 1890–1960, vol. V
Pollitt, Col Sir William, 1842–1908, vol. I
Pollitzer, Sir Frank Joseph Coleman, 1869–1944, vol. IV
Pollock, Sir Adrian Donald Wilde, 1867–1943, vol. IV
Pollock, Maj.-Gen. Arthur Jocelyn Coleman, 1891–1968, vol. VI
Pollock, Lt-Col Arthur Williamson Alsager, 1853–1923, vol. II
Pollock, Rt Rev. Bertram, 1863–1943, vol. IV
Pollock, Rev. Charles Archibald Edmund, 1858–1944, vol. IV
Pollock, Hon. Sir Charles Edward, 1823–1897, vol. I
Pollock, Maj.-Gen. Charles Edward, died 1929, vol. III
Pollock, Courtenay Edward Maxwell, died 1943, vol. IV
Pollock, Hon. Surg. Comdr Sir Donald; see Pollock, Hon. Surg. Comdr Sir J. D.
Pollock, Sir Edward James, 1841–1930, vol. III
Pollock, Rt Hon. Sir Frederick, 3rd Bt (cr 1866), 1845–1937, vol. III
Pollock, Sir (Frederick) John, 4th Bt (cr 1866), 1878–1963, vol. VI
Pollock, Sir Frederick Richard, 1827–1899, vol. I
Pollock, George Frederick, 1821–1915, vol. I
Pollock, Sir George Seymour Montagu-, 4th Bt, 1900–1985, vol. VIII
Pollock, Guy Cameron, 1878–1957, vol. V
Pollock, Harry Frederick, 1857–1901, vol. I
Pollock, Henry Brodhurst, 1883–1958, vol. V
Pollock, Hon. Sir Henry Edward, 1864–1953, vol. V
Pollock, Rev. Herbert Charles, 1852–1910, vol. I
Pollock, Rt Hon. Hugh McDowell, 1852–1937, vol. III

Pollock, J. Arthur, *died* 1922, vol. II

Pollock, James Edward, 1819–1910, vol. I

Pollock, James Huey Hamill, 1893–1982, vol. VIII

Pollock, Rev. Jeremy Taylor, 1850–1916, vol. II

Pollock, Sir John; *see* Pollock, Sir F. J.

Pollock, Lt-Col John Alsager, 1882–1941, vol. IV

Pollock, Maj.-Gen. John Archibald Henry, 1856–1949, vol. IV

Pollock, Hon. Surg. Comdr Sir (John) Donald, 1st Bt (*cr* 1939), 1868–1962, vol. VI

Pollock, Sir Montagu Frederick Montagu-, 3rd Bt (*cr* 1872), 1864–1938, vol. III

Pollock, Robert Erskine, 1849–1915, vol. I

Pollock, Sir Ronald Evelyn, 1891–1974, vol. VII

Pollock, Walter Herries, 1850–1926, vol. II

Pollock, William Barr Inglis, 1878–1953, vol. V

Pollock, William Rivers, 1859–1909, vol. I

Pollok Rev. Allan, 1829–1918, vol. II

Pollok, Maj.-Gen. Robert Valentine, 1884–1979, vol. VII

Pollok-M'Call, Brig.-Gen. John Buchanan, 1870–1951, vol. V

Pollok Morris, Col William, 1867–1936, vol. III

Polo de Bernabe, Don Luis, 1854–1929, vol. III

Polson, Cyril John, 1901–1986, vol. VIII

Polson, Milson George, 1917–1977, vol. VII

Polson, Col Sir Thomas Andrew, 1865–1946, vol. IV

Polson, Hon. Sir William John, 1875–1960, vol. V

Poltimore, 2nd Baron, 1837–1908, vol. I

Poltimore, 3rd Baron, 1859–1918, vol. II

Poltimore, 4th Baron, 1882–1965, vol. VI

Poltimore, 5th Baron, 1883–1967, vol. VI

Poltimore, 6th Baron, 1888–1978, vol. VII

Polunin, Oleg, 1914–1985, vol. VIII

Polwarth, 8th (styled 6th) Lord, 1838–1920, vol. II

Polwarth, 9th Lord, 1864–1944, vol. IV

Polwarth, Master of; Hon. Walter Thomas Hepburne-Scott, 1890–1942, vol. IV

Polybe, *see* Reinach, Joseph.

Pomare, Hon. Sir Maui, 1876–1930, vol. III

Pomeroy, F. W., *died* 1924, vol. II

Pomfret, Surgeon Rear-Adm. Arnold Ashworth, 1900–1984, vol. VIII

Pompidou, Georges Jean Raymond, 1911–1974, vol. VII

Ponce, Don Ignacio G.; *see* Gutierrez-Ponce.

Poncet, André F.; *see* François-Poncet.

Pond, Sir Desmond Arthur, 1919–1986, vol. VIII

Pond, James Burton, 1838–1903, vol. I

Poniatowski, Prince Louis Leopold Charles Marie André, 1864–1954, vol. V

Pons, Lily, 1898–1976, vol. VII

Ponsford, Brian David, 1938–1989, vol. VIII

Ponsonby of Shulbrede, 1st Baron, 1871–1946, vol. IV

Ponsonby of Shulbrede, 2nd Baron, 1904–1976, vol. VII

Ponsonby of Shulbrede, 3rd Baron, 1930–1990, vol. VIII

Ponsonby, Arthur Gordon, 1892–1978, vol. VII

Ponsonby, Hon. Bertie Brabazon, 1885–1967, vol. VI

Ponsonby, Col Sir Charles Edward, 1st Bt, 1879–1976, vol. VII

Ponsonby, Hon. Cyril Myles Brabazon, 1881–1915, vol. I

Ponsonby, Hon. Edwin Charles William, 1851–1939, vol. III

Ponsonby, Sir George Arthur, 1878–1969, vol. VI

Ponsonby, Hon. Gerald, 1829–1908, vol. I

Ponsonby, Rev. Gordon; *see* Ponsonby, Rev. S. G.

Ponsonby, Brig. Henry Chambré, 1883–1953, vol. V

Ponsonby, Maj.-Gen. Sir John, 1866–1952, vol. V

Ponsonby, Col Justinian Gordon, *died* 1929, vol. III

Ponsonby, Rev. Maurice George Jesser, 1880–1943, vol. IV

Ponsonby, Noel Edward, 1891–1928, vol. II

Ponsonby, Rev. (Stewart) Gordon, *died* 1938, vol. III

Ponsonby, Thomas Brabazon, *died* 1946, vol. IV

Ponsonby, Captain William Rundall, 1874–1919, vol. II

Ponsonby-Fane, Rt Hon. Sir Spencer Cecil Brabazon, 1824–1915, vol. I

Pontifex, Sir Charles, 1831–1912, vol. I

Ponting, Herbert George, *died* 1935, vol. III

Ponting, Brig. Theophilus John, 1886–1972, vol. VII

Pontoppidan, Henrik, 1857–1943, vol. IV

Pontypridd, 1st Baron, 1840–1927, vol. II

Pool, Arthur George, 1905–1963, vol. VI

Pool, Augustus Frank, 1872–1955, vol. V

Pool, Bernard Frank, 1896–1977, vol. VII

Pool, William Arthur, 1889–1969, vol. VI

Poole, Brig.-Gen. Arthur James, 1872–1956, vol. V

Poole, Austin Lane, 1889–1963, vol. VI

Poole, Major Cecil Charles, 1902–1956, vol. V

Poole, Charles Edward L.; *see* Lane Poole.

Poole, Edgar Girard Croker, 1891–1940, vol. III

Poole, Ernest, 1880–1950, vol. IV (A), vol. V

Poole, Rev. Frederic John, 1852–1923, vol. II

Poole, Maj.-Gen. Sir Frederick Cuthbert, 1869–1936, vol. III

Poole, Lt-Gen. Gerald Robert, 1868–1937, vol. III

Poole, Granville, 1885–1962, vol. VI

Poole, Henry, 1873–1928, vol. II

Poole, Brig. Ivan Maxwell Conway, 1878–1963, vol. VI

Poole, Sir James, 1827–1903, vol. I

Poole, John Hewitt Jellett, 1893–1976, vol. VII

Poole, Rev. Canon Joseph Weston, 1909–1989, vol. VIII

Poole, Maj.-Gen. Leopold Thomas, 1888–1965, vol. VI

Poole, Sir Lionel Pinnock, 1894–1967, vol. VI

Poole, Reginald Lane, 1857–1939, vol. III

Poole, Sir Reginald Ward Edward Lane, 1864–1941, vol. IV

Poole, Vice-Adm. Sir Richard Hayden Owen L.; *see* Lane-Poole.

Poole, Stanley L.; *see* Lane-Poole.

Poole, Lt-Col Sir Thomas G., 1859–1937, vol. III

Poole, Hon. Thomas Slaney, 1873–1927, vol. II

Poole, Maj.-Gen. William Henry Evered, 1902–1969, vol. VI

Poole, Wordsworth, 1868–1902, vol. I

Poole Hughes, Rt Rev. John Richard Worthington, 1916–1988, vol. VIII

Poole-Hughes, Rev. W. Worthington, 1865–1928, vol. II

Pooler, Ven. Lewis Arthur, 1858–1924, vol. II

Pooley, Charles Blois, 1881–1938, vol. III

Pooley, Sir Ernest Henry, 1st Bt, 1876–1966, vol. VI
Poore, Dennis; *see* Poore, R. D.
Poore, Sir Edward, 5th Bt, 1894–1938, vol. III
Poore, Maj.-Gen. Francis Harwood, 1841–1928, vol. II
Poore, George Vivian, 1843–1904, vol. I
Poore, Adm. Sir Richard, 4th Bt, 1853–1930, vol. III
Poore, Brig.-Gen. Robert Montagu, 1866–1938, vol. III
Poore, Major Roger Alvin, 1870–1917, vol. II
Poore, Roger Dennistoun, (Dennis), 1916–1987, vol. VIII
Pope, Col Albert Augustus, 1843–1909, vol. I
Pope, Alfred, 1842–1934, vol. III
Pope, Arthur Upham, 1881–1969, vol. VI
Pope, Arthur William Uglow, 1858–1927, vol. II
Pope, Sir Barton; *see* Pope, Sir S. B.
Pope, Lt-Col Edward Alexander, 1875–1919, vol. II
Pope, Frank Aubrey, 1893–1962, vol. VI
Pope, Sir George Reginald, 1902–1982, vol. VIII
Pope, Rev. George Uglow, 1820–1908, vol. I
Pope, Col Harold, 1873–1938, vol. III
Pope, Rev. Henry John, 1836–1912, vol. I
Pope, Rev. Hugh, 1869–1946, vol. IV
Pope, James Alister, 1883–1954, vol. V
Pope, Jessie, (Mrs Babington Lenton), *died* 1941, vol. IV
Pope, Rev. (John) Russell, 1909–1985, vol. VIII
Pope, John van Someren, 1850–1932, vol. III
Pope, Sir Joseph, 1854–1926, vol. II
Pope, Lt-Gen. Maurice Arthur, 1889–1978, vol. VII
Pope, Mildred Katherine, 1872–1956, vol. V
Pope, Col Philip Edward, 1842–1916, vol. II
Pope, Rev. Richard William Massy, 1849–1923, vol. II
Pope, Brig. Ronald James, 1924–1976, vol. VII
Pope, Rev. Russell; *see* Pope, Rev. J. R.
Pope, Samuel, 1826–1901, vol. I
Pope, Samuel, *died* 1935, vol. III
Pope, Sir (Sidney) Barton, 1905–1983, vol. VIII
Pope, Maj.-Gen. Sydney Buxton, 1879–1955, vol. V
Pope, Thomas Michael, 1875–1930, vol. III
Pope, Maj.-Gen. Vyvyan Vavasour, 1891–1941, vol. IV
Pope, Walter James M.; *see* Macqueen-Pope.
Pope, Sir William Jackson, 1870–1939, vol. III
Pope, Lt-Col William Wippell, 1857–1926, vol. II
Pope, Wilson, 1866–1953, vol. V
Pope-Hennessy, James, 1916–1974, vol. VII
Pope-Hennessy, Maj.-Gen. Ladislaus Herbert Richard, 1875–1942, vol. IV
Pope-Hennessy, Dame Una, *died* 1949, vol. IV
Popham, Arthur Ewart, 1889–1970, vol. VI
Popham, Francis William L.; *see* Leyborne-Popham.
Popham, Sir Henry Bradshaw, 1881–1947, vol. IV
Popham, Air Chief Marshal Sir (Henry) Robert (Moore) Brooke-, 1878–1953, vol. V
Popham, Margaret Evelyn, 1894–1982, vol. VIII
Popham, Air Chief Marshal Sir Robert Brooke-; *see* Popham, Air Chief Marshal Sir H. R. M. B.
Popham, Col Robert Stewart, 1876–1949, vol. IV
Popkess, Captain Athelstan, 1893–1967, vol. VI
Popplewell, Baron (Life Peer); Ernest Popplewell, 1899–1977, vol. VII

Popplewell, Patrick John Lyon, 1937–1983, vol. VIII
Porbandar, HH Maharaja of, 1901–1982, vol. VIII
Porcelli, Col Baron Alfred, 1849–1937, vol. III
Porcelli, Lt-Col Baron Ernest George Macdonald di S Andrea, 1886–1965, vol. VI
Porch, Col Edward Albert, 1879–1937, vol. III
Porges, Waldo William, 1899–1976, vol. VII
Porral, Albert, 1846–1918, vol. II
Porritt, Arthur, 1872–1947, vol. IV
Porritt, Lt-Col Austin Townsend, 1875–1956, vol. V
Porritt, Benjamin Dawson, 1884–1940, vol. III
Porritt, Edward, 1860–1921, vol. II
Porritt, Captain Richard W., 1910–1940, vol. III
Portal, 1st Viscount, 1885–1949, vol. IV
Portal of Hungerford, 1st Viscount, 1893–1971, vol. VII
Portal of Hungerford, Baroness (2nd in line), 1923–1990, vol. VIII
Portal, Brig.-Gen. Sir Bertram Percy, 1866–1949, vol. IV
Portal, Sir Francis Spencer, 5th Bt, 1903–1984, vol. VIII
Portal, Melville, 1819–1904, vol. I
Portal, Adm. Sir Reginald Henry, 1894–1983, vol. VIII
Portal, Sir Spencer John, 4th Bt, 1864–1955, vol. V
Portal, Sir William Wyndham, 2nd Bt, 1850–1931, vol. III
Portal, Sir Wyndham Spencer, 1st Bt, 1822–1905, vol. I
Portarlington, 5th Earl of, 1858–1900, vol. I
Portarlington, 6th Earl of, 1883–1959, vol. V
Portelli, Rt Rev. Angelo, *born* 1852, vol. II
Porteous, Alexander, 1855–1932, vol. III
Porteous, Alexander James Dow, 1896–1981, vol. VIII
Porteous, Col Charles Arkcoll, 1839–1929, vol. III
Porteous, Douglas Archibald, 1891–1974, vol. VII
Porteous, Lt-Col John James, 1857–1948, vol. IV
Porteous, Norman, 1881–1940, vol. III
Porter, Baron (Life Peer); Samuel Lowry Porter, 1877–1956, vol. V
Porter, Surg.-Col Alexander, 1841–1918, vol. II
Porter, Sir Alexander, 1853–1926, vol. II
Porter, Sir Alfred de Bock, 1840–1908, vol. I
Porter, Alfred Ernest, 1896–1987, vol. VIII
Porter, Rev. Alfred Stephenson, 1841–1914, vol. I
Porter, Alfred William, 1863–1939, vol. III
Porter, Rt Hon. Sir Andrew Marshall, 1st Bt (*cr* 1902), 1837–1919, vol. II
Porter, Annie, (Mrs H. B. Fantham), *died* 1963, vol. VI
Porter, Cecil George, 1887–1938, vol. III
Porter, Air Vice-Marshal Cedric Ernest Victor, 1893–1975, vol. VII
Porter, Charles, 1873–1952, vol. V
Porter, Rev. Charles Fleetwood, 1830–1914, vol. I
Porter, Cole, 1893–1964, vol. VI
Porter, Brig.-Gen. Cyril Lachlan, 1872–1951, vol. V
Porter, Edward, 1880–1960, vol. V
Porter, Edward Guss, 1859–1929, vol. III
Porter, Frederick, 1871–1949, vol. IV (A)
Porter, Gene Stratton-, 1868–1924, vol. II
Porter, Col Geoffrey M., 1854–1944, vol. IV

Porter, George, 1884–1973, vol. VII
Porter, Sir George Swinburne, 3rd Bt (*cr* 1889), 1908–1974, vol. VII
Porter, Sir Haldane; *see* Porter, Sir W. H.
Porter, Harold, 1879–1938, vol. III
Porter, Sir Harry Edwin Bruce B.; *see* Bruce-Porter.
Porter, Helen Kemp, 1899–1987, vol. VIII
Porter, Major Herbert Alfred, 1872–1939, vol. III (A), vol. IV
Porter, Rev. James, *died* 1900, vol. I
Porter, Sir James, *died* 1935, vol. III
Porter, John, 1838–1922, vol. II
Porter, John Bonsall, 1861–1944, vol. IV
Porter, Maj.-Gen. John Edmund L.; *see* Leech-Porter.
Porter, John Fletcher, 1873–1927, vol. II
Porter, Captain John Grey Archdale, 1886–1917, vol. II
Porter, John Porter, 1855–1939, vol. III
Porter, Sir John Scott Horsbrugh-, 2nd Bt (*cr* 1902), 1871–1953, vol. V
Porter, Joseph William Geoffrey, 1920–1983, vol. VIII
Porter, Katherine Anne, 1890–1980, vol. VII
Porter, Keith Ridley Douglas, 1913–1977, vol. VII
Porter, Sir Leslie Alexander Selim, 1854–1932, vol. III
Porter, Sir Ludovic Charles, 1869–1928, vol. II
Porter, Sir Neale, *died* 1905, vol. I
Porter, Raymond Alfred James, 1896–1988, vol. VIII
Porter, Major Reginald Whitworth, *died* 1902, vol. I
Porter, Maj.-Gen. Sir Robert, 1858–1928, vol. II
Porter, Sir Robert Evelyn, 1913–1983, vol. VIII
Porter, Robert P., 1852–1917, vol. II
Porter, Rev. Robert Waltham, *died* 1927, vol. II
Porter, Rodney Robert, 1917–1985, vol. VIII
Porter, Rose Henniker, (Mrs Adrian Porter); *see* Heaton, R. H.
Porter, Rt Hon. Samuel Clarke, 1875–1956, vol. V
Porter, Brig.-Gen. Thomas Cole, 1851–1938, vol. III
Porter, Thomas Cunningham, 1860–1933, vol. III
Porter, Col Thomas William, 1844–1920, vol. II
Porter, Sir (William) Haldane, 1867–1944, vol. IV
Porter, Sir William Henry, 2nd Bt (*cr* 1889), 1862–1935, vol. III
Porter, William Ninnis, *died* 1929, vol. III
Porter, William Smith, 1855–1927, vol. II
Porter, Hon. William Thomas, 1877–1928, vol. II
Porter Goff, Eric Noel; *see* Goff.
Porter-Phillips, John George, *died* 1946, vol. IV
Porteus, Rev. Canon Thomas Cruddas, 1876–1948, vol. IV
Portland, 6th Duke of, 1857–1943, vol. IV
Portland, 7th Duke of, 1893–1977, vol. VII
Portland, 8th Duke of, 1888–1980, vol. VII
Portland, 9th Duke of, 1897–1990, vol. VIII
Portlock, Rear-Adm. Ronald Etridge, 1908–1983, vol. VIII
Portman, 2nd Viscount, 1829–1919, vol. II
Portman, 3rd Viscount, 1860–1923, vol. II
Portman, 4th Viscount, 1864–1929, vol. III
Portman, 5th Viscount, 1898–1942, vol. IV
Portman, 6th Viscount, 1868–1946, vol. IV
Portman, 7th Viscount, 1875–1948, vol. IV

Portman, 8th Viscount, 1903–1967, vol. VI
Portman, Hon. Edward William Berkeley, 1856–1911, vol. I
Portman, Hon. Edwin Berkeley, 1830–1921, vol. II
Portman, Eric, 1903–1969, vol. VI
Portman, Guy Maurice Berkeley, 1890–1961, vol. VI
Portman-Dalton, Seymour Berkeley, 1838–1912, vol. I
Porto-Riche, Georges de, 1849–1930, vol. III
Portsea, 1st Baron, 1860–1948, vol. IV
Portsmouth, 6th Earl of, 1856–1917, vol. II
Portsmouth, 7th Earl of, 1859–1925, vol. II
Portsmouth, 8th Earl of, 1861–1943, vol. IV
Portsmouth, 9th Earl of, 1898–1984, vol. VIII
Portsmouth, Percy, 1874–1953, vol. V
Portway, Col Donald, 1887–1979, vol. VII
Poskitt, Frederick Richard, 1900–1983, vol. VIII
Poskitt, Rt Rev. Henry John, 1888–1950, vol. IV
Post, Emily, (Mrs Price Post), *died* 1960, vol. V
Post, Mrs Price; *see* Post, Emily.
Post, Rear-Adm. Simon Edward, 1910–1965, vol. VI
Postan, Sir Michael Moïssey, 1899–1981, vol. VIII
Postgate, John Percival, 1853–1926, vol. II
Postgate, Raymond William, 1896–1971, vol. VII
Postill, Ronald, 1907–1980, vol. VII
Postlethwaite, John Rutherfoord Parkin, 1883–1956, vol. V
Potez, Andrew Louis, 1920–1977, vol. VII
Po Tha, Sir Maung, *died* 1933, vol. III
Pothecary, Major Walter Frank, 1882–1958, vol. V
Potier, Gilbert George, 1915–1969, vol. VI
Pott, Anthony Percivall, 1904–1963, vol. VI
Pott, Col Douglas, 1888–1974, vol. VII
Pott, Francis Lister Hawks, 1864–1947, vol. IV
Pott, Sir (George) Stanley, 1870–1951, vol. V
Pott, Gladys Sydney, 1867–1961, vol. VI
Pott, H(enry) Percivall, 1908–1964, vol. VI
Pott, Rear-Adm. Herbert, 1886–1945, vol. IV
Pott, Sir Leslie, 1903–1985, vol. VIII
Pott, Sir Stanley; *see* Pott, Sir G. S.
Potter, Sir Alan Graeme, 1891–1969, vol. VI
Potter, Albert Knight, 1864–1948, vol. IV
Potter, Beatrice; *see* Webb, Mrs Sidney.
Potter, Ven. Beresford, 1853–1931, vol. III
Potter, Carlyle Thornton, *died* 1962, vol. VI
Potter, Lt-Col Claud Furniss, 1881–1965, vol. VI
Potter, Col Colin Kynaston, 1877–1964, vol. VI
Potter, Cora Urquhart, *died* 1936, vol. III
Potter, Cyril H., 1877–1941, vol. IV
Potter, David Morris, 1910–1971, vol. VII
Potter, Douglas Charles Loftus, 1903–1983, vol. VIII
Potter, Frank, 1856–1919, vol. II
Potter, Frederick Felix, 1882–1955, vol. V
Potter, George Richard, 1900–1981, vol. VIII
Potter, Harold, 1896–1951, vol. V
Potter, Rt Rev. Henry Codman, 1834–1908, vol. I
Potter, Sir Henry Steven, 1904–1976, vol. VII
Potter, Brig.-Gen. Herbert Cecil, 1875–1964, vol. VI
Potter, Howard Vincent, 1888–1970, vol. VI (AII)
Potter, Mrs J. Brown; *see* Potter, Cora Urquhart.
Potter, Lt-Col James Archer, 1875–1962, vol. VI
Potter, John, 1873–1940, vol. III
Potter, John Alexander, 1851–1929, vol. III
Potter, Rev. John Hasloch, 1847–1935, vol. III

Potter, Marian Anderson, (Mary), 1900–1981, vol. VIII

Potter, Mrs Mary; *see* Potter, Marian A.

Potter, Rev. Michael Cressé, 1858–1948, vol. IV

Potter, Air Marshal Sir Patrick Brunton L.; *see* Lee Potter.

Potter, Rev. Reginald Joseph William Henry, 1877–1941, vol. IV

Potter, Ven. Richard Harry, 1861–1931, vol. III

Potter, Rupert Barnadiston, 1899–1970, vol. VI

Potter, Simeon, 1898–1976, vol. VII

Potter, Stephen, 1900–1969, vol. VI

Potter, Thomas Bayley, 1817–1898, vol. I

Potter, Col William Allen, *died* 1953, vol. V

Pottinger, Lt-Gen. Brabazon Henry, 1840–1913, vol. I

Pottinger, David, 1843–1938, vol. III

Pottinger, Don; *see* Pottinger, J. I. D.

Pottinger, Lt-Col Eldred Thomas, 1840–1905, vol. I

Pottinger, Sir Henry, 3rd Bt, 1834–1909, vol. I

Pottinger, John Inglis Drever, (Don Pottinger), 1919–1986, vol. VIII

Pottinger, Lt-Col Robert Southey, 1870–1943, vol. IV

Pottle, Frederick Albert, 1897–1987, vol. VIII

Potts, Lt-Col Edmund Thurlow, 1878–1948, vol. IV

Potts, Edward Logan Johnston, 1915–1984, vol. VIII

Potts, Brig.-Gen. Frederick, 1866–1945, vol. IV

Potts, George, 1877–1948, vol. IV

Potts, John, *died* 1938, vol. III

Potts, Kenneth Hampson, 1921–1990, vol. VIII

Potts, William Alexander, 1866–1939, vol. III

Pouishnoff, Leff, 1891–1959, vol. V

Poulenc, Francis, 1899–1963, vol. VI

Poulett, 6th Earl, 1827–1899, vol. I

Poulett, 7th Earl, 1883–1918, vol. II

Poulett, 8th Earl, 1909–1973, vol. VII

Pouliot, Joseph Camille, 1865–1935, vol. III

Poultney, Alfred Henry, *died* 1906, vol. I

Poulton, Lt-Col Arthur Faulconer, 1858–1935, vol. III

Poulton, Sir Edward Bagnall, 1856–1943, vol. IV

Poulton, Edward Lawrence, 1865–1937, vol. III

Poulton, Edward Palmer, 1883–1939, vol. III

Poulton, Elgan Nathaniel George, 1881–1944, vol. IV

Poulton, Lt-Col Henry Mortimer, 1898–1973, vol. VII

Poulton, Rev. Canon John Frederick, 1925–1987, vol. VIII

Pouncey, Philip Michael Rivers, 1910–1990, vol. VIII

Pound, Admiral of the Fleet Sir (Alfred) Dudley (Pickman Rogers), 1877–1943, vol. IV

Pound, Sir Allen Leslie, 3rd Bt, 1888–1952, vol. V

Pound, Sir Derek Allen, 4th Bt, 1920–1980, vol. VII

Pound, Admiral of the Fleet Sir Dudley; *see* Pound, Admiral of the Fleet Sir A. D. P. R.

Pound, Ezra Weston Loomis, 1885–1972, vol. VII

Pound, Sir John, 1st Bt, 1829–1915, vol. I

Pound, Sir (John) Lulham, 2nd Bt, 1862–1937, vol. III

Pound, Sir Lulham; *see* Pound, Sir J. L.

Pound, Roscoe, 1870–1964, vol. VI

Pounds, Charles Courtice, 1862–1927, vol. II

Pounsett, Clement Aubrey, 1900–1968, vol. VI

Pountney, Arthur Meek, 1873–1940, vol. III

Povah, Rev. John Walter, 1883–1961, vol. VI

Powel, Thomas, 1845–1922, vol. II

Powell, Agnes B.; *see* Baden-Powell.

Powell, Alan Richard, 1894–1975, vol. VII

Powell, Sir Allan; *see* Powell, Sir G. A.

Powell, Rev. Canon Arnold Cecil, 1882–1963, vol. VI

Powell, Arthur, 1864–1926, vol. II

Powell, Arthur, 1853–1930, vol. III

Powell, Arthur Geoffrey, 1915–1982, vol. VIII

Powell, Rev. Astell Drayner, 1851–1934, vol. III

Powell, Col Atherton Ffolliott, 1858–1941, vol. IV

Powell, Major Baden Fletcher Smyth B.; *see* Baden-Powell.

Powell, Baden Henry B.; *see* Baden-Powell.

Powell, Cecil Frank, 1903–1969, vol. VI

Powell, Maj.-Gen. Sir Charles Herbert, 1857–1943, vol. IV

Powell, Ven. Dacre Hamilton, 1843–1912, vol. I

Powell, Lt-Col David Watson, 1878–1935, vol. III

Powell, Brig. Donald, 1896–1942, vol. IV

Powell, Lt-Col Sir Douglas, 2nd Bt (*cr* 1897), 1874–1932, vol. III

Powell, E. Alexander, 1879–1957, vol. V

Powell, Rt Rev. Edmund Nathanael, 1859–1928, vol. II

Powell, Edward, 1907–1982, vol. VIII

Powell, Brig.-Gen. Edward Weyland Martin, 1869–1954, vol. V

Powell, Ellis Thomas, 1869–1922, vol. II

Powell, Lt-Col Evelyn George Harcourt, 1883–1961, vol. VI

Powell, Sir Francis, 1833–1914, vol. I

Powell, Adm. Sir Francis, 1849–1927, vol. II

Powell, Francis Edward, *died* 1938, vol. III

Powell, Sir Francis Sharp, 1st Bt (*cr* 1892), 1827–1911, vol. I

Powell, Frank John, 1891–1971, vol. VII

Powell, Frank Smyth B.; *see* Baden-Powell.

Powell, Frederick York, 1850–1904, vol. I

Powell, Sir (George) Allan, *died* 1948, vol. IV

Powell, Vice-Adm. George Bingham, 1871–1952, vol. V

Powell, George Herbert, 1856–1924, vol. II

Powell, Sir George Smyth B.; *see* Baden-Powell.

Powell, Gillian Margot, 1934–1989, vol. VIII

Powell, Rt Rev. Grandage Edwards, 1882–1948, vol. IV

Powell, Helena Langhorne, 1862–1942, vol. IV

Powell, Henry Arthur, 1868–1944, vol. IV

Powell, Col Henry Lloyd, 1866–1941, vol. IV

Powell, Rear-Adm. James, 1887–1971, vol. VII

Powell, Col James Leslie Grove, 1853–1925, vol. II

Powell, Col John, 1876–1936, vol. III

Powell, Lt-Col John, 1856–1938, vol. III

Powell, Gp-Captain John Alexander, 1909–1944, vol. IV

Powell, Rt Hon. John Blake, *died* 1923, vol. II

Powell, Lawrence Fitzroy, 1881–1975, vol. VII

Powell, Sir Leonard; *see* Powell, Sir R. L.

Powell, Llewelyn, 1870–1934, vol. III

Powell, Michael Latham, 1905–1990, vol. VIII

Powell, Rev. Morgan Jones, 1863–1947, vol. IV

Powell, Dame Muriel, 1914–1978, vol. VII

Powell, Percival Herbert, *died* 1958, vol. V
Powell, Lt-Col Philip Lionel William, 1882–1959, vol. V
Powell, Raphael, 1904–1965, vol. VI
Powell, Ray Edwin, 1887–1973, vol. VII
Powell, Richard, 1889–1961, vol. VI
Powell, Richard Albert Brakell, 1892–1957, vol. V
Powell, Sir Richard Douglas, 1st Bt (*cr* 1897), 1842–1925, vol. II
Powell, Major Sir Richard George Douglas, 3rd Bt (*cr* 1897), 1909–1980, vol. VII
Powell, Sir (Robert) Leonard, 1853–1938, vol. III
Powell, Roger, 1896–1990, vol. VIII
Powell, Ronald Arthur, 1888–1966, vol. VI
Powell, Samuel M.; *see* Morgan-Powell.
Powell, Sidney, 1894–1964, vol. VI
Powell, Maj.-Gen. Sidney Henry, 1866–1945, vol. IV
Powell, Warington B.; *see* Baden-Powell.
Powell, Lt-Col William Bowen, 1868–1940, vol. III
Powell, Rev. William Hawkshaw, 1842–1930, vol. III
Powell, Col William Jackson, 1881–1961, vol. VI
Powell-Cotton, Percy Horace Gordon, 1866–1940, vol. III
Powell-Price, John Cadwgan, 1888–1964, vol. VI
Power, Sir Adam Clayton, 6th Bt (*cr* 1836), 1844–1903, vol. I
Power, Albert G., 1883–1945, vol. IV
Power, Admiral of the Fleet Sir Arthur John, 1889–1960, vol. V
Power, Vice-Adm. Sir Arthur Mackenzie, 1921–1984, vol. VIII
Power, Beryl Millicent le Poer, 1891–1974, vol. VII
Power, Charles Gavan, 1888–1968, vol. VI
Power, Sir D'Arcy, 1855–1941, vol. IV
Power, Air Vice-Marshal d'Arcy, 1889–1958, vol. V
Power, Eileen, 1889–1940, vol. III
Power, Sir Elliott Derrick le Poer, 5th Bt (*cr* 1836), 1872–1902, vol. I
Power, Sir George, 7th Bt (*cr* 1836), 1846–1928, vol. II
Power, Ven. George Edmund, *died* 1950, vol. IV (A), vol. V
Power, Gerald, 1891–1967, vol. VI
Power, Lt-Col Gervase Bushe, 1883–1974, vol. VII
Power, Harold Septimus, *died* 1951, vol. V
Power, Henry, *died* 1911, vol. I
Power, Hubert, *born* 1860, vol. II
Power, Sir Ivan McLannahan Cecil, 2nd Bt (*cr* 1924), 1903–1954, vol. V
Power, Sir James Douglas Talbot, 4th Bt (*cr* 1841), 1884–1914, vol. I
Power, Sir James Talbot, 5th Bt (*cr* 1841), 1851–1916, vol. II
Power, Sir John Cecil, 1st Bt (*cr* 1924), 1870–1950, vol. IV
Power, John Danvers, 1858–1927, vol. II
Power, Sir John Elliott Cecil, 4th Bt (*cr* 1836), 1870–1900, vol. I
Power, Sir John Patrick McLannahan, 3rd Bt, (*cr* 1924), 1928–1984, vol. VIII
Power, Sir John Talbot, 3rd Bt (*cr* 1841), 1845–1901, vol. I
Power, Mrs (John) Wyse, *died* 1941, vol. IV
Power, Adm. Sir Laurence Eliot, 1864–1927, vol. II

Power, Hon. Lawrence Geoffrey, 1841–1921, vol. II
Power, Adm. Sir Manley Laurence, 1904–1981, vol. VIII
Power, Rev. Patrick, 1862–1951, vol. V
Power, Patrick Joseph, 1850–1913, vol. I
Power, Patrick Joseph Mahon, 1826–1913, vol. I
Power, Sir Samuel Murray, 1863–1933, vol. III
Power, Gen. Thomas Sarsfield, 1905–1970, vol. VI
Power, Sir Thomas Talbot, 6th Bt (*cr* 1841), 1863–1930, vol. III
Power, William, 1873–1951, vol. V
Power, Sir William Henry, 1842–1916, vol. II
Power, Sir William Richard, 1861–1945, vol. IV
Power, Major William Sayer, 1859–1940, vol. III
Power, Mrs Wyse; *see* Power, Mrs John W.
Powers, Hon. Sir Charles, 1853–1939, vol. III
Powers, George Wightman, 1864–1932, vol. III
Powerscourt, 7th Viscount, 1836–1904, vol. I
Powerscourt, 8th Viscount, 1880–1947, vol. IV
Powerscourt, 9th Viscount, 1905–1973, vol. VII
Powicke, Frederick James, 1854–1935, vol. III
Powicke, Sir (Frederick) Maurice, 1879–1963, vol. VI
Powicke, Sir Maurice; *see* Powicke, Sir F. M.
Powis, 4th Earl of, 1862–1952, vol. V
Powis, 5th Earl of, 1889–1974, vol. VII
Powis, 6th Earl of, 1904–1988, vol. VIII
Powles, Col (Charles) Guy, 1872–1951, vol. V
Powles, Col Guy; *see* Powles, Col C. G.
Powles, Lewis Charles, 1860–1942, vol. IV
Powlett, Adm. Armund Temple, 1841–1925, vol. II
Powlett, Vice-Adm. Frederick Armand, 1873–1963, vol. VI
Powlett, Col Percy William, 1837–1910, vol. I
Powlett, Vice-Adm. Sir Peveril Barton Reibey Wallop W.; *see* William-Powlett.
Powley, Albert E., 1868–1937, vol. III
Powley, Edward B., 1887–1968, vol. VI
Pownall, Lt-Col Sir Assheton, 1877–1953, vol. V
Pownall, Adm. Charles Pipon B.; *see* Beaty-Pownall.
Pownall, George Henry, 1850–1916, vol. II
Pownall, Lt-Gen. Sir Henry Royds, 1887–1961, vol. VI
Pownall, John Cecil Glossop, 1891–1967, vol. VI
Pownall, Mary, *died* 1937, vol. III
Powter, John, 1881–1930, vol. III
Powys, Albert Reginad, 1881–1936, vol. III
Powys, John Cowper, 1872–1963, vol. VI
Powys, Llewelyn, 1884–1939, vol. III
Powys, Theodore Francis, *died* 1953, vol. V
Powys-Jones, Lionel, 1894–1966, vol. VI
Powys-Keck, Thomas Charles Leycester, 1871–1931, vol. III
Poy; *see* Fearon, Percy Hutton.
Poynder, Lt-Col Frederic Sinclair, 1893–1943, vol. IV
Poynter, Sir Ambrose Macdonald, 2nd Bt, 1867–1923, vol. II
Poynter, Sir Edward John, 1st Bt, 1836–1919, vol. II
Poynter, (Frederick) Noel (Lawrence), 1908–1979, vol. VII
Poynter, Sir Hugh Edward, 3rd Bt, 1882–1968, vol. VI
Poynter, Noel; *see* Poynter, F. N. L.
Poynting, John Henry, 1852–1914, vol. I
Poynton, Hon. Alexander, 1853–1935, vol. III

Poynton, Arthur Blackburne, 1867–1944, vol. IV
Poynton, Frederic John, 1869–1943, vol. IV
Poyntz, Rev. Newdigate, 1842–1931, vol. III
Poyser, Sir (Arthur Hampden) Ronald (Wastell), 1884–1957, vol. V
Poyser, Arthur Horatio, 1849–1923, vol. II
Poyser, Sir Kenneth Elliston, *died* 1943, vol. IV
Poyser, Col Richard, 1842–1919, vol. II
Poyser, Sir Ronald; *see* Poyser, Sir A. H. R. W.
Pozzi, Jean Samuel, 1849–1918, vol. II
Pozzoni, Mgr Dominico, 1861–1924, vol. II
Pradhan, Sir Govindrao Balwantrao, 1874–1943, vol. IV
Praed, Sir Herbert Bulkley Mackworth-, 1st Bt, 1841–1921, vol. II
Praed, Rosa Caroline Mackworth, 1851–1935, vol. III
Praeger, Robert Lloyd, 1865–1953, vol. V
Praeger, S. Rosamond, *died* 1954, vol. V
Praga, Alfred, *died* 1949, vol. IV
Pragnell, Sir George, 1863–1916, vol. II
Pragnell, Col Thomas Wykeham, 1883–1957, vol. V
Prain, Alexander Moncur, 1908–1989, vol. VIII
Prain, Lt-Col Sir David, 1857–1944, vol. IV
Prain, John Murray, 1902–1985, vol. VIII
Prain, Vyvyen Alice, 1895–1983, vol. VIII
Prance, Basil Camden, 1884–1948, vol. IV
Prance, Brig. Robert Courtenay, 1882–1966, vol. VI
Prang, Louis, 1824–1909, vol. I
Prasad, Ganesh, 1876–1935, vol. III
Prasad, Jagat, 1879–1957, vol. V
Prasad, Sir Jwala, 1875–1933, vol. III
Prasad, Rajendra, 1884–1963, vol. VI
Prater, Stanley Henry, 1890–1960, vol. V
Pratt, Col (Arthur) Spencer, 1855–1933, vol. III
Pratt, Sir Bernard; *see* Pratt, Sir E. B.
Pratt, Rear-Adm. Charles Bernard, 1907–1973, vol. VII
Pratt, David Doig, 1894–1962, vol. VI
Pratt, Maj.-Gen. Douglas Henry, 1892–1958, vol. V
Pratt, Sir (E.) Bernard, 1889–1975, vol. VII
Pratt, Edward Millard, 1865–1949, vol. IV
Pratt, Edward Roger Murray, 1847–1921, vol. II
Pratt, Edwin John, 1883–1964, vol. VI
Pratt, Brig.-Gen. (Ernest) St George, 1863–1918, vol. II
Pratt, Col Fendall William Harvey, 1892–1960, vol. V
Pratt, Rev. Canon Francis William, 1900–1971, vol. VII
Pratt, Frederick Greville, 1869–1949, vol. IV
Pratt, Col Henry Marsh, 1838–1919, vol. II
Pratt, Sir Henry Sheldon, 1873–1954, vol. V
Pratt, John, 1880–1935, vol. III
Pratt, John Lhind, 1885–1960, vol. V
Pratt, Sir John Thomas, 1876–1970, vol. VI
Pratt, Sir John William, 1873–1952, vol. V
Pratt, Joseph, 1843–1929, vol. III
Pratt, Brig. Reginald S.; *see* Sutton-Pratt.
Pratt, Rev. Ronald Arthur Frederick, 1886–1983, vol. VIII
Pratt, Brig.-Gen. St George; *see* Pratt, Brig.-Gen. E. St G.
Pratt, Col Spencer; *see* Pratt, Col A. S.

Pratt, William Henry; *see* Karloff, Boris.
Pratt, Surg.-Gen. William Simson, 1849–1917, vol. II
Pratt-Tynte, Fortescue Joseph; *see* Tynte.
Pratten, Herbert Edward, 1865–1928, vol. II
Pratz, Claire de, *died* 1934, vol. III
Prausnitz Giles, Carl, 1876–1963, vol. VI
Praz, Mario, 1896–1982, vol. VIII
Prebensen, Per Preben, 1896–1961, vol. VI
Preece, Sir Arthur Henry, 1867–1951, vol. V
Preece, Engr Vice-Adm. Sir George, *died* 1945, vol. IV
Preece, John Richard, 1843–1917, vol. II
Preece, Sir William Henry, 1834–1913, vol. I
Preedy, Rev. Arthur, *died* 1929, vol. III
Preedy, Digby C.; *see* Cotes-Preedy.
Preedy, George R.; *see* Long, M. G.
Preedy, Kenelm, *died* 1945, vol. IV
Preeston, Lt-Col Noel Percival Richard, 1880–1937, vol. III
Préfontaine, Hon. Joseph Raymond Fournier, 1850–1905, vol. I
Preller, Charles S. Du Riche, 1844–1929, vol. III
Prelooker, Jaakoff, 1860–1935, vol. III
Prem, Dhani Ram, 1904–1979, vol. VII
Premchand, Sir Kikabhai, 1883–1953, vol. V
Preminger, Otto Ludwig, 1906–1986, vol. VIII
Prempeh II, Otumfuo Sir Osei Agyeman, 1892–1970, vol. VI
Prendergast, Brig.-Gen. Charles Gordon, 1864–1930, vol. III
Prendergast, Brig.-Gen. Donald Guy, 1861–1938, vol. III
Prendergast, Hon. George Michael, 1854–1937, vol. III
Prendergast, Maj.-Gen. Guy Annesley, 1834–1919, vol. II
Prendergast, Gen. Sir Harry North Dalrymple, 1834–1913, vol. I
Prendergast, Hon. Sir James, 1828–1921, vol. II
Prendergast, Hon. James Emile Pierre, 1858–1945, vol. IV
Prendergast, Adm. Sir Robert John, 1864–1946, vol. IV
Prendergast, W. Dowling, 1862–1933, vol. III
Prendergast, William, 1868–1933, vol. III
Prenderville, Arthur de, *died* 1919, vol. II
Prendiville, Most Rev. Redmond, 1900–1968, vol. VI
Prentice, Bertram, 1867–1938, vol. III
Prentice, Frank Douglas, 1898–1962, vol. VI
Prentice, Brig.-Gen. Robert Emile Shepherd, 1872–1953, vol. V
Prentice, Sir William David Russell, *died* 1933, vol. III
Prescott, Caroline, (Mrs Cyril Prescott), *died* 1943, vol. IV
Prescott, Charles Barrow Clarke, 1870–1932, vol. III
Prescott, Charles John, 1857–1946, vol. IV
Prescott, Sir Charles William Beeston, 6th Bt (*cr* 1794), 1877–1955, vol. V
Prescott, Mrs Cyril; *see* Prescott, Caroline.
Prescott, E. Livingston, *died* 1901, vol. III
Prescott, Sir George Lionel Lawson Bagot, 5th Bt (*cr* 1794), 1875–1942, vol. IV
Prescott, Lt-Col Henry Cecil, 1882–1960, vol. V

Prescott, Hilda F. M., 1896–1972, vol. VII
Prescott, James Arthur, 1890–1987, vol. VIII
Prescott, James C., 1894–1964, vol. VI
Prescott, Ven. John Eustace, *died* 1920, vol. II
Prescott, Richard Gordon Bathgate, 1896–1963, vol. VI
Prescott, Sir Richard Stanley, 2nd Bt (*cr* 1938), 1899–1965, vol. VI
Prescott, Stanley; *see* Prescott, W. R. S.
Prescott, Sir Stanley Lewis, 1910–1978, vol. VII
Prescott, Col Sir William Henry, 1st Bt (*cr* 1938), 1874–1945, vol. IV
Prescott, (William Robert) Stanley, 1912–1962, vol. VI
Prescott-Davies, N., 1862–1915, vol. I
Prescott-Decie, Brig.-Gen. Cyril; *see* Decie.
Prescott-Westcar, Lt-Col Sir William Villiers Leonard, 7th Bt (*cr* 1794), 1882–1959, vol. V
Presgrave, Col Edward Robert John, 1855–1919, vol. II
Presland, John, (Gladys Bendit), *died* 1975, vol. VII
Press, Robert, 1915–1984, vol. VIII
Pressburger, Emeric, 1902–1988, vol. VIII
Pressly, David Leith, 1855–1922, vol. II
Prest, Alan Richmond, 1919–1984, vol. VIII
Prest, Major Edward Papillon, 1864–1932, vol. III
Prest, Stanley Faber, 1858–1931, vol. III
Prestage, Edgar, 1869–1951, vol. V
Prestige, Rev. Canon George Leonard, 1889–1955, vol. V
Prestige, Major Sir John Theodore, 1884–1962, vol. VI
Preston, Alan, 1929–1988, vol. VIII
Preston, Hon. Mrs Angela C.; *see* Campbell-Preston.
Preston, Arthur, 1864–1948, vol. IV
Preston, Major Arthur John, 1842–1930, vol. III
Preston, Rt Rev. Arthur Llewellyn, *died* 1936, vol. III
Preston, Aston Zachariah, 1925–1986, vol. VIII
Preston, Bryan Wentworth, 1905–1965, vol. VI
Preston, Col D'Arcy Brownlow, 1860–1932, vol. III
Preston, Lt-Col Sir Edward Hulton, 5th Bt, 1888–1963, vol. VI
Preston, Francis Noel Dykes, 1888–1957, vol. V
Preston, Frank Sansome, 1875–1970, vol. VI
Preston, Sir Frederick George Panizzi, *died* 1949, vol. IV
Preston, Rev. George, 1840–1913, vol. I
Preston, George Dawson, 1896–1972, vol. VII
Preston, George Frederic, *died* 1939, vol. III
Preston, Sir Harry John, 1860–1936, vol. III
Preston, Henry Edward, 1857–1924, vol. II
Preston, Herbert Sansome, *died* 1935, vol. III
Preston, Sir Jacob, 4th Bt, 1887–1918, vol. II
Preston, Lt-Col Jenico Edward, 1855–1940, vol. III
Preston, Joseph Henry, 1911–1985, vol. VIII
Preston, Kerrison, 1884–1974, vol. VII
Preston, Adm. Sir Lionel George, 1875–1971, vol. VII
Preston, Lt-Col Hon. Richard Martin Peter, 1884–1965, vol. VI
Preston, Col Rupert Lionel, 1902–1982, vol. VIII
Preston, Sidney, 1850–1938, vol. III
Preston, Thomas, 1860–1900, vol. I
Preston, Thomas, 1834–1901, vol. I

Preston, Col Thomas, 1886–1966, vol. VI
Preston, Thomas Alford H. B.; *see* Houston-Boswall-Preston.
Preston, Sir Thomas Hildebrand, 6th Bt, 1886–1976, vol. VII
Preston, Sir Walter Reuben, 1875–1946, vol. IV
Preston, William, 1874–1941, vol. IV
Preston, Sir William Edward, 1865–1939, vol. III
Preston, Lt-Col William John Phaelim, 1873–1943, vol. IV
Preston-Thomas, Herbert, *died* 1909, vol. I
Pretorius, Major Philip Jacobus, *died* 1945, vol. IV
Pretty, Eric Ernest Falk, 1891–1967, vol. VI
Pretty, Air Marshal Sir Walter Philip George, 1909–1975, vol. VII
Pretyman, Rt Hon. Ernest George, 1860–1931, vol. III
Pretyman, Frederic Henry, 1875–1939, vol. III
Pretyman, Wing-Comdr George Frederick, 1891–1937, vol. III
Pretyman, Maj.-Gen. Sir George Tindal, 1845–1917, vol. II
Pretyman, Sir Walter Frederick, 1901–1988, vol. VIII
Prevett, Comdr Harry, 1900–1972, vol. VII
Previté-Orton, Charles William, 1877–1947, vol. IV
Prevost, Sir Augustus, 1st Bt (*cr* 1903), 1837–1913, vol. I
Prevost, Sir Charles, 3rd Bt (*cr* 1805), 1831–1902, vol. I
Prevost, Sir Charles Thomas Keble, 4th Bt (*cr* 1805), 1866–1939, vol. III
Prevost, Francis; *see* Battersby, H. F. P.
Prevost, Captain Sir George James Augustine, 5th Bt, 1910–1985, vol. VIII
Prevost, Marcel, 1862–1941, vol. IV
Preziosi, Count Luigi, *died* 1965, vol. VI
Price, Col Adolphus James, 1846–1937, vol. III
Price, Albert Thomas, 1903–1978, vol. VII
Price, Allen, 1905–1970, vol. VI
Price, Sir Archibald Grenfell, 1892–1977, vol. VII
Price, Arnold Justin, 1919–1987, vol. VIII
Price, Aubrey Joseph, 1899–1978, vol. VII
Price, Bartholomew, 1818–1898, vol. I
Price, Hon. Brig.-Gen. Bartholomew George, 1870–1947, vol. IV
Price, Byron, 1891–1981, vol. VIII
Price, Maj.-Gen. Cedric Rhys George, 1905–1987, vol. VIII
Price, Maj.-Gen. Charles Basil, 1889–1975, vol. VII
Price, Charles Edward, *died* 1934, vol. III
Price, Sir Charles Frederick Rugge-, 7th Bt (*cr* 1804), 1868–1953, vol. V
Price, Brig.-Gen. Charles Henry Uvedale, 1862–1942, vol. IV
Price, Lt-Col Sir Charles James Napier Rugge-, 8th Bt (*cr* 1804), 1902–1966, vol. VI
Price, Captain Charles Lempriere, 1877–1914, vol. I
Price, Sir (Charles) Roy, 1893–1976, vol. VII
Price, Sir Charles Rugge-, 6th Bt (*cr* 1804), 1841–1927, vol. II
Price, Major Sir Charles William Mackay, 1872–1954, vol. V
Price, Rev. Clement, 1858–1937, vol. III
Price, Rev. Cyril, *died* 1943, vol. IV

Price, Col Cyril Uvedale, 1868–1956, vol. V
Price, Hon. Sir David William T.; *see* Tudor Price.
Price, Maj.-Gen. Denis Walter, 1908–1966, vol. VI
Price, Dennis, 1915–1973, vol. VII
Price, Dorothy Stopford, 1890–1954, vol. V
Price, Rt Rev. Dudley William Mackay, 1899–1971, vol. VII
Price, (Edith) Mary, 1897–1980, vol. VII
Price, Rev. Canon Edward Hyde B.; *see* Blackwood-Price.
Price, Edwin Lessware, 1874–1935, vol. III
Price, Ernest Griffith, 1870–1962, vol. VI
Price, Rev. Ernest Jones, 1882–1952, vol. V
Price, Sir Francis Caradoc Rose, 5th Bt (*cr* 1815), 1880–1949, vol. IV
Price, Frank Corbyn, *born* 1862, vol. III
Price, Sir Frederick; *see* Price, Sir J. F.
Price, Frederick George Hilton, 1842–1909, vol. I
Price, Frederick William, *died* 1957, vol. V
Price, G. Ward, *died* 1961, vol. VI
Price, Gabriel, 1879–1934, vol. III
Price, George Basil, *died* 1939, vol. III
Price, Brig.-Gen. George Dominic, 1867–1943, vol. IV
Price, Comdr George Edward, 1842–1926, vol. II
Price, Gwilym Ivor, 1899–1981, vol. VIII
Price, H. L., 1899–1943, vol. IV
Price, Harold Louis, 1917–1986, vol. VIII
Price, Harry, 1881–1948, vol. IV
Price, Henry Alfred, 1911–1982, vol. VIII
Price, Henry Habberley, 1899–1984, vol. VIII
Price, Sir Henry Philip, 1st Bt (*cr* 1953), 1877–1963, vol. VI
Price, Captain Henry Ryan, 1912–1986, vol. VIII
Price, Captain Henry Talbot, 1839–1915, vol. I
Price, Herbert Spencer, 1892–1976, vol. VII
Price, Rt Rev. Hetley; *see* Price, Rt Rev. S. H.
Price, Rt Rev. Horace MacCartie Eyre, 1863–1941, vol. IV
Price, Major Hubert Davenport, 1890–1958, vol. V
Price, Comdr Hugh Perceval, 1901–1983, vol. VIII
Price, Sir James Frederick George, 1873–1957, vol. V
Price, John Cadwgan P.; *see* Powell-Price.
Price, Sir (John) Frederick, 1839–1927, vol. II
Price, Sir John G.; *see* Green-Price.
Price, John Lloyd, 1882–1941, vol. IV
Price, John Playfair, 1905–1988, vol. VIII
Price, Rev. John Willis, 1872–1940, vol. III
Price, (Joseph) Thomas, 1902–1973, vol. VII
Price, Julius Mendes, *died* 1924, vol. II
Price, Sir Keith, 1879–1956, vol. V
Price, Langford Lovell F. R., 1862–1950, vol. IV
Price, (Lilian) Nancy (Bache), 1880–1970, vol. VI
Price, Marjorie Muriel, 1907–1946, vol. IV
Price, Mary; *see* Price, E. M.
Price, Morgan Philips, 1885–1973, vol. VII
Price, Nancy; *see* Price, L. N. B.
Price, Norman Stewart, 1907–1988, vol. VIII
Price, Lt-Col Owen Glendower H.; *see* Howell-Price.
Price, Col Sir Rhys Howell, 1872–1943, vol. IV
Price, Sir Richard Dansey G.; *see* Green-Price.
Price, Richard John Lloyd, 1843–1923, vol. II
Price, Robert; *see* Price, W. R.
Price, Major Sir Robert Henry G.; *see* Green-Price.

Price, Sir Robert John, 1854–1926, vol. II
Price, Very Rev. Robert Peel, 1905–1981, vol. VIII
Price, Sir Rose, 4th Bt (*cr* 1815), 1878–1901, vol. I
Price, Sir Rose Francis, 6th Bt (*cr* 1815), 1910–1979, vol. VII
Price, Sir Rose Lambart, 3rd Bt (*cr* 1815), 1837–1899, vol. I
Price, Sir Roy; *see* Price, Sir C. R.
Price, S. Warren, *died* 1944, vol. IV
Price, Seymour James, 1886–1959, vol. V
Price, Rt Rev. (Stuart) Hetley, 1922–1977, vol. VII
Price, Hon. Thomas, 1852–1909, vol. I
Price, Col Thomas, 1842–1911, vol. I
Price, Thomas; *see* Price, J. T.
Price, Brig.-Gen. Thomas Herbert Francis, 1869–1945, vol. IV
Price, Thomas Phillips, 1844–1932, vol. III
Price, Sir Thomas Rees, 1848–1916, vol. II
Price, Brig. Thomas Reginald, 1894–1978, vol. VII
Price, Brig.-Gen. Thomas Rose Caradoc, 1875–1949, vol. IV
Price, Thomas Slater, 1875–1949, vol. IV
Price, Major Vincent Walter, 1890–1976, vol. VII
Price, Walter Harrington C.; *see* Crawfurd-Price.
Price, Walter Robert, 1926–1987, vol. VIII
Price, Wilfrid, 1879–1961, vol. VI
Price, Willard De Mille, 1887–1983, vol. VIII
Price, Sir William, 1867–1924, vol. II
Price, Sir William, *died* 1938, vol. III
Price, Hon. Brig.-Gen. William, 1864–1952, vol. V
Price, Lt-Col William Herbert, 1877–1963, vol. VI
Price, Rev. William James, *died* 1928, vol. II
Price, William James, 1884–1973, vol. VII
Price, William Thomas, 1895–1982, vol. VIII
Price-Davies, Brig. Charles Stafford, 1892–1959, vol. V
Price-Davies, Maj.-Gen. Llewelyn Alberic Emilius, 1878–1965, vol. VI
Price Hughes, Mary Katherine H., 1853–1948, vol. IV
Price Thomas, Sir Clement, 1893–1973, vol. VII
Price-White, Lt-Col David Archibald, 1906–1978, vol. VII
Prichard, Rev. Alfred George, 1869–1945, vol. IV
Prichard, Arthur William, *died* 1926, vol. II
Prichard, Brig.-Gen. Charles Stewart, 1861–1942, vol. IV
Prichard, Harold Arthur, 1871–1947, vol. IV
Prichard, Herbert William, 1873–1951, vol. V
Prichard, Major (Hesketh Vernon) Hesketh, 1876–1922, vol. II
Prichard, Lt-Col Hubert Cecil, 1865–1942, vol. IV
Prichard, Sir John, 1887–1971, vol. VII
Prichard, Katharine Susannah, *died* 1969, vol. VI
Prichard, Sir Norman George Mollet, 1895–1972, vol. VII
Prichard, Rev. Canon Thomas Estlin, 1910–1975, vol. VII
Prichard, Brig. Walter Clavel Herbert, 1883–1965, vol. VII
Prichard-Jones, Sir John, 1st Bt, 1845–1917, vol. II
Prickard, Arthur Octavius, 1843–1939, vol. III
Prickard, Thomas Francis Vaughan, 1879–1973, vol. VII

Prickett, Brig. Charles Henry, 1881–1958, vol. V
Prideaux, Sir Francis; *see* Prideaux, Sir J. F. E.
Prideaux, Lt-Col Francis Beville, 1871–1938, vol. III
Prideaux, Sir (Joseph) Francis (Engledue), 1884–1959, vol. V
Prideaux, Rev. Canon Walter Archibald, 1882–1965, vol. VI
Prideaux, Rev. Walter Cross, 1845–1912, vol. I
Prideaux, Sir Walter Sherburne, 1846–1928, vol. II
Prideaux, Col William Francis, 1840–1914, vol. I
Prideaux-Brune, Charles Glynn, 1821–1907, vol. I
Prideaux-Brune, Col Charles Robert, 1848–1936, vol. III
Prideaux-Brune, Sir Humphrey Ingelram, 1886–1979, vol. VII
Pridham, Vice-Adm. Sir (Arthur) Francis, 1886–1975, vol. VII
Pridham, Vice-Adm. Sir Francis; *see* Pridham, Vice-Adm. Sir A. F.
Pridham, Col Geoffrey Robert, 1872–1951, vol. V
Pridham-Wippell, Adm. Sir Henry Daniel, 1885–1952, vol. V
Pridie, Sir Eric Denholm, 1896–1978, vol. VII
Pridmore, Albert Edward, 1864–1927, vol. II
Pridmore, Walter George, 1864–1943, vol. IV
Priebsch, Robert, 1866–1935, vol. III
Priest, Alfred, 1874–1929, vol. III
Priest, Maj.-Gen. Robert Cecil, *died* 1966, vol. VI
Priestley, Sir Arthur, 1864–1933, vol. III
Priestley, Briggs, 1832–1907, vol. I
Priestley, Sir Gerald William, 1888–1978, vol. VII
Priestley, Lt-Col Harold Edgar, *died* 1941, vol. IV
Priestley, Henry, 1884–1961, vol. VI
Priestley, Henry James, 1883–1932, vol. III
Priestley, Herbert Ingram, 1875–1944, vol. IV
Priestley, John Boynton, 1894–1984, vol. VIII
Priestley, Sir Joseph Child, 1862–1941, vol. IV
Priestley, Joseph Hubert, 1883–1944, vol. IV
Priestley, Sir Raymond Edward, 1886–1974, vol. VII
Priestley, Sir William Edwin Briggs, 1859–1932, vol. III
Priestman, Bertram, 1868–1951, vol. V
Priestman, Harold Eddey, 1888–1956, vol. V
Priestman, Howard, 1865–1931, vol. III
Priestman, Sir John, 1st Bt, *died* 1941, vol. IV
Priestman, Maj.-Gen. John Hedley Thornton, 1885–1964, vol. VI
Prime, Derek Arthur, 1932–1990, vol. VIII
Prime-Stevenson, Edward Irenaeus; *see* Stevenson.
Primo de Rivera, Duke of, *died* 1964, vol. VI
Primrose, Sir Alasdair Neil, 4th Bt, 1935–1986, vol. VIII
Primrose, Alexander, 1861–1944, vol. IV
Primrose, Vice-Adm. George Anson, 1849–1930, vol. III
Primrose, Rt Hon. Sir Henry William, 1846–1923, vol. II
Primrose, Sir John Ure, 1st Bt, 1847–1924, vol. II
Primrose, Sir John Ure, 1900–1974, vol. VII
Primrose, Sir John Ure, 3rd Bt, 1908–1984, vol. VIII
Primrose, Rt Hon. Neil James Archibald, 1882–1917, vol. II
Primrose, William, 1904–1982, vol. VIII

Primrose, Sir William Louis, 2nd Bt, 1880–1953, vol. V
Prince, Sir Alexander William, 1870–1933, vol. III
Prince, Edward Ernest, 1858–1936, vol. III
Prince, J.-E., 1851–1923, vol. II, vol. III
Prince, John Dyneley, 1868–1945, vol. IV
Prince, Leslie Barnett, 1901–1985, vol. VIII
Prince, Lt-Col Peregrine, 1882–1935, vol. III
Prince, Lt-Col Robert, *died* 1945, vol. IV
Prince-Smith, Sir Prince, 2nd Bt, 1869–1940, vol. III
Prince-Smith, Sir William, 3rd Bt, 1898–1964, vol. VI
Prinetti, Marchese Giulio, 1851–1908, vol. I
Pring, Hon. Robert Darlow, 1853–1922, vol. II
Pringle, Rev. Arthur, 1866–1933, vol. III
Pringle, Lt-Col David, *died* 1936, vol. III (A), vol. IV
Pringle, G. L. Kerr, *died* 1961, vol. VI
Pringle, Sir George, 1825–1911, vol. I
Pringle, George Taylor, 1890–1955, vol. V
Pringle, Brig. Hall Grant, 1876–1942, vol. IV
Pringle, Harold, *died* 1935, vol. III
Pringle, James Alexander, 1874–1935, vol. III
Pringle, James Hogarth, *died* 1941, vol. IV
Pringle, Sir James Scott, 1876–1951, vol. V
Pringle, Sir John, 1848–1923, vol. II
Pringle, Rev. John Christian, 1872–1938, vol. III
Pringle, John James, *died* 1922, vol. II
Pringle, John Mackay, 1888–1955, vol. V
Pringle, J(ohn) Seton Michael, 1909–1975, vol. VII
Pringle, Col Sir John Wallace, 1863–1938, vol. III
Pringle, John William Sutton, 1912–1982, vol. VIII
Pringle, Captain Lionel Graham, 1880–1915, vol. I
Pringle, Mia Lilly Kellmer, 1920–1983, vol. VIII
Pringle, Sir Norman Hamilton, 9th Bt, 1903–1961, vol. VI
Pringle, Sir Norman Robert, 8th Bt, 1871–1919, vol. II
Pringle, Maj.-Gen. Sir Robert, 1855–1926, vol. II
Pringle, Seton Sidney, 1879–1955, vol. V
Pringle, William Henderson, 1877–1967, vol. VI
Pringle, William Mather Rutherford, 1874–1928, vol. II
Pringle-Pattison, Andrew Seth; *see* Seth, Andrew.
Prinsep, Anthony Leyland, 1888–1942, vol. IV
Prinsep, Lt-Gen. Arthur Haldimand, 1840–1915, vol. I
Prinsep, Col Evelyn Siegfried MacLeod, 1892–1973, vol. VII
Prinsep, Hon. Sir Henry Thoby, 1836–1914, vol. I
Prinsep, Valentine Cameron, 1838–1904, vol. I
Prinz, Gerhard, 1929–1983, vol. VIII
Prioleau, John Randolph Hamilton, 1882–1954, vol. V
Prior, A. C. Vincent, 1881–1954, vol. V
Prior, Rev. Alfred Hall, *died* 1937, vol. III
Prior, Arthur Norman, 1914–1969, vol. VI
Prior, Sir (Charles) Geoffrey, *died* 1972, vol. VII
Prior, Col Hon. Edward Gawler, 1853–1920, vol. II
Prior, Edward Schroder, 1852–1932, vol. III
Prior, Sir Geoffrey; *see* Prior, Sir C. G.
Prior, George Thurland, 1862–1936, vol. III
Prior, Maj.-Gen. George Upton, 1843–1919, vol. II
Prior, Sir Henry Carlos, 1890–1967, vol. VI
Prior, Melton, 1845–1910, vol. I
Prior, Oliver Herbert Phelps, 1871–1934, vol. III

Prior, Comdr Redvers Michael, *died* 1964, vol. VI
Prior, Samuel Henry, 1869–1933, vol. III
Prior, Ven. William Henry, 1883–1969, vol. VI
Prior-Palmer, Maj.-Gen. George Erroll, 1903–1977, vol. VII
Prior-Palmer, Brig. Sir Otho Leslie, 1897–1986, vol. VIII
Priston, Rev. Stewart Browne, 1880–1960, vol. V
Pritchard, Sir Albert Edward, 1859–1937, vol. III
Pritchard, Sir Asa Hubert, 1891–1990, vol. VIII
Pritchard, Brig.-Gen. Aubrey Gordon, 1869–1943, vol. IV
Pritchard, Sir Charles Bradley, 1837–1903, vol. I
Pritchard, Brig. Charles Hilary Vaughan; *see* Vaughan, Brig. C. H. V.
Pritchard, Brig.-Gen. Clive Gordon, 1871–1948, vol. IV
Pritchard, Sir Edward Evan E.; *see* Evans-Pritchard.
Pritchard, Eric; *see* Pritchard, G. E. C.
Pritchard, Eric Alfred Blake, 1889–1962, vol. VI
Pritchard, Sir Fred Eills, 1899–1982, vol. VIII
Pritchard, Frederick Hugh Dalzel, 1905–1983, vol. VIII
Pritchard, (George) Eric (Campbell), *died* 1943, vol. IV
Pritchard, Maj.-Gen. Gordon Arthur Thomas, 1902–1957, vol. V
Pritchard, Lt-Gen. Sir Gordon Douglas, 1835–1912, vol. I
Pritchard, Sir Harry Goring, 1868–1962, vol. VI
Pritchard, Maj.-Gen. Harry Lionel, 1871–1953, vol. V
Pritchard, Lt-Col Hugh Robert Norman, 1879–1967, vol. VI
Pritchard, Col Hurlock Galloway, 1836–1909, vol. I
Pritchard, Ivor Mervyn, *died* 1948, vol. IV (A), vol. V
Pritchard, John Joseph, 1916–1979, vol. VII
Pritchard, Captain John Laurence, 1885–1968, vol. VI
Pritchard, Sir John Michael, 1921–1989, vol. VIII
Pritchard, Leslie Francis Gordon, 1918–1977, vol. VII
Pritchard, Robert Albion, *died* 1916, vol. II
Pritchard, Urban, 1845–1925, vol. II
Pritchard, Rev. William Charles, 1856–1931, vol. III
Pritchett, John Suckling, *died* 1941, vol. IV
Pritchett, Sir Theodore Beal, 1890–1969, vol. VI
Pritt, Denis Nowell, 1887–1972, vol. VII
Prittie, Hon. Terence Cornelius Farmer, 1913–1985, vol. VIII
Privett, Frank John, 1874–1937, vol. III
Probert, Arthur Reginald, 1909–1975, vol. VII
Probert, Rev. Lewis, 1841–1908, vol. I
Probert, Rhys Price, 1921–1980, vol. VII
Proby, Col Douglas James, 1856–1931, vol. III
Proby, Granville, 1883–1947, vol. IV
Proby, Major Sir Richard George, 1st Bt, 1886–1979, vol. VII
Probyn, Rt Hon. Sir Dighton Macnaghten, 1833–1924, vol. II
Probyn, Sir Lesley Charles, 1834–1916, vol. II
Probyn, Sir Leslie, 1862–1938, vol. III
Probyn, Lt-Col Percy John, *died* 1940, vol. III

Probyn-Jones, Sir Arthur Probyn, 2nd Bt, 1892–1951, vol. V
Probyn-Williams, Robert James, 1866–1952, vol. V
Procter, Rev. Arthur Herbert, 1890–1973, vol. VII
Procter, Rev. Charles James, *died* 1925, vol. II
Procter, Dod, *died* 1972, vol. VII
Procter, Ernest, *died* 1935, vol. III
Procter, Evelyn Emma Stefanos, 1897–1980, vol. VII
Procter, Henry Adam, 1883–1955, vol. V
Procter, Sir Henry Edward Edleston, 1866–1928, vol. II
Procter, Henry Richardson, 1848–1927, vol. II
Procter, Lt-Col James, 1884–1955, vol. V
Procter, Joan Beauchamp, 1897–1931, vol. III
Procter, Very Rev. John, 1849–1911, vol. I
Procter, Rev. John Mathias, 1835–1917, vol. II
Procter, Sir William, 1871–1951, vol. V
Procter-Gregg, Humphrey, 1895–1980, vol. VII
Proctor, Adam E., 1864–1913, vol. I
Proctor, Alexander Phimister, 1862–1950, vol. IV (A), vol. V
Proctor, Col Alfred Henry, *died* 1950, vol. IV
Proctor, Captain Andrew Weatherley Beauchamp, *died* 1921, vol. II
Proctor, Sir Dennis; *see* Proctor, Sir P. D.
Proctor, Sir (George) Philip, 1902–1986, vol. VIII
Proctor, Rev. Henry, *died* 1940, vol. III
Proctor, Mary, *died* 1957, vol. V
Proctor, Sir Philip; *see* Proctor, Sir G. P.
Proctor, Sir Philip Bridger, 1870–1940, vol. III
Proctor, Sir (Philip) Dennis, 1905–1983, vol. VIII
Proctor, Surg. Rear-Adm. Richard Louis Gibbon, 1900–1969, vol. VI
Proctor, William Thomas, 1896–1967, vol. VI
Proctor-Beauchamp, Col Sir Horace George; *see* Beauchamp.
Proctor-Beauchamp, Rev. Sir Ivor Cuthbert; *see* Beauchamp.
Proctor-Beauchamp, Rev. Sir Montagu Harry; *see* Beauchamp.
Proctor-Beauchamp, Sir Reginald William; *see* Beauchamp.
Proctor-Sims, Ernest William; *see* Sims.
Proe, Thomas, 1852–1922, vol. II
Proes, Lt-Col Ernest Marinus, 1871–1940, vol. III
Profeit, Col Charles William, 1870–1937, vol. III
Profumo, Albert Peter Anthony, 1879–1940, vol. III
Prokofieff, Serge Sergeyevich, 1891–1953, vol. V
Prokosch, Frederic, 1908–1989, vol. VIII
Prole, Lozania; *see* Bloom, Ursula.
Propert, Rev. P. S. G., 1861–1940, vol. III
Propsting, Hon. William Bispham, 1861–1937, vol. III
Prosser, (Albert) Russell (Garness), 1915–1988, vol. VIII
Prosser, Rt Rev. Charles Keith Kipling, 1897–1954, vol. V
Prosser, Rt Rev. David Lewis, *died* 1950, vol. IV
Prosser, David Russell, 1889–1974, vol. VII
Prosser, Ernest Albert, *died* 1933, vol. III
Prosser, Francis Richard W.; *see* Wegg-Prosser.
Prosser, Rev. Henry Paul, *died* 1932, vol. III
Prosser, Sir John, 1857–1945, vol. IV
Prosser, Russell; *see* Prosser, A. R. G.

Prosser, Seward, 1871–1942, vol. IV
Prosser, Thomas Vivian, 1908–1987, vol. VIII
Prothero, Adm. Arthur William Edward, 1850–1931, vol. III
Prothero, Sir George Walter, 1848–1922, vol. II
Prothero, Vice-Adm. Reginald Charles, 1849–1927, vol. II
Protheroe, Ven. James Havard, *died* 1903, vol. I
Protheroe, Maj.-Gen. Montagu, 1841–1905, vol. I
Protheroe-Beynon, Major Godfrey Evan Schaw, 1872–1958, vol. V
Protheroe-Smith, Lt-Col Sir Hugh Bateman, 1872–1961, vol. VI
Proud, Sir George, 1910–1976, vol. VII
Proudfoot, Alexander, 1878–1957, vol. V
Proudfoot, Col Frank Grégoire, 1869–1940, vol. III
Proudfoot, James, 1908–1971, vol. VII
Proudfoot, William, 1932–1990, vol. VIII
Proudman, Joseph, 1888–1975, vol. VII
Prout, Ebenezer, 1835–1909, vol. I
Prout, Henry Goslee, *died* 1927, vol. II, vol. III
Prout, Margaret F.; *see* Fisher Prout.
Prout, Sir William Thomas, *died* 1939, vol. III
Provand, Andrew Dryburgh, 1839–1915, vol. I
Provis, Edward, 1849–1941, vol. IV
Provis, Sir Samuel Butler, 1845–1926, vol. II
Prowde, Oswald Longstaff, 1882–1949, vol. IV
Prower, Brig. John Mervyn, 1885–1968, vol. VI
Prowse, Arthur Bancks, 1856–1925, vol. II
Prowse, Daniel Woodley, 1834–1914, vol. I
Prowse, Richard Orton, 1862–1949, vol. IV
Prowse, Richard Thomas, 1835–1921, vol. II
Prudden, T. Mitchell, 1849–1924, vol. II
Pruden, Arthur George, 1860–1936, vol. III
Prunty, Francis Thomas Garnet, 1910–1979, vol. VII
Prunty, Garnet; *see* Prunty, F. T. G.
Pryce, Daniel Merlin, 1902–1976, vol. VII
Pryce, Edward Calcott, 1885–1972, vol. VII
Pryce, Frederick Norman, 1888–1953, vol. V
Pryce, Howard Lloyd, *died* 1932, vol. III
Pryce, Very Rev. John, *died* 1903, vol. I
Pryce, Ven. Lewis Hugh Oswald, 1873–1930, vol. III
Pryce, Rev. R. Vaughan, 1834–1917, vol. II
Pryce, Richard, *died* 1942, vol. IV
Pryce, Very Rev. Shadrach, *died* 1914, vol. I
Pryce, Ven. Thomas P.; *see* Parry Pryce.
Pryce-Jones, Col Sir Edward; *see* Pryce-Jones, Col Sir P. E.
Pryce-Jones, Bt Col Henry Morris, 1878–1952, vol. V
Pryce-Jones, Sir Pryce, 1834–1920, vol. II
Pryce-Jones, Col Sir (Pryce) Edward, 1st Bt, 1861–1926, vol. II
Pryce-Jones, Sir Pryce Victor, 2nd Bt, 1887–1963, vol. VI
Pryde, David Johnstone, 1890–1959, vol. V
Pryde, George Smith, 1899–1961, vol. VI
Pryde, James, 1869–1941, vol. IV
Pryde, James Richmond Northridge, 1894–1980, vol. VII
Pryer, Major Alfred Amos, 1891–1943, vol. IV
Pryke, Sir Dudley; *see* Pryke, Sir W. R. D.
Pryke, Rev. William Emmanuel, 1843–1920, vol. II
Pryke, Sir William Robert, 1st Bt, 1847–1932, vol. III

Pryke, Sir (William Robert) Dudley, 2nd Bt, 1882–1959, vol. V
Pryn, Surg. Rear-Adm. Sir William Wenmoth, 1859–1942, vol. IV
Prynne, E. A. Fellowes, 1854–1921, vol. II
Prynne, Rev. George Rundle, 1818–1903, vol. I
Prynne, Brig. Harold Gordon Lusby, 1899–1976, vol. VII
Prynne, Col Harold Vernon, *died* 1954, vol. V
Prynne, Maj.-Gen. Michael Whitworth, 1912–1977, vol. VII
Pryor, Arthur Vickris, 1846–1927, vol. II
Pryor, Grafton Deen, 1883–1947, vol. IV
Pryor, Maurice Arthur, 1911–1969, vol. VI
Pryor, Rev. Michael, 1857–1929, vol. III
Pryor, Norman Selwyn, 1896–1982, vol. VIII
Pryor, Maj.-Gen. Sir Pomeroy Holland-, 1866–1955, vol. V
Pryor, Robert Nelson, 1921–1979, vol. VII
Pryor, S. J., 1865–1924, vol. II
Pryor, Lt-Col Walter Marlborough, 1880–1962, vol. VI
Prys, Rev. Owen, 1857–1934, vol. III
Prys Jones, David; *see* Jones, D. P.
Pryse, Sir Edward John Webley-Parry-, 2nd Bt, 1862–1918, vol. II
Pryse, Gerald Spencer, 1882–1956, vol. V
Pryse, Sir Lewes Thomas Loveden, 3rd Bt, 1864–1946, vol. IV
Pryse, Sir Pryse, 1st Bt, 1838–1906, vol. I
Pryse, Sir Pryse Loveden S.; *see* Saunders-Pryse.
Pryse-Rice, Dame Margaret Ker, *died* 1948, vol. IV
Pryse-Saunders, Sir George Rice, 4th Bt, 1870–1948, vol. IV
Ptolemy, William John, 1850–1920, vol. II
Puccini, Giacomo, 1858–1924, vol. II
Puckey, Sir Walter Charles, 1899–1983, vol. VIII
Puckle, Sir Frederick Hale, 1889–1966, vol. VI
Puckle, Lt-Col Frederick Kaye, 1880–1959, vol. V
Puckle, Lt-Col John, 1869–1917, vol. II
Puckle, Richard Kaye, 1830–1917, vol. II
Puckridge, Geoffrey Martin, 1895–1974, vol. VII
Puddester, Sir John Charles, 1881–1947, vol. IV
Puddicombe, Anne Adalisa, (Mrs Beynon Puddicombe); *see* Raine, Allen.
Pudner, Anthony Serle, 1917–1980, vol. VII
Pudney, John Sleigh, 1909–1977, vol. VII
Pudsey, Lt-Col Denison, 1876–1940, vol. III (A), vol. IV
Pudukota, Raja of, 1875–1928, vol. II
Pudumjee, Nowrojee, 1841–1930, vol. III
Puech, Albert G., 1859–1929, vol. III
Puech, Denys, 1854–1942, vol. IV
Pugh, Sir Alun; *see* Pugh, Sir J. A.
Pugh, Sir Arthur, 1870–1955, vol. V
Pugh, Lt-Col David Charles, 1859–1929, vol. III
Pugh, Rt Rev. Edward; *see* Pugh, Rt Rev. W. E. A.
Pugh, Ven. Edward William Wynn, *died* 1950, vol. IV
Pugh, Edwin William, 1874–1930, vol. III
Pugh, Sir (John) Alun, 1894–1971, vol. VII
Pugh, Rev. Canon John Richards, 1885–1961, vol. VI
Pugh, Leslie Mervyn, 1905–1978, vol. VII
Pugh, Leslie Penrhys, 1895–1983, vol. VIII
Pugh, Maj.-Gen. Lewis Owain, 1907–1981, vol. VIII

Pugh, Lewis Pugh, 1837–1908, vol. I

Pugh, Lewis Pugh Evans, 1865–1940, vol. III

Pugh, Ralph Bernard, 1910–1982, vol. VIII

Pugh, Rev. Canon T(homas) Jenkin, 1903–1980, vol. VII

Pugh, Rt Rev. William Edward Augustus, 1909–1986, vol. VIII

Pugh, Sir William John, 1892–1974, vol. VII

Pugh, William Thomas Gordon, *died* 1945, vol. IV

Pugno, Raoul, 1852–1914, vol. I

Pugsley, Rear Adm. Anthony Follett, 1901–1990, vol. VIII

Pugsley, Sir Reuben James, 1886–1975, vol. VII

Pugsley, Hon. William, 1850–1925, vol. II

Pulay, George, 1923–1981, vol. VIII

Pulbrook, Sir Eustace Ralph, 1881–1953, vol. V

Puleston, Sir John Henry, 1830–1908, vol. I

Pulford, Air Vice-Marshal Conway Walter Heath, *died* 1942, vol. IV

Pulford, Col Russell Richard, 1845–1920, vol. II

Pulitzer, Joseph, 1847–1911, vol. I

Pulitzer, Ralph, 1879–1939, vol. III

Pullan, Ayrton George Popplewell, 1879–1973, vol. VII

Pullan, Ayrton John Seaton, 1906–1967, vol. VI

Pullan, Rev. Leighton, 1865–1940, vol. III

Pullar, Hubert Norman, 1914–1988, vol. VIII

Pullar, Sir Robert, 1828–1912, vol. I

Pullar, Rufus D., 1861–1917, vol. II

Pullein, John, *died* 1948, vol. IV

Pullein-Thompson, Mrs Joanna; *see* Cannan, J.

Pulleine, Rt Rev. John James, 1841–1913, vol. I

Pullen, Rev. Henry William, 1836–1903, vol. I

Pullen, William le Geyt, 1855–1922, vol. II

Pullen-Burry, Bessie, 1858–1937, vol. III

Puller, Rev. Frederick William, 1843–1938, vol. III

Pulley, Col Charles, 1851–1925, vol. II

Pulley, Sir Charles Thornton, 1864–1947, vol. IV

Pulley, Sir Joseph, 1st Bt, 1822–1901, vol. I

Pulliblank, Engr-Rear-Adm. John Blackler, 1879–1951, vol. V

Pullicino, Anthony Alfred, 1917–1986, vol. VIII

Pullicino, Sir Philip, 1889–1960, vol. VI

Pullin, Victor Edward, *died* 1956, vol. V

Pulling, Alexander, 1857–1942, vol. IV

Pulling, Rev. Edward Herbert, 1859–1928, vol. II

Pulling, Martin John Langley, 1906–1988, vol. VIII

Pullinger, Frank, 1866–1920, vol. II

Pullinger, Henry Robert, 1884–1970, vol. VI

Pullinger, Thomas Charles Willis, 1867–1945, vol. IV

Pullman, Major Alfred Hopewell, *died* 1942, vol. IV

Pulsford, Rev. Edward John, 1878–1952, vol. V

Pulteney, Lt-Gen. Sir William Pulteney, 1861–1941, vol. IV

Pulvertaft, Robert James Valentine, 1897–1990, vol. VIII

Pumpelly, Raphael, 1837–1923, vol. II

Pumphrey, Richard Julius, 1906–1967, vol. VI

Punch, Arthur Lisle, *died* 1964, vol. VI

Punchard, Constance, (Mrs F. B. Punchard); *see* Holme, C.

Punchard, Rev. Elgood George, 1844–1917, vol. II

Punnett, Reginald Crundall, 1875–1967, vol. VI

Pupin, Michael Idvorsky, 1858–1935, vol. III

Purbrick, Reginald, 1877–1950, vol. IV

Purcell, Albert Arthur, 1872–1935, vol. III

Purcell, Denis; *see* Purcell, J. D.

Purcell, Sir Gilbert Kenelm Treffry, 1867–1934, vol. III

Purcell, Rev. Handfield Noel, *died* 1925, vol. II

Purcell, Hubert Kennett, 1884–1962, vol. VI

Purcell, (John) Denis, 1913–1990, vol. VIII

Purcell, Sir John Samuel, 1839–1924, vol. II

Purcell, Pierce Francis, 1881–1968, vol. VI

Purcell, Major Raymond John Hugo, 1885–1928, vol. II

Purcell, Ronald Herbert, 1904–1969, vol. VI

Purcell, Victor, 1896–1965, vol. VI

Purcell-Buret, Captain Theobald John Claud, 1879–1974, vol. VII

Purchas, Rev. Canon Alban Charles Theodore, 1890–1976, vol. VII

Purchase, Sir Bentley; *see* Purchase, Sir W. B.

Purchase, Edward James, *died* 1924, vol. II

Purchase, Henry George, 1873–1945, vol. IV

Purchase, Sir (William) Bentley, 1890–1961, vol. VI

Purchase, Sir William Henry, 1860–1924, vol. II

Puchon, William Sydney, 1879–1942, vol. IV

Purdie, Rev. Albert Bertrand, 1888–1976, vol. VII

Purdie, Edna, 1894–1968, vol. VI

Purdie, Thomas, 1843–1916, vol. II

Purdie, Wendy C.; *see* Campbell-Purdie.

Purdom, Charles Benjamin, 1883–1965, vol. VI

Purdom, Thomas Hunter, 1853–1923, vol. II

Purdon, Lt-Col David William, 1853–1948, vol. IV (A), vol. V

Purdon, Maj.-Gen. William Brooke, *died* 1950, vol. IV

Purdy, Lt-Col John Smith, 1872–1936, vol. III

Purdy, Richard Little, 1904–1990, vol. VIII

Purefoy, Richard Dancer, *died* 1919, vol. II

Purefoy, Adm. Richard Purefoy FitzGerald, 1862–1943, vol. IV

Purefoy, Wilfred Bagwell, 1862–1930, vol. III

Purey-Cust, Very Rev. Arthur Perceval; *see* Cust.

Purey-Cust, Adm. Sir Herbert Edward; *see* Cust.

Purey-Cust, Brig. Richard Brownlow, 1888–1958, vol. V

Purey Cust, Rev. Canon William Arthur; *see* Cust.

Purnell, Anthony Guy, 1944–1989, vol. VIII

Purnell, Charlotte, *died* 1944, vol. IV

Purnell, Christopher James, 1878–1959, vol. V

Purnell, David Cuthbert, 1932–1979, vol. VII

Purohit, Sir Gopinath Sahitya Bhusan, 1863–1935, vol. III

Purse, Benjamin Ormond, 1876–1950, vol. IV

Purser, Maj.-Gen. Arthur William, 1884–1953, vol. V

Purser, Frederick, 1840–1910, vol. I

Purser, John Mallet, 1839–1929, vol. III

Purser, Louis Claude, 1854–1932, vol. III

Pursey, Comdr Harry, 1891–1980, vol. VII

Purssell, Richard Stanley, 1882–1954, vol. V

Purucker, Gottfried von; *see* Purucker, H. L. G. von.
Purucker, (Hobart Lorenz) Gottfried von, 1874–1942, vol. IV
Purves, James Grant, 1911–1984, vol. VIII
Purves, James Liddell, 1843–1910, vol. I
Purves, Laidlaw; *see* Purves, W. L.
Purves, Sir Raymond Edgar, 1910–1973, vol. VII
Purves, Robert Egerton, 1859–1943, vol. IV
Purves, Col Sir Thomas Fortune, 1871–1950, vol. IV
Purves, William Donald Campbell Laidlaw, 1888–1964, vol. VI
Purves, (William) Laidlaw, *died* 1917, vol. II
Purves-Stewart, Sir James; *see* Stewart.
Purvis, Brig.-Gen. Alexander Burridge, 1854–1928, vol. II
Purvis, Rt Hon. Arthur Blaikie, 1890–1941, vol. IV
Purvis, Adm. Sir Charles Edward K.; *see* Kennedy-Purvis.
Purvis, Sir Robert, 1844–1920, vol. II
Purvis, Tom, *died* 1959, vol. V
Purvis-Russell-Montgomery, Lt-Col Henry Keith; *see* Montgomery.
Pusey, Philip Francis B.; *see* Bouverie-Pusey.
Putnam, George Haven, 1844–1930, vol. III
Putnam, Herbert, 1861–1955, vol. V
Putnam, Sir Thomas, 1862–1936, vol. III
Puttanna Chetty, Sir Krishnarajapur Palligondé, 1856–1938, vol. III
Puttick, Lt-Gen. Sir Edward, 1890–1976, vol. VII
Puxley, Henry Lavallin, 1834–1909, vol. I
Pybus, Sir John; *see* Pybus, Sir P. J.
Pybus, Sir (Percy) John, 1st Bt, *died* 1935, vol. III
Pycraft, W. P., 1868–1942, vol. IV
Pye, Sir David Randall, 1886–1960, vol. V
Pye, Joseph Patrick, *died* 1920, vol. II
Pye, Col William Edmund, 1872–1949, vol. IV
Pye-Smith, Arnold, 1847–1933, vol. III
Pye-Smith, Philip Henry, *died* 1914, vol. I
Pye-Smith, Rutherfoord John, 1848–1921, vol. II
Pyke, Air Cdre Alan, 1911–1977, vol. VII
Pyke, Cyril John, 1892–1976, vol. VII
Pyke, Joseph, 1884–1955, vol. V
Pyke, Lionel Edward, 1854–1899, vol. I
Pyke, Sir Louis Frederick, 1907–1988, vol. VIII
Pyke, Rev. R., 1873–1965, vol. VI
Pyke-Lees, Walter Kinnear, 1909–1978, vol. VII
Pyke-Nott, Comdr Sir James Grenvile, 1897–1972, vol. VII
Pyle, Howard, 1853–1912, vol. I
Pym, Barbara Mary Crampton, 1913–1980, vol. VII
Pym, Sir Charles Evelyn, 1879–1971, vol. VII
Pym, Charles Guy, 1841–1918, vol. II
Pym, Francis, 1849–1927, vol. II
Pym, Col Frederick Harry Norris, 1868–1944, vol. IV
Pym, Leslie Ruthven, 1884–1945, vol. IV
Pym, Rev. Thomas Wentworth, 1885–1945, vol. IV
Pyman, Frank Lee, 1882–1944, vol. IV
Pyman, Gen. Sir Harold English, 1908–1971, vol. VII
Pyne, Brig. Henry George, 1887–1945, vol. IV

Pyne, James Kendrick, 1852–1938, vol. III
Pyne, Hon. Robert Allan, 1855–1931, vol. III
Pyne, Sir Salter; *see* Pyne, Sir T. S.
Pyne, Thomas, 1843–1935, vol. III
Pyne, Sir (Thomas) Salter, 1860–1921, vol. II

Q

Qadir, Khan Bahadur Sheikh Sir Abdul, 1874–1951, vol. V
Quail, Jesse, *died* 1939, vol. III
Quain, Sir Richard, 1st Bt, 1816–1898, vol. I
Qualtrough, Sir Joseph Davidson, 1885–1960, vol. V
Quaranta di San Severino, Baron Bernardo, 1870–1934, vol. III
Quarles, Donald Aubrey, 1894–1959, vol. V
Quarmby, Sir John, 1868–1943, vol. IV
Quaroni, Pietro, 1898–1971, vol. VII
Quarrell, Arthur George, 1910–1983, vol. VIII
Quarrington, Rev. Edwin Fowler, *died* 1922, vol. II
Quartermaine, Sir Allan Stephen, 1888–1978, vol. VII
Quartermaine, Leon, 1876–1967, vol. VI
Quashie-Idun, Sir Samuel Okai, 1902–1966, vol. VI
Quasimodo, Salvatore, 1901–1968, vol. VI
Quass, Phineas, *died* 1961, vol. VI
Quastel, Juda Hirsch, 1899–1987, vol. VIII
Quayle, Sir Anthony; *see* Quayle, Sir J. A.
Quayle, Bronte Clucas, 1919–1986, vol. VIII
Quayle, Sir (John) Anthony, 1913–1989, vol. VIII
Quayle, Richard William, 1901–1973, vol. VII
Quayle, Thomas, 1884–1963, vol. VI
Quayle-Jones, Brig.-Gen. Morey, 1855–1946, vol. IV
Queen, Rt Rev. Carman John, 1912–1974, vol. VII
Queen, Ellery; *see* Dannay, Frederic and Lee, Manfred B.
Queenborough, 1st Baron, 1861–1949, vol. IV
Queensberry, 9th Marquess of, 1844–1900, vol. I (A)
Queensberry, 10th Marquess of, 1868–1920, vol. II
Queensberry, 11th Marquess of, 1896–1954, vol. V
Quekett, Sir Arthur Scott, 1881–1945, vol. IV
Quénet, Hon. Sir Vincent Ernest, 1906–1983, vol. VIII
Quenington, Viscount; Michael Hugh Hicks-Beach, 1877–1916, vol. II
Quennell, Charles Henry Bourne, 1872–1935, vol. III
Quennell, Marjorie, *died* 1972, vol. VII
Quennell, Rev. William, 1839–1908, vol. I
Querido, Israël, 1874–1932, vol. III
Queripel, Hon. Col Alfred Ernest, 1870–1921, vol. II
Queripel, Col Leslie Herbert, 1881–1962, vol. VI
Quex; *see* Nichols, George Herbert Fosdike.
Quibell, 1st Baron, 1879–1962, vol. VI
Quick, Hon. Sir John, 1852–1932, vol. III
Quick, Rev. Oliver Chase, 1885–1944, vol. IV
Quick, Richard, *died* 1939, vol. IV
Quick-Smith, George William, 1905–1986, vol. VIII
Quicke, Captain Noel Arthur Godolphin, 1888–1943, vol. IV
Quickswood, 1st Baron, 1869–1956, vol. V
Quidde, Ludwig, 1858–1941, vol. IV
Quig, Alexander Johnstone, 1892–1962, vol. VI

Quigley, Arthur Grainger, *died* 1945, vol. IV
Quigley, Hugh, 1895–1979, vol. VII
Quigley, Most Rev. James Edward, 1854–1916, vol. II
Quill, Albert William, *died* 1908, vol. I
Quill, Lt-Col Berkeley Crosbie, 1852–1932, vol. III
Quill, Col Raymond Humphrey, 1897–1987
Quill, Maj.-Gen. Richard Henry, 1848–1924, vol. II
Quiller-Couch, Sir Arthur Thomas, 1863–1944, vol. IV
Quilter, Sir Cuthbert; *see* Quilter, Sir W. C.
Quilter, Sir Cuthbert; *see* Quilter, Sir W. E. C.
Quilter, Harry, 1851–1907, vol. I
Quilter, Sir (John) Raymond (Cuthbert), 3rd Bt, 1902–1959, vol. V
Quilter, Sir Raymond; *see* Quilter, Sir J. R. C.
Quilter, Roger, 1877–1953, vol. V
Quilter, Sir (William) Cuthbert, 1st Bt, 1841–1911, vol. I
Quilter, Sir (William Eley) Cuthbert, 2nd Bt, 1873–1952, vol. V
Quin, Rt Rev. George Alderson, 1914–1990, vol. VIII
Quin, Sir Stephen, 1860–1944, vol. IV
Quin, Maj.-Gen. Thomas James, 1842–1919, vol. II
Quin, Captain Hon. Valentine Maurice W.; *see* Wyndham-Quin.
Quinan, Gen. Sir Edward Pellew, 1885–1960, vol. V
Quinan, Kenneth Bingham, 1878–1948, vol. IV
Quine, Rev. John, 1857–1940, vol. III
Quinlan, Hon. Timothy Francis, 1861–1927, vol. II
Quinn, Most Rev. Austin, 1892–1974, vol. VII
Quinn, Harley; *see* Thorley, Wilfrid.
Quinn, James, 1870–1951, vol. V
Quinn, John, 1870–1924, vol. II, vol. III
Quinn, Sir Patrick, 1855–1936, vol. III
Quinnell, Cecil Watson, 1868–1932, vol. III
Quinnell, Air Cdre John Charles, 1891–1983, vol. VIII
Quinton, Hon. Herman William, 1896–1952, vol. V
Quinton, Richard Frith, 1849–1934, vol. III
Quirk, Lt-Col Douglas, 1887–1941, vol. IV
Quirk, Rev. James Francis, 1850–1927, vol. II
Quirk, Rt Rev. Canon John Nathaniel, 1849–1924, vol. II
Quirk, Col John Owen, 1847–1928, vol. II
Quirk, Rev. Canon Robert, 1883–1949, vol. IV
Quirk, Roger Nathaniel, 1909–1964, vol. VI
Quirk, Ronald Charles, 1908–1973, vol. VII
Quist, Sir Emmanuel Charles, *died* 1959, vol. V
Quraishi, Khan Bahadur Nawab, *born* 1878, vol. VI
Qvist, George, 1910–1981, vol. VIII

R

Rabagliati, Andrea Carlo Francisco, 1843–1930, vol. III
Rabagliati, Herman Victor, 1883–1962, vol. VI
Raban, Brig.-Gen. Sir Edward, 1850–1927, vol. II
Rabett, Brig. Reginald Lee Rex, 1887–1966, vol. VI
Rabi, Isidor Isaac, 1898–1988, vol. VIII
Rabino, H. Louis, 1877–1950, vol. IV, vol. V

Raborn, Vice-Adm. William Francis, Jr, 1905–1990, vol. VIII
Raby, Frederic James Edward, 1888–1966, vol. VI
Raby, Henry James, 1827–1907, vol. I
Raby, Joseph Thomas, 1853–1916, vol. II
Raby, Sir Victor Harry, 1897–1990, vol. VIII
Race, Robert Russell, 1907–1984, vol. VIII
Rachmaninoff, Sergei Vassilievitch, 1873–1943, vol. IV
Rackham, Arthur, 1867–1939, vol. III
Rackham, Bernard, 1876–1964, vol. VI
Rackham, Clara Dorothea, *died* 1966, vol. VI
Rackham, Harris, 1868–1944, vol. IV
Radcliffe, 1st Viscount, 1899–1977, vol. VII
Radcliffe, Alexander Nelson, 1856–1944, vol. IV
Radcliffe, Very Rev. Bennett Samuel, *died* 1943, vol. IV
Radcliffe, Brig.-Gen. Sir Charles D.; *see* Delme-Radcliffe.
Radcliffe, Sir Clifford Walter, 1888–1965, vol. VI
Radcliffe, Sir David, 1834–1907, vol. I
Radcliffe, Sir Everard; *see* Radcliffe, Sir J. B. E. H.
Radcliffe, Sir Everard Joseph, 5th Bt, 1884–1969, vol. VI
Radcliffe, Francis Reynolds Yonge, 1851–1924, vol. II
Radcliffe, Sir Frederick Morton, 1861–1953, vol. V
Radcliffe, Brig.-Gen. Frederick Walter, 1873–1934, vol. III
Radcliffe, Geoffrey Reynolds Yonge, 1886–1959, vol. V
Radcliffe, Ven. Harry Sydney, 1867–1949, vol. IV
Radcliffe, Henry, *died* 1921, vol. II
Radcliffe, Major Jasper Fitzgerald, 1867–1916, vol. II
Radcliffe, John Ed., 1846–1919, vol. II
Radcliffe, Sir (Joseph Benedict) Everard (Henry), 6th Bt, 1910–1975, vol. VII
Radcliffe, Sir Joseph Edward, 4th Bt, 1858–1949, vol. IV
Radcliffe, Sir Joseph Percival Pickford, 3rd Bt, 1824–1908, vol. I
Radcliffe, Col Nathaniel Robert, 1870–1930, vol. III
Radcliffe, Gen. Sir Percy Pollexfen de Blaquiere, 1874–1934, vol. III
Radcliffe, Col Philip John Joseph, 1863–1943, vol. IV
Radcliffe, Sir Pollexfen; *see* Radcliffe, Sir W. P.
Radcliffe, Sir Ralph Hubert John D.; *see* Delme-Radcliffe.
Radcliffe, Lt-Gen. Robert Parker, 1819–1907, vol. I
Radcliffe, Vice-Adm. Stephen Herbert, 1874–1939, vol. III
Radcliffe, William, 1856–1938, vol. III
Radcliffe, Sir (William) Pollexfen, 1822–1897, vol. I
Radcliffe, Wyndham Ivor, *died* 1927, vol. II
Radcliffe-Brown, Alfred Reginald, 1881–1955, vol. V
Radcliffe-Cooke, Charles Wallwyn; *see* Cooke.
Radclyffe, Lt-Col Charles Edward, 1864–1915, vol. I
Radclyffe, Major (Charles Robert) Eustace, 1873–1953, vol. V
Radclyffe, Major Eustace; *see* Radclyffe, Major C. R. E.
Radden, Horace Gray, 1903–1966, vol. VI
Radford, Arthur, 1888–1963, vol. VI
Radford, Adm. Arthur William, 1896–1973, vol. VII

Radford, Basil, 1897–1952, vol. V
Radford, Sir Charles Horace, 1854–1916, vol. II
Radford, Air Cdre Dudley Spencer, 1910–1984, vol. VIII
Radford, Edmund Ashworth, 1881–1944, vol. IV
Radford, Edward, 1831–1920, vol. II
Radford, Sir George Heynes, 1851–1917, vol. II
Radford, Rt Rev. Lewis Bostock, 1869–1937, vol. III
Radford, Col Oswald Claude, 1850–1924, vol. II
Radford, Robert, 1874–1933, vol. III
Radhakrishnan, Sir Sarvepalli, 1888–1975, vol. VII
Radhanpur, Nawab Sahib of, 1889–1936, vol. III
Radice, Mrs A. H., (Sheila Radice), died 1960, vol. V
Radice, Evasio Hampden, 1866–1909, vol. I
Radice, Fulke Rosavo, 1888–1987, vol. VIII
Radice, Sheila; see Radice, Mrs A. H.
Radin, Max, 1880–1950, vol. IV (A), vol. V
Radley, Sir Gordon; see Radley, Sir W. G.
Radley, Brig. Hugh Poynton, 1891–1943, vol. IV
Radley, Oswald Alfred, 1887–1977, vol. VII
Radley, Sir (William) Gordon, 1898–1970, vol. VI
Radnor, 5th Earl of, 1841–1900, vol. I
Radnor, 6th Earl of, 1868–1930, vol. III
Radnor, 7th Earl of, 1895–1968, vol. VI
Rado, Richard, 1906–1989, vol. VIII
Radstock, 3rd Baron, 1833–1913, vol. I
Radstock, 4th Baron, 1859–1937, vol. III
Radstock, 5th Baron, 1867–1953, vol. V
Rae, Sir Alexander, 1849–1924, vol. II
Rae, Sir Alexander (Montgomery) Wilson, 1896–1978, vol. VII
Rae, Lt-Col Cecil, 1880–1945, vol. IV
Rae, Brig. Cecil Alexander, 1889–1966, vol. VI
Rae, Cecil Douglas, 1882–1942, vol. IV
Rae, Charles Robert Angus, 1922–1990, vol. VIII
Rae, Duncan McFadyen, 1888–1964, vol. VI
Rae, George Bentham Leathart, 1884–1958, vol. V
Rae, Henrietta; see Normand, Mrs Ernest.
Rae, Sir (Henry) Norman, 1860–1928, vol. II
Rae, Sir James, 1879–1957, vol. V
Rae, Captain Sir James Robert, 1859–1928, vol. II
Rae, Sir James Stanley, 1881–1956, vol. V
Rae, John, 1845–1915, vol. I
Rae, Sir Norman; see Rae, Sir H. N.
Rae, Sir Robert, 1894–1971, vol. VII
Rae, William, 1840–1907, vol. I
Rae, Lt-Col William, 1883–1973, vol. VII
Rae, William Fraser, 1835–1905, vol. I
Rae Smith, Sir Alan, 1885–1961, vol. VI
Raeburn, Agnes M., died 1955, vol. V
Raeburn, Sir Colin, 1894–1970, vol. VI
Raeburn, Sir Edward Alfred, 3rd Bt, 1919–1977, vol. VII
Raeburn, Sir Ernest Manifold, 1878–1922, vol. II
Raeburn, Henry Raeburn Macbeth-, 1860–1947, vol. IV
Raeburn, Walter Augustus Leopold, 1897–1972, vol. VII
Raeburn, Sir William Hannay, 1st Bt, 1850–1934, vol. III
Raeburn, Sir William Norman, 2nd Bt, 1877–1947, vol. IV
Raemaekers, Louis, 1869–1956, vol. V
Raffaelli, J. F., 1850–1924, vol. II

Raffan, Peter Wilson, 1863–1940, vol. III
Rafferty, Michael Harvey, 1877–1953, vol. V
Raffety, Frank Walter, 1875–1946, vol. IV
Raffety, Harold Vezey, 1873–1948, vol. IV
Raffles, Rev. Thomas Stamford, 1853–1926, vol. II
Raffles-Flint, Ven. Stamford R., 1847–1925, vol. II
Raffray, Sir Philippe, 1888–1975, vol. VII
Rafter, Sir Charles Haughton, died 1935, vol. III
Ragg, Rt Rev. Harry Richard, 1889–1967, vol. VI
Ragg, Sir Hugh Hall, 1882–1963, vol. VI
Ragg, Ven. Lonsdale, 1866–1945, vol. IV
Ragg, Air Vice-Marshal Robert Linton, 1901–1973, vol. VII
Ragg, Rev. William Henry Murray, 1861–1944, vol. IV
Raggatt, Sir Harold George, 1900–1968, vol. VI
Raghava Rau, G. Pantulu, 1862–1921, vol. II
Raghavendra Rao, E., died 1942, vol. IV
Raghunath Das Rai Bahadur, Diwan Bahadur Sir Chaube, 1849–1923, vol. II
Raghunath Rao Dinkar, Rao Raja, Mashir-i-Khas Bahadur, Madar-ul-Moham, born 1858, vol. II
Raglan, 3rd Baron, 1857–1921, vol. II
Raglan, 4th Baron, 1885–1964, vol. VI
Rahilly, Captain Denis Edward, 1887–1966, vol. VI
Rahim, Sir Abdur, 1867–1952, vol. V
Rahimtoola, Sir Fazal Ibrahim, 1895–1977, vol. VII
Rahimtoola, Sir Ibrahim, 1862–1942, vol. IV
Rahman, Shaikh Abdur, 1903–1979, vol. VII
Rahman, Sir Ahmed Fazlur, died 1945, vol. IV (A), vol. V
Rahman, Sheikh Mujibur, 1920–1975, vol. VII
Rahman Putra, Tunku (Prince) Abdul; see Abdul Rahman Putra.
Raikes, Captain Arthur E. H., 1867–1915, vol. I
Raikes, Arthur Stewart, 1856–1925, vol. II
Raikes, Vice-Adm. Cecil Dacre Staveley, 1874–1947, vol. IV
Raikes, Maj.-Gen. Charles Lewis, 1837–1919, vol. II
Raikes, Col David Taunton, 1897–1966, vol. VI
Raikes, Ernest Barkley, 1863–1931, vol. III
Raikes, Francis Edward, 1870–1922, vol. II
Raikes, Francis William, died 1906, vol. I
Raikes, Lt-Col Frederick Duncan, 1848–1915, vol. I
Raikes, Maj.-Gen. Sir Geoffrey Taunton, 1884–1975, vol. VII
Raikes, Maj.-Gen. George Leonard, 1878–1949, vol. IV
Raikes, Henry St John Digby, 1863–1943, vol. IV
Raikes, Sir (Henry) Victor (Alpin MacKinnon), 1901–1986, vol. VIII
Raikes, Humphrey Rivaz, died 1955, vol. V
Raikes, Col Lawrence Taunton, 1882–1932, vol. III
Raikes, Adm. Sir Robert Henry Taunton, 1885–1953, vol. V
Raikes, Gen. Robert Napier, 1813–1909, vol. I
Raikes, Sir Victor; see Raikes, Sir H. V. A. M.
Raikes, Rev. Walter Allan, 1852–1928, vol. II
Railing, Sir Harry, 1878–1963, vol. VI
Railing, Max John, 1868–1942, vol. IV
Railston, Lt-Col Henry George Moreton P.; see Pleydell-Railston.
Railton, Herbert, 1857–1910, vol. I
Railton, James, 1863–1949, vol. IV

Railton, Ven. Nathaniel Gerard, 1886–1948, vol. IV
Railton, Reid Antony, 1895–1977, vol. VII
Raimond, C. E.; *see* Robins, Elizabeth.
Rainals, Sir Harry Thomas Alfred, 1816–1899, vol. I
Rainbird, George Meadus, 1905–1986, vol. VIII
Raine, Allen, 1836–1908, vol. I
Raine, Sir Walter, 1874–1938, vol. III
Raines, Gen. Sir Julius Augustus Robert, 1827–1909, vol. I
Raines, Lt-Col Ralph Gore Devereux Groves-, 1877–1953, vol. V
Rainey, Lt-Col John Wakefield, 1881–1967, vol. VI
Rainey, Reginald Charles, 1913–1990, vol. VIII
Rainey, William, 1852–1936, vol. III
Rainey-Robinson, Col Robert Maximilian, 1861–1932, vol. III
Rainier, Adm. John Harvey, 1847–1915, vol. I
Rains, Claude, 1889–1967, vol. VI
Rainsford, Col Marcus Edward Read, 1853–1933, vol. III
Rainsford, Col Stephen Dickson, 1853–1920, vol. II
Rainsford, Col William John Read, 1852–1932, vol. III
Rainsford-Hannay, Brig.-Gen. Frederick, 1854–1950, vol. IV
Rainsford-Hannay, Col Frederick, 1878–1959, vol. V
Rainsford-Hannay, Col Ramsay William, 1844–1933, vol. III
Rainville, Hon. Henri B., 1852–1937, vol. III
Rainwater, James; *see* Rainwater, L. J.
Rainwater, (Leo) James, 1917–1986, vol. VIII
Rainy, Adam Rolland, 1862–1911, vol. I
Rainy, Sir George, 1875–1946, vol. IV
Rainy, Rev. Robert, 1826–1906, vol. I
Raisman, Sir (Abraham) Jeremy, 1892–1978, vol. VII
Raisman, Sir Jeremy; *see* Raisman, Sir A. J.
Raison, Rev. Herbert Chaplin, 1889–1952, vol. V
Raistrick, Harold, 1890–1971, vol. VII
Rait, Lt-Col Arthur John, 1839–1902, vol. I
Rait, Helen Anna Macdonald, *died* 1955, vol. V
Rait, Sir Robert Sangster, 1874–1936, vol. III
Rait Kerr, Col Rowan Scrope, 1891–1961, vol. VI
Raitt, Maj.-Gen. Sir Herbert Aveling, 1858–1935, vol. III
Rajadhyaksha, Ganpat Sakharam, 1896–1955, vol. V
Rajagopala, Sir Chariyar, Perungavur, 1862–1927, vol. II
Rajagopalachari, Sir Shrinivas Prasonna, 1883–1963, vol. VI
Rajagopalacharya, Chakravarti, 1878–1972, vol. VII
Rajapakse, Sir Lalita Abhaya, 1900–1976, vol. VII
Rajgarh, HH Rajah Bir Indra of, *died* 1936, vol. III
Rajkot, Thakore Saheb Shri Dharmendrasinhji Lakhaji Raj, 1910–1940, vol. III
Rajkot, Thakore Saheb Sir Lakhaji Raj Bawaji Raj, 1885–1930, vol. III
Rajpipla, Raja of, 1862–1915, vol. I
Rajpipla, Maharaja of, *died* 1951, vol. V
Rajwade, Maj.-Gen. Ganpatrao Raghunath Raja, Mushir-i-Khas Bahadur, Shaukat-Jung, 1884–1945, vol. IV
Rake, Alfred Mordey, 1906–1978, vol. VII
Raleigh, Cecil, *died* 1914, vol. I
Raleigh, Nigel Hugh C.; *see* Curtis-Raleigh.

Raleigh, Hon. Sir Thomas, 1850–1920, vol. II
Raleigh, Sir Walter Alexander, 1861–1922, vol. II
Ralfs, Maj.-Gen. Bertram George, 1905–1977, vol. VII
Ralli, Augustus John, 1875–1954, vol. V
Ralli, Constantine S.; *see* Scaramanga-Ralli.
Ralli, Sir Lucas Eustratio, 1st Bt, 1846–1931, vol. III
Ralli, Pandeli, 1845–1928, vol. II
Ralli, Sir Strati, 2nd Bt, 1876–1964, vol. VI
Ralph, Col Alfred Colyer, 1869–1932, vol. III
Ralph, Annabella, 1884–1962, vol. VI
Ralph, Helen Douglas Guest, 1892–1961, vol. VI
Ralph, Herbert Walter, 1885–1955, vol. V
Ralph, Ronald Seton, 1895–1985, vol. VIII
Ralph, William, *died* 1928, vol. II, vol. III
Ralphs, Sir (Frederick) Lincoln, 1909–1978, vol. VII
Ralphs, Sir Lincoln; *see* Ralphs, Sir F. L.
Ralston, Alexander Gerard, 1860–1932, vol. III
Ralston, Col Alexander Windeyer, 1885–1971, vol. VII
Ralston, Col Hon. James Layton, 1881–1948, vol. IV
Ralston, Maj.-Gen. William Henry, 1837–1914, vol. I
Ram, Abel John, 1842–1920, vol. II
Ram, Sir Granville; *see* Ram, Sir L. A. J. G.
Ram, Jagjivan, 1908–1986, vol. VIII
Ram, Rai Bahadur Sir Lala G.; *see* Ganga Ram.
Ram, Sir (Lucius Abel John) Granville, 1885–1952, vol. V
Ram, Rev. Robert Digby, 1844–1925, vol. II
Ram, Sir Shri, 1884–1963, vol. VI
Ram, Rev. Stephen Adye Scott, 1864–1928, vol. II
Ram, William Francis Willett, 1907–1968, vol. VI
Ram Chandra, 1889–1987, vol. VIII
Ramachandra Rao, Dewan Bahadur Sir M., 1868–1936, vol. III
Ramaciotti, Maj.-Gen. Gustave, 1861–1927, vol. II
Ramage, Cathleen Mary; *see* Nesbitt, C. M.
Ramage, Captain Cecil Beresford, 1895–1988, vol. VIII
Ramage, Sir Richard Ogilvy, 1896–1971, vol. VII
Ramakrishna, T., *born* 1854, vol. II
Raman, Sir (Chandrasekhara) Venkata, 1888–1970, vol. VI
Raman, Sir Venkata; *see* Raman, Sir C. V.
Ramanathan, Sir Ponnambalam, 1851–1930, vol. III
Ramasany Mudaliyar, Raja Sir Savalai, 1840–1911, vol. I
Ramaswami Aiyar, Sir C. P., 1879–1966, vol. VI
Rambaut, Arthur Alcock, 1859–1923, vol. II
Rambert, Dame Marie (Dame Marie Dukes), 1888–1982, vol. VIII
Ramée, Marie Louise De la; *see* Ouida.
Ramgoolam, Rt Hon. Sir Seewoosagur, 1900–1985, vol. VIII
Rammingen, Baron Luitbert Alexander George Lionel Alphons P.; *see* Pawel-Rammingen.
Rampal Singh, Raja, 1867–1909, vol. I
Rampolla, His Eminence Cardinal Mariano, 1843–1913, vol. I
Rampur, Nawab Sir Sayed Mohammad Hamid Ali Khan Bahadur, 1875–1930, vol. III
Rampur, Maj.-Gen. HH the Nawab, 1906–1966, vol. VI

Ramsay, Maj.-Gen. Sir Alan Hollick, 1895–1973, vol. VII

Ramsay, Alexander, 1822–1909, vol. I

Ramsay, Rev. Alexander, 1857–1935, vol. III

Ramsay, Sir Alexander, 1887–1969, vol. VI

Ramsay, Sir Alexander Burnett, 6th Bt (cr 1806), 1903–1965, vol. VI

Ramsay, Sir Alexander Entwisle, 4th Bt (cr 1806), 1837–1902, vol. I

Ramsay, Adm. Hon. Sir Alexander Robert Maule, 1881–1972, vol. VII

Ramsay, Allen Beville, 1872–1955, vol. V

Ramsay, Andrew Maitland, 1859–1946, vol. IV

Ramsay, Captain Archibald Henry Maule, died 1955, vol. V

Ramsay, Lt-Col Arthur Dennys Gilbert, 1872–1939, vol. III

Ramsay, Adm. Sir Bertram Home, 1883–1945, vol. IV

Ramsay, Hon. Charles Maule, 1859–1936, vol. III

Ramsay, Clyde Archibald, 1914–1974, vol. VII

Ramsay, Maj.-Gen. Frank William, 1875–1954, vol. V

Ramsay, Rev. Frederick Ernest, died 1913, vol. I

Ramsay, Sir George Dalhousie, 1828–1920, vol. II

Ramsay, George Gilbert, 1839–1921, vol. II

Ramsay, Gilbert Anderson, 1880–1915, vol. I

Ramsay, Graham Colville, 1889–1959, vol. V

Ramsay, Henry Havelock, 1863–1929, vol. III

Ramsay, Sir Herbert, 5th Bt (cr 1806), 1868–1924, vol. II

Ramsay, Maj.-Gen. Herbert Maynard, 1843–1917, vol. II

Ramsay, Comdr Hugh Malcolm, 1884–1975, vol. VII

Ramsay, Rev. Ivor Erskine St Clair, 1902–1956, vol. V

Ramsay, J. Grant, 1856–1940, vol. III

Ramsay, James, 1905–1959, vol. V

Ramsay, J(ames) Arthur, 1909–1988, vol. VIII

Ramsay, Sir James Douglas, 11th Bt (cr 1666), 1878–1959, vol. V

Ramsay, Lt-Col James Gordon, 1880–1952, vol. V

Ramsay, Sir James Henry, 10th Bt (cr 1666), 1832–1925, vol. II

Ramsay, Cdre Sir James Maxwell, 1916–1986, vol. VIII

Ramsay, Lt-Col Sir John, 1862–1942, vol. IV

Ramsay, Sir John, 1872–1944, vol. IV

Ramsay, Maj.-Gen. Sir John George, 1856–1920, vol. II

Ramsay, Dom Leander; see Ramsay, H. H.

Ramsay, Louis Eveleigh Bawtree C.; see Cobden-Ramsay.

Ramsay, Mabel Lieda, died 1954, vol. V

Ramsay, Sir Malcolm Graham, 1871–1946, vol. IV

Ramsay, Sir Neis Alexander, 12th Bt, 1909–1986, vol. VIII

Ramsay, The Lady Patricia, (Victoria Patricia Helena Elizabeth), 1886–1974, vol. VII

Ramsay, Hon. Sir Patrick William Maule, 1879–1962, vol. VI

Ramsay, Robert Anstruther, 1887–1975, vol. VII

Ramsay, Rt Rev. Ronald Erskine, 1882–1954, vol. V

Ramsay, Thomas Bridgehill Wilson, 1887–1956, vol. V

Ramsay, Sir William, 1852–1916, vol. II

Ramsay, Sir William Clark, 1901–1973, vol. VII

Ramsay, Sir William Mitchell, 1851–1939, vol. III

Ramsay-Fairfax, Lt-Col William George Astell, 1876–1946, vol. IV

Ramsay-Fairfax, Sir William George Herbert Taylor; see Fairfax.

Ramsay-Fairfax-Lucy, Major Sir Brian Fulke Cameron; see Fairfax-Lucy.

Ramsay-Fairfax-Lucy, Sir Henry William Cameron; see Fairfax-Lucy.

Ramsay-Steel-Maitland, Sir Keith Richard Felix; see Steel-Maitland.

Ramsbotham, Rt Rev. John Alexander, 1906–1989, vol. VIII

Ramsbottom, Edmund Cecil, 1881–1959, vol. V

Ramsbottom, John, 1885–1974, vol. VII

Ramsbottom, John William, 1883–1966, vol. VI

Ramsden, 1st Baron, 1883–1955, vol. V

Ramsden, Brig. Sir Arthur Maxwell, 1894–1957, vol. V

Ramsden, Sir Caryl Oliver Imbert, 8th Bt, 1915–1987, vol. VIII

Ramsden, Charles Frederick Ingram, 1888–1958, vol. V

Ramsden, Sir Geoffrey Charles Frescheville, 1893–1990, vol. VIII

Ramsden, George Taylor, 1879–1936, vol. III

Ramsden, Lady Guendolen; see Ramsden, Lady H. G.

Ramsden, Lady (Helen) Guendolen, 1846–1910, vol. I

Ramsden, Col Herbert Frecheville Smyth, 1856–1931, vol. III

Ramsden, John Charles Francis, 1835–1910, vol. I

Ramsden, Sir John Frecheville, 6th Bt, 1877–1958, vol. V

Ramsden, John Watkinson, 1880–1943, vol. IV

Ramsden, Sir John William, 5th Bt, 1831–1914, vol. I

Ramsden, Lt-Col Josslyn Vere, 1876–1952, vol. V

Ramsden, Omar, 1873–1939, vol. III

Ramsden, Lt-Col Vincent Basil, 1888–1936, vol. III

Ramsden, Walter, died 1947, vol. IV

Ramsden, Sir William, 1857–1928, vol. II

Ramsden, Maj.-Gen. William Havelock, 1888–1969, vol. VI

Ramsden, Major Sir William P.; see Pennington-Ramsden.

Ramsden-Jodrell, Dorothy Lynch, died 1958, vol. V

Ramsey of Canterbury, Baron (Life Peer); Rt Rev. and Rt Hon. Arthur Michael Ramsey, 1904–1988, vol. VIII

Ramsey, Alicia, died 1933, vol. III

Ramsey, Arthur Stanley, 1867–1954, vol. V

Ramsey, Adm. Sir Charles Gordon, 1882–1966, vol. VI

Ramsey, Col Colin Worthington Pope, 1883–1926, vol. II

Ramsey, Rt Rev. Ian Thomas, 1915–1972, vol. VII

Ramsey, Rt Rev. Kenneth Venner, 1909–1990, vol. VIII

Ramsey, Leonard Gerald Gwynne, 1913–1990, vol. VIII

Ramsey, Robert John, 1921–1986, vol. VIII
Ramsey, Stanley Churchill, 1882–1968, vol. VI
Ramson, Ven. John Luce, 1870–1944, vol. IV
Ramunni Menon, Sir Konkoth, 1872–1949, vol. IV
Ranalow, Frederick Baring, 1873–1953, vol. V
Ranasinha, Sir Arthur Godwin, 1898–1976, vol. VII (AII)
Ranbir Singh, Raja Sir, *died* 1916, vol. II
Rance, Maj.-Gen. Sir Hubert Elvin, 1898–1974, vol. VII
Rand, Benjamin, 1856–1934, vol. III
Rand, Ivan Cleveland, 1884–1969, vol. VI
Randall, Sir Alec Walter George, 1892–1977, vol. VII
Randall, Gp Captain Charles Russell Jekyl, 1879–1956, vol. V
Randall, Harry, 1860–1932, vol. III
Randall, Harry Enos, 1899–1976, vol. VII
Randall, Sir Henry Edward, 1847–1930, vol. III
Randall, Henry John, 1877–1964, vol. VI
Randall, Henry John, 1894–1967, vol. VI
Randall, J(ames) G(arfield), 1881–1953, vol. V
Randall, Rt Rev. James Leslie, *died* 1922, vol. II
Randall, John, 1810–1910, vol. I
Randall, Sir John Turton, 1905–1984, vol. VIII
Randall, John William, 1891–1979, vol. VII
Randall, Sir Richard John, 1906–1982, vol. VIII
Randall, Very Rev. Richard William, 1824–1906, vol. I
Randall, Terence George, 1904–1979, vol. VII
Randall Lane, Henry Jerrold; *see* Lane.
Randall-MacIver, David, 1873–1945, vol. IV
Randegger, Alberto, 1832–1911, vol. I
Randell, Major Charles Edmund, 1893–1961, vol. VI
Randell, David, 1854–1912, vol. I
Randell, Hon. George, 1830–1912, vol. I
Randell, John Bulmer, 1918–1982, vol. VIII
Randell, Wilfrid L., 1874–1952, vol. V
Randle, Herbert Niel, 1880–1973, vol. VII
Randles, Sir John Scurrah, 1857–1945, vol. IV
Randles, Rev. Marshall, 1826–1904, vol. I
Randolph, Lt-Col Algernon Forbes, 1865–1953, vol. V
Randolph, Rev. Berkeley William, 1858–1925, vol. II
Randolph, Cyril George, 1899–1985, vol. VIII
Randolph, Mrs Evelyn St L.; *see* St Leger, E.
Randolph, Rev. Francis Charles H.; *see* Hingeston-Randolph.
Randolph, George Boscawen, 1864–1951, vol. V
Randolph, Adm. Sir George Granville, 1818–1907, vol. I
Randolph, Rt Rev. John Hugh Granville, 1866–1936, vol. III
Randolph, Joseph Randolph, 1867–1936, vol. III
Randolph, Peter, 1920–1971, vol. VII
Randolph, Ven. Thomas Berkeley, 1904–1987, vol. VIII
Randolph-Rose, Walter Clerk, 1884–1938, vol. III
Randrup, Michael, 1913–1984, vol. VIII
Ranfurly, 5th Earl of, 1856–1933, vol. III
Ranfurly, 6th Earl of, 1913–1988, vol. VIII
Ranganathan, Shiyali Ramamrita, 1892–1972, vol. VII
Ranger, James, 1889–1975, vol. VII
Ranger, Sir Washington, 1848–1929, vol. III

Rangnekar, Hon. Sir Saiba Shankar, 1878–1949, vol. IV
Ranjitsinhji, Kumar Shri; *see* Nawanagar, Maharaja Jamsaheb of.
Rank, 1st Baron, 1888–1972, vol. VII
Rank, James Voase, 1881–1952, vol. V
Rank, Joseph, *died* 1943, vol. IV
Rankeillour, 1st Baron, 1870–1949, vol. IV
Rankeillour, 2nd Baron, 1897–1958, vol. V
Rankeillour, 3rd Baron, 1899–1967, vol. VI
Ranken, William Bruce Ellis, 1881–1941, vol. IV
Rankin, Lt-Col Allan Coats, 1877–1959, vol. V
Rankin, Dame Annabelle Jane Mary, *died* 1986, vol. VIII
Rankin, Archibald Aloysius, 1871–1951, vol. V
Rankin, Lt-Col (Arthur) Niall (Talbot), 1904–1965, vol. VI
Rankin, Brig.-Gen. Charles Herbert, 1873–1946, vol. IV
Rankin, Ethel Mary, 1893–1956, vol. V
Rankin, Rt Hon. Sir George Claus, 1877–1946, vol. IV
Rankin, Guthrie, 1854–1919, vol. II
Rankin, Maj.-Gen. Henry Charles Deans, 1888–1965, vol. VI
Rankin, Sir Hugh Charles Rhys, 3rd Bt, 1899–1988, vol. VIII
Rankin, Sir James, 1st Bt (*cr* 1898), 1842–1915, vol. I
Rankin, James Stuart, *died* 1960, vol. V
Rankin, John, 1845–1928, vol. II
Rankin, John, *died* 1973, vol. VII
Rankin, John Elliott, 1882–1960, vol. V
Rankin, John Eric, 1905–1976, vol. VII
Rankin, John Mitchell, 1924–1980, vol. VII
Rankin, Lt-Col Niall; *see* Rankin, Lt-Col A. N. T.
Rankin, Rev. Oliver Shaw, 1885–1954, vol. V
Rankin, Lt-Col Sir Reginald, 2nd Bt (*cr* 1898), 1871–1931, vol. III
Rankin, Sir Robert, 1st Bt (*cr* 1937), 1877–1960, vol. V
Rankin, Thomas, 1884–1959, vol. V
Rankin, William Brian, 1915–1976, vol. VII
Rankine, Alexander Oliver, 1881–1956, vol. V
Rankine, Sir John, 1846–1922, vol. II
Rankine, Sir John Dalzell, 1907–1987, vol. VIII
Rankine, Sir Richard Sims Donkin, *died* 1961, vol. VI
Rankine, Col Robert, 1868–1941, vol. IV
Ranking, Lt-Col George Speirs Alexander, 1852–1934, vol. III
Ranking, Maj.-Gen. Robert Philip Lancaster-, 1896–1961, vol. VI
Rankl, Karl, 1898–1968, vol. VI
Ranksborough, 1st Baron, 1852–1921, vol. II
Ransford, Col Sir Alister John, 1895–1974, vol. VII
Ransford, Ella, *died* 1968, vol. VI
Ransford, Rev. Robert Bolton, 1840–1914, vol. I
Ransom, Hon. Sir Alfred; *see* Ransom, Hon. Sir E. A.
Ransom, Rear-Adm. (S) Alfred Charles, 1871–1953, vol. V
Ransom, Charles Frederick George, 1911–1986, vol. VIII
Ransom, Hon. Sir (Ethelbert) Alfred, 1868–1943, vol. IV
Ransom, Herbert Charles, 1881–1960, vol. V

Ransom, William Henry, 1824–1907, vol. I
Ransome, Maj.-Gen. Algernon Lee, 1883–1969, vol. VI
Ransome, Arthur, 1834–1922, vol. II
Ransome, Arthur, 1884–1967, vol. VI
Ransome, Edward Coleby, 1864–1939, vol. III
Ransome, Sir Gordon Arthur, 1910–1978, vol. VII
Ransome, James, 1865–1944, vol. IV
Ransome, Maj.-Gen. Robert St George Tyldesley, 1903–1982, vol. VIII
Ransome, Stafford, 1860–1931, vol. III
Ranson, Col Wilson, 1870–1937, vol. III
Rapallo, Rt Rev. Edward, 1914–1984, vol. VIII
Raper, Agnes Madeline, *died* 1948, vol. IV
Raper, Alfred Baldwin, 1889–1941, vol. IV
Raper, Maj.-Gen. Allan Graeme, 1843–1906, vol. I
Raper, Vice-Adm. Sir George; *see* Raper, Vice-Adm. Sir R. G.
Raper, Henry Stanley, *died* 1951, vol. V
Raper, Sir John Hugh Francis, 1889–1955, vol. V
Raper, Sir Robert George, 1827–1901, vol. I
Raper, Vice-Adm. Sir (Robert) George, 1915–1990, vol. VIII
Raper, Robert William, 1842–1915, vol. I
Raphael, Francis Charles, 1871–1945, vol. IV
Raphael, Geoffrey G., 1893–1969, vol. VI
Raphael, Sir Herbert Henry, 1st Bt, 1859–1924, vol. II
Raphael, John N. (Percival), 1868–1917, vol. II
Rapp, Sir Thomas Cecil, 1893–1984, vol. VIII
Rappoport, Angelo Solomon, 1871–1950, vol. IV
Rapson, Edward James, 1861–1937, vol. III
Ras Mekonen, Sir, 1852–1906, vol. I
Rasch, Sir Carne; *see* Rasch, Sir F. C.
Rasch, Sir Frederic Carne, 1st Bt, 1847–1914, vol. I
Rasch, Sir (Frederic) Carne, 2nd Bt, 1880–1963, vol. VI
Rasch, Brig. Guy Elland Carne, 1885–1955, vol. V
Raschen, George H., 1889–1964, vol. VI
Rash, Dora Eileen A.; *see* Wallace, Doreen.
Rashbrook, Engr Rear-Adm. Henry Samuel, 1856–1942, vol. IV
Rashdall, Very Rev. Hastings, 1858–1924, vol. II
Rashleigh, Sir Colman Battie, 3rd Bt, 1846–1907, vol. I
Rashleigh, Sir Colman Battie Walpole, 4th Bt, 1873–1951, vol. V
Rashleigh, Sir Harry Evelyn Battie, 5th Bt, 1923–1984, vol. VIII
Rashleigh, Rev. John Kendall, 1847–1933, vol. III
Rashleigh, Major Philip, 1881–1949, vol. IV
Rashleigh, Captain Vernon Stanhope, 1879–1946, vol. IV
Rashleigh, Rev. William, 1867–1937, vol. III
Rasmussen, Knud, 1879–1933, vol. III
Rasmussen, Steen Eiler, 1898–1990, vol. VIII
Rason, Hon. Sir Cornthwaite Hector, 1858–1927, vol. II
Rason, Ernest Goldfinch, vol. II
Rassam, Hormuzd, 1826–1910, vol. I
Rastall, Robert Heron, 1871–1950, vol. IV
Rasul, Syed Alay, 1931–1987, vol. VIII
Ratcliff, Rev. Canon Edward Craddock, 1896–1967, vol. VI

Ratcliff, Robert Frederick, *died* 1943, vol. IV
Ratcliffe, Arthur, 1882–1963, vol. VI
Ratcliffe, Dorothy Una; *see* Phillips, Mrs McGrigor.
Ratcliffe, Henry Butler, *died* 1929, vol. III
Ratcliffe, John Ashworth, 1902–1987, vol. VIII
Ratcliffe, Reginald, 1908–1982, vol. VIII
Ratcliffe, Samuel Kerkham, 1868–1958, vol. V
Ratcliffe-Ellis, Sir Thomas Ratcliffe, 1842–1925, vol. II
Rathbone, Basil, 1892–1967, vol. VI
Rathbone, Eleanor, *died* 1946, vol. IV
Rathbone, Hugh Reynolds, *died* 1940, vol. III
Rathbone, John Rankin, 1910–1940, vol. III
Rathbone, Monroe Jackson, 1900–1976, vol. VII
Rathbone, Philip Richardson, 1913–1988, vol. VIII
Rathbone, William Gair, 1849–1919, vol. II
Rathborne, Air Cdre Charles Edward Harry, *died* 1943, vol. IV
Rathcavan, 1st Baron, 1883–1982, vol. VIII
Rathcreedan, 1st Baron, 1850–1930, vol. III
Rathcreedan, 2nd Baron, 1905–1990, vol. VIII
Rathdonnell, 2nd Baron, 1848–1929, vol. III
Rathdonnell, 3rd Baron, 1881–1937, vol. III
Rathdonnell, 4th Baron, 1914–1959, vol. V
Rathmore, 1st Baron, 1838–1919, vol. II
Rathom, John Revelstoke, 1868–1923, vol. II
Ratlam, Maj.-Gen. HH Maharaja Sir Sajjan Singhji, 1880–1947, vol. IV
Ratsey, Col Harold Edward, 1861–1953, vol. V
Ratten, Victor Richard, 1878–1962, vol. VI
Rattenbury, John Ernest, 1870–1963, vol. VI
Rattenbury, Robert Mantle, 1901–1970, vol. VI
Ratteray, Hon. Sir George Oswald, 1903–1980, vol. VII
Rattey, Engr-Rear-Adm. William, 1871–1939, vol. III
Ratti, Achille Ambrogio Damiano; *see* Pius XI.
Rattigan, Frank; *see* Rattigan, W. F. A.
Rattigan, Sir Henry Adolphus Byden, 1864–1920, vol. II
Rattigan, Sir Terence Mervyn, 1911–1977, vol. VII
Rattigan, (William) Frank (Arthur), 1879–1952, vol. V
Rattigan, Sir William Henry, 1842–1904, vol. I
Rattray, Rear-Adm. Sir Arthur Rullion, 1891–1966, vol. VI
Rattray, Brig.-Gen. Charles, 1868–1943, vol. IV
Rattray, Lt-Col Haldane Burney, 1870–1917, vol. II
Rattray, Lt-Gen. Sir James C.; *see* Clerk-Rattray.
Rattray, Col John Grant, 1867–1944, vol. IV
Rattray, Col Paul Robert Burn Clerk, 1859–1937, vol. III
Rattray, Robert Fleming, *died* 1967, vol. VI
Rattray, Captain Robert Sutherland, 1881–1938, vol. III
Rattray, Wellwood, 1849–1902, vol. I
Rattray Taylor, Gordon; *see* Taylor.
Ratter, John, 1908–1985, vol. VIII
Ratwatte, Sir Jayatilaka Cudah, *died* 1940, vol. III (A), vol. V
Rau, Sir Benegal Rama, 1889–1969, vol. VI
Rau, Bhimanakunté Hanumanta, 1855–1922, vol. II
Rau, Sir Narsing, 1887–1953, vol. V
Rau, Sir Raghavendra, 1889–1942, vol. IV

Ravel, Maurice, 1875–1937, vol. III

Raven, Rev. Berney Wodehouse, *died* 1911, vol. I

Raven, Rev. Charles Earle, 1885–1964, vol. VI

Raven, Edward, 1874–1952, vol. V

Raven, Rev. Edward Earle, 1889–1951, vol. V

Raven, Rev. John James, 1833–1906, vol. I

Raven, Rear-Adm. John Stanley, 1910–1987, vol. VIII

Raven, Martin Owen, 1888–1976, vol. VII

Raven, Sir Vincent Litchfield, 1859–1934, vol. III

Raven-Hart, Rev. William Roland, *died* 1919, vol. II

Raven-Hill, Leonard, 1867–1942, vol. IV

Ravenel, Mazyck P., *died* 1946, vol. IV

Ravenhill, Lt-Col Edgar Evelyn, 1859–1907, vol. I

Ravenhill, Brig.-Gen. Frederick Thornhill, 1865–1935, vol. III

Ravenhill, Col Harry Stuart, 1872–1930, vol. III

Ravenhill, Rev. Henry Everett, 1831–1913, vol. I

Ravenscroft, Edward William, 1831–1911, vol. I

Ravensdale, Baroness (2nd in line), 1896–1966, vol. VI

Ravensdale, Thomas Corney, 1905–1990, vol. VIII

Ravenshaw, Lt-Col Charles Withers, 1851–1935, vol. III

Ravenshaw, Maj.-Gen. Hurdis Secundus Lalande, 1869–1920, vol. II

Ravenshear, Ewart Watson, 1893–1959, vol. V

Ravenstein, Ernest George, 1834–1913, vol. I

Ravensworth, 2nd Earl, 1821–1903, vol. I

Ravensworth, 3rd Earl, 1833–1904, vol. I

Ravensworth, 5th Baron, 1837–1919, vol. II

Ravensworth, 6th Baron, 1869–1932, vol. III

Ravensworth, 7th Baron, 1902–1950, vol. IV

Raverat, Gwendolen Mary, 1885–1957, vol. V

Ravilious, Eric, *died* 1942, vol. IV

Raw, Brig. Cecil Whitfield, 1900–1969, vol. VI

Raw, Lt-Col Nathan, 1866–1940, vol. III

Raw, Rupert George, 1912–1988, vol. VIII

Raw, Vice-Adm. Sir Sydney Moffatt, 1898–1967, vol. VI

Rawcliffe, Gordon Hindle, 1910–1979, vol. VII

Rawden-Smith, Rupert Rawden, 1912–1985, vol. VIII

Rawdon, Rev. J. Hamer, *died* 1916, vol. II

Rawdon-Hastings, Paulyn Charles James Reginald; *see* Hastings.

Rawdon-Hastings, Hon. Paulyn Francis Cuthbert, 1856–1907, vol. I

Rawdon Smith, Edward Rawdon, 1890–1957, vol. V

Rawle, Francis, 1846–1930, vol. III

Rawling, Brig.-Gen. Cecil Godfrey, 1870–1917, vol. II

Rawling, Ven. John, 1869–1955, vol. V

Rawlings, Adm. Sir Bernard; *see* Rawlings, Adm. Sir H. B. H.

Rawlings, Edmund Charles, 1854–1917, vol. II

Rawlings, Francis Ian Gregory, 1895–1969, vol. VI

Rawlings, Gertrude Burford, *died* 1939, vol. III

Rawlings, Adm. Sir (Henry) Bernard (Hughes), 1889–1962, vol. VI

Rawlings, Rear-Adm. Henry Clive, 1883–1965, vol. VI

Rawlings, Justly John Gabriel, 1868–1950, vol. IV

Rawlings, Marjorie Kinnan, 1896–1953, vol. V

Rawlins, Maj.-Gen. Alexander Macdonell, 1838–1916, vol. II

Rawlins, Lt-Col Arthur Kennedy, 1868–1943, vol. IV

Rawlins, Evelyn Charles Donaldson, 1884–1971, vol. VII

Rawlins, Francis Hay, 1850–1920, vol. II

Rawlins, Morna Lloyd, 1882–1969, vol. VI

Rawlins, Percy Lionel Edwin, 1902–1977, vol. VII

Rawlins, Maj.-Gen. Stuart Blundell, 1897–1955, vol. V

Rawlins, Col Stuart William Hughes, 1880–1927, vol. II

Rawlins, William Donaldson, 1846–1920, vol. II

Rawlinson, 1st Baron, 1864–1925, vol. II

Rawlinson, Lt-Col Sir Alfred, 3rd Bt, 1867–1934, vol. III

Rawlinson, Rt Rev. Alfred Edward John, 1884–1960, vol. V

Rawlinson, Sir (Alfred) Frederick, 4th Bt, 1900–1969, vol. VI

Rawlinson, Sir Anthony Keith, 1926–1986, vol. VIII

Rawlinson, Rev. Bernard Stephen, 1865–1953, vol. V

Rawlinson, Lt-Col Charles Brooke, 1866–1919, vol. II

Rawlinson, Charles William, *died* 1910, vol. I

Rawlinson, Francis William, 1856–1944, vol. IV

Rawlinson, Sir Frederick; *see* Rawlinson, Sir A. F.

Rawlinson, Rev. Canon George, 1812–1902, vol. I

Rawlinson, Hugh George, 1880–1957, vol. V

Rawlinson, Rt Hon. John Frederick Peel, 1860–1926, vol. II

Rawlinson, Sir Joseph, 1897–1971, vol. VII

Rawlinson, Sir Robert, 1810–1898, vol. I

Rawlinson, Lt-Col Spencer Richard, 1848–1903, vol. I

Rawnsley, Col Claude, 1862–1944, vol. IV

Rawnsley, Edward Preston, 1851–1934, vol. III

Rawnsley, Col Gerald Thomas, 1865–1942, vol. IV

Rawnsley, Rev. Hardwicke Drummond, 1851–1920, vol. II

Raworth, Benjamin Alfred, 1849–1919, vol. II

Raws, Lt-Col Sir Lennon; *see* Raws, Lt-Col Sir W. L.

Raws, Lt-Col Sir (William) Lennon, 1878–1958, vol. V

Rawson, Sir Cooper, 1876–1946, vol. IV

Rawson, Brig. Creswell Duffield, 1883–1964, vol. VI

Rawson, Elizabeth Donata, 1934–1988, vol. VIII

Rawson, Frank, 1856–1928, vol. II

Rawson, Maj.-Gen. Geoffrey Grahame, 1887–1979, vol. VII

Rawson, Harry, 1862–1930, vol. III

Rawson, Adm. Sir Harry Holdsworth, 1843–1910, vol. I

Rawson, Col Herbert Edward, 1852–1924, vol. II

Rawson, Sir Rawson William, 1812–1899, vol. I

Rawson, Col Richard Hamilton, 1863–1918, vol. II

Rawson, Sir Stanley Walter, 1891–1973, vol. VII

Rawson-Shaw, William, 1860–1932, vol. III

Rawsthorne, Alan, 1905–1971, vol. VII

Rawstorne, Rt Rev. Atherton Gwillym, 1855–1936, vol. III

Rawstorne, Brig. George Streynsham, 1895–1962, vol. VI

Rawstorne, Lawrence, 1842–1938, vol. III

Rawstorne, Ven. Robert Atherton, 1824–1902, vol. I

Ray, Rt Rev. Chandu, *born* 1912, vol. VIII

Ray, Frederick Ivor, 1899–1983, vol. VIII

Ray, Gordon Norton, 1915–1986, vol. VIII

Ray, Maharaja Rao Sir Jogendra Narayan, *died* 1946, vol. IV

Ray, Maj.-Gen. Kenneth, 1894–1956, vol. V

Ray, Major MacCarthy Emmet, 1867–1906, vol. I

Ray, Mahendranath, 1862–1925, vol. II

Ray, Matthew Burrow, *died* 1950, vol. IV

Ray, Sir Prafulla Chandra, 1861–1944, vol. IV

Ray, Prithwis Chandra, 1870–1927, vol. II

Ray, Reginald Edwin Anthony, 1891–1972, vol. VII

Ray, Sidney Herbert, 1858–1939, vol. III

Ray, Ted, 1905–1977, vol. VII

Ray, Sir William, 1876–1937, vol. III

Ray-Jones, Raymond, 1886–1942, vol. IV

Raybould, Clarence, 1886–1972, vol. VI

Raybould, Sidney Griffith, 1903–1977, vol. VII

Rayburn, Sam, 1882–1961, vol. VI

Rayleigh, 3rd Baron, 1842–1919, vol. II

Rayleigh, 4th Baron, 1875–1947, vol. IV

Rayleigh, 5th Baron, 1908–1988, vol. VIII

Rayment, Instr Captain Guy Varley, 1878–1951, vol. V

Raymer, Rev. Robert Richmond, 1870–1948, vol. IV

Raymond, Air Vice-Marshal Adélard, 1889–1962, vol. VI

Raymond, E. T.; *see* Thompson, Edward Raymond.

Raymond, Ernest, 1888–1974, vol. VII

Raymond, Col Francis, 1854–1945, vol. IV

Raymond, George, *died* 1929, vol. III

Raymond, George Lansing, 1839–1929, vol. III

Raymond, Harold, 1887–1975, vol. VII

Raymond, Lt-Col Maurice Claud, 1884–1959, vol. V

Raymond, Sir Stanley Edward, 1913–1988, vol. VIII

Raymond, Walter, 1852–1931, vol. III

Raymont, John Edwin George, 1915–1979, vol. VII

Raymont, Thomas, 1864, 1953, vol. V

Rayner, Frank, 1866–1945, vol. IV

Rayner, Henry, 1841–1926, vol. II

Rayner, Vice-Adm. Herbert Sharples, 1911–1976, vol. VII

Rayner, Mabel Mary Cheveley, (Mrs W. N. Jones), *died* 1948, vol. IV

Rayner, Neville, 1914–1988, vol. VIII

Rayner, Brig. Sir Ralph, *died* 1977, vol. VII

Rayner, Sir Thomas Crossley, 1860–1914, vol. I

Raynes, Harold Ernest, 1882–1964, vol. VI

Raynes, John Richard, 1881–1944, vol. IV

Raynes, Rev. Raymond Richard Elliott, 1903–1958, vol. V

Raynes, William Robert, 1871–1966, vol. VI

Raynham, Eustace Frederick, *died* 1939, vol. III

Raynor, Geoffrey Vincent, 1913–1983, vol. VIII

Raynor, Rev. Philip Edwin, 1857–1930, vol. III

Raynor, Sir William Pick, 1854–1972, vol. II

Raynsford, Lt-Col Richard Montague, 1877–1965, vol. VI

Raza Ali, Sir Syed, 1882–1949, vol. IV

Razak bin Hussein, Hon. Tun Haji Abdul; *see* Abdul Razak.

Rea, 1st Baron, 1873–1948, vol. IV

Rea, 2nd Baron, 1900–1981, vol. VIII

Rea, Lady; (Lorna), 1897–1978, vol. VII

Rea, Alec Lionel, 1878–1953, vol. V

Rea, Cecil W., *died* 1935, vol. III

Rea, Edward Hugh, *died* 1901, vol. I

Rea, George Grey, 1858–1931, vol. III

Rea, Major John George Grey, 1886–1955, vol. V

Rea, Robert Lindsay-, 1881–1971, vol. VII

Rea, Rt Hon. Russell, 1846–1916, vol. II

Read, Alexander Llewellyn, 1877–1942, vol. IV

Read, Alfred Burgess, 1899–1973, vol. VII

Read, Sir Alfred Henry, 1871–1955, vol. V

Read, Col Alfred Howard, 1893–1977, vol. VII

Read, Arthur Avery, 1868–1943, vol. IV

Read, Vice-Adm. Arthur Duncan, 1889–1976, vol. VII

Read, Bertie L.; *see* Lees Read.

Read, Carveth, 1848–1931, vol. III

Read, Charles; *see* Read, Cyril N.

Read, Sir Charles David, 1902–1957, vol. V

Read, Sir (Charles) Hercules, 1857–1929, vol. III

Read, Clare Sewell, 1826–1905, vol. I

Read, Conyers Read, 1881–1959, vol. V

Read, Cyril Norman, (Charles), 1925–1987, vol. VIII

Read, Edward Harry H.; *see* Handley-Read.

Read, Ernest, 1879–1965, vol. VI

Read, Francis Charles Jennings, 1875–1958, vol. V

Read, Grantly Dick-, 1890–1959, vol. V

Read, Brig.-Gen. Hastings, 1852–1928, vol. II

Read, Rt Rev. Henry Cecil, 1890–1963, vol. VI

Read, Sir Herbert, 1893–1968, vol. VI

Read, Herbert Harold, 1889–1970, vol. VI

Read, Sir Herbert James, 1863–1949, vol. IV

Read, Sir Hercules; *see* Read, Sir C. H.

Read, John, 1884–1963, vol. VI

Read, (Sir) John Cecil, (styled 9th Bt *cr* 1641), 1820–1899, vol. I

Read, John Erskine, 1888–1973, vol. VII

Read, John Gordon, 1886–1958, vol. V

Read, Lt-Gen. Sir John Hugh Sherlock, 1917–1987, vol. VIII

Read, Opie, 1852–1939, vol. III (A), vol. IV

Read, Col Randulph Offley C.; *see* Crewe-Read.

Read, Col Richard Valentine, 1892–1964, vol. VI

Read, Simon Holcombe Jervis, 1922–1989, vol. VIII

Read, Thomas Talmage, 1893–1974, vol. VII

Read, Walter William, 1855–1907, vol. I

Read, William Henry McLeod, 1819–1909, vol. I

Read, (Sir) William Vero, (styled 10th Bt *cr* 1641), born 1839 (this entry was not transferred to Who Was Who).

Reade, Aleyn Lyell, 1876–1953, vol. V

Reade, Lt-Col Charles James, 1863–1912, vol. I, vol. III

Reade, Sir George Compton, 9th Bt, 1845–1908, vol. I

Reade, Rev George Edwin Pearsall, 1841–1937, vol. III

Reade, Sir George Franklin, 10th Bt, 1869–1923, vol. II

Reade, Herbert Taylor, 1828–1897, vol. I

Reade, Herbert Vincent, 1870–1929, vol. III

Reade, John, 1837–1919, vol. II

Reade, Surg. Maj.-Gen. Sir John By Cole, 1832–1914, vol. I

Reade, Sir John Stanhope, 11th Bt, 1896–1958, vol. V
Reade, Maj.-Gen. Raymond Northland Revell, 1861–1943, vol. IV
Reade, Robert Henry, *died* 1913, vol. I
Reader, Dame Audrey Tattie Hinchcliff, 1903–1989, vol. VIII
Reader, Ralph; *see* Reader, W. H. R.
Reader, (William Henry) Ralph, 1903–1982, vol. VIII
Readett-Bayley, Sir H. Dennis, 1878–1940, vol. III
Readhead, Sir James, 1st Bt, *died* 1930, vol. III
Readhead, Sir James Halder, 2nd Bt, 1879–1940, vol. III
Readhead, James Templeman, (3rd Bt), 1910–1988, vol. VIII
Reading, 1st Marquess of, 1860–1935, vol. III
Reading, 2nd Marquess of, 1889–1960, vol. V
Reading, 3rd Marquess of, 1916–1980, vol. VII
Reading, Marchioness of; (Stella); Baroness Swanborough (Life Peer), 1894–1971, vol. VII
Reading, Marchioness of; (Eva Violet), 1895–1973, vol. VII
Reading, Maj.-Gen. Arnold Hughes Eagleton, 1896–1975, vol. VII
Reading, Sir Claude Hill, 1874–1946, vol. IV
Reading, Joseph Lewis, 1907–1980, vol. VII
Reading, Martin Luther, 1869–1943, vol. IV
Readman, Maj.-Gen. Edgar Platt, 1893–1980, vol. VII
Ready, Gen. Sir Felix Fordati, 1872–1940, vol. III
Reakes, Charles John, 1865–1943, vol. IV
Reakes, George Leonard, 1889–1961, vol. VI
Real, Patrick, 1847–1928, vol. II
Reardon-Smith, Sir Willie; *see* Smith.
Reason, Richard Edmund, 1903–1987, vol. VIII
Reaume, Hon. Joseph Octave, 1856–1933, vol. III
Reavell, Arthur; *see* Reavell, J. A.
Reavell, (James) Arthur, 1872–1973, vol. VII
Reavell, Sir William, 1866–1948, vol. IV
Reay, 11th Lord, 1839–1921, vol. II
Reay, 12th Lord, 1870–1921, vol. II
Reay, 13th Lord, 1905–1963, vol. VI
Reay, Basil; *see* Reay, S. B.
Reay, Hon. Brig.-Gen. Charles Tom, 1857–1933, vol. III
Reay, George Adam, 1901–1971, vol. VII
Reay, Margaret Edith, 1876–1959, vol. V
Reay, (Stanley) Basil, 1909–1987, vol. VIII
Reay, Rev. Thomas Osmotherley, 1834–1914, vol. I
Rebbeck, Rear Adm. Sir Edward; *see* Rebbeck, Sir L. E.
Rebbeck, Sir Frederick Ernest, *died* 1964, vol. VI
Rebbeck, Rear-Adm. Sir (Leopold) Edward, 1901–1983, vol. VIII
Rébora, Piero, 1889–1963, vol. VI
Rebsch, Brig. William Knowles, 1885–1940, vol. III
Reckitt, Sir Harold James, 2nd Bt, 1868–1930, vol. III
Reckitt, Sir James, 1st Bt, 1833–1924, vol. II
Reckitt, Sir Philip Bealby, 3rd Bt, 1873–1944, vol. IV
Recknell, George Hugh, 1893–1975, vol. VII
Reclus, Jacques Elisée, 1830–1905, vol. I
Record, Edgar W., 1873–1943, vol. IV
Redcliffe-Maud, Baron (Life Peer); John Primatt Redcliffe Redcliffe-Maud, 1906–1982, vol. VIII

Reddaway, (Arthur Frederick) John, 1916–1990, vol. VIII
Reddaway, John; *see* Reddaway, A. F. J.
Reddaway, William Fiddian, 1872–1949, vol. IV
Reddick, Ven. Percy George, 1896–1978, vol. VII
Reddie, Brig.-Gen. Anthony Julian, 1873–1960, vol. V
Reddie, Cecil, 1858–1932, vol. III
Reddie, Charles Frederick, *died* 1931, vol. III
Reddie, Lt-Col Sir John Murray, 1872–1954, vol. V
Redding, Rt Rev. Donald Llewellyn, 1898–1969, vol. VI
Redding, John Magnus, 1889–1930, vol. III
Reddish, Sir Halford Walter Lupton, 1898–1978, vol. VII
Reddy, Sir C. Ramalinga, 1880–1951, vol. V
Reddy, Michael, *died* 1919, vol. II
Rede, Captain Roger L'Estrange Murray, *died* 1930, vol. III
Redesdale, 1st Baron, 1837–1916, vol. II
Redesdale, 2nd Baron, 1878–1958, vol. V
Redesdale, 3rd Baron, 1880–1962, vol. VI
Redesdale, 4th Baron, 1885–1963, vol. VI
Redfearn, Sir Herbert, 1915–1988, vol. VIII
Redfern, Sir (Arthur) Shuldham, 1895–1985, vol. VIII
Redfern, Sir Shuldham; *see* Redfern, Sir A. S.
Redfern, Rev. Thomas, 1853–1924, vol. II
Redfern, Thomas William, *died* 1924, vol. II
Redford, Arthur, 1896–1961, vol. VI
Redford, Sir Edward Pigott William, 1850–1933, vol. III
Redford, George Alexander, *died* 1916, vol. II
Redgrave, Sir Michael Scudamore, 1908–1985, vol. VIII
Redgrave, William Archibald, 1903–1986, vol. VIII
Redhead, Edward Charles, 1902–1967, vol. VI
Redhead, Captain Mahon, 1871–1940, vol. III
Redhead, Lt-Col Richard Henry M.; *see* Milne-Redhead.
Redington, Rt Hon. Christopher Talbot, 1847–1899, vol. I
Redington, Frank Mitchell, 1906–1984, vol. VIII
Redl, Lt-Col Ernest Arthur Frederick, 1869–1954, vol. V
Redlich, Rev. Canon Edwin Basil, 1878–1960, vol. V
Redlich, Hans Ferdinand, 1903–1968, vol. VI
Redman, Rev. Alfred, *died* 1927, vol. II
Redman, Brig. Arthur Stanley, 1879–1963, vol. VI
Redman, George Herbert, 1882–1959, vol. V
Redman, Lt-Gen. Sir Harold, 1899–1986, vol. VIII
Redman, Sir (Herbert) Vere, 1901–1975, vol. VII
Redman, Roderick Oliver, 1905–1975, vol. VII
Redman, Sir Vere; *see* Redman, Sir H. V.
Redmayne, Baron (Life Peer); Martin Redmayne, 1910–1983, vol. VIII
Redmayne, Sir Richard Augustine Studdert, 1865–1955, vol. V
Redmayne-Jones, Sir Edward, 1877–1963, vol. VI
Redmond, John Edward, 1851–1918, vol. II
Redmond, Lt-Gen. John Patrick Sutton, *died* 1902, vol. I
Redmond, Sir Joseph Michael, *died* 1921, vol. II

Redmond, Captain William Archer, 1886–1932, vol. III

Redmond, Major William Hoey Kearney, 1861–1917, vol. II

Redpath, Anne, 1895–1965, vol. VI

Redpath, Rev. Henry Adeney, 1848–1908, vol. I

Redpath, Robert, 1871–1960, vol. V

Redshaw, Sir Leonard, 1911–1989, vol. VIII

Redwood, Sir Boverton, 1st Bt, 1846–1919, vol. II

Redwood, Most Rev. Francis Mary, 1839–1935, vol. III

Redwood, Rev. Canon Frederick Arthur, 1891–1964, vol. VI

Redwood, Hugh; see Redwood, W. A. H.

Redwood, Sir Thomas Boverton, 2nd Bt, 1906–1974, vol. VII

Redwood, (William Arthur) Hugh, 1883–1963, vol. VI

Ree, Sir Frank, died 1914, vol. I

Reece, Sir Alan; see Reece, Sir L. A.

Reece, B(razila) Carroll, 1889–1961, vol. VI

Reece, Courtenay Walton, 1899–1984, vol. VIII

Reece, Francis Bertram, 1888–1971, vol. VII

Reece, Sir Gerald, 1897–1985, vol. VIII

Reece, John H.; see Holroyd-Reece.

Reece, Sir (Louis) Alan, 1906–1984, vol. VIII

Reece, Surg.-Col Richard James, 1862–1924, vol. II

Reed, Sir (Albert) Ralph, 1884–1958, vol. V

Reed, Sir Alfred Hamish, 1875–1975, vol. VII

Reed, Sir Andrew, 1837–1914, vol. I

Reed, Sir Arthur Conrad, died 1961, vol. VI

Reed, Arthur William, 1873–1957, vol. V

Reed, Austin Leonard, 1873–1954, vol. V

Reed, Bellamy Alexander C.; see Cash-Reed.

Reed, Sir Carol, 1906–1976, vol. VII

Reed, Col Charles, 1879–1958, vol. V

Reed, Clinton Austin, 1876–1954, vol. V

Reed, Douglas, 1895–1976, vol. VII

Reed, Edward, 1902–1953, vol. V

Reed, Sir Edward James, 1830–1906, vol. I

Reed, Edward Tennyson, 1860–1933, vol. III

Reed, Rt Rev. Ernest Samuel, died 1970, vol. VI

Reed, Hon. Sir Geoffrey Sandford, 1892–1970, vol. VI (AII)

Reed, Maj.-Gen. Hamilton Lyster, 1869–1931, vol. III

Reed, Haythorne, 1873–1934, vol. III

Reed, Henry, 1914–1986, vol. VIII

Reed, Henry Ashman, 1866–1935, vol. III

Reed, Col Henry Robert Baynes, 1880–1939, vol. III

Reed, Herbert Langford, 1889–1954, vol. V

Reed, Herbert Parker, died 1920, vol. II

Reed, Sir (Herbert) Stanley, 1872–1969, vol. VI

Reed, Lt-Col John Arthur Wemyss, 1864–1939, vol. III

Reed, Hon. Sir John Ranken, 1864–1955, vol. V

Reed, Sir John Seymour B.; see Blake-Reed.

Reed, Col Sir Joseph, 1867–1942, vol. IV

Reed, Joseph Martin, 1857–1932, vol. III

Reed, Langford; see Reed, H. L.

Reed, Rev. Martin, 1856–1926, vol. II

Reed, Maurice Ernest, 1908–1975, vol. VII

Reed, Michael, 1912–1985, vol. VIII

Reed, Philip Dunham, 1899–1989, vol. VIII

Reed, Sir Ralph; see Reed, Sir A. R.

Reed, Sir Reginald Charles, 1909–1982, vol. VIII

Reed, Rev. Samuel, 1844–1932, vol. III

Reed, Sir Stanley; see Reed, Sir H. S.

Reed, Thomas Brackett, 1839–1902, vol. I

Reed, William Henry, 1877–1942, vol. IV

Rees, Arthur J., died 1942, vol. IV

Rees, Sir Beddoe, died 1931, vol. III

Rees, Ven. David John, 1862–1924, vol. II

Rees, David Morgan, 1904–1980, vol. VII

Rees, Dame Dorothy Mary, born 1898, vol. VIII

Rees, E(dgar) Philip, 1896–1964, vol. VI

Rees, Lt-Col Evan Thomas, 1883–1955, vol. V

Rees, Sir Frederick; see Rees, Sir J. F.

Rees, Sir Frederick Tavinor, 1890–1976, vol. VII

Rees, Prof. Garnet, 1912–1990, vol. VIII

Rees, Geraint; see Rees, R. G.

Rees, Goronwy; see Rees, M. G.

Rees, Griffith Caradoc, 1868–1924, vol. II

Rees, Rev. Henry, 1844–1924, vol. II

Rees, Howell, 1847–1933, vol. III

Rees, Brig.-Gen. Hubert Conway, 1882–1948, vol. IV

Rees, Sir Hugh E.; see Ellis-Rees.

Rees, Sir (James) Frederick, 1883–1967, vol. VI

Rees, Sir John David, 1st Bt, 1854–1922, vol. II

Rees, Engr-Captain John David, 1861–1951, vol. V

Rees, Lt-Col John Gordon, 1884–1963, vol. VI

Rees, John Rawlings, 1890–1969, vol. VI

Rees, (John) Tudor, died 1956, vol. V

Rees, Sir Josiah, 1821–1899, vol. I

Rees, Leonard, 1856–1932, vol. III

Rees, Mrs Leonard, (Mary Emily MacLeod Moore), died 1960, vol. V

Rees, Gp Captain Lionel Wilmot Brabazon, 1884–1955, vol. V

Rees, Sir Milsom, 1866–1952, vol. V

Rees, (Morgan) Goronwy, 1909–1979, vol. VII

Rees, Richard Geraint, 1907–1986, vol. VIII

Rees, Sir Richard Lodowick Edward Montagu, 2nd Bt, 1900–1970, vol. VI

Rees, Rev. Thomas, 1869–1926, vol. II

Rees, Thomas Ifor, 1890–1977, vol. VII

Rees, Thomas James, 1875–1957, vol. V

Rees, Rev. Thomas Morgan, 1850–1937, vol. III

Rees, Maj.-Gen. Thomas Wynford, died 1959, vol. V

Rees, Rt Rev. Timothy, 1874–1939, vol. III

Rees, Tudor; see Rees, J. T.

Rees, Ven. Vaughan William Treharne, 1879–1948, vol. IV

Rees, William, 1887–1978, vol. VII

Rees, Rev. William Goodman Edwards, died 1936, vol. III

Rees, Adm. William Stokes, 1853–1929, vol. III

Rees-Davies, Sir Colin, 1867–1933, vol. III

Rees-Davies, Sir William; see Davies.

Rees-Mogg, Lt-Col Graham Beauchamp Coxeter, 1881–1949, vol. IV

Rees-Reynolds, Col Alan Randall, 1909–1982, vol. VIII

Rees-Thomas, Ruth, (Mrs William Rees-Thomas); see Darwin, R.

Rees-Thomas, William, 1887–1978, vol. VII

Reese, Frederick Focke, 1854–1924, vol. II

Reeve, Ada, 1874–1966, vol. VI

Reeve, Rt Rev. (Arthur) Stretton, 1907–1981, vol. VIII
Reeve, Charles Arthur, 1857–1936, vol. III
Reeve, Charles William, 1879–1965, vol. VI
Reeve, Rev. Edward Henry Lisle, *died* 1936, vol. III
Reeve, Henry Fenwick, 1854–1920, vol. II
Reeve, Maj.-Gen. John Talbot Wentworth, 1891–1983, vol. VIII
Reeve, Raymond Roope, 1875–1952, vol. V
Reeve, Russell, 1895–1970, vol. VI
Reeve, Simms, 1826–1919, vol. II
Reeve, Rt Rev. Stretton; *see* Reeve, Rt Rev. A. S.
Reeve, Rt Rev. William Day, 1844–1925, vol. II
Reeves, Amber; *see* Blanco White, A.
Reeves, Rt Rev. Ambrose; *see* Reeves, Rt Rev. R. A.
Reeves, Vice-Adm. Edward, 1869–1954, vol. V
Reeves, Edward Ayearst, 1862–1945, vol. IV
Reeves, Helen, (Mrs Henry Reeves); *see* Mathers, Helen.
Reeves, Henry Albert, *died* 1914, vol. I
Reeves, Col Henry Spencer Edward, 1843–1914, vol. I
Reeves, James, 1909–1978, vol. VII
Reeves, Col John, 1854–1904, vol. I
Reeves, John Sims, 1822–1900, vol. I
Reeves, Joseph, 1888–1969, vol. VI
Reeves, Rt Rev. (Richard) Ambrose, 1899–1980, vol. VII
Reeves, Hon. Sir William Conrad, 1838–1902, vol. I
Reeves, Hon. William Pember, 1857–1932, vol. III
Reeves-Smith, Sir George, *died* 1941, vol. IV
Refalo, Sir Michelangelo, 1876–1923, vol. II
Reford, John Hope, 1873–1957, vol. V
Regan, Charles Tate, 1878–1943, vol. IV
Regan, Col James Louis, 1888–1948, vol. IV
Regener, Erich, 1881–1955, vol. V
Regester, William, 1848–1929, vol. III
Regg, Ven. Thomas Richard, *died* 1930, vol. III
Regis, Sister Mary; *see* Morant, Dame Mary Maud.
Regis de Oliveira, Raul, *died* 1942, vol. IV
Regnart, Sir Horace Grece, 1841–1912, vol. I
Regnier, Henri François Joseph de, 1864–1936, vol. III
Rehan, Ada, 1860–1916, vol. II
Reiach, Herbert, 1873–1921, vol. II
Reich, Emil, 1854–1910, vol. I
Reichenbach, Henry-Béat de F.; *see* de Fischer-Reichenbach.
Reichardt, Charles Henry, 1851–1903, vol. I
Reichel, Sir Harry Rudolf, 1856–1931, vol. III
Reichel, Rev. Oswald Joseph, 1840–1923, vol. II
Reid, Baron (Life Peer); James Scott Cumberland Reid, 1890–1975, vol. VII
Reid, Surg.-Gen. Sir Adam Scott, 1848–1918, vol. II
Reid, Captain Alec Stratford C.; *see* Cunningham-Reid.
Reid, Alexander, 1843–1919, vol. II
Reid, Lt-Col Alexander, 1863–1927, vol. II
Reid, Sir Alexander James, 1889–1968, vol. VI
Reid, Maj.-Gen. Sir Alexander John Forsyth, 1846–1913, vol. I
Reid, Col Alexander Kirkwood, 1884–1948, vol. IV
Reid, Alfred Henry, 1845–1931, vol. III
Reid, Col A(ndrew) McKie, 1893–1973, vol. VII

Reid, Sir Archdall; *see* Reid, Sir G. A. O'B.
Reid, Archibald David, 1844–1908, vol. I
Reid, Sir Archibald Douglas, 1871–1924, vol. II
Reid, Arthur Beatson, 1888–1965, vol. VI
Reid, Sir Arthur Hay Stewart, 1851–1930, vol. III
Reid, Sir Charles, 1819–1901, vol. I
Reid, Charles, 1892–1961, vol. VI
Reid, Sir Charles Carlow, 1879–1961, vol. VI
Reid, Charles William, 1895–1983, vol. VIII
Reid, Dame Clarissa Guthrie, *died* 1933, vol. III
Reid, Clement, *died* 1916, vol. II
Reid, Sir David Douglas, 1st Bt (*cr* 1936), 1872–1939, vol. III
Reid, Lt-Col David Elder, 1864–1930, vol. III
Reid, Maj.-Gen. Denys Whitehorn, 1897–1970, vol. VI
Reid, Desmond Arthur, 1918–1983, vol. VIII
Reid, Donald Darnley, 1914–1977, vol. VII
Reid, Sir Douglas Neilson, 2nd Bt (*cr* 1922), 1898–1971, vol. VII
Reid, Sir Edward, 1819–1912, vol. I
Reid, Edward Douglas Whitehead, 1883–1930, vol. III
Reid, Sir Edward James, 2nd Bt (*cr* 1897), 1901–1972, vol. VII
Reid, Rt Rev. Edward Thomas Scott, 1871–1938, vol. III
Reid, Edward Waymouth, 1862–1948, vol. IV
Reid, Col Ellis Ramsay, 1850–1918, vol. II
Reid, Ven. Ernest Gordon, *died* 1966, vol. VI
Reid, Forrest, 1876–1947, vol. IV
Reid, Francis Alexander, 1915–1987, vol. VIII
Reid, Col Francis Maude, 1849–1922, vol. II
Reid, Brig. Sir Francis Smith, 1900–1970, vol. VI
Reid, Frank Aspinall, 1875–1961, vol. VI
Reid, Very Rev. G. R. S., 1871–1964, vol. VI
Reid, Sir George, 1841–1913, vol. I
Reid, George, *died* 1925, vol. II
Reid, George Agnew, 1860–1947, vol. IV
Reid, Sir (George) Archdall O'Brien, 1860–1929, vol. III
Reid, Col George Eric, *died* 1938, vol. III
Reid, Rt Hon. Sir George Houstoun, 1845–1918, vol. II
Reid, George Ogilvy, *died* 1928, vol. II
Reid, George Smith, 1904–1985, vol. VIII
Reid, Sir George Thomas, 1881–1966, vol. VI
Reid, Very Rev. George Thomson Henderson, 1910–1990, vol. VIII
Reid, Gordon Stanley, 1923–1989, vol. VIII
Reid, Harold Alexander, 1891–1974, vol. VII
Reid, Lt-Col Harry Avery, 1877–1947, vol. IV
Reid, Rt Rev. Harry Seymour, *died* 1943, vol. IV
Reid, Col Hector Gowans, 1881–1966, vol. VI
Reid, Helen Richmond Young, 1869–1941, vol. IV
Reid, Helen Rogers, (Mrs Ogden Reid), 1882–1970, vol. VI
Reid, Rev. Henry M. B., 1856–1927, vol. II
Reid, Sir Henry Valentine Rae, 4th Bt (*cr* 1823), 1845–1903, vol. I
Reid, Lt-Col Herbert Cartwright, 1864–1950, vol. IV
Reid, Vice-Adm. Howard Emerson, 1897–1962, vol. VI
Reid, Sir Hugh, 1st Bt (*cr* 1922), 1860–1935, vol. III

Reid, Sir Hugh Gilzean-, 1836–1911, vol. I
Reid, James, 1839–1908, vol. I
Reid, Sir James, 1st Bt (cr 1897), 1849–1923, vol. II
Reid, Rev. James, 1877–1963, vol. VI
Reid, James Robert, 1838–1908, vol. I
Reid, James Smith, 1846–1926, vol. II
Reid, Very Rev. James Watson, died 1904, vol. I
Reid, Sir John, 1861–1933, vol. III
Reid, John, 1874–1934, vol. III
Reid, John, 1906–1990, vol. VIII
Reid, John Alexander, 1895–1969, vol. VI
Reid, Hon. John Dowsley, 1859–1929, vol. III
Reid, Lt-Col John Garnet, 1878–1939, vol. III
Reid, Adm. Sir (John) Peter (Lorne), 1903–1973, vol. VII
Reid, John R., died 1926, vol. II
Reid, Sir John Thyne, 1903–1984, vol. VIII
Reid, Sir John Watt, 1823–1909, vol. I
Reid, Rev. Kenneth Lyle, 1873–1937, vol. III
Reid, Col Lestock Hamilton, 1857–1936, vol. III
Reid, Louis Arnaud, 1895–1986, vol. VIII
Reid, Sir Marshall Frederick, 1864–1925, vol. II
Reid, May, 1882–1980, vol. VII
Reid, Ogden, 1882–1947, vol. IV
Reid, Mrs Ogden; see Reid, Helen Rogers.
Reid, Patrick Robert, 1910–1990, vol. VIII
Reid, Col Percy Lester, 1882–1968, vol. VI
Reid, Adm. Sir Peter; see Reid, Adm. Sir J. P. L.
Reid, Rachel Robertson, 1876–1952, vol. V
Reid, Lt-Col Richard, died 1918, vol. II
Reid, Robert, 1922–1980, vol. VII
Reid, Robert Douglas, 1898–1983, vol. VIII
Reid, Robert Lawrence, 1858–1916, vol. II
Reid, Sir Robert Niel, 1883–1964, vol. VI
Reid, Robert Payton, 1859–1945, vol. IV
Reid, Robert Whyte, 1885–1929, vol. III
Reid, Robert William, died 1939, vol. III
Reid, Samuel, born 1854, vol. II
Reid, Stephen, 1873–1948, vol. IV
Reid, Stuart J., died 1927, vol. II
Reid, Thomas, 1881–1963, vol. VI
Reid, Thomas Bertram Wallace, 1901–1981, vol. VIII
Reid, Sir (Thomas) Wemyss, 1842–1905, vol. I
Reid, Walter, died 1917, vol. II
Reid, Col Walter Richard, 1880–1959, vol. V
Reid, Sir Wemyss; see Reid, Sir T. W.
Reid, Hon. Whitelaw, 1837–1912, vol. I
Reid, Major Sir William, died 1934, vol. III
Reid, William, died 1965, vol. VI
Reid, Sir William, 1906–1985, vol. VIII
Reid, William Allan, 1865–1952, vol. V
Reid, Rev. William Cawley, died 1933, vol. III
Reid, William Clarke, 1909–1956, vol. V
Reid, William David, 1883–1964, vol. VI
Reid, Sir William Duff, 1869–1924, vol. II
Reid, William Edwin Charles, 1870–1947, vol. IV
Reid, Sir William James, 1871–1939, vol. III
Reid, William Paton, 1854–1932, vol. III
Reid, William Sydney, 1880–1960, vol. V
Reid-Adam, Randle, 1912–1982, vol. VIII
Reid Dick, Sir W(illiam), 1879–1961, vol. VI
Reilly, Baron (Life Peer); Paul Reilly, 1912–1990, vol. VIII

Reilly, Lt-Col Sir Bernard Rawdon, 1882–1966, vol. VI
Reilly, Brian Thomas, 1924–1988, vol. VIII
Reilly, Col Charles Cooper, 1862–1926, vol. II
Reilly, Sir Charles Herbert, 1874–1948, vol. IV
Reilly, Sir D'Arcy; see Reilly, Sir H. D. C.
Reilly, E. Albert, 1868–1943, vol. IV
Reilly, Sir (Henry) D'Arcy (Cornelius), 1876–1948, vol. IV
Reilly, Joseph, 1889–1965, vol. VI
Reilly, Very Rev. Thomas, died 1921, vol. II
Reinach, Joseph, 1856–1921, vol. II
Reinach, Salomon, 1858–1932, vol. III
Reindorp, Rt Rev. George Edmund, 1911–1990, vol. VIII
Reinhardt, Max, 1873–1943, vol. IV
Reinold, Arnold William, 1843–1921, vol. II
Reinold, Vice-Adm. Harold Owen, 1877–1962, vol. VI
Reisner, George Andrew, 1867–1942, vol. IV
Reiss, Lt-Col Alec, 1871–1932, vol. III
Reiss, Charles, 1873–1949, vol. IV
Reiss, Sir John Anthony Ewart, 1909–1989, vol. VIII
Reiss, Richard Leopold, 1883–1959, vol. V
Reith, 1st Baron, 1889–1971, vol. VII
Reith, Rev. David, 1842–1909, vol. I
Reitlinger, Gerald Roberts, 1900–1978, vol. VII
Reitz, Col Deneys, 1882–1944, vol. IV
Reitz, Hon. Francis William, 1844–1934, vol. III
Réjane, Madame, (Gabrielle Réju), 1857–1920, vol. II
Relf, Ernest Frederick, 1888–1970, vol. VI
Relph, George, 1888–1960, vol. V
Relton, Arthur John, 1856–1946, vol. IV
Relton, Frederick Ernest, 1883–1963, vol. VI
Relton, Rev. Herbert Maurice, 1882–1971, vol. VII
Remarque, Erich Maria, 1898–1970, vol. VI
Remer, John Rumney, 1883–1948, vol. IV
Remington, Geoffrey Cochrane, 1897–1968, vol. VI
Remizov, Alexei, 1877–1957, vol. V
Remnant, 1st Baron, 1863–1933, vol. III
Remnant, 2nd Baron, 1895–1967, vol. VI
Remnant, Ernest, 1872–1941, vol. IV
Remnant, Hon. Peter Farquharson, 1897–1968, vol. VI
Remsen, Ira, 1846–1927, vol. II
Renals, Sir Herbert, 3rd Bt, 1919–1961, vol. VI
Renals, Sir James Herbert, 2nd Bt, 1870–1927, vol. II, vol. III
Renals, Sir Joseph, 1st Bt, 1843–1908, vol. I
Renard, Samuel, died 1924, vol. II
Renaud, Maj.-Gen. Ernest James, died 1967, vol. VI
Renault, Louis, 1843–1918, vol. II
Renault, Mary (Mary Challans), 1905–1983, vol. VIII
Rendall, Archibald, 1921–1989, vol. VIII
Rendall, Athelstan, 1871–1948, vol. IV
Rendall, Rev. Gerald Henry, 1851–1945, vol. IV
Rendall, Montague John, 1862–1950, vol. IV
Rendall, Philip Stanley, 1895–1983, vol. VIII
Rendall, Richard Antony, 1907–1957, vol. V
Rendall, Vernon Horace, 1869–1960, vol. V
Rendel, 1st Baron, 1834–1913, vol. I
Rendel, Sir Alexander Meadows, 1829–1918, vol. II
Rendel, George Wightwick, 1833–1902, vol. I

Rendel, Sir George William, 1889–1979, vol. VII
Rendel, Harry Stuart G.; see Goodhart-Rendel.
Rendell, Rev. Arthur Medland, 1842–1918, vol. II
Rendell, Rev. James Robson, 1850–1926, vol. II
Rendell, Col Walter Frederic, 1888–1951, vol. V
Rendell, William Reginald, 1868–1948, vol. IV
Rendle, Alfred Barton, 1865–1938, vol. III
Rendlesham, 5th Baron, 1840–1911, vol. I
Rendlesham, 6th Baron, 1868–1938, vol. III
Rendlesham, 7th Baron, 1874–1943, vol. IV
Renfrew, Thomas, 1901–1975, vol. VII
Renier, Gustaaf Johannes, 1892–1962, vol. VI
Renison, Sir Patrick Muir, 1911–1965, vol. VI
Renison, Most Rev. Robert John, 1875–1957, vol. V
Rennell, 1st Baron, 1858–1941, vol. IV
Rennell, 2nd Baron, 1895–1978, vol. VII
Rennenkampff, Gen.-Lt Paul Charles von, 1854–1918, vol. II
Rennert, Guenther, 1911–1978, vol. VII
Rennie, Sir Alfred Baillie, 1896–1987, vol. VIII
Rennie, Charles Robert, 1880–1969, vol. VI
Rennie, Compton Alexander, 1915–1987, vol. VIII
Rennie, Edward Henry, 1852–1927, vol. II
Rennie, Sir Ernest Amelius, 1868–1935, vol. III
Rennie, Francis Pepys, 1872–1946, vol. IV
Rennie, Col George Arthur Paget, 1872–1951, vol. V
Rennie, Col George Septimus, died 1930, vol. III
Rennie, Sir Gilbert McCall, 1895–1981, vol. VIII
Rennie, Lt-Col Horace Watt, died 1943, vol. IV
Rennie, James, 1814–1903, vol. I
Rennie, John, died 1960, vol. V (A)
Rennie, Major John George, 1865–1920, vol. II
Rennie, Sir John Ogilvy, 1914–1981, vol. VIII
Rennie, Sir Richard Temple, 1839–1905, vol. I
Rennie, Maj.-Gen. Robert, 1862–1949, vol. IV
Rennie, Col Samuel James, 1855–1935, vol. III
Rennie, Maj.-Gen. Tom Gordon, 1900–1945, vol. IV
Rennie, William, died 1957, vol. V
Renny, Brig. George Douglas, 1908–1971, vol. VII
Renny, Gen. Henry, 1815–1900, vol. I
Renny, Col Lewis Frederick, 1877–1955, vol. V
Renny, Maj.-Gen. Sidney Mercer, 1861–1921, vol. II
Renny-Tailyour, Col Thomas Francis Bruce, 1863–1937, vol. III
Renoir, Jean, 1894–1979, vol. VII
Renold, Sir Charles Garonne, 1883–1967, vol. VI
Renouf, Vice-Adm. Edward de Faye, 1888–1972, vol. VII
Renouf, Sir Peter le Page, 1822–1897, vol. I
Renouf, Winter Charles, 1868–1954, vol. V
Renouvin, Pierre, 1893–1974, vol. VII
Renshaw, Arthur Henry, died 1918, vol. II
Renshaw, Sir Charles Bine, 1st Bt, 1848–1918, vol. II
Renshaw, Sir (Charles) Stephen (Bine), 2nd Bt, 1883–1976, vol. VII
Renshaw, Hon. John Brophy, 1909–1987, vol. VIII
Renshaw, John W., 1877–1955, vol. V
Renshaw, Sir Stephen; see Renshaw, Sir C. S. B.
Renshaw, Walter Charles, 1840–1922, vol. II
Rentell, Henry William Sidney, 1864–1927, vol. II, vol. III
Renton, Major (Alexander) Leslie, 1868–1947, vol. IV
Renton, Sir Alexander Wood, 1861–1933, vol. III

Renton, Lady; Claire Cicely Renton, 1923–1986, vol. VIII
Renton, James Crawford, died 1919, vol. II
Renton, Brig. James Malcolm Leslie, 1898–1972, vol. VII
Renton, Major Leslie; see Renton, Major A. L.
Rentoul, Sir Gervais, 1884–1946, vol. IV
Rentoul, James Alexander, died 1919, vol. II
Rentoul, Rt Rev. John Laurence, 1846–1926, vol. II
Renwick, 1st Baron, 1904–1973, vol. VII
Renwick, Hon. Sir Arthur, 1837–1910, vol. I
Renwick, Sir Eustace Deuchar, 3rd Bt (cr 1921), 1902–1973, vol. VII
Renwick, Sir George, 1st Bt (cr 1921), 1850–1931, vol. III
Renwick, George Russell, 1901–1984, vol. VIII
Renwick, Major Gustav Adolph, 1883–1956, vol. V
Renwick, Sir Harry Benedetto, 1st Bt, 1861–1932, vol. III
Renwick, Sir John, 1901–1983, vol. VIII
Renwick, Sir John Robert, 2nd Bt (cr 1921), 1877–1946, vol. IV
Renwick, William Lindsay, 1889–1970, vol. VI
Renzis, Francesco de, Baron, died 1900, vol. I
Repington, Lt-Col Charles A'Court-, 1858–1925, vol. II
Repington, Charles Henry Wyndham A'C.; see A'Court Repington.
Repplier, Agnes, 1858–1950, vol. IV
Restler, Sir James William, died 1918, vol. II
Reston, Clifford Arthur, 1928–1979, vol. VII
Reszke, Jean de, 1853–1925, vol. II
Rettie, Middleton, died 1910, vol. I
Retie, Lt-Col William John Kerr, 1868–1939, vol. III
Retzius, Magnus Gustaf, 1842–1919, vol. II
Reuter, Baron de; Auguste Julius Clemens Herbert, 1852–1915, vol. I
Reuter, Baron de; Paul Julius, 1816–1899, vol. I
Reuther, Walter Philip, 1907–1970, vol. VI
Revans, Sir John, 1911–1988, vol. VIII
Revel, John Daniel, 1884–1967, vol. VI
Revell, Alfred Edgar, 1877–1932, vol. III
Revell, Daniel Graisberry, 1869–1954, vol. V
Revell-Smith, Maj.-Gen. William Revell, 1894–1956, vol. V
Revelstoke, 1st Baron, 1828–1897, vol. I
Revelstoke, 2nd Baron, 1863–1929, vol. III
Revelstoke, 3rd Baron, 1864–1934, vol. III
Reventlow, Count Eduard, 1883–1963, vol. VI
Revie, Donald, 1927–1989, vol. VIII
Reville, Rt Rev. Mgr Stephen, 1844–1916, vol. II
Revington, Air Cdre Arthur Pethick, 1901–1986, vol. VIII
Rew, Lt-Col Horace Edward, 1899–1967, vol. VI
Rew, Sir (R.) Henry, 1858–1929, vol. III
Rewa, Bandhvesh Ex-Maharaja of, Sir Gulab Singh Bahadur, 1903–1950, vol. IV
Rewah, HH Maharaja Venkat Raman Singh Bahadur, 1876–1918, vol. II
Rewcastle, Cuthbert Snowball, 1888–1962, vol. VI
Rewse, Rev. Gilbert Flesher S.; see Smith-Rewse.
Rewse, Col Henry Whistler, S.; see Smith-Rewse.
Rex, Marcus, 1886–1971, vol. VII
Rey, Lt-Col Sir Charles Fernand, 1877–1968, vol. VI

Rey, Jean, 1902–1983, vol. VIII

Reymont, Wladislaw Stanislaw, 1867–1925, vol. II

Reynard, Helene, 1875–1947, vol. IV

Reynard, Matthew Andrew, 1878–1946, vol. IV

Reynard, Robert Froding, 1857–1926, vol. II

Reynardson, Col Charles Birch-, 1845–1919, vol. II

Reynardson, Lt-Col Henry T. Birch, 1892–1972, vol. VII

Reynaud, Paul, 1878–1966, vol. VI

Reyne, Rear-Adm. Sir Cecil Nugent, 1881–1958, vol. V

Reyne, Lt-Col Gerard van Rossum, 1886–1940, vol. III

Reynell, Douglas, 1877–1949, vol. IV

Reynell, Walter Rupert, 1885–1948, vol. IV

Reynell-Pack, Arthur Denis Henry Heber, 1860–1937, vol. III

Reynolds, Col Alan Randall R.; *see* Rees-Reynolds.

Reynolds, Lt-Col Alan Boyd, 1879–1940, vol. III

Reynolds, Alan Lowe, 1897–1977, vol. VII

Reynolds, Sir Alfred, 1850–1931, vol. III

Reynolds, Alfred Charles, 1884–1969, vol. VI

Reynolds, Alice; *see* Cullen, A.

Reynolds, Rev. Bernard, 1850–1930, vol. III

Reynolds, Air Marshal Sir Bryan Vernon, 1902–1965, vol. VI

Reynolds, Cedric Lawton, 1888–1958, vol. V

Reynolds, Charles Henry, 1844–1908, vol. I

Reynolds, Clyde Albert M.; *see* Marshall-Reynolds.

Reynolds, Lt-Col Denys Walter, 1884–1940, vol. III

Reynolds, Doris Livesey, (Mrs Arthur Holmes), 1899–1985, vol. VIII

Reynolds, Major Douglas, 1881–1916, vol. II

Reynolds, Edward, 1874–1944, vol. IV

Reynolds, Emerson; *see* Reynolds, J. E.

Reynolds, Ernest Septimus, 1861–1926, vol. II

Reynolds, Sir Francis Jubal, 1857–1924, vol. II

Reynolds, Frank, 1876–1953, vol. V

Reynolds, Frank Neon, 1895–1952, vol. V

Reynolds, Sir Frank Umhlali, 1852–1930, vol. III

Reynolds, George McClelland, 1865–1940, vol. III

Reynolds, Rt Hon. Gerald William, 1927–1969, vol. VI

Reynolds, Adm. Harry Campbell, 1853–1949, vol. IV

Reynolds, Captain Henry, 1881–1948, vol. IV

Reynolds, Henry Osborne, 1883–1947, vol. IV

Reynolds, Herbert John, 1832–1916, vol. II

Reynolds, J. H., 1842–1927, vol. II

Reynolds, (James) Emerson, 1844–1920, vol. II

Reynolds, Lt-Col James Henry, 1844–1932, vol. III

Reynolds, Col Sir James Philip, 1st Bt, 1865–1932, vol. III

Reynolds, Sir Jeffrey Fellowes Crofts, 1893–1966, vol. VI

Reynolds, John Arthur, 1925–1990, vol. VIII

Reynolds, Lt-Col Sir John Francis Roskell, 2nd Bt, 1899–1956, vol. V

Reynolds, John Henry, 1874–1949, vol. IV

Reynolds, John Richardson, 1873–1934, vol. III

Reynolds, Sir Leonard William, 1874–1946, vol. IV

Reynolds, Mrs Louis Baillie, *died* 1939, vol. III

Reynolds, Louis George Stanley, *died* 1945, vol. IV

Reynolds, Osborne, 1842–1912, vol. I

Reynolds, Paul Kenneth Baillie, 1896–1973, vol. VII

Reynolds, Major Sir Percival Reuben, 1876–1965, vol. VI

Reynolds, Major Philip Guy, 1871–1936, vol. III

Reynolds, Quentin James, 1902–1965, vol. VI

Reynolds, Reginald Francis, *died* 1936, vol. III

Reynolds, Reginald Philip Neri, 1867–1936, vol. III

Reynolds, Richard Samuel, Jr, 1908–1980, vol. VII

Reynolds, Maj.-Gen. Roger Clayton, 1895–1983, vol. VIII

Reynolds, Russell John, 1880–1964, vol. VI

Reynolds, Seymour John Romer, 1911–1987, vol. VIII

Reynolds, Sidney Hugh, 1867–1949, vol. IV

Reynolds, Stephen, 1881–1919, vol. II

Reynolds, Warwick, 1880–1926, vol. II

Reynolds, William George Waterhouse, 1860–1928, vol. II

Reynolds, William Vaughan, 1908–1988, vol. VIII

Reynolds-Ball, Eustace Alfred, *died* 1928, vol. II

Reynolds-Stephens, Sir William, 1862–1943, vol. IV, HH

Rhayader, 1st Baron, 1862–1939, vol. III

Rhead, George Woolliscroft, *died* 1920, vol. II

Rheam, Henry Meynell, 1859–1920, vol. II

Rhigini, Madame de; *see* Russell, Ella.

Rhind, Donald, 1899–1982, vol. VIII

Rhind, Lt-Col Sir Duncan; *see* Rhind, Lt-Col Sir T. D.

Rhind, Edwin Scoby O.; *see* Oak-Rhind.

Rhind, John Massey, 1868–1936, vol. III

Rhind, Lt-Col Sir (Thomas) Duncan, 1871–1927, vol. II

Rhind, William Birnie, *died* 1933, vol. III

Rhine, Joseph Banks, 1895–1980, vol. VII

Rhoades, James, 1841–1923, vol. II

Rhoads, Cornelius Packard, 1898–1959, vol. V

Rhodes, Baron (Life Peer); Hervey Rhodes, 1895–1987, vol. VIII

Rhodes, Sir Campbell, 1874–1941, vol. IV

Rhodes, Rt Hon. Cecil John, 1853–1902, vol. I

Rhodes, Rev. Canon Cecil, 1910–1990, vol. VIII

Rhodes, Charles Kenneth, 1889–1941, vol. IV

Rhodes, Sir Christopher George, 3rd Bt, 1914–1964, vol. VI

Rhodes, Rev. Clifford Oswald, 1911–1985, vol. VIII

Rhodes, Hon. Edgar Nelson, 1877–1942, vol. IV

Rhodes, Sir Edward, 1870–1959, vol. V

Rhodes, Major Elmhirst, 1858–1931, vol. III

Rhodes, Col Francis William, 1851–1905, vol. I

Rhodes, Sir Frederick Edward, 4th Bt, 1843–1911, vol. I

Rhodes, Geoffrey William, 1928–1974, vol. VII

Rhodes, George, 1851–1924, vol. II

Rhodes, Sir George Wood, 1st Bt, 1860–1924, vol. II

Rhodes, Brig.-Gen. Sir Godfrey Dean, 1886–1971, vol. VII

Rhodes, Harold, 1885–1964, vol. VI

Rhodes, Harold Vale, *died* 1970, vol. VI

Rhodes, Harold William, 1889–1956, vol. V

Rhodes, Col Hon. Sir Heaton; *see* Rhodes, Col Hon. Sir R. H.

Rhodes, Helen, *died* 1936, vol. III

Rhodes, Rev. Herbert A., 1869–1956, vol. V

Rhodes, James Ford, 1848–1927, vol. II

Rhodes, Lt-Col Sir John Phillips, 2nd Bt, 1884–1955, vol. V

Rhodes, Kathlyn Mary, *died* 1962, vol. VI

Rhodes, Col Hon. Sir (Robert) Heaton, 1861–1956, vol. V

Rhodes, Col Stephen, *died* 1966, vol. VI

Rhodes, Stephen, 1918–1989, vol. VIII

Rhodes, Walter Harpham, 1888–1962, vol. VI

Rhondda, 1st Viscount, 1856–1918, vol. II

Rhondda, Viscountess (2nd in line), *died* 1958, vol. V

Rhondda, Viscountess; (Sybil), *died* 1941, vol. IV

Rhydderch, Sir William Edmund Hodges, 1890–1961, vol. VI

Rhyl, Baron (Life Peer); (Evelyn) Nigel (Chetwode) Birch, 1906–1981, vol. VIII

Rhys, Ernest, 1859–1946, vol. IV

Rhys, Jean, (Mrs Jean Hamer), 1894–1979, vol. VII

Rhys, Rt Hon. Sir John, 1840–1915, vol. I

Rhys, Keidrych, 1915–1987, vol. VIII

Rhys-Roberts, Thomas Esmôr Rhys, 1910–1975, vol. VII

Rhys Williams, Sir Brandon Meredith, 2nd Bt, 1927–1988, vol. VIII

Rhys Williams, Juliet Evangeline, (Lady Rhys Williams), 1898–1964, vol. VI

Rhys-Williams, Lt-Col Sir Rhys; *see* Williams.

Riach, Col William, 1873–1942, vol. IV

Riall, Air Cdre Arthur Bookey, 1911–1984, vol. VIII

Ribbentrop, Joachim von, 1893–1946, vol. IV

Ribblesdale, 4th Baron, 1854–1925, vol. II

Riberi, His Eminence Cardinal Antonio, 1897–1967, vol. VI

Ribot, Alexandre F., 1842–1923, vol. II

Ribton, Sir George, 4th Bt, 1842–1901, vol. I

Ricardo, Lt-Col Ambrose St Quintin, 1866–1923, vol. II

Ricardo, Adm. Arthur David, 1861–1931, vol. III

Ricardo, Col Francis Cecil, 1852–1924, vol. II

Ricardo, Halsey Ralph, 1854–1928, vol. II

Ricardo, Sir Harry Ralph, 1885–1974, vol. VII

Ricardo, Major Harry William Ralph, 1860–1945, vol. IV

Ricardo, Lt-Col Henry George, 1860–1940, vol. III

Ricardo, Col Horace, 1850–1935, vol. III

Ricardo, Col Percy Ralph, 1855–1907, vol. I

Ricci, Luigi, *died* 1915, vol. I

Rice, Alexander Hamilton, 1875–1956, vol. V

Rice, Alice Hegan, *died* 1942, vol. IV

Rice, (Benjamin) Lewis, 1837–1927, vol. II

Rice, Cale Young, 1872–1943, vol. IV (A), vol. V

Rice, Rt Hon. Sir Cecil Arthur S.; *see* Spring-Rice.

Rice, David Talbot, 1903–1972, vol. VII

Rice, Dominick S.; *see* Spring-Rice.

Rice, Air Vice-Marshal Sir Edward Arthur Beckton, 1893–1948, vol. IV

Rice, Sir Edward Bridges, 1819–1902, vol. I

Rice, Elmer, 1892–1967, vol. VI

Rice, Adm. Sir Ernest, 1840–1927, vol. II

Rice, Sir Frederick Gill, 1866–1935, vol. III

Rice, George Ritchie, 1881–1982, vol. VIII

Rice, George Samuel, 1866–1950, vol. IV

Rice, Col Henry James, 1894–1964, vol. VI

Rice, James, 1874–1936, vol. III

Rice, Joseph M., 1857–1934, vol. III

Rice, Lewis; *see* Rice, B. L.

Rice, Dame Margaret Ker P.; *see* Pryse-Rice.

Rice, Percy Christopher, 1877–1963, vol. VI

Rice, Roderick Alexander, 1922–1984, vol. VIII

Rice, Lt-Col Sidney Mervyn, 1873–1959, vol. V

Rice, Maj.-Gen. Sir Spring Robert, 1858–1929, vol. III

Rice, Stephen Edward S.; *see* Spring-Rice.

Rice, Thomas Edmund, *died* 1941, vol. IV

Rice, Walter Francis, *died* 1941, vol. IV

Rice, Wilfred Eric, 1898–1979, vol. VII

Rice, Sir William George, 1861–1936, vol. III

Rice, Rev. William Ignatius, 1883–1955, vol. V

Rice, Hon. and Rev. William Talbot, 1861–1945, vol. IV

Rice, Comdr William Victor, *died* 1932, vol. III

Rice-Jones, Benjamin Rowland, 1888–1978, vol. VII

Rice-Oxley, Sir Alfred James, 1856–1941, vol. IV

Rice-Oxley, Douglas George, 1885–1972, vol. VII

Rich, Adena M., (Mrs Kenneth F. Rich), *died* 1967, vol. VI

Rich, Alfred William, 1856–1922, vol. II

Rich, Sir Almeric Edmund Frederic, 5th Bt, 1859–1948, vol. IV

Rich, Sir Almeric Frederic Conness, 6th Bt, 1897–1983, vol. VIII

Rich, Sir Charles Henry Stuart, 4th Bt, 1859–1913, vol. I

Rich, Charles T., 1869–1940, vol. III

Rich, Edmund Milton, 1875–1954, vol. V

Rich, Col Edmund Tillotson, 1874–1937, vol. III

Rich, Edward Charles, 1895–1959, vol. V

Rich, Edwin Ernest, 1904–1979, vol. VII

Rich, Vice-Adm. Frederick St George, 1852–1914, vol. I

Rich, Rt Hon. Sir George Edward, 1863–1956, vol. V

Rich, Maj.-Gen. Henry Hampden, 1891–1976, vol. VII

Rich, Jacob Morris, 1897–1987, vol. VIII

Rich, Rev. John, 1826–1913, vol. I

Rich, Mrs Kenneth F.; *see* Rich, Adena M.

Rich, Rev. Leonard James, *died* 1920, vol. II

Rich, Rowland William, 1901–1981, vol. VIII

Rich, Roy, 1912–1970, vol. VI

Richard, Ven. Robert Henry, 1869–1929, vol. III

Richard, Timothy, 1845–1919, vol. II

Richards, Albert Edwin George, 1856–1942, vol. IV

Richards, Albert Elswood, 1848–1918, vol. II

Richards, Alfred Newton, 1876–1966, vol. VI

Richards, Audrey Isabel, 1899–1984, vol. VIII

Richards, Ceri Giraldus, 1903–1971, vol. VII

Richards, Brig. Collen Edward Melville, *died* 1971, vol. VII

Richards, Rev. Daniel, 1892–1989, vol. VIII

Richards, Dickinson Woodruff, Jr, 1895–1973, vol. VII

Richards, Edgar Lynton, (Tony Richards), 1912–1983, vol. VIII

Richards, Sir Edmund Charles, 1889–1955, vol. V

Richards, Edward Windsor, *died* 1921, vol. II

Richards, Sir Erle; *see* Richards, Sir H. E.

Richards, Major Francis Howe, 1890–1937, vol. III

Richards, Francis John, 1901–1965, vol. VI

Richards, Frank, 1875–1961, vol. VI

Richards, Frank Roydon, 1899–1978, vol. VII
Richards, Franklin Thomas Grant, 1872–1948, vol. IV
Richards, Fred C., died 1932, vol. III
Richards, Sir Frederick William, 1833–1912, vol. I
Richards, Hon. Sir Frederick William, 1869–1957, vol. V
Richards, Rear-Adm. G. E., 1852–1927, vol. II
Richards, Rev. George Chatterton, 1867–1951, vol. V
Richards, George Edward Fugl, 1891–1974, vol. VII
Richards, Maj.-Gen. George Warren, 1898–1978, vol. VII
Richards, Gertrude Mary, died 1944, vol. IV
Richards, Gilbert Stanley Nowell, 1912–1980, vol. VII
Richards, Sir Gordon, 1904–1986, vol. VIII
Richards, Lt-Col Harold Arthur David, 1874–1947, vol. IV
Richards, Harold Meredith, died 1942, vol. IV
Richards, Henry Caselli, 1884–1947, vol. IV
Richards, Henry Charles, 1851–1905, vol. I
Richards, Sir (Henry) Erle, 1861–1922, vol. II
Richards, Sir Henry George, 1860–1928, vol. II
Richards, Sir Henry Maunsell, 1869–1957, vol. V
Richards, Henry William, 1865–1956, vol. V
Richards, Herbert Arthur, 1866–1957, vol. V
Richards, Herbert Paul, 1848–1916, vol. II
Richards, Hugh Augustine, 1884–1949, vol. IV
Richards, Brig. Hugh Upton, 1894–1983, vol. VIII
Richards, Rt Rev. Isaac, 1859–1936, vol. III
Richards, Ivor Armstrong, 1893–1979, vol. VII
Richards, Engr-Captain John Arthur, 1865–1949, vol. IV
Richards, John Eugene, 1885–1951, vol. V
Richards, John Gower Meredith, 1900–1968, vol. VI
Richards, Very Rev. John Harold, 1869–1952, vol. V
Richards, John Henry, 1818–1901, vol. I
Richards, John Morgan, 1841–1918, vol. II
Richards, Rt Rev. John Richards, 1901–1990, vol. VIII
Richards, Sir Joseph, 1888–1968, vol. VI
Richards, Rev. Leyton, 1879–1948, vol. IV
Richards, Maurice John, 1894–1969, vol. VI
Richards, Hon. Mrs Noel Olivier, 1892–1969, vol. VI (AII)
Richards, Sir Norman Grantham Lewis, 1905–1977, vol. VII
Richards, Owain Westmacott, 1901–1984, vol. VIII
Richards, Owen, 1873–1949, vol. IV
Richards, Percy Andrew Ellis, 1868–1937, vol. III
Richards, Raymond, 1906–1978, vol. VII
Richards, Reginald James, died 1950, vol. IV
Richards, Robert, 1884–1954, vol. V
Richards, Rupert Peel, 1872–1941, vol. IV
Richards, Col Samuel Smith Crosland, 1841–1918, vol. II
Richards, Major Sidney, vol. III
Richards, Stephen Elswood, 1878–1950, vol. IV (A)
Richards, Theodore William, 1868–1928, vol. II, vol. III
Richards, Rt Hon. Thomas, 1859–1931, vol. III
Richards, Thomas Frederick, 1863–1942, vol. IV
Richards, Tony; see Richards, E. L.
Richards, Whitmore Lionel, 1869–1954, vol. V

Richards, William, 1863–1939, vol. III
Richards, Air Cdre William Edward Victor, 1897–1964, vol. VI
Richards, William James, 1915–1978, vol. VII
Richards, William John, 1903–1976, vol. VII
Richards, Maj.-Gen. William Watson, 1892–1961, vol. VI
Richardson, Very Rev. Alan, 1905–1975, vol. VII
Richardson, Sir Albert Edward, 1880–1964, vol. VI
Richardson, Air Marshal Sir (Albert) Victor (John), 1884–1960, vol. V
Richardson, Sir Albion Henry Herbert, died 1950, vol. IV
Richardson, Sir Alexander, 1864–1928, vol. II
Richardson, Alexander Stewart, 1897–1989, vol. VIII
Richardson, Maj.-Gen. Alexander Whitmore Colquhoun, 1887–1964, vol. VI
Richardson, Alfred, died 1934, vol. III
Richardson, Arnold Edwin Victor, 1883–1949, vol. IV
Richardson, Arthur, 1860–1936, vol. III
Richardson, Arthur, 1897–1980, vol. VII (AII)
Richardson, Arthur Johnstone, 1862–1940, vol. III
Richardson, Charles Arthur, 1918–1972, vol. VII
Richardson, Lt-Gen. Sir Charles William Grant, 1868–1929, vol. III
Richardson, Cyril Albert, 1891–1966, vol. VI
Richardson, Maj.-Gen. David Turnbull, 1886–1957, vol. V
Richardson, Dorothy M., (Mrs Alan Odle), died 1957, vol. V
Richardson, Sir Earl; see Richardson, Sir L. E. G.
Richardson, Sir Edward Austin Stewart-, 15th Bt (cr 1630), 1872–1914, vol. I
Richardson, Edward Gick, 1896–1960, vol. V
Richardson, E(dward) Ryder, 1901–1961, vol. VI
Richardson, Ven. Edward Shaw, 1862–1921, vol. II
Richardson, Lt-Col Edwin Hautonville, 1863–1948, vol. IV
Richardson, Emily Moore; see Hamilton, E. M.
Richardson, Foster, died 1942, vol. IV
Richardson, Major Francis James, 1866–1917, vol. II
Richardson, Sir Frank; see Richardson, Sir H. F.
Richardson, Frank, 1870–1917, vol. II
Richardson, Frederic Stuart, 1855–1934, vol. III
Richardson, Rev. Canon Frederick, 1885–1967, vol. VI
Richardson, Frederick Denys, 1913–1983, vol. VIII
Richardson, Rev. George Leyburn, 1867–1934, vol. III
Richardson, Lt-Gen. Sir George Lloyd Reily, 1847–1931, vol. III
Richardson, Maj.-Gen. Sir George Spafford, 1868–1938, vol. III
Richardson, Sir George Wigham, 3rd Bt, 1895–1981, vol. VIII
Richardson, Col Gerald, 1907–1974, vol. VII
Richardson, Major Guy; see Richardson, Major T. G. F.
Richardson, Harold Owen Wilson, 1907–1982, vol. VIII
Richardson, Harry, 1891–1966, vol. VI
Richardson, Harry Linley, 1878–1947, vol. IV
Richardson, Sir Henry; see Richardson, Sir J. H. S.
Richardson, Henry Gerald, died 1974, vol. VII

Richardson, Henry Handel, *died* 1946, vol. IV

Richardson, Henry Marriott, 1876–1936, vol. III

Richardson, Lt-Col Henry Sacheverell Carleton, 1883–1958, vol. V

Richardson, Hon. Horace Frank, 1854–1935, vol. III

Richardson, Sir (Horace) Frank, 1901–1983, vol. VIII

Richardson, Major Sir Ian Rorie Hay S.; *see* Stewart-Richardson.

Richardson, Ven. James Banning, 1843–1923, vol. II

Richardson, Col James Jardine, 1873–1942, vol. IV

Richardson, James Nicholson, 1846–1921, vol. II

Richardson, Ven. John, 1817–1904, vol. I

Richardson, Engr-Rear-Adm. John, 1862–1928, vol. II

Richardson, Major John, 1859–1935, vol. III

Richardson, Rt Rev. John, 1894–1978, vol. VII

Richardson, Most Rev. John Andrew, 1868–1938, vol. III

Richardson, Maj.-Gen. John Booth, 1838–1923, vol. II

Richardson, Maj.-Gen. John Dalyell, 1880–1954, vol. V

Richardson, Ven. John Gray, 1849–1924, vol. II

Richardson, John Henry, 1890–1970, vol. VI

Richardson, Sir (John) Henry (Swain), 1889–1980, vol. VII

Richardson, John I., 1836–1913, vol. I

Richardson, Very Rev. John Macdonald, 1880–1964, vol. VI

Richardson, Joseph, 1830–1902, vol. I

Richardson, Maj.-Gen. Joseph Fletcher, 1822–1900, vol. I

Richardson, Joseph Hall, 1857–1945, vol. IV

Richardson, Josephus Hargreaves, 1856–1932, vol. III

Richardson, Leopold John Dixon, 1893–1979, vol. VII

Richardson, Captain Leslie, 1885–1934, vol. III

Richardson, Sir Leslie Lewis, 2nd Bt, 1915–1985, vol. VIII

Richardson, Sir Lewis, 1st Bt (*cr* 1924), 1873–1934, vol. III

Richardson, Lewis Fry, 1881–1953, vol. V

Richardson, Linetta de Castelvecchio, *died* 1975, vol. VII

Richardson, Sir (Lionel) Earl (George), 1921–1990, vol. VIII

Richardson, Maggie; *see* Mitchell, Mrs G. J.

Richardson, Maurice Robert, 1884–1950, vol. IV

Richardson, Brig.-Gen. Morris Ernald, 1878–1929, vol. III

Richardson, Lt-Col Neil Graham Stewart-, 1881–1934, vol. III

Richardson, Sir Owen Willans, 1879–1959, vol. V

Richardson, Philip John Sampey, 1875–1963, vol. VI

Richardson, Lt-Col Sir Philip Wigham, 1st Bt (*cr* 1929), 1865–1953, vol. V

Richardson, Ralph, 1845–1933, vol. III

Richardson, Sir Ralph David, 1902–1983, vol. VIII

Richardson, Rev. Raymond William, 1909–1968, vol. VI

Richardson, Robert, 1862–1943, vol. IV

Richardson, Bt Lt-Col Robert Airth, 1864–1936, vol. III

Richardson, Rev. Canon Robert Douglas, 1893–1989, vol. VIII

Richardson, Maj.-Gen. Roland, 1896–1973, vol. VII

Richardson, Spencer William, 1869–1927, vol. II

Richardson, Sir Thomas, 1846–1906, vol. I

Richardson, Thomas, 1868–1928, vol. II

Richardson, Thomas, *died* 1956, vol. V

Richardson, Major (Thomas) Guy (Fenton), 1885–1966, vol. VI

Richardson, Sir Thomas William, 1865–1947, vol. IV

Richardson, Maj.-Gen. Thomas William, 1895–1968, vol. VI

Richardson, Air Marshal Sir Victor; *see* Richardson, Air Marshal Sir A. V. J.

Richardson, Violet Roberta S.; *see* Stewart-Richardson.

Richardson, Rt Rev. William Moore, 1844–1915, vol. I

Richardson, Sir William Robert, 1909–1986, vol. VIII

Richardson, William Rowson, 1892–1978, vol. VII

Richardson, Maj.-Gen. William Stewart, *died* 1901, vol. I

Richardson, Sir William Wigham, 2nd Bt (*cr* 1929), 1893–1973, vol. VII

Richardson, Col Sir Wodehouse Dillon, 1854–1929, vol. III

Richardson-Bunbury, Sir Mervyn William; *see* Bunbury.

Richardson-Cox, Major Eustace, 1862–1935, vol. III

Richardson-Drummond-Hay, Col James Adam Gordon; *see* Hay.

Richardson-Griffiths, Major Charles Du Plat, 1855–1925, vol. II

Riche, Georges de P.; *see* Porto-Riche.

Richepin, Jean, 1849–1926, vol. II

Riches, Sir Eric William, 1897–1987, vol. VIII

Riches, Lindsay Gordon, 1904–1972, vol. VII

Riches, Tom Hurry, 1846–1911, vol. I

Richet, Charles Robert, 1850–1935, vol. III

Richey, Lt-Col George Henry Mills, 1867–1949, vol. IV

Richey, James Alexander, 1874–1931, vol. III

Richey, Sir James Bellett, 1834–1902, vol. I

Richey, James Ernest, 1886–1968, vol. VI

Richmond, 7th Duke of, **and Gordon,** 2nd Duke of, 1845–1928, vol. II

Richmond, 8th Duke of, **and Gordon,** 3rd Duke of, 1870–1935, vol. III

Richmond, 9th Duke of, **and Gordon,** 4th Duke of, 1904–1989, vol. VIII

Richmond and Gordon, Duchess of; (Hilda Madeleine), *died* 1971, vol. VII

Richmond, Sir Arthur Cyril, 1879–1968, vol. VI

Richmond, Brig. Arthur Eaton, 1892–1961, vol. VI

Richmond, Sir Bruce Lyttelton, 1871–1964, vol. VI

Richmond, Sir Daniel; *see* Richmond, Sir R. D.

Richmond, Sir David, 1843–1908, vol. I

Richmond, Douglas Close, 1839–1930, vol. III

Richmond, Sir Frederick Henry, 1st Bt, 1873–1953, vol. V

Richmond, Rev. George Edward, 1859–1935, vol. III

Richmond, Adm. Sir Herbert W., 1871–1946, vol. IV

Richmond, Herbert William, 1863–1948, vol. IV

Richmond, Sir Ian, 1902–1965, vol. VI

Richmond, James, 1849–1914, vol. I
Richmond, Sir John Christopher Blake, 1909–1990, vol. VIII
Richmond, Sir John Ritchie, 1869–1963, vol. VI
Richmond, Lawrence, 1885–1968, vol. VI
Richmond, Leonard, *died* 1965, vol. VI
Richmond, Maurice Wilson, 1860–1919, vol. II
Richmond, Vice-Adm. Sir Maxwell, 1900–1986, vol. VIII
Richmond, Oliffe Legh, 1881–1977, vol. VII
Richmond, Sir (Robert) Daniel, 1878–1948, vol. IV
Richmond, Rev. Thomas Knyvett, *died* 1901, vol. I
Richmond, Rev. Wilfrid John, 1848–1938, vol. III
Richmond, Col Wilfrid Stanley, 1881–1962, vol. VI
Richmond, Sir William Blake, 1842–1921, vol. II
Richter, Eugen, 1838–1906, vol. I
Richter, Gisela M. A., 1882–1972, vol. VII
Richter, Hans, 1843–1916, vol. II
Richter, Hon. Sir Harold, 1906–1979, vol. VII
Richter, Herbert Davis, 1874–1955, vol. V
Richter, Jean Paul, 1847–1937, vol. III
Richter, Mrs Jean Paul; *see* Richter, Louise Marie.
Richter, Louise Marie, *died* 1938, vol. III
Rickaby, Father Joseph, 1845–1932, vol. III
Rickard, Sir Arthur, 1868–1948, vol. IV
Rickard, Charles Ernest, 1880–1961, vol. VI
Rickard, Rev. Herbert, *died* 1926, vol. II
Rickard, Jessie Louisa; *see* Rickard, Mrs Victor.
Rickard, Thomas Arthur, 1864–1953, vol. V
Rickard, Mrs Victor, (Jessie Louisa), *died* 1963, vol. VI
Rickards, Arthur George, 1848–1924, vol. II
Rickards, David Ayscough, 1912–1973, vol. VII
Rickards, George William, 1877–1943, vol. IV
Rickards, Maj.-Gen. Gerald Arthur, 1886–1972, vol. VII
Rickards, Rev. Marcus Samuel Cam, 1840–1928, vol. II
Rickards, Oscar Stanley Norman, 1893–1986, vol. VIII
Rickenbacker, Edward Vernon, 1890–1973, vol. VII
Ricketson, Staniforth, 1891–1967, vol. VI
Rickett, Arthur C.; *see* Compton-Rickett.
Rickett, Harold Robert Norman, 1909–1969, vol. VI
Rickett, Rt Hon. Sir Joseph C.; *see* Compton-Rickett.
Ricketts, Major Arthur, 1874–1968, vol. VI
Ricketts, Charles, 1866–1931, vol. III
Ricketts, Sir Claude Albert Frederick, 6th Bt, 1880–1937, vol. III
Ricketts, Rt Rev. Clement Mallory, 1885–1961, vol. VI
Ricketts, Sir Frederick William Rodney, 5th Bt, 1857–1925, vol. II
Ricketts, George Henry Mildmay, 1827–1914, vol. I
Ricketts, George William, 1864–1927, vol. II
Ricketts, Gordon Randolph, 1918–1968, vol. VI
Ricketts, Lt-Col Percy Edward, 1868–1940, vol. III
Rickford, Braithwaite; *see* Rickford, R. B. K.
Rickford, Richard Braithwaite Keevil, 1914–1990, vol. VIII
Rickman, Lt-Col Arthur Wilmot, 1874–1925, vol. II
Rickman, Captain William Edward, 1855–1927, vol. II

Rickmers, W. Rickmer, 1873–1965, vol. VI
Riddel, Vice-Adm. Daniel MacNab, *died* 1941, vol. IV
Riddel, James, 1857–1928, vol. II
Riddell, 1st Baron, 1865–1934, vol. III
Riddell, Sir (Alexander) Oliver, 1844–1918, vol. II
Riddell, Rt Rev. Arthur, 1836–1907, vol. I
Riddell, Athol George, 1917–1974, vol. VII
Riddell, Maj.-Gen. Charles James Buchanan, 1817–1903, vol. I
Riddell, Charlotte Eliza Lawson, (Mrs J. H. Riddell), 1832–1906, vol. I
Riddell, Cuthbert David Giffard, 1868–1937, vol. III
Riddell, Brig.-Gen. Sir Edward Pius Arthur, 1875–1957, vol. V
Riddell, Col Edward Vansittart Dick, 1873–1942, vol. IV
Riddell, Florence, *died* 1960, vol. V
Riddell, Captain George Hutton, 1878–1915, vol. I
Riddell, Mrs J. H.; *see* Riddell, C. E. L.
Riddell, Rev. John Gervase, 1896–1955, vol. V
Riddell, John Robertson, 1874–1941, vol. IV
Riddell, Col John Scott, 1864–1929, vol. III
Riddell, Sir John Walter Buchanan-, 11th Bt (*cr* 1628), 1849–1924, vol. II
Riddell, Sir Oliver; *see* Riddell, Sir A. O.
Riddell, Sir Rodney Stuart, 4th Bt (*cr* 1778), 1838–1907, vol. I
Riddell, Roland William, (Ronald), 1913–1984, vol. VIII
Riddell, Ronald; *see* Riddell, Roland W.
Riddell, Victor Horsley, *died* 1976, vol. VII
Riddell, Walter Alexander, 1881–1963, vol. VI
Riddell, Sir Walter Robert Buchanan-, 12th Bt (*cr* 1628), 1879–1934, vol. III
Riddell, William John Brownlow, 1899–1976, vol. VII
Riddell, William Renwick, 1852–1945, vol. IV
Riddell-Blount, Edward Francis; *see* Blount.
Riddell-Webster, Gen. Sir Thomas Sheridan, 1886–1974, vol. VII
Riddet, William, 1896–1958, vol. V
Riddick, Col John Galloway, 1879–1964, vol. VI
Ridding, Rt Rev. George, 1828–1904, vol. I
Riddle, Sir Ernest Cooper, 1873–1939, vol. III
Riddle, Sir George, 1875–1944, vol. IV
Riddle, John Wallace, 1864–1941, vol. IV
Riddoch, George, 1888–1947, vol. IV
Riddoch, John William, 1893–1969, vol. VI
Riddoch, William, 1862–1942, vol. IV
Ride, Sir Lindsay Tasman, 1898–1977, vol. VII
Rideal, Sir Eric Keightley, 1890–1974, vol. VII
Rideal, Samuel, *died* 1929, vol. III
Ridealgh, Mabel, 1898–1989, vol. VIII
Ridehalgh, Arthur, 1907–1971, vol. VII
Rideing, William Henry, 1853–1919, vol. II
Rideout, Maj.-Gen. Arthur Kennedy, 1835–1913, vol. I
Rideout, Maj.-Gen. Francis Goring, 1839–1913, vol. I
Rideout, Percy Rodney, 1868–1956, vol. V
Rider, Engr Rear-Adm. Sydney, *died* 1943, vol. IV
Rider, Thomas Francis, 1843–1922, vol. II
Ridge, Pett; *see* Ridge, W. P.

Ridge, (William) Pett, 1857–1930, vol. III
Ridgeway, Rt Rev. Charles John, 1841–1927, vol. II
Ridgeway, Rev. Charles Spencer-Churchill FitzGerald, (F.˙ Gerald Ridgeway), 1872–1958, vol. V
Ridgeway, Brig. David Graeme, 1879–1950, vol. IV
Ridgeway, Major Edward William Crawfurd, died 1917, vol. II
Ridgeway, F. Gerald; see Ridgeway, Rev. C. S.-C. F.
Ridgeway, Rt Rev. Frederick Edward, 1848–1921, vol. II
Ridgeway, Rt Hon. Sir (Joseph) West, 1844–1930, vol. III
Ridgeway, Col Richard Kirby, 1848–1924, vol. II
Ridgeway, Ven. S., 1872–1951, vol. V
Ridgeway, Rt Hon. Sir West; see Ridgeway, Rt Hon. Sir J. W.
Ridgeway, Sir William, 1853–1926, vol. II
Ridgway, Brig.-Gen. Richard Thomas Incledon, 1868–1939, vol. III
Riding, George Albert, 1888–1982, vol. VIII
Ridley, 1st Viscount, 1842–1904, vol. I (A)
Ridley, 2nd Viscount, 1874–1916, vol. II
Ridley, 3rd Viscount, 1902–1964, vol. VI
Ridley, Alice, (Lady Ridley), died 1945, vol. IV
Ridley, Arnold, 1896–1984, vol. VIII
Ridley, Brig.-Gen. Charles Parker, 1855–1937, vol. III
Ridley, Wing Comdr Claude Alward, 1896–1942, vol. IV
Ridley, Rt Hon. Sir Edward, 1843–1928, vol. II
Ridley, Col Edward Davenport, 1883–1934, vol. III
Ridley, Frederick Thomas, 1903–1977, vol. VII
Ridley, George, 1886–1944, vol. IV
Ridley, Guy, 1885–1947, vol. IV
Ridley, Henry Nicholas, 1855–1956, vol. V
Ridley, Hon. Sir Jasper Nicholas, 1887–1951, vol. V
Ridley, Maurice Roy, 1890–1969, vol. VI
Ridley, Nicholas Charles, 1863–1937, vol. III
Ridley, Samuel Forde, 1864–1944, vol. IV
Ridley, Rt Rev. William, 1836–1911, vol. I
Ridley, William Arnold; see Ridley, A.
Ridout, Maj.-Gen. Sir Dudley Howard, 1866–1941, vol. IV
Ridpath, Sir Henry, 1873–1950, vol. IV
Ridsdale, Arthur Francis, died 1935, vol. III
Ridsdale, Sir Aurelian; see Ridsdale, Sir E. A.
Ridsdale, Rt Rev. Charles Henry, 1873–1952, vol. V
Ridsdale, Sir (Edward) Aurelian, 1864–1923, vol. II
Ridsdale, Sir William, 1890–1957, vol. V
Riefler, Winfield William, 1897–1974, vol. VII
Rieger, Sir Clarence Oscar Ferrero, 1897–1978, vol. VII
Riesenfeld, Hugo, 1884–1939, vol. III (A), vol. IV
Rietchel, Julius, died 1963, vol. VI
Rieu, Charles Pierre Henri, 1820–1902, vol. I
Rieu, Emile Victor, 1887–1972, vol. VII
Rieu, Sir (Jean) Louis, 1872–1964, vol. VI
Rieu, Sir Louis; see Rieu, Sir J. L.
Rifaat, Kamal Eldin Mahmoud, 1921–1977, vol. VII
Rigby, Cuthbert, 1850–1935, vol. III
Rigby, Herbert Cecil, 1917–1986, vol. VIII
Rigby, Col Sir Hugh Mallinson, 1st Bt, 1870–1944, vol. IV

Rigby, Sir Ivo Charles Clayton, 1911–1987, vol. VIII
Rigby, Rt Hon. Sir John, 1834–1903, vol. I
Rigby, Brig. Thomas, 1897–1969, vol. VI
Rigg, Caroline E., died 1929, vol. III
Rigg, Sir Edward, 1850–1933, vol. III
Rigg, Harry Sibson Leslie, 1915–1976, vol. VII
Rigg, Herbert Addington, died 1924, vol. II
Rigg, James Harrison, 1821–1909, vol. I
Rigg, John, 1858–1943, vol. IV
Rigg, Major Richard, 1877–1942, vol. IV
Rigg, Sir Theodore, 1888–1972, vol. VII
Rigg, Ven. William Harrison, 1877–1966, vol. VI
Riggall, Major Arthur Horton, 1867–1929, vol. III
Riggall, Lt-Col Harold William, 1882–1930, vol. III
Riggall, Robert Marmaduke, 1881–1970, vol. VI
Riggs, Kate Douglas, (Mrs George Christopher Riggs); see Wiggin, K. D.
Righton, Thomas Edward Corrie Burns, died 1899, vol. I
Rignold, Hugo Henry, 1905–1976, vol. VII
Riis, Jacob A., died 1914, vol. I
Riley, Athelstan, 1858–1945, vol. IV
Riley, Ben, 1866–1946, vol. IV
Riley, Rt Rev. Charles Lawrence, 1888–1971, vol. VII
Riley, Most Rev. Charles Owen Leaver, 1854–1929, vol. III
Riley, Frederick Fox, died 1934, vol. III
Riley, Maj.-Gen. Sir Guy; see Riley, Maj.-Gen. Sir H. G.
Riley, Lt-Col Hamlet Lewthwaite, 1882–1932, vol. III
Riley, Harry Lister, 1899–1986, vol. VIII
Riley, Maj.-Gen. Sir (Henry) Guy, 1884–1964, vol. VI
Riley, James Whitcomb, 1849–1916, vol. II
Riley, Norman Denbigh, 1890–1979, vol. VII
Riley, Brig. Rupert Farquhar, 1873–1941, vol. IV
Riley, William, 1866–1961, vol. VI
Riley, William Edward, 1852–1937, vol. III
Riley, Engr Rear-Adm. William Henry, died 1926, vol. II
Rilot, Charles Frederick, 1864–1942, vol. IV
Rimington, A. Wallace, died 1918, vol. II
Rimington, Maj.-Gen. Joseph Cameron, 1864–1942, vol. IV
Rimington, Maj.-Gen. Sir Michael Frederic, 1858–1928, vol. II
Rimington-Wilson, Reginald Henry Rimington; see Wilson.
Rimmer, Edward Johnson, 1883–1962, vol. VI
Rind, Col Alexander Thomas Seton Abercromby, 1847–1925, vol. II
Rind, Lt-Col George Burnet Abercrombie, 1880–1958, vol. V
Rinder, Frank, 1863–1937, vol. III
Rinehart, Mary Roberts, died 1958, vol. V
Rinfret, Rt Hon. Thibaudeau, 1879–1962, vol. VI
Ring, George Alfred, died 1927, vol. II
Ring, Rev. Timothy J., 1858–1941, vol. IV
Ringer, Sydney, 1835–1910, vol. I
Ringham, Reginald, 1894–1973, vol. VII
Rink, George Arnold, 1902–1983, vol. VIII
Rintoul, Andrew, 1908–1984, vol. VIII

Riordan, Very Rev. Father James John, 1896–1959, vol. V

Riordan, Most Rev. Patrick William, 1841–1914, vol. I

Rios Urruti, Fernando de los, *born* 1879, vol. IV

Ripley, Lt-Col B., 1880–1958, vol. V

Ripley, Sir Edward, 2nd Bt (*cr* 1880), 1840–1903, vol. I

Ripley, Sir Frederick, 1st Bt (*cr* 1897), 1846–1907, vol. I

Ripley, Sir Frederick Hugh, 2nd Bt (*cr* 1897), 1878–1945, vol. IV

Ripley, Sir Geoffrey Arnold, 3rd Bt (*cr* 1897), 1883–1954, vol. V

Ripley, Gladys, (Mrs E. A. Dick), 1908–1955, vol. V

Ripley, Sir Henry William Alfred, 3rd Bt (*cr* 1880), 1879–1956, vol. V

Ripley, Rev. William Nottidge, *died* 1912, vol. I

Ripman, Walter, 1869–1947, vol. IV

Ripon, 1st Marquess of, 1827–1909, vol. I

Ripon, 2nd Marquess of, 1852–1923, vol. II

Ripper, Walter Eugene, 1908–1965, vol. VI

Ripper, William, 1853–1937, vol. III

Riquetti de Mirabeau, Sybille Gabrielle Marie Antoinette de; *see* Gyp, Sybille.

Riseley, George, 1845–1932, vol. III

Rishworth, Frank Sharman, 1876–1960, vol. V

Risk, (Charles) John, 1926–1985, vol. VIII

Risk, John; *see* Risk, C. J.

Risk, Captain Richard Henry Litle, 1857–1933, vol. III

Risley, Sir Herbert Hope, 1851–1911, vol. I

Risley, Sir John Shuckburgh, 1867–1957, vol. V

Rissik, Hon. Johann Friedrich Bernhardt, *died* 1925, vol. II

Ristori, Madame, 1822–1906, vol. I

Rita, (Mrs W. Desmond Humphreys), *died* 1938, vol. III

Ritchard, Cyril, 1898–1977, vol. VII

Ritchie of Dundee, 1st Baron, 1838–1906, vol. I

Ritchie of Dundee, 2nd Baron, 1866–1948, vol. IV

Ritchie of Dundee, 3rd Baron, 1902–1975, vol. VII

Ritchie of Dundee, 4th Baron, 1908–1978, vol. VII

Ritchie, Sir Adam Beattie, 1881–1957, vol. V

Ritchie, Alexander Brown, 1865–1936, vol. III

Ritchie, Ven. Andrew Binny, 1880–1956, vol. V

Ritchie, Anne Isabella, (Lady Ritchie), 1837–1919, vol. II

Ritchie, Maj.-Gen. Sir Archibald Buchanan, 1869–1955, vol. V

Ritchie, Arthur David, 1891–1967, vol. VI

Ritchie, Rev. Canon Charles Henry, 1887–1958, vol. V

Ritchie, Charles John, 1871–1950, vol. IV

Ritchie, David George, 1853–1903, vol. I

Ritchie, Rev. David Lakie, 1864–1951, vol. V

Ritchie, Sir Douglas; *see* Ritchie, Sir J. D.

Ritchie, Douglas Ernest, 1905–1967, vol. VI

Ritchie, Sir George, 1849–1921, vol. II

Ritchie, Hon. Sir George, 1864–1944, vol. IV

Ritchie, Major Hon. Harold, 1876–1918, vol. II

Ritchie, Harry; *see* Ritchie, Henry P.

Ritchie, Henry Parker, (Harry), 1919–1988, vol. VIII

Ritchie, Captain Henry Peel, 1876–1958, vol. V

Ritchie, Hugh, 1864–1948, vol. IV

Ritchie, James, 1864–1923, vol. II

Ritchie, James, 1882–1958, vol. V

Ritchie, Sir James Martin, 1874–1951, vol. V

Ritchie, Rear-Adm. James Stuart McLaren, 1884–1955, vol. V

Ritchie, Sir James Thomson, 1st Bt (*cr* 1903), 1835–1912, vol. I

Ritchie, Sir James William, 1st Bt *cr* 1918 (styled 2nd Bt), 1868–1937, vol. III

Ritchie, Maj.-Gen. John, 1834–1919, vol. II

Ritchie, Sir John, *died* 1947, vol. IV

Ritchie, John, 1882–1959, vol. V

Ritchie, John, 1913–1988, vol. VIII

Ritchie, Sir (John) Douglas, 1885–1983, vol. VIII

Ritchie, Sir John Neish, 1904–1977, vol. VII

Ritchie, Captain Sir Lewis Anselmo, 1886–1967, vol. VI

Ritchie, Gen. Sir Neil Methuen, 1897–1983, vol. VIII

Ritchie, R. L. Græme, 1880–1954, vol. V

Ritchie, Sir Richmond Thackeray Willoughby, 1854–1912, vol. I

Ritchie, Lt-Col Thomas Fraser, 1875–1931, vol. III

Ritchie, Sir Thomas Malcolm, 1894–1971, vol. VII

Ritchie, Maj.-Gen. Walter Henry Dennison, 1901–1984, vol. VIII

Ritchie, William, 1854–1931, vol. III

Ritchie, Col William Buchanan, 1877–1937, vol. III

Ritchie, William George Brookfield, 1875–1949, vol. IV

Ritchie, William Thomas, 1873–1945, vol. IV

Ritchie-Calder, Baron (Life Peer); Peter Ritchie Ritchie-Calder, 1906–1982, vol. VIII

Ritchie-Scott, A., 1874–1962, vol. VI

Ritson, Sir Edward Herbert, 1892–1981, vol. VIII

Ritson, Lt-Col John Anthony Sydney, 1887–1957, vol. V

Ritson, Rev. John Holland, 1868–1953, vol. V

Ritson, Joshua, 1874–1955, vol. V

Ritson, Lady Kitty, 1887–1969, vol. VI

Ritson, Muriel, 1885–1980, vol. VII

Ritson, Col William Henry, 1867–1942, vol. IV

Ritter, Gustave Albert, *died* 1914, vol. I

Ritter, His Eminence Cardinal Joseph Elmer, 1892–1967, vol. VI

Rivalland, Sir Michel Jean Joseph Laval, 1910–1970, vol. VI

Rivard, Adjutor, 1868–1945, vol. IV

Rivaz, Hon. Sir Charles Montgomery, 1845–1926, vol. II

Rivaz, Col Vincent, 1842–1924, vol. II

Riverdale, 1st Baron, 1873–1957, vol. V

Rivers, Lady; (Emmeline Laura), *died* 1918, vol. II

Rivers, Alfred Peter, 1906–1979, vol. VII

Rivers, Very Rev. Arthur Richard, 1857–1940, vol. III (A), vol. IV

Rivers, Augustus Henry Lane F. P.; *see* Fox-Pitt-Rivers.

Rivers, George Henry Lane Fox P.; *see* Pitt-Rivers.

Rivers, Georgia; *see* Clark, Marjorie.

Rivers, Rosalind Venetia P.; *see* Pitt-Rivers.

Rivers, William Halse R., 1864–1922, vol. II

Rivers Pollock, William; *see* Pollock.

Rives, Amélia, (Princess Pierre Troubetskoy), 1863–1945, vol. IV

Rivet, Raoul, 1896–1957, vol. V

Rivett, Sir (Albert Cherbury) David, 1885–1961, vol. VI

Rivett, Sir David; *see* Rivett, Sir A. C. D.

Rivett, Louis Carnac, 1888–1947, vol. IV

Rivett-Carnac, Charles James, 1853–1935, vol. III

Rivett-Carnac, Sir Claud James, 4th Bt, 1877–1909, vol. I

Rivett-Carnac, Rev. Sir George, 6th Bt, 1850–1932, vol. III

Rivett-Carnac, Sir Henry George Crabbe, 7th Bt, 1889–1972, vol. VII

Rivett-Carnac, Vice-Adm. James William, 1891–1970, vol. VI

Rivett-Carnac, Col John Henry, 1838–1923, vol. II

Rivett-Carnac, Col Percy Temple, 1852–1932, vol. III

Rivett-Carnac, Sir William Percival, 5th Bt, 1847–1924, vol. II

Rivière, A. Joseph, 1859–1946, vol. IV

Riviere, Briton, 1840–1920, vol. II

Riviere, Clive, 1872–1929, vol. III

Riviere, Hugh Goldwin, 1869–1956, vol. V

Rivington, Albert Gibson, 1883–1950, vol. IV

Rivington, Rev. Cecil Stansfeld, 1853–1934, vol. III

Rivington, Charles Robert, 1846–1928, vol. II

Rivington, Mme Hill, (Lady Holmes), *died* 1957, vol. V

Rivington, Gerald Chippindale, 1893–1977, vol. VII

Rivington, Rev. Thurston, 1848–1929, vol. III

Rivington, William John, 1845–1914, vol. I

Rix, Rt Rev. George Alexander, *died* 1945, vol. IV

Roach, Alfred Thomas, 1899–1946, vol. IV

Roach, Edward K.; *see* Keith-Roach.

Roach, Rt Rev. Frederick, 1856–1922, vol. II

Roach, Air Vice-Marshal Harold Jace, 1896–1977, vol. VII

Roach, Harry Robert, 1906–1979, vol. VII

Road, Sir Alfred, 1891–1972, vol. VII

Roaf, Herbert Eldon, 1881–1952, vol. V

Rob, John Vernon, 1915–1971, vol. VII

Robartes, Hon. Thomas Charles Reginald A.; *see* Agar-Robartes.

Robarts, Abraham John, 1838–1926, vol. II

Robarts, David John, 1906–1989, vol. VIII

Robarts, John, 1872–1954, vol. V

Robathan, Rev. Canon Frederick Norman, 1896–1986, vol. VIII

Robb, Alexander, *died* 1934, vol. III

Robb, Alfred Arthur, 1873–1936, vol. III

Robb, Andrew McCance, 1887–1968, vol. VI

Robb, Sir Douglas; *see* Robb, Sir G. D.

Robb, Maj.-Gen. Sir Frederick Spencer, 1858–1948, vol. IV

Robb, Sir (George) Douglas, 1899–1974, vol. VII

Robb, Hon. James Alexander, 1859–1929, vol. III

Robb, Air Chief Marshal Sir James Milne, *died* 1968, vol. VI

Robb, Rt Hon. John Hanna, 1873–1956, vol. V

Robb, Hon. John Morrow, 1876–1942, vol. IV

Robb, Leonard Arthur, 1891–1964, vol. VII (AI)

Robb, Michael Antony Moyse, 1914–1977, vol. VII

Robb, Nesca Adeline, 1905–1976, vol. VII

Robb, Ven. Percy Douglas, 1902–1976, vol. VII

Robb, William, 1885–1982, vol. VIII

Robb, William George, 1872–1940, vol. III

Robberds, Rt Rev. Walter John Forbes, 1863–1944, vol. IV

Robbins, Baron (Life Peer); Lionel Charles Robbins, 1898–1984, vol. VIII

Robbins, Alan Pitt, 1888–1967, vol. VI

Robbins, Sir Alfred Farthing, 1856–1931, vol. III

Robbins, Alfred Gordon, 1883–1944, vol. IV

Robbins, Dennis; *see* Robbins, J. D.

Robbins, Edgar Carmichael, 1911–1988, vol. VIII

Robbins, Sir Edmund, 1847–1922, vol. II

Robbins, John Dennis, 1915–1986, vol. VIII

Robbins, Rowland Richard, *died* 1960, vol. V

Robbins, Brig. Thomas, 1893–1981, vol. VIII

Roberson, Rev. Henry, 1858–1934, vol. III

Robert, Henri, 1863–1936, vol. III

Roberthall, Baron (Life Peer); Robert Lowe Roberthall, 1901–1988, vol. VIII

Roberton, Sir Hugh S., 1874–1952, vol. V

Roberton, Rev. Ivor Johnstone, 1865–1948, vol. IV

Roberton, Violet Mary Craig, 1888–1954, vol. V

Roberts, 1st Earl, 1832–1914, vol. I

Roberts, Countess (2nd in line), 1870–1944, vol. IV

Roberts, Countess (3rd in line), 1875–1955, vol. V

Roberts, Aled Owen, 1889–1949, vol. IV

Roberts, Rev. Alexander, 1826–1901, vol. I

Roberts, Lt-Col Sir Alexander Fowler, 1882–1961, vol. VI

Roberts, Hon. Alexander William, 1857–1938, vol. III

Roberts, Sir Alfred, 1823–1899, vol. I

Roberts, Ven. Alfred, 1853–1937, vol. III

Roberts, Sir Alfred, 1897–1963, vol. VI

Roberts, Allan, 1943–1990, vol. VIII

Roberts, Allan Arbuthnot Lane, 1884–1967, vol. VI

Roberts, Angus, 1893–1937, vol. III

Roberts, Arthur, 1852–1933, vol. III

Roberts, Rev. Arthur Betton, 1880–1961, vol. VI

Roberts, Sir Arthur Cornelius, 1869–1946, vol. IV

Roberts, Arthur James Rooker, 1882–1943, vol. IV

Roberts, Rt Rev. Basil Coleby, 1887–1957, vol. V

Roberts, Rev. Bleddyn Jones, 1906–1977, vol. VII

Roberts, Brian Birley, 1912–1978, vol. VII

Roberts, Brian Richard, 1906–1988, vol. VIII

Roberts, Bryn, 1897–1964, vol. VI

Roberts, Carl Eric Bechhofer, 1894–1949, vol. IV

Roberts, Cecil Edric Mornington, 1892–1976, vol. VII

Roberts, Cedric Sydney L.; *see* Lane-Roberts.

Roberts, Chalmers; *see* Roberts, H. C.

Roberts, Ven. Charles Frederic, *died* 1942, vol. IV

Roberts, Col Charles Fyshe, 1837–1914, vol. I

Roberts, Sir Charles George Douglas, 1860–1943, vol. IV

Roberts, Charles Henry, 1865–1959, vol. V

Roberts, Charles Hubert, *died* 1929, vol. III

Roberts, Hon. Charles James, 1846–1925, vol. II

Roberts, Rev. Charles Philip, 1842–1918, vol. II

Roberts, Charles Stuart, 1918–1989, vol. VIII

Roberts, Colin Henderson, 1909–1990, vol. VIII

Roberts, Cyril, 1871–1949, vol. IV

Roberts, Cyril Alfred, 1908–1988, vol. VIII

Roberts, Sir David Arthur, 1924–1987, vol. VIII
Roberts, Sir David Charles, 1859–1940, vol. III
Roberts, Ven. David Egryn, *died* 1935, vol. III
Roberts, David Lloyd, *died* 1920, vol. II
Roberts, David Thomas, *died* 1903, vol. I
Roberts, Denis; *see* Roberts, E. F. D.
Roberts, Denys K.; *see* Kilham-Roberts.
Roberts, Rev. E. Berwyn, 1869–1951, vol. V
Roberts, Col Edward, 1841–1904, vol. I
Roberts, Very Rev. Edward Albert Trevillian, 1877–1968, vol. VI
Roberts, Rev. Edward Dale, 1848–1927, vol. II
Roberts, Edward E.; *see* Emrys-Roberts.
Roberts, (Edward Frederick) Denis, 1927–1990, vol. VIII
Roberts, Ellis, 1860–1930, vol. III
Roberts, Emrys Owain, 1910–1990, vol. VIII
Roberts, Sir Ernest Handforth Goodman, 1890–1969, vol. VI
Roberts, Rev. Ernest Marling, 1873–1929, vol. III
Roberts, Rev. Ernest Stewart, 1847–1912, vol. I
Roberts, Francis Noel, 1893–1969, vol. VI
Roberts, Maj.-Gen. Frank Crowther, 1891–1982, vol. VIII
Roberts, Hon. Frederick Hugh Sherston, 1872–1899, vol. I
Roberts, Rt Hon. Frederick Owen, 1876–1941, vol. IV
Roberts, Frederick Thomas, *died* 1918, vol. II
Roberts, Geoffrey Dorling, 1886–1967, vol. VI
Roberts, Sir George, 1st Bt (*cr* 1930), 1859–1950, vol. IV
Roberts, George Augustus, 1875–1962, vol. VI
Roberts, George Charles L.; *see* Lloyd-Roberts.
Roberts, Col Sir George Fossett, 1870–1954, vol. V
Roberts, Rt Hon. George Henry, 1869–1928, vol. II
Roberts, George Lawrence, 1904–1967, vol. VI
Roberts, George Quinlan, 1860–1943, vol. IV
Roberts, Sir George William Kelly, 1907–1964, vol. VI
Roberts, Gervase Henry, *died* 1944, vol. IV
Roberts, Sir Gilbert, 1899–1978, vol. VII
Roberts, Captain Gilbert Howland, 1900–1986, vol. VIII
Roberts, Air Vice Marshal Glynn S.; *see* Silyn Roberts.
Roberts, Goronwy; *see* Baron Goronwy-Roberts.
Roberts, Very Rev. Griffith, 1845–1943, vol. IV
Roberts, Harold, 1884–1950, vol. IV
Roberts, Harold, 1879–1959, vol. V
Roberts, Rev. Harold, 1896–1982, vol. VIII
Roberts, Sir Harold Charles West, 1892–1983, vol. VIII
Roberts, Harry, 1871–1946, vol. IV
Roberts, (Henry) Chalmers, *died* 1949, vol. IV
Roberts, Henry David, 1870–1951, vol. V
Roberts, Lt-Col Henry Roger Crompton-, 1863–1925, vol. II
Roberts, Herbert Ainslie, 1864–1932, vol. III
Roberts, Brig.-Gen. Hereward Llewelyn, 1864–1947, vol. IV
Roberts, Sir Howard; *see* Roberts, Sir J. R. H.
Roberts, Col Sir Howland, 5th Bt (*cr* 1809), 1845–1917, vol. II

Roberts, Hugh Douglas, 1869–1942, vol. IV
Roberts, Hugh Gordon, 1885–1961, vol. VI
Roberts, Hugh Leslie-, 1860–1949, vol. IV
Roberts, Hugh Lloyd, *died* 1906, vol. I
Roberts, Isaac, 1829–1904, vol. I
Roberts, Rev. J. J., 1840–1914, vol. I
Roberts, Sir James, 1st Bt (*cr* 1909), 1848–1935, vol. III
Roberts, Hon. James, 1881–1967, vol. VI
Roberts, James Alexander, 1876–1945, vol. IV
Roberts, Sir James Denby, 2nd Bt (*cr* 1909), 1904–1973, vol. VII
Roberts, James Ernest Helme, *died* 1948, vol. IV
Roberts, James Frederick, 1847–1911, vol. II
Roberts, Sir (James Reginald) Howard, 1891–1975, vol. VII
Roberts, Lt-Col Sir James Reid, 1861–1941, vol. IV
Roberts, Dame Jean, *died* 1988, vol. VIII
Roberts, Dame Joan Howard, 1907–1990, vol. VIII
Roberts, Sir John, 1861–1917, vol. II
Roberts, Sir John, 1845–1934, vol. III
Roberts, Captain John, 1867–1943, vol. IV
Roberts, Sir John, 1876–1966, vol. VI
Roberts, John Alexander Fraser, 1899–1987, vol. VIII
Roberts, John Bryn, 1843–1931, vol. III
Roberts, Rev. John Edward, 1866–1929, vol. III
Roberts, John Gwyndeg H.; *see* Hughes-Roberts.
Roberts, Maj.-Gen. John Hamilton, 1891–1962, vol. VI
Roberts, John Keith, 1897–1944, vol. IV
Roberts, John Reginald, 1893–1971, vol. VII
Roberts, Sir John Reynolds, 1834–1917, vol. II
Roberts, John Varley, 1841–1920, vol. II
Roberts, Kate Winifred J.; *see* Jones-Roberts.
Roberts, Kenneth, 1885–1957, vol. V
Roberts, Lancelot, *died* 1950, vol IV (A), vol. V
Roberts, Sir Leslie, *died* 1976, vol. VII
Roberts, Llewelyn, 1881–1939, vol. III
Roberts, Major Marmaduke Torin Cramer-, 1880–1939, vol. III
Roberts, Captain Marshall Owen, 1878–1931, vol. III
Roberts, Martin, 1853–1926, vol. II, vol. III
Roberts, Michael, 1902–1948, vol. IV
Roberts, Michael Hilary Arthur, 1927–1983, vol. VIII
Roberts, Brig. Michael Rookherst, 1894–1977, vol. VII
Roberts, Morley, 1857–1942, vol. IV
Roberts, Sir Norman Stanley, 1893–1972, vol. VII
Roberts, Gen. Sir Ouvry Lindfield, 1898–1986, vol. VIII
Roberts, Sir Owen, 1835–1915, vol. I
Roberts, Owen Glynne, 1880–1947, vol. IV
Roberts, Owen Josephus, 1875–1955, vol. V
Roberts, Patrick Maxwell, 1895–1937, vol. III
Roberts, Paul Ernest, 1873–1949, vol. IV
Roberts, Peter Burman Moir, 1874–1956, vol. V
Roberts, Sir Peter Geoffrey, 3rd Bt, 1912–1985, vol. VIII
Roberts, Lt-Comdr Peter Scawen Watkinson, 1917–1979, vol. VII
Roberts, Rachel, 1927–1980, vol. VII
Roberts, Sir Randal Howland, 4th Bt (*cr* 1809), 1837–1899, vol. I

Roberts, Reginald Arthur, 1874–1940, vol. III
Roberts, Reginald Hugh, 1883–1955, vol. V
Roberts, Very Rev. Richard, 1874–1945, vol. IV
Roberts, Richard Arthur, 1851–1943, vol. IV
Roberts, Richard Ellis, 1879–1953, vol. V
Roberts, Rev. Richard Gwylfa, 1871–1935, vol. III
Roberts, Ven. Richard Henry, *died* 1970, vol. VI
Roberts, Sir Richard L.; *see* Lloyd-Roberts.
Roberts, Richard Owen, 1876–1929, vol. III
Roberts, Robert A.; *see* Alun Roberts.
Roberts, Robert David Valpo, 1906–1973, vol. VII
Roberts, Robert Davies, 1851–1911, vol. I
Roberts, Rev. Canon Robert Edwin, 1878–1940, vol. III
Roberts, Robert Herbert M.; *see* Mills-Roberts.
Roberts, Robert Lewis, 1875–1956, vol. V
Roberts, Robert Silyn, *died* 1930, vol. III
Roberts, Rev. Roger Lewis, 1911–1990, vol. VIII
Roberts, Rev. Canon Roland Harry William, 1894–1951, vol. V
Roberts, Samuel, 1852–1913, vol. I
Roberts, Rt Hon. Sir Samuel, 1st Bt (*cr* 1919), 1852–1926, vol. II
Roberts, Sir Samuel, 2nd Bt (*cr* 1919), 1882–1955, vol. V
Roberts, Sidney Morton Pearson, 1860–1930, vol. III
Roberts, Sir Stephen Henry, 1901–1971, vol. VII
Roberts, Lt-Col Stephen Richard Harricks, 1874–1943, vol. IV
Roberts, Stuart; *see* Roberts, C. S.
Roberts, Sir Sydney Castle, 1887–1966, vol. VI
Roberts, T. Stanley, *died* 1935, vol. III
Roberts, Thomas Arnold, 1911–1990, vol. VIII
Roberts, Most Rev. Thomas d'Esterre, 1893–1976, vol. VII
Roberts, Sir Thomas Edwards, 1851–1926, vol. II
Roberts, Thomas Esmôr Rhys R.; *see* Rhys-Roberts.
Roberts, Thomas Francis, 1860–1919, vol. II
Roberts, Col Sir Thomas Langdon Howland, 6th Bt (*cr* 1809), 1898–1979, vol. VII
Roberts, Sir Thomas Lee, 1848–1924, vol. II
Roberts, Tom, 1856–1931, vol. III
Roberts, W. J., *died* 1943, vol. IV
Roberts, Sir Walter St Clair Howland, 1893–1978, vol. VII
Roberts, Walter Stewart S.; *see* Stewart-Roberts.
Roberts, Sir Walworth Howland, 1855–1924, vol. II
Roberts, Sir William, 1830–1899, vol. I
Roberts, William, 1862–1940, vol. III
Roberts, Sir William, 1884–1971, vol. VII
Roberts, William, 1895–1980, vol. VII
Roberts, Rev. William Corbett, 1873–1953, vol. V
Roberts, Rev. William Henry, 1844–1921, vol. II
Roberts, Col William Henry, 1848–1926, vol. II
Roberts, Brig. William Henry, 1882–1954, vol. V
Roberts, William Lee Henry, 1871–1928, vol. II
Roberts, Rev. William Masfen, *died* 1927, vol. II
Roberts, Very Rev. William Page-, 1836–1928, vol. II
Roberts, William Poulter, 1874–1937, vol. III
Roberts, Col William Quincey, 1912–1980, vol. VII
Roberts, Rev. William Ralph Westropp, 1850–1935, vol. III
Roberts, William Rhys, 1858–1929, vol. III
Roberts, Col William Richter, 1888–1975, vol. VII

Roberts, William Stewart, *died* 1937, vol. III
Roberts, Ven Windsor, 1898–1962, vol. VI
Roberts-Austen, Sir William Chandler, 1843–1902, vol. I
Roberts-Wray, Sir Kenneth Owen, 1899–1983, vol. VIII
Roberts-Wray, Captain Thomas Henry; *see* Wray.
Robertshaw, Vice-Adm. Sir Ballin Illingworth, 1902–1971, vol. VII
Robertshaw, Sir Charles, 1874–1960, vol. V
Robertshaw, Wilfrid, 1893–1974, vol. VII
Robertson, Baron (Life Peer); James Patrick Bannerman Robertson, 1845–1909, vol. I
Robertson, Hon. Lord; Thomas Graham Robertson, 1881–1944, vol. IV
Robertson of Oakridge, 1st Baron, 1896–1974, vol. VII
Robertson, Alan, 1920–1989, vol. VIII
Robertson, Alan Murray, 1914–1984, vol. VIII
Robertson, Alasdair Stewart Struan-Robertson, 1863–1910, vol. I
Robertson, Rear-Adm. Albert John, 1884–1954, vol. V
Robertson, Alec; *see* Robertson, A. T. P. A. C.
Robertson, Rev. Alexander, 1846–1933, vol. III
Robertson, Alexander, *died* 1970, vol. VI
Robertson, Sir Alexander, 1896–1970, vol. VI
Robertson, Sir Alexander, 1908–1990, vol. VIII
Robertson, Brig.-Gen. Alexander Brown, 1878–1951, vol. V
Robertson, Alexander Thomas Parke Anthony Cecil, (Alec Robertson), 1892–1982, vol. VIII
Robertson, Algar Ronald Ward, 1902–1975, vol. VII
Robertson, Andrew, *died* 1977, vol. VII
Robertson, Rt Rev. Archibald, 1853–1931, vol. III
Robertson, Archibald Wallace, 1895–1966, vol. VI
Robertson, Cdre A(rthur) Ian, 1898–1961, vol. VI
Robertson, Sir Benjamin, 1864–1953, vol. V
Robertson, Sir Carrick Hey, *died* 1963, vol. VI
Robertson, Catherine Christian, 1886–1985, vol. VIII
Robertson, Maj.-Gen. Cecil Bruce, 1897–1977, vol. VII
Robertson, Rev. Charles, *died* 1921, vol. II
Robertson, Charles, 1874–1968, vol. VI
Robertson, Sir Charles Grant, 1869–1948, vol. IV
Robertson, Adm. Charles Hope, 1856–1942, vol. IV
Robertson, Lt-Col Charles Lonsdale, 1867–1943, vol. IV
Robertson, Very Rev. Charles R., 1873–1946, vol. IV
Robertson, Col Colin MacLeod, 1870–1951, vol. V
Robertson, Maj.-Gen. David, *died* 1913, vol. I
Robertson, Rev. David, 1838–1916, vol. II
Robertson, David, *died* 1925, vol. II
Robertson, David, 1875–1941, vol. IV
Robertson, David, *died* 1952, vol. V
Robertson, Sir David, 1890–1970, vol. VI
Robertson, Sir Dennis Holme, 1890–1963, vol. VI
Robertson, Lt-Col Sir Donald, 1847–1930, vol. III
Robertson, Maj.-Gen. Donald Elphinston, 1879–1953, vol. V
Robertson, Donald James, 1926–1970, vol. VI
Robertson, Col Donald Murdoch, 1859–1938, vol. III
Robertson, Donald Struan, 1885–1961, vol. VI

Robertson, Douglas Moray Cooper Lamb Argyll, 1837–1909, vol. I

Robertson, E. Arnot, (Lady Turner), *died* 1961, vol. VI

Robertson, Edith Anne, 1883–1973, vol. VII

Robertson, Air Cdre Edmund Digby Maxwell, 1887–1956, vol. V

Robertson, Edward, *died* 1964, vol. VI

Robertson, Eric Desmond, 1914–1987, vol. VIII

Robertson, Sir Frederick Alexander, 1854–1918, vol. II

Robertson, Frederick Ewart, 1847–1912, vol. I

Robertson, Sir Frederick Wynne, 1885–1964, vol. VI

Robertson, George, 1883–1956, vol. V

Robertson, George Matthew, 1864–1932, vol. III

Robertson, George Paterson, 1911–1982, vol. VIII

Robertson, Sir George Scott, 1852–1916, vol. II

Robertson, George Scott, 1893–1948, vol. IV

Robertson, Sir George Stuart, 1872–1967, vol. VI

Robertson, Hon. Gideon Decker, 1874–1933, vol. III

Robertson, Lt-Col Gordon McMahon, 1891–1932, vol. III

Robertson, Lt-Col Graham; *see* Robertson, Lt-Col J. H. G.

Robertson, Granville Douglas, 1891–1951, vol. V

Robertson, Sir Helenus Robert, 1841–1919, vol. II

Robertson, Sir Henry Beyer, 1862–1948, vol. IV

Robertson, Henry Robert, 1839–1921, vol. II

Robertson, Herbert, 1849–1916, vol. II

Robertson, Lt-Gen. Sir Horace Clement Hugh, 1894–1960, vol. V

Robertson, Sir Howard Morley, 1888–1963, vol. VI

Robertson, Engr-Comdr Hugh, *died* 1940, vol. III (A)

Robertson, Ian Gow, 1910–1983, vol. VIII

Robertson, Very Rev. James, 1837–1920, vol. II

Robertson, Rev. James, 1840–1920, vol. II

Robertson, Rev. James, 1855–1929, vol. III

Robertson, James, *died* 1938, vol. III

Robertson, Rev. James Alex., 1880–1955, vol. V

Robertson, Sir James Anderson, 1906–1990, vol. VIII

Robertson, Lt-Col James Archibald St George Fitzwarenne D.; *see* Despencer-Robertson.

Robertson, Brig.-Gen. James Campbell, 1878–1951, vol. V

Robertson, James Cassels, 1921–1978, vol. VII

Robertson, Lt-Col James Currie, 1870–1923, vol. II

Robertson, James Edwin, 1840–1915, vol. I

Robertson, Col James F.; *see* Forbes-Robertson.

Robertson, Lt-Col (James Herbert) Graham, *died* 1956, vol. V

Robertson, Maj.-Gen. James Howden, 1915–1987, vol. VIII

Robertson, Sir James Jackson, 1893–1970, vol. VI

Robertson, Group Captain James Leask, 1882–1945, vol. IV

Robertson, James Logie, *died* 1922, vol. II

Robertson, Col James Peter, 1822–1916, vol. II

Robertson, James Wilson, 1857–1930, vol. III

Robertson, Sir James Wilson, 1899–1983, vol. VIII

Robertson, Jean F.; *see* Forbes-Robertson.

Robertson, Rev. John, 1852–1913, vol. I

Robertson, Col John, 1837–1915, vol. I

Robertson, Rev. John, *died* 1925, vol. II

Robertson, John, 1867–1926, vol. II

Robertson, Sir John, 1862–1936, vol. III

Robertson, John, *died* 1937, vol. III

Robertson, Col John, 1878–1951, vol. V

Robertson, John, 1913–1987, vol. VIII

Robertson, John Archibald Campbell, 1912–1962, vol. VI

Robertson, John Arthur Thomas, 1873–1942, vol. IV

Robertson, Rev. John Charles, 1868–1931, vol. III

Robertson, John Charles, 1864–1956, vol. V

Robertson, John F.; *see* Forbes-Robertson.

Robertson, John G., 1867–1933, vol. III

Robertson, John Henry; *see* Connell, John.

Robertson, Captain John Hercules, 1864–1943, vol. IV

Robertson, John James, 1898–1955, vol. V

Robertson, John McKellar, 1883–1939, vol. III

Robertson, Rt Hon. John Mackinnon, 1856–1933, vol. III

Robertson, John Monteath, 1900–1989, vol. VIII

Robertson, Col John Richard Hugh, 1912–1977, vol. VII

Robertson, John Williamson, 1900–1969, vol. VI

Robertson, Sir Johnston F.; *see* Forbes-Robertson.

Robertson, Laurence, *died* 1945, vol. IV

Robertson, Lindesay John, 1861–1929, vol. III

Robertson, Sir MacPherson, 1860–1945, vol. IV

Robertson, Rt Hon. Sir Malcolm Arnold, 1877–1951, vol. V

Robertson, Margaret Ethel, 1861–1943, vol. IV

Robertson, Muriel, 1883–1973, vol. VII

Robertson, Norman Alexander, 1904–1968, vol. VI

Robertson, Norman Charles, 1908–1956, vol. V

Robertson, Maj.-Gen. Sir Philip Rynd, 1866–1936, vol. III

Robertson, Rae, 1893–1956, vol. V

Robertson, Sir Robert, 1869–1949, vol. IV

Robertson, Robert Burns, 1861–1938, vol. III

Robertson, Robert Spelman, 1870–1955, vol. V

Robertson, Robin Haskew, 1898–1952, vol. VI

Robertson, Stuart, *died* 1958, vol. V

Robertson, Thomas, *died* 1906, vol. I

Robertson, Thomas, 1842–1925, vol. II

Robertson, Thomas Atholl, *died* 1955, vol. V

Robertson, Thomas Dixon Marr Trotter, 1856–1913, vol. I

Robertson, Thomas Graham; *see* Robertson, Hon. Lord.

Robertson, Thomas Logan, 1901–1969, vol. VI

Robertson, Thorburn Brailsford, 1884–1930, vol. III

Robertson, Tom, 1850–1947, vol. IV

Robertson, Vernon Alec Murray, 1890–1971, vol. VII

Robertson, W. Graham, 1866–1948, vol. IV

Robertson, Major W. M., *died* 1902, vol. I

Robertson, Walter James, 1869–1942, vol. IV

Robertson, Watson A.; *see* Askew-Robertson.

Robertson, Wheatley Alexander, 1885–1964, vol. VI

Robertson, Sir William, 1856–1923, vol. II

Robertson, Rev. William, 1847–1936, vol. III

Robertson, Lt-Col William, 1865–1949, vol. IV

Robertson, William Albert, 1885–1942, vol. IV

Robertson, Sir William Charles Fleming, *died* 1937, vol. III

Robertson, William Chrystal, 1850–1922, vol. II

Robertson, William Francis, 1882–1939, vol. III

Robertson, William Haggerston A.; *see* Askew Robertson.

Robertson, Rev. William Lewis, 1860–1947, vol. IV

Robertson, William Nathaniel, *died* 1938, vol. III

Robertson, Field-Marshal Sir William Robert, 1st Bt, 1860–1933, vol. III

Robertson, William Walter Samuel, 1906–1989, vol. VIII

Robertson-Aikman, Col Thomas S. G. H.; *see* Aikman.

Robertson-Eustace, Major Charles Legge Eustace, 1867–1908, vol. I

Robertson-Eustace, Marjory Edith, *died* 1957, vol. V

Robertson-Eustace, Robert William Barrington, 1870–1935, vol. III

Robertson-Glasgow, Raymond Charles, 1901–1965, vol. VI

Robertson-Justice, James Norval Harald, 1905–1975, vol. VII

Robertson-Macdonald, Adm. David, 1817–1910, vol. I

Robertson Scott, John William, 1866–1962, vol. VI

Robeson, Ven. Hemming, *died* 1912, vol. I

Robeson, Paul Le Roy, 1898–1976, vol. VII

Robey, Edward George Haydon, 1899–1983, vol. VIII

Robey, Sir George, 1869–1954, vol. V

Robichaud, Most Rev. Norbert, 1905–1979, vol. VII (AII)

Robidoux, Joseph Emery,1843–1929, vol. III

Robieson, Sir William, 1890–1977, vol. VII

Robin, Maj.-Gen. Sir Alfred William, 1860–1935, vol. III

Robin, Rt Rev. Bryan Percival, 1887–1969, vol. VI

Robins, 1st Baron, 1884–1962, vol. VI

Robins, Rev. Arthur, 1834–1899, vol. 1

Robins, Daniel Gerard, 1942–1989, vol. VIII

Robins, Denise Naomi, 1897–1985, vol. VIII

Robins, Rt Rev. Edwin Frederick, 1870–1951, vol. V

Robins, Elizabeth, (Mrs George Richmond Parks; C. E. Raimond), 1862–1952, vol. V

Robins, G. M.; *see* Reynolds, Mrs Louis Baillie.

Robins, Very Rev. Henry Charles, 1882–1960, vol. V

Robins, Sir Reginald Edwin, 1891–1971, vol. VII

Robins, Ven. William Aubrey, 1868–1949, vol. IV

Robins, Rev. William Henry, 1847–1923, vol. II

Robins, William Palmer, 1882–1959, vol. V

Robinson, 1st Baron, 1883–1952, vol. V

Robinson, Albert, 1878–1943, vol. IV

Robinson, Rev. Canon Albert Gossage, 1863–1948, vol. IV

Robinson, Maj.-Gen. Alfred Eryk, 1894–1978, vol. VII

Robinson, Sir Alfred Theodore Vaughan, 1879–1945, vol. IV

Robinson, Andrew, 1858–1929, vol. III

Robinson, Rev. Archibald, *died* 1902, vol. I

Robinson, Sir Arnet, 1898–1975, vol VII

Robinson, Arnold; *see* Robinson, F. A.

Robinson, Sir Arnold Percy, 1879–1960, vol. V

Robinson, Hon. Sir Arthur, 1872–1945, vol. IV

Robinson, Arthur, 1862–1948, vol. IV

Robinson, Arthur, 1864–1948, vol. IV

Robinson, Sir Arthur; *see* Robinson, Sir W. A.

Robinson, Sir (Arthur) Douglas, 1878–1939, vol. III

Robinson, Arthur Hildyard, 1859–1939, vol. III

Robinson, Arthur Leyland, 1887–1959, vol. V

Robinson, Rev. Arthur William, 1856–1928, vol. II

Robinson, Rev. Cecil Lowes, 1869–1936, vol. III

Robinson, Charles, 1870–1937, vol. III

Robinson, Charles Edmund N.; *see* Newton-Robinson.

Robinson, Adm. Charles Grey, 1850–1934, vol. III

Robinson, Rev. Charles Henry, 1861–1925, vol. II

Robinson, Rev. Charles Kirkby, 1826–1909, vol. I

Robinson, Charles Napier, 1849–1936, vol. III

Robinson, Charles Stanley, 1887–1969, vol. VI

Robinson, Maj.-Gen. Sir Charles Walker, 1836–1924, vol. II

Robinson, Sir Christopher Henry L.; *see* Lynch-Robinson.

Robinson, Rt Rev. Christopher James Gossage, 1903–1988, vol. VIII

Robinson, Hon. Clifford William, 1866–1944, vol. IV

Robinson, Sir Clifton, 1849–1910, vol. I

Robinson, Rear-Adm. Sir Cloudesley Varyl, 1883–1959, vol. V

Robinson, Courtenay Denis Carew, 1887–1958, vol. V

Robinson, Rt Rev. Cuthbert Cooper, 1893–1971, vol. VII

Robinson, Sir David, 1904–1987, vol. VIII

Robinson, Captain David Lubbock, 1882–1943, vol. IV

Robinson, David Moore, 1880–1958, vol. V

Robinson, David Morrant, 1910–1977, vol. VII

Robinson, Cdre David Samuel, 1888–1972, vol. VII

Robinson, Sir Douglas; *see* Robinson, Sir A. D.

Robinson, Sir Douglas Innes, 6th Bt (*cr* 1823), 1863–1944, vol. IV

Robinson, Sir Dove-Myer, 1901–1989, vol. VIII

Robinson, Rev. Edward Colles, 1877–1956, vol. V

Robinson, Edward G., 1893–1973, vol. VII

Robinson, Edward Kay, 1857–1928, vol. II

Robinson, Sir Edward Stanley Gotch, *died* 1976, vol. VII

Robinson, Edwin Arlington, 1869–1935, vol. III

Robinson, Eric, 1908–1974, vol. VII

Robinson, Rear-Adm. Eric Gascoigne, 1882–1965, vol. VI

Robinson, Col Ernest, 1877–1935, vol. III

Robinson, Sir (Ernest) Stanley, 1905–1977, vol. VII

Robinson, Sir Ernest William, 5th Bt (*cr* 1823), 1862–1924, vol. II

Robinson, (Esmé Stuart) Lennox, 1886–1958, vol. V

Robinson, Forbes; *see* Robinson, P. F.

Robinson, Sir Foster Gotch, 1880–1967, vol. VI

Robinson, Frank Arnold, 1907–1988, vol. VIII

Robinson, Frederic Cayley-, 1862–1927, vol. II

Robinson, Sir Frederic Lacy, 1840–1911, vol. I

Robinson, Sir Frederick Arnold, 3rd Bt (*cr* 1854), 1855–1901, vol. I

Robinson, Sir (Frederick) Percival, 1887–1949, vol. IV

Robinson, Major Sir Frederick Villiers Laud, 10th Bt (*cr* 1660), 1880–1975, vol. VII

Robinson, Frederick William, 1830–1901, vol. I

Robinson, George Drummond, 1864–1950, vol. IV

Robinson, Sir George Gilmour, 1894–1985, vol. VIII

Robinson, Surg.-Gen. George Winsor, 1854–1929, vol. III

Robinson, Gerald Philip, 1858–1942, vol. IV

Robinson, Sir Gerald William Collingwood, 4th Bt (*cr* 1819), 1857–1903, vol. I

Robinson, Gilbert Wooding, 1888–1950, vol. IV

Robinson, Gleeson Edward, *died* 1978, vol. VII

Robinson, Godfrey, 1897–1961, vol. VI

Robinson, Lt-Col Godfrey Walker, 1863–1930, vol. III

Robinson, Maj.-Gen. Guy St George, 1887–1973, vol. VII

Robinson, Sir Harold Ernest, 1905–1979, vol. VII

Robinson, Sir Harold Francis C.; *see* Cartmel-Robinson.

Robinson, Harold Roper, 1889–1955, vol. V

Robinson, Sir Harry Perry, 1859–1930, vol. III

Robinson, Lt-Col Sir Heaton Forbes, 1873–1946, vol. IV

Robinson, Rt Rev. Hector Gordon, 1899–1965, vol. VI

Robinson, Henry, *died* 1901, vol. I

Robinson, Rev. Henry, 1849–1918, vol. II

Robinson, Rt Hon. Sir Henry Augustus, 1st Bt (*cr* 1920), 1857–1927, vol. II

Robinson, Henry Betham, 1860–1918, vol. II

Robinson, Henry Goland, 1896–1960, vol. V

Robinson, Captain Henry Harold, *died* 1919, vol. II

Robinson, Henry Morton, 1898–1961, vol. VI

Robinson, Maj.-Gen. Henry R.; *see* Rowan-Robinson.

Robinson, Rear-Adm. Sir Henry Russell, 1856–1942, vol. IV

Robinson, Rev. Henry Wheeler, 1872–1945, vol. IV

Robinson, Hon. Hercules Edward Joseph, 1895–1915, vol. I

Robinson, Sir (Hugh) Malcolm, 1857–1933, vol. III

Robinson, James, 1884–1956, vol. V

Robinson, Joan Violet, 1903–1983, vol. VIII

Robinson, Hon. Sir John, 1839–1903, vol. I

Robinson, Sir John, 1839–1929, vol. III

Robinson, Hon. John Alexander, 1862–1929, vol. III

Robinson, Rt Rev. John Arthur Thomas, 1919–1983, vol. VIII

Robinson, Sir John Beverley, 4th Bt (*cr* 1854), 1848–1933, vol. III

Robinson, Sir John Beverley, 6th Bt (*cr* 1854), 1885–1954, vol. V

Robinson, Sir John Beverley, 7th Bt (*cr* 1854), 1913–1988, vol. VIII

Robinson, Sir John Beverley Beverley, 5th Bt (*cr* 1854), 1895–1948, vol. IV

Robinson, Sir John Charles, 1824–1913, vol. I

Robinson, Sir John Edgar, 1895–1978, vol. VII

Robinson, John Foster, 1909–1988, vol. VIII

Robinson, John George, 1856–1943, vol. IV

Robinson, Sir John Holdsworth, 1855–1927, vol. II

Robinson, Rev. John Josiah, *died* 1916, vol. II

Robinson, John Lovell, 1849–1939, vol. III

Robinson, Col John Poole Bowring, 1881–1966, vol. VI

Robinson, John Robert, 1850–1910, vol. I

Robinson, John William Dudley, 1886–1967, vol. VI

Robinson, Joseph, 1905–1970, vol. VI

Robinson, Very Rev. Joseph Armitage, 1858–1933, vol. III

Robinson, Sir Joseph Benjamin, 1st Bt (*cr* 1908), 1840–1929, vol. III

Robinson, Sir Joseph Benjamin, 2nd Bt (*cr* 1908), 1887–1954, vol. V

Robinson, Joseph John, 1858–1939, vol. III

Robinson, Kenneth Dean, 1909–1987, vol. VIII

Robinson, Laurence Milner, 1885–1957, vol. V

Robinson, Lennox; *see* Robinson, E. S. L.

Robinson, Leonard Nicholas, 1869–1955, vol. V

Robinson, Sir Leslie Harold, 1903–1974, vol. VII

Robinson, Rev. Ludovick Stewart, 1864–1923, vol. II

Robinson, Lt-Col Macleod Bawtree, 1858–1935, vol. III

Robinson, Sir Malcolm; *see* Robinson, Sir H. M.

Robinson, Air Cdre Maurice Wilbraham Sandford, 1910–1977, vol. VII

Robinson, Sir Montague Arnet; *see* Robinson, Sir Arnet.

Robinson, Nigel Francis Maltby, 1906–1985, vol. VIII

Robinson, Very Rev. Norman, 1905–1973, vol. VII

Robinson, Sir Norman De Winton, 1890–1972, vol. VII

Robinson, Rev. Norman Hamilton Galloway, 1912–1978, vol. VII

Robinson, Maj.-Gen. Oliver Long, 1867–1947, vol. IV

Robinson, Most Rev. Mgr Paschal, 1870–1948, vol. IV

Robinson, Sir Percival; *see* Robinson, Sir F. P.

Robinson, Percival James, 1879–1944, vol. IV

Robinson, Brig.-Gen. Percy Morris, 1873–1949, vol. IV

Robinson, (Peter) Forbes, 1926–1987, vol. VIII

Robinson, Rev. Canon Reginald Henry, 1881–1970, vol. VI

Robinson, Sir Richard Atkinson, 1849–1928, vol. II

Robinson, Sir Richard Harcourt, 5th Bt (*cr* 1819), 1828–1910, vol. I

Robinson, Sir Robert, 1886–1975, vol. VII

Robinson, Col Robert Maximilian R.; *see* Rainey-Robinson.

Robinson, Robert Thomson, 1867–1926, vol. II

Robinson, Ronald Henry Ottywell Betham, 1896–1973, vol. VII

Robinson, Samuel, 1870–1958, vol. V

Robinson, Samuel, 1893–1967, vol. VI

Robinson, Sidney, 1863–1956, vol. V

Robinson, Stanford, 1904–1984, vol. VIII

Robinson, Sir Stanley; *see* Robinson, Sir E. S.

Robinson, Col Stapylton Chapman Bates, 1855–1927, vol. II

Robinson, Brig.-Gen. Stratford Watson, 1871–1962, vol. VI

Robinson, Sydney Allen, 1905–1978, vol. VII

Robinson, Sir Sydney Maddock, 1865–1948, vol. IV

Robinson, Sir Sydney Walter, 1876–1950, vol. IV

Robinson, Theodore Henry, 1881–1964, vol. VI

Robinson, Sir Thomas, 1827–1897, vol. I

Robinson, Sir Thomas, 1855–1927, vol. II

Robinson, Sir Thomas, *died* 1953, vol. V

Robinson, Lt-Col Sir Thomas Bilbe, 1853–1939, vol. III
Robinson, Sir Thomas William, 1864–1946, vol. IV
Robinson, Tom, *died* 1916, vol. II
Robinson, Ursula; *see* Bloom, U.
Robinson, Sir Victor Lloyd, 1899–1966, vol. VI
Robinson, Vincent Joseph, 1829–1910, vol. I
Robinson, Rt Rev. Mgr Walter Croke, 1839–1914, vol. I
Robinson, Rt Rev. Walter Wade, 1919–1975, vol. VII
Robinson, Maj.-Gen. Wellesley Gordon Walker, 1839–1908, vol. I
Robinson, Sir William, 1836–1912, vol. I
Robinson, Sir William, *died* 1932, vol. III
Robinson, William, 1838–1935, vol. III
Robinson, Sir William, 1879–1961, vol. VI
Robinson, William Albert, *died* 1949, vol. IV
Robinson, Brig.-Gen. William Arthur, 1864–1929, vol.III
Robinson, Sir (William) Arthur, 1874–1950, vol. IV
Robinson, Maj.-Gen. William Arthur, 1908–1982, vol. VIII
Robinson, Sir William Cleaver Francis, 1835–1897, vol. I
Robinson, William Cornforth, 1861–1931, vol. III
Robinson, William Edward, 1863–1927, vol. II
Robinson, Rev. W(illiam) Gordon, 1903–1977, vol. VII
Robinson, William Heath, 1872–1944, vol. IV
Robinson, Sir William Henry, *died* 1940, vol. III
Robinson, Sir William Henry, 1874–1964, vol. VI
Robinson, Maj.-Gen. William Henry Banner, 1863–1922, vol. II
Robinson, William Leefe,1895–1918, vol. II
Robinson, William Oscar James, 1909–1968, vol. VI
Robinson, William Sugden, *died* 1968, vol. VI
Robinson-Douglas, William Douglas; *see* Douglas.
Robiquet, Jean, 1874–1960, vol. V (A), vol. VI (AI)
Robison, Lionel MacDowall, 1886–1967, vol. VI
Robison, Robert, 1883–1941, vol. IV
Robjent, Frederick Pring, 1859–1938, vol. III
Robjohns, Sydney, 1878–1954, vol. V
Robley, Maj.-Gen. Horatio Gordon, 1840–1930, vol. III
Roblin, Hon. Sir Rodmond Palen, 1853–1937, vol. III
Roborough, 1st Baron, 1859–1938, vol. III
Robson, Baron (Life Peer); William Snowdon Robson, 1852–1918, vol. II
Robson, Air Vice-Marshal Adam Henry, 1892–1980, vol. VII
Robson, Albert Henry, *died* 1939, vol. III
Robson, Sir Arthur William Mayo-, 1853–1933, vol. III
Robson, Denis Hicks, 1904–1983, vol. VIII
Robson, Edward Robert, 1835–1917, vol. II
Robson, Dame Flora, 1902–1984, vol. VIII
Robson, Vice-Adm. Sir Geoffrey; *see* Robson, Vice-Adm. Sir W. G. A.
Robson, George, 1842–1911, vol. I
Robson, Hon. Harold Burge, 1888–1964, vol. VI
Robson, Sir Henry, 1848–1911, vol. I
Robson, Henry Naunton, 1861–1925, vol. II
Robson, Lt-Col Henry William Cumine, 1886–1942, vol. IV

Robson, Sir Herbert Thomas, 1874–1935, vol. III
Robson, Hugh Amos, 1871–1945, vol. IV
Robson, Sir Hugh Norwood, 1917–1977, vol. VII
Robson, Captain Humphrey Maurice, 1889–1940, vol. III
Robson, James, 1890–1981, vol. VIII
Robson, James Jeavons, 1918–1989, vol. VIII
Robson, Rev. John, 1836–1908, vol. I
Robson, John Henry Matthews, 1870–1945, vol. IV
Robson, John Michael, 1900–1982, vol. VIII
Robson, Juliette Louise; *see* Alvin, J. L.
Robson, Sir Kenneth, 1909–1978, vol. VII
Robson, Col Lancelot, 1855–1936, vol. III
Robson, Sir Lawrence William, 1904–1982, vol. VIII
Robson, Leonard Charles, 1894–1964, vol. VI
Robson, Philip Appleby, 1871–1951, vol. V
Robson, Robert, 1845–1928, vol. II
Robson, William, 1893–1975, vol. VII
Robson, William Alexander,1895–1980, vol. VII
Robson, Vice-Adm. Sir (William) Geoffrey (Arthur), 1902–1989, vol. VIII
Robson, Rev. William Henry Fairfax, 1834–1913, vol.I
Robson Brown, Sir William, *died* 1975, vol. VII
Robson-Scott, William Douglas, 1901–1980, vol. VII
Roby, Arthur Godfrey, 1862–1944, vol. IV
Roby, Henry John, 1830–1915, vol. I
Roch, Col Horace Sampson, 1876–1960, vol. V
Roch, Walter Francis, 1880–1965, vol. VI
Rochdale, 1st Baron,1866–1945, vol. IV
Roche, Baron (Life Peer); Alexander Adair Roche, 1871–1956, vol. V
Roche, Alexander, 1861–1921, vol.II
Roche, Alexander Ernest, 1896–1963, vol. VI
Roche, Hon. Alexis Charles Burke, 1853–1914, vol. I
Roche, Augustine, *died* 1915, vol. I
Roche, Sir David Vandeleur, 2nd Bt, 1833–1908, vol. I
Roche, Most Rev. Edward Patrick, 1874–1950, vol. IV (A)
Roche, Sir George, 1850–1932, vol. III
Roche, Col Henry John, 1864–1944, vol. IV
Roche, Most Rev. James J., 1870–1956, vol. V
Roche, John, 1848–1914, vol. I
Roche, Sir Standish Deane O'Grady, 3rd Bt, 1845–1914, vol. I
Roche, Sir Standish O'Grady, 4th Bt, 1911–1977, vol. VII
Roche, Col Hon. Ulick de Rupe Burke, 1856–1919, vol. II
Roche, Hon. William,1842–1925, vol. II
Roche, William, 1880–1942, vol. IV
Roche, Hon. William James, 1860–1937, vol. III
Rochefort, Henri, 1831–1913, vol. I
Rochefort-Lucay, Marquis de, Victor Henri; *see* Rochefort, Henri.
Rochester, 1st Baron, 1876–1955, vol. V
Rochford, James Donald Henry, 1921–1986, vol. VIII
Rochfort, Maj.-Gen. Sir Alexander Nelson, 1850–1916, vol. II
Rochfort, Sir Cecil Charles B.; *see* Boyd-Rochfort.
Rochfort, Captain George Arthur B.; *see* Boyd-Rochfort.

Rochfort-Boyd, Col Charles Augustus, 1850–1940, vol. III

Rochfort-Boyd, Lt-Col Henry Charles, 1877–1917, vol. II

Rocke, Col Cyril Edmund Alan, 1876–1968, vol. VI

Rocke, Maj.-Gen. James Harwood, 1829–1913, vol. I

Rocke, Col Walter Leslie, 1862–1932, vol. III

Rockefeller, John Davison, 1839–1937, vol. III

Rockefeller, John Davison, Jr, 1874–1960, vol. V

Rockefeller, John Davison, 3rd, 1906–1978, vol. VII

Rockefeller, Nelson Aldrich, 1908–1979, vol. VII

Rockhill, William Woodville, 1854–1914, vol. I

Rockley, 1st Baron, 1865–1941, vol. IV

Rockley, 2nd Baron, 1901–1976, vol. VII

Rockley, Lady; (Alicia-Margaret), *died* 1941, vol. IV

Rockliff, Percy, 1869–1958, vol. V

Rocyn-Jones, Arthur, *died* 1972, vol. VII

Rocyn-Jones, Sir David Thomas, 1872–1953, vol. V

Rod, Edouard, 1857–1910, vol. I

Rodd, Hon. Nancy, (Hon. Mrs Peter Rodd); *see* Mitford, N.

Rodda, Diwan Bahadur Shrinivas Konher, 1851–1929, vol. III

Roddan, Gilbert McMicking, 1906–1990, vol. VIII

Roddick, Sir Thomas George, 1846–1923, vol. II

Roddie, Lt-Col William Stewart, 1878–1961, vol. VI

Roddy, Col Henry Hugh, 1866–1932, vol. III

Roden, 5th Earl of, 1823–1897, vol. I

Roden, 6th Earl of, 1842–1910, vol. I

Roden, 7th Earl of, 1845–1915, vol I

Roden, 8th Earl of, 1883–1956, vol. V

Roden, Countess of; (Ada Maria), 1860–1931, vol. III

Roden, Sir Robert Blair, 1860–1939, vol. III

Rodenberg, Julius, 1831–1914, vol. I

Rodes Green, Brig.-Gen. Henry Clifford; *see* Green.

Rodger, Adam Keir, 1855–1946, vol. IV

Rodger, Alec, (Thomas Alexander), 1907–1982, vol. VIII

Rodger, Sir Alexander, *died* 1950, vol. IV

Rodger, Sir John Pickersgill, 1851–1910, vol. I

Rodger, Thomas Alexander; *see* Rodger, Alec.

Rodger, Thomas Ferguson, 1907–1978, vol. VII

Rodger, T(homas) Ritchie, 1878–1968, vol. VI

Rodger, Sir William Glendinning, 1912–1990, vol. VIII

Rodgers, Air Cdre Alexander Mitchell, 1906–1973, vol. VII

Rodgers, David John, 1890–1975, vol. VII

Rodgers, Gerald Fleming, 1917–1990, vol. VIII

Rodgers, Rt Rev. Harold Nickinson, *died* 1947, vol. IV

Rodgers, Richard, 1902–1979, vol. VII

Rodgers, William Robert, 1909–1969, vol. VI

Rodham, Brig. Cuthbert Harold Boyd, 1900–1973, vol VII

Rodham, Rear-Adm. (S) Harold, 1873–1947, vol. IV

Rodin, Auguste, 1840–1917, vol. II

Rodman, Adm. Hugh, 1859–1940, vol. III

Rodney, 7th Baron, 1857–1909, vol. I

Rodney, 8th Baron, 1891–1973, vol. VII

Rodney, Hon. James Henry Bartie, 1893–1933, vol. III

Rodocanachi, Emmanuel Michel, 1855–1932, vol. III

Rodrigo, Joseph Lionel Christie, *born* 1895, vol. VII

Rodrigo, Sir Philip; *see* Rodrigo, Sir S. T. P.

Rodrigo, Sir (Senapathige Theobald) Philip, *born* 1899, vol. VII

Rodway, James, 1848–1926, vol. II

Rodway, Leonard, 1853–1936, vol. III

Rodwell, Sir Cecil Hunter-, 1874–1953, vol. V

Rodwell, Brig.-Gen. Ernest Hunter, 1858–1937, vol. III

Rodwell, Air Cdre Robert John, 1897–1970, vol. VI

Rodzianko, Col Paul, *died* 1965, vol. VI

Rodzinski, Artur, 1894–1958, vol. V

Roe, 1st Baron, 1832–1923, vol. II

Roe, Sir Alliot Verdon-, 1877–1958, vol. V

Roe, Sir Charles Arthur, 1841–1927, vol. II

Roe, Brig.-Gen. Cyril Harcourt, 1864–1928, vol. II

Roe, Francis Reginald, 1869–1942, vol. IV

Roe, Fred, *died* 1947, vol. IV

Roe, Frederic Gordon, 1894–1985, vol. VIII

Roe, Frederick Charles, 1894–1958, vol. V

Roe, Harold Riley, 1883–1963, vol. VI

Roe, Humphrey Verdon, 1878–1949, vol. IV

Roe, Rev. Robert Gordon, 1860–1927, vol. II

Roe, Rev. Robert James, *died* 1921, vol. II

Roe, Brig. William C.; *see* Carden Roe.

Roe, Dep. Surg.-Gen. William Carden, 1834–1922, vol. II

Roe, Lt-Col William Francis, 1871–1925, vol. II

Roe, Maj.-Gen. Sir William Gordon, 1904–1969, vol. VI

Roe-Thompson, Edwin Reginald, 1894–1970, vol. VI

Roebuck, Alfred, 1889–1962, vol. VI

Roerich, Nicholas K., 1874–1947, vol. IV

Roff, William George, 1858–1926, vol. II

Roffey, Edgar Stuart, 1875–1957, vol. V

Roffey, Sir (George) Walter, 1870–1940, vol. III

Roffey, Sir James, *died* 1912, vol. I

Roffey, Sir Walter; *see* Roffey, Sir G. W.

Rogan, Lt-Col John M.; *see* Mackenzie-Rogan.

Rogan, Rev. William Henry, 1908–1987, vol. VIII

Roger, Alastair Forbes, 1916–1980, vol. VII

Roger, Sir Alexander, 1878–1961, vol. VI

Roger, Captain Archibald, *born* 1842, vol. II

Rogers, Arthur Kenyon, 1868–1936, vol. III

Rogers, Sir Arthur Stanley, 1883–1953, vol. V

Rogers, Arthur William, 1872–1946, vol. IV

Rogers, Benjamin, 1837–1923, vol. II

Rogers, Bertram Mitford Heron, 1860–1953, vol. V

Rogers, Bruce, 1870–1957, vol. V

Rogers, Charles Coltman Coltman, 1854–1929, vol. III

Rogers, Rev. Charles Fursdon, 1848–1928, vol. II

Rogers, Charles Gilbert, *died* 1937, vol. III

Rogers, Claude Maurice, 1907–1979, vol. VII

Rogers, Rev. Clement Francis, 1866–1949, vol. IV

Rogers, Brig. Edgar William, 1892–1973, vol. VII

Rogers, Edmund Dawson, 1823–1910, vol. I

Rogers, Edwin John, 1858–1951, vol. V

Rogers, Ven. Evan James Gwyn, 1914–1982, vol. VIII

Rogers, Captain Francis Caryer Campbell, 1883–1915, vol. I

Rogers, Francis Edward Newman, 1868–1925, vol. II

Rogers, Frederick, 1846–1915, vol. I

Rogers, Rev. Frederick Arundel, 1876–1944, vol. IV

Rogers, George Henry Roland, 1906–1983, vol. VIII
Rogers, Ven. George Herbert, *died* 1926, vol. II
Rogers, Col George William, 1843–1917, vol. II
Rogers, Graham, 1907–1973, vol. VII
Rogers, Rev. Guy; *see* Rogers, Rev. T. G.
Rogers, Ven. Gwyn; *see* Rogers, Ven. E. J. G.
Rogers, Sir Hallewell, 1864–1931, vol. III
Rogers, Lt-Col Henry, 1876–1931, vol. III
Rogers, Sir Henry Montagu, 1855–1931, vol. III
Rogers, Lt-Col Henry Schofield, 1869–1955, vol. V
Rogers, Henry Wade, 1853–1926, vol. II
Rogers, Herbert Lionel, 1871–1950, vol. IV
Rogers, Howard John, 1943–1987, vol. VIII
Rogers, Lt-Col Hugh Henry, 1858–1932, vol. III
Rogers, Rear-Adm. Hugh Hext, 1883–1955, vol. V
Rogers, Brig.-Gen. Hugh Stuart, 1878–1952, vol. V
Rogers, Rev. James Guinness, 1822–1911, vol. I
Rogers, John, *died* 1945, vol. IV
Rogers, John, 1878–1975, vol. VII
Rogers, Lt-Col Sir John Godfrey, 1850–1922, vol. II
Rogers, Lt-Col John Middleton, 1864–1945, vol. IV
Rogers, Brig. Joseph Bartlett, *died* 1940, vol. III
Rogers, Lambert Charles, 1897–1961, vol. VI
Rogers, Maj.-Gen. Sir Leonard, 1868–1962, vol. VI
Rogers, Leonard James, 1862–1933, vol. III
Rogers, Lindsay, 1891–1970, vol. VI (AII)
Rogers, Mark, 1848–1933, vol. III
Rogers, Muriel Augusta Gillian C.; *see* Coltman-Rogers.
Rogers, Neville William, 1908–1985, vol. VIII
Rogers, Maj.-Gen. Norman Annesley C.; *see* Coxwell-Rogers.
Rogers, Hon. Norman McLeod, 1894–1940, vol. III
Rogers, Sir Percival Halse, 1883–1945, vol. IV
Rogers, Rev. Percy, 1826–1910, vol. I
Rogers, Sir Philip, 1914–1990, vol. VIII
Rogers, Philip Graham, *died* 1958, vol. V
Rogers, Hon. Robert, 1864–1936, vol. III
Rogers, Lt-Gen. Sir Robert Gordon, 1832–1906, vol. I
Rogers, Sir Robert Hargreaves, 1850–1924, vol. II
Rogers, Robert Vashon, 1843–1911, vol. I
Rogers, Robert William, 1864–1930, vol. III
Rogers, Roland, 1847–1927, vol. II
Rogers, Thomas Arthur, 1897–1965, vol. VI
Rogers, Thomas Englesby, 1817–1912, vol. I
Rogers, Rev. (Travers) Guy, *died* 1967, vol. VI
Rogers, Major Vivian Barry, 1887–1965, vol. VI
Rogers, William Penn Adair, 1879–1935, vol. III
Rogerson, John, 1917–1990, vol. VIII
Rogerson, Captain John Edwin, 1865–1925, vol. II
Rogerson, Col Sidney, 1894–1968, vol. VI
Roget, F. F., 1859–1938, vol. III
Rogosinski, Werner Wolfgang, 1894–1964, vol. VI
Rohan, Duchesse de, (dowager); Herminie de Verteillac, *died* 1926, vol. II
Rohde, Eleanour Sinclair, *died* 1950, vol. IV
Rohlfs, Mrs Charles, (Anna Katharine Rohlfs), 1846–1935, vol. III
Rohmer, Sax, *died* 1959, vol. V
Roles, Francis Crosbie, 1867–1931, vol. III
Rolfe, Douglass Horace B.; *see* Boggis-Rolfe.
Rolfe, Eustace N.; *see* Neville-Rolfe.
Rolfe, Rev. Harry Roger, 1851–1924, vol. II

Rolfe, Captain Herbert Neville, 1854–1942, vol. IV
Rolfe, William James, 1827–1910, vol. I
Roll, Sir Cecil Ernest, 3rd Bt, 1878–1938, vol. III
Roll, Sir Frederick James, 2nd Bt, 1873–1933, vol. III
Roll, Grahame Winfield, *died* 1942, vol. IV
Roll, Sir James, 1st Bt, 1846–1927, vol. II
Rolland, Brig.-Gen. Alexander, 1871–1939, vol. III
Rolland, Very Rev. Sir Francis William, 1878–1965, vol. VI
Rolland, Major George Murray, 1869–1910, vol. I
Rolland, Romain, 1866–1944, vol. IV
Rolland, Brig.-Gen. Stewart Erskine, 1846–1927, vol. II
Rolland, Vice-Adm. William Rae, 1817–1904, vol. I
Rollason, Ernest Clarence, 1908–1972, vol. VII
Rolle, Hon. Mark George Kerr, 1835–1907, vol. I
Roller, Major George C., 1856–1941, vol. IV
Rolleston, Charles Ffranck, 1833–1913, vol. I
Rolleston, Francis Joseph, 1873–1946, vol. IV
Rolleston, Sir Humphry Davy, 1st Bt, 1862–1944, vol. IV
Rolleston, Iris Brenda, 1880–1948, vol. IV
Rolleston, John Davy, 1873–1946, vol. IV
Rolleston, Sir John Fowke Lancelot, 1848–1919, vol. II
Rolleston, Adm. John Philip, 1859–1936, vol. III
Rolleston, Col Sir Lancelot, 1847–1941, vol. IV
Rolleston, Thomas William, 1857–1920, vol. II
Rolleston, Sir William Gustavus Stanhope, 1862–1944, vol. IV
Rolleston, Col William Lancelot, 1905–1974, vol. VII
Rollett, Herbert, 1872–1932, vol. III
Rolling, Col Bernard Ismay, 1883–1937, vol. III
Rollins, John Wenlock, *died* 1940, vol. III
Rollit, Sir Albert Kaye, 1842–1922, vol. II
Rollo, 10th Lord, 1835–1916, vol. II
Rollo, 11th Lord, 1860–1946, vol. IV
Rollo, 12th Lord, 1889–1947, vol. IV
Rollo, Hon. Bernard Francis, 1868–1935, vol. III
Rollo, Hon. Eric Norman, 1861–1930, vol. III
Rollo, Lt-Col George, 1881–1944, vol. IV
Rollo, Gen. Hon. Sir Robert, 1814–1907, vol. I
Rollo, Rev. William, 1859–1949, vol. IV
Rolls, Hon. Charles Stewart, 1877–1910, vol. I
Rolls, Captain Sir John Courtown Edward S.; *see* Shelley-Rolls.
Rolo, Sir Robert, 1869–1944, vol. IV
Rolph, Sir Gordon Burns, 1893–1959, vol. V
Rolt, Bernard, 1874–1937, vol. III
Rolt, Very Rev. Cecil Henry, 1865–1926, vol. II
Rolt, James, 1860–1938, vol. III
Rolt, Lionel Thomas Caswall, 1910–1974, vol. VII
Rolt, Brig.-Gen. Stuart Peter, 1862–1933, vol. III
Rolt, Vivian, 1874–1933, vol. III
Romains, Jules, 1885–1972, vol. VII
Romanes, Ethel, *died* 1927, vol. II
Romanes, Mrs George; *see* Romanes, Ethel.
Romanis, William Hugh Cowie, 1889–1972, vol. VII
Romanne-James, Helena Constance, (Mrs H. C. Aylen), *died* 1966, vol. VI
Romanos, Athos, 1858–1940, vol. III
Rome, Brig.-Charles Leslie, 1878–1936, vol. III
Rome, Brig.-Gen. Claude Stuart, 1875–1956, vol. V

Rome, Maj.-Gen. Francis David, 1905–1985, vol. VIII

Rome, Thomas, 1852–1938, vol. III

Romer, Baron (Life Peer); Mark Lemon Romer, 1866–1944, vol. IV

Romer, Carrol, 1883–1951, vol. V

Romer, Gen. Sir Cecil Francis, 1869–1962, vol. VI

Romer, Rt Hon. Sir Charles Robert Ritchie, 1897–1969, vol. VI

Romer, Frank, 1871–1939, vol. III

Romer, Lt-Col Frederick Charles, 1854–1915, vol. I

Romer, Rt Hon. Sir Robert, 1840–1918, vol. II

Romer, Thomas Ansdell, 1848–1917, vol. II

Romer-Lee, Lt-Col H., 1874–1955, vol. V

Romeril, Herbert George, 1881–1963, vol. VI

Romilly, 3rd Baron, 1866–1905, vol. I

Romilly, 4th Baron, 1899–1983, vol. VIII

Romilly, Col Bertram Henry Samuel, 1878–1940, vol. III

Romilly, Eric Carnegie, (Frederic Carnegie Romilly), 1886–1953, vol. V

Romilly, Frederic Carnegie; *see* Romilly, E. C.

Romilly, Col Frederick William, 1854–1935, vol. III

Romilly, George, *died* 1933, vol. III

Romilly, Samuel Henry, 1849–1940, vol. III

Romiti, William, 1850–1936, vol. III

Romney, 4th Earl of, 1841–1905, vol. I

Romney, 5th Earl of, 1864–1933, vol. III

Romney, 6th Earl of, 1892–1975, vol. VII

Ronald, E. B.; *see* Barker, Ronald Ernest.

Ronald, Sir Landon, 1873–1938, vol. III

Ronald, Sir Nigel Bruce, 1894–1973, vol. VII

Ronalds, Andrew John, 1897–1978, vol. VII

Ronaldson, James Bruce, 1886–1952, vol. V

Ronaldson, Brig.-Gen. Robert William Hawthorn, 1864–1946, vol. IV

Ronaldson, Thomas Martine, 1881–1942, vol. IV

Ronan, Very Rev. Myles V., 1877–1959, vol. IV

Ronan, Rt Hon. Stephen, 1848–1925, vol. II

Ronayne, Thomas, 1848–1925, vol. II

Roncalli, Angelo Giuseppe; *see* John XXIII.

Roney, Sir Ernest, 1871–1952, vol. V

Roocroft, Col William Mitchell, 1859–1943, vol. IV

Rood, Felix Stephen, 1883–1933, vol. III

Rook, Air Vice-Marshal Sir Alan Filmer, *died* 1960, vol. V

Rook, John Allan Fynes, 1926–1987, vol. VIII

Rook, Sir William James, 1885–1958, vol. V

Rooke, Charles Eustace, 1892–1947, vol. IV

Rooke, Lt-Col Everard Home, 1875–1936, vol. III

Rooke, Col Harry William, 1842–1921, vol. II

Rooke, Ven. Henry, 1829–1926, vol. II

Rooke, Herbert K., 1872–1944, vol. IV

Rooke, Thomas Matthews, 1842–1942, vol. IV

Rooke, Maj.-Gen. William, 1836–1919, vol. II

Rooker, John Kingsley, 1887–1951, vol. V

Rooks, Maj.-Gen. Lowell W., 1893–1973, vol. VII

Rookwood, 1st Baron, 1826–1902, vol. I

Room, Thomas Gerald, 1902–1986, vol. VIII

Roome, Gen. Frederick, 1829–1907, vol. I

Roome, Engr-Rear-Adm. George W., 1865–1945, vol. IV

Roome, Henry Delacombe, 1882–1930, vol. III

Roome, Rear-Adm. Henry Stewart, 1896–1981, vol. VIII

Roome, Maj.-Gen. Sir Horace Eckford, 1887–1964, vol. VI

Rooney, Rt Rev. John, *died* 1927, vol. II

Rooney, Maj.-Gen. Sir Owen Patrick James, 1900–1972, vol. VII

Roos, Gustaf Ehrenreich, 1838–1928, vol. II

Roos-Keppel, Sir George; *see* Keppel.

Roose, (Edward Charles) Robson, 1848–1905, vol. I

Roosevelt, (Anna) Eleanor, (Mrs F. D. Roosevelt), 1884–1962, vol. VI

Roosevelt, Eleanor; *see* Roosevelt, A. E.

Roosevelt, Franklin Delano, 1882–1945, vol. IV

Roosevelt, Col Kermit, *died* 1943, vol. IV

Roosevelt, Robert Barnewell, 1829–1906, vol. I

Roosevelt, Col Theodore, 1858–1919, vol. II

Roosevelt, Theodore, 1887–1944, vol. IV

Root, Hon. Elihu, 1845–1937, vol. III

Root, Frederick James, 1906–1982, vol. VIII

Rootes, 1st Baron, 1894–1964, vol. VI

Rootes, Sir Reginald Claud, 1896–1977, vol. VII

Rooth, Henry Goodwin, 1861–1928, vol. II

Rooth, Ivar, 1888–1972, vol. VII

Rooth, John, 1864–1930, vol. III

Rootham, Cyril Bradley, 1875–1938, vol. III

Rootham, Jasper St John, 1910–1990, vol. VIII

Roots, Rt Rev. Logan Herbert, 1870–1945, vol. IV

Roots, William Lloyd, 1911–1971, vol. VII

Rope, Ellen Mary, *died* 1934, vol. III

Roper, Brig.-Gen. Alexander William, 1862–1940, vol. III

Roper, Edgar Stanley, 1878–1953, vol. V

Roper, Captain Edward Gregson, 1910–1983, vol. VIII

Roper, Edward Ridgill, 1885–1974, vol. VII

Roper, Freeman, 1862–1925, vol. II

Roper, Garnham, 1862–1940, vol. III

Roper, Sir Harold, 1891–1971, vol. VII

Roper, Henry Basil, 1846–1918, vol. II

Roper, Maj.-Gen. Henry Ernest, 1923–1982, vol. VIII

Roper, Most Rev. John Charles, 1858–1940, vol. III

Roper, Philip Hampden, 1906–1956, vol. V

Ropes, Arthur Reed, 1859–1933, vol. III

Ropner, Sir (Emil Hugo Oscar) Robert, 3rd Bt (*cr* 1904), 1893–1962, vol. VI

Ropner, Sir Guy; *see* Ropner, Sir W. G.

Ropner, Sir John Henry, 2nd Bt (*cr* 1904), 1860–1936, vol. III

Ropner, Leonard, 1873–1937, vol. III

Ropner, Col Sir Leonard, 1st Bt (*cr* 1952), 1895–1977, vol. VII

Ropner, Col Sir Robert, 1st Bt (*cr* 1904), 1838–1924, vol. II

Ropner, Sir Robert; *see* Ropner, Sir E. H. O. R.

Ropner, Sir Robert Desmond, 1908–1977, vol. VII

Ropner, Sir (William) Guy, 1896–1971, vol. VII

Rops, Henry D.; *see* Daniel-Rops.

Roques, Frederick William, 1898–1964, vol. VI

Roques, Mario Louis Guillaume, 1875–1961, vol. VI

Rorie, Col David, 1867–1946, vol. IV

Rorie, James, 1838–1911, vol. I

Rorimer, James J., 1905–1966, vol. VI

Rorison, Very Rev. Vincent Lewis, 1851–1910, vol. I

Rorke, Rev. Joseph, *died* 1932, vol. III
Rorke, Kate, (Mrs Douglas Cree), *died* 1945, vol. IV
Rosa, John Nogueira, 1903–1977, vol. VII
Rosay, Françoise, 1891–1974, vol. VII
Rosbotham, Sir Samuel Thomas, 1864–1950, vol. IV
Roscoe, (Edward) John (Townsend), 1913–1984, vol. VIII
Roscoe, Edward Stanley, 1849–1932, vol. III
Roscoe, Frank, 1870–1942, vol. IV
Roscoe, Rt Hon. Sir Henry Enfield, 1833–1915, vol. I
Roscoe, Rev. John, 1861–1932, vol. III
Roscoe, John; *see* Roscoe, E. J. T.
Roscoe, Kenneth Harry, 1914–1970, vol. VI
Roscoe, Air Cdre Peter Henry, 1912–1987, vol. VIII
Rose, Sir Alan Edward Percival, 1899–1975, vol. VII
Rose, Rt Rev. Alfred Carey Wollaston, *died* 1971, vol. VII
Rose, Algernon Sidney, *died* 1934, vol. III
Rose, Archibald; *see* Rose, C. A. W.
Rose, Hon. Lt-Col Sir Arthur; *see* Rose, Hon. Lt-Col Sir H. A.
Rose, Captain Arthur Martin Thomas, 1918–1987, vol. VIII
Rose, (Charles) Archibald (Walker), 1879–1961, vol. VI
Rose, Sir Charles Day, 1st Bt (*cr* 1909), 1847–1913, vol. I
Rose, Sir Charles Henry, 3rd Bt (*cr* 1909), 1912–1966, vol. VI
Rose, Clifford Alan, 1929–1983, vol. VIII
Rose, Sir Cyril Stanley, 3rd Bt (*cr* 1872), 1874–1915, vol. I
Rose, Sir David James Gardiner, 1923–1969, vol. VI
Rose, Edward, 1849–1904, vol. I
Rose, Edward, 1845–1910, vol. I
Rose, Gen. Edward Lee, 1841–1903, vol. I
Rose, (Edward) Michael, 1913–1986, vol. VIII
Rose, Lt-Col Ernest Albert, 1879–1976, vol. VII
Rose, Sir Francis Cyril, 4th Bt (*cr* 1872), 1909–1979, vol. VII
Rose, Francis Leslie, 1909–1988, vol. VIII
Rose, Frank Atcherley, 1873–1935, vol. III
Rose, Vice-Adm. Sir Frank Forrester, 1878–1955, vol. V
Rose, Frank Herbert, 1857–1928, vol. II
Rose, Sir Frank Stanley, 2nd Bt (*cr* 1909), 1877–1914, vol. I
Rose, Frederick, *died* 1932, vol. III
Rose, Frederick Campbell, 1865–1946, vol. IV
Rose, Geoffrey Keith,1889–1959, vol. V
Rose, George Pringle, 1855–1918, vol. II
Rose, Brig.-Gen. Henry Metcalfe, 1848–1909, vol. I
Rose, Herbert Jennings, 1883–1961, vol. VI
Rose, Dame Hilda Nora, 1891–1982, vol. VIII
Rose, Horace Arthur, 1867–1933, vol. III
Rose, Lt-Col Hugh, 1863–1946, vol. IV
Rose, Sir Hugh, 2nd Bt (*cr* 1935) 1902–1976, vol. VII
Rose, Major Hugh Alexander Leslie, *died* 1918, vol. II
Rose, Lt-Col Sir (Hugh) Arthur, 1st Bt (*cr* 1935), 1875–1937, vol. III
Rose, Hugh Edward, 1869–1945, vol. IV
Rose, Major James, 1820–1909, vol. I
Rose, John, 1841–1926, vol. II

Rose, John Donald, 1911–1976, vol. VII
Rose, John Holland, 1855–1942, vol. IV
Rose, Brig.-Gen. John Latham, 1867–1931, vol. III
Rose, Col John Markham, 1865–1942, vol. IV
Rose, Michael; *see* Rose, E. M.
Rose, Percy Jesse, 1878–1959, vol. V
Rose, Sir Philip Frederick, 2nd Bt (*cr* 1874), 1843–1919, vol. II
Rose, Captain Sir Philip Humphrey Vivian, 3rd Bt, 1903–1982, vol. VIII
Rose, Reginald Leslie S.; *see* Smith-Rose.
Rose, Col Richard Aubrey De Burgh, 1877–1962, vol. VI
Rose, Captain Thomas Allen, 1874–1914, vol. I
Rose, Sir Thomas Kirke, 1865–1953, vol. V
Rose, Walter Clerk R.; *see* Randolph-Rose.
Rose, Sir William, 2nd Bt (*cr* 1872), 1846–1902, vol. I
Rose, William, 1847–1910, vol. I
Rose, William, 1894–1961, vol. VI
Rose, William John, 1885–1968, vol. VI
Rose-Innes, Rt Hon. Sir James, 1855–1942, vol. IV
Rose-Innes, Sir Patrick, 1853–1924, vol. II
Rose-Miller, Brig. George Patrick; *see* Miller.
Rosebery, 5th Earl of, 1847–1929, vol. III
Rosebery, 6th Earl of, 1882–1974, vol. VII
Rosedale, Captain Rev. Honyel Gough, 1863–1928, vol. II
Rosenbach, Abraham S. Wolf, 1876–1952, vol. V
Rosenfeld, Léon, 1904–1974, vol. VII
Rosenhain, Walter, 1875–1934, vol. III
Rosenhead, Louis, 1906–1984, vol. VIII
Rosenheim, Baron (Life Peer); Max Leonard Rosenheim, 1908–1972, vol. VII
Rosenheim, Otto, 1871–1955, vol. V
Rosenman, Samuel Irving, 1896–1973, vol. VII
Rosenthal, Maj.-Gen. Sir Charles, 1875–1954, vol. V
Rosenthal, Harold David, 1917–1988, vol. VIII
Rosenthal, Moriz, 1862–1946, vol. IV
Roseveare, Sir Martin Pearson, 1898–1985, vol. VIII
Roseveare, Rt Rev. Reginald Richard, 1902–1972, vol. VII
Roseveare, Rev. Richard Polgreen, 1865–1924, vol. II
Roseveare, Richard Victor Harley, 1897–1968, vol. VI
Roseveare, William Nicholas, 1864–1948, vol. IV
Rosewater, Hon. Edward, 1841–1906, vol. I
Rosewater, Victor, 1871–1940, vol. III (A), vol. IV
Roseway, Sir David; *see* Roseway, Sir G. D.
Roseway, Sir (George) David, 1890–1969, vol. VI
Rosing, Vladimir, *died* 1963, vol. VI
Roskill, John, *died* 1940, vol. III
Roskill, Captain Stephen Wentworth, 1903–1982, vol. VIII
Rosling, Sir Edward, 1863–1946, vol. IV
Roslyn, Louis Frederick, 1878–1940, vol. III
Rosman, Alice Grant, *died* 1961, vol. VI
Rosmead, 1st Baron, 1824–1897, vol. I
Rosmead, 2nd Baron, 1866–1933, vol. III
Rosmer, Milton, 1882–1971, vol. VII
Ross of Marnock, Baron (Life Peer); William Ross, 1911–1988, vol. VIII
Ross, Adrian; *see* Ropes, A. R.
Ross, Brig. Alan Campbell, 1878–1937, vol. III
Ross, Alan Strode Campbell, 1907–1980, vol. VII

Ross, Alexander, 1845–1923, vol. II
Ross, Rev. Alexander, 1888–1965, vol. VI
Ross, Brig.-Gen. Alexander, 1880–1973, vol. VII
Ross, Alexander Carnegie, 1859–1940, vol. III (A), vol. IV
Ross, Alexander David, 1883–1966, vol. VI
Ross, Lt-Gen. Sir Alexander George, 1840–1910, vol. I
Ross, Rev. Alexander George Gordon, *died* 1938, vol. III
Ross, Alexander Howard, 1880–1965, vol. VI
Ross, Allan Dawson, 1909–1982, vol. VIII
Ross, Andrew, 1849–1925, vol. II
Ross, Archibald Hugh Houstoun, 1896–1969, vol. VI
Ross, Sir Archibald John Campbell, 1867–1931, vol. III
Ross, Brig.-Gen. Arthur Edward, 1870–1952, vol. V
Ross, Rt Rev. Arthur Edwin, 1869–1923, vol. II
Ross, Lt-Col Arthur Murray, 1879–1933, vol. III
Ross, Barnaby; *see* Dannay, Frederic and Lee, Manfred B.
Ross, Hon. Sir Bruce; *see* Ross, Hon. Sir D. B.
Ross, Maj.-Gen. Charles, 1864–1930, vol. III
Ross of that Ilk, Charles Campbell, yr, 1901–1966, vol. VI
Ross, Charles Griffith, 1885–1950, vol. IV
Ross, Sir Charles Henry Augustus Frederick Lockhart, 9th Bt (*cr* 1672), 1872–1942, vol. IV
Ross, Sir David; *see* Ross, Sir W. D.
Ross, Rev. David Morison, 1852–1927, vol. II
Ross, Sir David Palmer, 1842–1904, vol. I
Ross, Sir Denison; *see* Ross, Sir E. D.
Ross, Hon. Sir (Dudley) Bruce, 1892–1984, vol. VIII
Ross, Edward Alsworth, 1866–1951, vol. V
Ross, Sir Edward Charles, 1836–1913, vol. I
Ross, Sir (Edward) Denison, 1871–1940, vol. III
Ross, Edward Rowlandson, 1868–1941, vol. IV
Ross, Rt Rev. Mgr Canon Francis, 1873–1945, vol. IV
Ross, Hon. Frank Mackenzie, 1891–1971, vol. VII
Ross, Sir Frederick William L.; *see* Leith Ross.
Ross, Col George, 1853–1926, vol.II
Ross, Rev. George Alexander Johnston, 1865–1937, vol. III
Ross, George Edward Aubert, 1847–1931, vol. III
Ross, George Mabyn, 1883–1954, vol. V
Ross, Rear-Adm. George Parish, 1875–1942, vol. IV
Ross, George Robert Thomson, 1874–1959, vol. V
Ross, Col George Whitehill, 1878–1952, vol. V
Ross, Hon. Sir George William, 1841–1914, vol. I
Ross, Hon. Dame (Grace) Hilda, 1884–1959, vol. V
Ross, Col Harry, 1869–1938, vol. III
Ross, Lt-Col Henry, 1877–1958, vol. V
Ross, Sir Henry James, 1893–1973, vol. VII
Ross, Hon. Dame Hilda; *see* Ross, Hon. Dame G. H.
Ross, Howard Salter, 1872–1955, vol. V
Ross, Major Hugh Alexander,1880–1918, vol. II
Ross, Lt-Col Hugh Cairns Edward, 1884–1940, vol. III
Ross, Hugh Campbell, 1875–1926, vol. II
Ross, Captain Hugo Donald, 1880–1960, vol. V
Ross, Sir Ian C.; *see* Clunies-Ross.
Ross, Ven. James, 1836–1902, vol. I
Ross, James, 1848–1913, vol. I

Ross, James, *died* 1953, vol. V
Ross, Maj.-Gen. James George, 1861–1956, vol. V
Ross, Sir James Paterson, 1st Bt (*cr* 1960), 1895–1980, vol. VII
Ross, Sir James Stirling, 1877–1961, vol. VI
Ross, James Stiven, 1892–1975, vol. VII
Ross, Janet Anne, 1842–1927, vol. II
Ross, Gen. Sir John, 1829–1905, vol. I
Ross, Rev. John, 1842–1915, vol. I
Ross, Sir John, 1834–1927, vol. II
Ross, Sir John, 1838–1931, vol. III
Ross, Rt Hon. Sir John, 1st Bt (*cr* 1919), 1854–1935, vol. III
Ross, John, 1893–1967, vol. VI
Ross, Major John Alexander, 1893–1917, vol. II
Ross, Brig. John Ellis, 1893–1965, vol. VI
Ross, Sir John Foster George; *see* Ross-of-Bladensburg.
Ross, John Kenneth Murray, 1856–1939, vol. III
Ross, John M. E., 1870–1925, vol. II
Ross, Maj.-Gen. John Munro, 1877–1959, vol. V
Ross, Sir John Sutherland, 1877–1959, vol. V
Ross, Rev. John Trelawny T.; *see* Trelawny-Ross.
Ross, Joseph Thorburn,1849–1903, vol. I
Ross, Kenneth Brebner, 1901–1973, vol. VII
Ross, Rev. Kenneth Needham, 1908–1970, vol. VI
Ross, Martin; *see* Martin, Violet.
Ross, Rev. Neil, 1871–1943, vol. IV
Ross, Norah Cecil; *see* Runge, N. C.
Ross, Peter McGregor, 1919–1974, vol. VII
Ross, Philip Dansken, 1858–1949, vol. IV
Ross, Reginald James Blair, *born* 1871, vol. II
Ross, Robert, 1893–1969, vol. VI
Ross, Robert Baldwin, 1869–1918, vol. II
Ross, Brig.-Gen. Robert James, 1865–1943, vol. IV
Ross, Maj.-Gen. Robert Knox, 1893–1951, vol. V
Ross, Air Cdre Robert Peel, *died* 1963, vol. VI
Ross, Roderick, 1863–1943, vol. IV
Ross, Col Sir Ronald, 1857–1932, vol. III
Ross, Lt-Col Sir Ronald Deane, 2nd Bt (*cr* 1919), 1888–1958, vol. V
Ross, Rev. Spence,1843–1929, vol. III
Ross, Stanley Graham, 1888–1980, vol. VII
Ross, Thomas Arthur, 1875–1941, vol. IV
Ross, Rev. Thomas Harry, 1863–1943, vol.IV
Ross, Sir Thomas Mackenzie, *died* 1927, vol. II
Ross of Cromarty, Brig.-Gen. Sir Walter Charteris, 1857–1928, vol. II
Ross, Col Walter John Macdonald, 1914–1982, vol. VIII
Ross, Hon. William, 1825–1912, vol. I
Ross, Hon. William, 1850–1925, vol. II
Ross, William Alexander, 1891–1977, vol. VII
Ross, Captain William Alston, 1875–1944, vol. IV
Ross, Hon. William Benjamin, 1854–1929, vol. III
Ross, Sir (William) David, 1877–1971, vol. VII
Ross, Hon. William Donald, 1869–1947, vol. IV
Ross, William Henry, 1862–1944, vol. IV
Ross, William Munro, 1858–1914, vol. I (A), vol. III
Ross, Hon. William Roderick, 1869–1928, vol. II, vol. III
Ross-Brown, James William, *died* 1938, vol. III
Ross-Frames, Col Percival, 1863–1947, vol. IV

Ross-Johnson, Maj.-Gen. Cyril Maxwell, 1868–1934, vol. III
Ross-Johnson, Dennis, 1860–1941, vol. IV
Ross-Lewin, Rev. George Harrison, 1846–1913, vol. I
Ross-Lewin, Ven. Richard S., 1848–1921, vol. II
Ross-Lewin, Rev. Robert O'Donelan, 1850–1922, vol. II
Ross-of-Bladensburg, Sir John Foster George, 1848–1926, vol. II
Ross Skinner, Lt-Col Harry Crawley, 1896–1972, vol. VII
Ross-Taylor, Sir Joshua, 1878–1959, vol. V
Ross Taylor, Walter, 1877–1958, vol. V
Ross-Taylor, Walter, 1912–1983, vol. VIII
Ross Williamson, Hugh, 1901–1978, vol. VII
Ross Williamson, Reginald Pole, 1907–1966, vol. VI
Rosse, 4th Earl of, 1840–1908, vol. I
Rosse, 5th Earl of, 1873–1918, vol. II
Rosse, 6th Earl of, 1906–1979, vol. VII
Rosselli, (Ignace Adolphe) Jacques, 1907–1974, vol. VII
Rosselli, Jacques; see Rosselli, I. A. J.
Rossetti, Harold Ford, 1909–1983, vol. VIII
Rossetti, William Michael, 1829–1919, vol. II
Rossillon, Rt Rev. Peter, 1874–1947, vol. IV
Rossiter, James Leonard,1887–1963, vol. VI
Rossiter, Hon. Sir John Frederick, 1913–1988, vol. VIII
Rossiter, Leonard, 1926–1984, vol. VIII
Rosslyn, 5th Earl of, 1869–1939, vol. III
Rosslyn, 6th Earl of, 1917–1977, vol. IV
Rossmore, 5th Baron, 1853–1921, vol. II
Rossmore, 6th Baron, 1892–1958, vol. V
Rostand, Edmond, 1868–1918, vol. II
Rostand, Jean, 1894–1977, vol. VII
Rostern, Joseph, 1862–1930, vol. III
Rostovtzeff, Michael I., 1870–1952, vol. V
Rostron, Captain Sir Arthur Henry, 1869–1940, vol. III
Rostron, Rev. Sydney N.; see Nowell-Rostron.
Rotch, Abbott Lawrence, 1861–1912, vol. I
Roth, Cecil, 1899–1970, vol. VI
Roth, George Kingsley, 1903–1960, vol. V
Roth, Leon, 1896–1963, vol. VI
Roth, Paul Bernard, 1882–1962, vol. VI
Roth, Brig.-Gen. Reuter Emerich, 1858–1924, vol. II
Roth, Air Cdre Victor Henry Batten, 1904–1979, vol. VII
Rotha, Paul, 1907–1984, vol. VIII
Rothband, Sir Henry Lesser, 1st Bt, died 1940, vol. III (A), vol. IV
Rothenstein, Sir William, 1872–1945, vol. IV
Rothera, Sir Percy, 1877–1940, vol. III
Rotherham, 1st Baron, 1849–1927, vol. II
Rotherham, 2nd Baron, 1876–1950, vol. IV
Rotherham, Arthur, died 1946, vol. IV
Rothermere, 1st Viscount, 1868–1940, vol. III
Rothermere, 2nd Viscount, 1898–1978, vol. VII
Rotherwick, 1st Baron, 1881–1958, vol. V
Rothery, Guy Cadogan, 1863–1940, vol. III (A), vol. IV
Rothery, William Gurney, 1858–1930, vol. III
Rothery, William H.; see Hume-Rothery.
Rothes, 19th Earl of, 1877–1927, vol. II

Rothes, 20th Earl of, 1902–1975, vol. VII
Rothko, Mark, 1903–1970, vol. VI
Rothschild, 1st Baron, 1840–1915, vol. I
Rothschild, 2nd Baron, 1868–1937, vol. III
Rothschild, 3rd Baron, 1910–1990, vol. VIII
Rothschild, Alfred Charles de, 1842–1918, vol. II
Rothschild, Anthony Gustav de, 1887–1961, vol. VI
Rothschild, Baron Ferdinand James de, 1839–1898, vol. I
Rothschild, Baron Henri de, 1872–1947, vol. IV
Rothschild, James A. de, died 1957, vol. V
Rothschild, Leopold de, 1845–1917, vol. II
Rothschild, Lionel Nathan de, 1882–1942, vol. IV
Rothschild, Hon. Nathaniel Charles, 1877–1923, vol. II
Rothwell, Harry, 1902–1980, vol. VII
Rothwell, James Herbert, 1881–1944, vol. IV
Rothwell, Brig. Richard Sutton, 1882–1962, vol. VI
Rothwell, Lt-Col William Edward, 1879–1937, vol. III
Rotter, Rear-Adm. (S) Charles John Ehrhardt, 1871–1948, vol. IV
Rotter, Godfrey, 1879–1969, vol. VI
Rotton, Sir John Francis, 1837–1926, vol. II
Rotton, Brig.-Gen. John Guy, 1867–1940, vol. III
Rouault, Georges, 1871–1958, vol. V
Roughead, William, 1870–1952, vol. V
Roughton, Edmund W., 1861–1913, vol. I
Roughton, Francis John Worsley, 1899–1972, vol. VII
Roughton, Noel James, 1885–1953, vol. V
Rougier, George Ronald, 1900–1976, vol. VII
Rouillard, Frederic Melchoir Louis, 1866–1933, vol. III
Rouleau, His Eminence Cardinal Raymond Marie, 1866–1931, vol. III
Roullier, Jean Georges, 1898–1974, vol. VII
Roulston, Air Cdre Jack Fendick, 1913–1973, vol. VII
Roumania, Queen Elizabeth of; see Sylva, Carmen.
Round, Charles James, 1885–1945, vol. IV
Round, Francis Richard, 1845–1920, vol. II
Round, Rt Hon. James, 1842–1916, vol. II
Round, John Horace, 1854–1928, vol. II
Round-Turner, Vice-Adm. Charles Wolfran, died 1953, vol. V
Roundell, Charles Savile, 1827–1906, vol. I
Roundell, Christopher Foulis, 1876–1958, vol. V
Roundell, Richard Foulis, 1872–1940, vol. III
Roundway, 1st Baron, 1854–1925, vol. II
Roundway, 2nd Baron, 1880–1944, vol. IV
Rounsevell, Hon. William Benjamin, 1842–1923, vol. II
Rountree, Gilbert Harry, 1907–1962, vol. VI
Rountree, Harry, 1878–1950, vol. IV
Rountree, Rev. James Peter, 1846–1929, vol. III
Roupell, Lt-Col Ernest Percy Stuart, 1870–1938, vol. III
Roupell, Brig. George Rowland Patrick, 1892–1974, vol. VII
Rous, (Francis) Peyton, 1879–1970, vol. VI
Rous, Peyton; see Rous, F. P.
Rous, Sir Stanley Ford, 1895–1986, vol. VIII
Rous, William John, 1833–1914, vol. I
Rouse, Sir Alexander Macdonald, 1878–1966, vol. VI

Rouse, Arthur Frederick, 1910–1984, vol. VIII
Rouse, Harold Lindsay, 1887–1959, vol. V
Rouse, Col Hubert, 1864–1945, vol. IV
Rouse, William Henry Denham, 1863–1950, vol. IV
Rouse-Boughton, Sir Charles Henry; *see* Boughton.
Rouse-Boughton, Sir Edward Hotham; *see* Boughton.
Rouse-Boughton, Sir William St Andrew; *see* Boughton.
Rouse-Boughton-Knight, Charles Andrew, 1859–1947, vol. IV
Rousseau, Arthur, 1871–1934, vol. III
Rousseau, Pierre Marie W.; *see* Waldeck-Rousseau.
Roussin, Leander Gaspard, 1870–1936, vol. III
Routh, Amand J. McC., 1853–1927, vol. II
Routh, Augustus Crosbie, 1892–1982, vol. VIII
Routh, Edward John, 1831–1907, vol. I
Routh, Co. Guy Montgomery, 1882–1963, vol. VI
Routh, Harold Victor, 1878–1951, vol. V
Routh, Vice-Adm. Henry Peter, 1851–1944, vol. IV
Routh, Robert Gordon, 1869–1964, vol. VI
Routhier, Hon. Sir Adolphe Basile, 1839–1919, vol. II
Routledge, Rev. C. F., 1838–1904, vol. I
Routledge, Rev. Canon Graham; *see* Routledge, Rev. Canon K. G.
Routledge, Rev. Canon (Kenneth) Graham, 1927–1989, vol. VIII
Routledge, Robert M., *died* 1907, vol. I
Routledge, Scoresby, 1859–1939, vol. III
Routley, Rev. Erik Reginald, 1917–1982, vol. VIII
Routley, Frederick William, 1879–1951, vol. V
Routley, Thomas Clarence, 1889–1963, vol. VI
Roux, François C.; *see* Charles-Roux.
Row, Canchi Sarvothama, *born* 1856, vol. II
Row, Kodikal S.; *see* Sanjiva Row.
Row, Comdr Sir Philip John, *died* 1990, vol. VIII
Row, Paymaster Rear-Adm. Philip John Hawkins Lander, 1870–1932, vol. III
Row, Brig. Robert Amos, 1888–1959, vol. V (A)
Rowallan, 1st Baron, 1856–1933, vol. III
Rowallan, 2nd Baron, 1895–1977, vol. VII
Rowan, John, *died* 1948, vol. IV
Rowan, Sir Leslie; *see* Rowan, Sir T. L.
Rowan, Lt-Col Percy Stewart, 1882–1931, vol. III
Rowan, Ven. Robert Philip, 1870–1946, vol. IV
Rowan, Sir (Thomas) Leslie, 1908–1972, vol. VII
Rowan-Hamilton, Brig. Gawaine Basil, 1884–1947, vol. IV
Rowan-Hamilton, Col Gawin William; *see* Hamilton.
Rowan-Hamilton, Sir Orme, 1877–1949, vol. IV
Rowan-Robinson, Maj.-Gen. Henry, 1873–1947, vol. IV
Rowan-Thomson, Sir William, 1867–1929, vol. III
Rowand, Alexander, 1868–1936, vol. III
Rowatt, Hugh Howard, 1861–1938, vol. III
Rowatt, Thomas, 1879–1950, vol. IV
Rowbotham, Edgar Stanley, 1890–1979, vol. VII
Rowbotham, Sir Hanson; *see* Rowbotham, Sir S. H.
Rowbotham, Rev. John Frederick, 1859–1925, vol. II
Rowbotham, Sir (Samuel) Hanson, 1880–1946, vol. IV
Rowbotham, Sir Thomas, 1851–1939, vol. III
Rowcroft, Maj.-Gen. Sir Bertram; *see* Rowcroft, Maj.-Gen. Sir E. B.

Rowcroft, Maj.-Gen. Sir (Eric) Bertram, 1891–1963, vol. VI
Rowcroft, Major Ernest Cave, 1866–1916, vol. II
Rowcroft, Maj.-Gen. George Cleland, 1831–1922, vol. II
Rowden, Aldred William, *died* 1919, vol. II
Rowe, Albert Percival, *died* 1976, vol. VII
Rowe, Rev. Alfred William, *died* 1921, vol. II
Rowe, Charles Henry, 1869–1925, vol. II
Rowe, Charles Henry, *died* 1943, vol. IV
Rowe, Charles William Dell, 1893–1954, vol. V
Rowe, Edward Rowe F.; *see* Fisher-Rowe.
Rowe, Eric George, 1904–1987, vol. VIII
Rowe, Frederick Maurice, 1891–1946, vol. IV
Rowe, Col Herbert Mayow F.; *see* Fisher-Rowe.
Rowe, John Clifford, 1872–1944, vol. IV
Rowe, Ven. John Tetley, *died* 1915, vol. I
Rowe, Louise J.; *see* Jopling, Louise.
Rowe, Sir Michael Edward, 1901–1978, vol. VII
Rowe, Norman Francis, 1908–1990, vol. VIII
Rowe, Rt Rev. Peter Trimble, 1856–1942, vol. IV
Rowe, Sir Reginald P. P., *died* 1945, vol. IV
Rowe, Lt-Col Richard Herbert, 1883–1933, vol. III
Rowe, S. Grant, 1861–1928, vol. II
Rowe, Chief Engr William, *died* 1924, vol. II
Rowe, William Hugh Cecil, *died* 1939, vol. III(A), vol. IV
Rowe-Dutton, Sir Ernest, 1891–1965, vol. VI
Rowell, Sir Andrew Herrick, 1890–1973, vol. VII
Rowell, Sir Herbert Babington, 1860–1921, vol. II
Rowell, Sir (Herbert Babington) Robin, 1894–1981, vol. VIII
Rowell, Col James, 1851–1940, vol. III
Rowell, John Soulsby, 1846–1916, vol. II
Rowell, Hon. Newton Wesley, 1867–1941, vol. IV
Rowell, Percy Fitz-Patrick, 1874–1940, vol. III
Rowell, Sir Reginald Kaye, 1888–1964, vol. VI
Rowell, Sir Robin; *see* Rowell, Sir H. B. R.
Rowell, Lt-Gen. Sir Sydney Fairbairn, 1894–1975, vol. VII
Rowell, Thomas Irvine, 1840–1932, vol. III
Rowett, Geoffrey Charles, 1925–1986, vol. VIII
Rowett, John Quiller, 1876–1924, vol. II
Rowland, Rev. Alfred, 1840–1925, vol. II
Rowland, Christopher John Salter, 1929–1967, vol. VI
Rowland, Deborah Molly, 1913–1986, vol. VIII
Rowland, Ernest Daniel, 1858–1933, vol. III
Rowland, Francis George, 1883–1957, vol. V
Rowland, Frank Mortimer, 1866–1932, vol. III
Rowland, Sir Frederick, 1st Bt, 1874–1959, vol. V
Rowland, Sir John, 1877–1941, vol. IV
Rowland, Sir John Edward Maurice, 1882–1969, vol. VI
Rowland, Sir John Thomas Podger, 1878–1933, vol. III
Rowland, John William, 1852–1925, vol. II
Rowland, Sir Leonard Bromfield, 1862–1939, vol. III
Rowland, Col Michael Carmichael, 1862–1947, vol. IV
Rowland, Col Thomas, 1831–1914, vol. I
Rowland, Sir Wentworth Lowe, 2nd Bt, 1909–1970, vol. VI
Rowland, Sir William, 1858–1945, vol. IV

Rowland-Brown, Lilian Kate; *see* Brown.

Rowlands, Sir Alun; *see* Rowlands, Sir R. A.

Rowlands, Sir Archibald, 1892–1953, vol. V

Rowlands, Rev. David, 1836–1907, vol. I

Rowlands, Ernest Brown B.; *see* Bowen-Rowlands.

Rowlands, Sir Gwilym, 1878–1949, vol. IV

Rowlands, Horace, 1869–1954, vol. V

Rowlands, Gen. Sir Hugh, 1829–1909, vol. I

Rowlands, James, 1851–1920, vol. II

Rowlands, John Wilfred, 1869–1948, vol. IV

Rowlands, Moses John, 1876–1932, vol. III

Rowlands, Sir (Richard) Alun, 1885–1977, vol. VII

Rowlands, Robert Pugh, 1874–1933, vol. III

Rowlands, Rowland, *died* 1935, vol. III

Rowlands, W. S., *died* 1939, vol. III

Rowlands, William Bowen, *died* 1906., vol. I

Rowlandson, Edmund James, 1882–1962, vol. VI

Rowlandson, Sir Graham; *see* Rowlandson, Sir S. G.

Rowlandson, Sir (Stanley) Graham, 1908–1986, vol. VIII

Rowlatt, Charles James, 1894–1959, vol. V

Rowlatt, Sir Frederick Terry, 1865–1950, vol. IV

Rowlatt, Sir John, 1898–1956, vol. V

Rowlatt, Rt Hon. Sir Sidney Arthur Taylor, 1862–1945, vol. IV

Rowledge, A. J., *died* 1957, vol. V

Rowlette, Robert James, 1873–1944, vol. IV

Rowley, Baron (Life Peer); Arthur Henderson, 1893–1968, vol. VI

Rowley, Alec, 1892–1958, vol. V

Rowley, Adm. Charles John, 1832–1919, vol. II

Rowley, Lt-Col Charles Samuel, 6th Bt (*cr* 1786), 1891–1962, vol. VI

Rowley, Brig.-Gen. Frank George Mathias, 1866–1949, vol. IV

Rowley, Rev. Sir George Charles Augustus, 4th Bt (*cr* 1836), 1869–1924, vol. II

Rowley, Sir George Charles Erskine, 3rd Bt (*cr* 1836), 1844–1922, vol. II

Rowley, George Fydell, 1851–1933, vol. III

Rowley, Captain Sir George William, 5th Bt (*cr* 1836), 1896–1953, vol. V

Rowley, Rev. Harold Henry, 1890–1969, vol. VI

Rowley, Hercules Douglas Edward, 1859–1945, vol. IV

Rowley, Hon. Hercules Langford, 1828–1904, vol. I

Rowley, Captain Howard Fiennes Julius, 1868–1948, vol. IV

Rowley, Hon. Hugh, 1833–1908, vol. I

Rowley, Ven. Hugh Edward, *died* 1938, vol. III

Rowley, John Hewitt, 1917–1986, vol. VIII

Rowley, Sir Joshua Thellusson, 5th Bt (*cr* 1786), 1838–1931, vol. III

Rowley, Sir William Joshua, 6th Bt (*cr* 1836), 1891–1971, vol. VII

Rowley, Rev. William Walter, 1812–1907, vol. I

Rowley-Conwy, Rear-Adm. Rafe Grenville; *see* Conwy.

Rowntree, Arnold Stephenson, 1872–1951, vol. V

Rowntree, Arthur, 1861–1949, vol. IV

Rowntree, Benjamin Seebohm, 1871–1954, vol. V

Rowntree, Cecil, *died* 1943, vol. IV

Rowntree, Ernest William, 1877–1936, vol. III

Rowntree, Joseph, 1836–1925, vol. II

Roworth, Edward, 1880–1964, vol. VI

Rowse, Herbert James, *died* 1963, vol. VI

Rowse, William Crapo, 1883–1961, vol. VI

Rowsell, Mary Catharine, vol. II

Rowsell, Philip Foale, 1864–1946, vol. IV

Rowsell, Rev. Walter Frederick, 1837–1924, vol. II

Rowson, Edmund, *died* 1951, vol. V

Rowson, Guy, *died* 1937, vol. III

Rowson, Lionel Edward Aston, 1914–1989, vol. VIII

Rowton, 1st Baron, 1838–1903, vol. I

Roxburgh, Alexander Bruce, *died* 1953, vol. V

Roxburgh, Archibald Cathcart, 1886–1954, vol. V

Roxburgh, Eleanor Mary Ann, (Lady Roxburgh), *died* 1929, vol. III

Roxburgh, Francis, 1850–1935, vol. III

Roxburgh, Air Vice-Marshal Henry Lindsay, 1909–1989, vol. VIII

Roxburgh, Sir James; *see* Roxburgh, Sir T. J. Y.

Roxburgh, Sir John Archibald, 1854–1937, vol. III

Roxburgh, John Fergusson, 1888–1954, vol. V

Roxburgh, Sir Ronald Francis, 1889–1981, vol. VIII

Roxburgh, Sir (Thomas) James (Young), 1892–1974, vol. VII

Roxburgh, Sir Thomas Laurence, 1853–1945, vol. IV

Roxburghe, 8th Duke of, 1876–1932, vol. III

Roxburghe, 9th Duke of, 1913–1974, vol. VII

Roxburghe, Duchess of; (Anne Emily), *died* 1923, vol. II

Roxby, Rev. Edmund Lally, 1844–1912, vol. I

Roxby, Captain Herbert, 1848–1905, vol. I

Roxby, John Henry M.; *see* Maude-Roxby.

Roxby, Percy Maude, 1880–1947, vol. IV

Roy, Sir Asoka Kumar, 1886–1982, vol. VIII

Roy, Sir Bijoy Prosad S.; *see* Singh Roy.

Roy, Camille, 1870–1943, vol. IV

Roy, Catherine Murray, *died* 1976, vol. VII

Roy, Charles T., 1854–1897, vol. I

Roy, Donald Whatley, 1881–1960, vol. V

Roy, Ferdinand, 1873–1948, vol. IV

Roy, Sir Ganen, 1872–1943, vol. IV

Roy, James Alexander, *died* 1973, vol. VII

Roy, Brig.-Gen. John William Gascoigne, 1863–1941, vol. IV

Roy, Lt-Col Joseph Edensor Gascoigne, 1872–1935, vol. III

Roy, His Eminence Cardinal Maurice, 1905–1985, vol. VIII

Roy, Maurice Paul Mary, *born* 1899, vol. VIII

Roy, Most Rev. Paul Eugene, 1859–1926, vol. II

Roy, Comdr Robert Stewart, 1878–1924, vol. II

Roy, Sir Satyendra Nath, 1888–1955, vol. V

Royall, Kenneth Claiborne, 1894–1971, vol. VII

Royce, Sir (Frederick) Henry, 1st Bt, 1863–1933, vol. III

Royce, Sir Henry; *see* Royce, Sir F. H.

Royce, William Stapleton, 1857–1924, vol. II

Royde Smith, Naomi Gwladys, *died* 1964, vol. VI

Royden, 1st Baron, 1871–1950, vol. IV

Royden, (Agnes) Maude, (Mrs G. W. H. Shaw), 1876–1956, vol. V

Royden, Sir Ernest Bland, 3rd Bt, 1873–1960, vol. V

Royden, Sir John Ledward, 4th Bt, 1907–1976, vol. VII

Royden, Maude; *see* Royden, A. M.

Royden, Sir Thomas Bland, 1st Bt, 1831–1917, vol. II
Royds, Vice-Adm. Sir Charles William Rawson, 1876–1931, vol. III
Royds, Col Sir Clement Molyneaux, 1842–1916, vol. II
Royds, Sir Edmund, 1860–1946, vol. IV
Royds, Rev. F. C., 1825–1913, vol. I
Royds, Rev. Gilbert Twemlow, 1845–1933, vol. III
Royds, Adm. Sir Percy Molyneaux Rawson, 1874–1955, vol. V
Royds, William Massy, 1879–1951, vol. V
Roylance, Robert Walker, 1882–1962, vol. VI
Royle, Baron (Life Peer); Charles Royle, 1896–1975, vol. VII
Royle, Arnold, 1837–1919, vol. II
Royle, Rev. Canon Arthur, 1895–1973, vol. VII
Royle, Charles, 1872–1863, vol. VI
Royle, Elizabeth Jean, (Mrs J. A. C. Royle); *see* Harwood, E. J.
Royle, Sir George, 1861–1949, vol. IV
Royle, Adm. Sir Guy Charles Cecil, 1885–1954, vol. V
Royle, Rear-Adm. Henry Lucius Fanshawe, 1849–1906, vol. I
Royle, Joseph Ralph Edward John, 1844–1929, vol. III
Royle, Joseph Kenneth, 1924–1990, vol. VIII
Royle, Sir Lancelot Carrington, 1898–1978, vol. VII
Royle, Col Reginald George, 1887–1938, vol. III
Royle, Thomas Wright, 1882–1969, vol. VI
Royle, Rev. Vernon Peter Fanshawe Archer, 1854–1929, vol. III
Royston, Viscount; Philip Simon Prospero Lindley Rupert Yorke, 1938–1973, vol. VII
Royston, Brig.-Gen. John Robinson, 1860–1942, vol. IV
Royston, Rt Rev. Peter Sorenson, 1830–1915, vol. I
Roze, Marie, 1846–1926, vol. II
Roze, Raymond, 1875–1920, vol. II
Roze-Perkins, J. H. Raymond; *see* Roze, Raymond.
Rubbra, Arthur Alexander, 1903–1982, vol. VIII
Rubbra, Edmund, 1901–1986, vol. VIII
Rube, Charles, 1852–1914, vol. I
Rubens, Paul Alfred, 1875–1917, vol. II
Rubie, Rev. Alfred Edward, 1863–1948, vol. IV
Rubie, Lt-Col Claude Blake, 1888–1939, vol. III
Rubie, John Fonthill, *died* 1907, vol. I
Rubinstein, Arthur, 1887–1982, vol. VIII
Rubinstein, Harold Frederick, 1891–1975, vol. VII
Rubinstein, Helena, (Princess Gourielli), 1871–1965, vol. VI
Rubra, Edward John, 1902–1974, vol. VII
Ruck, Berta, (Mrs Oliver Onions), 1878–1978, vol. VII
Ruck, Maj.-Gen. Sir Richard Matthews, 1851–1935, vol. III
Ruck Keene, Vice-Adm. Philip, 1897–1977, vol. VII
Ruck Keene, Adm. William George Elmhirst, 1867–1935, vol. III
Rücker, Sir Arthur William, 1848–1915, vol. I
Ruckstull, Frederick Wellington, 1853–1942, vol. IV
Rudd, Surg. Rear-Adm. Eric Thomas Sutherland, 1902–1977, vol. VII

Rudd, G(eoffrey) Burkitt (Whitcomb), 1908–1975, vol. VII
Rudd, Col Thomas William, 1869–1943, vol. IV
Ruddell, Ven. Joseph, 1866–1941, vol. IV
Rudderham, Rt Rev. Joseph Edward, 1899–1979, vol. VII
Ruddle, Lt-Col Sir (George) Kenneth (Fordham), 1903–1979, vol. VII
Ruddle, Lt-Col Sir Kenneth; *see* Ruddle, Lt-Col Sir G. K. F.
Ruddock, Ven. David, *died* 1920, vol. II
Ruddock, Richard, 1837–1908, vol. I
Ruddock, Thomas Emerson, 1873–1932, vol. III
Rudgard, Rev. R. W., *died* 1933, vol. III
Rudgard, Ven. Richard Cuthbert, 1901–1985, vol. VIII
Rudge, Florence H.; *see* Haynes-Rudge.
Rudini, Antonio Starrabba, Marquis di, 1839–1908, vol. I
Rudkin, Brig.-Gen. Charles Mark Clement, 1872–1957, vol. V
Rudkin, George Drury, 1879–1929, vol. III
Rudkin, Brig.-Gen. William Charles Eric, 1875–1930, vol. III
Rudler, Frederick William, 1840–1915, vol. I
Rudler, Gustave, 1872–1957, vol. V
Rudmose-Brown, Robert Neal, 1879–1957, vol. V
Rudmose-Brown, Thomas Brown, 1878–1942, vol. IV
Rudolf, Rev. Edward de Montjoie, 1852–1933, vol. III
Rudolf, Robert Dawson, 1865–1941, vol. IV
Rudolf, Robert de Montjoie, 1856–1932, vol. III
Rudolph, Felix; *see* Scatcherd, F. R.
Rueff, Jacques, 1896–1978, vol. VII
Ruegg, Alfred Henry, *died* 1941, vol. IV
Ruegger, Paul J., 1897–1988, vol. VIII
Ruete, Hans Hellmuth, 1914–1987, vol. VIII
Ruff, Howard, *died* 1928, vol. II
Ruffer, Sir Marc Armand, 1859–1917, vol. II
Ruffside, 1st Viscount, 1879–1958, vol. V
Rugby, 1st Baron, 1877–1969, vol. VI
Rugby, 2nd Baron, 1913–1990, vol. VIII
Rugg, Sir (Edward) Percy, 1906–1986, vol. VIII
Rugg, Sir Percy; *see* Rugg, Sir E. P.
Rugge-Price, Sir Charles; *see* Price.
Rugge-Price, Sir Charles Frederick; *see* Price.
Rugge-Price, Lt-Col Sir Charles James Napier; *see* Price.
Ruggeri, Vincenzo G.; *see* Giuffrida-Ruggeri.
Ruggles, Maj.-Gen. John, 1827–1919, vol. II
Ruggles-Brise, Archibald Weyland, 1853–1939, vol. III
Ruggles-Brise, Col Sir Edward Archibald, 1st Bt, 1882–1942, vol. IV
Ruggles-Brise, Sir Evelyn John, 1857–1935, vol. III
Ruggles-Brise, Maj.-Gen. Sir Harold Goodeve, 1864–1927, vol. II
Ruggles Brise, Col Sir Samuel; *see* Brise.
Rugman, Sir Francis Dudley, 1894–1946, vol. IV
Rukidi III, HH Sir George David Kamurasi, 1906–1966, vol. VI
Rule, Frank Gordon, 1882–1965, vol. VI
Rule, Mollie, 1899–1965, vol. VI

Rumball, Air Vice-Marshal Sir Aubrey; *see* Rumball, Air Vice-Marshal Sir C. A.

Rumball, Air Vice-Marshal Sir (Campion) Aubrey, 1904–1975, vol. VII

Rumble, Sir Bertram Thomas, 1875–1949, vol. IV

Rumbold, Sir Anthony; *see* Rumbold, Sir H. A. C.

Rumbold, Captain Charles E. A. L., 1872–1943, vol. IV

Rumbold, Rev. Canon Charles Robert, *died* 1973, vol. VII

Rumbold, Etheldred, (Lady Rumbold), 1879–1964, vol. VI

Rumbold, Rt Hon. Sir Horace, 8th Bt, 1829–1913, vol. I

Rumbold, Sir (Horace) Anthony (Claude), 10th Bt, 1911–1983, vol. VIII

Rumbold, Rt Hon. Sir Horace George Montagu, 9th Bt, 1869–1941, vol. IV

Rumbold, Col William Edwin, 1870–1947, vol. IV

Rumboll, Arthur Charles, 1869–1935, vol. III

Rumford, R. Kennerley, 1870–1957, vol. V

Ruml, Beardsley, 1894–1960, vol. V

Rumney, Abraham Wren, 1863–1942, vol. IV

Rumsey, Almaric, 1825–1899, vol. I

Rumsey, Harry Victor, 1898–1971, vol. VII

Rumsey, Robert Murray, 1849–1922, vol. II

Runciman, 1st Baron, 1847–1937, vol. III

Runciman of Doxford, 1st Viscount, 1870–1949, vol. IV

Runciman of Doxford, 2nd Viscount, 1900–1989, vol. VIII

Runciman of Doxford, Viscountess, (Hilda), 1869–1956, vol. V

Runciman, Philip, *died* 1953, vol. V

Runcorn, Baron (Life Peer); Dennis Forwood Vosper, 1916–1968, vol. VI

Rundall, Lt-Col Charles Frank, 1871–1951, vol. V

Rundall, Sir Francis Brian Anthony, 1908–1987, vol. VIII

Rundall, Gen. Francis Hornblow, 1823–1908, vol. I

Rundall, Col Frank Montagu, 1851–1930, vol. III

Rundall, Matthew Adkins, 1856–1935, vol. III

Rundle, David John, 1938–1987, vol. VIII

Rundle, Col George Richard Tyrrell, 1860–1947, vol. IV

Rundle, Gen. Sir (Henry Macleod) Leslie, 1856–1934, vol. III

Rundle, Gen. Sir Leslie; *see* Rundle, Gen. Sir H. M. L.

Rundle, Rear-Adm. Mark, 1871–1958, vol. V

Runge, Rev. Charles Herman Schmettau, 1889–1970, vol. VI

Runge, Norah Cecil, (Mrs Thomas A. Ross), 1884–1978, vol. VII

Runge, Sir Peter Francis, 1909–1970, vol. VI

Runnett, Henry Brian, 1935–1970, vol. VI

Runtz, Sir John Johnson, 1842–1922, vol. II

Ruoff, Theodore Burton Fox, 1910–1990, vol. VIII

Rupp, Rev. (Ernest) Gordon, 1910–1986, vol. VIII

Rupp, Rev. Gordon; *see* Rupp, Rev. E. G.

Rusby, Lloyd; *see* Rusby, N. L.

Rusby, Norman Lloyd, 1905–1988, vol. VIII

Ruse, Harold Stanley, 1905–1974, vol. VII

Rush, (Edward Antisell) Michael (Stanistreet), 1933–1988, vol. VIII

Rush, Michael; *see* Rush, E. A. M. S.

Rushbrook Williams, Laurence Frederick; *see* Williams.

Rushbrooke, Vice-Adm. Edmund Gerard Noel, 1892–1972, vol. VII

Rushbrooke, Rev. James Henry, 1870–1947, vol. IV

Rushbrooke, William George, 1849–1926, vol. II

Rushbury, Sir Henry George, 1889–1968, vol. VI

Rushcliffe, 1st Baron, 1872–1949, vol. IV

Rushmore, Frederick Margetson, 1869–1933, vol. III

Rusholme, 1st Baron, 1890–1977, vol. VII

Rushout, Sir Charles Hamilton, 4th Bt, 1868–1931, vol. III

Rushton, Sir Arnold, 1870–1930, vol. III

Rushton, Vice-Adm. Edward Astley Astley-, 1879–1935, vol. III

Rushton, Frederick Alan, 1905–1982, vol. VIII

Rushton, George R., *died* 1948, vol. IV

Rushton, Major Harold P., 1895–1968, vol. VI

Rushton, Martin Amsler, 1903–1970, vol. VI

Rushton, Sir Reginald Fielding, *died* 1979, vol. VII

Rushton, William Albert Hugh, 1901–1980, vol. VII

Rushton, William S., 1850–1924, vol. II

Rushworth, Geoffrey Harrington, 1899–1969, vol. VI

Rusk, Robert Robertson, 1879–1972, vol. VII

Ruska, Ernst August Friedrich, 1906–1988, vol. VIII

Ruskin, John, 1819–1900, vol. I

Russ, Sidney, 1879–1963, vol. VI

Russel, James, 1858–1939, vol. III

Russell, 2nd Earl, 1865–1931, vol. III

Russell, 3rd Earl, 1872–1970, vol. VI

Russell, 4th Earl, 1921–1987, vol. VIII

Russell, Countess; (Elizabeth Mary), *died* 1941, vol. IV

Russell, 1st Baron, 1834–1920, vol. II

Russell, Hon. Lord; Albert Russell, 1884–1975, vol. VII

Russell, Baron (Life Peer); Charles Russell, 1832–1900, vol. I

Russell, Baron (Life Peer); Frank Russell, 1867–1946, vol. IV

Russell of Killowen, Baron (Life Peer); Charles Ritchie Russell, 1908–1986, vol. VIII

Russell of Liverpool, 2nd Baron, 1895–1981, vol. VIII

Russell, Alan, 1910–1986, vol. VIII

Russell, Albert; *see* Russell, Hon. Lord.

Russell, Captain Sir Alec Charles, 2nd Bt (*cr* 1916), 1894–1938, vol. III

Russell, Alexander, 1861–1943, vol. IV

Russell, Alexander David, 1864–1934, vol. III

Russell, Col Alexander Fraser, 1856–1938, vol. III

Russell, Hon. Sir (Alexander) Fraser, 1876–1952, vol. V

Russell, Lord Alexander George, 1821–1907, vol. I

Russell, Col Sir Alexander James Hutchison, 1882–1958, vol. V

Russell, Alexander Smith, 1888–1972, vol. VII

Russell, Brig.-Gen. Hon. Alexander Victor Frederick Villiers, 1874–1965, vol. VI

Russell, Sir Alexander West, 1879–1961, vol. VI

Russell, Alfred Ernest, 1870–1944, vol. IV

Russell, Rev. Alfred Francis, *died* 1936, vol. III

Russell, Sir Alison, 1875–1948, vol. IV

Russell, Maj.-Gen. Sir Andrew Hamilton, 1868–1960, vol. V

Russell, Archibald George Blomefield, 1879–1955, vol. V

Russell, Hon. Arthur, 1861–1907, vol. I

Russell, Sir Arthur Edward Ian Montagu, 6th Bt (*cr* 1812), 1878–1964, vol. VI

Russell, Audrey; *see* Russell, M. A.

Russell, Gen. Sir Baker Creed, 1837–1911, vol. I

Russell, Ben Harold, 1891–1979, vol. VII

Russell, Hon. Benjamin, 1849–1935, vol. III

Russell, Hon. Sir Charles, 1st Bt (*cr* 1916), 1863–1928, vol. II

Russell, Charles Alfred, 1855–1926, vol. II

Russell, Charles Barrett, 1823–1911, vol. I

Russell, Rev. Charles Dickinson, *died* 1915, vol. I

Russell, Rev. Charles Frank, 1882–1951, vol. V

Russell, Charles Gilchrist, 1840–1916, vol. II

Russell, Sir (Charles) Lennox (Somerville), 1872–1960, vol. V

Russell, Charles Pearce, 1887–1961, vol. VI

Russell, Charles Scott, 1912–1971, vol. VII

Russell, Charles Taze, (Pastor Russell), 1852–1916, vol. II

Russell, Hon. Claud Eustace H.; *see* Hamilton-Russell.

Russell, Sir Claud Frederick William, 1871–1959, vol. V

Russell, Hon. Cyril, 1866–1920, vol. II

Russell, Sir David, 1872–1956, vol. V

Russell, Dorothy Stuart, 1895–1983, vol. VIII

Russell, Lt-Gen. Sir Dudley, 1896–1978, vol. VII

Russell, Lt-Col Edmund Stuart Eardley Wilmot E.; *see* Eardley-Russell.

Russell, Rev. Edward Francis, 1844–1925, vol. II

Russell, Hon. Edward John, 1879–1925, vol. II

Russell, Sir (Edward) John, 1872–1965, vol. VI

Russell, Sir Edward Lechmere, 1818–1904, vol. I

Russell, Sir (Edward) Lionel, 1903–1983, vol. VIII

Russell, Edward Stuart, 1887–1954, vol. V

Russell, Madame Ella, 1864–1935, vol. III

Russell, Hon. (Francis Albert) Rollo, 1849–1914, vol. I

Russell, Maj.-Gen. Frank Shirley, 1840–1912, vol. I

Russell, Hon. Sir Fraser; *see* Russell, Hon. Sir A. F.

Russell, Hon. Frederick Gustavus H.; *see* Hamilton-Russell.

Russell, Frederick Vernon, 1870–1942, vol. IV

Russell, Sir Frederick Stratten, 1897–1984, vol. VIII

Russell, Sir George, 4th Bt, 1828–1898, vol. I

Russell, Sir George Arthur Charles, 5th Bt (*cr* 1812), 1868–1944, vol. IV

Russell, George Clifford Dowsett, 1901–1970, vol. VI

Russell, Maj.-Gen. George Neville, 1899–1971, vol. VII

Russell, Rev. George Stanley, *died* 1957, vol. V

Russell, George William, 1867–1935, vol. III

Russell, Rt Hon. George William Erskine, 1853–1919, vol. II

Russell, Adm. Gerald Walter, 1850–1928, vol. II

Russell, Sir Gordon; *see* Russell, Sir S. G.

Russell, Hon. Frederick Gustavus H.; *see* Hamilton-Russell.

Russell, Sir Guthrie; *see* Russell, Sir T. G.

Russell, Col Guy Hamilton,1882–1958, vol. V

Russell, Adm. Hon. Sir Guy Herbrand Edward, 1898–1977, vol. VII

Russell, Gyrth, 1892–1970, vol. VI

Russell, Hamer, *died* 1941, vol. IV

Russell, Harold G. Bedford, 1886–1957, vol. V

Russell, Harold John Hastings, 1868–1926, vol. II

Russell, Henry, 1813–1900, vol. I

Russell, Henry Blythe Westrap, 1868–1912, vol. I

Russell, Henry Chamberlain, 1836–1907, vol. I

Russell, Henry Norris, 1877–1957, vol. V

Russell, Henry Stanway, 1910–1985, vol. VIII

Russell, Rear-Adm. Sir (Henshaw) Robert, 1875–1957, vol. V

Russell, Air Vice-Marshal Herbert Bainbrigge, 1895–1963, vol. VI

Russell, Herbert John, 1890–1949, vol. IV

Russell, Sir Herbert William Henry, 1869–1944, vol. IV

Russell, Lt-Col Horatio Douglas, 1874–1931, vol. III

Russell, James, 1839–1923, vol. II

Russell, Sir James Alexander, 1846–1918, vol. II

Russell, James Burn, 1837–1905, vol. I

Russell, Rt Rev. James Curdie, 1830–1925, vol. II

Russell, James George, 1848–1918, vol. II

Russell, Captain James Reginald, 1893–1920, vol. II

Russell, James Samuel Risien, *died* 1939, vol. III

Russell, Sir John; *see* Russell, Sir E. J.

Russell, John Archibald, 1816–1899, vol. I

Russell, Air Vice-Marshal John Bernard, 1916–1978, vol. VII

Russell, Air Cdre John Cannan, 1896–1956, vol. V

Russell, Maj.-Gen. John Cecil, 1839–1909, vol. I

Russell, John Eaton Nevill, 1911–1970, vol. VI

Russell, John Francis Robert V.; *see* Vaughan-Russell.

Russell, Maj.-Gen. John Joshua, 1862–1941, vol. IV

Russell, Rt Rev. John Keith, 1916–1979, vol. VII

Russell, Sir John Weir, 1893–1978, vol. VII

Russell, Sir John Wriothesley, 1914–1984, vol. VIII

Russell, Sir Lennox; *see* Russell, Sir C. L. S.

Russell, Leonard, 1906–1974, vol. VII

Russell, Leonard James, 1884–1971, vol. VII

Russell, Hon. Leopold Oliver, 1907–1989, vol. VIII

Russell, Lilian M., 1875–1949, vol. IV

Russell, Sir Lionel; *see* Russell, Sir E. L.

Russell, Louis Pitman, 1850–1914, vol. I

Russell, Mabel; *see* Philipson, Mrs H.

Russell, Rev. Matthew, 1834–1912, vol. I

Russell, Maj. Gen. Sir Michael William, 1860–1949, vol. IV

Russell, (Muriel) Audrey, 1906–1989, vol. VIII

Russell, Brig. Nelson, 1897–1971, vol. VII

Russell, Hon. Sir Odo William Theophilus Villiers, 1870–1951, vol. V

Russell, Patrick Wimberley D.; *see* Dill-Russell.

Russell, Sir Peter Nicol, *died* 1905, vol. I

Russell, Col Reginald Edmund Maghlin, 1879–1950, vol. IV

Russell, Reginald James Kingston, 1883–1943, vol. IV

Russell, Reginald Pemberton, 1860–1917, vol. II

Russell, Richard Drew, 1903–1981, vol. VIII

Russell, Richard John, 1872–1943, vol. IV
Russell, Col Richard Tyler, 1875–1940, vol. III
Russell, Ritchie; *see* Russell, W. R.
Russell, Robert, 1843–1910, vol. I
Russell, Rear-Adm. Sir Robert; *see* Russell, Rear-Adm. Sir H. R.
Russell, Sir Robert Edwin, 1890–1972, vol. VII
Russell, Robert Tor, 1888–1972, vol. VII
Russell, Hon. Rollo; *see* Russell, Hon. F. A. R.
Russell, Sir Ronald Stanley, 1904–1974, vol. VII
Russell, Rosalind, (Mrs F. Brisson), 1911–1976, vol. VII
Russell, Captain Stuart Hugh Minto, 1909–1943, vol. IV
Russell, Sir (Sydney) Gordon, 1892–1980, vol. VII
Russell, Thomas, 1830–1904, vol. I
Russell, Sir (Thomas) Guthrie, 1887–1963, vol. VI
Russell, Rt Hon. Sir Thomas Wallace, 1st Bt, 1841–1920, vol. II
Russell, Sir Thomas Wentworth, 1879–1954, vol. V
Russell, Col Valentine Cubitt, 1896–1976, vol. VII
Russell, Rev. Vernon William, 1861–1953, vol. V
Russell, Hon. Victor Alexander Frederick Villiers, 1874–1965, vol. VI
Russell, Sir Walter Westley,1867–1949, vol. IV
Russell, Sir William, 3rd Bt (*cr* 1832), 1865–1915, vol. I
Russell, William, 1868–1931, vol. III
Russell, William, 1859–1937, vol. III (A), vol. IV
Russell, William, 1852–1940, vol. III
Russell, William Clark, 1844–1911, vol. I
Russell, Sir William Fleming, *died* 1925, vol. II
Russell, Sir William Howard, 1820–1907, vol. I
Russell, William James, 1830–1910, vol. I
Russell, Col William Kelson, 1873–1949, vol. IV
Russell, (William) Ritchie, 1903–1980, vol. VII
Russell, Captain Sir William Russell, 1838–1913, vol. I
Russell, Captain Wilmot Peregrine Maitland, 1874–1950, vol. IV
Russell-Astley, Bertram Frankland F.; *see* Astley.
Russell-Astley, Henry Jacob Delaval F.; *see* Astley.
Russell-Brown, Col Claude, 1873–1939, vol. III
Russell-Johnson, Lt-Col Walter, 1888–1940, vol. III
Russell-Smith, Dame Enid Mary Russell, 1903–1989, vol. VIII
Russell-Wells, Sir Sydney, 1869–1924, vol. II
Russia, Grand Duke Michael of, 1861–1929, vol. III
Russo, Sir Peter George, *born* 1899, vol. VIII
Russon, Sir Clayton; *see* Russon, Sir W. C.
Russon, Sir (William) Clayton, 1895–1968, vol. VI
Rust, William, 1903–1949, vol. IV
Rust, William Thomas Cutler, 1874–1937, vol. III
Rustomjee, Heerjeebhoy Manackjee, *died* 1904, vol. I
Ruston, Rev. Canon (Cuthbert) Mark, 1916–1990, vol. VIII
Ruston, Lt-Col Joseph Seward, 1869–1939, vol. III
Ruston, Rev. Canon Mark; *see* Ruston, Rev. Canon C. M.
Ruston, Col Reginald Seward, 1867–1963, vol. VI
Ruth, Rev. Thomas E., 1875–1956, vol. V
Ruthen, Sir Charles Tamlin, 1871–1926, vol. II
Rutherfoord, Captain J. B., *born* 1864, vol. II
Rutherford, 1st Baron, 1871–1937, vol. III

Rutherford, Hon. Alexander Cameron, 1857–1941, vol. IV
Rutherford, Col Charles, 1858–1922, vol. II
Rutherford, Very Rev. Claud Anselm, 1886–1952, vol. V
Rutherford, Sir David Carter, 1868–1948, vol. IV
Rutherford, Sir Ernest Victor Buckley, *died* 1929, vol. III
Rutherford, George, 1818–1904, vol. I
Rutherford, Gideon Campbell, 1888–1971, vol. VII
Rutherford, James Rankin, 1882–1967, vol. VI
Rutherford, Sir John, 1st Bt (*cr* 1916), 1854–1932, vol. III
Rutherford, Sir John George, 1886–1967, vol. VI
Rutherford, John Gunion, 1857–1923, vol. II
Rutherford, Sir John Hugo, 2nd Bt (*cr* 1923), 1887–1942, vol. IV
Rutherford, John Rutherford, 1904–1957, vol. V
Rutherford, Dame Margaret, 1892–1972, vol. VII
Rutherford, Mark; *see* White, William Hale.
Rutherford, Sir Robert, 1854–1930, vol. III
Rutherford, Sir Thomas George, 1886–1957, vol. V
Rutherford, Brig.-Gen. Thomas John, 1893–1975, vol. VII
Rutherford, Vickerman Henzell, 1860–1934, vol. III
Rutherford, Sir Watson; *see* Rutherford, Sir William W.
Rutherford, William, 1839–1899, vol. I
Rutherford, Rev. William Gunion, 1853–1907, vol. I
Rutherford, William John, 1868–1930, vol. III
Rutherford, Sir (William) Watson, 1st Bt (*cr* 1923), 1853–1927, vol. II
Rutherfurd, Andrew, 1835–1906, vol. I
Rutherfurd, James Hunter, 1864–1927, vol. II
Rutherfurd, Maj.-Gen. Thomas Walter, 1832–1918, vol. II
Rutherston, Albert Daniel, 1881–1953, vol. V
Ruthnaswamy, Miriadas, 1885–1977, vol. VII (AII)
Ruths, Johannes, 1879–1935, vol. III
Ruthven of Freeland, 9th Lord, 1838–1921, vol. II
Ruthven of Freeland, 10th (wrongly shown as 9th) Lord, 1870–1956, vol. V
Ruthven of Freeland, Lady (11th in line), (The Dowager Viscountess Monckton of Brenchley), 1896–1982, vol. VIII
Ruthven, Col Hon. (Christian) Malise Hore, 1880–1969, vol. VI
Ruthven, Col Hon. Malise Hore-; *see* Ruthven, Col. Hon. C. M. H.
Ruthven-Murray, Alan James; *see* Murray.
Rutkowski, Sir Miecislas de, 1853–1941, vol. IV
Rutland, 7th Duke of, 1818–1906, vol. I
Rutland, 8th Duke of, 1852–1925, vol. II
Rutland, 9th Duke of, 1886–1940, vol. III
Rutland, Duchess of; (Violet), *died* 1937, vol. III
Rutland, Charles, 1858–1943, vol. IV
Rutledge, Hon. Sir Arthur, 1843–1917, vol. II
Rutledge, Sir Guy; *see* Rutledge, Sir. J. G.
Rutledge, Sir (John) Guy, 1872–1930, vol. III
Rutledge, Wiley, 1894–1949, vol. IV
Ruttan, Robert F., 1856–1930, vol. III
Rutter, Frank V. P., 1876–1937, vol. III
Rutter, Sir Frederick William Pascoe, 1859–1949, vol. IV

Rutter, Herbert Hugh, 1905–1975, vol. VII
Rutter, Owen, 1889–1944, vol. IV
Rutter, W(illiam) Arthur, 1890–1980, vol. VII
Ruttledge, David Knox, 1865–1931, vol. III
Ruttledge, Hugh, 1884–1961, vol. VI
Ruttledge, Lt-Col Thomas Geoffrey, 1882–1958, vol. V
Ruvigny and Raineval, 9th Marquis of, 1868–1921, vol. II
Ruvigny and Raineval, 10th Marquis of, 1903–1941, vol. IV
Ruxton, Major U. FitzHerbert, 1873–1954, vol. V
Ryall, Sir Charles, died 1922, vol. II
Ryalls, Hon. Captain Harry Douglas, 1887–1964, vol. VI
Ryan, Alfred Patrick, 1900–1972, vol. VII
Ryan, Sir Andrew, 1876–1949, vol. IV
Ryan, Arthur James, 1900–1990, vol. VIII
Ryan, Sir Charles Lister, 1831–1920, vol. II
Ryan, Brig.-Gen. Charles Montgomerie, 1867–1935, vol. III
Ryan, Maj.-Gen. Sir Charles Snodgrass, 1853–1926, vol. II
Ryan, Cornelius John, 1920–1974, vol. VII
Ryan, Curteis Norwood, 1891–1969, vol. VI
Ryan, Captain Cyril Percy, 1875–1940, vol. III
Ryan, Major Denis George Jocelyn, 1885–1927, vol. II
Ryan, Sir Derek Gerald, 3rd Bt, 1922–1990, vol. VIII
Ryan, Most Rev. Dermot, 1924–1985, vol. VIII
Ryan, Edward Joseph, 1845–1923, vol. II
Ryan, Col Eugene, 1873–1951, vol. V
Ryan, Most Rev. Finbar, 1882–1975, vol. VII
Ryan, Adm. Frank Edward Cavendish, 1865–1945, vol. IV
Ryan, Bt Major George Julian, 1878–1915, vol. I
Ryan, Sir Gerald Ellis, 2nd Bt, 1888–1947, vol. IV
Ryan, Sir Gerald Hemmington, 1st Bt, died 1937, vol. III
Ryan, Hugh, 1873–1931, vol. III
Ryan, Most Rev. Hugh Edward, 1888–1977, vol. VII
Ryan, James, 1892–1970, vol. VI
Ryan, (James) Stewart, 1913–1990, vol. VIII
Ryan, John, 1894–1975, vol. VII
Ryan, Rt Rev. John A., 1869–1945, vol. IV
Ryan, John Francis, 1894–1978, vol. VII
Ryan, Rt Rev. Joseph Francis, 1897–1990, vol. VIII
Ryan, Mary, died 1961, vol. VI
Ryan, Mervyn Frederick, died 1952, vol. V
Ryan, Patrick Francis William, 1873–1939, vol. III
Ryan, Patrick John McNamara, 1919–1978, vol. VII
Ryan, Most Rev. Richard, 1881–1957, vol. V
Ryan, Lt-Col Rupert Sumner, 1884–1952, vol. V
Ryan, Stewart; see Ryan, J. S.
Ryan, Sir Thomas, 1879–1934, vol. III
Ryan, Thomas, born 1911, vol. VIII
Ryan, Thomas Joseph, 1876–1921, vol. II
Ryan, Wing-Comdr William John, 1883–1959, vol. V
Ryan, William Patrick, died 1942, vol. IV

Ryckman, Hon. Edmond Baird, 1866–1934, vol. III
Rycroft, Sir Benjamin William, 1902–1967, vol. VI
Rycroft, Charlotte Susanna, (Mrs W. N. Wenban-Smith), 1941–1990, vol. VIII
Rycroft, Bt Major Julian Neil Oscar, 1892–1928, vol. II
Rycroft, Sir Nelson Edward Oliver, 6th Bt, 1886–1958, vol. V
Rycroft, Sir Richard Nelson, 5th Bt, 1859–1925, vol. II
Rycroft, Maj.-Gen. Sir William Henry, 1861–1925, vol. II
Ryde, John Walter, 1898–1961, vol. VI
Ryde, Walter Cranley, 1856–1938, vol. III
Ryder, Rev. Alexander Roderick, 1852–1919, vol. II
Ryder, Charles Foster, died 1942, vol. IV
Ryder, Col Charles Henry Dudley, 1868–1945, vol. IV
Ryder, Lady Frances, 1888–1965, vol. VI
Ryder, Col Francis John, 1866–1920, vol. II
Ryder, Sir Gerard, 1909–1973, vol. VII
Ryder, Captain Robert Edward Dudley, 1908–1986, vol. VIII
Rydge, Sir Norman Bede, 1900–1980, vol. VII
Rye, Frank Gibbs, 1874–1948, vol. IV
Rye, Reginald Arthur, 1876–1945, vol. IV
Rye, Walter, 1843–1929, vol. III
Ryerson, Maj.-Gen. George Sterling, 1854–1926, vol. II
Rylah, Hon. Sir Arthur Gordon, 1909–1974, vol. VII
Ryland, Sir (Albert) William (Cecil), 1913–1988, vol. VIII
Ryland, Charles Ivor Phipson Smith, 1898–1929, vol. III
Ryland, Sir Charles Mortimer Tollemache S.; see Smith-Ryland.
Ryland, Edward Charles, 1864–1941, vol. IV
Ryland, Frederick, 1854–1902, vol. I
Ryland, Henry, died 1924, vol. II
Ryland, Sir William; see Ryland, Sir A. W. C.
Rylands, Louis Gordon, 1862–1942, vol. IV
Rylands, Sir Peter; see Rylands, Sir W. P.
Rylands, Sir (William) Peter, 1st Bt, 1868–1948, vol. IV
Ryle, Arthur Johnston, 1857–1915, vol. I
Ryle, George Bodley, 1902–1978, vol. VII
Ryle, Gilbert, 1900–1976, vol. VII
Ryle, Herbert, 1881–1966, vol. VI
Ryle, Rt Rev. Herbert Edward, 1856–1925, vol. II
Ryle, John Alfred, 1889–1950, vol. IV
Ryle, Rt Rev. John Charles, 1816–1900, vol.I
Ryle, Sir Martin, 1918–1984, vol. VIII
Ryle, Reginald John, 1854–1922, vol. II
Rylett, Rev. Harold, 1851–1936, vol. III
Ryley, Air Vice-Marshal Douglas William Robert, 1905–1985, vol. VIII
Ryley, Madeleine Lucette, 1868–1934, vol. III
Ryman, Brenda Edith, (Mrs Harry Barkley), 1922–1983, vol. VIII
Rymer, Sir Joseph Sykes, 1841–1923, vol. II

Rymill, Hon. Sir Arthur Campbell, 1907–1989, vol. VIII

Rymill, John Riddoch, 1905–1968, vol. VI

Ryner, Harry, 1872–1964, vol. VI

Ryrie, Maj.-Gen. Hon. Sir Granville de Laune, 1865–1937, vol. III

S

Sabatier, Paul, 1858–1928, vol. II

Sabatier, Paul, 1854–1941, vol. IV (A), vol. V

Sabatini, Rafael, 1875–1950, vol. IV

Sabelli, Humbert Anthony, 1878–1961, vol. VI

Sabin, Arthur Knowles, 1879–1959, vol. V

Sabiti, Most Rev. Erica, 1903–1988, vol. VIII

Sacher, Harry, 1881–1971, vol. VII

Sacher, Michael Moses, 1917–1986, vol. VIII

Sachin, Nawab of, 1886–1930, vol. III

Sachs, Maj.-Gen. Albert, 1904–1976, vol. VII

Sachs, Edwin O., 1870–1919, vol. II

Sachs, Rt Hon. Sir Eric, 1898–1979, vol. VII

Sachs, Nelly Leonie, 1891–1970, vol. VI

Sachse, Sir Frederic Alexander, 1878–1957, vol. V

Sackett, Alfred Barrett, 1895–1977, vol. VII

Sacks, Muriel Elsie, (Mrs Samuel Sacks); *see* Landau, M. E.

Sackville, 2nd Baron, 1827–1908, vol. I

Sackville, 3rd Baron, 1867–1928, vol. II

Sackville, 4th Baron, 1870–1962, vol. VI

Sackville, 5th Baron, 1901–1965, vol. VI

Sackville, Major Lionel Charles Stopford, 1891–1920, vol. II

Sackville, Lady Margaret, *died* 1963, vol. VI

Sackville, Col Nigel Victor S.; *see* Stopford Sackville.

Sackville, Sackville George Stopford, 1840–1926, vol. II

Sackville-West, Hon. V., (Victoria Mary), 1892–1962, vol. VI

Sacre, Rev. Arthur Joseph, 1862–1931, vol.III

Sadasiva Aiyar, Sir Theagaraja Aiyar, *died* 1927, vol. II

Sadat, Mohamed Anwar El; *see* El-Sadat, M. A.

Sadd, Sir Clarence Thomas Albert, 1883–1962, vol. VI

Sadhu, Rai Tarak Nath, 1875–1937, vol. III

Sadleir, Michael, 1888–1957, vol. V

Sadleir-Jackson, Brig.-Gen. Lionel Warren de Vere, 1876–1932, vol. III

Sadler, Adm. Arthur Hayes, 1863–1952, vol. V

Sadler, Arthur Lindsay, 1882–1970, vol. VI

Sadler, Herbert Charles, 1872–1948, vol. IV

Sadler, Lt-Col Sir James Hayes, 1851–1922, vol. II

Sadler, Sir Michael Ernest, 1861–1943, vol. IV

Sadler, Col Sir Samuel Alexander, 1842–1911, vol. I

Sadler, Walter Dendy, 1854–1923, vol. II

Sadlier, Rt Rev. William Charles, 1867–1935, vol. III

Sadul Singh, Col Rao Bahadur, Thakur, Sir, 1881–1937, vol. III

Safford, Sir Archibald, 1892–1961, vol. VI

Safford, Col Arthur Hunt, 1873–1933, vol. III

Safford, Frank, *died* 1929, vol. III

Safonoff, Wassily, 1852–1918, vol. II

Sagrada, Rt Rev. V. Emanuel, 1860–1939, vol. III

Sahni, Birbal, 1891–1949, vol. IV

Sahni, Rai Bahadur Daya Ram, 1879–1939, vol. III

Sailana, Raja of, 1864–1919, vol. II

Sailana, Raja of, 1891–1961, vol. VI

Sainsbury, Rev. Charles, 1837–1915, vol. I

Sainsbury, Air Vice-Marshal Thomas Audley L.; *see* Langford-Sainsbury.

Saint, Charles Frederick Morris, 1886–1973, vol. VII

Saint, Sir John; *see* Saint, Sir S. J.

Saint, Lawrence Bradford, 1885–1961, vol. VI

Saint, Captain Peter Johnson J.; *see* Johnston-Saint.

Saint, Sir (Sidney) John, 1897–1987, vol. VIII

Saint, Stafford Eric, 1904–1988, vol. VIII

Saint, Sir Thomas Wakelin, 1861–1928, vol. II

St Albans, 10th Duke of, 1840–1898, vol. I

St Albans, 11th Duke of, 1870–1934, vol. III

St Albans, 12th Duke of, 1874–1964, vol. VI

St Albans, 13th Duke of, 1915–1988, vol. VIII

St Albans, Duchess of; (Grace), *died* 1926, vol. II

St Aldwyn, 1st Earl, 1837–1916, vol. II

St Aubyn, Alan, *died* 1920, vol. II

St Aubyn, Hon. Edward Stuart, 1858–1915, vol. I

St Aubyn, Geoffrey Peter, *born* 1858, vol. II

St Aubyn, Sir Hugh M.; *see* Molesworth-St Aubyn.

St Aubyn, Sir John M.; *see* Molesworth-St Aubyn.

St Aubyn, Captain Hon. Lionel Michael, 1878–1965, vol. VI

St Aubyn, Rev. Sir St A. Hender M.; *see* Molesworth-St Aubyn.

St Audries, 1st Baron, 1853–1917, vol. II

St Audries, 2nd Baron, 1893–1971, vol. VII

Saint Aulaire, Comte de, 1866–1954, vol. V

Saint Brides, Baron (Life Peer); John Morrice Cairns James, 1916–1989, vol. VIII

Saint-Clair, George; *see* Coudurier de Chassaigne, Joseph.

St Clair, Maj.-Gen. George James Paul, 1885–1955, vol. V

St Clair, Col James Latimer Crawshay, 1850–1940, vol. III

St Clair, Hon. Lockhart Matthew, 1855–1930, vol. III

St Clair, William; *see* Ford, William.

St Clair, Lt-Col William Augustus Edmond, 1854–1923, vol. II

St Clair, William Graeme, 1849–1930, vol. III

St Clair, Adm. William Home Chisholme, 1841–1905, vol. I

St Clair, Major William Lockhart, 1883–1920, vol. II

St Clair-Ford, Maj.-Gen. Sir Peter, 1905–1989, vol. VIII

St Clair-Morford, Maj.-Gen. Albert Clarence, 1893–1945, vol.IV

St Cyres, Viscount; Stafford Harry Northcote, 1869–1926, vol. II

St Davids, 1st Viscount, 1860–1938, vol. III

St Davids, Viscountess; (Elizabeth Frances), 1884–1974, vol. VII

Saint-Denis, Michel Jacques, 1897–1971, vol. VII

St George, 6th Marquis of, *born* 1875, vol. III

St George, Sir Denis Howard, 8th Bt, 1902–1989, vol. VIII

St George, Air Vice-Marshal Douglas Fitzclarence, 1919–1985, vol. VIII
St George, Frederick Ferris Bligh, 1908–1970, vol. VI
Saint-George, Henry, 1866–1917, vol. II
St George, Sir John, 5th Bt, 1851–1938, vol. III
St George, Sir Robert Alan, 7th Bt, 1900–1983, vol. VIII
St George, Sir Theophilus John, 6th Bt, 1856–1943, vol. IV
St Germans, 5th Earl of, 1835–1911, vol. I
St Germans, 6th Earl of, 1890–1922, vol. II
St Germans, 7th Earl of, 1867–1942, vol. IV
St Germans, 8th Earl of, 1870–1960, vol. V
St Germans, 9th Earl of, 1914–1988, vol. VIII
St Helens, 1st Baron, 1912–1980, vol. VII
St Helier, 1st Baron, 1843–1905, vol. I
St Helier, Lady; (Mary), died 1931, vol. III
St John of Bletso, 17th Baron, 1876–1920, vol. II
St John of Bletso, 18th Baron, 1877–1934, vol. III
St John of Bletso, 19th Baron, 1917–1976, vol. VII
St John of Bletso, 20th Baron, 1918–1978, vol. VII
St John, Alfred, 1857–1939, vol. III
St John, Lt-Col Sir Beauchamp; see St John, Lt-Col Sir H. B.
St John, Charles Edward, 1857–1935, vol. III
St John, Col Edmund Farquhar, 1879–1945, vol. IV
St John, Vice-Adm. Francis Gerald, 1869–1947, vol. IV
St John, Sir Frederick Robert, 1831–1923, vol. II
St John, Geoffrey Robert, 1889–1972, vol. VII
St John, Brig.-Gen. George Francis William, 1861–1937, vol. III
St John, Lt-Col Sir (Henry) Beauchamp, 1874–1954, vol. V
St John, Adm. Henry Craven, died 1909, vol. I
St John, Henry Percy, 1854–1921, vol. II
St John, Hon. Joseph Wesley, 1854–1907, vol. I
St John, Mabel; see Cooper, H. St J.
St John, Rev. Maurice William Ferdinand, 1827–1914, vol. I
St John, Lt-Col Oliver Charles Beauchamp, 1907–1976, vol. VII
St John, Maj.-Gen. Richard Stukeley, 1876–1959, vol. V
St John, Hon. Rowland Tudor, 1882–1948, vol. IV
St John, Sir Spenser, 1825–1910, vol. I
St John-Brooks, Ralph Terence, 1884–1963, vol. VI
St John-Mildmay, Sir Anthony; see Mildmay.
St John-Mildmay, Sir Gerald Anthony Shaw-Lefevre; see Mildmay.
St John-Mildmay, Sir Henry Bouverie Paulet; see Mildmay.
St John-Mildmay, Sir Henry Gerald; see Mildmay.
St John-Mildmay, Rev. Sir Neville; see Mildmay.
St John-Mildmay, Major Wyndham Paulet; see Mildmay.
St John Perse; see Léger, Marie-René Alexis Saint-Léger.
St Johnston, Sir Eric; see St Johnston, Sir T. E.
St Johnston, Sir Reginald, 1881–1950, vol. IV
St Johnston, Sir (Thomas) Eric, 1911–1986, vol. VIII
St Just, 1st Baron, 1870–1941, vol. IV
St Just, 2nd Baron, 1922–1984, vol. VIII

St Laurent, Rt Hon. Louis Stephen, 1882–1973, vol. VII
St Lawrence, Julian Charles G.; see Gaisford-St Lawrence.
St Leger, Evelyn, died 1944, vol. IV
St Leger, Col Henry Hungerford, 1833–1925, vol. II
St Leger, Col Stratford Edward, 1878–1935, vol. III
St Leonards, 2nd Baron, 1847–1908, vol. I
St Leonards, 3rd Baron, 1890–1972, vol. VII
St Leonards, 4th Baron, 1950–1985, vol. VIII
St Levan, 1st Baron, 1829–1908, vol. I
St Levan, 2nd Baron, 1857–1940, vol. III
St Levan, 3rd Baron, 1895–1978, vol. VII
St Maur, Lord Ernest, 1847–1922, vol. II
St Maur, Lord Percy, 1847–1907, vol. I
St Oswald, 2nd Baron, 1857–1919, vol. II
St Oswald, 3rd Baron, 1893–1957, vol. V
St Oswald, 4th Baron, 1916–1984, vol. VIII
St Quintin, William Herbert, 1851–1933, vol. III
Saint-Saens, Camille, 1835–1921, vol. II
St Vigeans, Hon. Lord; David Anderson, 1862–1948, vol. IV
St Vincent, 5th Viscount, 1855–1908, vol. I
St Vincent, 6th Viscount, 1859–1940, vol. III
St Vincent Ferreri, 7th Marquis of, 1880–1945, vol. IV
Sainthill, Loudon, 1919–1969, vol. VI
Sainton, Charles Prosper, 1861–1914, vol. I
Saintsbury, George Edward Bateman, 1845–1933, vol. III
Saionji, Prince, died 1940, vol. III
Sait, Edward M'Chesney, 1881–1943, vol. IV
Saiyid, Fazl Ali, Sir, 1886–1959, vol. V
Sakharov, Andrei Dimitrievich, 1921–1989, vol. VIII
Saklatvala, Sir Nowroji, 1875–1938, vol. III
Saklatvala, Shapurji, 1874–1936, vol. III
Saklatvala, Sir Sorabji Dorabji, died 1948, vol. IV (A), vol. V
Sala, Antoni, 1893–1945, vol. IV
Salaman, Charles Kensington, 1814–1901, vol. I
Salaman, Malcolm Charles, 1855–1940, vol. III
Salaman, Redcliffe Nathan, 1874–1955, vol. V
Salandra, Antonio, 1853–1931, vol. III
Salas, Rafael Montinola, 1928–1987, vol. VIII
Salazar, Antonio de Oliveira, 1889–1970, vol. VI
Salberg, Major Frank James, 1884–1964, vol. VI
Sale, Charles Vincent, 1868–1943, vol. IV
Sale, Geoffrey Stead, 1907–1987, vol. VIII
Sale, George S., 1831–1922, vol. II
Sale, John Lewis, 1885–1973, vol. VII
Sale, Col Matthew Townsend, 1841–1913, vol. I
Sale, Richard, 1919–1987, vol. VIII
Sale, Sir Stephen George, 1852–1934, vol. III
Sale, Stephen Leonard, 1889–1958, vol. V
Sale, Ven. Thomas Rawlinson, 1865–1939, vol. III
Sale, Brig. Walter Morley, 1903–1976, vol. VII
Sale-Hill, Gen. Sir Rowley Sale, 1839–1916, vol. II
Saleeby, Caleb Williams, 1878–1940, vol. III
Salis-Schwabe, Maj.-Gen. George, 1843–1907, vol. I
Salisbury, 3rd Marquess of, 1830–1903, vol. I
Salisbury, 4th Marquess of, 1861–1947, vol. IV
Salisbury, 5th Marquess of, 1893–1972, vol. VII
Salisbury, Lt-Col Alfred George Grazier, 1885–1942, vol. IV

Salisbury, Sir Edward James, 1886–1978, vol. VII
Salisbury, Francis, 1850–1922, vol. II
Salisbury, Frank O., 1874–1962, vol. VI
Salisbury-Jones, Maj.-Gen. Sir (Arthur) Guy, 1896–1985, vol. VIII
Salisbury-Jones, Maj.-Gen. Sir Guy; see Salisbury-Jones, Maj.-Gen. Sir A. G.
Salles, Georges Adolphe, 1889–1966, vol. VI
Salmon, Alfred, 1868–1928, vol. II
Salmon, Amedee Victor, 1857–1919, vol. II
Salmon, Balliol, 1868–1953, vol. V
Salmon, Barnett Alfred, 1895–1965, vol. VI
Salmon, Lt-Col Hon. Charles Carty, died 1917, vol. II
Salmon, Cyril, 1924–1981, vol. VIII
Salmon, Air Vice-Marshal Sir Cyril John Roderic; see Salmon, Air Vice-Marshal Sir Roderic.
Salmon, Edward, 1865–1955, vol. V
Salmon, Ven. Edwin Arthur, 1832–1899, vol. I
Salmon, Sir Eric Cecil Heygate, 1896–1946, vol. IV
Salmon, Frederick John, 1882–1964, vol. VI
Salmon, Geoffrey Isidore Hamilton, 1908–1990, vol. VIII
Salmon, Col Geoffrey Nowell, 1871–1954, vol. V
Salmon, Rev. George, 1819–1904, vol. I
Salmon, Rev. Preb. Harold Bryant, 1891–1965, vol. VI
Salmon, Harry, 1881–1950, vol. IV
Salmon, Sir Isidore, 1876–1941, vol. IV
Salmon, John Cuthbert, 1844–1917, vol.II
Salmon, Sir Julian, 1903–1978, vol. VII
Salmon, Neil Lawson, 1921–1989, vol. VIII
Salmon, Admiral of the Fleet Sir Nowell, 1835–1912, vol.I
Salmon, Percy R., 1872–1959, vol. V
Salmon, Air Vice-Marshal Sir Roderic, 1911–1985, vol. VIII
Salmon, Sir Samuel Isidore, 1900–1980, vol. VII
Salmond, Air Chief Marshal Sir Geoffrey; see Salmond, Air Chief Marshal Sir W. G. H.
Salmond, Hubert George, 1889–1946, vol. IV
Salmond, Captain Hubert Mackenzie, 1874–1947, vol. IV
Salmond, Marshal of the Royal Air Force Sir John Maitland, 1881–1968, vol. VI
Salmond, Sir John William, 1862–1924, vol. II
Salmond, Robert Williamson Asher, 1883–1953, vol. V
Salmond, Rev. Stewart Dingwall Fordyce, 1838–1905, vol. I
Salmond, Rev. William, 1835–1917, vol. II
Salmond, Maj.-Gen. Sir William, 1840–1933, vol. III
Salmond, Air Chief Marshal Sir (William) Geoffrey (Hanson), 1878–1933, vol. III
Salmone, H. Anthony, 1860–1904, vol. I
Salomon, Sir Walter Hans, 1906–1987, vol. VIII
Salomons, Sir David Lionel Goldsmid-Stern-, 2nd Bt, 1851–1925, vol. II
Salomons, Hon. Sir Julian Emanuel, 1836–1909, vol.I
Saloway, Sir Reginald Harry, 1905–1959, vol. V
Salt, Dame Barbara, 1904–1975, vol. VII
Salt, Sir David Shirley, 5th Bt (cr 1869), 1930–1978, vol. VII
Salt, Sir Edward William, 1881–1970, vol. VI
Salt, Emmaline Juanita, 1910–1986, vol. VIII

Salt, Rev. Enoch, 1845–1919, vol. II
Salt, Maj.-Gen. Harold Francis, 1879–1971, vol. VII
Salt, Henry Edwin, died 1970, vol. VI
Salt, Henry Stephens, 1851–1939, vol. III
Salt, Sir John William Titus, 4th Bt (cr 1869), 1884–1953, vol. V
Salt, Sir Shirley Harris, 3rd Bt (cr 1869), 1857–1920, vol. II
Salt, Sir Thomas, 1st Bt (cr 1899), 1830–1904, vol. I
Salt, Sir Thomas Anderdon, 2nd Bt (cr 1899), 1863–1940, vol. III
Salt, Lt-Col Sir Thomas Henry, 3rd Bt (cr 1899), 1905–1965, vol. VI
Salter, 1st Baron, 1881–1975, vol. VII
Salter, Alfred, 1873–1945, vol. IV
Salter, Sir Arthur Clavell, 1859–1928, vol. II
Salter, Emma G.; see Gurney-Salter.
Salter, Frank Reyner, 1887–1967, vol. VI
Salter, Rev. Herbert Edward, 1863–1951, vol. V
Salter, Vice-Admiral Jocelyn Stuart Cambridge, 1901–1989, vol. VIII
Salter, Mortyn de Carle Sowerby, 1880–1923, vol. II
Salter Davies, Ernest, 1872–1955, vol. V
Salter Davies, Roy Dicker; see Davies.
Saltmarsh, Sir (Edward) George, 1869–1931, vol. III
Saltmarsh, Sir George; see Saltmarsh, Sir E. G.
Saltmarsh, John, 1848–1916, vol. II
Saltmarshe, Col Philip, 1853–1941, vol. IV
Saltoun, 18th Lord, 1851–1933, vol. III
Saltoun, 19th Lord, 1886–1979, vol. VII
Saltoun, Master of; Hon. Alexander Simon Fraser, 1921–1944, vol. IV
Saltus, Edgar Evertson, 1858–1921, vol. II
Salusbury, Charles Vanne, 1887–1969, vol. VI
Salusbury, Frederic George Hamilton Piozzi, 1895–1957, vol. V
Salusbury-Trelawny, Sir John William; see Trelawny.
Salusbury-Trelawny, Sir John William Robin Maurice; see Trelawny.
Salusbury-Trelawny, Sir William Lewis; see Trelawny.
Salvage, Sir Samuel Agar, 1876–1946, vol. IV
Salvemini, Gaetano, 1873–1957, vol. V
Salvesen, Rt Hon. Lord; Edward Theodore Salvesen, 1857–1942, vol. IV
Salvesen, Edward Theodore; see Rt Hon. Lord Salvesen.
Salvidge, Rt Hon. Sir Archibald Tutton James, 1863–1928, vol. II
Salvin, Gerard Thornton, 1878–1921, vol. II
Salvin, Henry; see Salvin, M. H.
Salvin, (Marmaduke) Henry, 1849–1924, vol. II
Salvin, Osbert, 1835–1898, vol. I
Salvini, Comdr Tommaso, died 1915, vol. I
Salwey, Rev. Herbert, 1842–1929, vol. III
Salwey, Rev. John, 1867–1943, vol. IV
Salzman, Louis Francis, 1878–1971, vol. VII
Samaldas, Sir Lalubhai, 1863–1936, vol. III
Samarth, Narayan Madhav, died 1926, vol. II
Sambell, Most Rev. Geoffrey Tremayne, 1914–1980, vol. VII
Sambon, Louis Westenra, died 1931, vol. III
Samborne-Palmer, Lt-Col Frederick Carey Stuckley, 1868–1950, vol. IV

Sambourne, Edward Linley, 1845–1910, vol. I
Sambrook, Henry Fabian, 1886–1935, vol. III
Samman, Lt-Col Charles Thomas, 1865–1939, vol. III
Samman, Sir Henry, 1st Bt, 1849–1928, vol. II
Samman, Sir Henry, 2nd Bt, 1881–1960, vol. V
Sammarco, Giuseppe Mario, 1873–1930, vol. III
Sammons, Albert E., 1886–1957, vol. V
Sammons, Herbert, 1896–1967, vol. VI
Sammut, Oscar, 1879–1959, vol. V
Sampayo, Sir Thomas Edward de, 1855–1927, vol. II
Sampson, Alexander Whitehead, 1859–1932, vol. III
Sampson, Col Sir Aubrey W.; *see* Wools-Sampson.
Sampson, Charles Henry, 1859–1936, vol. III
Sampson, Rev. Canon Christopher Bolckow, 1903–1967, vol. VI
Sampson, George, 1873–1950, vol. IV
Sampson, Rev. Gerald Victor, 1864–1928, vol. II
Sampson, Hon. Henry William, 1872–1938, vol. III
Sampson, Herbert E., 1871–1962, vol. VI
Sampson, Jack; *see* Sampson, Jacob Albert.
Sampson, Jacob Albert, (Jack Sampson), 1905–1976, vol. VII
Sampson, John, 1859–1925, vol. II
Sampson, Major Patrick, 1881–1922, vol. II
Sampson, Ralph Allen, 1866–1939, vol. III
Sampson, Hon. Victor, 1855–1940, vol. II, vol. III
Sampson, Rear Adm. William Thomas, 1840–1902, vol. I
Sampson-Way, Maj.-Gen. Nowell FitzUpton; *see* Way.
Sams, Sir Hubert Arthur, 1875–1957, vol. V
Samson, Col Arthur Oliver, 1888–1955, vol. V
Samson, Charles Leopold, 1853–1923, vol. II
Samson, Air Cdre Charles Rumney, 1883–1931, vol. III
Samson, Sir (Edward) Marlay, 1869–1949, vol. IV
Samson, Sir Frederick; *see* Samson, Sir W. F.
Samson, John, 1848–1905, vol. I
Samson, Lt-Col Louis Lort Rhys, 1866–1944, vol. IV
Samson, Sir Marlay; *see* Samson, Sir E. M.
Samson, Otto William, 1900–1976, vol. VII
Samson, Sir (William) Frederick, 1892–1974, vol. VII
Samthar, Maharaja of, 1865–1936, vol. III
Samuel, 1st Viscount, 1870–1963, vol. VI
Samuel, 2nd Viscount, 1898–1978, vol. VII
Samuel of Wych Cross, Baron (Life Peer); Harold Samuel, 1912–1987, vol. VIII
Samuel, Alexander L.; *see* Lyle-Samuel.
Samuel, Sir Edward Levien, 2nd Bt (*cr* (1898), 1862–1937, vol. III
Samuel, Sir Edward Louis, 3rd Bt (*cr* 1898), 1896–1961, vol. VI
Samuel, Col Frederick Dudley, 1877–1951, vol. V
Samuel, Harold, 1879–1937, vol. III
Samuel, Rt Hon. Sir Harry Simon, 1853–1934, vol. III
Samuel, Herbert Dawkin, 1904–1984, vol. VIII
Samuel, Howel Walter, 1881–1953, vol. V
Samuel, John Augustus, 1887–1965, vol. VI
Samuel, Sir John Oliver Cecil, 4th Bt (*cr* 1898), 1916–1962, vol. VI
Samuel, Sir John Smith, 1870–1934, vol. III
Samuel, Jonathan, 1853–1917, vol. II

Samuel, Marcus, 1873–1942, vol. IV
Samuel, Rev. Richard W.; *see* Wood-Samuel.
Samuel, Samuel, 1855–1934, vol. III
Samuel, Hon. Sir Saul, 1st Bt (*cr* 1898), 1820–1900, vol. I
Samuel, Sir Stuart Montagu, 1st Bt (*cr* 1912), 1856–1926, vol. II
Samuels, Rt Hon. Arthur Warren, 1852–1925, vol. II
Samuels, Albert Edward, 1900–1982, vol. VIII
Samuels, Sir Alexander, 1905–1986, vol. VIII
Samuels, Herbert David, 1880–1947, vol. IV
Samuels, Moss T.; *see* Turner-Samuels.
Samuelson, Berhard Martin, 1874–1921, vol. II
Samuelson, Rt Hon. Sir Bernhard, 1st Bt, 1820–1905, vol. I
Samuelson, Cecil Llewellyn, 1882–1950, vol. IV
Samuelson, Sir Francis, 3rd Bt, 1861–1946, vol. IV
Samuelson, Sir Francis Henry Bernard, 4th Bt, 1890–1981, vol. VIII
Samuelson, Godfrey Blundell, 1863–1941, vol. IV
Samuelson, Sir Henry Bernhard, 2nd Bt, 1845–1937, vol. III
Samuelson, Sir Herbert, 1865–1952, vol. V
Samut, Lt-Col Achilles, 1859–1935, vol. III
Samwell, Ven. Frederick William, 1861–1925, vol. II
San Giovanni, 12th Baron, 1866–1934, vol. III
San Giuliano, Antonino Paterno Castello, Marquis of, 1852–1914, vol. I
Sanchez-Gavito, Vicente, 1910–1976, vol. VII
Sanctuary, Rev. Charles Lloyd, 1854–1934, vol. III
Sand, Alec, 1901–1945, vol. IV
Sandall, Col Thomas Edward, 1869–1930, vol. III
Sandars, Lt-Col Edward Carew, 1869–1944, vol. IV
Sandars, George Edward Russell, 1901–1985, vol. VIII
Sandars, John Drysdale, 1860–1922, vol. II
Sandars, John Eric William Graves, 1906–1974, vol. VII
Sandars, Rt Hon. John Satterfield, 1853–1934, vol. III
Sandars, Vice-Adm. Sir (Reginald) Thomas, 1904–1975, vol. VII
Sandars, Vice-Adm. Sir Thomas; *see* Sandars, Vice-Adm. Sir R. T.
Sanday, Rev. William, 1843–1920, vol. II
Sandbach, Maj.-Gen. Arthur Edmund, 1859–1928, vol. II
Sandbach, Francis Edward, 1874–1946, vol. IV
Sandbach, John Brown, *died* 1951, vol. V
Sandberg, Christer Peter, 1876–1941, vol. IV
Sandberg, Nils Percy Patrick, 1881–1934, vol. III
Sandbrook, John Arthur, 1876–1942, vol. IV
Sandburg, Carl, 1878–1967, vol. VI
Sandeman, Albert George, 1833–1923, vol. II
Sandeman, Christopher, 1882–1951, vol. V
Sandeman, Condie, 1866–1933, vol. III
Sandeman, Col Donald George, 1884–1965, vol. VI
Sandeman, Edward, 1862–1959, vol. V
Sandeman, Rear-Adm. Henry George Glas, 1868–1928, vol. II
Sandeman, John Glas, 1836–1921, vol. II
Sandeman, Sir Nairne Stewart, 1st Bt, 1876–1940, vol. III
Sanders, Alan, 1878–1969, vol. VI

Sanders, Air Chief Marshal Sir Arthur Penrose Martyn, 1898–1974, vol. VII

Sanders, Rev. Charles Evatt, 1846–1927, vol. II

Sanders, Sir Charles John Ough, 1865–1938, vol. III

Sanders, Sir Edgar Christian, 1871–1942, vol. IV

Sanders, Rev. Ernest Arthur Blackwell, 1858–1917, vol. II

Sanders, Ven. Frederick Arthur, 1856–1930, vol. III

Sanders, Brig. Geoffrey Percival, 1880–1952, vol. V

Sanders, Brig. Gen. George Herbert, 1868–1935, vol. III

Sanders, Brig.-Gen. Gerard Arthur Fletcher, 1869–1941, vol. IV

Sanders, Col Gilbert Edward, 1863–1955, vol. V

Sanders, Sir Harold George, 1898–1985, vol. VIII

Sanders, Henry Arthur, 1868–1956, vol. V (A), vol. VI (AI)

Sanders, Rev. Henry Martyn, 1869–1963, vol. VI

Sanders, Rev. Canon Henry S., 1864–1920, vol. II

Sanders, Sir John Owen, 1892–1954, vol. V

Sanders, Sir Percy Alan, 1881–1962, vol. VI

Sanders, Rev. S. J. W., 1846–1915, vol. I

Sanders, Terence Robert Beaumont, 1901–1985, vol. VIII

Sanders, Thomas W., 1855–1926, vol. II

Sanders, Engr Rear-Adm. William Cory, 1868–1933, vol. III

Sanders, Captain William Stephen, 1871–1941, vol. IV

Sanderson, 1st Baron (cr 1905), 1841–1923, vol. II

Sanderson, 1st Baron (cr 1930), 1868–1939, vol. III

Sanderson of Ayot, 1st Baron, 1894–1971, vol. VII

Sanderson, Air Marshal Sir (Alfred) Clifford, 1898–1976, vol. VII

Sanderson, Lt-Col Aymor Eden, 1886–1932, vol. III

Sanderson, Sir Charles Claxton, 1864–1929, vol. III

Sanderson, Air Marshal Sir Clifford; see Sanderson, Air Marshal Sir A. C.

Sanderson, Rev. Edward, died 1930, vol. III

Sanderson, Rev. Edward Manners, 1847–1932, vol. III

Sanderson, Sir Frank Bernard, 1st Bt, 1880–1965, vol. VI

Sanderson, Frederick William, 1857–1922, vol. II

Sanderson, Harold Arthur, died 1932, vol. III

Sanderson, Sir Harold Leslie, 1890–1966, vol. VI

Sanderson, Col Henry Bristow, 1840–1915, vol. I

Sanderson, Sir John, 1868–1945, vol. IV

Sanderson, John Ellerslie, 1922–1985, vol. VIII

Sanderson, Sir John Scott B.; see Burdon-Sanderson.

Sanderson, Kenneth Francis Villiers, 1895–1973, vol. VII

Sanderson, Rt Hon. Sir Lancelot, 1863–1944, vol. IV

Sanderson, Captain Lancelot, 1889–1984, vol. VIII

Sanderson, Oswald, 1863–1926, vol. II

Sanderson, Sir Percy, 1842–1919, vol. II

Sanderson, Robert, 1881–1943, vol. IV

Sanderson, Rev. Robert Edward, 1828–1913, vol. I

Sanderson, Sibyl, 1865–1903, vol. I

Sanderson, Wilfrid Ernest, 1878–1935, vol. III

Sanderson, Rt Rev. Wilfrid Guy, 1905–1988, vol. VIII

Sanderson, William Allendale, 1913–1961, vol. VI

Sanderson, Col William Denziloe, 1868–1941, vol. IV

Sanderson, William Waite, 1868–1944, vol. IV

Sanderson-Wells, John Sanderson, 1872–1955, vol. V

Sanderson-Wells, Thomas Henry, 1871–1958, vol. V

Sandes, Alfred James Terence F.; see Fleming-Sandes.

Sandes, Lt-Col Edward Warren Caulfeild, 1880–1973, vol. VII

Sandes, Elise, 1851–1934, vol. III

Sandford, 1st Baron, 1887–1959, vol. V

Sandford, Arthur Wellesley, 1858–1939, vol. III

Sandford, Rt Rev. Charles Waldegrave, 1828–1903, vol. I

Sandford, Brig. Daniel Arthur, 1882–1972, vol. VII

Sandford, Ven. Ernest Grey, 1839–1910, vol. I

Sandford, Ven. Folliott George, 1861–1945, vol. IV

Sandford, Sir Folliott Herbert, 1906–1986, vol. VIII

Sandford, Captain Francis Hugh, 1887–1926, vol. II

Sandford, Brig. Francis Rossall, 1898–1962, vol. VI

Sandford, Sir George Ritchie, 1892–1950, vol. IV

Sandford, Hon. Sir (James) Wallace, 1879–1958, vol. V

Sandford, Kenneth Stuart, 1899–1971, vol. VII

Sandford, Thomas Frederick, 1886–1963, vol. VI

Sandford, Hon. Sir Wallace; see Sandford, Hon. Sir J. W.

Sandham, E., died 1944, vol. IV

Sandham, Henry, 1842–1910, vol. I

Sandhurst, 1st Viscount, 1855–1921, vol. II

Sandhurst, 3rd Baron, 1857–1933, vol. III

Sandhurst, 4th Baron, 1892–1964, vol. VI

Sandie, Brig. John Grey, 1897–1975, vol. VII

Sandiford, Charles Thomas, 1840–1919, vol. II

Sandiford, Peter, 1882–1941, vol. IV

Sandilands, George Sommerville, 1889–1961, vol. VI

Sandilands, Brig. Harold Richard, 1876–1961, vol. VI

Sandilands, Brig.-Gen. Henry George, 1864–1930, vol. III

Sandilands, Maj.-Gen. James Walter, 1874–1959, vol. V

Sandison, Sir Alfred, died 1906, vol. I

Sandlands, Paul Ernest, 1878–1962, vol. VI

Sandon, Frank, 1890–1979, vol. VII

Sandover, Sir (Alfred) Eric, 1897–1983, vol. VIII

Sandover, Sir Eric; see Sandover, Sir A. E.

Sandrey, John Gordon, 1903–1988, vol. VIII

Sands, Hon. Lord; Christopher Nicholson Johnston, 1857–1934, vol. III

Sands, Ven. Havilland Hubert Allport, 1896–1970, vol. VI

Sands, Rev. Hubert, 1855–1922, vol. II

Sands, Sir James Patrick, 1859–1925, vol. II

Sands, Percy Cooper, 1883–1971, vol. VII

Sands, Sir Stafford Lofthouse, 1913–1972, vol. VII

Sands, William Southgate, 1853–1924, vol. II

Sandwich, 8th Earl of, 1839–1916, vol. II

Sandwich, 9th Earl of, 1874–1962, vol. VI

Sandwith, Fleming Mant, 1853–1918, vol. II

Sandwith, Major Ralph Leslie, 1859–1920, vol. II

Sandwith, Thomas Backhouse, 1831–1900, vol. I

Sandys, 4th Baron, 1840–1904, vol. I

Sandys, 5th Baron, 1855–1948, vol. IV

Sandys, 6th Baron, 1876–1961, vol. VI

Sandys, Duncan Edwin; see Baron Duncan-Sandys.

Sandys, Hon. Edmund Arthur Marcus, 1860–1914, vol. I

Sandys, Lt-Col Edward Seton, 1872–1953, vol. V

Sandys, Frederick, 1832–1904, vol. I

Sandys, Captain George John, 1875–1937, vol. III

Sandys, George Owen, 1884–1973, vol. VII

Sandys, Sir John Edwin, 1844–1922, vol. II

Sandys, Oliver, *died* 1964, vol. VI

Sandys, Col Thomas Myles, 1837–1911, vol. I

Sandys, Brig.-Gen. William Bain Richardson, 1868–1946, vol. IV

Sandys-Lumsdaine, Edwin Robert John, 1864–1933, vol. III

Saner, Col John Arthur, 1864–1952, vol. V

Sanford, Col Edward Charles Ayshford, 1859–1923, vol. II

Sanford, Lt-Gen. George Edward Langham Somerset, 1840–1901, vol. I

Sangar, Owen Jermy, 1893–1972, vol. VII

Sanger, Sir Ernest, 1875–1939, vol. III

Sanger, Gerald Fountaine, 1898–1981, vol. VIII

Sanger, William, 1873–1948, vol. IV

Sangster, Sir Donald Burns, 1911–1967, vol. VI

Sangster, John Young, 1896–1977, vol. VII

Sangster, Leith, *died* 1962, vol. VI

Sangster, Margaret Elizabeth, 1838–1912, vol. I

Sangster, Maj.-Gen. Patrick Barclay, 1872–1951, vol. V

Sangster, Rev. William Edwin Robert, 1900–1960, vol. V

Sanguinetti, Frederick Shedden, 1847–1906, vol. I

Sanjiva Row, Kodikal, 1890–1951, vol. V

Sankaran Nair, Sir Chettur, 1857–1934, vol. III

Sankey, 1st Viscount, 1866–1948, vol. IV

Sankey, Col Harold Bantock, 1895–1954, vol. V

Sankey, Ira David, 1840–1908, vol. I

Sankey, Captain Matthew Henry Phineas Riall, 1853–1925, vol. II

Sankey, Sir Richard Hieram, 1829–1908, vol. I

Sankey, Col Sir Stuart, 1854–1940, vol. III

Sansar Chandra Sen, Rao Bahadur, 1846–1909, vol. I

Sansbury, Rev. Canon Graham Rogers, 1909–1980, vol. VII

Sansom, Arthur Ernest, 1838–1907, vol. I

Sansom, Col Charles Henry, 1886–1949, vol. IV

Sansom, Charles Lane, 1862–1951, vol. V

Sansom, Lt-Gen. Ernest William, *born* 1890, vol. VIII

Sansom, Sir George Bailey, 1883–1965, vol. VI

Sansom, George Samuel, 1888–1980, vol. VII

Sansom, William, 1912–1976, vol. VII

Sant, Raja of, 1881–1946, vol. IV

Sant, James, 1820–1916, vol. II

Sant, Captain Mowbray Lees, 1863–1943, vol. IV

Sant-Cassia, 7th Count, 1889–1947, vol. IV

Santa Cruz, Marqués de; José Fernandez Villaverde y Roca de Togores, 1902–1988, vol. VIII

Santa Cruz, Victor Rafael Andrés, 1913–1990, vol. VIII

Santayana, George, 1863–1952, vol. V

Santi, Philip Robert William de, *died* 1942, vol. IV

Santley, Sir Charles, 1834–1922, vol. II

Santos-Dumont, Alberto, 1873–1932, vol. III

Sao, Sir Moung, 1847–1926, vol. II

Sao Kin Maung, 1883–1936, vol. III

Sapara-Williams, Hon. Christopher Alexander, 1854–1915, vol. II

Sapellnikoff, Wassily, 1868–1941, vol. IV (A), vol. V

Sapper; *see* McNeile, Lt-Col Cyril.

Sapper, Laurence Joseph, 1922–1989, vol. VIII

Sapru, Rt Hon. Sir Tej Bahadur, *died* 1949, vol. IV

Sapsworth, Captain Charles Howard, 1883–1958, vol. V

Sapte, Ven. John Henry, 1821–1906, vol. I

Sara, Rt Rev. Edmund Willoughby, 1891–1965, vol. VI

Saragat, Giuseppe, 1898–1988, vol. VIII

Sarasate, Pablo Martin Meliton de, 1844–1908, vol. I

Saravanamuttu, Sir Ratnajoti, *died* 1949, vol. IV

Sarawak, Rajah of, 1829–1917, vol. II

Sarawak, Rajah of; *see* Brooke, Sir C. V.

Sarawak, HH Ranee Margaret Alice Lilly of, *died* 1936, vol. III

Sarbah, John Mensah, 1864–1910, vol. I

Sardou, Victorien, 1831–1908, vol. I

Sarel, Rear-Adm. Colin Alfred Molyneux, 1880–1954, vol. V

Sarel, Col George Benedict Molyneux, *died* 1953, vol. V

Sarel, Rev. Sydney Lancaster, *died* 1950, vol. IV

Sarel, William Samuel, 1861–1933, vol. III

Sarell, Philip Charles, 1866–1942, vol. IV

Sargant, Rt Hon. Sir Charles Henry, 1856–1942, vol. IV

Sargant, Ethel, 1863–1918, vol. II

Sargant, Thomas, 1905–1988, vol. VIII

Sargant, Walter Lee, *died* 1956, vol. V

Sargant, William Walters, 1907–1988, vol. VIII

Sargant-Florence, Mary, 1857–1954, vol. V

Sargeant, Sir Alfred Read, 1873–1949, vol. IV

Sargeaunt, Bertram Edward, 1877–1978, vol. VII

Sargeaunt, John, 1857–1922, vol. II

Sargeaunt, Margaret Joan, 1903–1978, vol. VII

Sargent, Rev. Canon Alexander, 1895–1989, vol. VIII

Sargent, Arthur J., 1871–1947, vol. IV

Sargent, Sir Charles, 1821–1900, vol. I

Sargent, Rt Rev. Christopher Birdwood Roussel, 1906–1943, vol. IV

Sargent, Sir Donald; *see* Sargent, Sir S. D.

Sargent, Rt Rev. Douglas Noel, 1907–1979, vol. VII

Sargent, Sir Frank Leyden, 1871–1940, vol. III

Sargent, Sir (Harold) Malcolm (Watts), 1895–1967, vol. VI

Sargent, Maj.-Gen. Harry Neptune, 1866–1946, vol. IV

Sargent, Very Rev. John Paine, 1838–1919, vol. II

Sargent, Sir John Philip, 1888–1972, vol. VII

Sargent, John Singer, 1856–1925, vol. II

Sargent, Sir Malcolm; *see* Sargent, Sir H. M. W.

Sargent, Sir Orme, 1884–1962, vol. VI

Sargent, Sir Percy, 1873–1933, vol. III

Sargent, Sir (Sidney) Donald, 1906–1984, vol. VIII

Sargison, Phillip Harold, 1920–1989, vol. VIII

Sargood, Hon. Lt-Col Sir Frederick Thomas, 1834–1903, vol. I

Sargood, Lilian Mary, 1879–1945, vol. IV

Sargood, Sir Percy Rolfe, 1865–1940, vol. III

Sargood, Richard, 1888–1979, vol. VII

Sarila, Maharaja of, 1898–1983, vol. VIII

Sarjant, Reginald Josiah, *died* 1965, vol. VI

Sarjeant, Frederick Arthur, 1861–1933, vol. III

Sark, Dame of; *see* Hathaway, Dame S. M.

Sarkar, Sir Jadunath, 1870–1958, vol. V

Sarkodee-Adoo, Julius, 1908–1971, vol. VII

Sarl, Arthur J., *died* 1946, vol. IV

Sarle, Sir Allen Lanyon, 1828–1903, vol. I

Sarle, Charles Spenser, *died* 1936, vol. III

Sarma, Rao Bahadur Sir Bayya N.; *see* Narasimha Sarma.

Sarma, Sir (Ramaswami) Srinivasa, 1890–1957, vol. V

Sarma, Sir Srinivasa; *see* Sarma, Sir R. S.

Sarnoff, David, 1891–1971, vol. VII

Sarolea, Charles, 1870–1953, vol. V

Saroyan, William, 1908–1981, vol. VIII

Sarrailh, Jean, 1891–1964, vol. VI

Sarsfield-Hall, Edwin Geoffrey, 1886–1975, vol. VII

Sarson, Col John Edward, 1844–1940, vol. III

Sarto, Giuseppe; *see* Pius X.

Sartoris, Alfred Urbain, 1826–1909, vol. I

Sartoris, Francis Charles, 1857–1923, vol. II

Sartorius, Maj.-Gen. Euston Henry, 1844–1925, vol. I

Sartorius, Col George, 1840–1912, vol. I

Sartorius, Maj.-Gen. Reginald William, 1841–1907, vol. I

Sartre, Jean-Paul, 1905–1980, vol. VII

Sarup, Anand, HH Sahabji Maharaj Sir, 1881–1937, vol. III

Sarvadhikary, Sir Deva Prasad, 1862–1935, vol. III

Sarzano, 11th Marquis of, 1847–1920, vol. II

Sasse, Captain Cecil Duncan, 1891–1934, vol. III

Sassoon, Arthur Abraham David, 1840–1912, vol. I

Sassoon, Sir Edward Albert, 2nd Bt (*cr* 1890), 1856–1912, vol. I

Sassoon, Sir Edward Elias, 2nd Bt (*cr* 1909), 1853–1924, vol. II

Sassoon, Sir (Ellice) Victor, 3rd Bt (*cr* 1909), 1881–1961, vol. VI

Sassoon, Eugenie Louise Judith, 1854–1943, vol. IV

Sassoon, Sir Jacob Elias, 1st Bt (*cr* 1909), 1844–1916, vol. II

Sassoon, Joseph S., 1855–1918, vol. II

Sassoon, Meyer Elias, 1855–1924, vol. II

Sassoon, Rt Hon. Sir Philip Albert Gustave David, 3rd Bt (*cr* 1890), 1888–1939, vol. III

Sassoon, Siegfried, 1886–1967, vol. VI

Sassoon, Sir Victor; *see* Sassoon, Sir E. V.

Sastri, Sir Calamur Viravalli Kumaraswami, 1870–1934, vol. III

Sastri, Rt Hon. Valangiman Sankaranarayana Srinivasa, 1869–1946, vol. IV

Sato, Eisaku, 1901–1975, vol. VII (AII)

Satow, Rt Hon. Sir Ernest Mason, 1843–1929, vol. III

Satow, Sir Harold Eustace, 1876–1969, vol. VI

Satow, Hugh Ralph, 1877–1967, vol. VI

Satow, Captain Lawrence de W., 1865–1948, vol. IV

Satow, Samuel Augustus Mason, 1847–1925, vol. II

Satterlee, Rt Rev. Henry Yates, 1843–1908, vol. I

Satterly, Air Vice-Marshal Harold Vivian, 1907–1982, vol. VIII

Satterly, John, 1879–1963, vol. VI

Satterthwaite, Rev. Charles James, 1834–1910, vol. I

Satterthwaite, Lt-Col Clement Richard, 1884–1953, vol. V

Satterthwaite, Col Edward, 1857–1932, vol. III

Sauber, Robert, 1868–1936, vol. III

Saudi Arabia, HM King of, 1905–1975, vol. VII

Sauer, Hon. J. W., *died* 1913, vol. I

Sauerwein, Jules Auguste, 1880–1967, vol. VI

Saugman, Christian Ditlev Trappaud, 1895–1976, vol. VII

Saul, Bazil Sylvester W.; *see* Wingate-Saul.

Saul, Sir Ernest Wingate W.; *see* Wingate-Saul.

Saul, Air Vice-Marshal Richard Ernest, *died* 1965, vol. VI

Saulles, G. W. de, *died* 1903, vol. I

Saumarez, Lt-Col Richard James, 1864–1943, vol. IV

Saundby, Robert, 1849–1918, vol. II

Saundby, Air Marshal Sir Robert Henry Magnus Spencer, 1896–1971, vol. VII

Saunders, Col Alan, 1886–1964, vol. VI

Saunders, Sir Alan Arthur, *died* 1957, vol. V

Saunders, Sir Alexander Morris C.; *see* Carr-Saunders.

Saunders, Arthur Leslie, 1862–1935, vol. III

Saunders, Benjamin James, 1856–1938, vol. III

Saunders, Lt-Col Cecil Howie, 1881–1954, vol V

Saunders, Sir Charles Edward, 1867–1937, vol. III

Saunders, Sir Charles James Renault, 1857–1931, vol. III

Saunders, Rt Rev. Charles John Godfrey, 1888–1973, vol. VII

Saunders, Lt-Col Cyril, 1875–1935, vol. III

Saunders, Edward, 1848–1910, vol. I

Saunders, Captain Edward Aldbrough, 1873–1934, vol. III

Saunders, Edward Arthur, 1866–1947, vol. IV

Saunders, Sir Edwin, 1814–1901, vol. I

Saunders, Major Frederick John, 1876–1916, vol. II

Saunders, Sir Frederick Richard, 1838–1910, vol. I

Saunders, George, 1823–1913, vol. I

Saunders, George, 1859–1922, vol. II

Saunders, Major George Frederick Cullen, 1869–1934, vol. III

Saunders, Sir George Rice P.; *see* Pryse-Saunders.

Saunders, Captain Harold Cecil Rich, 1882–1919, vol. II

Saunders, Sir Harold Leonard, 1885–1965, vol. VI

Saunders, Ven. Harry Patrick, 1913–1967, vol. VI

Saunders, Henry George Boulton, 1914–1984, vol. VIII

Saunders, Hilary Aidan St George, 1898–1951, vol. V

Saunders, Howard, 1835–1907, vol. I

Saunders, Air Chief Marshal Sir Hugh William Lumsden, 1894–1987, vol. VIII

Saunders, John O'Brien, *died* 1903, vol. I

Saunders, John Tennant, 1888–1965, vol. VI

Saunders, Maj.-Gen. Macan, 1884–1956, vol. V

Saunders, Margaret B.; *see* Baillie-Saunders.

Saunders, Margaret Marshall, 1861–1947, vol. IV

Saunders, Reginald George Francis, 1882–1947, vol. IV

Saunders, Col Robert Joseph Pratt, 1841–1908, vol. I

Saunders, Samuel Edgar, 1857–1933, vol. III

Saunders, Thomas Bailey, 1860–1928, vol. II
Saunders, Rev. Thomas Bekenn Avening, 1870–1950, vol. IV
Saunders, William, 1836–1914, vol. I
Saunders-Davies, Rt Rev. David Henry, 1894–1975, vol. VII
Saunders-Jacobs, Brig. John Conrad, 1900–1986, vol. VIII
Saunders-Pryse, Sir Pryse Loveden, 5th Bt, 1896–1962, vol. VI
Saunderson, Col Rt Hon. Edward James, 1837–1906, vol. I
Saurat, Denis, 1890–1958, vol. V
Sausmarez, Sir Havilland Walter de, 1st Bt, 1861–1941, vol. IV
Sauter, George, 1866–1937, vol. III
Sauve, Hon. Arthur, 1875–1944, vol. IV
Sauveur, Albert, 1863–1939, vol. III
Sauzier, Anatole, 1849–1920, vol. II, vol. III
Savage, Sir Alfred William Lungley, 1903–1980, vol. VII
Savage, Anthony, 1920–1989, vol. VIII
Savage, Col Arthur Johnson, 1874–1933, vol. III
Savage, Sir (Edward) Graham, 1886–1981, vol. VIII
Savage, Rev. Edwin Sidney, 1862–1947, vol. IV
Savage, Ernest A., 1877–1966, vol. VI
Savage, Rev. Canon Ernest Bickersteth, 1849–1915, vol. I
Savage, Rev. Francis Forbes, died 1932, vol. III
Savage, Sir Geoffrey Herbert, 1893–1953, vol. V
Savage, Sir George Henry, 1842–1921, vol. II
Savage, Col George Robert Rollo, 1849–1930, vol. III
Savage, Rt Rev. Gordon David, 1915–1990, vol. VIII
Savage, Sir Graham; see Savage, Sir E. G.
Savage, Henry, 1854–1912, vol. I
Savage, Very Rev. Henry Edwin, died 1939, vol. III
Savage, John Percival, 1895–1970, vol. VI
Savage, Rt Hon. Michael Joseph, 1872–1940, vol. III
Savage, Lt-Col Morris Boscawen, 1879–1958, vol. V
Savage, Raymond, died 1964, vol. VI
Savage, Rt Rev. Thomas Joseph, 1900–1966, vol. VI
Savage, Sir William George, 1872–1961, vol. VI
Savage, Col William Henry, 1863–1951, vol. V
Savage-Armstrong, Major Francis Savage Nesbitt, 1880–1917, vol. II
Savage-Armstrong, George Francis, 1845–1906, vol. I
Savary, Alfred William, 1831–1918, vol. II
Savary, Ven. T. W., 1878–1948, vol. IV
Savatard, Louis Charles Arthur, 1874–1962, vol. VI
Savery, Frank, 1883–1965, vol. VI
Savery, Sir S. Servington, died 1938, vol. III
Savi, Ethel Winifred, died 1954, vol. V
Savige, Lt-Gen. Sir Stanley George, 1890–1954, vol. V
Savile, 2nd Baron, 1853–1931, vol. III
Savile, Lady Anne; see Loewenstein-Wertheim, HSH Princess.
Savile, Brig. Clare Ruxton Uvedale, 1881–1949, vol. IV
Savile, Rev. E. S. Gordon, 1866–1937, vol. III
Savile, Hon. George, 1871–1937, vol. III
Savile, Bt Col George Walter Wrey, 1860–1936, vol. III

Savile, Col Henry Bourchier Osborne, 1819–1917, vol. II
Savile, Sir Leopold Halliday, 1870–1953, vol. V
Savile, Robert Stewart, 1863–1945, vol. IV
Savile, Lt-Col Robert Vesey, 1873–1947, vol. IV
Savile, Brig.-Gen. Walter Clare, 1857–1928, vol. II
Savill, Agnes F., 1875–1964, vol. VI
Savill, Lt-Col Alfred Cecil, 1897–1943, vol. IV
Savill, Sir Edwin, 1868–1947, vol. IV
Savill, Sir Eric Humphrey, 1895–1980, vol. VII
Savill, Ven. Leonard, 1869–1959, vol. V
Savill, Lt-Col Sydney Rowland, 1891–1967, vol. VI
Savill, Thomas Dixon, 1856–1910, vol. I
Saville, (Leonard) Malcolm, 1901–1982, vol. VIII
Saville, Malcolm; see Saville, L. M.
Savin, Lewis Herbert, 1901–1983, vol. VIII
Savorgnan, Count de; see Brazza, P. P. F. C. de.
Savory, Rev. Sir Borradaile, 2nd Bt, 1855–1906, vol. I
Savory, Sir Douglas Lloyd, 1878–1969, vol. VI
Savory, Rev. Edmund, died 1912, vol. I
Savory, Vice-Adm. Herbert Whitmore, 1857–1918, vol. II
Savory, Sir Joseph, 1st Bt, 1843–1921, vol. II
Savory, Major Kenneth Stevens, 1894–1939, vol. III
Savory, Lt-Gen. Sir Reginald Arthur, 1894–1980, vol. VII
Savory, Sir Reginald Charles Frank, 1908–1989, vol. VIII
Savory, Sir William Borradaile, 3rd Bt, 1882–1961, vol. VI
Saw, Hon. Athelstan John Henton, 1868–1929, vol. III
Saw, Ruth Lydia, 1901–1986, vol. VIII
Sawantwadi, Raja of, 1897–1937, vol. III
Saward, Maj.-Gen. Michael Henry, 1840–1928, vol. II
Saward, Sidney Carman, 1889–1967, vol. VI
Sawbridge, Henry Raywood, 1907–1990, vol. VIII
Sawbridge, Rear-Adm. Henry Richard, 1885–1956, vol. V
Sawbridge, Rev. John Sikes, died 1925, vol. II
Sawers, Maj.-Gen. James Maxwell, 1920–1988, vol. VIII
Sawers, Maj.-Gen. Max; see Sawers, Maj.-Gen. J. M.
Sawicki, Roman Mieczyslaw, 1930–1990, vol. VIII
Sawistowski, Henryk, 1925–1984, vol. VIII
Sawkins, Harold, 1888–1957, vol. V
Sawle, Sir Charles Brune Graves, 2nd Bt, 1816–1903, vol. I
Sawle, Sir Charles John Graves-, 4th Bt, 1851–1932, vol. III
Sawle, Col Sir Francis Aylmer Graves, 3rd Bt, 1849–1903, vol. I
Sawrey-Cookson, Sydney Spencer, 1876–1933, vol. III
Sawyer, Charles, 1887–1979, vol. VII
Sawyer, Col Charles Edward, 1848–1931, vol. III
Sawyer, Ethel V.; see Vaughan-Sawyer.
Sawyer, George Alexander, died 1944, vol. IV
Sawyer, Rev. Harold Athelstane Parry, 1865–1939, vol. III
Sawyer, Maj.-Gen. Henry Thomas, 1871–1955, vol. V
Sawyer, Sir James, 1844–1919, vol. II
Sawyer, James Edward Hill, 1874–1953, vol. V

Sawyer, Maj.-Gen. Richard Henry Stewart, 1857–1926, vol. II
Sawyer, Robert Henry, 1832–1905, vol. I
Sawyer, Sir William Phillips, 1844–1908, vol. I
Sawyerr, Rev. Canon Harry Alphonso Ebun, 1909–1986, vol. VIII
Saxby, Jessie Margaret Edmondston, 1842–1940, vol. III (A), vol. IV
Saxe-Weimar, HH Prince (William Augustus) Edward of, 1823–1902, vol. I
Saxl, Fritz, 1890–1948, vol. IV
Saxon Snell, Alfred Walter, 1860–1949, vol. IV
Saxton, John Arthur, 1914–1980, vol. VII
Saxton, Rev. William Isaac, 1891–1975, vol. VII
Sayce, Rev. Archibald Henry, 1845–1933, vol. III
Sayce, Col George Edward, 1857–1940, vol. III
Sayce, George Ethelbert, 1875–1953, vol. V
Saye and Sele, 17th (styled 14th) Baron, 1830–1907, vol. I
Saye and Sele, 18th Baron, 1858–1937, vol. III
Saye and Sele, 19th Baron, 1884–1949, vol. IV
Saye and Sele, 20th Baron, 1885–1968, vol. VI
Saye, Air Vice-Marshal Geoffrey Ivon Laurence, 1907–1959, vol. V
Sayer, Brig. Arthur Penrice, 1885–1962, vol. VI
Sayer, Ettie, died 1923, vol. II
Sayer, Vice-Adm. Sir Guy Bourchier, 1903–1985, vol. VIII
Sayer, Captain Humphrey, 1889–1943, vol. IV
Sayer, Captain M. B., died 1928, vol. II
Sayers, Dorothy Leigh, 1893–1957, vol. V
Sayers, Sir Edward George, 1902–1985, vol. VIII
Sayers, Sir Frederick, 1885–1977, vol. VII
Sayers, John Edward, 1911–1969, vol. VI
Sayers, Dame Lucile Newell, died 1959, vol. V
Sayers, Richard Sidney, 1908–1989, vol. VIII
Sayers, William Charles Berwick, 1881–1960, vol. V
Sayle, Robert, 1889–1971, vol. VII
Saywell, Rev. Preb. George Frederick, 1882–1956, vol. V
Sbarretti, His Eminence Cardinal Donatus, 1856–1939, vol. III
Scaddan, Hon. John, 1876–1934, vol. III
Scadding, Rt Rev. Charles, 1861–1914, vol. I
Scafe, Gen. Charles, 1844–1918, vol. II
Scafe, Lt-Col William Ernest, 1878–1951, vol. V
Scales, Francis Shillington, died 1927, vol. II
Scallan, Eugene Kevin, 1893–1966, vol. VI
Scallon, Gen. Sir Robert Irvin, 1857–1939, vol. III
Scammell, Lt-Col Alfred George, 1878–1941, vol. IV
Scamp, Sir (Athelstan) Jack, 1913–1977, vol. VII
Scamp, Sir Jack; see Scamp, Sir A. J.
Scanlan, Most Rev. Mgr James Donald, 1899–1976, vol. VII
Scanlan, Thomas, died 1930, vol. III
Scanlen, Hon. Sir Thomas Charles, 1834–1912, vol. I
Scannell, Rev. Thomas Bartholomew, 1854–1917, vol. II
Scaramanga-Ralli, Constantine, 1854–1934, vol. III
Scarborough, Harold, 1909–1988, vol. VIII
Scarbrough, 10th Earl of, 1857–1945, vol. IV
Scarbrough, 11th Earl of, 1896–1969, vol. VI
Scarbrough, John Impey, 1846–1929, vol. III
Scarfe, Francis Harold, 1911–1986, vol. VIII

Scarff, Robert Wilfred, 1899–1970, vol. VI
Scarfoglio, Carlo, 1887–1969, vol. VI
Scarisbrick, Sir Charles, 1839–1923, vol. II
Scarisbrick, Sir Everard Talbot, 2nd Bt, 1896–1955, vol. V
Scarisbrick, Sir Tom Talbot Leyland, 1st Bt, 1874–1933, vol. III
Scarles, Sir Edward John, 1871–1947, vol. IV
Scarlett, Air Vice-Marshal Francis Rowland, 1875–1934, vol. III
Scarlett, Maj.-Gen. Hon. Gerald, 1885–1957, vol. V
Scarlett, Lt-Col Henry A.; see Ashley-Scarlett.
Scarlett, Lt-Col James Alexander, 1877–1925, vol. II
Scarlett, Sir Peter William Shelley Yorke, 1905–1987, vol. VIII
Scarr, John Geoffrey Fearnley, 1910–1982, vol. VIII
Scarsdale, 2nd Viscount, 1898–1977, vol. VII
Scarsdale, 4th Baron, 1831–1916, vol. II
Scarth, Sir Charles, 1846–1921, vol. II
Scarth of Breckness, Col Henry William, 1899–1972, vol. VII
Scarth, Rev. John, 1826–1909, vol. I
Scarth, Lt-Col Robert, 1894–1966, vol. VI
Scatcherd, Felicia Rudolphina, died 1927, vol. II
Sceales, Col George Adinston M'Laren, 1878–1956, vol. V
Scebarras, Sir Fillipo, died 1928, vol. II
Scerri, Arthur J., 1921–1980, vol. VII
Schacht, Hjalmar Horace Greely, 1877–1970, vol. VI
Schacht, Joseph, 1902–1969, vol. VI
Schaeffer, Claude Frederic Armand, 1898–1982, vol. VIII
Schafer, Sir Edward Albert S.; see Sharpey-Schafer.
Schafer, Edward Peter S.; see Sharpey-Schafer.
Schalch, Col Vernon Ansdell, 1849–1935, vol. III
Schapiro, Leonard Bertram, 1908–1983, vol. VIII
Schärf, Adolf, 1890–1965, vol. VI
Scharff, Robert Francis, 1858–1934, vol. III
Scharlieb, Dame Mary Ann Dacomb, 1845–1930, vol. III
Scharrer, Irene, died 1971, vol. VII
Schaw, Maj.-Gen. Henry, 1829–1902, vol. I
Schechter, Solomon, died 1915, vol. I
Schelfhaut, Mgr Philip, 1850–1921, vol. II
Schelling, Ernest, died 1939, vol. III
Scherger, Air Chief Marshal Sir Frederick Rudolph Williams, 1904–1984, vol. VIII
Schermbrucker, Lt-Col Hon. Frederic, died 1904, vol. I
Schiaparelli, Mme Elsa, died 1975, vol. VII
Schick, Béla, 1877–1967, vol. VI
Schierwater, Harry Turner, 1876–1952, vol. V
Schiff, Sir Ernest Frederick, 1840–1918, vol. II
Schild, Heinz Otto, 1906–1984, vol. VIII
Schiller, Ferdinand Canning Scott, 1864–1937, vol. III
Schiller, Ferdinand Philip Maximilian, 1868–1946, vol. IV
Schilsky, Eric, 1898–1974, vol. VII
Schindler, Gen. Sir A. Houtum, died 1916, vol. II
Schipa, Tito, 1890–1965, vol. VI
Schlapp, Otto, 1859–1939, vol. III
Schlapp, Walter, 1898–1966, vol. VI
Schlesinger, Arthur Meier, 1888–1965, vol. VI

Schlesinger, Bernard Edward, 1896–1984, vol. VIII
Schlesinger, Frank, 1871–1943, vol. IV
Schleswig-Holstein, HH Major Prince Christian Victor of, 1867–1900, vol. I
Schleswig-Holstein, HRH Gen. Prince Frederick Christian Charles Augustus of, 1831–1917, vol. II
Schletter, Col Percy, 1855–1922, vol. II
Schley, Rear-Adm. Winfield Scott, 1839–1911, vol. I
Schlich, Sir William, 1840–1925, vol. II
Schlink, Sir Herbert Henry, 1883–1962, vol. VI
Schloesser, C. W. Adolph, 1830–1913, vol. I
Schmidt, Carl Friedrich, 1875–1948, vol. IV
Schmidt, Nathaniel, 1862–1939, vol. III (A), vol. IV
Schmidt-Isserstedt, Hans, 1900–1973, vol. VI
Schmiedel, Paul Wilhelm, 1851–1935, vol. III
Schmitt, Marchese Albert Félix; see Della Torre Alta.
Schmitt, Bernadotte Everly, 1886–1969, vol. VI
Schmitthoff, Clive Macmillan, 1903–1990, vol. VIII
Schmoller, Hans Peter, 1916–1985, vol. VIII
Schnabel, Artur, 1882–1951, vol. V
Schnadhorst, Francis, 1840–1900, vol. I
Schneider, Charles Eugene, 1868–1942, vol. IV
Schneider, Sir Gualterus Stewart, 1864–1938, vol. III
Schneider, Sir John William, 1824–1903, vol. I
Schober, Johannes, 1874–1932, vol. III
Schoenberg, Arnold; see Schönberg, A.
Schofield, Alfred Norman, 1903–1973, vol. VII
Schofield, Alfred Taylor, 1846–1929, vol. III
Schofield, Vice-Adm. Brian Betham, 1895–1984, vol. VIII
Schofield, Rt Rev. Charles de Veber, 1871–1936, vol. III
. Schofield, (Edward) Guy, 1902–1990, vol. VIII
Schofield, Lt-Col Frederick William, 1856–1949, vol. IV
Schofield, Guy; see Schofield, E. G.
Schofield, Lt-Col Harry Norton, 1865–1931, vol. III
Schofield, Herbert, 1883–1963, vol. VI
. Schofield, Ivor Frederick Wentworth, 1904–1979, vol. VII
Schofield, J. W., died 1944, vol. IV
Schofield, W. Elmer, 1867–1944, vol. IV
Schofield, Wentworth, 1891–1957, vol. V
Scholder, Charles Albert, 1861–1918, vol. II
Scholderer, (Julius) Victor, 1880–1971, vol. VII
Scholderer, Victor; see Scholderer, J. V.
Scholefield, Arthur, 1853–1930, vol. III
Scholefield, Guy Hardy, 1877–1963, vol. VI
Scholefield, Sir Joshua, died 1950, vol. IV
Scholes, Frank Victor Gordon, 1885–1954, vol. V
Scholes, G. E., died 1968, vol. VI
Scholes, Joseph, 1889–1983, vol. VIII
Scholes, Percy Alfred, 1877–1958, vol. V
Scholey, Harry, 1872–1945, vol. IV
Scholfield, Alwyn Faber, 1884–1969, vol. VI
Scholfield, Brig.-Gen. George Peabody, 1868–1952, vol. V
Scholte, Lieut-Col Frederick Lewellen, 1890–1984, vol. VIII
Schomberg, Rev. Edward St George, 1882–1952, vol. V
Schomberg, Gen. Sir George Augustus, 1821–1907, vol. I

Schomberg, Brig. Harold St George, 1886–1954, vol. V
Schomberg, Lt-Gen. Herbert St George, 1845–1915, vol. I
Schomberg, Col Reginald Charles Francis, died 1958, vol. V
Schönberg, Arnold, 1874–1951, vol. V
Schonell, Sir Fred Joyce, 1900–1969, vol. VI
Schöner, Josef A., 1904–1978, vol. VII
Schonland, Sir Basil Ferdinand Jamieson, 1896–1972, vol. VII
Schonland, Selmar, 1860–1940, vol. III
Schooles, Sir Henry Pipon, died 1913, vol. I
Schooling, Frederick, 1851–1936, vol. III
Schooling, John Holt, 1859–1927, vol. II
Schooling, Sir William, 1860–1936, vol. III
Schorr, Friedrich, 1888–1953, vol. V
Schorstein, Gustave, died 1906, vol. I
Schott, George Adolphus, 1868–1937, vol. III
Schotz, Benno, 1891–1984, vol. VIII
Schram, Emil, 1893–1987, vol. VIII
Schreiber, Col Acton Lemuel, 1865–1951, vol. V
Schreiber, Maj.-Gen. Brymer Francis, 1835–1907, vol. I
Schreiber, Sir Collingwood, 1831–1918, vol. II
Schreiber, Brig. Derek, 1904–1972, vol. VII
Schreiber, Lt-Gen. Sir Edmond Charles Acton, 1890–1972, vol. VII
Schreiber, Ricardo Rivera, 1892–1969, vol. VI
Schreiner, Olive Emilie Albertina, 1855–1920, vol. II
Schreiner, S. C. Cronwright; see Cronwright, S. C.
Schreiner, Rt Hon. William Philip, 1857–1919, vol. II
Schröder, Baron Bruno, 1867–1940, vol. III
Schroder, Helmut William Bruno, 1901–1969, vol. VI
Schröder, Sir John Henry William, 1st Bt, 1825–1910, vol. I
Schröder, Sir Walter, 1855–1942, vol. IV
Schroder, Captain William Henry, 1867–1945, vol. IV
Schrödinger, Erwin, 1887–1961, vol. VI
Schryver, Samuel Barnett, 1869–1929, vol. III
Schüddekopf, Albert Wilhelm, 1861–1916, vol. II
Schuler, Gottlieb Frederick Henry, 1854–1926, vol. II
Schultz, Donald Lorimer, 1926–1987, vol. VIII
Schumacher, Ernst F(riedrich), 1911–1977, vol. VII
Schuman, Robert, 1886–1963, vol. VI
Schumann, Elisabeth, 1885–1952, vol. V
Schunck, Henry Edward, 1820–1903, vol. I
Schurman, Jacob Gould, 1854–1942, vol. IV
Schuschnigg, Kurt von, 1897–1977, vol. VII
Schuster, 1st Baron, 1869–1956, vol. V
Schuster, Sir Arthur, 1851–1934, vol. III
Schuster, Ernest Joseph, 1850–1924, vol. II
Schuster, Sir Felix, 1st Bt, 1854–1936, vol. III
Schuster, Sir (Felix) Victor, 2nd Bt, 1885–1962, vol. VI
Schuster, Sir George Ernest, 1881–1982, vol. VIII
Schuster, Sir Victor; see Schuster, Sir F. V.
Schutt, William John, 1868–1933, vol. III
Schütze, Gladys Henrietta, (Mrs Harrie Schütze); see Leslie, Henrietta.
Schütze, Harrie Leslie Hugo, 1882–1946, vol. IV
Schütze, Henrietta; see Leslie, H.
Schwab, Charles M., 1862–1939, vol. III

Schwab, John Christopher, 1865–1916, vol. II
Schwabe, Maj.-Gen. George S.; see Salis-Schwabe.
Schwabe, Randolph, 1885–1948, vol. IV
Schwabe, Sir Walter George Salis, 1873–1931, vol. III
Schwartz, George Leopold, 1891–1983, vol. VIII
Schwarz, Ernest H. L., 1873–1928, vol. II
Schwarzenberg, Johannes Erkinger, 1903–1978, vol. VII
Schweinitz, E. A. de, died 1904, vol. I
Schweitzer, Albert, 1875–1965, vol. VI
Schwerdt, Captain Charles Max Richard, 1889–1968, vol. VI
Scicluna, Sir Hannibal Publius, 1880–1981, vol. VIII
Sciortino, Anthony, 1883–1947, vol. IV
Sclater, Charlotte Seymour, 1858–1942, vol. IV
Sclater, Edith Harriet, (Lady Sclater), died 1927, vol. II
Sclater, Gen. Sir Henry Crichton, 1855–1923, vol. II
Sclater, Very Rev. John Robert Paterson, 1876–1949, vol. IV
Sclater, Philip Lutley, 1829–1913, vol. I
Sclater, William Lutley, 1863–1944, vol. IV
Sclater-Booth, Hon. Charles Lutley, 1861–1931, vol. III
Sclater-Booth, Col Hon. Walter Dashwood, 1869–1953, vol. V
Scobell, Ven. Edward Chessall, 1850–1917, vol. II
Scobell, Maj.-Gen. Sir Henry Jenner, 1859–1912, vol. I
Scobell, Maj.-Gen. Sir John; see Scobell, Maj.-Gen. Sir S. J. P.
Scobell, Maj.-Gen. Sir (Sanford) John (Palairet), 1879–1955, vol. V
Scobie, Col Mackay John Graham, 1852–1930, vol. III
Scobie, Lt-Gen. Sir Ronald MacKenzie, 1893–1969, vol. VI
Scoble, Rt Hon. Sir Andrew Richard, 1831–1916, vol. II
Scoby-Smith, George, 1848–1929, vol. III
Scoggins, Air Vice-Marshal Roy, 1908–1970, vol. VI
Scogings, Very Rev. Frank, died 1976, vol. VII
Scollard, Clinton, 1860–1932, vol. III
Scollard, Rt Rev. David Joseph, 1862–1934, vol. III
Scoones, Gen. Sir Geoffry Allen Percival, 1893–1975, vol. VII
Scopes, Sir Frederick, 1892–1978, vol. VII
Scorgie, Mervyn Nelson, 1915–1986, vol. VIII
Scorgie, Sir Norman Gibb, 1884–1956, vol. V
Scorgie, Norman James, 1908–1958, vol. V
Scorrer, Aileen Mona, 1905–1984, vol. VIII
Scot-Skirving, Archibald Adam, 1868–1930, vol. III
Scothern, Col Albert Edward, 1882–1970, vol. VI
Scotland, Sir Colley Harman, 1818–1903, vol. I
Scotland, James, 1917–1983, vol. VIII
Scotland, Rear-Adm. John Earl, 1911–1978, vol. VII
Scotson, Frederick Hector, 1900–1955, vol. V
Scott, A. R.; see Ritchie-Scott.
Scott, Adrian Gilbert, 1882–1963, vol. VI
Scott, Agnes Catharine, 1875–1955, vol. V
Scott, Vice-Adm. Albert Charles, 1872–1969, vol. VI
Scott, Alexander, 1853–1947, vol. IV
Scott, Alexander MacCallum, 1874–1928, vol. II
Scott, Alfred Henry, 1868–1939, vol. III

Scott, Sir Andrew, 1857–1939, vol. III
Scott, Lt-Col Angel; see Scott, Lt-Col W. A.
Scott, Sir Angus Newton, 1876–1958, vol. V
Scott, Maj.-Gen. Anthony Gerald O'Carroll, 1899–1980, vol. VII
Scott, Very Rev. Archibald, 1837–1909, vol. I
Scott, Archibald Gifford, 1889–1980, vol. VII
Scott, Lt-Col Archibald Malcolm H.; see Henderson-Scott.
Scott, Sir (Arleigh) Winston, 1900–1976, vol. VII
Scott, Arthur, 1881–1953, vol. V
Scott, Maj.-Gen. Sir Arthur Binny, 1862–1944, vol. IV
Scott, Sir (Arthur) Guillum, 1842–1909, vol. I
Scott, Arthur William, 1846–1927, vol. II
Scott, Ven. Avison Terry, 1848–1925, vol. II
Scott, Sir Basil, 1859–1926, vol. II
Scott, Sir Benjamin, 1841–1927, vol. II
Scott, Benjamin Charles George, 1846–1929, vol. III
Scott, Sir Bernard Francis William, 1914–1987, vol. VIII
Scott, Col Bertal Hopton, 1863–1926, vol. II
Scott, Col Sir Buchanan, 1850–1937, vol. III
Scott, Catharine Amy D.; see Dawson Scott.
Scott, Charles, 1851–1934, vol. III
Scott, Rev. Charles Anderson, 1859–1941, vol. IV
Scott, Charles Clare, 1850–1925, vol. II
Scott, Rev. Canon Charles Harold, 1871–1940, vol. III (A), vol. IV
Scott, Maj.-Gen. Sir Charles Henry, 1848–1919, vol. II
Scott, Col Charles Inglis, 1866–1941, vol. IV
Scott, Charles Norman Lindsay Tollemache, 1852–1938, vol. III
Scott, Charles Paley, 1881–1950, vol. IV
Scott, Rt Rev. Charles Perry, 1847–1927, vol. II
Scott, Charles Prestwich, 1846–1932, vol. III
Scott, Charles Russell, 1898–1979, vol. VII
Scott, Rt Hon. Sir Charles Stewart, 1838–1924, vol. II
Scott, Charles Thomas, 1868–1953, vol. V
Scott, Lord Charles Thomas Montagu-Douglas-, 1839–1911, vol. I
Scott, Maj.-Gen. Charles Walker, 1875–1929, vol. III
Scott, Christopher Fairfax, 1894–1958, vol. V
Scott, Ven. Claud Syms, 1901–1983, vol. VIII
Scott, Clement William, 1841–1904, vol. I
Scott, Cyril, 1879–1970, vol. VI
Scott, David Aylmer, 1892–1971, vol. VII
Scott, Sir David John Montagu Douglas, 1887–1986, vol. VIII
Scott, Hon. David Lynch, 1845–1924, vol. II
Scott, David Robert, died 1943, vol. IV
Scott, David Russell, died 1954, vol. II
Scott, Denis Herbert, 1899–1958, vol. V
Scott, Sir Donald; see Scott, Sir R. D.
Scott, Douglas, 1913–1990, vol. VIII
Scott, Maj.-Gen. Douglas Alexander, 1848–1924, vol. II
Scott, Sir Douglas Edward, 7th Bt (cr April 1806), 1863–1951, vol. V
Scott, Col. Sir Douglas Winchester, 2nd Bt, 1907–1984, vol. VIII
Scott, Dukinfield Henry, 1854–1934, vol. III

Scott, Duncan Campbell, 1862–1947, vol. IV
Scott, Rev. Edward Anderson Seymour, 1865–1941, vol. IV
Scott, Sir Edward Arthur Dolman, 8th Bt (cr April 1806), 1905–1980, vol. VII (AII)
Scott, Edward B.; see Baliol Scott.
Scott, Sir Edward Dolman, 6th Bt (cr April 1806), 1826–1905, vol. I
Scott, Edward Hey L.; see Laughton-Scott.
Scott, Edward John Long, 1840–1918, vol. II
Scott, Edward Taylor, 1883–1932, vol. III
Scott, Elisabeth Whitworth, 1898–1972, vol. VII
Scott, Sir Eric, 1891–1982, vol. VIII
Scott, Sir Ernest, 1868–1939, vol. III
Scott, Ernest Findlay, 1868–1954, vol. V
Scott, Ernest Newey, died 1952, vol. V
Scott, Hon. Sir Ernest Stowell, 1872–1953, vol. V
Scott, Ethleen Mary, 1896–1985, vol. VIII
Scott, Eustace Lindsay, 1885–1956, vol. V
Scott, Major Finlay Forbes, died 1949, vol. IV
Scott, Francis Clayton, 1881–1979, vol. VII
Scott, Maj.-Gen. Sir Francis Cunningham, 1834–1902, vol. I
Scott, Sir Francis David Sibbald, 4th Bt (cr Dec. 1806), 1851–1906, vol. I
Scott, Lt-Col Lord Francis George Montagu-Douglas-, 1879–1952, vol. V
Scott, Sir Francis Montagu Sibbald, 5th Bt (cr Dec. 1806), 1885–1945, vol. IV
Scott, Francis Reginald Fairfax, 1897–1969, vol. VI
Scott, Frank, (Francis Reginald), 1899–1985, vol. VIII
Scott, Col Frederick Beaufort, 1839–1903, vol. I
Scott, Ven. Frederick George, 1861–1944, vol. IV
Scott, Gavin, 1876–1933, vol. III
Scott, Lt-Col George, 1859–1955, vol. V
Scott, Sir George; see Scott, Sir J. G.
Scott, George Alexander, 1862–1933, vol. III
Scott, George Barclay, 1928–1990, vol. VIII
Scott, George Batley, 1844–1932, vol. III
Scott, Sir George Edward, 1903–1989, vol. VIII
Scott, George Edwin, 1925–1988, vol. VIII
Scott, George Ian, 1907–1989, vol. VIII
Scott, Lt-Col George John, 1858–1925, vol. II
Scott, George Walter, 1896–1963, vol. VI
Scott, Lord George William Montagu-Douglas-, 1866–1947, vol. IV
Scott, Col Gerald Bassett, 1875–1964, vol. VI
Scott, Geraldine Edith, (Lady Scott); see Mitton, G. E.
Scott, G(ilbert) Shaw, 1884–1969, vol. VI
Scott, Sir Giles Gilbert, 1880–1960, vol. V
Scott, Sir Guillum; see Scott, Sir A. G.
Scott, Rev. G(uthrie) Michael, 1907–1983, vol. VIII
Scott, Guy Harden Guillum, 1874–1960, vol. V
Scott, Sir Harold; see Scott, Sir Henry H.
Scott, Sir Harold Richard, 1887–1969, vol. VI
Scott, Major Harvey, 1868–1912, vol. I
Scott, Henry Cooper, 1915–1977, vol. VII
Scott, Col Lord Henry Francis Montagu-Douglas-, 1868–1945, vol. IV
Scott, Henry George, 1875–1935, vol. III
Scott, Sir (Henry) Harold, 1874–1956, vol. V
Scott, Brig. Sir Henry Lawrence, 1882–1971, vol. VII

Scott, Sir (Henry) Maurice, 1910–1976, vol. VII
Scott, Sir Henry Milne, 1876–1956, vol. V
Scott, Hon. Henry Robert H.; see Hepburne-Scott.
Scott, Brig. Henry St George Stewart, 1880–1940, vol. III
Scott, Lord Herbert Andrew Montagu-Douglas-, 1872–1944, vol. IV
Scott, Sir Herbert Septimus, 1873–1952, vol. V
Scott, Hugh, 1885–1960, vol. V
Scott, Hugh Stowell; see Merriman, Henry Seton.
Scott, James, 1850–1920, vol. II
Scott, Sir James, 1838–1925, vol. II
Scott, James, died 1929, vol. III
Scott, James, 1876–1939, vol. III
Scott, Maj.-Gen. James Bruce, 1892–1974, vol. VII
Scott, James Cospatrick Hepburne-, 1882–1942, vol. IV
Scott, Sir (James) George, 1851–1935, vol. III
Scott, James Henderson, 1913–1970, vol. VI
Scott, J(ames) M(aurice), 1906–1986, vol. VIII
Scott, Sir James William, 1st Bt (cr 1909), 1844–1913, vol. I
Scott, Maj.-Gen. James Woodward, 1838–1914, vol. I
Scott, Col Sir Jervoise Bolitho, 1st Bt (cr 1962), 1892–1965, vol. VI
Scott, Sir John, 1814–1898, vol. I
Scott, John, 1830–1903, vol. I
Scott, Hon. Sir John, 1841–1904, vol. I
Scott, Rev. John, 1836–1906, vol. I
Scott, John, died 1919, vol. II
Scott, Sir John, 2nd Bt (cr 1907), 1854–1922, vol. II
Scott, Sir John, 1878–1946, vol. IV
Scott, Brig. John, 1887–1971, vol. VII
Scott, John Alexander, 1900–1965, vol. VI
Scott, Sir John Arthur G.; see Guillum Scott.
Scott, John Dick, 1917–1980, vol. VII
Scott, John Gordon Cameron, 1888–1946, vol. IV
Scott, John Halliday, died 1914, vol. I
Scott, Sir John Harley, died 1931, vol. III
Scott, John Healey, 1843–1925, vol. II
Scott, John Russell, 1879–1949, vol. IV
Scott, Maj.-Gen. John Walter Lennox, 1883–1960, vol. V
Scott, John Waugh, 1878–1974, vol. VII
Scott, Comdr John Wilfred, 1881–1926, vol. II
Scott, John William R.; see Robertson Scott.
Scott, Rev. Canon Joseph John, died 1931, vol. III
Scott, Kathleen, (Lady Scott); see Kennet, Lady.
Scott, Kenneth, died 1918, vol. II
Scott, Laurence Prestwich, 1909–1983, vol. VIII
Scott, Rt Hon. Sir Leslie Frederic, 1869–1950, vol. IV
Scott, Sir Lindsay; see Scott, Sir W. L.
Scott, Lt-Col Lothian Kerr, 1841–1919, vol. II
Scott, Hon. Louis Guy, 1850–1900, vol. I
Scott, Mackay Hugh Baillie, 1865–1945, vol. IV
Scott, Rear-Adm. Malcolm Maxwell-, 1883–1943, vol. IV
Scott, Col Sir Malcolm S.; see Stoddart-Scott.
Scott, Margaret, 1841–1917, vol. II
Scott, M(argaret) Audrey, 1904–1990, vol. VIII
Scott, Sir Maurice; see Scott, Sir H. M.
Scott, Hon. Mrs Maxwell, (Mary Monica), 1852–1920, vol. II

Scott, Rev. Melville, *died* 1929, vol. III

Scott, Ven. Melville Horne, 1827–1898, vol. I

Scott, Sir Michael Fergus M.; *see* Maxwell Scott.

Scott, Most Rev. Moses Nathanael Christopher Omobiala, 1911–1988, vol. VIII

Scott, Napier B.; *see* Baliol Scott.

Scott, Noel, 1890–1956, vol. V

Scott, Norman Carson, 1899–1975, vol. VII

Scott, Lt-Col Norman Emile Henry, 1875–1958, vol. V

Scott, Sir Oswald Arthur, 1893–1960, vol. V

Scott, Owen Stanley, 1852–1922, vol. II

Scott, Paul Mark, 1920–1978, vol. VII

Scott, Adm. Sir Percy Moreton, 1st Bt (*cr* 1913), 1853–1924, vol. II

Scott, Rev. Percy Richard, 1850–1906, vol. I

Scott, Peter, *died* 1972, vol. VII

Scott, Peter Duncan, 1914–1977, vol. VII

Scott, Peter Heathcote Guillum, 1913–1961, vol. VI

Scott, Sir Peter Markham, 1909–1989, vol. VIII

Scott, Brig.-Gen. Philip Clement J., 1871–1932, vol. III

Scott, Ralph Roylance, 1893–1978, vol. VII

Scott, Brig. Raymond S., *died* 1972, vol. VII

Scott, Richard, 1914–1983, vol. VIII

Scott, Rear-Adm. Richard James Rodney, 1887–1967, vol. VI

Scott, Hon. Sir Richard William, 1825–1913, vol. I

Scott, Sir Robert, 1903–1968, vol. VI

Scott, Sir Robert Claude, 7th Bt (*cr* 1821), 1886–1961, vol. VI

Scott, Sir (Robert) Donald, 1901–1974, vol. VII

Scott, Captain Robert Falcon, 1868–1912, vol. I

Scott, Very Rev. Robert Forrester Victor, 1897–1975, vol. VII

Scott, Sir Robert Forsyth, 1849–1933, vol. III

Scott, Robert George, 1857–1918, vol. II

Scott, Sir Robert Heatlie, 1905–1982, vol. VIII

Scott, Robert Henry, 1833–1916, vol. II

Scott, Robert Julian, 1861–1930, vol. III

Scott, Maj.-Gen. Robert Kellock, 1871–1942, vol. IV

Scott, Gen. Robert Nicholl D.; *see* Dawson-Scott.

Scott, Robert Pickett, 1856–1931, vol. III

Scott, Sir (Robert) Russell, 1877–1960, vol. V

Scott, Sir Robert Townley, 1841–1922, vol. II

Scott, Sir Ronald B.; *see* Bodley Scott.

Scott, Group Captain Roy Charles Edwin, 1918–1982, vol. VIII

Scott, Sir Russell; *see* Scott, Sir Robert R.

Scott, Rev. Samuel Cooper, 1838–1923, vol. II

Scott, Sir Samuel Edward, 6th Bt (*cr* 1821), 1873–1943, vol. IV

Scott, Rev. Samuel Gilbert, 1847–1916, vol. II

Scott, Sir Samuel Haslam, 2nd Bt (*cr* 1909), 1875–1960, vol. V

Scott, Sebastian Gilbert, 1879–1941, vol. IV

Scott, Sheila Christine, 1927–1988, vol. VIII

Scott, Rev. Sidney; *see* Scott, Rev. W. S.

Scott, Sydney Richard, *died* 1966, vol. VI

Scott, Rev. Thomas, 1831–1914, vol. I

Scott, Maj.-Gen. Thomas, 1897–1968, vol. VI

Scott, Rt Rev. Thomas Arnold, 1879–1956, vol. V

Scott, Thomas Bodley, *died* 1924, vol. II

Scott, Lt-Gen. Sir Thomas Edwin, 1867–1937, vol. III

Scott, Rev. Thomas Errington, *died* 1930, vol. III

Scott, Thomas Gilbert, 1874–1933, vol. III

Scott, Maj.-Gen. Thomas Patrick David, 1905–1976, vol. VII

Scott, Tom, 1854–1927, vol. II

Scott, Col Wallace Arthur, *died* 1949, vol. IV (A), vol. V

Scott, Sir Walter, 1st Bt (*cr* 1907), 1826–1910, vol. I

Scott, Hon. Walter, 1867–1938, vol. III

Scott, Sir Walter, 3rd Bt (*cr* 1907), 1895–1967, vol. VI

Scott, Sir Walter, 1903–1981, vol. VIII

Scott, Rev. Walter Henry, 1842–1931, vol. III

Scott, Maj.-Gen. Sir Walter Joseph Constable M.; *see* Maxwell-Scott.

Scott, Sir Walter Lawrence, 1880–1951, vol. V

Scott, Walter Montagu, 1867–1920, vol. II

Scott, Walter Samuel, 1870–1951, vol. V

Scott, Rev. (Walter) Sidney, 1900–1980, vol. VII

Scott, Sir (Warwick) Lindsay, 1892–1952, vol. V

Scott, Sir William, 1898–1965, vol. VI

Scott, William A., 1871–1918, vol. II

Scott, Lt-Col (William) Angel, 1857–1932, vol. III

Scott, Maj.-Gen. Sir William Arthur, 1899–1976, vol. VII

Scott, Col William Augustus, 1856–1930, vol. III

Scott, William Berryman, 1858–1947, vol. IV

Scott, William Coxon, 1895–1968, vol. VI

Scott, Sir William Dalgliesh, 1890–1966, vol. VI

Scott, Col Sir William Dishington, 1878–1952, vol. V

Scott, William Douglas R.; *see* Robson-Scott.

Scott, Ven. William Edward, *died* 1918, vol. II

Scott, William George, 1913–1989, vol. VIII

Scott, Rev. William Major, 1879–1932, vol. III

Scott, Sir William Monteath, 7th Bt (*cr* 1671), 1829–1902, vol. I

Scott, Rev. William Morris FitzGerald, 1912–1959, vol. V

Scott, William Robert, 1868–1940, vol. III

Scott, Maj.-Gen. William Walter Hopton, 1843–1906, vol. I

Scott, Lt-Col Lord William Walter Montagu-Douglas-, 1896–1958, vol. V

Scott, Winifred Mary, (Pamela Wynne), *died* 1959, vol. V

Scott, Sir Winston; *see* Scott, Sir A. W.

Scott-Barrett, Rev. Hugh, 1887–1958, vol. V

Scott-Batey, Rowland William John, 1913–1980, vol. VII

Scott Blair, George William, 1902–1987, vol. VIII

Scott-Brown, Walter Graham, 1897–1987, vol. VIII

Scott-Duff, Bt Lt-Col Arthur Abercromby, 1874–1951, vol. V

Scott-Elliot, Walter Travers, 1895–1977, vol. VII

Scott Fox, Sir David; *see* Scott Fox, Sir R. D. J.

Scott Fox, Sir (Robert) David (John), 1910–1985, vol. VIII

Scott-Gatty, Sir Alfred Scott, 1847–1918, vol. II

Scott Hall, Stewart, 1905–1961, vol. VI

Scott-Hill, Engr Rear-Adm. Walter, 1873–1963, vol. VI

Scott-James, Rolfe Arnold, 1878–1959, vol. V

Scott-Kerr, Brig.-Gen. Robert, 1859–1942, vol. IV

Scott Makdougall, Hugh James Elibank, 1861–1934, vol. III

Scott-Moncrieff, Adm. Sir Alan Kenneth, *died* 1980, vol. VII

Scott Moncrieff, Charles Kenneth, 1889–1930, vol. III

Scott-Moncrieff, Sir Colin Campbell, 1836–1916, vol. II

Scott-Moncrieff, Maj.-Gen. Sir George Kenneth, 1855–1924, vol. II

Scott-Moncrieff, Joanna Constance, 1920–1978, vol. VII

Scott-Moncrieff, William George, 1846–1927, vol. II

Scott O'Connor, Thomas Arthur Leslie, 1878–1944, vol. IV

Scott-Owen, Col Arthur Lewis, 1885–1944, vol. IV

Scott-Paine, Hubert, 1891–1954, vol. V

Scott-Smith, Sir Henry, 1865–1950, vol. IV

Scott-Taggart, Wing Comdr John, 1897–1979, vol. VII

Scott Thomson, Gladys, *died* 1966, vol. VI

Scotter, Sir Charles, 1st Bt, 1835–1910, vol. I

Scotter, Sir Frederick Charles, 2nd Bt, 1868–1911, vol. I

Scotter, Gen. Sir William Norman Roy, 1922–1981, vol. VIII

Scotti, Antonio, 1866–1936, vol. III

Scougal, Andrew E., 1846–1916, vol. II

Scourfield, Sir Owen Henry Philipps, 2nd Bt, 1847–1921, vol. II

Scovell, Sir Augustus Charles, 1840–1924, vol. II

Scovell, Lt-Col George Julian Selwyn, *died* 1948, vol. IV

Scovell, Rowley Fielding, 1902–1972, vol. VII

Scragg, Air Vice-Marshal Sir Colin, 1908–1989, vol. VIII

Scrase-Dickins, Col Spencer William; *see* Dickins.

Scrase-Dickins, Maj.-Gen. William Drummond, 1832–1914, vol. I

Scratchley, Herbert Arthur, 1855–1920, vol. II

Scratchley, Lt-Col Victor Henry Sylvester, 1870–1936, vol. III

Scriabin, Alexander, 1872–1915, vol. I

Scribner, Charles, 1890–1952, vol. V

Scrimgeour, H(ugh) Carron, 1883–1958, vol. V

Scrimgeour, James, 1903–1987, vol. VIII

Scrimgeour, John Stuart, 1887–1950, vol. IV

Scrimger, Lt-Col Francis Alexander Carron, 1880–1937, vol. III

Scriven, Ven. Augustine, *died* 1916, vol. II

Scrivener, Sir Patrick Stratford, 1897–1966, vol. VI

Scroggie, Rev. William Graham, 1877–1958, vol. V

Scroggie, Col William Reith John, 1876–1953, vol. V

Scroope, Arthur Edgar, *died* 1954, vol. V

Scrope, Henry Aloysius, 1862–1950, vol. IV

Scrutton, James Herbert, 1858–1938, vol. III

Scrutton, Sir Thomas Edward, 1856–1934, vol. III

Scrymgeour, Edwin, 1866–1947, vol. IV

Scrymgeour, Norval, 1870–1952, vol. V

Scrymsoure-Steuart-Fothringham, Walter Thomas James, 1862–1936, vol. III

Scudamore, Brig.-Gen. Charles Philip, 1861–1929, vol. III

Scudder, Horace Elisha, 1838–1902, vol. I

Scullard, Rev. Herbert Hayes, 1862–1926, vol. II

Scullard, Howard Hayes, 1903–1983, vol. VIII

Scullin, Rt Hon. James Henry, 1876–1953, vol. V

Scully, Harry, *died* 1935, vol. III

Scully, James Aloysius, 1856–1929, vol. III

Scully, Major Vincent Joseph, 1876–1941, vol. IV

Scully, Lt-Col Vincent Marcus Barron, 1881–1941, vol. IV

Scully, Vincent William Thomas, 1900–1980, vol. VII

Scupham, John, 1904–1990, vol. VIII

Scupham, Brig. Sir William Eric Halstead, 1893–1958, vol. V

Scurfield, Harold, 1863–1941, vol. IV

Scurr, John, 1876–1932, vol. III

Sea-Lion; *see* Bennett, Captain G. M.

Seaborne Davies, David Richard; *see* Davies, D. R. S.

Seabrook, John, 1896–1985, vol. VIII

Seabrook, William, 1886–1945, vol. IV

Seabrooke, Elliott, *died* 1950, vol. IV

Seabrooke, Sir James Herbert, 1852–1933, vol. III

Seaby, Allen W., 1867–1953, vol. V

Seafield, 11th Earl of, 1876–1915, vol. I

Seafield, Countess of (12th in line), 1906–1969, vol. VI

Seafield, Countess of; (Caroline), *died* 1911, vol. I

Seaford, Sir Frederick Jacob, *died* 1968, vol. VI

Seaforth, 1st Baron, 1847–1923, vol. II

Seaforth, Lady; (Mary Margaret), *died* 1933, vol. III

Seager, Basil William, 1898–1977, vol. VII

Seager, Most Rev. Charles Allen, 1872–1948, vol. IV

Seager, Ven. Edward Leslie, 1904–1983, vol. VIII

Seager, Captain John Elliot, 1891–1955, vol. V

Seager, Philip Samuel, 1845–1924, vol. II

Seager, Samuel Hurst, 1855–1933, vol. III

Seager, Sir William Henry, 1862–1941, vol. IV

Seago, Edward Brian, 1910–1974, vol. VII

Seagram, Brig.-Gen. Tom Ogle, 1872–1958, vol. V

Seal, Sir Brajendranath, 1864–1938, vol. III

Seal, Sir Eric Arthur, 1898–1972, vol. VII

Seale, A. Barney, *died* 1957, vol. V

Seale, Rev. E. G., 1870–1936, vol. III

Seale, Sir John Carteret Hyde, 4th Bt, 1881–1964, vol. VI

Seale, Sir John Henry, 3rd Bt, 1843–1914, vol. I

Sealy, Sir John, 1807–1899, vol. I

Sealy, Patrick Persse, 1853–1938, vol. III

Seaman, Clarence Milton Edwards, 1908–1974, vol. VII

Seaman, Col Edwin Charles, 1867–1919, vol. II

Seaman, Edwin de Grey, 1908–1983, vol. VIII

Seaman, Sir Owen, 1st Bt, 1861–1936, vol. III

Seaman, Paymaster-Captain Tom, *died* 1943, vol. IV

Seamer, Rev. Arthur John, *died* 1963, vol. VI

Searcy, Philip Roy, 1914–1983, vol. VIII

Searight, Major Hugh fforde, 1875–1942, vol. IV

Searle, Alfred Broadhead, 1877–1967, vol. VI

Searle, Maj.-Gen. Arthur Thaddeus, 1830–1925, vol. II

Searle, Rev. Charles Edward, 1828–1902, vol. I

Searle, Col Frank, *died* 1948, vol. IV

Searle, George Frederick Charles, 1864–1954, vol. V

Searle, Herbert Victor, 1892–1968, vol. VI

Searle, Humphrey, 1915–1982, vol. VIII

Searle, Sir Malcolm William, *died* 1926, vol. II

Searles-Wood, Herbert Duncan, 1853–1936, vol. III
Sears, Rear-Adm. Harold Baker, 1880–1959, vol. V
Sears, John Edward, 1857–1941, vol. IV
Sears, John Edward, 1883–1954, vol. V
Sears, William, *died* 1929, vol. III
Seath, Maj.-Gen. Gordon Hamilton, *died* 1952, vol. V
Seaton, 3rd Baron, 1854–1933, vol. III
Seaton, 4th Baron, 1863–1955, vol. V
Seaton, Albert Edward, 1848–1930, vol. III
Seaton, Rev. Douglas, 1839–1923, vol. II
Seaton, Edward Cox, 1847–1915, vol. I
Seaton, J. S., *died* 1929, vol. III
Seaton, Rt Rev. James Buchanan, 1868–1938, vol. III
Seaton, Reginald Ethelbert, 1899–1978, vol. VII
Seaver, Very Rev. Charles, 1820–1907, vol. I
Seaver, Very Rev. George, 1890–1976, vol. VII
Seaverns, Joel Herbert, 1860–1923, vol. II
Sebag-Montefiore, Edmund; *see* Montefiore.
Sebag-Montefiore, Sir Joseph; *see* Montefiore.
Sebastian, Rear-Adm. Brian Leonard Geoffrey, 1891–1983, vol. VIII
Sebastian, Erroll Graham, 1892–1978, vol. VII
Sebright, Sir Edgar Reginald Saunders, 11th Bt, 1854–1917, vol. II
Sebright, Sir Egbert Cecil Saunders, 10th Bt, 1871–1897, vol. I
Sebright, Lt-Col Sir Giles Edward, 13th Bt, 1896–1954, vol. V
Sebright, Sir Guy Thomas Saunders, 12th Bt, 1856–1933, vol. III
Sebright, Sir Hugo Giles Edmund, 14th Bt, 1931–1985, vol. VIII
Seccombe, Brig.-Gen. Archibald Kennedy, 1868–1931, vol. III
Seccombe, Thomas, 1866–1923, vol. II
Seccombe, Sir Thomas Lawrence, 1812–1902, vol. I
Secker, Martin, 1882–1978, vol. VII
Seckham, Lt-Col Bassett Thorne, 1863–1925, vol. II
Seckham, Lt-Col Douglas Thorne, 1873–1937, vol. III
Secombe, Maj.-Gen. Victor Clarence, 1897–1962, vol. VI
Secretan, Hubert Arthur, 1891–1969, vol. VI
Secretan, Walter Bernard, 1875–1966, vol. VI
Seddon, Charles Norman, 1870–1950, vol. IV
Seddon, Sir Harold, 1881–1958, vol. V
Seddon, Harry Sterratt, 1881–1944, vol. IV
Seddon, Sir Herbert John, 1903–1977, vol. VII
Seddon, James Andrew, 1868–1939, vol. III
Seddon, John Pollard, 1827–1906, vol. I
Seddon, Rt Hon. Richard John, 1845–1906, vol. I
Seddon-Brown, Lt-Col Sir Norman Seddon, 1880–1971, vol. VII
Sedgefield, W. J., 1866–1945, vol. IV
Sedgewick, Hon. George Herbert, 1878–1939, vol. III
Sedgwick, Adam, 1854–1913, vol. I
Sedgwick, Anne Douglas, 1873–1935, vol. III
Sedgwick, Rear-Adm. Cyril Gordon, 1885–1948, vol. IV
Sedgwick, Ellery, 1872–1960, vol. V
Sedgwick, Lt-Col Francis Roger, 1876–1955, vol. V
Sedgwick, Rev. Gordon, 1840–1921, vol. II
Sedgwick, Henry Dwight, 1861–1957, vol. V

Sedgwick, Patrick Cardinall Mason, 1911–1985, vol. VIII
Sedgwick, Richard Romney, 1894–1972, vol. VII
Sedgwick, Rev. S. N., 1872–1941, vol. IV
Sedgwick, William Thompson, 1855–1921, vol. II
Sedgwick, Rt Rev. William Walmsley, 1858–1948, vol. IV
See, Hon. Sir John, 1845–1907, vol. I
Sée, Peter Henri, 1910–1963, vol. VI
Seebohm, Baron (Life Peer); Frederic Seebohm, 1909–1990, vol. VIII
Seebohm, Frederic, 1833–1912, vol. I
Seebohm, Hugh Exton, 1867–1946, vol. IV
Seeds, Sir William, 1882–1973, vol. VII
Seefried, Irmgard Maria Theresia, 1919–1988, vol. VIII
Seel, Major Edward M.; *see* Molyneux-Seel.
Seel, Sir George Frederick, 1895–1976, vol. VII
Seeley, Edward Alexander, 1913–1979, vol. VII
Seeley, Ven. George Henry, *died* 1935, vol. III
Seeley, Harry Govier, 1839–1909, vol. I
Seely, Sir Charles, 1st Bt, 1833–1915, vol. I
Seely, Sir Charles Hilton, 2nd Bt, 1859–1926, vol. II
Seely, Sir Victor Basil John, 4th Bt, 1900–1980, vol. VII
Seers, Dudley, 1920–1983, vol. VIII
Seferiades, George, 1900–1971, vol. VII
Seferis, George; *see* Seferiades, G.
Sefton, 4th Earl of, 1835–1897, vol. I
Sefton, 5th Earl of, 1867–1901, vol. I
Sefton, 6th Earl of, 1871–1930, vol. III
Sefton, 7th Earl of, 1898–1972, vol. VII
Sefton, Anne Harriet, (Mrs Walter Sefton); *see* Fish, A. H.
Sefton-Cohen, Arthur, 1879–1968, vol. VI (AII)
Segal, Baron (Life Peer); Samuel Segal, 1902–1985, vol. VIII
Segar, George Xavier, 1838–1901, vol. I
Segar, Hugh William, 1868–1954, vol. V
Segonzac, André D. de; *see* Dunoyer de Segonzac.
Segovia Torres, Andrés, 1893–1987, vol. VIII
Segrave, Edmond, 1904–1971, vol. VII
Segrave, Brig.-Gen. Eric; *see* Segrave, Brig.-Gen. W. H. E.
Segrave, Major Sir Henry O'Neal Dehane, 1896–1930, vol. III
Segrave, Vice-Adm. John Roderick, 1871–1938, vol. III
Segrave, Captain Sir Thomas George, 1865–1941, vol. IV
Segrave, Brig.-Gen. (William Henry) Eric, 1875–1964, vol. VI
Segrè, Emilio, 1905–1989, vol. VIII
Séguel, George Gregory M., *died* 1954, vol. V
Segur, Marquis de; Pierre Marie Maurice Henri, 1853–1916, vol. II
Seifert, Jaroslav, 1901–1986, vol. VIII
Seigne, John Thomas, 1844–1922, vol. II
Seignobos, Charles, 1854–1942, vol. IV
Seillière, Baron Ernest, 1866–1955, vol. IV
Seitz, John Arnold, 1883–1963, vol. VI
Sekers, Miki; *see* Sekers, Sir N. T.
Sekers, Sir Nicholas Thomas, (Miki Sekers), 1910–1972, vol. VII

Sekon, George Augustus, 1867–1948, vol. IV
Selbie, Rev. John A., 1856–1931, vol. III
Selbie, Robert Hope, 1868–1930, vol. III
Selbie, Rev. William Boothby, 1862–1944, vol. IV
Selborne, 2nd Earl of, 1859–1942, vol. IV
Selborne, 3rd Earl of, 1887–1971, vol. VII
Selby, 1st Viscount, 1835–1909, vol. I
Selby, 2nd Viscount, 1867–1923, vol. II
Selby, 3rd Viscount, 1911–1959, vol. V
Selby, Arthur Laidlaw, 1861–1942, vol. IV
Selby, Maj.-Gen. Arthur Roland, 1893–1966, vol VI (AII)
Selby, Lt-Col Charles Westrope, 1883–1929, vol. III
Selby, Francis Guy, 1852–1927, vol. II
Selby, Francis James, 1867–1942, vol. IV
Selby, Harry, 1913–1984, vol. VIII
Selby, Percival Marchant, 1886–1955, vol. V
Selby, Rev. Thomas Gunn, 1846–1910, vol. I
Selby, Sir Walford Harmood Montague, 1881–1965, vol. VI
Selby, Lt-Col William, 1869–1916, vol. II
Selby, Rev. William John, 1858–1935, vol. III
Selby-Bigge, Sir Amherst; see Selby-Bigge, Sir L. A.
Selby-Bigge, Sir John Amherst, 2nd Bt, 1892–1973, vol. VII
Selby-Bigge, Sir (Lewis) Amherst, 1st Bt, 1860–1951, vol. V
Selby-Lowndes, Brig. Montacute William Worrall, 1896–1972, vol. VII
Selby-Lowndes, Col William; see Lowndes.
Seldon Truss, Leslie, 1892–1990, vol. VIII
Self, Sir (Albert) Henry, 1890–1975, vol. VII
Self, Sir Henry; see Self, Sir A. H.
Self, Sir Robert Carr, 1840–1926, vol. II
Selfe, Sir William Lucius, 1845–1924, vol. II
Selfridge, Harry Gordon, 1858–1947, vol. IV
Seligman, Sir Charles David, 1869–1954, vol. V
Seligman, Charles Gabriel, 1873–1940, vol. III
Seligman, Edwin Robert Anderson, 1861–1939, vol. III
Seligman, Brig.-Gen. Herbert Spencer, 1872–1951, vol. V
Selincourt, Agnes de, 1872–1917, vol. II
Sélincourt, Anne de; see Sedgwick, Anne Douglas.
Selincourt, Ernest de, 1870–1943, vol. IV
Selincourt, Hugh de, 1878–1951, vol. V
Selkirk, Countess of; (Cecely Louisa), died 1920, vol. II
Sell, Rev. Edward, 1839–1932, vol. III
Sell, William James, died 1915, vol. I
Sellar, Harry Harpham, 1893–1966, vol. VI
Sellar, Robert Watson, 1894–1965, vol. VI
Sellar, Lt-Col Thomas Byrne, 1865–1924, vol. II
Selleck, Sir Francis Palmer, 1895–1976, vol. VII
Sellers, Rt Hon. Sir Frederic Aked, 1893–1979, vol. VII
Sellers, Peter Richard Henry, 1925–1980, vol. VII
Sellers, Rev. Robert Victor, 1894–1973, vol. VII
Selley, Sir Harry Ralph, 1871–1960, vol. V
Sellheim, Maj.-Gen. Victor Conradsdorf Morisset, 1866–1928, vol. II
Sellon, Hugh Gilbert René, 1901–1974, vol. VII
Sellors, Sir Thomas Holmes, 1902–1987, vol. VIII
Sells, Arthur Lytton L.; see Lytton Sells.

Sells, Vice-Adm. William Fortescue, 1881–1966, vol. VI
Selous, Frederick Courteney, 1851–1917, vol. II
Selous, Gerald Holgate, 1887–1978, vol. VII
Selsdon, 1st Baron, 1877–1938, vol. III
Selsdon, 2nd Baron, 1913–1963, vol. VI
Seltman, Charles Theodore, 1886–1957, vol. V
Selway, Air Marshal Sir Anthony Dunkerton, 1909–1984, vol. VIII
Selway, Cornelius James, 1875–1948, vol. IV
Selwyn, Rev. Edward Carus, 1853–1918, vol. II
Selwyn, Very Rev. Edward Gordon, 1885–1959, vol. V
Selwyn, Rt Rev. George Theodore, 1887–1957, vol. V
Selwyn, Rt Rev. John Richardson, 1844–1898, vol. I
Selwyn, Rev. William, 1840–1914, vol. I
Selwyn, Rt Rev. William Marshall, 1880–1951, vol. V
Selwyn-Clarke, Sir Selwyn, 1893–1976, vol. VII
Selwyn-Lloyd, Baron (Life Peer); John Selwyn Brooke Selwyn-Lloyd, 1904–1978, vol. VII
Selznick, David Oliver, 1902–1965, vol. VI
Semenov, Nikolai Nikolaevich, 1896–1986, vol. VIII
Semon, Sir Felix, 1849–1921, vol. II
Semon, Henry, 1881–1971, vol. VII
Semper, Dudley Henry, 1905–1982, vol. VIII
Sempill, 17th Lord, 1836–1905, vol. I
Sempill, 18th Lord, 1863–1934, vol. III
Sempill, 19th Lord, 1893–1965, vol. VI
Sempill, Major Hon. Douglas F.; see Forbes-Sempill.
Semple, Lt-Col Sir David, 1856–1937, vol. III
Semple, Dugald, 1884–1964, vol. VI
Semple, John Edward, 1903–1969, vol. VI
Semple, John Greenlees, 1904–1985, vol. VIII
Semple, Patrick, 1875–1954, vol. V
Semple, Hon. Robert, 1873–1955, vol. V
Semple, William Hugh, 1900–1981, vol. VIII
Sen, Jitendranath, 1875–1945, vol. IV
Sen, K. Chandra, 1888–1981, vol. VIII
Sen, Nirmul Chunder, 1869–1936, vol. III
Sen, Susil C., died 1946, vol. IV
Sen, Sir Usha Nath, 1880–1959, vol. V
Senanayake, Rt Hon. Don Stephen, 1884–1952, vol. V
Senanayake, Hon. Dudley Shelton, 1911–1973, vol. VII
Sencourt, Robert, 1890–1969, vol. VI
Sendall, Sir Walter Joseph, 1832–1904, vol. I
Sender, Ramón José, 1902–1982, vol. VIII
Senier, Alfred, 1853–1918, vol. II
Senier, Sir Frederic William, 1869–1951, vol. V
Senior, Albert, 1867–1929, vol. III
Senior, Bernard, 1865–1934, vol. III
Senior, Derek, 1912–1988, vol. VIII
Senior, Col Henry William Richard, 1866–1935, vol. III
Senior, Mark, 1863–1927, vol. II
Senior, Ronald Henry, 1904–1988, vol. VIII
Senior, William, died 1920, vol. II
Senior, William Goodwin, 1894–1969, vol. VI
Senior, William Hirst, 1904–1984, vol. VIII
Senior, Hon. William Sidney, 1888–1938, vol. III
Senn, Charles Herman, died 1934, vol. III
Sennett, Sir Richard, 1862–1947, vol. IV
Senter, George, 1874–1942, vol. IV

Senter, Sir John Watt, 1905–1966, vol. VI
Sepeku, Rt Rev. John, *died* 1983, vol. VIII
Sephton, Ven. Arthur, 1894–1982, vol. VIII
Sequeira, James Harry, *died* 1948, vol. IV
Serao, Matilde, 1856–1927, vol. II
Serena, Arthur, *died* 1922, vol. II
Serena, Clara, *died* 1972, vol. VII
Sergeant, Adeline, 1851–1904, vol. I
Sergeant, Emily Frances Adeline; *see* Sergeant, Adeline.
Sergeant, Maj.-Gen. Frederick Cavendish H.; *see* Hilton-Sergeant.
Sergeant, (Herbert) Howard, 1914–1987, vol. VIII
Sergeant, Howard; *see* Sergeant, Herbert H.
Sergeant, Lewis, 1841–1902, vol. I
Sergent, René Edmond, 1904–1984, vol. VIII
Sergison, Captain Charles Warden, 1867–1911, vol. I
Sergison-Brooke, Lt-Gen. Sir Bertram Norman; *see* Brooke.
Serjeant, Sir David Maurice, *died* 1929, vol. III
Serjeant, Col Sir William Charles Eldon, 1857–1930, vol. III
Serle, Rev. Samuel Edward Bayard, 1866–1939, vol. III
Serocold, Brig.-Gen. Eric P.; *see* Pearce-Serocold.
Serocold, Oswald P.; *see* Pearce-Serocold.
Serpell, Henry Oberlin, 1853–1943, vol. IV
Serra Largo, Count de; Peter Alexander Cameron Mackenzie, 1856–1931, vol. III
Servaes, Vice-Adm. Reginald Maxwell, 1893–1978, vol. VII
Service, Hon. James, 1823–1899, vol. I
Service, Robert William, 1874–1958, vol. V
Seshadri, Tiruvenkata Rajendra, 1900–1975, vol. VII
Setalvad, Sir Chimanlal Harilal, *died* 1947, vol. IV
Setchell, Herbert Leonard, 1892–1976, vol. VII
Seth, Andrew, 1856–1931, vol. III
Seth, Arathoon, 1852–1918, vol. II
Seth, George, 1905–1990, vol. VIII
Seth, James, 1860–1924, vol. II
Seth-Smith, David, 1875–1963, vol. VI
Seth-Smith, Brig. Hugh Garden, 1885–1958, vol. V
Seth-Smith, W. H., 1852–1928, vol. II
Sethna, Hon. Sir Phiroze, 1866–1938, vol. III
Seton, Sir Alexander Hay, 10th Bt (*cr* 1663), 1904–1963, vol. VI
Seton, Anya, (Anya Seton Chase), *died* 1990, vol. VIII
Seton, Sir Bruce; *see* Seton, Sir C. B.
Seton, Col Sir Bruce Gordon, 9th Bt (*cr* 1663), 1868–1932, vol. III
Seton, Sir Bruce Lovat, 11th Bt (*cr* 1663), 1909–1969, vol. VI
Seton, Sir Bruce Maxwell, 8th Bt (*cr* 1663), 1836–1915, vol. I
Seton, Sir (Christopher) Bruce, 12th Bt, 1909–1988, vol. VIII
Seton, Sir Claud Ramsay Wilmot, 1888–1982, vol. VIII
Seton, Ernest Thompson, 1860–1946, vol. IV
Seton, George, 1822–1908, vol. I
Seton, Grace Gallatin Thompson, *died* 1959, vol. V
Seton, Captain Sir John Hastings, 10th Bt (*cr* 1683), 1888–1956, vol. V

Seton, Sir Malcolm Cotter Cariston, 1872–1940, vol. III
Seton, Miles Charles Cariston, 1874–1919, vol. II
Seton, Robert George, 1860–1939, vol. III
Seton, Robert S., *died* 1942, vol. IV
Seton, Walter Warren, 1882–1927, vol. II
Seton, Sir William Samuel, 9th Bt (*cr* 1683), 1837–1914, vol. I
Seton-Karr, Sir Henry, 1853–1914, vol. I
Seton-Karr, Heywood Walter, 1859–1938, vol. III
Seton Pringle, John; *see* Pringle, J. S. M.
Seton-Steuart, Sir Alan Henry; *see* Steuart.
Seton-Steuart, Sir Douglas Archibald; *see* Steuart.
Seton-Thompson; *see* Seton, E. T.
Seton-Watson, (George) Hugh (Nicholas), 1916–1984, vol. VIII
Seton-Watson, Hugh; *see* Seton-Watson, G. H. N.
Seton-Watson, Robert William, 1879–1951, vol. V
Settle, Alison, *died* 1980, vol. VII
Settle, Charles Arthur, 1905–1979, vol. VII
Settle, Lt-Gen. Sir Henry Hamilton, 1847–1923, vol. II
Settrington, Lord; Charles Henry Gordon-Lennox, 1899–1919, vol. II
Seuffert, Stanislaus, 1899–1986, vol. VIII
Ševčik, Otakar, 1852–1934, vol. III
Séverine, Madame, 1855–1929, vol. III
Severn, Arthur, *died* 1931, vol. III
Severn, Sir Claud, 1869–1933, vol. III
Severn, Walter, 1830–1904, vol. I
Seversky, Major Alexander P. de, 1894–1974, vol. VII
Sevestre, Robert, 1868–1949, vol. IV
Sewall, May Wright, *died* 1920, vol. II
Seward, Sir Albert Charles, 1863–1941, vol. IV
Seward, Sir Conrad; *see* Seward, Sir S. C.
Seward, Edwin, 1853–1924, vol. II
Seward, Sir Eric John, 1899–1981, vol. VIII
Seward, Sir (Samuel) Conrad, 1908–1976, vol. VII
Seward, Air Vice-Marshal Walter John, 1898–1972, vol. VII
Sewell, Rev. Archibald Hankey, 1874–1943, vol. IV
Sewell, Arnold Edward, 1886–1969, vol. VI
Sewell, Brig. Edgar Patrick, 1905–1957, vol. V
Sewell, Elizabeth Missing, 1815–1906, vol. I
Sewell, Col Evelyn Pierce, *died* 1960, vol. V
Sewell, Rev. Henry, 1847–1943, vol. IV
Sewell, Brig.-Gen. Horace Somerville, 1881–1953, vol. V
Sewell, Rev. James Edwards, 1810–1903, vol. I
Sewell, John Thomas Beadsworth, 1858–1930, vol. III
Sewell, Brig.-Gen. Jonathan William Shirley, 1872–1941, vol. IV
Sewell, Lt-Col Robert Beresford Seymour, 1880–1964, vol. VI
Sewell, Sir Sidney Valentine, 1880–1949, vol. IV
Sewell, Col Thomas Davies, 1832–1916, vol. II
Sexton, Frederic Henry, 1879–1955, vol. V
Sexton, Most Rev. Harold Eustace, 1888–1972, vol. VII
Sexton, Sir James, 1856–1938, vol. III
Sexton, Col Michael John, 1860–1922, vol. II
Sexton, Sir Robert, 1814–1901, vol. I

Sexton, T. M., *died* 1946, vol. IV (A), vol. V
Sexton, Thomas, 1848–1932, vol. III
Sexton, Walter, 1877–1941, vol. IV
Seyler, Athene, 1889–1990, vol. VIII
Seyler, Clarence Arthur, 1866–1959, vol. V
Seymour, Ven. Albert Eden, 1841–1908, vol. I
Seymour, Sir Albert Victor Francis, 2nd Bt (*cr* 1869), 1879–1949, vol. IV
Seymour, Alfred Wallace, 1881–1960, vol. V
Seymour, Very Rev. Algernon Giles, 1886–1933, vol. III
Seymour, Brig.-Gen. Archibald George, 1875–1933, vol. III
Seymour, Captain Arthur George, 1884–1935, vol. III
Seymour, Beatrice Kean, *died* 1955, vol. V
Seymour, Charles, 1885–1963, vol. VI
Seymour, Charles Derick, 1863–1935, vol. III
Seymour, Lt-Col Charles Hugh Napier, 1874–1933, vol. III
Seymour, Vice-Adm. Claude, 1876–1941, vol. IV
Seymour, Derek Robert Gurth, 1917–1986, vol. VIII
Seymour, Edgar William, 1868–1926, vol. II
Seymour, Major Sir Edward, 1877–1948, vol. IV
Seymour, Lord Edward Beauchamp, 1879–1917, vol. II
Seymour, Admiral of the Fleet Rt Hon. Sir Edward Hobart, 1840–1929, vol. III
Seymour, Lord Ernest James, 1850–1930, vol. III
Seymour, Sir George S.; *see* Seymour Seymour.
Seymour, Brig.-Gen. Lord Henry Charles, 1878–1939, vol. III
Seymour, Henry J., 1876–1954, vol. V
Seymour, Horace Alfred Damer, 1843–1902, vol.I
Seymour, Sir Horace James, 1885–1978, vol. VII
Seymour, Lady Katharine, 1900–1985, vol. VIII
Seymour, Leslie George, 1900–1976, vol. VII
Seymour, Sir Michael Culme-, 3rd Bt (*cr* 1809), 1836–1920, vol. II
Seymour, Vice-Adm. Sir Michael Culme-, 4th Bt (*cr* 1809), 1867–1925, vol. II
Seymour, Michael Richard, 1880–1936, vol. III
Seymour, Comdr Ralph Frederick, 1886–1922, vol. II
Seymour, Lt-Col Sir Reginald Henry, 1878–1938, vol. III
Seymour, Richard, 1903–1982, vol. VIII
Seymour, Richard Sturgis, 1875–1959, vol. V
Seymour, Air Cdre Roland George, 1905–1983, vol. VIII
Seymour, Rosalind Herschel; *see* Wade, R. H.
Seymour, Rev. Lord Victor Alexander, 1859–1935, vol. III
Seymour, Gen. Lord William Frederick Ernest, 1838–1915, vol. I
Seymour, Gen. Sir William Henry, 1829–1921, vol. II
Seymour, William Kean, 1887–1975, vol. VII
Seymour-Lloyd, Sir John Hall, 1873–1939, vol. III
Seymour Seymour, Sir George, 1880–1962, vol. VI
Seys, Roland Alex. W.; *see* Wood-Seys.
Seznec, Jean Joseph, 1905–1983, vol. VIII
Sforza, Count Carlo, 1873–1952, vol. V
Sgambati, Giovanni, 1843–1914, vol. I
Shackle, Major Ernest William, 1862–1938, vol. III
Shackle, Robert Jones, 1895–1950, vol. IV

Shackleton, Sir David James, 1863–1938, vol. III
Shackleton, Edith; *see* Heald, E. S.
Shackleton, Major Sir Ernest Henry, 1874–1922, vol. II
Shackleton, Sir Harry Bertram, 1878–1958, vol. V
Shackleton, Robert, 1919–1986, vol. VIII
Shackleton, William, 1872–1933, vol. III
Shackman, Ralph, 1910–1981, vol. VIII
Shadbolt, Ernest Ifill, 1851–1936, vol. III
Shadi Lal, Rt Hon. Sir, 1874–1945, vol. IV
Shadwell, Arthur, 1854–1936, vol. III
Shadwell, Charles Lancelot, 1840–1919, vol. II
Shadwell, Lionel Lancelot, 1845–1925, vol. II
Shadwell, William L.; *see* Lucas-Shadwell.
Shafi, Sir Muhammad, 1869–1932, vol. III
Shafter, William Rufus, 1835–1906, vol. I
Shaftesbury, 9th Earl of, 1869–1961, vol. VI
Shaftesley, John Maurice, 1901–1981, vol. VIII
Shafto, Captain Arthur Duncombe, 1880–1914, vol. I
Shah, Hon. Sir Lallubhai Asharam, 1873–1926, vol. II
Shah, Khan Bahadur Sir Sayyid Mehdi, *died* 1927, vol. II, vol. III
Shahan, Rt Rev. Thomas Joseph, 1857–1932, vol. III
Shahpura, Raja Sir Nahar Singh Dhiraj, 1855–1932, vol. III
Shahub-ud-Din, Khan Bahadur Sir Chaudhri, *died* 1949, vol. IV (A), vol. V
Shaikh, Lt-Col Abdul Hamid, 1890–1963, vol. VI
Shairp, Lt-Col Alexander, 1873–1944, vol. IV
Shakerley, Sir Charles Watkin, 2nd Bt, 1833–1898, vol. I
Shakerley, Major Sir Cyril Holland, 5th Bt, 1897–1970, vol. VI
Shakerley, Major Geoffrey Charles, 1869–1915, vol. I
Shakerley, Sir Geoffrey Peter, 1906–1982, vol. VIII
Shakerley, Sir George Herbert, 4th Bt, 1863–1945, vol. IV
Shakerley, Sir Walter Geoffrey, 3rd Bt, 1859–1943, vol. IV
Shakespear, Alexander Blake, 1873–1949, vol. IV
Shakespear, Brig. Arthur Talbot, 1884–1964, vol. VI
Shakespear, Dame Ethel Mary Reader, 1871–1946, vol. IV
Shakespear, Maj.-Gen. George Robert James, 1842–1926, vol. II
Shakespear, Lt-Col John, 1861–1942, vol. IV
Shakespear, Col Leslie Waterfield, 1860–1933, vol. III
Shakespeare, Rt Hon. Sir Geoffrey Hithersay, 1st Bt, 1893–1980, vol. VII
Shakespeare, Rev. John Howard, 1857–1928, vol. II
Shakespeare, William, 1849–1931, vol. III
Shams-ul-Huda, Nawab Sir Syded, 1864–1922, vol. II
Shamsher Singh, Sir Sardar, Sardar Bahadur, 1860–1920, vol. II, vol. III
Shanahan, Col Daniel Davis, 1863–1954, vol. V
Shanahan, Foss, 1910–1964, vol. VI
Shand, 1st Baron, 1828–1904, vol. I
Shand, Alexander Faulkner, 1858–1936, vol. III
Shand, Alexander Innes, 1832–1907, vol. I
Shand, Sir Charles Lister, 1846–1925, vol. II
Shand, Surg. Rear-Adm. Jonathan, 1865–1961, vol. VI

Shand, Philip Morton, 1888–1960, vol. V

Shand, Samuel James, 1882–1957, vol. V

Shand, Rev. Thomas Rodie, 1827–1914, vol. I

Shandon, 1st Baron, 1857–1930, vol. III

Shanker Shamsher Jang Bahadur Rana, Gen., 1909–1976, vol. VII

Shankland, Sir Thomas Murray, 1905–1986, vol. VIII

Shanks, Edward, 1892–1953, vol. V

Shanks, Michael James, 1927–1984, vol. VIII

Shanks, S(eymour) Cochrane, 1893–1980, vol. VII

Shanks, W(illiam) Somerville, 1864–1951, vol. V

Shann, Edward Owen Giblin, 1884–1935, vol. III

Shann, Sir Keith Charles Owen, 1917–1988, vol. VIII

Shann, Sir Thomas Thornhill, 1846–1923, vol. II

Shannan, A. M'F., *died* 1915, vol. I

Shannon, 6th Earl of, 1860–1906, vol. I

Shannon, 7th Earl of, 1897–1917, vol. I

Shannon, 8th Earl of, 1900–1963, vol. VI

Shannon, Alastair, 1894–1982, vol. VIII

Shannon, Charles, 1863–1937, vol. III

Shannon, Godfrey Eccleston Boyd, 1907–1989, vol. VIII

Shannon, Howard Huntley, 1892–1976, vol. VII

Shannon, Sir James Jebusa, 1862–1923, vol. II

Shannon, Brig.-Gen. Lewis William, 1859–1936, vol. III

Shansfield, William Newton, *died* 1925, vol. II

Shapcott, Brig. Sir Henry, 1888–1967, vol. VI

Shapcott, John Dufour, 1857–1923, vol. II

Shapcott, Louis Edward, 1877–1950, vol. IV

Shapland, Cyril Dee, 1899–1980, vol. VII

Shapland, Maj.-Gen. John Dee, 1897–1971, vol. VII

Shapland, Rev. Richard Henry Bowden, 1877–1937, vol. III

Shapley, Harlow, 1885–1972, vol. VII

Shapley, Rt Rev. Ronald Norman, 1890–1964, vol. VI

Shapurji, Sir Burjorji Broacha, *died* 1920, vol. II

Share, Sir Hamnet Holditch, 1864–1937, vol. III

Sharfuddin, Syed, *born* 1856, vol. II

Sharkey, Sir Seymour John, 1847–1929, vol. III

Sharman, Col Charles Henry Ludovic, 1881–1970, vol. VI

Sharman, Charlotte, 1832–1929, vol. III

Sharman, Thomas Charles, 1912–1990, vol. VIII

Sharman-Crawford, Col Rt Hon. Robert Gordon, 1853–1934, vol. III

Sharp, Baroness (Life Peer); Evelyn Adelaide Sharp, 1903–1985, vol. VIII

Sharp, Col Alexander Dunstan, 1870–1955, vol. V

Sharp, Air Vice-Marshal Alfred Charles Henry, 1904–1956, vol. V

Sharp, Alphonse, 1872–1942, vol. IV

Sharp, Rev. Arnold Mortimer, 1864–1938, vol. III

Sharp, Ven. Arthur Frederick, 1866–1960, vol. V

Sharp, Cecil James, 1859–1924, vol. II

Sharp, Clifford Dyce, 1883–1935, vol. III

Sharp, David, 1840–1922, vol. II

Sharp, Dorothea, *died* 1955, vol. V

Sharp, Sir Edward, 1st Bt (*cr* 1922), 1854–1931, vol. III

Sharp, Sir Edward Herbert, 3rd Bt, 1927–1985, vol. VIII

Sharp, Elizabeth Amelia, 1856–1932, vol. III

Sharp, Ernest Hamilton, *died* 1922, vol. II

Sharp, Evelyn, 1869–1955, vol. V

Sharp, Francis Everard, 1890–1972, vol. VII

Sharp, Lt-Col Frederick Leonard, 1867–1916, vol. II

Sharp, Geoffrey Newton, 1914–1974, vol. VII

Sharp, Most Rev. Gerald, 1865–1933, vol. III

Sharp, Gilbert Granville-, 1894–1968, vol. VI

Sharp, Harold Gregory, 1886–1972, vol. VII

Sharp, Sir Henry, 1869–1954, vol. V

Sharp, Henry Sutcliffe, 1910–1984, vol. VIII

Sharp, Sir Herbert Edward, 2nd Bt (*cr* 1922), 1879–1936, vol. III

Sharp, Janet A.; *see* Achurch, J.

Sharp, Rev. John, 1837–1917, vol. II

Sharp, Rev. John Alfred, 1856–1932, vol. III

Sharp, Gen. Sir John Aubrey Taylor, 1917–1977, vol. VII

Sharp, Rev. Canon John Herbert, 1887–1950, vol. IV

Sharp, Major John Reuben Philip, *died* 1922, vol. II

Sharp, Lauriston William, 1897–1959, vol. V

Sharp, Brig. Mainwaring Cato Ensor, 1897–1990, vol. VIII

Sharp, Sir Milton, 2nd Bt (*cr* 1920), 1880–1941, vol. IV

Sharp, Sir Milton Sheridan, 1st Bt (*cr* 1920), 1856–1924, vol. II

Sharp, Noel Farquharson, 1905–1978, vol. VII

Sharp, Sir Percival, 1867–1953, vol. V

Sharp, Rear-Adm. Philip Graham, 1913–1988, vol. VIII

Sharp, Ven. Richard Lloyd, 1916–1982, vol. VIII

Sharp, Robert Farquharson, 1864–1945, vol. IV

Sharp, Thomas, 1901–1978, vol. VII

Sharp, Thomas Herbert, 1840–1918, vol. II

Sharp, W. H. Cartwright, 1883–1950, vol. IV

Sharp, William, 1856–1905, vol. I

Sharp, Mrs William; *see* Sharp, Elizabeth Amelia.

Sharp, Rev. Canon William Hey, 1845–1928, vol. II

Sharpe, Sir Alfred, 1853–1935, vol. III

Sharpe, Charles W., *died* 1955, vol. V

Sharpe, Ven. Ernest Newton, *died* 1949, vol. IV

Sharpe, Sir Frank Victor, 1903–1988, vol. VIII

Sharpe, Rev. Harold Stephen, 1886–1960, vol. V

Sharpe, Rev. Henry Edmund, 1859–1939, vol. III

Sharpe, Joseph, 1859–1930, vol. III

Sharpe, Sir Montagu, 1856–1942, vol. IV

Sharpe, Phoebe Elizabeth, 1888–1941, vol. IV

Sharpe, Reginald Robinson, 1848–1925, vol. II

Sharpe, Richard Bowdler, 1847–1909, vol. I

Sharpe, Major Robert William, 1886–1943, vol. IV

Sharpe, Rev. Thomas Wetherherd, 1829–1905, vol. I

Sharpe, Major Wilfred Stanley, 1860–1917, vol. II

Sharpe, William Edward Thompson, 1834–1909, vol. I

Sharpe, Sir William Rutton Searle, 1881–1968, vol. VI

Sharpey-Schafer, Sir Edward Albert, 1850–1935, vol. III

Sharpey-Schafer, Edward Peter, 1908–1963, vol. VI

Sharpin, Ven. Frederick Lloyd, *died* 1921, vol. II

Sharples, Charles Norman, 1906–1954, vol. V

Sharples, Sir Richard Christopher, 1916–1973, vol. VII

Sharples, William Johnson, 1865–1948, vol. IV

Sharpley, Forbes Wilmot, 1897–1965, vol. VI
Sharrock, Rev. John Alfred, 1853–1932, vol. III
Sharrock, Roger Ian, 1919–1990, vol. VIII
Sharrock, Rev. Canon William R., *died* 1940, vol. III
Sharwood-Smith, Sir Bryan Evers, 1899–1983, vol. VIII
Sharwood-Smith, Edward, 1865–1954, vol. V
Shastri, Shri Lal Bahadur, 1904–1966, vol. VI
Shastri, Prabhu Dutt, *born* 1885, vol. IV
Shatford, Rev. Canon Allan P., 1873–1935, vol. III
Shattock, Clement Edward, 1887–1969, vol. VI
Shattock, Rear-Adm. Ernest Henry, 1904–1985, vol. VIII
Shattock, Samuel George, 1852–1924, vol. II
Shatwell, Kenneth Owen, 1909–1988, vol. VIII
Shaughnessy, 1st Baron, 1853–1923, vol. II
Shaughnessy, 2nd Baron, 1883–1938, vol. III
Shaw, Alan Frederick, 1910–1984, vol. VIII
Shaw, Albert, 1857–1947, vol. IV
Shaw, Alexander Malcolm, 1885–1974, vol. VII
Shaw, Sir Alexander William, 1847–1923, vol. II
Shaw, (Agnes) Maude; *see* Royden, A. M.
Shaw, Anne Gillespie, (Mrs J. H. Pirie), 1904–1982, vol. VIII
Shaw, Ven. Archibald, 1879–1956, vol. V
Shaw, Sir (Archibald) Douglas MacInnes, 1895–1957, vol. V
Shaw, Sir Archibald M'Innes, 1862–1931, vol. III
Shaw, Arnold John, 1909–1984, vol. VIII
Shaw, Rev. Arthur; *see* Shaw, Rev. B. A.
Shaw, Arthur, 1880–1939, vol. III
Shaw, Arthur Frederick Bernard, *died* 1947, vol. IV
Shaw, Arthur W.; *see* Winter-Shaw.
Shaw, Benjamin, 1906–1986, vol. VIII
Shaw, Bernard; *see* Shaw, G. B.
Shaw, Rev. (Bernard) Arthur, 1914–1988, vol. VIII
Shaw, Sir Bernard Vidal, 1891–1984, vol. VIII
Shaw, Byam; *see* Shaw, J. B. L.
Shaw, Sir Charles; *see* Shaw, Sir T. F. C. E.
Shaw, Very Rev. Charles Allan, 1927–1989, vol. VIII
Shaw, Charles James Dalrymple; *see* Baron Kilbrandon.
Shaw, Rev. Sir Charles John Monson, 8th Bt (*cr* 1665), 1860–1922, vol. II
Shaw, Charles Thomas K.; *see* Knox-Shaw.
Shaw, Clarice McNab, *died* 1946, vol. IV
Shaw, Captain (E) Cyril Arthur, 1894–1946, vol. IV
Shaw, Maj.-Gen. David G. Levinge, 1860–1930, vol. III
Shaw, Sir Douglas MacInnes; *see* Shaw, Sir A. D. M.
Shaw, Sir Doyle Money, 1830–1918, vol. II
Shaw, Rt Rev. Edward Domett, 1860–1937, vol. III
Shaw, Edward Wingfield, 1895–1916, vol. II
Shaw, Sir Evelyn Campbell, 1882–1974, vol. VII
Shaw, Sir Eyre Massey, 1830–1908, vol. I
Shaw, Col Francis Stewart Kennedy, 1871–1964, vol. VI
Shaw, Frank Howard, 1913–1990, vol. VIII
Shaw, Lt-Gen. Rt Hon. Sir Frederick Charles, 1861–1942, vol. IV
Shaw, Frederick John Freshwater, 1885–1936, vol. III
Shaw, Sir Frederick William, 5th Bt (*cr* 1821), 1858–1927, vol. II

Shaw, Geoffrey Mackintosh, 1927–1978, vol. VII
Shaw, Geoffrey Reginald Devereux, 1896–1960, vol. V
Shaw, Geoffrey Turton, 1879–1943, vol. IV
Shaw, George Anthony Theodore, 1917–1990, vol. VIII
Shaw, (George) Bernard, 1856–1950, vol. IV
Shaw, George Ernest, 1877–1958, vol. V
Shaw, George Ferdinand, 1821–1899, vol. I
Shaw, George Thomas, 1863–1938, vol. III
Shaw, Sir George Watson, 1858–1931, vol. III
Shaw, Rev. George William Hudson, *died* 1944, vol. IV
Shaw, Air Cdre Gerald Stanley, 1898–1976, vol. VII
Shaw, Harold Batty, 1867–1936, vol. III
Shaw, Harold K.; *see* Knox-Shaw.
Shaw, Harry Balmforth, 1899–1976, vol. VII
Shaw, Sir Havergal D.; *see* Downes-Shaw.
Shaw, Helen Brown, *died* 1964, vol. VI
Shaw, Henry Selby H.; *see* Hele-Shaw.
Shaw, Herman, 1891–1950, vol. IV
Shaw, Irwin, 1913–1984, vol. VIII
Shaw, Sir James Dods, *died* 1916, vol. II
Shaw, James Johnston, 1845–1910, vol. I
Shaw, John Byam Lister, 1872–1919, vol. II
Shaw, John C. Middleton, 1901–1961, vol. VI
Shaw, Sir John Charles Kenward, 7th Bt (*cr* 1665), 1829–1909, vol. I
Shaw, John Dennis Bolton, 1920–1989, vol. VIII
Shaw, Sir John Houldsworth, 1874–1962, vol. VI
Shaw, Sir John James Kenward B.; *see* Best-Shaw.
Shaw, Rev. John Mackintosh, 1879–1972, vol. VII
Shaw, Sir John Valentine Wistar, 1894–1982, vol. VIII
Shaw, John Woollands, 1875–1937, vol. III
Shaw, Joseph, 1856–1933, vol. III
Shaw, Kathleen Trousdell, 1870–1958, vol. V
Shaw, Lauriston Elgie, 1859–1923, vol. II
Shaw, Hon. Leslie Mortier, 1848–1932, vol. III
Shaw, Martin Fallas, 1875–1958, vol. V
Shaw, Mary, (Mrs Robert Shaw); *see* Ure, M.
Shaw, Maurice Elgie, 1894–1977, vol. VII
Shaw, Sir Napier; *see* Shaw, Sir W. N.
Shaw, Sir Patrick, 1913–1975, vol. VII
Shaw, Major Peter Stapleton-, 1888–1953, vol. V
Shaw, Philip Egerton, 1866–1949, vol. IV
Shaw, Reeves, 1886–1952, vol. V
Shaw, Richard James Herbert, 1885–1946, vol. IV
Shaw, Richard Norman, 1831–1912, vol. I
Shaw, Robert, 1927–1978, vol. VII
Shaw, Sir Robert de Vere, 6th Bt (*cr* 1821), 1890–1969, vol. VI
Shaw, Rt Hon. Sir Sebag, 1906–1982, vol. VIII
Shaw, Sinclair, *died* 1985, vol. VIII
Shaw, Sir (Theodore Frederick) Charles (Edward), 1st Bt (*cr* 1908), 1859–1942, vol. IV
Shaw, Surg. Rear-Adm. Thomas Brown, 1879–1961, vol. VI
Shaw, Thomas Claye, 1841–1927, vol. II
Shaw, Thomas Edward, 1888–1935, vol. III
Shaw, Thomas K.; *see* Knox-Shaw.
Shaw, Thomas Richard, 1912–1989, vol. VIII
Shaw, Rt Hon. Tom, 1872–1938, vol. III
Shaw, Trevor Ian, 1928–1972, vol. VII

Shaw, Sir Walter Sidney, 1863–1937, vol. III
Shaw, Captain Walter William, 1868–1927, vol. II
Shaw, Wilfred, 1897–1953, vol. V
Shaw, William Arthur, 1865–1943, vol. IV
Shaw, William Barbour, 1868–1930, vol. III
Shaw, William Boyd Kennedy, 1901–1979, vol. VII
Shaw, Sir William Fletcher, 1878–1961, vol. VI
Shaw, Rev. William Francis, *died* 1904, vol. I
Shaw, Rev. William Frederick, 1843–1931, vol. III
Shaw, Sir (William) Napier, 1854–1945, vol. IV
Shaw, William R.; *see* Rawson-Shaw.
Shaw, William Thomas, 1879–1965, vol. VI
Shaw-Hamilton, Very Rev. Robert James, 1840–1908, vol. I
Shaw-Mackenzie, John Alexander, 1857–1933, vol. III
Shaw-Stewart, Col Basil Heron, 1877–1939, vol. III
Shaw-Stewart, Sir Euan Guy, 10th Bt, 1928–1980, vol. VII
Shaw-Stewart, Lt-Col Sir Guy; *see* Shaw-Stewart, Lt-Col Sir W. G.
Shaw-Stewart, Sir Hugh; *see* Shaw-Stewart, Sir M. H.
Shaw-Stewart, Sir (Michael) Hugh, 8th Bt, 1854–1942, vol. IV
Shaw-Stewart, Sir Michael Robert, 7th Bt, 1826–1903, vol. I
Shaw-Stewart, Lt-Col (Walter) Guy, 9th Bt, 1892–1976, vol. VII
Shaw-Stewart, Walter Richard, 1861–1934, vol. III
Shaw-Zambra, William Warren, 1898–1971, vol. VII
Shawcross, Christopher Nyholm, 1905–1973, vol. VII
Shawe, Lt-Col Charles, 1878–1951, vol. V
Shawe, Henry Benjamin, 1864–1943, vol. IV
Shawyer, Arthur Frederic, 1876–1954, vol. V
Shawyer, Robert Cort, 1913–1989, vol. VIII
Shaylor, Joseph, 1844–1923, vol. II
Shea, Lt-Col Alexander Gallwey, 1880–1935, vol. III
Shea, Hon. Sir Edward Dalton, 1820–1913, vol. I
Shea, Gen. Sir John Stuart Mackenzie, 1869–1966, vol. VI
Shea, Patrick, 1908–1986, vol. VIII
Shead, Sir Samuel George, 1871–1948, vol. IV
Sheals, John Gordon, 1923–1989, vol. VIII
Shearburn, Rt Rev. Victor George, 1900–1975, vol. VII
Sheard, Thomas Frederick Mason, 1866–1921, vol. II
Shearer, Sir Bruce, 1888–1971, vol. VII
Shearer, Cresswell, 1874–1941, vol. IV
Shearer, E., *died* 1945, vol. IV
Shearer, Brig. Eric James, 1892–1980, vol. VII
Shearer, Sir James Greig, 1893–1966, vol. VI
Shearer, Sir John, 1843–1908, vol. I
Shearer, John Burt, 1904–1962, vol. VI
Shearer, Col Johnston, 1852–1917, vol. II
Shearer, Lt-Col Magnus, 1890–1961, vol. VI
Shearer, Rev. W(illiam) Russell, 1898–1987, vol. VIII
Shearing, Joseph; *see* Long, M. G.
Shearman, Arthur T., 1866–1937, vol. III
Shearman, Brig. Charles Edward Gowran, 1889–1968, vol. VI
Shearman, Sir Harold Charles, 1896–1984, vol. VIII
Shearman, Rt Hon. Sir Montague, 1857–1930, vol. III

Shearme, Edward, *died* 1920, vol. II
Shearme, Paymaster-Captain Edward Haweis, 1876–1925, vol. II
Shearme, Rev. John, 1842–1925, vol. II
Shears, Frederick Sidney, 1892–1932, vol. III
Shears, Maj.-Gen. Philip James, 1887–1972, vol. VII
Sheat, Sir Oliver; *see* Sheat, Sir W. J. O.
Sheat, Sir (William James) Oliver, 1864–1944, vol. IV
Shebbeare, Rev. Charles John, 1865–1945, vol. IV
Shebbeare, Edward Oswald, 1884–1964, vol. VI
Shedden, Sir Frederick Geoffrey, 1893–1971, vol. VII
Shedden, Sir George, 1856–1937, vol. III
Shedden, Sir Lewis, 1870–1941, vol. IV
Shedden, Rt Rev. Roscow George, 1882–1956, vol. V
Shedlock, John South, 1843–1919, vol. II
Shee, Sir George Richard Francis, 1869–1939, vol. III
Shee, Henry Gordon, 1847–1909, vol. I
Shee, Lt-Col Sir Martin A.; *see* Archer-Shee.
Sheean, (James) Vincent, 1899–1975, vol. VII
Sheean, Vincent; *see* Sheean, J. V.
Sheehan, Harold Leeming, 1900–1988, vol. VIII
Sheehan, Sir Henry John, 1883–1941, vol. IV
Sheehan, Most Rev. Michael, 1870–1945, vol. IV
Sheehan, Rev. Patrick Augustine, 1852–1913, vol. I
Sheehan, Most Rev. Richard Alphonsus, 1845–1915, vol. I
Sheehy, Sir Christopher, 1894–1960, vol. V
Sheehy, Sir John Francis, 1889–1949, vol. IV
Sheehy, Sir Joseph Aloysius, 1900–1971, vol. VII
Sheen, Alfred William, 1869–1945, vol. IV
Sheen, Engr-Rear-Adm. Charles C., 1871–1952, vol. V
Sheen, Most Rev. Fulton John, 1895–1979, vol. VII
Sheen, Air Vice-Marshal Walter Charles, 1907–1969, vol. VI (AII)
Sheepshanks, Rt Rev. John, 1834–1912, vol. I
Sheepshanks, Sir Thomas Herbert, 1895–1964, vol. VI
Sheepshanks, William, 1851–1928, vol. II
Sheffield, 3rd Earl of, 1832–1909, vol. I
Sheffield, 4th Baron, **and Stanley of Alderley**, 4th Baron, 1839–1925, vol. II
Sheffield, 6th Baron, **and Stanley of Alderley**, 6th Baron, 1907–1971, vol. VII
Sheffield, 7th Baron, **and Stanley of Alderley**, 7th Baron, 1915–1971, vol. VII
Sheffield, Sir Berkeley Digby George, 6th Bt, 1876–1946, vol. IV
Sheffield, Edmund Charles Reginald, 1908–1977, vol. VII
Sheffield, Maj.-Gen. John, 1910–1987, vol. VIII
Sheffield, Sir Robert Arthur, 7th Bt, 1905–1977, vol. VII
Sheffield, Robert Stoney O.; *see* Oliphant-Sheffield.
Shehyn, Hon. Joseph, 1829–1918, vol. II
Sheil, Charles Leo, 1897–1968, vol. VI
Sheil, James, 1829–1908, vol. I
Sheil, John Devonshire, 1855–1935, vol. III
Sheild, Arthur Marmaduke, 1858–1922, vol. II
Sheilds, Francis Ernest W.; *see* Wentworth-Sheilds.
Sheilds, Rt Rev. Wentworth Francis W.; *see* Wentworth-Sheilds.
Sheils, George Kinglsey, 1894–1953, vol. V

Shekleton, Brig.-Gen. Hugh Pentland, 1860–1938, vol. III

Sheldon, Charles Monroe, 1857–1946, vol. IV

Sheldon, Christine Mary, *died* 1970, vol. VI

Sheldon, John Prince, *died* 1913, vol. I

Sheldon, Sir Mark, 1871–1956, vol. V

Sheldon, Norman Lindsay, 1876–1946, vol. IV

Sheldon, Sir Wilfrid Percy Henry, 1901–1983, vol. VIII

Shelford, Frederic, 1871–1943, vol. IV

Shelford, Rev. Leonard Edmund, 1836–1914, vol. I

Shell, Rita, *died* 1950, vol. IV

Shelley, Col Bertram Arthur Graham, 1869–1947, vol. IV

Shelley, Sir Charles, 5th Bt (*cr* 1806), 1838–1902, vol. I

Shelley, Herbert John, 1895–1975, vol. VII

Shelley, Sir James, 1884–1961, vol. VI

Shelley, Sir John, 9th Bt (*cr* 1611), 1848–1931, vol. III

Shelley, Sir John Frederick, 10th Bt (*cr* 1611), 1884–1976, vol. VII

Shelley, Kew Edwin, 1894–1964, vol. VI

Shelley, Malcolm Bond, 1879–1968, vol. VI

Shelley, Sir Percy Bysshe, 7th Bt (*cr* 1806), 1872–1953, vol. V

Shelley, Sir Sidney Patrick, 8th Bt (*cr* 1806), 1880–1965, vol. VI

Shelley-Rolls, Captain Sir John Courtown Edward, 6th Bt (*cr* 1806), 1871–1951, vol. V

Shellshear, Joseph Lexden, 1885–1958, vol. V

Shelmerdine, Lt-Col Sir Francis Claude, 1881–1945, vol. IV

Shennan, Sir Alfred Ernest, 1887–1959, vol. V

Shennan, Hay, 1859–1937, vol. III

Shennan, Theodore, *died* 1948, vol. IV

Shenstone, Allen Goodrich, 1893–1980, vol. VII

Shenstone, William Ashwell, 1850–1908, vol. I

Shentall, Sir Ernest, 1861–1936, vol. III

Shenton, Edward Warren Hine, 1872–1955, vol. V

Shenton, Hon. Sir George, 1842–1909, vol. I

Shenton, Sir William Edward Leonard, 1885–1967, vol. VI

Shepard, Ernest Howard, 1879–1976, vol. VII

Shepard, Helen Gould, 1868–1938, vol. III (A), vol. IV

Shepardson, Whitney Hart, 1890–1966, vol. VI

Shephard, Cecil Yaxley, 1900–1959, vol. V

Shephard, Lt-Col Charles Sinclair, 1848–1930, vol. III

Shephard, Firth, 1891–1949, vol. IV

Shephard, Sir Horatio Hale, *died* 1921, vol. II

Shephard, Rev. John, 1837–1926, vol. II

Shephard, Sidney, 1894–1953, vol. V

Shepheard, Rex Beaumont, 1902–1980, vol. VII

Shepheard, Sir Victor George, 1893–1989, vol. VIII

Shepherd, 1st Baron, 1881–1954, vol. V

Shepherd, Rev. Ambrose, 1854–1915, vol. I

Shepherd, Arthur, 1884–1951, vol. V

Shepherd, Arthur Edmond, 1867–1942, vol. IV

Shepherd, Ven. Arthur Pearce, 1885–1968, vol. VI

Shepherd, Col Charles Herbert, 1846–1920, vol. II

Shepherd, Lt-Col Claude Innes, 1884–1960, vol. V

Shepherd, Sir (Edward Henry) Gerald, 1886–1967, vol. VI

Shepherd, E(dwin) Colston, 1891–1976, vol. VII

Shepherd, Eric Andres, *died* 1937, vol. III

Shepherd, F. H. S., *died* 1948, vol. IV

Shepherd, Francis John, 1851–1929, vol. III

Shepherd, Sir Francis Michie, 1893–1962, vol. VI

Shepherd, Sir Gerald; *see* Shepherd, Sir E. H. G.

Shepherd, Gilbert David, 1880–1958, vol. V

Shepherd, Brig. Gilbert John Victor, 1887–1969, vol. VI

Shepherd, Harold Richard Bowman A.; *see* Adie-Shepherd.

Shepherd, Sir (Harry) Percy, *died* 1946, vol. IV

Shepherd, Henry Bryan, 1917–1974, vol. VII

Shepherd, Very Rev. Henry Young, *died* 1947, vol. IV

Shepherd, James Affleck, 1867–1946, vol. IV

Shepherd, Joseph Wilfrid, 1885–1975, vol. VII

Shepherd, Dame Margaret Alice, 1910–1990, vol. VIII

Shepherd, Air Vice-Marshal Melvin Clifford Seymour, 1922–1989, vol. VIII

Shepherd, Sir Percy; *see* Shepherd, Sir H. P.

Shepherd, Very Rev. Robert Henry Wishart, 1888–1971, vol. VII

Shepherd, Sir Walker; *see* Shpherd, Sir William W. F.

Shepherd, William Kidd Ogilvy, 1888–1941, vol. IV

Shepherd, William Morgan, 1905–1987, vol. VIII

Shepherd, Rev. William Mutrie, 1832–1910, vol. I

Shepherd, Sir (William) Walker (Frederick), 1895–1959, vol. V

Shepherd-Barron, Wilfrid Philip, 1888–1979, vol. VII

Shepherd-Cross, Herbert, 1847–1916, vol. II

Shepherd-Folker, Horace, 1859–1938, vol. III

Sheppard, Alfred Tresidder, 1871–1947, vol. IV

Sheppard, Adm. Sir Dawson; *see* Sheppard, Adm. Sir T. D. L.

Sheppard, Rev. Canon Edgar, 1845–1921, vol. II

Sheppard, Col George Sidney, 1867–1936, vol. III

Sheppard, Brig.-Gen. Herbert Cecil, *died* 1953, vol. V

Sheppard, Very Rev. Hugh Richard Lawrie, 1880–1937, vol. III

Sheppard, Sir John Tresidder, 1881–1968, vol. VI

Sheppard, Leslie Alfred, 1890–1985, vol. VIII

Sheppard, Oliver, *died* 1941, vol. IV

Sheppard, Percival Albert, (Peter), 1907–1977, vol. VII

Sheppard, Peter; *see* Sheppard, Percival A.

Sheppard, Philip Macdonald, 1921–1976, vol. VII

Sheppard, Sir Richard Herbert, 1910–1982, vol. VIII

Sheppard, Major Samuel Gurney, 1865–1915, vol. I

Sheppard, Samuel Townsend, 1880–1951, vol. V

Sheppard, Maj.-Gen. Seymour Hulbert, 1869–1957, vol. V

Sheppard, Thomas, 1876–1945, vol. IV

Sheppard, Adm. Sir (Thomas) Dawson Lees, 1866–1953, vol. V

Sheppard, Vivian Lee Osborne, 1877–1963, vol. VI

Sheppard, Sir William Didsbury, 1865–1933, vol. III

Sheppard, William Vincent, 1909–1985, vol. VIII

Sheppard Fidler, Alwyn Gwilym, 1909–1990, vol. VIII

Shepperson, Claude Allin, 1867–1921, vol. II

Shepperson, Sir Ernest Whittome, 1st Bt, 1874–1949, vol. IV

Shepstone, Arthur Jesse, 1852–1912, vol. I

Shepstone, John Wesley, 1827–1916, vol. II
Shepstone, Theophilus, 1843–1907, vol. I
Shera, Arthur Geoffrey, 1889–1971, vol. VII
Shera, Frank Henry, 1882–1956, vol. V
Sherard, 10th Baron, 1849–1902, vol. I
Sherard, 11th Baron, 1851–1924, vol. II
Sherard, 12th Baron, 1858–1931, vol. III
Sherard, Col Ralph Woodchurch, 1860–1922, vol. II
Sherard, Robert Harborough, 1861–1943, vol. IV
Sheraton, Rev. James Paterson, 1841–1906, vol. I
Sherborne, 4th Baron, 1831–1919, vol. II
Sherborne, 5th Baron, 1840–1920, vol. II
Sherborne, 6th Baron, 1873–1949, vol. IV
Sherborne, 7th Baron, 1911–1982, vol. VIII
Sherborne, 8th Baron, 1898–1985, vol. VIII
Sherbrooke, Captain Henry Graham, 1877–1940, vol. III
Sherbrooke, Rev. Henry Nevile, 1846–1916, vol. II
Sherbrooke, Col Nevile Hugh Cairns, 1880–1944, vol. IV
Sherbrooke, Rear-Adm. Robert St Vincent, 1901–1972, vol. VII
Sherbrooke-Walker, Col Ronald Draycott, 1897–1984, vol. VIII
Sherburn, Sir John, 1851–1926, vol. II
Shercliff, John Arthur, 1927–1983, vol. VIII
Sherek, Major Henry, 1900–1967, vol. VI
Sherer, Brig.-Gen. James Donnelly, 1870–1959, vol. V
Sherer, John Walter, 1823–1911, vol. I
Sheridan, Algernon Thomas Brinsley, 1845–1931, vol. III
Sheridan, Charles Cahill, died 1941, vol. IV
Sheridan, Clare Consuelo, died 1970, vol. VI
Sheridan, Sir Dermot Joseph, 1914–1978, vol. VII
Sheridan, Edward, died 1949, vol. IV
Sheridan, Rear-Adm. Henry A., 1884–1959, vol. V
Sheridan, Sir Joseph, 1882–1964, vol. VI
Sheridan, Sir Philip Cahill, 1871–1949, vol. IV
Sheriff, Rev. Thomas Holmes, died 1923, vol. II
Sheringham, George, 1884–1937, vol. III
Sheringham, Rev. Harry Alsager, 1852–1907, vol. I
Sheringham, Hugh Tempest, 1876–1930, vol. III
Sheringham, Ven. John William, died 1904, vol. I
Sherlock, Sir Alfred Parker, 1876–1946, vol. IV
Sherlock, Col David John Christopher Eustace, 1879–1938, vol. III
Sherlock, David Thomas Joseph, 1881–1964, vol. VI
Sherlock, Frederick, 1853–1914, vol. I
Sherlock, Ven. William, died 1919, vol. II
Sherman, Gina, (Mrs Alec Sherman); see Bachauer, G.
Sherman, John, 1823–1900, vol. I
Sherman, Most Rev. Louis Ralph, 1886–1953, vol. V
Sherrard, Col James William, died 1926, vol. II
Sherren, James, died 1945, vol. IV
Sherriff, Lt-Gen. John Pringle, 1831–1911, vol. I
Sherriff, Robert Cedric, 1896–1975, vol. VII
Sherrill, Brig.-Gen. Charles H., 1867–1936, vol. III
Sherrill, Rt Rev. Henry Knox, 1890–1980, vol. VII
Sherrington, Sir Charles Scott, 1857–1952, vol. V
Sherston, Brig. John Reginald Vivian, 1888–1975, vol. VII
Sherston, Col William Maxwell, 1859–1925, vol. II

Sherston-Baker, Lt-Col Sir Dodington George Richard, 5th Bt, 1877–1944, vol. IV
Sherston-Baker, Sir Humphrey Dodington Benedict, 6th Bt, 1907–1990, vol. VIII
Sherwell, Arthur, 1863–1942, vol. IV
Sherwen, Ven. William, died 1915, vol. I
Sherwill, Sir Ambrose James, 1890–1968, vol. VI
Sherwin, Amy, died 1935, vol. III
Sherwin, Charles Edgar, 1909–1981, vol. VIII
Sherwin, Frederick George James, 1909–1984, vol. VIII
Sherwood, 1st Baron, 1898–1970, vol. VI
Sherwood, Col Sir Arthur Percy, 1854–1940, vol. III
Sherwood, Rev. Edward Charles, died 1947, vol. IV
Sherwood, Frederic William, 1864–1931, vol. III
Sherwood, George Henry, 1877–1935, vol. III
Sherwood, Harry Leslie, 1863–1946, vol. IV
Sherwood, Leslie Robert, 1889–1974, vol. VII
Sherwood, Robert Emmet, 1896–1955, vol. V
Sherwood, Will, 1871–1955, vol. V
Sherwood, William Albert, 1855–1919, vol. II
Sherwood, Rev. William Edward, 1851–1927, vol. II
Sherwood-Kelly, Lt-Col John; see Kelly.
Sheshadri Iyar, K., Sir, died 1901, vol. I
Shevill, Rt Rev. Ian Wotton Allnutt, 1917–1988, vol. VIII
Shewan, Henry Alexander, 1906–1990, vol. VIII
Shewell, Brig. Eden Francis, 1877–1964, vol. VI
Shewell-Cooper, Wilfred Edward, 1900–1982, vol. VIII
Shiel, Rt Rev. Joseph, 1873–1931, vol. III
Shiel, Matthew Phipps, 1865–1947, vol. IV
Shield, George William, 1876–1935, vol. III
Shield, Hugh, 1831–1903, vol. I
Shields, Sir Douglas Andrew, 1878–1952, vol. V
Shields, Frederick James, 1833–1911, vol. I
Shields, Harry G., 1859–1935, vol. III
Shields, John Veysie Montgomery, 1914–1966, vol. VI
Shields, Ronald McGregor Pollock, 1921–1987, vol. VIII
Shields, Hon. Tasman, 1872–1950, vol. IV
Shiels, Sir Drummond; see Shiels, Sir T. D.
Shiels, Sir (Thomas) Drummond, 1881–1953, vol. V
Shiffner, Rev. Sir George Croxton, 4th Bt, 1819–1906, vol. I
Shiffner, Major Sir Henry Burrows, 7th Bt, 1902–1941, vol. IV
Shiffner, Sir John, 5th Bt, 1857–1914, vol. I
Shiffner, Sir John Bridger, 6th Bt, 1899–1918, vol. II
Shigemitsu, Mamoru, 1887–1957, vol. V
Shillaker, James Frederick, 1870–1943, vol. IV
Shillidy, George Alexander, 1886–1968, vol. VI
Shillidy, John Armstrong, 1882–1952, vol. V
Shillington, Courtenay Alexander Rives, 1902–1983, vol. VIII
Shillington, Major Rt Hon. David Graham, 1872–1944, vol. IV
Shillito, Rev. Edward, 1872–1948, vol. IV
Shimeld, Kenneth Reeve, 1921–1984, vol. VIII
Shine, Eustace Beverley, 1873–1952, vol. V
Shine, Col James Mathew Forrest, 1861–1931, vol. III
Shine, Most Rev. Thomas, 1872–1955, vol. V

Shiner, Lt-Col Sir Herbert, 1890–1962, vol. VI
Shiner, Ronald Alfred, 1903–1966, vol. VI
Shingleton, Frederick, 1846–1938, vol. III
Shinkwin, Col Ion Richard Staveley, 1875–1961, vol. VI
Shinn, Frederick George, 1867–1950, vol. IV
Shinnie, Andrew James, 1886–1963, vol. VI
Shinwell, Baron (Life Peer); Emanuel Shinwell, 1884–1986, vol. VIII
Shipley, Sir Arthur Everett, 1861–1927, vol. II
Shipley, Brig.-Gen. Charles Orby, 1867–1934, vol. III
Shipley, Col Charles Tyrell, 1863–1933, vol. III
Shipley, Hammond Smith, 1858–1930, vol. III
Shipley, Orby, 1832–1916, vol. II
Shipley, Lt-Col Reginald Burge, died 1924, vol. II
Shipley, Sir William Alexander, died 1922, vol. II
Shipman, Louis Evan, 1869–1933, vol. III
Shippard, Sir Sidney Godolphin Alexander, 1837–1902, vol. I
Shipstone, Sir Thomas, 1851–1940, vol. III
Shipton, Eric Earle, 1907–1977, vol. VII
Shipway, Sir Francis Edward, 1875–1968, vol. VI
Shipwright, Sqdn Leader Denis E. B. K., 1898–1984, vol. VIII
Shipwright, Lottie Adelina de Lara; see de Lara, Adelina.
Shircore, John Owen, 1882–1953, vol. V
Shires, Sir Frank, 1899–1981, vol. VIII
Shirlaw, John Fenton, 1896–1975, vol. VII
Shirlaw, Matthew, 1873–1961, vol. VI
Shirley; see Skelton, Sir John.
Shirley, Evelyn Philip Sewallis, 1900–1978, vol. VII
Shirley, Rev. (Frederick) John, 1890–1967, vol. VI
Shirley, Herbert John, 1868–1943, vol. IV
Shirley, Rev. John; see Shirley, Rev. F. J.
Shirley, Hon. Ralph, 1865–1946, vol. IV
Shirley, Sewallis Evelyn, 1844–1904, vol. I
Shirley, Air Vice-Marshal Sir Thomas Ulric Curzon, 1908–1982, vol. VIII
Shirley, William, 1866–1930, vol. III
Shirley-Fox, John Shirley, died 1939, vol. III
Shirley-Smith, Sir Hubert, 1901–1981, vol. VIII
Shirras, George Findlay, 1885–1955, vol. V
Shirres, Major John Chivas, 1854–1899, vol. I
Shirtcliffe, Sir George, 1862–1941, vol. IV
Shoaib, Mohammad, 1905–1976, vol. VII
Shockley, Dr William Bradford, 1910–1989, vol. VIII
Shoenberg, Sir Isaac, 1880–1963, vol. VI
Shoesmith, Kenneth Denton, 1890–1939, vol. III
Sholl, Richard Adolphus, 1846–1919, vol. II
Sholokhov, Mikhail Aleksandrovich, 1905–1984, vol. VIII
Shone, Rt Rev. Samuel, 1820–1897, vol. I
Shone, Sir Terence Allen, 1894–1965, vol. VI
Shone, Lt-Gen. Sir William Terence, 1850–1938, vol. III
Shonfield, Sir Andrew Akiba, 1917–1981, vol. VIII
Shoobert, Sir Harold; see Shoobert, Sir W. H.
Shoobert, Sir (Wilfred) Harold, 1896–1969, vol. VI
Shoobridge, Hon. Sir Rupert Oakley, 1883–1962, vol. VI
Shoolbred, Frederick Thomas, 1841–1922, vol. II
Shoolbred, Lt-Col Rupert, 1869–1946, vol. IV

Shoosmith, Maj.-Gen. Stephen Newton, 1900–1956, vol. V
Shoosmith, Thurston Laidlaw, 1865–1933, vol. III
Shore, Bernard Alexander Royle, 1896–1985, vol. VIII
Shore, Lewis Erle, 1863–1944, vol. IV
Shore, Brig.-Gen. Offley Bohun Stovin Fairless, 1863–1922, vol. II
Shore, Robert S., died 1931, vol. III
Shore, Rev. Thomas Teignmouth, 1841–1911, vol. I
Shore, Thomas William, 1861–1947, vol. IV
Shore, W. Teignmouth, died 1932, vol. III
Shores, John Wallis, 1851–1935, vol. III
Shorrock, James Godby, 1910–1987, vol. VIII
Shorrock, William Gordon, 1879–1944, vol. IV
Short, Adrian Hugh H.; see Hassard-Short.
Short, Alfred, 1882–1938, vol. III
Short, Brig.-Gen. Anthony Holbeche, 1862–1940, vol. III
Shortt, Maj.-Gen. Arthur Charles, 1899–1984, vol. VIII
Short, Arthur Rendle, died 1953, vol. V
Short, Ernest Henry, 1875–1959, vol. V
Short, Lt-Col Ernest William George, 1877–1953, vol. V
Short, Sir Frank, 1857–1945, vol. IV
Short, Rev. Frank, 1895–1975, vol. VII
Short, Rev. Canon Frederick Winning H.; see Hassard-Short.
Short, Rev. Harry Lismer, 1906–1975, vol. VII
Short, Herbert Arthur, 1895–1967, vol. VI
Short, John, 1894–1967, vol. VI
Short, John Tregerthen, 1858–1933, vol. III
Short, Richard, 1841–1916, vol. II
Short, Thomas Sydney, died 1924, vol. II
Short, Vivian Augustus, 1883–1950, vol. IV
Short, Wilfrid Maurice, 1870–1947, vol. IV
Short, William, 1866–1929, vol. III
Short, Lt-Col William Ambrose, died 1917, vol. II
Shortall, Sir Patrick, 1872–1925, vol. II
Shorter, Clement King, 1857–1926, vol. II
Shorter, Dora, died 1918, vol. II
Shorthouse, Joseph Henry, 1834–1903, vol. I
Shortland, Adm. Edward George, 1855–1929, vol. III
Shortland, Captain Henry Vincent, died 1913, vol. I
Shorto, William Alfred Thomas, 1876–1951, vol. V
Shortt, Adam, 1859–1931, vol. III
Shortt, Rt Hon. Edward, 1862–1935, vol. III
Shortt, Col Henry Edward, 1887–1987, vol. VIII
Shortt, John, died 1932, vol. III
Shostakovich, Dmitry Dmitrievich, 1906–1975, vol. VII
Shott, Henry Hammond, 1877–1914, vol. I
Shotton, Frederick William, 1906–1990, vol. VIII
Shotwell, James Thomson, 1874–1965, vol. VI
Shoubridge, Harry Oliver Baron, 1872–1934, vol. III
Shoubridge, Maj.-Gen. Herbert; see Shoubridge, Maj.-Gen. T. H.
Shoubridge, Maj.-Gen. (Thomas) Herbert, 1871–1923, vol. II
Shove, Gerald Frank, 1887–1947, vol. IV
Shove, Captain Herbert William, 1886–1943, vol. IV
Shove, Ralph Samuel, 1889–1966, vol. VI
Shovelton, Sydney Taverner, 1881–1967, vol. VI

Showa, Emperor; *see* Hirohito, Emperor of Japan.
Showering, Sir Keith Stanley, 1930–1982, vol. VIII
Showers, Lt-Col Herbert Lionel, 1861–1916, vol. II
Shrapnell-Smith, Edward Shrapnell, 1875–1952, vol. V
Shreeve, George Harry, 1888–1960, vol. V
Shrewsbury and Waterford, 20th Earl of, 1860–1921, vol. II
Shrewsbury and Waterford, 21st Earl of, 1914–1980, vol. VII
Shrewsbury, J. F. D., 1898–1971, vol. VII
Shrimsley, Anthony, 1934–1984, vol. VIII
Shrubsall, Frank Charles, *died* 1935, vol. III
Shrubsole, Rear-Adm. Percy Joseph, 1875–1958, vol. V
Shuard, Amy, (Mrs Peter Asher), 1924–1975, vol. VII
Shuckburgh, Sir Charles Gerald Stewkley, 12th Bt, 1911–1988, vol. VIII
Shuckburgh, Evelyn Shirley, 1843–1906, vol. I
Shuckburgh, Sir Gerald Francis Stewkley, 11th Bt, 1882–1939, vol. III
Shuckburgh, Sir John Evelyn, 1877–1953, vol. V
Shuckburgh, Robert Shirley, 1882–1954, vol. V
Shuckburgh, Sir Stewkley Frederick Draycott, 10th Bt, 1880–1917, vol. II
Shufeldt, Major Robert Wilson, 1850–1934, vol. III
Shufflebotham, Frank, *died* 1932, vol. III
Shuffrey, Paul, 1889–1955, vol. V
Shuffrey, Rev. William Arthur, 1851–1932, vol. III
Shuldham-Legh, Col Harry Shuldham, 1854–1915, vol. I
Shurmer, Percy Lionel Edward, *died* 1959, vol. V
Shute, Gen. Sir Cameron Deane, 1866–1936, vol. III
Shute, Gen. Sir Charles Cameron, 1816–1904, vol. I
Shute, Lt-Col Cyril Aveling, 1886–1950, vol. IV
Shute, Geoffrey Gay, 1892–1951, vol. V
Shute, Col Henry Gwynn Deane, 1860–1909, vol. I
Shute, Col Sir John Joseph, *died* 1948, vol. IV
Shute, Nevil; *see* Norway, N. S.
Shuter, Comdr Joseph Armand, 1876–1915, vol. I
Shuter, Brig.-Gen. Reginald Gauntlett, 1875–1957, vol. V
Shutt, Frank Thomas, 1859–1940, vol. III
Shuttleworth, 1st Baron, 1844–1939, vol. III
Shuttleworth, 2nd Baron, 1913–1940, vol. III
Shuttleworth, 3rd Baron, 1917–1942, vol. IV
Shuttleworth, 4th Baron, 1917–1975, vol. VII
Shuttleworth, Alfred, 1843–1925, vol. II
Shuttleworth, Brig. Betham Wilkins, 1880–1937, vol. III
Shuttleworth, Maj.-Gen. Sir Digby Inglis, 1876–1948, vol. IV
Shuttleworth, Edward Cheke Smalley, 1866–1943, vol. IV
Shuttleworth, Edward James K.; *see* Kay-Shuttleworth.
Shuttleworth, Col Frank, 1845–1913, vol. I
Shuttleworth, George Edward, 1842–1928, vol. II
Shuttleworth, Rev. Henry Cary, 1850–1900, vol. I
Shuttleworth, Hon. Lawrence Ughtred K.; *see* Kay-Shuttleworth.
Shvernik, Nikolai Mikhailovich, 1888–1970, vol. VI
Siam, HM King of, Rama VI, 1881–1925, vol. II
Sibbald, Sir John, 1833–1905, vol. I

Sibbald, Rev. Samuel James Ramsay, 1869–1950, vol. IV
Sibbett, Cecil James, *died* 1967, vol. VI
Sibelius, Jean Julius Christian, 1865–1957, vol. V
Sibley, Walter Knowsley, 1862–1944, vol. IV
Sibly, Sir Franklin; *see* Sibly, Sir T. F.
Sibly, Sir (Thomas) Franklin, 1883–1948, vol. IV
Sibly, William Arthur, 1883–1959, vol. V
Siborne, Maj.-Gen. Herbert Taylor, 1826–1902, vol. I
Sibree, Rev. James, 1836–1929, vol. III
Sibthorpe, Surg.-Gen. Charles, 1847–1906, vol. I
Sichel, Alan William Stuart, 1886–1966, vol. VI
Sichel, Edith, 1862–1914, vol. I
Sichel, Walter, 1855–1933, vol. III
Sickert, Walter Richard, 1860–1942, vol. IV
Sicot, Marcel Jean, 1898–1981, vol. VIII
Sidaner, Henri Le, 1862–1939, vol. III
Siddall, Joseph Bower, 1840–1925, vol. II
Siddeley, John Tennant Davenport, (3rd Baron Kenilworth), 1924–1981, vol. VIII
Sidebotham, Herbert, 1872–1940, vol. III
Sidebotham, John Biddulph, 1891–1988, vol. VIII
Sidebotham, Joseph Watson, 1857–1925, vol. II
Sidebottam, Tom Harrop, *died* 1908, vol. I
Sidebottom, William, *died* 1933, vol. III
Sidey, John MacNaughton, 1914–1990, vol. VIII
Sidey, Sir Thomas Kay, 1863–1933, vol. III
Sidgreaves, Sir Arthur Frederick, 1882–1948, vol. IV
Sidgreaves, Rev. Walter, 1837–1919, vol. II
Sidgwick, Alfred, 1850–1943, vol. IV
Sidgwick, Arthur, *died* 1920, vol. II
Sidgwick, Cecily, *died* 1934, vol. III
Sidgwick, Eleanor Mildred, 1845–1936, vol. III
Sidgwick, Ethel, 1877–1970, vol. VI
Sidgwick, Henry, 1838–1900, vol. I
Sidgwick, Mrs Henry; *see* Sidgwick, Eleanor Mildred.
Sidgwick, Rear-Adm. John Benson, 1891–1983, vol. VIII
Sidgwick, Nevil Vincent, 1873–1952, vol. V
Sidmouth, 3rd Viscount, 1824–1913, vol. I
Sidmouth, 4th Viscount, 1854–1915, vol. I
Sidmouth, 5th Viscount, 1882–1953, vol. V
Sidmouth, 6th Viscount, 1887–1976, vol. VII
Sidney, Herbert, *died* 1923, vol. II
Sidney, Thomas Stafford, 1863–1917, vol. II
Sidney-Humphries, Sydney, 1862–1941, vol. IV
Sidney-Wilmot, Air Vice-Marshal Aubrey, 1915–1989, vol. VIII
Sidwell, Rt Rev. Henry Bindley, 1857–1936, vol. III
Sieff, Baron (Life Peer); Israel Moses Sieff, 1889–1972, vol. VII
Sieff, Joseph Edward, 1905–1982, vol. VIII
Sieff, Hon. Michael David, 1911–1987, vol. VIII
Siegbahn, (Karl) Manne (Georg), 1886–1978, vol. VII
Siegbahn, Manne; *see* Siegbahn, K. M. G.
Siegfried, André, 1875–1959, vol. V
Sieghart, Paul Henry Laurence Alexander, 1927–1988, vol. VIII
Siemens, Alexander, 1847–1928, vol. II
Sienkiewicz, Henryk, 1846–1916, vol. II
Siepmann, Charles Arthur, 1899–1985, vol. VIII
Siepmann, Harry Arthur, 1889–1963, vol. VI
Sieveking, Albert Forbes, 1857–1951, vol. V

Sieveking, Sir Edward Henry, 1816–1904, vol. I
Sieveking, Captain Lancelot de Giberne, 1896–1972, vol. VII
Sievier, Robert Standish, 1860–1939, vol. III
Sievwright, Andrew George Hume, 1885–1956, vol. V
Sievwright, J. D., 1863–1947, vol. IV
Sifton, Rt Hon. Arthur Lewis, 1858–1921, vol. II
Sifton, Hon. Sir Clifford, 1861–1929, vol. III
Sifton, Sir James David, 1878–1952, vol. V
Sifton, John William, 1925–1969, vol. VI
Sifton, Victor, 1897–1961, vol. VI
Sigerson, George, died 1925, vol. II
Siggers, Ven. William C.; see Curzon-Siggers.
Signoret, Simone, (Simone Henriette Charlotte Montand), 1921–1985, vol. VIII
Sigrist, Frederick, 1884–1956, vol. V
Sigsbee, Rear-Adm. Charles Dwight, 1845–1923, vol. II
Sigurdsson, Asgeir Thorsteinn, 1864–1935, vol. III
Sikes, Alfred Walter, 1869–1948, vol. IV
Sikes, Edward Ernest, 1867–1940, vol. III
Sikes, Francis Henry, 1862–1943, vol. IV
Sikes, Howard Lecky, 1881–1943, vol. IV
Sikkim, Maharaja Kumar Sidkeong Tulku of, 1879–1914, vol. I
Sikkim, Maharaja Sidkeong Tulku of, died 1914, vol. I
Sikkim, Maharaja of, 1893–1963, vol. VI
Sikorski, Gen. Wladyslaw Eugeniusz, 1881–1943, vol. IV
Sikorsky, Igor Ivan, 1889–1972, vol. VII
Silberrad, Oswald John, 1878–1960, vol. V
Silberrad, Una L., 1872–1955, vol. V
Silburn, Col Percy Arthur Baxter, 1876–1929, vol. III
Silcock, Arnold, 1889–1953, vol. V
Silcock, Arthur Quarry, 1855–1904, vol. I
Silcock, Henry Thomas, 1882–1969, vol. VI
Silcock, Thomas Ball, 1854–1924, vol. III
Silcox, Albert Henry, 1895–1971, vol. VII
Silk, Paymaster Rear-Adm. Ernest Edwin, 1862–1940, vol. III
Silk, John Frederick William, 1858–1943, vol. IV
Silkin, 1st Baron, 1889–1972, vol. VII
Silkin of Dulwich, Baron (Life Peer); Samuel Charles Silkin, 1918–1988, vol. VIII
Silkin, Rt Hon. John Ernest, 1923–1987, vol. VIII
Sillem, Maj.-Gen. Sir Arnold Frederick, 1865–1949, vol. IV
Sillery, Anthony, 1903–1976, vol. VII
Sillince, William Augustus, 1906–1974, vol. VII
Sillitoe, Sir Percy Joseph, 1888–1962, vol. VI
Sills, George, 1832–1905, vol. I
Silone, Ignazio, 1900–1978, vol. VII
Siloti, Alexander, 1863–1945, vol. IV
Silsoe, 1st Baron, 1894–1976, vol. VII
Silver, Albert Harlow, 1875–1954, vol. V
Silver, Alfred Jethro, 1870–1935, vol. III
Silver, Gertrude; see Kingston, G.
Silver, Lt-Col John Payzant, 1868–1957, vol. V
Silver, Vice-Adm. Mortimer L'E., 1869–1946, vol. IV
Silverman, Herbert Albert, 1896–1980, vol. VII (AII)
Silverman, (Samuel) Sydney, 1895–1968, vol. VI
Silverman, Sydney; see Silverman, S. S.
Silverstone, Arnold; see Baron Ashdown.

Silvester, Air Cdre James, 1898–1956, vol. V
Silvester, Norman Langton, 1894–1969, vol. VI (AII)
Silvester, Victor Marlborough, 1900–1978, vol. VII
Silvestri, Constantin, 1913–1969, vol. VI
Silyn Roberts, Air Vice-Marshal Glynn, 1906–1983, vol. VIII
Sim, Alastair, 1900–1976, vol. VII
Sim, Sir Alexander; see Sim, Sir G. A. S.
Sim, David, 1899–1987, vol. VIII
Sim, Sir (George) Alexander (Strachan), 1905–1980, vol. VIII
Sim, Brig. George Edward Herman, 1886–1952, vol. V
Sim, George Gall, 1878–1930, vol. III
Sim, Col George Hamilton, 1852–1929, vol. III
Sim, Henry Alexander, 1856–1928, vol. II
Sim, James Duncan Stuart, 1849–1912, vol. I
Sim, Sir Wilfrid Joseph, 1890–1974, vol. VII
Simcock, Rev. Canon James Alexander, 1897–1984, vol. VIII
Sime, John, 1842–1911, vol. I
Sime, William Arnold, 1909–1983, vol. VIII
Simenon, Georges, 1903–1989, vol. VIII
Simeon, Vice-Adm. Sir Charles Edward Barrington, 1889–1955, vol. V
Simeon, Sir Edmund Charles, 5th Bt, 1855–1915, vol. I
Simeon, Sir John Stephen Barrington, 4th Bt, 1850–1909, vol. I
Simeon, Sir John Walter Barrington, 6th Bt, 1886–1957, vol. V
Simeon, Stephen Louis, 1857–1937, vol. III
Simes, Charles Erskine Woollard, 1893–1978, vol. VII
Simey, Baron (Life Peer); Thomas Spensley Simey, 1906–1969, vol. VI
Simkin, Rt Rev. William John, 1883–1967, vol. VI
Simm, Matthew Turnbull, 1869–1928, vol. II
Simmonds, Arthur, 1892–1968, vol. VI
Simmonds, B(ernard) Sangster, 1886–1953, vol. V
Simmonds, Frederick, 1845–1921, vol. II
Simmonds, Herbert John, 1867–1950, vol. IV
Simmonds, Hugh Henry Dawes, 1886–1952, vol. V
Simmonds, Sir Oliver Edwin, 1897–1985, vol. VIII
Simmonds, Sidney, 1899–1977, vol. VI
Simmonds, William George, 1876–1968, vol. VI
Simmonds, William Henry, 1860–1934, vol. III
Simmons, Mrs Amy, died 1964, vol. VI
Simmons, Sir Anker; see Simmons, Sir W. A.
Simmons, Arthur Thomas, 1865–1921, vol. II
Simmons, Charles James, 1893–1975, vol. VII
Simmons, Ernest Bernard, 1913–1988, vol. VIII
Simmons, Ernest J., 1903–1972, vol. VII
Simmons, Maj.-Gen. Frank Keith, 1888–1952, vol. V
Simmons, Rev. Frederic Pearson Copland, 1902–1978, vol. VII
Simmons, Sir Frederick James, 1867–1955, vol. V
Simmons, Col George Francis Henry Le B.; see Le Breton-Simmons.
Simmons, Engr-Captain George Thomas, 1853–1933, vol. III
Simmons, George Thomas Wagstaffe, died 1954, vol. V
Simmons, Sir Ira Marcus, 1917–1974, vol. VII (AII)

Simmons, Sir John Lintorn Arabin, 1821–1903, vol. I
Simmons, Major Sir Percy Coleman, 1875–1939, vol. III
Simmons, Robert J., 1894–1985, vol. VIII
Simmons, Sir (William) Anker, 1857–1927, vol. II
Simmons, William Foster, 1888–1985, vol. VIII
Simms, Ven. Arthur Hennell, 1853–1921, vol. II
Simms, Captain Charles Edward, 1900–1963, vol. VI
Simms, Very Rev. John Morrow, 1854–1934, vol. III
Simms, Ven. William, 1845–1932, vol. III
Simner, Col Sir Percy Reginald Owen Abel, 1878–1963, vol. VI
Simnett, William Edward, 1880–1958, vol. V
Simogun, Sir Petar, 1900–1987, vol. VIII
Simon, 1st Viscount, 1873–1954, vol. V
Simon, Viscountess; (Kathleen), 1871–1955, vol. V
Simon of Wythenshawe, 1st Baron, 1879–1960, vol. V
Simon of Wythenshawe, Lady; (Shena Dorothy), 1883–1972, vol. VII
Simon, André Louis, 1877–1970, vol. VI
Simon, Rev. D. W., 1830–1909, vol. I
Simon, (Ernest Julius) Walter, 1893–1981, vol. VIII
Simon, Sir Francis Eugene, 1893–1956, vol. V
Simon, George Percival, 1893–1963, vol. VI
Simon, Rt Rev. Glyn; see Simon, Rt Rev. W. G. H.
Simon, Sir John, 1818–1897, vol. I
Simon, Sir John, 1816–1904, vol. I
Simon, Rev. John Smith, 1843–1933, vol. III
Simon, Sir Leon, 1881–1965, vol. VI
Simon, Col Maximilian St Leger, 1876–1951, vol. V
Simon, Oliver, 1895–1956, vol. V
Simon, Sir Robert Michael, 1850–1914, vol. I
Simon, Walter; see Simon, E. J. W.
Simon, Walter, died 1967, vol. VI
Simon, Rt Rev. (William) Glyn (Hughes), 1903–1972, vol. VII
Simond, Charles François, died 1957, vol. V
Simonds, 1st Viscount, 1881–1971, vol. VII
Simonds, Frank H., 1878–1936, vol. III
Simonds, Frederick Adolphus, 1881–1953, vol. V
Simonds, Lt-Gen. Guy Granville, 1903–1974, vol. VII
Simonds, John Hayes, 1879–1946, vol. IV
Simonds, Most Rev. Justin Daniel, 1890–1967, vol. VI
Simonds, William Barrow, 1820–1911, vol. I
Simons, Adm. Ernest Alfred, 1856–1928, vol. II
Simons, Very Rev. William Charles, died 1921, vol. II
Simonsen, Sir John Lionel, 1884–1957, vol. V
Simonson, Lee, 1888–1967, vol. VI
Simopoulos, Charalambos John, 1874–1942, vol. IV
Simpkin, Sir Oswald Richard Arthur, 1879–1936, vol. III
Simpkinson, Henry Walrond, 1853–1934, vol. III
Simpson, Lt-Col Adrian Francis Hugh Sibbald, 1880–1960, vol. V
Simpson, Rev. Alan Haldane, 1875–1941, vol. IV
Simpson, Rev. Albert Edward, 1868–1947, vol. IV
Simpson, Sir Alexander Russell, 1835–1916, vol. II
Simpson, Alfred Allen, 1875–1939, vol. III
Simpson, Alfred Muller, 1843–1918, vol. II
Simpson, Archibald Henry, 1843–1918, vol. II
Simpson, Sir Basil Robert James, 2nd Bt (cr 1935), 1898–1968, vol. VI
Simpson, Sir Benjamin, 1831–1923, vol. II

Simpson, Bertie Soutar, 1896–1972, vol. VII
Simpson, Rt Rev. Bertram Fitzgerald, 1883–1971, vol. VII
Simpson, Bertram Lenox; see Weale, Putnam.
Simpson, (Cedric) Keith, 1907–1985, vol. VIII
Simpson, Col Charles Napier, 1856–1933, vol. III
Simpson, Maj.-Gen. Charles Rudyerd, 1856–1948, vol. IV
Simpson, Charles Valentine George, 1900–1987, vol. VIII
Simpson, Charles Walter, 1885–1971, vol. VII
Simpson, Sir Clement Bell, 1866–1933, vol. III
Simpson, Rear-Adm. Cortland Herbert, 1856–1943, vol. IV
Simpson, Very Rev. Cuthbert Aikman, 1892–1969, vol. VI
Simpson, Sir Cyril; see Simpson, Sir J. C. F.
Simpson, Rev. David Capell, 1883–1955, vol. V
Simpson, Edward Sydney, 1875–1939, vol. III
Simpson, Ernest Smith, 1921–1989, vol. VIII
Simpson, Miss Evelyn Blantyre, 1856–1920, vol. II
Simpson, Dame Florence Edith Victoria, 1874–1956, vol. V
Simpson, Gen. Sir Frank Ernest Wallace, 1899–1986, vol. VIII
Simpson, Col Sir Frank Robert, 1st Bt (cr 1935), 1864–1949, vol. IV
Simpson, Fred Brown, 1886–1939, vol. III
Simpson, Rev. Frederick Arthur, 1883–1974, vol. VII
Simpson, Frederick Moore, died 1928, vol. II
Simpson, Maj.-Gen. George, 1845–1908, vol. I
Simpson, Sir George Bowen, 1838–1915, vol. I
Simpson, Sir George Clarke, 1878–1965, vol. VI
Simpson, Col George Selden, 1878–1971, vol. VII
Simpson, Rear-Adm. George Walter Gillow, 1901–1972, vol. VII
Simpson, Gerald Gordon, 1918–1979, vol. VII
Simpson, Maj.-Gen. Hamilton Wilkie, 1895–1986, vol. VIII
Simpson, Harold, 1876–1974, vol. VII
Simpson, Harry Butler, 1861–1940, vol. III
Simpson, Helen de Guerry, 1897–1940, vol. III
Simpson, Col Henry Charles, 1879–1943, vol. IV
Simpson, Col Henry Cuthbert Connell Dunlop, 1854–1942, vol. IV
Simpson, Henry Fife Morland, 1859–1920, vol. II
Simpson, Henry George, 1917–1988, vol. VIII
Simpson, Sir Henry Lunnon, 1842–1900, vol. I
Simpson, Captain Henry Valentine, 1864–1937, vol. III
Simpson, Herbert Clayton, 1872–1947, vol. IV
Simpson, Sir James, 1858–1934, vol. III
Simpson, James, 1874–1939, vol. III
Simpson, Sir James Dyer, 1888–1979, vol. VII
Simpson, Sir James Fletcher, 1874–1967, vol. VI
Simpson, Very Rev. James Gilliland, 1865–1948, vol. IV
Simpson, Rev. James Harvey, 1825–1915, vol. I
Simpson, James Herbert, 1883–1959, vol. V
Simpson, Sir James Hope, 1864–1924, vol. II
Simpson, Sir James Walter Mackay, 3rd Bt (cr 1866), 1882–1924, vol. II
Simpson, James Young, 1873–1934, vol. III
Simpson, John Alexander, 1892–1977, vol. VII

Simpson, Rt Rev. John Basil, *died* 1942, vol. IV
Simpson, Sir (John) Cyril (Finucane), 3rd Bt, 1899–1981, vol. VIII
Simpson, Rev. John E., 1905–1970, vol. VI
Simpson, Air Cdre John Herbert Thomas, 1907–1967, vol. VI
Simpson, Sir John Hope, 1868–1961, vol. VI
Simpson, Sir John Roughton, 1899–1976, vol. VII
Simpson, Sir John William, 1858–1933, vol. III
Simpson, Joseph, 1879–1939, vol. III
Simpson, Sir Joseph, 1909–1968, vol. VI
Simpson, Keith; *see* Simpson, C. K.
Simpson, Lightly Stapleton, *died* 1942, vol. IV
Simpson, Mary Goudie, *died* 1934, vol. III
Simpson, Sir Maurice George, 1866–1954, vol. V
Simpson, Maxwell, 1815–1902, vol. I
Simpson, Melville William H.; *see* Hilton-Simpson.
Simpson, Maj.-Gen. Noel William, 1907–1972, vol. VII
Simpson, Rev. Patrick Carnegie, 1865–1947, vol. IV
Simpson, Percy, 1865–1962, vol. VI
Simpson, Rev. Percy John, 1864–1944, vol. IV
Simpson, Peter Miller, 1921–1988, vol. VIII
Simpson, Pierce Adolphus, 1837–1900, vol. I
Simpson, Rayene Stewart, 1926–1978, vol. VII
Simpson, Richard Jefferson, 1874–1936, vol. III
Simpson, Rev. Robert, 1900–1977, vol. VII
Simpson, Robert Gordon, 1887–1958, vol. V
Simpson, Col Robert John Shaw, 1858–1931, vol. III
Simpson, Col Robert Mills, 1865–1945, vol. IV (A)
Simpson, Sir Robert Russell, 1840–1923, vol. II
Simpson, Samuel, 1876–1952, vol. V
Simpson, S(amuel) Leonard, 1900–1983, vol. VIII
Simpson, Scott, 1915–1981, vol. VIII
Simpson, Air Vice-Marshal Sturley Philip, 1896–1966, vol. VI
Simpson, Thomas, 1877–1964, vol. VI
Simpson, Thomas Blantyre, 1892–1954, vol. V
Simpson, Rear-Adm. (E) Thomas Harold, 1896–1952, vol. V
Simpson, Col Thomas Thomson, 1836–1916, vol. II
Simpson, Thomas Young, *died* 1963, vol. VI
Simpson, Trevor Claude, 1877–1929, vol. III
Simpson, Rev. W. J. Sparrow, 1859–1952, vol. V
Simpson, Sir Walter Grindlay, 2nd Bt (*cr* 1866), 1843–1898, vol. I
Simpson, Wilfred L., 1862–1937, vol. III
Simpson, William, 1823–1899, vol. I
Simpson, William Douglas, 1896–1968, vol. VI
Simpson, Col William George, 1876–1961, vol. VI
Simpson, Sir William John Ritchie, 1855–1931, vol. III
Simpson, William Marshall, 1868–1951, vol. V
Simpson, William Wynn, 1907–1987, vol. VIII
Simpson-Baikie, Brig.-Gen. Sir Hugh Archie Dundas; *see* Baikie.
Simpson-Hinchliffe, William Algernon, 1880–1963, vol. VI
Sims, Sir Alfred John, 1907–1977, vol. VII
Sims, Sir Arthur, 1877–1969, vol. VI
Sims, Arthur Mitford, 1889–1977, vol. VII
Sims, Charles, 1873–1928, vol. II
Sims, Ernest William Proctor-, 1868–1943, vol. IV
Sims, Francis John, 1856–1950, vol. IV

Sims, George Robert, 1847–1922, vol. II
Sims, Brig.-Gen. Reginald Frank Manley, 1878–1951, vol. V
Sims, Sir Thomas, 1858–1936, vol. III
Sims, Adm. William Sowden, 1858–1936, vol. III
Simson, Captain Sir Donald Petrie, *died* 1961, vol. VI
Simson, Harold F.; *see* Fraser-Simson.
Simson, Sir Henry John Forbes, 1872–1932, vol. III
Simson, Richard Arbuthnot, 1871–1958, vol. V
Simson, Col William Amor, 1872–1925, vol. II
Sinbad; *see* Dingle, Aylward Edward.
Sinclair, 15th Lord, 1831–1922, vol. II
Sinclair, 16th Lord, 1875–1957, vol. V
Sinclair of Cleeve, 1st Baron, 1893–1979, vol. VII
Sinclair of Cleeve, 2nd Baron, 1919–1985, vol. VIII
Sinclair, Alexander Garden, 1859–1930, vol. III
Sinclair, Lt-Col Alfred Law, 1853–1911, vol. I
Sinclair, Allan Fergus Wilson, 1900–1980, vol. VII (AII)
Sinclair, Archibald, 1866–1922, vol. II
Sinclair, Arthur Henry Havens, 1868–1962, vol. VI
Sinclair, Rev. Hon. Charles Augustus, 1865–1944, vol. IV
Sinclair, Hon. Sir Colin Archibald, 1876–1956, vol. V
Sinclair, Surg.-Gen. David, 1847–1919, vol. II
Sinclair, Dep. Surg.-Gen. Edward M., 1832–1916, vol. II
Sinclair, Adm. Sir Edwyn Sinclair A.; *see* Alexander-Sinclair.
Sinclair, George Robertson, 1863–1917, vol. II
Sinclair, Hugh; *see* Herman, E.
Sinclair, Adm. Sir Hugh Francis Paget, 1873–1939, vol. III
Sinclair, Hugh Macdonald, 1910–1990, vol. VIII
Sinclair, Col Hugh Montgomerie, 1855–1924, vol. II
Sinclair, James, 1832–1910, vol. I
Sinclair, John, 1860–1938, vol. III
Sinclair, John, 1898–1979, vol. VII (AII)
Sinclair, John Alexander, 1885–1961, vol. VI
Sinclair, Maj.-Gen. Sir John Alexander, 1897–1977, vol. VII
Sinclair, John Alexis Clifford Cerda A.; *see* Alexander-Sinclair.
Sinclair, Sir John George Tollemache, 3rd Bt (*cr* 1786), 1825–1899, vol. I
Sinclair, John Houston, 1871–1961, vol. VI
Sinclair, Rt Hon. John Maynard, 1896–1953, vol. V
Sinclair, Sir John Robert, 1850–1940, vol. III
Sinclair, Sir John Rollo Norman Blair, 9th Bt (*cr* 1704), 1928–1990, vol. VIII
Sinclair, Sir John Rose George, 7th Bt (*cr* 1704), 1864–1926, vol. II
Sinclair, Ven. John Stewart, 1853–1919, vol. II
Sinclair, Captain Sir Kenneth Duncan Lecky, 1889–1973, vol. VII
Sinclair, Sir Leonard, 1895–1984, vol. VIII
Sinclair, Louis, 1861–1928, vol. II
Sinclair, Lt-Col Malcolm Cecil, 1899–1955, vol. V
Sinclair, May, 1870–1946, vol. IV
Sinclair, Meurice, 1878–1966, vol. VI
Sinclair, Sir Robert Charles, 9th Bt (*cr* 1636), 1820–1899, vol. I

Sinclair, Major Sir Ronald Norman John Charles Udny, 8th Bt (*cr* 1704, shown as 1631), 1899–1952, vol. V
Sinclair, Rev. Canon Ronald Sutherland Brook, 1894–1953, vol. V
Sinclair, Shapton Donald, 1923–1974, vol. VII
Sinclair, Rt Hon. Thomas, 1838–1914, vol. I
Sinclair, Col Thomas, *died* 1940, vol. III
Sinclair, T(homas) Alan, 1899–1961, vol. VI
Sinclair, Col Thomas Charles, 1879–1948, vol. IV
Sinclair, Upton, 1878–1968, vol. VI
Sinclair, Lt-Col Sir Walrond Arthur Frank, 1880–1952, vol. V
Sinclair, Sir William, 1895–1976, vol. VII
Sinclair, William Angus, 1905–1954, vol. V
Sinclair, Sir William Japp, 1846–1912, vol. I
Sinclair, Ven. William Macdonald, 1850–1917, vol. II
Sinclair-Burgess, Maj.-Gen. Sir William Livingstone Hatchwell, 1880–1964, vol. VI
Sinclair Lockhart, Sir Graeme Alexander, 10th Bt (*cr* 1636); *see* Lockhart.
Sinclair-Lockhart, Sir Graeme Duncan Power, 12th Bt (*cr* 1636), 1897–1959, vol. V
Sinclair-Lockhart, Sir John Beresford, 13th Bt (*cr* 1636), 1904–1970, vol. VI
Sinclair-Lockhart, Sir Muir Edward, 14th Bt, 1906–1985, vol. VIII
Sinclair-Lockhart, Sir Robert Duncan, 11th Bt (*cr* 1636), 1856–1919, vol. II
Sinclair-Maclagan, Maj.-Gen. Ewen George, 1868–1948, vol. IV
Sinderson, Sir Harry Chapman, Pasha, 1891–1974, vol. VII
Sinding, Stephan, 1846–1922, vol. II
Sing, John Millington, 1863–1947, vol. IV
Sing, Roger Percy, 1865–1940, vol. III
Sing, Rt Rev. Tsae-Seng, 1861–1940, vol. III (A), vol. IV
Singer, Charles, 1876–1960, vol. V
Singer, Brig.-Gen. Charles William, 1870–1936, vol. III
Singer, Dorothea Waley, 1882–1964, vol. VI
Singer, Adm. Sir Morgan, 1864–1938, vol. III
Singer, Sir Mortimer, 1863–1929, vol. III
Singer, Rev. Canon Samuel Stanfield, 1920–1989, vol. VIII
Singer, Rev. Simeon, 1848–1906, vol. I
Singer, Washington Merritt Grant, 1866–1934, vol. III
Singers-Davies, Rev. R. W. F., *died* 1936, vol. III
Singh, Sardar Bahadur Sir D.; *see* Datar Singh.
Singh, Prince Frederick D.; *see* Duleep Singh.
Singh, Sir Ganesh Dutta, 1868–1943, vol. IV
Singh, Kanwar Jasbir, 1889–1942, vol. IV
Singh, Raja Sir Maharaj, 1878–1959, vol. V
Singh, Nagendra, 1914–1988, vol. VIII
Singh, Raja Sir Padam, 1873–1947, vol. IV
Singh, Prince Victor Albert Jay D.; *see* Duleep Singh.
Singh Bahadur, Maharawal Shri Sir Lakshman, 1908–1989, vol. VIII
Singh Roy, Sir Bijoy Prosad, 1894–1961, vol. VI
Singhateh, Alhaji Sir Farimang Mohamadu, 1912–1977, vol. VII (AII)
Singhji Bahadur, Karni; *see* Bikaner, Maharaja of.

Singleton, Esther, *died* 1930, vol. III
Singleton, Col Henry Townsend Corbet, 1874–1934, vol. III
Singleton, Rt Rev. Hugh, 1851–1934, vol. III
Singleton, Rt Hon. Sir John Edward, 1885–1957, vol. V
Singleton, Rev. John J., 1838–1917, vol. II
Singleton, Rear-Adm. Uvedale Corbet, 1838–1910, vol. I
Singleton, William Adam, 1916–1960, vol. V
Sington, Gerald Henry Adolphus, 1876–1946, vol. IV
Sinha, 1st Baron, 1864–1928, vol. III
Sinha, 2nd Baron, 1887–1967, vol. VI
Sinha, Narendra Prasanna, *born* 1858, vol. III
Sinha, Rajandhari, 1893–1976, vol. VII
Sinha, Sir Rajivaranjan Prashad, 1893–1948, vol. IV (A), vol. V
Sinker, Sir (Algernon) Paul, 1905–1977, vol. VII
Sinker, Rev. Canon Arthur, *died* 1940, vol. III
Sinker, Rev. Edmund, 1872–1941, vol. IV
Sinker, Rt Rev. George, 1900–1986, vol. VIII
Sinker, Very Rev. John, 1874–1936, vol. III
Sinker, Sir Paul; *see* Sinker, Sir A. P.
Sinker, Rev. Robert, 1838–1913, vol. I
Sinkinson, George, 1874–1939, vol. III
Sinnatt, Frank Sturdy, 1880–1943, vol. IV
Sinnatt, Oliver Sturdy, 1882–1965, vol. VI
Sinnett, Alfred Percy, 1840–1921, vol. II
Sinnott, Most Rev. Alfred A., 1877–1954, vol. V
Sinnott, Col Edward Stockley, 1868–1969, vol. VI
Sinnott, Ernest, 1909–1989, vol. VIII
Sinnott, John Joseph, 1882–1943, vol. IV
Sinton, Lt-Col John Alexander, 1884–1956, vol. V
Siqueland, Col Tryggve Albert, 1888–1937, vol. III
Sircar, Sir Nilratan, 1861–1943, vol. IV
Sircar, Sir Nripendra Nath, *died* 1945, vol. IV
Sire, Henry Alphonse, 1864–1947, vol. IV
Siriwardena, N. D. A. Silva-Wijayasinghe; *see* Wijayasinghe Siriwardena.
Sirmur (Nahan), Raja of, 1867–1911, vol. I
Sirmur, Maharaja of, 1888–1933, vol. III
Sirohi, HH Maharajadhiraj, 1888–1946, vol. IV
Sisam, Kenneth, 1887–1971, vol. VII
Sisley, Charles Percival, 1867–1934, vol. III
Sisnett, Sir Herbert Kortright McDonnell, 1862–1937, vol. III
Sisson, Charles Jasper, 1885–1966, vol. VI
Sisson, Marshall Arnott, 1897–1978, vol. VII
Sissons, Charles B., 1879–1965, vol. VI
Sissons, Ven. Gilbert Holme, 1870–1940, vol. III
Sita Ram, Rai Bahadur Sir, 1885–1972, vol. VII
Sitwell, Dame Edith Louisa, 1887–1964, vol. VI
Sitwell, Sir George Reresby, 4th Bt, 1860–1943, vol. IV
Sitwell, Maj.-Gen. Hervey Degge Wilmot, 1896–1973, vol. VII
Sitwell, Sir Osbert, 5th Bt, 1892–1969, vol. VI
Sitwell, Sir Sacheverell, 6th Bt, 1897–1988, vol. VIII
Sitwell, Sir Sidney Ashley Hurt, 1871–1956, vol. V
Sitwell, Brig.-Gen. William Henry, 1860–1932, vol. III
Sivagnanam Pillai, Diwan Bahadur Sir Tinnevelly Nelliappa Pillai, *died* 1936, vol. III
Sivell, Robert, 1888–1958, vol. V

Sivewright, Hon. Sir James, 1848–1916, vol. II

Sixsmith, Maj.-Gen. Eric Keir Gilborne, 1904–1986, vol. VIII

Sixsmith, Guy; see Sixsmith, P. G. D.

Sixsmith, (Philip) Guy (Dudley), 1902–1984, vol. VIII

Skae, Victor Delvine Burnham, 1914–1979, vol. VII

Skaife, Brig. Sir Eric Ommanney, 1884–1956, vol. V

Skaug, Arne, 1906–1974, vol. VII

Skeaping, John Rattenbury, 1901–1980, vol. VII

Skeat, Rev. Walter William, 1835–1912, vol. I

Skeats, Ernest Willington, 1875–1953, vol. V

Skeen, Gen. Sir Andrew, 1873–1935, vol. III

Skeen, Brig. Andrew, 1906–1984, vol. VIII

Skeffington, Arthur Massey, 1909–1971, vol. VII

Skeffington, Hon. Oriel John Clotworthy Whyte Melville Foster-, 1871–1905, vol. I

Skeffington Smyth, Lt-Col Geoffrey Henry Julian; see FitzPatrick, Lt-Col G. H. J.

Skeggs, Rev. Thomas Charles, died 1927, vol. II

Skelhorn, Sir Norman John, 1909–1988, vol. VIII

Skellerup, Sir Valdemar Reid, 1907–1982, vol. VIII

Skelmersdale, 5th Baron, 1876–1969, vol. VI

Skelmersdale, 6th Baron, 1896–1973, vol. VII

Skelton, Archibald Noel, 1880–1935, vol. III

Skelton, Rev. Charles Arthur, died 1913, vol. I

Skelton, Sir Charles Thomas, 1833–1913, vol. I

Skelton, Maj.-Gen. Dudley Sheridan, 1878–1962, vol. VI

Skelton, Rt Rev. Henry Aylmer, 1884–1959, vol. V

Skelton, Sir John, 1831–1897, vol. I

Skelton, Oscar Douglas, 1878–1941, vol. IV

Skelton, Engr Vice-Adm. Sir Reginald William, 1872–1956, vol. V

Skelton, Robert Lumley, 1896–1973, vol. VII

Skelton, Rev. Canon Thomas, 1834–1915, vol. I

Skemp, Arthur Rowland, 1882–1918, vol. II

Skemp, Frank Whittingham, 1880–1971, vol. VII

Skene, Macgregor, 1889–1973, vol. VII

Skene, Hon. Thomas, died 1910, vol. I

Skene, William Baillie, 1838–1911, vol. I

Skerrett, Hon. Sir Charles Perrin, 1863–1929, vol. III

Skerrington, Hon. Lord; William Campbell, 1855–1927, vol. II

Sketch, Ralph Yeo, 1877–1952, vol. V

Sketchley, Major Ernest Frederick Powys, 1881–1916, vol. II

Skevington, Sir Joseph Oliver, 1873–1952, vol. V

Skewes-Cox, Sir Thomas, 1849–1913, vol. I

Skey, Rev. Oswald William Laurie, 1878–1954, vol. V

Skidmore, Charles, 1839–1908, vol. I

Skiffington, Sir Donald Maclean, 1880–1963, vol. VI

Skikne, Larushka Mischa; see Harvey, Laurence.

Skilbeck, Dunstan, 1904–1989, vol. VIII

Skilbeck, William Wray, 1864–1919, vol. II

Skillicorn, Alice Havergal, 1894–1979, vol. VII

Skillicorn, William James Kinlay, 1883–1955, vol. V

Skimming, Ian Edward Bowring, 1920–1973, vol. VII

Skinnard, Frederick William, 1902–1984, vol. VIII

Skinner, Rev. Albert James, 1869–1949, vol. IV

Skinner, Allan Maclean, 1846–1901, vol. I

Skinner, Arthur Banks, 1861–1911, vol. I

Skinner, Maj.-Gen. Bruce Morland, 1858–1932, vol. III

Skinner, Burrhus Frederic, 1904–1990, vol. VIII

Skinner, C(harles) William, 1895–1971, vol. VII

Skinner, Clarence Farringdon, 1900–1962, vol. VI

Skinner, Colin Marshall, 1882–1968, vol. VI

Skinner, Cornelia Otis, (Mrs A. S. Blodget), 1901–1979, vol. VII

Skinner, Maj.-Gen. Sir Cyriac; see Skinner, Maj.-Gen. Sir P. C. B.

Skinner, Col Edmund Grey, 1850–1917, vol. II

Skinner, Ernest Harry Dudley, 1892–1985, vol. VIII

Skinner, Maj.-Gen. Frank Hollamby Jerry, 1897–1979, vol. VII

Skinner, Col Frederick St Duthus, 1859–1938, vol. III

Skinner, Col George John, 1841–1930, vol. III

Skinner, Sir Gordon; see Skinner, Sir T. G.

Skinner, Lt-Col Harry Crawley R.; see Ross Skinner.

Skinner, Sir Harry Ross, 1867–1943, vol. IV

Skinner, Hon. Sir Henry Albert, 1926–1986, vol. VIII

Skinner, Herbert Wakefield Banks, 1900–1960, vol. V

Skinner, Sir Hewitt; see Skinner, Sir T. H.

Skinner, Horace Wilfrid, 1884–1955, vol. V

Skinner, Rev. James Henry, died 1913, vol. I

Skinner, Col James Tierney, 1845–1902, vol. I

Skinner, Rev. John, 1851–1925, vol. II

Skinner, John William, 1890–1955, vol. V

Skinner, Most Rev. Patrick James, born 1904, vol. VIII

Skinner, Maj.-Gen. Sir (Percy) Cyriac Burrell, 1871–1955, vol. V

Skinner, Robert, 1877–1955, vol. V

Skinner, Robert Peet, 1866–1960, vol. V

Skinner, Robert Taylor, 1867–1946, vol. IV

Skinner, Sidney, 1863–1944, vol. IV

Skinner, Sir Sydney Martyn, 1864–1941, vol. IV

Skinner, Sir Thomas, 1st Bt, 1840–1926, vol. II

Skinner, Sir (Thomas) Gordon, 3rd Bt, 1899–1972, vol. VII

Skinner, Sir (Thomas) Hewitt, 2nd Bt, 1875–1968, vol. VI

Skinner, Waldo W., 1878–1943, vol. IV

Skinner, Walter Robert, 1851–1924, vol. II

Skinner, Rev. William, 1859–1942, vol. IV

Skinner, William Goudie, died 1935, vol. III

Skipton, Rev. Horace Pitt Kennedy, 1861–1943, vol. IV

Skipwith, Col Frederick George, 1870–1964, vol. VI

Skipwith, Sir Grey Humberston d'Estoteville, 11th Bt, 1884–1950, vol. IV

Skipwith, Vice-Adm. Harry Louis d'Estoteville, 1868–1955, vol. V

Skipworth, Frank Markham, 1854–1929, vol. III

Skira, Albert, 1904–1973, vol. VII

Skirmunt, Constantine, 1866–1939, vol. III

Skirrow, Major Arthur George Walker, 1862–1941, vol. IV

Skirving, Archibald Adam S.; see Scot-Skirving.

Sklodowska, Marie; see Curie, Madame.

Skottowe, Britiffe Constable, 1857–1925, vol. II

Skouras, Spyros Panayiotis, 1893–1971, vol. VII

Skrimshire of Quarter, Baroness (Life Peer); Margaret Betty Harvie Anderson, 1915–1979, vol. VII

Skrine, Sir Clarmont Percival, 1888–1974, vol. VII

Skrine, Francis Henry, 1847–1933, vol. III

Skrine, Henry Mills, 1844–1915, vol. I

Skrine, Rev. John Huntley, 1848–1923, vol. II

Skues, George Edward Mackenzie, 1858–1949, vol. IV

Skutsch, Otto, 1906–1990, vol. VIII

Skyrm, Llewellyn Sidgwick M., *died* 1964, vol. VI

Skyrme, Stanley James Beresford, 1912–1985, vol. VIII

Slack, Captain Charles, *died* 1925, vol. II

Slack, Sir John B.; *see* Bamford-Slack.

Slack, Rev. Kenneth, 1917–1987, vol. VIII

Slack, Samuel Benjamin, 1859–1955, vol. V

Slacke, Francis Alexander, 1853–1940, vol. III

Slacke, Sir Owen Randal, 1837–1910, vol. I

Sladden, Sir Julius, 1847–1928, vol. II

Slade, Sir Alfred Fothringham, 5th Bt, 1898–1960, vol. V

Slade, Col Cecil Townley M.; *see* Mitford-Slade.

Slade, Cecil William Paulet, 1863–1943, vol. IV

Slade, Sir Cuthbert, 4th Bt, 1863–1908, vol. I

Slade, Adm. Sir Edmond John Warre, 1859–1928, vol. II

Slade, Lt-Gen. Frederick George, 1851–1910, vol. I

Slade, George Penkivil, 1899–1942, vol. IV

Slade, Sir Gerald Osborne, 1891–1962, vol. VI

Slade, Gordon; *see* Slade, R. G.

Slade, Sir James Benjamin, 1861–1950, vol. IV

Slade, Maj.-Gen. Sir John Ramsay, 1843–1913, vol. I

Slade, Mead, 1894–1954, vol. V

Slade, Sir Michael Nial, 6th Bt, 1900–1962, vol. VI

Slade, Richard Gordon, 1912–1981, vol. VIII

Slade, Roland Edgar, 1886–1968, vol. VI

Slade, William Ball, 1843–1938, vol. III

Slade, Wyndham, 1826–1910, vol. I

Slade, Wyndham Neave, 1867–1941, vol. IV

Sladen, Arthur French, 1866–1944, vol. IV

Sladen, Brig.-Gen. David Ramsay, 1869–1923, vol. II

Sladen, Douglas Brooke Wheelton, 1856–1947, vol. IV

Sladen, Francis Farquhar, 1875–1970, vol. VI

Sladen, Major Gerald Carew, 1881–1930, vol. III

Sladen, Hugh Alfred Lambart, 1878–1962, vol. VI

Sladen, Col Joseph, 1840–1930, vol. III

Sladen, Joseph Maurice, 1896–1956, vol. V

Sladen, Lt-Comdr Sir Sampson, 1868–1940, vol. III

Slaney, Col Francis Gerald K.; *see* Kenyon-Slaney.

Slaney, George Wilson, 1884–1978, vol. VII

Slaney, Major Philip Percy K.; *see* Kenyon-Slaney.

Slaney, Major Robert Orlando Rodolph K.; *see* Kenyon-Slaney.

Slaney, Sybil Anges, K.; *see* Kenyon-Slaney.

Slaney, Maj.-Gen. Walter Rupert K.; *see* Kenyon-Slaney.

Slaney, Rt Hon. William Slaney K.; *see* Kenyon-Slaney.

Slater, Baron (Life Peer); Joseph Slater, 1904–1977, vol. VII

Slater, Sir (Alexander) Ransford, 1874–1940, vol. III

Slater, Arthur Edward, 1895–1982, vol. VIII

Slater, Charles, 1856–1940, vol. III

Slater, David A., 1866–1938, vol. III

Slater, Eliot Trevor Oakeshott, 1904–1983, vol. VIII

Slater, Ernest, *died* 1942, vol. IV

Slater, George, *died* 1941, vol. IV

Slater, George, 1874–1956, vol. V

Slater, Gilbert, 1864–1938, vol. III

Slater, Gordon Archbold, 1896–1979, vol. VII

Slater, Mrs Harriet, *died* 1976, vol. VII

Slater, John, 1847–1924, vol. II

Slater, John, 1889–1935, vol. III

Slater, Col John William, 1867–1936, vol. III

Slater, Col Owen, 1890–1976, vol. VII

Slater, Sir Ransford; *see* Slater, Sir A. R.

Slater, Adm. Sir Robin Leonard Francis D.; *see* Durnford-Slater.

Slater, Samuel Henry, 1880–1967, vol. VI

Slater, Hon. William, 1890–1960, vol. V

Slater, Rev. William Fletcher, 1831–1924, vol. II

Slater, William Henry, 1896–1962, vol. VI

Slater, Sir William Kershaw, 1893–1970, vol. VI

Slatin Pacha, Baron Rudolf Carl, 1857–1932, vol. III

Slator, Instr Captain Thomas, *died* 1961, vol. VI

Slatter, Air Marshal Sir Leonard Horatio, 1894–1961, vol. VI

Slattery, Rt Rev. Charles Lewis, 1867–1930, vol. III

Slattery, John, 1886–1958, vol. V

Slattery, Rear-Adm. Sir Matthew Sausse, 1902–1990, vol. VIII

Slaughter, James Cameron, 1902–1982, vol. VIII

Slaughter, Lt-Col Reginald Joseph, 1874–1968, vol. VI

Slaughter, Sir William Capel, 1857–1917, vol. II

Slayter, Col Edward Wheeler, 1869–1946, vol. IV

Slayter, Adm. William Firth, 1867–1936, vol. III

Slayter, Adm. Sir William Rudolph, 1896–1971, vol. VII

Sleator, James Sinton, *died* 1950, vol. IV

Slee, Frederick Abraham, 1882–1963, vol. VI

Slee, Comdr John Ambrose, 1878–1944, vol. IV

Slee, Col Percy Henry, 1861–1929, vol. III

Sleeman, Cyril Montagu, 1883–1971, vol. VII

Sleeman, Col Sir James Lewis, 1880–1963, vol. VI

Sleeman, John Herbert, 1880–1963, vol. VI

Sleep, Arthur, 1894–1959, vol. V

Sleigh, Charles William, 1863–1949, vol. IV

Sleigh, Sir Hamilton Morton Howard, 1896–1979, vol. VII

Sleigh, Sir William Lowrie, 1865–1945, vol. IV

Sleight, Major Sir Ernest, 2nd Bt, 1873–1946, vol. IV

Sleight, Sir George Frederick, 1st Bt, 1853–1921, vol. II

Sleight, Sir John Frederick, 3rd Bt, 1909–1990, vol. VIII

Slesinger, Edward Gustave, 1888–1975, vol. VII

Slesser, Rt Hon. Sir Henry Herman, 1883–1979, vol. VII

Slessor, Alexander Johnston, 1912–1954, vol. V

Slessor, Marshal of the Royal Air Force Sir John Cotesworth, 1897–1979, vol. VII

Sligo, 4th Marquess of, 1824–1903, vol. I

Sligo, 5th Marquess of, 1831–1913, vol. I

Sligo, 6th Marquess of, 1856–1935, vol. III

Sligo, 7th Marquess of, 1898–1941, vol. IV

Sligo, 8th Marquess of, 1867–1951, vol. V
Sligo, 9th Marquess of, 1873–1952, vol. V
Slim, 1st Viscount, 1891–1970, vol. VI
Slingo, Sir William, 1855–1935, vol. III
Sliwinski, Stanislaw, 1893–1940, vol. III (A), vol. IV
Sloan, Alexander, *died* 1945, vol. IV
Sloan, Alfred Pritchard, Jun., 1875–1966, vol. VI
Sloan, Hon. Gordon McGregor, 1898–1959, vol. V
Sloan, Maj.-Gen. John Macfarlane, 1872–1941, vol. IV
Sloan, John MacGavin, *died* 1926, vol. II
Sloan, Lawrence Gunn, 1859–1939, vol. III
Sloan, Robert Patrick, 1874–1947, vol. IV
Sloan, Sir Tennant, 1884–1972, vol. VII
Sloane, Maj.-Gen. John Bramley Malet, 1912–1990, vol. VIII
Sloane, Mary Annie, *died* 1961, vol. VI
Sloane, William Milligan, 1850–1928, vol. II
Sloane-Stanley, Ronald Francis Assheton, 1867–1948, vol. IV
Slocock, Francis Samuel Alfred, *died* 1945, vol. IV
Slocombe, George Edward, 1894–1963, vol. VI
Slocum, Captain Frank Alexander, 1897–1982, vol. VIII
Slocum, William Frederick, 1851–1934, vol. III
Sloggett, Col Arthur John Henry, 1882–1950, vol. IV
Sloggett, Lt-Gen. Sir Arthur Thomas, 1857–1929, vol. III
Sloley, Sir Herbert Cecil, 1855–1937, vol. III
Sloman, Rev. Arthur, 1851–1919, vol. II
Sloman, Very Rev. Ernest, *died* 1918, vol. II
Sloman, Harold Newnham Penrose, 1885–1965, vol. VI
Sloman, Brig.-Gen. Henry Stanhope, 1861–1945, vol. IV
Slot, Gerald Maurice Joseph, *died* 1972, vol. VII
Slotki, Israel Wolf, 1884–1973, vol. VII
Sly, Sir Frank George, 1866–1928, vol. II
Sly, Henry Edward, 1876–1932, vol. III
Sly, Richard Meares, 1849–1929, vol. III
Slyne, Denis, *died* 1928, vol. II
Slyth, Arthur Roy, 1910–1989, vol. VIII
Smail, James Cameron, 1880–1970, vol. VI
Smail, William Mitchell, 1885–1971, vol. VII
Smailes, Arthur Eltringham, 1911–1984, vol. VIII
Smaldon, Catherine Agnes, 1903–1980, vol. VII
Smale, Morton Alfred, 1847–1916, vol. II
Small, Sir Alexander Sym, 1887–1944, vol. IV
Small, Sir (Andrew) Bruce, 1895–1980, vol. VII (AII)
Small, Sir Bruce; *see* Small, Sir A. B.
Small, Sir Frank Augustus, 1903–1973, vol. VII
Small, James, 1889–1955, vol. V
Small, James, *died* 1968, vol. VI
Small, William, 1843–1929, vol. III
Small, Col William George, *died* 1931, vol. III
Small, William Watson, 1909–1978, vol. VII
Smallbones, Robert Townsend, 1884–1976, vol. VII
Smalley, Beryl, 1905–1984, vol. VIII
Smalley, George Washburn, 1833–1916, vol. II
Smalley, Sir Herbert, 1851–1945, vol. IV
Smalley-Baker, Charles Ernest, 1891–1972, vol. VII
Smallfield, F., *died* 1915, vol. I
Smallman, Lt-Col Arthur Briton, 1873–1950, vol. IV
Smallman, Sir George; *see* Smallman, Sir H. G.

Smallman, Sir (Henry) George, 1854–1923, vol. II
Smallwood, Arthur William, 1873–1938, vol. III
Smallwood, Edward, 1861–1939, vol. III
Smallwood, Lt-Col Frank Graham, 1867–1919, vol. II
Smallwood, Geoffrey Arthur John, 1900–1973, vol. VII
Smallwood, Maj.-Gen. Gerald Russell, 1889–1977, vol. VII
Smallwood, Henry Armstrong, 1869–1942, vol. IV
Smallwood, Norah Evelyn, 1909–1984, vol. VIII
Smallwood, Oliver Daniel, 1889–1962, vol. VI
Smallwood, Richard Coningsby, 1879–1933, vol. III
Smart, Archibald Guelph Holdsworth, 1882–1964, vol. VI
Smart, Borlase, 1881–1947, vol. IV
Smart, Brig.-Gen. Charles Allan, 1868–1937, vol. III
Smart, Douglas Ian, *died* 1970, vol. VI (AII)
Smart, E. Hodgson, *died* 1942, vol. IV
Smart, Lt-Gen. Edward Kenneth, 1891–1961, vol. VI
Smart, Sir Eric Fleming, 1911–1973, vol. VII
Smart, Sir Harold Nevil, 1883–1950, vol. IV
Smart, Henry C., 1878–1951, vol. V
Smart, Henry Walter, 1908–1990, vol. VIII
Smart, John, 1838–1899, vol. I
Smart, Joseph McCaig, 1882–1953, vol. V
Smart, Leslie Masson, 1889–1972, vol. VII
Smart, Comdr Sir Morton, 1878–1956, vol. V
Smart, Maj.-Gen. Robert Arthur, 1914–1986, vol. VIII
Smart, V. Irving, 1874–1940, vol. III
Smart, Sir Walter Alexander, 1883–1962, vol. VI
Smart, Wilfred Wilmot, 1876–1961, vol. VI
Smart, William, 1853–1915, vol. I
Smart, William Marshall, 1889–1975, vol. VII
Smart, William Wilkinson, *died* 1943, vol. IV
Smartt, Rt Hon. Sir Thomas William, 1858–1929, vol. III
Smartt, Rev. William Hanbury, 1854–1933, vol. III
Smeaton, Lt-Col (Charles) Oswald, 1862–1923, vol. II
Smeaton, Donald Mackenzie, 1848–1910, vol. I
Smeaton, Oliphant; *see* Smeaton, W. H. O.
Smeaton, Lt-Col Oswald; *see* Smeaton, Lt-Col C. O.
Smeaton, William Henry Oliphant, *died* 1914, vol. I
Smeddles, Thomas Henry, 1904–1987, vol. VIII
Smedley, Constance, *died* 1941, vol. IV
Smeed, Reuben Jacob, 1909–1976, vol. VII
Smeeton, Captain Samuel Page, 1842–1916, vol. II
Smele, William Smauel George, 1912–1976, vol. VII
Smellie, Alexander, 1857–1923, vol. II
Smellie, Elizabeth Lawrie, 1884–1968, vol. VI
Smellie, James Maclure, 1893–1961, vol. VI
Smellie, Kingsley Bryce Speakman, 1897–1987, vol. VIII
Smellie, R(obert) Martin S(tuart), 1927–1988, vol. VIII
Smeterlin, Jan, 1892–1967, vol. VI
Smethurst, Albert H., 1868–1935, vol. III
Smethurst, Rev. Canon Arthur Frederick, 1904–1957, vol. V
Smethurst, Sir Thomas, 1860–1935, vol. III
Smiddy, Timothy A., 1875–1962, vol. VI

Smijth, Sir William Bowyer-, 12th Bt (*cr* 1661), 1840–1916, vol. II

Smiles, Samuel, 1812–1904, vol. I

Smiles, Samuel, 1877–1953, vol. V

Smiles, Lt-Col Sir Walter Dorling, *died* 1953, vol. V

Smiles, William, 1824–1915, vol. I

Smiley, Sir Hugh Houston, 1st Bt, 1841–1909, vol. I

Smiley, Sir Hugh Houston, 3rd Bt, 1905–1990, vol. VIII

Smiley, Sir John, 2nd Bt, 1876–1930, vol. III

Smiley, Norman Bryce, 1909–1968, vol. VI

Smiley, Peter Kerr K.; *see* Kerr-Smiley.

Smillie, Robert, 1857–1940, vol. III

Smit, Hon. Jacob Hendrik, 1881–1959, vol. V

Smit, Jacobus Stephanus, 1878–1960, vol. V

Smith, A. Reginald, *died* 1934, vol. III

Smith, Abel, 1829–1898, vol. I

Smith, Abel Henry, 1862–1930, vol. III

Smith, Hon. Sir Abercrombie; *see* Smith, Hon. Sir C. A.

Smith, Adam, 1854–1920, vol. II

Smith, Sir Alan R.; *see* Rae Smith.

Smith, Albert, 1867–1942, vol. IV

Smith, Sir Albert, 1862–1944, vol. IV

Smith, Brig. Albert, 1896–1959, vol. V

Smith, Albert Hugh, 1903–1967, vol. VI

Smith, Albert William, 1863–1940, vol. III

Smith, Lt-Col Alexander Hugh Dickson, 1890–1960, vol. V

Smith, Sir Alexander Rowland, 1888–1988, vol. VIII

Smith, Alfred, *died* 1931, vol. III

Smith, Alfred Emanuel, 1873–1944, vol. IV

Smith, Alfred John, 1865–1925, vol. II, vol. III

Smith, Hon. Alfred Lee, *born* 1838, vol. II

Smith, Sir Alfred M.; *see* Mays-Smith.

Smith, Maj.-Gen. Alfred Travers Fairtlough, 1890–1965, vol. VI

Smith, Sir Alfred van W. L.; *see* Lucie-Smith.

Smith, Rt Rev. Alfred William, 1875–1958, vol. V

Smith, Lt-Col Algernon Fox Eric, 1857–1942, vol. IV

Smith, Alic Halford, 1883–1958, vol. V

Smith, Alick Drummond Buchanan-; *see* Baron Balerno.

Smith, Sir Allan Chalmers, 1893–1980, vol. VII

Smith, Allan Frith, 1857–1935, vol. III

Smith, Sir Allan Gordon G.; *see* Gordon-Smith.

Smith, Sir Allan Macgregor, *died* 1941, vol. IV

Smith, Allan Ramsay, 1875–1926, vol. II

Smith, Andrew, 1849–1914, vol. I

Smith, Sir Andrew, 1880–1967, vol. VI

Smith, Andrew Thomas, 1884–1943, vol. IV

Smith, Comdr Andrew W.; *see* Wilmot-Smith.

Smith, Dame Anne Beadsmore, 1869–1960, vol. V

Smith, Annie Shepherd; *see* Smith, Mrs Burnett.

Smith, Dame Annis; *see* Gillie, Dame A. C.

Smith, Sir Anthony Paul G.; *see* Grafftey-Smith.

Smith, Anthony Robert, 1926–1988, vol. VIII

Smith, Rt Hon. Sir Archibald Levin, 1836–1901, vol. I

Smith, (Arnold) John Hugh, 1881–1964, vol. VI

Smith, Arnold P.; *see* Pye-Smith.

Smith, Arthur C.; *see* Corbett-Smith.

Smith, Arthur Croxton, 1865–1952, vol. V

Smith, Rev. Arthur Edward, 1871–1952, vol. V

Smith, Lt-Gen. Sir Arthur Francis, 1890–1977, vol. VII

Smith, Vice-Adm. Arthur Gordon, 1873–1953, vol. V

Smith, Arthur H.; *see* Hopewell-Smith.

Smith, Arthur Hamilton, 1860–1941, vol. IV

Smith, Rev. Arthur Henderson, 1845–1932, vol. III

Smith, Sir Arthur Henry, 1905–1989, vol. VIII

Smith, Arthur Kirke, 1878–1937, vol. III

Smith, Arthur Lionel, 1850–1924, vol. II

Smith, Arthur Lionel Forster, 1880–1972, vol. VII

Smith, Arthur Llewellyn, 1903–1978, vol. VII

Smith, Lt-Col Arthur M.; *see* Murray-Smith.

Smith, Arthur Norman E.; *see* Exton-Smith.

Smith, Arthur William, 1880–1961, vol. VI

Smith, Sir Aubrey; *see* Smith, Sir Charles A.

Smith, Adm. Sir Aubrey Clare Hugh, 1872–1957, vol. V

Smith, Ven. Augustus Elder, *died* 1916, vol. II

Smith, Austin Geoffrey, 1918–1984, vol. VIII

Smith, Rev. Canon Basil Alec, 1908–1969, vol. VI

Smith, Basil Guy Oswald, 1861–1928, vol. II

Smith, Basil Thomas P.; *see* Parsons-Smith.

Smith, Gen. Bedell; *see* Smith, Gen. W. B.

Smith, Rt Hon. Sir Ben, 1879–1964, vol. VI

Smith, Benjamin Eli, 1857–1913, vol. I

Smith, Ven. Benjamin Frederick, *died* 1900, vol. I

Smith, Bernard, 1881–1936, vol. III

Smith, Bernard Joseph G.; *see* Gilliat-Smith.

Smith, Sir Berry C.; *see* Cusack-Smith.

Smith, Col Bertram Abel, 1879–1947, vol. IV

Smith, Captain Bertram Hornsby, 1874–1945, vol. IV

Smith, Lt-Col Bertram M.; *see* Metcalfe-Smith.

Smith, Sir Bracewell, 1st Bt (*cr* 1947), 1884–1966, vol. VI

Smith, Major Brooke H.; *see* Heckstall-Smith.

Smith, Hon. Bruce, 1851–1937, vol. III

Smith, Sir Bryan Evers S.; *see* Sharwood-Smith.

Smith, Mrs Burnett, 1860–1943, vol. IV

Smith, Sir Carl Victor, 1897–1979, vol. VII

Smith, Carlton A., 1853–1946, vol. IV

Smith, Cecil Archibald, *died* 1948, vol. IV

Smith, Rt Hon. Sir Cecil Clementi, 1840–1916, vol. II

Smith, Sir Cecil F.; *see* Furness-Smith.

Smith, Sir Cecil Harcourt-, 1859–1944, vol. IV

Smith, Maj.-Gen. Sir Cecil Miller, 1896–1988, vol. VIII

Smith, Mrs Cecil W.; *see* Woodham-Smith.

Smith, Charles, 1844–1916, vol. II

Smith, Hon. Sir (Charles) Abercrombie, 1834–1919, vol. II

Smith, Lt-Col Charles Aitchison, 1871–1940, vol. III

Smith, Captain Charles Appleton, 1864–1928, vol. II

Smith, Sir (Charles) Aubrey, 1863–1948, vol. IV

Smith, Col Sir Charles Bean Euan-, 1842–1910, vol. I

Smith, Charles Bennett, 1870–1939, vol. III (A), vol. IV

Smith, Sir Charles Cunliffe, 3rd Bt (*cr* 1804), 1827–1905, vol. I

Smith, Air Cdre Sir Charles Edward K.; *see* Kingsford-Smith.

Smith, Charles Emory, 1842–1908, vol. I

Smith, Captain Charles Futcher, *died* 1925, vol. II

Smith, Air Cdre Charles Gainer, 1880–1948, vol. IV

Smith, Sir Charles Garden A.; *see* Assheton-Smith.

Smith, Hon. Sir Charles George, *died* 1941, vol. IV
Smith, Charles George Percy; *see* Baron
Delacourt-Smith.
Smith, Charles H.; *see* Herbert-Smith.
Smith, Charles Harvard G.; *see* Gibbs-Smith.
Smith, Charles Henry C.; *see* Chichester Smith.
Smith, Sir (Charles) Herbert, 1871–1941, vol. IV
Smith, Maj.-Gen. Sir Charles Holled, 1846–1925,
vol. II
Smith, C(harles) Holt, 1903–1984, vol. VIII
Smith, Charles Howard, 1888–1942, vol. IV
Smith, Rev. Charles John, *died* 1940, vol. III
Smith, Charles Johnston, 1880–1943, vol. IV
Smith, Charles Michie, 1854–1922, vol. II
Smith, Charles Nugent C.; *see* Close-Smith.
Smith, Very Rev. Charles Pressley, 1862–1935,
vol. III
Smith, Sir (Charles) Robert, 1887–1959, vol. V
Smith, Rev. Charles Ryder, 1873–1956, vol. V
Smith, Charles Stewart, 1859–1934, vol. III
Smith, Captain Charles Valentine, 1854–1932,
vol. III
Smith, Mgr Charles William, 1873–1954, vol. V
Smith, Charlotte F.; *see* Fell-Smith.
Smith, Charlotte Susanna Wenban; *see* Rycroft, C. S.
Smith, Chilton Lind A.; *see* Addison-Smith.
Smith, Christopher Patrick Crawford, 1902–1984,
vol. VIII
Smith, Cicely Fox, *died* 1954, vol. V
Smith, Sir Clarence, 1849–1941, vol. IV
Smith, Rev. Clement, 1845–1921, vol. II
Smith, Lt-Gen. Clement John, 1831–1910, vol. I
Smith, Brig.-Gen. Clement Leslie, *died* 1927, vol. II
Smith, Sir Clifford Edward H.; *see* Heathcote-Smith.
Smith, Clifford P., 1869–1945, vol. IV
Smith, Colin, 1881–1940, vol. III
Smith, Sir Colville; *see* Smith, Sir P. C.
Smith, Surg.-Gen. Sir Colvin C.; *see* Colvin-Smith.
Smith, Constance Isabella Stuart, *died* 1930, vol. III
Smith, Cyril James, 1909–1974, vol. VII
Smith, Rev. David, 1866–1932, vol. III
Smith, David B.; *see* Baird-Smith.
Smith, David Bonner-, 1890–1950, vol. IV
Smith, Hon. David John, 1907–1976, vol. VII
Smith, David MacLeish, 1900–1986, vol. VIII
Smith, David Murray, *died* 1952, vol. V
Smith, David Nichol, 1875–1962, vol. VI
Smith, David S.; *see* Seth-Smith.
Smith, Hon. Sir David Stanley, 1888–1982, vol. VIII
Smith, Sir David Wadsworth, 1883–1948, vol. IV
Smith, Dempster, *died* 1953, vol. V
Smith, Desmond A.; *see* Abel Smith.
Smith, Dodie, 1896–1990, vol. VIII
Smith, Dorothy; *see* Smith, Dodie.
Smith, Douglas Alexander, 1915–1988, vol. VIII
Smith, Lt-Col Douglas Kirke, 1883–1923, vol. II
Smith, Sir Drummond Cospatric Hamilton-S., 5th Bt
(*cr* 1804); *see* Spencer-Smith.
Smith, Sir Drummond Cuncliffe, 4th Bt (*cr* 1804),
1861–1947, vol. IV
Smith, Sir Dudley S.; *see* Stewart-Smith.
Smith, Maj.-Gen. E. Davidson-, *died* 1916, vol. II
Smith, E. W.; *see* Whitney-Smith.
Smith, Ean Kendal S.; *see* Stewart-Smith.

Smith, Edgar Albert, 1847–1916, vol. II
Smith, Edgar Charles B.; *see* Bate-Smith.
Smith, Edgar Dennis, 1911–1986, vol. VIII
Smith, Maj.-Gen. Sir Edmund H.; *see* Hakewill
Smith.
Smith, Adm. Edmund Hyde, 1865–1939, vol. III
Smith, Edmund Robinson, 1856–1942, vol. IV
Smith, Sir Edmund Wyldbore-, 1877–1938, vol. III
Smith, Edward, 1839–1919, vol. II
Smith, Sir Edward, 1857–1926, vol. II
Smith, Edward B.; *see* Barclay-Smith.
Smith, Col Edward Castleman C.; *see*
Castleman-Smith.
Smith, Edward John Gregg, 1930–1989, vol. VIII
Smith, Edward Orford, 1841–1915, vol. I
Smith, Lt-Col Edward Osborne, 1864–1930, vol. III
Smith, Major Edward Pelham, 1868–1937, vol. III
Smith, Major Edward Pendarves D.; *see*
Dorrien-Smith.
Smith, Edward Percy, 1891–1968, vol. VI
Smith, Edward Rawdon R.; *see* Rawdon Smith.
Smith, Edward S.; *see* Sharwood-Smith.
Smith, Edward Shrapnell S.; *see* Shrapnell-Smith.
Smith, Edwin, 1870–1937, vol. III
Smith, Col Edwin Charles M.; *see*
Montgomery-Smith.
Smith, Hon. Sir Edwin Thomas, 1830–1919, vol. II
Smith, Rev. Edwin W., 1876–1957, vol. V
Smith, Lady Eleanor, *died* 1945, vol. IV
Smith, Ellis, 1896–1969, vol. VI
Smith, Dame Enid Mary Russell R.; *see*
Russell-Smith.
Smith, Captain Eric; *see* Smith, Captain Evan C. E.
Smith, Sir Eric; *see* Smith, Sir J. E.
Smith, Sir Eric Conran C.; *see* Conran-Smith.
Smith, Eric Martin, 1908–1951, vol. V
Smith, Eric Percival, 1890–1938, vol. III
Smith, Erik John, 1914–1972, vol. VII
Smith, Ernest, 1869–1945, vol. IV
Smith, Hon. Ernest D'Israeli, 1853–1948, vol. IV
Smith, Ernest Gardiner, *died* 1956, vol. V
Smith, Ernest T.; *see* Thornton-Smith.
Smith, Brig. Ernest Thomas Cobley, 1895–1977,
vol. VII
Smith, Sir Ernest Woodhouse, 1884–1960, vol. V
Smith, Eustace, *died* 1914, vol. I
Smith, Col Sir Eustace; *see* Smith, Col Sir T. E.
Smith, Eustace Abel, 1862–1938, vol. III
Smith, Captain Evan Cadogan Eric, 1894–1950,
vol. IV
Smith, Everard Reginald Martin, 1875–1938, vol. III
Smith, Florence Margaret; *see* Smith, Stevie.
Smith, Sir Francis Edward James, 1863–1950, vol. IV
Smith, Francis Edward Viney, 1902–1979, vol. VII
Smith, Sir Francis H.; *see* Harrison-Smith.
Smith, Francis Hopkinson, 1838–1915, vol. I
Smith, Francis Jagoe, 1873–1969, vol. VI
Smith, (Francis) Raymond (Stanley), 1890–1981,
vol. VIII
Smith, Francis St George M.; *see* Manners-Smith.
Smith, Sir Francis Villeneuve-, 1819–1909, vol. I
Smith, Sir Francis Whitmore, 1844–1931, vol. III
Smith, Francis William Head, 1886–1964, vol. VI
Smith, Hon. Sir Frank, *died* 1901, vol. I

Smith, Frank, 1854–1940, vol. III
Smith, Frank, 1882–1951, vol. V
Smith, Frank Braybrook, 1864–1950, vol. IV
Smith, Sir Frank Edward, 1879–1970, vol. VI
Smith, Sir Frank Edwin N.; *see* Newson-Smith.
Smith, Frank Guthrie, 1873–1932, vol. III
Smith, Frank Moffatt, 1872–1940, vol. III
Smith, Fred, 1880–1940, vol. III
Smith, Fred John, 1857–1919, vol. II
Smith, Frederic G.; *see* Gordon-Smith.
Smith, Frederic Marlett B.; *see* Bell-Smith.
Smith, Maj.-Gen. Sir Frederick, 1857–1929, vol. III
Smith, Col Frederick, 1858–1933, vol. III
Smith, Sir Frederick, 1859–1945, vol. IV
Smith, Frederick A., 1887–1943, vol. IV
Smith, Frederick Bonham, *born* 1837, vol. II
Smith, Rev. Frederick J. J.; *see* Jervis-Smith.
Smith, Col Frederick John, 1866–1915, vol. I
Smith, Lt Col Frederick Lawrence C.; *see* Coldwell-Smith.
Smith, Frederick Llewellyn, 1909–1988, vol. VIII
Smith, Sir Frederick William, 1861–1926, vol. II
Smith, Frederick William, 1896–1981, vol. VIII
Smith, Garden Grant, 1860–1913, vol. I
Smith, Col Sir Gengoult; *see* Smith, Sir H. G.
Smith, Geoffrey, 1878–1910, vol. I
Smith, Geoffrey Ellrington Fane, 1903–1987, vol. VIII
Smith, Geoffrey R. H., 1901–1964, vol. VI
Smith, Geoffrey Samuel A.; *see* Abel-Smith.
Smith, Vice-Adm. Sir Geoffrey T.; *see* Thistleton-Smith.
Smith, Ven. Geoffry Bertram, 1889–1957, vol. V
Smith, George, 1833–1919, vol. II
Smith, George, 1870–1934, vol. III
Smith, Sir George, 1858–1938, vol. III
Smith, George, 1867–1957, vol. V
Smith, George A.; *see* Armitage-Smith.
Smith, Very Rev. Sir George Adam, 1856–1942, vol. IV
Smith, George Barnett, 1841–1909, vol. I
Smith, Brig.-Gen. George Barton, 1860–1921, vol. II
Smith, Sir George Basil H.; *see* Haddon-Smith.
Smith, Sir George Bracewell, 2nd Bt (*cr* 1947), 1912–1976, vol. VII
Smith, George Charles Moore, 1858–1940, vol. III
Smith, George Douglas, 1865–1949, vol. IV
Smith, Brig.-Gen. George Edward, 1868–1944, vol. IV
Smith, Sir George Fenwick, 1914–1978, vol. VII
Smith, George Frederick Herbert, 1872–1953, vol. V
Smith, Rev. George Furness, 1849–1929, vol. III
Smith, George G.; *see* Gregory Smith.
Smith, George Geoffrey, 1885–1951, vol. V
Smith, Sir George Henry F.; *see* Fisher-Smith.
Smith, Rev. George Herbert, 1851–1923, vol. II
Smith, George Hill, 1833–1926, vol. II
Smith, Rt Rev. George John, 1840–1918, vol. II
Smith, Sir George John, 1845–1921, vol. II
Smith, Col George John, 1862–1946, vol. IV
Smith, George Lind A.; *see* Addison-Smith.
Smith, Rev. George Maberly, 1831–1917, vol. II
Smith, Lt-Col George Maciver Campbell, 1869–1946, vol. IV

Smith, Col George Moultrie B.; *see* Bullen-Smith.
Smith, George Munro, 1856–1917, vol. II
Smith, George Murray, 1859–1919, vol. II
Smith, Sir George R.; *see* Reeves-Smith.
Smith, George S.; *see* Scoby-Smith.
Smith, George Stuart G.; *see* Graham-Smith.
Smith, George Tulloch B.; *see* Bisset-Smith.
Smith, George W. Duff A.; *see* Assheton-Smith.
Smith, George William Q.; *see* Quick-Smith.
Smith, Major George Wilson, 1880–1940, vol. IV
Smith, Gerald Dudley, 1866–1936, vol. IV
Smith, Lt-Col Sir Gerard, 1839–1920, vol. II
Smith, Gerard Gustave L.; *see* Lind-Smith.
Smith, Brig.-Gen. Gilbert Boys, 1859–1937, vol. III
Smith, Rev. Gilbert Edward, *died* 1912, vol. I
Smith, Air Vice-Marshal Gilbert H.; *see* Harcourt-Smith.
Smith, Col Sir Gilbertson, 1867–1958, vol. V
Smith, Ven. Godfrey Scott, 1878–1944, vol. IV
Smith, Goldwin, 1823–1910, vol. I
Smith, Sir Gordon; *see* Smith, Sir W. G.
Smith, Sir Grafton Elliot, 1871–1937, vol. III
Smith, Graham Burrell, 1880–1975, vol. VII
Smith, Granville, 1859–1925, vol. II
Smith, Col Granville Roland Francis, 1860–1917, vol. II
Smith, Rev. Granville V. V., 1838–1929, vol. III
Smith, Guy B.; *see* Bassett Smith, N. G.
Smith, Sir Guy B.; *see* Bracewell-Smith.
Smith, Guy Basil G.; *see* Gilliat-Smith.
Smith, Guy Bellingham, 1865–1945, vol. IV
Smith, Rt Rev. Guy Vernon, 1880–1957, vol. V
Smith, Rev. Gwilym, 1881–1939, vol. III
Smith, H. Herbert, 1851–1913, vol. I
Smith, Sir Hamilton Pym F.; *see* Freer Smith.
Smith, Sir Harold, 1876–1924, vol. II
Smith, Col Sir Harold Charles T.; *see* Templar-Smith.
Smith, Harold Clifford, 1876–1960, vol. V
Smith, Col Sir (Harold) Gengoult, 1890–1983, vol. VIII
Smith, Harold Hamel, 1867–1944, vol. IV
Smith, Harold Octavius, 1882–1952, vol. V
Smith, Harold Ross, 1906–1956, vol. V
Smith, Harry, 1870–1940, vol. III
Smith, Rev. Harry, 1865–1942, vol. IV
Smith, Sir Harry, 1874–1949, vol. IV
Smith, Lt-Col Harry Cyril, 1888–1983, vol. VIII
Smith, Ven. (Harry Kingsley) Percival, 1898–1965, vol. VI
Smith, Maj.-Gen. Sir Harry Reginald Walter Marriott, 1875–1955, vol. V
Smith, Harry Worcester, 1865–1945, vol. IV
Smith, Harvey Hall, 1880–1958, vol. V
Smith, Rev. Haskett, 1847–1906, vol. I
Smith, Rt Hon. Hastings Bertrand L.; *see* Lees-Smith.
Smith, Helen Gregory, *died* 1956, vol. V
Smith, Hely, 1862–1941, vol. IV
Smith, Sir Henry, *died* 1919, vol. II
Smith, Lt-Col Sir Henry, 1835–1921, vol. II
Smith, Rev. Henry, 1857–1939, vol. III
Smith, Lt-Col Henry, 1862–1948, vol. IV
Smith, Henry B.; *see* Batty-Smith.

Smith, Sir Henry Babington, 1863–1923, vol. II
Smith, Henry Bompas, 1867–1953, vol. V
Smith, Maj.-Gen. Henry C.; *see* Coape-Smith.
Smith, Engr Rear-Adm. Henry Frank, 1875–1939, vol. III
Smith, Rev. Henry Gibson, *died* 1931, vol. III
Smith, Brig. Henry Gilbertson, 1896–1977, vol. VII
Smith, Lt-Col Henry Lockhart, 1859–1935, vol. III
Smith, Sir Henry Martin, 1907–1979, vol. VII
Smith, Sir Henry Moncrieff, 1873–1951, vol. V
Smith, H(enry) Norman, 1890–1962, vol. VI
Smith, Col Henry Robert, 1843–1917, vol. II
Smith, Henry Roy William, 1891–1971, vol. VII
Smith, Sir Henry S.; *see* Scott-Smith.
Smith, Sir Henry Sutcliffe, 1864–1938, vol. III
Smith, Sir Henry Thompson, 1905–1986, vol. VIII
Smith, Henry W.; *see* Whitby-Smith.
Smith, Sir Henry W.; *see* White-Smith.
Smith, Sir Henry W.; *see* Wilson Smith.
Smith, Henry Wood, 1865–1906, vol. I
Smith, Sir Herbert; *see* Smith, Sir C. H.
Smith, Sir Herbert, 1st Bt (*cr* 1920), 1872–1943, vol. IV
Smith, Herbert, 1881–1953, vol. V
Smith, Sir Herbert, 2nd Bt (*cr* 1920), 1903–1961, vol. VI
Smith, Herbert Alexander, 1896–1976, vol. VII
Smith, Herbert Arthur, 1885–1961, vol. VI
Smith, Col Herbert Austen, 1866–1949, vol. IV
Smith, Herbert Cecil, 1893–1981, vol. VIII
Smith, Col Herbert Francis, 1859–1948, vol. IV
Smith, Lt-Col Herbert Frederick Edgar, 1888–1940, vol. III
Smith, Herbert Greenhough, *died* 1935, vol. III
Smith, Maj.-Gen. Sir Herbert Guthrie, 1864–1930, vol. III
Smith, Rev. Herbert Maynard, 1869–1949, vol. IV
Smith, Herbert S.; *see* Somerville Smith.
Smith, Major Herbert Stoney-, 1868–1915, vol. I
Smith, Herbert Williams, 1919–1987, vol. VIII
Smith, Horace, 1836–1922, vol. II
Smith, Howard; *see* Smith, P. H.
Smith, Col Howard William, 1858–1905, vol. I
Smith, Brig. Hubert Clementi, 1878–1958, vol. V
Smith, Sir Hubert Llewellyn, 1864–1945, vol. IV
Smith, Sir Hubert S.; *see* Shirley-Smith.
Smith, Hon. Hugh Adeane Vivian, 1910–1978, vol. VII
Smith, Hugh Alexander McC.; *see* McClure-Smith.
Smith, Lt-Col Sir Hugh Bateman P.; *see* Protheroe-Smith.
Smith, Hugh Bellingham, 1866–1922, vol. II
Smith, Hugh Colin, 1836–1910, vol. I
Smith, Hugh Crawford, *died* 1907, vol. I
Smith, Captain Hugh D.; *see* Dalrymple-Smith.
Smith, Brig. Hugh Garden S.; *see* Seth-Smith.
Smith, Hugh William H.; *see* Heckstall-Smith.
Smith, Vice-Adm. Humphrey Hugh, 1875–1940, vol. III
Smith, Ida Phyllis B.; *see* Barclay-Smith.
Smith, Rev. Irton, 1855–1933, vol. III
Smith, Rev. Isaac A., *died* 1940, vol. III
Smith, Rev. Isaac Gregory, 1826–1920, vol. II
Smith, J. Allister, 1866–1960, vol. V

Smith, J. T., *died* 1937, vol. III
Smith, Sir James, 1847–1932, vol. III
Smith, Most Rev. James A., 1841–1928, vol. II
Smith, James Alexander George, *died* 1942, vol. IV
Smith, Very Rev. James Allan, 1841–1918, vol. II
Smith, Col James Aubrey, 1877–1955, vol. V
Smith, Sir James Brown, 1845–1913, vol. I
Smith, Sir James Cowlishaw, 1873–1946, vol. IV
Smith, James Cruickshank, 1867–1946, vol. IV
Smith, James David Maxwell, 1895–1969, vol. VI
Smith, James Dury H.; *see* Hindley-Smith.
Smith, Sir James Edward M.; *see* Masterton-Smith.
Smith, Sir (James) Eric, 1909–1990, vol. VIII
Smith, James Hamblin, 1827–1901, vol. I
Smith, Hon. Sir (James) Joynton, 1855–1943, vol. IV
Smith, Surg.-Rear-Adm. James Lawrence, 1862–1945, vol. III
Smith, James Lorrain, *died* 1931, vol. III
Smith, James Maclaren G.; *see* Gray-Smith.
Smith, Rt Hon. James Parker, 1854–1929, vol. III
Smith, Lt-Col Sir James Robert Dunlop, 1858–1921, vol. II
Smith, James Stewart, 1900–1987, vol. VIII
Smith, James Walter, 1868–1931, vol. III
Smith, Maj.-Gen. Jeremy Michael S.; *see* Spencer-Smith.
Smith, Rev. John, 1844–1905, vol. I
Smith, John, 1825–1910, vol. I
Smith, John, 1837–1922, vol. II
Smith, Very Rev. John, 1854–1927, vol. II
Smith, John, 1883–1964, vol. VI
Smith, John Alexander, 1863–1939, vol. III
Smith, Sir John Alfred L.; *see* Lucie-Smith.
Smith, Maj.-Gen. John Blackburne, 1865–1928, vol. II
Smith, John F.; *see* Forest Smith.
Smith, John George, 1881–1968, vol. VI
Smith, Sir John George Lawley V.; *see* Vassar-Smith.
Smith, John Gerald, 1907–1979, vol. VII
Smith, Lt-Col John Grant, *died* 1942, vol. IV
Smith, J(ohn) G(uthrie) Spence, 1880–1951, vol. V
Smith, John Henry E.; *see* Etherington-Smith.
Smith, John Hugh; *see* Smith, A. J. H.
Smith, John Hughes W.; *see* Wardle-Smith.
Smith, Sir John James, 1875–1957, vol. V
Smith, John Keats C.; *see* Catterson-Smith.
Smith, Lt-Col John Manners, 1864–1920, vol. II
Smith, John Mitchell Aitken, 1902–1974, vol. VII
Smith, John Obed, 1864–1937, vol. III
Smith, Rev. John Reader, *died* 1923, vol. II
Smith, Sir John Smalman, 1847–1913, vol. I
Smith, Rt Rev. John Taylor, 1860–1938, vol. III
Smith, John William, 1864–1926, vol. II
Smith, Sir Jonah W.; *see* Walker-Smith.
Smith, Joseph, 1855–1939, vol. III
Smith, Maj.-Gen. Joseph Barnard, 1839–1925, vol. II
Smith, Sir Joseph Benjamin George, 1878–1950, vol. IV
Smith, Rt Rev. Joseph Oswald, 1854–1924, vol. II
Smith, Hon. Sir Joynton; *see* Smith, Hon. Sir James J.
Smith, K. W. A., 1899–1951, vol. V
Smith, Sir Keith Macpherson, 1890–1955, vol. V
Smith, Col Kenneth, 1885–1971, vol. VII

Smith, Kenneth Brooke Farley, 1913–1943, vol. IV
Smith, Brig.-Gen. Kenneth John K.; *see* Kincaid-Smith.
Smith, Kenneth Manley, 1892–1981, vol. VIII
Smith, Kenneth Shirley, 1900–1987, vol. VIII
Smith, Lancelot Grey Hugh, 1870–1941, vol. IV
Smith, Launcelot Eustace, 1868–1948, vol. IV
Smith, Sir Laurence Barton G.; *see* Graffley-Smith.
Smith, Sir Leonard Herbert, 1907–1989, vol. VIII
Smith, Col Leonard Kirke, 1877–1941, vol. IV
Smith, Lewis, 1869–1944, vol. IV
Smith, Captain Sir Lindsey, 1870–1960, vol. V
Smith, Brig.-Gen. Lionel A.; *see* Abel-Smith.
Smith, Col Lionel Fergus, 1869–1945, vol. IV
Smith, Lionel Graham Horton H.; *see* Horton-Smith.
Smith, Logan Pearsall, 1865–1949, vol. IV
Smith, Louis L.; *see* Laybourne-Smith.
Smith, Sir Louis W., *died* 1939, vol. III
Smith, Rt Rev. Lucius, 1860–1934, vol. III
Smith, Sir Lumley, 1834–1918, vol. II
Smith, Lyman Cornelius, *died* 1910, vol. I
Smith, Sir Malcolm, *died* 1935, vol. III
Smith, Lt-Col Malcolm K.; *see* Kincaid-Smith.
Smith, Marcella, *died* 1963, vol. VI
Smith, Maria Constance, *died* 1930, vol. III
Smith, Marshall King, 1867–1946, vol. IV
Smith, Rt Rev. Martin Linton, 1869–1950, vol. IV
Smith, Martin Ridley, 1833–1908, vol. I
Smith, Mary Isobel Barr, *died* 1941, vol. IV
Smith, Mary Sybil, *died* 1952, vol. V
Smith, Sir Matthew Arnold Bracy, 1879–1959, vol. V
Smith, May, 1879–1968, vol. VI
Smith, Maynard, 1875–1928, vol. II
Smith, Maj.-Gen. Merton B.; *see* Beckwith-Smith.
Smith, Michael James B.; *see* Babington Smith.
Smith, Michael Seymour S.; *see* Spencer-Smith.
Smith, Michael Wharton, 1927–1989, vol. VIII
Smith, Hon. Miles Staniforth Cater, 1869–1934, vol. III
Smith, Montague Bentley Talbot P.; *see* Paske-Smith.
Smith, Morton William, 1851–1925, vol. II
Smith, Naomi Gwladys R.; *see* Royde Smith.
Smith, Sir Nathaniel B.; *see* Bowden-Smith.
Smith, Nevil Digby B.; *see* Bosworth-Smith.
Smith, (Newlands) Guy B.; *see* Bassett Smith.
Smith, Noel James Gillies, *born* 1899, vol. VI
Smith, Norman, 1877–1963, vol. VI
Smith, Norman Kemp, 1872–1958, vol. V
Smith, Norman Lockhart, 1887–1968, vol. VI
Smith, Sir Norman Percival Arthur, 1892–1964, vol. VI
Smith, Captain Norman Wesley, 1900–1977, vol. VII
Smith, Nowell Charles, 1871–1961, vol. VI
Smith, Lt-Gen. Octavius Ludlow, 1828–1927, vol. II
Smith, Olivia Mary, (Mrs R. D. Smith); *see* Manning, O. M.
Smith, Lt-Col Osbert Walter Dudley, 1898–1973, vol. VII
Smith, Sir Osborne Arkell, 1876–1952, vol. V
Smith, Very Rev. Oswin Harvard G.; *see* Gibbs-Smith.
Smith, Owen Hugh, *died* 1958, vol. V
Smith, Owen Maurice, 1888–1957, vol. V

Smith, Patrick, 1858–1930, vol. III
Smith, Patrick Wykeham M.; *see* Montague-Smith.
Smith, Ven. Percival; *see* Smith, Ven. H. K. P.
Smith, Major Percy George D.; *see* Darvil-Smith.
Smith, Percy John Delf, *died* 1948, vol. IV
Smith, Surg.-Rear-Adm. Sir Percy W. B.; *see* Bassett-Smith.
Smith, Peter Caldwell, 1858–1923, vol. II
Smith, Philip, 1853–1922, vol. II
Smith, Sir (Philip) Colville, *died* 1937, vol. III
Smith, Philip H. Law, 1866–1920, vol. II
Smith, Philip Henry P.; *see* Pye-Smith.
Smith, (Philip) Howard, 1845–1919, vol. II
Smith, Rear-Adm. P(hilip) Sydney, 1899–1973, vol. VII
Smith, Rev. Philip Vernon, 1845–1929, vol. III
Smith, Brig. Philip William Lilian B.; *see* Broke-Smith.
Smith, Phyllis B.; *see* Barclay-Smith.
Smith, Priestley, *died* 1933, vol. III
Smith, Sir Prince, 1st Bt (*cr* 1911), 1840–1922, vol. II
Smith, Sir Prince P., 2nd Bt (*cr* 1911); *see* Prince-Smith.
Smith, Ralph Henry H.; *see* Hammersley-Smith.
Smith, Ralph Henry T.; *see* Tottenham-Smith.
Smith, Ravenscroft Elsey, 1859–1930, vol. III
Smith, Raymond; *see* Smith, F. R. S.
Smith, Reginald, vol. II
Smith, Rev. Reginald, 1844–1936, vol. III
Smith, Reginald Allender, *died* 1940, vol. III
Smith, Reginald Arthur, 1904–1985, vol. VIII
Smith, Reginald Eccles, 1887–1963, vol. VI
Smith, Reginald Henry Macaulay A.; *see* Abel Smith.
Smith, Col Rt Hon. Sir Reginald Hugh D.; *see* Dorman-Smith.
Smith, Reginald John, 1857–1916, vol. II
Smith, Reginald John, 1895–1981, vol. VIII
Smith, Reginald Montagu B.; *see* Bosworth-Smith.
Smith, Reginald Norman M.; *see* Marsh Smith.
Smith, Rennie, 1888–1962, vol. VI
Smith, Richard Edwin, 1910–1978, vol. VII
Smith, Richard G.; *see* Gordon-Smith.
Smith, Richard Horton H.; *see* Horton-Smith.
Smith, Richard M.; *see* Mudie-Smith.
Smith, Maj.-Gen. Richard Talbot S.; *see* Snowden-Smith.
Smith, Sir Richard Vassar V.; *see* Vassar-Smith.
Smith, Sir Robert; *see* Smith, Sir C. R.
Smith, Robert Addison, *died* 1925, vol. II
Smith, Robert Allan, 1909–1980, vol. VII
Smith, Robert Cooper, 1859–1917, vol. II
Smith, Robert John, 1866–1942, vol. IV
Smith, Robert Macaulay, 1859–1927, vol. II
Smith, Sir Robert Murdoch, 1835–1900, vol. I
Smith, Robert Murray, 1831–1921, vol. II
Smith, Robert Paterson, 1903–1971, vol. VII
Smith, Robert Percy, *died* 1941, vol. IV
Smith, Robert Shingleton, 1845–1922, vol. II
Smith, Sir Robert Workman, 1st Bt (*cr* 1945), 1880–1957, vol. V
Smith, Rt Rev. Rocksborough Remington, 1872–1955, vol. V
Smith, Sir Roderick Philip, 1926–1981, vol. VIII
Smith, Gipsy Rodney, 1860–1947, vol. IV

Smith, Roger Thomas, 1863–1940, vol. III
Smith, Rev. Ronald Gregor, 1913–1968, vol. VI
Smith, Ronald Parkinson; *see* Parkinson, N.
Smith, Sir Ross G.; *see* Grey-Smith.
Smith, Sir Ross Macpherson, 1892–1922, vol. II
Smith, Sir Rudolph Hampden; *see* Smith, Sir T. R. H.
Smith, Col Rupert Alexander A.; *see* Alec-Smith.
Smith, Rupert Rawden R.; *see* Rawden-Smith.
Smith, Rutherfoord John P.; *see* Pye-Smith.
Smith, S. Catterson, 1849–1912, vol. I
Smith, Rt Hon. Samuel, 1836–1906, vol. I
Smith, Samuel, 1855–1921, vol. II
Smith, Samuel Harold, 1888–1971, vol. VII
Smith, Samuel Walter Johnson, 1871–1948, vol. IV
Smith, Sarah; *see* Stretton, Hesba.
Smith, Sheila K.; *see* Kaye-Smith.
Smith, Sidney, 1889–1979, vol. VII
Smith, Lt-Col Sidney Browning, *died* 1930, vol. III
Smith, Sidney Earle, 1897–1959, vol. V
Smith, Solomon Charles Kaines, *died* 1958, vol. V
Smith, Spence; *see* Smith, John G. S.
Smith, Stanley Alexander de; *see* de Smith.
Smith, Major Stanley Alwyn, 1882–1931, vol. III
Smith, Stanley G.; *see* Graham Smith.
Smith, Stanley Livingston, 1889–1958, vol. V
Smith, Stanley Parker, 1884–1953, vol. V
Smith, Stanley Wyatt-, 1887–1958, vol. V
Smith, Stephen Henry, 1865–1943, vol. IV
Smith, Col Steuart B.; *see* Bogle-Smith.
Smith, Stevie, (Florence Margaret Smith),
   1902–1971, vol. VII
Smith, Stuart Hayne G.; *see* Granville-Smith.
Smith, Captain Sutton, *died* 1938, vol. III
Smith, Sir Swire, 1842–1918, vol. II
Smith, Maj.-Gen. Sir Sydenham Campbell Urquhart,
   1859–1940, vol. III
Smith, Hon. Sydney, 1856–1934, vol. III
Smith, Sydney, 1900–1981, vol. VIII
Smith, Sir Sydney Alfred, *died* 1969, vol. VI
Smith, Sir Sydney Armitage A.; *see* Armitage-Smith.
Smith, Sydney David, 1873–1936, vol. III
Smith, Col Sydney Ernest, 1881–1943, vol. IV
Smith, Rev. Sydney Fenn, 1843–1921, vol. II
Smith, Sydney Herbert, 1885–1984, vol. VIII
Smith, Sydney Ure, 1887–1949, vol. IV
Smith, Sydney William, 1878–1963, vol. VI
Smith, T. Gilbert, *died* 1904, vol. I
Smith, Theobald, 1859–1934, vol. III
Smith, Theodore Clarke, 1870–1960, vol. V (A),
   vol. VI (AI)
Smith, Thomas, 1817–1906, vol. I
Smith, Sir Thomas, 1st Bt (*cr* 1897), 1833–1909, vol. I
Smith, Sir Thomas, 1875–1963, vol. VI
Smith, Thomas, 1883–1969, vol. VI
Smith, Thomas Algernon D.; *see* Dorrien-Smith.
Smith, Sir Thomas Brown, 1915–1988, vol. VIII
Smith, Major Thomas Close, 1878–1946, vol. IV
Smith, Sir Thomas Cospatric Hamilton-S., 6th Bt (*cr*
   1804); *see* Spencer-Smith.
Smith, Sir Thomas D. S.; *see* Straker-Smith.
Smith, Col Sir (Thomas) Eustace, 1900–1971,
   vol. VII
Smith, Rev. Canon Thomas G.; *see* Grigg-Smith.

Smith, Major Sir Thomas Gabriel Lumley L.; *see*
   Lumley-Smith.
Smith, Rt Rev. Thomas Geoffrey Stuart, 1901–1981,
   vol. VIII
Smith, Thomas I.; *see* Irvine Smith.
Smith, Sir Thomas James, *died* 1939, vol. III
Smith, Thomas James, 1905–1970, vol. VI
Smith, Thomas Roger, 1830–1903, vol. I
Smith, Sir (Thomas) Rudolph Hampden, 2nd Bt (*cr*
   1897), 1869–1958, vol. V
Smith, Sir Thomas Turner, 3rd Bt (*cr* 1897),
   1903–1961, vol. VI
Smith, (Thomas) Wareham, 1874–1938, vol. III
Smith, Thomas William, 1878–1946, vol. IV
Smith, Tom, 1886–1953, vol. V
Smith, Sir Tom Elder B.; *see* Barr Smith.
Smith, Mrs Toulmin; *see* Meade, L. T.
Smith, Trafford, 1912–1975, vol. VII
Smith, Vernon Russell, 1849–1921, vol. II
Smith, Victor, 1879–1931, vol. III
Smith, Vincent Arthur, 1848–1920, vol. II
Smith, Vivian Francis C.; *see* Crowther-Smith.
Smith, W. Harding, *died* 1922, vol. II
Smith, W. H. S.; *see* Seth-Smith.
Smith, W. P. Haskett-, *died* 1946, vol. IV
Smith, Sir Walter B.; *see* Buchanan-Smith.
Smith, Gen. (Walter) Bedell, 1895–1961, vol. VI
Smith, Walter Campbell, 1887–1988, vol. VIII
Smith, Rev. Walter Chalmers, 1824–1908, vol. I
Smith, Walter George, 1844–1932, vol. III
Smith, Rev. Walter Percy, 1848–1922, vol. II
Smith, Rev. Walter R., 1845–1921, vol. II
Smith, Walter Riddell, 1914–1984, vol. VIII
Smith, Walter Robert, 1872–1942, vol. IV
Smith, Walter Robert George, 1887–1966, vol. VI
Smith, Walter William Marriott, 1846–1944, vol. IV
Smith, Wareham; *see* Smith, T. W.
Smith, Watson, 1845–1920, vol. II
Smith, Wilfred, 1903–1955, vol. V
Smith, Maj.-Gen. Wilfrid Edward Bownas,
   1867–1942, vol. IV
Smith, Sir William, 1843–1916, vol. II
Smith, Maj.-Gen. William, 1835–1922, vol. II
Smith, William, 1859–1932, vol. III
Smith, Sir William Alexander, 1854–1914, vol. I
Smith, Col William Apsley, 1856–1927, vol. II
Smith, Vice-Adm. William B.; *see* Bowden Smith.
Smith, William Benjamin, 1850–1934, vol. III (A),
   vol. IV
Smith, William Binns, 1837–1911, vol. I
Smith, William Brownhill, *died* 1948, vol. IV
Smith, Sir William C.; *see* Cusack-Smith.
Smith, William Charles, 1849–1915, vol. I
Smith, William Charles Clifford, 1855–1931, vol. III
Smith, Maj.-Gen. Sir William Douglas, 1865–1939,
   vol. III
Smith, Maj.-Gen. William Dunlop, 1865–1940,
   vol. III
Smith, Sir William Edward, 1850–1930, vol. III
Smith, Hon. William Forgan, 1887–1953, vol. V
Smith, Sir William Frederick Haynes, 1839–1928,
   vol. II
Smith, William French, 1917–1990, vol. VIII
Smith, Sir William George Verdon, 1876–1957, vol. V

Smith, Sir (William) Gordon, 2nd Bt, 1916–1983, vol. VIII
Smith, William Henry, 1894–1968, vol. VI
Smith, William Herbert G.; see Guthrie-Smith.
Smith, Rev. William Hodson, 1856–1943, vol. IV
Smith, Brig.-Gen. William Hugh Usher, 1869–1940, vol. III
Smith, Captain William Humphrey, 1879–1942, vol. IV
Smith, Rev. William Isaac Carr, died 1930, vol. III
Smith, Sir William James, 1853–1912, vol. I
Smith, Sir William Joseph P.; see Pearman-Smith.
Smith, William Owen Lester, 1888–1976, vol. VII
Smith, Sir William P.; see Prince-Smith.
Smith, Sir William Proctor, 1891–1963, vol. VI
Smith, Sir William R., died 1932, vol. III
Smith, William Ramsay, 1859–1937, vol. III
Smith, Sir William Reardon, 1st Bt (cr 1920), 1856–1935, vol. III
Smith, Maj.-Gen. William Revell R.; see Revell-Smith.
Smith, Sir (William Robert) Dermot (Joshua) C.; see Cusack-Smith.
Smith, Sir William Rose, 1852–1934, vol. III
Smith, Most Rev. William Saumarez, 1836–1909, vol. I
Smith, William Sydney, 1866–1945, vol. IV
Smith, Sir William Sydney Winwood, 4th Bt (cr 1809), 1879–1953, vol. V
Smith, Sir William Wright, 1875–1956, vol. V
Smith, Willie; see Smith, H. W.
Smith, Sir Willie Reardon-, 2nd Bt (cr 1920), 1887–1950, vol. IV
Smith, Wilson, 1897–1965, vol. VI
Smith, Winifred L. B.; see Boys-Smith.
Smith-Bingham, Brig.-Gen. Oswald Buckley Bingham; see Bingham.
Smith-Bosanquet, Major George Richard Bosanquet, 1866–1939, vol. III
Smith-Carington, Herbert Hanbury; see Carington.
Smith-Carington, Neville Woodford, 1878–1933, vol. III
Smith-Dodsworth, Sir Claude Matthew, 7th Bt, 1888–1940, vol. III
Smith-Dorrien, Olive Crofton, (Lady Smith-Dorrien), died 1951, vol. V
Smith-Dorrien, Gen. Sir Horace Lockwood, 1858–1930, vol. III
Smith-Dorrien, Rev. Walter Montgomery, died 1924, vol. II
Smith-Gordon, Sir Lionel Eldred, 2nd Bt, 1833–1905, vol. I
Smith-Gordon, Sir Lionel Eldred Pottinger, 3rd Bt, 1857–1933, vol. III
Smith-Gordon, Sir Lionel Eldred Pottinger, 4th Bt, 1889–1976, vol. VII
Smith-Marriott, Rev. Sir Hugh Randolph Cavendish, 9th Bt, 1868–1944, vol. IV
Smith-Marriott, Sir John Richard Wyldbore, 7th Bt, 1875–1942, vol. IV
Smith-Marriott, Sir Ralph George Cavendish, 10th Bt, 1900–1987, vol. VIII
Smith-Marriott, Sir William, 8th Bt, 1865–1943, vol. IV

Smith-Marriott, Sir William Henry, 5th Bt, 1835–1924, vol. II
Smith-Marriott, Sir William John, 6th Bt, 1870–1941, vol. IV
Smith-Neill, Col James William, 1865–1935, vol. III
Smith-Pearse, Thomas Lawrence, 1893–1972, vol. VII
Smith-Pearse, Rev. Thomas Northmore Hart, 1854–1943, vol. IV
Smith-Rewse, Rev. Gilbert Flesher, died 1935, vol. III
Smith-Rewse, Col Henry Whistler, 1850–1930, vol. III
Smith-Rose, Reginald Leslie, 1894–1980, vol. VII
Smith-Ryland, Sir Charles Mortimer Tollemache, 1927–1989, vol. VIII
Smithard, Major Richard Glass, 1891–1939, vol. III
Smithe, Ida Elizabeth, died 1951, vol. V
Smithe, Major Percy Bourdillon, 1860–1912, vol. I
Smithells, Arthur, 1860–1939, vol. III
Smithers, Sir Alfred Waldron, 1850–1924, vol. II
Smithers, Sir Arthur Tennyson, 1894–1972, vol. VII
Smithers, Donald William, 1905–1986, vol. VIII
Smithers, Brig. Leonard Sueton Hirsch, 1879–1954, vol. V
Smithers, Sir Waldron, 1880–1954, vol. V
Smithson, Col Walter Charles, 1860–1938, vol. III
Smithwick, Rear-Adm. Algernon Robert, 1887–1948, vol. IV
Smithwick, John Francis, 1844–1913, vol. I
Smolka, H. P.; see Smollett, H. P.
Smollett, Maj.-Gen. Alexander Patrick Drummond T.; see Telfer-Smollett.
Smollett, Harry Peter, 1912–1980, vol. VII
Smollett, Captain James Drummond T.; see Telfer-Smollett.
Smoot, Reed, 1862–1941, vol. IV
Smout, Sir Arthur John Griffiths, 1888–1961, vol. VI
Smout, Charles Frederick Victor, 1895–1978, vol. VII
Smout, David Arthur Lister, 1923–1987, vol. VIII
Smuts, Field Marshal Rt Hon. Jan Christian, 1870–1950, vol. IV
Smuts, Johannes, 1865–1937, vol. III
Smylie, Air Cdre Gilbert Formby, 1895–1965, vol. VI
Smyly, Col Dennis Douglas Pilkington, 1913–1979, vol. VII
Smyly, J. Gilbert, 1867–1948, vol. IV
Smyly, Sir Philip Crampton, 1838–1904, vol. I
Smyly, Sir Philip Crampton, 1896–1953, vol. V
Smyly, William Cecil, 1840–1921, vol. II
Smyly, Sir William Josiah, 1850–1941, vol. IV
Smyth, Sir Alfred John Bowyer-, 13th Bt (cr 1661), 1850–1927, vol. II
Smyth, Austin Edward Arthur Watt, 1877–1949, vol. IV
Smyth, Col Charles Coghlan, 1842–1920, vol. II
Smyth, Charles Edward O.; see Owen-Smyth.
Smyth, Rev. Canon Charles Hugh Egerton, 1903–1987, vol. VIII
Smyth, David Henry, 1908–1979, vol. VII
Smyth, Dame Ethel Mary, 1858–1944, vol. IV
Smyth, Col Etwall Walter, 1843–1929, vol. III
Smyth, Lt-Col Geoffrey Henry Julian Skeffington; see FitzPatrick, Lt-Col G. H. J.
Smyth, George Watson, 1838–1910, vol. I

Smyth, Captain Gerald Brice Ferguson, 1885–1920, vol. II
Smyth, Hon. Gilbert Neville, 1864–1940, vol. III
Smyth, Rear-Adm. Harry Hesketh, 1872–1926, vol. II
Smyth, Lt-Col Henry, 1866–1943, vol. IV
Smyth, Gen. Sir Henry Augustus, 1825–1906, vol. I
Smyth, (Herbert) Warington, died 1943, vol. IV
Smyth, Major Humphrey Etwall, 1884–1927, vol. II
Smyth, James Richard, 1895–1953, vol. V
Smyth, John, 1864–1927, vol. II
Smyth, Brig.-Gen. John Ambard B.; see Bell-Smyth.
Smyth, John Andrew, 1893–1971, vol. VII
Smyth, Brig. Rt Hon. Sir John George, 1st Bt, 1893–1983, vol. VIII
Smyth, Lt-Col John Henry Graham Holroyd, 1846–1904, vol. I
Smyth, Sir John Henry Greville, 1st Bt, 1836–1901, vol. I
Smyth, Ven. John Paterson, died 1932, vol. III
Smyth, John William, 1880–1968, vol. VI
Smyth, Michael Joseph, died 1964, vol. VI
Smyth, Montague; see Smyth, W. M.
Smyth, Vice-Adm. Morris Henry, 1853–1940, vol. III
Smyth, Maj.-Gen. Sir Nevill Maskelyne, 1868–1941, vol. IV
Smyth, Col Owen Stuart, 1853–1923, vol. II
Smyth, Captain Sir Philip Weyland Bowyer-, 14th Bt, 1894–1978, vol. VII
Smyth, Sir Robert Middleton Watson, 1872–1939, vol. III
Smyth, Brig.-Gen. Robert Napier, 1868–1947, vol. IV
Smyth, Lt-Col Robert Riversdale, 1875–1946, vol. IV
Smyth, Sir Samuel Andrew, 1877–1953, vol. V
Smyth, Rev. Thomas Alexander, died 1936, vol. III
Smyth, Thomas Francis, 1875–1937, vol. III
Smyth, (Walter) Montague, 1863–1965, vol. VI
Smyth, Warington; see Smyth, H. W.
Smyth, Rev. William A. B.; see Blood-Smyth.
Smyth, William Bates, 1874–1946, vol. IV
Smyth, Rt Rev. William Edmund, 1858–1950, vol. IV
Smyth, Col William Ross, 1857–1932, vol. III
Smyth-Osbourne, Brig.-Gen. George Nowell Thomas, 1877–1942, vol. IV
Smyth-Osbourne, Air Cdre Sir Henry Percy, 1879–1969, vol. VI
Smyth-Pigott, Gp Captain (Joseph) Ruscombe (Wadham), 1889–1971, vol. VII
Smyth-Pigott, Gp Captain Ruscombe; see Smyth-Pigott, Gp Captain J. R. W.
Smythe, Albert Charles B.; see Butler-Smythe.
Smythe, Charles John, 1852–1918, vol. II
Smythe, Col David Murray, 1850–1928, vol. II
Smythe, Sir Edward Walter Joseph Patrick Herbert, 9th Bt, 1869–1942, vol. IV
Smythe, Rev. Canon Francis Henry Dumville, 1873–1966, vol. VI
Smythe, Francis Sydney, 1900–1949, vol. IV
Smythe, Henry James Drew-, 1916–1983, vol. VIII
Smythe, Sir (John) Walter, 8th Bt, 1827–1919, vol. II
Smythe, Lionel Percy, 1840–1918, vol. II
Smythe, Very Rev. Patrick Murray, 1860–1935, vol. III
Smythe, Sir Reginald Harry, 1905–1981, vol. VIII

Smythe, Lt-Col Rupert Cæsar, 1879–1943, vol. IV
Smythe, Sir Walter; see Smythe, Sir J. W.
Smythies, Evelyn Arthur, 1885–1975, vol. VII
Snadden, Sir William McNair, 1st Bt, 1896–1959, vol. V
Snagge, Vice-Adm. Arthur Lionel, 1878–1955, vol. V
Snagge, Sir Harold Edward, 1872–1949, vol. IV
Snagge, Sir Mordaunt; see Snagge, Sir T. M.
Snagge, Sir (Thomas) Mordaunt, 1868–1955, vol. V
Snagge, Sir Thomas William, 1837–1914, vol. I
Snaith, John Collis, 1876–1936, vol. III
Snaith, Gp Captain Leonard Somerville, 1902–1985, vol. VIII
Snaith, Rev. Norman Henry, 1898–1982, vol. VIII
Snaith, Stanley, 1903–1976, vol. VII
Snape, Henry Lloyd, 1861–1933, vol. III
Snark, The; see Wood, Starr.
Snead-Cox, John, 1855–1939, vol. III
Snedden, Rt Hon. Sir Billy Mackie, 1926–1987, vol. VIII
Snedden, Sir Richard, 1900–1970, vol. VI
Sneddon, Rev. James, 1871–1945, vol. IV
Snell, 1st Baron, 1865–1944, vol. IV
Snell, Alfred Walter S.; see Saxon-Snell.
Snell, Ven. Basil Clark, 1907–1986, vol. VIII
Snell, Rev. Bernard J., 1856–1934, vol. III
Snell, Rt Rev. Geoffrey Stuart, 1920–1988, vol. VIII
Snell, Harvie Kennard, 1898–1969, vol. VI
Snell, Captain Ivan Edward, 1884–1958, vol. V
Snell, J. Herbert, 1861–1935, vol. III
Snell, Sir John Francis Cleverton, 1869–1938, vol. III
Snell, Simeon, died 1909, vol. I
Snell, William Edward, 1902–1990, vol. VIII
Snell, William Thomas, died 1951, vol. V
Snelling, Maj.-Gen. Arthur Hugh Jay, 1897–1965, vol. VI
Snelus, Alan Roe, 1911–1990, vol. VIII
Snelus, George James, 1837–1906, vol. I
Sneyd, Ralph, 1863–1949, vol. IV
Sneyd, Vice-Adm. Ralph Stuart W.; see Wykes-Sneyd.
Sneyd, Maj.-Gen. Thomas William, 1837–1918, vol. II
Sneyd-Kynnersley, Charles Walter; see Kynnersley, C. W. S.
Snodgrass, William Robertson, 1890–1955, vol. V
Snow, Baron (Life Peer); Charles Percy Snow, 1905–1980, vol. VII
Snow, Lady; see Johnson, Pamela Hansford.
Snow, Rt Rev. George D'Oyly, 1903–1977, vol. VII
Snow, Edgar Parks, 1905–1972, vol. VII
Snow, Ernest Charles, 1886–1959, vol. V
Snow, Sir Frederick Sidney, 1899–1976, vol. VII
Snow, (George) Robert Sabine, 1897–1969, vol. VI
Snow, Sir Gordon Keith, 1898–1954, vol. V
Snow, Sir Harold Ernest, 1897–1971, vol. VII
Snow, Henry Martin, 1859–1931, vol. III
Snow, Herbert, 1847–1930, vol. III
Snow, Lt-Col Humphry Waugh, 1879–1969, vol. VI
Snow, Julian Ward; see Baron Burntwood.
Snow, Philip Chicheley Hyde, 1853–1931, vol. III
Snow, Robert Sabine; see Snow, G. R. S.
Snow, Sir Sydney, 1887–1958, vol. V

Snow, Lt-Gen. Sir Thomas D'Oyly, 1858–1940, vol. III

Snowden, 1st Viscount, 1864–1937, vol. III

Snowden, Viscountess; (Ethel), 1881–1951, vol. V

Snowden, Sir Arthur, 1829–1918, vol. II

Snowden, Arthur de Winton, 1872–1950, vol. IV

Snowden, Rev. Arthur Hillersdon, 1856–1940, vol. III

Snowden, Lt-Col Sir Eccles; see Snowden, Lt-Col Sir R. E.

Snowden, James; see Snowden, Keighley.

Snowden, Rev. John Hampden, 1828–1907, vol. I

Snowden, Joseph Stanley, 1901–1980, vol. VII

Snowden, Keighley, 1860–1947, vol. IV

Snowden, Lt-Col Sir (Robert) Eccles, 1880–1934, vol. III

Snowden, Tom, 1875–1949, vol. IV

Snowden-Smith, Maj.-Gen. Richard Talbot, 1887–1951, vol. V

Snoy, Baron Robert, 1879–1946, vol. IV

Snyder, John Wesley, 1895–1985, vol. VIII

Soady, Brig.-Gen. George Joseph FitzMaurice, 1863–1940, vol. III

Soame, Sir Charles Buckworth-Herne-, 9th Bt, 1830–1906, vol. I

Soame, Sir Charles Buckworth-Herne-, 10th Bt, 1864–1931 (this entry was not transferred to Who Was Who).

Soame, Sir Charles Burnett Buckworth-Herne-, 11th Bt, 1894–1977, vol. VII (inserted in error in vol. III)

Soames, Baron (Life Peer); Arthur Christopher John Soames, 1920–1987, vol. VIII

Soames, Major Alfred, 1862–1915, vol. I

Soames, Arthur Gilstrap, 1854–1934, vol. III

Soames, Arthur Wellesley, 1852–1934, vol. III

Soames, Geoffrey Ewart, 1881–1952, vol. V

Soar, Joseph, 1878–1971, vol. VII

Soar, Leonard Charles, 1899–1969, vol. VI

Soares, Sir Ernest Joseph, 1864–1926, vol. II

Sobha Singh, Hon. Sardar Bahadur Sir Sardar, 1890–1978, vol. VII

Sobry, Henri, 1861–1937, vol. III

Soddy, Frederick, 1877–1956, vol. V

Soddy, Kenneth, 1911–1986, vol. VIII

Soden, Freiherr Hermann von, 1852–1914, vol. I

Soden, Thomas Spooner, 1837–1920, vol. II

Söderblom, Nathan Lars Olof Jonathan, 1866–1931, vol. III

Soertsz, Sir Francis Joseph, 1886–1951, vol. V

Soheily, Ali, 1896–1958, vol. V

Sokhey, Maj.-Gen. Sir Sahib Singh, 1887–1971, vol. VII

Solberg, Thorvald, 1852–1949, vol. IV (A), vol. V

Soldene, Emily, died 1912, vol. I

Sole, Brig. Denis Mavesyn Anslow, 1883–1962, vol. VI

Sollas, William Johnson, 1849–1936, vol. III

Sollberger, Edmond, 1920–1989, vol. VIII

Solley, Leslie Judah, 1905–1968, vol. VI

Solloway, Rev. John, 1860–1946, vol. IV (A)

Solly, S. Edwin, 1845–1906, vol. I

Solly-Flood, Maj.-Gen. Arthur, 1871–1940, vol. III

Solly-Flood, Maj.-Gen. Sir Frederick Richard, 1829–1909, vol. I

Solly-Flood, Brig.-Gen. Richard Elles, 1877–1954, vol. V

Sologub, Feodor, 1864–1927, vol. II

Solomon, 1902–1988, vol. VIII

Solomon, Hon. Albert Edgar, 1876–1914, vol. I

Solomon, Sir (Aubrey) Kenneth, 1884–1954, vol. V

Solomon, Hon. Sir Edward Philip, died 1914, vol. I

Solomon, Edwin, 1914–1985, vol. VIII

Solomon, Frank Oakley, 1867–1941, vol. IV

Solomon, Sir Kenneth; see Solomon, Sir A. K.

Solomon, Sir Richard, 1850–1913, vol. I

Solomon, Saul, 1875–1960, vol. V

Solomon, Solomon Joseph, 1860–1927, vol. II

Solomon, Captain William Ewart Gladstone, 1880–1965, vol. VI

Solomon, Rt Hon. Sir William Henry, 1852–1930, vol. III

Solomons, Bethel, died 1965, vol. VI

Solomons, Estella Frances, died 1968, vol. VI

Solomons, Henry, 1902–1965, vol. VI

Soloveytchik, George Michael de, 1902–1982, vol. VIII

Soltau, Col Alfred Bertram, 1876–1930, vol. III

Soltau, Roger Henry, 1887–1953, vol. V

Soltau-Symons, Lt-Col George Algernon James, 1867–1947, vol. IV

Soltau-Symons, George William Culme, 1831–1916, vol. II

Soltykoff, HSH Prince Dimitri, died 1903, vol. I

Solvay, Ernest, 1839–1922, vol. II

Sombart, Werner, 1863–1941, vol. IV

Somerhough, Hon. Anthony George, 1906–1960, vol. V

Somerleyton, 1st Baron, 1857–1935, vol. III

Somerleyton, 2nd Baron, 1889–1959, vol. V

Somerleyton, Lady; (Phyllis), died 1948, vol. IV

Somers, 5th Baron, 1815–1899, vol. I

Somers, 6th Baron, 1887–1944, vol. IV

Somers, 7th Baron, 1864–1953, vol. V

Somers, Lady; (Finola), 1896–1981, vol. VIII

Somers, Thomas Peter Miller, 1877–1965, vol. VI

Somers-Cocks, Rev. Henry Lawrence, 1862–1940, vol. III

Somers Cocks, John Sebastian, 1907–1964, vol. VI

Somerset, 15th Duke of, 1846–1923, vol. II

Somerset, 16th Duke of, 1860–1931, vol. III

Somerset, 17th Duke of, 1882–1954, vol. V

Somerset, 18th Duke of, 1910–1984, vol. VIII

Somerset, Col Sir Alfred Plantagenet Frederick Charles, 1829–1915, vol. I

Somerset, Brig.-Gen. Charles Wyndham, 1862–1938, vol. III

Somerset, Lady Henry, (Isabel), 1851–1921, vol. II

Somerset, Henry Charles Somers Augustus, 1874–1945, vol. IV

Somerset, Rt Hon. Lord Henry Richard Charles, 1849–1932, vol. III

Somerset, Henry Robert Somers Fitzroy de Vere, 1898–1965, vol. VI

Somerset, John Henry William, 1848–1928, vol. II, vol. III

Somerset, Brig. Hon. Nigel FitzRoy, 1893–1990, vol. VIII

Somerset, Richard Gay, 1848–1928, vol. II, vol. III

Somerset, Raglan Horatio Edwyn Henry, 1885–1956, vol. V

Somerset, Sir Thomas, 1870–1947, vol. IV

Somerset-Thomas, William Edwin, 1867–1946, vol. IV

Somervell of Harrow, Baron (Life Peer); Donald Bradley Somervell, 1889–1960, vol. V

Somervell, Sir Arnold Colin, 1883–1957, vol. V

Somervell, Sir Arthur, 1863–1937, vol. III

Somervell, David Churchill, 1885–1965, vol. VI

Somervell, James, 1845–1924, vol. II

Somervell, Rupert Churchill Gelderd, 1892–1969, vol. VI

Somervell, Theodore Howard, 1890–1975, vol. VII

Somervell, William Henry, 1860–1934, vol. III

Somerville, Sir Annesley Ashworth, 1858–1942, vol. IV

Somerville, Arthur Fownes, 1850–1942, vol. IV

Somerville, Vice-Adm. Boyle; see Somerville, Vice-Adm. H. B. T.

Somerville, Daniel Gerald, 1879–1938, vol. III

Somerville, David Hughes, 1840–1918, vol. II

Somerville, Edith Anna Œnone, 1858–1949, vol. IV

Somerville, Col George Cattell, 1878–1959, vol. V

Somerville, Vice-Adm. (Henry) Boyle (Townshend), 1863–1936, vol. III

Somerville, Howard, 1873–1952, vol. V

Somerville, Vice-Adm. Hugh Gaultier-Coghill, 1873–1950, vol. IV

Somerville, Lt-Col James Aubrey Henry Bellingham, 1884–1950, vol. IV

Somerville, Admiral of the Fleet Sir James Fownes, 1882–1949, vol. IV

Somerville, Col John Arthur Coghill, 1872–1955, vol. V

Somerville, Sir John Livingston, 1885–1964, vol. VI

Somerville, (Katherine) Lilian, 1905–1985, vol. VIII

Somerville, Lilian; see Somerville, K. L.

Somerville, Mary, 1897–1963, vol. VI

Somerville, Comdr Philip, 1906–1942, vol. IV

Somerville, Rev. Richard Neville, 1864–1932, vol. III

Somerville, Col Thomas Cameron FitzGerald, 1860–1942, vol. IV

Somerville, Walter Harold, 1881–1959, vol. V

Somerville, Sir William, 1860–1932, vol. III

Somerville, Lt-Col William Arthur Tennison Bellingham, 1882–1951, vol. V

Somerville, William Dennistoun, 1842–1917, vol. II

Somerville Smith, Herbert, 1890–1967, vol. VI

Somjee, Mahomedbhoy Alladinbhoy, 1889–1942, vol. IV

Sommer, André D.; see Dupont-Sommer.

Sommerlad, Hon. Ernest Christian, 1886–1952, vol. V

Sommerville, David, died 1937, vol. III

Sommerville, Duncan M'Laren Young, 1879–1934, vol. III

Sommerville, Vice-Adm. Frederick Avenel, 1883–1962, vol. VI

Sommerville, Norman, 1878–1941, vol. IV

Sonbarsa, Maharaja of, 1846–1907, vol. I

Sondes, 2nd Earl, 1861–1907, vol. I

Sondes, 3rd Earl, 1866–1941, vol. IV

Sondes, 4th Earl, 1914–1970, vol. VI

Sondheimer, Franz, 1926–1981, vol. VIII

Song Ong Siang, Sir, died 1941, vol. IV

Sonnenschein, Edward Adolf, 1851–1929, vol. III

Sonneborn, Tracy Morton, 1905–1981, vol. VIII

Sonnino, Baron Sidney, 1847–1922, vol. II

Sontag, Raymond James, 1897–1972, vol. VII

Soothill, Alfred, 1863–1926, vol. II

Soothill, Ronald Gray, 1898–1980, vol. VII

Soothill, Rev. William Edward, 1861–1935, vol. III

Soper, Frederick George, 1898–1982, vol. VIII

Soper, George, 1870–1942, vol. IV

Soper, Harry Tapley Tapley-, 1875–1951, vol. V

Soper, J. Dewey, 1893–1982, vol. VIII

Sopoushek, Mrs Jan; see Greig, Maysie.

Sopwith, Douglas George, 1906–1970, vol. VI

Sopwith, Ven. Thomas Karl, 1873–1945, vol. IV

Sopwith, Sir Thomas Octave Murdoch, 1888–1989, vol. VIII

Sorabji, Cornelia, died 1954, vol. V

Sorby, Rev. Albert Ernest, 1859–1934, vol. III

Sorby, Henry Clifton, 1826–1908, vol. I

Sorel, Albert, 1842–1906, vol. I

Sorel Cameron, Brig. John, 1907–1986, vol. VIII

Sorell-Cameron, George Cecil Minett; see Cameron.

Sorensen, Baron (Life Peer); Reginald William Sorensen, 1891–1971, vol. VII

Sorine, Savely, 1886–1953, vol. V

Sorley, Herbert Tower, 1892–1968, vol. VI

Sorley, Air Marshal Sir Ralph Squire, 1898–1974, vol. VII

Sorley, William Ritchie, 1855–1935, vol. III

Sorn, Hon. Lord; James Gordon McIntyre, 1896–1983, vol. VIII

Sorokin, Pitirim Alexandrovitch, 1889–1968, vol. VI

Sorrell, Alan, 1904–1974, vol. VII

Sorsbie, Sir Malin, 1906–1988, vol. VIII

Sorsbie, Brig.-Gen. Robert Fox, 1866–1948, vol. IV

Sorsby, Arnold, 1900–1980, vol. VII

Sorsby, Maurice, 1898–1949, vol. IV

Soskice, Frank; see Baron Stow Hill.

Soteriades, Antis Georghios, 1924–1988, vol. VIII

Sotheby, Sir Edward Southwell, 1813–1902, vol. I

Sotheby, Lt-Col Herbert George, 1871–1954, vol. V

Sothern, Edward H., 1859–1933, vol. III

Sotheron-Estcourt, Rev. Edmund Walter, 1850–1938, vol. III

Sotheron-Estcourt, Captain Thomas Edmund, 1881–1958, vol. V

Sothers, Donald Bevan, 1889–1979, vol. VII

Souchon, Sir (Hippolyte) Louis (Wiehe du Coudray), 1865–1957, vol. V

Souchon, Sir Louis; see Souchon, Sir H. L. W. du C.

Soulbury, 1st Viscount, 1887–1971, vol. VII

Soulby, Rev. Charles Frederick Hodgkinson, 1881–1952, vol. V

Soule, Malcolm H., 1896–1951, vol. V

Soulsby, Sir Llewellyn T. G., 1885–1966, vol. VI

Soulsby, Sir William Jameson, 1851–1937, vol. III

Soundy, Hon. Sir John, 1878–1960, vol. V (A), vol. VI (AI)

Soundy, Sir John Thomas, 1851–1935, vol. III

Sousa, John Philip, 1854–1932, vol. III

Soustelle, Jacques Emile, 1912–1990, vol. VIII

Soutar, Andrew, 1879–1941, vol. IV

Soutar, Brig. John James Macfarlane, 1889–1956, vol. V

Soutar, William, 1898–1943, vol. IV

Souter, Alexander, 1873–1949, vol. IV

Souter, Sir Charles Alexander, 1877–1958, vol. V

Souter, Sir Edward Matheson, 1891–1959, vol. V

Souter, Col Hugh Maurice Wellesley, 1873–1941, vol. IV

Souter, Sir William Alfred, 1879–1968, vol. VI

Souter, William Lochiel Berkeley, 1865–1945, vol. IV

South, Richard, died 1932, vol. III

Southall, Joseph Edward, 1861–1944, vol. IV

Southall, Reginald Bradbury, 1900–1965, vol. VI

Southall, Thomas Frederick, 1898–1965, vol. VI

Southam, Alexander William, 1898–1981, vol. VIII

Southam, Rev. Eric George, 1884–1952, vol. V

Southam, Frederick Armitage, died 1927, vol. II

Southam, Harry Stevenson, died 1954, vol. V

Southampton, 4th Baron, 1867–1958, vol. V

Southampton, 5th Baron (disclaimed for life); see FitzRoy, Charles.

Southborough, 1st Baron, 1860–1947, vol. IV

Southborough, 2nd Baron, 1889–1960, vol. V

Southborough, 3rd Baron, 1897–1982, vol. VIII

Southby, Sir (Archibald) Richard (Charles), 2nd Bt, 1910–1988, vol. VIII

Southby, Comdr Sir Archibald Richard James, 1st Bt, 1886–1969, vol. VI

Southby, Sir Richard; see Southby, Sir A. R. C.

Southcott, Rev. Canon Ernest William, 1915–1976, vol. VII

Southee, Ethelbert Ambrook, 1890–1968, vol. VI

Southern, Sir James Wilson, 1840–1909, vol. I

Southern, Ralph Lang, 1893–1968, vol. VI (AII)

Southern, Richard, 1903–1989, vol. VIII

Southerton, Sydney James, 1874–1935, vol. III

Southesk, 9th Earl of, 1827–1905, vol. I

Southesk, 10th Earl of, 1854–1941, vol. IV

Southey, Hon. Charles William, 1832–1924, vol. II

Southey, Air Cdre Harold Frederic George, 1906–1979, vol. VII

Southey, Reginald, 1835–1899, vol. I

Southey, Sir Richard, 1808–1901, vol. I

Southey, Col Richard George, 1844–1909, vol. I

Southey, Maj.-Gen. William Melvill, 1866–1939, vol. III

Southgate, Bernard Alfred, 1904–1975, vol. VII

Southgate, Margaret Cecil Irene, 1918–1970, vol. VI

Southorn, Sir Thomas; see Southorn, Sir W. T.

Southorn, Sir (Wilfrid) Thomas, 1879–1957, vol. V

Southouse-Cheyney, Major Reginald Evelyn Peter; see Cheyney, Peter.

Southward, Rev. Walter Thomas, 1851–1919, vol. II

Southwark, 1st Baron, 1843–1929, vol. III

Southwell, 5th Viscount, 1872–1944, vol. IV

Southwell, 6th Viscount, 1898–1960, vol. V

Southwell, Sir (Charles Archibald) Philip, 1894–1981, vol. VIII

Southwell, Rt Rev. Henry Kemble, died 1937, vol. III

Southwell, Rev. Herbert Burrows, died 1922, vol. II

Southwell, Sir Philip; see Southwell, Sir C. A. P.

Southwell, Sir Richard Vynne, 1888–1970, vol. VI

Southwood, 1st Viscount, 1873–1946, vol. IV

Southwood, Albert Ray, died 1973, vol. VII

Souttar, Sir Henry, 1875–1964, vol. VI

Souttar, Robinson, 1848–1912, vol. I

Soutter, Francis William, 1844–1932, vol. III

Sovereign, Rt Rev. Arthur Henry, 1881–1966, vol. VI (AII)

Soward, Sir Alfred Walter, 1856–1949, vol. IV

Sowby, Rev. Cedric Walter, 1902–1975, vol. VII

Sowden, Sir William John, 1858–1943, vol. IV

Sowerby, (Amy) Millicent, 1878–1967, vol. VI (AII)

Sowerby, Arthur de Carle, 1885–1954, vol. V

Sowerby, Lt-Col Harry John, 1867–1935, vol. III

Sowerby, Katherine Githa, (Mrs John Kendall), died 1970, vol. VI

Sowerby, Millicent; see Sowerby, A. M.

Sowler, Col Harry, died 1962, vol. VI

Sowman, Air Cdre John Edward Rudkin, 1902–1979, vol. VII

Sowrey, Gp Captain Frederick, 1893–1968, vol. VI

Sowrey, Air Cdre William, 1894–1968, vol. VI

Sowter, Ven. Francis Briggs, died 1928, vol. II

Sowton, Charles, 1865–1932, vol. III

Spaak, Fernand Paul Jules, 1923–1981, vol. VIII

Spaak, Paul-Henri, 1899–1972, vol. VII

Spaatz, Gen. Carl Andrew, 1891–1974, vol. VII

Spackman, Air Vice-Marshal Charles Basil Slater, 1895–1971, vol. VII

Spackman, Cyril Saunders, 1887–1963, vol. VI

Spahlinger, Henry, 1882–1965, vol. VI

Spaight, James Molony, 1877–1968, vol. VI

Spain, Lt-Col George Redesdale Booker, 1877–1961, vol. VI

Spain, John Edward D.; see Dixon-Spain.

Spain-Dunk, Susan, 1880–1962, vol. VI

Spalding, Franklin Spencer, 1865–1914, vol. I

Spalding, Henry Norman, 1877–1953, vol. V

Spalding, Kenneth Jay, 1879–1962, vol. VI

Spalding, Col Warner, 1844–1920, vol. II

Spalding, William F., 1879–1963, vol. VI

Spanswick, Albert; see Spanswick, E. A. G.

Spanswick, (Ernest) Albert (George), 1919–1983, vol. VIII

Spanton, Rev. Ernest Frederick, 1871–1936, vol. III

Spargo, John, 1876–1966, vol. VI

Sparke, George Archibald, 1871–1970, vol. VI

Sparkes, Henry, 1871–1950, vol. IV

Sparkes, Sir James; see Sparkes, Sir W. B. J. G.

Sparkes, Rear-Adm. Robert C.; see Copland-Sparkes.

Sparkes, Stanley Robert, 1910–1976, vol. VII

Sparkes, Sir (Walter Beresford) James (Gordon), 1889–1974, vol. VII

Sparkes, Col William Spottiswoode, 1862–1906, vol. I

Sparkman, John Jackson, 1899–1985, vol. VIII

Sparks, Sir Ashley, 1877–1964, vol. VI

Sparks, Beatrice M., died 1953, vol. V

Sparks, Charles Pratt, 1866–1940, vol. III

Sparks, Sir Frederick James, 1881–1953, vol. V

Sparks, Col Hubert Conrad, 1874–1933, vol. III

Sparks, Joseph Alfred, 1901–1981, vol. VIII

Sparks, Nathaniel, 1880–1957, vol. V

Sparrow, Rev. David Alan, 1936–1981, vol. VIII

Sparrow, Col Richard, 1871–1953, vol. V

Sparrow, Walter Shaw, *died* 1940, vol. III
Sparshott, Margaret Elwin, 1870–1940, vol. III
Spater, Ernest George, 1886–1975, vol. VII
Spath, Leonard Frank, 1882–1957, vol. V
Spaul, Eric Arthur, 1895–1978, vol. VII
Speaight, Frederick William, 1869–1942, vol. IV
Speaight, Richard Langford, 1906–1976, vol. VII
Speaight, Richard Neville, 1875–1938, vol. III
Speaight, Robert William, 1904–1976, vol. VII
Speakman, Sir Harry, 1865–1946, vol. IV
Speakman, John Bamber, 1897–1969, vol. VI
Speakman, Lionel, *died* 1948, vol. IV
Spear, (Augustus John) Ruskin, 1911–1990, vol. VIII
Spear, Lt-Col Christopher Ronald, 1897–1942, vol. IV
Spear, Sir John Ward, 1848–1921, vol. II
Spear, Ruskin; *see* Spear, A. J. R.
Speares, Denis James, 1922–1970, vol. VI
Spearman, Sir Alexander Bowyer, 4th Bt, 1917–1977, vol. VII
Spearman, Sir Alexander Cadwallader Mainwaring, 1901–1982, vol. VIII
Spearman, Sir Alexander Young, 3rd Bt, 1881–1959, vol. V
Spearman, Charles E., 1863–1945, vol. IV
Spearman, Edmund Robert, 1837–1918, vol. II
Spearman, Sir Joseph Layton Elmes, 2nd Bt, 1857–1922, vol. II
Spears, Maj.-Gen. Sir Edward Louis, 1st Bt, 1886–1974, vol. VII
Spears, Mary, (Lady Spears); *see* Borden, Mary.
Speck, Rev. Jocelyn Henry, *died* 1922, vol. II
Spector, Walter Graham, 1924–1982, vol. VIII
Spedding, Major Charles Rodney, 1871–1915, vol. I
Spedding, Brig.-Gen. Edward Wilfrid, 1867–1939, vol. III
Speechly, Rt Rev. John Martindale, 1836–1898, vol. I
Speed, Sir Edwin Arney, 1869–1941, vol. IV
Speed, Sir Eric Bourne Bentinck, 1895–1971, vol. VII
Speed, Harold, 1872–1957, vol. V
Speed, James A.; *see* Andrews-Speed.
Speed, Lancelot, 1860–1931, vol. III
Speed, Marjorie Jane, 1903–1982, vol. VIII
Speelman, Sir Cornelis Jacob, 7th Bt, 1881–1949, vol. IV
Speelman, Sir Cornelis Jacob Abraham, 5th Bt, 1823–1898, did not have an entry in Who's Who.
Speelman, Sir Helenus, 6th Bt, 1852–1907, did not have an entry in Who's Who.
Speer, Rear-Adm. F. Shirley Litchfield-, 1874–1922, vol. II
Speer, Robert Elliott, 1867–1947, vol. IV
Speidel, Gen. Hans, 1897–1984, vol. VIII
Speight, Harold Edwin Balme, 1887–1975, vol. VII
Speight, Thomas Wilkinson, 1830–1915, vol. I
Speir, Col Guy Thomas, 1875–1951, vol. V
Speir, Wing Comdr Robert Cecil Talbot, 1904–1980, vol. VII
Speir, Robert Thomas Napier, 1841–1922, vol. II
Speirs, Alexander Archibald Hagart-, 1869–1958, vol. V
Spellman, Cardinal Francis J., 1889–1967, vol. VI
Spenale, Georges, 1913–1983, vol. VIII

Spence, Sir Alexander, 1866–1939, vol. III (A), vol. IV
Spence, Col Alexander Hierom Ogilvy, 1869–1936, vol. III
Spence, Allan William, 1900–1990, vol. VIII
Spence, Col Sir Basil Hamilton Hebden N.; *see* Neven-Spence.
Spence, Sir Basil Urwin, 1907–1976, vol. VII
Spence, Catherine Helen, 1825–1910, vol. I
Spence, Edward Fordham, 1860–1932, vol. III
Spence, Sir George Hemming, 1888–1962, vol. VI
Spence, Col Gilbert Ormerod, 1879–1925, vol. II
Spence, Henry Reginald, 1897–1981, vol. VIII
Spence, Sir James Calvert, 1892–1954, vol. V
Spence, James Knox, 1844–1919, vol. II
Spence, (James) Lewis (Thomas Chalmers), 1874–1955, vol. V
Spence, Ven. John, *died* 1914, vol. I
Spence, John, 1878–1949, vol. IV
Spence, John Bowring, 1861–1918, vol. II
Spence, John Deane, 1920–1986, vol. VIII
Spence, Lewis; *see* Spence, J. L. T. C.
Spence, Sir Reginald, 1880–1961, vol. VI
Spence, Robert, 1870–1964, vol. VI
Spence, Robert, 1879–1966, vol. VI
Spence, Robert, 1905–1976, vol. VII
Spence, Most Rev. Robert William, 1860–1934, vol. III
Spence, Thomas William Leisk, 1845–1923, vol. II
Spence, William Robert Locke, 1875–1954, vol. V
Spence-Colby, Col Cecil John Herbert, 1873–1954, vol. V
Spence-Jones, Very Rev. Henry Donald Maurice, 1836–1917, vol. II
Spencelayh, Charles, 1865–1958, vol. V
Spencer, 5th Earl, 1835–1910, vol. I
Spencer, 6th Earl, 1857–1922, vol. II
Spencer, 7th Earl, 1892–1975, vol. VII
Spencer, Countess; (Cynthia Ellinor Beatrix), 1897–1972, vol. VII
Spencer, Rev. Arthur John, 1850–1922, vol. II
Spencer, Lt-Col Aubrey Vere, 1886–1973, vol. VII
Spencer, Augustus, 1860–1924, vol. III
Spencer, Sir Baldwin; *see* Spencer, Sir W. B.
Spencer, Brian, 1922–1985, vol. VIII
Spencer, Sir Charles Gordon Spencer, 1869–1934, vol. III
Spencer, Col Charles Louis, 1870–1948, vol. IV
Spencer, Dorothy, *died* 1969, vol. VI
Spencer, Sir Ernest, 1848–1937, vol. III
Spencer, Brig. Francis Elmhirst, 1881–1972, vol. VII
Spencer, Frederic, 1861–1942, vol. IV
Spencer, Air Vice-Marshal Geoffrey Roger Cole, 1901–1969, vol. VI
Spencer, Ven. George, *died* 1926, vol. II, vol. III
Spencer, George Alfred, 1872–1957, vol. V
Spencer, Gilbert, 1893–1979, vol. VII
Spencer, Sir Harris, 1863–1934, vol. III
Spencer, Sir Henry Francis, 1892–1964, vol. VI
Spencer, Herbert, 1820–1903, vol. I
Spencer, Major Herbert Eames, 1871–1945, vol. IV
Spencer, Herbert Ritchie, 1860–1941, vol. IV
Spencer, Hugh, 1867–1926, vol. II
Spencer, James Frederick, 1881–1950, vol. IV

Spencer, Brig.-Gen. John Almeric Walter, 1881–1952, vol. V
Spencer, Col John H.; see Heatly-Spencer.
Spencer, Leonard James, 1870–1959, vol. V
Spencer, Surg.-Gen. Sir Lionel Dixon, 1842–1915, vol. I
Spencer, Col Maurice, 1863–1940, vol. III
Spencer, Noël, 1900–1986, vol. VIII
Spencer, Percival, 1864–1913, vol. I
Spencer, Rev. Percival L., 1845–1932, vol. III
Spencer, Captain Richard Austin, 1892–1956, vol. V
Spencer, Lt-Col Rowland Pickering, 1892–1965, vol. VI
Spencer, Sir Stanley, 1891–1959, vol. V
Spencer, Terence John Bew, 1915–1978, vol. VII
Spencer, Sir Thomas George, 1888–1976, vol. VII
Spencer, Sir (Walter) Baldwin, 1860–1929, vol. III
Spencer, Walter George, died 1940, vol. III
Spencer, William Kingdon, died 1955, vol. V
Spencer Chapman, Lt-Col Frederick, 1907–1971, vol. VII
Spencer-Churchill, Baroness (Life Peer); Clementine Ogilvy Spencer-Churchill, 1885–1977, vol. VII
Spencer-Churchill, Lord Edward; see Churchill.
Spencer-Churchill, Captain Edward George; see Churchill.
Spencer-Nairn, Sir Douglas Leslie; see Nairn.
Spencer-Nairn, Major Sir Robert, 1st Bt, 1880–1960, vol. V
Spencer-Phillips, Major John Charles, died 1937, vol. III
Spencer-Smith, Sir Drummond Cospatric Hamilton-, 5th Bt, 1876–1955, vol. V
Spencer-Smith, Maj.-Gen. Jeremy Michael, 1917–1985, vol. VIII
Spencer-Smith, Michael Seymour, 1881–1928, vol. II
Spencer-Smith, Sir Thomas Cospatric Hamilton-, 6th Bt, 1917–1959, vol. V
Spender, A. F., died 1947, vol. IV
Spender, Arthur Edmund, 1871–1923, vol. II
Spender, E. Harold, 1864–1926, vol. II
Spender, Hugh Frederick, 1873–1930, vol. III
Spender, John Alfred, 1862–1942, vol. IV
Spender, Hon. Sir Percy Claude, 1897–1985, vol. VIII
Spender, Lt-Col Sir Wilfrid Bliss, 1876–1960, vol. V
Spender-Clay, Lt-Col Rt Hon. Herbert Henry, 1875–1937, vol. III
Spengler, Oswald, 1880–1936, vol. III
Spenlove-Spenlove, Frank, 1868–1933, vol. III
Spens, 1st Baron, 1885–1973, vol. VII
Spens, 2nd Baron, 1914–1984, vol. VIII
Spens, Ven. Andrew N. W., 1844–1932, vol. III
Spens, Col Hugh Baird, 1885–1958, vol. V
Spens, Maj.-Gen. James, 1853–1934, vol. III
Spens, Janet, 1876–1963, vol. VI
Spens, J(ohn) Ivan, 1890–1964, vol. VI
Spens, Nathaniel, 1850–1933, vol. III
Spens, Sir Will, 1882–1962, vol. VI
Spenser, Harry Joseph, 1866–1937, vol. III
Spenser-Wilkinson, Sir Thomas Crowe, 1899–1982, vol. VIII
Sperling, Sir Rowland Arthur Charles, 1874–1965, vol. VI
Sperrin-Johnson, John Charles, 1885–1948, vol. IV

Sperring, Digby, 1897–1969, vol. VI
Sperry, Willard Learoyd, 1882–1954, vol. V
Speyer, Sir Edgar, 1st Bt, 1862–1932, vol. III
Spicer, Rt Hon. Sir Albert, 1st Bt, 1847–1934, vol. III
Spicer, Sir (Albert) Dykes, 2nd Bt, 1880–1966, vol. VI
Spicer, Sir Dykes; see Spicer, Sir A. D.
Spicer, Sir Evan, 1849–1937, vol. III
Spicer, Gerald Sydney, 1874–1942, vol. IV
Spicer, Henry Gage, 1875–1944, vol. IV
Spicer, Holmes W. T., 1860–1935, vol. III
Spicer, Sir Howard, 1872–1926, vol. II
Spicer, James Leonard, 1873–1949, vol. IV
Spicer, Hon. Sir John Armstrong, 1899–1978, vol. VII
Spicer, John Edmund Philip, 1850–1928, vol. II
Spicer, Rev. Canon John Maurice, died 1920, vol. II
Spicer, Lancelot Dykes, 1893–1979, vol. VII
Spicer, Robert Henry Scanes, died 1925, vol. II
Spicer, Roy Godfrey Bullen, 1889–1946, vol. IV
Spicer, Captain Sir Stewart Dykes, 3rd Bt, 1888–1968, vol. VI
Spicer, W. T. H.; see Spicer, Holmes W. T.
Spicer-Jay, Edith Katharine; see Prescott, E. Livingston.
Spickernell, Sir Frank Todd, 1885–1956, vol. V
Spidle, Rev. Simeon, 1867–1954, vol. V
Spielman, Sir Meyer A., 1856–1936, vol. III
Spielmann, Sir Isidore, 1854–1925, vol. II
Spielmann, Mabel Henrietta, 1862–1938, vol. III
Spielmann, Marion Harry Alexander, 1858–1948, vol. IV
Spielmann, Percy Edwin, 1881–1964, vol. VI
Spiers, Harry Ratcliff, 1883–1956, vol. V
Spiers, Richard Phené, 1838–1916, vol. II
Spiers, Victor Julian Taylor, died 1937, vol. III
Spiller, John Wyatt, 1878–1949, vol. IV
Spilsbury, Alfred John, 1874–1940, vol. III
Spilsbury, Sir Bernard Henry, 1877–1947, vol. IV
Spinelli, Altiero, 1907–1986, vol. VIII
Spingarn, J. E., 1875–1939, vol. III (A), vol. IV
Spink, John Stephenson, 1909–1985, vol. VIII
Spinks, Alfred, 1917–1982, vol. VIII
Spinks, Maj.-Gen. Sir Charlton Watson, 1877–1959, vol. V
Spinks, Frederick Lowten, 1816–1899, vol. I
Spinks, Rev. George Stephens, 1903–1978, vol. VII
Spinks, Major John Thomas, 1889–1969, vol. VI
Spinner, Alice; see Fraser, Mrs Augusta Zelia.
Spinney, George Franklin, 1852–1926, vol. II
Spinney, George Wilbur, 1889–1948, vol. IV
Spire, Frederick, 1863–1951, vol. V
Spitta, Edmund Johnson, 1853–1921, vol. II
Spitta, Harold Robert Dacre, 1877–1954, vol. V
Spittel, Richard Lionel, 1881–1969, vol. VI
Spitteler, Carl Friedrich Georg, 1845–1924, vol. II
Spoer, Mrs H. H.; see Goodrich-Freer, A. M.
Spofforth, Markham, 1825–1907, vol. I
Spokes, Arthur Hewett, 1854–1922, vol. II
Spokes, Sir Peter, 1830–1910, vol. I
Spong, Major Charles Stuart, 1859–1925, vol. II
Spooner, Brig. Gen. Arthur Hardwicke, 1879–1945, vol. IV
Spooner, Charles Edwin, 1853–1909, vol. I

Spooner, Edgar Clynton Ross, 1908–1976, vol. VII
Spooner, Very Rev. Edward, *died* 1899, vol. I
Spooner, Edwin George, 1898–1977, vol. VII
Spooner, Rear-Adm. Ernest John, 1887–1942, vol. IV
Spooner, Ven. George Hardwicke, *died* 1933, vol. III
Spooner, Henry John, 1856–1940, vol. III
Spooner, Rev. Henry Maxwell, *died* 1929, vol. III
Spooner, Rev. William Archibald, 1844–1930, vol. III
Spooner, Rt Hon. Sir William Henry, 1897–1966, vol. VI
Spoor, Rt Hon. Benjamin Charles, 1878–1928, vol. II
Sporborg, Henry Nathan, 1905–1985, vol. VIII
Spottiswoode, John Roderick Charles Herbert, 1882–1946, vol. IV
Spottiswoode, Col Robert Collinson D'Esterre, 1841–1936, vol. III
Spottiswoode, William Hugh, 1864–1915, vol. I
Spowers, Col Allan, 1892–1968, vol. VI
Spragg, Cyril Douglas, 1894–1986, vol. VIII
Spragge, Lt-Col Basil Edward, 1852–1926, vol. II
Spragge, Brig.-Gen. Charles Henry, 1842–1920, vol. II
Spraggett, Col Richard William, *died* 1976, vol. VII
Sprague, Oliver Mitchell Wentworth, 1873–1953, vol. V
Sprague, Thomas Bond, 1830–1920, vol. II
Sprankling, Rt Rev. Mgr James, 1860–1935, vol. III
Spratt, Most Rev. Michael J., 1854–1938, vol. III
Sprawson, Maj.-Gen. Sir Cuthbert Allan, 1877–1956, vol. V
Sprawson, Evelyn Charles, 1881–1955, vol. V
Spreckels, Claus, 1828–1908, vol. I
Spreckels, John Diedrich, 1853–1926, vol. II
Spreckley, Air Marshal Sir Herbert Dorman, 1904–1963, vol. VI
Spreckley, Herbert William, 1857–1950, vol. IV
Sprengel, Hermann Johann Philipp, 1834–1906, vol. I
Sprigg, Alfred Gordon, 1861–1921, vol. II
Sprigg, Rt Hon. Sir John Gordon, 1830–1913, vol. I
Sprigg, Stanhope William, *died* 1932, vol. III
Sprigge, Cecil Jackson Squire, 1896–1959, vol. V
Sprigge, Elizabeth Miriam Squire, 1900–1974, vol. VII
Sprigge, Sir Squire, 1860–1937, vol. III
Spriggs, Sir Edmund Ivens, *died* 1949, vol. IV
Spriggs, Sir Frank Spencer, 1895–1969, vol. VI
Spring, Sir Francis Joseph Edward, 1849–1933, vol. III
Spring, Brig.-Gen. Frederick Gordon, 1878–1963, vol. VI
Spring, Howard, 1889–1965, vol. VI
Spring-Rice, Rt Hon. Sir Cecil Arthur, 1859–1918, vol. II
Spring-Rice, Dominick, 1889–1940, vol. III
Spring-Rice, Stephen Edward, 1856–1902, vol. I
Springall, Harold Douglas, 1910–1982, vol. VIII
Springer, Axel Caesar, 1912–1985, vol. VIII
Springett, Rev. William Douglas, 1850–1928, vol. II
Springfield, George, 1861–1939, vol. III
Springfield, Lincoln, *died* 1950, vol. IV
Springhall, Brig. Robert John, 1900–1965, vol. VI
Springman, Dame Ann Marcella, 1933–1987, vol. VIII
Sprot, Col Sir Alexander, 1st Bt, 1853–1929, vol. III

Sprot, Lt-Gen. John, 1830–1907, vol. I
Sprot, Major Mark, 1881–1946, vol. IV
Sprott, Sir Frederick Lawrence, 1863–1943, vol. IV
Sprott, Rt Rev. John Chappell, 1903–1982, vol. VIII
Sprott, Rt Rev. Thomas Henry, *died* 1942, vol. IV
Sprott, Walter John Herbert, 1897–1971, vol. VII
Sproul, Robert Gordon, 1891–1975, vol. VII
Sproule, Brig. James Chambers, 1887–1955, vol. V
Sproule, Percy Julian, 1873–1954, vol. V
Sproule, Hon. Robert, *died* 1948, vol. IV
Sproule, Thomas Simpson, 1843–1917, vol. II
Sproull, Maj.-Gen. Alexander Wallace, 1892–1961, vol. VI
Sprules, Dorothy Winifred, 1883–1972, vol. VII
Spry, Charles Gordon, 1872–1940, vol. III
Spry, Constance, *died* 1960, vol. V
Spry, Maj.-Gen. Daniel Charles, 1913–1989, vol. VIII
Spry, Graham, 1900–1983, vol. VIII
Spry, Lt-Col Leighton Hume-, 1871–1934, vol. III
Spurgeon, Sir Arthur, 1861–1938, vol. III
Spurgeon, Caroline F. E., 1869–1942, vol. IV
Spurgeon, Christopher Edward, 1879–1951, vol. V
Spurgeon, Rev. John, 1810–1902, vol. I
Spurgeon, Rev. Thomas, 1856–1917, vol. II
Spurgin, Sir John Blick, 1821–1903, vol. I
Spurling, Antony Cuthbert, 1906–1984, vol. VIII
Spurling, Hon. Sir (Arthur) Dudley, 1913–1986, vol. VIII
Spurling, Hon. Sir Dudley; *see* Spurling, Hon. Sir A. D.
Spurling, Rev. Frederick William, 1844–1914, vol. I
Spurling, Maj.-Gen. John Michael Kane, 1906–1980, vol. VII
Spurling, Sir Stanley, 1879–1961, vol. VI
Spurr, Frederic Chambers, 1862–1942, vol. IV
Spurrell, Walter Roworth, 1897–1966, vol. VI
Spurrier, Alfred Henry, 1862–1935, vol. III
Spurrier, Sir Henry, 1898–1964, vol. VI
Spurrier, Rev. Horatio, 1832–1913, vol. I
Spurrier, John Marston, 1886–1973, vol. VII
Spurrier, Mabel Annie, *died* 1979, vol. VII
Spurrier, Steven, *died* 1961, vol. VI
Spyers, Roper, 1868–1961, vol. VI
Squair, John, 1850–1928, vol. II
Squire, Alice, *died* 1936, vol. III
Squire, Sir Giles Frederick, 1894–1959, vol. V
Squire, Herbert Brian, 1909–1961, vol. VI
Squire, Sir John Collings, 1884–1958, vol. V
Squire, John Edward, 1855–1917, vol. II
Squire, Rev. John Henry, *died* 1955, vol. V
Squire, John Rupert, 1915–1966, vol. VI
Squire, Sir Peter Wyatt, 1847–1919, vol. II
Squire, Ronald, 1886–1958, vol. V
Squire, Rose Elizabeth, 1861–1938, vol. III
Squire, William Barclay, 1855–1927, vol. II
Squire, William Henry, 1871–1963, vol. VI
Squires, Lt-Gen. Ernest Ker, 1882–1940, vol. III
Squires, Herbert Chavasse, 1880–1964, vol. VI
Squires, James Duane, 1904–1981, vol. VIII
Squires, Rt Hon. Sir Richard Anderson, 1880–1940, vol. III
Squirrell, Leonard Russell, 1893–1979, vol. VII
Sraffa, Piero, 1898–1983, vol. VIII

Srámek, Mgr Jan, 1870–1956, vol. V
Srawley, Rev. James Herbert, 1868–1954, vol. V
Srivastava, Sir Bisheshwar Nath, 1881–1938, vol. III
Srivastava, Sir Jwala Prasad, 1889–1954, vol. V
Staal, Baron de, 1822–1907, vol. I
Stabb, Sir Newton John, 1868–1931, vol. III
Stable, Daniel Wintringham, 1856–1929, vol. III
Stable, Maj.-Gen. Hugh Huntington, 1896–1985, vol. VIII
Stable, J. Joseph, 1883–1953, vol. V
Stable, Rt Hon. Sir Wintringham Norton, 1888–1977, vol. VII
Stableforth, Arthur Wallace, 1902–1978, vol. VII
Stabler, Harold, 1872–1945, vol. IV
Stabler, Phœbe, died 1955, vol. V
Stables, William G.; see Gordon-Stables.
Stacey, Sir Ernest, 1896–1973, vol. VII
Stacey, Major Gerald Arthur, 1881–1916, vol. II
Stacey, Air Chief Marshal Sir John; see Stacey, Air Chief Marshal Sir W. J.
Stacey, Reginald Stephen, 1905–1974, vol. VII
Stacey, Air Chief Marshal Sir (William) John, 1924–1981, vol. VIII
Stack, Austin, 1880–1929, vol. III
Stack, Rt Rev. Charles Maurice, 1825–1914, vol. I
Stack, Lt-Col Charles Spottiswoode, 1868–1943, vol. IV
Stack, Maj.-Gen. Sir Lee Oliver Fitzmaurice, 1868–1924, vol. II
Stackhouse, J. Foster, died 1915, vol. I
Stacpole, Col John, 1849–1916, vol. II
Stacpoole, Florence, died 1942, vol. IV
Stacpoole, Frederic, 1813–1907, vol. I
Stacpoole, Lt-Col George William Robert, 1872–1939, vol. III
Stackpoole, Henry de Vere Stacpoole, 1863–1951, vol. V
Stacton, David Derek, 1925–1968, vol. VI
Stacy, Lt-Col Bertie Vandeleur, 1886–1971, vol. VII
Stacy, Reginald Joseph William, 1904–1981, vol. VIII
Staddon, John Henry, died 1944, vol. IV
Stadler, Sir Sydney Martin, 1893–1976, vol. VII
Stafford, 11th Baron, 1833–1913, vol. I
Stafford, 12th Baron, 1859–1932, vol. III
Stafford, 13th Baron, 1864–1941, vol. IV
Stafford, 14th Baron, 1926–1986, vol. VIII
Stafford, Maj.-Gen. Boyle Torriano, 1828–1913, vol. I
Stafford, Hon. Sir Edward William, 1820–1901, vol. I
Stafford, Jack, 1909–1982, vol. VIII
Stafford, James William, 1884–1945, vol. IV
Stafford, Rev. John T. Wardle, 1861–1944, vol. IV
Stafford, Rt Hon. Sir Thomas, 1st Bt, 1857–1935, vol. III
Stafford, Brig.-Gen. William Francis Howard, 1854–1942, vol. IV
Stafford-King-Harman, Sir Cecil William Francis, 2nd Bt, 1895–1987, vol. VIII
Stagg, Cecil, died 1955, vol. V
Stagg, James Martin, 1900–1975, vol. VII
Stagg, Air Cdre Walter Allan, 1903–1984, vol. VIII
Stagni, Most Rev. Pellegrino Francesco, 1859–1918, vol. II

Staig, Sir Bertie Munro, 1892–1952, vol. V
Staine, Sir Albert Llewellyn, 1928–1987, vol. VIII
Stainer, George Henry, died 1901, vol. I
Stainer, Sir John, 1840–1901, vol. I
Staines, Donald Victor, 1897–1960, vol. V
Staines, Herbert J., died 1958, vol. V
Staines, Michael, 1885–1955, vol. V
Stainforth, Graham Henry, 1906–1987, vol. VIII
Stainforth, Lt-Col Herbert Graham, 1865–1916, vol. II
Stainton, Sir Anthony Nathaniel, 1913–1988, vol. VIII
Stainton, Sir John Armitage, 1888–1957, vol. V
Stair, 10th Earl of, 1819–1903, vol. I
Stair, 11th Earl of, 1848–1914, vol. I
Stair, 12th Earl of, 1879–1961, vol. VI
Stair, Alfred, 1845–1914, vol. I
Stairs, Gilbert S., 1882–1947, vol. IV
Stairs, Major Henry Bertram, 1871–1940, vol. III (A), vol. IV
Stalbridge, 1st Baron, 1837–1912, vol. I
Stalbridge, 2nd Baron, 1880–1949, vol. IV
Staley, Rt Rev. Thomas N., 1823–1898, vol. I
Staley, Rev. Vernon, 1852–1933, vol. III
Stalin, Generalissimo Joseph Vissarionovich, 1879–1953, vol. V
Stalker, Alexander Logie, 1920–1987, vol. VIII
Stalker, Alexander Mitchell, 1853–1932, vol. III
Stalker, Rev. James, 1848–1927, vol. II
Stallard, Col Hon. Charles Frampton, 1871–1971, vol. VII
Stallard, George, 1856–1912, vol. I
Stallard, Hyla Bristow, 1901–1973, vol. VII
Stallard, John Prince, 1857–1952, vol. V
Stallard, Lt-Col Sidney, 1870–1949, vol. IV
Stallard, Brig.-Gen. Stacy Frampton, 1873–1961, vol. VI
Stallwood, Frank, 1910–1978, vol. VII
Stallybrass, William Swan, 1855–1931, vol. III
Stallybrass, William Teulon Swan, 1883–1948, vol. IV
Stamer, Arthur Cowie, 1869–1944, vol. IV
Stamer, Sir Lovelace, 4th Bt, 1859–1941, vol. IV
Stamer, Rt Rev. Sir Lovelace Tomlinson, 3rd Bt, 1829–1908, vol. I
Stamer, Maj.-Gen. William Donovan, died 1963, vol. VI
Stamford, 9th Earl of, 1850–1910, vol. I
Stamford, 10th Earl of, 1896–1976, vol. VII
Stamford, Thomas William, 1882–1949, vol. IV
Stamfordham, 1st Baron, 1849–1931, vol. III
Stamm, Air Vice-Marshal William Percivale, 1909–1986, vol. VIII
Stammers, Arthur Dighton, 1889–1971, vol. VII
Stammers, Francis Alan Roland, 1898–1982, vol. VIII
Stamp, 1st Baron, 1880–1941, vol. IV
Stamp, 2nd Baron, 1904–1941 (died with 1st Baron and did not have an entry in Who's Who).
Stamp, 3rd Baron, 1907–1987, vol. VIII
Stamp, Alfred Edward, 1870–1938, vol. III
Stamp, Hon. (Arthur) Maxwell, 1915–1984, vol. VIII
Stamp, Rt Hon. Sir Blanshard; see Stamp, Rt Hon. Sir E. B.

Stamp, Sir Dudley; *see* Stamp, Sir L. D.
Stamp, Edward, 1928–1986, vol. VIII
Stamp, Rt Hon. Sir (Edward) Blanshard, 1905–1984, vol. VIII
Stamp, Ernest, 1869–1942, vol. IV
Stamp, Sir (Laurence) Dudley, 1898–1966, vol. VI
Stamp, Hon. Maxwell; *see* Stamp, Hon. A. M.
Stampa, George Loraine, 1875–1951, vol. V
Stampe, Sir William Leonard, 1882–1951, vol. V
Stamper, James William, 1873–1947, vol. IV
Stamper, Thomas Henry Gilborn, 1884–1980, vol. VII
Stanbridge, Air Vice-Marshal Reginald Horace, 1897–1986, vol. VIII
Stancomb, William, 1850–1941, vol. IV
Stancliffe, Very Rev. Michael Staffurth, 1916–1987, vol. VIII
Stancomb-Wills, Dame Janet Stancomb Graham, *died* 1932, vol. III
Standage, Lt-Col Robert Fraser, 1868–1927, vol. II
Standen, Rev. Canon Aubrey Owen, 1898–1961, vol. VI
Standen, Sir Bertram Prior, 1867–1947, vol. IV
Standen, Edward James, 1836–1921, vol. II
Standen, Rev. James Edward, 1865–1933, vol. III
Standford, Col William, *died* 1926, vol. II
Standing, Rev. George, 1875–1966, vol. VI
Standing, Comdr Sir Guy, 1873–1937, vol. III
Standing, Michael Frederick Cecil, 1910–1984, vol. VIII
Standing, Percy Cross, *died* 1931, vol. III
Standish, Henry Noailles Widdrington, 1847–1920, vol. II
Standish, Col Ivon Tatham, 1883–1967, vol. VI
Standish, Major William Pery, 1860–1922, vol. II
Standish-White, Robert, 1888–1961, vol. VI
Stanes, Sir Robert, 1841–1936, vol. III
Stanfield, Richard, 1863–1950, vol. IV (A), vol. V
Stanford, Bedell; *see* Stanford, W. B.
Stanford, Gp-Captain C. E. C.; *see* Cortis-Stanford.
Stanford, Sir Charles T.; *see* Thomas-Stanford.
Stanford, Sir Charles Villiers, 1852–1924, vol. II
Stanford, Ernest, 1894–1966, vol. VI
Stanford, Rt Rev. Frederic, 1883–1964, vol. VI
Stanford, John Keith, 1892–1971, vol. VII
Stanford, Ven. Leonard John, 1896–1967, vol. VI
Stanford, Col Hon. Sir Walter Ernest Mortimer, 1850–1933, vol. III
Stanford, (William) Bedell, 1910–1984, vol. VIII
Stanford-Tuck, Wing Comdr Robert Roland, 1916–1987, vol. VIII
Stanger, Henry Yorke, 1849–1929, vol. III
Stanham, Maj.-Gen. Sir Reginald George, 1893–1957, vol. V
Stanhope, 6th Earl, 1838–1905, vol. I
Stanhope, 7th Earl, 1880–1967, vol. VI
Stanhope, Ven. Hon. Berkeley Lionel Scudamore, 1824–1919, vol. II
Stanhope, Hon. Charles Hay Scudamore, 1864–1937, vol. III
Stanhope, Hon. Evelyn Theodore Scudamore, 1862–1925, vol. II
Stanhope, Hon. Henry Augustus, 1845–1933, vol. III
Stanhope, James Banks, 1821–1904, vol. I

Stanhope, Hon. Richard Philip, 1885–1916, vol. II
Stanhope, Col Sir Walter Thomas William Spencer, 1827–1911, vol. I
Stanier, Sir Beville, 1st Bt, 1867–1921, vol. II
Stanier, Robert Spenser, 1907–1980, vol. VII
Stanier, Roger Yate, 1916–1982, vol. VIII
Stanier, Sir William Arthur, 1876–1965, vol. VI
Staniforth, Joseph Morewood, 1863–1921, vol. II
Stanistreet, Maj.-Gen. Sir George Bradshaw, 1866–1941, vol. IV
Stanistreet, Rt Rev. Henry Arthur, 1901–1981, vol. VIII
Stanley of Alderley, 3rd Baron, 1827–1903, vol. I
Stanley of Alderley, 4th Baron; *see* Sheffield.
Stanley of Alderley, 5th Baron, **and Sheffield**, 5th Baron, 1875–1931, vol. III
Stanley, Lord; Edward Montagu Cavendish Stanley, 1894–1938, vol. III
Stanley, Albert, 1863–1915, vol. I
Stanley, Rt Rev. Mgr the Hon. Algernon Charles, 1843–1928, vol. II
Stanley, Col Hon. Algernon Francis, 1874–1962, vol. VI
Stanley, Hon. Sir Arthur, 1869–1947, vol. IV
Stanley, Arthur; *see* Megaw, Arthur Stanley.
Stanley, Brian Taylor, 1907–1983, vol. VIII
Stanley, Carleton Wellesley, 1886–1971, vol. VII
Stanley, Charles Orr, 1899–1989, vol. VIII
Stanley, Charles Sidney Bowen W.; *see* Wentworth-Stanley.
Stanley, Captain Sir Charles Wentworth, 1860–1939, vol. III
Stanley, Dorothy, (Lady Stanley), *died* 1926, vol. II
Stanley, Edward Arthur Vesey, 1879–1941, vol. IV
Stanley, Edward James, 1826–1907, vol. I
Stanley, Brig.-Gen. Hon. Ferdinand Charles, 1871–1935, vol. III
Stanley, Lt-Col Hon. Frederick William, 1878–1942, vol. IV
Stanley, Col Geoffrey, 1855–1943, vol. IV
Stanley, Lt-Col Rt Hon. Sir George Frederick, 1872–1938, vol. III
Stanley, George J., 1852–1931, vol. III
Stanley, Harry Merridew, 1865–1945, vol. IV
Stanley, Sir Henry Morton, 1841–1904, vol. I
Stanley, Sir Herbert James, 1872–1955, vol. V
Stanley, Herbert Muggleton, 1903–1987, vol. VIII
Stanley, Rev. Howard Spencer, 1901–1975, vol. VII
Stanley, Sir John, 1846–1931, vol. III
Stanley, Lt-Col Joseph Henry, 1864–1937, vol. III
Stanley, Hon. Maude Alethea, 1833–1915, vol. I
Stanley, Michael Charles, 1921–1990, vol. VIII
Stanley, Rt Hon. Oliver Frederick George, 1896–1950, vol. IV
Stanley, Lt-Col Hon. Oliver Hugh, 1879–1952, vol. V
Stanley, Hon. Richard Oliver, 1920–1983, vol. VIII
Stanley, Sir Robert Christopher Stafford, 1899–1981, vol. VIII
Stanley, Robert Crooks, 1876–1951, vol. V
Stanley, Ronald Francis Assheton S.; *see* Sloane-Stanley.
Stanley, Adm. Hon. Sir Victor Albert, 1867–1934, vol. III
Stanley, Wendell Meredith, 1904–1971, vol. VII

Stanley, Captain William Blakeney, 1878–1935, vol. III

Stanley-Clarke, Brig. Arthur Christopher Lancelot, 1886–1983, vol. VIII

Stanley-Wrench, Mollie Louise, *died* 1966, vol. VI

Stanmore, 1st Baron, 1829–1912, vol. I

Stanmore, 2nd Baron, 1871–1957, vol. V

Stannard, Mrs Arthur; *see* Stannard, H. E. V.

Stannard, H. Sylvester, 1870–1951, vol. V

Stannard, Henrietta Eliza Vaughan, 1856–1911, vol. I

Stannard, Henry, *died* 1920, vol. II

Stannard, Captain Richard Been, 1902–1977, vol. VII

Stannard, Rt Rev. Robert William, 1895–1986, vol. VIII

Stanner, William Edward Hanley, 1905–1981, vol. VIII

Stannus, Hugh Stannus, 1877–1957, vol. V

Stansbury, Captain Hubert, 1873–1949, vol. IV

Stansfeld, Maj.-Gen. Henry Hamer, 1839–1914, vol. I

Stansfeld, Rt Hon. Sir James, 1820–1898, vol. I

Stansfeld, Col James Rawdon, 1866–1936, vol. III

Stansfeld, Captain John, 1840–1928, vol. II

Stansfeld, Captain John Raymond Evelyn, 1880–1915, vol. I

Stansfeld, Captain Logan Sutherland, 1859–1936, vol. III

Stansfeld, Margaret, *died* 1951, vol. V

Stansfeld, Brig.-Gen. Thomas Wolryche, 1877–1935, vol. III

Stansfield, Alfred, *died* 1944, vol. IV

Stansfield, Sir Charles Henry Renn, 1856–1926, vol. II

Stansfield, Herbert, 1872–1960, vol. V

Stansfield, Knowles; *see* Stansfield, T. E. K.

Stansfield, (Thomas Edward) Knowles, 1862–1939, vol. III

Stansfield, Lt-Gen. Thomas Wolrich, 1829–1910, vol. I

Stansfield, Sir Walter, 1917–1984, vol. VIII

Stansfield, William, 1877–1946, vol. IV

Stansgate, 1st Viscount, 1877–1960, vol. V

Stantiall, William, 1865–1947, vol. IV

Stanton, Sir (Ambrose) Thomas, 1875–1938, vol. III

Stanton, Maj.-Gen. Anthony Francis, 1915–1988, vol. VIII

Stanton, Rev. Arthur Henry, 1839–1913, vol. I

Stanton, Blair Rowlands H.; *see* Hughes-Stanton.

Stanton, Charles Butt, 1873–1946, vol. IV

Stanton, Sir Edward, 1827–1907, vol. I

Stanton, Col Edward Alexander, 1867–1947, vol. IV

Stanton, Brig.-Gen. Frederick William Starkey, 1863–1930, vol. III

Stanton, Rt Rev. George Henry, 1835–1905, vol. I

Stanton, Major Harold James Clifford, 1859–1927, vol. II

Stanton, Maj.-Gen. Sir Henry Ernest, 1861–1943, vol. IV

Stanton, Sir Herbert H.; *see* Hughes-Stanton.

Stanton, Rev. Herbert Udny Weitbrecht, 1851–1937, vol. III

Stanton, Lt-Col John Percy, 1899–1974, vol. VII

Stanton, Lt-Col John Richard Guy, 1919–1990, vol. VIII

Stanton, Joseph, 1859–1935, vol. III

Stanton, Sir Joseph, 1884–1963, vol. VI

Stanton, Lionel William, 1843–1925, vol. II

Stanton, Sir Thomas, 1865–1931, vol. III

Stanton, Sir Thomas; *see* Stanton, Sir A. T.

Stanton, Rev. Vincent Henry, 1846–1924, vol. II

Stanton, Walter Kendall, 1891–1978, vol. VII

Stanton, Rev. William Henry, 1824–1910, vol. I

Stanton-Jones, Rt Rev. William, 1866–1951, vol. V

Stanuell, Lt-Col Herbert Stewart M'Cance, 1857–1930, vol. III

Stanway, Rt Rev. Alfred, 1908–1989, vol. VIII

Stanyforth, Lt-Col Edwin Wilfrid, 1861–1939, vol. III

Stanyforth, Lt-Col Ronald Thomas, 1892–1964, vol. VI

Stanyon, Sir Henry John, 1857–1934, vol. III

Stapf, Otto, 1857–1933, vol. III

Stapledon, Sir George; *see* Stapledon, Sir R. G.

Stapledon, Sir (Reginald) George, 1882–1960, vol. V

Stapledon, Sir Robert de Stapledon, 1909–1975, vol. VII

Stapledon, William Olaf, 1886–1950, vol. IV

Staples, Irene E. Toye W.; *see* Warner-Staples.

Staples, Sir John Molesworth, 11th Bt, 1847–1933, vol. III

Staples, Sir John Richard, 14th Bt, 1906–1989, vol. VIII

Staples, Sir Nathaniel Alexander, 10th (shown as 8th) Bt, 1817–1899, vol. I

Staples, Sir Robert George Alexander, 13th Bt, 1894–1970, vol. VI

Staples, Sir Robert Ponsonby, 12th Bt, 1853–1943, vol. IV

Stapleton, Sir Francis George, 8th Bt, 1831–1899, vol. I

Stapleton, Brig. Francis Harry, 1876–1956, vol. V

Stapleton, Air Vice-Marshal Frederick Snowden, 1912–1974, vol. VII

Stapleton, Henry Ernest, 1878–1962, vol. VI

Stapleton, Major Sir Miles Talbot, 9th Bt, 1893–1977, vol. VII

Stapleton-Bretherton, Frederick, 1841–1919, vol. II

Stapleton-Cotton, Adm. Richard Greville Arthur Wellington, 1873–1953, vol. V

Stapleton-Cotton, Col Hon. Richard Southwell George, 1849–1925, vol. II

Stapleton-Shaw, Major Peter; *see* Shaw.

Stapley, Sir Richard, 1842–1920, vol. II

Stapylton, Col Bryan Henry C.; *see* Chetwynd-Stapylton.

Stapylton, Granville Brian C.; *see* Chetwynd-Stapylton.

Stapylton, Lt-Gen. Granville George C.; *see* Chetwynd-Stapylton.

Stapylton, Rev. William C.; *see* Chetwynd-Stapylton.

Starey, Captain Stephen Helps, 1896–1972, vol. VII

Stark, Adm. Harold Raynsford, 1880–1972, vol. VII

Stark, Rev. James, 1838–1922, vol. II

Stark, John, 1865–1940, vol. III

Starke, Sir Hayden Erskine, 1871–1958, vol. V

Starke, Leslie Gordon Knowles, 1898–1984, vol. VIII

Starkey, James Sullivan; *see* O'Sullivan, Seumas.

Starkey, Sir John Ralph, 1st Bt, 1859–1940, vol. III

Starkey, Lewis Randle, 1836–1910, vol. I

Starkey, Thomas Albert, 1872–1939, vol. III (A), vol. IV

Starkey, William Joseph Starkey B.; *see* Barber-Starkey.

Starkey, Lt-Col Sir William Randle, 2nd Bt, 1899–1977, vol. VII

Starkie, Enid Mary, *died* 1970, vol. VI

Starkie, Rev. Preb. Le Gendre George H.; *see* Horton-Starkie.

Starkie, Le Gendre Nicholas, 1828–1899, vol. I

Starkie, Robert Fitzwilliam, 1855–1934, vol. III

Starkie, Walter Fitzwilliam, 1894–1976, vol. VII

Starkie, Rt Hon. William Joseph Myles, 1860–1920, vol. II

Starley, Hubert Granville, 1909–1984, vol. VIII

Starling, Ernest Henry, 1866–1927, vol. II

Starling, Frederick Charles, 1886–1962, vol. VI

Starling, Hubert John, 1874–1950, vol. IV

Starling, John Henry, 1883–1966, vol. VI

Starling, Brig. John Sieveking, 1898–1986, vol. VIII

Starmer, Sir Charles Walter, 1870–1933, vol. III

Starr, Clarence L., 1868–1928, vol. II

Starr, Frederic Newton Gisborne, 1867–1934, vol. III

Starr, Sir Kenneth William, 1908–1976, vol. VII

Starr, Col William Henderson, 1861–1947, vol. IV

Starte, Oliver Harold Baptist, 1882–1969, vol. VI

Startin, Adm. Sir James, 1855–1948, vol. IV

Statham, Hon. Sir Charles Ernest, 1875–1946, vol. IV

Statham, Rev. George Herbert, 1842–1922, vol. II

Statham, Heathcote Dicken, 1889–1973, vol. VII

Statham, Henry Heathcote, 1839–1924, vol. II

Statham, Ira Cyril Frank, 1886–1967, vol. VI

Statham, Col John Charles Barron, 1872–1933, vol. III

Statham, Sir Randulph Meverel, 1890–1944, vol. IV

Statham, Reginald Samuel Sherard, 1884–1959, vol. V

Staton, Air Vice-Marshal William Ernest, 1898–1983, vol. VIII

Staudinger, Hermann, 1881–1965, vol. VI

Staughton, Captain Samuel Thomas, 1876–1903, vol. I

Staunton, Hugh Geoffrey, 1871–1951, vol. V

Staunton, Most Rev. James, 1889–1963, vol. IV

Staunton, Lt-Col Reginald Kirkpatrick Lynch, 1880–1918, vol. II

Staveley, Adm. Cecil Minet, 1874–1934, vol. III

Staveley, Brig. Robert, 1892–1968, vol. VI

Staveley, Brig.-Gen. William Cathcart, 1865–1939, vol. III

Staveley-Hill, Henry Staveley, 1865–1946, vol. IV

Stavert, Sir William Ewen, 1861–1937, vol. III

Stavert, Rev. William James, 1858–1932, vol. III

Stavridi, Sir John, 1867–1948, vol. IV

Stawell, Sir Richard Rawdon, 1864–1935, vol. III

Stawell, Mrs Rodolph, *died* 1949, vol. IV

Stawell, Maj.-Gen. William Arthur Macdonald, 1895–1987, vol. VIII

Stayner, Brig. Gerrard Francis Hood, 1900–1980, vol. VII

Staynes, Percy Angelo, *died* 1953, vol. V

Steacie, Edgar William Richard, 1900–1962, vol. VI

Steacy, Rev. Richard Henry, 1869–1950, vol. IV

Stead, Alfred, 1877–1933, vol. III

Stead, Lt-Col Alfred James, 1845–1909, vol. I

Stead, Sir Charles, 1877–1961, vol. VI

Stead, Christina Ellen, 1902–1983, vol. VIII

Stead, Francis Bernard, 1873–1954, vol. V

Stead, Francis Herbert, 1857–1928, vol. II

Stead, Gilbert, 1888–1979, vol. VII

Stead, James Lister, 1864–1915, vol. I

Stead, John Edward, 1851–1923, vol. II

Stead, Kingsley Willans, 1883–1950, vol. IV

Stead, William Thomas, 1849–1912, vol. I

Steadman, Frank St J., 1880–1943, vol. IV

Steadman, W. C., 1851–1911, vol. I

Steane, Bruce Harry Dennis, 1866–1939, vol. III

Steavenson, Arthur Paget, 1872–1934, vol. III

Steavenson, Hon. Brig.-Gen. Charles John, 1867–1933, vol. III

Steavenson, David Fenwick, 1844–1920, vol. II

Steavenson, William Herbert, 1894–1975, vol. VII

Stebbing, Edward Percy, 1870–1960, vol. V

Stebbing, (Lizzie) Susan, 1885–1943, vol. IV

Stebbing, Susan; *see* Stebbing, L. S.

Stebbing, Rev. Thomas Roscoe Rede, 1835–1926, vol. II

Stebbing, William, *died* 1926, vol. II

Stebbings, Sir John Chalmer, 1924–1988, vol. VIII

Stedeford, Sir Ivan Arthur Rice, 1897–1975, vol. VII

Stedman, Edgar, 1890–1975, vol. VII

Stedman, Edmund Clarence, 1833–1908, vol. I

Stedman, Gen. Sir Edward, 1842–1914, vol. I

Stedman, Air Vice-Marshal Ernest W., 1888–1957, vol. V

Stedman, Sir George Foster, 1895–1985, vol. VIII

Stedman, Sir Leonard Foster, 1871–1948, vol. IV

Stedman, Ralph Elliott, *died* 1964, vol. VI

Steed, Henry Wickham, 1871–1956, vol. V

Steedman, Maj.-Gen. John Francis Dawes, 1897–1983, vol. VIII

Steeds-Bird, Elliott Beverley, 1881–1945, vol. IV

Steegman, John E. H., 1899–1966, vol. VI

Steel, Allan Gibson, 1858–1914, vol. I

Steel, Anthony Bedford, 1900–1973, vol. VII

Steel, Charles, 1847–1925, vol. II

Steel, Sir Christopher Eden, 1903–1973, vol. VII

Steel, Edward, 1906–1976, vol. VII

Steel, Major Edward Anthony, 1880–1919, vol. II

Steel, Flora Annie, 1847–1929, vol. III

Steel, Gerald, 1895–1957, vol. V

Steel, Gerald Arthur, *died* 1963, vol. VI

Steel, Sir James, 1st Bt (*cr* 1903), 1830–1904, vol. I

Steel, Air Chief Marshal Sir John Miles, 1877–1965, vol. VI

Steel, Sir (Joseph) Lincoln (Spedding), 1900–1985, vol. VIII

Steel, Sir Lincoln; *see* Steel, Sir J. L. S.

Steel, Lt-Col Matthew Reginald, 1896–1941, vol. IV

Steel, Col Richard Alexander, 1873–1928, vol. II

Steel, Robert, 1839–1903, vol. I

Steel, Major Sir Samuel Strang, 1st Bt (*cr* 1938), 1882–1961, vol. VI

Steel, William Strang, 1832–1911, vol. I

Steel-Maitland, Rt Hon. Sir Arthur Herbert Drummond Ramsay, 1st Bt, 1876–1935, vol. III

Steel-Maitland, Sir (Arthur) James (Drummond Ramsay-), 2nd Bt, 1902–1960, vol. V
Steel-Maitland, Sir James; *see* Steel-Maitland, Sir A. J. D. R.
Steel-Maitland, Sir Keith Richard Felix Ramsay-, 3rd Bt, 1912–1965, vol. VI
Steele, Bertram Dillon, 1870–1934, vol. III
Steele, Col Charles Edward Beevor, 1876–1940, vol. III
Steele, Air Marshal Sir Charles Ronald, 1897–1973, vol. VII
Steele, Maj.-Gen. Sir Clive Selwyn, 1892–1955, vol. V
Steele, Fanny; *see* Steele, Francesca Maria.
Steele, Francesca Maria, *died* 1931, vol. III
Steele, (Francis) Howard, 1929–1983, vol. VIII
Steele, Lt-Col Frederick William, 1858–1909, vol. I
Steele, Comdr Gordon Charles, 1892–1981, vol. VIII
Steele, Lt-Col Harwood Robert Elmes, 1897–1978, vol. VII
Steele, Sir Henry, 1879–1963, vol. VI
Steele, Howard; *see* Steele, F. H.
Steele, Gen. Sir James Stuart, 1894–1975, vol. VII
Steele, John, 1837–1922, vol. II
Steele, John Scott, 1870–1947, vol. IV
Steele, Maj.-Gen. Julian McCarty, 1870–1926, vol. II
Steele, Sir Kenneth Charles, 1913–1986, vol. VIII
Steele, Norman James, 1918–1977, vol. VII
Steele, Robert, 1860–1944, vol. IV
Steele, Col St George Loftus, 1859–1936, vol. III
Steele, Maj.-Gen. Sir Samuel Benfield, 1849–1919, vol. II
Steele, Thomas, 1905–1979, vol. VII
Steele, Col William Lawrence, 1878–1958, vol. V
Steell, David G., 1856–1930, vol. III
Steell, Graham, 1851–1942, vol. IV
Steen, Marguerite, 1894–1975, vol. VII
Steen, Robert Elsworth, 1902–1981, vol. VIII
Steen, Robert Hunter, 1870–1926, vol. II
Steen, Stephen Nicholas, 1907–1988, vol. VIII
Steenbock, Harry, 1886–1967, vol. VI
Steenkamp, Major William, 1868–1935, vol. III
Steer, Edward Pemberton, 1881–1938, vol. III
Steer, Francis William, 1912–1978, vol. VII
Steer, George Lowther, 1909–1944, vol. IV
Steer, Henry Reynolds, 1858–1928, vol. II
Steer, P. Wilson, 1860–1942, vol. IV
Steer, Captain T. Bruce, *died* 1904, vol. I
Steer, William Bridgland, 1867–1939, vol. III (A), vol. IV
Steere, Sir Ernest Augustus L.; *see* Lee Steere.
Steere, Henry Charles Lee, 1859–1933, vol. III
Steere, Hon. Sir James George Lee, 1830–1903, vol. I
Steers, James Alfred, 1899–1987, vol. VIII
Steevens, Maj.-Gen. Sir John, 1855–1925, vol. II
Stefansson, Vilhjalmur, 1879–1962, vol. VI
Steggall, Charles, 1826–1905, vol. I
Steggall, John Edward Aloysius, 1855–1935, vol. III
Steggall, Reginald, 1867–1938, vol. III
Steil, John Wellesley, 1899–1983, vol. VIII
Stein, Adolphe, 1878–1938, vol. III
Stein, Sir Aurel, 1862–1943, vol. IV
Stein, Gertrude, 1874–1946, vol. IV
Stein, John, 1922–1985, vol. VIII
Stein, John Alan, 1888–1982, vol. VIII

Stein, Leonard Jacques, 1887–1973, vol. VII
Stein, William Howard, 1911–1980, vol. VII
Steinaecker, Lt-Col Francis Christian Ludwig, Baron von, *born* 1854, vol. II
Steinbeck, John Ernst, 1902–1968, vol. VI
Steinberg, Sigfrid Henry, 1899–1969, vol. VI
Steinberg, William, 1899–1978, vol. VII
Steinhardt, Laurence A., 1892–1950, vol. IV
Steinitz, (Charles) Paul (Joseph), 1909–1988, vol. VIII
Steinitz, Paul; *see* Steinitz, C. P. J.
Steinlen, Theophile Alexander, 1859–1923, vol. II
Stemp, Major Charles Hubert, 1871–1948, vol. IV
Stenbock, Count Otto, 1838–1915, vol. I
Stengel, Erwin, 1902–1973, vol. VII
Stenhouse, Maj.-Gen. William, 1840–1914, vol. I
Stennett, Col Harry March, 1877–1941, vol. IV
Stenning, Sir Alexander Rose, 1864–1928, vol. II
Stenning, Ven. Ernest Henry, 1885–1964, vol. VI
Stenning, Rev. George Covey, 1840–1915, vol. I
Stenning, John Frederick, *died* 1959, vol. V
Stent, Percy John Hodsoll, 1888–1962, vol. VI
Stentiford, Charles Douglas, *died* 1920, vol. II
Stenton, Doris Mary, (Lady Stenton), 1894–1971, vol. VII
Stenton, Sir Frank Merry, 1880–1967, vol. VI
Step, Edward, 1855–1931, vol. III
Stephen, Sir Alastair Edward, 1901–1982, vol. VIII
Stephen, Captain Albert Alexander Leslie, 1879–1914, vol. I
Stephen, Sir Alexander Condie, 1850–1908, vol. I
Stephen, Sir Alexander Murray, 1892–1974, vol. VII
Stephen, Sir Andrew, 1906–1980, vol. VII
Stephen, Campbell, 1884–1947, vol. IV
Stephen, Col Charles Merton, 1874–1955, vol. V
Stephen, Sir Colin Campbell, 1872–1937, vol. III
Stephen, Edward Milner, 1870–1939, vol. III
Stephen, Col Fitzroy, 1835–1906, vol. I
Stephen, George, 1886–1972, vol. VII
Stephen, George Arthur, 1880–1934, vol. III
Stephen, Lt-Col Guy Neville, 1858–1932, vol. III
Stephen, Sir Harry Lushington, 3rd Bt, 1860–1945, vol. IV
Stephen, Sir Henry; *see* Stephen, Sir M. H.
Stephen, Sir Herbert, 2nd Bt, 1857–1932, vol. III
Stephen, Sir James Alexander, 4th Bt, 1908–1987, vol. VIII
Stephen, Katharine, 1856–1924, vol. II
Stephen, Sir Leslie, 1832–1904, vol. I
Stephen, Sir (Matthew) Henry, 1828–1920, vol. II
Stephen, Norman Kenneth, 1865–1948, vol. IV
Stephen, Rt Rev. Reginald, 1860–1956, vol. V
Stephen, Maj.-Gen. Robert Alexander, 1907–1983, vol. VIII
Stephen, Brig.-Gen. Robert Campbell, 1867–1947, vol. IV
Stephens, Maj.-Gen. Adolphus Haggerston, 1835–1916, vol. II
Stephens, Sir Alfred, 1871–1938, vol. III
Stephens, Alfred George Gower, *died* 1933, vol. III
Stephens, Berkeley John Byng, 1871–1950, vol. IV
Stephens, Sir David, 1910–1990, vol. VIII
Stephens, Sir Edgar; *see* Stephens, Sir L. E.
Stephens, Brig. Frederick, 1906–1967, vol. VI

Stephens, Frederick James, 1903–1978, vol. VII
Stephens, George Arbour, 1870–1945, vol. IV
Stephens, George Henry, 1855–1927, vol. II
Stephens, Rear-Adm. George Leslie, 1889–1979, vol. VII
Stephens, George Washington, 1866–1942, vol. IV
Stephens, Henry Morse, 1857–1919, vol. II
Stephens, Herbert John, 1875–1957, vol. V
Stephens, Surg. Rear-Adm. Horace Elliott Rose, 1883–1959, vol. V
Stephens, Ian Melville, 1903–1984, vol. VIII
Stephens, James, died 1950, vol. IV
Stephens, James Brunton, 1835–1902, vol. I
Stephens, James Henry, 1862–1937, vol. III
Stephens, John Edward Robert, 1869–1941, vol. IV
Stephens, Rev. John Otter, 1832–1925, vol. II
Stephens, John William Watson, 1865–1946, vol. IV
Stephens, Sir (Leon) Edgar, 1901–1977, vol. VII
Stephens, Engr Rear-Adm. Lindsay James, 1868–1958, vol. V
Stephens, Lockhart, 1858–1940, vol. III
Stephens, Rear-Adm. (S) Montague, died 1950, vol. IV
Stephens, Pembroke Scott, died 1914, vol. I
Stephens, Peter Scott, 1910–1981, vol. VIII
Stephens, Gen. Sir Reginald Byng, 1869–1955, vol. V
Stephens, Captain Richard Markham Tyringham, 1875–1967, vol. VI
Stephens, Lt-Col Rupert, 1884–1970, vol. VI
Stephens, Sir William, 1848–1929, vol. III
Stephens, William Francis, 1869–1963, vol. VI
Stephens, Sir William R.; see Reynolds-Stephens.
Stephens, Very Rev. William Richard Wood, 1839–1902, vol. I
Stephens Spinks, Rev. George; see Spinks.
Stephenson, Sir (Albert) Edward, 1864–1928, vol. II
Stephenson, Sir Albert Frederick, 1854–1934, vol. III
Stephenson, Lt-Col Arthur, died 1950, vol. IV
Stephenson, Sir Arthur George, 1890–1967, vol. VI
Stephenson, Sir Augustus Frederick William Keppel, 1827–1904, vol. I
Stephenson, Basil Ernest, 1901–1977, vol. VII
Stephenson, Ven. Edgar, 1894–1984, vol. VIII
Stephenson, Sir Edward; see Stephenson, Sir A. E.
Stephenson, Edward F., 1868–1948, vol. IV
Stephenson, Col Eric Lechmere, 1892–1978, vol. VII
Stephenson, Eric Seymour, 1879–1915, vol. I
Stephenson, Lt-Col Sir Francis; see Stephenson, Lt-Col Sir H. F. B.
Stephenson, Francis Lawrance, 1845–1920, vol. II
Stephenson, Rev. Frank, died 1936, vol. III
Stephenson, Gen. Sir Frederick Charles Arthur, 1821–1911, vol. I
Stephenson, George Robert, 1819–1905, vol. I
Stephenson, Vice-Adm. Sir Gilbert Owen, 1878–1972, vol. VII
Stephenson, Sir Guy, 1865–1930, vol. III
Stephenson, Sir Henry, 1826–1904, vol. I
Stephenson, Lt-Col Sir (Henry) Francis (Blake), 2nd Bt, 1895–1982, vol. VIII
Stephenson, Adm. Sir Henry Frederick, 1842–1919, vol. II
Stephenson, Lt-Col Sir Henry Kenyon, 1st Bt, 1865–1947, vol. IV

Stephenson, Rev. Henry Spencer, 1871–1957, vol. V
Stephenson, Sir Hugh Lansdown, 1871–1941, vol. IV
Stephenson, Sir Hugh Southern, 1906–1972, vol. VII
Stephenson, Rev. Jacob, 1844–1927, vol. II
Stephenson, Lt-Col John, 1871–1933, vol. III
Stephenson, Sir John Everard, 1893–1948, vol. IV
Stephenson, Air Vice-Marshal John Noel Tracy, 1907–1985, vol. VIII
Stephenson, Sir John Walker, died 1960, vol. V
Stephenson, Joseph, 1882–1965, vol. VI
Stephenson, Katharine J., 1874–1953, vol. V
Stephenson, Marjory, 1885–1948, vol. IV
Stephenson, Rt Rev. Percival William, 1888–1962, vol. VI
Stephenson, Sir Percy, 1909–1979, vol. VII
Stephenson, Lt-Col Robert, 1876–1959, vol. V
Stephenson, Sydney, 1862–1923, vol. II
Stephenson, Rev. T. Bowman, 1839–1912, vol. I
Stephenson, Maj.-Gen. Theodore Edward, 1856–1928, vol. II
Stephenson, Thomas, 1864–1938, vol. III
Stephenson, Thomas, 1889–1974, vol. VII
Stephenson, Thomas Alan, died 1961, vol. VI
Stephenson, Rev. Thomas Wilkinson, died 1936, vol. III
Stephenson, William, 1837–1919, vol. II
Stephenson, Sir William Haswell, 1836–1918, vol. II
Stephenson, Sir William Henry, 1811–1898, vol. I
Stephenson, William Lawrence, 1880–1963, vol. VI
Stephenson, Sir William Samuel, 1896–1989, vol. VIII
Stephenson, Willie, died 1938, vol. III (A), vol. IV
Stepney, Sir Emile Algernon Arthur Keppel C.; see Cowell-Stepney.
Steptoe, Harry Nathaniel, 1892–1949, vol. IV
Steptoe, Patrick Christopher, 1913–1988, vol. VIII
Sterling, Antoinette, 1843–1904, vol. I
Sterling, Herbert Harry, 1886–1959, vol. V
Sterling, Maj.-Gen. John Barton, 1840–1926, vol. II
Sterling, Sir Louis Saul, died 1958, vol. V
Sterling, Thomas Smith, 1883–1970, vol. VI
Stern, Lt-Col Sir Albert, 1878–1966, vol. VI
Stern, Sir Edward David, 1st Bt, 1854–1933, vol. III
Stern, Sir Frederick Claude, 1884–1967, vol. VI
Stern, Gladys Bertha, 1890–1973, vol. VII
Stern, Rev. Joseph Frederick, 1865–1934, vol. III
Stern, Philip, died 1933, vol. III
Stern-Salomons, Sir David Lionel Goldsmid-; see Salomons.
Sternberg, Hon. Joseph, 1855–1928, vol. II
Sternberg, Rudy; see Baron Plurenden.
Sterndale, 1st Baron, 1848–1923, vol. II
Sterndale, Robert Armitage, 1839–1902, vol. I
Sterndale-Bennett, T. C., died 1944, vol. IV
Sterne, Maurice, 1877–1957, vol. V
Sterrett, John Robert Sitlington, 1851–1914, vol. I
Sterry, Joseph A.; see Ashby-Sterry.
Sterry, Sir Wasey, 1866–1955, vol. V
Stettinius, Edward R., (Jr), 1900–1949, vol. IV
Steuart, Sir Alan Henry Seton-, 4th Bt, 1856–1913, vol. I
Steuart, Sir Douglas Archibald Seton-, 5th Bt, 1857–1930, vol. III
Steuart, Ethel Mary, died 1960, vol. V
Steuart, John Alexander, died 1932, vol. III

Steuart, Rev. Robert H. J., 1874–1948, vol. IV

Steuart-Fothringham, Walter Thomas James S.; *see* Scrymsoure-Steuart-Fothringham.

Steuart-Menzies, William George, 1858–1941, vol. IV

Steven, Temp. Captain Fraser; *see* Steven, Temp. Captain J. F.

Steven, Guy Savile, 1906–1980, vol. VII

Steven, Henry Marshall, 1893–1969, vol. VI

Steven, Temp. Captain (John) Fraser, *died* 1920, vol. II

Stevens, Air Marshal Sir Alick Charles, 1898–1987, vol. VIII

Stevens, Col Arthur Borlase, 1881–1965, vol. VI

Stevens, Col Arthur Cornish Jeremie, 1875–1962, vol. VI

Stevens, Bertram, *died* 1922, vol. II

Stevens, Hon. Sir Bertram Sydney Barnsdale, 1889–1973, vol. VII

Stevens, Air Vice-Marshal Cecil Alfred, 1898–1958, vol. V

Stevens, Lt-Col Cecil Robert, 1867–1919, vol. II

Stevens, Engr-Rear-Adm. Charles, 1869–1933, vol. III

Stevens, Sir Charles Cecil, 1840–1909, vol. I

Stevens, Col Charles Frederick, 1866–1944, vol. IV

Stevens, Charles John, 1857–1917, vol. II

Stevens, Clement Henry, 1870–1959, vol. V

Stevens, Hon. E. J., 1845–1922, vol. II

Stevens, E. S.; *see* Drower, Ethel May Stefana, (Lady Drower).

Stevens, Ernest Hamilton, 1864–1945, vol. IV

Stevens, Frank, 1850–1935, vol. III

Stevens, Lt-Col Sir Frank, 1877–1939, vol. III

Stevens, Frederick, 1840–1917, vol. II

Stevens, Frederick Guy, 1878–1944, vol. IV

Stevens, Frederick William, 1847–1900, vol. I

Stevens, Geoffrey Paul, 1902–1981, vol. VIII

Stevens, Brig.-Gen. George Archibald, 1875–1951, vol. V

Stevens, George Bridges, 1882–1937, vol. III

Stevens, George Cooper, 1905–1975, vol. VII

Stevens, Col Harold Raphael Gaetano, 1883–1961, vol. VI

Stevens, Sir Harold Samuel Eaton, 1892–1969, vol. VI

Stevens, Henry, 1885–1963, vol. VI

Stevens, Rev. Henry Bingham, 1835–1924, vol. II

Stevens, Hon. Henry Herbert, 1878–1973, vol. VII

Stevens, Herbert Lawrence, 1892–1978, vol. VII

Stevens, Maj.-Gen. Sir Jack Edwin Stawell, 1896–1969, vol. VI

Stevens, James Algernon, 1873–1934, vol. III

Stevens, Vice-Adm. Sir John Felgate, 1900–1989, vol. VIII

Stevens, Sir John Foster, 1845–1925, vol. II

Stevens, Engr Captain John Greet, 1857–1943, vol. IV

Stevens, Sir John Melior, 1913–1973, vol. VII

Stevens, Sir Joseph W.; *see* Weston-Stevens.

Stevens, Marshall, 1852–1936, vol. III

Stevens, Martin, 1929–1986, vol. VIII

Stevens, Lt-Col Nathaniel Melhuish Comins, 1868–1954, vol. V

Stevens, Norman Anthony, 1937–1988, vol. VIII

Stevens, Rt Rev. Percy, 1882–1966, vol. VI

Stevens, Sir Roger Bentham, 1906–1980, vol. VII

Stevens, Siaka Probyn, 1905–1988, vol. VIII

Stevens, Rt Rev. Thomas, 1841–1920, vol. II

Stevens, Thomas George, 1869–1953, vol. V

Stevens, Lt-Col Thomas Harry Goldsworthy, 1883–1970, vol. VI

Stevens, Thomas Terry Hoar; *see* Terry-Thomas.

Stevens, Thomas Wilson, 1901–1990, vol. VIII

Stevens, Walter Charles, 1904–1954, vol. V

Stevens, Rt Rev. William Bertrand, 1884–1947, vol. IV

Stevens, William C.; *see* Cleveland-Stevens.

Stevens, William Charles, 1900–1973, vol. VII

Stevens, William George, 1883–1971, vol. VII

Stevens, Maj.-Gen. William George, 1893–1974, vol. VII

Stevens, William Mitchell, 1868–1944, vol. IV

Stevens, William Oswald, 1891–1972, vol. VII

Stevenson, 1st Baron, 1873–1926, vol. II

Stevenson, Hon. Lord; James Stevenson, *died* 1963, vol. VI

Stevenson, Adlai Ewing, 1900–1965, vol. VI

Stevenson, Alan; *see* Stevenson, D. A.

Stevenson, Alan Leslie, 1901–1985, vol. VIII

Stevenson, Sir Alexander, 1860–1936, vol. III

Stevenson, Maj.-Gen. Alexander Gavin, 1871–1939, vol. III

Stevenson, Alexander James, 1901–1970, vol. VI

Stevenson, Alexander Wight, 1886–1954, vol. V

Stevenson, Allan, 1878–1948, vol. IV

Stevenson, Rt Hon. Sir (Aubrey) Melford (Steed), 1902–1987, vol. VIII

Stevenson, D. E., 1892–1973, vol. VII

Stevenson, Sir Daniel Macaulay, 1st Bt, 1851–1944, vol. IV

Stevenson, D(avid) Alan, 1891–1971, vol. VII

Stevenson, David Watson, 1842–1904, vol. I

Stevenson, Air Vice-Marshal Donald Fasken, 1895–1964, vol. VI

Stevenson, Sir Edmond Sinclair, 1850–1927, vol. II

Stevenson, Lt-Col Sir Edward Daymonde, 1895–1958, vol. V

Stevenson, Brig.-Gen. Edward Hall, 1872–1964, vol. VI

Stevenson, Edward Irenæus Prime-, 1868–1942, vol. IV

Stevenson, Edward Snead Boyd, 1849–1917, vol. II

Stevenson, Flora Clift, *died* 1905, vol. I

Stevenson, Frances; *see* Lloyd George of Dwyfor, Countess.

Stevenson, Col Francis, 1851–1922, vol. II

Stevenson, Francis Seymour, 1862–1938, vol. III

Stevenson, Sir George Augustus, 1856–1931, vol. III

Stevenson, George Hope, 1880–1952, vol. V

Stevenson, Col George Ingram, 1882–1958, vol. V

Stevenson, Surg.-Gen. Henry Wickham, 1857–1944, vol. IV

Stevenson, Dame Hilda Mabel, 1895–1987, vol. VIII

Stevenson, Sir Hubert Craddock, 1888–1971, vol. VII

Stevenson, Rev. J. Ross, 1866–1939, vol. III

Stevenson, Col James, 1838–1926, vol. II

Stevenson, James; *see* Stevenson, Hon. Lord.

Stevenson, James Alexander, 1881–1937, vol. III

Stevenson, James Arthur Radford, *died* 1974, vol. VII
Stevenson, James Cochran, 1825–1905, vol. I
Stevenson, James Verdier, 1858–1933, vol. III
Stevenson, Lt-Col John, 1895–1952, vol. V
Stevenson, Rear-Adm. John Bryan, 1876–1957, vol. V
Stevenson, John Horne, 1855–1939, vol. III
Stevenson, John Lynn, 1927–1971, vol. VII
Stevenson, Rev. John Sinclair, 1868–1930, vol. III
Stevenson, Air Vice-Marshal Leigh Forbes, 1895–1989, vol. VIII
Stevenson, Sir Malcolm, 1878–1927, vol. II
Stevenson, Margaret; *see* Stevenson, Mrs Sinclair.
Stevenson, Rt Hon. Sir Melford; *see* Stevenson, Rt Hon. Sir A. M. S.
Stevenson, Rev. Canon Morley, 1851–1930, vol. III
Stevenson, Gen. Nathaniel, 1840–1911, vol. I
Stevenson, R. Macaulay, *died* 1952, vol. V
Stevenson, Sir Ralph Clarmont Skrine, 1895–1977, vol. VII
Stevenson, Ralph Cornwallis, 1894–1967, vol. VI
Stevenson, Col Robert, 1845–1930, vol. III
Stevenson, Robert, 1905–1986, vol. VIII
Stevenson, Robert Alan Mowbray, 1847–1900, vol. I
Stevenson, Robert Scott, 1889–1967, vol. VI
Stevenson, Sir Roy Hunter, 1892–1963, vol. VI
Stevenson, Mrs Sinclair, (Margaret), 1875–1957, vol. V
Stevenson, Sir Thomas, 1838–1908, vol. I
Stevenson, Thomas Henry Craig, 1870–1932, vol. III
Stevenson, Maj.-Gen. Thomas Rennie, 1841–1923, vol. II
Stevenson, Walter Clegg, 1877–1931, vol. III
Stevenson, Sir William Alfred, *died* 1983, vol. VIII
Stevenson, William Barron, 1869–1954, vol. V
Stevenson, Lt-Col William David Henderson, *died* 1945, vol. IV
Stevenson, Maj.-Gen. William Flack, 1844–1922, vol. II
Stevenson, William Grant, 1849–1919, vol. II
Stevenson, Rt Rev. William Henry Webster, 1878–1945, vol. IV
Stevenson-Hamilton, Lt-Col James, 1867–1957, vol. V
Stevenson-Moore, Sir Charles James, 1866–1947, vol. IV
Steward, Rev. Edward, 1851–1930, vol. III
Steward, Maj.-Gen. Edward Harding, 1835–1918, vol. II
Steward, Maj.-Gen. Edward Merivale, 1881–1947, vol. IV
Steward, Francis James, *died* 1940, vol. III
Steward, Lt-Col Sir George, 1866–1920, vol. II
Steward, George Coton, 1896–1989, vol. VIII
Steward, George Frederick, 1884–1952, vol. V
Steward, Col Godfrey Robert Viveash, 1881–1969, vol. VI
Steward, Sir Harold Macdonald, 1904–1977, vol. VII
Steward, Sir Henry Allan Holden, 1865–1954, vol. V
Steward, Rt Rev. John Manwaring, 1874–1937, vol. III
Steward, Maj.-Gen. Reginald Herbert Ryrie, 1898–1975, vol. II

Steward, Sir William Arthur, 1901–1987, vol. VIII
Stewardson Edward Alfred, 1904–1973, vol. VII
Stewart, Hon. Lord; Ewan George Francis Stewart, 1923–1987, vol. VIII
Stewart of Alvechurch, Baroness (Life Peer); Mary Elizabeth Henderson Stewart, 1903–1984, vol. VIII
Stewart of Fulham, Baron (Life Peer); Robert Michael Maitland Stewart, 1906–1990, vol. VIII
Stewart, Lt-Col Albert Fortescue, *died* 1925, vol. II
Stewart, Very Rev. Alexander, 1847–1915, vol. I
Stewart, Rev. Alexander, *died* 1916, vol. II
Stewart, Sir Alexander, 2nd Bt (*cr* 1920, of Balgownie), 1886–1934, vol. III
Stewart, Sir Alexander Anderson, 1877–1956, vol. V
Stewart, Alexander Bernard, 1908–1974, vol. VII
Stewart, Alexander Boyd, 1904–1981, vol. VIII
Stewart, Alexander Carmichael, 1865–1944, vol. IV
Stewart, Maj.-Gen. Alexander Charles Hector, 1838–1917, vol. II
Stewart, Lt-Col Alexander Dron, 1883–1969, vol. VI
Stewart, Brig.-Gen. Alexander Edward, 1867–1940, vol. III
Stewart, Alexander G.; *see* Graham-Stewart.
Stewart, Alexander MacKay, 1878–1952, vol. V
Stewart, Alfred Walter, *died* 1947, vol. IV
Stewart, Major Algernon Bingham Anstruther, 1869–1916, vol. II
Stewart, Allan, 1865–1951, vol. V
Stewart, Andrew, 1895–1972, vol. VII
Stewart, Andrew, 1904–1990, vol. VIII
Stewart, Andrew Charles, 1907–1979, vol. VII
Stewart, Andrew Graham, 1901–1964, vol. VI
Stewart, Lt-Col Archibald Campbell, 1872–1936, vol. III
Stewart, Comdr Archibald Thomas, 1876–1968, vol. VI
Stewart, Arthur, 1877–1941, vol. IV
Stewart, Captain Arthur Courtenay, 1871–1958, vol. V
Stewart, Col Basil Heron S.; *see* Shaw-Stewart.
Stewart, Sir Bruce Fraser, 2nd Bt (*cr* 1920, of Fingask), 1904–1979, vol. VII (AII)
Stewart, Col Bryce, 1857–1936, vol. III
Stewart, Charles, 1840–1907, vol. I
Stewart, Charles, 1840–1916, vol. II
Stewart, Hon. Charles, 1868–1946, vol. IV
Stewart, Charles Cosmo Bruce, 1912–1988, vol. VIII
Stewart, Col Charles Edward, 1836–1904, vol. I
Stewart, Lt-Col Charles Edward, 1868–1916, vol. II
Stewart, Rev. Charles Henry Hylton, *died* 1922, vol. II
Stewart, Charles Hunter, 1854–1924, vol. II
Stewart, Charles Hylton, 1884–1932, vol. III
Stewart, Sir Charles John, 1851–1932, vol. III
Stewart, Charles John, *died* 1954, vol. V
Stewart, Charlotte, 1863–1918, vol. II
Stewart, Air Vice-Marshal Colin Murray, 1910–1990, vol. VIII
Stewart, Brig.-Gen. Cosmo Gordon, 1869–1948, vol. IV
Stewart, Daniel, 1836–1912, vol. I
Stewart, Sir David, 1835–1919, vol. II

Stewart, Col David Brown Douglas, 1862–1935, vol. III

Stewart, David Macfarlane, 1878–1950, vol. IV

Stewart, David Mitchell, 1853–1924, vol. II

Stewart, Desmond Stirling, 1924–1981, vol. VIII

Stewart, Donald, 1894–1976, vol. VII

Stewart, Sir Donald Martin, 1st Bt (cr 1881), 1824–1900, vol. I

Stewart, Sir Donald William, 1860–1905, vol. I

Stewart, Lt-Col Douglas, 1875–1943, vol. IV

Stewart, Sir Douglas Law, 3rd Bt (cr 1881), 1878–1951, vol. V

Stewart, Douglas Roy, 1886–1939, vol. III

Stewart, Col Dudley Strathearn, 1859–1933, vol. III

Stewart of Appin, Sir Dugald Leslie Lorn, 1921–1984, vol. VIII

Stewart, Duncan George, 1904–1949, vol. IV

Stewart, Edith Anne; see Robertson, E. A.

Stewart, Lt-Col Sir Edward, 1857–1948, vol. IV

Stewart, Sir Edward Orde MacTaggart-, 2nd Bt (cr 1892), 1883–1948, vol. IV

Stewart, Ellen Frances, died 1945, vol. IV

Stewart of Coll, Brig.-Gen. Ernest Moncrieff Paul, 1864–1942, vol. IV

Stewart, Sir Euan Guy S.; see Shaw-Stewart.

Stewart, Sir Findlater; see Stewart, Sir S. F.

Stewart, Frances Henrietta, (Lady Stewart), 1883–1962, vol. VI

Stewart, Sir Francis Hugh, 1869–1921, vol. II

Stewart, Francis William, 1885–1963, vol. VI

Stewart, Francis William Sutton C.; see Cumbrae-Stewart.

Stewart, Frank Ogilvie, 1893–1964, vol. VI

Stewart, Rev. Frank White, 1867–1933, vol. III

Stewart, Col Sir Frederick Charles, died 1950, vol. IV

Stewart, Sir Frederick Harold, 1884–1961, vol. VI

Stewart, Maj.-Gen. George, 1839–1927, vol. II

Stewart, Rt Rev. George Craig, 1879–1940, vol. III

Stewart, Rt Hon. George Francis, 1851–1928, vol. II

Stewart, George Innes, 1896–1968, vol. VI

Stewart, Lt-Col Sir George Powell, 5th Bt (cr 1803), 1861–1945, vol. IV

Stewart, Sir Gershom, 1857–1929, vol. III

Stewart, Gordon William, 1906–1988, vol. VIII

Stewart, Haldane Campbell, 1868–1942, vol. IV

Stewart, Sir Halley, 1838–1937, vol. III

Stewart, Sir Harry Jocelyn Urquhart, 11th Bt (cr 1623), 1871–1945, vol. IV

Stewart, Sir Hector Hamilton, 1901–1980, vol. VII (AII)

Stewart, Henrietta; see Shell, Rita.

Stewart, Henry Cockburn, 1844–1899, vol. I

Stewart, Ven. Henry John, 1873–1960, vol. V

Stewart, Lt-Col Henry King, 1861–1907, vol. I

Stewart, Sir Herbert Ray, 1890–1989, vol. VIII

Stewart, Maj.-Gen. Herbert William Vansittart, 1886–1975, vol. VII

Stewart, Howard Hilton, 1900–1961, vol. VI

Stewart, Lt-Col Hugh, 1872–1931, vol. III

Stewart, Hugh, 1884–1934, vol. III

Stewart, Rev. Hugh Fraser, 1863–1948, vol. IV

Stewart, Brig.-Gen. Sir Hugh Houghton, 4th Bt (cr 1803), 1858–1942, vol. IV

Stewart, Sir Hugh S.; see Shaw-Stewart.

Stewart, Brig.-Gen. Ian, 1874–1941, vol. IV

Stewart, Ian Struthers, 1876–1930, vol. III

Stewart, Sir Iain Maxwell, 1916–1985, vol. VIII

Stewart, James, 1846–1906, vol. I

Stewart, James, 1863–1931, vol. III

Stewart, James, 1867–1943, vol. IV

Stewart, Maj.-Gen. James Calder, 1840–1930, vol. III

Stewart, Brig.-Gen. James Campbell, 1884–1947, vol. IV

Stewart, Hon. James Charles, 1850–1931, vol. III

Stewart, Brig. James Crossley, 1891–1972, vol. VII

Stewart, Hon. James D., 1874–1933, vol. III

Stewart, James Douglas, 1869–1955, vol. V

Stewart, Sir James H.; see Henderson-Stewart.

Stewart, James King, 1863–1938, vol. III

Stewart, Maj.-Gen. Sir James Marshall, 1861–1943, vol. IV

Stewart, Sir James Purves-, 1869–1949, vol. IV

Stewart, Very Rev. James Stuart, 1896–1990, vol. VIII

Stewart, Sir James Watson, 1st Bt (cr 1920, of Balgownie), 1852–1922, vol. II

Stewart, Sir James Watson, 3rd Bt (cr 1920, of Balgownie), 1889–1955, vol. V

Stewart, Sir James Watson, 4th Bt (cr 1920, of Balgownie), 1922–1988, vol. VIII

Stewart, Sir Jocelyn Harry, 12th Bt, 1903–1982, vol. VIII

Stewart, Col John, 1833–1914, vol. I

Stewart, Sir John, 1st Bt (cr 1920, of Fingask), 1877–1924, vol. II

Stewart, Lt-Col John, 1869–1931, vol. III

Stewart, Col John, 1848–1933, vol. III

Stewart, Sir John, 1867–1947, vol. IV

Stewart, Sir John, 1887–1958, vol. V

Stewart, John Alexander, 1846–1933, vol. III

Stewart, John Alexander, 1882–1948, vol. IV

Stewart, John Alexander, 1915–1974, vol. VII

Stewart of Ardvorlich, John Alexander MacLaren, 1904–1985, vol. VIII

Stewart, Captain John Christie, 1888–1978, vol. VII

Stewart, John Graham, died 1917, vol. II

Stewart, Maj.-Gen. Sir (John Henry) Keith, 1872–1955, vol. V

Stewart, Sir (John) Keith (Watson), 5th Bt, 1929–1990, vol. VIII

Stewart, John McKellar, 1878–1953, vol. V

Stewart, Sir John Marcus, 3rd Bt (cr 1803), 1830–1905, vol. I

Stewart, John Philip, 1900–1984, vol. VIII

Stewart, Brig.-Gen. John Smith, 1877–1970, vol. VI

Stewart, Maj.-Gen. John William, 1862–1938, vol. III

Stewart, Rev. Joseph Atkinson, died 1913, vol. I

Stewart, Joseph Francis, 1889–1964, vol. VI

Stewart, Maj.-Gen. Sir Keith; see Stewart, Maj.-Gen. Sir J. H. K.

Stewart, Sir Keith; see Stewart, Sir J. K. W.

Stewart, Maj.-Gen. Sir Keith Lindsay, 1896–1972, vol. VII

Stewart, Sir Kenneth Dugald, 1st Bt (cr 1960), 1882–1972, vol. VII

Stewart, Louisa Mary, 1861–1943, vol. IV

Stewart, Sir Malcolm; see Stewart, Sir P. M.

Stewart, Sir Mark John MacTaggart, 1st Bt (*cr* 1892), 1834–1923, vol. II
Stewart, Very Rev. Matthew, 1881–1952, vol. V
Stewart, Matthew John, 1885–1956, vol. V
Stewart, Sir Michael Hugh S.; *see* Shaw-Stewart.
Stewart, Sir Michael Robert S.; *see* Shaw-Stewart.
Stewart, Major Noel St Vincent Ramsay, 1870–1940, vol. III
Stewart, Sir Norman Robert, 2nd Bt (*cr* 1881), 1851–1926, vol. II
Stewart, Major Oliver, 1895–1976, vol. VII
Stewart, Col Patrick Alexander Vansittart, 1875–1960, vol. V
Stewart, Rev. Percy, 1856–1934, vol. III
Stewart, Sir (Percy) Malcolm, 1st Bt (*cr* 1937), 1872–1951, vol. V
Stewart, Potter, 1915–1985, vol. VIII
Stewart, Rev. Ravenscroft, 1845–1921, vol. II
Stewart, Sir Richard Campbell, 1836–1904, vol. I
Stewart, Sir Robert, 1858–1937, vol. III
Stewart, Robert Bruce, 1863–1948, vol. IV
Stewart, Maj.-Gen. Robert Crosse, 1825–1913, vol. I
Stewart of Physgill, Adm. Robert Hathorn J.; *see* Johnston-Stewart of Physgill.
Stewart, Col Sir Robert King, 1854–1930, vol. III
Stewart, Gen. Sir Robert Macgregor, 1842–1919, vol. II
Stewart, Sir Robert Sproul, 1874–1969, vol. VI
Stewart, Robert Strother-, 1878–1954, vol. V
Stewart, Lt-Col Rupert, 1864–1930, vol. III
Stewart, Sir (Samuel) Findlater, 1879–1960, vol. V
Stewart, Sir Thomas Alexander, 1888–1964, vol. VI
Stewart, Brig. Thomas G.; *see* Grainger-Stewart.
Stewart, Thomas Grainger, *died* 1957, vol. V
Stewart, Valentine Peter Beardmore, 1882–1933, vol. III
Stewart, Lt-Col Sir Walter Guy S.; *see* Shaw-Stewart.
Stewart, Walter Richard S.; *see* Shaw-Stewart.
Stewart, Walter W., 1885–1958, vol. V
Stewart, Rt Rev. Weston Henry, 1887–1969, vol. VI
Stewart, Major William, 1859–1918, vol. II
Stewart, William, 1835–1919, vol. II
Stewart, William, 1856–1947, vol. IV (A), vol. V
Stewart, William, 1879–1964, vol. VI
Stewart, William, 1916–1975, vol. VII
Stewart, Lt-Col William Burton, 1872–1936, vol. III
Stewart, Hon. William Downie, 1878–1949, vol. IV
Stewart, William James, 1889–1969, vol. VI
Stewart, William John, 1849–1908, vol. I
Stewart, William John, *died* 1946, vol. IV
Stewart, William Joseph, *died* 1960, vol. V
Stewart, Air Vice-Marshal William Kilpatrick, 1913–1967, vol. VI
Stewart, William McCausland, 1900–1989, vol. VIII
Stewart, Lt-Col William Murray, 1875–1948, vol. IV
Stewart, Brig.-Gen. William Robert, 1862–1932, vol. III
Stewart, Maj.-Gen. William Ross, 1889–1966, vol. VI
Stewart, Hon. William Snodgrass, 1855–1938, vol. III (A), vol. IV
Stewart-Bam of Ards, Lt-Col Sir Pieter Canzius van Blommestein, 1869–1928, vol. II
Stewart-Brown, Ronald, 1872–1940, vol. III
Stewart-Brown, Ronald David, 1911–1963, vol. VI

Stewart-Clark, Sir John, 1st Bt, 1864–1924, vol. II
Stewart-Clark, Sir Stewart, 2nd Bt, 1904–1971, vol. VII
Stewart-Dick-Cunyngham, Sir William; *see* Cunyngham.
Stewart-Liberty, Captain Ivor; *see* Liberty.
Stewart-Richardson, Sir Edward Austin, 15th Bt; *see* Richardson.
Stewart-Richardson, Major Sir Ian Rorie Hay, 16th Bt, 1904–1969, vol. VI
Stewart-Richardson, Lt-Col Neil Graham; *see* Richardson.
Stewart-Richardson, Violet Roberta, 1882–1967, vol. VI
Stewart-Roberts, Walter Stewart, 1889–1975, vol. VII
Stewart-Smith, Sir Dudley, 1857–1919, vol. II
Stewart-Smith, Ean Kendal, 1907–1964, vol. VI
Stewart-Wallace, Sir John Stewart, *died* 1963, vol. VI
Stewart-Wilson, Sir Charles, 1864–1950, vol. IV
Stewartson, Keith, 1925–1983, vol. VIII
Steyn, Lucas Cornelius, 1903–1976, vol. VII
Steyn, Martinus Theunis, 1857–1916, vol. II
Sthamer, Friedrich, 1856–1931, vol. III
Stibbe, Edward Philip, 1884–1943, vol. IV
Stiebel, Sir Arthur, 1875–1949, vol. IV
Stiebel, Herbert Cecil, 1876–1941, vol. IV
Stiebel, Victor Frank, 1907–1976, vol. VII
Stiffe, Captain Arthur William, 1831–1912, vol. I
Stigand, Major Chauncey Hugh, *died* 1919, vol. II
Stigand, William, 1825–1915, vol. I
Stikeman, William Rucker, 1854–1927, vol. II
Stikker, Dirk Uipko, 1897–1979, vol. VII
Stileman, Rt Rev. Charles Harvey, 1863–1925, vol. II
Stileman, Rear-Adm. Sir Harry Hampson, 1860–1938, vol. III
Stileman, Maj.-Gen. William Croughton, *died* 1915, vol. I
Stiles, Charles Wardell, 1867–1941, vol. IV
Stiles, Lt-Col Sir Harold Jalland, 1863–1946, vol. IV
Stiles, Walter, 1886–1966, vol. VI
Stiles, Walter Stanley, 1901–1985, vol. VIII
Stilgoe, Henry Edward, *died* 1943, vol. IV
Still, Alexander William, 1860–1931, vol. III
Still, Dame Alicia Frances Jane Lloyd, *died* 1944, vol. IV
Still, Andrew, 1866–1939, vol. III
Still, Charles, 1849–1930, vol. III
Still, Sir George Frederic, 1868–1941, vol. IV
Still, Rev. John, *died* 1914, vol. I
Still, William Chester, 1878–1928, vol. II
Stillman, William James, 1828–1901, vol. I
Stilwell, Gen. Joseph Warren, 1883–1946, vol. IV
Stimson, Henry Lewis, 1867–1950, vol. IV
Stinson, Sir Charles Alexander, 1919–1989, vol. VIII
Stinton, T., 1886–1957, vol. V
Stirling, Mrs A. M. W., *died* 1965, vol. VI
Stirling, Brig. Alexander Dickson, 1886–1961, vol. VI
Stirling, Alfred T., 1902–1981, vol. VIII
Stirling, Adm. Anselan John Buchanan, 1875–1936, vol. III
Stirling, Brig.-Gen. Archibald, 1867–1931, vol. III
Stirling, Sir (Archibald) David, 1915–1990, vol. VIII
Stirling, Archibald William, *died* 1923, vol. II
Stirling, Carl Ludwig, 1890–1973, vol. VII

Stirling, Sir Charles Elphinstone Fleming, 8th Bt (*cr* 1666), 1831–1910, vol. I
Stirling, Sir Charles Norman, 1901–1986, vol. VIII
Stirling, Sir David; *see* Stirling, Sir A. D.
Stirling, Duncan Alexander, 1899–1990, vol. VIII
Stirling, Edward, 1891–1948, vol. IV
Stirling, Sir Edward Charles, 1848–1919, vol. II
Stirling, Col Sir George; *see* Stirling, Col Sir W. G.
Stirling, George Claudius Beresford, 1861–1929, vol. III
Stirling, Col Sir George Murray Home, 9th Bt (*cr* 1666), 1869–1949, vol. IV
Stirling, Gilbert, 1843–1915, vol. I
Stirling, Hon. Grote, 1875–1953, vol. V
Stirling, Rt Hon. Sir James, 1836–1916, vol. II
Stirling, Sir James; *see* Stirling, Sir R. J. L.
Stirling, Brig. James Erskine, 1898–1968, vol. VI
Stirling, James Heron, 1867–1928, vol. II
Stirling, James Hutchison, 1820–1909, vol. I
Stirling, Hon. Brig.-Gen. James Wilfred, 1855–1926, vol. II
Stirling, Sir John, 1893–1975, vol. VII
Stirling, John Ashwell, 1891–1965, vol. VI
Stirling, John Bertram, 1888–1988, vol. VIII
Stirling, Hon. Sir (John) Lancelot, 1849–1932, vol. III
Stirling, John W., 1859–1923, vol. II
Stirling, Hon. Sir Lancelot; *see* Stirling, Hon. Sir J. L.
Stirling, Sir (Robert) James (Lindsay), 1907–1974, vol. VII
Stirling, Viola Henrietta Christian, 1907–1989, vol. VIII
Stirling, Rt Rev. Waite Hockin, 1829–1923, vol. II
Stirling, Brig. Walter Andrew, 1883–1972, vol. VII
Stirling, Lt-Col Walter Francis, 1880–1958, vol. V
Stirling, Col Sir (Walter) George, 3rd Bt (*cr* 1800), 1839–1934, vol. III
Stirling, Gen. Sir William, 1835–1906, vol. I
Stirling, William, 1851–1932, vol. III
Stirling, Brig.-Gen. William, 1878–1949, vol. IV
Stirling, Gen. Sir William Gurdon, 1907–1973, vol. VII
Stirling-Hamilton, Sir Bruce, 13th Bt, 1940–1989, vol. VIII
Stirling-Hamilton, Captain Sir Robert William, *see* Hamilton.
Stirling-Hamilton, Sir William; *see* Hamilton.
Stirling Home Drummond, Lt-Col Henry Edward, 1846–1911, vol. I
Stirling-Maxwell, Sir John M.; *see* Maxwell.
Stirton, Rev. John, 1871–1944, vol. IV
Stitt, Rear-Adm. Edward Rhodes, 1867–1948, vol. IV
Stobart, Col George Herbert, 1873–1943, vol. IV
Stobart, Lt-Col Hugh Morton, 1883–1952, vol. V
Stobart, Mrs St Clair, (Mrs Stobart Greenhalgh), *died* 1954, vol. V
Stobie, Harry, 1882–1948, vol. IV
Stobie, William, 1886–1957, vol. V
Stoby, Sir Kenneth Sievewright, 1903–1985, vol. VIII
Stock, Allen Lievesley, 1906–1982, vol. VIII
Stock, Arthur Boy, *died* 1915, vol. I
Stock, Eugene, 1836–1928, vol. II
Stock, Henry John, 1853–1930, vol. III

Stock, James Henry, 1855–1907, vol. I
Stock, Keith Lievesley, 1911–1988, vol. VIII
Stock, Col Philip Graham, 1876–1975, vol. VII
Stock, Ralph, *died* 1962, vol. VI
Stockdale, Sir Edmund Villiers Minshull, 1st Bt, 1903–1989, vol. VIII
Stockdale, Frank Alleyne, 1910–1989, vol. VIII
Stockdale, Sir Frank Arthur, 1883–1949, vol. IV
Stockdale, Group Captain George William, 1932–1990, vol. VIII
Stockdale, Brig.-Gen. Herbert Edward, 1867–1953, vol. V
Stockdale, Herbert Fitton, 1868–1951, vol. V
Stockdale, Maj.-Gen. Reginald Booth, 1908–1979, vol. VII
Stockenström, Sir Anders Johan Booysen, 4th Bt, 1908–1957, vol. V
Stockenström, Sir Andries, 3rd Bt, 1868–1922, vol. II
Stockenström, Hon. Sir Gysbert Henry, 2nd Bt, 1841–1912, vol. I
Stocker, Edgar Percy, 1888–1959, vol. V
Stocker, Ven. Harry, *died* 1922, vol. II
Stocker, Richard Dimsdale, 1877–1935, vol. III
Stockil, Sir Raymond Osborne, 1907–1984, vol. VIII
Stockings, Major Arthur Perry, 1880–1943, vol. IV
Stockley, Brig.-Gen. Arthur Uniacke, 1869–1939, vol. III
Stockley, Lt-Col Charles Hugh, 1882–1955, vol. V
Stockley, Col Charles More, 1845–1923, vol. II
Stockley, Cynthia, *died* 1936, vol. III
Stockley, David Dudgeon, 1900–1980, vol. VII
Stockley, Brig.-Gen. Ernest Norman, 1872–1946, vol. IV
Stockley, Gerald Ernest, 1900–1981, vol. VIII
Stockley, Major Sir Harry Hudson Fraser, 1878–1951, vol. V
Stockley, Brig.-Gen. Hugh Roderick, 1868–1935, vol. III
Stockley, Rev. Joseph John Gabbett, 1862–1949, vol. IV
Stockley, William F. P., 1859–1943, vol. IV
Stockman, Henry Watson, 1894–1982, vol. VIII
Stockman, Ralph, 1861–1946, vol. IV
Stockman, Sir Stewart, 1869–1926, vol. II
Stocks, Baroness (Life Peer); Mary Danvers Stocks, 1891–1975, vol. VII
Stocks, Alfred James, 1926–1988, vol. VIII
Stocks, Sir (Andrew) Denys, 1884–1961, vol. VI
Stocks, Arthur Hudson, 1889–1940, vol. III
Stocks, Charles Lancelot, 1878–1975, vol. VII
Stocks, Sir Denys; *see* Stocks, Sir A. D.
Stocks, Francis W., 1873–1929, vol. III
Stocks, Harold Carpenter Lumb, 1884–1956, vol. V
Stocks, Rev. John Edward, 1843–1926, vol. II
Stocks, John Leofric, 1882–1937, vol. III
Stocks, Percy, 1889–1974, vol. VII
Stockton, 1st Earl of, 1894–1986, vol. VIII
Stockton, Rear-Adm. Charles Herbert, 1845–1924, vol. II
Stockton, Sir Edwin Forsyth, 1873–1939, vol. III
Stockton, Francis Richard, 1834–1902, vol. I
Stockwell, Brig.-Gen. Clifton Inglis, 1879–1953, vol. V

Stockwell, Hon. Maj.-Gen. George Clifton Inglis, 1863–1936, vol. III
Stockwell, Captain Henry, 1875–1962, vol. VI
Stockwell, Gen. Sir Hugh Charles, 1903–1986, vol. VIII
Stockwell, Col Ralph Frederick, 1885–1962, vol. VI
Stockwood, Ven. Charles Vincent, 1885–1958, vol. V
Stodart, Sqdn Ldr David Edmund, 1882–1938, vol. III
Stodart, James Carlyle, 1880–1956, vol. V
Stodart, Col Thomas, 1868–1934, vol. III
Stoddard, Charles Warren, 1843–1909, vol. I
Stoddard, Francis Hovey, 1847–1936, vol. III
Stoddard, Lothrop, 1883–1950, vol. IV (A)
Stoddart, Alexander Frederick Richard, 1904–1973, vol. VII
Stoddart, Andrew Ernest, 1863–1915, vol. I
Stoddart, Anna M., 1840–1911, vol. I
Stoddart, Adm. Archibald Peile, 1860–1939, vol. III
Stoddart, Sir Charles John, 1839–1913, vol. I
Stoddart, Jane T., died 1944, vol. IV
Stoddart, William Henry Butter, died 1950, vol. IV
Stoddart-Scott, Col Sir Malcolm, 1901–1973, vol. VII
Stoessel, Walter John, Jr, 1920–1986, vol. VIII
Stogdon, Rev. Edgar, 1870–1951, vol. V
Stoker, Abraham; see Stoker, Bram.
Stoker, Bram, 1847–1912, vol. I
Stoker, Col Claude Bayfield, 1875–1948, vol. IV
Stoker, George, 1855–1920, vol. II, vol. III
Stoker, George Herbert, 1874–1935, vol. III
Stoker, Graves, 1864–1938, vol. III
Stoker, Captain Hew Gordon Dacre, 1885–1966, vol. VI
Stoker, Robert Burdon, died 1919, vol. II
Stoker, Thomas, 1849–1925, vol. II
Stoker, Sir Thornley; see Stoker, Sir W. T.
Stoker, William Henry, died 1944, vol. IV
Stoker, Sir (William) Thornley, 1st Bt, 1845–1912, vol. I
Stokes, A. G. Folliott, died 1939, vol. III
Stokes, Adrian, 1887–1927, vol. II
Stokes, Adrian, 1854–1935, vol. III
Stokes, Adrian Durham, 1902–1972, vol. VII
Stokes, Brig.-Gen. Alfred, 1860–1931, vol. III
Stokes, Rev. Anson Phelps, 1874–1958, vol. V
Stokes, Sir Arthur, 2nd Bt, 1858–1916, vol. II
Stokes, Rev. Augustus Sidney, died 1922, vol. II
Stokes, Edith, died 1936, vol. III
Stokes, Eric Thomas, 1924–1981, vol. VIII
Stokes, Maj.-Gen. Sir Folliott Stuart Furneaux, 1849–1911, vol. I
Stokes, Sir (Frederick) Wilfrid Scott, 1860–1927, vol. II
Stokes, Sir Gabriel, 1849–1920, vol. II
Stokes, Sir George Gabriel, 1st Bt, 1819–1903, vol. I
Stokes, George Joseph, 1859–1935, vol. III
Stokes, Rev. George Thomas, 1843–1898, vol. I
Stokes, George Vernon, 1873–1954, vol. V
Stokes, Rear-Adm. Graham Henry, 1902–1969, vol. VI
Stokes, Haldane Day, 1885–1915, vol. I
Stokes, Sir Harold Frederick, 1899–1977, vol. VII
Stokes, Col Harold William Puzey, 1878–1949, vol. IV

Stokes, Sir Henry Edward, 1841–1926, vol. II
Stokes, Rev. Henry Paine, 1849–1931, vol. III
Stokes, Sir Hopetoun Gabriel, 1873–1951, vol. V
Stokes, Hugh, 1875–1932, vol. III
Stokes, Sir John, 1825–1902, vol. I
Stokes, Leonard Aloysius Scott, 1858–1925, vol. II
Stokes, Brig. Ralph Shelton Griffin, 1882–1979, vol. VII
Stokes, Rt Hon. Richard Rapier, 1897–1957, vol. V
Stokes, Sir Robert Baret, 1833–1899, vol. I
Stokes, Rear-Adm. Robert Henry Simpson, 1855–1914, vol. I
Stokes, Whitley, 1830–1909, vol. I
Stokes, Sir Wilfrid; see Stokes, Sir F. W. S.
Stokes, Sir William, 1839–1900, vol. I
Stokes, William Henry, 1894–1977, vol. VII
Stokowski, Leopold Boleslawowicz Stanislaw Antoni, 1882–1977, vol. VII
Stoll, Sir Oswald, 1866–1942, vol. IV
Stollery, Col John, 1852–1940, vol. III
Stone, Baron (Life Peer); Joseph Ellis Stone, 1903–1986, vol. VIII
Stone, Ven. Arthure Edward, 1852–1927, vol. II
Stone, Sir Benjamin; see Stone, Sir J. B.
Stone, Bertram Gilchrist, 1903–1978, vol. VII
Stone, Sir Charles, 1850–1931, vol. III
Stone, Christopher Reynolds, 1882–1965, vol. VI
Stone, Rev. Darwell, 1859–1941, vol. IV
Stone, Hon. Sir Edward Albert, 1844–1920, vol. II
Stone, Edward James, 1831–1897, vol. I
Stone, Brig.-Gen. Francis Gleadowe, 1857–1929, vol. III
Stone, George Frederick, 1855–1928, vol. II
Stone, Sir Gilbert, 1886–1967, vol. VI
Stone, Harlan F., 1872–1946, vol. IV
Stone, Rev. Henry Cecil Brough, died 1936, vol. III
Stone, Henry Walter James, 1877–1954, vol. V
Stone, Air Vice-Marshal James Ambrose, 1885–1966, vol. VI
Stone, Sir (John) Benjamin, 1838–1914, vol. I
Stone, Sir (John) Leonard, 1896–1978, vol. VII
Stone, John William, 1852–1936, vol. III
Stone, Sir Joseph Henry, 1858–1941, vol. IV
Stone, Julius, 1907–1985, vol. VIII
Stone, Sir Leonard; see Stone, Sir J. L.
Stone, Col Lionel George Tempest, 1874–1946, vol. IV
Stone, Marcus, 1840–1921, vol. II
Stone, Brig.-Gen. Percy Vere Powys, 1883–1959, vol. V
Stone, Reynolds, 1909–1979, vol. VII
Stone, Richard Evelyn, 1914–1980, vol. VII
Stone, Riversdale Garland, 1903–1985, vol. VIII
Stone, Lt-Gen. Robert Graham William Hawkins, 1890–1974, vol. VII
Stone, Rev. Samuel John, 1839–1900, vol. I
Stone, Thomas Archibald, 1900–1965, vol. VI
Stone, Rev. W. H., 1860–1920, vol. II
Stone, William, 1857–1958, vol. V
Stone, William George Rush, 1855–1939, vol. III
Stone, Very Rev. William Henry, died 1912, vol. I
Stone-Wigg, Rt Rev. Montagu John, 1861–1918, vol. II
Stoneham, Sir Ralph Thompson, 1888–1965, vol. VI

Stoneham, Robert Thompson Douglas, 1883–1962, vol. VI

Stonehaven, 1st Viscount, 1874–1941, vol. IV

Stonehewer Bird, Sir (Francis) Hugh (William), 1891–1973, vol. VII

Stonehewer Bird, Sir Hugh; *see* Stonehewer Bird, Sir F. H. W.

Stonehouse, Sir Edmund, 1854–1938, vol. III

Stonehouse, John Thomson, 1925–1988, vol. VIII

Stoneley, Robert, 1894–1976, vol. VII

Stoneman, Walter E., 1876–1958, vol. V

Stoner, Edmund Clifton, 1899–1968, vol. VI

Stones, Edward Lionel Gregory, 1914–1987, vol. VIII

Stones, Sir Frederick, 1886–1947, vol. IV

Stones, Hubert Horace, 1892–1965, vol. VI

Stones, James, *died* 1935, vol. III

Stones, William, 1904–1969, vol. VI

Stonestreet, George William, 1863–1940, vol. III

Stonex, Rev. Francis Tilney, 1857–1920, vol. II

Stoney, Bindon Blood, 1828–1909, vol. I

Stoney, Edith Anne, 1869–1938, vol. III

Stoney, Edward Waller, *died* 1931, vol. III

Stoney, Florence Ada, 1870–1932, vol. III

Stoney, George Gerald, 1863–1942, vol. IV

Stoney, George Johnstone, 1826–1911, vol. I

Stoney, Richard Atkinson, 1877–1966, vol. VI

Stoney-Smith, Major Herbert; *see* Smith.

Stonham, Baron (Life Peer); Victor John Collins, 1903–1971, vol. VII

Stonham, Charles, 1858–1916, vol. II

Stonham, Edwin Earle, 1867–1934, vol. III

Stonhouse, Sir Arthur Allan, 17th Bt, and 13th Bt, 1885–1967, vol. VI

Stonhouse, Sir Ernest Hay, 16th Bt, and 12th Bt, 1855–1937, vol. III

Stonhouse-Gostling, Maj.-Gen. Philip Le Marchant Stonhouse, 1899–1990, vol. VIII

Stonier, George Walter, 1903–1985, vol. VIII

Stonor, Most Rev. Mgr Hon. Edmund, 1831–1912, vol. I

Stonor, Hon. Edward Alexander, 1867–1940, vol. III

Stonor, Hon. Sir Harry, 1859–1939, vol. III

Stonor, Henry James, 1820–1908, vol. I

Stonor, Oswald Francis Gerard, 1872–1940, vol. III

Stoodley, Edwin Edward, 1844–1922, vol. II

Stooke, Sir George Beresford-, 1897–1983, vol. VIII

Stopes, Charlotte Carmichael, *died* 1929, vol. III

Stopes, Marie Charlotte Carmichael, *died* 1958, vol. V

Stopford of Fallowfield, Baron (Life Peer); John Sebastian Bach Stopford, 1888–1961, vol. VI

Stopford, Vice-Adm. Hon. Arthur, 1879–1955, vol. V

Stopford, Edward Kennedy, 1911–1983, vol. VIII

Stopford, Francis Powys, 1861–1935, vol. III

Stopford, Rear-Adm. Frederick Victor, 1900–1982, vol. VIII

Stopford, Lt-Gen. Hon. Sir Frederick William, 1854–1929, vol. III

Stopford, Captain Hon. Guy, 1884–1954, vol. V

Stopford, Hon. Horatia Charlotte Frances, 1835–1920, vol. II

Stopford, Rev. John Bird, 1859–1934, vol. III

Stopford, Maj.-Gen. Sir Lionel Arthur Montagu, 1860–1942, vol. IV

Stopford, Louise, *died* 1935, vol. III

Stopford, Gen. Sir Montagu George North, 1892–1971, vol. VII

Stopford, Robert Jemmett, 1895–1978, vol. VII

Stopford, Vice-Adm. Robert Wilbraham, 1844–1911, vol. I

Stopford, Rt Rev. and Rt Hon. Robert Wright, 1901–1976, vol. VII

Stopford Sackville, Col Nigel Victor, 1901–1972, vol. VII

Stopford-Taylor, Richard, 1884–1964, vol. VI

Stopp, Eric John Carl, 1894–1967, vol. VI

Stoppani, Rt Rev. Antonio, 1873–1940, vol. III (A), vol. IV

Stops, Col George, 1876–1940, vol. III

Storer, Bellamy, 1847–1922, vol. II

Storey, Charles Ambrose, 1888–1967, vol. VI

Storey, Major Charles Ernest, 1877–1943, vol. IV

Storey, Hon. Sir David, 1856–1924, vol. II

Storey, George Adolphus, 1834–1919, vol. II

Storey, Gladys; *see* Storey, M. G.

Storey, Harold Haydon, 1894–1969, vol. VI

Storey, Sir John Stanley, 1896–1955, vol. V

Storey, (Mary) Gladys, 1887–1978, vol. VII

Storey, Robert Holme, *died* 1956, vol. V

Storey, Samuel, 1840–1925, vol. II

Storey, Samuel; *see* Baron Buckton.

Storey, Sir Thomas, 1825–1898, vol. I

Storey, Sir Thomas James, 1851–1933, vol. III

Stork, Herbert Cecil, 1890–1983, vol. VIII

Stork, Joseph Whiteley, 1902–1990, vol. VIII

Storke, Arthur Ditchfield, 1894–1949, vol. IV

Storkey, Percy Valentine, 1893–1969, vol. VI

Storm, Lesley, *died* 1975, vol. VII

Stormonth-Darling, Hon. Lord; Moir Tod Stormonth-Darling, 1844–1912, vol. I

Stormonth-Darling, Major John Collier, 1878–1916, vol. II

Stormonth-Darling, Moir Tod; *see* Stormonth-Darling, Hon. Lord.

Storr, Francis, 1839–1919, vol. II

Storr, Lt-Col Lancelot, 1874–1944, vol. IV

Storr, Norman, 1907–1984, vol. VIII

Storr, Rev. Canon Vernon Faithfull, 1869–1940, vol. III

Storrar, Sir John, 1891–1984, vol. VIII

Storrar, Air Vice-Marshal Ronald Charles, 1904–1985, vol. VIII

Storrar, Air Vice-Marshal Sydney Ernest, 1895–1969, vol. VI

Storrs, Rt Rev. Christopher E., 1889–1977, vol. VII

Storrs, Very Rev. John, *died* 1928, vol. II

Storrs, Rear-Adm. Robert Francis, 1906–1968, vol. VI

Storrs, Sir Ronald, 1881–1955, vol. V

Storrs, William Hargrave, 1880–1964, vol. VI

Story, A. B. Herbert, *died* 1910, vol. I

Story, Alfred Thomas, 1842–1934, vol. III

Story, Arthur John, 1864–1938, vol. III

Story, Douglas, 1872–1921, vol. II

Story, Janet Leith, 1828–1926, vol. II

Story, John Benjamin, *died* 1926, vol. II

Story, Lt-Gen. Philip, 1840–1916, vol. II

Story, Very Rev. Robert Herbert, 1835–1907, vol. I

Story, Col William Frederick, *died* 1939, vol. III
Story, Adm. William Oswald, 1859–1938, vol. III
Story Maskelyne, Mervyn Herbert Nevil; *see* Maskelyne.
Stotesbury, Herbert Wentworth, 1916–1988, vol. VIII
Stothert, Sir Percy Kendall, 1863–1929, vol. III
Stott, Sir Arnold Walmsley, *died* 1958, vol. V
Stott, Edward, *died* 1918, vol. II
Stott, Sir George Edward, 2nd Bt, 1887–1957, vol. V
Stott, Maj.-Gen. Hugh, 1884–1966, vol. VI
Stott, May, (Lady Stott; May B. Lee), *died* 1977, vol. VII
Stott, Sir Philip Sidney, 1st Bt, 1858–1937, vol. III
Stott, Sir Philip Sidney, 3rd Bt, 1914–1979, vol. VII
Stott, Lt-Col William Henry, 1863–1930, vol. III
Stoughton, Rev. John, 1807–1897, vol. I
Stoughton, Raymond Henry, 1903–1979, vol. VII
Stourton, Col Hon. Edward Plantagenet Joseph Corbally, 1880–1966, vol. VI
Stourton, Sir Ivo Herbert Evelyn Joseph, 1901–1985, vol. VIII
Stourton, Rt Rev. Mgr Joseph, 1845–1921, vol. II
Stout, Alan Ker, 1900–1983, vol. VIII
Stout, Sir Duncan; *see* Stout, Sir T. D. M.
Stout, George Frederick, 1860–1944, vol. IV
Stout, Percy Wyfold, 1875–1937, vol. III
Stout, Rt Hon. Sir Robert, 1844–1930, vol. III
Stout, Sir (Thomas) Duncan (Macgregor), 1885–1979, vol. VII
Stow, Sir Alexander Montague, 1873–1936, vol. III
Stow, Sir Edmond Cecil P.; *see* Philipson-Stow.
Stow, Sir Elliot Philipson Philipson-, 2nd Bt, 1876–1954, vol. V
Stow, Sir Frederic Lawrence Philipson-, 3rd Bt, 1905–1976, vol. VII
Stow, Sir Frederic Samuel Philipson-, 1st Bt, 1849–1908, vol. I
Stow, Robert Frederic Philipson-, 1878–1949, vol. IV
Stow, Vincent Aubrey Stewart, 1883–1968, vol. VI
Stow Hill, Baron (Life Peer); Frank Soskice, 1902–1979, vol. VII
Stowe, Leonard, 1837–1920, vol. II
Stowell, Lt-Col Arthur Terence, 1873–1945, vol. IV
Stowell, Gordon William, 1898–1972, vol. VII
Stowell, Rev. Thomas Alfred, 1831–1916, vol. II
Stowell, Thomas Edmund Alexander, *died* 1970, vol. VI
Stowers, Arthur, 1897–1977, vol. VII
Strabolgi, 9th Baron, 1853–1934, vol. III
Strabolgi, 10th Baron, 1886–1953, vol. V
Stracey, Sir Edward Paulet, 7th Bt, 1871–1949, vol. IV
Stracey, Maj.-Gen. Henry, 1839–1930, vol. III
Stracey, Sir Michael George Motley, 8th Bt, 1911–1971, vol. VII
Stracey-Clitherow, Lt-Col John Bourchier, 1853–1931, vol. III
Strachan, Hon. Lord; James Frederick Strachan, 1894–1978, vol. VII
Strachan, Sir Andrew Henry, 1895–1976, vol. VII
Strachan, Douglas, 1875–1950, vol. IV
Strachan, Gilbert Innes, 1888–1963, vol. VI

Strachan, Lt-Col Harcus; *see* Strachan, Lt-Col Henry.
Strachan, Lt-Col Henry, 1884–1982, vol. VIII
Strachan, James, *died* 1917, vol. II
Strachan, James Frederick; *see* Strachan, Hon. Lord.
Strachan, John, 1838–1918, vol. II
Strachan, John, 1877–1934, vol. III
Strachan, Rev. Robert Harvey, 1873–1958, vol. V
Strachan, Robert Martin, 1913–1981, vol. VIII
Strachan, William Henry Williams, *died* 1921, vol. II
Strachan-Davidson, James Leigh, 1843–1916, vol. II
Strachey, Hon. Sir Arthur, 1858–1901, vol. I
Strachey, Sir Charles, 1862–1942, vol. IV
Strachey, Christopher, 1916–1975, vol. VII
Strachey, Sir Edward, 3rd Bt, 1812–1901, vol. I
Strachey, Rt Hon. (Evelyn) John (St Loe), 1901–1963, vol. VI
Strachey, (Giles) Lytton, 1880–1932, vol. III
Strachey, Jane Maria, (Lady Strachey), *died* 1928, vol. II
Strachey, Joan Pernel, 1876–1951, vol. V
Strachey, Sir John, 1823–1907, vol. I
Strachey, Rt Hon. John; *see* Strachey, Rt Hon. E. J. St L.
Strachey, John St Loe, 1860–1927, vol. II
Strachey, Lytton; *see* Strachey, G. L.
Strachey, Oliver, 1874–1960, vol. V
Strachey, Mrs Oliver; *see* Strachey, Ray.
Strachey, Philippa, 1872–1968, vol. VI
Strachey, Ray, 1887–1940, vol. III
Strachey, Lt-Gen. Sir Richard, 1817–1908, vol. I
Strachey, Col Richard John, 1861–1935, vol. III
Strachie, 1st Baron, 1858–1936, vol. III
Strachie, 2nd Baron, 1882–1973, vol. VII
Stradbroke, 3rd Earl of, 1862–1947, vol. IV
Stradbroke, 4th Earl of, 1903–1983, vol. VIII
Stradbroke, 5th Earl of, 1907–1983, vol. VIII
Stradling, Sir Reginald Edward, *died* 1952, vol. V
Strafford, 3rd Earl of, 1830–1898, vol. I
Strafford, 4th Earl of, 1831–1899, vol. I
Strafford, 5th Earl of, 1835–1918, vol. II
Strafford, 6th Earl of, 1862–1951, vol. V
Strafford, 7th Earl of, 1904–1984, vol. VIII
Strafford, Countess of; (Alice), 1830–1928, vol. II
Strafford, Air Marshal Stephen Charles, 1898–1966, vol. VI
Straghan, Col Abel, 1836–1914, vol. I
Strahan, Sir Aubrey, 1852–1928, vol. II
Strahan, Lt-Gen. Charles, 1843–1930, vol. III
Strahan, Frank, 1886–1976, vol. VII
Strahan, Lt-Col Geoffrey Carteret, 1886–1973, vol. VII
Strahan, Rev. James, 1863–1926, vol. II
Strahan, James Andrew, 1858–1930, vol. III
Straight, Sir Douglas, 1844–1914, vol. I
Straight, Major Douglas Marshall, 1869–1949, vol. IV
Straight, Whitney Willard, 1912–1979, vol. VII
Strain, Euphans H., *died* 1934, vol. III
Strain, Lt-Col Laurence Hugh, 1876–1952, vol. V
Straker, Herbert, 1856–1929, vol. III
Straker, John Coppin, 1847–1937, vol. III
Straker, William, 1855–1941, vol. IV

Straker-Smith, Sir Thomas Dalrymple, 1890–1970, vol. VI
Strakosch, Sir Henry, 1871–1943, vol. IV
Stralia, Elsa, *died* 1945, vol. IV
Stranders, Michael O'Connell, 1911–1973, vol. VII
Strang, 1st Baron, 1893–1978, vol. VII
Strang, Lady; (Barbara Mary Hope), 1925–1982, vol. VIII
Strang, Alexander Ronald, 1848–1926, vol. II
Strang, Barbara Mary Hope; *see* Strang, Lady.
Strang, Ian, 1886–1952, vol. V
Strang, John Martin, 1888–1970, vol. VI
Strang, William, 1859–1921, vol. II
Strang-Watkins, Watkin, 1869–1921, vol. II
Strange, 15th Baron, 1900–1982, vol. VIII
Strange of Knokin, Baroness; *see* St Davids, Viscountess.
Strange, Rev. Cresswell, 1842–1905, vol. I
Strange, Lt-Col Edward Fairbrother, 1862–1929, vol. III
Strange, Lt-Col Louis Arbon, 1891–1966, vol. VI
Strange, Brig.-Gen. Robert George, 1861–1949, vol. IV
Strange, Maj.-Gen. Thomas Bland, 1831–1925, vol. II
Stranger, Innes Harold, 1879–1936, vol. III
Stranger-Jones, Leonard Ivan, 1913–1983, vol. VIII
Strangman, James Gonville, 1902–1977, vol. VII
Strangman, Sir Thomas Joseph, 1873–1971, vol. VII
Strangways, Arthur Henry Fox, 1859–1948, vol. IV
Strangways, Mary, *died* 1945, vol. IV
Strangways, Maurice Walter F.; *see* Fox-Strangways.
Stranks, Ven. Charles James, 1901–1981, vol. VIII
Stranks, Donald Richard, 1929–1986, vol. VIII
Stransham, Sir Anthony Blaxland, 1805–1900, vol. I
Strasser, Sir Paul, *born* 1911, vol. VIII
Strategicus; *see* O'Neill, H. C.
Stratford, Brig.-Gen. Cecil Vernon W.; *see* Wingfield-Stratford.
Stratford, Esmé Cecil W.; *see* Wingfield-Stratford.
Stratford, Rt Hon. James, 1869–1952, vol. V
Strath, Sir William, 1906–1975, vol. VII
Strathalmond, 1st Baron, 1888–1970, vol. VI
Strathalmond, 2nd Baron, 1916–1976, vol. VII
Strathcarron, 1st Baron, 1880–1937, vol. III
Strathclyde, 1st Baron (*cr* 1914), 1853–1928, vol. II
Strathclyde, 1st Baron (*cr* 1955), 1891–1985, vol. VIII
Strathcona and Mount Royal, 1st Baron, 1820–1914, vol. I
Strathcona and Mount Royal, Baroness (2nd in line), 1854–1926, vol. II
Strathcona and Mount Royal, 3rd Baron, 1891–1959, vol. V
Strathearn, Sir John Calderwood, 1878–1950, vol. IV
Stratheden, 3rd Baron, **and Campbell,** 3rd Baron, 1829–1918, vol. II
Stratheden, 4th Baron, **and Campbell,** 4th Baron, 1899–1981, vol. VIII
Stratheden, 5th Baron, **and Campbell,** 5th Baron, 1901–1987, vol. VIII
Stratheden and Campbell, Lady; (Jean Helen), *died* 1956, vol. V
Strathie, Sir (David) Norman, 1886–1959, vol. V
Strathie, Sir Norman; *see* Strathie, Sir D. N.

Strathmore and Kinghorne, 13th Earl of, 1824–1904, vol. I
Strathmore and Kinghorne, 14th Earl of, 1855–1944, vol. IV
Strathmore and Kinghorne, 15th Earl of, 1884–1949, vol. IV
Strathmore and Kinghorne, 16th Earl of, 1918–1972, vol. VII
Strathmore and Kinghorne, 17th Earl of, 1928–1987, vol. VIII
Strathon, Eric Colwill, 1908–1988, vol. VIII
Strathspey, 4th Baron, 1879–1948, vol. IV
Straton, Rt Rev. Norman Dumenil John, 1840–1918, vol. II
Stratten, Thomas Price, 1904–1980, vol. VII
Strattmann, HSH Edmund B.; *see* Batthyany-Strattmann.
Stratton, Arthur, *died* 1955, vol. V
Stratton, Sir (Francis) John, 1906–1976, vol. VII
Stratton, Frederick John Marrian, 1881–1960, vol. V
Stratton, Hon. J. R., 1858–1916, vol. II
Stratton, Sir John; *see* Stratton, Sir F. J.
Stratton, Rev. Joseph, 1839–1917, vol. II
Stratton, Sir Richard James, 1924–1988, vol. VIII
Stratton, Lt-Col Wallace Christopher Ramsay, 1862–1942, vol. IV
Stratton, Lt-Gen. Sir William Henry, 1903–1989, vol. VIII
Stratton-Porter, Gene; *see* Porter.
Strauchon, John, 1848–1934, vol. III
Straus, Bertram Stuart, 1867–1933, vol. III
Straus, Nathan, 1848–1931, vol. III
Straus, Oscar, 1870–1954, vol. V
Straus, Oscar S., 1850–1926, vol. II
Straus, Ralph, 1882–1950, vol. IV
Strauss, Lady; Patricia Frances Strauss, 1909–1987, vol. VIII
Strauss, Arthur, 1847–1920, vol. II
Strauss, Edward Anthony, 1862–1939, vol. III
Strauss, Eric Benjamin, 1894–1961, vol. VI
Strauss, Franz Josef, 1915–1988, vol. VIII
Strauss, Adm. Joseph, 1861–1948, vol. IV
Strauss, Lewis L., 1896–1974, vol. VII
Strauss, Richard, 1864–1949, vol. IV
Stravinsky, Igor, 1882–1971, vol. VII
Streat, Sir (Edward) Raymond, 1897–1979, vol. VII
Streat, Sir Raymond; *see* Streat, Sir E. R.
Streatfeild, Frank Newton, 1843–1916, vol. II
Streatfeild, Sir Geoffrey Hugh Benbow, 1897–1979, vol. VII
Streatfeild, Mrs Granville, (Lucy Anne Evelyn Streatfeild), *died* 1950, vol. IV
Streatfeild, Col Sir Henry, 1857–1938, vol. III
Streatfeild, Rev. Henry Bertram, 1852–1922, vol. II
Streatfeild, Henry Cuthbert, 1866–1950, vol. IV
Streatfeild, Lucy Anne Evelyn; *see* Streatfeild, Mrs Granville.
Streatfeild, (Mary) Noel, 1895–1986, vol. VIII
Streatfeild, Noel; *see* Streatfeild, M. N.
Streatfeild, Richard Alexander, 1866–1919, vol. II
Streatfeild, Brig. Richard John, 1903–1952, vol. V
Streatfeild, Rt Rev. William Champion, 1865–1929, vol. III
Streatfield, Captain Eric, *died* 1902, vol. I

Street, Lt-Col Alfred William Frederick, 1852–1911, vol. I
Street, Arthur George, 1892–1966, vol. VI
Street, Sir Arthur William, 1892–1951, vol. V
Street, Lt-Col Ashton, 1864–1946, vol. IV
Street, Captain Edmund Rochfort, *died* 1916, vol. II
Street, Fanny, 1877–1962, vol. VI
Street, Brig. Hon. Geoffrey Austin, 1894–1940, vol. III
Street, George Slythe, 1867–1936, vol. III
Street, Col Harold Edward, *died* 1917, vol. II
Street, John Hugh, 1914–1977, vol. VII
Street, Harry, 1919–1984, vol. VIII
Street, Hon. Sir Kenneth Whistler, 1890–1972, vol. VII
Street, Hon. Sir Philip Whistler, 1863–1938, vol. III
Street, Reginald Owen, 1890–1967, vol. VI
Street, Robert William, 1860–1954, vol. V
Street, Maj.-Gen. Vivian Wakefield, 1912–1970, vol. VI
Street, William P. R., 1841–1906, vol. I
Streeter, Rev. Burnett Hillman, 1874–1937, vol. III
Streeter, Wilfrid A., 1877–1962, vol. VI
Streeton, Sir Arthur, 1867–1943, vol. IV
Streicher, Most Rev. Henry, 1863–1944, vol. IV
Streit, Clarence Kirshman, 1896–1986, vol. VIII
Strelcyn, Stefan, 1918–1981, vol. VIII
Stresemann, Gustav, 1878–1929, vol. III
Stretch, Rt Rev. John Francis, 1885–1919, vol. II
Strettell, Maj.-Gen. Sir C. B. Dashwood, 1881–1958, vol. V
Stretten, Charles James Derrickson, 1830–1919, vol. II
Stretton, Lt-Col Arthur John, 1863–1947, vol. IV
Stretton, Hesba, 1832–1911, vol. I
Stretton, Leonard Edward Bishop, 1893–1967, vol. VI
Strevens, Peter Derek, 1922–1989, vol. VIII
Stribling, Thomas Sigismund, 1881–1965, vol. VI
Strick, Col John, 1838–1903, vol. I
Strick, Maj.-Gen. John Arkwright, 1870–1934, vol. III
Strickland, 1st Baron, 1861–1940, vol. III
Strickland, Algernon Henry Peter, 1863–1928, vol. II
Strickland, Algernon Walter, 1891–1938, vol. III
Strickland, Rear-Adm. Sir Arthur Foster, 1882–1955, vol. V
Strickland, Barbara, (Lady Strickland), 1884–1977, vol. VII
Strickland, Sir Charles William, 8th Bt, 1819–1909, vol. I
Strickland, Claude Francis, 1881–1962, vol. VI
Strickland, Gen. Sir (Edward) Peter, 1869–1951, vol. V
Strickland, Maj.-Gen. Eugene Vincent Michael, 1913–1982, vol. VIII
Strickland, Frederic, 1867–1934, vol. III
Strickland, Henry H.; *see* Hornyold-Strickland.
Strickland, Hon. Mabel Edeline, 1899–1988, vol. VIII
Strickland, Hon. Mary Constance Elizabeth Christina H.; *see* Hornyold-Strickland.
Strickland, Captain Paul Sebring, 1885–1964, vol. VI

Strickland, Gen. Sir Peter; *see* Strickland, Gen. Sir E. P.
Strickland, Walter G., 1850–1928, vol. II
Strickland, Sir Walter William, 9th Bt, 1851–1938, vol. III
Strickland, Captain William Frederick, 1880–1954, vol. V
Strickland-Constable, Sir Henry Marmaduke, 10th Bt, 1900–1975, vol. VII
Striedinger, Col Oscar, 1875–1938, vol. III
Strijdom, Hon. Johannes Gerhardus, 1893–1958, vol. V
Strindberg, Auguste, 1849–1912, vol. I
Stringer, Most Rev. Isaac O., 1866–1934, vol. III
Stringer, John Daniel, 1914–1971, vol. VII
Stringer, Sir (Thomas) Walter, 1855–1944, vol. IV
Stringer, Sir Walter; *see* Stringer, Sir T. W.
Stritch, His Eminence Cardinal Samuel Alphonsus, 1887–1958, vol. V
Strobl, Kisfalud Sigismund de, 1884–1975, vol. VII
Strode, Edward David C.; *see* Chetham-Strode.
Strode, Warren C.; *see* Chetham-Strode.
Strode-Jackson, Col Arnold Nugent Strode, 1891–1972, vol. VII
Strohmenger, Sir Ernest John, 1873–1967, vol. VI
Stromeyer, Charles E., 1856–1935, vol. III
Stronach, Ancell, 1901–1981, vol. VIII
Stronach, Catherine Geddes, *died* 1962, vol. VI
Stronach, John Clark, 1887–1967, vol. VI
Strong, Lt-Col Addington Dawsonne, 1875–1930, vol. III
Strong, Sir Archibald Thomas, 1876–1930, vol. III
Strong, Austin, 1881–1952, vol. V
Strong, Rev. Charles, 1844–1942, vol. IV
Strong, Sir Charles Love, 1908–1988, vol. VIII
Strong, Maj.-Gen. Dawsonne Melancthon, 1841–1903, vol. I
Strong, Rev. Canon Edward Herbert, *died* 1960, vol. V (A), vol. VI (AI)
Strong, Emilia Francis; *see* Dilke, E. F.
Strong, Eugénie, 1860–1943, vol. IV
Strong, Lt-Col Henry Stuart, 1873–1949, vol. IV
Strong, Herbert A., *died* 1918, vol. II
Strong, Hugh W., 1861–1920, vol. II
Strong, John, 1868–1945, vol. IV
Strong, John Alexander, 1844–1917, vol. II
Strong, Maj.-Gen. Sir Kenneth William Dobson, 1900–1982, vol. VIII
Strong, Leonard Alfred George, 1896–1958, vol. V
Strong, Most Rev. Philip Nigel Warrington, 1899–1983, vol. VIII
Strong, Richard Pearson, 1872–1948, vol. IV
Strong, Rt Hon. Sir Samuel Henry, 1825–1909, vol. I
Strong, Sandford Arthur, 1863–1904, vol. I
Strong, Rt Rev. Thomas Banks, 1861–1944, vol. IV
Strong, Rt Hon. Sir (Thomas) Vezey, *died* 1920, vol. II
Strong, Rt Hon. Sir Vezey; *see* Strong, Rt Hon. Sir T. V.
Strong, Brig.-Gen. William, 1870–1956, vol. V
Stronge, Sir Charles Edmond Sinclair, 7th Bt, 1862–1939, vol. III
Stronge, Captain Rt Hon. Sir (Charles) Norman (Lockhart), 8th Bt, 1894–1981, vol. VIII

Stronge, Sir Francis William, 1856–1924, vol. II

Stronge, Sir Herbert Cecil, 1875–1963, vol. VI

Stronge, Brig. Humphrey Cecil Travell, 1891–1977, vol. VII

Stronge, Rt Hon. Sir James Henry, 5th Bt, 1849–1928, vol. II

Stronge, Sir John Calvert, 4th Bt, 1813–1899, vol. I

Stronge, Captain Rt Hon. Sir Norman; see Stronge, Captain Rt Hon. Sir C. N. L.

Stronge, Sir Walter Lockhart, 6th Bt, 1860–1933, vol. III

Stross, Sir Barnett, 1899–1967, vol. VI

Strother-Stewart, Robert; see Stewart.

Stroud, Lt-Gen. Edward James, 1867–1935, vol. III

Stroud, Frederick, 1835–1912, vol. I

Stroud, Henry, 1861–1940, vol. III

Stroud, William, 1860–1938, vol. III

Stroyan, John, 1856–1941, vol. IV

Struben, William Charles Marinus, 1856–1928, vol. II, vol. III

Strudwick, Ethel, 1880–1954, vol. V

Strudwick, J. M., 1849–1937, vol. III

Strugnell, Surg. Rear-Adm. Lionel Frederick, 1892–1962, vol. VI

Struther, Jan, (Mrs A. K. Placzek), 1901–1953, vol. V

Struthers, Sir John, 1823–1899, vol. I

Struthers, Sir John, 1857–1925, vol. II

Strutt, Alfred William, died 1924, vol. II

Strutt, Vice-Adm. Hon. Arthur Charles, 1878–1973, vol. VII

Strutt, Sir Austin; see Strutt, Sir H. A.

Strutt, Hon. Charles Hedley, 1849–1926, vol. II

Strutt, Hon. Charles Richard, 1910–1981, vol. VIII

Strutt, Hon. Edward Gerald, 1854–1930, vol. III

Strutt, Lt-Col Edward Lisle, 1874–1948, vol. IV

Strutt, Geoffrey St John, 1888–1971, vol. VII

Strutt, George Herbert, 1854–1928, vol. II

Strutt, Sir (Henry) Austin, 1903–1979, vol. VII

Strutt, Maj.-Gen. John Rootsey, 1831–1909, vol. I

Strutt, Hon. Richard, 1848–1927, vol. II

Strutt, Rt Rev. Rupert Gordon, 1912–1985, vol. VIII

Strutt, William, died 1915, vol. I

Struve, Otto, 1897–1963, vol. VI

Stryker, M. Woolsey, 1851–1929, vol. III

Strzygowski, Josef, 1862–1941, vol. IV

Stuart, Viscount; David Andrew Noel Stuart, 1921–1942, vol. IV

Stuart, Viscount; Robert John Ochiltree Stuart, 1923–1944, vol. IV

Stuart of Findhorn, 1st Viscount, 1897–1971, vol. VII

Stuart of Wortley, 1st Baron, 1851–1926, vol. II

Stuart, Alan, 1894–1983, vol. VIII

Stuart, Sir Alexander M.; see Moody-Stuart.

Stuart, Alexander Mackenzie, 1877–1935, vol. III

Stuart, Alexander Moody, died 1915, vol. I

Stuart, Andrew Edmund Castlestuart, died 1936, vol. III

Stuart, Maj.-Gen. Sir Andrew Mitchell, 1861–1936, vol. III

Stuart, Arthur Constable M.; see Maxwell Stuart.

Stuart, Col Burleigh Francis Brownlow, 1868–1952, vol. V

Stuart, Sir Campbell, 1885–1972, vol. VII

Stuart, Charles Allan, 1864–1926, vol. II

Stuart, Rear-Adm. Charles Gage, 1887–1970, vol. VI

Stuart, Sir Charles James, 2nd Bt (cr 1840), 1824–1901, vol. I

Stuart, Lt-Col Charles Kennedy-Craufurd-, died 1942, vol. IV

Stuart, Charles Maddock, 1857–1932, vol. III

Stuart, Charles Russell, 1895–1975, vol. VII

Stuart, Lord Colum Edmund C.; see Crichton-Stuart.

Stuart, Rt Rev. Cyril Edgar, 1892–1982, vol. VIII

Stuart, Brig.-Gen. Donald MacKenzie, 1864–1946, vol. IV

Stuart, Dorothy Margaret, died 1963, vol. VI

Stuart, Maj.-Gen. Douglas, 1894–1955, vol. V

Stuart, Dudley, 1861–1939, vol. III

Stuart, Rev. Edward Alexander, 1853–1917, vol. II

Stuart, Sir Edward Andrew, 3rd Bt (cr 1840), 1832–1903, vol. I

Stuart, Rt Rev. Edward Craig, 1827–1911, vol. I

Stuart, George Eustace B.; see Burnett-Stuart.

Stuart, George Moody, 1851–1940, vol. III

Stuart, Gerald Fitzgerald, 1897–1938, vol. III

Stuart, Major Godfrey Richard Conyngham, 1866–1955, vol. V

Stuart, Sir Harold Arthur, 1860–1923, vol. II

Stuart, Very Rev. Henry Venn, 1864–1933, vol. III

Stuart, Herbert Constable M.; see Maxwell-Stuart.

Stuart, Hilda Violet, died 1975, vol. VII

Stuart, Sir Houlton John, 8th Bt (cr 1660), 1863–1959, vol. V

Stuart, Ian Malcolm Bowen, 1902–1969, vol. VI

Stuart, Rev. James, 1841–1911, vol. I

Stuart, Rt Hon. James, 1843–1913, vol. I

Stuart, Rev. Sir James, 4th Bt (cr 1840), 1837–1915, vol. I

Stuart, John, 1836–1926, vol. II

Stuart, John, 1847–1931, vol. III

Stuart, Col John Alexander Man, 1841–1908, vol. I

Stuart, John Matthew Blackwood, 1882–1942, vol. IV

Stuart, Col John Patrick V.; see Villiers-Stuart.

Stuart, Gen. Sir John Theodosius B.; see Burnett-Stuart.

Stuart, John Windsor, 1846–1905, vol. I

Stuart, Lt-Gen. Kenneth, 1891–1945, vol. IV

Stuart, Leslie, 1866–1928, vol. II

Stuart, Rear-Adm. Leslie Creery, 1851–1908, vol. I

Stuart, Brig. Lionel Arthur, 1892–1959, vol. V

Stuart, Sir Louis, 1870–1949, vol. IV

Stuart, Captain Murray, 1882–1967, vol. VI

Stuart, Lord Ninian Edward C.; see Crichton-Stuart.

Stuart, Norman; see Teeling, Mrs Bartle.

Stuart, Maj.-Gen. Sir Robert Charles Ochiltree, 1861–1948, vol. IV

Stuart, Captain Hon. Robert Sheffield, 1886–1914, vol. I

Stuart, Captain Ronald Niel, 1886–1954, vol. V

Stuart, Ruth M'Enery, died 1917, vol. II

Stuart, Sir Simeon Henry Lechmere, 7th Bt (cr 1660), 1864–1939, vol. III

Stuart, Rt Rev. Simon; see Stuart, Rt Rev. C. E.

Stuart, Sir Thomas Anderson, 1856–1920, vol. II

Stuart, William C. S.; see Crawfurd-Stirling-Stuart.

Stuart, Maj.-Gen. William James, 1831–1914, vol. I

Stuart, Brig.-Gen. William V.; *see* Villiers-Stuart.

Stuart Black, (Ian) Hervey; *see* Black.

Stuart-Clark, Arthur Campbell, 1906–1973, vol. VII

Stuart-Forbes of Pitsligo, Sir Hugh; *see* Forbes of Pitsligo.

Stuart-Forbes-Trefusis, Hon. Henry Walter H.; *see* Trefusis.

Stuart-Forbes-Trefusis, Major Hon. John Frederick Hepburn; *see* Trefusis.

Stuart-Jones, Sir Henry, 1867–1939, vol. III

Stuart-Knill, Sir Ian, 3rd Bt, 1886–1973, vol. VII

Stuart-Low, William, 1857–1935, vol. III

Stuart-Menteth, Sir James; *see* Menteth.

Stuart-Menteth, Lt-Col Sir James Frederick; *see* Menteth.

Stuart-Menteth, Sir William Frederick; *see* Menteth.

Stuart Smith, Rt Rev. Thomas Geoffrey; *see* Smith.

Stuart Taylor, Sir Richard Laurence, 3rd Bt, 1925–1978, vol. VII

Stuart-Williams, Sir Charles; *see* Stuart-Williams, Sir S. C.

Stuart-Williams, Sir (Sydney) Charles, 1876–1960, vol. V

Stuart-Wortley, Lt-Gen. Hon. Sir (Alan) Richard Montagu-, 1868–1949, vol. IV

Stuart-Wortley, Hon. Clare Euphemia, 1889–1945, vol. IV

Stuart-Wortley, Maj.-Gen. Hon. Edward James Montagu-, 1857–1934, vol. III

Stuart-Wortley, Lt-Gen. Hon. Sir Richard; *see* Stuart-Wortley, Lt-Gen. Hon. Sir A. R. M.

Stuart-Wortley, Violet, (Hon. Mrs Edward Stuart Wortley), *died* 1953, vol. V

Stubber, Lt-Col John Henry H.; *see* Hamilton Stubber.

Stubbs, Albert Ernest, 1877–1962, vol. VI

Stubbs, Rev. Arthur James, 1861–1945, vol. IV

Stubbs, Rt Rev. Charles William, 1845–1912, vol. I

Stubbs, Sir Edward; *see* Stubbs, Sir R. E.

Stubbs, George, 1864–1940, vol. III

Stubbs, Brig.-Gen. Guy Clifford, 1883–1939, vol. III

Stubbs, Lawrence Morley, 1874–1958, vol. V

Stubbs, Sir (Reginald) Edward, 1876–1947, vol. IV

Stubbs, Roy, 1897–1951, vol. V

Stubbs, Stanley, 1906–1976, vol. VII

Stubbs, Sydney, 1861–1953, vol. V

Stubbs, Rt Rev. William, 1825–1901, vol. I

Stubbs, William, 1911–1967, vol. VI

Stubbs, William Frederick, 1902–1987, vol. VIII

Stuchbery, Arthur Leslie, 1903–1986, vol. VIII

Stuck, Ven. Hudson, 1863–1920, vol. II

Stuckey, Reginald Robert, 1881–1948, vol. IV

Stucley, Maj. Sir Dennis Frederic Bankes, 5th Bt, 1907–1983, vol. VIII

Stucley, Sir Edward Arthur George, 3rd Bt, 1852–1927, vol. II

Stucley, Sir George Stucley, 1st Bt, 1812–1900, vol. I

Stucley, Sir Hugh Nicholas Granville, 4th Bt, 1873–1956, vol. II

Stucley, John Humphrey Albert, 1916–1988, vol. VIII

Stucley, Sir Lewis; *see* Stucley, Sir W. L.

Stucley, Sir (William) Lewis, 2nd Bt, 1836–1911, vol. I

Studd, C. T., *died* 1931, vol. III

Studd, Sir Eric, 2nd Bt, 1887–1975, vol. VII

Studd, Brig.-Gen. Herbert William, 1870–1947, vol. IV

Studd, Sir (John Edward) Kynaston, 1st Bt, 1858–1944, vol. IV

Studd, Sir Kynaston; *see* Studd, Sir J. E. K.

Studd, Sir Kynaston; *see* Studd, Sir R. K.

Studd, Brig. Malden Augustus, 1887–1973, vol. VII

Studd, Sir (Robert) Kynaston, 3rd Bt, 1926–1977, vol. VII

Studdert, Ven. Augustine John de Clare, 1901–1972, vol. VII

Studdert, Maj.-Gen. Robert Hallam, 1890–1968, vol. VI

Studdy, Sir Henry, 1894–1975, vol. VII

Studer, Paul, 1879–1927, vol. II

Studholme, Sir Henry Gray, 1899–1987, vol. VIII

Studholme, Lt-Col John, 1863–1934, vol. III

Studholme, Sir Paul Henry William, 2nd Bt, 1930–1990, vol. VIII

Studholme, Sir Richard Home, 1901–1963, vol. VI

Stupart, Sir Frederic; *see* Stupart, Sir R. F.

Stupart, Sir (Robert) Frederic, 1857–1940, vol. III

Sturdee, Col Alfred Hobart, 1863–1939, vol. III

Sturdee, Admiral of the Fleet Sir Doveton; *see* Sturdee, Admiral of the Fleet Sir F. C. D.

Sturdee, Admiral of the Fleet Sir (Frederick Charles) Doveton, 1st Bt, 1859–1925, vol. II

Sturdee, Rear-Adm. Sir Lionel Arthur Doveton, 2nd Bt, 1884–1970, vol. VI

Sturdee, Rev. Robert James, 1879–1932, vol. III

Sturdee, Lt-Gen. Sir Vernon Ashton Hobart, 1890–1966, vol. VI

Sturdy, William Arthur, 1877–1958, vol. V

Sturge, Arthur Colwyn, 1912–1986, vol. VIII

Sturge, Arthur Lloyd, 1868–1942, vol. IV

Sturge, Raymond Wilson, 1904–1984, vol. VIII

Sturge, William Allen, 1850–1919, vol. II

Sturges, Hugh Murray, 1863–1952, vol. V

Sturges, Lt-Gen. Sir Robert Grice, 1891–1970, vol. VI

Sturgess, Paymaster Rear-Adm. Richard Ernest Stanley, *died* 1933, vol. III

Sturgis, Julian Russell, 1848–1904, vol. I

Sturgis, Sir Mark Beresford Russell G.; *see* Grant-Sturgis.

Sturley, Major Albert Avern, 1887–1922, vol. II

Sturrock, Alick Riddell, 1885–1953, vol. V

Sturrock, Hon. Claud; *see* Sturrock, Hon. F. C.

Sturrock, Hon. (Frederick) Claud, 1882–1958, vol. V

Sturrock, Brig. George Colleymore, *died* 1935, vol. III

Sturrock, John, 1845–1926, vol. II

Sturrock, Sir John Christian Ramsay, 1875–1937, vol. III

Sturrock, John Leng, 1878–1943, vol. IV

Sturrock, William Duncan, 1880–1942, vol. IV

Sturt, Maj.-Gen. Charles Sheppey, 1838–1910, vol. I

Sturt, George, 1863–1927, vol. II

Sturt, Hon. Gerard Philip Montagu Napier, 1893–1918, vol. II

Sturt, Lt-Col Robert Ramsay Napier, 1852–1907, vol. I

Stutchbury, George Frederick, 1844–1934, vol. III
Stutfield, Hugh E. M., 1858–1929, vol. III
Stuttaford, Hon. Richard, 1870–1945, vol. IV
Style, Sir Frederick Montague, 10th Bt, 1857–1930, vol. III
Style, Rev. George, died 1922, vol. II
Style, Sir William Frederick, 11th Bt, 1887–1943, vol. IV
Style, Sir William Henry Marsham, 9th Bt, 1826–1904, vol. I
Style, Sir William Montague, 12th Bt, 1916–1981, vol. VIII
Styles, (Herbert) Walter, 1889–1965, vol. VI
Styles, Walter; see Styles, H. W.
Suárez, Eduardo, 1895–1976, vol. VII
Suart, Evelyn, (Lady Harcourt), died 1950, vol. IV
Suart, Brig.-Gen. William Hodgson, 1850–1923, vol. II
Suckling, Rev. Charles William B.; see Baron-Suckling.
Suckling, Rev. Robert Alfred J., died 1917, vol. II
Sucksmith, Willie, 1896–1981, vol. VIII
Sucre-Trias, Juan Manuel, 1940–1983, vol. VIII
Sudborough, John Joseph, 1869–1963, vol. VI
Sudbury, Col Frederick Arthur, 1904–1983, vol. VIII
Sudeley, 4th Baron, 1840–1922, vol. II
Sudeley, 5th Baron, 1870–1932, vol. III
Sudeley, 6th Baron, 1911–1941, vol. IV
Sudermann, Hermann, 1857–1928, vol. II
Sudmerson, Frederick William, died 1953, vol. V
Sueter, Rear-Adm. Sir Murray Fraser, 1872–1960, vol. V
Suffield, 5th Baron, 1830–1914, vol. I
Suffield, 6th Baron, 1855–1924, vol. II
Suffield, 7th Baron, 1897–1943, vol. IV
Suffield, 8th Baron, 1907–1945, vol. IV
Suffield, 9th Baron, 1861–1946, vol. IV
Suffield, 10th Baron, 1865–1951, vol. V
Suffolk, 18th Earl of, and Berkshire, 11th Earl of, 1833–1898, vol. I
Suffolk, 19th Earl of, and Berkshire, 12th Earl of, 1877–1917, vol. II
Suffolk, 20th Earl of, and Berkshire, 13th Earl of, 1906–1941, vol. IV
Sugden, Alan Victor, 1877–1956, vol. V
Sugden, Sir Bernard, 1877–1954, vol. V
Sugden, General Sir Cecil Stanway, 1903–1963, vol. VI
Sugden, Charles, 1850–1921, vol. II
Sugden, Frank, 1852–1927, vol. II
Sugden, Maj.-Gen. Sir Henry Haskins Clapham, 1904–1977, vol. VII
Sugden, Kaye Aspinall Ramsden, 1880–1966, vol. VI
Sugden, Sir Morris; see Sugden, Sir T. M.
Sugden, Brig.-Gen. Richard Edgar, 1871–1951, vol. V
Sugden, Gp Captain Ronald Scott, 1896–1971, vol. VII
Sugden, Samuel, 1892–1950, vol. IV
Sugden, Sir (Theodore) Morris, 1919–1984, vol. VIII
Sugden, Sir Wilfrid Hart, died 1960, vol. V
Sugerman, Sir Bernard, 1904–1976, vol. VII
Suggia, Guilhermina, 1888–1950, vol. IV
Suhrawardy, Sir Abdulla Al-Mamun, died 1935, vol. III

Suhrawardy, Lt-Col Sir Hassan, 1884–1946, vol. IV
Suhrawardy, Huseyn Shaheed, 1893–1963, vol. VI
Suhrawardy, Sir Zahhadur Rahim Zahid, 1870–1949, vol. IV
Sukhdeo Prasad Kak, Rao Bahadur Pandit Sir, 1862–1935, vol. III
Sukuna, Sir Joseva Lalabalavu Vanaaliali, died 1958, vol. V
Sulaiman, Sir Shah Muhammad, 1886–1941, vol. IV
Sulivan, Col Ernest Frederic, 1860–1928, vol. II
Sulivan, Vice-Adm. Norton Allen, 1879–1964, vol. VI
Sullivan, Albert Patrick Loisol, 1898–1981, vol. VIII
Sullivan, Alexander Martin, 1871–1959, vol. V
Sullivan, Rev. Arnold Moon, 1878–1943, vol. IV
Sullivan, Sir Arthur Seymour, 1842–1900, vol. I
Sullivan, Basil Martin, 1882–1946, vol. IV
Sullivan, Bernard Ponsonby, 1891–1958, vol. V
Sullivan, Hon. Daniel Giles, 1882–1947, vol. IV
Sullivan, Donal, 1838–1907, vol. I
Sullivan, Edmund J., 1869–1933, vol. III
Sullivan, Rt Rev. Edward, died 1899, vol. I
Sullivan, Sir Edward, 2nd Bt (cr 1881), 1852–1928, vol. II
Sullivan, Brig.-Gen. Edward Langford, 1865–1949, vol. IV
Sullivan, Sir Edward Robert, 5th Bt (cr 1804), 1826–1899, vol. I
Sullivan, Francis Loftus, 1903–1956, vol. V
Sullivan, Sir Francis William, 6th Bt (cr 1804), 1834–1906, vol. I
Sullivan, Rev. Sir Frederick, 7th Bt (cr 1804), 1865–1954, vol. V
Sullivan, Henry Edward, 1830–1905, vol. I
Sullivan, James Frank, died 1936, vol. III
Sullivan, John William Navin, 1886–1937, vol. III
Sullivan, Joseph, 1866–1935, vol. III
Sullivan, Very Rev. Martin Gloster, 1910–1980, vol. VII
Sullivan, Sir Richard Benjamin Magniac, 8th Bt (cr 1804), 1906–1977, vol. VII
Sullivan, Timothy, 1874–1949, vol. IV
Sullivan, Timothy Daniel, 1827–1914, vol. I
Sullivan, Sir Wilfred; see Sullivan, Hon. Sir William W.
Sullivan, Sir William, 3rd Bt (cr 1881), 1860–1937, vol. III
Sullivan, Sir William, 1891–1967, vol. VI
Sullivan, William Charles, died 1926, vol. II
Sullivan, Sir William John, 1895–1971, vol. VII
Sullivan, Sir (William) Wilfred, 1843–1923, vol. II
Sully, James, 1842–1923, vol. II
Sully, Air Vice-Marshal John Alfred, 1892–1968, vol. VI (AII)
Sulman, Sir John, 1849–1934, vol. III
Sulte, Benjamin, 1841–1923, vol. II
Sulzbach, Herbert, 1894–1985, vol. VIII
Sulzberger, Arthur Hays, 1891–1968, vol. VI
Sulzberger, Mayer, 1843–1923, vol. II
Sumichrast, Frederick C. de, 1845–1933, vol. III
Summerbell, Thomas, 1861–1910, vol. I
Summerford, Engr Rear-Adm. Horace George, 1872–1963, vol. VI
Summerhayes, Sir Christopher Henry, 1896–1988, vol. VIII

Summerhayes, Lt-Col John Orlando, 1869–1942, vol. IV

Summerhays, Reginald Sherriff, 1881–1976, vol. VII

Summers, Rev. Alphonsus Joseph-Mary Augustus Montague, 1880–1948, vol. IV

Summers, Sir Geoffrey, 1st Bt, 1891–1972, vol. VII

Summers, Bt-Lt-Col Sir Gerald Henry, 1885–1925, vol. II

Summers, Sir (Gerard) Spencer, 1902–1976, vol. VII

Summers, James Woolley, 1849–1913, vol. I

Summers, Captain Joseph J., *died* 1954, vol. V

Summers, Sir Richard Felix, 1902–1977, vol. VII

Summers, Sir Spencer; *see* Summers, Sir G. S.

Summers, Thomas, *died* 1944, vol. IV

Summers, Walter Coventry, 1869–1937, vol. III

Summersby, Charles Harold, 1882–1961, vol. VI

Summerscale, Sir John Percival, 1901–1980, vol. VII

Summerskill, Baroness (Life Peer); Edith Summerskill, 1901–1980, vol. VII

Summerson, Thomas Hawksley, 1903–1986, vol. VIII

Summerville, Sir Alan; *see* Summerville, Sir W. A. T.

Summerville, Sir (William) Alan (Thompson), 1904–1980, vol. VII

Sumner, 1st Viscount, 1859–1934, vol. III

Sumner, Benedict Humphrey, 1893–1951, vol. V

Sumner, Captain Berkeley H.; *see* Holme-Sumner.

Sumner, Donald; *see* Sumner, W. D. M.

Sumner, Rt Rev. George Henry, 1824–1909, vol. I

Sumner, James Batcheller, 1887–1955, vol. V

Sumner, Sir John, 1856–1934, vol. III

Sumner, John Richard Hugh, 1886–1971, vol. VII

Sumner, (William) Donald (Massey), 1913–1990, vol. VIII

Sundar Singh Majithia, Sirdar Sir, 1872–1941, vol. IV

Sundarlal, Hon. Pandit, 1857–1918, vol. II

Sunday, Rev. William Ashley, 1863–1935, vol. III

Sunderland, Earl of; John David Ivor Spencer-Churchill, 1952–1955, vol. V

Sunderland, (George Frederick) Irvon, 1905–1984, vol. VIII

Sunderland, Irvon; *see* Sunderland, G. F. I.

Sunderland, J. E., 1885–1956, vol. V

Sunderland, Col Marsden Samuel James, 1841–1929, vol. III

Sunderland, Septimus Philip, *died* 1950, vol. IV

Sunley, Bernard, 1910–1964, vol. VI

Sunlight, Joseph, 1889–1978, vol. VII

Supervia, Conchita, 1899–1936, vol. III

Supomo, Raden, 1903–1958, vol. V

Supple, Col James Francis, 1843–1922, vol. II

Surfaceman; *see* Anderson, Alexander.

Surplice, Reginald Alwyn, 1906–1977, vol. VII

Surridge, Brewster Joseph, 1894–1982, vol. VIII

Surridge, Sir (Ernest) Rex (Edward), 1899–1990, vol. VIII

Surridge, Sir Rex; *see* Surridge, Sir E. R. E.

Surtees, Col Charles Freville, 1823–1906, vol. I

Surtees, Brig.-Gen. Sir Conyers, 1858–1933, vol. III

Surtees, Maj.-Gen. George, 1895–1976, vol. VII

Surtees, Major (Henry) Siward (Balliol), 1873–1955, vol. V

Surtees, Major Siward; *see* Surtees, Major H. S. B.

Surtees, Rt Rev. William F., 1871–1956, vol. V

Surveyer, Hon. Edouard-Fabre, 1875–1957, vol. V

Susman, Maurice Philip, 1898–1988, vol. VIII

Susskind, (Jan) Walter, 1913–1980, vol. VII

Susskind, Walter; *see* Susskind, J. W.

Sutch, Ven. Ronald Huntley, 1890–1975, vol. VII

Sutcliffe, Frank Edmund, 1918–1983, vol. VIII

Sutcliffe, Halliwell, 1870–1932, vol. III

Sutcliffe, Sir Harold, 1897–1958, vol. V

Sutcliffe, Joseph Richard, 1897–1985, vol. VIII

Sutcliffe, Bt Col Richard Douglas, *died* 1941, vol. IV

Sutcliffe, Tom, 1865–1931, vol. III

Sutcliffe, Air Cdre Walter Philip, 1910–1990, vol. VIII

Sutcliffe, Very Rev. William Ormond, 1856–1944, vol. IV

Suter, George Edward, 1869–1939, vol. III

Suter, Captain Roy Neville, 1884–1958, vol. V

Suther, Gen. Cuthbert Collingwood, 1839–1927, vol. II

Suther, Brig. Percival, 1873–1945, vol. IV

Sutherland, 4th Duke of, 1851–1913, vol. I

Sutherland, 5th Duke of, 1888–1963, vol. VI

Sutherland, Duchess of; (Millicent Fanny), 1867–1955, vol. V

Sutherland, Alexander Malcolm G.; *see* Græme-Sutherland.

Sutherland, Algernon Robert, 1854–1933, vol. III

Sutherland, Angus, 1848–1922, vol. II

Sutherland, Sir Arthur Munro, 1st Bt, 1867–1953, vol. V

Sutherland, Sir (Benjamin) Ivan, 2nd Bt, 1901–1980, vol. VII

Sutherland, (Carol) Humphrey (Vivian), 1908–1986, vol. VIII

Sutherland, Charles Leslie, 1839–1911, vol. I

Sutherland, D. M., *died* 1951, vol. V

Sutherland, David M., 1883–1973, vol. VII

Sutherland, Lt-Col David Waters, 1871–1939, vol. III

Sutherland, Lt-Col Hon. Donald Matheson, 1879–1949, vol. IV

Sutherland, Earl Wilbur, Jr, 1915–1974, vol. VII

Sutherland, Edward Davenport, 1853–1923, vol. II

Sutherland, Sir (Frederick) Neil, 1900–1986, vol. VIII

Sutherland, George Alexander, *died* 1939, vol. III

Sutherland, George Arthur, 1891–1970, vol. VI

Sutherland, Sir George Henry, 1866–1937, vol. III

Sutherland, Sir Gordon Brims Black McIvor, 1907–1980, vol. VII

Sutherland, Graham Vivian, 1903–1980, vol. VII

Sutherland, Halliday Gibson, 1882–1960, vol. V

Sutherland, Lt-Col Henry Homes, 1871–1940, vol. III

Sutherland, Humphrey; *see* Sutherland, C. H. V.

Sutherland, Sir Iain Johnstone Macbeth, 1925–1986, vol. VIII

Sutherland, Sir Ivan; *see* Sutherland, Sir B. I.

Sutherland, Hon. James, 1849–1905, vol. I

Sutherland, Joan, *died* 1947, vol. IV

Sutherland, Sir John Donald, 1865–1952, vol. V

Sutherland, John Ebenezer, *died* 1918, vol. II

Sutherland, Lewis Robertson, 1863–1933, vol. III

Sutherland, Dame Lucy Stuart, 1903–1980, vol. VII

Sutherland, Mary Elizabeth, *died* 1972, vol. VII

Sutherland, Monica La Fontaine, 1897–1982, vol. VIII

Sutherland, Sir Neil; *see* Sutherland, Sir F. N.

Sutherland, Rt Hon. Robert Franklin, 1859–1922, vol. II

Sutherland, Scott, 1910–1984, vol. VIII

Sutherland, Sir Thomas, 1834–1922, vol. II

Sutherland, Hon. William, 1857–1935, vol. III

Sutherland, William, *died* 1945, vol. IV

Sutherland, Rt Hon. Sir William, 1880–1949, vol. IV

Sutherland, Hon. William Charles, 1865–1940, vol. III

Sutherland-Dunbar, Sir George Cospatrick D.; *see* Duff-Sutherland-Dunbar.

Sutherland-Dunbar, Sir George D.; *see* Duff-Sutherland-Dunbar.

Sutherland-Gower, Rt Hon. Lord Ronald; *see* Gower.

Sutherland-Harris, Lt-Col Alexander Sutherland, 1865–1934, vol. III

Sutherland-Harris, Sir Jack Alexander, 1908–1986, vol. VIII

Sutherland-Leveson Gower, Major Lord Alastair St Clair; *see* Leveson Gower.

Suthers, Rev. Canon George, 1908–1965, vol. VI

Sutro, Alfred, 1863–1933, vol. III

Suttie, Sir George Grant-, 7th Bt, 1870–1947, vol. IV

Suttie, Col Hubert Francis Grant-, 1884–1973, vol. VII

Suttner, Baroness Bertha Felicie Sophie von, 1843–1914, vol. I

Sutton, Sir Abraham, 1849–1921, vol. II

Sutton, Maj.-Gen. Alexander Arthur, 1861–1941, vol. IV

Sutton, Col Alfred, *died* 1922, vol. II

Sutton, Rev. Alfred, 1851–1938, vol. III

Sutton, Sir Arthur, 7th Bt (*cr* 1772), 1857–1948, vol. IV

Sutton, Rev. Arthur Frederick, *died* 1925, vol. II

Sutton, Arthur Warwick, 1854–1925, vol. II

Sutton, Air Marshal Sir Bertine Entwisle, 1886–1946, vol. IV

Sutton, Engr Rear-Adm. Charles Edwin, 1880–1968, vol. VI

Sutton, Charles William, 1848–1920, vol. II

Sutton, Surg.-Rear-Adm. Edward, 1870–1940, vol. III

Sutton, Maj.-Gen. Evelyn Alexander, 1891–1964, vol. VI

Sutton, Maj.-Gen. F. A., 1884–1944, vol. IV

Sutton, Francis Henry Astley M.; *see* Manners-Sutton.

Sutton, Sir George, 1st Bt (*cr* 1922), 1856–1934, vol. III

Sutton, Sir George Augustus, 1st Bt, 1869–1947, vol. IV

Sutton, George Lowe, 1872–1964, vol. VI

Sutton, Hon. Sir George Morris, 1834–1913, vol. I

Sutton, Brig. George William, 1893–1971, vol. VII

Sutton, Sir Graham; *see* Sutton, Sir O. G.

Sutton, Sir Henry, 1845–1920, vol. II

Sutton, Rev. Henry, 1833–1921, vol. II

Sutton, Henry Cecil, 1868–1936, vol. III

Sutton, Maj.-Gen. Hugh Clement, 1867–1928, vol. II

Sutton, Janet Vida, (Mrs John Sutton); *see* Watson, J. V.

Sutton, John Edward, 1862–1945, vol. IV

Sutton, Sir John Smale, *died* 1942, vol. IV

Sutton, Leonard Goodhart, 1863–1932, vol. III

Sutton, Martin Hubert Foquett, 1875–1930, vol. III

Sutton, Martin John, 1850–1913, vol. I

Sutton, Sir (Oliver) Graham, 1903–1977, vol. VII

Sutton, Peter John, 1917–1982, vol. VIII

Sutton, Ralph, 1881–1960, vol. V

Sutton, Sir Richard Vincent, 6th Bt (*cr* 1772), 1891–1918, vol. II

Sutton, Ven. Robert, 1832–1910, vol. I

Sutton, Sir Robert Lexington, 8th Bt, 1897–1981, vol. VIII

Sutton, Stanley Cecil, 1907–1977, vol. VII

Sutton, William Godfrey, 1894–1985, vol. VIII

Sutton, Brig. William Moxhay, 1885–1949, vol. IV

Sutton Curtis, John, 1913–1988, vol. VIII

Sutton Nelthorpe, Col Oliver, 1888–1963, vol. VI

Sutton-Nelthorpe, Robert Nassau, 1850–1937, vol. III

Sutton-Pratt, Brig. Reginald, 1898–1962, vol. VI

Suttor, Hon. Sir Francis Bathurst, 1839–1915, vol. I

Suvorin, Alexis, 1834–1912, vol. I

Suyematsu, Viscount Kencho, 1855–1920, vol. II

Svenningsen, Nils Thomas, 1894–1985, vol. VIII

Swabey, Christopher, 1906–1972, vol. VII

Swabey, Vice-Adm. Sir George Thomas Carlisle Parker, 1881–1952, vol. V

Swabey, Brig.-Gen. Wilfred Spedding, 1871–1939, vol. III

Swaby, Ven. J. A. R., *died* 1944, vol. IV

Swaby, Rt Rev. John Cyril Emerson, 1905–1975, vol. VII

Swaby, Rt Rev. William Proctor, 1844–1916, vol. II

Swaffer, Hannen, 1879–1962, vol. VI

Swain, Rt Rev. Edgar Priestley, 1881–1949, vol. IV

Swain, Rev. Edmund Gill, 1861–1938, vol. III

Swain, Air Cdre (Francis) Ronald Downs, 1903–1989, vol. VIII

Swain, Freda Mary, 1903–1985, vol. VIII

Swain, Very Rev. George Lill, 1870–1955, vol. V

Swain, Hon. Col George Llewellyn Douglas, 1858–1924, vol. II

Swain, James, *died* 1951, vol. V

Swain, Joseph, 1857–1927, vol. II

Swain, Percival Francis, 1888–1924, vol. II

Swain, Air Cdre Ronald; *see* Swain, Air Cdre F. R. D.

Swain, Thomas Henry, 1911–1979, vol. VII

Swain, Walter, 1876–1945, vol. IV

Swaine, Col Charles Edward, 1844–1928, vol. II

Swaine, Maj.-Gen. Sir Leopold Victor, 1840–1931, vol. III

Swainson, Maj.-Gen. Frederick Joseph, 1911–1965, vol. VI

Swainson, Willan, *died* 1970, vol. VI

Swaish, Sir John, 1852–1931, vol. III

Swales, A. B., *died* 1952, vol. V

Swales, John Kirby, 1879–1956, vol. V

Swallow, Rev. Richard Dawson, 1847–1930, vol. III

Swamikannu Pillai, Louis Dominic, 1865–1925, vol. II

Swan, Sir Alexander Brown, 1869–1941, vol. IV

Swan, Alice Macallan, *died* 1939, vol. III

Swan, Annie Shepherd; *see* Smith, Mrs Burnett.

Swan, Col Charles Arthur, 1854–1941, vol. IV
Swan, Sir Charles Sheriton, 1870–1944, vol. IV
Swan, Captain Donald C.; *see* Cameron-Swan.
Swan, Rear-Adm. (S) Edgar Bocquet, 1874–1951, vol. V
Swan, Ernest William, 1883–1948, vol. IV
Swan, Harold Couch, 1890–1972, vol. VII
Swan, Henry Frederick, 1842–1908, vol. I
Swan, John Arthur Laing, 1877–1938, vol. III
Swan, John Edmund, 1877–1956, vol. V
Swan, John Macallan, 1847–1910, vol. I
Swan, Sir Joseph Wilson, 1828–1914, vol. I
Swan, Lt-Comdr Sir Kenneth Raydon, 1877–1973, vol. VII
Swan, Lionel Maynard, 1885–1969, vol. VI
Swan, Robert A., 1849–1937, vol. III
Swan, Robert Clayton, *died* 1929, vol. III
Swan, Russell Henry Jocelyn, 1876–1943, vol. IV
Swan, Sheriton Clements, 1909–1986, vol. VIII
Swan, Thomas, 1899–1981, vol. VIII
Swan, Lt-Col Sir William Bertram, 1914–1990, vol. VIII
Swan, Maj.-Gen. William Travers, 1861–1949, vol. IV
Swanborough, Baroness (Life Peer); *see* Reading, Marchioness of.
Swann, Baron (Life Peer); Michael Meredith Swann, 1920–1990, vol. VIII
Swann, Rev. Canon Alfred, *died* 1961, vol. VI
Swann, Rev. Cecil Gordon Aldersey, 1888–1969, vol. VI
Swann, Sir (Charles) Duncan, 2nd Bt, 1879–1962, vol. VI
Swann, Rt Hon. Sir Charles Ernest, 1st Bt, 1844–1929, vol. III
Swann, Sir Duncan; *see* Swann, Sir C. D.
Swann, Rev. Ernest Henry, 1869–1948, vol. IV
Swann, Frederick Samuel Philip, *died* 1921, vol. II
Swann, Harry Kirke, 1871–1926, vol. II, vol. III
Swann, Maj.-Gen. John Christopher, 1856–1939, vol. III
Swann, Louis Herbert H.; *see* Hartland-Swann.
Swann, Air Vice-Marshal Sir Oliver, 1878–1948, vol. IV
Swann, Peter Geoffrey, 1921–1988, vol. VIII
Swann, Robert Swinney, 1915–1986, vol. VIII
Swann, Rev. Sidney, 1862–1942, vol. IV
Swann, Rev. Canon Sidney Ernest, 1890–1976, vol. VII
Swann, William Francis Gray, 1884–1962, vol. VI
Swann-Mason, Rev. Richard Swann, *died* 1942, vol. IV
Swansea, 2nd Baron, 1848–1922, vol. II
Swansea, 3rd Baron, 1875–1934, vol. III
Swanson, Gloria May Josephine Swanson, 1899–1983, vol. VIII
Swanson, John Leslie, 1892–1974, vol. VII
Swanson, Sir John Warren, 1865–1924, vol. II
Swanston, Lt-Col Charles Oliver, 1865–1914, vol. I
Swanston, Comdr David, 1919–1987, vol. VIII
Swanston, John Francis Alexander, 1877–1958, vol. V
Swanwick, Anna, 1813–1899, vol. I
Swanwick, Betty, 1915–1989, vol. VIII

Swanwick, Harold, *died* 1929, vol. III
Swanwick, Helena Maria, 1864–1939, vol. III
Swanzy, Very Rev. Henry Biddall, 1873–1932, vol. III
Swanzy, Sir Henry Rosborough, 1843–1913, vol. I
Swanzy, Rev. Thomas Erskine, 1869–1950, vol. IV
Swarbrick, John, 1879–1964, vol. VI
Swarbrick, Thomas, 1900–1965, vol. VI
Swart, Hon. Charles Robberts, 1894–1982, vol. VIII
Swayne, Col Charles Henry, 1848–1925, vol. II
Swayne, Charles Richard, 1843–1921, vol. II
Swayne, Brig.-Gen. Sir Eric John Eagles, 1863–1929, vol. III
Swayne, Col Harald George Carlos, 1860–1940, vol. III
Swayne, Maj.-Gen. James Dowell, 1827–1916, vol. II
Swayne, Lt-Gen. Sir John George des Réaux, 1890–1964, vol. VI
Swayne, Walter Carless, 1862–1925, vol. II
Swayne, Rt Rev. William Shuckburgh, 1862–1941, vol. IV
Swaythling, 1st Baron, 1832–1911, vol. I
Swaythling, 2nd Baron, 1869–1927, vol. II
Swaythling, 3rd Baron, 1898–1990, vol. VIII
Sweatman, Most Rev. Arthur, 1834–1909, vol. I
Sweeney, Hon. Francis J., 1862–1921, vol. II, vol. III
Sweeney, Very Rev. Canon Garrett Daniel, 1912–1979, vol. VII
Sweeney, James Augustine, 1883–1945, vol. IV
Sweeney, Maj.-Gen. Joseph A., 1897–1980, vol. VII (AII)
Sweeny, Most Rev. James Fielding, 1857–1940, vol. III
Sweeny, Lt-Col Roger Lewis Campbell, 1878–1926, vol. II
Sweet, Lt-Col Edward Herbert, 1871–1966, vol. VI
Sweet, Henry, 1845–1912, vol. I
Sweet, Ven. John Hales Sweet, 1849–1929, vol. III
Sweet-Escott, Sir Bickham; *see* Sweet-Escott, Sir E. B.
Sweet-Escott, Sir (Ernest) Bickham, 1857–1941, vol. IV
Sweeting, Richard Deane, 1856–1913, vol. I
Sweetman, Sir Henry, 1858–1944, vol. IV
Sweetman, Seamus George, 1914–1985, vol. VIII
Sweny, Captain William Halpin Paterson, 1871–1951, vol. V
Swete, Henry Barclay, 1835–1917, vol. II
Swetenham, Clement William, 1852–1927, vol. II
Swettenham, Sir Alexander, 1846–1933, vol. III
Swettenham, Sir Frank Athelstane, 1850–1946, vol. IV
Swettenham, Lt-Col George Kilner, 1866–1933, vol. III
Swettenham, Lt-Col William Alexander Whybault, 1870–1947, vol. IV
Swift, Brig.-Gen. Albert Edward, 1870–1948, vol. IV
Swift, Sir Brian Herbert, 1893–1969, vol. VI
Swift, Herbert Walker, 1894–1960, vol. V
Swift, Sir Rigby Philip Watson, 1874–1937, vol. III
Swifte, Sir Ernest Godwin, 1839–1927, vol. II
Swinburn, Maj.-Gen. Henry Robinson, 1897–1981, vol. VIII
Swinburne, A. J., 1846–1915, vol. I

Swinburne, Algernon Charles, 1837–1909, vol. I
Swinburne, Hon. George, 1861–1928, vol. II
Swinburne, Sir Hubert, 8th Bt, 1867–1934, vol. III
Swinburne, Sir James, 9th Bt, 1858–1958, vol. V
Swinburne, Sir John, 7th Bt, 1831–1914, vol. I
Swinburne, Sir Spearman Charles, 10th Bt, 1893–1967, vol. VI
Swinburne, Lt-Col Thomas Robert, 1853–1921, vol. II
Swinburne-Hanham, John Castleman, 1860–1935, vol. III
Swinburne-Ward, Col Henry Charles, 1879–1966, vol. VI
Swindell, Rev. Frank Guthrie, 1874–1975, vol. VII
Swindell, Rev. Canon Frederic Smith, *died* 1941, vol. IV
Swindells, Rev. Bernard Guy, 1887–1977, vol. VII
Swindlehurst, Joseph Eric, 1890–1972, vol. VII
Swindley, Maj.-Gen. John Edward, 1831–1919, vol. II
Swiney, Brig.-Gen. Alexander John Henry, 1866–1933, vol. III
Swiney, Maj.-Gen. Sir (George Alexander) Neville, 1897–1970, vol. VI
Swiney, Maj.-Gen. John, 1832–1918, vol. II
Swiney, Maj.-Gen. Sir Neville; *see* Swiney, Maj.-Gen. Sir G. A. N.
Swinfen, 1st Baron, 1851–1919, vol. II
Swinfen, 2nd Baron, 1904–1977, vol. VII
Swing, Raymond, 1887–1968, vol. VI
Swingler, Rt Hon. Stephen Thomas, 1915–1969, vol. VI
Swinhoe, Lt-Gen. Frederick William, 1821–1907, vol. I
Swinley, Captain Casper Silas Balfour, 1898–1983, vol. VIII
Swinley, Maj.-Gen. George, 1842–1924, vol. II
Swinnerton, Frank Arthur, 1884–1982, vol. VIII
Swinnerton, Henry Hurd, 1875–1966, vol. VI
Swinnerton-Pilkington, Sir Thomas Edward Milborne-; *see* Pilkington.
Swinny, Shapland Hugh, 1857–1923, vol. II
Swinstead, Felix Gerald, 1880–1959, vol. V
Swinstead, Frank Hillyard, 1862–1937, vol. III
Swinstead, George Hillyard, *died* 1926, vol. II
Swinstead, Rev. John Howard, 1864–1924, vol. II
Swinton, 1st Earl of, 1884–1972, vol. VII
Swinton, Alan Archibald Campbell, 1863–1930, vol. III
Swinton, Brig. Alan Henry Campbell, 1896–1972, vol. VII
Swinton, Col Charles William, 1872–1935, vol. III
Swinton, Maj.-Gen. Sir Ernest Dunlop, 1868–1951, vol. V
Swinton, Lt-Col Francis Edward, 1866–1927, vol. II
Swinton, Captain George Herbert Tayler, 1852–1923, vol. II
Swinton, Captain George Sitwell Campbell, 1859–1937, vol. III
Swinton, John Edulf Blagrave, 1864–1941, vol. IV
Swinton, John Liulf Campbell, 1858–1920, vol. II
Swiny, Brig.-Gen. William Frederick, 1873–1950, vol. IV
Swire, John, 1861–1933, vol. III

Swire, John Kidston, 1893–1983, vol. VIII
Swire, Rev. S., 1866–1936, vol. III
Swire, William, 1862–1942, vol. IV
Swithinbank, Bernard Winthrop, 1884–1958, vol. V
Swithinbank, Harold William, 1858–1928, vol. II
Swords, William Francis, 1873–1964, vol. VI
Swynnerton, Annie Louisa, *died* 1933, vol. III
Swynnerton, Charles Francis Massy, 1877–1938, vol. III
Swynnerton, Maj.-Gen. Charles Roger Alan, 1901–1973, vol. VII
Sycamore, Thomas Andrew Harding, 1907–1986, vol. VIII
Sydenham of Combe, 1st Baron, 1848–1933, vol. III
Sydenham, Engr-Rear-Adm. Ernest Dickerson, 1875–1952, vol. V
Sydenham, Engr Rear-Adm. Frederick William, 1871–1946, vol. IV
Sydnor, Charles Sackett, 1898–1954, vol. V
Syed, Sir Ali Imam, 1869–1932, vol. III
Syed Sirdar Ali Khan, Nawab, 1879–1942, vol. IV
Syer, William George, 1913–1988, vol. VIII
Syers, Sir Cecil George Lewis, 1903–1981, vol. VIII
Syers, Rev. Henry S., 1838–1915, vol. I
Syfret, Adm. Sir (Edward) Neville, 1889–1972, vol. VII
Syfret, Adm. Sir Neville; *see* Syfret, Adm. Sir E. N.
Sykes, Sir Alan John, 1st Bt (*cr* 1917), 1868–1950, vol. IV
Sykes, Vice-Adm. Alfred Charles, 1868–1933, vol. III
Sykes, Sir Arthur, 7th Bt (*cr* 1781), 1871–1934, vol. III
Sykes, Arthur Alkin, *died* 1939, vol. III
Sykes, Brig. Arthur Clifton, 1891–1967, vol. VI
Sykes, (Arthur) Frank (Seton), 1903–1980, vol. VII
Sykes, Sir (Benjamin) Hugh, 2nd Bt (*cr* 1921), 1893–1974, vol. VII
Sykes, Sir Charles, 1st Bt (*cr* 1921), 1867–1950, vol. IV
Sykes, Sir Charles, 1905–1982, vol. VIII
Sykes, Christopher, 1831–1898, vol. I
Sykes, Christopher Hugh, 1907–1986, vol. VIII
Sykes, Brig.-Gen. Clement Arthur, 1871–1938, vol. III
Sykes, Rev. Edward, 1862–1937, vol. III
Sykes, Ella Constance, *died* 1939, vol. III
Sykes, Ernest, 1870–1958, vol. V
Sykes, Sir Francis Godfrey, 9th Bt, 1907–1990, vol. VIII
Sykes, Frank; *see* Sykes, A. F. S.
Sykes, Rev. Canon Frank Morris, 1879–1939, vol. III
Sykes, Sir Frederic Henry, 5th Bt (*cr* 1781), 1826–1899, vol. I
Sykes, Rev. Sir Frederic John, 8th Bt (*cr* 1781), 1876–1956, vol. V
Sykes, Maj.-Gen. Rt Hon. Sir Frederick Hugh, 1877–1954, vol. V
Sykes, Sir Henry, 6th Bt (*cr* 1781), 1828–1916, vol. II
Sykes, Sir Hugh; *see* Sykes, Sir B. H.
Sykes, James, 1857–1929, vol. III
Sykes, Sir John Charles Gabriel, 1869–1952, vol. V
Sykes, John Frederick Joseph, *died* 1913, vol. I
Sykes, Joseph, 1899–1967, vol. VI

Sykes, Lt-Col Sir Mark, 6th Bt (*cr* 1783), 1879–1919, vol. II

Sykes, Sir (Mark Tatton) Richard T., 7th Bt (*cr* 1783); *see* Tatton-Sykes.

Sykes, Very Rev. Norman, 1897–1961, vol. VI

Sykes, Brig.-Gen. Sir Percy Molesworth, 1867–1945, vol. IV

Sykes, Comdr Percy Stanley, 1878–1966, vol. VI

Sykes, Lt-Col Peter Thomas Wellesley, 1903–1975, vol. VII

Sykes, Reginald James, 1869–1940, vol. III

Sykes, Sir Richard Adam, 1920–1979, vol. VII

Sykes, Rev. Simon Joseph, 1867–1941, vol. IV

Sykes, Sir Tatton, 5th Bt (*cr* 1783), 1826–1913, vol. I

Sykes, Lt-Col William Ainley, 1857–1940, vol. III

Sykes, Sir William Edmund, 1884–1961, vol. VI

Sykes, William Stanley, 1894–1961, vol. VI

Sylva, Carmen, 1843–1916, vol. II

Sylvaine, Vernon, 1897–1957, vol. V

Sylvester, Albert James, 1889–1989, vol. VIII

Sylvester, Sir (Arthur) Edgar, 1891–1969, vol. VI

Sylvester, Sir Edgar; *see* Sylvester, Sir A. E.

Sylvester, George Oscar, 1898–1961, vol. VI

Sylvester, Asst Surgeon Henry Thomas, 1831–1920, vol. II

Sylvester, James Joseph, 1814–1897, vol. I

Sylvester, Rev. Samuel Augustus Kirwan, 1852–1928, vol. II

Sylvester-Bradley, Peter Colley, 1913–1978, vol. VII

Sym, John David, 1855–1931, vol. III

Sym, Maj.-Gen. Sir John Munro, 1839–1919, vol. II

Sym, William George, 1864–1938, vol. III

Syme, Sir Colin York, 1903–1986, vol. VIII

Syme, David, 1827–1908, vol. I

Syme, Sir Geoffrey, 1873–1942, vol. IV

Syme, Sir George Adlington, 1859–1929, vol. III

Syme, Sir Ronald, 1903–1989, vol. VIII

Symes, Sir Edward Spence, 1852–1901, vol. I

Symes, Lt-Col Sir (George) Stewart, 1882–1962, vol. VI

Symes, Maj.-Gen. George William, 1896–1980, vol. VII

Symes, Lt-Col Gustavus Phelps, 1857–1938, vol. III

Symes, Rev. John Elliotson, 1847–1921, vol. II

Symes, John Odery, 1867–1951, vol. V

Symes, Sir Robert Henry, 1837–1908, vol. I

Symes, Rev. Ronald, 1870–1935, vol. III

Symes, Lt-Col Sir Stewart; *see* Symes, Lt-Col Sir G. S.

Symes-Thompson, Edmund, 1837–1906, vol. I

Symes-Thompson, Henry Edmund, *died* 1952, vol. V

Symington, David, 1904–1984, vol. VIII

Symington, Herbert James, 1881–1965, vol. VI

Symington, John Alexander, 1887–1961, vol. VI

Symington, Johnson, 1851–1924, vol. II

Symington, Stuart; *see* Symington, W. S.

Symington, (William) Stuart, 1901–1988, vol. VIII

Symmers, W. St Clair, 1863–1937, vol. III

Symmons, Israel Alexander, 1862–1923, vol. II

Symon, Sir Alexander Colin Burlington, 1902–1974, vol. VII

Symon, Rev. Dudley James, 1887–1961, vol. VI

Symon, Col Frank, 1879–1956, vol. V

Symon, Harold, 1896–1971, vol. VII

Symon, Jocelyn, (Mrs David Symon); *see* Moore, Miss J. A. M.

Symon, Hon. Sir Josiah Henry, 1846–1934, vol. III

Symon, Lt-Col Walter Conover, 1874–1949, vol. IV

Symonds, Sir Alfred Percival, *died* 1929, vol. III

Symonds, (Arthur) Leslie, 1910–1960, vol. V

Symonds, Sir Aubrey Vere, 1874–1931, vol. III

Symonds, Sir Charles Putnam, 1890–1978, vol. VII

Symonds, Sir Charters James, 1852–1932, vol. III

Symonds, Captain F. C. Loder-, 1846–1923, vol. II

Symonds, Vice-Adm. Frederick Parland Loder-, 1876–1952, vol. V

Symonds, Rev. Henry Herbert, 1885–1958, vol. V

Symonds, Joseph Bede, 1900–1985, vol. VIII

Symonds, Leslie; *see* Symonds, A. L.

Symonds, Robert Wemyss, 1889–1958, vol. V

Symonds, Rev. William, 1832–1919, vol. II

Symonds-Tayler, Adm. Sir Richard Victor, 1897–1971, vol. VII

Symonette, Hon. Sir Roland Theodore, 1898–1980, vol. VII

Symons, Brig.-Gen. Adolphe, 1872–1954, vol. V

Symons, Albert James Alroy, 1900–1941, vol. IV

Symons, Arthur, 1865–1945, vol. IV

Symons, Col Charles Bertie Owen, 1874–1948, vol. IV

Symons, Rev. Charles Douglas, 1885–1949, vol. IV

Symons, Ernest Vize, 1913–1990, vol. VIII

Symons, Lt-Col Frank Albert, 1869–1917, vol. II

Symons, Lt-Col George Algernon James S.; *see* Soltau-Symons.

Symons, George James, 1838–1900, vol. I

Symons, George William Culme S.; *see* Soltau-Symons.

Symons, Maj.-Gen. Sir Henry; *see* Symons, Maj.-Gen. Sir T. H.

Symons, Hubert Wallace, 1890–1973, vol. VII

Symons, Noel Victor Housman, 1894–1986, vol. VIII

Symons, Sir Robert F.; *see* Fox-Symons.

Symons, Ronald Stuart, 1904–1977, vol. VII

Symons, Maj.-Gen. Sir (Thomas) Henry, 1872–1948, vol. IV

Symons, Captain Thomas Raymond, 1866–1922, vol. II

Symons-Jeune, John Frederic; *see* Jeune.

Sympson, Edward Mansel, 1860–1922, vol. II

Synge, Sir Francis Robert Millington, 6th Bt, 1851–1924, vol. II

Synge, John Millington, 1871–1909, vol. I

Synge, Major Mark, 1871–1921, vol. II

Synge, Sir Robert Follett, 1853–1920, vol. II

Synge, Sir Robert Millington, 7th Bt, 1877–1942, vol. IV

Synge, Victor Millington, 1893–1976, vol. VII

Synge-Hutchinson, Sir Edward; *see* Hutchinson, Sir E. S.

Synnot, Maj.-Gen. Arthur FitzRoy H.; *see* Hart-Synnot.

Synnot, Brig.-Gen. Arthur Henry Seton H.; *see* Hart-Synnot.

Synnot, Ronald Victor Okes H.; *see* Hart-Synnot.

Synnott, Nicholas Joseph, *died* 1920, vol. II

Synnott, Pierce Nicholas Netterville, 1904–1982, vol. VIII

Synnott, Bt Lt-Col Wilfrid Thomas, 1877–1941, vol. IV
Syrett, Herbert Sutton, *died* 1959, vol. V
Syrett, Netta, *died* 1943, vol. IV
Sysonby, 1st Baron, 1867–1935, vol. III
Sysonby, 2nd Baron, 1903–1956, vol. V
Szarvasy, Frederick Alexander, *died* 1948, vol. IV
Szczepanski, Maj.-Gen. Henry Charles Antony, 1841–1923, vol. II
Szent-Györgyi, Albert, 1893–1986, vol. VIII
Szeryng, Henryk, 1918–1988, vol. VIII
Szigeti, Joseph, 1892–1973, vol. VII
Szlumper, Alfred Weeks, 1858–1934, vol. III
Szlumper, Gilbert Savil, 1884–1969, vol. VI
Szlumper, Sir James Weeks, 1834–1926, vol. II

T

Taaffe, George Joseph, 1866–1923, vol. II
Tabor, James, 1869–1938, vol. III
Tabor, Margaret Emma, *died* 1954, vol. V
Tabor, Richard John, *died* 1958, vol. V
Tabouis, Geneviève, 1892–1985, vol. VIII
Tabrar, Joseph, 1857–1931, vol. III
Tabuteau, Maj.-Gen. George Grant, 1881–1940, vol. III
Tachie-Menson, Sir Charles William, 1889–1962, vol. VI
Tacon, Sir Thomas Henry, 1838–1922, vol. II
Tadema, Miss Anna A.; *see* Alma-Tadema.
Tadema, Laura Theresa A.; *see* Alma-Tadema.
Tadema, Miss Laurence A.; *see* Alma-Tadema.
Tadema, Sir Lawrence A.; *see* Alma-Tadema.
Tafawa Balewa, Alhaji Rt Hon. Sir Abubakar, 1912–1966, vol. VI
Taflia, 4th Marquis of, 1837–1921, vol. II
Taft, Charles Phelps, 1897–1983, vol. VIII
Taft, Lorado, 1860–1936, vol. III
Taft, Robert Alphonso, 1889–1953, vol. V
Taft, William Howard, 1857–1930, vol. III
Tagart, Edward Samuel Bourn, 1877–1956, vol. V
Tagart, Maj.-Gen. Sir Harold Arthur Lewis, 1870–1930, vol. III
Tagg, Sir Arundel; *see* Arundel, Sir A. T.
Taggart, Sir James, 1849–1929, vol. III
Taggart, Wing Comdr John S.; *see* Scott-Taggart.
Tagore, Abanindra Nath, 1871–1951, vol. V
Tagone, Maharaja Bahadur Sir Joteendro Mohun, 1831–1908, vol. I
Tagone, Hon. Majharaja Bahadur Sir Prodyot Coomar, 1873–1942, vol. IV
Tagore, Sir Rabindranath, 1861–1941, vol. IV
Tagore, Raja Sir Sourindro Mohun, 1840–1914, vol. I
Tahourdin, Peter Anthony Ivan, 1920–1983, vol. VIII
Taillon, Hon. Sir Louis Olivier, 1840–1923, vol. II
Tailyour, Gen. Sir Norman Hastings, 1914–1979, vol. VII
Tailyour, Col Thomas Francis Bruce R.; *see* Renny-Tailyour.
Tainsh, Lt-Col Joseph Ramsay, 1874–1954, vol. V

Tait, Andrew Wilson, 1876–1930, vol. III
Tait, Rev. Arthur James, 1872–1944, vol. IV
Tait, Adm. Sir Campbell; *see* Tait, Adm. Sir W. E. C.
Tait, Ven. Donald, 1862–1932, vol. III
Tait, Sir Frank Samuel, 1883–1965, vol. VI
Tait, George Hope, 1861–1943, vol. IV
Tait, Hugh Nimmo, 1888–1960, vol. V
Tait, James, 1863–1944, vol. IV
Tait, Sir James Blair, 1890–1985, vol. VIII
Tait, John, 1878–1944, vol. IV
Tait, Sir John, *died* 1972, vol. VII
Tait, Lt-Col John Spottiswood, 1875–1951, vol. V
Tait, Lawson, 1845–1899, vol. I
Tait, Sir Melbourne McTaggart, 1842–1917, vol. II
Tait, Peter Guthrie, 1831–1901, vol. I
Tait, Sir Thomas, 1864–1940, vol. III (A), vol. IV
Tait, Thomas Smith, 1882–1954, vol. V
Tait, Air Vice-Marshal Sir Victor Hubert, 1892–1988, vol. VIII
Tait, Adm. Sir (William Eric) Campbell, 1886–1946, vol. IV
Taite, Charles Davis, 1872–1948, vol. IV
Taitt, Rt Rev. Francis Marion, 1862–1943, vol. IV
Takamine, Jokichi, 1854–1923, vol. II
Talbot de Malahide, 5th Baron, 1846–1921, vol. II
Talbot de Malahide, 6th Baron, 1874–1948, vol. IV
Talbot de Malahide, 7th Baron, 1912–1973, vol. VII
Talbot of Malahide, 8th Baron, 1897–1975, vol. VII
Talbot of Malahide, 9th Baron, 1899–1987, vol. VIII
Talbot, Lt-Col Sir Adelbert Cecil, 1845–1920, vol. II
Talbot, Very Rev. Albert Edward, 1877–1936, vol. III
Talbot, Vice-Adm. Arthur George, 1892–1960, vol. V
Talbot, Rev. Arthur Henry, 1855–1927, vol. II
Talbot, Benjamin, 1864–1947, vol. IV
Talbot, Bertram, 1865–1936, vol. III
Talbot, Bridget Elizabeth, *died* 1971, vol. VII
Talbot, Vice-Adm. Sir Cecil Ponsonby, 1884–1970, vol. VI
Talbot, Charles Henry, 1842–1916, vol. II
Talbot, Rev. Edward Keble, 1877–1949, vol. IV
Talbot, Rt Rev. Edward Stuart, 1844–1934, vol. III
Talbot, Emily Charlotte, *died* 1918, vol. II
Talbot, Rt Rev. Ethebert, 1848–1928, vol. II
Talbot, Frank Heyworth, 1895–1990, vol. VIII
Talbot, George, 1823–1914, vol. I
Talbot, Lt-Col George James Francis, 1857–1941, vol. IV
Talbot, Rt Hon. Sir George John, 1861–1938, vol. III
Talbot, Sir Gerald Francis, 1881–1945, vol. IV
Talbot, Gustavus Arthur, 1848–1920, vol. II
Talbot, Howard, 1865–1928, vol. II
Talbot, John Ellis, 1906–1967, vol. VI
Talbot, Rt Hon. John Gilbert, 1835–1910, vol. I
Talbot, Matilda Theresa, 1871–1958, vol. V
Talbot, Dame Meriel Lucy, 1866–1956, vol. V
Talbot, Col Hon. Milo George, 1854–1931, vol. III
Talbot, Rt Rev. Neville Stuart, *died* 1943, vol. IV
Talbot, Lt-Gen. Sir Norman Graham Guy, 1914–1979, vol. VII
Talbot, Hon. Sir Patrick Wellington, 1817–1898, vol. I
Talbot, Percy Amaury, 1877–1945, vol. IV
Talbot, Maj.-Gen. Hon. Sir Reginald Arthur James, 1841–1929, vol. III

Talbot, Comdr Reginald George Chetwynd, 1881–1939, vol. III

Talbot, Hon. Reginald Gilbert Murray, 1849–1930, vol. III

Talbot, Very Rev. Reginald Thomas, 1862–1935, vol. III

Talbot, Sir Samuel Thomas, *died* 1931, vol. III

Talbot, Thomas, *died* 1929, vol. III

Talbot, Walter Stanley, 1869–1935, vol. III

Talbot, Sir William Henry, 1831–1919, vol. II

Talbot, Sir William J., 1872–1947, vol. IV

Talbot, William John, 1859–1923, vol. II

Talbot Rice, David; *see* Rice.

Tallack, Sir Hugh M.; *see* Mackay-Tallack.

Tallberg, Axel, 1860–1928, vol. II

Tallents, George William, 1856–1924, vol. II

Tallents, Philip Cubitt, 1886–1962, vol. VI

Tallents, Sir Stephen George, 1884–1958, vol. V

Tallerman, Kenneth Harry, 1894–1981, vol. VIII

Tallis, Sir George, 1869–1948, vol. IV

Tallis, Gillian Helen; *see* Mackay, G. H.

Talmage, Algernon, *died* 1939, vol. III

Tamagno, Francisco, 1851–1905, vol. I

Tamm, Igor Evgenievich, 1895–1971, vol. VII

Tamplin, Herbert Travers, 1853–1925, vol. II

Tan, Dato Sir Cheng-lock, 1883–1960, vol. V

Tancock, Lt-Col Alexander Charles, *died* 1966, vol. VI

Tancock, Rev. Charles Coverdale, 1851–1922, vol. II

Tancock, Col Osborne Kendall, 1866–1946, vol. IV

Tancock, Rev. Osborne William, 1839–1930, vol. III

Tancred, Vice-Adm. James Charles, 1864–1943, vol. IV

Tancred, Maj.-Gen. Thomas Angus, 1867–1944, vol. IV

Tancred, Sir Thomas Selby, 8th Bt, 1840–1910, vol. I

Tancred, Major Sir Thomas Selby L.; *see* Lawson-Tancred.

Tandy, Sir Arthur Harry, 1903–1964, vol. VI

Tandy, Brig. Sir Edward Aldborough, 1871–1950, vol. IV

Tandy, Brig.-Gen. Ernest Napper, 1879–1953, vol. V

Tandy, Col Maurice O'Connor, 1873–1942, vol. IV

Tang, Sir Shiu-kin, 1901–1986, vol. VIII

Tangley, Baron (Life Peer); Edwin Savory Herbert, 1899–1973, vol. VII

Tangney, Dame Dorothy Margaret, 1911–1985, vol. VIII

Tangye, Captain Sir Basil Richard Gilzean, 2nd Bt, 1895–1969, vol. VI

Tangye, Claude Edward, 1877–1952, vol. V

Tangye, Sir (Harold) Lincoln, 1st Bt, 1866–1935, vol. III

Tangye, Sir Lincoln; *see* Tangye, Sir H. L.

Tangye, Sir Richard, 1833–1906, vol. I

Tangye, Lt-Col Richard Trevithick Gilbertstone, 1875–1944, vol. IV

Tankerville, 6th Earl of, 1810–1899, vol. I

Tankerville, 7th Earl of, 1852–1931, vol. III

Tankerville, 8th Earl of, 1897–1971, vol. VII

Tankerville, 9th Earl of, 1921–1980, vol. VII

Tann, Florence Mary, 1892–1981, vol. VIII

Tanner, Archibald Gerard, 1895–1937, vol. III

Tanner, Charles Elliott, 1857–1946, vol. IV

Tanner, Sir Edgar Stephen, 1914–1979, vol. VII

Tanner, Maj.-Gen. Edward, 1839–1916, vol. II

Tanner, Dame Emmeline Mary, 1876–1955, vol. V

Tanner, Lt-Col Frederick Courtney, 1879–1965, vol. VI

Tanner, Frederick John Shirley; *see* Tanner, Jack.

Tanner, Col Sir Gilbert, 1877–1953, vol. V

Tanner, Sir Henry, 1849–1935, vol. III

Tanner, Henry, 1876–1947, vol. IV

Tanner, Henry William Lloyd, 1851–1915, vol. I

Tanner, Herbert George, 1882–1974, vol. VII

Tanner, Jack, (Frederick John Shirley Tanner), 1889–1965, vol. VI

Tanner, Brig.-Gen. John Arthur, 1858–1917, vol. II

Tanner, John Arthur Charles, 1854–1928, vol. II

Tanner, John Edward, 1834–1906, vol. I

Tanner, Joseph Robson, 1860–1931, vol. III

Tanner, Lawrence Edward, 1890–1979, vol. VII

Tanner, Norman Cecil, 1906–1982, vol. VIII

Tanner, Lt-Gen. Sir Oriel Viveash, 1832–1911, vol. I

Tanner, Lt-Col Richard Morrison, 1871–1936, vol. III

Tanner, William Edward, 1889–1951, vol. V

Tanner, Maj.-Gen. William Ernest Collins, 1875–1943, vol. IV

Tanqueray, Rev. Truman, 1888–1960, vol. V

Tanquerey, F. J., *died* 1942, vol. IV

Tansley, Sir Arthur George, 1871–1955, vol. V

Tapley, Harold Livingstone, 1875–1932, vol. III

Tapley, Maj.-Gen. James John Bonifant, 1877–1958, vol. V

Tapley-Soper, Harry Tapley; *see* Soper.

Taplin, Walter, 1910–1986, vol. VIII

Tapp, Norman Charles, 1925–1977, vol. VII

Tapp, Percy John Rutty, 1886–1964, vol. VI

Tapper, Sir Walter John, 1861–1935, vol. III

Tapps-Gervis-Meyrick, Sir George Augustus Eliott; *see* Meyrick.

Tapps-Gervis-Meyrick, Major Sir George Llewelyn; *see* Meyrick.

Tarbat, Sir John Allan, 1891–1977, vol. VII

Tarbet, Lt-Col Alexander Francis, 1860–1939, vol. III

Tarbet, Captain William Godfrey, 1878–1911, vol. I

Tarbolton, Harold Ogle, *died* 1947, vol. IV

Tardieu, André Pierre Gabriel Amedée, 1876–1945, vol. IV

Tardrew, Rev. Canon Thomas Hedley, 1889–1966, vol. VI

Targett, James Henry, *died* 1913, vol. I

Targett, Sir Robert William, 1891–1965, vol. VI

Tarkington, Booth, 1869–1946, vol. III

Tarleton, Captain Alfred Henry, 1862–1921, vol. II

Tarleton, Francis Alexander, 1841–1920, vol. II

Tarn, Sir William Woodthorpe, 1869–1957, vol. V

Tarrant, Dorothy, 1885–1973, vol. VII

Tarrant, Surg.-Gen. Thomas, 1830–1909, vol. I

Tarrant, William Charles, 1881–1941, vol. IV

Tarrant, Rev. William George, 1853–1928, vol. II

Tarring, Sir Charles James, 1845–1923, vol. II

Tarry, Frederick Thomas, 1896–1976, vol. VII

Tarte, Hon. Joseph Israel, 1848–1907, vol. I

Tarver, Maj.-Gen. Alexander Leigh, 1871–1941, vol. IV

Tarver, Maj.-Gen. Charles Herbert, 1908–1982, vol. VIII
Tarver, J. C., *died* 1926, vol. II
Tarver, Maj.-Gen. William Knapp, 1872–1952, vol. V
Tasadduk Rasul Khan, Raja Sir, *died* 1928, vol. II
Taschereau, His Eminence Cardinal Elzéar Alexander, 1820–1898, vol. I
Taschereau, Rt Hon. Sir Henri Elzéar, 1836–1911, vol. I
Taschereau, Sir Henri Thomas, 1841–1909, vol. I
Taschereau, Hon. Louis Alexandre, 1867–1952, vol. V
Taschereau, Rt Hon. Robert, 1896–1970, vol. VI
Tasker, Antony Greaves, 1916–1990, vol. VIII
Tasker, Rev. Canon Derek Morris Phipps, 1916–1978, vol. VII
Tasker, Rev. John Greenwood, 1853–1936, vol. III
Tasker, Rev. Randolph Vincent Greenwood, 1895–1976, vol. VII
Tasker, Major Sir Robert Inigo, 1868–1959, vol. V
Tasker, Sir Theodore James, 1884–1981, vol. VIII
Tasma; *see* Couvreur, Jessie.
Tassell, Alick James, 1865–1932, vol. III
Tata, Sir Dorabji Jamsetji, 1859–1932, vol. III
Tata, Jamsetjee Nasarwanji, 1839–1904, vol. I
Tata, Sir Ratanji Jamsetji, 1871–1918, vol. II
Tatchell, Sydney Joseph, 1887–1965, vol. VI
Tate, Col Alan Edmondson, 1859–1934, vol. III
Tate, Adm. Alban Giffard, 1853–1930, vol. III
Tate, Lt-Col Arthur Wignall, 1888–1939, vol. III
Tate, Charles James Gerrard, 1880–1951, vol. V
Tate, D'Arcy, 1866–1935, vol. III
Tate, Sir Ernest William, 3rd Bt, 1867–1939, vol. III
Tate, Frank, 1863–1939, vol. III
Tate, George Vernon, 1890–1955, vol. V
Tate, Col Gerard William, 1866–1937, vol. III
Tate, Maj.-Gen. Godfrey, 1873–1944, vol. IV
Tate, Harry, *died* 1940, vol. III
Tate, Sir Henry, 1st Bt, 1819–1899, vol. I
Tate, James William, 1875–1922, vol. II
Tate, Jonathan, 1899–1958, vol. V
Tate, Mavis Constance, *died* 1947, vol. IV
Tate, Phyllis Margaret Duncan, (Mrs Alan Frank), 1911–1987, vol. VIII
Tate, Col Robert Ward, 1864–1938, vol. III
Tate, Major Sir Robert William, 1872–1952, vol. V
Tate, Thomas Bailey, 1882–1957, vol. V
Tate, Walter William Hunt, 1865–1916, vol. II
Tate, Sir William Henry, 2nd Bt, 1842–1921, vol. II
Tatham, Brig.-Gen. Arthur Glanville, 1856–1933, vol. III
Tatham, Rev. Edward Henry Ralph, 1857–1938, vol. III
Tatham, Lt-Col Hon. Frederic Spence, 1865–1934, vol. III
Tati, Jacques, (Jacques Tatischeff), 1908–1982, vol. VIII
Tatischeff, Jacques; *see* Tati, J.
Tatlock, Robert Rattray, 1889–1954, vol. V
Tatlow, Frank, 1861–1934, vol. III
Tatlow, Joseph, 1851–1929, vol. III
Tatlow, Hon. Robert Garnett, 185–1910, vol. I
Tatlow, Rev. Canon Tissington, 1876–1957, vol. V

Tattersall, Creassey Edward Cecil, 1877–1957, vol. V
Tattersall, Lt-Col Edmund Harry, 1897–1968, vol. VI
Tattersall, John Lincoln, 1865–1942, vol. IV
Tattersall, Rev. Thomas Newell, 1879–1943, vol. IV
Tattersall, William, *died* 1914, vol. I
Tattersall, William Boothman, 1873–1943, vol. IV
Tatton-Sykes, Sir (Mark Tatton) Richard, 7th Bt, 1905–1978, vol. VII
Tatum, E(dward) L(awrie), 1909–1975, vol. VII
Tauber, Richard, 1892–1948, vol. IV
Taubman, Frank Mowbray, 1868–1946, vol. IV
Taunton, Agnes, 1877–1941, vol. IV
Taunton, Sir Ivon Hope, 1890–1957, vol. V
Taussig, Francis William, 1859–1940, vol. III (A), vol. IV
Taveggia, Rt Rev. Santino, 1855–1928, vol. II, vol. III
Taverner, Hon. Sir John William, 1852–1923, vol. II
Taverner, William Burgoyne, 1879–1958, vol. V
Taw Sein Ko, 1864–1930, vol. III
Tawney, Charles Henry, 1837–1922, vol. II
Tawney, Richard Henry, 1880–1962, vol. VI
Tawse, Col Harry Storey, 1889–1959, vol. V
Tay, Waren, *died* 1927, vol. II
Tayler, Albert Chevallier, 1862–1925, vol. II
Tayler, Lt-Col Francis Lionel, 1883–1933, vol. III
Tayler, Maj.-Gen. John Charles, 1834–1913, vol. I
Tayler, Adm. Sir Richard Victor S.; *see* Symonds-Tayler.
Taylor, Baron (Life Peer); Stephen James Lake Taylor, 1910–1988, vol. VIII
Taylor, Alan Carey, 1905–1975, vol. VII
Taylor, Alan John Percivale, 1906–1990, vol. VIII
Taylor, Rt Hon. Sir Alan Russell, 1901–1969, vol. VI (AII)
Taylor, Albert Booth, 1896–1971, vol. VII
Taylor, Alec C.; *see* Clifton-Taylor.
Taylor, Sir Alexander, 1826–1912, vol. I
Taylor, Alexander, 1872–1917, vol. II
Taylor, Alexander Burt, 1904–1972, vol. VII
Taylor, Sir Alexander Thomson, 1873–1953, vol. V
Taylor, Alfred Edward, 1869–1945, vol. IV
Taylor, Rear-Adm. Alfred Hugh, 1886–1972, vol. VII
Taylor, (Alfred) Maurice, 1903–1979, vol. VII
Taylor, Sir Allen, 1864–1940, vol. III
Taylor, Sir Andrew Thomas, 1850–1937, vol. III
Taylor, Brig.-Gen. Arthur Henry Mendle, 1870–1934, vol. III
Taylor, Lt-Col Arthur James, 1876–1949, vol. IV (A), vol. V
Taylor, Arthur John Ernest, 1913–1979, vol. VII
Taylor, Captain Arthur Lombe, 1882–1968, vol. VI
Taylor, Captain Arthur Trevelyan, 1864–1956, vol. V
Taylor, Lt-Col Arthur William Neufville, 1863–1930, vol. III
Taylor, Arthur Wood, 1909–1987, vol. VIII
Taylor, Austin, *died* 1955, vol. V
Taylor, Col Bertie Harry Waters, *died* 1946, vol. IV
Taylor, Rear-Adm. Bertram Wilfrid, 1906–1970, vol. VI
Taylor, Maj.-Gen. Sir Brian; *see* Taylor, Maj.-Gen. Sir G. B. O.
Taylor, Rev. Charles, 1840–1908, vol. I

Taylor, Charles Allison, 1885–1965, vol. VI
Taylor, Charles Bell, 1829–1909, vol. I
Taylor, Charles Edward, 1853–1924, vol. II
Taylor, Lt-Col Charles Newton, 1866–1949, vol. IV
Taylor, Rev. Charles Reeve, 1845–1931, vol. III
Taylor, Sir Charles Stuart, 1910–1989, vol. VIII
Taylor, Charles William, 1878–1960, vol. V
Taylor, Very Rev. Charles William Gray, 1879–1950, vol. IV
Taylor, Christopher Albert, 1915–1981, vol. VIII
Taylor, Claude, 1877–1957, vol. V
Taylor, Rev. Decimus A. G., 1871–1933, vol. III
Taylor, Desmond Maxwell, 1928–1978, vol. VII
Taylor, Dorothy Daisy C.; see Cottington-Taylor.
Taylor, Dorothy Mary, 1902–1983, vol. VIII
Taylor, Douglas, 1915–1971, vol. VII
Taylor, Col Edward, 1860–1931, vol. III
Taylor, Ven. Edward, 1921–1982, vol. VIII
Taylor, Lt-Col Edward Harrison Clough, 1849–1921, vol. II
Taylor, Edward Henry, died 1922, vol. II
Taylor, Edward Plunket, 1901–1989, vol. VIII
Taylor, Edward R., 1838–1911, vol. I
Taylor, (Edward) Wilfred, 1891–1980, vol. VII
Taylor, Edwin, 1881–1972, vol. VII
Taylor, Edwin, 1905–1973, vol. VII
Taylor, Elizabeth, (Mrs J. W. K. Taylor), 1912–1975, vol. VII
Taylor, Sir Eric Stuart, 2nd Bt (cr 1917), 1889–1977, vol. VII
Taylor, Vice-Adm. Sir Ernest Augustus, 1876–1971, vol. VII
Taylor, Ernest Edward, 1897–1974, vol. VII
Taylor, Col Ernest Fitzwilliam, 1867–1944, vol. IV
Taylor, Lt-Col Eustace Trevor Neave, 1894–1971, vol. VII
Taylor, Eva Germaine Rimington, died 1966, vol. VI
Taylor, Fanny Isabel, died 1947, vol. IV
Taylor, Lt-Col Hon. Fawcett Gowler, 1878–1940, vol. III (A), vol. IV
Taylor, Francis, 1845–1915, vol. I
Taylor, Sir Francis Edward W.; see Worsley-Taylor.
Taylor, Francis Henry, 1903–1957, vol. V
Taylor, Rt Rev. Francis John, 1912–1971, vol. VII
Taylor, Francis Maurice Gustavus D. P.; see Du-Plat-Taylor.
Taylor, Col Francis Pitt Stewart, 1869–1924, vol. II
Taylor, Frank Alwyn, 1890–1960, vol. V
Taylor, Frank Herbert Graham, 1890–1971, vol. VII
Taylor, F(rank) Sherwood, 1897–1956, vol. V
Taylor, Franklin, 1843–1919, vol. II
Taylor, Fred, 1875–1963, vol. VI
Taylor, Ven. Frederic Norman, 1871–1960, vol. V
Taylor, Frederic Richard, 1876–1929, vol. III
Taylor, Sir Frederick, 1st Bt (cr 1917), 1847–1920, vol. II
Taylor, Rt Rev. Frederick Adrian, 1892–1961, vol. VI
Taylor, Sir Frederick W.; see Williams-Taylor.
Taylor, Frederick William, 1909–1989, vol. VIII
Taylor, Sir Geoffrey Ingram, 1886–1975, vol. VII
Taylor, Hon. George, 1840–1919, vol. II
Taylor, Maj.-Gen. Sir (George) Brian (Ogilvie), died 1973, vol. VII

Taylor, George Francis, 1903–1979, vol. VII
Taylor, Sir George L.; see Langley-Taylor.
Taylor, George Paul, 1860–1917, vol. II
Taylor, George Reginald Thomas, 1876–1965, vol. VI
Taylor, George Simon Arthur W.; see Watson-Taylor.
Taylor, George William, 1864–1929, vol. III
Taylor, Rear-Adm. George William, 1883–1964, vol. VI
Taylor, Brig.-Gen. Gerald Kyffin-, 1863–1949, vol. IV
Taylor, Dame Gladys, 1890–1950, vol. IV
Taylor, Sir Gordon G.; see Gordon-Taylor.
Taylor, Gordon Rattray, 1911–1981, vol. VIII
Taylor, Griffith; see Taylor, T. G.
Taylor, Col H. Brooke, 1855–1923, vol. II
Taylor, H. Stanley, 1871–1959, vol. V
Taylor, Major Harold Blake, 1862–1936, vol. III
Taylor, Harold George K.; see Kirwan-Taylor.
Taylor, Rev. Harold Milman Strickland, 1890–1966, vol. VI
Taylor, Harold Victor, died 1965, vol. VI
Taylor, Harry Ashworth, died 1907, vol. I
Taylor, Harry Mead, 1872–1928, vol. II
Taylor, Harry Willoughby O.; see Oddin-Taylor.
Taylor, Col Haydon D'Aubrey Potenger, 1860–1939, vol. III
Taylor, Henry Archibald, died 1980, vol. VII
Taylor, Henry G.; see Gawan Taylor.
Taylor, Rev. Henry James, died 1945, vol. IV
Taylor, Henry Martyn, 1842–1927, vol. II
Taylor, Henry Osborn, 1856–1941, vol. IV
Taylor, Sir Henry Wilson W.; see Worsley-Taylor.
Taylor, Herbert, 1885–1970, vol. VI (AII)
Taylor, Captain Herbert Bardsley, 1884–1947, vol. IV
Taylor, Col Herbert James Cox-, 1872–1936, vol. III
Taylor, Sir Herbert John, 1865–1943, vol. IV
Taylor, Hobart Chatfield C.; see Chatfield-Taylor.
Taylor, Horace, 1881–1934, vol. III
Taylor, Lt-Col Hugh Neufville, 1859–1931, vol. III
Taylor, Sir Hugh Stott, 1890–1974, vol. VII
Taylor, Rev. Isaac, 1829–1901, vol. I
Taylor, Col Jack H.; see Hulme Taylor.
Taylor, Rev. Jackson, died 1929, vol. III
Taylor, James, 1871–1944, vol. IV
Taylor, James, 1859–1946, vol. IV
Taylor, James Benjamin, 1860–1944, vol. IV
Taylor, Sir James Braid, 1891–1943, vol. IV
Taylor, Air Vice-Marshal James Clarke, 1910–1978, vol. VII
Taylor, James Haward, 1909–1968, vol. VI
Taylor, James Henry, 1861–1926, vol. II
Taylor, James Monroe, 1848–1916, vol. II
Taylor, Lt-Col Sir James W.; see Worsley-Taylor.
Taylor, Joe, 1906–1989, vol. VIII
Taylor, Sir John, 1833–1912, vol. I
Taylor, John, 1834–1922, vol. II
Taylor, John, 1857–1936, vol. III
Taylor, John, 1861–1945, vol. IV
Taylor, Maj.-Gen. Sir John, 1884–1959, vol. V
Taylor, John, 1902–1962, vol. VI
Taylor, Sir John, 1876–1971, vol. VII

Taylor, Brig. John Alexander Chisholm, 1891–1981, vol. VIII

Taylor, Rev. John Edward, 1899–1966, vol. VI

Taylor, Captain Sir John Godfrey W.; *see* Worsley-Taylor.

Taylor, John Gray, 1890–1944, vol. IV

Taylor, John Hugh, 1916–1985, vol. VIII

Taylor, John Idowu Conrad, 1917–1973, vol. VII

Taylor, Sir John James, 1859–1945, vol. IV

Taylor, Col John Lowther Du Plat, 1829–1904, vol. I

Taylor, John Norman, *died* 1945, vol. IV

Taylor, Rt Rev. John Ralph Strickland, 1883–1961, vol. VI

Taylor, John T., 1840–1908, vol. I

Taylor, Sir John W.; *see* Wilson-Taylor.

Taylor, John William, 1851–1910, vol. I

Taylor, Sir John William, 1895–1974, vol. VII

Taylor, Mrs John William Kendell; *see* Taylor, Elizabeth.

Taylor, Joseph Charlton, 1913–1971, vol. VII

Taylor, Sir Joshua R.; *see* Ross-Taylor.

Taylor, Julian, 1889–1961, vol. VI

Taylor, Kenneth, 1923–1990, vol. VIII

Taylor, Kenneth Roy E.; *see* Eldin-Taylor.

Taylor, Most Rev. Leo Hale, 1889–1965, vol. VI

Taylor, Leonard Campbell, 1874–1969, vol. VI

Taylor, Leonard Whitworth, 1880–1979, vol. VII

Taylor, Sir Lionel Goodenough, 1871–1963, vol. VI

Taylor, Lionel Robert Stewart, 1915–1972, vol. VII

Taylor, Luke, 1876–1916, vol. II

Taylor, Rev. Malcolm Campbell, *died* 1922, vol. II

Taylor, Gen. Sir Malcolm Cartwright C.; *see* Cartwright-Taylor.

Taylor, Air Vice-Marshal Malcolm Lincoln, 1893–1970, vol. VI

Taylor, Hon. Mrs Margaret Sophia, 1877–1962, vol. VI

Taylor, Margerie Venables, 1881–1963, vol. VI

Taylor, Mark Ronald, *died* 1942, vol. IV

Taylor, Martin, 1885–1981, vol. VIII

Taylor, Maurice; *see* Taylor, A. M.

Taylor, Gen. Sir Maurice Grove, 1881–1960, vol. V

Taylor, Gen. Maxwell Davenport, 1901–1987, vol. VIII

Taylor, Myron C., 1874–1959, vol. V

Taylor, Captain Sir Patrick Gordon, *died* 1966, vol. VI

Taylor, Peter Athol, 1926–1976, vol. VII

Taylor, Peter John, 1929–1987, vol. VIII

Taylor, Col Philip Beauchamp, *died* 1939, vol. III

Taylor, Rear-Adm. Philip Cardwell, 1902–1965, vol. VI

Taylor, Rachel Annand, 1876–1960, vol. V

Taylor, Raymond Charles, 1926–1977, vol. VII

Taylor, Brig.-Gen. Reginald O'Bryen, 1872–1949, vol. IV

Taylor, Sir Reginald William, 1895–1971, vol. VII

Taylor, Brig.-Gen. Reynell Hamilton Baylay, 1858–1942, vol. IV

Taylor, Rev. Richard, *died* 1922, vol. II

Taylor, Sir Richard Chambré Hayes, 1819–1904, vol. I

Taylor, Sir Richard Laurence S.; *see* Stuart Taylor.

Taylor, Richard S.; *see* Stopford-Taylor.

Taylor, Richard Sanderson, *died* 1932, vol. III

Taylor, Sir Richard Stephens, 1842–1928, vol. II

Taylor, Richard Whately C.; *see* Cooke-Taylor.

Taylor, Sir Robert, 1855–1921, vol. II

Taylor, Robert, *died* 1969, vol. VI

Taylor, Robert Arthur, 1886–1934, vol. III

Taylor, Robert Bruce, 1869–1954, vol. V

Taylor, Robert George, 1932–1981, vol. VIII

Taylor, Rt Hon. Robert John, 1881–1954, vol. V

Taylor, Col Robert Lewis, 1822–1906, vol. I

Taylor, Sir Robert Mackinlay, 1912–1985, vol. VIII

Taylor, Very Rev. Robert Oswald Patrick, 1873–1944, vol. IV

Taylor, Robert Walter, 1883–1972, vol. VII

Taylor, Rupert Sutton, 1905–1986, vol. VIII

Taylor, Lt-Col St John Louis Hyde du Plat-, 1865–1936, vol. III

Taylor, Samuel C.; *see* Coleridge-Taylor.

Taylor, Rt Rev. Samuel Mumford, 1859–1929, vol. III

Taylor, Seymour, 1851–1931, vol. III

Taylor, Sidney Berald, 1900–1960, vol. V

Taylor, Stanley Grisewood, 1893–1980, vol. VII

Taylor, Stanley Shelbourne, 1875–1965, vol. VI

Taylor, Theodore Cooke, 1850–1952, vol. V

Taylor, Thomas, 1851–1916, vol. II

Taylor, Thomas, 1849–1938, vol. III

Taylor, Rev. Thomas, 1858–1938, vol. III

Taylor, Sir Thomas, 1876–1941, vol. IV

Taylor, (Thomas) Griffith, 1880–1963, vol. VI

Taylor, Sir Thomas Marris, 1871–1941, vol. IV

Taylor, Sir Thomas Murray, 1897–1962, vol. VI

Taylor, Rt Rev. Mgr Thomas N., *died* 1963, vol. VI

Taylor, Sir Thomas Wardlaw, 1833–1917, vol. II

Taylor, Sir Thomas Weston Johns, 1895–1953, vol. V

Taylor, Thomas Whiting, 1907–1981, vol. VIII

Taylor, Tom Lancelot, 1878–1960, vol. V

Taylor, Rev. Vincent, 1887–1968, vol. VI

Taylor, Walter R.; *see* Ross Taylor.

Taylor, Rev. Walter Ross, 1838–1907, vol. I

Taylor, Gen. Sir Walter William P.; *see* Pitt-Taylor.

Taylor, Wilfred; *see* Taylor, E. W.

Taylor, Surg.-Gen. Sir William, 1843–1917, vol. II

Taylor, Col Sir William, 1871–1933, vol. III

Taylor, William, 1865–1937, vol. III

Taylor, William, 1892–1977, vol. VII

Taylor, William Benjamin, 1875–1932, vol. III

Taylor, William Ernest, 1900–1965, vol. VI

Taylor, Ven. William Francis, *died* 1906, vol. I

Taylor, Lt-Col William Herbert, 1885–1959, vol. V

Taylor, Sir William Johnson, 1st Bt (*cr* 1963), 1902–1972, vol. VII

Taylor, Sir William Ling, 1882–1969, vol. VI

Taylor, William T., 1843–1933, vol. III

Taylor, Sir William Thomas, 1848–1931, vol. III

Tayside, Baron (Life Peer); David Lauchlan Urquhart, 1912–1975, vol. VII

Tchigorin, T., 1850–1908, vol. I

Teacher, Anthony Donald Macdonald, 1905–1969, vol. VI

Teacher, John Hammond, 1869–1930, vol. III

Teago, Frederick Jerrold, 1886–1964, vol. VI

Teague, Col John, 1896–1983, vol. VIII

Teague, Rev. John Jessop, 1856–1929, vol. III

Teakle, Laurence John Hartley, 1901–1979, vol. VII
Teale, Sir Edmund Oswald, 1874–1971, vol. VII
Teale, Sir Francis Hugo, *died* 1959, vol. V
Teale, Rear-Adm. Godfrey Benjamin, 1908–1978, vol. VII
Teale, Major Joseph William, 1876–1926, vol. II
Teale, Thomas Pridgin, 1831–1923, vol. II
Teall, Major George Harris, 1880–1939, vol. III
Teall, Sir Jethro Justinian Harris, 1849–1924, vol. II
Teare, Robert Donald, 1911–1979, vol. VII
Tearle, Sir Godfrey Seymour, 1884–1953, vol. V
Tearsdale, Sir John Smith, 1881–1962, vol. VI
Tebb, William, 1830–1918, vol. II
Tebbitt, Sir Alfred St Valery, *died* 1941, vol. IV
Tebbs, Herbert Louis, 1868–1940, vol. III
Tebbutt, Edward G. F., *died* 1934, vol. III
Tebbutt, Dame Grace, 1893–1983, vol. VIII
Tebbutt, Rev. Henry Jemson, *died* 1915, vol. I
Teck, HH the Duke of; Francis Paul Louis Alexander, 1837–1900, vol. I
Teck, HSH Prince Francis Joseph Leopold Frederick of, 1870–1910, vol. I
Tedder, 1st Baron, 1890–1967, vol. VI
Tedder, Sir Arthur John, 1851–1931, vol. III
Tedder, Henry Richard, 1850–1924, vol. II
Tee, Lt-Col James Henry Stanley, 1876–1951, vol. V
Teed, Frank Litherland, 1858–1937, vol. III
Teeling, Bartholomew, 1848–1921, vol. II
Teeling, Mrs Bartle, *died* 1906, vol. I
Teeling, Charles Hamilton, *died* 1921, vol. II
Teeling, Luke Alexander, 1856–1943, vol. IV
Teeling, Sir (Luke) William (Burke), 1903–1975, vol. VII
Teeling, Sir William; *see* Teeling, Sir L. W. B.
Teelock, Sir Leckraz, 1909–1982, vol. VIII
Teesdale, Rev. Frederic Dobree, 1845–1935, vol. III
Teetzel, James Vernal, 1853–1926, vol. II
Teevan, Thomas Leslie, 1927–1954, vol. V
Tegart, Sir Charles Augustus, 1881–1946, vol. IV
Tegetmeier, William Bernhard, 1816–1912, vol. I
Tehri, HH Raja Sir Keerti Shah, 1874–1913, vol. I
Tehri-Garhwal, Maharaja of, 1898–1950, vol. IV (A), vol. V
Teichman, Sir Eric, 1884–1944, vol. IV
Teichman, Major Oskar, 1880–1959, vol. V
Teichman-Derville, Major Max, 1876–1963, vol. VI
Teignmouth, 3rd Baron, 1840–1915, vol. I
Teignmouth, 4th Baron, 1844–1916, vol. II
Teignmouth, 5th Baron, 1847–1926, vol. II
Teignmouth, 6th Baron, 1881–1964, vol. VI
Teignmouth, 7th Baron, 1920–1981, vol. VIII
Teixeira de Mattos, Alexander Louis, 1865–1921, vol. II
Tek Chand, Sir, 1883–1962, vol. VI
Telfer, Rev. Andrew Cecil, 1893–1978, vol. VII
Telfer, Rev. Canon William, 1886–1968, vol. VI
Telfer-Smollett, Maj.-Gen. Alexander Patrick Drummond, 1884–1954, vol. V
Telfer-Smollett, Captain James Drummond, 1824–1909, vol. I
Telford, Evelyn Davison, 1876–1961, vol. VI
Telford, Rev. John, 1851–1936, vol. III
Tellier, Hon. Sir Joseph Mathias, 1861–1952, vol. V
Tellier, Louis, 1844–1935, vol. III

Telling, Harry George, 1880–1961, vol. VI
Tempany, Sir Harold Augustin, 1881–1955, vol. V
Tempel, Frederik Jan, 1900–1974, vol. VII
Temperley, Rev. Canon Arthur, 1850–1927, vol. II
Temperley, Maj.-Gen. Arthur Cecil, 1877–1940, vol. III
Temperley, Major Harold William Vazeille, 1879–1939, vol. III
Tempest, Major Adolphus V.; *see* Vane-Tempest.
Tempest, Lord Henry John V.; *see* Vane-Tempest.
Tempest, Lord Henry V.; *see* Vane-Tempest.
Tempest, Margaret Mary, (Lady Mears), *died* 1982, vol. VIII
Tempest, Dame Mary Susan, 1866–1942, vol. IV
Tempest, Norton Robert, 1904–1985, vol. VIII
Tempest, Sir Percy Crosland, 1861–1924, vol. II
Tempest, Sir Robert Tempest, 3rd Bt, 1836–1901, vol. I
Tempest, Brig.-Gen. Roger Stephen, 1876–1948, vol. IV
Tempest, Sir Tristram Tempest, 4th Bt, 1865–1909, vol. I
Tempest-Hicks, Brig.-Gen. Henry, 1852–1922, vol. II
Templar-Smith, Col Sir Harold Charles, 1890–1970, vol. VI
Temple of Stowe, 5th Earl, 1871–1940, vol. III
Temple of Stowe, 6th Earl, 1909–1966, vol. VI
Temple of Stowe, 7th Earl, 1910–1988, vol. VIII
Temple, Sir Alfred George, 1848–1928, vol. II
Temple, Maj.-Gen. Bertram, 1896–1973, vol. VII
Temple, Charles Lindsay, 1871–1929, vol. III
Temple, Edwin, *died* 1932, vol. III
Temple, Frances Gertrude Acland, (Mrs William Temple), 1890–1984, vol. VIII
Temple, Col Frank Valiant, 1879–1937, vol. III
Temple, Most Rev. and Rt Hon. Frederick, 1821–1902, vol. I
Temple, Frederick Charles, 1879–1957, vol. V
Temple, Comdr Grenville Mathias, 1897–1965, vol. VI
Temple, Rev. Henry, *died* 1906, vol. I
Temple, Lt-Col Henry Martindale, 1853–1905, vol. I
Temple, Hope, 1859–1938, vol. III
Temple, John, 1839–1922, vol. II
Temple, Lt-Gen. Reginald Cecil, 1877–1959, vol. V
Temple, Rt Hon. Sir Richard, 1st Bt, 1826–1902, vol. I
Temple, Lt-Col Sir Richard Carnac, 2nd Bt, 1850–1931, vol. III
Temple, Col Sir Richard Durand, 3rd Bt, 1880–1962, vol. VI
Temple, Lt-Col William, 1833–1919, vol. II
Temple, Most Rev. and Rt Hon. William, 1881–1944, vol. IV
Temple-Gore-Langton, Hon. Chandos Graham, 1873–1921, vol. II
Temple-Gore-Langton, Comdr Hon. Evelyn Arthur Grenville, 1884–1972, vol. VII
Temple-Morris, Sir Owen, 1896–1985, vol. VIII
Templeman, Geoffrey, 1914–1988, vol. VIII
Templeman, Philip George, 1910–1972, vol. VII
Templeman, Hon. William, 1844–1914, vol. I
Templemore, 2nd Baron, 1821–1906, vol. I
Templemore, 3rd Baron, 1854–1924, vol. II

Templemore, 4th Baron, 1880–1953, vol. V
Templer, Brig.-Gen. Cyril Frank, 1869–1947, vol. IV
Templer, Frederic Gordon, 1849–1918, vol. II
Templer, Field Marshal Sir Gerald Walter Robert, 1898–1979, vol. VII
Templer, Col J. L. B., 1846–1924, vol. II
Templer, Lt-Col Walter Francis, 1865–1942, vol. IV
Templeton, Archibald Angus, 1893–1969, vol. VI
Templeton, Charles Perry, 1884–1929, vol. III
Templeton, James Stanley, 1906–1977, vol. VII
Templeton, Col John Montgomery, 1840–1908, vol. I
Templeton, William Paterson, 1876–1938, vol. III
Templetown, 4th Viscount, 1853–1939, vol. III
Templetown, 5th Viscount, 1894–1981, vol. VIII
Templewood, 1st Viscount, 1880–1959, vol. V
Tenby, 1st Viscount, 1894–1967, vol. VI
Tenby, 2nd Viscount, 1922–1983, vol. VIII
Tengbom, Ivar Justus, 1878–1968, vol. VI
Tenison, Marika H.; see Hanbury Tenison.
Tenison, Lt-Col William Percival Cosnahan, 1884–1983, vol. VIII
Tennant, Sir Charles, 1st Bt, 1823–1906, vol. I
Tennant, Charles Coombe, 1852–1928, vol. II
Tennant, Hon. Sir David, 1829–1905, vol. I
Tennant, Francis John, 1861–1942, vol. IV
Tennant, Rev. Frederick Robert, 1866–1957, vol. V
Tennant, Rt Hon. Harold John, 1865–1935, vol. III
Tennant, Hercules, 1850–1925, vol. II
Tennant, Lt-Gen. James Francis, 1829–1915, vol. I
Tennant, Lt-Col John Edward, 1890–1941, vol. IV
Tennant, Major John Trenchard, 1841–1904, vol. I
Tennant, Sir Mark Dalcour, 1911–1990, vol. VIII
Tennant, May, 1869–1946, vol. IV
Tennant, Robert Hugh, 1860–1936, vol. III
Tennant, Adm. Sir William George, 1890–1963, vol. VI
Tennant, Sir William Robert, 1892–1969, vol. VI
Tennent, Thomas, 1900–1962, vol. VI
Tenney, John, 1856–1944, vol. IV
Tenniel, Sir John, 1820–1914, vol. I
Tennyson, 2nd Baron, 1852–1928, vol. II
Tennyson, 3rd Baron, 1889–1951, vol. V
Tennyson, Sir Charles Bruce Locker, 1879–1977, vol. VII
Tennyson, Frederick, 1807–1898, vol. I
Tennyson-d'Eyncourt, Edmund Charles, 1855–1924, vol. II
Tennyson d'Eyncourt, Adm. Edwin Clayton; see d'Eyncourt.
Tennyson d'Eyncourt, Sir (Eustace) Gervais, 2nd Bt, 1902–1971, vol. VII
Tennyson-d'Eyncourt, Sir Eustace Henry William, 1st Bt, 1868–1951, vol. V
Tennyson-d'Eyncourt, Sir Gervais; see Tennyson d'Eyncourt, Sir E. G.
Tennyson d'Eyncourt, Sir Giles Gervais, 4th Bt, 1935–1989, vol. VIII
Tennyson-d'Eyncourt, Sir Jeremy; see Tennyson-d'Eyncourt, Sir J. J. E.
Tennyson-d'Eyncourt, Sir (John) Jeremy (Eustace), 3rd Bt, 1927–1988, vol. VIII
Tenterden, 4th Baron, 1865–1939, vol. III
Tenzing Norgay, 1914–1986, vol. VIII

Ternan, Brig.-Gen. Trevor Patrick Breffney, 1860–1949, vol. IV
Terrell, Arthur Koberwein à Beckett, 1881–1956, vol. V
Terrell, Sir Courtney, 1881–1938, vol. III
Terrell, Edward, 1902–1979, vol. VII
Terrell, George, 1862–1952, vol. V
Terrell, Henry, 1856–1944, vol. IV
Terrell, Captain Sir Reginald; see Terrell, Captain Sir T. A. R.
Terrell, Thomas, died 1928, vol. II
Terrell, Captain Sir (Thomas Antonio) Reginald, 1889–1979, vol. VII
Terrey, Henry, died 1954, vol. V
Terrington, 1st Baron, 1852–1921, vol. II
Terrington, 2nd Baron, 1877–1940, vol. III
Terrington, 3rd Baron, 1887–1961, vol. VI
Terriss, William, 1852–1897, vol. I
Terrot, Brig. Charles Russell, died 1944, vol. IV
Terry, Sir Andrew Henry Bouhier I.; see Imbert-Terry.
Terry, Charles Sanford, 1864–1936, vol. III
Terry, Lt-Col Claude Henry Maxwell I.; see Imbert-Terry.
Terry, Major Sir Edward Henry Bouhier I.; see Imbert-Terry.
Terry, Edward O'Connor, 1844–1912, vol. I
Terry, Dame Ellen (Alice), 1847–1928, vol. II
Terry, Sir Francis William, 1877–1960, vol. V
Terry, Fred, 1863–1933, vol. III
Terry, Captain Frederic Bouhier Imbert-, 1887–1963, vol. VI
Terry, Rev. Canon George Frederick, 1864–1919, vol. II
Terry, George Percy Warner, 1867–1949, vol. IV
Terry, Harold; see Terry, J. E. H.
Terry, Lt-Col Sir Henry Bouhier I.; see Imbert-Terry.
Terry, Sir Henry Machu I.; see Imbert-Terry.
Terry, Captain Herbert Durell, 1847–1911, vol. I
Terry, Sir Joseph, 1827–1898, vol. I
Terry, (Joseph Edward) Harold, 1885–1939, vol. III
Terry, Joseph Pitches, 1880–1955, vol. V
Terry, Julia; see Neilson, J.
Terry, Marion, died 1930, vol. III
Terry, Michael, 1899–1981, vol. VIII
Terry, Phyllis N.; see Neilson-Terry.
Terry, Sir Richard Runciman, 1865–1938, vol. III
Terry, Major Robert Joseph Atkinson, 1869–1915, vol. I
Terry, Stephen Harding, 1853–1924, vol. II
Terry-Thomas, (Thomas Terry Hoar Stevens), 1911–1990, vol. VIII
Tertis, Lionel, 1876–1975, vol. VII
Teschemacher, Edward, 1876–1940, vol. III (A), vol. IV
Tesla, Nikola, 1857–1943, vol. IV
Tessier, Hon. Auguste, 1853–1938, vol. III
Tessier, Hon. Jules, 1852–1934, vol. III
Tester, Air Cdre John Andrews, 1907–1972, vol. VII
Tester, Leslie, 1891–1975, vol. VII
Teternikov, Feodor Kuzmich; see Sologub, Feodor.
Tetley, Rev. James George, 1843–1924, vol. II
Tetley, Brig. James Noel, 1898–1971, vol. VII
Tetrazzini, Luisa, 1871–1940, vol. III

Teunon, Sir William, 1863–1926, vol. II
Teversham, Brig. Mark Symonds, 1895–1973, vol. VII
Teversham, Col Richard Kinlock, 1856–1929, vol. III
Teviot, 1st Baron, 1874–1968, vol. VI
Tew, Lt-Col Harold Stuart, 1869–1945, vol. IV
Tew, Sir Mervyn Lawrence, 1876–1963, vol. VI
Tew, Percy, 1840–1921, vol. II
Tew, Thomas Percy, 1876–1953, vol. V
te Water, Charles Theodore, 1887–1964, vol. VI
Tewsley, Cyril Hocken, 1878–1950, vol. IV
Tewson, Sir (Harold) Vincent, 1898–1981, vol. VIII
Tewson, Sir Vincent; see Tewson, Sir H. V.
Tey, Josephine; see Daviot, Gordon.
Teyen, Charles St Leger, 1877–1947, vol. IV
Teynham, 18th Baron, 1867–1936, vol. III
Teynham, 19th Baron, 1896–1972, vol. VII
Teyte, Dame Maggie, (Dame Margaret Cottingham), 1888–1976, vol. VII
Thacker, Charles, 1897–1982, vol. VIII
Thacker, Maj.-Gen. Herbert Cyril, 1870–1953, vol. V
Thacker, Maj.-Gen. Percival Edward, 1873–1945, vol. IV
Thacker, Ransley Samuel, 1891–1965, vol. VI
Thacker, Thomas William, 1911–1984, vol. VIII
Thackeray, Col Charles Bouverie, 1875–1938, vol. III
Thackeray, Col Edward Francis, 1870–1956, vol. V
Thackeray, Col Sir Edward Talbot, 1836–1927, vol. II
Thackeray, Rev. Francis St John, 1832–1919, vol. II
Thackeray, Brig.-Gen. Frank Staniford, 1880–1960, vol. V
Thackeray, Lance, died 1916, vol. II
Thackersey, Sir Vithaldas Damodher, 1873–1922, vol. II
Thackstone, Howard Harrison, 1905–1969, vol. VI
Thackwell, Major Charles Joseph, 1870–1933, vol. III
Thackwell, Col Colquhoun Grant Roche, 1857–1931, vol. III
Thackwell, Gen. Joseph Edwin, 1813–1900, vol. I
Thackwell, Maj.-Gen. William de Wilton Roche, 1834–1910, vol. I
Thaddeus, Henry Jones, 1860–1929, vol. III
Thaine, Robert Niemann, 1875–1943, vol. IV
Thakorram Kapilram, Diwan Bahadur, born 1868, vol. V
Thakurdas, Sir Purshotamdas, 1879–1961, vol. VI
Thalben-Ball, Sir George Thomas, 1896–1987, vol. VIII
Thane, Sir George Dancer, 1850–1930, vol. III
Thankerton, Baron (Life Peer); William Watson, 1873–1948, vol. IV
Thant, U Maung, 1909–1974, vol. VII
Thapa, Hon. Captain Lalbahadur, 1907–1968, vol. VI
Thapar, Prem Nath, 1903–1982, vol. VIII
Tharp, Arthur Keane, 1848–1928, vol. II
Tharp, Philip Anthony, 1890–1958, vol. V
That; see Tate, James William.
Thatcher, J. Wells, 1856–1946, vol. IV
Thatcher, Sir Reginald Sparshatt, 1888–1957, vol. V
Thatcher, William Sutherland, 1888–1966, vol. VI
Thavenot, Alexander Frank Noel, 1883–1947, vol. IV
Thayer, William Sydney, died 1932, vol. III

Thayre, Albert Jesse, 1917–1988, vol. VIII
Theak, Air Vice-Marshal William Edward, 1898–1955, vol. V
Theaker, Harry G., 1873–1954, vol. V
Theiler, Sir Arnold, 1867–1936, vol. III
Theiler, Max, 1899–1972, vol. VII
Theis, Otto Frederick, 1881–1966, vol. VI
Thelwall, John Walter Francis, 1884–1934, vol. III
Thelwell, Sir Arthur Frederick, 1889–1966, vol. VI
Theobald, Rev. Charles, 1831–1930, vol. III
Theobald, Frederic Vincent, 1868–1930, vol. III
Theobold, Sir Henry Studdy, 1847–1934, vol. III
Theodore, Hon. Edward Granville, 1884–1950, vol. IV
Theorell, (Axel) Hugo (Teodor), 1903–1982, vol. VIII
Theorell, Hugo; see Theorell, A. H. T.
Theotonio Pereira, Pedro, 1902–1972, vol. VII
Theron, Maj.-Gen. François Henri, 1891–1967, vol. VI
Thesiger, Arthur Lionel Bruce, 1872–1968, vol. VI
Thesiger, Adm. Sir Bertram Sackville, 1875–1966, vol. VI
Thesiger, Lt-Gen. Hon. Charles Wemyss, 1831–1903, vol. I
Thesiger, Hon. Sir Edward Peirson, 1842–1928, vol. II
Thesiger, Ernest, 1879–1961, vol. VI
Thesiger, Brig.-Gen. George Handcock, 1868–1915, vol. I
Thesiger, Sir Gerald Alfred, 1902–1981, vol. VIII
Thesiger, Captain Hon. Wilfred Gilbert, 1871–1920, vol. II
Theunis, Georges, 1873–1966, vol. VI
Theunissen, Most Rev. John Baptist Hubert, 1905–1979, vol. VII (AII)
Theuriet, Claude André, died 1907, vol. I
Thew, Sir Edgar William, 1879–1942, vol. IV
Thibaudeau, Hon. Alfred Arthur, 1860–1926, vol. II
Thibault, Jacques Anatole François; see France, A.
Thibaut, George Frederick William, 1848–1914, vol. I
Thicknesse, Very Rev. Cuthbert Carroll, 1887–1971, vol. VII
Thicknesse, Rt Rev. Francis Henry, 1829–1921, vol. II
Thicknesse, Ven. Francis Norman, 1858–1946, vol. IV
Thiman, Eric Harding, 1900–1975, vol. VII
Thin, Robert, 1861–1941, vol. IV
Thirkell, Angela Margaret, (Mrs G. L. Thirkell), 1890–1961, vol. VI
Thirkell, Lancelot George, 1921–1989, vol. VIII
Thirkhill, Sir Henry, 1886–1971, vol. VII
Thirlmere, Rowland, 1861–1932, vol. III
Thirtle, James William, 1854–1934, vol. III
Thiselton-Dyer, Sir William Turner, 1843–1928, vol. II
Thistleton-Smith, Vice-Adm. Sir Geoffrey, 1905–1986, vol. VIII
Thoday, David, 1883–1964, vol. VI
Thom, Alexander, 1894–1985, vol. VIII
Thom, Donaldson Rose, died 1920, vol. II
Thom, Col George St Clair, died 1935, vol. III
Thom, Herbert James, 1895–1972, vol. VII
Thom, James Robert, 1910–1981, vol. VIII

Thom, Lt-Col Sir John Gibb, 1891–1941, vol. IV
Thom, Sir William, *died* 1939, vol. III
Thomas, Baron (Life Peer); William Miles Webster Thomas, 1897–1980, vol. VII
Thomas, Abel, 1848–1912, vol. I
Thomas, Sir (Abraham) Garrod, 1853–1931, vol. III
Thomas, Alan Ernest Wentworth, 1896–1969, vol. VI
Thomas, Rt Rev. Albert Reuben Edward, 1908–1983, vol. VIII
Thomas, Rev. Alexander, *died* 1918, vol. II
Thomas, Rev. Canon Alfred, *died* 1957, vol. V
Thomas, Sir (Alfred) Brumwell, 1868–1948, vol. IV
Thomas, Alfred Patten, 1860–1931, vol. III
Thomas, Sir Algernon Phillips Withiel, 1857–1937, vol. III
Thomas, Annie, 1838–1918, vol. II
Thomas, Brig. Arthur Frank Friend, 1897–1987, vol. VIII
Thomas, Col Arthur Havilland, 1860–1919, vol. II
Thomas, Arthur Hermann, 1877–1971, vol. VII
Thomas, Rt Rev. Arthur Nutter, 1869–1954, vol. V
Thomas, (Aubrey) Ralph, 1879–1957, vol. V
Thomas, Augustus, 1857–1934, vol. III
Thomas, Sir Ben Bowen, 1899–1977, vol. VII
Thomas, Bert, *died* 1966, vol. VI
Thomas, Bertie P.; *see* Pardoe-Thomas.
Thomas, Bertram Sidney, 1892–1950, vol. IV
Thomas, Brandon, 1849–1914, vol. IV
Thomas, Brian Dick Lauder, 1912–1989, vol. VIII
Thomas, Sir Brumwell; *see* Thomas, Sir A. B.
Thomas, Carmichael, 1856–1942, vol. IV
Thomas, Cecil, 1885–1976, vol. VII
Thomas, Cecil James, 1902–1973, vol. VII
Thomas, Maj.-Gen. Charles Frederick, *died* 1922, vol. II
Thomas, Sir (Charles) Inigo, 1846–1929, vol. III
Thomas, Lt-Col Sir Charles John Howell, 1874–1943, vol. IV
Thomas, Captain Charles William, 1854–1935, vol. III
Thomas, Claudius Cornelius, 1928–1987, vol. VIII
Thomas, Sir Clement P.; *see* Price Thomas.
Thomas, Daniel, 1880–1938, vol. III
Thomas, Sir Daniel Lleufer, 1863–1940, vol. III
Thomas, David Emlyn, 1892–1954, vol. V
Thomas, Rev. David John, 1862–1936, vol. III
Thomas, Ven. David Richard, *died* 1916, vol. II
Thomas, David Rowland, *died* 1955, vol. V
Thomas, Rev. David Walter, *died* 1905, vol. I
Thomas, Ven. David William, *died* 1951, vol. V
Thomas, David Winton, 1901–1970, vol. VI
Thomas, Rev. Canon Dennis Daven-, 1913–1973, vol. VII
Thomas, Dewi-Prys, 1916–1985, vol. VIII
Thomas, Dylan Marlais, 1914–1953, vol. V
Thomas, Ebenezer Rhys, 1885–1979, vol. VII
Thomas, Edgar, 1900–1979, vol. VII
Thomas, Edgar William, 1879–1963, vol. VI
Thomas, Edward; *see* Thomas, P. E.
Thomas, Brig.-Gen. Edward Algernon D'Arcy, 1858–1937, vol. III
Thomas, Edward Francis, 1880–1954, vol. V
Thomas, Elbert Duncan, 1883–1953, vol. V
Thomas, Sir Eric; *see* Thomas, Sir W. E.

Thomas, Ethel Nancy Miles, *died* 1944, vol. IV
Thomas, Sir Eustace; *see* Thomas, Sir W. E. R.
Thomas, Evan Kyffin, 1866–1935, vol. III
Thomas, Evan Lewis, *died* 1935, vol. III
Thomas, Rev. Evan Lorimer, 1872–1953, vol. V
Thomas, Wing Comdr Forest Frederick Edward Y.; *see* Yeo-Thomas.
Thomas, Rt Rev. Francis Gerard, 1930–1988, vol. VIII
Thomas, Col Francis Herbert Sullivan, 1862–1944, vol. IV
Thomas, Gen. Sir Francis William, 1832–1925, vol. II
Thomas, Lt-Col Frank S. W.; *see* Williams-Thomas.
Thomas, Frederic George, 1872–1937, vol. III
Thomas, Frederic William W.; *see* Watkyn-Thomas.
Thomas, Frederick Maginley, 1908–1984, vol. VIII
Thomas, Frederick William, 1867–1956, vol. V
Thomas, Sir Garrod; *see* Thomas, Sir A. G.
Thomas, Sir George Alan, 7th Bt (*cr* 1766), 1881–1972, vol. VII
Thomas, George Arthur, 1877–1950, vol. IV
Thomas, George H.; *see* Holt-Thomas.
Thomas, Sir George Hector, 1884–1965, vol. VI
Thomas, George Ross, 1876–1955, vol. V
Thomas, Sir George Sidney Meade, 6th Bt (*cr* 1766), 1847–1918, vol. II
Thomas, Gerwyn Pascal, 1895–1956, vol. V
Thomas, Gilbert Oliver, 1891–1978, vol. VII
Thomas, Rt Hon. Sir Godfrey John Vignoles, 10th Bt (*cr* 1694), 1889–1968, vol. VI
Thomas, Brig.-Gen. Sir Godfrey Vignoles, 9th Bt (*cr* 1694), 1856–1919, vol. II
Thomas, Sir Griffith, 1847–1923, vol. II
Thomas, Grosvenor, 1856–1923, vol. II
Thomas, Gwilym Ewart A.; *see* Aeron-Thomas.
Thomas, Gen. Sir (Gwilym) Ivor, 1893–1972, vol. VII
Thomas, Gwyn, 1913–1981, vol. VIII
Thomas, Brig.-Gen. Gwyn G.; *see* Gwyn-Thomas.
Thomas, Harold, 1847–1917, vol. II
Thomas, Rt Rev. Harry, 1897–1955, vol. V
Thomas, Sir Henry, 1878–1952, vol. V
Thomas, Henry Arnold, 1848–1924, vol. II
Thomas, Henry Hugh, 1904–1967, vol. VI
Thomas, Brig.-Gen. Henry Melville, 1870–1940, vol. III
Thomas, Herbert Henry, 1876–1935, vol. III
Thomas, Herbert J., 1892–1947, vol. IV
Thomas, Herbert James, 1882–1960, vol. V
Thomas, Herbert P.; *see* Preston-Thomas.
Thomas, Herbert Percival, 1879–1972, vol. VII
Thomas, Horatio Oritsejolomi, 1917–1979, vol. VII
Thomas, Howard, 1909–1986, vol. VIII
Thomas, Lt-Col Hubert St George, 1862–1936, vol. III
Thomas, Adm. Sir Hugh E.; *see* Evan-Thomas.
Thomas, Hugh Hamshaw, 1885–1962, vol. VI
Thomas, Major Sir Hugh James Protheroe, 1879–1924, vol. II
Thomas, Hugh Lloyd, 1888–1938, vol. III
Thomas, Hugh Whitelegge, *died* 1960, vol. V
Thomas, Sir Illtyd, 1864–1943, vol. IV
Thomas, Sir Inigo; *see* Thomas, Sir C. I.
Thomas, Iorwerth Rhys, 1895–1966, vol. VI
Thomas, Gen. Sir Ivor; *see* Thomas, Gen. Sir G. I.

Thomas, Sir Ivor Broadbent, 1890–1955, vol. V
Thomas, Ivor Cradock, 1861–1942, vol. IV
Thomas, Ivor Owen, 1898–1982, vol. VIII
Thomas, J. Havard, 1854–1921, vol. II
Thomas, Rt Hon. James Henry, 1874–1949, vol. IV
Thomas, James Jonathan, 1850–1919, vol. II
Thomas, Sir (James William) Tudor, 1893–1976, vol. VII
Thomas, Jeffrey, 1933–1989, vol. VIII
Thomas, Sir John, 1834–1920, vol. II
Thomas, John Aeron, 1850–1935, vol. III
Thomas, John Herbert, 1895–1960, vol. V
Thomas, Sir John L.; see Lynn-Thomas.
Thomas, Gen. Sir (John) Noel, 1915–1983, vol. VIII
Thomas, John Owen, 1862–1928, vol. II
Thomas, John Richard, 1897–1968, vol. VI
Thomas, Rev. John Roland Lloyd, 1908–1984, vol. VIII
Thomas, Lt-Gen. Sir John Wellesley, 1822–1908, vol. I
Thomas, Joseph Anthony Charles, 1923–1981, vol. VIII
Thomas, Rev. Joseph Llewelyn, died 1940, vol. III
Thomas, Joseph Silvers Williams-, 1848–1933, vol. III
Thomas, Hon. Josiah, 1863–1933, vol. III
Thomas, Ven. Lawrence, 1889–1960, vol. V
Thomas, Maj.-Gen. Lechmere Cay, 1897–1981, vol. VIII
Thomas, Leonard Charles, 1879–1964, vol. VI
Thomas, Sir Leslie Montagu, 1906–1971, vol. VII
Thomas, (Lewis John) Wynford V.; see Vaughan-Thomas.
Thomas, Col Lionel B.; see Beaumont-Thomas.
Thomas, Llewelyn E.; see Evan-Thomas.
Thomas, Lowell Jackson, 1892–1981, vol. VIII
Thomas, Sir Lynn U.; see Ungoed-Thomas, Sir A. L.
Thomas, Margaret, died 1929, vol. III
Thomas, Meirion, 1894–1977, vol. VII
Thomas, Melbourne, 1906–1989, vol. VIII
Thomas, Air Vice Marshal Meredith, 1892–1984, vol. VIII
Thomas, Captain Mervyn Somerset, 1900–1947, vol. IV
Thomas, Rt Rev. Nathaniel Seymour, 1867–1937, vol. III
Thomas, Gen. Sir Noel; see Thomas, Gen. Sir J. N.
Thomas, Oldfield, 1858–1929, vol. III
Thomas, Sir Patrick Muirhead, 1914–1990, vol. VIII
Thomas, Percy, died 1922, vol. II
Thomas, Sir Percy Edward, 1883–1969, vol. VI
Thomas, Percy Goronwy, 1875–1954, vol. V
Thomas, Major Peter David, 1873–1952, vol. V
Thomas, (Philip) Edward, 1878–1917, vol. II
Thomas, Philip Henry, 1854–1920, vol. II
Thomas, Philip Martin, 1924–1968, vol. VI
Thomas, Ralph; see Thomas, A. R.
Thomas, Rees Griffith, 1870–1934, vol. III
Thomas, Lt-Col Sir Reginald Aneurin, 1879–1975, vol. VII
Thomas, Lt-Col Reginald Silvers W.; see Williams-Thomas.
Thomas, Rt Rev. Richard, 1881–1958, vol. V
Thomas, Richard, 1890–1977, vol. VII
Thomas, Rev. Richard Albert, 1873–1943, vol. IV

Thomas, Richard Macaulay, 1857–1937, vol. III
Thomas, Ven. Richard Rice, died 1942, vol. IV
Thomas, Robert Antony C.; see Clinton-Thomas.
Thomas, Robert Clifford Lloyd, 1893–1969, vol. VI
Thomas, Brig. Robert Henry, 1877–1946, vol. IV
Thomas, Sir Robert John, 1st Bt (cr 1918), 1873–1951, vol. V
Thomas, Sir Robert Kyffin, 1851–1910, vol. I
Thomas, Sir Roger, 1886–1960, vol. V
Thomas, Ronald Hamilton Eliot, 1896–1977, vol. VII
Thomas, Ruth Rees-, (Mrs William Rees-Thomas); see Darwin, R.
Thomas, Ryland Lowell Degwel, 1914–1982, vol. VIII
Thomas, Salusbury Vaughan, 1856–1943, vol. IV
Thomas, Sir Samuel Joyce, died 1952, vol. V
Thomas, Sir Shenton; see Thomas, Sir T. S. W.
Thomas, Stephen Peter John Quao, 1904–1975, vol. VII
Thomas, Rev. Sutcliffe, died 1930, vol. III
Thomas, Terry; see Terry-Thomas.
Thomas, Terry, 1888–1978, vol. VII
Thomas, Theodore, 1835–1905, vol. I
Thomas, Sir Theodore Eastaway, 1882–1951, vol. V
Thomas, Theodore Lynam, 1900–1976, vol. VII
Thomas, Thomas; see Lewis, Richard.
Thomas, Thomas Henry, 1839–1915, vol. I
Thomas, Sir Thomas Powell, died 1932, vol. III
Thomas, Sir (Thomas) Shenton (Whitelegge), 1879–1962, vol. VI
Thomas, Trevor Cawdor, 1914–1985, vol. VIII
Thomas, Sir Tudor; see Thomas, Sir J. W. T.
Thomas, Maj.-Gen. Vivian Davenport, 1897–1984, vol. VIII
Thomas, Sir (Walter) Eric, 1889–1963, vol. VI
Thomas, Rt Rev. Wilfrid William Henry, died 1953, vol. V
Thomas, William, 1891–1958, vol. V
Thomas, William, 1890–1974, vol. VII
Thomas, Sir William Beach, 1868–1957, vol. V
Thomas, Sir William Bruce, 1878–1952, vol. V
Thomas, Rev. William Ceidrych, 1850–1937, vol. III
Thomas, William Edwin S.; see Somerset-Thomas.
Thomas, Sir (William) Eustace) (Rhyddlad), 2nd Bt (cr 1918), 1909–1957, vol. V
Thomas, Sir William Henry, 1859–1947, vol. IV
Thomas, Rev. William Henry Griffith, 1861–1924, vol. II
Thomas, William Herbert Evans, 1886–1979, vol. VII
Thomas, Sir William James, 1st Bt (cr 1919), 1867–1945, vol. IV
Thomas, William Luson, 1830–1900, vol. I
Thomas, William Moy, 1828–1910, vol. I
Thomas, William Norman, 1885–1960, vol. V
Thomas, William R.; see Rees-Thomas.
Thomas, William Stanley Russell, 1896–1957, vol. V
Thomas, William Thelwall, 1865–1927, vol. II
Thomas, Wynford V.; see Vaughan-Thomas, L. J. W.
Thomas-Stanford, Sir Charles, 1st Bt, 1858–1932, vol. III
Thomason, Maj.-Gen. Charles Simson, 1833–1911, vol. I
Thomasson, Lt-Col Franklin, died 1941, vol. IV
Thomasson, John Pennington, died 1904, vol. I

Thomlinson, Lt-Col Sir William, 1854–1943, vol. IV
Thompson, Col Albert George, *died* 1940, vol. III
Thompson, Alexander Hamilton, 1873–1952, vol. V
Thompson, Alexander M., 1861–1948, vol. IV
Thompson, Alfred Corderoy, *died* 1928, vol. II
Thompson, Captain Sir Algar de Clifford Charles M.; *see* Meysey-Thompson.
Thompson, Lt-Gen. Arnold Bunbury, 1822–1917, vol. II
Thompson, Rev. Arthur Charles, 1868–1933, vol. III
Thompson, Arthur Hugh, *died* 1937, vol. III
Thompson, Ven. Arthur Huxley, 1872–1951, vol. V
Thompson, Rev. Arthur Wellington, *died* 1937, vol. III
Thompson, Aubrey Denzil F.; *see* Forsyth-Thompson.
Thompson, Rev. Austin Henry, 1870–1941, vol. IV
Thompson, Brenda, (Mrs Gordon Thompson), 1935–1989, vol. VIII
Thompson, Lt-Col Cecil Henry Farrer, 1882–1975, vol. VII
Thompson, Charles Henry, 1865–1948, vol. IV
Thompson, Charles John S., *died* 1943, vol. IV
Thompson, Charles Paxton, 1911–1985, vol. VIII
Thompson, Comdr Charles Ralfe, 1894–1966, vol. VI
Thompson, Maj.-Gen. Charles William, 1859–1940, vol. III
Thompson, Captain Hon. Claude Henry M.; *see* Meysey-Thompson.
Thompson, Claude Metford, 1855–1933, vol. III
Thompson, Lt-Col Cyril Powney, 1864–1924, vol. II
Thompson, Daniel Varney, 1902–1980, vol. VII
Thompson, Sir D'Arcy Wentworth, 1860–1948, vol. IV
Thompson, Dorothy, 1894–1961, vol. VI
Thompson, Rev. Douglas Weddell, 1903–1981, vol. VIII
Thompson, Mrs E. Roffe; *see* Lejeune, C. A.
Thompson, Lt-Col Edgar Hynes, 1910–1976, vol. VII
Thompson, Edith Marie, *died* 1961, vol. VI
Thompson, Edmund S.; *see* Symes-Thompson.
Thompson, Edward, 1881–1954, vol. V
Thompson, Edward Charles, 1851–1933, vol. III
Thompson, Edward Herbert, 1860–1935, vol. III
Thompson, Edward John, 1886–1946, vol. IV
Thompson, Sir Edward Maunde, 1840–1929, vol. III
Thompson, Edward Raymond, 1872–1928, vol. II
Thompson, Edward Vincent, 1880–1976, vol. VII
Thompson, Sir Edward Walter, 1902–1989, vol. VIII
Thompson, Edwin, 1881–1967, vol. VI
Thompson, Edwin Reginald R.; *see* Roe-Thompson.
Thompson, Eric, 1905–1969, vol. VI
Thompson, Sir Eric; *see* Thompson, Sir J. E. S.
Thompson, Sir Ernest, 1865–1941, vol. IV
Thompson, Ernest Claude M.; *see* Meysey-Thompson.
Thompson, E(rnest) Heber, 1891–1971, vol. VII
Thompson, Estelle Merle O'Brien; *see* Oberon, Merle.
Thompson, Francis, 1859–1907, vol. I
Thompson, Francis L.; *see* Longstreth-Thompson.
Thompson, Frank Charles, 1890–1977, vol. VII
Thompson, Fred, 1884–1949, vol. IV
Thompson, Fred, 1883–1951, vol. V
Thompson, Frederick Charles, *died* 1919, vol. II

Thompson, Brig.-Gen. Frederick Hacket-, 1858–1944, vol. IV
Thompson, Sir Geoffrey Harington, 1898–1967, vol. VI
Thompson, Lt-Gen. Sir Geoffrey Stuart, 1905–1983, vol. VIII
Thompson, Rev. George, *died* 1941, vol. IV
Thompson, George Henry Main, 1882–1957, vol. V
Thompson, Rev. Gerald Alexander, 1868–1939, vol. III
Thompson, Gertrude C.; *see* Caton-Thompson.
Thompson, Gibson, *died* 1917, vol. II
Thompson, Gustav Weber, 1878–1944, vol. IV
Thompson, Captain Harold, 1881–1917, vol. II
Thompson, Sir Harold Warris, 1908–1983, vol. VIII
Thompson, Maj.-Gen. Sir Harry Neville, 1861–1925, vol. II
Thompson, Harry Sydney, 1878–1966, vol. VI
Thompson, Sir Henry, 1st Bt (*cr* 1899), 1820–1904, vol. I
Thompson, Rev. Henry, *died* 1916, vol. II
Thompson, Henry Edmund S.; *see* Symes-Thompson.
Thompson, Sir (Henry Francis) Herbert, 2nd Bt (*cr* 1899), 1859–1944, vol. IV
Thompson, Rt Rev. Henry Gregory, 1871–1942, vol. IV
Thompson, Henry Nilus, *died* 1938, vol. III
Thompson, Rev. (Henry) Percy, 1858–1935, vol. III
Thompson, Henry Yates, 1838–1928, vol. II
Thompson, Herbert, 1856–1945, vol. IV
Thompson, Herbert, 1870–1949, vol. IV
Thompson, Sir Herbert; *see* Thompson, Sir Henry F. H.
Thompson, Sir Herbert; *see* Thompson, Sir J. H.
Thompson, Herbert Marshall, *died* 1945, vol. IV
Thompson, Col Horace Cuthbert Rees, 1893–1975, vol. VII
Thompson, Hubert Charles M.; *see* Meysey-Thompson.
Thompson, Sir Ivan, 1894–1970, vol. VI
Thompson, J. Ashburton, 1846–1915, vol. I
Thompson, Sir James, 1835–1906, vol. I
Thompson, James Coulthred, *died* 1935, vol. III
Thompson, Rt Rev. James Denton, 1856–1924, vol. II
Thompson, Rev. James Matthew, 1878–1956, vol. V
Thompson, Maj.-Gen. John, 1830–1915, vol. I
Thompson, John Baird, 1868–1948, vol. IV
Thompson, John Crighton, 1902–1982, vol. VIII
Thompson, Sir (John) Eric (Sidney), 1898–1975, vol. VII
Thompson, John Fairfield, 1881–1968, vol. VI
Thompson, (John) Kenneth, 1913–1985, vol. VIII
Thompson, John McLean, 1887–1977, vol. VII
Thompson, John Ockelford, 1872–1940, vol. III
Thompson, Sir John Perronet, 1873–1935, vol. III
Thompson, John William Howard, *died* 1959, vol. V
Thompson, Sir (Joseph) Herbert, 1898–1984, vol. VIII
Thompson, Kenneth; *see* Thompson, J. K.
Thompson, Rt Rev. Kenneth George, 1909–1975, vol. VII
Thompson, Sir Kenneth Pugh, 1st Bt, 1909–1984, vol. VIII
Thompson, Sir Lionel; *see* Thompson, Sir Louis L. H.
Thompson, Llewellyn E., 1904–1972, vol. VII

Thompson, Sir (Louis) Lionel (Harry), 1893–1983, vol. VIII

Thompson, Sir Luke, 1867–1941, vol. IV

Thompson, Sir Matthew William, 3rd Bt (cr 1890), 1872–1956, vol. V

Thompson, Maurice, died 1901, vol. I

Thompson, Merrick Arnold Bardsley D.; see Denton-Thompson.

Thompson, Owen, 1868–1958, vol. V

Thompson, Rev. Sir Peile, 2nd Bt (cr 1890), 1844–1918, vol. II

Thompson, Sir Peile, 5th Bt, 1911–1985, vol. VIII

Thompson, Sir Peile Beaumont, 4th Bt (cr 1890), 1874–1972, vol. VII

Thompson, Adm. Percival Henry H.; see Hall-Thompson.

Thompson, Sir Percy, 1872–1946, vol. IV

Thompson, Rev. Percy; see Thompson, Rev. H. P.

Thompson, Peter, 1871–1921, vol. II

Thompson, Piers Gilchrist, 1893–1969, vol. VI

Thompson, Rev. Ralph Wardlaw, died 1916, vol. II

Thompson, Rt Hon. Sir Ralph Wood, 1830–1902, vol. I

Thompson, Reginald Campbell, 1876–1941, vol. IV

Thompson, Reginald Edward, 1834–1912, vol. I

Thompson, Rev. Reginald William, died 1953, vol. V

Thompson, Col Richard, 1852–1932, vol. III

Thompson, Col Richard Frederick M.; see Meysey-Thompson.

Thompson, Lt-Col Richard James Campbell, 1880–1946, vol. IV

Thompson, Maj.-Gen. Richard Lovell Brereton, 1874–1957, vol. V

Thompson, Rt Hon. Robert, 1839–1918, vol. II

Thompson, Robert Cyril, 1907–1967, vol. VI

Thompson, Sir Robert James, 1845–1926, vol. II

Thompson, Robert John, 1867–1951, vol. V

Thompson, Sir Robert Norman, 1878–1951, vol. V

Thompson, Lt-Col Roland-Wycliffe, 1864–1940, vol. III

Thompson, Lt-Col Rt Hon. S. H. H.; see Hall-Thompson.

Thompson, Samuel Nock, 1851–1938, vol. III

Thompson, Silvanus Phillips, 1851–1916, vol. II

Thompson, Major Stephen John, 1875–1955, vol. V

Thompson, Sylvia, (Mrs Peter Luling), 1902–1968, vol. VI

Thompson, Theodore, 1878–1935, vol. III

Thompson, Hon. Thomas, vol. II

Thompson, Sir Thomas Raikes, 3rd Bt (cr 1806), 1852–1904, vol. I

Thompson, Lt-Col Sir Thomas Raikes Lovett, 4th Bt (cr 1806), 1881–1964, vol. VI

Thompson, Maj.-Gen. Sir Treffry Owen, 1888–1979, vol. VII

Thompson, Viginti Tertius, 1862–1946, vol. IV

Thompson, Sir Walter, 1875–1951, vol. V

Thompson, Walter Scott, 1885–1966, vol. VI

Thompson, Rev. William, died 1909, vol. I

Thompson, Brig.-Gen. William Arthur Murray, 1866–1938, vol. III

Thompson, William David James C.; see Cargill Thompson.

Thompson, William George, 1863–1953, vol. V

Thompson, Brig.-Gen. William George Hemsley, 1871–1944, vol. IV

Thompson, William Harding, 1887–1946, vol. IV

Thompson, Sir William Henry, died 1918, vol. II

Thompson, William Hugh, 1885–1966, vol. VI

Thompson, Rt Rev. William Jameson, 1885–1975, vol. VII

Thompson, Sir William John, 1861–1929, vol. III

Thompson, William John, 1871–1959, vol. V

Thompson, William John, died 1971, vol. VII

Thompson, William Marcus, 1857–1907, vol. I

Thompson, Lt-Col William Maxwell, 1869–1934, vol. III

Thompson, Col William Oliver, 1844–1917, vol. II

Thompson, William Robin, 1887–1972, vol. VII

Thompson, William Whitaker, 1857–1920, vol. II

Thompson-McCausland, Lucius Perronet, 1904–1984, vol. VIII

Thompstone, Sir Eric Westbury, 1897–1974, vol. VII

Thompstone, Sydney Wilson, 1863–1935, vol. III

Thoms, Lt-Col Nathaniel William Benjamin Butler, 1880–1957, vol. V

Thomson, 1st Baron, 1875–1930, vol. III

Thomson, Hon. Lord; Alexander Thomson, 1914–1979, vol. VII

Thomson, Rt Hon. Lord; George Reid Thomson, 1893–1962, vol. VI

Thomson of Fleet, 1st Baron, 1894–1976, vol. VII

Thomson, Ada; see Merchant, Vivien.

Thomson, A(dam) Bruce, 1885–1976, vol. VII

Thomson, Addison Yalden, 1863–1931, vol. III

Thomson, Brig. Alan Fortescue, 1880–1957, vol. V

Thomson, Engr Captain Alan Leslie, 1890–1970, vol. VI

Thomson, Alexander; see Thomson, Hon. Lord.

Thomson, Lt-Col Alexander Guthrie, 1873–1953, vol. V

Thomson, Col Alexander M.; see Milne-Thomson.

Thomson, Hon. Alexander Macdonald, 1863–1924, vol. II

Thomson, Alexander Stuart Duff, 1854–1927, vol. II

Thomson, Alfred Reginald, died 1979, vol. VII

Thomson, Rev. Andrew, 1814–1901, vol. I

Thomson, Brig.-Gen. Andrew Graham, 1858–1926, vol. II

Thomson, Captain Anthony Standidge, 1851–1925, vol. II

Thomson, Arthur, 1858–1935, vol. III

Thomson, Sir Arthur; see Thomson, Sir J. A.

Thomson, Sir (Arthur) Landsborough, 1890–1977, vol. VII

Thomson, Sir Arthur Peregrine, 1890–1977, vol. VII

Thomson, Sir Basil Home, 1861–1939, vol. III

Thomson, Benjamin, died 1934, vol. III

Thomson, César, 1856–1931, vol. III

Thomson, Rev. Canon Clement R., 1870–1953, vol. V

Thomson, Sir Daniel, 1912–1976, vol. VII

Thomson, David, 1912–1970, vol. VI

Thomson, David Alexander, 1872–1922, vol. II

Thomson, David Couper, 1861–1954, vol. V

Thomson, David Croal, 1855–1930, vol. III

Thomson, Lt-Col David George, 1856–1923, vol. II

Thomson, David Landsborough, 1901–1964, vol. VI

Thomson, Donald F., 1901–1970, vol. VI (AII)

Thomson, Sir Douglas; *see* Thomson, Sir J. D. W.
Thomson, Hon. Dugald, 1848–1922, vol. II
Thomson, Edward William, 1849–1924, vol. II
Thomson, Elihu, 1853–1937, vol. III
Thomson, Eric Hugh, 1909–1973, vol. VII
Thomson, Vice-Adm. Evelyn Claude Ogilvie, 1884–1941, vol. IV
Thomson, Ewen Cameron, 1915–1988, vol. VIII
Thomson, Rt Rev. Francis, 1917–1987, vol. VIII
Thomson, Sir (Francis) Vernon, 1st Bt (*cr* 1938), 1881–1953, vol. V
Thomson, Frank David, 1877–1934, vol. III
Thomson, Sir Frederick Charles, 1st Bt (*cr* 1929), 1875–1935, vol. III
Thomson, Sir Frederick Whitley W.; *see* Whitley-Thomson.
Thomson, Surg.-Col Sir George, 1843–1903, vol. I
Thomson, George, *died* 1939, vol. III
Thomson, Major George, 1889–1970, vol. VI
Thomson, George Derwent, 1903–1987, vol. VIII
Thomson, George Ewart, 1897–1981, vol. VIII
Thomson, Rev. George Ian Falconer, 1912–1987, vol. VIII
Thomson, George Malcolm, 1848–1933, vol. III
Thomson, Sir George Paget, 1892–1975, vol. VII
Thomson, Rear-Adm. Sir George Pirie, 1887–1965, vol. VI
Thomson, Rt Hon. George Reid; *see* Thomson, Rt Hon. Lord.
Thomson, Lt-Col George Ritchie, *died* 1946, vol. IV
Thomson, Rev. George Thomas, 1887–1958, vol. V
Thomson, George Walker, 1883–1949, vol. IV
Thomson, George William, 1845–1928, vol. II
Thomson, Gladys S.; *see* Scott Thomson.
Thomson, Sir Godfrey Hilton, 1881–1955, vol. V
Thomson, Sir Graeme, 1875–1933, vol. III
Thomson, Harry Redmond, 1860–1917, vol. II
Thomson, Harry Torrance, 1868–1944, vol. IV
Thomson, Henry, 1840–1916, vol. II
Thomson, Maj.-Gen. Henry, 1851–1932, vol. III
Thomson, Henry Alexis, 1863–1924, vol. II
Thomson, Henry John, *died* 1966, vol. VI
Thomson, Henry Wagstaffe, 1874–1941, vol. IV
Thomson, Herbert Campbell, 1870–1940, vol. III
Thomson, Hugh, 1860–1920, vol. II
Thomson, Col Sir Hugh Davie W.; *see* White-Thomson.
Thomson, Maj.-Gen. Hugh Gordon, 1830–1910, vol. I
Thomson, Sir James, 1848–1929, vol. III
Thomson, Maj.-Gen. James, 1862–1953, vol. V
Thomson, James, 1895–1959, vol. V
Thomson, James Alexander Kerr, 1879–1959, vol. V
Thomson, Tun Sir James Beveridge, 1902–1983, vol. VIII
Thomson, Sir (James) Douglas (Wishart), 2nd Bt (*cr* 1929), 1905–1972, vol. VII
Thomson, James Frederick Gordon; *see* Hon. Lord Migdale.
Thomson, James Moffat, *died* 1953, vol. V
Thomson, Maj.-Gen. James Noel, 1888–1978, vol. VII
Thomson, James Oliver, 1889–1971, vol. VII
Thomson, James Park, 1854–1941, vol. IV

Thomson, Very Rev. James Sutherland, 1892–1972, vol. VII
Thomson, Lt-Col Sir James Wishart, 1871–1929, vol. III
Thomson, Captain Jocelyn Home, 1859–1908, vol. I
Thomson, John, 1856–1926, vol. II
Thomson, John, 1903–1974, vol. VII
Thomson, John A.; *see* Anstruther-Thomson.
Thomson, Sir (John) Arthur, 1861–1933, vol. III
Thomson, John Ebenezer Honeyman, 1841–1923, vol. II
Thomson, Lt-Col John Ferguson, 1880–1937, vol. III
Thomson, John Gordon, *died* 1937, vol. III
Thomson, Sir John Mackay, 1887–1974, vol. VII
Thomson, John Millar, 1849–1933, vol. III
Thomson, J(ohn) Murray, 1885–1974, vol. VII
Thomson, John Stuart, 1888–1973, vol. VII
Thomson, Sir Joseph John, 1856–1940, vol. III
Thomson, Sir Landsborough; *see* Thomson, Sir A. L.
Thomson, Rt Rev. Leonard Jauncey W.; *see* White-Thomson.
Thomson, Leslie, *died* 1929, vol. III
Thomson, Louis Melville M.; *see* Milne-Thomson.
Thomson, Mark Alméras, 1903–1962, vol. VI
Thomson, (Matthew) Sydney, 1894–1969, vol. VI
Thomson, Sir Mitchell M.; *see* Mitchell-Thomson.
Thomson, Gen. Sir Mowbray, 1832–1917, vol. II
Thomson, Brig.-Gen. Noel Arbuthnot, 1872–1959, vol. V
Thomson, Very Rev. P. D., 1872–1955, vol. V
Thomson, Col Sir Robert Thomas W.; *see* White-Thomson.
Thomson, Col Roger Gordon, 1878–1976, vol. VII
Thomson, Air Vice-Marshal Ronald Bain, 1912–1984, vol. VIII
Thomson, Sir Ronald Jordan, 1895–1978, vol. VII
Thomson, Roy Harry Goodisson, 1891–1974, vol. VII
Thomson, Sir St Clair, 1859–1943, vol. IV
Thomson, Col Samuel John, 1853–1936, vol. III
Thomson, Sydney; *see* Thomson, M. S.
Thomson, Theodore, 1857–1916, vol. II
Thomson, Rev. T(homas) B(entley) Stewart, 1889–1973, vol. VII
Thomson, Thomas Davidson, 1911–1989, vol. VIII
Thomson, Trevelyan, 1875–1928, vol. II
Thomson, Sir Vernon; *see* Thomson, Sir F. V.
Thomson, Walter Henry, 1856–1917, vol. II
Thomson, Sir Wilfrid Forbes Home, 1st Bt (*cr* 1925), 1858–1939, vol. III
Thomson, Sir William, 1843–1910, vol. I
Thomson, Sir William, 1856–1947, vol. IV
Thomson, Sir William, 1916–1971, vol. VII
Thomson, Sir William Brown, 1863–1937, vol. III
Thomson, William Archibald Robson, 1906–1983, vol. VIII
Thomson, Col William David, 1858–1941, vol. IV
Thomson, Sir William Gardner, 1874–1938, vol. III
Thomson, Sir William Johnston, 1881–1949, vol. IV
Thomson, Lt-Gen. Sir William Montgomerie, 1877–1963, vol. VI
Thomson, Sir William R.; *see* Rowan-Thomson.
Thomson, Sir William Willis Dalziel, *died* 1950, vol. IV

Thomson-Walker, Sir John William, *died* 1937, vol. III

Thorburn, Archibald, 1860–1935, vol. III

Thorburn, Col Harold Hay, 1882–1937, vol. III

Thorburn, J. Hay, 1848–1931, vol. III

Thorburn, James Jamieson, 1864–1929, vol. III

Thorburn, Sir Michael Grieve, 1851–1934, vol. III

Thorburn, Hon. Sir Robert, 1836–1906, vol. I

Thorburn, Septimus Smet, 1844–1924, vol. II

Thorburn, Thomas, *died* 1927, vol. II

Thorburn, Rev. Thomas James, 1858–1923, vol. II

Thorburn, Sir Walter, 1842–1908, vol. I

Thorburn, Sir William, *died* 1923, vol. II

Thorburn, Lt-Col William, 1881–1959, vol. V

Thorby, Hon. Harold Victor Campbell, 1888–1973, vol. VII

Thorley, George Earlam, 1830–1904, vol. I

Thorley, Sir Gerald Bowers, 1913–1988, vol. VIII

Thorley, Wilfrid, 1878–1963, vol. VI

Thorman, Rt Rev. Joseph, 1871–1936, vol. III

Thorn, Sir Jules, 1899–1980, vol. VII

Thorn-Drury, George; *see* Drury.

Thorndike, Dame (Agnes) Sybil, 1882–1976, vol. VII

Thorndike, (Arthur) Russell, 1885–1972, vol. VII

Thorndike, Russell; *see* Thorndike, A. R.

Thorndike, Dame Sibyl; *see* Thorndike, Dame A. S.

Thorne, Alfred Charles, 1870–1952, vol. V

Thorne, Gen. Sir Andrew; *see* Thorne, Gen. Sir A. F. A. N.

Thorne, Atwood, 1867–1932, vol. III

Thorne, Gen. Sir (Augustus Francis) Andrew (Nicol), 1885–1970, vol. VI

Thorne, Charles, *died* 1933, vol. III

Thorne, Edward Henry, 1834–1916, vol. II

Thorne, Rt Rev. Frank Oswald, 1892–1981, vol. VIII

Thorne, George Rennie, 1853–1934, vol. III

Thorne, Gordon, 1912–1965, vol. VI

Thorne, Guy; *see* Gull, Cyril Arthur Edward Ranger.

Thorne, Sir John Anderson, 1888–1964, vol. VI

Thorne, Sir Richard Thorne, 1841–1899, vol. I

Thorne, Air Vice-Marshal Walter, 1890–1960, vol. V

Thorne, Rt Hon. Will; *see* Thorne, Rt Hon. W. J.

Thorne, Sir William, 1839–1917, vol. II

Thorne, Sir William Calthrop, 1864–1935, vol. III

Thorne, William Hobart Houghton, 1875–1931, vol. III

Thorne, William Huxtable, 1882–1951, vol. V

Thorne, Rt Hon. William James, (Will), 1857–1946, vol. IV

Thorne-Waite, Robert, 1842–1935, vol. III

Thorneloe, Most Rev. George, 1848–1935, vol. III

Thornely, Sir Arnold, 1870–1953, vol. V

Thornely, P. Wilfrid, 1879–1926, vol. II

Thornely, Thomas, 1855–1949, vol. IV

Thorneycroft, Maj.-Gen. Alexander Whitelaw, 1859–1931, vol. III

Thorneycroft, Major George Edward Mervyn, 1883–1943, vol. IV

Thorneycroft, Harry, 1892–1956, vol. V

Thorneycroft, Thomas Hamo, *died* 1970, vol. VI

Thorneycroft, Wallace, 1864–1954, vol. V

Thornhill, Sir Anthony John Compton-, 2nd Bt, 1868–1949, vol. IV

Thornhill, Arthur Horace, 1895–1970, vol. VI

Thornhill, Arthur John, 1850–1930, vol. III

Thornhill, Col Cudbert John Massy, 1883–1952, vol. V

Thornhill, George, *died* 1908, vol. I

Thornhill, Col George B.; *see* Badham-Thornhill.

Thornhill, Lt-Col Sir Henry Beaufoy, 1854–1942, vol. IV

Thornhill, Noel, 1881–1955, vol. V

Thornhill, Dame Rachel; *see* Crowdy, Dame R. E.

Thornhill, Sir Thomas, 1st Bt, 1837–1900, vol. I

Thornhill, Thomas Bryan C.; *see* Clarke-Thornhill.

Thornley, Sir Colin Hardwick, 1907–1983, vol. VIII

Thornley, Sir Hubert Gordon, 1884–1962, vol. VI

Thornley, Reginald Ernest, 1872–1942, vol. IV

Thornley, Major Samuel Kerr, 1871–1947, vol. IV

Thornton, Alfred Henry Robinson, 1863–1939, vol. III

Thornton, Lt-Col Arthur Parry, 1848–1909, vol. I

Thornton, Rev. Augustus Vansittart, 1851–1913, vol. I

Thornton, Lt-Col Charles Edward, 1867–1946, vol. IV

Thornton, Charles Inglis, 1850–1929, vol. III

Thornton, (Clara) Grace, 1913–1987, vol. VIII

Thornton, Ven Claude Cyprian, *died* 1939, vol. III

Thornton, Edna, *died* 1964, vol. VI

Thornton, Rt Hon. Sir Edward, 1817–1906, vol. I

Thornton, Brig. Sir Edward Newbury, 1878–1946, vol. IV

Thornton, Sir Ernest Hugh, 1884–1951, vol. V

Thornton, Rev. Frederick Ferdinand Martin S., *died* 1938, vol. III

Thornton, George Edwin, 1899–1983, vol. VIII

Thornton, George Lestock, 1872–1951, vol. V

Thornton, Rev. George Ruthven, 1882–1964, vol. VI

Thornton, Sir Gerard; *see* Thornton, Sir H. G.

Thornton, Grace; *see* Thornton, C. G.

Thornton, Sir (Henry) Gerard, 1892–1977, vol. VII

Thornton, Air Vice-Marshal Henry Norman, 1896–1971, vol. VII

Thornton, Sir Henry Worth, 1871–1933, vol. III

Thornton, Rev. Herbert Parry, *died* 1923, vol. II

Thornton, Hugh Aylmer, 1872–1962, vol. VI

Thornton, Sir Hugh Cholmondeley, 1881–1962, vol. VI

Thornton, James Cholmondeley, 1906–1969, vol. VI

Thornton, Sir James Howard, 1834–1919, vol. II

Thornton, Col Leslie Heber, 1873–1937, vol. III

Thornton, Rev. Lionel Spencer, 1884–1960, vol. V

Thornton, Maxwell Ruthven, 1878–1950, vol. IV

Thornton, Michael James, 1919–1989, vol. VIII

Thornton, Percy Melville, 1841–1918, vol. II

Thornton, R. M., 1841–1913, vol. I

Thornton, Major Robert Lawrence, 1865–1947, vol. IV

Thornton, Hon. Robert Stirton, 1863–1936, vol. III

Thornton, Major Roland Hobhouse, 1892–1967, vol. VI

Thornton, Sir Ronald George, 1901–1981, vol. VIII

Thornton, Russel William, 1881–1966, vol. VI

Thornton, Rt Rev. Samuel, 1835–1917, vol. II

Thornton, Rev. Stephen Augustine Lawrence, 1871–1936, vol. III

Thornton, Swinford Leslie, 1853–1939, vol. III

Thornton, Sir Thomas, 1829–1903, vol. I
Thornton, Col Thomas Anson, 1887–1978, vol. VII
Thornton, Thomas Henry, 1832–1913, vol. I
Thornton, William Mundell, 1870–1944, vol. IV
Thornton-Berry, Trevor, 1895–1967, vol. VI
Thornton Cook, Elsie; see Cook.
Thornton-Duesbury, Rt Rev. Charles Leonard, 1867–1928, vol. II
Thornton-Duesbery, Rev. Canon Julian Percy, 1902–1985, vol. VIII
Thornton-Kemsley, Col Sir Colin Norman, 1903–1977, vol. VII
Thornton-Smith, Ernest T., 1881–1971, vol. VII
Thornycroft, Lt-Col Charles Mytton, 1879–1948, vol. IV
Thornycroft, Sir Hamo; see Thornycroft, Sir W. H.
Thornycroft, Sir John Edward, 1872–1960, vol. V
Thornycroft, Sir John Isaac, 1843–1928, vol. II
Thornycroft, John Ward, 1899–1989, vol. VIII
Thornycroft, Oliver, 1885–1956, vol. V
Thornycroft, Sir (William) Hamo, 1850–1925, vol. II
Thoroddsen, Thorvald, 1855–1921, vol. II
Thorogood, Horace Walter, died 1962, vol. VI
Thorogood, Stanley, 1873–1953, vol. V
Thorold, Algar Labouchere, 1866–1936, vol. III
Thorold, Rev. Ernest Hayford, 1879–1940, vol. III
Thorold, Sir Guy Frederick, 1898–1970, vol. VI
Thorold, Col Hayford Douglas, 1859–1934, vol. III
Thorold, Air Vice-Marshal Henry Karslake, 1896–1966, vol. VI
Thorold, Sir James Ernest, 14th Bt, 1877–1965, vol. VI
Thorold, Sir John George, 13th Bt, 1870–1951, vol. V
Thorold, Sir John Henry, 12th Bt, 1842–1922, vol. II
Thorold, Montague George, 1844–1920, vol. II
Thorold, William James, 1871–1942, vol. IV (A), vol. V
Thorold, Lt-Col Charles Julian, 1875–1939, vol. III
Thorp, Lt-Col Arthur Hugh, 1869–1955, vol. V
Thorp, Austin, 1873–1918, vol. II
Thorp, Adm. Charles Frederick, 1869–1954, vol. V
Thorp, Col Herbert Walter Beck, 1879–1934, vol. III
Thorp, J. Walter H., 1851–1912, vol. I
Thorp, Sir John Kingsmill Robert, 1912–1961, vol. VI
Thorp, Joseph Peter, 1873–1962, vol. VI
Thorp, Linton Theodore, 1884–1950, vol. IV
Thorp, Brig. Robert Allen Fenwick, 1900–1966, vol. VI
Thorp, William Henry, 1852–1944, vol. IV
Thorpe, A(rthur) Winton, 1865–1952, vol. V
Thorpe, Bernard, 1895–1987, vol. VIII
Thorpe, Sir Edward; see Thorpe, Sir T. E.
Thorpe, Brig.-Gen. Edward Ivan de Sausmarez, 1871–1942, vol. IV
Thorpe, Frank Gordon, 1885–1967, vol. VI
Thorpe, Col Sir Fred Garner, 1893–1970, vol. VI
Thorpe, Maj.-Gen. Gervase, 1877–1962, vol. VI
Thorpe, Harry, 1913–1977, vol. VII
Thorpe, James, 1876–1949, vol. IV
Thorpe, Sir Jocelyn Field, 1872–1940, vol. III
Thorpe, John Henry, 1887–1944, vol. IV
Thorpe, Ven. John Henry, died 1932, vol. III
Thorpe, Lewis Guy Melville, 1913–1977, vol. VII

Thorpe, Sir (Thomas) Edward, 1845–1925, vol. II
Thorpe, Surg. Rear-Adm. Vidal Gunson, 1864–1948, vol. IV
Thorpe, William Geoffrey, 1909–1975, vol. VII
Thorpe, William Homan, 1902–1986, vol. VIII
Thorson, Hon. Joseph T., 1889–1978, vol. VII
Thorvaldson, Gunnar S., 1901–1969, vol. VI
Thorvardsson, Stefan, 1900–1951, vol. V
Thoseby, William Martin, 1901–1959, vol. V
Thouless, Robert Henry, 1894–1984, vol. VIII
Threipland, Col William M.; see Murray-Threipland.
Threlfall, Sir Richard, 1861–1932, vol. III
Threlfall, Thomas, 1842–1907, vol. I
Threlford, Sir William Lacon, 1883–1958, vol. V
Thresh, John Clough, 1850–1932, vol. III
Thresher, Lt-Col James Henville, 1870–1943, vol. IV
Thrift, Sir John Edward, 1845–1926, vol. II
Thrift, William Edward, 1870–1942, vol. IV
Thring, 1st Baron, 1818–1907, vol. I
Thring, Sir Arthur Theodore, 1860–1932, vol. III
Thring, Captain Ernest Walsham Charles, 1875–1970, vol. VI
Thring, George Herbert, 1859–1941, vol. IV
Thring, Captain Walter Hugh Charles Samuel, 1873–1949, vol. IV
Throckmorton, Geoffrey William Berkeley, 1883–1976, vol. VII
Throckmorton, Sir Nicholas William George, 9th Bt, 1838–1919, vol. II
Throckmorton, Sir Richard Charles Acton, 10th Bt, 1839–1927, vol. II
Throckmorton, Sir Robert George Maxwell, 11th Bt, 1908–1989, vol. VIII
Throssell, Arthur Graham, 1881–1942, vol. IV
Throssell, Hon. George, 1840–1910, vol. I
Throssell, Hugo Vivian Hope, 1884–1933, vol. III
Thrower, Frank James, 1932–1987, vol. VIII
Thrower, Percy John, 1913–1988, vol. VIII
Thubron, John Brown Sydney, 1879–1949, vol. IV
Thuillier, Sir Henry Edward Landor, 1813–1906, vol. I
Thuillier, Maj.-Gen. Sir Henry Fleetwood, 1868–1953, vol. V
Thuillier, Sir Henry Ravenshaw, 1838–1922, vol. II
Thuillier, Lt-Col Henry Shakespear, 1895–1982, vol. VIII
Thuillier, Brig.-Gen. Willoughby, 1860–1941, vol. IV
Thulrai, Taluqdar of, 1865–1920, vol. II, vol. III
Thumboo Chetty, Amatyasiromani Sir Bernard T., 1877–1952, vol. V (A), vol. VI (AI)
Thunder, Lt-Col Stuart Harman Joseph, 1879–1948, vol. IV
Thurber, James Grover, 1894–1961, vol. VI
Thurburn, Edward Alexander, 1841–1915, vol. I
Thurburn, Col James White, 1848–1930, vol. III
Thurburn, Brig. Roy Gilbert, 1901–1990, vol. VIII
Thureau-Dangin, François, 1872–1944, vol. IV
Thureau-Dangin, Paul Marie Pierre, 1837–1913, vol. I
Thurles, Viscount; James Anthony Butler, 1916–1940, vol. III
Thurlow, 5th Baron, 1838–1916, vol. II
Thurlow, 6th Baron, 1869–1952, vol. V
Thurlow, 7th Baron, 1910–1971, vol. VII
Thurnam, Walter Digby, 1854–1934, vol. III

Thurnheer, Walter, 1884–1945, vol. IV
Thursby, Adm. Sir Cecil Fiennes, 1861–1936, vol. III
Thursby, Sir George James, 3rd Bt, 1869–1941, vol. IV
Thursby, Sir John Hardy, 1st Bt, 1826–1901, vol. I
Thursby, Sir John Ormerod Scarlett, 2nd Bt, 1861–1920, vol. II
Thursby-Pelham, James, 1869–1947, vol. IV
Thursfield, (Edward) Philip, 1876–1962, vol. VI
Thursfield, Rear-Adm. Henry George, 1882–1963, vol. VI
Thursfield, Hugh, died 1944, vol. IV
Thursfield, Sir James Richard, 1840–1923, vol. II
Thursfield, Philip; see Thursfield, E. P.
Thursfield, Captain (S) Raymond Spencer, 1882–1953, vol. V
Thurso, 1st Viscount, 1890–1970, vol. VI
Thurstan, Edward William Paget, 1880–1947, vol. IV
Thurstan, Violetta, died 1978, vol. VII
Thurston, Albert Peter, 1881–1964, vol. VI
Thurston, E. Temple, 1879–1933, vol. III
Thurston, Edgar, 1855–1935, vol. III
Thurston, Frederick John, 1901–1953, vol. V
Thurston, Gavin Leonard Bourdas, 1911–1980, vol. VII
Thurston, Sir George; see Thurston, Sir T. G. O.
Thurston, Rev. Herbert, 1856–1939, vol. III
Thurston, Col Hugh Champneys, 1862–1919, vol. II
Thurston, Col Hugh Stanley, 1869–1945, vol. IV
Thurston, Katherine Cecil, 1875–1911, vol. I
Thurston, Sir (T.) George (O.), died 1950, vol. IV
Thurtle, Ernest, 1884–1954, vol. V
Thwaite, Hartley, 1903–1978, vol. VII
Thwaites, Brian St George, 1912–1989, vol. VIII
Thwaites, Lt-Col Norman Graham, 1872–1956, vol. V
Thwaites, Gen. Sir William, 1868–1947, vol. IV
Thwing, Charles Franklin, 1853–1937, vol. III
Thyateira, Archbishop of; see Athenagoras, Archbishop.
Thyne, William, 1901–1978, vol. VII
Thynne, Lord Alexander George, 1873–1918, vol. II
Thynne, Major Algernon Carteret, 1868–1917, vol. II
Thynne, Col Hon. Andrew Joseph, 1847–1927, vol. II
Thynne, Rev. Arthur Barugh, 1840–1917, vol. II
Thynne, Rev. Arthur Christopher, 1832–1908, vol. II
Thynne, Captain Denis Granville, 1875–1955, vol. V
Thynne, Francis John, 1830–1910, vol. I
Thynne, Sir Henry, 1839–1915, vol. I
Thynne, Rt Hon. Lord Henry Frederick, 1832–1904, vol. I
Thynne, Maj.-Gen. Sir Reginald Thomas, 1843–1926, vol. II
Thynne, Col Ulric Oliver, 1871–1957, vol. V
Tiarks, Frank Cyril, 1874–1952, vol. V
Tiarks, Rt Rev. Geoffrey Lewis, 1909–1987, vol. VIII
Tiarks, Rt Rev. John Gerhard, 1903–1974, vol. VII
Tibbits, Vice-Adm. Charles, 1872–1947, vol. IV
Tibbits, Charles John, 1861–1935, vol. III
Tibbits, Sir Cliff; see Tibbits, Sir J. C.
Tibbits, Sir (Jabez) Cliff, 1884–1974, vol. VII
Tibble, John William, 1901–1972, vol. VII
Tibbles, Sydney Granville, 1884–1960, vol. V
Tibbles, William, 1859–1928, vol. II

Tichborne, Sir Anthony Joseph Henry Doughty Doughty-, 14th Bt, 1914–1968, vol. VI
Tichborne, Charles Robert, died 1905, vol. I
Tichborne, Rt Rev. Ford, died 1940, vol. III
Tichborne, Sir Henry Alfred Joseph Doughty-, 12th Bt, 1866–1910, vol. I
Tichborne, Sir Joseph Henry Bernard Doughty-, 13th Bt, 1890–1930, vol. III
Tickell, Lt-Col Edward James, 1861–1942, vol. IV
Tickell, Maj.-Gen. Sir Eustace Francis, 1893–1972, vol. VII
Tickell, Rear-Adm. Frederick, 1857–1919, vol. II
Tickell, Richard Hugh, died 1948, vol. IV
Tickle, Ernest William, 1882–1947, vol. IV
Tickler, Thomas George, 1852–1938, vol. III
Tidbury-Beer, Sir Frederick Tidbury, 1892–1959, vol. V
Tiddeman, Lizzie Ellen, died 1937, vol. III
Tidswell, Brig.-Gen. Edward Cecil, 1862–1937, vol. III
Tidy, Sir Henry Letheby, 1877–1960, vol. V
Tiegs, Oscar Werner, 1897–1956, vol. V
Tierney, Michael, 1894–1975, vol. VII
Tiffany, Stanley, 1908–1971, vol. VII
Tiffin, Arthur Ernest, 1896–1955, vol. V
Tigar, Edward, 1851–1937, vol. III
Tighe, Maj.-Gen. Anthony; see Tighe, Maj.-Gen. P. A. M.
Tighe, Edward Kenrick Banbury, 1862–1917, vol. II
Tighe, Henry, (Harry), 1877–1946, vol. IV
Tighe, Lt-Gen. Sir Michael Joseph, 1864–1925, vol. II
Tighe, Maj.-Gen. Patrick Anthony Macartan, 1923–1989, vol. VIII
Tighe, Thomas, 1829–1914, vol. I
Tighe, Major Vincent John, 1865–1919, vol. II
Tighe, Rear-Adm. Wilfred Geoffrey Stuart, 1905–1975, vol. VII
Tilbe, Douglas Sidney, 1931–1984, vol. VIII
Tilby, A. Wyatt, 1880–1948, vol. IV
Tilden, Philip Armstrong, 1887–1956, vol. V
Tilden, Sir William Augustus, 1842–1926, vol. II
Tilden, William Tatem, 1893–1953, vol. V
Tilea, Viorel Virgil, 1896–1972, vol. VII
Tillard, Col Arthur Basil, 1870–1938, vol. III
Tillard, Rear-Adm. Sir Aubrey Thomas, 1881–1952, vol. V
Tillard, Maj.-Gen. John Arthur, 1837–1928, vol. II
Tillard, Adm. Philip Francis, 1852–1933, vol. III
Tillett, Benjamin, 1860–1943, vol. IV
Tillett, Emmie Muriel, 1896–1982, vol. VIII
Tillett, John Varnell, 1868–1931, vol. III
Tillett, Louis John, 1865–1929, vol. III
Tilley, Arthur Augustus, 1851–1942, vol. IV
Tilley, Cecil Edgar, 1894–1973, vol. VII
Tilley, Sir George, 1866–1948, vol. IV
Tilley, George Reginald Louis, 1904–1963, vol. VI
Tilley, Herbert, died 1941, vol. IV
Tilley, Sir John, 1813–1898, vol. I
Tilley, Rt Hon. Sir John Anthony Cecil, 1869–1952, vol. V
Tilley, Leonard Percy De Wolfe, 1870–1947, vol. IV
Tilley, Vesta, (Lady de Frece; Matilda Alice), 1864–1952, vol. V

719

Tillich, Paul, 1886–1965, vol. VI
Tillie, Lt-Col William Kingsley, *died* 1939, vol. III
Tilling, Richard Stephen, 1851–1929, vol. III
Tillotson, Geoffrey, 1905–1969, vol. VI
Tilly, Maj.-Gen. Justice Crosland, 1888–1941, vol. IV
Tillyard, Eustace Mandeville Wetenhall, 1889–1962, vol. VI
Tillyard, Sir Frank, 1865–1961, vol. VI
Tillyard, Henry Julius Wetenhall, 1881–1968, vol. VI
Tillyard, Robin John, 1881–1937, vol. III
Tilman, Harold William, 1898–1977/8, vol. VII
Tilmouth, Michael, 1930–1987, vol. VIII
Tilney, Frederick Colin, 1870–1951, vol. V
Tilney, John Deane, 1841–1909, vol. I
Tilney, Lt-Col Norman Eccles, 1872–1950, vol. IV
Tilney, Brig. Robert Adolphus George, 1903–1981, vol. VIII
Tilsley, Frank, 1904–1957, vol. V
Tiltman, H(ugh) Hessell, 1897–1976, vol. VII
Tiltman, Brig. John Hessell, 1894–1982, vol. VIII
Timbury, Gerald Charles, 1929–1985, vol. VIII
Timins, Rev. Francis Charles, 1866–1941, vol. IV
Timmins, Samuel, *died* 1903, vol. I
Timmis, Col Reginald Symonds, 1884–1968, vol. VI
Timmis, Shirley Sutton, 1875–1957, vol. V
Timoshenko, Marshal Semyon Konstantinovich, 1895–1970, vol. VI
Timoshenko, Stephen, 1878–1972, vol. VII
Timpson, Sir John, 1863–1937, vol. III
Tims, Henry William Marett, 1863–1954, vol. V
Tims, Ven. John William, 1857–1945, vol. IV
Tinayre, Marcelle; *see* Tinayre, M. S. M.
Tinayre, (Marguerite Suzanne) Marcelle, *died* 1948, vol. IV
Tinbergen, Nikolaas, 1907–1988, vol. VIII
Tindal, Rev. William Strang, 1899–1965, vol. VI
Tindal-Carill-Worsley, Philip Ernest, 1881–1946, vol. IV
Tindall, Albert Alfred, 1840–1931, vol. III
Tindall, Benjamin Arthur, *died* 1963, vol. VI
Tindall, Christian, 1878–1951, vol. V
Tindall, Rt Rev. Gordon Leslie, *died* 1969, vol. VI
Tindall, Rev. Peter Francis, *died* 1931, vol. III
Tindall, William Edwin, 1863–1938, vol. III
Tindaro, Count del; *see* Rampolla, Cardinal Mariano.
Tingley, Katherine, 1852–1929, vol. III
Tinker, Brian, 1892–1977, vol. VII
Tinker, Chauncey Brewster, 1876–1963, vol. VI
Tinker, John Joseph, 1875–1957, vol. V
Tinkler, Charles Kenneth, 1881–1951, vol. V
Tinley, Col Gervase Francis Newport, 1857–1918, vol. II
Tinling, Rev. Edward Douglas, *died* 1898, vol. I
Tinne, John Abraham, 1877–1933, vol. III
Tinsley, Captain Richard Bolton, 1875–1944, vol. IV
Tinton, Major Ben Thomas, 1897–1966, vol. VI
Tinworth, George, 1843–1913, vol. I
Tipperah, Hill, Raja of, 1857–1909, vol. I
Tippet, Captain Arthur Grendon, 1885–1943, vol. IV
Tippetts, Sydney Atterbury, 1878–1946, vol. IV
Tipping, Col Robert Francis G.; *see* Gartside-Tipping.

Tippinge, Captain Leicester Francis Gartside, 1855–1938, vol. III
Tirard, Sir Nestor Isidore Charles, 1853–1928, vol. II
Tirebuck, William Edwards, *died* 1900, vol. I
Tireman, Henry Stainton, 1871–1951, vol. V
Tirikatene, Sir Eruera Tihema, 1895–1967, vol. VI
Tisdale, Lt-Col Hon. David, 1835–1913, vol. I
Tisdall, Col Arthur Lance, 1860–1927, vol. II
Tisdall, Rev. William St Clair, 1859–1928, vol. II
Tiselius, Arne Wilhelm Kaurin, 1902–1971, vol. VII
Tisserant, His Eminence Cardinal Eugène, 1884–1972, vol. VII
Titchmarsh, Edward Charles, 1899–1963, vol. VI
Titheradge, Madge, *died* 1961, vol. VI
Titheridge, Lieut Benjamin, *died* 1918, vol. II
Titman, Sir George Alfred, 1889–1980, vol. VII
Titmas, Air Cdre John Francis, 1898–1973, vol. VII
Titmuss, Richard Morris, 1907–1973, vol. VII
Tito, President (Josip Broz), 1892–1980, vol. VII
Tito, Pittore Ettore, 1860–1941, vol. IV
Titta, Commendatore Ruffo, 1877–1953, vol. V
Titterington, Meredith Farrar, 1886–1949, vol. IV
Titterton, Major David Maitland M.; *see* Maitland-Titterton.
Titterton, Sir Ernest William, 1916–1990, vol. VIII
Titterton, Frank, 1882–1956, vol. V
Tittle, Walter Ernest, 1883–1966, vol. VI
Tittoni, Tommaso, 1855–1931, vol. III
Titulesco, Nicolas, 1883–1941, vol. IV
Titus, Rev. Murray Thurston, 1885–1964, vol. VI
Titzell, Anne; *see* Parrish, A.
Tivey, Maj.-Gen. Edwin, 1866–1947, vol. IV
Tivey, Sir John Proctor, 1882–1968, vol. VI
Tivy, Henry Lawrence, 1848–1929, vol. III
Tiwana, Al-Haj Lt-Col Nawab Sir Malik Khizar Hayat Khan, 1900–1975, vol. VII
Tizard, Sir Henry Thomas, 1885–1959, vol. V
Tizard, Jack, 1919–1979, vol. VII
Tizard, Captain Thomas Henry, 1839–1923, vol. II
Tobias, Rt Rev. George Wolfe Robert, 1882–1974, vol. VII
Tobias, Stephen Albert, 1920–1986, vol. VIII
Tobin, Sir Alfred Aspinall, 1855–1939, vol. III
Tobin, Maurice J., 1901–1953, vol. V
Tobler, Adolf, 1835–1910, vol. I
Toby, MP; *see* Lucy, Sir Henry.
Tocher, Rev. Forbes Scott, 1885–1973, vol. VII
Tocher, James Fowler, 1864–1945, vol. IV
Tocker, Albert Hamilton, 1884–1964, vol. VI
Tod, Sir Alan Cecil, 1887–1970, vol. VI
Tod, Hunter F., *died* 1923, vol. II
Tod, James Niebuhr, 1876–1947, vol. IV
Tod, Col John Kelso, *died* 1946, vol. IV
Tod, Marcus Niebuhr, 1878–1974, vol. VII
Tod, Murray Macpherson, 1909–1974, vol. VII
Todd, Adam Brown, 1822–1915, vol. I
Todd, Alan Livesey Stuart, 1900–1976, vol. VII
Todd, Lt-Col Alfred John Kennett, 1890–1970, vol. VI
Todd, (Alfred) Norman, 1904–1990, vol. VIII
Todd, Col Arthur George, *died* 1954, vol. V
Todd, Arthur Henry Ashworth, 1884–1938, vol. III
Todd, Arthur James Stewart, 1895–1978, vol. VII
Todd, Arthur Ralph Middleton, *died* 1966, vol. VI

Todd, Sir Bryan James, 1902–1987, vol. VIII
Todd, Sir Charles, 1826–1910, vol. I
Todd, Charles, 1869–1957, vol. V
Todd, Col Charles Campbell, 1870–1956, vol. V
Todd, Sir Desmond Henry, 1897–1970, vol. VI
Todd, Frederick, *died* 1940, vol. III (A), vol. IV
Todd, Frederick Augustus, 1880–1944, vol. IV
Todd, Sir Geoffrey Sydney, 1900–1986, vol. VIII
Todd, George, 1844–1912, vol. I
Todd, George E.; *see* Eyre-Todd.
Todd, George William, 1886–1950, vol. IV
Todd, Guy Mansfield, 1883–1958, vol. V
Todd, Sir Herbert John, 1893–1985, vol. VIII
Todd, Howard, 1855–1925, vol. II
Todd, James Eadie, *died* 1949, vol. IV
Todd, James Maclean, 1907–1988, vol. VIII
Todd, John Aiton, 1875–1954, vol. V
Todd, John L., 1876–1949, vol. IV
Todd, (John) Spencer Brydges, 1840–1921, vol. II
Todd, John William, 1882–1957, vol. V
Todd, Sir Joseph White, 1st Bt, 1846–1926, vol. II
Todd, Margaret; *see* Travers, Graham.
Todd, Norman; *see* Todd, A. N.
Todd, Ronald Ruskin, 1902–1980, vol. VII
Todd, Spencer Brydges; *see* Todd, J. S. B.
Todd, Thomas Robert Rushton, 1895–1975, vol. VII
Todd, W. J. Walker, 1884–1944, vol. IV
Todd, Sir William Alexander Forster, *died* 1946, vol. IV
Todd, Hon. William Frederic, 1854–1935, vol. III
Todd, Captain Sir William Henry W.; *see* Wilson-Todd.
Todd, Captain Sir William Pierrepoint W.; *see* Wilson-Todd.
Todd-Jones, Sir Basil; *see* Todd-Jones, Sir G. B.
Todd-Jones, Sir (George) Basil, 1898–1980, vol. VII
Todhunter, Sir Charles George, 1869–1949, vol. IV
Todhunter, Brig. Edward Joseph, 1900–1976, vol. VII
Todhunter, Col Herbert William, 1875–1936, vol. III
Todhunter, John, 1839–1916, vol. II
Toft, Albert, 1862–1949, vol. IV
Toft, Alfonso, *died* 1964, vol. VI
Togo, Adm. Marquis Heihachiro, 1847–1934, vol. III
Tohill, Rt Rev. John, 1855–1914, vol. I
Toker, Maj.-Gen. Sir Alliston Champion, 1843–1936, vol. III
Tolansky, Samuel, 1907–1973, vol. VII
Tole, Hon. Joseph Augustus, *died* 1920, vol. II
Toler, Hector Robert Graham, 1847–1899, vol. I
Toler, Otway Scarlett Graham, 1886–1941, vol. IV
Tolerton, Sir Robert Hill, 1887–1956, vol. V
Tolkien, John Ronald Reuel, 1892–1973, vol. VII
Tollemache, 2nd Baron, 1832–1904, vol. I
Tollemache, 3rd Baron, 1883–1955, vol. V
Tollemache, 4th Baron, 1910–1975, vol. VII
Tollemache, Arthur Frederick Churchill, 1860–1923, vol. II
Tollemache, Sir (Cecil) Lyonel (Newcomen), 5th Bt, 1886–1969, vol. VI
Tollemache, David, *died* 1918, vol. II
Tollemache, Lt-Col Hon. Denis Plantagenet, 1884–1942, vol. IV
Tollemache, Hon. Douglas Alfred, 1862–1944, vol. IV

Tollemache, Maj.-Gen. Edward Devereux Hamilton, 1885–1947, vol. IV
Tollemache, Henry James, 1846–1939, vol. III
Tollemache, Maj.-Gen. Sir Humphry Thomas, 6th Bt, 1897–1990, vol. VIII
Tollemache, Hon. Lionel Arthur, 1838–1919, vol. II
Tollemache, Sir Lyonel; *see* Tollemache, Sir C. L. N.
Tollemache, Sir Lyonel Felix Carteret Eugene, 4th Bt, 1854–1952, vol. V
Tollemache, Lyonulph De Oreliana, 1892–1966, vol. VI
Tollemache, Hon. Mortimer Granville, 1872–1950, vol. IV
Tollemache, Hon. Stratford, 1864–1937, vol. III
Toller, Arthur Thomas, 1857–1899, vol. I
Toller, Ernst, 1893–1939, vol. III
Toller, Brig. Hamlet Bush, 1871–1950, vol. IV
Toller, William Stark, 1884–1968, vol. VI
Tollerfield, Albert Edward, 1906–1984, vol. VIII
Tolley, Major Cyril James Hastings, 1895–1978, vol. VII
Tolley, Louis, *died* 1959, vol. V
Tollinton, Henry Phillips, 1870–1937, vol. III
Tollinton, Rev. Richard Bartram, 1866–1932, vol. III
Tollinton, Richard Bartram Boyd, 1903–1978, vol. VII
Tollit, Percy Kitto, 1863–1942, vol. IV
Tollner, Col Barrett Lennard, 1839–1918, vol. II
Tolmie, Hon. James, 1862–1939, vol. III (A), vol. IV
Tolmie, Hon. Simon Fraser, 1867–1937, vol. III
Tolstoy, Alexandra, 1884–1979, vol. VII
Tolstoy, Count Leo, 1828–1910, vol. I
Tom, Henry, 1881–1937, vol. III
Tomasson, Captain Sir William Hugh, 1858–1922, vol. II
Tomb, John Walker, 1882–1948, vol. IV
Tomblings, Douglas Griffith, 1889–1970, vol. VI
Tombs, Robert Charles, 1842–1923, vol. II
Tomes, Sir Charles Sissmore, 1846–1928, vol. II
Tomes, Brig. Clement Thurstan, 1882–1972, vol. VII
Tomkins, Sir Alfred George, 1895–1975, vol. VII (AII)
Tomkins, Ernest William, 1872–1925, vol. II
Tomkins, Lt-Col Harry Leith, 1870–1926, vol. III
Tomkins, Herbert Gerard, 1869–1934, vol. III
Tomkins, Sir Lionel Linton, 1871–1936, vol. III
Tomkins, Stanley Charles, *died* 1946, vol. IV
Tomkins, William Douglas, 1882–1959, vol. V
Tomkins, Gen. William Percival, 1841–1922, vol. II
Tomkinson, Charles, 1893–1976, vol. VII
Tomkinson, Sir Geoffrey Stewart, 1881–1963, vol. VI
Tomkinson, Brig. Henry Archdale, 1881–1937, vol. III
Tomkinson, Joseph Goodwin-, *died* 1940, vol. III
Tomkinson, Michael, 1841–1921, vol. II
Tomkinson, Vice-Adm. Wilfred, 1877–1971, vol. VII
Tomley, John Edward, 1874–1951, vol. V
Tomlin of Ash, Baron (Life Peer); Thomas James Chesshyre Tomlin, 1867–1935, vol. III
Tomlin, Eric Walter Frederick, 1913–1988, vol. VIII
Tomlin, Vice-Adm. George Napier, 1875–1947, vol. IV
Tomlin, Rev. James William Sackett, 1871–1959, vol. V

Tomlin, Lt-Col Julian Latham, 1886–1960, vol. V
Tomlinson, Rev. Cyril Edric, 1886–1968, vol. VI
Tomlinson, Rt Hon. George, 1890–1952, vol. V
Tomlinson, Rt Rev. Mgr George Arthur, 1906–1985, vol. VIII
Tomlinson, Sir George John Frederick, 1876–1963, vol. VI
Tomlinson, H. M., 1873–1958, vol. V
Tomlinson, Harry, 1846–1938, vol. III
Tomlinson, Herbert, 1845–1931, vol. III
Tomlinson, Maj.-Gen. Sir Percy Stanley, 1884–1951, vol. V
Tomlinson, Reginald Robert, 1885–1978, vol. VII
Tomlinson, Robert Parkinson, *died* 1943, vol. IV
Tomlinson, Ruth, *died* 1972, vol. VII
Tomlinson, Sir Thomas, 1877–1957, vol. V
Tomlinson, Sir Thomas Symonds, 1877–1965, vol. VI
Tomlinson, Sir William Edward Murray, 1st Bt, 1838–1912, vol. I
Tomney, Frank, 1908–1984, vol. VIII
Tomonaga, Sin-itiro, 1906–1979, vol. VII
Tomory, Maj.-Gen. Kenneth Alexander Macdonald, 1891–1968, vol. VI
Tompkins, Engr Captain Albert Edward, 1863–1927, vol. II
Tompson, Col Hew Wakeman, 1870–1933, vol. III
Tompson, Rev. Reginald, 1845–1907, vol. I
Tompson, Maj.-Gen. Reginald Henry Dalrymple, 1879–1937, vol. III
Tompson, Maj.-Gen. William Dalrymple, 1833–1916, vol. II
Toms, Frederick, *died* 1900, vol. I
Tomson, Rev. John, *died* 1926, vol. II
Toner, Rt Rev. John, 1857–1949, vol. IV
Tong, Sir Walter Wharton, 1890–1978, vol. VII
Tonga, HM the Queen of; Queen Salote Tupou, 1900–1965, vol. VI
Tonge, Francis Henry, 1855–1936, vol. III
Tonge, George Edward, 1876–1956, vol. V
Tonge, George Edward, 1910–1979, vol. VII
Tonge, Col William Corrie, 1862–1943, vol. IV
Tonk, HH Amin-ud-Daula Wazir-ul Mulk Nawab Sir Hafiz Muhammad Ibrahim Ali Khan Bahadur, Saulat Jung, 1848–1930, vol. III
Tonk, HH Said-ud-Daulah Wazir-ul-Mulk Nawab Hafiz Sir Mohammed Saadat Ali Khan Bahadur Sowlat-i-Jung, 1879–1947, vol. IV
Tonkinson, Harry, 1880–1937, vol. III
Tonks, Rt Rev. Basil, *born* 1930, vol. VIII
Tonks, Ven. Charles Frederick, 1881–1957, vol. V
Tonks, Henry, 1862–1937, vol. III
Tonks, Rt Rev. Horace Norman Vincent, 1891–1959, vol. V
Tonnochy, Alec Bain, *died* 1963, vol. VI
Toogood, Col Cyril George, 1894–1962, vol. VI
Tookey, Geoffrey William, 1902–1976, vol. VII
Toole, John Lawrence, 1830–1906, vol. I
Toole, Joseph, 1887–1945, vol. IV
Tooley, Sarah A., *died* 1946, vol. IV
Toomer, Air Vice-Marshal Sydney Edward, 1895–1954, vol. V
Toone, Sir Frederick Charles, 1868–1930, vol. III
Toone, Rev. John, 1844–1934, vol. III
Toop, Engr-Rear-Adm. William, *died* 1950, vol. IV

Toosey, Sir Philip John Denton, 1904–1975, vol. VII
Tooth, Sir (Archibald) Leonard (Lucas) L.; *see* Lucas-Tooth.
Tooth, Hon. Sir Douglas; *see* Tooth, Hon. Sir S. D.
Tooth, Sir Edwin Marsden, 1886–1957, vol. V
Tooth, Howard Henry, 1856–1925, vol. II
Tooth, Sir Hugh Vere Huntly Duff M. L.; *see* Munro-Lucas-Tooth.
Tooth, Sir Robert Lucas L.; *see* Lucas-Tooth.
Tooth, Hon. Sir (Seymour) Douglas, 1904–1982, vol. VIII (A)
Toothill, Sir John Norman, 1908–1986, vol. VIII
Tootill, Robert, 1850–1934, vol. III
Toovey, Maj.-Gen. Cecil Wotton, 1891–1954, vol. V
Toovey, Rev. Henry, 1843–1922, vol. II
Tope, Maj.-Gen. Wilfrid Shakespeare, 1892–1962, vol. VI
Topham, Alfred Frank, 1874–1952, vol. V
Topham, Frank W. W., 1838–1924, vol. II
Topham, Rev. John, 1863–1955, vol. II
Topham, Lt-Col Thomas H.; *see* Harrison-Topham.
Topley, William Whiteman Carlton, 1886–1944, vol. IV
Toplis, James, 1876–1961, vol. VI
Topolski, Feliks, 1907–1989, vol. VIII
Topp, Charles Alfred, 1847–1932, vol. III
Topp, Brig.-Gen. Charles Beresford, 1893–1976, vol. VII
Topp, Wilfred Bethridge, 1891–1978, vol. VII
Toppin, Aubrey John, 1881–1969, vol. VI
Topping, Andrew, 1890–1955, vol. V
Topping, Sir (Hugh) Robert, 1877–1952, vol. V
Topping, Sir Robert; *see* Topping, Sir H. R.
Topping, Col Thomas Edward, 1871–1926, vol. II
Topping, Rt Hon. Walter William Buchanan, 1908–1978, vol. VII
Torphichen, 12th Lord, 1846–1915, vol. I
Torphichen, 13th Lord, 1886–1973, vol. VII
Torphichen, 14th Lord, 1917–1975, vol. VII
Torphichen, Master of; Hon. James Archibald Douglas Sandilands, 1884–1909, vol. I
Torr, Cecil, 1857–1928, vol. II
Torr, James Fenning, *died* 1915, vol. I
Torr, Rev. William Edward, 1851–1924, vol. II
Torr, Brig. (William) Wyndham (Torre), 1890–1963, vol. VI
Torr, Brig. Wyndham; *see* Torr, Brig. W. W. T.
Torrance, Sir A. M., *died* 1909, vol. I
Torre-Diaz, Count de; Brodie Manuel de Zulueta, 1842–1918, vol. II
Torrens, James Aubrey, 1881–1954, vol. V
Torres Bodet, Jaime, 1902–1974, vol. VII
Torrey, Charles Cutler, 1863–1956, vol. V
Torrey, Reuben Archer, 1856–1928, vol. II
Torriano, Col Charles Edward, 1833–1908, vol. I
Torrie, Lt-Col Claud Jameson, 1879–1936, vol. III
Torrington, 9th Viscount, 1886–1944, vol. IV
Torrington, 10th Viscount, 1876–1961, vol. VI
Tortelier, Paul, 1914–1990, vol. VIII
Tortise, Col Herbert James, *died* 1954, vol. V
Tory, Henry Marshall, 1864–1947, vol. IV
Tory, Hon. James Cranswick, *died* 1944, vol. IV
Toscanini, Arturo, 1867–1957, vol. V
Toseland, Charles Stephen, 1894–1971, vol. VII

Tostevin, Engr-Captain Harold Bertram, 1884–1956, vol. V

Tosti, Sir (Francesco) Paolo, 1847–1916, vol. II

Tosti, Sir Paolo; *see* Tosti, Sir F. P.

Tothill, Adm. Sir Hugh Henry Darby, 1865–1927, vol. II

Tothill, John Douglas, 1888–1969, vol. VI

Totman, Grenfell William, 1911–1986, vol. VIII

Tottenham, Sir Alexander Robert Loftus, 1873–1946, vol. IV

Tottenham, Major Charles Bosvile, 1869–1911, vol. I

Tottenham, Col Charles George, 1835–1918, vol. II

Tottenham, Charles Gore Loftus, 1861–1929, vol. III

Tottenham, Rear-Adm. Edward Loftus, 1896–1974, vol. VII

Tottenham, Adm. Sir Francis Loftus, 1880–1967, vol. VI

Tottenham, Very Rev. George, 1825–1911, vol. I

Tottenham, Sir (George) Richard (Frederick), 1890–1977, vol. VII

Tottenham, Adm. Henry Loftus, 1860–1950, vol. IV

Tottenham, Percy Marmaduke, 1873–1975, vol. VII

Tottenham, Sir Richard; *see* Tottenham, Sir G. R. F.

Tottenham, Richard E., *died* 1971, vol. VII

Tottenham-Smith, Ralph Henry, 1893–1971, vol. VII

Totterdell, Sir Joseph, 1885–1959, vol. V

Touche, Sir George Alexander, 1st Bt (*cr* 1920), 1861–1935, vol. III

Touche, Rt Hon. Sir Gordon Cosmo, 1st Bt (*cr* 1962), 1895–1972, vol. VII

Touche, Sir Norman George, 2nd Bt (*cr* 1920), 1888–1977, vol. VII

Toulmin, Sir George, 1857–1923, vol. II

Toulmin Smith, Elizabeth Thomasina; *see* Meade, L. T.

Tours, Berthold George, 1871–1944, vol. IV

Tours, Frank E., 1877–1963, vol. VI

Tours, Kenneth Cecil, 1908–1987, vol. VIII

Tout, Sir Frederick Henry, *died* 1950, vol. IV

Tout, Thomas Frederick, 1855–1929, vol. III

Tout, W. J., 1870–1946, vol. IV

Tovell, Brig. Raymond Walter, 1890–1966, vol. VI

Tovey, 1st Baron, 1885–1971, vol. VII

Tovey, Sir Donald Francis, 1875–1940, vol. III

Tovey, Lt-Col George Strangways, 1875–1943, vol. IV

Towell, Brig. Rowland Henry, 1891–1973, vol. VII

Tower, Bernard Henry, *died* 1933, vol. III

Tower, Charlemagne, 1848–1923, vol. II

Tower, Christopher Joan Hume, 1841–1924, vol. II

Tower, Adm. Cyril Everard, 1861–1929, vol. III

Tower, Comdr Francis FitzPatrick, 1859–1944, vol. IV

Tower, Vice-Adm. Sir Francis Thomas Butler, 1885–1964, vol. VI

Tower, Rev. Henry, 1862–1948, vol. IV

Tower, Rev. Henry Bernard, 1882–1964, vol. VI

Tower, Sir Reginald Thomas, 1860–1939, vol. III

Towers, Graham Ford, 1897–1975, vol. VII

Towers, Samuel, 1863–1943, vol. IV

Towers-Clark, James, 1852–1926, vol. II

Towle, Arthur Edward, 1878–1948, vol. IV

Towle, Lt-Col Sir Francis William, 1876–1951, vol. V

Towle, Margery; *see* Lawrence, M.

Towle, Sir William, 1849–1929, vol. III

Towler, Eric William, 1900–1987, vol. VIII

Town, Sir (Hugh) Stuart, 1893–1972, vol. VII

Town, Sir Stuart; *see* Town, Sir H. S.

Townend, Arnold Ernest, 1880–1970, vol. VI (AII)

Townend, Donald Thomas Alfred, 1897–1984, vol. VIII

Townend, Harry, 1872–1949, vol. IV

Townend, Sir Harry Douglas, 1891–1976, vol. VII

Townend, Herbert Patrick Victor, 1887–1950, vol. IV

Towner, Major Edgar Thomas, 1890–1972, vol. VII

Townesend, Air Cdre Ernest John Dennis, 1896–1975, vol. VII

Townesend, Stephen, *died* 1914, vol. I

Townley, Athol Gordon, 1907–1963, vol. VI

Townley, Rev. Charles Francis, 1856–1930, vol. III

Townley, Rev. Charles Gale, 1848–1942, vol. IV

Townley, Frank, 1924–1982, vol. VIII

Townley, Rt Rev. George Frederick, 1891–1977, vol. VII

Townley, Sir John Barton, 1914–1990, vol. VIII

Townley, Maximilian Gowran, 1864–1942, vol. IV

Townley, Reginald Colin, 1904–1982, vol. VIII

Townley, Sir Walter Beaupre, 1863–1945, vol. IV

Townroe, Bernard Stephen, 1885–1962, vol. VI

Townroe, Rev. James Weston, *died* 1934, vol. III

Townsend, Alexander Cockburn, 1905–1964, vol. VI

Townsend, Crewe Armand Hamilton, *died* 1954, vol. V

Townsend, Adm. Cyril Samuel, 1875–1949, vol. IV

Townsend, Surg.-Gen. Sir Edmond, 1845–1917, vol. II

Townsend, Major Edward Neville, 1871–1938, vol. III

Townsend, Brig. Edward Philip, 1909–1978, vol. VII

Townsend, Frederick Henry, 1868–1920, vol. II

Townsend, Rev. Henry, *died* 1955, vol. V

Townsend, Sir John Sealy Edward, 1868–1957, vol. V

Townsend, Sir Lance; *see* Townsend, Sir S. L.

Townsend, Rear-Adm. Michael Southcote, 1908–1984, vol. VIII

Townsend, Sir Reginald, 1882–1938, vol. III

Townsend, Stephen Chapman, 1826–1901, vol. I

Townsend, Sir (Sydney) Lance, 1912–1983, vol. VIII

Townsend, Thomas Sutton, 1847–1918, vol. II

Townsend, Air Vice-Marshal William Edwin, *born* 1916, vol. VIII

Townsend, Rev. William John, 1835–1915, vol. I

Townsend-Farquhar, Sir Robert; *see* Farquhar.

Townshend, 5th Marquess, 1831–1899, vol. I

Townshend, 6th Marquess, 1866–1921, vol. II

Townshend, Sir Charles James, 1844–1924, vol. II

Townshend, Maj.-Gen. Sir Charles Vere Ferrers, 1861–1924, vol. II

Townshend, Col Frederick Trench, 1838–1924, vol. II

Townshend, Captain Harry Leigh, 1842–1924, vol. II

Townshend, Hugh, 1890–1974, vol. VII

Townshend, James, *died* 1949, vol. IV

Townshend, Hon. Robert M.; *see* Marsham-Townshend.

Townshend, Samuel Nugent, 1844–1910, vol. I

Townshend, William Tower, 1855–1943, vol. IV

Towse, Captain Sir Beachcroft; *see* Towse, Captain Sir E. B. B.

Towse, Captain Sir (Ernest) Beachcroft Beckwith, 1864–1948, vol. IV

Towse, Sir (John) Wrench, 1848–1929, vol. III

Towse, Sir Wrench; see Towse, Sir J. W.

Towsey, Brig.-Gen. Francis William, died 1948, vol. IV

Toy, Carter; see Toy, F. C.

Toy, Crawford Howell, 1836–1919, vol. II

Toy, Francis Carter, 1892–1988, vol. VIII

Toy, Sir Henry, 1862–1939, vol. III

Toye, Brig. Alfred Maurice, 1897–1955, vol. V

Toye, Dudley Bulmer, 1888–1968, vol. VI

Toye, Major Edward Geoffrey, 1889–1942, vol. IV

Toye, Francis; see Toye, J. F.

Toye, Herbert Graham Donovan, 1911–1969, vol. VI

Toye, (John) Francis, 1883–1964, vol. VI

Toynbee, Arnold Joseph, 1889–1975, vol. VII

Toynbee, Brig. Guy Elliston, 1884–1947, vol. IV

Toynbee, Jocelyn Mary Catherine, 1897–1985, vol. VIII

Toynbee, Paget, 1855–1932, vol. III

Toynbee, Philip; see Toynbee, T. P.

Toynbee, (Theodore) Philip, 1916–1981, vol. VIII

Toyne, Rev. Frederick Elijah, died 1927, vol. II

Toyne, Stanley Mease, died 1962, vol. VI

Tozer, Basil, 1896–1949, vol. IV

Tozer, Beatrice Cordelia Auchmuty, (Mrs Basil Tozer); see Langley, B.

Tozer, Rev. Henry Fanshawe, 1829–1916, vol. II

Tozer, Hon. Sir Horace, 1844–1916, vol. II

Tozer, Major Sir James Clifford, 1889–1970, vol. VI

Tozer, Col William, 1894–1971, vol. VII

Tozer, Rt Rev. William George, died 1899, vol. I

Tracey, Herbert Trevor, 1884–1955, vol. V

Tracey, Sir Richard Edward, 1837–1907, vol. I

Tracy, Major Hon. Algernon Henry Charles H.; see Hanbury-Tracy.

Tracy, Frederick, 1862–1951, vol. V

Tracy, Hon. Frederick Stephen Archibald H.; see Hanbury-Tracy.

Tracy, Louis, 1863–1928, vol. II

Tracy, Spencer, 1900–1967, vol. VI

Tracy-Inglis, Col Russell; see Inglis.

Trafalgar, Viscount; Herbert Horatio Nelson, 1854–1905, vol. I

Trafford, Baron (Life Peer); Joseph Anthony Porteous Trafford, 1932–1989, vol. VIII

Trafford, Edward Southwell, 1838–1912, vol. I

Trafford, F. G.; see Riddell, C. E. L.

Trafford, Marcus Antonius Johnston de L.; see de Lavis-Trafford.

Trafford, Rt Rev. Ralph Sigebert, 1886–1976, vol. VII

Tragett, Margaret Rivers; see Larminie, M. R.

Trahan, Hon. Arthur, 1877–1950, vol. IV (A), vol. V

Trail, James William Helenus, 1851–1919, vol. II

Trail, Richard Robertson, 1894–1971, vol. VII

Traill, Anthony, 1838–1914, vol. I

Traill, Major Cecil James, 1888–1968, vol. VI

Traill, Maj.-Gen. George Balfour, 1833–1913, vol. I

Traill, Henry Duff, 1842–1900, vol. I

Traill, Lt-Col John Charles Merriman, 1881–1942, vol. IV

Traill, Peter; see Morton, Guy Mainwaring.

Traill, Major Thomas Balfour, 1881–1920, vol. II

Traill, Air Vice-Marshal Thomas Cathcart, 1899–1973, vol. VII

Traill, Lt-Col William Henry, 1871–1951, vol. V

Traill, Lt-Col William Stewart, 1868–1959, vol. V

Train, Arthur, 1875–1945, vol. IV

Train, George Francis, 1829–1904, vol. I

Train, Sir John, 1873–1942, vol. IV

Train, Rev. John Gilkison, 1847–1920, vol. II

Train, Sir (John) Landale, 1888–1969, vol. VI

Train, Sir Landale; see Train, Sir J. L.

Trainor, James P., 1914–1989, vol. VIII

Transjordan, King of; HH Abdullah Ibn Hussein, died 1951, vol. V

Trant, John Philip, 1889–1953, vol. V

Trapani, Lt-Col Alfred, 1859–1928, vol. II, vol. III

Trapnell, Alan Stewart, 1913–1986, vol. VIII

Trapnell, John Graham, died 1949, vol. IV

Trappes-Lomax, Michael Roger, 1900–1972, vol. VII

Trappes-Lomax, Brig. Thomas Byrnand, 1895–1962, vol. VI

Traquair, Harry Moss, 1875–1954, vol. V

Traquair, Ramsay, 1874–1952, vol. V

Traquair, Ramsay Heatley, 1840–1912, vol. I

Trask, Katrina, died 1922, vol. II

Tratman, David William, died 1953, vol. V

Tratman, Edgar Kingsley, 1899–1978, vol. VII

Travancore, Maharajah of, 1857–1924, vol. II

Travers, Ben, 1886–1980, vol. VII

Travers, Captain Francis Eaton, died 1953, vol. V

Travers, Lt-Col George Alfred, 1867–1950, vol. IV

Travers, Graham, 1859–1918, vol. II

Travers, Sir Guy Francis Travers Clarke-, 3rd Bt (cr 1804), 1842–1905, vol. I

Travers, Col Henry Cecil, died 1958, vol. V

Travers, Brig.-Gen. Jonas Hamilton du Boulay, 1861–1933, vol. III

Travers, Brig.-Gen. Joseph Oates, 1867–1936, vol. III

Travers, Sir Lancelot, see Travers, Sir W. L.

Travers, Morris William, 1872–1961, vol. VI

Travers, Lt-Gen. Sir Paul Anthony, 1927–1983, vol. VIII

Travers, Sir (Walter) Lancelot, 1880–1937, vol. III

Travis, Comdr Sir Edward Wilfrid Harry, 1888–1956, vol. V

Travis, Harry, 1858–1927, vol. II

Travis, Rev. James, 1840–1919, vol. II

Travis, Rev. William Travis, died 1924, vol. II

Travis-Clegg, Sir James Travis, 1874–1942, vol. IV

Trayner, Hon. Lord; John Trayner, 1834–1929, vol. III

Trayner, John; see Hon. Lord Trayner.

Treacher, Rev. Preb. Hubert Harold, 1891–1964, vol. VI

Treacher, Sir William Hood, 1849–1919, vol. II

Treacy, Rt Rev. Eric, 1907–1978, vol. VII

Treadgold, Group Captain Henry A., 1883–1941, vol. IV

Treadwell, Brig. John William Ferguson, 1901–1968, vol. VI

Treanor, Ven. James, died 1926, vol. II

Trease, George Edward, 1902–1986, vol. VIII

Treasure, Col Kenneth David, 1913–1983, vol. VIII

Treasure, William Houston, died 1916, vol. II

Treatt, Hon. Sir Vernon Haddon, 1897–1984, vol. VIII

Treble, Rev. Edmund John, *died* 1924, vol. II

Treble, Col George Walker, 1865–1929, vol. III

Tredcroft, Lt-Col Charles Lennox, 1832–1917, vol. II

Tredegar, 1st Viscount (*cr* 1905), 1830–1913, vol. I

Tredegar, 1st Viscount (*cr* 1926), 1867–1934, vol. III

Tredegar, 2nd Viscount (*cr* 1926), 1893–1949, vol. IV

Tredegar, 5th Baron, 1873–1954, vol. V

Tredegar, 6th Baron, 1908–1962, vol. VI

Tredennick, (George) Hugh (Percival Phair), 1899–1981, vol. VIII

Tredennick, Rev. George Nesbitt Haydon, 1860–1942, vol. IV

Tredennick, Hugh; *see* Tredennick, G. H. P. P.

Tredennick, Rev. John Nesbitt Ernest, 1892–1976, vol. VII

Tredgold, Alfred Frank, 1870–1952, vol. V

Tredgold, Sir Clarkson Henry, 1865–1938, vol. III

Tredgold, Joan Alison, 1903–1989, vol. VIII

Tredgold, Rt Hon. Sir Robert Clarkson, 1899–1977, vol. VII

Tredgold, Roger Francis, 1911–1975, vol. VII

Tree, Charles, *died* 1940, vol. III

Tree, Sir Herbert Beerbohm, 1853–1917, vol. II

Tree, Maud, (Lady Tree), 1864–1937, vol. III

Tree, Ronald, 1897–1976, vol. VII

Tree, Ven. Ronald James, 1914–1970, vol. VI

Treeby, Lt-Col Henry Paul, 1858–1935, vol. III

Treffry, Charles Ebenezer, 1842–1924, vol. II

Treffry, Col Edward, 1869–1942, vol. IV

Treffry, Mary Beatrice, 1865–1942, vol. IV

Trefgarne, 1st Baron, 1894–1960, vol. V

Trefle, Hon. John Louis, *died* 1915, vol. I

Trefusis, Hon. Henry Walter Hepburn-Stuart-Forbes-, 1864–1948, vol. IV

Trefusis, Major Hon. John Frederick Hepburn-Stuart-Forbes-, 1878–1915, vol. I

Trefusis, Col Hon. John Schomberg, 1852–1932, vol. III

Trefusis, Lady Mary, 1869–1927, vol. II

Trefusis, Rt Rev. Robert Edward, 1843–1930, vol. III

Tregarthen, John Coulson, 1854–1933, vol. III

Tregear, Edward, 1846–1931, vol. III

Tregear, Maj.-Gen. Sir Vincent William, 1842–1925, vol. II

Tregoning, Wynn Harold, 1876–1930, vol. III

Treharne, Kenneth John, 1939–1989, vol. VIII

Treharne, Reginald Francis, 1901–1967, vol. VI

Trehearne, Alfred Frederick Aldridge, 1874–1962, vol. VI

Trehearne, Frank William, 1881–1956, vol. V

Treherne, Rev. Charles Albert, 1856–1919, vol. II

Treherne, Maj.-Gen. Sir Francis Harper, 1858–1955, vol. V

Treherne, John Edwin, 1929–1989, vol. VIII

Trelawny, Horace Dormer, 1824–1906, vol. I

Trelawny, Maj.-Gen. John I.; *see* Iago-Trelawny.

Trelawny, Sir John William Robin Maurice Salusbury-, 12th Bt, 1908–1956, vol. V

Trelawny, Sir John William Salusbury-, 11th Bt, 1869–1944, vol. IV

Trelawny, Sir William Lewis Salusbury-, 10th Bt, 1844–1917, vol. II

Trelawny-Ross, Rev. John Trelawny, 1852–1935, vol. III

Treloar, Sir William Purdie, 1st Bt, 1843–1923, vol. II

Trematon, Viscount; Rupert Alexander George Augustus Cambridge, 1907–1928, vol. II

Tremayne, Lt-Col Arthur, 1827–1905, vol. I

Tremayne, Arthur, 1879–1954, vol. V

Tremayne, Harold, *died* 1908, vol. I

Tremayne, John, 1825–1901, vol. I

Tremayne, Air Marshal Sir John Tremayne, 1891–1979, vol. VII

Tremblay, Maj.-Gen. Thomas Louis, 1886–1951, vol. V

Tremellen, Norman Cleverton, 1895–1979, vol. VII

Tremlett, Charles Hugh, 1876–1939, vol. III

Tremlett, Col Colin Percy, 1880–1972, vol. VII

Tremlett, Maj.-Gen. Erroll Arthur Edwin, 1893–1982, vol. VIII

Trenam, Edwin, 1843–1909, vol. I

Trench, Anthony C.; *see* Chenevix-Trench.

Trench, Col Arthur Henry C.; *see* Chenevix-Trench.

Trench, Charles Godfrey C.; *see* Chenevix-Trench.

Trench, Hon. Cosby Godolphin, 1844–1925, vol. II

Trench, Sir David Clive Crosbie, 1915–1988, vol. VIII

Trench, Ernest Frederic Crosbie, 1869–1960, vol. V

Trench, Col Frederic John Arthur, 1857–1942, vol. IV

Trench, Hon. Frederic Sydney, 1894–1916, vol. II

Trench, Lt-Col Frederick Amelius Le P.; *see* Le Poer Trench.

Trench, Hon. Frederick Le P.; *see* Le Poer Trench.

Trench, Lt-Col George Frederick C.; *see* Chenevix-Trench.

Trench, Herbert, 1865–1923, vol. II

Trench, Col Lawrence C.; *see* Chenevix-Trench.

Trench, Brig. Ralph C.; *see* Chenevix-Trench.

Trench, Lt-Col Sir Richard Henry C.; *see* Chenevix-Trench.

Trench, Wilbraham Fitz-John, 1873–1939, vol. III

Trench, Hon. William Cosby, 1869–1944, vol. IV

Trench, William Launcelot Crosbie, *died* 1949, vol. IV

Trench, Col Hon. William Le-P.; *see* Le-Poer-Trench.

Trench, Rev. William Robert, 1838–1913, vol. I

Trenchard, 1st Viscount, 1873–1956, vol. V

Trenchard, 2nd Viscount, 1923–1987, vol. VIII

Trend, Baron (Life Peer); Burke St John Trend, 1914–1987, vol. VIII

Trend, John Brande, 1887–1958, vol. V

Trendell, Sir Arthur James Richens, 1836–1909, vol. I

Trendell, Herbert Arthur Previté, 1864–1929, vol. III

Trenholme, Norman William, 1837–1919, vol. II

Trent, 1st Baron, 1850–1931, vol. III

Trent, 2nd Baron, 1889–1956, vol. V

Trent, Col George Alexander, 1870–1930, vol. III

Trent, Group Captain Leonard Henry, 1915–1986, vol. VIII

Trent, Newbury Abbot, 1885–1953, vol. V

Trentham, Everard Noel Rye, 1888–1963, vol. VI

Trentham, George Percy, *died* 1940, vol. III

Treowen, 1st Baron, 1851–1933, vol. III

Tresidder, Lt-Col Alfred Geddes, 1881–1970, vol. VI

Tresidder, Captain Tolmie John, 1850–1931, vol. III

Treston, Hubert Joseph, 1888–1959, vol. V
Treston, Col Maurice Lawrence, 1891–1970, vol. VI
Trestrail, Major Alfred Ernest Yates, 1876–1935, vol. III
Trethowan, Hon. Sir Arthur King, 1863–1937, vol. III
Trethowan, Sir Ian; see Trethowan, Sir J. I. R.
Trethowan, Sir (James) Ian (Raley), 1922–1990, vol. VIII
Trevail, Silvanus, 1851–1903, vol. I
Trevan, John William, 1887–1956, vol. V
Trevaskis, Sir (Gerald) Kennedy (Nicholas), 1915–1990, vol. VIII
Trevaskis, Rev. Hugh Kennedy, 1882–1962, vol. VI
Trevaskis, Sir Kennedy; see Trevaskis, Sir G. K. N.
Trevelyan, Baron (Life Peer); Humphrey Trevelyan, 1905–1985, vol. VIII
Trevelyan, Rt Hon. Sir Charles Philips, 3rd Bt (cr 1874), 1870–1958, vol. V
Trevelyan, Edmond Fauriel, died 1911, vol. I
Trevelyan, Sir Ernest John, 1850–1924, vol. II
Trevelyan, George Macaulay, 1876–1962, vol. VI
Trevelyan, Rt Hon. Sir George Otto, 2nd Bt (cr 1874), 1838–1928, vol. II
Trevelyan, Hilda, died 1959, vol. V
Trevelyan, Janet Penrose, 1879–1956, vol. V
Trevelyan, Julian Otto, 1910–1988, vol. VIII
Trevelyan, Mary, 1897–1983, vol. VIII
Trevelyan, Robert Calverley, 1872–1951, vol. V
Trevelyan, Sir Walter John, 8th Bt (cr 1662), 1866–1931, vol. III
Trevelyan, Rev. William Bouverie, 1853–1929, vol. III
Trevelyan, Sir Willoughby John, 9th Bt (cr 1662), 1902–1976, vol. VII
Treves, Sir Frederick, 1st Bt, 1853–1923, vol. II
Trevethin, 1st Baron, 1843–1936, vol. III
Trevethin, 2nd Baron, 1879–1959, vol. V
Trevethin, 3rd Baron, and Oaksey 1st Baron, 1880–1971, vol. VII
Trevithick, Arthur Reginald, 1858–1939, vol. III
Trevor, 2nd Baron, 1852–1923, vol. II
Trevor, 3rd Baron, 1863–1950, vol. IV
Trevor, Lady; (Rosamond Catherine), 1857–1942, vol. IV
Trevor, Sir Arthur Charles, 1841–1920, vol. II
Trevor, Arthur Hill, 1858–1924, vol. II
Trevor, Lt-Col Arthur Prescott, 1872–1930, vol. III
Trevor, Sir Cecil; see Trevor, Sir Charles C.
Trevor, Sir Cecil Russell, 1899–1971, vol. VII
Trevor, Sir (Charles) Cecil, 1830–1921, vol. II
Trevor, Sir (Charles) Gerald, 1882–1959, vol. V
Trevor, David, 1906–1988, vol. VIII
Trevor, Surg.-Gen. Sir Francis Woollaston, 1851–1922, vol. II
Trevor, Frederick George Brunton, 1838–1924, vol. II
Trevor, Hon. George Edwyn Hill-, 1859–1922, vol. II
Trevor, Col George Herbert, 1840–1927, vol. II
Trevor, Sir Gerald; see Trevor, Sir C. G.
Trevor, Brig.-Gen. Herbert Edward, 1871–1939, vol. III
Trevor, Col Philip Christian William, 1863–1932, vol. III

Trevor, Rev. Thomas Warren, 1839–1924, vol. II
Trevor, Col William Herbert, 1872–1936, vol. III
Trevor, Maj.-Gen. William Spottiswoode, 1831–1907, vol. I
Trevor-Battye, Aubyn Bernard Rochfort, died 1922, vol. II
Trevor Jones, Alan; see Jones.
Trew, Brig.-Gen. Edward Fynmore, 1879–1935, vol. III
Trewavas, Joseph, 1835–1905, vol. I
Trewby, Vice-Adm. George, 1874–1953, vol. V
Trewin, John Courtenay, 1908–1990, vol. VIII
Trias, Juan Mannel S.; see Sucre-Trias.
Tribe, Sir Frank Newton, 1893–1958, vol. V
Trickett, Sir Henry Whittaker, 1857–1913, vol. I
Trickett, William, 1840–1928, vol. II, vol. III
Trickett, Hon. William Joseph, 1844–1916, vol. II
Triggs, H. Inigo, 1876–1923, vol. II
Triggs, William Henry, 1855–1934, vol. III
Trilling, Lionel, 1905–1975, vol. VII
Trimble, Brig. Arthur Philip, 1909–1984, vol. VIII
Trimble, Charles Joseph, 1856–1944, vol. IV
Trimble, S. Delmege, 1857–1947, vol. IV
Trimble, William Copeland, 1851–1941, vol. IV
Trimen, Roland, 1840–1916, vol. II
Trimingham, Sir Eldon Harvey, 1889–1959, vol. V
Trimlestown, 18th Baron, 1862–1937, vol. III
Trimlestown, 19th Baron, 1899–1990, vol. VIII
Trimmer, Sir George William Arthur, 1882–1972, vol. VII
Trimnell, Col William Duncan Conabeare, 1874–1953, vol. V
Trinder, Sir (Arnold) Charles, 1906–1989, vol. VIII
Trinder, Sir Charles; see Trinder, Sir A. C.
Trinder, Thomas Edward, 1909–1989, vol. VIII
Trine, Ralph Waldo, 1866–1958, vol. V
Trinkler, Emil, 1896–1931, vol. III
Tripp, Sir Alker; see Tripp, Sir H. A.
Tripp, Bernard Edward Howard, 1868–1940, vol. III (A), vol. IV
Tripp, George Henry, 1860–1922, vol. II
Tripp, Sir (Herbert) Alker, 1883–1954, vol. V
Tripp, Lt-Gen. William Henry Lainson, 1881–1959, vol. V
Trippe, Juan Terry, 1899–1981, vol. VIII
Trippel, Sir Francis, 1866–1930, vol. III
Tripura, Maharaja of, 1908–1947, vol. IV
Triscott, Col Charles Prideaux, 1857–1926, vol. II
Tristram, Ernest William, 1882–1952, vol. V
Tristram, Rev. Henry, 1881–1955, vol. V
Tristram, Rev. Henry Baker, 1822–1906, vol. I
Tristram, Henry Barrington, 1861–1946, vol. IV
Tristram, Rev. John William, died 1926, vol. II
Tristram, Katharine Alice Salvin, 1858–1948, vol. IV
Tristram, Thomas H., 1825–1912, vol. I
Tritton, Sir Alfred Ernest, 2nd Bt, 1873–1939, vol. III
Tritton, Arthur Henry, 1855–1936, vol. III
Tritton, Arthur Stanley, 1881–1973, vol. VII
Tritton, Sir (Charles) Ernest, 1st Bt, 1845–1918, vol. II
Tritton, Sir Ernest; see Tritton, Sir C. E.
Tritton, Major Sir Geoffrey Ernest, 3rd Bt, 1900–1976, vol. VII
Tritton, Herbert Leslie Melville, 1870–1940, vol. III

Tritton, Joseph Herbert, 1844–1923, vol. II
Tritton, Julian Seymour, 1889–1979, vol. VII
Tritton, Sir Seymour Biscoe, 1860–1937, vol. III
Tritton, Sir William Ashbee, 1876–1946, vol. IV
Trivedi, Sir Chandulal Madhavlal, 1893–1980, vol. VII (AII)
Trofimov, M. V., *died* 1948, vol. IV
Trollip, Arthur Stanley, 1888–1963, vol. VI
Trollope, Sir Anthony Owen Clavering, 16th Bt, 1917–1987, vol. VIII
Trollope, Lt-Col Sir Arthur Grant, 13th Bt, 1866–1937, vol. III
Trollope, Fabian George, 1872–1960, vol. V
Trollope, Sir Frederic Farrand, 14th Bt, 1875–1957, vol. V
Trollope, Sir Gordon Clavering, 15th Bt, 1885–1958, vol. V
Trollope, Sir Henry Cracroft, 12th Bt, 1860–1935, vol. III
Trollope, Brig. Hugh Charles Napier, 1895–1953, vol. V
Trollope, Rt Rev. Mark Napier, 1862–1930, vol. III
Trollope, Hon. Robert Cranmer, 1852–1908, vol. I
Trollope, Sir Thomas Ernest, 11th Bt, 1858–1927, vol. II
Trollope, Sir William Henry, 10th Bt, 1858–1921, vol. II
Troop, Rev. G. Osborne, 1854–1932, vol. III
Trotman, Arthur Edwin, 1906–1961, vol. VI
Trotman, Gen. Sir Charles Newsham, 1864–1929, vol. III
Trotman, Rev. Edward Fiennes, 1828–1910, vol. I
Trotman-Dickenson, Rev. Lenthall Greville, 1864–1931, vol. III
Trotsky, Lev Davidovich, 1879–1940, vol. III
Trott, Alan Charles, 1895–1959, vol. V
Trott, Charles Edmund, 1911–1984, vol. VIII
Trott, George Henry, 1889–1972, vol. VII
Trott, Hon. Sir Howard; *see* Trott, Hon. Sir W. J. H.
Trott, Hon. Sir (William James) Howard, 1883–1971, vol. VII
Trotter, Alexander Cooper, 1902–1975, vol. VII
Trotter, Alexander Pelham, 1857–1947, vol. IV
Trotter, Col Charles William, 1865–1931, vol. III
Trotter, Edith, *died* 1962, vol. VI
Trotter, Rev. Canon Edward Bush, 1842–1920, vol. II
Trotter, Major Edward Henry, 1872–1916, vol. II
Trotter, Col Gerald Frederic, 1871–1945, vol. IV
Trotter, Maj-Gen. Sir Henry, 1844–1905, vol. I
Trotter, Lt-Col Sir Henry, 1841–1919, vol. III
Trotter, Henry Alexander, 1869–1949, vol. IV
Trotter, Rev. Henry Eden, 1844–1922, vol. II
Trotter, Hugh, 1890–1965, vol. VI
Trotter, Maj.-Gen. Sir James Keith, 1849–1940, vol. III
Trotter, Rev. John Crawford, 1848–1942, vol. IV
Trotter, Rev. John George, 1848–1917, vol. II
Trotter, Lt-Col John Moubray, 1842–1924, vol. II
Trotter, Rev. Mowbray, 1848–1913, vol. I
Trotter, Col Sir Philip, 1844–1918, vol. II
Trotter, Reginald George, 1888–1951, vol. V
Trotter, Captain Richard Durant, 1887–1968, vol. VI
Trotter, Richard Stanley, 1903–1974, vol. VII

Trotter, Thomas, 1868–1944, vol. IV
Trotter, Thomas Henry Yorke, 1854–1934, vol. III
Trotter, Sir Victor Murray Coutts, 1874–1929, vol. III
Trotter, Wilfred, *died* 1939, vol. III
Trotter, William, 1839–1908, vol. I
Trotter, William Finlayson, 1871–1945, vol. IV
Troubetskoi, Prince, *died* 1915, vol. I
Troubetskoy, Princess Pierre; *see* Rives, Amélie.
Troubridge, Adm. Sir Ernest Charles Thomas, 1862–1926, vol. II
Troubridge, Laura, (Lady Troubridge), *died* 1946, vol. IV
Troubridge, Sir Peter, 6th Bt, 1927–1988, vol. VIII
Troubridge, Lt-Col Sir St Vincent; *see* Troubridge, Lt-Col T. St V. W.
Troubridge, Sir Thomas Herbert Cochrane, 4th Bt, 1860–1938, vol. III
Troubridge, Vice-Adm. Sir Thomas Hope, 1895–1949, vol. IV
Troubridge, Lt-Col Sir (Thomas) St Vincent (Wallace), 5th Bt, 1895–1963, vol. VI
Troughton, Rev. Arthur Perceval, 1858–1937, vol. III
Troughton, John Frederick George, 1902–1975, vol. VII
Trouncer, Cecil, 1898–1953, vol. V
Trouncer, Harold Moltke, 1871–1948, vol. IV
Troup, Lt-Col Alan Gordon, 1879–1931, vol. III
Troup, Sir (Charles) Edward, 1857–1941, vol. IV
Troup, Sir Edward; *see* Troup, Sir C. E.
Troup, Francis William, 1859–1941, vol. IV
Troup, Sir George Alexander, 1863–1941, vol. IV
Troup, James, 1840–1925, vol. II
Troup, Vice-Adm. Sir James Andrew Gardiner, 1883–1975, vol. VII
Troup, Robert Scott, 1874–1939, vol. III
Trousdale, Major Robert Cecil, 1876–1934, vol. III
Trout, Sir (Herbert) Leon, 1906–1978, vol. VII
Trout, Sir Leon; *see* Trout, Sir H. L.
Troutbeck, John, 1860–1912, vol. I
Troutbeck, Sir John Monro, 1894–1971, vol. VII
Trouton, Frederick Thomas, 1863–1922, vol. II
Trow, Albert Howard, *died* 1939, vol. III
Trowbridge, John Townsend, 1827–1916, vol. II
Trower, Col Courtney Vor, 1856–1947, vol. IV
Trower, Rt Rev. Gerard, 1860–1928, vol. II
Trower, John Henry Peter, 1913–1968, vol. VI
Trower, Sir Walter, 1853–1924, vol. II
Trower, Sir William Gosselin, 1889–1963, vol. VI
Troy, Hon. Michael Francis, 1877–1953, vol. V
Troyte, Sir Gilbert John A.; *see* Acland-Troyte.
Troyte-Bullock, Lt-Col Edward George, 1862–1942, vol. IV
Trubshaw, Dame Gwendoline Joyce, *died* 1954, vol. V
Trubshaw, Wilfred, 1870–1944, vol. IV
Trudeau, Edward Livingston, 1848–1915, vol. I
Truell, Maj.-Gen. Robert Holt, 1837–1900, vol. I
Trueman, Sir Arthur Elijah, 1894–1956, vol. V
Trueman, George Johnstone, 1872–1949, vol. IV
Trueta, Joseph, 1897–1977, vol. VII
Truffaut, François, 1932–1984, vol. VIII
Truman, Charles Edwin, *died* 1938, vol. III
Truman, Lt-Col Egerton Danford, *died* 1938, vol. III

Truman, Harry S., 1884–1972, vol. VII
Truman, Maj.-Gen. William Robinson, *died* 1905, vol. I
Trumble, Thomas, 1872–1954, vol. V
Trump, John, 1858–1941, vol. IV
Trumpler, Stephen Alfred Herman, 1879–1963, vol. VI
Truninger, Lionel, 1870–1961, vol. VI
Truro, 3rd Baron, 1856–1899, vol. I
Truscott, Sir Denis Henry, 1908–1989, vol. VIII
Truscott, Sir Eric Homewood Stanham, 2nd Bt, 1898–1973, vol. VII
Truscott, Sir George Wyatt, 1st Bt, 1857–1941, vol. IV
Truscott, Samuel John, 1870–1950, vol. IV
Truss, Leslie S.; *see* Seldon Truss.
Trust, Helen, *died* 1953, vol. V
Trustam, Sir Charles Frederick, 1900–1964, vol. VI
Trusted, Sir Harry Herbert, 1888–1985, vol. VIII
Trutch, Sir Joseph William, 1826–1904, vol. I
Truter, Sir Theodore Gustaff, 1873–1949, vol. IV
Trye, Captain John Henry, 1875–1959, vol. V
Tryhorn, Frederick Gerald, 1893–1972, vol. VII
Tryon, 1st Baron, 1871–1940, vol. III
Tryon, 2nd Baron, 1906–1976, vol. VII
Tschiffeley, Aimé Felix, 1895–1954, vol. V
Tschudi, Hugo von, 1851–1911, vol. I
Tsen, Rt Rev. P(hilip) Lindel, *died* 1954, vol. V
Tsibu Darku, Nana Sir, 1902–1982, vol. VIII
Tubb, Carrie, (Mrs A. J. E. Oliveira), 1876–1976, vol. VII
Tubb, Captain Frederick Harold, *died* 1917, vol. II
Tubbs, Francis Ralph, 1907–1980, vol. VII
Tubbs, Rt Rev. Norman H., 1879–1965, vol. VI
Tubbs, Percy Burnell, 1868–1933, vol. III
Tubbs, Sir Stanley William, 1st Bt, 1871–1941, vol. IV
Tubby, Alfred Herbert, 1862–1930, vol. III
Tuck, Sir Adolph, 1st Bt, 1854–1926, vol. II
Tuck, Maj.-Gen. George Newsam, 1901–1981, vol. VIII
Tuck, Col Gerald Louis Johnson, 1889–1966, vol. VI
Tuck, Gustave, 1857–1942, vol. IV
Tuck, Sir Raphael Herman, 1910–1982, vol. VIII
Tuck, Major Sir Reginald; *see* Tuck, Major Sir W. R.
Tuck, Wing Comdr Robert Roland S.; *see* Stanford-Tuck.
Tuck, William Henry, 1840–1922, vol. II
Tuck, Major Sir (William) Reginald, 2nd Bt, 1883–1954, vol. V
Tucker, Baron (Life Peer); Frederick James Tucker, 1888–1975, vol. VII
Tucker, Alexander Lauzun Pendock, 1861–1941, vol. IV
Tucker, Alfred Brook, 1861–1945, vol. IV
Tucker, Rt Rev. Alfred Robert, 1849–1914, vol. I
Tucker, Archibald Norman, 1904–1980, vol. VII
Tucker, Arthur, 1864–1929, vol. III
Tucker, Col Aubrey Hervey, 1833–1907, vol. I
Tucker, Rt Rev. Beverley Dandridge, 1846–1930, vol. III
Tucker, Lt-Gen. Sir Charles, 1838–1935, vol. III
Tucker, David Gordon, 1914–1990, vol. VIII
Tucker, Sir Edward George, 1896–1961, vol. VI

Tucker, Francis Ellis, 1844–1921, vol. II
Tucker, Frederick St George de Lautour B.; *see* Booth Tucker.
Tucker, Rev. George, 1835–1908, vol. I
Tucker, Gordon; *see* Tucker, D. G.
Tucker, Hon. Sir Henry James, 1903–1986, vol. VIII
Tucker, Howard Archibald, 1889–1963, vol. VI
Tucker, Sir James Millard, 1892–1963, vol. VI
Tucker, Rev. John Savile, 1866–1954, vol. V
Tucker, Keith Ravenscroft, 1890–1963, vol. VI
Tucker, Maj.-Gen. Louis Henry Emile, 1843–1925, vol. II
Tucker, Sir Norman Sanger, 1895–1965, vol. VI
Tucker, Norman Walter Gwynn, 1910–1978, vol. VII
Tucker, Captain S. N., 1876–1902, vol. I
Tucker, Thomas George, 1859–1946, vol. IV
Tucker, William, *died* 1909, vol. I
Tucker, Very Rev. William Frederic, 1856–1934, vol. III
Tucker, Maj.-Gen. William Guise, 1850–1906, vol. I
Tucker, William Kidger, 1857–1944, vol. IV
Tucker, Lt-Col William Kington, 1877–1956, vol. V
Tuckey, Rev. Canon James Grove White, 1864–1947, vol. IV
Tuckwell, Sir Edward George, 1910–1988, vol. VIII
Tuckwell, Gertrude Mary, 1861–1951, vol. V
Tuckwell, Rev. W., 1829–1919, vol. II
Tudball, Sir William, 1866–1939, vol. III
Tudhope, George Ranken, 1893–1955, vol. V
Tudor, Sir Daniel Thomas, 1866–1928, vol. II
Tudor, Hon. Frank Gwynne, 1866–1922, vol. II
Tudor, Adm. Sir Frederick Charles Tudor, 1863–1946, vol. IV
Tudor, Maj.-Gen. Sir H. Hugh, 1871–1965, vol. VI
Tudor-Craig, Major Sir Algernon Tudor, 1873–1943, vol. IV
Tudor Davies, William; *see* Davies.
Tudor-Evans, Rev. George Simon, 1867–1935, vol. III
Tudor Price, Hon. Sir David William, 1931–1986, vol. VIII
Tudsbery, Sir Francis Cannon Tudsbery, 1888–1968, vol. VI
Tudsbery, Col Henry Tudsbery, 1886–1946, vol. IV
Tudsbery, J. H. T., 1859–1939, vol. III
Tudsbery, Marmaduke Tudsbery, 1892–1983, vol. VIII
Tudway, Brig.-Gen. Robert John, 1859–1944, vol. IV
Tuer, Andrew White, 1838–1900, vol. I
Tuff, Charles, 1855–1929, vol. III
Tuff, Sir Charles, 1881–1961, vol. VI
Tuffier, Sir Theodore Martin, 1857–1929, vol. III
Tuffill, Comdr (S) Harold Birch, 1870–1950, vol. IV
Tufnell, Col Arthur Wyndham, *died* 1920, vol. II
Tufnell, Lt-Col Edward, 1848–1909, vol. I
Tufnell, Brig.-Gen. Lionel Charles Gostling, 1865–1941, vol. IV
Tufnell, Adm. Lionel Grant, 1857–1930, vol. III
Tufnell, Lt-Comdr Richard Lionel, 1896–1956, vol. V
Tufnell, Col William Nevill, 1838–1922, vol. II
Tufnell-Barrett, Hugh, 1900–1981, vol. VIII
Tufton, Hon. Charles Henry, 1879–1923, vol. II
Tufts, J. F., *died* 1921, vol. II
Tufts, James Hayden, 1862–1942, vol. IV

Tugendhat, Georg, 1898–1973, vol. VII
Tugwell, Rt Rev. Herbert, *died* 1936, vol. III
Tugwell, Ven. Lewen Greenwood, *died* 1937, vol. III
Tuite, Sir Brian Hugh Morgan, 12th Bt, 1897–1970, vol. VI
Tuite, Sir Denis George Harmsworth, 13th Bt, 1904–1981, vol. VIII
Tuite, James, 1849–1916, vol. II
Tuite, Sir Mark Anthony Henry, 10th Bt, 1808–1898, vol. I
Tuite, Sir Morgan Harry Paulet, 11th Bt, 1861–1946, vol. IV
Tuke, Anthony William, 1897–1975, vol. VII
Tuke, Lt-Col George Francis Stratford, 1876–1948, vol. IV
Tuke, Captain Godfrey, 1871–1944, vol. IV
Tuke, Henry Scott, 1858–1929, vol. III
Tuke, Sir John Batty, 1835–1913, vol. I
Tuke, Col John Melville, 1885–1958, vol. V
Tuke, Dame Margaret Janson, 1862–1947, vol. IV
Tuke, William Favill, 1863–1940, vol. III
Tuker, Lt-Gen. Sir Francis Ivan Simms, 1894–1967, vol. VI
Tull, Thomas Stuart, 1914–1982, vol. VIII
Tulloch, Maj.-Gen. Sir Alexander Bruce, 1838–1920, vol. II
Tulloch, Angus Alexander Gegorie, 1867–1932, vol. III
Tulloch, Maj.-Gen. Derek; *see* Tulloch, Maj.-Gen. Donald D. C.
Tulloch, Maj.-Gen. (Donald) Derek (Cuthbertson), 1903–1974, vol. VII
Tulloch, Major Hector, 1835–1922, vol. II
Tulloch, Brig.-Gen. James Bruce Gregorie, *died* 1946, vol. IV
Tulloch, Brig.-Gen. John Arthur Stamford, 1865–1946, vol. IV
Tulloch, Maj.-Gen. John Walter Graham, 1861–1934, vol. III
Tulloch, Rev. W. W., 1846–1920, vol. II
Tulloch, William John, 1887–1966, vol. VI
Tulloh, Maj.-Gen. John Stewart, 1827–1901, vol. I
Tully, Jasper, 1858–1938, vol. III
Tully, Kivas, 1820–1905, vol. I
Tully, Sydney Strickland, *died* 1911, vol. I
Tun, Hon. Sir Paw, *died* 1953, vol. V
Tunbridge, Sir Ronald Ernest, 1906–1984, vol. VIII
Tunbridge, Brig.-Gen. Walter Howard, 1856–1943, vol. IV
Tunnard, John Samuel, 1900–1971, vol. VII
Tunnecliffe, Hon. Thomas, 1869–1948, vol. IV
Tunnicliffe, Charles Frederick, 1901–1979, vol. VII
Tunnicliffe, Francis Whittaker, *died* 1928, vol. II
Tunstall, Brian; *see* Tunstall, W. C. B.
Tunstall, (William Cuthbert) Brian, 1900–1970, vol. VI
Tuohy, James M., 1859–1923, vol. II
Tuohy, Patrick Joseph, 1894–1930, vol. III
Tuominen, Leo Olavi, 1911–1981, vol. VIII
Tuplin, William Alfred, *died* 1975, vol. VII
Tupolev, Andrei Nikolaevich, 1888–1972, vol. VII
Tupou, Queen Salote; *see* Tonga, HM the Queen of.
Tupp, Alfred Cotterell, 1840–1914, vol. I
Tupper, Rt Hon. Sir Charles, 1st Bt, 1821–1915, vol. I

Tupper, Sir Charles, 3rd Bt, 1880–1962, vol. VI
Tupper, Hon. Sir Charles Hibbert, 1855–1927, vol. II
Tupper, Sir (Charles) Lewis, 1848–1910, vol. I
Tupper, Sir Charles Stewart, 2nd Bt, 1884–1960, vol. V
Tupper, Sir Daniel Alfred Anley, 1849–1922, vol. II
Tupper, Gen. Gaspard le Marchant, 1826–1906, vol. I
Tupper, J. Stewart, 1851–1915, vol. I
Tupper, Sir James Macdonald, 4th Bt, 1887–1967, vol. VI
Tupper, Sir Lewis; *see* Tupper, Sir C. L.
Tupper, Adm. Sir Reginald Godfrey Otway, 1859–1945, vol. IV
Tupper, William Johnston, 1862–1947, vol. IV
Tupper-Carey, Rev. Albert Darell, 1866–1943, vol. IV
Turbayne, Albert Angus, 1866–1940, vol. III
Turbervill, Edith P.; *see* Picton-Turbervill.
Turberville, Arthur Stanley, 1888–1945, vol. IV
Turck, Hermann, 1856–1933, vol. III
Turgeon, Hon. Adelard, 1863–1930, vol. III
Turgeon, Hon. William Ferdinand Alphonse, 1877–1969, vol. VI
Turing, Alan Mathison, 1912–1954, vol. V
Turing, Harvey Doria, 1877–1950, vol. IV
Turing, Henry, 1843–1922, vol. II
Turing, Sir James Walter, 9th Bt, 1862–1928, vol. II
Turing, Sir John Leslie, 11th Bt, 1895–1987, vol. VIII
Turing, Sir Robert Andrew Henry, 10th Bt, 1895–1970, vol. VI
Turing, Sir Robert Fraser, 8th Bt, 1827–1913, vol. I
Turle, Rear-Adm. Charles Edward, 1883–1966, vol. VI
Turle, Henry Bernard, 1885–1974, vol. VII
Turley, Henry, *died* 1929, vol. III
Turnbull, Col Alan William, 1893–1964, vol. VI
Turnbull, Sir Alexander Cuthbert, 1925–1990, vol. VIII
Turnbull, Sir Alfred Clarke, *died* 1962, vol. VI
Turnbull, Col Bruce, 1880–1952, vol. V
Turnbull, Dora Amy; *see* Turnbull, Mrs George.
Turnbull, Brig. Douglas John Tulloch, 1901–1973, vol. VII
Turnbull, Major Dudley Ralph, 1891–1917, vol. II
Turnbull, Edwin Laurence, 1888–1968, vol. VI
Turnbull, Sir Francis Fearon, (Sir Frank Turnbull), 1905–1988, vol. VIII
Turnbull, Mrs George, (Dora Amy), *died* 1961, vol. VI
Turnbull, George Henry, 1889–1961, vol. VI
Turnbull, Gilbert Learmonth, 1895–1981, vol. VIII
Turnbull, Herbert Westren, 1885–1961, vol. VI
Turnbull, Hubert Maitland, 1875–1955, vol. V
Turnbull, Lt-Col Sir Hugh Stephenson, 1882–1973, vol. VII
Turnbull, Cdre James, 1874–1964, vol. VI
Turnbull, Jane Holland, *died* 1958, vol. V
Turnbull, Col John, 1864–1937, vol. III
Turnbull, Ven. John William, 1905–1979, vol. VII
Turnbull, Sir March; *see* Turnbull, Sir R. M. K.
Turnbull, Maj.-Gen. Peter Stephenson, 1836–1921, vol. II
Turnbull, Sir (Reginald) March Kesterson, 1878–1943, vol. IV

Turnbull, Robert, 1823–1901, vol. I
Turnbull, Sir Robert, 1852–1926, vol. II
Turnbull, Sir Roland Evelyn, 1905–1960, vol. V
Turnbull, Lt-Col Thomas, *died* 1929, vol. III
Turnbull, Sir Winton George, 1899–1980, vol. VII
Turner, Sir Adolphus Hilgrove, *died* 1911, vol. I
Turner, Sir Alan George, 1906–1978, vol. VII (AII)
Turner, Alfred, 1874–1922, vol. II
Turner, Alfred, 1874–1940, vol. III
Turner, Sir Alfred Charles; *see* Turner, Sir V. A. C.
Turner, Maj.-Gen. Sir Alfred Edward, 1842–1918, vol. II
Turner, Rt Rev. Arthur Beresford, 1862–1910, vol. I
Turner, Arthur James, 1889–1971, vol. VII
Turner, Brig.-Gen. Arthur Jervois, 1878–1952, vol. V
Turner, Arthur Logan, 1865–1939, vol. III
Turner, Engr Rear-Adm. Arthur William, 1859–1928, vol. II
Turner, Col Augustus Henry, 1842–1925, vol. II
Turner, Beatrice Ethel, 1891–1964, vol. VI
Turner, Sir Ben, 1863–1942, vol. IV
Turner, Captain Bingham Alexander, 1877–1914, vol. I
Turner, Comdr Bradwell Talbot, 1907–1990, vol. VIII
Turner, Maj.-Gen. Cecil Douglas Lovett, 1898–1976, vol. VII
Turner, Sir Cedric Oban, 1907–1982, vol. VIII
Turner, Sir Charles Arthur, 1833–1907, vol. I
Turner, Major Charles Cyril, 1870–1952, vol. V
Turner, Col Charles Edward, 1876–1961, vol. VI
Turner, Brig. Charles Edward Francis, 1899–1990, vol. VIII
Turner, Charles George, 1838–1913, vol. I
Turner, Rt Rev. Charles Henry, 1842–1923, vol. II
Turner, Sir Charles William Aldis, 1879–1938, vol. III
Turner, Vice-Adm. Charles Wolfran R.; *see* Round-Turner.
Turner, Major Clarence Roy, 1891–1957, vol. V
Turner, Cuthbert Hamilton, 1860–1930, vol. III
Turner, Dawson, 1857–1928, vol. II
Turner, Douglas William, 1894–1977, vol. VII
Turner, Dudley Charles, 1885–1958, vol. V
Turner, E. A., (Lady Turner); *see* Robertson, E. Arnot.
Turner, E. L., *died* 1940, vol. III
Turner, Edmund Robert, 1826–1899, vol. I
Turner, Edward Beadon, 1854–1931, vol. III
Turner, Edward Raymond, 1881–1929, vol. III
Turner, Elston G.; *see* Grey-Turner.
Turner, Eric, 1918–1980, vol. VII
Turner, Sir Eric Gardner, 1911–1983, vol. VIII
Turner, Ernest George, 1874–1932, vol. III
Turner, Ernest James, 1877–1966, vol. VI
Turner, Maj.-Gen. Ernest Vere, *died* 1949, vol. IV
Turner, Ethel, (Mrs H. R. Curlewis), 1872–1958, vol. V
Turner, Eustace Ebenezer, 1893–1966, vol. VI
Turner, Dame Eva, 1892–1990, vol. VIII
Turner, Lt-Col Francis Charles, 1866–1942, vol. IV
Turner, Francis McDougall Charlewood, 1897–1982, vol. VIII
Turner, Frank Douglas, 1871–1957, vol. V
Turner, Franklyn Lewis, 1866–1933, vol. III

Turner, Fred, 1852–1939, vol. III
Turner, Frederick Bancroft, *died* 1966, vol. VI
Turner, Frederick Charles, 1872–1950, vol. IV
Turner, Vice-Adm. Sir Frederick Richard Gordon, 1889–1976, vol. VII
Turner, Sir George, *died* 1915, vol. I
Turner, Rt Hon. Sir George, 1851–1916, vol. II
Turner, George Charlewood, 1891–1967, vol. VI
Turner, Col George Frederick Brown, 1876–1941, vol. IV
Turner, George Grey, 1877–1951, vol. IV
Turner, George Henry, 1837–1903, vol. I
Turner, George James, *died* 1946, vol. IV
Turner, Sir George Robertson, 1855–1941, vol. IV
Turner, Sir George Wilfred, 1896–1974, vol. VII
Turner, Rt Rev. Gilbert Price Lloyd, 1888–1968, vol. VI
Turner, Maj.-Gen. Guy Roderick, 1889–1963, vol. VI
Turner, Harold Goodhew, 1906–1981, vol. VIII
Turner, Harold H.; *see* Horsfall Turner.
Turner, Captain Harry Gordon, *born* 1862, vol. III
Turner, Sir Harvey, 1889–1983, vol. VIII
Turner, Hawes Harison, 1851–1939, vol. III
Turner, Henry Blois Hawkins, 1839–1909, vol. I
Turner, Sir Henry Ernest, *died* 1961, vol. VI
Turner, H(enry) F(rederic) Lawrence, 1908–1977, vol. VII
Turner, Col Henry Fyers, 1840–1909, vol. I
Turner, Sir Henry Samuel Edwin, 1887–1978, vol. VII
Turner, Herbert Arthur, 1912–1972, vol. VII
Turner, Herbert Hall, 1861–1930, vol. III
Turner, Rt Rev. Herbert Victor, 1888–1968, vol. VI
Turner, Rev. Herbert William, 1846–1922, vol. II
Turner, Maj.-Gen. James Gibbon, 1859–1950, vol. IV
Turner, James Grant Smith, 1897–1985, vol. VIII
Turner, James Neil Frederick, 1932–1984, vol. VIII
Turner, Sir John, 1858–1931, vol. III
Turner, John Andrew, 1858–1922, vol. II
Turner, Ven. John Carpenter, 1867–1952, vol. V
Turner, Col John Eamer, 1880–1955, vol. V
Turner, Col Sir John Fisher, 1881–1958, vol. V
Turner, John Hastings, 1892–1956, vol. V
Turner, John Herbert, 1833–1923, vol. II
Turner, John Sidney, 1843–1920, vol. II
Turner, John William Aldren, 1911–1980, vol. VII
Turner, Sir Joseph, 1868–1939, vol. III
Turner, Joseph Harling, 1859–1942, vol. IV
Turner, Rear-Adm. Laurence, 1882–1963, vol. VI
Turner, Laurence Beddome, 1886–1963, vol. VI
Turner, Sir Llewelyn, 1823–1903, vol. I
Turner, Sir Mark; *see* Turner, Sir R. M. C.
Turner, Brig.-Gen. Martin Newman, 1865–1944, vol. IV
Turner, Maxwell Joseph Hall, 1907–1960, vol. V
Turner, Sir Michael William, 1905–1980, vol. VII
Turner, Sir Montagu Cornish, 1853–1934, vol. III
Turner, Brig.-Gen. Percy Alexander, 1868–1940, vol. III
Turner, Percy Frederick, 1878–1926, vol. II
Turner, Philip, 1873–1955, vol. V
Turner, Lt-Col Ralph Beresford, 1879–1972, vol. VII
Turner, Sir Ralph Lilley, 1888–1983, vol. VIII
Turner, Lt-Col Reginald, 1870–1953, vol. V

Turner, Col Reginald George, 1870–1953, vol. V
Turner, Lt-Gen. Sir Richard Ernest William, 1871–1961, vol. VI
Turner, Richard Whitbourn, 1867–1932, vol. III
Turner, Robert Noel, 1912–1987, vol. VIII
Turner, Vice-Adm. Sir Robert Ross, 1885–1977, vol. VII
Turner, Sir (Ronald) Mark (Cunliffe), 1906–1980, vol. VII
Turner, Sir Samuel, 1840–1924, vol. II
Turner, Sir Samuel, 1878–1955, vol. V
Turner, Maj.-Gen. Samuel Compton, died 1900, vol. I
Turner, Sir Sidney, 1882–1966, vol. VI
Turner, Sir Skinner, 1868–1935, vol. III
Turner, Sydney George, 1880–1967, vol. VI
Turner, Theodore Francis, 1900–1986, vol. VIII
Turner, Thomas, 1861–1951, vol. V
Turner, Sir Victor Alfred Charles, 1892–1974, vol. VII
Turner, Lt-Col Victor Buller, 1900–1972, vol. VII
Turner, Sir Walford Hollier, 1881–1962, vol. VI
Turner, Walter James Redfern, 1889–1946, vol. IV
Turner, Rt Rev. William, 1844–1914, vol. I
Turner, Sir William, 1832–1916, vol. II
Turner, William, 1856–1936, vol. III
Turner, Rt Hon. Sir William, 1872–1937, vol. III
Turner, Lt-Col William, 1859–1940, vol. III
Turner, William, died 1944, vol. IV
Turner, William Aldren, 1864–1945, vol. IV
Turner, William Ernest Stephen, 1881–1963, vol. VI
Turner, Lt-Gen. Sir William Francis Robert, 1907–1989, vol. VIII
Turner, Sir William Henry, 1868–1923, vol. II
Turner, William Hovell, 1891–1979, vol. VII
Turner, William Percy Whitford, 1884–1962, vol. VI
Turner-Samuels, Moss, died 1957, vol. V
Turney, Sir John, 1839–1927, vol. II
Turnor, Algernon, 1845–1921, vol. II
Turnor, Christopher Hatton, 1873–1940, vol. III
Turnor, Edmund, 1838–1903, vol. I, vol. III
Turnor, Lady Mary Katherine, died 1930, vol. III
Turnour, Rear-Adm. Edward Winterton, 1821–1901, vol. I
Turnour-Fetherstonhaugh, Hon. Keith; see Fetherstonhaugh.
Turpin, Edmund Hart, 1885–1907, vol. I
Turpin, George Sherbrooke, died 1948, vol. IV
Turpin, Sir William Gibbs, 1854–1940, vol. III
Turpin, Ven. William Homan, died 1920, vol. II
Turquan, Joseph, died 1928, vol. II
Turquet, André, died 1940, vol. III
Turquet, Gladys, died 1977, vol. VII
Turrell, Charles, 1846–1932, vol. III
Turrell, Harry Joseph, 1863–1936, vol. III
Turrell, Walter John, 1865–1943, vol. IV
Turrill, William Bertram, 1890–1961, vol. VI
Turton, Sir Edmund Russborough, 1st Bt, 1857–1929, vol. III
Turton, Col Ralph Douglas, 1862–1936, vol. III
Turton, Lt-Col William Harry, 1856–1938, vol. III
Turvey, Isaiah, 1845–1934, vol. III
Turville-Petre, Edward Oswald Gabriel, 1908–1978, vol. VII

Turville-Petre, Lt-Col Oswald Henry Philip, 1862–1941, vol. IV
Tushingham, Sidney, died 1968, vol. VI
Tuson, Alan Arthur Lancelot, 1890–1968, vol. VI
Tuson, Brig.-Gen. Harry Denison, 1866–1958, vol. V
Tuson, Sir Henry Brasnell, 1836–1916, vol. II
Tussaud, John Theodore, 1858–1943, vol. IV
Tute, Sir Richard Clifford, 1874–1950, vol. IV
Tute, Warren Stanley, 1914–1989, vol. VIII
Tutin, Thomas Gaskell, 1908–1987, vol. VIII
Tutt, James William, 1858–1911, vol. I
Tuttiett, Mary Gleed; see Gray, Maxwell.
Tuttle, Rt Rev. Daniel Sylvester, 1837–1923, vol. II
Tuttle, Sir Geoffrey William, 1906–1989, vol. VIII
Tuttle, Wilbur C., 1883–1969, vol. VI
Tutton, Alfred Edwin Howard, 1864–1938, vol. III
Tuxford, Brig.-Gen. George Stuart, 1870–1943, vol. IV
Twain, Mark, 1835–1910, vol. I
Tweddle, Sir William, 1914–1982, vol. VIII
Tweed, Rev. Henry Earle, 1827–1910, vol. I
Tweed, John, 1869–1933, vol. III
Tweed, Lt-Col Thomas Frederic, 1890–1940, vol. III
Tweedale, Rev. Charles L., died 1944, vol. IV
Tweedale, Violet, died 1936, vol. III
Tweeddale, 10th Marquess of, 1826–1911, vol. I
Tweeddale, 11th Marquess of, 1884–1967, vol. VI
Tweeddale, 12th Marquis of, 1921–1979, vol. VII
Tweeddale, Marchioness of; (Julia), died 1937, vol. III
Tweedie, Mrs Alec, died 1940, vol. III
Tweedie, Lt-Col David Keltie, 1878–1941, vol. IV
Tweedie, Adm. Sir Hugh Justin, 1877–1951, vol. V
Tweedie, Col John Lannoy, 1842–1920, vol. II
Tweedie, Hon. Lemuel John, 1849–1917, vol. II
Tweedie, Mary, 1875–1961, vol. VI
Tweedie, Maj.-Gen. Michael, 1836–1917, vol. II
Tweedie, Maj.-Gen. William, 1836–1914, vol. I
Tweedie, Col William John Bell, 1869–1929, vol. III
Tweedmouth, 2nd Baron, 1849–1909, vol. I
Tweedmouth, 3rd Baron, 1874–1935, vol. III
Tweedsmuir, 1st Baron, 1875–1940, vol. III
Tweedsmuir, Lady; (Susan Charlotte), 1882–1977, vol. VII
Tweedsmuir of Belhelvie, Baroness (Life Peer); Priscilla Jean Fortescue Buchan, 1915–1978, vol. VII
Tweedy, Ernest Hastings, 1862–1945, vol. IV
Tweedy, George Alfred, died 1934, vol. III
Tweedy, Sir John, 1849–1924, vol. II
Twells, Rt Rev. Edward, 1828–1898, vol. I
Twemlow, Col Francis Randle, 1852–1927, vol. II
Twemlow, George Fletcher Fletcher-, 1857–1935, vol. III
Twentyman, Col Augustus Charles, 1836–1913, vol. I
Twentyman-Jones, Hon. Percy Sydney, 1876–1954, vol. V
Twidale, Lt-Col Cecil; see Twidale, Lt-Col W. C. E.
Twidale, Lt-Col (William) Cecil Erasmus, 1877–1949, vol. IV
Twigg, Surg. Rear-Adm. Francis John Despard, 1888–1962, vol. VI
Twigg, Sir John, 1856–1935, vol. III
Twigg, John James, 1825–1920, vol. II
Twigg, Brig.-Gen. Robert Henry, 1860–1956, vol. V

Twinberrow, James Frederick, 1866–1931, vol. III

Twining, Baron (Life Peer); Edward Francis Twining, 1899–1967, vol. VI

Twining, Louisa, 1820–1911, vol. I

Twining, Gen. Nathan Farragut, 1897–1982, vol. VIII

Twining, Maj.-Gen. Sir Philip Geoffrey, 1862–1920, vol. II

Twining, Richard Haynes, 1889–1979, vol. VII

Twinn, Frank Charles George, 1885–1972, vol. VII

Twisaday, Major C. E. J., 1850–1925, vol. II

Twisden, Rev. Sir John Francis, 11th Bt, 1825–1914, vol. I

Twisden, Sir John Ramskill, 12th Bt, 1856–1937, vol. III

Twisleton-Wykeham-Fiennes, Gerard Francis Gisborne, 1906–1985, vol. VIII

Twisleton-Wykeham-Fiennes, Lt-Col Sir Ranulph; see Fiennes.

Twiss, Brig.-Gen. Francis Arthur, 1871–1952, vol. V

Twiss, Lt-Col George Edward, 1856–1921, vol. II

Twiss, Vice-Adm. Guy Ouchterlony, 1834–1918, vol. II

Twiss, Brig.-Gen. John Henry, 1867–1941, vol. IV

Twiss, Maj.-Gen. Sir William Louis Oberkirch, 1879–1962, vol. VI

Twist, Henry, 1870–1934, vol. III

Twitchell, Rt Rev. Thomas Clayton, 1864–1947, vol. IV

Twitchett, Ven. Cyril Frederick, 1890–1950, vol. IV

Twohig, Brig. Joseph Patrick O.; see O'Brien Twohig.

Twohig, Col Michael Joseph O.; see O'Brien-Twohig.

Twomey, Sir Daniel Harold Ryan, 1864–1935, vol. III

Twopeny, Richard Ernest Nowell, 1857–1915, vol. I

Twort, Frederick William, 1877–1950, vol. IV

Twyford, Sir Harry Edward Augustus, 1870–1967, vol. VI

Twyford, Thomas William, 1849–1921, vol. II

Twyman, Frank, died 1959, vol. V

Twynam, Sir Henry Joseph, 1887–1966, vol. VI

Twynam, Major Humphrey Martin, 1858–1913, vol. I

Twynam, Col Philip Alexander Anstruther, 1832–1920, vol. II

Twynam, Sir William Crofton, died 1922, vol. II

Twysden, Sir Anthony Roger Duncan, 11th Bt, 1918–1946, vol. IV

Twysden, Sir Louis John Francis, 9th Bt, 1831–1911, vol. I

Twysden, Sir Roger Thomas, 10th Bt, 1894–1934, vol. III

Twysden, Sir William Adam Duncan, 12th Bt, 1897–1970, vol. VI

Tyabji, Badruddin, 1844–1906, vol. I

Tyerman, Donald, 1908–1981, vol. VIII

Tylden, Brig.-Gen. William, died 1942, vol. IV

Tylden-Pattenson, Major Arthur Henry, 1856–1938, vol. III

Tylden-Pattenson, Lt-Col Edwin Cooke; see Pattenson.

Tylecote, Edward Ferdinando Sutton, 1849–1938, vol. III

Tylecote, Frank Edward, died 1965, vol. VI

Tylecote, Dame Mabel, 1896–1987, vol. VIII

Tyler, Sir Alfred, 1869–1936, vol. III

Tyler, Brig.-Gen. Arthur Malcolm, 1866–1950, vol. IV

Tyler, Sir Frederick Charles, 2nd Bt, 1865–1907, vol. I

Tyler, Froom; see Tyler, G. C. F.

Tyler, (George Charles) Froom, 1904–1983, vol. VIII

Tyler, Sir George Robert, 1st Bt, 1835–1897, vol. I

Tyler, Rev. Henry Francis Macdonald, 1846–1929, vol. III

Tyler, Sir Henry Hewey Francis M.; see Macdonald-Tyler.

Tyler, Sir Henry Whatley, 1827–1908, vol. I

Tyler, Brig.-Gen. James Arbuthnot, 1867–1945, vol. IV

Tyler, Sir John William, 1939–1913, vol. I

Tyler, Maj.-Gen. Trevor Bruce, 1841–1923, vol. II

Tylor, Alfred, 1888–1958, vol. V

Tylor, Sir Edward Burnett, 1832–1917, vol. II

Tylor, Sir Theodore Henry, 1900–1968, vol. VI

Tymms, Sir Frederick, 1889–1987, vol. VIII

Tymms, Ralph Vincent, 1913–1987, vol. VIII

Tymms, Rev. T. Vincent, 1842–1921, vol. II

Tynan, Katharine, 1861–1931, vol. III

Tynan, Kenneth Peacock, 1927–1980, vol. VII

Tyndale, Geoffrey Clifford, 1887–1966, vol. VI

Tyndale, Henry Edmund Guise, 1887–1948, vol. IV

Tyndale, Walter, 1855–1943, vol. IV

Tyndale, Lt-Col Wentworth Francis, 1874–1964, vol. VI

Tyndale-Biscoe, Rev. Cecil Earle, 1863–1949, vol. IV

Tyndale-Biscoe, Brig.-Gen. Julian Dallas Tyndale, 1867–1960, vol. V

Tyndall, Sir Arthur, 1891–1979, vol. VII

Tyndall, Arthur Mannering, 1881–1961, vol. VI

Tyndall, Rt Rev. Charles John, 1900–1971, vol. VII

Tyndall, Lt-Col Henry Stuart, 1875–1942, vol. IV

Tyndall, Maj.-Gen. William Ernest, 1891–1975, vol. VII

Tyndall, Lt-Col William Ernest Marriott, 1875–1916, vol. II

Tyner, Rt Rev. Richard, died 1958, vol. V

Tynte, Fortescue Joseph Pratt-, 1841–1907, vol. I

Tyrer, Anderson; see Tyrer, F. A.

Tyrer, (Frank) Anderson, died 1962, vol. VI

Tyrer, William Henry, 1876–1947, vol. IV

Tyrrell, 1st Baron, 1866–1947, vol. IV

Tyrrell, Col Charles Robert, 1859–1934, vol. III

Tyrrell, Sir Francis Graeme, died 1964, vol. VI

Tyrrell, Rev. George, 1861–1909, vol. I

Tyrrell, George Walter, 1883–1961, vol. VI

Tyrrell, Lt-Col Gerald Ernest, 1871–1917, vol. II

Tyrrell, Lt-Col Jasper Robert Joly, died 1951, vol. V

Tyrrell, Col John Frederick, 1872–1944, vol. IV

Tyrrell, Robert Yelverton, 1844–1914, vol. I

Tyrrell, Thomas, 1857–1929, vol. III

Tyrrell, Air Vice-Marshal Sir William, 1885–1968, vol. VI

Tyrrell, Brig. William Grant, 1882–1961, vol. VI

Tyrrell-Green, Rev. Edmund; see Green.

Tyrwhitt, Hon. Clement, 1857–1938, vol. III

Tyrwhitt, Captain Hon. Hugh, 1856–1907, vol. I

Tyrwhitt, Rev. Hon. Leonard Francis, 1863–1921, vol. II

Tyrwhitt, Adm. of the Fleet Sir Reginald Yorke, 1st Bt, 1870–1951, vol. V

Tyrwhitt, Adm. Sir St John Reginald Joseph, 2nd Bt, 1905–1961, vol. VI

Tyrwhitt, Walter Spencer-Stanhope, 1859–1932, vol. III

Tyrwhitt-Drake, Sir Garrard; *see* Drake.

Tyrwhitt-Drake, Hon. Montague W.; *see* Drake.

Tyser, Sir Charles Robert, 1848–1926, vol. II

Tyser, Granville, 1884–1970, vol. VI

Tyson, Dorothy Estelle Esmé W.; *see* Wynne-Tyson.

Tyson, Geoffrey William, 1898–1971, vol. VII

Tyson, George Alfred, 1888–1972, vol. VII

Tyson, Sir John Dawson, 1893–1976, vol. VII

Tyson, Moses, 1897–1969, vol. VI

Tyson, William Joseph, 1851–1927, vol. II

Tyssen, Air Vice-Marshal John Hugh Samuel, 1889–1953, vol. V

Tytler, Adam Gillies, 1845–1929, vol. III

Tytler, Edward Grant F.; *see* Fraser-Tytler.

Tytler, Maj.-Gen. Sir Harry Christopher, 1867–1939, vol. III

Tytler, Sir James Macleod Bannatyne F.; *see* Fraser-Tytler.

Tytler, Bt Col Neil F.; *see* Fraser-Tytler.

Tytler, Maj.-Gen. Robert Francis Christopher Alexander, *died* 1916, vol. II

Tytler, Sarah; *see* Keddie, Henrietta.

Tytler, William Howard, 1885–1957, vol. V

Tytler, Lt-Col Sir William Kerr F.; *see* Fraser-Tytler.

Tyzack, Group Captain John Edward Valentine, 1904–1979, vol. VII

U

Ubbelohde, (Alfred Rene John) Paul, 1907–1988, vol. VIII

Ubbelohde, Paul; *see* Ubbelohde, A. R. J. P.

Udaipur, HH Maharajahdhiraja Maharana of, 1849–1930, vol. III

Udaipur, HH Maharana of, 1884–1955, vol. V

Udal, (Nicholas) Robin, 1883–1964, vol. VI

Udal, Robin; *see* Udal, N. R.

Udny, John Henry Fullarton, 1853–1934, vol. III

Udny, Sir Richard, 1847–1923, vol. II

Uhr, Sir Clive Wentworth, *died* 1974, vol. VII

Uhthoff, John Caldwell, 1856–1927, vol. II

Ullah, Rev. Ihsan, 1857–1929, vol. III

Ullman, Maj.-Gen. Peter Alfred, 1897–1972, vol. VII

Ullmann, Stephen, 1914–1976, vol. VII

Ullmann, Walter, 1910–1983, vol. VIII

Ullswater, 1st Viscount, 1855–1949, vol. IV

Ulrich, Ruy E.; *see* Ennes Ulrich.

Umfreville, Col Percy, 1868–1922, vol. II

Umfreville, Lt-Col Ralph Brunton, *died* 1937, vol. III

Umfreville, William Henry, 1893–1984, vol. VIII

Umney, John Charles, 1868–1919, vol. II

Umpherston, Francis Albert, 1869–1940, vol. III

Unbegaun, Boris Ottokar, 1898–1973, vol. VII

Underdown, Emanuel Maguire, *died* 1913, vol. I

Underdown, Thomas H. J., 1872–1953, vol. V

Underhill, Sir Arthur, 1850–1939, vol. III

Underhill, Charles Edward, 1845–1908, vol. I

Underhill, Adm. Edwin Veale, 1868–1928, vol. II

Underhill, Evelyn, 1875–1941, vol. IV

Underhill, Rt Rev. Francis, 1878–1943, vol. IV

Underhill, Michael Thomas Ben, 1918–1987, vol. VIII

Underhill, Rev. Percy Cyril, 1883–1963, vol. VI

Underwood, Rev. Alfred Clair, 1885–1948, vol. IV

Underwood, Arthur Swayne, *died* 1916, vol. II

Underwood, Edgar Ashworth, 1899–1980, vol. VII

Underwood, Eric Gordon, *died* 1952, vol. V

Underwood, Eric John, 1905–1980, vol. VII

Underwood, John Ernest Alfred, 1886–1960, vol. V

Underwood, Brig. John Percy Delabene, 1882–1958, vol. V

Underwood, Leon, 1890–1975, vol. VII

Undset, Sigrid, 1882–1949, vol. IV

Unett, Captain John Alfred, 1868–1932, vol. III

Unger, Gladys Buchanan, *died* 1940, vol. III, vol. IV

Unger, Josef, 1912–1967, vol. VI

Ungoed-Thomas, Sir (Anwyn) Lynn, 1904–1972, vol. VII

Ungoed-Thomas, Sir Lynn; *see* Ungoed-Thomas, Sir A. L.

Uniacke, Lt-Gen. Sir Herbert Crofton Campbell, 1866–1934, vol. III

Uniacke-Penrose-Fitzgerald, Sir Robert; *see* Fitzgerald.

Unmack, Randall Carter, 1899–1978, vol. VII

Unstead, Robert John, 1915–1988, vol. VIII

Untermeyer, Louis, 1885–1977, vol. VII

Unwin, Edward, 1840–1933, vol. III

Unwin, Captain Edward, 1864–1950, vol. IV

Unwin, Francis Sydney, 1885–1925, vol. II

Unwin, Col Garton Bouverie, 1859–1928, vol. II

Unwin, Rear-Adm. John Harold, 1906–1970, vol. VI

Unwin, Joseph Daniel, 1895–1936, vol. III

Unwin, Sir Keith, 1909–1990, vol. VIII

Unwin, Nora Spicer, 1907–1982, vol. VIII

Unwin, Sir Raymond, 1863–1940, vol. III

Unwin, Sir Stanley, 1884–1968, vol. VI

Unwin, Thomas Fisher, 1848–1935, vol. III

Unwin, William Cawthorne, 1838–1933, vol. III

Upcher, Rev. Abbot Roland, 1849–1929, vol. III

Upcher, Rev. Arthur Charles Wodehouse, 1846–1938, vol. III

Upcher, Sir Henry Edward Sparke, 1870–1954, vol. V

Upcher, Henry Morris, 1839–1921, vol. II

Upcher, Ven. James Hay, *died* 1931, vol. III

Upcher, Maj.-Gen. Russell, 1844–1936, vol. III

Upcott, Ven. Arthur William, 1857–1922, vol. II

Upcott, Sir Frederick Robert, 1847–1918, vol. II

Upcott, Sir Gilbert Charles, 1880–1967, vol. VI

Updike, Daniel Berkeley, 1860–1941, vol. IV

Upington, Sir Thomas, 1844–1898, vol. I

Upjohn, Baron (Life Peer); Gerald Ritchie Upjohn, 1903–1971, vol. VII

Upjohn, Howard Emlyn, 1925–1980, vol. VII

Upjohn, Sir William George Dismore, 1888–1980, vol. VII

Upjohn, William Henry, 1853–1941, vol. IV

Upperton, Maj.-Gen. John, 1838–1924, vol. II

Upson, Rt Rev. Dom Wilfrid, 1880–1963, vol. VI

Upton, Charles B., 1831–1920, vol. II
Upton, Captain Edward James Gott, *died* 1943, vol. IV
Upton, Hon. Eric Edward Montagu John, 1885–1915, vol. I
Upton, Sir Everard; *see* Upton, Sir T. E. T.
Upton, Florence, *died* 1922, vol. II
Upton, James Bryan, 1900–1976, vol. VII
Upton, John Herbert, 1865–1930, vol. III
Upton, Leslie William Stokes, 1900–1979, vol. VII
Upton, Sir (Thomas) Everard (Tichborne), 1871–1937, vol. III
Upton, Rev. William Clement, *died* 1922, vol. II
Upward, Allen, 1863–1926, vol. II
Upward, Herbert, *died* 1944, vol. IV
Urban, Wilbur Marshall, 1873–1952, vol. V
Ure, Alexander; *see* Baron Strathclyde.
Ure, Mary Eileen (Mrs Robert Shaw), 1933–1975, vol. VII
Ure, Percy Neville, 1879–1950, vol. IV
Ure, Peter, 1919–1969, vol. VI
Uren, Reginald Harold, 1906–1988, vol. VIII
Urey, Harold Clayton, 1893–1981, vol. VIII
Urgüplü, Ali Suad Hayri, 1903–1981, vol. VIII
Uriburu, José Evaristo, *died* 1956, vol. V
Urich, John, 1849–1939, vol. III (A), vol. IV
Urling Clark, Sir Henry Laurence, 1883–1975, vol. VII
Urmson, George Harold, 1851–1907, vol. I
Urmson, Rev. Thomas, *died* 1926, vol. II
Urmston, Col Edward Brabazon, 1858–1920, vol. II
Urquhart, Alexander, 1867–1942, vol. IV
Urquhart, Sir Andrew, 1918–1988, vol. VIII
Urquhart, David Lanchlan; *see* Baron Tayside.
Urquhart, Lt-Col Francis Edward Romulus P.; *see* Pollard-Urquhart.
Urquhart, Francis Fortescue, 1868–1934, vol. III
Urquhart, Frederic Charles, 1858–1936, vol. III
Urquhart, George A., 1888–1951, vol. V
Urquhart, Sir James, 1864–1930, vol. III
Urquhart, John Leslie, 1874–1933, vol. III
Urquhart, Col Robert, 1845–1922, vol. II
Urquhart, Maj.-Gen. Robert Elliott, 1901–1988, vol. VIII
Urquhart, Sir Robert William, 1896–1983, vol. VIII
Urquhart, Maj.-Gen. Ronald Walton, 1906–1968, vol. VI
Urquhart, Rev. William Spence, 1877–1964, vol. VI
Urton, Sir William Holmes Lister, 1908–1982, vol. VIII
Urwick, Edward Johns, 1867–1945, vol. IV
Urwick, Col Frank Davidson, 1874–1936, vol. III
Urwick, Sir Henry, 1859–1931, vol. III
Urwick, Lyndall Fownes, 1891–1983, vol. VIII
Urwick, Sir Thomas Hunter, 1865–1939, vol. III
Urwin, Rt Hon. Thomas William, 1912–1985, vol. VIII
Usborne, Vice-Adm. Cecil Vivian, 1880–1951, vol. V
Usborne, Thomas, 1840–1915, vol. I
Usher, Col Charles Milne, 1891–1981, vol. VIII
Usher, Sir George Clemens, 1889–1963, vol. VI
Usher, Herbert Brough, 1892–1969, vol. VI
Usher, James Ward, *died* 1921, vol. II
Usher, Sir John, 1st Bt, 1828–1904, vol. I

Usher, Col Sir John Turnbull, 3rd Bt, 1891–1951, vol. V
Usher, Sir Peter Lionel, 5th Bt, 1931–1990, vol. VIII
Usher, Rev. Philip Charles Alexander, 1899–1941, vol. IV
Usher, Sir Robert, 2nd Bt, 1860–1933, vol. III
Usher, Sir (Robert) Stuart, 4th Bt, 1898–1962, vol. VI
Usher, Sir Stuart; *see* Usher, Sir R. S.
Usher, Brig. Thomas Clive, 1907–1982, vol. VIII
Usher-Wilson, Rt Rev. Lucian Charles, 1903–1984, vol. VIII
Usherwood, John F., *died* 1964, vol. VI
Usherwood, Kenneth Ascough, 1904–1988, vol. VIII
Usherwood, Ven. Thomas Edward, 1841–1939, vol. III
Usman, Sir Mahomed, 1884–1960, vol. V
Ussher, Col Allan Vesey, 1860–1941, vol. IV
Ussher, Captain Edward, *died* 1902, vol. I
Ussishkin, Menahem, *died* 1941, vol. IV
Uthwatt, Baron (Life Peer); Augustus Andrewes Uthwatt, 1879–1949, vol. IV
Uthwatt, Ven. William Andrewes, *died* 1952, vol. V
Utley, Clifton Maxwell, 1904–1978, vol. VII
Utley, Peter; *see* Utley, T. E.
Utley, Thomas Edwin, (Peter), 1921–1988, vol. VIII
Utrillo, Maurice, (Maurice Valadon), 1883–1955, vol. V
Utterson, Maj.-Gen. Archibald Hammond, 1836–1912, vol. I
Utterson-Kelso, Maj.-Gen. John Edward, 1893–1972, vol. VII
Utterton, Ven. Frank Ernest, *died* 1908, vol. I
Utting, Sir John, *died* 1927, vol. II
Uttley, Albert Maurel, 1906–1985, vol. VIII
Uttley, Alison, 1884–1976, vol. VII
Uttley, George Harry, 1879–1960, vol. V
Uvarov, Sir Boris Petrovitch, 1889–1970, vol. VI
Uvedale of North End, 1st Baron, 1885–1974, vol. VII
Unwins, Cyril Frank, 1896–1972, vol. VII
Uzanne, Octave, 1852–1931, vol. III
Uzès, Duchesse d', 1848–1933, vol. III
Uzielli, Herbert Rex, 1890–1961, vol. VI
Uzielli, Col Theodore John, 1882–1934, vol. III

V

Vacaresco, Helen, *died* 1947, vol. IV
Vachell, Benjamin Garnet L.; *see* Lampard-Vachell.
Vachell, Charles Francis, 1854–1935, vol. III
Vachell, Horace Annesley, 1861–1955, vol. V
Vachon, Most Rev. Mgr Alexandre, 1885–1953, vol. V
Vade-Walpole, Henry Spencer, 1837–1913, vol. I
Vade-Walpole, Thomas Henry Bourke, 1879–1915, vol. I
Vaghjee, Sir Harilal Ranchhordas, 1912–1979, vol. VII
Vaillancourt, Hon. Cyrille, 1892–1969, vol. VII (AI)
Vailland, Roger, 1907–1965, vol. VI
Vaisey, Dame Dorothy May, *died* 1969, vol. VI
Vaisey, Sir Harry Bevir, 1877–1965, vol. VI

Vaithianathan, Sir Kanthiah, 1896–1965, vol. VI

Vaizey, Baron (Life Peer); John Ernest Vaizey, 1929–1984, vol. VIII

Vaizey, Mrs G. de Horne, *died* 1927, vol. II

Vakil, Sardar Khan Bahadur Sir Rustom Jehangir, 1879–1933, vol. III

Valadier, Sir Auguste Charles, 1873–1931, vol. III

Valadon, Maurice; *see* Utrillo, M.

Valantine, Louis Francis, 1907–1977, vol. VII

Valdés, Armando P.; *see* Palacio Valdés.

Vale, Brig. Croxton Sillery, 1896–1975, vol. VII

Vale, Edmund; *see* Vale, H. E. T.

Vale, (Henry) Edmund (Theodoric), 1888–1969, vol. VI

Vale, Captain Seymour Douglas, 1865–1931, vol. III

Valentia, 11th Viscount, 1843–1927, vol. II

Valentia, 12th Viscount, 1883–1949, vol. IV

Valentia, 13th Viscount, 1875–1951, vol. V

Valentia, 14th Viscount, 1888–1983, vol. VIII

Valentine; *see* Pechey, Archibald T.

Valentine, Sir Alec, (Alexander Balmain Bruce Valentine), 1899–1977, vol. VII

Valentine, Alfred Buyers, 1894–1970, vol. VI

Valentine, Charles Wilfrid, 1879–1964, vol. VI

Valentine, David Henriques, 1912–1987, vol. VIII

Valentine, George Donald, 1877–1946, vol. IV

Valentine, Wing-Comdr George Engebret, 1909–1941, vol. IV

Valentine, William Alexander, 1869–1959, vol. V

Valéry, Paul, 1871–1945, vol. IV

Valintine, Thomas Harcourt Ambrose, 1865–1945, vol. IV

Vallance, Lt-Col Aylmer, (George Alexander Gerald Vallance), 1892–1955, vol. V

Vallance, David James, 1849–1915, vol. I

Vallance, George Alexander Gerald; *see* Vallance, Lt-Col Aylmer.

Vallance, William Fleming, 1827–1904, vol. I

Vallery-Radot Pasteur, Louis, 1886–1970, vol. VI

Valluy, Général d'Armée Jean Étienne, 1899–1970, vol. VI

Valon, Maj.-Gen. Albert Robert, 1885–1971, vol. VII

Valpy, Rev. Arthur Sutton, *died* 1909, vol. I

Valtorta, Rt Rev. Mgr Henry Paschal, 1883–1951, vol. V

Vambery, Arminius, 1832–1913, vol. I

van Allen, Rev. William Harman, 1870–1931, vol. III

van Anrooy, A., 1870–1949, vol. IV

Van Beinum, Eduard, 1900–1959, vol. V

Van Beneden, Edward, *died* 1910, vol. I, vol. III

van Boeschoten, Sir Johannes Gerard, 1862–1937, vol. III

van Broekhuizen, Herman Dirk, 1872–1953, vol. V

Vanbrugh, Dame Irene, 1872–1949, vol. IV

Vanbrugh, Violet, 1867–1942, vol. IV

Van Buren, Rt Rev. James Heartt, 1850–1917, vol. II

Vance, Very Rev. George Oakley, 1828–1910, vol. I

Vance, Rt Rev. John Gabriel, 1885–1968, vol. VI

Van Cuylenburg, Sir Hector, 1847–1915, vol. I

Vandal, Louis Jules Albert, 1853–1910, vol. I

Vandam, Albert Dresden, 1843–1903, vol. I

Vandeleur, Lt-Col Cecil Foster Seymour, 1869–1901, vol. I

Vandeleur, Captain Hector Stewart, 1836–1909, vol. I

Vandeleur, Brig. Henry Martley, 1875–1951, vol. V

Vandeleur, Maj.-Gen. John Ormsby, 1832–1908, vol. I

Vandeleur, Brig.-Gen. Robert Seymour, 1869–1956, vol. V

Vanden-Bempde-Johnstone, Hon. Sir Alan; *see* Johnstone.

Vandenberg, Arthur Hendrick, 1884–1951, vol. V

Van Den Berg, Frederick, 1893–1957, vol. V

Van den Bergh, Donald Stanley, 1888–1949, vol. IV

Van den Bergh, Henry, 1851–1937, vol. III

Van Den Bergh, James Philip, 1905–1988, vol. VIII

van den Heever, C. M., 1902–1957, vol. V

Vanden Heuvel, Frederick, 1885–1963, vol. VI

Vandepeer, Sir Donald Edward, 1890–1968, vol. VI

van der Bijl, Hendrik Johannes, 1887–1948, vol. IV

Vanderbilt, Alfred Gwynne, 1877–1915, vol. I

Vanderbilt, Brig.-Gen. Cornelius, 1873–1942, vol. IV

Vanderbilt, Cornelius, 1898–1974, vol. VII

Vanderbilt, Frederick William, 1856–1938, vol. III

Vanderbilt, George Washington, 1862–1914, vol. I

Vanderbilt, William Kissam, 1849–1920, vol. II

Van der Byl, Brig. John, 1878–1953, vol. V

van der Byl, Major Hon. Pieter Voltelyn Graham, 1889–1975, vol. VII

Vanderbyl, Captain P. B., 1867–1930, vol. III

Van Der Hoeve, Jan, 1878–1952, vol. V

Van der Kiste, Lt-Col Freegift William, 1875–1948, vol. IV

Vanderlip, Frank Arthur, 1864–1937, vol. III

Vanderlyn, Nathan, 1872–1946, vol. IV

van der Meulen, Daniel, 1894–1989, vol. VIII

Van der Meulen, Sir Frederick Alan, 1875–1935, vol. III

Vander-Meulen, Adm. Frederick Samuel, 1839–1913, vol. I

Vanderpant, Sir Harry Sheil Elster, 1866–1955, vol. V

Van der Poorten-Schwartz, Joost Marius Willem; *see* Maartens, Maarten.

van der Post, Jan Laurens, 1928–1984, vol. VIII

Van der Riet, Frederick John Werndly, *died* 1929, vol. III

Van der Smissen, William Henry, 1844–1929, vol. III

Van der Veer, John Conrad, 1869–1928, vol. II

Vandervelde, Emile, *died* 1938, vol. III

Vandervell, Harry, 1870–1956, vol. V

Van der Vlugt, W., 1853–1928, vol. II

Van der Waals, Johannes Diedevik, 1837–1923, vol. II

Vanderzee, Maj.-Gen. Francis Henry, 1841–1909, vol. I

Van Deventer, Hon. Lt-Gen. Sir Louis Jacob, *died* 1922, vol. II

Van de Weyer, Victor William Bates, 1839–1915, vol. I

Van de Weyer, Major William John Bates, 1870–1946, vol. IV

Van Dine, S. S.; *see* Wright, Willard Huntington.

Van Druten, John William, 1901–1957, vol. V

Vandry, Rt Rev. Mgr Ferdinand, 1887–1967, vol. VI (AII)

Van Dyck, Ernest Marie Hubert, 1861–1923, vol. II

Van Dyke, Rev. Henry, 1852–1933, vol. III

Vane, Major Sir Francis Patrick Fletcher, 5th Bt, 1861–1934, vol. III
Vane, Frederick William, 1852–1935, vol. III
Vane, Harry Tempest, *died* 1943, vol. IV
Vane, Captain Hon. Henry Cecil, 1882–1917, vol. II
Vane, Sir Henry Ralph Fletcher, 4th Bt, 1830–1908, vol. I
Vane, Hon. Ralph Frederick, 1891–1928, vol. II
Vane, Hon. William Lyonel, 1859–1920, vol. II
Vane-Tempest, Major Adolphus; *see* Vane-Tempest, Major F. A.
Vane-Tempest, Major (Francis) Adolphus, 1863–1932, vol. III
Vane-Tempest, Lord Henry; *see* Vane-Tempest, Lord Herbert L. H.
Vane-Tempest, Lord Henry John, 1854–1905, vol. I
Vane-Tempest, Lord (Herbert Lionel) Henry, 1862–1921, vol. II
Vangeke, Most Rev. Sir Louis, 1904–1982, vol. VIII
van Geyzel, Lt-Col John Lawrence, 1857–1932, vol. III
Van Heerden, Hon. H. C., 1862–1933, vol. III
van Heyningen, William Edward, 1911–1989, vol. VIII
Van Horne, William Cornelius, 1843–1915, vol. I
Van Hulsteyn, Sir Willem, 1865–1939, vol. III
Vanier, Gen. Rt Hon. Georges Philias, 1888–1967, vol. VI
Van Koughnet, Captain Edmund Barker, 1849–1905, vol. I
Van Lare, William Bedford, 1904–1969, vol. VI
van Loon, Hendrik Willem, *died* 1944, vol. IV
van Meerbeke, René Louis Joseph Marie, 1895–1983, vol. VIII
Van Miltenburg, Most Rev. Mgr Alcuin, 1909–1966, vol. VI
Vanneck, Hon. Andrew Nicolas Armstrong, 1890–1965, vol. VI
Van Neck, Captain Stephen Hugh, 1889–1963, vol. VI
Vanneck, Hon. William Arcedeckne, 1845–1912, vol. I
Van Notten-Pole, Sir Cecil Pery; *see* Pole.
Van Praagh, Dame Peggy, 1910–1990, vol. VIII
van Raalte, Charles, 1857–1907, vol. I
Van Reeth, Rt Rev. Joseph, 1843–1923, vol. II
Van Rhyn, Albertus Johannes Roux, 1890–1971, vol. VII
Van Roey, His Eminence Cardinal Joseph Ernest, 1874–1961, vol. VI
Van Ryneveld, Gen. Sir Pierre Helperus Andrias, 1891–1972, vol. VII
Vans Agnew, Lt-Col John, 1859–1943, vol. IV
Van Scoy, Thomas, 1848–1901, vol. I
Vansittart, 1st Baron, 1881–1957, vol. V
Vansittart, Arthur George, 1854–1911, vol. I
Vansittart, Col Eden, 1856–1936, vol. III
Vansittart, Adm. Edward Westby, 1818–1904, vol. I
Vansittart, Guy Nicholas, 1893–1989, vol. VIII
Vansittart, Ronald Arnold, 1851–1938, vol. III
Vansittart, Spencer Charles Patrick, 1860–1928, vol. II
Vansittart-Neale, Sir Henry James; *see* Neale.
Van Someren, William Taylor, 1855–1944, vol. IV

Van Someren, Major William Weymouth, 1876–1939, vol. III
Vanston, Sir George Thomas Barrett, 1853–1923, vol. II
van Straubenzee, Maj.-Gen. Sir Casimir Cartwright, 1867–1956, vol. V
van Straubenzee, Brig.-Gen. Casimir Henry Claude, 1864–1943, vol. IV
van Straubenzee, Maj.-Gen. Turner, 1838–1920, vol. II
Van Swinderen, Jonkheer Rene de Marees-, 1860–1955, vol. V
Van Vechten, Carl, 1880–1964, vol. VI
van Verduynen, (Edgar) Michiels, 1885–1952, vol. V
van Verduynen, Michiels; *see* van Verduynen, E. M.
Van Vleck, John Hasbrouch, 1899–1980, vol. VII
Van Wyck, Robert Anderson, 1849–1918, vol. II
van Zeeland, Paul, Vicomte, 1893–1973, vol. VII
Van Zyl, Rt Hon. Gideon Brand, 1873–1956, vol. V
Vapereau, Louis Gustave, 1819–1906, vol. I
Varcoe, Frederick Percy, 1889–1965, vol. VI
Vardon, Harry, 1870–1937, vol. III
Vardy, Rev. Albert Richard, 1841–1900, vol. I
Varin, René Louis, 1896–1976, vol. VII
Varjivandas, Sir Jugmohandas; *see* Jugmohandas Varjivandas.
Varley, Frank Bradley, *died* 1929, vol. III
Varley, George Copley, 1910–1983, vol. VIII
Varley-Haigh, Ernest; *see* Haigh.
Varrier-Jones, Sir Pendrill Charles, 1883–1941, vol. IV
Varvill, Michael Hugh, 1909–1988, vol. VIII
Vasey, Sir Ernest Albert, 1901–1984, vol. VIII
Vasey, Maj.-Gen. George Alan, 1895–1945, vol. IV
Vaskess, Henry Harrison, 1891–1969, vol. VI
Vassal, Gabrielle M., *died* 1959, vol. V
Vassall-Phillips, Father Oliver Rodie, *died* 1932, vol. III
Vassar-Smith, Sir John George Lawley, 2nd Bt, 1868–1942, vol. IV
Vassar-Smith, Sir Richard Vassar, 1st Bt, 1843–1922, vol. II
Vasse, Air Cdre Gordon Herbert, 1899–1965, vol. VI
Vatcher, Rev. James Raynold Morley, 1861–1931, vol. III
Vaucher, Paul, 1887–1966, vol. VI
Vaudin, William Marshall, 1866–1919, vol. II
Vaudrey, Sir William Henry, 1855–1926, vol. II
Vaudrey-Barker-Mill, William Claude Frederick, 1874–1916, vol. II
Vaughan, Rev. Bernard, 1847–1922, vol. II
Vaughan, Major Charles Davies, 1868–1915, vol. I
Vaughan, Charles Edwyn, 1854–1922, vol. II
Vaughan, Brig. (Charles) Hilary (Vaughan), 1905–1976, vol. VII
Vaughan, Col Charles Jerome, 1873–1948, vol. IV
Vaughan, Very Rev. Charles John, 1816–1897, vol. I
Vaughan, Hon. Crawford, 1874–1947, vol. IV
Vaughan, David, 1873–1938, vol. III
Vaughan, Rev. David James, 1825–1905, vol. I
Vaughan, David Thomas G.; *see* Gwynne-Vaughan.
Vaughan, David Wyamar, 1906–1982, vol. VIII
Vaughan, Brig.-Gen. Edward, 1866–1956, vol. V

Vaughan, Brig.-Gen. Edward James Forrester, 1875–1957, vol. V

Vaughan, Brig. Edward William Drummond, 1894–1953, vol. V

Vaughan, Ernest James, 1901–1987, vol. VIII

Vaughan, Major Eugene Napoleon Ernest Mallet, 1878–1934, vol. III

Vaughan, Francis Baynham, 1844–1919, vol. II

Vaughan, Rt Rev. Francis John, 1877–1935, vol. III

Vaughan, Captain George Augustus, 1833–1914, vol. I

Vaughan, Dame Helen Charlotte Isabella G.; see Gwynne-Vaughan.

Vaughan, Rev. Henry, 1848–1920, vol. II

Vaughan, His Eminence Cardinal Herbert, 1932–1903, vol. I

Vaughan, Very Rev. Herbert, 1874–1936, vol. III

Vaughan, Herbert Millingchamp, 1870–1948, vol. IV

Vaughan, Col Herbert Radclyffe, 1864–1947, vol. IV

Vaughan, Brig. Hilary; see Vaughan, Brig. C. H. V.

Vaughan, Hilda, (Mrs Charles Morgan), 1892–1985, vol. VIII

Vaughan, Maj.-Gen. Hugh Thomas J.; see Jones-Vaughan.

Vaughan, Sir James, 1814–1906, vol. I

Vaughan, Rev. Canon John, 1841–1918, vol. II

Vaughan, Rev. Canon John, 1855–1922, vol. II

Vaughan, Maj.-Gen. John, 1871–1956, vol. V

Vaughan, Sir (John Charles) Tudor (St Andrew-), 1870–1929, vol. III

Vaughan, John Edwards, 1863–929, vol. III

Vaughan, John Godfrey, 1916–1984, vol. VIII

Vaughan, John Henry, 1892–1965, vol. VI

Vaughan, John Howard, 1879–1955, vol. V

Vaughan, (John) Keith, 1912–1977, vol. VII

Vaughan, Sir John Luther, 1820–1911, vol. I

Vaughan, Rt Rev. John Stephen, 1853–1925, vol. II

Vaughan, Keith; see Vaughan, J. K.

Vaughan, Lt-Col Joseph Charles Stoelke, 1862–1932, vol. III

Vaughan, Lt-Gen. Sir Louis Ridley, 1875–1942, vol. IV

Vaughan, Margaret; see Vaughan, Mrs William Wyamar.

Vaughan, Reginald Charles, 1874–1935, vol. III

Vaughan, Reginald Charles, 1896–1960, vol. V

Vaughan, Sir Robert, 1866–1941, vol. IV

Vaughan, Robert Charles, 1883–1966, vol. VI

Vaughan, Maj.-Gen. Robert Edward, 1866–1946, vol. IV

Vaughan, Sir Tudor; see Vaughan, Sir J. C. T. St A.

Vaughan, Victor C., 1851–1929, vol. III

Vaughan, Rt Rev. William, 1814–1902, vol. I

Vaughan, William Hubert, 1894–1959, vol. V

Vaughan, William Wyamar, 1865–1938, vol. III

Vaughan, Mrs William Wyamar, (Margaret Vaughan), 1869–1925, vol. II

Vaughan-Hughes, Brig. Gerald Birdwood, 1896–1983, vol. VIII

Vaughan-Lee, Col Arthur Vaughan Hanning, 1862–1933, vol. III

Vaughan-Lee, Charles Guy, 1913–1984, vol. VIII

Vaughan-Lee, Adm. Sir Charles Lionel, 1867–1928, vol. II

Vaughan-Morgan, Sir Kenyon Pascoe, 1873–1933, vol. III

Vaughan-Russell, John Francis Robert, 1895–1958, vol. V

Vaughan-Sawyer, Ethel, 1868–1949, vol. IV

Vaughan-Thomas, (Lewis John) Wynford, 1908–1987, vol. VIII

Vaughan-Thomas, Wynford; see Vaughan-Thomas, L. J. W.

Vaughan Wilkes, Rev. John Comyn, 1902–1986, vol. VIII

Vaughan-Williams, Major Francis, 1856–1920, vol. II

Vaughan Williams, Ralph, 1872–1958, vol. V

Vautelet, Renée G., (Mme H. E. Vautelet), 1897–1980, vol. VII (AII)

Vaux of Harrowden, 7th Baron, 1860–1935, vol. III

Vaux of Harrowden, Baroness (8th in line), 1887–1958, vol. V

Vaux of Harrowden, 9th Baron, 1914–1977, vol. VII

Vaux, Lt-Col Ernest, 1865–1925, vol. II

Vaux, Lt-Col Henry George, 1883–1957, vol. V

Vaux, Sir Richard Augustus, 1869–1946, vol. IV

Vavasour, Sir Henry Mervin, 3rd Bt (cr 1801), 1814–1912, vol. I

Vavasour, Captain Sir Leonard Pius, 4th Bt (cr 1828), 1881–1961, vol. VI

Vavasour, Sir William Edward, 3rd Bt (cr 1828), 1846–1915, vol. I

Vavasseur, Josiah, 1834–1908, vol. I

Vawdrey, Col George, 1872–1961, vol. VI

Vawdrey, Rev. John Cossham, died 1931, vol. III

Veale, Sir Douglas, 1891–1973, vol. VII

Veale, Sir Geoffrey, 1906–1971, vol. VII

Veall, Harry Truman, 1901–1983, vol. VIII

Veasey, Brig. Harley Gerald, 1896–1982, vol. VIII

Veblen, Oswald, 1880–1960, vol. V

Vecqueray, Rev. Gerard Cokayne, 1851–1933, vol. III

Vedder, Elihu, 1836–1923, vol. II

Vedrenne, John E., 1867–1930, vol. III

Veidt, Conrad, 1893–1943, vol. IV

Veitch, Allan, 1900–1971, vol. VII

Veitch, George Stead, 1885–1943, vol. IV

Veitch, Sir Harry James, 1840–1924, vol. II

Veitch, Marian, (Mrs Donald Barnie), 1913–1973, vol. VII

Veitch, William, 1885–1968, vol. VI

Veitch, Maj.-Gen. William Lionel Douglas, 1901–1969, vol. VI

Velázquez, Carlos María, 1918–1970, vol. VI

Veley, Lilian Jane, 1861–1936, vol. III

Veley, Victor Herbert, 1856–1933, vol. III

Vella, Hon. Tom, born 1849, vol. II

Vella, Col Victor George, 1901–1963, vol. VI

Vellacott, Paul Cairn, 1891–1954, vol. V

Venables, Major Charles John, 1865–1915, vol. I

Venables, Rev. Canon E(dward) Malcolm, 1884–1957, vol. V

Venables, Rev. George, 1821–1908, vol. I

Venables, Harry Archbutt, 1858–1944, vol. IV

Venables, Oswald Eric, 1891–1960, vol. V

Venables, Sir Peter Percy Frederick Ronald, 1904–1979, vol. VII

Venables-Llewelyn, Sir Charles Leyshon Dillwyn-, 2nd Bt, 1870–1951, vol. V

Venables-Llewelyn, Brig. Sir (Charles) Michael Dillwyn-, 3rd Bt, 1900–1976, vol. VII

Venables-Llewelyn, Brig. Sir Michael Dillwyn-; *see* Venables-Llewelyn, Brig. Sir C. M. D.

Venables-Vernon, Sir William Henry; *see* Vernon.

Venis, Arthur, 1857–1918, vol. II

Venizelos, Eleutherios, 1864–1936, vol. III

Venkata Reddi Naidu, Sir Kurma, 1875–1942, vol. IV

Venkatagiri, Rajah of, 1857–1916, vol. II

Venkatagiri, Maharajah of, *died* 1937, vol. III

Venkatanarayana Nayudu, Diwan Bahadur J., 1875–1958, vol. V

Venkataratnam Nayudu, Sir R., 1862–1939, vol. III

Venkatasweta Chalapati Runga-Rao Bahadur, Maharajah Sir Ravu, Maharajah of Bobbili, 1862–1920, vol. II

Venmore, Arthur, 1883–1961, vol. VI

Venn, Albert John, 1840–1919, vol. II

Venn, Edward James Alfred, 1919–1989, vol. VIII

Venn, Air Cdre George Oswald, 1892–1984, vol. VIII

Venn, George William Cavendish, *died* 1933, vol. III

Venn, Rev. Henry, 1838–1923, vol. II

Venn, John, 1834–1923, vol. II

Venn, John Archibald, 1883–1958, vol. V

Venner, Sir Edwin John, 1871–1955, vol. V

Venner, John Franklyn, 1902–1955, vol. V

Venning, Alfred Reid, 1846–1927, vol. II

Venning, Sir Edgcombe, 1837–1920, vol. II

Venning, Brig. Francis Esmond Wingate, 1882–1970, vol. VI

Venning, Lieut Gordon Ralph, *died* 1902, vol. I

Venning, Gen. Sir Walter King, 1882–1964, vol. VI

Veno, Sir William Henry, 1866–1933, vol. III

Venour, Major Wilfred John, 1870–1914, vol. I

Venter, Gen. Christoffel Johannes, 1892–1977, vol. VII

Ventris, Maj.-Gen. Francis, 1857–1929, vol. III

Ventry, 4th Baron, 1828–1914, vol. I

Ventry, 5th Baron, 1861–1923, vol. II

Ventry, 6th Baron, 1864–1936, vol. III

Ventry, 7th Baron, 1898–1987, vol. VIII

Verco, Sir Joseph Cooke, 1851–1933, vol. III

Verdi, Guiseppe, 1813–1901, vol. I

Verdin, Sir Joseph, 1st Bt, 1838–1920, vol. II

Verdin, Lt-Col Sir Richard Bertram, 1912–1978, vol. VII

Verdin, William Henry, 1848–1929, vol. III

Verdon, Rt Rev. Michael, 1838–1918, vol. II

Verdon-Roe, Sir Alliott; *see* Roe.

Vere, James Charles H.; *see* Hope-Vere.

Vere, Very Rev. Langton George, 1844–1924, vol. II

Vere Hodge, John Douglass; *see* Hodge.

Vere-Laurie, Lt-Col George Halliburton Foster Peel, 1906–1981, vol. VIII

Vereker, Sir (George) Gordon (Medlicott), 1889–1976, vol. VII

Vereker, Sir Gordon; *see* Vereker, Sir G. G. M.

Vereker, Hon. Henry Prendergast, 1824–1904, vol. I

Veresmith, Daniel Albert, 1861–1932, vol. III

Veresmith, Emile, vol. III

Verestchagin, Vassili, 1842–1904, vol. I

Verey, David Cecil Wynter, 1913–1984, vol. VIII

Verey, Lt-Col Henry Edward, 1877–1968, vol. VI

Verey, Sir Henry William, 1836–1920, vol. II

Verey, Rev. Lewis, 1874–1961, vol. VI

Verhaeren, Emil, 1855–1916, vol. II

Verity, Gp Captain Conrad Edward Howe, 1901–1984, vol. VIII

Verity, Sir Edgar William, 1891–1975, vol. VII

Verity, Francis Thomas, *died* 1937, vol. III

Verity, George, 1867–1936, vol. III

Verity, Rev. Heron Beresford, *died* 1940, vol. III (A), vol. IV

Verity, Sir John, 1892–1970, vol. VI

Verne, Adela, 1886–1952, vol. V

Verne, Jules, 1828–1905, vol. I

Verner, Sir Edward Derrick Wingfield, 6th Bt, 1907–1975, vol. VII

Verner, Sir Edward Wingfield, 4th Bt, 1830–1899, vol. I

Verner, Captain Sir Edward Wingfield, 5th Bt, 1865–1936, vol. III

Verner, Maj.-Gen. Thomas Edward, 1845–1931, vol. III

Verner, Col William Willoughby Cole, 1852–1922, vol. II

Verneuil, Louis, 1893–1952, vol. V

Verney, Sir Edmund Hope, 3rd Bt (*cr* 1818), 1838–1910, vol. I

Verney, Ernest Basil, 1894–1967, vol. VI

Verney, Frank Arthur, 1874–1952, vol. V

Verney, Frederick William, 1846–1913, vol. I

Verney, Maj.-Gen. Gerald Lloyd, 1900–1957, vol. V

Verney, Sir Harry Calvert Williams, 4th Bt (*cr* 1818), 1881–1974, vol. VII

Verney, Sir Harry Lloyd, 1872–1950, vol. IV

Verney, Margaret Maria, (Lady Verney), 1844–1930, vol. III

Verney, Lt-Col Sir Ralph, 1st Bt (*cr* 1946), 1879–1959, vol. V

Verney, Air Cdre Reynell Henry, 1886–1974, vol. VII

Vernham, John Edward, 1854–1921, vol. II

Vernon, 7th Baron, 1854–1898, vol. I

Vernon, 8th Baron, 1888–1915, vol. I

Vernon, 9th Baron, 1889–1963, vol. VI

Vernon, Ambrose White, 1870–1951, vol. V

Vernon, Sir (Bowater) George (Hamilton), 2nd Bt (*cr* 1885), 1865–1940, vol. III

Vernon, Rev. Canon C. W., 1871–1934, vol. III

Vernon, Major Frank, 1875–1940, vol. III

Vernon, Air Cdre Frederick Edward, 1899–1963, vol. VI

Vernon, Sir George; *see* Vernon, Sir B. G. H.

Vernon, Rt Rev. Gerald Richard, 1899–1963, vol. VI

Vernon, Hon. Greville Richard, 1835–1909, vol. I

Vernon, Harold Anselm Bellamy, 1874–1945, vol. IV

Vernon, Sir Harry Foley, 1st Bt (*cr* 1885), 1834–1920, vol. II

Vernon, Brig.-Gen. Henry Albemarle, 1879–1943, vol. IV

Vernon, Sir Herbert; *see* Vernon, Sir J. H.

Vernon, Horace Middleton, 1870–1951, vol. V

Vernon, Captain Hubert Edward, 1867–1902, vol. I

Vernon, Rev. James Edmund, 1837–1928, vol. II

Vernon, Sir (John) Herbert, 2nd Bt (*cr* 1914), 1858–1933, vol. III

Vernon, Sir Norman; *see* Vernon, Sir W. N.
Vernon, Philip Ewart, 1905–1987, vol. VIII
Vernon, Roland Venables, *died* 1942, vol. IV
Vernon, Rupert Robert, 1872–1940, vol. III
Vernon, Sir Sydney, 1876–1966, vol. VI
Vernon, Sir Wilfred Douglas, 1897–1973, vol. VII
Vernon, Major Wilfrid Foulston, 1882–1975, vol. VII
Vernon, Sir William, 1st Bt (*cr* 1914), 1835–1919, vol. II
Vernon, Sir William Henry Venables-, 1852–1934, vol. III
Vernon, Sir (William) Norman, 3rd Bt (*cr* 1914), 1890–1967, vol. VI
Vernon Harcourt, Augustus George, 1834–1919, vol. II
Vernon-Harcourt, Leveson Francis, 1839–1907, vol. I
Vernon-Harcourt, Rt Hon. Sir William George Granville Venables; *see* Harcourt.
Vernon-Hunt, Ralph Holmes, 1923–1987, vol. VIII
Vernon-Jones, Vernon Stanley, 1875–1955, vol. V
Vernon-Wentworth, Captain Bruce Canning, 1862–1951, vol. V
Vernon-Wentworth, Captain Frederick Charles Ulick, 1866–1947, vol. IV
Veronese, Senator Giuseppe, *born* 1854, vol. II
Veronese, Vittorino, 1910–1986, vol. VIII
Verpilleux, Antoine Emile, 1888–1964, vol. VI
Verrall, Arthur Woollgar, 1851–1912, vol. I
Verrall, George Henry, 1848–1911, vol. I
Verrall, Sir Jenner; *see* Verrall, Sir T. J.
Verrall, Paul Jenner, 1883–1951, vol. V
Verrall, Sir (Thomas) Jenner, 1852–1929, vol. III
Verrett, Lt-Col Hector Bacon, 1874–1926, vol. II
Verrieres, Albert Claude, 1871–1940, vol. III
Verrill, Alpheus Hyatt, 1871–1954, vol. V
Verry, Frederick William, 1899–1981, vol. VIII
Verschoyle, Arthur Robert, 1859–1937, vol. III
Verschoyle, Beresford St George, *died* 1962, vol. VI
Verschoyle, Derek Hugo, 1911–1973, vol. VII
Verschoyle, James Kynaston Edwards, 1858–1907, vol. I
Verschoyle-Campbell, Maj.-Gen. William Henry McNeile, 1884–1964, vol. VI
Versey, Henry Cherry, 1894–1990, vol. VIII
Verstone, Philip Eason, 1882–1973, vol. VII
Verteillac, Herminie de; *see* Rohan, Duchess de.
Vertue, Rt Rev. John, 1826–1900, vol. I
Verulam, 3rd Earl of, 1852–1924, vol. II
Verulam, 4th Earl of, 1880–1949, vol. IV
Verulam, 5th Earl of, 1910–1960, vol. V
Verulam, 6th Earl of, 1912–1973, vol. VII
Verykios, Panaghiotis Andrew, 1910–1990, vol. VIII
Verwoerd, Hendrik Frensch, 1901–1966, vol. VI
Vesey, Captain Charles Nicholas C.; *see* Colthurst-Vesey.
Vesey, Ven. Francis Gerald, 1832–1915, vol. I
Vesey, Gen. Sir Ivo Lucius Beresford, 1876–1975, vol. VII
Vesey, Lt-Col Hon. Sir Osbert Eustace, 1884–1957, vol. V
Vesey, Sidney Philip Charles, 1873–1932, vol. III
Vesey, Col Hon. Thomas Eustace, 1885–1946, vol. IV
Vesey-Fitzgerald, Brian Percy Seymour, 1900–1981, vol. VIII

Vesey-Fitzgerald, James Foster-; *see* Fitzgerald.
Vesey-FitzGerald, John Foster, *died* 1932, vol. III
Vesey-FitzGerald, John Vesey, 1848–1929, vol. III
Vesey-Fitzgerald, Seymour Gonne, 1884–1954, vol. V
Vesnin, Victor, 1882–1950, vol. IV (A)
Vestal, Stanley; *see* Campbell, W. S.
Vestey, 1st Baron, 1859–1940, vol. III
Vestey, 2nd Baron, 1882–1954, vol. V
Vestey, Sir Edmund Hoyle, 1st Bt, 1866–1953, vol. V
Vestey, Ronald Arthur, 1898–1987, vol. VIII
Vetch, Col Robert Hamilton, 1841–1916, vol. II
Vetch, Maj.-Gen. William Francis, 1845–1910, vol. I
Vevers, Geoffrey Marr, 1890–1970, vol. VI
Veysey, Geoffrey Charles, 1895–1984, vol. VIII
Vezin, Hermann, 1829–1910, vol. I
Vial, Rev. Frank Gifford, 1872–1948, vol. IV
Vialls, Lt-Col Harry George, 1859–1918, vol. II
Vian, Admiral of the Fleet Sir Philip, 1894–1968, vol. VI
Viant, Samuel Philip, 1882–1964, vol. VI
Viardot, Michelle Pauline, 1821–1910, vol. I
Viaud, Louis Marie Julien; *see* Loti, Pierre.
Vibart, Col Henry Meredith, 1839–1917, vol. II
Vibart, Captain John Fleming, 1877–1948, vol. IV (A), vol. V
Vibart, Bt Lt-Col Noel Meredith, 1893–1935, vol. III
Vibert, Captain Frederick William, 1859–1935, vol. III
Vibert, McInroy Este, 1894–1986, vol. VIII
Vicars, Sir Arthur Edward, 1864–1921, vol. II
Vicars, Edward Robert Eckersall, 1869–1949, vol. IV
Vicars, Sir John, 1857–1936, vol. III
Vicars, Sir William, 1859–1940, vol. III
Vicary, Col Alexander Craven, 1888–1975, vol. VII
Viccars, John Ellis, 1882–1940, vol. III
Vick, Sir Godfrey Russell, 1892–1958, vol. V
Vick, Reginald Martin, *died* 1971, vol. VII
Vickers, Albert, 1838–1919, vol. II
Vickers, Allan Robert Stanley, 1901–1967, vol. VI
Vickers, Sir (Charles) Geoffrey, 1894–1982, vol. VIII
Vickers, Douglas, 1861–1937, vol. III
Vickers, Sir Geoffrey; *see* Vickers, Sir C. G.
Vickers, Harold James, 1895–1970, vol. VI
Vickers, Kenneth Hotham, 1881–1957, vol. V
Vickers, Col Thomas Edward, 1833–1915, vol. I
Vickers, Vincent Cartwright, 1879–1939, vol. III
Vickers, William John, 1898–1979, vol. VII
Vickers, Lt-Gen. Wilmot Gordon Hilton, 1890–1987, vol. VIII
Vickery, Col Charles Edwin, 1881–1951, vol. V
Vickery, Sir Philip Crawford, 1890–1987, vol. VIII
Vicky; *see* Weisz, Victor.
Victor, Rt Rev. Dennis, 1882–1949, vol. IV
Vidal, Col Francis Peter, 1879–1952, vol. V
Vidal, Rt Rev. Julian, 1846–1922, vol. II
Vidor, King Wallis, 1896–1982, vol. VIII
Viener, Rev. Harry Dan Leigh, 1868–1947, vol. IV
Vigne, Lt-Col Robert Austen, 1862–1940, vol. III
Vignoles, Charles Malcolm, 1901–1961, vol. VI
Vigors, Edward Cliffe, *died* 1945, vol. IV
Vigors, Captain Philip Urban, 1875–1917, vol. II
Vigors, Major Philip Urban Walter, 1863–1935, vol. III
Viljoen, Hon. Sir Antonie Gysbert, 1858–1918, vol. II

Viljoen, W. J., 1869–1929, vol. III
Villa-Urrutia, Marquis de, 1850–1933, vol. III
Villalobar, Marquis of, 1866–1926, vol. II
Villar, Captain George, 1887–1970, vol. VI
Villard, Oswald Garrison, 1872–1949, vol. IV
Villars, Henry G.; see Gauthier-Villars.
Villars, Paul, 1849–1935, vol. III
Villasante, Julian Martinez-Villasante y Navarro, 1876–1945, vol. IV
Villeneuve, Son Eminence le Cardinal J. M. Rodrigue, 1883–1947, vol. IV
Villeneuve-Smith, Sir Francis; see Smith.
Villiers, Alan John, 1903–1982, vol. VIII
Villiers, Hon. Arthur George Child, 1883–1969, vol. VI
Villiers, Lt-Col Charles Hyde, died 1947, vol. IV
Villiers, Rt Hon. Charles Pelham, 1802–1898, vol. I
Villiers, Lt-Col Charles Walter, 1873–1938, vol. III
Villiers, Sir Edward; see Villiers, Sir F. E. E.
Villiers, Rear-Adm. Edward Cecil, 1866–1939, vol. III
Villiers, Col Ernest, 1838–1921, vol. II
Villiers, Ernest Amherst, 1863–1923, vol. II
Villiers, Lt-Col Evelyn Fountaine, 1875–1955, vol. V
Villiers, Sir (Francis) Edward Earle, 1889–1967, vol. VI
Villiers, Rt Hon. Sir Francis Hyde, 1852–1925, vol. II
Villiers, Francis John, 1851–1925, vol. II
Villiers, Frederic, 1852–1922, vol. II
Villiers, Gerald Hyde, 1882–1953, vol. V
Villiers, Rev. Henry Montagu, 1837–1908, vol. I
Villiers, Vice-Adm. Sir (John) Michael, 1907–1990, vol. VIII
Villiers, Maria Theresa; see Earle, Mrs C. W.
Villiers, Vice-Adm. Sir Michael; see Villiers, Vice-Adm. Sir J. M.
Villiers, Richard J., 1850–1913, vol. I
Villiers, Brig. Richard Montagu, 1905–1973, vol. VII
Villiers, Sir Thomas Lister, 1869–1959, vol. V
Villiers-Stuart, Col John Patrick, 1879–1958, vol. V
Villiers-Stuart, Brig.-Gen. William, 1872–1961, vol. VI
Vinall, Joseph William Topham, 1873–1953, vol. V
Vinaver, Eugène, 1899–1979, vol. VII
Vince, Charles Anthony, 1855–1929, vol. III
Vincent, Sir Alfred, 1891–1967, vol. VI
Vincent, Sir Anthony Francis, 14th Bt (cr 1620), 1894–1936, vol. III
Vincent, Col Arthur Craigie Fitz-Hardinge, 1857–1929, vol. III
Vincent, Arthur Rose, 1876–1956, vol. V
Vincent, Brig.-Gen. Sir Berkeley, 1871–1963, vol. VI
Vincent, Rt Rev. Boyd, 1845–1935, vol. III
Vincent, Sir (Charles Edward) Howard, 1849–1908, vol. I
Vincent, Air Vice-Marshal Claude McClean, 1896–1967, vol. VI
Vincent, Eric Reginald Pearce, 1894–1978, vol. VII
Vincent, Ethel Gwendoline (Lady Vincent), 1861–1952, vol. III
Vincent, Sir Francis Erskine, 13th Bt (cr 1620), 1869–1935, vol. III
Vincent, Frank Arthur Money, 1875–1950, vol. IV

Vincent, Sir Frederick d'Abernon, 15th Bt (cr 1620), 1852–1936, vol. III
Vincent, George Edgar, 1864–1941, vol. IV
Vincent, Sir Graham; see Vincent, Sir H. G.
Vincent, Sir (Harold) Graham, 1891–1981, vol. VIII
Vincent, Sir Harry, 1874–1952, vol. V
Vincent, Brig.-Gen. Henry Osman, 1863–1945, vol. IV
Vincent, Sir Howard; see Vincent, Sir C. E. H.
Vincent, Sir Hugh Corbet, died 1931, vol. III
Vincent, James Edmund, 1857–1909, vol. I
Vincent, Rt Rev. John Dacre, 1894–1960, vol. V
Vincent, John Lewis, 1845–1915, vol. I
Vincent, Very Rev. John Ranulph, died 1914, vol. I
Vincent, Lady Kitty; see Ritson, Lady K.
Vincent, Sir Lacey Eric, 2nd Bt (cr 1936), 1902–1963, vol. VI
Vincent, Marvin Richardson, 1834–1922, vol. II
Vincent, Sir Percy, 1st Bt (cr 1936), 1868–1943, vol. IV
Vincent, Ralph, 1870–1922, vol. II
Vincent, Robert William Edward Hampe, 1841–1914, vol. I
Vincent, Rev. Samuel, 1839–1910, vol. I
Vincent, Air Vice-Marshal Stanley Flamank, 1897–1976, vol. VII
Vincent, Swale, 1868–1933, vol. III
Vincent, Sir William, 12th Bt (cr 1620), 1834–1914, vol. I
Vincent, Sir William Henry Hoare, 1866–1941, vol. IV
Vincent, William James Nathaniel, 1867–1953, vol. V
Vincent, Sir William Wilkins, 1843–1916, vol. II
Vincent-Gompertz, Frank Priestly, died 1968, vol. VI
Vincent-Jackson, Rev. William, died 1919, vol. II
Vinden, Brig. Frederick Hubert, 1898–1977, vol. VII
Vine, Rev. Aubrey Russell, 1900–1973, vol. VII
Vine, Francis Seymour, 1904–1961, vol. VI
Vine, Sir John Richard Somers, 1847–1929, vol. III
Vine, Laurence Arthur, 1885–1954, vol. II
Vine, Rev. Marshall George, 1850–1918, vol. II
Viney, Lt-Col Horace George, 1885–1972, vol. VII
Vine, Norman Douglas, 1890–1966, vol. VI
Vines, Col Clement Erskine, 1878–1964, vol. VI
Vines, Howard William Copland, 1893–1982, vol. VIII
Vines, Sydney Howard, 1849–1934, vol. III
Vines, Rev. Thomas Hotchkin, died 1928, vol. II
Viney, Col Oscar Vaughan, 1886–1976, vol. VII
Vining, Most Rev. Leslie Gordon, 1885–1955, vol. V
Vinogradoff, Sir Paul Gavrilovitch, 1854–1925, vol. II
Vinson, Frederick Moore, 1890–1953, vol. V
Vintcent, Sir Joseph, 1861–1914, vol. I
Vinter, Geoffrey Odell, 1900–1981, vol. VIII
Vintras, George Charles Louis Bartlett, 1864–1934, vol. III
Viollet, Paul, 1840–1914, vol. I
Vipan, Alfred, 1884–1947, vol. IV
Vipan, Major Charles, 1849–1921, vol. II
Vipan, Captain John Alexander Maylin, 1849–1939, vol. III
Virchow, Rudolf, 1821–1902, vol. I
Virgo, Charles G., 1843–1907, vol. I
Virgo, John James, 1865–1956, vol. V

Virtanen, Artturi Ilmari, 1895–1973, vol. VII
Virtue, Hon. Sir John Evenden, 1905–1986, vol. VIII
Vischer, Sir Hanns, 1876–1945, vol. IV
Visconti, Luchino, 1906–1976, vol. VII
Visetti, Albert, 1846–1928, vol. II
Visger, Mrs Owen; see Owen, Jean A.
Vissanji, Sir Mathuradas, 1881–1949, vol. IV
Visser't Hooft, Willem Adolf, 1900–1985, vol. VIII
Visvesvaraya, Sir Mokshagundam, 1861–1962, vol. VI
Viswa Nath, Rao Bahadur Bhagavatula, 1889–1964, vol. VI
Vivian, 4th Baron, 1878–1940, vol. III
Vivian, Adm. Algernon W. H.; see Walker-Heneage-Vivian.
Vivian, Captain Anthony Hamilton, 1880–1937, vol. III
Vivian, Arthur Henry Seymour, 1899–1985, vol. VIII
Vivian, Sir Arthur Pendarves, 1834–1926, vol. II
Vivian, Hon. Claud Hamilton, 1849–1902, vol. I
Vivian, Captain Gerald William, 1869–1921, vol. II
Vivian, Graham Linsell, 1887–1978, vol. VII
Vivian, Henry, 1868–1930, vol. III
Vivian, Herbert, 1865–1940, vol. III
Vivian, Vice-Adm. John Guy Protheroe, 1887–1963, vol. VI
Vivian, Preston G.; see Graham-Vivian, R. P.
Vivian, Lt-Col Ralph, 1845–1924, vol. II
Vivian, Sir Sylvanus Percival, 1880–1958, vol. V
Vivian, Lt-Col Valentine, 1880–1948, vol. IV
Vivian, Lt-Col Valentine Patrick Terrel, 1886–1969, vol. VI
Vivian, William Graham, 1827–1912, vol. I
Vizard, Brig.-Gen. Robert Davenport, 1861–1941, vol. IV
Vizetelly, Ernest Alfred, 1853–1922, vol. II
Vizetelly, Francis Horace, (Frank), 1864–1938, vol. III
Vizianagram, Rajkumar of, 1905–1965, vol. VI
Vlasto, Michael, 1888–1979, vol. VII
Vlieland, Alice Edith, died 1944, vol. IV
Vodden, Rt Rev. Henry Townsend, 1887–1960, vol. V
Voelcker, Arthur Francis, 1861–1946, vol. IV
Voelcker, Francis William, 1896–1954, vol. V
Voelcker, John Augustus, 1854–1937, vol. III
Vogel, Harry Benjamin, 1868–1947, vol. IV
Vogel, Hon. Sir Julius, 1835–1899, vol. I
Vogt, Alfred, 1879–1943, vol. IV
Vogt, Paul Benjamin, 1863–1947, vol. IV
Vogüé, Marquis Charles Jean Melchior de, 1829–1916, vol. II
Voigt, F. A., 1892–1957, vol. V
Vokes, Maj.-Gen. Christopher, 1904–1985, vol. VIII
Volkers, Robert Charles Francis, died 1929, vol. III
von Anrep, Boris, 1883–1969, vol. VI
Von Arnheim, Edward Henry Silberstein; see Arnheim.
von Berg, Clement, 1853–1936, vol. III
von Bibra, Major Sir Eric Ernest, 1895–1958, vol. V
von Braun, Wernher, 1912–1977, vol. VII
von Bülow, Prince Bernhard Henry Martin Charles, 1849–1929, vol. III
Von der Heyde, Brig. John Leslie, 1896–1974, vol. VII

von Donop, Lt-Col Pelham George, 1851–1921, vol. II
von Donop, Maj.-Gen. Sir Stanley Brenton, 1860–1941, vol. IV
von Euler, Ulf Svante, 1905–1983, vol. VIII
von Frisch, Karl Ritter, 1886–1982, vol. VIII
von Hagen, Victor Wolfgang, born 1908, vol. VIII
von Halle, Ernst, 1868–1909, vol. I
von Karajan, Herbert, 1908–1989, vol. VIII
Vonier, Rt Rev. Dom Anscar, 1875–1938, vol. III
von Karman, Theodore, 1881–1963, vol. VI
von Laue, Max Theodor Felix, 1879–1960, vol. V
von Neumann, John, 1903–1957, vol. V
von Neurath, Freiherr Constantin, 1873–1956, vol. V
Vonnoh, Bessie Potter, 1872–1955, vol. V
Vonnoh, Robert, 1858–1933, vol. III
von Nordenwall, Oswald Hans Carl Maria; see von Stroheim, Erich.
von Purucker, (Hobart Lorenz) Gottfried; see Purucker.
von Ribbentrop, Joachim; see Ribbentrop.
von Sauer, Emil, 1862–1942, vol. IV
von Schröder, Baron William Henry, 1841–1912, vol. I
von Seeckt, Gen., 1866–1936, vol. III
von Stroheim, Erich, (Oswald Hans Carl Maria von Nordenwall), 1885–1957, vol. V
Vonwiller, Oscar Ulrich, 1882–1972, vol. VII
Vora, Sir Manmohandas Ramji, 1857–1934, vol. III (A), vol. V
Vorley, Lt-Col John Stuart, 1898–1953, vol. V
Voronoff, Serge, 1866–1951, vol. V
Voroshilov, Kliment Efremovich, 1881–1969, vol. VI
Vorster, Hon. Balthazar Johannes, 1915–1983, vol. VIII
Vos, Philip, 1891–1948, vol. IV
Vosper, Dennis Forwood; see Baron Runcorn.
Vosper, Sydney Curnow, 1866–1942, vol. IV
Vouel, Raymond, 1923–1987, vol. VIII
Voules, Arthur Blennerhassett, 1870–1954, vol. V
Voules, Sir Francis Minchin, 1867–1947, vol. IV
Voules, Sir Gordon Blennerhassett, 1839–1924, vol. II
Voules, Horace St George, 1844–1909, vol. I
Vousden, William John, 1845–1902, vol. I
Vowden, Desmond Harvey Weight, 1921–1990, vol. VIII
Voynich, Wilfrid Michael, 1865–1930, vol. III
Voysey, Rev. Charles, 1828–1912, vol. I
Voysey, Charles C.; see Cowles-Voysey.
Voysey, Charles Francis Annesley, 1857–1941, vol. IV
Voysey, Violet Mary Annesley, 1880–1943, vol. IV
Vroom, Ven. Fenwick Williams, 1856–1944, vol. IV
Vulliamy, Colwyn Edward, 1886–1971, vol. VII
Vulliamy, Maj.-Gen. Colwyn Henry Hughes, 1894–1972, vol. VII
Vulliamy, Edward, 1876–1962, vol. VI
Vulliamy, Grace, 1878–1957, vol. V
Vyle, Sir Gilbert Christopher, 1870–1933, vol. III
Vyner, Clare George, 1894–1989, vol. VIII
Vyner, Robert Charles de Grey, 1842–1915, vol. I
Vynne, Nora, died 1914, vol. I
Vyse, Charles, 1882–1971, vol. VII

Vyse, Lt-Gen. Edward H.; *see* Howard-Vyse.

Vyse, Howard Henry H.; *see* Howard-Vyse.

Vyse, Maj.-Gen. Sir Richard Granville Hylton H.; *see* Howard-Vyse.

Vyshinsky, Andrei Yanuarievich, 1883–1954, vol. V

Vyvyan, Col Sir Courtenay Bourchier, 10th Bt, 1858–1941, vol. IV

Vyvyan, Captain Sir George Rawlinson, 1838–1914, vol. I

Vyvyan, Jennifer Brigit, 1925–1974, vol. VII

Vyvyan, Maj.-Gen. Ralph Ernest, 1891–1971, vol. VII

Vyvyan, Sir Richard Philip, 11th Bt, 1891–1978, vol. VII

Vyvyan, Major Richard Walter Comyn, 1859–1931, vol. III

Vyvyan, Air Vice-Marshal Sir Vyell, 1875–1935, vol. III

Vyvyan, Rev. Sir Vyell Donnithorne, 9th Bt, 1826–1917, vol. II

Vyvyan, Rt Rev. Wilmot Lushington, 1861–1937, vol. III

W

Waal, Hon. Sir Frederic de; *see* Waal, Hon. Sir N. F. de.

Waal, Hon. Sir (Nicholas) Frederic de, 1853–1932, vol. III

Wace, Alan John Bayard, 1879–1957, vol. V

Wace, Sir Blyth; *see* Wace, Sir F. B.

Wace, Brig.-Gen. Edward Gurth, 1876–1962, vol. VI

Wace, Col Ernest Charles, 1850–1927, vol. II

Wace, Ernest William Cornish, 1894–1977, vol. VII

Wace, Sir (Ferdinand) Blyth, 1891–1964, vol. VI

Wace, Very Rev. Henry, 1836–1924, vol. II

Wace, Herbert, *died* 1906, vol. I

Wace, Maj.-Gen. Richard, 1842–1920, vol. II

Wacha, Sir Dinsha Edulji, 1844–1936, vol. III

Wacher, David Mure, 1909–1989, vol. VIII

Wackett, Air Vice-Marshal Ellis Charles, 1901–1984, vol. VIII

Wackett, Sir Lawrence James, 1896–1982, vol. VIII

Waddams, Rev. Canon Herbert Montague, 1911–1972, vol. VII

Waddell, Hon. Sir (Charles) Graham, 1877–1960, vol. V (A)

Waddell, Gilbert, 1894–1967, vol. VI

Waddell, Hon. Sir Graham; *see* Waddell, Hon. Sir C. G.

Waddell, Helen, 1889–1965, vol. VI

Waddell, John J.; *see* Jeffrey-Waddell.

Waddell, Alexander Peddie-, 1832–1917, vol. II

Waddell, John, *died* 1923, vol. II

Waddell, John J.; *see* Jeffrey-Waddell.

Waddell, Lt-Col Laurence Austine, 1854–1938, vol. III

Waddell, Hon. Thomas, 1854–1940, vol. III

Waddell, William Gillan, 1884–1945, vol. IV

Waddilove, Douglas Edwin, 1918–1976, vol. VII

Waddilove, Sir Joshua Kelley, *died* 1920, vol. II

Waddington, Charles Willoughby, 1865–1946, vol. IV

Waddington, Conrad Hal, 1905–1975, vol. VII

Waddington, Sir (Eubule) John, 1890–1957, vol. V

Waddington, John, 1855–1935, vol. III

Waddington, Sir John; *see* Waddington, Sir E. J.

Waddington, Mary King, *died* 1923, vol. II

Waddington, Sir Robert, 1868–1941, vol. IV

Waddington, Samuel, 1844–1923, vol. II

Waddington, Maj.-Gen. Thomas, 1827–1921, vol. II

Waddington, Brig. Thomas Thelwall, 1888–1958, vol. V

Waddy, Bentley Herbert, 1893–1956, vol. V

Waddy, Dorothy Knight, 1909–1970, vol. VI

Waddy, Henry Turner, 1863–1926, vol. II

Waddy, Rev. Percival Stacy, 1875–1937, vol. III

Waddy, Samuel Danks, 1830–1902, vol. I

Wade, Baron (Life Peer); Donald William Wade, 1904–1988, vol. VIII

Wade, Sir Armigel de Vins, 1880–1966, vol. VI

Wade, Arthur Shepherd, *died* 1941, vol. IV

Wade, Hon. Sir Charles Gregory, 1863–1922, vol. II

Wade, Emlyn Capel Stewart, 1895–1978, vol. VII

Wade, Brig. Ernest Wentworth, 1889–1970, vol. VI

Wade, Hon. Frederick Coate, 1860–1924, vol. II

Wade, Surg.-Maj.-Gen. Frederick William, *died* 1906, vol. I

Wade, Col Sir George Albert, 1891–1986, vol. VIII

Wade, George Edward, 1853–1933, vol. III

Wade, Major George Frederick Dennis, 1899–1968, vol. VI

Wade, Rev. George Woosung, 1858–1941, vol IV

Wade, Sir Henry, 1877–1955, vol. V

Wade, Col Henry Oswald, 1869–1941, vol. IV

Wade, John Charles, 1908–1984, vol. VIII

Wade, John Roland, 1890–1984, vol. VIII

Wade, Philip Harold, 1860–1930, vol. III

Wade, Sir Robert Blakeway, 1874–1954, vol. V

Wade, Rosalind Herschel, (Mrs R. H. Seymour), 1909–1989, vol. VIII

Wade, Rt Rev. (Sydney) Walter, 1909–1976, vol. VII

Wade, Sqdn Ldr Trevor Sidney, 1920–1951, vol. V

Wade, Rt Rev. Walter; *see* Wade, Rt Rev. S. W.

Wade, Sir William, 1849–1935, vol. III

Wade, Sir Willoughby Francis, 1827–1906, vol. I

Wade-Evans, Rev. Arthur Wade, 1875–1964, vol. VI

Wade-Gery, Henry Theodore, 1888–1972, vol. VII

Wadel, William, 1868–1946, vol. IV

Wadely, Frederick William, 1882–1970, vol. VI

Wadeson, Maj.-Gen. Frederick William George, 1860–1920, vol. II

Wadham, Arthur, 1852–1923, vol. II

Wadham, Sir Samuel MacMahon, 1891–1972, vol. VII

Wadia, Sir Bomanji Jamsetji, 1881–1947, vol. IV

Wadia, Sir Cusrow, 1869–1950, vol. IV

Wadia, D. N., 1883–1969, vol. VI

Wadia, Sir Hormasji Ardeshir, *died* 1928, vol. II

Wadia, Sir Ness Nowrosjee, 1873–1952, vol. V

Wadley, Sir Douglas, 1904–1984, vol. VIII

Wadley, Lt-Col Edward John, 1880–1950, vol. IV

Wadley, Walter Joseph Durham, 1903–1982, vol. VIII

Wadsley, Olive, *died* 1959, vol. V

Wadson, Hon. Sir Thomas John, 1844–1921, vol. II

Wadsworth, Alfred Powell, 1891–1956, vol. V
Wadsworth, Edward Alexander, 1889–1949, vol. IV
Wadsworth, George, 1902–1979, vol. VII (AII)
Wadsworth, John, 1850–1921, vol. II
Wadsworth, Sir Sidney, 1888–1976, vol. VII
Waechter, Sir d'Arcy; *see* Waechter, Sir H. L. d'A.
Waechter, Sir Harry, 1st Bt, 1871–1929, vol. III
Waechter, Sir (Harry Leonard) d'Arcy, 2nd Bt, 1912–1987, vol. VIII
Waechter, Sir Max Leonard, 1837–1924, vol. II
Wager, Harold, 1862–1929, vol. III
Wager, Lawrence Rickard, 1904–1965, vol. VI
Wagg, Alfred Ralph, 1877–1969, vol. VI
Waggett, Ernest Blechynden, 1866–1939, vol. III
Waggett, Rev. Philip Napier, 1862–1939, vol. III
Waghorn, Brig.-Gen. Sir William Danvers, *died* 1936, vol. III
Wagner, Franz William, 1905–1985, vol. VIII
Wagner, Wieland Adolf Gottfried, 1917–1966, vol. VI
Wagner, Very Rev. William Wolfe, *died* 1937, vol. III
Wagstaff, Charles John Leonard, 1875–1981, vol. VIII
Wagstaff, Maj.-Gen. Cyril Mosley, 1878–1934, vol. III
Wagstaff, John Edward Pretty, 1890–1963, vol. VI
Wagstaff, Lt-Col Lewis Cecil, 1882–1951, vol. V
Wagstaff, William George, 1837–1918, vol. II
Wahab, Col Robert Alexander; *see* Wauhope, Col R. A.
Wahba, Sheikh Hafiz, 1889–1967, vol. VI
Wahlstatt, Blucher von, 3rd Prince, 1836–1916, vol. II
Waight, Leonard, 1895–1970, vol. VI
Waights, Rev. Kenneth Laws, 1909–1984, vol. VIII
Wain, Louis William, 1860–1939, vol. III
Wainewright, Brig.-Gen. Arthur Reginald, 1874–1970, vol. VI
Wainwright, Maj.-Gen. Charles Brian, 1893–1968, vol. VI
Wainwright, Desmond; *see* Wainwright, E. D.
Wainwright, (Edward) Desmond, 1902–1976, vol. VII
Wainwright, Elsie, *died* 1964, vol. VI
Wainwright, Rev. Frederick, *died* 1921, vol. II
Wainwright, Sir Gilbert Cochrane, 1871–1954, vol. V
Wainwright, Sir James Gadesden, 1837–1929, vol. III
Wainwright, Robert Everard, 1913–1990, vol. VIII
Wainwright, William J., 1855–1931, vol. III
Waistell, Adm. Sir Arthur Kipling, 1873–1953, vol. V
Wait, Air Vice-Marshal George Enoch, 1895–1972, vol. VII
Wait, Col Hugh Godfrey Killigrew, 1871–1948, vol. IV
Wait, Walter Ernest, 1878–1961, vol. VI
Waite, Arthur Edward, 1857–1942, vol. IV
Waite, Clifford, 1896–1974, vol. VII
Waite, Col Hon. Fred, 1885–1952, vol. V
Waite, Herbert William, 1887–1967, vol. VI
Waite, Rev. Joseph, 1824–1908, vol. I
Waite, Air Cdre Reginald Newnham, 1901–1975, vol. VII
Waite, Robert T.; *see* Thorne-Waite.
Waithman, Robert William, 1828–1914, vol. I

Waithman, William Sharp, 1853–1922, vol. II
Wake, Major Charles St Aubyn, 1861–1938, vol. III
Wake, Adm. Sir Drury St Aubyn, 1863–1935, vol. III
Wake, Lt-Col Edward St Aubyn, 1862–1944, vol. IV
Wake, Sir Herewald, 12th Bt, 1852–1916, vol. II
Wake, Herewald Crawfurd, 1828–1901, vol. I
Wake, Maj.-Gen. Sir Hereward, 13th Bt, 1876–1963, vol. VI
Wake, Hereward Baldwin Lawrence, 1900–1983, vol. VIII
Wake, Major Hugh St Aubyn, 1870–1914, vol. I
Wake, Joan, 1884–1974, vol. VII
Wake, Vice-Adm. Sir St Aubyn Baldwin, 1882–1951, vol. V
Wake, William St Aubyn, 1871–1900, vol. I
Wake-Walker, Adm. Sir William Frederic, 1888–1945, vol. IV
Wakefield, 1st Viscount, 1859–1941, vol. IV
Wakefield of Kendal, 1st Baron, 1898–1983, vol. VIII
Wakefield, Arthur John, 1900–1973, vol. VII
Wakefield, Sir Edward Birkbeck, 1st Bt, 1903–1969, vol. VI
Wakefield, George Edward Campbell, 1873–1944, vol. IV
Wakefield, Rt Rev. Henry Russell, 1854–1933, vol. III
Wakefield, Hubert George; *see* Wakefield, Hugh.
Wakefield, Maj.-Gen. Hubert Stephen, 1883–1962, vol. VI
Wakefield, Hugh, (Hubert George), 1915–1984, vol. VIII
Wakefield, Roger Cuthbert, 1906–1986, vol. VIII
Wakefield, Lt-Col Thomas Montague, 1878–1936, vol. III
Wakefield-Harrey, Cyril Ogden, 1894–1971, vol. VII
Wakeford, Edward Felix, 1914–1973, vol. VII
Wakeford, John Chrysostom Barnabas, 1898–1989, vol. VIII
Wakeford, Major Richard, 1921–1972, vol. VII
Wakeham, Rev. Charles Thomas, 1852–1931, vol. III
Wakehurst, 1st Baron, 1861–1936, vol. III
Wakehurst, 2nd Baron, 1895–1970, vol. VI
Wakelam, Lt-Col Henry Blythe Thornhill, 1893–1963, vol. VI
Wakeley, Sir Cecil Pembrey Grey, 1st Bt, 1892–1979, vol. VII
Wakely, Maj.-Gen. Arthur Victor Trocke, 1886–1959, vol. V
Wakely, Sir Clifford Holland, 1891–1976, vol. VII
Wakely, John, 1861–1942, vol. IV
Wakely, Sir Leonard Day, 1880–1961, vol. VI
Wakeman, Henry Offley, 1852–1899, vol. I
Wakeman, Sir Offley, 3rd Bt, 1850–1929, vol. III
Wakeman, Captain Sir Offley, 4th Bt, 1887–1975, vol. VII
Wakerley, Rev. John E., 1858–1923, vol. II
Wakley, Thomas, 1851–1909, vol. I
Wakley, Thomas Henry, 1821–1907, vol. I
Waksman, Selman Abraham, 1888–1973, vol. VII
Walbrook, Anton, 1900–1967, vol. VI
Walbrook, Henry Mackinnon, *died* 1941, vol. IV
Walby, Herbert Charles, 1897–1966, vol. VI
Walch, Sir Geoffrey Archer, 1898–1971, vol. VII
Walcot, Lt-Col Basil, 1880–1918, vol. II

Walcot, William, 1874–1943, vol. IV
Walcott, Charles Doolittle, 1850–1927, vol. II
Walcott, Captain Colpoys Cleland, 1878–1961, vol. VI
Walcott, Col Edmund Scopoli, 1842–1923, vol. II
Walcott, Sir Henry Barclay, 1866–1931, vol. III
Walde, Ernest Herman Stewart, 1874–1958, vol. V
Waldeck-Rousseau, Pierre Marie, 1846–1904, vol. I
Waldegrave, 9th Earl, 1851–1930, vol. III
Waldegrave, 10th Earl, 1882–1933, vol. III
Waldegrave, 11th Earl, 1854–1936, vol. III
Waldegrave, Countess; (Mary), 1850–1933, vol. III
Waldegrave-Leslie, Hon. George; *see* Leslie.
Walden, Alfred Edward, 1893–1968, vol. VI
Walden, Sir Robert Woolley, *died* 1929, vol. III
Walden, Stanley Arthur, 1905–1980, vol. VII
Walden, Trevor Alfred, 1916–1979, vol. VII
Walder, (Alan) David, 1928–1978, vol. VII
Walder, David; *see* Walder, A. D.
Walder, Hon. Sir Samuel Robert, 1879–1946, vol. IV
Waldersee, Field-Marshal Count Von, 1832–1904, vol. I
Waldie-Griffith, Sir Richard John; *see* Griffith.
Waldman, Milton, 1895–1976, vol. VII
Waldman, Ronald Hartley, 1914–1978, vol. VII
Waldman, Stanley John, 1923–1989, vol. VIII
Waldo, Frederick Joseph, 1852–1933, vol. III
Waldock, Sir (Claud) Humphrey (Meredith), 1904–1981, vol. VIII
Waldock, Sir Humphrey; *see* Waldock, Sir C. H. M.
Waldram, Percy John, 1869–1949, vol. IV
Waldron, Rev. Arthur John, 1868–1925, vol. II
Waldron, Brig.-Gen. Francis, 1853–1932, vol. III
Waldron, Rt Hon. Laurence Ambrose, 1858–1923, vol. II
Waldron, Sir John Lovegrove, 1909–1975, vol. VII
Waldron, Col Sir William James, 1876–1957, vol. V
Waldstein, Sir Charles; *see* Walston, Sir Charles.
Waldstein, Louis, 1853–1915, vol. I
Waldteufel, Emile, 1837–1915, vol. I
Waleran, 1st Baron, 1849–1925, vol. II
Waleran, 2nd Baron, 1905–1966, vol. VI
Wales, Sir (Alexander) George, 1885–1962, vol. VI
Wales, Rev. Arthur Philip, 1896–1964, vol. VI
Wales, Geoffrey, 1912–1990, vol. VIII
Wales, Sir George; *see* Wales, Sir A. G.
Wales, Horace Geoffrey Quaritch, 1900–1981, vol. VIII
Wales, Hubert, 1870–1943, vol. IV
Wales, Quaritch; *see* Wales, H. G. Q.
Waley, Sir David; *see* Waley, Sir S. D.
Waley, Alfred Joseph, 1861–1953, vol. V
Waley, Arthur David, 1889–1966, vol. VI
Waley, Sir Frederick George, 1860–1933, vol. III
Waley, Sir (Sigismund) David, 1887–1962, vol. VI
Walford, Maj.-Gen. Alfred Ernest, 1896–1990, vol. VIII
Walford, Col J. A., *died* 1903, vol. I
Walford, Lucy Bethia, 1845–1915, vol. I
Walkden, 1st Baron, 1873–1951, vol. V
Walkden, Evelyn, 1893–1970, vol. VI
Walkem, Joseph B., 1842–1938, vol. III
Walker, Hon. Lord; James Walker, 1890–1972, vol. VII

Walker, Sir Alan, *died* 1978, vol. VII
Walker, Major Alan Richard H.; *see* Hill-Walker.
Walker, Maj.-Gen. Albert Lancelot, 1839–1918, vol. II
Walker, Maj.-Gen. Alexander, 1838–1905, vol. I
Walker, Alexander, 1866–1945, vol. IV
Walker, Sir Alexander, 1869–1950, vol. IV
Walker, Sir Alexander Arthur, 2nd Bt (*cr* 1906), 1857–1932, vol. III
Walker, Alexander Neilson Strachan, 1921–1980, vol. VII
Walker, Andrew Barclay, 1865–1930, vol. III
Walker, Archibald, 1858–1945, vol. IV
Walker, Archibald Stodart, 1869–1934, vol. III
Walker, Sir Arnold Learoyd, *died* 1968, vol. VI
Walker, Rev. Arthur, *died* 1918, vol. II
Walker, Arthur George, 1861–1939, vol. III
Walker, Rear-Adm. Arthur Horace, 1881–1947, vol. IV
Walker, Air Chief Marshal Sir Augustus; *see* Walker, Air Chief Marshal Sir G. A.
Walker, Augustus Merrifield, 1880–1965, vol. VI
Walker, Sir Baldwin Wake, 2nd Bt (*cr* 1856), 1846–1905, vol. I
Walker, Bernard F.; *see* Fleetwood-Walker.
Walker, Bertram James, 1880–1947, vol. IV
Walker, Sir (Byron) Edmund, 1848–1924, vol. II
Walker, Major Sir Cecil Edward, 3rd Bt *cr* 1906, 1882–1964, vol. VI
Walker, Sir Charles, 1871–1940, vol. III
Walker, Charles Alfred le Maistre, 1873–1961, vol. VI
Walker, Charles Clement, 1877–1968, vol. VI
Walker, Charles Edward, *died* 1953, vol. V
Walker, Rear-Adm. Charles Francis, 1836–1925, vol. II
Walker, Vice-Adm. Sir (Charles) Peter (Graham), 1911–1989, vol. VIII
Walker, Col Charles William Garne, 1882–1974, vol. VII
Walker, Lt-Col Claude Edward Forestier-, *died* 1932, vol. III
Walker, Sir Clive Radzivill Forestier-, 5th Bt, 1922–1983, vol. VIII
Walker, Cyril Herbert, 1888–1970, vol. VI
Walker, Cyril Hutchinson, 1861–1955, vol. V
Walker, Daniel Pickering, 1914–1985, vol. VIII
Walker, David Esdaile, 1907–1968, vol. VI
Walker, Rev. Dawson D.; *see* Dawson-Walker.
Walker, Douglas Learoyd, 1894–1962, vol. VI
Walker, Dame Eadith Campbell, 1874–1937, vol. III
Walker, Sir Edmund; *see* Walker, Sir B. E.
Walker, Edmund W., 1832–1919, vol. II
Walker, Sir Edward Daniel, 1840–1919, vol. II
Walker, Rev. Edward Mewburn, 1857–1941, vol. IV
Walker, Sir Edward Noel-, 1842–1908, vol. I
Walker, Sir E(dward) Ronald, 1907–1988, vol. VIII
Walker, Sir Emery, 1851–1933, vol. III
Walker, Eric Anderson, 1886–1976, vol. VII
Walker, Ernest, 1870–1949, vol. IV
Walker, Maj.-Gen. Sir Ernest Alexander, 1880–1944, vol. IV
Walker, Ernest Octavius, 1850–1919, vol. II
Walker, Ernest William A.; *see* Ainley-Walker.

Walker, Dame Ethel, 1861–1951, vol. V
Walker, Sir Francis Elliot, 3rd Bt (*cr* 1856), 1851–1928, vol. II
Walker, Francis John, *died* 1940, vol. III
Walker, Rev. Francis Joseph, 1876–1933, vol. III
Walker, Francis S., 1848–1916, vol. II
Walker, Lt-Col Francis Spring, 1876–1941, vol. IV
Walker, Sir Francis William, 1887–1968, vol. VI
Walker, Frank Stockdale, 1895–1989, vol. VIII
Walker, Captain Frederic John, 1896–1944, vol. IV
Walker, Lt-Col Frederic William, 1870–1954, vol. V
Walker, Frederick James, 1835–1913, vol. I
Walker, Frederick William, 1830–1910, vol. I
Walker, Gen. Sir Frederick William Edward Forestier Forestier-, 1844–1910, vol. I
Walker, Sir G. Bernard L.; *see* Lomas-Walker.
Walker, Garrett William, 1856–1932, vol. III
Walker, Maj.-Gen. George, 1869–1936, vol. III
Walker, George Abram, 1879–1959, vol. V
Walker, Air Chief Marshal Sir (George) Augustus, 1912–1986, vol. VIII
Walker, Sir George Casson, 1854–1925, vol. II
Walker, George Edward Orr, 1909–1973, vol. VII
Walker, Sir George Ferdinand Forestier-, 3rd Bt (*cr* 1835), 1855–1933, vol. III
Walker, Major Sir George Ferdinand Forestier-, 4th Bt (*cr* 1835), 1899–1976, vol. VII
Walker, Major George Goold, *died* 1955, vol. V
Walker, Sir George Gustavus, 1831–1897, vol. I
Walker, Col George Gustavus, 1897–1972, vol. VII
Walker, George Henry, 1874–1954, vol. V
Walker, George Herbert Dacres, 1845–1929, vol. III
Walker, Col George Kemp, 1872–1942, vol. IV
Walker, Maj.-Gen. Sir George Townshend Forestier-, 1866–1939, vol. III
Walker, George Walker, 1874–1921, vol. II
Walker, Gen. George Warren, 1823–1920, vol. II
Walker, Rev. Gilbert George, 1858–1933, vol. III
Walker, Gilbert James, 1907–1982, vol. VIII
Walker, Sir Gilbert Thomas, 1868–1958, vol. V
Walker, Lt-Gen. Sir Harold Bridgwood, 1862–1934, vol. III
Walker, Adm. Sir Harold Thomas Coulthard, 1891–1975, vol. VII
Walker, Sir Henry, 1873–1954, vol. V
Walker, Henry; *see* Walker, R. St J.
Walker, Brig.-Gen. Henry Alexander, 1874–1953, vol. V
Walker, Henry Claude, 1851–1939, vol. III
Walker, Henry de Rosenbach, 1867–1923, vol. II
Walker, Sir Herbert Ashcombe, 1868–1949, vol. IV
Walker, Lt-Col Herbert Sutherland, 1864–1932, vol. III
Walker, Hirst, 1868–1957, vol. V
Walker, Sir (Horace) Alan; *see* Walker, Sir Alan.
Walker, Sir Hubert Edmund, 1891–1969, vol. VI
Walker, Hugh, 1855–1939, vol. III
Walker, Sir Hugh Selby N.; *see* Norman-Walker.
Walker, Ian Royaards, 1927–1985, vol. VIII
Walker, J. Wallace, *died* 1932, vol. III
Walker, Sir James, 1864–1933, vol. III
Walker, Sir James, 1863–1935, vol. III
Walker, Lt-Col James, *died* 1940, vol. III
Walker, James, *died* 1945, vol. IV

Walker, James; *see* Walker, Hon. Lord.
Walker, James Arthur H.; *see* Higgs-Walker.
Walker, James Atkinson, 1878–1954, vol. V
Walker, James Douglas, 1841–1920, vol. II
Walker, Maj.-Gen. James Grant Duff, 1842–1921, vol. II
Walker, Captain Sir James Heron, 3rd Bt (*cr* 1868), 1865–1900, vol. I
Walker, Sir James Lewis, 1845–1927, vol. II
Walker, Sir James Robert, 2nd Bt, 1829–1898, vol. I
Walker, Hon. James Thomas, 1841–1923, vol. II
Walker, Major James Thomas, *died* 1930, vol. III
Walker, Brig.-Gen. James Workman, 1873–1945, vol. IV
Walker, Jane Harriett, 1859–1938, vol. III
Walker, Rev. John, 1837–1910, vol. I
Walker, John, 1900–1964, vol. VII
Walker, John; *see* Thirlmere, Rowland.
Walker, Sir John, 1906–1984, vol. VIII
Walker, John Bayldon, 1854–1927, vol. II
Walker, John Brisben, 1847–1931, vol. III
Walker, John Crampton, 1890–1942, vol. IV
Walker, John Henry, 1915–1974, vol. VI
Walker, Col John Norman N.; *see* Norman-Walker.
Walker, John Reid, 1855–1934, vol. III
Walker, John Riddell Bromhead, 1913–1984, vol. VIII
Walker, Sir John William T.; *see* Thomson-Walker.
Walker, Kenneth, 1874–1947, vol. IV
Walker, Kenneth Macfarlane, *died* 1966, vol. VI
Walker, Kenneth Richard, 1931–1989, vol. VIII
Walker, Sir Leolin F.; *see* Forestier-Walker, Sir C. L.
Walker, Leonard, *died* 1964, vol. VI
Walker, Malcolm Thomas, 1915–1980, vol. VII
Walker, Sir Mark, 1827–1902, vol. I
Walker, Miles, *died* 1941, vol. IV
Walker, Sir Norman, 1862–1942, vol. IV
Walker, Norman, 1907–1963, vol. VI
Walker, Norman Macdonald Lockhart, 1889–1975, vol. VII
Walker, Norman Marshall, 1882–1956, vol. V
Walker, Oliver Ormerod, 1833–1914, vol. I
Walker, Patrick Chrestien G.; *see* Baron Gordon-Walker.
Walker, Vice-Adm. Sir Peter; *see* Walker, Vice-Adm. Sir C. P. G.
Walker, Sir Peter Carlaw, 2nd Bt (*cr* 1886), 1854–1915, vol. I
Walker, Raymond St John, (Henry), 1917–1980, vol. VII
Walker, Paymr Captain Reginald Phelps, 1871–1958, vol. V
Walker, Major Reginald Selby, 1871–1918, vol. II
Walker, Richard Cornelius Critchett, 1841–1903, vol. I
Walker, Richard Johnson, 1868–1934, vol. III
Walker, Robert, *died* 1910, vol. I
Walker, Robert, 1842–1920, vol. II
Walker, Sir Robert Bryce, 1873–1956, vol V
Walker, Ven. Robert Henry, 1857–1939, vol. III
Walker, Major Sir Robert James Milo, 4th Bt (*cr* 1868), 1890–1930, vol. III
Walker, Robert John, 1870–1936, vol. III
Walker, Robert Milnes, 1903–1985, vol. VIII

Walker, Lt-Col Robert Sandilands Frowd, 1850–1917, vol. II

Walker, Bt-Col Roland Stuart Forestier-, 1871–1938, vol. III

Walker, Sir Ronald; see Walker, Sir E. R.

Walker, Col Ronald Draycott S.; see Sherbrooke-Walker.

Walker, Sir Ronald Fitz-John, 1880–1971, vol. VII

Walker, Ronald Leslie, 1896–1984, vol. VIII

Walker, Rt Hon. Sir Samuel, 1st Bt (cr 1906), 1832–1911, vol. I

Walker, Samuel, 1875–1945, vol. IV

Walker, Samuel Richard, 1892–1989, vol. VIII

Walker, Air Cdre Sidney George, 1911–1975, vol. VII

Walker, Rev. Thomas, died 1929, vol. III

Walker, Hon. Thomas, 1858–1932, vol. III

Walker, Rev. Thomas Alfred, 1862–1935, vol. III

Walker, Very Rev. Thomas Gordon, died 1916, vol. II

Walker, Sir Thomas Gordon, 1849–1917, vol. II

Walker, Lt-Col Thomas Henry, 1877–1955, vol. V

Walker, Thomas Hollis, 1860–1945, vol. IV

Walker, Thomas Kennedy, 1893–1970, vol. VI

Walker, Thomas Leonard, 1867–1942, vol. IV

Walker, Adm. Thomas Philip, died 1932, vol. III

Walker, Timothy Ashley Peter, 1942–1988, vol. VIII

Walker, Very Rev. William, died 1911, vol. I

Walker, Sir William, 1863–1930, vol. III

Walker, Sir William, died 1961, vol. VI

Walker, William, 1920–1984, vol. VIII

Walker, William Anderson Macpherson, 1891–1962, vol. VI

Walker, Hon. William Campbell, 1837–1904, vol. I

Walker, Col William Eric, 1885–1949, vol. IV

Walker, William Eyre, 1847–1930, vol. III

Walker, Adm. Sir William Frederic W.; see Wake-Walker.

Walker, Maj.-Gen. William George, 1863–1936, vol. III

Walker, Sir William Giles Newsom, 1905–1989, vol. VIII

Walker, William Gregory, 1848–1910, vol. I

Walker, William Henry, 1864–1933, vol. III

Walker, William James Dickson, 1854–1926, vol. II

Walker, William James Stirling, 1897–1958, vol. V

Walker, Rev. William Lowe, 1845–1930, vol. III

Walker, William Sylvester, 1846–1926, vol. II

Walker-Heneage-Vivian, Adm. Algernon, 1871–1952, vol. V

Walker Lee, Rev. William; see Lee.

Walker-Okeover, Col Sir Ian Peter Andrew Monro, 3rd Bt, 1902–1982, vol. VIII

Walker-Smith, Sir Jonah, 1874–1964, vol. VI

Walkey, Rear-Adm. Howarth Seymour, 1900–1970, vol. VI

Walkey, Rev. James Rowland, 1880–1960, vol. V

Walkey, Maj.-Gen. John Christopher, 1903–1989, vol. VIII

Walkinton, John James Gordon, 1895–1968, vol. VI

Walkley, Arthur Bingham, 1855–1926, vol. II

Walkley, Sir William Gaston, 1896–1976, vol. VII

Walkling, Maj.-Gen. Alec Ernest, 1918–1988, vol. VIII

Wall, Baron (Life Peer); John Edward Wall, 1913–1980, vol. VII

Wall, Arnold, died 1966, vol. VI

Wall, Arthur Joseph, died 1927, vol. II

Wall, Rt Rev. Bernard Patrick, 1894–1976, vol. VII

Wall, (Charles) Patrick, 1933–1990, vol. VIII

Wall, Col Edward Watkin, 1866–1954, vol. V

Wall, Rt Rev. Francis Joseph, 1866–1947, vol. IV

Wall, Col Frank, 1868–1950, vol. IV

Wall, Sir Frederick Joseph, 1858–1944, vol. IV

Wall, Sir (George) Rolande (Percival), 1898–1972, vol. VII

Wall, Engr Rear-Adm. Henry, 1867–1950, vol. IV

Wall, John William, 1910–1989, vol. VIII

Wall, Patrick; see Wall, C. P.

Wall, Reginald Cecil Bligh, 1869–1947, vol. IV

Wall, Sir Rolande; see Wall, Sir G. R. P.

Wallace, Abraham, died 1930, vol. III

Wallace, Maj.-Gen. Sir Alexander, 1858–1922, vol. II

Wallace, Alexander Falconer, 1836–1925, vol. III

Wallace, Very Rev. Alexander Ross, 1891–1982, vol. VIII

Wallace, Alfred Russel, 1823–1913, vol. I

Wallace, Sir Arthur Robert, 1837–1912, vol. I

Wallace, Rev. Charles Hill, 1833–1912, vol. I

Wallace, Maj.-Gen. Charles John, 1890–1943, vol. IV

Wallace, Charles Redwood Vachel, 1877–1944, vol. IV

Wallace, Rev. Charles Stebbing, died 1914, vol. I

Wallace, Charles William, 1865–1932, vol. III

Wallace, Col the Hon. Clarence, 1894–1982, vol. VIII

Wallace, Sir Cuthbert Sidney, 1st Bt (cr 1937), 1867–1944, vol. IV

Wallace, Sir David, 1862–1952, vol. V

Wallace, Captain Rt Hon. (David) Euan, 1892–1941, vol. IV

Wallace, Major David Johnston, 1886–1965, vol. VI

Wallace, Denis Bowes J.; see Johnstone-Wallace.

Wallace, Sir Donald Mackenzie, 1841–1919, vol. II

Wallace, Doreen, (Mrs Dora Eileen A. Rash), 1897–1989, vol. VIII

Wallace, Edgar; see Wallace, R. H. E.

Wallace, Sir Edward Hamilton, 1873–1943, vol. IV

Wallace, Edward Wilson, 1880–1941, vol. IV

Wallace, Captain Rt Hon. Euan; see Wallace, Captain Rt Hon. D. E.

Wallace, Rev. Francis Huston, 1851–1930, vol. III

Wallace, George, 1854–1927, vol. II

Wallace, Col George Smith, 1878–1951, vol. V

Wallace, George Williamson, 1862–1952, vol. V

Wallace, Sir Gordon, 1900–1987, vol. VIII

Wallace, Harold Frank, 1881–1962, vol. VI

Wallace, Harry Wright, 1885–1973, vol. VII

Wallace, Henry Agard, 1888–1965, vol. VI

Wallace, Captain Henry Steuart Macnaghten H.; see Harrison-Wallace.

Wallace, Maj.-Gen. Hill, 1823–1899, vol. I

Wallace, Hugh Campbell, 1863–1931, vol. III

Wallace, Lt-Col Hugh Robert, 1861–1924, vol. II

Wallace, Irving, 1916–1990, vol. VIII

Wallace, Air Cdre James, 1918–1980, vol. VII

Wallace, James Sim, 1869–1951, vol. V

Wallace, Sir John, 1868–1949, vol. IV

Wallace, Air Vice-Marshal John Brown, 1907–1980, vol. VII
Wallace, John Henry, 1903–1960, vol. V
Wallace, John Madder, 1887–1975, vol. VII
Wallace, Sir John Stewart S.; *see* Stewart-Wallace.
Wallace, Col Sir Johnstone, 1861–1922, vol. II
Wallace, Sir Lawrence Aubrey, 1857–1942, vol. IV
Wallace, Gen. Lew, (Lewis), 1827–1905, vol. I
Wallace, Malcolm William, 1873–1960, vol. V
Wallace, Sir Martin Kelso, 1898–1978, vol. VII
Wallace, Sir Matthew Gemmill, 1st Bt (*cr* 1922), 1854–1940, vol. III
Wallace, Hon. Nathaniel Clarke, 1844–1901, vol. I
Wallace, Col Nesbit Willoughby, 1839–1931, vol. III
Wallace, O. C. S., 1856–1947, vol. IV
Wallace, Percy Maxwell, 1863–1943, vol. IV
Wallace, Philip Adrian H.; *see* Hope-Wallace.
Wallace, (Richard Horatio) Edgar, 1875–1932, vol. III
Wallace, Rear-Adm. Richard Roy, 1895–1963, vol. VI
Wallace, Robert, 1831–1899, vol. I
Wallace, Robert, 1878–1931, vol. III
Wallace, Sir Robert, 1850–1939, vol. III
Wallace, Robert, 1853–1939, vol. III
Wallace, Robert Charles, 1881–1955, vol. V
Wallace of that Ilk, Col Robert Francis Hurter, 1880–1970, vol. VI
Wallace, Col Rt Hon. Robert Hugh, 1860–1929, vol. III
Wallace, Robert John, 1846–1909, vol. I
Wallace, Robert Johnston, 1886–1967, vol. VI
Wallace, Sir Robert Strachan, 1882–1961, vol. VI
Wallace, Roger William, 1854–1926, vol. II
Wallace, Lt-Gen. Rowland Robert, 1830–1915, vol. I
Wallace, S. Williamson, 1855–1932, vol. III
Wallace, Samuel Thomas Dickson, 1892–1968, vol. VI
Wallace, Thomas, 1891–1965, vol. VI
Wallace, Thomas Brown, 1865–1951, vol. V
Wallace, Sir William, 1856–1916, vol. II
Wallace, William, 1843–1921, vol. II
Wallace, William, 1860–1922, vol. II
Wallace, William, 1860–1940, vol. III
Wallace, Sir William, 1881–1963, vol. VI
Wallace, William, 1891–1976, vol. VII
Wallace, William, 1911–1990, vol. VIII
Wallace, Col William Arthur James, 1842–1902, vol. I
Wallace, Lt-Col William Berkeley, *died* 1934, vol. III
Wallace, William Kelly, 1883–1969, vol. VI
Wallace, William Reeve, 1873–1966, vol. VI
Wallace, William Stewart, 1884–1970, vol. VI
Wallace-Copland, Harold, 1893–1973, vol. VII
Wallace-Hadrill, John Michael, 1916–1985, vol. VIII
Wallace Whitfield, Sir Cecil Vincent, 1930–1990, vol. VIII
Wallach, Lewis Charles, 1871–1964, vol. VI
Wallack, Maj.-Gen. Ernest Townshend, 1857–1932, vol. III
Wallas, Graham, 1858–1932, vol. III
Wallas, Katharine Talbot, 1864–1944, vol. IV
Waller, Alfred Rayney, 1867–1922, vol. II
Waller, Vice-Adm. Arthur Craig, 1872–1943, vol. IV

Waller, Augustus Désiré, 1856–1922, vol. II
Waller, Rev. Bolton Charles, 1890–1936, vol. III
Waller, Sir Charles, 6th Bt (*cr* 1780), 1835–1912, vol. I
Waller, Rev. Charles Cameron, 1869–1944, vol. IV
Waller, Very Rev. Charles Kempson, 1891–1951, vol. V
Waller, Sir David Grierson, 1872–1949, vol. IV
Waller, Sir Edmund, 6th Bt (*cr* 1815), 1871–1954, vol. V
Waller, Very Rev. Edward Hardress, 1859–1933, vol. III
Waller, Rt Rev. Edward Harry Mansfield, 1871–1942, vol. IV
Waller, Sir Francis Ernest, 4th Bt (*cr* 1815), 1880–1914, vol. I
Waller, Maj.-Gen. John Edmund, 1841–1934, vol. III
Waller, Captain John Hampden, 1839–1934, vol. III
Waller, Vice-Adm. John William Ashley, 1892–1975, vol. VII
Waller, Lewis, (William Waller Lewis), 1860–1915, vol. I
Waller, Mary Lemon, *died* 1931, vol. III
Waller, Sir Maurice Lyndham, 1875–1932, vol. III
Waller, Mervyn Napier, 1893–1972, vol. VII
Waller, Brig.-Gen. Richard Lancelot, 1875–1961, vol. VI
Waller, Sir Roland Edgar, 8th Bt (*cr* 1780), 1892–1958, vol. V
Waller, Ross Douglas, 1899–1988, vol. VIII
Waller, Samuel Edmund, 1850–1903, vol. I
Waller, Col Stainier, 1844–1930, vol. III
Waller, Sir Wathen Arthur, 5th Bt (*cr* 1815), 1881–1947, vol. IV
Waller, Sir William Edgar, 7th Bt (*cr* 1780), 1863–1943, vol. IV
Wallers, Sir Evelyn Ashley, 1876–1934, vol. III
Wallerston, Brig.-Gen. Francis Edward, 1856–1926, vol. II
Wallhead, Richard Collingham, 1869–1934, vol. III
Walling, Robert Alfred John, 1869–1949, vol. IV
Wallinger, Lt-Col Ernest Arnold, 1875–1934, vol. III
Wallinger, Sir Geoffrey Arnold, 1903–1979, vol. VII
Wallinger, Sir John Arnold, 1872–1931, vol. III
Wallingford, Air Cdre Sidney, 1898–1978, vol. VII
Wallington, Sir Edward William, 1854–1933, vol. III
Wallington, Hon. Sir Hubert Joseph, *died* 1962, vol. VI
Wallington, Col Sir John Williams, 1822–1910, vol. I
Wallis, Captain Arthur Hammond, 1903–1989, vol. VIII
Wallis, Arthur Henry, 1847–1929, vol. III
Wallis, Sir Barnes Neville, 1887–1979, vol. VII
Wallis, Major Charles Braithwaite, *died* 1945, vol. IV
Wallis, Charles Edward, *died*1927, vol. II
Wallis, Rev. Charles Steel, 1875–1959, vol. V
Wallis, Claude Edgar, 1886–1980, vol. VII
Wallis, Rt Rev. Frederic, 1853–1928, vol. II
Wallis, Sir Frederick Charles, 1859–1912, vol. I
Wallis, Frederick Samuel, 1857–1939, vol. III (A), vol. IV
Wallis, George Harry, *died* 1Wallis, Henry Aubrey Beaumont, *died* 1926, vol. II

Wallis, Henry Richard, 1866–1946, vol. IV
Wallis, Rt Hon. Sir John Edward Power, 1861–1946, vol. IV
Wallis, Rev. Canon John Eyre Winstanley, 1886–1957, vol. V
Wallis, Leonard George C.; *see* Coke Wallis.
Wallis, Mrs Ransome, 1858–1928, vol. II
Wallis, Sir Whitworth, 1855–1927, vol. II
Wallop, Hon. Frederick Henry Arthur, 1870–1953, vol. V
Walls, Hamish; *see* Walls, Henry J.
Walls, Henry James, 1907–1988, vol. VIII
Walls, Rev. John W., 1858–1924, vol. II
Walls, Tom, 1883–1949, vol. IV
Walls, William, 1860–1942, vol. IV
Wallscourt, 4th Baron, 1841–1918, vol. II
Wallscourt, 5th Baron, 1876–1920, vol. II
Walmesley White, Brig. Arthur, 1917–1985, vol. VIII
Walmsley, Allan, 1889–1963, vol. VI
Walmsley, Ben, 1871–1960, vol. V (A), vol. VI (AI)
Walmsley, Charles; *see* Walmsley, R. C.
Walmsley, Sir Hugh, 1871–1950, vol. IV
Walmsley, Air Marshal Sir Hugh Sydney Porter, 1898–1985, vol. VIII
Walmsley, Rt Rev. John, *died* 1922, vol. II
Walmsley, Air Cdre John Banks, 1896–1976, vol. VII
Walmsley, Kenneth Maurice, 1914–1977, vol. VII
Walmsley, Leo, 1892–1966, vol. VI
Walmsley, Robert Mullineux, *died* 1924, vol. II
Walmsley, (Ronald) Charles, 1909–1983, vol. VIII
Walmsley, Thomas, *died* 1951, vol. V
Waln, Nora, 1895–1964, vol. IV
Walpole, 9th Baron, 1913–1989, vol. VIII
Walpole, Sir Charles George, 1848–1926, vol. II
Walpole, George Frederick, 1892–1975, vol. VII
Walpole, Rt Rev. George Henry Somerset, 1854–1929, vol. III
Walpole, Henry Spencer V.; *see* Vade-Walpole.
Walpole, Sir Horatio George, 1843–1923, vol. II
Walpole, Sir Hugh Seymour, 1884–1941, vol. IV
Walpole, Kathleen Annette, 1899–1987, vol. VIII
Walpole, Ralph Charles, 1844–1928, vol. II
Walpole, Sir Spencer, 1839–1907, vol. I
Walpole, Rt Hon. Spencer Horatio, 1806–1898, vol. I
Walpole, Thomas Henry Bourke V.; *see* Vade-Walpole.
Walrond, Arthur Melville Hood, 1861–1946, vol. IV
Walrond, Col Henry, 1841–1917, vol. II
Walrond, Main Swete Osmond, 1870–1927, vol. II
Walrond, Hon. William Lionel Charles, 1876–1915, vol. I
Walsh, Hon. Sir Albert Joseph, *died* 1958, vol. V
Walsh, Arthur Donald, 1916–1977, vol. VII
Walsh, Sir Cecil, 1869–1946, vol. IV
Walsh, Sir Charles Arthur, 1869–1949, vol. IV
Walsh, Rt Hon. Sir Cyril Ambrose, 1909–1973, vol. VII
Walsh, Sir David Philip, 1902–1989, vol. VIII
Walsh, Ernest Herbert Cooper, 1865–1952, vol. V
Walsh, Ernst P.; *see* Pakenham-Walsh.
Walsh, Rt Rev. Francis, 1901–1974, vol. VII
Walsh, Maj.-Gen. Francis James, 1900–1987, vol. VIII
Walsh, Geoffrey, 1884–1946, vol. IV

Walsh, Maj.-Gen. George Peregrine, 1899–1972, vol. VII
Walsh, Air Vice-Marshal George Victor, 1893–1960, vol. V
Walsh, Hon. Gerald, 1864–1925, vol. II
Walsh, Rt Rev. Gordon John, 1880–1971, vol. VII
Walsh, Col Henry Alfred, 1853–1918, vol. II
Walsh, Henry Francis Chester, 1891–1977, vol. VII
Walsh, Rt Rev. Herbert Pakenham P.; *see* Pakenham-Walsh.
Walsh, Sir Hunt Henry Allen Johnson-, 5th Bt, 1864–1953, vol. V
Walsh, Very Rev. James Hornidge, *died* 1919, vol. II
Walsh, James J., 1865–1942, vol. IV
Walsh, James Joseph, 1880–1948, vol. IV
Walsh, James Morgan, 1897–1952, vol. V
Walsh, John, 1856–1925, vol. II
Walsh, Most Rev. Joseph, 1888–1973, vol. VII
Walsh, Langton Prendergast, 1856–1927, vol. II
Walsh, Leslie, 1903–1986, vol. VIII
Walsh, Brig. Mainwaring Ravell, 1876–1940, vol. III
Walsh, Maurice, 1879–1964, vol. VI
Walsh, Hon. Nigel Christopher, 1867–1931, vol. III
Walsh, Hon. Patrick Joseph Stanislaus, 1872–1943, vol. IV
Walsh, Ven. Philip, 1843–1914, vol. II
Walsh, Richard; *see* Walsh, W. H.
Walsh, Brig.-Gen. Richard Knox, 1873–1960, vol. V
Walsh, Maj.-Gen. Ridley P. P.; *see* Pakenham-Walsh.
Walsh, Ven. Robert, *died* 1917, vol. II
Walsh, Col Robert Henry, 1884–1968, vol. VI
Walsh, Rt Hon. Stephen, 1859–1929, vol. III
Walsh, Lt-Col Theobald Alfred, 1882–1935, vol. III
Walsh, Valentine John Hussey-, 1862–1925, vol. II
Walsh, Walter, 1847–1912, vol. I
Walsh, Rev. Walter, 1857–1931, vol. III
Walsh, Rt Rev. William, 1836–1918, vol. II
Walsh, Lt-Col William H.; *see* Hussey-Walsh.
Walsh, William Henry, 1913–1986, vol. VIII
Walsh, Most Rev. William J., 1841–1921, vol. II
Walsh, William Joseph, 1919–1978, vol. VII
Walsh, Hon. William Legh, 1857–1938, vol. III
Walsh, Rt Rev. William Pakenham, 1820–1902, vol. I
Walsham, Hugh, *died* 1924, vol. II
Walsham, Sir John, 2nd Bt, 1830–1905, vol. I
Walsham, Sir John Scarlett, 3rd Bt, 1869–1940, vol. III
Walsham, William Johnson, 1847–1903, vol. I
Walshe, Sir Francis Martin Rouse, *died* 1973, vol. VII
Walshe, Brig.-Gen. Frederick William Henry, *died* 1931, vol. III
Walshe, Lt-Col Henry Ernest, 1866–1947, vol. IV
Walshe, Lt-Col Sarsfield James Ambrose Hall, 1881–1959, vol. V
Walshe, Rt Rev. Mgr T. J., 1861–1938, vol. III
Walsingham, 6th Baron, 1843–1919, vol. II
Walsingham, 7th Baron, 1849–1929, vol. III
Walsingham, 8th Baron, 1884–1965, vol. VI
Walston, Sir Charles, 1856–1927, vol. II
Waltari, Mika, 1908–1979, vol. VII
Walter, Arthur, 1874–1921, vol. II
Walter, Arthur Fraser, 1846–1910, vol. I
Walter, Arthur James, *died* 1919, vol. II

Walter, Bruno, 1876–1962, vol. VI
Walter, Lt-Col Edmund, 1881–1951, vol. V
Walter, Sir Edward, 1823–1904, vol. I
Walter, Major Frederick Edward, 1848–1931, vol. III
Walter, Hubert, 1870–1933, vol. III
Walter, John, 1873–1968, vol. VI
Walter, Maj.-Gen. John McNeill, 1861–1951, vol. V
Walter, Rear-Adm. Keith McNeil C.; see Campbell-Walter.
Walter, Louis Heathcote, died 1922, vol. II
Walter, Madison Melville, 1897–1960, vol. V
Walter, Captain Philip Norman, 1898–1984, vol. VIII
Walter, Robert, died 1959, vol. V
Walter, William, 1852–1942, vol. IV
Walter, W(illiam) Grey, 1910–1977, vol. VII
Walters, Air Vice-Marshal Allan Leslie, 1905–1968, vol. VI
Walters, Arthur Melmoth, 1865–1941, vol. IV
Walters, Rev. Charles Ensor, 1872–1938, vol. III
Walters, Rev. David John, 1893–1979, vol. VII
Walters, Francis Paul, 1888–1976, vol. VII
Walters, Frank Bridgman, 1851–1899, vol. I
Walters, Rev. Harold Crawford, died 1958, vol. V
Walters, Henry Beauchamp, 1867–1944, vol. IV
Walters, Hubert Algernon, 1898–1969, vol. VI
Walters, Lt-Col Hubert de Lancey, 1868–1936, vol. III
Walters, John Cuming, died 1933, vol. III
Walters, Rt Hon. Sir (John) Tudor, 1868–1933, vol. III
Walters, Rt Hon. Sir Tudor; see Walters, Rt Hon. Sir J. T.
Walters, W. C. Flamstead, died 1927, vol. II
Walters, Rev. W. D., 1839–1913, vol. I
Walters, Ven. William, died 1912, vol. I
Walters, Col William Barker, 1839–1929, vol. III
Walters, Sir William Howell, 1857–1934, vol. III
Walters, William Melmoth, 1835–1925, vol. II
Walthall, Brig.-Gen. Edward Charles Walthall Delves, 1874–1961, vol. VI
Walther, David Philippe, 1909–1973, vol. VII
Walthew, Richard Henry, 1872–1951, vol. V
Walton, Allan, 1891–1948, vol. IV
Walton, Cecil Simpson, 1905–1955, vol. V
Walton, Col Sir Cusack, 1878–1966, vol. VI
Walton, Lt-Col Edgar Brocas, 1880–1964, vol. VI
Walton, Hon. Sir Edgar Harris, 1856–1942, vol. IV
Walton, Edward Arthur, 1860–1922, vol. II
Walton, Frank, 1840–1928, vol. II
Walton, Frederick Parker, 1858–1948, vol. IV
Walton, Frederick Thomas Granville, 1840–1925, vol. II
Walton, Brig. Sir George Hands, died 1976, vol. VII
Walton, Sir George O'Donnell, 1871–1950, vol. IV
Walton, Col Granville, 1888–1974, vol. VII
Walton, Henry George, 1876–1962, vol. VI
Walton, Rev. Herbert Arthur, died 1955, vol. V
Walton, Herbert Francis Raine, 1869–1929, vol. III
Walton, James, 1867–1924, vol. II
Walton, Sir James, 1881–1955, vol. V
Walton, James Ratcliffe, 1898–1973, vol. VII
Walton, John, 1895–1971, vol. VII
Walton, Sir John Charles, 1885–1957, vol. V

Walton, Sir John Lawson, 1852–1908, vol. I
Walton, Sir Joseph, 1845–1910, vol. I
Walton, Sir Joseph, 1st Bt, 1849–1923, vol. II
Walton, Kenneth, 1923–1979, vol. VII
Walton, Leslie Bannister, 1895–1960, vol. V
Walton, Norman Burdett, 1884–1950, vol. IV
Walton, Sir Raymond Henry, 1915–1988, vol. VIII
Walton, Sir Richmond, 1888–1971, vol. VII
Walton, Sir Robert, 1843–1914, vol. I
Walton, Lt-Col Robert Henry, 1877–1959, vol. V (A)
Walton, Sydney, 1882–1964, vol. VI
Walton, Sir William, 1844–1929, vol. III
Walton, Brig.-Gen. William Crawford, 1864–1937, vol. III
Walton, William Stanley, 1901–1979, vol. VII
Walton, Sir William Turner, 1902–1983, vol. VIII
Waltz, Jacques; see Hansi.
Walwyn, Algernon Edward Vere, 1888–1970, vol. VI
Walwyn, Eileen Mary, (Lady Walwyn), died 1973, vol. VII
Walwyn, Vice-Adm. Sir Humphrey Thomas, 1879–1957, vol. V
Walwyn, Rear-Adm. James Humphrey, 1913–1986, vol. VIII
Walzer, Richard Rudolf, 1900–1975, vol. VII
Wanamaker, John, 1838–1922, vol. II
Wanamaker, Rodman, died 1928, vol. II
Wand, Rt Rev. and Rt Hon. (John) William (Charles), 1885–1977, vol. VII
Wand, Solomon, 1899–1984, vol. VIII
Wand, Rt Rev. and Rt Hon. William; see Wand, Rt Rev. and Rt Hon. J. W. C.
Wandsworth, 1st Baron, 1845–1912, vol. I
Wang, Chunk-Yik, 1888–1930, vol. III
Wankaner, Maharana Raj Saheb of, 1879–1954, vol. V
Wanklyn, Lt-Comdr Malcolm David, 1911–1942, vol. IV
Wanless, Sir William James, 1865–1933, vol. III
Wanless-O'Gowan, Maj.-Gen. Robert, 1864–1947, vol. IV
Wanliss, Col David Sydney, 1864–1943, vol. IV
Wanliss, Captain Harold Boyd, 1891–1917, vol. II
Wannell, Lt-Col George Edward, 1882–1933, vol. III
Wannop, Rev. Thomas Nicholson, 1822–1910, vol. I
Wansbrough, George, 1904–1979, vol. VII
Wansbrough, Hon. Lt-Col Thomas Percival, 1875–1943, vol. IV
Wansbrough-Jones, Maj.-Gen. Llewelyn, 1900–1974, vol. VII
Wansbrough-Jones, Sir Owen Haddon, 1905–1982, vol. VIII
Wanstall, Rev. Walter, 1847–1918, vol. II
Wantage, 1st Baron, 1832–1901, vol. I
Wantage, Lady; (Harriet Sarah), 1837–1920, vol. II
Wapshare, Lt-Gen. Sir Richard, 1860–1932, vol. III
Warbey, William Noble, 1903–1980, vol. VII
Warburg, Frederic John, 1898–1981, vol. VIII
Warburg, Sir Oscar Emanuel, 1876–1937, vol. III
Warburg, Otto Heinrich, 1883–1970, vol. VI
Warburg, Sir Siegmund George, 1902–1982, vol. VIII
Warburton, A. Bannerman, 1852–1929, vol. III
Warburton, Eric John Newnham, 1904–1989, vol. VIII

Warburton, Geoffrey E.; *see* Egerton-Warburton.

Warburton, John E.; *see* Egerton-Warburton.

Warburton, John Paul, 1840–1919, vol. II

Warburton, Piers E.; *see* Egerton-Warburton.

Warburton, Col Sir Robert, *died* 1899, vol. I

Warburton, Lt-Col William Melvill, 1877–1952, vol. V

Warburton, Col William Pleace, 1843–1911, vol. I

Ward of North Tyneside, Baroness (Life Peer); Irene Mary Bewick Ward, 1895–1980, vol. VII

Ward of Witley, 1st Viscount, 1907–1988, vol. VIII

Ward, Sir Adolphus William, 1837–1924, vol. II

Ward, Col Sir (Albert) Lambert, 1st Bt (*cr* 1929), 1875–1956, vol. V

Ward, Ven. Algernon, 1869–1947, vol. IV

Ward, Anthony Edward Walter, 1905–1968, vol. VI

Ward, Arnold Sandwith, 1876–1950, vol. IV

Ward, Lt-Col Arthur, 1866–1935, vol. III

Ward, Lt-Col Arthur Blackwood, 1870–1950, vol. IV

Ward, Arthur Claud, 1878–1914, vol. I

Ward, Rev. Canon Arthur Evelyn, 1877–1944, vol. IV

Ward, (Arthur) Neville, 1922–1989, vol. VIII

Ward, Arthur Samuel, *died* 1952, vol. V

Ward, Arthur William, 1858–1919, vol. II

Ward, Sir Ashley Skelton, 1877–1959, vol. V

Ward, Sir Aubrey Ernest, 1899–1987, vol. VIII

Ward, Barbara; *see* Jackson of Lodsworth, Baroness.

Ward, Basil Robert, 1902–1976, vol. VII

Ward, Rt Rev. Mgr Bernard, 1857–1920, vol. II

Ward, Lt-Gen. Hon. Bernard Matthew, 1831–1918, vol. II

Ward, Col Bernard Rowland, 1863–1933, vol. III

Ward, Rear-Adm. (S) Cecil Arthur, 1881–1954, vol. V

Ward, Charles James, *died* 1913, vol. I

Ward, Rev. Charles Triffit, *died* 1925, vol. II

Ward, Cyril, 1863–1935, vol. III

Ward, Captain Hon. Cyril Augustus, 1876–1930, vol. III

Ward, Sir Cyril Rupert Joseph, 2nd Bt (*cr* 1911), 1884–1940, vol. III

Ward, David, 1922–1983, vol. VIII

Ward, Sir Deighton Harcourt Lisle, 1909–1984, vol. VIII

Ward, Denzil Anthony Seaver, 1909–1989, vol. VIII

Ward, Dudley, 1885–1957, vol. V

Ward, Ebenezer Thomas, 1879–1942, vol. IV

Ward, Edward, *died* 1921, vol. II

Ward, Lt-Col Edward Francis, 1870–1935, vol. III

Ward, Edward Rex, 1902–1984, vol. VIII

Ward, Captain Sir Edward Simons, 2nd Bt (*cr* 1914), 1882–1930, vol. III

Ward, Col Sir Edward Willis Duncan, 1st Bt (*cr* 1914), 1853–1928, vol. II

Ward, Edwin, 1880–1934, vol. III

Ward, Lt-Col Ellacott Leamon, 1873–1968, vol. VI

Ward, Enoch, 1859–1922, vol. II

Ward, F. K.; *see* Kingdon-Ward.

Ward, Francis Alan Burnett, 1905–1990, vol. VIII

Ward, Maj.-Gen. Francis William, 1840–1919, vol. II

Ward, Rev. Frederick Hubert, 1858–1918, vol. II

Ward, Frederick John, 1922–1986, vol. VIII

Ward, Frederick Josiah, 1861–1941, vol. IV

Ward, Frederick Temple B.; *see* Barrington-Ward.

Ward, Rev. Frederick William Orde, 1843–1922, vol. II

Ward, Genevieve, Countess de Guerbel, 1837–1922, vol. II

Ward, George, 1878–1951, vol. V

Ward, George Edgar Septimus, 1888–1969, vol. VI

Ward, Ven. George Herbert, 1862–1946, vol. IV

Ward, Hon. Gerald Ernest Francis, 1877–1914, vol. I

Ward, Lt-Col Guy Bernard Campbell, 1875–1933, vol. III

Ward, Col Harry, 1876–1939, vol. III

Ward, Harry Marshall, 1854–1905, vol. I

Ward, Henrietta Mary Ada, *died* 1924, vol. II

Ward, Col Henry Charles S.; *see* Swinburne-Ward.

Ward, Col Henry Constantine Evelyn, 1837–1907, vol. I

Ward, Maj.-Gen. Henry Dudley Ossulston, 1872–1947, vol. IV

Ward, Herbert, *died* 1919, vol. II

Ward, Herbert, 1866–1938, vol. III

Ward, Mrs Humphry, (Mary Augusta Ward), 1851–1920, vol. II

Ward, Ida Caroline, 1880–1949, vol. IV

Ward, James, 1851–1924, vol. II

Ward, James, 1843–1925, vol. II

Ward, Rt Rev. James, 1905–1973, vol. VII

Ward, Sir John, *died* 1908, vol. I

Ward, John, 1832–1912, vol. I

Ward, Lt-Col John, 1866–1934, vol. III

Ward, Col Sir John Chappell, 1877–1942, vol. IV

Ward, John Frederick, 1883–1954, vol. V

Ward, John Grosvenor B.; *see* Barrington-Ward.

Ward, Major Hon. Sir John Hubert, 1870–1938, vol. III

Ward, John Manning, 1919–1990, vol. VIII

Ward, Captain John Richard Le Hunte, 1870–1953, vol. V

Ward, Engr-Captain John Tom Hickman, *died* 1939, vol. III

Ward, Rev. John William, 1874–1938, vol. III

Ward, Joseph, *died* 1963, vol. VI

Ward, Rt Hon. Sir Joseph George, 1st Bt (*cr* 1911), 1856–1930, vol. III

Ward, Sir Joseph George Davidson, 3rd Bt (*cr* 1911), 1909–1970, vol. VI

Ward, Col Sir Lambert; *see* Ward, Col Sir A. L.

Ward, Sir Lancelot Edward B.; *see* Barrington-Ward.

Ward, Lt-Col Lancelot Edward Seth, 1875–1929, vol. III

Ward, Sir Leslie, 1851–1922, vol. II

Ward, Leslie Moffat; *see* Ward, P. L. M.

Ward, Lester F., 1841–1913, vol. I

Ward, Rev. Mark James B.; *see* Barrington-Ward.

Ward, Mary Augusta; *see* Ward, Mrs Humphry.

Ward, Comdr Sir Melvill Willis, 3rd Bt (*cr* 1914), 1885–1973, vol. VII

Ward, Sir Michael B.; *see* Barrington-Ward.

Ward, Neville; *see* Ward, A. N.

Ward, Philip, 1845–1916, vol. II

Ward, (Philip) Leslie Moffat, 1888–1978, vol. VII

Ward, Adm. Philip N.; *see* Nelson-Ward.

Ward, Captain Hon. Reginald, 1874–1904, vol. I

Ward, Gen. Sir Richard Erskine, 1917–1989, vol. VIII

Ward, Richard Percyvale, 1894–1945, vol. IV

Ward, Hon. Robert Arthur, 1871–1942, vol. IV

Ward, Robert De Courcy, 1867–1931, vol. III

Ward, Robert M'Gowan B.; see Barrington-Ward.

Ward, Robert Percy, 1868–1936, vol. III

Ward, Ronald, 1909–1973, vol. VII

Ward, Ronald Ogier, 1886–1971, vol. VII

Ward, Sarah Adelaide, died 1969, vol. VI

Ward, Captain Hon. Somerset Richard Hamilton Augusta, 1833–1912, vol. I

Ward, Stacey George, 1906–1980, vol. VII

Ward, Brig.-Gen. Thomas, 1861–1949, vol. IV

Ward, Thomas Humphry, 1845–1926, vol. II

Ward, Adm. Thomas Le Hunte, 1830–1907, vol. I

Ward, Sir Thomas Robert John, 1863–1944, vol. IV

Ward, Sir (Victor) Michael B.; see Barrington-Ward.

Ward, Col Walter, died 1948, vol. IV

Ward, Brig.-Gen. Walter Reginald, 1869–1952, vol. V

Ward, Wilfrid Arthur, 1892–1981, vol. VIII

Ward, Wilfrid Philip, 1856–1916, vol. II

Ward, Sir William, 1841–1927, vol. II

Ward, Rt Hon. William Dudley, 1877–1946, vol. IV

Ward, Sir William Erskine, 1838–1916, vol. II

Ward, Rev. William Hayes, 1835–1916, vol. II

Ward-Harrison, Maj.-Gen. John Martin Donald, 1918–1985, vol. VIII

Ward-Jackson, Major Charles Lionel Atkins, 1869–1930, vol. III

Ward-Perkins, John Bryan, 1912–1981, vol. VIII

Wardale, Edith Elizabeth, 1863–1943, vol. IV

Wardale, John Dobson, died 1958, vol. V

Warde, Beatrice Lamberton, 1900–1969, vol. VI

Warde, Lt-Col Charles Arthur Madan, 1839–1912, vol. I

Warde, Col Sir Charles Edward, 1st Bt, 1845–1937, vol. III

Warde, Rt Rev. Geoffrey Hodgson, 1889–1972, vol. VII

Warde, Lt-Col Henry Murray Ashley, 1850–1940, vol. III

Warde, Engr Rear-Adm. Thomas Herbert, 1882–1960, vol. V

Warde-Aldam, Col William St Andrew, 1882–1958, vol. V

Wardell, Lt-Col Henry, died 1933, vol. III

Wardell, John Henry, 1878–1957, vol. V

Wardell-Yerburgh, Rev. Oswald Pryor, 1858–1913, vol. I

Warden, Archibald A., 1869–1943, vol. IV

Warden, Florence; see James, Florence.

Warden, Herbert Lawton, 1877–1946, vol. IV

Warden, William Luck, died 1942, vol. IV

Warder, John Arthur, 1909–1989, vol. VIII

Wardington, 1st Baron, 1869–1950, vol. IV

Wardlaw, Hon. Alan Lindsay, 1887–1938, vol. III

Wardlaw, Rear-Adm. Alexander Livingston Penrose M.; see Mark-Wardlaw.

Wardlaw, Claude Wilson, 1901–1985, vol. VIII

Wardlaw, Sir Henry, 18th Bt, 1822–1897, vol. I

Wardlaw, Sir Henry, 19th Bt, 1867–1954, vol. V

Wardlaw, Sir Henry, 20th Bt, 1894–1983, vol. VIII

Wardlaw, Rev. James Tait P.; see Plowden-Wardlaw.

Wardlaw, William, 1892–1958, vol V

Wardlaw, Rear-Adm. William Penrose M.; see Mark-Wardlaw.

Wardlaw-Milne, Sir John Sydney, died 1967, vol. VI

Wardle, Air Cdre Alfred Randles, 1898–1989, vol. VIII

Wardle, Arthur, 1864–1949, vol. IV

Wardle, Captain Ernest Vivian Livesey, 1878–1931, vol. III

Wardle, George James, 1865–1947, vol. IV

Wardle, Sir Thomas, 1831–1909, vol. I

Wardle, Vice-Adm. Thomas Erskine, 1877–1944, vol. IV

Wardle, Ven. Walter Thomas, 1900–1982, vol. VIII

Wardle, Rev. William Lansdell, 1877–1946, vol. IV

Wardle-Smith, John Hughes, 1909–1968, vol. VI

Wardley, Donald Joule, 1893–1950, vol. IV

Wardrop, Maj.-Gen. Alexander, 1831–1908, vol. I

Wardrop, Gen. Sir Alexander, 1872–1961, vol. VI

Wardrop, Col Douglas, 1854–1937, vol. III

Wardrop, Col Frederick Meyer, 1847–1905, vol. I

Wardrop, Rev. James, died 1909, vol. I

Wardrop, Sir (John) Oliver, 1864–1948, vol. IV

Wardrop, Sir Oliver; see Wardrop, Sir J. O.

Wardrope, William Hugh, 1860–1947, vol. IV

Ware, Maj.-Gen. Sir Fabian Arthur Goulstone, 1869–1949, vol. IV

Ware, Sir Frank, 1886–1968, vol. VI

Ware, Lt-Col Frank Cooke W.; see Webb-Ware.

Ware, Lt-Col George William Webb, died 1943, vol. IV

Ware, Sir Henry Gabriel, 1912–1989, vol. VIII

Ware, Rev. Martin Stewart, died 1934, vol. III

Wareham, Arthur George, 1908–1988, vol. VIII

Wareing, Alfred, 1876–1942, vol. IV

Wareing, Eustace Bernard Foley, 1890–1958, vol. V

Warfield, Benjamin Breckinridge, 1851–1921, vol. II

Wargrave, 1st Baron, 1862–1936, vol. III

Waring, 1st Baron, 1860–1940, vol. III

Waring, Sir (Alfred) Harold, 2nd Bt, 1902–1981, vol. VIII

Waring, Col Anthony Henry, 1871–1941, vol. IV

Waring, Sir (Arthur) Bertram, 1893–1974, vol. VII

Waring, Captain Arthur Cunliffe Bernard C.; see Critchley-Waring.

Waring, Sir Bertram; see Waring, Sir A. B.

Waring, Lady Clementine; see Waring, Lady S. E. C.

Waring, Sir Douglas Tremayne, 1904–1980, vol. VII

Waring, Francis John, 1843–1924, vol. II

Waring, Sir Harold; see Waring, Sir A. H.

Waring, Sir Henry John, 1817–1903, vol. I

Waring, (Henry) William (Allen), 1906–1962, vol. VI

Waring, Herbert, 1857–1932, vol. III

Waring, Sir Holburt Jacob, 1st Bt, 1866–1953, vol. V

Waring, Rev. Canon John, 1890–1967, vol. VI

Waring, Margaret Alicia, 1887–1968, vol. VI

Waring, Lady (Susan Elizabeth) Clementine, died 1964, vol. VI

Waring, Col Thomas, died 1898, vol. I

Waring, Walter, 1876–1930, vol. III

Waring, William; see Waring, H. W. A.

Warington, Robert, 1838–1907, vol. I

Wark, Hon. Lord; John Lean Wark, 1877–1943, vol. IV

Wark, Anna Elisa, 1867–1944, vol. IV

Wark, Lt-Col Blair Anderson, 1894–1941, vol. IV

Wark, Sir Ian William, 1899–1985, vol. VIII

Wark, John Lean; *see* Wark, Hon. Lord.

Warleigh, Captain Percival H., 1873–1933, vol. III

Warlow, Ven. Edmund John, 1863–1937, vol. III

Warlow-Davies, Eric John, 1910–1964, vol. VI

Warman, Rt Rev. (Frederic Sumpter) Guy, 1872–1953, vol. V

Warman, Rt Rev. Guy; *see* Warman, Rt Rev. F. S. G.

Warmington, Sir Cornelius Marshall, 1st Bt, 1842–1908, vol. I

Warmington, Eric Herbert, 1898–1987, vol. VIII

Warmington, Sir Marshall Denham, 2nd Bt, 1871–1935, vol. III

Warne, Rt Rev. Francis Wesley, 1854–1932, vol. III

Warne, George Henry, 1881–1928, vol. II

Warne, Rear-Adm. Robert Spencer, 1903–1990, vol. VIII

Warne-Browne, Air Marshal Sir Thomas Arthur, 1898–1962, vol. VI

Warner, Hon. Sir Arthur George, 1899–1966, vol. VI

Warner, Brodrick Ashton, 1888–1942, vol. IV

Warner, Charles Dudley, 1829–1900, vol. I

Warner, Rev. Canon Charles Edward, 1868–1945, vol. IV

Warner, Sir Christopher Frederick Ashton, 1895–1957, vol. V

Warner, Sir Courtenay; *see* Warner, Sir T. C. T.

Warner, Col Sir Edward Courtenay Thomas, 2nd Bt, 1886–1955, vol. V

Warner, Edward Handley, 1850–1925, vol. II

Warner, Edwin Charles, 1900–1968, vol. VI

Warner, Francis, 1847–1926, vol. II

Warner, Sir Frank, 1862–1930, vol. III

Warner, Frederick Sydney, 1903–1987, vol. VIII

Warner, Sir George Frederic, 1845–1936, vol. III

Warner, Sir Geoge Redston, 1879–1978, vol. VII

Warner, Lt-Col Harry Granville L.; *see* Lee-Warner.

Warner, Jack, (Jack Waters), 1896–1981, vol. VIII

Warner, Rev. John, 1860–1933, vol. III

Warner, Sir Joseph Henry, 1836–1897, vol. I

Warner, Rt Rev. Kenneth Charles Harman, 1891–1983, vol. VIII

Warner, Leonard William, *died* 1959, vol. V

Warner, Sir Lionel Ashton Piers, 1875–1953, vol. V

Warner, Oliver, 1903–1976, vol. VII

Warner, Sir Pelham Francis, 1873–1963, vol. VI

Warner, Philip Henry L.; *see* Lee Warner.

Warner, Rex, 1905–1986, vol. VIII

Warner, Rev. Richard Edward, 1836–1910, vol. I

Warner, Robert Stewart Aucher, 1859–1944, vol. IV

Warner, Robert Townsend, 1868–1938, vol. III

Warner, Rev. Canon Stephen Mortimer, 1873–1947, vol. IV

Warner, Sydney Jeannetta, 1890–1979, vol. VII

Warner, Sylvia Townsend, 1893–1978, vol. VII

Warner, Sir (Thomas) Courtenay Theydon, 1st Bt, 1857–1934, vol. III

Warner, Sir William L.; *see* Lee-Warner.

Warner, Brig.-Gen. William Ward, 1867–1950, vol. IV

Warner-Staples, Irene E. Toye, *died* 1954, vol. V

Warnock, Rt Hon. Edmond, 1887–1971, vol. VII

Warnock, Frederick Victor, 1893–1976, vol. VII

Warnock, John, 1864–1942, vol. IV

Warnock, Rt Hon. (John) Edmond; *see* Warnock, Rt Hon. E.

Warnock, William Robertson Lyon, 1916–1971, vol. VII

Warr, Augustus Frederick, 1847–1908, vol. I

Warr, Very Rev. Charles Laing, 1892–1969, vol. VI

Warr, George Charles Winter, 1845–1901, vol. I

Warr, Sir George Godfrey, 1882–1943, vol. IV

Warr, George Michael, 1915–1989, vol. VIII

Warrack, Grace Harriet, 1855–1932, vol. III

Warrack, Guy Douglas Hamilton, 1900–1986, vol. VIII

Warrack, Sir James Howard, 1855–1926, vol. II

Warrand, Maj.-Gen. William Edmund, 1831–1910, vol. I

Warre, Rev. Edmond, 1837–1920, vol. II

Warre, Felix Walter, 1879–1953, vol. V

Warre, Rev. Francis, *died* 1917, vol. II

Warre, Captain George Francis, 1876–1957, vol. V

Warre, Lt-Col Henry Charles, 1866–1934, vol. III

Warre, Sir Henry James, 1819–1898, vol. I

Warren, Albert Henry, 1830–1911, vol. I

Warren, Alec Stephen, 1894–1982, vol. VIII

Warren, Sir Alfred Haman, 1856–1927, vol. II

Warren, Sir Alfred Henry, (Sir Freddie), 1915–1990, vol. VIII

Warren, Rt Rev. Alwyn Keith, 1900–1988, vol. VIII

Warren, Arthur, 1860–1924, vol. II

Warren, Maj.-Gen. Sir Arthur Frederick, 1830–1913, vol. I

Warren, Arthur George, 1887–1967, vol. VI

Warren, Sir (Augustus George) Digby, 7th Bt, 1898–1958, vol. V

Warren, Sir Augustus Riversdale, 5th Bt, 1833–1914, vol. I

Warren, Sir Augustus Riversdale John Blennerhasset, 6th Bt, 1865–1914, did not have an entry in Who's Who.

Warren, Gen. Sir Charles, 1840–1927, vol. II

Warren, Charles, 1868–1954, vol. V

Warren, Clarence Henry, 1895–1966, vol. VI

Warren, Cuthbert L.; *see* Leicester-Warren.

Warren, Maj.-Gen. Dawson Stockley, 1830–1908, vol. I

Warren, Sir Digby; *see* Warren, Sir A. G. D.

Warren, Douglas Daintry, 1897–1972, vol. VII

Warren, Earl, 1891–1974, vol. VII

Warren, Hon. Sir Edward Emerton, 1897–1983, vol. VIII

Warren, Brig. Edward Galwey, 1893–1975, vol. VII

Warren, Edward Prioleau, 1856–1937, vol. III

Warren, Ernest, 1871–1946, vol. IV

Warren, Falkland George Edgeworth, 1834–1908, vol. I

Warren, Sir Freddie; *see* Warren, Sir A. H.

Warren, Rev. Frederick Edward, 1842–1930, vol. III

Warren, Frederick Samuel Edward Wright, 1878–1952, vol. V

Warren, Major George Ernest, 1871–1942, vol. IV

Warren, Rear-Adm. Guy Langton, 1888–1961, vol. VI

Warren, Rev. Henry George, 1851–1942, vol. IV

Warren, Sir (Henry William) Hugh, 1891–1961, vol. VI

Warren, Sir Herbert; see Warren, Sir T. H.

Warren, Adm. Herbert Augustus, 1855–1926, vol. II

Warren, Howard Crosby, 1867–1934, vol. III

Warren, Sir Hugh; see Warren, Sir Henry W. H.

Warren, John, 1830–1919, vol. II

Warren, Vice-Adm. John Borlase, 1838–1919, vol. II

Warren, John Herbert, 1895–1960, vol. V

Warren, Lt-Col John Leighton Byrne L.; see Leicester-Warren.

Warren, Col John Raymond, 1888–1956, vol. V

Warren, Rev. John Shrapnel, died 1925, vol. II

Warren, Ven. Latham Coddington, died 1912, vol. I

Warren, Low, died 1941, vol. IV

Warren, Rev. Max Alexander Cunningham, 1904–1977, vol. VII

Warren, Sir Mortimer Langton, 1903–1972, vol. VII

Warren, Nigel Sebastian Sommerville, 1912–1967, vol. VI

Warren, Sir Norcot Hastings Yeeles, 1864–1947, vol. IV

Warren, Sir Pelham Laird, 1845–1923, vol. II

Warren, Col Peter, 1866–1952, vol. V

Warren, Philip David, 1851–1928, vol. II

Warren, Phillip; see Warren, W. P.

Warren, Richard, 1876–1957, vol. V

Warren, Robert Penn, 1905–1989, vol. VIII

Warren, Rt Hon. Robert Richard, 1817–1897, vol. I

Warren, Thomas Alfred, 1882–1968, vol. VI

Warren, Sir (Thomas) Herbert, 1853–1930, vol. III

Warren, Col Sir Thomas Richard Pennefather, 8th Bt, 1885–1961, vol. VI

Warren, Sir Victor Dunn, 1903–1953, vol. V

Warren, William Fairfield, 1833–1929, vol. III

Warren, William Henry, 1852–1926, vol. II

Warren, William Phillip, 1924–1988, vol. VIII

Warren, Hon. William Robertson, 1879–1927, vol. II

Warren, Col William Robinson, 1882–1969, vol. VI

Warrender, Sir George, 6th Bt, 1825–1901, vol. I

Warrender, Vice-Adm. Sir George John Scott, 7th Bt, 1860–1917, vol. II

Warrender, Lt-Col Hugh Valdave, 1868–1926, vol. II

Warrender, Lady Maud, 1870–1945, vol. IV

Warriner, John, 1860–1938, vol. III

Warrington of Clyffe, 1st Baron, 1851–1937, vol. III

Warrington, Anthony, 1929–1990, vol. VIII

Warrington-Morris, Air Cdre Alfred Drummond, 1883–1962, vol. VI

Warry, George Deedes, 1831–1904, vol. I

Warry, William Taylor, 1836–1906, vol. I

Warter, Sir Philip Allan, 1903–1971, vol. VII

Warton, Rear-Adm. John Fenwick, 1877–1950, vol. IV

Warwick, 5th Earl of, 1853–1924, vol. II

Warwick, 6th Earl of, 1882–1928, vol. II

Warwick, 7th Earl of, 1911–1984, vol. VIII

Warwick, Countess of; (Frances), 1861–1938, vol. III

Warwick, Countess of; (Marjorie), 1887–1943, vol. IV

Warwick, Cyril Walter, 1899–1985, vol. VIII

Warwick, Rt Rev. Mgr J. V., 1857–1939, vol. III

Warwick, Captain John Abraham, 1871–1937, vol. III

Warwick, Sir Norman Richard Combe, 1892–1962, vol. VI

Warwick, Walter Curry, 1877–1963, vol. VI

Warwick, Rev. William Geoffrey, 1898–1955, vol. V

Warwick, William Turner, 1888–1949, vol. IV

Washbourn, John Wichenford, 1863–1902, vol. I

Washbourn, Rear-Adm. Richard Everley, 1910–1988, vol. VIII

Washbourn, William, 1862–1959, vol. V

Washington, Vice-Adm. Basil George, died 1940, vol. III

Washington, Booker T., died 1915, vol. I

Washington, Horace Lee, 1864–1938, vol. III

Washington, Rev. Marmaduke, 1846–1935, vol. III

Wason, Rear-Adm. Cathcart Romer, 1874–1941, vol. IV

Wason, Rt Hon. Eugene, 1846–1927, vol. II

Wason, John Cathcart, 1848–1921, vol. II

Wason, Lt-Gen. Sydney Rigby, 1887–1969, vol. VI

Wass, Charles Alfred Alan, 1911–1989, vol. VIII

Wass, Samuel Hall, 1907–1970, vol. VI

Wassermann, Jakob, 1873–1934, vol. III

Watchorn, Col Edwin Thomas, 1856–1940, vol. III(A), vol. V

Waterer, Sir Bernard; see Waterer, Sir R. B.

Waterer, Sir (Robert) Bernard, 1891–1971, vol. VII

Waterfall, Sir Charles Francis, 1888–1954, vol. V

Waterfall, William Duncan, 1889–1970, vol. VI

Waterfield, Sir (Alexander) Percival, 1888–1965, vol. VI

Waterfield, Bt-Col Arthur Charles Mallison, 1866–1943, vol. IV

Waterfield, Sir Henry, 1837–1913, vol. I

Waterfield, Maj.-Gen. Henry Gordon, 1840–1901, vol. I

Waterfield, Lina, 1874–1964, vol. VI

Waterfield, Sir Percival; see Waterfield, Sir A. P.

Waterfield, Very Rev. Reginald, 1867–1967, vol. VI

Waterford, 6th Marquess of, 1875–1911, vol. I

Waterford, 7th Marquess of, 1901–1934, vol. III

Waterhouse, Alfred, 1830–1905, vol. I

Waterhouse, Captain Rt Hon. Charles, 1893–1975, vol. VII

Waterhouse, Charles Owen, 1843–1917, vol. II

Waterhouse, Eben Gowrie, 1881–1977, vol. VII

Waterhouse, Edwin, 1841–1917, vol. II

Waterhouse, Sir Ellis Kirkham, 1905–1985, vol. VIII

Waterhouse, Rev. Eric Strickland, 1879–1964, vol. VI

Waterhouse, Maj.-Gen. George Guy, 1886–1975, vol. VII

Waterhouse, Gilbert, 1888–1977, vol. VII

Waterhouse, Sir Herbert Furnivall, 1864–1931, vol. III

Waterhouse, J. W., died 1917, vol. II

Waterhouse, Maj.-Gen. James, 1842–1922, vol. II

Waterhouse, Michael Theodore, 1888–1968, vol. VI

Waterhouse, Sir Nicholas Edwin, 1877–1964, vol. VI

Waterhouse, Osborn, 1881–1945, vol. IV

Waterhouse, Paul, 1861–1924, vol. II

Waterhouse, Lt-Col Sir Ronald, 1878–1942, vol. IV

Waterhouse, Rupert, 1873–1958, vol. V

Waterhouse, Thomas, 1878–1961, vol. VI
Waterhouse, Walter Lawry, 1887–1969, vol. VI
Waterloo, Stanley, 1846–1913, vol. I
Waterlow, David Sydney, 1857–1924, vol. II
Waterlow, Sir Edgar Lutwyche, 3rd Bt (cr 1873), 1870–1954, vol. V
Waterlow, Sir Ernest Albert, 1850–1919, vol. II
Waterlow, Col Sir James; see Waterlow, Col Sir W. J.
Waterlow, Col James Francis, 1869–1942, vol. IV
Waterlow, Sir Philip Alexander, 4th Bt (cr 1873), 1897–1973, vol. VII
Waterlow, Sir Philip Hickson, 2nd Bt (cr 1873), 1847–1931, vol. III
Waterlow, Sir Sydney Hedley, 1st Bt (cr 1873), 1822–1906, vol. I
Waterlow, Sir Sydney Philip, 1878–1944, vol. IV
Waterlow, Sir Thomas Gordon, 3rd Bt, 1911–1982, vol. VIII
Waterlow, Sir William Alfred, 1st Bt (cr 1930), 1871–1931, vol. III
Waterlow, Col Sir (William) James, 2nd Bt (cr 1930), 1905–1969, vol. VI
Waterman, Sir Ewen McIntyre, 1901–1982, vol. VIII
Waterman, Rt Rev. Robert Harold, 1894–1984, vol. VIII
Watermeyer, Rt Hon. Ernest Frederick, 1880–1958, vol. V
Waterpark, 4th Baron, 1839–1912, vol. I
Waterpark, 5th Baron, 1883–1932, vol. III
Waterpark, 6th Baron, 1876–1948, vol. IV
Waters, Alfred Charles, 1848–1912, vol. I
Waters, Alwyn Brunow, 1906–1988, vol. VIII
Waters, Major Sir Arnold Horace Santo, 1886–1981, vol. VIII
Waters, Arthur George, 1888–1953, vol. V
Waters, Edwin George Ross, 1890–1930, vol. III
Waters, Rev. Francis Edward, 1847–1929, vol. III
Waters, Frank George, 1911–1974, vol. VII
Waters, Frank Henry, 1908–1954, vol. V
Waters, George, died 1905, vol. I
Waters, Sir George Alexander, 1880–1967, vol. VI
Waters, Sir Harry G., 1868–1946, vol. IV
Waters, Jack; see Warner, Jack.
Waters, James, died 1923, vol. II
Waters, John Dallas, 1889–1967, vol. VI
Waters, Lt-Col Robert, died 1927, vol. II
Waters, Rev. Thomas Brocas, died 1922, vol. II
Waters, Brig.-Gen. Wallscourt Hely-Hutchinson, 1855–1945, vol. IV
Waters, William Alexander, 1903–1985, vol. VIII
Waterson, Anthony Peter, 1923–1983, vol. VIII
Waterson, David, died 1942, vol. IV
Waterson, David, 1870–1954, vol. V
Waterson, Hon. Sidney Frank, 1896–1976, vol. VII
Waterston, David James, 1910–1985, vol. VIII
Wates, George Leslie, 1884–1958, vol. V
Wates, Sir Ronald Wallace, 1907–1986, vol. VIII
Wathen, Gerald Anstruther, 1878–1958, vol. V
Watherston, Lt-Col Alan Edward Garrard, 1867–1909, vol. I
Watherston, Charles Fell, 1875–1940, vol. III
Watherston, Sir David Charles, 1907–1977, vol. VII
Watkin, Sir Alfred Mellor, 2nd Bt, 1846–1914, vol. I

Watkin, Sir Edward William, 1st Bt, 1819–1901, vol. I
Watkin, Ernest Lucas, 1876–1951, vol. V
Watkin, Col Henry Samuel Spiller, 1843–1905, vol. I
Watkin, Sir Herbert George, died 1966, vol. VI
Watkin, Morgan, 1878–1970, vol. VI
Watkin, Thomas Morgan Joseph, 1856–1915, vol. I
Watkin-Davies, Rev. Francis Parry, 1862–1939, vol. III
Watkin-Jones, Rev. Howard, 1888–1953, vol. V
Watkin-Williams, Robert Thesiger, 1867–1953, vol. V
Watkins, Baron (Life Peer); Tudor Elwyn Watkins, 1903–1983, vol. VIII
Watkins, Arthur Ernest, 1898–1967, vol. VI
Watkins, Arthur Goronwy, 1903–1990, vol. VIII
Watkins, Brig. Bernard Springett, 1900–1977, vol. VII
Watkins, Col Charles Bell, 1859–1929, vol. III
Watkins, Ven. D. Glyn, 1844–1907, vol. I
Watkins, Frederick Charles, 1883–1954, vol. V
Watkins, Frederick Henry, 1859–1928, vol. II, vol. III
Watkins, Col Frederic Mostyn, 1873–1946, vol. IV
Watkins, Rear-Adm. Geoffrey Robert Sladen, 1885–1950, vol. IV
Watkins, Harold James, 1914–1983, vol. VIII
Watkins, Henry George, 1907–1932, vol. III
Watkins, Col Henry George, 1880–1935, vol. III
Watkins, Ven. Henry William, 1844–1922, vol. II
Watkins, Lt-Col Hubert Bromley, 1897–1984, vol. VIII
Watkins, Rt Rev. Ivor Stanley, 1896–1960, vol. V
Watkins, James William, 1890–1959, vol. V
Watkins, Rear-Adm. John Kingdon, 1913–1970, vol. VI
Watkins, Mary Gwendolen, 1905–1981, vol. VIII
Watkins, Sir Metford, 1900–1950, vol. IV
Watkins, Michael John, 1875–1945, vol. IV
Watkins, Ven. Oscar Daniel, 1848–1926, vol. II
Watkins, Lt-Col Oscar Ferris, 1877–1943, vol. IV
Watkins, Rev. Owen Spencer, 1873–1957, vol. IV
Watkins, Sir Percy Emerson, 1871–1946, vol. IV
Watkins, Stanley Heath, died 1967, vol. VI
Watkins, Rev. Thomas Benjamin, 1856–1933, vol. III
Watkins, Vernon Phillips, 1906–1967, vol. VI
Watkins, Watkin S.; see Strang-Watkins.
Watkins, William Henry, 1877–1964, vol. VI
Watkins-Pitchford, Denys James, 1905–1990, vol. VIII
Watkins-Pitchford, Lt-Col Herbert, died 1951, vol. V
Watkinson, Arnold Edwards, 1893–1953, vol. V
Watkinson, Sir (George) Laurence, 1896–1974, vol. VII
Watkinson, Sir Laurence; see Watkinson, Sir G. L.
Watkinson, William Henry, 1860–1932, vol. III
Watkinson, Rev. William L., 1838–1925, vol. II
Watkis, Gen. Sir Henry Bulckley Burlton, 1860–1931, vol. III
Watkyn-Thomas, Frederic William, died 1963, vol. VI
Watling, Col Francis Wyatt, 1869–1953, vol. V
Watlington, Sir Henry William, 1866–1942, vol. IV
Watmough, John Edwin, 1860–1939, vol. III
Watney, Col Charles Norman, 1868–1956, vol. V

Watney, Dendy, 1865–1955, vol. V

Watney, Col Sir Frank Dormay, 1870–1965, vol. VI

Watney, Sir John, 1834–1923, vol. II

Watney, Oliver Vernon, 1902–1966, vol. VI

Watney, Vernon James, 1860–1928, vol. II

Watson, Baron (Life Peer); William Watson, 1828–1899, vol. I

Watson, Aaron, 1850–1926, vol. II

Watson, Very Rev. Alan Cameron, 1900–1976, vol. VII

Watson, Alexandra Mary Chalmers, 1873–1936, vol. III

Watson, Alfred Edward Thomas, 1849–1922, vol. II

Watson, Sir Alfred Henry, 1874–1967, vol. VI

Watson, Sir Alfred William, 1870–1936, vol. III

Watson, Col Andrew Alexander, *died* 1931, vol. III

Watson, A(ndrew) Aiken, 1897–1969, vol. VI

Watson, Andrew Gordon, *died* 1949, vol. IV

Watson, Sir Angus; *see* Watson, Sir J. A.

Watson, Archibald, 1849–1940, vol. III(A), vol. IV

Watson, Sir Arthur, 1873–1954, vol. V

Watson, Arthur E., 1880–1969, vol. VI

Watson, Sir Arthur Egerton, 1882–1967, vol. VI

Watson, Arthur George, 1829–1916, vol. II

Watson, Ven. Arthur Herbert, 1864–1952, vol. V

Watson, Arthur Kenelm, 1867–1947, vol. IV

Watson, Sir Arthur Townley, 2nd Bt (*cr* 1866), 1830–1907, vol. I

Watson, Arthur William, 1874–1925, vol. II

Watson, Basil Bernard, *died* 1941, vol. IV

Watson, Benjamin Philip, 1880–1976, vol. VII

Watson, Vice-Adm. Bertram Chalmers, 1887–1976, vol. VII

Watson, Sir Bertrand, 1878–1948, vol. IV

Watson, Rear-Adm. Burges, 1846–1902, vol. I

Watson, Most Rev. Campbell West W.; *see* West-Watson.

Watson, Chalmers, 1870–1946, vol. IV

Watson, Sir Charles Cuningham, 1874–1934, vol. III

Watson, Brig.-Gen. Charles Frederic, 1877–1948, vol. IV

Watson, Maj.-Gen. Sir Charles G.; *see* Gordon-Watson.

Watson, Col Sir Charles Moore, 1844–1916, vol. II

Watson, Sir Charles Rushworth, 3rd Bt (*cr* 1866), 1865–1922, vol. II

Watson, Gen. Sir Daril G., 1888–1967, vol. VI

Watson, Maj.-Gen. Sir David, 1871–1922, vol. II

Watson, David, *died* 1940, vol. III

Watson, David Archibald Beverley, 1905–1971, vol. VII

Watson, Hon. David John, 1911–1959, vol. V

Watson, Sir David M.; *see* Milne-Watson.

Watson, David Meredith Seares, 1886–1973, vol. VII

Watson, Sir (David) Ronald M.; *see* Milne-Watson.

Watson, Dennis George, *died* 1977, vol. VII

Watson, Captain Sir Derrick William Inglefield Inglefield-, 4th Bt, 1901–1987, vol. VIII

Watson, Sir Duncan, 1873–1959, vol. V

Watson, Vice-Adm. Sir Dymock; *see* Watson, Vice-Adm. Sir R. D.

Watson, Edith Margaret, *died* 1953, vol. V

Watson, Edmund Henry Lacon, 1865–1948, vol. IV

Watson, Rev. Edward William, 1859–1936, vol. III

Watson, Elliot Lovegood Grant, 1885–1970, vol. VI

Watson, Rear-Adm. Fischer Burges, 1884–1960, vol. V

Watson, Lt-Col Forrester Colvin, 1878–1951, vol. V

Watson, Foster, 1860–1929, vol. III

Watson, Sir Francis, 1864–1947, vol. IV

Watson, Col Francis William, 1893–1966, vol. VI

Watson, Sir Frank Pears, 1878–1941, vol. IV

Watson, Rev. Frederick, 1844–1906, vol. I

Watson, Frederick, 1885–1935, vol. III

Watson, Frederick, 1880–1947, vol. IV

Watson, Rev. Frederick Vincent, 1869–1954, vol. V

Watson, Sir Geoffrey Lewin, 3rd Bt (*cr* 1918), 1879–1959, vol. V

Watson, George, 1845–1927, vol. II

Watson, George, 1872–1937, vol. III

Watson, Sir George; *see* Watson, Sir W. G.

Watson, George Lennox, 1851–1904, vol. I

Watson, George Spencer, 1869–1934, vol. III

Watson, Ven. George Wade, 1838–1915, vol. I

Watson, Sir George Willes, 1827–1897, vol. I

Watson, George William, 1877–1956, vol. V

Watson, Gilbert, *died* 1920, vol. II

Watson, Gilbert, 1864–1941, vol. IV

Watson, Gilbert, 1882–1987, vol. VIII

Watson, Maj.-Gen. Gilbert France, 1895–1976, vol. VII

Watson, G(ordon) G(raham) Gibbes, 1891–1971, vol. VII

Watson, Harold Argyle, 1884–1959, vol. V

Watson, Lt-Col Harold Farnell, 1876–1941, vol. IV

Watson, Harrison, 1864–1948, vol. IV

Watson, Harry, 1871–1936, vol. III

Watson, Maj.-Gen. Sir Harry Davis, 1866–1945, vol. IV

Watson, Henry Angus, 1863–1952, vol. V

Watson, Henry Brereton Marriott, 1863–1921, vol. II

Watson, Henry C.; *see* Cradock-Watson.

Watson, Sir Henry Edmund, 1815–1901, vol. I

Watson, Hon. Sir (Henry) Keith, 1900–1973, vol. VII

Watson, Rev. Henry Lacon, 1823–1903, vol. I

Watson, Brig. Henry Neville Grylls, 1885–1976, vol. VII

Watson, Rev. Henry William, 1827–1903, vol. I

Watson, Herbert Adolphus G.; *see* Grant Watson.

Watson, Rev. Herbert Armstrong, 1860–1937, vol. III

Watson, Herbert Edmeston, 1886–1980, vol. VII

Watson, Major Herbert Frazer, 1881–1937, vol. III

Watson, Herbert James, 1895–1988, vol. VIII

Watson, Homer, 1855–1936, vol. III

Watson, Captain Horace Cyril, 1876–1949, vol. IV

Watson, Hubert Digby, 1869–1947, vol. IV

Watson, Rev. Hubert Luing, 1892–1985, vol. VIII

Watson, Sir Hugh, 1897–1966, vol. VI

Watson, Adm. Sir Hugh Dudley Richards, 1872–1954, vol. V

Watson, Hugh Gordon, 1912–1989, vol. VIII

Watson, Sir Hugh Wesley Allen, 1875–1953, vol. V

Watson, Maj.-Gen. Hugh Wharton Myddleton, 1881–1938, vol. III

Watson, Sir James Anderson Scott, 1889–1966, vol. VI

Watson, Sir (James) Angus, 1874–1961, vol. VI

Watson, Lt-Col James Kiero, 1865–1942, vol. IV
Watson, James Murray, 1888–1955, vol. V
Watson, Very Rev. James P.; see Pitt-Watson.
Watson, James Wreford, 1915–1990, vol. VIII
Watson, Janet Vida, (Mrs John Sutton), 1923–1985, vol. VIII
Watson, Sir John, 1st Bt (cr 1895), 1819–1898, vol. I
Watson, Sir John, 2nd Bt (cr 1895), 1860–1903, vol. I
Watson, Rev. John, 1850–1907, vol. I
Watson, John, died 1908, vol. I
Watson, Sir John, 3rd Bt (cr 1895), 1898–1918, vol. II
Watson, Gen. Sir John, 1829–1919, vol. II
Watson, John, died 1928, vol. II
Watson, Rev. John, 1843–1930, vol. III
Watson, John, died 1936, vol. III
Watson, John, 1847–1939, vol. III
Watson, John Alfred, died 1931, vol. III
Watson, John Arthur Fergus, 1903–1978, vol. VII
Watson, Sir John Ballingall Forbes, 1879–1952, vol. V
Watson, Sir John Charles, 1883–1944, vol. IV
Watson, Hon. John Christian, 1867–1941, vol. IV
Watson, John Duncan, 1860–1946, vol. IV
Watson, Brig.-Gen. John Edward, 1859–1951, vol. V
Watson, John Harry, 1875–1944, vol. IV
Watson, Sir John Mathewson, died 1942, vol. IV
Watson, John Parker, 1909–1989, vol. VIII
Watson, (John) Steven, 1916–1986, vol. VIII
Watson, Lt-Col John William, 1874–1962, vol. VI
Watson, Hon. Sir Keith; see Watson, Hon. Sir H. K.
Watson, Laurence H.; see Hill Watson, Hon. Lord
Watson, Engr Rear-Adm. Lewis Jones, 1871–1942, vol. IV
Watson, Sir Logie Pirie, 1864–1933, vol. III
Watson, Malcolm, 1853–1929, vol. III
Watson, Sir Malcolm, 1873–1955, vol. V
Watson, Sir Norman James, 2nd Bt, 1897–1983, vol. VIII
Watson, Maj.-Gen. Norman Vyvyan, 1898–1974, vol. VII
Watson, P. F.; see Fletcher-Watson.
Watson, Sir Patrick Heron, 1832–1907, vol. I
Watson, Reginald Frank William, 1921–1989, vol. VIII
Watson, Reginald George, 1862–1926, vol. II
Watson, Captain Reginald James Newall, 1877–1930, vol. III
Watson, Sir Renny; see Watson, Sir W. R.
Watson, Hon. Robert, 1853–1929, vol. III
Watson, Hon. Robert, 1868–1930, vol. III
Watson, Robert, 1882–1948, vol. IV
Watson, Robert, 1894–1977, vol. VII
Watson, Rev. Robert A., 1845–1921, vol. II
Watson, Vice-Adm. Sir (Robert) Dymock, 1904–1988, vol. VIII
Watson, Rt Hon. Robert Spence, 1837–1911, vol. I
Watson, Robert William S.; see Seton-Watson.
Watson, Sir Ronald M.; see Milne-Watson, Sir D. R.
Watson, Col Ronald Macgregor, 1887–1936, vol. III
Watson, Samuel, 1898–1967, vol. VI
Watson, Lt-Col Stancliffe Wallace, 1889–1947, vol. IV
Watson, Sir Stephen John, 1898–1976, vol. VII
Watson, Steven; see Watson, J. S.

Watson, Lt-Col Sydney Twells, 1879–1936, vol. III
Watson, Thomas, 1844–1914, vol. I
Watson, Sir Thomas Aubrey, 4th Bt (cr 1866), 1911–1941, vol. IV
Watson, Lt-Col Thomas Colclough, 1867–1917, vol. II
Watson, Sir Thomas Edward, 1st Bt (cr 1918), 1851–1921, vol. II
Watson, Thomas J., 1847–1912, vol. I, vol. III
Watson, Thomas William, 1889–1957, vol. V
Watson, Ven. W. C., 1867–1916, vol. II, vol. III
Watson, Sir Wager Joseph, 4th Bt (cr 1760), 1837–1904, vol. I
Watson, Rev. Wentworth, 1848–1925, vol. II
Watson, Sir Wilfrid Hood, 2nd Bt (cr 1918), 1875–1922, vol. II
Watson, William, 1843–1909, vol. I
Watson, Sir William, 1842–1918, vol. II
Watson, William, 1868–1919, vol. II
Watson, Sir William, 1858–1935, vol. III
Watson, Major William, 1885–1942, vol. IV
Watson, Sir William, 1902–1984, vol. VIII
Watson, William; see Baron Thankerton.
Watson, Maj.-Gen. William Arthur, 1860–1944, vol. IV
Watson, Sir (William) George, 1st Bt (cr 1912), 1861–1930, vol. III
Watson, William Henry Lowe, 1891–1932, vol. III
Watson, William John, 1865–1948, vol. IV
Watson, William Law, 1883–1958, vol. V
Watson, William Livingstone, 1835–1903, vol. I
Watson, William McLean, 1874–1962, vol. VI
Watson, William Peter, died 1932, vol. III
Watson, Sir (William) Renny, 1838–1900, vol. I
Watson, William Trevor, 1886–1943, vol. IV
Watson, Lt-Col William Walter Russell, 1875–1924, vol. II
Watson, Wreford; see Watson, J. W.
Watson-Jones, Sir Reginald, 1902–1972, vol. VII
Watson-Kennedy, Lt-Col Thomas Francis Archibald, 1856–1935, vol. III
Watson Stewart, Sir James; see Stewart.
Watson-Taylor, George Simon Arthur, 1850–1942, vol. IV
Watson-Watt, Air Chief Comdt Dame Katherine Jane Trefusis, 1899–1971, vol. VII
Watson-Watt, Sir Robert Alexander, 1892–1973, vol. VII
Watson-Williams, Eric, 1890–1964, vol. VI
Watson-Williams, Patrick, 1863–1938, vol. III
Watt, Sir Alan Stewart, 1901–1988, vol. VIII
Watt, Lt-Col Alexander Fitzgerald, 1871–1957, vol. V
Watt, Alexander Pollock, died 1914, vol. I
Watt, Alexander Strahan, died 1948, vol. IV
Watt, Alexander Stuart, 1892–1985, vol. VIII
Watt, Very Rev. Archibald, 1901–1981, vol. VIII
Watt, David, 1932–1987, vol. VIII
Watt, Brig-Gen. Donald Munro, 1871–1942, vol. IV
Watt, Lt-Col Edward William, 1877–1955, vol. V
Watt, Commissary-Gen. FitzJames Edward, 1822–1902, vol. I
Watt, Francis, 1849–1927, vol. II
Watt, Francis Clifford, 1896–1971, vol. VII

Watt, Sir George, 1851–1930, vol. III
Watt, George, 1854–1940, vol. III
Watt, George Fiddes, 1873–1960, vol. V
Watt, George Percival Norman, 1890–1983, vol. VIII
Watt, Sir George Steven H.; *see* Harvie-Watt.
Watt, Harry Anderson, 1863–1929, vol. III
Watt, Henry J., 1879–1925, vol. II
Watt, Very Rev. Hugh, 1879–1968, vol. VI
Watt, Rt Hon. Hugh, 1912–1980, vol. VII
Watt, Ian Buchanan, 1916–1988, vol. VIII
Watt, James, 1867–1929, vol. III
Watt, Sir James, *died* 1935, vol. III
Watt, James, 1863–1945, vol. IV
Watt, James, 1870–1945, vol. IV
Watt, James Crabb, 1853–1917, vol. II
Watt, James Cromar, 1862–1940, vol. III(A), vol. IV
Watt, Rev. John, 1862–1930, vol. III
Watt, John Mitchell, 1892–1980, vol. VII
Watt, Dame Katherine Christie, 1886–1963, vol. VI
Watt, Air Chief Comdt Dame Katherine Jane Trefusis W.; *see* Watson-Watt.
Watt, Langmuir; *see* Watt, W. L.
Watt, Very Rev. Lauchlan MacLean, *died* 1957, vol. V
Watt, Rev. Lewis, 1885–1965, vol. VI
Watt, Michael Herbert, 1887–1967, vol. VI
Watt, Sir Robert Alexander W.; *see* Watson-Watt.
Watt, Robert Cameron, 1898–1983, vol. VIII
Watt, Sir Robert Dickie, 1881–1965, vol. VI
Watt, Samuel, 1876–1927, vol. II
Watt, Captain Samuel Alexander, 1876–1950, vol. IV
Watt, Theodore, 1884–1946, vol. IV
Watt, Hon. Sir Thomas, 1857–1947, vol. IV
Watt, Sir Thomas, 1882–1955, vol. V
Watt, (Walter) Langmuir, 1876–1953, vol. V
Watt, William, 1912–1985, vol. VIII
Watt, Rt Hon. William Alexander, 1871–1946, vol. IV
Watt, William Robert, 1888–1949, vol. IV
Watt, William Warnock, 1890–1963, vol. VI
Watterson, Hon. Henry, 1840–1921, vol. II
Watterston, David, 1845–1931, vol. III
Wattie, Sir James, 1902–1974, vol. VII
Wattie, James MacPherson, 1862–1943, vol. IV
Watts, Arthur, *died* 1935, vol. III
Watts, Arthur Francis, 1916–1972, vol. VII
Watts, Arthur Frederick, 1897–1970, vol. VI(AII)
Watts, Rev. Arthur Herbert, 1886–1960, vol. V
Watts, Charles Albert, 1858–1946, vol. IV
Watts, Maj.-Gen. Charles Donald Raynsford, 1871–1943, vol. IV
Watts, Rt Rev. Christopher Charles, *died* 1958, vol. V
Watts, Sir (Fenwick) Shadforth, 1858–1926, vol. II
Watts, Sir Francis, 1859–1930, vol. III
Watts, George Frederick, 1817–1904, vol. I
Watts, Gordon Edward, 1902–1974, vol. VII
Watts, Henry Edward, 1832–1904, vol. I
Watts, Lt-Gen. Sir Herbert Edward, 1858–1934, vol. III
Watts, Rt Rev. Horace Godfrey, 1901–1959, vol. V
Watts, Sir Hugh Edmund, 1888–1958, vol. V
Watts, James, 1903–1961, vol. VI
Watts, James T., *died* 1930, vol. III
Watts, John Hylton, 1890–1972, vol. VII

Watts, Leonard, 1871–1951, vol. V
Watts, Maurice Emygdius, 1878–1933, vol. III
Watts, Col Sir Philip, 1846–1926, vol. II
Watts, Rev. Robert Rowley, *died* 1911, vol. I
Watts, Sir Shadforth; *see* Watts, Sir F. S.
Watts, Rev. Sidney Maurice, 1892–1979, vol. VII
Watts, Sir Thomas, 1868–1951, vol. V
Watts, Weldon Patrick Tyrone, 1897–1972, vol. VII
Watts, Col Sir William, 1858–1922, vol. II
Watts, William John, 1923–1983, vol. VIII
Watts, William Marshall, 1844–1919, vol. II
Watts, William Walter, 1862–1948, vol. IV
Watts, William Whitehead, 1860–1947, vol. IV
Watts-Ditchfield, Rt Rev. John Edwin, 1861–1923, vol. II
Watts-Dunton, Walter Theodore, 1832–1914, vol. I
Wauchope, Gen. Sir Arthur Grenfell, 1874–1947, vol. IV
Wauchope, Lt-Col David Alexander, 1871–1929, vol. III
Wauchope, Mrs, (Jean Mary Wauchope), *died* 1942, vol. IV
Wauchope, Sir John Douglas Don-, 9th Bt, 1859–1951, vol. V
Wauchope, Sir Patrick George Don-, 10th Bt, 1898–1989, vol. VIII
Waugh, Alec, 1898–1981, vol. VIII
Waugh, Sir (Alexander) Telford, 1865–1950, vol. IV
Waugh, Arthur, 1866–1943, vol. IV
Waugh, Sir Arthur Allen, 1891–1968, vol. VI
Waugh, Ven. Arthur Thornhill, 1842–1922, vol. II
Waugh, Rev. Benjamin, 1839–1908, vol. I
Waugh, Evelyn Arthur St John, 1903–1966, vol. VI
Waugh, George Ernest, *died* 1940, vol. III
Waugh, Sir Telford; *see* Waugh, Sir A. T.
Waugh, William James, 1856–1931, vol. III
Waugh, William Templeton, 1884–1932, vol. III
Wauhope, Col Robert Alexander, 1855–1921, vol. II
Wauters, Emile, 1846–1933, vol. III
Wauton, Edric Brenton, 1883–1957, vol. V
Wavell, 1st Earl, 1883–1950, vol. IV
Wavell, 2nd Earl, 1916–1953, vol. V
Wavell, Maj.-Gen. Archibald Graham, 1843–1935, vol. III
Waverley, 1st Viscount, 1882–1958, vol. V
Waverley, 2nd Viscount, 1911–1990, vol. VIII
Waverley, Viscountess; (Ava), 1896–1974, vol. VII
Wavertree, 1st Baron, 1856–1933, vol. III
Wavertree, Lady; (Sophie Florence Lothrop), (Mrs F. M. B. Fisher), *died* 1952, vol. V
Way, Andrew Greville Parry, 1909–1974, vol. VII
Way, Arthur S., 1847–1930, vol. III
Way, Lt-Col Benjamin Irby, 1869–1932, vol. III
Way, Lt-Col Bromley George Vere, 1873–1940, vol. III
Way, Rev. Charles Parry, 1870–1949, vol. IV
Way, Christine Stella, 1895–1975, vol. VII
Way, Col George Augustus, 1837–1899, vol. I
Way, Gerald Oscar, 1875–1938, vol. III
Way, Rev. John Hugh, 1834–1912, vol. I
Way, Rev. John Pearce, 1850–1937, vol. III
Way, Maj.-Gen. Nowell FitzUpton Sampson-, 1838–1926, vol. II

Way, Rt Hon. Sir Samuel James, 1st Bt, 1836–1916, vol. II

Way, Rt Rev. Wilfrid Lewis Mark, 1905–1982, vol. VIII

Way, Captain William, 1847–1927, vol. II

Wayland, Edward James, 1888–1966, vol. VI

Wayland, Lt-Col Edward Robert, 1871–1939, vol. III

Wayland, Lt-Col Sir William Abraham, 1869–1950, vol. IV

Wayman, Lt-Col Harry Reginald Bland, 1877–1931, vol. III

Wayman, Lt-Col Sir Myers, 1890–1959, vol. V

Wayman, Thomas, 1833–1901, vol. I

Waymouth, Adm. Arthur William, 1863–1936, vol. III

Waymouth, Paymaster-Captain Frederick Richard, 1862–1927, vol. II

Wayne, Sir Edward Johnson, 1902–1990, vol. VIII

Wayne, Naunton, 1901–1970, vol. VI

Wayne, Richard St John Ormerod, 1904–1959, vol. V

Waynforth, Harry Morton, 1867–1916, vol. II

Wayte, Lt-Col Adrian Barclay, 1882–1934, vol. III

Wazir Hasan, Hon. Sir Saiyid, 1874–1947, vol. IV(A), vol. V

Weakley, Ernest, 1861–1923, vol. II

Weale, Putnam, 1877–1930, vol. III

Weale, W. H. James, 1832–1917, vol. II

Wear, Col Algernon Edward Luke, 1866–1941, vol. IV

Weardale, 1st Baron, 1847–1923, vol. II

Weare, Sir Henry Edwin, 1825–1898, vol. I

Wearing, John Frederick, 1922–1974, vol. VII

Weatherall, Col Henry Burgess, died 1917, vol. II

Weatherall, John Henry, 1868–1950, vol. IV

Weatherburn, Charles Ernest, 1884–1974, vol. VII

Weatherby, Sir Francis, 1885–1969, vol. VI

Weatherhead, Arthur Evelyn, 1880–1956, vol. V

Weatherhead, Rev. Arthur Swinton, 1866–1937, vol. III

Weatherhead, Sir Arthur Trenham, 1905–1984, vol. VIII

Weatherhead, Rev. Herbert Thomas Candy, 1875–1930, vol. III

Weatherhead, Very Rev. James, 1863–1944, vol. IV

Weatherhead, Rev. Leslie Dixon, 1893–1976, vol. VII

Weatherhead, Rev. Robert Johnston, 1839–1912, vol. I

Weatherill, Charles, 1874–1944, vol. IV

Weatherill, Rev. Canon David, 1866–1933, vol. III

Weatherill, Henry, 1868–1943, vol. IV

Weatherly, Frederic Edward, 1848–1929, vol. III

Weatherstone, Sir Duncan Mackay, 1898–1972, vol. VII

Weaver, Mrs Baillie, (Gertrude Weaver), died 1926, vol. II

Weaver, Gertrude; see Weaver, Mrs Baillie.

Weaver, Herbert Parsons, 1872–1945, vol. IV

Weaver, John Reginald Homer, 1882–1965, vol. VI

Weaver, Sir Lawrence, 1876–1930, vol. III

Weaver, Percy William, 1882–1943, vol. IV

Weaver, Warren, 1894–1978, vol. VII

Web-Gilbert, Charles, 1869–1925, vol. II

Webb, Rt Rev. Allan Becher, 1839–1907, vol. I

Webb, Sir (Ambrose) Henry, 1882–1964, vol. VI

Webb, Lt-Col Andrew Henry, 1873–1949, vol. IV

Webb, Sir Arthur Lewis, 1860–1921, vol. II

Webb, Col Sir (Arthur) Lisle Ambrose, 1871–1945, vol. IV

Webb, Sir Aston, 1849–1930, vol. III

Webb, Augustus D., 1880–1953, vol. V

Webb, Beatrice; see Webb, Mrs Sidney.

Webb, C. Locock, 1822–1898, vol. I

Webb, Cecil Richard, 1887–1974, vol. VII

Webb, Sir Charles Morgan, 1872–1963, vol. VI

Webb, Clement Charles Julian, 1865–1954, vol. V

Webb, Clifford, 1895–1972, vol. VII

Webb, Hon. Sir Clifton; see Webb, Hon. Sir T. C.

Webb, Douglas Edward, 1909–1988, vol. VIII

Webb, Francis Gilbert, 1853–1941, vol. IV

Webb, Frederick William, 1837–1919, vol. II

Webb, Geoffrey Fairbank, 1898–1970, vol. VI

Webb, Lt-Col George Ambrose Congreve, 1869–1942, vol. IV

Webb, Brig. George Clifford, 1905–1945, vol. IV

Webb, Lt-Col Sir Henry, 1st Bt, 1866–1940, vol. III

Webb, Sir Henry; see Webb, Sir A. H.

Webb, Mrs Henry Bertram Law; see Webb, Mary.

Webb, James, 1918–1982, vol. VIII

Webb, Col James B., see Baldwin-Webb.

Webb, John, 1885–1954, vol. V

Webb, John Curtis, 1868–1949, vol. IV

Webb, John Victor Duncombe, 1930–1983, vol. VIII

Webb, Katharine, (Katharine Adams), 1862–1952, vol. V

Webb, Col Sir Lisle; see Webb, Col Sir A. L. A.

Webb, Marion St John, died 1930, vol. III

Webb, Mary, 1881–1927, vol. III

Webb, Maurice, 1880–1946, vol. IV

Webb, Rt Hon. Maurice, 1904–1956, vol. V

Webb, Maurice Everett, 1880–1939, vol. III

Webb, Millicent Vere, 1878–1969, vol. VI

Webb, Sir Montagu de Pomeroy, 1869–1938, vol. III

Webb, Montague, 1847–1930, vol. III

Webb, Percy Henry, 1856–1937, vol. III

Webb, Philip George Lancelot, 1856–1937, vol. III

Webb, Adm. Sir Richard, 1870–1950, vol. IV

Webb, Robert Alexander, 1891–1978, vol. VII

Webb, Mrs Sidney, (Beatrice Webb), 1858–1943, vol. IV

Webb, Stella Dorothea, (Mrs A. B. Webb); see Gibbons, S. D.

Webb, Sir Sydney, 1816–1898, vol. I

Webb, Hon. Sir (Thomas) Clifton, 1889–1962, vol. VI

Webb, Thomas Ebenezer, 1827–1903, vol. I

Webb, Lt-Col Walter Edward, died 1934, vol. III

Webb, Col Walter George, 1838–1919, vol. II

Webb, Walter Prescott, 1888–1963, vol. VI

Webb, Lt-Col Wilfred Francis, 1897–1973, vol. VII

Webb, Wilfred Mark, 1868–1952, vol. V

Webb, William Flood, 1887–1972, vol. VII

Webb, William Harcourt, 1875–1968, vol. VI

Webb, William Seward, 1851–1926, vol. II

Webb, Rt Rev. William Walter, 1857–1934, vol. III

Webb-Bowen, Col Hildred Edward, 1882–1958, vol. V

Webb-Bowen, Air Vice-Marshal Sir Tom Ince, 1879–1956, vol. V

Webb-Johnson, 1st Baron, 1880–1958, vol. V

Webb-Johnson, Cecil, *died* 1930, vol. III
Webb-Johnson, Stanley, 1888–1965, vol. VI
Webb-Jones, James William, 1904–1965, vol. VI
Webb-Peploe, Rev. Hanmer William, 1837–1923, vol. II
Webb-Ware, Lt-Col Frank Cooke, 1866–1934, vol. III
Webbe, Alexander Josiah, 1855–1941, vol. IV
Webbe, Sir Harold, 1885–1965, vol. VI
Webber, Brig.-Gen. Adrian Beare I.; *see* Incledon-Webber.
Webber, Sir Arthur Frederick Clarence, 1873–1952, vol. V
Webber, Maj.-Gen. Charles Edmund, 1838–1904, vol. I
Webber, Lt-Col Godfrey Sturdy I.; *see* Incledon-Webber.
Webber, Harold Norris, 1881–1954, vol. V
Webber, Lt-Col Horace Armine William, 1880–1940, vol. III
Webber, Brig.-Gen. Norman William, 1881–1950, vol. IV
Webber, Robert Bryan, 1860–1934, vol. III
Webber, Sir Robert John, 1884–1962, vol. VI
Webber, William Downes, 1834–1924, vol. II
Webber, Sir William James Percival, 1901–1982, vol. VIII
Webber, William Southcombe L.; *see* Lloyd Webber.
Webber, Rt Rev. William Thomas Thornhill, 1837–1903, vol. I
Weber, F. Parkes, 1863–1962, vol. VI
Weber, Sir Herman, 1823–1918, vol. II
Weber, Col William Hermann Frank, 1875–1936, vol. III
Weber-Brown, Lt-Col Arthur Miles, 1898–1965, vol. VI
Webley-Parry-Pryse, Sir Edward John; *see* Pryse.
Webster, Adam Blyth, 1882–1956, vol. V
Webster, Amy Marjorie, 1901–1967, vol. VI
Webster, Col Arthur George, 1837–1916, vol. II
Webster, Hon. Arthur Harold, 1874–1902, vol. I
Webster, Sir Augustus Frederick Walpole Edward, 8th Bt, 1864–1923, vol. II
Webster, Benjamin, 1864–1947, vol. IV
Webster, Brian Mackenzie, 1938–1985, vol. VIII
Webster, Sir Charles Kingsley, 1886–1961, vol. VI
Webster, Sir David Lumsden, 1903–1971, vol. VII
Webster, David William Ernest, 1923–1969, vol. VI
Webster, Rev. Canon Douglas, 1920–1986, vol. VIII
Webster, Edmund Forster, *died* 1913, vol. I
Webster, Sir Francis, 1850–1924, vol. II
Webster, Rev. Francis Scott, *died* 1920, vol. II
Webster, George Frederick, 1889–1959, vol. V
Webster, George Henry, 1887–1955, vol. V
Webster, Rev. George Russell B.; *see* Bullock-Webster.
Webster, Rt Rev. Hedley, 1880–1954, vol. V
Webster, Herbert Cayley, *died* 1917, vol. II
Webster, Herman Armour, 1878–1970, vol. VII (AI)
Webster, Sir Hugh Calthrop, 1869–1941, vol. IV
Webster, Hugh Colin, 1905–1979, vol. VII (AII)
Webster, James Alexander, 1877–1964, vol. VI
Webster, James Mathewson, *died* 1973, vol. VII
Webster, John, 1891–1947, vol. IV

Webster, Captain John Alexander, 1874–1924, vol. II
Webster, John Clarence, 1863–1950, vol. IV
Webster, John Edward, 1870–1943, vol. IV
Webster, John Henry Douglas, 1882–1975, vol. VII
Webster, Sir Lonsdale; *see* Webster, Sir T. L.
Webster, Lorne C., 1871–1941, vol. IV
Webster, Margaret, 1905–1972, vol. VII
Webster, Dame May, 1865–1948, vol. IV
Webster, Very Rev. Reginald Godfrey Michael, 1860–1913, vol. I
Webster, Sir Richard James, 1913–1986, vol. VIII
Webster, Robert Grant, *died* 1925, vol. II
Webster, Sir Robert Joseph, 1891–1981, vol. VIII
Webster, Thomas Bertram Lonsdale, 1905–1974, vol. VII
Webster, Lt-Gen. Thomas Edward, 1830–1909, vol. I
Webster, Sir (Thomas) Lonsdale, 1868–1930, vol. III
Webster, Gen. Sir Thomas Sheridan R.; *see* Riddell-Webster.
Webster, Tom, 1890–1962, vol. VI
Webster, Walter Ernest, 1878–1959, vol. V
Webster, Col William, 1865–1934, vol. III
Webster, William, 1866–1953, vol. V
Webster, Major William Henry Albert, 1884–1968, vol. VI
Weck, Richard, 1913–1986, vol. VIII
Wedd, Major Aubrey Pattison Wallman, 1885–1945, vol. IV
Wedd, Nathaniel, *died* 1940, vol. III
Wedd, Brig. William Basil, 1890–1966, vol. VI
Weddell, (Alexander) Graham (McDonnell), 1908–1990, vol. VIII
Weddell, Graham; *see* Weddell, A. G. M.
Weddell, Col John Murray, 1884–1966, vol. VI
Wedderburn, Alexander, 1854–1931, vol. III
Wedderburn, Alexander Henry Melvill, 1892–1968, vol. VI
Wedderburn, Sir Ernest Maclagan, 1884–1958, vol. V
Wedderburn, Henry Scrymgeour, 1840–1914, vol. I
Wedderburn, Lt-Col Henry Scrymgeour, 1872–1924, vol. II
Wedderburn, Sir John Andrew O.; *see* Ogilvy-Wedderburn.
Wedderburn, Comdr Sir (John) Peter O.; *see* Ogilvy-Wedderburn.
Wedderburn, Joseph Henry Maclagan, 1882–1948, vol. IV
Wedderburn, Sir Maxwell MacLagan, 1883–1953, vol. V
Wedderburn, Sir William, 10th and 4th Bt, 1838–1918, vol. II
Wedderburn-Maxwell, Major James Andrew Colvile, 1849–1917, vol. II
Wedderspoon, Sir Thomas Adam, 1904–1987, vol. VIII
Wedgwood, 1st Baron, 1872–1943, vol. IV
Wedgwood, 2nd Baron, 1898–1959, vol. V
Wedgwood, 3rd Baron, 1921–1970, vol. VI
Wedgwood, Hon. Camilla Hildegarde, 1901–1955, vol. V
Wedgwood, Major Cecil, *died* 1916, vol. II
Wedgwood, Francis Hamilton, *died* 1930, vol. III
Wedgwood, Geoffrey Heath, 1900–1977, vol. VII (AII)

Wedgwood, Dame Ivy Evelyn, *died* 1975, vol. VII

Wedgwood, Sir John Hamilton, 2nd Bt, 1907–1989, vol. VIII

Wedgwood, Hon. Josiah, 1899–1968, vol. VI

Wedgwood, Julia, 1833–1913, vol. I

Wedgwood, Sir Ralph Lewis, 1st Bt, 1874–1956, vol. V

Wedlake, John, 1892–1958, vol. V

Wedmore, Edmund Basil, 1876–1956, vol. V

Wedmore, Sir Frederick, 1844–1921, vol. II

Weech, William Nassau, 1878–1961, vol. VI

Weedon, Augustus Walford, *died* 1908, vol. I

Weedon, Air Marshal Sir Colin Winterbotham, 1901–1975, vol. VII

Weedon, Hon. Sir Henry, 1859–1921, vol. II

Weekes, Ven. Christian William Hampton, 1880–1948, vol. IV

Weekes, Rev. George Arthur, 1869–1953, vol. V

Weekes, Col Henry Wilson, 1870–1943, vol. IV

Weekes, Paymaster Rear-Adm. Victor Herbert Thomas, 1873–1937, vol. III

Weekes, Rev. William Haye, 1867–1945, vol. IV

Weekley, Charles Montague, 1900–1982, vol. VIII

Weekley, Ernest, *died* 1954, vol. V

Weeks, 1st Baron, 1890–1960, vol. V

Weeks, Edward Augustus, 1898–1989, vol. VIII

Weeks, Engr Rear-Adm. Edward John, 1868–1954, vol. V

Weeks, Maj.-Gen. Ernest Geoffrey, 1896–1987, vol. VIII

Wegg-Prosser, Francis Richard, 1824–1911, vol. I

Weguelin, Mrs Arthur, *died* 1931, vol. III

Weguelin, John Reinhard, 1849–1927, vol. II

Wei Yuk, Sir Boshan, 1849–1921, vol. II

Weidlein, Edward Ray, 1887–1983, vol. VIII

Weigall, Albert Bythesea, 1840–1912, vol. I

Weigall, Lt-Col Sir Archibald; *see* Weigall, Lt-Col Sir W. E. G. A.

Weigall, Arthur Edward Pearse Brome, 1880–1934, vol. III

Weigall, Cecil Edward, 1870–1955, vol. V

Weigall, Henry, 1829–1925, vol. II

Weigall, Julian William Wellesley, 1868–1945, vol. IV

Weigall, Lady Rose Sophia Mary, 1834–1921, vol. II

Weigall, Theyre à Beckett, 1860–1926, vol. II

Weigall, Lt-Col Sir (William Ernest George) Archibald, 1st Bt, 1874–1952, vol. V

Weight, Rev. Thomas Joseph, 1845–1922, vol. II

Weightman, Sir Hugh, 1898–1949, vol. IV

Weightman, William Henry, 1887–1970, vol. VI

Weighton, Robert Lunan, 1851–1937, vol. III

Weill, David D.; *see* David-Weill.

Weinberger, Jaromir, 1896–1967, vol. VI

Weiner, Joseph Sidney, 1915–1982, vol. VIII

Weingartner, Felix, 1863–1942, vol. IV

Weinthal, Leo, 1865–1930, vol. III

Weipers, Sir William Lee, 1904–1990, vol. VIII

Weir, 1st Viscount, 1877–1959, vol. V

Weir, 2nd Viscount, 1905–1975, vol. VII

Weir, Archibald A. E., 1859–1935, vol. III

Weir, Sir Cecil McAlpine, 1890–1960, vol. V

Weir, Air Vice-Marshal Cecil Thomas, 1913–1965, vol. VI

Weir, Lt-Col Donald Lord, 1885–1921, vol. II

Weir, Gen. Sir George Alexander, 1876–1951, vol. V

Weir, George Moir, 1885–1949, vol. IV

Weir, Harrison William, 1824–1906, vol. I

Weir, Helen Stuart, *died* 1969, vol. VI

Weir, James Galloway, 1839–1911, vol. I

Weir, James George, 1887–1973, vol. VII

Weir, Lt-Col James Leslie Rose, 1883–1950, vol. IV

Weir, Sir John, 1879–1971, vol. VII

Weir, Sir John Charles, 1872–1936, vol. III

Weir, (Lauchlan) MacNeill, 1877–1939, vol. III

Weir, MacNeill; *see* Weir, L. MacN.

Weir, Neil Archibald Campbell, 1895–1967, vol. VI

Weir, Maj.-Gen. Sir Norman William McDonald, 1893–1961, vol. VI

Weir, Rt Rev. Mgr Peter John, 1831–1917, vol. II

Weir, Ralph Somerville, 1884–1962, vol. VI

Weir, Major Hon. Robert, 1882–1939, vol. III

Weir, Robert Fulton, 1838–1927, vol. II

Weir, Robert Hendry, 1912–1985, vol. VIII

Weir, Robert Stanley, 1856–1926, vol. II

Weir, Brig.-Gen. Stanley Price, 1866–1944, vol. IV

Weir, Maj.-Gen. Sir Stephen Cyril Ettrick, 1905–1969, vol. VI

Weir, Hon. William Alexander, 1858–1929, vol. III

Weir, Rev. Canon William Mortimer, 1868–1936, vol. III

Weirter, Louis, 1873–1932, vol. III

Weis-Fogh, Torkel, 1922–1975, vol. VII

Weisberg, Hyman, 1890–1976, vol. VII

Weismann, August, 1834–1914, vol. I

Weiss, Sir Eric, 1908–1990, vol. VIII

Weiss, Frederick Ernest, 1865–1953, vol. V

Weiss, Joseph J., 1907–1972, vol. VII

Weiss, Peter Ulrich, 1916–1982, vol. VIII

Weiss, Roberto, 1906–1969, vol. VI

Weisz, Victor, 1913–1966, vol. VI

Weitnauer, Albert, 1916–1984, vol. VIII

Weitzman, David, 1898–1987, vol. VIII

Weizmann, Chaim, 1874–1952, vol. V

Welbourne, Edward, 1894–1966, vol. VI

Welby, 1st Baron, 1832–1915, vol. I

Welby, Sir Alfred Cholmeley Earle, 1849–1937, vol. III

Welby, Charles Cornwallis Anderson P.; *see* Pelham Welby.

Welby, Sir Charles Glynne Earle, 5th Bt, 1865–1938, vol. III

Welby, Edward Montague Earle, 1836–1926, vol. II

Welby, Euphemia Violet, 1891–1987, vol. VIII

Welby, Sir George Earle, 1851–1936, vol. III

Welby, Hugh Robert Everard Earle, 1885–1970, vol. VI

Welby, John Earle, 1820–1905, vol. I

Welby, Sir Oliver Charles Earle, 6th Bt, 1902–1977, vol. VII

Welby, Rt Rev. Thomas Earle, 1811–1899, vol. I

Welby, Thomas Earle, 1881–1933, vol. III

Welby-Everard, Edward Everard Earle, 1870–1951, vol. V

Welch, Rev. Adam Cleghorn, 1864–1943, vol. IV

Welch, Charles, 1848–1924, vol. II

Welch, Col Sir Cullum; *see* Welch, Col Sir G. J. C.

Welch, Sir David Nairne, 1820–1912, vol. I

Welch, Rev. Edward Ashurst, 1860–1932, vol. III

Welch, Surg.-Rear-Adm. Sir George, 1858–1947, vol. IV

Welch, Col Sir (George James) Cullum, 1st Bt, 1895–1980, vol. VII

Welch, Col George Osbaldeston, 1861–1935, vol. III

Welch, Sir Gordon; *see* Welch, Sir H. G. G.

Welch, Sir (Henry George) Gordon, 1890–1960, vol. V

Welch, Henry John, 1872–1958, vol. V

Welch, James, 1865–1917, vol. II

Welch, James William, 1900–1967, vol. VI

Welch, John Joseph, 1871–1950, vol. IV

Welch, Lucy Elizabeth K.; *see* Kemp-Welch.

Welch, Brig.-Gen. Malcolm Hammond Edward, 1872–1946, vol. IV

Welch, Margaret K.; *see* Kemp-Welch.

Welch, Brig.-Gen. Martin K.; *see* Kemp-Welch.

Welch, William Henry, 1850–1934, vol. III

Welch, William Tom, 1910–1979, vol. VII

Welchman, Col Edmund Walter St George, 1857–1933, vol. III

Welchman, Edward Theodore, 1881–1914, vol. I

Welchman, Ven. William, 1866–1954, vol. V

Weld, Brig. Charles Joseph, 1893–1962, vol. VI

Weld, Francis Joseph, 1873–1958, vol. V

Weld, Rt Rev. George, 1883–1959, vol. V

Weld, Harry Porter, 1877–1970, vol. VI(AII)

Weld, Herbert, *died* 1935, vol. III

Weld, Reginald Joseph, 1842–1923, vol. II

Weld, Rev. Walter Joseph, 1881–1969, vol. VI

Weld-Blundell, Charles Joseph, 1845–1927, vol. II

Weld-Forester, Hon. Charles Cecil Orlando; *see* Forester.

Weld-Forester, Major Hon. Edric Alfred Cecil; *see* Forester.

Weld-Forester, Lt-Comdr Wolstan Beaumont Charles, 1899–1961, vol. VI

Weldon, Col Sir Anthony Arthur, 6th Bt, 1863–1917, vol. II

Weldon, Sir Anthony Crosdill, 5th Bt, 1827–1900, vol. I

Weldon, Sir Anthony Edward Wolseley, 7th Bt, 1902–1971, vol. VII

Weldon, Lt-Col Ernest Steuart, 1877–1946, vol. IV

Weldon, Major Francis Harry, 1869–1920, vol. II

Weldon, George, 1908–1963, vol. VI

Weldon, Surg.-Rear-Adm. Gerald; *see* Weldon, Surg.-Rear-Adm. S. G.

Weldon, Brig. Hamilton Edward Crosdill, 1910–1985, vol. VIII

Weldon, Surg.-Rear-Adm. (Samuel) Gerald, 1900–1958, vol. V

Weldon, Col Thomas, 1834–1905, vol. I

Weldon, Sir Thomas Brian, 8th Bt, 1905–1979, vol. VII

Weldon, Thomas Dewar, 1896–1958, vol. V

Weldon, Walter Frank Raphael, 1860–1906, vol. I

Weldon, Sir William Henry, 1837–1919, vol. II

Welford, Richard, 1836–1919, vol. II

Welford, Walter Thompson, 1916–1990, vol. VIII

Welham, David Richard, 1930–1989, vol. VIII

Welland, Rt Rev. Thomas James, 1830–1907, vol. I

Wellborne, Lt-Col Cyril de Montfort, 1884–1965, vol. VI

Wellcome, Sir Henry, 1853–1936, vol. III

Welldon, Rt Rev. James Edward Cowell, 1854–1937, vol. III

Weller, Major Bernard George, 1881–1941, vol. IV

Weller, Bernard Williams, 1870–1943, vol. IV

Weller, Rt Rev. John Reginald, 1880–1969, vol. VI

Weller, Rt Rev. Reginald Heber, 1857–1935, vol. III

Weller-Poley, Thomas, 1850–1924, vol. II

Welles, (George) Orson, 1915–1985, vol. VIII

Welles, Orson; *see* Welles, G. O.

Welles, Sumner, 1892–1961, vol. VI

Wellesley, Col Hon. Frederick Arthur, 1844–1931, vol. III

Wellesley, Lord George, 1889–1967, vol. VI

Wellesley, Sir George Greville, 1814–1901, vol. I

Wellesley, Lord Richard, 1879–1914, vol. I

Wellesley, Brig.-Gen. Richard Ashmore Colley, 1868–1939, vol. III

Wellesley, Sir Victor Alexander Augustus Henry, 1876–1954, vol. V

Wellesz, Egon Joseph, 1885–1974, vol. VII

Wellings, Milton, 1850–1929, vol. III

Wellington, 3rd Duke of, 1846–1900, vol. I

Wellington, 4th Duke of, 1849–1934, vol. III

Wellington, 5th Duke of, 1876–1941, vol. IV

Wellington, 6th Duke of, 1912–1943, vol. IV

Wellington, 7th Duke of, 1885–1972, vol. VII

Wellington, Arthur Robartes, 1877–1961, vol. VI

Wellington, Gilbert Trevor, 1882–1963, vol. VI

Wellington, Hubert Lindsay, 1879–1967, vol. VI

Wellington, Rt Rev. John, 1889–1976, vol. VII

Wellington, Sir Lindsay; *see* Wellington, Sir R. E. L.

Wellington, Sir (Reginald Everard) Lindsay, 1901–1985, vol. VIII

Wellish, Edward Montague, 1882–1948, vol. IV

Wellock, Wilfred, 1879–1972, vol. VII

Wells, Arthur Collings, 1857–1922, vol. II

Wells, Arthur Quinton, 1896–1956, vol. V

Wells, Sir Arthur Spencer, 2nd Bt (*cr* 1883), 1866–1906, vol. I

Wells, Carveth; *see* Wells, G. C.

Wells, Charles, *died* 1917, vol. II

Wells, Charles, 1859–1932, vol. III

Wells, Charles Alexander, 1898–1989, vol. VIII

Wells, Cyril Mowbray, 1871–1963, vol. VI

Wells, Rear-Adm. David Charles, 1911–1983, vol. VIII

Wells, Denys George, 1881–1973, vol. VII

Wells, Eugene, *died* 1925, vol. II

Wells, Frederick Arthur, 1901–1971, vol. VII

Wells, Sir Frederick Michael, 1st Bt (*cr* 1948), 1884–1966, vol. VI

Wells, Rt Rev. George Anderson, 1877–1964, vol. VI

Wells, George Philip, 1901–1985, vol. VIII

Wells, Vice-Adm. Sir Gerard Aylmer, *died* 1943, vol. IV

Wells, (Grant) Carveth, *died* 1957, vol. V

Wells, Air Cdre Hardy Vesey, 1877–1956, vol. V

Wells, Lt-Gen. Sir Henry, 1898–1973, vol. VII

Wells, Henry Bensley, 1891–1967, vol. VI

Wells, Henry Tanworth, 1828–1903, vol. I

Wells, Sir Henry Weston, 1911–1971, vol. VII

Wells, Herbert George, 1866–1946, vol. IV

Wells, Rev. Herbert Methuen, 1862–1931, vol. III

Wells, Rev. James, 1838–1924, vol. II
Wells, Sister Janet; *see* King J.
Wells, Brig.-Gen. John Bayford, 1881–1952, vol. V
Wells, John Sanderson S.; *see* Sanderson-Wells.
Wells, Captain John Stanhope Collings, 1880–1918, vol. II
Wells, Major John Stuart Kerr, 1873–1937, vol. III(A), vol. IV
Wells, Joseph, 1855–1929, vol. III
Wells, Rt Rev. Lemuel H., 1841–1936, vol. III
Wells, Captain Sir Lionel de Lautour, 1859–1929, vol. III
Wells, Adm. Sir Lionel Victor, 1884–1965, vol. VI
Wells, Madeline, *died* 1959, vol. V
Wells, Percy Lawrence, 1891–1964, vol. VI
Wells, Reginald F., 1877–1951, vol. V
Wells, Sir Richard; *see* Wells, Sir S. R.
Wells, Robert Douglas, 1875–1963, vol. VI
Wells, Sidney Herbert, 1865–1923, vol. II
Wells, Stanley Walter, 1887–1975, vol. VII
Wells, Sir Sydney R.; *see* Russell-Wells.
Wells, Sir (Sydney) Richard, 1st Bt (*cr* 1944), 1879–1956, vol. V
Wells, Thomas Bucklin, 1875–1944, vol. IV
Wells, Thomas Grantham, 1901–1943, vol. IV
Wells, Thomas Henry S.; *see* Sanderson-Wells.
Wells, Sir William Henry, 1871–1933, vol. III
Wells, William Page Atkinson, 1872–1923, vol. II
Wells, William Thomas, 1908–1990, vol. VII
Wells-Cole, Lt-Col Henry, 1864–1914, vol. I
Wells-Durrant, Frederick Chester, 1864–1934, vol. III
Wellstood, Frederick Christian, 1884–1942, vol. IV
Wellwood, William, 1893–1971, vol. VII
Welman, Captain Arthur Eric Pole, 1893–1966, vol. VI
Welman, Maj.-Gen. William Henry Dowling Reeves, 1828–1906, vol. I
Welpton, William P., 1872–1939, vol. III
Welsford, Sir Robert Mills, 1861–1933, vol. III
Welsh, Hon. Sir Allan Ross, 1875–1957, vol. V
Welsh, Brig. David, 1908–1987, vol. VIII
Welsh, David Arthur, *died* 1948, vol. IV
Welsh, Elizabeth, *died* 1921, vol. II
Welsh, Harry Lambert, 1910–1984, vol. VIII
Welsh, James, 1881–1969, vol. VI
Welsh, James C., 1880–1954, vol. V
Welsh, John, 1887–1950, vol. IV
Welsh, John Aitken, 1871–1940, vol. III
Welsh, Rt Rev. John Francis, *died* 1916, vol. II
Welsh, Dame Mary; *see* Welsh, Dame R. M. E.
Welsh, Rev. Robert E., 1857–1935, vol. III
Welsh, Dame (Ruth) Mary (Eldridge), 1896–1986, vol. VIII
Welsh, Rev. Thomas, *died* 1920, vol. II, vol. III
Welsh, Air Marshal Sir William Lawrie, *died* 1962, vol. VI
Welsh, Brig. William Miles Moss O'Donnell, 1888–1965, vol. VI
Welsted, Col Reginald Hugh P.; *see* Penrose-Welsted.
Welton, James, 1854–1942, vol. IV
Welwood, John Allan Maconochie, *died* 1934, vol. III
Wemyss, 10th Earl of, **and March,** 6th Earl of, 1818–1914, vol. I

Wemyss, 11th Earl of, **and March,** 7th Earl of, 1857–1937, vol. III
Wemyss, Gen. Sir Colville; *see* Wemyss, Gen. Sir H. C. B.
Wemyss, Sir Francis C.; *see* Colchester-Wemyss.
Wemyss, Gen. Sir (Henry) Colville (Barclay), 1891–1959, vol. V
Wemyss, Maj.-Gen. Henry Manley, 1831–1915, vol. I
Wemyss, Maynard Willoughby C.; *see* Colchester Wemyss.
Wemyss, Randolph Gordon Erskine, *died* 1908, vol. I
Wenban-Smith, Charlotte Susanna; *see* Rycroft, C. S.
Wendell, Barrett, 1855–1921, vol. II
Wenden, Henry Charles Edward, *died* 1919, vol. II
Wendover, Viscount; Albert Edward Samuel Charles Robert Wynn-Carrington, 1895–1915, vol. I
Wendt, Henry Lorenz, 1858–1911, vol. I
Wenger, Adolph Henry Charles, 1877–1954, vol. V
Wenger, Marjorie Lawson, 1910–1981, vol. VIII
Wenham, Edward Gordon, 1884–1956, vol. V
Wenham, Sir John Henry, 1891–1970, vol. VI
Wenley, Robert Mark, 1861–1929, vol. III
Wenlock, 3rd Baron, 1849–1912, vol. I
Wenlock, 4th Baron, 1856–1918, vol. II
Wenlock, 5th Baron, 1857–1931, vol. III
Wenlock, 6th Baron, 1860–1932, vol. III
Wenlock, Lady; (Annie Allen), *died* 1944, vol. IV
Wensinck, Arent Jan, 1882–1939, vol. III(A), vol. IV
Went, Rev. James, 1845–1936, vol. III
Wentworth, Baroness (14th in line), 1871–1917, vol. II
Wentworth, Baroness (15th in line), 1837–1917, vol. II
Wentworth, Baroness (16th in line), 1873–1957, vol. V
Wentworth, Captain Bruce Canning V.; *see* Vernon-Wentworth.
Wentworth, Captain Frederick Charles Ulick V.; *see* Vernon-Wentworth.
Wentworth, Patricia; *see* Turnbull, Mrs George.
Wentworth-Fitzwilliam, George Charles; *see* Fitzwilliam.
Wentworth-Fitzwilliam, Captain Hon. Sir (William) Charles; *see* Fitzwilliam.
Wentworth-Fitzwilliam, Hon. William Henry; *see* Fitzwilliam.
Wentworth-Sheilds, Francis Ernest, 1869–1959, vol. V
Wentworth-Sheilds, Rt Rev. Wentworth Francis, 1867–1944, vol. IV
Wentworth-Stanley, Charles Sidney Bowen, 1892–1960, vol. V
Wenyon, Charles Morley, *died* 1948, vol. IV
Wenyon, Herbert John, 1888–1944, vol. IV
Were, Cecil Allan Walter, 1889–1977, vol. VII
Were, Rt Rev. Edward Ash, 1846–1915, vol. I
Were, Major Harry Harris, 1865–1925, vol. II
Werfel, Franz, 1890–1945, vol. IV
Werner, Alfred, 1866–1919, vol. II
Werner, Alice, 1859–1935, vol. III
Werner, E. A., *died* 1951, vol. V
Werner, Edward Theodore Chalmers, 1864–1954, vol. V
Werner, Louis, *died* 1936, vol. III
Wernham, Archibald Garden, 1916–1989, vol. VIII

Wernher, Sir Derrick Julius, 2nd Bt, 1889–1948, vol. IV

Wernher, Hon. Maj.-Gen. Sir Harold Augustus, 3rd Bt, 1893–1973, vol. VII

Wernher, Sir Julius Charles, 1st Bt, 1850–1912, vol. I

Wertenbaker, Thomas Jefferson, 1879–1966, vol. VI

Werth, Albertus Johannes, 1888–1948, vol. IV

Werth, Alexander, 1901–1969, vol. VI

Wertheimer, Julius, *died* 1924, vol. II

Wesbrook, F. F., 1868–1918, vol. II

Wesselitsky, Gabriel de, 1841–1930, vol. III

Wessels, Hon. Sir Cornelius Hermanus, 1851–1924, vol. II

Wessels, Rt Hon. Sir Johannes Wilhelmus, 1862–1936, vol. III

West, Brig. Alexander Henry Delap, 1877–1959, vol. V

West, Alfred Slater, 1846–1932, vol. III

West, Rt Hon. Sir Algernon, 1832–1921, vol. II

West, Andrew F., 1853–1943, vol. IV

West, Anthony Panther, 1914–1987, vol. VIII

West, Rev. Arthur George Bainbridge, 1864–1952, vol. V

West, Cecil McLaren, 1893–1951, vol. V

West, Charles Ernest, *died* 1951, vol. V

West, Charles Henry, 1859–1923, vol. II

West, Christopher, 1915–1967, vol. VI

West, Maj.-Gen. Clement Arthur, 1892–1972, vol. VII

West, Daniel Granville; *see* Baron Granville-West.

West, David, *died* 1936, vol. III

West, Rev. Edward Courtenay, 1872–1938, vol. III

West, Air Cdre Ferdinand Maurice Felix, 1896–1988, vol. VIII

West, Fielding Reginald, 1892–1935, vol. III

West, Sir Frederick John, 1897–1971, vol. VII

West, Sir Frederick Joseph, 1872–1959, vol. V

West, Rt Rev. George Algernon, 1893–1980, vol. VII

West, Major George F. M. C.; *see* Cornwallis-West.

West, George Stephen, 1876–1919, vol. II

West, Gladys; *see* Young, G.

West, Sir Glynn Hamilton, 1877–1945, vol. IV

West, Sir Harold Ernest Georges, 1895–1968, vol. VI

West, Sir James Grey, 1885–1951, vol. V

West, John Henry Rickard, 1846–1920, vol. II

West, Col John Milns, 1897–1973, vol. VII

West, Maj.-Gen. John Weir, 1875–1949, vol. IV

West, Joseph Walter, *died* 1933, vol. III

West, Sir Leonard Henry, 1864–1950, vol. IV

West, Leonard R., 1859–1910, vol. I

West, Mary, (Mrs James West); *see* McCarthy, M.

West, Gen. Sir Michael Montgomerie Alston Roberts, 1905–1978, vol. VII

West, Ralph Winton, 1895–1968, vol. VI

West, Sir Raymond, 1832–1911, vol. I

West, Dame Rebecca, 1892–1983, vol. VIII

West, Samuel, 1848–1920, vol. II

West, Stewart Ellis Lawrence, 1890–1968, vol. VI

West, Hon. V. S.; *see* Sackville-West.

West, Sir Walter Wooll, 1861–1952, vol. V

West, William Cornwallis Cornwallis-, 1835–1917, vol. II

West, William Frederick, 1882–1954, vol. V

West-Watson, Most Rev. Campbell West, 1877–1953, vol. V

Westall, Bernard Clement, 1893–1970, vol. VI

Westall, Gen. Sir John Chaddesley, 1901–1986, vol. VIII

Westall, Rt Rev. Wilfrid Arthur Edmund, 1900–1982, vol. VIII

Westall, William Bury, 1834–1903, vol. I

Westaway, Katharine Mary, 1893–1973, vol. VII

Westbrook, Bernard Anson, 1884–1969, vol. VI

Westbrook, Trevor Cresswell Lawrence, 1901–1978, vol. VII

Westbury, 3rd Baron, 1852–1930, vol. III

Westbury, 4th Baron, 1914–1961, vol. VI

Westbury, Lt-Col Frederic Newell, 1877–1946, vol. IV

Westbury, Marjorie; *see* Westbury, R. M.

Westbury, (Rose) Marjorie, 1905–1989, vol. VIII

Westcar, Lt-Col Sir William Villiers Leonard P.; *see* Prescott-Westcar.

Westcott, Rt Rev. Brooke Foss, 1825–1901, vol. I

Westcott, Rt Rev. Foss, 1863–1949, vol. IV

Westcott, Ven. Frederick Brooke, 1857–1918, vol. II

Westcott, George Foss, 1893–1987, vol. VIII

Westcott, Rt Rev. George Herbert, *died* 1916, vol. II

Westcott, J. B., *died* 1907, vol. I

Westcott, Col Sinclair, 1859–1923, vol. II

Westcott, William Wynn, 1848–1925, vol. II

Westell, William Percival, 1874–1943, vol. IV

Wester Wemyss, 1st Baron, 1864–1933, vol. III

Westerman, Percy F., 1876–1959, vol. V

Westermann, Diedrich H., 1875–1956, vol. V

Westermarck, Edward Alexander, 1862–1939, vol. III

Western, Lt-Col Bertram Charles Maximilian, 1886–1942, vol. IV

Western, Col Charles Maximilian, *died* 1915, vol. I

Western, Rt Rev. Frederick James, 1880–1951, vol. V

Western, George Trench, 1877–1948, vol. IV

Western, Lt-Col James Halifax, 1842–1917, vol. II

Western, John Henry, 1906–1981, vol. VIII

Western, Col John Sutton Edward, *died* 1931, vol. III

Western, Sir Thomas Charles Callis, 3rd Bt, 1850–1917, vol. II

Western, Maj.-Gen. Sir William George Balfour, 1861–1936, vol. III

Westhoven, Joseph Charles, 1876–1957, vol. V

Westinghouse, George, 1846–1914, vol. I

Westlake, Alan Robert Cecil, 1894–1978, vol. VII

Westlake, Col Almond Paul, 1858–1927, vol. II

Westlake, Sir Charles Redvers, 1900–1972, vol. VII

Westlake, Rev. Herbert Francis, 1879–1925, vol. II

Westlake, John, 1828–1913, vol. I

Westlake, Nathaniel Hubert John, 1833–1921, vol. II

Westland, Sir James, 1842–1903, vol. I

Westley, Lt-Col Joseph Harold Stops, 1882–1959, vol. V

Westmacott, Brig.-Gen. Claude Berners, 1865–1948, vol. IV

Westmacott, Frederic Hibbert, 1867–1935, vol. III

Westmacott, Percy Graham Buchanan, 1830–1917, vol. II

Westmacott, Maj.-Gen. Sir Richard, 1841–1925, vol. II

Westmacott, Rev. Walter, 1853–1939, vol. III

Westmeath, 11th Earl of, 1870–1933, vol. III
Westmeath, 12th Earl of, 1880–1971, vol. VII
Westminster, 1st Duke of, 1825–1899, vol. I
Westminster, 2nd Duke of, 1879–1953, vol. V
Westminster, 3rd Duke of, 1894–1963, vol. VI
Westminster, 4th Duke of, 1907–1967, vol. VI
Westminster, 5th Duke of, 1910–1979, vol. VII
Westminster, Viola Dowager Duchess of; Viola Maud Grosvenor, 1912–1987, vol. VIII
Westmorland, 13th Earl of, 1859–1922, vol. II
Westmorland, 14th Earl of, 1893–1948, vol. IV
Westmorland, Brig.-Gen. Charles Henry, 1856–1916, vol. II
Westmorland, Lt-Col Percy Thuillier, 1863–1929, vol. III
Westoby, Jack Cecil, 1912–1988, vol. VIII
Weston, Dame Agnes Elizabeth, 1840–1918, vol. II
Weston, Rev. Arthur Ernest, 1890–1971, vol. VII
Weston, Captain Arthur Fullam, 1879–1962, vol. VI
Weston, Sir Arthur Reginald Astley, 1892–1969, vol. VI
Weston, Lt-Gen. Sir Aylmer H.; see Hunter-Weston.
Weston, Col Claude Horace, 1879–1946, vol. IV
Weston, Sir Eric, 1892–1976, vol. VII
Weston, Lt-Gen. Eric Culpeper, 1888–1950, vol. IV
Weston, Lt-Col Ernest Arthur, 1880–1940, vol. III
Weston, Rt Rev. Frank, 1871–1924, vol. II
Weston, Garfield; see Weston, W. G.
Weston, George, 1878–1956, vol. V
Weston, Maj.-Gen. Gerald Patrick Linton, 1910–1977, vol. VII
Weston, Lt-Col Gould H.; see Hunter-Weston.
Weston, Jessie Laidlay, died 1928, vol. II
Weston, Air Vice-Marshal Sir John Gerard Willsley, 1908–1979, vol. VII
Weston, Hon. Brig. John Leslie, 1882–1963, vol. VI
Weston, Sir John Wakefield, 1st Bt, 1852–1926, vol. II
Weston, Kenneth Southwold, 1899–1971, vol. VII
Weston, Laurence, 1909–1972, vol. VII
Weston, Lt-Col Reginald Salter, 1867–1944, vol. IV
Weston, Ronald, 1929–1990, vol. VIII
Weston, Brig.-Gen. Spencer Vaughan Percy, 1883–1973, vol. VII
Weston, Rev. Walter, 1861–1940, vol. III
Weston, (Willard) Garfield, 1898–1978, vol. VII
Weston, William Guy, 1907–1980, vol. VII
Weston-Stevens, Sir Joseph, 1861–1917, vol. II
Westphal, Bishop Augustus, 1864–1939, vol. III (A), vol. IV
Westrop, Brig. Sidney Albert, 1895–1979, vol. VII
Westropp, Col George O'C.; see O'Callaghan-Westropp.
Westropp, Col George Ralph Collier, 1859–1934, vol. III
Westropp, Col John M.; see Massy-Westropp.
Westropp, Maj.-Gen. Roberts Michael, 1824–1910, vol. I
Westropp, Maj.-Gen. Victor John Eric, 1897–1974, vol. VII
Westrup, Sir Jack Allan, 1904–1975, vol. VII
Westwood, 1st Baron, 1880–1953, vol. V
Westwood, Earle Cathers, 1909–1980, vol. VII (AII)
Westwood, John David, 1881–1964, vol. VI

Westwood, Rt Hon. Joseph, 1884–1948, vol. IV
Wetherall, Lt-Gen. Sir Edward; see Wetherall, Lt-Gen. Sir H. E. de R.
Wetherall, Lt-Gen. Sir (Harry) Edward de Robillard, 1889–1979, vol. VII
Wetherall, Rev. Canon Theodore Sumner, 1910–1990, vol. VIII
Wetherall, Col William Alexander, 1847–1935, vol. III
Wetherbee, George, 1851–1920, vol. II
Wethered, Ernest Handel Cossham, 1878–1975, vol. VII
Wethered, Lt-Col Francis Owen, 1864–1922, vol. II
Wethered, Frank Joseph, 1860–1928, vol. II
Wethered, Brig. Herbert Lawrence, 1877–1953, vol. V
Wethered, Col Joseph Robert, 1873–1942, vol. IV
Wethered, Thomas Owen, 1832–1921, vol. II
Wethered, Vernon, 1865–1952, vol. V
Wetherell, Col Robert May, 1874–1960, vol. V
Wetherill, Henry Buswell, 1876–1959, vol. V
Wethey, Captain Edwin Howard, 1887–1963, vol. VI
Wetmore, Hon. Edward Ludlow, 1841–1922, vol. II
Wetton, Henry Davan, 1862–1928, vol. II
Weyer, Deryk Vander, 1925–1990, vol. VIII
Weygand, Général Maxime, 1867–1965, vol. VI
Weyler y Nicolau, Valeriano, 1838–1930, vol. III
Weyman, Stanley John, 1855–1928, vol. II
Weymouth, Viscount; John Alexander Thynne, 1895–1916, vol. II
Whaite, Col Thomas du Bédat, 1862–1943, vol. IV
Whale, George, 1849–1925, vol. II
Whale, George Harold Lawson, 1876–1943, vol. IV
Whale, Philip Barrett, 1898–1950, vol. IV
Whale, Winifred Stephens, died 1944, vol. IV
Whalley, Frank Douglas, 1877–1932, vol. III
Whalley, Philip Guy Rothay, 1901–1950, vol. IV
Whalley, Major Richard Cyril Rae, 1896–1944, vol. IV
Wharhirst, Sir Robert William, 1885–1949, vol. IV
Wharncliffe, 1st Earl of, 1827–1899, vol. I
Wharncliffe, 2nd Earl of, 1856–1926, vol. II
Wharncliffe, 3rd Earl of, 1892–1953, vol. V
Wharncliffe, 4th Earl of, 1935–1987, vol. VIII
Wharry, Harry Mortimer, 1891–1933, vol. III
Wharton, 8th Baron, 1876–1934, vol. III
Wharton, 9th Baron, 1908–1969, vol. VI
Wharton, Baroness (10th in line), 1906–1974, vol. VII
Wharton, Anthony, 1877–1943, vol. III
Wharton, Sir Anthony; see Wharton, Sir G. A.
Wharton, Rev. Edgar, died 1936, vol. III
Wharton, Edith, 1862–1937, vol. III
Wharton, Sir (George) Anthony, 1917–1980, vol. VII
Wharton, Rt Hon. John Lloyd, 1837–1912, vol. I
Wharton, William Henry Anthony, 1859–1938, vol. III
Wharton-Duff, John Wharton; see Duff.
Whately, Ven. Herbert Edward, 1876–1947, vol. IV
Whately, William, died 1937, vol. III
Whateley, Dame Leslie Violet Lucy Evelyn Mary, 1899–1987, vol. VIII
Whates, Harry Richard, died 1923, vol. II
Whatham, Rev. William Laurence T., 1866–1938, vol. III
Whatley, Norman, 1884–1965, vol. VI

Whatman, George Dunbar, 1846–1923, vol. II
Whatman, Col William Douglas, 1860–1929, vol. III
Whatmough, Joshua, 1897–1964, vol. VI
Whayman, Engr Rear-Adm. William Matthias, 1871–1955, vol. V
Wheare, Sir Kenneth Clinton, 1907–1979, vol. VII
Wheatcroft, Edward Lewis Elam, 1896–1982, vol. VIII
Wheatcroft, Rev. Frank Elam, *died* 1930, vol. III
Wheatcroft, George Shorrock Ashcombe, 1905–1987, vol. VIII
Wheatcroft, Harry, 1898–1977, vol. VII
Wheatley, Baron (Life Peer); John Wheatley, 1908–1988, vol. VIII
Wheatley, Major Cyril Moreton, 1870–1942, vol. IV
Wheatley, Dennis Yates, 1897–1977, vol. VII
Wheatley, Edith Grace, *died* 1970, vol. VI
Wheatley, Frederick William, 1871–1955, vol. V
Wheatley, Henry Benjamin, *died* 1917, vol. II
Wheatley, Col Henry Spencer, 1851–1932, vol. III
Wheatley, Rt Hon. John, 1869–1930, vol. III
Wheatley, John, 1892–1955, vol. V
Wheatley, Joseph Larke, 1846–1932, vol. III
Wheatley, Brig.-Gen. Leonard Lane, 1876–1954, vol. V
Wheatley, Major Sir Mervyn James, 1880–1974, vol. VII
Wheatley, Maj.-Gen. Mervyn Savile, 1900–1979, vol. VII
Wheatley, Col Moreton John, 1837–1916, vol. II
Wheatley, Maj.-Gen. (Percival) Ross, 1909–1988, vol. VIII
Wheatley, Brig.-Gen. Philip, 1871–1935, vol. III
Wheatley, Robert Albert, 1873–1954, vol. V
Wheatley, Maj.-Gen. Ross; *see* Wheatley, Maj.-Gen. P. R.
Wheatley, Major William Prescott Ross, 1878–1925, vol. II
Wheatley, Sir Zachariah, 1865–1950, vol. IV
Wheeldon, Edward Christian, 1907–1980, vol. VII
Wheeldon, William Edwin, 1898–1960, vol. V
Wheeler, Rev. Alfred, *died* 1949, vol. IV
Wheeler, Sir Arthur, 1st Bt, 1860–1943, vol. IV
Wheeler, Sir Arthur F. P., 2nd Bt, 1900–1964, vol. VI
Wheeler, Arthur H., *died* 1935, vol. III
Wheeler, Rear-Adm. Aubrey John, 1894–1970, vol. VI
Wheeler, Burton Kendall, 1882–1975, vol. VII
Wheeler, Sir Charles Reginald, 1904–1975, vol. VII
Wheeler, Sir Charles Thomas, 1892–1974, vol. VII
Wheeler, Denis Edward, 1910–1977, vol. VII
Wheeler, Brig. Sir (Edward) Oliver, 1890–1962, vol. VI
Wheeler, Edwin Paul, 1897–1944, vol. IV
Wheeler, Lt-Comdr Sir (Ernest) Richard, 1917–1990, vol. VIII
Wheeler, Geoffrey, 1909–1987, vol. VIII
Wheeler, Lt-Col Geoffrey Edleston, 1897–1990, vol. VIII
Wheeler, Sir Henry, 1870–1950, vol. IV
Wheeler, Major Henry Littleton, 1868–1924, vol. II
Wheeler, Rev. Hugh Trevor, 1874–1949, vol. IV
Wheeler, Gen. Joseph, 1836–1906, vol. I
Wheeler, Sir Mortimer; *see* Wheeler, Sir R. E. M.

Wheeler, Maj.-Gen. Norman; *see* Wheeler, Maj.-Gen. T. N. S.
Wheeler, Dame Olive Annie, *died* 1963, vol. VI
Wheeler, Brig. Sir Oliver; *see* Wheeler, Brig. Sir E. O.
Wheeler, Brig. Ralph Pung, 1898–1977, vol. VII
Wheeler, Lt-Comdr Sir Richard; *see* Wheeler, Lt-Comdr Sir E. R.
Wheeler, Richard Vernon, 1883–1939, vol. III
Wheeler, Sir (Robert Eric) Mortimer, 1890–1976, vol. VII
Wheeler, Rev. Thomas Littleton, 1834–1910, vol. I
Wheeler, Maj.-Gen. (Thomas) Norman (Samuel), 1915–1990, vol. VIII
Wheeler, Thomas Sherlock, 1899–1962, vol. VI
Wheeler, Thomas Whittenbury, *died* 1923, vol. II
Wheeler, William, *died* 1926, vol. II
Wheeler, Sir William Ireland de Courcy, 1879–1943, vol. IV
Wheeler-Bennett, John Wheeler, *died* 1926, vol. II
Wheeler-Bennett, Sir John Wheeler, 1902–1975, vol. VII
Wheeler-Cuffe, Sir Charles Frederick Denny; *see* Cuffe.
Wheeler-Cuffe, Sir Otway Fortescue Luke; *see* Cuffe.
Wheelock, Frank E., 1877–1941, vol. IV
Wheelwright, Charles Apthorpe, 1873–1954, vol. V
Wheelwright, Rowland, 1870–1955, vol. V
Wheen, Rear-Adm. Charles Kerr Thorneycroft, 1912–1989, vol. VIII
Whelan, Air Cdre James Roger, 1914–1985, vol. VIII
Whelan, Leo, 1892–1956, vol. V
Whelan, Robert Ford, 1922–1984, vol. VIII
Wheldon, Sir Huw Pyrs, 1916–1986, vol. VIII
Wheldon, Robert William, 1893–1954, vol. V
Wheldon, Sir Wynn Powell, 1879–1961, vol. VI
Wheler, Sir Edward, 12th Bt (*cr* 1660), 1857–1903, vol. I
Wheler, Sir Granville Charles Hastings, 1st Bt (*cr* 1925), 1872–1927, vol. II
Wheler, Sir Trevor, 11th Bt (*cr* 1660), 1828–1900, vol. I
Wheler, Captain Sir Trevor Wood, 13th Bt, 1889–1986, vol. VIII
Whelpton, Rev. Henry Urling, 1860–1935, vol. III
Wherry, George Edward, 1852–1928, vol. II
Whetham, Rear-Adm. Edye Kington B.; *see* Boddam-Whetham.
Whetham, Major Sydney A. B.; *see* Boddam-Whetham.
Whettnall, Baron Edward Charles Stephen, 1840–1903, vol. I
Whetton, John Thomas, 1894–1979, vol. VII
Whewell, Herbert, 1863–1951, vol. V
Whibley, Charles, 1859–1930, vol. III
Whibley, Leonard, 1863–1941, vol. IV
Whichcote, Sir George, 9th Bt, 1870–1946, vol. IV
Whichcote, Sir Hugh Christopher, 10th Bt, 1874–1949, vol. IV
Whidden, Howard Primrose, 1871–1952, vol. V
Whiddington, Richard, 1885–1970, vol. VI
Whigham, Gen. Sir Robert Dundas, 1865–1950, vol. IV
Whigham, Walter Kennedy, 1878–1948, vol. IV
Whillis, James, 1900–1955, vol. V

Whinney, Sir Arthur, 1865–1927, vol. II
Whinney, Margaret Dickens, 1897–1975, vol. VII
Whipham, Thomas Rowland Charles, 1871–1945, vol. IV
Whipham, Thomas Tillyer, *died* 1917, vol. II
Whipple, Dorothy, *died* 1966, vol. VI
Whipple, Francis John Welsh, 1876–1943, vol. IV
Whipple, George Hoyt, 1878–1976, vol. VII
Whipple, Rt Rev. Henry Benjamin, 1823–1901, vol. I
Whipple, Robert Stewart, 1871–1953, vol. V
Whishaw, Sir Ralph, 1895–1976, vol. VII
Whiskard, Sir Geoffrey Granville, 1886–1957, vol. V
Whistler, Rev. Charles Watts, 1856–1913, vol. I
Whistler, Group Captain Harold Alfred, 1896–1940, vol. III
Whistler, James Abbott McNeill, 1834–1903, vol. I
Whistler, Gen. Sir Lashmer Gordon, 1898–1963, vol. VI
Whitaker, Col Sir Albert Edward, 1st Bt, 1860–1945, vol. IV
Whitaker, Sir Arthur; *see* Whitaker, Sir F. A.
Whitaker, Charles Kenneth, 1919–1981, vol. VIII
Whitaker, Sir Cuthbert Wilfrid, 1873–1950, vol. IV
Whitaker, Edgar, *died* 1903, vol. I
Whitaker, (Edgar) Haddon, 1908–1982, vol. VIII
Whitaker, Enid Rosamond, (Mrs G. C. F. Whitaker); *see* Love, E. R.
Whitaker, Ernest Gillett, 1903–1975, vol. VII
Whitaker, Frank, *died* 1962, vol. VI
Whitaker, Frank Howard, 1909–1987, vol. VIII
Whitaker, Sir (Frederick) Arthur, 1893–1968, vol. VI
Whitaker, Major George Cecil, 1880–1959, vol. V
Whitaker, George Herbert, 1862–1933, vol. III
Whitaker, Haddon; *see* Whitaker, E. H.
Whitaker, James, 1863–1946, vol. IV
Whitaker, Sir James Smith, 1866–1936, vol. III
Whitaker, Maj.-Gen. Sir John Albert Charles, 2nd Bt, 1897–1957, vol. V
Whitaker, William, 1836–1925, vol. II
Whitaker, William Ingham, 1866–1936, vol. III
Whitamore, Charles Eric, 1890–1965, vol. VI
Whitbread, Francis Pelham, 1867–1941, vol. IV
Whitbread, Col Sir Howard, 1836–1908, vol. I
Whitbread, Samuel, 1830–1915, vol. I
Whitbread, Samuel Howard, 1858–1944, vol. IV
Whitbread, Major Simon, 1904–1985, vol. VIII
Whitburgh, 1st Baron, 1874–1967, vol. VI
Whitby, Anthony Charles, 1929–1975, vol. VII
Whitby, Beatrice Janie, *died* 1931, vol. III
Whitby, Sir Bernard James, 1892–1973, vol. VII
Whitby, G. Stafford, 1887–1972, vol. VII
Whitby, Harry, 1910–1984, vol. VIII
Whitby, Sir Lionel Ernest Howard, 1895–1956, vol. V
Whitby, Rev. Thomas, 1835–1918, vol. II
Whitby-Smith, Henry, 1858–1934, vol. III
Whitchurch, Major Harry Frederick, 1866–1907, vol. I
Whitcombe, Maj.-Gen. Philip Sidney, 1893–1989, vol. VIII
Whitcombe, Rt Rev. Robert Henry, 1862–1922, vol. II
White, Adam Seaton, *died* 1950, vol. IV
White, Hon. Albert Scott, 1855–1931, vol. III
White, Alexander Hay, 1898–1975, vol. VII

White, Sir (Alfred Edward) Rowden, 1876–1963, vol. VI
White, Alfred George Hastings, 1859–1945, vol. IV
White, Hon. Sir Alfred John, 1902–1987, vol. VIII
White, Amber B.; *see* Blanco White.
White, Andrew Dickson, 1832–1918, vol. II
White, Anne Margaret Wilson, 1916–1976, vol. VII
White, Antonia, 1899–1980, vol. VII
White, Sir Archibald Woollaston, 4th Bt (*cr* 1802), 1877–1945, vol. IV
White, Col Archie Cecil Thomas, 1891–1971, vol. VII
White, Arnold, 1848–1925, vol. II
White, Sir Arnold; *see* White, Sir C. A.
White, Ven. Arthur, 1880–1961, vol. VI
White, Lt-Col Arthur Denham, 1879–1950, vol. IV
White, Arthur Silva, 1859–1932, vol. III
White, Maj.-Gen. Arthur Thomas, 1860–1947, vol. IV
White, Brig. Arthur W.; *see* Walmesley White.
White, Aubrey, *died* 1915, vol. II
White, Sir Bernard Kerr, 1888–1964, vol. VI
White, Sir Bruce Gordon, 1885–1983, vol. VIII
White, Gen. Sir Brudenell; *see* White, Gen. Sir C. B. B.
White, Maj.-Gen. Cecil Meadows Frith, 1897–1985, vol. VIII
White, Sir (Charles) Arnold, 1858–1931, vol. III
White, Charles Francis, 1890–1966, vol. VI
White, Charles Frederick, 1863–1923, vol. II
White, Charles Frederick, 1891–1956, vol. V
White, Major Hon. Charles James, 1860–1930, vol. III
White, Major Charles James B.; *see* Brooman-White.
White, Charles Percival, *died* 1928, vol. II
White, Charles Powell, 1867–1930, vol. III
White, Claude G.; *see* Graham-White.
White, Clifford, 1881–1957, vol. V
White, Gen. Sir (Cyril) Brudenell (Bingham), 1876–1940, vol. III
White, Cyril Grove C.; *see* Costley-White.
White, Cyril Montgomery, 1897–1980, vol. VII
White, Lt-Col David Archibald P.; *see* Price-White.
White, Sir Dennis Charles, 1910–1983, vol. VIII
White, Dudley, 1873–1930, vol. III
White, Sir Edward, 1847–1914, vol. I
White, Edward, *died* 1952, vol. V
White, Brig.-Gen. Edward Dalrymple, 1865–1929, vol. III
White, Edwin George, 1911–1988, vol. VIII
White, (Elizabeth) Evelyne (McIntosh), *died* 1972, vol. VII
White, Elwyn Brooks, 1899–1985, vol. VIII
White, Sir Eric Henry W.; *see* Wyndham White.
White, Very Rev. Eric M.; *see* Milner-White.
White, Sir (Eric) Richard Meadows, 2nd Bt (*cr* 1937), 1910–1972, vol. VII
White, Brig. Eric Stuart, 1888–1979, vol. VII
White, Sir Ernest, 1867–1949, vol. IV
White, Sir Ernest Keith, 1892–1983, vol. VIII
White, Lt-Col Ernest William, 1851–1935, vol. III
White, Errol Ivor, 1901–1985, vol. VIII
White, Ethelbert, 1891–1972, vol. VII
White, Evelyne; *see* White, Elizabeth E. M.

White, Col Frank Augustin Kinder, 1873–1948, vol. IV
White, Frank Faulder, 1861–1939, vol. III
White, Lt-Col Frederick, 1847–1918, vol. II
White, Col Frederick, 1861–1924, vol. II
White, Major Frederick Alexander, 1872–1919, vol. II
White, Frederick Meadows, 1829–1898, vol. I
White, Major Frederick Norman, 1877–1964, vol. VI
White, Gabriel Ernest Edward Francis, 1902–1988, vol. VIII
White, Geoffrey Charles, 1912–1961, vol. VI
White, Geoffrey Henllan, 1873–1969, vol. VI
White, Maj.-Gen. Geoffrey Herbert Anthony, 1870–1959, vol. V
White, Sir George, 1840–1912, vol. I
White, Sir George, 1st Bt (cr 1904), 1854–1916, vol. II
White, Brig.-Gen. George Francis, died 1938, vol. III
White, Brig. George Frederick Charles, 1882–1953, vol. V
White, George Gilbert, 1857–1916, vol. II
White, Air Vice-Marshal George Holford, 1904–1965, vol. VI
White, George Rivers Blanco, 1883–1966, vol. VI
White, Sir (George) Stanley, 2nd Bt (cr 1904), 1882–1964, vol. VI
White, Sir George Stanley Midelton, 3rd Bt, 1913–1983, vol. VIII
White, Field-Marshal Sir George Stuart, 1835–1912, vol. I
White, Col Hon. Gerald Verner, 1879–1948, vol. IV
White, Rt Rev. Gilbert, 1859–1933, vol. III
White, Gleeson, 1851–1898, vol. I
White, Lt-Col Sir Godfrey Dalrymple D.; see Dalrymple-White.
White, Ven. Graham, born 1884, vol. IV
White, Rt Hon. Graham; see White, Rt Hon. H. G.
White, Very Rev. Harold C.; see Costley-White.
White, Lt-Col Harold Fletcher, 1883–1971, vol. VII
White, Rt Rev. Harry Vere, 1853–1941, vol. IV
White, Sir Headley Dymoke, 3rd Bt (cr 1922), 1914–1971, vol. VII
White, Henrietta Margaret, died 1936, vol. III
White, Henry, 1850–1927, vol. II
White, Henry, 1890–1964, vol. VI
White, Sir Henry Arthur, 1849–1922, vol. II
White, Henry Bantry, died 1929, vol. III
White, Surg. Rear-Adm. Sir Henry Ellis Yeo, 1888–1976, vol. VII
White, Hon. Henry Frederic, 1859–1903, vol. I
White, Maj.-Gen. Henry George, 1835–1906, vol. I
White, Rt Hon. (Henry) Graham, died 1965, vol. VI
White, Lt-Col Henry Herbert Ronald, 1879–1939, vol. III
White, Henry James, 1898–1961, vol. VI
White, Very Rev. Henry Julian, 1859–1934, vol. III
White, Sir Henry M.; see Milner-White.
White, Herbert Arthur, 1876–1958, vol. V
White, Sir Herbert Edward, 1855–1947, vol. IV
White, Herbert Martyn Oliver, 1885–1963, vol. VI
White, Maj.-Gen. Herbert Southey Neville, 1862–1938, vol. III
White, Sir Herbert Thirkell, 1855–1931, vol. III
White, Horace, 1834–1916, vol. II

White, Horace Powell W.; see Winsbury-White.
White, Hugh Fortescue Moresby, 1891–1979, vol. VII
White, Air Vice-Marshal Hugh Granville, 1898–1983, vol. VIII
White, James, 1878–1927, vol. II
White, James, 1863–1928, vol. II
White, James, 1908–1988, vol. VIII
White, James Charles Napoleon, died 1923, vol. II
White, James Cobb, 1855–1927, vol. II
White, J(ames) Dundas, 1866–1951, vol. V
White, Col James G.; see Grove-White.
White, James Martin, 1857–1928, vol. II
White, James William, 1850–1916, vol. II
White, Jessie, 1865–1958, vol. V
White, John, 1839–1912, vol. I
White, Hon. John, 1852–1922, vol. II
White, John, 1851–1933, vol. III(A), vol. IV
White, Instr Captain John, 1870–1934, vol. III
White, Rt Rev. John, 1867–1951, vol. V
White, John B.; see Bazley-White.
White, Lt-Col John Baker, 1902–1988, vol. VIII
White, John Bell, 1857–1934, vol. III
White, Maj.-Gen. John Burton, 1874–1945, vol. IV
White, John Claude, died 1918, vol. II
White, Lt-Col John Henry, 1868–1942, vol. IV
White, Maj.-Gen. John Hubbard, 1834–1910, vol. I
White, John W., died 1919, vol. II
White, John Williams, 1849–1917, vol. II
White, Joseph Henry Lachlan, 1859–1940, vol. III
White, Lt-Col Joshua Chaytor, 1864–1924, vol. II
White, Kenneth James Macarthur, 1894–1969, vol. VI
White, Leslie Gordon, 1889–1979, vol. VII
White, Sir Luke, 1845–1920, vol. II
White, Margaret B.; see Bourke-White.
White, Maude Valérie, 1855–1937, vol. III
White, Lt-Gen. Sir Maurice Fitzgibbon G.; see Grove-White.
White, Michael James Denham, 1910–1983, vol. VIII
White, Air Vice-Marshal Michael William Langtry, 1915–1984, vol. VIII
White, Montagu, died 1916, vol. II
White, Maj.-Gen. Napier; see White, Maj.-Gen. P. N.
White, Rev. Newport John Davis, 1860–1936, vol. III
White, Norman Lewis, died 1978, vol. VII
White, Lt-Col Oliver Woodhouse, 1884–1940, vol. III
White, Oswald, 1884–1970, vol. VI
White, P. Bruce, died 1949, vol. IV
White, Patrick Victor Martindale, 1912–1990, vol. VIII
White, Paul Dudley, 1886–1973, vol. VII
White, Maj.-Gen. (Percival) Napier, 1901–1982, vol. VIII
White, Percy, 1852–1938, vol. III
White, Maj.-Gen. Percy C.; see Carr-White.
White, Philip Jacob, died 1929, vol. III
White, Col Reginald Strelley Moresby, 1893–1947, vol. IV
White, Sir Richard, died 1925, vol. II
White, Sir Richard; see White, Sir E. R. M.
White, Richard Charles B.; see Brooman-White.
White, Adm. Richard Dunning, 1813–1899, vol. I

White, Col Richard Stephen Murray, 1876–1942, vol. IV

White, Vice-Adm. Richard William, 1849–1924, vol. II

White, Sir Robert, 1827–1902, vol. I

White, Brig.-Gen. Hon. Robert, 1861–1936, vol. III

White, Robert, 1872–1959, vol. V

White, Sir Robert Eaton, 1st Bt (cr 1937), 1864–1940, vol. III

White, Robert George, 1885–1976, vol. VII

White, Robert George, 1917–1982, vol. VIII

White, Lt-Col Robert L; see Lynch-White.

White, Robert Prosser, 1855–1934, vol. III

White, Robert S.; see Standish-White.

White, Sir Rowden; see White, Sir A. E. R.

White, Sir Rudolph Dymoke, 2nd Bt (cr 1922), 1888–1968, vol. VI

White, Rt Rev. Russell Berridge, 1896–1978, vol. VII

White, Captain Samuel Albert, 1870–1954, vol. V

White, Lt-Col Samuel Robert Llewellyn, 1863–1925, vol. II

White, Sinclair, 1858–1920, vol. II

White, Stanford, 1853–1906, vol. I

White, Sir Stanley; see White, Sir G. S.

White, Stuart Arthur Frank, died 1951, vol. V

White, Sir Sydney Arthur, 1884–1958, vol. V

White, T. Charters, 1828–1916, vol. II

White, Terence Hanbury, 1906–1964, vol. VI

White, Sir Thomas, died 1938, vol. III

White, Rt Hon. Sir Thomas; see White, Rt Hon. Sir W. T.

White, Thomas Cyril, 1911–1981, vol. VIII

White, Group Captain Hon. Sir Thomas Walter, 1888–1957, vol. V

White, Sir Thomas Woollaston, 3rd Bt (cr 1802), 1828–1907, vol. I

White, Wilbert Webster, 1863–1944, vol. IV

White, Brig.-Gen. Wilfred Arthur, 1870–1935, vol. III

White, William, died 1912, vol. I

White, Rt Rev. William Charles, 1865–1943, vol. IV

White, Rt Rev. William Charles, 1873–1960, vol. V

White, Sir William H.; see Hale-White.

White, William Hale, 1831–1913, vol. I

White, William Harry, 1851–1914, vol. I

White, Sir William Henry, 1845–1913, vol. I

White, Col William Lambert, 1849–1929, vol. III

White, Brig.-Gen. William Lewis, 1856–1931, vol. III

White, William Lindsay, 1900–1973, vol. VII

White, Brig. William Nicholas, 1879–1951, vol. V

White, William Rogerson, 1850–1913, vol. I

White, Rt Hon. Sir (William) Thomas, 1866–1955, vol. V

White, Col William Westropp, 1862–1927, vol. II

White, Rev. Wilson Woodhouse, 1864–1941, vol. IV

White, Sir Woolmer Rudolph Donati, 1st Bt (cr 1922), 1858–1931, vol. III

White-Jervis, Sir Henry Felix Jervis; see Jervis.

White-Jervis, Col Sir John Henry Jervis; see Jervis.

White-Smith, Sir Henry, 1878–1943, vol. IV

White-Thomson, Col Sir Hugh Davie, 1866–1922, vol. II

White-Thomson, Rt Rev. Leonard Jauncey, 1863–1933, vol. III

White-Thomson, Col Sir Robert Thomas, 1831–1918, vol. II

White-Winton, Meryon, died 1921, vol. II

Whiteaves, Joseph Frederick, 1835–1909, vol. I

Whitechurch, Rev. Victor Lorenzo, 1868–1933, vol. III

Whitefoord, Rev. Canon Benjamin, 1848–1911, vol. I

Whitefoord, Maj.-Gen. Philip Geoffrey, 1894–1975, vol. VII

Whitehead, Alfred North, 1861–1947, vol. IV

Whitehead, Arnold Sydney, 1895–1966, vol. VI

Whitehead, Arthur Longley, died 1930, vol. III

Whitehead, Sir Charles, 1834–1912, vol. I

Whitehead, Rt Rev. Cortlandt, 1842–1922, vol. II

Whitehead, Sir Edgar Cuthbert Fremantle, 1905–1971, vol. VII

Whitehead, Comdr Edward, 1908–1978, vol. VII

Whitehead, Frank Henry, 1918–1988, vol. VIII

Whitehead, Vice-Adm. Frederic Aubrey, 1874–1958, vol. V

Whitehead, Frederick, died 1938, vol. III

Whitehead, Sir George Hugh, 2nd Bt, 1861–1931, vol. III

Whitehead, Maj.-Gen. Sir Hayward Reader, 1855–1925, vol. II

Whitehead, Henry, 1842–1921, vol. II

Whitehead, Sir Henry, 1859–1928, vol. II

Whitehead, Rt Rev. Henry, 1853–1947, vol. IV

Whitehead, Sir James, 1st Bt, 1834–1917, vol. II

Whitehead, James, died 1936, vol. III

Whitehead, Brig. James, 1880–1955, vol. V

Whitehead, Sir James Beethom, 1858–1928, vol. II

Whitehead, Col James Buckley, 1898–1983, vol. VIII

Whitehead, John Henry Constantine, 1904–1960, vol. V

Whitehead, Col John Herbert, 1869–1928, vol. II

Whitehead, Major Sir Philip Henry Rathbone, 4th Bt, 1897–1953, vol. V

Whitehead, Maj.-Gen. Robert Children, 1833–1905, vol. I

Whitehead, Sir Rowland Edward, 3rd Bt, 1863–1942, vol. IV

Whitehead, Rev. Silvester, 1841–1917, vol. II

Whitehead, Spencer, 1845–1922, vol. II

Whitehead, Thomas Alec, 1886–1959, vol. V

Whitehead, Thomas Henderson, 1851–1933, vol. III

Whitehead, Lt-Col Wilfred James, 1873–1934, vol. III

Whitehead, Lt-Col Wilfrid Arthur, 1898–1981, vol. VIII

Whitehill, Clarence Eugene, 1871–1932, vol. III

Whitehorn, Joseph Hammond, 1861–1935, vol. III

Whitehorn, Rev. Roy Drummond, 1891–1976, vol. VII

Whitehorne, James Charles, died 1905, vol. I

Whitehouse, Arthur Wildman, 1865–1944, vol. IV

Whitehouse, Cyril John Arthur, 1913–1982, vol. VIII

Whitehouse, Sir George, 1857–1938, vol. III

Whitehouse, Sir Harold Beckwith, 1882–1943, vol. IV

Whitehouse, John Howard, 1873–1955, vol. V

Whitehouse, Sir Julian Osborn, 1876–1942, vol. IV

Whitehouse, Rev. Owen Charles, 1849–1916, vol. II

Whitehouse, Wallace Edward, 1882–1963, vol. VI

Whitehouse, William Edward, 1859–1935, vol. III

Whitehouse, Major William Henry, 1873–1963, vol. VI

Whiteing, Richard, 1840–1928, vol. II

Whitelaw, Alexander, 1862–1938, vol. III

Whitelaw, Anne Watt, 1875–1966, vol. VI

Whitelaw, David, 1876–1971, vol. VII

Whitelaw, Græme Alexander Lockhart, 1863–1928, vol. II

Whitelaw, Maj.-Gen. John Stewart, 1894–1964, vol. VI

Whitelaw, Robert Pender, 1865–1934, vol. III

Whitelaw, Thomas, 1840–1917, vol. II

Whitelaw, William, 1868–1946, vol. IV

Whitelegge, Sir (B.) Arthur, 1852–1933, vol. III

Whiteley, Cecil, 1875–1942, vol. IV

Whiteley, Frank, 1856–1933, vol. III

Whiteley, Sir Gerald Charles, 1891–1958, vol. V

Whiteley, Sir Herbert Huntington-, 1st Bt, 1857–1936, vol. III

Whiteley, Captain Sir (Herbert) Maurice H.; *see* Huntington-Whiteley.

Whiteley, Gen. Sir John Francis Martin, 1896–1970, vol. VI

Whiteley, Brig. John Percival, *died* 1943, vol. VI

Whiteley, Martha Annie, 1866–1956, vol. V

Whiteley, Wilfrid, 1882–1970, vol. VI

Whiteley, Rt Hon. William, 1882–1955, vol. V

Whitelock, Dorothy, 1901–1982, vol. VIII

Whitelocke, R. Henry Anglin, 1861–1927, vol. II

Whiteman, George W., 1903–1974, vol. VII

Whiteman, William Meredith, 1905–1989, vol. VIII

Whiteside, Borras Noel Hamilton, 1903–1948, vol. IV

Whiteside, Sir Cuthbert William, 1880–1969, vol. VI(AII)

Whiteside, Surg. Rear-Adm. Henry Cadman, *died* 1949, vol. IV

Whiteside, Most Rev. Thomas, 1857–1921, vol. II

Whiteway, Ronald Harry Clift, 1885–1951, vol. V

Whiteway, Rt Hon. Sir William Vallance, 1828–1908, vol. I

Whitfeld, Hubert Edwin, 1875–1939, vol. III

Whitfield, Arthur, *died* 1947, vol. IV

Whitfield, Sir Cecil Vincent W.; *see* Wallace Whitfield.

Whitfield, George, 1891–1983, vol. VIII

Whitfield, Maj.-Gen. John Yeldham, 1899–1971, vol. VII

Whitfield-Jackson, John; *see* Jackson, J. W.

Whitford, Air Vice-Marshal Sir John, 1893–1966, vol. VI

Whitham, Rev. Arthur Richard, 1863–1930, vol. III

Whitham, Gilbert Shaw, 1889–1970, vol. VI

Whitham, Lt-Gen. John Lawrence, 1881–1952, vol. V

Whitham, Air Cdre Robert Parker Musgrave, 1895–1943, vol. IV

Whiting, Arthur John, *died* 1941, vol. IV

Whiting, Rev. Charles Edwin, 1871–1953, vol. V

Whiting, Frederic, *died* 1962, vol. VI

Whiting, John Robert, 1917–1963, vol. VI

Whiting, Maurice Henry, 1885–1984, vol. VIII

Whiting, William Henry, 1854–1927, vol. II

Whiting, William Robert Gerald, 1884–1947, vol. IV

Whiting, Winifred Ada, 1898–1979, vol. VII

Whitington, Ven. Frederick Taylor, 1853–1938, vol. III

Whitla, Sir William, 1851–1933, vol. III

Whitley, Brig.-Gen. Sir Edward Nathan, 1873–1966, vol. VI

Whitley, Very Rev. Henry Charles, 1906–1976, vol. VII

Whitley, Rt Rev. Jabez Cornelius, 1837–1904, vol. I

Whitley, Rt Hon. John Henry, 1866–1935, vol. III

Whitley, John Robinson, 1843–1922, vol. II

Whitley, Kate Mary, *died* 1920, vol. II

Whitley, Sir Michael Henry, 1872–1959, vol. V

Whitley, Sir Norman Henry Pownall, 1883–1957, vol. V

Whitley, William Thomas, 1858–1942, vol. IV

Whitley, William Thomas, 1861–1947, vol. IV

Whitley-Jones, Ernest, 1890–1965, vol. VI

Whitley-Thomson, Sir Frederick Whitley, 1851–1925, vol. II

Whitlock, Brand, 1869–1934, vol. III

Whitlock, Col George Frederic Ashford, 1868–1936, vol. III

Whitman, Alfred Charles, 1860–1910, vol. I

Whitman, Sidney, *died* 1925, vol. II

Whitmarsh, Gerald Edward Leaman, 1908–1980, vol. VII (AII)

Whitmarsh, Rev. Robert Thomas, *died* 1921, vol. II

Whitmee, Harold James Conder, 1901–1954, vol. V

Whitmore, Charles Algernon, 1851–1908, vol. I

Whitmore, Francis, 1903–1975, vol. VII

Whitmore, Col Sir Francis Henry Douglas Charlton, 1st Bt, 1872–1962, vol. VI

Whitmore, Hon. Col Sir George Stoddart, 1830–1903, vol. I

Whitnall, S. E., 1876–1950, vol. IV

Whitney, Sir Benjamin, 1833–1916, vol. II

Whitney, Caspar, 1864–1929, vol. III

Whitney, Sir Cecil Arthur, 1862–1956, vol. V

Whitney, George, 1885–1963, vol. VI

Whitney, Harry Payne, 1872–1930, vol. III

Whitney, Henry Ernest William F.; *see* Fetherstonhaugh-Whitney.

Whitney, Hon. Sir James Pliny, 1843–1914, vol. I

Whitney, James Pounder, 1857–1939, vol. III

Whitney, John Hay, 1904–1982, vol. VIII

Whitney, William Collins, 1841–1904, vol. I

Whitney, William Dwight, 1899–1973, vol. VII

Whitney-Smith, E., 1880–1952, vol. V

Whitsey, Rt Rev. Hubert Victor, 1916–1987, vol. VIII

Whitsey, Rt Rev. Victor; *see* Whitsey, Rt Rev. H. V.

Whitson, Sir Thomas Barnby, 1869–1948, vol. IV

Whittaker, Arnold, 1900–1984, vol. VIII

Whittaker, Sir Edmund Taylor, 1873–1956, vol. V

Whittaker, John Macnaghten, 1905–1984, vol. VIII

Whittaker, Sir (Joseph) Meredith, 1914–1984, vol. VIII

Whittaker, Sir Meredith; *see* Whittaker, Sir J. M.

Whittaker, Sir Meredith Thompson, 1841–1931, vol. III

Whittaker, Maj.-Gen. Robert Frederick Edward, 1894–1967, vol. VI

Whittaker, Thomas, 1856–1935, vol. III

Whittaker, Rt Hon. Sir Thomas Palmer, 1850–1919, vol. II

Whittaker, William Gillies, 1876–1944, vol. IV

Whittaker, William Joseph, 1868–1931, vol. III

Whittall, Sir (James) William, 1838–1910, vol. I

Whittall, Lionel Harry, 1907–1977, vol. VII

Whittall, Lt-Col Percival Frederick, 1877–1943, vol. IV

Whittall, Sir William; see Whittall, Sir J. W.

Whittard, Walter Frederick, 1902–1966, vol. VI

Whitten, Wilfred, died 1942, vol. IV

Whitten-Brown, Sir Arthur, 1886–1948, vol. IV

Whittet, Thomas Douglas, 1915–1987, vol. VIII

Whittick, Henry John, 1870–1937, vol. III

Whitting, Brig. Everard Le Grice, 1881–1953, vol. V

Whittingham, Col Charles Herbert, 1873–1932, vol. III

Whittingham, Rev. George Gustavus Napier, 1866–1941, vol. IV

Whittingham, Air Marshal Sir Harold Edward, 1887–1983, vol. VIII

Whittingham, Rt Rev. Walter Godfrey, died 1941, vol. IV

Whittingham, Engr-Rear-Adm. William, 1862–1940, vol. III

Whittingstall, Francis Herbert F.; see Fearnley-Whittingstall.

Whittingstall, William Arthur F.; see Fearnley-Whittingstall.

Whittington, Brig.-Gen. Cecil Henry, 1878–1934, vol. III

Whittington, Col George John Charles, 1836–1916, vol. II

Whittington, Rev. Richard, 1825–1900, vol. I

Whittington, Sir Richard, 1905–1975, vol. VII

Whittington-Ince, Captain Edward Watkins, 1886–1976, vol. VII

Whittle, Alfred Thomas, 1836–1913, vol. I

Whittle, Claude Howard, 1896–1986, vol. VIII

Whittle, Ven. John Tyler, 1889–1969, vol. VI

Whittome, Sir Maurice Gordon, 1902–1974, vol. VII

Whitton, Charlotte Elizabeth, 1896–1975, vol. VII

Whitton, Lt-Col Frederick Ernest, 1872–1940, vol. III

Whitton, James Reid, died 1919, vol. II

Whitty, Maj.-Gen. Henry Martin, 1896–1961, vol. VI

Whitty, Sir John Tarlton, 1876–1948, vol. IV

Whitty, Dame May; see Webster, Dame May.

Whitty, Brig. Noel Irwine, 1885–1964, vol. VI

Whitty, Sir Reginald Ramson, 1891–1960, vol. V

Whitwell, Edward Robson, 1843–1922, vol. II

Whitwell, Joseph Fry, 1869–1932, vol. III

Whitwell, William Fry, 1867–1942, vol. IV

Whitwill, Col Mark, 1889–1967, vol. VI

Whitworth, Arthur, 1875–1972, vol. VII

Whitworth, Charles Stanley, 1880–1963, vol. VI

Whitworth, Clifford, 1906–1983, vol. VIII

Whitworth, Cyril, 1904–1968, vol. VI

Whitworth, Brig. Dysart Edward, 1890–1974, vol. VII

Whitworth, Eric Edward Allen, died 1971, vol. VII

Whitworth, Geoffrey Arundel, 1883–1951, vol. V

Whitworth, Harry, 1870–1930, vol. III

Whitworth, Air Cdre John Nicholas Haworth, 1912–1974, vol. VII

Whitworth, Thomas, 1917–1979, vol. VII

Whitworth, Rev. William Allen, 1840–1905, vol. I

Whitworth, William Hervey Allen, died 1960, vol. V

Whitworth, Adm. Sir William Jock, 1884–1973, vol. VII

Whitworth Jones, Air Chief Marshal Sir John; see Jones.

Whorlow, Rev. Alfred, 1852–1937, vol. III

Whyatt, Sir John, 1905–1978, vol. VII

Whyham, William Henry, born 1848, vol. II

Whymper, Charles, 1853–1941, vol. IV

Whymper, Edward, 1840–1911, vol. I

Whymper, Josiah Wood, 1813–1903, vol. I

Whyte, Rev. Alexander, 1836–1921, vol. II

Whyte, Sir (Alexander) Frederick, 1883–1970, vol. VI

Whyte, Angus H.; see Hedley-Whyte.

Whyte, Frederic, 1867–1941, vol. IV

Whyte, Sir Frederick; see Whyte, Sir A. F.

Whyte, Gabriel Thomas, 1925–1986, vol. VIII

Whyte, Sir Hamilton; see Whyte, Sir. W. E. H.

Whyte, Ian, 1901–1960, vol. V

Whyte, J. Mackie, 1858–1930, vol. III

Whyte, James Wilkinson, 1852–1923, vol. II

Whyte, Jardine Bell, 1880–1954, vol. V

Whyte, Major John Nicholas, 1864–1906, vol. I

Whyte, Lewis Gilmour, 1906–1986, vol. VIII

Whyte, Ven. Richard Athenry, died 1917, vol. II

Whyte, Air Comdt Dame Roberta Mary, 1897–1979, vol. VII

Whyte, Sir William, 1843–1914, vol. I

Whyte, Sir William, died 1945, vol. IV

Whyte, Sir William Edward, died 1950, vol. IV

Whyte, Sir (William Erskine) Hamilton, 1927–1990, vol. VIII

Whyte, William Hamilton, 1885–1973, vol. VII

Whyte, Sir William Marcus Charles Beresford, 1863–1932, vol. III

Whytehead, Rev. Henry Robert, 1849–1937, vol. III

Whytehead, Rev. Canon Ralph Layard, 1883–1956, vol. V

Whytlaw-Gray, Robert Whytlaw, 1877–1958, vol. V

Wibberley, Charles, 1851–1929, vol. III

Wibberley, T., 1880–1930, vol. III

Wickenden, Keith David, 1932–1983, vol. VIII

Wickens, Charles Henry, 1872–1939, vol. III

Wickham, Rev. Archdale Palmer, 1855–1935, vol. III

Wickham, Lt-Col Sir Charles George, 1879–1971, vol. VII

Wickham, Very Rev. Edward Charles, 1834–1910, vol. I

Wickham, Lt-Col Edward Thomas Ruscombe, 1890–1957, vol. V

Wickham, Rev. Gordon Bolles, 1850–1920, vol. II

Wickham, Sir Henry, 1846–1928, vol. II

Wickham, Lt-Col Henry, 1855–1933, vol. III

Wickham, Col Henry Francis, 1874–1931, vol. III

Wickham, Brig. John Charles, 1886–1970, vol. VI

Wickham, Major Thomas Edmund Palmer, 1879–1917, vol. II

Wickham, Captain Thomas Strange, 1878–1914, vol. I

Wickham, William, 1831–1897, vol. I

Wickham, Col William James Richard, 1860–1932, vol. III

Wickham, William Reginald Lamplugh, 1908–1956, vol. V

Wickham-Boynton, Captain Thomas Lamplugh, 1869–1942, vol. IV

Wickins, Bt-Col George Cradock, 1884–1973, vol. VII

Wickins, Ven. William John, *died* 1933, vol. III

Wicklow, 7th Earl of, 1877–1946, vol. IV

Wicklow, 8th Earl of, 1902–1978, vol. VII

Wickremasinghe, N. Don Martino de Zilva, 1865–1937, vol. III

Wickremesinghe, Cyril Leonard, 1890–1945, vol. IV

Wicks, Frederick, 1840–1910, vol. I

Wicks, Sir James, 1909–1989, vol. VIII

Wicks, Margaret Campbell Walker, 1893–1970, vol. VI

Wicks, Pembroke, 1882–1957, vol. V

Wicksteed, Joseph Hartley, 1842–1919, vol. II

Wicksteed, Rev. Philip Henry, 1844–1927, vol. II

Wicksteed, Thomas Frederic, 1848–1901, vol. I

Widdess, Rev. Canon Arthur Geoffrey, 1920–1982, vol. VIII

Widdicombe, Lt-Col George Templer, 1867–1952, vol. V

Widdicombe, Rev. John, 1839–1927, vol. II

Widdows, Archibald Edwards, 1878–1942, vol. IV

Widdowson, Thomas William, 1877–1956, vol. V

Widdrington, Brig.-Gen. Bertram FitzHerbert, 1873–1942, vol. IV

Widdrington, Major Shallcross Fitzherbert, 1826–1917, vol. II

Widener, Joseph E., *died* 1943, vol. IV

Widener, Peter A. Brown, 1834–1915, vol. I

Widgery, Baron (Life Peer); John Passmore Widgery, 1911–1981, vol. VIII

Widgery, Alban Gregory, 1887–1968, vol. VI

Widor, Charles-Marie, 1847–1937, vol. III

Wieland, Heinrich Otto, 1877–1957, vol. V

Wieler, Brig. Leslie Frederic Ethelbert, 1899–1965, vol. VI

Wien, Hon. Sir Phillip Solly, 1913–1981, vol. VIII

Wiener, Leo, 1862–1939, vol. III(A), vol. IV

Wiener, Norbert, 1894–1964, vol. VI

Wiesner, Karel František, 1919–1986, vol. VIII

Wigan, Alfred Edmund, 1855–1940, vol. III

Wigan, Charles, 1860–1937, vol. III

Wigan, Sir Frederick, 1st Bt, 1827–1907, vol. I

Wigan, Sir Frederick Adair, 4th Bt, 1911–1979, vol. VII

Wigan, Sir Frederick William, 2nd Bt, 1859–1907, did not have an entry in Who's Who

Wigan, Brig.-Gen. John Tyson, 1877–1952, vol. V

Wigan, Sir Roderick Grey, 3rd Bt, 1886–1954, vol. V

Wigg, Baron (Life Peer); George Edward Cecil Wigg, 1900–1983, vol. VIII

Wigg, Rt Rev. Montagu John S.; *see* Stone-Wigg.

Wiggin, Alfred Harold, 1864–1933, vol. III

Wiggin, Arthur Francis Holme, 1892–1935, vol. III

Wiggin, Sir Charles Douglas, 1922–1977, vol. VII

Wiggin, Sir Charles Richard Henry, 3rd Bt, 1885–1972, vol. VII

Wiggin, Brig.-Gen. Edgar Askin, 1867–1939, vol. III

Wiggin, Sir Henry Samuel, 1st Bt, 1824–1905, vol. I

Wiggin, Sir Henry Arthur, 2nd Bt, 1852–1917, vol. II

Wiggin, Kate Douglas, 1856–1923, vol. II

Wiggin, Lt-Col Walter William, 1856–1936, vol. III

Wiggin, Lt-Col Sir William Henry, 1888–1951, vol. V

Wiggins, Rev. Clare Aveling, *died* 1965, vol. VI

Wiggins, Captain Joseph, 1832–1905, vol. I

Wiggins, William Denison Clare, 1905–1971, vol. VII

Wiggins, William Martin, 1870–1950, vol. IV

Wigglesworth, Air Cdre Cecil George, 1893–1961, vol. VI

Wigglesworth, Air Marshal Sir (Horace Ernest) Philip, 1896–1975, vol. VII

Wigglesworth, Air Marshal Sir Philip; *see* Wigglesworth, Air Marshal Sir H. E. P.

Wigglesworth, Walter Somerville, 1906–1972, vol. VII

Wigham, Eric Leonard, 1904–1990, vol. VIII

Wigham, Joseph Theodore, 1874–1951, vol. V

Wigham Richardson, Sir George; *see* Richardson.

Wight, Sir Gerald Robert, 1898–1962, vol. VI

Wight, Martin; *see* Wight, R. J. M.

Wight, (Robert James) Martin, 1913–1972, vol. VII

Wight-Boycott, Lt-Col T. A., 1872–1916, vol. II

Wightman, Sir Owen William, 1869–1948, vol. IV

Wightman, Ralph, 1901–1971, vol. VII

Wightwick, Humphrey Wolseley, 1889–1962, vol. VI

Wigley, Frederick George, 1855–1918, vol. II

Wigley, Sir George, 1837–1925, vol. II

Wigley, Sir Henry Rodolph, 1913–1980, vol. VII (AII)

Wigley, Rev. Henry Townsend, 1893–1970, vol. VI

Wigley, John Edwin Mackonochie, 1892–1962, vol. VI

Wigley, Sir Wilfrid Murray, 1876–1959, vol. V

Wigmore, John Henry, 1863–1943, vol. IV

Wignall, Frederick William, *died* 1939, vol. III

Wignall, James, 1865–1925, vol. II

Wignall, Joshua Jennings, 1859–1941, vol. IV

Wigram, 1st Baron, 1873–1960, vol. V

Wigram, Alfred Money, 1856–1899, vol. I

Wigram, Sir Charles Hampden, 1826–1903, vol. I

Wigram, Sir Edgar Thomas Ainger, 6th Bt, 1864–1935, vol. III

Wigram, Vice-Adm. Ernest, 1877–1944, vol. IV

Wigram, Maj.-Gen. Godfrey James, 1836–1908, vol. I

Wigram, Sir Henry Francis, 1857–1934, vol. III

Wigram, Gen. Sir Kenneth, 1875–1949, vol. IV

Wigram, Loftus Edward, 1877–1963, vol. VI

Wigram, Ralph Follet, 1890–1936, vol. III

Wigram, Rev. William Ainger, 1872–1953, vol. V

Wigram, Rev. Woolmore, 1831–1907, vol. I

Wijayasinghe Siriwardena, N. D. A. Silva-, 1888–1949, vol. IV(A)

Wijeyekoon, Sir Gerard, 1878–1952, vol. V

Wijeyeratne, Sir Edwin Aloysius Perera, 1890–1968, vol. VI

Wijeyewardene, Hon. Sir Arthur; *see* Wijeyewardene, Hon. Sir E. A. L.

Wijeyewardene, Hon. Sir (Edwin) Arthur (Lewis), 1887–1964, vol. VI

Wijhe, J. W. van, 1856–1935, vol. III

Wikeley, Thomas, 1902–1984, vol. VIII

Wilberforce, Ven. Albert Basil Orme, 1841–1916, vol. II

Wilberforce, Edward, 1834–1914, vol. I
Wilberforce, Rt Rev. Ernest Roland, 1840–1907, vol. I
Wilberforce, Col Harold Hartley, 1881–1943, vol. IV
Wilberforce, Brig.-Gen. Sir Herbert William, 1866–1952, vol. V
Wilberforce, Sir Herbert William Wrangham, 1864–1941, vol. IV
Wilberforce, Lionel Robert, 1861–1944, vol. IV
Wilberforce, Robert Francis, 1887–1990, vol. VIII
Wilberforce, Samuel, 1874–1954, vol. V
Wilberforce-Bell, Lt-Col Sir Harold, 1885–1956, vol. V
Wilbraham, Lt-Col Bernard Hugh, died 1942, vol. IV
Wilbraham, Edward; see Lathom, 3rd Earl of.
Wilbraham, Sir George Barrington Baker-, 5th Bt, 1845–1912, vol. I
Wilbraham, Hugh Edward, 1857–1930, vol. III
Wilbraham, Sir Philip Wilbraham Baker, 6th Bt, 1875–1957, vol. V
Wilbraham, Sir Randle John Baker, 7th Bt, 1906–1980, vol. VII
Wilbraham, Sir Richard, 1811–1900, vol. I
Wilby, Col (Arthur William) Roger, 1875–1942, vol. IV
Wilby, John Ronald William, 1906–1989, vol. VIII
Wilby, Col Roger; see Wilby, Col A. W. R.
Wilcher, Lewis Charles, 1908–1983, vol. VIII
Wilcock, Alfred William, died 1953, vol. V
Wilcock, Gp Captain Clifford Arthur Bowman, died 1962, vol. VI
Wilcock, John Stewart, 1905–1951, vol. V
Wilcocks, Hon. Carl Theodorus Muller, 1861–1936, vol. III
Wilcocks, C(harles), 1896–1977, vol. VII
Wilcockson, Rear-Adm. Kenneth Dilworth East, 1927–1986, vol. VIII
Wilcox, Rev. Arthur John, 1889–1960, vol. V
Wilcox, Bernard Herbert, 1917–1980, vol. VII
Wilcox, Claude Henry Marwood, 1908–1981, vol. VIII
Wilcox, Ella Wheeler, 1855–1919, vol. II
Wilcox, Dame (Florence) Marjorie; see Neagle, Dame Anna.
Wilcox, Herbert Sydney, 1892–1977, vol. VII
Wilcox, Sir Malcolm George, 1921–1986, vol. VIII
Wilcox, Dame Marjorie; see Neagle, Dame Anna.
Wild, Albert, 1899–1971, vol. VII
Wild, Maj.-Gen. Edward John, died 1914, vol. I
Wild, Sir Ernest Edward, 1869–1934, vol. III
Wild, F. Percy, died 1950, vol. IV
Wild, Frank, 1874–1939, vol. III
Wild, Captain Geoffrey Alan, 1904–1985, vol. VIII
Wild, Rt Rev. Herbert Louis, 1865–1940, vol. III
Wild, Rt Hon. Sir (Herbert) Richard (Churton), 1912–1978, vol. VII
Wild, Ira, 1895–1974, vol. VII
Wild, Jack, 1927–1988, vol. VIII
Wild, James Anstey, 1853–1922, vol. II
Wild, Rev. Marshall, 1834–1916, vol. II
Wild, Ralph Bagnall B.; see Bagnall-Wild.
Wild, Brig.-Gen. Ralph Kirkby B.; see Bagnall-Wild.
Wild, Rt Hon. Sir Richard; see Wild, Rt Hon. Sir H. R. C.

Wild, Robert Briggs, 1862–1941, vol. IV
Wild, Lt-Col Wilfrid Hubert, 1874–1953, vol. V
Wilde, Henry, 1833–1919, vol. II
Wilde, Johannes, 1891–1970, vol. VI
Wilde, Percy, 1857–1929, vol. III
Wilden-Hart, Bernard John, 1881–1932, vol. III
Wildenburg, Count Paul von H.; see Hatzfeldt-Wildenburg.
Wilder, Thornton Niven, 1897–1975, vol. VII
Wildey, Alexander Gascoigne, 1860–1934, vol. III
Wilding, Anthony Frederick, 1883–1915, vol. I
Wilding, Brig.-Gen. Charles Arthur, 1868–1953, vol. V
Wilding, Edward, 1875–1939, vol. III
Wilding, Longworth Allen, 1902–1963, vol. VI
Wilding, Michael, 1912–1979, vol. VII
Wilding, Captain Michael Henry, 1875–1933, vol. III
Wildish, Engr Rear-Adm. Sir Henry William, 1884–1973, vol. VII
Wildman-Lushington, Maj.-Gen. Godfrey Edward, 1897–1970, vol. VI
Wildy, (Norman) Peter (Leete), 1920–1987, vol. VIII
Wildy, Peter; see Wildy, N. P. L.
Wile, Frederic William, 1873–1941, vol. IV
Wileman, Alfred Ernest, 1860–1929, vol. III
Wilenski, Reginald Howard, 1887–1975, vol. VII
Wiles, Sir Gilbert, 1880–1961, vol. VI
Wiles, Sir Harold Herbert, 1892–1965, vol. VI
Wiles, Philip, 1899–1967, vol. VI
Wiles, Reid, 1919–1975, vol. VII
Wiles, Rt Hon. Thomas, died 1951, vol. V
Wiley, Very Rev. C. Ormsby, 1839–1915, vol. I
Wiley, Charles Joseph, 1873–1939, vol. III
Wiley, Louis, 1869–1935, vol. III
Wilford, Rev. Canon John Russell, 1877–1954, vol. V
Wilford, Sir Thomas Mason, died 1939, vol. III
Wilgar, Lt-Col William Percy, 1877–1940, vol. III(A), vol. IV
Wilgress, Rev. George Frederick, 1868–1953, vol. V
Wilgress, L. Dana, 1892–1969, vol. VI
Wilhelm, C.; see Pitcher, W. J. C.
Wilkes, Rev. John Comyn V.; see Vaughan Wilkes.
Wilkes, Richard Leslie Vaughan, 1904–1970, vol. VI
Wilkie, Alexander, 1850–1928, vol. II
Wilkie, Alexander Mair, 1917–1966, vol. VI
Wilkie, Rev. Arthur West, 1875–1958, vol. V
Wilkie, Daniel R., 1846–1914, vol. I
Wilkie, Sir David Percival Dalbreck, 1882–1938, vol. III
Wilkie, Hugh Graham, 1893–1969, vol. VI
Wilkie, James, 1890–1957, vol. V
Wilkie, James, 1896–1987, vol. VIII
Wilkie-Dalyell, Major Sir James Bruce; see Dalyell.
Wilkin, Sir Albert Scholick, 1883–1943, vol. IV
Wilkin, Vice-Adm. Henry Douglas, 1862–1931, vol. III
Wilkin, Sir Walter Henry, 1842–1922, vol. II
Wilkins, Augustus Samuel, 1843–1905, vol. I
Wilkins, Charles Timothy, 1905–1979, vol. VII
Wilkins, Major Cyril Francis, died 1935, vol. III
Wilkins, Frederick Charles, 1901–1987, vol. VIII
Wilkins, Rev. George, died 1920, vol. II
Wilkins, Sir (George) Hubert, 1888–1958, vol. V
Wilkins, Sir Henry John Arthur, died 1936, vol. III

772

Wilkins, Rev. Henry Russell, 1859–1924, vol. II
Wilkins, Sir Hubert; see Wilkins, Sir G. H.
Wilkins, Col James Sutherland, 1851–1916, vol. II
Wilkins, Mary E., died 1930, vol. III
Wilkins, Roland Field, 1872–1950, vol. IV
Wilkins, William Albert, 1899–1987, vol. VIII
Wilkins, William Henry, 1860–1905, vol. I
Wilkins, William Vaughan, 1890–1959, vol. V
Wilkinson, Col Arthur Clement, 1870–1950, vol. IV
Wilkinson, Rev. Arthur Henry, 1885–1973, vol. VII
Wilkinson, Rev. Arthur Rupert B.; see Browne-Wilkinson.
Wilkinson, Engr Rear-Adm. Brian John Hamilton, died 1963, vol. VI
Wilkinson, Rt Rev. (Charles Robert) Heber, 1900–1979, vol. VII
Wilkinson, Ven. Charles Thomas, 1823–1910, vol. I
Wilkinson, Col Charles William, 1868–1954, vol. V
Wilkinson, Clennell Anstruther, 1883–1936, vol. III
Wilkinson, Clennell Frank Massy D.; see Drew-Wilkinson.
Wilkinson, Cyril Hackett, 1888–1960, vol. V
Wilkinson, Cyril Theodore Anstruther, 1884–1970, vol. VI
Wilkinson, Sir David; see Wilkinson, Sir L. D.
Wilkinson, Edgar Riley, 1898–1977, vol. VII
Wilkinson, Edward Sheldon, 1883–1950, vol. IV
Wilkinson, Rt Hon. Ellen Cicely, 1891–1947, vol. IV
Wilkinson, Fanny Rollo, died 1951, vol. V
Wilkinson, Most Rev. Francis Oliver G.; see Green-Wilkinson.
Wilkinson, Frank, 1900–1970, vol. VI
Wilkinson, Frank Clare, 1889–1979, vol. VII
Wilkinson, Frederick, 1891–1978, vol. VII
Wilkinson, Frederick Edgar, 1871–1950, vol. IV
Wilkinson, Lt-Gen. Frederick G.; see Green-Wilkinson.
Wilkinson, George, 1867–1956, vol. V
Wilkinson, Col George Alexander Eason, 1860–1941, vol. IV
Wilkinson, Maj.-Gen. George Allix, 1828–1919, vol. II
Wilkinson, Sir George Henry, 1st Bt, 1885–1967, vol. VI
Wilkinson, Rt Rev. George Howard, 1833–1907, vol. I
Wilkinson, Sir Harold, 1903–1986, vol. VIII
Wilkinson, Rt Rev. Heber; see Wilkinson, Rt Rev. C. R. H.
Wilkinson, Hector Russell, 1888–1972, vol. VII
Wilkinson, Lt-Col Henry Benfield Des Vœux, 1870–1943, vol. IV
Wilkinson, Lt-Gen. Sir Henry Clement, 1837–1908, vol. I
Wilkinson, (Henry) Spenser, 1853–1937, vol. III
Wilkinson, Hiram Parkes, 1866–1935, vol. III
Wilkinson, Sir Hiram Shaw, 1840–1926, vol. II
Wilkinson, Ven. Hubert Seed, 1897–1984, vol. VIII
Wilkinson, Hon. James, 1854–1915, vol. I
Wilkinson, James Hardy, 1919–1986, vol. VIII
Wilkinson, Rev. John, 1856–1935, vol. III
Wilkinson, Brig. John Shann, 1884–1977, vol. VII
Wilkinson, Sir Joseph Loftus, 1845–1903, vol. I

Wilkinson, Vice-Adm. Julian Charles Allix, 1859–1917, vol. II
Wilkinson, Kenneth Douglas, 1886–1951, vol. V
Wilkinson, Kenneth Grahame, 1917–1990, vol. VIII
Wilkinson, Lancelot Craven, died 1923, vol. II
Wilkinson, (Lancelot) Patrick, 1907–1985, vol. VIII
Wilkinson, Sir (Leonard) David, 2nd Bt, 1920–1972, vol. VII
Wilkinson, Leslie, 1882–1973, vol. VII
Wilkinson, Brig.-Gen. Lewis Frederic G.; see Green-Wilkinson.
Wilkinson, Louis Umfreville, 1881–1966, vol. VI
Wilkinson, Dame Louisa Jane, 1889–1968, vol. VI
Wilkinson, Sir Martin; see Wilkinson, Sir R. F. M.
Wilkinson, Brig. Maurice Lean, 1873–1946, vol. IV
Wilkinson, Rev. Michael Marlow Umfreville, 1831–1916, vol. II
Wilkinson, Brig.-Gen. Montagu Grant, 1857–1943, vol. IV
Wilkinson, Major Sir Nevile Rodwell, 1869–1940, vol. III
Wilkinson, Norman, 1882–1934, vol. III
Wilkinson, Norman, 1878–1971, vol. VII
Wilkinson, Maj.-Gen. Osborn, 1822–1906, vol. I
Wilkinson, Patrick; see Wilkinson, L. P.
Wilkinson, Maj.-Gen. Sir Percival Spearman, 1865–1953, vol. V
Wilkinson, Peter, 1918–1981, vol. VIII
Wilkinson, Reginald Warren Hale, 1882–1973, vol. VII
Wilkinson, Richard Edward, 1901–1972, vol. VII
Wilkinson, Richard James, 1867–1941, vol. IV
Wilkinson, Sir (Robert Francis) Martin, 1911–1900, vol. VIII
Wilkinson, Sir Robert Pelham, 1883–1962, vol. VI
Wilkinson, Sir Russell Facey, 1888–1968, vol. VI
Wilkinson, Spenser; see Wilkinson, H. S.
Wilkinson, Stephen, 1876–1962, vol. VII
Wilkinson, Sydney Frank, 1894–1988, vol. VIII
Wilkinson, Sir Thomas Crowe S.; see Spenser-Wilkinson.
Wilkinson, Rt Rev. Thomas Edward, died 1914, vol. I
Wilkinson, Major Thomas Henry Des Vœux, 1858–1928, vol. II
Wilkinson, Rt Rev. Thomas W., 1825–1909, vol. I
Wilkinson, Walter Sutherland, 1875–1943, vol. IV
Wilkinson, William, 1882–1944, vol. IV
Wilkinson, William Dale, 1893–1973, vol. VII
Wilkinson, Rev. Canon William Evans, 1891–1967, vol. VI
Wilkinson, Sir William Henry, 1858–1930, vol. III
Wilkinson-Guillemard, Hugh; see Wilkinson-Guillemard, W. H. J.
Wilkinson-Guillemard, (Walter) Hugh (John), 1874–1939, vol. III
Wilks, Dick Lloyd, 1923–1985, vol. VIII
Wilks, Rev. William, 1843–1923, vol. II
Will, John Shiress, 1840–1910, vol. I
Will, Robert Ross, 1883–1968, vol. VI
Willan, Col Frank, 1846–1931, vol. III
Willan, Group Captain Frank Andrew, 1915–1981, vol. VIII
Willan, Brig.-Gen. Frank Godfrey, 1878–1957, vol. V
Willan, Sir Harold Curwen, 1896–1971, vol. VII

Willan, Healey, 1880–1968, vol. VI
Willan, Col Henry Percy Douglas, 1848–1912, vol. I
Willan, Col Robert Hugh, 1882–1960, vol. V
Willan, Robert Joseph, 1878–1955, vol. V
Willans, Sir Frederic Jeune, *died* 1949, vol. IV
Willans, Maj.-Gen. Harry, 1892–1943, vol. IV
Willans, Lt-Col Thomas James, 1872–1922, vol. II
Willans, William Henry, 1833–1904, vol. I
Willar, Paul; *see* Villars, Paul.
Willard, E. S. *died* 1915, vol. I
Willard, Frances Elizabeth, 1839–1898, vol. I
Willasey-Wilsey, Maj.-Gen. Anthony Patrick, 1920–1985, vol. VIII
Willcock, Rev. John, 1853–1931, vol. III
Willcock, Hon. John Collings, 1879–1956, vol. V
Willcock, Major Ralph, 1887–1969, vol. VI
Willcocks, G. Waller, *died* 1918, vol. II
Willcocks, Gen. Sir James, 1857–1926, vol. II
Willcocks, Sir William, 1852–1932, vol. III
Willcox, Arthur, 1909–1963, vol. VI
Willcox, Lt-Gen. Sir Henry Beresford Dennitts, 1889–1968, vol. VI
Willcox, Captain Howard James Lionel Walter Kox, *died* 1936, vol. III
Willcox, Lt-Col Walter Temple, 1869–1943, vol. IV
Willcox, Sir William Henry, 1870–1941, vol. IV
Willert, Sir Arthur, 1882–1973, vol. VII
Willert, Paul Ferdinand, 1844–1912, vol. I
Willes, Lt-Col Charles Edward, 1870–1952, vol. V
Willes, Adm. Sir George Lambart A.; *see* Atkinson-Willes.
Willes, Sir George Ommanney, 1823–1901, vol. I
Willes, Richard Augustus, 1881–1966, vol. VI
Willes, William, 1855–1924, vol. II
Willets, Lt-Col Charles Richard Edward, 1880–1931, vol. III
Willett, Alfred, 1837–1913, vol. I
Willett, Captain Basil Rupert, 1896–1966, vol. VI
Willett, Guy William, 1913–1990, vol. VIII
Willett, John Eddowes, 1853–1937, vol. III
Willett, Comdr William Basil, 1919–1976, vol. VII
Willey, Arthur, 1867–1942, vol. IV
Willey, Basil, 1897–1978, vol. VII
Willey, Rt Hon. Frederick Thomas, 1910–1987, vol. VIII
Willey, Octavius George, 1886–1952, vol. V
William-Powlett, Vice-Adm. Sir Peveril Barton Reibey Wallop, 1898–1985, vol. VIII
Williams, 1st Baron, 1892–1966, vol. VI
Williams of Barnburgh, Baron (Life Peer); Thomas Williams, 1888–1967, vol. VI
Williams, A. Franklyn, 1907–1979, vol. VII
Williams, Rt Rev. Aidan; *see* Williams, Rt Rev. Augustine A.
Williams, Sir Alan Meredith, 1909–1972, vol. VII
Williams, Captain Albert, 1864–1926, vol. II
Williams, (Albert) Clifford, *born* 1905, vol. VIII
Williams, Maj.-Gen. Sir Albert Henry Wilmot, 1832–1919, vol. II
Williams, Ven. Aldred; *see* Williams, Ven. E. D. A.
Williams, Alexander, *died* 1930, vol. III
Williams, Sir Alexander Thomas, 1903–1984, vol. VIII
Williams, Alfred Cecil, 1899–1976, vol. VII

Williams, Col Alfred Ernest, 1871–1941, vol. IV
Williams, Alfred Martyn, 1897–1985, vol. VIII
Williams, Alice Helena Alexandra, 1863–1957, vol. V
Williams, Rt Rev. Alwyn Terrell Petre, 1888–1968, vol. VI
Williams, Alyn, *died* 1941, vol. IV
Williams, Aneurin, 1859–1924, vol. II
Williams, Anna, *died* 1924, vol. II
Williams, Sir Anthony James, 1923–1990, vol. VIII
Williams, Rt Rev. Anthony Lewis Elliott, 1892–1975, vol. VII
Williams, Arnold, 1890–1958, vol. V
Williams, Rt Rev. Arthur Acheson, *died* 1914, vol. I
Williams, Brig.-Gen. Arthur Blount Cuthbert, 1860–1918, vol. II
Williams, Lt-Col Arthur Cecil, 1871–1940, vol. III
Williams, Ven. Arthur Charles, 1899–1974, vol. VII
Williams, Arthur de Coetlogon, 1890–1973, vol. VII
Williams, A(rthur) Emlyn, 1910–1976, vol. VII
Williams, (Arthur Frederic) Basil, 1867–1950, vol. IV
Williams, Col Arthur Frederick Carlisle, 1876–1934, vol. III
Williams, Arthur James, 1880–1962, vol. VI
Williams, Arthur John, 1835–1911, vol. I
Williams, Brig.-Gen. Sir Arthur John A.; *see* Allen-Williams.
Williams, Sir (Arthur) Leonard, 1904–1972, vol. VII
Williams, Rt Rev. Arthur Llewellyn, 1856–1919, vol. II
Williams, Rev. Arthur Lukyn, 1853–1943, vol. IV
Williams, Maj.-Gen. Arthur Nicholl, 1894–1982, vol. VIII
Williams, Sir (Arthur) Osmond, 1st Bt (*cr* 1909), 1849–1927, vol. II
Williams, Captain Ashley Paget Wilmot, 1867–1913, vol. I
Williams, Maj.-Gen. Aubrey Ellis, 1888–1977, vol. VII
Williams, Rt Rev. (Augustine) Aidan, 1904–1965, vol. VI
Williams, Brig. Augustus John, 1876–1945, vol. IV
Williams, B. Francis, 1845–1914, vol. I
Williams, Barbara M.; *see* Moray Williams.
Williams, Basil; *see* Williams, A. F. B.
Williams, Sir Benjamin Allen, *died* 1968, vol. VI
Williams, Benjamin H.; *see* Haydn Williams.
Williams, Captain Berkeley Cole Wilmot, 1865–1938, vol. III
Williams, Bernard Warren, 1895–1970, vol. VI
Williams, Sir Brandan Meredith R.; *see* Rhys Williams.
Williams, Lt-Col Brian Robertson, 1909–1980, vol. VII
Williams, Sir Burton Robert, 6th Bt (*cr* 1866), 1889–1917, vol. II
Williams, C. F. Abdy, 1855–1923, vol. II
Williams, Carrington Bonsor, 1889–1981, vol. VIII
Williams, Brig. Cecil James, 1898–1948, vol. IV
Williams, Charles, 1834–1900, vol. I
Williams, Charles, 1838–1904, vol. I
Williams, Rt Hon. Charles, 1886–1955, vol. V
Williams, Lt-Col Charles Augustus M; *see* Muspratt-Williams.
Williams, Rt Rev. Charles David, 1860–1923, vol. II

Williams, Major Charles Edward, 1873–1955, vol. V
Williams, Charles Frederick Victor, 1898–1984, vol. VIII
Williams, Charles Garrett, 1901–1976, vol. VII
Williams, Charles Hanson Greville, 1829–1910, vol. I
Williams, Charles Harold, 1895–1981, vol. VIII
Williams, Sir Charles Henry Trelease, (Sir Harry), 1898–1982, vol. VIII
Williams, Charles Riby, 1857–1924, vol. II
Williams, Sir Charles S.; see Stuart-Williams.
Williams, Captain Charles Shrine, 1895–1973, vol. VII
Williams, Charles Theodore, 1838–1912, vol. I
Williams, Charles Walter Stansby, 1886–1945, vol. IV
Williams, Charles Wodehouse, 1899–1957, vol. V
Williams, Chisholm, 1866–1928, vol. II
Williams, Christmas Price, died 1965, vol. VI
Williams, Christopher A.; see Addams Williams.
Williams, Hon. Christopher Alexander S.; see Sapara-Williams.
Williams, Christopher David, 1873–1934, vol. III
Williams, Clarence Faithfull M.; see Monier-Williams.
Williams, Clifford; see Williams, A. C.
Williams, Conrad Veale, 1903–1969, vol. VI
Williams, Major Craufurd Victor M.; see Monier-Williams.
Williams, Cyril Herbert, 1908–1983, vol. VIII
Williams, Daniel, 1876–1944, vol. IV
Williams, Sir (Daniel) Thomas, died 1973, vol. VII
Williams, David, 1877–1927, vol. II
Williams, Ven. David, 1841–1929, vol. III
Williams, Most Rev. David, 1859–1931, vol. III
Williams, Ven. David, 1862–1936, vol. III
Williams, David, 1865–1941, vol. IV
Williams, David, 1900–1978, vol. VII
Williams, David, 1898–1984, vol. VIII
Williams, David Davey, 1874–1954, vol. V(A)
Williams, Ven. David Edward, 1847–1920, vol. II
Williams, David Gwynne, 1886–1975, vol. VII
Williams, David James, 1897–1972, vol. VII
Williams, David L.; see Llewelyn-Williams.
Williams, David Parry, 1842–1909, vol. I
Williams, Sir David Philip, 3rd Bt (cr 1915), 1909–1970, vol. VI
Williams, Lt-Gen. David Walter, 1839–1909, vol. I
Williams, Sir Dawson, 1854–1928, vol. II
Williams, Denis John, 1908–1990, vol. VIII
Williams, Donald; see Williams, W. D.
Williams, Dorian Joseph George, 1914–1985, vol. VIII
Williams, Dorothy Sylvia L.; see Lloyd-Williams.
Williams, Captain Douglas, 1892–1975, vol. VII
Williams, D(ouglas) Graeme, 1909–1970, vol. VI
Williams, Hon. Sir Dudley, 1889–1963, vol. VI
Williams, E. C., 1892–1973, vol. VII
Williams, E. G. Harcourt, 1880–1957, vol. V
Williams, Edith, died 1919, vol. II
Williams, Rev. Edward Adams, 1826–1913, vol. I
Williams, Edward Cecil, 1867–1939, vol. III
Williams, Maj.-Gen. Edward Charles Ingouville, 1861–1916, vol. II

Williams, Sir Edward Charles Sparshott, 1831–1907, vol. I
Williams, Major Edward Ernest, 1875–1915, vol. I
Williams, Edward Francis; see Baron Francis-Williams.
Williams, Brig.-Gen. Edward George, 1867–1941, vol. IV
Williams, Rt Hon. Sir Edward John, 1890–1963, vol. VI
Williams, Sir Edward Leader, 1828–1910, vol. I
Williams, Brig. Edward Stephen Bruce, 1892–1977, vol. VII
Williams, Edward Wilmot, 1826–1913, vol. I
Williams, Rev. Eleazar, died 1905, vol. I
Williams, Lt-Col Eliot C.; see Crawshay-Williams.
Williams, Rt Hon. Sir Ellis H.; see Hume-Williams.
Williams, Emlyn; see Williams, G. E.
Williams, Eric, 1911–1983, vol. VIII
Williams, Eric Charles, 1915–1980, vol. VII
Williams, Rt Hon. Eric Eustace, 1911–1981, vol. VIII
Williams, Eric W.; see Watson-Williams.
Williams, Ernest Edwin, 1866–1935, vol. III
Williams, Sir Ernest H.; see Hodder-Williams, Sir J. E.
Williams, Sir Ernest Hillas, 1899–1965, vol. VI
Williams, (Ernest) Rohan, 1906–1963, vol. VI
Williams, Ethel Mary Nucella, 1863–1948, vol. IV
Williams, Sir Evan, 1st Bt (cr 1935), 1871–1959, vol. V
Williams, Ven. (Evan Daniel) Aldred, 1879–1951, vol. V
Williams, Evan James, 1903–1945, vol. IV
Williams, Sir (Evan) Owen, 1890–1969, vol. VI
Williams, Bt-Col Evelyn Hugh Watkin, 1884–1934, vol. III
Williams, F. Harald; see Ward, Rev. Frederick W. O.
Williams, Major Francis V.; see Vaughan-Williams.
Williams, Francis Wigley Greswolde G.; see Greswolde-Williams.
Williams, Surg. Rear-Adm. (D) Frank Reginald Parry, 1897–1965, vol. VI
Williams, Franklyn; see Williams, A. F.
Williams, Sir Frederic Calland, 1911–1977, vol. VII
Williams, Rev. Frederick Billingsley Ambrose, 1870–1932, vol. III
Williams, Brig. and Chief Paymaster Frederick Christian, 1891–1970, vol. VI
Williams, Rev. Frederick Farewell Sanigear, 1870–1956, vol. V
Williams, Sir Frederick Law, 7th Bt (cr 1866), 1862–1921, vol. II
Williams, Frederick Sims, 1855–1941, vol. IV
Williams, Sir Frederick William, 5th Bt (cr 1866), 1888–1913, vol. I
Williams, Brig.-Gen. G. Coventry, 1860–1947, vol. IV
Williams, Very Rev. Garfield Hodder, 1881–1960, vol. V
Williams, Geoffrey Milson John, 1923–1988, vol. VIII
Williams, Geoffrey Sydney, 1871–1952, vol. V
Williams, Sir George, 1821–1905, vol. I
Williams, George, 1879–1951, vol. V

Williams, Sir George Clark, 1st Bt (*cr* 1955), 1878–1958, vol. V

Williams, Comdr George Davies, 1879–1947, vol. IV

Williams, (George) Emlyn, 1905–1987, vol. VIII

Williams, Rev. George H., 1859–1926, vol. II

Williams, George L; *see* Lowsley-Williams.

Williams, Brig.-Gen. George Mostyn, 1868–1943, vol. IV

Williams, Gerald Wellington, 1903–1989, vol. VIII

Williams, Rt Rev. Gershom Mott, 1857–1923, vol. II

Williams, Gertrude, (Lady Williams), 1897–1983, vol. VIII

Williams, Gilbert Milner, 1898–1979, vol. VII

Williams, Maj.-Gen. Sir Godfrey, 1859–1940, vol. III

Williams, Godfrey Herbert, 1875–1956, vol V

Williams, Sir Griffith Goodland, 1890–1974, vol. VII

Williams, Gen. Sir Guy Charles, 1881–1959, vol. V

Williams, Gwilym, 1839–1906, vol. I

Williams, Sir Gwilym Ffrangcon, 1902–1969, vol. VI

Williams, Rt Rev. Gwilym Owen, 1913–1990, vol. VIII

Williams, Sir Gwilym Tecwyn, 1913–1989, vol. VIII

Williams, Gwyn, 1904–1955, vol. V

Williams, Gwynne Evan Owen, *died* 1958, vol. V

Williams, Harcourt; *see* Williams, E. G. H.

Williams, Harley; *see* Williams, J. H. H.

Williams, Lt-Gen. Sir Harold, 1897–1971, vol. VII

Williams, Harold Beck, 1889–1969, vol. VI

Williams, Very Rev. Harold Claude Noel, 1914–1990, vol. VIII

Williams, Harold H.; *see* Heathcote-Williams.

Williams, Sir Harold Herbert, 1880–1964, vol. VI

Williams, Sir Harry; *see* Williams, Sir C. H. T.

Williams, Hon. Sir Hartley, 1843–1929, vol. III

Williams, Henry, 1850–1933, vol. III

Williams, Col Henry David, 1854–1924, vol. II

Williams, Lt-Gen. Sir Henry Francis, 1825–1907, vol. I

Williams, Rt Rev. Henry Herbert, 1872–1961, vol. VI

Williams, Lt-Col Henry John, 1870–1935, vol. III

Williams, Sir Henry Morton Leech, 1913–1989, vol. VIII

Williams, Henry Owen, 1855–1943, vol. IV

Williams, Herbert, 1862–1916, vol. II

Williams, Sir Herbert Geraint, 1st Bt (*cr* 1953), 1884–1954, vol. V

Williams, Rt Rev. Herbert William, *died* 1937, vol. III

Williams, Howard, 1837–1931, vol. III

Williams, Sir Howell Jones, *died* 1939, vol. III

Williams, Hubert Llewelyn, 1890–1964, vol. VI

Williams, Rev. Hugh, 1843–1911, vol. I

Williams, Hugh Anthony Glanmore, 1904–1969, vol. VI

Williams, Maj.-Gen. Sir Hugh Bruce Bruce-, 1865–1942, vol. IV

Williams, Rev. Hugh Cernyw, 1843–1937, vol. III

Williams, Sir Hugh Grenville, 6th Bt (*cr* 1798), 1889–1961, vol. VI

Williams, Hugh L.; *see* Lloyd-Williams.

Williams, Hugh Noel, 1870–1925, vol. II

Williams, Adm. Hugh Pigot, 1858–1934, vol. III

Williams, Sir (I.) Thomas, 1853–1941, vol. IV

Williams, Sir Ifor, 1881–1965, vol. VI

Williams, Iolo Aneurin, 1890–1962, vol. VI

Williams, Isaac John, 1875–1939, vol. III

Williams, Ivor Maredydd B.; *see* Bankes-Williams.

Williams, J. H., 1855–1942, vol. IV

Williams, J. Lloyd, *died* 1945, vol. IV

Williams, Jack F.; *see* Fox-Williams.

Williams, James, 1851–1911, vol. I

Williams, James Alexander, *born* 1856, vol. II

Williams, Ven. James Evan, *died* 1953, vol. V

Williams, Captain James Evan L.; *see* Lloyd-Williams.

Williams, James Howard, 1897–1958, vol. V

Williams, James Leslie, 1870–1949, vol. IV

Williams, Hon. James Rowland, 1860–1916, vol. II

Williams, John, 1861–1922, vol. II

Williams, Sir John, 1st Bt, 1840–1926, vol. II

Williams, Lt-Col John, 1874–1942, vol. IV

Williams, John, *died* 1951, vol. V

Williams, John Basil, 1906–1953, vol. V

Williams, John Carvell, 1821–1907, vol. I

Williams, John Charles, 1861–1939, vol. III

Williams, Sir John Coldbrook H.; *see* Hanbury-Williams.

Williams, John David, 1853–1923, vol. II

Williams, John Elwyn, 1921–1990, vol. VIII

Williams, Sir John Fischer, 1870–1947, vol. IV

Williams, Sir John Francis, 1901–1982, vol. VIII

Williams, Very Rev. John Frederick, 1907–1983, vol. VIII

Williams, Maj.-Gen. Sir John H.; *see* Hanbury-Williams.

Williams, John H.; *see* Haynes-Williams.

Williams, (John Hargreaves) Harley, *died* 1974, vol. VII

Williams, John Haulfryn, 1908–1980, vol. VII

Williams, John Henry, 1870–1936, vol. III

Williams, Sir John Lias Cecil C.; *see* Cecil-Williams.

Williams, Sir (John Lloyd Vaughan) Seymour, 1868–1945, vol. IV

Williams, Rev. John Owen, 1853–1932, vol. III

Williams, Captain Sir John Protheroe, *born* 1896, vol. VIII

Williams, Sir John Rolleston L.; *see* Lort-Williams.

Williams, John Trevor, 1921–1987, vol. VIII

Williams, Maj.-Gen. John William C.; *see* Channing Williams.

Williams, Sir John William Collman, 1823–1911, vol. I

Williams, John Williams, 1885–1957, vol. V

Williams, Joseph Grout, 1848–1923, vol. II

Williams, Rt Hon. Joseph Powell, 1840–1904, vol. I

Williams, Rt Rev. Joseph Watkin, 1857–1934, vol. III

Williams, Rt Hon. Sir Joshua Strange, 1837–1915, vol. I

Williams, Katharine Georgina L.; *see* Lloyd-Williams.

Williams, Kenneth; *see* Williams, O. K.

Williams, Kenneth Charles, 1926–1988, vol. VIII

Williams, Lt-Col Kenneth Greville, 1892–1972, vol. VII

Williams, L. Gwendolen, *died* 1955, vol. V

Williams, Laurence Frederic Rushbrook, 1890–1978, vol. VII

Williams, Maj.-Gen. Lawrence Henry, 1834–1916, vol. II

Williams, Rt Rev. Lennox Waldron, 1859–1958, vol. V

Williams, Sir Leonard; *see* Williams, Sir A. L.

Williams, Leonard John, 1894–1975, vol. VII

Williams, Leonard Llewelyn Bulkeley, 1861–1939, vol. III

Williams, Col Leslie Gwatkin, 1878–1926, vol. II

Williams, Maj.-Gen. Sir Leslie Hamlyn, 1892–1965, vol. VI

Williams, Leslie Harry, 1909–1978, vol. VII

Williams, Leslie Herbert Whitby, 1893–1972, vol. VII

Williams, Leslie Thomas Douglas, 1905–1976, vol. VII

Williams, Lily, 1874–1940, vol. III

Williams, Llywelyn, 1911–1965, vol. VI

Williams, Margaret Lindsay, *died* 1960, vol. V

Williams, Mary, 1882–1977, vol. VII

Williams, Mary Atkinson, *died* 1949, vol. IV

Williams, Mary Bridget, 1933–1989, vol. VIII

Williams, Sir Michael Sanigear, 1911–1984, vol. VIII

Williams, Monier Faithfull M.; *see* Monier-Williams.

Williams, Sir Monier M.; *see* Monier-Williams.

Williams, Montagu Sneade Faithfull M.; *see* Monier-Williams.

Williams, Morgan Stuart, 1846–1909, vol. I

Williams, Captain Nevill Glennie G.; *see* Garnons Williams.

Williams, Neville John, 1924–1977, vol. VII

Williams, Rev. Norman Powell, 1883–1943, vol. IV

Williams, Brig.-Gen. Oliver de Lancey, 1875–1959, vol. V

Williams, Orlando Cyprian, (Orlo), 1883–1967, vol. VI

Williams, Sir Osmond; *see* Williams, Sir A. O.

Williams, Sir Owen; *see* Williams, Sir E. O.

Williams, Owen Gwyn Revell, 1886–1954, vol. V

Williams, Owen Herbert, 1884–1962, vol. VI

Williams, Owen John, 1850–1908, vol. I

Williams, (Owen) Kenneth, 1928–1984, vol. VIII

Williams, Lt-Gen. Owen Lewis Cope, 1836–1904, vol. I

Williams, Owen Thomas, 1877–1913, vol. I

Williams, Patrick W.; *see* Watson-Williams.

Williams, Penry, 1866–1945, vol. IV

Williams, Rev. Philip, *died* 1933, vol. III

Williams, Sir Philip Francis Cunningham, 2nd Bt (*cr* 1915), 1884–1958, vol. V

Williams, Philip Maynard, 1920–1984, vol. VIII

Williams, Sir Ralph Champneys, 1848–1927, vol. II

Williams, Ralph Paul, 1874–1939, vol. III

Williams, Ralph V.; *see* Vaughan Williams.

Williams, Ralph Wilfred H.; *see* Hodder-Williams.

Williams, Brig.-Gen. Raymond Burlton, 1855–1929, vol. III

Williams, Raymond Henry, 1921–1988, vol. VIII

Williams, Sir Reginald Lawrence William, 7th Bt (*cr* 1798), 1900–1971, vol. VII

Williams, Lt-Col Sir Rhys Rhys-, 1st Bt (*cr* 1918), 1865–1955, vol. V

Williams, Air Marshal Sir Richard, 1890–1980, vol. VII

Williams, Richard Aelwyn Ellis, 1901–1981, vol. VIII

Williams, Richard James, 1876–1964, vol. VI

Williams, Sir Richard John, 1853–1941, vol. IV

Williams, Richard Tecwyn, 1909–1979, vol. VII

Williams, Robert, 1881–1936, vol. III

Williams, Sir Robert, 1st Bt (*cr* 1928), 1860–1938, vol. III

Williams, Ven. Robert, 1863–1938, vol. III

Williams, Col Sir Robert, 1st Bt (*cr* 1915), 1848–1943, vol. IV

Williams, Robert Allan, *died* 1951, vol. V

Williams, Rev. Robert C.; *see* Camber-Williams.

Williams, Lt-Col Robert Carlisle, 1880–1964, vol. VI

Williams, Robert Emmanuel, 1900–1988, vol. VIII

Williams, Maj.-Gen. Robert Ernest, 1855–1943, vol. IV

Williams, Sir Robert Ernest, 9th Bt (*cr* 1866), 1924–1976, vol. VII

Williams, Robert James P.; *see* Probyn-Williams.

Williams, Robert Percy H.; *see* Hodder-Williams.

Williams, Robert Stenhouse, 1871–1932, vol. III

Williams, Robert Thesiger W.; *see* Watkin-Williams.

Williams, Rohan; *see* Williams, E. R.

Williams, Roland Edmund Lomax Vaughan, 1866–1949, vol. IV

Williams, Rt Hon. Sir Roland Lomax Bowdler Vaughan, 1838–1916, vol. II

Williams, Sir Rolf Dudley D.; *see* Dudley-Williams.

Williams, Romer, 1850–1942, vol. IV

Williams, Rt Rev. Ronald Ralph, 1906–1979, vol. VII

Williams, Major Ronald Samuel Ainslie, 1890–1971, vol. VII

Williams, Ronald Watkins, 1907–1958, vol. V

Williams, Sir Roy Ellis H.; *see* Hume-Williams.

Williams, Captain Rupert Stanley G.; *see* Gwatkin-Williams.

Williams, Ven. Samuel, 1822–1907, vol. I

Williams, Rev. Samuel Blackwell G.; *see* Guest Williams.

Williams, Samuel Charles Evans, 1842–1926, vol. II

Williams, Sir Seymour; *see* Williams, Sir J. L. V. S.

Williams, Stanley, 1911–1990, vol. VIII

Williams, Lt-Col. Stanley Price, 1885–1977, vol. VII

Williams, Stuart Graeme, 1914–1986, vol. VIII

Williams, Brig.-Gen. Sydney Frederick, 1866–1942, vol. IV

Williams, Tennessee, (Thomas Lanier Williams) 1911–1983, vol. VIII

Williams, Terrick, 1860–1936, vol. III

Williams, Theodore Rowland, 1889–1964, vol. VI

Williams, Rev. Thomas, *died* 1915, vol. I

Williams, Sir Thomas, 1893–1967, vol. VI

Williams, Sir Thomas; *see* Williams, Sir D. T.

Williams, Sir Thomas; *see* Williams, Sir I. T.

Williams, Sir Thomas; *see* Williams, Sir W. T.

Williams, Very Rev. Thomas Alfred, 1870–1941, vol. IV

Williams, Rev. Thomas Charles, *died* 1927, vol. II

Williams, Thomas Christopher, 1913–1972, vol. VII

Williams, Thomas; *see* Hudson-Williams.

Williams, Sir Thomas Herbert P.; *see* Parry-Williams.

Williams, Thomas Jeremiah, 1872–1919, vol. II

Williams, Ven. Thomas John, 1889–1956, vol. V

Williams, Thomas Lanier; *see* Williams, Tennessee.

Williams, Most Rev. Thomas Leighton, 1877–1946, vol. IV

Williams, Sir Thomas Marchant, 1845–1914, vol. I

Williams, Air Marshal Sir Thomas Melling, 1899–1956, vol. V

Williams, Rev. Thomas Rhondda, 1860–1945, vol. IV

Williams, Maj.-Gen. Thomas Rhys, 1884–1950, vol. IV

Williams, Lt-Col Thomas Samuel Beauchamp, 1877–1927, vol. II

Williams, Thurston Monier, 1924–1985, vol. VIII

Williams, Valentine, 1883–1946, vol. IV

Williams, Victor Erle N.; see Nash-Williams.

Williams, W. H.; see Howard-Williams.

Williams, W. Llewelyn, 1867–1922, vol. II

Williams, W. Phillpotts, 1860–1916, vol. II

Williams, Engr-Comdr Walter Kent, died 1914, vol. I

Williams, Maj.-Gen. Walter David Abbott, 1897–1973, vol. VII

Williams, Walter Nalder, 1880–1966, vol. VI

Williams, Rt Rev. Watkin Herbert, 1845–1944, vol. IV

Williams, Rev. Watkin Wynn, 1859–1944, vol. IV

Williams, Maj.-Gen. Weir De Lancey, 1872–1961, vol. VI

Williams, Very Rev. William, died 1930, vol. III

Williams, Engr-Captain William Arthur, 1882–1953, vol. V

Williams, William Daniel, 1888–1970, vol. VI

Williams, Surg.-Gen. Sir William Daniel Campbell, 1856–1919, vol. II

Williams, (William) Donald, 1919–1990, vol. VIII

Williams, Sir William Emrys, 1896–1977, vol. VII

Williams, Sir William Frederick, 4th Bt (cr 1866), 1886–1905, vol. I

Williams, Sir William Grenville, 4th Bt (cr 1798), 1844–1904, vol. I

Williams, William Henry, 1852–1941, vol. IV

Williams, Col William Hugh, 1857–1938, vol. III

Williams, Sir William John, 1828–1903, vol. I

Williams, William John, 1878–1952, vol. V

Williams, Lt-Col Sir William Jones, 1904–1976, vol. VII

Williams, Sir William Law, 8th Bt (cr 1866), 1907–1960, vol. V

Williams, Rt Rev. William Leonard, 1829–1916, vol. II

Williams, Hon. William Micah, died 1924, vol. II

Williams, William Owen, 1860–1911, vol. I

Williams, William Penry, 1892–1981, vol. VIII

Williams, Col William Picton B.; see Bradley-Williams.

Williams, Sir William Richard, 1879–1961, vol. VI

Williams, William Richard, 1895–1963, vol. VI

Williams, Sir William Robert, 3rd Bt (cr 1866), 1860–1903, vol. I

Williams, William St John F.; see Francis-Williams.

Williams, Sir (William) Thomas, 1915–1986, vol. VIII

Williams, Sir William Willoughby, 5th Bt (cr 1798), 1888–1932, vol. III

Williams-Bulkeley, Sir Richard Henry; see Bulkeley.

Williams-Drummond, Sir James Hamlyn Williams; see Drummond.

Williams-Drummond, Sir William Hugh Dudley; see Drummond.

Williams-Ellis, Amabel, (Lady Williams-Ellis); see Williams-Ellis, M. A. N.

Williams-Ellis, Sir (Bertram) Clough, 1883–1978, vol. VII

Williams-Ellis, Sir Clough; see Williams-Ellis, Sir B. C.

Williams-Ellis, Mary Annabel Nassau, (Amabel), (Lady Williams-Ellis), 1894–1984, vol. VIII

Williams-Freeman, Comdr Frederick Arthur Peere, 1889–1939, vol. III

Williams-Taylor, Sir Frederick, 1863–1945, vol. IV

Williams-Thomas, Lt-Col Frank S., 1879–1942, vol. IV

Williams-Thomas, Joseph Silvers; see Thomas.

Williams-Thomas, Lt-Col Reginald Silvers, 1914–1990, vol. VIII

Williams Wynn, Frederick R., 1865–1940, vol. III

Williams-Wynn, Col Sir Herbert Lloyd Watkin, 7th Bt, 1860–1944, vol. IV

Williams-Wynn, Col Sir (Owen) Watkin, 10th Bt, 1904–1988, vol. VIII

Williams-Wynn, Col Sir Robert William Herbert Watkin, 9th Bt, 1862–1951, vol. V

Williams-Wynn, Col Sir Watkin; see Williams-Wynn, Col Sir O. W.

Williams-Wynn, Sir Watkin, 8th Bt, 1891–1949, vol. IV

Williamson, Baron (Life Peer); Thomas Williamson 1897–1983, vol. VIII

Williamson, Captain Adolphus Huddleston, 1869–1918, vol. II

Williamson, Alec, 1886–1975, vol. VII

Williamson, Sir Alexander, 1879–1971, vol. VII

Williamson, Alexander William, 1824–1904, vol. I

Williamson, Air Comdt Dame Alice Mary, 1903–1983, vol. VIII

Williamson, Alice Muriel, 1869–1933, vol. III

Williamson, Andrew, died 1937, vol. III

Williamson, Rt Rev. Andrew Wallace, 1856–1926, vol. II

Williamson, Benjamin, 1827–1916, vol. II

Williamson, Bruce, 1893–1984, vol. VIII

Williamson, Mrs Catherine Ellis, 1896–1977, vol. VII

Williamson, Rev. Charles David Robertson, 1853–1943, vol. IV

Williamson, Sir Charles Hedworth, 10th Bt, 1903–1946, vol. IV

Williamson, Charles Norris, 1859–1920, vol. II

Williamson, Mrs Charles Norris; see Williamson, Alice Muriel.

Williamson, Colin Martin, 1887–1976, vol. VII

Williamson, David, 1868–1955, vol. V

Williamson, David, 1916–1980, vol. VII

Williamson, David Robertson, 1830–1913, vol. I

Williamson, Rt Rev. Edward William, 1892–1953, vol. V

Williamson, Francis John, 1833–1920, vol. II

Williamson, Brig.-Gen. Sir Frederic Herbert, 1876–1939, vol. III

Williamson, Frederick, 1891–1935, vol. III

Williamson, Sir George Alexander, 1898–1975, vol. VII

Williamson, George Charles, 1858–1942, vol. IV

Williamson, George Watkins, 1875–1957, vol. V

Williamson, Harold, 1872–1935, vol. III
Williamson, Sir Hedworth, 8th Bt, 1827–1900, vol. I
Williamson, Sir Hedworth, 9th Bt, 1867–1942, vol. IV
Williamson, Henry, 1895–1977, vol. VII
Williamson, Rev. Henry Drummond, 1854–1926, vol. II
Williamson, Rev. Henry Trevor, died 1940, vol. III
Williamson, Herbert, 1872–1924, vol. II
Williamson, Sir Horace, 1880–1965, vol. VI
Williamson, Gp Captain Hugh Alexander, 1885–1979, vol. VII
Williamson, Hugh R.; see Ross Williamson.
Williamson, Sir James, 1839–1932, vol. III
Williamson, Sir James, 1877–1959, vol. V
Williamson, James Alexander, 1886–1964, vol. VI
Williamson, John, 1915–1982, vol. VIII
Williamson, Col John Francis, 1851–1930, vol. III
Williamson, John Thoburn, 1907–1958, vol. V
Williamson, Kenneth Bertram, 1875–1959, vol. V
Williamson, Lawrence Collingwood, 1886–1955, vol. V
Williamson, Ven. Montague Blamire, 1863–1939, vol. III
Williamson, Oliver Key, died 1941, vol. IV
Williamson, Air Vice-Marshal Peter Greville Kaye, 1923–1982, vol. VIII
Williamson, Reginald Pole R.; see Ross Williamson.
Williamson, Richard Harcourt, 1879–1941, vol. IV
Williamson, Richard Thomas, 1862–1937, vol. III
Williamson, Col Robert Frederic, 1843–1938, vol. III
Williamson, Robert Wood, 1856–1932, vol. III
Williamson, Samuel, died 1950, vol. IV
Williamson, Stephen, 1827–1903, vol. I
Williamson, Thomas Bateson, 1915–1985, vol. VIII
Williamson, Thomas Broadwood, 1911–1963, vol. VI
Williamson, Victor Alexander, 1838–1924, vol. II
Williamson, Sir Walter James Franklin, 1867–1954, vol. V
Williamson, Rev. William, 1851–1936, vol. III
Williamson-Noble, Frederick Arnold, 1889–1969, vol. VI
Willingdon, 1st Marquis of, 1866–1941, vol. IV
Willingdon, 2nd Marquess of, 1899–1979, vol. VII
Willingdon, Marchioness of; (Marie Adelaide), 1875–1960, vol. V
Willink, Rt Hon. Sir Henry Urmston, 1st Bt, 1894–1973, vol. VII
Willink, Very Rev. John Wakefield, 1858–1927, vol. II
Willis, Sir Addington; see Willis, Sir W. A.
Willis, Hon. Albert Charles, 1876–1954, vol. V
Willis, Rt Rev. Alfred, 1836–1920, vol. II
Willis, Admiral of the Fleet Sir Algernon Usborne, 1889–1976, vol. VII
Willis, Anthony Armstrong, 1897–1976, vol. VII
Willis, Arthur d'Anyers, 1879–1953, vol. V
Willis, Charles Armine, 1881–1975, vol. VII
Willis, Col Charles Fancourt, 1854–1918, vol. II
Willis, Lt-Col Charles Hope, 1859–1940, vol. III
Willis, Maj.-Gen. Edward Henry, 1870–1961, vol. VI
Willis, Sir Edward William, 1849–1941, vol. IV
Willis, Ernest William, 1874–1939, vol. III
Willis, Rt Hon. Eustace George, 1903–1987, vol. VIII
Willis, Frank, 1865–1932, vol. III

Willis, Sir Frank; see Willis, Sir Z. F.
Willis, Captain Frank Reginald, 1881–1964, vol. VI
Willis, Rev. Frederic Earle d'Anyers, 1869–1940, vol. III
Willis, Rev. Frederic William, 1842–1930, vol. III
Willis, Sir Frederick James, 1863–1946, vol. IV
Willis, Rt Rev. Frederick Roberts, 1900–1976, vol. VII
Willis, Sir George Henry Smith, 1823–1900, vol. I
Willis, Col Sir George Henry, 1875–1940, vol. III
Willis, Paymaster Captain George Hughlings Armstrong, 1863–1934, vol. III
Willis, Harold Infield, 1902–1986, vol. VIII
Willis, Hector Ford, 1909–1989, vol. VIII
Willis, Hon. Henry, 1860–1950, vol. IV
Willis, John Christopher, 1868–1958, vol. V
Willis, Maj.-Gen. John Christopher Temple, 1900–1969, vol. VI
Willis, John Henry, 1887–1989, vol. VIII
Willis, Rt Rev. John Jamieson, 1872–1954, vol. V
Willis, Sir John Ramsay, 1908–1988, vol. VIII
Willis, John Robert, 1896–1982, vol. VIII
Willis, Joseph George, 1861–1924, vol. II
Willis, Olive Christine, (Lady Willis), 1895–1987, vol. VIII
Willis, Col Richard ffolliott, 1875–1960, vol. V
Willis, Major Richard Raymond, 1876–1966, vol. VI
Willis, Rupert Allan, 1898–1980, vol. VII
Willis, Samuel William Ward, 1870–1948, vol. IV
Willis, Sir (Walter) Addington, 1862–1953, vol. V
Willis, Sir William, 1821–1906, vol. I
Willis, William, 1835–1911, vol. I
Willis, Comdr William John Adlam, 1894–1982, vol. VIII
Willis, Ven. William Newcombe de Laval, 1846–1916, vol. II
Willis, William Outhwaite, 1870–1940, vol. III
Willis, Sir (Zwinglius) Frank, 1890–1974, vol. VII
Willis-Bund, John William, 1843–1928, vol. II
Willis-O'Connor, Col Henry; see O'Connor.
Willison, Brig. Arthur Cecil, 1896–1966, vol. VI
Willison, Herbert, died 1943, vol. IV
Willison, Sir John Stephen, 1856–1927, vol. II
Willkie, Wendell Lewis, 1892–1944, vol. IV
Willmer, Rt Hon. Sir Gordon; see Willmer, Rt Hon. Sir H. G.
Willmer, Rt Hon. Sir (Henry) Gordon, 1899–1983, vol. VIII
Willmore, Henry Horace Albert, 1871–1919, vol. II
Willmot, Joseph William, 1849–1929, vol. III
Willmot, Roger Boulton, 1892–1964, vol. VI
Willmott, Harry, 1851–1931, vol. III
Willmott, Sir Maurice Gordon, 1894–1977, vol. VII
Willock, Brig.-Gen. Frederick George, died 1955, vol. V
Willock, Air Vice-Marshal Robert Peel, 1893–1973, vol. VII
Willock-Pollen, Henry Court, 1860–1934, vol. III
Willott, Lt-Col Roland Lancaster, 1912–1984, vol. VIII
Willoughby de Broke, 18th Baron, 1844–1902, vol. I
Willoughby de Broke, 19th Baron, 1869–1923, vol. II
Willoughby de Broke, 20th Baron, 1896–1986, vol. VIII

Willoughby de Eresby, Lord; Timothy Gilbert Heathcote-Drummond-Willoughby, 1936–1963, vol. VI

Willoughby, Brig.-Gen. Hon. Charles Strathavon Heathcote-Drummond-, 1870–1949, vol. IV

Willoughby, Lt-Col Hon. Claud Heathcote-Drummond, 1872–1950, vol. IV

Willoughby, Col Hon. Claude Henry Comaraich, 1862–1932, vol. III

Willoughby, Col Douglas Vere, 1882–1949, vol. IV

Willoughby, Rear-Adm. Guy, 1902–1987, vol. VIII

Willoughby, Maj.-Gen. James Fortnom, 1844–1922, vol. II

Willoughby, Major Sir John Christopher, 5th Bt, 1859–1918, vol. II

Willoughby, Leonard Ashley, 1885–1977, vol. VII

Willoughby, Brig.-Gen. Michael Edward, 1864–1939, vol. III

Willoughby, Lt-Gen. Michael Weekes, 1833–1925, vol. II

Willoughby, Percival Robert Augustus, 1868–1913, vol. I

Willoughby, Wellington Bartley, 1859–1932, vol. III

Willoughby-Osborne, Col Arthur de Vere, 1869–1933, vol. III

Willox, Sir John Archibald, 1842–1905, vol. I

Wills, Rt Hon. Sir Alfred, 1828–1912, vol. I

Wills, Captain Arnold Stancomb, 1877–1961, vol. VI

Wills, Arthur Walters, 1868–1948, vol. IV

Wills, Lt-Col Caleb Shera, 1834–1906, vol. I

Wills, Cecil Upton, died 1954, vol. V

Wills, Charles James, 1842–1912, vol. I

Wills, Vice-Adm. Charles Samuel, died 1931, vol. III

Wills, Edith Agnes, 1892–1970, vol. VI

Wills, Lt-Col Sir Edward; see Wills, Lt-Col Sir Ernest E. de W.

Wills, Sir Edward Chaning, 2nd Bt (cr 1904), 1861–1921, vol. II

Wills, Sir Edward Payson, 1st Bt (cr 1904), 1834–1910, vol. I

Wills, Lt-Col Sir (Ernest) Edward (de Winton), 4th Bt, 1903–1983, vol. VIII

Wills, Sir Ernest Salter, 3rd Bt, (cr 1904), 1869–1958, vol. V

Wills, Sir Frank William, 1852–1932, vol. III

Wills, Sir Frederick, 1st Bt (cr 1897), 1838–1909, vol. I

Wills, Rev. Freeman, died 1913, vol. I

Wills, Sir George Alfred, 1st Bt (cr 1923), 1854–1928, vol. II

Wills, Sir (George) Peter (Vernon), 3rd Bt (cr 1923), 1922–1945, vol. IV

Wills, Sir George Vernon Proctor, 2nd Bt (cr 1923), 1887–1931, vol. III

Wills, Sir Gerald, 1905–1969, vol. VI

Wills, Henry Herbert, 1856–1922, vol. II

Wills, Herbert W., died 1937, vol. III

Wills, Dame Janet Stancomb Graham S.; see Stancomb-Wills.

Wills, John Joseph, 1877–1971, vol. VII

Wills, Joseph Lyttleton, born 1899, vol. VIII

Wills, Brig. Sir Kenneth Agnew, 1896–1977, vol. VII

Wills, Leonard Johnston, 1844–1979, vol. VII

Wills, Rev. Percival Banks, died 1936, vol. III

Wills, Sir Peter; see Wills, Sir G. P. V.

Wills, Philip Aubrey, 1907–1978, vol. VII

Wills, Richard Lloyd Joseph, 1914–1969, vol. VI

Wills, Dame Violet Edith, died 1964, vol. VI

Wills, Walter Kenneth, 1872–1968, vol. VI

Wills, Wilfrid Dewhurst, 1898–1954, vol. V

Wills, Major William Arthur, 1863–1937, vol. III

Willshire, Sir Arthur Reginald Thomas Maxwell-, 2nd Bt, 1850–1919, vol. II

Willshire, Sir Gerard Arthur Maxwell-, 3rd Bt, 1892–1947, vol. IV

Willson, Rev. Archdall Beaumont Wynne, died 1958, vol. V

Willson, Beckles, 1869–1942, vol. IV

Willson, Leslie, died 1924, vol. II

Willson, Maj.-Gen. Sir Mildmay Willson, 1847–1912, vol. I

Willson, Rt Rev. St J. Basil Wynne, 1868–1946, vol. IV

Willson, Rev. Thomas B., 1851–1932, vol. III

Willson, Thomas Olaf, 1880–1973, vol. VII

Willson, Sir Walter Stuart James, 1876–1952, vol. V

Willson, William Thomas C.; see Curtis-Willson.

Willway, Brig. Alfred Cedric Cowan, 1898–1980, vol. VII

Willway, Brig. Cedric; see Willway, Brig. A. C. C.

Willy; see Gauthier-Villars, Henry.

Willyams, Arthur Champion Phillips, 1837–1917, vol. II

Willyams, Edward Brydges, 1836–1916, vol. II

Willyams, Bt Col Edward Neynoe, 1891–1964, vol. VI

Wilmer, Brig. Eric Randal Gordon, 1882–1958, vol. V

Wilmer, Rev. John Kidd, died 1928, vol. II, vol. III

Wilmers, John Geoffrey, 1920–1984, vol. VIII

Wilmot of Selmeston, 1st Baron, 1895–1964, vol. VI

Wilmot, Hon. Alexander, 1836–1923, vol. II

Wilmot, Col Arthur E.; see Eardley-Wilmot.

Wilmot, Captain Sir Arthur Ralph, 7th Bt (cr 1759), 1909–1942, vol. IV

Wilmot, Air Vice-Marshal Aubrey S.; see Sidney-Wilmot.

Wilmot, Chester, (Reginald William Winchester Wilmot), 1911–1954, vol. V

Wilmot, Sir Henry, 5th Bt (cr 1759), 1831–1901, vol. I

Wilmot, Captain Cecil F. E.; see Eardley-Wilmot.

Wilmot, Rev. Ernest Augustus E.; see Eardley-Wilmot.

Wilmot, Harold, 1895–1966, vol. VI

Wilmot, Hugh Eden E.; see Eardley-Wilmot.

Wilmot, Sir John E.; see Eardley-Wilmot.

Wilmot, May E.; see Eardley-Wilmot.

Wilmot, Sir Ralph Henry Sacheverel, 6th Bt (cr 1759), 1875–1918, vol. II

Wilmot, Reginald William Winchester; see Wilmot, C.

Wilmot, Maj.-Gen. Revell E.; see Eardley-Wilmot.

Wilmot, Sir Robert Arthur, 8th Bt, 1939–1974, (cr 1759), vol. VII

Wilmot, Sir Robert Rodney, 6th Bt (cr 1772), 1853–1931, vol. III

Wilmot, Sir Sainthill E.; see Eardley-Wilmot.

Wilmot, Rear-Adm. Sir Sydney Marow E.; *see* Eardley-Wilmot.

Wilmot-Smith, Comdr Andrew, *died* 1937, vol. III

Wilmott, Alfred James, 1888–1950, vol. IV

Wilmshurst, Thomas Percival, *died* 1950, vol. IV

Wilsden, Rev. Joseph Samuel, 1835–1914, vol. I

Wilsey, Maj.Gen. Anthony Patrick W.; *see* Willasey-Wilsey.

Wilsey, Maj.-Gen. John Harold Owen, 1904–1961, vol. VI

Wilshaw, Sir Edward, 1879–1968, vol. VI

Wilshere, Alfred Henry, 1854–1927, vol. II, vol. III

Wilshire, Frederick Allen, 1868–1944, vol. IV

Wilsmore, Norman T. M., 1868–1940, vol. III

Wilson, 1st Baron, 1881–1964, vol. VI

Wilson of High Wray, Baron (Life Peer); Paul Norman Wilson, 1908–1980, vol. VII

Wilson of Radcliffe, Baron (Life Peer); Alfred Wilson, 1909–1983, vol. VIII

Wilson, Adam, 1882–1951, vol. V

Wilson, Alan, 1896–1959, vol. V

Wilson, Rear-Adm. Alan Christopher Wyndham, 1919–1985, vol. VIII

Wilson, Lt-Col Alban; *see* Wilson, Lt-Col J. A.

Wilson, Albert Edward, *died* 1960, vol. V

Wilson, Sir Alexander, 1st Bt (*cr* 1897), 1837–1907, vol. I

Wilson, Sir Alexander, 1843–1907, vol. I

Wilson, Maj.-Gen. Sir Alexander, 1858–1937, vol. III

Wilson, Alexander, 1917–1978, vol. VII

Wilson, Captain Alexander Guy Berners, 1890–1942, vol. IV

Wilson, Alexander Johnstone, 1841–1921, vol. II

Wilson, Alfred Harold, 1895–1984, vol. VIII

Wilson, Alpheus Waters, 1834–1916, vol. II

Wilson, Rev. Ambrose John, 1853–1929, vol. III

Wilson, Andrew, 1852–1912, vol. I

Wilson, Andrew, 1909–1974, vol. VII

Wilson, Rev. Canon Andrew, 1920–1985, vol. VIII

Wilson, Sir (Archibald) Duncan, 1911–1983, vol. VIII

Wilson, Archibald Wayet, *died* 1950, vol. IV (A), vol. V

Wilson, Lt-Col Sir Arnold Talbot, 1884–1940, vol. III

Wilson, Arthur, 1836–1909, vol. I

Wilson, Rt Hon. Sir Arthur, 1837–1915, vol. I

Wilson, Col Arthur Harry H.; *see* Hutton-Wilson.

Wilson, Adm. Sir Arthur Knyvet, 3rd Bt (*cr* 1857), 1842–1921, vol. II

Wilson, Arthur Stanley, 1868–1938, vol. III

Wilson, Sir Arton, 1893–1977, vol. VII

Wilson, Sir Austin George, 1906–1987, vol. VIII

Wilson, Rev. Barton Worsley, *died* 1920, vol. II

Wilsden, Rev. Bernard Robert, 1857–1909, vol. I

Wilson, Sir Bertram, 1893–1974, vol. VII

Wilson, Bertram Martin, 1896–1935, vol. III

Wilson, Beryl Charlotte Mary, *died* 1951, vol. V

Wilson, Maj.-Gen. Bevil Thomson, 1885–1975, vol. VII

Wilson, Col Campbell Aubrey Kenneth I.; *see* Innes-Wilson.

Wilson, Rt Rev. Cecil, 1860–1941, vol. IV

Wilson, Cecil Claude, 1885–1968, vol. VI

Wilson, Cecil Henry, 1862–1945, vol. IV

Wilson, Rt Rev. Cecil Wilfred, 1875–1937, vol. III

Wilson, Major Cecil William, 1870–1937, vol. III

Wilson, Charles Ashley C.; *see* Carus-Wilson.

Wilson, Mrs Charles Ashley C.; *see* Carus-Wilson.

Wilson, Captain Charles Benjamin, 1885–1957, vol. V

Wilson, Charles Edward, 1848–1938, vol. III (A), vol. IV

Wilson, Rev. Charles Edward, 1871–1956, vol. V

Wilson, Charles Edward, 1886–1972, vol. VII

Wilson, Charles Erwin, 1890–1961, vol. VI

Wilson, Sir Charles Henry, 1859–1930, vol. III

Wilson, Charles Henry, 1858–1937, vol. III

Wilson, Col Charles Henry Luttrell Fahie, 1858–1935, vol. III

Wilson, Charles Paul, 1900–1970, vol. VI

Wilson, Sir Charles Rivers, 1831–1916, vol. II

Wilson, Sir Charles S.; *see* Stewart-Wilson.

Wilson, Brig.-Gen. Charles Stuart, 1867–1933, vol. III

Wilson, Charles Thomson Rees, 1869–1959, vol. V

Wilson, Rev. Charles William Goodall, 1860–1948, vol. IV

Wilson, Christopher James, 1879–1956, vol. V

Wilson, Col Christopher Wyndham, 1844–1918, vol. II

Wilson, Claude, 1860–1937, vol. III

Wilson, Clive Henry Adolphus, 1876–1921, vol. II

Wilson, Clyde Tabor, 1889–1971, vol. VII

Wilson, Sir Courthope; *see* Wilson, Sir William C. T.

Wilson, Col Cyril Edward, 1873–1938, vol. III

Wilson, D. Forrester, *died* 1950, vol. IV

Wilson, Rev. Daniel Frederic, 1830–1918, vol. II

Wilson, Hon. Daniel Martin, 1862–1932, vol. III

Wilson, Sir David, 1838–1924, vol. II

Wilson, Sir David, 1st Bt (*cr* 1920), 1855–1930, vol. III

Wilson, David Alec, 1864–1933, vol. III

Wilson, Very Rev. David Frederick Ruddell, 1871–1957, vol. V

Wilson, David Mackay, 1863–1929, vol. III

Wilson, Rt Rev. Douglas John, 1903–1980, vol. VII

Wilson, Sir Duncan; *see* Wilson, Sir A. D.

Wilson, Sir Duncan Randolph, 1875–1945, vol. IV

Wilson, Major Duncan William, 1881–1935, vol. III

Wilson, Lt-Col Edmond Munkhouse, 1855–1921, vol. II

Wilson, Edmund, 1895–1972, vol. VII

Wilson, Edmund Beecher, 1856–1939, vol. III

Wilson, Col Edward Hales, 1845–1917, vol. II

Wilson, Edward Meryon, 1906–1977, vol. VII

Wilson, Brig. Edward William Gravatt, 1888–1971, vol. VII

Wilson, Edwin John B.; *see* Boyd-Wilson.

Wilson, Eleanora Mary C.; *see* Carus-Wilson.

Wilson, Ellis; *see* Wilson, H. E. C.

Wilson, Maj.-Gen. Erastus William, 1860–1922, vol. II

Wilson, Brig. Sir Eric Edward Boketon H.; *see* Holt-Wilson.

Wilson, Ernest, *died* 1932, vol. III

Wilson, Ernest Henry, 1876–1930, vol. III

Wilson, Florence Roma Muir; *see* Wilson, Romer.

Wilson, Forsyth James, 1880–1944, vol. IV

Wilson, Maj.-Gen. Francis Adrian, 1874–1954, vol. V

Wilson, Maj.-Gen. Francis Edward Edwards, 1839–1905, vol. I

Wilson, Hon. Frank, 1859–1918, vol. II

Wilson, Captain Sir Frank O'Brien, 1883–1962, vol. VI

Wilson, Frank Percy, 1889–1963, vol. VI

Wilson, Col Frank Walter, 1869–1953, vol. V

Wilson, Lt-Col Frederick Alfred, 1863–1932, vol. III

Wilson, Frederick James, 1858–1926, vol. II

Wilson, Maj.-Gen. Frederick Maurice, 1868–1956, vol. V

Wilson, Sir Frederick William, 1844–1924, vol. II

Wilson, Sir Garnet Douglas, 1885–1975, vol. VII

Wilson, Geoffrey; see Wilson, H. G. B.

Wilson, Maj.-Gen. Geoffrey Boyd, 1927–1984, vol. VIII

Wilson, Captain George, 1849–1932, vol. III

Wilson, Lt-Col George, 1869–1935, vol. III

Wilson, George, 1862–1943, vol. IV

Wilson, Sir George, 1900–1979, vol. VII

Wilson, George Ambler, 1906–1977, vol. VII

Wilson, George Bailey, 1863–1952, vol. V

Wilson, George Frederick, 1886–1970, vol. VI

Wilson, George Hamilton Bracher, 1895–1963, vol. VI

Wilson, Sir George Henry, 1869–1939, vol. III

Wilson, Rev. Canon George Herbert, 1870–1952, vol. V

Wilson, George Heron, 1868–1959, vol. V

Wilson, George Maryon Maryon-, 1861–1941, vol. IV

Wilson, Rev. Canon Sir George Percy Maryon M.; see Maryon-Wilson.

Wilson, Lt-Col George Robert Stewart, 1896–1958, vol. V

Wilson, Gerald Sidney, 1880–1960, vol. V

Wilson, Godfrey Harold Alfred, 1871–1958, vol. V

Wilson, Maj.-Gen. Sir Gordon, 1887–1971, vol. VII

Wilson, Lt-Col Gordon Chesney, 1865–1914, vol. I

Wilson, Grace Margaret, (Mrs Bruce Campbell), died 1957, vol. V

Wilson, Graham Malcolm, 1917–1977, vol. VII

Wilson, Sir Graham Selby, 1895–1987, vol. VIII

Wilson, Gregg, 1865–1951, vol. V

Wilson, Rear-Adm. Guy Austen Moore, 1906–1986, vol. VIII

Wilson, Rt Hon. Sir Guy Douglas Arthur Fleetwood, 1850–1940, vol. III

Wilson, Col Hon. Guy Greville, 1877–1943, vol. IV

Wilson, Rev. Canon Harold, 1919–1975, vol. VII

Wilson, Harold Albert, 1874–1964, vol. VI

Wilson, Harold Fitzhardinge Wilson, 1913–1984, vol. VIII

Wilson, Col Harold René, 1890–1941, vol. IV

Wilson, Harold William, died 1959, vol. V

Wilson, Harry, 1852–1928, vol. II

Wilson, (Harry) Ellis (Charter), 1899–1987, vol. VIII

Wilson, Rear-Adm. (S) Harry George, 1874–1947, vol. IV

Wilson, Harry Lawrence L.; see Lawrence-Wilson.

Wilson, Harry Leon, 1867–1939, vol. III

Wilson, Helen Russell, died 1924, vol. II

Wilson, Rt Rev. Henry Albert, 1876–1961, vol. VI

Wilson, Rev. Henry Austin, 1854–1927, vol. II

Wilson, Sir Henry Francis, (Harry), 1859–1937, vol. III

Wilson, Lt-Gen. Sir Henry Fuller Maitland, 1859–1941, vol. IV

Wilson, Field-Marshal Sir Henry Hughes, 1st Bt (cr 1919), 1864–1922, vol. II

Wilson, (Henry) James, 1916–1990, vol. VIII

Wilson, Col Henry James, 1904–1985, vol. VIII

Wilson, Henry Joseph, 1833–1914, vol. I

Wilson, Henry Leonard, 1897–1968, vol. VI

Wilson, Henry Wilcox, 1895–1974, vol. VII

Wilson, Herbert, 1862–1927, vol. II, vol. III

Wilson, Captain Herbert Haydon, 1875–1917, vol. II

Wilson, Sir Herbert W. L.; see Lush-Wilson.

Wilson, Herbert Wrigley, 1866–1940, vol. III

Wilson, Sir Horace John, 1882–1972, vol. VII

Wilson, Sir Hubert Guy Maryon M.; see Maryon-Wilson.

Wilson, Hubert Wilberforce, 1867–1949, vol. IV

Wilson, Sir Hugh; see Wilson, Sir L. H.

Wilson, (Hugh) Geoffrey (Birch), 1903–1975, vol. VII

Wilson, Hon. Sir Ian; see Wilson, Hon. Sir T. I. F.

Wilson, Rev. Canon Ian George MacQueen, 1920–1988, vol. VIII

Wilson, Sir Isaac Henry, died 1944, vol. IV

Wilson, Isabel Grace Hood, 1895–1982, vol. VIII

Wilson, Sir Jacob, 1836–1905, vol. I

Wilson, James; see Wilson, H. J.

Wilson, Rev. James, 1856–1923, vol. II

Wilson, James, 1847–1924, vol. II

Wilson, Sir James, 1853–1926, vol. II

Wilson, James, 1861–1941, vol. IV

Wilson, James, 1879–1943, vol. IV

Wilson, James, 1899–1978, vol. VII (AII)

Wilson, Lt-Col (James) Alban, 1865–1928, vol. II

Wilson, Rev. James Allen, 1827–1917, vol. II

Wilson, Sir James Arthur, 1877–1950, vol. IV

Wilson, Maj.-Gen. James Barnett, 1862–1936, vol. III

Wilson, Sir James Glenny, 1849–1929, vol. III

Wilson, Ven. James Maurice, 1836–1931, vol. III

Wilson, Sir James Robertson, 2nd Bt (cr 1906), 1883–1964, vol. VI

Wilson, Sir (James) Steuart, 1889–1966, vol. VI

Wilson, James Thomas, 1861–1945, vol. IV

Wilson, James Thomas Pither, 1884–1976, vol. VII

Wilson, Sir Jeremiah, died 1930, vol. III

Wilson, John, 1837–1915, vol. I

Wilson, Sir John, 1st Bt (cr 1906), 1844–1918, vol. II

Wilson, John, 1837–1928, vol. II

Wilson, John, 1860–1938, vol. III

Wilson, Rev. John, 1854–1939, vol. III

Wilson, John; see Ashmore, Hon. Lord.

Wilson, Sir John Carnegie Dove-, 1865–1935, vol. III

Wilson, John Dove, 1833–1908, vol. I

Wilson, John Dover, 1881–1969, vol. VI

Wilson, Col John George Yule, 1853–1935, vol. III

Wilson, Col John Gerald, 1841–1902, vol. I

Wilson, John Gideon, 1876–1963, vol. VI

Wilson, John Gray, 1915–1968, vol. VI

Wilson, J(ohn) Greenwood, 1897–1990, vol. VIII

Wilson, John Henry, 1862–1932, vol. III

Wilson, Rev. John Kenneth, 1890–1949, vol. IV

Wilson, Rt Rev. John Leonard, 1897–1970, vol. VI

Wilson, Sir John Menzies, 3rd Bt (*cr* 1906), 1885–1968, vol. VI

Wilson, Sir John Mitchell Harvey, 2nd Bt (*cr* 1920), 1898–1975, vol. VII

Wilson, Very Rev. John Skinner, 1849–1926, vol. II

Wilson, Col John Skinner, 1888–1969, vol. VI

Wilson, John Thomson, 1855–1930, vol. III

Wilson, Rt Hon. John William, 1858–1932, vol. III

Wilson, Joseph Havelock, 1859–1929, vol. III

Wilson, Rev. Joseph Kershaw, 1854–1930, vol. III

Wilson, Joseph Maitland, 1868–1940, vol. III

Wilson, Hon. Joseph Marcellin, 1859–1940, vol. III (A), vol. IV

Wilson, Joseph Vivian, 1894–1977, vol. VII

Wilson, Joseph William, 1851–1930, vol. III

Wilson, Sir Keith Cameron, 1900–1987, vol. VIII

Wilson, Kenneth Henry, 1885–1969, vol. VI

Wilson, Brig.-Gen. Lachlan Chisholm, 1871–1947, vol. IV

Wilson, Col Lancelot Machell, 1873–1950, vol. IV

Wilson, Sir Leonard, 1888–1980, vol. VII

Wilson, Sir (Leslie) Hugh, 1913–1985, vol. VIII

Wilson, Col Rt Hon. Sir Leslie Orme, 1876–1955, vol. V

Wilson, Rt Rev. Lucian Charles U.; *see* Usher-Wilson.

Wilson, Sir Mark, 1896–1956, vol. V

Wilson, Sir Mathew Amcotts, 3rd Bt (*cr* 1874), 1853–1914, vol. I

Wilson, Lt-Col Sir Mathew Richard Henry, 4th Bt (*cr* 1874), 1875–1958, vol. V

Wilson, Sir Mathew Wharton, 2nd Bt (*cr* 1874), 1827–1909, vol. I

Wilson, Matthew, 1854–1920, vol. II

Wilson, Maurice, 1862–1936, vol. III

Wilson, Sir Maurice B.; *see* Bromley-Wilson.

Wilson, Sir Michael Thomond, 1911–1983, vol. VIII

Wilson, Mona, 1872–1954, vol. V

Wilson, Morris W., 1883–1946, vol. IV

Wilson, Lt-Col Sir Murrough John, 1875–1946, vol. IV

Wilson, Lt-Col Nathaniel, *died* 1944, vol. IV

Wilson, Captain Neville Frederick Jarvis, 1865–1947, vol. IV

Wilson, Maj.-Gen. Nigel Maitland, 1884–1950, vol. IV

Wilson, Maj.-Gen. Norman Methven, 1881–1961, vol. VI

Wilson, Oscar, 1867–1930, vol. III

Wilson, P. Macgregor, *died* 1928, vol. II, vol. III

Wilson, Lt-Col Patrick Hogarth, 1874–1939, vol. III

Wilson, Percy, 1904–1986, vol. VIII

Wilson, Rev. Canon Sir Percy M.; *see* Maryon-Wilson.

Wilson, Lt-Col Percy Norton Whitestone, 1886–1933, vol. III

Wilson, Peter Cecil, 1913–1984, vol. VIII

Wilson, Peter Humphrey St John, 1908–1987, vol. VIII

Wilson, Philip Duncan, 1886–1969, vol. VI

Wilson, Philip Whitwell, 1875–1956, vol. V

Wilson, Rt Rev. Piers Holt, *died* 1956, vol. V

Wilson, Ralph Darrell, 1892–1967, vol. VI

Wilson, Reginald Appleby, 1878–1955, vol. V

Wilson, Rev. Reginald Francis, 1873–1937, vol. III

Wilson, Reginald Henry Rimington Rimington-, 1852–1927, vol. II

Wilson, Reginald Page, *died* 1950, vol. IV

Wilson, Hon. Sir (Reginald) Victor, 1877–1957, vol. V

Wilson, Col Richard Henry, 1886–1969, vol. VI

Wilson, Lt-Col Richard Henry Francis Wharton, 1855–1936, vol. III

Wilson, Richard Henry George, 1874–1944, vol. IV

Wilson, Rev. Richard Mercer, 1887–1976, vol. VII

Wilson, Robert, 1871–1920, vol. II

Wilson, Sir Robert, 1865–1943, vol. IV

Wilson, Captain Robert Amcotts, 1882–1960, vol. V

Wilson, Robert Andrew, 1905–1984, vol. VIII

Wilson, Hon. Sir Robert Christian, 1896–1973, vol. VII

Wilson, Lt-Col Robert Edward, 1884–1936, vol. III

Wilson, Robert Graham, 1917–1982, vol. VIII

Wilson, Rev. Robert James, *died* 1897, vol. I

Wilson, Robert John, 1865–1946, vol. IV

Wilson, Very Rev. Robert John, 1893–1981, vol. VIII

Wilson, Robert McNair, 1882–1963, vol. VI

Wilson, Sir (Roderick) Roy, 1876–1942, vol. IV

Wilson, Gen. Sir Roger Cochrane, 1882–1966, vol. VI

Wilson, Lt-Col Roger Parker, 1870–1943, vol. IV

Wilson, Sir Roland Knyvet, 2nd Bt (*cr* 1857), 1840–1919, vol. II

Wilson, Romer, 1891–1930, vol. III

Wilson, Sir Roy; *see* Wilson, Sir Roderick R.

Wilson, Sheriff Roy Alexander, 1927–1985, vol. VIII

Wilson, Sir Roy Mickel, 1903–1982, vol. VIII

Wilson, Sir Samuel, 1861–1937, vol. III

Wilson, Samuel Alexander Kinnier, 1874–1937, vol. III

Wilson, Brig.-Gen. Sir Samuel Herbert, 1873–1950, vol. IV

Wilson, Lady Sarah Isabella Augusta, 1865–1929, vol. III

Wilson, Sir Spencer Maryon Maryon, 10th Bt (*cr* 1661), 1829–1897, vol. I

Wilson, Sir Spencer Pocklington Maryon Maryon-, 11th Bt (*cr* 1661), 1859–1944, vol. IV

Wilson, Stanley Reginald, 1890–1973, vol. VII

Wilson, Stephen Shipley, 1904–1989, vol. VIII

Wilson, Sir Steuart; *see* Wilson, Sir J. S.

Wilson, Sydney Ernest, *died* 1973, vol. VII

Wilson, T. Henry, *died* 1941, vol. IV

Wilson, Theodora Wilson, *died* 1941, vol. IV

Wilson, Theodore Stacey, 1861–1949, vol. IV

Wilson, Col Thomas, 1831–1915, vol. I

Wilson, Sir Thomas, 1863–1930, vol. III

Wilson, Thomas, 1905–1988, vol. VIII

Wilson, Maj.-Gen. Thomas Arthur Atkinson, 1882–1958, vol. V

Wilson, Ven. Thomas Bowstead, 1882–1961, vol. VI

Wilson, Thomas Corby, *died* 1934, vol. III

Wilson, Captain Sir Thomas Douglas, 4th Bt, 1917–1984, vol. VIII

Wilson, Rev. Thomas Erskine, 1874–1951, vol. V

Wilson, Sir Thomas Fleming, 1862–1929, vol. III

Wilson, Sir Thomas George, 1876–1958, vol. V

Wilson, Sir (Thomas) George; *see* Wilson, Sir G.

Wilson, Maj.-Gen. Thomas Needham Furnival, 1896–1961, vol. VI

Wilson, (Thomas) Woodrow, 1856–1924, vol. II

Wilson, Hon. Sir (Tom) Ian (Findley), 1904–1971, vol. VII

Wilson, Hon. Sir Victor; *see* Wilson, Hon. Sir R. V.

Wilson, Gp Captain Walter Carandini, 1885–1968, vol. VI

Wilson, Walter Gordon, 1874–1957, vol. V

Wilson, Hon. Walter Horatio, 1839–1902, vol. I

Wilson, Sir Wemyss G.; *see* Grant-Wilson.

Wilson, William, 1884–1944, vol. IV

Wilson, William, 1875–1965, vol. VI

Wilson, William, 1920–1972, vol. VII

Wilson, Engr-Captain William Anderson, 1868–1957, vol. V

Wilson, William Combe, 1897–1974, vol. VII

Wilson, Sir (William) Courthope (Townshend), 1865–1944, vol. IV

Wilson, Surg.-Gen. Sir William Deane, 1843–1921, vol. II

Wilson, William Edward, 1851–1908, vol. I

Wilson, Sir William G.; *see* Grey-Wilson.

Wilson, Very Rev. William Hay, *died* 1925, vol. II

Wilson, Major William Herbert, *died* 1928, vol. II

Wilson, William James, 1879–1954, vol. V

Wilson, William Joseph Robinson, 1909–1982, vol. VIII

Wilson, William Lyne, 1843–1900, vol. I

Wilson, Gp Captain William Proctor, 1902–1980, vol. VII

Wilson, William Robert, 1844–1928, vol. II

Wilson, Sir William Tweedley, 1882–1942, vol. IV

Wilson, William Tyson, 1855–1921, vol. II

Wilson, William Wright, 1843–1919, vol. II

Wilson, Woodrow; *see* Wilson, T. W.

Wilson-Farquharson, Lt-Col David Lorraine; *see* Farquharson.

Wilson-Fox, Hon. Mrs Eleanor Birch, *died* 1963, vol. VI

Wilson-Fox, Henry; *see* Fox.

Wilson-Haffenden, Maj.-Gen. Donald James, 1900–1986, vol. VIII

Wilson-Johnston, Joseph; *see* Johnston.

Wilson-Johnston, Maj.-Gen. Walter Edward; *see* Johnston.

Wilson Smith, Sir Henry, 1904–1978, vol. VII

Wilson Taylor, Sir John, *died* 1943, vol. IV

Wilson-Todd, Captain Sir William Henry, 1st Bt, 1828–1910, vol. I

Wilson-Todd, Captain Sir William Pierrepoint, 2nd Bt, 1857–1925, vol. II

Wilsone, Arthur Henry, 1860–1939, vol. III

Wilthew, Gerard Herbert Guy, 1876–1913, vol. I, vol. III

Wilton, 4th Earl of, 1839–1898, vol. I

Wilton, 5th Earl of, 1863–1915, vol. I

Wilton, 6th Earl of, 1896–1927, vol. II

Wilton, Sir Ernest Colville Collins, 1870–1952, vol. V

Wilton, George Wilton, 1862–1964, vol. VI

Wilton, Herbert George, 1882–1959, vol. V

Wilton, Captain Sir James M., *died* 1946, vol. IV

Wilton, Gen. Sir John Gordon Noel, 1910–1981, vol. VIII

Wilton, John Raymond, 1884–1944, vol. IV

Wilton, Sir Thomas, 1861–1929, vol. III

Wiltshire, Aubrey Roy Liddon, 1891–1969, vol. VI

Wiltshire, Sir Frank H. C., 1881–1949, vol. IV

Wiltshire, Harold Waterlow, 1879–1937, vol. III

Wiltshire, Samuel Paul, 1891–1967, vol. VI

Wimberley, Col Charles Neil Campbell, 1867–1949, vol. IV

Wimberley, Maj.-Gen. Douglas Neil, 1896–1983, vol. VIII

Wimble, Ernest Walter, 1887–1979, vol. VII

Wimble, Sir John Bowring, 1868–1927, vol. II

Wimborne, 1st Baron, 1835–1914, vol. I

Wimborne, 1st Viscount, 1873–1939, vol. III

Wimborne, 2nd Viscount, 1903–1967, vol. VI

Wimperis, Arthur Harold, 1874–1953, vol. V

Wimperis, Harry Egerton, 1876–1960, vol. V

Wimshurst, James, 1832–1903, vol. I

Winans, Walter, *died* 1920, vol. II

Winant, Hon. John Gilbert, 1889–1947, vol. IV

Winby, Lt-Col Lewis Phillips, 1874–1956, vol. V

Winchell, Walter, 1897–1972, vol. VII

Winchester, 15th Marquess of, 1858–1899, vol. I

Winchester, 16th Marquess of, 1862–1962, vol. VI

Winchester, 17th Marquess of, 1905–1968, vol. VI

Winchester, Clarence Arthur C.; 1895–1981, vol. VIII

Winchester, Tarleton, 1895–1967, vol. VI

Winchilsea, 12th Earl of, **and Nottingham,** 7th Earl of, 1851–1898, vol. I

Winchilsea, 13th Earl of, **and Nottingham,** 8th Earl of, 1852–1927, vol. II

Winchilsea, 14th Earl of, **and Nottingham,** 9th Earl of, 1885–1939, vol. III

Winchilsea, 15th Earl of, **and Nottingham,** 10th Earl of, 1911–1950, vol. IV

Winckley, Rev. Canon Sidney Thorold, 1858–1937, vol. III

Winckworth, Chauncey P. Tietjens, 1896–1954, vol. V

Wincott, Harold Edward, 1906–1969, vol. VI

Wind, Edgar, 1900–1971, vol. VII

Windaus, Adolf Otto Reinhold, 1876–1959, vol. V

Winder, Sir Arthur Benedict, 1875–1953, vol. V

Winder, Col John Lyon C.; *see* Corbett-Winder.

Winder, Lt-Col Maurice Guy, *died* 1932, vol. III

Winder, Captain Robert Cecil, *died* 1920, vol. II

Winder, Very Rev. Thomas Edward, *died* 1926, vol. II

Winder, Major William John C.; *see* Corbett-Winder.

Windeyer, John Cadell, 1875–1951, vol. V

Windeyer, Rt Hon. Sir Victor; *see* Windeyer, Rt Hon. Sir W. J. V.

Windeyer, Sir William Charles, 1834–1897, vol. I

Windeyer, Rt Hon. Sir (William John) Victor, 1900–1987, vol. VIII

Windham, Vice-Adm. Charles, 1851–1916, vol. II

Windham, Lt-Col Charles Joseph, 1867–1941, vol. IV

Windham, Sir Ralph, 1905–1980, vol. VII

Windham, Comdr Sir Walter George, 1868–1942, vol. IV

Windham, Sir William, 1864–1961, vol. VI

Windham, William Evan, 1904–1977, vol. VII

Windle, Sir Bertram Coghill Alan, 1858–1929, vol. VII

Windlesham, 1st Baron, 1877–1953, vol. V

Windlesham, 2nd Baron, 1903–1962, vol. VI
Windlesham, Lady; *see* Glynn, P. L.
Windley, Sir Edward Henry, 1909–1972, vol. VII
Windsor, Viscount; Other Robert Windsor-Clive, 1884–1908, vol. I
Windsor, Bt-Col Arthur Herbert, 1880–1972, vol. VII
Windsor, Lt-Col Frank Needham, 1868–1951, vol. V
Windsor, Robert, 1916–1980, vol. VII
Windsor, Walter, *died* 1945, vol. IV
Windsor-Aubrey, Henry Miles, 1901–1986, vol. VIII
Windsor-Clive, Lt-Col George, 1878–1968, vol. VI
Windsor-Clive, Lt-Col Hon. George Herbert Windsor, 1835–1918, vol. II
Windsor Lewis, Brig. James Charles, 1907–1964, vol. VI
Winegarten, Asher, 1922–1979, vol. VII
Winfield, Rev. Benjamin, *died* 1933, vol. III
Winfield, Sir Percy Henry, 1878–1953, vol. V
Winfrey, Sir Richard, 1858–1944, vol. IV
Wing, Brig.-Gen. Frederick Drummond Vincent, 1860–1915, vol. I
Wing, Thomas Edward, 1853–1935, vol. III
Wingate, Col Alfred Woodrow Stanley, 1861–1938, vol. III
Wingate, Sir Andrew, 1846–1937, vol. III
Wingate, Col Basil Fenton, *died* 1940, vol. III
Wingate, Gen. Sir (Francis) Reginald, 1st Bt, 1861–1953, vol. V
Wingate, Col George, 1852–1936, vol. III
Wingate, Henry Smith, 1905–1982, vol. VIII
Wingate, Sir (James) Lawton, 1846–1924, vol. II
Wingate, Sir Lawton; *see* Wingate, Sir J. L.
Wingate, Captain Malcolm Roy, 1893–1918, vol. II
Wingate, Maj.-Gen. Orde Charles, 1903–1944, vol. IV
Wingate, Gen. Sir Reginald; *see* Wingate, Gen. Sir F. G.
Wingate, Sir Ronald Evelyn Leslie, 2nd Bt, 1889–1978, vol. VII
Wingate, William Granville, 1911–1990, vol. VIII
Wingate-Saul, Bazil Sylvester, 1906–1975, vol. VII
Wingate-Saul, Sir Ernest Wingate, 1873–1944, vol. IV
Winge, Ojvind, 1886–1964, vol. VI
Wingfield, Sir Anthony H., 1857–1952, vol. V
Wingfield, Sir Charles John FitzRoy Rhys, 1877–1960, vol. V
Wingfield, Sir Edward, 1834–1910, vol. I
Wingfield, Lt-Col John Maurice, 1863–1931, vol. III
Wingfield, Ven. John William, 1915–1983, vol. VIII
Wingfield, Maj.-Gen. Hon. Maurice Anthony, 1883–1956, vol. V
Wingfield, Maurice Edward, 1869–1937, vol. III
Wingfield, Mervyn Edward George Rhys, 1872–1952, vol. V
Wingfield, Major Walter Clopton, 1833–1912, vol. I
Wingfield, Rev. Lt-Col William Edward, 1867–1927, vol. II
Wingfield Digby, George F.; *see* Digby.
Wingfield-Stratford, Brig.-Gen. Cecil Vernon, 1853–1939, vol. III
Wingfield-Stratford, Esmé Cecil, 1882–1971, vol. VII
Wingrave, Vitruvius Harold Wyatt, 1858–1938, vol. III

Winks, William Edward, 1842–1926, vol. II
Winlaw, Ashley William Edgell, 1914–1988, vol. VIII
Winlock, Herbert Eustis, 1884–1950, vol. IV
Winmill, Thomas Field, 1888–1953, vol. V
Winn, Rt Hon. Sir (Charles) Rodger (Noel), 1903–1972, vol. VII
Winn, Air Vice-Marshal Charles Vivian, 1918–1988, vol. VIII
Winn, Godfrey Herbert, 1908–1971, vol. VII
Winn, Rt Hon. Sir Rodger; *see* Winn, Rt Hon. Sir C. R. N.
Winn, Lt-Comdr Sydney Thornhill, *died* 1924, vol. II
Winneke, Hon. Sir Henry Arthur, 1908–1985, vol. VIII
Winner, Dame Albertine Louise, 1907–1988, vol. VIII
Winnicott, Sir Frederick; *see* Winnicott, Sir J. F.
Winnicott, Sir (John) Frederick, 1855–1948, vol. IV
Winning, Theodore Norman, 1884–1946, vol. IV
Winnington, Sir Francis Salwey, 5th Bt, 1849–1931, vol. III
Winnington, Lt-Col John Francis Sartorius, 1876–1918, vol. II
Winnington Ingram, Rt Rev. and Rt Hon. Arthur Foley; *see* Ingram.
Winnington-Ingram, Ven. Arthur John, 1888–1965, vol. VI
Winnington-Ingram, Rev. Edward Henry; *see* Ingram.
Winsbury-White, Horace Powell, *died* 1962, vol. VI
Winser, Col Charles Rupert Peter, 1880–1961, vol. VI
Winser, (Cyril) Legh, 1884–1983, vol. VIII
Winser, Legh; *see* Winser, C. L.
Winsloe, Adm. Sir Alfred Leigh, 1852–1931, vol. III
Winsloe, Col Alfred Raynaud, 1868–1932, vol. III
Winsloe, Lt-Col Herbert Edward, 1873–1921, vol. II
Winsloe, Col Richard William Charles, 1835–1917, vol. II
Winslow, Rev. Forbes Edward, 1842–1913, vol. I
Winslow, L. Forbes, 1844–1913, vol. I
Winslow, Rev. William Copley, 1840–1925, vol. II
Winstanley, Denys Arthur, 1877–1947, vol. IV
Winstedt, Sir Richard Olaf, 1878–1966, vol. VI
Winster, 1st Baron, 1885–1961, vol. VI
Winston, Charles Edward, 1898–1989, vol. VIII
Wint, Hon. Dunbar Theophilus, 1879–1938, vol. III
Winter, Carl, 1906–1966, vol. VI
Winter, Col Clifford Boardman, 1869–1930, vol. III
Winter, Rt Rev. Colin O'Brien, 1928–1981, vol. VIII
Winter, Rev. Edward George Adlington, 1853–1933, vol. III
Winter, Edwin, 1840–1915, vol. I
Winter, Lt-Col Ernest Arthur, *died* 1925, vol. II
Winter, Hon. Sir Francis Pratt, 1848–1919, vol. II
Winter, Rev. Canon George Percival Thomas Horden, 1885–1953, vol. V
Winter, Hon. Henry Daniel, 1851–1927, vol. II
Winter, James Alexander, 1886–1971, vol. VII
Winter, Sir James Spearman, 1845–1911, vol. I
Winter, John Strange; *see* Stannard, H. E. V.
Winter, Keith, 1906–1983, vol. VIII
Winter, Hon. Sir Marmaduke George, 1857–1936, vol. III

Winter, Brig.-Gen. Sir Ormonde de l'Epée, 1875–1962, vol. VI

Winter, Reginald Keble, 1883–1955, vol. V

Winter, Robert Pearson, 1897–1973, vol. VII

Winter, Col Samuel Henry, 1854–1938, vol. III

Winter, Thomas, 1866–1912, vol. I

Winter, W. Tatton, *died* 1928, vol. II

Winter, William, 1836–1917, vol. II

Winter-Shaw, Arthur, *died* 1948, vol. IV

Winterbotham, Gp Capt. Frederick William, 1897–1990, vol. VIII

Winterbotham, Sir Geoffrey Leonard, *died* 1966, vol. VI

Winterbotham, Brig. Harold St John Lloyd, 1878–1946, vol. IV

Winterbotham, Sir Henry Martin, 1847–1932, vol. III

Winterbotham, Rev. Rayner, *died* 1924, vol. II

Winterbotham, Sir William Howard, 1843–1926, vol. II

Winterbottom, Lt-Col Archibald Dickson, 1885–1942, vol. IV

Winterbottom, Richard Emanuel, 1899–1968, vol. VI

Winters, Ellen Dorothea Margaret, 1894–1956, vol. V

Winterstoke, 1st Baron, 1830–1911, vol. I

Winterton, 5th Earl, 1837–1907, vol. I

Winterton, 6th Earl, 1883–1962, vol. VI

Winterton, George Ernest, 1873–1942, vol. IV

Winterton, Maj.-Gen. Sir John; *see* Winterton, Maj.-Gen. Sir T. J. W.

Winterton, Ralph; *see* Winterton, W. R.

Winterton, Maj.-Gen. Sir (Thomas) John (Willoughby), 1898–1987, vol. VIII

Winterton, (William) Ralph, 1905–1988, vol. VIII

Wintle, Col Charles Edmund Hunter, *died* 1969, vol. VI

Wintle, Col Frank Graham, 1852–1907, vol. I

Winton, Frank Robert, 1894–1985, vol. VIII

Winton, Meryon W.; *see* White-Winton.

Wintour, Maj.-Gen. Fitzgerald, 1860–1949, vol. IV

Wintour, Ulick Fitzgerald, 1877–1947, vol. IV

Wintringham, Col John Workman, 1894–1980, vol. VII

Wintringham, Margaret, *died* 1955, vol. V

Wintringham, Thomas, 1867–1921, vol. II

Wintringham, Thomas Henry, 1898–1949, vol. IV

Wintz, Adm. Lewis Edmund, 1849–1933, vol. III

Wintz, Dame Sophia Gertrude, *died* 1929, vol. III

Winwood, Lt-Col William Quintyne, 1873–1954, vol. V

Wippell, Adm. Sir Henry Daniel P.; *see* Pridham-Wippell.

Wippell, Rev. Canon John Cecil, 1883–1978, vol. VII

Wirgman, Ven. Augustus Theodore, 1846–1917, vol. II

Wirgman, T. Blake, *died* 1925, vol. II

Wirkkala, Tapio, 1915–1985, vol. VIII

Wisdom, Brig.-Gen. Evan Alexander, 1869–1945, vol. IV

Wisdom, George Evan Cameron, 1899–1958, vol. V

Wise, 1st Baron, 1887–1968, vol. VI

Wise, Alfred Gascoyne, 1854–1923, vol. II

Wise, Lt-Col Alfred Roy, 1901–1974, vol. VII

Wise, Hon. Bernhard Ringrose, 1858–1916, vol. II

Wise, Rear-Adm. Cyril Hubert Surtees, 1913–1982, vol. VIII

Wise, Edward Frank, 1885–1933, vol. III

Wise, Francis Hubert, 1869–1917, vol. II

Wise, Sir Fredric, 1871–1928, vol. II

Wise, Hon. George Henry, 1853–1950, vol. IV

Wise, Lt-Col Henry Edward Disbrowe Disbrowe-, 1868–1948, vol. IV

Wise, Rear-Adm. John; *see* Wise, Rear-Adm. C. H. S.

Wise, Sir John Humphrey, 1890–1984, vol. VIII

Wise, Sir Lloyd; *see* Wise, Sir W. L.

Wise, Gp Captain Percival Kinnear, 1885–1968, vol. VI

Wise, Rabbi Stephen S., 1874–1949, vol. IV

Wise, Thomas James, 1859–1937, vol. III

Wise, Sir (William) Lloyd, 1845–1910, vol. I

Wiseham, Sir Joseph Angus Lucien, 1906–1972, vol. VII

Wiseman, Arthur Maurice, 1893–1948, vol. IV

Wiseman, Christopher Luke, 1893–1987, vol. VIII

Wiseman, Gen. Clarence Dexter, 1907–1985, vol. VIII

Wiseman, Rev. Frederick Luke, 1858–1944, vol. IV

Wiseman, Very Rev. James, *died* 1925, vol. II

Wiseman, Air Cdre Percy John, 1888–1948, vol. IV

Wiseman, Robert Arthur, 1886–1955, vol. V

Wiseman, Stephen, 1907–1971, vol. VII

Wiseman, Sir William George Eden, 10th Bt, 1885–1962, vol. VI

Wiseman-Clarke, Lt-Gen. Somerset Molyneux, 1830–1905, vol. I

Wishart, D. J. Gibb, 1859–1934, vol. III

Wishart, George Macfeat, 1895–1958, vol. V

Wishart, John, 1898–1956, vol. V

Wishart, John, 1879–1970, vol. VI

Wishart, Rear-Adm. John Webster, 1892–1968, vol. VI

Wishart, Captain Robert, 1875–1938, vol. III (A), vol. IV

Wishart, Col Sir Sidney, 1854–1935, vol. III

Wiskemann, Elizabeth Meta, 1901–1971, vol. VII

Wissman, Major Herman von, 1853–1905, vol. I

Wister, Owen, 1860–1938, vol. III

Witham, Col James Kirkconnell Maxwell, 1848–1937, vol. III

Witham, Philip, *died* 1921, vol. II

Witherby, Harry Forbes, 1873–1943, vol. IV

Withers, Alfred, *died* 1932, vol. III

Withers, Col Charles M'Gregor, 1876–1958, vol. V

Withers, Captain Edgar Clements, 1883–1951, vol. V

Withers, Harry Livingston, 1864–1902, vol. I

Withers, Hartley, 1867–1950, vol. IV

Withers, Lt-Col Henry Hastings Cavendish, 1904–1948, vol. IV

Withers, Isobelle; *see* Dods-Withers.

Withers, Sir John James, 1863–1939, vol.III

Withers, Percy, 1867–1945, vol. IV

Withers, Lt-Col Samuel Henry, *died* 1942, vol. IV

Withycombe, Brig.-Gen. William Maunder, 1869–1951, vol. V

Witney, John Humphrey, 1879–1964, vol. VI

Witt, Sir John Clermont, 1907–1982, vol. VIII

Witt, Maj.-Gen. John Evered, 1897–1989, vol. VIII

Witt, John George, *died* 1906, vol. I

Witt, Sir Robert Clermont, *died* 1952, vol. V

Witt, Tansley, 1839–1915, vol. I

Witte, Count Sergius, 1849–1915, vol. I

Wittenham, 1st Baron, 1852–1931, vol. III

Wittenoom, Hon. Sir Edward Horne, 1854–1936, vol. III

Wittet, John, 1868–1952, vol. V

Wittewronge, Sir Charles L.; *see* Lawes-Wittewronge.

Wittewronge, Sir John Bennet L.; *see* Lawes-Wittewronge.

Wittewronge, Sir John Claud Bennet Lawes; *see* Lawes, Sir J. C. B.

Wittig, Georg, 1897–1987, vol. VIII

Wittgenstein, Ludwig, 1889–1951, vol. V

Wittkower, Rudolf, 1901–1971, vol. VII

Wittrick, William Henry, 1922–1986, vol. VIII

Witts, Rev. Francis Edward Broome, 1840–1913, vol. I

Witts, Brig. Frank Hole, 1887–1941, vol. IV

Witts, Maj.-Gen. Frederick Vavasour Broome, 1889–1969, vol. VI

Witts, Leslie John, 1898–1982, vol. VIII

Woakes, Claud Edward, 1868–1936, vol. III

Wodehouse, Hon. Armine, 1860–1901, vol. I

Wodehouse, Rev. Armine, 1860–1938, vol. III

Wodehouse, Edmond Henry, 1837–1923, vol. II

Wodehouse, Rt Hon. Edmond Robert, 1835–1914, vol. I

Wodehouse, Major Sir (Edwin) Frederick, 1851–1934, vol. III

Wodehouse, Major Ernest Charles Forbes, 1871–1915, vol. I

Wodehouse, Lt-Col Frederic William, 1867–1961, vol. VI

Wodehouse, Major Sir Frederick; *see* Wodehouse, Major Sir E. F.

Wodehouse, Helen Marion, 1880–1964, vol. VI

Wodehouse, Henry Ernest, 1845–1929, vol. III

Wodehouse, Gen. Sir Josceline Heneage, 1852–1930, vol. III

Wodehouse, Vice-Adm. Norman Atherton, 1887–1941, vol. IV

Wodehouse, Sir Pelham Grenville, 1881–1975, vol. VII

Wodehouse, Rev. Philip John, 1836–1917, vol. II

Wodehouse, Philip Peveril John, 1877–1951, vol. V

Wodeman, Guy Stanley, 1886–1970, vol. VI

Woden, George; *see* Slaney, G. W.

Woelmont, Henry, Baron de, 1881–1931, vol. III

Wofinden, Robert Cavill, 1914–1975, vol. VII

Woinarski, Casimir Julius Z.; *see* Zichy-Woinarski.

Wolf, Abraham, 1876–1948, vol. IV

Wolf, Lucien, 1857–1930, vol. III

Wolf-Ferrari, Ermanno, 1876–1948, vol. IV

Wolfe, Very Rev. Charles William, 1914–1980, vol. VII (AII)

Wolfe, Rev. Clarence Albert Edward, 1892–1967, vol. VI

Wolfe, Frederick John, *died* 1962, vol. VI

Wolfe, George, 1859–1941, vol. IV

Wolfe, Herbert Robert Inglewood, 1907–1970, vol. VI

Wolfe, Humbert, 1886–1940, vol. III

Wolfe, James Nathan, 1927–1988, vol. VIII

Wolfe, Nathan; *see* Wolfe, J. N.

Wolfe-Barry, Sir John Wolfe; *see* Barry.

Wolfe-Murray, Lt-Col Arthur Alexander, 1866–1918, vol. II

Wolfenden, Baron (Life Peer); John Frederick Wolfenden, 1906–1985, vol. VIII

Wolff, Hon. Sir Albert Asher, 1899–1977, vol. VII

Wolff, Lt-Co. Arnold Johnston, 1873–1941, vol. IV

Wolff, Edna; *see* Best, E.

Wolff, Ernest Charteris Holford, 1875–1946, vol. IV

Wolff, Eugene, 1896–1954, vol. V

Wolff, Frederick Ferdinand, 1910–1988, vol. VIII

Wolff, Gustav William, 1834–1913, vol. I

Wolff, Henry D.; *see* Drummond-Wolff.

Wolff, Rt Hon. Sir Henry Drummond Charles, 1830–1908, vol. I

Wolff, Henry William, 1840–1931, vol. III

Wolff, Johannes, *born* 1862, vol. IV

Wolff, John Arnold Harrop, 1912–1984, vol. VIII

Wolff, Michael, 1930–1976, vol. VII

Wolfflin, Heinrich, 1864–1945, vol. IV

Wolffsohn, Sir Arthur Norman, 1888–1967, vol. VI

Wolfit, Sir Donald, 1902–1968, vol. VI

Wollaston, Alexander Frederick Richmond, 1875–1930, vol. III

Wollaston, Sir Arthur Naylor, 1842–1922, vol. II

Wollaston, Sir Gerald Woods, 1874–1957, vol. V

Wollaston, Sir Harry Newton Phillips, 1846–1921, vol. II

Wollaston, Henry Woods, 1916–1989, vol. VIII

Wollaston, Vice-Adm. Herbert Arthur Buchanan-, 1878–1975, vol. VII

Wollen, Sir (Ernest) Russell (Storey), 1902–1986, vol. VIII

Wollen, Sir Russell; *see* Wollen, Sir E. R. S.

Wollen, William Barnes, 1857–1936, vol. III

Wolley, Sir Clive P.; *see* Phillipps-Wolley.

Wolley, Rev. Henry Francklyn, 1839–1915, vol. I

Wolley-Dod, Brig.-Gen. Owen Cadogan, 1863–1942, vol. IV

Wolmark, Alfred Aaran, 1877–1961, vol. VI

Wolmer, Viscount; William Matthew Palmer, 1912–1942, vol. IV

Wolpe, Berthold Ludwig, 1905–1989, vol. VIII

Wolrige-Gordon, Henry, 1831–1906, vol. I

Wolrige-Gordon, Col John Gordon, 1859–1925, vol. II

Wolrige Gordon, Captain Robert, *died* 1939, vol. III

Wolseley, 1st Viscount, 1833–1913, vol. I

Wolseley, Viscountess (2nd in line), 1872–1936, vol. III

Wolseley, Sir Capel Charles, 9th Bt (*cr* 1744), 1870–1923, vol. II

Wolseley, Sir Charles Michael, 9th Bt (*cr* 1628), 1846–1931, vol. III

Wolseley, Sir Edric Charles Joseph, 10th Bt (*cr* 1628), 1886–1954, vol. V

Wolseley, Garnet Ruskin, 1884–1967, vol. VI

Wolseley, Gen. Sir George Benjamin, 1839–1921, vol. II

Wolseley, Sir Reginald Beatty, 10th Bt (*cr* 1744), 1872–1933, vol. III

Wolseley, Rev. Sir William Augustus, 11th Bt (*cr* 1744), 1865–1950, vol. IV

Wolseley-Lewis, Mary, 1865–1955, vol. V

Wolstencroft, Frank, 1882–1952, vol. V

Wolstenholme, William, 1865–1931, vol. III

Wolverhampton, 1st Viscount, 1830–1911, vol. I

Wolverhampton, 2nd Viscount, 1870–1943, vol. IV

Wolverson, William Alfred, 1905–1974, vol. VII

Wolverton, 4th Baron, 1861–1932, vol. III

Wolverton, 5th Baron, 1904–1986, vol. VIII

Wolverton, 6th Baron, 1913–1988, vol. VIII

Wolvin, Roy Mitchell, 1880–1945, vol. IV

Wombwell, Lt-Gen. Arthur, 1821–1914, vol. I

Wombwell, Sir (Frederick) Philip (Alfred William), 6th Bt, 1910–1977, vol. VII

Wombwell, Sir George Orby, 4th Bt, 1832–1913, vol. I

Wombwell, Captain Sir Henry Herbert, 5th Bt, 1840–1926, vol. II

Wombwell, Sir Philip; *see* Wombwell, Sir F. P. A. W.

Womersley, J(ohn) Lewis, 1910–1990, vol. VIII

Womersley, Rt Hon. Sir Walter James, 1st Bt, 1878–1961, vol. VI

Wonham, Rear-Adm. (S) Charles Scrivener, 1870–1946, vol. IV

Wonnacott, Ven. Thomas Oswald, 1869–1957, vol. V

Wontner, Arthur, 1875–1960, vol. V

Wood, Sir Alexander, *died* 1924, vol. II

Wood, Rt Rev. Alexander, *died* 1937, vol. III

Wood, Alexander, 1879–1950, vol. IV

Wood, Major Alexander Vaughan Leipsic, 1867–1933, vol. III

Wood, Alfred, 1836–1906, vol. I

Wood, Sir Alfred, 1878–1960, vol. V

Wood, Alfred Cecil, 1896–1968, vol. VI

Wood, Ven. Alfred Maitland, 1840–1918, vol. II

Wood, Allan Fergusson, 1876–1966, vol. VI

Wood, Rev. Andrew, 1833–1917, vol. II

Wood, Rear-Adm. Arthur Edmund, 1875–1961, vol. VI

Wood, Arthur Henry, 1870–1964, vol. VI

Wood, Sir (Arthur) Michael, 1919–1987, vol. VIII

Wood, Sir Arthur Nicholas Lindsay, 2nd Bt (*cr* 1897), 1875–1939, vol. III

Wood, Captain Sir Basil Samuel Hill H.; *see* Hill-Wood.

Wood, Brooks Crompton, *died* 1946, vol. IV

Wood, Butler, 1854–1934, vol. III

Wood, Catherine Jane, *died* 1930, vol. III

Wood, Col Cecil Ernest, *died* 1932, vol. III

Wood, Cecil Godfrey, 1851–1906, vol. I

Wood, Rt Rev. Cecil John, 1874–1957, vol. V

Wood, Rev. Canon Cecil Thomas, 1903–1980, vol. VII

Wood, Sir (Charles) Edgar, 1877–1941, vol. IV

Wood, Charles Frederick, 1867–1937, vol. III

Wood, Charles Malcolm, 1846–1915, vol. I

Wood, Col Charles Michell Aloysius, 1873–1936, vol. III

Wood, Lt-Col Charles Peevor Boileau, *died* 1932, vol. III

Wood, Rt Rev. Claud Thomas Thellusson, 1885–1961, vol. VI

Wood, Lt-Col Cyril, 1852–1904, vol. I

Wood, Lt-Col David Edward, 1853–1927, vol. II

Wood, Sir David John Hatherley P., 7th Bt (*cr* 1837); *see* Page Wood.

Wood, Sir Edgar; *see* Wood, Sir C. E.

Wood, Rev. Edmund Gough De Salis, 1842–1932, vol. III

Wood, Edmund Walter Hanbury, 1898–1947, vol. IV

Wood, Sir Edward, 1839–1917, vol. II

Wood, Maj.-Gen. Edward Alexander, 1841–1898, vol. I

Wood, Brig.-Gen. Edward Allan, 1872–1930, vol. III

Wood, Sir (Edward) Graham, 1854–1930, vol. III

Wood, Edward Stephen, 1890–1948, vol. IV

Wood, Maj.-Gen. Sir Elliott, 1844–1931, vol. III

Wood, Eric Rawlinson, 1893–1977, vol. VII

Wood, Lt-Gen. Sir Ernest, 1894–1971, vol. VII

Wood, Ernest Clement, 1890–1970, vol. VI

Wood, Brig.-Gen. Ernest Joseph MacFarlane, 1867–1939, vol. III

Wood, Ethel Mary, *died* 1970, vol. VI

Wood, Field-Marshal Sir Evelyn; *see* Wood, Field-Marshal Sir H. E.

Wood, Hon. Col Evelyn Fitzgerald Michell, 1869–1943, vol. IV

Wood, Francis Derwent, 1871–1926, vol. II

Wood, Sir Frank, 1913–1974, vol. VII

Wood, Franklin Garrett, *died* 1978, vol. VII

Wood, Frederick Benjamin, 1849–1928, vol. II

Wood, Frederick Lloyd Whitfeld, 1903–1989, vol. VIII

Wood, George Arnold, 1865–1928, vol. II

Wood, Sir George Ernest Francis, 1900–1978, vol. VII (AII)

Wood, Maj.-Gen. George Neville, 1898–1982, vol. VIII

Wood, Gervase E., 1877–1954, vol. V

Wood, Sir Graham; *see* Wood, Sir E. G.

Wood, Harrie Dalrymple, 1869–1937, vol. III

Wood, Col Hastings St Leger, 1856–1933, vol. III

Wood, Haydn, 1882–1959, vol. V

Wood, Col Henry, 1835–1919, vol. II

Wood, Col Henry, 1872–1940, vol. III

Wood, Henry Ernest, 1868–1946, vol. IV

Wood, Field-Marshal Sir (Henry) Evelyn, 1838–1919, vol. II

Wood, Sir Henry Hastings Affleck, 1826–1904, vol. I

Wood, Sir Henry Joseph, 1869–1944, vol. IV

Wood, Rev. Henry Thellusson, *died* 1928, vol. II

Wood, Sir Henry Trueman, 1845–1929, vol. III

Wood, Herbert, 1893–1950, vol. IV

Wood, Herbert Duncan S.; *see* Searles-Wood.

Wood, Herbert George, 1879–1963, vol. VI

Wood, Hubert Lyon-Campbell, 1903–1982, vol. VIII

Wood, Hugh McKinnon, 1884–1955, vol. V

Wood, Rev. Hugh Singleton, 1859–1941, vol. IV

Wood, I. Hickory, *died* 1913, vol. I

Wood, Sir Ian Jeffreys, 1903–1986, vol. VIII

Wood, Captain Sir Ian Lindsay, 3rd Bt (*cr* 1897), 1909–1946, vol. IV

Wood, J. S. 1853–1920, vol. II

Wood, James, *died* 1936, vol. III

Wood, Lt-Col Sir James L.; *see* Leigh-Wood.

Wood, Sir James Lockwood, *died* 1941, vol. IV

Wood, James Maxwell, (Max Wood), 1914–1982, vol. VIII

Wood, Rev. John, 1833–1929, vol. III

Wood, Sir John, 1st Bt (*cr* 1918), 1857–1951, vol. V

Wood, John, 1880–1952, vol. V

Wood, Sir John Arthur Haigh, 2nd Bt (*cr* 1918), 1888–1974, vol. VII

Wood, Sir John Barry, 1870–1933, vol. III

Wood, Lt-Col John Bruce, *died* 1927, vol. II

Wood, Hon. John Dennistoun, 1829–1914, vol. I

Wood, John Gathorne, 1839–1929, vol. III

Wood, Captain John Lockhart, 1871–1915, vol. I

Wood, Lt-Col John Nicholas Price, 1877–1962, vol. VI

Wood, Major Sir John Page, 5th Bt (*cr* 1837), 1860–1912, vol. I

Wood, John Philip, *died* 1906, vol. I

Wood, Sir John Stuart Page, 6th Bt (*cr* 1837), 1898–1955, vol. V

Wood, John Vincent, 1905–1952, vol. V

Wood, Lt-Col John William Massey, 1855–1916, vol. II

Wood, Rev. Joseph, 1842–1921, vol. II

Wood, Josiah, 1843–1927, vol. II

Wood, Sir Kenneth Millns, 1909–1986, vol. VIII

Wood, Kenneth Spencer, 1897–1963, vol. VI

Wood, Rt Hon. Sir Kingsley, 1881–1943, vol. IV

Wood, Lawson, 1878–1957, vol. V

Wood, Leslie Stuart, 1873–1948, vol. IV

Wood, Sir Lindsay, 1st Bt (*cr* 1897), 1834–1920, vol. II

Wood, Rev. Llewellyn, *died* 1929, vol. III

Wood, Mary Hay, *died* 1934, vol. III

Wood, Sir Matthew, 4th Bt (*cr* 1837), 1857–1908, vol. I

Wood, Max; *see* Wood, J. M.

Wood, Metcalfe, *died* 1944, vol. IV

Wood, Sir Michael; *see* Wood, Sir A. M.

Wood, Major Sir Murdoch McKenzie, 1881–1949, vol. IV

Wood, Oswald Edward, 1899–1974, vol. VII

Wood, Lt-Col Oswald Gillespie, 1851–1902, vol. I

Wood, Paul Hamilton, 1907–1962, vol. VI

Wood, Philip Francis, 1858–1939, vol. III

Wood, Brig.-Gen. Philip Richard, 1868–1845, vol. IV

Wood, Ralph, 1921–1986, vol. VIII

Wood, Sir Richard, 1806–1900, vol. I

Wood, Gen. Robert E., 1879–1969, vol. VI

Wood, Robert Henry, 1860–1930, vol. III

Wood, Sir Robert Stanford, 1886–1963, vol. VI

Wood, Robert Williams, 1868–1955, vol. V

Wood, Roger L.; *see* Leigh-Wood.

Wood, R(onald) McKinnon, 1892–1967, vol. VI

Wood, Maj.-Gen. Sam; *see* Wood, Maj.-Gen. G. N.

Wood, Major Sir Samuel Hill H.; *see* Hill-Wood.

Wood, Starr, 1870–1944, vol. IV

Wood, Stuart Zachary Taylor, 1889–1966, vol. VI

Wood, Sydney Herbert, 1884–1958, vol. V

Wood, Rev. Theodore, 1862–1923, vol. II

Wood, Col Thomas, 1853–1933, vol. III

Wood, Thomas, 1892–1950, vol. IV

Wood, Rev. Thomas, 1919–1987, vol. VIII

Wood, Thomas Alfred, 1867–1944, vol. IV

Wood, Thomas Andrew Urquhart, 1914–1975, vol. VII

Wood, Thomas Barlow, 1869–1929, vol. III

Wood, Brig.-Gen. Thomas Birchall, 1865–1944, vol. IV

Wood, Rt Hon. Thomas McKinnon, 1855–1927, vol. II

Wood, Thomas Outterson, *died* 1930, vol. III

Wood, W. H., 1888–1954, vol. V

Wood, Walter, 1866–1961, vol. Vi

Wood, Walter Gunnell, 1861–1942, vol. IV

Wood, Sir Wilfred William Hill H.; *see* Hill-Wood.

Wood, Wilfrid Burton, 1883–1943, vol. IV

Wood, Rev. William, 1829–1919, vol. II

Wood, William Alfred Rae, 1878–1970, vol. VI

Wood, William Charles Henry, *died* 1947, vol. IV (A)

Wood, William Francis John, 1876–1934, vol. III

Wood, William Henry Heton A.; *see* Arden Wood.

Wood, William K.; *see* King-Wood.

Wood, William L.; 1879–1958, vol. V

Wood, William Thomas, 1877–1958, vol. V

Wood, Sir William Valentine, 1883–1959, vol. V

Wood, William Walter, 1896–1982, vol. VIII

Wood, William Wightman, 1846–1914, vol. I

Wood, Sir William Wilkinson, 1879–1963, vol. VI

Wood, Lt-Col Wyndham Madden Pierpoint, *died* 1950, vol. IV

Wood, Zachary Taylor, 1860–1915, vol. I

Wood-Martin, William Gregory, 1847–1917, vol. II

Wood-Samuel, Rev. Richard, *died* 1939, vol. III

Wood-Seys, Roland Alex., 1854–1919, vol. II

Woodall, Sir Corbet, 1841–1916, vol. II

Woodall, Col Frederic, 1866–1956, vol. V

Woodall, Lt-Col Harold Whiteman, 1872–1951, vol. V

Woodall, Lt-Gen. Sir John Dane, 1897–1985, vol. VIII

Woodall, Mary, 1901–1988, vol. VIII

Woodall, William, 1832–1901, vol. I

Woodard, Rev. Canon Alfred Lambert, 1880–1971, vol. VII

Woodard, Rev. Lambert, 1848–1924, vol. II

Woodberry, George Edward, 1855–1930, vol. III

Woodbridge, 1st Baron, 1867–1949, vol. IV

Woodburn, Rt Hon. Arthur, 1890–1978, vol. VII

Woodburn, Rev. George, 1867–1947, vol. IV

Woodburn, Hon. Sir John, 1843–1902, vol. I

Woodburn, Lt-Col Thomas Stanley, 1881–1965, vol. VI

Woodcock, Eric Charles, 1904–1978, vol. VII

Woodcock, Rt Hon. George, 1904–1979, vol. VII

Woodcock, Co. Herbert Charles, 1871–1950, vol. IV

Woodcock, Hubert Bayley Drysdale, 1867–1957, vol. V

Woodcock, John, 1920–1981, vol. VIII

Woodcock, T. A., 1897–1965, vol. VI

Woodcock, Brig.-Gen. Wilfrid James, 1878–1960, vol. V

Woodd, Ven. Henry Alexander, 1865–1954, vol. V

Woodeson, Sir James Brewis, 1917–1980, vol. VII

Woodfall, Robert, 1855–1920, vol. II

Woodfield, Ven. Samuel Percy, 1889–1983, vol. VIII

Woodford, Charles Morris, 1852–1927, vol. II

Woodford, Brig. Edward Cecil James, 1901–1988, vol. VIII
Woodford, James, 1893–1976, vol. VII
Woodford, Stewart Lyndon, 1835–1913, vol. I
Woodford, Thomas Gordon Charles, 1911–1962, vol. VI
Woodforde, Very Rev. Christopher, 1907–1962, vol. VI
Woodgate, Sir Alfred, 1860–1943, vol. IV
Woodgate, Maj.-Gen. Edward Robert Prevost, 1845–1900, vol. I
Woodgate, (Hubert) Leslie, 1902–1961, vol. VI
Woodgate, Leslie; see Woodgate, H. L.
Woodgate, Walter Bradford, 1840–1920, vol. II
Woodger, Joseph Henry, 1894–1981, vol. VIII
Woodhall, Lt-Comdr Eric Langton, 1899–1940, vol. III
Woodham-Smith, Cecil (Blanche), 1896–1977, vol. VII
Woodhams, Herbert Martin, 1890–1965, vol. VI
Woodhead, Arthur Longden, 1862–1957, vol. V
Woodhead, Ernest, 1857–1944, vol. IV
Woodhead, Sir German Simms, 1855–1921, vol. II
Woodhead, Henry George Wandesford, 1883–1959, vol. V
Woodhead, Sir John Ackroyd, 1881–1973, vol. VII
Woodhouse, Albert Cyril, 1887–1940, vol. IV
Woodhouse, Arthur William Webster, 1867–1961, vol. VI
Woodhouse, Adm. Sir Charles Henry Lawrence, 1893–1978, vol. VII
Woodhouse, Rev. Frederick Charles, 1827–1905, vol. I
Woodhouse, Brig. Harold Lister, 1887–1960, vol. V
Woodhouse, Rear-Adm. Hector Roy Mackenzie, 1889–1971, vol. VII
Woodhouse, Henry, 1913–1990, vol. VIII
Woodhouse, Rev. Henry George, 1852–1930, vol. III
Woodhouse, Herbert, 1859–1957, vol. V
Woodhouse, Rt Rev. John Walker, 1884–1955, vol. V
Woodhouse, Sir Percy, 1856–1931, vol. III
Woodhouse, Maj.-Gen. Sir Percy; see Woodhouse, Maj.-Gen. Sir T. P.
Woodhouse, Sir Stewart, 1846–1921, vol. II
Woodhouse, Thomas, 1862–1933, vol. III
Woodhouse, Maj.-Gen. Sir (Tom) Percy, 1857–1931, vol. III
Woodhouse, Vernon Kerslake, died 1936, vol. III
Woodhouse, William Bradley, 1873–1940, vol. III
Woodhouse, William John, 1866–1937, vol. III
Woodhull, Zula Maud, died 1940, vol. III
Woodifield, Rear-Adm. Anthony, 1912–1986, vol. VIII
Woodifield, Col Anthony Hudson, 1867–1946, vol. IV
Wooding, Rt Hon. Sir Hugh Olliviere Beresford, 1904–1974, vol. VII
Wooding, John Conrad, 1901–1954, vol. V
Woodland, Col Arthur Law, 1849–1921, vol. II
Woodland, Austin William, 1914–1990, vol. VIII
Woodland, William Norton Ferrier, 1879–1952, vol. V
Woodley, Sir (Frederick George) Richard, died 1971, vol. VII

Woodley, Sir Richard; see Woodley, Sir F. G. R.
Woodlock, Rev. Francis, 1871–1940, vol. III
Woodman, Sir George Joseph, 1847–1915, vol. I
Woodman, John, 1888–1971, vol. VII
Woodnutt, Harold Frederick Martin; see Woodnutt, Mark.
Woodnutt, Mark, (Harold Frederick Martin Woodnutt), 1918–1974, vol. VII
Woodroffe, Brig.-Gen. Charles Richard, 1878–1965, vol. VI
Woodroffe, Hon. James T., 1838–1908, vol. I
Woodroffe, Sir John George, 1865–1936, vol. III
Woodroffe, Paul Vincent, 1875–1954, vol. V
Woodrooffe, Very Rev. Henry Reade, 1834–1913, vol. I
Woodrow, Maj.-Gen. (Albert) John, 1919–1988, vol. VIII
Woodrow, Maj.-Gen. John; see Woodrow, Maj.-Gen. A. J.
Woodruff, Douglas; see Woodruff, J. D.
Woodruff, Harold Addison, died 1966, vol. VI
Woodruff, (John) Douglas, 1897–1978, vol. VII
Woodruff, Keith Montague Cumberland, 1891–1978, vol. VII
Woodruff, Timothy Lester, 1858–1913, vol. I
Woods, Albert, died 1944, vol. IV
Woods, Lt-Col Albert Edward, 1862–1938, vol. III
Woods, Sir Albert William, 1816–1904, vol. I
Woods, Rev. Vice-Adm. Alexander Riall Wadham, 1880–1954, vol. V
Woods, Alice, 1849–1941, vol. IV
Woods, Donald Devereux, 1912–1964, vol. VI
Woods, Maj.-Gen. Edward Ambrose, 1891–1957, vol. V
Woods, Rt Rev. Edward Sydney, 1877–1953, vol. V
Woods, Rt Rev. Frank Theodore, 1874–1932, vol. III
Woods, George David, 1901–1982, vol. VIII
Woods, Rev. George Frederick, 1907–1966, vol. VI
Woods, Rev. George Saville, 1886–1951, vol. V
Woods, Col Harold, 1879–1952, vol. V
Woods, Henry, 1846–1921, vol. II
Woods, Henry, 1868–1952, vol. V
Woods, Henry Charles, 1841–1931, vol. III
Woods, Henry Charles, 1881–1939, vol. III
Woods, Adm. Sir Henry Felix, 1843–1929, vol. III
Woods, Rev. Henry George, 1842–1915, vol. I
Woods, Hon. Henry John Bacon, 1842–1916, vol. II
Woods, Brig.-Gen. Hugh Kennedy, 1877–1964, vol. VI
Woods, Irene Charlotte, 1891–1976, vol. VII
Woods, Sir James Edward, 1850–1944, vol. IV
Woods, Hon. Lt-Col James Hossack, 1867–1941, vol. IV
Woods, Sir James William, died 1941, vol. IV
Woods, Sir John Harold Edmund, 1895–1962, vol. VI
Woods, Joseph Ainsworth, 1870–1947, vol. IV
Woods, Joseph Andrews, died 1925, vol. II
Woods, Margaret Louisa, 1856–1945, vol. IV
Woods, Matthew Snooke Grosvenor, 1838–1925, vol. II
Woods, Maurice Henry, 1882–1929, vol. III
Woods, Oliver Frederick John Bradley, 1911–1972, vol. VII
Woods, Percy, 1842–1922, vol. II

Woods, Col Philip James, 1880–1961, vol. Vi
Woods, Sir Raymond Wybrow, 1882–1943, vol. IV
Woods, Reginald Salisbury, (Rex Woods), 1891–1986, vol. VIII
Woods, Rex; *see* Woods, Reginald S.
Woods, Richard Lennox, 1838–1918, vol. II
Woods, Sir Robert Henry, 1865–1938, vol. III
Woods, Sir Robert Stanton, 1877–1954, vol. V
Woods, Samuel, 1846–1915, vol. I
Woods, Samuel Moses James, 1867–1931, vol. III
Woods, Maj.-Gen. Thomas Frederic Mackie, 1904–1982, vol. VIII
Woods, Walter Sainsbury, 1884–1960, vol. V(A)
Woods, Adm. Sir Wilfrid John Wentworth, 1906–1975, vol. VII
Woods, Sir Wilfrid Wentworth, 1876–1947, vol. IV
Woods, William, 1855–1932, vol. III
Woods, William Forster, 1865–1942, vol. IV
Woods, Col William Talbot, 1891–1975, vol. VII
Woods, William Wilson, 1884–1972, vol. VII
Woods Ballard, Lt-Col Basil, 1900–1980, vol. VII
Woodthorpe, John Frederick, 1897–1966, vol. VI
Woodthorpe, Ven. Robert Augustus, 1861–1931, vol. III
Woodthorpe, Col Robert Gosset, 1844–1898, vol. I
Woodville, Richard Caton, 1856–1927, vol. II
Woodward, Sir (Alfred) Chad (Turner), 1880–1957, vol. V
Woodward, Arthur Maurice, 1883–1973, vol. VII
Woodward, Sir Arthur Smith, 1864–1944, vol. IV
Woodward, Sir Chad; *see* Woodward, Sir A. C. T.
Woodward, Rt Rev. Clifford Salisbury, 1878–1959, vol. V
Woodward, Denys Cuthbert, 1902–1972, vol. VII
Woodward, Edward Gilbert, 1900–1950, vol. IV
Woodward, Lt-Col Edward Hamilton Everard, 1888–1976, vol. VII
Woodward, Maj.-Gen. Sir Edward Mabbott, 1861–1943, vol. IV
Woodward, Lt-Gen. Sir Eric Winslow, 1899–1967, vol. VI
Woodward, Sir (Ernest) Llewellyn, 1890–1971, vol. VII
Woodward, (Foster) Neville, 1905–1985, vol. VIII
Woodward, Col Francis Willoughby, 1872–1926, vol. II
Woodward, George Ernest, 1865–1939, vol. III
Woodward, Henry, 1832–1921, vol. II
Woodward, Rear-Adm. Sir Henry William, 1879–1959, vol. V
Woodward, Rev. Herbert Willoughby, 1854–1932, vol. III
Woodward, Horace Bolingbroke, 1848–1914, vol. I
Woodward, Joan; *see* Woodward, W. J.
Woodward, Joan, (Mrs L. T. Blakeman), 1916–1971, vol. VII
Woodward, Col John Henry, 1849–1918, vol. II
Woodward, Sir Lionel Mabbott, 1864–1925, vol. II
Woodward, Sir Llewellyn; *see* Woodward, Sir E. L.
Woodward, Marcus, *died* 1940, vol. III
Woodward, Neville; *see* Woodward, F. N.
Woodward, Oliver Holmes, 1885–1966, vol. VI
Woodward, Adm. Robert, 1838–1907, vol. I
Woodward, Robert Burns, 1917–1979, vol. VII

Woodward, Robert Simpson, 1849–1924, vol. II
Woodward, William Harrison, 1855–1941, vol. IV
Woodward, (Winifred) Joan, 1907–1981, vol. VIII
Woodward-Nutt, Arthur Edgar, 1902–1980, vol. VII
Woodwark, Sir (Arthur) Stanley, *died* 1945, vol. IV
Woodwark, Col (George) Graham, 1874–1938, vol. III
Woodwark, Col Graham; *see* Woodwark, Col George G.
Woodwark, Sir Stanley; *see* Woodwark, Sir A. S.
Woodwright, Surg. Rear-Adm. Charles Sharman, 1870–1949, vol. IV
Woodyatt, Maj.-Gen. Nigel Gresley, 1861–1936, vol. III
Woof, Rowsby, 1883–1943, vol. IV
Wookey, Eric Edgar, 1892–1985, vol. VIII
Woolacott, John Evans, 1862–1936, vol. III
Woolavington, 1st Baron, 1849–1935, vol. III
Woolcock, William James Uglow, 1878–1947, vol. IV
Wooldridge, George Henry, *died* 1957, vol. V
Wooldridge, Harry Ellis, 1845–1917, vol. II
Wooldridge, Henry, 1908–1975, vol. VII
Wooldridge, Sidney William, 1900–1963, vol. VI
Wooldridge, Walter Reginald, 1900–1966, vol. VI
Woolf, Albert Edward Mortimer, 1884–1957, vol. V
Woolf, Rev. Bertram Lee, *died* 1956, vol. V
Woolf, Charles H.; *see* Hyatt-Woolf.
Woolf, Leonard Sidney, 1880–1969, vol. VI
Woolf, Virginia, 1882–1941, vol. IV
Woolfe, Brig. Richard Dean Townsend, 1888–1966, vol. VI
Woolford, Sir Eustace Gordon, 1876–1966, vol. VI
Woolfryes, Surg.-Gen. Sir John Andrews, 1823–1912, vol. I
Woolgar, Alfred John, 1879–1968, vol. VI
Wooll, Edward, 1878–1970, vol. VI
Woollam, Rev. Canon J., 1827–1909, vol. I
Woollard, Herbert Henry, 1889–1939, vol. III
Woollcombe, Captain Charles George Ley, 1884–1962, vol. VI
Woollcombe, Lt-Gen. Sir Charles Louis, 1857–1934, vol. III
Woollcombe, Rt Rev. Henry St John Stirling, 1869–1941, vol. IV
Woollcombe, Dame Jocelyn May, 1898–1986, vol. VIII
Woollcombe, Adm. Louis Charles Stirling, 1872–1951, vol. V
Woollcombe, Major Malcolm Louis, 1891–1968, vol. VI
Woollcombe, Adm. Maurice, 1868–1930, vol. III
Woollcott, Alexander, 1887–1943, vol. IV
Woollen, James, 1854–1921, vol. II
Wooler, Arthur, 1912–1989, vol. VIII
Woolley, Baron (Life Peer); Harold Woolley, 1905–1986, vol. VIII
Woolley, Rev. (Alfred) Russell, 1899–1986, vol. VIII
Woolley, Charles, 1846–1922, vol. II
Woolley, Lt-Col Sir Charles Augustus, 1859–1936, vol. III
Woolley, Sir Charles Campbell, 1893–1981, vol. VIII
Woolley, Paymaster Rear-Adm. Charles Edward Allen, 1863–1940, vol. III
Woolley, Sir (Charles) Leonard, 1880–1960, vol. V

Woolley, Frank Edward, 1887–1978, vol. VII
Woolley, Rev. Geoffrey Harold, 1892–1968, vol. VI
Woolley, Howard Mark, 1879–1971, vol. VII
Woolley, Sir Leonard; *see* Woolley, Sir C. L.
Woolley, Rev. Reginald Maxwell, 1877–1931, vol. III
Woolley, Richard, 1916–1986, vol. VIII
Woolley, Sir Richard van der Riet, 1906–1986, vol. VIII
Woolley, Rev. Russell; *see* Woolley, Rev. A. R.
Woolley, Samuel Walter, 1865–1927, vol. II
Woolley, William Edward, 1901–1989, vol. VIII
Woolley-Hart, Arthur, 1859–1941, vol. IV
Woolmer, Rt Rev. Laurence Henry, 1906–1977, vol. VII
Woolmer, Ronald Francis, 1908–1962, vol. VI
Woolner, Alfred Cooper, *died* 1936, vol. III
Woolner, Maj.-Gen. Christopher Geoffrey, 1893–1984, vol. VIII
Woolnough, Rev. Canon Howard Frank, 1886–1973, vol. VII
Woolnough, Walter George, 1876–1958, vol. V
Woolrych, H. R., 1858–1917, vol. II
Wools-Sampson, Col Sir Aubrey, *died* 1924, vol. II
Woolston, Thomas Henry, 1855–1927, vol. II
Woolton, 1st Earl of, 1883–1964, vol. VI
Woolton, 2nd Earl of, 1922–1969, vol. VI
Woolveridge, Air Cdre Harry Leonard, 1887–1960, vol. V
Woon, Gen. Sir John Blaxall, 1856–1938, vol. III
Woosnam, Ven. Charles Maxwell, 1856–1930, vol. III
Woosnam, R. B., *died* 1915, vol. I
Wootten, Aubrey Francis Wootten, 1866–1923, vol. II
Wootten, Maj.-Gen. Sir George Frederick, 1893–1970, vol. VI
Wootten, Maj.-Gen. Richard Montague, 1889–1979, vol. VII
Wootton of Abinger, Baroness (Life Peer); Barbara Frances, 1897–1988, vol. VIII
Wootton, Harold Samuel, 1891–1989, vol. VIII
Wootton, Hubert Arthur, 1884–1947, vol. IV
Wootton-Davies, James Henry, 1884–1964, vol. VI
Worboys, Sir Arthur Thomas, *died* 1966, vol. VI
Worboys, Sir Walter John, 1900–1969, vol. VI
Worden, Alastair Norman, 1916–1987, vol. VIII
Wordie, Sir James Mann, 1889–1962, vol. VI
Wordingham, Charles Henry, 1866–1925, vol. II
Wordsworth, Rev. Christopher, 1848–1938, vol. III
Wordsworth, Dame Elizabeth, 1840–1932, vol. III
Wordsworth, Rt Rev. John, 1843–1911, vol. I
Wordsworth, Maj.-Gen. Robert Harley, 1894–1984, vol. VIII
Wordsworth, William, 1835–1917, vol. II
Wordsworth, William Christopher, 1878–1950, vol. IV
Wordsworth, Captain Sir William Henry Laycock, 1880–1960, vol. V
Worgan, Lt-Gen. John, 1821–1909, vol. I
Worgan, Brig.-Gen. Rivers Berney, *died* 1936, vol. III
Worgan, Col Sydney Drummond, 1872–1950, vol. IV
Workman, Charles Rufus Marshall, *died* 1942, vol. IV
Workman, Fanny Bullock, *died* 1925, vol. II
Workman, Harold, 1897–1975, vol. VII

Workman, Rev. Herbert Brook, 1862–1951, vol. V
Workman, Mark, 1864–1936, vol. III
Workman, Walter Percy, 1863–1918, vol. II
Workman, William Arthur, 1877–1956, vol. V
Workman, William Hunter, 1847–1937, vol. III
Workman, William Thomas, *died* 1971, vol. VII
Workman-Macnaghten, Rt Hon. Sir Francis Edmund; *see* Macnaghten.
Worley, Sir Arthur, 1st Bt, 1871–1937, vol. III
Worley, Frederick Palliser, 1880–1960, vol. V(A)
Worley, Sir Newnham Arthur, 1892–1976, vol. VII
Worlledge, Rev. Arthur John, 1848–1919, vol. II
Worlledge, Sir John Leonard, 1895–1968, vol. VI
Wormald, Francis, 1904–1972, vol. VII
Wormald, Sir John, 1859–1933, vol. III
Wormall, Arthur, 1900–1964, vol. VI
Wormell, Donald Ernest Wilson, 1908–1990, vol. VIII
Wormell, Richard, 1838–1914, vol. I
Worms, 2nd Baron de, 1829–1912, vol. I
Worms, 3rd Baron de, 1869–1938, vol. III
Worms, Percy George de, 1873–1941, vol. IV
Wornum, George Grey, 1888–1957, vol. V
Wornum, Ralph Selden, 1847–1910, vol. I
Worrall, Arthur Hardey, 1868–1960, vol. V
Worrall, Air Vice-Marshal John, 1911–1988, vol. VIII
Worrell, Most Rev. Clarendon Lamb, 1853–1934, vol. III
Worrell, Sir Frank Mortimer Maglinne, 1924–1967, vol. VI
Worrell, John Austin, 1852–1927, vol. II
Worsfold, Sir Thomas Cato, 1st Bt, *died* 1936, vol. III
Worsfold, William Basil, 1858–1939, vol. III
Worsley, Lord; Charles Sackville Pelham, 1887–1914, vol. I
Worsley, Lady; (Alexandra Mary Freesia), 1890–1963, vol. VI
Worsley, Rev. Edward, 1844–1923, vol. II
Worsley, Comdr Frank Arthur, 1872–1943, vol. IV
Worsley, Very Rev. Godfrey Stuart Harling, 1906–1990, vol. VIII
Worsley, Very Rev. Gordon; *see* Worsley, Very Rev. Godfrey S. H.
Worsley, Col Henry Robert Brown, 1833–1902, vol. I
Worsley, Lt-Gen. Sir John Francis, 1912–1987, vol. VIII
Worsley, Philip Ernest T. C.; *see* Tindal-Carill-Worsley.
Worsley, Ralph Marcus Meaburn, 1887–1939, vol. III
Worsley, Rev. Richard, 1889–1972, vol. VII
Worsley, Lt-Col Richard Stanley, 1879–1917, vol. II
Worsley, Major Ronald Henry Warton, 1886–1932, vol. III
Worsley, Col Sidney John, 1895–1974, vol. VII
Worsley, Col Sir William Arthington, 4th Bt, 1890–1973, vol. VII
Worsley, Sir William Cayley, 2nd Bt, 1828–1897, vol. I
Worsley, Sir William Henry Arthington, 3rd Bt, 1861–1936, vol. III
Worsley-Gough, Lt-Col Henry Worsley; *see* Gough.

Worsley-Taylor, Sir Francis Edward, 4th Bt, 1874–1958, vol. V

Worsley-Taylor, Sir Henry Wilson, 1st Bt, 1847–1924, vol. II

Worsley-Taylor, Lt-Col Sir James, 2nd Bt, 1872–1933, vol. III

Worsley-Taylor, Captain Sir John Godfrey, 3rd Bt, 1915–1952, vol. V

Worsnop, Bernard Lister, 1892–1980, vol. VII

Worster-Drought, Charles, *died* 1971, vol. VII

Worswick, Thomas, *died* 1932, vol. III

Wort, Sir Alfred William Ewart, 1883–1976, vol. VII

Worth, Arthur Hovenden, 1877–1955, vol. V

Worth, Claud, *died* 1936, vol. III

Wortham, Maj.-Gen. Geoffrey Christopher Hale, 1913–1967, vol. VI

Wortham, Col Harold Charles Webster Hale, 1878–1939, vol. III

Wortham, Hugh Evelyn, 1884–1959, vol. V

Wortham, Brig. Philip William Temple Hale, 1874–1955, vol. V

Worthington, Albert Octavius, 1844–1918, vol. II

Worthington, Arthur Furley, 1874–1964, vol. VI

Worthington, Arthur Mason, 1852–1916, vol. II

Worthington, Charles Edward, 1897–1970, vol. VI

Worthington, Col Edward Bruen, 1860–1945, vol. IV

Worthington, Col Sir Edward Scott, 1876–1953, vol. V

Worthington, Frank, 1874–1964, vol. VI

Worthington, Maj.-Gen. Frederic Frank, 1889–1967, vol. VI

Worthington, Henry Hugo, 1857–1924, vol. II

Worthington, Sir Hubert, 1886–1963, vol. VI

Worthington, John Morton, 1883–1956, vol. V

Worthington, Sir John Vigers, 1872–1951, vol. V

Worthington, Sir Percy Scott, 1864–1939, vol. III

Worthington, Rear-Adm. Roger Ernest, 1889–1967, vol. VI

Worthington, Thomas, 1850–1933, vol. III

Worthington, William Barton, 1854–1939, vol. III

Worthington-Evans, Rt Hon. Sir Laming, 1st Bt, 1868–1931, vol. III

Worthington-Evans, Sir Shirley; *see* Worthington-Evans, Sir W. S. W.

Worthington-Evans, Sir (William) Shirley (Worthington), 2nd Bt, 1904–1971, vol. VII

Wortley, Ben Atkinson, 1907–1989, vol. VIII

Wortley, Hon. Clare Euphemia S.; *see* Stuart-Wortley.

Wortley, Maj.-Gen. Hon. Edward James Montagu S.; *see* Stuart-Wortley.

Wortley, Rev. Edward Jocelyn, *died* 1928, vol. II

Wortley, Edward Jocelyn, 1884–1942, vol. IV

Wortley, Hon. Mrs Edward S.; *see* Stuart Wortley, Violet.

Wortley, Harry Almond Saville, 1885–1947, vol. IV

Wortley, Lt-Gen. Hon. Sir Richard Montagu S.; *see* Stuart-Wortley.

Worton, Albert Samuel, 1874–1940, vol. III

Wotherspoon, (George) Ralph (Howard), 1897–1979, vol. VII

Wotherspoon, Ralph; *see* Wotherspoon, G. R. H.

Wotherspoon, Robert Andrew, 1912–1975, vol. VII

Wragg, Sir Herbert, *died* 1956, vol. V

Wragg, Hon. Sir Walter Thomas, 1842–1913, vol. I

Wragge, Clement Lindley, 1852–1922, vol. II

Wragge, Robert Horton Vernon, 1854–1933, vol. III

Wraight, Ernest Alfred, 1879–1946, vol. IV

Wraith, Col Ernest Arnold, 1876–1937, vol. III

Wrangel, Count Herman, 1857–1934, vol. III

Wrangham, Cuthbert Edward, 1907–1982, vol. VIII

Wrangham, Dennis; *see* Wrangham, C. E.

Wrangham, Rev. Francis, *died* 1941, vol. IV

Wrangham, Sir Geoffrey Walter, 1900–1986, vol. VIII

Wratislaw, Albert Charles, 1862–1938, vol. III

Wratislaw, Adm. Henry Rushworth, 1832–1913, vol. I

Wraxall, 1st Baron, 1873–1931, vol. III

Wraxall, Sir Charles Frederick Lascelles, 7th Bt, 1896–1951, vol. V

Wraxall, Sir Morville William, 6th Bt, 1862–1902, did not have an entry in Who's Who.

Wraxall, Sir Morville William Lascelles, 8th Bt, 1922–1978, vol. VII

Wraxall, Sir Morville William Nathaniel, 5th Bt, 1834–1898, vol. I

Wray, Brig.-Gen. Cecil; *see* Wray, Brig.-Gen. J. C.

Wray, Vice-Adm. Fawcet, 1873–1932, vol. III

Wray, Rev. Frederick William, 1864–1943, vol. IV

Wray, Brig.-Gen. (John) Cecil, 1864–1947, vol. IV

Wray, Captain Kenneth Mackenzie, 1855–1927, vol. II

Wray, Sir Kenneth Owen R.; *see* Roberts-Wray.

Wray, Leonard, *died* 1942, vol. IV

Wray, Captain Thomas Henry Roberts-, *died* 1943, vol. IV

Wray, W. Fitzwater, *died* 1938, vol. III

Wreford, Sir Ernest Henry, 1866–1938, vol. III

Wreford, George, 1843–1919, vol. II

Wreford, James; *see* Watson, J. W.

Wreford-Brown, Captain Claude Wreford, 1876–1915, vol. I

Wren, Maj.-Gen. John, 1896–1958, vol. V

Wren, Percival Christopher, 1885–1941, vol. IV

Wren, Walter, *died* 1898, vol. I

Wrenbury, 1st Baron, 1845–1935, vol. III

Wrenbury, 2nd Baron, 1890–1940, vol. III

Wrench, Sir Charles Arthur, 1875–1948, vol. IV

Wrench, Edward Mason, 1833–1912, vol. I

Wrench, Sir Evelyn; *see* Wrench, Sir J. E. L.

Wrench, Rt Hon. Frederick Stringer, 1849–1926, vol. II

Wrench, Hylda Henrietta, (Lady Wrench), *died* 1955, vol. V

Wrench, Sir (John) Evelyn (Leslie), 1882–1966, vol. VI

Wrench, John Mervyn Dallas, 1883–1961, vol. VI

Wrench, Mollie Louise S.; *see* Stanley-Wrench.

Wrenfordsley, Sir Henry Thomas, *died* 1908, vol. I

Wrenn, Charles Leslie, 1895–1969, vol. VI

Wrey, Rev. Sir Albany Bourchier Sherard, 13th Bt, 1861–1948, vol. IV

Wrey, Sir Bourchier; *see* Wrey, Sir R. B. S.

Wrey, Sir Henry Bourchier Toke, 10th Bt, 1829–1900, vol. I

Wrey, Sir Philip Bourchier Sherard, 12th Bt, 1858–1936, vol. III

Wrey, Sir (Robert) Bourchier (Sherard), 11th Bt, 1855–1917, vol. II

Wrey, Captain William Bourchier Sherard, 1865–1926, vol. II

Wright, Baron (Life Peer); Robert Alderson Wright, 1869–1964, vol. VI

Wright of Ashton under Lyne, Baron (Life Peer); Lewis Tatham Wright, 1903–1974, vol. VII

Wright, Adam Henry, 1846–1930, vol. III

Wright, Alastair William, 1913–1985, vol. VIII

Wright, Albert Allen, 1846–1905, vol. I

Wright, Albert Ernest, 1902–1960, vol. V

Wright, Comdr Alexander Galloway, 1874–1943, vol. IV

Wright, Sir Alexander Kemp, 1859–1933, vol. III

Wright, Sir Almroth Edward, 1861–1947, vol. IV

Wright, Sir Andrew Barkworth, 1895–1971, vol. VII

Wright, Brig.-Gen. Archibald John Arnott, 1851–1943, vol. IV

Wright, Arnold, *died* 1941, vol. IV

Wright, Rev. Arthur, 1831–1920, vol. II

Wright, Rev. Arthur, 1843–1924, vol. II

Wright, Arthur Alban, 1887–1967, vol. VI

Wright, Sir Arthur Cory C.; *see* Cory-Wright.

Wright, A(rthur) Dickson, *died* 1976, vol. VII

Wright, Arthur Robinson, 1862–1932, vol. III

Wright, Lt-Col Bache Allen, 1874–1932, vol. III

Wright, Basil Charles, 1907–1987, vol. VIII

Wright, Bernard Arker, 1893–1973, vol. VII

Wright, Sir Bernard Swanwick, 1876–1961, vol. VI

Wright, Cecily Gertrude, *died* 1942, vol. IV

Wright, Col Sir Charles; *see* Wright, Col Sir W. C.

Wright, Charles Edward, *died* 1945, vol. IV

Wright, Charles Henry, 1864–1941, vol. IV

Wright, Charles Henry Conrad, 1869–1957, vol. V

Wright, Rev. Charles Henry Hamilton, 1836–1909, vol. I

Wright, Charles Ichabod, 1828–1905, vol. I

Wright, Sir Charles Seymour, 1887–1975, vol. VII

Wright, Sir Charles Theodore Hagberg, 1862–1940, vol. III

Wright, Sir Cory Francis C.; *see* Cory-Wright.

Wright, Dickson; *see* Wright, A. D.

Wright, Donald Arthur, 1911–1988, vol. VIII

Wright, Sir Douglas; *see* Wright, Sir R. D.

Wright, Dudley, 1868–1949, vol. IV

Wright, Dudley d'Auvergne, 1867–1948, vol. IV

Wright, Edward Fitwalter, 1902–1957, vol. V

Wright, Edward Fortescue, 1858–1904, vol. I

Wright, Edward Perceval, 1834–1910, vol. I

Wright, Rev. Edwin Henry, 1843–1937, vol. III

Wright, Eric Blackwood, 1860–1940, vol. III

Wright, Ernest, 1882–1974, vol. VII

Wright, Fowler; *see* Wright, S. F.

Wright, Frank, 1853–1922, vol. II

Wright, Frank Arnold, 1874–1961, vol. VI

Wright, Frank Joseph Henry, 1901–1970, vol. VI

Wright, Frank Lloyd, 1869–1959, vol. V

Wright, Frank Trueman W.; *see* Wynyard-Wright.

Wright, Frederick Adam, 1869–1946, vol. IV

Wright, Lt-Col Frederick William, 1850–1927, vol. II

Wright, Frederick Matthew, 1916–1990, vol. VIII

Wright, Sir Geoffrey C.; *see* Cory-Wright.

Wright, George, *died* 1913, vol. I

Wright, Sir George, *died* 1927, vol. II

Wright, Col George, 1860–1942, vol. IV

Wright, George Arthur, *died* 1920, vol. II

Wright, George Maurice, *died* 1956, vol. V

Wright, George Payling, 1898–1964, vol. VI

Wright, Rt Rev. George William, 1873–1956, vol. V

Wright, Lt-Col Guy Jefferys H.; *see* Hornsby-Wright.

Wright, H. C. Seppings, *died* 1937, vol. III

Wright, Harold, 1858–1908, vol. I

Wright, Harold Bell, 1872–1944, vol. IV

Wright, Harold Edward, 1868–1946, vol. IV

Wright, Rev. Harold Hall, 1859–1926, vol. II

Wright, Lt-Col Harry, 1856–1942, vol. IV

Wright, Major Hedley, 1859–1903, vol. I

Wright, Hedley Duncan, 1891–1942, vol. IV

Wright, Maj.-Gen. Henry Brooke Hagstromer, 1864–1948, vol. IV

Wright, Rev. Henry Dixon D.; *see* Dixon-Wright.

Wright, Sir Henry Edward, 1893–1966, vol. VI

Wright, Henry FitzHerbert, 1870–1947, vol. IV

Wright, Henry Robert, 1877–1951, vol. V

Wright, Henry Smith, 1839–1910, vol. I

Wright, Sir Herbert, 1874–1940, vol. III

Wright, Lt-Col Herbert James, 1888–1974, vol. VII

Wright, Huntley, 1869–1941, vol. IV

Wright, Sir James, 1823–1899, vol. I

Wright, James, *died* 1947, vol. IV

Wright, James Brown, 1861–1926, vol. II

Wright, John, 1857–1933, vol. III

Wright, Air Cdre John Allan Cecil C.; *see* Cecil-Wright.

Wright, Most Rev. John Charles, 1861–1933, vol. III

Wright, John George, 1897–1971, vol. VII

Wright, John Graham, 1873–1949, vol. IV

Wright, John Henry, 1910–1984, vol. VIII

Wright, John Moncrieff, 1884–1971, vol. VII

Wright, John Nicholson, 1896–1982, vol. VIII

Wright, Col Sir John Roper, 1st Bt, 1843–1926, vol. II

Wright, Sir Johnstone, 1883–1953, vol. V

Wright, Joseph, 1855–1930, vol. III

Wright, Joshua Butler, 1877–1939, vol. III

Wright, Kenneth Anthony, 1899–1975, vol. VII

Wright, Sir Leonard Morton, 1906–1967, vol. VI

Wright, Rev. Leslie, 1899–1972, vol. VII

Wright, Louis Booker, 1899–1984, vol. VIII

Wright, Louise, *died* 1944, vol. IV

Wright, Mabel Osgood, 1859–1934, vol. III

Wright, Mark Robinson, 1854–1944, vol. IV

Wright, Sir Michael Robert, 1901–1976, vol. VII

Wright, Rear-Adm. Noel, 1890–1975, vol. VII

Wright, Sir Norman Charles, 1900–1970, vol. VI

Wright, Orville, 1871–1948, vol. IV

Wright, Percy Malcolm, 1906–1959, vol. V

Wright, Peter Harold, 1916–1990, vol. VIII

Wright, Philip Arundell, 1889–1970, vol. VI

Wright, R. Ramsay, 1852–1933, vol. III

Wright, Hon. Sir Reginald Charles, 1905–1990, vol. VIII

Wright, Sir Robert Brash, 1915–1981, vol. VIII

Wright, Lt-Col Robert Ernest, 1884–1977, vol. VII

Wright, Sir Robert Patrick, 1857–1938, vol. III

Wright, Sir Robert Samuel, 1839–1904, vol. I

Wright, Col Robert Wallace, 1863–1928, vol. II

Wright, Sir (Roy) Douglas, 1907–1990, vol. VIII
Wright, Adm. Sir Royston Hollis, 1908–1977, vol. VII
Wright, Samson, *died* 1956, vol. V
Wright, Samuel, 1895–1975, vol. VII
Wright, Samuel John, 1899–1975, vol. VII
Wright, Sewall, 1889–1988, vol. VIII
Wright, Lt-Col Stephen, 1863–1936, vol. III
Wright, (Sydney) Fowler, 1874–1965, vol. VI
Wright, Sir Thomas, 1838–1905, vol. I
Wright, Gen. Sir Thomas, 1825–1910, vol. I
Wright, Thomas, 1859–1936, vol. III
Wright, Thomas Erskine, 1902–1986, vol. VIII
Wright, Thomas G., 1878–1929, vol. III
Wright, Thomas Rowland Drake, 1853–1926, vol. II
Wright, Uriah John, 1840–1914, vol. I
Wright, Brig.-Gen. Wallace Duffield, *died* 1953, vol. V
Wright, Walter Page, 1864–1940, vol. III
Wright, Wilfrid Thomas Mermoud, 1882–1946, vol. IV
Wright, Willard Huntington, 1888–1939, vol. III
Wright, William, 1862–1931, vol. III
Wright, William, 1874–1937, vol. III
Wright, William, 1918–1985, vol. VIII
Wright, William Alan, *born* 1895, vol. VIII
Wright, William Aldis, 1831–1914, vol. I
Wright, Col William Burgess, *died* 1930, vol. III
Wright, Col Sir (William) Charles, 2nd Bt, 1876–1950, vol. IV
Wright, Major William Gordon, 1883–1930, vol. III
Wright, William Hammond, 1871–1959, vol. V(A)
Wright, Rev. William Herbert Thomas, *died* 1929, vol. III
Wright, Rev. Canon William Joseph, 1881–1954, vol. V
Wright, Most Rev. William Lockridge, 1904–1990, vol. VIII
Wright, Sir William Owen, 1882–1951, vol. V
Wright, Gen. Sir William Purvis, 1846–1910, vol. I
Wright, Sir William Shaw, 1843–1914, vol. I
Wright, Lt-Col Rev. William Thomas, *died* 1938, vol. III
Wright-Henderson, Rev. Patrick Arkley, 1841–1922, vol. II
Wrighton, Edward, 1880–1937, vol. III
Wrightson, Captain Charles Archibald Wise, 1874–1953, vol. V
Wrightson, Edmund Harry Paul Garmondsway, 1919–1972, vol. VII
Wrightson, Sir Guy; *see* Wrightson, Sir T. G.
Wrightson, John, 1840–1916, vol. II
Wrightson, Sir John Garmondsway, 3rd Bt, 1911–1983, vol. VIII
Wrightson, Oliver, 1920–1987, vol. VIII
Wrightson, Sir Thomas, 1st Bt, 1839–1921, vol. II
Wrightson, Sir Thomas Garmondsway, (Sir Guy), 2nd Bt, 1871–1950, vol. IV
Wrightson, Walsh, 1852–1935, vol. III
Wrigley, Arthur Joseph, 1902–1983, vol. VIII
Wrigley, Hon. Brig.-Gen. Clement Carr, 1870–1934, vol. III
Wrigley, Fred, 1909–1982, vol. VIII
Wrigley, Sir John Crompton, 1888–1977, vol. VII

Wrigley, Rev. Joseph Henry, *died* 1938, vol. III
Wrigley, Leslie James, *died* 1933, vol. III
Wrinch, Dorothy, *died* 1976, vol. VII
Wrisberg, Lt-Gen. Sir (Frederick) George, 1895–1982, vol. VIII
Wrisberg, Lt-Gen. Sir George; *see* Wrisberg, Lt-Gen. Sir F. G.
Wrixon, Hon. Sir Henry John, 1839–1913, vol. I
Wrixon-Becher, Sir Eustace William Windham; *see* Becher.
Wrixon-Becher, Lt-Col Henry; *see* Becher.
Wrixon-Becher, Sir John; *see* Becher.
Wroblewski, Wladyslaw, 1875–1952, vol. V
Wrong, Edward Murray, 1889–1928, vol. II
Wrong, George Mackinnon, 1860–1948, vol. IV
Wrong, Humphrey Hume, 1894–1954, vol. V
Wrottesley, 3rd Baron, 1824–1910, vol. I
Wrottesley, 4th Baron, 1873–1962, vol. VI
Wrottesley, 5th Baron, 1918–1977, vol. VII
Wrottesley, Captain Francis Robert, 1877–1954, vol. V
Wrottesley, Rt Hon. Sir Frederic John, 1880–1948, vol. IV
Wroughton, Brig.-Gen. John Bartholomew, 1874–1940, vol. III
Wroughton, Philip, 1846–1910, vol. I
Wroughton, Major Philip Musgrave Neeld, 1887–1917, vol. II
Wroughton, William Musgrave, 1850–1928, vol. II
Wunderly, Sir Harry Wyatt, 1892–1971, vol. VII
Wurth, Wallace Charles, 1896–1960, vol. V(A)
Wurtzburg, Charles Edward, 1891–1952, vol. V
Wyard, Stanley, 1887–1946, vol. IV
Wyatt, Brig. Arthur Geoffrey, 1900–1960, vol. V
Wyatt, Vice-Adm. Sir (Arthur) Guy (Norris), 1893–1981, vol. VIII
Wyatt, Col Ernest Robert Caldwell, 1880–1957, vol. V
Wyatt, Major Francis Ogilvy, 1871–1919, vol. II
Wyatt, Vice-Adm. Sir Guy; *see* Wyatt, Vice-Adm. Sir A. G. N.
Wyatt, Harold Frazer, *died* 1925, vol. II
Wyatt, Horace Matthew, 1876–1954, vol. V
Wyatt, James Montagu, 1883–1953, vol. V
Wyatt, Rev. Joseph Light, 1841–1936, vol. III
Wyatt, Brig.-Gen. Louis John, 1874–1955, vol. V
Wyatt, Sir Myles Dermot Norris, 1903–1968, vol. VI
Wyatt, Rev. Paul Williams, 1856–1935, vol. III
Wyatt, Sir Stanley, 1877–1968, vol. VI
Wyatt, Thomas Henry, 1841–1920, vol. II
Wyatt, Travers Carey, 1887–1954, vol. V
Wyatt, Sir William Henry, 1823–1898, vol. I
Wyatt-Paine, Wyatt, *died* 1935, vol. III
Wyatt-Smith, Stanley; *see* Smith.
Wyburn, George McCreath, 1903–1985, vol. VIII
Wyche, Rev. Cyrill John, 1867–1945, vol. IV
Wycherley, Sir Bruce; *see* Wycherley, Sir R. B.
Wycherley, Sir (Robert) Bruce, 1894–1965, vol. VI
Wyeth, Paul James Logan, 1920–1982, vol. VIII
Wyeth, Rex, 1914–1978, vol. VII
Wyfold, 1st Baron, 1851–1937, vol. III
Wyfold, 2nd Baron, 1880–1942, vol. IV
Wyke, Rt Hon. Sir Charles Lennox, 1815–1897, vol. I
Wykeham-Martin, Cornwallis Philip; *see* Martin.

Wykeham-Musgrave, Herbert Wenman, 1871–1931, vol. III

Wykes, John Arthur, 1891–1970, vol. VI

Wykes-Finch, Rev. William Robert, 1855–1922, vol. II

Wykes-Sneyd, Vice-Adm. Ralph Stuart, 1882–1951, vol. V

Wyld, Rev. Edwin George, *died* 1919, vol. II

Wyld, Henry Cecil Kennedy, 1870–1945, vol. IV

Wyldbore-Smith, Sir Edmund; *see* Smith.

Wylde, Rt Rev. Arnold Lomas, 1880–1958, vol. V

Wylde, Col Charles Fenwick, 1867–1946, vol. IV

Wylde, Gen. Edward Andrée, 1858–1925, vol. II

Wylde, Everard William, *died* 1911, vol. I

Wylde, Rev. John, 1841–1941, vol. IV

Wylde, John Truro, 1849–1927, vol. II

Wylde, Rev. Robert, *died* 1927, vol. II

Wylde, William Henry, 1819–1909, vol. I

Wyler, William, 1902–1981, vol. VIII

Wyles, Lilian Mary Elizabeth, 1895–1975, vol. VII

Wyley, Col Sir William Fitzthomas, 1852–1940, vol. III

Wylie, Alexander, *died* 1921, vol. II

Wylie, Andrew, *died* 1935, vol. III

Wylie, Major Charles Hotham Montagu Doughty-, 1868–1915, vol. I

Wylie, David Storer, 1876–1965, vol. VI

Wylie, Sir Francis James, 1865–1952, vol. V

Wylie, Sir Francis Verner, 1891–1970, vol. VI

Wylie, Maj.-Gen. Henry, 1844–1918, vol. II

Wylie, Miss I. A. R., *died* 1959, vol. V

Wylie, James, 1875–1941, vol. IV

Wylie, James Hamilton, 1844–1914, vol. I

Wylie, Rt Hon. James Owens, 1845–1935, vol. III

Wylie, Brig.-Gen. James Scott, 1862–1937, vol. III

Wylie, John, *died* 1936, vol. III

Wylie, Major John Price, 1888–1939, vol. III

Wylie, Lt-Col Macleod, 1881–1952, vol. V

Wylie, Hon. William Evelyn, 1881–1964, vol. VI

Wyllarde, Dolf, *died* 1950, vol. IV

Wyllie, Lt-Col Alexander Keith, 1853–1928, vol. II

Wyllie, Charles W., *died* 1923, vol. II

Wyllie, Lt-Col Harold, 1880–1973, vol. VII

Wyllie, John, *died* 1916, vol. II

Wyllie, William Gifford, *died* 1969, vol. VI

Wyllie, Lt-Col Sir William Hutt Curzon, 1848–1909, vol. I

Wyllie, William Lionel, 1851–1931, vol. III

Wylly, Col Guy George Egerton, 1880–1962, vol. VI

Wylly, Col Harold Carmichael, 1858–1932, vol. III

Wylson, Oswald Cane, 1858–1925, vol. II

Wymark, Patrick Carl, (A. K. A. Cheeseman), 1926–1970, vol. VI

Wymer, Francis John, 1898–1976, vol. VII

Wyne-Harris, Sir Percy, 1903–1979, vol. VII

Wynch, Lionel Maling, 1864–1955, vol. V

Wyncoll, Col Charles Edward, 1857–1943, vol. IV

Wyndham, Sir Charles, 1837–1919, vol. II

Wyndham, Lt-Col Charles John, 1844–1930, vol. III

Wyndham, Rt Hon. George, 1863–1913, vol. I

Wyndham, Sir (George) Hugh, 1836–1916, vol. II

Wyndham, Col Guy Percy, 1865–1941, vol. IV

Wyndham, Major Guy Richard Charles, 1896–1948, vol. IV

Wyndham, Sir Harold Stanley, 1903–1988, vol. VIII

Wyndham, Henry Saxe, 1867–1940, vol. III

Wyndham, Horace Cowley, 1873–1970, vol. VI

Wyndham, Sir Hugh; *see* Wyndham, Sir G. H.

Wyndham, Mary, (Lady Wyndham); *see* Moore, Mary.

Wyndham, Sir Percy, 1864–1943, vol. IV

Wyndham, Percy, 1867–1947, vol. IV

Wyndham, Hon. Percy Scawen, 1835–1911, vol. I

Wyndham, Lady Sibell Mary; *see* Grosvenor, Countess.

Wyndham, Col Walter George Crole, 1857–1948, vol. IV

Wyndham, Captain William, 1842–1930, vol. III

Wyndham, Hon. William Reginald, 1876–1914, vol. I

Wyndham-Quin, Captain Hon. Valentine Maurice, 1890–1983, vol. VIII

Wyndham White, Sir Eric, 1913–1980, vol. VII

Wynford, 3rd Baron, 1826–1899, vol. I

Wynford, 4th Baron, 1829–1903, vol. I

Wynford, 5th Baron, 1834–1904, vol. I

Wynford, 6th Baron, 1871–1940, vol. III

Wynford, 7th Baron, 1874–1943, vol. IV

Wynn, Hon. Charles Henry, 1847–1911, vol. I

Wynn, Hon. Frederick George, 1853–1932, vol. III

Wynn, Frederick R. W.; *see* Williams Wynn.

Wynn, Rt Rev. Harold Edward, 1889–1956, vol. V

Wynn, Col Sir Herbert Lloyd Watkin W.; *see* Williams-Wynn.

Wynn, Col Sir (Owen) Watkin W.; *see* Williams-Wynn.

Wynn, Col Sir Robert William Herbert Watkin W.; *see* Williams-Wynn.

Wynn, Hon. Rowland Tempest Beresford, 1898–1977, vol. VII

Wynn, Rev. Walter, 1865–1951, vol. V

Wynn, Sir Watkin W.; *see* Williams-Wynn.

Wynn, William Henry, 1878–1956, vol. V

Wynn Parry, Hon. Sir Henry, 1899–1964, vol. VI

Wynn-Wynne, Major Reginald, 1857–1913, vol. I

Wynne, Hon. Agar, 1850–1934, vol. III

Wynne, Anthony; *see* Wilson, Robert McNair.

Wynne, Rev. Arthur Edwin, 1864–1964, vol. VI

Wynne, Gen. Sir Arthur Singleton, 1846–1936, vol. III

Wynne, Esmé; *see* Wynne-Tyson, D. E. E.

Wynne, Major Francis George, 1885–1918, vol. II

Wynne, Frederick Horton, 1877–1943, vol. IV

Wynne, Ven. G. R., 1838–1912, vol. I

Wynne, George, 1839–1912, vol. I

Wynne, Rt Hon. Sir Henry Arthur, 1867–1943, vol. IV

Wynne, Lt-Col Henry Ernest Singleton, 1877–1962, vol. VI

Wynne, May; *see* Knowles, Mabel Winifred.

Wynne, Pamela; *see* Scott, Winifred Mary.

Wynne, Major Reginald W.; *see* Wynn-Wynne.

Wynne, Sir Trevredyn Rashleigh, 1853–1942, vol. IV

Wynne, William Palmer, 1861–1950, vol. IV

Wynne, William Robert Maurice, 1840–1909, vol. I

Wynne-Edwards, Rev. John Rosindale, 1864–1943, vol. IV

Wynne-Edwards, Sir Robert Meredydd, 1897–1974, vol. VII

Wynne-Eyton, Alan John F.; *see* Fairbairn-Wynne-Eyton.

Wynne-Eyton, Mrs Frances; *see* Wynne-Eyton, Mrs S. F.

Wynne-Eyton, Mrs Selena Frances, 1898–1982, vol. VIII

Wynne Finche, Col John Charles, 1891–1982, vol. VIII

Wynne Finch, Col Sir William Heneage, 1893–1961, vol. VI

Wynne-Jones, Baron (Life Peer); William Francis Kenrick Wynne-Jones, 1903–1982, vol. VIII

Wynne-Jones, Major Charles Llewelyn, 1890–1974, vol. VII

Wynne-Jones, Very Rev. Llewelyn, *died* 1936, vol. III

Wynne-Jones, Tom Neville, 1893–1979, vol. VII

Wynne-Tyson, Dorothy Estelle Esmé, 1898–1972, vol. VII

Wynter, Bryan Herbert, 1915–1975, vol. VII

Wynter, Brig.-Gen. Francis Arthur, 1870–1942, vol. IV

Wynter, Maj.-Gen. Henry Douglas, 1886–1945, vol. IV

Wynter, Brig. Henry Walter, 1882–1959, vol. V

Wynter, Sir Luther Reginald, 1899–1984, vol. VIII

Wynter, Walter Essex, 1860–1945, vol. IV

Wynter-Morgan, Air Cdre Wilfred, 1894–1968, vol. VI

Wynyard, Diana, 1906–1964, vol. VI

Wynyard, Major Edward George, 1861–1936, vol. III

Wynyard, Col Rowley, 1855–1931, vol. III

Wynyard-Wright, Frank Trueman, 1884–1979, vol. VII

Wyon, Sir Albert William, 1869–1937, vol. III

Wyon, Allan, 1843–1907, vol. I

Wyon, Rev. Allan Gairdner, 1882–1962, vol. VI

Wyrall, Everard; *see* Wyrall, R. E.

Wyrall, Reginald Everard, 1878–1933, vol. III

Wyse, Andrew Nicholas B.; *see* Bonaparte-Wyse.

Wyse, Henry Taylor, 1870–1951, vol. V

Wyse, Marjorie Anne E.; *see* Erskine-Wyse.

Wyss, Sophie Adele, 1897–1983, vol. VIII

Wythes, Ernest James, 1868–1949, vol. IV

Wyvill, Marmaduke D'Arcy, 1849–1918, vol. II

Y

Yahuda, Abraham Shalom Ezekiel, 1877–1951, vol. V

Yahya Khan, Gen. Agha Muhammad, 1917–1980, vol. VII

Yain, Sir Lee Ah, 1874–1932, vol. III

Yakub, Moulvi Sir Mohammad, 1879–1942, vol. IV

Yaldwin, Lt-Col Alfred George, 1847–1905, vol. I

Yale, Col James Corbet, 1859–1936, vol. III

Yamagata, Aritomo, Field-Marshal Prince, 1838–1922, vol. II

Yamin Khan, Sir Mohammed, *died* 1966, vol. VI

Yapp, Sir Arthur Keysall, 1869–1936, vol. III

Yapp, Sir Frederick Charles, 1880–1958, vol. V

Yapp, Richard Henry, *died* 1929, vol. III

Yarborough, 4th Earl of, 1859–1936, vol. III

Yarborough, 5th Earl of, 1888–1948, vol. IV

Yarborough, 6th Earl of, 1893–1966, vol. VI

Yarborough, Countess of; (Marcia Amelia Mary); *see* Fauconberg and Conyers, Baroness.

Yarborough, George Eustace C.; *see* Cooke-Yarborough.

Yarborough, Rev. John James Cooke-, 1855–1941, vol. IV

Yarde, Air Vice-Marshal Brian Courtenay, 1905–1986, vol. VIII

Yarde-Buller, Brig.-Gen. Hon. Sir Henry, 1862–1928, vol. II

Yarde-Buller, Hon. Walter, 1859–1935, vol. III

Yardley, Captain John Henry Reginald, 1881–1938, vol. III

Yardley, Col John Watkins, 1858–1920, vol. II

Yardley, Samuel, 1839–1902, vol. I

Yarr, Maj.-Gen. Sir Thomas, 1862–1937, vol. III

Yarrow, Sir Alfred Fernandez, 1st Bt, 1842–1932, vol. III

Yarrow, Eleanor Cecilia, (Lady Yarrow), *died* 1953, vol. V

Yarrow, Sir Harold Edgar, 2nd Bt, 1884–1962, vol. VI

Yarwood, Dame Elizabeth Ann, 1900–1989, vol. VIII

Yarworth-Jones, Sir William, 1870–1953, vol. V

Yashiro, Yukio, 1890–1975, vol. VII

Yate, Lt-Col Arthur Campbell, 1853–1929, vol. III

Yate, Col Sir Charles Edward, 1st Bt, 1849–1940, vol. III

Yate, Rev. George Edward, *died* 1908, vol. I

Yate-Lee, Lawford, 1838–1901, vol. I

Yates, Col Clarence Montague, 1881–1952, vol. V

Yates, Lt-Gen. Sir David P.; *see* Peel Yates.

Yates, Lt-Col Donald, 1893–1960, vol. V (A), vol. VI (AI)

Yates, Dornford; *see* Mercer, Major Cecil William.

Yates, Dame Frances Amelia, 1899–1981, vol. VIII

Yates, Lt-Col Hubert Peel, 1874–1938, vol. III

Yates, Bt-Col James Ainsworth, 1883–1929, vol. III

Yates, John Ernest, 1887–1969, vol. VI

Yates, Joseph Maghull, 1844–1916, vol. II

Yates, Rev. Thomas, 1873–1936, vol. III

Yates, Sir Thomas, 1896–1978, vol. VII

Yates, Victor Francis, 1900–1969, vol. VI

Yates, Walter Baldwyn, *died* 1947, vol. IV

Yates, Rev. Canon William R., 1870–1951, vol. V

Yatman, Col Arthur Hamilton, 1874–1947, vol. IV

Yatman, Brig.-Gen. Clement, 1871–1940, vol. III

Yeabsley, Sir Richard Ernest, 1898–1983, vol. VIII

Yeaman, Sir Ian David, 1889–1977, vol. VII

Yeames, William Frederick, 1835–1918, vol. II

Yearsley, Macleod; *see* Yearsley, P. M.

Yearsley, (Percival) Macleod, *died* 1951, vol. V

Yeatman-Biggs, Rt Rev. Huyshe Wolcott, 1845–1922, vol. II

Yeats, Gerald Aylmer L.; *see* Levett-Yeats.

Yeats, Jack Butler, *died* 1957, vol. V

Yeats, John Butler, 1839–1922, vol. II

Yeats, William Butler, 1865–1939, vol. III

Yeats-Brown, Francis, 1886–1944, vol. IV

Yeats-Brown, Montagu, 1834–1921, vol. II

Yeatts, Maurice William Walter Murray, 1894–1950, vol. IV

Yeaxlee, Basil Alfred, 1883–1967, vol. VI
Yeilding, Col William Richard, 1856–1934, vol. III
Yeld, Edward, 1839–1921, vol. II
Yellowlees, Henry, 1888–1971, vol. VII
Yelverton, Adm. Bentinck John Davies, died 1959, vol. V
Yelverton, Hon. Roger Dawson, died 1912, vol. I
Yelverton, William Henry Morgan, 1840–1909, vol. I
Yen, W. W., 1877–1950, vol. IV(A), vol. V
Yencken, Arthur F., 1894–1944, vol. IV
Yendell, Rear-Adm. William John, 1903–1988, vol. VIII
Yeo, Sir Alfred William, 1863–1928, vol. II
Yeo, Gerald Francis, 1845–1909, vol. I
Yeo, Rt Rev. Mgr Henry D., 1872–1952, vol. V
Yeo, J. Burney, died 1914, vol. I
Yeo, Sir William, 1896–1972, vol. VII
Yeo-Thomas, Wing Comdr Forest Frederick Edward, 1901–1964, vol. VI
Yeoman, Rev. Alexander Ross, 1874–1956, vol. V
Yeoman, Ven. Henry Walker, died 1897, vol. I
Yerburgh, Rev. Oswald Pryor W.; see Wardell-Yerburgh.
Yerburgh, Richard Eustre, 1847–1939, vol. III
Yerburgh, Robert Armstrong, 1853–1916, vol. II
Yerbury, Francis Rowland, 1885–1970, vol. VI
Yerbury, Air Vice-Marshal Richard Olyffe, 1914–1971, vol. VII
Yerkes, Charles Tyson, 1837–1905, vol. I
Yerkes, Robert Mearns, 1876–1956, vol. V
Yetts, W. Perceval, 1878–1957, vol. V
Yew, Loke, died 1917, vol. II
Yexley, Lionel, 1861–1933, vol. III
Yglesias, V. P., died 1911, vol. I
Yolland, John Horatio, 1863–1944, vol. IV
Yonge, Sir (Charles) Maurice, 1899–1986, vol. VIII
Yonge, Charlotte Mary, 1823–1901, vol. I
Yonge, Sir Maurice; see Yonge, Sir C. M.
Yonge, Lt-Col Philip Caynton, 1877–1928, vol. II
Yool, Air Vice-Marshal William Munro, 1894–1978, vol. VII
York, Ven. George William, died 1944, vol. IV
York, Thomas John Pinches, 1898–1970, vol. VI
Yorke, Hon. Alexander Grantham, 1847–1911, vol. I
Yorke, Hon. Alfred Ernest Frederick, 1871–1928, vol. II
Yorke, Lt-Col Sir Arthur; see Yorke, Lt-Col Sir H. A.
Yorke, Curtis, died 1930, vol. III
Yorke, Dorothy, 1879–1946, vol. IV
Yorke, Francis Reginald Stevens, 1906–1962, vol. VI
Yorke, Lt-Col Sir (H.) Arthur, 1848–1930, vol. III
Yorke, Sir Henry Francis Redhead, 1842–1914, vol. I
Yorke, Henry Vincent; see Green, H.
Yorke, John Reginald, 1836–1912, vol. I
Yorke, Brig. Philip Gerard, 1882–1968, vol. VI
Yorke, Brig.-Gen. Ralph Maximilian, 1874–1951, vol. V
Yorke, Robert Langdon, 1887–1954, vol. V
Yorke, Simon, 1903–1966, vol. VI
Yorke, Vincent Wodehouse, 1869–1957, vol. V
Yorke, Warrington, 1883–1943, vol. IV
Yorston, Sir Keith; see Yorston, Sir R. K.
Yorston, Sir (Robert) Keith, 1902–1983, vol. VIII

Yorstoun, Brig.-Gen. Archibald Mordern C.; see Carthew-Yorstoun.
Yoshida, Shigeru, 1878–1967, vol. VI
Yost, Charles Woodruff, 1907–1981, vol. VIII
Youard, Very Rev. Wilfrid Wadham, 1869–1964, vol. VI
Youde, Sir Edward, 1924–1986, vol. VIII
Youens, Rev. Canon Fearnley Algernon Cyril, 1886–1967, vol. VI
Youens, Rt Rev. Laurence W., died 1939, vol. III
Youl, Sir James Arndell, 1809–1904, vol. I
Young, Rt Hon. Lord; George Young, 1819–1907, vol. I
Young, Sir Alastair Spencer Templeton, 2nd Bt (cr 1945), 1918–1963, vol. VI
Young, Sir Alban; see Young, Sir C. A.
Young, Hon. Sir Alexander; see Young, Hon. Sir J. A.
Young, Maj.-Gen. Alexander, 1915–1983, vol. VIII
Young, (Alexander Bell) Filson, 1876–1938, vol. III
Young, Alfred, died 1900, vol. I
Young, Rev. Alfred, 1873–1940, vol. III
Young, Alfred Harry, died 1912, vol. I
Young, Sir Alfred Karney, 1865–1942, vol. IV
Young, Rev. Allan, 1925–1979, vol. VII
Young, Sir Allen William, 1827–1915, vol. I
Yonng, Allyn Abbott, 1876–1929, vol. III
Young, Andrew, 1873–1937, vol. III
Young, Andrew, 1858–1943, vol. IV
Young, Rev. Canon Andrew John, 1885–1971, vol. VII
Young, Col Archibald, 1865–1931, vol. III
Young, Archibald, 1873–1939, vol. III
Young, Archibald Hope, 1863–1935, vol. III
Young, Lt-Col Arthur Davidson, 1862–1937, vol. III
Young, Col Sir Arthur Edwin, 1907–1979, vol. VII
Young, Captain Sir Arthur Henderson, 1854–1938, vol. III
Young, Arthur Primrose, 1885–1977, vol. VII
Young, Sir Arthur Stewart Leslie, 1st Bt (cr 1945), 1889–1950, vol. IV
Young, Rev. Augustus Blayney Russell, 1845–1941, vol. IV
Young, Maj.-Gen. Bernard Keith, 1892–1969, vol. VI
Young, Carmichael Aretas, 1913–1986, vol. VIII
Young, Rev. Canon (Cecil) Edwyn, 1913–1988, vol. VIII
Young, Sir (Charles) Alban, 9th Bt (cr 1769), 1865–1944, vol. IV
Young, Col Charles Augustus, 1863–1944, vol. IV
Young, Rev. Canon Charles Edgar, 1897–1977, vol. VII
Young, Charles Edward Baring, 1850–1928, vol. II
Young, Maj.-Gen. Charles Frederic Gordon, 1859–1956, vol. V
Young, (Charles) Kenneth, 1916–1985, vol. VIII
Young, Christopher Alwyne Jack, 1912–1978, vol. VII
Young, Clyde, 1871–1948, vol. IV
Young, Sir Cyril Roe Muston, 4th Bt (cr 1821), 1881–1955, vol. V
Young, Rev. Daniel Eliott, 1851–1935, vol. III
Young, Daniel Henderson Lusk, 1861–1921, vol. II
Young, Lt-Col David Douglas, 1857–1940, vol. III

Young, Rev. Dinsdale Thomas, 1861–1938, vol. III
Young, Douglas, 1882–1967, vol. VI
Young, Sir Douglas; see Young, Sir J. D.
Young, Sir Douglas; see Young, Sir W. D.
Young, Edith Isabella, 1904–1988, vol. VIII
Young, Rev. Canon Edwyn; see Young, Rev. Canon C. E.
Young, Rev. Egerton Ryerson, 1840–1909, vol. I
Young, Emily Hilda, 1880–1949, vol. IV
Young, Sir Eric; see Young, Sir T. E. B.
Young, Eric Edgar, 1912–1986, vol. VIII
Young, Eric William, 1896–1987, vol. VIII
Young, Ernest, 1869–1952, vol. V
Young, Brig.-Gen. Ernest Douglas, 1872–1957, vol. V
Young, Ernest Herbert, 1878–1921, vol. II, vol. III
Young, Evelyn Lucy, 1879–1960, vol. V
Young, F. E. Mills, died 1945, vol. IV
Young, Filson, see Young, A. B. F.
Young, Francis Brett, 1884–1954, vol. V
Young, Rev. Francis Samuel, 1871–1934, vol. III
Young, Francis Watson, 1851–1941, vol. IV
Young, Sir Frank George, 1908–1988, vol. VIII
Young, Lt-Col Sir Frank Popham, 1863–1940, vol. III
Young, Captain Sir Frederic William, 1859–1927, vol. II
Young, Sir Frederick, 1817–1913, vol. I
Young, Frederick, 1890–1948, vol. IV
Young, Col Frederick de Bude, 1865–1920, vol. II
Young, Frederick George Charles, 1877–1955, vol. V
Young, Frederick Hugh, 1892–1969, vol. VI
Young, Frederick Trestrail Clive, 1887–1982, vol. VIII
Young, Sir Frederick William, 1876–1948, vol. IV
Young, Geoffrey Winthrop, 1876–1958, vol. V
Young, Sir George, 3rd Bt (cr 1813), 1837–1930, vol. III
Young, Sir George, 4th Bt (cr 1813), 1872–1952, vol. V
Young, George; see Young, Rt Hon. Lord.
Young, Rt Hon. George Charles Gillespie, 1876–1939, vol. III
Young, Very Rev. George Edward, died 1937, vol. III
Young, Brig.-Gen. George Frederick, 1846–1919, vol. II
Young, George Kennedy, 1911–1990, vol. VIII
Young, George Malcolm, 1882–1959, vol. V
Young, Sir George Peregrine, 5th Bt (cr 1813), 1908–1960, vol. V
Young, Mrs George Washington; see Nordica, Lillian.
Young, Gerard Mackworth-, 1884–1965, vol. VI
Young, Gladys, 1887–1975, vol. VII
Young, Maj.-Gen. Gordon Drummond, 1896–1964, vol. VI
Young, Grace Chisholm, 1868–1944, vol. IV
Young, Most Rev. Sir Guilford Clyde, 1916–1988, vol. VIII
Young, Lt-Col Harry Norman, 1874–1944, vol. IV
Young, Brig.-Gen. Henry Alfred, 1867–1941, vol. IV
Young, Henry Alfred, died 1942, vol. IV
Young, Brig. Henry Ayerst, 1895–1952, vol. V
Young, Hon. Henry Esson, 1867–1939, vol. III
Young, Brig.-Gen. Henry George, 1870–1956, vol. V

Young, Hilda Beatrice, (Sister Pauline), died 1967, vol. VI
Young, Major Sir Hubert Winthrop, 1885–1950, vol. IV
Young, Maj.-Gen. Hugh A., 1898–1982, vol. VIII
Young, Hugh Hampton, 1870–1945, vol. IV
Young, Hugo Joseph, 1847–1929, vol. III
Young, James, 1883–1963, vol. VI
Young, James, 1887–1975, vol. VII
Young, Hon. Sir (James) Alexander, 1875–1956, vol. V
Young, James Barclay Murdoch, 1897–1957, vol. V
Young, James Carleton, 1856–1918, vol. II
Young, Maj.-Gen. James Charles, 1858–1926, vol. II
Young, Gen. James Nowell, 1824–1917, vol. II
Young, Sir James Reid, 1888–1971, vol. VII
Young, Maj.-Gen. James Vernon, 1891–1961, vol. VI
Young, John, 1835–1902, vol. I
Young, Rt Hon. John, 1826–1915, vol. I
Young, John, 1845–1925, vol. II
Young, Rev. John, 1844–1930, vol. III
Young, Major John Darling, 1910–1988, vol. VIII
Young, Sir (John) Douglas, 1883–1973, vol. VI
Young, Col Sir John Smith, 1843–1932, vol. III
Young, John Stirling, 1894–1971, vol. VII
Young, Sir John William Roe, 5th Bt, 1913–1981, vol. VIII
Young, Brig.-Gen. Sir Julian Mayne, 1872–1961, vol. VI
Young, Brig.-Gen. Julius Ralph, 1864–1961, vol. VI
Young, Karl, 1879–1943, vol. IV
Young, Brig. Keith de Lorentz, 1889–1962, vol. VI
Young, Keith Downes, 1848–1929, vol. III
Young, Kenneth; see Young, C. K.
Young, M'Gregor, 1864–1942, vol. IV
Young, Sir Mark Aitchison, 1886–1974, vol. VII
Young, Mary Lavinia Bessie, 1911–1986, vol. VIII
Young, Morris Yudlevitz, died 1950, vol. IV
Young, Major Norman Edward, 1862–1902, vol. I
Young, Norman Egerton, 1892–1964, vol. VI
Young, Norwood, 1860–1943, vol. IV
Young, Comdr Oliver, 1855–1908, vol. I
Young, Owen D., 1874–1962, vol. VI
Young, Patrick Charles, 1880–1951, vol. V
Young, Brig. Peter, 1915–1988, vol. VIII
Young, Ven. Peter Claude, 1916–1987, vol. VIII
Young, Maj.-Gen. Peter George Francis, 1912–1976, vol. VII
Young, Pierre Henry John, 1926–1985, vol. VIII
Young, Reginald Stanley, (Robert), 1891–1985, vol. VIII
Young, Rt Rev. Richard, 1843–1905, vol. I
Young, Robert; see Young, Reginald S.
Young, Rt Hon. Robert, 1822–1917, vol. II
Young, Robert, 1860–1932, vol. III
Young, Maj.-Gen. Robert, 1877–1953, vol. V
Young, Sir Robert, 1872–1957, vol. V
Young, Sir Robert Arthur, 1871–1959, vol. V
Young, Robert Fitzgibbon, died 1960, vol. V
Young, Robert Magill, 1851–1925, vol. II
Young, Ruth, 1884–1983, vol. VIII
Young, Samuel, 1822–1918, vol. II
Young, Stephen, 1894–1972, vol. VII
Young, Stuart, 1934–1986, vol. VIII

Young, Sydney, 1857–1937, vol. III
Young, Thomas, 1896–1977, vol. VII
Young, Maj.-Gen. Thomas, 1893–1979, vol. VII
Young, Sir (Thomas) Eric (Boswell), 1891–1973, vol. VII
Young, Thomas Moffat, 1873–1946, vol. IV
Young, Lt-Col Walter Herbert, *died* 1940, vol. III
Young, Sir Walter James, 1872–1940, vol. III
Young, Rev. William, 1840–1915, vol. I
Young, William, 1863–1942, vol. IV
Young, Sir William, 1875–1957, vol. V
Young, William, 1885–1965, vol. VI(AII)
Young, Sir William, 1905–1980, vol. VII
Young, William Arthur, 1867–1955, vol. V
Young, William Arthur, 1890–1955, vol. V
Young, Sir (William) Douglas, 1859–1943, vol. IV
Young, William Henry, 1863–1942, vol. IV
Young, William John, 1878–1942, vol. IV
Young, Sir William Lawrence, 8th Bt (*cr* 1769), 1864–1921, vol. II
Young, Sir William Mackworth, 1840–1924, vol. II
Young, Sir William Muston Need, 3rd Bt (*cr* 1821), 1847–1934, vol. III(A), vol. IV
Young, Rt Hon. William Robert, 1856–1933, vol. III
Young-Jamieson, Vice-Adm. Douglas, 1893–1955, vol. V
Younger of Leckie, 1st Viscount, 1851–1929, vol. III
Younger of Leckie, 2nd Viscount, 1880–1946, vol. IV
Younger, Brig. Arthur Allan Shakespear, 1881–1960, vol. V
Younger, Harry George, 1866–1951, vol. V
Younger, Sir James Paton, 1891–1974, vol. VII
Younger, Maj.-Gen. John Edward Talbot, 1888–1974, vol. VII
Younger, Rt Hon. Sir Kenneth Gilmour, 1908–1976, vol. VII
Younger, Maj.-Gen. Ralph, 1904–1985, vol. VIII
Younger, Robert; *see* Baron Blanesborough.
Younger, Robert Tannahill, 1860–1906, vol. I
Younger, Sir William, 1st Bt, 1862–1937, vol. III
Younger, Rev. William, 1869–1956, vol. V
Younger, Sir William Robert, 2nd Bt, 1888–1973, vol. VII
Younghusband, Arthur Delaval, 1854–1931, vol. III
Younghusband, Charles Wright, 1821–1899, vol. I
Younghusband, Dame Eileen Louise, 1902–1981, vol. VIII
Younghusband, Sir Francis Edward, 1863–1942, vol. IV
Younghusband, Maj.-Gen. Sir George John, 1859–1944, vol. IV
Younghusband, Maj.-Gen. John William, 1823–1907, vol. I
Younghusband, Maj.-Gen. Leslie Napier, *died* 1939, vol. III
Younghusband, Gen. Robert Romer, 1819–1905, vol. I
Younghusband, Romer Edward, 1858–1933, vol. III
Youngman, Annie Mary, *died* 1919, vol. II
Youngman, William, 1880–1963, vol. VI
Yousuf, Lt-Gen. Mohammed, 1908–1981, vol. VIII
Yoxall, Harry Waldo, 1896–1984, vol. VIII
Yoxall, Sir James Henry, 1857–1925, vol. II
Ypres, 1st Earl of, 1852–1925, vol. II

Ypres, 2nd Earl of, 1881–1958, vol. V
Ypres, 3rd Earl of, 1921–1988, vol. VIII
Ysaye, Eugene, 1858–1931, vol. III
Ystwyth, 1st Baron, 1840–1935, vol. III
Yuill, Lt-Col Harry Hogg, 1886–1935, vol. III
Yukawa, Hideki, 1907–1981, vol. VIII
Yule, Annie Henrietta, (Lady Yule), *died* 1950, vol. IV
Yule, Sir David, 1st Bt, 1858–1928, vol. II
Yule, George Udny, 1871–1951, vol. V
Yule, Col James Herbert, 1847–1920, vol. II
Yusuf, Sir Mohamad, *died* 1965, vol. VI(AII)
Yusuf, Nawab Sir Muhammad, *born* 1895, vol. VI
Yutang, Lin; *see* Lin Yutang.
Yves-Guyot, 1843–1928, vol. II

Z

Zacharewitsch, Michael, 1878–1953, vol. V
Zaehner, Robert Charles, 1913–1974, vol. VII
Zafar Ali, Sir, Khan Bahadur, Mirza, 1870–1942, vol. IV
Zafrulla Khan, Hon. Chaudhri Sir Muhammad, 1893–1985, vol. VIII
Zaharoff, Sir Basil, 1850–1936, vol. III
Zaimis, Eleanor, 1915–1982, vol. VIII
Zambra, William Warren S.; *see* Shaw-Zambra.
Zammit, Salvatore Cachia, *died* 1918, vol. II
Zammit, Sir Temistocle, 1864–1935, vol. III
Zamora y Torres, Don Niceto Alcalá, 1877–1949, vol. IV
Zanardelli, Guiseppe, 1829–1903, vol. I
Zangwill, Edith Ayrton, *died* 1945, vol. IV
Zangwill, Israel, 1864–1926, vol. II
Zangwill, Louis, 1869–1938, vol. III
Zangwill, Oliver Louis, 1913–1987, vol. VIII
Zanuck, Darryl Francis, 1902–1979, vol. VII
Zanzibar, Sultan of, *died* 1902, vol. I
Zanzibar, Sultan of, 1879–1960, vol. V
Zaphiro, Photius Philip Constantine, 1877–1933, vol. III
Zaroubin, Georgi Nikolaevitch, 1900–1968, vol. VI
Zavertal, Hon. Captain Ladislao Joseph Philip Paul, 1849–1942, vol. IV
Zeal, Hon. Sir William Austin, 1830–1912, vol. I
Zealley, Sir Alec Thomas Sharland, 1893–1970, vol. VI
Zeiller, Charles René, 1847–1915, vol. I
Zelie, Rev. John Sheridan, 1866–1942, vol. IV
Zepler, Eric Ernest, 1898–1980, vol. VII
Zeppelin, Count Ferdinand von, 1838–1917, vol. II
Zernike, Frits, 1888–1966, vol. VI
Zetland, 1st Marquess of, 1844–1929, vol. III
Zetland, 2nd Marquess of, 1876–1961, vol. VI
Zetland, 3rd Marquess of, 1908–1989, vol. VIII
Zeuner, Frederick Everard, 1905–1963, vol. VI
Zhukov, Marshal Georgi Konstantinovich, 1896–1974, vol. VII
Ziaur Rahman, General, 1935–1981, vol. VIII
Zichy-Woinarski, Casimir Julius, 1863–1935, vol. III
Ziegler, Karl, 1898–1973, vol. VII

Zielinski, Thaddeus, 1859–1944, vol. IV
Zigomala, Hilda, 1869–1946, vol. IV
Zilliacus, Konni, 1894–1967, vol. VI
Ziman, Herbert David, 1902–1983, vol. VIII
Zimbalist, Efrem, 1890–1985, vol. VIII
Zimmer, George Frederick, 1854–1935, vol. III
Zimmermann, Agnes Marie, 1847–1925, vol. II
Zimmern, Sir Alfred, 1879–1957, vol. V
Zimmern, Alice, 1855–1939, vol. III
Zimmern, Archibald, 1917–1985, vol. VIII
Zimmern, Helen, 1846–1934, vol. III
Zinkeisen, Anna Katrina, *died* 1976, vol. VII
Zinn, Maj. William Victor, 1903–1989, vol. VIII
Ziwer, Ahmad Pasha, 1864–1945, vol. IV
Zohrab, Gen. Sir Edward Henry, 1850–1909, vol. I
Zola, Emile Edouard Charles Antoine, 1840–1902, vol. I

Zoppi, Count Vittorio, 1898–1967, vol. VI
Zorn, Anders Leonard, 1860–1920, vol. II
Zouche, 15th Baron, 1851–1914, vol. I
Zouche, Baroness (16th in line), 1860–1917, vol. II
Zouche, Baroness (17th in line), 1875–1965, vol. VI
Zukor, Adolph, 1873–1976, vol. VII
Zulfikar Ali Khan, Sir, 1875–1933, vol. III
Zuloaga, Ignacio, 1870–1945, vol. IV
Zulu, Rt Rev. Alphaeus Hamilton, 1905–1988, vol. VIII
Zulueta, Francis de, 1878–1958, vol. V
Zulueta, Sir Philip Francis de, 1925–1989, vol. VIII
Zwar, Bernard T., 1876–1947, vol. IV
Zweig, Arnold, 1887–1968, vol. VI
Zweig, Stefan, *died* 1942, vol. IV
Zwemer, Rev. Samuel Marinus, 1867–1952, vol. V